Television Westerns Episode Guide:
All United States Series, 1949–1996

Television Westerns Episode Guide

All United States Series, 1949–1996

HARRIS M. LENTZ III

McFarland & Company, Inc., Publishers
Jefferson, North Carolina, and London

Harris M. Lentz III is also the author of numerous major reference books published by McFarland over more than 25 years, on such topics as assassinations, heads of states and governments, volcanos, feature films, television westerns, and professional wrestlers.

The present work is a reprint of the library bound edition of Television Westerns Episode Guide: All United States Series, 1949–1996, *first published in 1997 by McFarland.*

LIBRARY OF CONGRESS CATALOGUING-IN-PUBLICATION DATA

Lentz, Harris M., III
Television westerns episode guide : all United States series, 1949–1996 / Harris M. Lentz III.
p. cm.
Includes bibliographical references and index.

ISBN 978-0-7864-7386-1
softcover : acid free paper ∞

1. Westerns (Television programs)—United States—Catalogs.
I. Title.
PN1992.8.W4L46   2012
791.43'6278—dc21   97-10085

BRITISH LIBRARY CATALOGUING DATA ARE AVAILABLE

© 1997 Harris M. Lentz III. All rights reserved

No part of this book may be reproduced or transmitted in any form or by any means, electronic or mechanical, including photocopying or recording, or by any information storage and retrieval system, without permission in writing from the publisher.

On the cover: Dan Blocker, Lorne Greene, Michael Landon of *Bonanza*, 1959-1973; John Hart of *The Lone Ranger*, 1949-1957; Amanda Blake and Milburn Stone of *Gunsmoke*, 1955-1975 (all Photofest)

Manufactured in the United States of America

McFarland & Company, Inc., Publishers
Box 611, Jefferson, North Carolina 28640
www.mcfarlandpub.com

This book is dedicated to
Dr. and Mrs. Joe Garbarini

Acknowledgments

Special thanks go to Francis M. Nevins, who graciously provided me with much information on many of the more difficult series. Many thanks also to my mother, Helene Lentz, and my friends Tony Pruitt, Larry Tauber and Carla Clark. Also thanks to Fred Davis and the fine folks at the Memphis Film Festival, Bill Anchors at Epi-Log, and all my friends at Berretta's Spike and Rail. I am also grateful to Casey Jones, Laurie Graham, Jason Wilson, Jim Champ, Christin Augyes, DeAnna Scott, Bettye Dawson, Wesley Phillips, Jeff, Steve & Rusty Tackett, Patty Peterson, Tara Mann, Louis & Vicki Berretta, Bud Greene, Bobby Matthews, Kent Nelson, Jay Kelley, John Kelley, Mark & Nina Heffington, Paul Geary, Doy L. Daniels, Jr., Anne Taylor, Scott Graves, Joy Martin, John Hoffman and Tom Walters.

Table of Contents

Acknowledgments	vi
Introduction	1
Bibliography	3

Adventures of Brisco County, Jr.	7
The Adventures of Champion	8
The Adventures of Rin Tin Tin	9
The Alaskans	16
Alias Smith and Jones	18
Annie Oakley	20
Barbary Coast	24
Bat Masterson	25
Bearcats!	31
Best of the West	31
Big Hawaii	32
The Big Valley	32
Black Saddle	38
Bonanza	40
Boots and Saddles	60
Bordertown	61
Branded	61
Brave Eagle	64
Bret Maverick	64
Broken Arrow	65
Bronco	68
Buckskin	72
Buffalo Bill, Jr.	74
Cade's County	75
The Californians	77
Centennial	80
Cheyenne	81
The Chisholms	87
Cimarron City	87
Cimarron Strip	89
Circus Boy	90
The Cisco Kid	92
Cliffhangers — The Secret Empire	99
Colt .45	100
Cowboy G-Men	103
Cowboy in Africa	104
The Cowboys	106
Custer	106
The Dakotas	107
Daniel Boone (1960)	108
Daniel Boone (1964)	108
Davy Crockett	116
Death Valley Days	117
The Deputy	131
Desperado	134
Destry	134
Dirty Sally	135
Dr. Quinn, Medicine Woman	135
Dundee and the Culhane	140
Dusty's Trail	141
Empire	141
F Troop	143
Father Murphy	145
Frontier	146
Frontier Circus	148
Frontier Doctor	149
Fury	150
The Gabby Hayes Show	155
The Gambler	155
The Gene Autry Show	155
Great Adventure	159
Gun Shy	160
The Guns of Will Sonnett	160
Gunslinger	162
Gunsmoke	163
Have Gun Will Travel	194
Hawkeye	205
Hawkeye and the Last of the Mohicans	207
Hec Ramsey	208
Here Come the Brides	209
The High Chaparral	211
Hondo	216
Hopalong Cassidy	217
Hotel De Paree	219
How the West Was Won	220
Iron Horse	222
Jefferson Drum	224
Jim Bowie	226
Johnny Ringo	229
Judge Roy Bean	231
Kit Carson	232
Klondike	235
Kung Fu	236
Lancer	239
Laramie	242
Laredo	248
Lash of the West	251
The Law of the Plainsman	251
Lawman	252
Lazarus Man	259
Legend	260
The Legend of Jesse James	261
Life and Legend of Wyatt Earp	262
The Life and Times of Grizzly Adams	273
Little House: A New Beginning	274
Little House on the Prairie	275
The Lone Ranger	282
The Loner	293
Lonesome Dove: The Series	294
Lonesome Dove: The Outlaw Years	295
A Man Called Shenandoah	296
Man from Blackhawk	297
Man Without a Gun	299
The Marshal of Gunsight Pass	301

Table of Contents

Maverick	301	
The Men from Shiloh	308	
The Monroes	309	
My Friend Flicka	310	
Nakia	312	
Ned Blessing: The Story of My Life and Times	313	
The New Land	313	
Nichols	313	
Nine Lives of Effego Baca	314	
Northwest Passage	315	
The Oregon Trail	316	
The Outcasts	317	
The Outlaws (1960)	318	
Outlaws (1987)	321	
Overland Trail	321	
Paradise	322	
Pistols 'n' Petticoats	325	
Pony Express	326	
The Quest	327	
The Range Riders	327	
Rango	331	
Rawhide	332	
The Rebel	343	
Redigo	346	
The Restless Gun	347	
The Rifleman	351	
Riverboat	359	
The Road West	361	
Rough Riders	363	
The Rounders	365	
The Roy Rogers Show	365	
The Saga of Andy Burnett	370	
Sara	370	
Sergeant Preston of the Yukon	371	
Shane	374	
Shotgun Slade	375	
Sky King	376	
Stagecoach West	379	
Steve Donovan, Western Marshal	381	
Stoney Burke	383	
Stories of the Century	384	
Sugarfoot	386	
Tales of the Texas Rangers	389	
Tales of Wells Fargo	392	
The Tall Man	401	
Tate	405	
Temple Houston	405	
The Texan	407	
Texas John Slaughter	411	
Tomahawk	411	
Tombstone Territory	412	
Trackdown	416	
The Travels of Jaimie McPheeters	420	
26 Men	421	
Two Faces West	424	
Union Pacific	425	
The Virginian	426	
Wagon Train	438	
Walker — Texas Ranger	454	
Wanted — Dead or Alive	457	
The Westerner	461	
Whispering Smith	462	
Wichita Town	463	
Wide Country	464	
Wild Bill Hickok	466	
The Wild, Wild West	471	
Wildside	477	
Wrangler	477	
Yancy Derringer	478	
Young Dan'l Boone	479	
Young Maverick	480	
The Young Pioneers	480	
Young Riders	480	
Zane Grey Theater	483	
Zorro (1957)	491	
Zorro (1990)	495	
Zorro and Son	495	

Storyline Index 496
Personnel Index 499

Introduction

The scope of this book begins from the earliest days of episodic television in the late 1940s and early 1950s, covering such series as *The Lone Ranger* and *The Roy Rogers Show*, through the glory days of the television Western a decade later where such series as *Rawhide*, *Wagon Train* and *The Virginian* ruled the airwaves. The book also covers the lean years of the 1970s and 1980s, where only a handful of Westerns such as *Centennial* and *Paradise* debuted, through 1996, where a few Westerns such as *Dr. Quinn, Medicine Woman* and *Lazarus Man* remain on the air.

Many of the series covered in this book, such as *Bonanza*, *Gunsmoke* and *Maverick*, have retained their popularity in syndication over a quarter-of-a-century after the completion of their network run. Others, such as *26 Men* and *Shotgun Slade*, have languished in obscurity, remembered by only their most loyal fans. I have indexed 180 series in this work, both memorable and largely forgotten. The series covered are, for the most part, traditional Westerns, set in the American West in the latter half of the 19th century. These series dealt with the exploits of the men and women who were instrumental in the expansion of the American frontier. Other series which contain the traditional trappings of Westerns, though with a shift in locale, are also included. These series' settings range from the Alaskan gold rush (*Klondike*), to a cattle ranch in Hawaii (*Big Hawaii*) to an African game preserve (*Cowboy in Africa*). The time frames of these series also vary, including series dedicated to the early pioneer days (*Daniel Boone*) and the French and Indian War (*Hawkeye*), to such contemporary dramas as *Cade's County* and *Walker, Texas Ranger*. Though the series covered are primarily dramas, a few sitcoms that use the West as their backdrop are also included. These shows included many of the conventions found in Westerns, such as settlers, Indians and expanding frontiers, and seem to fit nicely with the scope of the book. I have included those series originally shown in syndication as well as network series. I have not included tele-films, unless the film was a pilot or follow-up to a series otherwise included or was itself part of a series (e.g., *Desperado* and *Kenny Roger's The Gambler*). I have also omitted specials and Western-themed episodes of non-Western series.

I have followed a consistent format with each series covered in this book. The series are arranged alphabetically. Each entry opens with a listing of the broadcast history of the series, including original network, day and time. This is followed by the regular cast listing and a brief premise of the series. I have then listed the individual episodes of the series, including title, original air date, leading guest stars and a brief synopsis of the episode. Some series, particularly those that originally aired in syndication, proved difficult to obtain a large amount of information on, and a few episodes will have "Title Unknown" in place of the title, when that information could not be discerned.

I hope that this book will not only serve its reference function but will also both rekindle fond memories among viewers who have been long-time television Western fans and stir interest in readers unfamiliar with a particular series.

Bibliography

Books

Adams, Les & Buck Rainey. *Shoot-Em-Ups*. New Rochelle, NY: Arlington House, 1978.

Anderson, Robert. *The Kung Fu Book*. Las Vegas, NV: Pioneer Books, 1994.

Barabas, SuzAnne, and Gabor Barabas. *Gunsmoke*. Jefferson, NC: McFarland, 1990.

Brooks, Tim. *The Complete Director of Prime Time TV Stars*. New York: Ballantine Books, 1987.

Buscombe, Edward, ed. *The BFI Companion to the Western*. New York: Atheneum, 1988.

Calder, Janni. *There Must Be a Lone Ranger*. London: Hamish Hamilton, 1974.

Erickson, Hal. *Syndicated Television*. Jefferson, NC: McFarland, 1989.

Gianakos, Larry James. *Television Drama Series Programming: A Comprehensive Chronicle, 1947–1959*. Metuchen, NJ: Scarecrow, 1980.

_____. _____, *1959–75*. Metuchen, NJ: Scarecrow, 1978.

_____. _____, *1975–80*. Metuchen, NJ: Scarecrow, 1981.

_____. _____, *1980–82*. Metuchen, NJ: Scarecrow, 1983.

_____. _____, *1982–84*. Metuchen, NJ: Scarecrow, 1987.

_____. _____, *1984–86*. Metuchen, NJ: Scarecrow, 1992.

Goldberg, Lee. *Unsold Television Pilots, 1955–89*. Jefferson, NC: McFarland, 1990.

Hardy, Phil. *The Western*. Woodstock, NY: Overlook Press, 1991.

Lovece, Frank. *The Television Yearbook*. New York: Perigee Books, 1992.

McDonald, Archie P., ed. *Shooting Stars*. Bloomington: Indiana University Press, 1987.

McNeil, Alex. *Total Television*. New York: Penguin Books, 1991.

Maltin, Leonard, ed. *Movie and Video Guide 1995*. New York: Signet Books, 1994.

Marill, Alvin H. *Movies Made for Television*. Westport, CT: Arlington House, 1980.

Parks, Rita. *The Western Hero in Film and Television*. Ann Arbor: UMI Research Press, 1982.

Parish, James Robert. *Actors' Television Credits 1950–1972*. Metuchen, NJ: Scarecrow, 1973.

Phillips, Robert W. *Roy Rogers: A Biography, Radio History, Television Career Chronicle, Discography, Filmography, Comicography, Merchandising and Advertising History, Collectibles Description, Bibliography and Index*. Jefferson, NC: McFarland, 1995.

Rothel, David. *The Gene Autry Book*. Madison, NC: Empire Publishing, 1988.

_____. *The Roy Rogers Book*. Madison, NC: Empire Publishing, 1987.

Terrace, Vincent. *Encyclopedia of Television Series, Pilots and Specials, 1937–1973*. New York: Zoetrope, 1986.

_____. *Encyclopedia of Television Series, Pilots and Specials, 1974–1984*. New York: Zoetrope, 1986.

Walker, John, ed. *Halliwell's Filmgoer's and Video Viewer's Companion*, 10th Edition. New York: HarperPerennial, 1993.

West, Richard. *Television Westerns: Major and Minor Series, 1946–1978*. Jefferson, NC: McFarland, 1987.

Woolley, Lynn, Robert W. Malsbary & Robert G. Strange, Jr. *Warner Bros. Television*. Jefferson, NC: McFarland, 1985.

Yoggy, Gary A. *Riding the Video Range: The Rise and Fall of the Western on Television*. Jefferson, NC: McFarland, 1995.

Bibliography

Periodicals

Classic Images (Muscatine, Iowa), 1985–.
The Commercial Appeal (Memphis, Tenn.), 1950–.
Epi-Log (Dunlap, Tenn.), 1990–95.
Epi-Log Journal (Dunlap, Tenn), 1992–92.
The New York Times (New York), 1950–.
TV Guide (Radnor, Penn.), 1953–.
Variety (New York), 1950–.

Episode Guide

1. *The Adventures of Brisco County, Jr.*

FOX. 60 minutes. Broadcast history: Friday, 8:00-9:00, Aug. 1993–July 1994.

Regular Cast: Bruce Campbell (Brisco County, Jr.), Julius Carry (Lord Bowler), Christian Clemenson (Socrates Poole).

Premise: This western series, set in the early 1890s, incorporated elements of fantasy and science fiction. Bounty hunter Brisco County, Jr., with the help of associates Lord Bowler and Socrates Poole, tries to hunt down the outlaws, led by the ruthless John Bly, who murdered Brisco's U.S. Marshal father. During the course of his quest he comes across a mystical orb that has strange powers. He and Bly often cross paths while attempting to recover the orb.

The Episodes

1.1 *Pilot.* Aug. 27, 1993. GS: Dan Gerrity, John Astin, Kelly Rutherford, Anne Tremko, Billy Drago, John Pyper-Ferguson, R. Lee Ermey, M.C. Gainey, Bert Remsen, Stuart Whitman, Rayford Barnes, Paul Brinegar, James Drury, Robert Fuller, Bill Bolender, Charles Noland, Mark Twogood, James Hong, Rick Dean, Peter Bromilow, Terry Funk. Brisco County, Jr. turns bounty hunter and agrees to hunt down the John Bly gang, who were responsible for the death of his lawman father.

1.2 *The Orb Scholar.* Sept. 3, 1993. GS: Kelly Rutherford, Brandon Maggart, Pat Skipper, Robert Picardo, Billy Drago, Ray Bumatai, Tom Simmons, Dewey Weber, Herman Poppe, David Youse. Brisco follows a lead on John Bly supplied by a childhood friend, and runs across a scholarly man in Colorado who somehow has gained possession of the orb.

1.3 *No Man's Land.* Sept. 10, 1993. GS: John Astin, Denise Crosby, Denis Forest, Judson Scott, Jeremy Roberts, Tracey Walter, Brook Susan Parker, Corey Everson, Cameo Kneuer, Tegan West, Jennifer McDonald, Sharren J. Mitchell, Andrew A. Rolfes, Thais Springer. Brisco follows the bank-robbing Swill brothers into No-Man's Land, an isolated community where only women live and work. Meanwhile, Lord Bowler is hired to find the missing prototype for a mobile battlewagon.

1.4 *Brisco in Jalisco.* Sept. 17, 1993. GS: Michael DeLorenzo, Miguel Perez, John Pyper-Ferguson, Kelly Rutherford, Frank Ronan, Paul Brinegar, Robert Fuller, Scott Lincoln, Albert Vasquez, Maraida Rios. Brisco and Socrates cross the border on the trail of a load of stolen guns, and find Dixie and themselves caught in the middle of the crossfire between a Mexican general and a revolutionary and his followers.

1.5 *Socrates' Sister.* Sept. 24, 1993. GS: John Astin, Judith Hoag, John Pyper-Ferguson, William Russ, Ashby Adams, Al Pugliese, Christopher Wynne, George "Buck" Flowers, Yvette Nipar, Owen Bush. Brisco rounds up a smooth talking crook, but things get a little sticky when Socrates' sister shows up to defend the scoundrel.

1.6 *Riverboat.* Oct. 1, 1993. GS: Xander Berkeley, Monte Russell, Don Stroud, John Shumski, John Pyper-Ferguson, Kelly Rutherford, Brandon Bluhm, Charles H. Hyman, Robert Prentiss, Charles Hutchins, Glenn Taranto. Brisco rides to the rescue in Louisiana when Socrates runs afoul of a riverboat gambler.

1.7 *Pirates.* Oct. 8, 1993. GS: Andrew Divoff, Robert O'Reilly, John Walcutt, Janel Moloney, Adam Wylie, James Greene, Yvette Nipar, Josh Lozoff, Michael Denney, Sarah Kim Heinberg, Josep Pilato. Brisco and Bowler pursues a displaced Caribbean pirate in the desert.

1.8 *Senior Spirit.* Oct. 15, 1993. GS: John Astin, Billy Drago, Jason Marsden, Steve Rankin, Yvette Nipar, James DiStefano, Adrian Sparks, Kort Falkenberg, Barbara Pilavin. Brisco receives some help from his late father as he tries to rescue the kidnapped son of a robber baron from John Bly.

1.9 *Brisco for the Defense.* Oct. 22, 1993. GS: Edward Blatchford, Felton Perry, Jensen Daggett, Carol Huston, Tony Jay, John Bellucci, Duane Tucker, Mark Bramhall, Carmen Filpi, James Harlow, Jack R. Orend. Brisco is drafted to defend an old friend, a doctor accused of murdering a prominent citizen in a Wild West town.

1.10 *Showdown.* Oct. 29, 1993. GS: Jessica Tuck, John P. Ryan, Richard Venture, Michael Bowen, Anthony Starke, John Hawkes, Vincent Klyn, James Staley, Holly Gagnier, Billie Worley. Brisco returns to his home town to help his childhood friend and his father defeat a cattle baron.

1.11 *Deep in the Heart of Dixie.* Nov. 5, 1993. GS: Kelly Rutherford, David Warner, Andrea Parker, James Greene, Ashby Adams, Deke Anderson, Joseph Anthony, Janet Rotblatt, Jose Perez, Michael Lowry. Brisco and Dixie find romance while trying to lose an assassin in hot pursuit of Dixie, who has incriminating evidence against a big-time politician.

1.12 *Crystal Hawks.* Nov. 12, 1993. GS: Sheena Easton, M.C. Gainey, Billy Drago, Rayford Barnes, Tom Dahlgren, James Gleason, Patrick Fischler, John Mueller, Adrienne Hampton. Brisco finds the tables turned when a pretty bounty hunter picks up his trail so she can bring him in for a killing.

1.13 *Iron Horses.* Nov. 19, 1993. GS: Don Michael Paul, Josh Richman, John Aston, James Greene, Geoffrey Blake, Brian Cousins, Dennis Fimple, Cameo Kneuer, Corey Everson, Kevin Lowe. Brisco and Bowler are assigned to catch a gang that is tracking the orb on stolen prototype motorcycles.

1.14 *Mail Order Brides.* Dec. 10, 1993. GS: Elizabeth Barondes, Romy Rosemont, Denis Forest, Jeremy Roberts, Tracey Walter, Kim Walker, Nan Martin, Abraham Alvarez, John Vargas. Outlaw brothers get into hot water with Brisco and Bowler when they steal the dowries of three mail-order brides.

1.15 *AKA Kansas.* Dec. 17, 1993. GS: Kelly Rutherford, Christopher Rich, Obba Babatunde, Andrea Parker, Ashby Adams, Robert Keith, Peter Dennis, Andreas Renell, Vaughn Armstrong, Zachary Mott. While undercover, Brisco learns that his girlfriend's ex-husband not only wants to steal government property, but also has his sights on Dixie.

1.16 *Bounty Hunter's Convention.* Jan. 7, 1994. GS: Jonathan Schaech, Clare Wren, Clement von Franckenstein, Morgan Woodward, Ian Ogilvy, Rex Linn, Luis Contreras, J.G. Hertzler, David Youse. Brisco, Bowler, and Socrates attend a bounty hunter convention to pool ideas about catching John Bly. They are soon involved in a mystery when the other bounty hunters start turning up dead.

1.17 *Fountain of Youth.* Jan. 14, 1994. GS: Billy Drago, Terri Ivens, Brandon Maggart, Wolf Larson, Dan Blom, Blake Bailey, James Hong, Greg Thomsen. Nothing is quite as it appears to be when Brisco and Bowler respond to what the think is a message from Prof. Coles and end up on a collision course with John Bly.

1.18 *Hard Rock.* Feb. 4, 1994. GS: Jo Nell Kennedy, Nicolas Surovy, Jeff Phillips, Gary Hudson, Hawthorne James, William Frankfather. Brisco and Bowler try to stop a man from harassing Bowler's old flame, who resists his attempt to extort protection money for her cafe in a town called Hard Rock.

1.19 *The Brooklyn Dodgers.* Feb. 11, 1994. GS: Michael Cade, Mercedes Alicia McNab, Clark Brolly, Kenneth Tigar, Ryan Cutrona, Scott Harlan, Sam Anderson, Devon O'Brien, Melissa Berger, Clyde Kusatsu. Brisco and Bowler escort a pair of urchins from Brooklyn to San Francisco, where the kids are headed to stake a claim on a gold mine. But they have to dodge a ruthless New York gang to do it.

1.20 *Bye Bly.* Feb. 18, 1994. GS: Melanie Smith, Billy Drago, Stewart Bick, Richard Herd, Kevin Lowe, Dennis Cockrum, Ryan Thomas Johnson. A figure from the future warns Brisco that John Bly is going to escape from his orb prison, and only Brisco can erase the dark chapter that is fated for the world.

1.21 *Ned Zed.* March 13, 1994. GS: Casey Siemaszko, Brenda Bakke, Ray Bumatai, James Drury, Tom McCleister, Charles Bailey-Gates, Michael Boston, Matt McColm, Vince Melocchi. Brisco pursues bank robber Ned Zed to the cold Northwest, where he encounters an old flame and a bear of a bad guy out for revenge.

1.22 *Stagecoach.* April 1, 1994. GS: Lisa Collins, Timothy Leary, Aries Spears, John Pyper-Ferguson, Debra Jo Rupp, Shelley Malil, Richard McGonagle, Robert Covarrubias, Pat Millicano. Brisco boards a stagecoach to escort a captured spy to the Mexican border for a prisoner exchange. To complicate matters there is an assassin along for the ride.

1.23 *Wild Card.* April 8, 1994. GS: Kelly Rutherford, Elaine Hendrix, Jeff Phillips, Louis Giambalvo, Paul Ben-Victor, Peter Dobson, Cosmo Canale. Dixie and her sister Dolly get Brisco dealt into a high-risk game against a family mob that wants to control the burgeoning gambling business in Reno.

1.24 *And Baby Makes Three.* April 22, 1994. GS: Tzi Ma, Kelly Rutherford, James Hong, John Pyper-Ferguson, Jeff Phillips, Peter Dennis, David Youse, Francois Chau, Gary Armagnac, Craig Ryan Ng. Brisco has a personal vendetta against a warlord who intends to kidnap the infant heir to the Chinese throne.

1.25 *Bad Luck Betty.* April 29, 1994. GS: Jeff Phillips, Annabella Price, Jane Sibbett, Jeff Doucette, Edith Fields, Don Keith Opper, Morgan Hunter, Dana Craig, Adam Hendershott. Socrates has an unwelcome birthday surprise when he is kidnapped by a man who is supposed to be dead.

1.26 *High Treason* **Part One.** May 13, 1994. GS: John Astin, John Pyper-Ferguson, Terry Bradshaw, Michael Fairman, Raye Birk, Andrew Hill Newman, Macon McCalman, Ely Pouget, Jeff Phillips, Gary Hudson. Brisco and Bowler are tried for high treason after trying to help the Army retrieve an heiress kidnapped by Mexican revolutionaries.

1.27 *High Treason* **Part Two.** May 20, 1994. GS: John Astin, John Pyper-Ferguson, Terry Bradshaw, Michael Fairman, Ely Pouget, Jeff Phillips, Gary Hudson, Victor Rivers, Ken Norton, Jr., Carl Banks, Jim Harbaugh, Richard Herd. Brisco and Bowler escape execution. Meanwhile, on secret orders for General Quarry, Colonel March leads an elite team of horsemen to hunt them down.

2. *The Adventures of Champion*

CBS. 30 min. Broadcast history: Friday, 7:30–8:00, Sept. 1955–March 1956.

Regular Cast: Barry Curtis (Ricky North), Jim Bannon (Sandy North), Francis McDonald (Will Calhoun), Ewing Mitchell (Sheriff Powers).

Premise: This series, set in the Southwest of the 1880s, dealt with the adventures of 12-year-old Ricky North, and his stallion Champion, the Wonder Horse.

The Episodes

2.1 *The Saddle Tramp.* Sept. 23, 1955. GS: William Tannen, Chris Alcaide.

2.2 *Crossroad Trail.* Sept. 30, 1955.

2.3 *Salted Ground.* Oct. 7, 1955. GS: Hal K. Dawson, Tristram Coffin, George J. Lewis, Melinda Plowman. Sandy, Ricky and Champion rescue a girl from a runaway buckboard. Later Sandy and Ricky come upon two men salting some ground and realize the girl's father is the victim of a land swindle.

2.4 *The Medicine Man Mystery.* Oct. 15, 1955. GS: Myron Healey, Harry Harvey, Sr., House Peters, Jr., Johnny Dallas. Sandy and Champion come to the rescue when Ricky's interest in a medicine show ventriloquist's dummy entangles him with jewel thieves.

2.5 *Lost River.* Oct. 23, 1955. GS: Ed Hinton, Rick Vallin, Edna Holland, Rhodes Reason.

2.6 *Renegade Stallion.* Oct. 29, 1955. GS: William Tannen, Chris Alcaide, Rex Lease. When an old prospector is found trampled to death by a herd of wild horses, the sheriff believes Champion is responsible. Ricky and Sandy try to save the stallion.

2.7 *Canyon of Wanted Men.* Nov. 7, 1955. GS: Tristram Coffin, George J. Lewis, Melinda Plowman, John Day. Ricky and Champion take a hand when an unscrupulous horse trader tries to get Sandy to sign a petition that would enble the trader to round up a wild horse herd and make a fat profit.

2.8 *Challenge of the West.* Nov. 8, 1955. Ricky and Champion try to clear an escaped convict's son who is accused of stealing money from Sandy.

2.9 *The Outlaw's Secret.* Nov. 15, 1955. GS: Leonard Penn, Howard J. Negley, Glenn Strange, Gregg Barton, Charlie Hayes, Grace Field. Ricky and Champion come upon a dying thief, shot by Sandy during a stagecoach holdup, who confesses to the robbery and claims he was acting under orders from a banker who was traveling in the coach.

2.10 *Hangman's Noose.* Nov. 22, 1955. GS: Hank Patterson, Frank Fenton, Keith Richards, Mauritz Hugo, I. Stanford Jolley, Stanley Blystone. Ricky and Champion uncover a pair of buried oil-soaked boots and find themselves the targets of the criminals who killed a rancher and framed a neighbor for the crime.

2.11 *King of the Rodeo.* Nov. 29, 1955. GS: Ed Hinton, Rick Vallin, Edna Holland, Rhodes Reason, Tex Palmer. Sandy and Ricky try to free Champion, who has been captured by the owner of a traveling carnival and offered as a prize to whoever can ride him.

2.12 *A Bugle for Ricky.* Dec. 6, 1955. GS: Harry Lauter, Edgar Dearing, Lane Bradford, Gregg Palmer, Terry Frost, John Parrish. When Ricky, Rebel and Champion are trapped in a barn by bank robbers, Ricky tries to attract help by using his bugle to blow a cavalry call.

2.13 *The Stone Heart.* Dec. 13, 1955. GS: James Best, Bill Henry, Don C. Harvey, Barbara Bestar. When Ricky and Champion discover a wounded man and return with his sister, all three are taken captive by a band of counterfeiters.

2.14 *The Deer Hunters.* Dec. 20, 1955. GS: Leonard Benn, Howard J. Ngeley, Glenn Strange, Gregg Barton, Kenne Duncan. Ricky and Champion incur the wrath of deer hunters from a railroad camp when they rescue a trapped fawn.

2.15 *The Golden Hoax.* Dec. 27, 1955. Ricky and Sandy become involved with stagecoach robbers after Champion discovers a deserted mine shaft in which the thieves hide their loot.

2.16 *Johnny Hands-Up.* Jan. 3, 1956. Ricky and Sandy join forces with Champion and Rebel in a scheme to clear the name of a young marshal who is being blamed for a mistake his predecessor made.

2.17 *Black Kachina.* Jan. 10, 1956. Ricky, Sandy and Champion fight a wicked medicine man who is trying to incite the Indians to war by holding the tribal chief as a hostage.

2.18 *Mystery Mountain.* Jan. 17, 1956. GS: Walter Reed, Duncan Richardson, Fred Sherman, Duane Thorsen, John McKee, Bob Woodward. Ricky, Sandy and Champion try to help a bright, but naive, young visitor from the East who has been fooled into performing gold assays for a swindler.

2.19 *Rails West.* Jan. 26, 1956. GS: Roy Barcroft, Mark Dana, Robin Short, Buzz Henry, John Cason. After Sandy and Ricky persuade the railroad to bypass the valley where Chamipon and his herd live, they have to fight some unscrupulous men who have found traces of gold in the valley and are trying to claim the land for themselves.

2.20 *The Real Unfriendly Ghost.* Feb. 1, 1956. Ricky, Sandy and Champion become involved with the eccentric sole resident of an empty town, a vanished politician and an apparent ghost.

2.21 *Andrew and the Deadly Double.* Feb. 13, 1956. GS: Bill Henry, Don C. Harvey, Bob Bice, Mary Jane Saunders, James Best, Jack Mulhall.

2.22 *Bad Men of the Valley.* Feb. 14, 1956. GS: Morgan Jones, Sally Fraser, Raphael Bennett, John Cliff.

2.23 *The Return of Red Cloud.* Feb. 24, 1956. GS: Alan Wells, Glenn Strange, Henry Rowland, Marshall Bradford, John War Eagle, Bob Swan, Mike Ragan.

2.24 *Brand of the Lawless.* Feb. 27, 1956. GS: Ann Doran, Walter Reed, Hank Patterson, Duane Thorsen, Jack Daly, Belle Mitchell, Sam Flint.

2.25 *The Die-Hards.* March 3, 1956. GS: Roy Barcroft, Bill Phipps, Kathleen Crowley, Mark Dana, Buzz Henry, Robin Short, Charlie Hayes, John Cason.

2.26 *Calhoun Rides Again.* March 3, 1956. GS: John Damler, Larry Hudson, Steve Conte. The tale-spinning old saddle tramp Will Calhoun returns to help Ricky, Sandy and Champion capture a gang of bank robbers.

The Adventures of Jim Bowie
see *Jim Bowie*

3. *The Adventures of Rin Tin Tin*

ABC. 30 min. Broadcast history: Friday, 7:30–8:00, Oct. 1954–Aug. 1959.

Regular Cast: Lee Aaker (Rusty), James L. Brown (Lt. Rip Masters), Joe Sawyer (Sergeant Aloysius "Biff" O'Hara), Rand Brooks (Corporal Randy Boone).

Premise: Rusty and his German Shepherd, Rin Tin Tin, are unofficially adopted by Lt. Rip Masters at Fort Apache in 1880s Arizona. The series depicts the exploits of Rusty and Rin Tin Tin with the 101st Cavalry.

The Episodes

3.1 *Meet Rin Tin Tin.* Oct. 15, 1954. GS: John Hoyt. U.S. Cavalry troops find Rin Tin Tin and his young master Rusty abandoned after an Indian raid. The men bring the boy and his dog back to Fort Apache with them but fear that Col. Barker, a strict disciplinarian who will arrive soon at the fort, will not allow the two to stay.

3.2 *Wolf Cry.* Oct. 22, 1954. GS: Leo Gordon, John Pickard. Rusty keeps pretending that the fort is being attacked, and his false alerts keep Lt. Masters busy. Finally, when the boy does witness a real crime, nobody believes him.

3.3 *Rin Tin Tin and the Flaming Forest.* Oct. 29, 1954. GS: Tim Considine, Roy Roberts. Tom Rogers, a trapper living near Fort Apache, has a wife and son living in Boston. When Mrs. Rogers dies, the boy Sydney comes West. Sydney meets but doesn't like Rusty and Rinty.

3.4 *Rin Tin Tin and the Raging River.* Nov. 5, 1954. Rusty and Rinty go along when the Fort Apache cavalry troops heads for Rifle River to blow up a clogged dam and release the water supply.

3.5 *Killer Cat.* Nov. 12, 1954. Rusty and Rinty are out searching for a stray mare when a mountain lion leaps on the boy.

3.6 *The Education of Corporal Rusty.* Nov. 19, 1954. GS: Robert Burton, John Cason. Rin Tin Tin takes an immediate dislike to the traveling teacher Lt. Masters enlists to give schooling to Rusty. The teacher seems to know a smuggler imprisoned in Masters' stockade.

3.7 *Rin Tin Tin and the Apache Chief.* Nov. 26, 1954. GS: Karen Greene, Fred Foote. Rusty's little friend, Susan, persuades him to leave Fort Apache.

3.8 *Rin Tin Tin, Outlaw.* Dec. 3, 1954. GS: Harry Hickox. A crooked trader is faced with exposure by an army investigator. He conceives a plan to save himself by getting ride of the man and putting the blame on Rinty.

3.9 *The Outcast of Fort Apache.* Dec. 10, 1954. GS: Richard Emory. Rusty's good friend, Lt. Masters, is accused of cowardice and drummed out of the Army because he refuses to lead his troops against a gang of horse smugglers.

3.10 *Rin Tin Tin and the Ancient Mariner.* Dec. 17, 1954. GS: William Fawcett. Rinty finds Capt. Longey wandering around on the desert deliriously muttering about a buried treasure. The man is brought to Fort Apache.

The Adventures of Rin Tin Tin

3.11 *Rin Tin Tin and the New Recruit.* Dec. 24, 1954. Rinty helps a new recruit adjust to life on the base.

3.12 *Rin Tin Tin and the Gold Bullion.* Dec. 31, 1954. A notorious gunman wins Rusty's friendship by stopping his men from shooting Rinty. Rusty becomes the man's champion without realizing the real reason behind the kind act.

3.13 *Blood Brothers.* Jan. 7, 1955. Rinty and Rusty save an Indian chief's son from a bear and help stop an Indian war.

3.14 *Rin Tin Tin and the Sacred Lance.* Jan. 14, 1955. Rusty is attacked by renegade Indians.

3.15 *Shifting Sands.* Jan. 21, 1955. Two thieves kill their brother when they learn that he has been cheating them out of some holdup loot. They then frame another man for the murder and organize a lynch mob to do away with him. But they reckon without Rusty, Rinty and Lt. Masters.

3.16 *Rusty Plays Cupid.* Jan. 28, 1955. Rusty is afraid he will be sent away from the fort to a proper home. In order to provide himself with a family to live with, the boy tries to find a wife for his pal, Lt. Rip Masters.

3.17 *Rin Tin Tin and the Medicine Man.* Feb. 4, 1955. A medicine man and his young daughter come to Fort Apache for refuge after being pursued by three outlaws.

3.18 *The Babe in the Woods.* Feb. 11, 1955. GS: Myron Healey, Roy Erwin, Connie Ceyon. Jesse Harkness and his two henchmen kill a miner to get possession of his claim. The claim papers however, are hidden on the victim's baby, who is found by Rinty in the woods.

3.19 *The Eagle's Nest.* Feb. 18, 1955. Since Rusty is an orphan, and his birth date is unknown, the soldiers at the fort decide to give him a surprise party on Lt. Masters' birthday. Rusty, meanwhile, is busy finding a suitable present for Rip.

3.20 *Rusty Resigns from the Army.* Feb. 25, 1955. GS: William Forrest, Edmund Hashim. While leading a reconnoitering patrol, Lt. Rip Masters is captured by Apache Indians. Upset by his friends capture, Rusty decides to resign from the army.

3.21 *The Legacy of Sean O'Hara.* March 4, 1955. GS: Lyle Talbot, Bobby Watson, Burt Mustin, Jameson Penrose. Soon after Sgt. O'Hara inherits a ranch from his uncle Sean, two desperadoes try to kill him. He and Lt. Masters ride to the ranch in an attempt to find the outlaws.

3.22 *The Barber of Seville.* March 11, 1955. GS: Nestor Paiva. The barber of San Carlos has been saving money to build an opera house in the town. The owner of the gambling house is opposed to it and tries to frighten the barber by setting fire to his shop.

3.23 *The Blushing Brides.* March 18, 1955. GS: Steve Conte, Edith Leslie. Rusty, Lt. Masters and Sgt. O'Hara head a patrol assigned to escort a group of girls through dangerous territory.

3.24 *The Guilty One.* March 25, 1955. GS: John Dierkes. Rusty and Rinty help a famous western marshal to recapture an outlaw prisoner.

3.25 *The Magic Box.* April 1, 1955. A news reporter who is writing a story on the Apache peace treaty, lets Rusty take some pictures with his camera. The photos turn out to be both valuable and dangerous.

3.26 *The Bandit Kingdom.* April 8, 1955. GS: Rudolfo Hoyos, Jr. An ambitious rancher, who dreams of a private kingdom in California, tries to enlist the aid of Lt. Masters.

3.27 *Rin Tin Tin and the Printer's Devil.* April 15, 1955. GS: Mildred von Holland, Robert Burton. A widowed newspaper publisher is the victim of a ruthless rival newspaper owner until Rusty and Rinty come to her aid.

3.28 *The Dead Man's Gold.* April 22, 1955. GS: Millie Doff, Lane Bradford. The widow of a gold prospector finds a clue to the location of his gold mine among his effects. She persuades Lt. Masters to help her find the lode.

3.29 *The Ghost Town.* April 29, 1955. An aged marshal is the victim of outlaws who want control of his property.

3.30 *O'Hara Gets Busted.* May 6, 1955. GS: Michael Carr. Rusty gets a practical lesson on the importance of obeying orders in the Army.

3.31 *The Bounty Hunters.* May 13, 1955. GS: Ed Hinton. Attacked by a mountain lion, Rinty is rescued by a doctor, who bandages the dog and then hurriedly rides away. It is later learned that the man is wanted for murder.

3.32 *Farewell to Fort Apache.* May 20, 1955. GS: Morris Ankrum, Paul Sorenson. A lawyer has proof that Rusty is really Ronald Barrington, believed killed in an Indian raid. Though Rusty appreciates his new found grandmother, he misses his pals at the fort.

3.33 *The Lost Scotchman.* May 27, 1955. GS: Lumsden Hare, Lee Roberts. Rusty and Rinty accompany a cavalry patrol headed by Lt. Masters. The group finds two prospectors who are searching for a lost gold man.

3.34 *The Lonesome Road.* June 4, 1955. GS: George Berkeley, Frank Sully. While in town with Rusty and Lt. Masters, Rinty is accidentally locked in a boxcar of a train bound for Kansas City.

Season Two

3.35 *The Bugle Call.* Sept. 9, 1955. GS: Ralph Moody, Richard Devon. Sgt. O'Hara and a new field gun are captured by the Indians. Lt. Rip Masters and Rinty set out to find them.

3.36 *Rin Tin Tin Meets Shakespeare.* Sept. 16, 1955. GS: Ian Keith, Myron Healey. When Odds-on O'Connor plots to steal the receipts of the Army widows benefit show, Shakespeare and Rin Tin Tin combine forces in an attempt to foil the plot.

3.37 *The Wild Stallion.* Sept. 23, 1955. GS: Pierre Watkin, Norman Leavitt. Chief, the black stallion leader of a herd of wild horses, is trapped by falling rocks. Rusty and Rinty find the animal in time to save him from an attack by Savage, a rebel horse. But Chief is hurt and under Savage's leadership the herd raids ranches.

3.38 *Rusty Volunteers.* Sept. 30, 1953. GS: Pamela Duncan, Mitchell Lawrence. Lt. Rip Masters poses as the U.S. Ambassador to Mexico to foil a rebel leader. Rip and Rusty join the decoy party on the dangerous trip south of the border.

3.39 *The Poor Little Rich Boy.* Oct. 7, 1955. GS: Ed Hinton, Harvey Grant, Jean Byron, Clancy Cooper, William Phipps. Judge Larrimore, heading a group seeking statehood for Arizona, is opposed by Wesley Parish. Parish provokes an argument with the judge and tries to shoot him.

3.40 *The White Buffalo.* Oct. 14, 1955. GS: Norman Fredric, Hal Hopper, Leo Gordon. The Chiracahua Indians extend an invitation to Rusty and Rinty to hunt in their territory. While they are hunting, Rusty runs into some white trespassers.

3.41 *Rin Tin Tin Meets Mister President*. Oct. 21, 1955. GS: Tony Barrett, Paul Birch. President Grant, on a visit to Mesa Grand, is in danger of being assassinated by a mysterious figure. Rusty and Rinty discover the plot.

3.42 *The Iron Horse*. Oct. 28, 1955. GS: Byron Keith, Brad Johnson, Lane Bradford. An ex-Army man, now one of a gang of desperadoes, plots to steal a gold shipment headed for Fort Apache. His meeting with Rusty and Rin Tin Tin changes his plans.

3.43 *Connecticut Yankees*. Nov. 4, 1955. GS: Dan Barton, Kenny Garcia, Paul Keast. Apaches capture the son of a prominent government official and demand a ransom for his return. Knowing that the money will go for guns, Lt. Rip Masters doesn't want the ransom paid.

3.44 *Higgins Rides Again*. Nov. 11, 1955. GS: William Fawcett, Ian MacDonald, Kenny Garcia. A ghost town is becoming a thriving community. Along with prosperity comes outlaws who plan to run one of their men for marshal. Rusty and Rinty foil the plot.

3.45 *Boone's Wedding Day*. Nov. 18, 1955. GS: J.P. O'Connell, Norman Fredric, Paul Richards, Cliff Carnell. On Boone's wedding day, the bride-to-be is held prisoner by the Cherokee Kid and his bandit gang.

3.46 *Rusty Goes to Town*. Nov. 25, 1955. GS: Lorna Thayer, Mildred Van Hollen, Stanley Andrews, Duane Thorsens. Rusty is appointed honorary mayor of Mesa Grande as first prize in an essay contest. During his term of office he learns a lot about good and bad government.

3.47 *The Lost Patrol*. Dec. 2, 1955; GS: Scott Wilder, Tommy Farrell. The sole survivor of an Indian raid is bitter about the career which has cost his father his life. The boy runs away from the protection of the fort in his resentment against Army life.

3.48 *The Star Witness*. Dec. 9, 1955. GS: Andy Clyde, Sheb Wooley, James Anderson. The star witness against a notorious bank robber sets off for the trial under the protection of Lt. Rip Masters. En route, the party is attacked by outlaws.

3.49 *The Last Chance*. Dec. 16, 1955. GS: Norman Frederic, Paul Richards, Cliff Carnell. A convicted murderer, a boyhood friend of Rip Masters, escapes just before he is to be hanged.

3.50 *Rin Tin Tin and the Christmas Story*. Dec. 23, 1955. GS: Steve Ritch, Serena Sands, George Keymas, Abel Fernandez. Rusty and Rinty join Lt. Rip Masters and his men in their search for a Christmas tree. On their way they meet Tahn-Te and his squaw who are being attacked by their chief and his braves.

3.51 *The Burial Ground*. Dec. 30, 1955. GS: John Cliff, John War Eagle. A gang of outlaws steals the jewelry buried with Apache braves. Lt. Masters tries to keep the Apaches from going on the warpath in revenge.

3.52 *The Missing Heir*. Jan. 13, 1956. GS: Bruce Weil, Mildred Von Hollen, William Bryant. Rusty finds evidence indicating that the son of an Apache chief is really the lost grandson of a wealthy white woman. The boy's re-education is made difficult by the interference of a jealous cousin.

3.53 *Rusty's Romance*. Jan. 20, 1956. GS: William Leslie, Adele Mara, Jim Hayward, Harry Hickox. Rusty tries to help a beautiful actress locate her fiance. The girl regrets providing him with a murder alibi and wants him to stand trial.

3.54 *The Tin Soldier*. Jan. 27, 1956. GS: Russell Johnson, Tony George. Rusty and Rinty are very unhappy when an arrogant lieutenant replaces Rip Masters, who has been ordered to another post. The new lieutenant refuses to allow Rusty and Rinty on patrol.

3.55 *The Big Top*. Feb. 3, 1956. GS: Douglas Fowley, Sheila Bromley, Frances Karath, George Lynn. A scoundrel with his eyes on the proceeds tries to turn one rival circus company against another and Rinty comes to the rescue.

3.56 *Rusty's Bank Account*. Feb. 20, 1956. A notorious robber reforms and becomes manager of the Salt River bank under a different name. Lt. Rip Masters is the only person in town who knows of his past and is impressed by the man's determination to live an honest life. But then the bank is robbed and the manager's identity is revealed, making him the chief suspect.

3.57 *Rin Tin Tin Meets O'Hara's Mother*. Feb. 17, 1956. Jane Darwell, Rico Alaniz, Hal Hopper, Harry Mackin. Sgt. Bif O'Hara's mother arrives at Fort Apache with a band of raging Utes in hot pursuit. Biff is taken prisoner by the tribe and his mother decides to offer herself as an exchange hostage.

3.58 *The Return of the Ancient Mariner*. Feb. 24, 1956. GS: William Fawcett. Treasure hunting Captain Longey returns to Fort Apache.

3.59 *The Failing Light*. March 2, 1956. The only son of an Army doctor is killed in an Indian battle. Seeking revenge, the father comes to Fort Apache and injures the friendly Chief Komawi.

3.60 *Rusty's Mystery*. March 9, 1956. GS: Ernest Sarracino. Capt. Creed, a government emissary, is joined by the Fort's staff in an investigation of Army script counterfeiters.

3.61 *The Third Rider*. March 16, 1956. GS: Leo Gordon, Louis Lettieri, Robert Keys, Stanley Andrews, Bruce Cowling. A retired gunman, who has vowed never to use his guns again, is forced to shoot it out with a crazed killer who has kidnaped his son.

3.62 *Rusty Surrenders*. March 23, 1956. War threatens when a young corporal mistakenly confesses to the accidental wounding of an Apache Brave.

3.63 *Rin Tin Tin and the Rainmaker*. March 30, 1956. GS: Myron Healey, Stanley Clements, George Meader, Edward Colmans, Hal Hooper. The farmers of the Fort Apache region mortgage their lands during a period of drought in order to hire a rainmaker. The landlord agrees to a horse race against Flame, Cpl. Bone's horse, with the farmers' lands as the stake. The farmers' cause looks hopeless, since Flame is a mudder and the rainmaker confesses that he is unable to produce a rainfall.

3.64 *Scotchman's Gold*. April 6, 1956.

3.65 *Attack on Fort Apache*. April 13, 1956. GS: Tom McKee, Ralph Moody, Peter Coe, Bob O'Neal, Abel Fernandez. The officer in charge of besieged Fort Apache is wounded by a poisoned arrow. Rinty is sent after the medicine that will save the man's life.

3.66 *Homer the Great*. April 20, 1956. GS: Andy Clyde, Ron Hagerthy, Mary Adams, Sam Flint, Syd Saylor, Harry Strong, Paul Keast. A stablehand had led his niece to believe he is Salt River's richest citizen, but he is accused of robbery on the eve of her visit.

3.67 *Rinty Finds a Bone*. April 27, 1956. GS: Otto Waldis, Franz Roehn, John Pickard, Rusty Wescoatt, Abel Fer-

The Adventures of Rin Tin Tin

nandez. Rin Tin Tin finds a bone belonging to a huge dinosaur. When he leads scientists to the spot where he dug up the bone, a pair of outlaws think that the scientists are searching for a vein of ore.

3.68 *Rusty Meets Mr. Nobody.* May 4, 1956. GS: Chubby Johnson, Rush Williams, Charles Stevens, Zon Murray. A hobo makes off with a $20,000 gold shipment which is being sent to the Kiowa Indians as part of a peace treaty.

3.69 *Circle of Fire.* May 11, 1956. GS: Adele Mara, Ed Hinton, Joey Hooker, Syd Saylor, George J. Lewis. A strong-willed and her young son drives into hostile Kiowa Indian territory with a wagon-load of guns. Rusty, Rinty and the girl's husband overtake her just as the Indians are preparing to attack.

3.70 *Hubert Goes West.* May 18, 1956. GS: Gordon Richards, Joel Ashley, Lee Roberts, Syd Saylor, Mildred Van Hollen. When an English butler buys the Salt River Hotel, a pair of desperadoes tries to drive him out of town.

3.71 *Lost Treasure.* May 25, 1956. GS: Benny Rubin, Philip Van Zandt, Syd Saylor, Henry Rowland, Chief Yowlachi. Two outlaws persuade an Indian friend of Rusty's to lead them to an underground chamber where Spanish treasure is hidden. The crooks tie up their guide, leave him to die and prepare to cart the treasure away.

3.72 *Rin Tin Tin and the Second Chance.* June 1, 1956. GS: Nan Leslie, John Crawford, Bruce Cowlin, John Reach, Bradford Johnson, William Tannen. An outlaw gang sets a trap for a U.S. marshal, who is trailing an accused murderer.

Season Three

3.73 *Forward Ho.* Sept. 7, 1956. GS: Bradford Jackson, Hal Hopper, Peter Coe. Reinforcements are hurried to Fort Apache to help in a threatened Indian attack. Then Maj. Swanson receives an unsigned letter from one of the new men in the fort. The writer accuses Lt. Rip Masters of murder and threatens revenge.

3.74 *Witch of the Woods.* Sept. 14, 1956. GS: Mildred Von Hollen, Lyle Talbot, Tiger Fafara, Joey Hooker, Syd Saylor. A man who wants to gain possession of an old woman's land pays a youngster to pretend she has cast a spell on him, hoping to run her out of the community for witchcraft.

3.75 *Sorrowful Joe.* Sept. 21, 1956. GS: Sterling Holloway, Syd Saylor, Richard Devon. The morale at Fort Apache hits a new low when a man known as the Army's worst jinx is transferred there. When Lt. Rip Masters leads his men against Kiowas who have captured a wagonload of rifles, he orders Joe the Jinx to stay at the fort and out of trouble.

3.76 *Return of the Chief.* Sept. 28, 1956. Jack Lambert, Norman Fredric, Dirk London, Paul Fierro. Lt. Rip Masters, Sgt. O'Hara and Chief Komawi go after a gang of horse rustlers who have stolen the prized herd belonging to the Chiracahuas.

3.77 *The Silent Battle.* Oct. 5, 1956. GS: Louis Lettieri, Tom McKee, William Forrest, Steven Ritch, George Keymas. Lt. Rip Masters permits a cattleman to use Indian land for his stock during a drought. One of the Indians is stricken with a cattle-borne disease, and unless the Army doctor can prove to the tribe the safety of an anti-toxin, they will go on the warpath. Rin Tin Tin and Chief Pokiwah are stricken by the dread cattle disease. Rusty bravely offers to be a guinea pig and test a new antitoxin for the disease.

3.78 *Yo-o Rinty.* Oct. 12, 1956. GS: Michael Ansara, Don Garrett, Hal Hopper. Geronimo attacks a Fort Mojave cavalry unit. The only survivor is Tioka, their Indian scout. He arrives at Fort Apache and offers to lead Lt. Rip Masters and his men to Geronimo.

3.79 *The White Wolf.* Oct. 19, 1956. GS: Ernest Sarracino, Patrick Whyte. On a trip to Canada, Lt. Rip Masters and Rusty meet a French trapper who has been losing most of his prized furs to a band of wolves.

3.80 *Return of Rin Tin Tin.* Oct. 26, 1956. GS: Patrick Whyte, Ralph Moody, Ernest Sarracino, X Brands. Rusty refuses to belive that Rinty has abandoned him and waits trustingly for his return.

3.81 *Boone's Grandpappy.* Nov. 2, 1956. GS: Chief Yowlachie, George Keymas. Cpl. Boone is a disgrace to his family's military tradition. He comes from a long line of military men, all of whom have been at least colonels. His grandfather enters him in West Point against his wishes.

3.82 *The Lost Puppy.* Nov. 9, 1956. GS: Tudor Owen, Kurt Katch, Terence de Marney. Rusty, Rinty and Cpl. Boone take care of an old Scotsman's shepherd dog and her pups while the man is away. One of the pups is missing, so Rusty and Rinty go to look for it.

3.83 *Presidential Citation.* Nov. 16, 1956. A ruthless general ignores the President's instructions and massacres an Apache village. Lt. Rip Masters sends his letter of resignation from the Army to Washington, but the arrival of President Grant changes things.

3.84 *Wagon Train.* Nov. 23, 1956. GS: Richard Avode, Nan Leslie, Hal Hopper, Tony McCoy. While escorting a wagon train to Oregon, Lt. Rip Masters runs into trouble with the leader, Bat Colby. He suspects Colby of being in league with marauding Indians.

3.85 *Fort Adventure.* Nov. 30, 1956. GS: Robert Lowery, Robert Bice, Don C. Harvey, Nan Leslie. Lt. Rip Masters and his patrol, which includes Rusty and Rin Tin Tin, are escorting a wagon train to Fort Adventure. One of their charges is a girl who plans to marry a major stationed at the fort. They arrive, only to find the man has disappeared.

3.86 *The Flaming Forest.* Dec. 7, 1956. GS: Tim Considine, Roy Roberts. After his mother's death, an Eastern youngster goes west to live with his trapper father. The man asks Rusty to come visit them and help him train his son in the ways of the woods.

3.87 *The Invaders.* Dec. 14, 1956. GS: Lane Bradford, Charlita, Tita Aragon, Rico Alaniz, X Brands. Mexican Indians have been making raids into the United States. Rip Masters is assigned to escort a Mexican dignitary across the border, but on hte way his party is attacked.

3.88 *Racing Rails.* Dec. 28, 1956. GS: Terry Frost, Ralph Moody. A race is on between a stagecoach and a railroad train. The night before, Rusty and Rinty discover the race is fixed.

3.89 *Higgins' Last Stand.* Jan. 4, 1957. GS: William Fawcett, Clem Bevans, Keith Richards, Joseph Turkel, Hal Hopper, Percy Helton. Four gunmen threaten the life of an old friend of Rusty and Rip Masters. Rusty and Rip come to his aid.

3.90 *The Indian Hater.* Jan. 11, 1957. GS: Clancy

Cooper, Rick Vallin, Jan Arvan, Dehl Berti, Joe Canutt. Rusty and Lt. Masters find an Indian lying in the woods wounded, and take him to the nearest cabin for first aid. The owner, however, refuses to admit them because he hates all Indians bitterly.

3.91 *The Southern Colonel.* Jan. 18, 1957. GS: Thurston Hall, Mildred von Hollen, Baynes Barron, William Tannen, William Griffith, Bud Osborne. An extremely clever con man swindles the citizens of Mesa Grande out of a considerable amount of money. Even Lt. Masters and Rusty are taken in by the fast talking of the man.

3.92 *The Warrior's Promise.* Jan. 25, 1957. GS: William Forrest, Monte Blue, Ward Wood, Hal Hooper, Dehl Berti. Trouble breaks out in the Mogollon Apache tribe after Chief Maco turns the leadership over to his son, Otonah. The new chief is a wise and peace-loving man, but another warrior, Tolque, determines to kill Otonah and become chief himself.

3.93 *Sorrowful Joe Returns.* Feb. 1, 1957. GS: Sterling Holloway, Willliam Forrest, Roscoe Ates, Frank Fenton, Bradford Jackson. Rusty goes to Apache Wells to visit Sorrowful Joe, called the Army's worst jinx, now in private business. As with everything Sorrowful attempts, this particular job is almost over, because the boss is going bankrupt.

3.94 *The Lieutenant's Lesson.* Feb. 8, 1957. GS: Clancy Cooper, Jerome Courtland, Glenn Strange, Larry Chance. Sgt. Walker is overjoyed because his son, a recent graduate of West Point, is assigned to his camp.

3.95 *Swedish Cook.* Feb. 15, 1957. GS: El Brendel. Fort Apache's new cook wants to be a soldier, but he serves such good food that no one is willing to help him achieve his goal.

3.96 *Rusty Gets Busted.* Feb. 22, 1957. GS: Don Haggerty, Barry Froner. An inspection tour brings an officer and his conceited young son to Fort Apache. The youngster tangles with Rusty. Both of them meet up with a band of hostile Indians, and Rusty is forced into rescuing the other boy in an unusual way.

3.97 *O'Hara's Gold.* March 1, 1957. GS: Hal Hopper, Byron Foulger, John Close, Syd Saylor. Sgt. O'Hara meets an old man who claims he has found a rich gold vein and wants to sell. When O'Hara inherits a sizable amount of money, he immediately decides to buy the mine.

3.98 *O'Hara Gets Culture.* March 8, 1957. GS: Nestor Paiva, Peggie Leon, Dehl Berti, Charles Stevens. Lt. Rip Masters and his men find out that the territory's orphanage is about to be closed because of lack of finances. They decide to give a show, with the proceeds going to the orphanage.

3.99 *The Frame-Up.* March 15, 1957. GS: Walter Reed, Roy Gordon, John Peach, John Pickard, George Eldredge. One of the Ft. Apache officers is accused of robbery and murder. He swears he is innocent, and Rusty and Cpl. Boone are the only ones who believe him.

3.100 *Boone's Commission.* March 22, 1957. GS: Charles Horvath, John Mitchum, Jerry Eskow. Cpl. Boone is given a commission which he takes very seriously. Left in command of the post, he decides to run Fort Apache according to the book, with disastrous results.

3.101 *The Silent Witness.* March 29, 1957. GS: Ron Hagerthy, Norma Jean Nilsson, Joseph Turkel, Stanley Andrews, Harry Strang, Roy Erwin. Cpl. Boone accuses the warehouse proprietor of cheating the Army on supplies. A battle ensues and the man tears a button from Boone's jacket. Later the man is found murdered, the button held tightly in his hand and Cpl. Boone is suspected of the crime.

3.102 *Indian Blood.* April 5, 1957. The Mescalero Kid, an Indian scout, arrives at Fort Apache to help stop Indian raids.

3.103 *The Old Soldier.* April 12, 1957. GS: Ralph Moody, Lee Roberts, Duane Grey. Unhappy about his retirement, a former master sergeant gets a job at Fort Apache. On the first day of his new job the ld man begins to suspect a merchant of cheating the Army on supplies. He tells Lt. Rip Masters of his suspicions.

3.104 *Stagecoach Sally.* April 19, 1957. GS: Ellen Corby, John Wilder, Lane Bradford, Terry Frost, Dennis Moore. A young man joins a gang of bandits who specialize in robbing stagecoaches. Then he learns that the gang plans to rob a coach belonging to the line operated by his mother. When he rebels, the leader threatens to kill him unless he carries out his part in the holdup.

3.105 *Bitter Medicine.* April 26, 1957. GS: Billy Miller. Laurindo, peace-loving medicine man of the Comanche Indian tribe, is exiled to live with his son Proud Arrow. His place is taken by Walking Bear, who is determined to lead the tribe on the warpath against the white man.

3.106 *Corporal Carson.* May 3, 1957. GS: William Forrest, Tommy Farrell, Jerry Eskow, Jan Arvan. The Army rejects a request from Maj. Swanson for more troops for Fort Apache. Instead, they send Cpl. Thaddeus Carson, grandson of the famous scout, in the belief that his name alone will hold off the Comanche Indians. But on his first assignment, Carson becomes hopelessly lost.

3.107 *Hubert's Niece.* May 10, 1957. GS: Anna MAria Nanasi, Gordon Richards, Tommy Farrell. Penelope Chatsworth comes to live with her Uncle Hubert, owner of the Salt River Hotel. Her governess, Miss Irmegarde, turns out to be a girl Hubert fell in love with years ago. Things are very pleasant until Sgt. O'Hara starts courting the pretty governess too.

3.108 *O'Hara Gets Amnesia.* May 17, 1957. GS: Tommy Farrell, Peter Coe, Joseph Waring. Sgt. Biff O'Hara disguises himself as a peddler and ventures into the Comanche camp to eavesdrop on a meeting of the tribal chieftains. It is rumored that Chief Stone Club is trying to persuade the Comanches to go on the warpath.

3.109 *Along Came Tubbs.* May 24, 1957. GS: Andy Clyde, Jim Bannon. A stablehand, old Mr. Tubbs, spins tall tales of his prowess as a gunfighter. When Rusty, Rinty and the citizens of Salt River find Mr. Tubbs, piston in hand, standing over the dead body of a notorious gunman, they believe the old man is as good as he says.

3.110 *Major Swanson's Choice.* May 31, 1957. GS: Frank de Kova, Norman Fredric. Learning that Maj. Swanson is leaving Fort Apache to take a post in Washington, Kiowa chief Culebra sees an opportunity to kill his enemy. He tries to get Apache chief Komawi to join him in the murder, but Komawi refuses and warns Swanson.

3.111 *The Gentle Kingdom.* June 7, 1957. GS: Jay Novello, Willis Bouchey, Tommy Ivo. A wealthy man brings his teenage son to the West, determined to make him as ruthless as himself. They trespass on the property of Carlos De La Marca,

The Adventures of Rin Tin Tin

who maintains his ranch as a wild-life sanctuary. But the boy loves animals and hates to hunt. When his father shoots and wounds a doe, the wounded animal is found by Rusty and Lt. Rip Masters.

3.112 *The Swapper.* June 14, 1957. A cavalryman, newly arrived at the fort, earns the nickname of Swapper because of his hobby of trading. He is given permission to trade with the Comanches, but while he is in their camp a crafty brave hides a peace talisman in the wagon, then claims it has been stolen.

3.113 *The Old Man of the Mountain.* June 21, 1957. GS: Robert Warwick, James Lanphier, Alan Wells. A railroad executive gets permission from the Topawa tribesmen to build a railroad across their barren lands. He is to give them a rich, fertile valley in exchange. The tribe prepares to leave for its new home, all except the elderly chief who insists he will stay.

Season Four

3.114 *Return to Fort Apache.* Sept. 20, 1957. GS: Frank de Kova, Tommy Farrell, Charles Horvath, Selmer Jackson. After all the Indian tribes in the Fort Apache area sign a peace treaty, the War Department orders the fort closed. All the men leave on furlough while waiting for reassignment. Then the Comanche chief, Okoma, takes over the fort and joins forces with Chief Black Cloud to raid the surrounding territory. Major Swanson is ordered to retake Fort Apache.

3.115 *The Courtship of Marshal Higgins.* Sept. 27, 1957. GS: William Fawcett, Cheerio Meredith, Toni Barrett, Dub Taylor, Bill Hale. Marshal Higgins and his deputy, Kid Hooker, start courting a charming widow. Hooker, who was once a desperado, decides to surrender his badge and return to a life of crime when he fears Higgins may marry the lady. Rusty and Lt. Rip Masters try to bring about an understanding between Hooker and Higgins.

3.116 *Rusty's Reward.* Oct. 4, 1957. When Sgt. Stan Powers learns that his wife has died and his children are about to be sent to an orphanage, he goes AWOL in an attempt to provide a home for his family.

3.117 *A Look of Eagles.* Oct. 11, 1957. GS: Tommy Farrell, Harry Strang, Natividad Vacio, Pierre Watkin. Lt. Rip Masters buys Red Eagle, a horse he believes will win the jumping competition between Fort Apache and Fort Comanche. But when Masters sets out after a bear, the enraged animals injures horse and rider.

3.118 *The Last Navajo.* Oct. 18, 1957. GS: Race Gentry, Robert Lowery, Robert Warwick, Hal Hopper, Robert Griffin, Bill Hale. The Navajo tribe agrees to leave its present lands for more fertile territory, and Chief Big Bear agrees to sign a treaty legalizing the exchange. But his brother Grey Fox refuses to leave the tribal grounds.

3.119 *Mother O'Hara's Marriage.* Oct. 25, 1957. GS: Connie Gilchrist, Harry Shannon, Jack Lomas, Tom McKee. A gang offers to buy a blacksmith shop owned by Mother O'Hara. They are anxious to acquire the property because it is next door to the U.S. Mint.

3.120 *Hostage of War Bonnet.* Nov. 1, 1957. GS: Ken Mayer, Bill Hale. A mysterious signal leads Rinty, Rusty, and Lt. Rip and their friends to a ghost town. There they find two brothers who have been attacked by Apaches and are holding a member of the tribe as hostage.

3.121 *Rodeo Clown.* Nov. 8, 1957. GS: Stacy Harris, Tiger Fafara, Bill Hale. A boy who has boasted to Rusty that his father is the top rodeo rider, runs off in humiliation when Rip introduces the man as the rodeo clown. The boy is ashamed because he thinks his father is a coward.

3.122 *Rusty's Strategy.* Nov. 15, 1957. GS: Robert Warwick. Gen. Tyne-Fyffe arrives from India to observe the operations of a frontier outpost To his dismay the general finds he cannot treat American Indians the way he did the people of India.

3.123 *Frontier Angel.* Nov. 22, 1957. GS: Claire Kelly. Fort Apache is without a doctor on the post, so Lt. Rip Masters arranges for a civilian physician to come to the post weekly. The doctor turns out to be a young lady, who is also the ex-fiancee of Lt. Ed Bassett.

3.124 *The Hunted.* Dec. 6, 1957. GS: Harry Harvey, Jr., John Cliff. Cpl. Boone invites Rinty, Rusty, Rip and O'Hara to vacation in Canada with him at his brother Jesse's forest cabin. But the former owner of the cabin comes to take vengeance on Jesse for a fancied offence.

3.125 *The White Chief.* Dec. 13, 1957. GS: Patrick Whyte. The Cree Indians in Canada hold Biff O'Hara as hostage, threatening to kill him unless the white men leave the territory. Rusty, Lt. Masters and Cpl. Boone plead with the Northwest Mounted Police to save O'Hara.

3.126 *Boundary Busters.* Dec. 20, 1957. GS: Bill Henry, Tracey Roberts. Bill and Ginny Anderson try to reclaim their land in a government land rush. They are blocked by ruthless men who want the land for themselves.

3.127 *River Chase.* Jan. 10, 1958. Sgt. O'Hara takes Rinty and Rusty with him on a gold-panning expedition to an abandoned gold mine. There they run into three desperadoes who have just robbed a bank.

3.128 *Top Gun.* Jan. 24, 1958. GS: John Duke, Anthony Jochim, Robert Jordan. When a gunfighter returns to his home town, his father, the ex-sheriff refuses to have anything to do with him. Lt. Rip Masters tries to help him.

3.129 *Tomahawk Tubbs.* Feb. 7, 1958. GS: Andy Clyde, Cyril Delevanti, Charles Stevens, Rudi Dana. Old Homer Tubbs tells Rusty how he save the life of Apache Chief Nan years before. Rusty doesn't really believe Homer, who is addicted to telling tall tales. Then Chief Nana arrives in Salt River to sign a treaty and Rusty decides to ask about Homer's story.

3.130 *The New C.O.* Feb. 14, 1958. GS: Les Tremayne, Guinn "Big Boy" Williams, Martin Balk, Tito Renaldo, Doyle Brooks. A new commanding officer arrives at the fort and decides to enforce rigid discipline. He refuses Lt. Masters' advice concerning a band of renegade Indians.

3.131 *Pritikin's Predicament.* Feb. 21, 1958. GS: Syd Saylor, Helene Heigh, Michael ye, Thom Carney, William Vaughn, Dick Elliott. Sgt. O'Hara is sent to Salt River to await the arrival of three new recruits. While waiting for the new men to arrive, O'Hara decides to help storekeeper Clem Pritikin, whose wife has accused him of cowardice.

3.132 *Rusty's Remedy.* Feb. 28, 1958. GS: Stacy Harris, Abel Fernandez, Steven Ritch, Mike Forest, Michael Carr. Lt. Rip Masters and Rusty find a starving, unkempt man at Salt River and take him back to Fort Apache. There they learn that the man is a former Army major who resigned because he feels responsible for leading his unit into an ambush.

3.133 *Spanish Gold.* March 7, 1958. GS: Jay Novello, Jean Howell, John Reach, Michael Carr. An elderly Spanish don has hidden a hoard of gold in a remote cave. He is keeping his treasure for his only living relative, his niece, whom he has not seen for years. The Lt. Rip Masters tells him the girl has been located in Kansas City and the old man sends for her.

3.134 *Bitter Bounty.* March 14, 1958. GS: Lynn Shubert, Manning Ross, Bud Osborne, Dehl Berti, Joseph Vitale. An Army patrol meets a bounty hunter who is holding a young Indian brave as a prisoner. The bounty hunter tells Lt. Rip Masters that the brave is wanted for murder and that he intends to collect the reward offered for him. Then the chief of the brave's tribe stops the patrol and tells Masters that unless the brave is released his tribe will go to war.

3.135 *Sorrowful Joe's Policy.* March 21, 1958. GS: Sterling Holloway, Lillian Bronson, Will Wright, Roy Erwin. When Sorrowful Joe complains that he never receives any mail, Rusty writes to Sorrowful's Uncle Herpo, telling him his nephew misses him. Uncle Herpo and family decide to visit Sorrowful, in the hopes of becoming the beneficiaries of his Army insurance.

3.136 *Border Incident.* March 28, 1958. GS: Lou Krugman, Jan Arvan, Mel Welles, Michael Vallon. The president of Mexico plans a trip to Washington to negotiate a much-needed loan for his country. After an attempt is made to assassinate the president, a lieutenant in the Mexican forces goes to Fort Apache to request an American escort for the Trip to Washington.

3.137 *Wind-Wagon McClanahan.* April 4, 1958. GS: Charles Irwin, Percy Helton, Oliver Blake, Syd Saylor. The men of Fort Apache are amazed when a wagon outfitted with sails, breezes through the gates of the fort. Excited over the new invention, they decide to invest money to have a whole fleet of the land boats made by the owner, one Terrance X. McClanahan.

3.138 *The Secret Weapon.* April 11, 1958. GS: Ernest Sarracino, Dehl Berti, John Harmon, Morris Ankrum, Les Tremayne. Sgt. Biff O'Hara is assigned to lead a group of volunteers to try out a new secret weapon. News of this reaches Walt Mathers, who sells the information to an Indian brave.

3.139 *Brave Bow.* April 18, 1958. GS: X Brands, Laurie Carroll, Larry Johns, Jack Mather, Tommy Farrell. The son and daughter of rival Indian chieftains fall in love, but the girl has been promised in marriage to a member of her own tribe. At the wedding celebration Rin Tin Tin helps the girl escape from her tent and guides her to the man she really loves.

Season Five

3.140 *The General's Daughter.* Sept. 19, 1958. GS: Morris Ankrum, Melinda Byron, Peter Walker, Russell Conklin. Indians attack a stagecoach carrying a brigadier general, his daughter April and a lieutenant. Rip Masters' patrol saves the. The lieutenant, annoyed by April's admiration for Rip, sets out alone to capture the Indian chief.

3.141 *Escape to Danger.* Sept. 26, 1958. GS: Harry Dean Stanton, Russell Thorson, Les Tremayne, Richard Gilden. A group of Army prisoners break out of the guardhouse at Fort Lincoln and Lt. Rip Masters recaptures them. He is commissioned to return the prisoners.

3.142 *Decision of Rin Tin Tin.* Oct. 3, 1958. GS: Harry Dean Stanton, Mildred Von Hollen, Hal Hopper, Rand Brooks. Lt. Rip Masters is kidnaped by a group of escaped Army prisoners led by Dirkson, a killer. While traveling back to Fort Apache, Rinty sees Masters with the gang and leads O'Hara to their hide-out.

3.143 *The Foot Soldier.* Oct. 10, 1958. GS: Onslow Stevens, Norman Alden, Morris Ankrum, Lee Roberts. Lt. Rip Masters saves Maj. Karn and his unit, who are trapped during the Mexican campaign. Masters is given a commission for his heroism, but the major is reprimanded for allowing his men to be trapped. He is convinced that he would have escaped from the trap without Masters aid.

3.144 *Rusty's Opportunity.* Oct. 17, 1958. GS: Douglas Fowley, Larry Chance. Rusty considers taking Rin Tin Tin and going on tour with P.T. Barnum. He is sure that Rinty and his tricks would be a great attraction.

3.145 *Running Horse.* Oct. 24, 1958. GS: Jan Arvan, Les Tremayne, Ernest Sarracino, Frank Lackteen, Jack Littlefield. Running Horse, the Sioux chief, signs a peace treaty with Maj. Stone. Later the chief's two sons are killed in a fight with a cavalry patrol and Running Horse holds Stone responsible. He sets out for Fort Apache to fight a duel with Stone.

3.146 *The Cloudbusters.* Oct. 31, 1958. GS: Jack Littlefield, Peter Mamakos, Herb Vigran, Harry Strang, Robert Easton. Prof. Wirt arrives in Salt River and sells tickets to the townspeople to watch him make an ascent in a balloon. But the balloon fails to rise and the sheriff insists that Wirt leave town.

3.147 *Deadman's Valley.* Nov. 7, 1959. GS: Chuck Courtney, Rayford Barnes, Harry Strang. Pvt. Jimmy Jersey can't adjust to Army life and tries to desert, but Rin Tin Tin stops him. Rusty persuades Lt. Rip Masters to give Jimmy another chance. Then the Salt River bank is held up by Jimmy's elder brother.

3.148 *Grandpappy's Love Affair.* Nov. 14, 1958. GS: Helen Spring, John Banner, John Hart, Jack Littlefield. Lt. Rip Masters, Sgt. O'Hara, Cpl Boone, Rusty and Rin Tin Tin are ordered to report for duty in Washington, D.C. When they arrive they learn that Cpl. Boone's grandfather, Col. Boone, has brought them to the capital to attend his wedding.

3.149 *The Epidemic.* Nov. 21, 1958. GS: Warren Oates, Tom McKee, Chuck Courtney, Bill Henry, Harry Strang, Don Devlin, Jerry Summers, Robert Fuller. During a bank holdup outlaw Deke Elston fires a shot which destroys the only bottle of anti-antrax vaccine. Deke's young brother Hall finds that he is unable to flee from the sene of the crime because he is suffering from the disease.

3.150 *The Best Policy.* Dec. 5, 1958. GS: Robert Lowery, Chubby Johnson, Craig Duncan. Jake Appleby, reformed ne'er-do-well, has just begun a career selling insurance. Jake sells his first customer a $20,000 policy and then learns that the man is an ex-marshal and is being hunted by the Martin gang.

3.151 *Miracle of the Mission.* Dec. 12, 1958. GS: Tommy Farrell, Joe Vitale, Carlos Romero, Iron Eyes Cody. Lt. Masters takes a patrol out to string telegraph wires between Fort Apache and the mission. Rip soon finds himself and his men in danger of attack.

3.152 *Star of India.* Jan. 2, 1959. GS: Robert Warwick, Patrick Whyte, Paul Picerni, George Keymas, Les Tremayne. Fort Apache's polo team, having won the Southwest championship, take Rusty and Rinty with them when they journey to India to play the champion British Army team at Fort Kaffir. Once there, however, the men from Fort Apache find themselves working to keep peace and prevent violence during a revolt.

3.153 *The Misfit Marshal.* Jan. 9, 1959. GS: George Hamilton, Ken Mayer. Lt. Rip Masters, Rusty and Rinty join forces to help Elwood Masterson, an inexperienced marshal, attain the position of a respected lawman.

3.154 *Ol' Betsy.* Jan. 16, 1959. GS: Stephen Pearson, Larry Chance, Ralph Moody. While out building a bridge, Lt. Rip Masters and a squad of troopers are captured by Comanches. Jeb Crawford, a hillbilly, decides to come to their rescue armed with an old turkey rifle.

3.155 *Stagecoach to Phoenix.* Jan. 23, 1959. GS: Keith Richards, Mary Beth Hughes, Tom McKee, Les Tremayne. Lt. Rip Masters is riding the stage to Phoenix along with two strangers, Dan Morris and his wife Lil. When the stage makes a stop in Mesa Grande, Dan and Lil rob the bank and decide to use the stage for their getaway.

3.156 *Major Mockingbird.* Jan. 30, 1959. GS: Willard Waterman, Louis Lettieri, Les Tremayne, Charles Evans, Monte Blue. Morton Mockingbird, a publicity agent in charge of recruiting, decides to raise the number of enlistments by touring the country with a pageant depicting a famous Apache uprising. Mockingbird wants to hold one performance of the pageant at Fort Apache with real soldiers and Apaches taking part.

3.157 *The Matador.* Feb. 6, 1959. GS: Michael Dante, Manning Ross, Miguel Landa, Vincent Padula. Lt. Rip Masters, Rusty and Rin Tin Tin meet Ramon Estrada, a famous matador. Estrada, recovering from a wound, receives a challenge from a competitor. Accepting the challenge, lest he be considered a coward, Estrada invites his new friends to accompany him to Mexico City.

3.158 *The Accusation.* Feb. 13, 1959. GS: Addison Richards, Harry Hickox, Steven Ritch, George Eldredge, Les Tremayne. Lt. Rip Masters is charged with mistreating a group of captured Indians and is brought up for court-martial.

3.159 *Royal Recruit.* Feb. 20, 1959. GS: Jack Diamond. Prince Michael of Cornvania runs away and joins the men at Fort Apache. When his father dies, the lad's life is threatened by a scheming prime minister.

3.160 *The Devil Rides Point.* Feb. 27, 1959. GS: Jud Taylor, Michael Pate. An Indian scout attached to Fort Apache is forced to lead a group of cavalrymen into an ambush.

3.161 *Pillajohn's Progress.* March 6, 1959. GS: Oliver Blake, Percy Helton, Les Tremayne, George Keymas, Iron Eyes Cody. The Comanches are ready to go on the warpath, but and epidemic hits their horses. Shortly thereafter, it is discovered that Seth Pillajohn and his horses are missing.

3.162 *The Ming Vase.* March 13, 1959. GS: Philip Ahn, James Hong, Jack Lomas, Don Devlin, Harry Strang. Not wanting to succeed his father in the business, a Chineses laundryman's son leaves home. Soon afterward the father's vase, containing his life savings, is found to be missing.

3.163 *Apache Stampede.* March 20, 1959. GS: Rayford Barnes, Jan Shepard, Sam Jackson, Stanley Andrews. Bill Masters works as a cowhand on a cattle drive as he travels to see his brother Lt. Rip Masters. At Fort Apache Bill learns that the foreman has changed his plans and intends to travel through Indian country.

3.164 *The Luck of O'Hara.* April 3, 1959. GS: Norman Alden, Monte Blue, Jack Littlefield, Emmett Lynn. A young Comanche brave spies the Fort Apache troops on maneuvers. They are staging a mock battle and the Indian thinks that they are actually warring among themselves.

3.165 *The Failure.* May 8, 1959. GS: Byron Foulger, Helene Heigh, Bill Henry, Harry Strang. Manley Barker, a man who thinks of himself as a failure, is accused of robbing a stagecoach. His friends Rusty and Rinty try to help prove him innocent of the crime.

4. *The Alaskans*

ABC. 60 min. Broadcast history: Sunday, 9:30-10:30, Oct. 1959–Sept. 1960.

Regular Cast: Roger Moore (Silky Harris), Dorothy Provine (Rocky Shaw), Jeff York (Reno McKee), Ray Danton (Nifty Cronin), Frank De Kova (Fantan).

Premise: This series was set in Alaska, during the gold rush the late 1890s. Adventurers Silky Harris and Reno McKee, and singer Rocky Shaw seek their fortune in the region, often coming into conflict with saloon owner Nifty Cronin.

The Episodes

4.1 *Gold Sled.* Oct. 4, 1959. GS: Allyn Joslyn, Hank Patterson. Silky Harris and Reno McKee are preparing to travel to the Klondike in search of gold. Entertainer Rocky Shaw, intrigued by a weird tale of gold buried in the snow, is eager to take the trip with the two men.

4.2 *Cheating Cheaters.* Oct. 11, 1959. GS: Frank Ferguson. Skagway saloon owner Nifty Cronin agrees to ship gold dust to the States for Silky Harris, Reno McKee and a number of other miners. En route the boat mysteriously sinks. When Silky threatens to investigate, Cronin admits that the gold was never placed on board.

4.3 *The Blizzard.* Oct. 18, 1959. GS: Andrea King, John Dehner, Walter Burke. Reno McKee is hauling a load of dynamite over a perilous trail to Nome when he is suddenly joined by three suspicious characters. Soon, a mighty blizzard threatens the group.

4.4 *The Petticoat Crew.* Oct. 25, 1959. Silky Harris dreams of a financial coup when he decides to ship a boatload of dancing girls and Thanksgiving turkeys from Seattle to Dawson. En route, Silky is surprised to encounter con man Nifty Cronin.

4.5 *Starvation Stampede.* Nov. 1, 1959. GS: James Westerfield, John Qualen, Allison Hayes, Joe di Reda, Dick Paul. A supply ship is trapped in an early freeze on its way to an isolated mining town. The greedy town storekeeper takes advantage of this mishap, forcing the miners to pay exorbitant prices for food and supplies.

4.6 *Big Deal.* Nov. 8, 1959. GS: John Dehner, Jesse White. Silky Harris and Reno McKee find a lost legal document and try to locate the owner. They stumble on a swindle scheme.

4.7 *Contest at Gold Bottom.* Nov. 15, 1959. GS: Archie

Duncan, George Dunn, Eddie Quillan, Patrick Westward, Monty Margetts, I. Stanford Jolley. Nifty Cronin threatens to foreclose a mortgage on Silky and Reno's mining property unless they can meet their next payment. Meanwhile, a baby is abandoned on their doorstep and, to raise the money, they decide to have a "Name the Baby" contest.

4.8 *Winter Song.* Nov. 22, 1959. GS: Marie Windsor, Alan Baxter, Jerome Cowan, George Wallace, Mickey Simpson. Silky, Reno and Rocky plan to stage a concert with opera star Maria Julien. Arriving in Eagle City to perform before a packed house, Miss Julien suddenly loses her voice.

4.9 *The Golden Fleece.* Nov. 29, 1959. GS: Beatrice Kay, Theodore Marcuse. Four men assault Silky Harris' partner Reno McKee and then purchase an apparently worthless gold mine.

4.10 *Doc Booker.* Dec. 6, 1959. GS: Julie Adams, Simon Oakland. Doc Booker and his new bride act to stop a typhoid epidemic. Then a woman tells the citizens that Booker isn't a real doctor.

4.11 *The Abominable Snowman.* Dec. 13, 1959. GS: Ruta Lee, Ray Teal, Robert Boon. A miner dies after being attacked by a weird monster. It is decided that the dead man's gold mine will go to the winner of a race between Silky Harris and another miner named Otto.

4.12 *Remember the Maine.* Dec. 20, 1959. GS: John Dehner. A con man named Soapy suddenly gets patriotic and organizes a special Skagway Guard to march off to the Spanish-American War. Silky Harris is suspicious of Soapy's motives.

4.13 *Million Dollar Kid.* Jan. 3, 1960. GS: Bart Bradley, Mort Mills. Reno McKee and Rocky Shaw encounter a young Indian named Kat who wants to go to the United States. The youth decides to trade some shares in a gold mine for the supplies he needs.

4.14 *The Trial of Reno McKee.* Jan. 10, 1960. GS: Efrem Zimbalist, Jr., Karen Steele, Fredd Wayne, Don O'Kelly, Bing Russell. Reno McKee is held for murder, although Silky Harris and Rocky Shaw know that someone else is responsible for the crime. The only way to keep Reno from hanging is to sober up a lawyer who can legally prove McKee's innocence.

4.15 *Gold Fever.* Jan. 17, 1960. GS: Gerald Mohr, Werner Klemperer, Susan Morrow, Wynn Pearce. Reno McKee's younger brother Danny comes to Skagway with his new bride. Reno wishes them well and offers a mine partnership to Danny, but the young man and his wife decide to strike out alone in the gold fields.

4.16 *The Challenge.* Jan. 24, 1960. GS: Don Dubbins, Robert Colbert, John Hoyt, Leonidas Ossetynski, Penny Edwards, Don Beddoe. The town is threatened by an impending avalanche, and Silky Harris volunteers to climb a mountain and set off some blasts which will divert the snowslide. As time runs short, Silky learns that a killer is trying to get rid of him and doom the town.

4.17 *The Long Pursuit.* Jan. 3, 1960. GS: Ruta Lee, Harold J. Stone, Mike Road, Rusty Lane, Dick Rich. Chicago detective Ed Bundy has traced a suspected murderess to an Alaskan village. On the trail to the town, Bundy saves Reno McKee's life, and the two men join forces to look for the girl.

4.18 *Spring Fever.* Feb. 7, 1960. GS: Rex Reason, Lynn Statten. Furious because Silky's taking her for granted, Rocky casts about for someone else to encourage. She comes up with a gentleman named Gordon Talbot, who is secretly after a gold claim that should be Rockys.

4.19 *Black Sand.* Feb. 14, 1960. GS: Karen Steele, Tom Drake, John Reach, Richard Reeves, Dan O'Kelly. Reno strikes out with Dan and Nora Weber to locate a lost gold mine. Along the trail, two other men join the group, and Reno becomes suspicious of Nora's behavior.

4.20 *The Seal Skin-Game.* Feb. 21, 1960. GS: Jacqueline Beer, Peter Whitney, Richard Sargent, Robert B. Williams. Silky, Reno and Rocky are conned into buying a bankrupt seal-raising business. Silky begins to sound like a con man himself when he tries to save the situation by promising some miners a huge return if they will take the business off his hands.

4.21 *Peril at Caribou Crossing.* Feb. 28, 1960. GS: Lee Van Cleef, Jerry Paris, Steve Brodie, Fay Spain, Vladimir Sokoloff. Weather drives Silky to shelter at an isolated cabin. He sees that his arrival has complicated a family quarrel, but before anything comes of it, two outlaws barge in bringing bigger trouble.

4.22 *Behind the Moon.* March 6, 1960. GS: Lee Patterson, Andra Martin, Hugh Sanders, Diane McBain. No sooner has a gold prospector made plans to marry an Indian girl than his backers plot to chase the Indians off the tribal land. It seems that gold has been discovered there.

4.23 *Partners.* March 13, 1960. GS: Jimmy Carter, Alan Hale, Jr., Warren Stevens. Rocky and Reno tell young Jimmy Hendricks that his father died a hero. But the lad overhears the less heroic truth about his father, and disappears.

4.24 *Disaster at Gold Hill.* March 20, 1960. GS: Madlyn Rhue, Rex Reason, Mike Road, Gil Rankin. Silky becomes involved in an explosive romantic triangle.

4.25 *The Last Bullet.* March 27, 1960. GS: Frank Cady, Gary Vinson, Andra Martin. Silky rescues a man from a pack of wolves and takes him to a trail house occupied by a pack of human wolves.

4.26 *A Barrel of Gold.* April 3, 1960. GS: Jean Allison, Ed Kemmer, Richard Evans, Jack Mather, Hal Baylor. A prospecting party started out to find gold, but death makes a strike and the only survivors report they were poisoned with spoiled meat.

4.27 *The Bride Wore Black.* April 10, 1960. GS: John Beal, Lee Bergere, Fay Spain, Keith Richards. Cass Wilson uses Silky's picture to win a mail-order bride. There is trouble when the girl arrives.

4.28 *Odd Man Hangs.* April 17, 1960. GS: Valerie French, Walter Sande, Myron Healey. Silky is one of the players in a strange game. He and two other men are jailed on a murder charge. Everyone is certain that one of them is a killer.

4.29 *Counterblow.* April 24, 1960. GS: Karen Steele, Horace MacMahon, Robert McQueeney. The Skookum Sentinel newspaper is handed over to Silky in payment of a debt. He finds himself with a ready-made crusade when his partner is killed by mobsters.

4.30 *Heart of Gold.* May 1, 1960. GS: Troy Donahue, Gary Vinson, Frank Ferguson, Paul Birch, Emory Parnell, Charles Stevens, Napua Wood, Bernie Fein, Jack Bighead. Pierre Duran is transporting thousands of dollars worth of the miners' gold dust to Yukon City. On the way, he is hijacked and left for dead.

4.31 *Kangaroo Court.* May 8, 1960. GS: Larry Pennell,

Joan O'Brien, Robert Lowery, Walter Burke. Traveling alone in barren and isolated country, Silky comes upon a girl entertainer and her male companion. They ask for a lift to a new gold-rush town.

4.32 *The Silent Land.* May 15, 1960. GS: Claude Akins, Richard Carlyle, Arthur Franz, Nancy Hsueh, Charles Stevens, Leonard Strong, Harry Swoger, W.T. Chang, Yaski Muneko. Loading supplies for a remote outpost, Pierre Duran meets a Mountie who is trailing a pair of fugitives. Later, traveling deep into the Arctic wilderness, Pierre encounters the Mountie again — this time marooned in the snow.

4.33 *Calico.* May 22, 1960. GS: Myrna Fahey, Rex Reason, Richard Webb, Tristram Coffin, Leo Gordon, Richard Cutting, Billy M. Greene, William Leicester. Silky Harris wins a half share in a gold mine. But there is a catch. His claim is forfeit unless he works it one day a week — and his partner vanishes without revealing the mine's location.

4.34 *Sign of the Kodiak.* May 29, 1960. GS: Lee Patterson, Pippa Scott, Chana Eden, Robert Armstrong, Leonid Kinskey. Traveling in mountain country, Pierre Duran narrowly escapes death from a hunter's bullet. The marksman seems obsessed with killing Big Mike, an elusive Kodiak bear.

4.35 *White Vengeance.* June 5, 1960. GS: Andra Martin, Peter Whitney, Robert Colbert, Tim Graham, Lynn Statten, Pat J. Renella, Carol Seffinger. Silky Harris heads for old Gil Hawkins' mountain cabin to tell him his son has made a gold strike. But before Silky can identify himself, the old man almost shoots him with a rifle.

4.36 *The Ballad of Whitehorse.* June 12, 1960. GS: Rex Reason, James Parnell, Jean Allison, Saundra Edwards, Ted White, Jack Shea, Ray Ballard, Lonnie Pierce, Frank Scannell. The Whitehorse saloon is decked out for a wedding. Robert Howard III, a drunken poet with six months to live, is marrying Yukon Kate, the queen of the dance hall girls. They ask Silky Harris to be best man.

4.37 *The Devil Made Five.* June 19, 1960. GS: Andrea King, Walter Burke, Susan Crane, Charles Fredericks, John Dehner, William Hunter, Kelly Thordsen, Richard Collier, Emory Parnell, Paul Wexler, George Cisar. Reno McKee is transporting dynamite over a perilous trail to Nome when he is suddenly joined by three suspicious characters. What is more, a mighty blizzard threatens the group.

5. *Alias Smith and Jones*

ABC. 60 min. Broadcast history: Thursday, 7:30-8:30, Jan. 1971–Sept. 1971; Thursday, 8:00-9:00, Sept. 1971–Aug. 1972; Saturday, 8:00–9:00, Sept. 1972–Jan. 1973.

Regular Cast: Ben Murphy (Kid Curry/Thaddeus Jones), Peter Duel (Hannibal Heyes/Joshua Smith) 1971, Roger Davis (Hannibal Heyes/Joshua Smith) 72-73.

Premise: The series was set in Kansas during the 1890s, and depicted the often comic adventures of reformed outlaws Kid Curry and Hannibal Heyes as they try to stay out of trouble while awaiting a pardon from the governor.

The Episodes

5.1 *Alias Smith and Jones.* Jan. 5, 1971. GS: Susan Saint James, James Drury, Earl Holliman, Forrest Tucker. Kid Curry and Hannibal Heyes are two bank robbers who are trying to go straight while working at excruciatingly tempting jobs in a bank.

5.2 *The McCreedy Bust.* Jan. 21, 1971. GS: Burl Ives, Cesar Romero, Edward Andrews, Mills Watson, Michael Murphy, Charles Wagenheim, Orville Sherman, Rudy Diaz, Duane Grey. A wealthy rancher involves the boys in the recovery of a stolen bust of Caesar, and some unusual high-stake card games.

5.3 *Exit from Wickenberg.* Jan. 28, 1971. GS: Susan Strasberg, Pernell Roberts, Slim Pickens, Ford Rainey, Mark Lenard, Dan Kemp, Johnny Lee, Lew Brown, Paul Kent, Michael Boles, Amzie Strickland. After finding good jobs in a saloon, Smith and Jones don't cotton to being ordered out of town. So they stick around to find out who is issuing the order, and why.

5.4 *The Wrong Train to Brimstone.* Feb. 4, 1971. GS: Beth Brickell, William Windom, J.D. Cannon, J. Pat O'Malley, Harry Hickox, William Mims. Heyes and Curry board a train that is loaded with gold, and with detectives disguised as passengers. It is all a gilded trap that has been set for them and their former gang.

5.5 *The Girl in Boxcar Number Three.* Feb. 11, 1971. GS: Heather Menzies, John Larch, Jack Garner, Claudia Bryar, Royal Dano, Conlan Carter, Alan Hale, Jr., Michael Carr, Sandy Ward, Raymond Guth, Liam Dunn. Heyes and Curry attempt to haul $50,000 to a town 400 miles away. Complicating their plan is a teenage girl who is riding the rails for kicks.

5.6 *The Great Shell Game.* Feb. 18, 1971. GS: Diana Muldaur, Sam Jaffe, Peter Breck, Vincent Beck, Ken Mayer, Jim Malinda, Paul Micale. Heyes appears to be setting up a well-to-do widow as a pigeon in an illegal gambling operation.

5.7 *Return to Devil's Hole.* Feb. 25, 1971. GS: Fernando Lamas, Diana Hyland, Brett Halsey, William McKinney, Dennis Fimple, Booth Colman, Robert B. Williams, Vaughn Taylor, Jon Lormer, Charlie Briggs, Sid Haig, Lee DeBroux. Outlaw leader Jim Santana must decide who is telling the truth: the woman Heyes has brought to his hideaway — or the gang member she is trying to kill.

5.8 *A Fistful of Diamonds.* March 4, 1971. GS: John McGiver, Sam Jaffe, Michelle Carey, Ken Scott, Clarke Gordon, Paul Sorenson, Mike Road, Lou Wagner. When an embezzling banker pins his crimes on Heyes and Curry, the boys attempt to clear themselves by playing on his greed.

5.9 *Stagecoach Seven.* March 11, 1971. GS: Keenan Wynn, Steve Ihnat, John Kellogg, L.Q. Jones, Dana Elcar, Randolph Mantooth, Mitzi Hoag, Bernard Green, Geoffrey Lewis, Sallie Shockley, Nick Benedict, Angela Clarke. Waystation manager Charlie Utley leads a battle against besieging outlaws who are after the reward on passengers Heyes and Curry, because he wishes to collect the reward himself.

5.10 *The Man Who Murdered Himself.* March 18, 1971. GS: Patrick MacNee, Juliet Mills, Maurice Hill, Charles Davis, Slim Pickens, Dennis Fimple, Walter Barnes, Don Keefer, Harry E. Northrup, Bill McKinney. Archaeologist Norman Alexander hires Heyes to guide an expedition into outlaw country, supposedly in search of Indian remains. But Heyes has his doubts as there is something phony about every member of the party.

5.11 *The Fifth Victim.* March 25, 1971. GS: Sharon

Acker, Joseph Campanella, Ramon Bieri, Sean Garrison, Frederick Downs, Boyd "Red" Morgan, Woodrow Parfrey, Lindsay Workman, Bill Quinn, Dennis Robertson, Barbara Rhodes, George Chandler. A friendly rancher invites the boy to a not-so-friendly game of poker. One of the players, taking unkindly to the discovery of a missing card, starts murdering the others one by one.

5.12 *The Root of It All*. April 1, 1971. GS: Tom Ewell, Judy Carne, Logan Ramsay, Victoria Thompson, Meg Wyllie, Mills Watson, C. Elliott Montgomery, Jerome Cowan, Walt Davis. Leslie O'Hara is a proper Philadelphia lady who can display most unladylike behavior when the occasion demands…which it frequently does in a wild and woolly hunt for a buried Army payroll.

5.13 *Journey from San Juan*. April 8, 1971. GS: Claudine Longet, Nico Minardos, Susan Oliver, Gregory Sierra, Dub Taylor, Med Florey, Curt Conway, Joaquin Martinez. A New Orleans chanteuse and a herd of scrawny cattle play a vital role in Heyes and Curry's secret mission to Mexico.

5.14 *Never Trust an Honest Man*. April 15, 1971. GS: Severn Darden, Robert Donner, Marj Dusay, Bill Fletcher, Burt Mustin, Glenn Dixon, Ford Rainey, Michael Carr, Robert Bruce Lane, Richard Anderson. Railroad magnate Oscar Harlingen, delighted when Smith and Jones return a fortune in jewels they picked up by accident, sends a posse after the boys when he learns that the gems are fake.

5.15 *The Legacy of Charlie O'Rourke*. April 22, 1971. GS: J.D. Cannon, Joan Hackett, Billy Green Bush, Guy Raymond, Erik Holland, Garry Van Orman, Hank Underwood, Steve Gravers. A saloon entertainer and a special agent are two among the many who take a special interest in Heyes and Curry's friendship with a condemned robber. Everyone thinks the man told them where he buried a stolen fortune in gold.

Season Two

5.16 *The Day They Hanged Kid Curry*. Sept. 16, 1971. GS: Walter Brennan, Robert Morse, Belinda J. Montgomery, Slim Pickens, Earl Holliman, Mickey Shaughnessy, Dennis Fimple, Henry Jones, Frank Maxwell, Paul Fix, Sid Haig, Vaughn Taylor, Booth Colman. Silky O'Sullivan is a con-man who masquerades as Curry's grandma to rescue a foolish youth from the gallows.

5.17 *How to Rob a Bank in One Hard Lesson*. Sept. 23, 1971. GS: Jack Cassidy, Joanna Barnes, Karen Machon, Greg Mullavey, Bobby Bass. Heyes and Curry are neatly trapped by a lady-in-distress gambit.

5.18 *Jailbreak at Junction City*. Sept. 30, 1971. GS: George Montgomery, Jack Albertson, James Wainwright, Kenneth Tobey, Bryan Montgomery, Angus Duncan, Thomas Bellin, Allen Emerson, William Bryant, Harry Hickox, Jon Lormer. Heyes and Curry find themselves in another bind courtesy of a sheriff they can't avoid and who is sure to recognize them.

5.19 *Smiler with a Gun*. Oct. 7, 1971. GS: Roger Davis, Will Geer, Barbara Stuart, Colby Chester, Harry Lauter, Milton Frome, Leo V. Gordon, Dick Haymes. A conflict-ridden party of treasure-seekers find themselves in the scorching desert.

5.20 *The Posse That Wouldn't Quit*. Oct. 14, 1971. GS: Vera Miles, Cindy Eilbacher, Lisa Eilbacher, Charles H. Gray, Richard X. Slattery, Russell Wiggins, Sidney Clute, Peter Brocco, Bert Holland. Belle Jordon is a strong-willed woman who provides Curry and Heyes with refuge from a relentless posse.

5.21 *Something to Get Hung About*. Oct. 21, 1971. GS: Monte Markham, Meredith MacRae, Roger Perry, Noah Beery, Jr., Ken Lynch, Paul Carr, Gary Van Orman. Curry and Heyes are hired to bring back a runaway wife and find they have stumbled into a romantic triangle.

5.22 *Six Strangers at Apache Springs*. Oct. 28, 1971. GS: Carmen Mathews, Sian Barbara Allen, John S. Ragin, Patricia Barry, Logan Ramsey. Hostile Chiricahua Apaches are threatening Heyes and Curry's attempt to retrieve a widow's hidden gold.

5.23 *The Night of the Red Dog*. Nov. 4, 1971. GS: Rory Calhoun, Jack Kelly, Joe Flynn, Paul Fix, Robert Pratt, Shannon Christie, Patricia Chandler. Heyes and Curry are involved in a marathon poker game in a snowbound cabin with the stakes $112,000 in gold dust.

5.24 *The Reformation of Harry Briscoe*. Nov. 11, 1971. GS: Jane Wyatt, J.D. Cannon, Jane Merrow, Joyce Jameson, Read Morgan. Curry and Heyes are drawn into a wild scramble over a hot $30,000.

5.25 *Dreadful Sorry, Clementine*. Nov. 18, 1971. GS: Sally Field, Keenan Wynn, Rudy Vallee, Don Ameche, Jackie Coogan, Ken Scott, Stuart Randall, Buddy Lester, William Benedict. Roguish Clementine Hale is trying to maneuver Heyes and Curry into a $50,000 swindle scheme.

5.26 *Shootout at Diablo Station*. Dec. 2, 1971. GS: Neville Brand, Howard Duff, Pat O'Brien, Steve Sandor, Anne Archer, Elizabeth Lane, Jim Antonio, Mike Road, Gary Van Orman, Bill Fletcher. Seven stagecoach passengers are held cative by outlaws who are setting a trap for a lawman.

5.27 *The Bounty Hunter*. Dec. 9, 1971. GS: Lou Gossett, Jr., Robert Donner, Geoffrey Lewis, Robert Middleton, R.G. Armstrong, Robert Easton, James McCallion. A black bounty hunter is determined to bring in prisoners Heyes and Curry.

5.28 *Everything Else You Can Steal*. Dec. 16, 1971. GS: Ann Sothern, Patrick O'Neal, Jessica Walter, David Canary, Kermit Murdock, Dennis Rucker, Parker West, Charles Dierkop, Allen Joseph, Robert Goodwin. Heyes and Curry are back in trouble with the law when they become involved with a fiery blackjack dealer.

5.29 *Miracle at Santa Marta*. Dec. 30, 1971. GS: Nico Minardos, Patricia Crowley, Ina Balin, Craig Stevens, Joanna Barnes, Gregory Walcott, Charles Tyner, Steven Gravers, Rudy Diaz, Fernando Escondas. Heyes does some sleuthing to clear his friend when Curry is the chief suspect in a murder rap.

5.30 *Twenty-One Days to Tenstrike*. Jan. 6, 1972. GS: Walter Brennan, Steve Forrest, Glenn Corbett, Joe Haworth, Pernell Roberts, Harry Harvey, Sr., Dick Cavett, Robert Colbert, Linda Marsh, Richard Wright, Paul Schott. Curry and Heyes become involved with a murder-ridden cattle drive.

5.31 *The McCreedy Bust — Going, Going, Gone*. Jan. 13, 1972. GS: Burl Ives, Cesar Romero, Bradford Dillman, Lee Majors, Ted Gehring, Paul Micale, Neil Russell, Mitch Carter, Robert P. Lieb. A gunman is forcing Curry into a showdown. It's part of a continuing battle over a bust of Caesar.

5.32 *The Man Who Broke the Bank at Red Gap.* Jan. 20, 1972. GS: Broderick Crawford, Rudy Vallee, Clarke Gordon, Ford Rainey, Bill Toomey, Dennis Fimple, Joe Schneider, Richard Wright. A banker dupes Curry and Heyes into a bum robbery rap.

5.33 *The Men That Corrupted Hadleyburg.* Jan. 27, 1972. GS: J.D. Cannon, Wally Cox, Sheree North, Dave Garroway, Andy Devine, Adam West, Gene Evans, David Gruner, Frederic Downs, Bill Anderson, Daniel F. Martin. Curry and Heyes try to help a family that captured them, and then broke them out of jail.

5.34 *The Biggest Game in the West.* Feb. 3, 1972. GS: Chill Wills, Jim Backus, Rod Cameron, Donald Woods, Dennis Fimple, Jackie Russell, Jon Lormer, Bill McKinney, Ford Rainey, X. Brands, Steven Gravers. Curry and Heyes again find themselves on the short end of another money-making stick when they become involved with counterfeit bills and a high stakes poker game.

5.35 *Which Way to the O.K. Corral?* Feb. 10, 1972. GS: Cameron Mitchell, Michele Lee, Neville Brand, Jackie Coogan, John Russell, Bill Fletcher, Burl Ives, William Mims, Walt Davis, Virginia Gregg, Bill Quinn, Tom Waters.

5.36 *Don't Get Mad, Get Even.* Feb. 17, 1972. GS: Michele Lee, John Banner, Robert Middleton, Walter Brennan, Gregg Palmer, Karen Smith, Eugene Shields, Monte Laird, Dave Morick. Heyes schemes to get back money he lost in a rigged poker game.

5.37 *What's in It for Mia?* Feb. 24, 1972. GS: Ida Lupino, Buddy Ebsen, George Robotham, Sallie Shockley, John Kellogg, Allen Pinson, Dud Wells. Heyes schemes to outfox a lady swindler.

5.38 *Bad Night in Big Butte.* March 2, 1972. GS: Arthur O'Connell, Michele Lee, Jack Elam, J.D. Cannon, Pat Buttram, Sam Jaffe, Mills Watson, Dave Willock, Robert Nicholas, Paul Schott, Frank Ferguson. A lovable rogue has a map to a hidden diamond, and a slick opportunist is hot on her trail.

Season Three

5.39 *The Long Chase.* Sept. 16, 1972. GS: James Drury, Frank Sinatra, Jr., J.D. Cannon, Larry Story, George Keymas, Dave Garroway. Smith and Jones elude a sheriff amid the canyons, arches and majestic spires of southeastern Utah.

5.40 *High Lonesome Country.* Sept. 23, 1972. GS: Rod Cameron, Buddy Ebsen, Marie Windsor, Walt Davis, Monty Laird. Bounty hunter Luke Billings track Curry and Heyes in Utah's Arches National Park.

5.41 *The McCreedy Feud.* Sept. 30, 1972. GS: Burl Ives, Cesar Romero, Katy Jurado, Dennis Fimple, Claudio Miranda, Rudy Diaz, Lou Peralta. Armendariz's aristocratic sister is the romantic key to a possible truce between him and his rancher rival McCreedy

5.42 *The Clementine Incident.* Oct. 7, 1972. Sally Field, Alejandro Rey, Ramon Bieri, Mills Watson, Joe Haworth, Cody Bearpaw. The outlaws' plan to retire in Mexico hit a snag when they encounter bounty hunters and lady con-artist Clementine Hale.

5.43 *Bushwack!* Oct. 21, 1972. GS: Christine Belford, Michael Conrad, Glenn Corbett, Frank Converse, Charles Gray, Ford Rainey, Mark Holly, Todd Martin, Buddy Foster, Sonny Shields. Smith and Jones sign on with a cattle drive plagued by a livestock association's hired guns.

5.44 *What Happened at the XST?* Oct. 28, 1972. GS: Keenan Wynn, Ed Nelson, Geoffrey Lewis, William Smith, Eve McVeagh, David Gruner, William D. Gordon, Dave Morick. An old friend ropes the boys into a scheme to dig up loot from a robbery which could cancel their promised amnesty.

5.45 *The Ten Days That Shook Kid Curry.* Nov. 4, 1972. GS: Shirley Knight, Edd Byrnes, Bill Fletcher, Ted Gehring, Frederick Downs, Barbara Bosson, Steve Gravers, Bill Quinn. Curry gets the blame for a bank robbery and kidnaping, but he is actually the victim, held in a mine by the two people who engineered the plot.

5.46 *The Day the Amnesty Came Through.* Nov. 25, 1972. GS: Lane Bradbury, John Russell, Brett Halsey, Robert Donner, Jeff Corey, Warren Vanders, Charles Dierkop, Sonny Shields, Gerald McRaney, Frank Stoll. Curry and Heyes plan to win their amnesty from the new territorial governor by rescuing a lady from her outlaw lover.

5.47 *The Strange Fate of Conrad Meyer Zulick.* Dec. 2, 1972. GS: David Canary, Sorrell Booke, Slim Pickens, John Kellogg, Michael Mikler, Dennis Rucker, Bert Santos, Annette Bravo, Laurie Ferrone. Curry and Heyes participate in the slightly illegal rescue of an American lawyer held under arrest in Mexico City.

5.48 *McGuffin.* Dec. 9, 1972. GS: Darleen Carr, Jackie Coogan, Clarke Gordon, Jack Manning, Walter Brooke, L.Q. Jones, Monty Laird, Alice Nunn, Mort Mills, Allen Joseph, Chuck Hicks, X Brands. When Curry and Heyes become involved with counterfeiters and the U.S. Treasury Department, their number one probem is telling the crooks from the cops.

5.49 *Witness to a Lynching.* Dec. 16, 1972. GS: John McGiver, Brenda Scott, G.D. Spradlin, Barry Cahill, Ann Doran, Kenneth Tobey, John Russell, Dick Whittington, Paul Schott. A witness to a lynching is held in protective custody by Curry and Heyes.

5.50 *Only Three to a Bed.* Jan. 13, 1973. GS: Dean Jagger, John Kerr, Jo Ann Pflug, Laurette Spang, Paul Fix, Dana Elcar, Janet Johnson, Pepper Martin, Gary Van Orman, Michael Rupert. During a wild-horse roundup Curry and Heyes encounter a husband-hunting singer and a hard-nosed ranger who accuse them of rustling.

6. *Annie Oakley*

Syndicated. 30 min. Broadcast history: Various, Jan. 1954–Feb. 1957.

Regular Cast: Gail Davis (Annie Oakley), Brad Johnson (Deputy Sheriff Lofty Craig), Jimmy Hawkins (Tagg Oakley).

Premise: Sharpshooter Annie Oakley and her brother, Tagg, assist Deputy Lofty Craig in rounding up badmen near her hometown of Diablo.

The Episodes

6.1 *Annie and the Brass Collar.* Jan. 9, 1954. GS: Robert Emmett O'Connor, Glase Lohman, Roy Barcroft, Paul E. Burns, Chris Alcaide. Annie and Sheriff Craig come to the aid of their old pal, stationmaster Dan Haywood, who is blamed for a series of train robberies.

6.2 *Annie Trusts a Convict.* Jan. 16, 1954. GS: Myron Healey, Harry Harvey, Jr., Gregg Barton, Steve Pendleton, Alan Bridge, Edward Earle. Annie and Tagg find a young escaped convict and believe him to be innocent of the crime.

6.3 *Gunplay.* Jan. 23, 1954. GS: Myron Healey, Ralph Sanford, Paul McGuire, Steve Pendleton, Gregg Barton, Francis McDonald, Bob Woodward. Annie is tricked by a gunman, but the outlaw makes a big mistake when he meets up with an old acquaintance.

6.4 *The Dude Stagecoach.* Jan. 30, 1954. GS: Maura Murphy, Tom London, House Peters, Jr., George Lewis, Bob Woodward. Annie, Tagg and Lofty try to persuade the spoiled rich girl who owns Diablo's unprofitable stage line to fight the outlaws who want to take it over.

6.5 *Ambush Canyon.* Feb. 6, 1954. GS: Robert B. Williams, Gloria Talbott, Marshall Reed, Sam Flint, William Fawcett, Mickey Simpson, Darwyn Greenfield. A young Indian girl, the adopted daughter of a gold mine owner, is put in an awkward position when he is murdered. Annie tries to help the girl make the right decision.

6.6 *Annie Calls Her Shots.* Feb. 13, 1954. GS: Alan Hale, Jr., Harry Lauter, Lane Bradford, Bud Osborne, Bob Woodward. When an embittered ex-convict, sent to prison for a crime he didn't commit, returns to Diablo and declares war on the town, Annie tries to prevent bloodshed between him and the man who prosecuted him.

6.7 *A Gal for Grandma.* Feb. 20, 1954. GS: Mabel Paige, Elizabeth Harrower, Christopher Cook, Myron Healey, Gregg Barton, Steve Mitchell, Bob Woodward. Annie becomes involved when a sour spinster who takes care of a rich, bitter and man-hating old invalid is courted by a handsome gunman who plans to marry the one woman and then kill them both.

6.8 *Annie and the Silver Ace.* Feb. 27, 1954. GS: Harry Lauter, Alan Hale, Jr., Mary Young, Lane Bradford, Jack Sterling, Bob Woodward, Bud Osborne. Annie tries to stop a likeable lad from opening a gambling hall. When gangsters try to move in, Annie makes a decision.

6.9 *Annie Finds Strange Treasure.* March 6, 1954. Don Harvey, Ric Vallin, Stanley Andrews, Bill Crandall, Sam Flint, Michael Vallon, Bob Woodward. Annie's trick shooting drives off three outlaws who have fatally wounded an old prospector while trying to learn where he hid his riches. Later the three lure Annie to an isolated shack and try to force the secret from her.

6.10 *The Cinder Trail.* March 13, 1954. GS: Robert Emmett O'Connor, Glase Lohman, Roy Barcroft, Paul E. Burns, Chris Alcaide, Bob Woodward. Annie, Tagg and Lofty battle a corrupt rancher who plans to take over the railroad and control the price of shipping cattle.

6.11 *Valley of the Shadows.* March 20, 1954. GS: Judy Nugent, Arthur Space, Forrest Taylor, Denver Pyle, Steve Darrell, John Cason. Annie helps a 12-year-old girl regain her eyesight in order to identify her father's killer.

6.12 *Annie and the Lily Maid.* March 27, 1954. GS: Maura Murphy, Tom London, House Peters, Jr., George J. Lewis, Bob Woodward. Annie is suspicious of the supposedly accidental death of a rancher. Her suspicions increase when the dead man's niece arrives in town.

6.13 *The Hardrock Trail.* April 3, 1954. GS: Kenneth MacDonald, Robert B. Williams, Alan Wells, William Fawcett. Annie lures Sheriff Luck MacTavish out of town to save him from the wrath of an ex-convict gunfighter, but it is Tagg's appetite for hard candy that causes the outlaw's downfall.

6.14 *Annie Gets Her Man.* April 10, 1954. GS: Darryl Hickman, John Eldredge, Steve Darrell, Clayton Moore, Hank Patterson, I. Stanford Jolley. Annie and Lofty use marked bullets to solve a bank robbery and murder.

6.15 *Justice Guns.* April 17, 1954. GS: Stanley Andrews, Rick Vallin, Damian O'Flynn, Sam Flint, Don C. Harvey, Bill Crandall, Bob Woodward. When a vicious young gunman provokes a proud old marshal into a shootout, Annie realizes that the old man is no match for the outlaw and uses her marksmanship to prevent a tragedy.

6.16 *Annie's Desert Adventure.* April 24, 1954. GS: Denver Pyle, Steve Darrell, John Cason, Forrest Taylor, Arthur Space, Francis McDonald. Annie, Tagg and Lofty come to the aid of an ex-convict who has been framed for a gold robbery just after his release from prison. At Annie's suggestion he takes up with the outlaws who accused him.

6.17 *Annie and the Mystery Woman.* May 1, 1954. GS: Virginia Lee, Fess Parker, Larry Chance, Dick Reeves, Edward Clark, Bob Woodward. A pretty dance hall queen, the key witness in a murder trial, hides out in Diablo when she is threatened by the suspected killer.

6.18 *Annie and the Texas Sandman.* May 8, 1954. GS: Fess Parker, Virginia Lee, Larry Chance, Dick Reeves, Pat O'Malley, Edward Clark, Isa Ashdown. Annie, Tagg and Lofty try to help a notorious Texas gunman who has put away his weapons and has come to Diablo to lead a peaceful life but has been followed by the revenge-driven brothers of a man he killed in self-defense.

6.19 *Annie Meets Some Tenderfeet.* May 15, 1954. GS: Kirk Alyn, Helene Marshall, Christopher Cook, Myron Healey, Gregg Barton, Alan Bridge. An Eastern banker comes to the attention of a local gambling king. The outlaw schemes to get his hands on the newcomer's money.

6.20 *Annie Joins the Cavalry.* May 22, 1954. GS: Keith Richards, Henry Rowland, Harry Harvey, Sr., Rodd Redwing, Karl Davis, Dick Jones, Kenne Duncan. Annie tries to prove that the Hopi Indians were not responsible for the ambush in which five cavalrymen and a bugle boy were killed.

6.21 *Bull's Eye.* May 29, 1954. GS: Kenneth MacDonald, Marshall Reed, Wade Crosby, William Fawcett, Robert B. Williams. A land-grabbing scheme involves poisoned water holes on rangeland set aside for wild animals.

6.22 *Annie Helps a Drifter.* June 5, 1954. GS: Dick Jones, Harry Harvey, Sr., Keith Richards, Henry Rowland, Karl Davis. Following her intuition, Annie helps a penniless young man who is arrested for petty larceny and is framed for the murder of his rich uncle.

6.23 *Sharpshooting Annie.* June 12, 1954. GS: George Pembroke, Mickey Simpson, Max Terhune, Terry Frost. Annie matches wits and guns with a mysterious masked bandit wanted for years by the law.

6.24 *Annie Makes a Marriage.* June 19, 1954. GS: Nancy Hale, Don Kennedy, Don C. Harvey, Mickey Simpson, Terry Frost. After reading some volumes of love poetry, Annie decides to play Cupid and help an ex-convict clear his name so he can marry the woman he loves.

Annie Oakley

6.25 *Outlaw Mesa.* June 26, 1954. GS: James Best, Jean Howell, Harry Lauter, Chris Alcaide, Rick Vallin, Duane Thorsen, Dick Elliott. Tagg's newest hobby, ventriloquism, comes in mighty handy when a young rancher refuses to testify against his outlaw brother.

6.26 *Annie and the Outlaw's Son.* July 3, 1954. GS: James Best, Jean Howell, Stanley Andrews, Duane Thorsen, Harry Lauter, Rick Vallin. Townspeople are baffled by a young rancher, who had the opportunity to stop fleeing bank robbers, and didn't shoot. Annie does some investigating.

Season Two

6.27 *Alias Annie Oakley.* July 10, 1954. GS: Nan Leslie, Harry Lauter, Lane Bradford, Tom Monroe, Bob Woodward, Carol Henry. A gun moll disguises herself as Annie Oakley and goes on a rampage of crime. Annie herself is in danger when she tries to track down the imposter.

6.28 *The Tomboy.* July 17, 1954. GS: David Alpert, Melinda Plowman, William Fawcett, Stanley Andrews, Gregg Barton, Joe Haworth, Mickey Little, Bob Woodward. Tagg Oakley is not too happy about playing host to Sheriff Craig's young niece. His objections disappear when the young lady proves herself quite a tomboy.

6.29 *The Runaways.* July 24, 1954. GS: Stuffy Singer, Bill Henry, Mike Ragan, Dennis Moore, Robert Bice, Fred Ritter. Annie allows Tagg and a young friend to run away from home and spend the night in a ghost town, not knowing that the town is the hideout of the notorious Shadow gang.

6.30 *Annie and the Six o'Spades.* July 31, 1954. GS: Dick Jones, Walter Reed, Jimmy Murphy, Gary Gray, Tom London. Tagg's slingshot saves the day when a 17-year-old with pretensions of being a sharpshooter takes it into his head to shoot it out with Annie.

6.31 *Escape from Diablo.* Aug. 7, 1954. GS: John Doucette, William Tannen, Red Morgan. Annie and Lofty search for Tagg, who has been captured by thieves while hunting for the cattle money they stole.

6.32 *The Iron Smoke Wagon.* Aug. 14, 1954. GS: Kirk Alyn, Sheila Ryan, John Patrick, Harry Harvey, Sr., Steve Pendleton, John Diehl. Annie tries to solve the bank robbery that followed the arrival of Diablo's first fire engine.

6.33 *Annie and the Chinese Puzzle.* Feb. 13, 1955. GS: Keye Luke, Lawrence Ryle, Craig Woods, William Tannen, Jack Ingram. Annie befriends a Chinese laundryman who has been having trouble with hostile townspeople and is being framed for a murder because he refuses to sell his property.

6.34 *Annie Breaks an Alibi.* Feb. 27, 1955. GS: Harry Cheshire, Lee Van Cleef, Keith Richards, Henry Rowland, John Damler, Lane Chandler. Annie battles two greedy cousins, neither of them satisfied with sharing the estate they inherited and each scheming to get it all for himself.

6.35 *Trigger Twins.* March 6, 1955. GS: Myron Healey, Eddie Dew, Lou Smith, Sue Smith, Charles Williams, Cecil Elliott, Carol Henry. Annie proves that she can compete on the dance floor as well as on the pistol range when she is challenged by a pair of attractive twin sisters, one a dancing teacher, the other a bandit.

6.36 *Diablo Doctor.* March 13, 1955. GS: David Alpert, Stanley Andrews, Melinda Plowman, William Fawcett, Gregg Barton, Joe Haworth, Harry Mackin, Bob Woodward. Annie tries to restore the self-confidence of a young doctor who was unable to save his dieing father.

6.37 *Dead Man's Bluff.* March 20, 1955. GS: Emile Meyer, Myron Healey, Eddie Dew, Pierre Watkin, Kenne Duncan, Grace Field. When panicky citizens of Diablo make a run on the town's failing bank, Annie, Tagg and Lofty set out to discover who is manipulating the financial crisis.

6.38 *Annie and the Junior Pioneers.* March 27, 1955. GS: Dick Jones, Walter Reed, Dorothy Adams, Gordon Gebert, Bob Woodward. Annie, Tagg and Lofty and the local Junior Pioneers club try to straighten out a juvenile delinquent, but the boy almost has a relapse when his older brother escapes from prison and comes home.

6.39 *Hard Luck Ranch.* April 3, 1955. GS: Lois Hall, Harry Lauter, Lane Bradford, Tom Monroe. Annie, Tagg and Lofty help a wheelchair-bound former rodeo stuntman when he and his wife are held prisoner at their ranch by two outlaws.

6.40 *Thunder Hill.* April 10, 1955. GS: Stanley Andrews, Barbara Woodell, Bill Henry, Stuffy Singer, Mike Ragan, Dennis Moore. Annie, Tagg and Lofty try to find out what is behind the unfriendliness of a newly arrived ranch family.

6.41 *Sure Shot Annie.* April 17, 1955. GS: Eve Miller, Rick Vallin, Harry Antrim, William Phipps, Paul Burns, Jean Lewis, Ruth Warren, Bob Woodward. Annie and Lofty go after a sultry siren who has come to Diablo and charmed her way inside the local bank vault.

6.42 *Annie and the Widow's Might.* April 24, 1955. GS: Barbara Woodell, Lawrence Ryle, Sammy Ogg, William Tannen. Annie saves a widow and her young son from a scheming schoolteacher and a greedy neighbor who are trying to make her sell her property.

6.43 *Trouble Shooter.* May 1, 1955. GS: Gene Reynolds, John Doucette, William Tannen, Joe Haworth, Selmer Jackson, Almira Sessions. Annie, Tagg and Lofty take the side of the underdog when Diablo's townspeople become incensed at a local rancher's hiring an ex-convict whose outlaw brother is still at large.

6.44 *Annie Takes a Chance.* May 8, 1955. GS: Gloria Jean, Douglas Kennedy, James Griffith, Marshall Bradford, Don C. Harvey, John Cason, Bob Woodward. Annie, Tagg and Lofty come to the rescue when a judge who has founded a rehabilitation ranch for ex-convicts is threatened by a gunfighter whose innocent brother the judge has sentenced to death.

6.45 *Annie and the Higher Court.* May 15, 1955. GS: Harry Cheshire, Lee Van Cleef, Henry Rowland, John Damler, Edna Holland, Sam Flint. Annie, Tagg and Lofty learn that a crooked banker has offered a bribe to Diablo's financially strapped judge if he will acquit the banker's arrested accomplice.

6.46 *Powder Rock Stampede.* May 22, 1955. GS: Gloria Jean, Douglas Kennedy, James Griffith, Marshall Bradford, Don C. Harvey, Bob Woodward. Annie contends with a land rush when the government opens the Powder Rock territory to homesteaders.

Season Three

6.47 *Sundown Stage.* June 3, 1956. GS: Walter Reed,

Helene Marshall, Barry Curtis, Carleton Young, Gabor Curtiz, Joel Ashley, Baynes Barron, Charlie Hayes, Bucko Stafford, Bob Woodward. Annie's brother Tagg finds an injured man wandering in a dazed condition outside of Diablo. The man has lost his memory but Annie finds a picture on the wanted list. He is accused of robbery and murder.

6.48 *Joker on Horseback.* June 10, 1956. GS: Robert Easton, Mary Ellen Kay, Myron Healey, William Tannen, Sam Flint, Frederick Ford, Reed Howes. Annie, Tagg and Lofty go after the practical joker who is responsible for a wave of robberies in Diablo.

6.49 *A Tall Tale.* June 17, 1956. GS: Sam Flint, Harry Lauter, Barry Froner, Joe Cranston, Douglas Grange, Paul Sorensen. An old prospector has written glowing letters of his exploits to his young grandson. When the youngster visits unexpectedly, he is afraid the boy's illusions will be destroyed. Annie, Tagg and Lofty conspire to help the old man out.

6.50 *Annie and the Twisted Trails.* June 24, 1956. GS: Carlyn Craig, Ewing Mitchell, Myron Healey, Barbara Knudson, Bill Phipps, Vaughn Meadows. Annie tries to help a young girl whose life is dominated by her overly-stern father. The man's sour outlook on life dates back to when the 18-year-old girl was a small child and her mother ran away and joined a rodeo.

6.51 *The Robin Hood Kid.* July 1, 1956. GS: William Fawcett, Roy Barcroft, Tyler MacDuff, L.Q. Jones, Buzz Henry, Howard Wright. Annie, Tagg and Lofty try to help a rich man's son who has taken the law into his own hands because the big ranchers are doing nothing to help their water-starved neighbors, but who finds himself accused of a bank robbery he didn't commit.

6.52 *Annie and the Bicycle Riders.* July 8, 1956. GS: Steven Clark, Lili Kardell, Keith Richards, Gregg Barton, John Parrish, Robert J. Wilke, Harry Mackin. Annie, Tagg and Lofty find a use for bicycles as they pursue the gunmen who mortally wounded a mailroom clerk during a robbery but who have to go on the run when the clerk manages to telegraph a description of them before he dies.

6.53 *Annie and the Lacemaker.* July 15, 1956. GS: Keith Richards, Lili Kardell, Steven Clark, Lisa Gaye, Gregg Barton, Paul E. Burns, Dick Alexander. When a man who refused to sell his ranch is murdered, Annie, Tagg and Lofty have to figure out which of the two young women claiming to be his daughter and heir is genuine and which is a fake.

6.54 *Annie and the First Phone.* July 22, 1956. GS: Peter Camlin, Harry Lauter, Frank Fenton, John War Eagle, Robert Cabal, X Brands, Bob Woodward. Annie, Tagg and Lofty use the first telephone seen in the West to organize the local settlers who are discouraged by failing crops and the menace of rampaging Indians.

6.55 *Indian Justice.* July 29, 1956. GS: Harry Lauter, Frank Fenton, John War Eagle, Robert Cabal, Jerry Summers, X Brand. A young veteran of Teddy Roosevelt's Rough Riders returns to Diablo intent on buying land in Senoquois Valley, but learns that the property has been taken over as an Indian reservation. Later, when an Indian is found murdered and the veteran is accused, Annie tries to capture him before the tribe does.

6.56 *Showdown at Diablo.* Aug. 5, 1956. GS: Roscoe Ates, Lane Bradford, Bill Henry, Stanley Andrews, Jacquelyn Park, Fritz Ford, Tyler McVey. A ruthless gang leader rides into Diablo determined to make trouble. The townspeople are baffled when Deputy Lofty Craig refuses to draw his gun and later turns in his badge. He is branded a coward, but Annie refuses to believe this.

6.57 *The Mississippi Kid.* Aug. 12, 1956. GS: Robert Easton, Mary Ellen Kay, Myron Healey, William Tannen, Frederick Ford. Annie, Tagg and Lofty encounter a tenderfoot from the South who has come West to live with his sister, and feels compelled to prove to everyone how brave he is.

6.58 *Renegade's Return.* Aug. 19, 1956. GS: Rick Vallin, Roy Barcroft, Mike Garrett, Maryellen Clemons, Kenne Duncan, Charlie Hayes, Bill Baucom. Annie, Tagg and Lofty become involved in an election campaign when a crooked politician threatens to tell an orphaned child being raised by her uncle that her father is not a dead hero, as she believes, but a live outlaw, unless her uncle drops out of the campaign.

6.59 *Sugarfoot Sue.* Aug. 26, 1956. GS: Roy Barcroft, Mike Garrett, Maryellen Clemons, Rick Vallin, Robert J. Wilke, Tom London, Ken Osmond. Annie and Lofty have to deal with a 10-year-old girl whose daydreams and wild yarns have been taken by Tagg for the truth.

6.60 *Annie and the Leprechauns.* Sept. 2, 1956. GS: Raymond Hatton, Walter Reed, Grace Field, Slim Pickens, Terry Frost. Annie, Tagg and Lofty try to prevent murder when an unscrupulous man hires a gunfighter to murder a friend and neighbor who has discovered gold on his property.

6.61 *Dilemma at Diablo.* Sept. 9, 1956. GS: Roy Barcroft, Tyler MacDuff, William Fawcett, Buzz Henry, L.Q. Jones. Annie, Tagg and Lofty try to help a young doctor who has returned to Diablo to hang out his shingle after his father has put him through medical school and equipped a new office for him.

6.62 *Outlaw Brand.* Sept. 16, 1956. GS: Leonard Penn, House Peters, Jr., Lane Bradford, Glenn Strange, Ken Christy, Sam Flint, Stuffy Singer. Annie, Tagg and Lofty try to help Tagg's young friend Johnny, the son of a slain deputy sheriff, who is being raised by a former outlaw, but believes his guardian is returning to his old ways and planning a robbery.

6.63 *Shadow at Sonoma.* Sept. 23, 1956. GS: Eve Miller, Harry Lauter, Baynes Barron, Frank Fenton, Gregg Barton, Henry Rowland, Bob Woodward. Lofty assumes the identity of a gunman and enters a shooting contest against Annie, while Tagg becomes captivated by a traveling magician.

6.64 *Western Privateer.* Sept. 30, 1956. GS: Bill Henry, Nancy Hale, Donald Curtis, Paul Fitzpatrick, Stanley Andrews, Charlie Hayes. John Boone and his young son are disliked by most of the inhabitants in Diablo. They claim that the man is responsible for the death of an old-timer who went with him on a treasure hunt.

6.65 *The Reckless Press.* Oct. 7, 1956. GS: Harry Lauter, Eve Miller, Baynes Barron, Frank Fenton, Gregg Barton, Henry Rowland, Pierre Watkin, Bob Woodward. Annie and Lofty pursue the bandits who robbed a bank and killed a sheriff while a wedding was taking place.

6.66 *Flint and Steel.* Oct. 14, 1956. GS: Jim Bannon, Lyle Talbot, Virginia Dale, Monte Blue, Helen Brown, Gregg Barton, Michael Taylor, Terry Frost, Frank Richards. Annie, Tagg and Lofty help some homesteaders who are being pressured to sell their land for half its value.

6.67 *Tagg Oakley, Sheriff.* Oct. 21, 1956. GS: Jim Bannon, Monte Blue, Frank Richards, Lyle Talbot, Michael Taylor. Annie and Lofty come to the rescue when Tagg is appointed Sheriff of Diablo County during National Boys Week and, by volunteering to help drive a shipment of supplies to Fort Yuma, unwittingly helps a criminal steal a wagonload of gunpowder.

6.68 *The Waco Kid.* Oct. 28, 1956. GS: Ron Hagerthy, Lizz Slifer, Roy Barcroft, Dick Reeves, Slim Pickens. Deputy Lofty Craig suspects an old beau of Annie's of being the notorious Waco Kid, for whom there is a wanted notice posted. When the man rides into town with another desperado, Annie steps in to arrest him, but is overpowered.

6.69 *The Saga of Clement O'Toole.* Nov. 4, 1956. GS: Tyler MacDuff, Frank Fenton, Sally Fraser, Edgar Dearing, Rick Vallin, Kenne Duncan, Bob Woodward. Annie, Tagg and Lofty try to help an innocent man mistaken by the townspeople for his double, a notorious outlaw.

6.70 *The Front Trail.* Nov. 11, 1956. GS: Tyler MacDuff, Edgar Dearing, Frank Fenton, Sally Fraser, Rick Vallin, Kenne Duncan, Harry Mackin, Hal K. Dawson, Bob Woodward. Annie, Tagg and Lofty try to help a retired U.S. Marshal confront his son, who runs a gambling house Annie would like to see closed.

6.71 *Annie Rides the Navajo Trail.* Nov. 18, 1956. GS: Victor Millan, Walter Reed, Bill Henry, John Beradino, Tita Aragon, George J. Lewis, Mike Ragan. Having been robbed of their handcrafts, the Navajo Indians meet to plan war. No outsider can get in to discuss peace, so Annie dons the garb of an Indian in an effort to halt war.

6.72 *Annie Rings the Bell.* Nov. 25, 1956. GS: Britt Lomond, Rob Barcroft, Ron Hagerthy, Slim Pickens, Dick Reeves, Edgar Dearing, X Brands, Tom Steele. Annie turns fight promoter for a contest held to raise funds for the town's new school, but is interrupted when desperadoes break out of jail and attempt to steel the boxoffice receipts.

6.73 *Santa Claus Wears a Gun.* Dec. 2, 1956. GS: Stanley Andrews, Keith Richards, Duane Grey, Paul E. Burns, Ewing Mitchell, Bob Woodward. A special agent who is guarding the delivery of an Army payroll, tells Annie he suspects that Snowy Kringle, an old circus sharpshooter, is after the money. When Kringle is arrested for the robbery, Annie an Tagg decide to help him prove his innocence.

6.74 *Amateur Outlaw.* Dec. 9, 1956. GS: George J. Lewis, Victor Millan, Walter Reed, Bill Henry, John Beradino, Dick Elliott, Mike Ragan, Tom London, Bob Woodward. Annie, Tagg and Lofty try to help an Indian who has inherited a mail-stage franchise from his white patron, but has also inherited the wrath of a few racist citizens of Diablo.

6.75 *Grubstake Bank.* Dec. 16, 1956. GS: Raymond Hatton, Walter Reed, Grace Field, Jose Gonzales Gonzales, Slim Pickens, Terry Frost, Frank Scannell. Everyone in Diablo is happy when an old prospector finally strikes gold. He plans to open a bank for other prospectors. Annie is suspicious when a stranger arrives and pays undue attention to the old man.

6.76 *Treasure Map.* Dec. 30, 1956. GS: Leonard Penn, Lane Bradford, House Peters, Jr., Glenn Strange, Shelley Fabares, Bob Woodward. Annie, Tagg and Lofty become involved when a man whose hobby is reading history finds a Spanish treasure map and is plagued by outlaws who want it for themselves.

6.77 *Annie and the Miser.* Jan. 20, 1957. GS: Roscoe Ates, Stanley Andrews, Lane Bradford, Bill Henry. An old miser who can't stand to throw anything away or give anything up, behaves very peculiarly when Annie and Deputy Craig question him about a robbery that took place near his shack. The robbers escaped without a trace and there is no sign of the missing money belonging to the Cattlemen's Association. Annie plays a hunch and visits the miner's shack and a talking parrot gives her the clue she needs.

6.78 *Tuffy.* Feb. 3, 1957. GS: Harry Lauter, Sam Flint, Joe Cranston, Barry Froner, Douglas George. When his father is killed, a young boy insists that he must continue on to his aunt's home in Colorado. Annie is mystified by the boy's insistence that he go by way of Traprock, which is a ghost town. Tagg goes with him to show him part of the way, and Annie realizes that both of the boys are in danger.

6.79 *Dude's Decision.* Feb. 10, 1957. GS: Bill Phipps, Myron Healey, Ewing Mitchell, Carolyn Craig, Robert Hinkle, Jock C. Watt. Annie, Tagg and Lofty try to help a young girl and her father who are delighted when a charming Bostonian turns up to look over their ranch, but who are unaware that the man is a young outlaw planning his first crime.

6.80 *The Dutch Gunmaker.* Feb. 17, 1957. GS: Gabor Curtiz, Helene Marshall, Walter Reed, Barry Curtis, Carleton Young, Baynes Barron, Joel Ashley, Bob Woodward. A newcomer to Dodge claims to have a gun like no one has ever seen before. The Dutchman has Annie test the gun and is delighted with her reaction. He tells her that he is going to give the gun to the Army to show his gratitude to his new country. But word of the fabulous gun spreads and a couple of rough characters scheme to get the valuable weapon.

6.81 *Desperate Men.* Feb. 24, 1957. GS: Bill Henry, Nancy Hale, Donald Curtis, Stanley Andrews, Charlie Hayes, Hank Patterson. Annie and Lofty pursue a man wanted for the murder of a sheriff while Tagg plays matchmaker for a beautiful, but painfully shy, schoolteacher.

7. *The Barbary Coast*

ABC. 60 min. Broadcast history: Monday, 8:00–9:00, Sept. 1975–Oct. 1975; Friday, 8:00–9:00, Oct. 1975–Jan. 1976.

Regular Cast: Doug McClure (Cash Conover), William Shatner (Jeff Cable), Richard Kiel (Moose Moran), Dave Turner (Thumbs), Francine York (Brandy), Bobbi Jordan (Flame), Brooke Mills (Sam, the bartender), Eddie Fontaine (Sam, the bartender), Jason Wingreen (casino waiter).

Premise: This series was set in San Francisco's Barbary Coast in the 1870s, and dealt with the exploits of special agent Jeff Cable and his ally, Golden Gate Casino owner Cash Conover.

The Episodes

7.1 *The Barbary Coast.* May 4, 1975. GS: Lynda Day George, Charles Aidman, Michael Ansara, Neville Brand, John Vernon, Leo V. Gordon, Bob Hoy, Terry Lester, Simon Scott, Todd Martin. Undercover agent Jeff Cable and casino owner Cash Canover work hand in glove to nab crooks on San Francisco's raucous Barbary Coast of the 1880s. They first team up to expose an extortion plot devised by a Confederate Army officer.

Season One

7.2 *Funny Money.* Sept. 8, 1975. GS: Pat Hingle, Kathleen Cody, William Bramley, David Macklin, Jeff Morris, Robert Foulk, Charles Macaulay. Cable and Conover target a banker who increased his account by $200,000 in countereit cash.

7.3 *Crazy Cats.* Sept. 15, 1975. GS: Eric Braeden, Joanna Miles, Andrew Prine, Zitto Kazann, Ian Wolfe, Sherry Jackson, Len Lesser, Bob Bass. Undercover agent Jeff Cable poses as a reporter for a game of cat-and-mouse with a millionaire rancher for possession of a $500,000 jade cat stolen from the Chinese government.

7.4 *Jesse Who?* Sept. 22, 1975. GS: Rosemary Forsyth, Lloyd Bochner, David Spielberg, Lance LeGault, Darrell Fetty, Carl Lee. Cable is put on the alert by a newspaper report that Jesse James has robbed a small California bank. The Missouri outlaw isn't apt to come so far and take so little unless he has something much bigger in mind.

7.5 *The Ballad of Redwing Jail.* Sept. 29, 1975. GS: Andrew Duggan, Ralph Meeker, James Cromwell, Roy Kelton, Marcy Lafferty, Paul Brinegar, Lawrence Casey. Cable poses as a wanted outlaw to liberate $20,000 hidden in a small-town jail managed by a money-grubbing sheriff.

7.6 *Guns for a Queen.* Oct. 6, 1975. GS: Joan Van Ark, Fred Beir, John Erickson, Nate Esformes, Seamon Glass, Joyce Jameson, Hal Baylor, Reggie Parton. Attempting to recover a hijacked shipment of rifles, Cash and Cable become involved with revolutionaries, cut-throats and a beautiful woman from their past.

7.7 *Irish Coffee.* Oct. 13, 1975. GS: William Daniels, Conny Van Dyke, Edward Andrews, Sandy Kenyon. A terrorist society plans to assassinate renowned Irish leader Charles Stewart Parnell as he tours San Francisco, and it's up to Cash and Cable to foil the attempt.

7.8 *Sauce for the Goose.* Oct. 20, 1975. GS: Joseph Campanella, Burr DeBenning, Martin E. Brooks, Simon Scott, Diane McBain, Charles Bateman. Playing on a corrupt civic leader's superstitious nature, Cable and Cash use pseudo-occult means in a scheme to con the man out of a book that lists political payoffs.

7.9 *An Iron-Clad Plan.* Oct. 31, 1975. GS: Tige Andrews, Louise Sorel, Severn Darden, Jacques Aubuchon, James Brown, Joan Bennett Perry, William Bryant. Posing as a sinister foreign agent, Cable tries to recover stolen blueprints for a top-secret ironclad submarine.

7.10 *Arson and Old Lace.* Nov. 14, 1975. GS: Gretchen Corbett, Dennis Patrick, Johnny Seven, Hal Baylor, William Jordan, Rudy Diaz, Jimmy Lannon. Cable and Cash try to uncover the identity of "The Shark", a waterfront racketeer who burns fishermen's boats if they don't pay him protection money.

7.11 *Sharks Eat Sharks.* Nov. 21, 1975. GS: Henry Gibson, Philip Bruns, Bernard Fox, Suzanne Charny, Karl Lukas, Tiger Joe Marsh. Cash and Cable set a couple of con men against a group of shakedown artists, with a phony diamond mine as the bone of contention.

7.12 *The Day Cable Was Hanged.* Dec. 26, 1975. GS: Tom Troupe, Anjanette Comer, John Dehner, Michael Blodgett, Booth Colman, Kelly Wilder, Monica Lewis, James Griffith. After bringing in a man believed to be John Wilkes Booth, Cable has second thoughts about the man's actual identity.

7.13 *Mary Had More Than a Little.* Jan. 2, 1976. GS: Judy Strangis, Kaz Garas, Whit Bissell, Don "Red" Barry, Phillip Pine, Robert Cornthwaite, Gene Tyburn. Attracted by a very pretty and very ladylike new dealer, Nob Hill gentlemen are packing the Golden Gate's gambling tables — and being robbed of their winnings on the way home.

7.14 *The Dawson Marker.* Jan. 9, 1976. GS: John Rubinstein, Udana Power, Billy Green Bush, Spencer Milligan, George Petrie, Douglas V. Fowley. The heirs of Confederate agents who stole a shipment of gold during the Civil War are meeting in San Francisco to recover the loot, but Cable hopes to get to the cache first.

8. *Bat Masterson*

NBC. 30 min. Broadcast history: Wednesday, 9:30-10:00, Oct. 1958–Sept. 1959; Thursday, 8:00-8:30, Oct. 1959–Sept. 1960; Thursday, 8:30–9:00, Sept. 1960–Sept. 1961.

Regular Cast: Gene Barry (Bat Masterson).

Premise: This series depicted highlights from the life of Bat Masterson, the debonair lawman with a gold-topped cane and derby hat, during the 1880s in his travels to uphold the law from Kansas to California.

The Episodes

8.1 *Double Showdown.* Oct. 8, 1958. GS: Robert Middleton, Jean Willes, Elisha Cook, Jr., Adele Mara, King Donovan, Charles Maxwell, K.L. Smith, William Vaughan. Bat Masterson goes to an Arizona town to help an old friend, the owner of a local saloon. He has nearly been put out of business by Big Keel Roberts, gambler and owner of a rival saloon. When Big Keel suggests that he and Bat solve the problem by a hand of showdown poker, Bat agrees.

8.2 *Two Graves for Swan Valley.* Oct. 15, 1958. GS: Broderick Crawford, Murvyn Vye, Bill Henry, Marcia Henderson, Patrick McVey. Gunman Ben Thompson is wounded when he saves Bat Masterson's life in a gunfight over a card game. Because of his wound, Thompson is unable to go through with his plan to help his brother Billy escape from jail. Ben claims the younger Thompson is not guilty. To repay Thompson for saving his life, Masterson offers to do the job himself.

8.3 *Dynamite Blows Two Ways.* Oct. 22, 1958. GS: Reed Hadley, Susan Cummings, Tyler McVey, Tom McKee, Jeff De Benning. Raoul Cummings, a ruthless rancher, has been preventing herds of cattle belonging to neighboring ranchers from reaching the Cheyenne stockyards. When Bat Masterson, who has just won some cattle in a poker game, joins with several other ranchers in a cattle drive to the market, Cummings threatens to kill both the man and their cattle.

8.4 *Stampede at Tent City.* Oct. 29, 1958. GS: William Conrad, James Best, Joan Marshall, Troy Melton. Bat answers a

Bat Masterson

plea from a former girl friend. She now lives in a tent city used as headquarters for cowmen who are herding and breaking wild horses for delivery to the Army. The girl tells Bat that the man she is in love with is accused of shooting a man in the back, and she fears a lynching.

8.5 *The Fighter.* Nov. 5, 1958. GS: Marie Windsor, Robert J. Wilke, Patrick Waltz, Ray Kellogg. To protect a young fighter against his unscrupulous manager, Bat Masterson wins the fighter's contract in a poker game. Bat then agrees to handle and train the boy for one fair fight and bets all his cash on the young fighter.

8.6 *Bear Bait.* Nov. 12, 1958. GS: James Westerfield, Milton Frome, Patricia Donahue, Bobby Hall, Wayne Burson. Bat Masterson accepts an offer to guide a bear-hunting party. During the trip, Bat discovers that the three people in the party are wanted for robbery and murder in the East.

8.7 *A Noose Fits Anybody.* Nov. 19, 1958. GS: Murvyn Vye, Bill Henry, Gary Vinson, Ernestine Clarke, Robert Swan, Jack Wagner, Les Hellman, Max Palmer. Gunman Ben Thompson is wounded when he saves Bat Masterson's life in a gunfight over a card game. Because of this, Thompson is unable to go through with his plan to help his brother Billy escape from jail. Ben claims the younger Thompson is not guilty. To repay Thompson for saving his life, Masterson offers to do the job himself.

8.8 *Dude's Folly.* Nov. 26, 1958. GS: Leo Gordon, Nancy Hadley, Joe Turkel, Allison Hayes, Jack Reitzen. Tough Joe Quince warns Jan and Woody Larkin that unless they sell him the hardware store they've inherited from their father, he will run them out of town. Jan asks Bat to teach her brother Woody how to use a gun.

8.9 *The Treasure of Worry Hill.* Dec. 3, 1958. GS: Audrey Dalton, Ross Martin, Harvey Stephens, Bob Anderson, Ken Drake. Three people are heirs to their uncle's estate, and each possesses one-third of a map showing the location of his huge treasure. Since they don't trust one another, each give his third of the map to Masterson and they hire him to guide them to the treasure site.

8.10 *Cheyenne Club.* Dec. 17, 1958. GS: Karl Swenson, Dean Harens, Louis Fletcher, William Tannen, Olan Soule, John Close, Frank Warren, Bill Catching, Lenny Geer, Joe Ferrente. Bat is sent for by John Conant, an influential figure in Cheyenne. Conant wants Bat to check on reports that Steven Haley, his daughter's fiance, is cheating at cards at the Cheyenne Club.

8.11 *Trail Pirate.* Dec. 31, 1958. GS: Gloria Talbott, Barry Atwater, James Bannon, Howard Wright, Hank Patterson, Charles MacDonald Heard. Bat Masterson answers a call for help sent by a friend in Salome. He finds that his friend has been killed while operating a wagon train. Bat sets out to avenge the man's death.

8.12 *Double Trouble in Trinidad.* Jan. 7, 1959. GS: Lance Fuller, Yvette Vickers, Dick Reeves, Richard Bakalyan, Johnny Silver, John Falvo, Charles Seel. Masterson learns that a man using his name has become sheriff of a town called Trinidad. Bat arrives in Trinidad incognito to investigate and learns that the impersonator is plotting to appropriate a gold shipment.

8.13 *Election Day.* Jan. 14, 1959. GS: Peter Hansen, Dan Sheridan, Kasey Rogers, Gene Roth, Vance Skarstedt, Ken Christy. Masterson, hired as trail boss of a cattle drive, runs into trouble in the town of Protection, Kansas. A local strongman demands a special cattle toll from Masterson before allowing him to move on. Bat refuses to pay and upon investigation discovers corruption in civic circles.

8.14 *One Bullet from Broken Bow.* Jan. 21, 1959. GS: H.M. Wynant, Joan O'Brien, Donna Martell, Susan Whitney, Charles Maxwell, Bob Shield. Gen. Phil Sheridan asks Bat Masterson to ride to Broken Bow, Kansas, to rescue the Rafferty sisters who have been kidnaped by the renegade Indian Stone Calf. Stone Calf and his war party kidnaped the girls after killing the rest of their family.

8.15 *A Personal Matter.* Jan. 28, 1959. GS: Alan Hale, Jr., Peggy Knudsen, Raymond Hatton, Dan Eitner, Robert Lynn, Dennis Moore, Tom London, Pierce Lyden. Outlaw Bailey Harper ambushes Bat Masterson and steals Bat's gun, money and horse. Bat warns Harper that he will track him down and regain his possessions, but the outlaw boasts that Masterson will never find him.

8.16 *License to Cheat.* Feb. 4, 1959. GS: Douglas Kennedy, Allison Hayes, William Phipps, Brett King, James Winslow, Frank Scannell, Jean Paul King, Moody Blanchard, Joel Riordan, Andy Albin. Bat stops off at Mason City to set up the only honest poker game in the town. However, he refuses to join the Protective Gamblers' Association, controlled by the sheriff, and finds himself behind bars.

8.17 *Sharpshooter.* Feb. 11, 1959. GS: Conrad Nagel, Lisa Gaye, Paul Dubov, Harry Fleer, Anne Dore. Unwittingly Bat Masterson makes an enemy of Harry Varden, owner of the largest saloon in Dodge City. Afraid that Bat is going to take some property away from him, Varden hires a man to kill Masterson.

8.18 *River Boat.* Feb. 18, 1959. GS: Jacques Aubuchon, Patricia Powell, Walter Barnes, Clark Howat, Brett Halsey, Bob Jellison. After boarding a Missouri river boat, Bat goes to the captain's cabin to deposit a large sum of money in the safe. Once inside, Bat is relieved of his cash by outlaw King Henry and his band, who are holding the captain prisoner.

8.19 *Battle of the Pass.* Feb. 25, 1959. GS: Wayne Morris, Will Wright, Roy Engel, Emile Meyer, Leo Needham. Ruthless Mace Pomeroy is engaged in a frantic attempt to lay tracks through a canyon faster than his rival, Gen. Moran. Bat turns down an offer to work for Pomeroy and helps Moran instead.

8.20 *Marked Deck.* March 11, 1959. GS: Denver Pyle, Cathy Downs, Phil Chambers, Richard Emory, Tom McKee, Ed Nelson, Ollie O'Toole, Charles Boaz, George Offerman. In a dishonest poker game, Bat loses a lot of money to Dan Morgan, strongman of the town of Morganville. Attempting to recover his money, Bat learns that Amelia and William Roberts, sister and brother, have also been swindled by Morgan.

8.21 *Incident in Leadville.* March 18, 1959. GS: Kathleen Crowley, Edward C. Platt, John Cliff, Jack Lambert, Jonathan Hole. Bat Masterson becomes furious when he reads a newspaper article, describing him as a notorious gunman who should be eliminated. He decides to have a talk with the author of the story, a charming woman named Jo Hart.

8.22 *The Tumbleweed Wagon.* March 25, 1959. GS: John Carradine, Paul Lambert, Fay Spain, Noel Drayton. Bat Masterson is deputized as a federal officer in order to transport outlaw Luke Steiger from Concho to Fort Smith. Steiger is to stand trial for killing one of Bat's friends. But the night before they are to leave, Steiger escapes.

8.23 *Brunette Bombshell.* April 1, 1959. GS: Gene Nelson, Rebecca Welles, Charles Fredericks, George Eldridge. Bat Masterson buys a Denver athletic club, but finds that it has been condemned and is being torn down by order of the fire commissioner. One of the firemen discloses that a gambling casino will replace it, and that Masterson had better not buck the commissioner.

8.24 *Deadline.* April 8, 1959. GS: Ken Lynch, Harry Dean Stanton, Eve Brent, Ralph Moody. En route to the state capital, Bat is pleased that his only stagecoach companion is lovely Lorna Adams. But his pleasure disappears when outlaws hold up the coach and steal the horses, and Lorna tells him that if she does not reach the capital by noon of the next day, an innocent man will be executed.

8.25 *Man of Action.* April 22, 1959. GS: Harold J. Stone, Joan Elan, Gavin Muir. Bat travels to Junction, New Mexico, to order some new clothes from his tailor, Oliver Jenkins. Masterson finds Oliver very busy with his new duties as head of a special citizens' committee.

8.26 *A Matter of Honor.* April 29, 1959. GS: Paula Raymond, John Vivyan, Stephen Bekassy, Kenneth MacDonald. Hurrying to invest in a new gambling casino, Bat Masterson pauses to engage in a roulette game. During this pause, an Austrian nobleman who is temporarily without funds, pulls a holdup.

8.27 *Lottery of Death.* May 13, 1959. GS: Warren Oates, John Sutton, Constance Ford, Myron Healey, Len Hendry, Bill Erwin, Jack Lester. During a poker game in Tucson, Arizona, Bat Masterson wins half of a lottery ticket. He is delighted to discover that the whole ticket is worth a great deal of money. But the man who has the other half is found dead, and his half of the ticket is missing.

8.28 *The Death of Bat Masterson.* May 20, 1959. GS: Claude Akins, Ruth Lee, Willard Waterman, Cliff Edwards. Bat returns to Bonanza, Colorado, to withdraw a large sum of money he had deposited in the bank there. The bank manager informs him that the account is closed and that Bat Masterson is dead.

8.29 *The Secret Is Death.* May 27, 1959. GS: John Larch, Allison Hayes, George Neise. Bat Masterson is given an assignment by the territorial administrator. He is to find out why the town of Cheyenne, Wyoming, has suddenly been hit by a crime wave.

8.30 *Promised Land.* June 10, 1959. GS: Gerald Mohr, Carol Ohmart, Arthur Space, Cal Tinney, Rance Howard, John Thye, Bill Walker. Bat Masterson is waylaid and taken to a town where the citizens are all reformed outlaws trying to live decent lives. The townspeople want Bat to open a bank there, as they don't trust themselves.

8.31 *The Conspiracy* Part One. June 17, 1959. GS: Arthur Shields, Diane Brewster, Paul Richards, Jerome Cowan, Ted de Corsia, Willis Bouchey, John Hart. Fifteen years after his acquittal, Lynn Harrison, Surratt's niece, asks Bat Masterson to help prevent the publication of a story signed by her uncle. The girl claims that Surratt is dead and the story is not factual.

8.32 *The Conspiracy* Part Two. June 24, 1959. GS: Arthur Shields, Diane Brewster, Paul Richards, Jerome Cowan, Ted de Corsia, Willis Bouchey, John Hart. Bat has discovered that John Watson, a bartender, poses as another man in order to sell a scandal-ridden story to a newspaper. After the discovery Bat finds Watson dead and realizes that his own life is in danger.

8.33 *The Black Pearls.* July 1, 1959. GS: James Coburn, Jacqueline Scott, Gerald Milton. Bat Masterson is accused of cheating at cards and is tossed in jail. He discovers that his cellmate is a murderer who also masterminded a train robbery in which a string of priceless black pearls were stolen.

8.34 *The Desert Ship.* July 15, 1959. GS: Karen Steele, John Wengraf, Jack Kruschen, Mike Forest. Anders Dorn and his niece Elsa have traveled from Holland in search of the legendary Santa Lucia, a Spanish ship supposed to have been wrecked many years ago when the Colorado River flowed through the lowlands to the Gulf. Bat Masterson attempts to discourage their quest because many have died trying to uncover the ship and her cargo of gold and jewels.

8.35 *The Romany Knives.* July 22, 1959. GS: Ray Danton, Frank Silvera, Chana Eden. Bat Masterson comes to the rescue of an old Gypsy who has aroused the wrath of a rancher in Dodge City. As a reward for his assistance, Masterson is offered some valuable gifts, including a girl.

8.36 *Buffalo Kill.* July 29, 1959. GS: John Doucette, Lisa Gaye, Ted Jacques. Incensed over some uncomplimentary remarks about his manner of dress by buffalo hunter Luke Simes, Bat Masterson temporarily puts Simes out of commission. But when Masterson discovers that Simes had been hired by a local hide buyer to obtain buffalo hides in dangerous Indian country, Bat takes on the assignment himself.

Season Two

8.37 *To the Manner Born.* Oct. 1, 1959. GS: Ernestine Barrier, Audrey Dalton, Jack Hogan, Myron Healey, David Thursby, James Hong. Mrs. Dwight Chancellor calls on her friend Bat Masterson for help. She is concerned about her daughter Abby, who has become involved with a cousin of dubious reputation.

8.38 *Wanted — Dead.* Oct. 15, 1959. GS: Bethel Leslie, Don Kennedy, John Dehner, Dabbs Greer, Dennis Moore. A gunman who is trying to reform borrows money from Bat Masterson. Later, learning that the gunman killed a man and ran away, Bat goes after him.

8.39 *No Funeral for Thorn.* Oct. 22, 1959. GS: Elisha Cook, Jr., Ray Teal, Joi Lansing, Dehl Berti. Bat learns that his good friend Thorn Loomis is dying in a town in Kansas.

8.40 *Shakedown at St. Joe.* Oct. 29, 1959. GS: Bruce Gordon, Joan O'Brien, Harvey Stephens, House Peters, Jr., Frank Wilcox, Frank Warren, Joe Guardino. Bat stops at St. Joseph, Missouri, to see Dora Miller, an old girl friend who's appearing as a singer at the local opera house. After arriving in town Bat comes to the aid of a local merchant who is being attacked.

8.41 *Lady Luck.* Nov. 5, 1959. GS: Dyan Cannon, Pamela Duncan, Don Haggerty. Casino owner Jess Porter plots a blackmail scheme against two sisters. Coming to the aid of the defenseless girls, Bat assumes a detective's role.

8.42 *Who'll Bury My Violence?* Nov. 12 1959. GS: Mort

Mills, Joanna Moore. Bat Masterson finds a town in the grip of Barney Kaster, who has a monopoly on the riverboats. Masterson devises a plan to break Kaster's hold on the shipping.

8.43 *Dead Men Don't Pay Debts.* Nov. 19, 1959. GS: Robert J. Wilke, Steven Terrell, Jeremy Slate, Jack Ging, Buck Young, June Blair. A feud between the Clements family and the Bassett brothers comes to a head. The Clements ride into town planning to shoot down the Bassetts, but Bat Masterson intercedes.

8.44 *Death and Taxes.* Nov. 26, 1959. GS: Richard Arlen, Don Kennedy, Susan Cummings. Sheriff Tim Lockhart asks Bat Masterson to help him collect the county taxes. They learn that some people are evading tax assessment by shipping their assets out of the county.

8.45 *Bat Plays a Dead Man's Hand.* Dec. 3, 1959. GS: Guy Prescott, Jan Harrison. Calculating Phil Hood holds the town in the palm of his hand and applies the law to suit himself. Bat Masterson assumes the role of a lawyer in an effort to break the tyrant's power.

8.46 *Garrison Finish.* Dec. 10, 1959. GS: Emile Meyer, John Gallaudet, Frankie Darro. General Moran is so sure that his Kentucky thoroughbred is a faster horse than Colonel Pierce's Western quarterhorse that he bets his railroad line on it. Later, the general has misgivings and goes to Bat Masterson for help.

8.47 *The Canvas and the Cane.* Dec. 17, 1959. GS: Joanna Moore, John Sutton, Dean Harens, Jack Reitzen, Patrick Whyte. Bat Masterson believes that a painting purchased by his friend Teresa Renault is real, and he backs up this opinion with a large wager. Discovering that the painting is a forgery, he tries to prove that he was tricked into making the bet.

8.48 *The Inner Circle.* Dec. 31, 1959. GS: Jean Willes, Marcia Henderson, Phillip Baird, Frank Ferguson. The members of the Inner Circle club are anxious to stop the women's suffrage movement. Bat Masterson agrees to help the women fight for their rights.

8.49 *The Pied Piper of Dodge City.* Jan. 7, 1960. GS: Donald Barry, King Calder, Evan MacNeil, Ron Hayes, Mel Bishop, Tom Montgomery, Matt Pelot, Robert Swan. To help pick up business at Luke Short's saloon, Bat Masterson hires a pretty piano player. A rival saloon owner plots to get the girl away from Short.

8.50 *A Picture of Death.* Jan. 14, 1960. GS: Patricia Donahue, Donald Woods, Howard Petrie, John Hart, Perry Cook, Dennis Moore, Pierre Watkin, Allen Jaffe, Charles Calvert. Masterson bets that a trotting horse's four feet are off the ground at the same time. To prove this assertion and win the wager, Bat tries to take a picture.

8.51 *Pigeon and Hawk.* Jan. 21, 1960. GS: Howard Petrie, Hugh Sanders, Rand Brooks, Lisa Montell. Two men attempt to corner the local market in mining stock by using former Pony Express riders to rush news to Denver ahead of their competition, broker Hugh Blaine. Blaine hires Bat Masterson to counter the move.

8.52 *Flume to the Mother Lode.* Jan. 28, 1960. GS: Paul Lambert, Miranda Jones, Jerome Cowan, Stephen Bekassy, Bobby Hall, John Baxter, Arnold Daly, Nick Nicholson, Frank Harding. Bat becomes a partner in a gold mine, but a millionaire competitor doesn't want Bat to do any mining. Masterson needs timber to shore up the tunnels of his mine, so his competitor starts buying up all the timber in the area.

8.53 *Death by the Half Dozen.* Feb. 4, 1960. GS: Ted De Corsia, Patrick Waltz, Willard Waterman, Norman Sturgis, Dorothy Johnson, William Vaughan, Terry Frost, Terry Rangno. Bat Masterson's effort to prevent a kidnaping are unsuccessful, and Bat is forced to deliver a ransom note.

8.54 *Deadly Diamonds.* Feb. 11, 1960. GS: Allison Hayes, Kenneth Tobey, William Tannen, William Schallert, Hank Peterson, Bill Catching. In the boom town of Leadville, Bat comes to the conclusion that a mine owner is putting over a hoax. To get proof, Bat invests some money in the mine.

8.55 *Mr. Fourpaws.* Feb. 18, 1960. GS: Paula Raymond, Gregory Walcott, Frank Gerstle, Les Hellman, Frank Scannell, Edmund Cobb. Bat is hired to find out what's behind some shortages that have been uncovered in a small-town bank. He finds a dead man and meets a stray dog which seems eager to help him with the investigation.

8.56 *Six Feet of Gold.* Feb. 25, 1960. GS: Carol Ohmart, James Coburn, Ronald Foster, William Fawcett, Woodrow Chambliss. Lisa Truex settles a debt with Bat by giving him a piece of wasteland, which he intends to turn into a cemetery. Double-dealing Lisa then forces the county clerk to alter the land deed so that Masterson appears to be a swindler.

8.57 *Cattle and Cane.* March 3, 1960. GS: Brad Dexter, Joyce Taylor, Dan White. Bat twirls his cane into a feud between ranchers and cattle barons. Using more lethal weapons, a callous cattleman decides to convince Bat he's on the wrong team.

8.58 *The Disappearance of Bat Masterson.* March 10, 1960. GS: Oscar Beregi, Erin O'Brien, Robert Karnes, Ray Kellogg. Herman the Great brings magic to the badlands, using sleight of hand to disarm a cowboy. Bandits think they might try the same trick on Bat Masterson.

8.59 *The Snare.* March 17, 1960. GS: Robert Ivers, Bill Henry, Marshall Reed. The murderous Yaqui Kid strikes again. When Sheriff Brady is ambushed and slain, his posse flees in panic—all but Bat Masterson.

8.60 *Three Bullets for Bat.* March 24, 1960. GS: Kent Taylor, Suzanne Lloyd, Tris Coffin, Miguel Landa. Bat is tricked into chasing some nonexistent gems to Mexico. By the time he learns he's been duped, he's facing a firing squad.

8.61 *The Reluctant Witness.* March 31, 1960. GS: Allison Hayes, Ronald Hayes, Harry Lauter, Donald Murphy, Charles Reade, Robert Swan, George Ross, Dave Perna, Chuck Bail. A reluctant witness is the only one who can prove Ellie Winters not guilty of murder. when the witness doesn't show, Bat figures she needs a good lawyer. He gets Wyatt Earp to pose as one.

8.62 *Come Out Fighting.* April 7, 1960. GS: Rhys Williams, Ken Mayer, Joan Granville, Steve Warren, Jean Paul King, Connie Buck, Alex Sharp. Bat's on the way to a championship fight when he gets into a battle of his own with Malachi Brody, the Fining Judge.

8.63 *Stage to Nowhere.* April 14, 1960. GS: Constance Ford, James Seay, Michael Forest, Craig Duncan. Bandits are making silver bullion disappear from stagecoaches. Bat has a plan to thwart the robbers, but when he puts it into effect, not just the bullion disappears, the stagecoach vanishes.

8.64 *Incident at Fort Bowie.* April 21, 1960. GS: Cathy

Downs, Robert J. Stevenson, Will Wright. Bat turns horse trade to sell a large herd to the Army. But before he can deliver them, a horse thief gets to them.

8.65 *Masterson's Arcadia Club.* April 28, 1960. GS: Morgan Jones, X Brands, Kasey Rogers, Larry Hudson, Lane Bradford. To lure the cash customers into his casino, a crooked gambler uses Bat Masterson's name, but Bat gets wind of the project.

8.66 *Welcome to Paradise.* May 5, 1960. GS: Robert Foulk, James Parnell, Ralph Taeger, Lonie Blackman, Charles Reade, Gerald Milton. It's illegal to carry firearms in Paradise, Colorado, and crooked officials impose staggering fines on strangers who unwittingly violate the law. One such stranger in Paradise is Bat Masterson.

8.67 *A Grave Situation.* May 12, 1960. GS: John Doucette, Howard Petrie, Lance Fuller. A huge herd of cattle dwindles overnight on a cattle ranch bought by Masterson's friend Hugh Blaine. Bat suspects a swindle by the agent who sold the property.

8.68 *Wanted—Alive Please.* May 26, 1960. GS: Steve Darrell, Diana Crawford, Joseph Turkel, H.M. Wynant, Douglas Dumbrille. Herds of diseased Mexican cattle are crossing the Rio Grande into the United States without authorization. Bat is sent to break up the smuggling.

8.69 *The Elusive Baguette.* June 2, 1960. GS: Leslie Parrish, Dan O'Kelly, Allison Hayes, Stanley Farrar, Frank Warren, Ralph Gray. A pretty widow hires Bat to be her personal escort. He is to prevent thieves from snatching the costly diamond she wears.

8.70 *The Big Gamble.* June 16, 1960. GS: Evan Thompson, Arch Johnson, Morgan Woodward, Gene Roth, Heather Ames, Anthony Dexter. Staked by Bat Masterson, Steve Fansler sets out for the Lost Dutchman Mine—and vanished without a trace. Bat learns that a long line of prospectors have disappeared the same way.

8.71 *Blood on the Money.* June 23, 1960. GS: Walter Coy, Page Slattery, Len Lesser, Paul Fierro, Kaye Elhardt. Bat is holding a bequest for Dane Holloway, and he advertises to learn his whereabouts. The ad brings an immediate offer of help, from a man who thinks Bat is out to kill Holloway.

8.72 *Barbary Castle.* June 30, 1960. GS: Jay Novello, Gloria Talbott, Stuart Bradley. Bat has heard of smugglers before, but this old gent has smuggled a castle. He's a Scottish sea captain, and he has brought his castle to San Francisco one stone at a time.

Season Three

8.73 *Debt of Honor.* Sept. 29, 1960. GS: Edgar Buchanan, Paul Langton, Gordon Hall, Hal Baylor, Page Slattery, Jack Lester. Prospector Cactus Charlie comes to town to repay a grubstake debt to Bat Masterson. He gives Bat two sacks of gold, tells the town that Bat is his new partner, and disappears.

8.74 *Law of the Land.* Oct. 6, 1960. GS: Howard Petrie, Leo Gordon, Allan Jaffe, Ray Teal, Barbara Lawrence, Buff Brady. Bat is called in by railroad president Hugh Blaine. Blaine's problem is that somebody has been stealing barbed wire fences along the right-of-way.

8.75 *Bat Trap.* Oct. 13, 1960. GS: Lon Chaney, Jr., Magie Pierce, Frank Ferguson, Jack Ging, Dick Ryan, Robin Riley. The Midas Creek town council hires Bat to see that their big turkey shoot will be on the up and up. But it seems that Rance Fletcher, the town troublemaker, is out to win the big prize any way he can.

8.76 *The Rage of Princess Ann.* Oct. 20, 1960. GS: Ron Hayes, Paul Lambert, Elaine Stewart. Bat is sorry he allowed his name to be listed as a partner in a mining venture. He gets a report that the mine in question is unsafe and the manager, Ulbrecht, is forcing the men to work it anyhow.

8.77 *The Hunter.* Oct. 27, 1960. GS: John Vivyan, Sue Randall, Mickey Simpson, Gerald Milton, Brett King. Sir Edward Marion, an Englishman, is firmly convinced that range is more vital than speed in shooting. He gets an unexpected chance to prove his theory when he accidentally kills a gunman.

8.78 *Murder Can Be Dangerous.* Nov. 3, 1960. GS: Tipp McClure, Kathleen Crowley, Ken Drake, Allison Hayes, Phil Dean. Bat finds out why his gambling establishment hasn't been doing so well. His partner Shad has been stealing some of the receipts.

8.79 *High Card Loses.* Nov. 10, 1960. GS: Joan O'Brien, Leatrice Leigh, Jean Blake, Paul Fierro, Marshall Reed, Francis J. McDonald, Don Douglas, Ray Ballard. A friend of Bat's is murdered while delivering three mail-order brides to Noble Creek, New Mexico. Bat becomes his replacement as escort and target.

8.80 *Dakota Showdown.* Nov. 17, 1960. GS: Tom Gilson, Kasey Rogers, Quentin Sondergaard, Les Hellman, James Best, James Seay. Jocko, Jeb and Gus Dakota have just killed the sheriff so they can operate freely in town. Town councilman Harry Cassidy sends for Bat to help select the next sheriff.

8.81 *The Last of the Night Raiders.* Nov. 24, 1960. GS: Paul Raymond, Don O'Kelly, Eugene Martin, Steve Mitchell, William Vaughn, Harry Clexx. Angie Pierce and her son escape from the Doolin gang, and ask Bat's help in eluding them.

8.82 *Last Stop to Austin.* Dec. 1, 1960. GS: Jan Merlin, Charles Reade, Robert Karnes, Susan Cummings, Charles Frederick. Bat thinks that Kid Jimmy Fresh, a young gunslinger, might be the orphaned son of a friend that killed in an Indian battle some years before. So he gets legal custody of Jimmy from another friend, the Governor of Texas.

8.83 *A Time to Die.* Dec. 15, 1960. GS: Robert Strauss, William Tannen, Jack Searl, Art Stewart, Leslie Parrish. A fellow named Smith murders one of Bat's buddies in a card game, and Bat is a witness at the trial. Smith's father has been scaring off the other witnesses and is anxious to add Masterson to his list.

8.84 *Death by Decree.* Dec. 22, 1960. GS: Paul Richards, June Blair, Allan Jaffe, Raymond Bailey, Robert F. Simon, Wayne Treadway. An old gambling rival of Bat's has willed Masterson his casino. But the place is heavily in debt and there's an early deadline for the payment.

8.85 *The Lady Plays Her Hand.* Dec. 29, 1960. GS: Wanda Hendrix, William Schallert, Robert Lynn, Johnny Seven, Judith Rawlins, Dave Cameron, Tom London. There's a slick Eastern gambler named Winston who is playing blackjack at Bat's casino. He keeps winning from dealer Daphne Kaye, and finally breaks the bank—putting Bat out of business and Daphne out of work.

8.86 *Tempest at Tioga Pass.* Jan. 5, 1961. GS: Hank Patterson, George Macready, John Burns, Jack Reitzen. Bat is helping Clyde Richards' road crew cut through the mountains from Nevada to California. Soda Smith, a miner who owns a cabin directly in the path of the proposed road, plants dynamite around his place to keep the crew from advancing.

8.87 *The Court Martial of Major Mars.* Jan. 12, 1961. GS: John Anderson, Peggy Knudsen, John Duke, Glen Gordon, Dick Wilson, Stephen Ellsworth. At Crazy Creek station there is no station master. In fact, when Bat and two fellow passengers, Lottie Tremaine and Major Liam Mars, arrive there by stage, they find only an Indian and a half-breed waiting to torture the major.

8.88 *The Price of Paradise.* Jan. 19, 1961. GS: Richard Arlen, Diane Cannon, Lance Fuller. In Paradise, Colorado, Bat tries to collect a gambling debt, but Walker Hayes, his debtor, doesn't like to pay bills. And Bat isn't the only one who gets thrown out of Haye's saloon — some poor tax assessor is too.

8.89 *End of the Line.* Jan. 26, 1961. GS: Liam Sullivan, Denver Pyle, Thom Carney, Paul Lukather. Bat is beset by trouble. He is in charge of a construction crew that is building a railroad through the Rockies. Rain, hail, fire and Indians are slowing up the works, and two wagonloads of expensive equipment go over a cliff, killing four men.

8.90 *The Prescott Campaign.* Feb. 2, 1961. GS: John Dehner, Philip Ober, George Sawaya, Valerie Allen, Emory Parnell, Joe Crehan. Bat gets to Prescott just in time to save Marshal Ben Holt from shooting Harry Sutton. Holt explains that Sutton works for a man who is trying to grab up land illegally. But Sutton tells a different story. He claims it is the marshal who is not on the side of the law.

8.91 *Bullwhacker's Bounty.* Feb. 16, 1961. GS: Jack Lambert, Will Wright, Jan Shepard, Rayford Barnes, J.L. Smith. Bat has been hired as guide for a wagon train carrying explosives. But the escort who is supposed to take him to the train is ambushed.

8.92 *A Lesson in Violence.* Feb. 23, 1961. GS: Virginia Gregg, Allan Jaffe, Richard Eastham, Larry Darr, Jerry Catron. In response to a telegram, Bat goes to the Grant farm in Beaumont, Texas. He is greeted by a lady behind a shotgun. Somehow Nora Grant, the girl with the gun, has decided that Bat is a hired killer.

8.93 *Run for Your Money.* March 2, 1961. GS: Ray Hamilton, Gerald Mohr, Jan Harrison, Carlyle Mitchell, Bob Swan, Dennis Moore, Harry Woods. When Crimp Ward, a saloonkeeper, challenges a local bank to back up its gold certificates, a stampede to cash in bank notes results.

8.94 *Terror on the Trinity.* March 9, 1961. GS: William Conrad, Lisa Lu, Mickey Morton, Billy Wells, Wally Campo. Bat wins a mining claim in a lottery. On his way to the claim site, he is attacked by a huge bearded man.

8.95 *Episode in Eden.* March 16, 1961. GS: Bek Nelson, Bob Rice, Ken Drake, Dan White. When Bat arrives in Eden, New Mexico, he finds that it is a long fall from Paradise. Gang-leader Sam Shanks imposes a local reign of terror.

8.96 *The Good and the Bad.* March 23, 1961. GS: Robert Ivers, Anna Navarro, Jeanette Nolan, Grace Lee Whitney. When masked bandits loot the stage to Tombstone, Mrs. Talbot is relieved of the medal of honor for which her husband gave his life. Bat produces a roll of hidden bills and offers to buy it back, but the bandits leave with both the money and the medal.

8.97 *No Amnesty for Death.* March 30, 1961. GS: Robert Blake, R.G. Armstrong, Betty Barry, DeForest Kelley. On his way into Las Tables, Bat finds Bill Bill MacWilliams, the marshal's son, playing his guitar in the graveyard. Bill Bill points out that the graveyard is less macabre than the town, where three hangings are about to take place.

8.98 *Ledger of Guilt.* April 6, 1961. GS: Jean Allison, Jack Hogan, Don Wilbanks, Barry Kelley, Trudy Ellison. Late one night in the mountain town of Meeker, Colorado, a terrified woman summons Bat away from the poker table. Before she can explain her problem, a shot is fired, an old man is killed, and the woman disappears.

8.99 *Meeting at Mimbers.* April 13, 1961. GS: Warren Oates, Harry Shannon, John Burns, Don O'Kelly. Cat and Jess Crail have devised a scheme for stealing horses which involves pitting members of two Indian tribes against each other. The Crails get their horses and the Army gets a lot of trouble when a war between the tribes becomes imminent. Sent by the Government, Bat rides in to assess the problem.

8.100 *Dagger Dance.* April 20, 1961. GS: George Eldredge, Ken Mayer, Marya Stevens, William Tannen, Byron Morrow, Tom Greenway. A peace conference with the Indians takes Colonel Downey from Fort Logan and leaves Major Whitsett in command. Bat rushes in with a message that the Indians plan an ambush. Whitsett, whose political career is blocked by Downey, fails to deliver the message to the colonel.

8.101 *The Fourth Man.* April 27, 1961. GS: George Kennedy, Dehl Berti, Audrey Dalton, Mickey Finn, Kevin Hagen. The friend Bat rides to meet in Lordsbury is dead when he arrives. It seems that the valley's three most powerful ranchers are killers, and they have a fourth man as their ally — the local sheriff.

8.102 *Dead Man's Claim.* May 4, 1961. GS: Charles Maxwell, Taffy Paul, Craig Duncan, Chuck Webster, Tyler McVey, John Close. The ghost town of Monument City springs back to life when a new silver strike is made. Bat rides in to investigate an old claim and runs up against Clay Adams and Harvey Mason, interlopers who accuse him of claim jumping.

8.103 *The Marble Slab.* May 11, 1961. GS: Erin O'Brien, Marvin Miller, Bob Rice, Rick Vallin. The Pinkerton Detective Agency hopes to expose John Kelso, head of a crime syndicate, and hires Bat to get evidence. Pretending to be a marble salesman, Bat plays upon Kelso's ego with the idea of erecting a statue of him in the town square.

8.104 *Farmer with a Badge.* May 18, 1961. GS: John Agar, Gregory Walcott, King Calder, Jackie Loughery. On his way into Tombstone, Bat is ambushed by outlaws and left to die. Marshal Sam Phelps rescues him, and Bat soon finds the chance to repay the favor. Killer Dinny Cave is waiting to murder the marshal in Rawhide.

8.105 *The Fatal Garment.* May 25, 1961. GS: Ron Hayes, Ed Nelson, Lisa Gaye, Les Hillman. Bat and Wyatt Earp are hired to guard the Oriental saloon in Tombstone. A hoodlum called Browder makes use of Bat's weakness for fine clothes to lure him away from his post.

8.106 *Jeopardy at Jackson Hole.* June 1, 1961. GS: Joan Tabor, Larry Pennell, Ron Foster, Paul Dubov, Harry Fleer, Nick Pawl. Kate Gannon asks Bat to help her avenge her father's death by setting himself up as a target to lure the killers.

9. Bearcats

CBS. 60 min. Broadcast history: Thursday, 8:00-9:00, Sept. 1971–Dec. 1971.

Regular Cast: Rod Taylor (Hank Brackett), Dennis Cole (Johnny Reach).

Premise: This adventure series, set in the Southwest during in 1914, dealt with the exploits of adventurers Hank Brackett and Johnny Reach, who travelled from case to case in a Stutz Bearcat.

The Episodes

9.1 *Pilot.* Sept. 16, 1971. GS: John Vernon, Kathy Lloyd, Paul Koslo, Sherry Bain, Julie Medina, Michael Masters, Evans Thornton. Troubleshooters Hank Brackett and Johnny Reach work from a Stutz Bearcat in the Southwest of 1914. They are assigned to stop a tank-driving bank robber.

9.2 *Dos Gringos.* Sept. 30, 1971. GS: Eric Braeden, Robert Tafur. Trouble-shooters Hank Brackett and Johnny Reach are assigned to lend covert assistance to a Mexican revolution.

9.3 *Title Unknown.* Oct. 7, 1971. GS: Henry Silva, Rex Holman, Katherine Justice. A Yaqui brave schemes to give the country back to the Indians.

9.4 *Hostages.* Oct. 14, 1971. GS: David Canary, Ed Flanders, Erin Moran, Sam Edwards, Gary McLarty. Hank and Johnny deal with an outlaw who is forcing the people of a small town to build a gallows. Maddeningly, he is not saying for whom.

9.5 *Conqueror's Gold.* Oct. 28, 1971. GS: Kevin McCarthy, Jane Merrow, Tom Nardini, Pepper Martin, Rod Cameron. The haunting ruins of New Mexico's ancient cliff dwellers set the scene as Hank and Johnny try to stop a bandit from stealing Indian artifacts.

9.6 *Blood Knot.* Nov. 4, 1971. GS: H.M. Wynant, Lauren Campbell, Leslie Parrish, X Brands, Lindsay Workman, Bob Hoy. Hank and Johnny are faced with vigilantes, renegade Indians and a hail of flaming arrows.

9.7 *Title Unknown.* Nov. 11, 1971. GS: Bruce Glover, Lincoln Kilpatrick, Edward Faulkner. The Bearcats job is to break into a prison to dislodge a German intelligence officer who has taken over the penitentiary to recruit saboteurs.

9.8 *Bitter Flats.* Nov. 18, 1971. GS: Keenan Wynn, Kathy Cannon, Rockne Tarkington. Hank and Johnny are involved in an adventure with a missing Army lieutenant and a barbaric rancher with a special cruelty for trespassers.

9.9 *Title Unknown.* Nov. 25, 1971. GS: Morgan Woodward, Lawrence Montaigne, Walter Brooke. The Bearcats are after an unusually dangerous quarry: an Army deserter-cum-mercenary who dynamites medical supply trains, kidnaps nurses and gets extra kicks hunting people.

9.10 *Title Unknown.* Dec. 2, 1971. GS: Leslie Nielsen, Morgan Paull. A vengeful Army deserter plots the destruction of a military convoy.

9.11 *Title Unknown.* Dec. 23, 1971. GS: Henry Darrow, Kathryn Hays, Brioni Farrell, William Smith, Richard Anders. The flying Jenny and adventurer Raoul Esteban return to help Hank and Johnny parachute into the camp of a hijack gang.

9.12 *Title Unknown.* Dec. 30, 1971. GS: John Anderson, Jeremy Slate, Luke Askew. Hank and Johnny are assigned to rescue a judge kidnaped by a sadistic outlaw. Their unlikely assistant is a convict who was sentenced by the judge.

10. Best of the West

ABC. 30 min. Broadcast history: Thursday, 8:30-9:00, Sept. 1981–Jan. 1982; Friday, 9:00-9:30, Feb. 1982; Monday, 8:00-8:30, June 1982–Aug. 1982.

Regular Cast: Joel Higgins (Sam Best), Carlene Watkins (Elvira Best), Meeno Peluce (Daniel Best), Leonard Frey (Parker Tillman), Tracey Walter (Frog), Tom Ewell (Doc Jerome Kullens), Valri Bromfield (Laney Gibbs), Macon McCalman (Mayor).

Premise: This comedy western told the story of Civil War veteran Sam Best, who brings his new wife and son westward in 1865. Best soon finds himself with the job of town marshal, which often brings him into conflict with wily saloonkeeper Parker Tillman.

The Episodes

10.1 *Pilot.* Sept. 10, 1981. GS: Christopher Lloyd, Brad Sullivan. Civil War vet Sam Best treks West to settle down in peace and run a general store. Unfortunately, his wife is inept, his young son is uncooperative and the man who sold him the store also owns the lawless town — and the protection racket Sam rashly turns down.

10.2 *The Prisoner.* Sept. 17, 1981. GS: Slim Pickens, Patrick Cranshaw, Richard Moll. A garrulous old sheriff takes sick on his way through town with a prisoner, leaving Sam to face the outlaw's mean, and many, brothers.

10.3 *Title Unknown.* Oct. 1, 1981. GS: Christopher Lloyd, Burton Gilliam. A weary Calico Kid, swearing never again to kill anything that can't be breaded and sauteed, hires on as cook at the Square Deal Saloon.

10.4 *Title Unknown.* Oct. 8, 1981. GS: Andy Griffith, Eve Brent Ashe, Bill Hart. Elvira's die-hard Confederate daddy puts up at the Square Deal Saloon during a reluctant visit to Copper Creek, while his wife tries to patch things up with their disowned daughter and despised Yankee son-in-law.

10.5 *They're Hanging Parker Tillman* Part One. Oct. 15, 1981. GS: Frank Marth, Al Lewis. Demanding due process, Sam goes out on a limb to save Tillman from a lynch mob, but promptly slips the noose back on with his clumsy testimony at the trial.

10.6 *They're Hanging Parker Tillman* Part Two. Oct. 22, 1981. GS: Frank Marth, Al Lewis. While a convicted Tillman awaits his hanging, a disguised Sam infiltrates an outlaw band to prove him innocent of cattle-rustling.

10.7 *Title Unknown.* Oct. 29, 1981. GS: Mark Withers. In a special election, Sam loses his marshal's badge to Tillman's squeaky-clean candidate.

10.8 *Title Unknown.* Nov. 5, 1981. GS: Barbara Whinnery, David Knell, Bruce Fischer. Daniel is surprised as anyone when a few innocent kisses with a nubile teenager lead to a shotgun wedding.

10.9 *Title Unknown.* Nov. 12, 1981. GS: Kevin Scannell. Laney is smitten with a smoothie who bids high for her at a social but turns out to be a low-down heel.

10.10 *The Railroad.* Nov. 19, 1981. GS: John Randolph. Sam and Tillman conduct a vigorous campaign to bring the railroad, and its economic benefits, to Copper Creek.

10.11 *Title Unknown.* Nov. 26, 1981. GS: Patrick Cranshaw. Sam's image as a sharp lawman loses some of its edge when a hastily built jail collapses around him. Shooting himself in the leg also doesn't help matters.

10.12 *Title Unknown.* Dec. 17, 1981. Sam pays little attention to Elvira's signs of discontent until the day he arrives home and finds her packed to leave.

10.13 *Frog Gets Lucky.* Jan. 7, 1982. GS: Barbara Babcock, Chuck Connors. A jilted woman rebounds with Frog, but neither is aware that her rawhide-tough lover wants her back.

10.14 *The Calico Kid Goes to School.* Jan. 14, 1982. GS: Christopher Lloyd, Barbara Byrne. A reformed Calico Kid hankers to be a U.S. marshal, a job requiring a third-grade education, which is something the Kid lacks.

10.15 *Title Unknown.* Jan. 21, 1982. GS: Robert Carnegie, John Dennis Johnston. The citizens of Copper Creek refuse to pay ransom for a kidnaped Tillman, much less attempt to rescue him.

10.16 *Mail Order Bride.* Jan. 28, 1982. GS: Betty White, Erik Holland, Ronald F. Hoiseck. Doc's mail-order bride has a past that matches her vivid personality and wilts the eagerness of her intended.

10.17 *Title Unknown.* Feb. 12, 1982. To get closer to her stepson, Elvira explores an abandoned outlaw cave with him, unaware that it is booby-trapped to seal itself shut.

10.18 *Title Unknown.* Feb. 19, 1982. GS: Jim Calvert, Jack O'Halloran. Daniel's refusal to confront a bully results in Sam locking horns with the bruiser's imposing father.

10.19 *The Pretty Prisoner.* Feb. 26, 1982. GS: Dixie Carter. Sam faces a ticklish overnight journey manacled to a flirtatious lady outlaw.

10.20 *Title Unknown.* June 14, 1982. A seduction scene he'd rather forget results from Tillman's efforts to wheedle clues out of a strange woman he suspects is threatening Sam.

10.21 *Title Unknown.* June 21, 1982. GS: Darrell Zwerling, Carlos Brown. To foil a holdup, Sam and Tillman stage a funeral for Frog, whose coffin contains the $20,000 targeted by the thieves.

11. Big Hawaii (A.K.A. "Danger in Paradise")

NBC. 60 min. Broadcast history: Wednesday, 10:00-11:00, Sept. 1977–Nov. 1977.

Regular Cast: Cliff Potts (Mitch Fears), John Dehner (Barrett Fears), Lucia Straler (Keke), Bill Lucking (Oscar), Elizabeth Smith (Auntie Lu), Moe Keale (Garfield), Remi Abellira (Kimo), Josie Over (Asita).

Premise: This series tells the story of wealthy landowner Barrett Fears and his family. The setting is the family's massive Paradise Ranch on the island of Hawaii.

The Episodes

11.1 *Gandy.* Sept. 21, 1977. GS: Don Johnson, Peter Marshall, Kimo Kakoano, Bill Edwards. Barrett Fears' niece Keke falls for a pilot who cons her out of a large sum of birthday money.

11.2 *Sun Children.* Sept. 28, 1977. GS: Cal Bellini, Tricia O'Neil, John Larch, Ted Shackelford, Tom Fujiwara. The islanders harass members of a new commune they blame for starting a typhoid epidemic.

11.3 *Pipeline.* Oct. 12, 1977. GS: Linda Gray, Stephen Macht. Mitch tries to protect a friend from her vicious ex-husband while at the same time keeping construction on schedule for a much-needed water pipeline.

11.4 *Red Midnight.* Oct. 19, 1977. GS: Charles Peck, Set Sakai. Mitch takes his convalescent father on a flight in his small plane, but they crash-land near an erupting volcano.

11.5 *Graduation Eve.* Oct. 26, 1977. GS: Marcy Lafferty, Sandy McPeak, Walter Brooke, Connie Sawyer, Michael Snedeker. While local lawmen are away on assignment, Mitch and Oscar are deputized to police the town on the eve of the high school's graduation.

11.6 *Sarah.* Nov. 23, 1977. GS: Pamela Bellwood.

11.7 *You Can't Lose 'Em All.* Nov. 30, 1977. GS: Richard Jaeckel, David Wayne, Rep Reiplinger. The sidekick of a fading rodeo star encourages Mitch to challenge the champ in a local competition, but plans the outcome to his own advantage.

12. The Big Valley

ABC. 60 min. Broadcast history: Wednesday, 9:00-10:00, Sept. 1965–July 1966; Monday, 10:00-11:00, July 1966–May 1969.

Regular Cast: Barbara Stanwyck (Victoria Barkley), Richard Long (Jarrod Barkley), Peter Breck (Nick Barkley), Lee Majors (Heath Barkley), Linda Evans (Audra Barkley), Napoleon Whiting (Silas), Charles Briles (Eugene Barkley) 65-66.

Premise: This Western series was set in the San Joaquin Valley in Stockton, California, in the late 1870s. It depicted the adventures of the Barkley family and their huge cattle ranch.

The Episodes

12.1 *Palms of Glory.* Sept. 15, 1965. GS: Malachi Throne, Vincent Gardenia, Len Wayland, Dennis Cross, Dallas McKennon, Miguel De Anda. The Barkley family has problems. The railroad has won legal rights to force the ranchers off their land, and a stranger has shown up claiming to be the son of the late Tom Barkley.

12.2 *Forty Rifles.* Sept. 22, 1965. Andrew Duggan, John Milford, Calvin Brown, Douglas Kennedy, Walker Edmiston, Allen Jaffe, Michael Fox. Heath has trouble with some of the hired hands, who don't like the idea of taking orders from the new member of the family.

12.3 *Boots with My Father's Name.* Sept. 29, 1965. GS: Jeanne Cooper, John Anderson, Richard Devon, Beah Richards, John Harmon. Victoria travels to Heath's birthplace to learn all she can about her late husband's relationship with Heath's mother.

12.4 *Young Marauders.* Oct. 6, 1965. GS: Sean Garrison, Buck Taylor, Virginia Christine, Kevin Hagen, James Patterson, Julie Payne, Mort Mills, Ken Lynch, Robert Porter,

James Gavin, J.P. Burns. Audra takes quite a fancy to the handsome young stranger who saved her life, unaware that her rescuer is the leader of an outlaw gang terrorizing the valley.

12.5 *The Odyssey of Jubal Tanner.* Oct. 13, 1965. GS: Arthur O'Connell, Jason Evers, Harlan Warde, Sheldon Golomb, Mort Mills, Ken Mayer, K.L. Smith, Tom Browne Henry. After many years, Jubal Tanner returns to the valley to claim the land promised him by the late Tom Barkley, land which has since become the proposed site for a dam.

12.6 *Heritage.* Oct. 20, 1965. GS: Anne Helm, Sherwood Price, Ford Rainey, John McLiam, Richard Hale, Harry Swoger, Brendan Dillon. There is trouble at the Barkley Sierra mine — trouble that includes a strike and a murder.

12.7 *Winner Lose All.* Oct. 27, 1965. GS: Katharine Ross, Henry Wilcoxon, Karl Swenson, Naomi Stevens, Robert Cabal, Gregg Palmer, Joe Higgins. Heath develops an attraction to Maria Montero, whose father, Don Alfredo Montero, says that a Spanish land grant gives him title to land the Barkleys sold to other ranchers.

12.8 *My Son, My Son.* Nov. 3, 1965. GS: Robert Walker, Jr., R.G. Armstrong, Katherine Bard, Ron Nicholas. The Miles and Barkley families have been friends for a long time, but not after young Evan Miles makes unwanted advances to Audra.

12.9 *Earthquake!* Nov. 10, 1965. GS: Charles Bronson, Alizia Gur, Wesley Lau, Audrey Dalton, Robert B. Williams, William Fawcett, John Craven, Robert Karnes. An earthquake traps Victoria in a church cellar with a forlorn unwed Indian girl who is about to give birth, and a surly ranch hand whom Nick fired for drinking.

12.10 *The Murdered Party.* Nov. 17, 1965. GS: Warren Oates, Larry D. Mann, Paul Fix, Fred Holliday, Paul Potash, Walter Woolf King, Jim Boles, Bill Quinn, Karl Held, Clegg Hoyt. Jake Kyles, head of the hated Kyles family, asks Jarrod to defend his son Korby in a murder case, despite the fact that Jarrod's brother Heath witnessed the killing.

12.11 *The Way to Kill a Killer.* Nov. 24, 1965. GS: Martin Landau, Rodolfo Acosta, Pepe Hern, Arthur Space, Carlos Rivero. Nick's Mexican friend Mariano Montoya is faced with losing the small herd of cattle he worked so hard to raise. While grazing on Nick's pasture, the cattle are stricken with anthrax, a deadly and highly contagious disease.

12.12 *Night of the Wolf.* Dec. 1, 1965. GS: Ronny Howard, Nancy Olson, Yuki Shimoda, Ted Gehring, Chubby Johnson, Russell Trent, Richard Wendley. Nick is bitten by a rabid wolf, but it may be two months before the doctor can determine whether the bite will be fatal.

12.13 *The Guilt of Matt Bentell.* Dec. 8, 1965. GS: John Anderson, Martine Bartlett, Anthony Zerbe, Morgan Woodward, Chuck Bail, Gene Dynarski, John Goff, Paul Sorensen. Introduced to the Barkley's timber camp foreman, Heath goes into a rage and attacks the man — accusing him of having been the inhuman commandant of a Confederate prison camp.

12.14 *The Brawlers.* Dec. 15, 1965. GS: Claude Akins, Noreen Corcoran, Eleanor Audley, J. Pat O'Malley, Olan Soule, Ken Lynch, Joe Higgins, John Harmon. Irish squatters have settled on Barkley land, which they insist they bought and paid for in San Francisco.

12.15 *Judgement in Heaven.* Dec. 22, 1965. GS: Lynn Loring, R.J. Porter, Nicolas Surovy, Ned Wever, Patrick Culliton, Frank Scannell, Kay Stewart, Ray Reynolds. Jarrod arranges for an outlaw's girl friend to be released from jail in his custody so she can spend Christmas with the Barkleys.

12.16 *The Invaders.* Dec. 29, 1965. GS: John Dehner, Yvonne Craig, Tom Fadden, Michael Green, Noah Keen, Pat Hawley, June Ellis, Claude Hall. Heath is bushwhacked by Daddy Cade and his murderous brood — who feel certain that he is worth more alive than dead.

12.17 *By Fires Unseen.* Jan. 5, 1966. GS: Diane Baker, Frank Scannell, King Johnson. Nick has fallen in love with Hester Converse, a beautiful Eastern socialite, whom he has known for only a few days.

12.18 *A Time to Kill.* Jan. 19, 1966. GS: William Shatner, Frank Marth, James Griffith, Jason Wingreen, Robert Cornthwaite, Bill Quinn, Rhoda Williams. After running into Brett Schuyler, an old friend from law school, Jarrod is visited by a Secret Service agent who suspects Schuyler of being part of a counterfeiting ring.

12.19 *Teacher of Outlaws.* Feb. 2, 1966. GS: Harold J. Stone, Steve Ihnat, Timothy Carey, Ken Lynch, Pepe Callahan, Richard Poston, Dennis Cross, Ken Drake. Gang leader Sam Beldon, who wants to learn to read and write, orders his men to kidnap a teacher, but the outlaws take Victoria by mistake.

12.20 *Under a Dark Sea.* Feb. 9, 1966. GS: Bruce Dern, Albert Salmi, K.T. Stevens, Chuck Francisco, Chuck Bail, Bert Whaley, Richard O'Brien, Robert B. Williams. Jarrod wants to help Keno Nash, who has been released from prison after serving nine years for a crime he didn't commit. Jarrod, as prosecuting attorney, helped put Nash behind bars.

12.21 *Barbary Red.* Feb. 16, 1966. GS: Jill St. John, George Kennedy, Donna Michelle, John Hoyt, Paul Sorensen, Bing Russell, John Orchard, Ric Roman. Nick Barkley celebrates his birthday at Barbary Red's waterfront saloon, where he is drugged and shanghaied.

12.22 *The Death Merchant.* Feb. 23, 1966. GS: James Whitmore, Royal Dano, Jim McMullan, Steve Whitaker, Pepe Hern, Michael Harris. The Barkley's, who are involved in a range feud, receive a visit from Handy Random, an old cowboy who killed the man who murdered Victoria's husband. But Heath knows something else about Random, and greets him only with silent hatred.

12.23 *The Fallen Hawk.* March 2, 1966. GS: Marlyn Mason, Peter Haskell, Paul Comi, Dennis Cross, Alexander Lockwood, Harry Swoger, Jim Boles. Heath, who feels responsible for an old friend's crippling injury, is determined to do all he can to help the man and his wife.

12.24 *Hazard.* March 9, 1960. GS: Robert Yuro, Lew Gallo, Bert Freed, Audrey Dalton, Frank Marth, Rex Holman, Mort Mills, John Rayborn, Alexander Lockwood, Larry J. Blake, Mike de Anda. Gil Anders, who comes to the Barkley ranch looking for Heath, is shot from ambush by two bounty hunters who claim he is wanted for murder.

12.25 *Into the Widow's Web.* March 23, 1966. GS: Kathleen Nolan, David Sheiner, Ken Lynch, Joe Higgins, King Donovan, Michael Harris, Lewis Charles, Harlan Warde. Heath's former love, Liberty Keane, is now married to a professional sharpshooter called the Great Ambrose, but Heath is still attracted to her.

12.26 *By Force and Violence.* March 30, 1966. GS: Bruce Dern, L.Q. Jones, Harry Dean Stanton. With Heath

The Big Valley

pinned beneath their overturned wagon, Victoria desperately searches for help. On the trail, she stops a man named Harry Dixon, who, without explaining why, refuses to give any assistance.

12.27 *The River Monarch.* April 6, 1966. GS: Chips Rafferty, Katherine Justice, John Rayner, Curt Conway, J.P. Burns, Sam Javis, Charles Land, Mark Levy. A Barkley river boat, sunk years before with a million dollars in Government gold aboard, has finally been located, but there is no trace of gold.

12.28 *The Midas Man.* April 13, 1966. GS: Tom Tryon, Richard O'Brien, Walker Edmiston, Hal Lynch. Audra is attracted to handsome Scott Breckenridge, a shrewd financier who has come to the valley to take advantage of a drought that has left most of the ranchers in need of loans.

12.29 *Tunnel of Gold.* April 20, 1966. GS: Warren Stevens, Jeanne Cooper, Malachi Throne, Paul Trinka, Don Diamond, Charles Wagenheim, Scott Peters, Joe Higgins. Bert and Elaine Jason's new general store is taken over by outlaws who plan to tunnel into the freight depot next door where a shipment of Barkley gold is to be stored.

12.30 *Last Train to the Fair.* April 27, 1966. GS: Richard Anderson, Karl Swenson, Tim McIntire, Ken Mayer, James McCallion, Hal Lynch, Nora Marlowe, Charles Horvath, Betty Harford. Audra is stricken with appendicitis on a train, and the only doctor on board has problems of his own. Two men are looking to kill him.

Season Two

12.31 *Lost Treasure.* Sept. 12, 1966. GS: Bruce Dern, John Milford, Buddy Hackett, Beah Richards, Dub Taylor. The Barkley family is shaken when a swindler named Charlie Sawyer claims that Heath is his long-lost son.

12.32 *Legend of a General* Part One. Sept. 19, 1966. GS: Nehemiah Persoff, Rudy Solari, Angela Dorian, Michael Davis, Carlos Romero, David Renard, Robert Karnes, Paul Comi, Pepe Hern, Don Dillaway, Rico Alaniz, Morgan Farley, John Hoyt, Than Wyenn, Pedro Gonzalez-Gonzalez. Attempting to avoid arrest by the Mexican Government, General Vicente Ruiz runs into good fortune when Heath offers Ruiz refuge at the Barkley ranch.

12.33 *Legend of a General* Part Two. Sept. 26, 1966. GS: Nehemiah Persoff, Rudy Solari, Angela Dorian, Michael Davis, Carlos Romero, David Renard, Robert Karnes, Paul Comi, Pepe Hern, Don Dillaway, Rico Alaniz, Morgan Farley, John Hoyt, Than Wyenn, Pedro Gonzalez-Gonzalez. Nick and Jarrod help General Ruiz return to Mexico, where Heath is about to go on trial for his life.

12.34 *Caesar's Wife.* Oct. 3, 1966. GS: Dianne Foster, Tim O'Kelly, Bert Freed, Bern Hoffman, Pat Wilkins, Michael Harris. Will Marvin, Audra's friend since childhood, is puzzled when his attractive young stepmother warns him not to get too involved with the Barkley girl.

12.35 *Pursuit.* Oct. 10, 1966. GS: James Gregory, Malachi Throne, Blaisdell McKee. At a desert mission, Victoria asks a cynical hard-drinking hunter to help find an Indian brave infected with measles before the frightened youth spreads the disease to his tribe.

12.36 *The Martyr.* Oct. 17, 1966. GS: Joseph Campanella, Nico Minardos, Clyde Ventura, Philip Bourneuf, Lori Scott, Graydon Gould, Jackson Weaver, William Mims, Charlie Briggs. Jarrod agrees to defend a young Basque sheepherder, who admits he is an anarchist, but insists that he has been falsely accused of murder.

12.37 *Target.* Oct. 31, 1966. GS: Julie Adams, James Whitmore, Sherwood Price, Strother Martin, Rudy Bukich, Paul Sorensen, Harlan Warde, Bill Quinn, Larry Domsin, Mel F. Allen, Walter Woolf King. Reform gubernatorial candidate Josh Hawks is stumping the valley and gaining a lot of attention. He is charging that the Barkleys are land grabbers.

12.38 *The Velvet Trap.* Nov. 7, 1966. GS: Laura Devon, Fred Beir, Kelly Thordsen, Hank Brandt, Chuck Bail, Richard Collier, Richard Harris, David Richards, J.P. Burns. During a storm, the Barkleys provide refuge for a frightened young woman who neglects to tell them about the mysterious rider who is pursuing her.

12.39 *The Man from Nowhere.* Nov. 14, 1966. GS: Sheree North, Anne Seymour, Gregory Walcott, Duane Chase, Arthur Space, Richard O'Brien, Howard Wendell, Robert Karnes, Bing Russell. Jarrod, who has lost his memory, is helping squatter Libby Mathews fight the cattlemen who want to evict her. But Libby doesn't know, and Jarrod doesn't remember, that he was hired by the cattlemen to persuade her to move on.

12.40 *The Great Safe Robbery.* Nov. 21, 1966. GS: Warren Oates, Christopher Cary, Kelton Garwood, Lee Krieger, Bill Quinn, Joe Higgins, Mark Tapscott, Earl Green. Three inept robbers carry a railroad strongbox, and hostages Victoria and Audra, into the hills. The crooks become impatient with their own fumbling attempts to open the safe, and their threats against the Barkley women grow more sinister.

12.41 *The Iron Box.* Nov. 28, 1966. GS: David Sheiner, Paul Picerni, Yaphet Kotto, Frank Marth, Walter Burke. Heath and Nick, held without trial on a rustling charge, undergo brutal treatment at the hands of a murderous stockade commander.

12.42 *Last Stage to Salt Flats.* Dec. 5, 1966. GS: Lamont Johnson, Norma Crane, Kevin Hagen, Steven Mines, Rex Holman, Dennis Cross, Fletcher Fist, Chuck Bail. Stage robbers leave Victoria, Jarrod, Heath and their companions to face death in the desert. The stranded travelers don't get much help from a cynical gun salesman who faced the same ordeal years before, and who is certain that everyone is going to die.

12.43 *A Day of Terror.* Dec. 12, 1966. GS: Colleen Dewhurst, Ross Hagen, Ken Swofford, Michael Burns, Amanda Harley, Tom Monroe, Gene O'Donnell. A ruthless woman and her outlaw sons turn the church into a prison for Audra, Victoria and the Bible-class children. The grim matriarch plans to use the church as a fortress until one of her boys recovers from a bullet wound.

12.44 *Hide the Children.* Dec. 19, 1966. GS: Stephen McNally, Royal Dano, Celia Lovsky, Chris Alcaide, Walter Coy, Rita Lynn, Eve Plumb, Jim Sheppard, John Gabriel, Jim Driskill, Warren Munson. Nick escorts three Gypsy women and finds plenty of trouble along the way. His problems include a band of thieves, hostile townsfolk and a small-town veterinarian who accuses the travelers of kidnapping.

12.45 *Day of the Comet.* Dec. 26, 1966. GS: Bradford Dillman, Douglas Kennedy, Chuck Bail, Ken Drake, Roberto

Contreras. Audra falls in love with Eric Mercer, a man being hunted by a band of ex-Union soldiers who blame him for the slaughter of 63 men.

12.46 *Wagonload of Dreams.* Jan. 2, 1967. GS: Tige Andrews, Dennis Safren, Karl Swenson, William Mims, James Gavin, Paul Sorensen, J.P. Burns, Harlan Warde. The Barkley brothers join a fiery tempered Greek farmer who is determined to bypass a crooked stationmaster's exorbitant railway rates. Peach grower Bodos loads his crop aboard a wagon and heads for market with the Barkleys, who are out to see that Bodos gets there safely.

12.47 *Image of Yesterday.* Jan. 9, 1967. GS: Dan O'Herlihy, Vincent Gardenia, Don Chastain, Sam Melville, Phil Arnold, Troy Melton, K.T. Stevens, Rayford Barnes. Victoria's feelings toward her former suitor change when he and his band of gunslingers make their headquarters at the Barkley ranch. The men, hired to rid the area of marauders, are now terrorizing the ranchers in the valley.

12.48 *Boy into Man.* Jan. 16, 1967. GS: Richard Dreyfuss, Diane Ladd, J. Pat O'Malley, John Harmon, Darby Hinton, Bryan O'Byrne, Larry Blake. Lud Akely is a teenager carrying a man's burden. Akely is determined to take care of his younger brother and sister without any help from the Barkleys, who are trying to find the children's missing mother.

12.49 *Down Shadow Street.* Jan. 23, 1967. GS: Robert Middleton, Dan Ferrone, James Gavin, Kam Fong, Jo Ann Pflug, Amzie Strickland. Victoria is plunged into a nightmare of terror when she witnesses a murder committed by her godson. The boy's father is taking steps to make sure that Victoria doesn't testify, by confining her in a madhouse.

12.50 *The Stallion.* Jan. 30, 1967. GS: Paul Fix, Brooke Bundy, Harry Swoger, Virginia Gregg, Jon Lormer, Harlan Warde. An old wrangler risks his life to regain his pride. Brahma is trying to prove his worth by capturing the wild stallion that nearly killed Nick.

12.51 *The Haunted Gun.* Feb. 6, 1967. GS: Andrew Duggan, Robert Ellenstein, Roger Davis, Joyce Jameson, Vincent Van Lynn, Lee Krieger, James Gavin. Senator Jud Robson's visit with the Barkleys is marred by his growing fear of assassination. The senator, once known as a tough lawman, is slowly being destroyed by his conviction that old enemies are out to kill him.

12.52 *Price of Victory.* Feb. 13, 1967. GS: Larry Pennell, Sandra Smith, Sandra Smith, Hal Baylor, Teddy Eccles, Walker Edmiston. Bare-knuckle boxer Jack Kilbain gives up fisticuffs for a job with the Barkleys. Kilbain then finds he can't resist returning to the ring for one more bout, even though he may lose his family and his life.

12.53 *Brother Love.* Feb. 20, 1967. GS: Robert Goulet, Strother Martin, Gavin MacLeod, Carolyn Conwell, Debi Storm, Phil Chambers. Faith healer Brother Love is out to fleece the people of the valley. The swindler is off to a good start when he finds an admiring disciple in Audra.

12.54 *Court Martial.* March 6, 1967. GS: Henry Jones, Alan Bergmann, David Renard, L.Q. Jones, Paul Comi, Clay Tanner. Five ex-soldiers turn the Barkley house into a courtroom to put Nick and his former Civil War commander on trial. The self-appointed judges accuse the pair of ordering a terrorist attacks on a helpless Southern town.

12.55 *Plunder at Hawk's Grove.* March 13, 1967. GS: Cloris Leachman, Dennis Hopper, Frank McGrath, Lonny Chapman, Rhodes Reason, James Gavin. Flood waters rise as a newly deputized Heath goes to protect a nearly evacuated town from looters. It is not long before he faces trouble in the form of four looters, who have teamed up to kill him.

12.56 *Turn of a Card.* March 20, 1967. GS: Joseph Campanella, Marayat Andriane, Don Chastain, Joe Higgins. Gentleman gambler Spider Martinson attaches himself to Heath, who is carrying $5000 in cash to a Barkley mine. Martinson tries to goad Heath into a game of poker, and he is not above using his lovely Tahitian companion as bait.

12.57 *Showdown in Limbo.* March 27, 1967. GS: Tom Lowell, Arch Johnson, L.Q. Jones, John Carter. Heath accompanies a U.S. marshal who is giving his Eastern educated son a taste of the lawman's life. The three escort a prisoner to Stockton, fully aware that his gang is following.

12.58 *The Lady from Mesa.* April 3, 1967. GS: Lee Grant, E.J. Andre, Frank Marth, Regan Wilson, Robert Cornthwaite. A saloon girl blames her dying father for ruining her life. Nick tries to soften Rosemary Williams by bringing her to the Barkley ranch, where her father stands little chance of recovering from a rustler's bullet.

12.59 *The Day of Grace.* April 17, 1967. GS: Bert Freed, Ellen McCrae, Karen Black.

12.60 *Cage of Eagles.* April 24, 1967. GS: Pernell Roberts, Harold Gould, John Pickard, Bing Russell, Paul Sorensen, John Harmon. Nick sparks a clash at a Barkley mine when he hires dynamiter Padraic Madigan, an Irish political fugitive whose presence infuriates a British engineer.

Season Three

12.61 *Joaquin.* Sept. 11, 1967. GS: Fabrizio Mioni, Douglas Kennedy, Robert Carricart, Margarita Cordova. A Barkley ranch hand believes that a wrangler is Joaquin Murietta, the infamous bandit supposedly killed years earlier. Tension builds when the suspicious ranch hand is found dead.

12.62 *Ambush.* Sept. 18, 1967. GS: James Gregory, L.Q. Jones, Toian Matchinga, Rex Holman, Ruben Moreno. At a desert mission, Victoria and buffalo hunter Simon Carter fight to protect three Yaqui Indian squaws from a trio of murderous scalp hunters.

12.63 *A Flock of Trouble.* Sept. 25, 1967. GS: Milton Berle, Robert Fuller, Eileen Baral. To pay off a gambling debt, sheepherder Josiah Freeman pawns off his flock on Nick, who stubbornly tries to tend the troublesome sheep, despite insults and threats from his fellow cattlemen.

12.64 *The Time After Midnight.* Oct. 2, 1967. GS: Lloyd Bochner, Shep Menken, Ed Bakey, Carol Booth. Jarrod's will to pursue justice is put to a severe test. After agreeing to prosecute a landgrabber, he loses his eyesight in an explosion. Despite his blindness, Jarrod decides to continue pressing the state's case.

12.65 *Night in a Small Town.* Oct. 9, 1967. GS: Susan Strasberg, James Whitmore, Kevin Hagen, Doug Lambert, Claudia Bryar, John J. Fox. Heath and the Barkley women are drawn into a conflict between a young woman and a puritanical sheriff. The lawman is obsessed with the thought that the attractive girl will somehow degrade his town.

12.66 *Ladykiller.* Oct. 16, 1967. GS: Marlyn Mason,

The Big Valley

Royal Dano, Anthony James, Roy Jenson, James Boles, Chris Alcaide, Jason Johnson. At a wayside inn, Nick Barkley enjoys a flirtation that may be his last. While young Belle Bleeck enthralls the unwary guest, her family plots to add Nick to the long list of people that they have robbed and murdered.

12.67 *Guilty.* Oct. 30, 1967. GS: Norman Alden, Robert Nichols, Joyce Ebert, Harlan Warde, Frankie Kabott, Rhonda Williams. Hysteria grips Stockton when an escaped murderer takes refuge in Audra's classroom, holding her and the children at gunpoint.

12.68 *The Disappearance.* Nov. 6, 1967. GS: Lew Ayres, Richard Anderson, John Milford, Walter Burke, Owen Bush, Gail Bonney. The Barkley women check into a hotel, and into a night of terror. Audra's sudden disappearance leaves Victoria unnerved, and completely dependent on the town's weak willed sheriff.

12.69 *A Noose Is Waiting.* Nov. 13, 1967. GS: Bradford Dillman, Martin Ashe, Ellen Corby, Lillian Adams, I. Stanford Jolley. The Barkleys put their trust in the town's new doctor, unaware that the man is a deranged killer who has hanged two people and is plotting the murder of a third — Victoria Barkley.

12.70 *Explosion!* Part One. Nov. 20, 1967. GS: Judy Carne, Stuart Erwin, Leticia Roman, Arlene Golonka, Carl Esmond, Eddie Firestone, Harry Swoger. As a raging forest fire threatens Stockton, the Barkley brothers prepare for a life-or-death mission transporting a wagonload of nitroglycerin to stop the fire.

12.71 *Explosion!* Part Two. Nov. 27, 1967. GS: Judy Carne, Stuart Erwin, Leticia Roman, Arlene Golonka, Carl Esmond, Eddie Firestone, Harry Swoger. Riding a hearse loaded with nitroglycerin, the Barkley brothers set out on a death-defying journey to stop a forest fire.

12.72 *Four Days to Furnace Hill.* Dec. 4, 1967. GS: Fritz Weaver, Bruce Dern, Don Chastain, Rafael Campos, Judi Reding. En route to the Barkley mine, Victoria is kidnaped by three men in the business of transporting criminals to prison. The trio intends to substitute Victoria for a lady prisoner they accidentally killed.

12.73 *Night of the Executioners.* Dec. 11, 1967. GS: David Sheiner, Dennis Hopper, Peter Whitney, Dabbs Greer. Only Heath can prevent town boss Gabe Simmons from getting away with murder. An old drunk has been framed for assassinating a congressman, but Heath saw the real killer.

12.74 *Journey into Violence.* Dec. 18, 1967. GS: Quentin Dean, Richard Peabody, Charles Tyner, Timothy Scott. A religious sect kidnaps Heath and cages him like an animal. Tried and convicted of murder by the nomadic group, the Barkley rancher is ordered to do penance as their slave.

12.75 *The Buffalo Man.* Dec. 25, 1967. GS: Albert Salmi, Lonny Chapman, Yaphet Kotto, Andreas Teuber. The Barkley ranch becomes a temporary honor farm for three convicts and their sadistic guard. But the penal experiment may end in disaster, thanks to the prisoners' plan for escape.

12.76 *The Good Thieves.* Jan. 1, 1968. GS: Russell Johnson, Charles Grodin, Flip Mark, Sam Gilman, Vinton Hayworth, Barbara Wilkins. Nick and Heath ride into the town of Sunflower, Nevada, in search of the Dunigan brothers, who seriously wounded Jarrod. The Dunigans, respected citizens of the town, are known elsewhere as murderous outlaws.

12.77 *Days of Wrath.* Jan. 8, 1968. GS: Michael Strong, Sandra Smith, Kevin Hagen, Peter Hobbs. Jarrod's surprise marriage has the Barkley family preparing a celebration, which turns to mourning when the new bride is murdered. Stricken by grief, Jarrod embarks on a burning trail of vengeance aimed at a paroled outlaw who threatened him.

12.78 *Miranda.* Jan. 15, 1968. GS: Barbara Luna, Don Randolph, Sherwood Price, Victor Millan. Miranda, a young anarchist from revolution-torn Mexico, comes to the Barkley ranch masquerading as an aristocrat. Her mission is to steal a treasured necklace that a fleeing royalist left with the Barkleys.

12.79 *Shadow of a Giant.* Jan. 29, 1968. GS: James Whitmore, Richard Evans, Walter Brooke, Ed Bakey, Stuart Randall, Rayford Barnes. Nick and Heath join a posse led by Marshal Seth Campbell. Past his prime, Campbell is pushing courage to a point that is endangering the lives of his deputies.

12.80 *Fall of a Hero.* Feb. 5, 1968. GS: Richard Anderson, Dennis Patrick, L.Q. Jones, Dub Taylor, Walter Burke. Accused murderer Heath Barkley goes on trial for his life, with his brother Jarrod as defense attorney. Hampered by Heath's cloudy memory, Jarrod must also contend with two witnesses who are crying for blood.

12.81 *The Emperor of Rice.* Feb. 12, 1968. GS: Julie Adams, Harry Townes, Kam Tong. A businessman and his wife make an effort to corner the rice market. When the Barkley's block the attempt, Victoria becomes a kidnap victim in the couple's vicious plot.

12.82 *Rimfire.* Feb. 19, 1968. GS: Van Williams, Mako, John Daniels, Lisa Lu, Robert Middleton. In the mining town of Rimfire, Jarrod jeopardizes a family business deal, and angers a wealthy mine owner, when he tries to protect the rights of a Chinese couple.

12.83 *Bounty on a Barkley.* Feb. 26, 1968. GS: Leslie Parrish, Peter Haskell, Mike Wagner, John J. Fox, Earl Nickel. Nick falls head over heals for newcomer Layle Johnson, an aloof lady who slowly warms to his attentions, but neglects to mention that she is married.

12.84 *The Devil's Masquerade.* March 4, 1968. GS: John Doucette, Anne Helm, Ray Danton. Rancher Jim North's mail-order bride-to-be impresses everyone but Heath, who becomes increasingly suspicious of the supposed Eastern-bred schoolteacher.

12.85 *Run of the Savage.* March 11, 1968. GS: Michael Burns, Grace Lee Whitney, Willard Sage, Carolyn Conwell, Harry Swoger. Nick tries to befriend an embittered 14-year-old who has been disowned by his parents. Armed with a gun, and contempt for everyone, the boy defies Nick by making him a captive in a condemned mine.

12.86 *The Challenge.* March 18, 1968. GS: James Gregory, Harold Gould, Regis Philbin. Victoria and Senator Jim Bannard, a long-time friend, are trapped in a smear campaign. Armed with a compromising photograph, Bannard's political foe puts on the pressure as Jarrod seeks a legal way to stop the trumped up scandal.

Season Four

12.87 *In Silent Battle.* Sept. 23, 1968. GS: Adam West, Don Knight. A mutual attraction between Audra and war hero Jonathan Eliot angers, and frightens, the officer's orderly, who threatens to expose Eliot's past if the friendship continues.

12.88 *They Called Her Delilah.* Sept. 30, 1968. GS: Julie London, Paul Lambert, Robert Nichols. A singer's arrival in Stockton sparks bitterness. A spy for the South during the Civil War, the lady is abused, threatened and charged with murder. Her only hope is former boy friend, Jarrod Barkley.

12.89 *Presumed Dead.* Oct. 7, 1968. GS: Lew Ayres, Gavin MacLeod, Richard O'Brien, Warren Vanders. A lonely cattle rustler gives amnesia victim Victoria Barkley an identity — that of his dead wife. Warmly, the man imposes his memories on the unwitting lady, fashioning a false present that spells danger for both.

12.90 *Run of the Cat.* Oct. 21, 1968. GS: Pernell Roberts, John Milford, Lisa Lu, Janis Hansen, Jon Lormer. Nick and professional hunter Ed Tanner form an uneasy alliance to track a marauding cougar. To Tanner, the quest is strictly a job, but Nick has a personal interest in the hunt as he was badly mauled by the cat.

12.91 *Deathtown.* Oct. 28, 1968. GS: Jason Evers, Antoinette Bower, Michael Dante, Frank Marth, Kathie Browne. In Baker City, Jarrod defies threats as he probes the circumstances behind the lynching of the Mendoza brothers. The men were hanged by the townspeople for the rape and murder of a housewife, a crime Jarrod is certain they didn't commit.

12.92 *The Jonah.* Nov. 11, 1968. GS: Marty Allen, Wayne Rogers. Audra takes a personal interest in the plight of Waldo Diefendorfer, a new hand on the Barkley harvest crew. Known as the valley's jinx, Waldo is living up to his reputation. Wherever he is, there is trouble, and his fearful co-workers are ready to walk out en masse.

12.93 *Hell Hath No Fury.* Nov. 18, 1968. GS: Carol Lynley, Don Dubbins, Conlan Carter, Steve Franken, Rayford Barnes, Chris Alcaide, Mark Tapscott. Dilly Shanks is a poker-playing outlaw leader who gives up robbery for romance. Her target is Heath Barkley, but the courtship is sadly one-sided. Heath is not at all serious about the girl, and knows nothing of her lawless past.

12.94 *The Long Ride.* Nov. 25, 1968. GS: Richard Anderson, Paul Petersen, Kevin Hagen, James Westerfield. On a stagecoach to Stockton, Victoria, Audra and four men face a nerve-shattering survival test. The group is being pursued by a killer who uses tricks and sabotage to strike a treacherous bargain. Give up one passenger — Audra — or all shall die.

12.95 *The Profit and the Lost.* Dec. 2, 1968. GS: Robert Loggia, Bert Freed. Heath risks his life to save gunman Vern Hickson from an ambush. When the hired killer recovers, the Barkley's learn an ironic truth. Hickson has a contract to kill Heath.

12.96 *A Stranger Everywhere.* Dec. 9, 1968. GS: Julie Harris, Richard Devon, Dennis Patrick. A writer's dime novel and front-page features turn a timid dressmaker into the sensation of Stockton. The stories claim that Jennie Hall was once an infamous bandit, a rumor that soon has the lady under investigation and a trio of thieves plotting to find her hidden loot.

12.97 *The Prize.* Dec. 16, 1968. GS: Bruce Dern, Peter Haskell, Ondine Vaughn, Noah Keen. Heath, Barkley and bounty hunter John Weaver take different paths after witnessing a young woman's death. While Heath cares for her infant son, Weaver sets a trap for the baby's father, outlaw Ben Rawlins.

12.98 *Hunter's Moon.* Dec. 30, 1968. GS: Lawrence Dobkin, Susan O'Connell, Bruce Glover, John Crawford, Don Chastain. Nick and two strangers are imprisoned by a fanatically jealous rancher who believes one of the men to be his wife's lover. With a death threat hanging over them, Nick's fellow captives decide to make him the scapegoat.

12.99 *Top of the Stairs.* Jan. 6, 1969. GS: Ron Harper, Jean Inness, Paul Fix, Robert Ellenstein, Walter Sande, Byron Morrow. On a visit to Abbottsville, the Barkley women are stunned by the news that Victoria's brother-in-law has been judged insane. Forbidden to see him, and puzzled by the mystery surrounding his illness, Victoria stays on to investigate.

12.100 *Joshua Watson.* Jan. 20, 1969. GS: Lou Rawls, Royal Dano, Greg Mullavey, Robert Sampson, Michael Bell, Mark Tapscott, Marvin J. Downey. Joshua Watson is a super cowboy who is riding for the Barkleys in a fiercely competitive rodeo. Their opponents are the Mortons, a mean and unscrupulous family whose plan for victory hinges on eliminating the spectacular rider.

12.101 *The Secret.* Jan. 27, 1969. GS: Simon Oakland, Nancy Malone, Kelly Corcoran. A wealthy and powerful rancher moves into Stockton to ruin the Barkley enterprises. His motive is intense hatred of Jarrod, who he thinks is having an affair with his young wife.

12.102 *The Twenty-five Graves of Midas.* Feb. 3, 1969. GS: Anne Baxter, Linda Marsh, Arch Johnson, Kevin Hagen, Gary Beban. Twenty-five men are killed in a mine cave-in. The Barkleys own the mine with town boss Webb Dutton, and the grieving townsfolk intend to take revenge for their tragic loss.

12.103 *Lightfoot.* Feb. 17, 1969. GS: Joe Don Baker, Amy Thomson, Harry Lauter, Walter Coy. Years of prejudice have taken their toll of Modoc Indian Tom Lightfoot, a young lawyer given to vitriolic outbursts against the white man. Accused of killing a bigoted rancher, Tom's outspoken anger makes him a lynch target and a difficult client for attorney Jarrod Barkley.

12.104 *Alias Nellie Handley.* Feb. 24, 1969. GS: Susan Oliver, Richard Anderson, Gavin MacLeod, Richard O'Brien. Victoria turns undercover agent to help probe conditions inside a women's prison. Masquerading as a tough-talking thief, the lady tries to get evidence against the sadistic warden in charge of the hell hole.

12.105 *The Royal Road.* March 3, 1969. GS: Kathy Garver, Sajid Kahn, Harold Gould. Jarrod steps in when romance blooms between his spirited ward Laura Hayden and a visiting Indian prince. The teenagers become too serious, too soon, and there is something fishy about the prince.

12.106 *A Passage of Saints.* March 10, 1969. GS: Fritz Weaver, Donna Baccala, Olive Dunbar, Paul Lambert, Mauritz Hugo. Jarrod acts as arbiter when bigots harass the Barkley's tenants — a stubborn Mormon farmer with two wives.

12.107 *The Battle of Mineral Springs.* March 24, 1969. GS: Jack Albertson, Dennis Patrick, Conlan Carter, Janis Hansen. The Barkleys make an effort to revive a dying town. Stiff opposition comes from a neighboring community, where the town boss rallies forces to crush the competition.

12.108 *The Other Face of Justice.* March 31, 1969. GS: John Crawford, James Gregory, Don Knight, Margarita Cordova. The valley is terrorized by a band of horse thieves whose violent rampage has left several dead and the sheriff wounded.

Taking up the pursuit, Nick and Heath try to enlist experienced, and legendary, ex-lawman Harry Bodine.

12.109 *Town of No Exit.* April 7, 1969. GS: Leslie Nielsen, John Carradine, Diana Ewing. Heath arrives in a dying desert town, only to find himself a visitor in a madhouse. His hosts are five deranged people who play bizarre and deadly games with their infrequent guests. Heath's role in their hellish fantasy is the accused, on trial for rape and murder.

12.110 *Danger Road.* April 21, 1969. GS: Maurice Evans, Anthony James, Logan Ramsey, Gilbert Green. When her wagon breaks down on the road, Victoria is forced to rely on, and soon clashes with, smooth-talking Edward Hewitt. The clash is over ethics. She is carrying supplies to an Indian school and he is smuggling whiskey onto the reservation.

12.111 *Flight from San Miguel.* April 28, 1969. GS: Gerald Mohr, Pat Delany, H.M. Wynant, Nate Esformes. Heath undertakes a dangerous trip to revolution-torn Mexico. His mission is to rescue a rebel leader who has been marked for execution by the Federales.

12.112 *Point and Counterpoint.* May 19, 1969. GS: Clifford David, Walter Burke, Russell Thorson. Jarrod agrees to defend the accused murderer of a Stockton banker, unaware of the savage irony at play. His client is carrying out a well-planned revenge, which has Victoria as the next murder victim.

13. *Black Saddle*

NBC/ABC. 30 min. Broadcast history: Saturday, 9:00–9:30, Jan. 1959–Sept. 1959; Friday, 10:30–11:00, Oct. 1959–Sept. 1960.

Regular Cast: Peter Breck (Clay Culhane), Anna-Lisa (Nora Travers), Russell Johnson (Marshal Gibson "Gib" Scott), Ken Patterson (Kelly, the bartender).

Premise: Set in the Southwest after the Civil War, this series tells of Clay Culhane's struggle to become a successful lawyer in spite of his reputation as an ex-gunfighter.

The Episodes

13.1 *Client: Travers.* Jan. 10, 1959. GS: Onslow Stevens, K.L. Smith. Clay Culhane goes to Latigo in the New Mexico Territory to defend his first client. He finds that the town is ruled by a vengeful rancher.

13.2 *Client: Meade.* Jan. 17, 1959. GS: Clu Gulager, Arvid Nelson, Joe Perry, Hampton Fancher, Ned Glass. Forced into a gunfight with the Tibbett brothers, Andy Meade kills one of them. Clay Culhane, believing that he has found a witness who can clear Andy, persuades the young man to surrender to Marshal Gib Scott. But the witness, intimidated by the Tibbett family, decides to change his testimony.

13.3 *Client: McQueen.* Jan. 24, 1959. GS: Basil Ruysdael, Lisa Gaye, Patrick Macnee, Charles Gray, Rex Ingram. Senator McQueen, once a wealthy rancher, has been dispossessed by members of his family of what is rightfully his. McQueen asks Clay for help. Clay answers the senator's request, but soon discovers that they differ on what methods to employ to regain the senator's holdings.

13.4 *Client: Dawes.* Jan. 31, 1959. GS: Phyllis Coates, Robert Gist, R.G. Armstrong, Mary Carver. Clay Culhane investigates the mysterious killing of Ben Dawes, a middle-aged bachelor who married a girl he selected from the pages of a matrimonial-bureau catalog. Ben's younger brother Milo disapproves of the girl and has been cut out of Ben's will. But circumstances point to the widow as the murderer.

13.5 *Client: Starkey.* Feb. 7, 1959. GS: Joan Camden, Tudor Owen, Parley Baer, John Mylong. June Starkey arrives in Latigo and persuades Clay Culhane to look for her missing husband. When the townspeople learn who June is, they regard her with open hostility.

13.6 *Client: Tagger.* Feb. 14, 1959. GS: Arthur Hunnicutt, Walter Sande, Wesley Lau, J. Pat O'Malley, Jan Stine. Roy Tagger is released from prison after serving a sentence for murder. He was imprisoned unjustly, and he brings his case to Clay Culhane.

13.7 *Client: Robinson.* Feb. 21, 1959. GS: Robert Blake, John Dehner, Ralph Votrian, Raymond Bailey, Bing Russell. Young Wayne Robinson is arrested by Marshal Gib Scott for brawling in a saloon. Clay Culhane tries to help him.

13.8 *Client: Martinez.* March 7, 1959. GS: Paul Richards, J. Pat O'Malley, Frank de Kova, Felipe Turich. Four Mexicans present Marshal Gib Scott with an extradition order that will allow them to take Mexican patriot Juan Martinez, a fugitive, back to his native country. Martinez tells Clay Culhane that the men intend to kill him.

13.9 *Client: Northrup.* March 14, 1959. GS: John Larch, Anne Barton, Charles Arnt, Lane Bradford. Ty Northrup, an ex-lawman turned renegade, and his wife arrive in Latigo, but Marshal Gib Scott orders them out of town. Northrup's wife, however, is unable to travel, and Clay Culhane tries to talk Scott into allowing them to stay until the woman is well enough to move on.

13.10 *Client: Steele.* March 21, 1959. GS: Scott Forbes, James Coburn, Warren Oates, Joel Ashley, Mark Tapscott, Lenny Geer. Lawyer Clay Culhane agrees to defend Bill Steele, one of three men being held by Marshal Gib Scott for robbery.

13.11 *Client: Mowery.* March 28, 1959. GS: Simon Oakland, Strother Martin, Barry Atwater. Marshal Gib Scott is forced to shoot Grat Mowery, a troublesome rancher. As he is dying, Mowery asks Clay Culhane to make out a will which leaves all his property to two outlaws, or to Scott on a survivor-take-all basis.

13.12 *Client: Braun.* April 4, 1959. GS: Barton MacLane, Eddie Firestone, Vic Perrin, Robert E. Griffin. A recluse hires Clay Culhane to obtain an injunction keeping trespassers off his property. While attending to this matter the lawyer is startled by an encounter with a famous general who is believed to have died heroically.

13.13 *Client: Banks.* April 11, 1959. GS: Lee Kinsolving, Vaughn Taylor, Amzie Strickland, Dabbs Greer, L.Q. Jones. Teenager Dick Banks maintains an interest in guns in spite of his father's opposition. Clay Culhane, who sees a similarity to the start of his own career as a gunfighter, befriends the youth. Then the elder Banks is murdered and Dick stalks the killer.

13.14 *Client: Jessup.* April 18, 1959. GS: Philip Abbott, Jeanette Nolan, J. Pat O'Malley, Sam Buffington, Barney Phillips. Rancher Lon Jessup is charged with robbery and murder by two Chicago detectives. Jessup tells Clay Culhane that he was involved in a robbery but had nothing to do with a murder.

13.15 *Client: Frome.* April 25, 1959. GS: Adam Williams, Michael Pate, Mary La Roche. Returning to Latigo, amnesia victim Clint Frome finds that he has been declared legally dead and his wife Lydia has remarried. Clint asks Clay Culhane to help him recover his property.

13.16 *Client: Nelson.* May 2, 1959. GS: Patrick McVey, James Best, Hampton Fancher. Clay Culhane encounters two men engaged in a fight. Each tells Clay that he is an officer of the law and that the other man is his prisoner. Marshal Gib Scott listens to their stories, takes one man into custody and sets the other free.

13.17 *Client: Neal Adams.* May 9, 1959. GS: James Drury, Charles Aidman, Walter Burke, Ken Patterson. An injured man arrives in Latigo and tells his friend Clay Culhane that he is being unjustly hunted. Clay learns that Adams is a wanted man and his pursuer is a bounty hunter.

13.18 *Client: Brand.* May 16, 1959. GS: Barry Atwater, Walter Burke, William Erwin, Gordon Polk. A Texan named Brand picks a fight with a cowboy and as the youth draws, Brand kills him. When Marshal Scott orders Brand to leave Latigo, the Texan tries to draw the marshal into a gunfight.

13.19 *Client: Reynolds.* May 23, 1959. GS: Madlyn Rhue, Don Kelly, Steve Roberts, J. Pat O'Malley, Roy Engel, Lorna Thayer. Clay Culhane is hired by Julie Reynolds when her employer, gambler Harry Briggs, refuses to give her back pay. During an argument with Clay, Briggs draws a gun but Julie uses a small knife to make him drop the weapon. Later Briggs is found murdered and Julie is the likely culprit.

13.20 *Client: Vardon.* May 30, 1959. GS: Richard Rust, Ed Nelson, Richard Shannon, J. Pat O'Malley, George Keymas, Dennis Cross, John Anderson. A dying outlaw says that Frank Vardon is planning to rob the bank where he works as a teller. Clay Culhane comes to Vardon's defense.

Season Two

13.21 *The Freebooters.* Oct. 2, 1959. GS: J. Pat O'Malley, Simon Scott, Walter Burke, Sam Buffington. A band of cavalrymen arrive in Latigo ready to defend the town against some Army deserters who have been looting the area. After Clay Culhane and Marshal Gib Scott give the soldiers a list of townsmen who can be of help, they learn that these men are really deserters.

13.22 *The Saddle.* Oct. 9, 1959. GS: Ralph Moody, Robert F. Simon, Brian Hutton. Clay Culhane helps Marshal Gib Scott apprehend three men who have escaped from prison and recognizes one of them as David Trench McKinney. McKinney's father, a judge, encouraged Clay's legal career.

13.23 *The Long Rider.* Oct. 16, 1959. GS: Suzanne Pleshette, Chris Alcaide, Perry Ivins, Stacy Harris, Bing Russell. While Marshal Gib Scott is riding to Albuquerque, his horse goes lame and the Marshal gets a ride with Pa Scale's wagon train. Scott, Pa Scales, and his son George come across two men, one of whom is injured, and a woman who identifies the injured man as a wanted criminal.

13.24 *The Hotel.* Oct. 23, 1959. GS: John Alderson. Nora Travers returns from a trip to San Francisco and decides to sell her hotel and settle there. Clay Culhane is upset when he learns that Big Sam Davis wants to buy the hotel.

13.25 *Client: Peter Warren.* Oct. 30, 1959. GS: John Lupton, Ed Nelson, Aneta Corseaut. Peter Warren is accused of murdering Priscilla Hayes, his estranged wife's wealthy aunt. Lawyer Clay Culhane agrees to take Warren's case.

13.26 *The Freight Line.* Nov. 6, 1959. GS: Frank Maxwell, Ben Wright. Nora Travers receives the government franchise to carry mail to and from Latigo. Soon after she begins her new enterprise her drivers and guards are the victims of repeated attacks.

13.27 *Murdock.* Nov. 13, 1959. GS: Charles Aidman, Michael McGreevey, Ralph Moody. A murderer is acquitted because of a lack of evidence. Gib Scott, realizing that the law can no longer touch the guilty man, resigns as marshal and endeavors to bring about justice as a private citizen.

13.28 *Apache Trail.* Nov. 20, 1959. GS: Mike Kellin, Roberta Haynes, DeForest Kelley, Connie Buck. Clay Culhane and Nora Travers set out to visit Indian agent Sam King. When they get to King's trading post, they find a group of Indians waiting to kill the agent.

13.29 *Four from Stillwater.* Nov. 27, 1959. GS: Karl Swenson, Barney Phillips, Duncan McLeod. Clay Culhane, traveling to a wedding in Stillwater, comes upon the body of the groom. Discovering that four men took part in the killing, the lawyer endeavors to prove them guilty.

13.30 *The Deal.* Dec. 4, 1959. GS: Frank Overton, Paul Carr. Nora Travers is kidnaped by Pete Hooker, brother of a bank robber imprisoned in the Latigo jail. Pete is willing to free Nora in exchange for his brother's release.

13.31 *Change of Venue.* Dec. 11, 1959. GS: Patricia Medina, Dean Harens, Willard Sage. Following a woman's murder, Marshal Gib Scott arrests Tom Brandon, the victim's suitor. Clay Culhane agrees to defend Brandon, but the dead woman's sister and brother-in-law say that they will hang Brandon before the trial.

13.32 *Blood Money.* Dec. 18, 1959. GS: Don Harvey, Mary Munday, William Schallert. A respected Latigo citizen is shot in the back by a stranger, and the enraged townspeople seek vengeance. Marshal Gib Scott learns that though the dead man appeared to be a solid citizen he was actually a wanted criminal.

13.33 *The Killer.* Jan. 1, 1960. GS: George Wallace, Eddie Firestone. A dog and four men die at the hands of an unknown killer. Unable to explain the murders, the townspeople live in constant fear.

13.34 *Letter of Death.* Jan. 8, 1960. GS: Adam Williams. Represented by lawyer Clay Culhane, Brad Pickard is awarded damages for false imprisonment. Then Clay, who believes Pickard was guilty of the crime, sets out to prove it.

13.35 *Mr. Simpson.* Jan. 22, 1960. GS: Paul Birch, John Newton. Clay Culhane learns that President Ulysses S. Grant will make an unpublicized stop at Latigo. When the President, traveling incognito, arrives in town, Clay and Marshal Gib Scott serve as bodyguards.

13.36 *Means to an End.* Jan. 29, 1960. GS: Patricia Donahue, Dennis McCarthy, Robert Knapp, Jack Ging. When Fran Whitney hires Clay Culhane he finds that she is more interested in his ability with a gun than in his legal services.

13.37 *The Indian Tree.* Feb. 19, 1960. GS: Dennis Cross, Nan Peterson. A client of Culhane's is hanged for robbery and murder, and the lawyer is accused of knowing where the stolen loot is hidden.

13.38 *The Apprentice.* March 11, 1960. GS: Buddy Ebsen, Richard Rust, Ben Wright. A gunman and his protege are hired by Culhane's client to settle his legal problems. Culhane tries to persuade the gunslingers to leave town.

13.39 *Burden of Guilt.* March 18, 1960. GS: John Marley, Wesley Lau, Ann McCrea, Harry Landers. Culhane helps to get an innocent man out of prison. Returning home, the man is murdered by an unseen killer.

13.40 *The Cabin.* April 1, 1960. GS: Gene Nelson, Mary Murphy, Lee Van Cleef, Debbie Megowan. Culhane trails his stolen horse to a cabin that is surrounded by a group of men who refuse to let anyone through their ranks. He learns that a sick child in need of a doctor is inside the cabin.

13.41 *The Return.* April 8, 1960. GS: Burt Douglas, John Kellogg. Marshal Scott breaks into an outlaw hideout and finds his brother Jamie there. Jamie claims to be a prisoner, but the outlaw leaders says he is one of the gang.

13.42 *A Case of Slow.* April 15, 1960. GS: John Dehner, Kay Stewart. Mary Forrest accuses her husband of trying to poison her so he could romance Nora Travers.

13.43 *The Penalty.* April 22, 1960. GS: James Franciscus, John Newton, Sam Edwards. A new employee tells Nora Travers how to run her freight line. She takes his advice, not suspecting he has got only his own interests at heart.

13.44 *End of the Line.* May 6, 1960. GS: Paul Burke, Paul Sorensen, Arch Duncan. Clay sides with the miners of Chloride when two brothers trying to take over the town force their leader into a gunfight.

14. Bonanza

NBC. 60 min. Broadcast history: Saturday, 7:30-8:30, Sept. 1959–Sept. 1961; Sunday, 9:00-10:00, Sept. 1961–Sept. 1971; Tuesday, 7:30-8:30, May 1972–Aug. 1972; Tuesday, 8:00-9:00, Sept. 1971–Jan. 1973.

Regular Cast: Lorne Greene (Ben Cartwright), Michael Landon (Little Joe Cartwright), Dan Blocker (Hoss Cartwright) 59-72, Pernell Roberts (Adam Cartwright) 59-65, Victor Sen Yung (Hop Sing), Ray Teal (Sheriff Roy Coffee) 60-72, David Canary (Candy) 67-70,72-73, Lou Frizzel (Dusty Rhoades) 70-72, Mitch Vogel (Jamie Hunter) 70-73, Tim Matheson (Griff King) 72-73.

Premise: This western adventure was set on the Ponderosa Ranch near Virginia City, Nevada, in the mid-1880s, and detailed the exploits of rancher Ben Cartwright and his three sons, Adam, Hoss and Little Joe.

The Episodes

14.1 *A Rose for Lotta.* Sept. 12, 1959. GS: Yvonne DeCarlo, George Macready. The powerful men of silver-rich Virginia City hire Lotta Crabtree, a famous entertainer, to lure Little Joe, the youngest Cartwright brother, into the city so that they can hold him prisoner and demand valuable timber from the Cartwrights as ransom.

14.2 *The Sun Mountain Herd.* Sept. 19, 1959. GS: Barry Sullivan, Leo Gordon, Bek Nelson, Karl Swenson. Mark Burdette, a slick opportunist from San Francisco, comes to Virginia City with his partner, Early Thorne, to seek gold and silver. Burdette and Thorne plan to make their money by killing off the Indian antelope herds and selling the meat to the luxury-starved miners at high prices.

14.3 *The Newcomers.* Sept. 26, 1959. GS: Inger Stevens, John Larch, Bob Knapp, Charles Maxwell. Blake McCall brings his lovely fiancee to the Ponderosa Ranch for her health. Hoss Cartwright feels a great tenderness for the frail girl, but he wonders about McCall's motives for visiting the ranch.

14.4 *The Paiute War.* Oct. 3, 1959. GS: Jack Warden, Anthony Caruso, Mike Forest. After mistreating two Indian women, trader Mike Wilson attempts to escape Indian reprisal by putting the blame on Adam Cartwright. A fierce war between the Paiute Indians and California militia results, and Adam is seized as a hostage by the Paiutes.

14.5 *Enter Mark Twain.* Oct. 10, 1959. GS: Howard Duff, John Litel, Dorothy Green, Ann Whitfield, Percy Helton, Patrick McVey. Before Samuel Langhorn Clemens became famous under the pen name Mark Twain, he worked as a reporter for the Virginia City Enterprise where he investigates suspected collusion between a judge and a railroad line.

14.6 *The Julia Bulette Story.* Oct. 17, 1959. GS: Janet Greet, Alexander Scourby, Harry Seymour, Robert Stevenson, Kem Dibbs. Despite warning from his father and brothers, young Joe Cartwright is fascinated by Julia Bulette, a cynical woman who does her gold digging above ground in Virginia City.

14.7 *The Saga of Annie O'Toole.* Oct. 24, 1959. GS: Ida Lupino, Alan Hale, Jr., Jon Patrick, Henry Lascoe, Richard Reeves, Ollie O'Toole. Annie O'Toole and her father arrive in the gold country with a claim filed by her suitor. When Annie's father dies, Adam Cartwright helps her start a restaurant in Virginia City to support her until she can settle her claim.

14.8 *The Diedeshiemer Story.* Oct. 31, 1959. GS: John Beal, Mala Powers, R.G. Armstrong, Charles Cooper, Paul Birch, Mae Marsh. Engineer Philip Diedeschiemer comes to Virginia City with a plan to make the deep silver mines safe from cave-ins. The mine owners oppose the plans.

14.9 *Mr. Henry Comstock.* Nov. 7, 1959. GS: Jack Carson, Joanna Sages, Terence De Marney, Jack Mather, Richard Cutting, Bruce Gordon, Charles Wagenheim, John Dierkes. Two miners rush into town with the news that they have staked a rich silver claim. Henry Comstock, hearing the news, does some fast talking and manages to get a half share of the claim for himself.

14.10 *The Magnificent Adah.* Nov. 14, 1959. GS: Ruth Roman, Don Megowan, Hal K. Smith, Mauritz Hugo. When a tour of Adah Menken's show brings the troupe to Virginia City, Adah stops to see her friend Ben Cartwright. Ben's sons begin to think the famous performer wants Ben to marry her.

14.11 *The Truckee Strip.* Nov. 21, 1959. GS: James Coburn, Carl Benton Reid, S. John Launer. Silver baron Jason Cauter wants to buy some timber which is growing on a disputed strip between the Cartwrights' Ponderosa ranch and Luther Bishop's land. Bishop won't sell until the ownership is established, but Carter impatiently takes action.

14.12 *The Hanging Posse.* Nov. 28, 1959. GS: Onslow Stevens, Adam Williams, Arthur Hunnicutt, Ray Hemphill. Flint Johnson forms a posse to track down the men who killed his wife. Fearing that the mob is out for blood, not justice, Adam and Little Joe join the posse.

14.13 *Vendetta.* Dec. 5, 1959. GS: Mort Mills, Simon Scott, William Quinn, William Pullen, Steve Rowland. During a bank holdup, Ben Cartwright is wounded, but he kills a member of the notorious Morgan gang. Carl Morgan announces that he will exact revenge.

14.14 *The Sisters.* Dec. 12, 1959. GS: Fay Spain, Malcolm Atterbury. Pretty Sue Ellen Terry is shot as she alights from Adam Cartwright's carriage. The town drunk says he saw Adam shoot her, and Adam is jailed on a murder charge.

14.15 *The Last Hunt.* Dec. 19, 1959. GS: Chana Eden, Steven Terrell, Carlyle Mitchell, Raymond Bailey. Hoss and Little Joe are in the mountains on a hunting expedition when they encounter an Indian girl about to give birth. With a winter blizzard and the baby both expected momentarily, the brothers quickly build a shelter.

14.16 *El Toro Grande.* Jan. 2, 1960. GS: Barbara Luna, Ricardo Cortez, Armand Alzamora, Jose Gonzalez Gonzalez, Alma Beltran. Ben Cartwright sends Hoss and Little Joe to California with a large sum of money to purchase a prize bull. The first night on the trail, the pair are ambushed by gunmen.

14.17 *The Outcast.* Jan. 9, 1960. GS: Susan Oliver, Jack Lord, Edward C. Platt, Mark Allen. After Leta Malvet's brother and father are hanged for murder the townspeople turn against the young girl. Desperately looking for someone she can trust, Leta turns to Clay Renton.

14.18 *House Divided.* Jan. 16, 1960. GS: Cameron Mitchell, Stacy Harris, Mickey Simpson, John Locke, Marianne Stewart, Howard Wendell. Southern sympathizer Fred Kyle comes to Nevada to purchase gold and silver for the Confederacy. He finds that the citizens of Virginia City are almost equally divided in the allegiance to the North and South.

14.19 *The Gunmen.* Jan. 23, 1960. GS: Henry Hull, Ellen Corby, Douglas Spencer, Jonathan Gilmore, George Mitchell. Climaxing a feud, the McFaddens hire the two vicious Slade brothers to kill the head of the Hadfield family. Unaware that they resemble the Slades, Hoss and Little Joe Cartwright ride into the midst of the feuders.

14.20 *The Fear Merchants.* Jan. 30, 1960. GS: Gene Evans, Pat Michon, Helen Westcott, Ray Stricklyn, Christopher Dark, Guy Lee. Frontier politician Andrew Fulmer runs for mayor of Virginia City on a platform of hatred for outsiders. Fulmer especially wants to get rid of the town's Chinese citizens, and he hires hoodlums to terrorize them.

14.21 *The Spanish Grant.* Feb. 6, 1960. GS: Patricia Medina, Sebastian Cabot, Paul Picerni, Mike Ragan. A pair of greedy swindlers employ a former dancing girl in a scheme to grab a large piece of Nevada land. The girl poses as the descendant of Spanish nobility, heir to the rich De la Cuesta land grant which includes part of the Cartwrights' Ponderosa ranch.

14.22 *Blood on the Land.* Feb. 13, 1960. GS: Everett Sloane, Ray Daley, Tom Reese. Driving his flock to the California market, sheepherder Jeb Drummond decides to fatten his animals on the rich Ponderosa grasslands. The Cartwrights warn Drummond to bypass their ranch, but the greedy sheepman ignores the warning.

14.23 *Desert Justice.* Feb. 20, 1960. GS: Claude Akins, Wesley Lau, Fintan Meyler, Ron Hayes, John Wengraf, Bud Osborne, Will Wright. Adam and Hoss decide they better go along to make sure that a murder suspect arrives safely in Los Angeles for his trial. The murder victim was the wife of Marshal Dowd, the suspect is a boy, and the man who's bringing him to trial is Dowd, who has shown his state of mind by beating and chaining the lad.

14.24 *The Stranger.* Feb. 27, 1960. GS: Lloyd Nolan, Robert Foulk, Joan Staley, Hal Baylor, Charles Tannen, Donald Foster. Nursing a personal grudge, New Orleans Police Inspector Charles Leduque tries to spoil Ben Cartwright's bid for the Nevada governorship. Leduque has brought a warrant for Cartwright's arrest.

14.25 *Escape to the Ponderosa.* March 5, 1960. GS: Joe Maross, Grant Williams, James Parnell, Gloria Talbott, Chris Alcaide, Dayton Lummis, Sherwood Price. Three escaped military prisoners bushwack Adam. The infuriated Cartwrights join the Army in pursuing the attackers.

14.26 *The Avenger.* March 19, 1960. GS: Vic Morrow, Jean Allison, Dan White, Nestor Paiva, Robert Griffin. Ben and Adam are convicted of murder, and a young stranger takes up their cause. His parents were lynch victims and he is determined that no one will share their fate.

14.27 *The Last Trophy.* March 26, 1960. GS: Hazel Court, Edward Ashley, Bert Freed, Ken Mayer. Lord and Lady Dunsford visit the Cartwrights. Once regarded as a top hunter, Dunsford now shies from the very mention of violence.

14.28 *San Francisco Holiday.* April 2, 1960. GS: Robert Nichols, O.Z. Whitehead, Murvyn Vye, Kathleen Crowley, David White, Richard Deacon, Herb Vigran. Ben declares a San Francisco holiday at the end of a cattle drive and cautions his cowhands about Barbaray Coast cutthroats. Even so two naive cowhands are shanghaied on a boat for Hong Kong.

14.29 *Bitter Water.* April 9, 1960. GS: Don Dubbins, Merry Anders, Robert F. Simon, Ken Becker. Neighbor Tod McKaren is about to sell his land to a miner, but the Cartwrights remind him that mining will pollute their water supply. Fearing McKaren will back out of the deal, the miner decides to force a decision.

14.30 *Feet of Clay.* April 16, 1960. GS: David Ladd, Logan Field, Robert Tetrick. Billy is a sullen and unfriendly youngster whose mother is dead and father is in prison. He seems to warm up to Hoss, until his father escapes from prison.

14.31 *Dark Star.* April 23, 1960. GS: Hugo Haas, Susan Harrison, Arthur Batanides, Lili Valenty. Tirza, a Gypsy, was born under a dark star. Her people think she is a witch — and Tirza thinks so too. When the Cartwrights find her hiding on their land, they try to return her to the Gypsy camp.

14.32 *Death at Dawn.* April 30, 1960. GS: Robert Middleton, Gregory Walcott, Morgan Woodward, Nancy Deale, Paul Carr, Peter Leeds, Hugh Sanders. Virginia City has fallen into the grip of organized crime. A gang is selling protection to town merchants, and dealing lethally with those who refuse to buy.

Season Two

14.33 *Showdown.* Sept. 10, 1960. GS: Ben Cooper, Jack Lambert, Jody Warner, John Maxwell, Norman Leavitt. After robbing the local bank, Sam Kirby and his gang hide out on the Ponderosa. Kirby then decides to get a job with the Cartwrights in order to keep his pals posted on the activities of the law in Virginia City.

14.34 *The Mission.* Sept. 17, 1960. GS: Henry Hull,

Peter Whitney, John Dehner, Harry Carey, Jr., Don Collier, Lane Bradford, Dale Van Sickel, Don Rhodes, Mike Ragan, Leo Needham. Charlie Trent has held himself responsible for the massacre of a troop of soldiers he was assigned to lead. Now he is a drunk and ridiculed by the people of Virginia City.

14.35 *Badge Without Honor.* Sept. 24, 1960. GS: Dan Duryea, Fred Beir, Christine White, Wendell Holmes, Richard Warren, James Hong, Bob Miles, Jr. Deputy Marshal Gerald Eskith is looking for Jason Blaine. He says he wants to escort Blaine to San Francisco to testify against the murderous Murdock gang.

14.36 *The Mill.* Oct. 1, 1960. GS: Claude Akins, Harry Townes, Dianne Foster. Crippled Tom Edwards spends him time drinking and gambling with Ezekiel, his hired hand. Somehow Ezekiel always wins, and Edwards gets deeper and deeper in debt.

14.37 *The Hopefuls.* Oct. 8, 1960. GS: Larry Gates, Patricia Donahue, Dennis Patrick, Charles Maxwell. A religious group led by Jacob Darien has pooled its money to buy land for a new home, and a special wagon train carries the people and the money across the Ponderosa. Darien's daughter Regina catches Adam's eye, so he and Hoss decide to escort the train.

14.38 *Denver McKee.* Oct. 15, 1960. GS: Franchot Tone, Natalie Trundy, Ken Mayer, Stephen Courtleigh, William Fawcett, Jack Lester, Bob Barker. Denver McKee is a friendly neighbor of the Cartwrights who has but one goal in life — to give his daughter Connie the best of everything. She has been attending an Eastern school for several years and now is coming home to her father's ranch.

14.39 *Day of Reckoning.* Oct. 22, 1960. GS: Ricardo Montalban, Madlyn Rhue, Karl Swenson, Anthony Caruso. An Indian named Matsou has saved Ben Cartwright's life, so Ben gratefully gives him a parcel of land on the Ponderosa. Neighbor Ike Daggett doesn't like Indians and starts trouble for Matsou.

14.40 *The Abduction.* Oct. 29, 1960. GS: Gerald Mohr, Jackie Russell, Barbara Lawrence, Jerry Oddo, Robert Maffei, Theodore Marcuse, Laurie Mitchell, Stafford Repp. Hoss and Little Joe take their dates for a night at the carnival. Phil Reed, the carnival owner, spots Jennifer Beale, Joe's pretty date, and decides he'd like to get better acquainted.

14.41 *Breed of Violence.* Nov. 5, 1960. GS: John Ericson, Val Avery, Hal Baylor, Norm Alden. Sheriff Kincaid is a strict father, and his daughter Dolly welcomes the chance to leave town with Vince Dagen — unaware that he has just robbed a bank.

14.42 *The Last Viking.* Nov. 12, 1960. GS: Neville Brand, Sonja Wilde, Al Ruscio, Louis Mercier, Ric Marlow, Herbert C. Lytton. Gunnar Borgstrom and his group of bandits are on their way to Canada to make a big raid. They stop overnight on the Ponderosa, and Borgstrom decides to pay a visit to his brother-in-law, Ben Cartwright.

14.43 *The Trail Gang.* Nov. 26, 1960. GS: Dick Davalos, James Westerfield, Edgar Buchanan, Robert J. Wilke, Linda Lawson. Outlaw Johnny Logan has sworn revenge on the sheriff who jailed him the year before. The sheriff's name is also Logan and is Johnny's father.

14.44 *The Savage.* Dec. 3, 1960. GS: Anna-Lisa, Hal Jon Norman, Vic Millan, Frank Sentry, Bob Wiensko, Maurice Jara, Larry Chance, Henry Wills. Haddon and McGregor, a pair of trappers, are killed by Shoshones when they stumble across a sacred burial ground. Soon after Adam comes along and overhears Chato, the chief, talking about a strange spirit woman who prevented the Indians from scalping their victims.

14.45 *Silent Thunder.* Dec. 10, 1960. GS: Stella Stevens, Albert Salmi, James Griffith, Kenneth MacKenna, Sherwood Price, Harry Swoger. Little Joe meets a deaf-mute named Ann Croft and attempts to teach her sign language. Ann's father, however, doesn't take kindly to Joe's efforts as he feels the two are getting much to interested in each other.

14.46 *The Ape.* Dec. 17, 1960. GS: Leonard Nimoy, Cal Bolder, Karen Sharpe, Rodolfo Hoyos, Charles Tannen. Arnie Gurne is a brute of a man with a childlike mentality. When Arnie manhandles Shari, the saloon girl, Adam and Little Joe come to her defense — only to be soundly thrashed. Then Hoss arrives and battles Arnie to a standoff. The trouble is that Hoss likes Arnie.

14.47 *The Blood Line.* Dec. 31, 1960. GS: Lee Van Cleef, Jan Sterling, David Macklin, Norman Leavitt, Allan Lane, Thomas B. Henry. Ben is forced to shoot down Luke Grayson when the man attacks in a drunken rage. Grayson's teenage son Todd soon arrives in Virginia City, bent on vengeance.

14.48 *The Courtship.* Jan. 7, 1961. GS: Julie Adams, Marshall Reed, Lyle Talbot, Paul Dubov. Helen Layton is beautiful, and she is the widow of a friend of the Cartwrights, so Hoss takes a shine to her.

14.49 *The Spitfire.* Jan. 14, 1961. GS: Katherine Warren, Jack Elam, Anita Sands, Steven Terrell, Don Harvey. Little Joe is riding on the Ponderosa when he comes across Jeb Hoad in the act of setting fire to a rich stand of timber. Jeb won't stop when Joe orders him to, so young Cartwright is forced to shoot.

14.50 *The Bride.* Jan. 21, 1961. GS: John McIntire, Adam West, Suzanne Lloyd, William Mims. Ben is away on business when a girl named Jennifer comes to the ranch and says that she is his new wife. She also presents a marriage license to prove it.

14.51 *Bank Run.* Jan. 28, 1961. GS: Ian Wolfe, Walter Burke, Dan Tobin, Wynn Pearce. Little Joe overhears a banker named Harrison plotting to close his establishment on pretense of insolvency, then make a fast foreclosure on some mining property. Joe and Hoss decide there is only one way to stop Harrison, so they rob the bank.

14.52 *The Fugitive.* Feb. 4, 1961. GS: Frank Silvera, Ziva Rodann, James Best, Will Wright, Veda Ann Borg, Arthur Batanides, Salvador Baguez. Neighbor Will Reagan gets word that his son Carl has died in Mexico. He asks Adam to bring the body home for burial and to find out how Carl died.

14.53 *Vengeance.* Feb. 11, 1961. GS: Adam Williams, Beverly Tyler, Keith Richards, Olan Soule, Roy Engle, Robert E. Griffin. Hoss defends himself against an attack by his neighbor Willie Twilight. But he defends himself too hard and kills Willie. Then Willie's brother Red goes after revenge.

14.54 *Tax Collector.* Feb. 18, 1961. GS: Eddie Firestone, Kathie Browne, Russ Conway, Charles Watts. Good for nothing Jock Henry, a neighbor of the Cartwright, finally lets himself be talked into going to work as the local tax collector. It suddenly occurs to Jock that he is the ultimate authority on how much taxpayers can be assessed.

14.55 *The Rescue.* Feb. 25, 1961. GS: Leif Erickson, Richard Coogan, Burt Douglas, Ron Hayes, Joe Partridge. A cow is stolen from the Ponderosa and Ben discovers the branded hide on the Tatum place. Josh Tatum and Ben get into a fight over the incident. When Ben returns home showing signs of the battle, his sons set out to even the score.

14.56 *The Dark Gate.* March 4, 1961. GS: James Coburn, CeCe Whitney, Med Flory, Harry Dean Stanton. Adam and his pal Ross Marquett get along famously until Ross accuses Adam of carrying on with his wife.

14.57 *The Duke.* March 11, 1961. GS: Maxwell Reed, Randy Stuart, J. Pat O'Malley, Jason Evers. An English prizefighter fancies himself a champion with his fists and with the girls. He and his manager Limey come to Virginia City in search of a worthy ring opponent and Hoss steps up to oblige.

14.58 *Cut-throat Junction.* March 18, 1961. GS: Robert Lansing, Shirley Ballard.

14.59 *The Gift.* April 1, 1961. GS: Martin Landau; Jim Davis, Jack Hogan, Joe Yrigoyen. Little Joe sets out on a hazardous journey through the desert. The object of the trip is a white Arabian stallion that Little Joe is set on getting as a birthday present for his Pa.

14.60 *The Rival.* April 15, 1961. GS: Peggy Ann Garner, Charles Aidman, Robert McQueeney. Although Hoss saw Jim Applegate riding away from the scene of a lynching, his sense of fair play keeps him from telling the Sheriff. Jim is his friendly rival for the affections of Cameo Johnson.

14.61 *The Infernal Machine.* April 22, 1961. GS: George Kennedy, Eddie Ryder, Willard Waterman, June Kenney, Nora Hayden. Hoss and his friend Daniel Pettibone offer the citizens of Virginia City a chance to get the inside track on the Automobile Age, by financing Pettibone's version of the horseless carriage. The two visionaries are roundly rejected, however, until a conman named Throckmorton appears in town and offers to help them out.

14.62 *Thunderhead Swindle.* April 29, 1961. GS: Parley Baer, Walter Coy, Ross Eliott, Judson Pratt, Vito Scotti. Mine owners Jack Cunningham and Frank Furnas announce a silver strike at Thunderhead Mine. But Ben learns that the mine's former owner has been murdered and suspects Cunningham and Furnas are up to something crooked.

14.63 *The Secret.* May 6, 1961. GS: Russell Collins, Crahan Denton, Stephen Joyce, Pat Michon, Dayton Lummis, Morgan Woodward, Sherwood Price, Bob Harris. Mary Parson is murdered, and Little Joe is arrested as the killer. Joe's best pal John Hardner says he saw them together just a few minutes before the murder, and Mary's father and brothers say she was planning to elope with Joe that night.

14.64 *The Dream Riders.* May 20, 1961. GS: Sidney Blackmer, Burt Douglas, Stuart Nisbet, Diana Millay, Jonathan Hole. Major Cayley says that man will some day be able to fly and the Cartwrights agree to let him use their ranch for a balloon experiment. As another part of the experiment two of the Major's fellow visionaries are busy casing a bank in Virginia City.

14.65 *Elizabeth, My Love.* May 27, 1961. GS: Geraldine Brooks, Torin Thatcher, Berry Kroeger, Richard Collier, Alex Sharpe, Bob Hopkins, Molly Roden, Max Staten, John Close, Jack Rice. In a nostalgic mood, Ben Cartwright recalls the days when he was first mate on a sailing ship, and how he met Adam's mother, Elizabeth.

14.66 *Sam Hill.* June 3, 1961. GS: Claude Akins, Ford Rainey, Edgar Buchanan, Robert Ridgely, Caroline Richter. Sam Hill is a traveling blacksmith of legendary strength and toughness. But Sam has his soft side. He refuses to sell the piece of land on which his mother is buried.

Season Three

14.67 *The Smiler.* Sept. 24, 1961. GS: Hershel Bernardi, Catherine McLeod, Bill Zuckert, Hy Terman, Scatman Crothers, Robert Foulk. Hoss gets into a fight with Arthur Bolling, whom he overhears insulting a woman. When Bolling is accidentally killed, his mild-mannered brother Clarence says he forgives Hoss, but secretly plans for revenge.

14.68 *Springtime.* Oct. 1, 1961. GS: John Carradine, John Qualen, Jena Engstrom, Claude Johnson, Denver Pyle. It's Springtime on the Ponderosa, and the Cartwright boys are acting as balmy as the weather until their horseplay accidentally injures old Jebediah, the hired hand.

14.69 *The Honor of Cochise.* Oct. 8, 1961. GS: Jeff Morrow, DeForest Kelley, Al Ruscio, Stacy Harris. Army Captain Johnson has aroused the anger of Cochise by killing some of the Indian chief's braves. Now pursued by the vengeful warrior, Johnson arrives at the Ponderosa, and begs for refuge.

14.70 *The Lonely House.* Oct. 15, 1961. GS: Paul Richards, Faith Domergue, Jim Beck, Vito Scotti. A wounded bandit named Trock eludes a posse by taking refuge in the home of widow Lee Bolden. But Little Joe happens to be visiting Lee, and recognizes Trock as a wanted man.

14.71 *The Burma Rarity.* Oct. 22, 1961. GS: Beatrice Kay, Wally Brown, Dave Willock. Con artists Henry Morgan and Phil Axe are in Virginia City searching for a sucker for the gem swindle they have concocted. Their pitch finally falls on the eager ears of former showgirl Clementine Hawkins.

14.72 *Broken Ballad.* Oct. 29, 1961. GS: Robert Culp, Ray Daley, Dabbs Greer, Abagail Shelton, Robert Christopher, Richard Rosmini, Cosmo Sardo. Former gunfighter Ed Payson rides into Virginia City for supplies, and news of his coming has proceeded him. Will Cass, proprietor of the general store and father of one of Payson's victims, refuses to sell him anything. Adam thinks Payson should have a chance to prove he has reformed, and buys the supplies for him.

14.73 *The Many Faces of Gideon Flinch.* Nov. 5, 1961. GS: Ian Wolfe, Arnold Stang, Sue Ane Langdon, Harry Swoger. Bullethead Burke is on the trail of investment broker Gideon Flinch, the man who bilked him in a mail-order deal. Bullethead doesn't know what Flinch looks like, and mistakes Little Joe for the shady operator.

14.74 *The Friendship.* Nov. 12, 1961. GS: Dean Jones, Janet Lake, Edward Faulkner, Norman Alden, Rusty Lane, Stafford Repp. Little Joe's horse bolts, and only the quick thinking of Danny Kidd, a chain-gang prisoner, saves him from being killed. Joe decides to repay the favor by getting Danny the one thing he wants most — his freedom.

14.75 *The Countess.* Nov. 19, 1961. GS: Maggie Hayes, John Anderson, Dan Sheridan. A wealthy widow, Lady Linda Chadwick, arrives on the Virginia City stage, but she is no stranger, at least to Ben. Linda rejected a proposal of marriage from him twenty years ago, and now she is ready to reconsider.

14.76 *The Horse Breaker.* Nov. 26, 1961. GS: Ben

Cooper, R.G. Armstrong, Addison Richards, Sue Randall, Don Burnett, John Cole. Bronco-buster Johnny Lightly is injured while working for the Cartwrights, and he loses the use of his legs. Dejected, Johnny doesn't want to live anymore — even though Dr. Kay tells him the injury may not be permanent.

14.77 Day of the Dragon. Dec. 3, 1961. GS: Lisa Lu, Richard Loo, Philip Ahn, Harry Lauter. Su Ling, a Chinese slave girl, has been brought to America by General Tsung. She is kidnaped by a pair of crooks named Gordon and Barrett, who anticipate a handsome ransom from the wealthy war lord. Then the kidnapers get into a poker game with Little Joe, who wins Sue Ling away from them.

14.78 The Frenchman. Dec. 10, 1961. GS: Andre Philippe, Erika Peters, Robert J. Stevenson. A stranger claiming to be a reincarnation of 15th-century poet Francois Villon arrives in Virginia City. Hoss makes it clear that he doesn't share Villon's enthusiasm for culture, and the gallant Gaul challenges him to a duel.

14.79 The Tin Badge. Dec. 17, 1961. GS: Vic Morrow, Karen Steele, John Litel, Robert Fortier, David Manley, Bill Catching. Mine owner Ab Brock and Mayor Goshen have joined forces in a hazardous project — murder. To insure the success of their plan they want to give the sheriff's job to someone who won't give them any trouble — someone like Little Joe.

14.80 Gabrielle. Dec. 24, 1961. GS: Diane Mountfort, John Abbott, Kevin Hagen. Riding homeward through the wintery mountains, the Cartwright men come upon young Gabrielle Wickham wandering alone through the snow. She says she is looking for her grandfather, a hermit known as Zachariah.

14.81 Land Grab. Dec. 31, 1961. GS: John McGiver, George Mitchell, Don Wilbanks. Mike Sullivan and his followers take over a section of the Ponderosa. When Ben tries to evict them, the settlers produce deeds to the property, bought fair and square from a man called John Zink.

14.82 The Tall Stranger. Jan. 7, 1962. GS: Sean McClory, Kathie Browne, Jacqueline Scott, Russell Thorson. Hoss Cartwright is interested in Margie Owens, the bankers daughter, but he has a formidable rival in Mark Connor. Margie, who has a bad case of wanderlust, is captivated by Connors' stories of his vast travels.

14.83 The Lady from Baltimore. Jan. 14, 1962. GS: Mercedes McCambridge, Audrey Dalton. Ambitious Deborrah Banning thought she had it made when she married promising Horace Banning, but Horace turned out to be a loser. Now she is determined that her daughter Melinda make up for her mistake by marrying one of the prosperous Cartwrights.

14.84 The Ride. Jan. 21, 1962. GS: Jan Merlin, Grace Gaynor, Hal Baylor, Chubby Johnson. A man wearing a hood robs the Goat Springs stage line and kills manager Toby Barker. Adam manages to catch a glimpse of the killer's face as he escapes, and is shocked to recognize his close friend Bill Enders.

14.85 The Storm. Jan. 28, 1962. GS: Brooke Hayward, Frank Overton. While Laura White and her father, an old friend of Ben Cartwright's, are visiting at the Ponderosa, Laura reveals her plans to marry her childhood sweetheart. But Laura's father is opposed to the match, and so is the childhood sweetheart — Little Joe.

14.86 The Auld Sod. Feb. 4, 1962. GS: Cheerio Meredith, James Dunn, Jeff DeBenning, Howard Wright. Danny Lynch has written his mother in Ireland a little blarney about his success in America, and about a huge ranch that he owns. Then he learns that she is coming to visit him, so the Cartwrights offer to pose as ranch hands while Danny acts as the owner of the Ponderosa.

14.87 Gift of Water. Feb. 11, 1962. GS: Royal Dano, Pam Smith, Majel Barrett. Some farmers who have been hit by a drought start eyeing the moist grassy highlands near the Ponderosa as a place to move their farming operations. But some of the Cartwrights' neighbors don't like the idea.

14.88 The Jacknife. Feb. 18, 1962. GS: Bethel Leslie, John Archer, Donald Losby, Robert H. Harris. The Cartwrights are after some rustlers and Adam is sent out to scout the area while the others set a trap. On the trail, he encounters a man named Mathew Grant, who says he was injured when his horse was frightened by a rattler.

14.89 The Guilty. Feb. 25, 1962. GS: Lyle Bettger, Charles Maxwell, Anne Benton, Edward C. Platt. Ben has some disturbing news for his old friend Lem Partridge. Right before his own eyes he saw ex-convict Jack Groat shoot down Lem's son. Lem is bitter and wonders if Ben was there, why didn't he do something about it.

14.90 The Wooing of Abigail Jones. March 4, 1962. GS: Eileen Ryan, Vaughn Monroe, Norma Varden, Diana Darrin. Ponderosa ranch hand Hank Meyers is romantically attracted to Abigail Jones, the local schoolmarm. Trouble is that Hanks is the shy type — so shy he is afraid to let her know his true feelings.

14.91 The Law Maker. March 11, 1962. GS: Arthur Franz, Les Tremayne, Charles Briggs, John Mitchum. Adam and Joe are having a chat in town with Sheriff Coffee, when they suddenly notice a hold-up gang hard at work in the Express office. The sheriff runs out to do his duty, and is run into the ground when the bandits stampede their horses.

14.92 Look to the Stars. March 18, 1962. GS: Douglas Lambert, William Schallert, Joe De Santis, Penny Santon. This story is based on the life of Albert Abraham Michelson, a Nobel Prize winning scientist. Young Albert Michelson, a brilliant student, is maligned by his teacher Mr. Norton, who appears to be jealous of the lad's ability.

14.93 The Gamble. April 1, 1962. GS: Charles McGraw, Ben Johnson, Robert Sampson, Raymond Greenleaf. On their way home from a profitable cattle drive, the Cartwrights stop overnight in the town of Alkali. The next morning they are met by the sheriff and townspeople, who accuse them of bank robbery, and point to a saddlebag full of money as proof.

14.94 Crucible. April 8, 1962. GS: Lee Marvin, Howard Ledig, Barry Cahill. Adam is off to the mountains for a few days of peace and quiet. Instead he gets Preston and Gann, a couple of crooks who make off with everything but the clothes on his back.

14.95 Inger, My Love. April 15, 1962. GS: Inga Swenson, James Philbrook, Jeremy Slate. Ben indulges in a nostalgic reverie about Hoss' deceased mother. Having worked his way West to Galesburg, Illinois, Ben is befriended by a girl named Inger, the fiancee of the tavern owner who gave him a job.

14.96 Blessed Are They. April 22, 1962. GS: Robert Brown, Ford Rainey, Leslie Wales, Irene Tedrow, Rory O'Brien. Virginia City is torn by a feud between the Mahans and the

Clarkes, and nearly a third of the town has chosen up sides. Ben is asked to bring the warring factions to terms.

14.97 *The Dowry.* April 29, 1962. GS: Steven Geray, Luciana Paluzzi, Lee Bergere, Ken Mayer, Roy Engel. Bandits hold up a stage and make off with a small chest belonging to Alexander Dubois, who claims it contained the dowry for his daughter's wedding.

14.98 *The Long Night.* May 6, 1962. GS: James Coburn, Bing Russell, Jack Chaplain, William Bramley, Whit Bissell. The Cartwrights' option in a business deal is about to expire and Adam races to the town of Bowlegs with a large bank draft to try and beat the deadline. A hitch develops when he is ambushed by an escaped convict.

14.99 *The Mountain Girl.* May 13, 1962. GS: Nina Shipman, Warren Oates, Carl Benton Reid, Nancy Hadley, Will Wright, Mary Treen. Trudy Harker was raised by her grandfather in the hill country. But now he is dead and Little Joe decides to take Trudy home to the Ponderosa and make a lady of her.

14.100 *The Miracle Worker.* May 20, 1962. GS: Ed Nelson, Patricia Breslin, Mort Mills, Jean Ingess, Tol Avery, Raymond Bailey. Susan Blanchard suffers a bad spill in a wagon crash and is unable to move her legs. But the doctors can find nothing wrong with her.

Season Four

14.101 *The First Born.* Sept. 23, 1962. GS: Barry Coe, Eddy Waller, Don Beddoe, Mike Ragan, Robert Karnes. Soon after Clay Stafford hires on at the Ponderosa, he and Little Joe become friends. When the sheriff orders him to leave town after a shooting, Clay lets Joe in on a secret. They were both born to the same mother.

14.102 *The Quest.* Sept. 30, 1962. GS: Grant Richards, James Beck, Frank Gerstle, Dan Riss, Charles Seel. Little Joe, tired of having his two brothers constantly watching over him, complains that he is never allowed to do anything on his own. So Ben gives his youngest son permission to strike out on his own—by securing an important contract to supply Ponderosa timber for a construction project by a mining company.

14.103 *The Artist.* Oct. 7, 1962. GS: Virginia Grey, Dan O'Herlihy, Arch Johnson, William Keene, S. John Launer. Stricken with blindness, artist Mathew Raine has withdrawn into a world of self-pity. But when Ben Cartwright strikes up a friendship, Raine appears to be losing some of his bitterness and becoming more like his former self.

14.104 *A Hot Day for a Hanging.* Oct. 14, 1962. GS: Denver Pyle, Olive Sturgess, Roy Roberts, Terry Becker, Kelly Thordsen. Hoss Cartwright is delivering a large amount of cash to his father when he is arrested by Sheriff Stedman. All that money he is carrying makes Hoss a suspect in a recent bank robbery in Stedman's town.

14.105 *The Deserter.* Oct. 21, 1962. GS: Claude Akins, Robert Sampson, Gale Garnett, Anthony Caruso, George Keymas. Col. Edward J. Dunwoody drops in at the Ponderosa to suggest that the Cartwrights may know the whereabouts of an Army deserter. When the Colonel shows them the picture of the man, they recognize him immediately as their neighbor Bill Winters.

14.106 *The Way Station.* Oct. 29, 1962. GS: Robert Vaughn, Dawn Wells, Trevor Bardette, Dorothy Green. With a storm coming up, Adam takes refuge in an isolated way station run by an old man named Jesse and his granddaughter Marty. But someone else is seeking shelter there—a killer named Luke Martin.

14.107 *The War Comes to Washoe.* Nov. 4, 1962. GS: Harry Townes, Joyce Taylor, Barry Kelley, Alan Caillou. Voters in the territory hold a statehood convention to choose whether to join the Union or the Confederacy. The Civil War has already turned brother against brother in the Cartwright home. Adam is furious because Little Joe plans to marry the daughter of an advocate of the Southern cause.

14.108 *Knight Errant.* Nov. 18, 1962. GS: John Doucette, Judi Meredith, Phil Chambers, Roy Engel, Tyler McVey, Tina Menard, George Robotham, Gil Perkins. The Cartwrights' friend and neighbor Walter Prescott applies to a magazine for a mail-order bride, but he hurts his leg just before he is supposed to pick her up. So Hoss agrees to ride out to meet the blushing bride.

14.109 *The Beginning.* Nov. 25, 1962. GS: Ken Lynch, Carl Reindel, Robert Burton. Ben brings a young man named Billy Horn to live at the Ponderosa. This will be Billy's first contact with white men since his childhood when he was abducted by Indians.

14.110 *The Deadly Ones.* Dec. 2, 1962. GS: Leo Gordon, Will Kuluva, Lee Farr, Jena Engstrom. The Ponderosa is invaded by a detachment of soldiers in the service of Mexico's General Juarez. One of the men, Forsythe, disobeys his orders to hold the Cartwrights hostage, and shoots Little Joe in the back.

14.111 *Gallagher Sons.* Dec. 9, 1962. GS: Eileen Chesis, Larrian Gillespie, Robert Strauss, Craig Curtis, Tom Greenway. Mr. Gallagher never had any sons, so he named his daughters Will and Charlie. When their father dies, the two little girls are left alone, until Hoss rides by their cabin.

14.112 *The Decision.* Dec. 16,1962. GS: DeForest Kelley, John Hoyt, Lisabeth Hush, Walter Sande, Eddie Quillan. Hoss suffers a bad fall from his horse and needs immediate medical attention. But when his kinfolk bring him to town, they learn that the only doctor in the vicinity is about to be hanged for murder.

14.113 *The Good Samaritan.* Dec. 23, 1962. GS: Jeanne Cooper, Don Collier, Noreen DeVita, Roy Engel. Hoss Cartwright decides to act the good Samaritan and introduce Wade Tyree to widow Abigail Hinton. The couple have several things in common. They are both lonely and they have both been jilted.

14.114 *The Jury.* Dec. 30, 1962. GS: Jack Betts, James Bell, Don Haggerty, Arthur Space, Tol Avery. The jury is out on accused murderer Jamie Wrenn, and all of the jurors have agreed to vote Warren guilty, except for one. The lone holdout is Hoss Cartwright, who believes that there is a reasonable doubt as to Wrenn's guilt.

14.115 *The Colonel.* Jan. 6, 1963. GS: John Larkin, Helen Westcott, Warren Kemmerling, Edward Platt, Mary Wickes. Ben meets his old Army buddy Frank Medford in Virginia City. Medford, a rather impoverished traveling salesman, notices that Ben is quite well off, and claims that he too is in the chips.

14.116 *Song in the Dark.* Jan. 13, 1963. GS: Edward

Andrews, Gregory Walcott, Virginia Christine, Mort Mills. Adam gives a guitar-strumming wanderer named Danny Morgan, who once saved Adam's life, a job on the Ponderosa. But Morgan doesn't sing for long, for he is arrested on suspicion of murder.

14.117 *Elegy for a Hangman.* Jan. 20, 1963. GS: Keir Dullea, Otto Kruger, Kevin Hagen, William Zuckert. Young Bob Jolley believes that his father was unjustly sentenced to be executed by a judge called "Hanging" Harry Whitaker. When Whitaker comes to Virginia City to visit Ben Cartwright, Jolley follows him to a local saloon and insults the judge's honor.

14.118 *Half a Rogue.* Jan. 27, 1963. GS: Slim Pickens, Judson Pratt, John Milford, Bing Russell. Big Jim Leyton tries to steal Hoss' horse, but passes out from a bullet wound in the process. He received the wound while busting out of jail.

14.119 *The Last Haircut.* Feb. 3, 1963. GS: Perry Lopez, Jered Barclay, Rex Holman, Alex Montoya, John Harmon. Gunslinger Duke Miller is the impatient type. When he goes to get a haircut and finds Carlos Rodriguez in the barber's chair, he shoots him to death.

14.120 *Marie, My Love.* Feb. 10, 1963. GS: Felicia Farr, George Dolenz, Lily Valenty, Richard Angarola, Jean Del Val. When Little Joe is hurt in a fall from his horse, Ben's memory wanders back to the time when he first met Marie, the woman who became his third wife and Joe's mother.

14.121 *The Hayburner.* Feb. 17, 1963. GS: William Demarest, Ellen Corby, Percy Helton, Howard Wright, Bing Russell, Paul Bryar. Adam and Hoss buy a thoroughbred race horse, which they hope to enter in the Virginia City Sweepstakes. When Hoss loses the animal in a card game, the boys are forced to borrow money from Little Joe to get the horse back.

14.122 *The Actress.* Feb. 24, 1963. GS: Patricia Crowley, Joey Scott, Lester Mathews, John Rodney, Robert J. Stevenson. Lovely Julia Grant, who has had no luck at capturing theater audiences, easily captures the heart of Little Joe.

14.123 *A Stranger Passed This Way.* March 3, 1963. GS: Signe Hasso, Robert Emhardt, Addison Richards, Robert Carricart, Dan White. After a blow on the head causes Hoss to lose his memory, he is adopted by an elderly couple who name him after the late son, Hendrick.

14.124 *The Way of Aaron.* March 10, 1963. GS: Aneta Corseaut, Ludwig Donath, Jason Wingreen, Harry Dean Stanton, Sarah Selby. Adam's romantic involvement with Rebecca Kaufmann, the daughter of a deeply religious peddler presents a problem. She is not of Adam's faith.

14.125 *A Woman Lost.* March 17, 1963. GS: Ruta Lee, Don Megowan, Harry Hickox, Roger Torrey, Bern Hoffman, Dick Miller, Don Edwards, John Indrisano. Rita Marlow, an alcoholic since the death of her husband and child, runs into Ben, an old friend, in a San Francisco saloon. He decides to take her to the Ponderosa and cure her.

14.126 *Any Friend of Walter's.* March 24, 1963. GS: Arthur Hunnicutt, Steve Brodie, Vic Werber, James Luisi, Katie Barrett, Robert Foulk. Hoss, an old prospector named Obie, and Obie's dog Walter are trapped in a mountain cabin, fighting off three outlaws who are trying to steal Obie's gold.

14.127 *Mirror of a Man.* March 31, 1963. GS: Ron Hayes, Ford Rainey, Nancy Rennick, Tris Coffin, Joseph Bree, Kathleen O'Malley, Eugene Martin. Rube Barnes steals a horse and kills a man in the process, but it is his twin brother Jud who gets arrested.

14.128 *My Brother's Keeper.* April 7, 1963. GS: Carolyn Kearney, Brendan Dillon, Ken Lynch. Adam becomes completely disgusted with the violent way of life in the West, when he accidentally shoots, and nearly kills, Little Joe.

14.129 *Five into the Wind.* April 21, 1963. GS: Kathleen Crowley, Betsy Jones Moreland, Kelly Thordsen, Mario Alcaide, Dabbs Greer. The coach bringing Little Joe back from the East breaks down 50 miles from civilization and fur trapper Howard Benson seems to be the only survivor who can lead the party to safety, if they can put up with his crudeness.

14.130 *The Saga of Whizzer McGee.* April 28, 1963. GS: George Brenlin, Jeanne Bal, Med Flory, Burt Mustin, Hal Baylor. Hoss takes a liking to pint-sized Whizzer McGee, who gets a lot of abuse because of his size, and makes things tougher with his rebellious attitude.

14.131 *The Thunder Man.* May 5, 1963. GS: Simon Oakland, Evelyn Scott, Harvey Stephens, Bing Russell, Bill Quinn, Toby Michaels. William Poole, an explosives expert, is on his way to the Ponderosa when he encounters a girl friend of Little Joe's, and then murders her.

14.132 *Rich Man, Poor Man.* May 12, 1963. GS: J. Pat O'Malley, John Fiedler, Florence Sundstrom, Jay Lanin. Try as he may, bungling Claude Miller just can't do anything right, until he stumbles onto a fortune in silver.

14.133 *The Boss.* May 19, 1963. GS: Carroll O'Connor, Denver Pyle, Judee Morton, Phil Ober, Chris Alcaide, William Tannen, Dan White, Roy Engel. Freight-line owner Tom Slayden is the boss in Virginia City. When one of his men catches Little Joe hauling lumber to the Ponderosa, he shoots him.

14.134 *Little Man — Ten Feet Tall.* May 26, 1963. GS: Ross Martin, Denver Pyle, James Anderson, Michael Davis, Lane Bradford, Bern Hoffman. Young Mario Biancci is studying to be a concert guitarist, but his thoughts turn to ranching when he and his father visit the Ponderosa.

Season Five

14.135 *She Walks in Beauty.* Sept. 22, 1963. GS: Gena Rowlands, Jeanne Cooper, Phil Chambers, Robert Adler, Craig Duncan. Ragan Miller's man-killing good looks have brought her nothing but unhappiness, men she never wanted and now Hoss, who has taken a shine to her.

14.136 *A Passion for Justice.* Sept. 29, 1963. GS: Jonathan Harris, Frank Albertson, Victor Maddern, Charles Irving, Sydney Smith, E.J. Andre, Alice Frost, Clegg Hoyt. Novelist Charles Dickens, in Virginia City for a visit, displays a passion for justice, but his arrogant attitude doesn't make him too popular with the townsfolk.

14.137 *Rain from Heaven.* Oct. 6, 1963. GS: John Anderson, Mickey Sholdar, Claudia Bryar, Eileen Chesis, Phil Chambers, Herb Lytton, Mary Newton. Rainmaker Tulsa Weems promises to deliver rain for drought-stricken Virginia City. But Weems, who has a very sick daughter on his hands, is charging $200 for his services.

14.138 *Twilight Town.* Oct. 13, 1963. GS: Davey Davison, Stacy Harris, Michael Mikler, Walter Coy, Andy Albin, Joseph Breen. A surprise birthday party awaits Little Joe at the

Ponderosa, but the honored guest may not be able to attend — his horse has been stolen and he is alone in desert country.

14.139 *The Toy Soldier.* Oct. 20, 1963. GS: Philip Abbott, Morgan Woodward, Trevor Bardette, Donna Martell, Michael Keep, Quinn Redeker. James Callan is a talented artist, but his heavy drinking and marriage to an Indian create quite a few problems for him.

14.140 *A Question of Strength.* Oct. 27, 1963. GS: Judy Carne, Ilka Windish, John Kellogg, Raymond Guth, James Jeter, I. Stanford Jolley. Hoss and two nuns are abandoned along the trail after their stage is attacked by bandits.

14.141 *Calamity Over the Comstock.* Nov. 3, 1963. GS: Stefanie Powers, Christopher Dark, Fifi D'Orsay, Bern Hoffman, Russ Bender, Big John Hamilton. Little Joe makes friends with Calamity Jane and her boy friend, gunman Doc Holliday, gets a little jealous.

14.142 *Journey Remembered.* Nov. 11, 1963. GS: Inga Swenson, Gene Evans, Kevin Hagen, Johnny Stephens, Dee Carroll, Ken Lynch, John Frederick. In a flashback, Ben recalls his journey West by wagon train with his second wife, Hoss's mother Inger.

14.143 *The Quality of Mercy.* Nov. 17, 1963. GS: Richard Rust, Nancy Rennick, Kitty Kelly, Ed Prentice, Bob Miles, Bill Clark. After a mine cave-in, Seth Pruitt kills his fiancee's father to put him out of his pain, and he asks Little Joe to share the secret.

14.144 *The Waiting Game.* Dec. 8, 1963. GS: Kathie Browne, Katie Sweet, Jacqueline Loughery, Wayde Preston, Bill Quinn, Craig Duncan. Adam is attracted to pretty Laura Dayton, a recently widowed mother who won't tell her daughter that her father is dead.

14.145 *The Legacy.* Dec. 15, 1963. GS: Robert H. Harris, Phillip Pine, Sandy Kevin, Jeanne Baird, Percy Helton, Rory Stevens, Dayton Lummis, James Doohan, Will J. White, John Mitchum. Adam, Hoss and Little Joe set out on separate trails to find the men who shot their father.

14.146 *Hoss and the Leprechauns.* Dec. 22, 1963. GS: Sean McClory, Robert Sorrells, Clegg Hoyt, Frank Delfino, Billy Curtis, Roger Arroya, Nels Nelson. Hoss brings home a strongbox full of gold and claims it belongs to a little feller in green.

14.147 *The Prime of Life.* Dec. 29, 1963. GS: Jay C. Flippen, Melora Conway, Dan Riss, Ralph Moody, Raymond Guth, Butch Patrick, Roy Engle, Roy Jenson. Ben competes with his old rival Barney Fuller to win the railroad's lumber contract.

14.148 *The Lila Conrad Story.* Jan. 5, 1964. GS: Andrew Duggan, Patricia Blair, Cathy O'Donnell, Lindsay Workman, Stuart Randall, Don O'Kelly. To escape the vengeful cohorts of the man she killed, dance-hall girl Lila Conrad hides in one of the Cartwrights' supply wagons.

14.149 *Ponderosa Matador.* Jan. 12, 1964. GS: Marianna Hill, Nestor Paiva, Frank Ferguson, Tol Avery, Mike Ragan. The boys are competing for the attentions of Senorita Dolores Tenino, who is visiting the ranch with her father.

14.150 *My Son, My Son.* Jan. 19, 1964. GS: Teresa Wright, Dee Pollack, Sherwood Price, Zon Murray. Ben and widow Katherine Saunders are considering marriage when Katherine's missing son shows up in town, and is promptly accused of murder.

14.151 *Alias Joe Cartwright.* Jan. 26, 1964. GS: Keenan Wynn, Douglas Dick, Owen Bush, Hugh Sanders, Joe Turkel, Dave Willock. Little Joe is unaware that he bears a striking resemblance to an Army deserter suspected of murder until he finds himself in custody, awaiting execution.

14.152 *The Gentleman from New Orleans.* Feb. 2, 1964. GS: John Dehner, Jean Willes, Sheldon Alman, Bern Hoffman, Harry Swoger. A prisoner claims to be the French-American pirate and hero Jean Lafitte, but he remains in jail until Hoss bails him out.

14.153 *The Cheating Game.* Feb. 9, 1964. GS: Kathie Browne, Peter Breck. A stranger tells Laura Dayton that she will receive a large sum from her late husband's insurance.

14.154 *Bullet for a Bride.* Feb. 16, 1964. GS: Marlyn Mason, Denver Pyle, Steve Harris, Grandon Rhodes, John Matthews, Gail Bonney. Little Joe wants to marry Tessa Caldwell, whom he blinded in a hunting accident.

14.155 *King of the Mountain.* Feb. 23, 1964. GS: Robert Middleton, Slim Pickens, Laurie Mitchell, Byron Foulger, Billy M. Greene. Hoss's mountaineer friend Jim Leyton is getting married, despite his long-standing feud with his girl's father.

14.156 *Love Me Not.* March 1, 1964. GS: Anjanette Comer, Jack Bighead, Gene Tyburn. An Indian chief presents Ben with a white girl held captive by the Paiutes for many years.

14.157 *The Pure Truth.* March 8, 1964. GS: Glenda Farrell, Lloyd Corrigan, Stanley Adams. Sent to pick up a prisoner, acting-deputy Hoss goes to the wrong town, and ends up accused of bank robbery.

14.158 *No Less a Man.* March 15, 1964. GS: Parley Baer, John Kellogg, Bill Zuckert, Justin Smith, Adrienne Marden, Ed Faulkner, Rush Williams. With the notorious Wagner gang on the loose, Virginia City's citizens decide to replace their aging sheriff.

14.159 *Return to Honor.* March 22, 1964. GS: Guy Williams, Arch Johnson, Robert J. Wilke, Hugh Sanders, I. Stanford Jolley, Ralph Montgomery. Ben hears that his nephew has been murdered in a neighboring town.

14.160 *The Saga of Muley Jones.* March 29, 1964. GS: Bruce Yarnell, Jesse White, Strother Martin, Jerome Cowan, Ken Drake, Bern Hoffman, Ralph Moody. The Cartwrights receive a visit from a guitar-strumming distant cousin whose vocal efforts are shattering.

14.161 *The Roper.* April 5, 1964. GS: Guy Williams, Scott Marlowe, Julie Sommars, John Hubbard, James Beck. Outlaws invade the ranch, rob Ben's safe and flee, taking Will Cartwright as a hostage.

14.162 *Pink Cloud Comes from Old Cathay.* April 12, 1964. GS: Marlo Thomas, Philip Ahn, Benson Fong, William Fawcett, Mike Ragan, Phil Chambers. The surprise Hoss ordered from a Chinese trading company finally arrives, and it turns out to be a beautiful woman labeled "wife".

14.163 *The Campaneros.* April 19, 1964. GS: Guy Williams, Faith Domergue, Frank Silvera, Roy Engel, Rico Alaniz, Rodolfo Hoyos, Anthony Carbone, Joe Yrigoyen, Pepe Hern. Will Cartwright's old friend Mateo wants him to return to Mexico to support President Juarez, who is in danger of being overthrown.

14.164 *Enter Thomas Bowers.* April 26, 1964. GS: William Marshall, Jason Wingreen, Ena Hartman, Kelly

Thordsen, Ken Renard, J. Edward McKinley, Dorothy Neumann, Robert P. Lieb. After a triumphant tour in Europe, a famous Negro singer encounters racial prejudice in Virginia City when he arrives for a concert.

14.165 *The Dark Past.* May 3, 1964. GS: Dennis Hopper, Susan Seaforth, Jim Boles, Ron Starr, Lewis Charles. Bounty hunter Dev Farnum isn't an easy person to get to know, and he makes it very clear that he doesn't want any friends.

14.166 *The Pressure Game.* May 10, 1964. GS: Kathie Browne, Joan Blondell, Katie Sweet, Robert Karnes, Charles Bateman. Adam's romance with widow Laura Dayton has reached the serious stage, and Laura's Aunt Lil thinks that Adam should hurry up and propose.

14.167 *Triangle.* May 17, 1964. GS: Guy Williams, Kathie Sweet, Grandon Rhodes. Will Cartwright finds himself falling in love with widow Laura Dayton, Adam's fiancee.

14.168 *Walter and the Outlaws.* May 24, 1964. GS: Arthur Hunnicutt, Steve Brodie, James Luisi, Vic Werber. A gang of outlaws are still after old prospector Obie's gold. They decide that the best way to get their hands on it is to dognap Walter, Obie's faithful pet.

Season Six

14.169 *Invention of a Gunfighter.* Sept. 20, 1964. GS: Guy Stockwell, Valerie Allen, Ron Foster, Bern Hoffman, John Hubbard. After Al Mooney forces Johnny Chapman to back down in a gunfight, the humiliated Johnny asks his friend Little Joe to teach him how to handle a gun.

14.170 *The Hostage.* Sept. 27, 1964. GS: Harold J. Stone, Conlan Carter, Buck Taylor, Bill Clark, Jacqueline Scott. Ben is kidnaped by outlaws, who demand a $100,000 ransom for his return.

14.171 *The Wild One.* Oct. 4, 1964. GS: Aldo Ray, Kathryn Hays. Gruff mountaineer Lafe Jessup is in the middle of a brawl with Hoss, when the Quaker wife he had deserted shows up.

14.172 *Thanks for Everything, Friend.* Oct. 11, 1964. GS: Rory Calhoun, Tom Skerritt, Barbara Wilkin, John Mitchum. Adam is saved from drowning by Tom Wilson, a handsome drifter who's quite an expert in dealing with cards and women.

14.173 *Logan's Treasure.* Oct. 18, 1964. GS: Dan Duryea, John Kellogg, Virginia Gregg, Tim McIntire, Russ Bender. Logan's treasure is the fortune in gold Sam Logan supposedly buried before going to prison, and now that Logan has been released, quite a few people have their eyes on him.

14.174 *The Scapegoat.* Oct. 25, 1964. GS: George Kennedy, Richard Devon, Sandra Warner, Jon Lormer, Troy Melton, Bill Catching. Waldo Watson, who has bungled two suicide attempts, is about to try again by jumping off a cliff, when Hoss intervenes.

14.175 *A Dime's Worth of Glory.* Nov. 1, 1964. GS: Walter Brooke, Bruce Cabot, Charles Maxwell, Dal Jenkins, Preston Pierce, James Bell. Ben says no to dime novelist Tobias Finch's request to write "The Saga of the Courageous Cartwrights". Sheriff Reed Laramore, however, would love Finch to write a book about him.

14.176 *Square Deal Sam.* Nov. 8, 1964. GS: Ernest Truex, Sandy Kenyon, Nydia Westman, Danny Flower. Square Deal Sam is nothing of the kind. He is a rascally old con artist who is planning to fleece the Cartwrights.

14.177 *Between Heaven and Earth.* Nov. 15, 1964. GS: Richard Jaeckel, Bill Moss, Bob Biheller. Little Joe is ornery and troubled because fear keeps him from climbing a near-by mountain.

14.178 *Old Sheba.* Nov. 22, 1964. GS: William Demarest, Clegg Hoyt, Henry Kulky, Phil Chambers. Old Sheba is an elephant, and Ben is aghast when Hoss and Little Joe bring the animal home in payment of a debt.

14.179 *A Man to Admire.* Dec. 6, 1964. GS: James Gregory, Booth Colman, Hal Baylor, William Mims, Michael Petit, Jason Johnson, Dave Willock, Jonathan Hole. There is no love lost between Hoss Cartwright and the Durfee brothers, especially after Hoss' testimony causes the Durfees to lose a big court case.

14.180 *The Underdog.* Dec. 13, 1964. GS: Charles Bronson, Tom Reese, Bill Clark. The Cartwrights offer a job on the Ponderosa to half-breed Harry Starr, a man who is continually the victim of prejudice.

14.181 *A Knight to Remember.* Dec. 20, 1964. GS: Henry Jones, Robert Sorrells, Charles Watts, Zeme North, Rodolfo Acosta. The stage Adam is returning home on is stopped by bandits, but the desperadoes promptly scatter when a knight in armor appears.

14.182 *The Saga of Squaw Charlie.* Dec. 27, 1964. GS: Anthony Caruso, Don "Red" Barry, Virginia Christine, Vickie Coe, Myron Healey, William Tannen. Squaw Charlie, an old Indian who is constantly being taunted and ridiculed, has as his only friends Ben Cartwright and a little girl named Angela.

14.183 *The Flapjack Contest.* Jan. 3, 1965. GS: Johnny Seven, Joan Huntington, Mel Berger, Howard Wendell, Olan Soule. Hoss is entered in a flapjack-eating contest, and Little Joe is trying to keep him on a diet to make sure the big fellow will be plenty hungry come the day of the competition.

14.184 *The Far, Far Better Thing.* Jan. 10, 1965. GS: Brenda Scott, X Brands, Warren Vanders, Jack Bighead, Stacy Harris. Little Joe and his friend Tuck are vying for the attentions of the same girl, a bookish young lady from the East.

14.185 *Woman of Fire.* Jan. 17, 1965. GS: Joan Hackett, Jay Novello, Cesare Danova, Susan Silo, Valentin De Vargas, Eugene Iglesias. Don Miguel, a guest at the Ponderosa, is having a hard time finding a husband for his daughter Margarita, an explosive senorita who manages to scare away all suitors.

14.186 *The Ballerina.* Jan. 24, 1965. GS: Barrie Chase, Warren Stevens, Douglas Fowley, Hugh Sanders, Read Morgan. Kellie Conrad did most of her dancing in saloons until she met former ballet star Paul Mandel.

14.187 *The Flannel-Mouth Gun.* Jan. 31, 1965. GS: Earl Holliman, Robert J. Wilke, Don Collier, Harry Carey, Jr. The local ranchers have been hit hard by cattle rustlers, and since the sheriff has been unable to put a stop to it, the ranchers decide to hire a professional gunman.

14.188 *Ponderosa Birdman.* Feb. 7, 1965. GS: Ed Wynn, Marlyn Mason. Prof. Phineas T. Klump has made a pair of handsomely feathered wings for his attempt at being the first man to fly, and Hoss has become his crew chief.

14.189 *The Search.* Feb. 14, 1965. GS: Lola Albright, Kelly Thordsen, Elaine Devry, Howard Wright, John Harding, Phil Chambers, Lindsay Workman. Adam learns that his exact look-alike is taking advantage of the resemblance to fatten his money belt.

14.190 *The Deadliest Game.* Feb. 21, 1965. GS: Cesar Romero, Ilze Taurins, Lili Valenty, Fabrizio Mioni. The troupe of aerial acrobats that just arrived in town may provide more than the expected excitement. The girl friend of one of the trapeze artist has taken a liking to Little Joe.

14.191 *Once a Doctor.* Feb. 28, 1965. GS: Michael Rennie, Ashley Cowen, Elizabeth Rogers, Bill Clark, Grandon Rhodes. Vengeful Thomas Crippin has traveled all the way from England to track down the doctor he claims murdered his wife.

14.192 *Right Is the Fourth R.* March 7, 1965. GS: Mariette Hartley, Everett Sloane. Adam comes to the rescue of the local school teacher. She has been tied to a stake by her unruly students.

14.193 *Hound Dog.* March 21, 1965. GS: Bruce Yarnell, Sue Ane Langdon, Chubby Johnson. The Cartwright's guitar strumming cousin Muley Jones pays a return visit to the Ponderosa. This time he brings along a pack of howling hound dogs.

14.194 *The Trap.* March 28, 1965. GS: Joan Freeman, Steve Cochran, Paul Lukather. Little Joe's former girlfriend thinks that Joe murdered her husband so that she could be free to marry him. The dead man's twin brother holds the same believe.

14.195 *Dead and Gone.* April 4, 1965. GS: Hoyt Axton, Susanne Cramer, Steve Ihnat. Adam tries to reform Howard Mead, a wandering troubadour who has the bad habit of taking what doesn't belong to him.

14.196 *A Good Night's Rest.* April 11, 1965. GS: Abigail Shelton, Robert Ridgley, Jean Willes, Jay Ripley, Eddie Firestone, Michael Forest, Lloyd Corrigan. A weary Ben, who can't seem to get a good night's rest at the Ponderosa, heads for town to take a room at the local hotel.

14.197 *To Own the World.* April 18, 1965. GS: Telly Savalas, Linda Lawson, Curt Conway, John Hubbard, J. Edward McKinley. Charles Hackett, the richest man in the world, figures there is a price on everything, including the Ponderosa.

14.198 *Lothario Larkin.* April 25, 1965. GS: Noah Beery, Jr., Dorothy Green, Jim Davis. Fun-loving Lothario Larkin is back in Virginia City and he is still irresistible to women, infuriating to fathers and a headache to the sheriff.

14.199 *The Return.* May 2, 1965. GS: Tony Young, Joan Blackman, John Conte, Dan Riss, Phil Chambers, Robert J. Stevenson. Ex-convict Trace Cordell has returned home to Virginia City, but banker Paul Dorn wants him driven out of town. The banker, who was crippled by Trace, is now married to Trace's former sweetheart.

14.200 *The Jonah.* May 9, 1965. GS: Andrew Prine, Angela Clarke, Erin O'Donnell, Dean Harens, Ken Mayer, Troy Melton. George Whitman has the reputation of being a jinx, and the Ponderosa ranch hands aren't very enthusiastic about his coming to work for the Cartwrights.

14.201 *The Spotlight.* May 16, 1965. GS: Viveca Lindfors, Ron Randell, Winnie Coffin, Jeanne Determann, Robert Foulk, Ian Wolfe, Victor Sen Yung. Retired opera star Angela Drake hasn't been in the spotlight for years, but Ben Cartwright, an old admirer, wants her to perform at Virginia City's anniversary ceremonies.

14.202 *Patchwork Man.* May 23, 1965. GS: Grant Williams, Bruce Gordon, Lane Bradford, Grandon Rhodes. In a ghost town, Hoss meets a self-demeaning recluse named Patch, whom he hires to work on the Ponderosa.

Season Seven

14.203 *The Debt.* Sept. 12, 1965. GS: Tommy Sands, Brooke Bundy, Ford Rainey. Because their father once swindled Ben, Wiley and Annie Kane arrive at the Ponderosa with intentions of working off the debt.

14.204 *The Dilemma.* Sept. 19, 1965. GS: Tom Tully, Elizabeth Perry, Anthony Call, Walter Sande, Kelly Thordsen, John Hubbard, Dayton Lummis. Ben, who has been named acting judge of Virginia City, has a problem. A man he once helped get paroled is suspected of robbing the bank.

14.205 *The Brass Box.* Sept. 26, 1965. GS: Ramon Novarro, Michael Dante, Adam Williams, Sydney Smith, Bill Clark, Roy Jenson. Although no one ever takes him seriously, old Jose Ortega is always spinning fanciful tales, including one about a Spanish land grant giving him ownership to the territory.

14.206 *The Other Son.* Oct. 3, 1965. GS: Ed Begley, Tom Simcox, Richard Evans, Bing Russell. To transport nitroglycerin to Virginia City, Ben hires an old friend, mule skinner Clint Watson, and Watson's sons.

14.207 *The Lonely Runner.* Oct. 10, 1965. GS: Gilbert Roland, Pat Conway, Roy Barcroft. Jim Acton isn't about to give up his prized mare, even though a judge has awarded the animal to another man.

14.208 *Devil on Her Shoulder.* Oct. 17, 1965. GS: Ina Balin, John Doucette, Peter Helm, Adrienne Marden. The Rev. Evan Morgan's brethren are having more than their share of trouble, and Morgan's wife says it is because Sarah Reynolds, one of their group, is possessed by Satan.

14.209 *Found Child.* Oct. 24, 1965. GS: Eileen Baral, Gerald Mohr. Hoss finds the sole survivor of a stagecoach robbery, a little girl who is in a state of shock.

14.210 *The Meredith Smith.* Oct. 31, 1965. GS: Strother Martin, Anne Helm, Robert Colbert, Guy Lee, Robert Sorrells, Winnie Coffin, Bert Mustin, Eddie Firestone, Kam Tong. With his dying breath, Jake Smith asks Ben to be the executor of his estate and to make certain that Meredith Smith, his next of kin, gets it all. But several Smiths turn up in Virginia City, each claiming to be the heir.

14.211 *Mighty Is the Word.* Nov. 7, 1965. GS: Glenn Corbett, Michael Whitney, Sue Randall. Former gunman Paul Watson has become a preacher, but Cliff Rexford refuses to let him forget the past. Rexford is gunning for Watson, who killed his brother five years earlier.

14.212 *The Strange One.* Nov. 14, 1965. GS: Louise Sorel, Robert McQueeney, Willard Sage. A woman, forced to leave a wagon train because the travelers think that she is a witch, is taken by Hoss and Little Joe to the Ponderosa, where she astounds the Cartwrights with her knowledge of their personal lives.

14.213 *The Reluctant Rebel.* Nov. 21, 1965. GS: Tim Considine, Royal Dano, Keith London, Craig Curtis, Janis Hansen, Mike Ragan, Ray Hemphill. Young Billy Penn tries to escape his humble origins by joining a gang of rustlers, but he has second thoughts about the outlaw life when he is caught stealing Cartwright cattle.

14.214 *Five Sundowns to Sunup.* Dec. 5, 1965. GS: Marie Windsor, Douglas Henderson, James Davidson, Jack Chaplain, G.B. Atwater, Stacy Harris, Tom Drake, Bruce Mars, William Tannen. Harry Lassiter is in jail awaiting hanging, and his murderous family will stop at nothing to get him out, including kidnaping local citizens.

14.215 *A Natural Wizard.* Dec. 12, 1965. GS: Eddie Hodges, Jacqueline Scott, Karl Swenson, Douglas Kennedy, Robert Rothwell. Skeeter Dexter loves animals, so much that he sets them free from the traps set by his stepfather.

14.216 *All Ye His Saints.* Dec. 19, 1965. GS: Clint Howard, Leif Erickson, Rodolfo Aosta, Simon Scott, Harvey Stephens. Told that only God can save his mortally wounded father, little Michael Thorpe sets out for the mountains to find the Almighty.

14.217 *A Dublin Lad.* Jan. 2, 1966. GS: Liam Sullivan, Maggie Mahoney, Tim McIntire, Paul Birch, Paul Genge, Bern Hoffman, Robert Carson. Irishman Terence O'Toole stands accused of robbery and murder, and all of the members of the jury are prepared to convict him, except for Little Joe.

14.218 *To Kill a Buffalo.* Jan. 9, 1966. GS: Jose De Vega, Grandon Rhodes, Sarah Selby, Ralph Moody, Trudy Ellison. Hoss is attacked when he comes to the aid of a badly injured Indian youth driven by a hatred for all white men.

14.219 *Ride the Wind* Part One. Jan. 16, 1966. GS: Victor Jory, Rod Cameron, DeForest Kelley, Tom Lowell, Wolfe Barzell, Stewart Moss, Warren Vanders, Richard Hale, S. Newton Anderson, Clay Tanner, Jack Bighead, Gilbert Green. Ben, who has offered financial support to the newly founded Pony Express, isn't pleased when Little Joe says he plans to become an Express rider, and the hostile Paiute Indians aren't happy about having Pony Express riders traveling across their land.

14.220 *Ride the Wind* Part Two. Jan. 23, 1966. GS: Victor Jory, Rod Cameron, DeForest Kelley, Tom Lowell, Wolfe Barzell, Stewart Moss, Warren Vanders, Richard Hale, S. Newton Anderson, Clay Tanner, Jack Bighead, Gilbert Green. Despite the Indians' increasing attacks on the Pony Express riders, Curtis Wade is determined to keep the Pony Express operating, and to complete the last leg of the route.

14.221 *Destiny's Child.* Jan. 30, 1966. GS: Dick Peabody, Walter Burke, Tim Stafford, Steve Raines, Lindsay Workman, Grandon Rhodes. Two strangers give Ben a hand when his wagon bogs down in mud, and Ben is only too glad to return the favor, by inviting the pair to dinner and trying to get jobs for them.

14.222 *Peace Officer.* Feb. 6, 1966. GS: Eric Fleming, Ray Stricklyn, Ron Foster, Ted Knight, Dee Pollock, Clyde Howdy, I. Stanford Jolley, Roy Barcroft. Sheriff Coffee is out of town during an outbreak of violence, so Virginia City's mayor hires a ruthless lawman to restore order.

14.223 *The Code.* Feb. 13, 1966. GS: George Montgomery, Robert Ellenstein, Jan Shepard, Gordon Wescourt, Zalman King, Bruno Ve Sota, Charles Wagenheim. Dan Taggert goads Joe into challenging him to a duel, and a man named Fitts, who is taking bets on the outcome, is putting all of his money on Taggert.

14.224 *Three Brides for Hoss.* Feb. 20, 1966. GS: Stuart Erwin, Danielle Aubrey, Majel Barrett, Mitzi Hoag, Claude Hall, Sharyl Locke. Hoss is as surprised and baffled as everyone else when widow Annie Slocum arrives from Kentucky and announces that Hoss sent for her to be his bride.

14.225 *The Emperor Norton.* Geb. 27, 1966. GS: Sam Jaffe, Parley Baer, John Napier, William Challee, Charles Irving, Tom Palmer, Audrey Larkin. To keep the self-styled "emperor" Joshua Norton from being committed to an asylum by San Francisco officials, a friend brings him to the Ponderosa. But the eccentric Norton soon stirs up a ruckus in Virginia City.

14.226 *Her Brother's Keeper.* March 6, 1966. GS: Nancy Gates, Wesley Lau, Grandon Rhodes, Ralph Montgomery, Norman Leavitt. Ben's romance with Claire Amory is complicated by her brother Carl, an unscrupulous invalid who relies on sympathy for his illness to use people.

14.227 *The Trouble with Jamie.* March 20. 1966. GS: Michael Burns, Ross Elliott, Tracy Olsen. When Ben's Eastern cousin Mathew brings his son Jamie for a visit to the Ponderosa, the Cartwrights are somewhat startled by the youngster. Jamie is a spoiled, arrogant little brat.

14.228 *Shining in Spain.* March 27, 1966. GS: Judi Rolin, Woodrow Parfrey, Gene Lyons, Hal Baylor, Robert B. Williams, Grandon Rhodes, Clint Sharp. Little Joe is attracted to Wendy Dant, but the stiff competition is getting him down. The most important man in Wendy's life is her father, whom she never stops talking about, and who will soon be coming to see her for the first time in several years.

14.229 *The Genius.* April 3, 1966. GS: Lonny Chapman, Jorja Curtwright, Salvador Baguez, Grandon Rhodes, Bruno Ve Sota, Troy Melton. Hoss, who has taken a liking to poetry-spouting Will Smith, takes it upon himself to help Will overcome his craving for liquor.

14.230 *The Unwritten Commandment.* April 10, 1966. GS: Wayne Newton, Anne Jeffreys, Malcolm Atterbury. Willard Walker, who isn't impressed with his son Andy's singing talent, says the boy should be doing more chores and less harmonizing.

14.231 *Big Shadow on the Land.* April 17, 1966. GS: Jack Kruschen, Brioni Farrell, Michael Stephani, Penny Santon, Hoke Howell, Robert Foulk. Little Joe is chased off Ponderosa land by a family of immigrant winegrowers who have decided the area would be an ideal site for their vineyards.

14.232 *The Fighters.* April 24, 1966. GS: Phillip Pine, Michael Conrad, Mari Aldon, Cal Bolder, Bruce Mars, Gene Tyburn. Hank Kelly, an over-the-hill professional boxer, is seriously injured when he is kayoed by challenger Hoss Cartwright.

14.233 *Home from the Sea.* May 1, 1966. GS: Alan Bergmann, Ivor Barry, Margaret Shinn, Wayne Heffley. Seaman Gilly Maples arrives in Virginia City with news of his shipmate Adam Cartwright, and Gilly, a lonely man who has never had a home or a family, is deeply moved by the Cartwrights' family-style welcome.

14.234 *The Last Mission.* May 8, 1966. GS: R.G. Armstrong, Tom Reese, Brendon Boone, Ken Mayer, George Keymas, Clay Tanner. Col. Keith Jarell, Ben's old Army companion, asks the elder Cartwright to accompany his small detachment on a peace-making mission to the hostile Paiute Indians.

14.235 *A Dollar's Worth of Trouble.* May 15, 1966. GS:

Sally Kellerman, Mabel Anderson, Elisha Cook, Jr., Hampton Fancher III. A palmist predicts that two persons will enter, and alter, Hoss' life. One is a blue-eyed blonde, and the other is a gunslinger with murder on his mind.

Season Eight

14.236 *Something Hurt, Something Wild.* Sept. 11, 1966. GS: Lyle Bettger, Lyn Loring, Erik Holland, Ron Foster, David Pritchard. The Cartwrights' long-standing friendship with the Fergusons ends when Laurie Ferguson accuses Little Joe of attacking her.

14.237 *Horse of a Different Hue.* Sept. 18, 1966. GS: Charles Ruggles, Skip Homeier, Julie Parrish, Johnny Silver, Joe Haworth, Steven Marlo. Colonel Fairchild and his granddaughter, Ben's friend from the South, ask the elder Cartwright to stage a horse race, but they neglect to tell him that they have agreed to fix the outcome.

14.238 *A Time to Step Down.* Sept. 25, 1966. GS: Ed Begley, Audrey Totter, Donald "Red" Barry, Sherwood Price, Renny McEvoy. Little Joe asks Ben to give veteran wrangler Dan Tolliver a less hazardous job, but the embittered old man turns down the offer and quits.

14.239 *The Pursued* Part One. Oct. 2, 1966. GS: Eric Fleming, Dina Merrill, Lois Nettleton, Vincent Beck, Booth Colman, Robert Brubaker, Jean Inness, Nelson Leigh, Byron Morrow. The Cartwrights are in Beehive, Nevada, to buy horses from rancher Heber Clawson, a Mormon settler who is determined to remain in the town, despite persecution for his religious beliefs.

14.240 *The Pursued* Part Two. Oct. 9, 1966. GS: Eric Fleming, Dina Merrill, Lois Nettleton, Vincent Beck, Booth Colman, Robert Brubaker, Jean Inness, Nelson Leigh, Byron Morrow. Hounded by hate mongers, Mormon Heber Clawson flees from his burned-out ranch with his two wives, one of whom is in desperate need of medical care.

14.241 *To Bloom for Thee.* Oct. 16, 1966. GS: Geraldine Brooks, Don Haggerty, Bing Russell, Robert B. Williams, Paul Micale. Cold and indifferent, Carol Attley seems to trust only one person in Virginia City — Hoss Cartwright, who has fallen for her.

14.242 *Credit for a Kill.* Oct. 23, 1966. GS: Don Collier, Luana Patten, Dean Harens, Charles Maxwell, Regina Gleason, Ed Faulkner, Troy Melton. Little Joe and rancher Morgan Tanner both shoot at a horse thief, but Joe claims credit for killing him.

14.243 *Four Sisters from Boston.* Oct. 30, 1966. GS: Vera Miles, Morgan Woodward, Owen Bush, Melinda Plowman, Lyn Edgington, Quentin Sondergaard, Rand Brooks. Four sisters arrive in Virginia City from Boston to claim an inherited ranch, but the girls don't have enough money to forestall the public sale of the debt-ridden property.

14.244 *Old Charlie.* Nov. 6, 1966. GS: John McIntire, Jeanette Nolan, Tim McIntire, Hal Baylor, Bill Fletcher, Dick Winslow. Old Charlie, a boastful teller of tall tales, doesn't credit Hoss with saving him from the knife-wielding youth outlaw who died in a hold-up attempt, not even when the brothers of the dead man come to town seeking revenge.

14.245 *Ballad of the Ponderosa.* Nov. 13, 1966. GS: Randy Boone, Ann Doran, Roger Davis, John Archer, Charles Irving. Fifteen years ago, Ben's testimony helped hang Colter Preston's father for murder. Now, young Colter comes to Virginia City as a balladeer whose bitter song denounces Ben Cartwright, forcing him to reopen the case.

14.246 *The Oath.* Nov. 20, 1966. GS: Tony Bill, Douglas Kennedy, Dallas McKennon. Half-breed Charlie Two is heading for Virginia City to carry out his oath to kill the Cartwright clan. Traveling the same trail is Little Joe, who is concealing his identity in an attempt to make Charlie change his mind.

14.247 *A Real Nice, Friendly Little Town.* Nov. 27, 1966. GS: Louise Latham, Mark Slade, Robert Doyle, Robert Foulk, Burt Mustin, Herb Vigran, Vaughn Taylor, Clegg Hoyt. A ricocheting bullet hits Little Joe where he sits, and leads Hoss into an encounter with a gun toting Willie Mae Rikeman and her two rascal sons.

14.248 *The Bridegroom.* Dec. 4, 1966. GS: Ron Hayes, Jeff Corey, Joanne Linville. Little Joe goes courting with Maggie Dowling. The lovers aren't lovers at all, just friends conspiring to make a widower jealous enough to ask for Maggie's hand.

14.249 *Tommy.* Dec. 18, 1966. GS: Teddy Quinn, Janet DeGore, Michael Witney. Jess Miller is terrorizing the Ponderosa. The vicious outlaw is determined to take his wife away from the Cartwrights' sanctuary, but he wants no part of their deaf-mute son.

14.250 *A Christmas Story.* Dec. 25, 1966. GS: Wayne Newton, Mary Wickes, Jack Oakie. Andy Walker has come home to sing at the orphans' Christmas benefit. Thadeus Cade, Andy's uncle and manager, is planning to take a big interest in the show — a 10 percent cut of the proceeds.

14.251 *Ponderosa Explosion.* Jan. 1, 1967. GS: Dub Taylor, Chick Chandler, Phil Chambers, Chubby Johnson. Hoss and Little Joe's investment in two rabbits will soon make them the bunny kings of Nevada. Complications multiply as quickly as the furry multitude when the Cartwrights find they haven't the heart to skin the little animals.

14.252 *Justice.* Jan. 8, 1967. GS: Beau Bridges, Shirley Bonne, Lurene Tuttle. Little Joe and his adoring fiancee Sally are eagerly awaiting their wedding day. But their happiness may be cut short by a shy young man named Horace, whose clumsy advances toward Sally conceal violent feelings.

14.253 *A Bride for Buford.* Jan. 15, 1967. GS: Lola Albright, Jack Elam, Richard Devon. Hoss Cartwright sets out to see if a saloon girl's sudden interest in a grubby miner is for love, or the man's new-found wealth.

14.254 *Black Friday.* Jan. 22, 1967. GS: John Saxon, Ford Rainey, Robert Phillips, James Davidson, Robert McQueeney, Robert Christopher. Little Joe risks his life to help a desperately ill gunfighter. A top gun has been stranded in a small town, where the vengeful citizens are planning to make him an easy target for a paid killer.

14.255 *The Unseen Wound.* Jan. 29, 1967. GS: Leslie Nielsen, Nancy Malone, Douglas Henderson, Bill Fletcher, Percy Helton. Ben tries to prevent wholesale tragedy when years of bloodshed finally take their toll on an old friend. Sheriff Rowen has gone berserk, barricaded himself in a stable and is shooting at everyone who crosses his sights.

14.256 *Journey to Terror.* Feb. 5, 1967. GS: John Ericson, Jason Evers, Kevin Hagen, Lory Patrick, Lindsay Work-

Bonanza

man, Richard Hale. Little Joe must fight for his life at the Blackwell farm, where he and the Blackwells have been imprisoned by a band of outlaws.

14.257 *Amigo.* Feb. 12, 1967. GS: Henry Darrow, Gregory Walcott, Anna Navarro, Warren Kemmerling, Tim Herbert, Grandon Rhodes. Amigo is a downtrodden Mexican who has been riding with a terrorist band. After Ben saves Amigo from lynching, the embittered outcast is torn between gratitude to Ben and loyalty to the terrorists.

14.258 *A Woman in the House.* Feb. 19, 1967. GS: Diane Baker, Paul Richards. Ben shelters young Mary Farnum from her drunken husband. The elder Cartwright has misgivings when the thankful girl mistakes her gratitude for love.

14.259 *Judgment at Red Creek.* Feb. 26, 1967. GS: John Ireland, Harry Carey, Jr., Bartlett Robinson, John Rayner, Martin West, James Sikking. Little Joe joins a posse hunting two men suspected of robbery and murder. Leading the manhunt is Rimbau, who is determined to exact his own justice without regard for the law.

14.260 *Joe Cartwright, Detective.* March 5, 1967. GS: Mort Mills, Ken Lynch. The youngest Cartwright has been reading British whodunits, and is fascinated by Scotland Yard techniques. His scheme to stop an impending bank robbery produces earth-shaking results, and several walking wounded.

14.261 *Dark Enough to See the Stars.* March 12, 1967. GS: Richard Evans, Linda Foster, Richard Eastham, Willard Sage, Grandon Rhodes, Rita Lynn, Steven Marlo, Baynes Barron. A ranch hand on the Ponderosa is torn between his love for visiting Jennifer Yardley, and his unexplained fear of her lawman father.

14.262 *The Deed and the Dilemma.* March 26, 1967. GS: Jack Kruschen, Donald Woods, Robert F. Lyons, Chris Alcaide. A dream comes true for immigrant Giorgio Rossi when Ben grants him land for a vineyard. But Giorgio's happiness is short-lived. A spiteful neighbor is cutting off the water supply.

14.263 *The Prince.* April 2, 1967. GS: Lloyd Bochner, Claire Griswold, Warren Stevens, Adam Williams, Noah Keen, Jerry Summers, Clyde Howdy, Gil Perkins. A royal romance and intrigue find their way from the Czar's court to the Ponderosa. The Cartwrights welcome a Russian count and countess, unaware that a mysterious outlaw is planning a reception of his own.

14.264 *A Man Without Land.* April 9, 1967. GS: Jeremy Slate, Royal Dano, Joan Marshall, James Gammon, Dorothy Neumann, Bing Russell. After Ben keeps a swindling foreman from bilking rancher Matt Jeffers, the foreman tries again by using the rancher's son and Little Joe as pawns in a grudge murder.

14.265 *Napoleon's Children.* April 16, 1967. GS: Michael Burns, Robert Biheller, Phyllis Hill, Woodrow Parfrey, Bing Russell. A young punk who fancies himself to be Napoleon leads an army of toughs against Virginia City, with special malice toward the Cartwrights.

14.266 *The Wormwood Cup.* April 23, 1967. GS: Frank Overton, Judi Meredith, Bing Russell, Will J. White, Myron Healey, Robert B. Williams. Two people are in Virginia City for the same purpose — to take revenge on Little Joe. One is a girl who is sure that Joe killed her brother. The second is the father of a man whom Little Joe shot in self-defense.

14.267 *Clarissa.* April 30, 1967. GS: Nina Foch, Roy Roberts, Robert Foulk, Ken Mayer, Louise Lorimer, Norman Leavitt. The Cartwrights ask for trouble when they welcome Cousin Clarissa, a snobbish and interfering Easterner. The trouble-making lady upsets everything at home and alienates most of the Cartwrights' friends.

14.268 *Maestro Hoss.* May 7, 1967. GS: Zsa Zsa Gabor, Kathleen Freeman, Del Moore, Doodles Weaver. A palm-reading con woman convinces gullible Hoss that he is a violin virtuoso, hands him a Stradivarius and predicts he will give his first concert within a week.

14.269 *The Greedy Ones.* May 14, 1967. GS: Robert Middleton, George Chandler, William Bakewell, Lane Bradford, Phil Chambers, Grandon Rhodes. Ben fights to keep his land from being ravaged by greedy gold seekers. Rumor has it that an old prospector's rich ore sampling came from the Ponderosa.

Season Nine

14.270 *Second Chance.* Sept. 17, 1967. GS: James Gregory, Joe De Santis, Bettye Ackerman, Douglas Kennedy, Olan Soule, Jane Zachary. Ben joins an Army patrol in an attempt to rescue his boys. Marauding Indians have forced Hoss and a badly wounded Little Joe to take refuge with a wagon party that includes thieves, two women, a dying man and a coward.

14.271 *Sense of Duty.* Sept. 24, 1967. GS: Gene Rutherford, Michael Forest, Ron Foster, Richard Hale. Ben Cartwright commands a militia unit escorting a rabble-rousing Indian fanatic to prison, with the demogogue's murderous followers close behind.

14.272 *The Conquistadors.* Oct. 1, 1957. GS: John Saxon, Eddie Ryder, John Kellogg, Mike De Anda, Brooke Bundy, Arch Johnson, Dabbs Greer, James Griffith, Robert Brubaker, Rusty Lane, Vaughn Taylor, Olan Soule. A $25,000 ransom paid to the Mexican kidnapers of Little Joe only puts him in deeper danger. A second bunch of scoundrels is out to hijack the ransom.

14.273 *Judgment at Olympus.* Oct. 8, 1967. GS: Barry Sullivan, Arch Johnson, Brooke Bundy, Vaughn Taylor. Little Joe and Hoss try to unravel a mystery as Candy stands trial for murder in a distant town. The sinister set-up includes a defense attorney in the pay of the victim's father, and an alleged eyewitness who will swear to anything for drinking money.

14.274 *Night of Reckoning.* Oct. 15, 1967. GS: Richard Jaeckel, Ron Hayes, Joan Freeman, Teno Pollock, William Jordan, Grandon Rhodes. Outlaws inflict a night of terror on the Ponderosa. The men are out to retrieve holdup money grabbed by a double-crossing partner who lies wounded in the Cartwright house.

14.275 *False Witness.* Oct. 22, 1967. GS: Davey Davison, Michael Blodgett, Robert McQueeney, Bill Fletcher, Russ Conway, Frank Gerstle. The sheriff of Sand Dust puts Little Joe, Hoss, Candy and a young woman under round-the-clock protection. As witnesses to a fatal shooting, the four have become targets for murder by the brothers of the accused killer.

14.276 *The Gentle Ones.* Oct. 29, 1967. GS: Robert Walker, Jr., Lana Wood, Pat Conway, Stuart Anderson, Douglas Henderson, Bing Russell. Horse trading at the Ponderosa develops into a human drama involving a gentle cowboy who loves animals, a British rancher, and an embittered widow who thinks the cowboy is a coward.

14.277 *Desperate Passage.* Nov. 5, 1967. GS: Tina Louise, Steve Forrest, Bing Russell. The Cartwrights fight their way through savage Paiutes with the sole survivors of an Indian massacre: a man charged with murder, and a woman who knows, but can't reveal, that he is innocent.

14.278 *The Sure Thing.* Nov. 12, 1967. GS: Kim Darby, Tom Tully, William Bryant. Ben has his own compassionate reasons for buying Trudy Loughlin's stallion from her drunken father. But he plans to let Trudy ride the horse in a big stakes race. Trudy must then decide whether she should throw the race because her father has fallen in with a crooked gambler.

14.279 *Showdown at Tahoe.* Nov. 19, 1967. GS: Richard Anderson, Sheila Larken, Kevin Hagen, Christopher Dark, Bing Russell. Jamison Fillmore plans to rob Ben's timber operation, then use his paddle-wheel steamboat to escape. When the vessel's captain is murdered, Candy takes the helm, and the initiative, to trap Fillmore.

14.280 *Six Black Horses.* Nov. 26, 1967. GS: Burgess Meredith, David Lewis, Judy Parker, Richard X. Slattery, Don Haggerty, Hal Baylor. An impish Irishman uses Tammany graft and a leprechaun's luck to give some greedy businessmen a lesson in one-upmanship.

14.281 *Check Rein.* Dec. 3, 1967. GS: Patricia Hyland, Ford Rainey, James MacArthur, Charles Maxwell, Robert Karnes. A quirk of fate involves the Ponderosa men in young Jace Fredericks' fight to save himself, and his inheritance, from the encroachments of a greedy uncle.

14.282 *Justice Deferred.* Dec. 17, 1967. GS: Simon Oakland, Nita Talbot, Carl Reindel, Shannon Farnum, John Hubbard, Claudia Bryar, Harlan Warde, Tol Avery, Byron Morrow. An anguished Hoss discovers that his testimony helped hang an innocent man accused of murder. As he struggles to bring the real killer to justice, Hoss must also combat the cowardice of another witness and the jury foreman, an influential banker.

14.283 *The Gold Detector.* Dec. 24, 1967. GS: Wally Cox, Paul Fix, Dub Taylor, Kelly Thordsen, Caroline Richter, Chubby Johnson, Mike de Anda. Hoss buys a gold detector sight unseen, then has an awful time proving its worth to skeptics and protecting it from greedy schemers.

14.284 *The Trackers.* Jan. 7, 1968. GS: Warren Stevens, Bruce Dern, Warren Vanders, Ted Gehring, Robert P. Lieb, James Sikking, Arthur Peterson, Christopher Shea. After a successful manhunt Ben, Candy and Hoss are forced to protect their prisoner, an ex-convict wanted for robbery and murder. The other members of the posse are trying to prevent a fair trail by conducting a lynching.

14.285 *A Girl Named George.* Jan. 14, 1968. GS: Sheilah Wells, Jack Albertson, Gerald Mohr, Fred Clark, Andy Devine, Patsy Kelly, Steve Raines. A group picture of the Ponderosa men provides a shocking development in a murder case. The photographer has doctored the photo, providing a perfect alibi for a murderer who committed his crime during the portrait session.

14.286 *The Thirteenth Man.* Jan. 21, 1968. GS: Albert Salmi, Richard Carlson, Kenneth Tobey, Anna Navarro, Myron Healey, Bill Quinn, John Zaremba, Jon Lormer. The Cartwrights and the Cattlemen's Association have grim second thoughts about a range detective hired to ferret out rustlers. The man is a fanatic who vents his unholy hatred by shooting suspects on sight.

14.287 *The Burning Sky.* Jan. 28, 1968. GS: Dawn Wells, Michael Murphy, Bobby Riha, Victor French, Iron Eyes Cody, Robert Foulk, Bill Clark. Tension mounts after the arrival of a new Ponderosa ranch hand and his Indian bride. Ben Cartwright, fearing tragic consequences from a neighbor's venomous reaction, moves quickly to get to the root of the matter.

14.288 *The Price of Salt.* Feb. 4, 1968. GS: Kim Hunter, James Best, John Doucette, Myron Healey, Dawn Wells, Michael Murphy, Robert Patten, Ken Drake, John Jay Douglas. A greedy woman turns the town of Spanish Wells into a powder keg. Ada Halle has a monopoly on the salt desperately needed by cattlemen, whose tempers flare as Ada raises the price.

14.289 *Blood Tie.* Feb. 18, 1968. GS: Robert Drivas, Conlan Carter, Leo Gordon, Peter Leeds. The Cartwrights are tricked into hiring Tracy Blaine, one of three men plotting to rob Ben. Blaine's partners soon carry out the next step. They wound Ben, then lure Hoss and Little Joe away from the Ponderosa.

14.290 *The Crime of Johnny Mule.* Feb. 25, 1968. GS: Noah Beery, Jr., Coleen Gray, Lee Patterson, Jack Ging, John Archer, John Lodge, Bruno Ve Sota. Hoss casts the vote that deadlocks a jury in the murder trial of Johnny Mule. The responsibility weighs heavily on Hoss when Johnny breaks jail to avoid retrial, before Hoss has a chance to prove the Johnny is innocent.

14.291 *The Late Ben Cartwright.* March 3, 1968. GS: Sidney Blackmer, Bert Freed, William Campbell, Simon Scott, George Gaynes, Tyler McVey. An assassin's bullet nearly ends Ben's battle to keep a tycoon's lackey out of the governor's chair. Ben plans to play dead until the nominating convention, but the plan hits a snag when a man is arrested for his murder.

14.292 *Star Crossed.* March 10, 1968. GS: Tisha Sterling, William Windom, Jean Willes. A blackmailing ex-marshal casts a long shadow over Candy's love for Laura Jean Pollard. The girl is harboring a secret guilt, which the former lawman sees as a chance for profit.

14.293 *Trouble Town.* March 17, 1968. GS: Robert J. Wilke, Elizabeth MacRae, Steve Brodie. The Cartwrights do some investigating in River Bend, where Candy is being held without bail on a minor charge. What they find is a town paralyzed by fear of the sheriff, who specializes in extortion and murder.

14.294 *Commitment at Angelus.* April 7, 1968. GS: Peter Whitney, Marj Dusay, Ivan Triesault, Ken Lynch, Greg Mullavey, Alan Reynolds. Little Joe gets embroiled in a miners' strike when its leader, a close friend, is accidentally killed. The miners are being driven to violence by corrupt officials of the company, and the Cartwrights are major stockholders.

14.295 *A Dream to Dream.* April 14, 1968. GS: Steve Ihnat, Julie Harris, Johnnie Whitaker, Michele Tobin. Rancher Josh Carter is a stranger in his own home, the result of drinking to drown guilty feelings about his son's death. Enter Hoss, whose warm, outgoing nature soon endears him to the children, and their unhappy mother.

14.296 *In Defense of Honor.* April 28, 1968. GS: Lou Antonio, Arnold Moss, Ned Romero, Cherie Latimer, Troy

Melton, John Lodge, Arthur Peterson. Treaty negotiations with the Indians are threatened when an outcast decides to rejoin the tribe he bitterly rejected for years. His love for an Indian girl incites tribesmen who despise him, and serves a grim purpose for bigots who are trying to wreck the peace pact.

14.297 *To Die in Darkness.* May 5, 1968. GS: James Whitmore, Noah Keen. John Postley seeks revenge against Ben, whose testimony unjustly sent him to prison. Cleared, Postley lures Ben and ranch hand Candy into a deserted mine shaft, where he keeps his prisoners alive on a diet of food, water and false hopes. A regimen that shackles Postley to his captives in a prison of his own making.

14.298 *The Bottle Fighter.* May 12, 1968. GS: Albert Dekker, Douglas Kennedy, Harlan Warde, Alan Baxter, Robert Sorrells, Charles Irving, Jon Lormer. Hoss is apparently a doomed murder suspect mired in circumstantial evidence. His memory damaged, Hoss is at the mercy of the only attorney who will take his case — a drunk.

14.299 *The Arrival of Eddie.* May 19, 1968. GS: Michael Vincent, Jim Davis, Bing Russell, Lincoln Demyan, Francis DeSales. Hoss buys trouble when he tries to atone for killing young Eddie Makay's father. Eddie signs on to work at the Ponderosa, intending to help a rancher who has a score to settle with the Cartwrights.

14.300 *The Stronghold.* May 26, 1968. GS: Michael Whitney, Paul Mantee, Lynda Day, James Davidson, William Bryant, Hal Baylor, Martin Blaine, Robert Brubaker, Ref Sanchez. Joe and Candy track the swindling Farrell brothers to their Arizona stronghold. As the pair make a bold move to get their money back, the Farrells' hatred for each other also comes to the fore.

14.301 *Pride of a Man.* June 2, 1968. GS: Morgan Woodward, Kevin Coughlin, Anne Helm, Steve Cory. Joe fills the unaccustomed role of schoolteacher. He faces a clash with two incorrigible boys and their father, who sees no point in educating his sons.

14.302 *A Severe Case of Matrimony.* July 7, 1968. GS: J. Carrol Naish, Susan Strasberg, Andre Philippe, Lili Valenty. The Cartwrights ride out a brief but hectic interlude with a wheeling-dealing band of gypsies. One of them is Rosalita, a tempestuous beauty determined to romance a Cartwright, any Cartwright, into backing her operatic career.

14.303 *Stage Door Johnnies.* July 28, 1968. GS: Kathleen Crowley, Walter Brooke, Mike Mazurki, Shug Fisher, Bruno Ve Sota, Ted Ryan, King Moody. Romantic rivalry for the new chanteuse at the Silver Dollar saloon embroils the Cartwrights in damage suits, and a crisis over the lady's lost dog.

Season Ten

14.304 *Different Pines, Same Wind.* Sept. 15, 1968. GS: Irene Tedrow, John Randolph, Herbert Voland, G.D. Spradlin, John L. Wheeler, George Murdock. Joe tries to save a lonely woman's timber stand from a ruthless lumber tycoon.

14.305 *Child.* Sept. 22, 1968. GS: John Marley, Harry Hickok, Yaphet Kotto, Henry Beckman, Frank DeVol, Robert Ball, Bruce Kirby, Charles Maxwell. Wrongly accused of murder and theft, Hoss breaks jail with the aid of cowboy Child Barnett. As the two men try to elude the posse, Hoss learns that his companion is an expert at the fugitive life.

14.306 *Salute to Yesterday.* Sept. 29, 1968. GS: Pat Conway, Sandra Smith, John Kellogg, Carlos Rivas, Richard Lapp, Troy Melton, Pepe Callahan. Trying to aid an army unit besieged by outlaws, Candy and the Cartwrights become involved in more than personal danger. The commanding officer is married to Candy's former wife.

14.307 *The Real People of Muddy Creek.* Oct. 6, 1968. GS: Joe Don Baker, Jean Hale, Ann Doran, Hal Lynch, Clifton James, Russell Thorson, Michael Vogel, Val Bisoglio, Jon Lormer, Ed Long. The Cartwrights go it alone in the town of Muddy Creek. Taking over for a murdered sheriff, Ben and Joe deliver outlaw Luke Harper to the Muddy Creek jail. The outlaw's threats, coupled with the impending arrival of his brothers, send everyone but the Cartwrights scurrying out of town.

14.308 *The Passing of a King.* Oct. 13, 1968. GS: Jeremy Slate, Denver Pyle, Diana Muldaur, Dan Tobin, Russ Conway. The Cartwrights battle ruthless Jeremy Roman, who takes advantage of his father's ill health to perpetrate a series of outrages.

14.309 *The Last Vote.* Oct. 20, 1968. GS: Tom Bosley, Wally Cox, Robert Emhardt, Bing Russell, Don Haggerty, Lane Bradford, Bruno Ve Sota. Bored to tears by the monotony of ranch life, Hoss and Joe Cartwright enter the political arena. On a bet, the two Cartwrights champion opposing candidates for the mayoralty of Virginia City, to the accompaniment of broken glass and ruined friendships.

14.310 *Catch as Catch Can.* Oct. 27, 1968. GS: Paul Richards, Slim Pickens, Robert Yuro, Arthur Malet, John Perch, John Quade. The Cartwrights are confronted by suspicion and anger in the town of Tinbucket. Candy is accused of cheating at cards, Joe is jailed as a pickpocket, and the whole town thinks Ben is bankrupt.

14.311 *Little Girl Lost.* Nov. 3, 1968. GS: Linda Sue Risk, Antoinette Bower, George Mitchell, Bob Padilla, Christian Anderson. The men of the Ponderosa become the cautious caretakers of a tough little tomboy named Samantha. She is a distant relative of Ben's, and the Cartwrights have their hands full trying to make her behave.

14.312 *The Survivors.* Nov. 10, 1968. GS: Mariette Hartley, John Carter, Martin Ashe, Harriet Medin, Lesley Woods, Ed Bakey. Ben helps a young mother fight bigotry in Virginia City. While a captive of the Paiutes, Alicia Pursell bore an Indian son. Now none of the town people, including her husband whom she hasn't seen in four years, will accept her.

14.313 *The Sound of Drums.* Nov. 17, 1968. GS: Jack Kruschen, Penny Santon, Brioni Farrell, Michael Stefani, Byron Morrow, Mark Tapscott, Debra Domasin. Despite Ben's warning, neighbor Giorgio Rossi invites a band of Indians to camp on his land, then learns the Indians think they have been invited to live there.

14.314 *Queen High.* Dec. 1, 1968. GS: Celeste Yarnell, Paul Lambert, Sandor Szabo, Dabney Coleman, Ken Drake, Edward Schaaf. Joe Cartwright, Candy and lively Kate Kelly become partners in an ore-processing mill. Joe and Candy work by day to get the mill in running order, with night devoted to outwitting each other and sparkin' Miss Kate.

14.315 *Yonder Man.* Dec. 8, 1968. GS: John Vernon, Melissa Murphy, Larry Ward, Pepper Martin. Candy has his doubts about Beaudry, a boisterous old friend of Ben's. He has stolen Joe's horse, gotten in a saloon brawl and sent Candy flying — all in fun.

14.316 *Mark of Guilt.* Dec. 15, 1968. GS: Dick Foran, Michael Vandever, Lou Frizzell, Alan Bergmann, Gordon Dilworth. Hoss and Hop Sing put together an unconventional case for the defense as they try to clear Joe Cartwright of murder.

14.317 *A World Full of Cannibals.* Dec. 2, 1968. GS: James Patterson, Linda March, Mark Richman, John Milford. Ben Cartwright invites trouble when he allows grand-jury witness Charles Ball to hide out at the Ponderosa. Ball plans to accuse seven men of fraud, and collect a rich fee from an equally guilty eighth man. But all eight men are gunning for the witness.

14.318 *Sweet Annie Laurie.* Jan. 5, 1969. GS: Joan Van Ark, James Olson, Lawrence Dane, James Jeter. Hoss tries to help Laurie Adams, a young woman who is desperately trying to break away from her husband, a wanted outlaw. Standing in her way in not so much the man himself, but his pride, which won't allow him to give her up.

14.319 *My Friend, My Enemy.* Jan. 12, 1969. GS: John Saxon, Woodrow Parfrey, Chick Chandler, Gregory Walcott, Ben Hammer, Raymond Guth, Sunshine Parker, Duane Grey. The Cartwrights try to clear Candy of a murder charge. Things couldn't be more difficult. The only witness is an elusive Indian horse thief, the defense will be handled by an unenthusiastic lawyer, and the case will be heard by a man known as the hanging judge.

14.320 *Mrs. Wharton and the Lesser Breeds.* Jan. 19, 1969. GS: Mildred Natwick, Oren Stevens, Jess Pearson, Jeffrey Morris, Chanin Hale, J.S. Johnson, Chuck Bail, Ollie O'Toole. Candy gets his lumps as he tries to help an uppity British matron ransom her valuables from a holdup gang.

14.321 *Erin.* Jan. 26, 1969. GS: Mary Fickett, Don Briggs, Michael Keep, Joan Tompkins. Hoss falls in love with Erin O'Donnell, an Irish girl raised by the Sioux. Hoss is determined to marry the girl, despite taunts from bigoted neighbors and a prophecy that she is fated to die in a battle between Indians and whites.

14.322 *Company of Forgotten Men.* Feb. 2, 1969. GS: James Gregory, Charles Maxwell, John Pickard, Ken Lynch, William Bryant, I. Stanford Jolley, Phil Chambers. Candy and the Cartwrights offer food and shelter to a ragged outfit of Army veterans, unaware they intend to rob the Carson City Mint.

14.323 *The Clarion.* Feb. 9, 1969. GS: Phyllis Thaxter, Simon Oakland, William Jordan, Hamilton Camp, Philip Kennally, Ken Mayer, Connie Sawyer, S. Newton Anderson, Ed McCready, James Jeter. Ben comes to the aid of Ruth Manning, a widowed newspaper publisher who is being forced out of business by town boss Seth Tabor.

14.324 *The Lady and the Mountain Lion.* Feb. 23, 1969. GS: Richard Haydn, Alyce Andrece, Rhae Andrece, Michael Keep, Dabbs Greer, Chet Stratton. A magician's twin daughters spell sweet confusion for the Cartwright boys. Joe and Hoss are unaware they are sparking two different girls — one a demure lass and the other a pool-playing cutie.

14.325 *Five Candles.* March 2, 1969. GS: Scott Thomas, Don Knight, Ted Gehring, Eddie Firestone, Louise Fitch, William Keene, Bobby Pickett, Tiffany Bolling. A mine explosion triggers the collapse of the Virginian City courthouse, trapping Ben Cartwright, a lawman, a miner accused of murder, a courthouse clerk and her beau — the chief witness in the case against the miner.

14.326 *The Wish.* March 9, 1969. GS: Ossie Davis, George Spell, Roy Jenson, Harry Page, Barbara Parrio, Charles Seel, Jerry Summers. Hoss postpones a fishing trip after meeting a young Negro whose father, ex-slave Sam Davis, is struggling to save his drought-stricken farm. Hoss wants to help, but charity would destroy Sam's self-respect, and Sam has no reason to trust Hoss or any other white man.

14.327 *The Deserter.* March 16, 1969. GS: Ford Rainey, Ellen Davalos, Ben Johnson, Duane Grey, Ken Drake, Todd Martin, Lincoln Demyan, Bing Russell. Candy befriends Sam Bellis, an Army sergeant who swears he is innocent of desertion and murder charges. With an Army patrol on their trail, the two seek evidence to clear Sam's name.

14.328 *Emily.* March 23, 1969. GS: Beth Brickell, Ron Hayes, David McLain, Bing Russell, Harry Holcombe, Byron Webster, Charles P. Thompson, Quentin Sondergaard. Emily McPhail is a capricious young beauty who was once Joe Cartwright's fiancée. Emily's sudden appearance in town sends Joe into delicious confusion, until the lady's lies land him in big trouble.

14.329 *The Running Man.* March 30, 1969. GS: Robert Pine, Will Geer, Jennifer Douglas, Larry Casey, Lee Farr, Ed Long. Candy and Little Joe grapple with a land baron who rules the town of Butlerville. Calvin Butler and his men have been burning out homesteaders. Now murder has been added to their list of crimes.

14.330 *The Unwanted.* April 6, 1969. GS: Bonnie Bedelia, Charles McGraw, Jan-Michael Vincent. Ben has his hands full trying to cope with Lorrie Mansfield, the headstrong young daughter of a lawman visiting the Ponderosa. While her father hunts for an escaped desperado, Lorrie forms a strong attachment for an ex-convict being held at the ranch.

14.331 *Speak No Evil.* April 20, 1969. GS: Patricia Smith, Kevin Burchett, Dana Elcar, Chick Chandler, Debbie Smaller, Ed Bakey, Ed Peck, Charles P. Thompson, Gregg Palmer. Ben and Hoss are drawn into a custody battle over a 14-year-old boy who inherited a gold mine from his late father. Stubborn and self-sufficient, the youngster equally disdains his greedy uncle and the mother who deserted him many years before.

14.332 *The Fence.* April 27, 1969. GS: J.D. Cannon, John Anderson, Lawrence Linville, Verna Bloom, Charles Dierkop, Frank Webb. Ben and Hoss are caught in a renewal of Civil War hostilities when they visit mine owner Sam Masters and his daughter. Masters commanded a Confederate prison where 500 men died, and now he is being hunted by an avenging ex-Union officer.

14.333 *A Ride in the Sun.* May 11, 1969. GS: Robert Hogan, Anthony Zerbe, Marj Dusay, Jack Collins, Harry Holcombe. The Cartwrights fall prey to a clever trio of swindlers who have worked out an audacious plan to rob the Virginia City bank.

Season Eleven

14.334 *Another Windmill to Go.* Sept. 14, 1969. GS: Laurence Naismith, Jill Townsend, Bart LaRue, Gregg Palmer, George Furth, Virgil Frye, Lee Jay Lambert, Bruce Watson. The sight of a dapper old man rowing a boat across dry grazing land is the quixotic scene that is bewildering all of Virginia

City. The Cartwrights are especially concerned, for they have leased the acreage and fear the gentleman may be engineering a swindle.

14.335 *The Witness.* Sept. 21, 1969. GS: Stefan Gierasch, Melissa Murphy, Connie Hines, Alan Baxter, Bo Hopkins, Wayne Storm, Matt Clark. A girl who claims she can identify a trio of murderous holdup men is offered refuge at the Ponderosa, where Candy and Joe become her willing guardians.

14.336 *Silence at Stillwater.* Sept. 28, 1969. GS: Pat Hingle, Strother Martin, Frank Marth, Eddie Ryder, Dan Kemp. Candy is jailed by the Stillwater sheriff, who refuses to tell him he is the prime suspect in a murder case, or let the Cartwrights know that their man is in his prison.

14.337 *A Lawman's Lot Is Not a Happy One.* Oct. 5, 1969. GS: Tom Bosley, Robert Emhardt, Melinda Dillon, Jay Novello. Hoss serves as temporary sheriff of Virginia City. The townsfolk are up in arms because Hoss is slow to jail an unruly citizen, but only too eager to jail an intrepid businessman.

14.338 *Anatomy of a Lynching.* Oct. 12, 1969. GS: Guy Stockwell, Walter Barnes, Ted Gehring, Mills Watson, Ellen Weston, Tyler McVey. The Cartwrights and Candy help Sheriff Coffee avert the lynching of Will Griner, who won acquittal on a charge of murder. The townspeople, certain that witnesses have been silenced, plan to implement vigilante justice.

14.339 *To Stop a War.* Oct. 19, 1969. GS: Steve Forrest, Miriam Colon, Warren Kemmerling, Bing Russell, Richard Bull, Chuck Bail, Ollie O'Toole, Alan Vint, John Tracy. The Cartwrights become involved with an impending range war, rustlers, and the man hired to clean things up, ex-sheriff Dan Logan. While he is cleaning up the range, Logan is working on another project, reforming a recalcitrant saloon girl.

14.340 *The Medal.* Oct. 26, 1969. GS: Dean Stockwell, Harry Townes, Susan Howard, Charles Briles, E.J. Schuster, John Beck, Remo Pisani, Sundown Spencer, James Rawley. Civil War hostilities are rekindled when Ben befriends a Yankee hero who is down on his luck. A Southerner whose home and family were lost in the war intends to drive the man away, or kill him.

14.341 *The Stalker.* Nov. 2, 1969. GS: Charlotte Stewart, Lloyd Battista, John Perak, Dorothy Konrad, Harry Holcombe. Candy tries to help the embittered wife of a rancher he was forced to kill in self-defense. Working at the ranch soon has him in a romantic entanglement, and his life threatened by a mysterious gunman.

14.342 *Meena.* Nov. 16, 1969. GS: Ann Prentiss, Victor French, Dub Taylor, Robert Donner, George Morgan. A pretty girl who lives at a remote gold mine saves Joe from certain death on the desert. But when she brings him home to meet her ornery father, Joe finds himself pegged as suitable marriage material. Also in on the action is a trio of bumbling outlaws after the gold.

14.343 *A Darker Shadow.* Nov. 23, 1969. GS: Gregory Walcott, Sandra Smith, Dabney Coleman, Bill Zuckert, Chick Chandler. Joe gives chase when bank employee Wade Turner abruptly calls off his impending marriage and leaves Virginia City. Bank funds are missing and Joe means to find out just how much trouble his friend is in.

14.344 *Dead Wrong.* Dec. 7, 1969. GS: Mike Mazurki, Arthur Hunnicutt, Robert Sorrells, Eric Christmas, Ivor Francis. Hoss is a big name in Sunville, thanks to tall-taleteller Salty Hubbard. Salty has spread the word that Hoss is a notorious bank robber. The result is that the townsfolk are preparing to fill his frame with holes.

14.345 *Old Friends.* Dec. 14, 1969. GS: Robert J. Wilke, Morgan Woodward, Rick Lamson. Ben intervenes when bounty hunter Jess Waddell goes after outlaw Charlie Sheppard. The elder Cartwrights knows both men, and while he tries to stay Waddell's itchy trigger finger, Ben is trying to insure the safety of Sheppard's prisoner — Hoss.

14.346 *Abner Willoughby's Return.* Dec. 21, 1969. GS: John Astin, Emmaline Henry, Irene Tedrow, Russell Schulman. A bemused Joe follows ex-miner Abner Willoughby as he searches for money he buried years before. A town has sprung up in the interim, and a widow, her son and mother now reside on the land holding Abner's cache.

14.347 *It's a Small World.* Jan. 4, 1970. GS: Michael Dunn, Edward Binns, Bing Russell, Angela Clarke, Carol Lawson. Ben tries to help a circus midget start a new life in Virginia City. Because of his size and background, no one wants to hire George Marshall, so the little man decides to turn lawbreaker.

14.348 *Danger Road.* Jan. 11, 1970. GS: Robert Lansing, Anna Novarro, William Sylvester, Jay Jones. Old animosities flare as Ben confronts a former Army gunnery officer who was branded for desertion. Ben can't bring himself to forgive Gunny Riley's past misdeeds, but he is willing to let the wagon driver get a fair chance to prove his skills.

14.349 *The Big Jackpot.* Jan. 18, 1970. GS: Walter Brooke, Robert F. Simon, Alan Caillou, Elizabeth Talbot-Martin, Al Checco, Nelson Olmsted, Robert Ball, Paula Mitchell, Remo Pisani, Leon Lontoc, Bruce Kirby. Candy inherits a small fortune and the wolves are on him in no time. Society folk, tradesmen and an unscrupulous land promoter all vie for his attention.

14.350 *The Trouble with Amy.* Jan. 25, 1970. GS: Jo Van Fleet, John Crawford, Donald Moffatt, Linda Watkins, Brian Wo, Elaine Giftos, Carl Pitts. Elderly Amy Wilder is a sharp-tongued widow who loves all animals, but can't abide a greedy land developer who is going to court to prove her senile.

14.351 *The Lady and the Mark.* Feb. 1, 1970. GS: Elaine Giftos, James Westerfield, Christopher Connelly, Lou Frizzell. The Cartwrights try to stop a band of swindling con men by setting up Chris Keller as a victim for the crooks. But the plan starts to skid when Chris gets a look at a new entry on the scene — a lovely con woman.

14.352 *Is There Any Man Here?* Feb. 8, 1970. GS: John McLiam, Mariette Hartley, Burr DeBenning, Vaughn Taylor, Roy Engel, Jon Lormer, Don Melvoin. A young lady who walked out on her wedding to an influential banker poses problems for Ben. Jennifer Carlis says she has been in love with Ben ever since she was a little girl, and now she intends to marry him.

14.353 *The Law and Billy Burgess.* Feb. 15, 1970. GS: Mercedes McCambridge, Les Tremayne, David Cassidy, Charles Maxwell. Ben battles Matilda Curtis, a wealthy widow who helped him open a school for Ponderosa youngsters. When the schoolmaster is murdered, Mrs. Curtis demands immediate punishment of Billy Burgess, the youth she holds responsible for the killing.

14.354 *Long Way to Ogden.* Feb. 22, 1970. GS: Kathleen

Freeman, Walter Barnes, James McCallion, Mark Tapscott, Billy Green Bush, Arthur Peterson, Tony Colti. A Chicago meat packer tries to force Ben and the other cattlemen to sell their herds at disastrously low prices. Emmett J. Whitney has the ranchers over a barrel as he has purchased the rights to every available railroad cattle car.

14.355 *Return Engagement.* March 1, 1970. GS: Joyce Bulifant, Sally Kellerman, Morgan Sterne, David McLean, Bart Robinson. Actress Lotta Crabtree arrives in Virginia City and sets off a ruckus when her leading man is murdered, and Hoss Cartwright accused of the crime.

14.356 *The Gold Mine.* March 8, 1970. GS: Tony De Costa, Bruce Dern, Ross Hansen, Charles P. Thompson. The Cartwrights befriend a Mexican boy who was sold into virtual slavery by his father. Because he has known only abuse from his two masters, the boy doesn't know who to tell about his good fortune — discovery of a vein of gold.

14.357 *Decision at Los Robles.* March 22, 1970. GS: William H. Bassett, Joe De Santis, Ted Cassidy, Anakorita, George D. Wallace, Ric Alaniz, Emile Meyer. Ben, wounded in an ambush, manages to gun down his attacker, town boss John Walker. Walker's son vows to avenge his father's death — even if he has to kill innocent townspeople to get at Ben.

14.358 *Caution, Easter Bunny Crossing.* March 29, 1970. GS: Marc Lawrence, Len Lesser, Vic Tayback, Art Metrano, Allyn Ann McLerie. Comic situations abound as four bumbling Brooklynites try to make it big as outlaws when they encounter Hoss, dressed in a rabbit costume to entertain at an orphanage.

14.359 *The Horse Traders.* April 5, 1970. GS: Dub Taylor, Ann Prentiss, Victor French, Lou Frizzell, George Morgan, Robert Donner, Jack Collins. Hoss and Joe figure to make some fast money by selling a herd of horses. They are in for a rude awakening, thanks to old acquaintance Luke Calhoun, a miner turned city slicker.

14.360 *What Are Pardners For?* April 12, 1970. GS: Slim Pickens, Dabbs Greer, John Beck, Richard Evans, Hamilton Camp, Bruce Glover, Tom Peters, Robert Cornthwaite, Tol Avery, Robert Padilla. Thrown in jail for complicity in a bank robbery, Hoss tries his darndest to prove he is innocent. His appeal loses believability when the bank robbers bust him out of jail.

14.361 *A Matter of Circumstance.* April 19, 1970. GS: Ted Gehring, Vincent Van Patten, Harry Holcombe. Joe is alone at the Ponderosa when he is trampled by a horse. Hobbled by pain and injuries, Joe fights to remain conscious and treat his wounds.

Season Twelve

14.362 *The Night Virginia City Died.* Sept. 13, 1970. GS: Angel Tompkins, Bing Russell, Phil Brown, Edith Atwater. Fear and anger grip the townspeople as the sheriff and his deputy fail to stop a rash of burnings that threaten to destroy Virginia City.

14.363 *A Matter of Faith.* Sept. 20, 1970. GS: Lou Frizzell, Bruce Gordon, Jack Collins, Geoffrey Lewis, Michael Hinn. Jamie, the junior member of a rainmaking team, figures that drought-stricken Virginia City is the perfect place to test his dead father's theories about precipitating precipitation.

14.364 *The Weary Willies.* Sept. 27, 1960. GS: Richard Thomas, Lee Purcell, Lonny Chapman, Elisha Cook, Jr. Hippie-like drifters who are wandering through the West after the Civil War temporarily take shelter at the Ponderosa. Their presence infuriates the people of Virginia City.

14.365 *The Wagon.* Oct. 5, 1970. GS: Denver Pyle, Salome Jens, George Murdock, Jonathan Lippe, Lee Jay Lambert. Hoss is manacled for delivery to prison to serve a five-year term. The brutal boss of a prison wagon has substituted the wounded Hoss for an escaped prisoner.

14.366 *The Power of Life and Death.* Oct. 11, 1970. GS: Rupert Crosse, Lou Frizzell, Larry Ward, Ted Gehring, Tina Menard. A fugitive killer is stranded at a water hole with a badly wounded Ben while Joe, alone and on foot, strikes out across the desert in search of help.

14.367 *Gideon the Good.* Oct. 18, 1970. GS: Richard Kiley, Terry Moore, A. Martinez, Carmen Zapata. A highly respected sheriff steps outside the law when he realizes that Joe Cartwright saw his wife kill a man. The sheriff sets out to silence the only witness.

14.368 *The Trouble with Trouble.* Oct. 25, 1970. GS: Gene Evans, E.J. Andre, G.D. Spradlin. Hoss takes over as the temporary sheriff of Trouble, California, a well-named community that thrives on rowdyism, frustrating Hoss' every effort to bring about law and order.

14.369 *Thorton's Account.* Nov. 1, 1970. GS: Gregory Walcott, Carl Reindel, Heather Menzies, Scott Walker, Jerry Gatlin, Chick Chandler, Harlan Warde. Seeking aid for a badly injured Ben, Joe becomes embroiled in a range feud, and with the gunmen who are terrorizing homesteaders.

14.370 *The Love Child.* Nov. 8, 1970. GS: Carol Lawson, Will Geer, Michael-James Wixted, Josephine Hutchinson. Etta Randolph is a dying unwed mother. She asks her parents to make a home for her young son, but Etta's embittered father will have nothing to do with her or the boy.

14.371 *El Jefe.* Nov. 15, 1970. GS: Rodolfo Acosta, Warren Stevens, Jaime Sanchez, Anna Navarro, Shug Fisher. Sheriff Vicente Aranda plays the gringo game against his own people, taking part in a land grab by helping to frame a Mexican rancher for murder.

14.372 *The Luck of Pepper Shannon.* Nov. 22, 1970. GS: Neville Brand, Walter Brooke, Dan Tobin, Arthur Peterson. In Virginia City to settle an old score, Pepper Shannon, an infamous stagecoach robber, becomes the object of intense hero worship from Jamie, who is jolted when Shannon is badly wounded and framed for attempted murder.

14.373 *The Imposters.* Dec. 13, 1970. GS: Strother Martin, Anthony Colti, Anthony James, Diane Shalet. Joad Bruder is holding the payroll his son stole from Hoss, while Hoss and Joe pose as the son's partners to get the money back.

14.374 *Honest John.* Dec. 20, 1970. GS: Jack Elam, Bing Russell, Bucklind Beery. Honest John is a misnamed vagrant who encounters the Cartwrights. The drifter is looking for a nest, and hopes to settle on the Ponderosa through his rapport with the newly adopted Jamie. But John's breakthrough with the boy must be weighed against the seamier side of his character.

14.375 *For a Young Lady* (airdate: December 27, 1970). GS: Jewel Blanch, Paul Fix, Madeleine Sherwood, William Bramley, Peggy Rea, Harry Holcombe. The Cartwrights team up to help Carri Sturgis, a frightened little girl who becomes the charge of a stern aunt and uncle.

14.376 *A Single Pilgrim.* Jan. 3, 1971. GS: Beth Brickell, Jeff Corey, John Schuck. Badly wounded in a hunting accident, Hoss faces death at the hands of a family of mountaineers. The tyrannical head of the clan fears that Hoss will seek revenge for the shooting.

14.377 *The Gold-Plated Rifle.* Jan. 10, 1971. A family crisis develops after young Jamie breaks one of Ben's prized guns.

14.378 *Top Hand.* Jan. 17, 1971. GS: Ben Johnson, Roger Davis, Walter Barnes, Jerry Gatlin, Richard Farnsworth, Bill Clark, Ed Jauregui. Kelly James, a soft-spoken veteran cowhand, is Ben's choice for trail boss on a major cattle drive. But Kelly is challenged by Bert Yates, a cocky young foreman spoiling for the job.

14.379 *A Deck of Aces.* Jan. 31, 1971. GS: Alan Oppenheimer, Linda Gaye Scott, Charles Dierkop, Jeff Morris, Tom Basham. Ben Cartwright meets his double, a hard-luck con man determined to cash in on his resemblance to the patriarch of the Ponderosa.

14.380 *The Desperado.* Feb. 7, 1971. GS: Lou Gossett, Marlene Clark, Ramon Bieri, Warren Vanders, Mike Mikler. Buck Walters is an embittered black man accused of murder. While fleeing from a posse, the man and his wife capture Hoss, on whom they plan to vent their hatred for whites.

14.381 *The Reluctant American.* Feb. 14, 1971. GS: Daniel Massey, Jill Haworth, J. Pat O'Malley, Daniel Kemp, Ronald Long, Bing Russell, Sandra Tgo. English banker Leslie Harwood arrives in Virginia City to manage a bank-owned ranch near the Ponderosa. His first task is to put a stop to cattle rustling, which proves to be a large order for a gentleman trained in the world of finance.

14.382 *Shadow of a Hero.* Feb. 21, 1971. GS: Dean Jagger, Laurence Luckinbill, John Randolph, Linda Watkins, Lane Bradford, Ruben Moreno. Gen. Ira Cloninger is a retired general being considered for the governorship. There is one dissident, a persistent reporter who is certain the general is guilty of murder.

14.383 *The Silent Killers.* Feb. 28, 1971. GS: Meg Foster, Harry Holcombe, Louise Latham, Ion Berger. Influenza is reaching epidemic proportions around Virginia City. The disease meets a formidable foe in Evangeline Woodtree, a doctor's wife with revolutionary ideas about medicine.

14.384 *Terror at 2:00.* March 7, 1971. GS: Steve Ihnat, Byron Mabe, Dabbs Greer. Gans is a psychopath who plans to kill all participants at a public treaty-signing between the Army and the Indians. To do so, he has smuggled a Gatling gun into a hotel room overlooking the signing site.

14.385 *The Stillness Within.* March 14, 1971. GS: Jo Van Fleet, Harry Holcombe, Jeannine Brown, Robert Noe. Ellen Dobbs is a teacher of the blind. She is summoned from San Francisco to teach Joe Cartwright, who has been blinded in an explosion. Joe's adjustment hinges on Ellen's ability to conceal the fact that she, too, is blind.

14.386 *A Time to Die.* March 21, 1971. GS: Vera Miles, Henry Beckman, Melissa Newman. April Christopher is the victim of an attack by an apparently rabid wolf. She can do nothing now but wait for the test results, or the first symptoms of rabies, to learn whether she will face a horrible death.

14.387 *Winter Kill.* March 28, 1971. GS: Glenn Corbett, Clifton James, Sheilah Wells.

14.388 *Kingdom of Fear.* April 4, 1971. GS: Alfred Ryder, Richard Mulligan, Luke Askew, Warren Finnerty. The Cartwrights and hired hand Candy are forced into a slave-labor gang working a gold mine after becoming victims of a phony trespassing charge.

14.389 *An Earthquake Called Callahan.* April 11, 1971. GS: Victor French, Sandy Duncan, Dub Taylor. Joe volunteers to bring an itinerant boxer back to Virginia City to testify for a friend. Unfortunately for Joe, big Tom Callahan is mighty hard to persuade.

Season Thirteen

14.390 *The Grand Swing.* Sept. 19, 1971. GS: Ralph Moody, Charlotte Stewart, Med Flory, Ted Gehring. Young Jamie learns a lesson in responsibility as he and Ben ride the Cartwright lands, from timber country to cattle ranges.

14.391 *Fallen Woman.* Sept. 26, 1971. GS: Susan Tyrrell, Arthur O'Connell, Ford Rainey, Johnny Lee, Lillian Field. Hoss becomes involved with an alcoholic who is determined to give her son a chance in life.

14.392 *Bushwacked.* Oct. 3, 1971. GS: Richard O'Brien, Peggy McCay, David Huddleston, Walter Barnes, Tony Colti, Bill Stevens. Little Joe has been found shot, near death and too delirious to provide a solid clue to who did it or why.

14.393 *Rock-a-Bye, Hoss.* Oct. 10, 1971. GS: Edward Andrews, Patricia Harty, Ellen Moss. Hoss finds himself judging a beautiful baby contest that is turning into all-out war. Virginia City is exploding with rivalries, and Hoss is in the middle.

14.394 *The Prisoners.* Oct. 17, 1971. GS: Michael Witney, Morgan Woodward, Manuel Padilla, Priscilla Garcia. Hank Simmons is a fugitive whose winning smile is a prelude to murder. He also has Joe Cartwright on his trail

14.395 *Cassie.* Oct. 27, 1971. GS: Lisa Gerritsen, Diane Baker, Jack Cassidy. A con man's relationship with his daughter determines the fate of a magnificent race horse.

14.396 *Don't Cry, My Son.* Oct. 31, 1971. GS: Richard Mulligan, Diana Shalet, Dan Ferrone, Ann Whitsett, Bing Russell. Dr. Mark Sloan is driven insane by senseless guilt and an unforgiving wife.

14.397 *Face of Fear.* Nov. 14, 1971. GS: Bradford Dillman, Chick Chandler, Donald Moffatt, Jewel Blanch, Athena Lorde, Bing Russell, Tom Gillerman, Susan Joyce. Bannon, a brutal murderer, has assumed his victim's identity, and is now hunting the teenage girl who witnessed the crime.

14.398 *Blind Hunch.* Nov. 21, 1971. GS: Rip Torn, Don Knight, Loretta Leversee, Charles Maxwell. A blind Civil War veteran is out to avenge his brother's murder.

14.399 *The Iron Butterfly.* Nov. 28, 1971. GS: Mariette Hartley, Stefan Gierasch, Allen Garfield. An affair of the heart has burly Hoss Cartwright risking his life to protect a lovely actress involved in a killing.

14.400 *The Rattlesnake Brigade.* Dec. 5, 1971. GS: Neville Brand, David Sheiner, Severn Darden, Don Keefer, Chris Beaumont, Richard Yniquez, Michele Nicholas. Ben is at the center of a kidnap drama as he and three other men have children trapped aboard a wagon being driven by an escaped murderer.

14.401 *Easy Come, Easy Go.* Dec. 12, 1971. GS: Dub Taylor, Ann Prentiss, Lyman Ward, Dan Scott, Channing Pollock. Ben becomes involved with a quixotic gambler when he attempts to purchase an important right of way.

14.402 *A Home for Jamie.* Dec. 19, 1971. GS: Will Geer, Ford Rainey. Jamie's long lost grandfather is putting a heavy burden on the boy's shoulders by forcing him to leave the only home he has ever know.

14.403 *Warbonnet.* Dec. 26, 1971. GS: Chief Dan George, Forrest Tucker, Linda Cristal, Patrick Adiarte, Russ Marin, Lee De Broux. Red Cloud and Ryan are the adversaries in a drama about the possession of a war bonnet lost in battle.

14.404 *A Lonely Man.* Jan. 2, 1972. GS: Kelly Jean Peters, Peter Hobbs, Henry Wills, Bing Russell. The growing love between Hop Sing and a Caucasian woman is threatened by prejudice.

14.405 *Second Sight.* Jan. 9, 1972. GS: Joan Hackett, Larry Ward, James Booth. Judith, a minister's fiancee, is tormented by her psychic powers. She is called upon to assist in a desperate search for young Jamie, who is lost in the wilderness.

14.406 *Saddle Stiff.* Jan. 16, 1972. GS: Buddy Ebsen, Don Collier, Charles H. Gray, Jay MacIntosh, Dick Farnsworth. Cactus Murphy is a crusty hired hand who challenges Ben Cartwright to prove that he could come up a winner without the power of his name and money. Ben attempts to prove his point by working incognito in the midst of a range war.

14.407 *Frenzy.* Jan. 30, 1972. GS: Kathleen Widdoes, Jason Karpf, Michael Pataki. An immigrant woman thinks that her husband may be out to kill her and her son.

14.408 *Customs of the Country.* Feb. 6, 1972. GS: Alan Oppenheimer, Pilar Seurat, Alfonso Arau, David Renard, Maria Grimm, Mike de Anda, Annette Cardona, Mallia Saint Duval. Hoss and Joe are imprisoned in an idyllic Mexican town, but are treated more like kings than prisoners.

14.409 *Shanklin.* Feb. 13, 1972. GS: Charles Cioffi, Woodrow Parfrey, Karl Lukas, Rance Howard, Clark Gordon. A brutal ex-Confederate officer has left Hoss near death as he awaits Ben's return with a fortune in tribute.

14.410 *Search in Limbo.* Feb. 20, 1972. GS: Albert Salmi, Pamela Payton-Wright, Lucille Benson, Lawrence Montaigne. Ben makes an agonizing attempt to recall a lost day and whether or not he killed a man he hated.

14.411 *He Was Only Seven.* March 5, 1972. GS: Roscoe Lee Browne, William Watson, Robert Doyle, Edward Crawford, Jeff Morris, Joseph Perry, Dick Farnsworth. Joshua is a crippled old man on an unlikely odyssey to nail his grandson's murderer.

14.412 *The Younger Brothers' Younger Brother.* March 12, 1972. GS: Strother Martin, Chuck McCann, Ted Gehring, Doc Severinsen, Henry Jones. Three outlaw brothers are bumbling their way back into crime after twelve years in jail.

14.413 *A Place to Hide.* March 19, 1972. GS: Suzanne Pleshette, Hurd Hatfield, Jodie Foster, Jon Cypher, John Perak. Rose is a worn Southerner picking up the pieces of a life shattered by the Civil War.

14.414 *A Visit to Upright.* March 26, 1972. GS: Alan Oppenheimer, Loretta Swit, Anne Seymour. The Cartwright brothers become involved in a business venture concerning a dilapidated saloon that might house a fortune.

14.415 *One Ace Too Many.* April 2, 1972. GS: Greg Mullavey, Kate Jackson, William Mims, Harry Holcombe. Ben Cartwright encounters his double, a roguish con man with an outlandish ploy to liquidate the Ponderosa during Ben's absence.

Season Fourteen

14.416 *Forever.* Sept. 23, 1972. GS: Bonnie Bedelia, Roy Jenson, Andy Robinson, Larry Golden. Joe Cartwright romances Alice Harper and the two young lovers plan their wedding.

14.417 *Heritage of Anger.* Sept. 19, 1972. GS: Robert Lansing, Fionnuala Flanagan, Warren Kemmerling, Len Lesser, Roydon Clark, Ed Long. An ex-con is out to prove that he served five years in prison on a frame-up.

14.418 *The Initiation.* Sept. 26, 1972. GS: Ronny Howard, James Chandler, Ed Bakey, Sean Kelly, Biff Elliot, William Bramley, Nicolas Beauvy. Jamie is involved in a boys' club initiation that has a tragic aftermath.

14.419 *Riot!* Oct. 3, 1972. GS: Aldo Ray, Tim Matheson, Marco St. John, Gregory Walcott, Barney Phillips, Denver Pyle. The inmates take over a Nevada penitentiary and threaten to kill their hostages, including Ben Cartwright.

14.420 *New Man.* Oct. 10, 1972. GS: Tim Matheson, Ronny Cox, Charles Dierkop. Griff King is paroled from prison to Ben Cartwright's custody. He is hired on as a new hand on the Ponderosa, but a chip on his shoulder promises trouble.

14.421 *Ambush at Rio Lobo.* Oct. 24, 1972. GS: James Olson, Albert Salmi, Sian Barbara Allen, Murray MacLeod, Douglas Dirkson. Teresa Burnside is a young woman in the advanced stages of a difficult pregnancy. Outlaws plan to use her as a pawn in a stage robbery.

14.422 *The 26th Grave.* Oct. 31, 1972. GS: Ken Howard, Dana Elcar, Stacy Keach, Sr., Phil Keanneally, Walter Burke, Staats Cotsworth, Richard Bull. Samuel Clemens goes muckraking in Virginia City. The gutsy editor claims the Government assayer is implicated in fraud and murder.

14.423 *Stallion.* Nov. 14, 1972. GS: Clu Gulager, Mitzi Hoag, Vincent Van Patten. The beautiful black thoroughbred that Ben gave Joe on his birthday is stolen.

14.424 *The Hidden Enemy.* Nov. 28, 1972. GS: Mike Farrell, Melissa Murphy, David Huddleston, Gary Busey, Harry Holcombe, Jason Wingreen, Russell Thorsen. Dr. Will Agar is a doctor whose addiction to morphine leads to the death of a patient.

14.425 *The Sound of Loneliness.* Dec. 5, 1972. GS: Jack Albertson, Timothy Marshall, Dan Feronne, John Randolph, Carol Lawson, Marty McCall. An old widower goes out on a limb to prevent the separation of two orphaned brothers.

14.426 *The Bucket Dog.* Dec. 19, 1972. GS: William Sylvester, John Zaremba, Don Knight, Ivan Bonar, Don Harris. Jamie's new bird dog is a beautiful specimen whose very life depends on winning a grueling three-hour field trial.

14.427 *First Love.* Dec. 26, 1972. GS: Pamela Franklin, Jordan Rhodes, Lisa Eilbacher, David Doremus, Steve Benedict, Michael Blake, Dennis Robertson, Eileen Ryan. Teenaged Jamie is swept off his feet by an older woman who happens to be married to Jamie's insanely jealous schoolteacher.

14.428 *The Witness.* Jan. 2, 1973. GS: Sally Kemp,

Stephen Nathan, Byron Mabe, William Wintersole, Shirley O'Hara. There is a murder charge against Candy, whose defense will depend on testimony by the killer's wife and the ability of a lawyer barely out of his teens.

14.429 *The Marriage of Theodora Duffy.* Jan. 9, 1973. GS: Richard Eastham, Ramon Bieri, Karen Carlson, Robert Yuro, Rayford Barnes, Willard Sage, Bill Clark, Jerry Gatlin, Hal Burton. Griff sets up housekeeping with a woman who is only pretending to be his wife.

14.430 *The Hunter.* Jan. 16, 1971. GS: Tom Skerritt, Phillip Avenetti, Peter O'Crotty. An unarmed Joe is pitted against a psychopath who specializes in hunting humans.

The Tele-films

14.431 *Bonanza: The Next Generation.* April 20, 1988. Cast: John Ireland, Robert Fuller, John Amos, Barbara Anderson, Michael Landon, Jr., Brian A. Smith, Peter Mark Richman. A new generation of Cartwrights arrive at the Ponderosa to take control of their legacy.

14.432 *Bonanza: The Return.* Nov. 28, 1993. Cast: Ben Johnson, Alistair McDougall, Brian Leckner, Michael Landon, Jr., Emily Warfield, Jack Elam, Dirk Blocker, Guy Stockell, Linda Gray, Stewart Moss. The descendants of the Cartwright clan return to the Ponderosa for a showdown with an unscrupulous tycoon.

14.433 *Bonanza: Under Attack.* Jan. 15, 1995. Cast: Ben Johnson, Michael Landon, Jr., Brian Leckner, Leonard Nimoy, Dennis Farina, Richard Roundtree, Emily Warfield, Jeff Phillips, Jack Elam, Sonja Satra, James Karen, Dirk Blocker, Ted Markland. The Cartwright descendants take on renegade Pinkerton agents who are unlawfully pursuing the once notorious outlaw Frank James.

15. *Boots and Saddles*

Syndicated. 30 min. Broadcast history: Various, Sept. 1957–May 1958.

Regular Cast: John Pickard (Captain Shank Adams), Patrick McVey (Lieutenant Colonel Hays), Gardner McKay (Lieutenant Kelly), Dave Willock (Lieutenant Binning), John Alderson (Sergeant Bullock), Michael Hinn (Luke Cummings).

Premise: This is the story of the adventurous life of the Fifth Cavalry, an Arizona battalion of the 1870's. The series dealt with the regiment's attempts to bring peace to the Arizona territory.

The Episodes

15.1 *The Gatling Gun.* Sept. 19, 1957. The future of both Colonel Hays and the Gatling Gun are threatened when Fort Lowell is visited on an inspection trip. It takes an over-age enlisted man and a surprise attack by the Indians to prove that experience counts more than regulations.

15.2 *The Repeater Rifle.* Sept. 26, 1957. A licensed trader sells repeater carbines to marauding Apache Indians. As a result, the Indians have a dangerous advantage over the U.S. Calvary troops at Fort Lowell.

15.3 *The Obsession.* Oct. 3, 1957. GS: Morris Ankrum, Natalie Norwick, Wright King, Mark Roberts. A new directive from Washington makes it possible for men from the ranks to apply for entrance to West Point. Pvt. Bennett makes all requirements for entrance to West Point, but his chances are blocked by the intolerant attitude of Lt. Hagan, a career officer.

15.4 *Private War.* Oct. 10, 1957. The Civil War is an all-too-recent memory. One Fort Lowell trooper has never mastered his hatred of the Confederacy. He starts trouble within the fort which develops to the point where the fort is a divided camp.

15.5 *Prussian Farmer.* Oct. 17, 1957. GS: Herbert Rudley. When Fort Lowell's main cavalry forces go out to recover supplies taken by the Apaches from a military supply train, the fort is left manned largely by recruits. A surprise attack on the fort causes the disorganized recruits to fall back to a nearby farm where the farmer, once a Prussian cavalry officer, reorganizes the men and leads a cavalry charge against the Apaches.

15.6 *The Paymaster.* Oct. 24, 1957. When the men of Fort Lowell finally receive four months back pay, they have a celebration that nearly levels the fort.

15.7 *Terror at Fort Lowell.* Oct. 31, 1957. Battle-weary and discouraged, Hank Swanson turns his misguided wrath on the Indian scout inside the fort.

15.8 *Border Raiders.* Nov. 7, 1957. Adams' patrol comes on the scene of a hanging affair. Two men are dead and a third is barely alive. Later, the patrol discovers a settler's ranch afire. Everything points to Apache raids, but Adams isn't convinced.

15.9 *The Deserter.* Nov. 14, 1957. GS: Paul Picerni. Captain Shank has never cared for Trooper Grimes. When he catches him feeding bad water to an Apache prisoner his dislike is underscored.

15.10 *Quiet Day at Fort Lowell.* Nov. 21, 1957. When Colonel Hays leaves for Lowell on a mission, he puts Captain Shank Adams in command. Shank's wisdom and understanding enable a young trooper, who feels guilty about a grave act of cowardice, to redeem himself and erase his complex.

15.11 *The Gift.* Dec. 5, 1957. On a routine patrol, Lt. Binning finds an injured Apache, helpless with a broken leg. He treats the Indian and sends him home. The next day the Apache sends Lt. Binning his daughter, Yellow Sky, as a gift.

15.12 *The Treasure.* Dec. 12, 1957. GS: Michael Emmett, Rebecca Welles, Edward Colemans, Johnny Western. A notorious Civil War renegade and bandit wills a fortune in hidden contraband to the U.S. Government. Cpl. Davis and Luke Cummings are assigned as escort for the Treasury man sent to claim the treasure. They run into trouble when the dead man's daughter contests her father's will.

15.13 *The Coward.* Dec. 19, 1957. Sgt. Bullock is proud as he awaits the arrival of his nephew, Jed, a young soldier. When Jed turns out to be a cocky kid Bullock is disappointed, but he is stunned when Jed appears to be a coward during an Apache raid.

15.14 *The Marquis of Donnybrook.* Dec. 26, 1957. GS: Joel Ashley, James Dobson, DeForest Kelley. The Fifth Cavalry is challenged to a boxing match by the nearby Seventh Cavalry. Captain Adams accepts because he believes Sergeant Bullock can win. The champion of the Seventh turns out to be an English ex-professional.

15.15 *Pound of Flesh.* Jan. 2, 1958. A new trooper at Fort Lowell acts arrogantly toward Captain Adams and gets away with it because he holds a secret with which he can bend Captain Adams to his will. It concerns the death of Colonel Hay's son and only the trooper and Adams know the details.

15.16 *The Strange Death of Trooper Jones.* Jan. 9, 1958. A young man with a minor law violation against him joins the cavalry to hide.

15.17 *The Duel.* Jan. 16, 1958. Lt. Dan Kelly, a reckless young officer, is challenged to a duel by a young Apache chief—lance versus sabre. The duel is stopped by Captain Adams and Kelly is warned not to engage in the practice again. But when an Apache crisis occurs in the desert, Adams finds that the only hope for his outnumbered patrol is to allow Kelly to re-engage the Apache chief as a means of winning peace by demonstrating the officer's courage and skill.

15.18 *The Last Word.* Jan. 23, 1958. GS: Joel Ashley, James Dobson. When a local editorial criticizes the town's businessmen for being too dependent on the military, Lt. Kelly makes a direct and forceful complaint.

15.19 *The Proud Condemned.* Jan. 30, 1958. Blaze, a well-loved horse, is condemned and sold for less than the value of his hide because of violent behavior in battle and on the post. Lt. Kelly becomes personally interested in Blaze's troubles.

15.20 *Female of the Species.* Feb. 6, 1958. Lt. Binning's patrol rescues an attractive young singer and escorts her back to the post.

15.21 *The Dispatch Rider.* Feb. 13, 1958. Pvt. Hatfield, who has not been considered a very good soldier, becomes of age during a dangerous duty.

15.22 *The Eight-for-Five Men.* Feb. 20, 1958. When a trooper is savagely beaten his fellow troopers go to Tucson to hunt for the assailants and put an end to an ugly loan racket.

15.23 *Late Arrival.* Feb. 27, 1958. The word circulates that "A" Company is about to be transferred to Vermont, with a company of Fort Ethan Allen to provide their replacements. Colonel Hays discovers that the new arrivals are a company he requested two years previously.

15.24 *Rescue of the Stranger.* March 6, 1958. With Colonel Hays leading the Fifth in the field, a small force has to protect a large, scattered group of Mormons, one small party of which has already been rescued from the Apaches. But Captain Adams' under-manned unit is further damaged by prejudice.

15.25 *The Cook.* March 13, 1958. GS: James Dobson. Pvt. Hatfield, a talented cook, violates military discipline and, as punishment, is assigned to cook. He hates the duty and goes AWOL to be along with his buddies on a night patrol.

15.26 *The Courtmartial.* March 20, 1958. Coming to the aid of a patrol commanded by Lt. Col. Claymore of the Third Cavalry, Lt. Kelly is made the scapegoat for a severe tactical blunder.

15.27 *The Lost Patrol.* March 27, 1958. On patrol for the first time, a green recruit is harassed by Sgt. Bullock who attempts to make him more soldierly.

15.28 *A Question of Duty.* April 3, 1958. Captain Shank Adams is under orders not to engage in any form of combat with hostile Apaches, while escorting a supply train back to Fort Lowell.

15.29 *One-Man War.* April 10, 1958. General Taylor and his daughter arrive at Fort Lowell on an inspection tour. The girl's thoughtlessness leads to her capture by Indians.

15.30 *The Indian Scout.* April 17, 1958. A major, while on an inspection tour, forces Captain Shank Adams to dispense with his much-needed Indian scouts.

15.31 *The Politician.* April 24, 1958. Captain Shank Adams uncovers evidence of incitement that points to a politician.

15.32 *The Recruit.* May 1, 1958. A young recruit's familiarity with Army regulations brings about the suspicion that he has had previous service experience.

15.33 *The Superstition.* May 8, 1958. Pvt. Mickey Spanner has a reputation as a jinx.

15.34 *Iron John.* May 15, 1958. A new recruit believes his methods of doing things to be better than the tried and true methods employed by a sergeant.

15.35 *The Holdout.* May 22, 1958. Pvt. Ben Wells is sent out to bring back Miss Lisa Emery, a fiery holdout who refuses to leave her ranch.

15.36 *Weight of Command.* May 29, 1958. When diphtheria strikes at Fort Lowell, Lt. Col. G.W. Hays must get word through to Fort Whipple before the Apaches learn of the situation.

16. Bordertown

Family Channel. 30 min. Broadcast history: Saturday, 6:00-6:30, Jan. 1989–June 1991.

Regular Cast: Richard Comar (Marshal Jack Craddock), John H. Brennan (Corporal Clive Bennett), Sophie Barjac (Marie Dumont).

Premise: This series was set in the 1880s in a border town near the United States and Canada. The town's location made cooperation necessary between law enforcement agents of both countries. Former gunfighter Jack Craddock was the U.S. Marshal and Corporal Clive Bennett represented the Canadian Mounties.

17. Branded

NBC. 30 min. Broadcast history: Sunday, 8:30-9:00, Jan. 1965–Sept. 1966.

Regular Cast: Chuck Connors (Jason McCord).

Premise: Jason McCord is a former Cavalry captain who wanders the west of the 1870s after being cashiered out of the Army for cowardice at the Battle of Bitter Creek.

The Episodes

17.1 *Survival.* Jan. 24, 1965. GS: Alex Cord, Janet De Gore, Valerie Szabo. McCord comes to the aid of Jed Colbee, whom he finds on foot and near death in the desert.

17.2 *The Vindicator.* Jan. 31, 1965. GS: June Lockhart, Claude Akins, John Litel, Harry Carey, Jr., Johnny Jensen, John Marley, John Pickard. A New York newspaperman tracks down McCord to learn why he was cashiered from the Cavalry.

17.3 *The Test.* Feb. 7, 1965. GS: Jason Evers, Joe De Santis, Michael Keep, Jay Silverheels. McCord inadvertently

Branded

involves a Catholic priest in a deadly encounter with four drunken Comanches.

17.4 *Elsie Brown*. Feb. 14, 1965. GS: Jeanne Cooper, Brad Weston, Russ Conway, Harry Bartell, L.Q. Jones. McCord comes to the aid of Elsie Brown, who once saved his life and is now, like McCord, trying to live down a bad reputation.

17.5 *The Bounty*. Feb. 21, 1965. GS: Pat Conway, Gene Evans, Michael Ansara, Julie Reding, Charles Maxwell, Reg Parton, Pete Kellett. A stranger lends McCord some much-needed help in a barroom brawl, and with good reason. He is out to collect the $5000 bounty placed on McCord's life.

17.6 *Leap Upon Mountains....* Feb. 28, 1965. GS: John Ireland, John Leslie, Chris Alcaide, Claude Hall, Mike Masters. McCord is hired by a Quaker widow who is being pressured by a neighboring rancher to sell her land.

17.7 *Coward Step Aside*. March 7, 1965. GS: Johnny Crawford, G.V. Homeier, Richard Arlen, Charla Doherty, Allen Jaffe, Loyal "Doc" Lucas, Melville Ruick, Harry Fleer. With the Jefferson City menfolk away at a silver strike, the local bank seems easy pickings to a gang of outlaws. The only people left in town are McCord, a teenage deputy, a one-legged bartender, old men, women and children.

17.8 *The Mission* Part One. March 14, 1965. GS: John Carradine, Cesar Romero, William Bryant, Kamala Devi, Macdonald Carey, Robert Q. Lewis, Peter Breck, H.M. Wynant, Jon Lormer, Rochelle Hudson, Wendell Corey, Patrick Wayne, Steven Marlo. At the urging of his former fiancee and her father, a U.S. senator, McCord returns to Washington, and finds that he is still front page news.

17.9 *The Mission* Part Two. March 21, 1965. GS: John Carradine, Cesar Romero, William Bryant, Kamala Devi, Macdonald Carey, Robert Q. Lewis, Peter Breck, H.M. Wynant, Jon Lormer, Rochelle Hudson, Wendell Corey, Patrick Wayne, Steven Marlo. President Grant asks McCord to risk the stigma of treason by infiltrating a band of marauding Mexican bandits.

17.10 *The Mission* Part Three. March 28, 1956. GS: John Carradine, Cesar Romero, William Bryant, Kamala Devi, Macdonald Carey, Robert Q. Lewis, Peter Breck, H.M. Wynant, Jon Lormer, Rochelle Hudson, Wendell Corey, Patrick Wayne, Steven Marlo. McCord succeeds in luring a band of Mexican brigands into a U.S. Army fort, but he can't convince the fort's commander that he is not one of the outlaws.

17.11 *The First Kill*. April 4, 1965. GS: Chad Everett, James Dunn, John Pickard, Pete Kellett, Howard Johnson. McCord meets a memory face to face — the exact double of the very first man he killed in battle.

17.12 *Very Few Heroes*. April 11, 1965. GS: Tom Drake, Kathryn Hays, Bing Russell, William Cort, Jay Jostyn, Bill Hickman. To avoid losing her ranch in a law suit, Christina Adams needs the testimony of McCord, a man she detests.

17.13 *One Way Out*. April 18, 1965. GS: John Dehner, Paul Brent, Jim Davis, Eddie Little Sky, Iron Eyes Cody. McCord is lured to a ghost town inhabited only by a religious zealot and his two brutish sons.

17.14 *That the Brave Endure*. April 25, 1965. GS: Marie Windsor, Tommy Sands, Willard Sage. West Point cadet Richard Bain, court-martialed for challenging the Army's verdict against McCord, is given 30 days to recant or resign from the Academy.

17.15 *A Taste of Poison*. May 2, 1965. GS: Carol Rossen, Walter Burke, Stuart Margolin, Clarke Gordon, Joseph Perry. On the way to a desert hospital, McCord, a woman doctor and a wounded Army officer stop at a way station recently raided by Indians.

17.16 *Price of a Name*. May 23, 1965. GS: Marilyn Maxwell, Keith Andes, Don Megowan, Jess Kirkpatrick, Don Douglas. After accepting a high-paying job from rancher Lucy Benson, McCord is jumped by three strangers and ordered to get out of town.

Season Two

17.17 *Judge Not*. Sept. 12, 1965. GS: Tom Drake, Warren Oates, Kathleen Crowley, Willard Sage, Harry Harvey, Sr., Clint Sharp, Lou Roberson. McCord hitches a ride on a stage carrying four passengers, including a prisoner who is headed for the gallows and an officer who was present at McCord's court-martial hearing.

17.18 *Now Join the Human Race*. Sept. 19, 1965. GS: Burt Reynolds, Noah Beery, Jr., James Anderson, Ann Morell, Jon Lormer, Ted Jordan. Red Hand, who has illegally left the reservation with his family, is cornered by the troops of cold-blooded Major Lynch. McCord, afraid that killing the Apache chief would set off an Indian war, offers to mediate Red Hand's surrender.

17.19 *Mightier than the Sword*. Sept. 26, 1965. GS: Lola Albright, Kevin Hagen, Michael Lane, Maureen Arthur, Charles Horvath, Ed McCready. McCord comes to the aid of newspaper publisher Ann Williams, who refuses to endorse cutthroat town boss Paul Mandell for an important political appointment.

17.20 *I Killed Jason McCord*. Oct. 3, 1965. GS: Bruce Bennett, Karen Steele, Larry Pennell. Footloose Tuck Fraser, unexpectedly the center of admiration for killing a man thought to be McCord, gets an unpleasant shock when McCord turns up alive.

17.21 *The Bar Sinister*. Oct. 10, 1965. GS: Stephen McNally, Michael Petit, Marian Seldes. McCord steps in when the cousins of an old friend's orphaned son attempt to take the boy away from the Indian housekeeper who raised him.

17.22 *Seward's Folly*. Oct. 17, 1965. GS: Coleen Gray, Ian Wolfe, J. Pat O'Malley, Charles Maxwell, Robert Hoy, Lulu Porter. Two unsavory characters plot to steal the maps McCord is making after his survey of the rich, recently purchased territory of Alaska.

17.23 *Salute the Soldier Briefly*. Oct. 24, 1965. GS: Michael Rennie, Jim Davis, John Pickard, Claude Hall, John Mitchum. McCord interrupts a miners' kangaroo court to save Charles Briswell, an accused murderer who claims he witnessed the battle at Bitter Creek and can clear McCord.

17.24 *The Richest Man in Boot Hill*. Oct. 31, 1965. GS: Lee Van Cleef, J. Pat O'Malley, Richard Bakalyan, Jack Lambert, Fred Carson, William Henry. McCord reluctantly agrees to help a small-town undertaker haul a coffin into town, unaware that it contains a live safecracker who plans to rob the Wells Fargo office.

17.25 *Fill No Glass for Me* Part One. Nov. 7, 1965. GS: Greg Morris, Michael Keep, Duncan McLeod, Davis Roberts, Harry Lauter, Pedro Gonzalez-Gonzalez. In a flashback to the days after he was cashiered from the Army, McCord recalls an encounter with Col. Johnny Macon, the inexperienced leader of a Cavalry patrol trapped by the Apaches.

17.26 *Fill No Glass for Me* **Part Two.** Nov. 14, 1965. Greg Morris, Michael Keep, Duncan McLeod, Davis Roberts, Harry Lauter, Pedro Gonzalez-Gonzalez. Cpl. Johnny Macon breaks out of jail to rescue McCord, unaware that the Indians are using McCord as bait.

17.27 *The Greatest Coward on Earth.* Nov. 21, 1965. GS: Pat O'Brien, James Chandler, Pamela Curran, I. Stanford Jolley, John Marley, Victor Izay. When McCord tries to collect the $50 prize offered for defeating a muscleman, circus owner P.T. Barnum decides to offer him a job, as the star of re-enactments of the Bitter Creek massacre.

17.28 *$10,000 for Durango.* Nov. 28, 1965. GS: Martha Hyer, John Agar, Gregg Palmer, Lloyd Bochner, Edwin Cook, James Drake. While McCord is cashing his employer's draft for $10,000, Frank Ross and his gang stage a holdup.

17.29 *Romany Roundup* **Part One.** Dec. 5, 1965. GS: Nico Minardos, Gary Merrill, Anna Capri, Joan Huntington, Don Collier, Alan Baxter, Ben Ari, Michael J. Pollard. McCord runs afoul of Aaron Shields when he stops the cattle baron from whipping Kolyan, leader of a band of Gypsies.

17.30 *Romany Roundup* **Part Two.** Dec. 12, 1965. GS: Nico Minardos, Gary Merrill, Anna Capri, Joan Huntington, Don Collier, Alan Baxter, Ben Ari, Michael J. Pollard. Cattle baron Aaron Shields learns that his daughter has given the Gypsies the money for McCord's bail bond, and he orders his men to wipe out the Gypsy band.

17.31 *A Proud Town.* Dec. 19, 1965. GS: Ludwig Donath, Ken Mayer, Pat Cardi, Pamelyn Ferdin, Carol Brewster, Robert Gross, Jay Jostyn. It's Christmas, but elderly tailor Julius Perrin, who provides a home for a flock of orphans, is being forced out of town. One of his youngsters has been accused of shooting the son of the community's leading citizen.

17.32 *The Golden Fleece.* Jan. 2, 1966. GS: Harry Townes, Bing Russell, William Phipps. Arrested by uniformed troopers, McCord is placed in a prison van with Randall Kirby, a former Confederate officer who is making plans to establish a military empire.

17.33 *The Wolfers.* Jan. 9, 1966. GS: Zeme North, Bruce Dern, Morgan Woodward, Charles Horvath. McCord finds a delirious white girl, wearing Indian dress, left tied in a clearing by wolf hunters.

17.34 *This Stage of Fools.* Jan. 16, 1966. GS: Martin Landau, Rex Ingram, Chris Alcaide. McCord goes to work as bodyguard to actor Edwin Booth, whose brother John Wilkes assassinated President Lincoln.

17.35 *A Destiny Which Made Us Brothers.* Jan. 23, 1966. GS: James MacArthur, William Bryant, Jan Merlin, Willard Sage, Buck Taylor. Army couriers awaken McCord at 3 A.M. to deliver a special letter which reminds McCord of an unexpected meeting with General Grant, also at 3 A.M., ten years earlier.

17.36 *McCord's Way.* Jan. 30, 1966. GS: Mona Freeman, Ben Johnson, Tom Reese, Willard Sage, Jim Beck, Robert Swan, Henry Capps. After killing a gunman, McCord is offered the job of sheriff in a town where three lawmen have been shot down within the past year.

17.37 *Nice Day for a Hanging.* Feb. 6, 1966. GS: James Anderson, Whitney Blake, Beau Bridges, Tiny Baskin, Rusty Lane, Dick Miller. In a town to witness the execution of a man who once saved his life, McCord meets the doomed man's son, who swears to take revenge on the townspeople.

17.38 *Barbed Wire.* Feb. 13, 1966. GS: Rod Cameron, Sherry Jackson, Leif Erickson, Lane Bradford. Cattleman Roy Beckwith hires McCord to fence his land, a move which marks the end of the open range and the beginning of the long war between cattlemen and farmers.

17.39 *Yellow for Courage.* Feb. 20, 1966. Patricia Medina, Michael Forest, Harry Harvey, Sr., Stuart Lancaster. McCord, stricken by diphtheria, risks his life to test a serum developed by a foreign lady doctor who is also an outcast.

17.40 *Call to Glory* **Part One.** Feb. 27, 1966. GS: David Brian, Robert Lansing, Michael Pate, Lee Van Cleef, Kathie Browne, H.M. Wynant, Felix Locher, William Bryant, John Pickard, Jacquelyn Hyde. President Grant asks McCord to find out why General Custer has attacked the Grant Administration over recent Indian outbreaks.

17.41 *Call to Glory* **Part Two.** March 6, 1966. GS: David Brian, Robert Lansing, Michael Pate, Lee Van Cleef, Kathie Browne, H.M. Wynant, Felix Locher, William Bryant, John Pickard, Jacquelyn Hyde. Soon after McCord prevents a clash between the soldiers and Indians, Chief Crazy Horse appears at a party for General Sheridan to plead for peace and fair treatment.

17.42 *Call to Glory* **Part Three.** March 13, 1966. GS: David Brian, Robert Lansing, Michael Pate, Lee Van Cleef, Kathie Browne, H.M. Wynant, Felix Locher, William Bryant, John Pickard, Jacquelyn Hyde. Chief Sitting Bull assures McCord that his braves did not kill the Indian agent — information that McCord must get back to General Custer to avert a full-scale battle.

17.43 *The Ghost of Murrieta.* March 20, 1966. GS: Dolores Del Rio, Jose De Vega, Rafael Campos, Linda Dangcil, Ben Welden, Robert Tafur. Los Angeles teenager Juan Molinera hopes to emulate the infamous bandit Murrieta by stealing the $50,000 in gold entrusted to McCord.

17.44 *The Assassins* **Part One.** March 27, 1966. GS: Peter Graves, Kamala Devi, William Bryant, Jim Davis, Carlos Rivas, Margarita Cordova, John Carradine. President Grant asks McCord to undertake a dirty job. He is assigned to infiltrate a group of men rumored to be plotting against Grant's life.

17.45 *The Assassins* **Part Two.** April 3, 1966. GS: Peter Graves, Kamala Devi, William Bryant, Jim Davis, Carlos Rivas, Margarita Cordova, John Carradine. McCord learns that the dagger with which he and President Grant were attacked came from the knife collection of Senator Ashley.

17.46 *Headed for Doomsday.* April 10, 1966. GS: Burgess Meredith, Robert Q. Lewis, Carol Ohmart, Bruno Ve Sota, Russ McCubbin, Leo V. Metrango. After saving famed newspaperman Horace Greeley from an assassin, McCord accepts a job as Greeley's armed social secretary.

17.47 *Cowards Die Many Times.* April 17, 1966. GS: Lola Albright, John Ireland, Bill Catching, Luke Saucier, William Benedict. Freight-line owner Tad Evers vows that he'll stop McCord from completing a survey for a railroad that would put him out of business.

17.48 *Kellie.* April 24, 1966. GS: Suzanne Cupito/Morgan Brittany, Lola Albright, John Carradine, Richard Webb, Billy Beck. Kellie, the spirited 11-year-old daughter of a bank robber, vows to get even with McCord for killing her father.

18. *Brave Eagle*

CBS. 30 min. Broadcast history: Wednesday, 7:30-8:00, Sept. 1955–June 1956.

Regular Cast: Keith Larsen (Brave Eagle), Kim Winona (Morning Star), Keena Nomkeena (Keena), Bert Wheeler (Smokey Joe).

Premise: This series dealt with the exploits of Brave Eagle, the young chief of the peaceful Cheyenne Indians, and his dealings with other Indian tribes and the encroachment of the white man.

The Episodes

18.1 *Blood Brother.* Sept. 28, 1955. Keena saves the life of a young Cree brave, and, according to Indian custom, the two youths become blood brothers.

18.2 *Cry of the Heron.* Oct. 5, 1955. An innocent jest almost causes war between the Cheyennes and the Blackfoot tribe.

18.3 *The Treachery of At-tat-tu.* Oct. 12, 1955. Against his chief's wishes, one of the Cheyenne braves kidnaps a white boy.

18.4 *Gold of Haunted Mountain.* Oct. 19, 1955. In their greed to find hidden gold, two white men bring violence and death to the historic and sacred grounds of the Cheyennes.

18.5 *Search for the Sun.* Oct. 26, 1955. Keena, young foster son of Brave Eagle, learns a renegade Indian tribe is acquiring guns in return for stolen gold.

18.6 *Moon Fire.* Nov. 2, 1955. Brave Eagle faces war against the white man.

18.7 *Mask of the Manitou.* Nov. 9, 1955. Young Keena makes a personal sacrifice in order to help a destitute Indian tribe in need of food.

18.8 *The Flight.* Nov. 16, 1955. War between the Cheyenne and the U.S. Cavalry appears unavoidable because of a stubborn and vindictive white man.

18.9 *Code of a Chief.* Nov. 23, 1955. Brave Eagle is taken into custody for the kidnaping of a young prospector. In order to clear himself of the charges, Brave Eagle must escape.

18.10 *Face of Fear.* Nov. 30, 1955. An unscrupulous trapper tries to use an ancient Indian superstition to increase his profits.

18.11 *Voice of the Serpent.* Dec. 7, 1955. At the pleading of an elderly squaw, Brave Eagle sets out to find her long-lost son. His search leads him into battle against a belligerent Cree chief.

18.12 *Shield of Honor.* Dec. 14, 1955. Brave Eagle finds he must win a deadly spear battle on horseback to uphold the honor of his tribe and to keep the trust of his son when Chief Great Bear tries to get the Cheyennes to join the Pawnees in the war against the Crows. As a part of his strategy to convince Brave Eagle that such a course is wise, Great Bear raids the tribe's herd.

18.13 *The Challenge.* Dec. 21, 1955. GS: Rick Vallin. In a duel to the death, Black Raven challenges Brave Eagle's right to rule the Cheyenne tribe.

18.14 *Medicine Drums.* Dec. 28, 1955. White outlaws masquerade as Indians and steal an Army payroll. Brave Eagle and Keena set out to find the guilty culprits in order to sop the impending war.

18.15 *The Spirit of Hidden Valley.* Jan. 4, 1956. GS: Cliff Darnell, Wally West. Smokey and his lovely daughter, Morning Star, are captured by Apaches and forced to lead them to the Cheyenne's hidden valley. Brave Eagle is sure Smokey had no choice in the matter, but Keena is not so sure, and cannond understand why his father wants to help an obvious traitor.

18.16 *Papoose.* Jan. 11, 1956. Brave Eagle, out to track down a couple of outlaws, meets Calvin Burns and his wife on a wagon trail. Frightened, and not understanding Brave Eagle's friendly gestures, they fire on him. The Burns horses panic and run away, leaving the couple stranded with the wagon. Then the outlaws arrive in search of booty. Brave Eagle is accused of kidnaping a child.

18.17 *The Storm Fool.* Jan. 18, 1956. GS: Benny Rubin. An Indian chief, eager for war with the white man, uses an alleged horse-theft to bring about a battle.

18.18 *The Gentle Warrior.* Jan. 25, 1956. GS: Edmund Hashim, Richard Avonde. A Comanche warrior, made chief after the death of his father, finds he must fight renegade forces that are seeking to take over the leadership of his tribe. He seeks refuge with Brave Eagle.

18.19 *The Strange Animal.* Feb. 1, 1956. When Brave Eagle is led into a trap by hostile Comanches, he is helped, unexpectedly, by an elephant brought into the territory to clear an area for an Army fort.

18.20 *White Medicine Man.* Feb. 8, 1956. Medical supplies, needed to halt an epidemic of smallpox, are stolen by an itinerant horse trader. Brave Eagle tries desperately to recover the medicine.

18.21 *Death Trap.* Feb. 15, 1956. A man disguised as an Indian conduct vicious attacks against traveling wagon trains.

18.22 *War Paint.* Feb. 22, 1956. Keena disobeys orders and follows his tribe on the warpath against renegade Indians who attacked a frontier settlement.

18.23 *Valley of Decision.* Feb. 29, 1956. A stubborn white settler refuses to let Brave Eagle's tribe pass through his property to harvest the corn they have planted.

18.24 *Witch Bear.* March 7, 1956. The tribe of Brave Eagle is terror-stricken by an unseen animal believed to be an evil spirit. Brave Eagle sets out to prove that it is a real animal.

18.25 *Trouble at Medicine Creek.* March 14, 1956. The efforts of two traitorous tribesmen to gain leadership leads to trouble.

18.26 *Ambush at Arrow Pass.* March 21, 1956. When a Cheyenne brave is spurned by a maiden, he kidnaps her and takes refuge with a Comanche tribe.

19. *Bret Maverick*

NBC. 60 min. Broadcast history: Tuesday, 9:00-10:00, Dec. 1981–March 1982; Tuesday, 8:00-9:00, March 1982–July 1982; Tuesday, 9:00-10:00, July 1982–Aug. 1982.

Regular Cast: James Garner (Bret Maverick), Darleen Carr (Mary Lou Sprigner), Ed Bruce (Sheriff Tom Guthrie), Stuart Margolin (Philo Sandine), Ramon Bieri (Elijah Crow), Tony Bush (Sturgess), John Shearin (Mitchell Dowd), Richard Hamilton (Cy Whitaker), David Knell (Rodney), Luis Delgado (Shifty).

Premise: Brett Maverick arrives in Sweetwater, Arizona, where he wins the Lazy Ace Ranch and the Red Ox saloon in a poker game. He decides to settle down as a gentleman rancher and saloon owner.

The Episodes

19.1 *The Lazy Ace.* Dec. 1. 1981. GS: Bill McKinney, Janis Paige, John McLiam, Billy Kerr. Bret wins $100,000 at poker and decides it is time to cash it in and settle down—until one of the losers robs the bank.

19.2 *Welcome to Sweetwater.* Dec. 8, 1981. GS: John Randolph, Russ Marin, Roger Torre, Priscilla Morrill. Bret suspects that a proposed railroad through Sweetwater is a scam, and schemes to save the overeager citizenry from embarrassment—and make a few dollars for himself.

19.3 *Anything for a Friend.* Dec. 15, 1981. GS: Lawrence Dobkin, Glenn Withrow, Charles Hallahan. Bret has problems on his ranch. He is missing parts for his prefabricated barn and he is harboring Billy the Kid in his root cellar.

19.4 *The Yellow Rose.* Dec. 22, 1981. GS: Marj Dusay, Keye Luke, Linda Lei, Marcia Rodd, Anthony Eisley, Priscilla Morrill. Woman's suffrage catches fire in Sweetwater and no one feels the heat more than Maverick, who has just won a Chinese girl in a poker game.

19.5 *Horse of Yet Another Color.* Jan. 5, 1982. GS: Simon Oakland, William Hootkins, Holly Palance, Allan Arbus. Bret wins a horse that turns out to be stolen, and is somehow connected to an Indian peace treaty.

19.6 *Dateline: Sweetwater.* Jan. 12, 1982. GS: Ed Nelson, Richard O'Brien, Joshua Bryant, Roy Jenson, Priscilla Morrill, Byron Morrow, Brady Rubin. Sweetwater's institutions, including the newspaper and the bank, are subjected to a ruthless takeover scheme on behalf of Eastern financial interests.

19.7 *The Mayflower Women's Historical Society.* Feb. 2, 1982. GS: Jenny O'Hara, David Young, Neva Patterson. To escape the hangman's noose, Bret Maverick must agree to sell his life story to an ambitious historian.

19.8 *Hallie.* Feb. 9, 1982. GS: Dixie Carter, Geoffrey Lewis, William Sanderson. An old flame of Bret's shows up in Sweetwater, pursued by two homicidal brothers she swindled.

19.9 *The Ballad of Bret Maverick.* Feb. 16, 1982. GS: James Whitmore, Jr., Sandy McPeak, Cliff Emmich, Howard Caine, Priscilla Morrill. A balladeer is writing a song about Bret, but it can't be completed until after Maverick's death.

19.10 *A Night at the Red Ox.* Feb. 23, 1982. GS: Savannah Smith, Paul Koslo, Murray Hamilton. Tom is accused of a 20-year-old murder and sentenced to death by a kangaroo court.

19.11 *The Not So Magnificent Six.* March 2, 1982. GS: Joseph Sirola, Ross Hagen, Kelly Ward, Art La Fleur, Jesse Vint. An Eastern writer proposes that six gunmen challenge Maverick. Whoever kills the gambler will have his life story immortalized in print.

19.12 *The Vulture Also Rises.* March 16, 1982. GS: Monte Markham, Peggy Walton-Walker, John Anderson, Maggie Malooly, Tomas Rosales. An apparent Apache attack on a stagecoach incites the town to call in the cavalry, but Phil suspects white men of the deed.

19.13 *The Eight Swords of Cyrus and Other Illusions of Grandeur.* March 12, 1982. GS: Cliff Potts, Sarah Rush, Sid Haig, W.T. Zacha. A crooked magician wants Maverick to disappear so he can work the Red Ox without Bret watching him.

19.14 *Faith, Hope and Clarity* Part One. April 13, 1982. GS: Robert Webber, James Staley, Richard Libertini, Marj Dusay, Simone Griffeth, Jameson Parker, Tony Burton. Bret sets up a sting to regain land taken from locals by an unscrupulous religious-cult leader.

19.15 *Faith, Hope and Clarity* Part Two. April 20, 1982. GS: Robert Webber, James Staley, Richard Libertini, Marj Dusay, Simone Griffeth, Jameson Parker, Tony Burton. Maverick's sting of a religious cult continues on schedule—unless Sandeen's "divine guidance" derails it.

19.16 *The Rattlesnake Brigade.* April 27, 1982. GS: Stanley Wells, Arlen Dean Snyder, J. Edward McKinley, Herb Armstrong. Maverick and Tom are suckered into protecting a gold shipment from a ruthless band of marauders.

19.17 *The Hidalgo Thing.* May 4, 1982. GS: Jack Kelly, Hector Elizondo, Dub Taylor, Marj Dusay, John Dennis Johnston. Bret tries to keep his $2 million scam from damaging Guthrie's campaign for sheriff.

20. Broken Arrow

ABC. 30 min. Broadcast history: Tuesday, 9:00-9:30, Sept. 1956–Sept. 1958.

Regular Cast: John Lupton (Tom Jeffords), Michael Ansara (Cochise).

Premise: This Western series was set in Tucson, Arizona, in the 1870s. It recounted the adventures of Indian Agent Tom Jeffords and Cochise, Chief of the Apaches.

The Episodes

20.1 *The Mail Riders.* Sept. 25, 1956. GS: Donald Randolph, Michael Pate, Tom Fadden, Ted de Corsia, Judith Ames. Tom Jeffords is faced with the problem of getting the mail through despite persistent attacks by the Apaches. He decides that the only practical move is to go directly to Cochise and plead for at least a temporary peace. In the face of disapproval from the white settlers in the area and possible death from the Apaches, Jeffords goes through with his plan.

20.2 *Battle at Apache Pass.* Oct. 2, 1956. GS: Michael Pate, Ross Elliott, Tom Fadden, Robert Warwick, Ted de Corsia. Angered because they think he has released information to Cochise, a group of settlers sets out to lynch mail carrier Tom Jeffords. Gen. Howard arrives just in time to turn back the mob.

20.3 *Indian Agent.* Oct. 9, 1956. GS: Michael Pate, Sue England, Tom Fadden. Geronimo leads an Indian attack on a stagecoach, and Tom Jeffords seeks help from Cochise in fighting off the renegade Indian band.

20.4 *The Captive.* Oct. 23, 1956. GS: Tom Fadden, Ray

Broken Arrow

Stricklyn, Trevor Bardette, Kathryn Card, Richard Wessel. Two whites kidnap a white boy who has been raised as an Apache. Cochise and his braves prepare to go on the warpath to get the boy back.

20.5 *Passage Deferred.* Oct. 30, 1956. GS: Chris Alcaide, Sean McClory, Henry Brandon, Pepe Hern. A poor Irishman is caught by Cochise mining gold in Apache territory. He is trespassing on forbidden territory and only the intervention of Tom Jeffords saves him from death. He is set free after he swears never to reveal the source of his gold.

20.6 *Medicine Man.* Nov. 13, 1956. When an Apache brave collapses at an Army post, the Army doctor diagnoses his ailment as smallpox. Investigation reveals that a major epidemic has broken out among the Apache tribesmen and the doctor is assigned to treat the stricken Indians. But the Apaches do not trust the white man's medicine and rely instead on Nochalo, their medicine man.

20.7 *Hermano.* Nov. 20, 1956. GS: Nick Venetoulis, Ray Teal, Kem Dibbs, Steve Conte. A young Indian is torn between loyalty to his brother, a member of Geronimo's band of renegade Indians, and his personal loyalty to the U.S. Army. He has to prove his worth to the whites by giving them information about Geronimo's activities.

20.8 *Justice* (A.K.A. "Caged"). Nov. 27, 1956. GS: Eugene Iglesias, Addison Richards, Robert Armstrong. An Indian friend of Tom Jeffords goes to San Francisco, believing he is to represent the Apaches at an Indian congress. It turns out to be a complete fraud, and the Indian is really being advertised as the star of a circus side show.

20.9 *Return from the Shadows.* Dec. 4, 1956. GS: Robert Cornthwaite, Marjorie Owens, Harry Harvey, Jr., Christopher Dark. An Army lieutenant who several years before lured five Indians into a trap by using a flag of truce, returns to admit his guilt. He has to face the only one who escaped the massacre.

20.10 *Cry Wolf.* Dec. 11, 1956. GS: Ricky Vera, Helen Wallace. The imaginative son of the town derelict reports that he witnessed a murder and saw two strange animals. One looked like a dinosaur, the other was a camel.

20.11 *The Conspirators.* Dec. 18, 1956. GS: Edgar Barrier, Angie Dickinson, Florenz Ames, Booth Coleman. Tom Jeffords makes a trip to San Francisco to find out what happened to an Apache clothing order supposedly sent by the government a month before.

20.12 *The Raiders.* Dec. 25, 1956. GS: Leo Gordon, William Phipps, Jean Howell. A general store owner, aided by three other men, campaigns to start war between the white settlers and the Apaches. The man wants the Army to send in troops to quell the war, so he will get the soldiers' trade.

20.13 *Apache Massacre.* Jan. 1, 1957. GS: Hal Smith, Peter Mamakos. After the renegade Geronimo makes two surprise attacks on white settlers, a white man leads a revengeful attack on an Indian village.

20.14 *The Rescue.* Jan. 8, 1957. GS: Kathy Nolan, Eddy Waller. Tom Jeffords rides from Fort Apache to Tucson to deliver a military dispatch to the Mexican Army forces. The information will aid them in their plan to trap the renegade Geronimo, if he gets there safely.

20.15 *Apache Dowry.* Jan. 15, 1957. GS: Howard Petrie, Maurice Jara, Strother Martin, Lisa Montell, Paul Birch. One of Cochise's Braves steals two horses from a rancher. Trouble develops between Tom Jeffords and Cochise, because both demand the right to punish the Brave.

20.16 *The Trial.* Jan. 22, 1957. GS: Damian O'Flynn, Don Beddoe, Arthur Space, Phil Van Zandt, Hal K. Dawson, Tamar Cooper. A young woman is shot while working in her father's store. The irate citizens, believing a young Indian brave is responsible, set up a posse to bring him to justice.

20.17 *The Missionaries.* Jan. 29, 1957. GS: Joan Camden, Chet Stratton, Don Beddoe, Manuel Rojas, Julian Rivero, Michael Granger, Jim Nusser. Jason Caldwell and his sister Amanda, both of whom are missionaries working in Indian territory, ask Tom Jeffords to help them obtain an Indian youngster. They want to educate and civilize a boy.

20.18 *The Challenge.* Feb. 5, 1957. GS: Anthony Caruso, Christopher Dark, Pat Hogan. One of the renegade Geronimo's allies asks Cochise to meet with him for a peace council. Against Tom Jeffords' advice, Cochise agrees to the meeting.

20.19 *Doctor.* Feb. 1, 1957. GS: Victor Millan, Robert Foulk, Gil Rankin, David Saber, Robert Cabal, Billy Milhil. Two youngsters, one an Indian, are injured seriously in an accident. The only doctor available is an Indian, and neither of the boy's fathers is willing to let him treat his son.

20.20 *Powder Keg.* Feb. 19, 1957. GS: Roland Winters, Lurene Tuttle, Bernie Gozier. A congressman visiting in Indian territory is shot and critically injured. Many years before, while in the Army, the man had ambushed an Apache tribal meeting. Therefore local authorities feel the Apaches may have chosen this method of getting even.

20.21 *Legacy of a Hero.* Feb. 26, 1957. GS: Ray Stricklyn, Ann Doran, Mort Mills, Joseph Turkel. A jury releases two men suspected of murder, but Tom Jeffords orders them out of the territory to forestall any further trouble. They decide to get revenge on Jeffords.

20.22 *Rebellion.* March 5, 1957. GS: John Beradino, Sally Fraser, Robert Burton. An Apache band, suffering from a malaria epidemic, becomes hostile to the settlers in the territory.

20.23 *Ghost Face.* March 12, 1957. GS: Robert F. Simon, Steven Ritch, Ken Christy, Steve Conte, Claire Du Brey. During the long winter, Cochise's Apache tribe is slowly starving. They ask help from Gen. Everitt, but it is refused.

20.24 *Johnny Flagstaff.* March 19, 1957. GS: James Craig. Indian agent Tom Jeffords is concerned when he learns that the superintendent of Indian affairs wants to move the Apaches to another area. He brings the superintendent, Flagstaff, to meet with Cochise, the Apache chief.

20.25 *The Desperado.* March 26, 1957. GS: Paul Richards, Francis McDonald. Bret Younger saves the life of Cochise when the Indian chief is threatened by a mountain lion. When Bret is wanted for homicide, Cochise feels honor-bound to protect him. Tom Jeffords is sent to bring Younger back to justice.

20.26 *Fathers and Sons.* April 2, 1957. GS: Willis Bouchey, Nico Minardos. A former Army general seeks to have the Chiricahua Apaches moved from their reservation to open up the land for white settlers. Nachise, son of Cochise, decides to take matters into his own hands, and kidnaps Indian agent Tom Jeffords and the ex-general.

20.27 *Quarantine.* April 9, 1957. GS: Eugene Martin,

Clancy Cooper, Robert Brubaker. Indian agent Tom Jeffords and Apache chief Cochise learn that a boy is driving a herd of infected cattle toward the Mexican border. They set out to track down the youngster before all the animals become infected.

20.28 *Ordeal.* April 16, 1957. GS: John Larch. Apache chief Cochise and Tom Jeffords set out to track down a killer. But during the pursuit Cochise is wounded, and when Tom captures the outlaw, both Tom's horse and Cochise's are killed. The three begin a torturous trek through the scorching desert.

20.29 *The Assassin.* April 23, 1957. GS: Charles Fredericks, Russ Bender, Tyler McVey. Indian agent Tom Jeffords hears of a plot to assassinate Cochise. There are only two strangers in town and he must determine which is the hired killer.

20.30 *The Archaeologist.* April 30, 1957. GS: Arthur Hanson, Anthony Eustrel, Richard Hale, Alex Montoya. Indian agent Tom Jeffords guides two archaeologists to the Apache reservation to record primitive Indian customs for their museum. But when the two archaeologists start probing into things the Indians regard as sacred, the Apaches take up arms against them.

20.31 *Apache Girl.* May 7, 1957. GS: Donna Martell, Miguel Landa, Jan Merlin. A beautiful Indian girl leaves the boy she loves and her home on the reservation to study in Tucson. She is convinced that education will enable her to be treated as a woman of intelligence. But in Tucson she meets a roughneck who begins to force his attentions upon her.

20.32 *The Broken Wire.* May 14, 1957. GS: Buzz Henry, George J. Lewis. Indian agent Tom Jeffords persuades Kotoy, chief of the Apaches, to permit the Army to string wire for the Western Union across his land. But when the crew boss's brother starts a fire that results in the death of a man, he blames the fire on the chief's son, Rano.

20.33 *Attack on Fort Grant.* May 21, 1957. GS: Hayden Rorke, Mae Clarke, Charles Horvath. Cochise learns Geronimo's plans to attack Fort Grant with a company of renegades. Cochise and Tom Jeffords go to the fort to warn the colonel in charge.

Season Two

20.34 *White Man's Magic.* Oct. 1, 1957. The renegade Indian Geronimo is wounded in a raid on a stagecoach and takes an Army doctor's fiancee as hostage. He sends word that in return for medical help, he will release the girl.

20.35 *Conquistador.* Oct. 8, 1957. GS: Trevor Bardette, Peter Mamakos, Sue England. Cochise receives permission from Don Mateo, a Spaniard, to graze his thirsty cattle near the water holes on Mateo's ranch. But a scheming Indian chief hoping to foment war between the Spanish settlers and the Apaches, sets a trap for Cochise.

20.36 *Apache Child.* Oct. 15, 1957. GS: Paul Picerni, Dan Casabian, Jill Jarmyn, Ken Christy. Tom Jeffords rescues the abandoned child of an exiled Chiricahua Apache Indian. To recover his offspring, the Indian kidnaps Jeffords.

20.37 *Ghost Sickness.* Oct. 22, 1957. GS: Armand Asamora. A young Apache boy sets out to clear the reputation of his dead father, who is regarded as a traitor. He feigns sickness in an attempt to expose the real traitor.

20.38 *Black Moment.* Oct. 29, 1957. Sp: William Phipps, Mort Mills, Steven Ritch, Frances McDonald, Peter Coe. An old miner is found dead and robbed of his most precious possession, a locket. Tom Jeffords and Cochise are accused of the crime.

20.39 *The Arsenal.* Nov. 5, 1957. GS: Harry Harvey, Jr., Howard Negley, John Holland. When the Apaches are accused of stealing guns and ammunition, Tom Jeffords and Cochise set out to find the outlaws actually responsible for the thefts.

20.40 *Devil's Eye.* Nov. 12, 1957. GS: Carl Millitaire, Louis Lettieri, Frank Cady. A photographer who has accompanied Indian agent Tom Jeffords to a reservation, is blamed for the death of a missing Indian boy because of his camera, which the Indians think is the devil's eye.

20.41 *The Teacher.* Nov. 19, 1957. GS: Phyllis Avery, Alan Roberts, Louis Lettieri, Hank Patterson, Charles Stevens. The government sends a young woman from the East to instruct the Chiricahua children, who live in the land of the Apaches. The teacher learns an object lesson herself before realizing the true needs of the children.

20.42 *The Bounty Hunters.* Nov. 26, 1957. GS: Ray Teal, Henry Rowland, Steven Ritch, Al Ferrara, Steven Darrell. Cochise and Tom Jeffords travel to Mexico to find white men who kill Apaches for their scalps.

20.43 *Renegades Return.* Dec. 3, 1957. GS: Jan Arvan, Manuel Rojas, Paul Langton, Greg Roman, Frank Nechero. Renegade Indians steal horses from the Chiricahua reservation, taking advantage of the fact that the Chiricahuas can't cross the boundary of the reservation. The Apache warriors revolt and pursue the horse thieves.

20.44 *Smoke Signal.* Dec. 10, 1957. GS: Gordon Jones, William Leicester, Tom London, Frank Wilcox, Merry Anders. Following the Civil War, a company of Confederate soldiers for whom the war never ended, steals cattle from the Apaches. Cochise is incited to the point of war.

20.45 *Son of Cochise.* Dec. 17, 1957. GS: Frank Wilcox, Robert Knapp, Jimmy Ogg. Cochise blows up an Army munitions wagon and refuses to explain why he did it. Tom Jeffords tries to find out the truth.

20.46 *White Savage.* Dec. 24, 1957. GS: Steven Ritch, Ralph Moody, Fred Graham, Paul Picerni, Gregg Palmer. An Indian-hating cavalry officer, pursued by hostile Apaches, is thrown from his horse and loses his memory. Found wandering by Cochise, the officer is regarded as a holy man and taken to the Chiricahua place of worship.

20.47 *Indian Medicine.* Dec. 31, 1957. GS: K.L. Smith, Harry Woods. A close friend of Tom Jeffords and Cochise is wasting away with a strange fever. They decide to administer an Indian medicine that Cochise is sure will cure their friend. When the man lapses into unconsciousness, Jeffords and Cochise are thrown into prison.

20.48 *Water Witch.* Jan. 7, 1958. GS: Emile Meyer, Phil Tead, Reed Howes, Jack Lomas, Steven Ritch, Jean Howell, Fred Graham. A drought plagues Arizona, and water has become a problem for Indians and ranchers alike. War threatens when a group of ranchers dynamite an Indian stream and divert the water for their thirsty cattle.

20.49 *Kingdom of Terror.* Jan. 14, 1958. GS: Lane Bradford, Eugenia Paul, Wilton Graff. Cochise and Indian Agent Tom Jeffords set out to rescue a young Apache who is being held prisoner on a tract of land in Arizona. The land, part of an old Spanish land grant, is the haven of outlaws and bandits.

20.50 *Bad Boy.* Jan. 21, 1959. GS: Peter Votrian, Denver Pyle, Isabel Winters, Russ Bender, Jason Robards, Sr. A young man, embarking on a life of crime, is taken to the Chiricahua reservation by Indian agent Tom Jeffords. There he is left to the care of Cochise in an attempt to effect a reformation.

20.51 *Massacre.* Jan. 28, 1958. GS: Paul Langton, Larry J. Blake, Frances McDonald. A small band of Apaches seeks protection at a fort and are shot down by soldiers. The chief and several of his followers manage to escape, and they begin a series of raids on the fort in retaliation for the massacre.

20.52 *Shadow of Cochise.* Feb. 4, 1958. GS: Strother Martin, Joseph Perry, Terry Frost. Tom Jeffords is kidnaped by a gang of outlaws who intend to kill him. Cochise rides out with a group of Apaches to rescue his blood brother.

20.53 *Warrant for Arrest.* Feb. 11, 1958. GS: Robert Einer, Booth Colman, Arthur Space. A U.S. marshal arrives in Tucson with a warrant for Tom Jeffords' arrest. Jeffords is charged with stealing Indian supplies.

20.54 *Escape.* Feb. 18, 1958. GS: Victor Millan, Pepe Hern, Steven Darrell, Tony Russo, Michael Kopcha. Cochise's eldest son is competing with another youth to decide which will be the chief of a tribal village. Cochise and Jeffords learn about a plot against the boy's life.

20.55 *Aztec Treasure.* Feb. 25, 1958. Sp.: Alex Stagg, Steven Ritch, Franco Corsaro, Jack Hogan. A Mexican commission comes to recover an ancient image of an Aztec god, taken many years before by Cochise and his Apaches during a raid into Mexico.

20.56 *Hired Killer.* March 4, 1958. GS: Renny McEvoy, George Cisar, Chris Alcaide, James Flavin. A group of businessmen in a small Arizona town believe that an uprising will bring in the military and also an upsurge in business. To provoke an uprising they decide to engage a professional gunman to kill the Apache chief Cochise.

20.57 *Panic.* March 11, 1958. An Apache, suspected of being a carrier of bubonic plague, is driven away by his people and flees to Tucson. The inhabitants of Tucson panic at the thought of the plague, and riots and violence break out.

20.58 *The Duel.* March 18, 1958. GS: John Wilder, Toni Gerry, Charles Fredericks, Charles Brill, X Brands. An Apache youth and a young settler both love an Apache girl. They decide on a battle to the death to determine who will marry the girl. Tom Jeffords tries to settle the feud between the two young men and avert bloodshed.

20.59 *Iron Maiden.* March 25, 1958. GS: Marya Stevens, Paul Dubov, George Sawaya, Lane Bradford. An Indian girl from the Oregon Territory arrives at the Chiricahua Reservation in Arizona. After her arrival trouble breaks out on the reservation.

20.60 *The Sisters.* April 1, 1958. Two nuns seek to restore a religious statue to an old mission on Chiricahua land. They endanger their lives and the life of Apache Chief Cochise.

20.61 *War Trail.* April 8, 1958. GS: John Archer, John Doucette, Don Kelly, Richard Collier. An Army officer who has embezzled government funds, decides to start an Indian war to avert discovery. He kidnaps and imprisons the Apache chief, Cochise.

20.62 *Turncoat.* April 15, 1958. GS: Laurie Carroll, John Beradino, H.M. Wynant, David Renard. Cochise exiles an Apache who deserted his tribe during a battle. Later, the Indian tries to return to his people.

20.63 *Power.* April 22, 1958. GS: Carlos Romero, James Drury, De Prentiss, Larry Perron. The Apache chief, Cochise, is wounded in battle and appoints a sub-chief to rule the Chiracahuas. The new leader, intoxicated with power, tries to lead the Apaches back to war.

20.64 *Bear Trap.* April 29, 1958. GS: Ralph Moody, Steven Ritch, House Peters, Jr., Robert Warwick, Robert Blake. An Apache youth loses his arm in a fight with a killer bear. He risks his life again when the bear attacks Cochise and Indian agent Tom Jeffords.

20.65 *Old Enemy.* May 6, 1958. GS: Marya Stevens, Paul Dubov, George Sawaya, Lane Bradford. A prospector who had been turned off the Indian reservation by Chief Cochise, returns. He is anxious to mine the gold he has discovered there.

20.66 *Blood Brothers.* May 13, 1958. GS: Hugh Sanders, Tom Fadden, Lee Roberts, Harry Carey, Jr., Robert Karnes. An Army general plans to occupy the Chiricahua Reservation, in violation of a treaty negotiated with Apache Chief Cochise. Cochise tells Indian agent Tom Jeffords that the move will cause full-scale war.

20.67 *The Courage of Ling Tang.* May 20, 1958. GS: Victor Sen Yung. Cochise rescues a Chinese cook who has been attacked by a band of renegades. The cook vows that he will one day repay the favor.

20.68 *Backlash.* May 27, 1958. GS: John Cliff, Ric Roman, Steve Conte, George Ross. The Pinal Apaches are on the warpath and Indian Agent Tom Jeffords travels to talk to their leader in an effort to avert war between the whites and the Indians. En route he is taken prisoner by the tribe.

20.69 *Manhunt.* June 3, 1958. GS: Bill Henry, James Philbrook, Valentin de Vargas. An Apache youth who believes he has committed a murder flees from the law. Indian Agent Tom Jeffords and Cochise try to find the young man.

20.70 *The Outlaw.* June 10, 1958. GS: Michael Hinn, George Milton, Hal J. Smith, Morgan Woodward, Stanley Clements. An outlaw sells whiskey to the Apaches which causes several deaths among the braves. Cochise begins a search for the outlaw.

20.71 *Jeopardy.* June 17, 1958. An Indian youth is killed and Indian Agent Tom Jeffords is accused of the killing. Jeffords risks his life to find the real killer and to clear his name with the Apaches.

20.72 *Transfer.* June 24, 1958. GS: Regis Toomey, Joel Smith, Tex Foster, Michael Galloway, Steven Ritch. Tom Jeffords goes to Colorado to help quell an Indian uprising. A new agent is sent to substitute for him in Arizona, and through his inhumane treatment of the Indian there, provokes an Apache uprising.

21. Bronco

ABC. 60 min. Broadcast history: Tuesday, 7:30-8:30, Sept. 1958–Sept. 1960; Monday, 7:30-8:30, Oct. 1960–Aug. 1962.

Regular Cast: Ty Hardin (Bronco Layne).

Premise: The Western series concerned the adventures of

Bronco Layne, a former Confederate army captain, in Texas during the 1860s.

Notes: *Bronco* alternated with *Sugarfoot* during its first season and aired with *Cheyenne* during its second season. It alternated with *Sugarfoot* and *Cheyenne* during its third season and alternated with *Cheyenne* during its final season.

The Episodes

21.1 *The Besieged.* Sept. 23, 1958. GS: Claude Akins, Sue Randall, Jack Elam, Allen Case, Robert Warwick, Terry Rangno. The Cabot family are members of a religious sect that refuses to use violence. While en route to their home in California they are attacked by gunmen who have learned there is gold on the Cabot property. Bronco Layne tries to save the family from certain death.

21.2 *Quest of the Thirty Dead.* Oct. 7, 1958. GS: Beverly Tyler, Ray Danton, Jay Novello, Tol Avery. A tragic train wreck takes the lives of 30 passengers, one of whom is a young man who was on his way to be married. On a tip from the man's grief-stricken fiancee, Bronco Layne sets out to learn who was responsible for the tragedy.

21.3 *The Turning Point.* Oct. 21, 1958. GS: Scott Marlowe, R.G. Armstrong, Walter Coy. After Bronco Layne saves a notorious gunfighter from death by snake bite, the gunfighter swears he will go straight. But two of his outlaw cousins persist in pinning their crimes on him.

21.4 *Four Guns and a Prayer.* Nov. 4, 1958. GS: Douglas Kennedy, Walter Barnes, Pamela Lincoln, John Hubbard, Gary Vinson. Bronco Layne is appointed marshal of a Texas town and tries to clear the town of the killers who control it. He hires several outside deputies in his efforts to get rid of the killers and then learns that the deputies are notorious gunslingers.

21.5 *The Long Ride Back.* Nov. 18, 1958. GS: Mort Mills, Kathleen Crowley, Gerald Mohr, Paul Fix, Charles Fredericks. Bronco Layne, an ex-Confederate captain, returns to his home town and learns that the residents blame him for the death of his sweetheart's brother while Layne and the brother were held as Union prisoners. The man who accuses Layne of the crime is a man who served with them.

21.6 *Trail to Taos.* Dec. 2, 1958. GS: Joanne Gilbert, Ed Kemmer, Frank Ferguson, Ron Hayes. The Post Office department hires Bronco Layne to track down a gang that has been stealing the U.S. mail from stagecoaches.

21.7 *Brand of Courage.* Dec. 16, 1958. GS: Anna-Lisa, Cheerio Meredith. A group of nuns fight desperately to keep their convent from falling into the hands of unscrupulous cattlemen. Bronco, who has been befriended by the nuns after suffering gunshot wounds, takes up their cause.

21.8 *Freeze-Out.* Dec. 30, 1958. GS: Grace Raynor, James Drury, Douglas Dick. Bronco is hired by a beautiful girl to guide her to a ghost town in the mountains. Her pretext for making the trip is that she is writing a book. But after an attempt is made on the lives of both, Bronco is convinced that the girl is concealing her real purpose.

21.9 *The Baron of Broken Lance.* Jan. 13, 1959. GS: William Reynolds, Shirley Knight, King Calder, Myron Healey, K.L. Smith, Betty Lynn. A young lady, the daughter of a cattle baron, runs away from home. With the help of Bronco Layne's friend Pete Loomis, she joins the wagon train that Bronco is leading through Wyoming. Layne has his hands full, however, when the girl's father and his henchmen attempt to kill Loomis.

21.10 *Payroll of the Dead.* Jan. 27, 1959. GS: John Dehner, James Coburn, Robert Warwick. Otis Dameyer asks Bronco to be his guide for a mission into Indian territory. Dameyer says that the Army has assigned him to recover government money stolen during an Indian massacre. Bronco resists his offer, saying that both of them will be killed, but is finally persuaded to accept.

21.11 *Riding Solo.* Feb. 10, 1959. GS: Robert Lowery, Ray Teal, Will Wright, Anne Anderson. Arriving in the town of Deepwater, Bronco Layne finds that word has spread that he is a friend of a man named Mike Kirk and involved in a stagecoach holdup and murder.

21.12 *Borrowed Glory.* Feb. 24, 1959. GS: Robert Vaughn, Andra Martin, Charles Cooper, William Reynolds. Bronco Layne, working as a deputy for Sheriff Lloyd Stover, learns that the sheriff lied about winning the Congressional Medal of Honor.

21.13 *The Silent Witness.* March 10, 1959. GS: Chris Alcaide, Russell Conway, Karl Davis, Karl Swenson. A man is killed, and Bronco Layne, who seems to have a motive, is accused of the crime.

21.14 *The Belles of Silver Flat.* March 24, 1959. GS: Pernell Roberts, Vaughn Taylor, John Beradino. Doc Moody hires a gunman to kill Bronco Layne, but the fast gun of Rev. David Clayton saves Bronco's life. Moody decides to take advantage of the Reverend's skill with a gun.

21.15 *Backfire.* April 7, 1959. GS: Barry Kelley, Troy Donahue, Don Beddoe, Jeff York, Joseph Holland, Carol Ohmart, Walter Coy, Kathleen O'Malley. Bronco Layne has taken a job as Sheriff Linc McKeever's deputy. After the sheriff is lured into a death trap and killed, Bronco sets out after the culprits.

21.16 *School for Cowards.* April 21, 1959. GS: Tommy Andre, Jeanne Cooper, Michael Connors, Yvette Dugay, Barry Atwater. While he is teaching at a military academy, Bronco Layne becomes involved in a family problem. Someone has tried to kill young Jamie Reynolds, whose mother is an Indian.

21.17 *Prairie Skipper.* May 5, 1959. GS: Arleen Howell, Lorne Greene, Bing Russell, Stephen Chase, Hank Patterson, Carlos Romero, Mickey Simpson. Working as trail boss on a cattle drive, Bronco Layne encounters former Navy captain Amos Carr, and his young wife. Traveling by land is unfamiliar to Carr, who is using his nautical training to guide him across the prairie.

21.18 *Shadow of a Man.* May 19, 1959. GS: Wayne Morris, Donald "Red" Barry, Rebecca Welles, George D. Wallace. Bronco Layne rescues a hobo from a pit of quicksand and then joins the man and his companion on their travels. When a stagecoach is robbed, the three are suspected of the crime.

21.19 *Hero of the Town.* June 2, 1959. GS: Lynn Bari, Ken Mayer, Karl Weber, Stephen Coit. Three masked men rob the local bank. When the confusion dies down, Tod Biggs is found dead holding Bronco Layne's gun in his hand. As Bronco attempts to clear his name, he finds his efforts hindered by Brigg's widow and the sheriff.

21.20 *Red Water North.* June 16, 1959. GS: Sarah Selby,

Burt Douglas, Hugh Sanders, Dorothy Provine, Michael Forest, Karl Swenson, Kelly Thordsen. Cargo-ship pilot Matt Crane, a friend of Bronco Layne's, is killed by members of a rival concern. Bronco signs on as Crane's replacement, working for the widow of a man he killed in a gunfight.

Season Two

21.21 *Game at the Beacon Club*. Sept. 22, 1959. GS: Patricia Crowley, Barry Kelley, Connie Hines, Gage Clarke. Bronco is introduced to San Francisco society and an exclusive card game. He in turn introduces a shy, card-playing schoolteacher into the game who surprises everyone.

21.22 *The Burning Spring*. Oct. 6, 1959. GS: Rhodes Reason, Suzanne Lloyd, Berry Kroeger, Adam West, John Qualen, Raymond Bailey. Lt. John Stoddard shoots at Bronco and is put on trial for attempted murder. During the trial, Bronco tells of a Civil War encounter in which he, a Confederate captain, clashed with Stoddard, a Union major.

21.23 *Bodyguard*. Oct. 20, 1959. GS: Alan Hale, Jr., Alan Baxter. Bronco Layne was hired by Frank Kelton to protect him from Dan Flood. Kelton is killed, but suspicion can't fall on Flood. He was with Bronco at the time of the murder.

21.24 *The Soft Answer*. Nov. 3, 1959. GS: Ray Stricklyn, Leo Gordon. Bronco Layne and Billy the Kid are working in Harmony for sheep rancher Barnaby Spence. When cattleman Mike Ransom, tries to harm Spence, Bronco and Billy join forces to help their employer.

21.25 *The Last Resort*. Nov. 17, 1959. GS: Kent Taylor, Marshall Thompson, Jean Allison, Ken Lynch, Vito Scotti. Carrying out a promise made to a dying man, Bronco Layne sets out to deliver some money to the notorious Billy Styles. Posing as an outlaw, Layne heads for a lawless town, hoping to find Styles there.

21.26 *The Devil's Spawn*. Dec. 1, 1959. GS: Troy Donahue, Mike Keene, Gary Vinson, Ray Teal. Bronco Layne is injured when a fleeing convict ambushes him. Taken in by the Donner family, Bronco learns that his assailant was one of the Donner boys.

21.27 *Flight from an Empire*. Dec. 15, 1959. GS: Karen Verne, Sasha Harden, Mary Tyler Moore, Barry Kelley. Bronco Layne comes to the aide of Ilse Von Weldenheim and her son Franz, who are being pursued by bandits.

21.28 *Night Train to Denver*. Dec. 29, 1959. GS: Brad Dexter, Myron Healey, Jacqueline McKeever, Robert Colbert. Bronco is guarding a body on a train to Denver. When a large sum of money is stolen from his railroad car, he is held for the theft. But two strangers, Al Simon and Matt Larker, pay his bail. Then Simon and Larker demand that Bronco give them the money.

21.29 *Shadow of Jesse James*. Jan. 12, 1960. GS: James Coburn, Jeanne Cooper, Richard Coogan, William Forrest, I. Stanford Jolley. In spite of Jesse James' senseless killing of innocent people, Cole Younger remains friendly with the notorious outlaw. Bronco Layne and Belle Starr attempt to get Younger to break off his friendship with James.

21.30 *The Masquerade*. Jan. 26, 1960. GS: Joel Grey, Chance Nesbitt, Jennifer West, Richard Evans, Rusty Lane, Frank Albertson, Clay Randolph, Paul Maxwell, Thad Swift. Bronco persuades four teenagers to postpone their holdup plans and take steady jobs. To keep them happy with their work, Bronco pretends to go along with the plans for a bigger holdup.

21.31 *Volunteers from Aberdeen*. Feb. 9, 1960. GS: Robert Reed, Susan Morrow, Regis Toomey. When Tom Fuller hears than an old girl friend wants to see him, he hastily leaves the cattle drive and heads for town. Bronco follows to look after his friend, but it isn't long before Tom lands in jail.

21.32 *Every Man a Hero*. Feb. 23, 1960. GS: Patricia Barry, Simon Oakland. Arriving at Fort Monument, Bronco Layne and Amy Carter find that the fort has been attacked by Indians, leaving five survivors. One survivor refuses to discuss the attack and Bronco learns that all five were awaiting court-martial.

21.33 *Death of an Outlaw*. March 8, 1960. GS: Stephen Joyce, Rhodes Reason, Alan Caillou, Miriam Colon, Jean Allison. In a fight with cattle thieves, Bronco gets an assist from Pat Garrett and Billy the Kid. But later, when Bronco tries to bring Billy to trial, Garrett is far from helpful.

21.34 *The Human Equation*. March 22, 1960. GS: Lawrence Dobkin, Herbert Rudley. To prevent an uprising, Bronco takes up the cause of the Osage Indians, restricted to an area of poor farm land.

21.35 *Montana Passage*. April 5, 1960. GS: Mala Powers, Mari Blanchard, Charles Cooper, Rex Reason, Robert Colbert, Hugh Sanders. Bronco is accused of murder and needs freedom to prove his innocence. So he stages his own death, assumes a fake name, complete with a fake wife, and begins his investigation.

21.36 *Legacy of Twisted Creed*. April 19, 1960. GS: Gustavo Rojo, John Anderson, Richard Hale, Henry Brandon, Robert B. Williams, Billy M. Greene, Dick Rich, Larry Chance, Bill Mims, Mike Sargent. Bronco, pursuing a fugitive Apache, is out to get his man alive. But the Indian's own tribesmen are also on his trail, and are out to kill him.

21.37 *Tangled Trail*. May 3, 1960. GS: Randy Stuart, Marc Lawrence, Arch Johnson, Bob Wiensko. Joe Russo has double trouble — Mark Tanner, whose hired guns have been terrorizing his ranch, and his wife Claire, who has been giving Bronco the eye.

21.38 *La Rubia*. May 1,7 1960. GS: Faith Domergue, Joan O'Brien, Rodolfo Acosta, Jack Mather, Carlos Romero, Fabrizio Mioni. An Indian attack on a stagecoach is foiled by the arrival of a Mexican bandit and his men, who take Brother Paul, Judith Castle and Bronco to their hideout. Then the leader offers the men freedom and announces his intention to marry the lady.

21.39 *Winter Kill*. May 31, 1960. GS: Virginia Grey, John Litel, Richard Rust, Edgar Buchanan, Merry Anders. Kate Crowley and her son Jack think that Pop Owens killed the oldest Crowley boy, and they intend to hang him for it. When Bronco and a marshal interfere, the Crowley's turn on them.

21.40 *End of a Rope*. June 14, 1960. GS: Robert Colbert, James Lydon, Horace MacMahon, Melora Conway, Joan Marshall. Allan Brierly is killed in his darkroom. Bronco discovers a clue in a photographic plate.

Season Three

21.41 *The Mustangers*. Oct. 17, 1960. GS: Mike Keene, Whitney Blake, Robert Ridgely, Kenneth Tobey. Broke, Bronco sings on as a cowhand at Abner Shelton's ranch. Shortly afterwards, Shelton is killed.

21.42 *Apache Treasure.* Nov. 7, 1960. GS: Mort Mills, Richard Hale, Buddy Ebsen, Chad Everett, Ed Prentiss. Bronco finds his mission of peace to the Apaches is falling flat. It is probably because a white man named Hickins is also making the rounds, killing Apaches and selling their scalps.

21.43 *Seminole War Pipe.* Dec. 12, 1960. GS: Robert Palmer, Anna Kashfi, Dean Fredericks, Robert Warwick, Don Wilbanks. Angry ranchers plan to hang an Indian couple. Bronco tries to calm the lynching party by relating a Civil War incident.

21.44 *Ordeal at Dead Tree.* Jan. 2, 1961. GS: Dorothy Neumann, Frank Ferguson, Merry Anders, Trent Dolan, Mary Newton, Lenmana Guerin. Marshal Bob Harrod believes Bronco is in cahoots with the murdering Welty gang, and jails him on suspicion of murder.

21.45 *The Invaders.* Jan. 23, 1961. GS: Gerald Mohr, Walter Sande, Shirley Knight, Joan Marshall, Gary Vinson. Outlaw Mace Tilsey holds Marshal Steve Durrock's daughter Molly as hostage, just to insure that the marshal won't stop his boys from having a good time in town.

21.46 *The Buckbrier Trail.* Feb. 20, 1961. GS: Michael Keep, Ray Danton, Mike Road, Paul Birch, Sandra Gale Bettin, Denver Pyle. Walter Ruick is in jail, awaiting trial for a local murder. But the townspeople are lynch crazy, and someone has to get Ruick out of town fast.

21.47 *Yankee Tornado.* March 13, 1961. GS: Will Hutchins, Tristram Coffin, Peter Breck, Whitney Blake, John Alvin, Don Haggerty, Lee Van Cleef. Bronco and Sugarfoot suspect that the men hunting buffalo are killing more than they should. Young Theodore Roosevelt finds out from Bronco what is going on, and he decides to do something about it.

21.48 *Manitoba Manhunt.* April 3, 1961. GS: Richard Garland, Jacqueline Beer, Felix Deebank. Bronco is asked to aid the Canadian Mounted Police in tracking down a bank robber who is heading for the wilds of western Canada. He is shocked to find that the fugitive's name is Dana Powell, his best friend.

21.49 *Stage to the Sky.* April 24, 1961. GS: Joan Marshall, Kent Taylor, Bing Russell, Charles Fredericks, Ron Corsi. Townspeople discover that the money they donated to build a new church has been stolen. Word gets around that their pastor, Rev. Billy Rawlins, was once a gunfighter. Angry at their loss and relieved to find a scapegoat, the citizens decide to lynch Rawlins.

21.50 *Guns of the Lawless.* May 8, 1961. GS: Denver Pyle, Fred Beir, Morris Ankrum. More than a decade earlier, Joe Spain and Petrie Munger started a cattle ranch. They agreed that Munger could have half the cattle if he wanted to nullify the agreement. Now that things are going well, Munger want half his cattle, and half the land to keep them on.

Season Four

21.51 *Cousin from Atlanta.* Oct. 16, 1961. GS: Anne Helm, Evan McCord, Kaye Elhardt. While awaiting the stagecoach arrival of his teenage cousin Amanda Layne, Bronco hears a gunshot from Logan's bar. Inside, he finds young gunslinger Tommy Dancer sipping beer, and learns that Tommy has just shot a man.

21.52 *The Prince of Darkness.* Nov. 6, 1961. GS: Efrem Zimbalist, Jr., Byron Keith, Donna Drew, John Howard, Denver Pyle, Keith Richards, Alan Reynolds. Although persecuted because his brother assassinated Lincoln, famed actor Edwin Booth responds to a call to aid his country. He joins Bronco Layne in trying to put down a rebellion started by former Confederate soldiers.

21.53 *One Came Back.* Nov. 27, 1961. GS: Robert McQueeney, Karen Steele, John Ramondetta. A group of investors, seeking to buy up Mexican ranchland, ask Bronco to guide them across the border. He is unaware that the investors are wanted for bank robbery and murder.

21.54 *The Equalizer.* Dec. 18, 1961. GS: Jack Nicholson, Steve Brodie, Sheldon Alman, Frank Albertson, Marie Windsor. All Bob Doolin and Ella Cassidy want to do is have a nice peaceful wedding. It is not going to be easy, though, because the Cassidy and Doolin gangs have been feuding for years.

21.55 *The Harrigan.* Dec. 25, 1961. GS: Jack Cassidy, Kathie Browne, Sean McClory, Wright King, Dick Graf, Ken Lynch. Bronco and his pal Terrence Harrigan hire on as cowpunchers at the Miller brothers' ranch. But they soon discover that the ranch is just a front for an outlaw hideout.

21.56 *Beginner's Luck.* Jan. 1, 1962. GS: Hayden Rourke, Keith Richards, Buzz Martin, Jean Willes. A group of cattlemen want the range land of homesteader Jim Gant. They figure they can get Gant's dander up by getting his son to draw on a professional gunfighter.

21.57 *Ride the Whirlwind.* Jan. 15, 1962. GS: Vaughn Taylor, Willis Bouchey, Edward Platt, George Petrie, Robert G. Anderson, Chad Everett. Dr. Miles Gillis has just finished a seven-year prison stretch and is headed for Willow Springs, home of the four men whose efforts put Gillis behind bars. One of the men, Judge Fowler, doesn't think Gillis means any harm, but the others aren't so sure.

21.58 *A Sure Thing.* Jan. 22, 1962. GS: Alan Hale, Jr., Mickey Simpson, Joan Taylor, Trevor Bardette. Bronco gets nothing but headaches when he wins a thousand head of cattle in a poker game.

21.59 *Trail of Hatred.* Feb. 5, 1962. GS: Kent Smith, Rian Garrick, Nina Shipman, James Griffith, Evan McCord. Cavalry lieutenant Steve Powell has been assigned the task of bringing back a deserter. Powell is grateful for this chance to clear his name — the deserter is Dana Powell, his father.

21.60 *Rendezvous with a Miracle.* Feb. 12, 1962. GS: Gloria Talbott, Mabel Albertson, Rico Alaniz, Paul Fierro. An attractive young woman named Valentine Ames, aboard the stagecoach bound for Santa Fe, doesn't know it but she is being followed. Her shadow happens to be Bronco, who's interest in her is anything but romantic.

21.61 *Destinies West.* Feb. 26, 1962. GS: Kathleen Crowley, Robert McQueeney, Leo Gordon, Donald "Red" Barry. Bronco is helping the Army search for LeBrec, an outlaw who stole a million-dollar gold shipment. His mission is made more difficult when he meets and falls for Belle Siddons, LeBrec's cohort.

21.62 *The Last Letter.* March 5, 1962. GS: Ernest Sarracino, Robert J. Wilke, Evan McCord, Doye O'Dell, Patricia Crest, Robert Colbert, Jean Allison, Arthur Space, Vito Scotti, Ken Lynch. Mexican patriot Benito Juarez and his men are trying to oust French Emperor Maximilian from the throne of their country. Juarez needs money and Bronco volunteers to smuggle a shipment of gold into Mexico.

21.63 *One Evening in Abilene.* March 19, 1962. GS: Lisa Gaye, Jack Cassidy, Jered Barclay, Tony Young, Lee Van Cleef. Donna Coe brings the body of her fiance, Will Morley, to his home town for burial. Morley was shot in Abilene by Marshal Bill Hickok, and Donna is obsessed with the thought of revenge.

21.64 *Until Kingdom Come.* March 26, 1962. GS: Jacqueline Beer, Philip Carey. Bronco helps the Duchess Eugenia and Prince Philip find asylum from Mexican revolutionaries. The Duchess then must protect the crown jewels from a crooked sheriff and a former newspaperman who seek to steal them.

21.65 *Moment of Doubt.* April 2, 1962. GS: Roxane Berard, Earl Hammond, Walter Brooke, Laurie Mitchell, Tol Avery, Doodles Weaver, Frank Wilcox, Bill Walker. Government officials suspect that a group of men are conspiring to overthrow the present administration by assassinating government officials. Bronco is dishonorably discharged from the Army in the hopes that he will be asked to join the conspiracy.

21.66 *A Town That Lived and Died.* April 9, 1962. GS: Anna Capri, Jolene Brand, Robert Rockwell. A woman named Emily is writing an article on ghost towns, and needs Bronco for a guide.

21.67 *The Immovable Object.* April 16, 1962. GS: William Fawcett, Mike Road, Maggie Pierce, George Neise, Bob Hogan, William Bell, J. Edward McKinley. Tom Christopher refuses to leave his home so that the Army can build a dam on the property. Old Tom says he will fight the whole U.S. Army before he will budge.

21.68 *Then the Mountains.* April 30, 1962. GS: Susan Seaforth, Gerald Mohr, Ken Mayer, James Best, Med Flory, Jim Boles. A horse trader sells Bronco several steeds, but it appears that he had an ulterior motive in doing business with Bronco — such as spying on him for a man called Bohannon.

22. *Buckskin*

NBC. 30 min. Broadcast history: Thursday, 9:30-10:00, July 1958–Sept. 1958; Friday, 7:30-8:00, Oct. 1958–Jan. 1959; Monday, 7:30-8:00, Jan. 1959–Sept. 1959.

Regular Cast: Tommy Nolan (Jody O'Connell), Sallie Brophy (Annie O'Connell), Mike Road (Sheriff Tom Sellers), Michael Lipton (Ben Newcomb), Marjorie Bennett (Mrs. Newcomb), Shirley Knight (Mrs. Newcomb).

Premise: This Western series concerned the adventures of young Jody O'Connell, whose widowed mother runs a hotel on the Montana frontier in 1880.

The Episodes

22.1 *The Lady from Blackhawk.* July 3, 1958. GS: Carolyn Kearney. Jody eagerly awaits the arrival of Marietta Flynn, who is coming to marry the local schoolmaster, Ben Newcomb. But after Marietta arrives she refuses to marry Ben and Jody tries to find out why.

22.2 *The Man Who Waited.* July 10, 1958. GS: Emerson Treacy, Stacy Harris. Jody finds a wounded man on the prairie and brings him back to the hotel, where Jody and his mother try to nurse him back to health. A friendship develops between Jody and the man, but Jody does not know that the man has a sinister reason for remaining on at the hotel even after he has recovered.

22.3 *The Outlaw's Boy.* July 17, 1958. GS: Tom Masters, Michael Lipton, Cheryl Callaway. An outlaw's son enters a spelling contest at Jody's school. When all of the other children withdraw from the contest in protest, Jody decides to do something about the situation.

22.4 *The Ballad of Gabe Pruitt.* July 24, 1958. GS: Margaret Lindsay, Tom Pittman, Vic Tayback. Dan Pruitt arrives in town to attend his father's funeral and stays at the O'Connell Hotel. The young man is upset over the fact that his mother and uncle married soon after his father's death. Then Jody hears a bystander say the word "Hamlet" at the funeral and tries to learn what the unfamiliar word means.

22.5 *The Trial of Chrissy Miller.* July 31, 1958. GS: Tharon Crigler, Myron Healey, Robert Fuller, Jeanne Bates. Jody promises not to tell when his friend Chrissy causes her father's prize mare to be injured. Chrissy returns home four hours late, and her parents and the townsfolk jump to wrong conclusions when the girl refuses to reveal where she has been. The girl's actions nearly lead to a hanging.

22.6 *Cash Robertson.* Aug. 7, 1958. GS: Willis Bouchey, Lurene Tuttle, Bill Henry, Reed Howes. Jody is anxious to buy a rifle from sheep trader Cash Robertson. He offers to sell his prize lamb to Robertson, but Robertson turns him down.

22.7 *Lament for Durango.* Aug. 14, 1958. GS: William Lundmark, Paul Lukather, Mike Road, Orville Sherman, Beverly Wills. Sheriff Tom Sellers loses the respect of the townsfolk when he guns down a killer, apparently without giving the desperado a chance to defend himself. The dead man's brother arrives to seek revenge.

22.8 *Tree of Death.* Aug. 21, 1958. GS: Michael Lipton, Emerson Treacy, Richard Karlan, Claudia Bryar. A quack doctor rides into town asking for a man called Yellowstone. Jody's mother recognizes the name of the doctor and becomes concerned that an unpleasant episode from the past will be brought out in the open.

22.9 *The Gold Watch.* Aug. 28, 1958. GS: Scott Morrow, Anna Marie Nanasi, Kathleen Freeman, Dorothea Lord, Dennis Moore, Ferris Taylor, Don Hi, Juanita Evers. Jody borrows the gold watch that belonged to his father and accidentally breaks it. When his mother finds it missing, she accuses a servant of stealing it.

22.10 *The Ghost of Balaclava.* Sept. 4, 1958. GS: Alan Marshal, Chris Roberts, Patrick Westwood, Orville Sherman. Jody is afraid to give a speech at school, but he learns a lesson in conquering fear from a survivor of the Charge of the Light Brigade.

22.11 *Hunter's Moon.* Sept. 11, 1958. GS: Walter Reed, Dayton Lummis, Marion Ross, Bill Henry. A detective arrives in town, looking for a man who once performed surgery without a license. His investigation leads to a homesteader whom Jody is helping to bait wolf traps.

22.12 *China Boy.* Sept. 18, 1958. Jody makes friends with a little Chinese boy whose parents come to Buckskin to open a laundry. But the owner of another laundry business instigates a boycott against his new competitor.

22.13 *Tell Me, Leonardo.* Sept. 25, 1958. GS: Chubby Johnson, Kathleen Freeman, Grant Richards, Rickey Kelman. The father of one of his friends is accused of murder and Jody seeks help from the town swami.

22.14 *A Picture of Pa.* Oct. 2, 1958. GS: Ben Morris, Natalie Masters, Tom Masters. Maggie Whitney, a lady photographer, arrives in town on a stagecoach that has just been held up. The holdup has an interest sequel when Maggie pays a professional call to photograph a sick man.

22.15 *The Money Man.* Oct. 9, 1958. GS: Melville Cooper. Old Man Sands, an eccentric printer working for the Gazette, is approached by George Cooke, a newcomer to the town. Sands thinks it would be nice if everyone could have lots of money, and Mr. Cooke convinces the elderly printer that he has a scheme that will make this possible.

22.16 *Miss Pringle.* Oct. 16, 1958. GS: Virginia Christine, Jim Bannon, Orville Sherman, Glen Vernon. Miss Pringle is a young music teacher who arrives in town and charms everybody in sight. They become quite fond of her, until the arrival of a traveling salesman causes them to question the young lady's past.

22.17 *A Permanent Juliet.* Oct. 23, 1958. GS: Jennifer West, Mary Beth Hughes, John Holland, Lillian Powell, Dennis Moore. A Shakespearean troupe arrives in Buckskin to perform "Romeo and Juliet". After an argument with her co-star, the leading lady leaves the troupe. Young Chrissie Miller, an aspiring actress who has been studying the part, offers to take her place.

22.18 *A Man from the Mountains.* Oct. 30, 1958. GS: Bern Hoffman, Harry O. Tyler, Gregg Palmer, Clancy Cooper. Marshal Tom Sellers arrests a mountain man on a charge of stealing from a mining firm. But the man claims that the company owed him money.

22.19 *The Bullnappers.* Nov. 6, 1958. GS: Richard Cutting, Rickey Kelman, James Flavin, Orville Sherman, Sandra Kelman. Jody and a friend nearly precipitate a range war when they hide a pet steer to prevent its being sold. As a result of the steer's disappearance, one rancher accuses another of rustling.

22.20 *The Greatest Man in History.* Jan. 5, 1959. GS: Michael Lipton, Stephen Chase, Hugh Corcoran, Amanda Webb, Richard Bermudez, Don Grady. Ben Newcomb hears a deathbed confession which implicates the mayor in a shooting. Respecting the dead man's religious beliefs, he must keep the information to himself.

22.21 *The Monkey's Uncle.* Jan. 12, 1959. GS: Carolyn Kearney, Scott Morrow, Vernon Rich. Teacher Ben Newcomb nearly loses his job for telling Jody about Darwin's theory of evolution.

22.22 *Mr. Rush's Secretary.* Jan. 19, 1959. GS: Jane Darwell, John Harmon, Roger Mobley. A lonely widow wants to leave town and return to her native Massachusetts, taking with her an antique desk which has been in her family for generations. But Jody and an orphan boy who needs a home, change her plans.

22.23 *Coup Stick.* Feb. 2, 1959. GS: Frank de Kova, Cris Roberts, Ted Markland. A reign of vandalism has struck the town. Coup sticks, carved Indian symbols of bravery, are found at the scene of each incident.

22.24 *Fry's Wife.* Feb. 9, 1959. GS: James Jonson, Suzanne Lloyd, Freeman Lusk, Addison Richards. Fry's wife is going to have a baby, so Marshal Sellers guarantees the outlaw temporary amnesty. But a posse from another town intends to try to take Fry into custody.

22.25 *Who Killed Pat Devlin?* Feb. 16, 1959. GS: House Peters, Jr., Marianne Stewart. Sheriff Devlin's wife isn't satisfied with her husband's job. She tries to push him to better things.

22.26 *Little Heathen.* Feb. 23, 1959. GS: Michael Lipton, Shirley Knight, Mark Douglas, Phyllis Standish. Jody meets a young Indian girl who asks him to take her tiny baby. When he refuses, she leaves the baby on a stump and runs away.

22.27 *The Knight Who Owned Buckskin.* March 2, 1959. GS: Robert Hardy, Mary Webster, Edmund Glover, J. Edward McKinley. A young Englishman has a deed to the entire town of Buckskin which was turned over to his family by Queen Victoria.

22.28 *Cousin Casey.* March 9, 1959. GS: Jimmy Murphy, Rusty Lane, Harry Strong. Jody's Cousin Casey arrives in Buckskin and proceeds to antagonize the townsfolk by his arrogance and quick temper. Then there is a bank robbery and he is the prime suspect.

22.29 *A Well of Gold.* March 16, 1959. GS: Roscoe Ates, Andy Clyde, Richard Rust. An old timer finally strikes gold and his ne'er-do-well sons come home to cash in on their father's good fortune.

22.30 *Act of Faith.* March 23, 1959. GS: James Griffith, Lyle Talbot, Freeman Lusk, Tyler McVey. An aloof and mysterious stranger rides into town and amazes the townsfolk with his facility at quoting the Bible.

22.31 *The Venus Adjourner.* March 30, 1959. GS: Tim Graham, Kathleen Freeman, David Leland. Ted Edegardh is always messing around with crackpot inventions, and his new one is the last straw for his wife.

22.32 *Charlie, My Boy.* April 6, 1959. GS: Edgar Stehli, Warren Oates, Freeman Lusk, John Milford. Charlie's father comes to Buckskin to see his son, who he thinks is a successful rancher. But Charlie's really a troublemaker who spends a lot of time in jail.

22.33 *Annie's Old Beau.* April 13, 1959. GS: Anthony Caruso, Clegg Hoyt, Paul Baxley, Scotty Morrow. Annie's old beau arrives in town—and asks for her hand in marriage. He is a handsome and wealthy man whom Annie had admired when she was a little girl.

22.34 *Mail-Order Groom.* April 20, 1959. GS: Jocelyn Brando, Dennis Patrick, Dave Willock, Abbey Sheltop. Determined to find the right husband for a friend, Annie O'Connell puts an ad in the paper.

22.35 *The Manager.* April 27, 1959. GS: Michael Lipton, Paul Newlan, Marjorie Bennett. Anne decides to take a vacation to visit her sister. She leaves Jody in full charge of the hotel while she is gone.

22.36 *I'll Sing at Your Wedding.* May 4, 1959. GS: Russell Arms, Bek Nelson, Dorothy Reese. A marriage counselor is retained to prepare Melissa Jenkins for the day her betrothed arrives in town.

22.37 *A Question of Courage.* May 11, 1959. GS: Pernell Roberts, Michael Lipton, Shirley Knight, Stephen Wootton. Schoolteacher Ben Newcomb discourages violence and exhorts his students to turn the other cheek. Then a local ruffian insults his wife.

22.38 Mary MacNamara. May 18, 1959. GS: Olive Sturgess, Murvyn Vye, Joseph Hamilton. Jody discovers Mary MacNamara lying unconscious in a ravine. She tells him her name but refuses to talk about the mysterious map she is carrying.

22.39 The Better Mouse Trap. May 25, 1959. GS: Rickey Kelman, Sandy Kelman, Orville Sherman, Richard Cutting. Jody and his friends have a plan to earn money to buy bicycles. By pressing grapes and adding sugar to the juice, they can make a very marketable beverage.

23. Buffalo Bill, Jr.

Syndicated. 30 min. Broadcast history: Various, March 1955–Sept. 1956.

Regular Cast: Dick Jones (Buffalo Bill, Jr.), Nancy Gilbert (Calamity), Harry Cheshire (Judge Ben Wiley).

Premise: Buffalo Bill, Jr. is the marshal of the town of Wileyville, Texas in the 1890s. He is assisted by his sister, Calamity, and his adopted father Judge Ben Wiley.

The Episodes

23.1 Fight for Geronimo. March 1, 1955. GS: Rodd Redwing, Harry Lauter, Robert Easton, Jack Daly, Wally West, Richard Cutting, Chief Thundercloud. Buffalo Bill, Jr., his kid sister Calamity and Judge Ben Wiley try to frustrate a plot to free the desperate Apache chief Geronimo as he is being transferred to a federal prison.

23.2 Runaway Renegade. March 1, 1955. GS: James Griffith, Walter Reed, Sammy Ogg, Lane Bradford. Bill and Calamity try to prove the innocence of a young boy's father who is accused of murdering the sheriff.

23.3 Empire Pass. March 3, 1955. GS: Bill Kennedy, Mauritz Hugo, Terry Frost, Mike Ragan. Bill and Calamity try to help an honest railroad man fight his crooked rival in the battle over a right of way.

23.4 Trail of the Killer. March 4, 1955. Chuck Courtney, Keith Richards, Henry Rowland. While Bill and everyone else in Wileyville are out hunting for Billy the Kid, he shows up in town and Calamity recognizes him.

23.5 The Black Ghost. March 12, 1955. GS: Bill Henry, Denver Pyle, Claudia Barrett, Dennis Moore, Ewing Mitchell, Budd Buster. Bill and Calamity try to expose a lovely young woman who is scheming with a notorious outlaw to take over her uncle's property.

23.6 The Death of Johnny Ringo. March 22, 1955. GS: Harry Lauter, George J. Lewis, Eddie Dew, James Best, Angie Dickinson, Dick Elliott. While Bill is out helping some Cavalry troopers find a missing messenger, the outlaw Johnny Ringo comes to town and captures Calamity and Judge Ben.

23.7 Boomer's Blunder. April 1, 1955. GS: Stanley Andrews, Lee Van Cleef, Don C. Harvey, Ben Welden, Kenne Duncan. Bill and Calamity try to keep Judge Ben and a friend of his from being cheated out of valuable land.

23.8 The Rain Wagon. April 8, 1955. GS: Lyle Talbot, John Doucette, Dick Elliott, Lane Bradford. Bill brings a traveling rainmaker to Wileyville to counter a destructive drought, but then has to capture a masked bandit who uses the rainmaker's experiments to cover his theft of the express office cashbox.

23.9 Tough Tenderfoot. April 14, 1955. GS: Leo Britt, Fred Coby, Nacho Galindo, Gregg Barton, Charlie Hayes, Fred Krone. A feud between an immigrant Scotsman and his visiting cousin helps Bill solve a lawyer's murder.

23.10 First Posse. April 18, 1955. GS: Walter Reed, James Griffith, Lane Bradford, Stanley Price. After not being allowed to ride in a posse because he is too young, Bill makes up for his disappointment by digging up plenty of trouble at home.

23.11 Hooded Vengeance. April 22, 1955. GS: Bill Henry, Denver Pyle, Claudia Barrett, Dennis Moore, Ewing Mitchell. Bill and Calamity go after a band of hooded riders who are terrorizing the local ranchers.

23.12 A Bronc Called Gunboat. May 11, 1955. GS: George J. Lewis, Eddie Dew, Stanley Andrews, Harry Lauter, Chris Alcaide, Bob Woodward. Bill has to master a bronco in order to capture an escaped criminal.

23.13 The Calico Kid. May 15, 1955. GS: Hank Patterson, Mollie McCart, Don C. Harvey, Lee Van Cleef, Ben Welden. Bill and Calamity conspire with the rest of Wileyville to convince a broken-down old prospector's 18-year-old daughter that her father is a wealthy mine owner.

23.14 Pawnee Stampede. May 19, 1955. GS: Leonard Penn, Myron Healey, Rick Vallin, Sandy Sanders, John War Eagle, Bob Woodward. Bill is unexpectedly helped by a fighting parson when he tries to make sure that the government's opening of the Pawnee Strip takes place without a hitch.

23.15 The Six-Gun Symphony. May 24, 1955. GS: Lyle Talbot, John Doucette, Lane Bradford, Dick Shackleton, Loie Bridge, Kathryn Sheldon, Hal K. Dawson. Bill and Calamity use an old music box to clear up a gambling scandal.

23.16 Grave of the Monsters. May 24, 1955. GS: Walter Reed, Tom Monroe, Glenn Strange, Joseph Michaels, Fred Libby. Bill and Calamity try to stop land grabbers from taking over Navajo land while the Indians are performing their sacred rites.

23.17 Lucky Horseshoe. May 27, 1955. GS: Richard Powers, William Fawcett, Jack Ingram, Chief Yowlachie, Ruth Robinson. When Judge Ben is almost run out of business by a rival storekeeper, Bill and Calamity try to find out how the other man can afford to sell his goods so cheaply.

23.18 Red Hawk. May 28, 1955. GS: Stanley Andrews, Michael Hall, Bill Henry, Dennis Moore, Steve Mitchell, Kenne Duncan, Bob Woodward. Bill comes to the aid of an old man and his adopted Indian son when a corrupt stage line owner tries to take their silver hauling contract away from them.

23.19 Redskin Gap. June 22, 1955. GS: Harry Lauter, Hank Patterson, Gregg Barton, Edwin Parker, Bob Woodward. Bill and Calamity try to stop a stagecoach robber who has escaped with a fortune in Canadian money but is heading in the opposite direction from Canada.

23.20 Legacy of Jesse James. June 23, 1955. GS: Carleton Young, House Peters, Jr., Buzz Henry, William Fawcett, Julian Rivero. Bill and Calamity try to track down three James gang survivors who have returned to Wileyville to dig up the loot Jesse buried there years before.

23.21 The Devil's Washbowl. July 27, 1955. GS: Leonard Penn, Myron Healey, Rick Vallin, Grace Field, Sandy Sanders,

Nina Varela, Bob Woodward. Bill and Calamity become suspicious of a stranger who comes to Wileyville and announced plans to build a hotel near the local hot springs.

23.22 *The Fight for Texas.* July 27, 1955. GS: Richard Powers, Steve Pendleton, William Fawcett, Jack Ingram, Jack Daly. Bill steps in when a cattle rustler forces Calamity to send a telegraph message that will disband the Texas Rangers.

23.23 *Apache Raid.* July 27, 1955. GS: Walter Reed, Glenn Strange, Joseph Michaels, Tom Monroe, Tom Humphrey, Mike Ragan, Rusty Wescoatt. Bill and Calamity try to help their young Apache friend Red Wolf, whom an Indian-hating rancher has accused of cattle rustling.

23.24 *Rails Westward.* July 30, 1955. GS: Stanley Andrews, Michael Hall, Bill Henry, Fran Bennett, Dennis Moore, Steve Mitchell, Bob Woodward, Dick Alexander. Bill, Calamity and Judge Ben unwittingly become involved in a scheme to sell a worthless stagecoach line to a stranger in town.

23.25 *The Little Mavericks.* Aug. 1, 1955. GS: Virginia Dale, House Peters, Jr., Carleton Young, Sharon Brand, Frances Karath, Bernadette Withers. Calamity and her playmates in the Mavericks Club try to capture two wanted outlaws so that the $1,000 price on their heads can pay for an operation for a crippled child.

23.26 *Fugitive from Injustice.* Aug. 13, 1955. GS: Harry Lauter, Peter Votrian, Hank Patterson, Edwin Parker, Henry Rowland. Bill, Calamity, Judge Ben and their friend Tinker Jones team up to help an illiterate Mexican boy.

Season Two

23.27 *Ambush at Lizard Rock.* April 27, 1956. GS: Stacy Harris, Syd Saylor, Terry Frost, X Brands, Reba Waters. In order to protect a prosecution witness from a shady gambler and a crooked aspiring politician, Bill sets a trap with himself as bait.

23.28 *The Assassins.* April 27, 1956. GS: Mike Garrett, Michael Bryant, Hal K. Dawson, Gregg Barton, Dennis Moore, Edgar Dearing, Rico Alaniz, Maria Monay, Billy Miller, Jack Mauck. Bill comes to the aid of a young deputy marshal who is trying to thwart the plans of his father's murderers.

23.29 *The Jayhawker.* April 27, 1956. GS: Mike Garrett, Michael Bryant, Lee Erickson, Hal K. Dawson, Gregg Barton, Don Bender. Bill and Calamity help a misguided teenager back on the right track when the youth tries his hand at lawbreaking.

23.30 *Trouble Thompson.* May 11, 1956. GS: Syd Saylor, Stacy Harris, Terry Frost, X Brands, Joe Greene, Jack Daly, Tom Noel. Bill and Calamity try to help an elderly circus clown who believes he is a jinx, but matters are complicated by a bank robbery and a case of the measles.

23.31 *The Golden Plant.* May 15, 1956. GS: Walter Reed, Keye Luke, House Peters, Jr., Billy Lee, Charlie Hayes, Barbara Jean Wong. Bill and Calamity use a shipment of firecrackers to clear a Chinese youth who is accused of the murder of his grandfather.

23.32 *Kid Curry — Killer.* May 18, 1956. GS: Walter Reed, Rodd Redwing, House Peters, Jr., Louis Lettieri, Bob Woodward, Charlie Hayes. Bill and Calamity go after the outlaw who has dynamited a train and murdered a marshal.

23.33 *Secret of the Silverado.* May 21, 1956. GS: Bill Henry, Keith Richards, Neyle Morrow, Rosa Rey, Henry Rowland, Steve Conte, Mike Ragan, Bob Woodward. Bill and Calamity join forces with a Mexican friend in a scheme to penetrate a silver smuggling ring.

23.34 *Angelo Goes West.* May 29, 1956. GS: Tito Vuolo, Bill Henry, Keith Richards, Henry Rowland, Steve Conte, Bob Woodward. Bill and Calamity try to help an Italian immigrant who has been framed for robbery by men who want to take over the land on which he is planting an olive orchard.

23.35 *Kansas City Lady.* July 23, 1956. GS: James Seay, Renee Godfrey, William Fawcett, George J. Lewis, Brad Morrow, Slim Pickens, Charlie Hayes. Two stagecoach robberies are blamed on a newcomer to Wileyville, Linda Abbott, new stepmother to a 10-year-old boy. Buffalo Bill, Jr., burns dubious newspaper clippings about Linda's past, believing her innocent, and sets out to uncover the real criminal.

23.36 *A Diamond for Grandpa.* July 23, 1956. GS: William Fawcett, Brad Morrow, Renee Godfrey, George J. Lewis, James Seay, Slim Pickens, Mauritz Hugo. When an eccentric old prospector finally thinks he has found a diamond mine, nobody pays much attention. He has boasted of striking it rich in gold and silver mines too often.

23.37 *The Lady and the Judge.* Aug. 1, 1956. GS: Louise Lorimer, Rick Vallin, Ed Hinton, Stanley Andrews, Fred Sherman, Fred Krone. Bill and Calamity try to discover why a woman recently arrived in Wileyville is playing up to Judge Ben and trying to persuade him to buy some stocks.

23.38 *Double-Cross Money.* Aug. 8, 1956. GS: Stanley Andrews, Louise Lorimer, Rick Vallin, Ed Hinton, Fred Krone, Charlie Hayes. Bill and Calamity become involved when gunmen are hired to rob a stagecoach.

23.39 *Silver Mine Mystery.* Aug. 16, 1956. GS: Stacy Harris, Edgar Dearing, Carolyn Craig, Gayne Whitman, Kirk Alyn, Dennis Moore. A man discovers a method of cheating mine owners of part of their silver ore shipments. Buffalo Bill, Jr. and Calamity soon learn of his crookedness and try to expose him.

23.40 *Blazing Guns.* Aug. 24, 1956. GS: Kirk Alyn, Gayne Whitman, Stacy Harris, Dennis Moore, Helen Brown, Edgar Dearing. Calamity's interest in dressmaking helps Bill find out how holdup men are getting inside information on money shipments.

23.41 *Gun-Talk.* Sept. 14, 1956. GS: Harry Lauter, Barry Curtis, Lane Bradford, X Brands, Bob Woodward, Chuck Cason. Bill and Calamity go after an outlaw who has stolen a fine horse, just recovering from pneumonia, from a reformed bandit's young son.

23.42 *Rough-Shod.* Sept. 21, 1956. GS: Harry Woods, Harry Lauter, Julian Rivero, Victor Millan, Lane Bradford, X Brands, Bob Woodward, Bill Baucom. Bill and Calamity try to protect a sheep rancher and his animals from a masked gang who have been raiding his property in order to make him sell out cheaply.

24. *Cade's County*

CBS. 60 min. Broadcast history: Sunday, 9:30–10:30, Sept. 1971–Aug. 1972; Monday, 10:00–11:00, Aug. 1972–Sept. 1972.

Cade's County

Regular Cast: Glenn Ford (Sam Cade), Edgar Buchanan (Senior Deputy J.J. Jackson), Taylor Lacher (Deputy Arlo Pritchard), Victor Campos (Deputy Rudy Davilo), Peter Ford (Pete), Betty Ann Carr (Betty Ann Sundown).

Premise: This contemporary Western series was sent in Madrid County, California, and dealt with the adventures of Sheriff Sam Cade, the law enforcement officer for the county.

The Episodes

24.1 *Homecoming*. Sept. 19, 1971. GS: Darren McGavin, Richard Anderson, H.M. Wynant, Loretta Swit, Jean Fowler, Ralph James, Myron Healey. Courtney Vernon is an old pal of Sheriff Sam Cade, but Sam doesn't know that his friend is out to kill him.

24.2 *Company Town*. Sept. 26, 1971. GS: Will Geer, Flora Plumb, Pippa Scott, Alan Vint, John McLiam, Richard Peabody, Arthur Space, Raymond Guth, Lucille Benson. An affably ruthless town boss uses his power to thwart Sheriff Cade's search for a missing miner.

24.3 *Safe Deposit*. Oct. 3, 1971. GS: Martin Sheen, Laraine Stephens, James Callahan, Elaine Giftos, James B. Sikking, Nora Marlowe, Dennis Fimple, Geoffrey Lewis, Mike Delano, Timothy Brown, Dal Jenkins. Cade investigates a bank robbery that is planned with the precision of a commando raid.

24.4 *Crisscross*. Oct. 10, 1971. GS: James Gregory, Rodolfo Acosta, Simon Scott, Linda Dangcil, Richard Yniguez, Margaret Markov, Michael Stokey, Bert Santos. A powerful rancher clashes with Cade over a murder investigation.

24.5 *Violent Echo*. Oct. 24, 1971. GS: Pat Harrington, John Anderson, William Windom, John Calvin, Ann Whitsett, Tony Perez, Calvin Chrane, Julian Rivero, Gordon Jump, Barney Phillips. A seamy abortionist is a key figure in Cade's last-ditch effort to save a condemned murderer.

24.6 *Gray Wolf*. Oct. 31, 1971. GS: John Savage, Cameron Mitchell, Tom Nardini, Sharon Acker, Jay Silverheels, Douglas Kennedy, James Luisi. A ruthless murderer calls on his Comanche cunning, and former training as Cade's deputy, to elude capture.

24.7 *The Armageddon Contract*. Nov. 7, 1971. GS: William Shatner, Mariette Hartley, Eric Christmas, Dan Ferrone, Norman Alden, John Zaremba, Lee J. Casey, Sammy Jackson. Cade's county is in for a face lifting when a saboteur plans to detonate the nuclear warheads at a missile site.

24.8 *The Mustangers*. Nov. 14, 1971. GS: George Maharis, Brenda Scott, Charles Dierkop, Jack Starrett, John Quade, Barney Phillips, Julian Rivero. A cold-blooded mustanger injects murder into his illegal roundup and sale of wild horses.

24.9 *Delegate at Large*. Nov. 21, 1971. GS: Dane Clark, Burr De Benning, L.Q. Jones, Charlotte Stewart, Lee Weaver, Irene Tsu, Dub Taylor, Richard Arlen. Los Angeles provides Sheriff Cade with an unwelcome change of scenery as he teams up with a veteran cop. Their mission is to find Cade's deputy, J.J., who has been kidnaped by kill-happy jewel thieves.

24.10 *A Gun for Billy*. Nov. 28, 1971. GS: Bobby Darin, Linda Cristal, Leif Garrett, Warren Kemmerling, Richard Kelton, David Doyle, Sandy Kevin. The legend of Billy the Kid takes a grim twist as a deranged ex-con thinks that he is the infamous outlaw and that Cade is Sheriff Pat Garrett.

24.11 *Requiem for Miss Madrid*. Dec. 12, 1971. GS: John Payne, Broderick Crawford, Johnny Crawford, Charles Robinson, E.J. Peaker, James Lydon, Gina Alvarado, Eric Mason, Jerry Daniels, Roberta Collins. A hotel detective and a congressman are both anxious, for different reasons, to pin a beauty queen's murder on a drunken broncobuster.

24.12 *The Alien Land*. Dec. 19, 1971. GS: Forrest Tucker, Heidi Vaughn, Fred Sadoff, Lou Gossett, Jr., Al Alu, Kathy Cannon, Mike Road, Sandra Ego, Betty Ann Carr. Middle East tension reaches the Southwest when an Arab college student is charged with the murder of a ranch foreman.

24.13 *Shakedown*. Jan. 9, 1972. GS: Judy Carne, Anthony Zerbe, Lonny Chapman, Milt Kamen, Richard Eastham, John Gruber, Barney Phillips. Cade poses as a blackmailer to nail the kingpin of a gold smuggling operation.

24.14 *One Small, Acceptable Death*. Jan. 16, 1972. GS: David Wayne, Michael Baseleon, William Smithers, Mike Road, Sid Grossfeld, S. John Launer, Sandy Kevin, James McCallion. A drunken bum is the only witness to a back-alley incident that led to the murder of his best friend.

24.15 *The Brothers*. Jan. 23, 1972. GS: Christopher Stone, Edmond O'Brien, Michael Pataki, Elliot Street, Cheryl Lynn Miller, Ted Gehring, Frank Maxwell. Deputy Arlo's black-sheep brother is planning the perfect crime.

24.16 *Slay Ride* Part One. Jan. 30, 1972. GS: Tony Bill, Gerald S. O'Loughlin, Leslie Parrish, John Schuck, Anne Seymour, Sam Chew, Bernie Casey, Mark Jenkins, Jill Banner, Dehl Berti, Pedro Regas, Hunter Von Leer, Harry Lauter. Cade has reason to doubt a hostile Apache's murder confession.

24.17 *Slay Ride* Part Two. Feb. 6, 1972. GS: Tony Bill, Gerald S. O'Loughlin, Leslie Parrish, John Schuck, Anne Seymour, Sam Chew, Bernie Casey, Mark Jenkins, Jill Banner, Dehl Berti, Pedro Regas, Hunter Von Leer, Harry Lauter. Cade attempts to solve a murder and clear a chronic confessor.

24.18 *Dead Past*. Feb. 13, 1972. GS: Simon Oakland, Steve Ihnat, Bridget Hanley, Jan Merlin, Michael C. Gwynne, Ken Sansom, Don Dubbins, Woodrow Parfrey, William Peterson, William Wintersole. An archaeology professor is the unlikely target of a syndicate murder plot.

24.19 *Inferno*. Feb. 27, 1972. GS: Scott Marlowe, Jeanette Nolan, Shelly Novack, Lou Antonio, Kathie Browne, Bart LaRue, Tracy Bogart. A son's vengeance against his overbearing mother takes the form of a campaign aimed at destroying the family's business.

24.20 *Ragged Edge*. March 5, 1972. GS: Kathryn Hays, Russ Tamblyn, Jack Carter, Harry Townes, Tom Falk, Troy Melton, Lori Busk, Suzanne Roth, Bob Hoy. An imprisoned drug pusher is the ransom demanded for a kidnaped child.

24.21 *Jessie*. March 12, 1972. GS: Barbara Rush, Bobby Sherman, Fredd Wayne, Robert Patten, Harold J. Stone, Bill Hayes, Kenneth Tobey, Bill Bryant, Bill Shannon. An accused murderer is trapped in a web of circumstantial evidence.

24.22 *Blackout*. March 19, 1972. GS: O.J. Simpson, Rosemary Forsyth, Don Porter, George Murdock, Joe Turkel, William Hansen. An ex-con art student's resentment at being refused a grant propels him into art forgery.

24.23 *The Fake*. March 26, 1972. Shelley Fabares, Edward Asner, Felice Orlandi, Larry Casey, Ed Flanders, William H. Bassett, Philip Kenneally, Anne Randall, Gene LeBell. An ex-syndicate boss is set up for an elaborately planned assassination.

24.24 *The Witness.* April 9, 1972. GS: Chief Dan George, Eric Braeden, Barney Phillips, Stewart Moss, Jennifer Kulik, Joe Renteria. A philosophical old Indian refuses to identify a killer. The old man believes that doing so would only promote further violence.

25. The Californians

NBC. 30 min. Broadcast history: Tuesday, 10:00-10;30, Sept. 1957–March 1959; Tuesday, 9:00-9:30, April 1959–June 1959; Thursday, 7:30-8:00, July 1959–Aug. 1959.

Regular Cast: Adam Kennedy (Dion Patrick) 57-58, Sean McClory (Jack McGivern) 57-58, Nan Leslie (Martha McGivern) 57-58, Herbert Rudley (Sam Brennan) 57-58, Richard Coogan (Matthew Wayne), Howard Caine (Schaab) 57-58, Carole Mathews (Wilma Fansler) 58-59, Arthur Fleming (Jeremy Pitt) 58-59.

Premise: This series was set during the San Francisco Gold Rush in the 1850s. The first season dealt mainly with the exploits of Irishman Dion Patrick, who worked as a reporter for Sam Brennan's newspaper and assisted Jack McGivern's vigilante group. Later episodes focused primarily on Sheriff Matthew Wayne's attempts to clean up crime in San Francisco.

The Episodes

25.1 *The Vigilantes Begin.* Sept. 24, 1957. Dion Patrick has come to San Francisco in search of gold and adventure. He makes friends with storekeeper Jack McGivern and his wife. They caution him to be careful, but Patrick decides to head for the Mother Lode country in Northern California, and search for gold. As he leaves the store he is attacked by a gang trying to shanghai a crew for a boat heading for China.

25.2 *All That Glitters.* Oct. 1, 1957. Dion Patrick goes into partnership with another prospector, Steve Thompson. Then Thompson is cheated.

25.3 *The Noose.* Oct. 8, 1957. GS: Darlene Field. After striking gold, Dion Patrick is robbed and beaten on his way to San Francisco. He joins up with the vigilantes and they seize a suspect whom they decide to hang. But some members of the vigilantes plead for a court trial.

25.4 *The Avenger.* Oct. 15, 1957. GS: Frank Gerstle, Judith Ames, Lowell Gilmore. A young newspaper reporter crusades against the lawless elements in the California of 1850. He is killed by a gang of criminals he has exposed in his paper and Dion Patrick, incensed by the brutal murder, decides to avenge the reporter.

25.5 *The Search for Lucy Manning.* Oct. 22, 1957. GS: Carolyn Craig, Fay Roope. In lawless San Francisco, a minister denounces the gangs of bandits from the pulpit. His courage inspires a young girl to leave her stepmother, who is a member of a vice ring. Dion Patrick and Jack McGivern try to help the young woman elude her enemies.

25.6 *The Lost Queue.* Oct. 29, 1957. GS: Aki Aleong, Michi Kobi, Robert Griffin. Lee Sing, a Chinese immigrant, and his fiancee Wan try to find their place in early San Francisco. A group of Chinese buy a piece of land on which to settle, but a gang of thugs threatens to get back the land by force.

25.7 *The Regulators.* Nov. 5, 1957. GS: Marie Windsor, Ray Kellogg, Lane Chandler. Vigilantes led by Jack McGivern and newspaper reporter Dion Patrick capture James Sloat, an outlaw leader. But McGivern's wife is kidnaped, and witnesses at Sloat's trial refuse to testify, fearing the gang will kill her.

25.8 *Man from Boston.* Nov. 12, 1957. GS: Robert Cornthwaite, Peg Hillias, Ted de Corsia. Vigilante leader Jack McGivern has been shot by a renegade and is in serious need of medical attention. Dion Patrick goes to find a doctor who deserted his practice in San Francisco to prospect for gold. But the doctor's wife salutes Patrick's arrival with gunfire.

25.9 *The Barber's Boy.* Nov. 19, 1957. GS: Bobby Hyatt, Steven Geray, Kem Dibbs, Kelly Thordsen. German settlers of early San Francisco are forced to pay off the Regulators, a vicious gang, or suffer destruction of their property. But the young son of a barber agrees to help Dion Patrick and Jack McGivern of the vigilantes to combat them.

25.10 *The Magic Box.* Nov. 26, 1957. Dion Patrick and the vigilantes believe that politician Martin Donovan is behind the murder of the man who was running against him for city council position, but they can't prove it.

25.11 *Little Lost Man.* Dec. 3, 1957. GS: Tommy Kirk, John Doucette, George Alexander, John Archer, Lynne Millan. Dion Patrick campaigns in his newspaper against a wave of teenage crime in San Francisco, when his money envelope is stolen by Billy Kilgore. His efforts gain momentum when he finds that the boys are being coached by the notorious Regulators' gang.

25.12 *Strange Quarantine.* Dec. 10, 1957. GS: Henry Daniell, Audrey Totter, Howard Dayton. Awaiting the arrival of a certain Dr. Kendall from the East, Dion Patrick and Jack McGivern are surprised to find that the doctor is a woman. She has an additional problem — doctors are in a bad repute in the area because of the activities of a charlatan named Rodman.

25.13 *Truce of the Tree.* Dec. 17, 1957. GS: Melville Cooper, Peter Whitney, Stacy Keach, Sr. In early San Francisco, violence threatens because of the intolerance of native Americans toward immigrants. Lord Charlie, loved and respected by all, seeks a solution.

25.14 *The PO 8.* Dec. 31, 1957. GS: Robert Ellenstein, Paul Bryar. Dion Patrick and Jack McGivern set out after a Robin Hood-type bandit with a flair for poetry. From circumstantial evidence they conclude that a local banker is their man.

25.15 *The Coward.* Jan. 7, 1958. GS: Sidney Blackmer, Jean Willes, Stacy Keach, Sr. Dion Patrick and Jack McGivern help elect Hector Jones Justice of the Peace. They believe that Jones will help clean out the lawless elements in San Francisco. They don't know that Jones can't stand physical pain.

25.16 *Panic on Montgomery Street.* Jan. 14, 1958. GS: Claudia Barrett, Willis Bouchey, Mabel Albertson, Nick Durrell. When a run on the bank is threatened, Patrick and McGivern get appeals for help from both the banker in charge and his daughter.

25.17 *China Doll.* Jan. 21, 1958. GS: Maria Tsien. While on the track of a killer, Dion Patrick visits a gambling hall on San Francisco's waterfront. There he becomes involved in a poker game with a wealthy Chinese, who loses all his money to Patrick.

25.18 *Mr. Valejo.* Jan. 28, 1958. GS: Salvador Baguez, Georgette Duval. Dion Patrick and Jack McGivern become embroiled in the feud between the American and Spanish set-

The Californians

tlers in California. The two men are investigating charges that Don Mariano Valejo is leading raids on the Yankee settlements.

25.19 *The Alice Pritchard Case.* Feb. 4, 1958. GS: Dan Haggerty, Richard Hale, Theodore Newton, John Gallaudet, Lillian Bond. Dion Patrick and Jack McGivern discover that a newspaper publisher plans to blackmail the wife of a respected judge. They try to thwart the publisher's plan.

25.20 *The Man from Paris.* Feb. 11, 1958. GS: Robert Cornthwaite, James Westerfield, Lilyan Chauvin. Charle Girard, a French dressmaker, arrives in San Francisco to establish a fashion shop. But the local residents think his profession is unmanly and subject him to some cruel criticism.

25.21 *The Duel.* Feb. 18, 1958. GS: Dorothy Green, Jeffrey Stone, Ralph Sanford. When Claude Talbot, a crack pistol shot, kills a number of prominent citizens in a series of duels, Dion Patrick and Jack McGivern suspect Talbot is using his skill for legal murder.

25.22 *Sorley Boy.* Feb. 25, 1958. GS: John Alderson, Charles Horvath, Mora O'Mahoney. In a saloon fight Sorley Boy McDonald, a muscle man, battles with Tully O'Neil, advertised as the champion fighter of England. Jack McGivern, who witnesses their fight, decides to promote a fight between the two men.

25.23 *Gentleman from Philadelphia.* March 4, 1958. GS: Ken Lynch, Patricia Donahue. Matt Wayne sees his mining partner shot down in cold blood and sets out to find the murderer. The vigilantes, believing Wayne is a member of a crooked mining syndicate, obstruct him in his search.

25.24 *The Marshal.* March 11, 1958. GS: Douglas Dumbrille, Billy Chapin, Sheppard Strudwick, John Alderson, Bob Steele, Robert Burton, Gil Perkins, Hubie Kerns, Robert Karnes. After Father Holzer, a friend of Matt Wayne's, is murdered, Matt accepts the post of marshal of San Francisco in an effort to capture the killers. Jack McGivern aids Wayne in smashing a crime ring.

25.25 *Death by Proxy.* March 18, 1958. GS: Philip Ahn, Michi Kobi, Robert Riordan, Kam Tong, Wendell Holmes. A Chinese laundryman is robbed of his savings and is unable to send money to his starving relatives in China. For a price he agrees to confess to a murder, and Marshal Wayne is forced to jail him even though he believes the man is innocent.

25.26 *The Street.* March 25, 1958. GS: R.G. Armstrong, Chris Alcaide. When Marshal Matt Wayne tries to protect the rights of the law-abiding citizens of San Francisco, an unscrupulous man decides to have Wayne killed.

25.27 *J. Jimmerson Jones, Inc.* April 1, 1958. GS: John Qualen, John Archer, John McNamara, Emmett Lynn. A successful gold prospector incorporates himself and sells shares in his enterprise. When the man is murdered and his gold hoard stolen, Marshal Matt Wayne starts an investigation.

25.28 *Skeleton in the Closet.* April 8, 1958. GS: Cathy O'Donnell, Lurene Tuttle, Roberto Cabal, Alex Montoya. A disbarred lawyer attempts to blackmail the wife of a California senator and is shot to death in the woman's home. Marshal Matt Wayne arrives to find that the body has disappeared.

25.29 *Pipeline.* April 22, 1958. GS: Whit Bissell, Mayo Loiseaux, Howard Petrie, Robert Fuller. A doctor complains about the unsanitary conditions of the local water supply. The man who controls the water retaliates by kidnaping the doctor's daughter. Marshal Matt Wayne is called in to locate the girl.

25.30 *The Foundling.* April 29, 1958. GS: Steve Wooten, Luis Van Rooten, Lorna Thayer. Marshal Matt Wayne finds he has trouble on his hands when he meets Martin Van Buren Hicks. Hicks, son of a notorious troublemaker, seems to be following in his father's footsteps.

25.31 *Second Trial.* May 6, 1958. GS: James Bronte, Mason Curry, Jean R. Maxey, Vici Raaf. Terrence Buchanan, a respected citizen of San Francisco, is found murdered. Accused of the killing, a man insists that Buchanan had a gun, but Buchanan's wife insists that he was unarmed. Convinced that the accused man is guilty, vigilantes decide to mete out justice.

25.32 *The Inner Circle.* May 13, 1958. GS: Peg Hillias, Robert P. Lieb, Howard Curry. Marshal Matt Wayne believes that a respected San Francisco businessman is a member of a crime syndicate preying on other merchants. He has the man brought into court on a charge of keeping stolen goods in his warehouse, but the judge dismisses the charge. Later the businessman is murdered.

25.33 *The Golden Bride.* May 20, 1958. GS: Jeffrey Stone, Helen Mowery, Edgar Buchanan. A reckless prospector falls in love with a pretty girl and asks her to marry him. When she doesn't seem to be interested in him, he offers a dowry of gold equal to her weight. The girl's boy friend thinks it's a fine idea and urges her to encourage the prospector.

25.34 *Murietta.* May 27, 1958. GS: Douglas Dumbrille, Anna Navarro, William Ching, William Quinn, Jerry Oddo. A beautiful Mexican girl falls in love with Jordan, an American banker. They must secure permission to marry from the girl's brother, Juan. Remembering the indignities to which Mexicans have been subjected by Americans in California, Juan swears to kill Jordan before he will agree to the marriage.

25.35 *Shanghai Queen.* June 3, 1958. GS: Paula Raymond, Peter Whitney, Ashley Cowan. An old sea captain learns of a gang that shanghais sailors for ships bound for the Orient. He goes to Marshal Matt Wayne, and Matt sets out to track down the gang's leader. He learns the leader is a beautiful woman.

25.36 *Bridal Bouquet.* June 10, 1958. GS: Rebecca Welles, John Alderson. A young woman who has journeyed to California to be married, rebels against her new husband. She goes to Marshal Matt Wayne, complaining that the house her husband has for her is not what she expected.

25.37 *Golden Grapes.* June 17, 1958. A young man refuses to work for his father, a wealthy vintner. Instead he goes to San Francisco to operate a fishing boat. When the young man is accused of a robbery, Marshal Matt Wayne tires to help him.

Season Two

25.38 *Dishonor for Matt Wayne.* Sept. 23, 1958. Marshal Matt Wayne is charged with running a crooked gambling house and put in jail. He engaged attorney Jeremy Pitt, a new arrival in San Francisco, to defend him. But after talking with Pitt he can't decide whether the lawyer sides with him.

25.39 *Mutineers from Hell.* Sept. 30, 1958. GS: Charles Aidman, Jean Allison, Dan Riss, Edwin Jerome, Robert Burton, Chet Stratton, Clive Holliday. Lawyer Jeremy Pitt is approached by Coffin, officer of a ship whose crew mutinied. Coffin plans to appear as a defense witness when the mutineers are tried, and he wants Pitt to become the defense attorney. Shortly before the trial, Coffin disappears and Marshal Matt Wayne tries to find him.

25.40 *Lola Montez.* Oct. 7, 1958. GS: Patricia Medina, Paul Lambert. The beautiful adventuress Lola Montez arrives in San Francisco and soon has every eligible male at her feet. Marshal Matt Wayne becomes concerned when his friend Jack McGivern falls in love with Lola and views with another young man for her attentions.

25.41 *A Girl Named Sam.* Oct. 14, 1958. GS: Sue George, Robert Cornthwaite. Marshal Matt Wayne finds a teenager, Samantha Jackson, after her wagon has been plundered by the notorious Bandanna Gang. He takes her to a mining camp where they meet a group of settlers anxious to go to San Franciscom but afraid of the Bandanna Gang. Matt agrees to escort them.

25.42 *The Salted Gold Mine.* Oct. 21, 1958. Troy Selby arrives in San Francisco and persuades Jeremy Pitt and Wilma Fansler to buy stock in a mine he owns, and also to sell more stock to other people. But Marshal Matt Wayne is convinced that Selby is a confidence man.

25.43 *Overland Mail.* Oct. 28, 1958. GS: Grace Raynor, Russell Johnson. Matt Wayne is sworn in as deputy U.S. Marshal to investigate the wrecking of stagecoach lines. Then a friend of Matt's, Wilma Fansler, comes to him and tells him that her cousin was a passenger on the stage that was just waylaid.

25.44 *Prince of Thieves.* Nov. 11, 1958. GS: John Sutton, Helen Spring. An Englishman named Sam Crawford arrives in San Francisco and tells Matt Wayne that he is known as the prince of thieves. Later, Matt learns that Crawford plans to lead an attack on a stagecoach and arrests him at a ball. But even though he is imprisoned, Crawford manages to carry out his plan for the robbery.

25.45 *Hangtown.* Nov. 18, 1958. GS: Anna Navarro, John Anderson, Jeff York, Ray Teal, Reed Howes, Ken Lynch. Matt Wayne and his friend Abe Sanchez are ambushed while traveling on a stage and Sanchez is killed. Before he dies Sanchez asks Wayne to deliver his money to his father in El Dorado County.

25.46 *Dangerous Journey.* Nov. 25, 1958. GS: Robert Osborne, Carolyn Craig, Addison Richards, George Brenlin. After a San Francisco bank is robbed, one of the witnesses accuses young Corey Harris of being a member of the holdup gang. Marshal Matt Wayne goes to arrest Harris and finds that he has just been married and appears to be a respectable citizen.

25.47 *Halfway House.* Dec. 2, 1958. GS: Joan Tompkins, Ann Daniels. Marshal Matt Wayne learns that a number of travelers have disappeared after stopping at an ancient inn, midway between San Francisco and Monterey. With his friend Jeremy Pitt, Matt rides out to investigate the inn.

25.48 *The Painless Extractionist.* Dec. 9, 1958. GS: Hans Conried, Penny Edwards, Frank De Kova. Painless Pepper, claiming to be a painless extractionist, arrives in San Francisco complete with his medicine show. Matt becomes suspicious when he notices Pepper showing an interest in the contents of the bank's vault.

25.49 *Old Sea Dog.* Dec. 16, 1958. GS: William Keene, David Post. Construction of a Navy base is constantly being interrupted by outlaws who are ambushing supply parties. Discovering that the outlaws are being tipped off by someone on the inside, Marshal Matt Wayne begins an investigation.

25.50 *The Long Night.* Dec. 23, 1958. GS: Chris Warfield, Robert Blake, Patricia Michon, Hal Baylor, Araceli Ray, Charles Arnt, William Tannen. Johnny Vonn, witness to a murder, is placed in protective custody by Marshal Wayne. Johnny escapes to join his wife, who is about to give birth to a baby, and jeopardizes his life, for three men have vowed to kill him.

25.51 *The Man Who Owned San Francisco.* Dec. 30, 1958. GS: Carlos Romero, Julian Rivero, Lisa Gaye. Jose Limantour claims he has title to two square miles of land in the heart of San Francisco. When Limantour hires lawyer Jeremy Pitt to help him claim the land, the townspeople, realizing they may lose their property, resort to violence.

25.52 *The First Gold Brick.* Jan. 6, 1959. GS: Don Megowan, J. Pat O'Malley, Mary Anderson, Walter Baldwin, Gretchen Thomas, Patrick Lawless, Patrick Whyte, Thomas Dillon. Matt is suspicious when Clay Kendall lays plans to sell stock in a gold mine and asks permission to display a gold brick from the mine in the bank window.

25.53 *The Painted Lady.* Jan. 13, 1959. GS: John Warburton, Don Kennedy, Lurene Tuttle, Dusty Anders. Cyrus Draton, a member of San Francisco society, is being blackmailed by Big Corny. Corny threatens to make known information about Draton's past.

25.54 *Bella Union.* Jan. 20, 1959. GS: Veda Ann Borg, Frank Albertson, Gail Kobe. Angry miners hold a protest gathering outside the luxurious Bella Union Hotel, from which they have been excluded. While they are staging the protest, the owner of the hotel is killed by a stray bullet. Molly Wallis, a friend of the dead man, is certain that the shooting was no accident.

25.55 *Crimps' Meat.* Jan. 27, 1959. GS: Charles Aidman, Billy House, Robert Burton, Jean Allison. Young Joy Ryan, a sailor, comes to San Francisco to find the man who shanghaied him. Ryan attacks Papa Kelly, the man responsible for his abduction, but Kelly, surprisingly, refuses to press charges.

25.56 *Corpus Delicti.* Feb. 3, 1959. GS: Philip Terry. Marshall Matt Wayne deputizes gambling-house owner Wilma Fansler in an attempt to prove a man guilty of murder.

25.57 *A Turn in the Trail.* Feb. 17, 1959. GS: Judith Ames, Jack Lambert, George Mitchell, Ruth Lee. Marshal Matt Wayne is on the trail of an outlaw. He rescues Madge Dorsett, a former Boston society girl, who was stranded when the outlaw took her horse.

25.58 *Wolf's Head.* Feb. 24, 1959. GS: Bruce Gordon, Alexander Campbell, Daniel White, Tom Trout. Charles Savage, a demented criminal, escapes just before he is to be hanged. Intent upon revenge against Matt Wayne and Jeremy Pitt, he puts a diabolic plan into action.

25.59 *Cat's Paw.* March 3, 1959. GS: Steve Roberts, Harlan Warde, Don Haggerty. When Lorraine Lathrop is knifed to death Marshal Matt Wayne deputizes Wilma Fansler to help him investigate.

25.60 *Gold-Tooth Charlie.* March 10, 1959. GS: James Hong, Michi Kobi, Sammee Tong, Henry Daniell, Kelly Thordsen, Bob Steele. Young Charlie Wong wants to break with his family and his heritage. His father, however, fears Charlie will become involved in the underworld.

25.61 *Stampede at Misery Flats.* March 17, 1959. GS: John Qualen, Stafford Repp, James Anderson. Vinegar Pete Jones, an old prospector, helps Marshal Matt Wayne's investigation of a gold embezzlement scheme.

25.62 *Guns for King Joseph.* March 24, 1959. GS: Jerry Oddo, Anna Navarro, Victor Magana, Jr. When lawyer Jeremy Pitt aids an Indian outlaw, he incurs the disfavor of Marshal Matt Wayne.

25.63 *Deadly Tintype.* March 31, 1959. GS: Vito Scotti, Dick Kallman, Charity Grace, Dan Riss. Marshal Matt Wayne asks lawyer Jeremy Pitt to help him in his investigation of a case of maritime larceny.

25.64 *A Hundred Barrels.* April 21, 1959. GS: Jennifer Raine, Alan Caillou. Marshal Matt Wayne sets out after men who are dealing in human slaves from the Orient.

25.65 *The Fugitive.* April 28, 1959. GS: Booth Colman, Rebecca Welles, Olin Howlin, Claire DuBrey. Marshal Matt Wayne and Jeremy Pitt become involved in an extradition case as they attempt to prove the innocence of a man accused of murder.

25.66 *The Fur Story.* May 5, 1959. GS: James Callahan, Dolores Donlon, Jack Lambert, Donald Randolph. Marshal Matt Wayne begins an investigation when American fur traders cause the vigilantes to run Russian fur dealers out of San Francisco.

25.67 *One Ton of Peppercorns.* May 12, 1959. GS: James Coburn, Edgar Buchanan, Marjorie Bennett, John McNamara. Marshal Wayne's gullible country cousin is victimized by swindlers during his visit to San Francisco.

25.68 *The Bell Tolls.* May 19, 1959. GS: Michael Connors, Rita Lynn, Henry Daniell. When California's attorney general is murdered, the culprit claims that he shot in self-defense. But aroused vigilantes form a lynching posse.

25.69 *Act of Faith.* May 26, 1959. GS: James Coburn, Robert Crawford, Maria Palmer, Mike Keene, Hal Baylor. A little boy is a witness to a murder. Deputy Anthony Wayne, cousin of Marshal Matt Wayne who is out of town, questions the youngster. But the lad, loyal to some unknown person, refuses to answer.

26. Centennial

NBC. 26 hours (total running time). Broadcast history: Saturday & Sunday, various times, Oct. 1978–Feb. 1979.

Regular Cast: Michael Ansara (Lame Beaver), William Atherton (Jim Lloyd), Raymond Burr (Herman Bockweiss), Barbara Carrera (Clay Basket), Richard Chamberlain (Alexander King), Robert Conrad (Pasquinel), Richard Crenna (Col. Frank Skimmerhorn), Timothy Dalton (Oliver Secombe), Cliff DeYoung (John Skimmerhorn), Chad Everett (Capt. Maxwell Mercy), Sharon Gless (Sidney Andermann), Andy Griffith (Prof. Lewis Venor), Merle Haggard (Cisco Calendar), Gregory Harrison (Levi Zendt), David Janssen (Paul Garrett/Narrator), Alex Karras (Hans Brumbaugh), Brian Keith (Sheriff Axel Dumire), Sally Kellerman (Lise Bockweiss), Stephen McHattie (Jacques Pasquinel), Lois Nettleton (Maude Wendell), Donald Pleasence (Samuel Purchase), Cristina Raines (Lucinda McKeag Zendt), Lynn Redgrave (Charlotte Buckland), Robert Vaughn (Morgan Wendell), Clint Walker (Joe Bean), Dennis Weaver (R.J. Poteet), Anthony Zerbe (Mervin Wendell), Robert Walden (Dr. Richard Butler), Kario Salem (Marcel Pasquinel), Chief Dan George (Old Sioux), Henry Darrow (Alvarez), Reb Brown (Jim Bridger), Maria Potts (Blue Leaf), Robert Tessier (Rude Water), Pernell Roberts (General Asher), Ray Tracey (Young Lame Beaver), Jorge Rivero (Broken Thumb), Stephanie Zimbalist (Elly Zendt), Irene Tedrow (Mother Zendt), Debi Richter (Rebecca Stolfitz), Laura Winston (Laura Lou Booker), Karen Carlson (Lisette Mercy), James Sloyan (Spade Larkin), Mark Harmon (John McIntosh), Morgan Woodward (General Wade), Nick Ramus (Lost Eagle), Barney McFadden (Abel Tanner), Rafael Campos (Nacho Gomez), Glynn Turman (Nate Person), Robby Weaver (Gompert), Jesse Vint (Amos Calendar), Les Lannom (Bufe Coker), Scott Hylands (Laseter), Greg Mullavey (Mule Canby), Michael LeClair (Young Jim Lloyd), Jay W. MacIntosh (Emmna Lloyd), Robert Douglas (Claude Richards), Adrianna LaRusso (Clemma Zendt), Clint Ritchie (Messmore Garrett), Mark Neely (Martin Zendt), Art Metrano (Muerice), Clive Revill (Finlay Perkin), Doug McKeon (Philip Wendell), A Martinez (Tranquilino Marquez), Silvana Gallendo (Serafina Marques), Robert Phalen (Reverend Holly), Lou Frizzell (Mr. Norris), Claude Earl Jones (Matt), Tiger Thompson (Beeley Garrett), Sandy McPeak (Soren Sorenson), Claude Jarman (Earl Grebe), Julie Sommars (Alice Grebe), Bo Brundin (Magnes Volkema), Lynn Borden (Vesta Volkema), Geoffrey Lewis (Sheriff Bogardus), Dana Elcar (Judge Hart), William Bogert (William Bellamy), Alex Colon (Truinfador Marquez), Alan Vint (Beeley Garrett as an Adult), Morgan Paull (Philip Wendell as an Adult), Joaquin Martinez (Colonel Salcedo), Gale Sondergaard (Aunt Agusta), Karmin Murcelo (Flor Marquez), Robert DoQui (Nate Person III), James Hampton (Defense Attorney), James McMullen (Prosecutor), Marshall Thompson (Dennis), Rene Enriquez (Manolo Marquez), Royce D. Applegate (Holmes), Richard O'Brien (Judge), James Best (Hank Garvey).

Premise: This epic mini-series was based on the James Michener novel and dramatized the growth of Colorado from the 1750s through the 1970s.

The Episodes

26.1 *Only the Banks Live Forever.* Oct. 1, 1978. French-Canadian trapper Pasquinel, who befriends an honorable Arapaho leader, forms an uneasy alliance with warlike Pawnees and strikes an unlikely partnership with a fugitive Scotsman.

26.2 *The Yellow Apron.* Oct. 8, 1978. In the midst of his desperate quest for gold, Pasquinel raises his two sons by the Arapaho woman named Clay Basket and returns to St. Louis for a bittersweet reunion with his wife.

26.3 *The Wagon and the Elephant.* Oct. 29, 1978. A wagon train bound westward from St. Louis in 1845 includes a Mennonite outcast and his wife, an Army captain, and a grizzled guide.

26.4 *For as Long as the Water Flows.* Nov. 4, 1978. Broken treaties imperil relations between Indians, settlers and the Army during the period from 1846 to 1860.

26.5 *The Massacre.* Nov. 11, 1978. A fanatical Army colonel commands a massacre of unarmed Indians, precipitating a wave of revenge and recriminations.

26.6 *The Longhorns.* Dec. 3, 1978. A seasoned trail boss recruits a motley crew of greenhorns and old hands to herd some 3,000 longhorns from Texas to a sprawling Colorado ranch.

26.7 *The Shepherds.* Dec. 10, 1978. The town of Centennial, Colorado, is born in 1876 as a range war threatens to erupt between independent farmers and the English owners of the six-million-acre Venneford Ranch.

26.8 *The Storm.* Jan. 14, 1979. The circus comes to Centennial, Levi Zendt returns to Pennsylvania to visit his Mennonite family, and Oliver Seccombe worries that measures he took to keep the ranch solvent will come under the disapproving eye of a Scottish accountant hired by the Venneford's owners.

26.9 *The Crime.* Jan. 21, 1979. The loss of most of the Venneford herd in a raging blizzard prompts a weary Oliver Seccombe to relinquish his duties as general manager. Meanwhile, con artists Mervin and Maude Wendell swindle the local minister out of his home, but not without arousing the suspicion of Sheriff Dumire.

26.10 *The Winds of Fortune.* Jan. 28, 1979. Jim Lloyd proposes to Charlotte Seccombe. Sheriff Dumire remains bent on proving that the Wendells are murderers, and an outlaw gang shows up to revenge the deaths of two members years earlier.

26.11 *The Winds of Death.* Feb. 3, 1979. Centennial attracts homesteaders in the 1920s, but their promised land is ravaged by drought and dust storms, and their future threatened by the onset of depression.

26.12 *The Scream of Eagles.* Feb. 4, 1979. History professor Lewis Vernor visits modern day Centennial, where he is told the history of the area.

27. *Cheyenne*

ABC. 60 min. Broadcast history: Tuesday, 7:30-8:30, Sept. 1955–Sept. 1959; Monday, 7:30-8:30, Sept. 1959–Dec. 1962; Friday, 7:30-8:30, April 1963–Sept. 1963.

Regular Cast: Clint Walker (Cheyenne Bodie), L.Q. Jones (Smitty) 55-56.

Premise: The Western series was set in the West during the 1860s and concerned the exploits of frontier scout Cheyenne Bodie.

Notes: During the 1955-56 season *Cheyenne* alternated with *Casablanca* and *King's Row* as part of *Warner Brothers Presents*. *Cheyenne* returned for the 1956-57 season and alternated with *Conflict*. *Cheyenne* alternated with *Sugarfoot* during the 1957-58 season. The series was off the air during the 1958-59 season because of a contract dispute with Clint Walker and *Sugarfoot* and *Bronco* rotated as part of *The Cheyenne Show*. *Cheyenne* returned in the 1959-60 season as a solo series, but in 1960-61 it again alternated with *Sugarfoot* and *Bronco* as part of *The Cheyenne Show*. During the 1961-62 season *Cheyenne* alternated with *Bronco*, then returned for a half season as a solo in fall of 1962.

The Episodes

27.1 *Mountain Fortress.* Sept. 20, 1955. GS: Anne Robinson, Robert J. Wilke, James Garner, Jeff Silver. Scout Cheyenne and mapmaker Smitty help rescue a young woman from a stagecoach attacked by Indians, only to be trapped in a mountain hideaway manned by a band of desperadoes.

27.2 *Julesburg.* Oct. 11, 1955. GS: Adele August, Ray Teal, David Albert. A herd of cattle is stolen from a wagon train lost en route to the cavalry post. Cheyenne and Smitty set out for the nearest town and the desperadoes they believe did the rustling.

27.3 *The Argonauts.* Nov. 1, 1955. GS: Rod Taylor, Steve Conte, Edward Andrews. Two prospectors are aided in their search for a rich gold mine by Cheyenne. A band of renegade Indians try to rob the small group of its ore and provisions. They tell Cheyenne he is needed at the Indian camp to aid a white woman.

27.4 *Border Showdown.* Nov. 22, 1955. GS: Myron Healey, Lisa Montell, Julian Rivero, Adele Mara. Cheyenne and his sidekick Smitty discover that the bandits responsible for the killing of a friend of theirs now hold an entire village under their thumb. The two men enlist the aid of the padre to inspire the townspeople to rebel against the gang.

27.5 *The Outlander.* Dec. 13, 1955. GS: Leo Gordon, Doris Dowling, Onslow Stevens. Cheyenne learns that the wife of the owner of the largest ranch in the territory is an ex-prostitute. Because Cheyenne has information on the operations of a blackmailing gang, he is beaten severely by three thugs. When Cheyenne returns to find one of the desperadoes, he is tried on a trumped-up charge.

27.6 *The Traveler.* Jan. 3, 1956. GS: James Gleason, Robert Armstrong, Diane Brewster, Morris Ankrum, Dennis Hopper. An old man is unjustly accused of murder and dragged off by a lynch mob. He is saved from hanging, but his rescuer is later shot.

27.7 *The Black Hawk War* (A.K.A. "Decision"). Jan. 24, 1956. GS: Nancy Hale, Richard Denning, Ray Teal, James Garner. Cheyenne faces the prospect of a court-martial when he warns the commander of Fort Wilderness that Indian tribes have combined under one leader to go on the warpath. Cheyenne feels he must disobey some unwise orders then issued by the commander.

27.8 *The Storm Riders.* Feb. 7, 1956. GS: Regis Toomey, Anne Whitfield, Barton MacLane, Beverly Michaels. When Cheyenne is ruthlessly run down by the hired hand of a wealthy cattleman, his wounds are treated by a friendly rancher. Cheyenne learns this rancher, too, is a victim of the cattleman's greedy schemes.

27.9 *Rendezvous at Red Rock.* Feb. 21, 1956. GS: Gerald Mohr, Douglas Fowley, Steve Darrell, Leo G. Carroll. Three men hold Cheyenne captive for a shooting he didn't do. There is a double twist when the notorious gunslinger who was responsible for the crime unexpectedly frees him.

27.10 *West of the River.* March 20, 1956. GS: Stepanie Griffin, Lois Collier, Trevor Bardette. With no regular troops available, Cheyenne is forced to lead a raiding party of renegade guardhouse cavalrymen to a Kiowa Indian village where two girls are held captive.

27.11 *Quicksand.* April 3, 1956. GS: Dennis Hopper, Norman Frederic, Peggy Webber, John Alderson. Marauding Comanches attack a party on its way through dangerous Indian territory. The leader of the party, Indian Scout Cheyenne

Cheyenne

Bodie, challenges the Comanche chief to battle for his life in a bed of quicksand.

27.12 *Fury at Rio Hondo.* April 17, 1956. GS: Ralph Moody, Peggy Castle, Karen Kadler, Tom Hernandez, Carl Esmond. Cheyenne makes the long trek to Mexico with a herd of cattle only to learn when he arrives that his client has disappeared. His problems are multiplied by a pretty girl who is trying to work her way back to the United States, and by the Frenchman Maximilian whose troops are attempting to take over all of Mexico.

27.13 *Star in the Dust.* May 1, 1956. GS: Don Megowan, Adele Mara. Cheyenne takes on his new duties as deputy sheriff. He soon learns the sheriff has no qualms about taking care of outlaws, but a pretty young woman provides unexpected trouble.

27.14 *Johnny Bravo.* May 15, 1956. GS: Carlos Rivas, Harry Shannon, Penny Edwards, Mort Mills. When Cheyenne signs up as the new foreman at Matt Crowley's ranch, he finds that he has more to contend with than cow-punching. Crowley, bitter and sharp-tempered, secretly wants Cheyenne to marry his beautiful daughter, the strong-willed Molly. Cheyenne also discovers that his pal Johnny Bravo is in love with Molly, but that the bigoted Crowley despises Johnny's ancestry and keeps the couple apart.

27.15 *The Last Train West.* May 29, 1956. GS: Barbara Lawrence, James Garner, Barbara Eiler. When he is framed for a murder he didn't commit, Cheyenne avoids both the law and the Comanches by boarding a train bound for California. In order to avoid suspicion when all single men are required to present identification, Cheyenne claims the pretty passenger standing next to him is his wife.

27.16 *Decision.* June 5, 1956. GS: Richard Denning, James Garner, Nancy Hale, Clegg Hoyt. While guiding a Cavalry troop through Indian territory, Cheyenne finds it necessary to lead a rebellion in order to avert a disaster. The Cavalry captain doesn't realize that Indians do not always fight by the Army's rule book.

Season Two

27.17 *The Dark Rider.* Sept. 11, 1956. GS: Diane Brewster, Myron Healey, Kurt Heinz, Gilchrest Stuart. Cheyenne is talked out of three hundred dollars by a woman who takes the money and then leaves town. Cheyenne's search for her leads him to a herd of cattle being taken to market.

27.18 *The Long Winter.* Sept. 25, 1956. GS: Tom Pittman, Robert J. Wilke, Fay Spain, Hayden Rorke. Cheyenne is left to guard a winter camp when bad weather catches up with the cattle train en route to Canada. When Cheyenne has a run-in with one of the cattle-drivers, the man pulls out and joins a band of rustlers.

27.19 *Death Deals This Hand.* Oct. 9, 1956. GS: Pat Tiernan, Arthur Hunnicut, Leo Gordon. Cheyenne falls for a schoolteacher aboard a riverboat bound for St. Louis. But she turns out to be the pawn of gamblers who try to take Hoot Hollister's money away from him.

27.20 *The Bounty Killer.* Oct. 23, 1956. GS: Andrew Duggan, James Gavin, Howard Petrie, Gail Kobe. Cheyenne unwittingly joins forces with a trigger-happy marshal who has a habit of not bringing prisoners back alive.

27.21 *The Law Man.* Nov. 6, 1956. GS: Andrea King, Grant Withers, Paul Engle, Charles Horvath, Stafford Repp. Local ranchers are sure that they have captured all the members of a gang of rustlers. But Cheyenne is equally sure that there are a few still on the lose.

27.22 *The Mustang Trail.* Nov. 20, 1956. GS: Diane Brewster, Ross Elliott, Robert J. Wilke, Lane Bradford, Paul Fierro, Nestor Paiva. Friends of Cheyenne's learn that several hundred horses are running wild in Mexico. They don't have anyone's brand on them, so are free for the taking to anyone willing to risk tangling with the Indian renegade who controls that part of the Mexican range. Cheyenne's friends ask him to go with them to round up and claim the herd.

27.23 *Lone Gun.* Dec. 4, 1956. GS: Nancy Hale, Paul Brinegar, Trevor Bardette, Hal Baylor, Bob Steele. The owner of a herd of cattle asks Cheyenne for help in getting his cattle to Dodge City. En route, the owner drowns and Cheyenne determines to get them through by himself, despite the opposition of the crew.

27.24 *The Trap.* Dec. 18, 1956. GS: Maggie Hayes, Rhodes Reason, Sally Fraser, Kenneth MacDonald. Corrupt Sheriff Gaffey claps Cheyenne in chains and puts him in a silver mine to work for a gang of outlaws. In an attempt to escape, Cheyenne plays on the sympathy of two women in the gang.

27.25 *The Iron Trail.* Jan. 1, 1957. GS: Dani Crayne, Dennis Hopper, Sheb Wooley, Sydney Smith, Almira Sessions. On a mail train heading west, Cheyenne and his pretty traveling companion are captured by a band of young bandits intent on robbing the mail.

27.26 *Land Beyond the Law.* Jan. 15, 1957. GS: Andrew Duggan, Jennifer Howard, James Griffith, Dan Blocker. In his determination for a showdown with a wanted bandit, Cheyenne rides into the stronghold of a band of dangerous outlaws.

27.27 *Test of Courage.* Jan. 29, 1957. GS: Mary Castle, George Neise, John Archer, Mickey Simpson, Britt Lomond. Cheyenne is caught in the cross fire between the United States Cavalry and a band of horse thieves.

27.28 *War Party.* Feb. 12, 1957. GS: Angie Dickinson. Cheyenne gets entangled in a dispute with a gold prospector and a band of renegades, and then faces capture by a tribe of vengeful Sioux.

27.29 *Deadline.* Feb. 26, 1957. GS: John Qualen, Mark Roberts, Bruce Cowling, Ann Robinson, Charlita, Lane Chandler. A crook wants control of a small-town newspaper and Cheyenne is drawn into the controversy. He learns that the publisher's wife is a girl he once loved.

27.30 *Big Ghost Basin.* March 12, 1957. GS: Robert Hover, Merry Anders, Buddy Baer. Ranchers and their families are terrorized by a mysterious killer. Cheyenne's job of tracking down the murderer is somewhat complicated when a young man becomes jealous of Cheyenne's attentions to his fiancee.

27.31 *Born Bad.* March 26, 1957. GS: Wright King, Jil Jarmyn, Robert F. Simon, Nestor Paiva. Working as a small town sheriff, Cheyenne is taken with one of the local beauties. Her father is the former sheriff and her brother is a wanted killer.

27.32 *The Brand.* April 9, 1957. GS: Edward Byrnes, Sue George, Darryl Duran, Benny Baker. In a search for his partner and his lost herd of horses, Cheyenne has an unexpected encounter with a young gunman who is sought by a posse. The fleeing desperado has hidden his brother and sister in an isolated mountain cabin, and fears discovery by the posse.

27.33 Decision at Gunsight. April 23, 1957. GS: John Carradine, Patrick McVey, Marie Windsor. Cheyenne faces a showdown with the leader of a protection racket that has just moved into town. Matters are complicated when Cheyenne makes the acquaintance of a pretty young woman who is part of the band.

27.34 The Spanish Grant. May 7, 1957. GS: Douglas Kennedy, Peggy Castle, Anthony George. Cheyenne learns that his ex-boss was responsible for the murder of a baby's father, and intends to do away with the tiny orphan as well in an attempt to make a claim on some land.

27.35 Hard Bargain. May 21, 1957. GS: Richard Crenna, Regis Toomey, Dawn Richard. While bringing back a bank robber, Cheyenne Bodie gets caught in a bear trap and is at the mercy of his prisoner.

27.36 The Broken Pledge. June 4, 1957. GS: John Dehner, Jean Byron, Norman Frederic, Paul Birch. A woman reporter unwittingly sends Chief Sitting Bull's tribe on the warpath. In her eagerness to get a story, she leads a band of renegade white men to an Indian accused of killing one of them. The woman believes the white men intend only to capture the Indian and hold him for trial. But the renegades are intent on meting out their own brand of justice.

Season Three

27.37 Incident at Indian Springs. Sept. 24, 1957. GS: Dan Barton, Carlyle Mitchell, Bonnie Bolding, John Cliff, Chris Olsen. A schoolmaster who killed a gang leader wants the reward. But he may get more than he bargained for. The gang attacks the schoolhouse, threatening the teacher and pupils.

27.38 The Conspirators. Oct. 8, 1957. GS: Joan Weldon, Guinn Williams, Tom Conway. Cheyenne is assigned as an Army undercover agent to help stamp out a ring of Confederate seditionists. He assumes the identity of an actor, Jim Merritt, who, in reality, is a friend of one of the traitors.

27.39 The Mutton Puncher. Oct. 22, 1957. GS: Robert J. Wilke, Marie Windsor, Lane Bradford, Gil Rankin, Billy Gray, Lauren Chapin. Cheyenne quits his job as Ben Creed's foreman but changes his mind after Creed saves him from an ambush. Then Creed gambles with a pretty ranch owner and offers his foreman as the stake.

27.40 Border Affair (A.K.A. "Traveling Princess"). Nov. 5,1957. GS: Erin O'Brien, Michael Pate, Sebastian Cabot, Joy Page, Linda Watkins. Cheyenne intervenes when a European princess is about to be married to an aged French general.

27.41 Devil's Canyon. Nov. 19, 1957. GS: Robert Foulk, Ainslie Pryor, Joanna Barnes, Jack LaRue, Mark Cavell, Myron Healey, Tom McKee, Gene Roth. Cheyenne soon learns that the fortune hunters he is guiding in their search for some diamonds want them at any price. Then he discovers that the diamonds are religious relics.

27.42 Town of Fear. Dec. 3, 1957. GS: Walter Coy, Alan Wells, Steve Darrell, Kathleen Crowley, John Doucette. Cheyenne was a local hero when he brought in a wanted outlaw. But the townsfolk have turned against him. The townsfolk do not agree with Cheyenne when he maintains that his friend Sheriff Townley is innocent of murder.

27.43 Hired Gun. Dec. 17, 1957. GS: Don Megowan, Alan Hale, Jr., Whitney Blake, Douglas Spencer, Russell Thorson, Michael Dante. Cheyenne gets involved in a murder plot when he signs on at the Bridgeman Ranch. Bridgeman thinks Cheyenne is a gunman his wife has hired to kill him.

27.44 Top Hand. Dec. 31, 1957. GS: Peter Brown, Jeanne Cooper, Walter Barnes, Paul Savage, Ed Prentiss. In an attempt to avoid entanglement in the feuds of three ranchers, Cheyenne turns down job offers from each of them. But when he heads out of the territory. Cheyenne is ambushed by one of the outfits and left without horse, water or food in the middle of desert country.

27.45 The Last Comanchero. Jan. 14, 1958. GS: Harold J. Stone, Edward Byrnes, Virginia Aldridge, Jonathan Hole. A renegade has been caught selling guns and alcohol to the Indians. Cheyenne fights to save him from a lynch mob.

27.46 The Gamble. Jan. 28, 1958. GS: Evelyn Ankers, James Seay, Theodora Davitt, Charles Fredericks, Raymond Hatton. The lady owner of a saloon asks Cheyenne's help when she learns that her daughter is returning home from Boston. She asks Cheyenne to take over the management of the saloon to keep the girl from learning that her mother is a saloon keeper.

27.47 Renegades. Feb. 11, 1958. GS: Bartlett Robinson, Peter Brown, Olive Sturgess, Steven Durrell. Col. Ralph Donovan claims that the only good Indian is a dead one. Cheyenne tries to keep the colonel's attitude from ruining peace negotiations with a hostile tribe.

27.48 The Empty Gun. Feb. 25, 1958. GS: Audrey Totter, John Russell, Sean Garrison. Matt Reardon is forced to kill his partner in a gun duel. When he offers the dead man's widow her share of the mine he finds that she nurses a deep and bitter hatred and that the dead man's son has sworn to kill him. Cheyenne agrees to help.

27.49 White Warrior. March 11, 1958. GS: Michael Landon, Peter Whitney, Randy Stuart, Richard Garland, Morris Ankrum. Cheyenne is employed to lead a wagon train through wild frontier territory. En route then encounter some Apache braves who have captured a teenage boy. Cheyenne buys the boy from his captors, bringing upon himself and the boy the wrath of the wagon train boss.

27.50 Ghost of Cimarron. March 25, 1958. GS: Patrick McVey, Peter Brown, Vaughn Taylor, Russ Conway, Wright King, Isabelle Dawn. During an ambush, Doc Johnson and his band of gunmen capture Cheyenne Bodie. They force him to accompany them to a hideout and order him to remove a bullet from the leg of their leader.

27.51 Wagon Tongue North. April 8, 1958. GS: Ann McCrae, Howard Petrie, Frank de Kova. Cheyenne assumes an alias to take a job as a trail boss for the widow of an ex-convict he was forced to kill. The rebellious cowhands try to deliver the herd of cattle to a crooked land baron.

27.52 The Long Search. April 22, 1958. GS: Claude Akins, Norman Frederic, Randy Stuart, Kim Chaney, Gail Kobe, Tommy Farrell. A Sioux brave is accused of kidnaping a white boy and is thrown in jail. Cheyenne alone proclaims the innocence of the Indian and finds himself facing the threats of an angry mob.

Cheyenne

27.53 *Standoff.* May 6, 1958. GS: Rodolfo Acosta, Richard Garland, Joy Page, H.M. Wynant, Joe Dominguez. Cheyenne helps a wounded man to a Mexican village. Then he learns he has aided a killer, who plans to destroy the entire town if the man who shot two of his henchmen won't give himself up.

27.54 *Dead to Rights.* May 20, 1958. GS: John Russell, Michael Connors, Joanna Barnes, Don Megowan, Donald "Red" Barry. Cheyenne's partner in a mining venture is murdered, and a suave attorney, Saylor Hornbrook, is bent on keeping the killer's identity a secret.

27.55 *Noose at Noon.* June 3, 1958. GS: Charles Quinlivan, Theona Bryant, Robert Bray. Cheyenne tries to save friend Jim O'Neil from being hanged. O'Neil was convicted of a murder he didn't commit, but he is afraid to tell what he knows because of a threat to his wife.

27.56 *The Angry Sky.* June 17, 1958. GS: Adele Mara, Joan Evans, Andrew Duggan. On the trail of an escaped murderer, Cheyenne is shot and left for dead on the trail. He is found by a woman who takes Cheyenne to her sister's cabin. When the sister's husband returns from a trip to town he seems taken aback at seeing Cheyenne.

Season Four

27.57 *Blind Spot.* Sept. 21, 1959. GS: Robert Crawford, Jean Byron, Barry Kelley, Adam West, Jon Litel, Dan Sheridan. Attempting to reunite a father and his young son Gerald, who took opposing sides during the Civil War, Cheyenne uncovers a scheme to take over cotton-rich land.

27.58 *Reprieve.* Oct. 5, 1959. GS: Connie Stevens, Don Megowan, Tim Considine, Edgar Stehli. Cheyenne Bodie is hired to find bank robber Wes McQueen and recover the money that McQueen has stolen. Wes has decided to return the money, but before he can do so, he is killed by outlaws. Cheyenne, continuing his search for the money, decides to assume McQueen's identity.

27.59 *The Rebellion.* Oct. 12, 1959. GS: Rodolfo Acosta, Frank De Kova, Joe De Santis, Faith Domergue, John Marley, Paul Dubov, Carlos Romero, Carmen Austin. Cheyenne Bodie is hired to guard some freight that is being shipped by train to a Mexican patriot named Manuel. During the trip, Luis Cardenas overpowers Cheyenne and flees with the cargo, making it appear that Manuel is a traitor.

27.60 *Trial by Conscience.* Oct. 26, 1959. GS: Jeff York, Pat Crowley, Richard Garland, Don Beddoe, John Holland. Nick Avalon, boss of a frontier town, knows the location of a murdered man's grave. Following a performance of "Hamlet", Cheyenne Bodie decides to employ some of the methods used in the play to gain information and strip Avalon of his power.

27.61 *The Imposter.* Nov. 2, 1959. GS: Robert McQueeney, Peter Whitney, James Drury. Texas cattleman Sam Magruder is murdered and an impostor takes over his name and his business. Suspicious, Cheyenne gets a job as a cowhand on the ranch.

27.62 *Prisoner of Moon Mesa.* Nov. 16, 1959. GS: Robert F. Simon, Chuck Wassil, Madlyn Rhue, Bill Cord, Russ Bender, George Kennedy. Replacing Clay Mason as foreman of a large cattle ranch, Cheyenne meets resistance from neighboring ranchers who are bitter about the circumstances surrounding Mason's dismissal.

27.63 *Gold, Glory and Custer — Prelude.* Jan. 4, 1960. GS: Julie Adams, Liam Sullivan, Lorne Greene, Barry Atwater, Ed Kemmer, Yvette Dugan, Andra Martin. As an Indian scout with Col. George Custer's regiment, Cheyenne Bodie helps search for gold on a Sioux reservation. Cheyenne fears that news of a gold strike would cause bloodshed.

27.64 *Gold, Glory and Custer — Requiem.* Jan. 11, 1960. GS: Julie Adams, Liam Sullivan, Lorne Greene, Barry Atwater, Ed Kemmer, Yvette Dugan, Andra Martin. Colonel Custer's regiment is wiped out in the battle of the Little Bighorn. Risking a charge of desertion, Cheyenne decides to appear at Maj. Marcus Reno's court martial.

27.65 *Riot at Arroyo Soco.* Feb. 1, 1960. GS: Wynn Pearce, Whitney Blake, Harry Lauter, Frank Ferguson, Don Hagerty, Willis Bouchey, James Bell. During his duty as Sheriff of Arroyo Soco, Cheyenne arrests a man for murder. When the townspeople form a lynch mob, Cheyenne is forced to shoot their leader, the son of a prominent citizen.

27.66 *Apache Blood.* Feb. 8, 1960. GS: Scott Marlowe, Lisa Montel. Mickey Free, who was raised by Indians, comes to town to live among his own people. He finds the townspeople hostile, but Cheyenne stands by him.

27.67 *Outcast of Cripple Creek.* Feb. 29, 1960. GS: Whit Bissell, Rhodes Reason, Robert J. Wilke, Lisa Gaye, Tol Avery, Hal Baylor, Emory Parnell. Cheyenne is hired as a marshal to help keep rambunctious cowboys in line. Fed up with the cowboys' behavior, Cheyenne quits and is whisked off to jail.

27.68 *Alibi for a Scalped Man.* March 7, 1960. GS: Mala Powers, R.G. Armstrong, Richard Coogan, Ross Elliott, Tom Gilson, Saundra Edwards, Ottola Nesmith, Harry Hines. Cheyenne travels to Emmetsville to attend his friend's wedding. The wedding plans are suddenly changed when the bridegroom mysteriously disappears, and Cheyenne is jailed on a faked murder charge.

27.69 *Home Is the Brave.* March 14, 1960. GS: John Howard, John Archer, Paula Raymond, Donna Martell, Brad Johnson. Cheyenne returns the body of a war hero to his hometown. But a prominent citizen, John Thompson, refuses to allow the body to be buried within the city limits.

Season Five

27.70 *The Long Rope.* Oct. 3, 1960. GS: Donald May, Merry Anders, Peter Whitney, Alan Baxter, James Hurst, Frank Albertson, Dick Bellis. Riding into the town of High Point, Cheyenne remembers a scene from his boyhood days—the lynching of Jeff Pierce by a band of masked men.

27.71 *Counterfeit Gun.* Oct. 10, 1960. GS: Robert Lowery, Lisa Gaye, Vito Scotti, Ray Teal, K.L. Smith, William Mims, Jack Reitzen. Cheyenne is guarding a shipment of gold when a gang of thieves steal the gold and kill a man. But Cheyenne has a clue—he thinks the gang leader's voice is familiar.

27.72 *Road to Three Graves.* Oct. 31, 1960. GS: Alan Hale, Jr., Joe De Santis, Jason Evers, Jean Byron, James Seay. Three wagonloads of equipment have to be delivered to a mine owned by a man named Tuk. But the road is dangerously close to the property of a competing mine owner.

27.73 Two Trails to Santa Fe. Oct. 28, 1960. GS: Sonja Wilde, Robert Colbert, Richard Webb, Randy Stuart, Walter Reed, Gayla Graves, Darlene Fields, Robert G. Anderson, John Harmon, Robert Carricart. Alleah, an Apache woman, was to be tortured to death for marrying a white woman. Cheyenne rescues her, and the enraged Apaches ride to attack a nearby mining settlement.

27.74 Savage Breed. Dec. 19, 1960. GS: Ray Danton, Charlie Briggs, Carlyle Mitchell, Walter Coy, Robert Clarke, Patricia Huston. Dodge City's marshal, Al Lestrade, is on vacation, supposedly hunting buffalo. But when someone fires a shot intended to stampede an approaching herd, the cartridge is traced to Lestrade's weapon.

27.75 Incident at Dawson Flats. Jan. 9, 1961. GS: Gerald Mohr, Joan O'Brien, Jock Gaynor, Hampton Fancher, Morris Ankrum. Cheyenne rides into Dawson Flats, all set to celebrate a friend's wedding. On arrival, he's attacked by Lafe Dawson and later Dawson is found dead.

27.76 Duel at Judas Basin. Jan. 30, 1961. GS: Ty Hardin, Will Hutchins, Jacques Aubuchon, Alan Caillou, Sheldon Allman, Ken Mayer, Ed Prentiss, Terry Frost. Cheyenne is trail boss of a cattle drive going to Fort Benton. After one of his cowhands is murdered, and someone takes a pot shot at him from an alley, Cheyenne realizes that someone doesn't want his herd to reach its destination.

27.77 The Return of Mr. Grimm. Feb. 13, 1961. GS: R.G. Armstrong, Anita Sands, Stephen Roberts, Maurice Manson, Sherwood Price, Orville Sherman, Myron Healey. A wealthy mine-owner named Grimm turns up in town, bent on one purpose—revenge on Cheyenne. Grimm's son was killed while resisting arrest by Sheriff Bodie.

27.78 The Beholden. Feb. 27, 1961. GS: Don Megowan, Patrice Wymore, Hanley Stafford, Sheldon Allman, John Hubbard, Max Baer, Robert Foulk. Deputy Marshal Bodie does a heap of work tracking down and bringing in a bank robber. Then Cheyenne learns that Tom Grant, the town marshal, has released the culprit from jail.

27.79 The Frightened Town. March 20, 1961. GS: Andrew Duggan, Myron Healey, James Griffith, Greg Palmer, Max Baer, Angela Greene, Lane Chandler, Bob Dunlap, William Fawcett, Tim Graham, John Ramondetta. A gang of outlaws take over the town of Kingsburg, but none of the townspeople are willing to help Marshal Delaney drive them out. With no opposition in sight, the badmen decide to have some fun with the town—by burning it down.

27.80 Lone Patrol. April 10, 1961. GS: Robert McQueeney, Evan McCord, Stacy Keach, Brad Weston, Harry Holcombe, Clyde Howdy. Cheyenne warns Army Captain Duquesne against starting his supply train out across the range. There is a restless Shawnee Indian party waiting in the hills. But Duquesne turns a deaf ear to the advice.

27.81 Massacre at Gunsight Pass. May 1, 1961. GS: Sherwood Price, X Brands, Jack Elam, I. Stanford Jolley, Rory Mallinson, John Alonzo. Traveling by stagecoach, Cheyenne is taking deserter Johnny Eldorado back to face an Army tribunal. While still far from any signs of civilization, the stage is brought to a halt by Indians on the warpath.

27.82 The Greater Glory. May 15, 1961. GS: William Sargent, Susan Crane, Tod Griffin, Ray Stricklyn, William Phipps. If Roy and Mary Wiley can drive their cattle to Salt Lake City in time to sell at the best prices, they can pay off the mortgage on their ranch. But ranch owner Rafe Donovan would prefer to have them fail since gold and silver deposits have been found on their land.

Season Six

27.83 Winchester Quarantine. Sept. 25, 1961. GS: Susan Cummings, Ross Elliott, Steve Brodie, William Fawcett, I. Stanford Jolley, Rory Mallinson, John Alonzo. Herds in the Texas Panhandle are being depleted by an unknown, but deadly, fever. The ranchers conclude that the disease is being brought in by cattle from the south.

27.84 Trouble Street. Oct. 2, 1961. GS: Mala Powers, Patrick McVey, James Coburn, Lee Van Cleef, Tom Drake, Anna Capri, Gilman Rankin. While passing through Colton City, Cheyenne stops to grab some grub. A man named Kell provokes him into a fight.

27.85 Cross Purpose. Oct. 9, 1961. GS: Edmon Ryan, Frank DeKova, Michael Forest, Walter Brooke, Joyce Meadows, Richard Tatro, Mickey Simpson, I. Stanford Jolley, Frank Gerstle, Dick Rich, Art Stewart. The townspeople of Clairmont have erected a statue to Col. Charles De Vier, believing he died at the hands of Apache torturers. But two prospectors happen to uncover the hero's body and bring it back to town. It seems the De Vier was shot in the head with Army bullets.

27.86 The Young Fugitives. Oct. 23, 1961. GS: Richard Evans, Trevor Bardette, Dayton Lummis, Anne Whitfield, Don Haggerty, Paul Langton. While former Sheriff Frank Collins wastes away in a wheel chair because of a bullet in his spine, his teenage son Gilby does pretty much as he pleases. The boy's passion is guns, and he has built one of his own.

27.87 Day's Pay. Oct. 30, 1961. GS: Rudolph Acosta, Ellen McRae/Burstyn, Evan McCord, Jim Boles, Willard Waterman, Trevor Bardette, Tom Gilson, John Durren, John Ramondetta. Cheyenne stops a lynching party in its tracks, and saves Luis Boladas from the hangman's noose. Cheyenne is only returning a favor, as Boladas once saved his life.

27.88 Retaliation. Nov. 13, 1961. GS: John Anderson, Jason Evers, Randy Stuart, John Rodney, Kelly Thordsen. The townspeople of Lehigh are not unhappy when the bank is robbed. Most of the money belonged to tycoon Thackeray Smith, not the good-neighbor type. Cheyenne receives a share of the town's hostility when he insists on raising a posse to chase the bandits.

27.89 Storm Center. Nov. 20, 1961. GS: Robert Crawford, Jr., Harry Shannon, Dorothy Green, Don Megowan, Mario Siletti, Jack Hogan. Young Frank Garcia lives at Father Paul's Orphanage, but he believes that his parents are alive. He begs Cheyenne to help locate them, and then he disappears.

27.90 Legacy of the Lost. Dec. 4, 1961. GS: Richard Hale, Peter Whitney, Peter Breck, William Windom, Jolene Brand. Cheyenne, who was raised by Chief Red Cloud, learns to his surprise that his father, Lionel Abbott, is still alive. He sets out to locate his long-lost parent.

27.91 The Brahma Bull. Dec. 11, 1961. GS: George D. Wallace, John Cliff, Owen Orr, Kevin Hagen, Suzi Carnell, Clyde Howdy. Cheyenne sets out with an impressive bankroll to buy a Brahma bull—a gift for a sick child. But the Hawker

Brothers, three good for nothings, get wind of the plan and intend to head him off at the pass.

27.92 *The Wedding Rings.* Jan. 8, 1962. GS: Harold J. Stone, Margarita Cordova, Raoul De Leon, Nestor Paiva, Ana Maria Majalca, Pedro Gonzales Gonzales. With the aid of his private army, a ruthless bandit named Perez has become virtual dictator of a Mexican province. He hopes to extort enough money from the peasants to buy himself a position in the national government.

27.93 *The Idol.* Jan. 29, 1962. GS: Jeff Morrow, Leo Gordon, Roger Mobley, Jean Byron, Robert Williams, Craig Duncan, Don Wilbanks. The three Kirby brothers don't need much of an excuse to kill any man, but gunfighter Ben Shelby they are determined to get. The trouble with their latest maneuver is that they haven't cornered Ben Shelby at all, but instead have encountered Cheyenne.

27.94 *One Way Ticket.* Feb. 19, 1962. GS: Philip Carey, Maureen Leeds, Lillian Bronson, Bob Anderson, Roxanne Arlen, Ronnie Dapo. Outlaw Cole Younger is being transported by train to the Denver jail, and Cheyenne is guarding him. Cheyenne would like to get acquainted with fellow passenger Laura Barrington, but Laura is also closely guarded, by staunch dowager Mrs. Frazier.

27.95 *The Bad Penny.* March 12, 1962. GS: Susan Seaforth, Robert Hogan, Richard Webb, Don Haggerty, Jeff De Benning, Carol Nicholson. When four men receive notes threatening their lives, Cheyenne suggests the notes may have come from the town's latest newcomer. This gets a hearty laugh, because the new arrival is pretty young Penelope Piper.

27.96 *A Man Called Ragan.* April 23, 1962. GS: Arch Johnson, Chad Everett, Jack Elam, Larry Ward, Mike Greene, Jeanne Cooper. Dakota Territorial Marshal Frank Ragan rides into Stark City to see his buddy Johnny Wilson. But cattle baron Ben Stark tells Ragan that Wilson has disappeared, and that Ragan had better do the same. *Note*: Clint Walker does not appear in this episode.

Season Seven

27.97 *The Durango Brothers.* Sept. 24, 1962. GS: Sally Kellerman, Jack Elam, Mickey Simpson, Ellen Corby, Charles Briggs, Warren Douglas, Chuck Hicks, Alex Sharpe. Cheyenne beats Homer Durango in a test of strength and thereby becomes a candidate for the hand of the Durango boys' old-maid sister Lottie. He soon learns that other likely suitors have refused the honor and haven't been seen since.

27.98 *Satonka.* Oct. 1, 1962. GS: Andrew Duggan, Susan Seaforth, James Best, Bill Zuckert. Satonka is the Indian name for the Evil One, and local citizens are applying it to a mysterious creature living on Desolation Mountain. While passing through the area, Cheyenne finds a dead body with huge footprints leading away from the scene.

27.99 *Sweet Sam.* Oct. 8, 1962. GS: Robert McQueeney, Ronnie Haran, Roger Mobley, James Best, Denver Pyle. Soon after Sam Pridemore arrives in Rock Springs, he disarms a killer and becomes the town hero. But Cheyenne remembers Sam as an unscrupulous boy and suspects that his real interest lies in a quarter of a million dollars worth of gold that is stashed in the bank.

27.100 *Man Alone.* Oct. 15, 1962. GS: Kathy Bennett, Carl Reindel, Steve Brodie, Sherwood Price, John Milford. Cheyenne helps a wounded cowboy suffering from amnesia. He suspects that the cowpoke, who calls himself Billy, was a member of the gang that robbed the cattlemen's association.

27.101 *The Quick and the Deadly.* Oct. 22, 1962. GS: Mike Road, Chris Alcaide, Jeanne Cooper. At Jud Ainley's murder trial, lawman Harry Thomas is not only discredited as a witness, he is charged with robbery.

27.102 *Indian Gold.* Oct. 29, 1962. GS: Peter Breck, Trevor Bardette, H.M. Wynant. Indian gold lures prospector Charlie Teeney and his followers onto the Sioux reservation when they see White Crow bring two sacks of the mineral into town. Sheriff Kilgore asks Cheyenne to help him keep this breach of the peace treaty from erupting into a full-scale Indian uprising.

27.103 *Dark Decision.* Nov. 5, 1962. GS: Diane Brewster, Peter Breck, Robert Brubaker, Barry Kelley. Nathan Alston keeps his money in a safe, but apparently it is not safe enough. He is found dead near the open steel box. A drifter named Tony Chance accuses Cheyenne of quarreling with Alston just before the murder.

27.104 *Pocketful of Stars.* Nov. 12, 1962. GS: Peter Brown, Robert Foulk, Frank De Kova, Lisa Lu. Based on information from his friend, surveyor Ross Andrews, Cheyenne assures Red Knife and his Shoshone braves that the railroad right of way will bypass the Indian burial ground.

27.105 *The Vanishing Breed.* Nov. 19, 1962. GS: Regis Toomey, Roy Roberts, Vaughn Taylor. Cheyenne would like to help preserve the vanishing buffaloes for the Indians against the onslaught of hunters. His chance comes when a vacancy occurs in the State Senate.

27.106 *Vengeance Is Mine.* Nov. 26, 1962. GS: Van Williams, Jean Willes, George Gaynes. Appointed as sheriff, Cheyenne finds his most pressing task is stopping a range war before it begins. It seems that his friend Ray Masters is out to get rancher Rod Delaplane, who Masters claims double-crossed him into jail

27.107 *Johnny Brassbuttons.* Dec. 3, 1962. GS: Philip Carey, Tony Young, Adam Williams, Angela Dorian, Michael Pate. Warrior-turned-soldier Johnny Brassbuttons is under suspicion when the Army unit he is with runs into an Apache ambush. Johnny is accused of leading the troops into a trap, but Cheyenne and Major Frank Nolan are determined to establish his innocence.

27.108 *Wanted for the Murder of Cheyenne Bodie.* Dec. 1, 1962. GS: Richard Webb, Ruta Lee, Dick Foran, Robert Knapp, Brad Weston. Sheriff Bigelow pick up a suspect for the murder of Cheyenne Bodie. The man they have arrested seems completely confused by the charge, an attitude which isn't hard to explain since he happens to be Cheyenne Bodie.

27.109 *Showdown at Oxbend.* Dec. 17, 1962. GS: Joan Caulfield, Andrew Duggan, Ray Teal, James Griffith. In the heart of cattle country, Cheyenne is surprised to find a herd of sheep, under armed guard, making themselves at home on the range.

28. The Chisholms

CBS. 60 min. Broadcast history: Thursday, 8:00-9:00, March 1979–April 1979; Saturday, 8:00-9:00, Jan. 1980–March 1980.

Regular Cast: Robert Preston (Hadley Chisholm), Rosemary Harris (Minerva Chisholm), Ben Murphy (Will Chisholm), Brian Kerwin (Gideon Chisholm) 1979, Brett Cullen (Gideon Chisholm) 1980, Jimmy Van Patten (Bo Chisholm), Stacey Nelkin (Bonnie Sue Chisholm) 1979, Glynnis O'Connor (Elizabeth Chisholm) 1979, Sandra Griego (Kewedinok Chisholm) 1979, Brian Keith (Andrew Blake) 1979, Delta Burke (Bonnie Sue Chisholm) 1980, David Hayward (Timothy Oates) 1979, Susan Swift (Annabel Chisholm) 1979, Susan Swift (Mercy Howell) 1980, Maureen Steindler (Millie Bain) 1979, Dennis Kennedy (Benjamin Lowery) 1979, James Harrell (Doc Simpson) 1979, Don Shanks (Enapay) 1979, Geno Silva (Ferocious Storm) 1979, Joe Garcia (Howahkan), Charles L. Campbell (Judge Wilson) 1979, Kate Hantley (Sarah Comybns) 1979, Jerry Hardin (Jonah Comyns) 1979, Tom Taylor (Harlow Cooper) 1979, Doug Kershaw (Fiddler Ephraim) 1979, Charles Frank (Lester Hackett) 1979, Devon Ericson (Betsy O'Neil) 1980, Reid Smith (Lester Hackett) 1980, Victoria Racimo (Kewedinok Chisholm) 1980, Mitchell Ryan (Cooper Hawkins) 1980.

Premise: This series, initially a 4-part mini-series, dealt with the saga of the pioneering Chisholm family and their trek from Virginia to Fort Laramie, Wyoming. During the second season, the family continued their journey by wagon train on to California.

The Episodes

28.1 *Part One.* March 29, 1979. GS: Anthony Zerbe, James D. O'Reilly, Gavin Troster, David Allen, Dean Hill. Hadley Chisholm, a stubborn, God-fearing farmer, is driven from his land by feuding neighbors and family tragedy. He leads his family west. As they travel down the Ohio River, their trek is endangered by shaky agreements with hard-bitten guides.

28.2 *Part Two.* April 5, 1979. GS: Peg Small, Katie Hanley, Jack Wallace. On the road to Independence, Missouri, romance blossoms between Bonnie Sue and Lester.

28.3 *Part Three.* April 12, 1979. Perilous river crossings and encounters with hostile Indians mark the family's continuing trek to Fort Laramie.

28.4 *Part Four.* April 19, 1979. GS: Christopher Allport, Billy Drago, Richard L. Jamison, Roger Frazier. After Annabel is killed by Indians, the family pushes on to Fort Laramie, Wyoming, where Bonnie Sue is reunited with Lester.

Season Two

28.5 *Part One.* Jan. 19, 1980. GS: Chief Standingbear. The Chisholm family prepare to continue west as Fort Laramie comes under Indian siege.

28.6 *Part Two.* Jan. 26, 1980. GS: Nick Ramos. Grain promised to the Indians is used to feed livestock after a prairie fire destroys their grazing. Betsy O'Neal exploits Bo and Gideon's sibling rivalry for her affection.

28.7 *Part Three.* Feb. 2, 1980. GS: Donald Moffat, Frank Noel. The Chisholms break with the wagon train, choosing the uncharted desert passage to California, and taking mischief-maker Betsy O'Neal with them at Gideon's behest.

28.8 *Part Four.* Feb. 9, 1980. GS: Guich Koock, Les Lannom. Hawkins and Betsy's brothers return with conflicting stories of a massacre, which are resolved in a showdown that ends up drawing Hadley's blood.

28.9 *Part Five* (A.K.A. "Death in the Sierras"). Feb. 16, 1980. GS: Donald Moffat, Ben Piazza. Violence, starvation and a shattering loss mark the Sierra Nevada crossing as the wagon train, paralyzed by heavy snows, awaits the outcome of Will's desperate supply mission to Fort Sutter.

28.10 *Part Six.* Feb. 23, 1980. GS: Don Chastain. In the aftermath of Hadley's death, Minerva wants to settle right there in the foothills, while her family wants to go on.

28.11 *Part Seven.* March 1, 1980. GS: Leslie Nielsen, E.J. Andre, Ruben Moreno, Jeanne Bates. Only Will thinks a wealthy trader is too good to be true when he courts Minerva and her family by lavishing gifts upon them.

28.12 *Part Eight* (A.K.A. "Chains"). March 8, 1980. GS: J.A. Preston, Ben Piazza, William Bryant, Michael Swan. As Minerva goes about starting her apple orchard, a runaway slave is found hiding at the ranch.

28.13 *Part Nine* (A.K.A. "The Siren Song"). March 15, 1980. GS: Donnelly Rhodes. The conscience of devoutly Baptist Minerva is tried by the friendship of Bo and a Franciscan padre who is paying him to help build a chapel.

29. Cimarron City

NBC. 60 min. Broadcast history: Saturday, 9:30-10:30, Oct. 1958-Sept. 1959; Friday, 7:30-8:30, June 1960–Sept. 1960.

Regular Cast: George Montgomery (Matthew Rockford), Audrey Totter (Beth Purcell), John Smith (Lane Temple), Claire Carleton (Alice Purdy), Fred Sherman (Burt Purdy), Dan Blocker (Tiny Budinger), Wally Brown (Jed Fame), Addison Richards (Banker Martin Kingsley), Stuart Randall (Sheriff Art Simpson).

Premise: This Western series, set in the 1880s, depicted the growth of Cimarron City, Oklahoma, as seen by cattle baron, and former mayor, Matthew Rockford.

The Episodes

29.1 *I, the People.* Oct. 11, 1958. GS: Fred MacMurray, Jason Robards, Sr., John Banner, Tom Fadden, Rick Vallin, Mary Alan Hokanson. Laird Garner arrives in town and helps to foil a robbery. He then opens a bank, and the townspeople, impressed with his bravery, elect him mayor. But after his election Laird begins to show his true colors.

29.2 *Terror Town.* Oct. 18, 1958. GS: Dan Duryea, Barbara Lawrence, Don Megowan, Jonathan Haze. On his way back to Cimarron City, Matt Rockford is taken prisoner by Roy Budinger and his brothers. They force him to work in an abandoned silver mine which they are convinced will pay off.

29.3 *To Become a Man.* Oct. 25, 1958. GS: Robin Riley, William Talman, Jason Robards, Sr. Matt Rockford tries to arrest a thief and in the ensuing struggle the man's gun goes off and he is killed. Matt is shocked when he recognizes the thief

Cimarron City

as an old friend. He tries to help the dead man's two sons, but one, a rebellious teenager, vows to hunt down the man responsible for his father's death.

29.4 *Twelve Guns.* Nov. 1, 1958. GS: Nick Adams, Luana Patten, John Dehner, Kay Stewart. Twelve gunmen ride into Cimarron City and try to extort money from the townspeople. Matt Rockford, Lane Temple and Beth Purcell band together and refuse to pay the gunmen.

29.5 *Medicine Man.* Nov. 8, 1958. GS: Gary Merrill, June Lockhart. Joshua Newton, an ex-Army doctor, arrive in Cimarron City with his wife Emily. Newton, who was accused of malpractice by his commanding officer, wants to make a new life for himself. But men who knew him in the Army arrive in town and start making trouble for him.

29.6 *Hired Hand.* Nov. 15, 1958. GS: Michael Connors, Elizabeth Montgomery. Cimarron City's water supply is suddenly cut off when the river is dammed by a rancher. A man sent to investigate the matter disappears and Matt Rockford decides to take a job as a hired hand on the ranch.

29.7 *Kid on a Calico Horse.* Nov. 22, 1958. GS: Linda Darnell, Dean Stockwell, Edgar Buchanan, John Litel, Douglas Kennedy, Walter Coy, Jason Robards, Sr. A young man is accused of a murder although he claims that he was forced to kill in self-defense. Matt Rockford, afraid of what the hostile townspeople may do, races against time in an effort to save the youth.

29.8 *The Beast of Cimarron.* Nov. 29, 1958. GS: Don Megowan, George Dunn. Beth Purcell is kidnaped and the townspeople of Cimarron City believe that a legendary monster has carried her off. Matt Rockford and Lane Temple lead a search party to find Beth.

29.9 *A Respectable Girl.* Dec. 6, 1958. GS: Dorothy Malone, Glenda Farrell, Harold J. Stone, Walter Sande, John Berardino. Nora Atkins and her mother settle in Cimarron City intent on starting a new life. Nora finds it a difficult task when her past and deputy Lane Temple interfere.

29.10 *The Bloodline.* Dec. 13, 1958. GS: J. Carrol Naish, Richard Jaeckel. Outlaw Rafe Crowder comes to town in search of his son. The boy is faced with a struggle between loyalty to his father and his notion of right behavior.

29.11 *Cimarron Holiday.* Dec. 20, 1958. GS: Tim Hovey, George Dunn, Peter Dunn, Dinah Shore, Missy Montgomery, John D. Montgomery. The townspeople of Cimarron City get together to produce a Western version of Charles Dickens' "Christmas Carol." After the performance the townspeople join in some festivities.

29.12 *McGowan's Debt.* Dec. 27, 1958. GS: Larry Pennell, William Phipps, Kathleen Crowley. Drew McGowan has just been released from prison where he served time for a crime he didn't commit. Seeking revenge, McGowan arrives in Cimarron City intent on finding the two people who framed him.

29.13 *The Bitter Lesson.* Jan. 3, 1959. GS: Dorothy Provine, Richard Travis, Gregg Palmer. Deputy sheriff Lane Temple is infatuated with the lovely schoolteacher who has just arrived in Cimarron City. Beth suspects, however, that the teacher is spending her after school hours helping to rob gold shipments.

29.14 *A Legacy for Ossie Harper.* Jan. 10, 1959. GS: Carlton Carpenter, Judi Meredith, James Seay. Ossie Harper is a young man who spends his time doing little more than singing for whisky. That is, until the day a land grant is found, giving Ossie title to Cimarron City, and Ossie decides to carry out his vengeance on the town and its people.

29.15 *Child of Fear.* Jan. 17, 1959. GS: John Carradine, Luana Anders, Tom Pittman, Jeanne Bates. Two youngsters find their romance threatened by the girl's father, Jared Tucker. A religious fanatic, Tucker has been successful in hiding his bizarre past.

29.16 *Burn the Town Down.* Jan. 24, 1959. GS: Dennis McCarthy, Wally Brown, George Dunn, Pete Dunn. Sheriff Lane Temple has jailed a member of an unidentified outlaw gang. In an attempt to force Temple to release the prisoner, the outlaws set fire to Cimarron City. Temple wants to keep the outlaw in jail and try to trap the gang, but his plan is opposed by frightened townspeople.

29.17 *Runaway Train.* Jan. 31, 1959. GS: Diane Brewster, Isabel Randolph, Myron Healey, Lyle Talbot. Mayor Matt Rockford meets Lisa Caldwell on a train and begins to fall in love with her. On the same train are a group of prisoners and a man Lisa once knew.

29.18 *The Beauty and the Sorrow.* Feb. 7, 1959. GS: Debra Paget, George Hamilton, Grant Richards, Terry Becker. A young lady breaks an engagement and then marries another man, a moody choirmaster. After the wedding two of her old beaus are found dead.

29.19 *Return of the Dead.* Feb. 14, 1959. GS: Brad Dexter, Tom Drake, John Goddard. Beth Purcell's husband, assumed dead for a number of years, rides into Cimarron City pursued by the man who supposedly had killed him.

29.20 *Blind Is the Killer.* Feb. 21, 1959. GS: Robert Fuller. Young gunslinger Joe Cole shoots Matt Rockford, and as a result Matt may lose his sight.

29.21 *The Unaccepted.* Feb. 28, 1959. GS: Judith Ames, Peter Graves. Matt Rockford and Jens, a Danish immigrant, are rivals for the affections of young widow Emmy Barton. This makes Beth jealous, and she decides to help Jens win Emmy. But Jens must face the enmity of the townspeople of Cimarron City, who are bitter about the influx of Danish immigrants.

29.22 *The Ratman.* March 7, 1959. GS: Everett Sloan, Dennis McCarthy. Dr. Eckhardt attempts to warn the townspeople of the dangers of bubonic plague, but he meets skepticism and ridicule.

29.23 *Have Sword, Will Duel.* March 14, 1959. GS: John Baragrey, Pernell Roberts, Gloria Talbott. Mayor Matt Rockford is kept busy when Grand Duke Nicolai, a dashing Russian, comes to Cimarron City. It seems that the Duke has an affinity for trouble and pretty women.

29.24 *Chinese Invasion.* March 21, 1959. GS: John McIntire, Robert Lowery, Lisa Lu, Dennis McCarthy. A foreman in charge of a Chinese work gang has terrorized the workers, who are building a railroad spur near Cimarron City. Mayor Matt Rockford and Sheriff Lane Temple look into the foreman's activities.

29.25 *The Town Is a Prisoner.* March 28, 1959. GS: George Dolenz, Rita Moreno, Penny Edwards, Robert Armstrong, Lee Van Cleef. A band of Mexican soldiers and U.S. Cavalry renegades ride into Cimarron City and take over the town. They plan to invade Texas.

29.26 *The Evil One.* April 4, 1959. GS: Eduard Franz, Olive Carey, Daria Massey, Dennis McCarthy. Mayor Matt

Rockford encounters Prof. King, a man who claims that he possesses supernatural powers.

30. *Cimarron Strip*

CBS. 90 min. Broadcast history: Thursday, 7:30-9:00, Sept. 1967–Sept. 1968; Tuesday, 8:30-10:00, July 1971–Sept. 1971.

Regular Cast: Stuart Whitman (Marshal Jim Crown), Randy Boone (Francis Wilde), Percy Herbert (MacGregory), Jill Townsend (Dulcey Coppersmith).

Premise: In the Oklahoma Territory in the 1880's Marshal Jim Crown's job is to keep the peace in an area where cattlemen and homesteaders clash over range rights.

The Episodes

30.1 *Journey to a Hanging.* Sept. 7, 1967. GS: John Saxon, Henry Silva, Michael Strong, Shug Fisher, William Bramley, Gregg Palmer, Rex Holman, Robert Sorrells. Crown leads a posse after outlaws headed by Ace Coffin, who murdered a gang member to keep him from talking. Outgunned and outnumbered, the posse is also endangered by a deputy called the Screamer, whose only interest is the price on Coffin's head.

30.2 *The Legend of Jud Star.* Sept. 14, 1967. GS: Beau Bridges, Darren McGavin, Barbara Luna, Ken Renard, Roy Jenson, Kelly Thordsen, Richard Anderson, Ford Rainey, Roy Barcroft, Percy Helton, Warren Vanders, Rex Bond, Morgan Challes, Scott Hale, Lew Brown, Al Wyatt. Marshal Crown has his hands full trying to capture Jud Starr. Jud is hiding in a Cherokee camp with his half-breed girl friend and a gang hankering to hit Cimarron.

30.3 *Broken Wing.* Sept. 21, 1967. GS: Pat Hingle, Steve Forrest, Arch Johnson, Larry Gates, Tim O'Kelly, Karl Swenson, Warren Vanders, Harry Harvey, Sr., Royal Dano, Joel Fluellen. Marshal Crown struggles to keep peace when a wealthy rancher's son wounds the local parson. The town is up in arms, and a rabble-rousing saloon owner is spreading lynch talk.

30.4 *The Battleground.* Sept. 28, 1967. GS: Telly Savalas, Warren Oates, R.G. Armstrong, Robert J. Wilke, Andrew Duggan, L.Q.Jones, John Milford, Arthur Bernard, Link Wyler, Natividad Vacio, Richard Farnsworth, Hal Needham. A range war is about to erupt as Crown struggles to mediate between the cattlemen and scores of newly arrived squatters willing to risk their lives for land.

30.5 *The Hunted.* Oc. 5, 1967. GS: David Carradine, Steve Ihnat, James Gregory, Arthur Batanides, Tom Palmer, Bill Fletcher, Vic Tayback, Richard Angarola, Dennis Cross, Joel Fluellen, Charles Wagenheim. Gunmen Felix and Gene Gauge turn themselves in to Marshal Crown, who has promised them a fair trial. But a wealthy cattleman doesn't intend to wait for the court's decision. He has hired two bounty hunters to kill the outlaws.

30.6 *The Battle of Blood Stone.* Oct. 12, 1967. GS: Michael J. Pollard, Gene Evans, Henry Wilcoxon, Richard X. Slattery, Tom Nardini, James Hampton, Elisha Cook, Jr., Robert Viharo, Roy E. Glenn, Jr., Richard Lapp, Karl Swenson, Hank Patterson. Marshal Crown must prevent a showdown between an old Indian chief and the flamboyant star of a Wild West show. The chief's son was killed after challenging the show's fictionalized version of a battle in which his father fought.

30.7 *Whitey.* Oct. 19, 1967. GS: Peter Kastner, John Anderson, Fred Coby, Robert B. Williams, James Almanzar, Meg Wyllie, Glen Vernon, Paul Sorensen, Michael Mikler, Russ Bender. Dulcey's life is in the hands of a vengeance-crazed outlaw. After escaping from Marshal Crown, the young bandit holds Dulcey hostage while he plots to get back at Crown and the gang leader who double-crossed him.

30.8 *The Roarer.* Nov. 2, 1967. GS: Richard Boone, Andrew Duggan, Robert Duvall, Morgan Woodward, Ed Flanders, Steven Beck, Lindsay Workman, Med Florey, Rayford Barnes, Ed McCready. A strapping Cavalry veteran's hell-raising escapades cause death and destruction in Cimarron. As Crown tries to control a lynch-minded mob, the brazen soldier continues to flout both the law and the vigilantes.

30.9 *The Search.* Nov. 9, 1967. GS: Joseph Cotten, Martha Scott, Zalman King, Jonathan Lippe, Jim Davis, L.Q. Jones, Harry Lauter, Amzie Strickland, Richard O'Brien, Charles Seel, James Gavin. Dulcey is forced to rely on a cynical quack in her desperate search for the wounded Marshal Crown, who is also being hunted by an outlaw's family.

30.10 *Till the End of the Night.* Nov. 16, 1967. GS: Suzanne Pleshette, Clifton James, Victor French, Harry Dean Stanton, James Nusser, Eddie Quillan. Framed for murder and sentenced to hang, MacGregor makes plans to cheat the gallows. The canny Scot and a lady prisoner decide to try an escape, even though they are handcuffed together.

30.11 *The Beast That Walks Like a Man.* Nov. 30, 1967. GS: Leslie Nielsen, Royal Dano, Simon Oakland, Lola Albright, Paul Carr, Gail Kobe, Woodrow Chambliss, Athena Lorde, Karl Swenson, Christopher Held. Defying Marshal Crown, Federal law and local taboos, a clan of squatters heads for the Mocane Valley, where it is said that a mysterious killer-beast slaughters all trespassers.

30.12 *Nobody.* Dec. 7, 1967. GS: Warren Oates, William C. Watson, Hal Smith, Richard Bakalyan, Ken Swofford, Ted Gehring, Dabbs Greer, Joe Haworth, Anne Barton, Clyde Howdy, Vince Barnett, Tony Epper, Robert Karnes, William Zuckert, Karl Swenson. A slow-witted cowboy named Mobeetie spells trouble for Marshal Crown, who is trying to move a load of dynamite safely out of town. Mobeetie, duped by two thieves, has agreed to kill the marshal.

30.13 *The Last Wolf.* Dec. 14, 1967. GS: Albert Salmi, Morgan Woodward, Denver Pyle, Tom Reese, Robert J. Wilke, Lane Bradford, Laurie Mock, Eddie Firestone, John Pickard, Stanley Clements, Read Morgan, Mary Wilcox. Marshal Crown tries to stem open warfare on the prairie. Hunter Sam Gallatin and his band, embittered and impoverished by the disappearance of game, are wreaking their vengeance on cattlemen and farmers alike.

30.14 *The Deputy.* Dec. 21, 1967. GS: J.D. Cannon, Lyle Bettger, Larry Pennell, Marj Dusay, Anthony James, Gregg Palmer, Tom Brown, James Tartan, Burt Mustin, Robert B. Williams, Victor Izay, William Tannen. Bo Woodard hires on as Marshal Crown's deputy, with plans to use his badge as a shield for murder. The targets of his revenge are former cohorts who left him for dead after a payroll robbery.

30.15 *The Judgment.* Jan. 4, 1968. GS: James Stacy, Burr De Benning, Don Keefer, Leonard Stone, Kip Whitman, Solomon Sturges, John Orchard, Charles Dierkop, James Chandler, Jon Silo. Marshal Crown makes jobless cowboy Joe Bravo the deputy marshal of a neighboring town. The experiment works well until Bravo's cronies get out of jail.

30.16 *The Assassin* (A.K.A. "Fool's Gold"). Jan. 11, 1968. GS: Robert Lansing, Slim Pickens, Bob Random, Russell Thorson, William Bramley, Lew Brown, Joshua Bryant, Harry Harvey, Sr., Karl Swenson, Edward Faulkner, Red Morgan. Three thieves hit the Cimarron bank for a $56,000 Army payroll, but their escape is hampered by a cagey old horse trader. Meanwhile, Marshal Crown and MacGregor begin to close in on their quarry.

30.17 *Heller.* Jan. 18, 1968. GS: Tuesday Weld, Bernie Hamilton, Robert Phillips, Morgan Woodward, Ken Renard. A young orphan cares for a seriously wounded Marshal Crown. As her infatuation for the lawman increases, so does the danger to her own life. The girl's self-appointed guardian is leading a band of sadists who shot Crown and intend to finish the job.

30.18 *Knife in the Darkness* (A.K.A. "Killer with a Knife"). Jan. 25, 1968. GS: Jennifer Billingsley, David Canary, Jeanne Cooper, Philip Carey, Tom Skerritt, Patrick Horgan, George Murdock, Ron Soble, Karl Swenson, William Phipps, Cal Bolder, Grace Lee Whitney. In a fog-shrouded Cimarron, Crown tries to prevent panic as he investigates the mutilation murder of two women. The mystery deepens as reporter Wilde suggests a startling suspect—Britain's Jack the Ripper.

30.19 *Sound of a Drum.* Feb. 1, 1968. GS: Steve Forrest, Gerald S. O'Loughlin, Lloyd Gough, John Milford, Rayford Barnes, Harry Carey, Jr., David Renard. Sgt. Clay Tyce, a flashy former Indian fighter, and Sgt. Maj. Boyd Chambers, a stern disciplinarian, have a conflict of values. Vengeance dominates the clash after Chambers has Tyce court-martialed for flouting regulations.

30.20 *Big Jessie.* Feb. 8, 1968. GS: Mariette Hartley, Donnelly Rhodes, Eddie Hodges, Jack Elam, Timothy Carey, Richard O'Brien, Jesslyn Fax, K.L. Smith, Ken Drake, Burt Mustin. Crown is forced into the unaccustomed role of the pursued after he is bushwhacked and stripped of his badge. Mistaken for a killer, the lawman becomes the quarry of a lynch-minded posse and a wily bounty hunter.

30.21 *The Blue Moon Train.* Feb. 15, 1968. GS: Broderick Crawford, Donald "Red" Barry, Kevin Hagen, Robert Foulk, Norman Leavitt. A cagey ex-con intends to free a trainload of his prisoner buddies. The outlaw lures Marshal Crown to a ghost town where he plans to stop the train, with the marshal's aid.

30.22 *Without Honor.* Feb. 29, 1968. GS: Chester Morris, Andrew Duggan, Jon Voight, Paul Mantee, Don Pedro Colley, George Sperdakos, Ed Bakey, James Davidson, John Nealson, Dallas Mitchell, John McKee, Boyd Santell. Dressed as saddle bums, Marshal Crown and Maj. Ben Covington set out to apprehend the major's son, an Army deserter who has joined a band of murdering marauders.

30.23 *The Greeners.* March 7, 1968. GS: Mark Lenard, David Brian, Dub Taylor, Peter Jason, Dan Ferrone, Donna Baccala, Shug Fisher, Robert Sorrells, Charles Horvath, Roy Jenson, Harry Lauter, Olan Soule, Gregg Palmer. Marshal Crown must persuade a fear-stricken family of sodbusters to help pin a murder charge on a wealthy cattleman. The newly arrived farmers witnessed the death of two derelicts, but refuse to identify the killer.

31. Circus Boy

NBC/ABC. 30 min. Broadcast history: Sunday, 7:30–8:00, Sept. 1956–Sept. 1957; Thursday, 7:30–8:00, Sept. 1957–Sept. 1958.

Regular Cast: Mickey Braddock/Mickey Dolenz (Corky), Robert Lowery (Big Tim Champion), Noah Beery, Jr. (Uncle Joey), Guinn Williams (Pete).

Premise: This series depicted the adventures of young Corky, who traveled the frontier near the turn of the century with Big Tim Champion's circus.

The Episodes

31.1 *Meet Circus Boy.* Sept. 23, 1956. GS: Leo Gordon, Billy Barty, Olin Howlin, Eddie Marr. Big Tim Champion buys the circus and arrives at the big top to find a full-fledged brawl in progress. He learns that the brawl was started by a group of men trying to collect money owed them by the previous owners of the circus.

31.2 *The Fabulous Colonel Jack.* Sept. 30, 1956. GS: Andy Clyde, Billy Barty. Corky persuades Big Tim to give a job to his new pal, Colonel Jack.

31.3 *The Great Gambino.* Oct. 7, 1956. GS: Anthony Caruso, Michael Ross, Eddie Garr. Big Tim buys a ferocious lion named Nuba to replace one that died. On the day of the lion's arrival, lion-tamer Gambino decides to use Nuba in the evening performance.

31.4 *The Amazing Mr. Sinbad.* Oct. 14, 1956. GS: Don Diamond, Raymond Hatton, Kenne Duncan. The star attraction of the circus is horseback rider Ben Ali. He threatens to quit if Corky stays.

31.5 *Corky and the Circus Doctor.* Oct. 21, 1956. GS: Stanley Andrews, Russell Johnson, Jim Hayward, George Chandler. When the big top's veterinarian seems unable to control an epidemic which is affecting the circus animals and nearby cattle, Big Tim decides to hire another animal doctor.

31.6 *Casey Rides Again.* Nov. 4, 1956. GS: Ralph Moody. Casey Perkins, retired railroad engineer, comes to the aid of Big Tim Chapion when a flood threatens the circus with ruin.

31.7 *The Little Fugitive.* Nov. 11, 1956. GS: John Hubbard, Millie Doff, Harvey Grant. Joey the Clown tries to help his friend Arthur win the hand of a widow with a young son. The boy, who worships prizefighters, doesn't think Arthur is courageous enough.

31.8 *The Proud Pagliacci.* Nov. 18, 1956. GS: Otto Waldis, Judy Short, Grant Withers, Slim Pickens, Jay Brooks. Old Fritz, once a circus headliner, tries to impress the circus gang by telling them he owns a farm. But when Corky and Joey visit the farm, the real owner's daughter destroys the illusion.

31.9 *White Eagle.* Nov. 25, 1956. GS: Ralph Moody, James Anders, Fred Letuli, Eugenia Paul. Chief Spotted Horse is hated by Taylor, the head groom. Big Tim fires Taylor when the groom makes an attempt on Spotted Horse's life.

31.10 *The Little Gypsy.* Dec. 2, 1956. GS: Norman

Fredric, Mary Ellen Kaye, Louis Lettieri, Martin Garralaga. The Gypsy king's son attends the circus. He is accompanied by one of the tribe, who recognizes the lovely equestrienne as a runaway Gypsy girl. Big Tim, Corky and Joey hurry to her aid when she is kidnaped.

31.11 *The Masked Marvel.* Dec. 9, 1956. GS: Bradford Jackson, John Reach, John Crawford, Stanley Andrews. Earl Stanton lures his brother Billy, the circus trick-shot artist, to a hideout and ties him up.

31.12 *The Good Samaritans.* Dec. 23, 1956. GS: Robert Foulk, Percy Helton, William Lally. Ben Farmer, Hayfield's wealthiest citizen, urges the townspeople to tell Big Tim that his circus is not welcome. To make matters worse, Farmer's young son picks a fight with Corky.

31.13 *Daring Young Man.* Dec. 30, 1956. GS: Rand Brooks, Helene Marshall, Wendell Niles. When the high-diving star leaves the circus, Corky persuades young Cal Jones to take the job. But first Cal must overcome a major obstacle — his fear of heights.

31.14 *Farewell to the Circus.* Jan. 6, 1957. GS: Irene Hervey, Harry Hickox, Bill Walker. Wealthy Martha Neilson discovers that Corky is her nephew and decides to take the boy away from the circus and raise him herself Corky is terribly upset at having to leave his circus friends.

31.15 *Elmer the Aeronaut.* Jan. 13, 1957. GS: Sterling Holloway, Hal Hopper, Harry Strang, Elaine Haslett. Corky helps Elmer, a circus emloyee, build a passenger balloon. Though Big Tim forbids them to continue, the two launch their creation and take off.

31.16 *The Remarkable Ricardo.* Jan. 20, 1957. GS: Richard Avonde, Ray Teal, Jack Daly. Ricardo, an escape artist, is suspected of being a thief. Corky follows the performer one night to see if the story is true.

31.17 *Big Top Angel.* Jan. 27, 1957. GS: Jane Darwell, Jan Shepard, Manning Ross, Hal Taggart. Mamie, the circus wardrobe-mistress, is working hard to put her grandson Ken through medical school. But after spending a summer at the circus, Ken decides that he would rather marry Estelle, the trapeze artist, than finish his education.

31.18 *The Return of Colonel Jack.* Feb. 10, 1957. GS: Andy Clyde, Ollie O'Toole, Ed Hinton. While Big Tim Chapmion is away from the circus on business, Colonel Jack decides to take over. He attempts to save the Big Top from bankruptcy by floating a huge loan, which results in chaos for the circus.

31.19 *The Knife Thrower.* Feb. 17, 1959. GS: Rick Vallin, Eugene Iglesias, Whitney Blake, Hal Taggart, Tom McKee. Firpo the knife thrower injures his eye while saving Corky's life during a storm, but he makes the boy promise not to tell anyone about it.

31.20 *Joey's Wedding Day.* Feb. 24, 1957. GS: Angela Stevens. Joey decides to find himself a wife so that Corky can have a mother's care. Pete, the lion tamer, send for his unmarried sister Sue to meet Joey.

31.21 *Man from Cimarron.* March 3, 1957. GS: William Fawcett, Dehl Berti. An old cowboy who repairs harnesses for the circus has Corky enthralled with his tales of the Old West. But when the cowboy refuses to identify the criminals after he is an eyewitness to a bank robbery, Corky is a disillusioned youngster.

31.22 *The Great Gambino's Son.* March 10, 1957. GS: Anthony Caruso, John Wilder. Tony, the teenage son of lion-tamer Gambino, joins his father at the circus after being brought up by his grandmother in Boston. Gambino's plans to include his son in his act are upset when the boy shows that he is contemptuous of all circus people and afraid of Papa's trained lions. Ashamed, and ready to leave the circus, he learns that one of the big cats has escaped.

31.23 *Corky's Big Parade.* March 24, 1957. GS: Ralph Moody, Roy Barcroft, Steve Warren, Ken Osmond, Richard Emory. Matt Flint, the racket boss of Titusville, is determined to keep the circus out of town until he is paid a bribe. But the circus people pitch their tents in a neighboring field.

31.24 *The Lady and the Circus.* March 31, 1957. GS: Frances Robinson, Thomas B. Henry, Jack W. Harris, Paul Keast. Big Tim has announced his engagement to his childhood sweetheart, the daughter of an oil and mining tycoon. But now he thinks the hardships of circus life are too much to ask her to share.

31.25 *Counterfeit Clown.* April 7, 1957. GS: Lee Patrick, Philip Van Zandt, Don Beddoe, Darlene Fields, Leonard Carey. Minerva Murdock, a wealthy widow, hires the circus to perform at her engagement party. She intends to announce her engagement to Gerald Van Dorne at the party, but her oldest friend is suspicious of Van Dorne's motive.

31.26 *The Pawnee Strip.* April 14, 1957. GS: Chubby Johnson, Jason Johnson, Daniel White, Grace Albertson, Coca Dolenz, Scott Morrow. Corky talks the circus people into joining a land rush. After staking their claim, they learn that they must farm the land to keep it.

31.27 *The Cub Reporter.* April 21, 1957. GS: Noreen Corcoran, Brad Johnson, James Seay, Kirby Smith, Elaine Haslett. Corky becomes a cub reporter and his editor lectures him on newspaper ethics. Then Corky gets a scoop.

31.28 *General Pete.* April 28, 1957. GS: Edward Cassidy, Lee Trent. Pete is joining the Rough Riders for the Spanish-American War. He promises to ask Teddy Roosevelt to enlist Corky as a drummer boy.

31.29 *The Tumbling Clown.* May 5, 1957. GS: Tom Brown, Barton MacLane, Emil Sitka. A performer who left the circus when his young bride met with an accident returns and attempts to pick up where he left off. A few days later a detective visits the circus looking for a bank robber.

31.30 *Death Defying Dozetti.* May 12, 1957. GS: Richard Benedict, Nan Leslie, Don Brodie. Dozetti is the star of a high-wire act, and his wife, an aerialist in her own right, is kept out of the limelight. Then Dozetti is injured in a fall, and is stunned to see his wife successfully take his place.

31.31 *Colonel Jack's Brother.* May. 19, 1957. GS: Andy Clyde. Before leaving for Africa, Col. Jack Bixby warns his brother Jonathan not to attempt to collect the money the circus owes them. As soon as Colonel Jack leaves, however, Jonathan begins to interfere in the circus's affairs.

31.32 *The Swamp Man.* May 26, 1957. GS: Race Gentry, John Majulin. While the circus is playing in Louisiana, Corky meets Jean Giroux, a teenage Cajun boy. Corky goes to visit Jean's cabin in the swamp and is asked to read a piece of paper left for the young boy by his grandfather, but the writing is in French.

31.33 *Hortense the Hippo.* June 2, 1957. GS: Hal Peary, Frank Jenks, Edward S. Brophy, Rusty Wescoatt. Corky gets a substantial present from Colonel Jack — Hortense the Hippo. She brings the boy some good luck — and a heap of trouble.

31.34 *The Fortuneteller.* June 9, 1957. GS: Mary Young, Barry Bernard, Baynes Barron, Jerome Landfield, Gloria Grant. Mrs. Lilly, the new cook at the circus, has a flair for reading tea leaves. But the circus people take her predictions seriously. They won't go to work when she says things are going wrong.

31.35 *The Gentle Giant.* June 16, 1957. GS: Buddy Baer, Effie Laird, Kubla Khan, Herb Vigran. The circus loses its strong man Abdullah to Gabby McDougall's medicine show. Big Tim persuades Hector Buford to take Abdullah's place. McDougall, seeing a chance to ruin the circus, challenges Hector to wrestle Abdullah, with both the circus and medicine show going to the winner's backer.

31.36 *Little Vagabond.* June 23, 1957. Ricky Vera, Paul Picerni, Yvette Dugay, Edmond Cobb. Gene, a homeless boy, is given a home with Big Tim's circus. Gene's usually belligerent attitude softens for the first time when he comes into contact with the horses of the equestrian act.

Season Two

31.37 *Elmer, Rainmaker.* Sept. 19, 1957. GS: Sterling Holloway. The circus arrives in a drought-stricken area where Elmer the Rainmaker volunteers his services. He and Corky ascend in the circus baloon to salt the clouds.

31.38 *Royal Roustabout.* Sept. 26, 1957. GS: Peter Votrian, Robert Warwick, Grant Withers, Pamela Beaird. The teenage heir to the throne of Corvania runs away from his country's embassy in Washington and joins the circus. He falls in love with a young equestrienne named April and joins her act.

31.39 *Bimbo Jr.* Oct. 3, 1957. GS: William Griffith, Sydney Mason. A baby elephant joins the circus, and Corky christens it Bimbo, Jr. Old Bimbo promptly gets jealous and refuses to perform.

31.40 *Alex the Great.* Oct. 10, 1957. GS: John Duke, Patrick Waltz, Don Diamond, Joyce Vanderveen, Fred Kohler. Aerialist Alex Conrad feels guilty in connection with the death of the Flying Falcons, Corky's parents. Now, years later, Joey the Clown sees Alex in the audience and persuades him to rejoin the circus.

31.41 *Return of Casey Perkins.* Oct. 17, 1957. GS: Ralph Moody, Will Wright, George Keymas, Joseph Vitale. The circus comes to the aid of an old friend, Casey Perkins, who is competing against another company to bring the first railroad into a cattle-shipping town. The rival concern has hired all available help, so the circus people help lay the track.

31.42 *Major Buffington.* Oct. 24, 1957. GS: Thurston Hall, Jesse White, Willard Waterman, Phil Tead. Con man Major Buffington and his partner Spike are leaving town fast. They climb into a boxcar that has already got a passenger — a tiger headed for the circus. They soon join the big top in the hopes of stealing the boxoffice receipts.

31.43 *The Clemens Boys.* Oct. 31, 1957. After seeing the circus, Lem Clemens decides that this is the life for him. Lem's younger brother Jody wants to go with Lem to join the circus, but Lem refuses to let him come along.

31.44 *The Magic Lantern.* Nov. 7, 1957. GS: Sterling Holloway, Ed Hinton, Karl Swenson, Lee Giroux. Big Tim gives Corky and Joey money to buy supplies in town. But instead the boys use the money to get their old friend, Elmer Purdy, out of jail. Elmer is considered a crackpot because he believes he can invent a machine to show moving pictures.

31.45 *The Dancing Bear.* Nov. 14, 1957. GS: Alex Gerry, George Eldredge. Karl Hofer brings his bear Mitzi to Big Tim in hopes of getting a job with the circus. Years before, Big Tim had reason to mistrust Hofer, and he refuses to employ him.

31.46 *The Marvelous Manellis.* Nov. 21, 1957. GS: Manning Ross, Norm Alden, Linda Gay. Tim Champion signs up the Marvelous Manellis, a good high-wire act. When they arrive at the circus, however, one of thir number is missing, supposedly because of an injury. Corky is trapped in a forest fire with Marie Manelli, a member of the troupe.

31.47 *Uncle Cyrus.* Nov. 28, 1957. GS: Lucien Littlefield, Lorna Thayer, Harry Hickox. Pete, one of the roustabouts working for the big top, receives news that his uncle is about to visit him. He is worried because he has told his uncle that he owns the circus.

31.48 *The Judge's Boy.* Dec. 5, 1957. GS: Ralph Clanton, Page Engle, Bill Phipps, Ed Hinton. Judge Sheldon's son Carlton leaves home to join the circus. Then the judge is attacked and Big Tim saves his life, so Carlton decides he is needed at home.

31.49 *The Return of Buffalo Bill.* Dec. 12, 1947. GS: Dick Foran, Ann Nagel, Anna Marie Nanasi. Buffalo Bill feels that his connection with the circus was somehow responsible for his son's death. Even when Big Tim's circus starts losing money and can only be saved by a big name like Buffalo Bill's, Bill refuses to appear.

32. *The Cisco Kid*

Syndicated. 30 min. Broadcast history: Various, Sept. 1950–March 1956.

Regular Cast: Duncan Renaldo (the Cisco Kid), Leo Carrillo (Pancho).

Premise: This series, based on a character created by O. Henry, depicted the exploits of the Cisco Kid in New Mexico territory of the 1890s. Known as "The Robin Hood of the West", the suave Mexican adventurer traveled the range with his trusty sidekick, Pancho.

The Episodes

32.1 *Boomerang.* Sept. 5, 1950. GS: Jane Adams, Byron Foulger, Stephen Chase, Edmund Cobb, Lee Phelps, Dave Sharpe, George De Normand. The Cisco Kid and Pancho find themselves wanted by the law after a prominent real estate broker has two gunmen impersonate them and rob the Mesa Verde bank.

32.2 *Counterfeit Money.* Sept. 12, 1950. GS: Peggy Stewart, Forrest Taylor, Luther Crockett, Riley Hill, Robert Livingston, George De Normand, Art Dupuis, Fred Kohler, Jr. Cisco and Pancho hunt a brother-sister team of counterfeiters who are using a secret room in a bank as their headquarters and forcing the banker to pass their phony money.

32.3 *Rustling.* Sept. 19, 1950. GS: Christine Larson, Raymond Hatton, Jonathan Hale, Douglas Evans, Frank Matts,

George De Normand. Cisco and Pancho are charged with murder when a rancher who secretly heads a rustling ring kills a suspicious neighbor and frames Cisco for the crime.

32.4 *Big Switch.* Sept. 26, 1950. GS: Pamela Blake, Sarah Padden, Nelson Leigh, Fred Kohler, Jr., Carol Henry, Jack Ingram, Pierre Watkin. Cisco and Pancho help the niece of a secretly murdered cattleman outwit a clever forger who closely resembles the woman's uncle.

32.5 *Convict Story.* Oct. 3, 1950. GS: Gail Davis, Riley Hill, Robert Livingston, Fred Kohler, Jr., Forrest Taylor. Cisco and Pancho try to help an escaped convict who stole Pancho's clothes and horse while Pancho was swimming, and then tried to kill the mine owner he says framed him.

32.6 *Oil Land.* Oct. 10, 1950. GS: Peggy Stewart, Fred Kohler, Jr., Robert Livingston, Luther Crockett, Earle Hodgins. When a rancher who has just discovered oil on his property is murdered by one of his hands, suspicion falls on Cisco and Pancho.

32.7 *Chain Lightning.* Oct. 14, 1950. GS: Noel Neill, Don C. Harvey, Edmund Cobb, Dave Sharpe, Lee Phelps. After being sent to prison by Cisco and Pancho with the help of stage line owner Bill Shannon, gunfighter Jim Brent is released and sets out for revenge on all three.

32.8 *Medicine Flats.* Oct. 17, 1950. GS: Christine Larson, Raymond Hatton, Jonathan Hale, Douglas Evans, Frank Matts, George De Normand. Suspecting a gambling-house owner of being behind the gang of rustlers that framed them for murder, Cisco and Pancho convince him that they are wanted for killing a sheriff and try to break up the gang from within.

32.9 *Railroad Land Rush.* Oct. 28, 1950. GS: Pamela Blake, Pierre Watkin, Nelson Leigh, Fred Kohler, Jr., Forrest Taylor, George De Normand, Carol Henry, Jack Ingram. Cisco and Pancho pursue the con man who killed a suspicious railroad detective and is using an innocent real estate dealer to foster a phony land promotion scheme.

32.10 *The Will.* Oct. 31, 1950. GS: Gail Davis, Riley Hill, Art Dupuis, Fred Kohler, Jr., Robert Livingston, Eddie Parker, Forrest Taylor, George De Normand. Cisco and Pancho stop two gunmen from killing a young freight wagon driver who has just been released from prison after serving time for a strongbox robbery. Then they set out to prove that the young man was framed.

32.11 *Cattle Quarantine.* Nov. 7, 1950. GS: Peggy Stewart, Earle Hodgins, Robert Livingston, Fred Kohler, Jr., Forrest Taylor, Art Dupuis, Luther Crockett, Riley Hill. Cisco and Pancho fight a crooked cattle buyer who is trying to gain control of a ranch by using the county livestock inspector as his tool to create a phony epidemic.

32.12 *Renegade Son.* Nov. 21, 1950. GS: Pamela Blake, Pierre Watkin, Fred Kohler, Jr., Nelson Leigh, Carol Henry, Jack Ingram. Cisco and Pancho try to save a young woman who has been convicted of the poison murder of her wealthy uncle.

32.13 *False Marriage.* Nov. 28, 1950. GS: Gail Davis, Mary Gordon, Sarah Padden, Robert Livingston, Russell Hicks, Fred Kohler, Jr., Luther Crockett, Forrest Taylor, Earle Hodgins. Cisco and Pancho try to help a wealthy rancher prevent his niece's marriage to a notorious gambler, but when the rancher is killed they are accused of his murder.

32.14 *Wedding Blackmail.* Dec. 5, 1950. GS: Phyllis Coates, Bill Kennedy, Mike Ragan, David Bruce, Tom Tyler. Cisco and Pancho help out a young bank cashier whose forthcoming marriage to the bank president's daughter is endangered when two gunmen who know he is an ex-convict try to blackmail him.

32.15 *Lynching Story.* Dec. 12, 1950. GS: Carol Forman, Richard Emory, Marshall Reed, Frank Matts, Victor Cox, Lane Chandler, I. Stanford Jolley. When a mine owner is murdered by three employees who have been stealing gold from him, Cisco and Pancho stop a mob from lynching the dead man's prospective son-in-law for the crime.

32.16 *Newspaper Crusaders.* Dec. 19, 1950. GS: Ellen Hall, Dennis Moore, Bill Henry, Steve Clark, Ted Adams, Ferris Taylor. Cisco and Pancho help a newspaper editor in his crusade against a crooked gambler and his cronies.

32.17 *Dog Story.* Dec. 26, 1950. GS: Tanis Chandler, Tristram Coffin, Zon Murray, Frank McCarroll, Hank Patterson, Kenne Duncan. Cisco, Pancho and a dead prospector's dog hunt the crooked gambler who murdered the prospector for refusing to tell the location of his secret gold mine.

32.18 *Confession for Money.* Jan. 2, 1951. GS: Carol Forman, Richard Emory, Marshall Reed, Frank Matts, Victor Cox, Lane Chandler, I. Stanford Jolley. A lovely young lady asks Cisco and Pancho to help her fiance, who has confessed to a bank robbery and murder in return for the money needed for surgery on his mother.

32.19 *The Old Bum.* Jan. 9, 1951. GS: Tanis Chandler, Tristram Coffin, Zon Murray, Frank McCarroll, Hank Patterson, Kenne Duncan. Cisco and Pancho help out a penniless derelict who unwittingly becomes a front man for rustlers when he pretends to be a wealthy rancher so as to impress his visiting daughter.

32.20 *Haven for Heavies.* Jan. 13, 1951. GS: Phyllis Coates, Bill Kennedy, Mike Ragan, Tom Tyler. Cisco follows the murderer of a U.S. marshal to the haven of Twin Buttes, where outlaws enjoy immunity from the law.

32.21 *Pancho Hostage.* Jan. 16, 1951. GS: Carol Forman, Richard Emory, Marshall Reed, Frank Matts, Victor Cox, Lane Chandler, I. Stanford Jolley. Having jailed a bank robber, Cisco and Pancho are taken prisoners by his sister, who threatens to kill Pancho unless her brother is released.

32.22 *Freight Line Feud.* Jan. 27, 1951. GS: Ellen Hall, Dennis Moore, Bill Henry, Steve Clark, Ted Adams. Cisco and Pancho try to expose the outlaws who are attacking Bittercreek's freight line and putting the blame on a competing stage line owner.

32.23 *Phoney Sheriff.* Feb. 6, 1951. GS: Phyllis Coates, Bill Kennedy, Mike Ragan, David Bruce, Tom Tyler. Cisco and Pancho go after a cattle buyer who used a fake sheriff and deputies to trick them into turning over a friend's cattle herd.

32.24 *Uncle Disinherits Niece.* Feb. 13, 1951. GS: Phyllis Coates, Bill Kennedy, Mike Ragan, David Bruce, Tom Tyler, Bud Osborne. When a crooked lawyer murders a rancher who had threatened to disinherit his niece unless she stopped seeing her boyfriend, Cisco and Pancho try to clear the young man.

32.25 *Phoney Heiress.* Feb. 13, 1951. GS: Lyn Thomas, Vivian Mason, Jack Reynolds, Robert Bice, Mauritz Hugo, Charles Watts, Joseph Granby. Cisco and Pancho try to save a young woman's inherited property from a crooked lawyer who has hired an impostor to pose as the rightful owner.

The Cisco Kid

32.26 Water Rights. Feb. 20, 1951. GS: Tanis Chandler, Zon Murray, Tristram Coffin, Frank McCarroll, Hank Patterson, Kenne Duncan. Cisco and Pancho try to expose a crooked banker and lawyer who are scheming to sabotage the ranchers' water project and then foist their own project on the valley.

Season Two

32.27 Performance Bond. Sept. 3, 1951. GS: Ellen Hall, Bill Henry, Dennis Moore, Ted Adams, Steve Clark, Ferris Taylor. Cisco and Pancho help a freight line owner who is in danger of forfeiting a $20,000 performance bond because of "accidents" preventing him from delivering ore to a smelter.

32.28 Stolen Bonds. Sept. 10, 1951. GS: Jean Dean, Reed Howes, Pierce Lyden, Bill Holmes, Jim Diehl, Stanley Andrews, Bud Osborne. While pursuing a man who stole $25,000 in bonds from their friend, Cisco and Pancho come to suspect that a young woman working as cook in a hotel is in league with the thief.

32.29 Postal Inspector. Sept. 17, 1951. GS: Maris Wrixon, Edward Keane, Myron Healey, Dick Rich, Rory Mallinson, Steve Pendleton. When Cisco and Pancho mail a letter in the town of Baxter Center, they are arrested as part of a gang of mail robbers.

32.30 Jewelry Store Fence. Sept. 24, 1951. GS: Kay Morley, Michael Whalen, Michael Mark, Robert Wood, George Offerman, Steve Clark, Therese Lyon. While hunting for a purchaser of stolen jewelry, Cisco and Pancho encounter a crazy old man who tries to kill them with a crossbow built into an ornate clock.

32.31 Foreign Agent. Oct. 1, 1951. GS: Ann Zika, Carl Milletaire, Paul Hogan, Terry Frost, William M. McCormick, John Merton, Garnett A. Marks. Cisco uses a coded musical score to outwit foreign spies who are trying to take over a vast deposit of tungsten.

32.32 Medicine Man Show. Oct. 8, 1951. GS: Wanda McKay, Stephen Chase, Dennis Moore, Ray Hyke, Cactus Mack, George Davis, Claudia Drake, Rodd Redwing, Charles Soldani. While tracing a trunk containing guns being smuggled to the Comanches, Cisco learns that the trunk belongs to a young woman.

32.33 Ghost Story. Oct. 15, 1951. GS: Lyn Thomas, Jack Reynolds, Robert Bice, Mauritz Hugo, Charles Watts, Joseph Granby. Cisco and Pancho go after a pair of silver smugglers who killed their nervous partner, a rancher, when he tried to break with them.

32.34 Protective Association. Oct. 22, 1951. GS: Jean Dean, Reed Howes, Pierce Lyden, Bill Holmes, Jim Diehl, Bud Osborne, Stanley Andrews. Cisco and Pancho help a rancher and his daughter fight a gang of protection racketeers.

32.35 Kid Sister Trouble. Oct. 29, 1951. GS: Maris Wrixon, Edward Keane, Ilse Mader, Myron Healey, Dick Rich, Rory Mallinson, Steve Pendleton. After encountering a woman gambling-house dealer doing target practice, Cisco and Pancho become involved with counterfeiters.

32.36 Water Toll. Nov. 5, 1951. GS: Kay Morley, Michael Whalen, Michael Mark, Robert Wood, George Offerman, Steve Clark, Brad Johnson. Cisco and Pancho help a woman rancher fight a greedy cattleman who is making unsuspecting drovers pay him for watering their stock,

32.37 The Bates Story. Nov. 12, 1951. GS: Ann Zika, Paul Hogan, Terry Frost, William M. McCormick, John Merton, Anna Demetrio. Cisco and Pancho are forced to switch clothes with two escaped convicts helped by a female accomplice and are later arrested as the fugitives themselves.

32.38 Water Well Oil. Nov. 13, 1951. GS: Lyn Thomas, Jack Reynolds, Robert Bice, Mauritz Hugo, Charles Watts, Joseph Granby. Cisco and Pancho are shot at by a young hothead who thinks they tried to kill him because he has found oil on his ranch.

32.39 Ride On (A.K.A. "Black Lightning"). Nov. 19, 1951. GS: Wanda McKay, Stephen Chase, Dennis Moore, Ray Hyke, Cactus Mack, George Davis, Chester Clute. Cisco and Pancho stop a young woman from killing the wild stallion she believes has been stealing her mares, then try to find the human thieves who framed the horse.

32.40 Vigilante Story. Dec. 4, 1951. GS: Lois Hall, Bill George, Craig Hunter, Hugh Prosser, James Kirkwood, Earle Hodgins, Edmund Cobb. Disguised as a gambler and an organ grinder, Cisco and Pancho try to break up the band of masked vigilantes terrorizing the town of Buffalo Flats.

32.41 Hidden Valley. Dec. 11, 1951. GS: Virginia Herrick, Tristram Coffin, Wee Willie Davis, I. Stanford Jolley, Keith Richards, George Eldredge. Cisco and Pancho get lost in the wilderness and discover a hidden valley run by a tyrannical ex-sea captain.

32.42 Carrier Pigeon. Dec. 18, 1951. GS: Sherry Moreland, Leonard Penn, Milburn Morante, John Cason, Ted Mapes, Garry Garrett. Cisco and Pancho become involved with a woman claiming to be an insurance investigator on the trail of a stolen diamond necklace.

32.43 Hypnotist Murder. Dec. 25, 1951. GS: Marsha Jones, Riley Hill, Joe Forte, Doris Merrick, Denver Pyle, Zon Murray, Tom Holland. Cisco and Pancho try to stop a former carnival hypnotist who gets tired of waiting for her wealthy father-in-law to die and mesmerizes her husband into a murder attempt.

32.44 Romany Caravan. Jan. 8, 1996. GS: Dolores Castle, Sondra Rodgers, Craig Woods, Peter Coe, Milburn Morante, Jack George. Cisco visits a Gypsy camp and gets involved in a knife fight over a woman while a dancing bear terrifies Pancho.

32.45 Robber Crow. Jan. 15, 1952. GS: Mary Dean Moss, Michael Vallon, Raphael Bennett, Karl Davis, Mickey Simpson, Kermit Maynard, Teddy Infuhr. Cisco and Pancho intervene in a feud between the gunmen who are guarding a placer mine and the workers from town who are suspected by the guards of stealing gold.

32.46 Sleeping Gas. Jan. 22, 1952. GS: Lois Hall, Bill George, Hugh Prosser, James Kirkwood, George Eldredge, Franklyn Farnum. A bank holdup while Pancho is cashing a check involves Cisco with an outlaw family whose modus operandi includes a high-pitched fiddle and an ornamental globe full of sleeping gas.

32.47 Quarter Horse. Jan. 29, 1952. GS: Virginia Herrick, Tristram Coffin, I. Stanford Jolley, Keith Richards, George Eldredge, Stanley Blystone, Eddie Nash. Cisco steps into a revenge-motivated plot to fix a race pitting four quarter horses against a thoroughbred.

32.48 Jewelry Holdup. Feb. 5, 1952. GS: Sherry Moreland, Leonard Penn, Helene Millard, John Cason, Milburn Morante, Ted Mapes. Cisco and Pancho step in when jewel thieves who mailed some loot to themselves try to retrieve their package by force from an officious postal clerk.

32.49 *Ghost Town.* Feb. 12, 1952. GS: Marsha Jones, Riley Hill, Joe Forte, Doris Merrick, Denver Pyle, Zon Murray. In an empty town, Cisco and Pancho meet a young woman searching for proof of her identity, a crazy hotel proprietor, an eloping young couple and some weird menaces.

32.50 *Quicksilver Murder.* Feb. 12, 1952. GS: Lois Hall, Bill George, Hugh Prosser, James Kirkwood, Joe Forte, Hunter Gardner. Cisco goes after the corrupt public prosecutor who steals quicksilver shipments and uses chemical means to commit murder.

32.51 *Buried Treasure.* Feb. 19, 1952. GS: Dolores Castle, Sondra Rodgers, Craig Woods, Peter Coe, Milburn Morante, Jack George. Cisco encounters an ancient witch-like hag and her sons, who resort to torture and murder while hunting the lost treasure of Jean Lafitte.

32.52 *Spanish Dagger.* Feb. 19, 1952. GS: Mary Dean Moss, Michael Vallon, Raphael Bennett, Karl Davis, Mickey Simpson, Kermit Maynard. While Cisco is rescuing a prospector from an explosion, he unearths a jeweled dagger bearing a curse which begins to work when it is stolen.

Season Three

32.53 *Monkey Business.* Aug. 3, 1952. GS: Poodles Hanneford, Grace Hanneford, Marshall Reed, Zon Murray, Jack Ingram. Cisco and Pancho are arrested for robbery after some stolen money is planted on them by three thieves using an equestrian clown show as their cover.

32.54 *The Puppeteer.* Aug. 10, 1952. GS: Leonard Penn, Raymond Hatton, Mike Ragan, Joel Marston, Ted Mapes, Louise Manley. Cisco and Pancho wonder why the notorious Ghost Gang has never robbed the wealthiest town in Peaceful Valley. When they find out, they use Pancho's uncle's puppet show to get word to the sheriff.

32.55 *The Talking Dog.* Aug. 17, 1952. GS: Gail Davis, Paul Livermore, Bruce Payne, Allen Pinson, Ferris Taylor, Cactus Mack. The first telephone in the West falls into the hands of bandits who use it to alert members of their gang when gold is being shipped. Without realizing it, Cisco and Pancho are the only ones who can break the gang's scheme.

32.56 *Pancho and the Pachyderm.* Oct. 5, 1952. GS: Carole Mathews, Tom London, House Peters, Jr., Sheb Wooley, James Parnell. When Cisco and Pancho thwart the holdup of a one-wagon medicine show, they find themselves involved in the mystery of a stolen jade idol.

32.57 *Kid Brother.* Oct. 12, 1952. GS: Edward Clark, Linda Johnson, Keith Richards, Robert Wilke, Kermit Maynard, Teddy Infuhr. In an apparently abandoned shack, Cisco and Pancho come upon a wounded teenage boy who tells them that outlaws murdered his brother.

32.58 *Face of Death.* Oct. 19, 1952. GS: Gloria Saunders, Billy Griffith, Robert Cabal, Tom Monroe, William Bakewell, Wesley Hudman, Don Mahin, Paul Marion, Watson Downs. Cisco and Pancho avenge an archaeologist who was murdered by his guides when on the verge of discovering the tomb of an Aztec high priest.

32.59 *Big Steal.* Oct. 19, 1952. GS: Gail Davis, Paul Livermore, Bruce Payne, John Cason. Cisco and Pancho run into a phony U.S. land commissioner and a crooked homesteading project when they try to help their friend Don Miguel Escobar settle a dispute with a neighbor over water rights.

32.60 *Laughing Badman.* Oct. 26, 1952. GS: Marshall Reed, Zon Murray, Jack Ingram, Billy Curtis. Cisco and Pancho discover a murdered deputy sheriff whose saddlebags are stuffed with $50 bills. A strange laugh, tiny footprints and a ventriloquist with a live dummy set them on the trail of the two counterfeiters who are responsible.

32.61 *Canyon City Kid.* Nov. 2, 1952. GS: Leonard Penn, Raymond Hatton, Mike Ragan, Joel Marston, Ted Mapes, Louise Manley. Cisco becomes suspicious of a group staying in Canyon City. They intercept his letter of inquiry about them and then try to manipulate a local boy into challenging Cisco to a gunfight.

32.62 *Dutchman's Flat.* Nov. 9, 1952. GS: Carole Mathews, Tom London, House Peters, Jr., Sheb Wooley, James Parnell, Guy Wilkerson. After being grubstaked by Cisco and Pancho, prospector Cactus Bronson strikes it rich. But he is murdered for his mine and his son thinks Cisco and Pancho are the killers.

32.63 *Mad About Money.* Nov. 16, 1962. GS: Edward Clark, Linda Johnson, Keith Richards, Robert J. Wilke, Kermit Maynard. When an eccentric old man starts giving away bags of gold coins, he is suspected of murder. Cisco and Pancho try to prove his innocence.

32.64 *Lost City.* Nov. 23, 1952. GS: Gloria Saunders, Billy Griffith, Robert Cabal, Tom Monroe, William Bakewell. Cisco and Pancho try to stop three men from making off with part of the treasure from a lost Inca city.

32.65 *Thunderhead.* Nov. 30, 1952. GS: Almira Sessions, Richard Barron, Edward Colmans, Everett Glass, Augie W. Gomez. Cisco and Pancho open the eyes of absentee landowner Kathy Kerrigan to the corrupt practices of her ranch manager, who then holds her captive.

32.66 *Bell of Santa Margarita.* Dec. 14, 1952. GS: Almira Sessions, Richard Barron, Rodolfo Hoyos, Jr., Edward Colmans, Everett Glass, Augie W. Gomez. When the good-luck bell of Santa Margarita is stolen by El Puma and his gang, Cisco and Pancho try to recover it in time for the wedding of a friend's daughter.

32.67 *Lodestone.* Dec. 21, 1952. GS: Peggy Stewart, Gordon Clark, Bud Osborne, Hal K. Dawson, Henry Rowland, Marshall Bradford. Cisco and Pancho go after a Kansas City dude who tries to kidnap the wife and daughter of a wealthy rancher and hold them for ransom.

32.68 *Dead by Proxy.* Dec. 28, 1952. GS: Anne Kimbell, Lee Roberts, Peter Leeds, Hank Patterson, John Hamilton. When a gunman hired to kill the owner of a general store is himself killed instead, Cisco persuades the intended victim to play dead as part of a scheme to flush out whoever hired the killer.

32.69 *The Devil's Deputy.* Jan. 4, 1953. GS: Myron Healey, Earle Hodgins, Salvador Baguez, Eddie Parker. A crooked businessman hires a gunman named Lopez to impersonate Colonel Lucky Gonzales, who is to be the town's new marshal. Then Cisco and Pancho ride into town, and Pancho is mistaken by the townspeople for Gonzales and by the crooks for Lopez.

32.70 Church in the Town. Jan. 11, 1953. GS: Tom Bernard, Bennie Bartlett, Forrest Taylor, Marshall Reed, Davison Clark, Lillian Albertson. Cisco and Pancho help a fighting parson build a new church, overcome the town banker's opposition and convert a sinful community.

32.71 Gun Totin' Papa. Jan. 18, 1953. GS: Gordon Clark, Bud Osborne, Hal K. Dawson, Henry Rowland, Marshall Bradford. A meek little bookkeeper leaves home with his prize possession, a shotgun that once belonged to the notorious outlaw Shotgun Miller. When the gun is recognized, Cisco and Pancho try to help the man prove he is not Miller.

32.72 The Fire Engine. Jan. 25, 1953. GS: Ezelle Poule, Bill Henry, Lee Roberts, Peter Leeds, Hank Patterson, John Hamilton. Cisco and Pancho become involved when an old miner who has always wanted to be a fire chief buys a fire engine for his town and unwittingly interferes with the schemes of the local banker.

32.73 The Census Taker. Feb. 1, 1953. GS: Roscoe Ates, Kyle James, Steve Wayne, Alex Sharp, William Fawcett, Edmund Cobb. Cisco and Pancho go after outlaws who pose as census takers to gather information on their potential victims.

32.74 Smuggled Silver. Feb. 8, 1953. GS: John Damler, Bill Hale, Gail Bonney, Harvey Dunn, Bobby Blake. Cisco and Pancho set out after a band of silver smugglers who seem to know all their pursuers' moves in advance.

32.75 The Runaway Kid. Feb. 15, 1953. GS: John Pickard, Harry Harvey, Jr., Robert Bice, B.G. Norman, James Harrison. Cisco and Pancho encounter an eight-year-old boy running away from home and a band of outlaws looking for the hidden loot from an old crime.

32.76 Fear. Feb. 22, 1953. GS: Anne Kimball, Ezelle Poule, Bill Henry, Lee Roberts, Peter Leeds, John Hamilton. Cisco and Pancho become involved in an "old dark house" mystery in which a dead man's ghost terrorizes the heirs who are required by his will to live on his ranch.

32.77 The Photo Studio. March 1, 1953. GS: Rand Brooks, James Seay, Madeleine Burkette, Walter McGrail, Charles Williams, Sandy Sanders, Frank Jenks. A rancher is shot to death while posing for a photograph. Cisco and Pancho try to clear the chief suspect, an ex-convict in love with the dead man's daughter.

32.78 The Commodore Goes West. March 8, 1953. GS: Edward Clark, Linda Johnson, Keith Richards, Robert Wilke, Kermit Maynard. On their way south to attend the wedding of Pancho's cousin, Cisco and Pancho stop to help a young woman who is worried about her arrogant father, who is a former Navy officer, and his embattled freight line.

Season Four

32.79 Bodyguard. Oct. 1, 1953. GS: Keith Richards, Steve Clark, John Merton, Riley Hill, Virginia Mullen. The wife of a cantankerous old rancher asks Cisco and Pancho to watch out for her husband while he is carrying a tote-bag full of money.

32.80 Pancho and the Wolf Dog. Oct. 8, 1953. GS: Gloria Talbott, John Doucette, Francis MacDonald, Robert Livingston, Bill Catching. Cisco and Pancho encounter a wild dog as they try to help an eccentric Frenchman who has built the first refrigeration plant in the West.

32.81 Bullets and the Booby Trap. Oct. 15, 1953. GS: Rory Mallinson, Billy Halop, Bobby Blake, Lillian Albertson, Troy Melton. Cisco and Pancho chase an outlaw gang into a ghost town inhabited only by a teenage inventor and his shotgun-toting grandmother.

32.82 The Gramophone. Oct. 22, 1953. GS: William Tannen, William Boyett, Iron Eyes Cody, Lyle Talbot, Rosa Turich. Cisco and Pancho combat a rancher who uses a primitive record player to scare the Sioux into fighting the coming of the railroad.

32.83 Freedom of the Press. Oct. 29, 1953. GS: Frank Wilcox, Paul Marion, I. Stanford Jolley, Richard Avonde, Bill Catching. Cisco and Pancho help out an old newspaper editor who is caught in the middle of a hotly contested election battle between a corrupt mayor and a young reformer.

32.84 Battle of Red Rock Pass. Nov. 5, 1953. GS: Rory Mallinson, William Fawcett, Red Morgan, Nan Leslie, Troy Melton. Cisco and Pancho try to help a retired Union Army artillery sergeant who spends his old age guarding a toll road with an old cannon but develop amnesia after being hit on the head by the outlaw Cisco is chasing.

32.85 Bandaged Badman. Nov. 12, 1953. GS: Christine Larson, Bill Henry, Reed Howes, Forrest Taylor, Marshall Bradford, Keith Richards, Lee Roberts. When a gunman hired to kill Cisco is blown up in an explosion, Cisco has a doctor cover his face with bandages and identify the corpse as Cisco himself.

32.86 Chinese Gold. Nov. 19, 1953. GS: Keith Richards, Steve Clark, Judy Dan, John Merton. Cisco and Pancho try to help a community of Chinese miners who are being systematically robbed by a masked bandit.

32.87 The Faded General. Nov. 26, 1953. GS: Gloria Talbott, John Doucette, Francis McDonald, Robert Livingston, Bill Catching. While trailing a gang of bank robbers who wear linen dusters, Cisco and Pancho are captured by a senile general and put in his private jail.

32.88 The Fugitive. Dec. 3, 1953. GS: Rory Mallinson, Billy Halop, Harry Strang, Troy Melton. Cisco and Pancho hunt for a plague-stricken Mexican youth and run into a wealthy rancher's plot to contaminate land with infected animals so he can buy it cheaply.

32.89 Indian Uprising. Dec. 10, 1953. GS: William Tannen, William Boyett, Iron Eyes Cody, Lyle Talbot. Cisco and Pancho go after the white men who are impersonating Chief Sky Eagle and his braves and terrorizing the farmers so they will sell out to a local realtor for a few cents on the dollar.

32.90 The Raccoon Story. Dec. 17, 1953. GS: Frank Wilcox, Paul Marion, I. Stanford Jolley, Almira Sessions, Claudia Barrett, Bill Catching. Cisco and Pancho are asked to deliver miner Gus Brown's death certificate to his partner in the town of Sweetwater, and soon learn that Brown's will left all his property to his dog.

32.91 Outlaw's Gallery. Dec. 24, 1953. GS: Rory Mallinson, William Fawcett, Red Morgan, Nan Leslie, John Damler. Cisco and Pancho use an express rider's hobby of painting and sketching to bait a trap for a robber gang plaguing the town of Dry River Falls.

32.92 The Black Terror. Dec. 31, 1953. GS: Christine Larson, Bill Henry, Reed Howes, Forrest Taylor, Lee Roberts. Cisco invents a masked-bandit personality for himself and uses it to join the notorious Barton Brothers gang so he can break it up from within.

32.93 Sky Sign. Jan. 7, 1954. GS: Jan Bryant, Mort Mills, Mike Ragan, Steve Clark. Cisco and Pancho run out of ammunition and stop at a country store where an escaped convict and his gang are hiding.

32.94 Cisco Meets the Gorilla. Jan. 14, 1954. GS: Robert Clarke, Russ Conway, Max Wagner, Troy Melton, Bill Catching. Cisco and Pancho go after the bandits who have pulled off a series of robberies while everyone in town was searching for an escaped carnival gorilla.

32.95 Not Guilty. Jan. 21, 1954. GS: Jose Gonzales Gonzales, Peter Coe, Tristram Coffin, Lyle Talbot, Troy Melton. Cisco and Pancho take a hand when Pancho's nephew witnesses a murder and one of the killer's pals impersonates the circuit judge in a scheme to free his friend.

32.96 Rodeo. Jan. 28, 1954. GS: Keith Richards, Marshall Reed, Shirley Lucas, John Cason, Bill Catching, Sharon Lucas. Cisco and Pancho try to protect two daredevil-riding sisters from a confidence man who is promoting a phony rodeo.

32.97 Marriage by Mail. Feb. 4, 1954. GS: Jan Bryant, Mort Mills, Mike Ragan, Steve Clark. Cisco wins a bride when Pancho enters his picture in a matrimonial lottery, but the lottery turns out to be an outlaw gang's ruse to empty the town.

32.98 The Iron Mask. Feb. 11, 1954. GS: Dan White, John Crawford, Michael Whalen. Cisco and Pancho try to rescue a sheriff who has been captured by outlaws and imprisoned in an iron mask.

32.99 Double Deal. Feb. 18, 1954. GS: Bill Henry, Edmund Cobb, William Phipps, Frank Hagney, Charles Watts, Bill Catching. Cisco finds himself a fugitive after an old enemy of his hires an actor to dress up as Cisco and commit a series of robberies.

32.100 Horseless Carriage. Feb. 25, 1954. GS: Jose Gonzales Gonzales, Peter Coe, Tristram Coffin, Jeanne Dean, William Fawcett, Bill Catching. Cisco and Pancho try to help Pancho's nephew, whose newly purchased horseless carriage is used as a getaway vehicle by bank robbers.

32.101 The Steel Plow. March 4, 1954. GS: Keith Richards, Marshall Reed, Shirley Lucas, John Cason, Bill Catching, Kermit Maynard. Cisco helps an inventive blacksmith make a steel plow to help the local farmers cultivate the stony soil.

32.102 The Ventriloquist. March 11, 1954. GS: Robert Clarke, Russ Conway, Max Wagner, Rankin Mansfield. Cisco uses Pancho's voice-throwing skill to expose a crooked assayer who kidnaps prospectors after they have filed their claims.

32.103 Powder Trail. March 18, 1954. GS: Bill Henry, Edmund Cobb, William Phipps, Frank Hagney, Shirley Tegge, Patsy Moran. Cisco and Pancho try to find out why outlaws are stealing wagonloads of the petrified-wood curios on which the economy of the virtual ghost town of Padera depends.

32.104 Cisco Plays the Ghost. March 25, 1954. GS: Dan White, John Crawford, Michael Whalen, Bennie Bartlett, Byron Foulger, Troy Melton. Cisco uses a player piano and spook effects to convince a superstitious killer that he is being haunted by his victim's ghost.

Season Five

32.105 A Six-Gun for No-Pain. Sept. 25, 1954. GS: Dennis Moore, Earle Hodgins, Henry Rowland, Joey Ray, Mickey Simpson, Zon Murray. Cisco enlists the aid of a traveling dentist to track down a notorious killer who has set up a new identity as a cattle dealer.

32.106 The Haunted Stage Stop. Oct. 2, 1954. GS: Nan Leslie, John Cason, Bill Kennedy, Myron Healey, Bob Woodward. What purports to be the ghost of way station master Angus MacPherson summons Cisco and Pancho to trace the gold shipment that vanished when Angus did.

32.107 Gold Strike. Oct. 9, 1954. GS: Jacquelyn Park, Sandy Sanders, James Anderson, Marshall Reed, Ed Hinton. Cisco and Pancho are escorting a safecracker to jail when their stagecoach is captured by bandits who take all the passengers to a ghost town.

32.108 Trouble in Tonopah. Oct. 16, 1954. GS: Edwin Parker, Kenneth MacDonald, Gregg Barton, Kermit Maynard, Edward Clark, Dan White. Cisco and Pancho try to outwit a robber who has somehow learned the combination to the express office's burglar-proof safe and pulled off a series of baffling thefts.

32.109 Harry the Heir. Oct. 23, 1954. GS: I. Stanford Jolley, Fay Morley, James Parnell, Leonard Penn, Keith Richards. While trying to save an egotistical actor who has confessed to a bank robbery and murder, Cisco and Pancho find that the grave of the supposed murder victim is empty.

32.110 The Lowest Bidder. Oct. 30, 1954. GS: Bill George, Kenneth Terrell, Lane Bradford, Eddy Waller, Jack Ingram. Cisco and Pancho confront a scheming well-digger who is out to steal the funds a thirsty town has raised to secure a water supply.

32.111 Mining Madness. Nov. 6, 1954. GS: Raymond Hatton, Marshall Reed, Ted Mapes, Lee Roberts. When an old prospector friend of theirs is cheated by a crooked gambler, Cisco and Pancho kidnap the gambler and make him work a worthless, but salted, gold claim.

32.112 Sundown's Gun. Nov. 13, 1954. GS: Dennis Moore, Henry Rowland, Earle Hodgins, B.G. Norman. Cisco and Pancho try to straighten out a 12-year-old boy who is disappointed in his father, a workmanlike sheriff, and worships his dead grandfather, a famous gunfighter.

32.113 Pot of Gold. Nov. 20, 1954. GS: Nan Leslie, John Cason, Bill Kennedy, Myron Healey, Hank Patterson, William Vedder, Bob Woodward. When a half-crazy old man is killed by a deputy sheriff trying to make him reveal the location of a buried Civil War treasure, Cisco and Pancho and a traveling snake-oil peddler help the dead man's daughter find the fortune.

32.114 Caution of Curley Thompson. Nov. 27, 1954. GS: Jacquelyn Park, Sandy Sanders, James Anderson, Marshall Reed, Ed Hinton. Cisco and Pancho help an ex-convict track down the leader of his old gang, who has started a new life as the owner of a general store.

32.115 Fool's Gold. Dec. 4, 1954. GS: Edwin Parker, Kenneth MacDonald, Gregg Barton, Kermit Maynard, Karolee Kelly. Cisco and Pancho trap some outlaws by making them believe that their hideout is the center of a major gold rush.

32.116 The Hospital. Dec. 11, 1954. GS: Bill George, Kenneth Terrell, Lane Bradford, Eddy Waller, Jack Ingram. Cisco and Pancho help a doctor who has been framed for attempted murder by a fund-embezzling trustee of the town hospital.

32.117 *Three Suspects.* Dec. 18, 1954. GS: Lee Roberts, Marshall Reed, Raymond Hatton, Red Mapes. With his only clue a bandit's hat found near the scene of a robbery, Cisco tries to figure out which of three suspects is the bandit.

32.118 *Pancho's Niece.* Dec. 25, 1954. GS: J.P. O'Donnell, John Pickard, Julian Rivero, William Tannen, Roy Engel. Cisco has Pancho pose as the uncle of a half-Mexican young woman whose banker father apparently killed himself after losing most of the bank's money.

32.119 *Extradition Papers.* Jan. 1, 1955. GS: John Beradino, Dayton Osmond, Mitchell Kowal, Henry Rowland, Sam Flint. While taking a captured bandit leader to trial, Cisco and Pancho are ambushed by his gang while passing through a ghost town.

32.120 *New Evidence.* Jan. 8, 1955. GS: Sandy Sanders, Edwin Parker, Fay Morley, Earle Hodgins, Edmund Cobb. When a rancher is murdered and his daughter's boyfriend is put on trial for the crime, Cisco uses a Farmer's Almanac and a full moon and the Army signal system to trap the real killer.

32.121 *Doorway to Nowhere.* Jan. 15, 1955. GS: Lillian Albertson, Nan Leslie, Kenneth MacDonald, Lane Chandler. Cisco escorts a wealthy old Boston lady to her daughter-in-law's ranch but is charged with kidnapping and robbery when both women disappear.

32.122 *Stolen River.* Jan. 22, 1955. GS: Nancy Hale, I. Stanford Jolley, Zon Murray, Thayer Roberts, Rory Mallinson. Arriving at the ranch of their old friend Wayne Barbour, Cisco and Pancho find that Wayne has been murdered and that his widow is ready to sell the ranch and go back east.

32.123 *Son of a Gunman.* Jan. 29, 1955. GS: John Beradino, Mitchell Kowal, Sam Flint, Henry Rowland. When the son of a famous gunfighter is run out of town, Cisco and Pancho try to help the young man outlive his father's reputation.

32.124 *Juggler's Silver.* Feb. 3, 1955. GS: Fortune Gordien, Rodd Redwing, Leonard Penn, Kenneth MacDonald. Cisco and Pancho are shot at by a former circus juggler who bought what he claims is a worthless mine.

32.125 *The Kidnapped Cameraman.* Feb. 10, 1955. GS: Tom Irish, Terry Frost, Keith Richards, Kermit Maynard, Chuck Carson. When a photographer inadvertently takes a picture of a murder at the Lone Mountain mine, Cisco uses the lantern slide to trap the killer.

32.126 *Cisco and the Giant.* Feb. 17, 1955. GS: Dennis Moore, Glenn Strange, Rex Thorsen, Kenneth Terrell, Patricia Tiernan. A huge and dim-witted man who thinks he has killed his lawman brother-in-law takes refuge with an outlaw gang. Then Cisco and Pancho join the gang in an attempt to solve a series of well-planned stagecoach robberies.

32.127 *Montezuma's Treasure.* Feb. 24, 1955. GS: Thayer Roberts, I. Stanford Jolley, Zon Murray, Ferris Taylor. A professor, hunting for the Aztec emperor's fabulous treasure, discovers its location but is attacked by outlaws and wounded. A coded message on a deck of cards leads Cisco and Pancho to the treasure.

32.128 *Vendetta.* March 3, 1955. GS: Alan Wells, Claudia Barrett, Kenneth MacDonald, Leonard Penn. Cisco and Pancho try to settle an old family feud between neighboring ranchers which has been secretly fanned by a mercenary uncle.

32.129 *The Two-Wheeler.* March 10, 1955. GS: Tom Irish, Sally Fraser, Keith Richards, Terry Frost. Cisco and Pancho help out a quick-tempered bicycle-riding young Easterner who has struck it rich with a gold claim but is being cheated by claim jumpers.

32.130 *The Tumblers.* March 17, 1955. GS: Loren Janes, Ward James, Harry Cody, Maureen Cassidy, William Fawcett. Cisco and Pancho teach an acrobat some riding and shooting skills so he can fight the bully who runs the town of Smoky Gap.

Season Six

32.131 *A Quiet Sunday Morning.* Oct. 6, 1955. GS: Frank Richards, Richard Castle, Elsie Baker, Margie Moran, Chuck Cason. Cisco and Pancho go after three robbers — one of the a teenage boy on his first job — who killed the sheriff while making their getaway.

32.132 *Arroyo Millionaire's Castle.* Oct. 13, 1955. GS: Wayne Mallory, Britt Wood, Mort Mills, Gene Covelli. While hunting the gunman who murdered a young prospector, Cisco and Pancho find an eccentric millionaire living in a castle in the desert.

32.133 *Witness.* Oct. 20, 1955. GS: Tristram Coffin, Terry Frost, Russell Whitney, Melinda Plowman. Cisco and Pancho try to persuade a teenage girl who witnessed a robbery to admit that she recognized the bandit leader as her uncle.

32.134 *Choctaw Justice.* Oct. 27, 1955. GS: Bill Pullen, Margaret Cahill, Paul Fierro, James Anderson, Chief Yowlachie. Cisco receives an urgent letter asking him to follow Choctaw custom and serve as the executioner of his friend Charlie Ponca, who has been convicted of murder by an Indian court. Instead he and Pancho set out to prove Charlie's innocence.

32.135 *New York's Finest.* Nov. 3, 1955. GS: Tristram Coffin, Terry Frost, Charles Maxwell, Anna Navarro. Cisco and Pancho help a young New York policeman who has come west to search for the murderer of his former commander.

32.136 *Cisco and the Tappers.* Nov. 3, 1955. GS: Wayne Mallory, Britt Wood, Mort Mills, Bill Catching. Cisco and Pancho help an old sheriff and his young deputy capture a group of outlaws who tap telegraph wires to learn of gold shipments.

32.137 *Young Blood.* Nov. 10, 1955. GS: Richard Castle, Elsie Baker, Gerald Olken, Tim Johnson. Cisco and Pancho help a widow whose young hired hand is associating with a pair of teenage bandits.

32.138 *School Marm.* Nov. 17, 1955. GS: Elaine Riley, Sydney Mason, Marshall Reed, Joel Ashley, Kenneth Miller. Cisco and Pancho try to rescue the town of Madera's new schoolteacher, who has been kidnapped and held for ransom.

32.139 *Bounty Men.* Nov. 24, 1955. GS: Frosty Royce, Earle Hodgins, Zon Murray, Mickey Simpson. Cisco and Pancho trail a wanted killer to an Army recruiting station where they encounter a corrupt military doctor who enlists outlaws in the service under dead men's names

32.140 *Quick on the Trigger.* Dec. 1, 1955. GS: Peter Mamakos, Robin Short, John Compton, Sue England. Cisco and Pancho try to help an expectant father who stole back the horse he sold to a crooked animal dealer in order to pay for medical care for his pregnant wife.

32.141 *Gold, Death and Dynamite.* Dec. 8, 1955. GS: Elaine Riley, Steven Clark, Marshall Reed, Joel Ashley, Sydney Mason. Cisco and Pancho become involved when the desperate owner of a stagecoach line substitutes dynamite for a gold shipment in hope of blowing up the outlaws who have been robbing his coaches.

32.142 *Jumping Beans.* Dec. 15, 1955. GS: Earle Hodgins, Robert Strong, Zon Murray, Mickey Simpson, Frosty Royce. Cisco and Pancho arrive in Rimtown too late to prevent a robbery by three escaped convicts, but try to catch the trio by using a handful of Mexican jumping beans as a lie detector.

32.143 *Ambush.* Dec. 22, 1955. GS: Paul Fierro, Bill Pullen, James Anderson, Joe Dominguez, Anna Navarro. Cisco encounters three rival outlaws who have joined forces to do away with him by using Pancho as bait for a clever ambush.

32.144 *Six Gun Cupids.* Dec. 29, 1955. GS: Robin Short, Paula Houston, John Compton, Jackie Loughery, Peter Mamakos. Cisco and Pancho learn that a wealthy old woman has forbidden her son to associate with the housemaid he loves, and try to help the young couple find happiness.

32.145 *Strangers.* Jan. 5, 1956. GS: John Cliff, Pierce Lyden, John Halloran, Don Gardner. Cisco and Pancho are ambushed and their horses stolen, but when they try to buy fresh horses everyone drives them away.

32.146 *The Joker.* Jan. 12, 1956. Terry Frost, John Beradino, Lee Morgan, Joyce Jameson. Cisco and Pancho go after a prankster who has made a fortune selling ranches he doesn't own.

32.147 *Man with the Reputation.* Jan. 19, 1956. GS: Steven Clark, Marilyn Saris, Paul Hahn, Joel Smith, Lane Bradford. A newspaper editor accuses Cisco and Pancho of taking bribes from a criminal in order to get them into town so he can ask their help in cleaning up local political corruption.

32.148 *The Epidemic.* Jan. 26, 1956. GS: George Meader, Leo Needham, Jack Littlefield, Ward C. James, John B. Duncan. Cisco and Pancho pursue the outlaws who are holding a bottle of vital smallpox vaccine for ransom.

32.149 *Mr. X.* Feb. 2, 1956. GS: Diana Welles, Gene Roth, Pierce Lyden, Don Gardner. Cisco rescues a mine owner who has been buried alive in a collapsed tunnel, then discovers that the apparent accident was a murder attempt and is himself trapped by the killer.

32.150 *Roundup.* Feb. 9, 1956. GS: Joyce Jameson, John Beradino, Terry Frost, Lee Morgan. Cisco and Pancho help a young woman who has come west to take control of the ranch she inherited, only to encounter trouble in the shape of a jealous foreman and some rustlers.

32.151 *He Couldn't Quit.* Feb. 16, 1956. GS: Lillian Molieri, Charles Maxwell, James Seay, William Fawcett. Cisco and Pancho become involved when an outlaw who is in love with a Gypsy palmist returns to town to visit his now respectable ex-partner in crime and collect his share of the loot from their last robbery.

32.152 *Kilts and Sombreros.* Feb. 23, 1956. GS: Ian Murray, Barry Froner, Sydney Mason, Lane Bradford, Joel Smith. Cisco and Pancho help a Scotsman who was fired from his job as a Wells Fargo courier after being ambushed by bandits.

32.153 *West of the Law.* March 1, 1956. GS: John B. Duncan, Leo Needham, Ward C. James, Fay Morley. Cisco and Pancho help a friendless young man who has been accused of stealing an opera singer's jewelry.

32.154 *Dangerous Shoemaker.* March 8, 1956. GS: Sandy Sanders, Keith Richards, Bruce Payne, Glenn Strange. Cisco and Pancho stop off at a shoemaker's shop to get Pancho's boots fixed and become entangled in a plot by the shoemaker to blackmail a man who thinks he is a murderer.

32.155 *The Magician of Jamesville.* March 15, 1956. GS: Earle Hodgins, Charles Maxwell, William Fawcett, James Seay, Bert Rumsey. Cisco uses a boomerang from a traveling magician's kit to expose a crooked mayor and a mysterious blowgun killer.

32.156 *Tangled Trails.* March 22, 1956. GS: William Vaughan, Ann Duncan, Don Mathers, Max Wagner, Lee Morgan. Cisco and Pancho try to clear an old friend who has disappeared along with a shipment of money.

33. Cliffhangers: The Secret Empire

NBC. 60 min. Broadcast history: Tuesday, 8:00-9:00, Feb. 1979–May 1979.

Regular Cast: Geoffrey Scott (Marshal Jim Donner), Diane Markoff (Tara), Stepfanie Kramer (Tara), Tiger Williams (Billy), Charlene Watkins (Millie), Jay Robinson (Demeter), Mark Lenard (Thorval), Peter Breck (Keller), S. Newton Anderson (Kalek), Pamela Brull (Maya), Sean Garrison (Yannuck), Peter Tomaren (Roe).

Premise: This science fiction-western tells the tale of Marshal Jim Donner who, in 1880 Wyoming, encounters a futuristic society beneath the earth. The evil leader Thorval plans to conquer the earth, and it is up to Donner and his allies to thwart his plans.

Notes: *The Secret Empire* shared the *Cliffhangers* series hour with the non-Westerns *Stop Susan Williams* and *The Curse of Dracula*.

The Episodes

33.1 *Plunge into Mystery.* Feb. 27, 1979. While investigating a series of gold shipment thefts, U.S. Marshal Jim Donner discovers a futuristic society of aliens who live inside the earth in the city of Chimera.

33.2 *Prisoner of the Empire.* March 6, 1979. The evil Tara offers to save Marshal Donner from an icy death in return for his enslavement.

33.3 *The Mind Twisters.* March 13, 1979. Empowered to control minds, the underworld emperor seeks to bend Marshal Jim's will.

33.4 *Seeds of Revolt.* March 20, 1979. Donner attempts to make his escape as Thorval prepares his plan to dominate the surface.

33.5 *Attack of the Phantom Riders.* March 27, 1979. The marshal is unaware that the Phantom Riders have taken Billy hostage as he plans to stop their next raid.

33.6 *Sizzling Threat.* April 3, 1979. Disguised as a Phantom Rider to thwart a gold-mine raid, the marshal is mistaken for a raider, captured and thrown into his own jail.

33.7 *Mandibles of Death.* April 10, 1979. Thorval orders the execution of Billy in the compression tube.

33.8 *The Last Gasp.* April 17, 1979. Thorval strikes a deal with Keller and orders an attack on the Partisans' stronghold.

33.9 *Return to Chimera.* April 24, 1979. A surprise rescuer comes to the aid of Maya, who is perishing in the surface atmosphere.

33.10 *Powerhouse.* April 31, 1979. Donner needs the reversal unit to undo the effects of the Compliatron on the captured Partisans.

34. *Colt .45*

ABC. 30 min. Broadcast history: Friday, 10:00–10:30, Oct. 1957–Dec. 1957; Friday, 8:30–9:00, Jan. 1958–April 1958; Sunday, 9:00–9:30; Oct. 1958–Sept. 1959; Sunday, 7:00–7:30, Oct. 1959–March 1960; Tuesday, 9:30–10:00, April 1960–Sept. 1960.

Regular Cast: Wayde Preston (Christopher Colt), Donald May (Sam Colt, Jr.) 59-60.

Premise: Christopher Colt is a government agent who poses as a salesman for the Colt .45 repeater in his efforts to ensure justice in the West of the 1880s.

Note: Wayde Preston left the series during the middle of the second season and was replaced by Donald May, playing the character of Sam Colt, Jr., Christopher Colt's nephew.

The Episodes

34.1 *The Peacemaker* (A.K.A. "Judgment Day"). Oct. 18, 1957. GS: Peter Brown, Erin O'Brien, Andrew Duggan, Helen Brown. Chris Colt arrives in Cottonwood, Arizona, to show his new guns. He is confronted by a young missionary who berates him for being a man of violence.

34.2 *A Time to Die.* Oct. 25, 1967. GS: Wayne Morris, Kenneth R. MacDonald, Dan Blocker, John Day, Edwin Parker. Chris Colt recognizes a prospective buyer of his firearms as Jim Girad, wanted for an Army payroll robbery. Colt takes Girad into custody and begins the trek to Fort Lawson with his prisoner. But en route they are attacked by Indians and Colt gives Girad a gun to defend himself. When the attackers are routed, Colt finds Girad has the drop on him. His assailant takes his weapons and his horse and leaves Colt to die. Colt vows to cross the desert and capture the robber.

34.3 *The Three Thousand Dollar Bullet.* Nov. 1, 1957. GS: Richard Garland, Harlan Warde, Toni Gerry, Michael Dante, John Beradino. A notorious gunman whom Colt is trying to capture, is shot down in a saloon after he maliciously shoots a young man. Three men who fired at him claim the reward. Colt arrives and pretends to be a friend of the dead man, but another outlaw recognizes him.

34.4 *Gallows at Granite Gap.* Nov. 8, 1957. GS: Stuart Randall, Virginia Gregg, John Smith, William Henry, Harry Antrim. When the notorious outlaw Comanche Kid is captured by Chris Colt, the townspeople of Granite Gap are determined to hang him. But an elderly woman pleads for the outlaw's life because she believes he is her long-lost son.

34.5 *Small Man.* Nov. 15, 1957. GS: Jay Novello, Paul Burns, Charles Fredericks, Vici Raaf, Rayford Barnes. Government agent Chris Colt finds his life threatened by a quiet Easterner who directs the operations of an outlaw gang.

34.6 *Final Payment.* Nov. 22, 1957. GS: Dick Foran, James Nolan, John Cliff, Walter Barnes. Government agent Chris Colt and his new assistant Tuck Degan set out to collect back taxes. Colt soon discovers a smuggling operation and learns that Degan is not working for him alone.

34.7 *One Good Turn.* Nov. 29, 1957. GS: Lisa Montell, William Phipps, Alma Beltran, Michael Healey. Christopher Colt attempts to save a badly wounded young outlaw from the wrath of a Mexican town.

34.8 *Last Chance.* Dec. 6, 1957. GS: Stacy Keach, Willard Sage, Tina Carver, Kent Taylor, Aline Towne. Colt rides into a frontier town to go bear-hunting with his friend Sheriff Ben Mason. When he arrives at Mason's office, a woman runs in to report that her accountant has been shot.

34.9 *Young Gun.* Dec. 13, 1957. GS: Charles Bronson, Lurene Tuttle, James Anderson, Hugh Sanders, Jaclynne Greene. Young Jimmy Benedict is determined to shoot Danny Gordon, the man who killed his father during a bank holdup. Gordon attempts to avoid a showdown with the boy until people start calling him a coward.

34.10 *Rebellion.* Dec. 20, 1957. GS: Robert Warwick, Leslie Bradley, Mary Beth Hughes, Fran Bennett. A rebellion is planned against the United States Government. Chris Colt's clue is a peso marked with a mysterious black cross.

34.11 *The Gypsies.* Dec. 27, 1957. GS: Lyn Thomas, Steve Darrell, Don Megowan, Paul Picerni. The girl friend of a deputy marshal elopes with the leader of a Gypsy band. Chris Colt is called in to prevent bloodshed between the Gypsy band and the residents of the town where the girl lived.

34.12 *Sign in the Sand.* Jan. 3, 1958. GS: James Lydon, William Tannen, Charles Tannen, Kenneth MacDonald, Francis De Sales. A dying government agent draws Indian pictures in the sand to help Chris Colt track down the bandits who robbed a government wagon train.

34.13 *The Mirage.* Jan. 10, 1958. GS: Ann Maria Majalca, Frank Puglia, John Vivyan, Valentin de Vargas, Donald "Red" Barry. A renegade band of soldiers tries to drive off a group of Mexicans who have settled by a water hole in the desert. The Mexicans appeal to Chris Colt for help in keeping their homes.

34.14 *Blood Money.* Jan. 17, 1958. GS: Jerry Paris, Randy Stuart, John Cliff. Chris Colt tries to help a man he has sworn to return to jail. The criminal wants Colt to claim the reward money offered for his capture and turn it over to the girl he loves.

34.15 *Dead Reckoning.* Jan. 24, 1958. GS: Richard Webb, Joan Vohs, Jason Robards, Sr., Lee Van Cleef, Kenneth MacDonald. Chris Colt poses as a paroled prisoner in an attempt to uncover a gang of bandits. Then he is confronted by the wife of the man he is impersonating.

34.16 *Decoy.* Jan. 31, 1958. GS: Kathleen Crowley, Pierre Watkin, Christopher Dark, Ernestine Barrier. Chris Colt sets out after a band of Mexican outlaws who have stolen a cargo of Colt firearms.

34.17 *Rare Specimen.* Feb. 7, 1958. GS: Kasey Rogers, Charles Cooper, Frank Ferguson. Chris Colt is wounded during a train robbery. A woman passenger uses a piece of her needlework to patch his bullet-torn jacket. Later the needlework provides a valuable clue for Colt.

34.18 *Mantrap.* Feb. 14, 1958. GS: Venetia Stevenson, Peter Whitney, Donald "Red" Barry, Travis Bryan, Robert Fortier. The notorious Birdwell brothers kidnap Chris Colt. They feel that their younger sister needs a husband and that Colt is the most likely candidate.

34.19 *Ghost Town.* Feb. 21, 1958. GS: Joanna Barnes, Bing Russell, Arthur Space, John Litel. Chris Colt struggles with a bank robber who has taken Colt's girl friend hostage. The girl's father is also on their trail with a posse.

34.20 *Golden Gun.* Feb. 28, 1958. GS: Paul Fix, Edd Byrnes, Dawn Richard. On the trail of an old gunfighter, Chris Colt finds his quarry dying. He tries desperately to get the old man to reveal where he has hidden his cache of stolen money.

34.21 *Circle of Fear.* March 7, 1958. GS: Tol Avery, Joan Weldon, Jean Willes, Harvey Stephens, Sean Garrison. Hostile Apaches attack a coach carrying Chris Colt and six other passengers. The passengers seek refuge in a mountain pass and look to Colt to lead them to safety.

34.22 *Split Second.* March 14, 1958. GS: Richard Garland, Elaine Edwards, Arthur Batanides, Dan Riss. The murder of his wife embitters a marshal and turns him into a vicious gunslinger. Chris Colt learns that the marshal has located the murderer and tries to avert bloodshed.

34.23 *Point of Honor.* March 21, 1958. GS: Cameron Mitchell, Marcia Henderson, Emile Meyer, John Smith. On the trail of a gang of bank robbers, Chris Colt winds up in a small frontier town. When a young woman doctor arrives and treats the leader of the outlaws, Colt believes that she is part of the gang.

34.24 *The Deserters.* March 28, 1958. GS: Angie Dickinson, Michael Dante, Myron Healey, Obie Venner, Robert Foulk. Chris Colt trails a number of deserts from an Army post to learn why they deserted. He finds out that a crooked gang of fur traders is responsible.

34.25 *The Manbuster.* April 4, 1958. GS: Chris Warfield, Jaclynne Greene, George Keymas, Gil Perkins, Don Beddoe, Gregg Barton, Jody Angelo. A bitter young man is tempted to become an outlaw. He unknowingly aids Chris Colt's search for a gang of bank robbers.

34.26 *Long Odds.* April 11, 1958. GS: Paul Engle, Charmienne Harker, Karl Swenson, Robert J. Wilke, John Hubbard. Chris Colt tries to help an elderly ex-sheriff clear his name. The lawman has been stripped of authority.

Season Two

34.27 *The Escape.* April 5, 1959. GS: Adam West, Myrna Fahey, Peter Miles, Robert Griffin, Sandy Kenyon, Bern Hoffman. Chris Colt apprehends Sgt. Ed Kallen, wanted for trial by the Army. After Colt turns his prisoner over to the Army he falls victim to a pretty girl's scheme to free the sergeant.

34.28 *Dead Aim.* April 12, 1959. GS: John Doucette, Jaclynne Greene, Bing Russell, James Maloney. Tracking down a bandit, Chris Colt comes upon Lou Gore, a bounty hunter. Knowing Gore is after the same man, Colt marks a hoof of Gore's horse and follows his trail.

34.29 *The Magic Box.* April 19, 1959. GS: Vaughn Taylor, Michael Carr, Dan Sheridan, Barbara Stuart, Maurice Manson. Chris Colt believes that an Indian youth is not guilty of the crime for which he will soon be hanged. Colt enlists the aid of Oliver Pate, a photographer, to try to prove the youth's innocence.

34.30 *The Confession.* April 26, 1959. GS: Dallas Mitchell, Dorothy Provine, Charles Aidman, Don C. Harvey. Chris Colt becomes suspicious of rancher Joe Donnelly's willing confession of a stagecoach robbery.

34.31 *The Man Who Loved Lincoln.* May 3, 1959. GS: Robert McQueeney, Hugh Sanders, Roxane Berard, Donald Buka, Allen Case. When actor Edwin Booth arrives in Virginia City to give a performance, he finds the townspeople hostile toward him because of his brother's assassination of President Lincoln.

34.32 *The Sanctuary.* May 10, 1959. GS: Lyle Talbot, Harry Lauter, Andra Martin, Van Williams. A killer sought by Chris Colt hides out in a small town, aided by the paid cooperation of the sheriff. Without the lawman's help, Colt tries a little game in order to get his prisoner.

34.33 *The Saga of Sam Bass.* May 17, 1959. GS: Alan Hale, Jr., Ann Doran, House Peters, Jr., Mickey Simpson, Ken Clark, Jr. In order to learn where the loot from a robbery has been stashed, Chris Colt has himself jailed with the chief robbery suspect. To win the man's trust, Colt escapes from jail with him.

34.34 *Amnesty.* May 24, 1959. GS: Robert Conrad, Willis Bouchey, Wayne Heffley, Barbara Darrow. At the governor's request, Chris Colt travel into the Black Hills to offer Billy the Kid a pardon. Because of the interference of an embittered sheriff, the Kid is suspicious of Colt's mission.

34.35 *The Pirate.* May 31, 1959. GS: Neil Hamilton, Patti Kane, Lance Fuller, Robert Foulk. Chris Colt is sent by the Government to regain federal money stolen by seafaring Captain Johnson. On board the Captain's ship, Colt finds himself a prisoner just outside of American territorial waters.

34.36 *Law West of the Pecos.* June 7, 1959. GS: Frank Ferguson, Lisa Gaye, William Lally, Douglas Kennedy, Jack Lambert. Attempting to clear an innocent man accused of stealing an Army payroll, Chris Colt finds himself jailed on a phony charges.

34.37 *Don't Tell Joe.* June 14, 1959. GS: Adam West, James Anderson, Mary Webster, Charles Fredericks. Trying to learn the identity of a killer, Chris Colt arrives in the town of Green Rock. He learns that an infamous gunslinger is trying to pin the murder on Marshal Joe Benjamin, a friend of Colt's.

34.38 *Return to El Paso.* June 21, 1959. GS: Robert Lowery, Paul Picerni, Kasey Rogers, James Lydon. Government agent Chris Colt is sent to El Paso to impound some rifles. When Colt arrives, he learns that the guns have been bought at an auction by a wealthy rancher.

34.39 *Night of Decision.* June 28, 1959. GS: Edith Evanson, Leonard Nimoy, Dallas Mitchell, Jory Raymond. Chris Colt, held hostage by Ma Thorpe and outlaw Luke Reid, tries to talk Ma into setting him free and letting him apprehend her son Ben, who is wanted by the law.

Season Three

34.40 *Queen of Dixie.* Oct. 4, 1959. GS: John Alderson, Tol Avery, Dale Johnson, George Cisar. Chris Colt, aboard a Mississippi gambling boat, clashes with a counterfeiting ring.

Colt .45

34.41 *The Reckoning.* Oct. 11, 1959. GS: Jack Mather, Joe di Reda, Buzz Martin, Kelly Thordsen. Trailing three unidentified killers, Colt meets Father Knox, a desert priest. Father Knox gives Colt a clue to the whereabouts of the killers, but refuses to give him their names or tell him exactly where they are hiding.

34.42 *The Devil's Godson.* Oct. 18, 1959. GS: Adam West, Ann Morriss, Billy Wells, Alan Dexter, Forrest Lewis, Lane Bradford, Nick Paul. Chris Colt uses the notorious Doc Holliday to bait a trap for a killer. Colt is trying to prevent harm to a small boy.

34.43 *The Rival Gun.* Oct. 25, 1959. GS: Robert McQueeney, George Kennedy, Dick Rich, Stephen Chase, Natividad Vacio. Colt is checking on a shipment of guns that failed to reach a Montana Territory Army post. He is pitted against the Duke, a supplier of guns to hostile Indians.

34.44 *The Hothead.* Nov. 1, 1959. GS: Troy Donahue, John McCann, K.L. Smith. Two outlaws and a girl are framing a young bank clerk for a bank robbery. Chris colt sets out to save the clerk, but the youth's infatuation for the young lady makes him uncooperative.

34.45 *A Legend of Buffalo Bill.* Nov. 8, 1959. GS: Britt Lomond, Lindsay Workman. On a train, Chris Colt meets two famous Westerners, Buffalo Bill Cody and writer Ned Buntline. The train is attacked by hijackers.

34.46 *Yellow Terror.* Nov. 15, 1959. GS: Richard Devon, Kaye Elhardt, Andy Clyde, Brad Dexter. Chris Colt and his prisoner are aboard a river boat when the prisoner is killed. Then a yellow fever panic seizes the passengers, and Colt hopes that fear will cause the killer to reveal himself.

34.47 *Tar and Feathers.* Nov. 22, 1959. GS: Sal Ponti, Jennifer Lea, Howard Petrie. Government agent Chris Colt is assigned to protect Andre Bourdette, a young foreign diplomat touring the West. While Bourdette romances the daughter of John Porter, a vicious landowner, Colt works to loosen Porter's stranglehold on the area.

34.48 *Alias Mr. Howard.* Dec. 6, 1959. GS: Mike Road, Howard Ledig, Jane Nigh, Harry Harvey, Sr. Sam Colt trails outlaw Woodie Keene to the house of a Mr. Howard. He soon learns that Howard is actually the notorious Jesse James.

34.49 *Calamity.* Dec 13, 1959. GS: Joan Taylor, Dody Heath. Driving the Deadwood stage through Indian country, Colt finds out that two female passengers, namely Calamity Jane and Dr. Ellen McGraw, can be more trouble than Indians.

34.50 *Under False Pretenses.* Jan. 10, 1960. GS: Suzanne Lloyd, Joe Partridge, Tim Graham, Jack Hogan. Sam Colt Jr. is on a stagecoach, guarding a shipment of money. Two men hold him up, he kills one, but the other rides off with the money. Noting the brand on the dead man's horse, Colt goes after the fleeing bandit.

34.51 *Impasse.* Jan. 31, 1960. GS: Sandy Koufax, Harry Lauter, Linda Lawson, Roy Engel, Ann Doran, Ron Haggerty, Mike Ragan, Randy Sparks. Sam Colt Jr. and Johnny, a soldier, go to turn over an Army payroll to three waiting soldiers. But the trio turn out to be bandits.

34.52 *Arizona Anderson.* Feb. 14, 1960. GS: Michael Road, Catherine McCleod, Allan Lane, Arthur Space, Donald "Red" Barry. Sam Colt Jr. dons the guise of a gambler and tries to force Arizona Anderson into revealing the whereabouts of stolen government money. Suddenly two outlaws appear on the scene to collect their part of the stolen funds.

34.53 *The Cause.* Feb. 28, 1960. GS: Rodolfo Hoyos, Tristram Coffin, Miguel Landa, Julia Montoya, Jay Novello. Col. Willis Murdock, in Mexico working with a band of revolutionaries, is wanted by the United States Government. Colt attempts to bring Murdock back by making a deal with Martinez, the rebel leader.

34.54 *Phantom Trail.* March 13, 1960. GS: John Archer, John McCann, Donald "Red" Barry, Walter Maslow. Chris and Sam are out to get the men who have been rustling Government cattle. Chris works in the open as a Government agent, but Sam assumes the role of a gunslinger willing, for a fee, to eliminate Chris.

34.55 *Breakthrough.* March 27, 1960. GS: Faith Domergue, Archie Duncan, Charles Cooper. Colt tries to prevent a gang of hijackers from holding up a stagecoach loaded with gold.

34.56 *Chain of Command.* April 5, 1960. GS: Alan Baxter, Ross Elliot, Gordon Jones, Jean Blake, Gary Vinson. There is no water on the route that Colonel Bealey has set. Colt risks a court-martial when he questions the colonel's plans.

34.57 *Alibi.* April 12, 1960. GS: Dan Haggerty, James Bell, Claudia Barrett, Jock Gaynor. Colt is on his way to Yucca Wells, where a prisoner claims to be innocent of a murder charge. When he arrives, he finds the prisoner gone and the townspeople unwilling to talk.

34.58 *Absent Without Leave.* April 19, 1960. GS: Gary Conway, Tyler McVey, Andra Martin, Steve Brodie. Col. Ben Williams is convinced that his son Charles, a lieutenant, went AWOL because he feared a Sioux attack. Chris Colt finds the lieutenant and learns another reason.

34.59 *Strange Encounter.* April 26, 1960. GS: Vaughn Taylor, Robert Colbert, Kasey Rogers, Frank Albertson, Mike Ragan. Colt is escorting a couple of murderers to jail, and on the way he finds two badly injured men. The prisoners may be killers, but one of them is a doctor.

34.60 *Trial by Rope.* May 3, 1960. GS: Lurene Tuttle, Pamela Duncan, Ed Kemmer, Don Chastain. In Harker City, matriarch Lottie Strong's word is law. And she says that Ben Anderson is guilty of murder.

34.61 *The Gandy Dancers.* May 10, 1960. GS: Charles Fredericks, Joan Lora, Elaine Edwards, John Wengraf. An outlaw gang is victimizing immigrant railroad workers, taking half their pay. Colt tries to put an end to the extortion.

34.62 *Martial Law.* May 17, 1960. GS: Margaret Whiting, Ray Daley, Robert Foulk, Merrit Bohn, Paul Picerni, Percy Helton, Joseph Ruskin. Sam Colt Jr. is sent to High Card to clean up the gambling and investigate two murders. It isn't long before he comes up against strong-willed Vinnie Berkeley, owner of the town's biggest gambling den.

34.63 *Attack.* May 24, 1960. GS: Robert Colbert, Richard Garland, Sharon Hugueny, Frank Gerstle, Glenn Strange. Acting as temporary Indian agent, Sam Colt Jr. is caught in a conflict between aggressive miners and determined Sioux Indians, owners of ore-rich land.

34.64 *Bounty List.* May 31, 1960. GS: Ray Danton, Janet Lake, Ron Foster, Harp McGuire, J. Edward McKinley. Kane is after the bounty offered for his former partners in crime. Sam Colt Jr. wants the same men but, unlike Kane, seeks to bring them in alive.

34.65 *Appointment in Agoura.* June 7, 1960. GS: Rhodes Reason, Hal Torey, Chris Robinson, Steve Drexel, Alan Reynolds. Ben Thompson has shot the youngest of the Sanger clan in self-defense. Colt tries to get him out of town before the rest of the Sangers can gun him down.

34.66 *Showdown at Goldtown.* June 14, 1960. GS: Ruta Lee, Robert Colbert, Harry Shannon, Jerry Barclay. Ex-con Johnny Moore has been paroled in Colt's custody. Now Johnny is assigned to drive a stage containing a shipment of gold dust — and Tip Cooper, his mortal enemy, is planning a holdup.

34.67 *The Trespasser.* June 21, 1960. GS: Ray Teal, Lee Van Cleef, Pamela Duncan, Arthur Space, Gary Vinson. Mike O'Tara's Indian wife was killed by a soldier. In his desire for vengeance, he waits outside Fort Brazo with an Indian confederate to ambush all persons who venture outside its walls. Sam Colt is assigned to tame him.

35. *Cowboy G-Men*

Syndicated. 30 min. Broadcast history: Various, Sept. 1952–June 1953.
Regular Cast: Russell Hayden (Pat Gallagher), Jackie Coogan (Stoney Crockett).
Premise: This series dealt with the exploits of United States Government undercover agents Pat Gallagher and Stoney Crockett in California during the 1880s.

The Episodes

35.1 *Ozark Gold.* Sept. 13, 1952. GS: El Brendel, Phil Arnold, Richard Travis, Mary Ann Edwards, Lane Bradford, Lee Roberts. Pat and Stoney are sent to the Ozarks to recover bullion stolen from the Army.

35.2 *Chinaman's Chance.* Sept. 20, 1952. GS: Phil Arnold, John Vosper, Robert Bice, Tom Monroe, Fred Libby, Judy Dan, Spencer Chan. Pat and Stoney investigate when Chinese gold miners in California are outrageously taxed by corrupt officials and terrorized by a racist White Dragon organization.

35.3 *The Golden Wolf.* Sept. 27, 1952. GS: Robert Lowery, Timothy Carey, Jonathan Hale, Stanley Andrews. Pat and Stoney encounter a gang of swindlers who are using the same assortment of wolf pelts to collect multiple bounties from various communities.

35.4 *The Secret Mission.* Oct. 4, 1952. Pat and Stoney use a pair of twins to carry secret documents into newly opened territory.

35.5 *Chippewa Indians.* Oct. 11, 1952. GS: Lyle Talbot, Phil Arnold, Lillian Porter, Rick Vallin, Robert Bice. Pat and Stoney take a hand when the Wisconsin Chippewas around Lac du Flambeau are victimized by unscrupulous lumber brokers.

35.6 *Center Fire.* Oct. 18, 1952. GS: Madge Meredith, Lyle Talbot, Rick Vallin, Robert Bice, George De Normand. Pat and Stoney go after a crooked veterinarian who has started an anthrax epidemic so that he can sell serum to the ranchers at ten times its value.

35.7 *Beware! No Trespassing.* Oct. 1, 1952. GS: Robert Lowery, Timothy Carey, Edward Colmans, Rick Vallin, Gil Barreto. Pat and Stoney are called in to help when a man-made malaria epidemic halts production at a vital tungsten mine in Mexico.

35.8 *Pixilated.* Oct. 8, 1952. GS: Florence Lake, John Eldredge, Phil Arnold, Richard Travis, Marshall Reed. Pat and Stoney investigate the leakage of secret information about land for a railroad.

35.9 *Running Iron.* Nov. 15, 1952. GS: Jim Davis, Phil Arnold, John Eldredge, Brad Johnson, Edith Leslie, Claudia Barrett, Tom Monroe, George Gregg, Bob Carson. Pat and Stoney try to clear a government cattle buyer who is accused of purchasing stolen herds on behalf of the United States.

35.10 *Bounty Jumpers.* Nov. 22, 1952. GS: John Cason, Ford Rainey, Warren McGregor, Scott Lee, Gordon Barnes. Pat and Stoney investigate when two deserters ambush an Army messenger and steal the military payroll vouchers he was carrying.

35.11 *Gunslingers.* Nov. 29, 1952. GS: Robert Lowery, Phil Arnold, Pamela Duncan, Robert Bray, Alfred Monroe, John Cason, Stephen Carr, Jack Ingram. Pat and Stoney are caught in an ambush while guarding a shipment of government gold.

35.12 *Koniackers.* Dec. 6, 1952. GS: Robert Bray, Walter McGrail, Stanley Andrews, Ed Heath, Mervin Williams, Phil Arnold, Chuck Roberson, Lee Morgan, Joel Smith, Warren MacGregor. Pat and Stoney investigate when the currency in a bank vault is mysteriously replaced with counterfeit money.

35.13 *Ghost Bushwacker.* Dec. 13, 1952. GS: Phil Arnold, James Seay, Stephen Carr, Gloria Talbott, Rick Vallin, James Macklin, Wes Hudman. Pat and Stoney join forces with a Mexican government agent to combat a band of outlaws dressed as Mexicans who are terrorizing the newly organized Arizona territory.

35.14 *Salted Mines.* Dec. 20, 1952. GS: Archie Twitchell, Kenneth MacDonald, Gloria Marshall, Tom London, Tom Tyler, Denver Pyle. Pat and Stoney help a mine broker who has been accused of selling the townspeople salted mines.

35.15 *Frontier Smugglers.* Dec. 27, 1952. GS: Robert J. Wilke, Harry Lauter, Drake Smith, John Cason, Riley Hill, Brad Johnson. Pat and Stoney team up with a Canadian Mountie to track down a gang of smugglers who are hiding diamonds inside rifle shells.

35.16 *Mysterious Decoy.* Jan. 3, 1953. GS: Morris Ankrum, Phil Arnold, Tristram Coffin, Rick Vallin, Gregg Barton, Kenneth McDonald, William Fawcett. Pat and Stoney visit a halfway house which is the center of a boundary dispute between Utah and Arizona and encounter a gang of hooded vigilantes.

35.17 *Ridge of Ghosts.* Jan. 10, 1953. GS: El Brendel, Richard Travis, Sunny Burdette, Lane Bradford, Lee Roberts. Pat and Stoney help an old prospector when some townspeople try to make him tell where his gold mine is located.

35.18 *Hang the Jury.* Jan. 17, 1953. GS: Morris Ankrum, Tristram Coffin, Rick Vallin, Helen Chapman. Pat and Stoney investigate when outlaws conspire with a corrupt frontier judge to collect the rewards for their own capture.

35.19 *Silver Shotgun.* Jan. 24, 1953. GS: Jim Davis, Phil Arnold, John Eldredge, Brad Johnson, Claudia Barrett, Tom Monroe, George Gregg. Pat and Stoney trail a mysterious shotgun killer into the private domain of a dictatorial sheriff.

35.20 *Rawhide Gold.* Jan. 31, 1953. GS: Virginia Herrick, Myron Healey, Marshall Reed, Pierce Lyden, Lee Roberts, Ted Adams. Undercover Federal agents Pat Gallagher and Stoney Crockett are sent to the town of Rawhide to track down a murder and recover the government gold he stole.

35.21 *The Run Down.* Feb. 7, 1953. GS: Valerie Vernon, George Eldredge, John Vosper, Tom Monroe, Fred Libby. Pat and Stoney hunt down the mysterious leader of a gang of cattle rustlers.

35.22 *Rawhiders.* Feb. 14, 1953. GS: John Eldredge, Madge Meredith, Richard Travis, Tom Monroe, Marshall Reed. Pat and Stoney battle Eastern schemers who are trying to take over a legal lottery in the state of Washington.

35.23 *General Delivery.* Feb. 21, 1953. GS: Madge Meredith, Lyle Talbot, Phil Arnold, Robert Bice, Rick Vallin, George De Normand, Lee Roberts. Pat and Stoney investigate the disappearance of a postal inspector and run into an insurance swindle aimed at the mail system.

35.24 *Gypsy Traders.* Feb. 28, 1953. GS: Charlita, James Seay, Phil Arnold, Gregg Barton, Harry Hickox, John Cason. Pat and Stoney are sent in after a Federal judge who has helped some local Gypsies is run out of town by bandits.

35.25 *Safe Crackers.* March 7, 1953. GS: Mae Clarke, John Vosper, Tom Monroe, Sam Flint, Pierce Lyden. Pat and Stoney go after a safecracking ring headed by a typewriter saleswoman.

35.26 *Silver Fraud.* March 14, 1953. GS: Paul Keasy, Robert J. Wilke, Brad Johnson, Harry Lauter, John Cason, Riley Hill. Pat and Stoney are called in when the U.S. Mint in Denver discovers that it has been purchasing silver which has been diluted with a large amount of lead.

35.27 *Hangfire.* March 21, 1953. GS: Phil Arnold, James Seay, Dorothy Patrick, James Macklin, Byron Foulger, Ruth Whitney. Pat and Stoney receive orders to clean up an outlaw town but their papers are stolen from them before they can act. Posing as fugitives, they ride into the outlaw town and try to recover the documents.

35.28 *Hush Money.* March 28, 1953. GS: Phil Arnold, James Seay, Jackie Cooper, Jr., Byron Foulger, Rick Vallin, James Macklin, Stephen Carr, Ella Ethridge. Pat and Stoney run into a seven-year-old murder and a plot to kill a young boy while they are working to clear title to a ranch that is needed for a government irrigation project.

35.29 *Ghost Town Mystery.* April 4, 1953. GS: El Brendel, Roy Barcroft, Florence Lake. Pat and Stoney are sent to find out why a government order for a million dollars' worth of silver hasn't been filled.

35.30 *Empty Mailbags.* April 11, 1953. GS: Robert Lowery, Phil Arnold, Robert Bray, Alfred Monroe, John Cason, Stephen Carr, George Gregg. Pat and Stoney are assigned to locate two missing postal inspectors and to breakup a mail fraud ring operating a large number of post offices in ghost towns.

35.31 *Sawdust Swindle.* April 18, 1953. GS: Robert Lowery, Phil Arnold, Robert Bice, Pamela Duncan, Alfred Monroe, John Cason. Pat and Stoney go after the gang responsible for hijacking goods from Indian trading posts.

35.32 *Spring the Trap.* April 25, 1953. GS: Phil Arnold, George Eldredge, Richard Travis, Marshall Reed, Tom Monroe, Madge Meredith, X Brands. Pat and Stoney devise a play for Pat to impersonate a dead outlaw he closely resembles while the two agents hunt along the Mexican border for the government gold the dead man stole and hid.

35.33 *Sidewinder.* May 2, 1953. GS: El Brendel, Dorothy Patrick, Roy Barcroft, Harry Hickox, X Brands, John Cason. Pat and Stoney trail a fugitive who tries to escape by trapping Pat in quicksand.

35.34 *Indian Traders.* May 9, 1953. GS: Wade Crosby, Bob Peyton, Sherwood Gell, Chief Willowbird, Eileen Rowe, Charles Harvey, George Pembroke. Pat and Stoney investigate Indians' claims that they are being fleeced by trading post proprietors.

35.35 *Stolen Dynamite.* May 16, 1953. GS: Jim Davis, Phil Arnold, Helen Parrish, John Eldredge, Brad Johnson, Tom Monroe, George Gregg. Pat and Stoney tangle with a syndicate that is trying to steal the formula for an underwater explosive.

35.36 *The Woman Mayor.* May 23, 1953. GS: Morris Ankrum, Jean Parker, Phil Arnold, Tristram Coffin, Florence Lake. Pat and Stoney help a hot-tempered woman mayor bring law and order to brawling Nugget City.

35.37 *Double Crossed.* May 30, 1953. GS: Jim Davis, Robert Bray, Jonathan Hale, Gary Garrett. Pat and Stoney come to Texas on a hunt for the forgers who sold the state several million dollars' worth of counterfeit U.S. gold bonds.

35.38 *High Heeled Boots.* June 6, 1953. GS: Jean Parker, Richard Travis, Phil Arnold, Rick Vallin, John Cason. Pat and Stoney go after a gang of counterfeiters led by a lovely woman saloonkeeper.

35.39 *The California Bullets.* June 13, 1953. GS: James Seay, Charlita, Gregg Barton, John Cason, Harry Hickox. Pat and Stoney are almost killed while investigating the mystery of the short-weight coins intended for the U.S. Mint.

36. *Cowboy in Africa*

ABC. 60 min. Broadcast history: Monday, 7:30–8:30, Sept. 1967–Sept. 1968.

Regular Cast: Chuck Connors (Jim Sinclair), Tom Nardini (John Henry), Ronald Howard (Howard Hayes), Gerald G. Edwards (Samson).

Premise: Champion rodeo rider Jim Sinclair and his Navajo sidekick John Henry join forces with Wing Commander Hayes, an African game rancher, who is determined to prove that wild animal ranching is Africa's best defense against the ravages caused by uncontrolled cattle grazing.

The Episodes

36.1 *The New World.* Sept. 11, 1967. GS: Frank Marth, Antoinette Bower. Jim Sinclair and John Henry assist Commander Hayes in his plan to domesticate wild animals in a game preserve, despite violent opposition from cattlemen.

36.2 *Kifaru! Kifaru!* Sept. 18, 1967. GS: Joanna Moore, Peter Bromilow, Dodie Marshall, Mel Scott. A rare white rhinoceros sparks a grim duel between two highly principled men. Jim is undertaking a suicidal rescue attempt of the wounded animal while a professional hunter bears down to put the rhino out of its misery.

36.3 *Incident at Derati Wells.* Sep. 25, 1967. GS: Yaphet

Kotto, Rupert Crose. Musa, the crafty chief of a nomadic tribe, plots to ambush the game ranchers in Northern Kenya, and force them to rope and corral horses for his tribe.

36.4 *What's an Elephant Mother to Do?* Oct. 2, 1967. GS: Lynda Day, Torin Thatcher, Paul Winfield. A reckless girl photographer stuns the game ranchers with her disregard for safety. Courting disaster, she separates a mother elephant from its calf.

36.5 *Search for Survival.* Oct. 9, 1967. GS: Anne Baxter, Izack Fields, Khalil Bezaleel, Cynthia Eilbacher. Erica Holloway is the pitiless owner of a ranch oasis, who refuses to offer the natives relief from a drought. Jim tries to melt the icy woman's refusal to provide water for dying men and animals.

36.6 *Stone Age Safari.* Oct. 16, 1967. GS: James McEachin, Emily Banks, Anthony Ghazio, Sr., Chips Robinson. Jim uses science to combat tribal superstition when young Samson has been accused of harboring an evil spirit and causing a boy's mysterious death.

36.7 *The Adopted One.* Oct. 23, 1967. GS: William Mims, Lisa Pera. A playful lion cub creates problems for Jim, who gave the cub to Samson in the belief that it was an orphan. The cub's mother is terrorizing the countryside in a search for her missing baby.

36.8 *Fang and Claw.* Oct. 30, 1967. GS: James Gregory, Louis Gossett, Jr., Arthur Adams. The Kenya Rifles assist Jim in his search for Hayes and John Henry. They have been kidnaped by a man whose quest for ransom is second only to his desire to crush Hayes' spirit.

36.9 *The Time of the Predator.* Nov. 6, 1967. GS: Ken Gampu, Chester Washington, Carl Thompson, Bill Russell. A distinguished African's tour of the ranch could mean heartbreak for Jim and Samson. The official is seeking a promising Kikuyu boy for schooling abroad, and his choice is Samson.

36.10 *Lake Sinclair.* Nov. 13, 1967. GS: Rockne Tarkington, Gloria Calomee, Albert Popwell, Ken Renard, Earl T. Smith, Zara Cully. All hands pitch in to help Mageela and Jacob, young lovers whose elopement caravan is being hounded by tribal hostility and plain bad luck.

36.11 *Tomorrow on the Wind.* Nov. 20, 1967. GS: Cicely Tyson, Richard Elkins. Jim and an American schoolteacher clash with the strong-willed Kisawa chief, who refuses to let his tribe's youngsters attend classes.

36.12 *Little Boy Lost.* Nov. 27, 1967. GS: Todd Martin, Charles Lampkin, Stan Duke, Kenneth Lupper, Tony White, Kyle Johnson. Jim faces two desperate crises. A rancher is baiting predatory animals with poisoned meat and Samson is off on an endurance test, with some of the meat in his pack.

36.13 *The Man Who Has Everything.* Dec. 4, 1967. GS: Edward Mulhare, James Wainwright, Hagan Beggs. Jim clashes with a wealthy man who wants to change the way the ranch operates.

36.14 *To Build a Beginning.* Dec. 11, 1967. GS: Kamala Devi, Kay Kuter, Don Megowan, Chester Washington, Bob Rhodes. John Henry and Samson desperately try to find Jim, who has been lost in a plane crash. As the search progresses, a grieving John Henry recalls his first meeting with Jim and the rocky beginnings of their friendship.

36.15 *The Hesitant Hero.* Dec. 18, 1967. GS: Brooke Bundy, Richard Eastham. John Henry falls in love with a timid girl who fears for his safety. His self-confidence corroded, the overcautious John Henry breeds danger when he and Jim set out to rope some buffalo.

36.16 *African Rodeo* Part One. Jan. 15, 1968. GS: Jan Murray, Alejandro Rey, Michael Conrad, Ronald Feinberg, Michael Jackson, Tom Kelly, Bob Morgan, Albert Popwell. An unscrupulous sports promoter provokes Jim into participating in an African game rodeo. Competing with the Yanks are two South American vaqueros with a style, and motives, of their own.

36.17 *African Rodeo* Part Two. Jan. 22, 1968. GS: Jan Murray, Alejandro Rey, Michael Conrad, Ronald Feinberg, Michael Jackson, Tom Kelly, Bob Morgan, Albert Popwell. Jim becomes increasingly edgy as the day of the wild-game rodeo nears. A smell of greed looms over the proceedings, whose participants include a sharp promoter and two vaqueros with motives as gamey as the beasts in the ring.

36.18 *First to Capture.* Jan. 29, 1968. GS: James Whitmore, Michael Burns, Alex Dreier, Rex Holman. Jim tries to curb the brutal tactis of Ryan Crose, a veteran game hunter who refuses to adapt to a changing Africa. Jim's quarrel with Crose conflicts with an old friendship between Crose and Hayes, and causes a clash between the hunter and his son.

36.19 *The Red Hand of Michael O'Neill.* Feb. 5, 1968. GS: Timothy Carey, Bonnie Beecher, Mac McLaughlin. The O'Neill family, newly arrived settlers, means trouble for game ranchers Hayes and his helpers. When mercenaries rob and pillage the settlers' property, the fiery O'Neills strike back — at Hayes and John Henry.

36.20 *The Quiet Death.* Feb. 19, 1968. GS: Lou Gossett, Jr., Len Birman, Bob DoQui, Arthur Adams, Davis Roberts, Izack Fields. Hayes clashes head-on with an African demagogue who is exploiting an epidemic of cattle disease to drive out the game ranchers.

36.21 *A Man of Value.* Feb. 26, 1968. GS: James Edwards, John Alderson, Patrick Horgan, Michael St. Clair. John Henry and Samson become pawns in a dangerous waiting game. Alone at the ranch, they unwittingly take in three kidnapers who intend to deliver a political hostage to his enemies in Hayes' plane.

36.22 *Search and Destroy.* March 4, 1968. GS: Cliff Osmond, Jeff Burton, Jason Wingreen, Don Drysdale. Friend and foe are thrown together in an emotion charged hunt for escaped game-ranch zebras. The animals — including Samson's pet — are carrying an infectious disease.

36.23 *Work of Art.* March 11, 1968. GS: Madlyn Rhue. Jim has a chance reunion with his former sweetheart, artist Christie Blaine. Their romance resumes under the hurt glances of Samson, who sees it as a threat to his place in Jim's life.

36.24 *John Henry's Eden.* March 18, 1968. GS: Harvey Jason, William Tannen. Upheaval looms at the game ranch when John Henry gets the mistaken idea that he's low man on the totem pole. Jim and Hayes watch in amazement as the Navajo's burning resentment involves him in a gargantuan effort to turn a wasteland into his private Eden.

36.25 *The Lions.* March 25, 1968. GS: Antoinette Bower, Royal Dano, Guy Edwards. Past, present and future are at issue as the ranchers work feverishly to capture a pride of lions. Two archeologists want to shoot the encroaching predators.

36.26 *The Kasubi Death.* April 1, 1968. GS: Michael Ansara, Rex Ingram, Sue England. As John Henry lies dying from a poisoned arrow, Hayes risks his own life to obtain the antidote from a poacher who rigged the lethal crossbow.

37. The Cowboys

ABC. 30 min. Broadcast history: Wednesday, 8:00-8:30, Feb. 1974–Aug. 1974.

Regular Cast: Jim Davis (Marshal Bill Winter), Diana Douglas (Kate Andersen), Moses Gunn (Nightlinger), Robert Carradine (Slim), A Martinez (Cimarron), Sean Kelly (Jimmy), Kerry MacLane (Homer), Clint Howard (Steve), Mitch Brown (Hardy), Clay O'Brien (Weedy).

Premise: Seven youngsters between the ages of nine and seventeen work as cowhands on a widow's ranch in New Mexico Territory in the 1870s.

The Episodes

37.1 *David Done It.* Feb. 6, 1974. GS: DeForest Kelley, Robert Hoy. In the New Mexico Territory of the 1870s, seven adolescent cowhands return with their black range cook to the widow's ranch where they work, not knowing that two outlaws are waiting at the ranch to steal the proceeds from their cattle drive.

37.2 *Death on a Fast Horse.* Feb. 13, 1974. GS: Brett Parker, Bill Shannon, Kevin Hagen. The young cowboys use a team of relay horses to break the alibi of a man suspected of killing a friend of theirs.

37.3 *The Long Rider.* Feb. 20, 1974. GS: Richard Kelton, Jennifer Lesko. An engaging visitor to the ranch charms all the youthful cowhands except Cimarron, who suspects that their guest is a killer.

37.4 *Many a Good Horse Dies.* Feb. 27, 1974. GS: John Carradine, Lurene Tuttle, Kelly Thordsen. Twelve-year-old Weedy tries desperately to buy an old cavalry horse which he is convinced belonged to his dead father.

37.5 *The Avenger.* March 6, 1974. GS: Gregory Walcott, John Harmon. A mysterious stranger from the black cook Nightlinger's past comes to Spanish Wells, boding ill for everyone on the ranch.

37.6 *The Accused.* March 13, 1974. GS: Walter Brooke, Roberto Contreras, Felipe Turich, John R. McKee, Ian Wolfe. The young cowboys try to clear the names of two innocent men who were hanged as horse thieves.

37.7 *A Matter of Honor.* March 20, 1974. GS: Pippa Scott, Monica Gayle, Robert Foulk, Stafford Repp. The young cowboys come to the aid of a woman visitor who has been accused, unfairly they think, of cheating at cards.

37.8 *The Ordeal.* March 27, 1974. Nightlinger and his young helpers try desperately to rescue Homer and Weedy from an underground tunnel where they have been trapped by a cave-in.

37.9 *The Remounts.* April 3, 1974. GS: Michael Keep, Myron Healey. Hope and disappointment ride on a captured wild pinto that Cimarron plans to tame and sell to the Army.

37.10 *The Trap.* April 1, 1974. A well-concealed coyote trap and a youngster planning a practical joke come close to causing tragedy for the young cowboys.

37.11 *The Indian Givers.* May 1, 1974. GS: Richard Hale, Cal Bellini. A barter session with a band of young Comanches gives the youthful cowboys a memorable lesson in horse trading.

37.12 *Requiem for a Lost Son.* May 8, 1974. GS: Ted Gehring, Irene Tedrow, Belinda Balaski, Jerry Wills, Skip Riley. The cowboys confront a family seeking vengeance for the death of one of their members.

38. Custer

ABC. 60 min. Broadcast history: Wednesday, 7:30-8:30, Sept. 1967–Dec. 1967.

Regular Cast: Wayne Maunder (Lt. Col. George Armstrong Custer), Slim Pickens (California Joe Milner), Peter Palmer (Sgt. James Bustard), Grant Woods (Captain Myles Keogh), Michael Dante (Crazy Horse), Robert F. Simon (Terry), Hick Hill (Rio).

Premise: The series dealt with the career of General George Armstrong Custer in the West from the end of the Civil War until a year before his death at the Battle of the Little Big Horn in 1876.

The Episodes

38.1 *Sabres in the Sun.* Sept. 6, 1967. GS: Mary Ann Mobley, Alex Davion. Lt. Col. George Armstrong Custer assumes command of the 7th Cavalry. Saddled with ragtag misfits, Custer is faced with the task of whipping his soldiers into shape.

38.2 *Accused.* Sept. 13, 1967. GS: Chris Robinson, James Daly, Jack Hogan. Defying General Terry, Custer braves the hostile Sioux to rescue Lt. Tim Rudford, the headstrong son of an influential newspaper publisher who is attacking Custer as a vainglorious murderer.

38.3 *Glory Rider.* Sept. 20, 1967. GS: Ralph Meeker. Contempt and smoldering resentment spell danger as Custer's men join Kermit Teller's drovers for a cattle drive across the Sioux-infested plains. Teller has a long-standing grudge against all Cavalrymen, and the troops smart at the notion of wet-nursing a herd of cows.

38.4 *To the Death.* Sept. 27, 1967. GS: Larry Pennell, Art Lund. A Cheyenne war chieftain's escape from Army custody leads to double trouble for Custer, who must fight both the Indian and a general uprising among the tribes.

38.5 *Massacre.* Oct. 4, 1967. GS: Philip Carey, Arthur Franz, Jan Arvan. The odds pile up against Custer and his men as they take a secret shipment through Sioux territory. Crazy Horse has learned what the wagon train is carrying and where it's going.

38.6 *War Lance and Saber.* Oct. 11, 1967. GS: James Craig, Bob Beck, R.G. Armstrong. A common enemy forces Colonel Custer and the Sioux war chief Crazy Horse to call a temporary truce in their personal war. Captured by the Blackfeet, the two mortal foes must forge an unlikely alliance to effect their escape.

38.7 *Suspicion.* Oct. 18, 1967. GS: Robert Loggia, Pierre Jalbert, Paul Peterson. Suspicion among Custer's men imperils a mission intended to split the Arapahoes from their Sioux allies.

Suspected of spying for the Indians is Lt. Carlos Moreno, a Kiowa whose tribe is also allied with the Sioux.

38.8 *Breakout.* Nov. 1, 1967. GS: Ray Walston, Gene Evans, Burr de Benning, Kathleen Nolan. At a remote relay station, Custer and other stagecoach passengers are besieged by Indians. Not all of the danger is from the outside, as two of the party are cold-blooded killers.

38.9 *Desperate Mission.* Nov. 8, 1967. GS: Lloyd Bochner, Darren McGavin, Bill Gray, Charles Dierkop. Custer raids the stockade to get troops for a desperate mission of mercy. Thieves, swindlers and murderers join the colonel in a race to stop the spread of smallpox among the Pawnee.

38.10 *Under Fire.* Nov. 15, 1967. GS: William Windom, John Nealson, James McCallion, John Cliff. A renegade scout makes a deal with Crazy Horse. In exchange for access to the gold of the Black Hills, he will lead Colonel Custer into a Sioux ambush.

38.11 *Death Hunt.* Nov. 22, 1967. GS: Patricia Harty, William Smith, Barbara Hale. A vengeful Cheyenne chief and a crusading woman journalist both seek Custer's scalp after his men inadvertently massacre an Indian hunting party.

38.12 *Blazing Arrows.* Nov. 29, 1967. GS: Rory Calhoun, Adam Williams, Stacy Harris, Rod Redwing, Hal Lynch. Custer is caught between Rebel and redskin when he escorts a survey party through a community of ex-Confederates menaced by the Crow. The Colonel must uphold Federal law without starting an Indian uprising, or reviving the Civil War.

38.13 *Dangerous Prey.* Dec. 6, 1967. GS: Albert Salmi, Robert Doyle, Donnelly Rhodes. Surviving an Indian attack at a remote relay station, Custer and two other officers employ strategy and counter-strategy to escape their pursuer, the brilliant tactician War Cloud.

38.14 *Spirit Woman.* Dec. 13, 1967. GS: Agnes Moorehead, James Whitmore, Read Morgan, Chick Casey, Eugene Martin, Christopher Milo. A Sioux mystic defies tribal warmongers to seek peace. Custer's job is to protect the woman from her enemies, both white and red.

38.15 *The Gauntlet.* Dec. 20, 1967. GS: Edward Mulhare, Barbara Rush, Dennis Patrick, Brett Pearson. Custer contends with Indians and a British officer's arrogance to raid a band of Irish fanatics planning an invasion of Canada.

38.16 *The Raiders.* Dec. 27, 1967. GS: Yvonne DeCarlo, Peter Adams, Jeff Scott, Henry Beckman. In a turnabout of Western tradition, the Indians ride to the Cavalry's rescue. Convinced that the Kiowas are unjustly being blamed for wagon-train raids, Custer asks the Indian's help in finding the real culprits.

39. *The Dakotas*

ABC. 60 min. Broadcast history: Monday, 7:30-8:30, June 1963–Sept. 1963.

Regular Cast: Larry Ward (Marshal Frank Ragan), Chad Everett (Deputy Del Stark), Jack Elam (Deputy J.D. Smith), Michael Green (Deputy Vance Porter).

Premise: This Western series, set in the Dakota Territory, depicts the efforts of a team of U.S. marshals to maintain law and order on a wild frontier.

The Episodes

39.1 *Return to Drydock.* Jan. 7, 1963. GS: Edward Binns, Richard Hale, Natalie Trundy, Howard Smith, Robert Ellin. One man wasn't hostile to J.D. when he was run out of his home town as a gunfighter. That man has been killed, and J.D. intends to avenge the slaying, with or without Ragan's approval.

39.2 *Red Sky Over Bismarck.* Jan. 14, 1963. GS: Andrew Duggan, Constance Ford, Chris Robinson. Deborah James sends for Marshal Ragan when it appears that her half-breed son Chino may receive harsh judgement from Colonel Withers, the local justice of the peace. But when Ragan arrives, Deborah changes her story.

39.3 *Mutiny at Fort Mercy.* Jan. 21, 1963. GS: George Macready, Jeanne Cooper, Anthony Bart, Russell Johnson, William Bramley, Lew Gallo, Hal Baylor, Stewart Bradley. Deputies Del Stark and Vance Porter return an Army escapee to the stockade at Fort Mercy, commanded by the merciless Captain Ridgeway. When the captain puts the prisoner in solitary confinement, the other inmates, irked by Ridgeway's brutality, stage and uprising and seize Del as a hostage.

39.4 *Trouble at French Creek.* Jan. 28, 1963. GS: Mercedes McCambridge, Michael Constantine, Joan Freeman, John Kellogg, Jere Barclay, Stephen Joyce, Allen Jaffe. Jay French, in an attempt to build the mining empire which her husband once envisioned, drives her workers too hard and they go out on strike. Marshal Ragan is called in to maintain order in a very tense situation. Jay has hired some gunslingers to keep the strikers at bay.

39.5 *Thunder in Pleasant Valley.* Feb. 4, 1963. GS: Gregory Walcott, Patricia Huston, Karl Swenson, Lee Van Cleef, Cliff Osmond, Chris Alcaide, Lane Allan. Rancher Harry McNeill's daughter has been abducted by outlaws who demand a ransom. Marshal Ragan doesn't want McNeill to pay, but McNeil cares about his daughter, and not about catching crooks.

39.6 *Crisis at High Banjo.* Feb. 11, 1963. GS: Karen Sharpe, Ed Peck, Warren Stevens, David Lewis, Robert J. Wilke, Michael Pate, Ed Prentiss, Percy Helton. When Marshal Ragan recognizes convict Johnny Fox as one of the men who murdered his wife five years before, he goes berserk and almost kills Fox. Fox admits someone hired him to kill Ragan's wife, but refuses to identify his employers.

39.7 *Requiem at Dancer's Hill.* Feb. 18, 1963. GS: Dennis Hopper, Dick Foran, Anne Whitefield, Milton Frome, Herb Vigran, Alan Reed, Jr., Milton Parsons, Gail Bonney. Marshal Ragan is investigating Ross Kendrick, the leader of a posse which captured Morgan Jackson and executed him.

39.8 *Fargo.* Feb. 25, 1963. GS: David Brian, Richard Jaeckel, Diane Brewster, Ted de Corsia, Tim Graham, Don O'Kelly, Victor French. J.D. tries to reform Sheriff Fargo, a lawman who has set up a little hometown kingdom where he exacts tribute from the local merchants.

39.9 *Incident at Rapid City.* March 4, 1963. GS: Bert Freed, Maggie Pierce, Dennis Patrick, Russ Conway, Willis Bouchey, William Fawcett. A renegade Cavalry band creates an incident at Rapid City by demanding that Del turn over Lloyd Mitchell to them. The fugitive soldiers claim Mitchell supplied them with spoiled food, which poisoned some of their men.

39.10 *Justice at Eagle's Nest.* March 11, 1963. GS: Everett Sloane, Joanna Moore, Harry Shannon, Karl Held, Gregory Gay, Laurence Mann, Ken Mayer, Gene Roth, Delbert Monroe. The farmers near the town of Eagle's Nest don't like cattlemen, so they bring in tough old Judge Daniel Harvey to enforce the law. It soon becomes a case of farmer vs. cowboys, and Marshal Ragan decides to investigate the judge's methods.

39.11 *Walk Through the Badlands.* March 18, 1963. GS: Ed Nelson, Strother Martin, Steve Brodie, Tom Drake, Lane Bradford, Michael Vandever, Lou Robb, James Waters. Marshal Ragan and his deputies, pursued by an army of outlaws, flee to the waterless wilderness, where they come upon some Cavalry troopers escaping from the same gunmen.

39.12 *Trial at Grand Forks.* March 25, 1963. GS: Werner Klemperer, Susanne Cramer, Robert F. Simon, Bartlett Robinson, Pat Rosson, Ross Elliott, Barbara Woodell, Anthony Call. A trial at Grand Forks ends in a death sentence for German countess Maria Hoenig, accused of murdering her husband, a Prussian general. Marshal Ragan wants to know why the countess refused to testify in her own defense, but he risks and international incident if he delays the execution.

39.13 *Reformation at Big Nose Butte.* April 1, 1963. GS: Telly Savalas, DeForest Kelley, Sue Randall, Hayden Rorke, Mickey Simpson, Wallace Rooney, Richard Cutting, Roy Lennert. Deputy J.D. Smith was once an outlaw and now his new way of life faces the test. His former gang leader, Jake Volet, has been released from prison and has summoned his men to rejoin him.

39.14 *One Day in Vermillion.* April 8, 1963. GS: Carlos Rivas, Whit Bissell, Med Flory, Eugene Iglesias. Ragan escorts Sioux chief Takanta and his son into town for the signing of a peace treaty, but the three of them walk right into a nest of trouble.

39.15 *Terror at Heart River.* April 15, 1963. GS: Royal Dano, Coleen Gray, Gene Lyons, Sean McClory. Abandoned by the railroad and repulsed by the residents of Heart River, a savage, starving gang of railworkers threatens to pillage the town.

39.16 *The Chooser of the Slain.* April 22, 1963. GS: Claude Akins, Beverly Garland, Richard Loo, Corey Allen, William Zuckert, Justin Smith, Dayton Lummis, E.J. Andre, Don Kennedy, Bill Walker. When Del and Vance admit to killing a man in self-defense, Ragan must find a mysterious woman witness to the slaying, or his deputies will be hanged.

39.17 *Feud at Snake River.* April 29, 1963. GS: Harry Townes, James Westerfield, Joseph Ruskin, Roger Mobley, Barry Kelley, Don Keefer, Brendan Dillon, Harlan Warde. Ragan persuades George Deus to oppose his ruthless, empire-building brother Simon. When Simon drives a farm family off its land, Ragan marshals the rest of the farmers behind George.

39.18 *Sanctuary at Crystal Springs.* May 6, 1963. GS: James Anderson, Les Tremayne, Norman Alden, Joe DiReda, John Hoyt, Charles Irving, Woodrow Parfrey, Myron Healey, Bill Erwin. The townspeople are incensed when Del and J.D. gun down two of the murderous Barton brothers in a church. The third Barton, Stan, is holding the pastor hostage in exchange for the deputies.

39.19 *A Nice Girl from Goliah.* May 13, 1963. GS: Audrey Dalton, Frank De Kova, John Carlyle, Elisha Cook, Jr., Sheldon Allman, Diane Sayer, Vinton Hayworth. Ronnie Kane's slightly perjured testimony sends Beau Kellog to the gallows. Then Ronnie talks Del into defending her from Beau's revenge-minded, gunslinging brother.

40. Daniel Boone

ABC. 60 min. Broadcast history: Sunday, 6:30-7:30, Dec. 1960–March 1961.

Regular Cast: Dewey Martin (Daniel Boone), Mala Powers (Rebecca Boone), Richard Banke (Squire Boone), Eddy Waller (John Finley), Kevin Corcoran (James), Diane Jergens (Maybelle Yancy), William Herrin (Bud Yancy), Dean Fredericks (Crowfeather), Anthony Caruso (Chief Blackfish).

Premise: This series depicted the exploits of the legendary frontiersman Daniel Boone and his trek to lead a group of pioneers to Kentucky.

Notes: This mini-series was broadcast as four segments of *Walt Disney Presents*.

The Episodes

40.1 *The Warrior's Path.* Dec. 4, 1960. GS: Alex Gerry. Lured by stories about the fertile lands of Kentucky, Boone and a band of men begin an exploratory expedition, starting with a trip along a secret Indian path.

40.2 *...And Chase the Buffalo.* Dec. 11, 1960. GS: Brian Corcoran, George Wallace, Whit Bissell, Alex Gerry, Don Dorrell. Twelve years have gone by, and Daniel Boone and his family are now farming in a North Carolina Valley. Taxes are high, the settlers are restless, and Boone feels there is going to be a run-in with the law.

40.3 *The Wilderness Road.* March 12, 1961. Daniel Boone and his band of settlers cross the Cumberland Gamp into Kentucky. Their passage is threatened by the attacks of his old enemy Crowfeather.

40.4 *Promised Land.* March 19, 1961. Most of the members of Daniel Boone's wagon train, tired of Indian attacks, head back to North Carolina. Boone and a handful of loyal followers push on to Kentucky.

41. Daniel Boone

NBC. 60 min. Broadcast history: Thursday, 7:30-8:30, Sept. 1964–Aug. 1970.

Regular Cast: Fess Parker (Daniel Boone), Patricia Blair (Rebecca Boone), Veronica Cartwright (Jemima Boone), Darby Hinton (Israel Boone), Albert Salmi (Yadkin) 64-65, Ed Ames (Mingo) 64-68, Dallas McKennon (Cincinatus) 68-70, Jimmy Dean (Josh Clements) 67-69, Robert Coogan (Jericho Jones).

Premise: The series concerned the adventures of frontiersman Daniel Boone and his attempts to protect the settlement of Boonesborough, Kentucky.

The Episodes

41.1 *Ken-Tuck-E.* Sept. 24, 1964. GS: Robert F. Simon, Arch Johnson, Stephen Courtleigh, George Lindsey, Gregory Morton. George Washington sends Daniel and his side-kick into Ken-tuck-e, the dark and bloody hunting ground of four Indian nations, to find a site for a fort.

41.2 *Tekawitha McLeod.* Oct. 1, 1964. GS: Lynn Loring, Chris Alcaide, Edna Skinner, Robert Foulk, David Cadiente, Donald O'Rourke. A renegade half-breed kidnaps an Indian princess and offers her to the Boonesville settlers for a jug of rum. His offer is at first refused, but then Boone discovers that the princess really is no Indian.

41.3 *My Brother's Keeper.* Oct. 8, 1964. GS: Ford Rainey, Peter Coe, Adam Williams. Yadkin insists that the Creeks who wounded him and killed an unarmed Cherokee were led by none other than Mingo.

41.4 *The Family Fluellen.* Oct. 15, 1964. GS: Bethel Leslie, Harold J. Stone, Donald Losley, Cindy Cassell, Suzanne Cupito/Morgan Brittany, Judson Pratt. Daniel and Yadkin's search for poachers unearths unexpected culprits: a widowed Welshwoman and her three children, who are determined to settle in the midst of hostile Shawnee territory.

41.5 *The Choosing.* Oct. 29, 1964. GS: David Brian, Richard Devon, Larry Chance. Daniel intends their trip into the wilderness to be a pleasant jaunt for Jemima, but he wounds himself with an axe and his daughter is kidnaped by a band of Indians.

41.6 *Lac Duquesne.* Nov. 5, 1964. GS: Emile Genest, James Griffith. Daniel, Yadkin and Mingo pursue Lac Duquesne, a river pirate who has stolen a shipment of rifles from some Boonesville settlers.

41.7 *The Sound of Wings.* Nov. 12, 1964. GS: Michael Rennie, Frank de Kova, Michael Pate, Ralph Moody. A Redcoat officer slugs Boone and assumes his identity so that he can persuade the Indians to back the British.

41.8 *A Short Walk to Salem.* Nov. 19, 1964. GS: James Westerfield, Charles Briggs, Dean Stanton, Robert Sorrells, William Fawcett. Simon Girty plays dirty, and so do his three hard-hearted sons. They plan to relieve the Boonesville settlers of their season's take of furs.

41.9 *The Sisters O'Hannrahan.* Dec. 3, 1964. GS: Fay Spain, Nina Shipman, Don Megowan, Sig Ruman, Larry J. Blake, Maudie Prickett, Hal Baylor. Daniel inadvertently becomes the owner of two indentured servant girls when Yadkin gets involved with an auctioneer.

41.10 *Pompey.* Dec. 10, 1964. GS: Brock Peters, Peter Whitney, Joe Perry. Daniel notices that a reward is being offered for the return of a runaway slave named Pompey, but he pays little attention until he discovers that some of his new blacksmith tools have been stolen.

41.11 *Mountain of the Dead.* Dec. 17, 1964. GS: Leslie Nielsen, Ed Peck, John McLiam, Kelly Thordsen. A man Boone thought dead and a trio of Britons appear out of nowhere, and they all want to be led to the site of a bloody Indian massacre.

41.12 *Not in Our Stars.* Dec. 31, 1964. GS: Walter Pidgeon, John Vivyan, Abraham Sofaer, J.B. Brown, Tim Graham. Lord Dunsmore, the British Governor General, orders the Boonesborough settlers out of Kentucky within thirty days.

41.13 *The Hostages.* Jan. 7, 1965. GS: Madlyn Rhue, Ellen Corby, Rhodes Reason. There is something unusual about the band of Senecas that kidnap Rebecca and burn the Boone cabin. They are led by a Loyalist officer.

41.14 *The Returning.* Jan. 14, 1965. GS: Pat Hingle, George Lewis, Robert G. Anderson, Pat Hogan, Carmen D'Antonio. The Boonesborough settlers offer a warm welcome to Daniel's old friend Will Carey when he enters the settlement with a load of pelts. They never dream that he got them by murdering three Cherokee braves.

41.15 *The Prophet.* Jan. 21, 1965. GS: John Russell, Kevin Hagen, Patricia Huston, Joe De Santis, Ric Roman, Hank Worden. The prophet is an Indian holy man who asks the Shawnee to join other tribes in driving the white settlers out of Kentucky. When the Shawnee hesitate, he promises to deliver Boone into their hands.

41.16 *The First Stone.* Jan. 28, 1965. GS: Geraldine Brooks, Kurt Russell, Gene Evans, Morgan Woodward. Daniel gives shelter to Esther Craig and her sons when they are found wandering in the wilderness. But signs indicate that Esther may be a witch.

41.17 *A Place of 1000 Spirits.* Feb. 4, 1965. GS: Macdonald Carey, Claude Akins, Ted White, I Stanford Jolley. Two Shawnee braves enter a Salem tavern and abduct a terrified British lieutenant at gunpoint.

41.18 *The Sound of Fear.* Feb. 11, 1965. GS: Dan Duryea, Peter Duryea, Jack Elam, Jacques Aubuchon. Daniel and his family are held prisoner by the murderous Simon Perigore, who drives a hard bargain — the lives of Daniel's wife and children in exchange for his help in starting an Indian war.

41.19 *The Price of Friendship.* Feb. 18, 1965. GS: Lloyd Nolan, Kurt Russell, Myrna Fahey, Lane Bradford, William Phipps, John Pickard. Daniel runs into some unusual river pirates — an old man, his daughter and an orphan — who steal all they can, provided that they don't hurt anyone in the process.

41.20 *The Quietists.* Feb. 25, 1965. GS: Alexander Scourby, Mary Jayne Saunders, Eve McVeagh, Bob Random, Jay Silverheels. Nothing Boone says can dissuade an unarmed pacifist Quaker family from moving onto the farm they bought — on the edge of dangerous Cherokee country.

41.21 *The Devil's Four.* March 4, 1965. GS: Bruce Cabot, James Best, Sean McClory, Gordon Jump, Charles Horvath, Whit Bissell. Yadkin finds four manacled felons to drive the wagons over the bandit-infested Cumberland Gap.

41.22 *The Reunion.* March 11, 1965. GS: John McIntire, Marvin Brody, Hank Patterson, Bebe Kelly, James Hayes. After years of searching for his daughter Rebecca, itinerant peddler Timothy Patrick Bryan finally finds her — married to Daniel. But Rebecca will have nothing to do with the old man.

41.23 *The Ben Franklin Encounter.* March 18, 1965. GS: Edward Mulhare, Laurie Main, Anna Lee, Vikki Harrington, James Forrest, Albert Carrier, Alan Simpson. After returning from a trip to Virginia, Daniel tells his family how he and Mingo met a famous Colonial insurgent, and almost got themselves shipped off to England.

41.24 *Four-Leaf Clover.* March 25, 1965. GS: George Gobel, Frank de Kova, Dick Wessel, Alvy Moore, Isa Crino. Daniel and Yadkin rescue the driver of an overturned buggy and discover he is Francis Clover, Boonesborough's bumbling new schoolteacher.

41.25 *Cain's Birthday* Part One. April 1, 1965. GS: Cesare Danova, Ted de Corsia, Connie Gilchrist, Maurice Marsac, Abel Fernandez, Shug Fisher, Alan Napier, Booth Colman. Daniel mysteriously orders the Boonesborough men,

Daniel Boone ['64]

working at a salt-making camp, to surrender to an Indian war party — which leaves only women and children to defend the fort.

41.26 *Cain's Birthday* **Part Two.** April 8, 1965. GS: Cesare Danova, Ted de Corsia, Connie Gilchrist, Maurice Marsac, Abel Fernandez, Shug Fisher, Alan Napier, Booth Colman. With water running low and no sign of help from the militia, the besieged Boonesborough defenders see little chance of repelling the Indians — especially after French Colonel Michelet blows up the fort's powder magazine.

41.27 *Daughter of the Devil.* April 15, 1965. GS: Pilar Seurat, Frank Silvera, Mario Alcaide, Orville Sherman, Pearl Shear, Norman Leavitt. Cajun travelers Marcel Bouvier and his daughter Marie arrive in Boonesborough just about the time that a black panther starts making murderous forays.

41.28 *Doll of Sorrow.* April 22, 1965. GS: Edward Binns, Chris Williams, Eddie Little Sky, Adrienne Hayes. Daniel feels responsible for the loss of itinerant tradesman Seth Jennings' wagonload of goods, and for Jennings' subsequent scandalous behavior in Boonesborough.

41.29 *The Courtship of Jericho Jones.* April 29, 1965. GS: Robert Logan, Anne Helm, Stuart Randall, Joe Canut, Russ McCubbin. When Jericho Jones elopes with a Creek princess, relations between the settlers and the Indians are put in jeopardy.

Season Two

41.30 *Empire of the Lost.* Sept. 16, 1965. GS: Edward Mulhare, George Backman, Abel Fernandez, Tom Browne Henry, Orville Sherman. Daniel returns from a journey to find Boonesborough evacuated by order of British colonel Marcus Worthing, who says he is battling a rebellion and that he wants Boone to turn over the fort.

41.31 *The Tortoise and the Hare.* Sept. 23, 1965. GS: Laurie Main, James Griffith, Orville Sherman, Shug Fisher, Ken Del Conte, Peter Mamakos. Daniel, the fort's best runner, sprains an ankle, which spells bad news for the settlers who have bet on him to win the hotly contested annual foot race with the Indians.

41.32 *The Mound Builders.* Sept. 30, 1965. GS: Henry Silva, Simon Oakland. Daniel and Mingo intercept a band of Shawnee pursuing a stranger, who is dressed in the regalia of an Aztec chieftain.

41.33 *My Name Is Rawls.* Oct. 7, 1965. GS: Rafer Johnson, Michael Conrad, Lawrence Montaigne, Orville Sherman, Harold Goodwin. Daniel sets out to trap an unusual fur thief — a huge runaway slave who makes a point of telling his victims who he is.

41.34 *The Old Man and the Cave.* Oct. 14, 1965. GS: Cyril Delevanti, Val Avery, Hal Jon Norman. In rescuing a starving old Indian from a scared burial cave, Israel unwittingly violates a tribal custom and arouses the wrath of the medicine man — an old enemy of Boone.

41.35 *The Trek.* Oct. 21, 1965. GS: Aldo Ray, John Lupton, Ted White, Roy C. Jenson, Charles Horvath. Daniel goes after the notorious renegade John Benton, a brawling drunkard who sells defective guns to the Indians, and then burns their villages when they refuse to pay.

41.36 *The Aaron Burr Story.* Oct. 28, 1965. GS: Leif Erickson, Michael St. Clair, Michael Ragan. Former Vice President Aaron Burr shows up in Boonesborough looking for a guide to the mouth of the Cumberland River. When Daniel turns him down, Burr hires impressionable young Jericho Jones.

41.37 *Cry of Gold.* Nov. 4, 1965. GS: Sarah Marshall, Maxwell Reed, William O'Connell, Kenneth MacDonald. Two land developers hire champion English boxer Thomas Cromwell to dispose of Boone, who has frustrated their efforts to buy Boonesborough property.

41.38 *The Peace Tree.* Nov. 11, 1965. GS: Liam Redmond, Larry Domasin, Peter Oliphant, Nestor Paiva, Harold Goodwin, Ted White, Abel Fernandez. Against Daniel's advice, a Scottish clan builds a settlement on the Cherokee hunting grounds, and the highlanders refuse to vacate their new home, despite an Indian war threat.

41.39 *The Thanksgiving Story.* Nov. 25, 1965. GS: John McIntire, Abraham Sofaer, Rodolfo Acosta, Ted White. As Daniel and Jericho return to Boonesborough for Thanksgiving, a rider brings news that promises a grim holiday. Choctaw chief Gabriel is on the warpath.

41.40 *A Rope for Mingo.* Dec. 2, 1965. GS: George Kennedy, Gloria Manon, Peter Coe, Leo Gordon, Peggy Stewart, Ray Montgomery, Med Flory, Bob Random. Near a burning wagon, Jericho finds a murdered family of three, with Mingo's knife in one of the victims.

41.41 *The First Beau.* Dec. 9, 1965. GS: Fabian Forte, Sam Jaffe, Myron Healey. Jemima feels the pangs of first love when young David Ellis comes to Boonesborough.

41.42 *Perilous Journey.* Dec. 16, 1965. GS: Steve Ihnat, Alan Napier, John Orchard, Stacy Harris, Albert Carrier. Daniel and Rebecca's long delayed honeymoon is interrupted by an officer of the Continental Army, who is shot by British agents as he gives Daniel a Presidential message to deliver to New Orleans.

41.43 *The Christmas Story.* Dec. 23, 1965. GS: Alizia Gur, Morgan Woodward, John Crawford, Valentin de Vargas, Eve McVeagh, Jay Silverheels, Sue England. As a blizzard rages, Boone tries to persuade the settlers to give food and shelter to an Indian brave and his expectant wife.

41.44 *The Tamarack Massacre Affair.* Dec. 30, 1965. GS: Dina Merrill, Robert Lansing, Charles Bateman, James O'Hara, Russ McCubbin, Michael Keep. Daniel is getting ready to negotiate a friendship treaty with the Iroquois Indians — but Madeline Lorne says that the Iroquois are guilty of a massacre of which she is the sole survivor.

41.45 *Gabriel.* Jan. 6, 1966. GS: Cesar Romero, Carlos Romero, Jacqueline Beer, Vincent Beck, Mike Mazurki. On the way to a French trading post, Daniel and Mingo are captured by a Spanish Army captain who says Daniel is an escaping French revolutionary.

41.46 *Seminole Territory.* Jan. 13, 1966. GS: Leonard Nimoy, Diana Ladd, Channing Pollack, Richard Devon, Judson Pratt, Russ Conway. While scouting in Florida, Daniel and Mingo make the mistake of trespassing on forbidden Seminole territory, where they encounter Fletcher the Flamboyant, an itinerant magician who dazzles the Indians with his tricks.

41.47 *The Deserter.* Jan. 20, 1966. GS: Slim Pickens, Dick Sargent, Henry Brandon, Rudy Robbins, Bob Terhune, Bruce Jacobs, Ted White. Tracking two army deserters, a bounty hunter finds one of them with Daniel, whom he mistakes for the other runaway.

41.48 *Crisis by Fire.* Jan. 27, 1966. GS: Rhodes Reason, George Sanders, Jeanne Cooper, John Crawford, Marvin Brody, Barbara Knudson, Hal Jon Norman. While Daniel is away from the fort, ambitious colonel Roger Barr takes advantage of an outbreak of small pox to seize power in Boonesborough.

41.49 *The Gun.* Feb. 3, 1966. GS: Robert Middleton, Milton Selzer, Warren Vanders, Dee Carroll, Ken Renard. Two thieves plan to steal Daniel's quipu, a kind of Indian passport, that guarantees his safety while he is in hostile Shawnee country.

41.50 *The Prisoners.* Feb. 10, 1966. GS: Warren Stevens, Chris Alcaide, Gregory Morton, Kelton Garwood, Rick Vallin. Convicted traitor Edward Eliot kidnaps the Boone children in an attempt to force Daniel to help him murder Colonel Callaway, who commanded the firing squad that executed Eliot's brother.

41.51 *The Fifth Man.* Feb. 17, 1966. GS: Cameron Mitchell, John Hoyt, John McLiam, Orville Sherman, George C. Fisher. To carry out an important military mission for Governor Patrick Henry. Daniel needs safe passage through hostile Tuscarora territory, which only the tribe's embittered chief can guarantee.

41.52 *Gun-Barrel Highway.* Feb. 24, 1965. GS: John Kellogg, Arthur Space, Dennis Cross, Timothy Scott, Fred Carson, Walter Reese, Bob Homel. Chief Red Hand promises not to drive out the road builders who have violated tribal hunting grounds, providing Daniel halts the project and no Indians are harmed. The agreement seems firm, until the construction boss accidentally kills a Shawnee boy.

41.53 *The Search.* March 3, 1966. GS: Nita Talbot, Michael Ansara, Douglas V. Fowley, Willard Sage, Russ McCubbin, Red Morgan. While taking furs to New Orleans, Daniel is jumped by a stranger who shoots him and takes his boat, leaving behind a leather pouch containing a French pirate's diary.

41.54 *Fifty Rifles.* March 10, 1966. GS: Henry Wilcoxon, William Mims, Christopher Dark. Daniel sets out to recover 50 stolen rifles stolen by his one-time friend William Blunt, a former British officer turned renegade. Daniel must find the weapons before Blunt peddles them to the murderous Shawnee.

41.55 *The Trap.* March 17, 1966. GS: Lloyd Bochner, Jack Lambert, Orville Sherman, Marc Cavell, Robert Donner. Daniel sets out after renegade scalp hunter Rafe Todd and his gang who terrorized Daniel's womenfolk and looted his house.

41.56 *The Accused.* March 24, 1966. GS: Jerome Thor, Joanna Moore, Ken Scott, E.J. Andre, Vaughn Taylor, Buck Young, Walker Edmiston, Eddie Quillan. Daniel, who had a disagreement with a fur trader, is accused of murdering him, and burning his store to destroy the evidence.

41.57 *Cibola.* March 31, 1966. GS: Royal Dano, Alejandro Rey, Jose Hector Galindo, Alexander D'Arcy. Half delirious with hunger, old Matty Brenner staggers into Daniel and Mingo's camp, dragging along a boy who claims to live in Cibola, one of the legendary seven cities of gold.

41.58 *The High Cumberland* **Part One.** April 14, 1966. GS: Jacqueline Evans, Armando Silvestre, Roy Jenson, Charles Horvath, Barbara Turner De Hubp, Bob Terhune, Chuck Roberson. In a look back at Daniel's early life, Daniel meets Rebecca Brian, a bonded servant on the wagon train he is taking to Kentucky. Daniel also saves the life of Jim Santee, who decides to join the train after meeting Rebecca.

41.59 *The High Cumberland* **Part Two.** April 21, 1966. GS: Jacqueline Evans, Armando Silvestre, Roy Jenson, Charles Horvath, Barbara Turner De Hubp, Bob Terhune, Chuck Roberson. Daniel drives his Boonesborough bound wagons into a narrow canyon where he takes a stand against pursuers who want the precious supplies.

Season Three

41.60 *Dan'l Boone Shot a B'ar.* Sept. 15, 1966. GS: Dick Foran, Slim Pickens, Chick Chandler, Claude Hall. Daniel is confronted by Cletus Mott and the bear that killed Mott's father and brother. Cletus is determined to hunt the bear down, and he threatens to shoot anyone who interferes with his revenge.

41.61 *The Allegiances.* Sept. 22, 1966. GS: Paul Fix, Michael Pate, Angela Clarke, Walter Kray. With British help, the Indian tribes unite too drive the settlers out of their country, even though the warpath may lead to the death of the Indians friend Daniel Boone.

41.62 *Goliath.* Sept. 29, 1966. GS: Woody Strode, Jack Oakie, Ed Peck, Jerome Cowan, Cal Bolder, Bea Bradley, Sheldon Allman. Horse trader Otis Cobb promised to surprise the settlers who commissioned him to buy draft horses, and Otis keeps his word. He returns with only a huge slave.

41.63 *Grizzly.* Oct. 6, 1966. GS: Rodolfo Acosta, Jeff York, Orville Sherman, Harold Goodwin, William Tannen, Phil Chambers, Gary Travis, Percy Helton, June Ellis. Israel rides into Boonesborough on the shoulders of his father's old friend, Big Zack, who is being sought by the Shawnee for killing one of their braves.

41.64 *First in War, First in Peace.* Oct. 13, 1966. GS: Michael Rennie, Lane Bradford, John Hoyt, Ivor Barry, Henry Corden, Bryan O'Byrne, Eddie Quillan. Daniel is honored when President Washington accepts his invitation to tour Kentucky, but he is also puzzled because he didn't send the invitation.

41.65 *Run a Crooked Mile.* Oct. 20, 1966. GS: Arthur Hunnicutt, Peter Graves, Myron Healey, Harry Harvey, Sr., Doodles Weaver, Ken Renard, Stanley Clements, Marvin Brody, Harry Raybould. Daniel and Israel are passengers on a coffin-carrying stagecoach which is waylaid by a band of body snatchers.

41.66 *The Matchmaker.* Oct. 27, 1966. GS: Laurie Main, Brenda Benet, Peter Mamakos, Waldon Norman, James J. Griffith, Larry Chance, Charles Roberson. To avert a tribal war, Daniel tries to arrange a marriage between the son of a Shawnee chief and a rebellious Creek princess, who is dead set against the union.

41.67 *Onatha.* Oct. 3, 1966. GS: Raymond St. Jacques, Alan Baxter, Virginia Capers, Rayford Barnes, Lila Perry, Kim Hamilton. Daniel and Mingo tangle with two slave hunters who claim legal ownership of Onatha, a small Negro girl Daniel saved from drowning.

41.68 *The Loser's Race.* Nov. 10, 1966. GS: Cameron Mitchell, Richard Devon, Douglas Henderson, Barbara Perry.

Daniel Boone ['64]

While visiting distant Williamsburg, Virginia, Daniel learns that the Boonesborough settlers have only two weeks to pay delinquent taxes or lose their land.

41.69 *The Enchanted Gun.* Nov. 17, 1966. GS: Michael Ansara, Robert J. Wilke, Ken Mayer, William Tannen, Tom Browne Henry, Bara Byrnes, X Brands. After giving Shawnee warrior Red Sky a rifle, Daniel faces a difficult task. He must dissuade Red Sky from his belief that the gun is magical and more powerful than the law.

41.70 *Requiem for Craw Green.* Dec. 1, 1966. GS: John Crawford, Jeffrey Hunter, Sabrina Scharf, Malcolm Atterbury, John Alvar, Frank Hagney, Bruno Ve Sota. Half-breed Mingo, posing as a white man, investigates the mysterious disappearance of a Cherokee Indian, last seen in a settlement run by bigoted Roark Logan.

41.71 *The Lost Colony.* Dec. 8, 1966. GS: Kathryn Walsh, Buck Taylor, John McLiam, Joseph Hoover. Elizabeth Corbett disappears from Boonesborough as suddenly as she appeared, involving Daniel and Mingo in a 100-year-old mystery.

41.72 *River Passage.* Dec. 15, 1966. GS: Leif Erickson, Jim Davis, Robert Brubaker. Brawling boatman Bill Sedley agrees to help Daniel run a cargo of gunpowder downriver to Kentucky. Only two things stand in the war — warring Indians and Big Bill himself, who would just as soon steal the gunpowder as deliver it.

41.73 *When a King Is a Pawn.* Dec. 22, 1966. GS: Cesare Danova, George Wallace, Morgan Mason, Lilyan Chauvan.

41.74 *The Symbol.* Dec. 29, 1966. GS: Ricardo Montalban, Jeff Morrow, David Peel, Carole Cook, Jon Locke, Mike Ragan. Impoverished Count Afonso De Borba strikes a bargain with the British. In exchange for 2000 gold crowns and a commission in the British Army, De Borba promises to deliver the Revolutionaries symbolic Liberty Bell, with Boone tied to the clapper.

41.75 *The Williamsburg Cannon* Part One. Jan. 12, 1967. GS: Keith Andes, Warren Stevens, Arch Johnson, Jack Lambert, Richard X. Slattery, Booth Colman, Michael Blodgett, George Backman, Byron Foulger, Dave Morick, Leo V. Matra. Daniel and Mingo set out to recruit three fighting backwoodsmen to help an arrogant artillery officer drag a heavy cannon 1000 miles through enemy-infested wilderness.

41.76 *The Williamsburg Cannon* Part Two. Jan. 19, 1967. GS: Keith Andes, Warren Stevens, Arch Johnson, Jack Lambert, Richard X. Slattery, Booth Colman, Michael Blodgett, George Backman, Byron Foulger, Dave Morick, Leo V. Matra. Daniel and his small band, hauling a heavy cannon to the Continental forces on the Western frontier, have no choice but to force their way through the redcoat lines.

41.77 *The Wolf Man.* Jan. 26, 1967. GS: R.G. Armstrong, Kenneth Tobey, Don Haggerty. Boonesborough faces the issue of slavery. The decision rests upon the actions of Daniel, a cold-hearted councilman and a frontiersman with a pet wolf.

41.78 *The Jasper Ledbedder Story.* Feb. 2, 1967. GS: Sidney Blackmer, Corey Fischer, Kate Murtagh, William Tannen, Abel Fernandez, Frank S. Hagney. An old codger with a sad tale leads Daniel and Mingo on a dangerous chase into hostile Shawnee country. But cagey Jasper Ledbedder's story about the Indians abducting his family conceals the real object of his search.

41.79 *When I Became a Man, I Put Away Childish Things.* Feb. 9, 1967. GS: Richard Sargent, Mala Powers. A pet fawn helps teach Israel the meaning of growing up. When the deer destroys a neighbors crops, the lad must face the painful prospect of seeing his pet destroyed.

41.80 *The Long Way Home.* Feb. 16, 1967. GS: William Marshall, Lawrence Montaigne, Richard Webb, Joel Ashley, Brett Pearson. Daniel hunts an escaped Army prisoner who is wanted for murder. The fugitive is Birch Kendall, and he may start an Indian uprising. His knife was the weapon that killed an Indian chief.

41.81 *The Young Ones.* Feb. 23, 1967. GS: Claire Wilcox, Kurt Russell, Jeanne Cooper, Bob Anderson, Frankie Kabott. Three young survivors of an Indian massacre brew up a storm for Daniel. The orphans tell the members of a wagon train that Daniel is their father.

41.82 *Delo Jones.* March 2, 1967. GS: Jimmy Dean, Lyle Bettger, John Orchard. Delo Jones, a banjo-strumming woodsman, is fleeing from a murder charge. Delo asks for Daniels' help, certain that the pursuing officer is the real killer.

41.83 *The Necklace.* March 9, 1967. GS: Philip Carey, Laurie Main, James J. Griffith, Kelly Thorsen. Daniel begins a journey to New Orleans, carrying a pearl necklace that will exonerate a wrongly convicted man. His trip is imperiled by three woodsmen who are determined to steal the jewelry.

41.84 *Fort West Point.* March 23, 1967. GS: Kent Smith, Bill Fletcher, Hampton Fancher, Robert Miller Driscoll, Alan Caillou. Gen. Hugh Scott, commander of Fort West Point, plans to turn over his vital post to the British, but the traitor neglects to consider Daniel's suspicious nature.

41.85 *Bitter Mission.* March 30, 1967. GS: Simon Oakland, Cesar Romero, Berry Kroeger, Mark Bailey. To prevent war, a badly wounded Daniel begins a long trek with a dangerous traitor as his prisoner. The man is a retired general who is pitting Virginia against Kentucky in hopes of getting Boonesborough for himself.

41.86 *Take the Southbound Stage.* April 6, 1967. GS: Torin Thatcher, Arnold Moss, Henry Darrow, Paul Brinegar, Mabel Albertson, Alan Carney, Sarah Marshall, Robert Donner, Doodles Weaver. Rebecca disobeys Daniel's orders to stay in Philadelphia while he undertakes a dangerous secret mission. After learning that Daniel is delivering ransom money for a kidnaped President Adams, Rebecca buys a gun and takes off in pursuit.

41.87 *The Fallow Land.* April 13, 1967. GS: John Ireland, Michael Forest, Steve Darrell, John Lodge, Ralph Maurer. Daniel sets out to stop an Indian war instigated by three trappers who persist in poaching on Cherokee land.

Season Four

41.88 *The Ballad of Sidewinder and Cherokee.* Sept. 14, 1967. GS: Victor Buono, Forrest Tucker, Vito Scotti, Victor French, Richard Hoyt. Daniel clashes with a river pirate who has stolen a shipment of furs. To retrieve the pelts, he enlists the aid of crafty Joe Snag, also a pirate.

41.89 *The Ordeal of Israel Boone.* Sept. 21, 1967. GS: Jim Davis, Teddy Eccles, Billy Corcoran, Rory O'Brien. A lesson in self-reliance becomes a terrible ordeal for young Israel Boone. After a rattlesnake fells Daniel, the 10-year-old defies hostile Indians and wild animals to go after help.

41.90 *The Renegade.* Sept. 28, 1967. GS: Mark Richman, Gregory Walcott, Phyllis Avery, Ric Natoli. Daniel and Mingo help protect a frontier couple and their adopted Indian son. The boy's real father is a renegade who is mobilizing his outlaws to recapture the youth.

41.91 *Tanner.* Oct. 5, 1967. GS: Neville Brand, John Pickard, James Dobson, James Alders. Daniel searches the forest for Tanner, a deranged outcast who has seized Israel. He must find th man before a pursuing mob of hysterical settlers frightens him into harming the boy.

41.92 *Beaumarchais.* Oct. 12, 1967. GS: Maurice Evans, Robert Wolders, Louise Sorel, Ivor Barry, Hugh Langtry. Undertaking a dangerous mission, French novelist Pierre Augustin Caron de Beaumarchais poses as a flamboyant head of a traveling troupe to smuggle gold through the British lines.

41.93 *The King's Shilling.* Oct. 19, 1967. GS: Barbara Hershey, Mort Mills, Peter Bromilow, Jeff Pomerantz, Robie Porter, John Orchard, Jack Bannon, Morgan Jones, Claude Johnson. As unrest boils in the Colonies, Daniel moves to prevent two executions that could trigger open warfare. The prisoners are revolutionary zealot Davey Hubbard, who is a captive of the British, and Redcoat Tom Chapin, held as a hostage by Davey's father.

41.94 *The Inheritance.* Oct. 26, 1967. GS: Royal Dano, Hank Patterson, Edwin Mills, Harold Goodwin. A foreboding old mansion holds unpleasant surprises for Rebecca, who has gained the house through an inheritance. With young Israel at her side, she sets out to explore the mansion and learns there is good reason for its reputation as a haunted house.

41.95 *The Traitor.* Nov. 2, 1967. GS: Kelly Thordsen, Lyn Peters, Joe Jenckes, Rex Holman, Patrick O'Moore. To escape execution as a traitor, Daniel volunteers to save a British colonel's daughter from her Shawnee captors. The task entails teaching the difficult art of Indian-fighting to the tradition-bound Redcoats.

41.96 *The Value of a King.* Nov. 9, 1967. GS: James Gregory, Ken Gampu, Dort Clark. To secure freedom for a band of runaway slaves, Daniel battles distrust, a determined slaver and marauding Indians.

41.97 *The Desperate Raid.* Nov. 16, 1967. GS: Jacques Bergerac, Hampton Fancher, William Mims, Jack Lambert. Escaped convicts and wharf rats are hired by Daniel and a young Army lieutenant. Their mission is to deliver a boatload of supplies to a besieged fort. Their main obstacle is a British cannon commanding a stretch of the river.

41.98 *The Spanish Horse.* Nov. 23, 1967. GS: Michael Burns, Henry Jones, Robert Emhardt, Bill Williams, Russ McCubbin, Jimmy Murphy. Daniel lends a guiding hand to orphan Cal Trevor, whose dying father left him with a lame thoroughbred and an admonition: "Take care of the horse, and some day he may take care of you."

41.99 *Chief Mingo.* Dec. 7, 1967. GS: John Larch. The brutal murder of a Cherokee chief puts Mingo and Daniel on a collision course. Mingo demands a tribal trial for the prime suspect, an Indian-hating trapper. Daniel, equally determined, insists on white man's justice.

41.100 *The Secret Code.* Dec. 14, 1967. GS: David Opatoshu, Lloyd Bochner, Edward Mulhare. Daniel is ordered to rescue the Continental Army's top code expert, or kill him before the Redcoats' Indian allies can make him talk. Daniel is put through an elaborate Ottawa ritual, in which the prisoner is alternately tortured and treated as a guest of honor.

41.101 *A Matter of Blood.* Dec. 28, 1967. GS: William Smith, Adrienne Hayes, Harry Bellaver, Mme. Spivy, Ben Andrews, Berry Kroeger, Lesley Woods, Walter Coy. Daniel helps an Indian princess, reared as a white, prove herself worthy to become queen of the Delawares. Besides bridging the culture gap, the woman must overcome Catoga, a would-be chief who challenges her right to rule.

41.102 *The Scrimshaw Ivory Chart.* Jan. 4, 1968. GS: James Westerfield, Jim Backus, Ted Cassidy, Percy Helton, Sid Haig. An amiable pirate involves the Boone family in a dangerous quest for buried treasure.

41.103 *The Imposter.* Jan. 18, 1968. GS: Jimmy Dean, Lloyd Bochner, Harold Gould. A backwoodsman poses as a British major's orderly in a plot to deny a new rapid-action rifle to the Redcoats. Filling the major's boots is an Oxford-educated Mingo, who brazenly sashays into a British fort to steal the guns.

41.104 *The Witness.* Jan. 25, 1968. GS: John Carradine, Virginia Gregg, Sheldon Collins, Jon Walmsley. A badly frightened Israel is caught in a terrible quandary. No one believes that he witnessed a killing, except the killer.

41.105 *The Flaming Rocks.* Feb. 1, 1968. GS: Jimmy Dean, Dorothy Green, R.G. Armstrong, Michael Witney. Daniel intercedes to prevent Indian reprisals when a hard-headed Welsh immigrant seizes Tuscarora land for coal mining.

41.106 *Then Who Will They Hang from the Yardarm if Willy Gets Away?* Feb. 8, 1968. GS: Wilfrid Hyde-White, Martin Horsey, Jack Bannon, Alan Caillou, Eddie Quillan, Joe Smith, Marinda French, David Peel, Jon Locke. A young British sailor is being sought as a mutineer and is being blackmailed by a wily old salt looking for a meal ticket.

41.107 *Fort New Madrid.* Feb. 15, 1968. GS: Gary Conway, Theo Marcuse, Ken Swofford, Richard Angarola, Hank Brandt. Daniel sets out to sabotage a Spanish fort being built on American soil. Allowing himself to be captured and placed on the forced-labor crew, his first task is to ferret out an informer who could wreck the scheme.

41.108 *Heroes Welcome.* Feb. 22, 1968. GS: Charles Drake, Sarah Marshall, Robert J. Wilke. En route to Philadelphia, Daniel stops at a settlement to clear up a mystery. Why has Revolutionary War hero Simon Jarvis become a drunken outcast, unfit to care for his wife and child?

41.109 *Orlando, the Prophet.* Feb. 29, 1968. GS: Hans Conried, Anthony Alda. Orlando is a self-proclaimed prophet who plans to profit by Daniel's absence from Boonesborough. As Orlando prepares to fleece the trappers, Israel and Mingo set about freeing his young Gypsy bond servant.

41.110 *The Far Side of Fury.* March 7, 1968. GS: Don Pedro Colley, Ezekial Williams, Med Flory, Johnny Cardos. An old trapper grimly seeks an eye for an eye from the Boones after his only son is kidnaped while in Daniel's care.

41.111 *Nightmare.* March 14, 1968. GS: Hans Wedemeyers. After saving Daniel from death by Shawnee torture, young Israel and his weakened father try every backwoods trick to elude their relentless pursuers.

Daniel Boone ['64]

41.112 *Thirty Pieces of Silver.* March 28, 1968. GS: Herbert Anderson, Warren Kemmerling, Andrew Prine, Virginia Christine, Susan Albert. The treachery of a young frontiersman endangers the mission and lives of Daniel and Mingo, who are out to deliver guns and ammunition to Boonesborough.

41.113 *Faith's Way.* April 4, 1968. GS: Julie Harris, Jeff Morrow, Claude Woolman. A schoolteacher is blessed, and cursed, with a strange ability to communicate with animals. She faces death from Indians who believe she is a witch, responsible for the forays of a killer panther.

Season Five

41.114 *Be Thankful for the Fickleness of Women.* Sept. 19, 1968. GS: Sean McClory, Brooke Bundy, James Davidson, Tom Fadden, John Goddard, Ollie O'Toole. Woodsman Josh Clements' problem is fending off an adoring young bond servant, whom he bought by mistake, and a huge unkempt trapper who wants the girl for himself.

41.115 *The Blackbirder.* Oct. 3, 1968. GS: Don Pedro Colley, Timothy Carey, Jim McMullan. Daniel's old friend Gideon, a freeborn Negro trapper, battles bigotry to escape a bounty hunter. Mistaken for a runaway slave, Gideon is led away in leg irons, chained to a deserter who can't stand blacks.

41.116 *The Dandy.* Oct. 10, 1968. GS: David Watson, Johnny Cardos, Sheldon Allman. David Scott, a dandified painter, is foisted on Dan for two month's training in the art of becoming a man. The apprenticeship takes on special significance when David is abducted by Longknife, a Shawnee seeking a replacement for the tribal artist.

41.117 *The Fleeing Nuns.* Oct. 24, 1968. GS: Kathleen Freeman, Brioni Farrell, Jim McMullan, Marcel Hillaire, William Phipps, Ollie O'Toole, Richard Angarola, Maurice Marsac. Daniel and trapper Mason Pruitt help a young French noblewoman and her elderly servant escape from New Orleans disguised as nuns. Hot on their trail are two revolutionaries and six mercenaries who plan for the ladies to keep a date with the guillotine.

41.118 *The Plague That Came to Ford's Run.* Oct. 31, 1968. GS: Charles Drake, Gail Kobe, Kevin Hagen, Richard Devon, John Todd Roberts, Ted White, Pete Logan. Josh stubbornly investigates the mysterious disappearance of his old friend, a German guitar maker, in a town suspicious of foreigners and strangers.

41.119 *The Bait.* Nov. 7, 1968. GS: Skip Ward, Kelly Thordsen, Lois Nettleton, Med Flory, James Daris, Robert Adler, Hank Patterson. Sulie and Davey, a backwoods Bonnie and Clyde, ride their separate ways after relieving Daniel and a constable of their money and guns. Unarmed, the lawman trails Davey while Daniel concentrates on Davey's wildcat partner.

41.120 *Big, Black and Out There.* Nov. 14, 1968. GS: Yaphet Kotto, Don Pedro Colley, Harry Basch, Art Jenoff, Claude Johnson, Tom Drury, Ezekiel Williams. Daniel's Negro friend Gideon struggles with conflicting loyalties when he and Dan go after a runaway slave who has been stealing food and guns in the odd guise of an Indian.

41.121 *Flag of Truce.* Nov. 21, 1968. GS: William Smith, Mort Mills, Mark Miranda, H.M. Wynant, Russ Conway, Pilar Del Rey, Joe Jenckes, David Farrow. An unprincipled general uses Daniel in a treacherous scheme to end a blood war with the Wyandots — by playing on Daniel's friendship with their chief.

41.122 *The Valley of the Sun.* Nov. 28, 1968. GS: Mariette Hartley, Severn Darden. A deer hunt becomes a bizarre adventure when Josh is captured by Sir Hubert Spencer, a mad English butterfly collector. Sir Hubert drags Josh deep into a Stygian maze of underground caverns, where he keeps a woman prisoner amid the dazzling splendor of Aztec treasure.

41.123 *The Patriot.* Dec. 5, 1968. GS: Ford Rainey, Tom Lowell, Teddy Eccles, John Anthony Epper, David Wendel. The real meaning of the Revolution comes under scrutiny when ex-Tory John Gist returns to Boonesborough with his young son, to live again among settlers he had fought against.

41.124 *The Return of Sidewinder.* Dec. 12, 1968. GS: Forrest Tucker, Rex Holman, Charles Dierkop, Robert Cornthwaite, Joseph Perry, Bob Adler. Joe Snag is a river pirate extraordinaire, and a friendly enemy of Dan's. He is currently employing scraggly bandits to plunder supply wagons, but Joe has to fight off both Daniel and his own men to get at the Boonesborough wagon.

41.125 *Minnow for a Shark.* Jan. 2, 1969. GS: Henry Jones, Ivor Barry, George Keymas, Jack Bannon, Morry Ogden, Orwin Harvey. Sly old sea captain Jonas Morgan's friendship with Israel reaps danger for the Boones. By helping Jonas retrieve a stolen government dispatch box, Israel involves his father with the Crown and attracts the deadly attention of the real thief.

41.126 *To Slay a Giant.* Jan. 9, 1969. GS: Don Pedro Colley, Torin Thatcher, Lee Jay Lambert. Things look mighty bleak for Daniel's Negro friend, Gideon, who has been accused of murder. Oddly, his chief accuser is the victim's indentured servant, a mistreated youth whom Gideon had tries to help.

41.127 *A Tall Tale of Prater Beasely.* Jan. 16, 1969. GS: Burl Ives, Lyle Bettger, Jeff Donnell, Rory Stevens. Peter Beasely, a teller of tall tales, pops up in Boonesborough with a very wise, and invisible, bear, By sugar-coating simple truths in outlandish stories, Prater helps a lame boy learns about self-reliance.

41.128 *Copperhead Izzy.* Jan. 30, 1969. GS: Vincent Price, J. Pat O'Malley, Butch Patrick, Sheldon Collins, Olan Soule, Randy Lane, Natalie Core, Tom Drury, Danny Rees. Dr. Thaddeus Morton is a teacher of young felons. It is Israel's unfortunate lot to fall in with Morton's pupils, a pick-pocketing ragtag of orphaned urchins with unlimited talent for thievery.

41.129 *Three Score and Ten.* Feb. 6, 1969. GS: Burgess Meredith, Paul Fix, James Wainwright, Warren Vanders, Clint Ritchie, John McCann, Luanne Roberts. Alex Hemmings is an old war horse who is determined not to be turned out to pasture in his search for usefulness. The 70-year-old gunsmith joins the Shawnee who show great respect for his age and his skill at making rifles.

41.130 *Jonah.* Feb. 13, 1969. GS: Yaphet Kotto, Michael Lane. Josh inherits a parcel of Kentucky land and a slave named Jonah from an uncle determined to transform Josh into a proper, upstanding planter whether he likes it or not.

41.131 *Bickford's Bridge.* Feb. 20, 1969. GS: Simon Oakland, Kurt Russell, Peter Jason. Ordered to destroy all bridges before the advancing British, Daniel meets uncompromising resistance from a farmer who need the last standing structure to get his crops to market.

41.132 *A Touch of Charity.* Feb. 27, 1969. GS: Shelley Fabares, John Davidson, Donald "Red" Barry, Richard Peabody. Jimmy McGill is a settler smitten with sweet Charity Brown. She has been promised to an austere man of means, forcing Jimmy to draw on his own riches, old-fashioned Yankee ingenuity.

41.133 *For Want of a Hero.* March 6, 1969. GS: Richard Anderson, Arch Johnson. The Boones ride into danger when they enter a fort recently attacked by Indians. Survivors of the raid are five soldiers whose interest in gravedigging covers a search for Army gold.

41.134 *Love and Equity.* March 13, 1969. GS: Victor French, Burl Ives, Med Flory, Liam Sullivan, Fran Ryan. Prater Beasely returns and he is charged with fraud by fortune-hunting brothers, who claim his love potion didn't work on wealthy widow Jones.

41.135 *The Allies.* March 27, 1969. GS: Dick Foran, Ronne Troup, Ben Archibek. Daniel and two friends conscript three improbable allies to help blow up a British wagon train. They include crafty Simon Doggett, his son and adopted daughter, who have already stolen Daniel's pack horses, but lost them to raiding Indians.

41.136 *A Man Before His Time.* April 3, 1969. GS: Ronny Howard, Warren Vanders, James Wainwright, Claire Wilcox. Daniel lends a guiding hand to an embittered orphan, who refuses to believe his father was a thief and murderer, and resolves to get even with the settler who killed him.

41.137 *For a Few Rifles.* April 10, 1969. GS: Michael Dante, Ted De Corsia, Donald Losby, Myron Healey, Ken Renard, Warren Vanders. Israel is kidnaped by Indians who offer to release him for twenty rifles, guns that would be used against the settlers. Daniel's decision is to ignore the trade and rescue his son.

41.138 *Sweet Molly Malone.* April 17, 1969. GS: Barbara Bel Geddes, Jack Kruschen, Stafford Morgan, Tom Drury, Jack Garner. Hard-shelled Molly Malone, a former cannoneer, shows up in Boonesborough to claim her veteran's land grant. The Boones undertake the humanization of Sergeant Molly by pairing her off with Herman Bloedel, a lonely tinker with a yen to farm.

41.139 *A Pinch of Salt.* May 1, 1969. GS: Joan Hackett, Bo Svenson, David Watson, Donna Baccala. While on a land survey, Daniel and a young artist friend are swept into a wild frontier-style love spat between a headstrong, rifle-wielding woman and a proud, domineering man.

Season Six

41.140 *A Very Small Rifle.* Sept. 18, 1969. GS: Roger Miller, Eddie Little Sky, Johnny Jensen, Armando Silvestre, Kevin Hagen. Gentle Jonny Appleseed is caught between white man and red when the accidental shooting of a Cherokee youth threatens to trigger reprisals.

41.141 *The Road to Freedom.* Oct. 2, 1969. GS: Floyd Patterson, Jim Davis, Warren Vanders, John Milford, Roy Jenson. Israel uses all his backwoods ingenuity to help the son of a runaway slave elude a trio of pursuers.

41.142 *Benvenuto ... Who?* Oct. 9, 1969. GS: Marj Dusay, Leon Askin, Richard Kiel, Aram Katcher. In New Orleans to sell furs, Daniel and Josh are swept into a petite mademoiselle's scheme to make off with a stolen diamond pendant. Her plot involves hiding the bauble in Josh's guitar to keep it from her hulking fellow thieves.

41.143 *The Man.* Oct. 16, 1969. GS: George Backman, Gene Evans, Kevin O'Neal. Daniel recruits Gabe Cooper, an escaped slave-turned-Indian chief, and three malcontents — a coward, a felon and a British deserter, to destroy the British cannon commanding the Ohio River.

41.144 *The Printing Press.* Oct. 23, 1969. GS: Fredd Wayne, Peter Bromilow, Woodrow Parfrey, Alan Caillou. Benjamin Franklin is conspiring with Daniel to bilk the British. With a makeshift printing press and homebrewed ink, Ben counterfeits the five-pound notes Dan needs for supplies.

41.145 *The Traitor.* Oct. 30, 1969. GS: Jill Ireland, Ed Flanders, Richard Devon, James Wainwright, John Orchard. Daniel is ordered to work with a defecting British officer offering the defense plans to British-held Fort Detroit. Still, a traitor is a traitor, and Dan can't help but be suspicious.

41.146 *The Grand Alliance.* Nov. 13, 1969. GS: Cesar Romero, Armando Silvestre, Carlos Rivas, Joel Fluellen. A land-locked pirated claims that Spain is plotting to conquer the United States. He persuades Josh and Gabe to help him steal the plans.

41.147 *Target Boone.* Nov. 20, 1969. GS: Will Geer, Kurt Russell, Ron Soble. Religious fanatic Adam Jarrett, blaming Daniel for the death of his wife, vows that Boone shall suffer terror before meeting death at the end of a rope.

41.148 *A Bearskin for Jamie Blue.* Nov. 27, 1969. GS: Christopher Connelly, Bernard Fox. Daniel undertakes the humanization of Jamie Blue, the 18-year-old indentured servant he bought for a bearskin. It is a tall order as Jamie was born in prison and all he knows is a dog-eat-dog existence.

41.149 *The Cache.* Dec. 4, 1969. GS: Alex Karras, John Kellogg, Vaughn Taylor, Richard Peabody, Robert Sorrells, James Doohan. Josh is headed for Kentucky's highest hanging tree unless Daniel nails the poachers who framed him for murdering a trapper and hiding his pelts.

41.150 *The Terrible Tarbots.* Dec. 11, 1969. GS: Strother Martin, Zalman King, Anthony Costello. Three members of the fearsome Tarbot family commandeer a chest of Army gold entrusted to Daniel for transport, and kidnap Israel for insurance.

41.151 *Hannah Comes Home.* Dec. 25, 1969. GS: Teddy Eccles, Mary Fickett, Ford Rainey, Ted de Corsia, William O'Connell, Ted White. Daniel persuades a white woman long held by Indians to return to the husband she believed dead. But fifteen years have made a difference, especially since she now has a half-breed son proud of his Indian heritage.

41.152 *An Angel Cried.* Jan. 8, 1970. GS: Mariette Hartley, Carlos Rivas. Trapped in hostile Indian country, Josh struggles to save himself and a novitiate nun, the only survivor of a massacre. In the course of their ordeal, Josh falls in love and begs her to reconsider taking her final vows.

41.153 *Perilous Passage.* Jan. 15, 1970. GS: Gloria Grahame, John Davidson, Liam Sullivan. Captured by the British, Daniel and Gabe escape with a young rebel also condemned to the gallows. The trio heads home through territory infested by redcoats and Tories, aided by a chain of American agents, a variety of disguises, and recognition signals from "Poor Richard's Almanack."

41.154 *The Sunshine Patriots.* Jan. 22, 1970. GS: Gail Kobe, Laurie Main, Ian Ireland. Ordered to kidnap a British lord, Josh and Gabe turn the mission into a comedy of errors. Not only do they abduct the wrong Sir George, an eccentric inventor sympathetic to their cause, but they are saddled with his daughter, a spunky lady not at all sympathetic.

41.155 *Mamma Cooper.* Feb. 5, 1970. GS: Ethel Waters, Michael-James Wixted, Tyler McVey. Gabe finds his long-lost mother, a sick old woman living on a Southern plantation. He and Daniel learn that she probably won't life to realize her dream — to die on free soil.

41.156 *Before the Tall Man.* Feb. 12, 1970. GS: Marianna Hill, Burr DeBenning, Harlan Warde, Tony Gange. The Boones play matchmaker for Tom Lincoln and Nancy Hanks, but it is no easy task. A practical-minded, quick-tempered carpenter, Tom distrusts Nancy's imaginative notions — like reading books and fulfilling a prophecy that she will have a "a boy baby who will sit in high places."

41.157 *Run for the Money.* Feb. 19, 1970. GS: Jack Albertson, Peter Mamakos, Ji-Tu Cumbuka, Dino Washington. Double-dealing Shem Sweet hits on a perfect scheme to hornswoggle both the Indians and the white in their annual two-man foot race. For a handsome fee and a percentage of the bets, he offers each side the services of a fleet-footed slave who looks like a sure winner.

41.158 *A Matter of Vengeance.* Feb. 26, 1970. GS: Linda Marsh, Jim McMullan, David McLean, Ramon Bieri. Daniel takes dramatic steps to cool off a young man simmering with hate. Mason Pruitt is determined to exact vengeance on a trapper he believes murdered his parents fifteen years before.

41.159 *The Landlords.* March 5, 1970. GS: Lloyd Bochner, Victor French, Med Flory, Robert Cornthwaite, James Wainwright, Wilbur Plaughter. Daniel poses as an infamous river pirate to get the goods on a chameleon-like con artist. Aristocratic Churchill James, master counterfeiter and forger, has deeded all of Boonesborough to two bumbling brothers.

41.160 *Readin', Ritin', and Revolt.* March 12, 1970. GS: Tony Davis, William O'Connell, Billy Corcoran, Arthur Batanides, Rory O'Brien. Inspired by a Tuscarora lad in their school, the children of Boonesborough petition their schoolmaster to teach them Indian culture. When he refuses, the little rebels take action.

41.161 *Noblesse Oblige.* March 26, 1970. GS: Philip Proctor, Murray MacLeod, Elizabeth Bauer, Virginia Christine, David Watson. The Boonesborough settlers whip up a royal reception for a visiting French prince. But they are in for a jolt because His Highness has switched places with his cook.

41.162 *The Homecoming.* April 9, 1970. GS: David Opatoshu. The Boones take in Tamenund, the last of the Piqua Indians. They are unaware that the frail old man plans to exact revenge on the white enemy who destroyed his people.

41.163 *Bringing Up Josh.* April 16, 1970. GS: Ty Wilson, Jodie Foster, Loretta Leversee. Josh assumes the role of foster father to two children foisted off on him by a woman in New Orleans. Remembering his own fatherless childhood, the backwoods bachelor takes the job with an enthusiasm undampened by inexperience.

41.164 *How to Become a Goddess.* April 30, 1970. GS: Paul Mantee, Ruth Warrick, Victor French, Med Flory, Anakorita. Thanks to two bumbling brothers, redheaded Rebecca is delivered to Indians awaiting a goddess with hair "as red as flame." They intend to marry her to an Indian brave.

41.165 *Israel and Love.* May 7, 1970. GS: Tim O'Connor, Robin Mattson. A traveling wood carver poses problems for the Boones. Flamboyant James Secord is becoming a permanent house guest, and his pretty daughter Brae is giving Israel a bad case of puppy love.

42. *Davy Crockett*

ABC. 60 min. Broadcast history: Wednesday, 7:30–8:30, Dec. 1954–Dec. 1955.

Regular Cast: Fess Parker (Davy Crockett), Buddy Ebsen (George Russell), Helen Stanley (Polly Crockett), Eugene Brindle (Billy Crockett), Ray Whiteside (Johnny Crockett), Hans Conried (Thimbelrig), Nick Cravat (Bustedluck), Jeff York (Mike Fink), Kenneth Tobey (Jim Bowie), Mike Mazurki (Big Foot Mason), William Blackwell (Major Norton), Basil Ruysdael (General Andrew Jackson), William Bakewell (Major Tobias Norton), Pat Hogan (Red Stick), Don Megowan (William Travis), Kenneth Tobey (Jocko), Clem Bevans (Captain Cobb), Irvin Ashkenazy (Moose), Mort Mills (Sam Mason) Paul Newlan (Big Harp), Frank Richards (Little Harp).

Premise: This series chronicled the life of legendary frontiersman Davy Crockett in the early 1880s.

Notes: This series aired as segments of Walt Disney's *Disneyland* series.

The Episodes

42.1 *Davy Crockett, Indian Fighter.* Dec. 15, 1954. Gen. Andrew Jackson commissions Maj. Norton to find Davy Crockett and enlist his aid against the raiding Creek Indians.

42.2 *Davy Crockett Goes to Congress.* Jan. 26, 1955. When Davy finds out that a gang of Tennesseans is depriving the Indians of their rights, he turns his career to politics in order to uphold justice. He rises from backwoods magistrate to a member of the U.S. House of Representatives.

42.3 *Davy Crockett at the Alamo.* Feb. 23, 1955. In the year 1836 a handful of Texans make up their minds to die rather than surrender the Alamo, the fort of San Antonio, to the overwhelming forces of Mexican General Santa Anna.

42.4 *Davy Crockett and the Keelboat Race.* Nov. 16, 1955. Davy engages in a race with Mike Fink down the Ohio and Mississippi Rivers to New Orleans. Along the way, Fink provokes an Indian attack and generally makes trouble for Davy's landlubber crew.

42.5 *Davy Crockett and the River Pirates.* Dec. 14, 1955. Davy teams up with his old nemesis Mike Fink to clean out Cave-In Rock, a hideout used by Ohio River pirates. Among the ruffians they have to contend with are the two Harpe brothers, outlaw Sam Mason and the wily Colonel Plug.

43. Death Valley Days

Syndicated. 30 min. Various, Fall 1952–Spring 1970.

Hosts: Stanley Andrews 52-65, Ronald Reagan 65-66, Robert Taylor 66-68, Dale Robertson 68-72.

Premise: This anthology series dramatized incidents in the lives of individuals involved in the Nevada and California areas during the late 1800s.

The Episodes

43.1 *Swamper Ike.* Feb. 3, 1952.
43.2 *How Death Valley Got Its Name.* Oct. 1, 1952.
43.3 *The Death Valley Kid.* Oct. 10, 1952.
43.4 *The Little Bullfrog Nugget.* Oct. 15, 1952.
43.5 *The Lost Pegleg Mine.* Oct. 17, 1952.
43.6 *The Little Dressmaker of Bodie.* Nov. 12, 1952.
43.7 *She Burns Green.* Nov. 14, 1952.
43.8 *Self Made Man.* Dec. 12, 1952.
43.9 *The Chivaree.* Jan. 7, 1953.
43.10 *The Lady with the Blue Silk Umbrella.* Jan. 9, 1953.
43.11 *The Rival Hash Houses.* Feb. 3, 1953. GS: Gordon Jones. Steve Bassett had a full house at his cafe until a beautiful blonde widow opened another across the street.
43.12 *Cynthy's Dream Dress.* March 3, 1953.
43.13 *The Belle of San Gabriel.* March 17, 1953.
43.14 *Claim Jumpin' Jennie.* March 31, 1953. GS: Irene Barton, Karen Sharpe. Linda is in for a shock when she pays an unexpected visit to her mother who is a rough gold prospector.
43.15 *The Bandits of Panamint.* March 31, 1953.
43.16 *Sego Lillies.* April 28, 1953. GS: Robert Hutton, Sally Mansfield, Ella Ethridge, John Dierkes, Hank Patterson. A group of Mormons, hand-picked by their leaders, is sent into an undeveloped area of Utah to build a community and clear the land for the raising of sugar and cotton. In the party is a young woman who finds life in the wilderness intolerable because of its lack of beauty.
43.17 *Little Oscar's Millions.* April 28, 1953. A middle-aged man goes to Rawhide, Nevada, and invests his last 10 dollars in a town lot which turns into a gold mine.
43.18 *Land of the Free.* May 26, 1953. GS: Felix Nelson, Gail Davis. Two slaves persuade their owner to let them go West and pan gold to earn their freedom papers.

Season Two

43.19 *The Diamond Babe.* Sept. 29, 1953. GS: Ann Savage, Jil Jarmyn. The townspeople of Gold Hill, Nevada, have nothing but scorn for a dance hall queen and her profession until an epidemic strikes the town.
43.20 *Little Washington.* Oct. 1, 1953. GS: John Eldredge, Louise Arthur. The newly appointed director of the Carson City mint finds his worst fears realized when he arrives in the crude Western town after years of elegant living in Washington.
43.21 *Solomon in All His Glory.* Oct. 27, 1953. GS: James Griffith. An ex-newspaperman who has become the town drunkard tries to reform.
43.22 *Which Side of the Fence?* Oct. 29, 1953. GS: Lynn Thomas. A man and the woman he loves are caught up in the dispute over the California-Nevada state boundary.
43.23 *Whirlwind Courtship.* Nov. 21, 1953. GS: Michael Hathaway, Robert Lowery. During the California gold rush, a young attorney has 24 hours to woo and win a bride.
43.24 *Dear Teacher.* Nov. 24, 1953. GS: Nancy Hale, Michael Moore. A new schoolmarm wins the respect of her unruly pupils by demonstrating her skill with a six shooter. Then one of the students starts a vicious rumor about the young teacher.
43.25 *One in a Hundred.* Dec. 23, 1953. GS: Michael Forest, Linda Watkins, Robert Griffin, George Mitchell. A new rifle changes a man's character and nearly results in horrible death for a pioneer family.
43.26 *Little Papeete.* Jan. 2, 1954. GS: Emily Heath, Richard Avonde, Regina Gleason. A woman in love with the fire chief of a California town finds her rival is a flashy red fire truck.
43.27 *Lotta Crabtree.* Jan. 5, 1954. GS: Gloria Jean, Sharon Baird. A little girl grows up to be the Golden West's gift to vaudeville.
43.28 *Yaller.* Jan. 30, 1954. GS: Ray Boyle, Jan Shepard. A young man who has claustrophobia tries to work in his father's mine. His phobia brings taunts from the other miners who dub him yellow.
43.29 *The Twelve Pound Nugget.* Jan. 30, 1954. GS: Betsy Wilson. The discovery of a nugget weighing twelve pounds causes an uproar in a California gold town.
43.30 *Jimmy Dayton's Treasure.* Feb. 29, 1954. GS: Harry Cody, Barbara Knudson. When love first comes to elderly Jimmy Dayton, he buys a toupee and a set of store teeth, hoping to win the hand of a gold-digging dance-hall queen.
43.31 *Snowshoe Thompson.* Feb. 29, 1954. GS: Don Kennedy, Jane Hampton. An immigrant volunteers to don snowshoes and carry mail across the mountains.
43.32 *Husband Pro Tem.* March 27, 1954. GS: Jock Mahoney, Gloria Marshall. A young mining engineer is sent to negotiate a peace treaty with Indians who refuse to let a railroad cross their lands. A young woman complicates matters for the engineer.
43.33 *The Kickapoo Run.* April 10, 1954. GS: Fess Parker, Nancy Hale. A U.S. marshal, who helps patrol the gigantic rush for free Government land, meets a courageous girl who wants to stake her claim in order to recoup the family fortunes.
43.34 *Sixth Sense.* May 8, 1954. GS: Jeanne Cooper, William Hudson. A fellow boarder urges a blind girl to learn a trade that will make her feel useful. She becomes a telegrapher, and while she is traveling is held up by masked bandits.
43.35 *The Rainbow Chaser.* May 15, 1954. GS: Arthur Space, Kay Stewart. An irresponsible husband leaves his family for long periods of time to go off and find a grubstake. The family finds that it profits in its self-sufficiency.
43.36 *Mr. Godiva.* June 17, 1954. GS: Rusty Morris. To win the hand of the girl he loves, a brash newspaperman bets her father that he can amass a fortune in three days.

Season Three

43.37 *The Saint's Portrait.* Sept. 24, 1954. GS: Eugenia

Death Valley Days

Paul, Rico Alaniz, Maurice Jara, Martin Garralaga. Two Indian tribes feud over a portrait of St. Joseph, which they belive has the power to bring prosperity to their people and fertility to their lands.

43.38 *Eleven Thousand Miners Can't Be Wrong.* Sept. 25, 1954. GS: Bill Kennedy, Bill Boyett. An ambitious politician exploits a murder case to help him prove to the government that the town of Columbia should become California's capital city.

43.39 *Halfway Girl.* Oct. 22, 1954. GS: Barbara Bestar, Steven Clark, Bill Kennedy. Two young lovers are involved in a feud between their families which results in tragedy and broken romance until a secret is revealed.

43.40 *Black Bart.* Oct. 26, 1954. GS: Don Beddoe, Helen Brown. A frontier schoolteacher stages a holdup as a practical joke. It works out so well, however, that he decides to become a highwayman.

43.41 *The Light on the Mountain.* Nov. 19, 1954.

43.42 *To Big Charlie from Little Charlie.* Dec. 6, 1954. GS: Don Megowan, Douglas Henderson, William O'Neal, Maureen Stephenson. When a desert prospector hits pay dirt, he becomes a man of fashion of 1885.

43.43 *Sequoia.* Dec. 31, 1954. GS: Angie Dickinson, Lane Bradford, Eileen Howe, Carol Thurston. Sequoyah, a self-sacrificing Cherokee Indian, spent twelve years developing an alphabet for his people. He was recognized later as a great contributor to Indian culture.

43.44 *Lola Montez.* Jan. 4, 1955. GS: Paula Morgan, James Lilburn, Michael Ferris. This is the tale of glamorous Lola Montez, whose great beauty was acclaimed by such famous men as Franz Liszt, Alexandre Dumas and Victor Hugo.

43.45 *The Big Team Rolls.* Jan. 27, 1955. GS: Damian O'Flynn, Lucille Barkley. In an attempt to prove to the girl he loves that he is a rugged and brave he-man, a young Easterner decides to be a swamper.

43.46 *Death and Taxes.* Feb. 3, 1955. GS: Wayne Mallory, Jean Lewis, Wes Hudman. A young deputy has some strange experiences when he attempts to collect taxes from outlaws.

43.47 *Riggs and Riggs.* Feb. 24, 1955. GS: Jack Daly, Ella Ethridge. How to spend $70,000 in nine months is an undertaking successfully managed by a middle-aged rascal, while his patient wife toils at prospecting to discover more gold ore.

43.48 *Million Dollar Wedding.* March 1, 1955. GS: Virginia Lee, James Best. Two miners offer their friend a great deal of money if he will wed the homely waitress, Aggie Filene. In reality the whole plan is just a practical joke, and the mine shares they give their pal are worthless.

43.49 *Love 'Em and Leave 'Em.* March 29, 1955. GS: Bill Sheldon, Helen Marshall. After two years of prospecting in Nevada, a young adventurer makes a gold strike and plans to return home to marry his fiancee.

43.50 *The Seventh Day.* April 21, 1955. GS: Alan Wells, Michael Moore, Barbara Lang. A gold prospector, elected head of a wagon train bound for California, runs into resistance when he insists that Sunday be kept a day of rest.

43.51 *The Mormon's Grindstone.* April 28, 1955. GS: Clark Howat. Prospectors suspect that an assayer is overestimating their finds to promote his business.

43.52 *Death Valley Scotty.* April 29, 1955. GS: Rusty Morris, Yvonne Cross, Emile Meyer. The story of one of the most colorful characters of the West, whose unlimited financial resources were a mystery to everyone.

43.53 *The Crystal Gazer.* June 4, 1955. GS: Natalie Norwick, Morgan Jones, Michael Ferris, Michael Monroe. Eilley, a Scottish immigrant, believes it is her destiny to go to Nevada and become a mining camp washwoman. Soon she meets and marries a miner. They come into possession of part of the fabulous Comstock Lode.

43.54 *I Am Joaquin.* June 7, 1955. GS: Cliff Field, Steve Conte, John Damler, Jeanne Cooper. The reign of terror visited upon the West by one of history's most famous desperadoes, Joaquin Murieta, is brought to life. Joaquin boards an ill-fated ship and finds a tiny baby in the captain's cabin.

Season Four

43.55 *Reno.* Sept. 23, 1955. GS: William Schallert, Stanley Clements, Frank Griffin. During the war with Mexico in 1847, Lt. Jessie Lee Reno — the man for whom Reno, Nevada, was named — becomes the idol of his men.

43.56 *The Valencia Cake.* Sept. 26, 1955. GS: Robert Tafur, Ariana Cole. The U.S. Land Office finds an ancient deed for a historic Spanish family.

43.57 *A Killing in Diamonds.* Oct. 20, 1955. GS: Michael Vallon, Robin Short, Baynes Barron, Emmett Vogan. Two miners announce the discovery of a diamond mine in the desert. After selling their interest in the fake mine, one of them disappears.

43.58 *The Homeliest Man in Nevada.* Oct. 24, 1955. GS: Paul Wexler, Pat Joiner. A young miner accepts good-naturedly the title of the state's least handsome citizen until a beautiful woman comes to town.

43.59 *Miracle of the Sea Gulls.* Nov. 14, 1955. GS: Peter Dane. A counterfeiter making a compulsory departure from town, joins a wagon train of Mormons.

43.60 *Wildcat's First Piano.* Nov. 21, 1955. GS: Michael Garth, Marilyn Saris. Culture comes to a Nevada mining town in the 1890's with the arrival of a piano. The only problem now is finding someone who knows how to play the instrument.

43.61 *California's First Ice Man.* Dec. 12, 1955. GS: Rhodes Reason, I. Stanford Jolley, Donna Drew. A malicious promoter capitalizes on fever victims by hauling snow from the mountains and selling it to them at exorbitant prices.

43.62 *The Hangman Waits.* Dec. 19, 1955. GS: Percy Helton, Ken Christy, Clark Howat, Claire Weeks. More than fifteen years go by before a man is accused and brought to trial for a murder. A prominent lawyer, fearful of competition, assigns an inexperienced young lawyer to the defense, hoping he will lose the case.

43.63 *Gold Is Where You Find It.* Jan. 9, 1956. GS: Claudia Barrett, George Mathews. A detective on the Wells Fargo Line enroute to San Francisco, is accused of being involved in the holdup of his coach.

43.64 *The Man Who'd Bet on Anything.* Jan. 16, 1956. GS: Mark Bennett, Helen Gilbert. Abe Curry is known as a man who will bet on anything. He wagers Nevada's capital, Carson City, into being with a bet.

43.65 *The Baron of Arizona.* Feb. 6, 1956. GS: Ken

Harp, Jack Gardner, Audrey Conti. A crusading reporter in 1880 investigates the legitimacy of the Baron. From the archives of the U.S. government comes the real story of the titled land grabber who turned the homesteaders into virtual slaves.

43.66 *Nevada's Plymouth Rock.* Feb. 13, 1956. GS: Liam Sullivan, Bobby Beekman, Charmienne Harker. A New England family travels west to a booming Nevada gold camp in 1863. But when the hardships of frontier life seem too hard to bear, the wife wants to take her young son back to New England.

43.67 *The Hoodoo Mine.* March 2, 1956. GS: Tyler McDuff, Duane Thorsen, Linda Brent. A young prospector is left by his partner to die from thirst after staking out a rich claim. He is found by a Piute Indian girl who takes him to her village.

43.68 *Mr. Bigfoot.* March 12, 1956. GS: Charles Martin, Duane Thornsen, Ann McCrea. When the same giant footprints for which Ownes Valley is noted suddenly turn up in Death Valley, who would suspect it was Cupid.

43.69 *Escape.* March 30, 1956. GS: Mark Dana, Beverly Tyler. A couple, on the verge of divorce, is menaced for twelve harrowing hours by an escaped killer.

43.70 *Two Bits.* April 7, 1956. GS: Harry Mackin, Charlie Heard. A broken-down race horse becomes a hero during an Apache uprising in Arizona territory in 1864.

43.71 *Bill Bottle's Birthday.* April 27, 1956. GS: Don Kent, Barbara Lang, Camille Franklyn, Homer Clayton. A pompous prospector puts an ad in the paper inviting anyone bearing the distinguished name of Bottle to attend his birthday party.

43.72 *The Sinbuster.* May 4, 1956. GS: Peter Thompson, Lyn Thomas, Don Kelly. An itinerant preacher arrives in a California desert town and is given a hostile greeting by the miners and cowhands who life there. His mettle is put to the test when the townspeople try to take the law into their own hands.

43.73 *Pay Dirt.* May 25, 1956. GS: Barbara Lang, Bradford Jackson, Paul McGuire. A pair of newlyweds heads west, hoping to strike it rich. When the husband is tricked into buying a phony gold mine, the hoax threatens to break up the marriage.

43.74 *The Longest Beard in the World.* June 1, 1956. GS: Guy Prescott, Patricia Donahue. Lawyer Barnaby Taylor is running for Congress, but is persuaded to attend the World's Fair in Chicago. He is billed as the man with the longest beard in the world, challenging all comers.

43.75 *Emperor Norton, 1st.* June 15, 1956. GS: Parker Garvie, Pat O'Hara, Mauritz Hugo, Leonard Penn. A prosperous San Francisco merchant hears a rumor that China is going to ban the export of rice. He and his partners corner the rice market only to discover the rumors are not true.

Season Five

43.76 *Faro Bill's Layout.* Sept. 14, 1956. GS: Britt Lomond, Diane Brewster. When a handsome gambling boss rescues the town belle from a bully called Sidewinder, the latter swears revenge.

43.77 *The Bear Flag.* Sept. 21, 1956. GS: Don Harvey, Robert Tafur. A wealthy Spaniard tries to get his family out of Mexican California when he learns that a group of American rebels are on its way to the town.

43.78 *Pat Garrett's Side of It.* Oct. 22, 1956. GS: Joel Collins, Mack Williams. Sheriff Pat Garrett is assigned the task of bringing in Billy the Kid. The outlaw has flagrantly refused to accept a full pardon by the governor of the territory of New Mexico.

43.79 *The Hidden Treasure of Cucamonga.* Nov. 5, 1956. GS: Anna Navarro, Richard Gilden, Tony Lawrence. A man, worried about a possible war between California and Mexico, hides his money with a friend of his. But the friend dies suddenly and no one knows the whereabouts of the money.

43.80 *The Loggerheads.* Nov. 17, 1956. GS: Bill Catching, Camille Franklin, Gregg Palmer. A young man wins a log-rolling contest, for which he is to receive a medal and a kiss from the lumber queen.

43.81 *The Rose of Rhyolite.* Dec. 3, 1956. GS: Lee Rhodes, Regina Gleason, Jeff Alexander. The gold-digging ways of a dance-hall queen in Rhyolite, Nevada, have a powerful affect on the efficiency of the railroad.

43.82 *The Last Letter.* Dec. 8, 1956. GS: William Pullen, Clint Eastwood. In exchange for gold, California's first mailman delivers the mail to his subscribers. His income soars until competition steps in. Then he must make a big decision.

43.83 *Year of Destiny.* Dec. 31, 1956. GS: Craig Hill, Doreen Dare. Author Bret Harte arrives in the West.

43.84 *Mercer Girl.* Jan. 7, 1957. GS: Norma Ward, Brad Jackson, Peggy O'Connor. Five hundred women make a long sea journey from Boston to Washington state under the care of Asa Mercer.

43.85 *California's Paul Revere.* Jan. 28, 1957. GS: Don C. Harvey. Mexican troops counterattack the fort at Los Angeles.

43.86 *The Trial of Red Haskell.* Feb. 25, 1957. GS: Chuck Robertson, Gregg Palmer. A notorious gunman, finding that he has a double, talks the man into impersonating him.

43.87 *The Washington Elm.* March 4, 1957. GS: Duane Cress, Eric Bond. A graduate student studying at Harvard is taken with the idea of the campus' Washington Elm.

43.88 *The Rosebush of Tombstone.* March 11, 1957. GS: Daria Massey, Peter Thompson. A Scottish lass is acutely indignant about the lack of law and order in a town.

43.89 *The Luck of the Irish.* March 25, 1957. GS: Bill Boyett, John Sorrentino, Rosemary Ace. After discovering an Indian chief dying in the desert Dr. Edward Wilson takes him to the Piute Village. There he finds a terrible epidemic seriously endangering the bribe.

43.90 *Lady Engineer.* April 1, 1957. GS: Allison Hayes, Greg Palmer, Frederick Ford. Beautiful Mary Granger is working on her father's mining property as an engineer in Death Valley. Paul Evans is ruthlessly determined to get her mining property, but Cramer, another young mining man, is in love with Mary.

43.91 *Train of Events.* April 22, 1957. GS: Craig Hill, Audrey Conti, Anne Gwynne. Wells Fargo messenger Mac Farlane is aboard a Montana-bound train in 1886, when it is held up by the famous Clayton gang led by the attractive Belle Clayton.

43.92 *The Man Who Was Never Licked.* April 29, 1957. GS: Bill Hudson, Daria Massey. In 1853 Elias Jackson Baldwin heads for California and the gold rush in the hopes of making a fortune. His love of horses leads him to open livery stables in San Francisco and then he begins investing in mining stocks.

Death Valley Days

Season Six

43.93 California Gold Rush in Reverse. Sept. 30, 1957. GS: Doug McClure, Stanley Lachman, Roy W. Gordon, Guy Prescott, I. Stanford Jolley, Mabel Rea. Army-Navy competition reaches its peak when two lieutenants from the rival branches are delegated to be the first to deliver some California gold to Washington, D.C.

43.94 Camel Train. Oct. 1, 1957. GS: William Reynolds, Stanley Lachman, Hadji Ali. On a scouting trip into the present Death Valley area in 1847, Lt. Edward F. Beale promotes the idea of using camels instead of horses in the southwestern deserts. He interests a senator in his scheme.

43.95 California's First Schoolmarm. Oct. 12, 1957. GS: Dorothy Granger, Richard Keith, Shera Stennette. The schoolteacher wife of a pioneer assembles her first class in the ruins of an old mission.

43.96 Arsenic Springs. Oct. 14, 1957. GS: Louis Zito, Bert Hanson, Joan Swift. A bank teller is accused of embezzlement and almost lynched. Believing him innocent, a co-worker and his fiancee aid in his escape.

43.97 Fifty Years a Mystery. Oct. 30, 1957. GS: Pat Waltz, John Holland, Rosemary Ace. Charlie Bates dreams of a stagecoach holdup. When it is learned that such a holdup actually did happen, Charlie becomes the prime suspect.

43.98 Fifteen Paces to Fame. Nov. 7, 1957. GS: Paul Donovan, Doug McClure, Gene O'Donnell. Mark Twain, while a Virginia City Enterprise reporter in 1864, arouses the jealousy of rival newspaperman Ganse Taylor. This occurs when Ganse's fiancee takes an interest in Twain.

43.99 The Calico Dog. Nov. 29, 1957. GS: Carol Nugent, Robert Beneveds, Steve Conte. Nancy Drake breaks her engagement to miner Dave Chapman because she is jealous of his dog, Colonel. Upset, but unwilling to give up his valuable dog, Dave goes off to work his mining claim in nearby Bismarck.

43.100 Rough and Ready. Dec. 7, 1957. GS: Ronald Foster, Philip Van Zandt, Maralou Gray. The gold-mining town of Rough and Ready has been trying to keep newcomers out. But a Massachusetts man tricks landowner Joe Sweigart into signing a contract which permits him to dig for gold in the area.

43.101 The Last Bad Man. Dec. 9, 1957. GS: Jean Moorehead, Roy Gordon, Morgan Sha'an, Amanda Alzamora. Pretty Harriet Warner is wounded when Tiburcio Vasquez, a notorious bandit, attempts to kidnap her. This prompts the California governor to assign manhunter Harry Morse to track down Vasquez.

43.102 The Greatest Scout of All. Jan 2, 1958. GS: Bruce Kaye, Frank Richards, Maureen Hingert. Fronk Grouard, a mail rider, has been captured by Sitting Bull but is spared from death. After marrying a Sioux girl, Grouard must leave her when Sitting Bull prepares war on the whites.

43.103 Empire of Youth. Jan. 13, 1958. GS: Gregg Palmer, Virginia Lee. Coming West in 1849, young, energetic William T. Coleman becomes a merchant in virtually lawless San Francisco. After becoming famous for his mighty contributions to the building of the city, he is offered his greatest honor, the candidacy for President of the United States.

43.104 Wheel of Fortune. Jan. 23, 1958. GS: William Hudson. Boarding with the friendly Groves family, tinsmith Lester Pelton takes pity on Margaret, the wife and mother, as she labors over her old foot-treadle sewing machine. He contrives a water-powered wheel to drive the sewing machine, but is not satisfied. He tinkers further until he stumbles on a principle destined to inscribe his name imperishable in the annals of world industry.

43.105 Man on the Run. Jan. 30, 1958. GS: Billy Nelson, Mary Field. A young drifter leaves town to avoid marrying his determined landlady. He moves to another town, but after a few days the woman shows up again.

43.106 Birth of a Boom. Jan. 31, 1958. GS: Roy Barcroft, Keith Byron. A burro which strays during the night leads his searching owner to a gold-and-silver strike that creates the city of Tonopah, Nevada.

43.107 Yankee Pirate. Feb. 13, 1958. GS: Ken Clark, Pamela Duncan, Edward Colmans. The crew of a French pirate ship raids one of California's great coastal ranches.

43.108 Ten in Texas. Feb. 14, 1958. GS: Harry Strang. Four Chicago businessmen find themselves owner of the biggest ranch in the country. The foreman is sure it can't be altered by rustlers but a wily young Mexican-American quickly proves that it can be.

43.109 Auto Intoxication. Feb. 24, 1958. GS: Raymond Hatton, Lizz Slifer. On his 30th anniversary, a grizzled prospector takes $4000 and buys his wife an automobile.

43.110 Two-Gun Nan. Feb. 27, 1958. GS: Penny Edwards, William O'Neal. Joining Buffalo Bill's Wild West Show as the bride of a trick roper, a Montana cowgirl decides to ride across the nation.

43.111 Cockeyed Charlie Parkhurst. March 13, 1958. GS: Frank Gerstle, Glenn Strange. A 10-year-old boy runs away from an orphanage.

43.112 The Great Amulet. March 14, 1958. GS: Don Reardon. Falling in love with a girl in France, and later learning of her miserable life with a husband in Monterey, California, Robert Lewis Stevenson travels to her aid.

43.113 The Telescope Eye. March 27, 1958. An impoverished clerk lends his meager savings to a friend. The friend dies before the loan is repaid.

43.114 The Mystery of Suicide Gulch. March 28, 1958. GS: Stephen Chase, Lee Anthony. When a sheep-rancher breaks an ankle, his 15-year-old son drives a herd of sheep to market for his father. At an overnight camp, 71 of the sheep die mysteriously.

43.115 The Big Rendezvous. April 5, 1958. GS: Peter Walker, Gardner McKay, Laurie Carroll. Kit Carson fights to protect a pretty Indian girl and win himself a wife.

43.116 The Girl Who Walked with a Giant. April 12, 1958. GS: Stephen Chase, Nancy Rennick. Sam Houston, middle-aged hero of the battle of Texas independence, marries young Margaret Lea against her parents' protests.

43.117 Jerkline Jitters. June 6, 1958. GS: Clay Randolph, Audrey Conti. To win his sweetheart Enid, Brad Tyson rides out on a desert trek.

Season Seven

43.118 Head of the House. Sept. 29, 1958. GS: Harold T. Daye, Morgan Jones. The death of their parents leaves seven pioneer children alone in the savage West.

43.119 *The Capture.* Oct. 2, 1958. GS: Irene Barton, Nancy Hale, Molly McGowan, Earl Robie. A white squaw helps a frontier widow regain children stolen by Comanche Indians.

43.120 *Ship of No Return.* Oct. 9, 1958. GS: David Frankham, Nyra Monsour. Edward Peel, an English sailor, is shanghaied onto a Mexican pearl-diving expedition.

43.121 *The Moving-Out of Minnie.* Oct. 13, 1958. An old servant proves a problem for a rancher.

43.122 *The Red Flannel Shirt.* Oct. 27, 1958. GS: Ewing Mitchell. A young miner plans to cash in on a secret when a rich vein is fund on the Comstock Lode.

43.123 *Big Liz.* Oct. 30, 1958. GS: Hope Emerson, Percy Helton. A tough woman prospector and the meek little man whose life she saved strike a rich gold find in Nevada.

43.124 *Thorn of the Rose.* Nov. 10, 1958. GS: Virginia Lee, Will White, Walter Barnes. An ex-bandit queen refuses to let her past ruin her new life.

43.125 *The Jackass Mail.* Nov. 12, 1958. GS: John Pickard, Maura Murphy, Frank Gerstle. Friendly Indians turn unfriendly and a stage driver hunts the cause.

43.126 *Perilous Cargo.* Nov. 24, 1958. GS: Gregg Palmer, Jean Carson. Tom Horn agrees to kidnap some mail-order brides and deliver them to a group of religious fanatics as wives. When he has a change of heart and decides to escape with the girl, the fanatics block the road with an avalanche.

43.127 *The Gambler and the Lady.* Nov. 27, 1958. GS: Kathy Case, Mark Dana. The new schoolmarm in Joshua accuses the local gambler and saloonkeeper of stealing the money for the new schoolhouse. The gambler decides to teach her a lesson of his own.

43.128 *Quong Kee.* Nov. 27, 1958. GS: Victor Sen Yung. A politician tries to create a scandal about a Senatorial candidate, who supposedly was in love with a dance-hall girl.

43.129 *Old Gabe.* Dec. 8, 1958. GS: Harry Shannon, Ron Hagerthy. Indian scout Jim Bridger returns from Army duty and discovers he is losing his sight. But in order to earn money to keep his home he accepts an Army offer to fight a Sioux uprising.

43.130 *The Gunsmith.* Dec. 11, 1958. GS: Anthony Caruso, Anita Gordon. A trick-short artist threatens to kill the fiance of the girl who was once his human target unless she rejoins his act. The fiance, a gunsmith, devises a dangerous and daring plan to foil the ace shot.

43.131 *A Piano Goes West.* Jan. 2, 1959. GS: Wally Brown, Britt Lomond. On a trip to Europe, wealthy miner Hank Braun orders a custom-made silver piano. When the salesman arrives in New Mexico with the instrument, he finds Braun his disappeared very mysteriously.

43.132 *A Bullet for the Captain.* Jan. 3, 1959. GS: Michael Emmett, John Parrish, Laurie Carroll. Capt. Owen Manners' patrol is wiped out by the Sioux, but he escapes.

43.133 *A Town Is Born.* Jan. 16, 1959. GS: Albert Carrier, Than Wyenn, Jean Howell. An American couple, who run a frontier store, are forced to pay illegal taxes to an army officer of Emperor Maximilian of Mexico.

43.134 *Sailor on a Horse.* Jan. 17, 1959. GS: Robert Dix, Roy Engel. A Navy lieutenant assigned to chart the Missouri River encounters an unreasonable Army major.

43.135 *Gold Lake.* Jan. 30, 1959. GS: Harry Lauter, Jack Lomas. As a practical joke, an old prospector tells an editor friend a tall tale about a lake of gold. The newspaper prints the story, but fails to realize the power of the press and the greed of the local people.

43.136 *Wheelbarrow Johnny.* Jan. 31, 1959. GS: Harry Lauter, Gil Lasky, Robert Ellis. A hopeful gold prospector arrives in California and in a few hours has lost his wagon and his savings.

43.137 *Stagecoach Spy.* Feb. 13, 1959. GS: Brad Johnson, Claudia Barrett, George Neise. The beautiful victim of a stagecoach robbery volunteers to act as a spy until the outlaw band is apprehended.

43.138 *Eruption at Volcano.* Feb. 14, 1959. GS: Stephen Chase, I. Stanford Jolley. The Civil War splits the town of Volcano. A group of Southerners, led by Bart Taylor, plans to take over the town and send its gold to aid the Confederacy.

43.139 *Price of a Passport.* Feb. 27, 1959. GS: Dan Barton, Rodolfo Hoyos. Imprisoned as spies by a Mexican governor, a band of trappers are unable to secure its release until a seaman dies of smallpox.

43.140 *Pioneer Circus.* Feb. 28, 1959. GS: Doug Odney, Joyce Vanderveen, Joanna Lee, John Holland. A circus owner sends Dan Rowland to make contact with a star rider, Juliette Bonet. The present equestrienne, jealous of losing her star billing and unable to win Dan, tells the owner of a rival circus of the plan.

43.141 *The Invaders.* March 13, 1959. GS: Nestor Paiva, Anthony Caruso, Chris Warfield, Jil Jarmyn. An Italian citizen submits to the extortion demands of a Mafia gangster until his son decides to fight back.

43.142 *The Blonde King.* March 14, 1959. GS: Lane Bradford, Brad Johnson. A trader, revered as an Indian king, opposes a mining agent who schemes to take over tribal gold claims. While leading a military expedition to settle the trouble, the trader becomes the first white man to see Yosemite Valley.

43.143 *The Newspaper That Went to Jail.* March 27, 1959. GS: Richard Vath, Larry Johns. A mining inspector gets Judge Clinton to hand down a court order closing a mine as unsafe. A newspaper editor accuses a judge of stupidity.

43.144 *Old Blue.* March 28, 1959. GS: Richard Cutting, Frank Killmond, Barbara Beaird. A homesteader arrives in Fort Sumner and decides to settle down with his family. One day his daughter arrives home with a pet, which turns out to be the valuable lead steer of a tough cattleman who hates homesteaders.

43.145 *Perilous Refuge.* April 10, 1959. GS: Gregg Palmer, Anthony George. Cattleman John Brewster claims a large part of the old Spanish land grant of Carlos Otega. After an argument over a land grant, the ambitious cattleman fatally wounds a Spanish ranch owner.

43.146 *The Talking Wire.* April 11, 1959. GS: Michael Emmet, Arthur Space, Morris Ankrum, Molly McGowan. When a man comes to install a long-distance phone line for a gold-mine owner, he finds that his employer has been denying much-need water to the farmers.

43.147 *RX—Slow Death.* April 24, 1959. GS: Sumner William, Charles Watts, Pamela Duncan. A little boy sinks into a coma after swallowing a compound sold by a traveling medicine man. His mother asks the town apothecary for aid.

Death Valley Days

43.148 *Half a Loaf.* April 25, 1959. GS: Richard Crane, Mason Alan Dinehart, Mauritz Hugo. Agreeing to split any profits, two brothers separate, one going to the Nevada gold mines and the other to Kentucky with a race horse.

43.149 *Valley of Danger.* May 8, 1959. GS: Don Wilbanks, John Merrick, Angela Stevens, Gregg McCabe. A man staggers into the trading post of the Warners' and tells of escaping from Indians. They nurse him back to health and make him manager of the post. They do not realize that he is plotting with the Indians to attack their ranch and steal their gold.

43.150 *Forty Steps to Glory.* May 9, 1959. GS: Don Megowan, Gregg Palmer. Saloon owner Buff McCloud has the town in his grip because he is the fastest draw. A stranger comes to town and threatens McCloud's domination with an unusual weapon.

Season Eight

43.151 *Olvera.* Oct. 13, 1959. GS: Cesar Romero, Michael Dante. The story of Don Augustine Olvera who played an important part in bringing California under the American flag is told.

43.152 *Gates Ajar Morgan.* Oct. 20, 1959. GS: Don Wilson. Gates Morgan arrives in a small western town to preach his gospel and replenish his empty purse.

43.153 *Sam Kee and Uncle Sam.* Oct. 27, 1959. GS: Benson Fong, Jim Douglas. A Chinese immigrant tries to prevent an entire Army garrison from deserting, and Fort Huachuca from falling into the hands of the Apache Indians.

43.154 *The Grand Duke.* Nov. 3, 1959. GS: John Lupton, Alex Davion. Answering a call from General Sheridan, Buffalo Bill receives orders to protect the life of Duke Alexis of Russia.

43.155 *Fair Exchange.* Nov. 13, 1959. GS: George Mitchell, Robert E. Griffin. Charlie Stoner and Major Bullock join forces to hunt for gold. Everything goes smoothly until the Major's possessions begin to disappear.

43.156 *The Scalpel and the Gun.* Nov. 17, 1959. GS: Lin McCarthy, Richard Shannon. A doctor whose devotion to gambling costs him the life of a patient, becomes an outcast. After joining a gang of outlaws, he is given a chance to redeem himself.

43.157 *Indian Emily.* Nov. 26, 1959. GS: Jolene Brand, Meg Wyllie, Burt Metcalf. After a battle with the Apaches, a wounded Indian girl is taken prisoner by the cavalry. She is quickly befriended by Lt. Tom Easton and his mother.

43.158 *Hang 'Em High.* Nov. 26, 1959. GS: Paul Birch, Laurie Carroll, William Schallert, Arthur Space. When President Lincoln orders the building of the first transcontinental telegraph, two companies vie with each other for a huge bonus prize.

43.159 *Tribal Justice.* Dec. 10, 1959. GS: Richard Angarola, Joe Perry. Comanche chiefs Quanah Parker and Yellow Bear, who are bitter enemies, come to Fort Worth to meet with cattlemen.

43.160 *The Little Trooper.* Dec. 10, 1959. GS: Lennie Bremen, Tom Palmer, Bryan Russell. A four-year-old boy and an Army sergeant become friends.

43.161 *Ten Feet of Nothing.* Dec. 24, 1959. GS: James Drury, Preshy Marker, Lew Gallo, Hank Patterson. A dance-hall boss, a song and a supposedly worthless mine combine to make a man a target for murder.

43.162 *Lady of the Press.* Dec. 24, 1959. GS: Mary Webster, Don Beddoe, James Franciscus. A female editor lacking in writing ability wins the editor of a rival newspaper to her side in an attempt to battle a crooked politician.

43.163 *The Reluctant Gun.* Dec. 26, 1959. GS: Ross Elliott, Alan Reed, Jr. The lawyer son of a famous man is determined to make a name for himself. His chance comes in a dramatic murder trial.

43.164 *His Brother's Keeper.* Jan. 9, 1960. GS: Harry Townes, Jack Mather. After Lincoln's assassination, actor Edwin Booth moves to California, but people are unfriendly to him because of his brother's crime.

43.165 *The Devil's Due.* Jan. 21, 1960. GS: Bob Knapp, June Dayton, Brett King, Pamela Duncan. In 1885 a bank robber decides to go straight, but hides $20,000 from his last job on the ranch.

43.166 *Money to Burn.* Jan. 22, 1960. GS: Lloyd Corrigan. A hobo's life takes a turn for the better when he discovers a fortune in stolen gold hidden by bandits in a hobo jungle.

43.167 *Dogs of the Mist.* Feb. 6, 1960. GS: James Douglas, Eleanor Barry. Steve Hewitt shoots a couple of wildcats one misty night, only to find they are the dogs of the legendary Joe Tule and that each carried a note asking for help.

43.168 *A Wedding Dress.* Feb. 13, 1960. GS: Brad Johnson. In 1894, Marshal Bill Tilghman is almost fired for trying to reclaim a stolen wedding dress instead of searching for the notorious Doolin gang.

43.169 *Shadow on the Window.* Feb. 18, 1960. GS: Dayton Lummis, Martin Braddock. Gen. Lew Wallace, governor of the New Mexico Territory, promises amnesty to Billy the Kid if he will turn state's evidence.

43.170 *The Battle of Mokelumne Hill.* Feb. 19, 1960. GS: Marcel Dalio, Diane DuBois, H.M. Wynant. A tax collector and a Frenchman, both interested in the same girl, settle a tax issue by slugging it out.

43.171 *The Strangers.* March 3, 1960. GS: Warner Anderson, Phyllis Hill, Robert Gist, Claudia Bryar. A family finally succeeds in carving a prosperous home out of the Wyoming wilderness. Then one night a strange wagon stops by their home and their happiness is threatened.

43.172 *Goodbye Five Hundred Pesos.* March 3, 1960. GS: Rafael Campos, Than Wyenn. During the years following the conquest of California, the Army commandant in charge of the Santa Barbara areas has considerable trouble with the local population. A brass cannon is washed ashore after the sinking of an American ship.

43.173 *Forbidden Wedding.* March 17, 1960. GS: Ted Otis, Ziva Rodann. Two men who want to marry the same woman try to outwit each other.

43.174 *One Man Tank.* March 17, 1960. GS: John Bleifer, Dabbs Greer, John Harmon. A man who struck out when everyone else was hunting for gold attempts to support his motherless family on his meager earnings.

43.175 *Man on the Road.* March 30, 1960. GS: John Raitt, Kevin Jones. Jim Dandy has just been confronted by Pete Rawson, a small, hungry boy wielding a rifle.

43.176 *The Man Everyone Hated.* April 1, 1960. GS:

James Craig, Charles Davis, Ken Mayer, Richard Gilden, Sonya Wilde. White man and Indian alike despise General Edward F. Beale for creating the Indian Reservation Act of 1852. The settlers feel that the state's choicest land has been given away, and the Indians feel imprisoned.

43.177 *The General Who Disappeared.* April 8, 1960. GS: Howard Petrie. Things get tough on corrupt politicians when the Governor of Montana insists they introduce reform bills.

43.178 *The Million Dollar Pants.* April 13, 1960. GS: Red Buttons, Richard Carlyle, Lisa Gaye. Levi Strauss turns a business reversal into a financial success when he makes a pair of canvas trousers for himself.

43.179 *Pirates of San Francisco.* April 14, 1960. GS: H.M. Wynant, George Wallace, Ann McCrea. A first mate hunts for a new crew when his sailors make a dash for the gold fields without stopping to unload the cargo.

43.180 *A Woman's Rights.* May 1, 1960. GS: Bethel Leslie, Dean Harens. A victim of corrupt politics loses his savings and decides to quit town.

43.181 *Eagle in the Rocks.* May 10, 1960. GS: Ricardo Montalban, Jack Kruschen. A Mexican outlaw is accused of killing four miners. The townspeople denounce all Mexicans.

43.182 *Cap'n Pegleg.* May 12, 1960. GS: Douglas Fowley, William Schallert, Paul Burke. A sailor who lost a leg to the sharks seeks revenge on the six men who abandoned him.

43.183 *Emma Is Coming.* May 24, 1960. GS: Erin O'Brien. A singer from Austin, Nevada, performs in Europe and is given a diamond necklace by Queen Victoria. But her greatest desire is to appear in her home town.

43.184 *Human Sacrifice.* June 2, 1960. GS: Christopher Dark, Herman Rudin, Arline Sax. When an Indian chief dies the fanatic medicine man tries to persuade the tribe to perform a an ancient ritual and kill the chief's young wife.

43.185 *Pete Kitchen's Wedding Night.* June, 7 1960. GS: Cameron Mitchell, Barbara Luna. Apaches have taken over the Arizona territory. But even though his life is in danger, a prosperous rancher refuses to leave.

43.186 *Mission to the Mountains.* June 9, 1960. GS: Harry Lauter, George Keymas, John Hoyt. On a peace mission, a Nevada rancher and an Indian chief meet a prospector who is convinced they are after his gold.

43.187 *The Great Lounsberry Scoop.* June 29, 1960. GS: John Clarke. Before General Custer leaves for a campaign against the Sioux, he selects Colonel Lounsberry to be the only newspaperman on the mission.

Season Nine

43.188 *Pamela's Oxen.* Sept. 24, 1960. GS: Ida Lupino, James Coburn. Pamela Mann's team of oxen are badly needed in the war against Mexico, but Pamela absolutely refuses to relinquish them.

43.189 *Splinter Station.* Sept. 25, 1960. GS: Jane Russell, Claude Akins, Raymond Guth, Chuck Roberson. Caleb Luck and Mel Frazer, two Confederate calvarymen, break into the home of Yankee Mary Taylor, intending to kill her.

43.190 *Queen of the High-Graders.* Oct. 2, 1960. GS: Larry Pennell, Wanda Shannon. Romer Maxwell comes to the Cripple Creek gold mine to investigate a robbery.

43.191 *Devil's Bar.* Oct. 3, 1960. GS: Ron Hayes, Terry Loomis, William Mims. Don and Marry Bartlett amaze the town of Murphy Flats by their refusal to use guns Then they save the town from a possible disaster.

43.192 *Learnin' at Dirty Devil.* Oct. 24, 1960. GS: Grant Richards, Philip Grayson, Robert Elston. Outlaw Hank Lanier's son is acquiring high ideals from his teacher, Ralph Edmunds.

43.193 *Yankee Confederate.* Oct. 24, 1960. GS: Tod Andrews, Elaine Davis. A Union officer tries to curb the activities of Belle Waverly.

43.194 *The Gentle Sword.* Nov. 7, 1960. GS: Roy Engel, Robert Montgomery, Jr., Karen Green. The outlaw Merced gang tries to take over Col. John Freemont's mine and traps Freemont and his miners inside it.

43.195 *Extra Guns.* Nov. 20, 1960. GS: Guy Madison, Wilton Graff. The mayor of Dodge City is determined to run reformed gangster Luke Short out of town.

43.196 *The White Healer.* Nov. 21, 1960. GS: Lee Philips, Allen Jaffe, Harry Holcombe, Joseph Bassett, Thomas Coley, Joe Lo Presti. Lieutenant Wood, a cavalry doctor, saves the Apache Hamaz from the plague and sets him free. Hamaz returns to Geronimo with the message that the doctor will help the Apaches if they will surrender.

43.197 *The Wind at Your Back.* Dec. 5, 1960. GS: June Dayton, Steve Terrell. In a hospital, outlaw Johnny Carter asks Sister Mary Francis to write a letter to his partner about a fortune in gold dust he has laid claim to.

43.198 *3-7-77.* Dec. 14, 1960. GS: Joel Crothers, Ralph Neff, Sheldon Allman. An old miner plays on the sympathy of young Jim Badger, and persuades him to steal a bag of gold.

43.199 *A Girl Named Virginia.* Dec. 18, 1960. GS: Patty McCormick, John Anderson, Edward Platt. Jim Reed, accused of murder, is banished by his party of wagon trains and left to starve.

43.200 *City of Widows.* Dec. 19, 1960. GS: Stan Young, Ann Carroll, Dayton Lummis. A pollution in the air and a mining engineer's refusal to employ proper mining methods is slowly killing off an entire community.

43.201 *The Young Gun.* Dec. 27, 1960. GS: Arthur Franz, David Howe, Reid Hammond. A man convicted and sent to jail decides to give his infant son up for adoption. Years later he returns and discovers that his son is being held on suspicion of robbery.

43.202 *The Lady Was an M.D.* Jan. 1, 1961. GS: Yvonne De Carlo, John Vivyan. Dr. Clare Reed learns the hard way that the public in the late 19th Century will not accept a woman doctor.

43.203 *The Salt War.* Jan. 15, 1961. GS: Lenore Roberts, Jeffrey Stone. An Eastern woman moves to a huge ranch in Texas and decides to sell the salt on her land.

43.204 *The Madstone.* Jan. 18, 1961. GS: Myron Healey, Eloise Hardt. Big Matt Denby, hit by ill luck, decides to move his family. But bad fortune follows when his son is bitten by a rabid animal and his wife leaves him.

43.205 *Deadline at Austin.* Jan. 29, 1961. GS: David Janssen, Harry Shannon, Jan Harrison, Stephen Chase. The governor of Nevada is bent on getting even with the whole town of Austin because its mayor once insulted him.

43.206 *South of Horror Flats.* Jan. 31, 1961. GS: Jimsey

Death Valley Days

Somers, John Lupton, Stephen Ellsworth. Abigale Britton, troubled by ghosts, hires a detective to take her and her fortune in gold to San Francisco.

43.207 *Gamble with Death.* Feb. 10, 1961. GS: Ken Murray, Dick Sargent, Eddie Quillan. Old Dave Eldridge wants to strike gold before he dies. But he can't get a stake because the people of Goldfield, Nevada, think he is a jinx.

43.208 *White Gold.* Feb. 15, 1961. GS: Paul Bryar, Charles Gray. Charles "Doughy" Lucas, a wealthy merchant, tells the townspeople that there will be scarcity of flour, and he jacks up the price of the available supply.

43.209 *Dead Man's Tale.* GS: Feb. 26, 1961. GS: Peter Hanson, Russell Johnson, Valerie Starrett. Dr. Allen Camden wants to know why anyone would want to harm Grant Noble, a well-liked storekeeper. A man with a hook on his arm has attacked Noble for no apparent reason.

43.210 *Who's for Divide?* GS: March 1, 1961. GS: Peter Whitney. Joe Meeks asks the settlers of Divide whether Oregon should join the United States or the British Empire.

43.211 *Dangerous Crossing.* March 12, 1961. GS: William Lundigan, Annelle Hayes. Nathaniel Norgate loves his wife, but he is unable to conform to her strict religious beliefs.

43.212 *Death Ride.* March 15, 1961. GS: Robert Rockwell, Marion Ross, William Flaherty, Rafael Lopez, Thayer Roberts. Lawyer William Thorne decides to defend Martha Sayles, who is accused of poisoning her son. The entire town is convinced of Martha's guilt.

43.213 *Loophole.* March 25, 1961. GS: Arthur Shields, Bruce Gordon, Alex Davion, Cynthia Patrick. Jebal McSween is being cheated of his gold and Hobert Mitchell employs his tacts as a lawyer to help him get it back.

43.214 *The Red Petticoat.* March 29, 1961. GS: H.M. Wynant, Allen Jaffe, Laura Shelton, Tim Bolton. Lt. Philip Sheridan heads an Army post that is at war with the Indians.

43.215 *The Stolen City.* April 9, 1961. GS: Darren McGavin, Gregory Morton, Sarita Vara. Jose Limantour has land claims that make him owner of practically all of San Francisco. Chemist Zacharias Gurney is determined to remedy the situation.

43.216 *A General Without Cause.* April 12, 1961. GS: Lisa Gaye, William Boyett, Jack Elam. Miles Owens is attacked by notorious bandit Juan Cortina as he tries to cross the Mexican desert.

Season Ten

43.217 *Queen of Spades.* Oct. 2, 1961. GS: Gloria Talbot. Beautiful Mary Kileen has a mental quirk. She likes to see men die for her.

43.218 *The Hold-Up Proof Safe.* Oct. 2, 1961. GS: Regis Toomey, John Ashley, Susan Crane. The hold-up proof safe in Gus Lammerson's store proves to be otherwise.

43.219 *Lieutenant Bungle.* Oct. 2, 1961. GS: Philip Ober, Ed Mallory. Major Galloway and his scouts find army life hectic.

43.220 *The Third Passenger.* Oct. 2, 1961. GS: Robert Palmer, Sandra Marsh, Tyler McVey. Lew Sayres, the local mail carrier, insists that Bill Gentry give up gambling before he marries Susan Sayres.

43.221 *Trial by Fear.* Oct. 2, 1961. GS: Eddie Quillan, Ed Peck. Two hoodlums overhear a conversation between some wealthy businessmen. They decide to make the most of what they have heard.

43.222 *Alias James Stuart.* Oct. 13, 1961. GS: Robert Culp, Eleanor Berry. Thomas Burdue's incredible resemblance to killer James Stuart lands him in a pack of trouble.

43.223 *Storm Over Truckee.* Oct. 23, 1961. GS: Jenna Engstrom, Fredrick Downs. Maggie Woolf and her father take refuge in an abandoned cabin during a snow storm. They soon have some uninvited company—two murderers.

43.224 *Treasure of Elk Creek Canyon.* Oct. 30, 1961. GS: Dennis Cross, Alan Hale, Jr., John Considine. The renegade Reynolds brothers hold up Abe Williamson's stage and take his last few cents.

43.225 *The Watch.* Dec. 4, 1961. GS: Dorothy Malone, Steve Clinton, Bing Russell. Polish immigrant Rafe Pegarski is learning to read and write for his citizenship test.

43.226 *A Bullet for the D.A.* Nov. 13, 1961. GS: Carole Mathews, Don Haggerty. Belle Starr vows revenge when District Attorney Frank Clayton makes a fool of her husband.

43.227 *Miracle at Boot Hill.* Dec. 11, 1961. GS: John Carradine, Penny Edwards, Peter Hansen, Chris Waterfield. A stranger in a small mining town professes the power to resurrect the dead.

43.228 *The Truth Teller.* Jan. 1, 1962. GS: Edward Kemmer, Barney Phillips. General Hancock is reported to be selling the Indians guns and supplies in exchange for their property.

43.229 *Sponge Full of Vinegar.* Jan. 15, 1962. GS: Lloyd Corrigan, Paul Birch. Townspeople aren't too fond of shabby storyteller Dorsey Bilger. They think he is setting a bad example for their children.

43.230 *Experiment in Fear.* Jan. 25, 1962.

43.231 *Miracle at Whiskey Gulch.* Jan. 26, 1962. GS: Fess Parker, George Kennedy, Hal Baylor, Eddie Firestone. Armed with a Bible, new arrival Rev. Joel Todd has plans to build a church. But saloonowner Steamboat Sully sees the preacher as a threat to his way of life.

43.232 *Feud at Dome Rock.* Jan. 29, 1962. GS: Michael Pate. An old Indian is killed while trying to stop outlaws from running off with his horses.

43.233 *Justice at Jackson Creek.* Jan. 30, 1962. GS: Arthur Franz, Dub Taylor. Disillusioned lawyer Payne P. Prim forsakes his career, becomes an alcoholic, and moves to a western mining camp.

43.234 *Preacher with a Past.* Feb. 1, 1962. GS: Neville Brand, Jean Gillespie, Richard Devon. A reformed outlaw moves to a new town, assumes a new name, and becomes a preacher.

43.235 *Abel Duncan's Dying Wish.* Feb. 3, 1962. GS: Eduard Franz, Tyler McVey. Abel Duncan's wish is to have an ordained Man of God conduct his burial service.

43.236 *A Matter of Honor.* Feb. 12, 1962. GS: Vic Morrow, Shirley Ballard. Lt. Robert Benson is torn between love and duty. The girl he loves wants him to accept a bribe and give out secret government information.

43.237 *The Breaking Point.* March 1, 1962. GS: DeForest Kelley, William Schallert, Dick Foran. Prospector Shad Cullen has hit a vein, and he is not going to share it with anyone—not even his unsuspecting partner, Dave Meiser.

43.238 *Girl with a Gun.* March 8, 1962. GS: Anne

Helm, Garry Walberg, Ken Mayer, Josh Peine, Ray Daley. Seeking revenge on Marshal Hobe Martin, teenager Jenny Metcalf joins a gang of outlaws.

43.239 *Way Station.* March 9, 1962. GS: Dennis Day, Merry Anders, Theona Bryant, Frank Wilcox. Bookkeeper Jason Barnes comes West to learn all about the railroad business. Jason intends to marry a railroad executive's daughter.

43.240 *The Unshakable Man.* May 6, 1962. GS: Tony Martin, Nick Dennis. Realizing that honest working men need a place to keep their savings, Amadeo Giannini founds the Bank of Italy.

43.241 *Showdown at Kamaaina Flats.* May 15, 1962. GS: John Vivyan, Jose DeVega. Five Hawaiian slaves escape from the schooner Escapade off the California coast.

43.242 *La Tules.* May 21, 1962. GS: Katy Jurado. Although the U.S. Army is advancing toward Santa Fe, a Mexican woman refuses to return to her native country.

Season Eleven

43.243 *Hangtown Fry.* Oct. 1, 1962. GS: Fabrizo Mioni, Nancy Rennick, Don Haggerty. Paul Duval has created an elaborate omelette to delay his execution for murder.

43.244 *The $275,000 Sack of Flour.* Oct. 1, 1962. GS: James Best, Booth Colman. Ruel Gridley pays off a bet by donating a bag of flour to the fund for the wounded of the Civil War.

43.245 *Suzie.* Oct. 3, 1962. GS: Jeffrey Hunter, Lenice Haywood, Aneta Corsaut. Suzie is the sole survivor of an Apache massacre.

43.246 *Fort Bowie: Urgent.* Oct. 8, 1962. Ed Nelson. The message must get through to Fort Bowie that Frank Girard has escaped from Yuma Prison.

43.247 *The Hat That Won the West.* Oct. 23, 1962. Alan Young, Don Haggerty, Lee Van Cleef. Plagued by tuberculosis, John Stetson is advised to go to Colorado.

43.248 *The Last Shot.* Oct. 25, 1962. GS: Johnny Seven, Richard Shannon, Grace Lee Whitney. Carlo Farelli, an immigrant farmer, runs into trouble when he tries to start a new life.

43.249 *To Walk with Greatness.* Nov. 12, 1962. GS: Jody McCrea. Newly-graduated from West Point, Lt. John F. Pershing becomes a hero of the old West by tracking down white renegades.

43.250 *The Grass Man.* Nov. 13, 1963. GS: Keenan Wynn, Alvy Moore. Botanist David Douglas crosses the Atlantic in search of a pine tree.

43.251 *Davy's Friend.* Nov. 14, 1962. GS: Tommy Rettig, George Mitchell, Ronnie Haran. Fifteen-year-old Joel Robinson joins the American fighting to avenge the death of his friend Davy Crockett. But he can't bring himself to bayonet a Mexican soldier, and is called a coward.

43.252 *Bloodline.* Dec. 17, 1962. GS: Paul Richards, Abraham Sofaer, Anthony Hall, Patricia Huston. Physician Max Richter is fighting for an unpopular cause when he uses transfusions instead of bleeding his patients. Then a princess visiting San Francisco becomes very ill and his services are requested.

43.253 *The Vintage Years.* Dec. 19, 1962. GS: Ralph Bellamy, Merry Anders, William Bryant. Lorna Erickson and her boyfriend plan to rob Daniel Quint of the large deposit he is taking to the bank.

43.254 *The Private Mint of Clark, Gruber and Company.* Dec. 28, 1962. GS: John Lupton, Jerry Paris. Two Denver bankers solve the problem of frequent gold robberies.

43.255 *Loss of Faith.* Dec. 31, 1962. GS: Rhonda Fleming, Don Collier, Jim Davis. A scorned woman comes between two friends who also happen to be the town's lawmen.

43.256 *Pioneer Doctor.* Jan. 2, 1963. GS: John Agar, Dick Foran, Marie Worsham. Young Doctor Edwards moves to a town on the California frontier. But he is kept from practicing by the town's old doctor.

43.257 *Stubborn Mule Hill.* Jan. 25, 1963. GS: David McLean. Riding through a desolate area, Kit Carson finds an exhausted man and takes him back to the Army post.

43.258 *A Gun Is Not a Gentleman.* Feb. 8, 1963. GS: Carroll O'Connor, Brad Dexter. Politics lead a U.S. Senator and a Supreme Court Justice to settle their difference in a gun duel.

43.259 *The Lion of Idaho.* Feb. 18, 1963. GS: Steve Forrest, Audrey Dalton. The career of William E. Borah, a lawyer who became the senator, from Idaho is dramatized.

43.260 *The Debt.* Feb. 20, 1963. GS: Alejandro Rey, Alan Caillou, Leo Gordon. A bandit's friendship with a teamster brings justice to enslaved miners.

43.261 *The Train and Lucy Tutaine.* Feb. 22, 1963. GS: Joan Blondell, Noah Beery, Jr. A widow takes on the Mountain Pacific Railroad when one of its trains kills her cow.

43.262 *Grotto of Death.* March 8, 1963. GS: Robert Colbert, Gilbert Green. Yank Van Duzen, crew chief of the Alta mine, quits when his foreman won't take necessary precautions against a cave-in.

43.263 *Diamond Jim Brady.* April 4, 1963. GS: Howard Keel, Charles Cooper. Confident that he will win a $50,000 bet, Brady spends $20,000 of the money on a party. But angry opponents plan to blast his scheme sky high.

43.264 *Phantom Procession.* March 12, 1963. Tony Young. In a haunted valley, a cowboy is thrown from his horse and knocked unconscious.

43.265 *With Honesty and Integrity.* April 18, 1963. GS: Michael Keep, Denver Pyle Crow Dog is acquitted of murder, but Lucius Baarkey wants to hang him.

43.266 *Coffin for a Coward.* April 21, 1963. GS: DeForest Kelley, Joseph Ruskin, Elinor Berry, Rusty Lane. Returning from the Civil War, Clint Rogers finds his home town ruled by terrorists.

43.267 *Shadow of Violence.* April 24, 1963. GS: James Caan. Two brothers spend their nights digging at an unattended grave.

43.268 *The Melancholy Gun.* April 26, 1963. GS: Ken Scott. Johnny Ringo tells how he came to be the greatest gunslinger in the West.

Season Twelve

43.269 *Thar She Blows.* Sept. 30, 1963. GS: George Gobel, Evan Evans, Dan Haggerty. When Baylor Thomas' mule dies, he has to drop out of the wagon train, but he continues his journey in an odd contraption — a sailing wagon.

43.270 *Measure of a Man.* Oct. 1, 1963. GS: Rory Calhoun, Michael Pate, Bing Russell, Robert P. Lieb, Chick Chandler, Richard Webb. Burt Mossman, Captain of the Arizona

Death Valley Days

Rangers, refuses to give up his position until he captures a renegade Indian.

43.271 Kingdom for a Horse. Oct. 1, 1963. GS: Gilbert Roland, Butch Patrick, Andrea Darvi, Patricia Huston, William Zuckert. Brazilian Don Pedro, the Emperor of Brazil, is accidentally deserted by his train at an isolated water stop. Then two imaginative youngsters take him prisoner.

43.272 Diamond Field Jack. Oct. 1, 1963. GS: Frank Sutton, Edward Binns, Don Hammer. Jack Davis is arrested for the murder of two sheep herders, but he seems more concerned about preserving his reputation as a gunman than saving his skin.

43.273 Deadly Decision. Oct. 8, 1963. GS: James Caan, Roger Mobley. A father decides between life and death for his outlaw son who is feared by townspeople for his temper.

43.274 The Man Who Died Twice. Oct. 8, 1963. GS: Don Collier, Robert J. Wilke, Chris Alcaide, Sue Randall. After peaceloving Jack Slade is nearly killed by a thief, he changes into a vengeful gunman.

43.275 The Holy Terror. Oct. 22, 1963. GS: Dick Foran, Penny Singleton, Sharon Farrell. Prospector Bill Franklin accidentally discovers a rich gold vein and names it after his wife, Holy Terror.

43.276 The Peacemaker. Oct. 29, 1963. GS: Don Haggerty, Richard Webb, David Brian. A cattle rancher orders the massacre of a peaceful Indian party which has crossed his ranch.

43.277 Three Minutes to Eternity. Dec. 11, 1963. GS: Forrest Tucker, Jim Davis, Tom Skerritt. The Dalton brothers stage a simultaneous robbery of two banks in Coffeyville, Kansas.

43.278 The Red Ghost of Eagle Creek. Dec. 29, 1963. GS: Paul Birch, Sarah Selby, Adrienne Hayes. A mysterious animal with tracks three times as large as a horse, starts attacking people on the Arizona frontier.

43.279 Graydon's Charge. Jan. 5, 1964. GS: Denver Pyle, Ken Curtis, Lyle Bettger, Cathy Lewis. Freighter Ortho Williams donates his partner's mules to the Union Army.

43.280 Little Cayuse. Jan. 7, 1964. GS: Ken Murray, Larry Damison, George Keymas, George Mitchell. Stagecoach depot manager Whipsaw McGee gives his Bowie knife to renegade Indians.

43.281 The Wooing of Perilous Pauline. Jan. 7, 1964. GS: Paula Raymond, Ray Danton, Ed Ryker. Pauline is being wooed by Jere Fryer, a newcomer to Arizona.

43.282 Sixty-Seven Miles of Gold. Jan. 14, 1964. GS: Gene Evans, James Best, Jack Albertson. Miner Winfield Stratton strikes gold, just after he options his mine to a syndicate.

43.283 The Paper Dynasty. March 1, 1964. GS: Barry Kelly, James Hampton, Lory Patrick, James Lamphier.

43.284 The Westside of Heaven. March 1, 1964. GS: Steve Cochran, Gilbert Green, Walter Brooke. Father Patrick Manogue, a miner turned priest, has as much trouble with his temper as he has with his parishioners.

43.285 Hastings Cut-off. March 3, 1964.

43.286 The Law of the Round Tent. March 3, 1964. GS: John Anderson, Walter Burke. Ex-convict George Kelsey becomes judge of the mining camp because he has the largest tent.

43.287 The Bigger They Are. March 10, 1964. GS: Dewey Martin, Strother Martin, Ron Soble, Gloria Talbott. Because John Wheeler has lost the will to live, he isn't afraid to take Arkie Monson's side in a fight with gunslinger Roy Beckett.

43.288 The Last Stagecoach Robbery. March 17, 1964. GS: Anne Francis, Jesse Pearson. Pearl Hart emigrates from Canada with one ambition — to commit the last stagecoach robbery in history.

43.289 A Book of Spanish Grammar. April 21, 1964. GS: David McLean, Rodolfo Acosta. Open hostility breaks out between Stephen Austin and his traveling companion.

43.290 Trial at Belle's Springs. April 21, 1964. GS: Ken Scott, Lynn Bari. Wyatt Earp's brother disguises himself as a bandit to gain access to a farm where outlaws are living.

43.291 After the O.K. Corral. April 28, 1964. GS: Jim Davis, John Clarke, Jeff Morris, Dan Stafford, Susan Seaforth, Billy Tannen, Stewart Bradley. The only survivors of the gunfight at the O.K. Corral are the Earp brothers and Doc Holliday.

43.292 The Quiet and the Fury. April 28, 1964. GS: Skip Homeier. Doc Holliday is forced to kill a man.

43.293 See the Elephant and Hear the Owl. April 28, 1964. GS: Steve Forrest, Roy Roberts, Sue Randall. A poor cowpoke loves the daughter of a powerful and haughty rancher.

43.294 The Streets of El Paso. May 5, 1964. GS: Marshall Thompson, Steve Ihnat. Mayor Ben Dowell sells the streets of El Paso to a saloon owner in an effort to raise money to clean up the town's water supply.

Season Thirteen

43.295 Honor the Name Dennis Driscoll. Oct. 1, 1964. GS: John Pickard, Don Haggerty, Tom Skerritt, Michael Keep. A recruit and his pet mule are the only hope for a Cavalry patrol.

43.296 The Lucky Cow. Oct. 1, 1964.

43.297 Big John and the Rainmaker. Oct. 1, 1964. GS: Denver Pyle, Jim Davis, Roy Engel, James Seay. Drought plagued ranchers feud over the services of a charlatan rainmaker named Feinmore Bleek.

43.298 From the Earth, a Heritage. Oct. 8, 1964. GS: John Alderson, Marianna Hill, Peter Whitney. Nat Halper wants to buy Joe Meek's Indian wife.

43.299 The Other White Man. Oct. 8, 1964. GS: James Edwards, Lisa Gaye, Rudolfo Acosta, Roy Engel, Valentine de Vargas, Don Haggerty. The Sioux warn all white men off treaty land, but one won't leave because he has found gold.

43.300 Hero of Fort Halleck. Oct. 9, 1964. GS: Annabel Garth, James Best, William Arvin, Michael T. Miller, Don Haggerty, Michael Keep, John Pickard. The presence of pretty Elsie Berringer stirs a rivalry between cowboy Jim Campbell and Lieutenant Harper.

43.301 The Left Hand Is Damned. Oct. 29, 1964. GS: Peter Haskell, Phyllis Coates, Judson Pratt, Stephen Roberts. In order to take vengeance on the man who crippled his right hand, Slim Kennedy learns to shoot with his left.

43.302 There Was Another Dalton Brother. Dec. 10, 1964. GS: Don Collier, Laura Shelton, William Zuckert, Robert Easton, Strother Martin. George Johnson doesn't approve of his daughter's romance with Frank Dalton, who has returned to his home town as a deputy U.S. Marshal.

43.303 *Tribute to the Dog.* Dec. 24, 1964. GS: Ronald Reagan, Carter Johnson, Danny Flower, Ralph Moody, William Zuckert, Kay Stewart, Walter Brooke. Lawyer George Vest, a candidate for the U.S. Senate, files suit against a man who recklessly shot a young boy's dog.

43.304 *The $25,000 Wager.* Dec. 24, 1964. GS: Hedley Mattingly, Diane Brewster, Charles Cooper, Harry Holcomb, Lew Brown. Does a running horse have all four feet off the ground? When a group of men bet on this, a young photographer begins a project which will decide the bet and create a new art form — movies.

43.305 *A Bargain Is for Keeping.* Dec. 30, 1964. GS: Robert Colbert, Sue Randall, Karl Swenson. A woman agrees to work for the owner of a trading post if he will return the harp her sister left in his store a year ago.

43.306 *Peter the Hunter.* Dec. 31, 1964. GS: Peter Whitney, Julie Sommars, Anthony Costello, Jenny Maxwell, Margaret Mason. A bear hunter and his three daughters help an injured young Easterner regain his health.

43.307 *Paid in Full.* Jan. 1, 1965. GS: Keith Andes, Michael Constantine, Aneta Corsaut, Gregg Palmer. A former Confederate officer tries to help the family of one of his late soldiers.

43.308 *A Bell for Volcano.* Jan. 11, 1965. GS: Jay Novello, Jean Willes, Russell Thorson, Dick Simmons, Robert Carricart. By the draw of a card, a petty thief is designated to go to San Francisco to purchase a new bell for the church in Volcano.

43.309 *The Trouble with Taxes.* Jan. 14, 1965. GS: Royal Dano, Alan Reed, Jr., Angela Clarke, Sheb Wooley, Joseph Sirola, Charles Fredericks. A man riding to the county seat to pay off a debt is pursued by robbers.

43.310 *The Race at Cherry Creek.* Jan. 20, 1965. GS: Jerome Courtland, Nancy Rennick, Walter Sande, Alvy Moore, Gene Roth. Two frontier editors compete to give Denver its first newspaper.

43.311 *Death in the Desert.* March 10, 1965. GS: David McLean, Don Megowan, Valentin de Vargas, Tom Nardini. After an Indian murders a mail rider, Dan Burgess demands that the tribe surrenders the guilty brave — or face the destruction of their village.

43.312 *Raid on the San Francico Mint.* March 10, 1965. GS: Ronald Reagan, Judson Pratt, Vaughn Taylor, John Clarke. Rumors of a gold reserve shortage threaten to cause financial panic in San Francisco.

43.313 *Magic Locket.* March 17, 1965. GS: June Lockhart, Kathy Garver, Sean McClory, Irene Tedrow, Dennis Robertson. Librarian Ina Coolbrith tries to encourage a young writer.

43.314 *The Battle of San Francisco Bay.* March 18, 1965. GS: Ronald Reagan, June Dayton, William Bramley, Hal Torey. As a young Navy captain, David Farragut is confronted by a vigilante mob that hs taken over San Francisco.

43.315 *The Wild West's Biggest Train Holdup.* March 18, 1965. GS: Charles Bateman, Roy Barcroft, Gilbert Green, Pat Priest. Deputy Jim Brand comes up with a plan to thwart a corrupt railroad lawyer.

43.316 *No Gun Behind His Badge.* March 25, 1965. GS: Ronald Reagan, Barry Kelley, Shary Marshall, Leo Gordon, Michael Witney. Bear River Smith tires to enforce the law in Abilene without a gun.

43.317 *The Fighting Sky Pilot.* March 25, 1965. GS: Skip Homeier, Carol Brewster, Sheldon Allman.

43.318 *The Journey.* March 29, 1965. GS: Wayne Rogers, Robert J. Wilke, Leonard Nimoy, Michael Keep, Steve Marlo, Coby Denton. Lt. Richard H. Pratt is transporting a group of captured Indian warriors to a stockade where they steal some rifles and escape.

43.319 *Kate Melville and the Law.* May 4, 1965. GS: Dick Foran, Gloria Talbott, Richard Anderson, Gregg Palmer, Rex Holman. After her father is jailed for contempt of court, Kate Melville takes over his job as sheriff.

43.320 *Birthright.* May 6, 1965. GS: R.G. Armstrong, Jason Evers, Susan Flannery. The citizens of the mining community of Rough and Ready vote to secede from the United States.

Season Fourteen

43.321 *Temporary Warden.* Sept. 30, 1965. GS: Ronald Reagan, George Murdoch, Charles Francisco, Rudolfo Acosta, Jim Bannon. A prison warden is determined to recapture three escaped convicts who have been terrorizing the state.

43.322 *The Captain Dick Mine.* Oct. 1, 1965. GS: Lisa Gaye, Gene Lyons, Steve Greavers, Dennis Cross. When a prospector is killed by claim-jumpers, his Indian wife plans revenge.

43.323 *The Lawless Have Laws.* Oct. 1, 1965. GS: Ronald Reagan, Tim McIntire, Shary Marshall. A Cavalry officer helps a bitter young man search for his sister.

43.324 *The Great Turkey War.* Oct. 7, 1965. GS: Parley Baer. Newspaper editor Horace Greeley goes on a crusade to bring law and order to Colorado.

43.325 *The Rider.* Oct. 7, 1965. GS: Jess Pearson, Lisa Gaye, John Reilly, Dennis Cross, Charles Briggs. A pretty widow decides to advertise for a husband.

43.326 *Traveling Trees.* Oct. 7, 1965. GS: Royal Dano, Robert Yuro, Tim McIntire. A Quaker farmer with a wagonload of appletree seedlings decides to leave the faster moving wagon train.

43.327 *No Place for a Lady.* Oct. 21, 1965. GS: Ronald Reagan, Linda Marsh, Simon Scott, Maidie Norman, Joel Fluellen. Susan Magoffin, accompanying her husband west, becomes the first woman to travel the perilous Santa Fe Trail.

43.328 *A City Is Born.* Oct. 22, 1965. GS: Ronald Reagan, James Seay, Jack Lambert, Oscar Beregi, June Lockhart, Tod Hunter. A stubborn ferry operator blocks mining engineer Charles Poston's efforts to get a loan.

43.329 *The Book.* Oct. 28, 1965. GS: Tom Skerritt, George Takei. A young miner uses astrological forecasts to break the bank at a gambling casino.

43.330 *Mrs. Romney and the Outlaws.* Dec. 23, 1965. GS: Rosemary De Camp, Willard Sage. Newspaper editor Caroline Romney launches a campaign against the outlaws terrorizing the town of Durango, Colorado.

43.331 *Dry Water Sailors.* Dec. 23, 1965. GS: Walter Brooks, Aneta Corsaut, Burt Douglas, Roy Engel, Ann Elder. Jason Howard Refuses to abandon his amphibious wagon when it bogs down in the Arizona desert.

43.332 *Devil's Gate.* Dec. 23, 1965.

43.333 *The Red Shawl.* Dec. 30, 1965. GS: Marietta

Death Valley Days

Hartley, Ken Scott, John Pickard, Roy Engel, Aneta Corsaut. Mormon emigrant Jessica Scott loses her baby while crossing a rough stream.

43.334 A Picture of a Lady. Dec. 30, 1965. GS: Peter Whitney, Francine York. Texas Judge Roy Bean names his town after a British actress whom he worships from afar.

43.335 Canary Harris vs. the Almighty. Dec. 30, 1965. GS: Rosemary De Camp, Gilbert Green, Robert Cornthwaite. A Colorado widow decides to sue God after meteorites destroy her front porch.

43.336 The Fastest Nun in the West. Jan. 20, 1966. GS: Julie Sommars, Michael Constantine, Don Haggerty, Willard Sage, John Clarke, Rex Holman, Michael Clarke. In the brawling frontier town of Trinidad, Colorado, Sister Blandina tries to stop a hanging.

43.337 The Fight San Francisco Never Forgot. March 17, 1966. GS: James Davison, John McLiam, Vicki Harrington, Scott Graham. James Corbett is a bank clerk who became heavyweight champion.

43.338 The Courtship of Carrie Huntington. March 17, 1966. GS: Sue Randall, Jess Pearson, Harry Holcomb, Herman Rudin, Bebe Kelly, Richard Gilder. A young freigh hauler, who married a wealthy girl by mistake, is given one week to court her before the marriage is annulled.

43.339 The Water Bringer. March 17, 1966. GS: Rory Calhoun, Lita Baron, Wil Kuluva. First Mate William Richardson, in San Francisco to get supplies, falls in love with the daughter of the Mexican commandante.

43.340 Crullers at Sundown! March 22, 1966. GS: Anthony Costello, Peter Whitney, Ann Elder, Ted de Corsia, Guy Wilkerson. A cowboy becomes an expert baker while competing for the daughter of the ranch boss.

43.341 Hugh Glass Meets the Bear. March 24, 1966. GS: John Alderson, Carl Reindel, Tris Coffin, Morgan Woodward, Victor French. In hostile Indian territory, a mountaineer is attacked by a bear and left for dead by his comrades.

43.342 The Firebrand. March 24, 1966. GS: Will Kuluva, Gerald Mohr, Arthur Batanides, Charles Cooper, Angela Clarke, Robert G. Anderson, Gregg Barton. Pio Pico, the last Mexican governor of California, fights to preserve peace in California.

43.343 The Hat That Huldah Wore. April 7, 1966. GS: Anna-Lisa, Carl Reindel, Tris Coffin, Laurence Haddon, Richard Gilden, Herman Rudin, Edgar Winston, Dub Taylor. Huldah Swanson is traveling west to meet her fiance with her $1000 dowry sewn in her hat.

43.344 The Four Dollar Law Suit. April 14, 1966. GS: Strother Martin, J. Pat O'Malley, Anthony Costello, Woodrow Parfrey. A law suit is brought against an insurance company by a farmer who claims he was cheated.

43.345 An Organ for Brother Brigham. April 28, 1966. GS: Hedley Mattingly, Morgan Woodward, Lew Brown, John Alderson, Byron Morrow. Carpenter Joseph Ridges insists on taking a pipe organ on the long trek to Salt Lake City.

43.346 Lady of the Plains. May 5, 1966. GS: Sherry Jackson, DeForest Kelley, Ken Mayer, Kathy Garver, Sherry O'Neil, Irene Tedrow, Howard Wright, Bobby Byles. A society lady takes over the wagon train when the wagonmaster is killed in an Indian raid.

Season Fifteen

43.347 The Day All Marriages Were Cancelled. Sept. 2, 1966. GS: Robert Taylor, Oscar Beregi, Willard Sage. The self-appointed mayor of Tucson is told that the marriages he has solemnized are all illegal.

43.348 The Solid Gold Cavity. Oct. 1, 1966. Paul Brinegar, Thomas Peters. A prospector finds a dentist who has been beaten and robbed by Mexican bandits.

43.349 The Resurrection of Deadwood Dick. Oct. 1, 1966. GS: Denver Pyle, Don Haggerty, Tol Avery, Hal Baylor, Winifred Coffin, Bern Hoffman, John Pickard. The mayor of Deadwood, South Dakota, comes up with a manufactured Western hero to lure tourists into his dying town.

43.350 Brute Angel. Oct. 5, 1966. GS: Robert J. Wilke, Sherwood Price, Jim Davis, Jean Engstrom, Bill Zuckert. A murderer draws attention to himself by bullying a livery stable owner.

43.351 Sense of Justice. Oct. 6, 1966. GS: Tom Skerritt, Tris Coffin. The warnings of San Diego mayor Josh Bean have no effect on his brother when the younger man gets involved in a rivarly over a pretty girl.

43.352 The Lady and the Sourdough. Oct. 8, 1966. GS: Paul Brinegar, Stanley Adams, Amzie Strickland, Fred Graham. A food loving miner offers a chef partnership in a mine in return for his culinary services.

43.353 The Kid from Hell's Kitchen. Oct. 20, 1966. GS: Robert Blake, John Alderson, Lane Bradford. The story of the friendship between the legendary outlaw Billy the Kid and English-born cattle-baron John Tunstall.

43.354 Samaritans, Mountain Style. Oct. 27, 1966. GS: Phillip Pine, Michael Pate, Dick Simmons. Two survivors of a massacre tell of losing their livestock to the Indians. Frontier scouts Kit Carson and French Gody try to regain the stolen livestock.

43.355 One Fast Injun. Dec. 21, 1966. GS: Don Collier, Diana Frothingham, Jan Clayton, Paul Fix. After an Indian attack, wounded Josiah Wilbarger is left for dead, but his friend Kate is sure he is alive. All she has to do is convince her father and the doctor that she knows where to find Josiah.

43.356 The Jolly Roger and Wells Fargo. Dec. 23, 1966. GS: Lloyd Bochner, Mark Anthony. Robert Lewis Stevenson is exploring a deserted mine with his son when they discover a Wells Fargo strong box.

43.357 The Hero of Apache Pass. Dec. 24, 1966. GS: Dub Taylor, Don Haggerty, Walter Burke, Joe Perry. A likeable old miner starts to lose all his friends when he starts winning bets.

43.358 The Gypsy. Dec. 28, 1966. GS: Lisa Gaye. Opportunist Monte Dunning decides to use the predictions of a gypsy fortune teller to intimidate his fellow miners.

43.359 A Calamity Called Jane. Dec. 29, 1966. GS: Fay Spain, Rhodes Reason, Ed Peck, Ron Doyle, Mike Wagner, Nancy Howard. Boisterous Calamity Jane joins Wild Bill Hickok in a Wild West show.

43.360 Doc Holliday's Gold Bard. Dec. 30, 1966. GS: Warren Stevens, Tol Avery, Jack Lambert. Doc Holliday, looking for some cash to finance his gambling, tries to con an eastern banker out of $20,000.

43.361 Silver Tombstone. Feb. 26, 1967. GS: Strother

Martin. Ed Schieffelin discovers the skeletons of two ambushed prospectors.

43.362 *The Man Who Didn't Want Gold.* March 1, 1967. GS: Hal Smith, Guy Wilkerson, Ken Del Conte. A wounded fugitive gives two prospectors a rich gold strike in return for aid and an alibi.

43.363 *Halo for a Badman.* March 2, 1967. GS: Robert Taylor, Don Megowan, Marion Ross, Roy Barcroft. Porter Stockton, a reformed gunman, is on the spot.

43.364 *A Wrangler's Last Ride.* March 3, 1967. GS: Robert Taylor, Don Megowan, Susan Brown. A dramatization of an incident from the life of Western artist Charles M. Russell.

43.365 *The Man Who Wouldn't Die.* March 4, 1967. GS: Patricia Huston, Jim Davis. Belle Monteverdi wants to help her outlaw brother, who was wounded in a stage robbery. She also wants to help the lawman she loves recover the loot.

43.366 *The Saga of Dr. Davis.* March 18, 1967. GS: Joby Baker, Mark Anthony, Judi Meredith. On her deathbed, Jenny Davis asks her magician-husband to take care of the 10-year-old orphan Tad, but the brokenhearted Davis decides to return the boy to the orphanage.

43.367 *Major Horace Bell.* April 26, 1967. GS: Robert Taylor, John Perry, Susan Hart, Lonnie Chapman. Major Horace Bell is a Los Angeles attorney who defends a man falsely accused of murder.

43.368 *The Day They Stole the Salamander.* April 28, 1967.

43.369 *Siege at Amelia's Kitchen.* May 3, 1967.

43.370 *Solid Foundation.* May 5, 1967.

43.371 *Along Came Mariana.* May 11, 1967. GS: Julie Parrish, Henry Beckman, Clyde Ventura, Carlos Romero, Arthur Peterson, E.J. Andre. Mariana Jaramilio is a peon with a passion for justice. She is determined to get the custom of servitude outlawed.

43.372 *A Man Called Abraham.* June 21, 1967. GS: Yaphet Kotto, Rayford Barnes, Ken Mayer. A missionary in Apache country engages in a philosophical battle with his captor, an escaped murderer.

Season Sixteen

43.373 *Shanghai Kelly's Birthday Party.* Oct. 7, 1967. GS: Robert Taylor, Mary Murphy, Robert Bice. Kelly is a saloonkeeper who kidnaps crewmen for sailing ships.

43.374 *Chicken Bill.* Oct. 14, 1967. GS: Dub Taylor, Don Haggerty, Jim Wainwright, Dick Simmons. A spiteful prospector tries to swindle a silver baron by selling him a salted mine.

43.375 *Let My People Go.* Oct. 21, 1967. GS: Michael Keep, Jay Novello, Ruben Moreno. An Indian leads his people in a revolt against tyrannical Spaniards.

43.376 *The Lone Grave.* Oct. 28, 1967. GS: Robert Taylor, Susan Brown, Kay Stewart. A farmer undertakes a lonely journey to deliver a headstone for his dead wife.

43.377 *The Girl Who Walked the West.* Nov. 4, 1967. GS: Angela Dorian/Victoria Vetri, Don Matheson. The story of Sacajawea, the Indian woman who helped explorers Lewis and Clark.

43.378 *The Informer Who Cried.* Nov. 11, 1967. GS: Mariette Hartley, Matt Clark, Tom Heaton, Gilbert Green, Bill Gwinn. A frontier nun faces rejection by the townspeople when she tries to help a wounded thief.

43.379 *Spring Rendezvous.* Nov. 18, 1967.

43.380 *Lost Sheep in Trinidad.* Dec. 30, 1967.

43.381 *The Saga of Sadie Orchard.* Jan. 13, 1968. GS: Patricia Huston, John Pickard. Sadie Orchard, the West's first freight-line driver, must get through with a silver shipment or she and her husband will lose their hauling contract.

43.382 *The Indian Girl.* Jan. 20, 1967. GS: James MacArthur, Gregg Palmer. Kit Carson is challenged by a renegade trapper for the hand of an Indian girl.

43.383 *Prince of the Oyster Pirates.* Jan. 28, 1967. GS: Dennis Whitcomb. Drama about the San Francisco waterfront, recreating an incident from the early life of author Jack London.

43.384 *The Friend.* Feb. 17, 1968. GS: Rudy Vallee; Robert Taylor.

43.385 *The Great Diamond Mines.* Feb. 23, 1968. GS: Gavin MacLeod, John Fiedler, Tod Andrews. Two prospectors pull a hoax banker, who wants the claim to their mine.

43.386 *Count Me In, Count Me Out.* Feb. 24, 1968.

43.387 *Dress for a Desert Girl.* March 1, 1968.

43.388 *Britta Goes Home.* March 2, 1968.

43.389 *Bread on the Desert.* March 2, 1968. GS: Richard Beymer, Mariette Hartley.

43.390 *Green Is the Color of Gold.* March 6, 1968.

43.391 *Out of the Valley of Death.* March 7, 1968. GS: Arch Johnson, Grace Lee Whitney, Cliff Norton, Bobby Byles, Joseph Mell. A trapper's short temper gets him into trouble, and out of it.

43.392 *The Gold Mine on Main Street.* March 15, 1968. GS: John Astin, Lita Baron, Dave Renard, Duane Grey. Jesse Martin stirs up everyone in town with his stories about a payload of gold lying right beneath Main Street.

43.393 *A Friend Indeed.* April 5, 1968.

43.394 *The Thirty-Calibre Town.* April 12, 1968.

43.395 *The Other Side of the Mountain.* April 13, 1968. GS: Royal Dano, Lisa Gaye, Chubby Johnson, Bella Bruck.

43.396 *By the Book.* May 10, 1968. GS: Jim Davis, Bing Russell, Lee Bergere, Harry Lauter, Douglas Fowley, Edward Colmans. Two members of a wagon train try to reach help before their group dies of starvation.

43.397 *The Pieces of the Puzzle.* May 11, 1968.

43.398 *Tall Heart, Short Temper.* May 17, 1968.

Season Seventeen

43.399 *The Secret of the Black Prince.* Sept. 28, 1968.

43.400 *The Leprechaun of Last Chance.* Sept. 28, 1968. GS: Denny Miller. A young Irish immigrant seeks his fortune, convinced that an old prospector is a leprechaun who will lead him to gold.

43.401 *Ton of Tin.* Sept. 28, 1968.

43.402 *The Sage Hen.* Oct. 1, 1968. GS: Collin Wilcox. Left alone while her husband is away, a clever wife defends herself against two blundering outlaws.

43.403 *The Other Cheek.* Oct. 4, 1968. GS: Robert Dunlap, Hal Baylor, Manuela Theiss, John Pickard. An easily intimidated cowhand seeks peace with his bullying foreman.

Death Valley Days

43.404 *A Mule, Like the Army's Mule.* Oct. 5, 1968.

43.405 *Lottie's Legacy.* Oct. 27, 1968. GS: Lisa Gaye, John Clarke. A schoolteacher engaged to a minister tries to hide the fact that she gambles.

43.406 *Lady with a Past.* Nov. 19, 1968. GS: Robert Taylor, Mariette Hartley, Brioni Farrell, Valerie De Camp. Dance-hall queen Tiger Lil tries to trade her fans and feathers for the quiet life.

43.407 *Short Cut Through Tombstone.* Nov. 22, 1968.

43.408 *Up the Chimney.* Nov. 30, 1968.

43.409 *The World's Greatest Swimming Horse.* Dec. 17, 1968. GS: Jess Pearson, J. Pat O'Malley, Janice Hansen, Christine Bancheri. Citizens of Los Angeles turn out in droves when a man comes to towon with a horse named Hippopotamus, and claims the pony will swim the Catalina Channel.

43.410 *The Day Millionaires.* Dec. 21, 1968.

43.411 *The Restless Man.* Jan. 2, 1969.

43.412 *A Gift.* Jan. 10, 1969.

43.413 *Solomon's Glory.* Jan. 17, 1969.

43.414 *The Understanding.* Jan. 28, 1969.

43.415 *Long Night at Fort Lonely.* Feb. 15, 1969.

43.416 *Here Stands Bailey.* Feb. 18, 1969.

43.417 *Angel of Tombstone.* March 8, 1969.

43.418 *A Full House.* March 14, 1969.

43.419 *How to Beat a Badman.* March 18, 1969.

43.420 *A Key for the Fort.* March 26, 1969.

43.421 *Dropout.* April 25, 1969.

43.422 *The Oldest Law.* May 2, 1969.

43.423 *Lucia Darling and the Ostrich.* May 11, 1969.

43.424 *Jimmy Dayton's Bonanza.* June 21, 1969.

Season Eighteen

43.425 *The Taming of Trudy Bell.* Oct. 2, 1969. GS: Valerie de Camp, Buck Taylor, Lew Brown, Bob Anderson, John Fox. A lumberjack refuses to indulge his boss' already pampered daughter.

43.426 *Tracy's Triumph.* Oct. 4, 1969. GS: Dale Robertson, Lisa Gaye, Richard Simmons, Roy Engel, Marshall Reed. The tale of a convict released from prison, but not from his past.

43.427 *Old Stape.* Oct. 4, 1969. GS: Don Haggerty, Eddie Firestone, Peggy Rea, John Pickard, Lew Brown.

43.428 *The Tenderfoot.* Oct. 9, 1969. GS: Kevin Burchett, Mitch Vogel, Erin Moran, Chubby Johnson, Ken Mayer. Orphaned, three children continue their dead parents' quest for California gold.

43.429 *Biscuits and Billy the Kid.* Oct. 10, 1969. GS: Ben Cooper, Emily Banks, Erin Moran, Valentin De Vargas, Ken Mayer.

43.430 *Son of Thunder.* Oct. 26, 1969. Gregg Palmer, Bing Russell, Ivalou Redd, Paul Sorensen, Clyde Howdy.

43.431 *The Lady Doctor.* Oct. 27, 1969. Maura McGivney, John Carter, Frank De Kova, Michael Keep.

43.432 *The Great Pinto Bean Gold Hunt.* Nov. 16, 1969. GS: Don Haggerty, Eddie Firestone, Paul Sorensen, Clyde Howdy, Michael Keep. Two gold prospectors find gold nuggets in a bag of purchased beans.

43.433 *The Visitor.* Nov. 17, 1969. GS: Eddie Little Sky, Ivalou Redd, Kevin Burchett, Mark Tapscott, Jana Redd. A peace-seeking Indian scout aids pioneers besieged by renegades.

43.434 *The King of Uvalde Road.* Jan. 1, 1970. GS: Dale Robertson, Robert Yuro, Brenda Benet, Pepe Callahan. A trouble-shooter must establish a U.S. mail route in bandit territory.

43.435 *The Mezcla Man.* Jan. 2, 1970. GS: Jess Pearson, Royal Dano, Karen Carlson, Roy Engel, Marshall Reed. Jess Ivy searches desperately for hidden gold. His pretty girl won't have him without it.

43.436 *Pioneer Pluck.* Jan. 3, 1970. GS: Irene Tedrow, Karen Carlson, Robert Zuckert, Roger Erwin. An outlaw finds more fire than fear in victim Granny Colvin.

43.437 *A Simple Question of Justice.* Jan. 12, 1970. Lane Bradford, Michael Margotta, Roy Dano, Murray McLeod, Veronica Cartwright.

43.438 *The Wizard of Aberdeen.* Jan. 17, 1970. GS: Conlan Carter, Beverlee McKinsey, William Zuckert, Robert Sorrells, Jennifer Edwards. This biographical tale of misadventure focuses on Frank Baum's penning of the "Wonderful World of Oz".

43.439 *The Dragon of Gold Hill.* Jan. 24, 1970. GS: Momo Yashina, Soon-Taik Oh, Bill Smith, Mark Jenkins, Frontis Chandler. Plague ridden ranchers pinpoint a Japanese settlement as the source of their affliction.

43.440 *The Biggest Little Post Office in the World.* Feb. 7, 1970. GS: Dale Robertson, Patrick O'Moore, Walter Brooke, Maria Desti, William Fawcett. A wily postmaster wheels and deals in stamps.

43.441 *A Saint of Travellers.* Feb. 14, 1970. GS: David McLean, Scott Graham, Jan Wilson, Ned Romero, Robert Ellenstein. Indians reject the doctrines of Christianity in this biographical tale of missionary priest Jean Baptiste Lamy.

43.442 *Talk to Me, Charley.* Feb. 15, 1970. GS: Sean McClory, Susan Brown, Lane Bradford, Phil Chambers.

43.443 *Amos and the Black Bull.* Feb. 28, 1970. GS: Anthony Caruso, Heidi Vaughn, Richard Bull, Steve Cory, Valentin De Vargas. A young cowboy and an Indian brave combine efforts to secure dowries for their respective sweethearts.

43.444 *The Man Who Planted Gold in California.* March 16, 1970. GS: Richard Angarola. A flamboyant San Diego sheriff schemes to gain an interest in California's wine industry.

43.445 *The Solid Gold Pie.* April 1, 1970. GS: John McLiam, June Dayton, Raymond Guth, Ted Gehring, George Neise.

43.446 *A Gift from Father Tapis.* April 7, 1970. GS: Ned Romero, David McLean, Joaquin Martinez, Reuben Moreno. Rampaging Indians threaten a mission.

43.447 *Clum's Constabulary.* April 9, 1970. GS: Sam Melville, Tris Coffin, William Gwinnn, James Seay, John Considine. Rookie Apache policemen try to solve the murder of a white settler before vigilantes raid their reservation.

43.448 *The Contract.* April 18, 1970. GS: William Smith, Richard Bull, Arlene McQuade, Don Megowan, Joe Perry. Outlaw-turned-lawman Hendry Brown is confronted by a tempting proposition.

43.449 *The Duke of Tombstone.* April 21, 1970. GS: Robert Colbert, Victoria Shaw, Bill Gwinn, Tris Coffin, Tom Peters.

43.450 *Early Candle Lighten.* April 24, 1970. GS: John McLiam, George Paulson, Ted Gehring, Raymond Griffith.

44. The Deputy

NBC. 30 min. Broadcast history: Saturday, 9:00-9:30, Sept. 1959–Sept. 1961.

Regular Cast: Henry Fonda (Marshal Simon Fry), Allen Case (Clay McCord), Betty Lou Keim (Fran McCord) 59-60, Read Morgan (Sergeant Hapgood Tasker) 60-61, Wallace Ford (Marshal Herk Lamson) 59-60.

Premise: This Western series depicted the exploits of Marshal Simon Fry in Silver City, Arizona, in the 1880s.

The Episodes

44.1 *The Deputy.* Sept. 12, 1959. GS: Robert J. Wilke, James Griffith, Steven Ritch, Quentin Sondergaard, Earl Hansen. Marshal Simon Fry is on the trail of two train robbers. He concocts a ruse to get his men, and tricks a young storekeeper into helping him carry it out.

44.2 *The Wild Wind.* Sept. 19, 1959. GS: Richard Shannon, John Ashley, Gary Vinson, Joel Colin. Marshal Fry encounters three teenagers who are under the influence of rustler Bull Ward. Suspecting that the boys are already implicated in the theft of some sheep, Fry nevertheless decides to entrust one of them with a gold shipment. But he has storekeeper Clay McCord watch over the youths.

44.3 *Back to Glory.* Sept. 26, 1959. GS: Frank De Kova, Marie Windsor, Carol Leigh, Jack Lambert. An escaped killer and his two confederates have escaped custody and gone separate ways. Marshal Fry sets out after the two henchmen, and old deputy marshal Herk Lamson gets storekeeper Clay McCord to help him track down the killer.

44.4 *Shadow of the Noose.* Oct. 3, 1959. GS: Clu Gulager, Denver Pyle, John McKee. Marshal Fry holds a prisoner whom an angry mob is anxious to lynch. Knowing that Fry must transport his prisoner to another town, the mob follows, waiting to surprise the marshal if he falls asleep.

44.5 *Powder Keg.* Oct. 10, 1959. GS: Onslow Stevens, Christopher Dark, Read Morgan, Ben Bigelow. Simon Fry has Lamson take Tom Deaver to Prescott to stand trial for supplying the Apaches with gunpowder. But Clay McCord learns that the Indians have been getting gunpowder from other sources.

44.6 *Like Father.* Oct. 17, 1959. GS: Fred Beir, James Westerfield, Tom Laughlin, Paul Engle, Mickey Simpson. Brad Vantage, son of Ches Vantage, arrives in town to become the new veterinarian. Clay McCord grows suspicious of a traveling gunman, fearing that Brad's life is in danger.

44.7 *Proof of Guilt.* Oct. 24, 1959. GS: Harry Stephens, Whitney Blake, Roy Barcroft, Mark Tapscott. Joe Carey, a reformed outlaw, comes back to Silver City and learns that his son has taken part in a gold robbery. Carey decides to take the blame himself.

44.8 *The Johnny Shanks Story.* Oct. 31, 1959. GS: Skip Homeier. Marshal Fry figures on trouble when three bounty hunters come to Silver City on the trail of con man Johnny Shanks. Fran McCord doesn't want her brother Clay involved with Fry's plans, so she gets Clay a job as a guide to some settlers who are leaving town.

44.9 *Focus of Doom.* Nov. 7, 1959. GS: Eduard Franz, Dennis Patrick, Vic Perrin. When the marshals of three neighboring towns are murdered, Chief Marshal Simon Fry moves to protect Silver City Marshal Herk Lamson by sending him on a vacation. Fry then sets himself up as a decoy for the killers.

44.10 *The Big Four.* Nov. 14, 1959. GS: Henry Brandon, Richard Bakalyan, Gerald Milton, Charles Fredericks. Clay McCord bumps into outlaws Curly Bill Brocius, Johnny Ringo, Billy the Kid and Ike Clanton. McCord joins them and tries to tip Chief Marshal Simon Fry to their plans.

44.11 *The Next Bullet.* Nov. 28, 1959. GS: Brad Weston. A note pinned to a murder victim marks Marshal Herk Lanson as the killer's next target. Chief Marshal Fry arrests the most likely suspect in town.

44.12 *The Deal.* Dec. 5, 1959. GS: Kelly Thordson, Mel Welles, Robert Osterloh, David Halper. Outlaws kidnap Fran McCord and force her brother Clay to agree to help them rob a mine payroll. Chief Marshal Fry suspects that Clay will go through with the deal to save his sister's life.

44.13 *Land Greed.* Dec. 12, 1959. GS: Vivian Vance. Widow Emma Gant approaches Chief Marshal Fry with evidence that she and her son Billy are being forced off their land. She claims that neighboring ranchers want her property.

44.14 *Man of Peace.* Dec. 19, 1959. GS: Robert Warwick, Edgar Buchanan. After Apaches steal some rifles, Simon Fry sends for the Army. Clay McCord believes that he can prevent war if he talks with the Apache chief.

44.15 *The Orphans.* Dec. 26, 1959. GS: Carol Kelly, Dennis Rush, Lane Bradford, Karl Lukas, Fred Sherman. Chief Marshal Fry plans to help three youngsters, orphaned by the murder of their parents, by raffling off a prize. Fry arranges to fix the raffle in order to bait a trap for the killers.

44.16 *Backfire.* Jan. 2, 1960. GS: Paula Raymond, Charles Cooper. Silver City Marshal Herk Lamson is forced to shoot an escaped convict in the back. The man's widow hires two gunmen to avenge the shooting, and Lamson finds that he has lost the townspeople's respect.

44.17 *Hang the Law.* Jan. 9, 1960. GS: Martha Hyer. Clay McCord is sentenced to hang for shooting a man in what witnesses claim was an unfair gun battle. Simon Fry concocts a desperate plan to prove McCord's innocence.

44.18 *Silent Gun.* Jan. 23, 1960. GS: Dean Fredericks, Marcia Henderson, Grandon Rhodes, Howard Wright, Herbert C. Lytton, James Parnell. A silent stranger comes to Silver City and allows his gun to do his talking. A few terrified citizens know the reason for the man's visit.

44.19 *The Hidden Motive.* Jan. 30, 1960. GS: Roxane Berard, Jeremy Slate, Charlie Briggs, Paul Sheriff. After Clay McCord is forced to kill a man in a gunfight, he attempts to console the man's widow by offering his services as a handyman on her ranch. But the widow misinterprets McCord's intentions.

44.20 *Lawman's Blood.* Feb. 6, 1960. GS: Phillip Pine, Willis Bouchey, Ronnie Burns. Dr. Landy, a Silver City physician, is kidnaped by outlaws and taken to treat their leader, who was shot by Marshal Fry. Deputy Clay McCord attempts a rescue.

44.21 *The Return of Simon Fry.* Feb. 13, 1960. GS: Stacy Keach, Hugh Sanders, Peter Mamakos, Larry Johns, Frank Richards. A hired gunslinger is killed when he tries to shoot down Simon Fry. The dead man is erroneously identified as Fry, and the marshal remains under cover to trap the killer.

44.22 *Queen Bea.* Feb. 20, 1960. GS: Phyllis Avery, Paul

The Deputy

Dubov, Kim Spalding. Protection racketeers move into Silver City. Their leader, Beatrice Vale, plans to ruin the small merchants so that she can set up a chain of stores in Arizona.

44.23 *The Two Faces of Bob Claxton.* Feb. 27, 1960. GS: Robert Montgomery, Jr., Bob Hopkins, Johnny Seven, Ron Soble. Teenager Bob Claxton is wounded and captured during a bank robbery attempt. Clay McCord and his sister Fran try to rehabilitate the youth.

44.24 *Lady with a Mission.* March 5, 1960. GS: Jan Clayton, Carleton Young, James Lanphier, Tod Griffin. A suffragette arrives in Silver City, but some of the local males are violently opposed to her campaign.

44.25 *The Border Between.* March 12, 1960. GS: Anna Kashfi, Leo Gordon, Laurie Mitchell, Steve Mitchell. Simon and Clay are held captive by a Mexican landowner whose daughter has eloped. The captor's terms are that Clay must find the girl or Simon will be killed.

44.26 *Final Payment.* March 19, 1960. GS: Gerald Mohr, Kevin Hagen, Mari Aldon, Charles Seel. A paralysis victim is out to get Clay and Fran McCord. He holds their father responsible for his condition.

44.27 *Dark Reward.* March 26, 1960. GS: Jean Willes, Richard Garland, John Dennis, Frances Morris. Local businessmen have a plan to put an end to bank robbers. They offer a reward for dead ones. So a gang of outlaws make dead bank robbers its specialty.

44.28 *Marked for Bounty.* April 2, 1960. GS: Ron Hayes, Alan Baxter, Edward Earle, Charles Seel, Raymond Hatton, Regis Toomey. Ralph Jenson escapes from prison to visit his dying father. But a bounty hunter plans to kill him and collect the reward.

44.29 *The Truly Yours.* April 9, 1960. GS: James Coburn, Miriam Colon, Adeline Pedroza, Anthony Caruso, Harry Townes, Arthur Batanides. Outlaws burn Clay McCord's store, then rob the bank. Infuriated, Clay decides to become a full-time deputy marshal.

44.30 *A Time to Sow.* April 23, 1960. GS: Richard Crenna, Coleen Gray, Frank Ferguson, Howard J. Negley, Dick Rich. Clay keeps a watchful eye out for a hired killer. He doesn't suspect that boyish Andy Willis could be the man he is looking for.

44.31 *Last Gunfight.* April 30, 1960. GS: Charles McGraw, Paul Clark, Robert Redford, Monica Lewis, Perry Ivins, Phil Tully. A self-confident young gunman thinks he can put the crowning touch on his reputation by luring a reformed gunfighter into a duel.

44.32 *The Chain of Action.* May 7, 1960. GS: Lee Patterson, Bek Nelson, Francis DeSales. Condemned to die, Lige Schofield stills refuses to tell where he hid the loot from a robbery. Part of the money was to be used for an operation to save a boy from blindness.

44.33 *Lucifer Urge.* May 14, 1960. GS: George Tobias, Nancy Valentine, James Bell, Vito Scotti, Ralph Moody. Barney Wagner rides into town and announces that he is the man who killed Clay McCord's father years before. Making himself more unpopular, he begins a legal fight to dispossess the Silver City ranchers.

44.34 *Palace of Chance.* May 21, 1960. GS: Karen Steele, Lee Van Cleef, Dennis Cross, Steve Brodie. A gambling hall comes to Silver City, bringing with it the girl friend of an outlaw. Thinking that her presence will bring the bandit to town, McCord refuses to stop the gambling.

44.35 *The X Game.* May 28, 1960. GS: John Hoyt, Howard Wendell, Tom McKee, Carlos Rivera, Don Gordon, Edward Foster. Two fast-talking cowpokes encourage an illiterate farmer to make his mark on a piece of paper. Too late, the farmer discovers that he has signed away his land.

44.36 *The Standoff.* June 11, 1960. GS: Alan Hale, Jr., Ann McCrea, Addison Richards, Vito Scotti. Simon Fry falls prey to a trap laid by an escaped criminal. Severely wounded, he just manages to reach Clay McCord's office before he collapses.

44.37 *Trail of Darkness.* June 18, 1960. GS: Donald Woods, Gregg Palmer, Vito Scotti, Clu Gulager, Addison Richards. Clay McCord captures a member of the Brainard gang and turns him over to Simon Fry for safekeeping. Fearful that the captive will talk, Brainard sends two henchmen into town to free him — or silence him.

44.38 *The Choice.* June 25, 1960. GS: Rex Holman, Vince Edwards, Chris Alcaide, Addison Richards. Dory Matson is back from jail, and lets it be known that he wants to reform. But the folks in town don't believe him.

44.39 *Ma Mack.* July 9, 1960. GS: Nina Varela, Jack Hogan, Douglas Kennedy. Ma Mack is an old friend of the family. So when she arrives in Silver City, Clay agrees to help her look for her son.

Season Two

44.40 *The Deadly Breed.* Sept. 24, 1960. GS: Susan Oliver, Lyle Bettger, Robert P. Lieb, Francis DeSales. A girl named Julie and a man named Aces Thompson are just a pair of petty swindlers. But Marshal Fry follows them to Silver City. Clay McCord wonders why his boss is taking such an interest in a routine matter.

44.41 *Meet Sergeant Tasker.* Oct. 1, 1960. GS: Joan O'Brien, Richard Cutting, Rayford Barnes, Phil Tully. Assigned to duty in Silver City, Sergeant Tasker is the victim of a trio of thieves. Simon and Clay try to stop him from reclaiming his cash by force.

44.42 *The Jason Harris Story.* Oct. 8, 1960. GS: Jeff Morrow, Dianne Foster, Myron Healey, Robert J. Stevenson. All the evidence seems to indicate that Marshal Harris has been tipping off stage robbers about the dates of gold shipments. Much as they regret it, Fry, McCord and Tasker have to confront their fellow lawman with the evidence.

44.43 *The Fatal Urge.* Oct. 15, 1960. GS: Kathleen Crowley, Ron Starr, Tony Young, Addison Richards, Argentina Brunetti. A wealthy man is killed in a holdup attempt, and Clay suspects Phil Jackson, the victims nephew. But Phil's sister Martha refuses to buy Clay's theory.

44.44 *Mother and Son.* Oct. 29, 1960. GS: James Franciscus, Josephine Hutchinson, Arthur Kendall, Robert Karnes, Pitt Herbert, Joe Yrigoyen. Outlaw William Stanhope is behind bars in Silver City, but his mother is coming from Boston to visit her beloved son.

44.45 *Bitter Root.* Nov. 5, 1960. GS: Virginia Gregg, Don Megowan, Zon Murray, Paul Sorensen. Fry, McCord and Tasker trail Tim Brandon, a wounded killer, to an isolated desert shack. They are met at the door by Hester Macklin, who says she kicked Tim off the land when he didn't have the money to buy water.

44.46 *The Higher Law.* Nov. 12, 1960. GS: H.M. Wynant, John Larch, Addison Richards, Lewis Martin. An Indian named Blackwing has been shot, but he refuses to tell McCord and Tasker who the gunman was. Blackwing doesn't believe in the white man's justice and wants and eye for an eye.

44.47 *Passage to New Orleans.* Nov. 19, 1960. GS: Patrice Wymore, Carl Benton Reid, George Douglas, Saul Gorss, Harvey Dunn. Clay is escorting pretty Lucy Ballance to New Orleans, where she is to appear as a murder witness. They no sooner board the riverboat than they are shot at from shore.

44.48 *The World Against Me.* Nov. 26, 1960. GS: Dennis Joel, Henry Rowland, Joseph Bassett, Harry Clexx, Fred Kruger. Young Tommy White's grandfather has been killed by bandits because he refused to tell them the location of his gold mine. Now they are after Tommy, and just about to catch him, when Sergeant Tasker rides up.

44.49 *Lady for a Hanging.* Dec. 3, 1960. GS: Fay Spain, William Fawcett, Don O'Kelly. Clay has to escort convicted murderess Sally Tornado to Yuma for hanging. Seems like a routine job, except that Sally rather likes Clay.

44.50 *Three Brothers.* Dec. 10, 1960. GS: Cathy Case, Jack Ging, Lew Gallo, Minga Mitchell, Carmen Phillips, Buzz Martin. Silver City has been plagued by a series of bank robberies, and McCord and Tasker are taking their sweet time about solving them. When violence erupts in the town, the boys wake up.

44.51 *Day of Fear.* Dec. 17, 1960. GS: Tyler McVey, Mary Tyler Moore, Robert Osterloh, Anne Barton. Clay brings a murderer into town. The outlaw has a fever, and the rumor spreads that he has smallpox.

44.52 *Second Cousin to the Czar.* Dec. 24, 1960. GS: Carl Esmond, George D. Wallace, Clancy Cooper, Phil Tully. Royalty comes to Silver City in the person of Dmitri, the Duke of Tiflis. And the Duke is a sporting fellow. He challenges Clay to a horse race.

44.53 *Judas Town.* Dec. 31, 1960. GS: Roy Roberts, Ed Nelson, Duane Cress, Ed Prentiss, Phil Tully, Dan White. Pete McCurdy has been arrested, and his father, a wealthy cattleman, offers Clay a bribe to free the boy. McCord refuses the deal, so McCurdy threatens to boycott Silver City's business enterprises.

44.54 *Duty Bound.* Jan. 7, 1961. GS: Frank Maxwell, Ron Harper, Pat McCaffrie, Joe Yrigoyen. Simon, Clay and Sarge are escorting a pair of murder suspects back to Silver City. One of them, Jay Elston, insists he isn't the man they want. But Mel Ricker, the other prisoner, insists that Elston was his partner.

44.55 *The Lesson.* Jan. 14, 1961. GS: Harry Lauter, Wanda Hendrix, Steven Darrell, Kevin O'Neal. Mary Willis has been teaching school in Silver City, and hiding from Lex Danton, her outlaw husband, at the same time. Then Danton shows up with his gang.

44.56 *Past and Present.* Jan. 21, 1961. GS: Arthur Franz, Murvyn Vye, Mary Beth Hughes, Vince Williams, Steven Peck. Bank clerk Herb Caldwell offers no resistance to outlaw Calico Bill, and permits him to escape during an attempted holdup. For this spineless demonstration, Caldwell gets thrown in jail.

44.57 *The Hard Decision.* Jan. 28, 1961. GS: Marc Lawrence, George Brenlin, Olan Soule, John Dennis, George Lynn. Murderer Jimmie Burke awaits execution in the Silver City jail, but his young brother Alvy is busy elsewhere. He takes Marshal Fry as a hostage.

44.58 *The Dream.* Feb. 4, 1961. GS: Dick Foran, Carolyn Craig, John McLaine, Mary Munday, Francis MacDonald. Clint Hammer returns to Silver City to accept the inheritance left by his father. Disappointed because the bequest isn't in cash, Clint decides to convert the holdings into wealth by firing loyal ranch hands and forcing the payment of old debts.

44.59 *The Shackled Town.* Feb. 11, 1961. GS: Robert Brubaker, Reed Hadley, Eugene Iglesias, Carla Alberghetti, Ralf Harolde. Fry arranges for Clay and Tasker to take a vacation. The boys are happy about having some time off in the town of Vista Grande, but they are soon thrown in jail.

44.60 *The Lonely Road.* Feb. 18, 1961. GS: Edward Binns, Constance Ford. Paroled convict Shad Billings returns to Silver City. Things are peaceful until he learns that his wife Meg has been unfaithful.

44.61 *The Challenger.* Feb. 25, 1961. GS: Hal Baylor, Stafford Repp, Paul Gilbert, Don Heitgert. Tasker learns that Clay is in financial difficulty, and he wants to help him. A traveling boxing champion named Titan is in town, so Tasker volunteers to go six rounds with him for $500.

44.62 *The Edge of Doubt.* March 4, 1961. GS: Richard Chamberlain, Floy Dean Smith, Bigelow C. Sayre, George Chandler, Tommy Jackson. Parolee Jerry Kirk travels to see his fiancee Annie Jenner in Silver City. Will Jenner, Annie's father, opposes the marriage, and a short time later he is found dead.

44.63 *Two-way Deal.* March 11, 1961. GS: Billy Gray, Ted De Corsia, Kenneth MacDonald, Nacho Galindo. Slade Blatner brings in a young outlaw and is anxious to collect the reward. The outlaw is Blatner's son Johnny.

44.64 *The Means and the End.* March 18, 1961. GS: Phyllis Love, DeForest Kelley, Justice Watson, Robert E. Griffin, Richard Warren, Don Heitgert. Outlaw Josie Styles is in jail awaiting trial. The main witness against her is murdered, and Fry suspects that Josie's husband is the killer.

44.65 *The Example.* March 25, 1961. GS: Denver Pyle, Jack Chaplain, Ricky Sorensen, Reedy Talton, Robert C. Ross. Deputy Clay McCord succeeds in putting outlaw Frank Barton behind bars — but only because Barton wants it that way. The outlaw has become alarmed at his son's desire to emulate him.

44.66 *Chechez la Femme.* April 1, 1961. GS: Lisa Montell, Phil Tully, Edward C. Platt. A rough character starts pestering pretty Rosaria Martinez, and Sarge steps in to protect her. But when Tasker accidentally kills the man and is charged with murder, he finds that Rosaria, his alibi, has disappeared.

44.67 *Tension Point.* April 8, 1961. GS: John Marley, Jerome Thor, Virginia Christine, William Stevens, Donald Losby, Bern Hoffman. Fry is visiting Zeb Baker and his family when three desperadoes burst into the cabin. Fry conceals his identity, knowing harm may come to the Bakers if the men recognize him as a marshal.

44.68 *Brother in Arms.* April 15, 1961. GS: Lon Chaney, Jr., Denny Miller, Bill Hale. Bill Jason, a boy who grew up with Clay McCord, returns to Silver City, and brings with him a killer's reputation.

44.69 *The Return of Widow Brown.* April 22, 1961. GS: Norma Crane, Richard Shannon, Dennis Holmes. Amelia

Brown's outlaw husband stashed some loot away before he was killed, and now everyone thinks Amelia knows where it is. Clay believes she is innocent, but to clear her name he will have to find the money.

44.70 Spoken in Silence. April 29, 1961. GS: Robert Burton, Frances Helm, Sydney Pollack, Hal K. Dawson. Mike Rogers needs money for an operation on his deaf-mute daughter, Laura. In a deal to get it, he agrees to help fugitive Chuck Johnson elude Marshal Fry.

44.71 Enemy of the Town. May 6, 1961. GS: Whit Bissell, Ray Kellogg, Stephen Roberts. A new tannery brings added prosperity to Silver City until Clay closes it down when it appears that it is polluting the water supply. The deputy is besieged by angry citizens who demand that he reopen the place.

44.72 The Legend of Dixie. May 20, 1961. GS: Gregory Walcott, Stanley Adams, Harry Fleer, King Calder. Silver City's leading ne'er-do-well, Dixie Miller, is found standing with his drawn gun beside the bodies of a pair of fugitive bandits. The happy citizens eagerly proclaim Dixie a hero.

44.73 The Deathly Quiet. May 27, 1961. GS: Johnny Cash, Robert Foulk, Michael Garrett, Chubby Johnson. Bo Braddock and Con Hawkins trade the Army life for lives of crime, with the aid of some high-powered Gatling guns. The pickings are pretty good around Silver City, especially since Fry and McCord's six-guns are no match for the Gatlings.

44.74 Brand of Honesty. June 10, 1961. GS: George Dolenz, Elisha Cook, Jr., J. Edward McKinley, Robert Osterloh, Norman Willis. Ramon Ortega and his sidekick Miller are supposed to have gone straight. But there is a strong feeling in the town that the two former crooks are behind a recent series of robberies.

44.75 Lorinda Belle. June 24, 1961. GS: Claude Akins, Frank Overton, Andy Albin. No one like brutish Jason Getty very much and someone hates him enough to have slipped him some poison. Getty learns he has only two days to live, and vows to find his assassin in the time that is left.

44.76 Lawman's Conscience. July 1, 1961. GS: Russell Johnson, Tracey Roberts, Jason Robards, Sr., Jerry LaZarre, Roy Wright. On his deathbed, rancher Rufus Hayden confesses to the murder for which Albee Beckett was sentenced to life imprisonment. Then Beckett comes home, with a chip on his shoulder.

45. Desperado

NBC. 120 min. Broadcast history: Various, April 1987–Dec. 1989.

Regular Cast: Alex McArthur (Duell McCall).
Premise: This series of tele-films depicted the adventures of loner Duell McCall on a quest to clear his name in the old West.

The Tele-films

45.1 Desperado. April 27, 1987. GS: Lise Cutter, David Warner, Yaphet Kotto, Robert Vaughn, Donald Moffat, Sydney Walsh, Pernell Roberts, Dirk Blocker, Gladys Knight. Duell McCall teams with a homesteader's spirited daughter to challenge a pack of land-grabbers.

45.2 The Return of Desperado. Feb. 15, 1988. GS: Robert Foxworth, Billy Dee Williams, Marcy Walker, Victor Love, Vanessa Bell, Charles Boswell, J. Jay Saunders. Duell McCall, now with a price on his head, runs afoul of a land grabber in New Mexico.

45.3 Desperado: Avalanche at Devil's Ridge. May 24, 1988. GS: Lise Cutter, Alic Adair, Hoyt Axton, Rod Steiger, Dwier Brown, Lee Paul. Duell McCall escapes hanging by agreeing to lead a posse after the kidnaped daughter of a wealthy rancher.

45.4 Desperado: The Outlaw Wars. Oct. 10, 1989. GS: Lise Cutter, Richard Farnsworth, Whip Hubley, Brad Dourif, James Remar, Deon Richmond, Brion James, Buck Taylor. Duell McCall becomes involved with a feud between warring outlaw factions.

45.5 Desperado: Badlands Justice. Dec. 17, 1989. GS: John Rhys-Davies, James B. Sikking, Gregory Sierra, Robert O'Reilly, Patricia Charbonneau. Duell McCall's quest to clear his name is side-tracked when he encounters corruption in a mining town.

46. Destry

ABC. 60 min. Broadcast history: Friday, 7:30-8:30, Feb. 1964–Sept. 1964.

Regular Cast: John Gavin (Harrison Destry).
Premise: The series, set in the 1860s, depicted the adventures of Harrison Destry, the peace-loving son of a famed lawman, who searches the west in an attempt to clear his name of a bogus robbery charge.

The Episodes

46.1 The Solid Gold Girl. Feb. 14, 1964. GS: Neville Brand, Tammy Grimes, Broderick Crawford, Claude Akins, Ken Mayer, Don Haggerty, William Fawcett. Robber Johnny Washburn is about to be hanged, and the townsfolk are sure he told Destry where he hid his loot.

46.2 Destry Had a Little Lamb. Feb. 21, 1964. GS: Fess Parker, David White, Lee Van Cleef, Barbara Stuart, Dabbs Greer, Edward Faulkner, Olan Soule, Max Wagner. Destry sets out to track down the man who framed him. He gets sidetracked as he meets a man named Clarence and the two of them, against Destry's better judgment, head off to clean up the town of Slipknot.

46.3 Law and Order Day. Feb. 28, 1964. GS: Una Merkel, Elisha Cook, Jr., Jerome Cowan, Ben Gage, Warren Kemmerling, Ken Drake, Ken Mayer. It is Law and Order Day in Waybuck, and elderly bank teller Granny Farrell celebrates it by stuffing her knitting bag with money and heading for the railroad station.

46.4 Stormy Is a Lady. March 6, 1964. GS: Janet Blair, Eileen Chesis, John Hoyt, Robert Cornthwaite, Myron Healey, Charles Macaulay. Eight-year-old Stormy has been brought up as a saloonkeeper's daughter.

46.5 The Nicest Girl in Gomorrah. March 13, 1964. GS: Albert Salmi, Patricia Barry, Marie Windsor, John McGiver, Richard Hale, Gage Clarke. A dying prospector names Destry executor of his will, which provides a jar of gold dust for the most deserving person in town.

46.6 *Big Deal at Little River.* March 20, 1964. GS: Katherine Crawford, Richard Devon, Frank Albertson, Stuart Randall, Mauritz Hugo, John Mitchum, Rush Williams. Melinda Carter clears Destry of a robbery charge and then asks him to be her escort while she tries out her system for beating the odds at a local gambling house.

46.7 *Go Away, Little Sheba.* March 27, 1964. GS: Joyce Bulifant, James Best, Paul Birch, Med Flory, Don Wilbanks, George Murdock, Brad Weston, Boyd Red Morgan. Impulsive Sheba Hannibal, aware that her enraged father will hang the man with whom she planned to elope, decides to protect him by claiming that Destry was the groom.

46.8 *Deputy for a Day.* April 3, 1954. GS: John Abbott, J. Pat O'Malley, Charles Ruggles, John Fiedler, Olive Sturgess, El Brendel, Ken Lynch, Arte Johnson. When Destry accepts a $50-a-day lawman's job, he is interested in the money, with nary a though given to coping with badmen, such as the two mayhem-minded jailbreakers now heading for town.

46.9 *Ride to Rio Verde.* April 1, 1964. GS: Lawrence Dobkin, Charles McGraw, Angela Dorian, John Alonzo, Chris Alcaide, Dal Jenkins. In a flashback, Destry recalls how he got a job with a photographer, and then hunted down the bank robbers who killed his employer.

46.10 *Blood Brother-in-Law.* April 17, 1964. GS: Shary Marshall, Ron Hayes, Paul Newlan, James McMullan, Frank Ferguson, Ellen Corby, Burt Mustin, Jack Searl, Cal Bolder, Warren Vanders, Nesdon Booth. After receiving a transfusion from Jethro Jellico, Destry automatically gets involved in a blood feud.

46.11 *Red Brady's Kid.* April 24, 1964. GS: Charles Drake, Roger Mobley, John Milford, William Bramley. Outlaw Red Brady's kid is 13-year-old Toby, who shows his contempt for the law by holding off a posse while his dad escapes.

46.12 *The Infernal Triangle.* May 1, 1964. GS: John Astin, Marlyn Mason, Conlan Carter, Tom Reese, Arthur Malet, Richard Bull, Carmen Phillips. A triangle begins when a bachelor friend hires Destry to protect him from a young woman with just one thing on her mind—marriage.

46.13 *One Hundred Bibles.* May 8, 1964. GS: Susan Oliver, Torin Thatcher, Gary Walberg, Chet Stratton, Jerry Campeau, Ratna Assan. Destry delivers one hundred bibles to a preacher who is planning to convert the hostile Comanches, secure in the belief that the Indians won't harm a hair on his head.

47. *Dirty Sally*

CBS. 30 min. Friday, 8:00-8:30, Jan. 1974–July 1974.

Regular Cast: Jeanette Nolan (Sally Fergus), Dack Rambo (Cyrus Pike).

Premise: This series concerned the adventures of hard-drinking Sally Fergus and her companion, the young ex-gunfighter Cyrus Pike as the duo head west to the California gold fields.

The Episodes

47.1 *Right of Way.* Jan. 11, 1974. GS: John McIntire, Scott Brady, Michele Carey, Irwin Charone, Bernard Fox, Jon Locke, Glen Vernon. Sally tries to protect a seedy pig farmer from a land-grabbing railroad baron.

47.2 *Title Unknown.* Jan. 18, 974. GS: Vincent Van Patten, Patti Cohoon. A family of five kids are struggling to run a farm on their own, and that isn't easy when their only mule is at death's door.

47.3 *The Old Soldier.* Jan. 25, 1974. GS: Gene Evans, Roger Bowen, Francine York. A retired cavalry sergeant has been drowning his blues in booze ever since the Army turned him out to pasture.

47.4 *Title Unknown.* Feb. 1, 1974. GS: Billy Green Bush, Millie Perkins, Mills Watson, Tara Talboy, Allen Price. A runaway convict strikes a bargain with Sally and Pike. He will let them turn him in for a reward if they will give him the chance to visit his expectant wife.

47.5 *Title Unknown.* Feb. 8, 1974. GS: Denver Pyle, Jon Lormer. Pike tries to outfox a sly old rancher in a horse trading deal.

47.6 *Title Unknown.* Feb. 15, 1974. GS: John J. Fox.

47.7 *Title Unknown.* Feb. 22, 1974. GS: Sarah Kennedy, Jack Collins. A distressed maiden wraps gullible Pike around her little finger. Sally, on the other hand, is suspicious of the girl, all the more because she openly admits that she's a cheat.

47.8 *Title Unknown.* March 8, 1974. GS: Beulah Bondi. A blind old woman is living for the return of her grandson from the Army, and he is already long overdue.

47.9 *Wimmen's Rights.* March 15, 1974. GS: Anthony Caruso, Ken Swofford, Maudie Prickett, Madeleine Adams, Bern Hoffman. Sally starts a war for women's right after being ejected from a men-only saloon.

47.10 *Title Unknown.* March 22, 1974. GS: Paul Stevens, Doreen Lang, Woodrow Chambliss, Gaye Nelson. A critically ill preacher, afraid that he is dying, asks Sally to carry a confession to his flock: he was never ordained as a minister.

47.11 *My Fair Laddie.* March 29, 1974. GS: Annette O'Toole, Robert Totten, Ric Carrott, David Barton. Playing Pygmalion, Sally tries to transform a tomboyish young farm girl into an attractive young lady.

47.12 *The Hanging of Cyrus Pike.* April 5, 1974. GS: Jackie Coogan, John Fiedler, Thelma Pelish. Sally must prove that Pike was framed of a horse-stealing charge before he is hanged.

47.13 *Title Unknown.* April 12, 1974. GS: Harold Gould, Julie Cobb, Virginia Baker, John Harmon. While preparing for his acting debut in a melodrama, Pike grows so conceited that Sally wonders how she ever will cure the ham.

47.14 *Title Unknown.* April 19, 1974. GS: Kathleen Cody, David Huddleston, George Keymas, Nicholas Hammond. Sally, pretending that she is the mother of Billy the Kid, plans to teach a few lessons to a gang of crooked poker players.

48. *Dr. Quinn, Medicine Woman*

1993–. CBS. 60 min. Broadcast history: Saturday, 8:00-9:00, Jan. 1993–Current.

Regular Cast: Jane Seymour (Dr. Michaela "Mike" Quinn), Jim Knobeloch (Jake Slicker), Joe Lando (Byron Sully), Chad Allen (Matthew Cooper), Erika Flores (Colleen Cooper)

Dr. Quinn, Medicine Woman

93–94, Jessica Bowman (Colleen Cooper) 94–, Shawn Toovey (Brian Cooper), Geoffrey Lower (Rev. Johnson), Orson Bean (Loren Bray), Frank Collison (Horace), William Shockley (Hank), Jonelle Allen (Grace), Helen Udy (Myra), Barbara Babcock (Dorothy Jennings), Gail Strickland (Olive Davis), Larry Sellers (Cloud Dancing), Andrea Bakkum (Alice), Melissa Flores (Missy), Jennifer Youngs (Ingrid), Henry G. Sanders 94–, Jason Leland Adams (Preston A. Lodge III) 95–.

Premise: Michaela "Mike" Quinn is a doctor from Boston sets up a medical practice in the Colorado Territory in the late 1860s.

The Episodes

48.1 *Dr. Quinn, Medicine Woman.* Jan. 1, 1993. GS: Diana Ladd, Colm Meaney, Guy Boyd, Verna Bloom, Adrian Sparks, Ivory Ocean, Larry Sellers, Heidi Kozak. Dr. Quinn gets off to a rocky start in Colorado Springs, where some folks don't like the notion of having a woman as the town doctor.

48.2 *Epidemic.* Jan. 2, 1993. GS: Taylor Nichols, Ashley Jones. Mike works feverishly against an influenza epidemic that isolates the town and causes panic among the townspeople.

48.3 *The Visitor.* Jan. 9, 1993. GS: Jane Wyman, George Furth. Mike's estranged mother Elizabeth visits from Boston, but she and Mike are still miles apart. Meanwhile, Robert E is seriously injured in a fire, and Mike may lose her clinic to foreclosure.

48.4 *Law of the Land.* Jan. 16, 1993. GS: Johnny Cash, Christopher Keene Kelly, Jeremy Brown, David Brooks, Endre Hules, Byron Hayes, Steven Hack. Kid Cole is a retired gunslinger looking for a quiet town to hang up his guns, but Colorado Springs is itching to lynch a young Swedish immigrant for cattle rustling and Cole gets involved.

48.5 *The Healing.* Jan. 23, 1993. GS: Heidi Kozak, Christopher Kriesa, Haylie Johnson. While coping with a potentially fatal hernia, Loren decides to cause Sully some pain by vindictively seeking to take away his homestead.

48.6 *Father's Day.* Jan. 30, 1993. GS: Ben Murphy, Deka Beaudine, Terrence McNally, Haylie Johnson. As Dr. Quinn struggles to persuade the townspeople that smallpox vaccinations are necessary, the father of her adopted children arrives in town. Meanwhile, Sully tries to learn how to ride a horse.

48.7 *Bad Water.* Feb. 6, 1994. GS: Michael Cavanaugh, Jared Rushton, R. Leo Schreiber, Michael Shamus Wiles. Mike and Sully meander up a creek to get a water sample near a mining baron's gold mill, which Mike believes is poisoning the water supply.

48.8 *Great American Medicine Show.* Feb. 13, 1993. GS: Robert Culp, Pato Hoffman, Seth Dillon, Jack Ray Stevens, Christopher Kriesa. Mike doesn't buy the sales pitch of an exploitative medicine-show man, especially when she is facing a real medical crisis involving Myra.

48.9 *A Cowboy's Lullaby.* Feb. 20, 1993. GS: John Schneider, Scotch Beverley, Charles Gunning, Kort Falkenberg, Elizabeth Reilly. A cowpoke reaches the end of his rope trying to care for his ailing infant, so he leaves the baby in the care of Mike.

48.10 *Progress.* Feb. 27, 1993. GS: Andrew Prine, Don Stroud, James Burdoff. An unscrupulous businessman tries to buffalo the townsfolk into selling their property to make way for the railroad, while Sully physically pays a big price for railing against bison hunters.

48.11 *The Prisoner.* March 13, 1993. GS: Andrew Prine, Darren Dalton, Tim DeZarn, Donn Berdahl, Jon Spradley, Joe Sikorra. A sinister General Custer intends to execute Cheyenne medicine man Cloud Dancing, but Sully and Mike have a plan to save the Indian. Meanwhile, Matthew has his eye on a potential dance partner.

48.12 *Happy Birthday.* March 27, 1993. GS: Christopher Kriesa, Teddy Haggerty, Tom Summers, John Fountain. Mike's loneliness surfaces as her birthday approaches, and Jake goes on a binge after his negligence leads to the death of a barbershop customer.

48.13 *Rite of Passage.* April 10, 1993. GS: James Encinas. Matthew is intent on proving to Mike that he is an adult when Dr. Quinn forbids him to pursue his plans to marry Ingrid.

48.14 *Heroes.* May 1, 1993. GS: David Tom, Tantoo Cardinal, Larisa Oleynik, Juney Smith. Colleen, with her mind filled with dime romances, gets a crush on Sully after he saves her from a runaway wagon. But her plan to have him rescue her again puts her in real peril. Meanwhile, Hank bellyaches about Grace's restaurant when he feels ill, putting her business in jeopardy.

48.15 *The Operation.* May 8, 1993. When Brian suffers a serious head injury and complications arise, the strain takes an emotional toll on Mike and the townspeople.

48.16 *The Secret.* May 15, 1993. GS: Joseph Gordon-Levitt, Matthew Speare, Jack Verbois, Thomas Rosales. Mike draws out the dark secrets about the developmentally disabled boy she finds hiding in a deceased patient's house, but the boy's artistic talents are exhibited to Brian.

48.17 *Portraits.* May 22, 1993. GS: Kenny Rogers, Heidi Kozak, Cathy Worthington, Jeff Ramsey, John Sexton, Rosemary Murphy. Mike discovers that a former Civil War photographer is battling severe diabetes and the loss of his sight.

Season Two

48.18 *The Race.* Sept. 25, 1993. GS: Jerry Hardin, Tantoo Cardinal, Blake Gibbons. Mike is eager to ride in a horse race, but she is thrown when she learns that women aren't allowed. She is also rebuffed by another doctor over her efforts to diagnose an injured rider.

48.19 *Sanctuary.* Oct. 2, 1993. GS: Tantoo Cardinal, Wayne Grace, Gary Herschberger. Loren's sister-in-law escapes from her abusive husband and finds a sensitive advocate in Mike.

48.20 *Halloween.* Oct. 30, 1993. GS: David Tom, Megan Gallivan, Tom Poston, Richard Lindheim. On Halloween, the town is spooked by a man who appears to be dead, disappears and then shows up again. Meanwhile, Brian suspects that Dorothy is a witch and Mike is haunted by the spirit of Sully's deceased wife.

48.21 *The Incident.* Nov. 6, 1993. GS: Pato Hoffman, Eric Balfour. Sully and Mike search for the truth about a hunting accident involving Jake and the death of a Cheyenne brave, which makes for tension between the town and Indians seeking justice.

48.22 *Saving Souls.* Nov. 13, 1993. GS: Johnny Cash, June Carter Cash, Heath Kizzier, Robert Keith. Ailing gunsling

Kid Cole meets a spirited faith healer, whose fire and brimstone gets a cold reception from Dr. Quinn. Meanwhile, Grace and Robert E plan to marry, but some in the town propose they look somewhere other than the church to hold the ceremony.

48.23 *Where the Heart Is.* Nov. 20, 1993. GS: Georgann Johnson, Alley Mills, Elinor Donahue, Anne Lockhart, Nancy Youngblut, Richard Herd, Edward Albert, David St. James, Pamela Kosh, Kathleen Tipton, Jessica Dollarhide. Mike returns to Boston on learning that her mother is ill. Her mother's stuffy doctor thinks she has cancer, but Mike concludes that she actually has hepatitis, and with the support of the doctor's partner, Dr. William Burke, Dr. Quinn administers a Cheyenne remedy. Meanwhile, Sully follows Mike to Boston, where he finds her becoming more at home, escpeially with Dr. Burke.

48.24 *Giving Thanks.* Nov. 27, 1993. Thanksgiving goodwill dries up in the drought-stricken town. Mike and Sully begin to cultivate their relationship by searching for common ground.

48.25 *Best Friends.* Dec. 4, 1993. GS: Thomas Ian Nicholas, Haylie Johnson. Dorothy shows symptoms of menopause, with complications, and the first blush of romance is on the cheek of Colleen, who is smitten with a boy who is also liked by her new best friend.

48.26 *Sully's Choice.* Dec. 11, 1993. GS: Tim DeZarn, Will Egan, Eric Briant Wells. While Mike is away treating an influenza outbreak in another town, Sully ends up with a bullet in his back and a bounty on his head after trying to quell violence between renegade Indians and the Cavalry.

48.27 *Mike's Dream — A Christmas Tale.* Dec. 18, 1993. GS: Diane Ladd, Brendan Burns, Sarah Kim Heinberg, Jeff Weatherford, Ron Melendez, Pamela Kosh, Paul Sand. On Christmas Eve Mike tends to a pregnant young woman during a long labor. The ghost of Charlotte Cooper appears and escorts Mike on a tour of Christmases past, present and future.

48.28 *Crossing the Line.* Jan. 1, 1994. GS: Peter Jason, Rodney Saulsberry, Christopher Keene Kelly, Stephen Posner, Edward Rote. Willing to take a risk to earn money, Matthew puts himself in jeopardy when he crosses the picket line of miners striking over unsafe working conditions.

48.29 *The Offering.* Jan. 8, 1994. GS: Tantoo Cardinal, Nick Ramus, John Reger, John Glenn Bishop, Brien Varady, Zahn McClarnon. Mike is wrapped up in a medical and emotional crisis when blankets she encourages the Cheyenne to accept from the Army prove to have been infected with typhus.

48.30 *The Circus.* Jan. 15, 1994. GS: Fionnula Flanagan, Lisa Rieffel, Katie Canty. The circus comes to town in the form of a whimsical woman and her adopted daughter, who invite the townsfolk to show off their talents in a little show.

48.31 *Another Woman.* Jan. 22, 1994. GS: Sheryl Lee, Tim DeZarn. A white woman who was raised by Indians finds a kindred spirit in Sully. Meanwhile, Loren is dispirited over Dorothy's attraction to Jake.

48.32 *Orphan Train.* Jan. 29, 1994. GS: Tar Subkoff, Thomas Leon Chaney, Aaron Michael Metchik, Shannon MacPherson, Blumen Young, Lyndsey Fields, Bob Swain. Mike works closely with several orphans who come to town, leaving Brian, Colleen and Matthew feeling neglected. Meanwhile, Myra's concerned when Hank has a business proposition for an orphaned girl.

48.33 *Buffalo Soldiers.* Feb. 5, 1994. GS: Dorian Harewood, Spencer Garrett, Keith Cameron, Sabrina Wiener. Mike makes room at the clinic for some buffalo soldiers before learning that they were involved in a massacre. But close quarters prove advantageous when Cloud Dancing asks her and Sully to spy on the men to prevent more bloodshed.

48.34 *Luck of the Draw.* March 5, 1994. GS: Craig Wasson, Alex Zonn. Matthew needs money, and bets he can get it by learing high-stakes poker from a card sharp. Meanwhile, Brian is upset with Loren for keeping an eagle in a cage at the store.

48.35 *Life and Death.* March 12, 1994. GS: Matthew Letscher. Dorothy is happy to welcome home her war-hero son Tom, but his ongoing battle with morphine addiction leads to a violent incident involving Mike and the family.

48.36 *The First Circle.* March 26, 1994. GS: George Furth. Racial hatred flares up and the Ku Klux Klan comes calling when Robert E and Grace buy a home in town.

48.37 *Just One Lullaby.* April 9, 1994. GS: Sherry Hursey, Christopher Masterson, Eric Balfour, Lyndsey Fields, Nancy Gilmour, Bob Swain, Jerry Giles, Ross Malinger, Haylie Johnson. Rev. Johnson is in love with the town's new schoolteacher, while Mike is concerned about the woman's wanton use of corporal punishment in the classroom.

48.38 *The Abduction.* April 30, 1994. GS: Jason Leland Adams, Tim DeZarn, Zahn McClarndon, Jeff O'Haco, Jules Desjarlais, Mary Rings. Mike's refusal to cover up an attack on an Army detachment by Cheyenne dog soldiers brings the wrath of the renegades down on the town.

48.39 *The Campaign.* May 7, 1994. GS: Kaye Kattrell, Steve Blackwood, J. Marvin Campbell, Dawn Hudson, John Naehrlich. Mike runs against Jake for mayor, and the election becomes a referendum on women's rights.

48.40 *The Man in the Moon.* May 14, 1994. GS: Jesse Dillon Miller, Susan Bambara. When Myra decides to leave the business, Hank is injured in a violent tirade. But when Hank lapses into a coma, Myra is the only one who seems to care.

48.41 *Return Engagement.* May 21, 1994. GS: Maxwell Caulfield. Horace and Myra plan their wedding day, and Mike happily accepts Sully's marriage proposal. But then Mike realizes the true identity of a visiting naturalist — he is her former fiance David, whom she presumed had been killed in the war.

Season Three

48.42 *The Train.* Sept. 24, 1994. GS: Allan Royal, Eric Michael Zee, Larry Sellers, Philip Persons, John Petlock, Ted Hayden, Melissa Flores. Mike favors the railroad coming to Clorado, but Sully doesn't, and the issue derails their relationship.

48.43 *Fathers and Sons.* Oct. 1, 1994. Feeling old, Loren leaves town to look for adventure in Bolivia. Meanwhile, Brian begins his journey into puberty and becomes curious about girls.

48.44 *The Cattle Drive* Part One. Oct. 8, 1994. GS: Casper Van Dien. Loren's sister Olive has died, and her cattle are bequeathed to Matthew, who takes the reins as trail boss to drive the doggies back to Colorado Springs.

48.45 *The Cattle Drive* Part Two. Oct. 15, 1994. GS: Casper Van Dien. Matthew resists Sully's advice as he struggles to bring the cattle home to Colorado Springs.

48.46 *The Library.* Oct. 22, 1994. Mike donates her father's book collection to start a town library, but Rev. Johnson has moral objections to some of the volumes.

48.47 *Halloween II.* Oct. 29, 1994. GS: Richard Moll. Brian befriends a disfigured man who is viewed by the townspeople as a monster, and Mike offers her surgical expertise to help him.

48.48 *The Washington Affair.* Nov. 5, 1994. GS: Dennis Lipscomb, Nicholas Pryor, Kathleen Lloyd, Gregory Sierra. Mike and the family are joined by Sully and Cloud Dancing on a mission to Washington, D.C., to lobby Congress on behalf of the Cheyenne.

48.49 *Money Trouble.* Nov. 12, 1994. GS: Joel Brooks. Sully can't afford to meet the expenses on the new house, but Mike can — and that causes a problem. Meanwhile, Myra begins sleepwalking.

48.50 *Thanksgiving.* Nov. 19, 1994. GS: Johnny Cash, June Carter Cash, Pepper Sweeney, Kristin Davis, Vince Melocchi. Mike and Sully meet newlyweds Kid Cole and Sister Ruth in Denver and ask them to return home with them for Thanksgiving. But on the way back their stagecoach is robbed in Dog Soldier territory.

48.51 *Ladies Night* Part One. Nov. 26, 1994. GS: Patrick St. Espirit, Tracy Fraim, Mary Rings. Mike detects a possible cancerous lump in Dorothy's breast, but Dorothy resists Mike's advice to have it treated.

48.52 *Ladies Night* Part Two. Dec. 3, 1994. GS: Patrick St. Espirit, Tracy Fraim, Mary Fings. Dorothy insists that the decision whether to have breast cancer surgery is hers, not Mike's.

48.53 *A First Christmas.* Dec. 10, 1994. GS: Trisha Yearwood, Bruce Nozick, Bari Hochwald, J.D. Daniels. A Jewish-immigrant family arrives in town at Christmastime, bringing their own seasonal traditions and competition for Loren's dry-goods business.

48.54 *The Indian Agent.* Jan. 7, 1995. GS: James Sloyan, Nick Ramus. Sully is sworn in as an Indian Agent, but his sincere efforts on behalf of the Cheyenne are undercut by bureaucratic corruption that leaves the tribe without food or supplies.

48.55 *The End of the World.* Jan. 14, 1995. A newspaper report of a comet's imminent collision with Earth causes hysteria in the town over the possible end of the world.

48.56 *Pike's Peak.* Jan. 28, 1995. GS: Eve Brenner. Mike finds a kindred spirit in a strong-willed Bostonian who is determined to scale Pike's Peak alone. Meanwhile, Grace acts bitterly toward Myra as Myra's due date approaches.

48.57 *Cooper vs. Quinn.* Feb. 4, 1995. GS: Ben Murphy, Kaitlin Hopkins. Mike and Sully decide to initiate a formal adoption of Colleen and Brian, but the kids' father and his young new wife challenge them for custody.

48.58 *What Is Love?* Feb. 11, 1995. Dorothy wants to stage Shakespeare's "Romeo and Juliet" for Valentine's Day. Meanwhile, Mike and Sully plan to celebrate the holiday together until Sully's job as an Indian Agent interferes.

48.59 *The Things My Father Never Gave Me.* Feb. 18, 1995. GS: Allan Royal, Eric Michael Zee, Ping Wu. In the most important job of his life, Robert E is hired to repair a steam engine to keep the construction of the railroad on track.

48.60 *Baby Outlaws.* Feb. 25, 1995. GS: Melissa Clayton, Ian Bohen, Donnie Jeffcoat. An ornery young woman is wounded while trying to rob the saloon. Mike offers to help her recuperate at the homestead, but Mike has never seen the likes of Belle Starr before.

48.61 *Bone of Contention.* March 11, 1995. GS: John Savage. A greedy paleontologist finds an excavation site that could yield a wealth of dinosaur fossils, but it is also a sacred Cheyenne burial ground.

48.62 *Permanence of Change.* April 8, 1995. GS: Doren Fein, Arthur Taxier. While filling in as a substitute teacher, Mike becomes aware that a new girl in school is being neglected and abused at home. Meanwhile, townsfolk are riled when Mike introduces the theory of evolution to the children.

48.63 *Washita.* April 29, 1995. GS: Jason Leland Adams, Larry Sellers, Nick Ramus, Tantoo Cardinal. Starvation among the Cheyenne hastens an increase in raids on settlers, and General Custer and his men arrive to quell the outbreak.

48.64 *Sully's Recovery.* May 6, 1995. Sully leaves town to resign from his position as Indian agent and, on the road, finds an injured Loren, who has been scouting for property in the former Cheyenne lands. Meanwhile, Brian is determined to build a flying machine.

48.65 *Ready or Not.* May 13, 1995. As their wedding day nears, Mike and Sully reflect on the ups and downs of their relationship.

48.66 *For Better or Worse.* May 20, 1995. GS: Georgann Johnson, Alley Mills, Elinor Donahue, Larry Sellers. Mike and Sully are ready to tie the knot, but not before they tie up some loose ends. They include Mike's frayed relationships with her mother and troubled sister, and Sully's imperiled bond with his best man.

Season Four

48.67 *A New Life.* Sept. 23, 1995. The newlyweds Mike and Sully must adust to life in a changing Colorado Springs where Bostonian Preston A. Lodge III establishes the town's first bank. Meanwhile, Sully's Cheyenne friend Cloud Dancing begins a new chapter when he agrees to move to a reservation.

48.68 *Travelling All Stars.* Sept. 30, 1995. GS: Joel Anderson, Johnny Moran. Colorado Springs fields a baseball team to play against a squad of touring professionals.

48.69 *Mothers and Daughters.* Oct. 7, 1995. GS: Johnny Moran, Haylie Johnson, Andrea Bakkum, R.J. Knoll. Mike is surprised by the depth of her passion for Sully. Meanwhile, Colleen becomes rebellious.

48.70 *Brother's Keeper.* Oct. 14, 1995. GS: Jennifer Youngs. Tragedy strikes when Brian's rabies-infected dog bites Matthew's fiancee, Ingrid.

48.71 *Halloween III.* Oct. 28, 1995. GS: Billy L. Sullivan, William Newman. As the town prepares for its annual Halloween celebration, a scary tale by a classmate spooks Brian. Meanwhile, an arthritic man seeks a cure in the hot sprigns, and Mike is afraid to tell him that any relief he might feel is psychological.

48.72 *Dorothy's Book.* Nov. 4, 1995. GS: John Valentine, Michael Rothhaar. Dorothy is thrilled by the publication of her book about the town, but the townsfolk, including Mike, read her depiction of them much differently than she intended.

48.73 *Promises, Promises.* Nov. 11, 1995. Loren proposes to Dorothy, but he suffers a stroke before she can give him her answer. Meanwhile, Sully is obliged to act upon an old friend's written request to help him set up a mining operation in Nevada.

48.74 *The Expedition.* Nov. 18, 1995. Mike guides Dorothy, Myra and Grace on a hiking expedition up Pike's Peak. Meanwhile back in town, Preston plots to build a hotel-casino with help from his partner Jake, and Robert E is bothered by an encounter with a bounty hunter.

48.75 *One Touch of Nature.* Nov. 25, 1995. GS: Richard Garon, Ingrid Beer, Edmund L. Shaffe. At Thanksgiving time, Mike faces the possibility that she might be infertile, while Jake struggles with the fact that he has no family to share the day with.

48.76 *Hell on Wheels.* Dec. 9, 1995. GS: Eric Michael Zee, John Doman, Kaz Garas. The family finds Matthew running a saloon at a railroad camp, where his grief over losing Ingrid drives him to volunteer for a dangerous blasting job.

48.77 *Fifi's First Christmas.* Dec. 16, 1995. GS: Susanna Thompson, Janna Michaels, Billy L. Sullivan. As Colorado Springs prepares for Christmas, the family receives a rambunctious toy poodle from Mike's mother in Boston, and Brian has a case of puppy love for a new girl in town.

48.78 *Change of Heart.* Jan. 6, 1996. GS: Brenden Jefferson, Charlotte Chatton, Suzanne Ventulett. Grace and Robert E take in an orphaned boy, who is afflicted with a strange malady Mike can't diagnose. Meanwhile, efforts are made to fix up Matthew with a new girl.

48.79 *Tin Star.* Jan. 13, 1996. GS: Travis Tritt, John Christian Graas, Bob McCracken. Increasing lawlessness in Colorado Springs sparks a demand for a new sheriff, and Matthew feels he is just the man for the job.

48.80 *If You Love Somebody.* Jan. 20, 1996. GS: Charlotte Chatton. Matthew falls for an independent young woman, but the fact that she is a prostitute complicates their blooming romance. Meanwhile, Preson offers Myra a job at the bank, but Horace opposes her taking it.

48.81 *The Iceman Cometh.* Jan. 27, 1996. GS: Brandon Douglas, Anthony Lee, Brenden Jefferson. Swindlers come to town seeking investors in a bogus home-refrigeration enterprise, which the townsfolk warmly receive.

48.82 *Dead or Alive* Part One. Feb. 3, 1996. GS: Lawrence Pressman, Jerry Hardin, Victoria Racimo, Denny Miller. The son of a politician who favors statehood for Colorado is kidnapped by a mountain man who opposes it, and Sully guides a posse to the high country to save the boy. Meanwhile, Mike suffers pregnancy complications.

48.83 *Dead or Alive* Part Two. Feb. 10, 1996. GS: Lawrence Pressman, Jerry Hardin, Victoria Racimo, Denny Miller. Matthew is taken hostage in the aftermath of a shootout with McBride, intensifying the hunt for the mountain man by Sully and Preston.

48.84 *Deal with the Devil.* Feb. 17, 1996. GS: Fred Rogers. Rev. Johnson's ministry mentor's imminent arrival leads the reverend to borrow money from devilish Hank to make repairs on the church.

48.85 *Eye for an Eye.* Feb. 24, 1996. GS: Geoffrey Blake, Charlotte Chatton, Paul Francis. An irredeemable murderer and rapist is sentenced to be hanged in Colorado Springs, and Mike has no objections to the execution.

48.86 *Hearts and Minds.* March 9, 1996. GS: Joseph Ashton. Rev. Johnson opens a school for Native American children on the reservation, but soon learns his methods don't mesh with tribal customs. Meanwhile, Dorothy negotiates with Preston about expanding her newspaper.

48.87 *Reunion.* March 23, 1996. GS: Christine Healy. Mike's college chum Miriam visits Colorado Springs, and their subtle rivalry is renewed. Meanwhile, Dorothy tries to get a handle on her new printing press.

48.88 *Woman of the Year.* April 6, 1996. GS: Bibi Besch, Gloria Le Roy, Haylie Johnson. A suffragist informs Mike that she is a Woman of the Year nominee. Meanwhile, Hank cleans up his act when his ailing grandmother visits.

48.89 *Last Chance.* April 13, 1996. GS: Charlotte Chatton, James Sloyan, Jeff O'Haco, Patrick Kilpatrick. Sully's method of handling conditions on the reservation displeases the Indian Superintendent. Meanwhile, Mike tends to Emma after she is injured by a rough customer.

48.90 *Fear Itself.* April 27, 1996. GS: Denise Crosby. An ebullient painter comes to town, where she tries to hide her unfortunate and misunderstood condition of having leprosy.

48.91 *One Nation.* May 4, 1996. GS: Patrick Kilpatrick. When Cloud Dancing takes the blame for shooting a soldier on the reservation, Sully insists he be tried by the Indians. However, Sgt. O'Connor thoroughly objects.

48.92 *When the Child Is Born* Part One. May 11, 1996. GS: Georgann Johnson, Alley Mills, Brandon Douglas, Patrick Kilpatrick. Mike's mother and sisters arrive, with a young doctor in tow, to help with Mike's imminent delivery. Meanwhile, the town prepares for the groundbreaking for Preston's health resort, and Sgt. O'Connor gets marching orders to move the Indians to different reservations.

48.93 *When a Child Is Born* Part Two. May 18, 1996. GS: Georgann Johnson, Alley Mills, Brandon Douglas, Patrick Kilpatrick. Mike and Cloud Dancing go deep into the woods, where they find Sully seriously wounded after his fight with Sgt. O'Connor. The sergeant manages to apprehend the wanted Cloud Dancing, and Mike, left alone in the forest with Sully, begins to have contractions.

Season Five

48.94 *Runaway Train.* Sept. 21, 1996. After negotiating Cloud Dancing's release from Army detention, Sully boards a homebound train with his friend, but robbers are also aboard. Meanwhile, Mike returns to work after maternity leave.

48.95 *Having It All.* Sept. 28, 1996. While Mike tries to juggle work and child-care responsibilities, Colleen prepares to leave town after she is accepted to college in Denver.

48.96 *Malpractice.* Oct. 5, 1996. GS: Joseph Dean Vachon, Michelle Joyner, Stacy Keach, Sr., Charlotte Chatton. A sick baby dies while under Mike's care, and the child's parents sue her for malpractice.

48.97 *All That Glitters.* Oct. 12, 1996. GS: Charlotte Chatton, Fred Applegate, Barbara Mandrell. Colleen returns from college in Denver in the company of Gilda St. Clair, a dazzling singing star who wows the town.

48.98 *Los Americanos.* Oct. 19, 1996. GS: Michelle Bonilla, S.J. Rio. Tragedy strikes Mexican-American newlyweds who purchase the ranch near the homestead, Robert E and

Grace consider formally adopting Anthony, and Mike and Sully must choose godparents for Katie.

48.99 *Last Dance.* Oct. 26, 1996. Sully is offered a job surveying the land in the new Yellowstone National Park, Matthew and Emma's relationship reaches a turning point, Dorothy asks Cloud Dancing if she can write a book about him, and Brian ponders how to ask a girl to the Sweetheart's Dance.

48.100 *Right or Wrong.* Nov. 2, 1996. While Jake and Preston campaign for mayor of Colorado Springs, Sully bravely elects, despite Mike's misgivings, to rescue a Pueblo Indian being held prisoner by the Army.

48.101 *Remember Me.* Nov. 9, 1996. GS: Ray Walston. An ailing, old gold miner turns out to be Jake's father, who abandoned his family years ago. Now, his memory is gone, but Jake remembers him, with bitterness. Meanwhile, Horace wishes to bury his past with Myra.

48.102 *Legend.* Nov. 16, 1996. GS: Willie Nelson. After a ruthless gang robs Preston's bank, Mike, Sully and Matthew team up with a legendary lawman to track down the bad guys. Meanwhile, Brian plays Cupid for Teresa and Jake.

48.103 *Tempest.* Nov. 23, 1996. GS: Jon Cypher. With a storm on the horizon, Mike's buffeted by news that Andrew's opening his own practice at Preston's hotel, and Preston's icy father blows into town for the resort's Thanksgiving Day opening.

48.104 *Separate But Equal.* Dec. 7, 1996. GS: Phillip Van Dyke, Pat Skipper. Grace and Robert E's efforts to enroll Anthony in the town school run into racial obstacles. Meanwhile, Jake and Hank compete with Preston for hotel customers.

48.105 *A Place to Die.* Dec. 14, 1996. GS: Brandon Douglas. A deadly outbreak is traced to Mike's clinic, and it threatens to destroy her medical practice. Meanwhile, Preston prescribes more business and less doctoring for Andrew.

48.106 *Season of Miracles.* Dec. 21, 1996. The joy of the Christmas season is diminished by Rev. Johnson's sudden blindness, a condition for which Mike can find no miraculous cure.

49. *Dundee and the Culhane*

1967. CBS. 60 min. Broadcast history: Wednesday, 10:00-11:00, Sept. 1967–Dec. 1967.

Regular Cast: John Mills (Dundee), Sean Garrison (the Culhane).

Premise: The series depicted the adventures of urbane British attorney Dundee and his apprentice lawyer, the Culhane, as they traveled the West in the late 19th century to aid the cause of justice.

The Episodes

49.1 *The Turn the Other Cheek Brief.* Sept. 6, 1967. GS: Warren Oates, John Drew Barrymore, Mark Allyson, Michael Constantine. Dundee and the Culhane travel to a Quaker community where outlaw Royal Bodie and his gang are extorting money from the farmers.

49.2 *The Vasquez Brief.* Sept. 13, 1967. GS: Donnelly Rhodes, Frank Silvera, Neil Burstyn, Angela Clarke, Benson Fong. In Mexico, Dundee depends on all of his legal wiles in an attempt to keep a client from being shot on the spot. Michael Vasquez is being tried for the inhuman acts committed by his late father, a brutal landowner.

49.3 *The Cat in the Bag Brief.* Sept. 20, 1967.

49.4 *The Murderer Stallion Brief.* Sept. 27, 1967. GS: Roy Poole, Walter Gregg, Eddie Firestone, Matt Clark. Dundee urges the people of a small town to stand up to tyrannical Zack Carson. To prove it can be done, Dundee defends an unusual client—a horse accused of killing Zack's son.

49.5 *The Dead Man's Brief.* Oct. 4, 1967. GS: David Canary, John McIntire, Sally Kellerman, Douglas V. Fowley, Don Keefer. An Army fort under Indian attack provides Dundee with the opportunity of re-opening a murder trial he has already lost.

49.6 *The Jubilee Raid Brief.* Oct. 18, 1967. GS: Simon Oakland, Evi Marandi, Julie Sommars, Tige Andrews, Dabney Coleman. More than one life is at stake as Dundee defends a client accused of murdering his own son. A bandit chieftain has sworn to wipe out the town if Dundee's client goes free.

49.7 *The 1000 Feet Deep Brief.* Oct. 25, 1967. Ralph Meeker, Michael Burns, Michael Pataki, Ingrid Pitt, Bing Russell, Jim Boles, Irene Tedrow, William Phipps, John Pickard. Dundee goes 1000 feet below ground to defend a mine owner whose men blame him for the death of seven miners. The proceeding is a grim ordeal for the lawyer, who once spent eight hours trapped in a cave-in.

49.8 *The Duelist Brief.* Nov. 1, 1967. GS: Louise Troy, Ed Baker, Carroll O'Connor. Dundee takes the case of a gentleman duelist being sued for $50,000 by his victim's wet-eyed widow. he lawyer's first mistake is thinking that he can prove the widow isn't a widow.

49.9 *The 3:10 to a Lynching Brief.* Nov. 8, 1967. GS: George Coulouris, Dub Taylor, Larry Perkins, Lonny Chapman, Joaquin Martinez. A poker game aboard a westbound train end in murder. Dundee is railroaded into defending the chief suspect, an Irish friend of Culhane's.

49.10 *The Death of a Warrior Brief.* Nov. 15, 1967. GS: John Anderson, James Dunn, Clyde Ventura, Maggie Thrett, Gus Trikonis. Dundee and the Culhane square off in a kangaroo court presided over by an old Indian chief. Dundee is the prosecutor as Culhane defends a prospector charged with murdering a brave.

49.11 *The Thy Brother's Keeper Brief.* Nov. 22, 1967. GS: William Windom, Mitch Vogel, Dallas McKennon. The death of a gold miner leads to acute discomfort for Dundee, who has been named legal guardian of the miner's young son. When the boy is kidnaped, the erudite attorney is forced into the unfamiliar role of gun-toting cowboy.

49.12 *The Widow's Weeds Brief.* Nov. 29, 1967. GS: Dana Wynter, Fred J. Scollay, William Campbell. Dundee battles small-town hostility and a politically ambitious sheriff as he tries to clear his client, a young woman charged with murdering her aged, and wealthy, husband.

49.13 *The Catch a Thief Brief.* Dec. 13, 1967. GS: Steve Ihnat, June Harding, Sam Melville. Culhane and bounty hunter Ben Murcheson chase a thief who pretended an interest in the banker's daughter—and got away with $175,000 from the bank's safe.

50. Dusty's Trail

Syndicated. 30 min. Broadcast history: Various, Fall 1973.

Regular Cast: Bob Denver (Dusty), Forrest Tucker (Mr. Callahan), Ivor Francis (Mr. Brookhaven), Lynn Wood (Mrs. Brookhaven), Jeannine Riley (Lulu McQueen), Lori Saunders (Betsy), Bill Cort (Andy).

Premise: This Western-comedy set in the 1880s depicted the comic adventures of a wagon train headed to California.

The Episodes

50.1 *Title Unknown.* Sept. 11, 1973. GS: Taylor Lacher, Dick Peabody. Dusty's toothache becomes a headache for all when a search for a dentist turns into a skirmish with outlaws.

50.2 *There Is Nothing Like a Dame.* Sept. 18, 1973. GS: Dennis Fimple, John Quade. Two cattle thieves try to rustle up some women.

50.3 *Lariat on the Loose.* Sept. 25, 1973. GS: Jim Gammon, Buck Young, Donald Barry. Dusty accidentally ropes a wild Appaloosa whose owner is hung up on hangings.

50.4 *Title Unknown.* Oct. 2, 1973. Dust's newly found treasure map brings out the worst in his friends — their greed.

50.5 *Title Unknown.* Oct. 9, 1973. GS: Reuben Moreno, Rudy Diaz. Brookhaven is ready to fight a duel when he comes to believe there is hanky-panky going on between his wife and Callahan.

50.6 *Title Unknown.* Oct. 16, 1973. GS: Janos Prohaska. The campsite's latest invader is an escapee from behind bars — a gorilla that broke away from his confining circus cage and master.

50.7 *Title Unknown.* Oct. 23, 1973. GS: Gary Vinson, Bob Phillips. Andy and Betsy are on a first aid mission with a wanted outlaw as the ailing victim.

50.8 *How Not to Be a Good Samaritan.* Oct. 30, 1973. GS: Eddie Little Sky, Ernesto Esparza III. The wagon train picks up an injured little Indian brave whose relatives are on the warpath.

50.9 *Title Unknown.* Nov. 6, 1973. GS: Ted Lehmann, Ed Bakey. When the group sees a wanted poster with a bearded Callahan as an outlaw they wonder if it is a lookalike coincidence or a good case of concealing the past.

50.10 *Title Unknown.* Nov. 13, 1973. GS: Ken Renard, Ivan Naranjo, Iron Eyes Cody. An Indian chief believes that his long lost son has finally come home when he spots a birthmark on Dusty and mistakes him for his missing offspring.

50.11 *Title Unknown.* Nov. 20, 1973. GS: Paul Wexler, Jim Burk. Dusty and Callahan are given the choice of getting married or getting shot when two gun-toting strangers seek husbands for their sisters.

50.12 *Title Unknown.* Nov. 27, 1973. A fugitive is loose in the campsite. He is wanted on several counts, including murder.

50.13 *Title Unknown.* Dec. 4, 1973. GS: Billy Barty, Cesare Danova. A traveling magician visits the wagon train and soon the Brookhavens' jewels disappear.

50.14 *Title Unknown.* Dec. 11, 1973. GS: Janos Prohaska, William Bryant. Dusty's latest friend is a grizzly bear who has followed him back to camp.

51. Empire

NBC. 60 min. Broadcast history: Tuesday, 8:30–9:30, Sept. 1962–Sept. 1963.

Regular Cast: Richard Egan (Jim Redigo), Terry Moore (Constance Garret), Anne Seymour (Lucia Garret), Ryan O'Neal (Tal Garret).

Premise: This Western centers on the industries which thrive on a vast modern ranch in New Mexico.

The Episodes

51.1 *The Day the Empire Stood Still.* Sept. 25, 1962. GS: Charles Bronson, Denver Pyle, Oliver McGowan, Paul Tripp, Vic Perrin. Ranch hand Paul Moreno is accused of killing the daughter of a co-worker. Redigo insists on standing by him despite the fact that the rest of the hands threaten to quit.

51.2 *Ballard Number One.* Oct. 2, 1962. GS: Ed Begley, George Matthews, Gilbert Green, Frederick Downs. The only man in the world that Redigo hates is Dan Ballard, whose embezzling sent Redigo's father to prison. Now after many years Ballard is back and he is digging for oil on property next to the Garret ranch.

51.3 *A Place to Put a Life.* Oct. 9, 1962. GS: Chris Robinson, James Griffith, Cathy Lewis, James Anderson. An argument with Tal serves to remind Redigo that the Garret spread is not his property. He returns to the small ranch his father left him to discover it is being farmed by teenager Arnold Koenig, who thinks he owns it.

51.4 *Ride to a Fall.* Oct. 16, 1962. GS: Victor Jory, Claude Akins. Milo Dahlbeck brings an uninvited guest, Joe Horvath, to a party at the ranch. Redigo notices that Dahlbeck is afraid of Horvath and wonders what hold he has over Dahlbeck.

51.5 *Long Past, Long Remembered.* Oct. 23, 1962. GS: Tom Tully, Richard Jordan, Paul Birch, Noah Keen, Michael Fox, Vincent St. Cyr. Wealthy rancher Tom Cole pays a friendly visit to the Garret spread during a severe drought. Redigo suspects that Cole is acting chummy because he wants to buy the ranch.

51.6 *Walk Like a King.* Oct. 30, 1962. GS: Ralph Meeker, Joanne Linville. When former employee Barney Swanton returns to the Garret ranch a rich man, he makes a great display of showing off his wealth. But Barney can't quit hide his jealousy of Redigo.

51.7 *The Fire Dancer.* Nov. 13, 1962. GS: Frank Gorshin, Roy Barcroft, Susan Silo, Jan Arvan, Kelly Thordsen, James Chandler. An oil well catches fire and Redigo can't find enough men to fight it. Then a young man named Billy Roy Fix appears and claims he will snuff out the fire for a fat fee.

51.8 *The Tall Shadow.* Nov. 20, 1962. GS: Bethel Leslie, Frank Overton, Mickey Sholdar, Ray Teal, Leo Gordon, Duane Grey. Facing the prospect of a forest fire during a severe drought, Redigo is anxiously awaiting the arrival of engineer Charles Pierce. Rumor has it that Pierce can find water even in a rock, but he is three days overdue.

51.9 *The Earth Mover.* Nov. 27, 1962. GS: Dan O'Herlihy, Linda Bennett, Eddy Waller, Max Showalter. The future seems bright for the town of Mesa when builder Glenn Kassin decides to construct a model industrial city nearby. But there is one piece of land Kassin can't get his hands on — homesteaders Abel Saunders refuses to sell.

51.10 *Pressure Lock.* Dec. 4, 1962. GS: Cathleen Nesbitt, Carolyn Kearney, Ford Rainey, Harvey Korman. In the midst of negotiating for the oil rights to Hettie Burton's land, Redigo is suddenly called out of town. This leaves Tal with the responsibility of carrying on the bargaining until Redigo returns.

51.11 *Echo of a Man.* Dec. 12, 1962. GS: John Dehner, Glenn Turnbull, Claire Griswold, Kelton Garwood, Wayne Heffley. Dan Tabor, chief engineer at the Garret ranch, is a good hand, but he has made a few mistakes of late. It may have something to do with worry over his pretty young ward Ellen, who is creating quite a stir.

51.12 *When the Gods Laugh.* Dec. 18, 1962. GS: James Gregory, Roger Mobley, James Maxwell. Sharecropper Theron Haskell doesn't want his son Kieran to get an education, and one morning he tries to stop him from going to school. The boy manages to reach his classroom, but Haskell follows him and threatens to beat him.

51.13 *Green, Green Hills.* Dec. 25, 1962. GS: Arthur O'Connell, Joanna Moore, Leonard Stone, Dayton Lummis. At the sight of the barren property they have just purchased, con artist Clayton Dodd and his daughter Althea realize that they have been cheated. But when Redigo offers to buy their land at a fair price, Dodd decides to hold out for more money.

51.14 *Stopover on the Way to the Moon.* Jan. 1, 1963. GS: Keir Dullea, Sharon Farrell, Mark Allen, Harold Gould, Armand Alzamora. Redigo takes young Skip Wade to court for damaging a chuck wagon at the Garret ranch. The pride and determination displayed by the young man convince Redigo that, with guidance, Skip could be made a useful citizen.

51.15 *The Four Thumbs Story.* Jan. 8, 1963. GS: Ray Danton, Rudy Solari, Barry Atwater, Don Diamond, George Gaynes, Joseph A. Vitale, Stuart Nisbet. A Navajo Indian named Four Thumbs served under Redigo during the Korean War and now he has become quite a problem. He is living in the past and refuses to get off the warpath, and he must be kept under restraint in a veterans' hospital.

51.16 *End of an Image.* Jan. 15, 1963. GS: Richard Jordan, Gail Kobe, Stefan Gierasch, Billy Mumy, Oliver McGowan, Nellie Burt, Leonard Stone, William Bryant, Dabbs Greer, Melora Conway. Jay Bee Fowler and Tal give a lift to Janet Rainey and her young son, who are leaving town, suitcase in hand. When Jay Bee pulls into a gas station, Janet first tries to hide from attendant Jack Morgan and, when he sees her, tells him that she is just out on a shopping trip.

51.17 *The Loner.* Jan. 22, 1963. GS: Jeremy Slate, Clarke Gordon, Warren Vanders, Allan Melvin, Michael Trekilis. Hoping to star his own ranch eventually, Mike Novak wants his choice of any mare on the Garret ranch, and he is willing to work until it is paid for. But the horse he picks is Tal's favorite.

51.18 *Where the Hawk Is Wheeling.* Jan. 29, 1963. GS: Robert Culp, Walter Burke, John Duke, Carlos Romero, Lew Brown, Michael Mikler, Arthur Marshall. When Tal balks at the strict rules Redigo has set up at the ranch, Connie explains to him why their mother chose Redigo as ranch foreman.

51.19 *No Small Wars.* Feb. 5, 1963. GS: Robert Vaughn, Walter Brooke, Otis Greene, Ronnie Knox, Jim Bowles, John McLiam, Stewart Bradley. On his way out of the hospital after an injury, Redigo meets an old friend, Capt. Paul Terman. Terman is in a wheelchair, his face contorted with pain, and he refuses to recognize Redigo.

51.20 *The Tiger Inside.* Feb. 12, 1963. GS: Harold J. Stone, Joyce Bulifant, Philip Abbott, Richard Evans, William Woodson, Dennis Patrick. Monte Clifford needs money, so he attacks and robs his boss Al Pope. Monte runs away with his girl Betty, unaware of the seriousness of Pope's injuries and the posse that is tracking him.

51.21 *Season of Growth.* Feb. 19, 1963. GS: Pat Conway, James Stapleton, Arch Johnson, Davy Davison, Frederic Downs, Nick Nicholson. When Dan Bishop, Connie's old flame, comes to the Garret spread, he expresses interest in her plan to mine potash on the ranch and also renews his romantic interest in her.

51.22 *Seven Days on Rough Street.* Feb. 26, 1963. GS: Frank Sutton, Clegg Hoyt, Suzi Carnell, Jerry Douglas, John Davis Chandler, Jack Searl. Tal claims that he can get along without his mother or Redigo, so Moreno takes him to the wide open town of Delgado and bets that he can't stay there for one week.

51.23 *A House in Order.* March 5, 1963. GS: Virginia Gregg, James Callahan, Oliver McGowan, Russell Thorson, James Doohan, Jason Johnson, Don Harvey. Lucia learns that she has a fatal disease and, before she dies, she is determined to establish a better working relationship between her son and Redigo.

51.24 *Down There, the World.* March 12, 1963. GS: Joanna Barnes, John Vivyan, Dayton Lummis, Oliver McGowan, Philip Ober, William Quinn, Bern Hoffman, Herb Armstrong, Ken Drake, Paul Fierro. The Garret mining operation shuts down when a vital processing plant falls into the hands of a beautiful enchantress who is determined to buy the Garret mine.

51.25 *Burnout.* March 19, 1963. GS: Gunnar Hellstrom, John Milford, Karen Steele, Joseph Gallison, Burt Douglas, Byron Morrow, Nancy Hadley. Forest Ranger Tom Barton has problems. The Garret logging operation is violating the timber contract with the Forest Service and logging foreman Chris Norden is a tough guy to deal with.

51.26 *Hidden Asset.* March 26, 1963. GS: Lon Chaney, Jr., William Windom, Barbara Bain, John Matthews, Willard Sage, Joseph Hoover. If he wants a bank loan, Redigo will have to cut the ranch's oversized payroll, but he hasn't reckoned with the opposition he will face from Tal and Moreno.

51.27 *Arrow in the Sky.* April 9, 1963. GS: Telly Savalas, Ilka Windish, Russell Johnson, Michael Davis, Don Diamond. Tibor, a former Hungarian freedom fighter, crosses the U.S.-Mexican border illegally and asks Moreno for work, believing that his wife is staying at the Garret ranch.

51.28 *Nobody Dies on Saturday* (A.K.A. "Breakout"). April 16, 1963. GS: William Schallert, Dean Stanton, Don Gordon, Jean Innes, Willard Sage, Jon Lormer, Jim Galante, Hugh Lawrence. Quinn Serrato and his pals stabbed a guard during their breakout from prison and now they are looking for Redigo, Quinn's former boss and the man who turned him in.

51.29 *Miles Is a Long, Long Way.* April 23, 1963. GS: Claude Akins, Jena Engstrom, Woodrow Parfrey, Ann Carroll, Hank Patterson, Robert J. Stevenson. Redigo and two other cattle owners are forced to drive their herds to market by a long route. A certain Mrs. Sangster is demanding too much money for the right to cross her property.

51.30 Duet for Eight Wheels. April 30, 1963. GS: Inger Stevens, Lawrence Dobkin, Noah Keen, Lauren Gilbert, Don Wilbanks, Gil Rankin. After he is trampled by a wild stallion, Redigo becomes paralyzed from the waist down and is confined to a wheelchair.

51.31 Between Friday and Monday. May 7, 1963. GS: Joan Hackett, William Mims, Naomi Stevens, Dort Clark, Maida Severn, Harvey Johnson, Peggy Adams. The day before Dolores Lanza is to begin life in a convent, she is stranded in a town filled with cowboys on a weekend spree.

51.32 The Convention. May 14, 1963. GS: Diane Brewster, Rudy Bond, Alan Hale, Jr., Anne Helm, L.Q. Jones, Jean Willes, William Bramley, Robert Anderson, Doye O'Del. Redigo has agreed to accompany Tal and Moreno to the convention on two conditions — Moreno must stay away from gambling and Tal must swear off women.

52. *F Troop*

ABC. 30 min. Broadcast history: Tuesday, 9:00-9:30, Sept. 1965–Aug. 1966; Thursday, 8:00-8:30, Sept. 1966–Aug. 1967.

Regular Cast: Ken Berry (Captain Wilton Parmenter), Forrest Tucker (Sergeant Morgan O'Rourke), Larry Storch (Corporal Randolph Agarn), Melody Patterson (Wrangler Jane), Edward Everett Horton (Roaring Chicken), Frank DeKova (Wild Eagle), James Hampton (Dobbs), Bob Steele (Duffy), Joe Brooks (Vanderbilt), John Mitchum (Hoffenmueller), Donald Diamond (Crazy Cat), Ivan Bell (Duddleson).

Premise: This Western situation comedy was set at Fort Courage in the days after the Civil War and depicted the antics of the bumbling Captain Parmenter and his troop of incompetent soldiers.

The Episodes

52.1 Scourge of the West. Sept. 14, 1965. GS: Alan Hewitt, Jay Sheffield, Barry Kelley. Private Parmenter is rewarded with the rank of captain and given command of Fort Courage.

52.2 Don't Look Now, One of Our Cannons Is Missing. Sept. 21, 1965. GS: Donald "Red" Barry. As a favor to his Indian friends, O'Rourke plans to smuggle a cannon out of the fort. His business associates want to borrow it for a festival.

52.3 The Phantom Major. Sept. 28, 1965. GS: Bernard Fox, John Holland, Willis Bouchey, Bella Bruck. Major Bentley-Royce of the Bengal Lancers has been dispatched to Fort Courage to teach the troopers his famed tactics of camouflage and infiltration.

52.4 Corporal Agarn's Farewell to the Troops. Oct. 5, 1965. GS: Forrest Lewis, Vic Tayback, Robert G. Anderson, Georgia Simmons, Buff Brady. Agarn gets his medical diagnosis mixed up with that of a horse and becomes convinced that he hasn't long to live.

52.5 The Return of Bald Eagle. Oct. 12, 1965. GS: Don Rickles. A renegade Indian tries to go straight, but finds it difficult.

52.6 Dirge for the Scourge. Oct. 19, 1965. GS: Jack Elam, Benny Baker, Harvey Perry. Parmenter is in serious trouble when he makes an enemy of Sam Urp, the fastest gun in the territory.

52.7 The Girl from Philadelphia. Oct. 26, 1965. GS: Linda Marshall. Jane and an Easterner vie for Captain Parmenter's affection.

52.8 Old Ironpants. Nov. 2, 1965. GS: John Stephenson. Sergeant O'Rourke, left in charge of Fort Courage while Parmenter attends command school, immediately embarks O'Rourke Enterprises on a new venture — selling mail-order brides.

52.9 Me Heap Big Injun. Nov. 9, 1965. Agarn's hitch is up in a week, and Captain Parmenter wants him to re-enlist, but Sergeant O'Rourke thinks Agarn would be more useful as a civilian.

52.10 She's Only a Built in a Girdled Cage. Nov. 16, 1965. GS: Patrice Wymore. Famous dancehall singer Laura Lee comes to Fort Courage to entertain the troops.

52.11 A Gift from the Chief. Nov. 23, 1965. GS: Mae Clarke. Captain Parmenter saves the Chief's life and is given a baby as a reward.

52.12 Honest Injun. Nov. 30, 1965. GS: John Dehner, Lou Wills. A con man muscles in on O'Rourke's enterprises.

52.13 O'Rourke vs. O'Reilly. Dec. 7, 1965. GS: Lee Meriwether. O'Rourke owns the only saloon within miles — until beautiful Lily O'Reilly decides to open one across the street.

52.14 The 86 Proof Spring. Dec. 14, 1965. GS: Parley Baer. Captain Parmenter launches a search for the Indian's whiskey supply.

52.15 Here Comes the Tribe. Dec. 21, 1965. GS: Laurie Sibbald. F Troop comes to the rescue when the Chief's daughter is kidnapped.

52.16 Iron Horse Go Home. Dec. 28, 1965. GS: Allyn Joslyn. The Hekawis sell their land and move into the fort in order to make room for the railroad.

52.17 Our Hero — What's His Name. Jan. 4, 1966. GS: Mike Mazurki, Jackie Joseph, William Woodson. Agarn has lost his girl friend to a horse-car conductor in the East, but O'Rourke thinks Agarn can win her back by telling her how he killed Geronimo.

52.18 Wrongo Starr and the Lady in Black. Jan. 11, 1966. GS: Henry Gibson, Sarah Marshall. Ill-starred is the word for the two newest arrivals at Fort Courage. Private Wrongo Starr, a well-known jinx, and Hermione Gooderly, whose four soldier husbands have all died under mysterious circumstances.

52.19 El Diablo. Jan. 18, 1966. GS: Hal England, Tony Martinez, Benny Baker. Corporal Agarn intends to clear the family name by personally capturing El Diablo, his notorious bandit cousin.

52.20 Go for Broke. Jan. 25, 1966. GS: George Gobel, Del Moore. The inspector general is due at the fort to check F Troop's pension fund, which O'Rourke has just gambled away.

52.21 The New I.G. Feb. 8, 1966. GS: Andrew Duggan, Ed Prentiss. Indian hating Major Chester Winchester plans to wipe out the friendly Hekawi Indians with the new rifle he has invented, the Chestwinster 76.

52.22 Spy, Counterspy, Counter Counterspy. Feb. 15,

1966. GS: Abbe Lane, Pat Harrington, Jr., William Woodson, Robert P. Lieb. Fort Courage is infiltrated by spies when F Troop is selected to test a secret bulletproof vest.

52.23 *The Courtship of Wrangler Jane.* Feb. 22, 1966. O'Rourke figures he could make more money from his illegal business enterprises if Captain Parmenter weren't around so much, so he plots to get the captain married off to Wrangler Jane.

52.24 *Play, Gypsy, Play.* March 1, 1966. GS: Zsa Zsa Gabor, Jackie Loughery, Angela Korens. Marika, a cunning Hungarian Gypsy, thinks she has found an easy source of revenue in Corporal Agarn.

52.25 *Reunion for O'Rourke.* March 8, 1966. GS: Ben Gage, Eve McVeagh, Marjorie Bennett, Richard Reeves. Captain Parmenter plans a reunion for the sergeant's old friends and throws a surprise party to celebrate O'Rourke's 25 years of military service.

52.26 *Captain Parmenter — One Man Army.* March 15, 1966. Because of a technicality, the men of F Troop aren't legally bound to remain in the Army, so they leave Captain Parmenter as the only defender of Fort Courage.

52.27 *Don't Ever Speak to Me Again.* March 22, 1966. F Troop is due to receive a citation for its high morale, but you would never guess it as everyone is feuding with just about everyone else.

52.28 *Too Many Cooks Spoil the Troop.* March 29, 1966. Although Corporal Agarn doesn't know beans about cooking, Sergeant O'Rourke makes him the company cook. O'Rourke plans to fatten his pocketbook by having Agarn pad the supply list.

52.29 *Indian Fever.* April 5, 1966. GS: Victor Jory, Lou Wills. Corporal Agarn reports seeing an Indian prowling around the fort at night.

52.30 *Johnny Eagle Eye.* April 12, 1966. GS: Paul Peterson, Cathy Lewis. O'Rourke plans to make a bundle betting on the young Indian sharpshooter he has entered as F Troop's representative in a marksmanship contest.

52.31 *A Fort's Best Friend Is Not a Mother.* April 19, 1966. GS: Jeanette Nolan. Captain Parmenter's bossy mother arrives for a visit and immediately begins telling Wilton how to run the fort.

52.32 *Lieutenant O'Rourke, Front and Center.* April 26, 1966. GS: James Gregory. Major Duncan wants to make Sergeant O'Rourke an officer, but the promotion would jeopardize O'Rourke's illegal business enterprises.

52.33 *The Day the Indians Won.* May 3, 1966. GS: Lou Krugman. As far as the Hekawis are concerned, a tomahawk is something to be sold as a souvenir, so the peace-loving braves are perplexed when the Council of Indian Nations orders them to go on the warpath.

52.34 *Will the Real Captain Try to Stand Up?* May 10, 1966. GS: Frank McHugh, Linda Foster, Benny Baker. Charlie, the town drunk, is down in the dumps. His daughter is coming to visit and she thinks her father is the commander of the fort.

Season Two

52.35 *The Singing Mountie.* Sept. 8, 1966. GS: Paul Lynde, Larry Storch. Corporal Agarn's cousin, a fur trapper named Lucky Pierre Agarniere, comes to the fort, followed by a Canadian Mountie who claims that Lucky Pierre is a notorious fur thief.

52.36 *How to Be F Troop Without Really Trying.* Sept. 15, 1966. GS: George Tyne, Les Brown, Jr. Corporal Agarn will be the only F Trooper left at Fort Courage unless Captain Parmenter can get Washington to rescind the transfer orders for himself and the rest of the men.

52.37 *Bye, Bye, Balloon.* Sept. 22, 1966. GS: Harvey Korman. F Troop may join the U.S. Balloon Corps. Col. Heinrich Von Zeppel, a stern Prussian balloonist, has arrived at the fort to inspect his prospective personnel.

52.38 *Reach for the Sky, Pardner.* Sept. 29, 1966. GS: Charles Lane, Paul Sorenson, Mary Young, George Barrows. The town banker has a good chance to repossess O'Rourke's saloon. O'Rourke's payroll has been stolen and his bank note is due.

52.39 *The Great Troop Robbery.* Oct. 6, 1966. GS: Milton Berle. Wise Owl, a medicine man specializing in psychiatry, tries to help Agarn after a bump on the head costs the corporal his memory.

52.40 *The West Goes Ghost.* Oct. 13, 1966. GS: Don Beddoe. Four F Troop stalwarts resign from the Army to homestead a ghost town. O'Rourke has them convinced that they will get rich quick when the railroad comes through.

52.41 *Yellow Bird.* Oct. 20, 1966. GS: Julie Newmar, Jacques Aubuchon. O'Rourke expects a handsome return on the money he paid Wild Eagle to locate a girl kidnaped years before by the Apaches since the girl's father is a mining tycoon.

52.42 *The Ballot of Corporal Agarn.* Oct. 27, 1966. GS: Tol Avery, Lew Parker, Luana Patten. Derby Dan McGurney, candidate in a tied election for mayor of Corporal Agarn's home town, carries his campaign to the Fort, and to his constituent, whose absentee ballot can break the deadlock.

52.43 *Did Your Father Come from Ireland?* Nov. 3, 1966. O'Rourke's father arrives from the Emerald Isle, and promptly turns Fort Courage into an Irish home away from home.

52.44 *For Whom the Bugle Tolls.* Nov. 10, 1966. GS: Richard X. Slattery. An inspector general who thinks a fort is only as good as its buglers is headed for Fort Courage, which is blessed with the world's worst bugler.

52.45 *Miss Parmenter.* Nov. 17, 1966. GS: Patty Regan, Dennis Troy. Captain Parmenter's aggressive, husband-hunting sister breezes into the fort, where she sets her sights on bugler Dobbs.

52.46 *La Dolce Courage.* Nov. 24, 1966. GS: Letitia Roman, Jay Novello, Joby Baker. Agarn once again demonstrates his uncanny ability to do something stupid. The Romeo of the Old West unwittingly comes between a beautiful Sicilian girl and her jealous suitor, who happens to belong to a secret terrorist society.

52.47 *Milton, the Kid.* Dec. 1, 1966. GS: Sterling Holloway, Tom Williams. A notorious crook called Kid Vicious is terrorizing the fort and the outlaw is a dead ringer for Captain Parmenter.

52.48 *The Return of Wrongo Starr.* Dec. 8, 1966. GS: Henry Gibson. The Fort Courage troopers are terrified by the return of Private Wrongo Starr, fastest jinx in the West. Wrongo just may blow the fort sky high as Captain Parmenter has ordered the foul-up to guard a load of dynamite.

52.49 *Survival of the Fittest.* Dec. 15, 1966. GS: George Furth. Parmenter and Agarn face death in the wilderness. The two F Troopers have been ordered to pass a survival test, armed only with a knife, canteen cups and a confusing Army manual.

52.50 *Bring on the Dancing Girls.* Dec. 22, 1966. GS: Peter Leeds. The F Troop foul-ups fight back when a smooth-talking blackmailer takes over O'Rourke's illegal saloon.

52.51 *The Loco Brothers.* Dec. 29, 1966. GS: Med Flory. The troopers ride out to save their beloved leader Parmenter when he is whisked away from Fort Courage by the maladjusted Loco Brothers, two renegade Indians who are more lonesome than dangerous.

52.52 *From Karate with Love.* Jan. 5, 1967. GS: Mako, Miko Mayana. Fort Courage and its men are in danger of being chopped to bits by the mighty karate blows of a samurai warrior, who has stormed the fort in pursuit of a beautiful Japanese girl.

52.53 *The Sergeant and the Kid.* Jan. 12, 1967. GS: Peter Robbins, Pippa Scott. A runaway boy aspires to be the best trooper at the fort when he tries to join the Cavalry.

52.54 *Where Were You at the Last Massacre?* Jan. 19, 1967. GS: Phil Harris. Flaming Arrow, a 147-year-old chieftain intends to reclaim all the land taken from his people. The fiery elder begins by laying siege to Fort Courage, where he plans to starve the troopers into surrendering.

52.55 *A Horse of Another Color.* Jan. 26, 1967. Everyone gets tied up in Captain Parmenter's new project. He is taking lasso lessons to rope a wild stallion for Wrangler Jane. It is a horse of a different color for O'Rourke, who is out to corral the animal for a circus.

52.56 *V Is for Vampire.* Feb. 2, 1967. GS: Vincent Price. The troopers are convinced that creepy Count Sfoza, a transplant for Transylvania, is responsible for the disappearance of Wrangler Jane.

52.57 *That's Show Biz.* Feb. 9, 1967. GS: The Factory Rock Quartet. Corporal Agarn resigns from the army to manage the Bedbugs, a long-haired musical group that is years ahead of its time.

52.58 *The Day They Shot Agarn.* Feb. 16, 1967. GS: Victor French, Fred Clark. Agarn faces an F Troop firing squad for the killing of Sergeant O'Rourke.

52.59 *Only One Russia Is Coming! Only One Russian Is Coming!* Feb. 23, 1967. Corporal Agarn's visiting Russian cousin Dmitri Agarnoff's old-world charm so enthralls Wrangler Jane that she may jilt Parmenter and head for Russia.

52.60 *Guns, Guns, Who's Got the Guns?* March 2, 1967. GS: Arch Johnson. Fort Courage is besieged by suspicion and espionage. A no-nonsense colonel informs Parmenter that there is a traitor in the fort. Someone is secretly selling guns to the Apaches.

52.61 *Marriage, Fort Courage Style.* March 9, 1967. GS: Mary Wickes, Joyce Jameson. Agarn and O'Rourke get a bitter taste of married life in a dream sequence, then rush to rescue Parmenter from a marriage broker.

52.62 *Carpetbagging, Anyone?* March 16, 1967. GS: James Gregory. F Troop faces eviction from Fort Courage when a wealthy carpetbagger takes over the town. After Big Jim Parker orders the troopers to vacate, they decide to scare him off by staging an Indian attack.

52.63 *Majority of Wilton.* March 23, 1967. Parmenter catches cold on the eve of his promotion examination. That is when his friends rush to his bedside with their sure-fire remedies.

52.64 *Our Brave in F Troop.* March 30, 1967. GS: Cliff Arquette, Hal England. Chief Wild Eagle sneaks into the fort for free dental care, but his visit soon gets out of hand. General Sam Courage decides that Wild Eagle is officer material, and good enough to command F Troop.

52.65 *Is This Fort Really Necessary?* April 6, 1967. GS: Charles Drake, Patrice Wymore, Amzie Strickland. The troopers face the loss of their lucrative operations when an efficiency-minded major arrives at Fort Courage with the authority to close it down.

53. *Father Murphy*

NBC. 60 min. Broadcast history: Tuesday, 8:00-9:00, Nov. 1981–March 1982; Sunday, 7:00-8:00. March 1982–July 1982; Tuesday, July 1982–Dec. 1982.

Regular Cast: Merlin Olsen (John Michael Murphy), Moses Gunn (Moses Gage), Katherine Cannon (Mae Woodward Murphy), Timothy Gibbs (Will Adams), Lisa Trusel (Lizette Winkler), Scott Mellini (Ephram Winkler), Charles Tyner (Howard Rodman), Chez Lister (Eli) 1982, Ivy Bethune (Miss Tuttle), Richard Bergman (Father Joe Parker), Warren Munson (Dr. Thompson), Charles Cooper (Sheriff).

Premise: This series was set in the 1870s in the town of Jackson in the Dakota Territory. It recounted the adventures of drifter John Murphy who poses as a priest to give legitimacy to a frontier orphanage.

The Episodes

53.1 *Father Murphy.* Nov. 3, 1981. GS: Burr De Benning, Spencer Milligan, Naomi White, Darrell Sandee, Michael Pataki, Dave Adams, Roy Jenson. John Michael Murphy is an 1870s frontiersman who runs afoul of a greedy town boss when he turns the tables on a crooked roulette wheel. The boss responds with a scheme to acquire Murphy's successful gold-mining claim.

53.2 *Eggs, Milk and a Dry Bed.* Nov. 10, 1981. GS: Erwin Fuller. Murphy's patience is tested by the school's newly ordained priest, who tries to run the school on his own when he learns of Murphy's charade.

53.3 *Establish Thou the Work of Our Hands.* Nov. 17, 1981. GS: Myron Williamson, Austin Judson. Moses accepts responsibility for a bitter black teenager whose hostility moves Murphy to challenge the youth to a manly test.

53.4 *A Horse from Heaven.* Nov. 24, 1981. GS: Christina Applegate, Tom Clancy, Erwin Fuller. Strapped for funds, the school is forced to sell off some livestock, but instead of cash, Father Parker returns with a horse that is guaranteed to win the $1000 Founder's Day race.

53.5 *By the Bear That Bit Me* Part One. Dec. 1, 1981. GS: Jack Elam, Shannon Doherty, Duncan McLeod, Lois Hall, Donald Craig. Ephram has a crush on a girl who only has eyes for Will.

53.6 *By the Bear That Bit Me* Part Two. Dec. 8, 1981. GS: Jack Elam, Shannon Doherty, Duncan McLeod, Lois Hall,

Donald Craig. Murphy and Eli devise a plan to free Dru, Will and Ephram from the workhouse.

53.7 *False Blessings.* Dec. 15, 1981. GS: Graham Jarvis, Jordan Rhodes, Laura Wallace-Rhodes. Rodman suggests state aid for the financially troubled school, a move that would require severing ties with the Church, and with Father Murphy.

53.8 *The Ghost of Gold Hill.* Dec. 22, 1981. GS: Steve Levitt. An eccentric with a deed to the school property plans to reopen the mine, and close the school if he makes a strike.

53.9 *Graduation.* Jan. 5, 1982. GS: Douglas V. Fowley, Amzie Strickland, Colin Drake, Grant Owens. An old miner asks Mae for book learnin' to court a genteel widow, but Rodman and Tuttle are shocked by his unorthodox contributions to the community.

53.10 *Will's Surprise.* Jan. 12, 1982. GS: Michael Pataki, Taylor Lacher, Suanne Atkins, Will Hunt. Will is kidnaped by his estranged father who is convinced that the youth has more gold than the nugget he cashed in town.

53.11 *Keys to Happiness.* Jan. 19, 1982. GS: Tracy Gold, Don Knight, Fran Ryan, Mickey Jones. With Murphy and Mae away, the children play a piano, acquired as payment for the use of the school as a casino.

53.12 *Knights of the White Camelia.* Feb. 2, 1982. GS: Randy Morton, Roger Torrey, Ned Wilson, Jennifer Beck. A 16-year-old Confederate Army veteran joins the school community, and a local racist group that issues an ultimatum to Moses.

53.13 *The Parable of Amanda.* Feb. 9, 1982. Juanin Clay, Randolph Powell, Elizabeth Hoy, Paul Barseou. As the sole survivor of a stagecoach accident, a swindler's accomplice assumes the identity of one of the victims, a nun assigned to inspect the Gold Hill School.

53.14 *The Spy.* Feb. 16, 1982. GS: Charles Tyner, Jason Tomarken. The school's future is threatened when a surly new orphan is discovered to have a father — Rodman.

53.15 *The Heir Apparent.* Feb. 23, 1982. GS: Brenda Benet, Ivor Barry. A wealthy widow from New York seeks to adopt Will, offering him all the material advantages Murphy can't provide.

53.16 *The Dream Day.* March 14, 1982. GS: Neil Billingsley, Tina Yothers, Matt Freeman, Darien Dash. An open house for prospective parents alarms brothers Matt and David, who face separation, and causes the others to wonder what appeals to a parent.

53.17 *Laddie.* March 21, 1982. GS: John Schulman, Ann Doran, Jerry Gatlin, Tom Roy Lowe. Moses and the children run up against horse thieves when they seek to retrieve a horse inadvertently sold for slaughter.

53.18 *Matthew and Elizabeth.* March 28, 1982. GS: Amanda Peterson, Wilfrid Hyde-White, C. Lindsay Workman. Matt falls for the daughter of new town boss Garrett, whose greedy rule of his late brother's businesses prompts the local drivers to start their own freight line.

53.19 *The First Miracle* Part One. April 4, 1982. GS: Burr De Benning, Donna Wilkes, Jerry Hardin, Brooke Bundy. Garrett thwarts Father Parker's efforts to find a church site in Jackson, and a troubled teenager develops a crush on Murphy.

53.20 *The First Miracle* Part Two. April 11, 1982. GS: Burr De Benning, Donna Wilkes, Jerry Hardin, Brooke Bundy. Murphy deceives Garrett to obtain a building for the new parish, but the Church withdraws its support of the parish when Emma reveals Murphy's priestly imposture.

Season Two

53.21 *Happiness Is....* Sept. 28, 1982. GS: Charles Lampkin, Lee Crawford, William Bryant, Fred Pinkard. The Gold Hill children work hard to allow the newlywed Murphys a honeymoon in Omaha, where they meet Mae's former beau and a hustling 11-year-old making book on a big horse race.

53.22 *The Father Figure.* Oct. 5, 1982. GS: Katie Hanley-Creore, James Hess, Ted Markland, Joseph Massengale. After accidentally killing a man in self-defense, Murphy must deal with his own grief, Garrett's taunting henchmen, and the hatred of the man's 12-year-old son.

53.23 *Stopover in a One-Way Horse Town.* Oct. 26, 1982.

53.24 *Outrageous Fortune.* Nov. 9, 1982. GS: John Fiedler, Happy La Shelle, Peter Haskell, Walter Baines. A detective identifies a Gold Hill girl as the heir to a fortune, but the man's a fraud hired to hide the girl until a time limit expires, giving the inheritance to a ne'er-do-well cousin.

53.25 *The Reluctant Runaway* Part One. Nov. 16, 1982. GS: James Cromwell, Heather McAdams. The secrecy surrounding Mae's pregnancy proves an embarrassment for Will. He assumes the new bedroom Murphy is building is for him.

53.26 *The Reluctant Runaway* Part Two. Nov. 23, 1982. GS: James Cromwell, Heather McAdams. In St. Louis, Murphy enlists Farley's help to search for Will, who has been taken in by a woman who trains children to be thieves.

53.27 *Buttons and Beaux.* Nov. 30, 1982. GS: Mary Robin-Redd, Todd Lookinland. Working as a dressmaker's apprentice in town, Lizette is charmed by a boy with a faster life style than she is used to.

53.28 *John Michael Murphy, R.I.P.* Dec. 7, 1982. GS: Eddie Quillan, Dub Taylor, Bruce M. Fischer, Jay Fletcher, Pat Buttram, Fred Stuthman, Parley Baer. A codger's tall tale and some circumstantial evidence identify Murphy and Moses as notorious bank robbers, just before the real outlaws hit the town.

53.29 *Title Unknown.* Dec. 14, 1982. GS: Davis Kaufman, Edith Fellows, Robert O'Reilly, Ned Bellamy. Matt recognizes a robber as a friend who is struggling to support his ailing mother, and agrees to keep silent, unless it happens again.

53.30 *Blood Right.* Dec. 21, 1982. GS: Adam Postil, Bob G. Anthony. A famous gunfighter just out of prison and intent on living within the law, comes to the orphanage for his son, who believes his father is dead.

53.31 *Title Unknown.* Dec. 28, 1982. GS: Mary Beth Evans, Jennifer Beck, Robert Darnell. After the sudden death of her aunt, a youngster forms an attachment to a troubled girl brought to the orphanage after an apparent drowning accident.

54. Frontier

NBC. 30 min. Broadcast history: Sunday, 7:30–8:00, Oct. 1955–Sept. 1956.

Regular Cast: Water Coy (Narrator).

Premise: This anthology series recounted tales of men and women facing hardship in the Western frontier.

The Episodes

54.1 *Paper Gunman.* Sept. 25, 1955. GS: King Donovan, John Smith, Carol Thurston, Scott Forbes. A newspaper reporter sent out west is to write a series on famous gunslingers. Finding that real gunmen are scarce he decides to invent one, and picks as his subject a village idler who yearns to be an outlaw.

54.2 *Tomas and the Widow.* Oct. 2, 1955. GS: Laura Elliot, Mike Connors, Sean McClory. A man accidentally kills his neighbor in a quarrel.

54.3 *A Stillness in Wyoming.* Oct. 16, 1955. GS: Peter Votrian, James Griffith, Lee Erickson, Walter Coy. The bitter war between sheepmen and cattlemen forces two young boys to keep their friendship a secret.

54.4 *The Shame of a Nation.* Oct. 23, 1955. GS: Scott Forbes, George Keymas, Hayden Rorke, Barry Atwater. Col. J.M. Chivington, of the U.S. cavalry, orders his men to massacre hundreds of friendly Cheyenne Indians, even though they had done nothing against Army instructions.

54.5 *The Founding of Omaha, Nebraska.* Oct. 30, 1955. GS: Sally Brophy, Jeff Morrow. En route by wagon train to Oregon, a young couple lose their baby. Unable to leave the place where the child is buried, they stay on.

54.6 *The Suspects.* Nov. 6, 1955. GS: John Bromfield, Stanley Jones. During a wave of bank robberies executed by two distinguished-looking bandits, Sheriff Morgan suspects a pair watching a local bank. He investigates and plans a trap.

54.7 *King of the Dakotas.* Nov. 13, 1955 & Nov. 20, 1955. GS: Tom Tryon, Phyllis Coates. A ruthless tycoon has built an empire for himself in the Dakotas. He is forced to flee to France when the cattlemen he has mistreated rebel.

54.8 *Cattle Drive to Casper.* Nov. 27, 1955. GS: Ray Teal, Beverly Garland, Stuart Randall. A young wife insists on going with her husband on a 600-mile cattle drive.

54.9 *Romance of Poker Alice.* Dec. 11, 1955. GS: Joan Vohs, Barry Atwater, Larry Arnold. An English girl accompanies her father west to a mining town. When he is killed in a mine disaster she turns to gambling.

54.10 *Ferdinand Meyer's Army.* Dec. 18, 1955. GS: Richard Karlan, Jack Elam, Donna Martell, Leo Gordon, Herb Butterfield. Elected mayor of his town, one of the first Jews to settle in New Mexico leads the Mexicans in a struggle against unscrupulous land grabbers. One of his staunchest supporters is a Catholic priest.

54.11 *The Long Road to Tucson.* Dec. 25, 1955. GS: Sally Brophy. A group of nuns sets out by wagon to travel to Arizona. They arrive on Christmas Day, 1870, and start the first hospital.

54.12 *The Texicans.* Jan. 8, 1956. GS: Paul Richards, John Dehner, Richard Garland, Coleen Gray, Jay Novello, Helen Kleeb, James Best. The entire male population of a town in Texas volunteers to infiltrate the enemy lines, one of whom becomes the only American deserter at the Battle of the Alamo.

54.13 *Mother of the Brave.* Jan. 15, 1956. GS: Peggy Webber, Stuart Towers, John Cliff, Terry Rangno, Denver Pyle, James Goodwin, Rod Redwing. When ranching proves unprofitable, the Horn family begins a long trek across western plains enroute to their native England. They fall prey to a band of Comanche Indians who kill the husband and take the children. The mother then sets out to rescue her children.

54.14 *The Ten Days of John Leslie.* Jan. 22, 1956. GS: Richard Crenna, Gloria Talbott, Claude Akins, Robert Burton. A young man is accused by townsfolk of having committed a murder. When even his wife becomes suspicious, he protests their hasty judgment and is given ten days to prove his innocence.

54.15 *The Devil and Doctor O'Hara.* Feb. 5, 1956. GS: J.M. Kerrigan, Tommy Kirk, Dorothy Addams. Sean Michael Xavier O'Hara has but two friends in the mining town of Plentywood, Montana — a young boy and his old goat Sam. The ostracized doctor, who loves bourbon and fears Satan, finds himself instrumental in the outcome of a crucial footrace on which all the townspeople have placed their money.

54.16 *The Captivity of Joe Long.* Feb. 12, 1956. GS: Jan Merlin, Tamar Cooper, John Miljan. A trapper is captured by a band of hostile Indians. Their efforts to pray to the spirits for much needed rain have failed. They want the trapper to pray to his great white father to end the drought.

54.17 *The Voyage of Captain Castle.* Feb. 19, 1956. GS: Donald Murphy, Gloria Saunders, Jan Arvan, Trevor Bardette, Eleanore Kent, John Merrick. During the Texas fight for independence from Mexico, Sam Houston sanctions the shanghaiing of a Naval officer. The Texans need a knowledgeable leader for their one-schooner navy.

54.18 *Assassin.* March 4, 1956. GS: Chuck Connors, John Hoyt, Isa Childers. Though guilty of other crimes, a man is hanged for a murder he did not commit.

54.19 *The Hanging at Thunder Butte Creek.* March 11, 1956. GS: Donald MacDonald, Vic Perrin, Robert Bray. In 1882 an Indian named Ogala is sentenced to hang for the killing of another Indian. Prior to the scheduled execution he is given the run of the town, where he becomes the favorite of the children.

54.20 *The Big Dry.* March 18, 1956. GS: Scott Forbes, Maura Murphy, Sally Corner, Paul Richards, K.L. Smith, Leo Gordon. In 1849 a married couple and an elderly woman set out across the desert in search of a shorter route to the California goldfields. In desperation they combine forces with three strangers.

54.21 *The Ballad of Pretty Polly.* April 1, 1956. GS: Nancy Hadley, Rhodes Reason, Richard Garland, Bill Bryant. A sailor waits too long to return home from the War of 1812 and learns his sweetheart is engaged to another.

54.22 *The Well.* April 8, 1956. GS: Christopher Dark, Don Kelly, Bob Anderson, Strother Martin. Two young men discharged from Fort Apache go into the hills to hunt for gold. In their greed they turn against each other, but find something even more previous than gold — water.

54.23 *Salt War.* April 22, 1956. GS: Richard Boone, Carol Thurston, Paul Richards, Maura Murphy, Scott Forbes. A Mexican War veteran and his bride settle down on the land grant given them by the U.S. government. In need of salt, the new settlers quarrels with another man who claims the salt supply on his land is not public domain, but is for sale at the price he can command.

54.24 *Patrol.* April 29, 1956. GS: Don Kennedy, James Griffith, Christopher Dark, Phil Barnes, Herb Ellis, Strother Martin, Marjorie Owens, Gil Rankin. When a patrol of nine men learns belatedly that the Civil War has broken out, the Southern and Northern factions in the party split and stage their own Civil War.

Frontier Circus

54.25 *A Somewhere Voice.* May 6, 1956. GS: Jeanne Moody, Don Kelly, Bob Anderson. Two brothers set up a homestead in Oklahoma in 1889. The older brother is unable to leave the homestead to bring back his fiancee, so he sends his brother to fetch her from her home 200 miles away. Trouble develops when the girl and the younger brother fall in love.

54.26 *The Hunted.* May 13, 1956. GS: Jack Kelly, Jan Merlin, Joan Hotchkis. After speaking out against one of his confederates, an outlaw flees in fear. A young woman who gives him sanctuary tries to get him to overcome his cowardice and make an appearance in court.

54.27 *Georgia Gold.* June 10, 1956. GS: John Dehner, Catherine McLeod. A Welshman brings his family to Georgia, where he wins a parcel of land in a lottery. Dissension arises in the family when it is rumored there is gold on the property.

54.28 *Out from Taos.* June 24, 1956. GS: Kenneth Tobey, Ted de Corsia, Jim Best. The father of a 17-year-old boy is accidentally killed in a saloon brawl. The two men responsible for the father's death steal the boy's wagon, which is loaded with all his possessions, and trade it for trapping gear.

54.29 *The Return of Jubal Dolan.* Aug. 26, 1956. GS: Jack Kelly, Robert Vaughn, Jean Willes. A gunman returns to his home ranch in Arizona after seven years, determined to give up gunfighting forever. His crippled brother, Cliff, has been living in the reflected glory of his famous brother, and cannot understand why Jubal wants to become an ordinary cowpoke.

54.30 *The Hostage.* Sept. 9, 1956. GS: Jack Kelly, Ted de Corsia, Kenneth Tobey. A bank clerk is taken hostage by three robbers.

55. *Frontier Circus*

CBS. 60 min. Broadcast history: Thursday, 7:30-8:30, Oct. 1961–Jan. 1962; Thursday, 8:00-9:00, Feb. 1962–Sept. 1962.

Regular Cast: Chill Wills (Col. Casey Thompson), John Derek (Ben Travis), Richard Jaeckel (Tony Gentry).

Premise: This series dealt with Col. Casey Thompson's T&T Circus, which travelled throughout the Southwest in the 1880s.

The Episodes

55.1 *The Depths of Fear.* Oct. 5, 1961. GS: Aldo Ray, James Gregory, Bethel Leslie, Vito Scotti, Bern Hoffman. While Ben is arranging the purchase of a mountain bear in a nearby town, he sees drifter Toby Mills cringe under the attack of a bully named Bannister. Ben takes care of Bannister, then advises Toby to stand on his own two feet — which he does by applying for a job with the circus.

55.2 *The Smallest Target.* Oct. 12, 1961. GS: Barbara Rush, Brian Keith, Brad Herman, Roy Barcroft, Mike Ragan, Dean Moray. Sharpshooter Bonnie Stevens is the circus' star attraction, but rancher Dan Osborne doesn't seem to be one of her fans. He tears down a poster with Bonnie's pictures on it, then orders the circus to get off his land.

55.3 *Lippizan.* Oct. 19, 1961. GS: Vera Miles, Otto Kruger, H.M. Wynant, Gordon Jones. Pursuing bandits who have just help up the box office, Ben jumps on the first horse at hand — the specially trained mount of blind equestrienne Maureen McBride.

55.4 *Dr. Sam.* Oct. 26, 1961. GS: Irene Dunne, Ellen Corby, J. Pat O'Malley, Norman Leavitt, Jon Locke, Jean Howell, Bob Wolmier. Colonel Thompson has sent for a doctor to join his traveling troupe. But when Tony returns with Dr. Sam, the circus people are shocked because Dr. Sam is a woman.

55.5 *The Hunter and the Hunted.* Nov. 2, 1961. GS: Eddie Albert, Rip Torn, Jocelyn Brando, Cloris Leachman, John Anderson. Colonel Thompson is hurt in an accident and Tony rides ahead to find a doctor. But Dr. Jordan is busy with another patient, the brother of notorious outlaw Jess Evans.

55.6 *Karina.* Nov. 9, 1961. GS: Elizabeth Montgomery, Barbara Stuart, Tod Andrews, Brian Hutton, J. Pat O'Malley, Albert Paulson. Colonel Thompson helps a young woman named Karina, who was injured in a spat with her husband. The circus men don't know that Karina's husband has some injuries of his own — Karina shot him.

55.7 *Journey from Hannibal.* Nov. 16, 1961. GS: Thelma Ritter, Arte Johnson, Clem Bevans. Colonel Thompson goes to Hannibal, Missouri, to buy an elephant, also named Hannibal, from a woman named Bertha Beecher. Bertha's a tough businesswoman. She won't let the Colonel or the elephant out of her sight until she is paid for her pachyderm.

55.8 *Winter Quarters.* Nov. 23, 1961. GS: Robert J. Wilke, Alex Viespi, Walter Sande, Roy Barcroft. Colonel Casey wants to get his wagons into sunny California before winter hits. But just as the circus reaches the crest of the mountains, horse thieves run off with their stock.

55.9 *The Patriarch of Purgatory.* Nov. 30, 1961. GS: Royal Dano, Robert Sampson, Carolyn Kearney, Jane Chang, George Barrows. The circus arrives in the mining town of Purgatory and finds the place almost deserted. Ben and Tony start to investigate and wind up working in a mine as slave laborers.

55.10 *The Shaggy Kings.* Dec. 7, 1961. GS: Dick York, Lorrie Richards, Dan Duryea, Michael Pate, Jack Lambert, Frank de Kova. When Molly the high-wire artist collapses from food poisoning, it is discovered that the last of the food supply has gone band and the next town is two weeks away.

55.11 *Coals of Fire.* Jan. 4, 1962. GS: Sammy Davis, Jr., R.G. Armstrong. Casey and Ben learn that Cata, an ex-slave recently hired as a roustabout, is looking for his master's killer. Cata figure that work with the circus will take him to different parts of the country, where he can continue his search.

55.12 *The Balloon Girl.* Jan. 11, 1962. GS: Stella Stevens, Chick Chandler, Stacy Morgan, Claude Akins. Balloonist Katy Cogswell is a girl with a dream. She believes that air travel is the coming thing. Then her lighter-than-air craft hits the big top's main tent pole, and Katy becomes a down-to-earth girl in a hurry.

55.13 *Mr. Grady Regrets.* Jan. 25, 1962. GS: Charles Ruggles, Anne Helm, Lillian Bronson, Michael Forest, Richard Lepore. When old friend Will Grady is paroled from the territorial prison, Casey greets him with a job offer. Grady accepts, but then it looks like there may be a change in his plans.

55.14 *Quick Shuffle.* Feb. 1, 1962. GS: Gilbert Roland, Patricia Barry, George Mitchell, Carl Benton Reid, Richard Reeves, Pat O'Malley, Wally Blair. Ben takes part in a card game in an attempt to get the circus out of the red. In no time at all he owes gambler Luke Santos a large sum of money.

55.15 *The Courtship.* Feb. 15,1962. GS: Jo Van Fleet, Henry Jones, Jeanette Noland. Tony arrive in the prairie town of New Atlanta and learns that Marshal Longstreet refuses to permit the circus to give a performance there. But Casey won't take no for an answer and rides back to town with Tony to argue the point.

55.16 *Stopover in Paradise.* Feb. 22, 1962. GS: Carolyn Jones, Robert Simon, Adam Kennedy, Don Hix, Robert Hinkle, James Anderson. As the circus approaches the town of Paradise, they are met by Tony, their advance man. Tony says prospects for a long run look pretty good, but the problem of supplies is another matter. There is no fresh meat in the town.

55.17 *Calamity Circus.* March 8, 1962. GS: Mickey Rooney, Nico Minardos, Inva Victor, Parley Baer, Howard McNear. Business hasn't been too good and now the star aerialist, the Great Roberto, is indisposed and can't go on. Ben, who fills in for the aerialist at the last minute, suddenly plunges into the safety net when the rigging gives way, and then discovers that it was cut deliberately.

55.18 *The Inheritance.* March 15, 1962. GS: Marc Marno, Tsuruko Kobayashi, Alan Hale, Jr., J. Pat O'Malley. The circus is headed for the town of Primrose, where it will take on the new act Colonel Thompson has booked, a Japanese acrobat team consisting of Yuki Yamoto and his sister Hideko. But when the Colonel arrives he learns that Yuki doesn't confine his stunts to the circus ring.

55.19 *Naomi Champagne.* March 29, 1962. GS: Constance Ford, Richard Conte, Neil Hamilton. Colonel Thompson and Ben foil the holdup of a stage coach, and since the driver has been killed, Ben agrees to take over the reins. He is not too eager, though three of the passengers didn't seem very happy about being rescued.

55.20 *Mighty Like Rogues.* April 5, 1962. GS: Glenda Farrell, Joby Baker, Roger Mobley, Jena Engstrom, J. Pat O'Malley, Renee Godfrey. That young girl who rides up to the circus wagons is Betsy Ross Jukes and her story about being lost on the desert with her family is very moving. It is also a big lie.

55.21 *Never Won Fair Lady.* April 12, 1962. GS: Red Buttons, Gloria Talbott, Christopher Dark, Paul Newlan, Richard Reeves. Casey remembers his old commanding officer, General Youngblood, as a blood-and-thunder type. But none of this has apparently rubbed off on the General's mild-mannered and scholarly son Earl — and now Earl show up at the circus with instructions from home for Casey to toughen him up.

55.22 *The Good Fight.* April 19, 1962. GS: Ray Daley, George Macready, Elizabeth Hush, Jason Evers, Stephanie Hill, Kenneth Tobey, Gordon Jones. Casey discovers that the new man he has hired, Luke Sanders, has a reputation for being hand with his fist. Luke isn't too happy about it. His religion forbids violence.

55.23 *The Clan MacDuff.* April 26, 1962. GS: James Barton. The circus encounters a large Irish family.

55.24 *The Race.* May 3, 1962. GS: Edward Andrews, Skip Homeier, James McMullan, Harry Carey, Jr., Jeff Bell, Don Haggerty. The circus is setting up at Grand Island, Nebraska, but the usual mob of eager kids is missing. Tony thinks he knows the reason. An entertainer who calls himself Duke Felix Otway has all the children at his show on the other side of town.

55.25 *The Daring Durandos.* May 17, 1962. GS: Nehemiah Persoff. A new aerial act joins the circus.

55.26 *Incident at Pawnee Gun.* Sept. 6, 1962. GS: Joe Maross, Robert Lowery, Kathie Browne, John Pickard, Dick Haynes. Thompson is traveling back to the circus after picking up a trained chimp in New Orleans. He doesn't know that there is a posse on his trail and that they are burning to the ground every building where Casey and the ape have stopped off.

56. *Frontier Doctor*

Syndicated. 30 min. Broadcast history: Various, Sept. 1958–June 1959.

Regular Cast: Rex Allen (Dr. Bill Baxter).

Premise: This series depicted the adventures of Bill Baxter, the doctor of the pioneer town of Rising Springs, Arizona, in the early days of the 20th century.

The Episodes

56.1 *Queen of the Cimarron.* Sept. 26, 1958. GS: Jean Willes, Glenn Strange, Gregory Walcott. Dr. Bill Baxter attempts to stop a ruthless dance hall queen from selling a herd of diseased cattle.

56.2 *San Francisco Story.* Oct. 4, 1958. GS: Lane Bradford. Dr. Baxter is framed for the murder of a man whose badly wounded leg he treated.

56.3 *Three Wanted Men.* Oct. 11, 1958. Dr. Baxter is captured by a gang of outlaws who need him to patch up a wound.

56.4 *The Crooked Circle.* Oct. 18, 1958. GS: Gregg Palmer, Don Harvey. Dr. Baxter finds himself caught in a frame-up when a spoiled, ruthless young lady attempts to murder her wealthy grandfather who stands in her way.

56.5 *The Apache Uprising.* Oct. 25, 1958. Dr. Baxter attempts to effect a truce between residents of Rising Springs and their Apache neighbors.

56.6 *Double Boomerang.* Nov. 1, 1958. GS: William Bryant. Dr. Baxter is perturbed by the many mine casualties he is being called on to treat.

56.7 *Mystery of the Black Stallion.* Nov. 8, 1958. GS: Stacy Harris. Two crooks conspire.

56.8 *The Outlaw Legion.* Nov. 15, 1958. GS: Joe Sawyer, Michael Ansara. A gang of outlaws plans to blow up a reservoir dam.

56.9 *Fury in the Big Top.* Nov. 22, 1958. GS: Robert Quarry. Dr. Bill Baxter attempts to help a girl regain her speech.

56.10 *The Desperate Game.* Nov. 29, 1958. GS: Taylor Holmes. Dr. Baxter attempts to upset the plans of a gambler who has been blackmailing a respected doctor into signing false death certificates.

56.11 *Great Stagecoach Robbery.* Dec. 6, 1958. GS: Lee Van Cleef, Mary Beth Hughes. Dr. Baxter teaches an actress that she cannot outsmart a bandit.

56.12 *Iron Trail Ambush.* Dec. 13, 1958. GS: Gloria Saunders. Dr. Baxter foils a sabotage plot against a railroad project in Arizona.

56.13 *Shotgun Hattie.* Dec. 20, 1958. Dr. Baxter risks his life and reputation to stop an eccentric widow and her accomplices from declaring her stepson insane.

56.14 Trouble in Paradise Valley. Dec. 27, 1958. GS: John Hoyt. Dr. Baxter goes against a town's prejudice and helps a young man.

56.15 Shadows of Belle Starr. Jan. 3, 1959. GS: Michael Landon, Frank Gorshin. Dr. Baxter saves an adolescent boy from juvenile delinquency.

56.16 Illegal Entry. Jan. 10, 1958. When a patient dies of cholera, Dr. Baxter sets out to find the carriers of the disease.

56.17 Sabotage. Jan. 17, 1959. GS: Morris Ankrum. A meatpacking company has been supplying American soldiers with contaminated meat rations.

56.18 Belle of Tennessee. Jan. 24, 1959. When a colorful frontier woman is murdered, Dr. Baxter, introducing the fingerprint technique, sets out to find the murderer.

56.19 Bittercreek Gang. Jan. 31, 1959. GS: Slim Pickens, Jack Lambert. Baxter poses as an ex-convict to aid the law in tracking down a gang.

56.20 Broken Barrier. Feb. 7, 1959. A girl outsmarts a shrewd operator who is trying to run her out of town.

56.21 Woman Who Dared. Feb. 14, 1959. An unreasonable mother threatens her daughter's happiness when she opposes the girl's forthcoming marriage.

56.22 Storm Over King City. Feb. 21, 1959. GS: Jack LaRue. Dr. Baxter learns he has inherited a half interest in a gold mine.

56.23 Law of the Badlands. Feb. 28, 1959. GS: Harry Woods, Diane Brewster. Attending to the wounded of both sides in a battle between the U.S. Cavalry and renegade Apaches, Dr. Baxter almost loses his life.

56.24 The Big Gamblers. March 7, 1959. GS: Montie Montana, Mary Castle. Two unscrupulous brothers attempting to set up illegal gambling in a peaceful town are stopped by the local sheriff. Then the law officer suffers a stroke and is helpless.

56.25 Strangers in Town. March 14, 1959. Dr. Baxter delivers a baby and discovers that the mother is the wife of a man who has fled to Mexico.

56.26 Big Frame-up. March 21, 1959. A girl announces that her husband and his brother have quarreled and killed each other. But Dr. Baxter is suspicious and starts an investigation.

56.27 Drifting Sands. March 28, 1959. GS: Ann Doran. The son of a rich rancher returns from medical school on his vacation. A destructive series of fires break out and Dr. Baxter suspects his young friend of setting them.

56.28 The Homesteaders. April 4, 1959. GS: Donald Curtis, Rhodes Reason, Ron Hagerthy. A young cowpoke finds himself caught in a range war with his girl friend's homesteading family.

56.29 Danger Valley. April 11, 1959. GS: Kenneth MacDonald, Angela Greene. Dr. Bill Baxter attempts to capture a fugitive wanted for robbery and murder. The man is also a carrier of the deadly disease, diphtheria.

56.30 South of the Rio Grande. April 18, 1959. GS: Pedro Gonzales-Gonzales, Lita Baron. Dr. Baxter meets up with a gang of outlaws when he attempts to bring some needed typhoid vaccine into Mexico.

56.31 A Twisted Road. April 25, 1959. Robert Vaughn. The townspeople of Rising Springs become worried when two girls have been strangled without any apparent motive.

56.32 Gringo Pete. May 2, 1959. GS: Ted DeCorsia, Robert Shayne. An outlaw is released from prison suffering from diabetes. He promises Dr. Baxter he will aid him in rounding up the rest of his gang.

56.33 Superstition Mountain. May 9, 1959. GS: Don Haggerty, Robert Dix. Dr. Baxter makes a hazardous trip into Comanche country to give medical aid to a cavalry trooper.

56.34 Elkton Lake Feud. May 16, 1959. GS: John Ashley. After feuding for two generations as to ownership of a lake, two families have almost annihilated themselves.

56.35 Strange Cargo. May 23, 1959. GS: Morgan Woodward. Dr. Baxter learns that an epidemic of bubonic plague is ready to break out.

56.36 Man to Man. May 30, 1959. A young boy is accused of trying to assassinate a political figure.

56.37 The Confidence Gang. June 6, 1959. GS: Carleton Young. A well-known writer and patient of Dr. Baxter's meets an attractive girl and almost loses his life.

56.38 The Counterfeiters. June 13, 1959. GS: Yvette Dugay, Ken Mayer. Dr. Baxter risks his life and reputation by assuming the guilt for the death of a captain of the Texas Rangers.

56.39 Flaming Gold. June 20, 1959. GS: Gloria Winters. Stopping at a small town, Dr. Baxter goes to see an old friend, but learns he died a week ago.

57. Fury

NBC. 30 min. Broadcast history: Saturday mornings, Oct. 1955–March 1960.

Regular Cast: Bobby Diamond (Joey Newton), Peter Graves (Jim Newton), William Fawcett (Pete), Roger Mobley (Packy Lambert), Jimmy Baird (Rodney "Pee Wee" Jenkins), Ann Robinson (Helen Watkins), Nan Leslie (Harriet Newton), James Seay (Sheriff Davis), Mike Taylor (Ted/Frankie) 55-56.

Premise: This series depicts the adventures of an orphaned boy, Joey, who is adopted by rancher Jim Newton and raised at the Broken Wheel Ranch. Newton gives the boy a black stallion, Fury, to instill in him a since of responsibility.

The Episodes

57.1 Joey Finds a Friend. Oct. 15, 1955. Rancher Jim Newton captures a wild black stallion which he names Fury. While in town, the widower meets a youngster wrongly accused of breaking a window. Jim clears the boy and brings him back to the ranch.

57.2 Killer Stallion. Oct. 22, 1955. GS: Walter Reed. Fury is suspected of raiding the horses of neighboring ranchers. Only Joey, who has seen the real raider at work, has faith in the wild stallion.

57.3 The Horse Coper. Oct. 29, 1955. GS: Parley Baer, Jim Hayward, Donald MacDonald. Joey tries to help Jim Newton raise some money to pay a bank loan due on the Broken Wheel Ranch. A crooked horse dealer offers to buy Fury, but Jim refuses. The dealer then resorts to trickery to obtain the horse.

57.4 Joey Goes Hunting. Nov. 5, 1955. GS: Russ Conway, Jim Hayward. Jim Newton presents Joey with a hunting rifle as a reward for his good report card. While tracking deer in the woods, Joey and a pal come across a dangerous escaped criminal.

57.5 *Scorched Earth.* Nov. 12, 1955. GS: Edward Penney, Dick Wessel, David Kasday. In an effort to cut down forest fires, Joey is asked by a forest ranger to help. Joey finds a hunter and his son using a fire in the closed forest area and gives them a warning. Joey and a buddy are trapped by flames in a forest fire started by a carelessly tossed cigarette.

57.6 *Joey's Dame Trouble.* Nov. 19, 1955. Joey is unhappy when Fury neglects him in favor of a white mare. In a rash moment, Joey releases the mare into open range land.

57.7 *Joey and the Gypsies.* Nov. 26, 1955. GS: Pierre Watkin, Anthony Caruso, Louis Lettieri, Jacqueline Way. Joey makes friends with a Gypsy boy who is appearing at a local fair with his family. When horse thieves begin stealing stock from Jim Newton and his neighbors, the ranchers suspect the Gypsies.

57.8 *Joey's Father.* Dec. 3, 1955. GS: Denver Pyle, Ernie Dotson, John Phillips. A man who claims to be Joey's real father pays an unexpected visit to Jim's ranch and demands custody of the boy.

57.9 *Joey Saves the Day.* Dec. 10, 1955. GS: Keith Richards, Erik Nielsen, Stanley Andrews, Harry Tyler, Richard Travis. Just as a welfare worker pays a visit to Jim Newton to check on Joey's progress, circumstantial evidence points to Joey as the one responsible for a theft of $20.

57.10 *The 4-H Story.* Dec. 17, 1955. GS: Robert B. Williams, Charles Watts. After raising a prize lamb for entry in the 4-H Club competition, Joey is put out when he realizes that his friend Frankie's lamb stands a better chance to win. When Frankie's lamb is lost in the wilderness, Joey learns a lesson in good sportsmanship.

57.11 *Junior Rodeo.* Dec. 24, 1955. GS: Sammy Ogg, Jimmy Karath, Harlan Warde, Robert B. Williams, Rod O'Connor. Joey is faced with some underhanded methods when he enters a rodeo competition. The local champion arranges to have an outlawed horse put in Joey's shute.

57.12 *Ghost Town.* Dec. 31, 1955. GS: Will Wright, Robert Karlan, Steve Conte, Dick Reeves. On a treasure hunt to a deserted old town, Joey finds real loot from a bank robbery hidden there by the thieves.

57.13 *The Hobo.* Jan. 7, 1956. GS: Wes Hudman, Larry Hudson, Dan Riss, William Hopper. A likeable transient who stops at Jim Newton's ranch looking for work, is discovered to be a veterinarian fleeing from a charge of manslaughter. Jim is faced with the decision of whether or not to turn him over to the law.

57.14 *Tungsten Queen.* Jan. 14, 1956. GS: Eddy Waller, Harry Lauter, Joe Hayworth, Dan Riss. When the owner of a tungsten mine is injured, he comes to Jim's ranch to recuperate. Unknown to him, his unscrupulous assistants are keeping the mine open, intending to steal the ore themselves.

57.15 *Joey Sees It Through.* Jan. 21, 1956. GS: Beverly Washburn, Elaine Riley, House Peters, Jr., Nolan Leary. A 10-year-old girl, whose widowed mother is remarrying, stays on the Broken Wheel Ranch until her mother returns from her honeymoon. Her misdeeds almost wreck her mother's chances for happiness.

57.16 *Stolen Fury.* Jan. 28, 1956. GS: Roy Barcroft, Frank Richards, John Cliff, Guy Teague. When horse rustlers raid Jim Newton's ranch, they take Joey captive to insure their safety. He escapes and tries to find the bandits' hideout, where he was taken blindfolded.

57.17 *The Choice.* Feb. 4, 1956. GS: Jean Byron, Ross Elliot, Robert Lynn. After he has been in an accident, Joey's eyesight is impaired. Jim, who is in financial straits, must sell Fury to get the money necessary for an operation.

57.18 *The Boy Scout Story.* Feb,. 11, 1956. GS: Helen Brown, Stuffy Singer. Joey tries to convince a young friend he should join with him in local scouting activities. But the boy feels he is too busy with part-time work helping his widowed mother.

57.19 *Search for Joey.* Feb. 18, 1956. GS: Bill Henry, Don C. Harvey. Joey is bitten by a dog. Later Jim and Pete learn that the dog was rabid. Joey is in serious trouble when he gets lost while on a camping trip and cannot receive the Pasteur treatment.

57.20 *The Miracle.* Feb. 25, 1956. GS: John Hart. Jim invites a world-champion cowboy, who has been crippled by a rodeo accident, to stay at the Broken Wheel. The champ, believing that he will never walk again, becomes bitter and downhearted until a near-tragedy changes the course of his life.

57.21 *The Test.* March 3, 1956. GS: Bill Chapin, Louis Jean Heydt. Joey befriends a new classmate whose father believes in all work and no play. Overemphasis on scholastic achievement causes the boy to steal an examination paper, but Joey finds himself blamed for the theft.

57.22 *Fury Runs to Win.* March 10, 1956. GS: Stanley Clements, Walter Woolf King, Andy Clyde. Jim agrees to a match race between Fury and a broken-down race horse belonging to a neighbor. He does not know that the neighbor plans to substitute a ringer, a champion thoroughbred, for his own entry.

57.23 *Timber.* March 17, 1956. GS: Bruce Cowling, John Pickard, Paul Sorenson. Joey and Jim learn that a friend who operates a lumber company is the victim of saboteurs. A rival company is after his lease and the timber.

57.24 *Wonder Horse.* March 24, 1956. GS: Gordon Jones, Sid Tomack, Billy Wayne. Two unscrupulous carnival operators attempt to steal Fury to use him as a star attraction.

57.25 *Pirate Treasure.* March 31, 1956. GS: Alan Hale, Jr. Joey and his friend Ben construct a raft and imagine themselves as daring pirates. Their adventures are interrupted by the appearance of a stranger who claims to be a real pirate and swears the boys to secrecy.

57.26 *The Baby.* April 7, 1956. GS: Claudia Barrett, Mark Scott. Joey and Frankie find a baby who has crawled away from her parents' trailer.

Season Two

57.27 *The Runaway.* Oct. 6, 1956. Fury becomes involved when a boy runs away.

57.28 *Joey and the Little League.* Oct. 13, 1956. GS: Roger Broadus, Robert Foulk. Joey rounds up a baseball team but runs into a snag when one of the youngsters refuses to play unless he pitches.

57.29 *Earthquake.* Oct. 20, 1956. A volcano long thought to be inactive, erupts following an earthquake. The flow of boiling lave separates Joey from Fury when he goes back for Jim, who was injured hen he was thrown from his frightened horse.

57.30 *Trial by Jury.* Oct. 27, 1956. GS: Pamela Baird, Ray Montgomery. Joey's girl friend's father is suspected of cattle rustling. The youngsters set out to find evidence to prove his innocence.

57.31 *Joey and the Wolf Pack.* Nov. 3, 1956. Jim has been losing a number of his horses to a pack of wolves. He finds an orphaned colt in the wilderness and brings it back to the ranch, but Fury leads the young horse away again.

57.32 *Indian Mountain.* Nov. 17, 1956. Jim, Pete and Joey come across an archaeologist who has been hurt in a landslide in his search for a buried Aztec village.

57.33 *Flying Saucer.* Nov. 24, 1956. Joey and one of his buddies attempt to convince Pete that flying saucers have been hovering near the ranch. When an unidentified object does come to earth, the two boys are trapped before they are able to notify Jim or the sheriff.

57.34 *Joey and the Stranger.* Dec. 1, 1956. GS: George Chandler, Rayford Barnes, Mark Bennett, Richard Towers. With the assistance of a ventriloquist, Joey is able to aid in the capture of two thieves.

57.35 *Pete's Folly.* Dec. 15, 1956. GS: Harry Tyler, Philip Van Zandt. Jim's ranch hand innocently invests all his money in a phony uranium-stock deal.

57.36 *Boy's Day.* Dec. 22, 1956. GS: Darryl Duran. On boys' day, Joey and his friend Buzz are named respectively sheriff and mayor of Twin Forks. They mistakenly jail a robbery witness as a desperado.

57.37 *The Feud.* Jan. 5, 1957. GS: Frances McDonald, Paul Burns. Joey tries to intervene when a disagreement between two rangers threatens to cut off a valuable water supply.

57.38 *Loco Weed.* Jan. 12, 1957. A poisonous weed causes Fury to turn against Joey and disappear into the nearby hills.

57.39 *The Horse Caper.* Jan. 19, 1957. Joey learns that Jim is in financial difficulty, so he plans to enter Fury in a traveling circus to raise money.

57.40 *Joey Shows the Way.* Jan. 26, 1957. GS: Peter Votrian. Joey befriends a young crippled boy in his class and helps him regain his self-confidence.

57.41 *Nature's Engineers.* Feb. 2, 1957. GS: Hal Baylor, Henry Rowland, John Cason. Joey discovers that poachers are responsible for a drop in the valuable water supply to Jim's ranch. They are raiding beaver colonies for the valuable pelts.

57.42 *The Strong Man.* Feb. 16, 1957. GS: Mickey Simpson, Barry Froner. An ex-seaman, who refuses to fight a smaller man, is branded a coward. Joey finds that when he befriends the sailor, his friends avoid him too.

57.43 *The Scientists.* Feb. 23, 1957. GS: Robert Keith. Jim orders Joey and his friend to conduct their chemistry experiments away from the ranch, but the boys put their elementary scientific knowledge to use when Pete is trapped in a collapsed well.

57.44 *My Horse Ajax.* March 9, 1957. GS: David Saber, Dabbs Greer, Ray Walker. A child star plots to take Fury away from Joey when the boy sees Fury outperform his own famed movie horse. He gets Joey to agree to let him take Fury back to Hollywood to finish a picture.

57.45 *The Tomboy.* March 16, 1957. Joey and his friends are distressed by the arrival of a pretty girl in town. She proves she can beat any of the boys in their games.

57.46 *Joey, Junior Lifeguard.* March 30, 1957. Joey learns the hard way not to ignore warnings against using the old swimming hole.

Season Three

57.47 *Fire Prevention Week.* Oct. 12, 1957. Joey is appointed national junior fire chief in his county. The training he receives come in handy when a neighbor's house catches fire.

57.48 *The Racers.* Oct. 19, 1957. GS: Gregory Howard. Joey enters the local soapbox derby. Another entrant, Bobby, is determined to win. In fact Bobby even tampers with Joey's racer to make sure Joey will not win.

57.49 *The Community Chest.* Oct. 26, 1957. Jim accepts the chairmanship of the Community Chest Drive, and Joey heads the junior committee. When Joey asks his friend Kenny Watson to help him, Kenny claims he is too busy. But Joey finds that the real reason is that Kenny's father lacks interest in the project.

57.50 *Mercy Flight.* Nov. 2, 1957. Jim helps the sheriff form an Aero Squadron for the valley. The squadron will work with the Civil Air Patrol.

57.51 *The Renegade.* Nov. 9, 1957. GS: Malcolm Atterbury. Joey and Pee Wee turn a small dog loose to prevent its being killed by its cruel master. The dog is blamed for the destruction of chickens and eggs in the neighborhood.

57.52 *Pee Wee Grows Up.* Nov. 16, 1957. Pee Wee is overly conscious of his size and tired of the teasing of bigger boys. At his own expense, Joey sends away for a body-building course for Pee Wee.

57.53 *The Fourth Estaters.* Nov. 23, 1957. Joey is working at the local newspaper with editor Pop Grayson. The paper's biggest advertiser, Mr. Allerdice, tries to force Pop to support an issue that will be beneficial to Allerdice, but not to the town.

57.54 *The Tornado.* Nov. 30, 1957. A series of tornadoes strikes near the McLaughlin ranch. Joey and Pee Wee dig a shelter that is large enough to accommodate people, but there is no room for Fury.

57.55 *The Pinto Stallion.* Dec. 7, 1957. Joey and Pee Wee are almost run down when a pinto stallion, trying to take over a herd, causes a stampede.

57.56 *Bike Road-eo.* Dec. 14, 1957. GS: Ernie Dotson. The sheriff and Jim organize a bicycle-safety program. But one bike hot-rodder, Carl Page, refuses to cooperate.

57.57 *The Wayfarer.* Dec. 21, 1957. Jim and Pete become worried about Joey and Pee Wee's reaction to Christmas. They feel that the youngsters are only interested in the gifts they will receive and not in the true spirit of Christmas.

57.58 *$1000 Reward.* Dec. 28, 1957. Joey and Pee Wee read the wanted notices in the post office. They are convinced that a stranger in the community is a wanted criminal.

57.59 *Operation CD.* Jan. 4, 1958. Charlie Fields, a neighboring rancher, refuses to take part in the local civil defense program because he believes it is childish. Then floods threaten the inhabitants of the valley.

57.60 *The Break-Up.* Jan. 11, 1958. After a very bad season, Jim blames Pete for the ranch's problems and the loss of a badly needed order for horses.

57.61 *Joey's First Crush.* Jan. 18, 1958. The new substitute teacher is a very pretty young woman. Joey gets a crush on her and is so preoccupied he is in a constant daze.

57.62 *Pee Wee's Problem.* Jan. 25, 1958. When Pee Wee's father decides to give up his ranch and take a job in South America, Joey is dismayed to learn that his friend will be sent away to boarding school.

57.63 *The Lost Herd.* Feb. 1, 1958. During a severe drought, a herd of wild horses has gone far north in search of water. Joey, Jim and Pete set out to find the herd.

57.64 *The Baby Sitters.* Feb. 8, 1958. GS: Richard Garland, Barbara Ann Knudson, Ray Ferrell, Bill Henry, Tom London. Joey and Pee Wee agree to baby-sit for Martha Michell's five-year-old son Mark. Two tramps come to the house and Joey learns that one of them is Martha's husband who deserted her years before.

57.65 *The Horse Nobody Wanted.* Feb. 15, 1958. GS: Hal K. Dawson, I. Stanford Jolley. A horse trainer named Sam learns that a horse he once trained for the circus is about to be sold to a glue factory. Feeling sorry for the animal, he sets him free to graze on the range.

57.66 *The Bounty Hunters.* Feb. 22, 1958. GS: Rocky Lundy, James Bannon. Joey and his friends want to hunt a cougar, but their parents insist they learn more about rifles first. One young man, however, is convinced that the adults want to win the bounty on the cougar themselves, and sets out to hunt on his own.

57.67 *The Meanest Man.* March 1, 1958. GS: Will Wright. Joey and Pee Wee are barred from swimming in their usual place when Daniel Malakey, the new owner of the Rocking Y Ranch, dams up one of his streams.

57.68 *A Fish Story.* March 8, 1958. GS: Ben Weldon, Richard Karlan, James Bannon. Joey and Pee Wee go fishing in a lake near the ranch. They meet two novice fishermen and try to give them some advice. Then they discover that their new acquaintances are wanted jewel thieves.

57.69 *Rogues and Squares.* March 15, 1958. Two young hooligans, Chuck and Vince, injure a horse by accident. Joey and Pee Wee are witnesses and the toughs accuse them of tattling to the sheriff.

57.70 *Robbers' Roost.* March 22, 1958. GS: Lane Bradford, James Gavin, Harlan Warde. Rustlers have been stealing horses from the broken Wheel Ranch, and Jim and Pete decide to keep a watch on the herd. Then Joey and Pee Wee go camping and accidentally discover the cave where the rustlers are hiding the horses.

57.71 *Second Chance.* March 29, 1958. GS: John Baer, Harlan Warde. Pete objects when Jim hires a handyman with a criminal record. Then Pete's wallet disappears and he is convinced that the new employee is to blame.

57.72 *The Claim Jumpers.* April 5, 1958. GS: Francis McDonald, Gregg Barton, Fred Coby. Joey and Pee Wee decide to take a picture of an old prospector to enter in a picture contest. They take the photograph just as the old man is staking a claim. Later the prospector is attacked by two claim jumpers.

Season Four

57.73 *The Littlest Horse Thief.* Oct. 11, 1958. Packy wants to buy a horse on the McLaughlin ranch, but his mother refuses to let him. When the horse disappears, Packy is accused of stealing it.

57.74 *Palomino.* Oct. 18, 1958. Jim tries to break a Palomino horse named Sunburst, but the animal is so wild it is impossible to ride him. Packy decides to make friends with the horse.

57.75 *Halloween.* Oct. 25, 1958. Joey and Packy decide to give a Halloween party. But two of the guests are practical jokers who set out to frighten everybody.

57.76 *Jailbreak.* Nov. 1, 1958. A cowboy is accused of armed robbery. Joey and his friend Packy try to prove the young man's innocence.

57.77 *Aunt Harriet.* Oct. 8, 1958. GS: Maudie Prickett. Aunt Harriet visits the Broken Wheel Ranch and decides that Jim and Joey need some discipline.

57.78 *The Fire Watchers.* Nov. 15, 1958. Packy and Joey, part-time fire watchers in the forests near their ranches, spot a fire. Learning that two lumbermen are trapped, the boys send Fury for help.

57.79 *The Ornithologists.* Nov. 22, 1958. Two competing ornithology professors come to the Broken Wheel Ranch in search of a rare bird — the yellow-tailed grosbeak. Joey and Packy try to help the men.

57.80 *The Unwanted Shepherd.* Nov. 29, 1958. A rancher tries to take over a shepherd's property. Joey and Jim decide to give the shepherd a helping hand.

57.81 *Troubles Have Wings.* Dec. 6, 1958. Fury makes friends with a raven, and when Pete's life is in danger the bird comes to the rescue.

57.82 *The Model Plane.* Dec. 20, 1958. Packy unintentionally breaks a model plane that Joey is readying for a contest. Packy blames the accident on Fury and then, ashamed of himself, runs away.

57.83 *The Will.* Dec. 27, 1958. GS: Diane Mountford. Penny Blaine's father was left instructions in a will to perform the mercy killing of a cat. Penny, fearing that her father will carry out the instructions, decides to hide with the cat. Hearing that Penny is missing, Joey and Packy help search for her.

57.84 *The Pulling Contest.* Jan. 3, 1959. GS: William Leslie, John Compton. Chris Lambert decides that there is only one way he can get enough money to save the farm. He must sell Packy's horse Lucky. But this leaves him with Dan, his plow horse, as the only entry in a pulling contest.

57.85 *Ten Dollars a Head.* Jan. 17, 1959. Jim leaves the ranch to pick up supplies, and Joey and Packy are left alone. While Jim is away, a rustler comes to the ranch and starts rounding up the horses.

57.86 *Feeling His Oats.* Jan. 24, 1959. Fury's colt, Thunder, continually trespasses on a neighbor's property. The neighbor tells Jim and Joey that if Thunder isn't kept tied, he will kill the colt.

57.87 *Bad Medicine.* Jan. 31, 1959. GS: Peter Votrian. Young Arthur Patton, an asthma sufferer is spending the summer at Broken Wheel Ranch. While on a camping trip with Joey and Packy, Arthur has a coughing spell and reaches for pills, unaware that they are poison.

57.88 *Sonic Boom.* Feb. 7, 1959. GS: Walter Reed. Miles Jackson attempts to arouse other ranchers in a protest against the presence of a nearby jet base.

57.89 *An Old Indian Trick.* Feb. 14, 1959. GS: Paul Picerni, Lars Henderson. While doing exploratory work on the Broken Wheel Ranch, a Pawnee Indian and his crippled son come across an outlaw hiding in a cave.

57.90 *The Relay Station.* Feb. 21, 1959. GS: Ben Harris, Walter Maslow. Jim's been swindled out of payment for some horses. He joins the sheriff's posse in search of the men who tricked him.

57.91 *Black Gold.* Feb. 28, 1959. GS: Andy Clyde, Robert Foulk, Robert Bice. Two wildcat oilmen learn that there is oil on Fred Farnum's ranch. The wildcatters seize Farnum's deed and plot to kill him.

57.92 *Girl Scout.* March 7, 1959. GS: Karen Green. Boy Scouts Joey and Pee Wee and Girl Scout Sally Ann Johnson get lost during an expedition in the mountains.

57.93 *House Guests.* March 14, 1959. Joey, out for a ride on Fury, comes across two injured men in a wrecked car. Believing the two men to be hunters, Joey takes them back to the ranch. Later, Joey learns the true identity of his guests.

57.94 *Joey's Jalopy.* April 4, 1959. GS: Lee Erickson, Dennis Moore. Joey and Pee Wee buy an old car on credit and put Fury up as their collateral.

Season Five

57.95 *Junior Achievement.* Oct. 10, 1959. GS: Buddy Hart. Joey and Packy decide to go into business. Their first venture is to buy some junk from a man at a bargain price.

57.96 *The Big Leaguer.* Oct. 17, 1959. GS: Charles Aidman. Joey and Packy are hoping to become members of the Little League baseball team.

57.97 *Trail Drive.* Oct. 24, 1959. GS: John Milford, John Pickard. On the trail drive to a cattle auction, Fury is the lead horse, and the driver encounters rustlers.

57.98 *Man-Killer.* Oct. 31, 1959. GS: Lane Bradford, Mike Ragan. Fury's son Thunder is stolen from the ranch. The thieves disguise the big horse and put him in a rodeo.

57.99 *Visiting Day.* Nov. 7, 1959. Packy is disappointed when his parents are too busy to visit his school during National Education Week. He runs away from home and joins a band of hoboes.

57.100 *Timber Walker.* Nov. 14, 1959. GS: Harry Lauter, Tony Young. Joey and Packy try to prevent the cutting down of a cluster of trees. If they are cut, nearby ranches would be vulnerable to floods.

57.101 *Turkey Day.* Nov. 21, 1959. To make sure that his pet turkey isn't the main course for Thanksgiving dinner, Packy hides the bird in the woods.

57.102 *The Map.* Nov. 28, 1959. An old prospector with a treasure map arrives at the Broken Wheel Ranch. Joey and Packy join the treasure hunt, but the group runs into unexpected trouble as three thugs plan to steal the map and the treasure.

57.103 *The Rocketeers.* Dec. 5, 1959. GS: Billy Chapin, Forrest Compton. A rocket scientist helps Joey, Packy and Vic Rockwell build a rocket. But Vic's father doesn't want him wasting his time with rockets.

57.104 *The Fort.* Dec. 12, 1959. GS: Lew Gallo, Jonathan Hole. Jim establishes homestead rights on some property. But two men scheme to appropriate the land, believing it will become the site of a new missile plant.

57.105 *The Vanishing Blacksmith.* Dec. 19, 1959. GS: Peter Whitney, John Conwell, Lewis Martin, Phil A. Dean. Blacksmith Eli Kane is threatened with eviction, so Jim attempts to raise money to pay the landlord.

57.106 *The Big Brothers.* Dec. 26, 1959. GS: Tony Haig, Syd Saylor. Jim is a member of the Big Brothers organization, which helps children in need. He brings an underprivileged boy to the Broken Wheel Ranch, and soon after Pete discovers that some of his money is missing.

57.107 *Packy, the Lion Tamer.* Jan. 2, 1960. GS: John Compton, Paul Picerni. After seeing the circus, Packy decides he wants to be a lion tamer. His ambition is put to the test when a lion escapes and comes to the area near the ranch.

57.108 *Private Eyes.* Jan. 9, 1960. GS: Sid Cassell, K.L. Smith. Joey and Packy are engrossed in a book entitled "How to Be a Detective." They put the book to use when burglars steal Fury's new saddle.

57.109 *The Witch.* Jan. 16, 1960. GS: Roy Kellogg, Hope Summers, Jess Kirkpatrick. Joey and Packy find a horse trapped in a mud hole. They seek the help of the Society for the Prevention of Cruelty to Animals.

57.110 *Gymkhana.* Jan. 23, 1960. GS: Stephen Hammer, Bartlett Robinson, Russ Whiteman, Tom Hanlon. Joey wants to win the Capitol City Gymkhana, a cross-country race. But Danny Hughes has been ordered by his father to win the race at any cost.

57.111 *A Present for Packy.* Jan. 30, 1960. GS: Russ Conway, Gary Roark. Joey gives Packy a rifle for his birthday and teaches the younger boy safety rules. The two then go into the woods, unaware that an escaped convict is hiding there.

57.112 *Trottin' Horse.* Feb. 6, 1960. GS: Maudie Prickett, Robert Burton, Brad Von Beltz, Ken Clayton. A man named Norden buys a children's camp and plans to change it into a ranch and raise trotting horses there. But local citizens protest, so Norden agrees to a match race to decide if the camp will reopen.

57.113 *Packy's Dilemma.* Feb. 13, 1960. GS: Doodles Weaver, Wendy Winkleman, Gregory Irvin. Young Packy thinks it is a boy's world, and he decides to prove it to Willie Jones, a girl who lives nearby. He challenges her to a horse race.

57.114 *Gaucho.* Feb. 20, 1960. GS: Carlos Vera, Paul Engel. Packy becomes jealous when a young South American visitor threatens to monopolize Joey's friendship. When a valuable horse disappears, Packy blames the boy for leaving a pasture gate open.

57.115 *The Skin Divers.* Feb. 27, 1960. GS: Burt Metcalfe, Lee Erickson, Stephen Hammer. A sporting-goods store owner volunteers to teach skin-diving to the boys in the area. One of the boys is a smart aleck who insists on horsing around during the class, and someone is hurt.

57.116 *Packy's Dream.* March 19, 1960. GS: Gordon Hebert, Carole Wells, Bucko Stafford. Packy admires the slam-bang methods of TV cowboys. He is disgusted when Jim advises Joey to settle an argument peaceably.

58. The Gabby Hayes Show

NBC/ABC. 30 min. Broadcast history: Saturday mornings, Dec. 11, 1950–Jan. 1, 1954 (NBC); May 12, 1956–July 14, 1956 (ABC).

Regular Cast: Gabby Hayes (Host).

Premise: In this series Western sidekick Gabby Hayes told tales to the kids as the Double Bar M Ranch about exploits in the West, often using abridged clips from B-Western films.

59. Gambler

Regular Cast: Kenny Rogers (Brady Hawkes).

Premise: This series of tele-films and mini-series depicted the adventures of gambler Brady Hawkes, who usually finds himself in dangerous predicaments while pursuing card games in the old west.

The Tele-films

59.1 *The Gambler.* April 8, 1980. GS: Bruce Boxleitner, Christine Belford, Harold Gould, Clu Gulager, Lance LeGault, Lee Purcell, Noble Willingham, Ronnie Scribner. Gambler Brady Hawkes boards a train to Yuma to aid a son he never knew he had. He encounters young Billy Montana en route and they assist a reformed prostitute named Jennie Reed escape from the unwelcome advances of a railroad baron. Hawkes' two new friends assist him in his confrontation with his son's cruel stepfather at the end of the journey.

59.2 *The Gambler, Part II — The Adventure Continues.* Nov. 28, 1983 & Nov. 29, 1983. GS: Bruce Boxleitner, Linda Evans, Johnny Crawford, Charlie Fields, David Hedison, Bob Hoy, Brion James, Paul Koslo, Cameron Mitchell, Mitchell Ryan, Gregory Sierra, Harold Gould, Ken Swofford, Macon McCalman. Brady Hawkes and Billy Montana track vicious outlaw leader Charlie McCourt, who has kidnaped Hawkes' son. hey are assisted by saloon singer Kate Muldoon, who is actually a quick-triggered bounty hunter.

59.3 *The Gambler, Part III — The Legend Continues.* Nov. 22, 1987 & Nov. 24, 1987. GS: Bruce Boxleitner, Linda Gray, Melanie Chartoff, Matt Clark, Jeffrey Jones, George American Horse, Marc Alaimo, Richard Chaves, Michael Berryman, George Kennedy, Dean Stockwell, Charles Durning. Brady Hawkes and Billy Montana try to protect Chief Sitting Bull and the Sioux Indians from Government corruption in North Dakota in the 1890s.

59.4 *The Gambler Returns: The Luck of the Draw.* Oct. 10, 1992 & Oct. 12, 1992. GS: Kenny Rogers, Reba McEntire, Rick Rossovich, Patrick Macnee, Park Overall, Claude Akins, Gene Barry, David Carradine, Chuck Connors, Johnny Crawford, Brian Keith, Jack Kelly, Hugh O'Brian, Clint Walker, James Drury, Paul Brinegar, Doug McClure, Linda Evans, Mickey Rooney, Zelda Rubinstein, Sheryl Lee Ralph, Dub Taylor. Brady Hawkes travels across the country to participate in a winner-take-all poker game in San Francisco.

59.5 *The Gambler V: Playing for Keeps.* Oct. 2, 1994 & Oct. 4, 1994. GS: Kris Kamm, Scott Paulin, Brett Cullen, Mariska Hargitay, Dixie Carter, Richard Riehle, Loni Anderson, Geoffrey Lewis, Martin Kove, Bruce Boxleitner, Dave Cass. Hawkes is on the trail of his estranged son, who is running with outlaws Butch Cassidy and the Sundance Kid. Hawkes follows the gang to Bolivia, with Pinkerton detectives hard on his trail.

60. The Gene Autry Show

CBS. 30 min. Broadcast history: Sunday, 7:00-7:30, July 1950–July 1953; Tuesday, 8:00-8:30, July 1953–Sept. 1954; Saturday, 7:00-7:30, Sept. 1954–Aug. 1956.

Regular Cast: Gene Autry (Gene Autry), Pat Buttram (Pat Buttram).

Premise: Singing cowboy Gene Autry, his horse Champion, and his sidekick Pat Buttram travel the Southwest to help maintain law and order.

The Episodes

60.1 *Head for Texas.* July 23, 1950. GS: Jim Frasher, George J. Lewis, House Peters, Jr., Ben Weldon, Ray Bennett. Gene returns from a trip to find that the new ranch hands working for his boss are really rustlers in disguise. When the rustlers decide to rebrand the herd and frame Gene, the trouble begins.

60.2 *Gold Dust Charlie.* July 30, 1950. GS: Sheila Ryan, Steve Darrell, Ralph Sanford, Alan Hale, Jr., Tom London, Gregg Barton, Sam Flint, Frankie Marvin, Bob Woodward, The Cass County Boys. Gene happens upon a murdered prospector and finds gold while digging the old man's grave. When he reports this, however, he is arrested on suspicion of murder.

60.3 *The Silver Arrow.* Aug. 6, 1950. GS: Jim Frasher, George J. Lewis, Gregg Barton, Ben Weldon, Robert Livingston, Sandy Sanders. When Gene finds a former witness against a young mine owner murdered, he suspects a frameup. Gene goes to the sheriff and when the two men investigate they find that a second murder is in the making.

60.4 *The Doodle Bug.* Aug. 13, 1950. GS: Sheila Ryan, Steve Darrell, Minerva Urecal, Gregg Barton, Alan Hale, Jr., Tommy Ivo, Tom London. While Gene and Pat are out investigating numerous holdups, they narrowly escape a landslide trap.

60.5 *The Star Toter.* Aug. 20, 1950. GS: Bill Gray, Barbara Stanley, George J. Lewis, House Peters, Jr., Robert Livingston, Wes Hudman, Frankie Marvin, Beatrice Gray. Gene dons a sheriff's badge to pursue a homicidal bank robber. A ten-year-old wayward son is thought to be the outlaw.

60.6 *The Double Switch.* Aug. 27, 1950. GS: Steve Darrel, Alan Hale, Jr., Sam Flint, Tom London, Gregg Barton, Frankie Marvin. Gene and Pat unmask an unexpected bandit leader when they investigate some stage coach robberies.

60.7 *Blackwater Valley Feud.* Sept. 3, 1950. GS: Stanley Andrews, Gail Davis, William Haade, Francis McDonald, Harry Lauter, Jack Ingram. A disguised crook tries to break up a neighboring ranch and put the blame on Autry's boss.

60.8 *Doublecross Valley.* Sept. 10, 1950. GS: Gail Davis, Stanley Andrews, Harry Lauter, William Haade, Francis McDonald, Michael Ragan, Wade Crosby, Bob Cason, Frankie

Marvin, Charles Lyon. Gene sets out after a mysterious gang which has been trying to gain possession of a local ranch. During his investigation, he stumbles upon a legend of buried gold.

60.9 *The Posse.* Sept. 17, 1950. GS: Wendy Waldron, Francis Ford, John Doucette, Bud Osborne, Robert J. Wilke, Bob Cason, Bob Woodward, Frankie Marvin. When Gene comes to the aid of a former outlaw, several of the outlaw's friends try to get him to assist them in robbing Gene's safe.

60.10 *The Devil's Brand.* Sept. 24, 1950. GS: Wendy Waldron, Gail Davis, John Doucette, Bud Osborne, Bob Cason, Francis Ford, Robert J. Wilke, George Lloyd, Wes Hudman. Foreman Gene Autry leads a manhunt for the killer of his boss, owner of the Rocking-R Ranch. Autry sends for the ranch owner's niece and heir, but the outlaw killers have some plans of their own for the ranch.

60.11 *Six Shooter Sweepstakes.* Oct. 1, 1950. GS: James Frazier, Harry Harvey, Virginia Merrick, Kenne Duncan, Zon Murray, Tom Neal, Wes Hudman, Louis Morphy, Frankie Marvin. Gene's horse, Champion, helps the cowboy track down some outlaws when the horse is entered in what turns out to be a fixed race.

60.12 *The Poisoned Waterhole.* Oct. 8, 1950. GS: Sheila Ryan, Bill Henry, Leonard Penn, Cheif Thundercloud, Don C. Harvey, Tom London, Frankie Marvin, Wes Hudman. Gene and his friend Pat come across a poisoned waterhold while out on a hunting trip. Attempting to find the culprit, Gene runs into some trouble with an Indian tribe and a railroad camp.

60.13 *Last Chance.* Oct. 15, 1950. GS: Zon Murray, Don Pietro, Kenne Duncan, Harry Harvey, Sr., Tom Neal, Wes Hudman, Frankie Marvin, Louis Morphy, George Steele, Keene Cooper. Gene tries to help a little Mexican boy out of a difficult situation. The boy is captured by a gang of outlaws who believe he knows the way to a legendary gold mine.

60.14 *The Black Rider.* Oct. 22, 1950. GS: Sheila Ryan, Tom London, Don C. Harvey, Bill Henry, Wes Hudman, Leonard Penn, Frank Downing, Frank Urton, Bob Woodward. Gene tangles with the mysterious Black Rider, who has been terrorizing the whole town. The desperate outlaw plans revenge on everyone connected with the execution of a killer.

60.15 *Gun Powder Range.* Oct. 29, 1950. Gail Davis, Dick Jones, George J. Lewis, Kenneth MacDonald, Dick Alexander, Lee Phelps, Chuck Roberson, Wes Hudman, Frank Matts, Rand Brooks, B. Naylor, Frankie Marvin. Gene and Pat risk disgrace and death in a desperate attempt to convince a boy that there is nothing heroic about the life of an outlaw.

60.16 *The Breakup.* Nov. 5, 1950. GS: Rand Brooks, Lynne Roberts, Jim Bannon, Paul Campbell, Alan Hale, Jr., I. Stanford Jolley, Wes Hudman, Edgar Dearing, Bob Woodward, Beatrice Gray, Carl Sepulveda. Gene and his pal Pat help a wounded rancher and learn that the man's son-in-law is suspected of the shooting.

60.17 *Twisted Trails.* Nov. 12, 1950. GS: Lynne Roberts, Jim Bannon, Billy Gray, Paul Campbell, Edgar Dearing, Alan Hale, Jr., Rand Brooks, Wes Hudman, I. Stanford Jolley, Boyd Stockman, Carl Sepulveda. When an outlaws tries to steal Champion, he gets into more trouble than he bargained for.

60.18 *Fight at Peaceful Mesa.* Nov. 19, 1950. GS: Gail Davis, Kenneth MacDonald, George J. Lewis, Lee Phelps, Dick Alexander, Wes Hudman, Chuck Roberson. Autry and Pat find a dying rancher while in search of a masked gang. The two cowboys witness the rancher's oral will but find themselves in danger when trying to carry it out.

60.19 *Hot Lead.* Nov. 26, 1950. GS: Don C. Harvey, Alan Hale, Jr., Jim Frasher, Harry Lauter, Harry Cheshire, Marshall Reed, Kenne Duncan, Frankie Marvin. Autry befriends a young boy and a mistreated palomino and his kindness is repaid in a strange and unexpected way while the cowboy is trailng some bank robbers.

60.20 *Gray Dude.* Dec. 3, 1950. GS: James Griffith, Reed Howes, Chill Wills, Robert Filmer, Kermit Maynard, Art Dillard, Tom Monroe, Sam Flint. Autry's best friend is killed by an outlaw called the Gray Dude and Gene sets out to capture the killer. But when a sheriff refuses to cooperate in the search Gene begins to suspect the lawman.

60.21 *Killer Horse.* Dec. 10, 1950 GS: Hal K. Dawson, Bill Kimbley, Alan Hale, Jr., Don C. Harvey, Kenne Duncan, Harry Cheshire, Marshall Reed, Frankie Marvin, Bob Woodward. Gene protects a young boy's unbroken horse when the animal is accused of killing an old prospector. Though evidence indicates that the horse is at fault, Gene sets out to find the real killer

60.22 *The Peace Maker.* Dec. 17, 1950. GS: Chill Wills, Sam Flint, James Griffith, Peggy Stewart, Robert Filmer, Reed Howes, Russell Hayden, Kermit Maynard, Art Dillard, George Steele, John Kee, Tom Monroe. When Gene is knocked unconscious by an outlaw, his horse Champion starts to enforce his own laws.

60.23 *The Sheriff of Santa Rosa.* Dec. 24, 1950. GS: Fuzzy Knight, Dick Jones, Mira McKinney, Stanley Andrews, Nan Leslie, Chuck Roberson, Dick Curtis, James Harrison, Boyd Stockman, Al Wyatt. Sheriff Gene Autry lets a young ranch owner, who is suspected of horse stealing, escape from jail.

60.24 *T.N.T.* Dec. 31, 1950. GS: Fuzzy Knight, Stanley Andrews, Eileen Janssen, Dick Curtis, Chuck Roberson, James Harrison. Gene gets in unexpected trouble when he befriends an apparently homeless little girl.

60.25 *The Raiders.* April 14, 1951. GS: Fuzzy Knight, George Cooper, Nan Leslie, Raymond Hatton, Reed Howes, Gregg Barton, Bill Kennedy, Jack Ingram, Michael Ragan, Wes Hudman, Boyd Stockman. A notorious outlaw fools even his own fiancee until Gene takes matters into his own hands. Gene plans a trap for the gangster when he suspects the plot.

60.26 *Double Barrelled Vengeance.* April 21, 1951. GS: Fuzzy Knight, Raymond Hatton, Nan Leslie, Jack Ingram, Gregg Barton, Bob Cason, Bill Kennedy, Michael Ragan. As special investigator for an express company, Gene has to turn outlaw to find soem money which has been stolen.

60.27 *Ghost Town Raiders.* Oct. 6, 1951. GS: William Fawcett, Wendy Waldron, Sam Flint, George J. Lewis, Raphael Bennett, Reed Howes, Kermit Maynard, Art Dillard, Bob Woodward. Gene risks his life to track down bandits.

60.28 *Frontier Guard.* Oct. 13, 1951. GS: James Craven, Francis McDonald, Donna Martell, Ewing Mitchell, Denver Pyle, Gregg Barton, Riley Hill, Tom Monroe. As a member of the Border Patrol, Gene helps a rancher who is being terrorized. Autry and his sidekick Pat prevent the attempted kidnaping of the ranch owner's daughter, and then investigate the attacks.

60.29 *Silver Dollars.* Oct. 20, 1951. GS: Wendy Waldron, William Fawcett, Louise Lorimer, Ray Bennett, George J. Lewis, Art Dillard, Kermit Maynard. Gene and his pal Pat join forces with the sheriff in order to find the outlaws who have killed and robbed a wagon driver.

60.30 *Killer's Trail.* Oct. 27, 1951. GS: Donna Martell, Francis McDonald, James Craven, Denver Pyle, Ewing Mitchell, Tom Monroe, Gregg Barton, Riley Hill, Bob Woodward. Autry and Pat Buttram find out the true identity of El Avengador, when they rescue a girl being pursued by three men.

60.31 *Frame for Trouble.* Nov. 3, 1951. GS: Gail Davis, Dick Curtis, Dennis Moore, John Halloran, Don C. Harvey, Marshall Reed. Gene is charged with murder when he keeps a captured gunslinger's secret rendezvous.

60.32 *Warning! Danger!* Nov. 10, 1951. GS: Dick Jones, Gloria Winters, Teddy Infuhr, Gordon Jones, Harry Lauter, Leonard Penn, Bill Kennedy. Gene and Put encounter a dangerous train robber.

60.33 *Revenge Trail.* Nov. 17, 1951. GS: Gail Davis, Dick Curtis, John Halloran, Don C. Harvey, Dennis Moore, Marshall Reed, Bob Woodward. Pat helps U.S. Marshal Gene Autry solve a series of mysterious murders.

60.34 *The Bandits of Boulder Bluff.* Nov. 24, 1951. GS: Dick Jones, Anne O'Neal, Leonard Penn, Harry Lauter, Bill Kennedy, Gordon Jones. Marshal Gene Autry aids Pat in exposing the murderer in a gold dust robbery. Gene and Pat search for the killer after an innocent man is accused of murder.

60.35 *Outlaw Escapes.* Dec. 1, 1951. GS: James Craven, Gail Davis, Ewing Mitchell, Robert Peyton, Ben Weldon, Myron Healey, Lee Morgan. Town boss Brad Bidwell arranges for the election of Pat Buttram as sheriff so that his illegal schemes may proceed undeterred. Pat contacts his friend Gene Autry to assist him bring the outlaws to justice.

60.36 *The Kid Comes West.* Dec. 8, 1951. GS: William Fawcett, Sherry Jackson, Steve Pendleton, Keith Richards, Craig Woods, Sandy Sanders. When his daughter dies, an elderly rancher sends for her child, whom he plans to make his heir. Gene and Pat go to meet the boy's stage, but find some unexpected trouble in store for them.

60.37 *The Return of Maverick Dan.* Dec. 15, 1951. GS: Carole Nugent, Ben Weldon, James Craven, Myron Healey, Ewing Mitchell, Lee Morgan, Robert Peyton. Gene is on the trail of Maverick Dan when he comes upon the man's sister. The girl believes her brother is innocent and asks Gene to investigate. When he does, he comes up with some surprising results.

60.38 *Galloping Hoofs.* Dec. 22, 1951. GS: Gail Davis, George J. Lewis, Denver Pyle, Harry Harvey, Belle Mitchell. Gene learns that a convicted embezzler has escaped from jail. The thief accuses his partner of double crossing him and Autry intervenes to see that justice is done.

60.39 *Heir to the Lazy L.* Dec. 29, 1951. GS: Gail Davis, Alan Hale, Jr., Sandy Sanders, Helen Servis, Hugh Prosser, Terry Frost. Gene inherits half of a ranch from an uncle but is attacked by masked men on his way to the Lazy L. When he learns that the owner of the other half plans to sell, Gene suspects a plot.

60.40 *Melody Mesa.* Jan. 4, 1952. GS: Gail Davis, Ewing Mitchell, Denver Pyle, Harry Harvey, Belle Mitchell, George J. Lewis, Riley Hill, Jim Brittain. A sheriff friend of Gene's asks the cowboy to pose as a music teacher to trap a counterfeiting gang.

60.41 *Horse Sense.* Jan. 11, 1952. GS: Gail Davis, Alan Hale, Jr., Dick Jones, Hugh Prosser, Terry Frost, Sandy Sanders, Bob Woodward. Gene and Pat are hired by a young rancher and her brother to help train horses.

60.42 *Rocky River Feud.* Jan. 18, 1952. GS: Sherry Jackson, William Fawcett, Craig Woods, Sandy Sanders, Keith Richards, Steve Pendleton. Pat inherits a stage line from a distant relative and Gene goes to the town with him.

60.43 *The Lawless Press.* Jan. 25, 1952. GS: Roy Gordon, James Anderson, George Pembroke, Dennis Moore, Gregg Barton, Ed Hinkle, Bruce Norman, Frankie Marvin. Gene discovers th solution to an attempt on his life in a very strang place when he is ambushed after being elected Sheriff. He finds a clue to his attacker when he sees a smudge on his shirt.

60.44 *The Western Way.* Feb. 1, 1952. GS: Mira McKinney, Dick Jones, Steve Clark, Harry Lauter, Robert J. Wilke, Don C. Harvey. Gene and Pat capture a bank robber and find that he is the son of their friend Ma Walker.

60.45 *Ruthless Renegade.* Feb. 8, 1952. GS: Dennis Moore, Roy Gordon, Jane Frazee, James Anderson, Bruce Norman, Ed Hinkle, Gregg Barton, Frankie Marvin. While riding through a lawless frontier town, U.S. Marshal Gene Atury and deputy Pat Buttram are drawn into the conflict between the decent citizens and a ruthless outlaw leader.

60.46 *Hot Lead and Old Lace.* Feb. 15, 1952. GS: Steve Clark, Mira McKinney, Harry Lauter, Don Harvey, Robert J. Wilke, Bob Woodward. Gene and Pat help a courageous old lady defend a ranch after the owner is murdered. The two cowboys investigate to find out why the ranch is so valuable to the gunmen.

60.47 *Blazeaway.* Feb. 22, 1952. GS: Mary Treen, Richard Travis, Pierre Watkin, Kermit Maynard, Robert Bice, Sandy Sanders, Bob Woodward. Gene, as a cavalry officer, helps to prove the innocence of an Indian tribe.

60.48 *Bullets and Bows.* March 2, 1952. GS: Elaine Riley, Denver Pyle, John Doucette, Gregg Barton, Myron Healey, Bob Woodward. Gene's friend Pat, owner of the town's tailor shop, gets a shipment of ladies' clothing by mistake. The error provides a local big shot with a way to get property.

60.49 *Trouble at Silver Creek.* March 9, 1952. GS: Barbara Stanley, Francis McDonald, Leonard Penn, Steve Conte, George Pembroke, Tom Tyler, Craig Woods. Gene and Pat foil the attempts of a rich and unscrupulous man to poison the cattle of a ranch owner. When Pat's boss is killed by a hired gunman, Gene helps his friend to track down the real criminal.

60.50 *Six Gun Romeo.* March 16, 1952. GS: Elaine Riley, Mary Treen, Richard Travis, Kermit Maynard, Robert Bice, Pierre Watkin, Frankie Marvin. A spinster determined to marry and a crook who covets a gold shipment provide some problems for Gene.

60.51 *The Sheriff Is a Lady.* March 23, 1952. GS: Elaine Riley, Denver Pyle, Dick Jones, Myron Healey, John Doucette, Gregg Barton. As a member of the Texas Border Patrol, Gene is assigned the task of finding the man responsible for gun smuggling.

60.52 *Trail of the Witch.* March 30, 1952. GS: Almira Sessions, Francis McDonald, Bill George, Leonard Penn, Steve

The Gene Autry Show

Conte, Tom Tyler, Craig Woods, George Pembroke, Bob Woodward. Gene and Pat are ambushed while trailing a gang of outlaws. The cowboys are called in by a young sheriff to help stop the series of mine shipment robberies by an unknown gang.

60.53 *Thunder Out West.* July 14, 1953. GS: Wendy Waldron, Lyle Talbot, William Fawcett, Lane Chandler, Harry Lauter, Bob Woodward, Tom Tyler, George Slocum, Larry Hudson. A clever safe cracker uses a mail-order telescope to get the information he needs to commit his crimes. Gene sets a trap for the man, but has a surprise when the crook is finally revealed.

60.54 *Outlaw Stage.* July 21, 1953. GS: Harry Mackin, Don C. Harvey, Edmund Cobb, Frank Jacquet, Pierce Lyden, Julian Upton, Steve Conte, Kermit Maynard. Autry attempts to clear a young stage driver in the fatal holdup of a jewelry salesman carrying a fortune in precious stones.

60.55 *Ghost Mountain.* July 28, 1953. GS: Eileen Janssen, Ross Ford, Clayton Moore, John Doucette, Ewing Brown, Sandy Sanders. Gene finds himself battling some very lifelike ghosts when he gets involved with an archaeologist and a clever outlaw.

60.56 *The Old Prospector.* Aug. 4, 1953. GS: Lyle Talbot, Myron Healey, Terry Frost, Bernard Szold, Ewing Mitchell, Sandy Sanders. Gene saves an old man from a gang of outlaws who believe the old man has found a gold mine.

60.57 *Narrow Escape.* Aug. 11, 1953. GS: Sheila Ryan, Rick Vallin, David Coleman, Bill Henry, George Pembroke, Marshall Reed, Frankie Marvin. Gene attempts to solve the mysterious holdups of stages carrying silver bullion.

60.58 *Border Justice.* Aug. 18, 1953. GS: Sheila Ryan, Pierce Lyden, Steve Conte, Don C. Harvey, Edmund Cobb, Julian Upton. Gene and Pat help the Mexican government when they go on the trail of smugglers.

60.59 *Gypsy Wagon.* Aug. 25, 1953. GS: Gloria Talbot, Lyle Talbot, Bernard Szold, Myron Healey, Ewing Mitchell, Terry Frost, Sandy Sanders, Herman Hack. When an old Gypsy and his granddaughter surprise outlaws in the act of robbing a stage, the outlaws try to kidnap the girl.

60.60 *Bandidos.* Sept. 1, 1953. GS: Wendy Waldron, Harry Lauter, William Fawcett, Lane Bradford, Tom Tyler, Larry Hudson, Bob Dominquez, Lane Chandler. A senator aids Gene in battling an outlaw gang. The outlaws are trying to swindle the townspeople into putting up money for a new dam.

60.61 *Dry Gulch at Devil's Elbow.* Sept. 8, 1953. GS: John Doucette, Clayton Moore, Joe McGuinn, Sandy Sanders, Ross Ford, Ewing Brown. Gene is called in to help a sheriff who is having trouble with a band of outlaws. It is Pa, though, who stumbles on a lead when he tells some tall tales which are believed.

60.62 *Cold Decked.* Sept. 15, 1953. GS: Stanley Andrews, Alan Bridge, William Fawcett, Henry Rowland, Gregg Barton, Kenne Duncan, Myron Healey, Ted Mapes, Bob Woodward, Terry Frost. Gene fights for justice when a local banker, who is believed to have embezzled bank funds, is threateend by a half-crazed lynch mob.

60.63 *Steel Ribbon.* Sept. 22, 1953. GS: Gail Davis, John Hamilton, Robert Lowery, Dick Emory, Terry Frost, Rusty Wescoatt, Tom London, Frankie Marvin, Bob Woodward. Gene and Pat are assigned to put an end to a series of railroad robberies.

60.64 *Rio Renegades.* Sept. 29, 1953. GS: Sheila Ryan, Stanley Andrews, Effie Laird, Myron Healey, Lee Van Cleef, Harry Harvey. Pat gets himself and Gene into trouble becuase he can't resist bragging.

60.65 *Ransom Cross.* Oct. 6, 1953. GS: Gail Davis, John Hamilton, Robert Lowery, Terry Frost, Rusty Wescoatt, Tom London, Frankie Marvin, Bob Woodward. When thieves steal an archeologist's treasure, Sheriff Gene Autry comes to the rescue and battles the crooks for the ancient relic.

60.66 *Santa Fe Raiders.* July 6, 1954. GS: Gloria Saunders, Dick Jones, Tom London, Henry Rowland, Stanley Andrews, Al Bridge, Myron Healey, Gregg Barton, Kenne Duncan, Terry Frost, Frankie Marvin, Bob Woodward. Gene comes to the aid of an old freight line operator and, subsequently, helps the son take over the business after the old man is murdered.

60.67 *Johnny Jackaroo.* July 13, 1954. GS: B.G. Norman, Ann Doran, William Fawcett, Harry Lauter, Henry Rowland, Denver Pyle, Gregg Barton. Johnny, the incorrigible eleven-year-old nephew of Gene and Pat's boss, ranch owner Lynne Moore, so irritates Pat that he plans a make-believe stage holdup to frighten some sense into the boy. Two disgruntled ranch hands intervene, however, and carry out a real robbery in the guise of Pat and Gene.

60.68 *The Hold-Up.* Dec. 14, 1952. GS: William Fawcett, Arthur Space, Rochelle Stanton, Rory Mallinson, James Best, Forrest Taylor, Gregg Barton, Red Morgan, Frankie Marvin. An old telegraph operator helps Gene round up a crooked oil promoter and his gang.

60.69 *Prize Winner.* July 27, 1954. GS: Sheila Ryan, George Pembroke, Louise Lorimer, Ferris Taylor, Rick Vallin, Marshall Reed, Edgar Dearing, Bob Woodward, Frankie Marvin. Pat's rooster leads Pat and Gene into an adventure at the county fair.

60.70 *Sharp Shooter.* Aur. 3, 1954. GS: Dick Jones, Margaret Field, Stanley Andrews, Henry Rowland, Denver Pyle, Tex Terry, Frankie Marvin. Gene and Pat come to the rescue of a young boy framed into a murder rap by a vicious sheriff. The three attempt to trap the sheriff.

60.71 *Talking Guns.* Aug. 10, 1954. GS: William Fawcett, Dee Pollock, Jim Bannon, Harry Lauter, I. Stanford Jolley, Pierce Lyden, Emmett Lynn. Gene discovers that the town gossip is far more dangerous than she seems.

60.72 *The Hoodoo Canyon.* Aug. 17, 1956. GS: James Best, Arthur Space, Rochelle Stanton, Forrest Taylor, William Fawcett, Rory Mallinson, Gregg Barton. The owner of a seemingly jinxed stageline enlists the help of Autry and his pal Pat to find the real cause of a series of robberies and damages which have been plaguing the stageline.

60.73 *The Carnival Comes West.* Aug. 24, 1954. GS: Ann Doran, Clayton Moore, William Fawcett, Denver Pyle, Henry Rowland, Harry Lauter, Gregg Barton, Pat Mitchell. The social leader of a small Western town goes to surprising lengths to guard the secret of her past life.

60.74 *Battle Axe.* Aug. 31, 1954. GS: Mira McKinney, Francis McDonald, Rick Vallin, Peter Votrian, Kenne Duncan, Gregg Barton, Terry Frost, Wes Hudman, Frankie Marvin, The Cass County Boys. When an old mai known as Battle Axe takes over as sheriff of Jimtown, Gene has trouble cleaning up an outlaw gang.

60.75 *Outlaw of Blue Mesa.* Sept. 7, 1954. GS: Denver Pyle, Claire Carleton, Dick Jones, Margaret Field, Hank Patterson, Henry Rowland, Tex Terry. Enroute to a conference with a banker, Gene and Pat save a young man from being hanged by three heavies.

60.76 *Civil War at Deadwood.* Sept. 14, 1954. GS: William Fawcett, Emmett Lynn, Gail Davis, Jim Bannon, Stanley Andrews, Harry Lauter, I. Stanford Jolley, Pierce Lyden, Frankie Marvin. A feud between a Union Army veteran and a Confederate Army veteran gets out of hand when the two men accuse each other of a robbery and a shooting.

60.77 *Boots and Ballots.* Sept. 25, 1954. GS: Kenne Duncan, Mira McKinney, Rick Vallin, Terry Frost, Gregg Barton, Howard McNeely, Frankie Marvin, Bob Woodward. The fight for mayor in a small-town election gets out of hand when a killing takes place. Gene takes matters into his own hands as he fights for a decent community.

60.78 *Outlaw Warning.* Oct. 2, 1954. GS: Sheila Ryan, Stanley Andrews, Myron Healey, Lee Van Cleef, Gregg Barton, Mickey Little, Melinda Plowman, Francis McDonald, Harry Harvey, Budd Buster, Bob Woodward. A killer, convicted on evidence given by Pat Buttram, swears revenge on Pat and the judge.

60.79 *The Million Dollar Fiddle.* Oct. 1, 1955. GS: Peter Votrian, Nestor Paiva, Jean Howell, Harry Lauter, Joe Besser, Frank Jenks, Mike Ragan. A boy violinist falls into the hands of crooks when he runs away from home and the concert stage to visit Gene's ranch.

60.80 *Stage to San Dimas.* Oct. 8, 1955. GS: Barbara Knudson, Keith Richards, George J. Lewis, Myron Healey, Steve Conte, Jack Daly, Edward Clark, Jacquelyn Park, Frankie Marvin. A stage is robbed, and a bejeweled dancer and a wounded cavalryman are among the victims of the attack.

60.81 *The Portrait of White Cloud.* Oct. 15, 1955. GS: Glenn Strange, Jack Daly, Dick Rich, John Close, Steve Raines, Terry Frost, Joseph Michaels, The Cass County Boys. Autry attempts to trap an artist who has been framing his subjects in more ways than one.

60.82 *Law Comes to Scorpion.* Oct. 22, 1955. GS: Arthur Space, Sydney Mason, Myron Healey, Lisa Montell, Richard Avonde, Earl Hodgins, Bob Cason. Autry attempts to clean up a ring of gamblers and crooked politicians, and is accused of murder as a result.

60.83 *The Golden Chariot.* Oct. 29, 1955. GS: Junius Matthews, Jean Howell, Harry Lauter, Elizabeth Harrower, Ralph Sanford, Bob Woodward, Frankie Marvin, Byron Foulger. Gene enters his matched bays in a carnival chariat race and puts to rout a band of unscrupulous carnival operators.

60.84 *Guns Below the Border.* Nov. 5, 1955. GS: Myron Healey, Keith Richards, Lane Bradford, George J. Lewis, Eugenia Paul, David Leonard, Steve Conte, David Saber. Gene is on the trail of an arms-smuggling gang. He follows them to the Mexican border where he joins with a law-enforcement officer in an effort to stop their crooked operations.

60.85 *Ghost Ranch.* Nov. 12, 1955. GS: Sally Fraser, Harry Harvey, Maxine Gates, Bob Woodward, The Cass County Boys. A hard-headed businesswoman finds that efficiency is not the only consideration when she takes over the ranch on which Autry is foreman.

60.86 *Go West, Young Lady.* Nov. 19, 1955. GS: Nan Leslie, John Close, Dick Rich, Jack Daly, Muriel Landers, Isabelle Dwan, Terry Frost, The Cass County Boys. Gene Autry investigates and tries to expose a Lonely Hearts Club racket.

60.87 *Feuding Friends.* Nov. 26, 1955. GS: Arthur Space, Myron Healey, Sydney Mason, Richard Avonde, Dennis Moore, Reed Howes, Brad Morrow, Bob Cason. Autry is on the trail of a confident threesome—a banker, a hotel owner and a counterfeiter, who think they have a perfect crime setup.

60.88 *Saddle Up.* Dec. 3, 1955. GS: Leonard Penn, Sally Mansfield, Sammy Ogg, Gregg Barton, Will Crandall, The Cass County Boys. Autry takes over as manager of a ranch for wayward boys and gets involved with a missing boy and a stray horse.

60.89 *Ride, Rancheros.* Dec. 10, 1955. GS: Leonard Penn, Emile Meyer, Sally Mansfield, Sammy Ogg, Peter Votrian, Kenne Duncan, Gregg Barton, Will Crandall, Bob Woodward, The Cass County Boys. Autry tries to reform a confirmed criminal, but the man turns out to be his own worst enemy.

60.90 *The Rangerette.* Dec. 17, 1955. GS: Leonard Penn, Emile Meyer, Sally Mansfield, Nancy Gilbert, Sammy Ogg, Peter Votrian, Kenne Duncan, Gregg Barton, Will Crandall, The Cass County Boys. Autry is pitted against a hardened band of crooks who try everything from arson to kidnaping.

60.91 *Dynamite.* Dec. 24, 1955. GS: Francis McDonald, Sally Fraser, Glenn Strange, Robert Bice, Harry Harvey, Sr., John Boutwell, Bob Woodward, The Cass County Boys. An empty stagecoach prompts Gene Autry to investigate a recent mine disaster.

61. Great Adventure

CBS. 60 min. Broadcast history: Friday, 7:30–8:30, Sept. 1963–Sept. 1964; Friday, 8:30–9:30, March 1965–April 1965.

Regular Cast: Van Heflin (Narrator).

Premise: This anthology series dramatized tales from American history, several of which dealt with the American West.

The Episodes

61.1 *The Death of Sitting Bull.* Oct. 4, 1963. GS: Ricardo Montalban, Anthony Caruso, Joseph Cotten, James Dunn, Lloyd Nolan, Claude Akins, Kent Smith, Noah Beery, Jr., Miriam Colon, Rodolfo Acosta, Eddie Little Sky. It has been fourteen years since Sitting Bull defeated Custer at the Little Bighorn, and now the suppressed Indian nations are planning an uprising. A fanatical religious cult called the Ghost Dancers expect a messiah who will bury the white man, but they wind up burying Sitting Bull instead.

61.2 *Massacre at Wounded Knee.* Oct. 11, 1963. GS: Ricardo Montalban, Anthony Caruso, Joseph Cotten, James Dunn, Lloyd Nolan, Claude Akins, Kent Smith, Noah Beery, Jr., Miriam Colon, Rodolfo Acosta, Eddie Little Sky. With the great Sioux leader dead, the Army is ordered to transfer the tribe to a new reservation. They get as far as Wounded Knee, where hatred turns to open rebellion.

61.3 *The Outlaw and the Nun.* Dec. 6, 1963. GS: Joan

Hackett, Andrew Prine, Leif Erickson, Sallie Brophy, Marion Ross, Richard Carlyle. Sister Blandina arrives in the rowdy Western town of Trinidad, Colorado, in 1870 to teach school. She soon finds that only two children in the area are attending classes.

61.4 *Wild Bill Hickok—the Legend and the Man.* Jan. 3, 1964. GS: Lloyd Bridges, Sheree North, Tom Reese, James Griffith, Len Lesser, Ed Knight, Leo Gordon, Neil Nephew. For many years Wild Bill Hickok was a U.S. marshal in the Old West, a position that called for his legendary prowess with a gun.

61.5 *Teeth of the Lion.* Jan. 17, 1964. GS: Earl Holliman, Collin Wilcox, Donald Losby, Jesse Pearson, Julie Sommars, Katie Sweet, Steven Marlo. Sodbusters Will and Elizabeth Cross have carried on a long, lonely struggle against fire, illness, weather and hostile Indians. Now they hope to persuade homesteaders Tom and Meg Jethro to settle nearby.

61.6 *The Testing of Sam Houston.* Jan. 31, 1964. GS: Robert Culp, Victor Jory, Mario Alcaide, Katherine Crawford, Robert Emhardt, Kent Smith, David White, Ralph Moody, Tom Palmer, June Vincent, Francis De Sales, Ken Drake, Robert Riordan, Edwin Mills, Bill Arvin, Dick Wilson. The early days of Sam Houston's life are depicted from his days as a lieutenant under Andrew Jackson in the War of 1812, through the start of his political career.

61.7 *The Special Courage of Captain Pratt.* Feb. 14, 1964. GS: Paul Burke, Ivan Dixon, Antoinette Bower, John Marley, Denver Pyle, Valentin de Vargas. In 1875, a group of the most dangerous renegade Indian leaders are ordered into exile in Florida, and Captain Richard Pratt is assigned to escort them, commanding members of the all-Negro 10th Cavalry.

61.8 *The Pathfinder.* March 6, 1964. GS: Rip Torn, Channing Pollock, Carroll O'Connor, Arthur Batanides, Joe De Santis, Don Dubbins, Robert F. Simon, David White, Paul Birch, Noel Drayton, Craig Duncan, John Garwood, Harry Carter, Daniel Nunez, Francisco Ortega, Elizabeth Perry. In the winter of 1844, Lt. John C. Fremont and scout Kit Carson lead their survey team over the High Sierras and down into Mexican-held California, where they have to take refuge on Johann Sutter's personal 150,000 acre empire.

61.9 *Kentucky's Bloody Ground.* April 3, 1964. GS: Peter Graves, Andrew Duggan, David McCallum, Peggy McCay, Judee Morton, Arthur Hunnicutt, Richard Lupino, Stuart Cooper, Laurie Mock, Teddy Eccles. In the mid-1770s, Daniel Boone and a party of settlers establish a settlement in the wilderness west of the Alleghenies.

61.10 *The Siege of Boonesborough.* April 10, 1964. GS: Peter Graves, Andrew Duggan, David McCallum, Peggy McCay, Judee Morton, Arthur Hunnicutt, Richard Lupino, Stuart Cooper, Laurie Mock, Teddy Eccles. Although the Indians have killed his son and kidnaped his daughter and two other girls, Daniel Boone is forced to negotiate with the red men to win the captives' release and prevent an attack on the settlement.

Grizzly Adams see *The Life and Times of Grizzly Adams*

62. Gun Shy

CBS. 30 min. Broadcast history: Tuesday, 8:30-9:00, March 1983–April 1983; Tuesday, 8:00-8:30, April 1983.

Regular Cast: Barry Van Dyke (Russell Donovan), Keith Mitchell (Clovis), Adam Rich (Clovis), Bridgette Anderson (Celia), Geoffrey Lewis (Amos), Tim Thomerson (Theodore), Henry Jones (Homer McCoy), Pat McCormick (Colonel Mound), Janis Paige (Nettie McCoy).

Premise: Russell Donovan, a gambler, settles in Quake City, California, with two children he won in a poker game and their two feckless outlaw pals.

The Episodes

62.1 *Title Unknown.* March 15, 1983. GS: Bernard Fox. Donovan gives his new son a horse he won at cards, unaware that the animal is a fabled English Derby winner.

62.2 *Title Unknown.* March 22, 1983. The red carpet is rolled out everywhere in town for Theodore and Amos when it is learned that only their shack stands in the way of Quake City becoming a railroad stop.

62.3 *Title Unknown.* March 29, 1983. GS: Lyle Waggoner. A legendary gunfighter summoned to rid Quake City of an outlaw band seems to have developed a bad case of nerves.

62.4 *Title Unknown.* April 5, 1983. GS: Henry Polic II. Donovan is banned from the gaming tables after the kids start a fire while he is out gambling—a rash decision that benefits a card shark.

62.5 *Title Unknown.* April 12, 1983. GS: Ruth Buzzi. Donovan is dragooned into riding shotgun on the stagecoach line run by Colonel Mound and his stage-driving mother after repeated ambushes by robbers.

Guns of Paradise see *Paradise*

63. The Guns of Will Sonnett

ABC. 30 min. Broadcast history: Friday, 9:30-10:00, Sept. 1967–May 1969; Monday, 8:30-9:00, June 1969–Sept. 1969.

Regular Cast: Walter Brennan (Will Sonnett), Dack Rambo (Jeff Sonnett), Jason Evers (James Sonnett).

Premise: Will Sonnett and his grandson Jeff comb the West looking for his long-missing son.

The Episodes

63.1 *The Guns of Will Sonnett.* Sept. 8, 1967. GS: Claude Akins, Paul Fix, J. Pat O'Malley, Perry Cook, Rex Holman. The Sonnetts encounter a revenge-seeker who lost an arm to the bullets of the elusive James Sonnett.

63.2 *A Bell for Jeff Sonnett.* Sept. 15, 1967. GS: Charles Grodin, Ford Rainey, Paul Wexler, Rayford Barnes, Charles Seel. A tiny bell tolls deadly for Jeff, who faces his first gunfight alone. He is up against fast gun Bells Pickering, who sews a silver bell on his holster for every victim.

63.3 *A Grave for James Sonnett.* Sept. 22, 1967. Jay Novello, Don Diamond. After finding the grave of James Sonnett, Will and Jeff set out to even the score with his killer, a marauding Mexican whom James was hired to gun down.

63.4 *The Natural Way.* Sept. 29, 1967. GS: Wendell Corey, Myron Healey, Bartlett Robinson, Hal Baylor, Charla Doherty, Jack Catron. In a Kansas town, the Sonnetts come to the aid of Sheriff Morg Braham, Will's old fighting buddy. Now a tired, weak-willed drinker, Morg can't begin to handle a band of Texas drovers who intend to tear up the town.

63.5 *Of Lasting Summers and Jim Sonnett.* Oct. 6, 1967. GS: Peter Whitney, Paul Richards, James Anderson, Michael Carr. A terrible choice faces young Jeff Sonnett, who must decide whether to help a man destined to hang.

63.6 *Message at Noon.* Oct. 13, 1967. GS: Strother Martin, Sam Melville, Lonny Chapman. James Sonnett is being followed by a young hothead bent on killing him.

63.7 *A Son for a Son.* Oct. 20, 1967. GS: Royal Dano, Virginia Gregg, Jack Elam. Paraphrasing a Biblical maxim, rancher Vance Murdock demands a son for a son. He insists that Jeff take the place of his own boy, who was killed by James Sonnett.

63.8 *Meeting at Devil's Fork.* Oct. 27, 1967. GS: James Best, Dean Stanton, Bill Foster, Claudia Bryar, Arthur Peterson, Tom Reese, Janice Yarbrough. Will uses divide and conquer strategy to unspring a trap that four gunmen are setting for James Sonnett, using Will and Jeff as bait.

63.9 *First Love.* Nov. 3, 1967. GS: Cherie Latimer, James Westmoreland, Harry Harvey, Sr., Hank Patterson, Pitt Herbert. Love finds Jeff in a Wyoming cow town. Despite a hostile reception from the townsfolk, the young wanderer is thinking about settling down.

63.10 *The Favor.* Nov. 10, 1967. GS: Stephen McNally, Tom Tully. In a ghost town, the Sonnetts lay their lives on the line to defend a wounded outlaw from a murderous trio of bounty hunters.

63.11 *Ride the Man Down.* Nov. 17, 1967. GS: Kevin McCarthy, Vaughn Taylor, Charlie Brooks. Will and Jeff join a sheriff's posse that is gunning for accused murderer James Sonnett. The pair are out to insure justice for their kin, if and when he is found.

63.12 *The Turkey Shoot.* Nov. 24, 1967. GS: R.G. Armstrong, David Macklin, Paul Sorensen. Jeff Sonnett buys a lot of trouble for 50 cents, the fee paid to enter a turkey shoot that has been dominated for years by a rugged rancher and his sharpshooting son.

63.13 *And a Killing Rode into Town.* Dec. 1, 1967. GS: Cloris Leachman, James Wainwright, Eddie Quillan, Jack Williams. Psychology is Will's weapon as he tries to disprove a saloon woman's claim that she is Jeff's mother.

63.14 *Find a Sonnett, Kill a Sonnett.* Dec. 8, 1967. GS: J.D. Cannon, Dennis Hopper, Rex Holman, Robert Karnes, Jim Boles, James McCallion. Unable to get help for the sheriff or townspeople, Will tries desperately to enlist the town drunk's help to save Jeff from a pair of killers.

63.15 *Sunday in Paradise.* Dec. 15, 1967. GS: Joan Blondell, Ed Bakey, Jonathan Hole, Norman Leavitt, Robert Foulk, Rosemary Eliot, Janice Yarbrough, Pat Patterson. In the town of Paradise, the Sonnetts help a saloon girl realize a dream. Feeling that Paradise is lost without a church, Miss Lottie is willing to donate the land if Will can persuade the self-centered townsfolk to provide materials and labor.

63.16 *The Secret of Hangtown Mine.* Dec. 22, 1967. GS: Jean Willes, Sam Gilman, Norman Alden, Ruben Moreno, Ceil Cabot. The Sonnetts gratefully accept lodging from a man and woman who are awfully glad to see them. The pair just happen to need a corpse, and Will Sonnett fits the bill.

63.17 *The Hero.* Dec. 29, 1967. GS: Robert J. Wilke, Patricia Barry. Jeff rides into hostile Apache country, determined to track down the bank robbers who gravely wounded his grandfather. He is joined by Sheriff Dan Butler, who seems surprisingly indifferent to bringing in the fugitives.

63.18 *What's in a Name?* Jan. 5, 1968. GS: Ross Hagen, Edward Andrews, Bo Hopkins, Harry Swoger. A trick-shooting flatterer is masquerading as Will Sonnett. The real Will holds off nailing the faker until he can find out what the man is up to.

63.19 *End of the Rope.* Jan. 12, 1968. GS: Richard Devon, Don Haggerty, William Smith, Don Keefer. For the first time in his life, Jeff sees his father — behind bars. Come morning, James Sonnett is due to be hanged for a murder that he didn't commit, which leaves Will and Jeff very little time to find the man who did the framing.

63.20 *And He Shall Lead the Children.* Jan. 19, 1968. GS: Ann Doran, Bert Freed, Soloman Sturges, Bing Russell. Will's kindness to a woman he once-loved impels her to take a new look at her life with a wanted outlaw and its effects on their children.

63.21 *Look for the Hound Dog.* Jan. 26, 1968. GS: William Schallert, Robert Donner, John Alderson, Dub Taylor, Laurie Main. Jeff goes on trial for murder in a peaceful, law-abiding town. With no legal counsel available, Jeff must rely on his grandfather to defend him.

63.22 *Stopover in a Troubled Town.* Feb. 2, 1968. GS: Anna Capri, Karl Swenson. Will Sonnett resorts to a bit of deception to get a dance-hall girl back into her father's good graces.

63.23 *Alone.* Feb. 9, 1968. GS: Noam Pitlik, Patrick Horgan, John Alderson, Pepper Martin. While waiting for young Jeff in a lonely ghost town, Will is wounded by a shadowy gunman. Groping through a haze of hallucinations, the old man relives much of his past as he fights against the unknown and his relentless assailant.

63.24 *The Sins of the Father.* Feb. 23, 1968. GS: Torin Thatcher, Annette Andre. A lead to James Sonnett's whereabouts promises to burden Will and Jeff with unexpected responsibilities. An unwed mother claims that her baby is James Sonnett's son.

63.25 *The Warriors.* March 1, 1968. GS: Denver Pyle, Jim Davis, Richard Webb, Anthony Caruso. The Army gives Will Sonnett a chance to exercise his acting talents. Posing as a prisoner, Will must find out where two jailed gunrunners have hidden their rifles.

63.26 *A Fool and His Money.* March 8, 1968. GS: Paul Brinegar, Heather Angel, Nina Shipman. Will tries to help an old friend wriggle out of a masquerade that promises nothing but heartaches and headaches. Charlie Moss has passed himself off as wealthy, gained the interest of a young woman, and incurred the wrath of two ex-partners who think Charlie's been welshing on them.

Season Two

63.27 *Reunion.* Sept. 27, 1968. GS: Tim O'Kelly. Will

The Gunslinger

and Jeff encounter Billy Delver. The young man is equally anxious to find James Sonnett, but for a well-concealed, and sinister, reason.

63.28 *The Trap.* Oct. 4, 1968. GS: Royal Dano, Robert DoQui, Arthur Malet, Walter Burke. There is little hope of escape when a burlesque of justice lands Will and Jeff on a slave-labor gang digging a railroad tunnel.

63.29 *Chapter and Verse.* Oct. 11, 1968. GS: Henry Jones, Rex Holman. Will and Jeff cross paths with a preacher and a bounty hunter, unholy partners who gun down wanted men for diverse reasons. And according to the posters, James Sonnett is wanted dead or alive, for murder.

63.30 *Pariah.* Oct. 18, 1968. GS: Ellen Corby, Paul Fix, Harry Lauter, Dennis Cross. Will walks into a festering situation when he stops off to see old pal Buck Cobb. Cobb is the town pariah because he was hospitable to James Sonnett, who was unfairly accused of killing a little girl.

63.31 *Joby.* Nov. 1, 1968. GS: Strother Martin. Joby, a weasel of a saloon swamper, gets his kicks from dime novels about gunfighters. But what really turns him on are real showdowns, like the one he has set for the unsuspecting Sonnetts.

63.32 *The Straw Man.* Nov. 8, 1968. GS: Madlyn Rhue, Walter Burke. In Dayton Wells, Will encounters a straw man, the effigy of James Sonnett, hanged for shooting an innocent man in the bank.

63.33 *A Difference of Opinion.* Nov. 15, 1968. GS: Lonny Chapman, Myron Healey, James Wainwright. A lesson in judgment awaits Jeff in Pleasant City, where a pair of bullies are trading on James Sonnett's name to bilk the local citizenry.

63.34 *Home Free.* Nov. 22, 1968. GS: Malcolm Atterbury, Richard Evans, Hal Baylor, Victoria Thompson. Will and Jeff try to bridge a gap between two people in need of each other — lonely old Asa Campbell and his former employee Ben Harper, who served a full term in prison to pay for the food he stole from Asa.

63.35 *Guilt.* Nov. 29, 1968. GS: Bo Hopkins, Robert Donner, Charlie Briggs, Robert Karnes, Larry D. Mann, Don Wilbanks, Duane Grey, Claude Hall. The arrival of Will and Jeff in a quiet farm community panics the three Merceen brothers. Big, hulking Lyle Merceen is sure the pair are after him for killing James Sonnett.

63.36 *Meeting in a Small Town.* Dec. 6, 1968. GS: Robert J. Wilke, Ford Rainey. Perhaps he is psychic, maybe foolish, but Jeff insists on checking out a disturbing dream — a nightmare that had his father ambushed by a sniper hidden in a Mexican bell tower.

63.37 *The Fearless Man.* Dec. 13, 1968. GS: Paul Richards, William Smith. Jeff finds a hero in Dave Henry, a wanderer who rescued Jeff and Will from outlaws. Dave stands up to every conceivable danger, but, although grateful, Will is certain there has got to be something wrong with a man completely devoid of fear.

63.38 *Where There's Hope.* Dec. 20, 1968. GS: Cindy Eilbacher, Jean Howell. Will and Jeff try to find a home for Hope, a little orphaned girl who doesn't laugh or cry.

63.39 *Join the Army.* Jan. 3, 1969. GS: Robert Pine, Tom Tully, Parley Baer, Jesse Pearson, Dennis Cross, Chuck Horne, Boyd Stockman. The wanton and illegal slaughter of the great buffalo herds that formed the Indians main source of food are the focus of this tale.

63.40 *Time Is the Rider.* Jan. 10, 1969. SP.: James Griffith, Rayford Barnes, Douglas V. Fowley, Allen Jaffe. Three stage robbers take Jeff hostage to secure cooperation from the youth's famous gunslinging father.

63.41 *Robber's Roost.* Jan. 17, 1969. GS: James Best, Jess Walton. Will and Jeff ride into Mesa, Mexico, a festering robbers' nest run by outlaw Harley Bass. Their appearance is a real windfall for Bass as he needs more guns to spring his men from jail.

63.42 *Trail's End.* Jan. 31, 1969. GS: Ruta Lee, Morgan Woodward, Jack Searl, Bill Foster, Ted de Corsia. Will and Jeff see a possible end to their trail in a drab little cowtown. One of two persons may lead them to James — Fan, a weary and tight-lipped bar girl, or Wilk, a deranged hulk of a man who is gunning for James.

63.43 *A Town in Terror* Part One. Feb. 7, 1969. GS: Sean McClory, Harry Lauter, Mort Mills, William Zuckert, Richard Hale, Don Wilbanks, Chuck Horne, Carlos Romero. The Sonnetts ride into a town on the brink of a range war. Both sides are waiting for gunmen. The cattlemen have hired killer Frank Corbett and the sheepmen await James Sonnett.

63.44 *A Town in Terror* Part Two. Feb. 14, 1969. GS: Sean McClory, Harry Lauter, Mort Mills, William Zuckert, Richard Hale, Don Wilbanks, Chuck Horne, Carlos Romero. With the range war imminent, father finally meets son and the results are catastrophic. Jeff inadvertently gives away his father's cover as the cattlemen's hired gun.

63.45 *Jim Sonnett's Lady.* Feb. 21, 1969. GS: Norma Crane, Peter Leeds, Bruce Glover, Mel Gallagher, Percy Helton, Bobby Byles, James McCallion. An intercepted telegram tips off Will and Jeff that James Sonnett is riding into an ambush. What they don't know is that the trap is baited by a lovely lady saloonkeeper who enjoys James' complete trust.

63.46 *The Trial.* Feb. 28, 1969. GS: Phillip Pine, Eddie Firestone. Will and Jeff work behind the scenes to help James Sonnett, who is defying a town of hired guns to defend a man framed for murder.

63.47 *One Angry Juror.* March 7, 1969. GS: John Milford, Judson Pratt, Susanne Cramer, Erik Holland, Kevin Hagen, Ed Bakey, Ben Wright, Henry Hunter. Will deadlocks a jury in an apparently open and shut murder case. The defendant is a sullen young farmer who pleads not guilty, but refuses to testify.

63.48 *The Marriage.* March 14, 1969. GS: Jacqueline Scott, Don Dubbins, Teddy Eccles, Bartlett Robinson. The Sonnetts try marital fence-mending. Sodbuster Burt Damon is trying to scratch a living out of the earth. His wife Emily yearns for civilization, and their 12-year-old son is caught helplessly in between.

63.49 *The Man Who Killed James Sonnett.* March 21, 1969. GS: Jay Novello, Robert F. Simon, Joan Van Ark, John Crawford, Harry Swoger, John Hale. Will and Jeff take a turn on stage to put the lie to a play titled "The Man Who Killed Jim Sonnett."

64. The Gunslinger

CBS. 60 min. Broadcast history: Thursday, 9:00–10:00, Feb. 1961–Sept. 1961.

Regular Cast: Tony Young (Cord), Preston Foster (Captain Zachary Wingate), Charles Gray (Pico McGuire), Dee Pollock (Billy Urchin), Midge Ware (Amby Hollister), John Pickard (Sgt. Major Murdock).

Premise: Set in the West shortly after the Civil War, the series concerns the exploits of Cord the Gunslinger, who works as an undercover agent for the cavalry.

The Episodes

64.1 *Border Incident* (A.K.A. "The Buried People"). Feb. 9, 1961. GS: Royal Dano, Fay Spain, Roy Barcroft. It is Cord's job to find Col. Carson Clayborne, notorious for his cruelty to prisoners during the war. In a Mexican town, Cord runs across a man he suspects is Clayborne — practicing medicine and being kind to the poor.

64.2 *The Hostage Fort.* Feb. 16, 1961. GS: Jack Elam, Jena Engstrom, Vaughn Taylor, Stafford Repp, Ron Soble, Charles Tannen, Raymond Guth. The folks of Borden's Crossing are about to lynch Clint Gannet. Then Cord arrives and whisks Gannet away. It seems that Gannet and his gang stole the Army payroll at Fort Scott.

64.3 *Appointment in Cascabel.* Feb. 12, 1961. GS: Antony Caruso, Charlita, Sarita Vara. Fort Scott is offering a reward for the capture of Mexican bandit Manuel Garcia, who kidnaps Amby and asks for a ransom equal to the price on his head.

64.4 *The Zone.* March 2, 1961. GS: Addison Richards, Sandy Kenyon, Anne Graves, Ernest Sarracino, Charles Fredericks. The town of Arroyo Seco, caught in a border dispute between the U.S. and Mexico, is overrun with lawless gunmen who take advantage of the confused jurisdiction. Cord is sent there to investigate.

64.5 *Rampage.* March 16, 1961. GS: Jock Mahoney, Jan Shepard, Lew Gallo, Steve Mitchell, Theodore Newton, Allen Jaffe, Zon Murray. Four renegades help their leader Halsey Roland escape from the Fort Scott jailhouse. After stealing Army uniforms, they ride out intent upon pillaging the countryside. When they encounter Cord, he momentarily mistakes them for friends, until he is shot.

64.6 *The Recruit.* March 23, 1961. GS: Gene Evans, John Howard, Stanley Clements, Ron Hagerthy, Jan Stine, Jay Silverheels. Cord discovers a private who has been beaten within an inch of his life, and Sergeant Croft and his men happen by and offer to take care of him. Cord goes on alone, and later Croft brings the private back to the fort — dead.

64.7 *Road of the Dead.* March 30, 1961. GS: Mari Blanchard, Paul Lambert, Carlos Romero, Hugh Sanders, Hardie Albright, Jack Searl, Jan Arvan, Norman Leavitt, Madeline Holmes, Bob Bice. The Army sends Cord and Pico to investigate a case of mass death-by-drowning involving a group of settlers from Mexico. The search leads them first to a beautiful contessa, and then to a man named Pritchard — the person responsible for selling the Mexicans the land on which they had hoped to settle.

64.8 *Golden Circle.* April 13, 1961. GS: Buddy Ebsen, John Hoyt, Pamela Britton, William Tannen, Tyler McVey, Milton Frome, Jay Jostyn, Byron Morrow. Yuma Prison releases Jed Spangler hoping he will lead them to the cash he helped steal from the Army during the War. Cord, assigned to accompany Spangler, has a particular interest in the case — Spangler killed the sentry who replaced him at the time of the robbery.

64.9 *The Diehards.* April 20, 1961. GS: Lloyd Corrigan, Arlene Sax, William Boyett. Sgt. Major Murdock rides ahead of his patrol to scout, and when he returns his men have been ambushed and killed. Murdock returns to Ft. Scott and is arrested. Wingate suspects his convenient absence had something to do with the attack.

64.10 *Johnny Sergeant.* May 4, 1961. GS: Jock Gaynor, Phyllis Coates, Sonya Wilde, Don Harvey, Peter Adams, Duane Gray, William Schallert, Harry Ellerbe, Hal Baylor. The citizens of Las Flores resent the soldiers in their midst because of their riotous off-duty behavior. When Indian soldier Johnny Sergeant is accused of annoying Teresa Perez, the angry community demands quick punishment.

64.11 *The Death of Yellow Singer.* May 11, 1961. GS: Henry Brandon, Barbara Luna, Vitina Marcus, Celia Lovsky, Edward Colmans, Michael Morgan, Eddie Little Sky, Bob Gunderson. Clea, an Indian girl, has been accused by her own people of killing their chief, Yellow Singer. When tribesmen bring her to Fort Scott as a prisoner, Cord recognizes the girl and tells Wingate he can't believe she is guilty.

64.12 *The New Savannah Story.* May 18, 1961. GS: Dorothy Green, Anne Helm, Frank De Kova, Jim Davis, Ron Hagerthy, William Vaughan, Otto Waldis. After the Civil War, Ella and Ruth St. Clair try to establish a cotton plantation in Arizona. But Don Ignacio Alesandro says their property is really his by right of a Spanish land grant. The Army sends Cord to prevent the dispute from growing into open warfare.

65. Gunsmoke

CBS. 30 min./60 min. Broadcast history: Saturday, 10:00–10:30, Sept. 1955–Sept. 1961; Saturday, 10:00–11:00, Sept. 1961–Sept. 1967; Tuesday, 7:30–8:30, Oct. 1961–June 1964; Monday, 7:30–8:30, Sept. 1967–Sept. 1971; Monday, 8:00–9:00, Sept. 1971–Sept. 1975.

Regular Cast: James Arness (Marshal Matt Dillon), Dennis Weaver (Chester B. Goode) 55–64, Amanda Blake (Kitty Russell), Milburn Stone (Doc Galen Adams), Ken Curtis (Festus Haggen) 64–75, Burt Reynolds (Quint Asper) 62–65, Roger Ewing (Thad Greenwood) 65–67, Buck Taylor (Newly O'Brian) 67–75, Glenn Strange (Sam the Bartender) 62–74, James Nusser (Louie Pheeters), Dabbs Greer (Jonas Jones, the storekeeper) 55–60, Charles Seel (Barney Danches, the telegraph agent), Hank Patterson (Hank, the stableman), Howard Culver (Howie, the hotel clerk), Sarah Selby (Ma Smalley) 62–75, Woodrow Chambliss (Mr. Lathrop, the storekeeper) 66–75, Roy Roberts (Mr. Bodkin) 66–75, Tom Brown (Ed O'Connor), Ted Jordan (Nathan Burke, the freight agent) 64–75, Charles Wagenheim (Halligan) 67–75, John Harper (Perry Crump).

Premise: This long-running series related the adventures of U.S. Marshal Matt Dillon in Dodge City, Kansas, during the 1860s.

The Episodes

65.1 *Matt Gets It.* Sept. 10, 1955. GS: Paul Richards, Malcolm Atterbury, Robert Anderson. Dan Grat, a gunman

Gunsmoke

hunted by Texas authorities, seeks refuge in Dodge City. Marshal Dillon goes into action against this outlaw who shoots before he talks.

65.2 *Hot Spell.* Sept. 17, 1955. GS: John Dehner, James Westerfield, Marvin Bryan. A notorious gunman swears to go straight after he is released from jail. His life is not made easier by lynching parties of Dodge City ranchers. Marshal Matt Dillon has his hands full protecting the ex-con.

65.3 *Word of Honor* (A.K.A. "Marked Man"). Oct. 1, 1955. GS: Robert Middleton, Claude Akins, Ray Boyle, Will Wright, Dick Paxton, Thom Carney. Matt Dillon comes to the aid of a friend involved in a murder. The witness is sought by both the killers and outraged friends of the victim.

65.4 *Home Surgery.* Oct. 8, 1955. GS: Joe De Santis, Gloria Talbott, Wright King. While riding through the desert, Marshal Dillon and Deputy Chester come upon a lonely ranch and find a frightened girl trying to save her dying father. Though the injuries seem to be the result of an accident, Dillon is suspicious.

65.5 *Obie Tater.* Oct. 15, 1955. GS: Royal Dano, John Shepodd, Kathy Adams, Pat Conway. Marshal Matt Dillon takes action against a brutal gang of killers which tries to force information from an old prospector reported to know of a hidden cache of gold.

65.6 *Night Incident.* Oct. 29, 1955. GS: Peter Votrian, Robert Foulk, Amzie Strickland, Anne Warren, Lance Warren, Jeanne Bates, Lou Vernon. Townsfolk ignore the story of a young boy who claims he overheard a highwayman and his wife plan a series of robberies. The youngster is too well-known for some previous tall tales.

65.7 *Smoking Out the Nolans.* Nov. 5, 1955. GS: John Larch, Ainslie Pryor, Jeanne Bates, Ed Platt. Marshal Dillon tries to avert a range war between a landowner and a homesteader. The landowner wants to evict the homesteader from land he claims for himself.

65.8 *Kite's Reward.* Nov. 12, 1955. GS: Adam Kennedy, James Griffith. There is still a price on the head of an outlaw who is making an honest effort to go straight. But he is forced to defend himself when a mercenary bounty hunter decides to collect the reward.

65.9 *The Hunter.* Nov. 26, 1955. GS: Peter Whitney, Richard Gilden, Lou Vernon, Robert Keene. A buffalo hunter defies Marshal Dillon and insists on invading sacred Indian hunting grounds. He does not reckon with the vengeance of the Indians.

65.10 *The Queue.* Dec. 3, 1955. GS: Sebastian Cabot, Keye Luke, Robert Gist, Devlin McCarthy. An unemployed Chinese cook arouses the prejudice of some trouble-makers in Dodge City. A faction of narrow-minded citizens wants to run him out of town.

65.11 *General Parsley Smith.* Dec. 10, 1955. GS: Raymond Bailey, James O'Rear, John Alderson, Wilfred Knapp. Parsley Smith, who calls himself a general, is known for his reputation for tall tales. When he claims that the town banker plans to abscond with money belonging to investors, no one pays any attention to him. Then Matt Dillon notes that the banker has acquired a new crony—a notorious gunslinger.

65.12 *Magnus* (A.K.A. "The Uncivilized"). Dec. 24, 1955. GS: Robert Easton, James Anderson, Than Wyenn, Tim Graham, Dorothy Schuyler. Matt Dillon's deputy, Chester, tries to teach his antisocial brother a lesson. Chester thinks his brother's life as a hunter and trapper is somewhat uncouth.

65.13 *The Reed Survives.* Dec. 31, 1955. GS: Lola Albright, John Carradine, James Drury, Virginia Arness. An ex-dance hall girl falls in love with another man and plots to do away with her husband.

65.14 *Professor Lute Bone.* Jan. 7, 1956. GS: John Abbott, Jester Hairston, Gloria Castillo, Don Gardner, Strother Martin, Sally Corner. Marshal Dillon has a job on his hands subduing a group of incensed citizens who are bent on revenge. The object of their ire is a peddler whose patent medicines prove fatal.

65.15 *No Handcuffs.* Jan. 21, 1956. GS: Vic Perrin, Charles Gray, Mort Mills, Marjorie Owens, Herbert Lytton, Cyril Delevanti. Marshal Matt Dillon is forced into a showdown with the vicious lawman of a neighboring frontier town. An innocent man has been ordered arrested to cover up the sheriff's misdeeds.

65.16 *Reward for Matt.* Jan. 28, 1956. GS: Paul Newlan, Helen Wallace, Val Dufour, Jean Inness, John G. Lee. When Marshal Dillon is forced to shoot a man who resists arrest, the man's embittered widow offers a reward for Dillon's life.

65.17 *Robin Hood.* Feb. 4, 1956. GS: James McCallion, Nora Marlowe, Wilfred Knapp, Barry Atwater, S. John Launer. Marshal Dillon comes up against a blank wall when witnesses refuse to testify against a notorious highwayman. The outlaw is reputed to rob only the wealthy.

65.18 *Yorky.* Feb. 18, 1956. GS: Jeff Silver, Mary Gregory, Howard Petrie, Dennis Cross, Malcolm Atterbury. A young white boy, raised by the Indians, goes outside the law to seek vengeance against horse thieves.

65.19 *20-20.* Feb. 25, 1956. GS: Martin Kingsley, Pitt Herbert, Wilton Graff. Once renowned for his prowess as one of the fastest guns in the West, a former lawman is now in fear of his life. An enemy has learned of his failing eyesight and plots to involve him in a gun duel.

65.20 *Reunion '78.* March 3, 1956. GS: Val Dufour, Maurice Manson, Marion Bransh, Joe Perry, Mason Curry. A vengeful cowboy vows to take the life of an outlaw who wronged him years before. He does so, but claims he shot in self-defense.

65.21 *Helping Hand.* March 17, 1956. GS: Ken L. Smith, James Nusser, Brett Halsey, Michael Granger, Russell Thorson. A would-be tough guy picks on the wrong man in an attempt to make a name for himself. He tries to involve Marshal Matt Dillon by staging a street fight.

65.22 *Tap Day for Kitty.* March 24, 1956. GS: John Dehner, Mary Adams, John Patrick, Evelyn Scott, Dorothy Schuyler, Charlene Brooks. Nip Cullers, a wealthy, eccentric miner, announces that he is going to marry Kitty, although she denies it. Later Nip is blasted by a shotgun, and he blames Kitty. In desperation, Kitty asks Matt to help her.

65.23 *Indian Scout.* March 31, 1956. GS: Eduard Franz, DeForest Kelley, William Vaughan, Pat Hogan, Tommy Hart. Will Bailey, bitter over the death of his cavalryman brother in a Comanche ambush, tries to start trouble with Amos Cartwright, an Indian scout. Bailey accuses Cartwright of being responsible for the killing.

65.24 *The Pest Hold.* April 14, 1956. GS: Patrick O'Moore, Howard McNear, Norbert Schiller, Evelyn Scott. Marshall Dillon and Dodge City's only doctor have a full-scale panic on their hands when word of a typhoid epidemic leaks out.

65.25 *The Big Broad.* April 28, 1956. GS: Dee J. Thompson, Joel Ashley, Terry Becker, Heinie Brock. Unpredictable Lena Wave, a woman who stands six feet tall, and her henpecked husband arrive in Dodge City to start up a card game. Before Lena is through, she beats up Chester for accusing her of running a crooked game, and kills a man she says attempted to kill her.

65.26 *Hack Prine.* May 12, 1956. GS: Leo Gordon, George Wallace, Hal Baylor, Wally Cassell, Tyler McVey. A former friend, turned outlaw, meets Marshal Dillon now as his mortal enemy. The gunman enters Dodge City as a hired killer.

65.27 *Cooter.* May 19, 1956. GS: Brett King, Strother Martin, Robert Vaughn, Vinton Hayworth. A mentally retarded youth is enraged when he realizes he's been made a victim in a plot to discredit Marshal Dillon. Armed with a gun, the youth goes berserk.

65.28 *The Killer.* May 26, 1956. GS: Charles Bronson, David Chapman. An overbearing migrant takes a heavy toll of human life by deliberately provoking others to battle. Marshal Matt Dillon decides to meet the man on his own terms.

65.29 *Doc's Revenge.* June 9, 1956. GS: Ainslie Pryor, Harry Bartell, Chris Alcaide. Marshal Dillon is faced with a difficult decision when his long-time friend Doc is accused of a shooting.

65.30 *The Preacher.* June 16, 1956. GS: Chuck Connors, Royal Dano, Paul Dubov, Jim Hyland. Seth Tandy, a newcomer to Dodge City, runs into trouble with cruel Sam Keeler. In order to avoid a serious fight between the two men, Matt Dillon challenges Keeler himself.

65.31 *How to Die for Nothing.* June 23, 1956. GS: Mort Mills, James Nolan, Maurice Manson, Laurence Dobkin, Bill White, Jr. Marshal Dillon finds himself marked for death by the brother of a man who lost a gun fight to the marshal.

65.32 *Dutch George.* June 30, 1956. GS: Robert Middleton, Tom Pittman. Matt Dillon comes face to face with his boyhood idol. The man is now the leader of a notorious gang of horse thieves. Matt, as marshal, must bring him to justice.

65.33 *Prairie Happy.* July 7, 1956. GS: Robert Ellenstein, Anne Barton, Tyler McVey, Bruce Holland, Jack Holland, Roy Engel. An embittered and sadistic old man deliberately terrorizes the entire population of Dodge City with a false story of an imminent Indian raid.

65.34 *Chester's Mail Order Bride.* July 14, 1956. GS: Mary Carver, Joel Ashley, Russell Thorson. Chester finds himself a reluctant prospective bridegroom when a young girl leaves her Philadelphia home to accept his letter of proposal.

65.35 *The Guitar.* July 21, 1956. GS: Aaron Spelling, Charles Gray, Jacques Aubuchon, Duane Thorson, Bill Hale, Joseph Mell. Veterans of the Civil War breed violence and death in Dodge City when Confederate and Union conflicts are revived.

65.36 *Cara.* July 28, 1956. GS: Jorja Curtwright, Charles Webster, Douglas Odney. Marshal Dillon renews his acquaintance with a former girl friend. But now she is on the opposite side of the law.

65.37 *Mr. and Mrs. Amber.* Aug. 4, 1956. GS: Ainslie Pryor, Paul Richards, Dabbs Greer, Gloria McGhee, Bing Russell. A penniless farmer marries the daughter of a self-styled religious prophet, who makes life unbearable for the young couple. The harassed farmer is forced to go outside the law to try to solve his dilemma.

65.38 *Unmarked Grave.* Aug. 18, 1956. GS: Ron Hagerthy, Helen Kleeb, William Hopper, Joe Scudero, Thann Wyenn. An elderly woman, who is unaware of his background, befriends a young but ruthless outlaw. The shrewd desperado uses the woman as a pawn in his desperate battle for freedom.

65.39 *Alarm at Pleasant Valley.* Aug. 25, 1956. GS: Lew Brown, Dorothy Schuyler, Bill White, Jr., Helen Wallace, Dan Blocker. A last-minute decision by a homesteader to leave his remote encampment for the safety of Dodge City is made too late. En route to town he and his family are ambushed by a band of renegade Indians.

Season Two

65.40 *Cow Doctor.* Sept. 8, 1956. GS: Robert H. Harris, Dorothy Adams, Tommy Kirk, Gage Clarke. Doc is furious when he is called to the ranch of his long-time enemy Ben Pitcher and learns that the patient is a cow. Doc is further enraged when he returns to Dodge City and finds that a woman died for lack of treatment because he was away at the Pitcher ranch.

65.41 *Brush at Elkador.* Sept. 15, 1956. GS: Gage Clarke, Paul Lambert, Alfred Linder, Dennis Cross, Malcolm Atterbury. Because of insufficient evidence, Matt Dillon has to set a murderer free. However, fate plays an ironic trick on the man after the marshal turns him loose.

65.42 *Custer.* Sept. 22, 1956. GS: Brian Hutton, Richard Keith, Herbert Lytton. A friend of Matt Dillon's is murdered. Matt sets out to find the murderer and his motive.

65.43 *The Round Up.* Sept. 29, 1956. GS: Barney Phillips, Jacques Aubuchon, John Dierkes, Michael Hinn, Mason Curry, Sam Schwart, John Patrick. Dodge City merchants ask Matt Dillon to deputize twenty men to protect the town against the escapades of a horde of celebrating cowhands. Dillon refuses and finds himself facing a mob of riotous cowboys alone.

65.44 *Young Man with a Gun.* Oct. 20, 1956. GS: Jack Diamond, Fredd Wayne, Clegg Hoyt, Sid Clute. After his outlaw brother is killed in a Dodge City gun battle, a young man swears revenge on Marshal Dillon.

65.45 *Indian White.* Oct. 27, 1956. GS: Peter Votrian, Marian Seldes, Alexander Lockwood, Abel Fernandez, Clegg Hoyt, Stanley Adams, Kenneth Alton. A young boy faces a problem when he must choose between the primitive way of the Indian and his rightful place in civilized society. Though born of white parents, the boy has been raised by a band of Cheyennes.

65.46 *How to Cure a Friend.* Nov. 10, 1956. GS: Andrew Duggan, Simon Oakland, Joseph Mell, Jess Kirkpatrick. A former friend of Matt Dillon is now a notorious gambler. The man tries to use his acquaintance with Dillon to fleece local townsfolk.

65.47 *Legal Revenge.* Nov. 17, 1956. GS: Cloris Leachman, Philip Bourneuf, Robert Strong. Doc Adams discovers a man and woman in an isolated prairie cabin. Each is afraid the other is going to kill him if he sleeps.

65.48 *The Mistake.* Nov. 24, 1956. GS: Michael "Touch"

Gunsmoke

Connors, Gene O'Donnell, Cyril Delevanti, Robert Hinkle. Marshal Dillon is faced with a problem after a gambler is killed in Dodge City. If he trails the man suspected of the killing, he will have to leave the town unprotected.

65.49 *Greater Love.* Dec. 1, 1956. GS: Claude Akins, Ray Bennett, Amzie Strickland, Frank de Kova. An outlaw whose buddy is near death threatens to take Doc's life if he fails to save the wounded man. Marshal Dillon tries to prevent bloodshed by placing himself at the mercy of the gunman.

65.50 *No Indians.* Dec. 8, 1956. GS: Dick Rich, Herbert Rudley, Mickey Simpson, Fintan Meyler, Joel Ashley, K.L. Smith. Marshal Dillon and Chester set themselves up as decoys in an attempt to ambush a band of Indian renegades.

65.51 *Spring Team.* Dec. 15, 1956. GS: Ross Ford, Paul Newlan, Harry Townes, Jack Kruschen, Stanley Adams, Clayton Post. A man is shot down on Dodge City's Front Street. During his investigation, Marshal Dillon discovers that he himself was the intended target.

65.52 *Poor Pearl.* Dec. 22, 1956. GS: Constance Ford, Michael Emmet, Denver Pyle, Jess Kirkpatrick, John Hamilton, John McGough. Two men who are in love with the same girl determine to shoot it out. Matt Dillon learns of the plans and intervenes.

65.53 *Cholera.* Dec. 29, 1956. GS: Paul Fix, Bartlett Robinson, Stuart Whitman, Peg Hillias, Gordon Gebert. An unscrupulous landowner attempts violence to evict a homesteader and his family from their claim.

65.54 *Pucket's New Year.* Jan. 5, 1957. GS: Edgar Stehli, Grant Withers, Richard Deacon, Rocky Shahan. Matt Dillon and Chester find an old buffalo hunter who has been left to die by his partner. They save the old man's life but have to cope with his bitterness. He now stalks his former partner, intent upon murder.

65.55 *The Cover-Up.* Jan. 12, 1957. GS: Roy Engle, Vivi Janiss, Tyler McVey, Theodore Marcuse, Malcolm Atterbury. Marshal Dillon seeks the answer when an unknown assailant shoots down defenseless homesteaders at the doors of their remote cabins.

65.56 *Sins of the Father.* Jan. 19, 1957. GS: Peter Whitney, Angie Dickinson, Gage Clark, Paul Wexler. An enraged hunter vows revenge after his Indian wife is brutally attacked.

65.57 *Kick Me.* Jan. 26, 1957. GS: Robert H. Harris, Frank de Kova, Julie Van Zandt, Paul Lambert. A bank robber poses as a respectable citizen of Dodge City, but overestimates his hold on an illiterate Indian guide on whom he perpetrated a cruel hoax.

65.58 *The Executioner.* Feb. 2, 1957. GS: Robert Keys, Michael Hinn, Liam Sullivan. A ruthless young gunslinger kills an older man in a senseless duel. The victim's brother, realizing he is unable to meet the slayer on equal terms, goes to avenge the death unarmed.

65.59 *Gone Straight.* Feb. 9, 1957. GS: Carl Betz, Tige Andrews, Marianne Stewart, Joe de Santis, John Dierkes. Marshal Dillon and Chester attempt to serve a warrant for arrest of a man in a nearby frontier town, but are stopped by townspeople, who refuse to identify him. The ex-outlaw, now a law-abiding citizen, wants to go straight.

65.60 *Bloody Hands.* Feb. 16, 1957. GS: Joe Perry, Larry Dobkin, Russell Johnson, Ed Platt. Marshall Dillon decides to turn in his badge after he is force to shoot a man down in the name of the law.

65.61 *Skid Row.* Feb. 23, 1957. GS: Susan Morrow, Joseph Sargent, Guinn Williams. A girl makes the long arduous trip west to meet the man who has asked her to be his wife. She arrives in Dodge City, only to have the man refuse to see her. A promising homesteader when he proposed, the young man is now destitute.

65.62 *Sweet and Sour.* March 2, 1957. GS: Karen Sharpe, John Alderson, Walter Reed, Ken Mayer, John Mitchum. A dance-hall queen newly arrived in Dodge City causes trouble for Marshal Matt Dillon. She deliberately goads admirers into gunfights over her affections.

65.63 *Cain.* March 9, 1957. GS: Mark Roberts, Paul Dubov, Harry Bartell, Dan Riss, Howard Ludwig. A wealthy Dodge City rancher must reckon with his unsavory past as a gun fighter when an embittered man challenges him to a showdown.

65.64 *Bureaucrat.* March 16, 1957. GS: John Hoyt, Ned Glass, Bill Bryant, Al Toigo, Ken Lynch. A politically-minded official arrives from Washington, D.C. He decides to take over the law enforcement of Dodge City against Marshal Dillon's warnings. The man suddenly finds an angry mob rebelling against his dictatorial methods.

65.65 *The Last Fling.* March 23, 1957. GS: Florenz Ames, Anne O'Neal, Frank de Kova, Susan Morrow. Kitty, hostess and part owner of the Long Branch Saloon, finds the attentions of one of her customers annoying, and rebuffs him. Later, the man is found shot, and Kitty is suspected of murder.

65.66 *Chester's Murder.* March 30, 1957. GS: Murray Hamilton, Peggy Castle, Tom Greenway, Gage Clarke, Charles Conrad, Tim Graham. Marshal Dillon is forced to take his friend Chester into custody when irate townspeople threaten violence. A jealous cowboy who had threatened Chester in public was later found dead. Evidence points to Chester as the guilty party.

65.67 *The Photographer.* April 6, 1957. GS: Sebastian Cabot, Norman Fredericks, Charles Horvath, Ned Glass, Dorothy Schuyler. Marshal Dillon's warnings to a brash photographer from the East fall on deaf ears. To satisfy his curiosity about the violent Wild West, the photographer trespasses on sacred Indian ground.

65.68 *Wrong Man.* April 13, 1957. GS: Don Keefer, Catherine McLeod, Robert Griffin. A man takes the life of another whom he mistakenly believes is a criminal with a price on his head. He learns he has made a tragic error when the dead man's friend vows vengeance.

65.69 *Big Girl Lost.* April 20, 1957. GS: Michael Pate, Gloria McGhee, Judson Pratt, Gerald Melton. A young woman now working in a Dodge City saloon is trying to avoid her ex-fiance. When the man arrives in town, he hires a gunman to try to force Marshal Dillon into revealing her whereabouts.

65.70 *What the Whiskey Drummer Heard.* April 27, 1957. GS: Vic Perrin, Robert Karnes, Robert Burton. When an attempt is made on his life, Marshal Dillon feigns death by staying out of sight, thinking to draw his assailant into the open. But a town braggart spoils the plan, and Dillon does not know when or where the next attack will come.

65.71 *Cheap Labor.* May 4, 1957. GS: Andrew Duggan, Peggy Webber, Robert F. Simon, Alan Emerson, Tom Gleason.

A man who has turned his back on violence tries to avoid getting involved in any more gunfights. But the brother of the girl he wants to marry deliberately provokes trouble.

65.72 *Moon.* May 11, 1957. GS: Rebecca Welles, Phillip Pine, Stafford Repp, Thomas Palmer, Jane Ray. Marshal Dillon and the gunman friend of a gambler try to gather evidence on a poker dealer suspected of killing the gambler after winning high stakes.

65.73 *Who Lives by the Sword.* May 18, 1957. GS: Steve Terrell, Robert C. Ross, Harry Wood, Harold J. Stone, Sheila Noonan. Marshal Dillon is faced with a real problem when a trigger-happy gunman finds a certain amount of immunity from the law by supposedly shooting his victims in self-defense. His method is to goad a man into drawing against him.

65.74 *Uncle Oliver.* May 25, 1957. GS: Earle Hodgins, Paul Wexler, Charles Bronson. Matt Dillon stalks a would-be killer who ambushed his friend Chester. In order to draw the gunman into the open, Dillon is forced to ask two of his closest friends to act as decoys.

65.75 *Daddy-O.* June 1, 1957. GS: John Dehner, Judson Pratt. Kitty's father, whom she has not seen since childhood, visits her in Dodge City. He tries to persuade her to make her home with him in New Orleans.

65.76 *The Man Who Would Be Marshal.* June 15, 1957. GS: Herbert Rudley, Alex Sharp, Clancy Cooper, Rusty Wescoatt. A retired Army officer seeks to get himself named as Marshal Dillon's replacement in Dodge City. In an attempt to recapture the old excitement of military duty, the man finally succeeds in talking Dillon into deputizing him. But he fails to impress frontier residents with his methods.

65.77 *Liar from Blackhawk.* June 22, 1957. GS: Denver Pyle. A brash young man considers himself a gunslinger, and in an attempt to impress the frontiersmen of Dodge City, he provokes a gun battle with a drunken man. When a genuine gunslinger arrives in town, the pretender is in real trouble.

65.78 *Jealousy.* July 6, 1957. GS: Than Wyenn, Jack Kelly, Joan Tetzel. A wily Dodge City gambler who has a grudge against Matt Dillon, incites trouble by convincing a hot-tempered husband that his wife and Dillon have been seeing each other.

Season Three

65.79 *Crack-Up.* Sept. 14, 1957. GS: John Dehner, Jess Kirkpatrick, Jean Vaughn. Matt Dillon is worried when a gunman known as a professional assassin, comes to Dodge City.

65.80 *Gun for Chester.* Sept. 21, 1957. GS: Thomas Coley, George Selk, Clayton Post. Chester dons gun and holster when he recognizes Asa Ledbetter, who has just arrived in town, as the man who vowed to kill him. Afraid to tell Dillon, he lives in constant fear of death until an unforeseen incident occurs.

65.81 *Blood Money.* Sept. 28, 1957. GS: James Dobson, Vinton Hayworth, Lawrence Green. Harry Spencer is thrown from his horse while riding on the prairie. He is rescued by Joe Harpe, who takes Spencer into Dodge City, where the two become friends. But Spencer learns that his rescuer is a wanted bank robber with a price on his head, and he decides to collect the reward.

65.82 *Kitty's Outlaw.* Oct. 5, 1957. GS: Ainslie Pryor, Chris Alcaide, Jack Mann. An old boy friend of Kitty's turns outlaw and robs the bank in Dodge City. The townspeople believe that she is covering up for the bandit.

65.83 *Potato Road.* Oct. 12, 1957. GS: Tom Pittman, Robert F. Simon, Jeanette Nolan. Young Budge Grilk tells Matt Dillon that his father has killed a man. Dillon rides out with the young man to investigate the charge, but finds that he has ridden into a trap.

65.84 *Jesse.* Oct. 19, 1957. GS: James Maloney, George Brenlin, Edward Binns, George Selk, Brick Sullivan. Marshal Dillon encounters a wrathful young man who has come to Dodge City in search of the man who killed his father. Only after he has made friends with Dillon does the youngster learn that the marshal was responsible for his father's death.

65.85 *Mavis McCloud.* Oct. 26, 1957. GS: Fay Spain, Casey Adams, Kelly Thordsen, Robert Cornthwaite, Dan Sheridan. A young woman arrives in Dodge City to wed a local rancher. Shortly after her marriage, the woman is shot. Marshal Dillon investigates the shooting.

65.86 *Born to Hang.* Nov. 2, 1957. GS: Anthony Caruso, Ken Lynch, Wright King, Mort Mills. A drifter who is miraculously saved from hanging plans revenge within the law against his would-be lynchers.

65.87 *Romeo.* Nov. 9, 1957. GS: Robert Vaughn, Barry Kelley, Barbara Eden, Robert McQueeney, Tyler McVey. Matt Dillon nearly has a range war on his hands when the daughter of Jake Pierce, a powerful cattle baron, and the son of Pierce's arch rival fall in love. Pierce threatens to ravage the whole town unless Dillon reveals the whereabouts of the young couple.

65.88 *Never Pester Chester.* Nov. 16, 1957. GS: Buddy Baer, Tom Greenway. Marshal Dillon is out for revenge after he finds his deputy Chester almost fatally injured from being dragged down Front St. behind the horses of transients Stobo and Treavitt. Matt puts aside his badge and prepares for a no-holds barred fight.

65.89 *Fingered.* Nov. 23, 1957. GS: John Larch, Virginia Christine, John Launer, Karl Swenson. There are dark hints around Dodge City about the mysterious disappearance of Jim Corbett's first wife, when his second wife, Lila, newly arrived from the East, also vanishes. Marshal Matt Dillon investigates.

65.90 *How to Kill a Woman.* Nov. 30, 1957. GS: June Lockhart, Grant Withers, Peg Hillias, Ruth Storey. Matt and Chester suspect collusion when a masked gunman robs the Overland Stage and wantonly murders two passengers, one of whom is a young woman.

65.91 *Cows and Cribs.* Dec. 7, 1957. GS: Val Avery, Kathy Browne, Judson Taylor. Marshall Matt Dillon faces a showdown with a drunken homesteader who has a mysterious source of income, yet refuses to provide for the needs of his family. He is suspected of murder and cattle theft.

65.92 *Doc's Reward.* Dec. 14, 1957. GS: Jack Lord. Marshal Matt Dillon faces public resentment when he refuses to jail his friend Doc Adams, although Adams has made a confession of murder. Dillon suspects that a stranger in town is out to kill Adams, and learns the identity of the man with the help of Kitty.

65.93 *Kitty Lost.* Dec. 21, 1957. GS: Warren Stevens, Gage Clarke, Brett King, Steve Ellsworth, George Selk. Kitty Russell, hostess of the Long Branch saloon, finds herself in danger when she is abandoned on a desolate plain by an Eastern dude.

65.94 *Twelfth Night.* Dec. 28, 1957. GS: William Schallert, James Griffith, Rose Marie, Dick Rich. Eben Hakes arrives in Dodge City bent on killing a homesteader named Joth Monger. The two are the surviving members of feuding families. Monger declines Marshal Dillon's help.

65.95 *Joe Phy.* Jan. 4, 1958. GS: Paul Richards, Morey Amsterdam, William Kendis. Matt Dillon learns from Cicero Grimes, the town drunk, that the acting marshal of a nearby town is not a fast draw. Dillon knows that his fellow lawman has been keeping the peace in the town solely on the strength of his reputation as a gunslinger.

65.96 *Buffalo Man.* Jan. 11, 1958. GS: Jack Klugman, John Anderson, Patricia Smith. Matt Dillon and his deputy Chester are held hostage by two buffalo hunters, and become involved in a plains war between Indians and the white hunters.

65.97 *Kitty Caught.* Jan. 18, 1958. GS: Bruce Gordon, Pat Conway, William Keene, John Compton. Two desperate bank robber brothers, Jed and Billy Gunter, carry Kitty off as a hostage. Marshal Dillon and Chester set out after them.

65.98 *Claustrophobia.* Jan. 25, 1958. GS: James Winslow, Will Sage, Vaughn Taylor, Joe Maross, Lynn Shubert, Jason Johnson. Two scheming land-grabbers attempt to oust a squatter from his land by killing his livestock and destroying his camp. Marshal Dillon tries to stop a gunfight between the squatter and the land-grabbers.

65.99 *Ma Tennis.* Feb. 2, 1958. GS: Nina Varela, Ron Hagerthy, Corey Allen. The mother of a fugitive from justice tells Marshal Matt Dillon that she has killed her son because he wanted to give himself up. Dillon is skeptical and decides to make a further investigation.

65.100 *Sunday Supplement.* Feb. 8, 1958. GS: Jack Weston, Werner Klemperer, Ed Little, David Whorf. Two sharp newspapermen from New York go to Dodge City hoping to uncover some colorful stories about the Wild West. Their search touches off an Indian uprising that results in a bloody battle between the U.S. Cavalry and the Pawnee Indians.

65.101 *Wild West.* Feb. 15, 1958. GS: Paul Engel, Phyllis Coates, Philip Bourneuf, Murray Hamilton, Robert Gift. Young Yorky Kelly tells Matt Dillon that he fears his elderly father has been kidnaped by outlaws. Hattie, an ex-dance-hall girl, laughs at her stepson's imaginative tale, but Matt decides to investigate the boy's story.

65.102 *The Cabin.* Feb. 22, 1958. GS: Harry Dean Stanton, Claude Akins, Patricia Barry. Seeking shelter from a raging blizzard, Marshal Matt Dillon stumbles into a cabin and finds himself the captive of two hunted bank robbers. They decide to leave him on the prairie to freeze to death.

65.103 *Dirt.* March 1, 1959. GS: June Lockhart, Wayne Morris, Gail Kobe, Ian MacDonald, Barry McGuire, Tyler McVey. Just as a young man and his bride are leaving on their honeymoon, the groom is shot and killed. Matt Dillon tries to track down the killer.

65.104 *Dooley Surrenders.* March 8, 1958. GS: Strother Martin, Ken Lynch, James Maloney, Ben Wright. Emmett Dooley is afraid that during a recent hunting party, he got drunk and was responsible for the death of one of his companions. Matt Dillon disproves his story and sets out to find the real murderer.

65.105 *Joke's on Us.* March 15, 1958. GS: Virginia Gregg, Bartlett Robinson, Michael Hinn, James Kevin, Herbert C. Lytton, Craig Duncan. Three ranchers are convinced that a neighbor is a horse thief, and a lynching results. Later, they discover the man is innocent.

65.106 *Bottleman* (A.K.A. "Tom Cassidy"). March 22, 1958. GS: John Dehner, Ross Martin, Peggy McKay. Dodge City is shocked when the usually peaceful town drunk, Tom Cassidy, threatens to kill a newcomer. In an attempt to avert the murder, Matt Dillon uncovers a tragic secret in Tom's past.

65.107 *Laughing Gas.* March 29, 1958. GS: Dean Harens, June Dayton, Jess Kirkpatrick, Val Benedict. A reformed gunfighter arrives in town with his traveling medicine show. He finds it difficult to refrain from taking to his guns again when the Marsh brothers, the town bullies, give him a beating.

65.108 *Texas Cowboys.* April 5, 1958. GS: Clark Gordon, Allan Lane, Ned Glass, Stafford Repp, John Mitchum. A Texan trail rider is murdered, and his friends take it upon themselves to decide who the murderer is. In an attempt to reason with the gang, Matt Dillon is forced to take a stand which makes him unpopular with the townspeople.

65.109 *Amy's Good Deed.* April 12, 1958. GS: Jeanette Nolan, Lou Krugman. Matt faces an unusual predicament when a bitter old woman sets out to gun him down. She has vowed revenge on Dillon for having shot her brother.

65.110 *Hanging Man.* April 19, 1958. GS: Zine Provendie, Robert Osterloh, Luis Van Rooten, Helen Kleeb, Dick Rich, K.L. Smith. A Dodge City merchant is found hanged in his office, apparently a suicide. But Marshal Matt Dillon believes the man has been murdered.

65.111 *Innocent Broad.* April 26, 1958. GS: Myrna Fahey, Joe Bassett, Ed Kemmer. On the way to town in a stagecoach, a gunslinger attempts to force his attentions on Linda Bell, who is coming to Dodge City to marry Lou Paxon. Learning of this, Paxon demands a showdown with the gunman.

65.112 *The Big Con.* May 3, 1958. GS: Joe Kearns, Alan Dexter, Raymond Bailey. Three confidence men attempt to escape from Dodge City with $20,000 they have stolen from the bank. To be sure Matt Dillon won't try to stop them, they take Doc Adams as hostage.

65.113 *Widow's Mite.* May 10, 1958. GS: Marshall Thompson, Katharine Bard, Ken Mayer. Matt Dillon shoots and kills an express office robber, but is unable to locate the stolen loot. Later, when Leach Fields marries the robber's widow, Dillon suspects Fields is interested only in finding out where the money is hidden.

65.114 *Chester's Hanging.* May 17, 1958. GS: Charles Cooper, Walter Barnes, Sam Edwards. After jailing a wanted stagecoach robber, Matt learns that the man's accomplice is planning a rescue attempt. The robber has hired a gunman and intends to raid the jail.

65.115 *Carmen.* May 24, 1958. GS: Ruta Lee, Robert Patten, Tommy Farrell, Ray Teal, Alan Gifford. Three cavalrymen are killed during an Army payroll robbery. The Fort Dodge commandant gives Marshal Matt Dillon just 48 hours to find the guilty party, or Dodge City will be put under martial law.

65.116 *Overland Express.* May 31, 1958. GS: Simon Oakland, Peter Mamakos, Clem Bevans, James Gavin, Forrest

Stanley, Jan Arvan, Jimmy Cross. Matt Dillon and Chester are taking Jim Nation, by way of the overland stage, to Dodge City to face a murder charge. Dillon is suddenly forced to trust the fugitive with the lives of all the passengers aboard the stagecoach when a highwayman gets the drop on him.

65.117 *The Gentleman.* June 7, 1958. GS: Timothy Carey, Virginia Baker, Jack Cassidy, Henry Corden. A gentleman gambler and Boni Damon, one of Kitty's hostesses, have fallen in love. Because a jealous teamster has threatened to kill anyone who associates with Boni, Matt Dillon attempts to persuade the gambler and Boni to leave town to avoid trouble.

Season Four

65.118 *Matt for Murder.* Sept. 13, 1958. GS: Robert J. Wilke, Bruce Gordon, Elisha Cook, Jr. Cattleman Red Samples' partner has been murdered. Samples accuses Matt Dillon of the deed, and brings a witness to prove it. Matt is suspended as U.S. marshal. Then he learns that his old friend Wild Bill Hickok, sheriff of Abilene, is coming to arrest him.

65.119 *The Patsy.* Sept. 20, 1958. GS: Peter Breck, Jan Harrison, Martin Landau, John Alderman, Ken Lynch. When young Dave Thorp is murdered, a hostess at the Long Branch Saloon identifies Fly Hoyt as the killer. Hoyt surrenders to Matt Dillon in an attempt to clear himself, but the murdered boy's older brother is determined to kill Hoyt, and not wait for the laws decision.

65.120 *Gunsmuggler.* Sept. 27, 1958. GS: Paul Langton, Frank de Kova. An entire family living on an isolated ranch is wiped out in what looks like an Indian massacre. Major Evans of the Army wants to call out his troops to track down the white men responsible for smuggling illegal arms to the Indians. But Matt convinces the major it would be wiser to let him take the responsibility.

65.121 *Monopoly.* Oct. 4, 1958. GS: Harry Townes, J. Pat O'Malley, Robert Gist. A stranger named Ivy moves into Dodge and proceeds to buy out all the local freight lines. Only old Joe Trimble refuses to sell. Not long afterwards, Trimble's home is set afire, and his wife is killed in the blaze.

65.122 *Letter of the Law.* Oct. 11, 1958. GS: Clifton James, Mary Carver, Harold J. Stone, Bartlett Robinson. Matt receives a court order saying he must evict Brandon Teek, a reformed gunslinger, and his wife from their home. But Teek refuses to move and threatens to protect his property with a gun. Matt decides to ride to Wichita to see the district judge on Teek's behalf.

65.123 *Thoroughbreds.* Oct. 18, 1958. GS: Ron Randell, Walter Barnes, Dan Blocker. Matt's suspicions about Jack Portis, a slick newcomer to Dodge City, are seemingly confirmed when Kitty claims she saw him draw first in a gunfight with two cowboys.

65.124 *Stage Hold-Up.* Oct. 25,1958. GS: Bob Morgan, John Anderson, Charles Aidman, Sandy Kenyon, Robert Brubaker. Caught in a stagecoach holdup, Matt and Chester see one of the bandits wounded in the arm during the getaway. Back in Dodge City, Matt recognizes the voice of a man trying to get medicine from Doc for a wounded friend. Matt is certain that the man is one of the bandits.

65.125 *Lost Rifle.* Nov. 1, 1958. GS: Charles Bronson, Paul Engel, Lew Gallo, Tom Greenway. Andy Spangler finds the body of Will Gibbs, and suspects Ben Tiple of the murder because Gibbs and Tiple were enemies. But Tiple, a good friend of Matt Dillon's, denies the murder, and Matt tries to help him.

65.126 *Land Deal.* Nov. 8, 1958. GS: Dennis Patrick, Nita Talbot, Murray Hamilton, Ross Martin. Matt Dillon is suspicious of Trumbill, a land agent who has made a deal with a group of settlers. Trumbill has agreed to obtain for them some acreage belonging to a railroad. Dillon decides to investigate.

65.127 *Lynching Man.* Nov. 15, 1958. GS: George Macready, Bing Russell, Charles Gray, O.Z. Whitehead. Two saddle tramps kill a would-be homesteader and steal his horse. Dodge City seethes over the incident and one man warns Matt Dillon he must find the criminals.

65.128 *How to Kill a Friend.* Nov. 22, 1958. GS: James Westerfield, Philip Abbott, Pat Conway. Matt refuses the bribe offered him by two gamblers and runs them out of town. The gamblers hire a gunman to get rid of Matt.

65.129 *Grass.* Nov. 29, 1958. GS: Philip Coolidge, Charles Fredericks, Chris Alcaide. Matt Dillon advises meek homesteader Harry Pope to get a rifle to protect himself from the Indians whom he insists he hears each night. Pope gets the rifle and unwittingly kills a cowboy. The cowboy's partner then decides to kill Pope.

65.130 *The Cast.* Dec. 6, 1958. GS: Robert F. Simon, Ben Carruthers. While doctor-hating rancher Shell Tucker is away on a wolf hunt, his wife accidentally swallows a nail. Her son brings Doc Adams to help, but despite his efforts, the woman dies. Matt realizes he will have to protect his friend Doc from the wrath of Tucker.

65.131 *Robber Bridegroom.* Dec. 13, 1958. GS: Burt Douglas, Jan Harrison, Donald Randolph, Frank Maxwell, Clem Fuller, Tex Terry, Dan Sheridan. En route to Dodge City to marry her fiance, a girl is abducted by a band of outlaws who have robbed the stage on which she was traveling. When the kidnaper rides into town with the girl, Dillon places him in jail, but the girl refuses to testify against him.

65.132 *Snakebite.* Dec. 20, 1958. GS: Andy Clyde, Warren Oates, Charles Maxwell. While riding into Dodge City, two drifters kill a dog belonging to elderly Poney Thompson. The old man swears revenge, and the next morning one of the drifters is found with his throat slashed. Circumstantial evidence points to Thompson.

65.133 *The Gypsum Hills Feud.* Dec. 27, 1958. GS: Anne Barton, William Schallert, Albert Linville, Hope Summers, Sam Edwards. Matt and Chester are hunting antelope in remote hill country when the are fired upon by an unseen assailant. Upon investigation, they discover two hostile mountain couples engaged in a bitter feud which has already claimed two lives.

65.134 *Young Love.* Jan. 3, 1959. GS: Joan Taylor, Jon Lormer, Wesley Lau, Charles Cooper, Stephen Chase. Matt Dillon is faced with a complicated situation when he discovers that the young widow of a murdered cattleman is in love with the man suspected of killing him.

65.135 *Marshal Proudfoot.* Jan. 10, 1959. GS: Dabbs Greer, Charles Fredericks, Earl Parker, Robert Brubaker. Marshal Dillon goes along with a hoax when Chester's aging Uncle Wesley arrives for a visit. Wesley thinks Chester is the marshal

65.136 Passive Resistance. Jan. 17, 1959. GS: Carl Benton Reid, Alfred Ryder, Read Morgan. During a range war, two cowmen kill all the sheep belonging to Gideon Seek and then burn the man's home and wagon. Seek, a deeply religious man, refuses to reveal the identity of his tormentors to Marshal Matt Dillon.

65.137 Love of a Good Woman. Jan. 24, 1959. GS: Kevin Hagen, Jacqueline Scott. Paroled convict Coney Thorn returns to Dodge City to kill Matt, who originally arrested him. Before Thorn can complete his task, he is stricken with brain fever. He is put in the care of a pretty widow who nurses his body and soul back to health.

65.138 Jayhawkers. Jan. 31, 1959. GS: Jack Elam, Ken Curtis, Chuck Hayward, Lane Bradford, Earl Parker, Brad Payne. Paul Jacks, who is riding with Dolph Quince's Texas herd, comes into Dodge City to tell Matt Dillon that his group fears a raid by renegades. Matt and Chester go with Jacks to investigate.

65.139 Kitty's Rebellion. Feb. 7, 1959. GS: Barry McGuire, Addison Powell, Robert Brubaker, Ben Wright. The younger brother of a long-time friend of Kitty's arrives in Dodge City. Shocked to discover that Kitty works as a hostess in a saloon, the young man appoints himself her bodyguard.

65.140 Sky. Feb. 14, 1959. GS: Allen Case, Charles Thompson, Linda Watkins, Olive Blakeney, Patricia Huston. One of the Longbranch girls is murdered and evidence points to young Billy Daunt as the murderer. Stealing a horse, the young man flees, and Marshal Matt Dillon and Chester set out to find him.

65.141 Doc Quits. Feb. 21, 1959. GS: Wendell Holmes, Fiona Hale, Bartlett Robinson, Jack Grinnage, Jack Younger, Bert Rumsey. A new doctor comes to Dodge City and opens a practice. Doc Adams claims that the man is a charlatan, but the townspeople won't listen because they believe Doc is jealous.

65.142 The Bear. Feb. 28, 1959. GS: Denver Pyle, Norma Crane, Grant Williams, Russell Johnson, Guy Wilkerson. Gentle Mike Blocker, a rancher, is planning to marry an ex-saloon girl, Tilda. Joe Plummer, once a friend of Tilda's, jealously plots against Mike.

65.143 The Coward. March 7, 1959. GS: Barry Atwater, Jim Beck, House Peters, Jr., William Phipps, Barney Phillips, Sheldon Allman. A rancher who bears an uncanny resemblance to Matt Dillon is found murdered. Matt is sure that the killer mistook the rancher for the man he really wanted to kill — Matt Dillon.

65.144 The F.U. March 14, 1959. GS: Bert Freed, Joe Flynn, Fay Roope, Steve Raines, Ed Faulkner. After a quarrel between Al Clovis and Onie Becker, Becker is found dead. Clovis immediately takes a train out of Dodge City, and Marshal Matt Dillon and Chester follow him.

65.145 Wind. March 21, 1959. GS: Whitney Blake, Mark Miller, Roy Engel, Walter Burke, Allen Lurie, Guy Teague. A new girl is working at one of the saloons in town and Matt Dillon suspects that she is a shill for a gambler. After two arguments over the girl result in two deaths, Matt determines to run the gambler and the girl out of town.

65.146 Fawn. April 4, 1959. GS: Peggy Stewart, Robert Rockwell, Robert Karnes, Wendy Stewart. Matt Dillon frees a squaw and her daughter who have been enslaved by a band of Indians. He then discovers that the squaw is really a white woman who was captured by the Indians some years earlier.

65.147 Renegade White. April 11, 1959. GS: Barney Phillips, Michael Pate, Bob Brubaker. Ord Spicer leaves Dodge City after Marshal Matt Dillon frees him for a murder charge by proving self-defense. Later Dillon hears that Spicer may be selling rifles to the Indians, so the Marshal rides out to question him.

65.148 Murder Warrant. April 18, 1959. GS: Ed Nelson, Onslow Stevens, Mort Mills, Fay Roope. Deputy Jake Harbin of Baker City sets up an ambush and almost kills Lee Prentice, who's wanted for murder. Prentice appeals to Marshal Dillon, claiming that he acted in self-defense and is not a murderer.

65.149 Change of Heart. April 25, 1959. GS: James Drury, Ken Curtis, Lucy Marlowe. Jerry Cass and dance-hall girl Bella Grant fall in love and plan to be married. Jerry's brother, however, is furious when he hears the news and he warns Jerry that he'd better change his wedding plans.

65.150 Buffalo Hunter. May 2, 1959. GS: Harold J. Stone, Lou Krugman, Garry Walberg, Scott Stevens, Sam Buffington. Two buffalo skinners are the victims of a brutal murder. Another skinner tells Marshal Dillon that the boss of the buffalo-hunting party might know something about their deaths.

65.151 The Choice. May 9, 1959. GS: Darryl Hickman, Robert Brubaker, Charles Maxwell, Dick Rich. Friendly Andy Hill, a new arrival in Dodge City, is hired as a guard by the stagecoach line. Soon after, another stranger, a known criminal, comes to town. Marshal Dillon learns that both men are on the wanted list.

65.152 There Never Was a Horse. May 16, 1959. GS: Jack Lambert, Joseph Sargent, Bill Wellman, Jr. Kin Creed, crack shot and troublemaker, coaxes a drunk into a gunfight. Creed kills the man and explains to Matt Dillon that he shot in self-defense. Knowing that Dillon won't arrest him, Creed attempts to goad the marshal into a showdown.

65.153 Print Asper. May 23, 1959. GS: J. Pat O'Malley, Ted Knight, Lew Brown, Robert Ivers. Print Asper decides to turn over his ranch to his two sons, and he asks a lawyer to draw up a deed. But the unscrupulous attorney takes over the title himself. When Asper learns of the deception, he threatens the lawyer.

65.154 The Constable. May 30, 1959. GS: John Larch, Pitt Herbert, Strother Martin, William Bryant, Joel Ashley, Scott Peters, Dan Sheridan, John Mitchum, Lee Winters, Vic Lundin. Cowboys from the Drag R ranch get so rough in Dodge City that Marshal Matt Dillon is forced to reprimand them. The boss of the cowboys tells Dillon to let his boys alone, or he and his men will boycott the town.

65.155 Blue Horse. June 6, 1959. GS: Gene Nelson, Michael Pate, Bill Murphy, Monte Hale. While taking a prisoner back to Dodge City, Marshal Matt Dillon and his deputy Chester are stopped by an Army patrol. The patrol is looking for some Indians who have run away from the reservation.

65.156 Cheyennes. June 13, 1959. GS: Walter Brooke, Chuck Robertson, Ralph Moody, Eddie Little Sky, Tim Brown. Marshal Dillon and his deputy Chester find the bodies of some settlers who have been killed by Indians. When an overly ambitious Army officer sets out after the Indians, Dillon fears that there will be an Indian uprising unless he reaches the killers first.

Season Five

65.157 Target. Sept. 5, 1959. GS: Darryl Hickman, John Carradine, Susan Lloyd, Frank De Kova. Young Danny Kadar has fallen in love with a Gypsy girl, one of a group who have camped near Dodge City. Danny and the girl want to marry, but his father and the Gypsies are strongly opposed to such a marriage.

65.158 Kitty's Injury. Sept. 19, 1959. GS: Don Dubbins, Karl Swenson, Anne Seymour. While riding with Marshal Matt Dillon, Kitty is thrown from her horse and badly injured. Dillon carries her to a nearby shack for help, but encounters a hostile family who are unwilling to give assistance. As Kitty's fever mounts, Dillon is forced to take action.

65.159 Horse Deal. Sep. 26, 1959. GS: Bartlett Robinson, Harry Carey, Jr., Trevor Bardette, Michael Hinn, Fred Grossinger, Bill Catching. Some ranchers near Dodge City buy horses which, they learn later, were stolen from a cowboy named Charlie Deesha. Marshal Dillon seems unwilling to track down the horse thief, and the enraged ranchers threaten to organize a lynch mob.

65.160 Johnny Red. Oct. 3, 1959. GS: James Drury, Josephine Hutchinson, Abel Fernandez, Dennis McMullen. A young man comes to Dodge City and identifies himself as Billy Crale. Matt Dillon recognizes him as a ruthless criminal called Johnny Red but he is unable to run him out of town because he has no concrete evidence.

65.161 Kangaroo. Oct. 10, 1959. GS: Peter Whitney, John Crawford, Richard Rust, Lew Brown, Clem Fuller. Matt Dillon and Chester rescue a cowboy from a flogging at the hand of the Scurlocks. The demented father and his two sons vow revenge, and kidnap Chester.

65.162 Tail to the Wind. Oct. 17, 1959. GS: Harry Townes, Alice Backes, Harry Swoger, Alan Reed, Jr. Big Burke Reese and his son Harlow want to buy a small farm from Pezzy Neller, but Neller refuses to sell. Reese and Harlow then prepare to run Neller and his wife off their land.

65.163 Annie Oakley. Oct. 24, 1959. GS: Florence MacMichael, George Mitchell, John Anderson. Because her husband pays too little attention to her, Kate Kinsman tricks him into fighting over her with a neighbor. Matt Dillon stops the fight, but Kate's husband is later found shot to death.

65.164 Saludos. Oct. 31, 1959. GS: Connie Buck, Gene Nelson, Jack Elam, Robert J. Wilke. A wounded half-breed girl rides into town and tells Marshal Dillon that she was shot by a man while traveling through the Choctaw Basin. Matt and Chester go after the culprit, but they find three suspects at their destination.

65.165 Brother Whelp. Nov. 7, 1959. GS: Lew Gallo, Ellen Clark, John Clarke. After some old robbery charges against him are dropped, Sted Rutger rides back to Dodge City and finds that his former fiancee has married his brother. Rutger tells Marshal Dillon that he intends to kill his brother.

65.166 The Boots. Nov. 14, 1959. GS: John Larch, Richard Eyer, Wynn Pearce. Zeno, the town character and salesclerk in the general story, is befriended by a young boy. Then a stranger comes to town who threatens to break up their friendship.

65.167 Odd Man Out. Nov. 21, 1959. GS: Elisha Cook, Jr., William Phipps, Elizabeth York, Dallas Mitchell. Cyrus Tucker tells Marshal Dillon that his wife has left him after many years of marriage. Checking around, Matt and Chester find that no one has seen Mrs. Tucker leave town.

65.168 Miguel's Daughter. Nov. 28, 1959. GS: Fintan Meyler, Simon Oakland, Wesley Lau, Ed Nelson. A pair of rough trail hands accost pretty Chavela Ramirez in town, but Kitty intervenes before they can harm the girl. Matt and Chester escort Chavela to her home, where they are met by an angry father.

65.169 Box O'Rocks. Dec. 5, 1959. GS: Vaughn Taylor, Howard McNear, Larry Blake, William Fawcett, Gertrude Flynn. Marshal Dillon attends funeral services for prospector Packy Rountree. When Dillon looks into the coffin, he finds that it is full of gold ore.

65.170 False Witness. Dec. 12, 1959. GS: Wright King, Wayne Rogers, Robert Griffin, Len Hendry, Richard Sinatra, Norman Sturgis, Brad Trumbull. A man is shot and killed by an unknown gunman in Dodge City. Seeing a chance to become important, Rumey Crep claims that he saw young Tom Morey shoot the man.

65.171 Tag, You're It. Dec. 19, 1959. GS: Paul Langton, Madlyn Rhue, Gregg Stewart, Harold Goodwin. Hired gunman Karl Killion rides into Dodge City. The townspeople are fearful, but Marshal Dillon is powerless to arrest Killion until he breaks the law.

65.172 Thick 'n' Thin. Dec. 26, 1959. GS: Robert Emhardt, Percy Helton, Tina Menard. Two old ranchers who have been partners for many years tire of their venture. Each comes separately to Marshal Dillon to demand the eviction of the other from their ranch.

65.173 Groat's Grudge. Jan. 2, 1960. GS: Ross Elliot, Thomas Coley, Ben Wright. Ex-Rebel Lee Grayson comes to Dodge City and announces that he intends to kill cowboy Tom Haskett. Grayson says Haskett was responsible for his wife's death during Sherman's march through Georgia.

65.174 Big Tom. Jan. 9, 1960. GS: Harry Lauter, Don Megowan, Robert J. Wilke, Howard Caine, Gregg Palmer, Rand Harper. Clay Cran, conniving manager of a bare-knuckle fighter, is looking for a way to make some quick money. He tricks a former boxer, who has retired because of a heart condition, into accepting a match.

65.175 Till Death Do Us. Jan. 16, 1960. GS: Milton Selzer, Mary Field, Rayford Barnes. Eccentric Jezra Cobb and his wife are the targets of an unsuccessful murder attempt in Dodge City. Marshal Dillon finds that some of Kitty's dance-hall girls hate Cobb enough to have hired a killer.

65.176 The Tragedian. Jan. 23, 1960. GS: John Abbott, Stanley Clements, Harry Woods, Howard McNear. Edward Vanderman, an unemployed actor, is caught using a marked deck in the Longbranch saloon. Marshal Matt Dillon takes pity on the old trouper and finds him a job.

65.177 Hinka Do. Jan. 30, 1960. GS: Nina Varela, Walter Burke, Mike Green, Richard Reeves, Bob Hopkins, Ric Roman. Overnight, Dodge City's Lady Gay saloon changes hands. The new owner is a woman who is handy with a six-gun.

Gunsmoke

65.178 *Doc Judge.* Feb. 6, 1960. GS: Barry Atwater, Dennis Cross. Matt Dillon is out of town and Doc, up to his usual tricks, needles Chester, remarking that he is useless. Then Doc's life is threatened by a gunslinger, and it is up to Chester to protect him.

65.179 *Moo Moo Raid.* Feb. 13, 1960. GS: Raymond Hatton, Lane Bradford, Robert Karnes, Richard Evans, Tyler McVey, Ron Hayes, John Close. Racing to deliver the first herd of the season to Dodge, the trail bosses of the two cattle drives meet at a rain-swollen river. They discover a scraggly old cow which could lead a heard across the river and clash over which herd should go first.

65.180 *Kitty's Killing.* Feb. 20, 1960. GS: Abraham Sofaer, John Pickard. Kitty hears that deranged Jacob Leech is planning to kill a rancher. It's too late to get help, so Kitty jeopardizes her own life in an attempt to warn the intended victim.

65.181 *Jailbait Janet.* Feb. 27, 1960. GS: John Larch, Nan Peterson, Bartlett Robinson, Steve Terrell, Jon Lormer. A bandit's two teenage children assist him in a train robbery. As they make their escape, one of the youngsters kills the baggage clerk.

65.182 *Unwanted Deputy.* March 5, 1960. GS: Charles Aidman, Mary Carver, Marlowe Jenson, Dick Rich, Ed Faulkner, Dick London, Craig Fox. The brother of a convicted killer plots revenge. He starts a campaign to unseat Dillon as United States Marshal.

65.183 *Where'd They Go?* March 12, 1960. GS: Jack Elam, Betty Harford. Jonas the storekeeper is positive it was farmer Clint Dodie who robbed his place. Matt and Chester can't believe that the shiftless Dodie pulled the job, but they head out to pick him up.

65.184 *Crowbait Bob.* March 26, 1960. GS: Shirley O'Hara, John Apone, Ned Glass. Old Crowbait draws up a will naming Kitty as his sole heir. Sensing unsuspected riches, his ravenous relatives circle around their prey.

65.185 *Colleen So Green.* April 2, 1960. GS: Joanna Moore, Harry Swoger, Robert Brubaker, Percy Ivins. A southern belle arrives in Dodge City, and Chester, Doc and buffalo skinner Bull Reeger fall all over themselves trying to protect the helpless lass.

65.186 *The Ex-Urbanites.* April 9, 1960. GS: Ken Curtis, Lew Brown, Robert J. Wilke. Chester gets a chance to show the stuff he is made of. When Doc is shot, Chester is left with two jobs — nursing his old enemy and holding off a pair of killers.

65.187 *I Thee Wed.* April 16, 1960. GS: Allyn Joslyn, Alice Frost. Matt Dillon tosses Sam Lackett into jail on his umpteenth charge of wife-beating. But Mrs. Lackett promptly pays Sam's fine.

65.188 *The Lady Killer.* April 23, 1960. GS: Jan Harrison, Ross Elliott, Harry Lauter, Charles Starrett. There is a new girl at the Longbranch saloon, and she sure makes a strong impression on the customers. She shoots a cowboy, then lines up Matt Dillon as her next victim.

65.189 *Gentleman's Disagreement.* April 30, 1960. GS: Adam Kennedy, Fintan Meyler, Val Dufour, Tom Reese. It looks like a showdown between Wells the blacksmith and a gunman who once courted his wife. Mrs. Wells begs Matt to protect her husband.

65.190 *Speak Me Fair.* May 7, 1960. GS: Douglas Kennedy, Ken Curtis, Perry Cook, Chuck Roberson. Out hunting, Matt, Doc and Chester find an Indian youth crawling through the brush. The boy has been savagely beaten.

65.191 *Belle's Back.* May 14, 1960. GS: Nita Talbot, Nancy Rennick, Daniel White, Gage Clark. Belle Ainsley turns up in Dodge City and gets a cool reception. Three years earlier she skipped town in the company of a wanted criminal.

65.192 *The Bobsy Twins.* May 21, 1960. GS: Ralph Moody, Morris Ankrum, Jean Howell, Buck Young, John O'Malley, Richard Chamberlain, Paul Hahn. A pair of killers from the hills have set themselves a lunatic goal — to rid the countryside of Indians.

65.193 *Old Flame.* May 28, 1960. GS: Marilyn Maxwell, Lee Van Cleef, Peggy Stewart, Hal Smith. An old friend of Matt's comes to Dodge City to ask his protection. She says her husband isn't far behind and that he intends to kill her.

65.194 *The Deserter.* June 4, 1960. GS: Rudy Solari, Joe Perry, Jean Inness, Henry Brandon, Charles Fredericks. The Army payroll looks good to Cpl. Lurie Janus, so he plots with a civilian to steal it.

65.195 *Cherry Red.* June 11, 1960. GS: Joanna Moore, Arthur Franz, Douglas Kennedy, Cliff Ketchum. Marshal Dillon gets word that prospector Slim O'Dell was killed while robbing a stage coach, but refrains from telling the widow until he can locate the dead man's partner in crime.

Season Six

65.196 *Friend's Pay-Off.* Sept. 3, 1960. GS: Mike Road, Tom Reese, Jay Hector. Before Joe Leeds dies he accuses Ab Butler of being a bank robber. Matt Dillon has a tough job ahead because Butler is his friend.

65.197 *The Blacksmith.* Sept. 17, 1960. GS: Anna-Lisa, George Kennedy, Bob Anderson, Wesley Lau, Herb Patterson. Emile, Dodge City's blacksmith, is getting married to Gretchen, his mail-order bride. But a rancher named Tolman, who wants Emil's property, tries to disrupt the wedding party.

65.198 *Small Water.* Sept. 24, 1960. GS: Trevor Bardette, Rex Holman, Warren Oates. Marshal Dillon is forced to kill Leroy Pickett when he tries to evade arrest. The Pickett family plots revenge.

65.199 *Say Uncle.* Oct. 1, 1960. GS: Richard Rust, Harry Lauter, Gene Nelson, Dorothy Green, Roy Barcroft. Lee Nagle's father died in an accident. But Lee suspects his drifter Uncle Hutch had something to do with causing it.

65.200 *Shooting Stopover.* Oct. 8, 1960. GS: Anthony Caruso, Patricia Barry, Paul Guilfoyle, Robert Brubaker. Matt and Chester are riding the stage to Wichita with killer Bud Gurney. Also on board is a young schoolteacher named Laura, a minister named Beckett, and a big gold shipment.

65.201 *The Peace Officer.* Oct. 15, 1960. GS: Lane Bradford, Susan Cummings, John Zaccaro, John Close. Sheriff Clegg Rawlins has taken over the town of Tuscosa, so the fearful citizens send for Matt for help. Dillon fires the sheriff from his job, but he is hardly out of town before Rawlins starts his revenge.

65.202 *Don Matteo.* Oct. 22, 1960. GS: Lawrence Dobkin, Bing Russell, Ben Wright. Grave Tabor causes a ruckus in the Longbranch Saloon, so Matt runs him out of town. Just in time too, for pretty soon Esteban Garcia rides into town with the intention of gunning Tabor down.

65.203 *The Worm.* Oct. 29, 1960. GS: Kenneth Tobey, H.M. Wynant, Ned Glass, Stewart Bradley, Gage Clark. Spadden is a brute of a man who likes to throw his weight around. But Archer, his newest victim, stands up to Spadden's bullying.

65.204 *The Badge.* Nov. 12, 1960. GS: John Dehner, Conlan Carter, Harry Swoger, Mike Mikler, Allan Lane. Matt chases two killers, one vicious and the other not too bright. There is a posse close behind, so Rack and Augie, the killers, wound Matt and take him hostage.

65.205 *Distant Drummer.* Nov. 19, 1960. GS: Jack Grinnage, George Mitchell, Bruce Gordon, William Newell, Phil Chambers. Two mule skinners named Grade and Sloat delight in tormenting young Raffie Bligh, a former wartime drummer boy. They force Raffie to play his drums on the streets of Dodge City and Raffie threatens to kill them.

65.206 *Ben Toliver's Stand.* Nov. 26, 1960. GS: John Lupton, Roy Barcroft, Jean Ingram. Jake Creed doesn't take kindly to hired hand Ben Tolliver's interest in his daughter Nancy, so they argue and Ben is fired. When he leaves, he takes a horse he captured and broke, but Jake accuses him of being a horse thief.

65.207 *No Chip.* Dec. 3, 1960. GS: John Hoyt, Rex Holman, Leo Gordon, Mark Allen, Guy Stockwell. Jeff Mossman and his son Pete run some stray cattle off their land. The stock belongs to the tough Dolan brothers, and Big Hutch Dolan swears he'll get the Mossmans.

65.208 *The Wake.* Dec. 10, 1960. GS: Denver Pyle, Anne Seymour, Joel Ashley, Gregg Schilling, Michael Hinn. Drifter Gus Mather arrives in Dodge with the body of a citizen named Boggs, and he wants a real high-class wake and funeral for his dear pal. But then Mrs. Boggs arrives, and claims she never heard her husband mention anyone named Gus.

65.209 *The Cook.* Dec. 17, 1960. GS: Guy Stockwell, Gene Benton, Harry Swoger, Sue Randall, John Pickard, Ken Mayer, Tom Greenway, John Milford, Brad Trumbull, Craig Duncan. The food is pretty bad at the local eatery, and since a drifter named Sandy is out of work and hungry, he is hired as cook to improve the situation. Everyone is impressed with Sandy's ability, except a buffalo hunter named Fisher who doesn't like the eggs.

65.210 *Old Fool.* Dec. 24, 1960. GS: Buddy Ebsen, Hope Summers, Linda Watkins, Hampton Fancher. Widow Elsie Hedgepeth takes a romantic interest in farmer Hannibal Bass and seeks to break up his marriage to his wife Della.

65.211 *Brother Love.* Dec. 31, 1960. GS: Lurene Tuttle, Kevin Hagen, Gene Lyons, Jack Grinnage, Jan Harrison. A Dodge City storekeeper named Gus is gunned down and dies with the name of Cumbers on his lips. But there are two men named Cumbers, Nate and Frank.

65.212 *Bad Sheriff.* Jan. 7, 1961. GS: Russell Arms, Ken Lynch, Harry Carey, Jr., Lane Chandler, Don Keefer. Trying to escape from Matt and Chester, a stagecoach robber named Gance runs smack into an ambush set by another desperado named Hark. When the lawmen arrive, Hark introduces himself as a sheriff.

65.213 *Unloaded Gun.* Jan. 14, 1961. GS: William Redfield, Lew Brown, Greg Dunn, James Malcolm, Rik Nervik. Matt's after a couple of desperadoes when he suddenly develops a fever. He manages to gun down one of the fugitives, but barely makes it back to Dodge City before collapsing.

65.214 *The Trapper.* Jan. 21, 1961. GS: Tom Reese, Strother Martin, Jan Shepard. Rowley and his wife Tassie ask for shelter at the camp of a solitary trapper named Ben. Ben extends his hospitality, but next day Tassie is found beaten to death.

65.215 *Love Thy Neighbor.* Jan. 28, 1961. GS: Jeanette Nolan, Jack Elam, Ken Lynch, Warren Oates, David Kent. Little Peter Scooper flees from the Galloway place with a sack of potatoes, and runs smack into a barbed-wire fence. The Galloways catch him, but decide not to punish him — this time.

65.216 *Bad Seed.* Feb. 4, 1961. GS: Ann Helm, Roy Barcroft, Burt Douglas. Trudy Trent comes up to Matt and begs him to take her to Dodge City. It seems that her father is a drunken brute and she just can't go on living with him. Matt tells her to give it another try.

65.217 *Kitty Shot.* Feb. 11, 1961. GS: George Kennedy, Christopher Gray, Rayford Barnes, Joseph Mell. Two miners named Jake and George are whooping it up in the Long Branch Saloon, and get into a fight. Jake shoots George, and one of the stray bullets hits Kitty. While Doc operates on Kitty, Matt goes after the culprit.

65.218 *About Chester.* Feb. 25, 1961. GS: Charles Aidman, House Peters, Jr., Mary Munday, Harry Shannon, George Eldredge. Doc's dour face hasn't been seen around town for a few days and Kitty is worried. He was supposed to set Jake Wirth's boy's broken leg, but he never showed up.

65.219 *Harriet.* March 4, 1961. GS: Suzanne Lloyd, Joseph Hamilton, Tom Reese, Ron Hayes. Schoolteacher James Horne and his daughter Harriet are on their way to Colorado when Horne is killed by two gunmen. Harriet escapes and walks all the way to Dodge City.

65.220 *Potshot.* March 11, 1961. GS: Karl Swenson, Gage Clark, Joseph Mell, Dallas Mitchell. Matt receives a telegram from a neighboring sheriff about two bank robbers who are on their way to Dodge. Soon afterward, Chester is bushwhacked and badly wounded and Matt sets out to find the attackers.

65.221 *Old Faces.* March 18, 1961. GS: James Drury, Jan Shepard, George Keymas, Ron Hayes. Tom Cook and his bride Tilda plan to settle in Dodge City. Chester thinks he has seen Tilda in Texas, and gunman Ed Ivers is sure he saw her on a Mississippi gambling boat.

65.222 *Big Man.* March 25, 1961. GS: John McLiam, George Kennedy, Chris Alcaide, Sandy Kenyon, Rayford Barnes, Barney Phillips. Pat Swarner tries to force his attentions on Kitty, but Matt sends him on his way. Later that night, Swarner is found beaten to death, and Jud Sloan thinks he saw the marshal do it.

65.223 *Little Girl.* April 1, 1961. GS: Susan Gordon, Wright King, Billy McLean, Ann Morrison, Rickie Weaver, Robby Weaver, Rusty Weaver, Megan King, Michael King, Rip King. Matt and Chester happen upon the smoldering ruins of a prairie cabin fire. A little girl named Charity comes up to them and says that the burned shack was her home and that her father perished in the fire.

65.224 *Stolen Horses.* April 8, 1961. GS: Jack Lambert, Guy Raymond, Henry Brandon, Shirley O'Hara. Jed Cuff's eyes are poor, but not so bad that he can't see horse thieves Tebow and Acker murder his pal Jim Redigo. Jed hightails it for Dodge to report the killing.

65.225 *Minnie.* April 15, 1961. GS: Virginia Gregg, Alan

Gunsmoke

Hale, Jr., Matthew McCue, Barry Cahill, Robert Human. Minnie Higgens seems to prefer buckskins to frilly frocks. But, while Doc is patching up a minor bullet wound for her, she takes a good look at him and love comes to her.

65.226 *Bless Me Till I Die.* April 22, 1961. GS: Ronald Foster, Phyllis Love, Vic Perrin. Townsman Nat Bush says that travelers Cole and Beth Treadwell aren't welcome in Dodge City, and he tries to scare off their horses. Then Matt sends Bush off to jail and the bully swears vengeance on the Treadwells.

65.227 *Long Hours, Short Pay.* April 29, 1961. GS: John Larch, Dawn Little Sky, Lalo Rios, Allan Lane, Steve Warren, Frank Sentry, Fred McDougall. Selling guns to the Indians is the way a man named Serpa makes his living. But he seems to have rung up his last sale. Matt spies him closing a deal with some Pawnees and, after waiting for the Indians to leave, arrests the gunrunner.

65.228 *Hard Virtue.* May 6, 1961. GS: Lia Waggner, Lew Brown, Robert Karnes, James Maloney. After Ed Fallon gives Andy Coe a job, he secretly makes a pass at Andy's wife, Millie. Andy becomes suspicious, and starts carrying a gun.

65.229 *The Imposter.* May 13, 1961. GS: Jim Davis, Virginia Gregg, Garry Walberg, Paul Langton, Harp McGuire. The new arrival in town is Ab Stringer, a Texas sheriff in search of a fleeing outlaw — or so Matt has been led to believe. Doubts arise when Matt learns that a Texas sheriff by the same name has been found murdered.

65.230 *Chester's Dilemma.* May 20, 1961. GS: Patricia Smith, John Van Dreelen. Chester takes an interest in pretty Edna Walstrom's arrival in Dodge. And Edna is interested in Chester, especially in his daily trips to pick up Marshal Dillon's mail.

65.231 *The Love of Money.* May 27, 1961. GS: Cloris Leachman, Warren Kemmerling, Tod Andrews. Dillon's friend Nate Tatham is a former lawman who turned in his badge when his nerve ran out. Now on his way to California and a new life, he stops off in Dodge where he meets Boni Van Deman, a homely Longbranch hostess.

65.232 *Melinda Miles.* June 3, 1961. GS: Diana Millay, Burt Douglas, Walter Sande, Christopher Gray, Rand Brooks. Melinda Miles is the cause of bad blood between cowhand Tom Potter and ranch foreman Ray Tayloe. Melinda loves Potter, but her father thinks his old friend Tayloe would make a better son-in-law.

65.233 *Colorado Sheriff.* June 17, 1961. GS: Wright King, Robert Karnes, Kelton Garwood, Wayne West. Two arrivals from Colorado turn up in Dodge City, and both of them have been wounded. Shortly after Rod Ellison is found with a bullet in his back, Deputy Sheriff Ben Witter rides into Dodge with a slug in his shoulder.

Season Seven

65.234 *Perce.* Sept. 30, 1961. GS: Ed Nelson, Chuck Bail, Chuck Hayward, Alex Sharp, Norma Crane, Ken Lynch. Marshal Dillon is riding toward Dodge and meets badman Perce McCall. When three outlaws try to gun Matt down they naturally expect that Perce will lend a hand — but the badman decides to help the marshal.

65.235 *Old Yellow Boots.* Oct. 7, 1961. GS: Warren Stevens, Joanna Linville, Harry Dean Stanton, Steve Brodie, Bing Russell. Dowdy Beulah Parker says the Parker Ranch belongs to her, a statement that makes a cowhand named Cassidy take a sudden interest. Cassidy's interest wanes when he learns that Beulah's brother Leroy is actually the owner. Then Leroy is murdered.

65.236 *Miss Kitty.* Oct. 14, 1961. GS: Roger Mobley, Harold J. Stone, Linda Watkins, John Lasell, Frank Sutton. Kitty is off to a mysterious errand in the dead of night — to intercept the stage and take custody of a youngster by the name of Thad. Dillon and Chester hear all about it the next day from storekeeper Jonas, and can't understand why Kitty is keeping them in the dark.

65.237 *Harper's Blood.* Oct. 21, 1961. GS: Peter Whitney, Dan Stafford, Conlan Carter, Evan Evans, Warren Kemmerling, William Yip, Moira Turner. On her deathbed, Sarah Cooley tells her husband Gip that she is the granddaughter of a notorious murderer. This means that their sons Kyle and Jeff have bad blood, and Cooley resolves that they will have a strict upbringing. They do, and grow up resenting their father.

65.238 *All That.* Oct. 28, 1961. GS: John Larch, Buddy Ebsen, Francis Helm, Guy Raymond, Gage Clarke. Cliff Shanks, who has come upon hard times, tries to sell his cattle to pay the mortgage on his ranch. There are no takers, so Shank's landlord, Jim Redfield, orders Cliff and his wife to vacate the place by sundown.

65.239 *Long, Long Trail.* Nov. 4, 1961. GS: Barbara Lord, Alan Baxter, Peggy Stewart, Mabel Albertson, Robert Dix. Young Sarah Drew wants to go to Fort Wallace to join her fiance, but she is having her problems. There is no stage, the Army can't provide her an escort, and even Marshal Dillon seems to have other things to do.

65.240 *The Squaw.* Nov. 11, 1961. GS: John Dehner, Vitina Marcus, Paul Carr, Bob Hastings, Jet McDonald, Jack Orrison, Bill Erwin. Fun-loving rancher Hardy Tate was long held in check by his narrow-minded wife. But now she is dead, and Hardy is trying to make up for lost time. The party is soon broken up by his son Cully, who seems to be as strait-laced as his mother was.

65.241 *Chesterland.* Nov. 18, 1961. GS: Sondra Kerr, Earle Hodgins, Arthur Peterson, Dal McKennon. Love comes to Chester Good in the form of Miss Daisy Fair, and she seems to be equally smitten with him. Then Chester decides that if he is going to become a family man, he should also become a man of property.

65.242 *Milly.* Nov. 25, 1961. GS: Jena Engstrom, Billy Hughes, Malcolm Atterbury, Don Dubbins, Sue Randall. Teenager Milly Glover and her young brother Joey are in a sorry state because their sodden father refuses to provide adequate food or clothing for them. But Milly is too proud to accept charity, and she vows to solve the problem on her own, by marrying the first available bachelor.

65.243 *Indian Ford.* Dec. 2, 1961. GS: R.G. Armstrong, Pippa Scott, Robert Dix, John Newton. Mary Tabor, missing daughter of a Dodge City storekeeper, was reportedly seen with some Arapaho Indians. The officer assigned to head an Army investigation is Captain Benter — a violent Indian-hater.

65.244 *Apprentice Doc.* Dec. 9, 1961. GS: Ben Cooper, Crahan Denton, Robert Sorrells. Doc is kidnaped by a pair of outlaws who want him to treat a member of their gang. But when Doc arrives, he finds that his services aren't required. Pitt, a young member of the gang, seems to have a natural talent as a doctor.

65.245 *Nina's Revenge.* Dec. 16, 1961. GS: Lois Nettleton, William Windom, Ron Foster, Johnny Seven. Rancher Lee Sharky thought he struck it rich when he and his wife Nina got married, since Nina's father is loaded. But the old man has yet to come through with a dime, and Sharkey doesn't let Nina forget it.

65.246 *Marry Me.* Dec. 12, 1961. GS: Don Dubbins, Warren Oates, Taylor McPeters, Garry Walberg. Sweet Billy Cathcart is all set to marry his girl friend Lou Ella until his Pa reminds him of a family custom. It seems the elder brother, Orkey, has to marry first, and Orkey hasn't found himself a girl yet.

65.247 *A Man a Day.* Dec. 30, 1961. GS: Val Dufour, Fay Spain, Leonard Nimoy, Garry Walberg, Roy Wright, Anne Morell, Arthur Peterson. A band of outlaws, led by a man named Cooner, intends to steal a gold shipment in Dodge City. Cooner sends a warning to Dillon. The gang will kill a man a day until Dillon leaves town.

65.248 *The Do-Badder.* Jan. 6, 1962. GS: Abraham Sofaer, Strother Martin, Warren Oates, Mercedes Shirley, H.M. Wynant, James Anderson, Adam Williams. Cowpokes Sam Smith and Bert Case change their minds about leaving Dodge when they hear prospector Harvey Easter is headed for town with ore from a rich gold strike. Instead, they ride out to meet Harvey and ambush him.

65.249 *Lacey.* Jan. 13, 1962. GS: Sherry Jackson, Jeremy Slate, Dorothy Green, Oliver McGowan, Nora Hayden. In spite of objections from her family, Lacy Parcher wants to marry farm hand Jess Ayley. But then the chief obstacle to their union, Lacey's father, is removed — permanently.

65.250 *Cody's Code.* Jan. 20, 1962. GS: Anthony Caruso, Gloria Talbott, Robert Knapp, Wayne Rogers, Ken Becker, Richard Bartell, Don Russell, Tom Hennesey, Guy Prescott. Cody Durham is planning to marry Rose Loring and is building a house in Dodge City for himself and his intended. Everyone wishes him well, except cowboy Sam Dukes, who intends to take Rose for himself.

65.251 *Old Dan.* Jan. 27, 1962. GS: Edgar Buchanan, Philip Coolidge, William Campbell, Dorothy Neumann, Sharon Wiley, Sandra Joslyn. Doc finds Dan Witter, an old alcoholic, along the road and decides to try to reform him. He gets Dan a job in Jonas' store, and then asks all Dodge City's saloon keepers to refuse to serve him.

65.252 *Catawomper.* Feb. 10, 1962. GS: Sue Ane Langdon, Dick Sargent, Roy Wright, Frank Sutton, Warren Vanders, Harold Innocent. Kate Tassel really loves Bud Bones, but she is fed up with his constant clowning and devil-may-care attitude toward her. So she begins to welcome attention from some of Dodge City's other eligible young bachelors.

65.253 *Half Straight.* Feb. 17, 1962. GS: John Kerr, Elizabeth MacRae, William Bramley, J. Edward McKinley, Lee Sabinson. The grimy Golden Bell Saloon in Cimarron isn't ideal for high living, but it is great for low scheming. It is there that Grant Hatcher hires Lute Willis to ride to Dodge City and kill Marshal Dillon.

65.254 *He Learned About Women.* Feb. 24, 1962. GS: Barbara Luna, Robert J. Wilke, Claude Akins, Ted de Corsia, Miriam Colon. Marshal Dillon sets out to investigate after receiving word of a prairie disaster. A band of ruthless comancheros, in search of horses, raided a camp and made off with a half-breed girl named Chavela after murdering the other inhabitants.

65.255 *The Gallows.* March 3, 1962. GS: Jeremy Slate, Robert J. Stevenson, William Challee, Joseph Ruskin. Ax Parsons tells Pruit Dover he will have to wait until nightfall to be paid for the merchandise he has just delivered. That is alright with Pruit, only if Parsons doesn't come across then, Pruitt says he will kill him.

65.256 *Reprisal.* March 10, 1962. GS: Dianne Foster, Jason Evers, Tom Reese, George Lambert, Joe di Reda, Brad Trumbull, Grace Lee Whitney. Oren Conrad's weekdays may be spent at his ranch with his wife, but when Saturday rolls around Oren heads for town and a little diversion named Pearl. But this week Oren arrives later than usual and Pearl says she can't spend much time with him because she has another date.

65.257 *Coventry.* March 17, 1962. GS: Joe Maross, Paul Birch, Mary Field, Don Keefe, Walter Burke, Helen Wallace, John Harmon. Jessie Ott and his expectant wife are on their way to Dodge City when their horse is injured, leaving them stranded on the prairie. The sudden appearance of Dean Beard doesn't improve matters either, because Beard just isn't interested in helping them.

65.258 *The Widow.* March 24, 1962. GS: Joan Hackett, Alan Reed, Jr., J. Edward McKinley, Alexander Lockwood. Drunken Emil Peck has cut quite a swatch down Dodge City's main street, leaving Doc knocked out cold and Kitty flopping in a horse trough. And Kitty's spirits aren't helped by the once-over she gets from Mady Arthur, the new girl in town.

65.259 *Durham Bull.* March 31, 1962. GS: Andy Clyde, Ricky Kelman, John Kellogg, Gilbert Green, George Keymas. A gang led by Silva is having a bad day of it. First the stagecoach they hold up turns out to be lootless, and then one of the men is recognized. Silva thinks their luck might change if they moved on to some other place, like Dodge City.

65.260 *Wagon Girls.* April 7, 1962. GS: Arch Johnson, Kevin Hagen, Ellen McRae, Constance Ford, Joan Marshall, Rayford Barnes. While on the trail of a couple of thieving cowpokes, Matt encounters a young lady alone on the prairie. She says her name is Polly and she is trying to get away from wagonmaster Karl Feester.

65.261 *The Dealer.* April 14, 1962. GS: Judi Meredith, Gary Clarke, George Mathews, Jess Kirkpatrick. In spite of cowpoke Johnny Cole's romantic overtures toward her, Lily Baskin's feelings about him remain tepid. But when Johnny is forced to kill her father in self-defense, her mood changes to bitter hate.

65.262 *The Summons.* April 21, 1962. GS: Bethel Leslie, John Crawford, Cal Bolder, Robert J. Stevenson, Myron Healey, Shug Fisher, Percy Helton, Tom Hennesey, Joyce Jameson. Marshal Dillon has some bad news for outlaw Loy Bishop. Just when Bishop thought he had made a legitimate dollar by killing his partner and asking the Marshal for a bounty, Dillon says the dead man wasn't wanted, and Loy is a murderer.

65.263 *The Dreamers.* April 28, 1962. GS: Liam Redmond, J. Pat O'Malley, Valerie Allen, Cece Whitney, Gage Clarke, Shug Fisher. Two old miners who have finally struck it rich, stop off in Dodge City on their way to Memphis. One of them gets a look at Kitty and decides he doesn't want to leave town.

65.264 *Cale.* May 5, 1962. GS: Carl Reindel, Robert Karnes, Joseph Hamilton, Peter Ashley. A young rider name Cale slips into Nick Archer's barn and fall asleep. Awakened by an argument between Archer and a horse thief, Cale is wounded when Archer mistakes him for one of the thief's friends.

65.265 *Chester's Indian.* May 12, 1962. GS: Jena Engstrom, Karl Swenson, Eddie Little Sky, Peggy Rea, Lew Brown, Garry Walberg, Michael Barrier, Shug Fisher. Storekeeper Adam Dill thinks his daughter Callie is flirting every time she waits on a male customer, so he takes Callie out of the store and shuts her up at home.

65.266 *The Prisoner.* May 19, 1962. GS: Andrew Prine, Nancy Gates, Conrad Nagel, Ed Nelson, William Phipps. When military prisoner Billy Joe Arlen escapes from a rock pile quarry near Dodge City, his first destination is the Longbranch Saloon.

65.267 *The Boys.* May 26, 1962. GS: Malcolm Atterbury, George Kennedy, Harry Dean Stanton, May Heatherton, Michael Parks. A snake-oil pitchman who calls himself Professor Eliot shows up in Dodge with his sons Hug, Nate and Park. Business doesn't look too good, but one thing is certain. If there is any money around, Eliot is sure to figure out a way to get it.

Season Eight

65.268 *The Search.* Sept. 15, 1962. GS: Carl Reindel, Ford Rainey, Virginia Gregg, Raymond Guth, Leonard Nimoy, Mike Ragan, Fred Coby, Mickey Morton. A young man named Cale may have earned Marshal Dillon's respect, but Tate Gifford isn't impressed.

65.269 *Call Me Dodie.* Sept. 22, 1962. GS: Kathy Nolan, Jack Searl, Mary Patton, Diane Mountford, Carol Seffinger, Dallas MacKennon, Joby Baker, Bob Hastings, Wallace Rooney, Nesdon Booth. Floyd Bagge and his sister Addie are a heartless pair who run their orphanage like a prison. One of the inmates, a teenage girl called Dodie, has had enough. She overpowers Addie and escapes.

65.270 *Quint Asper Comes Home.* Sept. 29, 1962. GS: Angela Clarke, Bill Zuckert, Earle Hodgins, Harry Carey, Jr., Michael Keep, Lane Bradford, Myron Healey, Robert Hinkle, Foster Brooks, Henry Beckman, John Vari, James Doohan, Ed Peck. Half-breed Quint Asper returns home to find that two white men have just shot his father and are terrorizing his Indian mother. Quint kills the men, then joins his mother's Comanche tribe, vowing vengeance on all white men.

65.271 *Root Down.* Oct. 6, 1962. GS: Sherry Jackson, John Dehner, Robert Doyle, Howard McNear, Michael Carr, Ollie O'Toole. Aggie Dutton is husband-hunting and Chester is the first eligible bachelor she meets in Dodge City.

65.272 *Jenny.* Oct. 13, 1962. GS: Ruta Lee, Ron Hayes, John Duke, Monte Montana, Jr., Ken Hudgins. After Zel Meyers robs a bank, he and his girl Jenny head for Dodge City. Jenny gets a job in Kitty's saloon, but her salary doesn't cover Zel's losses at Kitty's gambling tables.

65.273 *Collie's Free.* Oct. 20, 1962. GS: Jason Evers, Jacqueline Scott, James Halferty, William Bramley. After eight years in prison Collie Patten is released. He blames Matt for his prison term and tells the Marshal that he has spent the last eight years devising ways to get even.

65.274 *The Ditch.* Oct. 27, 1962. GS: Joanne Linville, Jay Lanin, Christopher Dark, Hardie Albright, Dehl Berti, Alex Sharp. After Susan Bart's father died, she decides to continue his project to cut off the homesteaders' water supply. She starts work on a ditch that will divert the path of a creek on her ranch, knowing that she might be starting a range war.

65.275 *The Trappers.* Nov. 3, 1962. GS: Strother Martin, Richard Shannon, Doris Singleton, Robert Lowery, Lane Chandler, Chal Johnson, Robert Brubaker. Tug Marsh and Billy Logan have been setting traps together for a long time. When Indians set a trap of their own, Billy runs for his life leaving the wounded Tug to die.

65.276 *Phoebe Strunk.* Nov. 10, 1962. GS: Joan Freeman, Virginia Gregg, Don Megowan, Dick Peabody, Gregg Palmer, Harry Raybould. Phoebe Strunk has raised four sons in her own image. They are all cold-blooded killers. Marshal Dillon is on the trail of the family after then engage in the activities of murder and robbery.

65.277 *The Hunger.* Nov. 17, 1962. GS: Ellen Willard, Robert Middleton, Hampton Fancher, Linda Watkins, Joe Flynn, Byron Foulger, Kelton Garwood, Henrietta Moore, Robert McQuain. Claude Dorf is big and mean and he rules his family with an iron hand. When his daughter Althea disobeys him, he locks her in the cellar and refuses to feed her.

65.278 *Abe Blocker.* Nov. 24, 1962. GS: Chill Wills, Wright King, Miranda Jones, Harry Carey, Jr., Robert Adler, Marshall Reed, Lane Bradford, Wallace Rooney, Chuck Roberson. Abe Blocker is a tough, old-time frontiersman, whose intense hatred for homesteaders keeps getting worse. In fact, he has just ordered Bud and Mary Groves to get off their ranch or he will kill them.

65.279 *The Way It Is.* Dec. 1, 1962. GS: Claude Akins, Garry Walberg, Virginia Lewis, Duane Grey, Bob Murphy. Angered when Matt breaks their date, Kitty decides to leave Dodge and visit some friends. On the trail she finds Ad Bellem, who is in bad shape after a fall from his horse.

65.280 *Us Haggens.* Dec. 8, 1962. GS: Ken Curtis, Denver Pyle, Elizabeth MacRae, Billy Hughes, Howard Wright. Matt is being assisted in his search for a killer named Black Jack Haggen by Fergus Haggen, who says he has reasons of his own for wanting to catch up with his uncle.

65.281 *Uncle Sunday.* Dec. 15, 1962. GS: Henry Beckman, Joyce Bullifant, Ed Nelson, Wallace Rooney. Chester's uncle, Sunday Meachem, is coming to Dodge for a visit and that means trouble. Sunday is really the weak end of the family. Chester decides to give his no-good relative some money as soon as he arrives, in the hope that he won't take long to leave.

65.282 *False Front.* Dec. 22, 1962. GS: William Windom, Andrew Prine, Art Lund, Charles Fredericks, Sharry Marshall, Wallace Rooney, Robert Fortier, Brett King, K.L. Smith, William Bryant, Roy Thinnes, Michael Mikler. Paul Nill believes that if a man is a good actor, he can fool people into believing that he is a fast gun. Hill bets gambler Nick Heber that Clay Tatum can get away with the kind of masquerade in Dodge City despite the fact that he has never even fired a six-gun.

65.283 *Old Comrade.* Dec. 29, 1962. GS: J. Pat O'Malley, Frank Sutton, Ralph Moody, Wayne Heffley, Vitina Marcus, Dick Whittinghill. Col. Gabe Wilson has come to Dodge in search for Gen. Kip Marston's son Billy. The General is dying and wants to see the boy for the last time, but Wilson soon discovers that Billy is known as the village fall guy.

65.284 *Louie Pheeters.* Jan. 5, 1963. GS: Larry Ward, John Larkin, Gloria McGehee, Woodrow Parfrey. In trying to distract her husband's attention from her romance with Murph Moody, Clara claims that salesman Tom Wiggins forced his attentions on her. Her husband promptly goes out and drowns Wiggins in the river.

65.285 *The Renegades.* Jan. 12, 1963. GS: Audrey Dalton, Ben Wright, Jack Lambert, Don "Red" Barry, John Pickard. Lavinia Pate, daughter of an Army colonel, thinks all Indians are bad, and her opinion includes half-breed Quint Asper. Quint further angers Lavinia when he tells her father that a band of white renegades are causing the latest uprising by plying the Indians with liquor and tempting them with money.

65.286 *Cotter's Girl.* Jan. 19, 1963. GS: Mariette Hartley, Roy Barcroft, John Clarke, Jesslyn Fax. An old man named Cotter dies in Dodge City and leaves Matt an envelope to be delivered to his daughter Clarey. Matt finds Clarey, but she isn't at all like the sweet little girl pictured in Cotter's photographs. She is an uninhibited, unrestrained, teenage nature-girl.

65.287 *The Bad One.* Jan. 26, 1963. GS: Chris Robinson, Dolores Sutton, Booth Colman, Michael Mikler, Ken Kenopka, Gil Lamb, Sue Casey, Robert Gravage. When young Willie Jett holds up a stagecoach, he steals a pleasant kiss from passenger Jenny Parker. Apparently Jenny will kiss, but she won't tell. Matt suspects Jett, but Jenny fails to identify him as the bandit.

65.288 *The Cousin.* Feb. 2, 1963. GS: Michael Forest, Gloria Talbott, John Anderson, Joseph Perry. Chance Hopper and Matt Dillon were raised by the same foster parents, but ended up on different sides of the law. Now Chance has been released from prison and he heads for Dodge to find out if Matt is really the man everyone says he is.

65.289 *Shona.* Feb. 9, 1963. GS: Miriam Colon, Robert Bray, John Crawford, Robert Palmer, Bart Burns, Steve Stevens. A series of Indian raids around Dodge has put the townsfolk in an ugly mood, so when Quint Asper's friend Gib brings his ailing Indian wife to town for treatment, the citizens plan to make big trouble.

65.290 *Ash.* Feb. 16, 1963. GS: John Dehner, Anthony Caruso, Dee Hartford, Adam West, Sheldon Allman. Ben Galt was one of Dodge City's friendliest citizens, until a head injury changed him into the meanest man in town.

65.291 *Blind Man's Bluff.* Feb. 23, 1963. GS: Will Hutchins, Crahan Denton, John Alderson, Herbert Lytton, Gregg Palmer. Before he dies, Bud Hays tells Matt that his assailant was Billy Poe. While Matt is searching for Billy, an attack by a trio of badmen leaves his eyesight impaired.

65.292 *Quint's Indian.* March 2, 1963. GS: Will Corey, James Brown, Patrick McVey, James Griffith, Rand Brooks. When the evidence indicates Quint Asper is a horse thief, some of Dodge's citizens take the law into their own hands and beat him up. Quint disgustedly decides to leave Dodge for good.

65.293 *Anybody Can Kill a Marshal.* March 9, 1963. GS: Warren Stevens, Milton Selzer, James Westerfield, Brenda Scott, Joyce Van Patten. Outlaws Cleed and Lucas fail in their attempt to murder Marshal Dillon, but they aren't easily discouraged. They hire a man named Painter to try again.

65.294 *Two of a Kind.* March 16, 1963. GS: Richard Jaeckel, Michael Higgins, Kent Smith, Garry Walberg, Ben Wright, John Mitchum, Earle Hodgins, Bee Tompkins. Immigrants Sean O'Ryan and Tim Finnegan were the best of friends until a woman parted them. And now their constant feuding is becoming a problem for Matt Dillon.

65.295 *I Call Him Wonder.* March 23, 1963. GS: Ron Hayes, Edmund Vargus, Sandy Kenyon, Leonard Nimoy, Duane Grey, Harry Bartell, William Zuckert, Eddie Little Sky, Alex Sharp. Drifter Jud Sorrell rides into Dodge with an orphaned Indian boy he picked up on the trial. But his charitable act gains him no thanks from the townspeople. Sorrell won't even be able to get a job until he gets rid of the boy.

65.296 *With a Smile.* March 30, 1963. GS: R.G. Armstrong, James Best, Dick Foran, Linden Chiles, Sharon Farrell, Dan Stafford. Dal Creed, the spoiled son of a powerful rancher, is used to getting what he wants and he wants pretty Lottie Foy, but she doesn't want him.

65.297 *The Far Places.* April 6, 1963. GS: Angela Clarke, Rees Vaughn, Bennye Gatteys, Orville Sherman, Dennis Cross. Carrie Newcomb wants to sell her ranch and send her son Jeff back East, but Jeff objects. He would rather keep the ranch and stay near Millie Smith, the girl he plans to marry.

65.298 *Panacea Sykes.* April 13, 1963. GS: Nellie Burt, Dan Tobin, Charles Watts, Lindsay Workman, Charlie Briggs, John Clarke, Jan Brooks, Carl Prickett. Panacea Sykes seems like a sweet old lady, but she is really a conniving crook who doesn't mind stealing from her friend Kitty.

65.299 *Tell Chester.* April 20, 1963. GS: Lonny Chapman, Mitzi Hoag, Jo Helton, Sara Taft. Chester has a crush on pretty Polly Donahue, but Polly is sweet on Wade Stringer, who neglected to tell her that he has a wife.

65.300 *Quint-Cident.* April 27, 1963. GS: Mary La Roche, Ben Johnson, Don Keefer, Catherine McLeod. Widow Willa Devlin is romantically interested in Quint Asper, but Quint doesn't feel the same way about Willa.

65.301 *Old York.* May 4, 1963. GS: Edgar Buchanan, H.M. Wynant, Robert Knapp, Ed Madden, Alex Sharp, Michael Constantine, Rudy Dolan. When Matt Dillon was very young, his life was saved by an outlaw named Dan York. Now they meet again, and Dan is still an outlaw.

65.302 *Daddy Went Away.* May 11, 1963. GS: Mary Carver, Suzanne Cupito/Morgan Brittany, William Schallert. Chester is paying a lot of attention to seamstress Lucy Damon, a widow who has recently arrived in Dodge with her young daughter.

65.303 *The Odyssey of Jubal Tanner.* May 18, 1963. GS: Beverly Garland, Peter Breck, Denver Pyle, Gregg Palmer, Kevin Hagen. Saloon girl Leah Brunson and drifter Jubal Tanner both have a score to settle with Collie Fletcher, who murdered Leah's fiance and, while fleeing Dodge, shot up Tanner and stole his horse.

65.304 *Jeb.* May 25, 1963. GS: Jim Hampton, Roy Thinnes, Emile Genest, William Hunt, Buck Young. Farm boy Jeb Willis sells a horse, which he found, to Ab Singleton. But a hunter named Chouteau accuses Ab of stealing the animal from his partner, and kills him.

Gunsmoke

65.305 *The Quest for Asa Janin.* June 1, 1963. GS: Anthony Caruso, Richard Devon, Gene Darfler, George Keymas, Joseph Sirola, Harry Carey, Jr., Jack Lambert. Matt Dillon's friend Dave Ingalls has been sentenced to hang for murder. Matt believes that Ingalls is innocent and sets out to find the guilty party.

Season Nine

65.306 *Kate Heller.* Sept. 28, 1963. GS: Tom Lowell, Mabel Albertson, Betsy Jones-Moreland, Robert Knapp, Harry Bartell, Duane Eddy. Young Andy Heller murders one man for his money, and then shoots down Matt in ambush.

65.307 *Lover Boy.* Oct. 5, 1963. GS: Ken Curtis, Sheree North, Alan Baxter, Carol Byron, Dorothy Konrad, Richard Coogan, Allan Hunt. Kyle Kelly is quite the ladies' man. He broke the heart of one girl, and now he has taken up with married Avis Fisher.

65.308 *Don't Sleep.* Oct. 12, 1963. GS: Hope Summers, William Talman, Scott Marlowe, Robert Bice, Alan Dexter, Ken Kenopka, Don Haggerty. Released from prison, famed gunslinger Race Fallon meets an admirer, a young upstart named Britt.

65.309 *Tobe.* Oct. 19, 1963. GS: Mary La Roche, Harry Townes, Philip Abbott, L.Q. Jones, Harry Dean Stanton, John Newton, S. John Launer. Mae Young runs out on her gambler boy friend, changes her name and takes a job in Kitty's saloon, where she makes fast friends with easygoing Tobe Hostader.

65.310 *Easy Come.* Oct. 26, 1963. GS: Andrew Prine, Carl Reindel, George Wallace, Dave Willock, Charles Briggs, Orville Sherman. Elmo Sippy doesn't look like a very dangerous cowpoke, but underneath that easygoing, unimpressive exterior lies a cold-blooded killer.

65.311 *My Sisters' Keeper.* Nov. 2, 1963. GS: Nancy Wickwire, James Broderick, Jennifer Billingsley. Grief-stricken after the death of his wife, Pete Sievers takes a job as a hired hand for two spinster sisters.

65.312 *Quint's Trail.* Nov. 9, 1963. GS: Everett Sloane, Don Haggerty, Sharon Farrell, Shirley O'Hara. Cyrus Neff and his family want to get to Oregon, but their trail guide runs out on them — taking along the money Neff gave him to finance the journey.

65.313 *Carter Caper.* Nov. 16, 1963. GS: Jeremy Slate, William Phipps, Rayford Barnes, Anjanette Comar, Michael Fox, I. Stanford Jolley, William Fawcett, Jess Kirkpatrick. When Joe Stark meets Billy Hargin in Dodge, he plans to even the score because Billy gave Stark a severe beating for trying to steal his horse.

65.314 *Ex-Con.* Nov. 30, 1963. GS: Jeanne Cooper, John Kellogg, Raymond Guth, Richard Devon, Howard Wendell, Harry Lauter. Leo Pitts, released from prison, brings his bride to Dodge city, and a bullet with Dillon's name on it.

65.315 *Extradition* Part One. Dec. 7, 1963. GS: Gilbert Roland, Gene Evans, Alex Montoya, Anna Novarro, Walter Burke, Miguel Landa, Pepe Hern, Rico Alaniz, Andy Albin. Matt heads for Texas to try to capture outlaw Charlie Hacker, wanted in Dodge for murder and robbery.

65.316 *Extradition* Part Two. Dec. 14, 1963. GS: Gilbert Roland, Gene Evans, Alex Montoya, Anna Novarro, Walter Burke, Miguel Landa, Pepe Hern, Rico Alaniz, Andy Albin. Matt's prisoner is behind bars in a Mexican jail, and so is Matt.

65.317 *The Magician.* Dec. 21, 1963. GS: Lloyd Corrigan, Brooke Bundy, Crahan Denton, Tom Simcox, William Zuckert, Ken Tiliesas, Sheldon Allman. An elderly traveling medicine man arrives in Dodge with his daughter, and is promptly accused of cheating at cards.

65.318 *Pa Hack's Brood.* Dec. 28, 1963. GS: Lynn Loring, James Hampton, Charles Kuenstle, Milton Selzer, Marianna Hill, Russell Thorson, George Lindsey. Pa Hack has never done much for his children, but he figures he will be well provided for if he can arrange a marriage between his daughter and rancher Jeb Willis.

65.319 *The Glory and the Mud.* Jan. 4, 1964. GS: Kent Smith, Marsha Hunt, James Best, Robert Sorrells, Joseph Hamilton, Rick Murray, Jenny Lee Arness. Sam Bell says he wants to be a deputy so he can get experience as a lawman, but Matt suspects that Sam only wants to build a reputation as a fast gun.

65.320 *Dry Well.* Jan. 11, 1964. GS: Bill Henry, Karen Sharpe, Tom Simcox, Ned Glass, John Hanek. As soon as Dave Linz goes to fetch supplies in Dodge, his young bride Yuma welcomes Web Vickers for a visit.

65.321 *Prairie Wolfer.* Jan. 18, 1964. GS: Noah Beery, Jr., Don Dubbins, Frank Coby, Holly McIntire, James Drake. Ranchers have been blaming wolves for slaughtering their cattle, and that is why Nate Guthrie doesn't want wolf-hunter Festus Haggen around. Haggen saw him butcher some of the same cattle.

65.322 *Friend.* Jan. 25, 1964. GS: Tom Reese, Ben Wright, Jan Shepard, Ralph Moody, Butch Patrick, George Keymas. Matt travels to a neighboring town to investigate the mysterious death of a friend.

65.323 *Once a Haggen.* Feb. 1, 1964. GS: Slim Pickens, Elizabeth MacRae, Kenneth Tobey, Roy Barcroft, John Hudson. Festus Haggen and his pal Bucko get cleaned out in a poker game, and when the game's big winner is found murdered, the evidence points to Bucko.

65.324 *No Hands.* Feb. 8, 1964. GS: Strother Martin, Denver Pyle, Kevin Hagen, Rayford Barnes, Wright King. The ruthless Ginnis clan doesn't like to be kept waiting, and they get plenty mad when Doc insists on finishing with another patient before seeing them.

65.325 *May Blossoms.* Feb. 15, 1964. GS: Laurie Peters, Charles Gray, Roger Torrey, Richard X. Slattery, Mary Munday. Cousin Mayblossom arrives in Dodge to tell Festus that he must marry her, as part of a pact their fathers once made.

65.326 *The Bassops.* Feb. 22, 1964. GS: Robert J. Wilke, Warren Oates, Eunice Pollis, Mickey Sholdar, James Griffith, Ollie O'Toole, Robert Bice, Patricia Joyce. Some hillbillies find Matt and his prisoner stranded on the prairie, handcuffed to each other, and both claiming to be the marshall.

65.327 *The Kite.* Feb. 29, 1964. GS: Lyle Bettger, Michael Higgins, Betsy Hale, Allyson Ames. The man who killed Letty Cassidy's mother doesn't know that the girl can identify him as the killer, and Dillon wants to make sure he doesn't find out.

65.328 *Comanches Is Safe.* March 7, 1964. GS: Kathy Nolan, Don Megowan, Robert Gravage, Dean Stanton, Rex Holman. After a wild night on the town in Wichita, Quint and

Festus are confronted by a saloon girl who says they invited her to come back to Dodge.

65.329 *Father's Love.* March 14, 1964. GS: Ed Nelson, Shary Marshall, Robert F. Simon, Anthony Caruso, Edith Evanson, Ben Wright, Hickman Hill. A bride discovers that her husband's uncle is the man who has been trying to force his attentions on her.

65.330 *Now That April's Here.* March 21, 1964. GS: Elizabeth MacRae, Royal Dano, Vic Perrin, Hal Baylor. Festus' girl friend claims she witnessed a killing, but nobody believes her except the killers.

65.331 *Caleb.* March 28, 1964. GS: John Dehner, Ann Loos, Lane Bradford, Dorothy Green, Vickie Cos, Christopher Barrey, Dennis Robertson. Farmer Caleb Marr is tired of the soil, the toil and the boredom. He wants to live a little, so he leaves his wife at home and heads for Dodge.

65.332 *Owney Tupper Had a Daughter.* April 4, 1964. GS: Jay C. Flippen, Andrea Darvi, Noreen Corcoran, Steven Gaynor, James Seay, Berkeley Harris, Alice Backes, Howard Wendell, Orville Sherman. The judge says kindly old widower Owney Tupper must give up custody of his daughter till he can provide a proper home for her.

65.333 *Bently.* April 11, 1964. GS: Jan Clayton, Charles McGraw, June Dayton, Bill Erwin, Gene Lyons. A jury found Ned Wright innocent of murder, but on his deathbed he makes a confession to Chester.

65.334 *Kitty Cornered.* April 18, 1964. GS: Jacqueline Scott, Shug Fisher, Joseph Sirola, Vici Raaf. There is not enough room in Dodge for both newcomer Stella Damon and Kitty, who has turned down Stella's offer to buy the Longbranch Saloon.

65.335 *The Promoter.* April 25, 1964. GS: Vic Perrin, Allen Case, Robert Fortier, Don Dollier, Larry J. Blake, Wilhelm Von Homburg. Former farmer Henry Huckaby comes up with a two-fisted way to make his fortune in Dodge City.

65.336 *Trip West.* May 2, 1964. GS: Herbert Anderson, Sharon Farrell, H.M. Wynant, Vinton Hayworth, Henry Rowland, Angela Clarke. Told by a patent-medicine peddler that he has only a short time to live, timid bank clerk Elwood Hardacre finds the courage to tell off his tyrannical boss, take his first drink of liquor and get friendly with a young lady.

65.337 *Scot Free.* May 9, 1964. GS: Patricia Owen, Anne Barton, Julie Sommars, Harry Bartel, Jay Lanin, Robert Bice. Rob Scot has left his wife and five children and is all set to take up with Nora Brand. But first he must dispose of the body of Nora's husband.

65.338 *Cool Dawn* (A.K.A. "The Warden"). May 16, 1964. GS: Julie Parrish, George Kennedy, Anthony Caruso, Christopher Connelly. After Indian maiden Cool Dawn is sold by her father to a man named Stark, she runs away and seeks refuge with Festus Haggen.

65.339 *Homecoming.* May 23, 1964. GS: Harold J. Stone, Phyllis Coates, Jack Elam, Tom Lowell, Emile Genest. A stranger named Orval Bass has some bad news for Hector Lowell. Bass claims that he is Mrs. Lowell's ex-husband, and that the Lowells' home, land and business rightfully belong to him.

65.340 *The Other Half.* May 30, 1964. GS: Lee Kinsolving, Donna J. Anderson, Paul Fix. Attractive Nancy Otis has long been a close friend of the Bartell twins, and everyone wonders which one she will marry.

65.341 *Journey for Three.* June 6, 1964. GS: William Arvin, Michael J. Pollard, Mark Goddard, Margaret Bly. On their trip to California, Adam and Cyrus Gifford are joined by Boyd Lambert, a cocky fellow whom Adam soon beings to resent, although Cyrus takes a strong liking to the newcomer.

Season Ten

65.342 *Blue Heaven.* Sept. 26, 1964. GS: Tim O'Connor, Kurt Russell, Diane Ladd, Karl Swenson, Jan Merlin, Eddie Hice. Two tough hombres meet on the trail and decide to join forces. One is Kip Gilman, who is fleeing the law, and the other is young Packy Kerlin, a runaway.

65.343 *Crooked Mile.* Oct. 3, 1964. GS: Katharine Ross, George Kennedy, Royal Dano. Cyrus Degler takes a bullwhip to Quint, just to warn him to stay away from his daughter.

65.344 *Old Man.* Oct. 10, 1964. GS: Ed Peck, Robert Hogan, Rayford Barnes, Howard Wendell. Joe Silva has enemies who have sworn to kill him, but when Silva does meet his death, the wrong man is arrested for the murder.

65.345 *The Violators.* Oct. 17, 1964. GS: Denver Pyle, James Anderson, Arthur Batanides, Michael Pate, Amzie Strickland, Garry Walberg, Martin Blaine. Hatred of Indians soars in Dodge after a man who wouldn't harm a fly is slain and scalped.

65.346 *Doctor's Wife.* Oct. 24, 1964. GS: James Broderick, Phyllis Love, Harold Gould, Anne Barton, Helen Kleeb, Robert Biheller. Physician Wesley May has arrived in Dodge to practice medicine, and his wife Jennifer figures that the best way to line up patients is to spread malicious gossip about Doc Adams.

65.347 *Take Her, She's Cheap.* Oct. 31, 1964. GS: Laurie Peters, Willard Sage, Mort Mills, Linda Watkins, Harry Dean Stanton. On the trail, Matt stops to fix the Carp family's broken-down wagon. The Carps are so grateful that they offer him daughter Allie as a bride.

65.348 *Help Me, Kitty.* Nov. 7, 1964. GS: Betty Conner, Jack Elam, James Frawley, Burt Douglas, Peggy Stewart, Hal Shaw, Joe Conley, Larry J. Blake. Miss Hope Farmer, the daughter of an old friend, is going to have a baby, and she comes to Kitty for advice.

65.349 *Hung High.* Nov. 14, 1964. GS: Robert Culp, Harold J. Stone, Scott Marlowe, Ed Asner, George Lindsey, Elisha Cook, Jr., Michael Conrad, Clegg Hoyt, Buck Young, Karl Lukas. A hatred for all lawmen prompts young Tony Serpa to gun down Matt's old friend, retired marshal Jim Downey.

65.350 *Jonah Hutchison.* Nov. 21, 1964. GS: Robert F. Simon, Richard Anderson, June Dayton, Tommy Alexander, Claude Johnson, David Macklin, Roy Barcroft, William Fawcett. Thirty years in prison hasn't changed ruthless Jonah Hutchison one bit. He returns home determined to rebuild his ranching empire using any means necessary.

65.351 *Big Man, Big Target.* Nov. 28, 1964. GS: Mariette Hartley, J.D. Cannon, Mike Road, Harry Lauter, John McLiam, Frank Ferguson. Pike Beechum is involved with Joe Merchant's wife and to get Merchant out of the way, Pike frames him on a horse-theft charge.

65.352 *Chicken.* Dec. 5, 1964. GS: Glenn Corbett, Gigi Perreau, John Lupton, L.Q. Jones, Lane Chandler, Chubby Johnson, Dave Willock, Lane Bradford. People are wrong in thinking that Dan Collins singlehandedly killed four outlaws, but he decides to live the lie and bask in the adoration bestowed on him.

65.353 *Innocence.* Dec. 12, 1964. GS: Bethel Leslie, Michael Forest, Claude Akins, Jason Evers, Jacque Shelton, Lee Krieger, Ric Roman. Cowboys Bob Sullins and Art McLane are enemies, but they have the same taste in girls. Both like Kitty's new saloon hostess Elsa Poe.

65.354 *Aunt Thede.* Dec. 19, 1964. GS: Jeanette Nolan, Dyan Cannon, James Stacy, Howard McNear, Frank Cady, Jenny Lee Arness. Festus' gun-toting Aunt Thede and young Ivy Norton both are desperate to get married. Thede's problem is finding a man and Ivy's is getting rid of her oppressive father.

65.355 *Hammerhead.* Dec. 26, 1964. GS: Arch Johnson, Linda Foster, Chubby Johnson, John Fiedler, William Henry, Peter Dunn, Don Briggs, Tommy Richards, Gene Redfern, Bill Catching. Gambler Big Jim Ponder is in Dodge to buy some horses, and Festus claims that a friend's quarter-horses are the fastest animals afoot in the West. A statement he will have to prove as rival horse trader Fitch Tallman suggests a race to Cheyenne, nearly 350 miles away, and he backs his challenge with a bet.

65.356 *Double Entry.* Jan. 2, 1965. GS: Forrest Tucker, Cyril Delevanti, Mel Gallagher, Nora Marlowe. Because he is an old friend of Matt's, newcomer Brad McClain has the complete trust of Dodge's citizens—a fact he plans to capitalize on.

65.357 *Run, Sheep, Run.* Jan. 9, 1965. GS: Burt Brinckerhoff, Davey Davison, Peter Whitney, Arthur Malet. Young Tom Stocker and his wife are planning to head for California just as soon as they collect the money due them for the sale of their ranch. But buyer Dan Braden has tricked them. He doesn't intend to pay up for a whole year.

65.358 *Deputy Festus.* Jan. 16, 1965. GS: Denver Pyle, Royal Dano, Shug Fisher, Carl Reindel, Don Beddoe, William Zuckert, Michael Petit, Ken Mayer, Harold Ensley. While filling in for Matt, Festus is surprised to find that the three drunken trappers locked up in jail are his cousins.

65.359 *One Killer on Ice.* Jan. 23, 1965. GS: John Drew Barrymore, Anne Helm, Philip Coolidge, Dennis Hopper, Richard Carlyle. Bounty hunter Anderson and his partner have managed to capture a dangerous outlaw, but they are afraid to bring him into town because of a possible ambush. Instead Anderson asks Matt for help.

65.360 *Chief Joseph.* Jan. 30, 1965. GS: Victor Jory, Robert Loggia, Joe Maross, Leonard Stone, Michael Keep. Trouble begins when a famous Indian chief tries to get a room at the Dodge House.

65.361 *Circus Trick.* Feb. 6, 1965. GS: Elizabeth MacRae, Walter Burke, Warren Oates, Ken Scott, Isabelle Jewell, Roy Barcroft. The carnival is in town and Festus is upset. His girl friend April has been hired to assist in one of the acts.

65.362 *Song for Dying.* Feb. 13, 1965. GS: Theodore Bikel, Robert F. Simon, Ford Rainey, Sheldon Allman, Roger Ewing, Lee Majors, Russel Thorson. A wandering minstrel known as the Singer arrives in Dodge pursued by the Lukens clan, who are intent on killing him.

65.363 *Winner Take All.* Feb. 20, 1965. GS: Tom Simcox, Margaret Bly, John Milford, H.M. Wynant, Nestor Paiva, Allen Jaffe, Red Rowe. A feud brewing between the Renner brothers boils over when the younger one refuses to turn over the money from a cattle sale to his brother.

65.364 *Eliab's Alm.* Feb. 27, 1965. GS: James Hampton, Dee J. Thompson, Donald O'Kelly, Gregg Palmer. Festus' mountaineer nephew comes to town asking his uncle to enforce the code of the Haggens.

65.365 *Thursday's Child.* March 6, 1965. GS: Jean Arthur, Scott Marlowe, Joe Raciti, Suzanne Benoit, Roy Barcroft, Fred Coby. Kitty is delighted when Julie Blane, her friend and former employer, makes a stopover in Dodge. Julie, who is on her way to Wichita where her son's wife is expecting a child, makes a big hit with Doc, so naturally both Doc and Kitty are puzzled and hurt when Julie disappears in the middle of the night without so much as saying goodbye.

65.366 *Breckinridge.* March 13, 1965. GS: Elisha Cook, Jr., Ben Cooper, Robert Sorrells, John Warburton. When Matt orders a barroom brawler out of town, a young Eastern lawyer questions the marshal's authority and whether the ruffian is being denied his rights.

65.367 *Bank Baby.* March 20, 1965. GS: Jacques Aubuchon, Gail Kobe, Virginia Christine, Hampton Fancher, Harry Carey, Jr. When he learns that some God-fearing pilgrim families are camped nearby, brutal Bert Clum decides to see if they possess anything worth stealing.

65.368 *The Lady.* March 27, 1965. GS: Katharine Ross, Eileen Heckart, R.G. Armstrong, Walter Sande, Clifton James, Michael Forest. Hattie Silks, a sophisticated, and once wealthy, lady from New Orleans, is on her way to San Francisco with her niece Liz. But a shortage of funds forces her to take a temporary job as hostess at the Long Branch Saloon.

65.369 *Dry Road to Nowhere.* April 3, 1965. GS: James Whitmore, Julie Sommars, John Saxon, Read Morgan, L.Q. Jones. Kitty's Long Branch Saloon can expect trouble when temperance preacher Amos Campbell arrives in town. And Campbell can expect trouble from gunman Dingo Tebbetts, who has a score to settle.

65.370 *Twenty Miles from Dodge.* April 10, 1965. GS: Darren McGavin, Everett Sloane, Aneta Corsaut, Gerald S. O'Loughlin, Tony Haig, Pat Cardi, Val Avery, Stafford Repp, William Fawcett, Noam Pitlik, Paul Barselow, Jennifer Lea, Danny Fowler. Kitty is among the unfortunate passengers kidnapped from a stagecoach by a gang of outlaws.

65.371 *The Pariah.* April 17, 1965. GS: John Dehner, Ilka Windish, Donald Losby, Steve Ihnat, Tom Reese, Lee Van Cleef, Don Keefer. After immigrant farmer Paolo Scanzano kills an outlaw, life seems to take a turn for the better.

65.372 *Gilt Guilt.* April 24, 1965. GS: Jan Clayton, Andrew Duggan, Peter Brooks, William Phipps, William Boyett. Festus' young friend Sully Rice collapses and Doc's investigation reveals that both Sully and his mother are suffering from scurvy.

65.373 *Bad Lady from Brookline.* May 1, 1965. GS: Betty Hutton, Claude Akins, Billy Bowles, John Hubbard, Jonathan Kidd, Ollie O'Toole, Jan Peters, Eddie Hice. Molly McConnell arrives in Dodge with her young son, and learns that her husband has been killed in a gunfight.

65.374 *Two Tall Men.* May 8, 1965. GS: Ben Cooper, Harry Townes, George Lindsey, Jay Ripley. After Doc is found battered and unconscious by buffalo hunter Abihu Howell,

Festus goes in search of the two men Howell is convinced are responsible.

65.375 *Honey Pot.* May 16, 1965. GS: Rory Calhoun, Joanna Moore, John Crawford, Dick Wessel, Harry Bartell, Harry Lauter, Roy Barcroft, Charles Maxwell. Matt's old friend Ben Stack arrives in Dodge and is immediately attracted to saloon girl Honey Dare. But Honey already has a gentleman friend.

65.376 *The New Society.* May 22, 1965. GS: Jeremy Slate, James Gregory, Elizabeth Perry, Sandy Kenyon, Jack Weston. Matt rides into Ridge Town to reopen an old murder case and is met with hostility from the small community's alarmed citizens.

65.377 *He Who Steals.* May 29, 1965. GS: Russ Tamblyn, Harold J. Stone, Len Wayland, Stanley Adams, Larry Ward, Roger Torrey. Cowboy Billy Walters admires veteran buffalo hunter Jeff Sutro, so much so that he doesn't want to tell his employer that Sutro has stolen one of his calves.

Season Eleven

65.378 *Seven Hours to Dawn.* Sept. 18, 1965. GS: John Drew Barrymore, Johnny Seven, Anthony Lettier, Jerry Douglas, Michael Vandever, Bernadette Hale, Gary Pagett, Joseph Perry, Rusty Lane, Allen Jaffe, Morgan Woodward. Outlaw Mace Gore and his gang ride into Dodge City, capture Marshal Dillon and proceed to take over the town.

65.379 *The Storm.* Sept. 25, 1965. GS: Forrest Tucker, Tim McIntire, Richard Evans, Ruth Warrick, Kelly Thorsden, Mary Lou Taylor, Victor Izay, Willard Sage, Steven Darrell. Buffalo hunter Mel Woodley is about to be hanged for murder, but the killers are the young Benteen brothers, whose family and Marshal Dillon are long-time friends.

65.380 *Clayton Thaddeus Greenwood.* Oct. 2, 1965. GS: Robert Sorrells, Roger Ewing, Jack Elam, William Henry, Paul Fix, Sherwood Price, Allen Jaffe. Young Clayton Thaddeus Greenwood sets out after the four toughs who humiliated his father, and caused the old man to have a fatal heart attack.

65.381 *Ten Little Indians.* Oct. 9, 1965. GS: Nehemiah Persoff, Warren Oates, Bruce Dern, Zalman King, Nina Roman, Rafael Campos, Stanja Lowe, Don Ross, John Marley. After killing a young gunman on the road, Matt finds three more gunfighters waiting for him in Dodge.

65.382 *Taps for Old Jeb.* Oct. 16, 1965. GS: Ed Begley, Wayne Rogers, Morgan Woodward, Arthur Batanides, Don Keefer, Rudy Sooter. After years of searching for gold, prospector Jeb Crater finally strikes it rich. Crater, who doesn't trust the banks, hires a bodyguard to protect his wealth.

65.383 *Kioga.* Oct. 23, 1965. GS: Neville Brand, Teno Pollick, John War Eagle, Ken Renard, John Hubbard, Nina Roman, Catherine Wyles. Wounded and on foot, a young Indian brave stalks the fur trader who murdered his father and attacked his sister.

65.384 *The Bounty Hunter.* Oct. 30, 1965. GS: Robert Lansing, Bert Freed, Gregg Palmer, Hal Lynch, Jon Kowal, Wright King, Lisabeth Hush, Amber Flower, James Anderson, Victor Izay, Jason Johnson. Wealthy rancher Chris Thornton asks retired bounty hunter Luke Frazer to strap on his gun and track down the man who killed his son.

65.385 *The Reward.* Nov. 6, 1965. GS: James Whitmore, David Ladd, Fred J. Scollay, Peter Whitney, Julio Medina, Gil Rankin, Berkeley Harris, Norman Burton. Convicted gold-mine swindler Jim Forbes returns from prison to resume mining operations, with money that his victims say is rightfully theirs.

65.386 *Malachi.* Nov. 13, 1965. GS: Harry Townes, Edward Andrews, Jack Elam, Robert Sorrells, Joey Wilcox, Rex Holman. Malachi Harper is trying to impress his visiting brother by posing as Dodge City's marshal, unaware that the marshal is being hunted down by a killer.

65.387 *The Pretender.* Nov. 20, 1965. GS: Tom Simcox, Tom Skerritt, Gregg Palmer, Julie Sommars, Rusty Lane, Rudy Sooter, Nehemiah Persoff, Athena Lorde, Sam Edwards, Harry Davis, Allen Jaffe, Ed McCready. After serving time for rustling, Frank and Edmund Dano return to an unhappy homecoming. Their mother is dying and their bitter father refuses to forgive Frank for teaching his younger brother to steal.

65.388 *South Wind.* Nov. 27, 1965. GS: Pat Cardi, Bruce Dern, Bob Random, Michael Davis, Ryan Hayes, Michael Whitney, Gregg Palmer, Michelle Breeze. Young Homer Bonney goes into hiding after he sees his father murdered by the man the Bonneys were traveling with.

65.389 *The Hostage.* Dec. 4, 1965. GS: Darren McGavin, Simon Oakland, Tom Reese, Vito Scotti, I. Stanford Jolley, Willis Bouchey, Jimmy Cross. Matt is taken hostage by four escaped convicts who are fleeing to Mexico.

65.390 *Outlaw's Woman.* Dec. 11, 1965. GS: Lane Bradbury, Vincent Beck, Lonny Chapman, Lou Antonio, Gene Tyburn, Peggy Rae. While pursuing a gang of train robbers, Matt manages to wound one of them — a woman.

65.391 *The Avengers.* Dec. 18, 1965. GS: John Saxon, James Gregory, Les Brown, Jr., Olan Soule, Ed McCready, X. Brands. Judge Calvin Storm and his two sons plan to even the score with Festus and Kitty, whom they accuse of murdering one member of their family.

65.392 *Gold Mine.* Dec. 25, 1965. GS: Tom Nardini, John Anderson, Paul Carr, Michael Vandever, Argentina Brunetti, Russ Bender. To lay claim to the gold mine she has inherited, Kitty travels to a rough mining town, where she is befriended by a young mute boy.

65.393 *Death Watch.* Jan. 8, 1966. GS: Albert Salmi, Willard Sage, Frank Silvera, Richard Evans. Bounty hunters Walker and Holly ride into Dodge with wounded outlaw John Drago, who is worth $30,000 in Mexico, dead or alive.

65.394 *Sweet Billy, Singer of Songs.* Jan. 15, 1966. GS: Bob Random, Brooke Bundy, Royal Dano, Slim Pickens, Shug Fisher, Judy Carne, Alice Backes, Diane Ladd. Festus' mountaineer relatives descend on Dodge City seeking Festus' help in finding a wife for Sweet Billy Haggen, his young nephew.

65.395 *The Raid* Part One. Jan. 22, 1966. GS: Gary Lockwood, Richard Jaeckel, Jeremy Slate, Michael Conrad, John Anderson, John Kellogg, Jim Davis, Preston Pierce, Roy Engel, Percy Helton, Tony Haig. After robbing the Sedalia bank, ruthless Jim Stark and his outlaw band make plans to hit Dodge City.

65.396 *The Raid* Part Two. Jan. 29, 1966. GS: Gary Lockwood, Richard Jaeckel, Jeremy Slate, Michael Conrad, John Anderson, John Kellogg, Jim Davis, Preston Pierce, Roy Engel, Percy Helton, Tony Haig. Doc is held hostage by Jim

Stark's outlaw gang, which is fleeing Dodge after robbing the bank and setting fire to the town.

65.397 *Killer at Large.* Feb. 5, 1966. GS: Geraldine Brooks, Robert Ballew, Craig Hundley, Tim O'Kelly, Hardie Albright, Cyril Delevanti, John Pickard, Stuart Erwin, James Beggs, Gilman Rankin, Jonathan Lippe, Morgan Jones. Festus makes uncomplimentary remarks about the marksmanship of a medicine-show sharpshooter, who angrily challenges Festus to a duel.

65.398 *My Father's Guitar.* Feb. 21, 1966. GS: Beau Bridges, Charles Dierkop, Steve Ihnat, William Bramley, Dub Taylor, Robin Blake. Jason, a young wanderer, considers his guitar his most valuable possession, and important enough to kill for when a rancher takes it away from him.

65.399 *Wishbone.* Feb. 19, 1966. GS: Lew Gallo, Victor French, Lyle Waggoner, Billy Beck, Michael Fox, Don Happy, Natalie Masters. Matt is on the trail of three bandits who robbed a stagecoach and murdered the driver and guard.

65.400 *Sanctuary.* Feb. 26, 1966. GS: Richard Bradford, Sean Garrison, Joan Blackman, Virginia Gregg, Larry Wood, Bill Hart, Martin Place, Jack Grinnage, Marshal Blakesley. After robbing the bank, a wounded outlaw takes refuge in a church, holding the pastor and two women hostage.

65.401 *Honor Before Justice.* March 5, 1966. GS: France Nuyen, Noah Beery, Jr., Michael Ansara, Barton MacLane, Harry Bartell, Richard Gilden, George Keymas, Ken Renard, James Almanzar. An Indian maiden asks Thad to intervene in a tribal matter. She claims her father has been sentenced to die for a murder he didn't commit.

65.402 *The Brothers.* March 12, 1966. GS: Scott Marlowe, Bobby Crawford, Joseph Hoover, Mark Sturges, Eddie Firestone, Tom Reese, Warren Vanders, Edmund Hashim. After a young outlaw is wounded and imprisoned by Matt, the boy's older brother Ed vows to set him free.

65.403 *Which Dr.* March 19, 1966. GS: George Lindsey, R.G. Armstrong, Shelley Morrison, Gregg Palmer, Claire Wilcox, Elizabeth Frazer. On a fishing trip, Doc and Festus are abducted by a clan of shabby buffalo hunters.

65.404 *Harvest.* March 26, 1966. GS: James MacArthur, Lesley Ann Warren, George Kennedy, Karl Swenson, Alma Platt, Fred Colby. Rancher Ben Payson doesn't intend to let go of his land or his daughter, but he may lose both. Scottish homesteaders have settled near his ranch, and one of them is attracted to young Betsy Payson.

65.405 *By Line.* April 9, 1966. GS: Chips Rafferty, Denver Pyle, Ted de Corsia, Stefan Arngrim, Maudie Prickett, Gertrude Flynn. Festus is working as a reporter for Dodge City's new paper, despite the fact that he can't read or write.

65.406 *Treasure of John Walking Fox.* April 16, 1966. GS: Leonard Nimoy, Richard Webb, Jim Davis, Lloyd Gough, Ted Gehring, Tom McCauley. Buffalo hunters Jacob Beamus and John Walking Fox have been the best of friends for many years, but some people in Dodge don't like the idea of a close friendship between a white man and an Indian.

65.407 *My Father, My Son.* April 23, 1966. GS: Jack Elam, Teno Pollick, Lee Van Cleef, Zalman King, Charles Kuenstle, Del Monroe, James Gammon, John McLiam, Scott Hale, Billy Halop. Gunman Jim Barrett shoots down a young challenger who was out to gain a reputation, which causes his victim's entire family to seek revenge.

65.408 *Parson Comes to Town.* April 30, 1966. GS: Sam Wanamaker, Lonny Chapman, John McLiam, Joan Granville, Kevin Burchett, Kelton Garwood. A man wearing a frock coat of a murdered preacher arrives in Dodge and announces that he has come to town to watch someone die.

65.409 *Prime of Life.* May 7, 1966. GS: Douglas Kennedy, Joe Don Baker, Martin West, Jonathan Lippe, Victor French, Cal Naylor, Lyn Edington. Kyle Stoner comes to Dodge to visit his girl Wilma, and when he sees her with another man he is ready to kill.

Season Twelve

65.410 *Snap Decision.* Sept. 17, 1966. GS: Claude Akins, Michael Strong, Michael Cole, Sam Gilman, Orville Sherman. Matt doesn't have much use for his job after he is forced to kill a horse thief who was once his friend. Matt decides to turn in his badge.

65.411 *The Goldtakers.* Sept. 24, 1966. GS: Martin Landau, Denver Pyle, Roy Jenson, Brad Weston, Charles Francisco, Michael Greene, William Bramley, John Boyer. Matt is off fishing when a band of outlaws, dressed in Army uniforms, ride into Dodge to melt down the gold shipment they have stolen.

65.412 *The Jailer.* Oct. 1, 1966. GS: Bette Davis, Bruce Dern, Robert Sorrells, Zalman King, Tom Skerritt, Julie Sommars. Six years earlier, Matt Dillon arrested Etta Stone's husband and three sons. The sons went to prison and the husband went to the gallows. Now that the boys have served their time vindictive matriarch Etta seeks revenge by hanging Matt.

65.413 *The Mission.* Oct. 8, 1966. GS: Bob Random, Robert F. Simon, Warren Oates, Steve Ihnat, Jim Davis, Robert Tafur, Rafael Campos, Arch Johnson. In Mexico, a trio of American thieves plot to rob Matt, unaware that he is a United States Marshal.

65.414 *The Good People.* Oct. 15, 1966. GS: Tim Simcox, Morgan Woodward, Allen Case, Fred Reiser, Shug Fisher, Frederic Downs, James O'Hara, Clyde Howdy. Seth Rucker intends to bury a man unjustly hanged for rustling. But when he arrives at the hanging site, Seth finds that the man has been cut down and carried away.

65.415 *Gunfighter, R.I.P.* Oct. 22, 1966. GS: Darren McGavin, France Nuyen, Allen Emerson, Stefan Gierasch, Michael Conrad, H.T. Tsiang, Don Hanmer. In Dodge, a Chinese girl takes loving care of wounded gunfighter Joe Bascome. Equally concerned with Bascome's well-being are two brothers, who had hired the gunslinger to kill Matt Dillon.

65.416 *The Wrong Man.* Oct. 29, 1966. GS: Carroll O'Connor, Clifton James, Kevin O'Neal, Charles Kuenstle, James Anderson, James Almanzar, Mel Gaines, Gilman Rankin, Victor Izay, Terry Frost. Farmer Hootie Kyle is poor enough to take a loan from Matt and foolish enough to think he can run his money up in a poker game. He then faces a murder charge when the cardsharp is found slain.

65.417 *The Whispering Tree.* Nov. 12, 1966. GS: John Saxon, Jacqueline Scott, Edward Asner, Morgan Woodward, Donald Losby, Christopher Pate, Rex Holman, Allen Jaffe, Kathleen O'Malley. After spending eight years in prison for robbery, Virgil Stanley returns to his farm and family, and is faced with two problems — searching the radically changed farm for the $40,000 he hid before going to prison and dealing with the relentless lawman from whom he stole the money.

65.418 *The Well.* Nov. 19, 1966. GS: Guy Raymond, Joan Payne, Lawrence Casey, Elizabeth Rogers, Ted Gehring, Karl Lucas, Pete Kellett, Robert Ballew. Spirits in drought-stricken Dodge are about as low as the water level in the town's only well. While Festus looks for a new source of water, Matt uses a rain maker to give the townspeople hope.

65.419 *Stage Stop.* Nov. 26, 1966. GS: John Ireland, Anne Whitfield, Jack Ging, Steve Raines, Michael Vandever, Joseph Ruskin, Sid Haig, Andy Albin. At a stage stop, Doc, a pregnant woman and a blind man makes a desperate stand against the bandits who unsuccessfully ambushed them and who have returned to finish the job.

65.420 *The Newcomers.* Dec. 3, 1966. GS: Karl Swenson, Ben Wright, James Murdock, Laurence Aten, Jon Voight, Robert Sorrells, Charles Dierkop, John Pickard, Daniel Ades. Traveling West with his father, Swedish immigrant Peter Karlgren accidentally kills a cowboy in a fight. Unfortunately for Peter, the only witness is a blackmailer.

65.421 *Quaker Girl.* Dec. 10, 1966. GS: William Shatner, Ariane Quinn, Liam Sullivan, Ben Johnson, Warren Vanders, Timothy Carey, Anna Karen, Nancy Marshall, William Bryant, Ed McCready, Joseph Breen, Tom Reese. Mistaken identities and a gang of cutthroats threaten a deputized Thad with losing his prisoner and his life.

65.422 *The Moonstone.* Dec. 17, 1966. GS: Mike Kellin, Tom Skerritt, Gail Kobe, Warren Kemmerling, Jeff Palmer, Larry Barton, Fred Coby, Fred Dale, Chick Sheridan. Chad Timpson, whose criminal past is hidden beneath a new life, may be exposed by a violent conflict surrounding three people: a former partner in crime, Chad's sweetheart and his halfwit brother.

65.423 *Champion of the World.* Dec. 24, 1966. GS: Alan Hale, Jr., Dan Tobin, Ralph Rose, Jane Dulo, Gale Robbins, Arthur Peterson, John McLiam, Jr., Don Keefer, Pete Kellett, Troy Melton. Bull Bannock is a swaggering ex-boxing champ with more brass than brains. To bulldoze Kitty into selling the Long Branch, he unwittingly teams up with an old man known to everyone as a con artist.

65.424 *The Hanging.* Dec. 31, 1966. GS: Tom Stern, Kit Smythe, Robert Knapp, Henry Darrow, Anna Navarro, Richard Bakalyan, Edmund Hashim, Larry Ward, Morgan Woodward, Byron Foulger. Matt has been ordered to carry out the hanging of a vicious killer who brags he will never stand on the gallows. Neither Matt nor the condemned man foresees just how a few former partners intend to stop their friend's hanging.

65.425 *Saturday Night.* Jan. 7, 1967. GS: Leif Erickson, William C. Watson, Victor French, Dub Taylor, Link Harget, Rudy Sooter, Frederick Downs. Virgil Powell and his drovers save Matt and his prisoner from certain death on the trail. But Matt doesn't know that one of Powell's men is plotting to free his crazed prisoner when the cattle drive reaches Dodge.

65.426 *Mad Dog.* Jan. 14, 1967. GS: George Lindsey, Denver Pyle, George Murdock, Iggie Wolfington, Hoke Howell, Sammy Reese, Butch Patrick, Dub Taylor. In the town of Bucklin, Festus is mistaken for gunslinger Jim Travers. The dying Travers gave Festus his gaudy saddle, and no amount of talk will convince the townsfolk that peaceable Festus isn't a hired gunman.

65.427 *Muley.* Jan. 21, 1967. GS: Zalman King, Lane Bradbury, Anthony Call, Marc Cavell, Ross Hagen. You need your wits about you when you go gunning for Matt Dillon, but a gunman named Muley can't keep his mind on the job. The vengeful outlaw's thoughts keep wandering in the direction of a pretty saloon girl.

65.428 *Mail Drop.* Jan. 28, 1967. GS: Eddie Hodges, John Anderson, Bing Russell, Steve Raines, Ted French, Pete Kellett, Fred McDougall, Chick Sheridan, Robert Miles, Jr. A boy may provide a clue to the whereabouts of his father, an outlaw who is being hunted by Marshal Dillon.

65.429 *Old Friend.* Feb. 4, 1967. GS: Fritz Weaver, Delphi Lawrence, William Benedict, Valentin de Vargas, Carlos Rivas, David Renard, Lew Brown, Pat Cardi, Robert B. Williams. The search for an outlaw band brings an Arizona lawman to Dodge. Marshal Burl Masters isn't about to lose his quarry, even if it means shooting first and asking questions later.

65.430 *Fandango.* Feb. 11, 1967. GS: Mario Alcaide, Torin Thatcher, Diana Muldaur, Paul Fix, Shug Fisher, Joe Higgins, Walter Baldwin, Fletcher Brian. Matt may be forced to arm the murderer he is bringing in. Both the marshal and his prisoner are the targets of a rancher who is determined to avenge the death of his brother and three ranch hands.

65.431 *The Returning.* Feb. 18, 1967. GS: Michael Ansara, Lois Nettleton, Steve Sanders, Johnnie Whittaker, Jonathan Lippe, Richard Webb, Kenneth Mars, Roy Barcroft, Billy Halop, Troy Melton. Amy Todd is an honest woman who faces temptation when her husband, a former outlaw, returns to a life of crime. Luke Todd is on the run, but he has left Amy with $20,000 in loot, money that she desperately needs.

65.432 *The Lure.* Feb. 25, 1967. GS: Stephen McNally, Kim Darby, Warren Vanders, John Pickard, Paul Picerni, Fred Coby, Len Wayland, Martin Brooks, Val Avery, Troy Melton. An outlaw kidnaps Kitty, who makes a bid for freedom by trying to turn the fugitive's daughter against him.

65.433 *Noose of Gold.* March 4, 1967. GS: Vincent Gardenia, Steve Ihnat, Sam Gilman, Jan Shepard, Barton MacLane, Michael Preece, Jack Bailey, Harry Basch, Robert B. Williams. Matt risks his life to help an old friend, outlaw John Farrow. An ambitious state official is trading on Matt's friendship with Farron in an attempt to capture the outlaw and nearly $10,000 in reward money.

65.434 *The Favor.* March 11, 1967. GS: James Daly, William Bramley, Diane Ladd, Troy Melton, Shirley Wilson, Fred J. Scollay, Lew Gallo. Kitty is torn between her loyalty to Marshal Dillon and the man he is searching for, a killer who once saved her from an Indian attack.

65.435 *Mistaken Identity.* March 18, 1967. GS: Albert Salmi, Hal Lynch, Ken Mayer, Sam Melville. A fugitive has been hiding from the law by using cowboy Mel Gates' identity. Now, the fugitive may have to commit murder. Matt has ridden into town with the injured Gates.

65.436 *Ladies from St. Louis.* March 25, 1967. GS: Claude Akins, Josephine Hutchinson, Aneta Corsaut, Kelly Jean Peters, Venita Wolf, Lois Roberts, Henry Darrow, John Carter, Ralph Roberts, Lew Brown, Vic Tayback. After outlaw Worth Sweeney saves a group of nuns from being murdered, the grateful sisters take their wounded protector into Dodge without revealing his criminal past.

65.437 *Nitro!* **Part One** (A.K.A. "Tiger by the Tail"). April 8, 1967. GS: David Canary, Bonnie Beecher, Tom Reese, Eddie Firestone, Robert Rothwell, Dub Taylor, Sue Collier, Michelle Breeze, Rudy Sooter, Anthony Redondo, John Breen, Scott Hale. Drifter George McClaney picks a dangerous way to finance his courtship of a saloon girl. He accepts an offer from a robbery gang to extract nitroglycerin from sticks of dynamite.

65.438 *Nitro!* **Part Two.** April 15, 1967. GS: David Canary, Bonnie Beecher, Tom Reese, Eddie Firestone, Robert Rothwell, Dub Taylor, Sue Collier, Michelle Breeze, Rudy Sooter, Anthony Redondo, John Breen, Scott Hale. Matt tries to track down a gang of bank robbers who use nitroglycerin for their illegal exploits. Meanwhile, a down-and-out drifter reluctantly agrees to mix one last batch of nitro for the gang.

Season Thirteen

65.439 *The Wreckers.* Sept. 11, 1967. GS: Edmund Hashim, Warren Oates, Warren Vanders, Rex Holman, Gene Rutherford, Charles Kuenstle, Trevor Bardette, James Almanzar, Lew Brown, Joe Haworth, Joe Yrigoyen. Matt, Kitty and an unconscious outlaw have been hauled from a wrecked stagecoach by a hold-up gang. To hide Matt's identity, Kitty pins his badge on the outlaw and prays that he won't regain consciousness.

65.440 *Cattle Barons.* Sept. 18, 1967. GS: Forrest Tucker, Robert J. Wilke, Brad Johnson, John Milford, Lew Brown, Robert Sampson, Fred Colby, Roy Barcroft, Clyde Howdy. Matt Dillon tenses for trouble as a cattle drive nears Dodge. The marshal's fear is well-founded. Two feuding cattle barons are claiming ownership of the herd.

65.441 *The Prodigal.* Sept. 25, 1967. GS: Lew Ayres, Charles Robinson, Richard Evans, Lamont Johnson, Lee Kreiger, Ted Gehring, Kelly Thordsen. A sensation-seeking journalist and the vengeful sons of a dead gunman ask Marshal Dillon to reopen a case he closed twelve years before. The journalist thinks the gunman was shot by Matt, who has never disclosed the killer's name.

65.442 *Vengeance* **Part One.** Oct. 2, 1967. GS: John Ireland, James Stacy, Morgan Woodward, James Anderson, Buck Taylor, Kim Darby, Paul Fix, Royal Dano, Victor French, Sandy Kevin, Rudy Sooter. Matt tries to help a young drifter, whose friends were trampled by a rancher's horsemen. Instead of pressing charges, the drifter is waiting for his moment of revenge.

65.443 *Vengeance* **Part Two.** Oct. 9, 1967. GS: John Ireland, James Stacy, Morgan Woodward, James Anderson, Buck Taylor, Kim Darby, Paul Fix, Royal Dano, Victor French, Sandy Kevin, Rudy Sooter. Matt arrests Bob Johnson for the murder of town boss Parker. Johnson intends to prove his innocence, aided by a servant girl from the hotel.

65.444 *A Hat.* Oct. 16, 1967. GS: Chill Wills, Gene Evans, Tom Simcox, H.M. Wynant, Robert Sorrells, Scott Hale, Gene O'Donnell, Bill Erwin, Ed McCready, Lee De Broux, Don Happy, Shirley Wilson. A stray bullet that ruined a frontiersman's hat sets off a chain reaction of bloodshed and retribution in Dodge City.

65.445 *Hard Luck Henry.* Oct. 23, 1967. GS: John Astin, Royal Dano, Ken Drake, Michael Fox, Mary Lou Taylor, Bobby Riha, Anthony James, John Shank, Charles Kuenstle, Bo Hopkins, Mayf Nutter, Warren Douglas. Festus deserts Dodge City for Pratt County, where his less intelligent kinfolk are feuding over a chest filled with Confederate gold while battling greedy neighbors.

65.446 *Major Glory.* Oct. 30, 1967. GS: Carroll O'Connor, Victor French, Robert F. Lyons, Link Wyler, Lawrence Mann, Don G. Ross, Cal Naylor, Chris Stephens, Russ Siler, William L. Sumper. Major Vanscoy, a strong-willed Army officer, is heading for a showdown with Matt. Both men claim jurisdiction in a case concerning Festus' alleged knifing of a sergeant.

65.447 *The Pillagers.* Nov. 6, 1967. GS: John Saxon, Joseph Schneider, Vito Scotti, Paul Picerni, William Bramley, Allen Jaffe, Harry Harvey, Sr. Kitty and gunsmith Newly O'Brien are kidnaped by a robbery gang who think that Newly is a doctor. Ordered to operate on a wounded outlaw, Newly proceeds as best he can while planning his and Kitty's escape.

65.448 *Prairie Wolfers.* Nov. 13, 1967. GS: Charles McGraw, Jon Voight, Lou Antonio, Kelly Jean Peters, I. Stanford Jolley, Matt Emery. Acting marshal Festus Haggen has a crime on his hands. Two trappers have stolen $20,000 from a fur trader who refused to buy their pelts.

65.449 *Stranger in Town.* Nov. 20, 1967. GS: Pernell Roberts, Jacqueline Scott, R.G. Armstrong, Henry Jones, Eric Shea, Jon Kowal, Billy Halop. A gunfighter is hired to kill a Dodge City businessman. Dave Reeves finds his interest in the assignment overshadowed by the presence of the wife who deserted him, and a young son he has never seen.

65.450 *Death Train.* Nov. 27, 1967. GS: Dana Wynter, Morgan Woodward, Norman Alden, Ed Bakey, Mort Mills, Trevor Bardette, Zalman King, Sam Melville. Matt enforces a quarantine on a private railroad car while Doc treats the passengers for a fever that could spread to Dodge. Panic spreads as the townspeople listen to the rantings of a fire and brimstone preacher.

65.451 *Rope Fever.* Dec. 4, 1967. GS: Ralph Bellamy, Anna Lee, George Murdock, Sam Gilman, Ken Mayer, Ted Gehring, Dennis Cross, Hal Baylor, Gertrude Flynn. An aging sheriff enjoys a new-found glory when he shoots a bank robber and jails Festus. He refuses to belive Festus is innocent of any wrongdoing.

65.452 *Wonder.* Dec. 18, 1967. GS: Tony Davis, Warren Berlinger, Richard Mulligan, Ken Swofford, Norman Alden, Jackie Russell, Fay Spain. An Indian boy insists that Matt help him search for his friend, a drifter who is being hounded by a trio of disgruntled cowboys.

65.453 *Baker's Dozen.* Dec. 25, 1967. GS: Denver Pyle, Peggy Rea, Harry Carey, Jr., Harry Lauter, Mitzi Hoag, Ed McCready, Sam Greene, Phyllis Coghlan, Tyler MacDuff, William Murphy, Dana Dillaway, Keith Schultz, Gary Grimes. Doc delivers three baby boys, but is unable to save their mother. Determined to find a home for the triplets, the grizzled old doctor begins a battle to keep them from being separated and kept out of an orphanage.

65.454 *The Victim.* Jan. 1, 1968. GS: Beverly Garland, James Gregory, Cliff Osmond, John Kellogg, Kevin Hagen, Warren Vanders, Edmund Hashim, Roy Jenson, Gregg Palmer, Tim O'Kelly, Willis Bouchey. Marshal Dillon helps the frightened sheriff of Martin's Bend keep lynch-minded citizens at bay, and an accused murderer alive, as they await the arrival of a circuit judge.

65.455 *Deadman's Law.* Jan. 8, 1968. GS: John Dehner, Gunnar Hellstrom, Eddie Little Sky, Craig Curtis, Ralph Manza, Gregg Palmer, Robert Brubaker, Steve Raines, Baynes Barron, Alex Sharp, Jonathan Harper. Marshal Dillon is missing. While Festus conducts a search, a Dodge City cattleman sets up a vigilante law enforcement band, and the carnage begins.

65.456 *Nowhere to Run.* Jan. 15, 1968. GS: J. Robert Porter, Bob Random, Dan Ferrone, Mark Lenard, Ilka Windish, Michael Burns, Harry Harvey, Sr., William Tannen. Two teenage boys pay close attention as Matt and Festus head for the Stonecipher ranch. The youngsters, who have pulled a robbery, fear that they will be exposed by their partner, who lies wounded at the bottom of a well.

65.457 *Blood Money.* Jan. 22, 1968. GS: Nehemiah Persoff, Anthony Zerbe, Donna Baccala, James Anderson, Hank Brandt, Mills Watson, Lee De Broux, Troy Melton. Furious because his son Nick has become a gunfighter, Alex Skouras maims the boy by putting a bullet through his gun hand. The old man then faces the wrath of three killers bent on settling a score with Nick.

65.458 *Hill Girl.* Jan. 29, 1968. GS: Lane Bradbury, Victor French, Anthony James, Burt Mustin. Newly frees a hill country girl from her brutish half-brothers, but trouble dogs the girl when the men follow her to Dodge City.

65.459 *The Gunrunners.* Feb. 5, 1968. GS: Michael Constantine, Dan Ferrone, Jim Davis, Dick Peabody, John McLiam, James Griffith, X Brands. Despite Matt's warning, an old trapper insists on meting out justice to a gang of Army deserters who wounded the trapper's Indian companion.

65.460 *The Jackals.* Feb. 12, 1968. GS: Paul Richards, Tige Andrews, Joe De Santis, Felice Orlandi, Ward Wood, Michael Vandever, Alex Montoya, David Renard, Martin Garralaga, Rico AP aniz, Jorge Moreno, Ruben Moreno, Ellen Davalos, Carmen Austin, Olga Velez. Matt rides into Mexico, relentlessly pursing the man who engineered a murder. The victim was Matt's old friend Sheriff Mark Handlin, who was gunned down on the day he retired.

65.461 *The First People.* Feb. 19, 1968. GS: Todd Armstrong, Gene Evans, Jack Elam, James Almanzar, James Lydon, Richard Hale, Felix Locher, Bill Erwin, Eddie Little Sky. Thomas Evans, an ambitious Indian agent, summons a Federal investigation and charges Marshal Dillon with complicity in a murder committed on the Elm Fork reservation.

65.462 *Mr. Sam'l.* Feb. 26, 1968. GS: Ed Begley, Mark Richman, Sandra Smith, Larry Pennell, Duke Hobbie. Mr. Sam'l, a water witcher, stirs up hope in drought-stricken Dodge. While the ranchers let him search for water, a murderous land swindler takes steps to see he doesn't find it.

65.463 *A Noose for Dobie Price.* March 4, 1968. GS: Chill Wills, Shug Fisher, Sheldon Allman, Robert Donner, E.J. Andre, Rose Hobart, Owen Bush, Michael Greene, Raymond Mayo, John "Bear" Hudkins, Bob Herron. Matt is on the trail of a condemned killer who broke out of the Dodge City jail. He deputizes ex-outlaw Elihu Gorman to assist him, but the likeable conman's bad habits keep getting in Matt's way.

Season Fourteen

65.464 *Lyle's Kid.* Sept. 23, 1968. GS: Morgan Woodward, Robert Pine, Joe De Santis, Charlotte Considine, Lew Palter, Mills Watson, I. Stanford Jolley, Jonathan Harper. Marshal Dillon tries to keep a crippled ex-lawman from using his son to settle a long-standing quest for vengeance.

65.465 *The Hide Cutters.* Sept. 30, 1968. GS: Joseph Campanella, Michael Burns, Conlan Carter, Cliff Osmond, Eddie Firestone, Ken Swofford, Gregg Palmer, Steve Raines, Mike Howden. Matt joins a cattle drive to avert bloodshed between trail boss McKee and a handful of evil-minded hide-cutters.

65.466 *Zavala.* Oct. 7, 1968. GS: Miriam Colon, Manuel Padilla, Jr., Jim Davis, Jonathan Lippe, Larry D. Mann, Rex Holman, Rico Alaniz, Robert Sorrells, Warren Vanders, Nacho Galindo, Jose Chavez, Elizabeth Germaine, Bobby E. Clark. Trailing outlaws to a small Mexican village, Matt is taken in tow by Paco, a youngster who plans to use the marshal's gunmanship in a scheme of his own.

65.467 *Uncle Finney.* Oct. 14, 1968. GS: Victor French, Anthony James, Burt Mustin, Lane Bradbury, Steve Raines, John Dolan, Monte Hale, Pete Kellett, Margaret Bacon. While their 103-year-old uncle lolls in the Dodge City jail, two hill men open a saloon, and begin tunnelling into the local freight office.

65.468 *Slocum.* Oct. 21, 1968. GS: Dub Taylor, Will Geer, James Wainwright, Ross Hagen, Lee Lambert, Mills Watson, Steve Sandor, Bill Erwin, Lew Brown, Charles Kuenstle. An old friend of Matt's vows to save the marshal from an unexpected source of danger — a Bible-spouting, moonshine-swilling rancher and his sons.

65.469 *O'Quillian.* Oct. 28, 1968. GS: John McLiam, Victor French, Lou Antonio, Vaughn Taylor, Ken Drake, Anthony James, Steve Raines, Iron Eyes Cody, Peggy Rea, Jerry Summers, Roy Barcroft. An exasperated Matt is sworn to protect the life and limb of Leary O'Quillian, an Irishman whose forte is making trouble. When he is not causing fights at the Longbranch, O'Quillian is on the lookout for a man who vowed to kill him.

65.470 *9:12 to Dodge.* Nov. 11, 1968. GS: Todd Armstrong, Joanne Linville, Frank Marth, Tom Water, Robert Emhardt, Harry Lauter, Troy Melton, Link Wyler, Fred Coby, Lee De Broux, William Murphy, Harry Harvey, Sr., Ed Long, Dan Terranova, Rush Williams, Johnny Haymer. A tense train ride is in store for Marshal Dillon and Doc as they return an escaped prisoner to Dodge. The other passengers include an influential woman who thinks the prisoner is being mistreated, and men waiting a chance to free their friend.

65.471 *Abelia.* Nov. 18, 1968. GS: Jacqueline Scott, Jeremy Slate, Tom Stern, Jack Lambert, Gregg Palmer, Mike Durkin, Susan Olsen, Jack Chaplain. Festus is forced to pose as a widow's husband when an outlaw gang returns to her home to hide from Matt Dillon's posse.

65.472 *Railroad.* Nov. 25, 1968. GS: Shug Fisher, Jim Davis, Buck Holland, Ramon Bieri, Roy Jenson, Don Hanmer, James McCallion. Marshal Dillon butts heads with burly Wes Cameron, a railroad boss who has been stopped in his tracks by a homesteader who refuses to sell his property.

65.473 *The Miracle Man.* Dec. 2, 1968. GS: Don Chastain, Sandra Smith, William Bramley, Joey Walsh, Bruce Watson, Margie de Meyer, Lisa Gerritsen, Kevin Cooper, John Crawford, Christopher Knight. Festus keeps a skeptical eye on

Bob Sullivan, a smooth talking salesman who has given up peddling to work on a widow's farm. The deputy is sure Sullivan is scheming to cheat the lady.

65.474 *Waco.* Dec. 9, 1968. GS: Victor French, Harry Carey, Jr., Louise Latham, Tom Reese, Lee De Broux, Mills Watson, Lawrence Mann, Pat Thompson, Joy Fielding, Liz Marshall. Fate seems determined to prevent Matt from taking a prisoner back to Dodge. He is being trailed by the outlaw's partners, and slowed down by an encounter with a pregnant Indian girl in need of medical help.

65.475 *Lobo.* Dec. 16, 1968. GS: Morgan Woodward, David Brian, Sheldon Allman, Sandy Kenyon, Ken Swofford, Eddie Firestone, Fred Coby, William Murphy. Matt joins mountain man Luke Brazo to hunt an elusive renegade wolf. The old friends must also contend with angry cattlemen, greedy bounty hunters and the certainty that this will be their last ride together.

65.476 *Johnny Cross.* Dec. 23, 1968. GS: Jeff Pomerantz, Harry Dean Stanton, John Crawford, Shug Fisher, Charles Thompson, Kelly Jean Peters. Newly O'Brien intervenes when two bounty hunters try to kill Johnny Cross, a wanted desperado who claims he is innocent of the murder charges that put a price on his head.

65.477 *The Money Store.* Dec. 30, 1968. GS: Eric Shea, Pamelyn Ferdin, William Schallert, Charles Aidman, Virginia Vincent, Ralph James. Two small children turn bank robbers to help their poverty stricken father. The victim is their uncle, a tightwad banker who refuses their father's plea for a loan.

65.478 *The Twisted Heritage.* Jan. 6, 1969. GS: John Ericson, Virginia Gregg, Lisa Gerritsen, Nora Marlowe, Conlan Carter, Charles Kuenstle, Richard O'Brien, David McLean, Robert Luster, Steve Raines, Robert Karns, Joshua Bryant. After saving the life of rancher Blaine Cooperton, Kitty becomes involved in the man's domestic problems. Copperton's tyrannical mother is stirring up trouble by dominating the household, ignoring the widower's young daughter, and dealing harshly with a family of squatters.

65.479 *Time of the Jackals.* Jan. 13, 1969. GS: Leslie Nielsen, Beverly Garland, Jonathan Lippe, Edmund Hashim, Robert Knapp, Charles Maxwell, Sid Haig, Art Stewart, Kip Whitman. Marshal Matt Dillon is marked for death as he searches for escaped killer Jess Trevor. The maniacal gunman has convinced his followers that with the lawman dead, the Southwest can be opened up for a crime wave. Central to the case is a woman who knew Matt years before, and whose life is in danger because she ran out on Trevor.

65.480 *Mannon.* Jan. 20, 1969. GS: Steve Forrest, Michelle Breeze. Will Mannon, a sharpshooter who rode with Quantrill's Raiders, terrorizes Dodge City as he waits for Matt to return and face him in a showdown.

65.481 *Gold Town.* Jan. 27, 1969. GS: Lou Antonio, Anthony James, Lane Bradbury, Kathryn Minner, Harry Davis, Chubby Johnson, Paul Wexler, Jack Searl, Pete Kellett, Jimmy Bracken, Eve Plumb. Run out of town by Matt Dillon, two sharpsters find a new way to swindle the townsfolk by salting an abandoned gold mine.

65.482 *The Mark of Cain.* Feb. 3, 1969. GS: Nehemiah Persoff, Louise Latham, Robert Totten, Kevin Coughlin, Stanley Clements, Olan Soule, Robert DoQui, Roy Barcroft. Shock and dissension divide Dodge when it is learned that a respected rancher was a Civil War prison commandant responsible for the death of 700 men.

65.483 *The Commandment.* Feb. 10, 1969. GS: Joe Don Baker, Eunice Christopher, I. Stanford Jolley, John Pickard, Dennis Cross, Jack Lambert. Doc Adams becomes a marked man after he saves a killer's life and attends a woman whose baby is born dead. Outraged because the child was lost, her husband vows to kill Doc, and so does the man Doc saved.

65.484 *The Long Night.* Feb. 17, 1969. GS: Bruce Dern, Lou Antonio, Russell Johnson, Susan Silo, Robert Totten, Robert Brubaker, Rex Holman, Matt Emery, Vic Tayback. Four of Matt's friends anxiously await his return to Dodge. They are being held hostage by bounty hunters determined to recapture Matt's prisoner, and $10,000 in reward money.

65.485 *The Night Riders.* Feb. 24, 1969. GS: Jeff Corey, Robert Pine, Bob Random, Norman Alden, Warren Vanders, Robert Karns, Scott Hale, Ed Bakey. Acting deputy Festus Haggen faces a showdown with a band of Missouri renegades who are seizing any excuse to exact revenge for property lost during the Civil War.

65.486 *The Intruders.* March 3, 1969. GS: Charles Aidman, John Kellogg, Gail Kobe, Eric Shea, Ralph James, Robert Gravage. Deputy Festus Haggen brings his wounded prisoner to the home of rancher Henry Decker. Neither the brutish rancher nor Festus is aware of the singular circumstances of the visit. Decker's wife was once married to the outlaw.

65.487 *The Good Samaritans.* March 1, 1969. GS: Brock Peters, Rex Ingram, L.Q. Jones, Sam Melville, Hazel Medina, Paulene Myers, Robert DoQui, Davis Roberts, Lyn Hamilton, Dan Ferrone, John Brandon, Pepe Brown. Matt's life depends on a family of ex-slaves, who shelter the wounded lawman from bounty hunters willing to kill to get the valuable papers he is carrying.

65.488 *The Prisoner.* March 17, 1969. GS: Jon Voight, Ramon Bieri, Kenneth Tobey, Ned Glass, Paul Bryar, Jan Peters, David Fresco, Don Happy. After a bounty hunter's prisoner risks his life to save Kitty, the grateful lady returns the favor. She wins the man in a loaded poker game before she learns why he has a $5000 price on his head.

65.489 *Reardon.* March 24, 1969. GS: Steve Ihnat, Kaz Garas, Brandon Carroll, William Bramley, Lane Bradford, Sarah Hardy, Hank Brandt. Ex-lawman Frank Reardon's methodical annihilation of the men who murdered his pregnant wife brings him to Dodge for a showdown with the three remaining members of the gang.

Season Fifteen

65.490 *The Devil's Outpost.* Sept. 22, 1969. GS: Robert Lansing, Jonathan Lippe, Karl Swenson, Sheila Larkin, Ken Swofford, Warren Vanders, Val de Vargas, Charles Kuenstle, I. Stanford Jolley, Sabrina Scharf, Troy Melton, Joe Higgins, Sam Edwards, William Tannen, Joe Haworth. Yancy Tyce is a wily outlaw leader who gives chase when Matt captures his brother during an attempted stage robbery.

65.491 *Stryker.* Sept. 29, 1969. GS: Morgan Woodward, Joan Van Ark, Royal Dano, Andy Devine, Mills Watson, Walter Sande, Ted French, Don Happy. Matt faces a showdown with former Dodge City marshal Josh Stryker, who has been released from prison after serving fifteen years for murder.

Stryker holds Matt responsible for the loss of his arm and the years he spent behind bars.

65.492 *Coreyville.* Oct. 6, 1969. GS: Nina Foch, Ruth Roman, Jo Ann Harris, Bruce Glover, Kevin Coughlin, Thomas Hunter, John Schuck, James Almanzar, Charles Fredericks, Bill Erwin, Pete Kellett, Bill Catching, Gary Combs. In a decaying cowtown, Marshal Dillon investigates the murder of a saloon girl. An innocent cowboy is being railroaded for the crime, while the real killer's identity is being kept secret by a wealthy widow and her bitter enemy, saloon owner Flo Watson.

65.493 *Danny.* Oct. 13, 1969. GS: Jack Albertson, Scott Brady, Vito Scotti, Frank Marth, Rayford Barnes, Jonathan Harper, Steve Raines. Danny, a con man, is on his way out due to a heart condition. Anxious to meet his maker in style, Danny needs $2000 to arrange the loudest wake and grandest funeral ever. That is the exact amount offered for the contract killing of Marshal Dillon.

65.494 *Hawk.* Oct. 20, 1969. GS: Brendon Boone, Louise Latham, Michael-James Wixted, Hilarie Thompson, Robert Brubaker, X Brands, Bill Hart, Hal Needham, Glen Randal, Jr. A white woman's refusal to accept her half-breed son, a product of her hated Apache captivity, is the theme of this drama. Festus is unaware of their tortured relationship when he brings the man, bleeding and unconscious, to her farm.

65.495 *A Man Called Smith.* Oct. 27, 1969. GS: Earl Holliman, Jacqueline Scott, Susan Olsen, Michael Durkin, Val Avery, Sid Haig, William Fawcett, Margarita Cordova. Abelia, the young widow who saved Festus' life, returns. But she isn't really a widow, as she learns when her outlaw husband shows up with plans to force her to exchange his stolen gold for cash.

65.496 *Charlie Noon.* Nov. 3, 1969. GS: James Best, Miriam Colon, Ronny Howard, Edmund Hashim, Kip Whitman. Marshal Dillon, his hardened prisoner, and an Indian widow and her white stepson are tracked by Comanches as they cross the desert. The Indians mean to kill them all, unless they hand over the woman, who jilted a Comanche leader years before.

65.497 *The Still.* Nov. 10, 1969. GS: Lane Bradbury, Anthony James, Shug Fisher, James Westerfield, J. Edward McKinley, Trent Lehman. Festus gets mixed up with a loony clan of hillbillies, who hide a moonshine still, and a kidnaped prize bull, in the cellar of the local school.

65.498 *A Matter of Honor.* Nov. 17, 1969. GS: John Anderson, Katherine Justice, Tom Simcox, Dan Ferrone, Richard Bakalyan, Walter Sande, Jack Bailey, Lawrence Mann, Bob Burrows. Festus finds Louie Pheeters, Dodge City's resident drunk, at the scene of a murder. The victim's last words implicate the oldster, who is too intoxicated to remember the scene he witnessed.

65.499 *The Innocent.* Nov. 24, 1969. GS: Eileen Heckart, Barry Atwater, Anthony James, Lee de Broux, Robert B. Williams, Eddie Little Sky, Manuel Padilla, Jr., Tom Nolan, Rush Williams. Festus volunteers to act as a guide and driver for a greenhorn missionary teacher en route to her first assignment. The trail they are riding is a tricky one, with a murderous hillbilly family just waiting for an opportune moment to strike.

65.500 *Ring of Darkness.* Dec. 1, 1969. Tom Drake, Pamela Dunlap, John Crawford, Anthony Caruso, Rex Holman. To help his blind daughter, farmer Ben Hurley stole horses for an outlaw gang. He faces a moral dilemma when deputy Newly O'Brian arrives at his farm, followed by the outlaws.

65.501 *MacGraw.* Dec. 8, 1969. GS: J.D. Cannon, Diana Ewing, Michael Larrain, Sam Melville, Charles Kuenstle, Ned Wertimer, Sid Haig, Allen Jaffe, Bobby Hall, Sam Edwards. Dodge City buzzes with excitement when ex-gunslinger Jake MacGraw comes to town after twenty years in prison. Folks are sure Jake is up to something, but he only shows an interest in two people: a young cowhand and a pretty saloon hostess.

65.502 *Roots of Fear.* Dec. 15, 1969. GS: John Anderson, Louise Latham, Warren Vanders, Cliff Osmond, Jody Foster, Walter Burke, Arthur Peterson, Robert Karnes, Paul Micale, Hank Wise. Dirt farmer Amos Sadler faces the loss of his new home when a panic closes down the Dodge City bank. To get the money for his final payment on the property, Amos and his kin plan to break into the bank and recover their hard-earned savings.

65.503 *The Sisters.* Dec. 29, 1969. GS: Jack Elam, Lynn Hamilton, Susan Batson, Gloria Calomee, Erica Petal, Chris Hundley, Cece Whitney. Trapper Pack Landers is astonished to find his cabin occupied by three nuns and two youngsters he has never seen before. The good sisters are honoring their promise to Landers' late wife by bringing the children to their father. Landers seeks a way to get the sisters money, and wriggle out of his parental responsibility.

65.504 *The War Priest.* Jan. 5, 1970. GS: Richard Anderson, Forrest Tucker, John Crawford, Richard Hale, Sam Melville, Link Wyler, Tom Sutton, Pete Kellett, Vincent Deadrick. Cavalry sergeant Emmett Holly, a whisky-soaked veteran, is on the verge of retirement. Only scant hours remain before he becomes a civilian, but that doesn't keep Holly from going AWOL to recapture an Apache prisoner who is making a break for freedom with Kitty as his hostage.

65.505 *The Pack Rat.* Jan. 12, 1970. GS: William C. Watson, Loretta Swit, Manuel Padilla, Jr., Heidi Vaughn, Robert Rothwell, Robert Brubaker, Bill Catching, Tom Sutton. A young thief holds the key to Matt Dillon's life. Only Sancho knows that Dillon is headed for a trap when he leaves Dodge City to return an escaped prisoner to custody.

65.506 *The Judas Gun.* Jan. 19, 1970. GS: Ron Hayes, Peter Jason, Richard X. Slattery, Laurie Mock, Sean McClory, Margarita Cordova, William Fawcett, Brad David, Ralph Neff. The long-running feud between the Haimes and Bolden families heads toward a showdown when a hired gunman enters the scene.

65.507 *Doctor Herman Schultz, M.D.* Jan. 26, 1970. GS: Benny Rubin, Pete Kellett. Herman Chultz is an expert hypnotist who uses his skill to steal lots of money. Dodge City poses a hurdle for Schultz, who must deal with the redoubtable Festus Haggen.

65.508 *The Badge.* Feb. 2, 1970. GS: Beverly Garland, Henry Jones, John Milford, Roy Jenson, Jack Lambert, William O'Connell, Mary Angela, John Finn, Fred Coby. Kitty is heartsick when Matt is wounded in a gun battle. She has seen it happen too many times before, so she leaves Dodge City and heads for a new town where a different kind of trouble awaits.

65.509 *Albert.* Feb. 9, 1970. GS: Milton Selzer, Patricia

Barry, L.Q. Jones, Bob Random, William Schallert, Dorothy Neumann, Natalie Masters. Trouble prays on Albert Schiller, an aging bank teller who foils a robbery, steals $5000 and then blames the unsuccessful thieves. When they learn of his success, the outlaws return to Dodge to try again, this time with Albert's help.

65.510 *Kiowa!* Feb. 16, 1970. GS: Dub Taylor, Victor French, John Beck, Lucas White, Joyce Ames, Jean Allison, Richard Lapp, Richard Angarola, Angela Carroll. Matt Dillon and a whisky-swilling preacher join rancher Ed Vail and his rambunctious sons as they track a Kiowa raiding party. The Indians made off with Vail's teenage daughter, and Matt suspects that Vail's pride hides the reason for the kidnaping.

65.511 *Celia.* Feb. 23, 1970. GS: Cliff Osmond, Melissa Murphy, Frank Marth, George Petrie, Walker Edmiston. Newly O'Brian gets his lumps as he tries to prove that a lovely girl is a con woman out to fleece blacksmith Ben Sommars.

65.512 *Morgan.* March 2, 1970. GS: Steve Forrest, Hank Brandt, Charlotte Stewart, Ed Long, Mills Watson, Jonathan Lippe, Jack Garner, I. Stanford Jolley, Fletcher Bryant, Read Morgan. Outlaw Cole Morgan and his men take over Dodge City, awaiting Matt Dillon's arrival with a large gold shipment. Although certain of success, Morgan is in a murderous mood after being disfigured in a fight with Kitty.

65.513 *The Thieves* (A.K.A. "The Fifth Horseman"). March 9, 1970. GS: Michael Burns, Bill Callaway, Timothy Burns, Royal Dano, Daphne Field, John Schuck. Sam, the Longbranch bartender, takes an interest in a delinquent boy. Eric Tabray, on probation, is being badgered by a county officer who believes he is a confirmed criminal.

65.514 *Hackett.* March 16, 1970. GS: Earl Holliman, Morgan Woodward, Jennifer West, Ken Swofford, Robert Totten, Bill Erwin, Allen Jung. A surly ex-con named Hackett spells trouble for farmer Quent Sargent. Years before, Sargent ran out on Hackett during a train robbery. Now Hackett means to try again, with Sargent's aid.

65.515 *The Cage.* March 23, 1970. GS: Steve Carlson, Laura Figueroa, Hank Brandt, Jorge Moreno, Paul Stewart, Gregg Palmer, Ken Mayer, Robert Swan, Allen Jaffe, Joaquin Martinez, Renata Vanni, Pedro Vegas, Araceli Rey. Matt leads a posse to New Mexico in search of murderous gold thieves. Helping the lawman is young Roy Stewart, who is out to kill the man who murdered his brother.

Season Sixteen

65.516 *Chato.* Sept. 14, 1970. GS: Ricardo Montalban, Miriam Colon, William Bryant, Peggy McCay, Pedro Regas, Rodolfo Hoyos, Robert Knapp, Jim Sheppard. Marshal Dillon travels to New Mexico to track down Chato, a wily killer who specializes in murdering lawmen. Dillon's first step is to take Chato's woman as prisoner.

65.517 *The Noose.* Sept. 21, 1970. GS: Tom Skerritt, William Fawcett. A stranger arrives in Dodge to settle an old score. Who he is and what he is after are a mystery that slowly begins to unfold when he kidnaps Kitty.

65.518 *Stark.* Sept. 28, 1970. GS: Richard Kiley, Suzanne Pleshette, Henry Wilcoxon, Shelly Novack, Bob Burrows, Rusty Lane. Bounty hunter Lewis Stark has struck it rich. His prisoner is the son of a wealthy rancher and his plans involve blackmail.

65.519 *Sam McTavish, M.D.* Oct. 5, 1970. GS: Vera Miles, Arch Johnson, Dee Carroll, Lisa Gerritsen, Amzie Strickland, Tom Fadden, Kathleen O'Malley, Harry Harvey, Sr., Read Morgan, Robert Rothwell, Lance Thomas, Glenn Redding. Crusty old Doc Adams is distressed, angered, and ultimately charmed, by Dr. Sam McTavish, a lady doctor who came to Dodge in response to Doc's ad for a temporary replacement.

65.520 *Gentry's Law.* Oct. 12, 1970. GS: John Payne, Peter Jason, Robert Pine, Don Keefer, Louise Latham, Shug Fisher, Darlene Conley, John Flinn, Robert Totten. Amos Gentry is a land baron who makes his own law, and who is doing everything in his power to protect two sons who accidentally hanged a squatter.

65.521 *Snow Train* Part One. Oct. 19, 1970. GS: Clifton James, Gene Evans, Ken Lynch, Roy Engel, Pamela Dunlap, Richard Lapp, Loretta Swit, Tim Considine, Richard Kelton, John Milford, Dana Elcar, Ron Hayes, X Brands. A train is besieged by Sioux hunting for the white passengers who sold them poisoned whiskey.

65.522 *Snow Train* Part Two. Oct. 26, 1970. GS: Clifton James, Gene Evans, Ken Lynch, Roy Engel, Pamela Dunlap, Richard Lapp, Loretta Swit, Tim Considine, Richard Kelton, John Milford, Dana Elcar, Ron Hayes, X Brands. A kangaroo court, an imminent birth and Matt's capture by Indians all figure into the conclusion of a drama about a train besieged by vengeful Sioux.

65.523 *Luke.* Nov. 2, 1970. GS: Morgan Woodward, Anthony Costello, Katherine Justice, Rex Holman, Victor Izay. A wounded outlaw, his trusty sidekick and a saloon hostess with a heart of gold are the protagonists in a drama that involves the outlaw's dying wish to see his long-lost daughter one last time.

65.524 *The Gun.* Nov. 9, 1970. GS: Kevin Coughlin, L.Q. Jones, Patricia Morrow, Robert Phillips, Sam Melville, Ken Mayer, Stanley Clements, Jack Garner, Foster Brooks, Marie Mantley. St. Louis newspaperman Sumner Pendleton hopes to exploit a teenager who accidentally shot down a famous gunfighter.

65.525 *The Scavengers.* Nov. 16, 1970. GS: Yaphet Kotto, Cicely Tyson, Slim Pickens, Roy Jenson, Link Wyler, Victor Holchak, Steve Raines, James Almanzar, Eddie Little Sky, Victor Izay. Piney Biggs claims to have survived an Indian massacre. Colley is a ghoulish buffalo hunter who captured the Indians, and can claim his reward only if Piney sticks to his story.

65.526 *The Witness.* Nov. 23, 1970. GS: Harry Morgan, Tim O'Connor, I. Stanford Jolley, Dack Rambo, Barry Brown, Robert Swan, June Dayton, Annette O'Toole, Ray Young, Herb Vigran. Osgood Pickett disposed of one witness against his murderous son. He now intends to silence another.

65.527 *McCabe.* Nov. 30, 1970. GS: Dan Kemp, Mitch Vogel, Jim Davis, Tani Phelps, David Brian, Jon Lormer, Robert Sorrells, Mills Watson, Lew Brown, Marie Cheatham, Trevor Bardette. In a town called Bowie Flats, Matt learns that his prisoner, held for robbery, has an old murder charge over his head. The townspeople mean to see the prisoner led to the gallows and their efforts are aided by the man's bitter young son.

65.528 *The Noonday Devil.* Dec. 7, 1970. GS: Anthony

Zerbe, John Dullaghan, Warren Vanders, Ernst Sarracino, Annette Cardona, Natividad Vacio, Bert Madrid, Pepe Callahan, Anthony Cordova, Fred Coby, Tony Davis, Julio Medina. A murderer is confronted by his twin brother, a priest trying to save the killer's soul.

65.529 *Sergeant Holly.* Dec. 14, 1970. GS: Forrest Tucker, Albert Salmi, Victor Eberg, Gregg Palmer, Vito Scotti, David Renard, Med Flory. Sergeant Holly, a heavy-drinking cavalryman, is framed for stealing an Army payroll. Holly defies regulations to track the outlaws who did him wrong.

65.530 *Jenny.* Dec. 28, 1970. GS: Lisa Gerritsen, Steve Ihnat, Rance Howard, Steve Rains, Bob Burrows. Deputy Newly tries to reunite little Jenny Pritchard with a father she doesn't know is a fugitive.

65.531 *Captain Sligo.* Jan. 4, 1971. GS: Richard Basehart, Salome Jens, Royal Dano, Stacy Harris, Robert Totten, Bob Eilbacher, Geri Reischl, Larry Finley, Matt Emery, Brian Foley, Boyd "Red" Morgan, Fred Stromsoe, Troy Melton, Bob Herron. Captain Sligo is a retired whaling skipper who drops anchor in Kansas and begins a stormy courtship with widow Josephine Burney. Josephine does not wish to share his company, especially after the Captain announces that he expects her to bear him ten sons

65.532 *Mirage.* Jan. 11, 1970. GS: John Anderson, Gary Wood, Mary Rings, William Zuckert, Harry Raybould, Robert Knapp, Dan White, Kevin Burchett. Festus returns from a desert shootout with his memory clouded by the heat, and his jumbled story making no sense at all to the family of the men he buried.

65.533 *The Tycoon.* Jan. 25, 1971. GS: Shug Fisher, John Beck, Nora Marlowe, James Minotto, Gwynne Gilford, Herman Poppe, Walker Edmiston. The usually penniless Festus inherits $500. He dudes himself up and goes into the freight business, where he falls into the clutches of a frontier woman hunting a husband for her daughter.

65.534 *The Convict.* Feb. 1, 1971. GS: Eric Braeden, Julie Gregg, Mia Bendien, John Crawford, Vic Tayback, James Chandler, Scott Edmonds, Bob Golden. Carl Jaekel is a pardoned convict who returns to Dodge to claim the woman he killed for. He finds that she is now married and has a child.

65.535 *Murdoch.* Feb. 8, 1971. GS: Jack Elam, Bob Random, Jim Davis, Anthony Caruso, Clint Howard, Tom Waters, Tim Burns, Liz Marshall, Bobby Clark, Gary Combs. U.S. Marshal Lucas Murdoch is an aging lawman with a heart of stone. Armed with an execution warrant, Murdoch uses a gold shipment to bait the notorious Carver gang, unaware that his own son is riding with them.

65.536 *Cleavus.* Feb. 15, 1971. GS: Robert Totten, Arthur Hunnicutt, William Challee, Robert Cornthwaite, Robert B. Williams, Henry Wise. Cleavus Lukens is as long on pride as he has always been short on luck. His luck changes in Dodge when he jumps a dead miner's claim and starts to court Kitty.

65.537 *Lavery.* Feb. 22, 1971. GS: Anthony Costello, Judi West, David Carradine, Karl Swenson, Ken Swofford, David Huddleston, Chanin Hale, Jack Perkins. Keith Lavery, home from prison with a five-year probation hanging over his head, just can't wait to resume chasing rainbows with the same friends who got him in trouble in the first place.

65.538 *Pike* Part One. March 1, 1971. GS: Jeanette Nolan, Dack Rambo, Cliff Osmond, William Murphy, Ross Hagen, William Mims, Jim Boles, Jon Jason Mantley, Maria Mantley, John Puglia, Billy McMickle. Sally Fergus is a crusty old woman who collects prairie junk. She takes home Cyrus Pike, a badly wounded robber.

65.539 *Pike* Part Two. GS: Jeanette Nolan, Dack Rambo, Cliff Osmond, William Murphy, Ross Hagen, William Mims, Jim Boles, Jon Jason Mantley, Maria Mantley, John Puglia, Billy McMickle. Old Sally Fergus is slowly beginning to like the ornery young outlaw she saved from death. The feeling is mutual, but the relationship promises to be shortlived. Sally wants no part of stolen money, and the robber's ex-partners are hot on his trail.

Season Seventeen

65.540 *The Lost.* Sept. 13, 1971. GS: Laurie Prange, Mercedes McCambridge, Royal Dano, Link Wyler, Charles Kuenstle, Dee Carroll, Harry Carey, Jr., Peggy Rea, Jerry Brown, Jon Jason Mantley, Maria Mantley, Heather Cotton. Stranded miles from civilization, Kitty seeks help from an unapproachable girl who has survived alone in the wilderness.

65.541 *Phoenix.* Sept. 20, 1971. GS: Glenn Corbett, Mariette Hartley, Gene Evans, Ramon Bieri, Frank Corsentino. Phoenix is an ex-con who is trying, like the legendary bird, to start a new life from the ashes of his past. This bird is bankrolling the future by hiring himself out as a killer.

65.542 *Waste* Part One. Sept. 27, 1971. GS: Ruth Roman, Jeremy Slate, Ellen Burstyn, Johnnie Whittaker, David Sheiner, Lieux Dressler, Shug Fisher, Rex Holman, Merry Anders. Matt's search for an outlaw involves him with a motherless boy and a wagonload of back-biting saloon women.

65.543 *Waste* Part Two. Oct. 4, 1971. GS: Ruth Roman, Jeremy Slate, Ellen Burstyn, Johnnie Whittaker, David Sheiner, Lieux Dressler, Shug Fisher, Rex Holman, Merry Anders. Outlaws have trapped Matt, an abandoned boy, an old man and five saloon women in a deserted and waterless fort. At the same time, one of the women is struggling with her conscience because she knows that the youngster is her son.

65.544 *New Doctor in Town.* Oct. 11, 1971. GS: Pat Hingle, Lane Bradford, Jon Lormer. John Chapman is the doctor trying to fill the unfillable shoes of Doc Adams. Something of a curmudgeon himself, Chapman finds acceptance hard to come by.

65.545 *The Legend.* Oct. 18, 1971. GS: Kim Hunter, Jan-Michael Vincent, Pat Hingle, Richard D. Kelton, Greg Mullavey, Lloyd Nelson, Pat Dennis-Leigh, Victor Izay, Michael Greene, Read Morgan, Bryan O'Byrne, Ken Mayer, Red Currie. Travis Colter is courting trouble in Dodge. The young man is heading down the path of his outlaw brothers.

65.546 *Trafton.* Oct. 25, 1971. GS: Victor French, Clay Tapper, Bill Catching, Fred Stromsoe, Sharon Acker, John Dullaghan, Mike Mazurki, Marie Windsor, Philip Carey, Jon Lormer, Patti Cohoon, Paul Stevens, Manuel Padilla, Jr. Trafton is a vicious outlaw doomed by a victim's compassion. The worlds "I forgive you," spoken by a dying priest, are somehow taking the killing instinct out of the killer.

65.547 *Lynott.* Nov. 1, 1971. GS: Richard Kiley, Peggy McCay, Pat Hingle, Anthony Caruso, Jonathan Lippe, Gregg Palmer, William Bramley. Tom Lynott is an easy-going former lawman who becomes involved in law and order in Dodge City.

65.548 *Lijah.* Nov. 8, 1971. GS: Denny Miller, Pat Hingle, Lane Bradford, Erin Moran, Harry Townes, William Wintersole, Herb Vigran, Pete Kellett, Dan Flynn, Jr. A mountain man is wrongly accused of a triple slaying. To make matters worse for himself, he has run off with the only survivor, a ten year old girl.

65.549 *My Brother's Keeper.* Nov. 15, 1971. GS: John Dierkes, Pat Hingle, Malcolm Atterbury, Pippa Scott, Charles McGraw. Insights into the Old West clash of white and Indian cultural values are the essence of this story about an old Indian who wants to die in peace, and Festus' compassionate, but misguided, efforts to keep him alive.

65.550 *Drago.* Nov. 22, 1971. GS: Buddy Ebsen, Ben Johnson, Edward Faulkner, Mitchell Silverman, Del Monroe, Rick Gates, Tani Phelps Guthrie, Pat Hingle. Drago is a grizzled scout who travels with a vicious hound at his side. He is hunting a murderer and plans to extract a terrible revenge.

65.551 *Gold Train: The Bullet* Part One. Nov. 29, 1971. GS: Eric Braeden, Alejandro Rey, Katherine Justice, Robert Hogan, Pepe Callahan, Sian Barbara Allen, Warren Kemmerling, Walter Sande, Harry Carey, Jr., Sam Melville, Eddie Firestone, Robert Sorrells, John Crawford, Jonathan Lippe, Mills Watson, Harry Harvey, Sr. Doc Adams returns to Dodge in time to save a wounded Matt Dillon.

65.552 *Gold Train: The Bullet* Part Two. Dec. 6, 1971. GS: Eric Braeden, Alejandro Rey, Katherine Justice, Robert Hogan, Pepe Callahan, Sian Barbara Allen, Warren Kemmerling, Walter Sande, Harry Carey, Jr., Sam Melville, Eddie Firestone, Robert Sorrells, John Crawford, Jonathan Lippe, Mills Watson, Harry Harvey, Sr. Bandits delay wounded Matt Dillon's journey to Denver.

65.553 *Gold Train: The Bullet* Part Three. Dec. 13, 1971. GS: Eric Braeden, Alejandro Rey, Katherine Justice, Robert Hogan, Pepe Callahan, Sian Barbara Allen, Warren Kemmerling, Walter Sande, Harry Carey, Jr., Sam Melville, Eddie Firestone, Robert Sorrells, John Crawford, Jonathan Lippe, Mills Watson, Harry Harvey, Sr. Matt Dillon is the patient in an emergency operation to remove the bullet lodged perilously near his spine.

65.554 *Murry Christmas.* Dec. 27, 1971. GS: Jeanette Nolan, Jack Elam, Patti Cohoon, Jodie Foster, Eric Moran, Josh Albee, Brian Morrison, Willie Aames, Todd Lookinland, Herb Vigran. Seven orphans, a drifter, and the citizens of Dodge warm up the cold-hearted headmistress of an orphanage.

65.555 *No Tomorrow.* Jan. 3, 1972. GS: Sam Groom, Pamela McMyler, H.M. Wynant, Steve Brodie, Henry Jones, Richard Hale, Herb Vigran, Liam Dunn, Robert Nichols, Joe Haworth, Leo Gordon, Dan Flynn, Allan Fudge. A homesteader is wrongly convicted of horse-stealing and then falsely accused of murdering a prison guard.

65.556 *Hidalgo.* Jan. 10, 1972. GS: Alfonso Arau, Thomas Gomez, Fabian Gregory, Linda Marsh, Stella Garcia, David Renard, Julio Medina, Edward Colmans. Mando is an arrogant outlaw who leaves a wounded Matt Dillon to die in the blazing desert of north Chihuahua.

65.557 *Tara.* Jan. 17, 1972. GS: Michele Carey, L.Q. Jones, Lawrence Delaney, James McCallion, Ken Mayer, Ken Swofford. Newly is hooked by a charming young widow who is proving adept at playing him against a vicious gunman. At stake is $5000 originally stolen by her late husband.

65.558 *One for the Road.* Jan. 24, 1972. GS: Jeanette Nolan, Jack Albertson, Victor Holchak, Melissa Murphy, Herb Vigran, Dorothy Neumann, Jack Perkins. Fate throws together toothless Sally Fergus and Lucius Prince, the drunkest drunk who ever staggered across the prairie, as Lucius tries to escape a socialite daughter intent on returning him to Philadelphia and respectability.

65.559 *The Predators.* Jan. 31, 1972. GS: Claude Akins, Jacqueline Scott, Jodie Foster, Brian Morrison, George Murdock, Mills Watson, Lew Brown, Read Morgan. Abelia's ranch is beset by two predator. Her children's dog, Cobie, who was a pup when he ran away, has become a killer after living in the wild for three years. Ex-gunman Howard Kane, who is seeking revenge against Cole Matson, also appears at the ranch.

65.560 *Yankton.* Feb. 7, 1972. GS: James Stacy, Forrest Tucker, Nancy Olson, Pamela Payton-Wright, Margaret Bacon, Tom Sutton, Bill Hart, Bennie Dobbins. Will Donavan is a powerful rancher with an aristocratic wife. Their quiet and plain daughter is courted by a saddle tramp who openly admits that he is courting the girl for her father's money.

65.561 *Blind Man's Buff.* Feb. 21, 1972. GS: Anne Jackson, Victor French, George Lindsey, Charles Kuenstle. Jed Frazer is a wounded mountaineer who unwittingly falls into the tender trap of a love-starved spinster.

65.562 *Alias Festus Haggen.* March 6, 1972. GS: Ramon Bieri, Lieux Dressler, Robert Totten, Booth Colman, Gregg Palmer, William Bryant, Rayford Barnes, Herb Vigran, Jon Lormer, Bill Erwin, Tom McFadden, Rusty Lane, Ed McCready, Louie Elias, Lloyd Nelson. An entire town thinks that Festus is Frank Eaton, an outlaw wanted for murder.

65.563 *The Wedding.* March 13, 1972. GS: Morgan Woodward, Sam Elliott, Melissa Murphy, James Chandler, Lane Bradford, Fran Ryan, Larry Barton, George Wallace, Byron Mabe, Troy Melton, Jason Wingreen. A young couple is determined to wed despite the opposition of an implacable parent.

Season Eighteen

65.564 *The River* Part One. Sept. 11, 1972. GS: Slim Pickens, Jack Elam, Miriam Colon, Clay O'Brien, Patti Cohoon, Roger Torrey, Read Morgan, Jerry Gatlin. Outlaws pursue Marshal Matt Dillon, who takes to a raft with two runaway children.

65.565 *The River* Part Two. Sept. 18, 1972. GS: Slim Pickens, Jack Elam, Miriam Colon, Clay O'Brien, Patti Cohoon, Roger Torrey, Read Morgan, Jerry Gatlin. Marshal Dillon remains aboard a raft in Oregon's Rogue River with two runaway children, two thieves and a bag full of money, heading down river towards rapids and a gang of waiting outlaws.

65.566 *Bohannan.* Sept. 25, 1972. GS: Richard Kiley, Linda Marsh, Vincent Van Patten, Ed Bakey, Helen Kleeb, Regis Cordic, Elizabeth Harrower. Bohannan is a charismatic itinerant with a special gift — the power to heal through the laying on of hands. The faith healer, certain that he has cured crippling ailments in the past, is now torn with doubt. Can he save a child who is actually dying and risk defying God's will?

65.567 *The Judgement.* Oct. 2, 1972. GS: Ramon Bieri, William Windom, Katherine Helmond, Tim O'Connor, Mariette Hartley, Richard Kelton, Jon Locke, Melissa Gilbert.

Dodge City's drunken Ira Spratt is the center of a deadly dilemma. Either the townspeople hand Spratt over to a gunman, or the killer will murder a respected member of the community.

65.568 *The Drummer.* Oct. 9, 1972. GS: Victor French, Fionnula Flanagan, Brandon Cruz, Bruce Glover, Kiel Martin, Herb Armstrong. Daniel Shay is a salesman forced to face up to a past he would rather forget.

65.569 *Sarah.* Oct. 16, 1972. GS: Anne Francis, Anthony Caruso, Jonathan Lippe, Michael Lane, John Orchard, Kay E. Kuter, Rex Holman, George Keymas, Larry Duran. Matt's old flame, a robbers' roost saloon owner, passes off Matt as her outlaw husband. It is only a ploy that throws the marshal in with a gang just as they are planning to rob a gold stage.

65.570 *The Fugitives.* Oct. 23, 1972. GS: James Olson, Darrell Larson, Vic Tayback, Russell Johnson, Troy Melton. Doc and Festus are captured by outlaws and Doc is ordered to save the life of a desperado in critical condition or forfeit his own.

65.571 *Eleven Dollars.* Oct. 30, 1972. GS: Susan Oliver, Josh Albee, Ike Eisenmann, Diane Shalet, Roy Engle, E.J. Andre. Festus is sent on a journey to settle an estate of $11. Along the way two slightly larcenous lads plan to surprise their widowed mama on her wedding day.

65.572 *Milligan.* Nov. 6, 1972. GS: Harry Morgan, Joseph Campanella, Lynn Carlin, Sorrell Booke, Patti Cohoon, Scott Walker, John Pickard, Lew Brown, Read Morgan, Gene Tyburn, Charles Macaulay. The townsfolk call the farmer who gunned down a Robin Hood-style bank robber a back shooter, and now they plan to make him pay.

65.573 *Tatum.* Nov. 13, 1972. GS: Gene Evans, Ana Korita, Sandra Smith, Jay MacIntosh, Sheila Larkin, Jeff Pomerantz, Kenneth Tobey, Lloyd Nelson, Neil Summers. A dying gunman begins a long, sad journey to try and reach his three estranged daughters.

65.574 *The Sodbusters.* Nov. 20, 1972. GS: Morgan Woodward, Alex Cord, Katherine Justice, Leif Garrett, Dawn Lyn, Harrison Ford, Robert Viharo, Richard Bull, Joe di Reda, Jim Boles, Colin Male. A dispute over water rights erupts into a range war between cattlemen and farmers.

65.575 *The Brothers.* Nov. 27, 1972. GS: Steve Forrest, Joe Silver, Angus Duncan, Richard O'Brien, Regis J. Cordic, Eddie Ryder, Edward Faulkner, Terry Wilson, Jon Kowal. A cold-blooded avenger is in search of a drifter named Brown and Miss Kitty, who he holds responsible for the killing of his brother.

65.576 *Hostage!* Dec. 11, 1972. GS: William Smith, Geoffrey Lewis, Marco St. John, Stafford Repp, Nina Roman, James Chandler, Hal Baylor, Sandra Kent. Kitty's life for a killer's: that is the deal offered to Matt by the condemned man's brother, the vicious leader of a terrorist gang.

65.577 *Jubilee.* Dec. 18, 1972. GS: Tom Skerritt, Scott Brady, Alan Hale, Jr., Collin Wilcox-Horne, Lori Rutherford, Todd Cameron, Whitey Hughes. A poor sodbuster neglects his farm and family to race his prized quarter horse.

65.578 *Arizona Midnight.* Jan. 1, 1973. GS: Billy Curtis, Stanley Clements, Mills Watson, Ken Mayer, Sandye Powell. Dodge City is visited by a midget who says that he will turn into an elephant at midnight.

65.579 *Homecoming.* Jan. 8, 1973. GS: Richard Kelton, Robert Pratt, Ivy Jones, Stuart Margolin, Lurene Tuttle, Lynn Marta, Claudia Bryar. There is a bad scene for Doc Adams at a farm woman's death bed. Her outlaw sons are back and with them is a killer who will stop at nothing to insure their safe flight to Mexico.

65.580 *Shadler.* Jan. 15, 1973. GS: Earl Holliman, Diana Hyland, Denver Pyle, Linda Watkins, Alex Sharp, Pat Conway, Ken Lynch, James Jeter, Donald "Red" Barry, Meg Wyllie. A condemned man who is posing as a priest is forced into a strange alliance with Newly to help the people in a tragedy-struck town.

65.581 *Patricia.* Jan. 22, 1973. GS: Jess Walton, Ike Eisenmann, John Baer, Gail Bonney, Donald Elson, Richard Lundin. Newly O'Brien is preparing to wed a girl who is afflicted with leukemia.

65.582 *A Quiet Day in Dodge.* Jan. 29, 1973. GS: Margaret Hamilton, Leo Gordon, Shug Fisher, Douglas V. Fowley, John Fiedler, Helen Page Camp, J. Pat O'Malley, Walker Edmiston, Herb Vigran, Willie Aames. With no sleep for 36 hours Matt must deal with a vicious prisoner, a nine-year-old thief, a brawl at the Longbranch and the silent treatment from Kitty.

65.583 *Whelan's Men.* Feb. 5, 1973. GS: Robert Burr, William Bramley, Noble Willingham, Harrison Ford, Frank Ramirez, Gerald McRaney, Seamon Glass. A gang of killers take over Dodge while Matt is away and it is up to Kitty's poker prowess to save the town.

65.584 *Kimbro.* Feb. 12, 1973. GS: John Anderson, Doreen Lang, Michael Strong, William Devane, Rick Weaver, Tom Falk, Lisa Eilbacher. Adam Kimbro was Matt's first mentor. The ex-lawman is now on the skids since he was put out to pasture. Matt plans to help by deputizing him for a dangerous assignment.

65.585 *Jesse.* Feb. 19, 1973. GS: Brock Peters, Jim Davis, Regis J. Cordic, Don Stroud, Leonard Stone, Robert Pine, Ted Gehring, Lloyd Nelson, Norman Bartold, Larry Finley. Festus encounters an old pal who is an escaped convict bound for life in prison if Festus brings him in.

65.586 *Talbot.* Feb. 26, 1973. GS: Anthony Zerbe, Salome Jens, Peter Jason, Bill Williams, Charles Macauley, Robert Totten, Chanin Hale. Talbot is an outlaw sidetracked by love. His growing attraction for the woman he widowed is upsetting his carefully laid plan to rob the Dodge City Bank.

65.587 *The Golden Land.* March 5, 1973. GS: Paul Stevens, Victor French, Richard Dreyfuss, Bettye Ackerman, Joseph Hindy, Wayne McLaren, Scott Selles, Kevin Coughlin. Moshe Gorofsky is a Russian Jew who immigrates to Kansas to escape the horror of the pogroms and finds more injustice on the frontier. Moshe's son dies before his eyes after being attacked by drunken cowboys, and Talmudic law forbids him to accuse the men.

Season Nineteen

65.588 *Women for Sale* Part One. Sept. 10, 1973. GS: James Whitmore, Shani Wallis, Nicholas Hammond, Kathleen Cody, Sally Kemp, Dan Ferrone, Gregory Sierra, Dawn Lyn, Lieux Dressler, Larry D. Mann. Matt Dillon targets Timothy Fitzpatrick, a white slave trader who kidnaps women and children for the purpose of selling them in Mexico.

Gunsmoke

65.589 *Women for Sale* **Part Two.** Sept. 17, 1973. GS: James Whitmore, Shani Wallis, Nicholas Hammond, Kathleen Cody, Sally Kemp, Dan Ferrone, Gregory Sierra, Dawn Lyn, Lieux Dressler, Larry D. Mann. A saloon woman, a motherless girl and a renegade who is falling in love with his captive are the human complications that are involved in Matt's pursuit of white slave traders.

65.590 *Matt's Love Story.* Sept. 24, 1973. GS: Michael Learned, Victor French, Keith Andes, Jonathan Lippe, William Schallert, Richard Lundin, Neil Summers. A romance between Matt and Mike Yardner is complicated by amnesia and a dangerous gunman.

65.591 *The Boy and the Sinner.* Oct. 1, 1973. GS: Ron Moody, Vincent Van Patten, Warren Vanders, John Crawford, Ken Lynch, Read Morgan, Florida Friebus, Hal Baylor, Victor Izay. Noah Beal is an old man who is willing to trade his honor for booze, despite a young farm boy who cares enough to try and stop him.

65.592 *The Widow-Maker.* Oct. 8, 1973. GS: Steve Forrest, Barra Grant, David Huddleston, Randolph Roberts, Rand Bridges, Jerry Gatlin, J.R. Clark. Scott Coltrane is a quiet man who is unable to live down his reputation as the ultimate gunslinger. He attracts challengers like gnats, and that won't do at all in Matt Dillon's Dodge City.

65.593 *Kitty's Love Affair.* Oct. 22, 1973. GS: Richard Kiley, Leonard Stone, Christopher Connelly, Paul Picerni, Don Keefer, Jack Perkins, Gerald McRaney, Del Monroe, Virginia Baker. A long-running romantic standoff between Matt and Kitty is the dramatic theme as another man enters her life. Will Stambridge is the newcomer, a reformed gunfighter who saved Kitty from holdup men.

65.594 *The Widow and the Rogue.* Oct. 29, 1973. GS: James Stacy, Beth Brickell, Clay O'Brien, Helen Page Camp, Monica Svensson, Walker Edmiston, Paul Sorensen. J.J. Honegger is a roguish thief who is long on charm but a bit short on ethics. His real test of character comes on a long, adversity-plagued journey to Dodge with his captor Festus.

65.595 *A Game of Death ... An Act of Love* **Part One.** Nov. 5, 1973. GS: Morgan Woodward, Donna Mills, Paul Stevens, Whitney Blake, John Pickard, Geoffrey Horne, X Brands, Ivan Naranjo, Michael Learned, Garry Walberg, Herb Vigran. Frontier justice goes on trial as a strong-willed cattleman seeks his own brand of revenge against the Indians he thinks murdered his wife.

65.596 *A Game of Death ... An Act of Love* **Part Two.** Nov. 12, 1973. GS: Morgan Woodward, Donna Mills, Paul Stevens, Whitney Blake, John Pickard, Geoffrey Horne, X Brands, Ivan Naranjo, Michael Learned, Garry Walberg, Herb Vigran. A murder trial witness has a small but pivotal role in this drama about justice on the Kansas frontier.

65.597 *Lynch Town.* Nov. 19, 1973. GS: David Wayne, Mitch Vogel, Scott Brady, Warren Kemmerling, Ken Swofford, Norman Alden, Julie Cobb, Nancy Jeris. An alcoholic judge is completely content to play the town boss' puppet, until a lynching takes place.

65.598 *The Hanging of Newly O'Brien.* Nov. 26, 1973. GS: Billy Green Bush, Jimmy Van Patten, Jessamine Milner, Jan Burrell, Rusty Lane, Deborah Dozier, Walter Scott. Doc sends Newly out to check on some families in the back country. He is frustrated by the poor response he receives from his patients and his life is threatened when an operation he performs results in the death of a patient.

65.599 *Susan Was Evil.* Dec. 3, 1973. GS: Kathleen Nolan, Art Lund, Kathy Cannon, George Di Cenzo, Henry Olek, Jim Gammon, Robert Brubaker. The appearance of a wounded outlaw proves a crucible of character for two women at a remote stagecoach way station. The elder, a strong-willed widow who runs the station, feels morally bound to help the man, but her niece can think only of leaving the place for the big city.

65.600 *The Deadly Innocent.* Dec. 17, 1973. GS: Russell Wiggins, Charles Dierkop, Herb Vigran, Danny Arnold, William Shriver. A young man has the mind and innocence of a child. Moved to violence by the sight of anything being hurt, he faces a dim future in the adult world.

65.601 *A Child Between.* Dec. 24, 1973. GS: Sam Groom, Alexandra Morgan, John Dierkes, Eddie Little Sky. Fugitive Lew Harrod kidnaps Newly at gunpoint to treat his sick baby. Harrod's wife refuses to take Newly's advice and endangers the baby's life by taking him to a Comanche shaman for help.

65.602 *A Family of Killers.* Jan. 14, 1974. GS: Glenn Corbett, Anthony Caruso, Mills Watson, Morgan Paull, Zina Bethune, Stuart Margolin, George Keymas, Frank Corsentino. A U.S. marshal is on a personal vendetta against the outlaw family who shot one of his deputies and cut up another.

65.603 *Like Old Times.* Jan. 21, 1974. GS: Nehemiah Persoff, Gloria de Haven, Dan Travanty, Charles Haid, Victor Izay, Robert Brubaker, Rhodie Cogan, Hal Bokar. Ben Rando is a reformed safecracker who after twelve years in prison battles enormous odds to weave the threads of his old life into a new pattern.

65.604 *The Town Tamers.* Jan. 28, 1974. GS: Jim Davis, Jean Allison, Ike Eisenmann, Rex Holman, Leo Gordon, Sean McClory, James Jeter, Kay E. Kuter, James Chandler, Don Megowan, Ed Call, Mary Betten. Bringing law and order to a wide-open frontier town is the dangerous task facing Matt and a fellow marshal.

65.605 *The Foundling.* Feb. 11, 1974. GS: Kay Lenz, Bonnie Bartlett, Donald Moffat, Dran Hamilton, Don Collier, Jerry Hardin. Matt makes an effort to find a proper loving home for a baby girl rejected by her family.

65.606 *The Iron Blood of Courage.* Feb. 18, 1974. GS: Lloyd Bochner, Eric Braeden, Mariette Hartley, Patti Cohoon, Gene Evans, Miriam Colon, John Milford, Bing Russell, Elizabeth Harrower, Nick Ramus. William Talley is a gentlemanly gunfighter hired by the ranchers in a confrontation over water rights.

65.607 *The Schoolmarm.* Feb. 25, 1974. GS: Sondra Blake, Lin McCarthy, Todd Lookinland, Scott Walker, Janet Nichols. An unwed schoolteacher is made pregnant by a rapist. To add to the tragedy, she is locking out of her life the very people who love and want to help her.

65.608 *Trail of Bloodshed.* March 4, 1974. GS: Kurt Russell, Tom Simcox, Harry Carey, Jr., Janit Baldwin, Larry Pennell, Nina Roman. A farm youth pursues his father's killer, a gunfighter who was also his father's brother.

65.609 *Cowtown Hustler.* March 11, 1974. GS: Jack Albertson, Jonathan Lippe, Nellie Bellflower, Henry Beckman, Lew Brown, John Davis Chandler, Richard O'Brien. Moses

Darby is a has-been pool hustler whose comeback trail is made a little rockier by the opportunistic young partner who serves as his bodyguard and shill.

65.610 *To Ride a Yellow Horse.* March 18, 1974. GS: Louise Latham, Kathleen Cody, Thomas Leopold, John Reilly, Parker Stevenson, Herb Vigran, Simon Scott. A mother makes an effort to secure a good life for her children, no matter what the cost to them.

65.611 *Disciple.* April 1, 1974. GS: Dennis Redfield, Frank Marth, Marco St. John, Paul Picerni, R.L. Armstrong, David Huddleston, Claire Brennan. A badly wounded arm effects drastic changes in the life of Matt Dillon. Unable to use a gun, he no longer can defend either himself or the citizens of Dodge.

Season Twenty

65.612 *Matt Dillon Must Die!* Sept. 9, 1974. GS: Morgan Woodward, Joseph Hindy, William Lucking, Henry Olek, Douglas Dirkson, Frederick Herrick, Elaine Fulkerson. Marshal Dillon is the captive of a crazed killer who, with his four sons, plans to avenge a fifth son's death.

65.613 *A Town in Chains.* Sept. 16, 1974. GS: Ramon Bieri, Gretchen Corbett, Lance Le Gault, Ron Soble, Don Stroud, Russell Wiggins, Med Flory, John Crawford, Thad Hall, Lloyd Nelson. Five brazen bank robbers, all former Johnny Rebs, don Union uniforms and take over a town for one last heist before going into legitimate business.

65.614 *The Guns of Cibola Blanca* Part One. Sept. 23, 1974. GS: Harold Gould, Dorothy Tristan, Richard Anderson, Michael Christofer, James Luisi, Jackie Coogan, Henry Beckman, Gloria Le Roy, Shug Fisher. An outlaws' hideaway deep in the desert becomes a prison for Doc and a woman friend who are captured while traveling from Santa Fe to Dodge.

65.615 *The Guns of Cibola Blanca* Part Two. Sept. 30, 1974. GS: Harold Gould, Dorothy Tristan, Richard Anderson, Michael Christofer, James Luisi, Jackie Coogan, Henry Beckman, Gloria Le Roy, Shug Fisher. Matt and his deputies masquerade as desperadoes to infiltrate a band of outlaws who have captured Doc and a woman friend.

65.616 *Thirty a Month and Found.* Oct. 7, 1974. GS: Gene Evans, Nicholas Hammond, Van Williams, David Brian, Ford Rainey, Kim O'Brien, Victor Izay, Hal Baylor. Three down-and-out cattle drovers have logged the hard and lonely miles of cattle drivers for $30 a month. Now, the railroad is putting them out of work and the men, increasingly frustrated and reckless, desperately try to hold on to their past.

65.617 *The Wiving.* Oct. 14, 1974. GS: Henry Morgan, Fran Ryan, Karen Grassle, John Reilly, Linda Sublette, Herman Poppe, Michelle Marsh. Farmer Jed Hockett orders his three sons to go to town and find their future brides. When the three brothers arrive in Dodge City they find the women unresponsive to their country ways and resort to kidnapping as a solution to the problem of matrimony.

65.618 *The Iron Man.* Oct. 21, 1974. GS: Cameron Mitchell, John Russell, Barbara Colby, George Murdock, William Bryant, Marc Alaimo, Paul Gehrman, Alec Murdock. Matt undertakes the rehabilitation of his old friend Chauncey Demon, an almost legendary ex-lawman who lost his family in an Indian attack and has been courting the bottle ever since.

65.619 *The Fourth Victim.* Nov. 4, 1974. GS: Biff McGuire, Leonard Stone, Paul Sorensen, Victor Killian, Lloyd Perryman. A mysterious killer is loose in Dodge. He is picking off his victims at night with a .30-calibre rifle and no one hears the shots.

65.620 *The Tarnished Badge.* Nov. 11, 1974. GS: Victor French, Ruth McDevitt, Pamela McMyler, Nick Nolte. Matt confronts a sheriff who once saved a town from desperadoes and now rules it like a feudal despot.

65.621 *In Performance of Duty.* Nov. 18, 1974. GS: Eduard Franz, David Huddleston, Paul Koslo, Rance Howard, Martin Kove, Michael MacRae. A lack of hard evidence frustrates Matt's efforts to nail an outlaw family that stays beyond the law's reach by killing all the witnesses to its crimes.

65.622 *Island in the Desert* Part One. Dec. 2, 1974. GS: Strother Martin, William C. Watson, Regis J. Cordic, Hank Brandt. Festus, wounded while tracking a killer across the desert, is rescued by a half-loco old hermit who is also on a search. He is looking for the partner who left him to die on the desert many years before.

65.623 *Island in the Desert* Part Two. Dec. 9, 1974. GS: Strother Martin, William C. Watson, Regis J. Cordic, Hank Brandt. A half-crazed hermit, determined to find the partner who left him to die on the desert many years before, forces Festus to pack gold across the arid wastes.

65.624 *The Colonel.* Dec. 16, 1974. GS: Lee J. Cobb, Julie Cobb, Richard Ely, Randolph Roberts, Roy Jenson, Robert Brubaker, Todd Lookinland, Dan Travanty. A former Army officer who is now the town drunk is faced with the upcoming marriage of his daughter to a respected businessman.

65.625 *The Squaw.* Jan. 6, 1975. GS: John Saxon, Arlene Martel, Tom Reese, Morgan Paull, X Brands, William Campbell, Harry Middlebrooks. A squaw unwanted by her tribe plays a vital role in an outlaw's flight across the badlands to escape the partners he outwitted.

65.626 *The Hiders.* Jan. 13, 1975. GS: Ned Beatty, Lee de Broux, Sierra Bandit, Damon Douglas, Robert Donner, Ellen Blake. Festus invites retribution when he urges a teenager to break ranks with a group of hiders, men who make a living by cutting skins from dead range cattle.

65.627 *Larkin.* Jan. 20, 1975. GS: Richard Jaeckel, Anthony Caruso, Robert Gentry, Robert Sorrells, Kathleen Cody, Maggie Malooly, Michael Le Clair. Newly bucks great odds to take a prisoner to Dodge. His captive is a professional killer, and they are being pursued by a band of bounty hunters.

65.628 *The Fires of Ignorance.* Jan. 27, 1975. GS: John Vernon, Allen Garfield, Lance Kerwin, Diane Shalet, Herb Vigran, George Di Cenzo, Karen Oberdiear, John Pickard. A child's right to an education becomes the underlying issue in an assault case brought by a dedicated teacher against a farmer determined to keep his son, a promising scholar, out of school.

65.629 *The Angry Land.* Feb. 3, 1975. GS: Carol Vogel, Eileen McDonough, Dayton Lummis, Bruce M. Fischer. A girl orphaned by the murder of her parents meets rejection from her only living relative, an aunt who has been battered by life and will not accept the responsibility of raising a child.

65.630 *Brides and Grooms.* Feb. 10, 1975. GS: Harry Morgan, David Soul, Amanda McBroom, Michele Marsh, Dennis Redfield, Spencer Milligan, Ray Girardin, Jim Backus,

Fran Ryan. Many a hitch develops in a farmer's plans to marry his three sons to three women in a triple wedding ceremony.

65.631 *Hard Labor.* Feb. 24, 1975. GS: John Colicos, Hal Williams, William Smith, Kevin Coughlin, Ben Piazza, Gregory Sierra, Gerald McRaney, Don Megowan, Jackie Russell. Illegally convicted of murdering a fugitive from justice, Matt is sentenced to life imprisonment at hard labor in the judge's silver mine.

65.632 *I Have Promises to Keep.* March 3, 1975. GS: David Wayne, Tom Lacy, Ken Swofford, Ken Renard, Trini Tellez, Fran Ryan, John Wheeler. Festus lends a much-needed hand to an ill and aging Eastern preacher who is determined to build a church for the Comanches despite strong opposition from both whites and Indians.

65.633 *The Busters.* March 1, 1975. GS: Gary Busey, John Beck, Lynn Benesch, Gregg Palmer, Randy Boone. A bronco buster is unaware that he will die from a head injury in a matter of days. But his partner knows, and he vows to show his friend a time that he will still be talking about two days after he's dead.

65.634 *Manolo.* March 17, 1975. GS: Nehemiah Persoff, Robert Urich, Mark Shera, Fran Ryan, Brian James, Claudio Martinez, Michael Gregory. A Basque sheepherder is both puzzled and shamed by his older son's aversion to fighting, especially since custom dictates that the younger man eventually must defeat his father to prove himself a man.

65.635 *The Sharecroppers.* March 31, 1975. GS: Susanne Benton, Terry Williams, Victor French, Jacques Aubuchon, Bruce Boxleitner, Graham Jarvis, Lisa Eilbacher. A comedy of errors puts Festus behind a plow, farming for a family of shiftless sharecroppers.

The Tele-films

65.636 *Gunsmoke: Return to Dodge.* Sept. 26, 1987. Cast: James Arness, Amanda Blake, Steve Forrest, Earl Holliman, Buck Taylor, Fran Ryan, Ken Olandt, W. Morgan Sheppard, Patrice Martinez, Tantoo Cardinal, Mickey Jones, Frank M. Totino, Robert Koons, Walter Kaase. Set fifteen years after the final episode, Matt Dillon is now retired and living as a mountain man and guardian to a group of Indian children. An ex-con tracks Matt down looking for vengeance, but Matt outdraws him. Matt is stabbed by some scavengers while bringing the outlaw back to Dodge and barely survives his injuries. After his recovery he is forced into a showdown with another former, outlaw Will Mannon, who has just been released from prison.

65.637 *Gunsmoke: The Last Apache.* March 18, 1990. Cast: James Arness, Richard Kiley, Amy Stock-Poynton, Michael Learned, Joe Lara, Hugh O'Brian, Geoffrey Lewis, Joaquin Martinez, Peter Murnik, Blake Boyd, Sam Vlahos, Robert Covarrubias, Ned Bellamy, Dave Florek, Kevin Sifuentes, Robert Brian Wilson, James Milanesa. In 1886 Matt Dillon no longer wears a badge and is about to take the law into his own hands. A renegade Apache named Wolf has abducted the daughter Dillon never knew he had. He and an ornery Army scout named Chalk Brighton break out Geronimo's two teenage sons from an Army stockade to be used as bargaining chips for the return of his daughter.

65.638 *Gunsmoke: To the Last Man.* Oct. 27, 1991. Cast: James Arness, Pat Hingle, Amy Stock-Poynton, Matt Mulhern, Jason Lively, Joseph Bottoms, Morgan Woodward, Mills Watson, James Booth, Amanda Wyss, Jim Beaver, Herman Poppe, Ken Swofford. Matt teams with his spirited daughter to battle a bloody range war in the Arizona Territory of the 1880s.

65.639 *Gunsmoke: The Long Ride.* May 8, 1993. Cast: James Arness, Ali McGraw, James Brolin, Amy Stock-Poynton, Christopher Bradley, Patrick Dollaghan, Don McManus, Marco Sanchez, Tim Choate, Michael Greene, Stewart Moss, Jim Beaver, Sharon Mahoney, Richard Dano, Victor Izay. Matt is on the trail of a trio of robber-murderers to clear his name. He is also being pursued by a posse convinced that he is responsible for the crime.

65.640 *Gunsmoke: One Man's Justice.* Feb. 10, 1994. Cast: James Arness, Bruce Boxleitner, Amy Stock-Poynton, Christopher Bradley, Alan Scarfe, Mikey Lebeau, Apesanahkwat, Hallie Foot, Clark Brolly, Don Collier, Ed Ames, Wayne Anthony, Bing Blenman. Matt is joined by a traveling salesman in his quest to find a fifteen-year-old boy who is chasing the robbers who killed his mother.

66. Have Gun, Will Travel

CBS. 30 min. Broadcast history: Saturday, 9:30-10:00, Sept. 1957–Sept. 1963.

Regular Cast: Richard Boone (Paladin), Kam Tong (Hey Boy), Lisa Lu (Hey Girl).

Premise: Paladin is a former U.S. Army officer whose gun is for hire in the rugged West of the 1870s. His symbol is the white knight, a chessman, which is on his black holster.

The Episodes

66.1 *Three Bells to Perdido.* Sept. 14, 1957. GS: Janice Rule, Jack Lord, Harry Shannon, Francis McDonald, Christian Drake, Ted Marcuse, Judson Pratt, Gene Roth, Martin Garralaga. Paladin is hired by a New Mexican rancher and given the assignment of bringing back the rancher's young daughter who has eloped with a gunfighter.

66.2 *The Outlaw.* Sept. 21, 1957. GS: Charles Bronson, Grant Withers, Warren Parker, Barry Cahill, Steve Mitchell, Peggy Stewart. Paladin is hired by a banker to trail an escaped outlaw. Manfred Holt has broken out of jail, killing two deputies. The outlaw has sworn to get rid of the banker, who is the only witness against him in a forthcoming trial.

66.3 *The Great Mojave Chase.* Sept. 28, 1957. GS: Lawrence Dobkin, Claude Akins, Earl Hodgkins, William Fawcett, Hal Smith, Jonathan Hole, Walter Reed. Paladin reads about a contest in which a sportsman offers big odds for a man to elude a posse in the Mojave Desert for a certain length of time. He decides to enter and rides into the desert township with a camel. The sportsman, knowing Paladin will win the contest, decides to have him killed.

66.4 *Winchester Quarantine.* Oct. 5, 1957. GS: Leo V. Gordon, Anthony Caruso, Robert Karnes, Don Keefer, Vic Perrin, Carol Thurston, Rocky Shahan, Jim Parnell. When the stage coach in which he is traveling stops in a small Western town, Paladin observes a fight between an Indian rancher and a cowman. The Indian is holding his own, until the cowman enlists the aid of several of his friends. They beat the Indian unmercifully and ride off. Paladin offers his services to the beaten man.

66.5 *A Matter of Ethics.* Oct. 12, 1957. GS: Harold J. Stone, Roy Barcroft, Steven Terrell, Angie Dickinson, Willis Bouchey, Peter Brocco, Strother Martin. Paladin reads of the capture of Bart Holgate, wanted for a killing in Bender, Wyoming. The newspaper article carries a statement by Holgate that he is afraid he will not reach Bender alive. Paladin offers his services to the prisoner. He will receive his fee only if he delivers Holgate alive to the court.

66.6 *The Bride.* Oct. 19, 1957. GS: Bruce Gordon, Michael Connors, Marian Seldes, Barry Cahill. A mail-order bride travels from Philadelphia to a western ranch to marry a man she has never seen. Paladin is aboard the coach, and when they stop in a deserted area the young woman gets off. Realizing that she is waiting for her fiance, Paladin decides to wait with her.

66.7 *Strange Vendetta.* Oct. 26, 1957. GS: June Vincent, Michael Pate, Onslow Stevens, Ned Glass, Gerald Milton, Rodolfo Acosta. Paladin comes to the aid of Maria Rojas, whom he meets in the lobby of his hotel in San Francisco. The lady wants tickets for the evening performance of the opera. Paladin invites the lady and her husband to share his box. At the opera, Maria's husband is attacked by an assassin.

66.8 *High Wire.* Nov. 2, 1957. GS: Strother Martin, John Dehner, Buddy Baer, Jack Albertson, Fay Spain. A hobo, who was once a circus acrobat, bets a gambler that he can walk a tightrope stretched across a saloon. Paladin, who is an interested spectator, sees the gambler's henchman cut the rope just as the hobo is about to complete the stunt.

66.9 *Show of Force.* Nov. 9, 1957. GS: Vic Perrin, Peter Coe, Rodolfo Acosta, Ned Glass, Russ Conway, Joe Bassett, Walter Brennan, Jr. Paladin wins fifty rifles in a poker game and makes use of them in a range war between two ranches.

66.10 *The Long Night.* Nov. 16, 1957. GS: Kent Smith, William Schallert, James Best, Michael Granger, Kenneth Alton. A cattle baron, seeking to avenge his wife's death, claims she was shot by a stranger, wearing dark clothes, who trespassed on his land. Paladin and two other men fitting the description are held by the rancher, who threatens that one of them will hang at sunrise.

66.11 *The Colonel and the Lady.* Nov. 23, 1957. GS: Robert F. Simon, Denver Pyle, June Vincent, Fay Nuell. Paladin is hired by a retired Army officer to locate a one-time silver-camp queen so he can complete the history of the West he is writing. Paladin learns that the last man sent on this mission never returned.

66.12 *No Visitors.* Nov. 30, 1957. GS: June Lockhart, Grant Withers, Peg Hillias, Ruth Storey, Whit Bissell, John Anderson, Johnny Western. Paladin finds a woman and her sick child abandoned by a wagon train master, who claimed the baby had typhoid. Paladin rides to the nearest settlement, where a woman doctor agrees to treat the child. But the wagonmaster intervenes.

66.13 *The Englishman.* Dec. 7, 1957. GS: Tom Helmore, Murvyn Vye, Alix Talton, Ted DeCorsia, Clinton Sundberg, Abel Fernandez, Robert Bice. Englishman James Brunswick hires Paladin to protect him and his cousin Felicia on their journey to his new ranch in Montana. On their arrival, an angered trader plots against the newcomers.

66.14 *The Yuma Treasure.* Dec. 14, 1957. GS: Warren Stevens, Henry Brandon, Harry Landers, Barry Cahill, Russell Thorson. At a small military outpost in Arizona, Paladin meets a Major Wilson, commander of a cavalry troop, who claims he knew Paladin at West Point. He seeks Paladin's help in quieting down some restless Yuma Apaches.

66.15 *The Hanging Cross.* Dec. 21, 1957. GS: Abraham Sofaer, Johnny Crawford. Paladin is hired by a rancher to help find his son who was kidnaped several years earlier during the Sioux wars. The embittered rancher believes that his boy is held by a Pawnee chief, and Paladin sets out to talk to the suspected kidnaper.

66.16 *Helen of Abajnian.* Dec. 28, 1957. GS: Harold J. Stone, Lisa Gaye, Wright King, Vladimir Sokoloff, Nick Dennis, Naomi Stevens. The daughter of a wealthy vintner becomes romantically involved with a cowboy despite the objections of her father. After the girl and the cowhand disappear, the vintner employs Paladin to find the girl and break up the romance.

66.17 *Ella West.* Jn. 4, 1958. GS: Norma Crane, Earle Hodgens, William Swan, Mike Mazurki. Paladin meets an old friend of his, Tomahawk Carter, proprietor of a Wild West Show. He asks Paladin to help him make a lady of his newest star, Ella West.

66.18 *The Reasonable Man.* Jan. 11, 1958. GS: Barry Atwater. While in a barbershop, Paladin witnesses a gun battle between a man and a teenager. He intervenes in an attempt to save the youngster's life.

66.19 *The High Graders.* Jan. 18, 1958. GS: Susan Cabot, Robert Steele. When a friend of Paladin's is killed shortly after purchasing a gold mine, Paladin sets out to investigate the murder. He learns that the dead man's heirs are being systematically robbed and killed.

66.20 *The Last Laugh.* Jan. 25, 1958. GS: Jean Allison, Stuart Whitman, Murray Hamilton, Peter Whitney. A ranch hand who has been fired bears a grudge against his former employer. He persuades a slow-witted man to place a burr under the saddle of a horse owned by the rancher. Then the horse throws the rancher's wife and the blame falls on Paladin, who had helped the lady to mount.

66.21 *The Bostonian.* Feb. 1, 1958. GS: Harry Townes, Joe de Santis, Constance Ford, Chris Alcaide, Louis Gomez, Frederick Ford. After a Bostonian buys a cattle ranch in the West and settles down to making a new life for himself and his wife, he gets embroiled in a feud with a veteran cattleman. Paladin steps in when gunplay ensues between the two enemies.

66.22 *The Singer.* Feb. 8, 1958. GS: Richard Long, Joan Weldon, Denver Pyle. A cowboy asks Paladin for help in his romance. He tells Paladin that the woman he loves has been forced to marry a rancher and is being held prisoner against her will.

66.23 *Bitter Wine.* Feb. 15, 1958. GS: Eduardo Ciannelli, Richard Shannon, Rita Lynn. Paladin is asked to be judge of a wine exhibit. Later, the winning vintner asks his aid in saving his vineyard from the ravages of a nearby oil rig.

66.24 *The Girl from Piccadilly.* Feb. 22, 1958. GS: Betsy von Furstenberg, Fintan Meyler. Paladin answers the advertisement of a wealthy San Franciscan, Marth Westrope. He is hired to find out the whereabouts of the man's missing daughter-in-law.

66.25 The O'Hare Story. March 1, 1958. GS: Victor McLaglen, John Doucette, Herbert Rudley, Christine White. Paladin is hired by a wealthy landowner to prevent the construction of a dam. After a fight with the engineer in charge of the dam's construction, Paladin begins to wonder about his employer's motives.

66.26 Birds of a Feather. March 8, 1958. GS: Robert H. Harris, James Craig. An agent for a railroad hires Paladin to bring peace to a Colorado town where two factions battle for a disputed right of way. But Paladin learns soon after his arrival that the man who hired him is a fraud.

66.27 The Teacher. March 15, 1958. GS: Carl Benson, Marian Seldes. Paladin rides into a small western town to find that a rancher has threatened to burn down the school unless the teacher retracts some remarks. After a meeting with the teacher, Paladin decides to rally the townspeople against the rancher.

66.28 Killer's Widow. March 22, 1958. GS: Barbara Baxley, Fay Roope, Roy Barcroft. Paladin is accused of taking stolen money from a bank robber he killed some months before. He visits the dead man's widow in an attempt to find the money and prove his innocence.

66.29 Gun Shy. March 29, 1958. GS: Jeanette Nolan, Lisa Gaye, Corey Allen. Paladin travels to a small border town in Montana to intercept bandits who have committed a robbery. While waiting for the bandits to arrive, Paladin stays at a boarding house and becomes involved with the landlady's pretty daughter.

66.30 The Prize Fight Story. April 5, 1958. GS: Hal Baylor, Don Megowan, King Calder, Gage Clarke, George E. Stone. Paladin helps to promote a prize fight in a mining town. But when the man he has supported is arrested by the local sheriff, Paladin is forced to take his place in the ring.

66.31 Hey Boy's Revenge. April 12, 1958. GS: Pernell Roberts, Philip Ahn, Bruce Cowling, David Leland, Dennis Cross, Harold Fong, Olan Soule. The houseboy at Paladin's San Francisco hotel receives word from his brother at a railroad camp in Utah that he fears he is about to be killed. The houseboy journeys to Utah but arrives too late. When he tries to avenge his brother's death he is jailed. Paladin tries to help.

66.32 The Five Books of Owen Deaver. April 26, 1958. GS: James Olson, Lurene Tuttle, Tyler McVey, Walter Barnes, Paul Lukather. Paladin saves the life of a young sheriff during a gun battle with two badmen. One of the gunmen escapes, and the sheriff seeks out Paladin believing that his rescuer is a wanted outlaw.

66.33 The Silver Queen. May 3, 1958. GS: Lita Milan, Earle Hodgins, Whit Bissell. Paladin introduces a San Francisco music-hall star to a lonesome prospector. After the man dies, he leaves his wealth to the girl, but his partner moves to nullify the will in court. Then an attempt is made to kill both Paladin and the girl.

66.34 Three Sons. May 10, 1958. GS: Paul Jasmin, Jacquline Mayo, Parker Fennelly, Warren Oates, Kevin Hagen, S. John Launer. Paladin gives up his hotel suite to a pair of newlyweds. The next morning he learns that the bridegroom's half-brothers have threatened the life of their father. Paladin rides into the range country to try to warn the old man.

66.35 Twenty-four Hours to North Fork. May 17, 1958. GS: June Lockhart, Grant Withers, Charles Aidman, Johnny Western, John Anderson, Sam Gilman. Called in to treat a sick ranch cook, Dr. Phyllis Thackeray diagnoses the illness as smallpox. She informs the ranch owner that all the ranch employees will have to be vaccinated, but the man refuses to allow this. Paladin tries to help the doctor.

66.36 Deliver the Body. May 24, 1958. GS: Morris Ankrum, Adeline deWalt Reynolds, Wayne Heffley, Jacqueline Scott, Karl Swenson, Harry Shannon, Brad Dexter. In a prairie town, Milo Culligan threatens to take over the prosperous farm of Max Bruckner, a Mennonite. Learning of Culligan's plan, Bruckner appeals to Paladin for help.

66.37 Silver Convoy. May 31, 1958. GS: Donald Randolph. Paladin stops for water at a Mexican hacienda and talks with the wealthy Spaniard who owns the property. The Spaniard asks Paladin to escort a shipment of silver through bandit country.

66.38 The Manhunter. June 7, 1958. GS: R.G. Armstrong, Robert Gist, James Francisco, Madeline Rhue. Paladin is summoned by the mayor of a small town in Nevada. His assignment is to track down the man accused of murdering the sheriff. The mayor tells Paladin that the accused man has recently been acquitted of a murder charge.

66.39 The Statue of San Sebastian. June 14, 1958. GS: John Carradine, Simon Oakland, Judson Pratt, Bart Bartley. Paladin arrives in a small town of San Sebastian. There he meets Ian Crown, a Scotsman who is anxious to capture Sancho Fernandez, the bandit who has been preying on the townspeople and ranchers. Later, when Paladin's wallet is stolen by a small boy, he learns that the child wants to buy a statue that Fernandez has stolen from the mission church.

Season Two

66.40 In an Evil Time. Sept. 13, 1958. GS: Joseph Calleia, David Whorf, Steve Colt, Hampton Fancher, Martin Balsam, Joe Perry, Rusty Lane. Hired to track down and bring back a killer to stand trial in Kansas City, Paladin is forced to kill his quarry when he tries to shoot it out. But the sheriff and the townspeople don't believe the killer was shot in self-defense.

66.41 The Man Who Wouldn't Talk. Sept. 20, 1958. GS: Hank Patterson, William Stevens, Charles Horvath. Paladin trails Pappy French, an aging bank robber who deserted his gang during a robbery, taking a fortune with him. When Paladin finally catches up with Pappy, he discovers that the old man has a broken leg. Pappy offers to split the stolen money with Paladin, if he will help him get away.

66.42 The Gentleman. Sept. 27, 1958. GS: Charles Bronson, Grace Raynor, Edmund Johnson, Harry Carey, Jr., Junius Matthews, Marion Collier. Paladin learns that a tough rancher, Chris Sorenson, is in love with Maria DeCastro, a pretty young woman who owns the adjoining ranch. He decides to teach Chris the ways of a gentleman so that he may win Maria. But then Paladin discovers that Maria's foreman plans to get possession of her ranch at any cost.

66.43 The Hanging of Roy Carter. Oct. 4, 1958. GS: Scott Marlowe, Robert Armstrong, Paul Birch, John Larch, John Duke. Paladin rides to the state penitentiary to ask the warden to delay the execution of a young man convicted of murder. The young man is cleared of the crime but the warden, believing him guilty, orders a lynching. Paladin attempts to save the man's life.

66.44 *Duel at Florence.* Oct. 11, 1958. GS: Dean Harens, Bonnie Bolding. Paladin agrees to help a timid young barber who asks him to stop a local gunfight between two men over a girl. But when he learns that the girl has encouraged the fight simply to make the barber jealous, Paladin decides to make a hero of the barber.

66.45 *The Protege.* Oct. 18, 1958. GS: Peter Breck, Ken Mayer, George Mitchell, William Meigs, Mel Welles, Cy Malls, Charles Tannen. Paladin teaches a shy young man to use a gun to protect himself. He later discovers that this same shy youngster has turned into a gunslinger who kills without provocation.

66.46 *The Road to Wickenberg.* Oct. 25, 1958. GS: Christine White, Harry Carey, Jr., Rayford Barnes, Ed Faulkner, Mickey Finn, Don "Red" Barry, Mike Forest. Beaten up and robbed, Paladin finds that his enemy is a crooked sheriff who lets his family run the town. Unable to leave town because of the loss of his horse, money and gun, Paladin is helped to reclaim his possessions by a beautiful dance-hall girl. In return Paladin has to promise to take her with him when he leaves.

66.47 *A Sense of Justice.* Nov. 1, 1958. GS: Barrie Chase, Virginia Gregg, Karl Swenson. Paladin rides into a Western town and finds that the townspeople are planning to lynch a man accused of murder. He learns that the accused man knows very little about the crime and begins to suspect a pretty girl who is a good friend of the sheriff's.

66.48 *Young Gun.* Nov. 8, 1958. GS: Paul Carr, Dick Foran, Robert F. Simon, Meg Wylie, Abby Dalton, Frederick Miller, Gene Roth. A group of ranchers, desperately needing water for their livestock, hire Paladin to reason with a retired gunfighter. He refuses to allow his neighbors access to the water on his property.

66.49 *The Lady.* Nov. 15, 1958. GS: Patricia Medina, Robert Karnes, George Richardson, Earl Parker. Intrigued by a lovely English girl, Paladin agrees to escort her to her brother's ranch. After they arrive, they discover that her brother and his family have been murdered by Comanche Indians. Paladin realizes that he and the girl will be in serious danger if they do not leave the ranch immediately.

66.50 *A Share for Murder.* Nov. 22, 1958. GS: Harry Bartell, Harry Morgan, Joel Ashley, Ron Hagerthy. Paladin seeks to learn the identity of an unknown gunman whose target is one of the partners in a gold mine. Each partner suspects the other of planning his murder in order to become sole owner of the mine.

66.51 *The Ballad of Oscar Wilde.* Dec. 6, 1958. GS: John O'Malley, Roy Engel, Jack Hogan, Richard Shannon, Chet Stratton. Paladin is hired as a bodyguard for Oscar Wilde, the English author, who is visiting American on a lecture tour. While carrying out his assignment, Paladin is beaten up, his credentials are stolen, and he is thrown into San Francisco Bay to drown.

66.52 *The Solid Gold Patrol.* Dec. 13, 1958. GS: Sean McClory, Don Keefer, Michael Hagen, Michael Carr, Mike Kellin. Paladin learns that an Army corporal holds the winning ticket in a lottery and has only a short time in which to ride to New Orleans to claim the money. But when Paladin arrives at the Army post, he learns that the corporal is with a patrol that has been ambushed by a tribe of Indians.

66.53 *Something to Live For.* Dec. 20, 1958. GS: Rayford Barnes, John Anderson, Tom Brown, Don Megowan, Vaughn Taylor, Nancy Hadley. On his way to a job at the Evans Ranch, Paladin encounters Harleigh Preston, a wealthy young man who has been robbed and deserted by his guide. Paladin decides to help the young man and suggests that Preston accompany him to the ranch.

66.54 *The Moor's Revenge.* Dec. 27, 1958. GS: Patricia Morison, Vincent Price, Morey Amsterdam, Richard Shannon, Joe Perry. Among a group of Shakespearean players scheduled to appear in San Diego during Roundup Weeks are two friends of Paladin's. Paladin, however, fears violence from raucous celebrants, because thespians Victoria Vestris and Charles Matthews have been misrepresented as a veil dancer and comic.

66.55 *The Wager.* Jan. 3, 1959. GS: Denver Pyle, Jacqueline Scott, Steve Gravers, Ken Lynch. Paladin is hired to escort wealthy Sid Morgan and his fiancee to Silver City. Morgan wants protection from outlaw Howard Gorman, who has threatened to kill him.

66.56 *The Taffeta Mayor.* Jan. 10, 1959. GS: Edward Platt, Robert Karnes, Norma Crane, Jeanne Bates, Bobby Hall. Paladin rides into a small Wyoming town to begin a new assignment, aiding John Kellaway in his campaign for mayor, only to discover that Kellaway has been killed. Paladin persuades Kellaway's widow to run in his stead.

66.57 *Lady on the Stagecoach.* Jan. 17, 1959. GS: Dolores Vitina, Fay Baker, Raymond Bailey, Ward Wood, Mark Dana, Warren Parker. Paladin and an Apache Indian princess, educated in New England, are aboard a stagecoach when it is held up. One of the outlaws offers to let the other passengers go free but decides to take the Indian girl with him.

66.58 *Treasure Trail.* Jan. 24, 1959. GS: Henry Brandon, Bruce Gordon, Dean Stanton, Willard Sage. In a poker game Paladin wins a portion of a torn map. When intact, the map showed the location of a cache of money. Paladin becomes wary when he learns that the hidden money was stolen from the Army.

66.59 *Julie.* Jan. 31, 1959. GS: Miranda Jones, John Beradino, Allen Case, Earle Hodgins, Ronald Greene, Tex Terry. Paladin decides to protect a young girl who is involved in a feud and marked for murder. The girl, however, misinterprets Paladin's gallant gesture.

66.60 *The Man Who Lost* (A.K.A. "The Avengers"). Feb. 7, 1959. GS: Robert J. Wilke, James Drury, Madlyn Rhue, Ric Rodman, Mark Tapscott. Paladin attempts to settle a feud between two brothers but soon becomes a target for death himself. The brothers are bitter enemies because the younger eloped with the intended bride of the elder, a powerful cattle baron.

66.61 *The Scorched Feather.* Feb. 14, 1959. GS: Lon Chaney, Jr., Mario Alcaide, Sy Malis, Mike Steele. Paladin is hired by Robert Ceilbleu to protect his father, an Indian scout, whose life has been threatened by a Comanche war chief named Hotanitan. Paladin soon discovers that Robert has a split personality, his other self being Hotanitan.

66.62 *The Return of the Lady.* Feb. 21, 1959. GS: Patricia Medina, Gene Nelson, Theodore Marcuse, Pilar del Rey. Beautiful Diana Coulter enters Paladin's life again. He receives a wire from her saying that she is to marry a Texas landowner and asks Paladin to give the bride away. Paladin arrives at the Texan's ranch and discovers another reason for the telegram.

66.63 *The Monster of Moon Ridge.* Feb. 28, 1959. GS: Barney Phillips, Natalie Norwick, Ralph Moody, Walter Coy, Robert Forster. Paladin is hired to investigate a monster which is terrorizing the people of Moon Ridge, Colorado. He finds a set of giant tracks and follows them.

66.64 *The Long Hunt.* March 7, 1959. GS: Stephen Roberts, Lane Bradbury, Anne Barton, Anthony Caruso. Paladin is hired by John Dundee to help track down a half-breed who has murdered two peace officers. When he discovers that Dundee is holding the hunted man's wife as a hostage, Paladin begins to suspect his motives.

66.65 *Death of a Gunfighter.* March 14, 1959. GS: Suzanne Pleshette, Russell Arms, Christopher Dark, Larkin Ford, Tom Greenway, Joe Bassett, I. Stanford Jolley. Juan Morita, a reformed gunman, plans to return to his native village and marry his childhood sweetheart. He hires Paladin to escort him to the village. When they arrive, Paladin learns that the girl plans to marry another man.

66.66 *Incident at Borasca Band.* March 21, 1959. GS: Jacques Aubuchon, Perry Cook, Ben Wright, Ted Markland. Paladin rides into a small temporary town to return a pouch of gold to its owner. He suddenly finds himself charged with murder and standing trial in a kangaroo court.

66.67 *Maggie O'Bannion.* April 4, 1959. GS: Marion Marshall, Peggy Rea, Don Haggerty, George Cisar, Paul Sorensen, Mickey Simpson. While traveling on a job, Paladin is ambushed and beaten. At a ranch, he talks Maggie O'Bannion, the owner, into hiring him. When he discovers that the foreman is stealing her cattle, Paladin tries to get Miss O'Bannion to take more of an interest in the ranch, but she takes an interest in Paladin instead.

66.68 *The Chase.* April 11, 1959. GS: Olive Sturgess, Paul Birch, Adam Williams, Paul Richards, Wright King, Lee Farr. A beautiful woman asks Paladin to prove that her husband, who is wanted for a bank holdup and murder, is innocent. Paladin agrees to help.

66.69 *Alaska.* April 18, 1959. GS: Richard Shannon, Karl Swenson, Elizabeth York, Allen Case, Fay Roope. An old furtrapping friend of Paladin's becomes embroiled in a claims dispute in Alaska. Paladin journeys north by dogsled and learns that the man's life has been threatened.

66.70 *Hunt the Man Down.* April 25, 1959. GS: Mort Mills, Ed Nelson, Rodolfo Acosta, Jack Elam, Marilyn Hanold. The Gage Brothers hire Paladin to find the men who committed a brutal crime involving their sister and her husband.

66.71 *The Return of Roy Carter.* May 2, 1959. GS: Clu Gulager, Larry Blake, Brad Von Beltz, Diana Crawford, Craig Duncan. Roy Carter owes his life to the gallant act of a prison chaplain. Learning that the chaplain has gone into mountainous snow country in an attempt to bring back an escaped convict, Carter hires Paladin to go after him.

66.72 *The Sons of Aaron Murdock.* May 9, 1959. GS: Philip Coolidge, Lee Kinsolving, Elizabeth York, Wesley Lau, Bill Shaw. A man is suspected of protecting his son, who is a murderer. Paladin comes to the man's defense and discovers that his services are needed for another reason.

66.73 *Commanche.* May 16, 1959. GS: Shirley O'Hara, Larry Pennell, Susan Cabot, Roy Barcroft, Robert Anderson. Paladin is hired to find a young cavalryman who deserted his company and disappeared with his sweetheart.

66.74 *Homecoming.* May 23, 1959. GS: Lewis Martin, Ed Nelson, Don Megowan, Dick Rich. Will Stanhope beseeches Paladin to protect him from a youth who has just been released from prison. Investigating, Paladin learns that the young man was jailed unjustly because of Stanhope's testimony.

66.75 *The Fifth Man.* May 30, 1959. GS: John Emery, Ward Wood, Leo Gordon, Clarke Alexander, Ben Wright, Walter Burke. Paladin learns that killer Bert Talman, who swore that he would kill the five men who once tried to lynch him, has carried out his threat against four of the men. Paladin decides to offer his services to the fifth man.

66.76 *Heritage of Anger.* June 6, 1959. GS: Carol Hill, Ricky Vera, Peter Coe, James Gavin, Carol Thurston, Roberto Contreras. Paladin is asked to protect the Avery family from Garcia, a Mexican bandit. He learns that Garcia is plaguing the family because he has a special interest in the Avery's adopted son.

66.77 *The Haunted Trees.* June 13, 1959. GS: Doris Dowling, Roy Barcroft, Jane Chang, Brad Trumbull, Duane Grey. A lovely widow tells Paladin that her stepson has threatened her life. She says that he is also attempting to destroy the lumber business which her late husband left to her.

66.78 *Gold and Brimstone.* June 20, 1959. GS: Eduardo Ciannelli, Philip Pine, Alan Reed, William Vaughan. Riding through a sudden cloud of smoke, Paladin encounters an old miner. The superstitious old man thinks Paladin is the Devil's emissary and asks him to help file the claim for a gold mine he has just discovered.

Season Three

66.79 *First, Catch a Tiger.* Sept. 12, 1959. GS: Harry Bartell, John Anderson, King Calder, Don Megowan, Pamela Lincoln. Stopping at a public house along the trail, Paladin encounters the bitter father of a desperado he recently sent to the gallows. Learning that the man has hired a gunman to kill him, Paladin is forced into a showdown with four men, not knowing which is the hired killer.

66.80 *Episode in Laredo.* Sept. 19, 1959. GS: Eugene Lyons, Norma Crane, J. Pat O'Malley, Johnny Eimen. In Laredo, Texas, Paladin runs into Sam Tuttle, a notorious gunman who has apparently slipped into town to see his wife and small son. Tuttle, feeling he must uphold his reputation, decides to challenge Paladin to a showdown.

66.81 *Les Girls.* Sept. 26, 1959. GS: Roxane Berard, Danielle DeMetz, Helene Stanley, Mabel Albertson. Paladin is hired for a rather unusual job — he is to deliver a group of mail-order brides to their prospective husbands. Paladin is pleasantly surprised to find that the girls are all lovely French mademoiselles.

66.82 *The Posse.* Oct. 3, 1959. GS: Perry Cook, Harry Carey, Jr., Denver Pyle, Ken Curtis, Paul Sorensen, Bill Wellman, Jr. While traveling to Santa Fe, Paladin stops to share another traveler's camp. A posse rides up, and the traveler points to Paladin as the murderer they have been chasing.

66.83 *Shot by Request.* Oct. 10, 1959. GS: John Abbott, Malcolm Atterbury, Sue Randall, John Holland, Robert Gist, Greg Dunne. A hired gun with a cultural background very similar to Paladin's, asks Paladin to stage a fair gunfight with him

Carson City. He wants Paladin to wound him in the hand so that he can retire without loss of prestige.

66.84 *Pancho.* Oct. 24, 1959. GS: Rafael Campos, Rico Alaniz, Luis Montell, Eduard Colmans. Paladin is hired by a wealthy Mexican rancher, Don Luis Ortega, to escort his daughter to the Unite States. During the trip Paladin discovers a young boy buried in an ant hill.

66.85 *Fragile.* Oct. 31, 1959. GS: Werner Klemperer, Jacqueline Scott, Alan Caillou, Gregg Palmer, William Boyett, Douglas Bank. Elegance is on its way to the California gold-mining town of Panamint. It is coming in the form of the town's first plate-glass window, provided Paladin can deliver the delicate item without it going to pieces.

66.86 *The Unforgiven.* Nov. 7, 1959. GS: David White, Hampton Fancher, Joel Ashley, Hank Patterson, Linda Lawson, Luciana Paluzzi, William Phipps, Paul Burke. Wealthy General Crommer, against whom Paladin bears and old grudge, summons the gunfighter to his bedside. As a dying request the general begs Paladin to bear a message of forgiveness to another man who hates Crommer.

66.87 *The Black Handkerchief.* Nov. 14, 1959. GS: Ed Nelson, Joe Perry, Terrence De Marney, Svea Grunveld, Gordon Polk. Paladin is hired by the proud Deverall family to vindicate their son Pierre, who is sentenced to hang for a stagecoach robbery and murder. The smug prisoner assures Paladin that the authorities wouldn't dare hang a Deverall.

66.88 *The Gold Toad.* Nov. 21, 1959. GS: Lorna Thayer, David White, Bill Wellman, Jr., Paul Sorensen, Kevin Hagen. Paladin investigates rumors of ancient Indian treasure in an Arizona valley. He soon finds that homesteader Ben Webster is at odds with rancher Doris Golemon in a race to discover the riches.

66.89 *Tiger.* Nov. 28, 1959. GS: Parley Baer, Elsa Cardenas, Paul Clark. A wealthy man who has just returned from a hunting trip is afraid that a tiger curse has been put on him. He hires Paladin to travel to his home in Houston and protect him.

66.90 *Champagne Safari.* Dec. 5, 1959. GS: William Mims, Patric Knowles, Valerie French, Lou Krugman, Gil Rankin, Vic Perrin. An enterprising guide has arranged a buffalo safari, complete with mock Indian attack, for a party of wealthy European hunters. One of the party is killed by an arrow, and the guide comes to Paladin for help.

66.91 *Charley Red Dog.* Dec. 12, 1959. GS: Scott Marlowe, Raymond Bailey, Kelton Garwood, Edmund Glover, William Bryant. A group of prominent businessmen hire Paladin to rid their town of outlaws. On his way to the town, Paladin meets a young Indian who claims to be a United States marshal.

66.92 *The Naked Gun.* Dec. 19. 1959. GS: Robert J. Wilke, Lane Chandler, Ken Curtis, Dallas Mitchell, Hal Needham. Looking for a fight, a rough trail boss challenges Paladin. But Paladin refuses to be goaded into a fight.

66.93 *One Came Back.* Dec. 26, 1959. GS: James Coburn, Tommy Cook, Strother Martin, George Mathews, Robert Dorough. Ben Harvey, who was a vicious outlaw leader during the Civil War, is released from prison. He hires Paladin to accompany him and a wagonload of supplies to a town where he and his family intend to get a fresh start.

66.94 *The Prophet.* Jan. 2, 1960. GS: Sheppard Strudwick, Barney Phillips, Lorna Thayer, Eddie Little Sky, Brad Von Beltz, Florence Martin. Soon after an Army colonel disappears in Apache country, it is reported that a white man is organizing the Indians for an attack on settlers and soldiers. The Army hires Paladin to find the colonel.

66.95 *The Day of the Bad Man.* Jan. 9, 1960. GS: William Joyce, Eleanor Audley, Harry Fleer, Norman Shelley, Sue Randall, Hal Needham, Don O'Kelly. Rancher Cynthia Palmer hires Paladin to rout troublemaker Amos Saint's gang and clean up the town of Cedar Wells. She also wants Paladin to send her meek nephew to the East.

66.96 *The Pledge.* Jan. 16, 1960. GS: Robert Gist, Charles Gray, Brad Weston, Susan Davis, Joe Hamilton. A rough frontier Irishman tells Paladin that his wife is being held prisoner by some renegade Indians. He wants Paladin to guide him to the renegades' camp so that he can trade a wagon load of food and blankets for the safe return of his wife.

66.97 *Jenny.* Jan. 23, 1960. GS: Ellen Clark, Peter Leeds, Phil Chambers, Quentin Sondergaard, Trevor Bardette, Ben Brogan, Olan Soule, Bud Osborne, Hal Needham. Jenny Lake has two problems. She is pursued by an unwelcome suitor and she has a packet of counterfeit money. She calls on Paladin to help her.

66.98 *Return to Fort Benjamin.* Jan. 30, 1960. GS: Anthony Caruso, Herbert Patterson, Charles Aidman, Robert J. Wilke. Paladin is hired by an Indian chief to go to Fort Benjamin and make sure that the chief's son, sentenced to hang for murder, receives proper tribal rites. At the fort, Paladin learns some facts pointing to the Indian's innocence.

66.99 *The Night the Town Died.* Feb. 6, 1960. GS: Barry Cahill, Robert J. Stevenson, Mary Gregory, Arthur Space, Barney Phillips, Sally Singer, Vic Perrin. Released from military prison, Aaron Bell starts for home with only one thought in mind — revenge against the people who hung his brother some years earlier. One of the townspeople asks Paladin to help prevent violence.

66.100 *The Ledge.* Feb. 13, 1960. GS: Richard Shannon, Don Beddoe, John Hoyt, Richard Rust. Paladin and his traveling companions witness a landslide that traps a man on a precarious ledge. The travelers must decide which of them will risk his life to find out whether the man is alive.

66.101 *The Lady on the Wall.* Feb. 20, 1960. GS: Howard Petrie, Ralph Clanton, Hank Patterson, James Stone, Perry Ivins, Lillian Bronson. A pretty girl's picture disappears from over the bar of a mining-camp saloon. Some of the old-timers liked that painting pretty well, and favor hiring Paladin to find it.

66.102 *The Misguided Father.* Feb. 27, 1960. GS: Harry Carey, Jr., Douglas Kennedy, Hampton Fancher, Gregg Palmer, Lee Sands. One of Paladin's friends is found dead in his hotel room. Paladin accompanies the body back to the man's home town, figuring that the key to the murder lies there.

66.103 *The Hatchet Man.* March 5, 1960. GS: Lisa Lu, Allen Jung, Nolan Leary, Benson Fong, Fuji. Joe Tsin, a Chinese-American detective on the San Francisco force has been threatened with death by a local tong. Paladin, hired to protect him, runs up against the Chinese code of honor.

66.104 *Fight at Adobe Wells.* March 12, 1960. GS: Ken Lynch, Miranda Jones, Sandy Kenyon, Brad Weston, Dorothy Dells, Gregg Palmer. Commodore Guilder has a money-making deal cooking in Indian territory. He hires Paladin to help him evade an old enemy, the Comanche leader.

66.105 *The Gladiators.* March 19, 1960. GS: Dolores Donlon, Paul Cavanagh, George Neise, James Coburn, Chet Stratton. Paladin comes to New Orleans to clear up a confused affair of honor. Too late, he learns he has been tricked into replacing one of the duelists.

66.106 *Love and a Bad Woman.* March 26, 1960. GS: Geraldine Brooks, Lawrence Dobkin, Ed Faulkner, Bob Hopkins, Sherwood Keith, Edwin Mills. An attractive widow lets it be known that she's available for matrimony. But there's a catch — her husband isn't dead.

66.107 *An International Affair.* April 2, 1960. GS: Ziva Rodann, Fintan Meyler, David Janti, Henry Corden, Oscar Beregi, Harold Innocent, Olan Soule. A prince from the Sandwich Islands is slaughtered in Paladin's doorway. Anyone on a list of international suspects might have wanted to kill him.

66.108 *Lady with a Gun.* April 9, 1960. GS: Jack Weston, Paula Raymond, Jean Eager, Ron Soble. The staid atmosphere of the Carleton Hotel lobby is ruffled when a guest ducks for cover. His reason is a gun-wielding young lady.

66.109 *Never Help the Devil.* April 16, 1960. GS: Jack Lambert, Kelton Garwood, Lewis Martin, Dick Rich, Bill Wellman, Jr. Gunman Doggie Kramer is slipping. He got his man, but was wounded in the process. And it looks like just a question of time before he's wiped out by his victim's brother. Paladin takes on the role of bodyguard.

66.110 *Ambush.* April 23, 1960. GS: Alan Dexter, Michael Ferris, Natalie Norwick, George Macready, Dan Barton, Hal Needham. On their way to San Francisco, Paladin and a prisoner are ambushed by a gunman who just tells them to wait. Then three more travelers are captured, but the gunman still gives no reason for holding them.

66.111 *Black Sheep.* April 30, 1960. GS: Pat Wayne, Stacy Harris, June Vincent, Suzanne Lloyd, Ed Faulkner, Ross Sturlin. Paladin heads for Mexico to find a youth who's just inherited a vast estate. The young man may be reluctant to return because he is wanted for robbery and manslaughter.

66.112 *Full Circle.* May 14, 1960. GS: Adam Williams, Barbara Baxley, Stewart Bradley, Raymond Hatton, Howard Dayton, Bobby Rose, Hal Needham. Three years back, Simon Quill faced certain death, until he got the bright idea of letting Paladin die in his place. Now Quill is about to be hanged, and he writes his friend Paladin for help.

66.113 *The Twins.* May 21, 1960. GS: Brian Hutton, Jennifer Lea, Lane Chandler, Sonia Warren, Tony Reagan. Adam Mirakian is wanted for murder. He surrenders, but swears the killer is his twin brother, and asks Paladin to prove it.

66.114 *The Campaign of Billy Banjo.* May 28, 1960. GS: Jacques Aubuchon, Rita Lynn, Charles Davis, Vic Perrin, Stewart East, Brad Von Beltz. Mrs. Billy Banjo has her heart set on seeing her husband elected to the Wyoming State Senate. Billy hires Paladin to prevent her from killing the rival candidate.

66.115 *Ransom.* June 4, 1960. GS: Valerie French, Robert H. Harris, Gene Roth, Tom Palmer, Alex Davion, Denver Pyle. Financier Carter wants to locate a man with a missing document, but the job sounds dull to Paladin and he turns it down. Then the beautiful Secura seeks the same man, and the job seems more interesting.

66.116 *The Trial.* June 11, 1960. GS: Robert F. Simon, Bud Slater, Raymond Hatton, Hal Smith, John Thye, Harry Antrim, Tom Jackson. Morgan Gibbs has a job for Paladin. His son David ran away after killing a woman, and Gibbs wants the boy brought back alive.

66.117 *The Search.* June 18, 1960. GS: Wright King, Earl Hodgins, Perry Cook, Lillian Bronson, Charles Aidman, Peggy Rae, Tex Lambert. Paladin is summoned to a San Francisco hospital by an elderly patient. She asks him to find her son, who ran away from home years ago.

Season Four

66.118 *The Fatalist.* Sept. 10, 1960. GS: Martin Gabel, Roxane Berard, Regina Gleason, Robert Blake, John Close, Lee Sands. Russian immigrant Nathan Shotness is the only witness who can convict an ex-con named Smollet of murder. Nathan's daughter is concerned for her father's safety, so she hires Paladin to protect him.

66.119 *Love's Young Dream.* Sept. 17, 1960. GS: Ken Curtis, Lorna Thayer, Mike Mazurki. A trail tramp named Monk is a man Paladin had hoped to forget. But now he shows up in San Francisco and wants Paladin to help him establish a claim on an inheritance.

66.120 *A Head of Hair.* Sept. 24, 1960. GS: Ben Johnson, George Kennedy, Donna Brooks, Chuck Hayward, Trevor Bardette. The Nez Perce Indians have kidnaped a young girl, and Paladin is sent to rescue her. Stopping at an Army post, he discovers the only guide who knows where the kidnapers are is John Anderson, himself part Indian.

66.121 *Out at the Old Ball Park.* Oct. 1, 1960. GS: John Larch, J. Pat O'Malley, Jack Albertson, Ted Hamilton, Sandy Kenyon, Perry Cook. There's bloodshed at the ball game in Whiskey Slide. Mayor Whiteside calls an armistice and Paladin comes in to umpire the rest of the game.

66.122 *Saturday Night.* Oct. 8, 1960. GS: Martin Balsam, Joanne Linville, Denny Miller, Rudy Solari, Terence De Marney, Raoul De Leon. Paladin gets kayoed in a saloon brawl. He wakes up in jail with three other men and a corpse.

66.123 *The Calf.* Oct. 15, 1960. GS: Denver Pyle, Parker Fennelly, Don Grady, Carl Henry, Hal Needham. There's a long fence which stretches along one border of rancher George Advent's land. It's straight, except for one little three-foot jog, and that's the thing that drives Advent to call on Paladin.

66.124 *The Tender Gun.* Oct. 22, 1960. GS: Jeanette Nolan, Don Keefer, Hank Patterson, Tony Reese, Lou Antonio. Sheriff M.J. Smuggley sends Paladin a letter asking his help in ridding a town of some land-grabbing schemers. Paladin doesn't know the the sheriff is a woman.

66.125 *The Shooting of Jesse May.* Oct. 29, 1960. GS: Robert Blake, William Talman, Hari Rhodes, Rayford Barnes, Barney Phillips, John Milford. During the Civil War, Jessie Turnbow's father was suspected of being a Rebel spy, and was slain by the local townspeople. Jessie sets out to even the score.

66.126 *The Poker Friend.* Nov. 12, 1960. GS: Jack Weston, Betsy Jones-Moreland, James Boles, Peter Falk, Warren Oates, Brett Somers, Leo Penn, Tony Haig. There is a poker fiend by the name of Neal who has already lost a half million dollars in a game. But he is still going strong. Neal's wife offers Paladin fifty grand to pry her husband loose from the game.

66.127 *Crowbait.* Nov. 19, 1960. GS: Russell Collins, Jacqueline Scott, Gordon Polk, Eddie Little Sky. A prospector named Crowbait once got some silver from a friendly Piute chief. Now Crowbait wants some more for his daughter, but the old chief is gone and the new one is decidedly unfriendly.

66.128 *The Marshal's Boy.* Nov. 26, 1960. GS: Ken Lynch, Andrew Prine, Harry Carey, Jr., Hal Needham. Billy, the marshal's son, is wanted for murder and it's his dad's job to get him. But the fatherly instinct is too strong. The marshal asks Paladin to find the boy, while he stalls off an angry posse.

66.129 *Fogg Bound.* Dec. 3, 1960. GS: Patric Knowles, Peter Whitney, Arlene McQuade, Jon Silo. Phileas Fogg arrives in San Francisco with his servant Passepartout while trying to journey around the world in eighty days. Fogg hires Paladin to escort them to Reno.

66.130 *The Legacy.* Dec. 10, 1960. GS: George Kennedy, Chuck Roberson, Harry Lauter, Harry Carey, Jr. Rancher Sam Tarnitzer takes justice into his own hands and hangs a boy who stole one of his cows. Paladin is hired by irate citizens to find Tarnitzer.

66.131 *The Prisoner.* Dec. 17, 1960. GS: Buzz Martin, Barry Kelley, George Mitchell, Liam Sullivan, Narda Onyx, Howard McNear. The only living member of the Groton gang is young Justin, imprisoned by the law since he was thirteen. Justin was sentenced to be hanged, and the law has been waiting for him to reach 21. Now he has reached it.

66.132 *The Puppeteer.* Dec. 24, 1960. GS: Crahan Denton, Natalie Norwick, Denver Pyle, Peter Boone. Paladin is stranded without his horse, but Jack Burnaby gives him a lift in his wagon. The wagon is filled with puppets and Burnaby's cynical philosophy.

66.133 *Vernon Good.* Dec. 31, 1960. GS: John Mauldin, James Anderson, Albert Salmi, Leo Gordon, Oscar Beregi. Paladin is on his way to Monterey when he meets a group of unfriendly gents, who let him pass when he says he knows nothing of a man named Vernon Good. Then Paladin rides into a mission and finds that Vernon Good is there.

66.134 *A Quiet Night in Town* Part One. Jan. 7, 1961. GS: Robert Carricart, Robert Emhardt, Phyllis Love, James Best, Sydney Pollock, Fredd Wayne, Kevin Hagen, William Challee. Paladin arrives in the Texas border town of Jody with a murder suspect named Joselito Kincaid. Their appearance creates an air of tension because they are in cow country and Kincaid is a sheepherder.

66.135 *A Quiet Night in Town* Part Two. Jan. 14, 1961. GS: Robert Carricart, Robert Emhardt, Phyllis Love, James Best, Sydney Pollock, Fredd Wayne, Kevin Hagen, William Challee. Joe Culp, Roy Smith and the Silmser brothers have all come into the town of Jody looking for a good time. Seeing Paladin with his prisoner, Joselito Kincaid, the boys decide a hanging is in order.

66.136 *The Princess and the Gunfighter.* Jan. 21, 1961. GS: Arline Sax, Ben Wright, Shirley O'Hara, Earl Parker, Hal Needham, Ross Sturlin. Princess Serafina, a member of European royalty, has come to San Francisco on business. But members of her court say she has disappeared, and they fear she may have been kidnaped.

66.137 *Shadow of a Man.* Jan. 28, 1961. GS: Kent Smith, Dianne Foster, Mike Kellin, Walter Burke, Robert Karnes. Marion Sutter sends an urgent message to Paladin, imploring him to save her Virginia-born husband from the tyranny of rebel-hating Logan Adcock.

66.138 *Long Way Home.* Feb. 4, 1961. GS: William Talman, Ivan Dixon, Rayford Barnes, John Milford. Isham Spruce is really wanted. There is a price of five grand on his head. Paladin is not alone on the hunt. Some bounty hunters have been hired by an unscrupulous sheriff who will stop at nothing to get Spruce.

66.139 *The Tax Gatherer.* Feb. 11, 1961. GS: Roy Barcroft, Harry Carey, Jr., Raymond Hatton, Stewart East, John Hopkins, Bob Woodward, Hal Needham. In the town of Bad Dog three men have tried to collect delinquent cattle taxes — and died trying. Paladin is then hired as tax collector.

66.140 *The Fatal Flaw.* Feb. 25, 1961. GS: Allyn Joslyn, Royal Dano, Jena Engstrom, Miguel de Anda. A sudden blizzard finds Paladin sharing a cabin refuge with Marshal McKendrick and his prisoner, Curley Ashburne. As the storm rages, Ashburne tries to prevail on the marshal to set him free.

66.141 *Fandango.* March 4, 1961. GS: Robert Gist, Karl Swenson, Andrew Prine, Jerry Summers, Rudolf Acosta. A couple of teenagers named Bobby Olson and James Horton have escaped from Texas where they were sentenced to hang for murder. Soon after he has read about the case in the papers, Paladin runs into young Olson in the desert.

66.142 *The Last Judgment.* March 11, 1961. GS: Harold J. Stone, Donald Randolph, Leo Gordon, James Anderson, Robert J. Stevenson. Judge Greenleaf holds court in the local saloon, and hanging is the only sentence he is known to hand out. Next on his docket is a murder charge against Dr. Simeon Loving, a man Paladin thinks is innocent.

66.143 *The Gold Bar.* March 18, 1961. GS: John Fiedler, Jena Engstrom, Val Avery, Chet Stratton. A banker named Throckton comes to Paladin in a rage. It seems a gold bar is missing from his establishment as well as a clerk named Turner.

66.144 *Everyman.* March 25, 1961. GS: Barry Kelley, Vic Perrin, David White, June Vincent, Roy Engel, Suzi Carnel, Loyal "Doc" Lucas, Lawrence Dutchison. Paladin's plans for a peaceful night of slumber in a mining camp come to naught. He becomes the target for a vengeance bent character named Danceman.

66.145 *The Siege.* April 1, 1961. GS: Mike Kellin, Perry Lopez, David J. Stewart, Brad Weston, Robert Karnes, Russ Bender. The Brent brothers are a truly nasty lot, who extort money from Arizona farmers by threatening to put poison in their water. A reward for the capture of the Brents arouses Paladin's interest in the case.

66.146 *The Long Weekend.* April 8, 1961. GS: Roy Barcroft, Ralph Moody, Paige Adams, Clegg Hoyt, Stephen Roberts, Ned Glass. A wealthy mine owner named Montrose appears twice a year to paint the town red. The citizens like his money, but not his manners, so they hire Paladin to tame him.

66.147 *El Paso Stage.* April 15, 1961. GS: Buddy Ebsen, Karl Swenson, Jeremy Slate, Hank Patterson, Mary Munday. Marshal Elmo Crane has bent the law to suit his purposes, but now the town citizens are fed up and they hire Paladin to straighten out the crooked lawman.

66.148 *Duke of Texas.* April 22, 1961. GS: Scott Marlowe, Eduard Franz, Robert Carricart, Albert Cavens, Roberto

Contreras. Austrian Prince Franz, inspired to follow in the footsteps of his cousin Maximilian, plans to invade Mexico, and insists that Paladin accompany him. Paladin demures, but learns that royalty is used to having its way.

66.149 *Broken Image.* April 29, 1961. GS: Kenneth Tobey, June Vincent, Johnny Eiman, Bob Woodward, Hal Needham, Ted Smile, Stewart East, Joan Dupuis. Tim Decker has quite a reputation among his relatives and friends for being handy with a gun. But when a gang of bank bandits raid the town and ride off with their loot, Tim seems reluctant to give chase.

66.150 *My Brother's Keeper.* May 6, 1961. GS: Wright King, Ben Wright, Karl Swenson, Betsy Jones-Moreland, Otto Waldis, Allen Wood. Paladin has been badly mauled by a mountain lion. A couple of drifters named Cull and Boggs happen along and, instead of helping Paladin, they help themselves to his horse and guns.

66.151 *Bear Bait.* May 13, 1961. GS: Judi Meredith, Richard Rust, Martin West, Ralph Reed, Stephen Roberts, Frank Ferguson, Ollie O'Toole, James Maloney. A brute named Sim and his cronies Bunk and Burt have cowed an entire town through violence and threats. When Paladin stops in the local saloon, they try to goad him into a gunfight, but Paladin stick to trading insults.

66.152 *The Cure.* May 20, 1961. GS: Norma Crane, Jerry Wayne, Jeanne Vaughn, Craig Duncan, Olan Soule. The body found on a sofa in the lobby at Paladin's hotel appears to be that of a dead man. But the male attire conceals the form of once-famous Martha "Calamity Jane" Conroy, who is very much alive, if somewhat immobilized by drink.

66.153 *The Road.* May 27, 1961. GS: Gene Lyons, Trevor Bardette, Perry Cook, Joel Crothers, Ben Wright, George Kennedy. Weary Paladin reluctantly stops at a trail-side flop house where he gets into an argument with a man named Merton. A little later, Merton and his cronies rob Paladin of his belongings and force him to start across the mountain trail on foot and without food.

66.154 *The Uneasy Grave.* June 3, 1961. GS: Pippa Scott, Werner Klemperer, Lillian Bronson, Wolfe Barzell, Don Beddoe, Steve Warren. Paladin is traveling to Johnsonville when he encounters young Kathy Rousseau engaged in an unlikely pursuit — gravedigging. She says the grave is for her fiance, killed by a man named Leander Johnson.

66.155 *Soledad Crossing.* June 10, 1961. GS: Ed Faulkner, Ken Curtis, Natalie Norwick, Chuck Roberson, Walter Edmiston. When Paladin learns that the brother of prisoner Bud McPhater has apparently died of diphtheria, he decides to hole up at Soledad Crossing until the report is verified. Others at Soledad also hear the news and soon are gripped with fear that Bud may be carrying the dread disease.

Season Five

66.156 *The Vigil.* Sept. 16, 1961. GS: Mary Fickett, George Kennedy, Dan Stafford. Nurse Adella Forsyth is determined to go to a wild frontier town, even though she is warned that the citizens want a doctor, not a nurse. She gets a chance to test her determination when she and Paladin meet a pair of unkempt roughnecks along the trail.

66.157 *The Education of Sara Jane.* Sept. 23, 1961. GS: Jena Engstrom, Duane Eddy. Paladin is riding toward Portland when he comes upon the corpse of a man who has just been shot. Then he meets the dead man's young daughter, Sarah Jane Darrow. Sarah says there is a feud between the Darrows and the Whitneys, and she intends to avenge her fathers death by killing a Whitney, any Whitney.

66.158 *The Revenger.* Sept. 30, 1961. GS: Anthony Caruso, Rayford Barnes, Janet Lake, Russell Arms, Shug Fisher, Harry Carey, Jr. Paladin gets a message, accompanied by half of a $500 bill and a stage ticket to Yuma — and it takes him straight to a bandit chief.

66.159 *Odds for a Big Red.* Oct. 7, 1961. GS: Richard Ney, Hope Holiday, Virginia Capers, Ollie O'Toole, Robert Karnes, Perry Cook. In search of a killer, Paladin visits Big Red's Roundup, a saloon where his quarry hangs out. Sure enough, he's there, and in the ensuing showdown Big Red, the lady saloonkeeper, is seriously wounded.

66.160 *A Proof of Love.* Oct. 14, 1961. GS: Charles Bronson, George Kennedy, Shirley O'Hara, Chana Eden, Jack Marshal. The life of Henry Grey is bounded by his farming chores on one side and his domineering mother on the other. He expected the arrival of his mail-order bride, a girl named Callie, to help change all that, until neighbor Rud Saxon lures Callie over to his place.

66.161 *The Gospel Singer.* Oct. 21, 1961. GS: Suzi Carnell, John McLiam, Ed Peck, Noah Keen, Brad Weston, Roy Engel. The citizens of Bugbear are on a cleanup campaign. They have changed the name of the town to Elysium, and called in Paladin to help clear out the undesirables. On his way to his new job, Paladin encounters Melissa Griffin, who also intends to improve the moral climate of Elysium as a missionary.

66.162 *The Race.* Oct. 28, 1961. GS: Ben Johnson, Michael Pate, Stuart East. Offered a large sum to ride for unscrupulous Sam Crabbe in a Comanche horse race, in which anything goes, Paladin discovers Crabbe has bet his ranch against the entire Indian Reservation. Seeing that the Comanches will be at Crabbe's mercy if they lose, Paladin refuses the job and offers to ride for the Indians instead.

66.163 *The Hanging of Aaron Gibbs.* Nov. 4, 1961. GS: Rupert Crosse, Odetta, Barry Cahill, Ed Faulkner, Hal Needham, Roy Barcroft, Stuart East, Peggy Rea. Paladin meets Sarah Gibbs, whose husband, Aaron, has been sentenced to hang for murder. Sarah wants a last visit with her husband before he is executed, but the marshal says Aaron isn't allowed to have visitors.

66.164 *The Piano.* Nov. 11, 1961. GS: Keith Andes, Antoinette Bower, Richard Reeves, Gertrude Flynn, Arny Freeman, Erin Leigh. European pianist Franz Lister has been brought to America by wealthy Mona Lansing, a frontier hostess turned social climber. Then Lister's piano is stolen and held for ransom.

66.165 *Ben Jalisco.* Nov. 18, 1961. GS: Charles Bronson, Coleen Gray, John Litel, Chuck Roberson, Rick Silver, Lane Chandler. Ben Jalisco, a notorious murderer, has broken out of prison and there is not much doubt that he is looking for two people — his wife Lucy, who betrayed him — and Paladin who captured him.

66.166 *The Brothers.* Nov. 25, 1961. GS: Buddy Ebsen, Paul Hartman, Stuart East, Peggy Stewart, Edward Faulkner,

Hal Needham. A calculating beauty named Edna Raleigh wants to hire Paladin to kill Bram Holden, the man who murdered her husband and is now the power behind the throne in the town of Thornberg. Paladin refuses to accept Edna's plan, but he agrees to bring Holden back for trial.

66.167 *A Drop of Blood.* Dec. 2, 1961. GS: Martin Gabel, Roxanne Berard, Mike Kellin, Regina Gleason, Noah Keen, Red Morgan, Milton Selzer. Paladin is to be the best man at Rivka Shotness' wedding, but when he arrives he finds the place in great turmoil. Billy Buckstone, a killer the groom helped to convict, is free and on his way back.

66.168 *A Knight to Remember.* Dec. 9, 1961. GS: Hans Conried, Robert Carricart, Dolores Donlon, Wright King. Alessandro Caloca hires Paladin to find his lost father Don Esteban. Paladin locates the old man, charging around the country costumed as Don Quixote.

66.169 *Blind Circle.* Dec. 16, 1961. GS: Susan Davis, Hank Patterson, Ellen Atterbury, Harrison Lewis, Bob Jellison, Gerald Gordon. Law and order have finally come to the range and the cattlemen's association has forgiven the last of the rustlers who used to plague them. This means that old Jess Larker, the stockmen's bounty hunter, will have to retire, but Jess isn't in a forgiving mood and he doesn't intend to retire.

66.170 *Squatter's Rights* (A.K.A. "The Kid"). Dec. 23, 1961. GS: Flip Mark, Jacques Aubuchon, Roy Engel, Eleanor Audley, Ollie O'Toole. A tough miner named Moriarity is having a run of bad luck in a poker game with Paladin. Trying to get even, Moriarity puts up his final stakes — the right to his "Silver Strike" for a month. It turns out that Silver Strike is a he and not an it.

66.171 *Justice in Hell.* Jan. 6, 1962. GS: Strother Martin, Dabbs Greer, Chris Alcaide, L.Q. Jones, Gaylord Cavallero, Gerald Gordon. On the trail, Paladin meets a pair of rollicking prospectors who say they are searching for a man named Boise Peabody. They look innocent enough to Paladin, except for one thing. They are carrying a chorus girl's costume with them.

66.172 *The Mark of Cain.* Jan. 13, 1962. GS: Betsy Hale, Don Beddoe, William Schallert, Alan Carney, John Alderson, Larry Brightman. Paladin hears an odd story from Salem Wagner's ten-year-old granddaughter, Anne Marie, a recent survivor of an Indian massacre. The little girl says the leader of the attack on the wagon train was a white man named Doggett, the train's former wagon master.

66.173 *Lazarus.* Jan. 20, 1962. GS: Phil Coolidge, Roy Barcroft, Iphigenie Castiglioni, Olive Carey. Dr. Avatar claims that criminal tendencies can be determined by measuring a man's skull. He offers Paladin one thousand dollars to find a likely specimen, and Paladin thinks Jake Trueblood fills the bill.

66.174 *The Exiles.* Jan. 27, 1962. GS: Gerald Price, Jay Novello, Vivi Janiss, Richard Bermudez, Joan Tabor. Paladin is hired by Mexican General Ortega to find the Count and Countess Casares, exiles from the old Maximilian regime. Ortega says that they took with them a fortune in government bonds.

66.175 *The Hunt.* Feb. 3, 1962. GS: Leonid Kinskey, Joan Elan, Hank Patterson, Edward Faulkner, John Mitchum. When Paladin learns that Vanessa Stuart is about to lose her timberlands in Oregon, he goes to help her. Upon arriving, however, he discovers that Vanessa's story was only the bait used by a Russian prince, Radachev, who offers Paladin a large sum of money to match hunting skills with him.

66.176 *Dream Girl.* Feb. 10, 1962. GS: Hal Needham, Peggy Ann Garner, Joseph Dimmitt, Fred Hakim, Chuck Couch. A young prospector named Buddy has hit it rich, and now he intends to make his dreams come true. One of his dreams is to court a young lady named Ginger whom he met some years ago. But in order to do so, he must find her.

66.177 *One, Two, Three.* Feb. 17, 1962. GS: Robert F. Simon, Jack Elam, Lloyd Corrigan, Eve McVeagh, Barbara Pepper, Dorothy Dells, William Woodson, Dean Smith. Samuel H. Keel wants Paladin to find a man named Seth Carter. Keel has backed Carter in a big lottery, and astrological charts show that the missing man is destined to win.

66.178 *The Waiting Room.* Feb. 24, 1962. GS: James Griffith, Dean Stanton, George Cisar, Byron Foulger. Paladin answers a newspaper call for help. It seems that the Wilder brothers have to be taken from their jail cell in the Dakota Territory to the gallows in Texas, and so far every lawman who has agreed to try it has been killed by the Wilders' friends.

66.179 *The Trap.* March 3, 1962. GS: Jeanette Nolan, Frank Sutton, Crahan Denton, Ed Peck. Paladin, who is on the trail of a vicious killer, stops for the night at Jeri Marcus' trail lodge. It seems that Jeri also has two other guests, Marshal Jim Buell and his prisoner Davey Walsh, and somehow the marshal gets the idea that Paladin is there to help Walsh escape.

66.180 *Don't Shoot the Piano Player.* March 10, 1962. GS: George Kennedy, James Callahan, Fintan Meyler, Virginia Gregg, Mike Mazurki. Emily Eubanks asks Paladin to help locate her fiance Albert, a musician, who she thinks is hiding out somewhere along San Francisco's Barbary Coast. And Emily literally means help — because she intends to lead the search into the tough saloon area, and only wants Paladin as an escort.

66.181 *Alive.* March 17, 1962. GS: Jena Engstrom, Jeanette Nolan, Richard Shannon, Mary Gregory, William Stevens, Perry Cook. Paladin is approached by a girl named Maya who wants him to locate her mother. Maya, who has been attending school in the East, says she became alarmed when her tuition was cut off, just after her mother's letters suddenly changed in tone.

66.182 *The Man Who Struck Moonshine.* March 24, 1962. GS: William Conrad, Phyllis Avery. Moses Kadish is disappointed after he levels his buffalo gun at his target, squeezes the trigger and misses. But Paladin isn't, since he was the target.

66.183 *Silent Death.* March 31, 1962. GS: Robert Emhardt, John Holland, Michael Pate. Paladin is sent to find Courtney Burgess, a fellow who is reputed to be something of a bounder. Paladin's only clue is a letter Burgess wrote to his family from Sacramento, seven years earlier.

66.184 *Hobson's Choice.* April 7, 1962. GS: Milton Selzer, Parley Baer, Ollie O'Toole, Olan Soule, Titus Moede, Harrison Lewis, Jan Peters, Shawn Michaels. The Swedish inventor Alfred Nobel has moved into the hotel where Paladin lives in San Francisco. But when Mr. Cartwright, the manager, learns that Nobel is carrying samples of his latest creation, nitroglycerin, he wants the inventor to get out of the hotel.

66.185 *Coming of the Tiger.* April 14, 1962. GS: Marc

Have Gun, Will Travel

Marno, Teru Shimada, James Hong, Fuji, Bob Okazaki, Beulah Quo, Setsukuo Yamaji, Gerald Milton, William Wellman, Jr. Paladin learns from his friend Takura that militarists in the Japanese government are plotting war against the United States and intend to lay the groundwork by setting up a spy ring.

66.186 *Darwin's Man.* April 21, 1962. GS: Kent Smith, Richard Rust, Buzz Martin, Bud Osborne. There is trouble in the Coombs family. Tully send word that his father and his brother Jayce are trying to kill him. But the father, Avery Coombs, warns Paladin off.

66.187 *Invasion.* April 28, 1962. GS: Robert Gist, Lew Brown, Douglas Lambert, Roy Roberts, Robert Gibbons, Vicki Benet. The State Department asks Paladin for help with a delicate matter. He must explain to Irish patriot Gavin O'Shea that he cannot use the United States as a base for his invasion of Canada.

66.188 *Cream of the Jest.* May 5, 1962. GS: Stanley Adams, Jeff Davis, Catherine McLeod, Naomi Stevens, Peter Brocco. It's Paladin to the rescue when Caleb Musgrove announces that he has swallowed some poisoned water. But Caleb isn't grateful, he is only amused. This was his idea of a big practical joke.

66.189 *Bandit.* May 12, 1962. GS: Natalie Norwick, Robert Adler, Charles Couch, Jerry Gatlin, Hal Needham. Paladin searches for a stagecoach bandit who not only has earned a reputation as a killer, but who also has another distinction. The bandit is a woman.

66.190 *Pandora's Box.* May 19, 1962. GS: Martin West, Lorna Thayer, Ken Curtis, Lewis Martin, Mary Munday, Robert J. Stevenson, Jamie Brothers. A government official has a secret mission for Paladin. He is sent to find the official's son, whom he has never seen and who is wanted for murder.

66.191 *The Jonah.* May 26, 1962. GS: Crahan Denton, Richard Shannon, Harry Carey, Jr., Dorothy Dells. Carl Soddenberg was adjudged insane at a murder trial and committed to a mental institution. But now Carl's rehabilitation is almost complete and he appears well enough to re-enter society.

66.192 *The Knight.* June 2, 1962. GS: Jay Novello, Will Corey, Charles Kuenstle, Jean Innes. Family tradition has left Otto von Albrecht with a stern code of honor. But Otto is crippled and when he suffers an affront from Carl Frome, he goes to Paladin for help.

Season Six

66.193 *Genesis.* Sept. 15, 1962. GS: Richard Boone, James Mitchum, William Conrad, Parley Baer, Ann Morrison. After an unsuccessful attempt on his life, Paladin remembers a similar incident when he was a young gunfighter.

66.194 *Taylor's Woman.* Sept. 22, 1962. GS: Kathie Browne, Harry Carey, Jr., Tom Hennessey, Olan Soule. A reluctant Thad Taylor is about to marry his housekeeper Lydia. Thad, the timid type, is used to taking orders from Lydia, and she has ordered him to marry her.

66.195 *The Fifth Bullet.* Sept. 29, 1962. GS: Ben Johnson, Peter Boone, Dorothy Dells, Shug Fisher. Eight years earlier Paladin broke a promise to John Bartlett and since that time Bartlett has been in prison. Now he is being released. To make up for his breach of faith, Paladin promises to protect Bartlett from trouble on the trail home.

66.196 *A Place for Abel Hix.* Oct. 6, 1962. GS: Kevin Hagen, Robert Blake, Paul Tripp, Jean Engstrom, Linda Cordova. Paladin receives a request for help from aged gunfighter Abel Hix. But when he arrives in Hix's home town, Paladin discovers he has come a little late. Hix is about to be buried.

66.197 *Beau Beste.* Oct. 13, 1962. GS: Paul Richards, Faith Domergue, Henry Beckman, Ray Guth. Sheriff John Dobbs, reputed to be the West's fastest-drawing lawman, has announced his retirement. But now that he is no longer the law, gunmen are coming from all over to get even with him.

66.198 *The Bird of Time.* Oct. 20, 1962. GS: George Mathews, John Hoyt. Paladin and a man named Stryker are both on the trail of outlaw Ahab Tyson. Paladin wants to bring Tyson back alive, but Stryker is determined to shoot him on sight.

66.199 *Memories of Monica.* Oct. 27, 1962. GS: Judi Meredith, Bing Russell, Larry Ward, Hal Needham. While Ben Turner was in prison, his girl friend Monica married Sheriff Reagan. Now Turner is being released and he sends Reagan a message. He is coming back for Monica and the sheriff had better leave town before he and his gang arrive.

66.200 *The Predators.* Nov. 3, 1962. GS: Richard Jaeckel, Ellen Willard, Lester Maxwell. Paladin goes up against a ruthless young outlaw

66.201 *Shootout at Hogtooth.* Nov. 10, 1962. GS: Patrick McVey, Les Damon, Doodles Weaver, Ralph Bernard, Steven Piccaro. The citizen's council of Hogtooth City hired three tough gunslingers to impose law and order and rid the town of bad elements. Now the townsfolk have to find a way to get rid of the trio of gunmen, so they hire Paladin.

66.202 *A Miracle for St. Francis.* Nov. 17, 1962. GS: Rafael Campos, David Garner, Miriam Goldyn. A treasured statue is stolen from the San Luis Rey mission and Father Clare asks Paladin to recover it.

66.203 *Marshal of Sweetwater.* Nov. 24, 1962. GS: David White, Kathie Browne, Gordon Jones, Booth Colman, Paul Birch, John Matthews. Paladin's friend Tom Carey has become marshal of Sweetwater, but he is acting more like a dictator than a servant of the people. When Paladin comes to town, there is a possibility of a showdown, and Cary is one man who has always been able to beat Paladin to the draw.

66.204 *Man in an Hourglass.* Dec. 1, 1962. GS: Edgar Buchanan, Jim Stacy, Morgan Woodward, Alan Baxter, Jerry Gatlin. Young Johnny Tully is on the trail of a veteran gunfighter named Cardiff, who the boy believes murdered his father. Paladin's friend, Dr. Moody, wants Johnny headed off before he becomes a killer or a corpse.

66.205 *Penelope.* Dec. 8, 1962. GS: Joanna Barnes, Lawrence Dobkin, Jack Donner, Ivan Bonar. A year earlier, Col. Oliver Lacey left his wife Penelope to seek his fortune. Now he has returned home to find that Penelope has been seeking too. She hasn't been without male company while he was gone.

66.206 *Trial at Tablerock.* Dec. 15, 1962. GS: Sherwood Price, Barry Kelley, William Mims, Gregg Palmer, John Damier, Joey Higgins. Gunslinger Virge Beech is the most hated man in Tablerock and when Beech kills a man, he is charged with murder, even though everyone in Tablerock knows it was self-defense.

66.207 *Be Not Forgetful to Strangers.* Dec. 22, 1962. GS: Duane Eddy, Josie Lloyd, Roy Barcroft, Pat Newby,

Robert J. Stevenson, Ed Faulkner, Hal Needham. A young cowboy and his wife arrive in a small town during the Christmas season and are unable to obtain lodgings for the night. The woman is due to have a baby at any moment and, as a last resort, Paladin gets the saloon keeper to let the young couple stay in his storeroom.

66.208 *The Treasure.* Dec. 29, 1962. GS: Jeanne Cooper, Jim Davis, DeForest Kelley, Lee Van Cleef, Bob Woodward, Buck Taylor. Jess Harden is being released from prison, and his wife Edna is to meet him in the ghost town where he supposedly hid some stolen money. Edna hires Paladin to protect her interests in case anyone else tries to get the loot.

66.209 *Brotherhood.* Jan. 5, 1963. GS: Charles Bronson, Michael Keep, Max Mellinger, Shug Fisher, Dawn Little Sky, Warren Joslin. Indian sheriff Jim Redrock has offered a $200 reward for the capture of his brother Abe — and Abe has offered a $500 reward to anyone who captures his lawman brother.

66.210 *Bob Wire.* Jan. 12, 1963. GS: Woodrow Parfrey, Irish McCalla, Chris King, James Bell, Hal Baylor. Salesman Bob Wire discovers that there is money to be named selling his namesake — barbed wire. But cattlemen don't like range fences, and Wire is afraid that they might string him up, so he hires Paladin to protect him.

66.211 *The Debutante.* Jan. 19, 1963. GS: Robert Emhardt, Wayne Rogers, Eleanor Audley, Gale Garnett, L.Q. Jones. Wealthy Mrs. Quincy of Nob Hill believes that a girl in a small mining town upstate may be her missing granddaughter. Paladin locates the girl for Mrs. Quincy, but learns she is definitely not the type to hobnob with Nob Hill society.

66.212 *Unforgiving Minute.* Jan. 26,1963. GS: Patricia Medina, Al Ruscio. Sabina, the beautiful wife of a penurious potter named Machado is disgusted with her life of poverty. Sabina wants to start enjoying the luxuries that money can provide, and she feels that Paladin may be the answer to her problem.

66.213 *American Primitive.* Feb. 2, 1963. GS: Harry Morgan, Robert J. Wilke, Pitt Herbert, Peggy Rea. Sheriff Ernie Backwater asks his old friend Paladin to go hunting with him. The prey is Will Tybee, a vicious killer who escaped from jail and badly wounded Ernie in the process.

66.214 *The Burning Tree.* Feb. 9, 1963. GS: Elinor Donahue, Whit Bissell, Paul Fix. Paladin is bringing in a killer named Fairchild, but the citizens of Osage Springs demand that he turn the prisoner over to them. The nearby Osage Indians demand a white man's scalp every time one of their chiefs dies — and one just has.

66.215 *Cage at McNaab.* Feb. 16, 1963. GS: Lon Chaney, Jr., Christopher Dark, Jacqueline Scott, John Harmon. Paladin agrees to visit Nora Larson's husband, who is awaiting execution, and unwittingly becomes part of an escape plot that sees him trading places with the prisoner.

66.216 *Caravan.* Feb. 23, 1963. GS: Miriam Colon, Dolores Faith, Cliff Osmond, Hal Needham, John Alderson. Paladin is hired to protect Skiri, a Nepalese princess, who is in danger of assassination by killers from her homeland.

66.217 *The Walking Years.* March 2, 1963. GS: Ellen Willard, Jacqueline Wilson, Satenio Donigan, Fred Hakim, Stewart East, Hal Needham. Paladin, an alcoholic named Alice, and a gentleman named Wiggen are sharing the same peculiar fate. Someone has imprisoned them in a San Francisco warehouse.

66.218 *Sweet Lady of the Moon.* March 9, 1963. GS: Crahan Denton, Richard Shannon, Dorothy Dells, Harry Carey, Jr., Robert J. Stevenson. Paladin is escorting homicidal maniac Carl Soddenberg to an asylum, but the relatives of one of Soddenberg's victims don't intend to let him get there alive.

66.219 *The Savages.* March 16, 1963. GS: Patric Knowles, Judi Meredith, James Griffith. French art collector August Pireaux persuades Paladin to help him find a famous English sculptor named Spencer, who has sought seclusion in the wilderness.

66.220 *The Eve of St. Elmo.* March 23, 1963. GS: Warren Stevens, Brett Somers, George Kennedy, Chris Alcaide, P.L. Smith, Jerry Summers. Colonel Draco, paralyzed after a gunfight with Brock March, wants revenge and he wants Paladin to do the job for him.

66.221 *The Lady of the Fifth Moon.* March 30, 1963. GS: Bethel Leslie, William Schallert. When the members of a Chinese tong demand that Kim Sing serve as payment for the debts of her deceased father, Kim Sing's grandmother asks Paladin to protect the girl.

66.222 *Two Plus One.* April 6, 1963. GS: Susan Silo, Gail Kobe, Ken Hudgkins, Rex Holman. En route to a rendezvous with his old sweetheart Francine, Paladin rescues an Indian girl from outlaws — a girl who tells him that she belongs to him now, and will never leave him.

66.223 *The Black Bull.* April 13, 1963. GS: Carlos Romero, Faith Domergue, Lita Marsell. Revenge brings matador Nino Ybarra out of retirement for one last fight in the arena, with Paladin as his intended prey.

66.224 *Face of a Shadow.* April 20, 1963. GS: Enid Jaynes, Lee Van Cleef, Nestor Paiva, Richard Reed, Harry Carey, Jr., Rayford Barnes, Roy Barcroft, William Woodson. A bank hires Paladin to pick up a large sum of money from rancher Dan Tibner, but Tibner is murdered and the money stolen, and the chief suspects are a band of Gypsies.

66.225 *The Sanctuary.* June 22, 1963. GS: Harry Carey, Jr., Hank Patterson, Jerry Summers. A fortune in gold bullion, dumped in Crystal Lake during a holdup, is perfectly visible through the clear water though it can be reached only with deep-sea diving equipment.

66.226 *The Mountebank.* Aug. 3, 1963. GS: Warren Stevens, Robert J. Stevenson, Natalie Norwick, Carlos Romero, Sandy Kenyon, Warren Joslin. To settle the score with a squatter who ran him off his land, a rancher named Costigan organizes a small army of gunmen, one of whom is Paladin.

67. Hawkeye

Syndicated. 60 min. Broadcast history: Various, Sept. 1994–Aug. 1995.

Regular Cast: Lee Horsley (Hawkeye), Lynda Carter (Elizabeth Shields), Rodney A. Grant (Chingachgook), Garwin Sanford (Capt. Taylor Shields), Lochlyn Munro (McKinney), Jed Rees (Peevey).

Premise: This series was set in New York's Hudson Valley during the French and Indian War in the 1750s and depicted the adventures of James Fenimore Cooper's legendary pathfinder Hawkeye.

The Episodes

67.1 *Pilot* Part One. Sept. 14, 1994. GS: Eric Keenleyside, Richard Sali, Michael Berry, Rick Burgess, David MacKay. Hawkeye saves Virginia merchant William Shields and his wife, Elizabeth, when they are ambushed by hostile Indians.

67.2 *Pilot* Part Two. Sept. 21, 1994. GS: Eric Keenleyside, Richard Sali, Michael Berry, Rick Burgess, David MacKay. Hawkeye and Elizabeth get a taste of the French and Indian War when they head off to negotiate for the release of Elizabeth's husband, who has been captured by the French.

67.3 *The Bear.* Sept. 28, 1994. GS: Andrew Kavadas, Tom McBeath, Mitch Kosterman, Forbes Angus, Ian Black, Luc Corbeil, Kirk Jarrett, John McLaren. Elizabeth's lesson in wilderness-survival skills, and Hawkeye's reading lesson, are interrupted by ammunition thieves bent on selling their stolen goods to the French.

67.4 *The Furlough.* Oct. 5, 1994. GS: Jill Teed, Eli Gabay, Annie Charles, Kate Twa, David McKay, David MacNiven, Lorne Cardinal. Hawkeye saves a settler from the French trader who kidnapped her, and kills him in the process, prompting revenge from the trader's Huron allies.

67.5 *The Siege.* Oct. 12, 1994. GS: Duncan Fraser, John Novak, Barry Greene, Peter Kelamis, Robert Lewis, Christopher Newton. All is gloomy at Fort Bennington. The French are laying siege and, rumor has it, will soon be reinforced with a huge cannon.

67.6 *The Child.* Oct. 19, 1994. GS: Tamsin Kelsey, Chris Humphreys, Byron Chief-Moon, Gungarie O'Sullivan. Hurons kidnap an infant from Fort Bennington and an attempt to get the child back could spark a war.

67.7 *The Vision.* Nov. 2, 1994. GS: Daniel Richer, D. Martin Pera, Jesse Moss, Sandra Ferens, Beverly Elliott, Margo Kane, Dave "Squatch" Ward. Chingachgook has a fatal vision of Hawkeye being killed by hostile Indians.

67.8 *Out of the Past.* Nov. 9, 1994. GS: Ron Ely, Evan Adams, Dave "Squatch" Ward, Simon Baker, Oliver Becker, Janet Craig, Margo Kane, Nick Misura. Hawkeye's old mentor arrives at Fort Bennington — not for a reunion but for revenge — and Elizabeth is his bait.

67.9 *Warrior.* Nov. 16, 1994. GS: Duncan Fraser, Jonathan Scarfe, Garry Chalk, Philip Hayes, Mark Abbott, Robin Mossley, Mark Saunders. Elizabeth's nephew realizes his dream of becoming a soldier, but when his courage fails in battle, Hawkeye and Chingachgook step in to help.

67.10 *The Quest.* Nov. 23, 1994. GS: Lindsey Ginter, Zoltan Buday, Richard Faraci, Dave "Squatch" Ward. When a stranger offers — for a hefty fee — to lead Elizabeth to William, a suspicious Taylor and Hawkeye insist on going along.

67.11 *The Ally.* Jan. 19, 1995. GS: Eric Schweig, Marianne Jones. A provoked attack on Taylor prompts the captain to ban the Delaware tribe, Chingachgook included, from Fort Bennington.

67.12 *The Boxer.* Jan. 26, 1995. GS: Edward Albert, Ken Kirzinger, Braun McAsh. An enigmatic French prisoner intrigues Hawkeye, who begins to believe that the soldier may not be what he seems.

67.13 *The Traitor.* Feb. 2, 1995. GS: Duncan Fraser, Scott McNeil, Jason Gray-Stanford, Hrothgar Mathews, Darren Adam, Andrew Airlie, Forbes Angus, Patrick Madden, Rob Morton. Taylor has Hawkeye tried for treason when the captain is shot soon after a heated argument between the two men. But Hawkeye's sense of honor hinders Elizabeth's efforts to prove his innocence.

67.14 *Amnesty.* Feb. 9, 1995. GS: Anthony DeLongis, Dmitry Chepovetsky, Demetri Goritsas, David MacNiven, Vince Metcalfe. Hawkeye fumes when Taylor grants a pardon to a recalcitrant soldier in exchange for crucial information about the French.

67.15 *Vengeance Is Mine.* Feb. 23, 1995. GS: Michael Horse, Renae Morriseau, Chilton Crane, Myles Ferguson, Robin Hildred, David Justason, David MacNiven, Dan Shea, Norman Browning, Bill Croft. The capture of a Huron chief's wife leads Hawkeye to his parent's killer, and even Elizabeth may not be able to stop him from taking revenge.

67.16 *The Plague.* March 2, 1995. GS: Larry Sellers, Andrew Wheeler, Margo Kane, Stefany Mathias, D. Martin Pera. A chief blames Elizabeth for a smallpox epidemic that spreads shortly after her inadvertent violation of sacred Indian ground.

67.17 *Fly with Me.* March 29, 1995. GS: Robert Wisden, Roger R. Cross, Danny Virtue, Dave "Squatch" Ward, David MacKay, Mark Abbott, Simon Baker, Fred McKenzie, Milton Murrill, Topaz Hasfal-Schou. Hawkeye and Chingachgook conspire to help two runaway slaves being returned to their owner by a Virginia gentleman.

67.18 *Hester.* April 26, 1995. GS: Charlene Fernetz, Doug Abrahams, James Bell, Ron Cook, Patrick T. Gorman, Mark Hildreth, Simon Juan Sobolewski, Malcolm Stewart, Simon Juan. A Massachusetts woman with mysterious healing powers struggles to save Fort Bennington from an epidemic, only to be branded a witch.

67.19 *The Bounty.* May 3, 1995. GS: Sara Sawatsky, Lori Ann Triolo, Tom Cavanaugh, Robert Lewis, Marc Baur, Michael Dobson, Don Shea, Michael Tiernan. An old friend appeals to Hawkeye to help free her brother-in-law from his captors, but, to complicate matters, the enemy has put a bounty on Hawkeye's head.

67.20 *The Return.* May 10, 1994. GS: Michael Berry, Yvan LaBelle. William Shields comes home, but while Elizabeth struggles to make a decision about her future, Chingachgook questions William's association with a shaman who practices black arts.

67.21 *The Visit.* May 24, 1995. GS: James Cromwell, Oliver Becker, Shaun Johnston, Beverly Elliott, Patrick Madden, Inez Point, Jim Smith, Michael Terry. Elizabeth resists her father's efforts to bring her back to Virginia — even after Taylor produces new evidence about her missing husband.

67.22 *The Escape.* Aug. 16, 1995. GS: Steve Makaj. The brother of a man Taylor had executed seeks revenge by luring the captain and Elizabeth on a business expedition that will lead to their capture by the French.

68. Hawkeye and the Last of the Mohicans

Syndicated. 30 min. Broadcast history: Various, April 1957–Dec. 1957.

Regular Cast: John Hart (Hawkeye), Lon Chaney, Jr. (Chingachgook).

Premise: This series was set in New York's Hudson Valley during the French and Indian War in the 1750s and depicted the adventures of James Fenimore Cooper's legendary pathfinder Hawkeye and his Indian blood brother Chingachgook, the last member of the Mohican tribe.

The Episodes

68.1 *Hawkeye's Homecoming.* April 3, 1957. GS: Michael Ansara, Lili Fontaine. Hawkeye returns to his home.

68.2 *The Threat.* April 10, 1957. A group of settlers from England head for the wilderness guided by two scouts. In the depths of the Huron territory they find themselves at the mercy of the two men. Hawkeye and Chingachgook, suspicious when the settlers are not heard from, set out to find them.

68.3 *Franklin Story.* April 17, 1957. GS: Stan Francis. Hawkeye and Chingachgook call on Ben Franklin for help to prevent a dictator from taking over a frontier town.

68.4 *The Wild One.* April 24, 1957. GS: Fred Euringer. Hawkeye and Chingachgook come to the aid of a young Indian doctor who attempts to practice in an intolerant frontier town.

68.5 *The Delaware Hoax.* May 1, 1957. GS: William Walker, Alex Denaszody. Hawkeye and Chingachgook learn that the Delaware tribe has been framed for the murder of several white men.

68.6 *The Coward.* May 8, 1957. A father and son are attacked while going for help during an Indian raid. When the boy flees, leaving his father for dead, the man thinks his son is a coward.

68.7 *Ethan Allen Story.* May 15, 1957. Hawkeye and Chingachgook are sent to investigate the complaint of Sheriff Peterson that Ethan Allen and his boys are committing crimes.

68.8 *The Witch.* May 22, 1957. GS: Arch McDonell. Weird incidents terrorize a frontier town. In spite of Hawkeye's efforts to disprove the witch stories, strange murders increase the settlers horror.

68.9 *The Medicine Man.* May 29, 1957. Hawkeye and Chinyachgook find an old medicine man of the Conestoga tribe wandering in the wilderness. He tells them he hwas been driven out by the Shenahbe of the same tribe.

68.10 *The Servant.* June 5, 1957. GS: Len Ontkean, Iris Krangle. Hawkeye and Chingachgook are given authority to investigate the claims that servants are being sold into bondage. They learn that an unscrupulous farmer is behind the illegal transactions.

68.11 *The Search.* June 12, 1957. GS: Larry Solway. After rescuing an elderly white woman from two Indian warriors, Hawkeye and Chingachgook learn that she has been a slave since her husband was killed.

68.12 *Snake Tattoo.* June 19, 1957. GS: Daryl Masters, Bob Ellison, Richmond Nairne. Hawkeye and Chingachgook try to help a young Indian boy who has been raised by the white man. They learn that the youngster is really the son of the Cree chief.

68.13 *False Witness.* June 26, 1957. Hawkeye and Chingachgook are assigned to investigate a series of robberies of Army payrolls.

68.14 *Powder Keg.* July 3, 1957. GS: William Walker. An unscrupulous fur trader organizes the hostile Huron tribes.

68.15 *The Scapegoat.* July 10, 1957. GS: Jonathan White, Bruce Webb. Hawkeye tries to help his friend, the Chief of the Tuscarora tribe, who is threatened with starvation in a rugged winter.

68.16 *Way Station.* July 17, 1957. Hawkeye and Chingachgook are taken prisoner by a band of armed warriors. They learn they are blamed for wounding a young brave.

68.17 *The Brute.* July 24, 1957. GS: Bill Walker. A kindly man with the mentality of a child is forced to join a gang of marauding desperadoes.

68.18 *Stubborn Pioneer.* July 31, 1957. A leader of a group of settlers ignores warnings and leads his people into hostile Huron territory.

68.19 *The Promised Valley.* Aug. 7, 1957. GS: William Walsh, Larry O'Connor. A fierce and unscrupulous brave of the Tuscarora tribe plots to overthrow Chief Tawenduma. Hawkeye and Chingachgook come onto the scene in time to save the Chief from ambush.

68.20 *The Girl.* Aug. 14, 1957. GS: Peegen Rose, Peter Humphreys. An unscrupulous girl uses trickery to anger the Iroquois tribe into war against the whites.

68.21 *The Soldier.* Aug. 21, 1957. GS: Mike Julian. Hawkeye and Chingachgook are called upon to investigate a problem between the Indians and the army.

68.22 *Huron Tomahawk.* Aug. 28, 1957. GS: Brian Smyth. A young man on his way to be married, finds that his fiancee and her family have been massacred, apparently by marauding Huron braves.

68.23 *Tolliver Gang.* Sept. 4, 1957. GS: John Vernon. Hawkeye and Chingachgook join a pirate band to rescue two women.

68.24 *The Colonel and His Lady.* Sept. 11, 1957. Hawkeye and Chingachgook attempt to prove that Chief Black Wolf and his tribe are innocent of attacking white settlers.

68.25 *Washington Story.* Sept. 18, 1957. GS: Rodney Bunker, Dawn Losley. Hawkeye and Chingachgook save a pretty girl and a young prospector from angry trappers who feel that the newcomers are threatening their hunting and trapping preserves.

68.26 *Winter Passage.* Sept. 25, 1957. When a party of women insist on taking a legendary pass to join their husbands, Hawkeye attempts to save them from treachery.

68.27 *The Reckoning.* Oct. 2, 1957. A young lieutenant comes home to find his boyhood friend an enemy.

68.28 *La Salle's Treasure.* Oct. 9, 1957. GS: Rodney Bunker, John Harding. Three greedy fortune hunters hire Hawkeye and Chingachgook to locate a treasure.

68.29 *The Prisoner.* Oct. 16, 1957. While taking a lieutenant accused of violating an Indian treaty to trial, Hawkeye and Chingachgook stop at an Indian village.

68.30 *False Faces.* Oct. 23, 1957. GS: William Walsh, Peter Humphreys, Larry Mann, Helen Gilbert. A gang of desperadoes raids trappers and isolated settlers.

68.31 *The Morristown Story.* Oct. 30, 1957. GS: Powys Thomas, George Barnes, Beryl Braithwaite, Juan Root. Hawkeye and Chingachgook are barred from entering a city because of a plague.

68.32 *Revenge.* Nov. 6, 1957. A Shawnee war chief kills the parents of a young lieutenant, who then swears vengeance.

68.33 *The Contest.* Nov. 13, 1957. GS: Jim Barron. When two thieves masquerade as Hawkeye and Chingachgook, the woodman and his friend have ten days to prove their innocence.

68.34 *The Truant.* Nov. 20, 1957. Hawkeye and Chingachgook accompany an orphaned boy, the heir to a silver mine, to his new frontier home.

68.35 *The Royal Grant.* Nov. 27, 1957. GS: Brian Smyth, Iris Krangle. A young couple who own a trading post is terrorized by Millard Cressing, who claims to own the territory by royal grant.

68.36 *The Long Rifles.* Dec. 4, 1957. Angry settlers blame gunsmith Eben Cotton and his daughter Beth for illegally selling rifles to the Ojibwas.

68.37 *The Printer.* Dec. 11, 1957. Hawkeye and Chingachgook arrive in a frontier town to deliver type from Ben Franklin.

68.38 *The Indian Doll.* Dec. 18, 1957. A medicine man, wishing to bring discredit to the whites, drugs the chief's daughter. He blames a gift from Hawkeye for casting the spell on the child.

68.39 *Circle of Hate.* Dec. 25, 1957. A young Army lieutenant whose family has been wiped out by Indians, nurses a bitter hatred for the Redmen.

69. Hec Ramsey

NBC. 90 min. Broadcast history: Sunday, 8:30–10:00, Oct. 1972–Aug. 1974.

Regular Cast: Richard Boone (Hec Ramsey), Richard Lenz (Sheriff Oliver B. Stamp), Harry Morgan (Doc Amos B. Coogan), Dennis Rucker (Arne Tornquist), Sharon Acker (Norma Muldoon), Brian Dewey (Andy Muldoon).

Premise: Hec Ramsey is an aging lawman in turn-of-the-century Oklahoma. He has hung up his old six-gun and uses his brain and the primitive beginnings of early-day criminal science.

Notes: This series rotated with *Columbo*, *McMillan and Wife* and *McCloud* as part of the *NBC Sunday Mystery Movie*.

The Episodes

69.1 *The Century Turns.* Nov. 8, 1972. GS: R.G. Armstrong, Robert Pratt, Ray Middleton, Dick Van Patten, William Vint, Robert Phillips. Hec Ramsey accepts a job as the new deputy in New Prospect, Oklahoma. When the stagecoach he is riding in to his new job his held up, he is arrested because of his gunslinger past. To clear himself Ramsey puts his scientific expertise to use when a double murder gives the West its first look at a ballistics test.

69.2 *Hangman's Wages.* Oct. 29, 1972. GS: Stella Stevens, Steve Forrest, Lee H. Montgomery, Perry Lopez, Abner Biberman, Murray Matheson, Richard Roat. The electric chair's Western debut awaits a captured killer, but someone is out to spoil the show. Anonymous threats are made that there will be a murder a day until the condemned prisoner is released.

69.3 *The Green Feather Mystery.* Dec. 17, 1972. GS: Rory Calhoun, Lorraine Gary, Alan Hewitt, Morgan Woodward, Lloyd Bochner, Marie Windsor. Hec is out to clear some innocent Indians and catch the real killers of three ranchers. Color blindness plays the bizarre key to solving the mystery.

69.4 *The Mystery of the Yellow Rose.* Jan. 28, 1973. GS: Diana Muldaur, Claude Akins, David Brian, Don Stroud, Philip Bourneuf, Ian Wolfe, Virginia Gregg, Francine York, Ken Renard. Hec plays lawyer for a former girlfriend. His old flame is accused of killing the son of the richest man in New Mexico, a man who controls both the sheriff and the judge.

69.5 *The Mystery of Chalk Hill.* Feb. 18, 1973. GS: Pat Hingle, Bruce Davison, Jeanette Nolan, Bernie Hamilton, Louise Latham, John Anderson, Lee Paul, Henry Jones, Robert Fuller. Hec begins a personal vendetta when he hunts for his fiancee's murderer. She and her son were killed during a stagecoach robbery. His chief suspect is the son of an old friend and fellow lawman.

Season Two

69.6 *A Hard Road to Vengeance.* Nov. 25, 1973. GS: Stuart Whitman, Ruth Roman, Keenan Wynn, Rita Moreno, James G. Richardson, Jean Allison, Harry Hickox, Fred Brookfield. A dead man becomes a legend and the ex-marshal who shot him becomes a pariah. The young folk hero was really a cold-blooded killer, but the worshipful townsfolk refuse to believe it. Hec tries to expose the dead man for the psychopathic killer that he was.

69.7 *The Detroit Connection.* Dec. 30, 1973. GS: Angie Dickinson, Kim Hunter, Luther Adler, Richard Jordan, Marshall Thompson, Frank Campanella, Kelly Thordsen. Ramsey is pitted against a crime syndicate who are victimizing impoverished oil-drillers who find themselves in trouble when they naively accept loans from the organization's henchmen.

69.8 *Dead Heat.* Feb. 3, 1974. GS: Jackie Cooper, Sheree North, Art Lund, John Anderson, Russell Wiggins, Tani Phelps Guthrie, Alfred Ryder, Dennis Rucker, Dee Carroll. An apparently healthy young man has died of heart failure, but skeptical Hec is not convinced that it happened naturally. Despite opposition from the townsfolk, he tries to prove that the man was murdered.

69.9 *Scar Tissue.* March 10, 1974. GS: Kurt Russell, Chill Wills, Dick Haymes, Charles Aidman, William Campbell, Hilarie Thompson, Albert Salmi, Jason Evers, Tom Drake. A hotheaded young gunslinger comes into town with a violent quest for revenge. He is bent on finding and killing his footloose father, who deserted his mother many years before. When the father is murdered Hec tries to prove that the young man is not the guilty party.

69.10 *Only Birds and Fools.* April 7, 1974. GS: Robert Foxworth, Cliff Potts, Charles Aidman, Fionnuala Flanagan, Harold J. Stone. A turn-of-the-century town is buzzing over an impossible dream — man in flight. The furor is created by two characters who have arrived to test out a glider, and have become suspects in the murder of a rival flier.

70. Here Come the Brides

ABC. 60 min. Broadcast history: Wednesday, 7:30-8:30, Sept. 1968–Sept. 1969; Friday, 9:00-10:00, Sept. 1969–Sept. 1970.

Regular Cast: Robert Brown (Jason Bolt), David Soul (Joshua Bolt), Bobby Sherman (Jeremy Bolt), Mark Lenard (Aaron Stempel), Henry Beckman (Clancey), Joan Blondell (Lottie Hatfield), Bridget Hanley (Candy Pruitt), Susan Tolsky (Biddie Cloom), Mitzi Hoag (Essie), Hoke Howell (Ben Jenkins), Bo Svenson (Big Swede), Carol Shelyne (Franny), Cynthia Hull (Ann), Robert Biheller (Corky), Lindsay Workman (Reverend Adams), Eric Chase (Christopher Pruitt) 69-70, Patti Cohoon (Molly Pruitt) 69-70.

Premise: Logging camp operator Jason Bolt and his two brothers, Jeremy and Joshua, bring over one hundred prospective brides to their disgruntled workers in the Seattle timberlands in the 1870s.

The Episodes

70.1 *Here Come the Brides*. Sept. 25, 1968. GS: James Almanzar, Dick Balduzzi, Barry Cahill, Buck Kartalian, Andy Romano, Vic Tayback, Gordon Jump, Diane Sayer, Elaine Joyce, Judy Cassmore, Karen Carlson, Jeanne Sheffield. Threatened with a walkout at his Seattle logging camp, Jason Bolt promises his men what they want — brides. But making good on the deal means a trip to Massachusetts, where Jason and his brothers must find 100 marriageable women and persuade them to make the return voyage.

70.2 *A Crying Need*. Oct. 2, 1968. GS: Kathleen Widdoes, Arthur Space, Dolores Mann, Karen Wolff, Pat Delaney, Buck Kartalian. Demands for a doctor in Seattle send Jason to San Francisco, where the only available medic turns out to be a sharp-tongued woman. Meanwhile, back at the camp, the younger Bolts face a monumental log jam.

70.3 *And Jason Makes Five*. Oct. 9, 1968. GS: Jennifer West, Bill Zuckert, Linda Sue Risk, Maralee Foster, Barry Cahill, James Almanzar, Diane Sayer, Eric Shea, Susan Michaels, Hollis Morrison, Dick Balduzzi. A freewheeling female fur-trapper with three children in tow, arrives in Seattle, determined to snare a husband. Her choice is Jason Bolt, who has a lot of explaining to do when the girl claims he fathered her little ones.

70.4 *Man in the Family*. Oct. 16, 1968. GS: William Schallert, Loretta Leversee, Stefan Arngrim, Elaine Joyce, Angel Tompkins, Karl Lukas, Elaine Fielding, Don Kennedy. A camp-wide crises occurs when bride-to-be Polly Black turns out o be a widow with a son who opposes his mother's planned marriage.

70.5 *A Hard Card to Play*. Oct. 23, 1968. GS: Sheree North, Phil Burns, Allen Jaffe, Helen Page Camp, Christopher Stone. Gambling fever grips the loggers when a trio of professionals sets up business in Seattle. A petition is soon circulated to stop the action, as the men ignore their jobs, and the brides, to try their luck at the gaming tables.

70.6 *Letter of the Law*. Oct. 30, 1968. GS: John Marley, Larry D. Mann, James Almanzar, Heidy Hunt, Michael Murphy, Buck Kartalian. Seattle's first sheriff starts a clean-up campaign that has the whole camp protesting. The unbending lawman has imposed a curfew, closed the saloon and infuriated the town leaders who signed him to an ironclad contract.

70.7 *Lovers and Wanderers*. Nov. 6, 1968. GS: Majel Barrett, Mills Watson, Hollis Morrison, Dick Balduzzi, Karen Carlson, Andy Romano. The romance of Swede and Miss Essie hits the skids and so may the Bolts' logging business. Swede has left town, the other loggers are talking strike, and time is running out on an all-important lumber contract.

70.8 *A Jew Named Sullivan*. Nov. 20, 1968. GS: Dan Travanty, Linda Marsh, Kristina Holland, Mary Wilcox, George Renschler. Jason has his hands full trying to aid the rocky romance of a hard-drinking logger and a lovely young bride. It seems the only thing the couple have in common is their Jewish faith.

70.9 *Stand Off*. Nov. 27, 1968. GS: Don Pedro Colley, Gary Dubin, Gordon De Vol, Buck Kartalian, Stefanianna Christopherson. Seattle is the combat area when the loggers take on Stempel's hired guards over rights to a roadway. To quell the fighting, the brides borrow a gambit from the Greek comedy "Lysistrata", denying the men any and all signs of affection.

70.10 *A Man and His Magic*. Dec. 4, 1968. GS: Jack Albertson, George Simms, Darryl Seman. Merlin, a drummer, brings elixirs, goods and magic to flood-threatened Seattle. Merlin sets up shop in town where his incantations coincide with a break in the weather to bring out some confident customers, including Jeremy who hopes to cure his stuttering.

70.11 *A Christmas Place*. Dec. 18, 1968. GS: Dolores Mann, Michael Bell, Erica Petal, Christie Matchett. All Seattle joyously awaits a baby's birth on Christmas Day, except for two little sisters. In their innocent confusion, they fear the infant may share the same fate as Jesus.

70.12 *After a Dream Comes Mourning*. Jan. 1, 1969. GS: Marvin Silbersher, Karen Carlson. The brides' early days in Seattle are recalled — the Bolts try to build a dormitory, despite Stempel's scheming, the ladies suffer homesickness, and they run into a stubborn Captain Clancey.

70.13 *The Log Jam*. Jan. 8, 1969. GS: Sam Melville, Pamela Dunlap, Todd Garrett, Dick Balduzzi. Waning romantic interest on the part of the loggers, and a broken engagement between Candy and Jeremy, prompts the brides to stage a freeze, interspersed with threats to return East.

70.14 *The Firemaker*. Jan. 15, 1969. GS: Monte Markham, Edward Asner, Hagan Beggs, Stefani Warren, James McCallion, Joan Dolan. Jason is wagering that one of his loggers will beat out Stempel's accountant for the hand of Lulu Bright. But Jason's chances dwindle when the man he is backing is suspected of arson and flees Seattle.

70.15 *Wives for Wakando*. Jan. 22, 1969. GS: Michael Ansara, Susan Howard, William Smith, William H. Bassett, Diane Sayer, Hollis Morrison, Karen Carlson, Mary Angela, Bert Santos. Jason and his brothers plot a trick mission — rescuing three brides who have been kidnaped by Chief Wakando. The chief's peaceful tribe is suffering a familiar problem — a dearth of females.

70.16 *A Kiss Just for You*. Jan. 29, 1969. GS: Kathryn Hays, Michael Forest, Rhys Williams, Gary Pillar, Barry Williams, Ralph Mara. Amish settlers stopping in Seattle cause a series of crises for Jason. The immigrants dress and manner create resentment, prejudice and fear, and their presence adds fuel to the strike plans of a militant logger. Added to all this is Jason's attraction to a beautiful Amish schoolteacher.

70.17 *Democracy Inaction.* Feb. 5, 1969. GS: Logan Ramsey, Raymond Kark, Bill Erwin. Loggers, brides and mill workers alike leap into politics, as Seattle seeks to become a legal community. The first venture, is a vigorous campaign for mayor with three candidates — Joshua Bolt, Aaron Stempel, and schoolteacher Essie, who is being supported by the newly-enfranchised females.

70.18 *One Good Lie Deserves Another.* Feb. 12, 1969. GS: Lew Ayres, Gene Tyburn. Smooth-talking Matthew Muncey intends to take Seattle by storm, and by fraud. First the con man romances Lottie into selling him part of the saloon, then he zeroes in on the brides and their newly acquired parcels of land.

70.19 *None to a Customer.* Feb. 19, 1969. GS: Peter Jason, Tina Holland, James Almanzar, Buck Kartalian. Mormon rancher Adam Wilson sends a shock wave through Seattle when he starts courting not one bride, but several. Trouble begins when five ladies, intent on making the loggers jealous, decide to accept the polygamist's proposals.

70.20 *A Dream That Glitters.* Feb. 26, 1969. GS: Will Geer, Buck Kartalian, Ed McCready, Mary Angela. Joy mixes with melancholy after Candy's grandad arrives. The old man, tired and ill, has come to the Northwest on a seemingly hopeless quest for gold.

70.21 *The Crimpers.* March 5, 1969. GS: Rosemary De Camp, Ben Alish, Dennis Fimple, Warren Munson, Jack Perkins. With the aid of Clancey and Stempel, Jason whips up a scheme to rescue his brothers, who've been shanghaied. The trio sets sail on the risky mission, unaware that their ship is carrying stowaway Candy and Biddie.

70.22 *Mr. and Mrs. J. Bolt.* March 12, 1969. GS: Henry Jones, Mary Jo Kennedy, Shorty Rogers. Joshua pretends he has wed one of the girls to prevent her from being shipped back East. The scheme backfires when her crafty guardian sees the marriage as a financial windfall, and tries to grab part of the Bolts' logging camp.

70.23 *A Man's Errand.* March 19, 1969. GS: John Anderson, Jeff Pomeranz, Larry D. Mann, Ceil Cabot. Jeremy is in San Francisco to bid on a logging contract, and girl friend Candy has all of Seattle buzzing. She is being seen in the company of a handsome logger.

70.24 *Loggerheads.* March 26, 1969. GS: Hal England, Alan Oppenheimer, Christopher Stone, Bill Zuckert. A policy fight between Jason and Joshua ripens them for a pair of swindling lawyers. The shysters' plan is to widen the chasm between the brothers and open the way for a Stempel takeover.

70.25 *Marriage Chinese Style.* April 9, 1969. GS: Linda Dangcil, Bruce Lee, Richard Loo Jeff De Benning, Nora Marlowe, Helen Kleeb, Weaver Levy, Myra De Groot, Hideo Imamura, Jack Perkins. A lovely Chinese girl unwittingly makes life miserable for Jeremy Bolt, who saved her life. Toy Quan feels honorbound to be Jeremy's devoted woman, which has Candy fuming and a tong society plotting revenge.

70.26 *The Deadly Trade.* April 16, 1969. GS: R.G. Armstrong, Jacqueline Scott, Ross Hagen, Murray MacLeod, X Brands, William Bassett, Christopher Shea, Ronald Feinberg. All of Seattle, especially the Bolts, face threats of violence from a vengeful old trapper whose son was killed in a logging accident.

Season Two

70.27 *A Far Cry from Yesterday.* Sept. 26, 1969. GS: William Schallert, Scoey Mitchlll. Candy is suddenly thrust into the role of guardian when word of her mother's death reaches Seattle — just after the arrival of her young sister and brother.

70.28 *The Wealthiest Man in Seattle.* Oct. 3, 1969. GS: Bernard Fox, Mills Watson, Ken Swofford, Felton Perry, Hagan Beggs, Dick Balduzzi. Seattle unites to transform booze hound Clancey into the town's classiest, wealthiest citizen. The purpose is to impress his visiting brother, a priest. Unfortunately, three bandits, taken in by the hoax, plan to rob the phony old moneybags.

70.29 *The Soldier.* Oct. 10, 1969. GS: Steve Ihnat, James Sikking, Christopher Stone, George Clifton, William Engel, Robert Bilheiler. The killing of a grizzly turns from triumph to tragedy for Jeremy Bolt, who shot the wrong bear. His prey was the tame mascot of a near-by Cavalry unit, and its death has spurred a soldier to swear revenge.

70.30 *Next Week, East Lynne.* Oct. 17, 1969. GS: Donald Moffat, Jayne Meadows, Susan Silo, Paul Marin, Ira Ireland, Gordon De Vol, Peter Lawrence, William Phillips. The brides joyfully believe culture has come to Seattle with the arrival of a Shakespearean troupe. But the thespians are thieves planning to pilfer as well as perform.

70.31 *A Wild Colonial Boy.* Oct. 24, 1969. GS: Art Lund, Brenda Scott, Donnelly Rhodes, Allan Arbus. Seattle's very existence is shaken by the arrival of three Irishmen and a lovely young lass. The four are firebrand rebels plotting an armed invasion of Canada, with Seattle as their base of operations.

70.32 *Hosanna's Way.* Oct. 31, 1969. GS: Ric Natoli, Eddie Firestone, Joe Perry, Roy Engel, Kelly Thordsen, Jon Shank, Paul Sorensen. The Bolt brothers create a tense situation when they house an Apache boy whose family was murdered. The youngster is intensely distrustful of whites, and most of Seattle fears the boy.

70.33 *The Road to the Cradle.* Nov. 7, 1969. GS: John Anderson, Ross Hagen, Dal Jenkins, Susannah Darrow, Henry Wills, Charles Seel, Michael Stanwood. Lottie and Jeremy embark on a rugged trip through the wilderness to act as midwives at a mission. Their journey is endangered by an uninvited companion, a sly whisky trader being pursued by bounty hunters.

70.34 *The Legend of Big Foot.* Nov. 14, 1969. GS: Paul Fix, Edward Asner, Richard Bull, Noam Pitlik, Mickey Morton, Larry Haddon, Sonny Jones. The reported appearance of Big Foot, a legendary man-beast, starts an epidemic of fear in Seattle. The frightened citizens' anger is increasingly directed at Caleb Balter, an old hermit who supposedly takes care of the monster.

70.35 *Land Grant.* Nov. 21, 1969. GS: Lou Antonio, Michael Baseleon, William Wintersole, Ken Swofford, Dave Cass, Jim Goodwin, Bill Zuckert. Bridal Veil Mountain is the center of a raging controversy between the Bolts, and some Greek immigrants who have claimed the property. Although the squatters' land documents are questionable, they are receiving wholehearted support from the softhearted brides.

70.36 *The Eyes of London Bob.* Nov. 28, 1969. GS: Peter

Whitney, Michael Forest, Richard Peabody, Joseph Bernard. In primitive timberland, Jason faces a perilous ordeal as the hostage of London Bob, a half-blind old convict who has escaped from prison to retrieve a cache of stolen money. Trailing the pair are the Bolt brothers, and former cronies of Bob's, also seeking the hidden fortune.

70.37 *The Fetching of Jenny.* Dec. 5, 1969. GS: Mala Powers, Alan Hale, Jr., Ivor Francis, Paul Lambert, Byron Morrow, Jack Bannon, Allison McKay. An appearance by singer Jenny Lind is the prize in a fierce rivalry between Seattle and Tacoma. When civic leaders from both towns are bilked by a con man posing as Miss Lind's manager, Jason Bolt and company set sail for San Francisco, hoping to sign up the Swedish nightingale on the spot.

70.38 *His Sister's Keeper.* Dec. 12, 1969. GS: Katherine Crawford, William Lucking. The bitterness between Jason and Stempel increases rapidly when the logger starts courting Stempel's sister. The two men sling fiery insults at each other, pushing their feud to a knock-down-drag-out fight.

70.39 *Lorenzo Bush.* Dec. 19, 1969. GS: Ronald Feinberg, Denis Cooney, Ken Kane, Lawrence Montaigne, David Draper. The Bolts' lucrative lumber contract with a construction company is being jeopardized by gun-toting Lorenzo Bush, a towering man of the forest who believes the newcomers are literally killing the land.

70.40 *A Bride for Obie Brown.* Jan. 9, 1970. GS: George Stanford Brown, Cicely Tyson, Ketty Lester. Ace logger Obie Brown delivers an ultimatum—find him a black bride of he will quit. With skill and skullduggery, Captain Clancey manages to import a lovely San Francisco dancer. Problems begin when the lady discovers why she has been brought to Seattle.

70.41 *Break the Bank of Tacoma.* Jan. 16, 1970. GS: Larry Linville, Harold Gould, Julian Burton, Billy Mumy, Ed Gilbert, Geraldine Wall, Sid Haig, Felton Perry. Jeremy and Joshua are duped into taking ownership of Tacoma's Red Rose casino, a joint in debt to the tune of $10,000. As the brothers seek a way out of their dilemma, the men who swindled them plots yet another fraud—to take control of Bridal Veil mountain.

70.42 *Debt of Honor.* Jan. 23, 1970. GS: Jennifer West, Pat Harrington, Jr., Guy Raymond, Leon Lontoc, Vic Tayback. Hillbilly Holly Houston returns to town with a bankroll generous enough to buy expensive gifts for her friends. But the boom is short-lived when her money turns out to be counterfeit. Holly's only hope is to trap the crooked gambler who duped her and collect the price on his head.

70.43 *The Sea-Bear.* Jan. 30, 1970. GS: Robert Cummings, Jay C. Flippen, Logan Ramsey, Ned Glass, Gene Rutherford. Lottie's dead-beat ex-husband Jack Crosse is a surprise visitor to Seattle. The whole town is gravely concerned when Crosse exhibits an almost evil hold on Lottie, making threatening demands for money.

70.44 *Another Game in Town.* Feb. 6, 1970. GS: Diahn Williams, Steve Gravers, Barbara Noonan, Nadia Sanders, Claire Hagen, Roberta Collins. Patricia Vanderhoff and her dancehall troupe bring competition to the brides and Lottie. The loggers are dazzled by the newcomers and Stempel is being wooed to insure backing for Patricia's proposed dance emporium.

70.45 *Candy and the Kid.* Feb. 13, 1970. GS: James Davidson, Ken Tilles, Porter Fowler. Jeremy faces a grim irony when cowboy Kid Holiday settles down in Seattle. The Kid saved Jeremy's life and now he has designs on his girl.

70.46 *Two Worlds.* Feb. 20, 1970. GS: Meg Foster, Ronald Feinberg, Don Hanmer, Rance Howard, John Czingland. While a raucous trapper's conclave gets under way in Seattle, Joshua Bolt opts for a quieter experience—arranging for Blind Callie Marsh to travel to San Francisco for an operation that could restore her sight.

70.47 *To the Victor.* Feb. 27, 1970. GS: Lou Antonio, Michael Baseleon, Arlene Martel, James Sikking, Eddie Ryder, Shepherd Sanders. Excitement stirs Seattle as Joshua and a young Greek farmer train for a bar-knuckles boxing match. The winner's prize is the companionship of beautiful Astasia.

70.48 *How Dry We Are.* March 6, 1970. GS: Alan Oppenheimer, Monica Evans, Marcel Hillaire, Johnny Seven, Timothy Scott, Quinn Redecker, Lou Robb, Carolye Shelyne. A lack of whiskey in Seattle has the citizenry considering a chancy plan to buy Canadian booze. Meanwhile, Biddie and Clancey distill their own, and get potted in the process.

70.49 *Bolt of Kilmaren.* March 13, 1970. GS: Denver Pyle, Bobby Hall, Ken Kane. Uncle Duncan, the blustery head of the Bolt clan, comes for a visit. Excitement over the old gent's arrival dims when he turns troublemaker, disrupting the logging camp and opposing Jeremy's romance.

70.50 *Absalom.* March 20, 1970. GS: Steve Ihnat, Mitch Vogel, Mills Watson, Mitzi Hoag, Don Steele. A maltreated mute boy has been willed to Jason. The child becomes the personal concern of Jeremy, who is determined to help the boy speak—and save him from commitment to an asylum.

70.51 *The Last Winter.* March 27, 1970. GS: Jeanette Nolan, Zooey Hall, Richard Hale, Robert Foulk, Bart LaRue, Joshua Bryant, William Zuckert, Bill Erwin. Friction between the Bolts and a family of trappers reaches it zenith when Jeremy is charged with murder. His eyewitness accuser is the youngest son in the rival clan.

70.52 *Two Women.* April 3, 1970. GS: Jane Wyatt, Lynda Day. A wealthy spinster and her niece come to Seattle to realize a dream, or so it seems. The lady has hired the Bolts to rebuild her family's mansion, but a series of troubling events becloud the project, and hint at more sinister motives.

71. *The High Chaparral*

NBC. 60 min. Broadcast history: Sunday, 10:00–11:00, Sept. 1967–Sept. 1968; Friday, 7:30–8:30, Sept. 1968–Sept. 1971.

Regular Cast: Leif Erickson (Big John Cannon), Linda Cristal (Victoria), Mark Slade (Billy Blue Cannon), Cameron Mitchell (Buck Cannon), Henry Darrow (Manolito Montoya), Frank Silvera (Don Sebastian Montoya), Don Collier (Sam), Roberto Contreras (Tedro), Rodolfo Acosta (Vaquero), Ted Markland (Reno), Bob Hoy (Joe), Rudy Ramos (Wind) 70-71.

Premise: This western series, set during the 1870s in Tucson, Arizona, depicted the story of the Cannon family, who ran the High Chaparral Ranch.

The Episodes

71.1 *The High Chaparral* (A.K.A. "Destination Tucson" & "The Arrangement"). Sept. 10, 1967. GS: Joan Caulfield, Erin O'Donnell, Henry Wills, Evelyn King, X Brands, Jorge Moreno, Mike de Anda, Rico Alaniz. The Cannon family is menaced by marauding Apaches, warned off by the Army and threatened by a Mexican cattle baron who tries to seize their cattle.

71.2 *The Ghost of Chaparral.* Sept. 17, 1967. GS: Patrick Horgan, Carlos Rivas, Joaquin Martinez. Big John Cannon is faced with rebellion from his wife and son. At the same time, he must deal with a possible Indian attack and a wealthy Englishman who wants to marry his wife.

71.3 *Best Man for the Job.* Sept. 24, 1967. GS: Warren Stevens, Ron Hagerthy, Lane Bradford, Steve Raines, Rush Williams. Indian disturbances prompt the arrival of a pig-headed Cavalry officer who soon stirs up more trouble with the Apaches. To undo the damage, Big John Cannon sends Billy Blue on a hazardous mission.

71.4 *A Quiet Day in Tucson.* Oct. 1, 1967. GS: Marie Gomez, Richard Devon, Vaughn Taylor. Manolito, Buck and Blue lose their shirts, and shooting irons, on a shopping trip to Tuscon. Brawls, poker games and wild women are just a few of the dangers the heroes face.

71.5 *Young Blood.* Oct. 8, 1967. GS: Alex Montoya, Mike de Anda. The volatile relationship between Manolito and Don Sebastian threatens to collapse John Cannon's dreams of an empire. Don Sebastian, certain that he has been tricked into giving up a prize bull, dispatches a bandit gang to steal the Cannon cattle.

71.6 *Shadows on the Land.* Oct. 15, 1967. GS: Kevin Hagen, Jan Arvan, Ronald Trujillo, John Pickard, Myron Healey, William Tannen. John Cannon risks everything to end Dolf Tanner's reign of terror over the ranchers. Tanner is using guerrilla tactics, and Apaches to corner the cattle market.

71.7 *The Fillibusteros.* Oct. 22, 1967. GS: Dan O'Herlihy, Beverly Hills, Anthony James, Roger DeKoven, Abel Franco. Buck, Victoria and Manolito are trapped with Don Sebastian when his ranch is overrun by an army of freebooters whose power-mad leader is out to grab all the neighboring ranches for his own tyrannical domain.

71.8 *The Doctor from Dodge.* Oct. 29, 1967. GS: Jack Kelly, Richard Angarola, John Davis Chandler. Mild-mannered Doc Henry saves Blue's life with a lightning draw. But the itinerant dentist then hatches a plan to deliver Blue to ransom-hungry outlaws.

71.9 *Sudden Country.* Nov. 5, 1967. GS: John Kerr, Jan Shepard, King Moody, Anthony Dexter, Robert Hernandez. The Cannons bend over backwards to help newcomers Creed and Meg Hallock, whose attempts at cattle ranching are disastrously inept. As Big John tries to head off catastrophe, Buck makes matters worse by falling for the married woman.

71.10 *A Hanging Offense.* Nov. 12, 1967. GS: Denver Pyle, Alan Bergmann, Ken Drake, Don Eitner, Paul Fix, Anna Navarro. Blue is ramrodded into an illegal Army trial for killing a general's son. While John defends his son, Buck searches for the Apache girl Blue was protecting from attack.

71.11 *The Pride of Revenge.* Nov. 19, 1967. GS: Ralph Meeker, Geraldine Brooks. Determined to control the High Chaparral, widow Fay Layton hires a gunman to poison the Cannons' cattle and destroy the rangeland.

71.12 *The Widow from Red Rock.* Nov. 26, 1967. GS: Patricia Barry, Carlos Romero, I. Stanford Jolley, Dick Gazinga. Buck signs on as temporary foreman for a beautiful widow. Before long, the woman is luring Buck into marriage, while secretly dealing with outlaws.

71.13 *Mark of the Turtle.* Dec. 10, 1967. GS: Robert Lansing, Anthony Caruso. Dissension erupts as a U.S. marshal leads Cannon's men to hunt desperadoes on Don Montoya's land. Buck defies the marshal's authority, while Manolito takes off to deal with the squatters in his own way.

71.14 *The Terrorist.* Dec. 17, 1967. GS: Henry Silva, Pilar Seurat, Paul Bryar, Lalo Rios, Gilbert Frye, Walt LaRue, John Cardos. A condemned Mexican revolutionary is whisked away to the Cannon ranch by Manolito. The young Montoya doesn't know that the man he saved is planning to kill an expected visitor, exiled president Juarez.

71.15 *The Firing Wall.* Dec. 31, 1967. GS: Fernando Lamas, Barbara Luna, Rico Alaniz, Pedro Gonzales Gonzales, Robert Carricart, Charles Horvath. The men of the High Chaparral are lured across the Mexican border into the clutches of a power-hungry bandit. El Caudillo plans to whip up revolutionary frenzy with an impressive display — the public execution of his prisoner.

71.16 *The Assassins.* Jan. 7, 1968. GS: X Brands, James Almanzar, Robert Bolger, Derrick Lewis, Geoffrey Deuel. A state of siege grips the High Chaparral, where Apache terrorists are trying to wreck peace talks between John and an emissary from Cochise.

71.17 *Survival.* Jan. 14, 1968. GS: Robert Phillips, James Almanzar. Big John and Blue face an ordeal of survival in a parched desert hell when their horses are stolen by Apaches. While Buck and Manolito search for the Cannons, Big John and Blue can only hope that a surly captive knows where to find water.

71.18 *Gold Is Where You Leave It.* Jan. 21, 1968. GS: Leo Gordon, Dean Stanton, Ted Gehring, Eddie Little Sky, William Tannen, Shelby Grant. John runs gold poachers of his land, then sends his wife and brother for explosives to seal up the abandoned mine. The fateful trip leads the couple to confused personal emotions, and a confrontation with death.

71.19 *The Kinsman.* Jan. 28, 1968. GS: Jack Lord, Rayford Barnes, William C. Watson, Jack Searl, Raymond Guth, William Tannen. The Cannons ask for trouble when they take in a wounded relative, unaware that he is a wanted man sought by bounty hunters.

71.20 *The Champion of the Western World.* Feb. 4, 1968. GS: Charles Aidman, Walter Brooke, Charles H. Gray, Maria Gomez. A comic fiasco mushrooms during a four-day trip to Tucson. The ranch hands break everything except records in a rodeo. Blue strikes up a friendship with a wild Irishman, and a sinister plot endangers Victoria's Paris chapeau.

71.21 *Ride the Savage Land.* Feb. 11, 1968. GS: Mary Jo Kennedy, George Keymas, Claire Wilcox, Gregg Palmer, Rockne Tarkington, Murray MacLeod. Buck and Manolito try to rescue two sisters from the Apaches, but get only one. Defying Big John and the Cavalry, the two cowboys go back unarmed, to bargain with their lives for the other girl's release.

71.22 *Bad Day for a Thirst.* Feb. 18, 1968. GS: Jose De Vega, Dennis Safren, Adam Williams, Robert Carson. Buck is determined to turn two Apaches into wranglers. His efforts reap gratifying rewards until prejudice takes its toll. A murder at the High Chaparral is blamed on the Indians by ranchers out for blood.

71.23 *Tiger by the Tail.* Feb. 25, 1968. GS: Ricardo Montalban, Noah Keen, Daniel Ades. A wounded desperado's forced confinement at High Chaparral puts everyone in danger. A mob is out to lynch the outlaw, and his brother will kill to free him.

71.24 *The Peacemaker.* March 3, 1968. GS: Victor Jory, Barbara Hershey, Paul Fix, Ron Foster, David Renard. Blue escorts a peace envoy and his adopted Apache daughter to a meeting with Cochise. Tragedy looms when the young people fall in love.

71.25 *The Hair Hunter.* March 10, 1968. GS: Richard Evans, James Gregory, Kelly Thordsen, James Almanzar. Revulsion and outrage incite Big John to attack the decayed conscience of Jake Stoner, who makes a grisly living by ambushing and scalping Apaches.

71.26 *A Joyful Noise.* March 24, 1968. GS: Ramon Novarro, Laurie Mock, Robert Yuro, Penny Santon, Angela Clarke. A priest causes a tragi-comic impasse when he settles in at the High Chaparral. The padre, two nuns and a lovely postulant are fleeing a tormentor who drove them out of Mexico.

71.27 *Threshold of Courage.* March 31, 1968. GS: Pat Hingle, Ron Hayes, Rex Holman, Charles Maxwell, Frank Puglia. A disfigured Confederate veteran kidnaps Victoria as the first step in a mad plan of revenge. Finley Carr is out to reap a full measure of justice from John Cannon, whom he blames for his wartime disgrace and disfigurement.

Season Two

71.28 *The Stallion.* Sept. 20, 1968. GS: Clive Clerk, Michael Keep. Disputed ownership of a wild stallion involves Blue Cannon in a fight with an Indian youth that could lead to a full-scale uprising.

71.29 *Ten Little Indians.* Sept. 27, 1968. GS: Armando Islas. Two by two they come to the Cannon ranch, ten little Apaches fleeing rampaging Pimas. Eldest of the children is Choddi, grandson of the Pimas' arch-enemy Geronimo, who chose the ranch haven in the innocent believe that Big John was the apostle he heard about at the mission school.

71.30 *Follow Your Heart.* Oct. 4, 1968. GS: Ed Begley, Miriam Colon, Abraham Sofaer, Jeff Pomerantz, Greydon Gould, Roy Jenson, Annette Cardona. A mysterious letter moves foreman Sam to quit the ranch to kill a man. One by one, the rancheros follow, knowing Sam's motives are rooted in memories of a happy marriage wrecked by bigotry.

71.31 *Tornado Frances.* Oct. 11, 1968. GS: Kathryn Hays, Charles Robinson, Dub Taylor, Tom Nolan, Harry Hickox, Ellen Corby. Buck faces formidable foes when he buys a saloon that has been hit by pretty teetotaler Frances O'Toole. Frances, leader of an army of rock-tossing temperance ladies, is planning to continue the siege.

71.32 *The Covey.* Oct. 18, 1968. GS: Anthony Caruso, Kelly Thordsen, Sara Vardi, Lane Bradford. The Cannons' heavily-laden supply train heads from Tucson into an ambush. El Lobo, an escaped Mexican bandit, risks recapture for the pleasure of attacking the High Chaparral men, especially his old nemesis Manolito.

71.33 *The Promised Land.* Oct. 25, 1968. GS: Alex Montoya, Natividad Vacio, Joe Maross, Jorge Moreno. The feud between Manolito and his father re-ignites during the crisis that follows the don's broken promise to sell a village to its people.

71.34 *Ebenezer.* Nov. 1, 1968. GS: John McGiver, Willard Sage, Alex Montoya, Tom Reese, Leonard Stone, Helen Kleeb, George Ostos, Robert Lusier. A crusading journalist is bent on founding Arizona's first newspaper. Under John Cannon's sponsorship, Binns blandly ignores the bullets whizzing around him as frantic Cannon men battle outlaws who menace his determination to go to press.

71.35 *North to Tucson.* Nov. 8, 1968. GS: Kevin McCarthy, Jack Elam, David Renard, Jorge Russek, Bee Tompkins. Left for dead after a desert stagecoach holdup, Victoria is brought to the chilling realization that the delirious man who shares her struggle for survival planned to kill her husband.

71.36 *The Deceivers.* Nov. 15, 1968. GS: Robert Loggia, Bonnie Bedelia. High Chaparral is marked for obliteration by a half-breed who has recruited an army of outcasts to destroy the society that shut him out. A growing threat to his plan is Tina, a lovely accomplice who is a generation removed from his hatred, and too close to Manolito's charm.

71.37 *The Buffalo Soldiers.* Nov. 22, 1968. GS: Yaphet Kotto, Morgan Woodward, Charles H. Gray, Robert DoQui, Charles Maxwell, William Jordan, Jess Riggle, Don Starr, Izark Fields. Lawlessness in Tucson brings martial law and the 10th Cavalry, a Negro regiment, into open conflict with the town's white populace and an army of outlaws.

71.38 *For What We Are About to Receive.* Nov. 29, 1968. GS: Christopher Dark, Marie Gomez, Ned Romero, Don Starr, Hal Jon Norman, Barry Sadler, Francesca Jarvis. A turkey shoot, Manolito's romantic entanglements and a random band of Indians are but a few of the ingredients in this Thanksgiving saga. Everyone but the U.S. Cavalry figures in the Cannon's calamity-strewn campaign to find a proper roasting bird in wild fowl country.

71.39 *A Way of Justice.* Dec. 13, 1968. GS: Anthony Caruso, Frank De Kova, Denny Miller, Mills Wason, Kathleen Freeman. While John Cannon stands trial for murder in a Mexican-style kangaroo court, a ranch search party finds an inarticulate lummox dressed in John's clothing, the only lead to John's whereabouts.

71.40 *Our Lady of Guadalupe.* Dec. 20, 1968. GS: Ricardo Montalban, Jan Shepard, Bill Fletcher, Mike de Anda, Norbert Schiller. For years, Father Sanchez has provided for the poor through collections he claimed were for the recovery of a sacred relic. But the well-intended scheme backfires. The Cannons make a donation so large that the padre must produce the relic, or confess his deception.

71.41 *Sea of Enemies.* Jan. 3, 1969. GS: Paul Winfield, John Pickard. Blue takes a calculated risk to help a deserting Negro cavalryman who carries scars of brutal maltreatment for his trouble. Blue is assaulted and taken hostage by the soldier, whose behavior becomes homicidal.

71.42 *Shadow of the Wind.* Jan. 10, 1969. GS: Luke Askew, Fabrizio Mioni, Chuck Bail, Fred Krone, Red Morgan, Charles Horvath, Julio Montoya. A chilling development mars a fiesta celebrating territorial peace. Into the merrymaking ride five Tombstone badmen, including Johnny Ringo, who have gone into the scalp-hunting business with an old friend of the Montoya family.

The High Chaparral

71.43 *No Irish Need Apply.* Jan. 17, 1969. GS: John Vernon, Eddie Firestone, Robert Cornthwaite, Charles Tyner, Ed Peck, Garry Walberg, William Tannen. The ranchers take up the cudgels for a group of miners striking against miserable working conditions. The first knell of tragedy is tolled when the hot-tempered strike leader locks horns with a blindly prejudiced mine manager.

71.44 *The Last Hundred Miles.* Jan. 24, 1969. GS: Robert Clary, Tom Tully, Walter Brooke, Jack Searl, Michael Keep, James Gavin, Dave Sharpe, Olga Velez. Lucien Charot in the unscrupulous owner of a freight-hauling monopoly. Trying to break Charot's hold, John Cannon learns that the sky-high profits will be used to restore Napoleonic domination in Mexico.

71.45 *The Glory Soldiers.* Jan. 31, 1969. GS: Elizabeth Allen, Anthony Caruso, Sean McClory, Heidi Vaughn, Jorge Moreno, John Quade. Manolito tries his darndest to resume a life of reckless pursuits. Pilfering from his father, fleecing a fellow bandito and keeping ahead of the law are easy. Dodging Capt. Ellie Strong and her ubiquitous Salvation Army soul savers becomes an incredibly complicated matter.

71.46 *Feather of an Eagle.* Feb. 7, 1969. GS: Quentin Dean, Frank Ramirez, Alicia Bond. An act of misguided gallantry gets Blue and the ranchers in serious trouble. Against the advice of his elders, Blue frees a white squaw from the Apaches and is captured for his efforts.

71.47 *Once, on a Day in Spring.* Feb. 14, 1969. GS: Kathleen Crowley, Martin Garralaga. Marital strife and romantic intrigues crop up at Don Sebastian's hacienda. A lovely noblewoman appears to brighten Don Sebastian's days, but the idyll is promptly shattered by the arrival of Victoria, who has left her husband, and Manolito, the don's fiercest rival in all things.

71.48 *Stinky Flanagan.* Feb. 21, 1969. GS: Frank Gorshin, Richard X. Slattery, Ken Mayer, Marie Gomez, Mike Wagner. Ordered to shoot Tillie, a beloved camel, Cavalry trooper Flanagan and his humpbacked friend go AWOL on a freedom march that be will indelibly etched in memory at High Chaparral.

71.49 *Surtee.* Feb. 28, 1969. GS: John Dehner, Christopher Dark, Chief Geronimo Kuth Le, Jerry Daniels, Susannah Darrow. A Government agent assigned to establish an Indian reservation humiliates the peaceful tribe the Cannons led into the compound. Trying to right the wrong, John locks horns with the flinty veteran of Indian wars who has been reduced to civilian status.

71.50 *A Fella Named Kilroy.* March 7, 1969. GS: Bert Freed, Ron Hayes, Chuck Bail, Bill Shannon, Sandy Rosenthal. All hands are agog when a saddle tramp who wandered onto the ranch proves to be an ace horseman, crack shot, chess wizard and amateur herpetologist among other things. He is also a thief being tailed by the gun-toting man he fleeced.

71.51 *No Bugles, No Women.* March 14, 1969. GS: Bethel Leslie, William Sylvester, Pamelyn Ferdin, Gregory Walcott. Buck yields to memories of a past love when his former flame arrives unexpectedly. Joy is short-lived when Buck learns that what she wants is the husband who deserted her. What Buck gets is the dangerous job of tracking down the recalcitrant man.

71.52 *The Lion Sleeps.* March 28, 1969. GS: Brenda Benet, Jorge Russek, Rico Alaniz, Luis de Cordova, Albert Monte, Martin Garralaga. A sorrowing clan gathers at Don Sebastian's death bed shortly before a miraculous, and slyly concealed, recovery. Unaware that the old fox is now shamming, Manolito, John and Victoria suffer agonies of conscience over his last wish. A diabolical ploy to marry off Manolito and swindle Cannon out of High Chaparral.

71.53 *For the Love of Carlos.* April 4, 1969. GS: Michael Ansara, Armando Islas, Fernando Pereira, Pamelyn Ferdin, Sara Vardi, Kevin Burchett. Victoria triumphs in her bid to provide a home for a hostile young vagrant. But her troubles aren't over. The boy is marking time until his lawbreaking father comes to fetch him.

Season Three

71.54 *Time of Your Life.* Sept. 19, 1969. GS: James Mitchum, Ted Gehring, Duane Grey, David Farrow, Gene Shane, Lani O'Grady. An accidental brush in a saloon is a trigger-happy gunfighter's excuse to hound Blue Cannon into the inevitable, face-saving tragedy — a showdown.

71.55 *A Time to Laugh, a Time to Cry.* Sept. 26, 1969. GS: Donna Baccala, Julio Medina, Argentina Brunetti, Victor Campos. Love comes to Manolito when a former childhood playmate arrives at Dn Sebastian's hacienda. Threatening the affair is a Mexican cattle-thief who hates the younger Montoya.

71.56 *The Brothers Cannon.* Oct. 3, 1969. GS: Lou Frizzell. Another family crisis flares over John's autocratic ruling of the roost. Cantankerous Buck finally bolts when he sees his position completely undermined, and young Blue defects when his father refuses to see Buck's side of things.

71.57 *A Piece of Land.* Oct. 10, 1969. GS: Lou Frizzell, Miguel Landa, John Zaremba. Buck and Manolito wheel and deal for the down payment on a ranch where Buck found a silver deposit. With the deed in their hands, they learn the silver is low-grade ore not worth transporting. What is worse is they are about to be raided by Comacheros.

71.58 *Bad Day for Bad Men.* Oct. 17, 1969. GS: Marianna Hill, Malachi Throne, Robert Yuro, Saadoren Bayati, Mark Tapscott. The ranchers follow a false trail as they track outlaws who robbed Manolito of Cannon's bankroll. The girl who helped trap Manolito has fled with the loot and is headed, unknowingly, for High Chaparral.

71.59 *To Stand for Something More.* Oct. 24, 1969. GS: Don Diamond, Gino Conforti, Mike DeAnda, Rico Cattani. Things go from bad to worse when Blue is finally put in charge of the ranch. He leaves High Chaparral open to a raid by horse thieves as he rides off to Tucson to round up his carousing ranch hands.

71.60 *Trail to Nevermore.* Oct. 31, 1969. GS: Milton Selzer, Bo Svenson, Rayford Barnes, Fabian Dean. Their wagon wrecked in an ambush, Manolito and Victoria harness themselves to a jerry-built rig to haul the unconscious John Cannon to the nearest haven. Awaiting them is an eerie interlude in a ghost town where an eccentric sheriff has kept a lonely vigil for many years.

71.61 *Apache Trust.* Nov. 7, 1969. GS: Chief Dan George, Ronald Feinberg, Evans Thornton, Mike Jenkins. Blue is captured by Apaches moments after witnessing a raid on a Cavalry wagon. As John goes into the enemy camp to rescue his son, Manolito follows his own hunch that the Indians were not the raiders.

71.62 *Lady Fair.* Nov. 14, 1969. GS: Joanna Moore, Dub Taylor, Joseph Ruskin. The Cannons lend vigorous support as Charly Converse, the pretty boss of a freight service, fights a vicious competitor with a gutsy spirit that hides her lack of confidence as a woman and her tender feelings for Buck.

71.63 *The Lost Ones.* Nov. 21, 1969. GS: Richard Lapp, Christopher Dark. Victoria nurses a wounded Apache back to health, little realizing that she may have signed her death warrant and his. The brave returns to his people convinced that she has magic powers and pledges his life that Victoria can save the chief's grievously wounded son.

71.64 *The Legacy.* Nov. 28, 1969. GS: Pamela Dunlap, John Dehner. John and Blue Cannon play into the hands of a father-daughter team of swindlers. The engaging couple has a scheme that will relieve John of a year's profits and leave Blue sadder, but infinitely wiser, about the ladies.

71.65 *Alliance.* Dec. 12, 1969. GS: Robert Viharo, Donald Buka, Jay Jones. Manolito plays for deadly stakes when he seeks to prevent an Indian uprising. He forms an alliance with Johnny Ringo, a feared bounty hunter hired by the Army to bring in an Apache fugitive, dead or alive. If the Indian is killed, High Chaparral could be destroyed in the ensuing carnage.

71.66 *The Little Thieves.* Dec. 26, 1969. GS: Jo Ann Harris, Heather Menzies, William Sylvester, William Vint, Alan Vint, Dick Haynes, John McKee. Annie and Bet are apparently rootless girls who stole Buck and Mano's horses. What the boys don't know is that the teenage terrors are from a den of thieves run by a man who can think of nothing nicer than having his novices acquire social polish at High Chaparral.

71.67 *The Long Shadow.* Jan. 2, 1970. GS: Richard Anders, Gregory Sierra, Don Kemp, Paul Sorensen, William Vaughn, Steve Raines, Dick Farnsworth. One by one the ranchers have near fatal encounters with an unseen enemy stalking the range. John Cannon must find out who is trying to destroy him before growing fear and suspicions among his men do the enemy's work for him.

71.68 *The Journal of Death.* Jan. 9, 1970. GS: John Colicos, Morgan Woodward. John Cannon faces an agonizing decision when Victoria is wounded during a fight between a United States marshal and a doctor he has been trailing for years. The avenging lawman judges his prisoner responsible for many wartime surgical deaths—and it may take surgery to save Victoria.

71.69 *Friends and Partners.* Jan. 16, 1970. GS: Howard Caine, Miguel Landa. Buck and Manolito spend some time on their own ranch to get the place in shape. Before long, they are too immersed in domestic chores and petty bickering to note that they are being watched by horse thieves waiting for the right moment to strike.

71.70 *Jelks.* Jan. 23, 1970. GS: Mitchell Ryan, Don Melvoin, Henry Wills. Joe's first official act as the new foreman is a calculated risk that endangers the ranch. He knowingly hires a shady character whose suspicious behavior leads to a showdown with John Cannon.

71.71 *The Guns of Johnny Rondo.* Feb. 6, 1970. GS: Steve Forrest, Mel Gallagher, Kurt Russell, Roy Jenson, Patrick Sullivan, Jim Nolan, Wayne Storm. An ex-gunfighter tries to bury a tragic past and signs on at High Chaparral with his 17-year-old son. Unaware that bloodthirsty avengers are dogging his trail, Rondo has forbidden the boy to wear a gun.

71.72 *Mi Casa, Su Casa.* Feb. 20, 1970. GS: Lew Palter, Pedro Gonzalez Gonzalez, William Bagdad, Michael Keep. John Cannon nearly bursts a blood vessel during his father-in-law's first visit. Aside from arriving with a mountain of luggage and a retinue of servants, the old hidalgo begins to run the place like his own hacienda.

71.73 *The Lieutenant.* Feb. 27, 1970. GS: Robert Pine, Donald Moffat, Renne Jarrett, Garry Walberg, Sandy Rosenthal, Stuart Randal. Blue defies Government and parental authority to help Henry Simmons, who has been wanted for years on an unjust desertion charge. Now, with an Army search party bearing down on them, Simmons' daughter wants her father to stand and fight.

71.74 *The Reluctant Deputy.* March 6, 1970. GS: Charles Durning, Robert Donner. Blue repays the prankish Buck and Mano for having him deputized. He arrests them for brawling, then is duped into stashing stolen money in the sheriff's safe, shortly before the jail doors reveal a tendency to pop open.

71.75 *New Hostess in Town.* March 20, 1970. GS: Jim Davis, Ed Bakey, Mills Watson, Todd Martin, Natividad Vacio, Paul Fierro. Victoria is kidnaped and made to work as a saloon girl. After would-be rescuer Buck arrives on the scene, the unlikely couple pose as husband and wife to escape from the saloon owner who runs the town.

71.76 *Too Many Chiefs.* March 27, 1970. GS: Noah Beery, Jr., Sandy Rosenthal, Monte Landis, Sherry Miles, Margaret Louise, Michael Keep, Richard Peel. John and Victoria spend a delayed honeymoon enjoying the high life in San Francisco. Meanwhile, back at the ranch, crises mushroom under the upright management of Blue.

71.77 *Auld Lang Syne.* April 10, 1970. GS: Gregory Walcott, Jonathan Lippe, Tony Epper. Things take a very nasty turn after Buck agrees to escort an old army buddy carrying a payroll to Yuma. It is government gold all right, but the man's destination is Mexico.

71.78 *Generation.* April 17, 1970. GS: Aspa Nakopoulou, Dick Meyers. Ridicule and rebukes greet Blue's new-found talent as an artist. The young man, embarrassed and frustrated, finds his love of sketching stifled until a surprising development offers him a chance to quit the ranch.

71.79 *No Trouble at All.* May 5, 1970. GS: William C. Watson, Tony Russel, Felice Orlandi. Victoria insists on crossing dangerous Indian country on an errand of mercy. She is captured by an Apache and is subsequently rescued by a trio who refuse to take her to her designation where a woman is about to give birth.

Season Four

71.80 *An Anger Greater Than Mine.* Sept. 18, 1970. GS: Alejandro Rey, Nate Esformes, Val de Vargas, Nico de Silva. Revolutionary leader Diego De la Paula, Victoria's rejected suitor, plots to destroy the Cannon and Montoya ranches.

71.81 *Spokes.* Sept. 25, 1970. GS: William Conrad, Vincent Van Patten, E.J. Andre, Larry D. Mann, Solomon Sturges, Walter Barnes, Tom Toner, Don Keefer, Ollie O'Toole. In a town called Spokes, Buck finds his life in jeopardy after he befriends a trapper wounded in a shoot-out. The trapper gunned down the son of the area's most powerful rancher.

71.82 Only the Bad Come to Sonora. Oct. 2, 1970. GS: Bruce Dern, Margarita Cordova, James Gammon, Ed Bakey, Joaquin Martinez, Ralph Manza, Paul Fierro, Than Wyenn. In Mexico, Manolito poses as a peasant to find the men who stole his father's prize stallion.

71.83 Wind. Oct. 9, 1970. GS: Scott Brady, R.G. Armstrong, Tyler McVey, Mark Tapscott, Dan White, Steve Raines, Henry Wills. Wind is a half-breed who owes his life to John Cannon. Wind gets a chance to repay the debt when a powerful rancher tries to destroy the Cannons.

71.84 A Matter of Survival. Oct. 16, 1970. GS: Barry Sullivan. Hard-bitten oldtimer Dan Casement and his infant grandson narrowly escaped death at the hands of an Apache war party. With the Apaches still menacing, Dan intends to escape on his own. He must be convinced at gunpoint to join Victoria and two Chaparral hands in a dash for freedom.

71.85 It Takes a Smart Man. Oct. 23, 1970. GS: Richard Bradford, Garry Walberg, Carl Benson, Wes Bishop, Sam Javis. Gunslinger Tulsa Red comes to Chaparral on a business errand. He wants $5000 from John Cannon in return for Buck's life.

71.86 A Good, Sound Profit. Oct. 30, 1970. GS: Harold Gould, Joe De Santis, Edward Colmans. John angers the members of his family when he decides to sell guns and horses to revolutionaries planning to overthrow Juarez' government in Mexico.

71.87 Too Late the Epitaph. Nov. 6, 1970. GS: Monte Markham, Mayf Nutter, Willard Sage, John Myhers, Jerry Wills, John Gilgreen. Things go from bad to worse for Manolito when he is mistaken for a holdup man, arrested, then released from jail so he can be framed for murder.

71.88 The Forge of Hate. Nov. 13, 1970. GS: Robert Loggia, Michael Baseleon, Ted de Corsia, Alan Caillou, Raymond Mayo. The Chaparral becomes the proving ground for two opposing Apache leaders. The two leaders are Two Pony, an advocate of peace with the white man, and Grey Wolf, head of a warring splinter group.

71.89 Fiesta. Nov. 20, 1970. GS: Nehemiah Persoff, Miguel Alejandro, Rodolfo Hoyos, Daniel Kemp, Felipe Turich, Julio Medina, Ken Mayer, Rico Alaniz. In Mexico, Buck jeopardizes his life to help an eleven-year-old boy escape a ruthless gang which makes its living off a gruesome sport called boy fighting.

71.90 A Matter of Vengeance. Nov. 27, 1970. GS: Barry Sullivan, Warren Kemmerling, Priscilla Pointer, Robert Donner, William Lucking, John J. Fox. Sam tries to prevent Dan Casement from gunning down the men who burned his home and killed his infant grandson.

71.91 Pale Warrior. Dec. 11, 1970. GS: Frank Webb, Harry Lauter, Henry Wills, X Brands. The Cannons employ a white man who claims to have escaped from the Apaches after fifteen years of captivity. But Wind, who has been observing the stranger, is certain that the man is a fraud.

71.92 The Badge. Dec. 18, 1970. GS: Morgan Woodward, Alan Oppenheimer, Jonathan Lippe, Lew Brown, Gary Busey, Henry Wills, Robert Broyles. This story recounts a time when the Cannon brothers were on opposite sides of the law. John was a U.S. marshal and Buck was a suspected bank robber.

71.93 The New Lion of Sonora. Feb. 19, 1971. GS: Gilbert Roland, Albert Paulsen, Eddra Gale, Roger C. Carmel, Val de Vargas. Domingo is the new head of the Montoya empire, but his empire will crumble unless his negligence is halted.

71.94 Sangre. Feb. 26, 1971. GS: Pat Renella, Kaz Garas, Charles Maxwell, Evans Thornton, Jerry Wills, Dave Cass. Apache Indians surround a group of cowboys and Manolito must bring back help.

71.95 The Hostage. March 5, 1971. GS: Edmond O'Brien, Joe Don Baker, Woodrow Parfrey, Bobby Riha, Tani Phelps, Rick Gates, Ted Gehring, Kermit Murdoch, Ken Drake. An aging outlaw, his son and his knife-wielding partner are trapped in a bank with their hostages.

71.96 A Man to Match the Land. March 12, 1971. GS: Albert Salmi, Michael Keep, Jennifer Rhodes, Allen Dexter, Myron Healey. John Cannon, badly in need of horses, arranges a unique agreement with the Indians that includes the exchange of hostages.

72. *Hondo*

ABC. 60 min. Broadcast history: Friday, 8:30-9:30, Sept. 1967–Dec. 1967.

Regular Cast: Ralph Taeger (Hondo Lane), Noah Beery, Jr. (Buffalo Baker), Kathie Brown (Angie), Buddy Foster (Johnny Dow), Michael Pate (Apache Chief Vittoro), Gary Clarke (Captain Richards).

Premise: In the Arizona Territory in 1869 Hondo Lane is an ex-Cavalry scout, Confederate soldier, widower of an Apaches princess, and newly hired trouble-shooter for the Army. This series was based on the 1953 John Wayne film.

The Episodes

72.1 Hondo and the Eagle Claw. Sept. 8, 1967. GS: Robert Taylor, John Smith, Gary Merrill, Randy Boone. Hondo's first assignment is to make peace with Apache Chief Vittoro, whose daughter, Hondo's wife, was killed by the Cavalry.

72.2 The War Cry. Sept. 15, 1967. GS: Michael Rennie, Robert Taylor, Randy Boone. Hondo must deal with a renegade Indian whose attacks against the settlers are threatening peace talks with Chief Vittoro.

72.3 Hondo and the Singing Wire. Sept. 22, 1967. GS: Perry Lopez, Pat Conway, Donald Woods. Hondo tracks Delgado, a half-breed killer strangely dedicated to destroying vital telegraph lines. The mystery deepens when a member of Hondo's patrol shows more interest in killing Delgado than in saving the lines.

72.4 The Superstition Massacre. Sept. 29, 1967. GS: Robert Reed, Nancy Malone. In a shattering moment, Hondo meets the man he has sworn to kill. Frank Davis, who killed Hondo's Apache wife, is the Government surveyor he must now lead into Apache territory.

72.5 The Savage. Oct. 6, 1967. GS: Nico Minardos, Charles McGraw. Hondo sees red when a stiff-necked general on an inspection tour initiates a get-tough policy with the Indians. After refusing to buy horses from the impoverished Apaches, the general orders the flogging of Ponce Coloradas, a friend of Hondo's and a prince of the Apache nation.

72.6 Hondo and the Apache Kid. Oct. 13, 1967. GS: Farley Granger, Nick Adams, Danielle Roter, Stan Barrett, Sofia-Marie, James Beck, William Benedict. A hot-shot reporter stirs up public outrage at the white man's injustice to the Indian. His prime target is Hondo, who has set out to recapture his own blood-brother, an escaped renegade.

72.7 Hondo and the War Hawks. Oct. 20, 1967. GS: John Carroll, Lawrence Montaigne, Glenn Langan, Jim Davis. Hondo faces and explosive situation. While the announced confiscation of Apache hunting weapons threatens to cause a breach with Chief Vittoro, two merchants are supplying a murderous renegade with guns for a nice, profitable war.

72.8 Hondo and the Mad Dog. Oct. 27, 1967. GS: James MacArthur, Royal Dano, James Beck, Ben Wright, William Benedict, Michael Harris. Trooper Jud Barton tries to capitalize on a rabies scare to get Hondo's dog destroyed. Barton has murdered a man and Hondo's dog known where the body is buried.

72.9 Hondo and the Judas. Nov. 3, 1967. GS: John Agar, John Carradine, Ricky Nelson, Forrest Tucker, Roger Perry. Hondo rejoins a group of outlaws summoned to a reunion by their former commander, a Rebel officer believed dead. The Colonel, regrouping his men for one last raid, is determined to find he man who shot him in the back.

72.10 Hondo and the Commancheros. Nov. 10, 1967. GS: Fernando Lamas, Marie Gomez. Hondo takes a desperate lone chance to bargain for Angie Dow's life. The young widow has been taken to Mexico by scoundrels who traffic in lives with the Comanches.

72.11 Hondo and the Sudden Town. Nov. 17, 1967. GS: Gene Raymond, Rod Cameron, Leonard Stone, Tom Reese, Glenn Langan. Hondo suspects fraud and bloodshed when an ex-senator reactivates an abandoned silver mine. The depleted mine is smack in the middle of the Apache hunting grounds, which the Indians will fight to keep.

72.12 The Ghost of Ed Dow. Nov. 24, 1967. GS: David Brian, Chris Alcaide, Ted Jordan, June Dayton. Angie's bereaved father-in-law draws the ugly conclusion that Hondo and the young widow conspired to kill her husband. Angry and disgusted, he arranges to kidnap Angie's son, unaware that his accomplices are hardened criminals.

72.13 Hondo and the Death Drive. Dec. 1, 1967. GS: Alan Hale, Jr., L.Q. Jones, J. Pat O'Malley, Terry Wilson, Reed Hadley. Long-standing hatreds create hazards for Hondo, who is under orders to escort a sheep drive to Apache country. The scout is unaware that the head drover is in on a cattleman's scheme to have renegade Indians stage an ambush.

72.14 Hondo and the Hanging Town. Dec. 8, 1967. GS: Dan O'Herlihy, Gary Crosby, Morgan Woodward, Denver Pyle. In a lynch-minded town, Hondo tries to clear a soldier suspected of murder. Defending the soldier before a hanging judge is a former Boston attorney, now a whiskey-guzzling salesman of patent medicines.

72.15 The Gladiators. Dec. 15, 1967. GS: Claude Akins, Barton MacLane, Richard Hale. Hondo is having his troubles protecting a Government peace envoy to the Apaches, and dealing with a personal dilemma: the kidnaping of his dog Sam by a sadist bent on turning the canine into a pit fighter.

72.16 The Apache Trail. Dec. 22, 1967. GS: Nick Adams, Annette Funicello, David Nelson, Ed McCready, Tony Epper, Pete Dunn, Roy Sickner. The murderous Apache Kid escapes as Hondo is taking him in for an Army trial. In hot pursuit, Hondo discovers more atrocities committed by the Kid, and promises Chief Vittoro he will deal with the killer the Apache way.

72.17 The Rebel Hat. Dec. 29, 1967. GS: Jack Elam, Rafael Campos, Rudy Battaglia, Linda Dangcil, Eugene Iglesias, John Indrisano. A horse-trading mission goes off-course when Hondo's cherished Rebel hat is stolen. In his efforts to reclaim it, Hondo copes with renegade Indians, Mexican terrorists, and a woman badly in need of a midwife.

73. Hopalong Cassidy

Syndicated. 30 min. Broadcast history: Various, Sept. 1952–April 1954.

Regular Cast: William Boyd (Hopalong Cassidy), Edgar Buchanan (Red Connors).

Premise: This series depicted the adventures of Hopalong Cassidy, the owner of the Bar 20 Ranch.

Notes: William Boyd starred as Hopalong Cassidy in over sixty films between 1935 and 1948. These were packaged as a 60 minute syndicated series in 1948 and were picked up by NBC the following year. The success of the series led Boyd to recreate the character for this syndicated series.

The Episodes

73.1 Guns Across the Border. Sept. 19, 1952. GS: Myra Marsh, Keith Richards, Henry Rowlands. While tracing Army rifles stolen for Mexican revolutionists, Hoppy is confronted by a fast-shooting lady marshal.

73.2 The Knife of Carlos Valero. Sept. 25, 1952. GS: Harry Cording, John Crawford, Olin Howlin, Victor Millan, Lillian Moliere, Byron Foulger. Hoppy and Red hide an innocent young Mexican from a lynch mob and then go after the murderer who framed the boy.

73.3 The Trap. Sept. 26, 1952. GS: Howard Negley, Lane Bradford, Bill Henry, Cajan Lee, Maudie Prickett. Hoppy tries to help an ex-convict, hoping to go straight, who is being blackmailed into joining a plot to rob the Cattlemen's Association.

73.4 Alien Range. Oct. 1, 1952. GS: Otto Waldis, Maria Palmer, Glenn Strange, James Griffith. Hoppy and his pal, Red Connors, must fight desperately to hold off two desperadoes who team up with a fake U.S. marshal. Hoppy shows himself to be a true friend to an immigrant ranching family who are being driven from their lands by the crooks.

73.5 The Feud. Oct. 28, 1952. GS: Hugh Beaumont, Lucia Carroll, Steve Darrell, Harold Goodwin, Herbert Lytton. The owners of the Diamond E Ranch and another rancher are feuding. Hoppy saves an innocent man from hanging and tracks down a murderer who is manipulating the feud between the two rival ranchers.

73.6 Ghost Trails. Oct. 28, 1952. GS: Frank Ferguson,

Hopalong Cassidy

Edward Clark, Jack Harden, Ted Mapes, John Cason, Charles F. Seel, Frank Jaquet, Tom London. Hoppy tries to prove that a traveling preacher is behind a series of robberies by three men who have a habit of vanishing into thin air.

73.7 *Marked Cards.* Oct. 28, 1952. GS: Tommy Ivo, George D. Wallace, Crane Whitney, James Diehl, Emmett Vogan, John Deering. Hoppy uses an incriminating letter and a crooked card deck to hunt down the murderers of a small boy's parents.

73.8 *Don Colorado.* Dec. 1, 1952. GS: Nelson Leigh, George D. Wallace, Noreen Nash, Stanley Blystone, Bud Osborne, John Frank. Hoppy's efforts to save a young woman's mine from swindlers are complicated when Red Connors develops amnesia and claims to be a Spanish nobleman.

73.9 *Black Waters.* Dec. 1, 1952. GS: Rick Vallin, Marilyn Nash, Walter Reed, Morris Ankrum, Clarence Straight, Malcolm Beggs. Hoppy uses an intricately carved bracelet to trap some oil-rich reservation lands.

73.10 *Blind Encounter.* Dec. 1, 1952. GS: Pepe Hern, Denver Pyle, Robert Bice, Donna Martell, John Halloran, Philip Van Zandt, Argentina Brunetti. A blind Mexican woman asks Hoppy to help her fugitive son, who has been falsely accused of murder.

73.11 *The Promised Land.* Dec. 10, 1952. GS: John Crawford, Maura Murphy, Thurston Hall, Edwin Parker, Sandy Sanders, William Fawcett. When Red Connors buys some arid land on the strength of a promised irrigation project, Hoppy investigates and learns that the promoters of the scheme are guilty of forgery, embezzlement and murder.

73.12 *The Vanishing Herd.* Dec. 12, 1952. GS: Betty Ball, Edward Colmans, Keith Richards, Lee Roberts, Pierce Lyden, Edgar Carpenter. Hoppy and Red Conners helps government agents search for a herd of over 600 stolen horses intended for the Spanish-American War, but when he finds the animals he has to save them from a grass fire.

73.13 *Black Sheep.* Dec. 26, 1952. GS: Richard Crane, Richard Travis, Claire Carleton, Antoinette Gerry, Edwin Parker, Ted Mapes, Sam Flint, Wheaton Chambers. Hoppy and Red try to settle a dispute between cattle ranchers and sheep grazers.

73.14 *Lawless Legacy.* Dec. 31, 1952. GS: Claudia Barrett, Steve Rowland, Clayton Moore, Marshall Reed, Tim Graham, Edgar Dearing. Hoppy helps a young man and woman who are framed as counterfeiters just before they are to claim their uncle's estate.

Season Two

73.15 *The Devil's Idol.* Oct. 9, 1953. GS: Ron Hagerthy, Nolan Leary, Don C. Harvey, Harry Harvey, Danny Mummert. Hoppy helps a minister convince a young boy who has just committed his first holdup that his gunman idol has feet of clay.

73.16 *The Sole Survivor.* Oct. 16, 1953. GS: Richard Reeves, Kenneth MacDonald, Dorothy Green, David Bruce, Harry Hines. Hoppy and Red are shot at when they ride into an apparently deserted town. They then discover the town's only resident, also shot and left for dead.

73.17 *Valley Raiders.* Oct 23, 1953. GS: Lyle Talbot, Henry Rowland, Harte Wayne. Hoppy and Red are riding to Stone Valley to see the sheriff when they find him ambushed by two riders. Ranchers are threatened by the group trying to sell their valley for a cavalry post.

73.18 *Twisted Trails.* Oct. 30, 1953. GS: Herbert Lytton, Richard Farmer, Gloria Talbott, Lane Bradford, George Spaulding, Wheaton Chambers, Rusty Wescoatt. Hoppy seems to be the victim of amnesia as he tries to save the ranchers from embezzlement by their own cattlemen's association.

73.19 *The Last Laugh.* Nov. 6, 1953. GS: Edward Clark, Edgar Dearing, Alan Wells, John Crawford, Jeanne Dean. Hoppy, posing as a cattle buyer, rides to Dorado to break up a ring of thieves who are stealing gold from the smelting plant.

73.20 *The Jinx Wagon.* Nov. 13, 1953. GS: Thurston Hall, Steve Conte, Myron Healey, Paul Burns, Kathleen Case, Michael Thomas. Bank robbers think that an old wagon in the deserted Twin Rivers livery stable is a perfect place to hide their money, but then the wagon is sold.

73.21 *Illegal Entry.* Nov. 20, 1953. GS: Emerson Treacy, Harry Lauter, Frank Hagney, Spencer Chan, Paul Marion, Larry Hudson. Hoppy and Red help the U.S. Immigration Service investigate the death of smuggled Chinese aliens and find that a limping man is the betrayer.

73.22 *Gypsy Destiny.* Nov. 27, 1953. GS: Robert Cabal, Pilar del Rey, Belle Mitchell, Paul Richards, John Merton, Frank Lackteen. Hoppy aids Cupid in trying to prove that a Gypsy boy's dead father was not a thief so that the boy will be free to marry his sweetheart.

73.23 *Arizona Troubleshooters.* Dec. 4, 1953. GS: Richard Avonde, Mort Mills, Howard Negley, Gregg Barton, Nan Leslie, Ned Davenport. While assigned to guard the workers building Arizona's first telegraph line, Hoppy discovers that a supposedly retired man, who owns a number of stores, stands to lose a fortune if the line is constructed. Hoppy uses wiretapping to foil the man's sabotage scheme

73.24 *Death by Proxy.* Dec. 11, 1953. GS: Paul Richards, Fred Sherman, Duane Thorsen, Pierce Lyden, Charles Cane, John Deering. Hoppy clears the name of a convicted killer and, with the aid of Red Connors and a health tonic, traps the real slayer.

73.25 *Frontier Law.* Dec. 18, 1953. GS: Bill Henry, Barbara Knudson, Robert Griffin, Pierre Watkin, Marshall Reed, Dan White. Hoppy and Red run into fireworks when they try to conduct an honest election in outlaw territory. The outlaws retaliate by getting Hoppy's nephew into trouble.

73.26 *Don't Believe in Ghosts.* Dec. 25, 1953. GS: Anthony Sydes, Aline Towne, Carleton Young, Steve Pendleton, Almira Sessions, Stanley Blystone. Rancher Tom Murdock has disappeared and is presumably dead. Events indicate, however, that he is very much alive. Hoppy risks death to convince the man's family and friends that the rancher has not returned from the dead to haunt them.

73.27 *The Renegade Press.* Jan. 1, 1954. GS: Rick Vallin, William Fawcett, Terry Frost, William Phillips, Lou Nova, I. Stanford Jolley. In his search for a counterfeiting gang, Hoppy discovers that the Twin Rivers newspaper is printing more than the news. Red assumes a disguise to break up the ring of counterfeiters.

73.28 *Double Trouble.* Jan. 8, 1954. GS: Victor Millan, Charlita Roeder, Sam Flint, Robert Knapp, John Pickard, Donald Novis. A young man's knife is found at the scene of the murder of a banker, but Hoppy believes the young Mexican laborer is innocent.

73.29 *Copper Hills.* Jan. 15, 1954. GS: Joseph Waring, George D. Wallace, Edwin Rand, Lee Roberts, Earle Hodgins, Paul Birch. While investigating raids by white men dressed as Indians, Hoppy and Red find valuable copper on the Indians' land.

73.30 *New Mexico Manhunt.* Jan. 22, 1954. GS: Raymond Hatton, Russ Conway, Leslie O'Pace, Douglas Kennedy, Dolores Mann, House Peters, Jr. An old man finds that he has stolen gold in his possession. Hoppy tries to clear the old prospector when he is accused of complicity in a train robbery.

73.31 *The Outlaw's Reward.* Jan. 29, 1954. GS: Harlan Warde, John Alvin, Griff Barnett, Elaine Riley, Denver Pyle, William Haade. Hoppy steps in when a notorious outlaw tries to force his honest father and brother to help him collect the reward for his own capture.

73.32 *Grubstake.* Feb. 5, 1954. GS: Christopher Dark, Percy Helton, Gladys George, Robert Paquin, Timothy Carey, Michael Fox. Hoppy helps an old prospector whose discover of gold has earned him several new friends and enemies.

73.33 *Steel Trails West.* Feb. 12, 1954. GS: Richard Powers, Robert Bice, Lewis Martin, Donald Kennedy. Hoppy steps in when the nephew of a contractor building a railroad is killed and all the construction plans stolen.

73.34 *Silent Testimony.* Feb. 19, 1954. GS: Hank Patterson, James Best, Vici Raaf, Richard Cutting, Keith Richards, Steve Clark. Hoppy comes to the aid of an old man who lost his ranch in a crooked card game.

73.35 *3-7-77.* Feb. 26, 1954. GS: James Anderson, James Seay, Ted Stanhope, Leonard Penn, Dick Rich, Bud Osborne. Hoppy frightens an outlaw gang by writing in prominent places the code numbers 3-7-77, the symbol of a band of vigilante terrorists.

73.36 *Masquerade for Matilda.* March 5, 1954. GS: Hazel Keener, Phil Tead, George Keymas, Zon Murray, Roy Barcroft, Frank Marlowe. Hoppy tries to trick an elderly woman's kidnapers by inducing Red Connors to wear her clothes.

73.37 *Frame-Up for Murder.* March 12, 1954. GS: Bill Henry, Ray Walker, Robert Knapp, Harry Hayden. Hoppy and Red arrests a young man whom they find wounded near the body of his uncle, but they soon learn that he is suffering from amnesia and try to clear him.

73.38 *The Black Sombrero.* March 19, 1954. GS: Rick Vallin, Cajan Lee, Morris Ankrum, Duane Thorsen, Larry Hudson, Edward Colmans, Forrest Taylor, Tony Roux. When a Mexican rancher accuses an innocent man of murder, Hoppy uses a black sombrero to clear the frame-up victim and save a wealthy young heiress.

73.39 *The Emerald Saint.* March 26, 1954. GS: George D. Wallace, Don Alvarado, Anna Navarro, Jack Ingram, Salvador Baguez, Ted Bliss, Julia Montoya. While chasing a murderer, Hoppy and Red are locked in a shrine with an emerald religious statue during a Mexican festival.

73.40 *Tricky Fingers.* April 2, 1954. GS: Marjorie Lord, Mark Dana, Stanley Andrews. Hoppy and Red are trapped in a burning house by a lovely young woman who has robbed a bank while posing as an old lady.

74. Hotel de Paree

CBS. 30 min. Broadcast history: Friday, 8:30-9:00, Oct. 1959–Sept. 1960.

Regular Cast: Earl Holliman (Sundance), Jeanette Nolan (Annette Devereaux), Judi Meredith (Monique Devereaux), Strother Martin (Aaron Donager).

Premise: The Hotel de Paree is a hotel in Georgetown, Colorado in the 1870s, which is owned by an ex-gunfighter, the Sundance Kid.

The Episodes

74.1 *Sundance Returns.* Oct. 2, 1959. GS: Theodore Bikel. Sundance returns to his home town after a prison term. He is looking for a place to settle down, but he is also interested in finding out what happened to a large sum of money he left behind when he was imprisoned.

74.2 *Juggernaut.* Oct. 9, 1959. GS: Brian Donlevy. Tough Sean McElroy rides into Georgetown claiming to represent a land company. He wants the town merchants to sell him land.

74.3 *Vein of Ore.* Oct. 16, 1959. GS: Royal Dano, Martin Milner, Trevor Bardette, Mark Tapscott. A man who has been severely beaten tells Sundance that a gang beat him to prevent him from reaching a mine that is rich with precious ore. He offers Sundance a share if he will help mine for the ore.

74.4 *The High Cost of Justice.* Oct. 23, 1959. GS: Leif Erickson. After the body of a dance-hall girl is found near the cabin of trapper Gurney Mills, he is accused of murder. Sundance hides the trapper from the posse because he is not convinced that the man is guilty.

74.5 *Return of Monique.* Oct. 30, 1959. GS: Mark Richman. Monique Devereaux returns to Georgetown from France accompanied by her fiance whom Sundance recognizes as an ex-convict.

74.6 *A Rope Is for Hanging.* Nov. 6, 1959. GS: Peter Whitney, Lindsay Workman, Nora Marlowe, Richard Bakalyan, K.L. Smith, Kelton Garwood, Russ Conklin. The ruthless Wyatt gang intends to hang a storekeeper friend of Sundance's. Because of his testimony, one of their men was convicted of murder.

74.7 *A Fool and His Gold.* Nov. 13, 1959. GS: James Barton, Sebastian Cabot. Prospector Cully Jackson rushes into Georgetown with the news that he has finally struck gold.

74.8 *The Only Wheel in Town.* Nov. 20, 1959. GS: Peggy Joyce, Kathleen Hughes.

74.9 *The Man Who Believed in Law.* Nov. 27, 1959. GS: Charles McGraw, Alice Frost, King Donovan, Bill Bryant, Bob Steele, Hugh Sanders. Georgetown is struck by a sudden crime wave and the people are anxious to put a stop to it. Sundance advises them to hire lawman Martin Wood.

74.10 *Sundance and the Hostiles.* Dec. 11, 1959. GS: Allyn Joslyn, Harry Swoger, John Pickard, Jason Johnson, Robin Riley. At county fair time, only Sundance and a few others are in Georgetown. Then six escaped convicts stage an invasion.

74.11 *Sundance and the Violent Siege.* Dec. 18, 1959. Three desperate men wanted for robbery and murder, take over the Hotel de Paree. They hold several hostages while they wait for their loot to be delivered.

74.12 *Sundance and the Blood Money.* Jan. 1, 1960. GS: Darryl Richard, Russ Conway, Ken Becker. An innocent-looking stranger comes to town and lays claim to the reward money offered for a killer. Sundance and his friends are happy to oblige until they discover the stranger's true identity.

74.13 *Sundance and the Bare-Knuckled Fighters.* Jan. 8, 1960. GS: Ken Lynch, Mike Lane, Gregg Palmer, Hal Baylor, Bob Steele. Hoping to create a little local excitement, Sundance arranges a boxing match. There is some heavy betting — then the money disappears.

74.14 *Sundance and the Kid from Nowhere.* Jan. 15, 1960. GS: Scott Marlowe, Dick Rich, John Close, George Graham. A boastful young gunman brazenly admits beating and robbing an old miner. Sundance locks him in the hotel basement to await the marshal.

74.15 *Sundance Goes to Kill.* Jan. 22, 1960. GS: Ron Hayes, Madlyn Rhue, Val Dufour, Bob Nash. Dave Carter is mortally wounded escaping from prison. Before he dies, he tells Sundance the name of the man who framed him for murder.

74.16 *Sundance and the Boat Soldier.* Feb. 5, 1960. GS: Judson Pratt, Edward Kemmer. Marine Lieutenant Booth arranges a cattle buying trip to Georgetown so that he can see Monique. He plans to propose to her.

74.17 *Sundance and the Man in Room Seven.* Feb. 12, 1960. GS: Fintan Meyler, Walter Reed, Robert Bray, Lee Van Cleef. Sundance watches as four nervous passengers get off the stage and check into the hotel. Their nervousness increases when a lone rider follows them into town.

74.18 *Hard Luck for Sundance.* Feb. 19, 1960. GS: Jacques Aubuchon, Walter Coy, Lew Gallo, Len Lesser, Irving Mitchell, Peggy Stewart, Wayne Heffley. Tired of being awakened in the middle of the night to register incoming guests, Sundance decides to hire a night clerk. His choice is Harry Holcombe, an old prospector who has had a streak of bad luck.

74.19 *Sundance and the Greenhorn Trader.* Feb. 26, 1960. GS: Richard Ney, Richard Devon. When a trapper doesn't return to Georgetown during a wintry blizzard, Sundance and Aaron head into the hills to find him.

74.20 *Sundance and Useless.* March 4, 1960. GS: Bruce Gordon, Read Morgan. Useless is the name of Sundance's dog. When a bounty hunter checks into the hotel with his catch, the prisoner finds Useless useful in a bid for freedom. He adds dognapping to his list of crimes.

74.21 *Sundance and the Hero of Bloody Blue Creek.* March 11, 1960. GS: Jerome Cowan, Frank De Kova, William Newell. A self-styled hero of the Indian wars returns to the scene of his triumphs to run for political office.

74.22 *Sundance and the Marshal of Water's End.* March 18, 1960. GS: Karl Swenson, Stewart Bradley, Buck Young, Oliver McGowan, Dick Meyers. Gunmen are in hot pursuit of elderly Marshal Jed Holmes. Sundance offers to hid the lawman at the hotel.

74.23 *Sundance and the Black Widow.* April 1, 1960. GS: Patricia Medina, Dennis Cross, Carole Kent, Russell Bender. Sundance has had a wild time in Denver, but he is a little hazy about what went on. Then Sabrina steps off the stage and reminds him that he promised to marry her.

74.24 *Vengeance for Sundance.* April 8, 1960. GS: J. Pat O'Malley, Lane Bradford, Ed Faulkner, H.M. Wynant. A fleeing bank bandit stops to help Sundance, who has been bitten by a rattlesnake.

74.25 *Sundance and the Man in the Shadows.* April 15, 1960. GS: Philip Abbott, Oliver McGowan, Wayne Heffley. There is a mad killer running amok in Georgetown. After he tries to kill Annette, Sundance leads the search to unmask him.

74.26 *Sundance and the Long Trek.* April 22, 1960. GS: Denver Pyle, Paul Burke, Harry Carey, Jr. Sundance is charged with the murder of a dance hall girl. There is a disagreement between the three posse members about where to take him to trial.

74.27 *Bounty for Sundance.* April 29, 1960. GS: King Donovan, Richard Shannon, Catherine McLeod. An old friend arrives at the hotel with a bounty hunter close on his heels. He wants Sundance to turn him in and collect the reward.

74.28 *Sundance and the Good-Luck Coat.* May 6, 1960. GS: Russ Bender, Robert Gist, Harry Swoger, O.Z. Whitehead, Dick Meyers. A coat was left behind by a guest who took off without paying six day's room and board. Sundance puts it on and immediately hits a streak of luck.

74.29 *Sundance and the Cattlemen.* May 13, 1960. GS: Brad Trumbull, David White, Robert Lowery, Rudolph Anders. A group of strangers come to Georgetown. They are wealthy cattle buyers, they say, and they are going to turn the place into a prosperous cattle center.

74.30 *Sundance and the Barren Soil.* May 20, 1960. GS: Joanne Linville, James Lydon, Don Keefer, Stephen Roberts, Marc Platt, Gordon Polk. Sundance wins some land in a poker game. Described as fertile land by Turkey Crowder, its former owner, it proves to be an arid waste, and Jennifer and Lowell Wheatley, a destitute young couple, are living on it.

74.31 *Sundance and the Fallen Sparrow.* May 27, 1960. GS: Patricia Breslin, Kevin Hagen, Rex Holman. Ellie has allowed alcohol to control her life, but now she is struggling to stay on the wagon. Annette suggests to Sundance that they help her out with a job as waitress at the hotel.

74.32 *Sundance and the Delayed Gun.* June 3, 1960. GS: Henry Silva, Albert Salmi, Barry McGuire. A hulking brute of a man rolls into the hotel and demands a room. Sundance senses something odd about his guest — beneath the swagger, he is quaking with fear.

75. How the West Was Won

ABC. 60/120 min. Broadcast history. Sunday, 8:00-9:00, Feb. 1978–Aug. 1978; Monday, 9:00-11:00, Jan. 1979–April 1979.

Regular Cast: James Arness (Zeb Macahan), Fionnula Flanagan (Aunt Molly Culhane), Bruce Boxleitner (Luke Macahan), Kathryn Holcomb (Laura Macahan), William Kirby Cullen (Josh Macahan), Vicki Schreck (Jessie Macahan).

Premise: This series depicted the adventures of rugged mountain man Zeb Macahan, who is left to care for his brother's four children. Later episodes dealt with the Macahans as they begin a ranch in the Tetons to raise Appaloosa horses.

The Episodes

75.1 *Episode One.* Feb. 6, 1977. GS: Anthony Zerbe, Don Murray, Brit Lind, Royal Dano, John Dehner. Set in the mid-1860s, the series interweaves the stories of three principal characters: Kate Macahan, a widow whose romantic feelings are rekindled by a disarming cowboy; her eldest son Luke, an Army deserter on the run; and her brother-in-law Zeb, the saddle-hardened patriarch who sets out to track Luke down.

75.2 *Episode Two.* Feb. 7, 1977. GS: Don Murray, Royal Dano, David Huddleston, Robert Padilla, Richard Angarola, John Dehner. Zeb joins a hard-bitten mountain man named Cully to search for Cully's son, held captive by Arikara Indianas. This episode also traces the growing fondness of Erica for Luke and of Kate for Anderson, who is challenged to fight for her by a Shoshone brave.

75.3 *Episode Three.* Feb. 14, 1977. GS: Don Murray, Britt Lind, Bridget Hanley, Jack Elam, Parley Baer, Paul Fix, Bebe Kelly. Indian war threatens the Macahan homestead. Meanwhile, Zeb continues his search for Luke, and so does a bounty hunter.

Season Two

75.4 *Episode One.* Feb. 12, 1978. GS: Lloyd Bridges, Ricardo Montalban, Horst Buchholz, Elyssa Davalos, Christopher Lee, Brian Keith. Zeb Macahan is tapped to mediate between the Army and the Sioux, who are posed for war after visiting Russian royalty slaughtered buffalo on their reservation. Meanwhile, Chicago-bred Molly Culhane arrives after her sister's death to join the now motherless Macahan siblings on their Great Plains homestead.

75.5 *Episode Two.* Feb. 19, 1978. GS: Richard Basehart, Elyssa Davalos, Ricardo Montalban, Lloyd Bridges, Horst Buchholz, Cameron Mitchell, Tim Matheson, Brian Keith, Mel Ferrer. Zeb sides with the Sioux after a Russian dies in a skirmish over a treaty violation. Laura accepts a marriage proposal from Mormon polygamist Jeremiah Taylor, and Luke joins up with bandits.

75.6 *Episode Three.* Feb. 26, 1978. GS: Lloyd Bridges, Elyssa Davalos, Vera Miles, Richard Basehart, Tim Matheson, Kristopher Marquis. Luke escapes from a thieving band of ex-Confederates to warn Sheriff Gant of their robbery scheme. Zeb is unexpectedly reunited with an old love he rescues from abductors, and Laura reconsiders her plans to wed Jeremiah Taylor.

75.7 *Episode Four.* March 5, 1978. GS: Vera Miles, Lloyd Bridges, Richard Basehart, Tim Matheson, Warren Kemmerling, William Shatner. A physician is summoned to treat Jessie, who lies comatose from bee-sting poisoning. Luke cannot avert a gold-shipment robbery by ex-Confederates. Zeb grows skeptical of Beth's claims about her past.

75.8 *Episode Five.* March 12, 1978. GS: Vera Miles, William Shatner. Beth is reunited with her husband, and Zeb returns to the Macahan homestead, where the family opposes his proposal to take a deathly ill Jessie to an Arapaho medicine man.

75.9 *Episode Six.* March 26, 1978. GS: Harris Yulin, Slim Pickens, Pat Petersen, Robert J. Wilke, Ray Tracey. Led by Luke and Zeb, Indian braves hope to buy cattle in Texas to feed their starving tribe. Meanwhile, Molly and Jessie are involved in a stagecoach mishap while en route to Santa Fe.

75.10 *Episode Seven.* April 9, 1970. GS: Pat Petersen, Slim Pickens, Ray Tracey, Harris Yulin, Robert J. Wilke, Warren Vanders. Zeb and Luke lead the Indians on a cattle drive to their starving tribe in Colorado. Meanwhile, Molly hires a drifter to help search for Jessie, who disappeared after a stagecoach accident.

75.11 *Episode Eight.* April 16, 1978. GS: Warren Kemmerling, Ray Tracey, Harris Yulin, Slim Pickens, Michael Conrad, Ed Lauter. Zeb and an old friend comes up with a plan that might secure a pardon for Luke. Meanwhile, Jessie and her Indian friend are captured by two slave traders.

75.12 *Episode Nine.* April 23, 1978. GS: Harris Yulin, Warren Kemmerling, Slim Pickens. During a cattle drive, Zeb and Indian braves are ambushed by renegade Arapahos intent on stealing the herd. Meanwhile, Teel-O is kidnaped by slavers.

75.13 *Episode Ten.* April 30, 1978. GS: Harris Yulin, Kay Lenz, Slim Pickens, Pat Petersen, Michael Conrad, Eric Braeden. Rustlers stalk the cattle drive led by Zeb. Josh sets out to deliver money for legal fees to a jailed Luke, and Molly, Laura and Jessie discover gold on the Macahan homestead.

75.14 *Episode Eleven.* May 7, 1978. GS: Harris Yulin, Kay Lenz, Pat Petersen, Slim Pickens, Jared Martin. Zeb accosts a band of thieves in a saloon. Josh romances an attractive bar girl. Deek Peasley schemes to profit from a gold find on the Macahan homestead.

75.15 *Episode Twelve.* May 14, 1978. GS: Eric Braeden, Harris Yulin, Stephen Elliott, Michael Conrad, Warren Kemmerling, Ed Lauter. On the cattle drive, Zeb must deal with rebellious Indian braves after water becomes scarce. At Luke's murder trial, a letter claiming Luke once cavorted with outlaws is introduced. Doreen tries to discredit Josh's testimony.

75.16 *Episode Thirteen.* May 21, 1978. GS: Harris Yulin, Ed Lauter, Jared Martin, Stephen Elliott, Kay Lenz, Michael Conrad. As Luke and Josh are tracked by a posse, Zeb learns of their plight and temporarily leaves the cattle drive to help them. Meanwhile, at the Macahan homestead, Molly questions Deek Peasley about his previous run-in with Zeb.

Season Three

75.17 *The Gunfighter.* Jan. 15, 1979. GS: Jared Martin, Burton Gilliam, Richard Wright, Morgan Woodward. The focus of this story is professional gunfighter Frank Gayson, hired by a local land baron to persuade neighboring homesteaders, including the Macahans, to vacate his valley. Grayson is an impassive but charismatic sort who captivates young Laura Macahan, despite the threat he embodies. She senses that beneath his callous exterior lies warmth and humanity, and it is her faith in him that bring him to question his assignment.

75.18 *The Rustler.* Jan. 22, 1979. GS: Vincent Van Patten, Taylor Lacher, Jeff East, Keith McDermott, Guy Stockwell, Skip Homeier. Jessie's new heartthrob turns out to be one of a trio of young rustlers Zeb catches making off with some Macahan horses.

75.19 *The Enemy.* Feb. 5, 1979. GS: Kip Niven, Denver Pyle, Lee Bryant, Paul Koslo, William Bryant, Duane Loken, Douglas Dirkson, Richard Moll. On a mission to track down Indians who have been plundering freight wagons, Zeb and a pair of Army scouts become involved in an ongoing war between the Crow and Blackfoot tribes.

75.20 *The Innocent.* Feb. 12, 1979. GS: Perry Lang, Bibi Besch, Charles Tyner, Ron Hayes, Barney McFadden, Fredric

Lehne, George Petrie. Josh befriends a widowed ferry operator and her son, an overprotected innocent with a knack for getting into serious trouble.

75.21 *Hillary.* Feb. 26, 1979. GS: Elyssa Davalos, Ken Curtis, Sean Thomas Roche, Luke Askew, Wilford Brimley, Richard Kelton. Luke's attempt to clear himself of an old murder charge involves not only taking after the killer, but also taking up with a former girl friend.

75.22 *L'Affaire Riel.* March 5, 1979. GS: David Dukes, Laura Cambell, Bill Lucking, Ramon Bieri, Jeff David, Titos Vandis, Philip Bruns, Paul Henry Itkin. Louis Riel, an historical French-Canadian insurrectionist, seeks refuge in the American West, only to be pursued by Canadian vigilantes and by Zeb, on a mission for the U.S. Army.

75.23 *The Scavengers.* March 12, 1979. GS: John Beck, Carol Vogel, Lance LeGault, Lee de Broux, Katy Kurtzman, Mitch Carter, Jack Stauffer, Davis Roberts. After an attack by river pirates, Zeb is left for dead, but Laura and Molly are rescued by a romantic Southern gentleman.

75.24 *The Forgotten.* March 19, 1979. GS: Kenneth Marshall, Bradford Dillman, Laurie Prange, Missy Gold. The Macahans take in a Confederate veteran who has just come out of the mountains, unaware that the Civil War has been long over.

75.25 *Luke.* April 2, 1979. GS: Belinda J. Montgomery, George DiCenzo, James Best, Mills Watson, Ken Swofford, Russell Wiggins, Gerald McRaney. With a price on his head, Luke flees from unrelenting bounty hunters.

75.26 *China Girl.* April 17, 1979. GS: Keye Luke, Rosalind Chao, Robert Ito, Soon-Teck Oh, Bill Fletcher, Alvin Ing. This story focuses on a Chinese family sent to a mine on land leased from the Macahans. Patriarch Leong Chung Hua, faithful to his homeland and traditions, his obedient wife Ah Kam, enterprising son Chuk, and daughter Li Sin, who carries the child of an American seaman who raped her aboard the transport — a source of deep shame to Leong, who vows that the tainted infant cannot be allowed to live.

75.27 *The Slavers.* April 23, 1979. GS: Fernando Lamas, Kim Cattrall, Joaquin Martinez, John Doucette, Beverly Garland, Luise Heath, Roy Jenson, Richard Evans, Dick Davalos. Zeb and Josh search for an old friend's daughter in Mexico, but find the locals strangely uncooperative.

76. Iron Horse

ABC. 60 min. Monday, 7:30–8:30, Sept. 1966–Sept. 1978; Saturday, 9:30–10:30, Sept. 1967–Jan. 1968.

Regular Cast: Dale Robertson (Ben Calhoun), Roger Torrey (Nils Torvald), Gary Collins (Dave Tarrant), Bob Random (Barnabas Roberts), Ellen McRae (Julie Parsons).

Premise: This series depicted the exploits of Ben Calhoun, who won a railroad in a poker game in Wyoming during the 1870s.

The Episodes

76.1 *Joy Unconfined.* Sept. 12, 1966. GS: Diana Hyland, David Sheiner, Steve Ihnat, Woodrow Parfrey, Herb Voland, Harry Swoger, Richard Bull, Stephanie Hill. After winning a railroad in a poker game, Ben Calhoun faces his first problem. Ben's former partner, Luke Joy, claims that the line is rightfully his.

76.2 *The Dynamite Driver.* Sept. 19, 1966. GS: Malachi Throne, Tom Reese, Paul Sorensen, Joel Fluellen, Richarde Lapp, Jon Kowal, James Hong, William Saito, Russ McCubbin. Unless Ben delivers Royal McClintock's 1100 steers to Kansas City within three weeks Ben will go into bankruptcy, and McClintock will be able to take over the railroad. McClintock tries to insure that Ben misses the deadline.

76.3 *High Devil.* Sept. 26, 1966. GS: Louise Sorel, James Best, Rex Holman, Charles Gray, Dal Jenkins, Fred Dale, Hardie Albright, George Winters. Obtaining a right of way through a mountain pass presents a problem for Ben. The owner is the notorious Jez Santeen, who greets her visitors with volleys of rifle fire.

76.4 *Right of Way Through Paradise.* Oct. 3, 1966. GS: Sean McClory, Hoyt Axton, E.J. Andre. Ben's poker prowess wins him the services of four Confederate veterans, Ben's former comrade Beau Sidell and Sidell's sidekicks — all good soldiers who never tired of fighting.

76.5 *Pride at the Bottom of the Barrel.* Oct. 10, 1966. GS: Rod Cameron, Victor Jory, Nina Shipman, Gene Evans, Jock Gaynor, Richard Gilden. Ben gets involved with a band of starving Apaches who left their reservation, and a detachment of misfit troopers who want to force the Indians back.

76.6 *Broken Gun.* Oct. 17, 1966. GS: Leigh Chapman, Robert Lyons, Strother Martin, Philip Ober, Kelly Jean Peters, James Almanzar, Steve Raines, Chuck Webster. Crystal Cochran and her uncle want Dave to stay at their ranch and protect them, but Crystal won't say why.

76.7 *Cougar Man.* Oct. 24, 1966. GS: Henry Darrow, Richard Hale, Morgan Woodward, Rodolfo Acosta. Ben goes after Cougar Man, an Apache who has slain several railroad workers to rid himself of a curse that forces him to keep killing until someone kills him.

76.8 *War Cloud.* Oct. 31, 1966. GS: Stephen McNally, Milton Selzer, John Pickard, Abel Fernandez, Marion Thompson. Ben hopes that a smooth, luxurious train trip will impress a banker and his daughter, but Ben's plans are threatened by a trouble-making Indian who is traveling as an Army prisoner.

76.9 *No Wedding Bells for Tony.* Nov. 7, 1966. GS: David Brian, Jeff Morrow, Virginia Field, Susan Browning, Warren Vanders. Ben's patience is worn thin after a long journey to attend a friend's wedding. The friend is nowhere to be found, and the townspeople warn Ben to stop asking questions and go home.

76.10 *The Man from New Chicago.* Nov. 14, 1966. GS: Madlyn Rhue, John Milford, James Anderson, Duane Gray. Ben passes himself off as a notorious gunslinger to gain entrance to New Chicago, a well-fortified outlaw refuge where Dave is being held prisoner.

76.11 *Explosion at Waycrossing.* Nov. 21, 1966. GS: Burr De Benning, Tol Avery, Michael T. Mikler, Mort Mills, Toian Matchinga. Ben becomes an outlaw to recover the $50,000 stolen from one of his baggage cars, and to save the life of footloose Curly Webb, who has been sentenced to hang for committing the robbery.

76.12 *Through Ticket to Gunsight.* Nov. 28, 1966. GS: Sandra Smith, John Pickard, Rayford Barnes, K.T. Stevens. Dave agrees to escort Nora Murphy to her newly acquired gold mine, unaware that a mysterious Captain Miles is determined to prevent the girl from reaching her destination.

76.13 *Town Full of Fear.* Dec. 5, 1966. GS: William Windom, Richard Evans, Antoinette Bower, Dennis Cross, Sid Haig. Ben lays his life on the line when he tries to buy a right-of-way through a nearly deserted mining town. The few remaining inhabitants are harboring a secret, and they will kill to keep it.

76.14 *Big Deal.* Dec. 12, 1966. GS: Hazel Court, Michael Ansara, Pat Conway, Woodrow Parfrey. Ben and his engineer hunt for the man who kidnaped financier Gillingham Conner from Ben's private coach. The search is strictly a man's job, but spirited Elizabeth Conner is determined to help find her husband.

76.15 *A Dozen Ways to Kill a Man.* Dec. 19, 1966. GS: Ford Rainey, Skip Homeier, Royal Dano, Sheree North, Lawrence D. Mann, William Bramley, Dick Shane, Rush Williams, Paul Sorensen, Owen Bush. Ben tries to find out why someone arranged a phony gold strike to lure his men away from the railroad.

76.16 *Hellcat.* Dec. 26, 1966. GS: Arlene Martel, Vincent Beck, Harry Landers, John War Eagle, Tony Young. Ben, in search of land for his railroads, hires a tempestuous Indian woman to guide him to the land of the Sioux. The pair undertake their journey through hostile Cheyenne and Crow country, tracked by greedy hunters and a mysterious Indian warrior.

76.17 *Welcome for the General.* Jan. 2, 1967. GS: Royal Dano, Lisabeth Hush, David Macklin, James J. Griffith, James Almanzar. At a tiny whistle stop, Dave searches for a way to prevent the murder of Civil War general Sherman. Dave, in town to photograph the Union hero, unwillingly joins the townsfolk locked up by a Confederate army veteran, who is preparing a deadly welcome for the general.

76.18 *The Pembrooke Blood.* Jan. 9, 1967. GS: Bert Freed, Sharon Farrell, Tim McIntire, Martin Ashe, Charles Grodin, Bob Morrison. Ben is forced into staking the company payroll and his life on the outcome of a card game. Sitting across the table is Breed Pembrooke, a vengeful land baron whose son was accidentally killed while stealing from Ben's railroad.

76.19 *Volcano Wagon.* Jan. 16, 1967. GS: Lane Bradbury, Dean Harens, Arthur Peterson. Ben undertakes a hazardous journey with a wagon-load of nitroglycerin. He is out to free two men and a child trapped by a rock slide, but he may be stopped by citizens who fear that he will blow up their towns.

76.20 *The Bridge at Forty-Mile.* Jan. 23, 1967. GS: Elena Verdugo, Douglas Kennedy, Richard X. Slattery, Katherine Justice, Clint Kimbrough. Dave, Nils and lumberman Amos Morgan search the brush country for Morgan's vanished brother. Their top suspects are a pair of renegade half-breeds, who trailed the man out of the railroad's construction camp.

76.21 *Shadow Run.* Jan. 30, 1967. GS: Mary Ann Mobley, Richard Devon, Frank Marth, Renny McEvoy. Ben is mistaken for a gunfighter and hired to kill himself. After boarding a train, the railroad president learns that several other passengers are also out to insure his death.

76.22 *Banner with a Strange Device.* Feb. 6, 1967. GS: Bob Random, Jeff York, Brenda Benet, Jorja Curtwright, Anthony Zerbe, Dean Pollack. Barnabas, who grew up in an orphanage, risks his life to learn his true identity. A remarkable resemblance to an arrogant Southerner places the teenager in the middle of a deadly family feud.

76.23 *Appointment with an Epitaph.* Feb. 13, 1967. GS: Gloria Grahame, John Ireland, Susan Howard, Lew Gallo, Bill Bixby, Robert Emhardt, Austin E. Roberts. Carl Mobley, a hired gun known as the Executioner, boards the train for Scalplock on business. Each of the seven passengers, including Ben, has reason to believe that he is the killer's intended victim.

76.24 *The Red Tornado.* Feb. 20, 1967. GS: Michael Rennie, Tony Davis, Jock Gaynor, Anne Karen, Blaisdell Makee. An Indian ultimatum puts a heavy responsibility on Ben's shoulders. The Shoshone are threatening to wipe out a Wyoming town unless Ben hands over the eight-year-old survivor of an Arapaho raiding party.

76.25 *Decision at Sundown.* Feb. 27, 1967. GS: Joan Huntington, Russ Tamblyn, Gus Trikonis, Celia Kaye, Victor French, Sam Reese. Dave plays for time to outsmart a gang of cold-blooded killers. The outlaws are after a shipment of valuable bonds, but they have hijacked the wrong train. Now they are holding the passengers and crew until the next train comes through.

76.26 *The Passenger.* March 6, 1967. GS: Mark Richman, Linda Cristal, Alejandro Rey. A special passenger creates special problems for Ben Calhoun. Frenchman Pierre Le Druc is being sought by the Mexican Government and protected by the U.S. Government, which places Ben's railroad right in the middle.

76.27 *The Execution.* March 13, 1967. GS: Julie Gregg, Noam Pitlik, Michael Whitney, Paul Brinegar, Joseph Perry. The sons of a wagon freightline owner hire an outlaw to help them rob one of Ben's trains. The reason is that Ben beat them out of a lucrative freight contract.

76.28 *Death by Triangulation.* March 20, 1967. GS: Gigi Perreau, Monte Markham, George Murdock, Christopher Dark, Allison Hayes. Ben pursues three sore losers who dropped $50,000 to him in a poker game, and then stole it back.

76.29 *The Golden Web.* March 27, 1967. GS: Gerald Mohr, David Sheiner, Patricia Barry, Woodrow Parfrey, Stanley Clements. Ben unwittingly becomes an accessory to a gold swindle. He allows a promoter to sell surplus railroad land, unaware that the promoter has rigged a phony gold strike on the property.

76.30 *Sister Death.* April 3, 1967. GS: Barbara Stuart, Mark Lenard, Bridget Hanley, Rita D'Amico, Lurene Tuttle, James Hong, John Alderman, Hal Baylor, Richard Crane, Sandy Kevin, Norman Rambo, Don Keefer. Influential Charlie Cuke has hired professional assassins to silence one of Ben's passengers, a lady prisoner who can testify to Charlie's crimes.

Season Two

76.31 *Diablo.* Sept. 16, 1967. GS: Strother Martin, Lloyd Gough, Harry Raybould. Three con artists sucker Ben into buying a share of Diablo, the speediest thoroughbred in the West.

76.32 *Consignment, Betsy the Boiler.* Sept. 23, 1967. GS: Michael Constantine, Linda Marsh, Warren Vanders, Paul Lambert. Ben must buy a badly needed boiler named Betsy, but three obstacles stand in his way: a lack of cash and two groups of determined rival buyers.

76.33 *Gallows for Bill Pardew.* Sept. 30, 1967. GS: Tom Heaton, Jeff Corey, David Lewis, John Marley, Bill Zuckert. Ben turns to a lawyer to help a railroad worker who faces trial for murder. The case, built on circumstantial evidence, is being heard by an unfriendly jury and a hanging judge.

76.34 *Five Days to Washtiba.* Oct. 7, 1967. GS: John Anderson, Louise Troy, Richard Hale, Lane Bradford. Ranchers have murder on their minds as Ben exercises his right of way through their lands. To shepherd a band of starving Indians home, he must travel through a deadly gauntlet 75 miles long and only 30 feet wide.

76.35 *The Silver Bullet.* Oct. 14, 1967. GS: Steve Ihnat, Peter Haskell, Ken Lynch, Ellen Madison. Dave is caught in the middle when a bounty hunter launches a campaign of terror to find killer Joel Tanner. Dave promised Tanner's estranged wife that he wouldn't reveal the outlaw's whereabouts.

76.36 *Grapes of Grass Valley.* Oct. 21, 1967. GS: Lonny Chapman, Emile Genest, Laurie Main, Marie Gomez, Victor Millan, Chuck Hicks, Charles Horvath, Mercedes Alberti, John Mitchum, Michael Abelar. Ben helps French monks establish vineyards in beaver country. Trapper Ike Bridger and his men are violently opposed to any inroads into their last refuge from civilization.

76.37 *Leopards Try, but Leopards Can't.* Oct. 28, 1967. GS: Gene Hackman, Sam Melville, Roy Barcroft. Changing spots proves difficult for bounty hunter Harry Wadsworth, who has come to Scalplock to start a new life. Killing is in Harry's blood, and it surfaces when he sees Ben as a rival for Julie's hand.

76.38 *The Return of Hode Avery.* Nov. 4, 1967. GS: Warren Oates, Susan Howard, Myron Healey. A rancher is up in arms because the trains are spooking his cattle and a troublemaker from Ben's Army days has shows up with murder on his mind.

76.39 *Four Guns to Scalplock.* Nov. 11, 1967. GS: Warren Stevens, Joan Hotchkiss, Simon Scott, Stanley Beck. On the long run to Scalplock, Ben faces a problem of lethal proportions. Four of his passengers are killers transporting a coffin filled with stolen gold.

76.40 *Steel Chain to a Music Box.* Nov. 18, 1967. GS: Harold J. Stone, Paul Peterson, Anna Capri, Tom Baker, Ken Mayer, Anna Wainwright. An accidental shooting brings Ben into conflict with tyrannical Josh Wyatt and his browbeaten sons. Wyatt takes his injured son off the train and hold Barnabas hostage, vowing to kill him is his son dies.

76.41 *Six Hours to Sky High.* Nov. 25, 1967. GS: Gavin MacLeod, Joe Maross, Fay Spain, Sherwood Price, Rex Holman, Bryan O'Byrne. Ben tries to defuse an employee's plot to dynamite a payroll train. Ironically, Ben's ally is the plotter himself, who has learned that his wife and child are passengers on the train.

76.42 *T Is for Traitor.* Dec. 2, 1967. GS: Peter Whitney, Kenneth Tobey, Woodrow Parfrey. To get a gold shipment out of town, a shorthanded Ben is forced to trust his old comrade in arms Matthew Kelsoe, who was literally branded a traitor in the Civil War. Ben doesn't know that the heavy drinking Kelsoe still commands a band of marauders.

76.43 *Dealer's Choice.* Dec. 9, 1967. GS: Jack Kelly, Douglas V. Fowley, Lee Meriwether, Duane Gray, Bill Quinn, William Challee, Hank Worden, Buck Buchanan. Ben employs a bit of poker strategy to outwit two swindlers who conned him out of $10,000 for a worthless bill.

76.44 *Wild Track.* Dec. 16, 1967. GS: Joanna Moore, Whit Bissell, Alan Hewitt, Judson Pratt, Sidney Clute. A dispute over ownership of a posh railway car forces Ben to hijack the car and its wealthy, poker-playing passengers. This results in a wild run from the law, and from outlaws with hijacking plans of their own.

76.45 *Death Has Two Faces.* Dec. 23, 1967. GS: Joyce Van Patten, John Abbott, Dabney Coleman, Norm Alden, William Bramley. The railroad may be stopped dead in its tracks unless Ben can overcome a mountain of spite that is keeping him from buying a necessary right of way.

76.46 *The Prisoners.* Dec. 30, 1967. GS: Edward Asner, Karen Black, Jim McMullan, Henry Beckman, Willard Sage, Harlan Warde, Mike Ragan. A train ride to Doan's Junction is disrupted by two passengers traveling against their will — a killer being brought to trial, and a shy woman who is being forced into marriage.

76.47 *Dry Run to Glory.* Jan. 6, 1968. GS: J.D. Cannon, Leslie Parrish, Dennis Cooney, Joel Fluellen, Allen Jaffe, Jess Kirkpatrick, John McKee. Ben attempts to outmaneuver Victor Lamphier, who has hijacked the train and crew to kidnap the hard-drinking son of a wealthy cattleman.

77. *Jefferson Drum*

NBC. 30 min. Broadcast history: Friday, 8:00-8:30, April 1958-Sept. 1958; Friday, 7:30-8:00, Sept. 1958–Oct. 1958; Thursday, 7:30-8:00, Oct. 1958–April 1959.

Regular Cast: Jeff Richards (Jefferson Drum), Eugene Martin (Joey Drum), Cyril Delevanti (Lucius Coin), Robert J. Stevenson (Big Ed).

Premise: Jefferson Drum is a newspaper editor who is equally adept with a pen and a gun in the lawless gold-mining town of Jubilee in the 1850s.

The Episodes

77.1 *Arrival.* April 25, 1958. GS: John Ashley, Hal Smith, Harry Hickox. Jefferson Drum arrives in the town of Jubilee with his small son and plans to book passage to San Francisco. He is an embittered man — his wife has been murdered and his newspaper wiped out, and he plans to start life again in a new locale. But when he encounters a local gunslinger who has murdered the publisher of Jubilee's paper, Drum decides to stay and fight him.

77.2 *The Bounty Man.* May 2, 1958. GS: John Larch, John Shay, Barbara Stuart, Martin Smith. Jefferson Drum saves a man from an Indian attack, not knowing that the man is a notorious gunslinger. Jeff's son Joey regards the gunman as a hero. The gunman gets into a quarrel and kills a man in self-defense.

77.3 *Law and Order.* May 9, 1958. GS: R.G. Armstrong, Hal Smith, Robert P. Lieb, Lyn Thomas, Charles Courtney. A self-righteous man kills the town's chief troublemaker, and the people of Jubilee choose him as their sheriff. The man, a fanatic, breaks up the romance between a mine owner's son and a barmaid. Then he warns the townspeople that if they do not attend the church services he is going to conduct he will punish them.

77.4 *Bad Day for a Tinhorn.* May 16, 1958. GS: Bruce Gordon, Rita Lynn, Edward McNally, Bill Catching. A group of pretty dance-hall hostesses arrive in Jubilee and open up a saloon. Jefferson Drum runs the ad announcing their arrival in town, but later reports in his newspaper that the customers at the saloon are being fleeced.

77.5 *The Cheater.* May 23, 1958. GS: Andrew Duggan, Philip Ahn, Paul Sorensen, Rex Lease. Two belligerent miners force George McGowan into a card game. When McGowan wins, one of the miners tries to stab him, but Jefferson Drum intervenes. The McGowan claims that he is an ex-gambler, now a preacher, who has come to Jubilee to build a church.

77.6 *A Very Deadly Game.* May 30, 1958. GS: Gerald Milton, Jean Byron, Russell Johnson, Jim Bannon, Kathryn Card. A young woman arrives in Jubilee to marry her fiance. She learns that the man has been murdered and soon after she begins to see a miner who wants to marry her. Editor Jefferson Drum becomes suspicious when the woman's supposedly dead fiance suddenly returns.

77.7 *Madame Faro.* June 6, 1958. GS: Karen Steele, Rick Vallin, Hal Smith. Kathy Evans, one of the West's most successful gamblers, is known as Madam Faro. She comes to Jubilee, and shortly thereafter an attempt is made on her life. In trying to protect the young woman, Jefferson Drum is shot and seriously wounded.

77.8 *Bandidos.* June 13, 1958. GS: Rodolfo Acosta, Than Wyenn, Lita Milan. Jefferson Drum is attacked by three bandits while bringing a new printing press back to Jubilee. They take his horse and buckboard, leaving him to make his way back to town on foot.

77.9 *The Outlaw.* June 20, 1958. GS: Sue George, Martin Balk, Robert Griffin, Harry Hickok, Barbara Stuart. Jefferson Drum finds a young girl on the open prairie who is dressed as a boy. He takes her back to Jubilee and learns that her name is Kate Sparks. Although he tries to win the girl's confidence, he can't learn anything else from her until an outlaw is brought through town on his way to be hanged.

77.10 *Wheel of Fortune.* June 27, 1958. GS: Richard Webb, Jeanne Cooper, Robert Foulk, Ned Glass, Douglas Fowley. Jefferson Drum inherits a share in a gold mine. He learns that three other men and an attractive woman also own shares in the venture. The woman wants to put the mine on a paying basis, but the other shareholders try to buy out both the woman and Drum.

77.11 *The Post.* July 4, 1958. GS: Skip Homeier, James Anderson, Hal Smith. Jefferson Drum writes an editorial about the murderous career of Spade Ritter, notorious gunslinger. Soon after, Kading, a gunman with a grudge against Ritter, arrives in Jubilee. Drum learns that Kading is waiting to kill Ritter.

77.12 *A Matter of Murder.* July 11, 1958. GS: Joe Maross, William Schallert, Joel Ashley, John Harmon. Peter Norse arrives in the town of Jubilee and launches a number of enterprises. Jefferson Drum does some investigating and learns that the man is a swindler. Then Norse threatens to kill Drum if he makes the information public.

77.13 *The Lawless.* July 18, 1958. GS: Robert Anderson, Richard Cutting, Karl Swenson, Frank Gerstle. The town of Jubilee is terrorized by a band of outlaws. Three citizens, led by a man named Varner, form a black-hooded secret society and run the outlaws out of town. But once the outlaws are disposed of the society does not disband.

77.14 *The Hanging of Joe Lavetti.* Aug. 1, 1958. GS: Virginia Gregg, Hal Smith, Harry Lauter, Russell Thorson, Richard Reeves, Greg Barton, Jan Arvan. After years of prospecting, the three Meeker brothers finally strike pay dirt. When a man tries to jump their claim, the Meekers kill him. The following day a woman arrives in town and announces that she was engaged to the dead man.

Season Two

77.15 *Showdown.* Sept. 26, 1958. GS: Paul Richards, Irene Tedrow, Gardner McKay, Dennis Cross. Les Groves is ambushed one night by two men. He manages to escape in the darkness but not before he has killed one of the men. The dead man is a member of the Easton family, who demand revenge. They trail Groves to Jefferson Drum's office.

77.16 *The Keeney Gang.* Oct. 3, 1958. GS: Brad Dexter, Judith Braun, L.Q. Jones, Andy Clyde, Joseph Turkel. While attempting to rob the assayer's office, Scott Keeney and his gang are captured. They are placed in a dry well for safe keeping until the marshal arrives. But Scott Keeney's girl friend helps him escape, and the two take Jefferson Drum with them as a hostage.

77.17 *Stagecoach Episode.* Oct. 10, 1958. GS: Dan Blocker, Helen Westcott, Lane Bradford, John Carson, Dan Sheridan, Henry Rowland. While returning to Jubilee with a large sum of money, Jefferson Drum becomes friendly with a young woman passenger in the stagecoach. Then the stagecoach is stopped and Craig, a circus strongman, climbs aboard. Drum learns that the woman has been running away from Craig.

77.18 *Obituary.* Oct. 16, 1958. GS: Robert Bray, Peggy Maley, Charles Tannen, Frank Scannell, Robert Foulk. Jefferson Drum is given an obituary to run in his newspaper and is shocked when he reads it and finds that it says he will die on a certain day. When the day comes, a traveling carnival arrives in town and the owner, Jack Page, confesses that he wrote the obituary as a publicity stunt to keep the people in town until his show arrived.

77.19 *Band of Iron.* Oct. 23, 1958. GS: Mary La Roche, Gregg Palmer, Peter Hornsby, Rand Brooks. Jefferson Drum worries when two settlers who live outside of town don't show up to buy supplies. He rides out to their house to investigate and finds the husband wounded and his wife terrified. Drum learns that two men shot the husband in the back and then stole the couple's horses.

77.20 *Return.* Oct. 30, 1958. GS: James Griffith, Robert Vaughn, Anna Karen. Troy Bendick, a wanted outlaw, returns to Jubilee to see his wife, who has settled there under another name. Bendick forces Jefferson Drum to give him directions to his wife's home. After Drum has left with Bendick, Shelly Poe, a bounty hunter, arrives in town and forces Drum's son to disclose Bendick's whereabouts.

77.21 *The Captive.* Nov. 6, 1958. GS: Baynes Barron, Sydney Mason, John Reach, Ron Hansen. While taking a killer to jail, Marshal Regan is fatally wounded. Before dying, Regan deputizes Jefferson Drum and gives him the job of taking the killer in.

77.22 *$50 for a Dead Man.* Nov. 13, 1958. GS: Kenneth Tobey, Hal Baylor, Frances De Sales, Dehl Berti. A group of Indians make their living by capturing wanted criminals, for which they are paid a reward. When they come to Jubilee they mistake Jefferson Drum for the sheriff and force him to pay them for the body of Totts Weeb, one of three escaped killers.

77.23 *Pete Henke.* Nov. 20, 1958. GS: Strother Martin, Frank Wolff, Bert Remsen. An elderly mine owner feels like a jinx because all of his partners have died. When he takes on a new partner, young Jim Ford, he hopes to conquer the jinx, but Ford becomes the target of a notorious gunslinger.

77.24 *Thicker Than Water.* Nov. 27, 1958. GS: Abby Dalton, Douglas Kennedy, Ron Hagerthy. Eloise and Will Barton go to Jubilee with their baby and plan to make a home. Will, who is a double for the notorious Billy the Kid, is first surprised, then intrigued, when he learns that the townspeople are afraid of him.

77.25 *Prison Hill.* Dec. 4, 1958. GS: Denver Pyle, Judson Pratt, Nancy Hadley, Charles Fredericks, John Beradino. Jeff and a prison chaplain are captured by the girl friend of a condemned killer, with the help of another boy friend of hers. They are told they must get the prisoner released.

77.26 *Simon Pitt.* Dec. 11, 1958. GS: Michael Connors, Ted de Corsia, Ken Mayer, Patrice Wymore, Alexander Campbell. Jefferson Drum and his son Joey journey to the town of Jackson to pick up some newsprint. Once there, they met lawyer Simon Pitt, who saves Drum's life when Drum is threatened by the town boss.

78. Jim Bowie

ABC. 30 min. Broadcast history: Friday, 8:00-8:30, Sept. 1956–Aug. 1958.

Regular Cast: Scott Forbes (Jim Bowie).

Premise: This series recounted the life and exploits of legendary frontiersman Jim Bowie. It was set during the 1830s in New Orleans.

The Episodes

78.1 *The Birth of the Blade.* Sept. 7, 1956. GS: Walter Sande, Robert Foulk, Kem Dibbs. This episode relates the circumstances that originally led Bowie to invent the famous Bowie knife.

78.2 *The Squatter.* Sept. 14, 1956. GS: Jeanne Moody, Steven Geray, Virginia Christine, George Eldredge. Regina, a landowner, is about to throw a German immigrant couple off her land. Jim Bowie goes to the woman to talk her out of this decision, only to learn she is the same woman he had an argument with that morning.

78.3 *An Adventure with Audubon.* Sept. 21, 1956. GS: Robert Cornthwaite, Barbara Eller, Jacques Scott, Booth Colman. Bowie comes to the aid of naturalist-painter John James Audubon, who is sought by both royalist and revolutionary French forces. The French belive Audubon is their long-lost dauphin.

78.4 *Deputy Sheriff.* Sept. 28, 1956. GS: Michael Landon, Josie Wyler, Maurice Marsac. Bowie accepts a temporary appointment as a deputy sheriff. His duties are to guard a prisoner, the son of a member of a French society at odds with the government. The prisoner insists that he is innocent, and Bowie determines to find out the facts.

78.5 *Trapline.* Oct. 5, 1956. GS: Ross Elliott, Lisa Gaye, Booth Colman. The Cajun fur trappers of Louisiana refuse to trade with Jim Bowie. They have been convinced by a fur company that they cannot trade with anyone not a member of that company. Bowie finally talks one of the trappers into dealing with him. The next morning he is found dead.

78.6 *Broomstick Wedding.* Oct. 12, 1956. GS: Mike Connors, Yvette Dugan, Paul Bryar. Jim Bowie trades horses with his neighbor, Rafe Bradford. This starts a chain of events resulting in Bowie being mistaken for Rafe by an irate father.

78.7 *Natchez Trace.* Oct 19, 1956. GS: Ross Elliott, Brad Morrow, Havis Davenport, John Bryant. A band of greenhorns headed for Natchez asks Jim Bowie for help. They are afraid of being robbed by a highwayman named Hawk.

78.8 *Jim Bowie Comes Home.* Oct. 26, 1956. GS: Kem Dibbs, Minerva Urecal, Peter Hansen. On his return home from a business trip, Jim Bowie finds the town in an uproar. A gang of young hoodlums has taken over and is terrorizing the citizens.

78.9 *The Ghost of Jean Battoo.* Nov. 2, 1956. GS: Ann Codee, Joe Conley, Kem Dibbs. An old crone and her son demand and get protection money from a group of superstitious Louisiana farmers. They claim that Jean Battoo, a long-dead pirate, has returned to haunt the territory.

78.10 *The Secessionist.* Nov. 9, 1956. GS: Marilyn Saris, Robert Lynn, Nestor Paiva, Jacques Gallo. President Andrew Jackson learns that Louisiana's French planters are planning to secede from the Union. He assigns a friend of Jim Bowie to stop the revolt before it can snowball into open rebellion.

78.11 *Land Jumpers.* Nov. 16, 1956. GS: Willard Waterman, Val Dufour, Narda Onyx, Peter Hansen. Jim and his brother Rezin sell a large tract of land belonging to them. They suspect a forgery when an unscrupulous French speculator appears bearing prior title to the property. But a relative of Jim's, Judge Koford, assures them that the document is genuine.

78.12 *The Select Females.* Nov. 23, 1956. GS: Roger Etienne, Eleanor Audley, Joyce Vanderveen. After one of her students is kidnaped, the headmistress of Miss Peabody's Select Female Academy sets off to rescue her. En route, she meets Jim Bowie and enlists his assistance.

78.13 *Jim Bowie and His Slave.* Nov. 30, 1956. GS: Joel Fluellen, Rita Lynn, Anthony Warde, Ivan Triesault, Booth Colman, Maurice Marsac, Richard Benedict. Bowie discovers one of the slaves he has freed is being sent to a slave auction. He attempts to separate this man from the others.

78.14 *Outlaw Kingdom.* Dec. 7, 1956. GS: Rita Lynn, Mike Mazurki, Charles Watt, Minerva Urecal, Maurice Marsac. Jim Bowie goes in search of valuable goods stolen from him by river pirates. The trail leads him into a trap set by his long-time enemy, Pierre Jouvin.

78.15 *The Swordsman.* Dec. 14, 1956. GS: Jeanne Moody, Lilyan Chauvin, Michael Landon, Richard Avonde. Jim Bowie goes to New Orleans to buy an estate, but loses sight of his objective after he meets the owner.

78.16 *The Return of the Alciblade.* Dec. 21, 1956. GS: Ivan Triesault, Judi Boutin, Johnny Lee, Ramsay Hill, Ernestine Wade, Peter Walker. Jim Bowie remains in New Orleans for Christmas, but to make up for his absence from home buys an expensive gift for his mother. Before he can send it to her, it is stolen, and he sets out to locate the thief.

78.17 *Monsieur Francois.* Dec. 28, 1956. GS: Paul Playdon, Joyce Vanderveen, Roger Til, James Fairfax, Franz Roehn, Paul Thompson, Lane Bradford. A ten-year-old marquis arrives in New Orleans from Paris. Jim Bowie learns that the youngster and his aunt are the marked victims of a confidence ring.

78.18 *A Horse for Old Hickory.* Jan. 4, 1957. GS: Denver Pyle, Ian Wolfe, Peter Mamakos, Vicki Bakken, Addison Richards, Ernest Sarracino, Frank Yaconelli, Ralph Smiley. Jim Bowie bids for a racing mare to present to President Andrew Jackson. What he doesn't know is that the unknown person bidding against him is his old friend Sam Houston.

78.19 *The Beggar of New Orleans.* Jan. 11, 1957. GS: John Hoyt, Robert Cornthwaite, Joyce Vanderveen, Morris Ankrum, Lorna Thayer, Paul Playdon. Jim Bowie learns why a former fencing champion has now become a beggar and tries to do something to help the man.

78.20 *Osceola.* Jan. 18, 1957. GS: Abel Fernandez, Josie Wyler, Peter Hansen, George Chester, Luis Cabello, Victor Magana. Jim Bowie gets into an argument with the U.S. Army over the rights of the Seminole Indians. The Army wants to move the tribe out of its traditional home into another more barren area.

78.21 *Master at Arms.* Jan. 25, 1957. GS: Peter Mamakos, Denver Pyle, John Miljan, Carol Ann Daniels, Paul Playdon, Joyce Vanderveen. Jim Bowie is sold a lottery ticket by a French swordsman. When Jim turns out to be the winner, the swordsman then attempts to rob and murder the frontiersman.

78.22 *Convoy Gold.* Feb. 1, 1957. GS: Sean McClory, King Donovan, Jacques Scott, Bob Cunningham, Anthony Eustral. Jim Bowie sets out for New Orleans with a precious cargo, a fortune in gold.

78.23 *Spanish Intrigue.* Feb. 8, 1957. GS: Lewis Charles, Lisa Gaye, Ivan Triesault, Dick Avonde, Val Dufour, Argentina Brunetti. During his business trip to New Orleans, Jim becomes involved with Simon Bolivar's plan to liberate Latin America from the Spanish.

78.24 *Bayou Tontine.* Feb. 15, 1957. GS: Robert Cornthwaite, Edward Colmans, Carol Leigh, John Cliff, Fay Roope, Speir Martin, George Chester. Naturalist James Audubon asks Jim Bowie to help him protect a young girl who has inherited a large fortune. Her life has been threatened.

78.25 *German George.* Feb. 22, 1957. GS: Wanda D'Ottoni, Fred Sherman, Paul Frees. Jim Bowie's partner is cheated out of most of his money by a crooked gambler, then murdered. Just before he dies, he gives Jim a clue as to the identity of the killer.

78.26 *An Eye for an Eye.* March 1, 1957. Jim makes a desperate effort to stop the Cherokee Indians from going on the warpath. His one mistake is telling an Indian princess the story of John Smith and Pocahontas.

78.27 *The Captain's Chimp.* March 8, 1957. GS: Lita Milan, William Schallert, Peter Mamakos, John Rogers. A chimpanzee who has been trained to climb in windows and steal, picks Jim Bowie as his victim. Jim starts a search for the animal and his owner, and finds he is not the only one looking for them.

78.28 *Jackson's Assassination.* March 15, 1957. GS: Leslie Kimmell, Perry Lopez. Jim Bowie unwittingly joins in a plot to assassinate President Andrew Jackson. When the first attempt to shoot the President fails, Jim realizes he is being used as a pawn and tries to save the President's life.

78.29 *Rezin Bowie, Gambler.* March 22, 1957. GS: Peter Hansen, Minerva Urecal, Grant Richards, Nancy Saunders, Robert Tafur. Jim's younger brother, Rezin, wins a large sum of money at the gambling tables. He is convinced that the life of a gambler is the only profession, and moves to New Orleans to live in style. Jim does some investigating and learns his brother is being set up for a killing by a group of professional gamblers, and he sets out to rescue the boy.

78.30 *Thieves' Market.* March 29, 1957. GS: Joyce Vanderveen, Pam Beaird, Paul Playdon, Kem Dibbs, Kay E. Kuter, Chester Jones. Jim's young friend Francois persuades Jim to take him to the notorious Thieves' Market in New Orleans. He is anxious to purchase a gift for his aunt, and finally decides on some jewelry. But the jewels are the real thing, and the leader of the thieves decides Jim and Francois must pay with their lives.

78.31 *The Pearl and the Crown.* April 5, 1957. GS: William Schallert, Marcel Rousseau, Frank Wilcox, Russ Bender. Jim Bowie arrivers in New Orleans to confront an editor with a poem written about Bowie. Shortly after the meeting the editor is found murdered, and Jim is accused of the crime.

78.32 *The General's Disgrace.* April 12, 1957. GS: Ray Stricklyn, Dayton Lummis, Carole Mathews, Pauline Myers. The owner of a New Orlean's gambling house tells Jim that a general's son has begun gambling and has incurred heavy losses. Jim feels there is a connection between recent holdups and the young man's debts.

78.33 *The Lottery.* April 19, 1957. GS: Howard Wendell, Myrna Dell. In an effort to help an orphanage, Jim engages several men to organize a lottery. Unknown to Jim they plan to fix the drawing so that they will win the grand prize as well as collect a fee for their services.

78.34 *The Intruder.* April 26, 1957. GS: Paul Playdon, Lee Erickson, Joyce Vanderveen, Harry Lauter. A youthful burglars is injured while robbing the home of Jim's young friend Francois. Francois' sister takes pity on the young man and decides to take care of him until he recovers. Meanwhile Jim does some investigating, finds the boy's father is to blame and tries to help the youngster.

78.35 *Country Cousin.* May 3, 1957. GS: Manning Ross, Howard McNear, Jay Jostyn. Trying to help a young relative visiting him, Jim cuts him in on a business deal that turns out to be a swindle. His relative believes that Jim is in on the racket.

78.36 *The Bound Girl.* May 10, 1957. GS: Jeanne Moody, Robert J. Wilke, Lurene Tuttle, Austin Green. When the wife of an unpopular resident dies, the husband immediately brings in an Irish girl under a bondage contract. Hearing of the girl's efforts to escape her bondage, Bowie gets involved

78.37 *The Bounty Hunter.* May 17, 1957. GS: William Schallert, William Ching, Eddy Waller, Mel Dowd, Reginald Sheffield, Louis Lettieri. Jim and his friend Justy Tebbs unwit-

Jim Bowie

tingly befriend a fugitive from justice. They in turn are also pursued by law officers.

78.38 *Gone to Texas.* May 24, 1957. GS: Rodolfo Hoyos, Jr., Virginia Core, Douglas Kennedy, Vincent Padula. Jim runs into passport difficulties when he tries to cross over into Mexico. Then he uncovers a plot to kill him.

Season Two

78.39 *Epitaph for an Indian.* Sept. 6, 1957. GS: Peggy McCay, Henry Brandon, Peter Whitney, Lyn Osborn. In order to keep his promise to a dead Indian friend, Jim Bowie travels to the town where his friend lived to visit his father. He learns that the man has been shot in a fight between the town's residents and some Indians.

78.40 *Flowers for McDonogh.* Sept. 13, 1957. Jim Bowie is in New Orleans to transact an important real-estate deal that promises to make him a rich man. But Jim is beaten out on the deal by wily Scotsman John McDonough.

78.41 *The Irishman.* Sept. 20, 1957. GS: Sean McClory. Jim Bowie takes over the bond contract of an indentured Irishman in an effort to help the man. But Jim finds himself in trouble when the Irishman almost convinces an innkeeper that Jim is the indentured servant and the Irishman the master.

78.42 *Counterfeit Dixie.* Sept. 27, 1957. GS: Gordon Jones, Nick Dennis, Sid Cassel, Penny Santon. In an attempt to break up a gang of counterfeiters, Jim Bowie enlists the aid of an ex-pickpocket and an ex-horsethief.

78.43 *Bullet Metal.* Oct. 4, 195. Jim Bowie tries to buy a lead mine from a Quaker. But the man fears the lead will be used to make bullets.

78.44 *The Quarantine.* Oct. 11, 1957. Joyce Vanderveen, Paul Playdon, Frank Tweddell, Jonathan Hole, James Fairfax. A group of thieves steals a shipment of smallpox vaccine and holds it for ransom. Jim Bowie risks his life to recover the vital vaccine and save the city of New Orleans from an epidemic.

78.45 *A Fortune for Madame.* Oct. 18, 1957. GS: Elizabeth Patterson, Fay Baker, Ellen Corby, Antony Eustrel. Jim Bowie begins negotiations for a valuable piece of property that will net him a good profit. But before the transaction is completed, he learns that the owner's niece, who holds a power of attorney for the owner, has been persuaded to sell to a swindler. Bowie decides to recover the deed and return it to the rightful owner.

78.46 *House Divided.* Oct. 25, 1957. Jim Bowie stops at a friend's cabin while on a hunting trip, but is shot and wounded as he approaches the dwelling. Later he regains consciousness in a luxurious mansion, where a young woman pleads with him not to reveal who shot him.

78.47 *The Whip.* Nov. 1, 1957. Jim Bowie learns of a plot to force prisoners to work on Texas plantations without payment, and is on his way to disclose the knowledge to the authorities when he is trapped in a warehouse by a man with a bullwhip.

78.48 *The Pearls of Talimeco.* Nov. 8, 1957. GS: Regis Toomey, June Carter, Ted de Corsia. Jim Bowie and Cow Chief, an Indian friend, attempt to send tightwad Charles Ike Snavely on a wild goose chase, but the plan backfires.

78.49 *Charivari.* Nov. 15, 1957. GS: Lloyd Corrigan, Amzie Strickland, Jean Howell. Jim Bowie investigates the death of an elderly bridegroom on his wedding night.

78.50 *Hare and Tortoise.* Nov. 22, 1957. GS: Josanna Mariani, Myron Healey, Addison Richards, William Allyn. Landowners plot to move the capital of Louisiana from New Orleans to a small Mississippi town to increase the value of their land.

78.51 *The Bridegroom.* Nov. 29, 1957. GS: Dee Humphrey, Edwin Jerome, Alan Reed, Charles Meredith. Fleeing from a waterfront gang, Jim Bowie hides in a home in the French Quarter, where he finds himself a prospective bridegroom.

78.52 *The Alligator.* Dec. 6, 1957. GS: Edward Ashley, Abraham Sofaer, Larry Dobkin. Jim Bowie buys a doll for a little girl's birthday and finds in it a clue to a homicide plot.

78.53 *Country Girl.* Dec. 13, 1957. GS: June Carter, Miguel Landa. In New Orleans, Jim Bowie and his brother's fiancee Rachel are duped by a beautiful swindler and her partner. They tell Bowie they need money to release a relative imprisoned in Mexico.

78.54 *Mexican Adventure.* Dec. 20, 1957. GS: Peter Mamakos, Whit Bissell, Rodolfo Hoyos. Joel Poinsette, American minister to Mexico, is captured by Gen. Santa Ana, leader of revolutionary forces. Jim Bowie and the pirate Jean Lafitte set out to rescue him. They reach him but are cut off from the escape. They seek refuge in an inn where the people are celebrating Christmas. The true story of the naming of the Christmas flower, the poinsettia, is told.

78.55 *Silk Purse.* Dec. 27, 1957. GS: Peggy McCay, Chubby Johnson, Gladys Hurlbut, Leonard Bell. In a poker game a man offers his young daughter as a stake and Bowie decides to teach him a lesson. He wins the man's daughter and then places her in a finishing school to make a lady out of her.

78.56 *Choctaw Honor.* Jan. 3, 1958. GS: Morey Amsterdam, Robert Warwick, Stewart Bradley, Rose Marie, Alex Stagg. When Jim Bowie is robbed, he learns that the man who robbed him is also wanted by an Indian tribe for murder.

78.57 *The Close Shave.* Jan. 10, 1958. GS: William Schallert, Charles Halton, Charles Meredith, Percy Helton, Strother Martin. An assassin, intent on killing Jim Bowie, mistakes another man for his victim and shoots him. When he realizes he has killed the wrong man he starts out again after Bowie.

78.58 *Pirate on Horseback.* Jan. 17, 1958. GS: Don Randolph, Lawrence Dobkin, Joyce Compton, Basil Howes. Jim Bowie learns that a member of a cutthroat's gang has committed a crime in his name. He sets out to track down the entire band to avenge his honor.

78.59 *Curfew Cannon.* Jan. 24, 1958. GS: Peter Hansen, Lisa Montell, Maurice Marsac, Karl Swenson. When Jim Bowie and his brother Rezin learn of a plot to rob the bank they own in New Orleans, they have little time to prevent the robbery. They steal the curfew gun belonging to the city in an attempt to foil the robbers.

78.60 *Home Sweet Home.* Jan. 31, 1958. GS: William Schallert, Jean Hamilton, James Westerfield, Grant Richards. Jim's newspaper friend Justy Tebbs arranges a public stage appearance for the composer John Howard Payne. Bowie learns that some rough characters are planning to attend the event and goes along to avert bloodshed.

78.61 *Deaf Smith.* Feb. 7, 1958. GS: Victor Perrin, Edgar

Buchanan, Paul Fierro, Lewis Martin, Doris Wiss. Jim Bowie is on the trail of three notorious outlaws who are terrorizing Texas. When the outlaws threaten his life, Bowie appeals to a scout, Deaf Smith, for help, but the scout has a strange reason for refusing.

78.62 *Ursula.* Feb. 14, 1958. GS: Sidney Blackmer, Tita Aragon, Eugenia Paul, Nan Boardman, Eugene Iglesias. While trying to obtain permission from the Mexican government to build a cotton mill in Texas, Jim Bowie is attracted to the daughter of the vice-governor.

78.63 *Apache Silver.* Feb. 21, 1958. GS: Sidney Blackmer, Richard Hale, George Keymas, Felix Locher. Jim Bowie accidentally comes across information giving the location of a lost silver mine. But hostile Apaches and a Mexican official stand in the way of his search for the mine.

78.64 *A Grave for Jim Bowie.* Feb. 28, 1958. GS: Robert Ellenstein, Victor Sutherland, Ralph Moody, Claude Akins, Lyn Osborn. When Johnny Appleseed is kidnaped by criminals who believe the little man has hidden some gold, Jim Bowie tries to rescue him.

78.65 *Up the Creek.* March 7, 1958. GS: Manning Ross, Olin Howlin, Barbara Lawrence. Jim Bowie, who felt sorry for a hillbilly family, learns that he has been swindled by them. Setting out to get revenge, he further complicates matters by almost getting his cousin married into the family.

78.66 *The Lion's Cub.* March 14, 1958. GS: Roy Hughes, William Challee, Kay E. Kuter, Forrest Lewis. Jim Bowie is refused entry to Texas and is forced to take a position as a valet to an Englishman in order to enter. Once across the border the pair find themselves under attack by white renegades and hostile Comanches.

78.67 *Horse Thief.* March 21, 1958. GS: Sidney Blackmer, Chuck Connors, Eugenia Paul, Richard Hale. Jim Bowie runs into an old friend of his while in Texas. But the friend's thievery almost loses Jim the friendship of the governor of Texas.

78.68 *Jim Bowie, Apache.* March 28, 1958. GS: Chuck Connors. While trying to locate a lost silver mine, Jim Bowie becomes a blood brother of the Lipan Apaches, who he believes know the whereabouts of the mine. But and old friend of Bowie's Cephas K. Ham, becomes the blood brother of the Comanches, who also knows the mine's whereabouts.

78.69 *The Brothers.* April 4, 1958. GS: Wilton Graff, Charles MacArthur, Forrest Lewis, James Pemberton. Jefferson Davis wants to join Jim Bowie in his search for the lost San Saba mine. But his elder brother Joe hears of his plans, quarrels with Bowie and then challenges him to a duel.

78.70 *Patron of the Art.* April 11, 1958. GS: Hans Conried, Lois Corbett, Dan Seymour, Richard Reeves. Jim Bowie intends to buy his mother a plantation. But he meets an art dealer, and decides to invest in paintings instead.

78.71 *Bad Medicine.* April 18, 1958. GS: Doug McClure, Michael Cane, Trevor Bardette, Brett Halsey. Jim Bowie obeys a request by President Jackson to take a doctor to aid an ailing Indian boy whose recovery is vital to a program for relocating the Choctaw tribe. When the doctor turns out to be an inexperienced young man fresh from medical school, Jim's life and the success of the project are threatened.

78.72 *A Night in Tennessee.* April 25, 1958. GS: George Dunn, Tom Brown, Jason Johnson, Joe Barry. Jim Bowie meets Davy Crockett when Bowie decides to run for Congress.

Crockett is his opponent and Bowie is shocked by Crockett's tactics.

78.73 *Bowie's Baby.* May 2, 1958. GS: Hal Torey, Linda Watkins, James Westerfield, Lorna Thayer. A baby is the sole survivor of an Indian raid, and Jim Bowie tries to locate a home for it. But an unsympathetic sheriff in Natchez blocks Bowie's attempts.

78.74 *The Cave.* May 9, 1958. GS: Maureen Cassidy, John Compton, Ed Prentiss, Ruby Goodwin. The bride of Jim Bowie's cousin disappears on her wedding day. An investigation reveals that the woman was last seen with a hypnotist.

78.75 *Man on the Street.* May 16, 1958. GS: Romney Brent, Iphigenie Castiglioni. After a dice game, Jim Bowie learns that a man who gave him an IOU for $5000 is penniless, but owns a great deal of land in New Orleans. Bowie decides to make the man an offer for his land.

78.76 *The Puma.* May 23, 1958. GS: Joe Partridge, Nacho Galindo, Donald Randolph, Martin Garralaga, Pamela Duncan. As a favor to his friend Jim Bowie, Jess Miller travels to Texas, where he is to collect a large sum of money owed to Bowie. But the Mexicans think he is Bowie, and send out the army to capture him.

79. *Johnny Ringo*

CBS. 30 min. Broadcast history: Thursday, 8:30-9:00, Oct. 1959–Sept. 1960.

Regular Cast: Don Durant (Johnny Ringo), Karen Sharpe (Laura Thomas), Mark Goddard (Cully), Terence de Marney (Case Thomas).

Premise: Johnny Ringo was a former gunfighter who served as sheriff of Velardi, Arizona. With the assistance of his deputy, Cully, he help bring law and order to the area.

The Episodes

79.1 *The Arrival.* Oct. 1, 1959. GS: James Coburn. Gunfighter Johnny Ringo accepts the proposal of the people of Velardi, Arizona, and becomes their sheriff. He then appoints the town drunk as his deputy.

79.2 *Cully.* Oct. 8, 1959. GS: Bruce Gordon. A traveling show comes to town featuring a young gunman named Cully. While displaying his ability to the townspeople he attracts the attention of Sheriff Johnny Ringo.

79.3 *The Accused.* Oct. 15, 1959. GS: Robert Gist, Ron Howard, William Schallert. When a murder suspect is acquitted of the charge, angry townspeople insist on a hanging.

79.4 *A Killing for Cully.* Oct. 22, 1959. In the line of duty Deputy Sheriff Cully is forced to kill a man. Cully is conscience-stricken because he has taken a life.

79.5 *The Hunters.* Oct. 29, 1959. GS: Richard Devon. Johnny Ringo is perplexed by a request from Jess Meade, an old friend. Meade asks Ringo to put him in jail.

79.6 *The Posse.* Nov. 5, 1959. Ringo gets the assistance of the townspeople when he goes after a band of outlaws.

79.7 *Ghost Coach.* Nov. 12, 1959. An old Civil War wagon with a skeleton on board is found near town. After Ringo wires the Army to come and investigate, two mysterious killings take place.

Johnny Ringo

79.8 *Dead Wait.* Nov. 19, 1959. Elisha Cook, Jr., Peter Whitney. Sheriff Johnny Ringo is taking two escaped prisoners back to the Arizona State Prison by stagecoach. During the journey, an avalanche wrecks the coach and Ringo is seriously injured.

79.9 *The Rain Man.* Nov. 26, 1959. GS: John Carradine. After a very dry spell in Velardi an unusual man comes to town and claims that he can produce rain.

79.10 *The Cat.* Dec. 3, 1959. GS: Cecil Kellaway, Archie Duncan. An eccentric millionaire from the East arrives in Arizona. The man has brought a Bengal tiger with him and he plans to conduct a tiger hunt.

79.11 *Love Affair.* Dec. 17, 1959. GS: Gloria De Haven, Gerald Mohr. Deputy Sheriff Cully admires Rosemary Blake, but an outlaw also has taken a special interest in her. The gunman comes to town to take Rosemary away with him, and Cully tries to persuade her to stay.

79.12 *Kid with a Gun.* Dec. 24, 1959. GS: Liza Minzies, Robert F. Simon, Vic Morrow. A little girl comes into Cason's general store to buy a gun. The child tells Ringo that her father has been murdered and she is going to find his killer.

79.13 *Bound Boy.* Dec. 31, 1959. GS: Tim Considine, James Westerfield. A young boy runs away from a man who held him in virtual slavery. The lad comes to Arizona to find asylum from his tormentor, but soon becomes the object of an intensive search.

79.14 *East Is East.* Jan. 7, 1960. GS: Debra Paget, Harry Landers, John Pickard, Mike Green. Agnes St. John, a sophisticated author from the East, witnesses murder and violence on a trip through the West. She intends to write a sensational expose of frontier life based on these observations.

79.15 *Poster Incident.* Jan. 14, 1960. GS: Gene Raymond. Politician Arthur Tobias kills two men and claims self-defense. But Ringo is suspicious of his claim.

79.16 *Die Twice.* Jan. 20, 1960. GS: Gene Evans, Brett King, Paul Sorensen, Jean Allison, Cecil Smith, Joe Haworth. Several robbery victims report that the leader of the outlaws who victimized them was a man named Boone Hackett. Hackett has supposedly been dead and buried for many years. Johnny Ringo decides to exhume Hackett's body to start his investigation.

79.17 *Four Came Quietly.* Jan. 28, 1960. GS: L.Q. Jones, Jay C. Flippen, Gordon Polk, Wayne Tucker. Johnny comes to Laura's defense and is forced to kill Billy Boy Jethro. Jethro's family vows revenge.

79.18 *The Liars.* Feb. 4, 1960. GS: Wally Brown, John Larch, Ken Mayer, Alvy Moore, Richard Newton. Posing as a condemned killer, Johnny Ringo is locked up with four other men in death row. Ringo's job is to determine which of the four is innocent.

79.19 *Mrs. Ringo.* Feb. 11, 1960. GS: Mona Freeman, Grant Richards. Ringo receives a shock when a young woman arrives in town and claims she is his wife.

79.20 *The Assassins.* Feb. 18, 1960. GS: Akim Tamiroff, Dennis McMullen. Fleeing the Russian Czar's secret police, Andrevich Baranov, arrives in Velardi, Arizona. Ringo learns that Baranov's pursuers are under orders to assassinate him.

79.21 *The Reno Brothers.* Feb. 25, 1960. GS: Jacques Aubuchon, Ben Cooper, Jim Beck, Charles Fredericks. An Eastern writer shows up with two would-be assassins hot on his trail. Not knowing that the writer is really a wanted murderer, Ringo agrees to help defend him.

79.22 *The Raffertys.* March 3, 1960. GS: Lon Chaney, Jr., Richard Bakalyan, Roxanne Berard, Charles Cooper. Johnny Ringo gets wind of a greedy bounty hunter's plan to kill murder suspect Ben Rafferty, guilty or not. Johnny tries to arrest Rafferty for his own safety before the ruthless bounty hunter gets him.

79.23 *Uncertain Vengeance.* March 10, 1960. GS: Don Dubbins, Stella Stevens, Sarah Selby, Wesley Lau. Out to avenge the death of his killer brother, Harley Krale captures Sheriff Ringo. Then, before the eyes of his mother and his dead brother's girl, Harley reveals his awful plan.

79.24 *Border Town.* March 17, 1960. GS: Matt Dennis, Paul Carr, Ed Nelson, Joyce Meadows. Ringo trails a killer to Mexico and finds him hiding out in a casino called the Garden of Eden.

79.25 *The Gunslinger.* March 24, 1960. GS: Dean Stanton, Fred Krone, Howard Petrie, Judy Howard, Natalie Masters. Two brothers are out to kill Sheriff Ringo and avenge a third brother who was killed by Johnny in a gunfight.

79.26 *The Vindicator.* March 31, 1960. GS: Paul Richards, Robert Griffin, Jean Inness, Dee Pollack, Richard Rust. An escaped prisoner is bent on avenging his wife's death. But his intended victim is in jail under Sheriff Ringo's watchful eye.

79.27 *Black Harvest.* April 7, 1960. GS: Royal Dano, Aneta Corseaut, William Phipps, Craig Duncan, Michael Hinn. A black harvest of revenge is planned by a deranged rancher. He doesn't know that Ringo is looking for the man he is holding prisoner.

79.28 *Judgment Day.* April 14, 1960. GS: Harry Townes, Wright King, Brett King. It's judgment day for Circuit Judge Bentley, out to get a sheriff's eye view of law-enforcement problems. Ringo pins a deputy's badge on him, and they start on the trail of some desperadoes.

79.29 *The Killing Bug.* April 28, 1960. GS: Buddy Ebsen, Joe Perry, Michael Hinn, Maureen Leeds, Wayne Rogers. Three jovial Texans ride into Velardi, but their air of gaiety isn't catching. Soon after their appearance Ringo finds a man's body hanging from a lamp post.

79.30 *Soft Cargo.* May 5, 1960. GS: Steven Marlo, Michael Fox, Sally Todd, Diana Spencer, Maggie Brooks. Outlaws kill the manager of a traveling show and kidnap the showgirls. But one of them escapes and finds her way to Johnny Ringo.

79.31 *Single Debt.* May 12, 1960. GS: Warren Oates, Alvy Moore, Ralph Thomas. A peaceable Chinese family settles on the land adjoining the Scanlon property. In blind hatred, the Scanlons plot to wipe out their new neighbors.

79.32 *The Stranger.* May 19, 1960. GS: Charles Aidman, Susan Cummings, Burt Reynolds. The stranger in Velardi is suave Jeffrey Blake. Dressed like a real Eastern dude, Blake is the butt of the cowboys' jokes.

79.33 *The Derelict.* May 26, 1960. GS: Martin Landau, John Anderson, Enid Janes, John Newton, John Maxwell. The town bank refuses to lend Wes Tymon money to provide medical attention for his wife. When Mrs. Tymon died, West goes for the town banker.

79.34 *Shoot the Moon.* June 2, 1960. GS: Frank Silvera, Theona Bryant, Walter Sande, Ken Patterson, George Keymas.

A townsman brings an Italian astronomer and his daughter to Ringo's office. He found the pair trespassing atop Superstition Mountain, sacred burial ground of the Yaqui Indians, and the incident might set the tribe on the warpath.

79.35 *Killer, Choose a Card.* June 9, 1960. GS: Lurene Tuttle, Mort Mills, Barry Kelley, Whit Bissell, William Schallert, King Calder. Mamie Murphy, Broken Wagon's hard-bitten saloonkeeper, is accused of murder. She telegraphs her old friend Johnny Ringo to save her from hanging.

79.36 *Coffin Sam* (A.K.A. "Reputation for Murder"). June 16, 1960. GS: Alan Hale, Jr., Richard Easton, Michael Hinn, Hank Patterson, Abbagail Shelton. Coffin Sam Sabine, a notorious gunfighter, comes to Velardi looking for trouble. He announces that Ringo will be the next notch on his gun.

79.37 *Lobo Lawman.* June 23, 1960. GS: Karl Swenson, Rodolfo Hoyos, Robert Carricart, Michael Hinn, Joe Perry. A U.S. Marshal brings a Mexican bandit to the Velardi jail. Sheriff Ringo faces a problem. The outlaw boasts that his gang will demolish the whole town to rescue him, and the lawman killed Ringo's uncle ten years earlier.

79.38 *Cave-In.* June 30, 1960. GS: Robert Culp, Ralph Moody, Lane Bradford, Hank Post. A gun-toting stranger rides up to Old Man Cobb's mine, invites himself to dinner and announces he is going to take the place over for a few days. He then hands Cobb a note and orders him to deliver it to Johnny Ringo.

80. *Judge Roy Bean*

Syndicated. 30 min. Broadcast history: Various, Sept. 1955–Sept. 1956.

Regular Cast: Edgar Buchanan (Judge Roy Bean), Jackie Loughery (Letty Bean), Jack Beutel (Jeff Taggard), Russell Hayden (Texas Ranger Steve).

Premise: This series depicted the exploits of Roy Bean, the self-appointed judge of Langtry, Texas, who was known as "the law west of the Pecos."

The Episodes

80.1 *The Judge of Pecos Valley.* Sept. 10, 1955. GS: Jean Lewis, Tristram Coffin, Bill Murphy, Donald Novis, Hal Hopper, X Brands. Judge Roy Bean, his niece Letty and his deputy Jeff Taggart try to help the judge's friend Old Sam, who is heartbroken at his son's having turned out to be a killer, but feels it is his duty to bring the boy to justice.

80.2 *Family Ties.* Oct. 1, 1955. GS: Jose Gonzales Gonzales, Lillian Porter, Robert Lowery, Pierce Lyden, Allegra R. Varron. Judge Roy defends a Mexican family against crooked real estate operators who have inside information that a railroad wants the family's land and who are trying to cheat the family out of the property.

80.3 *The Horse Thief.* Oct. 1, 1955. GS: X Brands, Tristram Coffin, Pierce Lyden, Robert Lowery, Ralph Kingston. When a rancher is accused of horse stealing, Judge Roy fights to keep mob violence from ruling the town of Langtry.

80.4 *Sunburnt Gold.* Oct. 1, 1955. GS: John Warburton, Bill Henry, Lane Bradford, Billy Baucom. Judge Roy goes after some criminals who are trying to make their stolen gold coins look like raw gold nuggets.

80.5 *The Wedding of Old Sam.* Oct. 1, 1955. GS: Tristram Coffin, Hazel O. Keener, Robert Lowery, Pierce Lyden, X Brands. Judge Roy is almost sued for breach of promise when a woman arrives in Langtry claiming that he promised to marry her.

80.6 *The Runaway.* Oct. 15, 1955. GS: John Carpenter, Richard Powers, X Brands, Sandra Hayden, Christopher Angell. Judge Roy goes after a crooked rancher who has contracted with businessmen to deliver a herd of cattle to the railroad on a certain day, and then delays them by force.

80.7 *Slightly Prodigal.* Oct. 15, 1955. GS: X Brands, Bernadene Hayes, Richard Powers, John Carpenter. Judge Roy meets Mrs. Brown, who has come to Langtry in search of her son, but finds that he has turned outlaw and was one of the gang that robbed the coach on which his mother was traveling.

80.8 *Black Jack.* Nov. 1, 1955. GS: Allan Nixon, X Brands, John Warburton, John Carpenter. Judge Roy pursues a notorious train robber who escaped from prison and then murdered the fence who he thought had betrayed him.

80.9 *Judge Declares a Holiday.* Nov. 1, 1955. GS: John Warburton, Allan Nixon, Roy Erwin, Fred Bailes, Doris Simons. Judge Roy encounters a man who visits Western towns, sets up horse races and then disappears with the money collected from bets.

80.10 *Citizen Romeo.* Dec. 1, 1955. GS: Ralph Manza, John Carpenter, George Mather, Leonard Penn. An organ grinder's monkey helps Judge Roy break up a plot to smuggle guns and ammunition to the Indians.

80.11 *Connie Comes to Town.* Dec. 1, 1955. GS: Doris Simons, Allan Nixon, X Brands. Judge Roy goes after three Easterners, two men and a young woman, who has fled from a robbery and plan to split the loot.

80.12 *The Fugitive.* Dec. 1, 1955. GS: Bill Henry, X Brands, Lane Bradford, John Warburton. Judge Roy helps out a respected rancher who is being blackmailed by three crooks claiming to be newspapermen.

80.13 *Letty Leaves Home.* Dec. 1, 1955. GS: John Warburton, Bill Henry, Lane Bradford, X Brands. Judge Roy's niece decides to leave Langtry when her riding and shooting skills cause the townsfolk to overlook her femininity.

80.14 *Murder in Langtry.* Dec. 1, 1955. GS: Leonard Penn, George Mather, John Carpenter, Ralph Kingston. Judge Roy steps in when his deputy, Jeff Taggart, is framed for the murder of a horse trader who had cheated him in a business deal.

80.15 *Vinegarone.* Dec. 1, 1955. GS: Jose Gonzales Gonzales, Joe Herrera, John Carpenter, Richard Powers/Tom Keene, X Brands. Judge Roy goes after two con men who are claiming that a young man has invalid title to the silver mine he inherited from his father.

80.16 *Ah Sid, Cowboy.* Jan. 1, 1956. GS: Sammee Tong, Glenn Strange, Keith Richards. Judge Roy helps out his friend, Ah Sid, who is being compelled to translate a map which two outlaws stole from Chinese gold miners.

80.17 *Checkmate.* Jan. 1, 1956. GS: Earle Hodgins, Myron Healey, Teri York, Robert Swan, Hal Hopper, Ralph Kingston. Judge Roy is almost fooled by the phony death and funeral of a wanted killer who was wounded while trying to steal a payroll.

80.18 *Desperate Journey.* Jan. 1, 1956. Judge Roy leads a posse to hunt down the Indians who kidnapped the adopted son of a wealthy rancher.

80.19 *The Eyes of Texas.* Jan. 1, 1956. GS: Earle Hodgins, Myron Healey, Robert Swan, Orlando Rodriguez, Hal Hopper, Ralph Kingston, Duke Sun Chief. Judge Roy temporarily loss his sight, but still manages to uncover a plot to steal Indian reservation land.

80.20 *Gunman's Bargain.* Jan. 1, 1956. GS: Lash LaRue, Dennis Moore, X Brands, Bill Baucom. Judge Roy tries to persuade a wanted killer to surrender and clear his name.

80.21 *The Hidden Truth.* Jan. 1, 1956. GS: Glenn Strange, Keith Richards, X Brands. Judge Roy tries to clear an ex-convict who is innocently involved in a murder and robbery.

80.22 *The Judge's Dilemma.* Jan. 1, 1956. GS: Glenn Strange, X Brands, Keith Richards, Carlos Victor. Judge Roy launches a campaign against swindlers who are trying to take control of Langtry.

80.23 *The Katcina Doll.* Jan. 1, 1956. GS: Lash LaRue, Myron Healey, Jose Gonzales Gonzales, Kitty Lysen. Judge Roy tries to help the residents of a Mexican Indian village recover their sacred idol, which has been stolen by outlaws.

80.24 *Outlaw's Son.* Jan. 1, 1956. Mason Alan Dinehart III, Lash LaRue, X Brands, Stanley Andrews, Bill French, Ralph Kingston, Bernadene Hayes, Dennis Moore. Judge Roy helps the son of an outlaw choose between right and wrong after his father is murdered.

80.25 *The Reformer.* Jan. 1, 1956. GS: Lash LaRue, Bernadene Hayes, X Brands, Dennis Moore. Judge Roy locks horns with a fanatical female reformer who is determined to remake the town of Langtry to her own liking.

80.26 *The Travelers.* Jan. 1, 1956. GS: Earle Hodgins, Myron Healey, Robert Swan, Hal Hopper, Ralph Kingston, Bernadene Hayes, Jean Vachon. Judge Roy's quick thinking saves the witness to a murder from meeting the same fate as the first victim.

80.27 *The Elopers.* GS: Morgan Jones, John Warburton, John Cason, Teri York. Judge Roy becomes involved in matrimonial mayhem when an irate father takes the law into his own hands and hunts the young man who eloped with his daughter.

80.28 *Spirit of the Law.* April 11, 1956. GS: John Warburton, John Cason, Morgan Jones, John Mitchum. Judge Roy pursues a pair of outlaws who are trying to force two brothers to sell their cattle ranch cheaply.

80.29 *Bad Medicine.* June 1, 1956. GS: Lash LaRue, Teri York, Earle Hodgins, Tom Monroe, Bill French, Ralph Kingston. Judge Roy goes after twin brothers who have confused the authorities by giving each other alibis for their holdups.

80.30 *The Defense Rests.* June 1, 1956. GS: Lash LaRue, Earle Hodgins, Byron Foulger, Tom Monroe, Bill Baucom, Hal Hopper, Ralph Kingston, Fred Kohler, Jr., Bill French. When his deputy Jeff is arrested and accused of a robbery, Judge Roy tries to prove the young man's innocence.

80.31 *Deliver the Body.* June 1, 1956. GS: Rick Vallin, Gregory Gay, May Morgan, John Cason, Reg Browne. Judge Roy tries to clean up the corruption in a town near Langtry.

80.32 *The Hypnotist.* June 1, 1956. GS: Rick Vallin, Reg Browne, Ralph Kingston. Ghosts and blackmail keep Langtry in jitters until Judge Roy brings the situation under control.

80.33 *Terror Rides the Trail.* June 1, 1956. GS: Karen Scott, Gregory Gay, Rick Vallin, John Cason, Reg Browne, Bill French. Judge Roy gives a wagon ride to the wife of a wounded bank robber and winds up being held hostage by the gang.

80.34 *Border Raiders.* July 1, 1956. GS: Tristram Coffin, Glenn Strange, Sandra Hayden, Christopher Angell, Glenn Smith. Judge Roy goes after a white man who is leading renegade Indians on a rampage of killing.

80.35 *The Cross Draw Kid.* July 1, 1956. GS: Frankie Darro, Tristram Coffin, Glenn Strange, Glenn Smith, Bill French, Ralph Kingston. Judge Roy tries to help a young killer who wants to mend his ways after learning that his father is still alive.

80.36 *Four Ladies from Laredo.* July 1, 1956. GS: Gloria McGhee, Gloria Winters, Norma Brooks, Valley Keene, Hal Hopper. Judge Roy and Jeff are captivated by four young women who, unknown to the men, are involved in a recent series of holdups.

80.37 *Luck O' the Irish.* July 1, 1956. GS: John Warburton, Madge Meredith, Morgan Jones, John Cason, John Mitchum. Judge Roy helps a young couple whose life savings have been stolen by bandits.

80.38 *The Refugee.* July 1, 1956. GS: Frankie Darro, Tristram Coffin, Glenn Strange, Hal Hopper, Glenn Smith. Judge Roy saves a Mexican political refugee from being executed for the reward money on his head.

80.39 *Lone Star Killer.* Aug. 1, 1956. GS: Tom Monroe, Lash LaRue, Earle Hodgins, Hal Hopper, Fred Kohler, Jr., Hank Calia. Judge Roy and Jeff are temporarily outwitted by outlaws posing as Texas Rangers.

81. Kit Carson, The Adventures of

Syndicated. 30 min. Broadcast history: Various, Aug. 1951–Aug. 1955.

Regular Cast: Bill Williams (Kit Carson), Don Diamond (El Toro).

Premise: This series depicted the adventures of frontiersman and Indian scout Kit Carson, who roamed the West in the 1880s with his Mexican sidekick, El Toro.

The Episodes

81.1 *California Outlaws.* Aug. 11, 1951. GS: Peter Mamakos, Lillian Molieri, Rico Alaniz, Victor Millan. Kit and El Toro try to trap the bandits who have been robbing stagecoaches.

81.2 *Prince of Padua Hills.* Aug. 18, 1951. GS: Kenneth MacDonald, Glenn Strange, Rita Conde, Frank Hagney, Edwin Parker, Tom London. Kit Carson and El Toro protect the heir of a large ranch, after the cowboy has several near fatal accidents.

81.3 *The Road to Monterey.* Aug. 25, 1951. Kit and El Toro try to protect a senator whose life has been threatened.

81.4 *The Padre's Treasure.* Sept. 1, 1951. One of the west's most feared bandits, El Cougar, steals a shipment of quinine which is vitally needed to stop an epidemic. Kit Carson and El Toro go after him.

81.5 *The Murango Story.* Sept. 8, 1951. GS: John Hamilton, Dee Pollock, Wesley Hudman, Virginia Dale, Margot Guilford, Tony Marsh. Kit Carson is appointed as one of the three guardians of a murdered miner's orphan. He joins the other two in trying to find the young boy's inheritance.

81.6 *Riders of Capistrano.* Sept. 15, 1951. GS: Paul Marion, Donna Martell, Riley Hill, William Tannen, Baynes Barron, Edward Cassidy, Harry Vejar. War is threatened between Mexico and the U.S. when the silver bell of a Mexican mission is stolen.

81.7 *Enemies of the West.* Sept. 22, 1951. GS: Rico Alaniz, Davison Clark, Sherry Moreland, Alan Keys. Kit Carson and El Toro escort the lawyer carrying a pardon for a condemned man about to hang.

81.8 *Law of the Six Guns.* Sept. 29, 1951. GS: Jack Mulhall, Jane Adams, Kenneth McDonald, John Cason. While riding across a mountainside, Kit and El Toro find a runaway horse dragging a lifeless rider.

81.9 *The Devil of Angel's Camp.* Oct. 6, 1951. A young boy is accused of murdering a wagon driver for his gold. Carson and El Toro believe he is innocent.

81.10 *Law of the Frontier.* Oct. 13, 1951. GS: Gordon Barnes, Ford Rainey, Stephen Chase, Patricia Michon, Stanley Farrar, Bert Arnold, Rube Schaffer, Gloria Grant. Colonel Gage, the new sheriff of Green Valley is held up and badly wounded by an outlaw, who impersonates the sheriff and tries to steal a shipment of gold bars.

81.11 *The Road to El Dorado.* Oct. 20, 1951. GS: Raymond Bond, Jo Gilbert, Stanley Andrews, Bill Hale. Judge Warren and Margie Jason, partners in crime, waylay stage coaches carrying gold dust from the El Dorado mines.

81.12 *Fury at Red Gulch.* Oct. 27, 1951. GS: Robert Peyton, William Fawcett, Reed Howes, Mara Corday, Burt Mustin, John Cason. A newspaper man who is trying to outlaw gambling is framed for a killing by an enemy. Kit Carson and El Toro try to save him.

81.13 *The Outlaws of Manzanita.* Nov. 3, 1951. Kit and El Toro are sent by the first American governor of California to tell a family of notorious outlaws that they are no longer fugitives.

81.14 *The Desperate Sheriff.* Nov. 10, 1951. GS: Ross Ford, Movita, William Tannen, John Cason, Jack Ingram, Troy Melton. A young sheriff captures a notorious bandit leader singlehanded.

81.15 *The Hero of Hermosa.* Nov. 17, 1951. GS: Donna Martell, Jan Arvan, Paul Marion, John Mansfield, John Sebastian. The Mexican government is aided by Carson and El Toro in tracking down some diamond smugglers.

81.16 *A Ticket to Mexico.* Nov. 24, 1951. A prize-winning ticket in the Mexican national lottery is stolen from a struggling art dealer. Kit and El Toro start out to catch the thief.

81.17 *The Return of Trigger Dawson.* Dec. 1, 1951. Marjorie Lord, Noralee Norman, Bob Cason, Gabriel Dubrey, Stanley Andrews, Riley Hill. Trigger Dawson, a notorious bandit, escapes from jail and tries to blackmail his former wife, now a schoolteacher.

81.18 *The Teton Tornado.* Dec. 8, 1951. GS: Linda Stirling Carson's suspicions are aroused when a seemingly slow horse wins a race.

81.19 *Bad Man of Briscoe.* Dec. 15, 1951.

81.20 *Spoilers of California.* Dec. 22, 1951.
81.21 *Feud in San Filipe.* Dec. 29, 1951.
81.22 *The Trap.* Jan. 5, 1952.
81.23 *Border Corsairs.* Jan. 12, 1952. GS: Robert Bice, John Eldredge, Martin Garralaga, Alex Montoya, Charlita, Pilar del Rey, Mara Corday, Guy Teague.
81.24 *Curse of the Albas.* Jan. 19, 1952.

Second Season

81.25 *Snake River Trapper.* Aug. 2, 1952.
81.26 *The Baron of Black Springs.* Aug. 9, 1952. GS: Tris Coffin, Marshall Reed, Terry Frost, Sandy Sanders, Barbara Bestar, Nolan Leary, Gregg Barton, Bud Osborne.
81.27 *Danger Trail.* Aug. 16, 1952. GS: Robert Peyton, Lois Hall, Virginia Dale, Sammie Reynolds, Rusty Wescoatt.
81.28 *Wild Horses of Pala.* Aug. 23, 1952. GS: Jean Howell, Lyle Talbot, Keith Richards, William Haade, Charles Stevens, Baynes Barron.
81.29 *Trail to Ft. Hazard.* Aug. 30, 1952. GS: Jim Bannon, Myron Healey, Charlita, Paul McGuire, Fred Graham, Boyd Stockman.
81.30 *Warwhoop.* Sept. 6, 1952. GS: John Eldredge, Duane Thorsen, Carol Thurston, Edward Colmans, David Colmans, Charles Stevens, George M. Lynn, Bob Woodward. The friendly Indians of Padre Diego are threatened by a man who hates Indians. Kit and El Toro learn of the Indians' danger while at a California mission.
81.31 *Outlaw Paradise.* Sept. 13, 1952.
81.32 *Powdersmoke Trail.* Sept. 20, 1952.
81.33 *Trouble in Tuscarora.* Sept. 27, 1952.
81.34 *Trail to Old Sonora.* Oct. 4, 1952.
81.35 *Road to Destiny.* Oct. 11, 1952.
81.36 *Border City.* Oct. 18, 1952. GS: Harry Lauter, Elaine Williams, Lillian Molieri, Zon Murray, Charles Stevens, Julian Rivero.
81.37 *Roaring Challenge.* Oct. 25, 1952. GS: Patricia Michon, Kenneth MacDonald, Ted Mapes, John Cason.
81.38 *Range Master.* Nov. 1, 1952. GS: Jack Halliday, Kenneth MacDonald, Jane Adams, Rick Vallin, John Cason, Cactus McPeters.
81.39 *Thunder Over Inyo.* Nov. 8, 1952. GS: Jeri James, Raymond Bond, Reed Howes, John Cason, Robert Bray.
81.40 *Pledge to Danger.* Nov. 15, 1952. GS: Kenneth Patterson, Gil Donaldson, Kathleen Case, Carol Thurston, Dorothy Adams, Sally Payne, Boyd Stockman, Carol Henry.
81.41 *Golden Snare.* Nov. 22, 1952. GS: James Craven, Gail Davis, Richard Avonde, Raymond Hatton, Ewing Mitchell, William Tannen.
81.42 *Singing Wires.* Nov. 29, 1952.
81.43 *Mojave Desperados.* Dec. 6, 1952.
81.44 *Highway to Doom.* Dec. 13, 1952.
81.45 *Hideout.* Dec. 20, 1952.
81.46 *Broken Spur.* Dec. 27, 1952.
81.47 *Venture Feud.* Jan. 3, 1953.
81.48 *Bad Men of Marysville.* Jan. 10, 1953. GS: Jo Carroll Dennison, John Dehner, Maudie Prickett, Ferris Taylor, Kit Guard, Jack Ingram, Rube Schaffer, John Cason, Chuck Cason.
81.49 *Claim Jumpers.* Jan. 17, 1953. GS: Kenneth Patter-

son, Kathleen Case, Dorothy Adams, Gil Donaldson, Harry Strang, Tom London, Boyd Stockman, Carol Henry. Carson and El Toro try to help a schoolmistress defend her right to a gold mine.

Third Season

81.50 *Outlaw Trail.* Aug. 1, 1953. GS: Myron Healey, James Craven, Nan Leslie, Dale Van Sickel, Robert Bice, Rusty Wescoatt, Lane Chandler.

81.51 *Savage Outpost.* Aug. 8, 1953. GS: John Doucette, Richard Garland, Tris Coffin, Gil Warren, Harry Woods, Archie Twitchell, Elaine Edwards, Gracia Narciso. Carson disguises himself as a notorious outlaw and El Toro poses as a Mexican Ambassador as the two lawmen are assigned to foil the plot of some international gangsters.

81.52 *Hawk Raiders.* Aug. 15, 1953. GS: Tol Avery, Richard Reeves, Pierre Watkin, Howard Negley, Sheb Wooley, Anna Navarro. Kit and El Toro masquerade as members of the Hawk Raiders, a gang of outlaws, who have been stealing horses and cattle from ranchers.

81.53 *The Widow of Indian Wells.* Aug. 22, 1953. GS: Ann Tyrell, Rick Vallin, Nancy Hale, Wallis Clark, Gregg Barton, George Pembroke, Don C. Harvey.

81.54 *Law of Boot Hill.* Aug. 29, 1953. GS: Roy Barcroft, George Chandler, Rand Brooks, Lee Van Cleef, Jeanne Cooper, Bob Woodward.

81.55 *Trouble at Fort Mojave.* Sept. 5, 1953. GS: John Eldredge, Duane Thorsen, Carol Thurston, Charles Stevens, David Colmans, Joel Whitecloud, George M. Lynn, Bob Rose.

81.56 *Powdersmoke Law.* Sept. 12, 1953.

81.57 *Secret Sheriff.* Sept. 19, 1953. GS: Pierre Watkin, Sheb Wooley, Tol Avery, Anna Navarro, Dick Reeves, Rankin Mansfield, Mike McHale.

81.58 *Outlaw Army.* Sept. 26, 1953. Kit Carson and El Toro are sent to capture a renegade who, with his own army, is attempting to conquer California.

81.59 *Lost Treasure of Panamint.* Oct. 3, 1953. Carson and El Toro clash with the masked El Chambergo and his gang. The outlaws are in the midst of robbing a stagecoach when Carson and El Toro arrive on the scene.

81.60 *Frontier Mail.* Oct. 10, 1953. Kit Carson is summoned to investigate a series of murders of private postmen employed by mine owners to carry the mail to the surrounding villages.

81.61 *Open Season.* Oct. 17, 1953.

81.62 *Renegade Wires.* Oct. 24, 1953. GS: Denver Pyle, Francis McDonald, Barbara Bestar, Chris Alcaide, Marshall Reed, Bruce Payne.

81.63 *Ambush.* Oct. 31, 1953.

81.64 *Gunsmoke Justice.* Oct. 7, 1953. GS: Roy Barcroft, George Chandler, Rand Brooks, Lee Van Cleef, Jeanne Cooper, Boyd Stockman.

81.65 *Challenge to Chance.* Nov. 14, 1953. A ranch owner is shot while sending an urgent telegram to Carson. The unfinished wire brings Kit and El Toro into town to find the killer.

81.66 *Marshal of Guntown.* Nov. 21, 1953.

81.67 *Uprising at Pawhuska.* Nov. 28, 1953.

81.68 *Army Renegades.* Dec. 5, 1953. GS: Jean Howell, Henry Rowland, Harry Lauter, Harry Harvey, Sr., Frank Fenton, Bob Woodward. Carson has his pal El Toro pose as Army messengers in order to catch a gang of outlaws, led by two Army renegades.

81.69 *Badman's Escape.* Dec. 12, 1953. GS: Rick Vallin, Wallis Clark, Ann Tyrell, Nancy Hale, Gregg Barton, Mort Mills, Dick Rich, Ted Stanhope. A psychopathic killer escapes from prison and heads for the home of the sheriff who convicted him. When Kit Carson and his Mexican friend El Toro arrive on the scene, the convict and his men are holding the sheriff's family hostage.

81.70 *The Haunted Hacienda.* Dec. 19, 1953.

81.71 *Gunsmoke Valley.* Dec. 26, 1953. GS: Myron Healey, Robert Bice, Nan Leslie, Dale Van Sickel, James Craven, Lane Chandler, Rusty Wescoatt. Kit and El Toro come into town to attend a wedding, but arrive in time to see the bridegroom about to be lynched by an angry crowd.

81.72 *Dry Creek Case.* Jan. 9, 1954. An ex-convict is released from prison after serving a term for robbery. When he sets out to look for the money he stole and hid, Kit and El Toro follow the man.

81.73 *Copper Town.* Jan. 16, 1954. GS: Myron Healey, Robert Bice, Nan Leslie, Dale Van Sickel, James Craven, Lane Chandler. Kit is after a gang of stagecoach bandits. He gets a lead when one of the victims recognizes a member of the gang.

81.74 *Counterfeit County.* Jan. 23, 1954. GS: Denver Pyle, Dick Elliot, Barbara Bestar, Francis McDonald, Marshall Reed, Chris Alcaide. Kit and El Toro witness the murder of an unidentified man. Kit links the death with a crooked bond deal planned in a nearby city.

81.75 *The Cache.* Jan. 30, 1954.

Fourth Season

81.76 *Trails Westward.* July 31, 1954.

81.77 *Stampede Fury.* Aug. 7, 1954.

81.78 *Bullets of Mystery.* Aug. 14, 1954. GS: Nan Leslie, Henry Rowland, Peter Mamakos, Denver Pyle, Pamela Duncan, Lyle Talbot, Edward Colmans, Kermit Maynard.

81.79 *The Wrong Man.* Aug. 21, 1954.

81.80 *The Gatling Gun.* Aug. 28, 1954.

81.81 *Powder Depot.* Sept. 4, 1954. GS: George Wallace, Tris Coffin, Don C. Harvey, Sally Payne, Francis McDonald, Pat O'Malley, Paul McGuire.

81.82 *The Hermit of Indian Ridge.* Sept. 11, 1954.

81.83 *Riders of the Hooded League.* Sept. 18, 1954. GS: Phyllis Coates, Richard Simmons, Dennis Moore, Rex Thorsen, Ted Mapes, Boyd Stockman.

81.84 *Frontier of Challenge.* Sept. 25, 1954. GS: George Wallace, Sally Payne, Don C. Harvey, Tris Coffin, Francis McDonald, Charlita.

81.85 *Trail to Bordertown.* Oct. 2, 1954.

81.86 *No Man's Law.* Oct. 9, 1954.

81.87 *The Missing Hacienda.* Oct. 16, 1954. GS: Linda Stirling, Lee Van Cleef, Richard Garland, Harry Harvey, Sr., Glen Kilburn, James Diehl, Virginia Carroll, Pete Dunn.

81.88 *Renegades of Rejo.* Oct. 23, 1954. GS: Bill Henry, Myron Healey, Pierce Lyden, Elaine Williams, Kenne Duncan, Pat O'Malley.

81.89 *Ghost Town Garrison.* Oct. 30, 1954. GS: Bill

Henry, Pierce Lyden, Myron Healey, Elaine Williams, Kenne Duncan.

81.90 *Eyes of the Outlaw.* Nov. 6, 1954. GS: Suzanne Ta Fel, Gregg Barton, Richard Avonde, Tom Irish, Terry Frost, John Pickard, Jerome Sheldon.

81.91 *Valiant Outlaw.* Nov. 13, 1954.

81.92 *Judge of Black Mesa.* Nov. 20, 1954.

81.93 *Frontier Empire.* GS: Anne Kimball, Steve Darrell, Mauritz Hugo, James Best, Terry Frost, Virginia Carroll, Ted Stanhope.

81.94 *Trouble in Sundown.* Dec. 4, 1954. GS: Chris Alcaide.

81.95 *Outlaw's Justice.* Dec. 11, 1954. GS: Jan Shepard, Hal K. Dawson, Terry Frost, Chris Alcaide, Larry Hudson.

81.96 *The Golden Ring of Cibola.* Dec. 18, 1954.

81.97 *Overland Stage.* Dec. 25, 1954.

81.98 *Devil's Remuda.* Jan. 1, 1955. GS: Suzanne Ta Fel, Richard Avonde, Tom Irish, Gregg Barton, William Fawcett, Sheb Wooley, Tom London, John Damler.

81.99 *The Phantom Uprising.* Jan. 8, 1955. GS: Anne Kimball, James Bell, Steve Darrell, Mauritz Hugo, William Fawcett, Jack Mulhall, Fred Carson.

81.100 *Mission to Alkali.* Jan. 15, 1955.

81.101 *Incident at Wagontire.* Jan. 22, 1955. GS: Linda Stirling, Lee Van Cleef, Harry Harvey, Sr., Richard Garland, Joe Haworth, X Brands.

82. *Klondike*

NBC. 30 min. Broadcast history: Monday, 9:00–9:30, Oct. 1960–Feb. 1961.

Regular Cast: Ralph Taeger (Mike Halliday), James Coburn (Jeff Durain), Mari Blanchard (Kathy O'Hara), Joi Lansing (Goldie).

Premise: Set during the Alaskan gold rush of the late 1890s, this series depicted the exploits of adventurer and gold miner Mike Halliday, who was often pitted against gambler Jeff Durain in the Alaskan town of Skagway.

The Episodes

82.1 *Klondike Fever.* Oct. 10, 1960. GS: Karl Swenson, Ray Teal, Sam Edwards, Bob Bryant. Adventurer Mike Halliday and hotel proprietess Kathy O'Hara are on a ship bound for Skagway. They meet slick Jeff Durain and his companion Goldie who proceed to set up a fixed poker game.

82.2 *River of Gold.* Oct. 24, 1960. GS: Forrest Lewis, L.Q. Jones, Larry Blake, Charles Reade. Jeff Durain's bag of slick and greedy tricks includes a way to aid Kathy O'Hara's hotel to his holdings.

82.3 *Saints and Stickups.* Oct. 31, 1960. GS: Whit Bissell, Virginia Gregg, L.Q. Jones. Evangelist Josiah Harless and his wife Harmony are soliciting donations to build a church in Skagway. Durain greedily eyes the flowing cash and decides he can put it to better use.

82.4 *The Unexpected Candidate.* Nov. 7, 1960. GS: Judson Pratt, Robert E. Griffin, L.Q. Jones, Georgia Ellis, Hal K. Dawson. Jeff Durain is the only one who is running for mayor. Naturally, Halliday and Kathy don't like it. They decide to bring in their own candidate.

82.5 *Keys to Trouble.* Nov. 14, 1960. GS: Wallace Ford, Charles Fredericks, William Hickman, Donald Kerr. Halliday buys Kathy an imported piano, but she doesn't get to enjoy it long — the only other piano in Skagway is wrecked in a brawl and Durain wants to buy Kathy's.

82.6 *Swoger's Mules.* Nov. 21, 1960. GS: Claude Akins, Jeanette Nolan, William Challee, Frank Cady. Durain and a hot-tempered partner named John Conrad are out to buy up all the mules in town. But there is one holdout — Henry Swoger wants to keep his.

82.7 *Sure Thing, Men.* Nov. 28, 1960. GS: Larry Pennell, Tyler McVey, Jack Albertson, Jan Stine, William Woodson. Outlaw Rufe Lukas arrives in Skagway, and Mike is sure he is up to no good. He is even surer when Rufe opens a telegraph office which does a thriving business right off the bat.

82.8 *Taste of Danger.* Dec. 5, 1960. GS Phillip Pine, Harry Lauter, Frank Ferguson, Steven Gravers. Jeff Durain doesn't care how he makes a buck. His latest is a plan to auction off food to the citizens of Skagway — food off a ship ravaged by typhoid.

82.9 *Bare Knuckles.* Dec. 12, 1960. GS: J. Pat O'Malley, Richard Kiel. Kathy's Uncle Jonah turns up in Skagway with a large assortment of watches and sundry other items.

82.10 *Halliday's Club.* Dec. 19, 1960. GS: Jackie Coogan, Hugh Sanders, Charles Herbert, Charles Tannen, Joseph Mell. Young Seth Bailey is caught stowing away on a ship bound for Skagway, and is forced into hard labor by the tough first mate. As soon as they hit port, Seth escapes and runs to Mike Halliday for refuge.

82.11 *Bathhouse Justice.* Dec. 26, 1960. GS: Walter Burke, Nora Marlowe, Brett, King, Britt Lomond, Milton Frome, Jerome Cowan, Claude Stroud, N.J. Davis. Bathhouse proprietor Sam Bronson goes prospecting and strikes it rich. But he gets into a poker game and loses his gold and the bathhouse.

82.12 *Swing Your Partner.* Jan. 9, 1961. GS: Chuck Webster, George Kennedy, James Griffith, Troy Melton, Karl Swenson. Two new miners, Buck and his not so-bright partner Ira, blow into Skagway on their way to the gold fields. They ask Mike to come along.

82.13 *The Golden Burro.* Jan. 16, 1961. GS: Edgar Buchanan, Robert F. Simon, Howard McNear, Robert Karnes. Mike sets up the Halliday Gold Protection Company, a vault for miners' gold dust. A sneaky customer named Ed Nash scents a good set-up for a robbery.

82.14 *Queen of the Klondike.* Jan. 23, 1961. GS: Hank Patterson, Jack Elam, Lane Bradford, John Qualen, Tudor Owen. While Skagway lies under a heavy blanket of snow, an ornery miner named Spunky ambles into town with a mean yen for eggs. Unfortunately the last egg in town is being devoured by Eli Roper at that very moment.

82.15 *The Man Who Owned Skagway.* Jan. 30, 1961. GS: Lawrence Dobkin, Emory Parnell, Ralph Moody, Raymond Hatton. Once upon a time, Mike grubstaked a miner who was down on his luck. Now the man has sent Mike an inheritance — a bundle of papers.

82.16 *Sitka Madonna.* Feb. 6, 1961. GS: Patric Knowles, Ron Hayes. On his way back from a hunting trip, Mike runs into a man who shoots at him, then collapses. Mike discovers the man wears the clothing of a Russian Orthodox priest.

82.17 *The Hostages.* Feb. 13, 1961. GS: Lon Chaney, Jr., Chris Alcaide, Michael Raffetto, Jack Petruzzi. Some robbers blow into Skagway and attempt to track down bank president Arnold Jackson to get the combination for the bank's vault. Jackson gets out of town, but he leaves the sought after knowledge with Mike.

83. *Kung Fu*

ABC. 60 min. Broadcast history: Saturday, 8:00–9:00, Oct. 1972–Nov. 1972; Thursday, 9:00–10:00, Jan. 1973–Aug. 1974; Saturday, 9:00–10:00, Sept. 1974–Oct. 1974; Friday, 8:00–9:00, Nov. 1974– Jan. 1975; Saturday, 8:00–9:00, Jan. 1975–June 1975.

Regular Cast: David Carradine (Kwai Chang Caine), Keye Luke (Master Po), Philip Ahn (Master Kan), Radames Pera (Young Caine).

Premise: Kwai Chang Caine is a Buddhist monk who flees from China when he is accused of murder and comes to the American West. Trained in the martial arts, he searches for his long-lost brother while avoiding American bounty hunters and Chinese agents.

Notes: A 1992 syndicated series, *Kung Fu— The Legend Continues*, also starring David Carradine, followed the descendants of Kwai Chang Caine into modern times.

The Episodes

83.1 *Kung Fu.* Feb. 22, 1972. GS: Barry Sullivan, Albert Salmi, Wayne Maunder, Benson Fong, Richard Loo, Victor Sen Yung, Keith Carradine, Roy Fuller, Robert Ito, John Leong, David Chow. Caine escapes a murder charge in China and goes to the American West, where he finds himself embroiled in the lives of those he meets.

Season One

83.2 *King of the Mountain.* Oct. 14, 1972. GS: John Saxon, Lara Parker, Brandon Cruz, Mills Watson, Ken Lynch, Ivy Bethune, Robert Hoy, Gary McLarty, Paul Harper, Mark Allen, Richard Loo. Caine, who is wanted for a murder he committed in China, is a magnet for greedy bounty hunter. His presence endangers those who he befriends.

83.3 *Dark Angel.* Nov. 11, 1972. GS: John Carradine, Robert Carradine, Dean Jagger, Adrienne Marden, Paul Harper, James Griffith, Richard Loo, Charles Bail, Robert Herron, Bill McLean, Jim Weatherill, Tim Haldeman. A mendicant preacher is driven by his own greed to blindness. Caine teaches the old man to see with his other sense.

83.4 *Blood Brother.* Jan. 18, 1973. GS: Clu Gulager, John Anderson, Benson Fong, Robert Urich, Scott Hylands, Kathleen Gackle, Frank Michael Liu, Kermit Murdock, Robert Emhardt, Beulah Quo, Paul Bryar. Caine is looking for a fellow priest in a town where all Chinese are held in contempt.

83.5 *An Eye for an Eye.* Jan. 25, 1973. GS: Lane Bradbury, Harry Townes, Tim McIntire, Robert J. Wilke, L.Q. Jones, Parley Baer, Clay Tanner, Judson Pratt, Ross Elliott, John War Eagle. Caine becomes involved in a young woman's quest for vengeance against the soldier who raped her.

83.6 *The Tide.* Feb. 1, 1973. GS: Andrew Duggan, Tina Chen, James Hong, Brian Tochi, Mako, Kenneth O'Brien, Robert Donner, Rosalind Chao. Caine is forced to rely on an enigmatic Chinese girl for protection from bounty hunters.

83.7 *The Soul Is the Warrior.* Feb. 8, 1973. GS: Pat Hingle, Shelly Novack, John Doucette, Robert Foulk, Jim Davis, Les Lannom, John Pickard, Robin Raymond, John Cliff. Caine's involvement with a sheriff facing death brings to light the nature of fear and a chilling test of courage.

83.8 *Nine Lives.* Feb. 15, 1973. GS: Geraldine Brooks, Albert Salmi, Merlin Olsen, Royal Dano, Dana Elcar, Ross Hagen, Michael Cameron. A burly Irish miner is in search of a beardrinking tomcat. It is an exasperating quest for Sahwn Mulhare as he has been banished from his diggings until he replaces the camp mascot he accidentally killed.

83.9 *Sun and Cloud Shadows.* Feb. 22, 1973. GS: Morgan Woodward, Richard Lawrence Hatch, Soon-Taik Oh, Aimee Eccles, Yuki Shimada, Ronald Feinberg, John Mamo, Clyde Kusatsu, Tad Horino. Caine acts as a peacemaker in a potentially explosive dispute between a small Chinese mining community and a powerful rancher claiming ownership of their mine.

83.10 *Chains.* March 8, 1973. GS: Michael Greene, Warren Vanders, Geoffrey Lewis, Larry Bishop, Robert Bralver, Ben Frank, Norm Stephens. Caine exerts a quiet influence on the brute he is chained to as they attempt to elude a pursuing provost marshal.

83.11 *Alethea.* March 15, 1973. GS: Jodie Foster, Kenneth Tobey, Byron Mabe, Charles Tyner, Khigh Dhiegh, Regis J. Cordic, William Mims, Frank Wilcox, Dale Ishimoto, Alex Henteloff. A twelve-year-old girl who testifies at Caine's murder trial honestly believes that he fired the fatal bullet.

83.12 *A Praying Mantis Kills.* March 22, 1973. GS: Norman Alden, Wendell Burton, William Schallert, Don Knight, Dennis Redfield, Bill Fletcher, Jason Wingreen, Murray MacLeod, Victor Sen Yung, Karen Morley. A youth, on the threshold of manhood, is heading for a showdown with a gang of killers.

83.13 *Superstition.* April 5, 1973. GS: Ford Rainey, Fred Sadoff, Roy Jenson, Woodrow Parfrey, Don Dubbins, Mike Mazurki, Larry J. Blake. Caine and other unfortunates have been railroaded into slave gangs at a silver mine.

83.14 *The Stone.* April 12, 1973. GS: Moses Gunn, Kelly Jean Peters, Gregory Sierra, William Lucking, Ike Eisenmann, Sean Marshall, Brian Andrews, Kiel Martin. Caine's adventures in a rough mining town hinge on three different elements: a former slave from Brazil, a huge uncut diamond, and three boys seeking revenge against the man who spurned their mother.

83.15 *The Third Man.* April 26, 1973. GS: Sheree North, Robert Hoy, Ed Nelson, Barbara Stuart, Fred Beir, Vic Perrin, Steve Chambers. Caine becomes involved with a mysterious gunman who seemed to come out of nowhere and finish off a gambler already wounded by two thieves.

83.16 *The Ancient Warrior.* May 3, 1973. GS: Will Geer, Chief Dan George, Kenneth O'Brien, Denver Pyle, Victor French, G.D. Spradlin, Clay Tanner, William Katt, Gary Busey. A dying Indian warrior is journeying to his predestined burial place. The trouble is that the site is now in the middle of Purgatory, a town seathing with hatred for Indians.

Season Two

83.17 *The Well.* Sept. 27, 1973. GS: Hal Williams, Jim Davis, Tim McIntire, Mae Mercer, George Spell, Ta-Ronce Allen, Robert Karnes, Jane Lambert, Chuck Hayward. Sickened by poisoned water, Caine is given reluctant haven by an ex-slave jealously guarding a water supply.

83.18 *The Assassin.* Oct. 4, 1973. GS: Dana Elcar, Nobu McCarthy, James Keach, William Glover, Beverly Kushida, Douglas V. Fowley, Robert Ito, Wayne Storm, Phil Chambers, Wayne Foster. A violent feud is threatening to drown two families in blood.

83.19 *The Chalice.* Oct. 11, 1973. GS: William Smith, Gilbert Roland, Charles Dierkop, Lee Paul, Pepe Serna, Victor Millan, Victor Arco, Stafford Repp, Steve Chambers. Caine promises a dying priest that he will try to return the golden chalice which the cleric stole from a mission and then lost to outlaws.

83.20 *The Brujo.* Oct. 25, 1973. GS: Emilio Fernandez, Henry Darrow, Maria Elena Cordero, Julio Medina, Rodolfo Hoyos, Benson Fong, Felipe Turich, Fernando Escandon. Caine, wandering in Mexico, is put to the task of breaking a warlock's spell by somehow convincing the villagers that they are victims of their own superstition.

83.21 *The Squaw Man.* Nov. 1, 1973. GS: Jack Elam, Elliott Street, Logan Ramsey, Rosana Soto, Booth Colman, Rex Holman, Eddie Firestone, James Hong, Victor Sen Yung. A simple farmer is kept low on the social totem pole because of his marriage to an Indian woman. A whole new world opens after he shoots an outlaw's son and finds himself elevated to the dizzying role of hero.

83.22 *The Spirit Helper.* Nov. 8, 1973. GS: Bo Svenson, Scott Hylands, Khigh Dhiegh, Don Johnson, James A. Watson, Jr., Rita Rogers, Rock Walker, Fred Lerner, Everett L. Creach, Steve D. Chambers. Caine, long a disciple of wise teachers, now teaches in turn. His pupil is an Indian lad faced with the man-sized task of rescuing his mother from the renegades who murdered his father.

83.23 *The Tong.* Nov. 15, 1973. GS: Diana Douglas, Richard Loo, Carey Wong, Tad Horino, Kinji Shibuya, David Chow. Caine champions the cause of a Chinese orphan who is seeking refuge from an underworld lord. The action brings Caine into conflict with the dreaded tong, the Mafia-like society of Chinese communities.

83.24 *The Soldier.* Nov. 29, 1973. GS: Tim Matheson, Myron Healey, John Dennis, Douglas Dirkson, Margaret Fairchild, Frank Whiteman, Wayne Heffley, Skip Riley, Kip Whitman. An Army lieutenant searches his soul to determine whether he is cut out for the uniform. He is ridden with guilt because he cannot bring himself to kill.

83.25 *The Salamander.* Dec. 6, 1973. GS: David Huddleston, Ed Flanders, Ramon Bieri, James Lee Reeves, Bill McLean, Richard Chien, K.C. Shieh. A philosophical question about the line that divides reality from illusion lies at the heart of this drama about a young man who fears he is going mad.

83.26 *The Hoots.* Dec. 13, 1973. GS: Anthony Zerbe, Howard Da Silva, Laurie Prange, Jock Mahoney, Rance Howard, Tom Waters, Link Wyler, Ed McCready, John Mamo. A dispute over water rights leads to persecution of a religious sect that believes in nonresistance, even in self-defense.

83.27 *The Elixir.* Dec. 20, 1973. GS: Diana Muldaur, David Canary, Don Megowan, Matt Clark, Richard Caine, Walter Barnes, Jerry Fujikawa, Henry Wills, Gary Epper. A glamorous medicine-wagon hawker's yearning for complete independence blinds her to her own selfishness, especially toward her hunchback sister.

83.28 *The Gunman.* Jan. 3, 1974. GS: Andrew Prine, Katherine Woodville, Jack Riley, Sandy Kenyon, Alan Fudge, Herbert Nelson, James Weatherill, Jonathan Wong. Caine becomes involved with a fugitive wanted for murder and a proud woman whose life he once saved by killing her husband.

83.29 *Empty Pages of a Dead Book.* Jan. 10, 1974. GS: Robert Foxworth, Slim Pickens, Nate Esformes, Bruce Carradine, James Storm, Doreen Lang, Carlos Romero, Tim Haldeman. A Texas rangers zealous adherence to the letter of the law blinds him to its spirit. He comes to appreciate the distinction after he and Caine are charged with murder.

83.30 *A Dream Within a Dream.* Jan. 17, 1974. GS: Howard Duff, Sorrell Booke, John Drew Barrymore, Ruth Roman, Tina Louise, Mark Miller, Bennie Dobbins, Fred Lerner, Tony Epper. Caine becomes involved with a sculptor of memorial statuary in this ghostly mystery about the disappearance of a corpse that Caine first saw hanging in a thick marshland fog.

83.31 *The Raiders* (A.K.A. "The Way of Violence Has No Mind"). Jan. 24, 1974. GS: Victor Sen Yung, Ron Soble, Fritz Weaver, Robert Ito, Gary Merrill, June Vincent, Jesse Dizon, William Traylor, Ted Gehring. Latter day Chinese Robin Hoods are out to turn the tables on the men who stole their gold mine.

83.32 *In Uncertain Bondage.* Feb. 7, 1974. GS: Warren Vanders, Judy Pace, Lynda Day George, Roger Mosely. A proud Southern belle is kidnaped by servants.

83.33 *Night of the Owls, Day of the Doves.* Feb. 14, 1974. GS: Barry Atwater, Anne Francis, Claire Nono, Rayford Barnes, Julie Andelman, Arlene Farber, Nancy Juno Dawson, Ted White, Ken Swofford, Paul Harper, George Dzundza. A madam is under attack by vigilantes. The night riders, motivated more by greed than moral indignation, are after a will that deeds a valuable parcel of land to the madam and her brood.

83.34 *Cross-ties.* Feb. 21, 1974. GS: Barry Sullivan, Denver Pyle, Andy Robinson, John Anderson, Harrison Ford, Dennis Fimple, Eric Server, Rolfe Sedan. Caine is caught in an uncompromising war between angry farmers dispossessed by the railroad and detectives hired to bring them to justice.

83.35 *The Passion of Chen Yi.* Feb. 28, 1974. GS: Bethel Leslie, Marianna Hill, Robert Middleton, Soon-Taik Oh, Arch Johnson, Bart Burns, Ivor Francis, James Hong, Robert Cornthwaite.Caine tries to save an old acquaintance who has myteriously confessed to a murder that Caine is sure he did not commit.

83.36 *Arrogant Dragons.* March 14, 1974. GS: Richard Loo, Jocelyne Lew, Clyde Kusatsu, James Hong, Nathan Jung, Hubert Wing, Dalton Leong, Edward Walsh, Yuki Shimada, Tommy Lee, Russ Grieve. Challenging the tong, a dreaded Chinese society in the Old West, Caine stands up for an aging leader who has been judged a traitor and condemned to death because he wishes to return home to China.

83.37 *The Nature of Evil.* March 21, 1974. GS: John Carradine, Morgan Woodward, Shelly Novack, Barbara Colby, Kelly Thordsen, Bartlett Robinson, James Gammon, Robert Donley, Larry Robb. A shadowy killer, the virtual embodiment of pure evil, is the adversary in this drama of a blind man's quest to avenge the murder of a friend.

83.38 *The Centoph* Part One. April 4, 1974. GS: Nancy Kwan, Stefan Gierasch, Ned Romero, Robert Ridgely, Milton Parsons, Michael Pataki, Don Hanmer, Ben Cooper, Ed Baker, Ivan Naranjo, Irene Tedrow, James Weatherill, Frank Ferguson, Tim Haldeman. Love is a common element in two interwoven stories. One, told in flashback, follows Caine's growing enchantment with an emperor's favorite concubine. The other, set in the Old West, concerns a slightly mad Scotsman on a mysterious burial odyssey.

83.39 *The Centoph* Part Two. April 11, 1974. GS: Nancy Kwan, Stefan Gierasch, Ned Romero, Robert Ridgely, Milton Parsons, Michael Pataki, Don Hanmer, Ben Cooper, Ed Baker, Ivan Naranjo, Irene Tedrow, James Weatherill, Frank Ferguson, Tim Haldeman. The tales of Caine's love for an emperor's concubine and a Scotsman who tries to bury his wife on Indian holy ground conclude.

Season Three

83.40 *Blood of the Dragon.* Sept. 14, 1974. GS: Patricia Neal, Season Hubley, Eddie Albert, Edward Albert, Clyde Kusatsu, Tom Reese, Kerry MacLane, Kay E. Kuter, Jake Sheffield, Wilbur Chang, Tad Horino. Caine searches for his grandfather's murderer and encounters the Order of the Avenging Dragon, whose members are sworn to destroy the fugitive priest.

83.41 *A Small Beheading.* Sept. 21, 1974. GS: William Shatner, Rosemary Forsyth, France Nuyen, James Hong, Robert Brubaker, Kinji Shibuya, Yuki Shimada, Frances Fong. The fugitive Caine considers an imperial offer: returning to China for a pardon at the cost of losing a finger.

83.42 *This Valley of Terror.* Sept. 28, 1974. GS: Sandra Locke, Howard Duff, Jan Sterling, Joe Renteria, Bill Catching, Ken Swofford, James Hong, John Quade, Bobby E. Clark. Caine gives protection and guidance to a young woman terrified by visions of future events that always seem to come true.

83.43 *The Predators.* Oct. 5, 1974. GS: Cal Bellini, Anthony Zerbe, George DiCenzo, Robert Phillips, Frank Michael, Robert Sorrells, Richard Narita. An Apache bent on vengeance jeopardizes Caine's efforts to clear himself of a murder charge. The Indian intends to kill the scalphunter whose testimony is essential to Caine's defense.

83.44 *My Brothers, My Executioner.* Oct. 12, 1974. GS: Carol Lawrence, A Martinez, James Wainwright, John Vernon, Richard Kelton, Beulah Quo, John Fujioka, Clay Tanner, Adrienne Marden. A seeress predicts that Caine finally will find his half-brother, but she warns that others also will find him and that death will be close behind.

83.45 *Cry of the Night Beast.* Oct. 19, 1974. GS: Albert Salmi, Don Stroud, Stefanie Powers, Alex Henteloff, Victor Jory, John War Eagle, Kenneth O'Brien, Jim Boles, Don Keefer. The supernatural cry of a child begging to be saved draws Caine into a strange adventure involving an unweaned buffalo calf and a hunter determined to kill it.

83.46 *The Garments of Rage.* Nov. 8, 1974. GS: James Shigeta, James Olson, James Hong, Harrison Page, Michael Francis Blake, Larry J. Blake, Lincoln Demyan, Jon Yune. Caine faces the task of stopping the vendetta of a Shaolin master, a former teacher of nonviolence, who is blowing up railroad tracks to avenge the death of a nephew crushed by a train.

83.47 *Besieged* Part One (A.K.A. "Death on Cold Mountain"). Nov. 15, 1974. GS: Barbara Hershey, Victor Sen Yung, Richard Narita, Khigh Dhiegh, Yuki Shimada, Sam Hiona, Brian Fong, Richard Loo, George Chiang. The priests of Caine's temple invite attack by a warlord when they offer sanctuary to fellow priests whom he was sent to destroy.

83.48 *Besieged* Part Two (A.K.A. "Cannon at the Gate"). Nov. 22, 1974. GS: Barbara Hershey, Victor Sen Yung, Richard Narita, Khigh Dhiegh, Yuki Shimada, Sam Hiona, Brian Fong, Richard Loo, George Chiang. As a warlord lays siege to the Shaolin temple, the defending priests must contend not only with his cannon at the gates, but also with a traitor in their midst.

83.49 *The Devil's Champion.* Nov. 29, 1974. GS: Soon-Taik Oh, Frank Michael Liu, John Fujioka, Victoria Racimo, Richard Loo, Dale Ishimoto, Jennifer Ann Lee, Richard Lee-Sung, Tad Horino, Gerald Jann. In China, a warrior mystically imbued with superhuman strength demands a ritualistic battle to the death with venerable Master Kan.

83.50 *The Demon God.* Dec. 13, 1974. GS: Brian Tochi, Michael Greene, Victor Sen Yung, Tad Horino, Brenda Venus, Robert Tessier, Kansuma Fujima. Young Caine has a brush with death that recurs in his adult life.

83.51 *The Vanishing Image.* Dec. 20, 1974. GS: Lew Ayres, Tom Nardini, Benson Fong, Bill Saito, Jonathan Hole. Caine's continuing search for his half-brother involves him with an aging photographer and with a vengeful Indian youth who beleves that the photographer stole his spirit.

83.52 *A Lamb to the Slaughter.* Jan. 11, 1975. GS: Barbara Luna, Alejandro Rey, Joe Santos, Richard Yniquez, Julio Medina, Roberto Contreras, Bill Fletcher, Stephen Manley. Caine is drawn into a conflict between Mexican villagers and the leader of a band that protects them from bandits, but at a terrible cost in tribute.

83.53 *Forbidden Kingdom.* Jan. 18, 1975. GS: James Shigeta, Clyde Kusatsu, Adele Yoshioka, Evan C. Kim, Wendy Tochi, Jesse Dizon, Bob Okazaki, Jerry Fujikawa, Tommy Lee. In China, the fugitive Caine is betrayed by a woman desperate to save her brother from being killed by the emperor's soldiers.

83.54 *One Step to Darkness.* Jan. 25, 1975. GS: Leslie Charleson, Byron Mabe, Bruce Carradine, Lloyd Kino, David Huddleston, Stephen Manley, Frances Fong, Wilford Brimley, Allen Melvin, Jay Jones. Caine finds that exorcising a personal demon is somehow connected with the baffling behavior of an Army officer's wife.

83.55 *Battle Hymn.* Feb. 8, 1975. GS: Jose Feliciano, Julian "Cannonball" Adderley, Beverly Garland, Joe Maross, John Bennett Perry, James Victor, Chuck Hicks. A map hidden in a dead man's watch triggers a treasure hunt that may prove lethal to Caine and two minstrel musicians who join him.

83.56 *Barbary House* Part One. Feb. 15, 1975. GS:

Leslie Nielsen, Lois Nettleton, John Blythe Barrymore, Ji-Tu Cumbuka, Tim McIntire, Ted Gehring, John Vernon, Val de Vargas, Maidi Norman, Juanita Moore, John Fujioka, John Lupton, Don Keefer, Ned Romero, Carl Weather, Jacques Aubuchon, Al Checco. Caine's search for his half-brother Danny leads to a Barbary Coast entertainment palace, where the owner is holding Danny's son in a revenge plot against the father.

83.57 *Flight to Orion* **Part Two.** Feb. 22, 1975. GS: Leslie Nielsen, Lois Nettleton, John Blythe Barrymore, Ji-Tu Cumbuka, Tim McIntire, Ted Gehring, John Vernon, Val de Vargas, Maidi Norman, Juanita Moore, John Fujioka, John Lupton, Don Keefer, Ned Romero, Carl Weather, Jacques Aubuchon, Al Checco. As Caine, his half-brother's son and the boy's mother take flight across the desert, a Barbary Coast casino owner offers a reward of $10,000 for the return of the boy alive and Caine dead.

83.58 *The Brothers Cain* **Part Three.** March 1, 1975. GS: Leslie Nielsen, Lois Nettleton, John Blythe Barrymore, Ji-Tu Cumbuka, Tim McIntire, Ted Gehring, John Vernon, Val de Vargas, Maidi Norman, Juanita Moore, John Fujioka, John Lupton, Don Keefer, Ned Romero, Carl Weather, Jacques Aubuchon, Al Checco. Caine and his nephew Zeke compete with professional bounty hunters to find Caine's half-brother Danny, who has a $10,000 price on his head. Danny's hiding place is known only to one woman, and she is offering the information to the highest bidder.

83.59 *Full Circle* **Part Four.** March 15, 1975. GS: Leslie Nielsen, Lois Nettleton, John Blythe Barrymore, Ji-Tu Cumbuka, Tim McIntire, Ted Gehring, John Vernon, Val de Vargas, Maidi Norman, Juanita Moore, John Fujioka, John Lupton, Don Keefer, Ned Romero, Carl Weather, Jacques Aubuchon, Al Checco. Caine and his half-brother ride to San Francisco to wrest Danny's son from the boy's wealthy grandfather.

83.60 *The Thief of Chendo.* March 29, 1975. GS: James Hong, Harushi, Clare Nono, John Fujioka, Beulah Quo, Jeanne Joe, Dale Ishimoto, Tad Horino, Bill Saito, Arthur Song. In China, Caine joins forces with a thief to aid a grand duke deposed by his evil cousin.

83.61 *Ambush.* April 5, 1975. GS: John Carradine, Rhonda Fleming, Timothy Carey, Pat Morita, Kay E. Kuter, Bill Mims, Gene Dynarski, Fred Borden, Randy Boone, Suzannah Brin, R.L. Armstrong. Caine serves as the eyes for his blind friend Serendipity Johnson when the old man responds to a mysterious summons from a woman who once robbed him of $1000.

83.62 *The Last Raid.* April 26, 1975. GS: Hal Williams, L.Q. Jones, Charles Aidman, Charles Haid, Mae Mercer, George Spell, Craig Hundley, Anne Seymour, Hoke Howell, Ta-Ronce Allen, Ivy Bethune. Renegade raiders led by a vengeful ex-Confederate officer kidnap two youngboys, the son of a white doctor and the son of a former slave.

The Tele-films

83.63 *Kung Fu: The Movie.* Feb. 1, 1986. Cast: David Carradine, Keye Luke, Kerrie Keane, Mako Iwamtsu, William Lucking, Luke Askew, Benson Fong, Brandon Lee, Martin Landau, Robert Harper, Calista Carradine, Ellen Geer. Kwai Chang Caine continues to roam the west in the late 1880s, where he goes up against an evil Chinse warlord involved in the opium trade and a young Manchu assassin.

84. Lancer

CBS. 60 min. Broadcast history: Tuesday, 7:30-8:30, Sept. 1968–June 1970.

Regular Cast: Andrew Duggan (Murdoch Lancer), Wayne Maunder (Scott Lancer), James Stacy (Johnny Madrid Lancer), Elizabeth Baur (Teresa O'Brien), Paul Brinegar (Jelly Hoskins).

Premise: This Western series concerned the attempts of Murdoch Lancer and his two sons to control the Lancer Ranch in California's San Joaquin Valley during the 1870s.

The Episodes

84.1 *The High Riders* (A.K.A. "The Homecoming"). Sept. 24, 1968. GS: Joe Don Baker, Anthony Caruso, Paul Fierro, Sean McClory, Lisa Jak, Ruben Moreno, Robert Adler, Stanley Waxman, Ref Sanchez, Chuck Roberson. Rancher Murdoch Lancer offers his two long-estranged sons a tantalizing proposition. Each will get a third of the huge Lancer spread for help against the land pirates who are infesting the area. The sons are Boston dandy Scott and his cynical half-brother Johnny.

84.2 *Blood Rock.* Oct. 1, 1968. GS: John Anderson, J.D. Cannon, Barry Williams, Charles Dierkop, Rayford Barnes, Jack Bannon, Tracy Morgan, Jon Lormer. The Lancers arrange for ten-year-old Ben Wallace to finally meet his outlaw father, a setup that settles well with the sheriff of Blood Rock, an ambitious man with a twisted sense of ethics.

84.3 *Chase a Wild Horse.* Oct. 8, 1968. GS: Robert J. Wilke, James Gammon, Bobby Clarke, Lloyd Haynes, Vaughn Taylor, Hick Hill, Brick Huston. A character study of Johnny equates the rebellious young man with the superb wild stallion he is determined to break.

84.4 *Foley.* Oct. 15, 1968. GS: R.G. Armstrong, Lynn Loring, Don Quine, Joe Perry, Rosa Turich, Harper Flaherty, Lorne McKellar, June Dayton, Bert Santos, Arvo Ojala. Scott gambles everything to save a pregnant woman from the clutches of her father-in-law. Gant Foley, patriarch of a notorious outlaw clan, promises to destroy anyone who stands between him and the baby, his only direct descendant.

84.5 *The Lawman.* Oct. 22, 1968. GS: James Gregory, Robert Doyle, Jack Garner, John Milford, Lloyd Haynes. Leathery old Marshal Barker is riding his last trail as he stops by the Lancers with two deputies and a murder suspect. With nothing to show for twenty years of service, Barker is weighing his future as a charity case against the $5000 bribe he has been offered by the prisoner.

84.6 *Julie.* Oct. 29, 1969. GS: Susan Strasberg, Bruce Dern, Val Avery, John Kellogg, Lincoln Tate, Frederic Downs, Clint Sharp. Johnny goes after the girl who framed Scott to protect her fugitive brother. Time is short as the girl has convinced two bounty hunters that Scott is their prize.

84.7 *The Prodigal.* Nov. 12, 1968. GS: Phyllis Thaxter, Kevin Hagen, Johnny Crawford, Del Monroe, Stewart Bradley, Paul Picerni, Roy Engel, Ray Kellogg, Jason Wingreen. Widow Marcy Dane is an old flame who starts a few fires on the Lancer ranch. One is in Murdoch's heart, the other is far more dangerous. Marcy is followed by her son, a young army deserter charged with murder.

84.8 *Jelly.* Nov. 19, 1968. GS: Ronny Howard, James Wainwright, Ken Lynch, Russell Thorson, Teddy Quinn, Chris Hundley, George Ostos, Mark Robert Brown, William Bryant. Cagey old codger Jelly Hoskins is caring for an astonishing brood of orphans — eight varieties of human flotsam in every size and color. Jelly helps them by helping himself to anything he can lay hands on, including a money bag lifted from a dead bank robber.

84.9 *The Last Train for Charlie Poe.* Nov. 26, 1968. GS: Harold Gould, Dub Taylor, Mary Fickett, Frank Marth, George Keymas, William Bryant, Harry Swoger, Robert Cornthwaite, Ian Wolfe, Hank Worden, Bob Dodson. Johnny and Scott scheme to rob a Sacramento bound express in an effort to halt a land grab. Compounding their foolishness, the pair enlist two retired train robbers who yearn for a return to easy pickings.

84.10 *Glory.* Dec. 10, 1968. GS: Brenda Scott, Laurence Naismith, Johnny Seven, Walter Baldwin, Matt Emery, Vic Perrin, Anthony Redondo. Desperately needing money to cover her grandfather's gambling debt, Glory unleashes her charms on the Lancer family, especially Scott, who seems least likely to melt.

84.11 *The Heart of Pony Alice.* Dec. 17, 1968. GS: Andrew Prine, Eve Plumb, Jeanne Cooper, James Griffith, Tom Fadden, Jack Perkins. Johnny sets out to even accounts with Wilf Guthrie, a crafty horse trader who unloaded an old nag on him. He gets hoodwinked the second time around when Wilf puts his little orphaned niece up for auction.

84.12 *The Escape.* Dec. 31, 1968. GS: Dan Travanty, Lynda Day George, Wayne Rogers, Robert Bieheller, Joe DeSantis, John Zaremba. Unrelenting hate pits three revenge-bent ex-soldiers against Scott, whom they blame for betraying a wartime escape attempt. Their leader, Lt. Dan Cassidy, faces a terrifying turn of events when the full truth of the incident comes to light.

84.13 *The Wedding.* Jan. 7, 1969. GS: Bo Svenson, Brioni Farrell, Brooke Bundy, Lawrence Dane, Robert Foulk, Steve Vincent, Harry Harvey, John Zaremba. Feelings of guilt spur Scott to join his friend Josh in pursuit of Dave Macall, an escaped outlaw who kidnaped Josh's bride at the wedding. Scott refrains from telling Josh that the woman used to work for Macall as a dance-hall girl, and may not want to be rescued after all.

84.14 *Death Bait.* Jan. 14, 1969. GS: James Olson, Tom Selleck, Bern Hoffman, Sam Elliot. Murdoch, Teresa and Jelly endure a night of terror when Alton Gannett, a former lawman, appears to even an old score. Gannett, who is as much wolf as his snarling half-breed dog, is stalking Jelly to avenge the loss of a hand many years earlier.

84.15 *The Black McGloins.* Jan. 21, 1969. GS: Jonathan Harris, Stefanie Powers, Peter Palmer, Nydia Westman, George Mitchell, William Bryant, Byron Morrow. Padraic McGloin, sporting a thick brogue and mutton-chop sideburns, finds a perfect patsy in Scott Lancer. Whining that he is just a poor put-upon immigrant, Paddy gains Scott's support while he robs the county blind, threatening the other ranchers with arson unless they acquiesce.

84.16 *Yesterday's Vendetta.* Jan. 28, 1969. GS: Teresa Wright, Lin McCarthy, Robert Sorrells, Ray Kellogg, Ted Gehring. Scott and Johnny are mystified by their father's sudden disappearance from the ranch. They are unaware that he has decided to bury the hatchet, one way or another, with Sheriff Judd Haney, his bitter enemy of 25 years. Ellen Haney, the lawman's wife, plays a pivotal role in resolving the long-standing feud.

84.17 *Warburton's Edge.* Feb. 4, 1969. GS: Arthur Hill, Burr DeBenning, Susan O'Connell, Richard Devon, Del Monroe, Buck Young, Alma Beltram. Johnny's loyalties are torn between his father and an adventurer in a cattlemen's dispute that finds plenty of wrongdoing, and violence, on both sides.

84.18 *The Fix-It Man.* Feb. 11, 1969. GS: Frank McHugh, Linden Chiles, Barry Atwater, Mark Allen, Dean Harens, Ted Gehring, Wayne Heffley. Old Charlie Wingate, the town drunk and sometimes fix-it man, resolves to do one constructive thing in his life — build a jailhouse for lawless Morro Coyo. But Charlie faces opposition from interests determined to keep law and order out of town.

84.19 *Angel Day and Her Sunshine Girls.* Feb. 25, 1969. GS: Cloris Leachman, Mark Richman, Joyce Bullifant, Carolyn Fleming, Don Briggs, Ray Fine, David McLean. Saloon entertainer Angel Day turns up at the Lancer ranch with a court order to claim Teresa, the daughter she once abandoned. Planned as an extortion scheme by her husband, the maneuver fails to consider Angel's maternal instincts.

84.20 *The Great Humbug.* March 4, 1969. GS: Lisa True Gerritson, William Windom, Morgan Woodward, Alan Oppenheimer, Sam Elliot, William Wintersole, Joseph Perry. The Lancers unwittingly play host to a swindler and the wealth of problems created by his fraudulent land-buying scheme.

84.21 *Juniper's Camp.* March 11, 1969. GS: Shelley Fabares, Dennis Cole, Walter Brooke, Ross Hagen, William Lucking, Duane Grey, Chuck Harrold. Scott and Johnny ride into a hornet's nest when they try to rescue a Boston miss supposedly kidnaped by a miner. The truth is she wants to marry the man, and is in no mood to be rescued.

84.22 *The Knot.* March 18, 1969. GS: Tom Skerritt, Martin Sheen, Wright King, Richard X. Slattery, Jack Williams. After being rescued from kidnapers, Teresa refuses to identify a former captor who had been kind to her. Her own kindness may reap a bitter reward. The man has sworn to kill Murdoch.

84.23 *The Man Without a Gun.* March 25, 1969. GS: Guy Stockwell, Warren Oates, Harry Harvey, Sr., Woodrow Parfrey, William Vaughn, Buck Young, Henry Wills, Joseph Ferrante, Tony Davis. Clay Criswell is a polished gentleman outlaw who doesn't carry a gun, yet plans to rob the town. His ingenious scheme is to replace the sheriff and then, in the name of civilized progress, disarm the townfolk.

84.24 *Child of Rock and Sunlight.* April 1, 1969. GS: Rex Holman, Johnnie Whitaker, Virginia Christine, Patty McCormack, Mary Jackson, Craig Hundley, Gary Walberg. Stranded on the blazing desert, Scott Lancer goes from frying pan into fire when he stumbles half blind onto an abandoned mine occupied by the Sickles family. Outlaw Luke Sickles sees a chance to shake the law by killing Scott and passing off the corpse as himself. Scott's only hope lies in Luke's nephew, Andy-Jack, a knowledge-hungry lad torn between family loyalty and a fierce desire for schooling.

84.25 ***The Measure of a Man.*** April 8, 1969. GS: Victor French, Ronny Howard, Julie Sommars, Roger Perry, Craig Hundley, Richard O'Brien, Debi Storm, Scott James. Strangely enough, it is Johnny, an untaught ex-gunfighter, who serves as a substitute teacher. He is helping a school marm prove the value of education to ranchers dead set against sending their children to school.

84.26 ***Devil's Blessing.*** April 22, 1969. GS: Beverly Garland, Joseph Campanella, Noah Beery, Jr., Victor Tayback, Charles Dierkop, Arthur Franz, E.J. Andre, John Harmon, William A. Henry. Smarting from accusations that he is suffering from age, Murdoch single-handedly takes on lawless elements in an ugly mining town misnamed Blessing.

Season Two

84.27 ***Blind Man's Bluff.*** Sept. 23, 1969. GS: L.Q. Jones, Melissa Murphy, Robert Doyle, Russell Thorson, James Gammon, Charles Irving, Frank Gerstle. Johnny, blinded by a sniper's bullet, must rely on a mute girl to help him escape his pursuers.

84.28 ***Zee.*** Sept. 30, 1969. GS: Stefanie Powers, Vaughn Taylor, Richard Evans, Jack Elam, Ellen Corby, Dub Taylor, William Bryant, Charles Irving, Ian Wolfe. Scott is deputized to keep watch over Zee, a tomboyish young hellion caught robbing a store, and a resourceful bundle of trouble for her hapless custodian.

84.29 ***The Kid.*** Oct. 7, 1969. GS: Billy Mumy, Bert Freed, Richard X. Slattery, Jennifer Douglas, Dabbs Greer, Lee Farr, Don Wilbanks, Vic Perrin. Johnny Lancer reverts to his former identity of gunslinger Johnny Madrid to teach a youngster the power of hate. The lad hires Johnny, for a rock-bottom fee of $26.37, to kill two ranchers he blames for the death of his father.

84.30 ***The Black Angel.*** Oct. 21, 1969. GS: Antoinette Bower, Gavin MacLeod, Tim Weldon. Old Jelly falls beard over boots in love with Angeline Ferris, a beguiling widow half his age. It is Murdoch who has reservations about the May-December pairing, and well he might. Angeline is part of an insurance scheme that pegs Jelly's life at $10,000.

84.31 ***The Gifts.*** Oct. 28, 1969. GS: Sharon Acker, Mary Jo Kennedy, Will Kuluva, June Dayton, Jim Woodall, Tom Lowe, Don Wilbanks, Jan Arvan, John Gallaudet. Three birthday gifts are intended for Murdoch—Scott's stereopticon, Johnny's priceless rifle, and Jelly's prize sow—but strange events befall each before delivery.

84.32 ***Cut the Wolf Loose.*** Nov. 4, 1969. GS: Brooke Bundy, Joe Don Baker, Vic Tayback, Ned Romero, Kevin O'Neall, Ned Glass, Dehl Berti, Arvo Ojala, Harvey Gold. Johnny battles unusual and formidable rivals for the love of missionary Laura Thompson, Laura's first concern is the frontier's human flotsam: the old men, cripples, derelicts and feckless town Indians she is struggling to reach.

84.33 ***Jelly Hoskins' American Dream.*** Nov. 11, 1969. GS: Frank Marth, James Griffith, David McLean, George Keymas, Harry Hickok, Mary Jackson, Shannon Farnon. Sentimental old Jelly becomes the laughingstock of cattledom when he buys a real bovine misfit—a ponderous, humpbacked bull like no one has ever seen. But for some reason, one of the cattlemen isn't laughing. If he can't have the gentle beast, then no one else will.

84.34 ***Welcome to Genesis.*** Nov. 18, 1969. GS: Pernell Roberts, Richard Carlson, Joanne Linville, Teddy Eccles, Bill Zuckert, Nellie Burt, David Macklin, Sundown Spencer. Theodore Banning, a frontier doctor of doubtful ethics and a dubious future, is jailed for practicing without a license. But Banning is the best Murdoch can find to treat a badly mauled Jelly and the long-neglected people of a forgotten mining town.

84.35 ***A Person Unknown.*** Nov. 25, 1969. GS: Agnes Moorehead, Quentin Dean, Ramon Bieri, Bruce Dern. A Southern gentlewoman is reduced to farming, but is determined to improve her daughter's lot. Opportunity knocks when the girl brings home Johnny, badly wounded and carrying a price on his head for murder.

84.36 ***Legacy.*** Dec. 9, 1969. GS: George Macready, Katherine Justice, Dal Jenkins, Teno Pollick, Kathleen Freeman, Jason Wingreen, Eddie Frank, Jack Turley. Harlan Garrett, Scott's maternal grandfather, has come West to resume a no-holds-barred battle with Murdoch for Scott's affections.

84.37 ***A Scarecrow at Hacket's.*** Dec. 16, 1969. GS: Pat Hingle, Sean Kelly, James Griffith, Ian Wolfe. A dying man, feeling his land accursed, wills it to the devil. Oddly enough, a claimant shows up, a softly sinister Absolem Weir, a gentleman with a slightly sulfurous air.

84.38 ***Little Darling of the Sierras.*** Dec. 30, 1969. GS: Cloris Leachman, Don Francks, Bayn Johnson. When mining-camp entertainer Penny Rose's father dies, Murdoch tries to find the fortune she supposedly has inherited, while helping the little trouper start a new life with her stuffy aunt from San Francisco.

84.39 ***Shadow of a Dead Man.*** Jan. 6, 1970. GS: Lynn Loring, Michael James Wixted, Harry Swoger. Investigating a forgotten piece of property, Johnny finds it occupied by a rifle-toting woman who claims to be a Lancer and wants no truck with strangers. With good reason, for she is being sought by a man with an easy smile, and the reflexes of a gunfighter.

84.40 ***Blue Skies for Willie Sharpe.*** Jan. 13, 1969. GS: Keenan Wynn, Clint Howard, Alfred Ryder, Sam Elliot, William Wintersole. For the sake of young Willie Sharpe, Scott tries to restore luster to the badly tarnished image of the boy's legendary grandfather. Once a town tamer, Kansas Bill Sharpe is now the town drunk. He is also the favorite clown of a sadistic town boss.

84.41 ***Chad.*** Jan. 20, 1970. GS: John Beck, Zina Bethune, Mills Watson, Robert Gravage. Entanglements multiply when Johnny helps a brother and sister who have come from the hills of Kentucky to settle an old family feud. With a band of desperadoes in deadly pursuit, Johnny slowly realizes that the girl is falling for him, and that the family they are seeking is his own.

84.42 ***The Lorelei.*** Jan. 27, 1970. GS: Anthony Eisley, Winifred Coffin, Leonard Stone, Roy Benson, Arthur Malet, Nina Shipman, Debi Storm. All that's gold doesn't necessarily glitter, as Jelly discovers upon acquiring a gold mine. Profitable mining of the vein requires blasting that will dam a stream vitally needed by he Lancers.

84.43 ***The Lion and the Lamb.*** Feb. 3, 1970. GS: Andrew Prine, Donna Mills, Donald Moffat, Ross Hagen, Hal Holmes, Jerry Strickler, John Harmon, Ray Kellogg. Gentle Gabe Lincoln, a sheepherder of Biblical mien, saves Johnny from a raging bull. In return, the young cowhand offers refuge for Gabe's sheep on Lancer land—an action that stirs fires of fanaticism among the neighboring cattlemen.

84.44 *The Experiment.* Feb. 17, 1970. GS: Scott Marlowe, Scott Brady, Richard Peabody, Charles Dierkop, Martin Huston, John McLiam, Ed Bakey, Stanley Adams, Alice Backes, Paul Sorenson. Testing an idea born before its time, Murdoch oversees an experimental prison farm for first-time offenders. Striving to remain firm, but fair, he grapples with skepticism from the six sullen convicts, the hard-nosed guards and hypocritical members of the prison board.

84.45 *Splinter Group.* March 3, 1970. GS: Ken Swofford, Tim O'Connor, Diana Ewing, William Mims, Jason Wingreen, Eileen Baral, Frances Spanier, Charles Wagenheim. Scott goes after supplies to help starving families of miners fleeing the law. The fugitives are exposed to great danger when the sheriff learns of their presence, and the foodstuffs turn out to be contaminated.

84.46 *Lamp in the Wilderness.* March 10, 1970. GS: Pippa Scott, Manuel Padilla, Michael Ansara, Melanie Craig, Mark Tapscott, George Ostos, Gloria Chavez, Ira Augustein. Murdoch lends a helping hand to a teacher working with Indian children. Rebecca Brown need the help as she has no understanding of the Indians culture, and her classes are being disrupted by an embittered brave.

84.47 *The Buscaderos.* March 17, 1970. GS: Warren Oates, Brenda Scott, Rex Holman, David McLean, Joseph Perry. Backed by desperadoes and a Gatling gun, the bandit Drago takes over the Lancer ranch, intent on stealing local tax monies. Jealous of his girl friend's one-time love for Johnny Lancer, Drago plans to humiliate Johnny before her eyes. But Drago picks on Scott by mistake, and vents his long-held fury on him.

84.48 *Dream of Falcons.* April 7, 1970. GS: John Beck, Harold Gould, Richard X. Slattery, Del Monroe, Don Wilbanks, Frank Christi. Chad Lancer, the hillbilly addition to the clan, helps an inventor give wings to an idea. Despite ridicule and opposition, old Otto Mueller is determined to test his tomfool notion that man can fly.

84.49 *Goodbye, Lizzie.* April 28, 1970. GS: Nan Martin, Victor Campos, James Best, Bill Vint, Annette Molen, Charles Briggs. Murdoch's old friend Lizzie Cramer is making a mighty effort to quit her outlaw band. But the past, like a shadow, is hard to leave behind.

84.50 *The Rivals.* May 5, 1970. GS: Rory Calhoun, Mary Fickett. Buck Addison, a ruthless land baron, is trying to squeeze out Murdoch. Addison's interests aren't entirely in land. He also considers Murdoch a rival in love.

84.51 *Lifeline.* May 19, 1970. GS: Donald Knight, Barbara Luna, Peter Palmer, Stewart Bradley, Arthur Bernard, Jim Burk. The Lancers experience an unnerving brush with the occult. A young seer's predictions of doom seem to be coming true. Jelly comes down with a strange sickness, and the cattle start dying likes flies.

85. *Laramie*

NBC. 60 minutes. Broadcast history: Tuesday, 7:30-8:30, Sept. 1959–Sept. 1963.

Regular Cast: John Smith (Slim Sherman), Robert Fuller (Jess Harper), Hoagy Carmichael (Jonesy) 59-60, Bobby Crawford, Jr. (Andy Sherman), Don Durant (Gandy) 60-63, Arch Johnson (Wellman) 60-63, Dennis Holmes (Mike) 61-63, Spring Byington (Daisy Cooper) 61-63, Eddy Waller (Mose Shell), Stuart Randall (Mort Corey) 60-63.

Premise: Three men and a boy operate a ranch and a stagecoach station for the Great Overland Mail Stage Lines near the town of Laramie in the 1880s.

The Episodes

85.1 *Stage Stop.* Sept. 15, 1959. GS: Dan Duryea, Everett Sloan. Outlaw Bud Carlin stops off at the Sherman ranch before carrying out a bold plan to free another gunslinger who was recently captured.

85.2 *Glory Road.* Sept. 22, 1959. GS: Eddie Albert, Nanette Fabray, Ray Teal. Traveling preacher Essie Bright is on the road to Laramie with her moody wagon driver. When they stop at the Sherman ranch to rest, the driver reveals the reason for his behavior.

85.3 *Circle of Fire.* Sept. 22, 1959. GS: Marsha Hunt, Ernest Borgnine, Robert F. Simon, Frank Ferguson, Eddy Waller, John Pickard, Frank de Kova. In a moment of unreasoning terror, stagecoach passenger Martha Chambers shoots and kills the son of a Pawnee chief. Infuriated by the killing of their chief's son, a group of Indians swear revenge on the woman responsible. The woman takes refuge at the Sherman Ranch.

85.4 *Fugitive Road.* Oct. 6, 1959. GS: Clu Gulager. Fed up because he has been persecuted, cavalryman Gil Brady deserts. Planning to flee to Canada, he seeks the aid of his brother-in-law, Jess Harper. But he is being followed by a sadistic Army Sergeant.

85.5 *The Star Trail.* Oct. 13, 1959. GS: Lloyd Nolan, Patricia Barry, Mildred Van Hollen, William Bryant. Jess Harper is upset to hear that his friend Tully Hatch took part in a bank robbery. Because Hatch once saved Harper's life and later made him deputy sheriff, Jess feels he must do something to help his friend.

85.6 *The Lawbreakers.* Oct. 20, 1959. GS: James Best, John McIntire, Christopher Dark, Rayford Barnes. To break up a robbery ring, Jess Harper poses as an outlaw. He is hired as a guide for the gang as they try to locate their loot.

85.7 *The Iron Captain.* Oct. 27, 1959. GS: Edmond O'Brien. Renegade Army captain Sam Prado and his gang take Slim Sherman and Jess Harper prisoner. Prado tells them he is looking for a dancer named Lita.

85.8 *The Run to Tumavaca.* Nov. 10, 1959. GS: Gena Rowlands, John Archer, Robert J. Wilke, John Alderson, Kevin Hagen, Harry Lauter. An old friend of Jess Harper's tells him that her husband is planning to kill her—and persuades him to help her escape to Mexico.

85.9 *The General Must Die.* Nov. 17, 1959. GS: Brian Keith, John Hoyt, Read Morgan, Don "Red" Barry, Gil Rankin, Kenneth MacDonald. Two ex-Army officer have a bizarre plan to kill Gen. William Tecumseh Sherman. And part of their plot is to seize Slim Sherman's ranch.

85.10 *Dark Verdict.* Nov. 24, 1959. GS: Thomas Mitchell, Warren Stevens, L.Q. Jones, Harry Dean Stanton, Grant Richards. An innocent man is jailed on circumstantial evidence, and a retired judge stirs up sentiment for a lynching.

85.11 Man of God. Dec. 1, 1959. GS: James Gregory, Bill Williams, Douglas Kennedy, Kathleen O'Malley, Sam Edwards. Father Elliot, a crusading priest, arrives with a peaceful plan to stop Sitting Bull's Indian wars. But the Army insists on using force.

85.12 Bare Knuckles. Dec. 8, 1959. GS: Don Megowan, Wally Brown, Eddy Waller, Hal Baylor. Jonesy tries to raise mortgage money by playing the piano at a local saloon. He inadvertently involves Slim Sherman in a shady boxing match.

85.13 The Lonesome Gun. Dec. 15, 1959. GS: Gary Merrill. Ed Farrell nurses a grudge against Slim Sherman and plots revenge. Jonesy sizes up the situation and goes into action to stop Farrell.

85.14 Night of the Quiet Man. Dec. 22, 1959. GS: Lyle Bettger, Carl Benton Reid, Read Morgan, Anthony Caruso, Robert Knapp. Ex-marshal John McCambridge intends to dedicate his life to the rehabilitation of outlaws. Slim and Jess lend a hand and they establish a haven for reformed gunmen in Laramie.

85.15 The Pass. Dec. 29, 1959. GS: Madlyn Rhue, Richard Shannon, John Pickard, Walter Sande. Army troops are preparing an all-out campaign against the Sioux. But the plans are delayed when Slim Sherman discovers that the Indians are holding a girl captive.

85.16 Trail Drive. Jan. 12, 1960. GS: Jim Davis. In order to meet financial obligations at the ranch, Slim, Jess and Jonesy hire on as hands in a cattle drive. Then they discover that trail boss Hake Ballard plans to kill them.

85.17 Day of Vengeance. Jan. 19, 1960. GS: John Larch, Adele Mara, Phillip Pine, Harry Bartell, Vinton Hayworth. Cabe Reynolds is accused of killing his wife, and a stage is bringing him to Laramie for trial. On the way, the coach is ambushed by a gang that doesn't want Reynolds to testify.

85.18 The Legend of Lily. Jan. 26, 1960. GS: Kent Taylor, Constance Moore, Patsy Kelly, George Tobias, William Tannen, Harry Lauter. Once the toast of three continents, actress Lily Langford is now reduced to performing in frontier saloons. Her husband, angered by her loss of prestige and earning power, torments Lily.

85.19 Death Wind. Feb. 2, 1960. GS: Claude Akins, Nancy Gates, Stacy Harris, Chris Alcaide, James Anderson, William Fawcett. The death wind, a raging tornado, drives escaped prisoner Tom Cole and his wife to seek shelter at the Sherman ranch. But the storm drives another party to the same shelter — Cole's pursuers, who intend to kill him.

85.20 Company Man. Feb. 9, 1960. GS: John Dehner, James Best, Rad Fulton, Olive Sturgess, Bing Russell. Jack Slade, the new superintendent for the stagecoach line arrives in Laramie with ambitious ideas for cleaning up the company. Objecting to Jess's background he intends to have him fired.

85.21 Rope of Steel. Feb. 16, 1960. GS: Harry Townes, Mari Blanchard, George Mitchell, Bartlett Robinson. A robber and his victim kill each other, and Mace Stringer is the only witness. He impulsively steals the money, but angry townspeople believe Jonesy and Slim Sherman have looted the bodies.

85.22 Duel at Alta Mesa. Feb. 23, 1960. GS: Douglas Dumbrille, Tom Drake, Fay Spain, Alan Dexter, Don O'Kelly, George Kennedy, Pamela Duncan. T.J. Patterson's stage line has been robbed, and he suspects Tom Mannering. Mannering admits he has a lot of money, but claims he won it in a poker game.

85.23 Street of Hate. March 1, 1960. GS: Charles Bronson, Dean Fredericks, Barton MacLane, Kathleen Crowley. The murderer of one of Laramie's most popular citizens is released on parole. Against the wishes of the townspeople, Slim Sherman agrees to be responsible for him.

85.24 Ride or Die. March 8, 1960. GS: Simon Oakland, Robert Clarke, Sue England, Steve Darrell, Howard Wright. Slim pursues outlaw Vernon Kane into the desert. Kane encounters Jack and Deborah Farnum and convinces them that Slim is a criminal.

85.25 Hour After Dawn. March 15, 1960. GS: Bruce Bennett, Ben Johnson, Gloria Talbott, Robert Osterloh, Anne Barton, Irving Bacon. Guilty of robbery and murder, Bill Pardee is slated to hang. But he isn't too worried about his fate. He is sure that his half-brother, Con Creighton, will come to his rescue.

85.26 The Protectors. March 22, 1960. GS: Vince Edwards, Herbert Rudley, Mari Aldon, Robert Bray, William Phipps, Baynes Barron, Ted de Corsia. Cattlemen around Laramie are supporting gunmen to run the settlers out. Then the newcomers hire their own gunslinger.

85.27 Saddle and Spur. March 29, 1960. GS: Beverly Garland, Edgar Buchanan, Richard Devon, Walter Coy. Slim and Jess make a brief stop in a small Kansas town. Before they can get under way again, they are elected temporary marshals.

85.28 Midnight Rebellion. April 5, 1960. GS: Bruce Gordon, Michael Pate, Ed Kemmer, Marian Collier. For reasons of his own, Jess Harper joins a gang of terrorists plotting against the Government and planning to set up a state of their own.

85.29 Cemetery Road. April 12, 1960. GS: Dennis Patrick, Read Morgan, Jocelyn Brando. Slim Sherman has done everything he could to prevent violence, but a member of a passing wagon train shoots the village blacksmith.

85.30 Men of Defiance. April 19, 1960. GS: Bing Russell, Don Megowan, Edgar Buchanan, Dennis Miller, John Pickard. Ambushed by an outlaw gang, Jess Harper is saved by Reb O'Neil. Then the gang takes O'Neil hostage, and will release him only in exchange for Jess.

Season Two

85.31 Queen of Diamonds. Sept. 20, 1960. GS: Julie London, Claude Akins, Tony Young, Brad Weston, Eddy Waller, Mike Ragan. Slim Sherman is in love with June Brown, a winsome stranger. But Jess recognizes the girl as a professional blackjack dealer.

85.32 The Track of the Jackal. Sept. 27, 1960. GS: Stephen McNally, Robert J. Wilke, Jeanne Bates, Stacy Harris. As acting deputy sheriff, Jeff Harper questions a murder charge against Sumner Campbell. But bounty hunter Luke Wiley, positive of Campbell's guilt, is determined to track him down and collect the reward.

85.33 Three Road West. Oct. 4, 1960. GS: Vera Miles, Myron Healey, Phyllis Love, Jan Merlin, Denver Pyle, Ross Elliott. Slim has been hired by a stage line to deliver a bushel of company money to agent Jack Adams. The mission is accomplished, but there is trouble to come. Stage driver Frank Skinner shoots Adams and makes off with the cash.

85.34 Ride the Wild Wind. Oct. 11, 1960. GS: Ernest Borgnine, Vivi Janiss, James Anderson, Ed Prentiss, Robert J.

Laramie

Stevenson. Slim is ready to sell Andy's horse, so the boy takes his palomino and runs away from home. The horse leads him to the camp of Boone Caudle, a wanted bank robber.

85.35 *Ride into Darkness.* Oct. 18, 1960. GS: Charles Drake, Phyllis Avery, Jason Robards, Sr, Kevin Pratt, Brad Weston. Jess is looking for prospector Dan Preston, who has mysteriously disappeared. He enters a town that is under the thumb of a man named Matt Jessup, who makes it clear he would like Jess to knuckle under too.

85.36 *The Long Riders.* Oct. 25, 1960. GS: Dan Duryea, John Anderson, Fred Coby. Slim and Jess rescue a happy-go-lucky cowpoke named Luke Gregg from a band of Indians. Then they give him a job on the ranch. But there is something about Gregg that Jess doesn't like.

85.37 *The Dark Trail.* Nov. 1, 1960. GS: Robert Vaughn, Gigi Perreau, Harold J. Stone. Ranch hand Sandy Kayle doesn't get along too well with his boss Sam Bronson. But he gets along fine with Bronson's daughter Celie.

85.38 *Calibre.* Nov. 15, 1960. GS: George Nader, Anna-Lisa, Lee Van Cleef, Katherine Warren, John Pickard, Charlie Briggs. A deputy marshal is killed by the vicious Torrey gang, and Wells Clark is sent to replace him. Clark swears he'll get the gang, but no one, including Jess, is inclined to help him.

85.39 *License to Kill.* Nov. 22, 1960. GS: R.G. Armstrong, Denny Miller, William Fawcett, Kem Dibbs. A bounty hunter named Sam Jarrad is after Jess, and finds him. He claims Jess has a price on his head and he aims to collect.

85.40 *Drifter's Gold.* Nov. 29, 1960. GS: Rod Cameron, Judi Meredith, Gregory Walcott, Sandra Knight, Don Kennedy. Tom Bedloe spreads a phony gold-rush rumor to get the men out of town. He then plans to rob the local bank.

85.41 *No Second Chance.* Dec. 6, 1960. GS: Jeff Richards, Fay Spain, Richard Coogan. Kem Backer wants Slim and Jess to switch their way station affiliation to his stagecoach line. When the boys refuse, Backer sends some brawny persuaders to help change their minds.

85.42 *Duel at Parkison Town.* Dec. 13, 1960. GS: Henry Hull, Murray Matheson, Ron Harper, Don Beddoe, Bartlett Robinson, Michael Vallon, Edward G. Robinson, Jr. The blood feud between the Parkisons and Shermans still rages. Ben Parkison thinks that Slim Sherman murdered his boy, and challenges him to a pistol duel.

85.43 *A Sound of Bells.* Dec. 27, 1960. GS: Kim Hector, Ross Martin, Robert J. Wilke, Dick Foran, Rachel Ames, Mara Corday, Ben Johnson. Indians pursue a stagecoach full of orphans on Christmas Eve. The coach finds refuge at the Sherman ranch, but despite his rescue little Neil Hunter is unhappy.

85.44 *The Passing of Kuba Smith.* Jan. 3, 1961. GS: John McIntire, Walter Sande, Gloria Talbott, Bartlett Robinson, Harry Tyler. Outlaw Kuba Smith kills a sheriff who looks just like him, and he plants the body where Slim and Jess will find it. Since the boys have been gunning for Smith, they think they have killed him.

85.45 *Man from Kansas.* Jan. 10, 1961. GS: Jock Mahoney, Jocelyn Brando, George Mitchell, Vinton Hayworth, Adam West, Kelly Thordsen. Outlaw Clay Jackson escapes a trap set by Slim, and in the process murders a deputy. The angry townspeople blame Smith for the deputy's death.

85.46 *Killer Without Cause.* Jan. 24, 1961. GS: Dayton Lummis, Onslow Stevens, James Westerfield, Rex Holman. Slim's Indian friend is shot by Carl Vail. Carl is put on trial, but nobody takes the murder seriously because the victim was an Indian.

85.47 *Stolen Tribute.* Jan. 31, 1961. GS: Jan Merlin, Dennis Patrick, Edgar Buchanan. Clint Wade, whom Jess helped imprison, is now out on parole. Wade finds Jess and forces him onto the desert to look for a bundle of money stolen years earlier.

85.48 *The Lost Dutchman.* Feb. 14, 1961. GS: Robert Emhardt, Robert Armstrong, Karen Steele, George Keymas, Rayford Barnes. Slim is convicted of prospector George Lake's murder. Jess comes to his aid, finds that Lake supposedly had a map to a lost gold mine, and suspects that the real killer is the man who now has the map.

85.49 *Cactus Lady.* Feb. 21, 1961. GS: Anita Sands, Arthur Hunnicutt, Harry Dean Stanton, L.Q. Jones, Grandon Rhodes, Katharine Warren. Slim is taken with the charms of lovely Troy McCanles, and won't heed the advice of Jess, who tells him that she is a member of a wild outlaw family. Troy tells Slim she is all through with lawbreaking. Then her family shows up.

85.50 *Riders of the Night.* March 7, 1961. GS: Richard Coogan, Norman Leavitt, James Griffith, Chuck Roberson, Gregg Barton, Hal Baylor. Slim and his friends, Doc Kingsly and Sandy, are forced at gun point to go to a cave, where Doc is told he must operate on an outlaw's leg.

85.51 *The Mark of the Maneaters.* March 14, 1961. GS: James Coburn, Charles McGraw, Marguerite Chapman. Gil Spanner is staying at the Sherman Ranch when he is called to testify for the prosecution in a murder case. The defendant's friends surround the place intending to kill Spanner.

85.52 *Rimrock.* March 21, 1961. GS: Lyle Bettger, Mort Mills, Susan Cummings, Tom London. Justice seems to have taken a holiday. Jess lands in jail after accusing Marshal Grant McClintock of covering up a murder, committed by McClintock himself.

85.53 *Run of the Hunted.* April 4, 1961. GS: Charles Bronson, R.G. Armstrong, Harry Lauter, Kevin Hagen, Leonard Geer, Harry Harvey, Jr., Gregg Barton. Cory Lake, a friend of Slim's, is committed by his relatives to an insane asylum, although he does not appear to be mentally disturbed. Slim suspects that Lake's kin are more interested in his ranch than his health, and are using his hospitalization as means to seize control.

85.54 *Two for the Gallows.* April 11, 1961. GS: Warren Oates, Donald Woods, Richard Evans, Eddy Waller. Bandit Morgan Bennett has found an excellent mountain hiding place for his loot. It is so good, in fact, that now even he can't find it. Realizing his need for an experienced guide, Bennett offers Slim the job.

85.55 *The Debt.* April 18, 1961. GS: Harry Carey, Jr., Jason Evers, Monica Lewis, Vaughn Taylor, Roy Barcroft, Emile Meyer. Jess' first act after hiring on as a deputy is to let murder suspect Harry Markle escape. Markle, it seems, once saved Jess from the noose.

85.56 *Killer's Odds.* April 25, 1961. GS: John Lupton, Russell Johnson, Lee Van Cleef, Pat Michon. Slim and Jess hire a drifter named Fred Powers to work on the farm. The job, however, doesn't seem to help Fred's restlessness. Finally he admits that hired killers are on his trail.

85.57 *Bitter Glory.* May 2, 1961. GS: Dick Foran, Ed Nelson, Dianne Foster, Paul Birch. Jess hears that his friend Billy Jacobs has gone AWOL with the fort's payroll. Jess makes a deal with Billy's commander, Major Stanton. The major won't report the theft until Jess has had a chance to persuade Billy to return with the money.

85.58 *The Tumbleweed Wagon.* May 9, 1961. GS: Jack Elam, Steve Darrell, Robert Crosson, Elisha Cook, Jr. Slim is waylaid and captured by two destitute farmers who, hoping to cash in on reward money, pass Slim off to federal marshals as an escaped fugitive.

85.59 *Trigger Point.* May 16, 1961. GS: Gregory Walcott, Mary Murphy, Lori Nelson, Willard Waterman. Riding shotgun on a stage hauling a large gold shipment, Jess is shot and beaten when bandits hold up the coach. The gang takes the gold, and the stage, leaving Jess and the passengers in the desert.

85.60 *Badge of the Outsider.* May 23, 1961. GS: Roy Barcroft, George Wallace, Jan Shepard. Outlaw Doc Longley is wanted for murder, but protests his innocence. Slim, whose life Longley once saved, talks the fugitive into a safe stay behind bars, while he hunts for the real killer.

85.61 *Men in Shadows.* May 30, 1961. GS: Rod Cameron, Joan Tabor, Dennis Patrick, Ken Christy. Howard Gallery is a gambler on the run, but it is Jess Harper who takes the chances when he hides Gallery and his pretty traveling companion, Julie. Jess believes his old friend is wanted only for another gambling escapade, then the sheriff shows up with a murder warrant.

85.62 *Strange Company.* June 6, 1961. GS: Bill Tennant, Jim Brown, Mark Dana, Christopher Dark, Denver Pyle, Dick Wessel. Slim and a crew of men are working to repair an old trail that bypasses dangerous Indian country. But the route appears to have perils of its own. Slim's workmen are being killed one by one.

85.63 *Widow in White.* June 13, 1961. GS: Sue England, Richard Coogan, Ed Prentiss, Rayford Barnes, Ben Johnson, George Keymas, Ross Elliott. Slim is hired by a young widow named Sheila Dawson as foreman of her ranch. It looks like a pretty attractive job, but Slim soon runs into labor-management problems — three of the ranch hands try to kill him.

Season Three

85.64 *Dragon at the Door.* Sept. 26, 1961. GS: Robert Kino, Nobu McCarthy, Teru Shimada, Anita Loos, Ed Nelson, K.L. Smith, Larry Perron. When a traveling Japanese circus has a wagon breakdown along the trail, Slim and Jess tow the wagon to the ranch. There the Oriental show folk ask them to look after ten-year Mike Williams, an orphan, whom they rescued from the scene of an Indian attack.

85.65 *Ladies Day.* Oct. 3, 1961. GS: Gloria Talbott, Jock Mahoney, James Anderson, William Bryant, Eddy Waller, Norman Leavitt, Carl Benton Reid. Slim and Jess are in the market for a housekeeper so they can keep guardianship of young Mike. The next stagecoach provides two candidate — widow Daisy Cooper and young Sally Malone. Mrs. Cooper is dismayed to find that the property she came to claim doesn't exist.

85.66 *Siege at Jubilee.* Oct. 10, 1961. GS: Lin McCarthy, Ruta Lee, Ted DeCorsia, L.Q. Jones, Percy Helton, Denver Pyle. In Cheyenne, Slim captures bank robber Hobey Devon when the crook eludes the Sheriff. Then Daisy volunteers Slim's services for additional duty, as a deputy to escort Devon back to Laramie.

85.67 *The Mountain Men.* Oct. 17, 1961. GS: Dan Duryea, Jason Evers, Alex Viespi, Fred Coby, John Cliff. Ben Sanford and his boys are out to avenge the death of their kinsman Warren. They think the law has been too easy on accused killer Joe Vance, and they plan to intercept the stage carrying Vance to Fort Leavenworth.

85.68 *The Fatal Step.* Oct. 24, 1961. GS: Gary Clarke, Dennis Patrick, Robert J. Wilke, Allison Hayes, Pat O'Malley, Tom Fadden, Raymond Greenleaf, Raymond Bailey, Olan Soule. Young Tad Kimball, who needs the wherewithal to get married, agrees to go along with Wes Darrin's plan to rob a stage coach, even though he knows his friend Jess will be riding in it.

85.69 *The Last Journey.* Oct. 31, 1961. GS: Rod Cameron, Sandra Knight, Richard Davalos, Mort Mills, Gene Roth, Dani Lynn, Mary Bishop. John Cole, just out of prison, rides into the Sherman ranch with a wounded, and unconscious, U.S. marshal. Slim finds it hard to believe Cole's story that the marshal was wounded by a bushwhacker.

85.70 *Deadly Is the Night.* Nov. 7, 1961. GS: Lloyd Nolan, Harry Lauter, Charles Robinson, Olive Carey, Vinton Hayworth, Don Harvey, George D. Wallace. Matt Dyer and his gang have held up the bank in Granite City, and the countryside is swarming with trigger-happy deputies. But Dyer is holed up in the home of the bank president, right under the town's collective nose.

85.71 *The Accusers.* Nov. 14, 1961. GS: Charles Drake, Joanne Linville, William Challee, Carmen Phillips, Harry Fleer, Kelly Thordsen. Allen Winter, county supervisor of the Overland Stage line, is a respected citizen of Laramie. But saloon hostess Carla Morton seems to have become an influence in Winter's life — a bad influence.

85.72 *Wolf Cub.* Nov. 21, 1961. GS: Robert Blake, Arthur Hunnicut, Kenneth MacDonald, Frank DeKova, Hardie Albright, Addison Richards. Wolf Cub is the name of a crippled Indian boy Jess has rescued from the hands of ruthless bounty hunter Earl Droody. While searching for a doctor to fix the boy's leg, Jess, Daisy and Mike shelter him — and violate Army regulations against harboring Indians.

85.73 *Handful of Fire.* Dec. 5, 1961. GS: George Macready, Karen Sharpe, Myron Healey, John Pickard, Herb Vigran, Maurice Manson, Ross Elliott, Doodles Weaver. Col. John Barrington, a believer in total war against the Indians, refuses to obey an order to cancel a planned attack. His decision results in a court-martial.

85.74 *The Killer Legend.* Dec. 12, 1961. GS: Pat Conway, Dick Foran, Joan Evans, Kevin Hagen, Harry Lauter, Hal Smith, Norman Leavitt. Jess Harper is filling in during the absence of Sheriff Mort Corey, but it looks as though the job may become permanent. A man named Tom Wade has just been released from prison and he is gunning for Corey.

85.75 *The Jailbreakers.* Dec. 19, 1961. GS: Charles Aidman, R.G. Armstrong, Jan Shepard, Erin O'Brien, James Anderson, Millicent Patrick, Will Wright, Frank Sully. Ex-convict Gil Martin returns to Cheyenne to see his girl friend. But Marshal Al Dawson, who had warned Martin to stay out of town, shows up and accidentally kills Gina in the ensuing struggle.

85.76 *The Lawless Seven.* Dec. 26, 1961. GS: Lyle Bettger, Jena Engstrom, Dorothy Green, Biff Elliott. Jess is angry when he finds out that some horses he ordered from a rancher named Gorman were sold to the Army instead. The next day, Jess is overtaken by a posse and charged with Gorman's murder.

85.77 *The Perfect Gift.* Jan. 2, 1962. GS: Lisa Gaye, Eugene Iglesias, Russell Johnson, Steve Warren, Michael Pate, Pamela Curran. When two men, Wayne and Lon Cady, try to kill Winona, a beautiful Indian girl, Slim appears in time to save her life. It is a noble deed, and according to tribal law, it gives him ownership of Winona for life.

85.78 *The Barefoot Kid.* Jan. 9, 1962. GS: Rafael Campos, Joanna Barnes, Richard Coogan, Oliver McGowan, Mary Sinclair, Harry Carey, Jr., Lennie Geer, Henry Rowland. Young Juan De La O is jailed in the town of Dry Springs for stealing Harper's horse. The citizens are enraged by the youth's act, and the court sentences him to hang.

85.79 *Shadows in the Dust.* Jan. 16, 1962. GS: Susan Oliver, Dennis Patrick, Francis J. McDonald, Walter Sande, Ed Prentiss, Tru Garrett. After a long chase, Slim finally corners a fleeing rustler. A vicious gunfight ensues, Slim is wounded, but he is able to capture the culprit, who turns out to be a beautiful girl named Jean Lavelle.

85.80 *The Runaway.* Jan. 23, 1962. GS: James Best, Jack Chaplain, Trevor Bardette, Will Wright, Hal Baylor, Hal K. Dawson, Barry Brooks. Teenager Bill Watkins gets mixed up with two saddle tramps named Johnny Best and Samson. In search of a little excitement, the trio decide to rustle some cattle at the Sherman ranch.

85.81 *The Confederate Express.* Jan. 30, 1962. GS: John Larch, Steve Brodie, Peggy Webber, Harry Dean Stanton, Gage Clarke, James Beck, Don Beddoe, George Cisar. Matt Grundy comes tearing into the Sherman ranch and says that there are three bandits right behind him. After Slim and Jess escort Grundy to safety in town, Jess is attacked by the trio, and learns that Grundy is wanted for bank robbery.

85.82 *The High Country.* Feb. 6, 1962. GS: Barton MacLane, Frank Overton, Anita Sands, William Wellman, Jr., Warren Kemmerling, Don Harvey. Slim is on the trail of a horse thief when he encounters cattleman Mel Bishop and his boys in a full-fledged range war with Jason Duncan's gang.

85.83 *A Grave for Cully Brown.* Feb. 13, 1962. GS: David McLean, Karen Steele, Karl Swenson, Barry Kelley, John Anderson, Will Wright, Fred Graham. Jess arrives in a small town on a business trip and finds that he has been expected. The sheriff thinks he is a man named Cully Brown, who is wanted for murder.

85.84 *The Runt.* Feb. 20, 1962. GS: Leonard Nimoy, Ben Cooper, Michael Forest, Sue England, George Keymas, Gregg Barton, Lane Bradford, Raymond Bailey, Susan Hart, Stacy M. Morgan. Sandy Catlin has tried to live peaceably apart from his outlaw family. But when Sandy hedges about helping his fugitive stepbrothers, the boys burn his crops and then threaten to kill his wife Marcy.

85.85 *The Dynamiters.* March 6, 1962. GS: Russell Johnson, Mark Andrews, Jean Allison, Stephen Barringer, Willis Bouchey, Myron Healey, Pamela Curran, Norman Leavitt. A large gold shipment is due to leave Laramie by stage and the authorities are making a final check on the plans to protect the valuable cargo. Meanwhile, outlaws Bob Murkland and Dave Boyd are putting the final touch to their scheme to steal the shipment by placing a timebomb aboard the stage.

85.86 *The Day of the Savage.* March 13, 1962. GS: John Lupton, Michael Pate, Lane Bradford, Gary Vinson, X Brands, Jay Silverheels, Tom Greenway, Boyd Stockman. Glenn Colton is waiting at the Sherman Relay Station for the stage to arrive bearing his fiance. He doesn't find the wait too boring though, because he is attacked by a gang of Indians.

85.87 *Justice in a Hurry.* March 20, 1962. GS: Diana Millay, Hugh Sanders, Robert J. Wilke, Kathleen Freeman, George D. Wallace, Dabbs Greer, Paul Birch, Gregg Barton, Dal McKennon, Nolan Leary. It is general knowledge that Ev Keleher is looking for Arney Jackson, who he thinks poisoned his water-hole and killed some cattle. So when Jackson is found murdered the sheriff arrested Keleher as the leading suspect.

85.88 *The Replacement.* March 27, 1962. GS: Richard Coogan, L.Q. Jones, Roberta Shore, Chuck Courtney, Addison Richards, John Harmon, WIlliam Fawcett, Paul E. Burns, Hank Patterson. Slim, Jess and Sheriff Corey shoot down an outlaw who turns out to be a teenager. When the townspeople learn that their sheriff has been shooting down children, they think it is time to replace him.

85.89 *The Turn of the Wheel.* April 3, 1962. GS: Lyle Bettger, Erin O'Brien, Anthony Caruso, Paul Geary, Sean McClory, Henry Beckman. Frank Mannus arrives in Laramie, only to learn that his reputation has preceded him. Billy O'Neill, for instance, knows how his sister Abbey was once treated by Mannus, and intends to kill him for it.

85.90 *Trial by Fire.* April 10, 1962. GS: Cloris Leachman, Karl Swenson, Jan Merlin, Jason Evers. Dancehall girl Zoie Carter thinks marriage will put her on the road to respectability. So when Lars Carlson's mail-order bride doesn't show up, Zoie decides to take her place.

85.91 *Fall into Darkness.* April 17, 1962. GS: Jean Byron, Harry Lauter, Rayford Barnes, Robert J. Wilke, Gina Gillespie. Slim rushes to help when he learns from Ben and Jack Frances that their sister Norma is trapped in a well. Slim rescues the girl, and is left trapped in Norma's place when he discovers that they are really outlaws.

Season Four

85.92 *Among the Missing.* Sept. 25, 1962. GS: Ivan Dixon, Claude Akins, Dolores Michaels, Jan Merlin, L.Q. Jones, William Bramley, William Boyett. Young Mike is wounded by a trio of desperados as they rob the Laramie bank. The bandits escape and Jess joins Sheriff Corey in their pursuit, determined to avenge the shooting.

85.93 *War Hero.* Oct. 2, 1962. GS: Lloyd Nolan, Joanna Barnes, Herbert Rudley, Mort Mills, Keith Richards, K.L. Smith, Maurice Manson. Jess is bodyguard for Gen. George Barton, a Union Army hero campaigning for the Presidential nomination. Barton, tired of riding in a coach, continues on horseback, followed by Jess and four would-be assassins.

85.94 *The Fortune Hunter.* Oct. 9, 1962. GS: Ray Danton, Carolyn Craig, Peter Whitney, Pat Krest, Parley Baer, Eddy Waller, Cathie Merchant, Willis Bouchey. Slim's lovely fiancee Kitty McAllen is stolen away by suave newcomer Vince Jackson. Jackson convinces her to leave town with him, but his motives are far from romantic.

85.95 *Shadow of the Past*. Oct. 16, 1962. GS: Jacqueline Scott, Jim Davis, Hugh Sanders, Ron Hayes, L.Q. Jones, Andy Romano, Olan Soule, John Qualen, Hal K. Dawson, Norman Leavitt. Jess has believed that his sister was dead for the past four years, but now she turns up in Laramie to bury her husband, a notorious gunfighter.

85.96 *The Long Road Back*. Oct. 23, 1962. GS: Yvonne Craig, Edgar Buchanan, James McMullen, Gregg Palmer, Sol Gorss, Robert Adler. Slim, acting as deputy, is escorting bank robber Virgil Walker back to Laramie. But, with the help of a girl named Ginny, he is overpowered by the outlaw on the trail and left tied up in a cave.

85.97 *Lost Allegiance*. Oct. 30, 1962. GS: Rod Cameron, Myrna Fahey, Walter Sande, Lee Farr, Harry Carey, Jr., Tru Garrett, Don Harvey. While tracking rustlers Jess is injured and finds himself face to face with one of the outlaws, and the face is a familiar one.

85.98 *The Sunday Shoot*. Nov. 13, 1962. GS: Burt Brinckerhoff, Jena Engstrom, Gregory Walcott, Dan White, Chris Alcaide, William Fawcett, Charles Seel, Barry Brooks. Hobey Carson comes down from the hills to enter a marksmanship contest in Laramie. Hobey is confident of winning, but his first target is cash for the entry fee, and he persuades Slim to lend it to him.

85.99 *Double Eagles*. Nov. 20, 1962. GS: Russell Johnson, Dick Foran, Charles Robinson, Emile Genest, Danielle Aubry, George D. Wallace, James Beck, James Griffith, Stacy Harris, Pamela Curran, Valera Noland, William Bryant, Norman Leavitt. Outlaws, who murdered their latest victim in the process of stealing a bank draft, have changed the loot into gold coins. When Jess learns of the crime he organizes a posse, hoping to catch up with the heavily laden bandits.

85.100 *Beyond Justice*. Nov. 27, 1962. GS: Lyle Bettger, David McLean, Fred Coby, Kathie Browne, Myron Healey, Margaret Hamilton, Brian Hutton, James McMullen. Slim has been deputized to protect Steven Collier, who is being held for trial on a charge of murder. Someone wants to kill Collier before he can testify and, to make matters, worse, Collier's lawyer seems reluctant for the case to come to trial.

85.101 *Bad Blood*. Dec. 4, 1962. GS: Jean Byron, John Anderson, Stephen Barringer, Barry Cahill, Joe Haworth, Lew Brown, Jan Sheppard, Leonard P. Geer, Brad Weston. Gunman Leo McCall has deserted his wife and son, Skip, but the boy still believes that there is some good in his father. There is no other way to settle matters, so his mother asks Jess to locate Skip's disreputable dad.

85.102 *Time of the Traitor*. Dec. 11, 1962. GS: Lew Ayres, R.G. Armstrong, Paul Carr, Harry Carey, Jr., Anne Whitfield, Lane Bradford, Don Harvey, William Fawcett. Young Steve Prescott is in serious need of medical treatment but the boy's father recognizes the physician as Samuel Mudd, who was imprisoned for treating John Wilkes Booth after Lincoln's assassination.

85.103 *Gun Duel*. Dec. 25, 1962. GS: DeForest Kelley, Ben Cooper, Richard Devon, Nick Nicholson, Gail Kobe, Jack Elam, Carole Wells, Dal McKennon, Olan Soule, Ed Prentiss. After a robbery in Casper, Del Shamley, Ray Vincent and Bart Collins agree to meet in Laramie to split the loot. But when Vincent doesn't show up, Ray and Bart are rather upset since he is the one carrying the cash.

85.104 *Naked Steel*. Jan. 1, 1963. GS: John Doucette, Charles Maxwell, Robert Cornthwaite, Joan Swift, Gage Clark, James Beck, Harlan Warde, Gloria Talbott, Gene Roth, James Flavin. Sheriff Tate guns down one bank robber, and the other one drops the loot in escaping. All of that available cash begins to give the lawman ideas. It reminds him of a certain pretty dance-hall girl with expensive tastes.

85.105 *Vengeance*. Jan. 8, 1963. GS: Fay Spain, Denver Pyle, John Milford, Lee Van Cleef, Kelly Thordsen, James Anderson, Norman Leavitt, Raymond Guth. Jess confronts a robbery suspect and accuses him of having the money on his person. A fight ensues and Jess is forced to shoot the man in self-defense, but the victim claims that he was shot in the back.

85.106 *Protective Custody*. Jan. 15, 1963. GS: David Brian, Gregory Walcott, Ron Hayes, Anne Helm, Jason Johnson, Martin Eric. When Walt Douglas, one of the managers of a stagecoach line, fires a young man named Willard he lets himself in for a lot of trouble. Willard and his pal Cass decide to steal a large shipment of gold.

85.107 *The Betrayers*. Jan. 22, 1963. GS: Adam West, Kathie Browne, Dennis Patrick, Don Kennedy, Fred Coby, George Orrison, George Selk, Harry Dean Stanton, Frank Jenks. Jess warns Sheriff Douglas that Kett Darby plans to hold up a train. So the sheriff rides off to stop him, and Darby and his gang rob the local bank without any interference.

85.108 *The Wedding Party*. Jan. 29, 1963. Barton MacLane, Jacqueline Scott, Ed Nelson, Ronald Foster, Russ Bender, Barbara Parkins, William Boyett, Chuck Courtney, Leonard P. Geer, Bill Catching. Gil Harrison doesn't want his former wife Stacey to marry Lee Taylor. So Gil has his old pal Slim brought to him, forcibly, and orders him to warn Stacey not to hold the wedding.

85.109 *No Place to Run*. Feb. 5, 1963. GS: Tom Skerritt, Ellen McRae/Burstyn, Richard Coogan, John Lodge, Frank Gerstle, Don Kennedy, Robert Hoy. Jess rescues reformed safecracker Gandy Ross from Indians, but Gandy has another problem. An outlaw named Wellman is trying to get him to resume his former profession.

85.110 *The Fugitives*. Feb. 12, 1963. GS: Phyllis Avery, Jan Merlin, Hal Baylor, Mark Dana, Bartlett Robinson, Ford Rainey, Charles Fredericks. Outlaw Joel Greevy bushwacks Slim and leave him dying on an isolated mountain ledge. Jess catches up with Greevy, and the gunslinger refuses to reveal Slim's whereabouts until he is freed.

85.111 *The Dispossessed*. Feb. 19, 1963. GS: Arthur Hunnicut, Carl Reindel, Robert Bray, Richard Shannon, Bennye Gatteys, Gail Kobe, Michael Forest, Jim Davis, Katherine Warren. On their way to horse-trade with the Beldens, Slim and Jess meet two pretty girls traveling with some very seedy gentlemen. Later, the Beldens suggest that maybe the girls are actually captives of the Comancheros.

85.112 *The Renegade Brand*. Feb. 26, 1963. GS: Lori Patrick, Jeanette Nolan, Ken Lynch. Slim tracks down gunman Hank McGovern, who wounded Jess in a robbery. He is forced to kill him in self-defense, a story which a local posse won't believe.

85.113 *The Violent Ones*. March 5, 1963. GS: John

Anderson, Dawn Wells, Paul Carr, Jack Blayne, Jack Chaplain, James Anderson. After gunning down a rival, Bill Blayne continues his amorous advances toward a saloon hostess, but she is not interested. When Jess steps in, Bill is ready to slap leather again.

85.114 *The Unvanquished.* March 12, 1963. GS: Frank De Kova, Jock Gaynor. When one of Slim's ranch hands is killed, the local citizens are quick to blame an Indian named Tah-sa, but Slim thinks there is more to the case than meets the eye.

85.115 *The Sometime Gambler.* March 19, 1963. GS: James Gregory, Jacqueline Scott, Michael Forest, Bing Russell. Honesty may not be the best policy for a reformed outlaw named Richards, who refused to join his former cronies in a bank robbery. The gang finds the vault empty and, thinking that Richards beat them to it, decides to shoot him.

85.116 *Edge of Evil.* April 2, 1963. GS: Ron Harper, Suzanne Lloyd, Alan Hale, Jr., Harry Lauter, Quinn Redeker. Farmer Stede Rhodes has found a cache of freshly mined gold, and he doesn't plan to give it up. When Jess tells him to find the rightful owner, Stede abandons him in the desert without water or weapons.

85.117 *Broken Honor.* April 9, 1963. GS: Rod Cameron, Donald "Red" Barry, Peggy McCay, Vinton Hayworth, Richard Bakalyan. Outlaw Dave Byrnie offers to pay Jess to keep him from riding shotgun on a stage line's payroll shipment, and Jess turns him in. But the line agent doesn't back Jess up, in fact, he fires him.

85.118 *The Last Battleground.* April 16, 1963. GS: John Hoyt, Frank Overton, Brett King, Robert Knapp, Dee Pollack. In self-defense, Jess kills a man who claims to be searching for a hidden cache of gold, then Slim reveals that the cache is real, and his father was branded a traitor because of it.

85.119 *The Stranger.* April 23, 1963. GS: Geraldine Brooks, Dewey Martin, Karl Swenson, Lee Van Cleef, L.Q. Jones, Ed Prentiss. Someone has been stealing food from the Sherman ranch and leaving money behind for it, and then a posse shows up, claiming to have tracked escaped killer Emil Viktor to the area.

85.120 *The Marshals.* April 30, 1963. GS: Reginald Gardiner, David McLean, William Bryant, Robert J. Wilke, Dennis Patrick. Jess is seriously wounded while warning Marshal Branch McGary on an ambush set up by Clint Buckner and his gang. Clint wants the lawman's prisoner, and McGary is forced to play into his hands. To save Jess' life, he must take him to a doctor in a town controlled by Buckner.

85.121 *Badge of Glory.* May 7, 1963. GS: Lin McCarthy, Jo Morrow, Gregg Palmer, Tru Garrett, Sheldon Allman. Fatally wounded by Jess in a robbery attempt, Sam Logan makes a final gesture by persuading a needy preacher named John Holby to collect a bounty on him. But Logan's brother believes that Holby killed Sam, and vows revenge.

85.122 *Trapped.* May 14, 1963. GS: Tommy Sands, Barton MacLane, Jim Davis, Claude Akins, Joan Freeman, Paul Lukather, James Kline. Slim is trapped and taken prisoner by wealthy rancher Owen Richards, who thinks he is one of the men who kidnaped his daughter.

85.123 *The Road to Helena.* May 21, 1963. GS: Henry Hull, Maggie Pierce, Robert Colbert, John Pickard, Don Krohn. Wounded David Franklin and his daughter Ruth are on the road to Helena, where Franklin plans to pay back the money he stole from the bank. But they are followed by a lawman named Ross, who wants the money for himself.

86. *Laredo*

NBC. 60 min. Broadcast history: Thursday, 8:30–9:30, Sept. 1965–Sept. 1966; Friday, 10:00–11:00, Sept. 1966–Sept. 1967.

Regular Cast: Neville Brand (Ranger Reese Bennett), Peter Brown (Ranger Chad Cooper), William Smith (Ranger Joe Riley), Philip Carey (Captain Edward Parmalee).

Premise: This western series depicted the adventures of three rowdy Texas Rangers stationed in Laredo, Texas, in the post–Civil War era.

The Episodes

86.1 *We've Lost a Train.* April 21, 1965. (This pilot to *Laredo* aired as an episode of *The Virginian*). GS: Doug McClure, Ida Lupino, Fernando Lamas, Rhonda Fleming, L.Q. Jones, Carol Bryon, Ross Elliott, Hal Baylor, George Sawaya, Alberto Morin. Trampas is sent to Mexico on an errand and, in the border town of Laredo, he gets into brawls with three Texas Rangers. *Note*: This episode was later released as the feature film *Backtrack*.

Season One

86.2 *Lazyfoot, Where Are You?* Sept. 16, 1965. GS: Burgess Meredith, Beverly Garland, Mario Alcaide, Harry Hickox, Leo Gordon, Bern Hoffman, Dorothy Dells, Henry Wills, Ron Burke. To keep tabs on the elusive Indian raider Lazyfoot, Ranger Captain Parmalee sends out Reese, Chad and Joe disguised as prospectors.

86.3 *I See By Your Outfit.* Sept. 23, 1965. GS: James Farentino, Vito Scotti, John Marley, James Doohan, Carlos Romero, Roberto Contreras, Ric Roman, Maurice McEndree, Seymour Cassel. The rangers are sent to the border town of Profirio to check on reported Mexican raiders, who welcome them by sacking the town and kidnaping Reese.

86.4 *Yahoo.* Sept. 30, 1965. GS: Martin Milner, Cliff Osmond, Dub Taylor, Shelly Morrison, Bill Walker, Marianne Gordon, Sam Edwards, Jon Cliff, X Brands, John Mitchum, William Vaughn. Clendon MacMillan joins the Rangers to give them the benefit of his nine years as deputy constable in New Hampshire, and just in time to show Reese, Chad and Joe how to hunt down the Indian raider Running Antelope.

86.5 *Rendezvous at Arillo.* Oct. 7, 1965. GS: Julie Harris, Donnelly Rhodes, Bruce Dern, Woodrow Parfrey, Don Stewart, Kim Kristofer Hector, Cindy Eilbacher. Under the pretext of investigating a widow's disputed land claim, the Rangers head for the outlaw town of Arillo to find a gang of silver thieves.

86.6 *Three's Company.* Oct. 14, 1965. GS: David Brian, Myrna Fahey, Estelita, Richard Reeves, James Seay. Chad's former sweetheart shows up in Laredo with her father, a railroad baron who has a tempting job offer for Chad.

86.7 *Anybody Here Seen Billy?* Oct. 21, 1965. GS: Joan Staley, Mickey Finn, Robert Hoy, John McCann. Chad sneaks into the Rangers barracks late at night, battered and bruised, all the work of Laurie Martin, girl friend of the prisoner he was taking to El Paso.

86.8 *A Question of Discipline.* Oct. 28, 1965. GS: Barbara Nichols, Marlyn Mason, Barbara Werle, Douglas V. Fowley, Vincent Van Lynn, Clinton Sundberg, George Keymas, Norman Leavitt. As punishment for brawling, Reese, Chad and Joe are ordered to escort a wagon load of foul-smelling buffalo hides, which conceal additional cargo that no one had counted on.

86.9 *The Golden Trail.* Nov. 4, 1965. GS: Jeanette Nolan, Jim Davis, Arthur Hunnicutt, Tom Reese, Gregg Palmer, Roy Barcroft, Adair Jameson, Troy Melton, Paul Baxley. Reese is sent to Red River to receive an important shipment — which rumors indicate is $100,000 in gold.

86.10 *A Matter of Policy.* Nov. 11, 1965. GS: Robert F. Simon, Charles Gray, Mickey Finn, Jon Locke, Mike Ragan, I. Stanford Jolley, Gil Perkins. Captain Parmalee, anxious to make a good impression on state senator Sparks, gets off to a bad start. After walking all the way to Laredo when their stage is robbed, they find Reese, Chad and Joe engaged in a street brawl.

86.11 *Which Way Did They Go?* Nov. 18, 1965. GS: Eve Arden, Myron Healey, Rex Holman, Lyle Talbot, Grandon Rhodes, Doodles Weaver. Librarian Emma Bristow is financing her trip to California with cultural lectures for the frontier folk, who are uniformly unappreciative, with the exception of Reese.

86.12 *Jinx.* Dec. 2, 1965. GS: Albert Salmi, Shelley Morrison, Richard Devon, John Abbott, Ralph Manza, Richard Collier, Roy Barcroft. Reese persuades his friend Cletus Grogan to ride with the Rangers against their old nemesis Linda Little Trees, despite the fact that Grogan has a way of attracting disaster.

86.13 *The Land Grabbers.* Dec. 9, 1965. GS: Fred Clark, Audrey Dalton, Alan Napier, Bart Burns, Keith Jones. With new territory being opened up, the Rangers are assigned to police a homesteaders land run. They come to grips with a bureaucratic commissioner, a retired Bengal Lancer, and the Sparr gang, who plan to beat the homesteaders out of the valuable river properties.

86.14 *Pride of the Rangers.* Dec. 16, 1965. GS: George Kennedy, Mickey Shaughnessy, Henry Gibson, Robert Cornthwaite, Mike Mazurki, K.L. Smith. The Rangers are certain, to the extent of a month's pay, that they have someone who can outbox the Cavalry champ, and now all they need is a contender to protect their bet.

86.15 *The Heroes of San Gill.* Dec. 23, 1965. GS: Lonny Chapman, Rodolfo Hoyos, Theo Marcuse, William Phipps, Doodles Weaver, Jo Marie Ward, Francine Pyne. Chad and Joe alter a telegram to Parmalee, making it appear that a wanted outlaw is heading for the same town as the Rangers' female acquaintances.

86.16 *A Medal for Reese.* Dec. 30, 1965. GS: Stacy Harris, Emile Genest, Robert Phillips, Pete Dunn, Robert Boon. The Rangers match tactics with an unusual gang of payroll hijackers. Dressed in French army uniforms, the thieves conduct their heists like a military operation.

86.17 *The Callico Kid.* Jan. 6, 1966. GS: George Chandler, Mimsy Farmer, Wesley Lau, Harry Hickox, Lalo Rios, Charles Horvath. After Chad and Joe wipe out a gang of outlaws, the citizens of Guarded Wells can't do enough to show their appreciation, so the high-living Rangers scheme to delay their return to dreary Laredo.

86.18 *Above the Law.* Jan. 13, 1966. GS: Jack Lord, Lola Albright, John Kellogg, Myron Healey, Laraine Stephens, Hal Baylor, Jonathan Hole. Ruth Phelps, convinced that her condemned husband is not a killer, hires Jab Heller to clear his name before the hanging. To find the real killer, Heller engineers the escape of murderer Brad Scanlon.

86.19 *That's Noway, Thataway.* Jan. 20, 1966. GS: Peter Graves, Marlyn Mason, Chad Stuart, Jeremy Clyde, Arch Johnson, Jack Bighead. Rescued from their creditors by Chad and Joe, penniless English actors Newton Weekes and Dudley Leicester plan to raise cash by bringing religion to Whiskey Flats.

86.20 *Limit of the Law Larkin.* Jan. 27, 1966. GS: Claude Akins, John Hoyt, Jacques Aubuchon, Joan Marshall, Whit Bissell, Bea Bradley, Tom Fadden, Dub Taylor. Ranger Cotton Buckmeister seems strangely reluctant to carry a box of court records back to the town of Uvalde, where they were salvaged from a fire started by citizens enraged at a corrupt judge.

86.21 *Meanwhile, Back at the Reservation.* Feb. 10, 1966. GS: Kurt Russell, Robert Yuro, J. Pat O'Malley, K.L. Smith, Rayford Barnes, John Harmon, Ray Kellogg, Jon Lormer. The Rangers plan to release Grey Smoke, a teenage Indian who rode with outlaws, but he is in no hurry to return to the reservation.

86.22 *The Treasure of San Diablo.* Feb. 17, 1966. GS: Claude Akins, Jan Arvan, Pedro Gonzalez Gonzalez, George Lewis, Ray Ballard, Carmen Phillips, Lane Bradford, Princess Livingston. After Reese and Buckmeister subdue two terrorists in a Mexican town, Reese agrees to stay and teach the farmers to defend themselves.

86.23 *No Bugles, On Drum.* Feb. 24, 1966. GS: Shelley Morrison, Richard Devon, Michael Conrad, Ralph Manza, Mike Ragan, Russ McCubbin. Outlaw Linda Littletrees has a crush on Joe, so Reese suggests using Joe to trap the licorice-chewing squaw.

86.24 *Miracle at Massacre Mission.* March 3, 1966. GS: Barbara Rush, Tina Holland, Eddie Little Sky, Henry Brandon, Christopher Dark, Ken Mayer, Robert S. Carson. Reese escorts two nuns who are heaven-bent on reopening an old Indian mission where two priests have already been massacred.

86.25 *It's the End of the Road, Stanley.* March 10, 1966. GS: Fernando Lamas, Jeanette Nolan, Jack Weston, Sheilah Wells, Marian Moses, Warren Kemmerling. Life gets hectic at Martha's dusty stage stop when three outlaws capture Reese and take over the place.

86.26 *A Very Small Assignment.* March 17, 1966. GS: Richard Haydn, Ken Lynch, Paul Mantee, Stuart Nisbet, Len Lesser, Hank Patterson, Claudia Bryar, June C. Ellis. Reese, who is too embarrassed to admit his job is to locate a mere schoolmaster, boasts about the importance of his mission. Unfortunately, he is overheard by outlaws, who become convinced that the teacher is a VIP and well worth kidnaping.

86.27 *Quarter Past Eleven.* March 24, 1966. GS: Lee Van Cleef, Stanley Adams, Roy Roberts. Reese wants to throw a party for Captain Parmalee, but his plans are upset by the lack of a cake and sundry outlaws who have gone on the rampage.

86.28 *The Deadliest Kid in the West.* March 31, 1966. GS: Jack Kelly, Gina Gillespie, David Perna. The Rangers trail train robber Lancy Mabray to his ranch, where he is met by his daughter Kim, a runaway from finishing school who knows nothing of her father's outlaw career.

86.29 *Sound of Terror.* April 7, 1966. GS: John Carradine, DeForest Kelley, Tom Simcox, Virginia Christine, Larraine Stephens, Kay E. Kuter, Tiger Joe Marsh. A strangler is loose in Laredo, and Parmalee's list of suspects is embarrassingly long, especially since it includes one of his Rangers.

86.30 *The Would-Be Gentleman of Laredo.* April 14, 1966. GS: Donnelly Rhodes, Madlyn Rhue, Barry Kelley, Joe De Santis, John Lawrence. A group of well-bred Spanish con artists select Reese as their dupe in a plan to claim ownership of Laredo and the surrounding county.

86.31 *A Taste of Money.* April 28, 1966. GS: Charles Ruggles, Noah Beery, Jr., Robert Yuro, Robert Cornthwaite, Jim Goodwin, Byron Foulger, Richard Reeves. At the Rangers' request, Major John Cane opens a jammed bank vault with ease, showing a mechanical ingenuity that isn't lost on bank robber Ezekial Fry.

Season Two

86.32 *The Legend of Midas Mantee.* Sept. 16, 1966. GS: Rex Holman, Cliff Osmond, Maura McGiveney, Howard Wendel, K.L. Smith, John Truax. Reese complicates matters for rookie Ranger Erik Hunter, who is posing as an outlaw to infiltrate the gang of the infamous gold thief Midas Mantee.

86.33 *The Dance of the Laughing Death.* Sept. 23, 1966. GS: Abraham Sofaer, Myron Healey, Diane Roter, Julie Edwards, Peter Dawson. A power-hungry Indian chief has trained his braves to fight like soldiers, and is attacking military outposts to obtain modern weapons.

86.34 *A Double Shot of Nepenthe.* Sept. 30, 1966. GS: Will Kuluva, Warren Kemmerling, Robert B. Williams, Leonard P. Geer, Shug Fisher, Bern Hoffman. Two men who would assassinate Captain Parmalee slip Reese a drug that renders the roustabout gentle and open to any suggestion, including murder.

86.35 *Coup de Grace.* Oct. 7, 1966. GS: Barbara Luna, Arnold Moss, John Hoyt, Fabian Dean, Louise Lawson. The Rangers have allowed Mexican rebel leader Juan Morales, who was given asylum in the United States, to be kidnaped and returned to Mexico, and they have only a short time to rectify their politically embarrassing mistake.

86.36 *The Land Slickers.* Oct. 14, 1966. GS: Gene Raymond, Anna Capri, Leo Gordon, Alan de Witt, Ron Russell, Byron Foulger. Reese's plan to give up rangering for ranching hits a slight snag. The land that he bought is at the bottom of a lake.

86.37 *Finnegan.* Oct. 21, 1966. GS: Malachi Throne, Ken Lynch, John Harmon, Stuart Anderson, K.L. Smith, Roy Roberts. The Rangers run up against a new breed of criminal in Sean Finnegan, who is recruiting outlaws for his college of crime.

86.38 *Any Way the Wind Blows.* Oct. 28, 1966. GS: Melodie Johnson, Michael Evans, Tiger Joe Marsh, Jay Della, Mike Wagner, Bill Quinn, Harry Harvey, Sr., Melville Ruick. Erik hires on as magician with a traveling circus that always seems to be in town when the bank is burglarized.

86.39 *The Sweet Gang.* Nov. 4, 1966. GS: Ellen Corby, Kathie Browne, Robert Beecher, Lennie Weinrib, Michael Masters. It looks like a routine assignment when the Rangers set out to deliver a mine payroll, until Ma Sweet and her outlaw brook block the only trail to the mine.

86.40 *One Too Many Voices.* Nov. 18, 1966. GS: Whitney Blake, Jim Goodwin. The Rangers set a trap for a gang of kidnapers, and they bait it with Reese, disguised as a gravel-voiced millionaire.

86.41 *Road to San Remo.* Nov. 25, 1966. GS: Claire Wilcox, Dabbs Greer, Val Avery. The Rangers try to solve two mysteries. Why is an Indian trying to kill the orphan girl they are escorting to San Remo, and why does the little girl's arrival upset the few residents of the nearly deserted town?

86.42 *The Last of the Caesars—Absolutely.* Dec. 2, 1966. GS: Jack Weston, E.J. Andre, Sid Haig, Joan Huntington. The Rangers go after Hannibal Rex, a modern-day Caesar who is enslaving and murdering settlers in an effort to carve a Roman-type empire out of the Texas wilderness.

86.43 *A Prince of a Ranger.* Dec. 9, 1966. GS: Peter Brown, Mimsy Farmer, Lisabeth Hush, Ivor Barry, John S. Ragin. Ranger Chad meets his identical twin, a visiting Balkan prince who is being pursued by assassins.

86.44 *Oh Careless Love.* Dec. 23, 1966. GS: Thomas Gomez, Ken Scott, Larry Chance, Peggy Mando. Chief Kicking Bear holds Reese and Joe hostage. The chief is threatening to go on the warpath unless Reese marries his plump daughter Lost Bird.

86.45 *Leave It to Dixie.* Dec. 30, 1966. GS: Donald "Red" Barry, Peter Dunhill, Clint Howard, Barbara Werle, George Keymas. Rangers Reese and Erik will need all their wits to outmaneuver a formidable group of opponents—four little orphaned boys who are dead set on joining a notorious bank robber.

86.46 *The Seventh Day.* Jan. 6, 1967. GS: Alfred Ryder, Wesley Lau, William Bramley, Michael Vandever, Michael Fox, Bunny Summers. Rangers Chad and Erik, posing as evangelists, join Joe to free a border town controlled by smuggler Clay Morgan. Clay, who has already driven out one minister, is dead set on keeping the new arrivals from bringing religion, law and order to the corrupt town.

86.47 *Scourge of San Rosa.* Jan. 20, 1967. GS: Robert Yuro, Kathleen Freeman, Rodolfo Acosta, Pedro Gonzalez Gonzalez, Robert Hoy, Fred Krone. In Mexico, Ranger Reese unwittingly sets a trap for a notorious killer. The lawman, suffering from amnesia, has been mistaken for outlaw Johnny Rhodes, who is due in town to help hijack a gold shipment.

86.48 *The Short, Happy Fatherhood of Reese Bennett.* Jan. 27, 1967. GS: Rick Natoli, Michael Greene. Hard-boiled Ranger Reese starts looking after an orphaned Indian lad. Two problems complicate Reese's foster parent hood. He is AWOL, and the boy is determined to find his father's killer.

86.49 *The Bitter Yen of General Ti.* Feb. 3, 1967. GS: Henry Silva, Philip Ahn, Lawrence Montaigne, Irene Tsu. The Rangers tangle with old Chinese customs when Joe rescues the unwilling fiancee of an exiled opium lord.

86.50 *The Other Cheek.* Feb. 10, 1967. GS: Barbara Anderson, Malcolm Atterbury, Edward Faulkner, Robert F. Simon, Ric Roman, Clay Tanner. The usually rowdy Reese is trying friendly persuasion to keep a cattleman's hired guns from terrorizing a family of sheepherders.

86.51 *Enemies and Brothers.* Feb. 17, 1967. GS: Jack Kelly, Mary Murphy, Barbara Werle. The capture of killer Bart Cutler forces the Rangers to hoodwink Captain Parmalee. The captain must never know that the outlaw is his brother Frank, who supposedly died a hero's death in the Civil War.

86.52 *Hey Diddle Diddle.* Feb. 24, 1967. GS: Claude Akins, Marilyn Erskine, Jacques Aubuchon, Carl Ballantine, Michael Forest, Michael Keep. A dying printer draws Ranger Cotton Buckmeister into a mystery. The mortally wounded man begs Buckmeister to deliver a satchel full of money and recite a nursery rhyme to his niece.

86.53 *The Small Chance Ghost.* March 3, 1967. GS: Jeanne Cooper, Edward Binns, Ted Cassidy, Shug Fisher. It is too bad that Reese doesn't scare easily, otherwise he would get out of Small Chance. A saloon owner and her boy friend have kept their gold strike a secret by frightening everyone out of town with a phony ghost, and murdering those too dumb to go.

86.54 *A Question of Guilt.* March 10, 1967. GS: Claude Akins, Walter Burke, Vaughn Taylor, Lisa James, Ed Peck, Claude Woolman. The Rangers battle frontier prejudice to guarantee a fair trail for an Indian accused of knifing a white woman.

86.55 *Like One of the Family.* March 24, 1967. GS: Jeanette Nolan, Parley Baer, Don Beddoe. Southern hospitality frustrates the Rangers' efforts to evict a charming but stubborn family from railroad land before the railroad men resort to violence.

86.56 *Walk Softly.* March 31, 1967. GS: Joe Flynn, Claude Akins, George Furth.

86.57 *Split the Difference.* April 7, 1967. GS: Shelley Morrison, Monica Lewis, Gerald Mohr, Myron Healey, Ralph Manza. A killer named Ringo leaves his estate to Captain Parmalee and a group of cutthroats. To collect their shares, the heirs must spend one night under the same roof, where each stands to profit from the others' deaths.

87. *Lash of the West*

Syndicated/ABC. 15 min. Broadcast history: Various, 1951–1952; Sunday, 6:30–6:45, Jan. 1953–April 1953.

Regular Cast: Lash LaRue (Marshal Lash LaRue).

Premise: This series depicted modern-day U.S. Marshal Lash LaRue as he told tales about his ancestor in the old west illustrated by clips from Lash's films made in the 1940s.

88. *Law of the Plainsman*

NBC. 30 min. Broadcast history: Thursday, 7:30–8:00, Oct. 1959–Sept. 1960.

Regular Cast: Michael Ansara (Sam Buckhart), Robert Harland (Deputy Billy Lordan), Dayton Lummis (Marshal Andrew Morrison), Gina Gillespie (Tess Logan), Nora Marlowe (Martha Cominter).

Premise: The Western was set in New Mexico territory during the 1880s and related the exploits of Sam Buckhart, an Indian U.S. Marshal.

The Episodes

88.1 *Prairie Incident.* Oct. 1, 1959. GS: Richard Devon, J. Pat O'Malley, William D. Gordon, Harry Swoger, Nora Marshall. Patrolling the plains, Marshal Sam Buckhart discovers a wagon containing a murdered man and his eight-year-old daughter. The girl is able to give Buckhart a description of the killer.

88.2 *Full Circle.* Oct. 8, 1959. GS: Lyle Bettger, Gail Kobe, Wayne Rogers. For years Sam Buckhart has been looking for a bank robber. He is stunned to discover that the thief is Sheriff Max Chafee, who Sam believed to be honest and straightforward.

88.3 *A Matter of Life or Death.* Oct. 15, 1959. GS: Gustavo Rojo, Jean Allison. Marshal Sam Buckhart, who has been searching for outlaw Charlie Slade for many years, finally locates his hideout. Before Buckhart can take the outlaw prisoner, Slade's henchmen overpower him.

88.4 *The Hostiles.* Oct. 22, 1959. GS: Ann Benton, Peter Whitney, Suzanne Lloyd, Dabbs Greer, Dorothy Adams. A man who lives in the mountains kills a young girl. Sam Buckhart is assigned to find the murderer.

88.5 *Passenger to Mescalero.* Oct. 29, 1959. GS: Brian G. Hutton, Richard Gaines, Hope Summers, Eddie Quillan, Rayford Barnes, Bud Osborne, John Pickard, Alice Backes. Deputy Marshal Sam Buckhart is assigned to bring a dangerous outlaw to the prison at Mescalero. During the journey a band of outlaws ambush the stagecoach.

88.6 *Blood Trails.* Nov. 5, 1959. GS: Chris Alcaide, Michael Hinn, Fiona Hale, Mike Vandever. Deputy Marshal Sam Buckhart receives a difficult assignment. He is to go into Apache territory and bring back a member of his own tribe.

88.7 *Desperate Decision.* Nov. 12, 1959. GS: Robert J. Wilke, Donald Buka, John Marley, Bill Catching, Tom McDonough, Manuel Lopez. Sam Buckhart tracks down a fugitive and starts to return home with him. The marshal and his prisoner run into Mexican bandits.

88.8 *Appointment in Santa Fe.* Nov. 19, 1959. GS: John Anderson, Michael Raffetto, Joseph Ruskin. Deputy Warden Clyde Santee demands custody of a prisoner held by Marshal Morrison. Remembering Santee's wartime record of brutality, Morrison refuses to hand over his prisoner.

88.9 *The Gibbet.* Nov. 26, 1959. GS: Robert F. Simon, Mort Mills, Patrick Riley, Walter Burke, William Erwin, Dee Pollack, George Mitchell. An outlaw gang rides into a small Western town, planning to take it over. The townspeople form a vigilante group to oppose the gang, and Marshal Sam Buckhart is sent to prevent open warfare.

88.10 *The Dude.* Dec. 3, 1959. GS: Robert Vaughn, Peter Whitney, Clegg Hoyt, Earle Hodgins, Ralph Moody, Barry Brooks, Wayne Tucker, Sam Reese. Young Teddy Roosevelt is determined to recover a ring that was taken from him by a gang of thugs. Deputy Marshal Sam Buckhart decides to ride with Roosevelt and protect the dude.

88.11 *The Innocents.* Dec. 10, 1959. GS: Robert Vaughn, Elena Verdugo, Clancy Cooper, Carter De Haven, Jr., Olive Carey, John Harrison, John Newton. Sam Buckhart's friend Ross Drake has been arrested for murder. To evade a lynch mob, Buckhart transfers him to another town for a fair trail.

88.12 *Clear Title.* Dec. 17, 1959. GS: John Dehner, Lee

Van Cleef, Jack Kruschen, Jean Allison, Garry Walberg, Steve Gravers, Brian Russell. Deputy Marshal Sam Buckhart is sent to Shannonville to investigate a shooting. The townspeople, afraid of town boss Walter Shannon, are unwilling to help Buckhart.

88.13 *Toll Road.* Dec. 24, 1959. GS: Bert Freed, Maggie Pierce, Phil Chambers, Jeanne Wood, Richard Rust, Robert Morris, Paul Fix. For years Dan Dawson and his wife have worked to build a toll road. Just as the road is completed, a pair of outlaws brutally murder the Dawsons.

88.14 *Calculated Risk.* Dec. 31, 1959. GS: Don Grady, Chris Alcaide, Lane Bradford, Wayne Rogers. Deputy Marshal Sam Buckhart shoots a bank robber in the presence of the outlaw's son. Buckhart tries to explain the incident to the boy, but is spurned by the bitter youth.

88.15 *Fear.* Jan. 7, 1960. GS: Stephen Talbot, John Larch, Peggy Webber. While on a camping trip with Sam Buckhart, a young girl falls into an abandoned well. Unable to get her out by himself, Buckhart goes to a nearby farmhouse for help but is mistaken for a renegade Indian and shot.

88.16 *Endurance.* Jan. 14, 1960. GS: John Anderson, Robert Osterloh, J. Pat O'Malley. Young Tess sees two outlaws murder a priest and then escape. Deputy Marshal Sam Buckhart goes after the killers.

88.17 *The Comet.* Jan. 21, 1960. GS: Jacques Aubuchon, Ned Glass, Wayne Tucker, Charity Grace, Enid Janes, Dan Sheridan, George Revink. A man claiming to be a minister tells the residents of a small town that the world is coming to an end. Another man appears at the same time, selling pills which he says will ward off the disaster

88.18 *The Rawhiders.* Jan. 28, 1960. GS: John Milford, Joe De Santis, Peter Whitney, Alex Gerry. Lije Wesley, one of a group of Western Gypsies hated by local landowners, is accused of murdering a rancher. Deputy Marshal Sam Buckhart's investigation turns up evidence indicating that Wesley is innocent.

88.19 *The Imposter.* Feb. 4, 1960. GS: Harry Landers, Lawrence Dobkin, John Hoyt, Francis J. McDonald, Mickey Finn, Tyler McVey, Lane Bradford, Ted Lehman. Sam Buckhart has taken the notorious Kid Remick into custody in Santa Fe to await the arrival of a Colorado marshal. When the lawman rides into town, an old-timer points out that his horse doesn't appear to have traveled very far.

88.20 *Common Ground.* Feb. 11, 1960. GS: Michael Pate, Richard Harland, Jess Kirkpatrick. Wounded during a holdup attempt, killer Frank Deegan hides out in Martha's rooming house. When Sam Buckhart stops by the house, Martha and Tess, terrorized by Deegan, try to get rid of him.

88.21 *The Matriarch.* Feb. 18, 1960. GS: Lynn Bari, Denver Pyle, Alan Reed, Michael Hinn, Patrick Troughton. Constance Valeri claims that she shot a ranch hand, but Sam Buckhart is suspicious of her confession.

88.22 *A Question of Courage.* Feb. 25, 1960. GS: Claude Akins, Patricia Donahue, Ken Mayer, Ken Drake. Sam Buckhart is stunned when a sheriff allows two outlaws to beat him. Buckhart finds that the new lawman is in the badmen's power.

88.23 *Dangerous Barriers.* March 10, 1960. GS: Arch Johnson, Steve Marlo, Frank Puglia, John Zaccaro, Ray Kellogg, Percy Helton, Wayne Rogers, Jovan Montell. Apache marshal Sam Buckhart offers to help a boy in his feud with a rancher who has killed his father and wants his land. The offer is rejected because the boy hates Apaches.

88.24 *The Show-Off.* March 17, 1960. GS: Scott Marlowe, Leo Gordon, Jess Kirkpatrick. Young Clancy Jones feels that he is a nobody, so he picks a Billy the Kid to imitate.

88.25 *Rabbit's Fang.* March 24, 1960. GS: Don Dubbins, Constance Ford, Christopher Dark, Peter Brocco. Slow-witted but fast on the draw, Mite Rankin worships Miss Jessie from afar. When Jessie's ex-husband shows up demanding quick cash, Mite decides to do something about it.

88.26 *Stella.* March 31, 1960. GS: Gloria Talbot, Richard Devon, Charlie Briggs, Wesley Lau, William Fawcett. Stella Meeker, one of a gang of bank robbers, makes friend with Sam Buckhart. She doesn't know he is a lawman.

88.27 *Amnesty.* April 7, 1960. GS: Chris Alcaide, Robert Warwick, Biff Elliott, Paul Sorensen, Natalie Norwick, Fred Graham. Amnesty is declared by the territorial governor, and a vicious killer escapes a murder rap Then Sam Buckhart hires him as a lawman.

88.28 *Jeb's Daughter.* April 14, 1960. GS: John Anderson, Suzanne Lloyd, Tom Reese, John Clarke. Jeb Wicken's daughter has been a burden to him long enough. So he decides to sell her into slavery. It is all legal, but legal or not, Buckhart won't uphold the sale.

88.29 *Cavern of the Wind.* April 21, 1960. GS: Paul Langton, Richard Anderson, Enid James, George Keymas, J. Pat O'Malley, Charles Stevens. A group of gold-hungry prospectors capture Sam Buckhart and force him to head their expedition. At the destination are Apaches waiting for the man who killed one of their braves.

88.30 *Trojan Horse.* May 5, 1960. GS: Gene Nelson, James Westerfield, Murvyn Vye, Joe Perry, Perry Cook, Diana Darrin. Sam Buckhart borrows a plan from the Greeks to penetrate the hideout of the notorious Seed gang. Having no wooden horse at hand, he rents a traveling show wagon.

89. *Lawman*

ABC. 30 min. Broadcast history: Sunday, 8:30-9:00, Oct. 1958–April 1962; Sunday, 10:30-11:00, April 1962–Oct. 1962.

Regular Cast: John Russell (Marshal Dan Troop), Peter Brown (Deputy Johnny McKay), Peggie Castle (Lilly Merrill) 59-62, Dan Sheridan (Jake, the Bartender), Bek Nelson (Dru Lemp) 58-59, Barbara Lang (Julie Tate) 1959.

Premise: Marshal Dan Troop and Deputy Johnny McKay seek to establish and maintain law and order in Laramie, Wyoming, during the 1870s.

The Episodes

89.1 *The Deputy.* Oct. 5, 1958. GS: Edward Byrnes, Jack Elam, Lee Van Cleef. Dan Troop is appointed marshal of Laramie and is warned that the last lawman was murdered. Troop sets out to find a deputy and then to solve the killing of his predecessor.

89.2 *The Prisoner.* Oct. 12, 1958. GS: John Doucette, William Henry, Henry Cheshire. A gunman provokes men to fight him and then kills them. Marshal Dan Troop realizes that the only way to deal with the gunslinger is to meet him on his own terms in a gunfight.

89.3 *The Joker.* Oct. 19, 1958. GS: Jeff York. Young

Johnny McKay becomes convinced that he is the son of a notorious outlaw. He decides to turn in his badge as deputy to Marshal Dan Troop.

89.4 *The Oath.* Oct. 26, 1958. GS: Barbara Stuart, Whit Bissell, Stephen Courtleigh, Don Kelly, Betty Lynn. Marshal Dan Troop and his deputy Johnny McKay are bringing in two prisoners. One is a man wanted for murder, the other a doctor who shot a man during an argument. When the two lawmen come upon a group of stagecoach passengers who are very ill and try to help them, the prisoners see their opportunity to escape.

89.5 *The Outcast.* Nov. 2, 1958. GS: Martin Landau. Bob Ford, the man who shot Jesse James, is marked for death by an old friend of Jesse's. Marshal Dan Troop is obliged to protect Ford to prevent a lynching.

89.6 *The Jury.* Nov. 9, 1958. GS: Jean Willes. A beautiful woman who leads a life of crime continually escapes justice when the all-male juries refuse to find her guilty. Marshal Troop decides to resort to an unusual scheme to make the woman pay for her crimes.

89.7 *Wanted.* Nov. 16, 1958. GS: Patrick McVey, Russell Thorson, Robert J. Wilke, Ralph Reed, Kelly Thordsen, I. Stanford Jolley. A vicious bounty hunter arrives in Laramie. He kills a fugitive from justice and then tries to take a prisoner away from Deputy Johnny McKay in order to collect the reward in a nearby town.

89.8 *The Badge.* Nov. 23, 1958. GS: Gary Vinson, Wesley Lau, Venetia Stevenson. Young Bill Andrews is accused of attempted murder and put in jail. Johnny McKay refuses to believe that Andrews is guilty of the crime, although the townspeople are sure that Andrews is a killer because his father and brother were criminals.

89.9 *Bloodline.* Nov. 30, 1958. GS: Will Wright, Paul Langton, Chuck Courtney. A young man who is a fast gun decides to kill his father to prove to his family that he is a faster draw. Marshal Dan Troop tries to stop the young man from carrying out his plan.

89.10 *The Intruders.* Dec. 7, 1958. GS: Frances Fong, Philip Ahn, John Hoyt. Marshal Dan Troop and Johnny McKay begin an investigation when a Chinese laborer is murdered. Eventually, the dead man's wife tells them that her husband was forced to pay half his salary to two men who killed him when he protested.

89.11 *Short Straw.* Dec. 14, 1958. GS: Jack Lambert, Ted de Corsia. Finding Marshal Troop's enforcement of the law too severe, a group of men hire a gunman to kill him. When the hired gun fails, the men draw straws to determine which one will try to kill Troop.

89.12 *Lady in Question.* Dec. 21, 1958. GS: Dorothy Provine, Michael Connors, Harry Cheshire. Deputy Johnny McKay's childhood girl friend Julie Preston comes to town. Julie's new boy friend draws a gun on Johnny, and Marshal Dan Troop finds himself arresting Johnny for a killing a man.

89.13 *The Master.* Dec. 28, 1958. GS: Wayne Morris. Marshal Dan Troop is surprised when Tod Horgan, the man he served under as a deputy, comes into town employed as a hired gunman by a cattle association. When Horgan kills a homesteader, Troop realizes he must bring the former lawman in.

89.14 *The Outsider.* Jan. 4, 1959. GS: Miranda Jones, Barry Kelley, Rosa Rey. The townspeople join rancher Josh Teller in discriminating against Rene Lebeau and her widowed Indian mother. Marshal Troop and Johnny McKay decide to help the two women who have recently been denied credit for supplies.

89.15 *The Captives.* Jan. 11, 1959. GS: Edgar Buchanan, James Bell, Michael Dante. Deputy Marshal Johnny McKay takes Doc Stewart out to treat Jess Miller. On their arrival at Miller's farmhouse, they are taken captive by a killer.

89.16 *The Encounter.* Jan. 18, 1959. GS: Louise Fletcher, Russell Johnson, Donald Buka. While trailing Ward Horgan and Cole Hawkins through the woods, Marshal Dan Troop is attacked and injured by a bear. Horgan's sister Betty finds Troop and brings him to her home to convalesce. When Betty learns who Troop is, and what his mission was, she must decide whether or not to kill him.

89.17 *The Brand Release.* Jan. 25, 1959. GS: R.G. Armstrong, Russell Thorson, Lee Farr, Stewart Bradley. A wounded man arrives in Laramie, followed shortly by a sheriff. The wounded man tells Marshal Dan Troop that the newly arrived sheriff sells cattle to newcomers and then accuses them of rustling.

89.18 *The Runaway.* Feb. 1, 1959. GS: Hugh Sanders, James Kirkwood, Jr., Joyce Taylor. Marshal Dan Troop sets out to find a young Army deserter who is hiding in Laramie with a dance-hall singer.

89.19 *Warpath.* Feb. 8, 1959. GS: Murvyn Vye, William Fawcett, Lew Gallo, Howard Caine. Marshal Dan Troop is about to apprehend a group of buffalo hunters who have killed an old man. But he is caught in the cross fire between the hunters and a tribe of Indians.

89.20 *The Gunmen.* Feb. 15, 1959. GS: Richard Arlen, Gordon Jones, Hal Baylor, Frank Scully, Dorothy Partington. Marshal Dan Troop tries to avert violence when Chalk Hennessey attempts to taunt a reformed gunslinger into a gun fight.

89.21 *The Big Hat.* Feb. 22, 1959. GS: Jon Lormer, Robert B. Williams. A peace-loving Laramie editor is shot while attending a wedding. The groom is Big Hat Anderson, and the victim was wearing a 10-gallon hat given to him by Anderson.

89.22 *The Chef.* March 1, 1959. GS Sig Ruman, Lee Patrick, John Doucette. Harry Dorn, proprietor of the Laramie Hotel and Restaurant, is overjoyed at the business brought in by his new chef, Hans Steinmayer, recently arrived from Germany. Complications arise when pompous Mrs. Young claims that she hired Hans during her trip to Europe and accuses Dorn of stealing the chef from her.

89.23 *The Posse.* March 8, 1959. GS: Michael Macready, Jean Allison, Tol Avery, Emerson Treacy, Pernell Roberts. Tracy Hunter is wanted by a lynch-minded posse for a crime he didn't commit. Marshal Dan Troop saves Hunter from the posse, but only temporarily.

89.24 *The Visitor.* March 15, 1959. GS: Charles Cooper, Roscoe Ates, Vivi Janiss, Stephen Talbot. Gunslinger Jack Rollins comes to Laramie to reclaim the son he deserted. Marshal Dan Troop tells Rollins to leave the boy where he is and get out of town.

89.25 *Battle Scar.* March 22, 1959. GS: Catherine McLeod, Walter Coy, R.G. Armstrong, Robert Conrad. Rancher Ben Rogers, former Army major, has violent spells of rage. His wife Cynthia, unable to cope with his outburst, turns to Marshal Dan Troop for help.

89.26 The Gang. March 29, 1959. GS: James Drury, Karl Davis, Roscoe Ates, Emory Parnell. A cowboy travels a great distance to tell Marshal Dan Troop that the Hayes gang, who were jailed by Marshal Troop, are headed for Laramie to exact revenge.

89.27 The Souvenir. April 5, 1959. GS: Don Kelly, Jan Harrison, Jeanette Nolan, Brett King. When a killer pistol whips Deputy Johnny McKay and escapes from jail, the citizens of Laramie demand that Marshal Dan Troop fire the deputy.

89.28 The Young Toughs. April 12, 1959. GS: Tom Gilson, Van Williams, Eric Morris. While Marshal Dan Troop is out of town, Deputy Johnny McKay is responsible for keeping law and order in Laramie. He faces trouble when three trigger happy youths ride into town anxious for a showdown with the deputy.

89.29 Riding Shotgun. April 19, 1959. GS: Allen Case, Paul Fix, Jack Lomas, Ron Soble. Larry Delong, a reformed outlaw, is suspected of shooting a stagecoach driver.

89.30 The Journey. April 26, 1959. GS: Robert J. Wilke, J. Pat O'Malley, Willis Bouchey, Harry Millard. Marshal Dan Troop rides out to help a friend and is ambushed.

89.31 The Huntress. May 3, 1959. GS: Andra Martin, Olive Sturgess, Keith Byron, John Pickard. Dance-hall girl Loma Williams arrives in Laramie set on exacting revenge against the brother of the man who killed her brother.

89.32 The Return. May 10, 1959. GS: Frank Albertson, Burt Douglas, Nan Peterson. A wealthy rancher's daughter falls in love with ex-convict Ben Adams. When her father tries to run Adams out of town, Marshal Troop intervenes.

89.33 The Senator. May 17, 1959. GS: Jack Elam, Donald "Red" Barry, Ted de Corsia, Grandon Rhodes, Bill Richmond, Edgar Buchanan. A senator scheduled to visit Laramie is unaware that his life is endangered by three hired gunslingers. Marshal Troop hears of the assassination plan less than an hour before the senator's train is due to arrive.

89.34 The Ring. May 24, 1959. GS: Richard Long, Roy Baker, Hillary Brooke, Byron Palmer. When a dance-hall girl is murdered, Marshal Troop finds only one clue to her killer's identity. As Troop checks out the lead, one of the chief suspects becomes the unknown murderer's second victim.

89.35 The Bandit. May 31, 1959. GS: Skip Homeier, Anne Anderson, Jimmy Baird, Don Beddoe, Lurene Tuttle. Tracking down a bank-robbery suspect, Marshal Troop and Deputy Johnny McKay find him in a farmhouse caring for a woman and her brother who are critically ill.

89.36 The Wayfarer. June 7, 1959. GS: Adam West, Jeff York, Ken Becker, Debby Hengen, Emory Parnell. Marshal Dan Troop decides to protect Doc Holliday from revenge-seeking Sam Cates even though Cates has warned Troop not to meddle.

89.37 Conclave. June 14, 1959. GS: Denver Pyle, Lawrence Dobkin, Carl Milletaire, Lee Van Cleef. When Marshal Dan Troop jails a drunk, he learns of an impending stagecoach robbery. Troop decides to use his prisoner as a decoy in an attempt to foil the plot.

89.38 Red Ransom. June 21, 1959. GS: Francis J. McDonald, George D. Wallace. When Chief Red Horse's son is killed, the Indians hold Deputy Johnny McKay. Racing against time, Marshal Dan Troop must bring in the boy's killer before the Indians take their revenge by murdering McKay.

89.39 The Friend. June 28, 1959. GS: Robert Fuller, Nestor Paiva, Robert F. Simon, Emory Parnell, Brad Von Beltz. Buck Harmon, childhood friend of Deputy Johnny McKay, is a member of a gang of outlaws. When Harmon learns that the gang is going to rob the Laramie bank, he tells them that he won't take part in the crime.

Season Two

89.40 Lily. Oct. 4, 1959. GS: Ray Danton, Nan Peterson, Dan Sheridan, Clancy Cooper. Lily Merrill arrives in Laramie to open a saloon. But she comes up against Marshal Troop, who suspects her of aiding an outlaw.

89.41 The Hunch. Oct. 11, 1959. GS: Tom Drake, Howard Petrie, Strother Martin. Accused of robbing the Overland Bank, Frank Judson is jailed. But Marshal Dan Troop, who arrested Judson, is keeping an eye on an ex-deputy who seems to have acquired a lot of money.

89.42 Shackled. Oct. 18, 1959. GS: Robert McQueeney, Kasey Rogers. Johnny McKay's assignment is to deliver criminal Ben Ryan to the state prison. Although McKay has handcuffed the prisoner to him, when the wagon breaks down along the way Ryan tries to escape. McKay throws away the key to the chain lock in order to prevent the escape.

89.43 The Exchange. Oct. 25, 1959. GS: Mike Road. Frank Quinlivan, a stranger in town, arrives at the Birdcage Saloon and tries to blackmail Lily Merrill. Lily decides to tackle the blackmailer without Marshal Dan Troop's help.

89.44 The Last Man. Nov. 1, 1959. GS: Henry Brandon, Steven Darrell. Awaiting the arrival of General Mider for the surrender of the Sioux Indians, Marshal Dan Troop is told that Joshua Haney, the Sioux chief's blood-brother, is plotting a mass murder.

89.45 The Breakup. Nov. 8, 1959. GS: Donald Buka. Upset because he had to kill two of his friends, Deputy Johnny McKay decides to resign.

89.46 Shadow Witness. Nov. 15, 1959. GS: Herbert Rudley, Percy Helton. When a dance-hall girl is killed, Marshal Dan Troop and Deputy Johnny McKay plot to have the killer give himself away.

89.47 The Prodigal. Nov. 22, 1959. GS: Tony Young, Clancy Cooper. Young Mark McQueen and his friends, looking for action, pose a problem for Marshal Don Troop and his deputy. Mark, the brains of the teenage gang, is the son of a friend of the lawmen.

89.48 The Press. Nov. 29, 1959. GS: Robert J. Wilke, Vinton Hayworth, Robert Riordan, Wendell Holmes. Lal Hoard controls the town of Laramie. But Marshal Troop can't interfere with his activities because he is careful to stay within the law.

89.49 9:05 to North Platte. Dec. 6, 1959. GS: Harry Shannon, Jimmy Baird, Richard Rust, Charlie Briggs. Pa Jute's son is a prisoner of the law. Old man Jute kidnaps Lily and young Joey Buckner, and tells Marshal Troop he will release them if Troop sets his son free.

89.50 The Hoax. Dec. 20, 1959. GS: Willard Waterman, John Hubbard. Marshal Troop becomes suspicious of two clergymen when they begin to collect money to rebuild a burned church.

89.51 The Shelter. Dec. 27, 1959. GS: Chris Alcaide.

While escorting a killer to justice, Marshal Dan Troop, Deputy Johnny McKay and their prisoner are caught in a storm. The three men take shelter in a cabin occupied by an escaped convict.

89.52 Last Stop. Jan. 3, 1960. GS: Richard Arlen, Jonathan Gilmore. Marshal Troop advises Bill Jennings to tell his son about the boy's mother, who is now dead. Jennings disregards this advice and soon he is confronted by his son — armed with a gun.

89.53 The Showdown. Jan. 10, 1960. GS: James Coburn, John Howard. Arriving in Laramie, gunfighter Blake Carr tells Marshal Dan Troop that he has come to kill Lance Creedy, his ex-partner. Troop, who knows that Creedy has vowed never to use a gun again, tries to keep Carr from carrying out his plan.

89.54 The Stranger. Jan. 17, 1960. GS: Ian Wolfe, Clancy Cooper, Roscoe Ates. Soon after Marshal Dan Troop kills a drunken gunslinger, he receives several unsigned letters informing him that he has one week to live. Deputy Johnny McKay sets out to learn the identity of the writer of the letter.

89.55 The Wolfer. Jan. 24, 1960. GS: Archie Duncan, Jack Mather, Spence Carlisle. Pike Reese kills Alf Betts for refusing to pay him for capturing a sheep-killing wolf. Dan Troop sets out to stalk Reese, but soon learns that Reese is stalking him.

89.56 The Hardcase. Jan. 31, 1960. GS: Dody Heath, Don Drysdale, Robert Armstrong, William Challee. Marshal Dan Troop asks Beth Denning to stay at home when a group of rowdy cowboys come to town, but Beth defies the marshal's request.

89.57 To Capture the West. Feb. 7, 1960. GS: Warren Stevens, Henry Brandon, Mickey Simpson. Stopping in Laramie, painter Frederick Jameson tells Marshal Troop that a murderer and his men are on his trail.

89.58 The Ugly Man. Feb. 14, 1960. GS: Eve McVeagh, Ted Knight, Mina Vaughn, Joyce Otis. Lily Merrill is the midnight target for an unseen gunman. He misses her, but he hits Josie, a girl working in Lily's saloon. Marshal Troop and Johnny McKay then stand guard over Lily.

89.59 The Kids. Feb. 21, 1960. GS: Evelyn Rudie, Tom Drake, Rick Roman. With no one to care for them, Dodie Weaver and her two brothers are held in the Laramie jail waiting for their outlaw father to claim them. An uncle asks the three youngsters to come home with him, but they insist on waiting for their father to show up.

89.60 The Thimblerigger. Feb. 28, 1960. GS: DeForest Kelley, Richard Reeves, Doodles Weaver. A stranger arrives in town and states that he will destroy a man without using a weapon. While the stranger plays a shell game which he claims will reveal his intended victim, Marshal Dan Troop tries to stay one step ahead of the newcomer.

89.61 The Truce. March 6, 1960. GS: Don O'Kelly, Robert McQueeney. Sheriff Jess Hahn is interested only in glory and would just as soon take his man dead or alive. He is after outlaw O.C. Coulsen — whom Marshal Troop tries to protect.

89.62 Reunion in Laramie. March 13, 1960. GS: William Schallert, Murvyn Vye. Reed Smith, a pianist with a bad conscience, works at the Birdcage Saloon. Marshal Dan Troop keeps a close watch, waiting for a meeting between the pianist and a man he fears.

89.63 Thirty Minutes. March 20, 1960. GS: Jack Elam. The afternoon quiet is shattered when Jake Wilson, a wanted killer, pulls a gun on everyone in the Birdcage Saloon.

89.64 Left Hand of the Law. March 27, 1960. GS: John Anderson, Robert Reed, Regis Toomey. Lloyd Malone lost his right arm in a gunfight with Marshal Troop. Now Malone's son wants to take a crack at the lawman. Troop decides to take him on, with his right hand tied behind his back.

89.65 Belding's Girl. April 3, 1960. GS: Susan Morrow, Donald "Red" Barry, Emile Meyer, Dermot Cronin. Meg Belding runs away from home and gets a job at the Birdcage Saloon. The law has to step in when her father comes after her.

89.66 Girl from Grantsville. April 10, 1960. GS: Suzanne Lloyd, Burt Douglas. Jenny Miles arrives in town and deputy Johnny McKay decides he is in love. He wants to get married right away, but Marshal Troop and Lily advise him to wait.

89.67 The Surface of Truth. April 17, 1960. GS: Peter Whitney, Richard Hale, Maurice Jara. Trapper Lucas Beyer, pickled with drink, becomes petrified with fear when he hears that an Indian is looking for him. The trapper is accused of killing his Indian wife, and Troop agrees to let her tribe decide whether he is guilty.

89.68 The Salvation of Owny O'Reilly. April 24, 1960. GS: Joel Grey, Donald Murphy, Bill Leicester. The people of Laramie have befriended young Owny O'Reilly. But he still won't tell the hiding place of the gold stolen by his older brother.

89.69 The Lady Belle. May 1, 1960. GS: Joan Marshall, Vinton Hayworth, Doodles Weaver. A lady bandit comes into town to case the bank and charm the people, including Marshal Troop.

89.70 The Payment. May 8, 1960. Troy Donahue, Robert McQueeney, Catherine McLeod. A reformed gunman wants to help the wife and son of one of his victims. But the boy wants to even the score.

89.71 The Judge. May 15, 1960. GS: John Hoyt, Diane McBain, Randy Stuart. Judge Loren Grant is the victim of a split personality. Driven to murder, he wounds Dan Troop and then tries to label the marshal a killer.

89.72 Man on a Wire. May 22, 1960. GS: Gustavo Rojo, Karen Steele. Lily has hired a husband and wife aerialist team to attract customers to the Birdcage saloon. The man, threatened with death by a secret society, seeks Troop's protection.

89.73 The Parting. May 29, 1960. GS: Kenneth Tobey, Nancy Valentine, Mike Road, Doodles Weaver. An escaped killer wants to make a deal. While Marshal Troop considers the offer, someone tries to blackmail the outlaw.

89.74 The Swamper. June 5, 1960. GS: Luana Anders, J. Pat O'Malley, Emory Parnell, Ken Becker. The town bum suddenly is in the chips, and Dan Troop wants to find out where he got the money.

89.75 Man on a Mountain. June 12, 1960. GS: Richard Garland, Lee Van Cleef, Dick Rich, Steve Pendleton, Christopher Essay. Ben Jaegers tried to get the money to save his sick wife by robbing a stage. Now a posse is out to kill him, but Marshal Troop rides out to save him.

89.76 Fast Trip to Cheyenne. June 19, 1960. GS: King Calder, Suzanne Storrs, Bill Dolan. Troop makes a trip to Cheyenne to save an innocent man from hanging.

Season Three

89.77 The Town Boys. Sept. 18, 1960. GS: Tom Rettig,

Richard Evans, Hank Patterson. Four young men are about to be jailed on delinquency charges when Deputy McKay steps in and asks Marshal Troop to put the boys in his custody. Johnny has a plan, but it isn't the same one he tells the boys.

89.78 *The Go-Between.* Sept. 26, 1960. GS: Paul Comi, Tom Gilson, Larry Blake, Lane Bradford, Charles Fredericks. Johnny McKay arrives in town, bloody and blindfolded. Outlaw Cole Reese has given him instructions for Marshal Troop — how much money to bring and where to go to get Lily Merrill back alive.

89.79 *The Mad Bunch.* Oct. 2, 1960. GS: Edward Byrnes, Nick Dennis, Asa Maynor, Harry Antrim, Frank Ferguson, Jack Hogan, Frederick Crane. Joe Knox quits a gang of cattle rustlers when they murder a young man who is trying to get a doctor for his wife. Then he risks the gang's revenge by bringing the woman to see Doc Shea.

89.80 *The Old War Horse.* Oct. 9, 1960. GS: Lee Patrick, Arch Johnson, Vinton Hayworth, Grady Sutton, Jim Hayward, Charles Alvin Bell. Jason McQuade, Bess Harper's finagling manager from her music hall days, is the brains behind her suit contesting her late husband's will. The money was left to the town of Laramie.

89.81 *The Return of Owny O'Reilly.* Oct. 16, 1960. GS: Joel Grey, Lee Van Cleef, William Fawcett, Bill Foster. At McKay's request, Troop reluctantly deputizes teenager Owny O'Reilly. Sure enough, Owny tries to be a hero and attempts to bring in Jack Saunders, a desperate outlaw.

89.82 *Yawkey.* Oct. 23, 1960. GS: Ray Danton, Don Sheridan, David McMahon, Martin Eric. A bitter, young outlaw strides into the Birdcage and says he will kill the town's marshal within the next half hour, though he gives no reason.

89.83 *Dilemma.* Oct. 30, 1960. GS: Tom Drake, John Beradino, James Anderson, Harry Antrim, John McCann. Dr. Sam Burbage treats a bullet wound for one of the Carmody gang. But the outlaws know that Sam must report all gunshot wounds, and they don't take kindly to the prospect.

89.84 *The Post.* Nov. 6, 1960. GS: Don Megowan, Bernard Fein, Saundra Edwards. Now that Troop has captured fugitive Rafe Curry, his next problem is to take Rafe from Wyoming to New Mexico.

89.85 *Chantay.* Nov. 13, 1960. GS: Sharon Hugueny, Dean Fredericks, Milton Parsons. Chantay, a proud Sioux maiden, confesses to the murder of Great Bear, a reservation policeman. But McKay's not convinced. His follow-up nets him a strange clue — a bag of candy.

89.86 *Samson the Great.* Nov. 20, 1960. GS: Walter Burke, Mickey Simpson, Charles Horvath, Mina Vaughn. Fight manager Jimmy Fresco brings Samson the Great to Laramie. The boxer beats everyone who gets into the ring, then starts on those outside the ring.

89.87 *The Second Son.* Nov. 27, 1960. GS: Kim Charney, Warren Oates, Harry Shannon, Fred Crane. An army paymaster is ambushed and robbed. Young Charlie May says he did it, but Troop is sure he is shielding someone else.

89.88 *The Catcher.* Dec. 4, 1960. GS: James Coburn, Robert Armstrong, Med Flory. A sheep drover dubbed Catcher is awakened in the middle of the night, told he murdered someone while drunk the night before and hurried on his way out of town.

89.89 *Cornered.* Dec. 11, 1960. GS: Frank De Kova, Tom Troupe, Harrison Lewis, Guy Wilkerson, Frank Kreig. Gunman Jed Barker draws on McKay while drunk and is shot dead. McKay has something to fret about as Jed's son is expected in town shortly.

89.90 *The Escape of Joe Kilmer.* Dec. 18, 1960. GS: Lenore Roberts, Wynn Pearce, Ken Lynch, Joe Ruskin. Troop is just a bit wary when Donna Killmer turns her wounded outlaw husband over to the law. She asks that he be given medical care, and that she be given the reward money.

89.91 *Old Stefano.* Dec. 25, 1960. GS: Gregg Palmer, John Qualen, Vladimir Sokoloff, Frank Mitchell. There is a newcomer in Laramie, Tracy McNeil, who seems to rub Troop the wrong way. First, he's flashy, second, he's arrogant, and third, he's courting Lily Merrill.

89.92 *The Robbery.* Jan. 1, 1961. GS: Robert Ridgely, Hal Torey, Warren Kemmerling. Troop becomes wary when three strangers appear in town just before the Army payroll is due.

89.93 *Firehouse Lil.* Jan. 8, 1961. GC: Sheldon Allman, Vinton Hayworth, I. Stanford Jolley, Jean Stine. The new chief of the Laramie Volunteer Fire Brigade is Lily Merrill. As she is celebrating her appointment in the Birdcage, bandits set a fire in a livery stable.

89.94 *The Frame-Up.* Jan. 15, 1961. GS: Randy Stuart, Dabbs Greer, Ric Roman, William Mims. Jessica Kindle's husband was sent to the gallows on evidence from Troop. But Jessica claims her husband was innocent, and hires lawyer Les Courtney to prove it.

89.95 *Marked Man.* Jan. 22, 1961. GS: Jeff De Benning, Andrew Duggan, Miranda Jones, Douglas Odney. Troop becomes a marked man when he closes down Ross Darby's Empire Saloon. The place ran crooked games, sold watered whisky, and a couple of traveling cowboys got outnumbered in a gunfight.

89.96 *The Squatters.* Jan. 29, 1961. GS: DeForest Kelley, Tom Gilson, Nina Shipman, King Calder, Hal K. Dawson, Stephen Ellsworth. Before he died, a kindly Wyoming cattleman gave Ad Prentice a tract of land to start a ranch. Prentice's hired hand, Brent Carr, hopes to gain possession of the land by proving the transaction was illegal.

89.97 *Homecoming.* Feb. 5, 1961. GS: Marc Lawrence, Ray Stricklyn, Adrienne Marsden. Frank Walker swore long ago that he would have his revenge on Marshal Troop. Now Walker has broken out of prison and is expected to arrive in Laramie any hour.

89.98 *Hassayampa.* Feb. 12, 1961. GS: John Anderson, Donald "Red" Barry, George D. Wallace, Harry Cheshire, Gail Bonney. Hassayampa Edwards arrives in Laramie preaching temperance. The Laramie Ladies Tuesday Club responds to the call and forces the Birdcage Saloon to close — but not before Hassayampa is jailed for wrecking the bar.

89.99 *The Promoter.* Feb. 19, 1961. GS: John Van Dreelen, Don Beddoe, Frank Gerstle, J. Edward McKinley. Malcolm Tyler De Vries is convinced he can take control of Laramie by buying up all the saloons. Most of the owners don't give him much trouble. Then he tries to buy the Birdcage and comes up against a determined Lily.

89.100 *Detweiler's Kid.* Feb. 26, 1961. GS: Otto Waldis, Joyce Meadows, Chad York, Harry Cheshire, Harrison Lewis. An old farmer named Detweiler instructs his daughter,

Elfrieda, to shoot anybody trespassing on their property. The first two trespassers are Deputy McKay and cowhand Jim Austin.

89.101 *The Inheritance.* March 5, 1961. GS: Will Wright, Lurene Tuttle, Rex Holman, Fuzzy Knight. Old Tecumsah Pruitt gives his friends advice on investments. His son Owlie finds out and figures Pa has a fortune stashed away. So Owlie buys some new boots and sends the bill to dad.

89.102 *Blue Boss and Willie Shay.* March 12, 1961. GS: Sammy Davis, Jr., Richard Jaeckel. Willie, a lonesome cowpoke, and a steer named Blue Boss become fast friends. But Blue Boss gets a little ornery sometimes and Willie's trail boss, Al Janaker, isn't going to stand for it.

89.103 *The Man from New York.* March 19, 1961. GS: Mike Road, Richard Arlen, John Cliff, Sheila Bromley. Foster, a detective from New York, wants Troop to arrest townsman Fred Stiles on a legal technicality. Foster suspects Stiles of a robbery committed years ago.

89.104 *Mark of Cain.* March 26, 1961. GS: Coleen Gray, John Kellogg, Theodore Newton, James Waters, Fred Sherman, Bruce MacFarlane. Rena Kennedy is convinced that her brother-in-law Chad killed her husband, even though he stood trial for the crime and was acquitted. Determined to make him pay, she sees a chance to frame him for murder in what was really an accidental death.

89.105 *Fugitive.* April 2, 1961. GS: Keith Richards, Catherine McLeod, Michael Davis. When Casey Cormack skips town, it strengthens Troop's suspicion that he is guilty of a stagecoach robbery. Casey's young son Joey could throw some light on the subject, but he won't talk.

89.106 *The Persecuted.* April 9, 1961. GS: Adam Williams, Jean Willes, Evan McCord. Though Burley Keller is an old acquaintance of Marshal Troop's, that doesn't stop Troop from bringing him to justice. But at the trial, the jury acquits the offender, who then decides he would like Lily for his girl.

89.107 *The Grubstake.* April 16, 1961. GS: Frank Ferguson, Heather Angel, Philip Terry, Robert Cornthwaite. An old prospector named Rainbow Jack tries to get money from Troop and McKay. They turn him down, but he gets the money anyway — from Stephanie Collins, an entertainer at the Birdcage Saloon.

89.108 *Whiphand.* April 23, 1961. GS: Med Florey, Peggy McCay, Leo Gordon. Big Bull Nickerson misunderstands innocent banter that peddler Jed Pennyman exchanges with Nickerson's wife. Bill threatens Jed with certain death if he doesn't leave town immediately.

89.109 *The Threat.* April 30, 1961. GS: Whit Bissell, Russ Conway, Don O'Reilly, Walter Reed. James Chase has been shot down by gunman Kurt Swan and James's brother Edgar sets out to avenge the murder. Being a gentle, non-violent man, Edgar decides to use psychology instead of gunplay.

89.110 *The Trial.* May 7, 1961. GS: Richard Sakal, Ray Teal, Shirley Knight, Tim Graham, Claudia Bryar. Dexter Watson was still a boy when a judge named Whitehall sentenced his father to hang for murder. Now Weston has his chance to even the score with the judge.

89.111 *Blind Hate.* May 14, 1961. GS: Mala Powers, Ted De Corsia, Jason Evers, John Qualen. Shag Warner sees Lucy Pastor, decides he'll pay her court, and gets bullwhipped for his trouble by Lem Pastor, Lucy's father. The more Shag thinks about this humiliation the more certain he is that Lem has lived long enough.

89.112 *The Break-In.* May 21, 1961. GS: Sheldon Allman, James Anderson, Maurice Manson, Chubby Johnson. There is an attractive price on the head of outlaw Walt Hudson. So irresistible, in fact, that Hudson decides he will turn himself in, collect the reward and set the cash aside for freer days. Now all he has to do is sell the idea to Troop.

89.113 *Conditional Surrender.* May 28, 1961. GS: Robert F. Simon, Claire Griswold, Tyler MacDuff, Hampton Fancher. Outlaw Pa Beason offers Troop a complete confession of all his crimes, if the marshal will promise to see that Beason's daughter Iona goes to finishing school in the East.

89.114 *Cold Fear.* June 4, 1961. GS: Frank Overton, Chris Alcaide, Maggie Mahoney, Jerry Barclay. Storekeeper Brad Turner, once a marshal, killed a gunman named Quade in the line of duty. The victim's older brothers avenge the death by kidnaping Turner's wife.

89.115 *The Promise.* June 11, 1961. GS: Robert Palmer, Carolyn Komant, Charles Tannen, Don Haggerty, Ken Lynch, Ben Wright. The promise that outlaw Jed Barrister makes before his death on the gallows is that Troop will be killed by a member of his gang before the week is out. McKay decides to make careful note of all newcomers in town.

Season Three

89.116 *Trapped.* Sept. 17, 1961. GS: Peter Breck, Vinton Hayworth, House Peters, Jr., Grady Sutton. Outlaw leader Hale Connors arrives in Laramie to notify Troop that the stage won't be arriving on schedule because Connors is holding the passengers for ransom.

89.117 *The Juror.* Sept. 24, 1961. GS: Jack Hogan, Larry Blake, Jim Hayward. Some members of a train-robbing gang are caught in a town near Laramie. The remaining gang members terrorize the townspeople so thoroughly that the court can't find twelve people willing to serve on the jury.

89.118 *The Four.* Oct. 1, 1961. GS: Jack Elam, Evan McCord, Norm Alden, Dorothy Konrad, Richard Gardner. Four strange men are stationed at strategic points in Laramie, each one holding a carbine. Troop learns that they are after a psychopathic killer named Lee Darragh, and they think that Darragh is in town.

89.119 *The Son.* Oct. 8, 1961. GS: Chad Everett, James Westerfield. Young Cole Herod was the only witness to his brother's murder. The boy is blind, but he heard the killer's voice.

89.120 *Owny O'Reilly, Esq.* Oct. 15, 1961. GS: Joel Grey, Roberta Shore, Mort Mills, Barry Kelley, Grady Sutton. A young girl who calls herself Millie Cotton tries to get a job singing in the Birdcage saloon. Troop soon learns that she is the runaway daughter of the territorial governor.

89.121 *The Substitute.* Oct. 22, 1961. GS: Whit Bissell, Dee Carrol, Kathleen Freeman. Schoolteacher Trilby Johnson isn't getting any younger, and any description would have to include the word plain. Now she has had an offer of marriage and wants to take it, but school is still in session.

89.122 *The Stalker.* Oct. 29, 1961. GS: Peter Whitney, Donald "Red" Barry, Harry Lauter. Alteeka McClintoch, a powerful, but good-natured trapper, is minding his own business in the Birdcage when Jess Schaeffer, a bullying cowboy, forces him to drink some whiskey at gunpoint, and then pulls the trigger.

89.123 The Catalog Woman. Nov. 5, 1961. GS: Herb Vigran, Vinton Hayworth, William Fawcett. Rancher Walter Perkins and his mail-order bride vanish and are never seen again. Troop wonders what will happen if he writes to the same people the Perkins did to get his wife.

89.124 The Cold One. Nov. 12, 1961. GS: Michael Pate, Joyce Meadows, Tom Bilson, Ric Marlow. King Harris, a notorious killer, has escaped from a territorial prison. His first objective is to settle the score with the woman who betrayed him—his wife.

89.125 Parphyrias Lover. Nov. 19, 1961. GS: Lance Fuller, Jeanne Vaughn, Benny Baker. Lily is terrified to learn that Galt Stevens is being released from prison. It was Stevens who killed one of her suitors and it was Lily's testimony that sent him to jail.

89.126 The Appointment. Nov. 26, 1961. GS: Kent Smith, John Kellogg, Grady Sutton. An old friend of McKay's, Major Jason Leeds, has secured an appointment for him to the U.S. Military Academy at West Point. But when Troop doesn't encourage him to take the opportunity, McKay hesitates, and incurs the Major's anger.

89.127 The Lords of Darkness. Dec. 3, 1961. GS: Arch Johnson, Jim De Closs, Corey Allen, Ellen Willard. Andrew Lord's two sons come home, with murder in their past and Troop on their trail. Their father, an arrogant and powerful rancher, refuses to turn them over to the lawman.

89.128 Tarot. Dec. 10, 1961. GS: Robert McQueeney, William Zuckert, K.L. Smith. Amateur fortuneteller Joe Wyatt takes a look at what is in the cards for himself, Lily, Troop and McKay. The answer is death for one of them.

89.129 The Prodigal Mother. Dec. 17, 1961. GS: Catherine McLeod, Billy Booth, Mina Brown, King Calder. As an infant, Tad Coleson was abandoned by his mother and a childless ranch couple, the McCallans, took him in and raised him. Now, nine years later, Tad's mother returns, with a court order, to reclaim her son.

89.130 By the Book. Dec. 24, 1961. GS: Lyle Talbot, Sheldon Allman. The U.S. Marshal's office of the Wyoming Territory has sent Orville Luster to Laramie to investigate Troop's methods. Luster is disturbed by Troop's flexible ways of enforcement.

89.131 The Trojan Horse. Dec. 31, 1961. GS: Kenneth Tobey, Richard Bakalyan, Charles Briggs. Troop evacuates Laramie so road engineer Duncan Clooney can bring his wagonload of nitroglycerin through town without risking injury to anyone.

89.132 The Locket. Jan. 7, 1962. GS: Julie Van Zandt, Robert Colbert, Boyd Morgan. Lily's friend Marcia Smith is expected on the next stagecoach. She arrives, injured and unconscious, in a driverless coach.

89.133 A Friend of the Family. Jan. 14, 1962. GS: Frank Ferguson, Vinton Hayworth. McKay is stunned when he discovers that one of the two bank bandits he and Troop have caught is old Joe Henny, a friend from McKay's childhood.

89.134 The Vintage. Jan. 21, 1962. GS: Kevin Hagen, Armand Alzamora, Ernest Sarracino. A couple of cowboys named Kulp and Joe get to slugging away outside the Birdcage saloon. During the struggle, a wagon parked nearby is overturned. Spilled out on the ground are the grapevines that Antonio Lazarino has carefully brought all the way from Italy.

89.135 The Tarnished Badge. Jan. 28, 1962. GS: Lon Chaney, Jr., Marshall Reed, Jack Searl. Marshal Jess Bridges was the childhood idol of Deputy McKay, and even Troop learned the ropes as the marshal's deputy. But Bridges isn't a marshal any longer and when he rides into Laramie behind the badge, it is a part of a ruse in his plan to rob the stage.

89.136 No Contest. Feb. 4, 1962. GS: Guy Stockwell, Dawn Wells, Richard Rogers, Frank Watkins. McKay's Boston cousin Jeff Allen arrives in Laramie for a visit. The first thing that Troop notices about the young man is that he bears a remarkable resemblance to Billy the Kid.

89.137 Change of Venue. Feb. 11, 1962. GS: Philip Carey, Jan Shepard, Roy Barcroft. The townspeople of Laramie are determined that captured gunman Barron Shaw receive the ultimate punishment for killing one of their favorite citizens. When word gets around that Shaw's trial has been transferred to another town an angry mob forms in front of the jail.

89.138 The Hold-Out. Feb. 18, 1962. GS: Arch Johnson, Addison Richards, Larry Ward, Harry Cheshire, Joseph Ruskin, Tom Munroe. The Territorial Vigilantes, led by a man called Logan, want Blake Stevens to join their group—and give him a beating when he refuses. Troop asks Stevens to testify against Logan's gang, but Stevens refuses.

89.139 The Barber. Feb. 25, 1962. GS: Pitt Herbert, Vinton Hayworth, Gail Bonney. Sylvester O'Toole says he bought Ed Carruthers' barber shop when Ed had to leave town in a hurry. But Ed, it seems, is still around, bound and gagged in the back of the shop.

89.140 The Long Gun. March 4, 1962. GS: John Dehner, George Dunn. Marshal Ben Wyatt rides into town leading a pack horse carrying the body of a dead man. Wyatt tells Troop that the man's name was Billy Bodeen, and that he killed him.

89.141 Clootey Hutter. March 11, 1962. GS: Virginia Gregg, Jack Hogan, Jack Elam, Justin Smith. Clootey Hutter is mild-mannered, calm and confident that she is the fasted gun in the West. When the body of Earl Henry, a notorious fast gun, is found Clootey confesses that she bested him in a fair fight.

89.142 Heritage of Hate. March 18, 1962. GS: Kathie Browne, Roy Roberts, William Joyce. Laurie Kemper was accused of killing her husband, and served time for manslaughter. Now that she is out of prison, Troop is anxious to help her—but John Kemper is just as anxious to see that his former daughter-in-law gets no help at all.

89.143 Mountain Man. March 25, 1962. GS: Med Florey, William Fawcett, Rusty Wescoatt. Lex Buckman doesn't leave his mountain home very often to visit Laramie, but when he does it is usually for a specific reason. The reason for his latest visit is to find a wife, and the minute he spots Lily, Buckman's mind is made up.

89.144 The Bride. April 1, 1962. GS: Jo Morrow, L.Q. Jones, William Mims. Wealthy young rancher Ollie Earnshaw is thrilled when Melanie Wells, a newcomer in town, agrees to marry him. But Troop, after doing a bit of research on Melanie, suspects that her only interest in Ollie is his money.

89.145 The Wanted Man. April 8, 1962. GS: Marie Windsor, Jan Stine, Dick Foran, Ralph Moody. Young Ben Jesse's mother is seriously ill and about to have a baby. Ben brings her to Laramie, but he can't afford a hospital. He asks Doc Greer to deliver the child in a stable.

89.146 *Sunday.* April 15, 1962. GS: Andrew Duggan, Richard Evans, Greg Benedict, Buzz Henry. Troop plans to hold outlaw Billy Deal for the Federal authorities, but it isn't going to be easy. A number of people in Laramie are determined to get their hands on Deal.

89.147 *The Youngest.* April 22, 1962. GS: Olive Carey, Evan McCord, Tom Gilson, Charles Briggs. Ma Martin comes to Laramie with her three sons. Her mission is revenge on Troop for killing her outlaw husband.

89.148 *Cort.* April 29, 1962. GS: Kevin Hagen, Harry Carey, Jr., Ralph Moody. A stranger rides into town, and collapses. After the doctor's examination, Troop tries to question him, but gets nowhere. All the stranger will say is that there is going to be a lot of trouble around sundown.

89.149 *The Doctor.* May 6, 1962. GS: Eloise Hardt, Charles Lane, Sherwood Price, Whit Bissell. Troop arrives in a mining town to bring Will Evans to Laramie, where he must act as witness at a trial. But Evans doesn't want to go and Troop has to force him at gunpoint.

89.150 *The Man Behind the News.* May 13, 1962. GS: Hal Baylor, Clinton Sundberg, Harry Cheshire, Peggy Mondo. Luther Boardman, Laramie's new newspaper editor, has a strange hobby. He is obsessed with criminals. Boardman tells Troop he intends to join every posse the marshal organizes.

89.151 *Get Out of Town.* May 20, 1962. GS: Bill Williams, Vinton Hayworth, Tim Graham, John Hubbard. Jim Bushrod arrives in Laramie with plans to open a saloon. Troop's friend, Amos Hall, tries to stop the newcomer because Bushrod has been selling whiskey and guns to the Indians.

89.152 *The Actor.* May 27, 1962. GS: John Carradine, Mary Anderson, Warren Kemmerling, Harry Harvey, Sr., Ray Mayo. Fading actor Geoffrey Hendon recites a particularly romantic passage from Shakespeare, and Martha Carson is convinced that Hendon is speaking directly to her.

89.153 *Explosion.* June 3, 1962. GS: Gary Vinson, Miranda Jones, John Qualen, Denver Pyle, Milton Parsons. Jess Billings, a hired hand on the Murdoch ranch, shoots his employer and heads for the hills. Doc Shay tries to explain that Jess' criminal action is the result of a brain injury, but the posse has already left.

89.154 *Jailbreak.* June 10, 1962. GS: Peter Breck, Pamela Austin, James Griffith, Frank Ferguson. A girl named Little Britches is wild about her fiance, killer Pete Bole. Her one consuming ambition is to get Bole out of jail.

89.155 *The Unmasked.* June 17, 1962. GS: Dabbs Greer, Angela Greene, Barry Atwater, Charles Maxwell, Jack Albertson. Carter Banks and Sam Davidson arrive in Laramie, pretending that they are looking for their cousin. But hotel owner Joe Brockway tells Troop that the two men are bounty hunters looking for the man who shot John Wilkes Booth.

89.156 *The Witness.* June 24, 1962. GS: John Agar, Jay Novello, Sarah Selby. A woman named Mrs. Adams is murdered, and it looks as though Troop's friend Jim Martin is in plenty of trouble. The dead woman's sister, Anna, swears she saw Martin kill Mrs. Adams.

90. *The Lazarus Man*

Syndicated. 60 min. Broadcast history: Various, Jan. 1996–Nov. 1996.

Regular Cast: Robert Urich (Lazarus), Natalija Nogulich (Joe de Winter), Wayne Grace (Derby Hat Man), Isabelle Townsend (the Dark-Haired Woman).

Premise: In the post-Civil War era, an amnesiac searches for his identity.

The Episodes

90.1 *Awakening* Part One. Jan. 20, 1996. GS: John Christian Graas, Elizabeth Dennehy, John Diehl. Lazarus awakes in a grave to find he has no memory of his past. He recuperates at the home of Natt and Lizbette Patchett, where flashbacks reveal pieces of his past.

90.2 *Awakening* Part Two. Jan. 27, 1996. GS: John Christian Graas, Elizabeth Dennehy, John Diehl, Walter Addison. Lazarus is mistaken for a sharp-shooter named Jack Prussard and, while attempting to help Natt, becomes involed in a plot to assassinate Ulysses S. Grant.

90.3 *The Palace of Dreams.* Feb. 3, 1996. GS: Carl Lumbly. Desperate for clues to his forgotten past, Lazarus meets an eccentric card shark with a mysterious grudge and ends up playing a high-stakes match, for life or death.

90.4 *Purgatory.* Feb. 10, 1996. GS: Stephen McHattie. Despite his clouded memory, Lazarus recognizes a Confederate veteran once under his command—a man who has set out to destroy him.

90.5 *The Conspirator.* Feb. 17, 1996. GS: Tom Mason, James Pickens, Jr., Laurie O'Brien. A Federal agent with a vendetta against Lazarus has him arrested and sentenced to death on trumped-up charges of aiding in the Lincoln assassination.

90.6 *The Boy General.* Feb. 24, 1996. GS: Maxwell Caulfield, Alicia Coppola, Arthur Hanket. George Armstrong Custer hires Lazarus as a scout to sniff out threats against him, not from the Sioux but from his own troops, who bristle at his harsh discipline.

90.7 *Cattle Drive.* March 2, 1996. GS: Tom Wright, Tony Amendola, Jim Haynie. As he struggles to save a black cowhand from a trumped-up racist murder charge, Lazarus must fend off enemies of his own who emerge from the hazy past.

90.8 *Panorama.* March 9, 1996. GS: Anthony Rapp. To his horror, Lazarus finds that he has become legendary as the man who can't be killed, and his life is in constant peril, as gunslingers lineup to challenge him.

90.9 *The Wallpaper Prison.* March 16, 1996. GS: Michael Harris, Kate Hodge, Bill McKinney, Annie Oringer, Becky Herbst. Lazarus finds a kindred spirit in a forlorn, world-weary prostitute and urges her to break free from the brutal bawdyhouse owner who rules her life.

90.10 *The Catamount.* March 30, 1996. GS: Nicholas Surovy, Cari Shayne, Zahn McClamon, Leon Russom, Saginaw Grant, Dan Bell. A malicious cavalry officer plans to mete out justice to the Navajo after grave robbers plundering a sacred burial ground end up clawed to death, as if by a mountain cat.

90.11 *Among the Dead.* April 20, 1996. GS: Marc Miles, Tobin Bell, Jennifer Nash, Robert Foxworth. After being shot at by three strangers, a wounded Lazarus is entrusted with the golden chalice his dying companion hoped to use to rebuild a war-ravaged town.

90.12 *The Journal.* April 27, 1996. GS: Anna Gunn, Jeremy Lelliott. A prospector is murdered after striking it rich, and Lazarus runs into a coverup in a silent town ruled by a ruthless saloon owner and graced by a lovely but dangerous barmaid. His only ally in the town is a thirteen-year-old street urchin.

90.13 *Jehovah and Son, Inc.* May 4, 1996. GS: Armin Shimerman, William Lucking, Bruce Wright. An unbalanced man shoots a U.S. Senator with Lazarus' gun, which puts Lazarus in grave danger of being lynched when he is fingered as the mastermind.

90.14 *The Rescue.* May 11, 1996. GS: Kellie Overbey, Mark Rolston, David Paul Midthunder. A Comanche brave battles the militia over a white woman, raised by the tribe, who has been seized by the soliders against her will and returned to civilization.

90.15 *Killer.* May 18, 1996. GS: Tomas Arana, Joshua Bryant. Lazarus takes a liking to a fellow Civil War veteran turned bounty hunter, and becomes his partner, only to discover that the war has made the old soldier a little too fond of killing.

90.16 *The Hold-Up.* Oct. 12, 1996. GS: Darrel Larson, Elpidia Carillo, Scott Kraft, Jeff Kober. When Lazarus defends a stagecoach owner, the grateful man gives him a job that ultimately tests his loyalty.

90.17 *The Penance.* Oct. 19, 1996. GS: Dorie Barton. Lazarus tries to protect a pacifist sect of farmes from the wrath of cattlemen who are determined to keep them from settling on good grazing land.

90.18 *The Sheriff.* Oct. 26, 1996. GS: Max Gail. A hotheaded young gunslinger returns to punish his hometown, seething with bitter memories, and faces an aging sheriff who has tormented the boy with guilt over the events that made the boy mean.

90.19 *Angel Maker.* Nov. 2, 1996. A mail-order bride who disposes of her husbands and pockets their money bears an uncanny resemblance to the photo that Lazarus carries in his locket.

90.20 *Quality of the Enemy.* Nov. 9, 1996. GS: Marcus Gilbert, Jake Walker, Ed Adams, Tony Frank, Wayne DeHart. A cynical, amoral bounty hunter, contemptuous of the human race, learns something about honor when he is hired to track down Lazarus and instead becomes his ally.

90.21 *Title Unknown.* Nov. 16, 1996. An eccentric doctor dabbling in mesmerism tries to restore Lazarus' memory of the hidden events of Lincoln's assassination, but the surviving plotters realize the threat he poses.

90.22 *Dance with Shadows.* Nov. 23, 1996. GS: Isabelle Townsend. Lazarus reunites with his long-lost wife, but on his enemies' terms. They are using her as bait to lure him into a trap.

91. Legend

UPN. 60 min. Broadcast history: Tuesday, 8:00–9:00, April 1995–July 1995.

Regular Cast: Richard Dean Anderson (Ernest Pratt/Nicodemus Legend), John de Lancie (Prof. Janos Bartok), Jarrad Paul (Skeeter), Robert Donner (Mayor Chamberlain Brown), Mark Adair Rios (Ramos), Robert Shelton (Grady).

Premise: Hard-drinking dime novelist Ernest Pratt assumes the identity of the hero of his books, Nicodemus Legend, and, with the assistance of inventor Janos Bartok, brings life to the legend in the West of the 1870s.

The Episodes

91.1 *Pilot.* April 18, 1995. GS: Stephanie Beacham, Katherine Moffat, Jon Pennel, Tim Thomerson, Pete Schrum, Betsy Beard, Stephane Copperman. Legend helps a group of immigrant farmers protect themselves from a greedy landowner.

91.2 *Mr. Pratt Goes to Sheridan.* April 25, 1995. GS: Stephen Baldwin, Michael Moss, Randy Oglesby, Lily Nielsen, Rusty Ferracane, John Chappel. A notorious bank robber who is accused of murder announces that he will give himself up, but only to Legend. Meanwhile, Pratt has trouble adhering to his literary creation's lifestyle.

91.3 *Legend on His President's Secret Service.* May 2, 1995. GS: Fionnula Flanagan, G.W. Bailey, Ken Jenkins, Leah Lail, Alan Brooks. Pratt must thwart a plot to assassinate President Ulysses S. Grant hatched by a group of Texans unhappy with the outcome of the Civil War.

91.4 *Custer's Next to Last Stand.* May 9, 1995. GS: Alex Hyde-White, Ashley Lawrence, Richard Cox, Ted Parks, Pato Hoffman, Fritz Sperberg. While a mysterious figure from his past stalks him, Pratt helps General Custer expose corruption inside the War Department.

91.5 *The Life, Death, and Life of Wild Bill Hickok.* May 16, 1995. GS: John Pyper-Ferguson, Debbie James, William Russ, Clark Ray, Ed Adams, Mike Faherty, Adam Beech. Having lost much of his eyesight and confidence, Wild Bill Hickok enlists the help of Legend in bringing down a band of train robbers.

91.6 *Knee-High Noon.* May 23, 1995. GS: Andrew Hill Newman, Mary-Margaret Humes, Michael Patrick Carter, Ray McKinnon, Courtney Gains, Don Collier, Dick Bellerue, Harlan Knudson. An aggressive stage mother manipulates Pratt into promoting the career of her bratty son, who fancies the role of Legend Junior. Meanwhile, Pratt investigates a pair of cattle rustlers.

91.7 *The Gospel According to Legend.* June 12, 1995. GS: Robert Englund, Tim Considine, Phillip Connery, Hamilton Mitchell, Tina Peeler, Brendan Kinkade. A preacher encourages the townspeople to reject Bartok's scientific experiments as the devil's work, but his motives are less than divine.

91.8 *Bone of Contention.* June 20, 1995. GS: Beth Toussaint, Patrick Kilpatrick, Douglas Rowe, Bruce Gray, Ana Auther, Robert Toeves. Bartok and Pratt suspect a petroleum company is behind a paleontologist's murder, and things get slippery when someone steals their only clue — a bag of valuable dinosaur bones.

91.9 *Revenge of the Herd.* July 4, 1995. GS: Rodney A. Grant, Bob Balaban, Reiner Schone, Christian Arin, John Chappell, Deryle Lunan, Mike Casper, Dick Bellerue. Pratt and Bartok concoct a scheme to stop a German hunting party from slaughtering a buffalo herd prized by an Arapaho Indian tribe.

91.10 *Fall of a Legend.* July 18, 1995. GS: Douglas Rowe, Andrew Hill Newman, Lisa Akey, John Dennis Johnston, Michael Ruud, Hamilton Mitchell, Dick Bellerue. Pratt ends up on a sheriff's most wanted list after he is erroneously incriminated in a murder and finds there is no safe place when everyone knows his face.

91.11 *Clueless in San Francisco.* July 25, 1995. GS: Molly Hagan, Janis Paige, Patty Maloney, James Hong. Pratt goes home to San Francisco to help a woman who was raised by Indians find her biological parents, but some folks there would prefer she didn't succeed in her search.

91.12 *Skeletons in the Closet.* Aug. 8, 1995. A skeleton wearing an Aztec ring awakens Ramos' sense of Mexican heritage, sending him on a search for the killer that leads to a town full of racial discord.

92. *The Legend of Jesse James*

ABC. 30 min. Broadcast history: Monday, 8:30–9:00, Sept. 1965–Sept. 1966.

Regular Cast: Christopher Jones (Jesse James), Allen Case (Frank James), Ann Doran (Mrs. James), Robert J. Wilke (Sam Corbett), John Milford (Cole Younger), Tim McIntire (Bob Younger).

Premise: This series, set in Missouri in the 1860s, related the exploits of Frank and Jesse James, who embark on a life of crime after their mother is killed when she refuses to sell their land to the railroad.

The Episodes

92.1 *Three Men from Now.* Sept. 13, 1965. GS: Jack Elam, Virginia Gregg, Robert McQueeney, Bob Random, Buff Brady, David Carlile. An outlaw called the Deacon disobeys Jesse's orders and holds up the bank in St. Joseph, killing the sheriff in cold blood.

92.2 *The Dead Man's Hand.* Sept. 20, 1965. GS: Lloyd Bochner, Buck Taylor, Susan Lee Albert, William Phipps, John Mitchum, Richard Travis. A young farmer is beaten and robbed after winning heavily in a poker game.

92.3 *Put Me in Touch with Jesse.* Sept. 27, 1965. GS: Michael Anderson, Jr., Tom Fadden, Roy Sickner. Young railroad employee Cass Pritchard wants to contact his hero Jesse. Pritchard has information about a gold shipment that should interest the outlaw.

92.4 *The Pursuers.* Oct. 11, 1965. GS: Eddie Firestone, Willard Sage, Ayllene Gibbons, Dennis Cross, Kathleen O'Malley, Joe McGuinn, Rory Stevens. Bandits posing as the James gang hold up a bank and run down a woman as they make their getaway.

92.5 *The Raiders.* Oct. 18, 1965. GS: Peter Whitney, Warren Vanders, Carol Brewster. Jesse and Frank ride into a town that has been taken over by William Clarke Quantrill, a former Confederate guerrilla leader who has become an outlaw.

92.6 *Vendetta.* Oct. 25, 1966. GS: Gene Evans, James Anderson, Lyle Talbot. Convict Jake Burnett, who once rode with the James boys, has been promised money and a pardon to help trap Jesse.

92.7 *The Quest.* Nov. 1, 1965. GS: John Cassavetes, Marie Windsor, Chanin Hale, Tris Coffin, Richard H. Cutting, Joe Higgins. Tired of being continually hunted, Jesse says farewell to Frank and heads for California, where he hopes he is not so well known.

92.8 *The Judas Boot.* Nov. 8, 1965. GS: Zalman King, Richard Reeves, John Dennis, Rusty Westcoatt. Jesse and his men are getting low on money and luck. An ambush awaits them everytime they pull a job.

92.9 *Jail Break.* Nov. 15, 1965. GS: Royal Dano, Don Haggerty. Jesse's brother Frank is wounded, tired of being hunted, and determined to give himself up.

92.10 *One Too Many Mornings.* Nov. 22, 1965. GS: Douglas Kennedy, Edith Atwater, Dal Jenkins, Lawrence Mann. After robbing a Union Army paymaster, the James boys seek refuge at the farm of an old and trusted friend.

92.11 *Manhunt.* Nov. 29, 1965. GS: Zeme North, John Marley, Woodrow Parfrey, Douglas Kennedy, Edith Atwater. Jesse and Frank turn in their guns, but certain railroad workers still have a score to settle with them.

92.12 *The Celebrity.* Dec. 6, 1965. GS: Jan Merlin, Merrie Spaeth, Harry Carey, Jr., Ken Mayer, Shug Fisher, Guy Wilkerson. Jesse rides into a town where a man in the saloon is claiming to be Jesse, and has so fascinated young Ellie Lou Kane that she has made up her mind to become Mrs. Jesse James.

92.13 *The Man Who Was.* Dec. 13, 1965. GS: Robert F. Simon. Jesse and Frank are taken prisoner by a Chicago detective who was brought up by the James brothers uncle, and is a wanted criminal.

92.14 *The Widow Fay.* Dec. 20, 1965. GS Ann Sothern, Stanley Adams, Robert Osterloh. Fleeing a posse, Jesse arrives at the farm of the Widow Fay who thinks Jesse is her missing son.

92.15 *The Man Who Killed Jesse.* Dec. 27, 1965. GS: Alvy Moore, Tom Tully, Del Monroe, Charles Seel. Jesse returns home and learns that everyone thought he was dead and that brother Frank has set out after his alleged killer.

92.16 *The Empty Town.* Jan. 3, 1966. GS: Nehemiah Persoff, Miriam Colon, Mike DeAnda. Jesse and Frank enter a Mexican town that appears to be all set for a fiesta, but is also deserted.

92.17 *Reunion.* Jan. 10, 1966. GS: Susan Strasberg, Gary Lockwood, Christopher Dark. Badly wounded, Jesse seeks refuge at the home of an old girl friend, whose husband is a member of the posse that is searching for Jesse.

92.18 *The Colt.* Jan. 17, 1966. GS: Claude Akins, Kurt Russell. Jesse and Frank are trying to outrun a posse, so Frank objects when Jesse stops to admire, and buy, a handsome colt.

92.19 *A Real Tough Town.* Jan. 24, 1966. GS: Paul Hartman, Gregg Palmer, Emile Meyer, Thom Carney, Don Eitner, David Fresco, Al Dunlap, Tim Donnelly, Eva Monty. Jesse and Frank, seeking peace and quiet, ride into a town that is being torn up by a gang of cowboys.

92.20 *Return to Lawrence.* Jan. 31, 1966. GS: George Kennedy, Jean Hale, Strother Martin. To inform a gang member's wife of her husband's death, Jesse travels to Lawrence, Kansas, site of the Civil War attack by Quantrill's Raiders, with whom Jesse once rode.

92.21 *The Cave.* Feb. 7, 1966. GS: Richard Chambers, Robert Yuro, Peter Helm, Lou Procopio, Claude R. Casey. Jesse and a wounded Frank are holed up in a cave by a posse that is combing the surrounding countryside.

92.22 South Wind. Feb. 14, 1966. GS: Warren Stevens, Dennis Hopper, Whitney Blake, Mickey Shaughnessy, J. Pat O'Malley, David Richard, Armand Alzamora, Dean Smith. The James gang has plans for the bank in Laprairie, where the only lawman is a one-armed sheriff who doesn't carry a gun.

92.23 The Lonely Place. Feb. 21, 1966. GS: Albert Salmi, Sally Kellerman, Alan Baxter, Sondra Kerr. Jesse has been captured at Paul Mason's ranch by Sheriff Pat Davis. The outlaw figures that his one chance for freedom lies in getting Davis and Mason to argue over the reward money.

92.24 Benjamin Bates. Feb. 28, 1966. GS: Liam Sullivan, Hank Patterson, Duncan McLeod, Robert G. Anderson, Mike Ragan, Jennifer Reilly, Patrick Creamer. Benjamin Bates seems to be a harmless little soul, but underneath his cherubic exterior lies a cold-blooded bounty hunter who has made Jesse his next target.

92.25 The Chase. March 7, 1966. GS: Charles Bronson. A sadistic bounty hunter named Cheyney is stalking Jesse, and he is determined to make the outlaw suffer before killing him.

92.26 Things Don't Just Happen. March 14, 1966. GS: Victor Jory, Vaughn Taylor, Regis Toomey, Kevin O'Neil, Sydney Smith, Jan Peters. Jesse's kindness to orphan Jimmy Andrews results in the boy's being shot and accused of being a member of the James gang.

92.27 As Far As the Sea. March 21, 1966. GS: John Carradine, David Richards, Todd Martin. The James gang is being hunted by a strange adversary, an old seaman named Noah, armed with a harpoon, who wants to get back the whaler's talisman Cole Younger stole during a stagecoach robbery.

92.28 1863. March 28, 1966. GS: John Howard, Rex Holman, Don "Red" Barry, J. Edward McKinley. Angered by what Eastern reporter Jason Smith has written about him, Jesse corners Smith on a train and tells his version of how he got started on a life of crime.

92.29 The Last Stand of Captain Hammel. April 4, 1966. GS: Joseph Wiseman, Richard Cutting. Seeking refuge from the law in what they believe to be an abandoned Union fort, Jesse and Frank are taken prisoner by a demented Army captain whose outfit was massacred by Quantrill's Raiders.

92.30 The Hunted and the Hunters. April 11, 1966. GS: Glenn Corbett, John Anderson, Ted Jacques. Jesse and Frank are being pursued by a posse which includes the kin of a boy Jesse killed.

92.31 Dark Side of the Moon. April 18, 1966. GS: Robert Doyle, Kevin Tate, Ann Williams, Barry Cahill, David Richards, Christopher Milo, David Perna. Jesse loses his sight after being shot by an unknown assailant.

92.32 A Field of Wild Flowers. April 25, 1966. GS: Jeffrey Hunter, Michael Burns, Harold J. Stone, Chuck Courtney. An old friend of Jesse and Frank who is now a lieutenant in the Union Army brings word that the Army wants to meet with the boys to discuss an amnesty.

92.33 Wanted: Dead and Only. May 2, 1966. GS: Slim Pickens, Kelly Thordsen, E.J. Andre, John McLiam, Kay Stewart. Marshal Corbett is shot while reading a wanted poster that calls for the death of Corbett and two other men. The signatures at the bottom of the poster are Jesse and Frank James.

92.34 A Burying for Rosey. May 9, 1966. GS: Kevin McCarthy, Mariette Hartley, Pamelyn Ferdin, Walter Burke, Harry Swoger. Jesse promises young Rosey Bryant that he will deliver a letter to her father, an old friend who is about to be hanged.

93. The Life and Legend of Wyatt Earp

ABC. 30 min. Broadcast history: Tuesday, 8:30–9:00, Sept. 1955–Sept. 1961.

Regular Cast: Hugh O'Brian (Wyatt Earp), Douglas Fowley (Doc Holliday) 57-61, Myron Healey (Doc Holliday) 58-59, Morgan Woodward (Shotgun Gibbs) 58-61, Alan Dinehart III (Bat Masterson) 55-59, Ralph Sanford (Mayor Jim "Dog" Kelley) 58-59, Paul Brinegar (Mayor Jim "Dog" Kelley) 56-58, Dirk London (Morgan Earp) 58-61, John Anderson (Virgil Earp) 58-61, Ross Elliott (Virgil Earp) 1959, Douglas V. Fowley (Doc Fabrique) 55-56, Randy Stuart (Nellie Cashman) 59-60, Carol Stone (Kate Holliday) 57-58, Stacy Harris (Mayor John Clum) 60-61, Lash LaRue (Sheriff John Behan) 1959, Steve Brodie (Sheriff John Behan) 59-61, Trevor Bardette (Old Man Clanton) 59-61, Carol Thurston (Emma Clanton) 59-60, Steve Rowland (Phin Clanton) 59-61, John Milford (Ike Clanton) 59-61, Rayford Barnes (Ike Clanton) 59-61, Damian O'Flynn (Judge Tobin) 56-59, Damian O'Flynn (Dr. Goodfellow) 59-61, James Seay (Judge Spicer) 59-61, Britt Lomond (Johnny Ringo) 60-61, William Phipps (Curly Bill Brocius) 59-61, William Tannen (Deputy Harold Norton) 57-58, Don Haggerty (Marsh Murdock) 55-56, Rodd Redwing (Mr. Brother) 56-57, Rico Alaniz (Mr. Cousin) 56-59, Denver Pyle (Ben Thompson) 55-56, Margaret Hayes (Dora Hand) 55-56, Norman Alden (Johnny Ringo) 1961.

Premise: This series related the exploits of U.S. Marshal Wyatt Earp as he strived to enforce the law in Dodge City and Tombstone in the 1870s.

The Episodes

93.1 Mr. Earp Becomes a Marshal. Sept. 6, 1955. GS: Marshall Bradford, Gloria Talbott, Alan Dinehart III, Hal Baylor, Denver Pyle, Richard Travis, Howard Wright, Arthur Space, Don C. Harvey, Robert Spencer, Dabbs Greer, Phil Chambers. A gunman comes gunning for Earp, who exposed his crooked card game. But the killer's bullet strikes down Earp's pal, Sheriff Whitney. Earp then accepts the marshal's badge he turned down earlier.

93.2 Mr. Earp Meets a Lady. Sept. 13, 1955. GS: Gloria Talbott, Alan Dinehart III, Denver Pyle, Hal Baylor, Richard Travis, Kim Dibbs. Earp is disturbed because Marshal Bat Masterson has fallen for a lady Earp knows is the girl friend of a notorious outlaw. Earp bans all guns in Ellsworth in an effort to find the lady's boy friend.

93.3 Bill Thompson Gives In. Sept. 20, 1955. GS: Hal Baylor, Denver Pyle, Alan Dinehart III, Richard Travis, Kim Dibbs, Rodd Redwing, Rico Alaniz. The angry townspeople insist that Marshal Earp form a posse to find killer Bill Thompson. Earp fears that this will cause needless slaughter. He wants to use Indian scouts to track Thompson down.

93.4 *Marshal Earp Meets General Lee.* Sept. 27, 1955. GS: Alan Dinehart III, Don Haggerty, Emlen Davies. The famous frontier marshal eases post-war tensions after the Civil War. Texas cowboys decide that Gen. Lee has been insulted by the townspeople of Ellsworth, Kansas. Earp is afraid that bloodshed will result.

93.5 *Marshal Earp's Romance* (A.K.A. "Wyatt Earp Comes to Wichita"). Oct. 4, 1955. GS: Colette Lyons. A local dancehall queen falls into disfavor with some dangerous outlaws because of a favor she granted Wyatt Earp. But no one wants to argue with the fast-drawing marshal when he lets it be known the woman is his girl friend.

93.6 *The Man Who Lied.* Oct. 11, 1955. GS: Rick Vallin, House Peters, Jr., Don Haggerty, Douglas Fowley. Marshal Earp finds himself the target of a gunman in need of cash when outlaws put a price on his head.

93.7 *The Gambler.* Oct. 18, 1955. GS: William Bryant, J.P. O'Donnell, House Peters, Jr. A young southern Confederate veteran is conned into a crooked roulette game with the aid of a pretty dance-hall girl.

93.8 *The Killer.* Oct. 25, 1955. GS: House Peters, Jr., Don Haggerty, Claire Carleton, Lane Bradford, Robert Bray. Marshal Earp orders a crooked gambler to leave town. The man plans revenge by hiring an assassin to kill the law man.

93.9 *John Wesley Hardin.* Nov. 1, 1955. GS: Phillip Pine, Barbara Bestar. One of the West's most vicious killers seeks revenge for a cousin whom Wyatt Earp had beaten in a fight.

93.10 *The Bank Robbers.* Nov. 8, 1955. GS: Rita Lynn, Leonard Penn, Robert Lowery, Douglas Fowley. A band of desperadoes decide to pull off a robbery without giving its wounded leader any part of the loot. When the leader's wife discovers the plot, she reports it to Wyatt Earp.

93.11 *King of the Cattle Trails.* Nov. 15, 1955. GS: Roy Roberts, Lynne Roberts, Don Haggerty. A wealthy gambler tries every means to get Wyatt Earp to join forces with him. The gambler even imports a beautiful lady from Kansas City to entreat the reluctant Earp.

93.12 *The Big Baby Contest.* Nov. 22, 1955. GS: Michael Connors, Carleton Young, Douglas Fowley. Questionable rules and ingenious gamblers make it difficult for Marshal Earp to conduct a local contest.

93.13 *Frontier Journalism Was Fearless.* Nov. 29, 1955. GS: Don Haggerty. Gamblers contrive a scheme to control the mayor's office and so get rid of Marshal Wyatt Earp. An honest newspaperman is threatened when he backs Earp.

93.14 *Trail's End for a Cowboy.* Dec. 6, 1955. GS: Tommy Cook, Morris Ankrum, George Eldredge, Tristram Coffin, Bob Steele, Hal Girard, George J. Lewis. Fear of his domineering father leads a cowboy into trouble when he loses money gambling. In order to gain back the money he has lost, the rash cowpoke tries to take the law into his own hands.

93.15 *Rich Man's Son.* Dec. 13, 1955. GS: Lee Erickson, Roy Barcroft, Bob Steele, Don Haggerty, Sam Flint. The son of a rich Chicago tycoon causes trouble when he runs away. Two railroad detectives arrive in Wichita searching for the rebellious teenager.

93.16 *The Buntline Special.* Dec. 20, 1955. GS: Lloyd Corrigan, Don Haggerty, Douglas Fowley. Famed showman Ned Buntline tries to sign up Wyatt Earp for a Wild West Show. The Marshal jails Buntline instead, for carrying an oversized pistol.

93.17 *Ben Thompson Returns.* Dec. 27, 1955. GS: Denver Pyle, Don Haggerty, Douglas Fowley. A troublesome outlaw surprises Earp by joining forces with the law. Because Earp had once treated him fairly, Thompson lends a hand in saving the marshal's life.

93.18 *Marshal Earp Plays Cupid.* Jan. 3, 1956. Howard Negley, Jan Shepard, Gordon Jones, Don Haggerty, Douglas Fowley. Earp encourages a romance in a very unusual manner. He fakes a killing in order to protect a young cowboy from real killers.

93.19 *The Assassins.* Jan. 10, 1956. GS: Dirk London, Ray Montgomery, Harry Lauter. Miffed because Marshal Earp has been making trouble for them, gamblers put a price on his head. Things, do not turn out as planed, however, when the hired killers arrive in Wichita and turn out to be Wyatt's brothers.

93.20 *It's a Wise Calf.* Jan. 17, 1956. GS: Bill Henry, Marvin Press, Tom Brown. When an innocent man faces lynching as a rustler Marshal Earp applies the old law of nature that a cow will ignore a calf not her own.

93.21 *Mr. Cousin and Mr. Brother.* Jan. 24, 1956. GS: Rico Alaniz, Rodd Redwing, Don Haggerty, Douglas Fowley. Earp goes on the trail of smugglers who are supplying illegal arms to the Indians. Earp enlists the aid of two friendly Indians and disguises himself as a traveling medicine man.

93.22 *The Bribe.* Jan. 31, 1956. GS: Colette Lyons, Douglas Fowley, Don Haggerty. A deputy who accepts a bribe in gold from a gambler, also accepts the job of doing away with Wyatt Earp.

93.23 *The Frontier Theatre.* Feb. 7, 1956. GS: Mark Dana, Angela Greene, Joan Freeman, Glenn Strange, Don Haggerty. Irked because Wyatt Earp closed down his peep show, the impresario tries to force the shutdown of the performance at Wichita's legitimate theater.

93.24 *Killing at Cowskin Creek.* Feb. 14, 1956. GS: Henry Rowland, Mike Ragan, Robert Nichols, Alan Wells. With the help of a courageous volunteer who is willing to risk his life, Wyatt Earp combats a group of robbers who are plotting to steal the winnings from lucky cowboys who beat the gambling games in Wichita.

93.25 *The Englishman.* Feb. 21, 1956. Don C. Harvey, Michael Emmett, Julie Van Zandt, Louise Arthur. An outlaw uses a visiting Britisher as the target for a swindle racket and plans to get rid of Wyatt Earp as well.

93.26 *The Desperate Half-Hour.* Feb. 28, 1956. GS: Trevor Bardette, Barry Truex, Elizabeth Harrower, George Chandler, Ken Christy. Wyatt Earp steps in to stop the lynching of a teenage boy accused of murder. The real culprits are urging the mob on in order to throw suspicion off themselves.

93.27 *The Necktie Party.* March 6, 1956. A man actually responsible for a horse theft tries to throw the blame on a band of roving Gypsies.

93.28 *One of Jesse's Gang.* March 13, 1956. GS: John Craven, Angie Dickinson, Grady Sutton, Roy Kellogg. A man thought to be a respectable citizen of Wichita is discovered to be a one-time outlaw.

93.29 *The Pinkertons.* March 20, 1956. GS: Douglas Evans, Michael Garrett, Tom Monroe, Sam Flint. Allan Pinkerton, well-known railroad detective, clashes with Earp over the latter's method of recovering the loot from a train robbery and apprehending the thieves. The difference of opinion costs Earp his badge and his job if only temporarily.

93.30 *The Suffragette.* March 27, 1956. GS: Linda Stirling, Howard Wendell, Douglas Fowley, Don Haggerty. Wyatt Earp takes his life in his hands when he comes between two opposing factions in the matter of women's suffrage.

93.31 *Hunt the Man Down.* April 3, 1956. GS: Walter Reed, Rico Alaniz, Douglas Fowley, Ray Kellogg, Carleton Young, Gregg Barton. In a dangerous cat-and-mouse game, Wyatt Earp trails a wanted man into rugged terrain, only to find himself the object of the hunt.

93.32 *The War of the Colonels.* April 10, 1956. GS: Pamela Duncan, Forrest Taylor, Stanley Andrews, Harry Harvey. When a range war seems dangerously imminent, Wyatt Earp finds it necessary to make mass arrests of cowboys carrying guns on the streets of Wichita.

93.33 *Bat Masterson Again.* April 17, 1956. GS: Alan Dinehart III, Jean Willes, Peter Adams. Masterson is upset when he learns a desperado is bent on taking his girl away from him. But Earp teaches Bat a few gun tricks he can use to show up his rival.

Season Two

93.34 *Wichita Is Civilized.* Aug. 18, 1956. GS: Alan Dinehart III, Ralph Sanford, Damian O'Flynn, Walter Coy, John Vivyan. Just as he is about to leave Wichita to take over as marshal of the new rail center, Dodge City, Earp is confronted by cowhands who make one last attempt to take the law into their own hands.

93.35 *Dodge City Gets a New Marshal.* Sept. 4, 1956. GS: Paul Brinegar, Selmer Jackson. Wyatt Earp goes to Dodge City to take over as the new marshal, and is greeted by a gang of would-be assassins.

93.36 *Fight or Run.* Sept. 11, 1956. GS: Paul Brinegar. Dodge City is being terrorized by cattle owners who use the town as a shipping center. Wyatt Earp backs a town code that will check the cattlemen's power.

93.37 *The Double Life of Dora Hand.* Sept. 18, 195. GS: Margaret Hayes, Paul Brinegar. Dora Hand, who runs a dance-hall during the weeks and sings in the church on Sunday, causes a near-battle between opposing factions in the town.

93.38 *Clay Allison.* Sept. 25, 1956. GS: Myron Healey, Charles Fredericks, Paul Brinegar, William Tannen. Wyatt Earp learns that his arch enemy in Dodge City has hired a gunman to shoot him down. He tracks the gunman to a saloon where he is drinking himself into a killing mood.

93.39 *Wyatt's Love Affair.* Oct. 2, 1956. GS: Nancy Hale, Gordon Richards, Paul Brinegar. Wyatt Earp's desire to get married is thwarted by his sweetheart's father. He convinces Wyatt that a man in his profession shouldn't even consider marriage.

93.40 *A Quiet Day in Dodge City.* Oct. 9, 1956. GS: Brad Morrow, Donald Curtis, Paul Brinegar, Selmer Jackson. Wyatt is anxious to make a good impression on a New York reporter visiting Dodge City. He wants the newsman to take home the idea that the community is a peaceful place to live in.

93.41 *The Almost Dead Cowhand.* Oct. 2, 1956. GS: Christian Drake, Camile Franklin, Sam Flint, Michael Bryant, Ray Kellogg, William Tannen, Wes Hudman. A Texas cowhand decides to take the law into his own hands after his bankroll is taken from him by Dodge City's crooked gamblers.

93.42 *The Reformation of Jim Kelley.* Oct. 30, 1956. GS: Paul Brinegar, Charles Fredericks, Margaret Hayes. An unscrupulous promoter attempts to rid Dodge City of Wyatt Earp by forging his name to the ownership papers of a gambling saloon.

93.43 *So Long, Dora, So Long.* Nov. 13, 1956. GS: Margaret Hayes, Paul Brinegar, Joseph Turkel, William Tannen. Dora Hand is killed by a stray bullet on the eve of her marriage to Jim Kelley. Wyatt Earp resolves to bring in the gunman responsible for her death.

93.44 *Bat Masterson Wins His Star.* Nov. 20, 1956. GS: Alan Dinehart III, George J. Lewis, Kasey Rogers. After applying for a job with Wyatt Earp, hot-tempered Bat Masterson gets himself into a shooting scrape. In an attempt to vindicate himself, Bat tries to help in solving a Santa Fe holdup.

93.45 *The Lonesomest Man in the World.* Nov. 27, 1956. GS: Alan Dinehart III, Helen Gilbert, Selmer Jackson, Charles Martin. Wyatt Earp takes Bat Masterson to task when the trigger-happy young man inadvertently shoots one of the townsmen. To add to Bat's troubles, Bat finds himself a target for revenge by the wounded man's family.

93.46 *Take Back Your Town.* Dec. 4, 1956. GS: Alan Dinehart III, Henry Rowland, William Phipps, Selmer Jackson. When Wyatt Earp rides out of Dodge City in pursuit of an outlaw, Bat Masterson is left alone to face a band of renegades who plan on taking over the town.

93.47 *Nineteen Notches on His Gun.* Dec. 11, 1956. GS: Alan Dinehart III, Gregg Barton, Rick Vallin. In an effort to trap a band of outlaws, Wyatt and Bat Masterson disguise themselves as Texas outlaws.

93.48 *The Hanging Judge.* Dec. 18, 1956. GS: Damian O'Flynn, Lewis Charles, Alan Dinehart III, Hal Gerard, Don C. Harvey, Terry Frost, I. Stanford Jolley, Lou Rhodes. A new judge in Dodge City goes overboard passing out sentences. To teach him a lesson, Earp frames the judge for a crime and puts him on trial.

93.49 *Justice.* Dec. 25, 1956. GS: Alan Dinehart III, Rico Alaniz, Rodd Redwing, John Close, Don Diamond, Keith Richards, Charles Fredericks. The leader of the Cheyennes threatens to take his tribe on the warpath after two white men murder an Indian.

93.50 *Shootin' Woman.* Jan. 1, 1957. GS: Ellen Corby, Bill Baucom, Alan Dinehart III, Mike Ragan, Paul Gary. A frontier woman doesn't trust banks, so she hides a cache of gold nuggets at home. She intends the gold to be her granddaughter's dowry, but robbers have a different idea.

93.51 *The Man Who Rode with Custer.* Jan. 8, 1957. GS: Mauritz Hugo, Bill Pullen, Alan Dinehart III, Emlen Davies, Steve Pendleton. A group of dishonest agents of the Government Indian Bureau plans a new way to make money out of the Indians. Wyatt learns of the plot and intervenes.

93.52 *Wyatt and the Captain.* Jan. 15, 1957. GS: James Seay, Bob Ellis, Harry Harvey, Iron Eyes Cody, Ron Kennedy, Tristram Coffin. Wyatt, intending to give him a civil trial, arrests an Army sergeant who murdered an Indian. The Army intervenes in the person of a battle-fatigued captain, who demands an Army trial for the soldier.

93.53 *Witness for the Defense.* Jan. 22, 1957. GS: William Henry, Denver Pyle, Vici Raaf, William Tannen, Damian O'Flynn. Wyatt's old friend, Ben Thompson, arrives in Dodge City and, as usual, he's in trouble with the law. Ben insists he is innocent of the charges brought against him, and asks Wyatt to be a character witness.

93.54 *The Sharpshooter.* Jan. 29, 1957. GS: Henry Rowland, Trevor Bardette, Elizabeth Harrower, Susan Seaforth. A renegade white man who intends to ransack Dodge City is thwarted by Wyatt Earp. The man then plans a revenge on the sheriff.

93.55 *Siege at Little Alamo.* Feb. 5, 1957. GS: William Phipps, Tom Monroe, Forrest Taylor, Alan Dinehart III, Hank Patterson. The Wells Fargo Company asks Wyatt's help in catching a gang that has been looting its stages.

93.56 *Vengeance Trail.* Feb. 12, 1957. GS: Jan Merlin, William Tannen, Jan England, Charles Evans, Leonard Penn, Michael Vallin. Fred Colby comes to Dodge City, determined to avenge the murder of his brother. Wyatt attempts to stop him, or at least see that he stays within the limits of the law.

93.57 *Command Performance.* Feb. 19, 1957. GS: Ray Kellogg, Steve Rowland, Lloyd Corrigan, Rex Lease, Harry Fleer. Buffalo Bill and Ned Buntline bring a foreign prince to Dodge City, intending to show him the sights of the Wild West.

93.58 *They Hired Some Guns.* Feb. 26, 1957. GS: Lane Chandler, Howard Wendell, Alan Dinehart III, Damian O'Flynn, Aline Towne, Art Millan, Selmer Jackson. Wyatt Earp tries to prevent a shooting war between gunmen hired by rival railroads. Both groups seek possession of Raton Pass.

93.59 *Bat Masterson for Sheriff.* March 3, 1957. GS: Alan Dinehart III, James Lamphier, William Tannen, Jean Howell, Butler Hixon, Syd Saylor, Joseph Waring. Wyatt's friend Bat Masterson runs for sheriff of Ford County, Kansas, at Wyatt's suggestion. As the campaign moves toward a close, Wyatt learns that his sponsorship of Bat is losing the young man votes.

93.60 *Hang 'Em High.* March 12, 1957. GS: Toni Gerry, Darryl Hickman, Alan Dinehart III, Carleton Young. A group of terrorists who call themselves the White Caps frame a young man on a murder charge. Bat Masterson is almost forced into carrying out the sentence.

93.61 *The Vultures.* March 19, 1957. GS: Stacy Harris, Mort Mills, Gordon Clark, Lane Bradford, Helen Warno, Richard Avonde. Dodge City gets two new citizens, both unwanted by Wyatt Earp and the other residents. They new men make their livings by finding and turning in former outlaws who have reformed.

93.62 *Young Guns.* March 26, 1957. GS: Ralph Reed, Frank Fenton, William Tannen, Russell Bender. A teenager who considers himself the best gunman in the area, comes to Wyatt looking for a job. Wyatt turns him down because of his youth, but the young man is determined to work with him anyway.

93.63 *The Nice Ones Always Die First.* April 2, 1957. GS: Brad Johnson, Alan Dinehart III, John Cliff, Zon Murray, John Mitchum. Wyatt hires Bat Masterson's brother Ed as a deputy. Ed's philosophy holds that if they would sit down and talk with outlaws, there would be less trouble in the West.

93.64 *Old Jake.* April 9, 1957. GS: Bob Cunningham, Francis J. McDonald, Ewing Mitchell, George J. Davis, William Tannen, Carol Thurston. An old friend of Wyatt Earp's shows up in Dodge City. He is determined to find his wife's murderer and get even.

93.65 *The Equalizer.* April 16, 1957. GS: Elisha Cook, Jr., John Pickard, Lynne Millan, Paul Brinegar, Phil Schumacher. Wyatt attempts to keep peace between a little guy who wears guns because it makes him feel as big and strong as anybody else, and the town bully, who is always taunting the smaller man about his size.

93.66 *Wyatt Meets Doc Holliday.* April 23, 1957. GS: Douglas Fowley, Don Diamond, Frank Scannel, Carol Stone, John Cason. While tracking down a notorious holdup gang, Wyatt is almost killed. He is saved by gunman, gambler and graduate dentist Doc Holliday.

93.67 *Beautiful Friendship.* April 30, 1957. GS: Douglas Fowley, Paul Brinegar, Dennis Moore, Alan Dinehart III. Wyatt's new friend Doc Holliday gets himself involved in a Dodge City gun battle. Wyatt is forced to throw him into jail, and Doc's wife shows up to get him released.

93.68 *Dull Knife Strikes for Freedom.* May 7, 1957. GS: Ian McDonald, Steve Pendleton, Bill Cassady, George Baxter, Rico Alaniz. The government has restricted a group of Cheyennes led by Dull Knife to a reservation in Oklahoma. But a few of them raid settlers' homes and soon the whole tribe is in trouble with the Government.

93.69 *The Gold Brick.* May 14, 1957. GS: Douglas Fowley. A gold brick from a Wells Fargo stagecoach robbery shows up in Dodge City. Wyatt discovers that Doc Holliday is mixed up in the acquisition of the brick.

93.70 *The Wicked Widow.* May 21, 1957. GS: Paul Dubov, Gloria Saunders, Thomas Palmer, William Tannen, Lyn Guild. A Dodge City dressmaker gets herself involved with a group of outlaws. She refuses to heed Wyatt's warning that this association could lead to her own disaster.

93.71 *They Think They're Immortal.* May 28, 1957. GS: Dirk London, William Phipps, Douglas Fowley, John Pickard, Paul Brinegar. Wyatt's younger brother Morgan arrives in Dodge City looking for a job. The job he has in mind is deputy sheriff, but Wyatt has other ideas.

93.72 *The Time for All Good Men.* June 4, 1957. GS: Richard Devon, Grant Withers, Douglas Fowley, Carol Stone, Alan Dinehart III, Kem Dibbs, Mike Ragan. A group of outlaws traps Wyatt Earp at Adobe Springs. The word is passed that Wyatt is badly in need of help, and a group of men assembles to rescue him.

Season Three

93.73 *Call Me Your Honor.* Sept. 17, 1957. GS: Paul Brinegar, Ralph Sanford, Rex Lease, Steve Dunhill. Dog Kelley, a friend of Wyatt Earp's, decides to run for the office of mayor. The other candidate is backed by gamblers and outlaws who are determined to elect their own man in an effort to get rid of Wyatt.

93.74 *The Big Bellyache.* Sept. 24, 1957. An old friend of Wyatt Earp's, Doc Fabrique, is forced at gunpoint to treat Shanghai Pierce, a crooked cattle baron. Wyatt resents the man and his hired gunslingers.

The Life and Legend of Wyatt Earp

93.75 *Pinkytown.* Oct. 1, 1957. GS: Douglas Fowley. When Dodge City decides to annex nearby Pinkytown in order to tax more citizens, Doc Holliday objects. Wyatt finds himself in a tangle with his old friend.

93.76 *Shoot to Kill.* Oct. 8, 1957. GS: Myron Healey, Douglas Dick, Paul Brinegar, Barbara Bestar. The notorious McAlester Brothers ride into Dodge City. When they start quarreling over a pretty girl, Wyatt Earp intervenes.

93.77 *Wells Fargo vs. Doc Holliday.* Oct. 15, 1957. GS: Douglas Fowley, Carol Stone, Paul Brinegar, Damian O'Flynn. When bandits star robbing the Wells Fargo stagecoaches operating between Dodge City and Hay, Kansas, Wyatt's good friend Doc Holliday is suspected of being a gang member.

93.78 *Warpath.* Oct. 22, 1957. GS: Donald Murphy, Monte Blue, Michael Carr, Rico Alaniz, Rodd Redwing. Wyatt steps in when a band of renegades sells several cases of guns to a tribe of Indians. The Army intelligence officers sent in to prevent an Indian uprising find themselves in trouble.

93.79 *Hung Jury.* Oct. 29, 1957. GS: Holly Harris, Jonathan Hole, Hal Gerard, Mark Dana. A well-known rancher is murdered, and Wyatt Earp conducts an investigation. He is soon faced with the prospect of arresting one of Dodge City's leading citizens as a suspect.

93.80 *Little Pistol.* Nov. 5, 1957. GS: Carol Stone, Tina Thompson, Douglas Fowley, Glenn Strange, Glenn Turnbull. Susan Leonard, a legendary female bandit, arouses unexpected parental instincts in Doc Holliday and his wife.

93.81 *The Magic Puddle.* Nov. 12, 1957. GS: Douglas Fowley, Carol Stone, Paul Brinegar. Wyatt has trouble with his scheming friend Doc Holliday. Oil is discovered on a homestead, and Doc has some not-too-honest ideas for putting it to use.

93.82 *Mr. Buntline's Vacation.* Nov. 19, 1958. GS: Lloyd Corrigan, Robert Lowery, Jim Bannon. Ned Buntline, Wyatt's old friend, arrives in Dodge City and tells him he has given a rubber check to a gambler. When the gambler arrives in town, he professes no knowledge of Buntline.

93.83 *Fortitude.* Nov. 26, 1957. GS: Carol Stone, Douglas Fowley, Paul Brinegar, Bill Henry, Virginia Dale, Damian O'Flynn. Kate Holliday warns Wyatt of a plot to kill him while he speaks at a cattleman's convention. Wyatt goes ahead with the speaking arrangements even though he doesn't know the identity of the would-be killer.

93.84 *The Good and Perfect Gift.* Dec. 3, 1957. GS: Douglas Fowley, Carol Stone, Tiger Fafara, Damian O'Flynn, William Tannen. Doc Holliday is taken aback when a juvenile would-be badman tries to emulate Holliday as a gunslinger. Doc and his wife Kate welcome Wyatt's attempts to straighten out the boy.

93.85 *Indian Wife.* Dec. 10, 1957. GS: Richard Garland, Carol Thurston, Sheb Wooley, Lane Bradford, Rico Alaniz, Rodd Redwing, William Tannen. Dick Melaney, a settler, encounters prejudice when he brings his Indian wife and son to Dodge City. His father-in-law, an Indian chief, refuses to speak to his daughter. Wyatt attempts to help the couple.

93.86 *Woman Trouble.* Dec. 17, 1957. GS: Alan Dinehart III, Nancy Hadley, Rex Lease, Paul Brinegar. From Jennie Brant's hints, Wyatt gets the idea that she would welcome a marriage proposal from him. But he is suspicious, since she reputedly belongs to the True Lighters, and he knows that this religious sect doesn't advocate matrimony.

93.87 *Shadow of a Man.* Dec. 24, 1957. GS: William Tannen, Alan Dinehart III. Hal Norton, successor to Wyatt's deputy Bat Masterson, faces a crisis when he is left in charge at Dodge City.

93.88 *Bad Woman.* Dec. 31, 1957. GS: Fay Baker, Don Hayden, Christian Drake, Paul Brinegar, William Tannen, Damian O'Flynn. Wyatt faces the wrath of a woman outlaw, Marie Burden, when he prevents her from staging a holdup in Dodge City.

93.89 *One-Man Army.* Jan. 7, 1958. GS: Bob Anderson, Sue George, Mauritz Hugo, Fred Sherman, Paul Brinegar, William Tannen, Bill Phipps. A Dodge City newspaper prints libelous material about Wyatt Earp. The editor hopes to blacken Earp's name and drive him out of office.

93.90 *The General's Lady.* Jan. 14, 1958. GS: Dorothy Green, Robert Carson, Bob Hopkins, Bing Russell, John Goddard, Joseph Vitale, William Tannen. Wyatt Earp tries to convince the widow of Gen. Custer that despite his faults, Custer was a courageous man.

93.91 *The Manly Art.* Jan. 21, 1958. GS: Alan Dinehart III, Ed Hinton, Tom Brown, Morgan Woodward, Ron Haggerthy, Roy Barcroft. Wyatt is goaded by his enemies to fight a traveling boxer. Wyatt doesn't want to fight, but he also doesn't want to look like a coward.

93.92 *Sweet Revenge.* Jan. 28, 1958. GS: Marjorie Owens, John Marshall, William Challee, Robert Patton. A man and a woman slip into Dodge City on a mission to shoot Wyatt Earp. Wyatt disarms the woman, but the man escapes and begins stalking him.

93.93 *The Imitation Jesse James.* Feb. 4, 1958. GS: Keith Richards, Fred Sherman, Bud Osborne, Sam Flint. A stage robber's unique method of operation makes it difficult for Earp to trap him.

93.94 *The Kansas Lily.* Feb. 11, 1958. GS: Peggy Knudsen, Zon Murray, Craig Duncan, Alan Dinehart III. A former lady spy for the Confederate Army seeks refuge in Dodge City and warns Wyatt Earp that his life is in danger.

93.95 *Wyatt Earp Rides Shotgun.* Feb. 18, 1958. GS: Isabelle Randolph, Harry Fleer, Tom Monroe, William Tannen, Alan Dinehart III, Will J. White, Don Kennedy. Wyatt Earp returns to his old job with an express company to stop the raids by a band of outlaws.

93.96 *Wyatt Fights.* Feb. 25, 1958. GS: Grant Richards, Damian O'Flynn, Alan Dinehart III, Leonard Penn. Wyatt faces a difficult decision when two saloon groups begin quarreling violently. He has to explain to the townspeople that he can't intervene in the quarrel until an actual crime is committed.

93.97 *Ballad and Truth.* March 4, 1958. GS: Mike Ragan, Henry Rowland, Frank Wilcox, Tyler McVey, Ralph Sanford, George Baster. Wyatt Earp is inadvertently drawn into a feud between cattlemen and railroad men. He ultimately finds himself defending an outlaw's right.

93.98 *The Schoolteacher.* March 11, 1958. GS: Virginia Core, Rico Alaniz, Bill Cassady, Douglas Dick, William Bryant. A stagecoach is robbed, and the driver ruthlessly slain. Wyatt Earp makes a special effort to find the murderer because of the grief of the victim's fiancee.

93.99 *When Sherman Marched Through Kansas.* March 18, 1958. GS: Thayer Roberts, Brad Morrow, Tyler McVey, Sally Hughes. Now commander of the Western Armies in Indian territory, Gen. Sherman plans a visit to the post at Dodge. When news of his arrival precedes him, Wyatt discovers he must contend with a small army of newspapermen and local dignitaries who want to see the General.

93.100 *Big Brother Virgil.* March 25, 1958. GS: John Anderson, Joanna Hayes, Michael Emmet, Alan Dinehart, Marc Platt. Susan Dodd arrives in Dodge City shortly after her divorce. Her fiance, Larry Herrick, accompanies her. When Susan's relatives send friends to check on her romance they get the impression that Wyatt's brother Virgil is courting her.

93.101 *It Had to Happen.* April 1, 1958. GS: Alan Dinehart III, Paul Brinegar, Marjorie Stapp, William Tannen, Alan Wells. Wyatt Earp is taunted into a gunfight by a cowboy. Unable to keep to his usual code of only wounding a man, Earp is forced to shoot to kill.

93.102 *County Seat War.* April 8, 1958. GS: Carolyn Craig, Paul Brinegar, Frank Scannell, Ralph Peters. Marshal Earp finds himself in the middle of an argument when local politician begin battling for authority. In the midst of the confusion a young lady arrives in town who fancies herself in love with Wyatt.

93.103 *One.* April 15, 1958. GS: Rico Alaniz, Hal Baylor, Tommy Cook, Alan Dinehart III, Walter Maslow, William Tannen, Rodd Redwing, Hank Patterson. In the first of a four-part story, Wyatt's two good Indian friends Mr. Cousin and Mr. Brother are ambushed by four men. Mr. Brother is killed and Wyatt swears vengeance against the murderers.

93.104 *The Underdog.* April 22, 1958. GS: Myron Healey, Brad Johnson, Peggy Stewart, Fay Roope, Dennis Moore, John Cliff. A young artist falls in love with a girl whose family objects to the romance. Later, he is accused of a murder and he tries to prove his innocence.

93.105 *Two.* April 29, 1958. GS: Walter Maslow, Tommy Cook, Alan Dinehart III, Hal Baylor, Stuart Randall. In the second of a four-part series Wyatt searches for three of the men who ambushed his Indian friends. He runs into complications when an eager-beaver Army lieutenant tries to help.

93.106 *Doc Holliday Rewrites History.* May 6, 1958. GS: Myron Healey, Robert Nichols, Paul Brinegar, Damian O'Flynn. A county historian runs afoul of Doc Holliday when he arrives to do research on local celebrities. Wyatt steps in to prevent the historian from ending up at Boot Hill.

93.107 *Three.* May 13, 1958. G: Rico Alaniz, Michael Carr, Tommy Cook, Walter Maslow, Alan Dinehart III, Hal Baylor, Morgan Woodward. In the third of a four-part series, Marshal Earp has tracked down two of the three men responsible for the ambush killing of one of his Indian friends. On the trail of number three, he calls on the Texas Rangers for help when the renegade takes refuge in their territory.

93.108 *Dig a Grave for Ben Thompson.* May 20, 1958. GS: Denver Pyle, Myron Healey, Adele Mara, Lorna Thayer, Paul Brinegar, Paul Fierro. Wyatt's friend Ben Thompson comes to Dodge City to hide from two women who claim they are in love with him. Not knowing what to do about the women, Ben appeals to Doc Holliday, who offers an unusual solution.

93.109 *Four.* May 27, 1958. GS: Stuart Randall, Trevor Bardette, Shawn Smith, Alan Dinehart III, Rico Alaniz, Michael Carr. In the conclusion of a four-part series Wyatt Earp travels to Texas to capture the last of the men who ambushed and killed one of his Indian friends. When he arrives in Texas, Earp finds that the outlaw is holed up in a ranch, protected by some friends.

93.110 *The Frame-Up.* June 3, 1958. GS: Myron Healey, Peter Mamakos, Gregg Barton, John Hubbard, Paul Brinegar, Damian O'Flynn. When Wyatt Earp's saddle bags are found to be loaded with money, the town believes that he has been taking bribes. Doc Holliday is the only one of Wyatt's friends who believes that he is innocent.

93.111 *My Husband.* June 10, 1958. GS: Myron Healey, Carol Stone, Paul Brinegar, Damian O'Flynn. Mayor Kelley and Judge Tobin become concerned about Wyatt's friendship with the dissolute Doc Holliday. They decide to persuade Kate Holliday to leave Dodge City and take Doc with her.

Season Four

93.112 *The Hole Up.* Sept. 16, 1958. GS: Morgan Woodward, Walter Maslow, Ralph Sanford, Bill Henry. In an attempt to track down Blackie Sanders, a sadistic gunman and robber, Marshal Wyatt Earp assumes the identity of a wanted outlaw and enters Brown's Hole, the favorite hideout of outlaws.

93.113 *The Peacemaker.* Sept. 23, 1958. GS: Morgan Woodward, William Phipps, Donald Murphy, Walter Maslow, Damian O'Flynn, Bill Baucom, Bill Catching. When Wyatt Earp is out of town on a special assignment, a gang of hoodlums, headed by Curly Brocius and Johnny Ringgold, attacks Dodge City. With Earp gone, the townspeople look to peace-loving frontiersman Shotgun Gibbs for leadership.

93.114 *The Bounty Killer.* Sept. 30, 1958. GS: Ashley Cowan, Steve Pendleton, Trevor Bardette, Jean G. Harvey, Hal Baylor, Roy Barcroft. Wyatt is called to Fort Lewis by his Army buddy, Col. Benteen, to help track down a murderer who has killed nine men. Wyatt is forced to deputize several notorious outlaws in his efforts to find the killer.

93.115 *Caught by a Whisker.* Oct. 7, 1958. GS: Morgan Woodward, Paul Dubov, Christian Drake, Hal H. Thompson, Lester Dorr, Sam Flint. Half-brothers Matt and Clint Dunbar successfully rob the state national bank, and make off with a large sum. Because their careful plot makes immediate identification impossible, Wyatt Earp resorts to unorthodox methods in an attempt to capture the robbers.

93.116 *The Mysterious Cowhand.* Oct. 14, 1958. GS: Morgan Woodward, Tom London, Robert Anderson, Frank Scannell, Don C. Harvey, Burt Nelson. When Wyatt Earp's cousin, U.S. Marshal Nate Strathearn, is killed, Earp disguises himself as a cowhand and joins a cattle outfit in an attempt to track down Nate's killer. Wyatt suspects the cattle outfit's leader.

93.117 *The Gatling Gun.* Oct. 21, 1958. GS: Richard Garland, Charles Fredericks, Rico Alaniz, William Pullen. Wyatt Earp receives orders from Gen. Sherman sending him on a mission to regain one of the historic Gatling guns which is in the possession of the Nez Perce Indians.

93.118 *Cattle Thieves.* Oct. 28, 1958. GS: Morgan Woodward, Ralph Sanford, Rex Lease, Dorothy Green, Thomas Palmer. Marshal Earp's attempts to strengthen the laws against cattle rustling are nearly thwarted when it's discovered that the mule belonging to his chief deputy was itself stolen.

93.119 *Remittance Man.* Nov. 4, 1958. GS: Michael Emmet, Douglas Evans, Judith Ames, Jonathan Hale, Howard Wendell, Buck Sullivan. Jonathan Milton, a young English nobleman, has come to Dodge City and is slowly drinking himself to death. While attempting to help the young man, Wyatt runs into difficulty with a noted gambler.

93.120 *King of the Frontier.* Nov. 11, 1958. GS: Morgan Woodward, Lloyd Corrigan, Ralph Sanford, Harry Fleer, Grant Withers. Wyatt meets his old friend Ned Buntline, and learns that Ned has written a book describing Earp as "King of the Frontier". Because of the flattering endorsement, Wyatt is forced to enter a rodeo and prove he is worthy of Buntline's praise.

93.121 *Truth About Gunfighting.* Nov. 18, 1958. GS: Morgan Woodward, Ralph Reed, Larry Thoras, James Bannon, Carolyn Craig, Brett King, Terry Frost. A young gunfighter is anxious to become foreman of the ranch where he is working. But a rough gang also working at the ranch is bitterly opposed to him, and repeatedly forces him into gunfights hoping to kill him. Marshal Earp hears about the situation and decides to help the young man.

93.122 *Frontier Woman.* Nov. 25, 1958. GS: Morgan Woodward, Jean Howell, Tom Monroe, Ed Hinton, Carleton Young, Don Dillaway. Marshal Wyatt Earp tries to help beautiful Martha Hildreth after her parents are slain by hoodlums. Martha, in a state of shock, is hiding in a cave, and threatens to kill herself.

93.123 *Santa Fe War.* Dec. 2, 1958. GS: Don Haggerty, Ralph Sanford, John C. Becher, Tyler McVey. The territorial farmers are ready to fight to stop the Western railroad people from expanding. Wyatt Earp travels to Garden City, Kansas, in an attempt to effect a compromise between the bitterly opposed factions.

93.124 *Plague Carrier.* Dec. 9, 1958. GS: Bill Cassady, Phillip Pine, Russ Bender, Larry Blake, Jimmy Noel, George Haywood, Virginia Christine. Marshal Earp is faced with a difficult problem when a smallpox epidemic strikes Dodge City. The only doctor available is a young man who is practicing medicine without the necessary credentials.

93.125 *Kill the Editor.* Dec. 16, 1958. GS: Morgan Woodward, Myron Healey, Ralph Sanford, Robert Patten, Mark Dana, Claire Carleton. Jim Murdock takes over as editor of the Dodge City Glove just at the time Marshal Earp is framed for the murder of a woman dance-hall owner. Wyatt attempts to clear his own name and still maintain a free press.

93.126 *Little Brother.* Dec. 23, 1958. GS: Dirk London, Myron Healey, Morgan Woodward, John Doucette, Collette Lyons, Joe Waring. Morgan Earp, Wyatt's younger brother, pays a visit to Dodge City and becomes embroiled in a scheme of Doc Holliday's to rescue outlaw Smiley Dunlap from the Greg Norton gang.

93.127 *The Reformation of Doc Holliday.* Dec. 30, 1958. GS: Myron Healey, Collette Lyons, Richard Devon, Bill Cassady, Ralph Sanford. To please his wife, Doc Holliday promises to try to reform his character. In an attempt to help his friend, Wyatt Earp becomes Doc's bodyguard.

93.128 *A Good Man.* Jan. 6, 1959. GS: Morgan Woodward, Denver Pyle, Frank Gerstle. Marshal Earp finds himself acting as referee when a new preacher arrives in Dodge City intent on ridding the town of its evil elements.

93.129 *Death for a Stolen Horse.* Jan. 13, 1959. GS: Morgan Woodward, John Milford, Myron Healey, Rico Alaniz, Carol Thurston, Damian O'Flynn. Horse trader Joe Riva and his daughter Helen are accused of stealing horses. To protect father and daughter, Marshal Wyatt Earp is forced to face a lynch-crazy mob.

93.130 *Last Stand at Smoky Hill.* Jan. 20, 1959. GS: Morgan Woodward, Alan Dinehart III, Rico Alaniz, I. Stanford Jolley. Word spreads that a large herd of buffalo is near the Smoky River. Hunters view with Apache Indians for the buffalo pelts and Marshal Wyatt Earp tries to prevent the two forces from fighting.

93.131 *The Muleskinner.* Jan. 27, 1959. GS: Morgan Woodward, Whit Bissell, Francis J. McDonald. Marshal Earp runs into an old friend, Sam McGuffin. Wyatt soon finds it necessary to restrain his friend, who has discovered that one of the men who works for him is a crook.

93.132 *Earp Ain't Even Wearing Guns.* Feb. 3, 1959. GS: Nancy Hale, Charles Evans, Ralph Sanford, Damian O'Flynn, Morgan Woodward, Bill Coontz. Marshal Earp and his deputy, Shotgun Gibbs, try to avoid bloodshed between Confederate sympathizers and Yankees in Dodge City. They decide to set an example by going out without their guns.

93.133 *Bat Jumps the Reservation.* Feb. 10, 1959. GS: Alan Dinehart III, Morgan Woodward, Sally Fraser, Keith Richards, Mae Clarke, Earl Parker. Unable to resist the charms of a lovely lady, Bat Masterson gets embroiled with a crooked mob. Wyatt tries to help his friend.

93.134 *The Truth About Rawhide Geraghty.* Feb. 17, 1959. GS: Eddy Waller, Edith Evanson, John Close, Lane Chandler. Wyatt Earp rides shotgun for Rawhide Geraghty, one of the frontier's greatest stage drivers, on a rough trip through dangerous Indian territory.

93.135 *She Almost Married Wyatt.* Feb. 24, 1959. GS: Ann Daniels, Ralph Sanford, Alan Dinehart III, Rico Alaniz, Bill Cassady, Helen Marr Van Tuyl, Elizabeth Harrower. A young woman, the victim of a recent beating, rides into town. Shocked to learn that the girl is practically a slave to a shiftless family, Marshal Wyatt Earp tries to help her.

93.136 *Horse Race.* March 3, 1959. GS: Stuart Randall, Paul Picerni, Tommy Cook, Morgan Woodward. Wyatt fears trouble when a horse race is scheduled between Milt Canyon's grat stallion and Chief Bullhead's pinto pony.

93.137 *Juveniles—1878.* March 10, 1958. GS: Jack Diamond, Gregg Barton, James Bronte, Ralph Sanford, Morgan Woodward, John Baxter, Robert Carson, Claudia Bryar. Wyatt Earp must contend with a youthful arrival from the East. The young man has a loaded six-gun and some false notions about the Wild West.

93.138 *One Murder—Fifty Suspects.* March 17, 1959. GS: Pamela Duncan, Douglas Fowley, Bill Cassady, Morgan Woodward. Skinner Smith, Dodge City loan shark, is found murdered. The man who disliked, and Marshal Wyatt Earp realizes that many people had motives and opportunities to kill him.

93.139 *How to Be a Sheriff.* March 24, 1959. GS: Morgan Woodward, Rand Brooks, Peggy Stewart, Ralph Sanford. Del Mathey, a likable rancher, is elected to succeed Bat Masterson as sheriff of Ford County, Kansas. He thinks the job is simple until he realizes that Marshal Wyatt Earp's authority doesn't extend beyond the Dodge City limits and that serving summonses is the least of his responsibilities.

93.140 *The Judas Goat.* March 31, 1959. GS: Robert Fuller, Penny Edwards, Buck Young, Damian O'Flynn, Morgan Woodward, Ralph Sanford, Francis De Sales. A deputy United States marshal from Kansas City contrives a scheme aimed at netting him a large Wells Fargo reward. He talks some unemployed cowhands into staging a gold-bullion robbery.

93.141 *Doc Fabrique's Greatest Case.* April 7, 1959. GS: Douglas Fowley, Bill Cassady, Enid Baine, Sam Flint, James Douglas, Freeman Morse, Harry Harvey, Jr., Ashley Cowan, Morgan Woodward. Doc Fabrique comes to Dodge City at the request of Marshal Earp. He finds a most unusual and exasperating case awaiting him.

93.142 *The Actress.* April 14, 1959. GS: Carol Ohmart, Peter Mamakos, Don Megowan, Michael Vallin, Louise Lorimer, Bill Cassady, Morgan Woodward. Cora Campbell, a famous actress, comes to Dodge City. Her visit creates an air of excitement which reaches its climax in murder.

93.143 *Love and Shotgun Gibbs.* April 21, 1959. GS: Morgan Woodward, Barbara Perry, Helene Heigh, Francis De Sales, Bill Cassady, Tom London. Marshal Wyatt Earp is disturbed to hear that his deputy Shotgun Gibbs has fallen victim to the charms of Dodge City's milliner. Wyatt doesn't trust the lady, and he cautions Shotgun.

93.144 *Dodge Is Civilized.* April 28, 1959. GS: Alan Dinehart III, Walter Coy, John Vivyan, Ralph Sanford. Wyatt finds it hard to convince some of his friends that Dodge City has become a reputable town.

93.145 *Little Gray Home in the West.* May 5, 1959. GS: Myron Healey, Randy Stuart, Larry Hudson, William Phipps, Donald Murphy. A successful round of poker rewards Doc Holliday with the dubious prize of a deserted ranch. He and Wyatt Earp go to look it over and discover that it actually isn't deserted.

93.146 *The Cyclone.* May 12, 1959. GS: Sandra Stone, Gordon Wynn, Pauline Drake, Ray Farrell, Morgan Woodward. A cyclone hits Dodge City in 1878, and Marshal Earp must maintain order in a town full of panic-stricken citizens.

93.147 *Kelley Was Irish.* May 19, 1959. GS: Ralph Sanford, Morgan Woodward, Myron Healey, Damian O'Flynn. Mayor Kelley and Marshal Earp have a disagreement, and Kelley's temper flares. When the mayor shows no signs of simmering down, Earp resigns his post and ends his friendship with Kelley.

93.148 *Arizona Comes to Dodge.* May 26, 1959. GS: Dirk London, Myron Healey, Bob Woodward, Steve Darrell. Marshal Wyatt Earp's brothers Morgan and Virgil arrive in Dodge City. They plan to take Wyatt back to Arizona.

Season Five

93.149 *Dodge City — Hail and Farewell.* Sept. 1, 1959. GS: Dirk London, Ross Elliott, Ralph Sanford. Wyatt Earp's brothers Morgan and Virgil finally persuade the marshal to join them in the Arizona Territory. As he prepares to leave Dodge City, the citizens honor Wyatt with a testimonial which prompts him to recall some of the memorable events in his career as marshal of Dodge City.

93.150 *The Trail to Tombstone.* Sept. 8, 1959. GS: Ross Elliott, Dirk London, Myron Healey, Frank Wilcox, Douglas Kennedy, Jack Pickard, Rush Williams, Paul Gary, Dick Foote, Bob Swan, Scott Peters. Wyatt Earp and his brothers leave Dodge City and hit the trail for Arizona Territory. On the way they encounter a group of ruthless outlaws, each of whom wants to kill Wyatt.

93.151 *Tombstone.* Sept. 15, 1959. GS: Douglas Fowley, Randy Stuart, Trevor Bardette, Carol Thurston, Damian O'Flynn. Wyatt leaves his guns with Doc Holliday and rides into Tombstone, Arizona as a land agent for Earp Brothers, Inc. He encounters belligerent miners who mistake him for a cowboy, and the unarmed Earp finds theat he is caught in a feud between the miners and ranchers.

93.152 *Wyatt's Decision.* Sept. 22, 1959. GS: Douglas Fowley, Randy Stuart, Frank Gerstle, Arthur Space, Sam Flint, Trevor Bardette, Carol Thurston. Disgusted by the corruption in Tombstone, Wyatt decides to join his brothers in Prescott, Arizona. But the Clanton family plot to ambush and kill him and honest townspeople plead with Earp to stay on as a deputy sheriff.

93.153 *Lineup for Battle.* Sept. 29, 1959. GS: Douglas Fowley, Randy Stuart, Trevor Bardette, Carol Thurston, Damian O'Flynn, Lou Krugman, John Milford, Howard Negley. In the new job as Deputy Sheriff of Tombstone, Wyatt is sent out to arrest Old Man Clanton for stealing horses and bushwhacking a trader. The lawless Clanton family plans to make him unwelcome.

93.154 *The Nugget and the Epitaph.* Oct. 6, 1959. GS: Douglas Fowley, Randy Stuart, Carol Thurston, Damian O'Flynn, William Foster, Kelly Thorsden, Stanley Clements, Sam Flint. In a rugged frontier town, a small newspaper battles to retain its high ideals and still stay in business. Impressed with the honesty of the publication, Marshal Wyatt Earp decides to help with the fight.

93.155 *The Perfidy of Shotgun Gibbs.* Oct. 13, 1959. GS: Morgan Woodward, Douglas Fowley, Randy Stuart, Trevor Bardette, Marshall Bradford, James Seay, Damian O'Flynn, Stacy Harris. During an election for the judgeship of Tombstone, Wyatt is confronted by the infamous Ten Percent Ring as well as the Clanton Gang. As he prepares for battle, Wyatt is joined by his old friend Shotgun Gibbs.

93.156 *You Can't Fight City Hall.* Oct. 20, 1959. GS: Lash LaRue, Douglas Fowley, Morgan Woodward, Carol Thurston, Trevor Bardette. Tombstone's sheriff Johnny Behan is a hero to the townspeople because of his efforts in raising money for a new hospital. But Wyatt believes that Behan is more villain than hero.

93.157 *Behan Shows His Hand.* Oct. 27, 1959. GS: Trevor Bardette, Damian O'Flynn, Stacy Harris, Lash LaRue, Charles Fredericks. Still attempting to get crooked Sheriff Johnny Behan to make a mistake, Wyatt Earp finds that Behan has taken four prisoners and put them under heavy guard. Earp must face a hundred guns when he seeks to release the prisoners.

93.158 *The Ring of Death.* Nov. 3, 1959. GS: Charles Fredericks, I. Stanford Jolley, Stuart Randall, Randy Stuart, Morgan Woodward, Douglas Fowley. Wyatt Earp continues to thwart the criminal efforts of the Ten Percent Ring in Tombstone. The leader, Dan Priddy, plots Earp's murder.

93.159 *Wyatt Wins One.* Nov. 10, 1959. GS: Trevor Bardette, John Milford, Steve Rowland, Mike Keene, Morgan Woodward. Old Man Clanton places a large claim with the

The Life and Legend of Wyatt Earp

Army for some cattle he says were rustled by young Geronimo and the Apaches. Wyatt Earp thinks the claim is phony and sets out to prove it.

93.160 *The Fugitive.* Nov. 17, 1959. GS: Armand Alzamora, Michael Carr, John Carradine, Anna Navarro, James Seay, Felix Locher, Orville Sherman. Wyatt Earp tracks down and captures a young Mexican wanted for murder. The youth claims that they are in Mexican territory and that Earp can't legally arrest him.

93.161 *The Noble Outlaws.* Nov. 24, 1959. GS: Lloyd Corrigan, Morgan Woodward, James Coburn, Robert Nichols, Carol Thurston, Trevor Bardette, Steve Rowland. Writer Ned Buntline presents Wyatt Earp with another wild idea. He tells the Marshal that the Clanton family of outlaws are really Robin Hoods.

93.162 *The Paymaster.* Dec. 1, 1959. GS: Clancy Cooper, Don Diamond, Mark Dana, Paula Raymond, Morgan Woodward, Roberto Contreras. An Army paymaster is assigned to deliver a Government payroll to Benson. Wyatt Earp agrees to ride with the paymaster as extra protection.

93.163 *The Clantons' Family Row.* Dec. 8, 1959. GS: Peter Thompson, William Phipps, Morgan Woodward, Peter Miller, Douglas Fowley, Carol Thurston, Stacy Harris, James Coburn. Gunfighters Curly Brocius and Johnny Ringo come to Tombstone. Marshal Wyatt Earp learns that they have come to settle a feud.

93.164 *The Matchmaker.* Dec. 15, 1959. GS: Morgan Woodward, Randy Stuart, Trevor Bardette, John Milford, Steve Rowland, Carol Thurston. Wyatt's friend, Shotgun Gibbs, decides that Earp ought to get married. Shotgun tries to promote a match between Wyatt and Nellie Cashman.

93.165 *Get Shotgun Gibbs.* Dec. 22, 1959. GS: Morgan Woodward, Fred Villani, Robert Gunderson, John Maxwell, Richard Reeves, Lash LaRue. Wyatt Earp's political enemies, unsuccessful in their efforts to get rid of him, turn their attention to Shotgun Gibbs, the chief deputy.

93.166 *Wells Fargo Calling Marshal Earp.* Dec. 29, 1959. GS: Morgan Woodward, John Baxter, Dehl Berti, Robert B. Williams, John Gallaudet, Don Kennedy, Ray Kellogg. Wyatt Earp is approached by his former employer, The Wells Fargo Company. The company wants him to stop the frequent stagecoach robberies in the Arizona Territory.

93.167 *A Murderer's Return.* Jan. 5, 1960. GS: Denver Pyle, Morgan Woodward, Carleton G. Young, Rachel Ames, Randy Stuart. Dobie Jenner, who is trying to go straight after serving a term for murder, rides into Tombstone. Because of his reputation, he is unwelcome in the town, and Wyatt Earp is forced to defend him from angry citizens.

93.168 *The Big Fight at Total Wreck.* Jan. 12, 1960. GS: Randy Stuart, Damian O'Flynn, Frank Gerstle, Duncan Lamont, Clancy Cooper, Dick Wilson. Welch and Irish miners clash at Nellie Cashman's saloon. Nellie asks Marshal Earp to help keep the peace.

93.169 *Frontier Surgeon.* Jan. 19, 1960. GS: Damian O'Flynn, Andy Albin, Lane Bradford, John Gallaudet, Rick Vallin, James Noel, Douglas Fowley, Morgan Woodward. Marshal Earp's strict observance of the legal code sometimes clashes with Dr. Goodfellow's medical ethics. The conflict appears to be leading to a violent showdown.

93.170 *Let's Hang Curly Bill.* Jan. 26, 1960. GS: Carol Thurston, Trevor Bardette, William Phipps, Sam Flint, Stacy Harris, Damian O'Flynn, James Seay, Morgan Woodward, Douglas Fowley. Dodge City gunslinger Curly Bill Brocius takes a vacation. He goes to Tombstone to celebrate his birthday.

93.171 *Silver Dollar.* Feb. 2, 1960. GS: Dusty Anders, Leslie Bradley, Randy Stuart, Morgan Woodward, Douglas Fowley, Robert Riordan, Tom Palmer, James Seay, Damian O'Flynn. Tombstone's Bird Cage gambling hall acquires a new cashier whose soft beauty doesn't square with her reputation. Marshal Earp wants to learn more about the girl.

93.172 *The Case of Senor Huerto.* Feb. 9, 1960. GS: Penny Santon, Joseph Sonessa, Paul Fierro, Douglas Fowley. A woman and her son arrive in Tombstone and make inquires about Juan Huerta. The woman tells Marshal Earp that he received a letter stating that her husband Juan had been murdered in Tombstone.

93.173 *The Arizona Lottery.* Feb. 16, 1960. GS: Tom Monroe, Thom Carney, Ron Foster, Patricia Donahue, Lester Vil, John Maxwell, James Seay, Morgan Woodward, Douglas Fowley, Michael Emmett. The Arizona lottery is started by the Ten Percent Ring, who promise a huge prize. When Wyatt investigates, he uncovers a murder.

93.174 *Don't Get Tough with a Sailor.* Feb. 23, 1960. GS: John Litel, Madge Kennedy, Lash LaRue, Trevor Bardette, Morgan Woodward, Douglas Fowley. An ex-Navy officer brings his gang of rough tough old salts inland to settle.

93.175 *The Scout.* March 1, 1960. GS: Charles McGraw, Stacy Harris, Rico Alaniz, Francis DeSales, Richard Warren. The Indian wife of scout Tom Barrows is knifed in the back by an unknown assailant. Her Apache relatives threaten a full-scale uprising.

93.176 *The Buntline Special.* March 8, 1960. GS: Gary Gray, Carol Thurston, Steve Rowland, Trevor Bardette, Charles Wagenheim, Robert Rawlings, Morgan Woodward. Already plagued by more than enough outlaw Clantons, Wyatt hopes to prevent young Billy Clanton from going bad. He gets unexpected help from Billy's older sister.

93.177 *China Mary.* March 15, 1960. GS: Carl Benson, Paul McGuire, Anna May Wong, Aki Aleong, Morgan Woodward. A large group of Chinese move into Tombstone, and Marshal Earp must deal with the prejudice of townspeople.

93.178 *His Life in His Hands.* March 22, 1960. GS: Mike Ragan, Steve Pendleton, Trevor Bardette, John Milford. Wyatt Earp risks his life to help a couple of undercover Wells Fargo men. He has to defend them from lawmen and outlaws alike.

93.179 *Behan's Double Game.* March 29, 1960. GS: Lash LaRue, Trevor Bardette, Orville Sherman, Mike Ragan, Steven Pendleton, Morgan Woodward, Douglas Fowley. Tombstone's crooked sheriff has openly opposed Marshal Earp. Now he gets even bolder. He challenges Wyatt to a gunfight.

93.180 *The Salvation of Emma Clanton.* April 5, 1960. GS: Carol Thurston, Sam Gilman, Trevor Bardette, Randy Stuart, Morgan Woodward, Douglas Fowley. Wyatt is proud of the fact he has been forced to kill only one man in the line of duty, but Gringo Hawkby wants Earp to kill again.

93.181 *John Clum, Fighting Editor.* April 12, 1960. GS: Stacy Harris, Trevor Bardette, Del Monroe, Lash LaRue, Randy Stuart, Morgan Woodward, John Baxter, Bill Simms. John Clum is under fire from local politicians, and Wyatt springs to his defense. Then he learns there are outlaws to contend with.

93.182 *The Judge.* April 19, 1960. GS: Douglas Fowley, Stacy Harris, Anthony Warde, Randy Stuart, Morgan Woodward. There is a business boom in Tombstone, and greedy outlaws want to get in on the easy money.

93.183 *The Court vs. Doc Holliday.* April 26, 1960. GS: Trevor Bardette, James Seay, Glen Holtzman, Douglas Fowley, Morgan Woodward, Forrest Lewis, Steve Pendleton, Preston Hanson, William Foster. Doc is in trouble. He is accused of looting the Wells Fargo office. Wyatt steps in for the defense of his old friend.

93.184 *Roscoe Turns Detective.* May 3, 1960. GS: Jock Gaynor, Paul Jasmin, Clancy Cooper, John Hackett, James Seay, Damian O'Flynn, Morgan Woodward, William Keene, Dan Riss, William Vaughn, Robert Swan. Roscoe the mule is a witness to the theft of some horses and mules.

93.185 *The Posse.* May 10, 1960. GS: Ron Ely, Jeanne Vaughn, Peter Mamakos, Douglas Fowley, Morgan Woodward, Clark Howat, Pat Hawley. Wyatt Earp leads a posse that sets out for a bloody battle with the notorious San Berdoo gang. Riding with Wyatt is a young Easterner who has never seen a dead man.

93.186 *The Confidence Man.* May 17, 1960. GS: Stacy Harris, Randy Stuart, Bill Cord, Nancy Hadley, Stewart Bradley, Pitt Herbert, Lester Dorr. Billy Costane arrives in Tombstone to meet the girl he has wooed by mail. He mailed her the money to come back East and marry him and hasn't heard a word from her since.

93.187 *The Toughest Judge in Arizona.* May 24, 1960. GS: James Seay, Peter Thompson, Trevor Bardette, Angela Greene, Robert Hutton, Sam Flint, Douglas Fowley, Morgan Woodward, I. Stanford Jolley, William Pullen. A cousin of the notorious Johnny Ringo is arrested on a robbery charge and Judge Spicer is scheduled to try him. Ringo sends the judge an ultimatum—free his cousin or die.

93.188 *My Enemy—John Behan.* May 31, 1960. GS: Lash LaRue, Trevor Bardette, James Seay, Randy Stuart, Robert Gothie, John Milford, Enid Janes, Steve Pendleton, Morgan Woodward. A reward is offered for the person or persons who held up a Wells Fargo office and killed the agent. Tombstone's crooked sheriff finds a way to collect the money by framing young Will Morris for the crime.

93.189 *Wyatt's Bitterest Enemy.* June 7, 1960. GS: Dirk London, Jeff De Benning, Steve Pendleton, William Phipps, John Milford, Trevor Bardette, Morgan Woodward, Douglas Fowley, Robert Nash. Old man Clanton decrees that Wyatt Earp must die. Fearful of a showdown in Tombstone, the Clantons hatch a plot to draw Wyatt out into the open.

Season Six

93.190 *The Truth About Old Man Clanton.* Sept. 27, 1960. GS: Trevor Bardette, Anthony Caruso, Britt Lomond, William Phipps, Howard Petrie, Rayford Barnes, Steve Rowland, Henry Rowland, Ralph Reed. Clanton, Wyatt's old nemesis, is sending men south of the border to hijack the herds and silver ore trains of Don Sebastian, a Mexican range tycoon.

93.191 *The Doctor.* Oct. 4, 1960. GS: Damian O'Flynn, Walter Coy, Sarah Selby, Gregory Walcott, Joe McGuinn, Morgan Woodward, Douglas Fowley. Doc Goodfellow, Tombstone's only doctor, is critically wounded. To save Doc's life, Earp looks for Henry Mason, a doctor turned gold prospector.

93.192 *Johnny Behind the Deuce.* Oct. 11, 1960. GS: Jack Ging, Britt Lomond, Carolyn Craig, Lane Bradford, Morgan Woodward, Douglas Fowley. Ringo is gunning for Johnny O'Rourke, a hero-worshiping flunky for Doc Holliday. O'Rourke has been rounding up poker games for Doc, and Ringo doesn't like it.

93.193 *Shoot to Kill.* Oct. 18, 1960. GS: Dirk London, Howard Petrie, James Seay, Barney Phillips, Diane Millay, Tyler McVey, William Kruse, Don Harvey, Frank Gerstle, Fern Berry, Douglas Fowley, Morgan Woodward, Damian O'Flynn. Arizona Governor Gosper issues a shoot to kill mandate to the lawmen. Earp objects to the impending slaughter.

93.194 *Study of a Crooked Sheriff.* Oct. 25, 1960. GS: Steve Brodie, Trevor Bardette, Henry Rowland, Paul Wexler, Pierce Lydon, Morgan Woodward, Douglas Fowley. John Behan is old man Clanton's hand-picked choice for the representative of the law in Tombstone. Clanton wants Behan to help smash Earp's legal power once and for all.

93.195 *Big Brother.* Nov. 1, 1960. GS: Dirk London, Sue Randall, Sherwood Price, John Anderson, Morgan Woodward, Douglas Fowley, Trevor Bardette. Morgan Earp's romances with an unending chain of dance hall girls is a matter of concern to big brother Wyatt. He decides the brotherly thing to do is to introduce young Morgan to a girl of quality—saleswoman Lucy Tedder.

93.196 *Woman of Tucson.* Nov. 15, 1960. GS: Lloyd Corrigan, Rita Lynn, William Vaughn, William Mims, Morgan Woodward, James Nolan, Lennie Geer. Dime-novelist Ned Buntline shows up again in Tombstone. This time he has come to write an expose of the Ten Percent Ring's Arizona operations, based on information supplied by Amy Jones, the widow of one of the gang's leaders. Earp warns Buntline not to talk to Amy or he'll jeopardize her life.

93.197 *The Fanatic.* Nov. 22, 1960. GS: Harold J. Stone, Mort Mills, Jeanne Bates, Morgan Woodward. It looks like religious persecution when Hiram Grant is beset by a mob that wants to burn him off his ranch. But after Wyatt saves Grant, he learns the citizens weren't opposed to Grant's religion. They say the cultists was the instigator of a massacre.

93.198 *He's My Brother.* Nov. 29, 1960. GS: Wesley Lau, Robert Sampson, Stacy Harris, Ray Kellogg, James Seay, Damian O'Flynn, Morgan Woodward, Ethan Laidlaw. Marshal Pritchard is trying to demonstrate the use of a straight jacket, and he starts to strap Cully Dray into it. Before he can finish, Cully shoots him.

93.199 *The Too Perfect Crime.* Dec. 6, 1960. GS: Nina Shipman, Denver Pyle, Ed Nelson, David Carlile, Douglas Fowley, Damian O'Flynn. Leone Simpson's father doesn't like any of her beaus. The he is murdered. Then one of the beaus is murdered and Wyatt Earp must determine if one of Leone's suitors is on a rampage.

93.200 *Johnny Ringo's Girl.* Dec. 13, 1960. GS: Britt Lomond, Suzanne Lloyd, Rayford Barnes, Trevor Bardette, Lee Farr, Alan Wells, Glenn Strange, Morgan Woodward, Douglas Fowley. Mary Turner, Johnny Ringo's girlfriend, is trying to make a good man out of Johnny. So Ringo tells Old Man Clanton that he wants to quit.

93.201 *Miss Sadie.* Dec. 20, 1960. GS: Susan Cummings, Alan Baxter, George Keymas, Jimmy Murphy, Damian O'Flynn, Duke Norton, Fred Krone, Sam Flint. Miss Sadie takes her boyfriend, wounded bank robber Ben Roberts, from Jacob Birch's outlaw hideout into Tombstone for medical attention. Unhampered by their disabled partner, Birch and his cronies plan on an outing in town, with a little bank-robing to keep things humming.

93.202 *Winning Streak.* Dec. 27, 1960. GS: Dirk London, John Anderson, Walter Reed, Gloria Winters, Douglas Fowley. Morgan Earp is on a hot winning streak. An he won't listen to anyone who tries to make him quit while he is ahead.

93.203 *Billy Buckett, Incorporated.* Jan. 3, 1961. GS: Andy Clyde, Ann Robinson, Bartlett Robinson, Dan Sheridan, Barney Phillips, Damian O'Flynn, Morgan Woodward. Old prospector Billy Buckett staggers into the Tombstone Saloon. He says he has been robbed of his money, then collapses on the floor.

93.204 *Horse Thief.* Jan. 10, 1961. GS: Ralph Reed, Trevor Bardette, Dirk London, Steve Brodie, James Seay, Norman Leavitt, Douglas Fowley, Morgan Woodward. Wyatt jails the McLowery brothers for suspected mail robbery. But the brothers work for Old Man Clanton, so Sheriff Behan releases them from jail.

93.205 *Terror in the Desert.* Jan. 24, 1961. GS: Richard Crane, Jacqueline Scott, Steve Brodie, James Seay, Francis McDonald, Richard Reeves, Stanley Clements, Peter Mamakos, Dave Fresco. Tom Grover is convicted of theft, and sentenced to a term in Yuma prison. His wife tries to convince Wyatt the Sheriff Johnny Behan framed Grover.

93.206 *Old Slanders Never Die.* Jan. 31, 1961. GS: Trevor Bardette, Stacy Harris, James Seay, Charles Watts, Hal Dawson, Rita Duncan, Ann Bellamy, Douglas Fowley, Damian O'Flynn. Wyatt saves old man Clanton's life, but the leader of the Ten Percent Ring isn't grateful. To get rid of Wyatt, he puts the pressure on a local newspaper to start a smear campaign.

93.207 *Loyalty.* Feb. 7, 1961. GS: Richard Benedict, Brett King, Paula Winslowe, Douglas Fowley, Morgan Woodward. Doc has a long streak of good luck. He wins at cards, she he buys some mining stock. Its value goes up, then he buys some railroad stock, and that goes up too. Figuring he can't lose, Doc decides to buy the local hotel and become a respectable businessman.

93.208 *Johnny Behan Falls in Love.* Feb. 14, 1961. GS: Steve Brodie, Jean Allison, Trevor Bardette, Andy Albin, Lennie Geer, Morgan Woodward. Sheriff Behan falls in love with traveling actress Minna Marlin, and after an evening of champagne and Minna's company, Behan reveals a little too much about the activities of the Clinton gang.

93.209 *Casey and the Clowns.* Feb. 21, 1961. GS: Willard Sage, L.Q. Jones, Ken Drake, Zon Murray, R.G. Armstrong, Kenneth MacDonald, Sam Flint, Stacy Harris, Trevor Bardette, Morgan Woodward. One of the most successful gang of bank robbers are known as the Harlequins because they disguise themselves as clowns. They show up to rob the Tombstone Bank.

93.210 *Doc Holliday Faces Death.* Feb. 28, 1961. GS: Steve Brodie, Gregg Palmer, George D. Wallace, Damian O'Flynn, Douglas Fowley, Morgan Woodward. Doc Holliday is warned that his life is in jeopardy if he doesn't ease up on his fast living and fast drinking. Wyatt hits on a scheme to reduce Doc's drinking by watering down his whiskey.

93.211 *Apache Gold.* March 7, 1961. GS: George Keymas, Robert Cabal, Steve Rowland, Rayford Barnes, Stacy Harris, Trevor Bardette, Morgan Woodward. Chief Natchez is afraid that his Apache warriors will go on the warpath if they continue drinking the bootleg booze the Clanton gang has been selling them.

93.212 *The Good Mule and the Bad Mule.* March 14, 1961. GS: William Mims, Stephen Wootton, Daniel White, Damian O'Flynn, Morgan Woodward, Clancy Cooper, Stacy Harris, Norman Leavitt. The Tombstone newspaper doesn't care for Wyatt or his friends and would print anything to run down his reputation. The big chance comes when a kid named Ollie claims that a mule, owned by Shotgun Gibbs, kicked him and broke his leg.

93.213 *Clanton and Cupid.* March 21, 1961. GS: Carol Thurston, Harlan Warde, Trevor Bardette, Steve Rowland, Douglas Fowley. Emma, who is just about the only respectable member of the Clanton family, has her eye on a lawyer named Ware as a likely prospect for a husband.

93.214 *Wyatt Takes the Primrose Path.* March 28, 1961. GS: Gene Roth, William Thourlby, Gordon Wynn, Lyn Thomas, X Brands, Peter Coe, Red Morgan, Al Wyatt, Douglas Fowley, Morgan Woodward. When a wagon train is attacked by outlaws, the Apaches are afraid they will be blamed. Chief Natchez hits on a plan to let Wyatt know the Indians are innocent.

93.215 *The Convict's Revenge.* April 4, 1961. GS: Warde Donovan, Janet Lake, Robert Harland, Ken Mayer, Robert Carson, Morgan Woodward. Ex-con Jed Lorimer is trying to go straight, but Phil Davies, the brother of his girl friend, keeps throwing him a curve. Phil, who takes a sour view of his sister's suitor, is a big gambler with big troubles, and he plans to palm them off on Jed.

93.216 *Until Proven Guilty.* April 11, 1961. GS: Steve Brodie, Britt Lomond, Stacy Harris, Kasey Rogers, James Seay, Trevor Bardette, William Phipps, Morgan Woodward, Douglas Fowley, James Lydon, Steve Pendleton. Dissension develops in the local criminal set when badmen Ringo and Brocius object to corrupt Sheriff Behan extending his tax-collecting powers to their illegal profits. The boys intend to frame Behan and ask Doc Holliday for his help.

93.217 *The Shooting Starts.* April 18, 1961. GS: Barney Phillips, Diane Jergens, Leo Gordon, Joseph Bassett, Edith Leslie, Troy Melton, Douglas Fowley, Morgan Woodward, Steve Raines, Dale Van Sickel. Business picks up in Lou Rickabaugh's saloon when his niece Edith starts giving poetry recitations for the patrons. This infuriates rival tavern owner Miggles Hannegan, who orders Rickabaugh to sell out—lock, stock, barrel and poetry act.

93.218 *Wyatt Earp's Baby.* April 25, 1961. GS: Marie Windsor, Sean McClory, Frank Ferguson, William Tracy, Barbara Bestar, Sherman Sanders, Ollie O'Toole. Wyatt faces an unexpected problem when he takes custody of the infant survivor of an Indian massacre. He can't find anyone in Tucson to take the baby off his hands. In desperation he leaves it temporarily with saloon hostess Lily Henry.

93.219 *The Law Must Be Fair.* May 2, 1961. GS: Louise Fletcher, Gregg Palmer, George D. Wallace, William Phipps,

Trevor Bardette, Stacy Harris, Douglas Fowley, Pat Moran. Old man Clanton sends his top guns, the McLowery brothers, down to take over the O.K. Corral and run it as a livery stable until he is ready to use it as a fortress in his war with Earp. But the boys no sooner arrive than a body is found in the stable, and Earp takes them into custody.

93.220 *A Papa for Butch and Ginger.* May 9, 1961. GS: Dorothy Green, Kevin Brodie, Debbie Megowan, Stacy Harris, Douglas Fowley, Morgan Woodward, Kem Dibbs, I. Stanford Jolley. Widow Amy Byfield has become the object of saddle tramp Whiskers Brown's unsolicited attention. When Gibbs drives the molester off, the widow's children regard Gibbs as their savior, and maybe their new papa.

93.221 *Hiding Behind a Star.* May 23, 1961. GS: Gloria Talbott, James Griffith, Roy Engel, Charles Wagenheim, James Seay, Damian O'Flynn, Stacy Harris, Douglas Fowley. There has never been any love lost between Doc Holliday and his former in-laws, Martha and Tim Connell. And when Doc generously recommends Tim for deputy's job, things don't get any friendlier. Martha says she doesn't want a lawman for a husband.

93.222 *Requiem for Old Man Clanton.* May 30, 1961. GS: Trevor Bardette, Don Haggerty, Norman Alden, William Phipps, Robert Bice, Gordon Wynn, Rodolfo Hoyos, Reuben Moreno, Joe Dominguez, Carlos Rivero, Manuel Lopez, Douglas Fowley. The Clanton gang has been skirmishing with Mexican bandits along the border, and Earp wants to put a stop to it before Old Man Clanton gets killed. He knows that Clanton's death would result in a struggle for power among his gunslinging followers.

93.223 *Wyatt's Brothers Join Up.* June 6, 1961. GS: Dirk London, John Anderson, Adele Mara, James Seay, Rayford Barnes, Don Wilbanks, Lennie Geer, Troy Melton, Dale E. Johnson, Steve Brodie. Doc Holliday has a plan to help Wyatt in his struggle with the Clantons, and he talks Earp's brothers into assisting him. There is only one thing Wyatt may not like about the scheme — it is illegal.

93.224 *Just Before the Battle.* June 13, 1961. GS: Norman Alden, William Phipps, Dirk London, John Anderson, Ralph Reed, Rayford Barnes, Gregg Palmer, George D. Wallace, Douglas Fowley, James Anderson. A stage-line holdup provides Wyatt with an opportunity to turn the rival factions of the Clanton mob against each other. The danger is when the fighting starts, the lawmen might get caught in the middle.

93.225 *Gunfight at the O.K. Corral.* June 20, 1961. GS: Dirk London, John Anderson, Ralph Reed, Rayford Barnes, Gregg Palmer, George D. Wallace, James Seay, Stacy Harris, Steve Brodie, Damian O'Flynn, Douglas Fowley. Ike Clanton and his followers come to town planning to shoot it out with the Earps. Wyatt hopes he will be able to arrest the men individually, and avoid an open battle.

93.226 *The Outlaws Cry Murder.* June 27, 1961. GS: Dirk London, John Anderson, Norman Alden, William Phipps, Rayford Barnes, Charles Watts, Stacy Harris, Freeman Lusk, Douglas Fowley, Steve Brodie. Tombstone is in an uproar after the O.K. Corral battle. A murder charge has been brought against Wyatt, and his surviving enemies are prepared to supplement the legal action with more gunfire.

94. *The Life and Times of Grizzly Adams*

NBC. 60 min. Wednesday, 8:00-9:00, Feb. 1977–July 1978.
Regular Cast: Dan Haggerty (James "Grizzly" Adams), Denver Pyle (Mad Jack), Don Shanks (Nakuma).
Premise: This series depicted the exploits of James Adams, a man unjustly accused of a crime, who sought refuge away from society in the wilderness of the West in the late 1800s.

The Episodes

94.1 *Adam's Cub.* Feb. 9, 1977. GS: Kristen Curry, Hank Kendrick. Adams exposes himself to capture by trying to find the parents of an eight-year-old girl he found stranded in the wilderness.

94.2 *Blood Brother.* Feb. 16, 1977. Adams tells an eight-year-old boy the story of how he saved the life of his Indian blood brother Nakuma and found Ben the bear.

94.3 *The Fugitive.* Feb. 23, 1977. GS: Ken Berry, Jason Clark, Patrick Wright. Fugitive mountain man Adams rescues a traveling salesman from a river, unaware that the fellow is being pursued by a posse.

94.4 *Unwelcome Neighbor.* March 2, 1977. GS: Ronny Cox, John Bishop. Adams and Nakuma try to befriend a pugnacious settler who shows little regard for the ways of nature.

94.5 *Howdy-Do, I'm Mad Jack.* March 9, 1977. Adams, believing his buddy Mad Jack has drowned, pages through the parts of the crusty old mountain man's diary that recount the beginning of their friendship.

94.6 *Adam's Ark.* March 16, 1977. GS: Don Galloway. Adams risks arrest to save his animal friends from an erupting volcano rather than hide from the famous lawman Allan Pinkerton.

94.7 *The Redemption of Ben.* March 23, 1977. GS: Charles Young, Norman Fell, Hayes Stewart, Earl Smith, Jane Harrison. Ben the bear, lonely and depressed after the apparent death of Adams, is captured by a brutal animal trainer.

94.8 *The Tenderfoot.* March 30, 1977. GS: Charles Martin Smith. Mad Jack and Adams keep company with a sickly but determined tenderfoot who is trying to learn how to survive in the wilderness.

94.9 *The Rivals.* April 6, 1977. GS: Betty Ann Carr. Mad Jack discovers gold in the stream that runs through Adams' valley.

94.10 *The Unholy Beast.* April 20, 1977. GS: Slim Pickens, George Aguilar. Mad Jack, Adams and Nakuma hunt a mysterious beast that is terrifying wildlife.

94.11 *Beaver Dam.* April 27, 1977. Mad Jack helps Adams save his cabin from possible flooding after beavers construct a dam nearby.

94.12 *Home of the Hawk.* May 5, 1977. GS: Margaret Willock, Jack Kruschen. Adams and Mad Jack help a fifteen-year-old nurse her overbearing father, a traveling salesman with a broken leg.

94.13 *The Storm.* May 11, 1977. Adams braves a bitter storm to search for an Indian girl who disappeared after her horse supposedly was spooked by a legendary mountain ghost.

Season Two

94.14 *Hot Air Hero.* Sept. 28, 1977. GS: Gino Conforti. Adams' buddy Mad Jack takes a potshot at a monstrous flying critter, and bags the airship of a famed French balloonist.

94.15 *Survival.* Oct. 12, 1977. GS: John Bishop, James Wainwright. A lost and frightened Adams wanders through the wilderness after a bump on the head induces amnesia.

94.16 *A Bear's Life.* Oct. 19, 1977. GS: Eugene George Standing, Oscar G. Rowland, Elaine Daniels. A severe thunderstorm sets Ben roaming the countryside while Adams repairs damage to his cabin.

94.17 *The Trial.* Oct. 26, 1977. GS: John War Eagle. Adams has to prove Ben's innocence after the bear is falsely accused of stealing an Indian chief's catch of fish.

94.18 *The Orphans.* Nov. 2, 1977. GS: Tiger Thompson, Jodee Jetton, James Griffith. Mad Jack and Adams come across two orphan children who have run away to the mountains because their superintendent wouldn't let them have pets.

94.19 *The Search.* Nov. 9, 1977. GS: Paul Brinegar. A helpless cougar cub wanders the wilderness after its mother is injured in a trapper's pitfall.

94.20 *Gold Is Where You Find It.* Nov. 23, 1977. GS: Larry Storch, Forrest Tucker. Two bumbling prospectors try to find a gold mine with a map they bought for $10.

94.21 *Track of the Cougar.* Dec. 14, 1977. Nakuma's tribe orders him to hunt down and destroy the cougar that he helped to raise.

94.22 *The Choice.* Dec. 21, 1977. GS: John Bishop. While Adams consoles a boy whose pet deer ran away, Nakuma and Mad Jack try to catch a wild burro.

94.23 *Woman in the Wilderness.* Dec. 21, 1977. GS: Tiffany Bolling. A woman set on shooting the black bear that killer her father dupes Adams into helping her track down the animal.

94.24 *The Spoilers.* Jan. 4, 1978. GS: Ken Lynch, Walter Wanderman. The reckless mining techniques of two prospectors threaten the ecology of the valley.

94.25 *Marvin the Magnificent.* Jan. 11, 1978. GS: Edward Andrews. Adams and Ben befriend a traveling magician and his pet bear, an aging critter that has never had a chance to roam the wilderness.

94.26 *A Time of Thirsting.* Jan. 18, 1978. Wildlife in the valley is threatened by a major drought that shows no sign of letup.

94.27 *The Seekers.* Jan. 25, 1978. GS: Keenan Wynn. An aging ex-cavalryman with dreams of living out his days as a farmer roams the mountains searching for the land he purchased sight unseen.

94.28 *A Gentleman Tinker.* Feb. 8, 1978. GS: Henry Beckman. A retired sea captain and his crew, consisting of a chimp and a parrot, sail their prairie schooner into the valley.

94.29 *The Runaway.* Feb. 22, 1978. GS: Roger Mosley. Adams helps an escaped slave in his run for freedom.

94.30 *The Great Burro Race.* March 1, 1978. GS: Jack Elam. Mad Jack schemes to get his burro back after losing it to a wily old woodsman in a game of horseshoes.

94.31 *The Littlest Greenhorn.* March 15, 1978. GS: Walter Burke, Al Hansen. Driven by the legend of leprechaun gold, Mad Jack goes on a merry chase after what he believes to be one of the wee people.

94.32 *The Renewal.* March 22, 1978. GS: Patrick Wayne, Ned Romero, John Bishop. Adams and his friends celebrate Easter in conjunction with the Indians' festival of Potlatch.

94.33 *The Stranger.* April 5, 1978. GS: Mark Slade. Nakuma teaches an Indian boy how to be a brave, and Adams befriends an Army surveyor — Captain Ulysses S. Grant.

94.34 *The Quest.* April 26, 1978. GS: David Carson, Roy Applegate. The Department of the Interior sends a representative into the wilderness to determine which predatory animals should have bounties on their heads.

94.35 *The Skyrider.* May 5, 1978. GS: Russ Tamblyn. An inventor uses the mountains as the test site for his human-powered aircraft.

94.36 *The World's Greatest Bounty Hunter.* May 12, 1978. Delirious from fever, Mad Jack imagines himself the world's greatest bounty hunter.

94.37 *Once Upon a Starry Night.* Dec. 19, 1978. GS: Ken Curtis, Jack Kruschen, Steven Robertson, Linda Arbizu. Adams and Mad Jack help save the holidays for two stranded pioneer children who want nothing more than to spend Christmas with their parents.

95. *Little House: A New Beginning*

NBC. 60 min. Broadcast history: Monday, 8:00-9:00, Sept. 1982–March 1983.

Regular Cast: Melissa Gilbert (Laura Ingalls Wilder), Dean Butler (Almanzo Wilder), Stan Ivar (John Carter), Pamela Roylance (Sarah Carter), Lindsay Kennedy (Jeb Carter), David Friedman (Jason Carter), Victor French (Isaiah Edwards), Nicholas Pryor (Royal Wilder), Shannen Doherty (Jenny Wilder), Leslie Landon (Etta Plum), Richard Bull (Nels Oleson), Katherine MacGregor (Harriet Oleson), Jonathan Gilbert (Willie Oleson), Allison Balson (Nancy Oleson), Ketty Lester (Hester Sue), Sam Edwards (Bill Anderson), Kevin Hagen (Dr. Baker), Dabbs Greer (Rev. Robert Alden).

Premise: This series, a sequel to *Little House on the Prairie*, was set in 1887, and continued the story of Laura Ingalls Wilder, now a teacher, in Plumb Creek, Minnesota.

The Episodes

95.1 *Times Are Changing* Part One. Sept. 27, 1982. GS: Nicholas Pryor, Michael Landon. Charles leaves Walnut Grove for good, selling his house to the Carters. Meanwhile, the Wilders receive an unexpected visit from Almanzo's ailing brother Royal and niece Jenny, and the town gets a new schoolmarm.

95.2 *Times Are Changing* Part Two. Oct. 4, 1982. GS: Nicholas Pryor. Feeling responsible for her father's death, a withdrawn Jenny fights guilt and loneliness. Meanwhile, Jeb battles his fear of water.

95.3 *Welcome to Olesonville.* Oct. 11, 1982. GS: Lew Ayres, Charles Lane. All is quiet on the political front until a town founder steps in to prevent Mrs. Oleson from turning Walnut Grove into a fiefdom of her own called Olesonville.

95.4 *Rage.* Oct. 18, 1982. GS: Robert Loggia, Tammy

Lauren, Michelle Marsh. Terror strikes the community when an enraged, and armed, neighbor of the Wilders goes berserk.

95.5 *Little Lou.* Oct. 25, 1982. GS: Billy Barty, Susan French. A midget promises his dying wife that he will give up the circus and settle down to raise their infant daughter.

95.6 *The Wild Boy* Part One. Nov. 1, 1982. GS: Jonathan Hall Kovacs, David Hooks, Anthony Zerbe, Walter Brooke. A boy billed as wild and dangerous escapes from a traveling medicine show during its stopover in Walnut Grove.

95.7 *The Wild Boy* Part Two. Nov. 8, 1982. GS: Jonathan Hall Kovacs, David Hooks, Anthony Zerbe, Walter Brooke. The sadistic McQueen returns for the mute orphan he once displayed as a wild boy in his traveling medicine show.

95.8 *The Return of Nellie.* Nov. 15, 1982. GS: Allison Arngrim. The attention lavished on Nellie when she returns for her birthday has Nancy fuming.

95.9 *The Empire Builders.* Nov. 22, 1982. GS: Stephen Elliott, Taylor Lacher, James O'Sullivan. The coming of the railroad holds great promise for the citizens of Walnut Grove, except for the Wilders and the Carters, who stand to lose their farm.

95.10 *Love.* Nov. 29, 1982. GS: Jill Schoeler. A May-December relationship blossoms between middle-aged Isaiah and a blind nineteen-year-old who has returned to Walnut Grove.

95.11 *Alden's Dilemma.* Dec. 6, 1982. GS: David Huffman. Shocks are in store for Almanzo and John on their first trip to rough-and-tumble San Francisco, and also for Reverend Alden, who is playing host to a minister sent by the diocese.

95.12 *Marvin's Garden.* Jan. 3, 1983. GS: Helen Kleeb, Ralph Bellamy. An accident leaves Jenny with impaired speech, mobility and use of her hands, and little hope for recovery.

95.13 *Sins of the Fathers.* Jan. 10, 1983. GS: John McLiam. Sarah's strong-willed publisher father tries to persuade the Carters to move to New York, and exerts a maleficent influence on Sarah's little country weekly.

95.14 *The Older Brothers.* Jan. 17, 1984. GS: Geoffrey Lewis, Robert Donner, Timothy Scott, Sunshine Parker. While trying to thwart a stagecoach robbery, Edwards is mistaken for one of the robbers, three bumbling brothers out of prison trying to rebuild their reputation as outlaws.

95.15 *Once Upon a Time.* Jan. 24, 1983. GS: Ralph Manza, Ron Doyle, Kay Howell. A contest spurs Laura to write the first of her "Little House" books.

95.16 *Home Again.* Feb. 7, 1983. GS: Georgia Schmidt, Claude Earl Jones, Charles Tyner. Charles and Albert return to Walnut Grove to straighten out Albert, who has fallen in with a bad crowd in the city.

95.17 *A Child with No Name.* Feb. 14, 1983. Doc Baker is ostracized by the community after Laura blames him for the cradle death of her newborn son.

95.18 *Ruthie.* Feb. 21, 1983. GS: Vera Miles, Eric Christmas. A close relationship develops between Jason and a childless woman who hires him to help her handyman.

95.19 *For the Love of Blanche.* March 7, 1983. GS: Eddie Quillan, Don Collier. Edwards promises a dying man that he will find a proper home for his three-year-old Blanche, unaware that the child in question is an impish orangutan.

95.20 *May I Have This Dance?* March 14, 1983. GS: Sherri Stoner, Jack Ging. Upon graduating from high school, Willie gives his domineering mother a double jolt. He refuses to go to college and he insists on getting married.

95.21 *Hello and Goodbye.* March 21, 1983. GS: Robert Casper, Jonathan Hall Kovacs, Sherri Stoner, Robert Darnett. Lives are changed by two new arrivals—Matthew's father who abandoned the boy when he was two, and a brilliant writer whose superior airs border on the unbearable.

The Tele-films

95.22 *Look Back to Yesterday.* Dec. 12, 1983. GS: Michael Landon, Melora Harden, James T. Callahan, Charles Cypher, Dabbs Greer, Sherri Stoner, Victor French, Melissa Gilbert, Dean Butler, Richard Bull, Kevin Hagen. Walnut Grove battles a recession and Albert battles a virulent blood disease.

95.23 *The Last Farewell.* Feb. 6, 1984. GS: James Karen, Dennis Robertson, Roger Torry, Michael Landon, Karen Grassle, Kevin Hagen, Victor French, Richard Bull, Leslie Landon, Stan Ivar, Lindsay Kennedy. Charles and Caroline Ingalls return to find that Walnut Grove is being taken over by a mining entrepreneur, and the townsfolk are taking up arms to defend their land.

95.24 *Bless All the Dear Children.* Dec. 17, 1984. GS: Melissa Gilbert, Dean Butler, Victor French, Patricia Pearcy, David Freidman, Robert Casper, Leslie Landon, Joel Graves, Shannen Doherty, Richard Bull, Kevin Hagen, Robin Clark. In Walnut Grove at Christmas, the Wilders' infant daughter has been abducted.

96. *Little House on the Prairie*

NBC. 60 min. Broadcast history: Wednesday, 8:00-9:00, Sept. 1974-Sept. 1976; Monday, 8:00-9:00, Sept. 1976-Sept. 1982.

Regular Cast: Michael Landon (Charles Ingalls), Karen Grassle (Caroline Ingalls), Melissa Sue Anderson (Mary Ingalls), Melissa Gilbert (Laura Ingalls), Lindsay and Sidney Greenbush (Carrie Ingalls), Wendi and Brenda Turnbeaugh (Grace Ingalls) 77-82, Victor French (Isaiah Edwards) 74-77, Bonnie Bartlett (Grace Edwards) 74-77, Richard Bull (Nels Oleson), Katherine MacGregor (Harriet Oleson), Jonathan Gilbert (Willie Oleson) 75-82, Alison Arngrim (Nellie Oleson) 74-81, Charlotte Stewart (Miss Beadle) 74-77, Dabbs Greer (Reverend Robert Alden), Ted Gehring (Ebenezer Sprague) 75-76, Kevin Hagen (Doc Baker), Tracie Savage (Christy), Merlin Olsen (Jonathan Garvey) 77-81, Hersha Parady (Alice Garvey) 77-80, Patrick Laborteaux (Andy Garvey) 77-81, Linwood Boomer (Adam Kendall) 77-82, Matthew Laborteaux (Albert) 78-82, Dean Butler (Almanzo Wilder) 79-82, Lucy Lee Flippin (Eliza Jane Wilder) 79-82, Steve Tracy (Percival Dalton) 80-81, Missy Francis (Cassandra) 81-82, Jason Bateman (James) 81-82, Allison Balson (Nancy) 81-82.

Premise: This series, based on the books by Laura Ingalls Wilder, followed the experiences of the Ingalls family, who homesteaded in the frontier of Walnut Grove, Minnesota, in the 1870s.

The Episodes

96.1 *Harvest of Friends.* Sept. 11, 1974. GS: Ramon

Little House on the Prairie

Bieri. The Ingalls family purchases land to farm in southwestern Minnesota, but there is no money left to buy a plow and seed from the local merchant.

96.2 *Country Girls.* Sept. 18, 1975. GS: Robert Hoffman. A lesson in snobbery awaits the Ingalls children on their first day at school. Some of their classmates take particular delight in calling them country girls.

96.3 *The 100 Mile Walk.* Sept. 25, 1974. GS: Don Knight, William Zuckert, Richard Hurst, Celia Kaye, Lance Kerwin, Terry Lumley. Hail flattens the wheat crop, forcing Pa Ingalls, like his equally distressed neighbors, to hit the road in a desperate search for work.

96.4 *Mr. Edwards' Homecoming.* Oct. 2, 1974. GS: Victor French, Robert Swann, Bonnie Bartlett. Ma cheerfully turns matchmaker when Pa brings home their still-unmarried former neighbor from Kansas.

96.5 *The Love of Johnny Johnson.* Oct. 9, 1974. GS: Mitch Vogel. Johnny Johnson, the shy new boy at school, captures little Laura's fancy.

96.6 *If I Should Wake Before I Die.* Oct. 23, 1974. GS: Josephine Hutchinson, Ruth McDevitt, Henry Olek, Betty Lynn. Convinced that only a funeral will gather her family, elderly Amy Hearn fakes her own death and arranges a wake for her 80th birthday.

96.7 *Town Party, Country Party.* Oct. 30, 1974. GS: Kim Richards, Jan Merlin. A twisted ankle gives Laura insight into the plight of a schoolmate often left out of games because of one short leg. And it's Laura who comes up with an observation that leads to a big change in her crippled friend's life.

96.8 *Ma's Holiday.* Nov. 6, 1974. GS: Victor French, Olive Dunbar, Bonnie Bartlett, Norma Connelly. The Ingalls' go to the city for a few days, but their time would be more carefree if Ma Ingalls could only forget that their three lively girls are in the well-intentioned, but inexperience, care of their bachelor friend Mr. Edwards.

96.9 *School Mom.* Nov. 13, 1974. GS: Dirk Blocker, Kelly Thordsen. Substituting for the injured schoolteacher, Caroline finds her biggest challenge in a shy, uneducated fifteen-year-old who is too embarrassed to continue school because he never learned to read or write.

96.10 *The Raccoon.* Nov. 20, 1974. GS: Tracie Savage. Laura's heart is stolen by a little masked bandit, a baby raccoon she tries to tame despite her father's warning that keeping a wild animal can lead to trouble.

96.11 *The Voice of Tinker Jones.* Dec. 4, 1974. GS: Chuck McCann, Wayne Heffley, Eileen Ryan, Jim Jeter. A mute, traveling coppersmith plays a key role in resolving a community squabble over the best way to obtain a bell for the church.

96.12 *The Award.* Dec. 11, 1974. GS: Eddie Rayden, Ruth Foster. Mary's life is filled with unexpected complications as she prepares for a special scholarship exam. The first occurs during a late-night study session when she accidentally sets fire to the barn.

96.13 *The Lord Is My Shepherd.* Dec. 18, 1974. GS: Ernest Borgnine, Bill Cort, Dabbs Greer, Victor French, Bonnie Bartlett. A son is born to the Ingalls and everyone rejoices, except Laura. She is afraid that the baby will replace her in her father's affection.

96.14 *Christmas at Plum Creek.* Dec. 25, 1974. Short on cash but long on ingenuity, the members of the Ingalls family hunt for special gifts to celebrate their first Christmas at Plum Creek.

96.15 *Family Quarrel.* Jan. 15, 1975. GS: Dabbs Greer. After one fight too many, the bickering Olesons finally separate, and neither will budge an inch to patch up their differences.

96.16 *Doctor's Lady.* Jan. 22, 1975. GS: Anne Archer, Steve Kunze, Bea Morris, Douglas Dirkson. A December-May romance blossoms between Walnut Grove's middle-aged bachelor doctor and Mrs. Oleson's visiting niece.

96.17 *Plague.* Jan. 29, 1975. GS: Victor French, Helen Clark, Bradley Greene, Matt Clark. A grain-dealer's acquisition of half-priced cornmeal brings an unexpected scourge. The grain is infested with typhus-bearing rats.

96.18 *The Circus Man.* Feb. 5, 1975. GS: Red Buttons. A charming charlatan comes to town with a bag of magic tricks that includes secret powders that he claims have miraculous healing powers.

96.19 *Child in Pain.* Feb. 12, 1975. GS: Harris Yulin, Johnny Lee, Wayne Heffley. The family members take a personal interest in the rehabilitation of an alcoholic farmer who habitually beats his motherless son.

96.20 *Money Crop.* Feb. 19, 1975. GS: Julie Cobb, Alan Fudge, Lew Brown, Art Lund, John Alderson, Ted Gehring, Jocelyn Brando, Wayne Heffley. Hope turns to concern and then to anger as the days pass without a sign of the young agronomist whom the farmers sent to Minneapolis to bring back a load of promising new seed corn.

96.21 *Survival.* Feb. 26, 1975. GS: Jack Ging, Robert Tessier, Carl Pitti. The Ingalls family, trapped in an abandoned cabin by an unseasonable blizzard, becomes involved in a U.S. marshal's vindictive pursuit of what he calls a Sioux renegade.

96.22 *To See the World.* March 5, 1975. GS: Mitch Vogel, Jane Alice Brandon, Victor French, James Griffith, Bob Hoy. Farm boy Johnny Johnson runs off to see the world, and one of the first sights is a beguiling barmaid who is scarcely older than he.

96.23 *Founder's Day.* May 7, 1975. GS: Forrest Tucker, Ann Doran, Wayne Heffley, Georgia Schmidt. A proud but aging logger puts his pride on the line in the log-chopping contest at the community's annual Founder's Day celebration.

Season Two

96.24 *The Richest Man in Walnut Grove.* Sept. 10, 1975. GS: Kelly Thordsen, Queenie Smith. Due to the bankruptcy of his employer's main customer, Charles is unable to collect two month's of back wages.

96.25 *Four Eyes.* Sept. 17, 1975. GS: Ford Rainey. Mary is falling behind at school, and no one can understand why. Always a good student, she has been studying harder than ever, but still her grades continue to slip.

96.26 *Ebenezer Sprague.* Sept. 24, 1975. GS: Ted Gehring. Charles needs a bank loan to buy more land, but he must deal with a new banker whose heart is as hard as the door of his vault.

96.27 *In the Big Inning.* Oct. 1, 1975. GS: Karl Lukas, Chuck Hayward, June Dayton, Gregory Walcott. The annual baseball game with the Sleepy Eye Greenstockings is coming up, and the men of Walnut Grove still lack a pitcher to avenge their 36-0 loss of the year before.

96.28 *Haunted House.* Oct. 8, 1975. GS: John Anderson, Steffen Zacharias, Lisa Lyon. Taunted by her friends, Laura warily investigates a scary old house they say is occupied by a maniac.

96.29 *The Spring Dance.* Oct. 29, 1975. GS: Clay O'Brien, Bonnie Bartlett. Laura and the Widow Snider resort to the old make-'em-jealous ploy to get the dates they want for the spring dance.

96.30 *Remember Me* **Part One.** Nov. 5, 1975. GS: Patricia Neal, Kyle Richards, Brian Part, Jim Goodwin, Sheldon Allman, Gerry Gaylor. A terminally ill widow must find a home for her three children in the short time she has to live.

96.31 *Remember Me* **Part Two.** Nov. 12, 1975. GS: Patricia Neal, Kyle Richards, Brian Part, Jim Goodwin, Sheldon Allman, Gerry Gaylor. Charles Ingalls must find a home for three children whose widowed mother has died.

96.32 *The Camp-Out.* Nov. 19, 1975. Afraid that the Ingalls children will outpace her own in collecting leaves for school, snobbish Mrs. Oleson packs up her family and her tea service, and joins the Ingalls in what was meant to be a pleasant weekend camp-out.

96.33 *At the End of the Rainbow.* Dec. 10, 1975. GS: Shane Sinutko. Visions of great riches dance in the heads of Laura and a school chum after they find flecks of shiny metal at their favorite fishing hole.

96.34 *The Gift.* Dec. 17, 1975. GS: Lurene Tuttle, David Byrd, Heather Totten. To buy a particularly fine Bible for Reverend Alden's birthday, Laura and Mary gamble the Sunday school's funds on patent medicines that they hope to sell for double their investment.

96.35 *His Father's Son.* Jan. 7, 1976. GS: E.J. Andre, Neil Russell, Peter Haas. A crisis threatens to divide Mr. Edwards' newly acquired family. He wants to make a hunter out of his eldest adopted son, a boy who wouldn't kill any living thing.

96.36 *The Talking Machine.* Jan. 14, 1976. GS: George Furth, Eric Shea. The newly invented phonograph plays a large, and sometimes unnerving, role in Laura's pursuit of a classmate who aspires to become a scientist.

96.37 *The Pride of Walnut Grove.* Jan. 28, 1976. GS: John Howard, Beth Howland, Gracia Lee. A statewide championship in mathematics gives the Ingalls girls a chance to shine. Mary is traveling with her mother to the finals in Minneapolis, and Laura is playing lady of the house at home.

96.38 *A Matter of Faith.* Feb. 4, 1976. GS: Kenneth Tobey, K.T. Stevens, John Alderson, Morgan Jones. Left alone on the farm for a day, Caroline fights for her life as a minor scratch on the leg flares into a major infection.

96.39 *The Runaway Caboose.* Feb. 11, 1976. GS: Sean McClory, Don Collier, Arch Johnson, Parley Baer, Larry Blake. Laura and Mary are also aboard when Mr. Edwards' son Carl accidentally uncouples a caboose from a train, and it begins to run free on a downhill grade nearly 30 miles long.

96.40 *Troublemaker.* Feb. 25, 1976. GS: Richard Basehart, Cooper Huckabee, Sean Kelly, Jack McCulloch. Concerned about unruly behavior in Miss Beadle's classroom, the school board replaces her with a strict disciplinarian whose regimen comes down hardest on Laura.

96.41 *The Long Road Home.* March 3, 1976. GS: Lou Gossett, Richard Jaeckel, Bill Quinn, John Mitchum, Robert Bodeen. Forced by plummeting grain prices to seek additional income, Charles and Mr. Edwards find employment hauling volatile nitroglycerin over rough mountain roads.

96.42 *For My Lady.* March 10, 1976. GS: Mariette Hartley, Karl Swenson, Ted Gehring, Richard Collier. Even Laura and Mary grow suspicious when their father, who is working overtime to surprise his wife with a gift of china, begins spending long hours at the home of an attractive widow.

96.43 *Centennial.* March 17, 1976. GS: Theodore Bikel, William Schallert, Ike Eisenmann, Lisa Pera. Indignant over high taxes and road assessments, the citizens of Walnut Grove consider canceling their Centennial celebration, until they hear from a recent Russian immigrant who lost everything in the old country.

96.44 *Soldier's Return.* March 24, 1976. GS: Richard Mulligan, Queenie Smith, Kelly Jean Peters, Michael James Wixted. A bugler wounded at Shiloh twelve years before returns home to Walnut Grove hoping to teach music, but still deeply troubled by his experience in battle.

96.45 *Going Home.* March 31, 1976. GS: Randames Pera, E.J. Andre, Lurene Tuttle. Discouraged over the loss of his crop to a tornado, Charles prepares to sell the farm and move the family back to Wisconsin.

Season Three

96.46 *The Collection.* Sept. 27, 1976. GS: Johnny Cash, June Carter Cash, Hope Summers, Queenie Smith. A wandering con man believes in the adage that the Lord helps those who help themselves. Taking advantage of Reverend Alden's illness, he dons the minister's clothing and goes to Walnut Grove to collect money and goods intended for the victims of a burned-out town.

96.47 *To Ride the Wind* **Part One.** Oct. 4, 1976. GS: Jim Jeter, Walter Brooke. Scheming Nellie Oleson, knocked from her horse after an argument with Laura, pretends to be crippled so she can turn guilt-stricken Laura into her personal handmaiden.

96.48 *The Race* **Part Two.** Oct. 11, 1976. GS: Jim Jeter, Walter Brooke. While Laura labors to have her horse properly shod and trained for the annual township race, her rival Nellie simply pouts until her mother buys her a thoroughbred racer.

96.49 *Bunny.* Oct. 18, 1976. GS: Walter Edmiston, Kyle Richards. A former engineer, who is now a drunken derelict, may be the Ingalls family's only hope of rescuing their youngest daughter from the depths of a crumbling old well.

96.50 *The Monster of Walnut Grove.* Nov. 1, 1976. GS: Milton Parsons, Charlotte Stewart, Brian Part. Laura gets a Halloween scare — while soaping a window at the Mercantile, she spies an angry Mr. Oleson apparently beheading his wife with a long steel sword.

96.51 *Journey in the Spring* **Part One.** Nov. 15, 1976. GS: Arthur Hill, Jan Sterling, Matthew Laborteaux, Hersha Parady, Jim Boles. The death of Charles' mother sends him back to Wisconsin to persuade his proud and stubborn father to come to Walnut Grove.

96.52 *Journey in the Spring* **Part Two.** Nov. 22, 1976. GS: Arthur Hill, Jan Sterling, Matthew Laborteaux, Hersha

Parady, Jim Boles. Grandfather Ingalls is adjusting nicely to his new life in Walnut Grove when a promise he makes to Laura threatens to shatter their increasingly warm relationship.

96.53 *Fred.* Nov. 29, 1976. GS: Arthur Space, Don "Red" Barry, Joan Tompkins. Laura acquires a new pet, a billy goat whose indiscriminate appetite and nasty disposition make it impossible to keep — or foist off on anyone else.

96.54 *The Bully Boys.* Dec. 6, 1976. GS: Geoffrey Lewis, Roy Jenson, Rayford Barnes, Michael Le Clair. The trusting and forbearing people of Walnut Grove are victimized by three brothers who lie, steal and bully anyone who dares to stand up to them.

96.55 *The Hunters.* Dec. 20, 1976. GS: Burl Ives, Paul Brinegar, Johnny Crawford, Michael Rouges. Laura must turn to a blind recluse trapper for help after accidentally wounding her father on a hunting trip deep in the forest.

96.56 *Blizzard.* Jan. 3, 1977. GS: John Carter, Luana Anders, Don Dubbins, Helen Stenberg, Robert Gibbons. The sudden rise of a blinding, wind-whipped blizzard traps many of the Walnut Grove children on their way home from school.

96.57 *Little Girl Lost.* Jan. 10, 1977. GS: John Ireland, Dabbs Greer. Thirteen-year-old Mary no sooner accepts a marriage proposal from Mr. Edwards' eldest son John, than the youth is offered a university scholarship that will take him away from her for four long years.

96.58 *Quarantine.* Jan. 17, 1977. GS: Marshall Kent, Rance Howard. Although the citizens of Walnut Grove are put under strict quarantine when a deadly fever strikes a neighboring town, Mr. Edwards inadvertently brings the disease home after visiting the stricken community.

96.59 *Little Women.* Jan. 24, 1977. GS: Warren Vanders, Kay Peters, Rachel Lonaker, Roger Bowen. Nellie has most of the lines in a school play, but the player who gets the most from the show is the daughter of a reclusive widow who uses the production to bring her mother back into society.

96.60 *Injun Kid.* Jan. 31, 1977. GS: George Murdock, Caesar Ramirez, Ivy Jones, Willie Aames. A white woman's half-Indian son meets with bigotry from classmates and rejection by his grandfather when the boy and his widowed mother move to the old man's farm.

96.61 *To Live with Fear* Part One. Feb. 14, 1977. GS: Ivan Bonar, Darrell Zwerling, Naomi Ross, James Sikking, John McLiam, James Shigeta, Sheldon Coburn. Mary contracts an infection that requires immediate, and expensive, surgery at a distant hospital.

96.62 *To Live with Fear* Part Two. Feb. 21, 1977. GS: Ivan Bonar, Darrell Zwerling, Naomi Ross, James Sikking, John McLiam, James Shigeta, Sheldon Coburn. To earn money for Mary's next operation, Charles and Mr. Edwards take a job dynamiting for the railroad.

96.63 *The Wisdom of Solomon.* March 7, 1977. GS: Todd Bridges, David Downing, Frederic Downs, Maidie Norman, Don Pedro Colley. A black youth offers to sell himself into slavery to obtain money for an education.

96.64 *The Music Box.* March 14, 1977. GS: Fred Stuthman, Katy Kurtzman, Linda Kristen. Nellie says she won't snitch on Laura for stealing her music box if Laura promises to do anything Nellie wishes, like embarrassing Laura's new friend, a girl who stutters.

96.65 *The Election.* March 21, 1977. GS: Eric Olson, Charles Aidman, Mitzi Hoag, John Herbsleb. The election of a class president becomes a three-way race among Mary, Nellie and a gentle, slow-witted boy who was nominated as a cruel joke.

96.66 *Gold Country.* April 4, 1977. GS: E.J. Andre, Wil Albert, Larry Golden, Robert Forward, Larry Pennell. Flood-ruined crops send Charles Ingalls and Isaiah Edwards packing up their families for the South Dakota gold fields, where high hopes — and even some luck — prove small defense in a climate of greed and violence.

Season Four

96.67 *Castoffs.* Sept. 12, 1977. GS: Hermione Baddeley. An eccentric wanderer comes to settle down in Walnut Grove, and unsettles everyone but the children with her fantasy life in a burned-out house.

96.68 *Times of Change.* Sept. 19, 1977. GS: Randames Pera, John Milford, Herbert Nelson, Paula Shaw, Richard Stanley, Lisa Reeves. Excitement grips Charles and Mary on their first trip to Chicago. He is representing Walnut Grove at the Grange convention, and she will be reunited with her fiance at a cotillion.

96.69 *My Ellen.* Sept. 26, 1977. GS: Corrine Michaels, James Wainwright, Ken Johnson, Bryce Berg, Mia Bendixsen. Laura is imprisoned in a root cellar by a grief-stricken woman who thinks she is her drowned daughter.

96.70 *The Handyman.* Oct. 3, 1977. GS: Gil Gerard, Hermione Baddeley. Caroline hires a handyman to complete the new kitchen Charles left unfinished when he was called away for two weeks on a job. Capable and gentle, the man also chows an interest in Caroline that is not lost on gossipy Mrs. Oleson or on resentful daughter Mary.

96.71 *The Wolves.* Oct. 17, 1977. GS: Don "Red" Barry, Hersha Parady, Patrick Laborteaux. Farmer Garvey reluctantly allows his son to keep an injured wolf and her pups at a time when wolves are being blamed for numerous livestock killings.

96.72 *The Creeper of Walnut Grove.* Oct. 24, 1977. GS: Bernard Behrens, Johnny Doran. Amateur sleuths Laura and her friend Andy crib ideas from penny dreadfuls to track down a sneak thief who seems to take nothing but food.

96.73 *To Run and Hide.* Oct. 31, 1977. GS: Collin Wilcox, Burr De Benning, Michael Pataki, Queenie Smith, Eddie Quillan. After losing a patient, Dr. Baker decides to retire, leaving the care of the deceased's pregnant widow, who has already lost two babies, to an uncaring new doctor.

96.74 *The Aftermath.* Nov. 7, 1977. GS: Dennis Rucker, John Bennett Perry, Frank Marth, Troy Melton, Tony Markes, Michael Conrad. The infamous James Brothers, Jesse and his wounded brother Frank, hide out in Walnut Grove in the guise of well-to-do land speculators.

96.75 *The High Price of Being Right.* Nov. 14, 1977. GS: Eddie Quillan, Denver Mattson, Carl Pitti. Although a fire has destroyed the Garvey's corn crop, a proud Jonathan would rather divorce his wife than let her take a job.

96.76 *The Fighter.* Nov. 21, 1977. GS: Moses Gunn, Ketty Lester, Raymond St. Jacques, Daryl Roach. When Garvey is injured, Charles takes his place in the ring against a touring boxer who is in no condition to fight.

96.77 *Meet Me at the Fair.* Nov. 28, 1977. GS: Dick

DeCoit, Michael Morgan, Dick Armstrong. The Ingalls and Oleson families spend a day at the fair in Mankato.

96.78 *Here Come the Bridges.* Dec. 5, 1977. GS: Joshua Bryant, Bob Marsic, Ivor Francis, Montana Smoyer. It's love at first sight for Miss Beadle and Nellie Oleson when they set eyes on Walnut Grove's latest arrivals: a simple hog farmer and his big, barefoot teenage son.

96.79 *Freedom Flight.* Dec. 12, 1977. GS: Richard O'Brien, Nick Ramus, Vivian Brown, Chief Geronimo, Kuthie Guillermo, San Juan, Brett Ericson. Risking the fury of Indian-hating neighbors, Charles hides a reservation-jumping chief who suffered a stroke while leading his people to new lands.

96.80 *The Rivals.* Jan. 9, 1978. GS: Chris Petersen, Seeley Ann Theimann, Leon Belasco, Sam Gilman, Sam Starr. Laura competes with a new girl for a boy's attention. Meanwhile, Charles and Garvey challenge professional drivers in a freight-hauling contest.

96.81 *Whisper Country.* Jan. 16, 1978. GS: Anita Dangler, John McLiam, Sandy McPeak, Linda McMillan, Dee Craxton, Mark Neely. Mary takes her first teaching job in a small, isolated community dominated by a strong-willed spinster who regards teachers and education as works of the devil.

96.82 *I Remember, I Remember.* Jan. 23, 1978. GS: Matthew Laborteaux, Katy Kurtzman, David Considine, Sorrell Booke, Adam Gunn. While Charles is delayed getting home for his anniversary, Caroline recalls the first times he kept her waiting, in the earliest days of their sputtering courtship.

96.83 *Be My Friend.* Jan. 30, 1978. GS: Donald Moffat, Lenora May, Michael Mullins, Dan McBride, Woodrow Parfrey, John Craig. A message in a bottle leads Laura to an abandoned infant she promptly takes into her heart and home.

96.84 *The Inheritance.* Feb. 6, 1978. GS: Allan Rich, Michael Prince. The death of a barely remembered uncle leaves Charles heir to a fortune.

96.85 *The Stranger.* Feb. 20, 1978. GS: Nehemiah Persoff, Michael Starett. The Olesons take in the only son of a cousin who sent the boy West to learn a sense of down-to-earth values.

96.86 *A Most Precious Guest.* Feb. 27, 1978. GS: Lili Valenty. Caroline's joy at being pregnant again is tempered by a fear that the baby won't by the boy she is sure Charles wants.

96.87 *I'll Be Waving As You Drive Away* Part One. March 6, 1978. GS: Rob Kenneally, David Opatoshu, Linwood Boomer. Charles is given the shattering news that Mary is going blind, and there is nothing medicine can do to prevent it.

96.88 *I'll Be Waving As You Drive Away* Part Two. March 13, 1978. GS: Rob Kenneally, David Opatoshu, Linwood Boomer. As Mary learns to cope with her blindness at an Iowa school, citizens of Walnut Grove face economic disaster in the form of a railroad embargo.

Season Five

96.89 *As Long As We're Together* Part One. Sept. 11, 1978. GS: Leon Charles, Cletus Young, David Hooks, Jodean Lawrence. Hard times on the farm force the Ingalls to move to the city of Winoka in Dakota, and a vastly different way of life.

96.90 *As Long As We're Together* Part Two. Sept. 18, 1978. GS: Leon Charles, Cletus Young, David Hooks, Jodean Lawrence. The Garveys and the Olesons also arrive in Winoka, a city that doesn't even have a public school.

96.91 *The Winoka Warriors.* Sept. 25, 1978. GS: Brad Wilkin, John Ireland, J. Andrew Kenny, Leon Charles, Peter Canon. A farmer sees no future for his blind son, a neither does the boy, until the husky youth plays in an unusual football game between the rich and poor schools of Winoka.

96.92 *The Man Inside.* Oct. 2, 1978. GS: Cliff Emmich, Julie Anne Haddock, Kate Woodville, Walter Edmiston. A fat man ashamed of his size hides from his family and the public by taking up residence where he works, and where he will never be seen, at the school for the blind.

96.93 *There's No Place Like Home* Part One. Oct. 9, 1978. GS: Ray Bolger, Leon Charles, Karl Swenson. An old man is cheated out of his $5000 lottery prize by Charles' unfeeling employer. It's the last straw for many Walnut Grove exiles, who seriously consider returning home.

96.94 *There's No Place Like Home* Part Two. Oct. 16, 1978. GS: Ray Bolger, Leon Charles, Karl Swenson. The exiles return to Walnut Grove, only to find the town dying.

96.95 *Fagin.* Oct. 23, 1978. GS: Kraig Metzinger, Hal Riddle, James Mendenhall. Laura smarts as Charles devotes his attention to his new "son" Albert, even buying the boy a calf to raise for the fair.

96.96 *Harriet's Happenings.* Oct. 30, 1978. GS: John Hellerman, King Moody, Ike Eisenmann. Mrs. Oleson plumbs new depths of yellow journalism as the gossip columnist for Walnut Grove's new newspaper.

96.97 *The Wedding.* Nov. 6, 1978. GS: Lou Fast, David Hooks, Michelle Downey. Wedding bells may peal for Mary, who accepts Adam's proposal but then has a tearful change of heart over the prospect of a blind couple raising a family.

96.98 *Men Will Be Boys.* Nov. 13, 1978. GS: Charles Cooper, Dorothy Konrad, Gus Peters. Charles and Garvey send their sons off to fend for themselves for three days in the wilderness, intending to monitor the test of manhood from a discreet distance.

96.99 *The Cheaters.* Nov. 20, 1978. Andy Garvey, the schoolmarm's son, may be doing poorly in school, but one lesson he quickly learns is not to accept tutoring from stellar student Nellie.

96.100 *Blind Journey* Part One. Nov. 27, 1978. GS: Moses Gunn, Leon Charles, David Hooks, Don "Red" Barry. The Winoka Academy for the Blind is sold, forcing Mary and Adam to seek a new home for their students.

96.101 *Blind Journey* Part Two. Dec. 4, 1978. GS: Moses Gunn, Leon Charles, David Hooks, Don "Red" Barry. Mrs. Oleson joins the blind students journeying to meet a similar group heading for their new school in Walnut Grove.

96.102 *The Godsitter.* Dec. 18, 1978. GS: Tom Clancy, Dolph Sweet, George D. Wallace. Lonely for her father, who is away on a job, little Carrie dreams up a friend who takes her on wonderful make-believe adventures.

96.103 *The Craftsman.* Jan. 8, 1979. GS: John Bleifer, Don "Red" Barry, Frank De Kova, Tony Becker, Alvin Kupperman, Christian Berrigan. Albert learns lessons in pride and prejudice as an apprentice to an elderly Jewish coffin maker.

96.104 *Blind Man's Bluff.* Jan. 15, 1979. GS: Ronnie Scribner, Bert Kramer, Kathryn Leigh Scott. After an accident temporarily impairs a youngster's vision, he resorts to a literal

Little House on the Prairie

blindman's bluff, pretending to have lost all sight, to prevent his parents from going ahead with their plans for divorce.

96.105 *Dance with Me.* Jan. 22, 1979. GS: Ray Bolger, Eileen Heckart, Ysabel MacCloskey, Sean Frye, Ketty Lester. Hard-drinking drifter Toby Noe returns and finds the road to romance not only rocky, but positively boulder-strewn as he tries to court a prim and proper Southern spinster.

96.106 *The Sound of Children.* Feb. 5, 1979. GS: Philip Abbott, Ellen Regan, Dan C. Turner, Ketty Lester, Martha Nix. Mary is pregnant, and the news not only brings Adam's estranged father from New York, but moves him to make an offer: to take them back with him so Adam can attend law school.

96.107 *The Lake Kezia Monster.* Feb. 12, 1979. GS: Hermione Baddeley. When Mrs. Oleson takes possession of a run-down house owned by the elderly eccentric Kezia, the Ingalls children come to the old lady's rescue — with a literally monstrous scheme suggested by one of her tales.

96.108 *Barn Burner.* Feb. 19, 1979. GS: Don "Red" Barry, Moses Gunn, Jeff Corey, Joan Tompkins. When Garvey embarrasses the hot-tempered town bigot Judd Larrabee in front of his family, Larrabee seeks revenge, and finds himself on trial for burning Garvey's barn and injuring his son Andy.

96.109 *The Enchanted Cottage.* Feb. 26, 1979. GS: Nathan Adler, Ketty Lester. Mary announces she can tell light from dark, raising hopes that she may be regaining her sight.

96.110 *Someone Please Love Me.* March 5, 1979. GS: Charles Cioffi, Jenny Sullivan, Bobby Rolofson, Kyle Richards, Eddie Quillan. While on a horse-buying trip, Charles stays at the home of a rancher who raises beautiful horses, but who, since the death of a favorite son, has become a drunk, and a stranger to his wife and remaining two children.

96.111 *Mortal Mission.* March 12, 1979. GS: Matt Clark, Jerry Hardin, Ketty Lester, Peter Kelman. The sale of mutton from diseased sheep creates an outbreak of deadly anthrax in Walnut Grove.

96.112 *The Odyssey.* March 19, 1979. GS: Bill Ewing, Steve Shaw, Melinda Cordell, Joe Young, Ken O'Brien. Laura and Albert must leave home to help a dying friend realize a dream to see the ocean.

Season Six

96.113 *Back to School.* Sept. 17, 1979. GS: Lucy Lee Flippen. Two newcomers arrive in Walnut Grove, schoolmarm Eliza Jane Wilder and her brother Almanzo, whom Laura instantly senses is the man she is going to marry.

96.114 *Laura's Love Story.* Sept. 24, 1979. GS: Lucy Lee Flippen. In their ongoing rivalry for Almanzo's affections, Nellie finds a particularly sneaky way to avenge a dirty trick played on her by Laura.

96.115 *The Family Tree.* Oct. 1, 1979. GS: Michael Pataki, John Zaremba. Charles runs into an unexpected roadblock when he files papers to legally adopt Albert.

96.116 *The Third Miracle.* Oct. 8, 1979. GS: Leslie Landon. A stagecoach accident in a remote area leaves only Mary unscathed to find help for the other passengers, including a young woman in labor.

96.117 *Annabelle.* Oct. 15, 1979. GS: Harriet Gibson, Ken Berry, Billy Barty, Wendy Schaal. A traveling circus brings joy to everyone but Nels Oleson, who recognizes the gargantuan fat lady as the sister he was always ashamed of.

96.118 *The Preacher Takes a Wife.* Oct. 22, 1979. GS: Iris Korn, William Schallert, Ketty Lester, Jon Lormer. Claiming that a minister is already married to his work, Mrs. Oleson threatens to have Reverend Alden dismissed if he proceeds with plans to wed a widowed parishioner.

96.119 *The Halloween Dream.* Oct. 29, 1979. GS: Philip Carey, Frank DeKova, Dick Alexander, Henry K. Bal. Albert and Laura are costumed as war-painted Indians for a Halloween party. After reading a book about Indian escapades, Albert dreams he is mistaken for the son of a chief and is given command of a tribe surrounding Walnut Grove.

96.120 *The Return of Mr. Edwards.* Nov. 5, 1979. GS: Victor French, Bonnie Bartlett, Kyle Richards, Eddie Quillan. The Ingalls old friend Mr. Edwards is now a success in the logging business, until a crippling accident destroys his will to live.

96.121 *The King Is Dead.* Nov. 12, 1979. GS: Ray Walston, Leo Gordon, John Robert Yeats, Nora Meerbaum. A crooked promoter tricks Jonathan into playing the patsy in a wrestling match.

96.122 *The Faith Healer.* Nov. 19, 1979. GS: James Olson, Tom Rosqui, Joey Seifers, Francesca Jarvin. A faith healer mesmerizes the people of Walnut Grove with his apparent ability to cure by the laying on of hands.

96.123 *Author, Author.* Nov. 26, 1979. GS: Barry Sullivan. Caroline's father arrives in Walnut Grove dispirited over the recent death of his wife. As a kind of therapy, the family urges him to put his lifetime of stories into a book.

96.124 *Crossed Connection.* Dec. 10, 1979. GS: Merlin Olson, Hersha Parady, Royal Dano, Sam Edwards, Marie Denn. The installation of a telephone exchange at the hotel gives the operator, gossipy Mrs. Oleson, a direct line to Walnut Grove's secrets, one of which threatens the Garveys' marriage.

96.125 *The Angry Heart.* Dec. 17, 1979. GS: Timothy Wead, Mary Hamill, Susan French, Malcolm Atterbury, Richard Donat. A hostile teenager, emotionally scarred by a brutal father, comes to live with his grandparents in Walnut Grove, where he gets off to a bad start by stealing Charles' watch.

96.126 *The Werewolf of Walnut Grove.* Jan. 7, 1980. GS: Tod Thompson, Sandy Ward. A newcomer to Miss Wilder's classroom is a wealthy farmer's strapping, spoiled son, who quickly becomes a holy terror to teacher and students alike.

96.127 *Whatever Happened to the Class of '56?* Jan. 14, 1980. GS: James Gallery, Liam Sullivan, Lynn Benesch, Phillip Pine, Mary Elizabeth Corrigan. Charles and Caroline set off for the Grange convention in Milwaukee, and to attend the reunion party of their high-school class of 1856.

96.128 *Darkness Is My Friend.* Jan. 21, 1980. GS: James McIntire, Jonathan Banks, Larry Golden, Toni Mele. Three escaped convicts seek shelter from a storm in the school where Mary and Laura are alone with the blind children.

96.129 *Silent Promises.* Jan. 28, 1980. GS: Alban Branton. Laura throws herself into teaching sign language to a deaf friend.

96.130 *May We Make Them Proud.* Feb. 4, 1980. A fire at the school for the blind claims the lives of Mary's baby and

Jonathan's wife, and lays a terrible burden of guilt on the person responsible.

96.131 *Wilder and Wilder.* Feb. 11, 1980. GS: Charles Bloom, Stacy Sipes, Kay Howell, Bill Cross. The arrival of Almanzo's younger brother raises Charles' hopes that Laura might fall for someone closer to her own age.

96.132 *Second Spring.* Feb. 18, 1980. GS: Suzanne Rogers, Tom Clancy. Fed up with his overbearing family, Oleson takes to the road, where he meets a beguiling colleen who almost makes him forget his age and his wife.

96.133 *Sweet Sixteen.* Feb. 25, 1980. GS: Lucille Benson, Parley Baer, Tim Maier. Teaching certificate in hand, Laura is driven to a nearby town to take over an injured teacher's class. Her driver, Almanzo, knows she is only sixteen, but somehow Laura Ingalls no longer seems like a kid.

96.134 *He Loves Me, He Loves Me Not* Part One. May 5, 1980. GS: Steve Tracy, Dub Taylor. Laura accepts Almanzo's marriage proposal, but Charles insists they wait two years to wed.

96.135 *He Loves Me, He Loves Me Not* Part Two. May 12, 1980. GS: Steve Tracy, Dub Taylor. The road to romance is rocky for Laura, who spots Almanzo rubbing a saloon-girl's back, and for Nellie, whose boy friend says he is leaving.

Season Seven

96.136 *Laura Ingalls Wilder* Part One. Sept. 22, 1980. Laura finally sets her wedding date, and Miss Wilder, the spinster schoolmarm, finds love for the first time in her life.

96.137 *Laura Ingalls Wilder* Part Two. Sept. 29, 1980. Laura's wedding prospects fade and Miss Wilder's prospects disappear altogether.

96.138 *A New Beginning.* Oct. 6, 1980. John Larch, Patrick Laborteaux, John Dukakis, Harry Carey, Jr., Med Flory, Milton Selzer. Widower Garvey and his son move to Sleepy Eye to start a new life and a freight business, but are harassed by a thieving gang of young toughs.

96.139 *Fight, Team, Fight.* Oct. 13, 1980. GS: William Traylor, James Carnagin, Irene O'Conor, Ron Doyce. Walnut Grove's new football coach believes that a game is akin to war, and that winning is the only thing that counts.

96.140 *The Silent Cry.* Oct. 20, 1980. GS: Dub Taylor, David Faustino, David Hollander, Ivan Bonar, George Dickerson. An elderly caretaker at the school for the blind shelters two runaway orphaned brothers who are facing separation: a couple wants to adopt the older boy, but not his silent brother.

96.141 *Portrait of Love.* Oct. 27, 1980. GS: Madeline Stowe, Mariclaire Costello, Paul Napier, Constance Pfeifer, Jim Antonio, Ward Costello. News of a blind artist's first exhibition moves the girl's natural mother to renew contact with the daughter she abandoned as a child.

96.142 *Divorce, Walnut Grove Style.* Nov. 10, 1980. GS: Tisch Raye. Laura rages with jealousy and moves back with her parents when a pretty acquaintance reenters Almanzo's life.

96.143 *Dearest Albert, I'll Miss You.* Nov. 17, 1980. GS: Diane Shalet, Suzy Gilstrap. Albert spins tall tales about himself to impress a pen pal in Minneapolis, unaware that she is confined to a wheelchair and is likewise stretching the truth.

96.144 *The In-Laws.* Nov. 24, 1980. GS: Eddie Quillan, Terence Evans. As partners in a new freight-hauling venture, Charles and Almanzo agree on a race to decide the better route between Walnut Grove and Sleepy Eye.

96.145 *To See the Light* Part One. Dec. 1, 1980. GS: Peter Hobbs, Ketty Lester, Donald Petrie, Donald Hotton. New horizons open up for Adam after a concussion restores his sight, but Mary grows increasingly apprehensive that the change may threaten their marriage.

96.146 *To See the Light* Part Two. Dec. 8, 1980. GS: Peter Hobbs, Ketty Lester, Donald Petrie, Donald Hotton. Adam has regained his sight but he fails to still Mary's fears when he leaves for Minneapolis to compete for a law-school scholarship.

96.147 *Oleson Versus Oleson.* Jan. 5, 1981. GS: Kay Howell. A petition demanding property rights for wives sets off a battle of the sexes in Walnut Grove.

96.148 *Come, Let Us Reason Together.* Jan. 12, 1981. GS: E.M. Margolese, Bea Silvern. The impending arrival of Nellie and Percival's firstborn sparks a battle over the child's religious upbringing between Nellie's Christian mother and Percival's Jewish father.

96.149 *The Nephews.* Jan. 19, 1981. GS: Rossie Harris, Woody Enery, Ham Larson, Aileen Fitzpatrick, Jack Alley. Laura and Almanzo are saddled with two young nephews who possess a genius for making mischief.

96.150 *Make a Joyful Noise.* Jan. 26, 1981. GS: Moses Gunn, Keith Mitchell, Mel Stewart, Starletta Du Pois. Joe Kagan returns and discovers he has a dapper rival for Hester-Sue's affections when he sells his farm in Walnut Grove and moves to Sleepy Eye to court her.

96.151 *Goodbye Mrs. Wilder.* Feb. 2, 1981. GS: Walker Edmiston, Dennis Dimster, Cletus Young, Gillian Grant. Stung by criticism of her teaching ability and choice of curriculum, Laura quits and turns the class over to her critic.

96.152 *Sylvia* Part One. Feb. 9, 1981. GS: Olivia Barash, Royal Dano, Richard Jaeckel. A fourteen-year-old girl lives in fear and humiliation after being sexually assaulted by a masked rapist.

96.153 *Sylvia* Part Two. Feb. 16, 1981. GS: Olivia Barash, Royal Dano, Richard Jaeckel. Albert resolves to marry Sylvia despite their tender ages, the false rumors that he sired her unborn child, and her father's determination to take her away.

96.154 *Blind Justice.* Feb. 23, 1981. GS: Jeff Corey, John Zaremba, Barbara Ballentine, Dub Taylor, Peter Hobbs. Adam accepts a highly unpopular first client in a land speculator accused of defrauding Walnut Grove investors.

96.155 *I Do Again.* March 2, 1981. GS: James Gallery, Sarah Miller, Dolores Albin, Hugh Warden. Both Laura and Caroline are happy to announce that they are expecting, but Doc Baker has sad news for Caroline.

96.156 *The Lost Ones* Part One. May 4, 1981. GS: E.J. Andre, Ketty Lester, Len Wayland, Barbara Tarbuck. Charles takes it upon himself to find a home for two children orphaned by a wagon accident.

96.157 *The Lost Ones* Part Two. May 11, 1981. GS: E.J. Andre, Ketty Lester, Len Wayland, Barbara Tarbuck. Charles and Caroline are uneasy about the humorless couple who agree to adopt orphaned James and Cassandra.

Season Eight

96.158 *The Reincarnation of Nellie* Part One. Oct. 5, 1981. GS: Laurence Bane, Melora Hardin. Charles and Caroline have adopted two orphans, and Mary, Adam, Percival and Nellie have moved to New York. It's Nellie's departure that devastates Mrs. Oleson, prompting her to seek a replacement.

96.159 *The Reincarnation of Nellie* Part Two. Oct. 12, 1981. GS: Laurence Bane, Melora Hardin. The Olesons' adopted daughter Nancy turns out to be even nastier than Nellie when she schemes to gain the lead in the school pageant.

96.160 *Growin' Pains.* Oct. 19, 1981. GS: Aaron Fletcher. The strain of having five youngsters living in one house takes its toll on James, who begins to feel that he really doesn't belong.

96.161 *Dark Sage.* Oct. 26, 1981. GS: Donald James Marshall, Marlene Warfield, John Shearin, Anne E. Curry. Even Doc Baker is surprised, and apprehensive, when his new associate shows up to serve the community as its first black doctor.

96.162 *A Wiser Heart.* Nov. 2, 1981. GS: Patrick Collins, Joe Lambie, Darlene Conley, Kathryn Fuller, Lucy Lee Flippen. Laura's failure to land an expected tutoring job is just the first in a series of events that sours her stay in Arizona for a summer class.

96.163 *Gambini the Great.* Nov. 9, 1981. GS: Jack Kruschen, Gloria Manos, Stephen Manley, Robert Torti. The death-defying stunts of an aging daredevil fascinate Albert, who tries to duplicate them.

96.164 *The Legend of Black Jake.* Nov. 16, 1981. GS: Todd Sussman, Royce D. Applegate, Sam Edwards. Oleson is kidnaped by two bumbling crooks who demand a $100 ransom, and Mrs. Oleson refuses to pay.

96.165 *Chicago.* Nov. 23, 1981. GS: Victor French, M. Emmet Walsh, Chez Lister, John Lawrence, Gene Ross. Charles joins Isaiah Edwards in Chicago to claim the body of Isaiah's adopted son, a newspaper copy boy reported killed in a street accident.

96.166 *For the Love of Nancy.* Nov. 30, 1981. GS: J. Brennan Smith, Elizabeth Rogers. An obese new student adores Nancy, who couldn't care less about him, but isn't above taking advantage of his interest.

96.167 *Wave of the Future.* Dec. 7, 1971. GS: Laurie Main. Mrs. Oleson bites off more than she can chew when she contracts for a franchise with a restaurant chain.

96.168 *A Christmas They Never Forgot.* Dec. 21, 1981. GS: Newell Alexander, Tom Lester, Eddy C. Dyer, Heibi Zuroe. Snowbound on Christmas Eve, Hester-Sue and the Ingalls family recall Christmases past.

96.169 *No Beast So Fierce.* Jan. 4, 1982. GS: Peter Billingsley, Dennis Howard, Jennifer Rhoades, Robert Patton. Two lonely creatures take a liking to James — a wild dog encountered on a trip to Minneapolis, and a new boy with a bad stammer.

96.170 *Stone Soup.* Jan. 18, 1982. While Almanzo and Charles are away, a pregnant Laura struggles alone to save a newly planted orchard from a drought.

96.171 *The Legacy.* Jan. 25, 1982. GS: Robert Boon, Claude Earl Jones, J.S. Young. Charles leaves the farm for the city to pursue a career as a cabinetmaker.

96.172 *Uncle Jed.* Feb. 1, 1982. GS: E.J. Andre, Claude Woolman, Wiley Harker. James and Cassandra are implored by their granduncle to live with him now that he is wealthy enough to give them anything they want.

96.173 *Second Chance.* Feb. 8, 1982. GS: Ketty Lester, J.A. Preston, Marguerite De Lain. Hester-Sue's ex-husband, a hard-drinking gambler who left her for another woman, shows up claiming he is reformed and hoping for a reconciliation.

96.174 *Days of Sunshine, Days of Shadow* Part One. Feb. 15, 1982. GS: Sam Edwards. The Wilders are looking forward to their first-born and a bountiful harvest, then hail destroys the crop and a stroke fells Almanzo.

96.175 *Days of Sunshine, Days of Shadow* Part Two. Feb. 22, 1982. GS: Sam Edwards. A tornado flattens the Wilders' house, injuring new mother Laura and further depressing Almanzo, who is still paralyzed.

96.176 *A Promise to Keep.* March 1, 1982. GS: Dabbs Greer. Isaiah Edwards, driven from his family because of his drunkenness, returns to Walnut Grove, but doesn't stop drinking.

96.177 *A Faraway Cry.* March 8, 1982. GS: Ruth Silveira, Calvin Bartlett, Brion James, James Griffith, Betty McGuire, Dennis Lipscomb. Doc Baker and Caroline answer a plea for help from Caroline's childhood friend, a woman about to give birth in an influenza-ridden mining camp.

96.178 *He Was Only Twelve* Part One. May 3, 1982. GS: Don Beddoe, John Dennis Johnston, Tom Roy Lowe, Hal Smith, Bill Vint, R.P. Call. Charles and Mr. Edwards set out after the outlaws who gravely wounded James during a bank robbery.

96.179 *He Was Only Twelve* Part Two. May 10, 1982. GS: Don Beddoe, John Dennis Johnston, Tom Roy Lowe, Hal Smith, Bill Vint, R.P. Call. Neglecting both family and work, Charles prays full time for a miracle to save his comatose son James.

97. *The Lone Ranger*

ABC. 30 min. Broadcast history: Thursday, 7:30-8:00, Sept. 1949–Sept. 1957.

Regular Cast: Clayton Moore (the Lone Ranger), Jay Silverheels (Tonto), John Hart (the Lone Ranger) 1951.

Premise: John Reid, the lone survivor of an attack on six Texas Rangers by the Butch Cavendish Hole in the Wall Gang, dons a mask and, with his Indian friend Tonto, attempts to maintain law and order in the West during the 1800s.

The Episodes

97.1 *Enter the Lone Ranger.* Sept. 15, 1949. GS: Glenn Strange, George Lewis, Tristram Coffin, Jack Clifford, Walter Sande, George Chesebro, Ralph Littlefield. While tracking down the Butch Cavendish gang, a patrol of six Texas Rangers is ambushed. The outlaws believe all six are killed, but an Indian discovers that one Ranger, though badly wounded, still lives. He carries him to a cave and tries to nurse the man back to health.

97.2 *The Lone Ranger Fights On.* Sept. 22, 1949. GS: Glenn Strange, Walter Sande, George Chesebro, Ralph Littlefield, George J. Lewis, Jack Clifford. The Lone Ranger and Tonto pursue the Cavendish gang to a town where they have killed several prominent citizens and replaced them with their own agents.

97.3 *The Lone Ranger's Triumph.* Sept. 29, 1949. GS: Glenn Strange, Walter Sande, George Chesebro, Jack Clifford. The Lone Ranger and Tonto organize the honest townsmen into a fighting force and ride out for the last battle with Cavendish and his gang.

97.4 *Legion of Old Timers.* Oct. 6, 1949. GS: DeForest Kelley, Emmett Lynn, Norman Willis, Lane Bradford, Sandy Sanders, Hank Patterson. A young Easterner has inherited a ranch, but gangsters want to take it away from him. The crooked foreman fires all the hands and hires his outlaw pals. The Lone Ranger and Tonto join forces with a small army of elderly cowhands to help the young man reclaim his ranch.

97.5 *Rustler's Hideout.* Oct. 13, 1949. GS: Harry Lauter, Kay Morley, Joseph Crehan, Dickie Jones, Fred Kohler, Jr. When a group of ranchers capture Pete Madden, leader of an outlaw gang, the outlaws retaliate by kidnaping a rancher's son.

97.6 *War Horse.* Oct. 20, 1949. GS: Leonard Penn, Jean DeBriac, John Merton, Ed Cassidy, Bob Cason, Chief Yowlachie. Chief Lame Bear's horse Red Cloud is in danger of being abducted by Madrigo, a vengeful hunter. The Lone Ranger and Tonto try to prevent an Indian war when Madrigo and his men steal the horse in order to sell it to a circus.

97.7 *Pete and Pedro.* Oct. 27, 1949. GS: Rufe Davis, Don Diamond, Sheila Ryan, John Parrish, Bill Lester, Fred Graham. The Lone Ranger, Tonto and pair of perpetually feuding cowboys help a young woman who is being forced to sell her ranch to the biggest cattleman in the area.

97.8 *Renegades.* Nov. 3, 1949. GS: Gene Roth, Harry Harvey, Ralph Moody, Kenneth MacDonald, Michael Ross, Wheaton Chambers, Lane Chandler. Tonto visits his old friend Chief Swift Eagle. The Lone Ranger steps in when a corrupt Indian agent and a group of deserters try to kill them.

97.9 *The Tenderfeet.* Nov. 10, 1949. GS: Rand Brooks, Ross Ford, Ray Bennett, Hank Worden, Monte Blue. The Lone Ranger tries to prove the innocence of the Larabee brothers, newcomers to the West, who have been accused of committing crimes.

97.10 *High Heels* (A.K.A. "Rustlers of Redstone"). Nov. 17, 1949. GS: James Sheldon, Stanley Andrews, Earle Hodgins, Johnny Berkes, Michael Whalen, Eric Alden. Pat St. Ives is a proud little man, so sensitive about his height that he wears special shoes to make him taller. Monk Gow plays on his pride to stir up trouble and the Lone Ranger and Tonto come to the rescue.

97.11 *Six-Gun Legacy.* Nov. 24, 1949. GS: Don Haggerty, James J. Hickman, Ian Wolfe, Hal Price, Jimmy Dundee, Chuck Roberson. Outlaws stop a stagecoach, steal Bob Walker's identification papers and leave him half dead beside the trail. They plan to substitute an impostor for the young man before he claims his inheritance.

97.12 *Return of the Convict* (A.K.A. "Western Vengeance"). Dec. 1, 1949. GS: John Kellogg, Robert Emmett Keane, Steve Clark, John Day, George Lloyd. John Ames is an ex-convict, jailed for a crime he didn't commit. He returns home, bitter about having been convicted by false testimony and hoping to clear himself.

97.13 *Finders Keepers.* Dec. 8, 1949. GS: Carol Thurston, Arthur Franz, Francis McDonald, Pedro de Cordova, Keith Richards, David Leonard. Vic Crowley and Wade Turner blackmail Nat Parker into robbing a bank for them. Nat returns to Desert City after serving a prison sentence for the robbery and attempts to recover the loot he hid.

97.14 *The Masked Rider.* Dec. 15, 1949. GS: John Doucette, Nan Leslie, Ed Rand, John Alvin, Sailor Vincent, George Slocum, Nolan Leary, Margarita Martin. A ruthless outlaw disguises himself as the Lone Ranger and sets out on the path of crime. When the imposter commits a murder, the Lone Ranger must bring the man to justice to clear his own name.

97.15 *Old Joe's Sister.* Dec. 22, 1949. GS: Anne O'Neal, Joel Friedkin, Lester Sharpe, Wade Crosby, Clancy Cooper. Old Joe is attacked by two outlaws while painting his house in anticipation of meeting a sister he hasn't seen in thirty years. The crooks push Old Joe over a cliff, hoping to find his house packed with hoarded money.

97.16 *Cannonball McKay.* Dec. 29, 1949. GS: Louise Lorimer, Leonard Strong, Charles Meredith, Tristram Coffin, Ralph Peters, Mack Williams, Fred Murray. Lady stagecoach driver Cannonball McKay has ex-convict Clem Jones for an assistant. Trouble arises when the ex-con is framed for a robbery. She calls on the Lone Ranger and Tonto to help her prove his innocence.

97.17 *The Man Who Came Back.* Jan. 5, 1950. GS: Emmett Lynn, Roy Gordon, Martha Hyer, Robert Carson, Robert J. Wilke. The Lone Ranger and Tonto stop to visit Joe Crawford at his ranch. They find that Joe is gone, and a man named Gavin claims that he owns the ranch.

97.18 *Outlaw Town.* Jan. 12, 1950. GS: John Eldredge, Greta Granstedt, Gene Reynolds, Marshall Bradford. Jack Buke runs Outlaw Town, a refuge for all the criminals in the surrounding territory. Jack's wife stands silently by, until the day he tries to frame young Jim Andrews.

97.19 *Greed for Gold.* Jan. 19, 1950. GS: Keene Duncan, Duke York, Lane Bradford, Kermit Maynard, Tudor Owen, Margaret Field. Greed for gold leads an outlaw to seek control of a rich gold mine. Along the way he finds it necessary to kill a friend of the Lone Ranger's

97.20 *Man of the House.* Jan. 26, 1950. GS: Esther Somers, Stanley Farrar, Tim Graham, Lane Chandler, William Tannen, Dick Curtis, John McGuire. Casper, a small timid man, is bullied by his wife. The Lone Ranger and Tonto help Casper overcome his wife's domination by taking him with them as they pursue an outlaw gang.

97.21 *Barnaby Boggs, Esquire.* Feb. 2, 1950. Hal Price, Gene Roth, Holly Bane, Bill Kennedy, Bob Kellard. An outlaw has been able to fool the townspeople, who know nothing of his illegal activities. He learns, however, that a quack doctor has found out about him, and he decides to kill the man.

97.22 *Sheep Thieves.* Feb. 9, 1950. GS: Chuck Courtney, Jimmy Ogg, Pedro de Cordova, Russ Conway, Almira Sessions, Harry Cording, John Day. The Lone Ranger's nephew, Dan Reid, poses as the grandson of a rich cattleman. A band of rustlers, believing the ruse, kidnap Dan and hold him for ransom.

97.23 *Jim Tyler's Past.* Feb. 16, 1950. GS: Rand Brooks, House Peters, Jr., Ray Bennett, Peter Mamakos. The Lone Ranger and Tonto discover a secret in lawman Jim Tyler's past, but give him another chance to go straight and help them trap a former partner.

97.24 *The Man with Two Faces.* Feb. 23, 1950. GS: Earle Hodgins, Stanley Andrews, Mira McKinney, Chris Drake, Steven Clark. A one-eyed outlaw robs three banks owned by Joshua Blaine. When it is suspected that one of Blaine's two nephews is the culprit, the Lone Ranger and Tonto begin an investigation.

97.25 *Buried Treasure.* March 2, 1950. GS: David Bruce, Gail Davis, William Challee, William Gould, Bob Kellard. An escaped outlaw forces his brother and sister-in-law to hide him in their house. The Lone Ranger and Tonto use a mirror trick to recapture the convict.

97.26 *Troubled Waters.* March 9, 1950. GS: Harry Lauter, Dick Alexander, Eula Morgan, Byron Foulger, Luther Crockett. A restaurant owner who holds the mortgage on a ranch learns that there is oil on the property and tries to prevent the rancher from paying off his debt.

97.27 *Gold Train.* March 16, 1950. GS: Frank Fenton, Bob Cason, DeForest Kelley, Erville Alderson, Billy Bletcher, Hank Patterson, Bob Kellard, Bob Woodward. As the result of mistaken identity, the Lone Ranger is thrown into jail as a masked desperado. He must convince the authorities of his innocence.

97.28 *Pay Dirt.* March 23, 1950. GS: Emmett Lynn, Martin Milner, Zon Murray, George Lewis, Walter Sande, George Lynn. The Lone Ranger and Tonto go after a gang of claim jumpers who have committed murder in order to get their hands on a rich strike.

97.29 *Billie the Great.* March 30, 1950. GS: Minerva Urecal, Steve Clark, James Flavin, Ward Blackburn, Bob Woodward, Matt McHugh, George Meader. Outlaws plan to steal the town's money, which is kept in a safe owned by a lady barber named Billie.

97.30 *Never Say Die.* April 6, 1950. GS: Glenn Strange, Joseph Crehan, David Hoyt, Lee Phelps, Cecil Spooner, Marjorie Eaton, Ray Teal. When Butch Cavendish makes his escape from jail by taking the warden's son hostage, the Lone Ranger sets out to find the outlaw.

97.31 *Gold Fever.* April 13, 1950. GS: John Doucette, Francis Ford, Leonard Strong, Harold Goodwin, John A. Butler, Elaine Retey, George Lewis. The Lone Ranger has reason to suspect that a notorious outlaw is seeking more than money when he holds up a stagecoach.

97.32 *Death Trap.* April 20, 1950. GS: James Griffith, Kenne Duncan, Jeff York, Lucien Littlefield, Lee Shumway, Steve Clark. When three deputies, escorting prisoners from Petersville to Abilene, mysteriously disappear, the Lone Ranger starts an investigation. His search leads him to the cabin of a harmless old prospector.

97.33 *A Matter of Courage.* April 27, 1950. GS: Edmund Cobb, James Arness, Don Haggerty, Juan Duvall, Raymond Largay, Dick Curtis. The Lone Ranger and Tonto, accompanied by a timid barber, set out to capture two outlaws who are fleeing to the border.

97.34 *Rifles and Renegades.* May 4, 1950. GS: Robert Kent, Robert Bice, I. Stanford Jolley, Gene Roth, Bill Ward, Frank Marlowe, Russ Conklin, John Hart. The Lone Ranger suspects an Army storekeeper of being in cahoots with a gang that steals rifles from the Army and sells them to an Indian chief. The Lone Ranger allows himself to be taken prisoner in order to expose the storekeeper.

97.35 *Bullets for Ballots.* May 11, 1950. GS: Craig Stevens, Marjorie Lord, Frederic Tozere, Frank Jacquet, John Alvin, Holly Bane, Phil Tead, Wade Blackburn. The Lone Ranger and Tonto arrive in a Western town in the midst of a mayoralty election. They intervene when a ruthless mob tries to gain control.

97.36 *The Black Hat.* May 18, 1950. GS: John Eldredge, Jeff York, Ed Hinton, George Pembroke, William Ruhl. On the trail of fleeing outlaws who have stolen gold and slain two guards, the Lone Ranger and Tonto have a strange clue to follow.

97.37 *Devil's Pass.* May 25, 1950. GS: Jim Bannon, Gene Evans, Marshall Brady, Jimmy Lloyd, Jeb Dooley. The Lone Ranger and Tonto notice two red-headed men acting suspiciously. Then they hear reports of a red-headed man at the scene of a bank robbery and decide to investigate.

97.38 *Spanish Gold.* June 1, 1950. GS: Gail Davis, Ross Ford, Steve Clark, Kenneth Tobey, Bruce Hamilton. The Lone Ranger and Tonto come to the aid of a young girl and her sweetheart when they are threatened by a band of outlaws. They learn that the outlaws have framed the girl's father.

97.39 *Damsels in Distress.* June 8, 1950. GS: John Banner, Phyllis Kennedy, Gloria Winters, Peggy McIntire, Tom Tyler, Phil Tead, Lee Tung Foo. In order to trap a criminal who is threatening three young ladies, the Lone Ranger adopts a clever disguise.

97.40 *Man Without a Gun.* June 15, 1950. GS: Dick Jones, Eddie Dunn, James Harrison, Ralph Moody, House Peters, Jr., Bob Kellard. While attempting to avert bloodshed between Indians and homesteaders, the Lone Ranger and Tonto find themselves trapped between the two opposing forces.

97.41 *Pardon for Curley.* June 22, 1950. GS: Douglas Kennedy, Stephen Chase, Marion Martin, Harry Harvey, Paul Hogan, John Cliff, Earle Hodgins, Dick Alexander. A dangerous outlaw whom the Lone Ranger sent to prison vows revenge. He breaks out of jail and sets out to make good his threat.

97.42 *Eye for an Eye.* June 29, 1950. GS: Steve Clark, Sue England, Chris-Pin Martin, Johnny Day. When they find out that the governor's daughter is in danger from a notorious outlaw, the Lone Ranger and Tonto try to protect her. Then they learn the outlaw plans to kill them both.

97.43 *Outlaws of the Plains.* July 6, 1950. GS: Jack Lee, Jay Morley, Bernie Marcus, Stanley Blystone, Edward Cassidy, Bert Arnold, Steve Dunhill. The Lone Ranger sets out to expose a dishonest sheriff who is head of a gang of cattle rustlers.

97.44 *White Man's Magic.* July 13, 1950. GS: Ralph Moody, Lane Bradford, Bill Kennedy, Jane Frazee, Charles Stevens, Bill Ward, Pierre Watkin. An artist, who defies an Indian tradition by painting the chief's portrait, finds his life in danger from the irate tribesmen. The Lone Ranger and Tonto attempt to rescue the painter.

97.45 *Trouble for Tonto.* July 20, 1950. GS: Gene Roth, Robert Arthur, Russ Conklin, Byron Foulger, Jimmy Dundee, Bill Ward, Lyle Talbot. Disguised as an Indian chief to help the Lone Ranger capture a bank robber, Tonto finds himself in trouble when the robber sees through his disguise.

97.46 *Sheriff of Gunstock.* July 27, 1950. GS: John

Doucette, John Hart, Walter Sande, William Vincent, Mira McKinney, Tom Irish, Jack Kenney. The Lone Ranger and Tonto suspect that Gunstock's sheriff is mixed up in a protection racket, but then learn that the criminals are holding his son hostage.

97.47 *The Wrong Man.* Aug. 3, 1950. GS: Don Beddoe, Paul Maxey, Glen Vernon, Nan Leslie, Richard Crane, Almira Sessions, Ted Adams, Walter Shumway. The Lone Ranger and Tonto champion the cause of a man they believe has been unjustly accused of murder.

97.48 *The Beeler Gang.* Aug. 10, 1950. GS: Robert Rockwell, Beverly Campbell, B.G. Norman, Ralph Peters, Hugh Prosser, Fred Graham, William Haade, George Slocum, Tim Graham. The Beeler gang kidnaps a sheriff's small son to force him to resign. The Lone Ranger tries to rescue the boy.

97.49 *The Star Witness.* Aug. 17, 1950. GS: Gene Evans, William H. Vedder, Ray Bennett, Henry Rowland, Michael Chapin, Clarence Straight, Charles Watts, Sarah Padden. No one will believe a twelve-year-old's tale that he witnessed a murder until the Lone Ranger uses a clever ruse.

97.50 *The Black Widow.* Aug. 24, 1950. GS: John Alvin, George Pembroke, Peter Mamakos, Lane Chandler Tony Rorex, Holly Bane, Michael Whalen. A vest which belonged to a man who is now dead provides the Lone Ranger with a lead to the whereabouts of an infamous outlaw and a large sum of stolen money.

97.51 *The Whimsical Bandit.* Aug. 31, 1950. GS: Chuck Courtney, Nestor Paiva, Bud Osborne, Sheila Ryan, Norman Willis, William Ruhl, John Cliff. To apprehend outlaw Juan Branco and his followers, the Lone Ranger uses a bullwhip and an unusual ring.

97.52 *Double Jeopardy.* Sept. 7, 1950. GS: Jack Ingram, Marin Sais, Rick Roman, James Kirkwood, Christine Larson, Riley Hill, Brad Slavin, Douglas Wood. A man is about to go on trial for murder. To secure his release his wife and two sons kidnap the judge's daughter.

97.53 *Million Dollar Wallpaper.* Sept. 14, 1950. GS: Emmett Lynn, Lucien Littlefield, Paul Fix, Kim Spalding, Duke York, Edmund Cobb. An old-timer finds that the stock he thought was worthless and papered the walls of his room with has become valuable.

97.54 *The Mission Bells.* Sept. 21, 1950. GS: Tristram Coffin, Walter Sande, James Griffith, Hal Fieberling/Baylor, Lee Roberts, Rosa Turich. The Lone Ranger and Tonto come upon the body of a crooked land speculator. A missing page from a 300-year-old journal and two mission bells are involved in the mystery.

97.55 *Dead Man's Chest.* Sept. 28, 1950. GS: William Vedder, Myron Healey, Frank Sully, George Lloyd, Harry Lauter, Stephen Chase, Natividad Vacio, Ray Montgomery. An old prospector carries a wooden chest with him constantly. He is murdered by outlaws who are looking for gold.

97.56 *Outlaw's Revenge.* Oct. 5, 1950. GS: Larry J. Blake, Kenneth MacDonald, Bill Haade, Larry Johns, Steven Clark, Richard Beach. A respected banker in town is leading a double life. As outlaw Trigger Taylor, he determines to avenge the death of one of his henchmen — a man the Lone Ranger sent to the gallows.

97.57 *Danger Ahead.* Oct. 12, 1950. GS: Don Haggerty, Max Terhune, William E. Green, Jack Briggs, Mike Ragan. A traveling ventriloquist named Boswell sees an outlaw murder Sheriff Roberts. A steaming cup of coffee gives the Lone Ranger a clue to the killer.

97.58 *Crime in Time.* Oct. 19, 1950. GS: Lane Bradford, John A. Butler, Monte Blue, Fred Libby. A crooked jeweler named Feeny McArdle is held up by the Watkins brothers. McArdle kills one of the brothers — and hires the other as his henchman.

97.59 *Drink of Water.* Oct. 26, 1950. GS: Stanley Andrews, Harlan Briggs, Bill Kennedy, Mitchell Kowal, Mickey Simpson, Arthur Stone, Linda Johnson, Gregg Barton. Thieves posing as rainmakers arrive in the town of Greenville in the middle of a dry spell. Their plans include murdering the Lone Ranger and Tonto.

97.60 *Thieves' Money.* Nov. 2, 1950. GS: John Doucette, Jack Briggs, Ward Blackburn, David McMahon, Charles Watts. The Lone Ranger and Tonto try to protect government funds from Dumont, a counterfeiter, who is posing as a federal agent.

97.61 *The Squire.* Nov. 9, 1950. GS: Dave Willock, Carol Thurston, Stuart Randall, Edmund Cobb, Lane Chandler, Peter Mamakos, Gregg Rogers, Bert Arnold. The Lone Ranger investigates when it appears that the town's most respected citizen is the man behind a series of robberies.

97.62 *Masked Deputy.* Nov. 16, 1950. GS: Stuart Randall, Dave Willock, Carol Thurston, Edmund Cobb, Peter Mamakos, Gregg Rogers, Bert Arnold, Lane Arnold. Large-scale cattle rustling operations are masterminded by a prosperous business man who tries to get rid of his many enemies.

97.63 *Banker's Choice.* Nov. 23, 1950. GS: Phyllis Morris, David Bruce, John Merton, Mickey Simpson, Bud Osborne, Jack Mower. After a quarrel with his son, a wealthy banker is approached by three masked men who convince him that his son is a thief and attempt to extort money from him.

97.64 *Desert Adventure.* Nov. 30, 1950. GS: House Peters, Jr., Charles Horvath, Bob Cason, Lane Bradford, Lee Shumway, Kermit Maynard. The Lone Ranger and Tonto are tracking down the notorious bandit, the Yuma Kid. Their search leads them into the desert.

97.65 *One Jump Ahead.* Dec. 7, 1950. GS: Robert Rockwell, Richard Crane, John Eldredge. The Lone Ranger and Tonto trail a pair of confidence men who pose as a professor and a soldier as they defraud the parents of Civil War victims.

97.66 *Bad Medicine.* Dec. 14, 1950. GS: Dick Curtis, Hal Baylor, Bob Cason, Harry Harvey, Sr., Greta Granstedt, Bob Kellard, Sandy Sanders, James Guilfoyle. Two bank robbers kill a clerk as they make their getaway. One of the bandits is hurt and must get to a doctor. The Lone Ranger and Tonto set out to investigate the offices of the doctors in town.

97.67 *Paid in Full.* Dec. 21, 1950. GS: Larry J. Blake, Harry Lauter, Johnny Day, Wanda McKay, Emmett Lynn, Charles Watts. A man tries to swindle Jim Craig out of his ranch when he learns that there is a rich deposit of borax on it. The Lone Ranger and Tonto risk their lives in order to thwart the man's plan.

97.68 *Lady Killer.* Dec. 28, 1950. GS: Nan Leslie, Robert Kent, I. Stanford Jolley, Fred Libby, Russell Trent, Ray Montgomery, Billy Vincent. Sheriff John Markum falls in love with pretty actress Lela Anson. The Lone Ranger believes that Lela is a murderess and the leader of a band of outlaws.

97.69 *Letter of the Law.* Jan. 4, 1951. GS: Robin Short,

Ed Hinton, Warren Douglas, Douglas Wood, Noel Neill, Monte Blue, John Halloran. Jeff Niles, once an outlaw, has now settled on a ranch with his wife. Then Sam Slater, an outlaw Jeff once knew, arrives at the ranch and demands that Jeff give him sanctuary.

97.70 *Silent Voice.* Jan. 11, 1951. GS: Ross Ford, Mike Ragan, Hal Baylor, Mira McKinney, John Morgan, Christine Larson. Three criminals think that they will go unpunished because the only witness to their crime is a deaf-and-dumb old woman. But the Lone Ranger finds a way to communicate with her.

97.71 *The Outcast.* Jan. 18, 1951. GS: Robert Rockwell, Denver Pyle, Pierre Watkin, Stephen Chase, Fred Libby, Mickey Simpson, Lane Bradford, Edmund Cobb, Gregg Barton. A group of Texas Rangers find they must enlist the aid of the Lone Ranger in order to bring a gang of outlaws to justice.

97.72 *Mister Trouble.* Jan. 25, 1951. GS: Robert Rockwell, Larry J. Blake, Earle Hodgins, John Bannon, Harry Harvey, Sr., David McMahon, Paul Campbell, Russell Trent, House Peters, Jr., Bob Kellard. The Lone Ranger and Tonto attempt to help in the completion of a railroad when a friend is in danger of losing his franchise.

97.73 *Behind the Law.* Feb. 1, 1951. GS: Bob Carson, Marshall Bradford, George Chesebro, James Guilfoyle, Gene Evans, Gene Roth, Ward Blackburn, Clarence Straight. Big Jim Folsom and his gang are living a double life. Considered outlaws in San Carlo County, they live as law-abiding citizens in San Pedro.

97.74 *Trouble at Black Rock.* Feb. 8, 1951. GS: Emmett Lynn, Wanda McKay, George Lewis, John Alvin, Michael Ansara, Constance Purdy. Elderly Jim Neely discovers a cache of gold coins. Neely is unaware that the coins were hidden by McCarty, a fugitive from prison.

97.75 *Two Gold Lockets.* Feb. 15, 1951. GS: Darryl Hickman, Dwayne Hickman, Stanley Andrews, Ben Welden, Tom Powers, Duke York, Greta Granstedt, John Cliff. The Lone Ranger and Tonto help reunite a lawman with the son who was stolen from him as a child and raised by outlaws. Two lockets are instrumental in saving the boy from a life of crime.

97.76 *The Hooded Men.* Feb. 22, 1951. GS: Walter Sande, Mira McKinney, John Doucette, Mort Thompson, Denver Pyle, Lane Bradford. In an effort to trap a gang of outlaws, the Lone Ranger adopts the same disguise that the crooks have used.

97.77 *Friend in Need.* March 1, 1951. GS: John McGuire, Robert Bice, Gail Davis, Stephen Clark, Edmund Cobb, Salvador Baguez, David Leonard, Paul Fierro, Joe Dominguez, Ed Clark. The Lone Ranger poses as a revolutionary and heads in to Mexico as he attempts to trap a homicidal outlaw and save an innocent man from hanging.

97.78 *Backtrail.* March 8, 1951. GS: Riley Hill, Robert Bice, Kim Spaulding, Rex Lease, Herbert Lytton, Bud Osborne. The Lone Ranger puts his own life and Tonto's in danger when he reports to Walter Mason that Mason's express shipments have been looted.

Season Two

97.79 *Outlaw's Son.* Sept. 11, 1952. GS: Robert Rockwell, Irene Vernon, Robert Arthur, John Pickard, Paul Fierro, William Haade. The Lone Ranger and Tonto pursue an outlaw who is trying to break with his gang and return to the wife and son he deserted years ago.

97.80 *Outlaw Underground.* Sept. 18, 1952. GS: Robert Clarke, Lois Hall, Lester Dorr, Richard Reeves, Michael Ansara, James Parnell, John Downey. The Lone Ranger and Tonto encounter an ambitious newspaper reporter from the East who is posing as an outlaw in order to penetrate a network of hideouts for fugitives.

97.81 *Special Edition.* Sept. 25, 1952. GS: Judd Holdren, Nan Leslie, Larry J. Blake, Hal K. Dawson, John Close, Marshall Ruth. The Lone Ranger and Tonto team up with the owner of Cave Creek's weekly newspaper in order to expose three confidence men who are peddling worthless stock.

97.82 *Desperado at Large.* Oct. 2, 1952. GS: Steven Clark, Lee Van Cleef, Douglas Kennedy, James Brown. The Lone Ranger and Tonto help an undercover federal agent escape the lynch mob stirred up against him by the criminal he is hunting.

97.83 *Through the Wall.* Oct. 9, 1952. GS: Dabbs Greer, Mike Ragan, Douglas Evans, George Lynn, Monte Blue, Phil Tead, Raymond Largay, George Slocum. The Lone Ranger and Tonto help an old stone mason right the wrong he committed thirty years earlier when he built a secret exit in a wall of the Granite City jail.

97.84 *Jeb's Gold Mine.* Oct. 16, 1952. GS: Raymond Greenleaf, Lane Bradford, Stephen Chase, Robert Bray, B.G. Norman, Syd Saylor, Rory Mallinson. The Lone Ranger and Tonto try to save an old homesteader's property from schemers who have learned that the old man's grandson has unwittingly discovered gold on the land.

97.85 *Frame for Two.* Oct. 23, 1952. GS: Richard Crane, John Damler, Robert Livingston, James Parnell, Robert B. Williams. The Lone Ranger and Tonto expose a crooked moneylender who has taken advantage of a feud between two ranchers to murder one and frame the other for the crime.

97.86 *Ranger in Danger.* Oct. 30, 1952. GS: Douglas Kennedy, Robert Arthur. While pursuing an outlaw who has sworn to kill them, the Lone Ranger and Tonto are led into a trap by a teenage boy under the badman's influence.

97.87 *Delayed Action.* Nov. 6, 1952. James Griffith, Ben Welden, Billy Vincent, Stanley Andrews, Robert Foulk, Gordon Wynne. On a trail of an outlaw gang, the Lone Ranger and Tonto are accused of the gang's latest bank robbery by a dimwit sheriff.

97.88 *The Map.* Nov. 13, 1952. GS: Frank Wilcox, Steve Darrell, Lanny Rees, Geraldine Wall, Marshall Reed, Harlan Warde. A thirteen-year-old boy whose hobby is chemistry helps the Lone Ranger and Tonto outwit the crooks who have waylaid a surveyor and stolen a map showing where the railroad will come through.

97.89 *Trial by Fire.* Nov. 20, 1952. GS: Ross Ford, Pierre Watkin, Gail Davis, Stanley Andrews, Robert J. Wilke, Mickey Simpson, Emerson Treacy, Marshall Bradford, Ralph Peters. The Lone Ranger and Tonto pursue the outlaw family responsible for shooting a man whose son has been charged with the crime.

97.90 *The Pledge* (A.K.A. "Word of Honor"). Nov. 27, 1952. GS: Ross Elliott, Hayden Rorke, Harry Cheshire, Sam Flint. The Lone Ranger and Tonto try to clear an honest young rancher who has been framed for a crime and then tricked into leaving the sheriff's custody by a false story that his mother is seriously ill.

97.91 *Treason at Dry Creek.* Dec. 4, 1952. GS: Frank Fenton, Ann Doran, Britt Wood, Paul Fierro, Rand Brooks, Charles Evans, Robert Carson. A drop of sealing wax helps the Lone Ranger and Tonto trap a crooked Pony Express station agent who has been intercepting Army dispatches and selling them to the Indians.

97.92 *The Condemned Man.* Dec. 11, 1952. GS: Don Beddoe, Russell Hicks, Monte Blue, Myron Healey, Maurice Jara, Charles Gibbs, Rusty Westcoatt. When Chief Lone Eagle's son is killed by an Indian agent, the Lone Ranger and Tonto try to expose the murderer in time to prevent an Indian uprising.

97.93 *The New Neighbor.* Dec. 18, 1952. GS: John Alvin, Walter Sande, B.G. Norman, Barbara Woodell, Robert Forrest, Larry Hudson, Edward Clark, John Phillips. The Lone Ranger and Tonto try to abort a range war over a selfish rancher's refusal to share water with his neighbors.

97.94 *Best Laid Plans.* Dec. 25, 1952. GS: House Peters, Jr., John Bryant, Ralph Sanford, Judd Holdren, John Pickard, Cathy Downs. The Lone Ranger and Tonto intervene in a war between the ranchers and homesteaders of Sunset Valley and thwart the plan of a gang leader to have one of his men elected sheriff.

97.95 *Indian Charlie.* Jan. 1, 1953. GS: Walter Reed, Alan Wells, Glenn Strange, Sally Corner, Harry Harvey, John Cason. The Lone Ranger and Tonto encounter an Indian boy, raised by whites, who seems to have turned against those who brought him up and to have become an outlaw.

97.96 *The Empty Strongbox.* Jan. 8, 1953. GS: Robert Carson, James Todd, Ed Rand, Dan Mahin, Hugh Prosser, Bud Osborne. The Lone Ranger and Tonto set a trap to catch a gang of stage robbers but are almost killed when a bomb is planted inside the strongbox they are using for bait.

97.97 *Trader Boggs.* Jan. 15, 1953. GS: Hal Price, I. Stanford Jolley, Aline Towne, Zon Murray, John Crawford, Kenne Duncan. The Lone Ranger and Tonto oppose a price-gouging merchant who is determined to stop their old friend Barnaby Boggs from opening a competing general store in the town of Larabee.

97.98 *Bandits in Uniform.* Jan. 22, 1953. GS: Gil Donaldson, John Doucette, I. Stanford Jolley, Robert Bray, James Parnell, George Douglas. The Lone Ranger and Tonto defend Mexican settlers who are being robbed and oppressed by an American military dictator and his tax-collecting thugs.

97.99 *Godless Men.* Jan. 29, 1953. GS: Hugh Beaumont, Hugh Sanders, Ray Page, Keith Richards. The Lone Ranger aids the Rev. Randy Roberts, a young preacher, recover the funds to build a church in Gold City which were stolen by corrupt powers intent on keeping religion out of the town.

97.100 *The Devil's Bog.* Feb. 5, 1953. GS: Hugh Prosser, Val DeSautels, Harry Harvey, Sr., Barbara Woodell, Bruce Edwards, Ferris Taylor, Frank Richards. Tonto comes down with a severe fever believed caused by mosquitoes from a nearby swamp. The Lone Ranger tries to help a doctor whose plans for draining the swamp are being inexplicably sabotaged.

97.101 *Right to Vote.* Feb. 12, 1953. GS: John Damler, Douglas Kennedy, Dick Elliott, Ben Welden, Richard Avonde. The Lone Ranger and Tonto race against time to recover a stolen petition calling for an election to rid a Western town of crooked officials.

97.102 *The Sheriff's Son.* Feb. 19, 1953. GS: Alan Wells, Emerson Treacy, Claudia Barrett, Hugh Prosser, William Haade, Walter Bonn. The Lone Ranger and Tonto try to stop a young man just released from prison from taking vengeance on his own father, the sheriff who arrested him.

97.103 *Tumblerock Law.* Feb. 26, 1953. GS: Richard Crane, Steve Brodie, Tom London, Bill Slack, Byron Foulger, Paul Birch, Kim Spaulding. When the sheriff of Tumblerock is murdered, the Lone Ranger and Tonto try to save the kidnapped witness who can break the power of the town political boss.

97.104 *Sinner by Proxy.* March 5, 1953. GS: Ross Elliott, Hugh Sanders, Russ Conway, Stephen Chase, Paul Hagen, Greta Granstedt, Dee Pollack, Mickey Simpson. When an outlaw posing as the Lone Ranger robs the Johnsville bank, the masked man and Tonto try to clear themselves and another innocent man who falsely confessed.

97.105 *A Stage for Mademoiselle.* March 12, 1953. GS: Noreen Nash, Frank Wilcox, Edmund Cobb, Emmett Lynn, Lane Bradford, Douglas Evans. The Lone Ranger and Tonto become involved when a glamorous opera star, scheduled to appear in the town of Red Pine, plans a fake robbery of her jewels as a publicity stunt only to have the gems stolen by real thieves.

97.106 *Son by Adoption.* March 19, 1953. GS: Frank Richards, Russ Conway, Dennis Ross, William Challee, Peter Mamakos. The Lone Ranger and Tonto try to keep a young man, adopted long ago by a generous family, from discovering that his real father is not a dead hero, but a living outlaw leader.

97.107 *Mrs. Banker.* March 26, 1953. GS: Esther Somers, Robert Neil, Dan White, Steve Mitchell, Harmon Stevens. The Lone Ranger disguises himself as an old prospector while he and Tonto try to solve a series of stagecoach robberies.

97.108 *Trouble in Town.* April 2, 1953. GS: Dayton Lummis, Lyle Talbot, Ross Ford, Jim Moloney, William Fawcett, Fred Essler, Mira McKinney, John Cason. Banker Wilkins faces trouble when ugly rumors cause the townspeople to fear that his bank is about to close its doors.

97.109 *Black Gold.* April 9, 1953. GS: Jim Hayward, Robert Shayne, Todd Karns, William Vedder. The Lone Ranger and Tonto go after the murderers trying to take over the land on which a young geologist has discovered oil.

97.110 *The Durango Kid.* April 16, 1953. GS: James Griffith, Judd Holdren, Nan Leslie, Lee Shumway, Fred Libby, Pierre Watkin. The Lone Ranger and Tonto try to help a young woman from the East who has become the unwitting accomplice of a notorious outlaw she falsely believes to be her long-lost brother.

97.111 *The Deserter.* April 23, 1953. GS: Chuck Courtney, Rand Brooks, Robert Foulk, Keith Richards, Gene Roth, Lane Bradford. A sensitive young man who has deserted the Army tries to redeem himself by helping the Lone Ranger, Tonto and Dan Reid capture the gang of renegades he has joined.

97.112 *Embezzler's Harvest.* April 30, 1953. GS:

Stephen Chase, Lois Hall, Harry Harvey, Sr., Leonard Freeman. The Lone Ranger and Tonto become suspicious of two men involved in embezzling funds from an irrigation project. With the use of a watch chain, they try to clear a third man who has been implicated in the crime.

97.113 *El Toro.* May 7, 1953. GS: Chuck Courtney, Eugene Wessen, Richard Avonde, Jim Hayward, Robert Spencer, Stan Blystone. Peter Casper, a member of El Torro's gang, goes gunning for the Lone Ranger, Tonto, and Dan Reid, in a vengeful attack. Only faithful Silver can save the day.

97.114 *The Brown Pony.* May 14, 1953. GS: Lee Van Cleef, Charles Stevens, Dennis Ross, Adele Longmire. The Lone Ranger and Tonto try to help a boy whose mother plans to sell his beloved pony and turn over the money to two escaped convicts who claim to have proof of her imprisoned husband's innocence.

97.115 *Triple Cross.* May 21, 1953. GS: John Cliff, Judy Nugent, Jack Ingram, Fred Coby, James Todd, Joe Haworth. The Lone Ranger and Tonto protect a young woman who witnessed two outlaws killing a third man whom they had helped to escape from prison and followed to where he buried the loot from a Wells Fargo robbery.

97.116 *The Wake of War.* May 28, 1953. GS: Don Beddoe, Richard Crane, Sheb Wooley, Hugh Prosser, John Crawford. The Lone Ranger and Tonto try to clear an innocent man framed for murder by gamblers who want to keep Union and Confederate veterans of the Civil War feuding with each other.

97.117 *Death in the Forest.* June 4, 1953. GS: Raymond Greenleaf, John Damler, Judd Holdren, DeForest Kelley, Lee Roberts, Edwin Rand, Phil Tead, Mickey Simpson. The Lone Ranger and Tonto learn from a dying man that a gang of crooks want to assassinate the state's governor. They must prevent the murder at all cost.

97.118 *The Gentleman from Julesberg.* June 11, 1953. GS: Eddy Waller, Walter Reed, Peter Mamakos, Robert Neil, Robert Filmer, Nan Leslie, Fred Libby. The Lone Ranger and Tonto try to save a young man framed for a robbery by enlisting the aid of an old hobo with an uncanny resemblance to a legendary gambler.

97.119 *Hidden Fortune.* June 18, 1953. GS: Steve Darrell, Bruce Payne, I. Stanford Jolley, Hugh Prosser, Ann Doran. The Lone Ranger and Tonto try to stop two criminals, just released after ten years in prison, who are desperate to get inside the house built over the spot where they buried their loot.

97.120 *The Old Cowboy.* June 25, 1953. GS: Russell Simpson, Steve Brodie, Frank Fenton, Bill Slack, Terry Frost, Denver Pyle. The Lone Ranger and Tonto try to prove that an old-timer, too proud to admit that his eyes are failing, has been tricked by crooks who want his land into thinking he is responsible for a railroad agent's murder.

97.121 *The Woman from Omaha.* July 2, 1953. GS: Chubby Johnson, Glenn Strange, Mauritz Hugo, Frank Richards, Herb Lytton, Susan Blystone. The Lone Ranger and Tonto help Nell Martin, a middle-aged woman, who has just taken over her late brother's stagecoach line and whose manager is working with a rival company to bankrupt her.

97.122 *Gunpowder Joe.* July 9, 1953. GS: Chubby Johnson, Glenn Strange, Frank Richards, Mauritz Hugo, Herbert Lytton, Stanley Blystone. The Lone Ranger and Tonto befriend Gunpowder Joe, an old explosives expert, who doesn't realize that the Cavendish gang is using his blasting skill to help them locate treasure.

97.123 *The Midnight Rider.* July 16, 1953. GS: Darryl Hickman, Harry Woods, Steve Darrell, Harry Cheshire, Hal K. Dawson, Mickey Simpson, Guy E. Hearn, Billy Vincent. Young Bob Jessup becomes the Midnight Rider to steal money from a mining company to finance an investigation of his father's death.

97.124 *Stage to Estacado.* July 23, 1953. GS: Sheb Wooley, Phyllis Coates, Lee Van Cleef, Ian McDonald, Monte Blue, Douglas Evans. The Lone Ranger and Tonto help a young couple keep their stage line franchise from being taken over by a crooked competitor.

97.125 *The Perfect Crime.* July 30, 1953. GS: Phyllis Coates, Robert Coates, Robert Bray, Edna Holland, Hayden Rorke, Richard Avonde, Terry Frost. The Lone Ranger and Tonto foil the attempted abduction of a young schoolmistress who has learned that an intellectual outlaw posing as a teacher is planning to rob the town bank.

97.126 *The Ghost of Coyote Canyon.* Aug. 6, 1953. GS: Lucien Littlefield, John Pickard, Richard Alexander, Marshall Reed, Tom London, Hank Worden. The Lone Ranger and Tonto track down a gang of thieves who have convinced the citizens of Crooked Ford that a nearby canyon is haunted.

97.127 *Old Bailey.* Aug. 13, 1953. GS: Phil Tead, Bruce Cowling, John Crawford, Ray Montgomery, Steve Pendleton. The Lone Ranger and Tonto try to expose the professional gamblers who murdered a wealthy rancher over a poker debt and framed an old derelict for the crime.

97.128 *Prisoner in Jeopardy.* Aug. 20, 1953. GS: Richard Crane, Frank Wilcox, Dorothy Patrick, Steve Bystrom, Jerome Sheldon, House Peters, Jr., Dick Rich. The Lone Ranger and Tonto try to clear a young man who, on the way home after serving time for a crime he didn't commit, is captured by outlaws and framed again.

97.129 *Diamond in the Rough.* Aug. 27, 1953. GS: Leo Britt, Emory Parnell, House Peters, Jr., Harry Lauter. The Lone Ranger and Tonto try to recover a stolen diamond which has been hidden in the head of a ventriloquist's dummy.

97.130 *The Red Mark.* Sept. 3, 1953. GS: Paul Bryar, Steve Roberts, Frank Fenton, Alan Wells, Tom London. Tonto helps the Lone Ranger disguise himself as an Indian thirsting for firewater as the masked man and his companion hunt a pair of stagecoach robbers who stole a shipment of red-marked money.

Season Three

97.131 *The Fugitive.* Sept. 9, 1954. GS: Denver Pyle, John Doucette, Charlita, Paul Langton, Griff Barnett. Clay Trowbridge is falsely accused of murder. He escapes from jail when a mob threatens him and then he gets involved with a gang of outlaws.

97.132 *Ex-Marshal.* Sept. 16, 1954. GS: Ray Teal, Tyler McVey, Glenn Strange, Stanley Clements, House Peters, Jr., Bob Cason. Former law officer Frank Dean was supposed to have lost his courage. But he joins the Lone Ranger to battle the notorious Compton gang.

97.133 *Message to Fort Apache.* Sept. 23, 1954. GS: Chick Chandler, Nancy Hale, Robert Livingston, Scott Elliott,

Lane Bradford, Fay Roope, Sheb Wooley, Harry Harvey, Charles Meredith. The Army has learned the identity of some outlaws who are selling guns to hostile Indians.

97.134 *The Frightened Woman.* Sept. 30, 1954. Emlen Davies, Ricky Murray, Richard Travis, Bruce Cowling, Don Harvey, Zon Murray, Emmett Lynn. Jenny Houston, a widow who witnessed a robbery, finds her life endangered. When it becomes apparent that the known robber is not threatening her, the Lone Ranger and Tonto suspect that the crook had a partner in crime.

97.135 *Gold Town.* Oct. 7, 1954. Myron Healey, Pierre Watkin, Earle Hodgins, Edward Ashley, James Craven, James Parnell, Anthony Sydes. Prospector Sam Bates dies and leaves half of his money to the Lone Ranger and the other half to Edgar Wellington. Outlaw Kirk Meacham poses as Wellington to claim the inheritance.

97.136 *Six-Gun Sanctuary.* Oct. 14, 1954. GS: Don Beddoe, Douglas Kennedy, Harry Harvey, Jr., Robert B. Williams, Frank Fenton, Hal Baylor. Reidsville is a perfect sanctuary for outlaws, thanks to Whittaker, the proprietor of the general store. The Lone Ranger and Tonto help a sheriff to bring law to the town.

97.137 *Outlaw's Trail.* Oct. 21, 1954. GS: Jack Elam, Robert Bice, Christian Drake, Hugh Sanders, Clarence Straight, Robert Bray, Rory Mallinson. Two gunmen, Joe Tarbuck and Reno Lawrence, visit the frontier town of Painted Post and meet an old friend — the sheriff.

97.138 *Stage to Tishomingo.* Oct. 28, 1954. GS: Lane Bradford, Don Megowan, Ben Welden, Kenneth Patterson, Robert Carson, Robert Foulk, Hank Worden, Si Jenks, Mira McKinney. Robberies of the stage to Tishomingo greatly please merchant Harper. He wouldn't mind seeing the stage line go out of business.

97.139 *Texas Draw.* Nov. 4, 1954. GS: Barry Kelley, Marion Ross, Christopher Dark, James Westerfield, Joe Haworth, Frank Richards. Gunman Crane Dillon knows that a certain piece of land has rich copper deposits. But John Thorpe, a circuit-riding preacher, has just bought the land for an orphanage.

97.140 *Rendezvous at Whipsaw.* Nov. 11, 1954. GS: Jean Inness, John Doucette, Hugh Sanders, Paul Brinegar, Don Beddoe, Clancy Cooper, William Haade. Outlaws are posing as respectable citizens of the own of Whipsaw. The Lone Ranger and Tonto come to the aid of a brother and sister who are being sought by the outlaw gang.

97.141 *Dan Reid's Fight for Life.* Nov. 18, 1954. GS: Chuck Courtney, Mickey Simpson, John Stephenson, Henry Kulky, Nestor Paiva, Nacho Galindo. The leader of the notorious Cardoza gang keeps his identity a secret. Attempting to capture the gang, the Lone Ranger and Tonto allow Dan Reid to be taken prisoner by the bandits.

97.142 *Tenderfoot.* Nov. 25, 1954. GS: Robert Horton, Dan Riss, Hal Baylor, William Forrest, George Chandler, Martin Garralaga. Jim Ferris is slated to sell his ranch to an Easterner. But before he can make the sale he is kidnaped.

97.143 *A Broken Match.* Dec. 2, 1954. GS: Phil Tead, Glen Gordon, Don Harvey, Robert Quarry, Whit Bissell, Paul Keast, Nan Leslie, Fred Coby. When an ex-convict is unjustly accused of robbing a bank, the Lone Ranger and Tonto set out to find the men responsible for the crime.

97.144 *Colorado Gold.* Dec. 9, 1954. GS: Robert Shayne, Gil Donaldson, Claudia Barrett, Gene Roth, George Barrows. When the Marybelle Mine begins producing some rich ore, neighboring miner Luther Gage decides he is going to cut himself in.

97.145 *Homer with a High Hat.* Dec. 16, 1954. GS: Chick Chandler, Kathleen Crowley, Minerva Urecal, Peter Hansen, Tom Brown, Rex Thorson, Terry Frost, Fred Libby. Homer Virgilius Potts, a superior gentleman from the East, come to Modoc City to visit his niece Cindy. Just to bring Potts down to size, Cindy's fiance, the town marshal, throws him into jail on a trumped-up charge. He lands in a cell housing an outlaw gang who have hidden the government gold that they stole.

97.146 *Two for Juan Ringo.* Dec. 23, 1954. GS: Lyle Talbot, John Hoyt, Bob Cason, Robert Bray, Dennis Moore, Bert Holland. The Lone Ranger adopts the identity of outlaw Juan Ringo to learn more about the activities of the Englishman who runs Border City.

97.147 *The Globe.* Dec. 30, 1954. GS: Frank Ferguson, Gregg Palmer, Stuart Randall, Michael Whalen, Phil Tead, Phil Chambers. Bank clerk Stan Ammons is worried about some unusual loans his bank is making. With the help of the Lone Ranger and Tonto, he investigates.

97.148 *Dan Reid's Sacrifice.* Jan. 6, 1955. GS: Chuck Courtney, Percy Helton, Mickey Knox, Fred Graham, John Cliff, Bill Kennedy. Attempting to help the Lone Ranger and Tonto put a stop to the work of a band of rustlers, Dan Reid is captured by the outlaw gang.

97.149 *Enfield Rifle.* Jan. 13, 1955. GS: Walter Coy, Frank Ferguson, Maurice Jara, Rand Brooks, Rico Alaniz, Peter Mamakos, Booker Ben Ali. During a visit to an Army fort in Montana, the Lone Ranger and Tonto become targets of a young Indian brave's gun. The renegade Indian shoots at them, thus getting them mixed up in a planned Indian uprising.

97.150 *The School Story.* Jan. 20, 1955. GS: Lee Aaker, Dick Elliott, John Doucette, Norman Keats, Stanley Andrews, Paul Birch, Raymond Meurer, Madge Meredith. The Lone Ranger and Tonto try to get a young boy to agree to attend the school soon to be built in his town.

97.151 *The Quiet Highwayman.* Jan. 27, 1955. GS: Chuck Courtney, Francis McDonald, Harry Harvey, Kathryn Card, Hugh Sanders. A U.S. marshal asks the Lone Ranger and Tonto to help him capture a gang of desperadoes who have been terrorizing the countryside.

97.152 *Heritage of Treason.* Feb. 3, 1955. GS: Charles Halton, Peter Whitney, Stuart Randall, Ed Hinton, Burt Mustin, Don Haggerty. A gang of confidence men and an Arizona cattle king connive to take possession of the entire territory.

97.153 *The Lost Chalice.* Feb. 10, 1955. GS: James Griffith, Joseph Turkel, William Challee, Julian Rivero, Edward Colmans, Argentina Brunetti. While the Lone Ranger and Tonto help the padre of Mission Valley locate water, escaped convicts plot to steal a gold chalice from the padre's mission.

97.154 *Code of the Pioneers.* Feb. 17, 1955. GS: Chuck Courtney, Emlen Davies, Walter Reed, Billy Curtis, Paul Keast, Lyle Talbot, Harry Lauter, Ron Sharan, Bill Kennedy. The townspeople know which man they want for sheriff but are too lazy to go to the polls. The Lone Ranger helps a newspaperwoman get out the vote.

The Lone Ranger

97.155 *The Law Lady.* Feb. 24, 1955. GS: Marjorie Lord, Peter Hansen, Richard Travis, Don Garrett. After a man is killed, his young wife replaces him as sheriff of a frontier town. The Lone Ranger and Tonto come to her assistance in finding her husband's killer and restoring peace to the Wyoming town.

97.156 *Uncle Ed.* March 3, 1955. GS: Will Wright, June Whitley, Nadene Ashdown, Bruce Cowling, Peter Mamakos, Ed Hinton, Frank Hagney, John Damler. When his son-in-law is robbed of his life savings, Uncle Ed finds that the Lone Ranger and Tonto are there to help him.

97.157 *Jornada Del Muerto.* March 10, 1956. GS: Joseph Vitale, Rick Vallin, Richard Crane, Steven Ritch, John Hubbard, Ray Montgomery, Marshall Bradford, Raymond Meurer. The Lone Ranger and Tonto set out after an outlaw who is living with the Apaches. They have learned that the man is responsible for a series of Indian uprisings.

97.158 *Sunstroke Mesa.* March 17, 1955. GS: Chuck Courtney, Dwayne Hickman, John Pickard, Joseph Crehan, Don Harvey, John Mansfield. While trapping a band of outlaws, the Lone Ranger and Tonto also are able to help a misguided teenager solve some of his personal problems.

97.159 *Sawtelle Saga's End.* April 24, 1955. GS: Robert Foulk, Peter Hansen, Frances Bavier, Paul Keast, William Forrest. Looking for the mastermind of a series of bank robberies, the Lone Ranger and Tonto are surprised to find that the trail ends at Aunt Maggie's farm.

97.160 *The Too-Perfect Signature.* March 31, 1955. GS: Ray Teal, Katherine Warren, Stacy Keach, Will White, Charles Meredith Glenn Strange, Terry Frost. An attorney wants to get legal possession of a ranch owner's land so he can sell it to the railroad, so he forges the man's name to a deed.

97.161 *Trigger Finger.* April 7, 1955. GS: Chuck Courtney, Douglas Kennedy, Stacy Keach, Steve Dunhill, Laura Elliott, Keith Richards, Mickey Simpson, Taggart Casey. The local paper blasts Sheriff Trent for killing an innocent man. But the sheriff claims that the dead man was a gang leader.

97.162 *The Tell-Tale Bullet.* April 14, 1955. GS: Roy Roberts, Mason Alan Dinehart, Anthony Caruso, Dennis Weaver, Bob Cason. The son of a country doctor is forced to join up with a gang of bank robbers. He is wounded by one of the Lone Ranger's silver bullets while escaping from a holdup.

97.163 *False Accusation.* April 21, 1955. GS: Michael Whalen, Harry Harvey, Whit Bissell, Robert Bray, Marshall Reed, Bruce Cowling. An outlaw, dressed as the Lone Ranger, robs a bank. Tonto helps the Ranger when his friend is mistaken for the bank robber.

97.164 *Gold Freight.* April 28, 1955. GS: Chuck Courtney, Ted DeCorsia, House Peters, Jr., Richard Wessel, Kenneth MacDonald, Fred Libby, Kenne Duncan, James Diehl. A mining town is in an uproar when a stagecoach is robbed. The Lone Ranger and Tonto set out to track down the robbers when it seems as if the wrong man is being accused of the crime.

97.165 *Wanted — the Lone Ranger.* May 5, 1955. GS: Richard Travis, Jesse White, Sheb Wooley, James Courtney, Al Jackson, Ray Saunders, William Challee, Mike Dengate. Seeking out the leader of a gang that is terrorizing a Western town, the Lone Ranger poses as a clown in a medicine show.

97.166 *The Woman in the White Mask.* May 12, 1955. GS: Chuck Courtney, Phyllis Coates, Denver Pyle, Richard Reeves, Gregg Barton, Jack Diamond, Peter Thompson. A young brother and sister seek revenge against a miner they hold responsible for their father's murder. The Lone Ranger and Tonto try to save the miner.

97.167 *Bounty Hunter.* May 19, 1955. GS: Richard Reeves, Russ Conway, Pierre Watkin, Gil Fallman. While pursuing a desperate outlaw, the Lone Ranger and Tonto meet a friendly stranger. They soon learn he is not to be trusted and find themselves at the mercy of a pair of cutthroats.

97.168 *Showdown at Sand Creek.* May 26, 1955. GS: Paul Burke, Robert B. Williams, Stacy Keach, Phil Tead, Christian Drake, Nancy Hale. The sheriff is murdered and his brother plans to take over his job and capture his killer. But first he has got to learn to handle a gun.

97.169 *Heart of a Cheater.* June 2, 1955. GS: Chuck Courtney, Eddy Waller, Tommy Ivo, Natalie Masters, John Pickard, William Challee. The Lone Ranger and his nephew, Dan Reid, trail a pair of bank robbers to the ranch house of a retired outlaw. His nephew is kidnaped by a band of outlaws and held as hostage.

97.170 *The Swami.* June 9, 1955. GS: Chuck Courtney, Earle Hodgins, Eddy Waller, Lou Krugman, Kem Dibbs, Chuck Carson. An elderly prospector, a friend of the Lone Ranger, is robbed of his life savings by a swami traveling with a general store on wheels. He asks the Lone Ranger for help.

97.171 *Sheriff's Sale.* June 16, 1955. GS: Peter Hanson, Larry Blake, Helen Seamon, Thurston Hall, Larry Hudson, Aaron Saxon. A ruthless man takes over a town and the new sheriff finds himself unable to minister justice. The Lone Ranger and Tonto set out to expose the man.

97.172 *Six-Gun Artist.* June 23, 1955. GS: Elaine Riley, Norman Willis, Guy Williams, Mort Mills, Emmett Lynn. An attractive girl has been seen painting landscapes while a lady gunslinger and her henchman have been getting away with numerous stage robberies.

97.173 *Death Goes to Press.* June 30, 1955. GS: Peter Hanson, Frank Ferguson, Guy Sorel, Kenneth MacDonald, Addison Richards. A newspaper editor is killed by his assistant and the town lawyer who plan to take over the town. The Lone Ranger and Tonto try to find evidence to expose the pair.

97.174 *The Return of Dice Dawson.* July 7, 1955. GS: Harry Carey, Jr., James Todd, Harry Lauter, Barbara Eiler, Herbert Heyes, Al Wyatt. Jay Thomasson, a respected rancher in Elliott City, had been an outlaw named Dice Dawson. A pair of black dice was left at the scene of a series of murders, and Dawson thinks he might be falsely associated with the crimes.

97.175 *Adventure at Arbuckle.* July 14, 1955. GS: Ray Teal, Nan Leslie, Lou Krugman, James Griffith, William Challee, Paul Keast. After her father is slain, Susan Starr wants to leave the town that is ruled by a gang leader and his men. But the Lone Ranger decides to expose the killers and Susan helps him get the goods on the crooks who run the town of Arbuckle.

97.176 *The Return.* July 21, 1955. GS: Yvette Dugay, Christopher Dark, Frank Wilcox, Terry Frost, Reed Howes. Talana, a mission-educated Indian girl, returns to her people, hoping to become their first schoolteacher. But her brother, Kat Kem, stirs up trouble within the tribe.

97.177 *Framed for Murder.* July 28, 1955. GS: James

Best, David Bruce, Whit Bissell, Robert Carson, Jan Shepard, Marshall Bradford. Young Jim Blake has come West and struck gold. John Carter plots to murder Blake and frame Tonto for the crime.

97.178 *Trapped.* Aug. 4, 1955. GS: Frank Ferguson, Taggart Casey, John Doucette, Robert Ellis, Marshall Bradford. Gaff Morgan and his sidekick escape from prison with the help of a deputy sheriff and head for Gainsville to rob a bank. Later the sheriff regrets his part in the escape and tells the Lone Ranger what has happened.

97.179 *The Bait: Gold.* Aug. 11, 1955. GS: George Neise, Richard Avonde, John Phillips, Michael Whalen, Joan Hovis, Hank Worden. Outlaws have been hijacking mine owner Harding's gold shipments and he is about to lose the mine for an unpaid mortgage. The Lone Ranger and Tonto set out to capture the robbers and recover the ore.

97.180 *The Sheriff's Wife.* Aug. 18, 1955. GS: Jack Elam, Joseph Turkel, John Bryant, Elaine Edwards, Hugh Sanders. When Sheriff Russell is shot by killers, his wife rides out after them. The Lone Ranger and Tonto attempt to rescue her.

97.181 *Counterfeit Redskins.* Aug. 25, 1955. GS: Paul Langton, John Doucette, Harry Lauter, Russell Johnson, Mel Welles, Peter Mamakos, Wayne Schatter. Beau Slate and his counterfeit redskins attack a new homesteader and destroy his house. But their horses don't disguise too well. The Lone Ranger and Tonto risk their lives in an attempt to capture the bandits.

97.182 *One Nation Indivisible.* Sept. 1, 1955. GS: Tyler MacDuff, Don Garner, Lyle Talbot, Roy Barcroft, Rand Brooks, Watson Downs. The Lone Ranger exposes a man stealing jewels and money originally given to help in the Civil War. Fred Loban, banker and swindler, plans to frame two Confederate Army veterans with the theft.

Season Four

97.183 *The Wooden Rifle.* Sept. 13, 1956. GS: Sydney Mason, Paul Engle, Rand Brooks, Barbara Ann Knudson, William Challee, Frank Scannell. The Lone Ranger impersonates a patent medicine salesman as he attempts to get to the bottom of a shooting of a farmer.

97.184 *The Sheriff of Smoke Tree.* Sept. 20, 1956. GS: Slim Pickens, Ron Haggerty, Tudor Owen, John Beradino, Mickey Simpson. The Lone Ranger and Tonto come to the help of part-time sheriff Buck Webb when outlaws run him out of town.

97.185 *The Counterfeit Mask.* Sept. 27, 1956. GS: Sydney Mason, John Cliff, Paul Engle, William Challee. The Lone Ranger and Tonto set out to capture an outlaw who is masquerading as the Lone Ranger. The Ranger disguises himself as an old prospector to capture him.

97.186 *No Handicap.* Oct. 4, 1956. GS: Will Wright, Gary Marshall, John Beradino, Jim Parnell, Ron Hagerthy, Tudor Owen. The Lone Ranger and Tonto set out to find Cole Douglas, whose gang blinded Marshal Griff Allison in a gunfight.

97.187 *The Cross of Santo Domingo.* Oct. 11, 1956. GS: Denver Pyle, Johnny Crawford, Gregg Barton, Jeanne Bates, Lane Bradford, Ric Roman, Larry Johnson. On the desert, the Lone Ranger and Tonto rescue two priests who have been captured by outlaws hunting for a fabulous jeweled cross.

97.188 *White Hawk's Decision.* Oct. 18, 1956. GS: Charles Stevens, Ed Hashim, Robert Swan, Harry Lauter, Louis Lettieri. The youngest son of an Indian chief hates all white men. When rich deposits fo silver are found on the tribal lands, he joins up with a band of outlaws, believing he will prevent the white race from profiting.

97.189 *The Return of Don Pedro O'Sullivan.* Oct. 25, 1956. GS: Tudor Owen, Maria Manay, Joseph Vitale, John Beradino, Mickey Simpson, George J. Lewis. The Lone Ranger and Tonto don disguises as they try to help a Mexican patriot return to Mexico to fight General Santoro, the dictator in power.

97.190 *Quicksand.* Nov. 1, 1956. GS: Ric Roman, Denver Pyle, Henry Rowland, Robert Burton. The Lone Ranger and Tonto are ambushed by a renegade Indian and an unscrupulous lawyer who are searching for hidden gold scheduled to be used to build a school for Indians.

97.191 *Quarterhorse War.* Nov. 8, 1956. GS: George Mather, Mae Morgan, William Tannen, Harry Lauter, Charles Stevens. During a horse race between a Cheyenne Indian and a white gambler, the wagered money is entrusted to a schoolteacher. The Cheyennes are enraged when the money disappears.

97.192 *The Letter Bride.* Nov. 15, 1956. GS: Victor Sen Yung, Joe Vitale, Dennis Moore, Slim Pickens, Claire Carleton, Tudor Owen, Judy Dan. The Lone Ranger and Tonto try to find a Chinese laundryman's missing mail-order bride.

97.193 *Hot Spell in Panamint.* Nov. 22, 1956. GS: Rand Brooks, Barbara Ann Knudson, Sydney Mason, William Challee, John Cliff. The Lone Ranger and Tonto come to the aid of a sheriff who has become the target of an outlaw and his gang.

97.194 *The Twisted Track.* Nov. 29, 1956. GS: Gregg Barton, Robert Burton, Bill Henry, Tyler MacDuff. The Lone Ranger tries to stop two brothers, ex-soldiers of the Confederacy, from exacting vengeance on the owner of a railroad by planting explosives under a train.

97.195 *Decision for Chris McKeever.* Dec. 6, 1956. During a stagecoach robbery, the McKeever gang captures the Lone Ranger and Tonto, forcing them to travel with the outlaws to the nearest city. Their only hope of escape lies with Chris, the youngest member of the gang.

97.196 *Trouble at Tylerville.* Dec. 13, 1956. GS: Tom Brown, John Pickard, Mary Ellen Kay, Francis McDonald, Charles Aldredge, Ben Welden. The Lone Ranger and Tonto come to the aid of an ex-convict who is about to be hanged by angered townspeople.

97.197 *Christmas Story.* Dec. 20, 1956. GS: Jimmy Baird, Bill Henry, Aline Towne, Robert Burton, Mary Newton, Lane Bradford. The Lone Ranger and Tonto set out to locate a missing saddle maker and return the man to his family in time for Christmas.

97.198 *Ghost Canyon.* Dec. 27, 1956. GS: Robert Swan, Charles Stevens, Harry Lauter, Mike Ragan, Edmund Hashim. The Lone Ranger and Tonto pursue three outlaws into Indian ceremonial grounds and find that the bandits have captured the tribal chief's son.

97.199 *Outlaw Masquerade.* Jan. 3, 1957. GS: House

Peters, Jr., Richard Crane, Steven Ritch, Joseph Crehan. The Long Ranger, posing as a famous outlaw, helps a band of robbers escape from prison in an attempt to learn the location of the gold shipment they stole.

97.200 *The Avenger.* Jan. 10, 1957. GS: Alan Wells, Tristram Coffin, Francis McDonald, Dennis Moore, Roy Barcroft. A man campaigns to have the local townspeople drive out the outlaws who have taken over their town. When the man is killed by the outlaws, his son vows vengeance

97.201 *The Courage of Tonto.* Jan. 17, 1957. GS: Francis McDonald, Maurice Jara, Joel Ashley, Ewing Mitchell, Jim Bannon. The Lone Ranger and Tonto attempt to settle a dispute between Chief Gray Horse and Lew Pearson. But Pearson kills the Indian chief and holds the Lone Ranger and Tonto hostage.

97.202 *The Breaking Point.* Jan. 24, 1957. GS: Charles Wagenheim, Brad Morrow, Richard Crane, Keith Richards, House Peters, Jr. A young boy and his dog set out to find the boy's father, who is being held by outlaws to learn the whereabouts of the man's mine. The Lone Ranger and Tonto try to help the youngster.

97.203 *A Harp for Hannah.* Jan. 31, 1957. GS: Trevor Bardette, Louise Lewis, Bob Roark, Pierce Lyden, Ralph Sanford. Walter Dubbs is a farmer who has worked hard and managed to save a good deal of money. On his way into town, Dubbs is robbed and beaten by a gang of young men led by the spoiled son of a rich man.

97.204 *A Message from Abe.* Feb. 7, 1957. GS: James Griffith, Maggie O'Byrne, Mauritz Hugo, Harry Strang, Don Harvey. A man who has paid for his past crimes asks the Lone Ranger and Tonto to help him lead a good life when he is desperate for money to cure his sick wife.

97.205 *Code of Honor.* Feb. 14, 1957. GS: Paul Engle, Helene Marshall, John Maxwell, Rand Brooks, John Cliff. The Lone Ranger and Tonto devise a plan to catch an outlaw gang believed to be led by a missing Army officer. The outlaws disguise themselves as cavalrymen in order to hoodwink a group of miners.

97.206 *The Turning Point.* Feb. 21, 1957. GS: Paul Campbell, Margaret Stewart, Pierce Lyden, George Barrows. A young rancher tries to take the law into his own hands and soon finds himself accused of murder.

97.207 *Dead-Eye.* Feb. 28, 1957. GS: William Fawcett, Zon Murray, Myron Healey. A retired lawman decides to come out of retirement to round up a group of badmen. The Lone Ranger and Tonto learn of a plot by two outlaws to ambush the lawman and try to help him.

97.208 *Clover in the Dust.* March 7, 1957. GS: Harry Strang, Dan Barton, Sydney Mason, Don C. Harvey. A rancher's son is murdered while tracking down a gang of rustlers. He draws a clover leaf in the dust before he dies as a clue to his murderer.

97.209 *Slim's Boy.* March 14, 1957. GS: Trevor Bardette, Louise Lewis, Bob Roark, Pierce Lyden. The Lone Ranger learns that a band of outlaws plans to rob a gold refinery and kill an aging marshal. He disguises himself as a deaf Mexican and goes o work for the outlaws. While undercover he attempts to bring a young man back to the side of the law.

97.210 *Two Against Two.* March 21, 1957. GS: Baynes Barron, Guy Murray, Eugenia Paul. An escaped robber sets out to gain revenge on the Lone Ranger, who sent him to prisoner. He succeeds in luring the masked man and Tonto into a trap.

97.211 *Ghost Town Fury.* March 28, 1957. GS: Baynes Barron, Richard Crane, House Peters, Steve Ritch. The Lone Ranger and Tonto look for three escaped outlaws who are on a robbery spree. They go to their old friend Blackhawk for information about hiding places in the badlands and find unexpected allies in two brave youngsters.

97.212 *The Prince of Buffalo Gap.* April 4, 1957. GS: Robert Crossan, Jim Bannon, Gabor Curtiz, Michael Winkleman. Prince Maximilian, heir to his country's throne, is on a visit to Buffalo Gap. The Lone Ranger and Tonto intervene when they learn of a plot by the Prince's uncle to have the royal visitor assassinated.

97.213 *The Law and Miss Aggie.* April 11, 1947. GS: Florence Lake, Dennis Moore, Brad Johnson, Joe Vitale, Max Baer. When two Indians cross her property on their way to sign a peace treaty, Miss Aggie has her ranch hands ambush them. The embittered woman's husband was killed by Indians years before and she has vowed revenge. The Lone Ranger tries to reason with her.

97.214 *The Tarnished Star.* April 18, 1957. GS: Myron Healey, Mercedes Shirley, Paul Engle, Zon Murray, William Fawcett. A band of masked robbers rides into town of Peaceful Valley and begins a reign of terror. The marshal seems unable to cope with them. The Lone Ranger and Tonto learn that the leader has a strange hold over him.

97.215 *Canuck.* April 25, 1957. GS: Peter Miles, Virginia Christine, Tristram Coffin, Richard Benedict, Jason Johnson, Roy Barcroft. A group of French-Canadian settlers is terrorized by a band of outlaws. The Lone Ranger and Tonto come to the rescue.

97.216 *Mission for Tonto.* May 2, 1957. GS: Tyler MacDuff, Robert Burton, Florence Lake, Lane Bradford, Gregg Barton. An ambitious mother and her two ex-convict sons attempt to take a ranch away from a law-abiding citizen. When the young heir to the ranch is shot and left for dead he is rescued by Tonto, and treated by the Lone Ranger. When Tonto rides to warn the boy's grandfather, he is ambushed and beaten. The Lone Ranger sets out after the would-be killers.

97.217 *Journey to San Carlos.* May 9, 1957. GS: Myron Healey, Joe Sargent, Harry Strang, Rick Vallin, Melinda Byron. The Lone Ranger and Tonto help two young men — one who has been branded a coward, the other an Indian chief who stood by while his renegade tribesmen attacked settlers.

97.218 *The Banker's Son.* May 16, 1957. GS: Jim Bannon, Ewing Mitchell, Pat Lawless, Don Haggerty, Hank Worden. Tonto overhears a fight between a banker and his son in which one of them is wounded by a bullet. Tonto reports the incident to a marshal but finds that the banker, his son and the marshal all deny the fact.

97.219 *The Angel and the Outlaw.* May 23, 1957. GS: Dennis Moore, Florence Lake, Brad Jackson, Carlos Vera, Linda Wrather. With the help of the Lone Ranger and Tonto, an elderly lady tries to discourage one of the orphan children in her care from a life of crime.

97.220 *Blind Witness.* May 30, 1957. GS: William Fawcett, Kay Riehl, Byron Foulger, Myron Healey. Robbers, caught in the act by the Lone Ranger and Tonto, accuse the Masked Man and his friend of the crime. The only witnesses to the robbery are a five-year-old boy and an elderly rancher who is suddenly struck blind.

97.221 *Outlaws in Grease Paint.* June 6, 1957. GS: Tom Brown, Mary Ellen Kay, John Pickard. The Lone Ranger encounters bandits who have been stealing shipments of gold from Wells Fargo, and then vanishing mysteriously. The Lone Ranger and Tonto pursue two crooked actors who are wearing Shakespearean costumes.

98. *The Loner*

CBS. 30 min. Broadcast history: Saturday, 9:30–10:00, Sept. 1965–April 1966.

Regular Cast: Lloyd Bridges (William Colton).

Premise: At the close of the Civil War, William Colton resigns his Union Army commission and heads west to forget the horror of battle.

The Episodes

98.1 *An Echo of Bugles.* Sept. 18, 1965. GS: Tony Bill, Whit Bissell, John Hoyt, Lou Krugman, Stephen Roberts, Gregg Palmer. Colton comes to the aid of a Confederate veteran who's being humiliated by a young tough.

98.2 *The Vespers.* Sept. 25, 1965. GS: Jack Lord, Joan Freeman, Ron Soble, Bill Quinn. The Rev. Mr. Booker, Colton's friend and a onetime gunfighter, is being hunted by the brother of two of his victims, but Booker refuses to defend himself.

98.3 *The Lonely Calico Queen.* Oct. 2, 1965. Tina Hermensen, Jeanne Cooper, Edward Faulkner, Tracy Morgan, Lyzanne LaDue, Breena Howard. Colton sets out to locate Miss Angela Wheeler after finding a letter from her on the body of a man killed by a bounty hunter.

98.4 *The Kingdom of McComb.* Oct. 9, 1965. GS: Leslie Nielsen, Tom Lowell, Ken Drake, Ed Peck, Robert Phillips. Colton rescues a young Amish boy who is about to receive a beating from the thugs of town boss McComb.

98.5 *One of the Wounded.* Oct. 16, 1965. GS: Anne Baxter, Lane Bradford, Paul Richards, Steve Gravers. Colton goes to work for Agatha Phelps, who has her hands full trying to run a farm and care for her husband, a battle-shocked veteran of the Civil War.

98.6 *The Flight of the Arctic Tern.* Oct. 23, 1965. GS: Janine Gray, Tom Stern, Larry Ward. Colton's friend Rob Clark is getting married soon, but he is beginning to suspect that there is something between his fiancee and Colton.

98.7 *Widow on the Evening Stage.* Oct. 30, 1965. GS: Katharine Ross, Lloyd Gough, Bill Zuckert, Alan Baxter, Ann Staunton, Rafael Lopez, John Damler. Sue Sullivan is unaware that her husband has been killed in a recent Indian raid, and her father-in-law wants Colton to help break the news to the widow when she arrives on the stage. But his feelings toward the girl change when he learns that she is a full-blooded Indian.

98.8 *The House Rules at Mrs. Wayne's.* Nov. 6, 1965. GS: Nancy Gates, Lee Philips, Lindy Davis, Dick Wilson, Jonathan Kidd. Colton stops to call on an old friend, and is shocked to learn that the man has been murdered.

98.9 *The Sheriff of Fetterman's Crossing.* Nov. 13, 1965.

GS: Allan Sherman, Harold Peary, Robin Hughes, Dub Taylor. Colton takes a job as deputy to a bungling sheriff who is credited with single handedly capturing thirty Confederate soldiers during the Civil War.

98.10 *The Homecoming of Lemuel Stove.* Nov. 20, 1965. GS: Brock Peters, Russ Conway, Don Keefer, John Pickard. Union Army veteran Lemuel Stove saves Colton from hostile Indians, and Colton agrees to join the man on his journey home.

98.11 *Westward the Shoemaker.* Nov. 27, 1965. GS: David Opatoshu, Warren Stevens. Colton befriends Hyman Rabinovitch, an immigrant shoemaker who plans to use his life savings to set up a shop.

98.12 *The Oath.* Dec. 4, 1965. GS: Barry Sullivan, Joby Baker, Viviane Ventura. Gunslinger Billy Ford faces death unless his inflamed appendix is removed, but there is no medical aid available, except for a drunken, one-armed doctor who doesn't want to be bothered.

98.13 *Hunt the Man Down.* Dec. 11, 1965. GS: Burgess Meredith, Tom Tully, Jason Wingreen, Bert Freed, James Drum. Colton joins a posse that is tracking an old mountain man, but it seems one of the men is out to kill the fugitive.

98.14 *Escort for a Dead Man.* Dec. 18, 1965. GS: Sheree North, Corey Allen, Jack Lambert, Hal Lynch, Sal Gorss, Thomas E. Jackson. A Deserter from Colton's old Army outfit wants to turn himself in, but he needs Colton's help to get past three gunmen who are waiting for him.

98.15 *The Ordeal of Bud Windom.* Dec. 25, 1965. GS: Sonny Tufts, Jeff Bridges, Allen Jaffe, Bryan O'Byrne. While transporting a prisoner to jail, Colton is confronted by the man's gun-wielding teenage son, who is determined to rescue his father.

98.16 *To the West of Eden.* Jan. 1, 1966. GS: Ina Balin, Stewart Moss, Zalman King. Against his better judgment, Colton finally gives in to a young Mexican girl's plea to travel with him across the desert.

98.17 *Mantrap.* Jan. 8, 1966. GS: Bethel Leslie, Pat Conway, Melville Ruick. Ellen Jameson brings Colton into her home after he is shot while fleeing from a gang of outlaws who want to kill him because he was the sole witness to a double murder.

98.18 *A Little Stroll to the End of the Line.* Jan. 15, 1966, GS: Dan Duryea, Robert Emhardt, Bart Burns. Colton neither likes nor respects the man he has been deputized to protect — a rabble-rousing preacher who fears death from an ex-convict.

98.19 *The Trial in Paradise.* Jan. 22, 1966. GS: Robert Lansing, Edward Binns, Deanna Lund, Curt Conway, Joe Mantell. Former Union Army Major Dichter finds himself reunited with three maimed survivors of his old command who have brought him to a ghost town and imminent execution. Dichter is charged with giving a foolish order that resulted in the death of nearly one hundred men.

98.20 *A Question of Guilt.* Jan. 29, 1966. GS: James Gregory, Jean Hale, Phil Chambers, Frank Gerstle. After learning that the assailant he killed was an Army officer, Colton tries to find out why the man attacked him.

98.21 *The Mourners for Johnny Sharp* Part One. Feb. 5, 1966. GS: Beau Bridges, James Whitmore, Pat Hingle, Joyce Van Patten, John Doucette, Skip Homeier. Young gunman

Johnny Sharp lies dying in a cave, while ruthless Bob Pierson waits outside hoping to get his hands on Johnny's loot.

98.22 *The Mourners for Johnny Sharp* Part Two. Feb. 12, 1966. GS: Beau Bridges, James Whitmore, Pat Hingle, Joyce Van Patten, John Doucette, Skip Homeier. Following the late Johnny Sharp's instructions, Colton has arranged for the four people who were closest to the gunman to meet at the undertaker's parlor.

98.23 *Incident in the Middle of Nowhere.* Feb. 19, 1966. GS: Mark Richman, Beverly Garland, Cindy Bridges, George Ramsey, Lennie Geer. Colton encounters a little girl riding his horse, which was stolen from Colton during a stagecoach robbery in which he was shot and left for dead.

98.24 *Pick Me Another Time to Die.* Feb. 26, 1966. GS: Martin Brooks, Ed Peck, Lewis Charles, Joan Adams, Mike Mazurki, Steven Darrell. Deputy Chris Meegan murder Sheriff Walter Cantrell, but Colton, who finds the sheriff's body, is arrested for the slaying.

98.25 *The Burden of the Badge.* March 5, 1966. GS: Victor Jory, Lonnie Chapman, Eloise Hardt, Dorothy Rice, John Daniels, Bill Henry, Buff Brady, Bill Hart. A community of reformed criminals asks Colton's help in their fight against a cattle baron who is trying to drive them off their land.

98.26 *To Hang a Dead Man.* March 12, 1966. GS: Bruce Dern, Howard Da Silva, Beverly Allyson. Colton tries to hunt down the bandits he thinks have captured a friend, and who have left the town of Mecca a smoking, burned-out ruin.

99. *Lonesome Dove: The Series*

Syndicated. 60 min. Broadcast history: Various, Sept. 1994–Sept. 1995.

Regular Cast: Scott Bairtow (Newt Dobbs Call), Christianne Hirt (Hannah Peale Call), Eric McCormack (Col. Francis Clay Mosby), Paul Johansson (Austin Peale), Bret Hart (Luther).

Premise: This series was based on the the 1989 mini-series and its 1993 sequel and dramatized the exploits of Newt Dobbs Call in Montana.

The Episodes

99.1 *Pilot* Part One. Oct. 2, 1994. GS: Billy Dee Williams, Diahann Carroll, Graham Greene, Robert Culp, Paul LeMat, Dennis Weaver, David Cubitt, John Gilbert, Gordon Tootoosis, Stephen Miller, Gary Chalk, Lorne Cardinal. Newt comes to the aid of a scout's wife who is being attacked by thieves.

99.2 *Pilot* Part Two. Oct. 9, 1994. GS: Billy Dee Williams, Diahann Carroll, Graham Greene, Robert Culp, Paul LeMat, Dennis Weaver, David Cubitt, John Gilbert, Gordon Tootoosis, Stephen Miller, Gary Chalk, Lorne Cardinal. Aaron seeks revenge on Ida's attackers. Red Hawk is ambushed by Sotted Elk. Robert learns of Mosby's love for Hannah.

99.3 *Pilot* Part Three. Oct. 16, 1994. GS: Billy Dee Williams, Diahann Carroll, Graham Greene, Robert Culp, Paul LeMat, Dennis Weaver, David Cubitt, John Gilbert, Gordon Tootoosis, Stephen Miller, Gary Chalk, Lorne Cardinal. Josiah gives reluctant permission for Newt and Hannah to marry, but their wedding is interrupted by Mosby's gang.

99.4 *Wild Horses.* Oct. 23, 1994. GS: Judge Reinhold. A convicted swindler en route to jail escapes and poses as a lawman. Meanwhile, Newt and Hannah tend to a traumatized boy.

99.5 *The Trial.* Oct. 30, 1994. GS: David Cubitt, George Kennedy. Mosby sticks his neck out to save Robert, who may be hanged for murder if Judge J.T. "Rope" Calder has his way.

99.6 *Duty Bound.* Nov. 6, 1994. GS: Jaimz Woolvett, Kenneth Welsh. Newt takes a job as an Army scout to earn some money, but didn't count on having to help catch deserters. Mosby and Hannah tend to settlers.

99.7 *Long Shot.* Nov. 13, 1994. GS: Helene Udy. Both Newt and Mosby have their own separate reasons for going after illegal-whiskey traders, while Ida takes in the homeless girlfriend of one of the gang.

99.8 *Last Stand.* Nov. 20, 1994. GS: Dennis Weaver, Adam Beach, August Schellenberg. Buffalo Bill makes a return visit to offer Newt a job, and the two promptly get caught up in a dispute between a Cheyenne chief and the army.

99.9 *Ballad of Gunfighter.* Nov. 27, 1994. GS: Michael Martin Murphey, Allison Hossack, Robert King. A friendship with an undercover police officer and Austin's duel with a gunfighter results in Newt being forced to pose as a bank robber.

99.10 *The Cattle Drive.* Dec. 4, 1994. GS: Olivia Hussey, Philip Granger, Anna Hagen. Newt and Austin ride after cattle rustlers who made off with the town's investment, while Mosby is visited by an old friend who sparks Josiah's interest.

99.11 *Firebrand.* Feb. 5, 1995. GS: Greg Ellwand, Rae Dawn Chong. A down-on-his-luck stranger loses his possessions at Mosby's gambling club, so Newt uses a winning of his own to help the man.

99.12 *High Lonesome.* Feb. 12, 1995. GS: Matthew Walker, Jack Elam, Alana Stewart, David McNally, Tony Rosato, Terri Hawkes, David Everhart, Philip Hayes, Peter Skagen. A trip to Sweetwater for some rest and relaxation turns into a nightmare when Austin is wrongly imprisoned by a lawman.

99.13 *Law and Order.* Feb. 19, 1995. GS: Denny Miller, Olivia Hussey, Eli Gabay, Brent Stait. The new sheriff of Curtis Wells comes to the aid of townspeople, including Newt and Hannah, who are being pressured by thugs into selling their land.

99.14 *The Road Home.* Feb. 26, 1995. GS: Gordon Pinsent, Judith Buchan, Andre Roy. Newt and other members of a stagecoach are terrorized by a sniper targeting one of them.

99.15 *Title Unknown.* March 5, 1995. GS: Georgie Collins, Denny Miller, Jeremy Ratchford, Art Hindle, Paul LeMat, Larry Reese, Rod Wilson, Pamela Sears, Mathew Lerigny, Stephen McIntyre, Wayne Hemmings. Hannah and Austin's childhood friend returns from prison and finds that townspeople are aware of his intentions to lead an honest life.

99.16 *Title Unknown.* April 30, 1995. GS: Dennis Weaver, Linda Sorensen. The Calls visit Buffalo Bill to see his Wild West show and end up giving him financial assistance, but they can't help Bill's marriage when his wife learns he has had an affair.

99.17 *The Traveler.* May 7, 1995. GS: Annette O'Toole. Hannah is quite taken with a new resident, a photographer with a wild streak. But Newt gets a report that paints a different picture of the woman — she may be a fugitive from the law.

99.18 *Rebellion.* May 14, 1995. GS: Winston Rekert, Katharine Isobel. Bullies terrorize the townspeople of Sweetwater, and the daughter of a corrupt sheriff gets caught in the middle. Meanwhile, a wounded Robert Shelby seeks help from Mosby.

99.19 *The List.* May 21, 1995. GS: Richard Comar. As gold fever rises, Austin leaves the paper to go prospecting, Josiah gets the story of a lifetime, and Mosby thinks he has met the man who killed his wife.

99.20 *Ties That Bind.* May 28, 1995. GS: Diahann Carroll, Lee Majors. Newt's disappearance, followed by the discovery of a corpse dressed in his clothes, leads townspeople to assume that he is dead, but Hannah and Newt's visiting father refuse to believe it.

99.21 *Title Unknown.* June 4, 1995. GS: Ron White. Hannah confesses her dalliance with Mosby to Newt, but the three must put aside their differences when the townspeople of Curtis Wells are terrorized by a band of criminals.

100. *Lonesome Dove: The Outlaw Years*

Syndicated. 60 min. Broadcast history: Various, Oct. 1995–March 1996.

Regular Cast: Scott Bairtow (Newt Dobbs Call), Eric McCormack (Mosby), Bret Hart (Luther), Tracy Scoggins (Amanda Carpenter), Kelly Rowan (Mattie).

Premise: In this sequel to *Lonesome Dove: The Series*, the widowed Newt returns to Curtis Wells after a two-year absence.

The Episodes

100.1 *The Return.* Oct. 1, 1995. GS: Dean Haglund, Doug Lennox, Paul LeMat. Newt learns that Mosby has corrupted Curtis Wells and may have killed his friend, a fellow bounty hunter.

100.2 *The Hanging.* Oct. 8, 1995. GS: Devon Sawa, Ann Warn Pegg, Robert Clothier, James Baker. A sixteen-year-old boy accused of cattle rustling will be hanged unless Call can prove he is innocent. Meanwhile, Mattie takes on the thankless job of town undertaker.

100.3 *Fear.* Oct. 15, 1995. GS: Peter MacNeil, John Pyper-Ferguson, Zook Matthews. The usually fearless Mosby is terrified when he receives threats from a mystery person, attributing them to the wrong man, despite Call's observation that it could have been anyone.

100.4 *The Alliance.* Oct. 22, 1995. GS: Nigel Bennett, Joel Wyner. Mosby goes into partnership with a wealthy man whose son, Deek, begins terrorizing the townspeople. But Deek picks the wrong target in Mattie, who kills him in self-defense when he attacks her.

100.5 *Nature of the Beast.* Oct. 29, 1995. GS: Frank C. Turner, Lisa Vultaggio, Esther Purves-Smith, Sam Khouth. The murder of a prostitute shuts down the town bordello, to Mosby's dismay, sends an innocent man to prison, and triggers memories of Hannah for Josiah and Call.

100.6 *Providence.* Nov. 5, 1995. Drifter Amanda Carpenter becomes Mosby's worthy rival after purchasing the Lonesome Dove Hotel. But her success, and her new life, are soon threatened.

100.7 *Badlands.* Nov. 12, 1995. GS: Sandra Oh. Mosby finds himself stranded on his way back to Curtis Wells, and reluctantly accompanies three prostitutes on a rough journey to Twyla's. Meanwhile, Austin takes charge of the town in Mosby's absence.

100.8 *Redemption.* Nov. 19, 1995. Townspeople turn against Mosby after an accident at his new copper mine results in numerous deaths, prompting Mosby to investigate what really led to the disaster.

100.9 *Thicker Than Water.* Nov. 26, 1995. GS: Douglas H. Arthurs. The tables are turned on former bounty hunter Call when a stranger claims that Call was responsible for the murder of an entire family.

100.10 *Day of the Dead.* Dec. 3, 1995. GS: Monica Parker, Earl Pastko, Scott McClelland. A traveling carnival visits Curtis Wells, bringing with it nightmares about her father for Mattie, and a curse on the town when a practical joke on the fortuneteller takes a tragic turn.

100.11 *Angel.* Dec. 10, 1995. A beautiful, mysterious bounty hunter comes to town to meet her brother, only to discover he's dead, and the town is hiding the truth of what happened behind a massive cover-up.

100.12 *Bounty.* Dec. 17, 1995. GS: Raoul Trujillo, Guylaine St. Onge. Call pursues a large bounty offered for a killer's capture. But the death toll starts to mount, and Call finds his own life in danger as he gets nearer to solving the crimes.

100.13 *Lover's Leap.* Dec. 24, 1995. GS: Nicholas Lea, Page Fletcher, Christopher Gray. Mattie falls deeply in love with the town's new schoolteacher, but Amanda's accidental knowledge of the man's past threatens to ruin Mattie's happiness, although it works to Amanda's advantage.

100.14 *Cattle War.* Jan. 13, 1996. GS: Robert Norsworthy. The simmering antagonism between Call and Mosby boils over when Call agrees to help the cattle rancher Mosby's trying to railroad for breach of contract.

100.15 *The Bride.* Jan. 21, 1996. GS: Matt Clark. Call is hired to search for a kidnapped mail-order bride, but ends up trying to protect her from her intended husband. Meanwhile, a preacher stirs up trouble for Mosby's brothel and saloon.

100.16 *Betrayal.* Jan. 28, 1996. GS: Peter Outerbridge. The already tense relationship between Austin and Newt is furthered strained when Austin begins to feel that townspeople, and his father, favor Newt over him.

100.17 *Hideout.* Feb. 4, 1996. Mattie and Amanda are kidnapped by a stranger who feels Mosby owes him and his friends money for the mine explosion.

100.18 *Partners.* Feb. 11, 1996. GS: Barry Pepper, Eugene A. Clark, Tom Heaton. Austin's ineffectiveness as a lawman is revealed when a gang of toughs threatens to destroy the town unless he pays them a substantial sum of money.

100.19 *The Robbery.* Feb. 18, 1996. GS: Paul LeMat, Bruce McFee. Mosby is robbed and savagely beaten by three men, one of whom may be a Curtis Wells resident. Soon, all clues point to Austin, who vehemently denies his involvement.

100.20 *When She Was Good.* Feb. 25, 1996. A young woman appeals to Call for help when she's the prime suspect in the brutal murder of her parents.

100.21 *Medicine.* March 3, 1996. GS: Katherine Kelly Lang, Bruce McFee. The death of a Lakota chief coincides with a visit from bounty hunter Enona whom Call remembers meeting, but who claims to have no memory of knowing him.

100.22 *Love and War.* March 10, 1996. GS: Alan C. Peterson. Amanda loses everything when Mosby blows the whistle on her card-cheating ways, and she soon learns the price she will have to pay to get it all back. Meanwhile, UnBob tries to play matchmaker for Mattie and Newt.

101. *A Man Called Shenandoah*

ABC. 30 min. Broadcast history: Monday, 9:00-9:30, Sept. 1965–Sept. 1966.

Regular Cast: Robert Horton (Shenandoah).

Premise: This series, set in the 1860s, concerned a man who is found by two bounty hunters after having been left to die on the prairie. He is nursed back to life by a saloon girl, but finds that he is suffering from amnesia. Calling himself Shenandoah, he attempts to learn his identity and the reason why someone tried to kill him.

The Episodes

101.1 *The Onslaught.* Sept. 23, 1965. GS: Beverly Garland, Noah Keen, Richard Devon, Robert Foulk, Steve Gravers. A stranger, shot down and left to die on the prairie, is found by two buffalo hunters, who haul the half-dead man to town on the chance that he is an outlaw with a price on his head.

101.2 *Survival.* Sept. 20, 1965. GS: Jeanne Cooper, John Davis Chandler, Dennis Patrick, John Anderson, Adam Williams. After buying a horse from a woman in a lonely cabin, Shenandoah rides into town, where he finds himself accused of the woman's murder.

101.3 *The Fort.* Sept. 27, 1965. GS: Edward Binns, Warren Oates, Milton Selzer. Shenandoah arrives at an Army post looking for the sergeant who answered his ad offering a reward to anyone recognizing his picture, but the sergeant is headed for the firing squad and Shenandoah is arrested as his accomplice.

101.4 *The Caller.* Oct. 11, 1965. GS: Cloris Leachman, David Sheiner, Kent Smith. Shenandoah is held for murder, and the only witness who could clear him is the victim's young daughter, who has been shocked speechless by the crime.

101.5 *The Debt.* Oct. 18, 1965. GS: Charles McGraw, Paul Carr, Whit Bissell, Harry Dean Stanton. Arriving in a strange town, Shenandoah is attacked by a man who says that Shenandoah was the Union Army officer who killed his brother during the Civil War.

101.6 *Obion—1866.* Oct. 25, 1965. GS: Claude Akins, James Griffith, Robert G. Anderson, Ken Lynch. At a wayside railroad station, a cigar-smoking salesman flees in terror after spotting Shenandoah in the coach.

101.7 *The Verdict.* Nov. 1, 1965. GS: Edward Asner, Bruce Dern, Harry Townes, Bill Zuckert, Richard Carlyle, Tom Greenway, James Gavin, Bing Russell, Robert S. Carson. After robbing the express office, Bobby Ballantine kills the marshal in his escape attempt. But he doesn't get past Shenandoah, who shoots him down and then protects him from a lynch mob.

101.8 *Town on Fire.* Nov. 8, 1965. GS: Elinor Donahue, Don Megowan, Henry Jones, Simon Scott. In prison, Johnny Kyle promised to kill the founder of Wade City and burn the town to the ground. Now Kyle is back to make good his threat, and Shenandoah and a has-been doctor are the only two men standing in his way.

101.9 *Incident at Dry Creek.* Nov. 15, 1965. GS: Leif Erickson, Michael Burns, Nina Shipman, Kelly Thordsen. Shenandoah applies for the job of deputy in a gold strike town where several deputies have already been killed.

101.10 *The Locket.* Nov. 22, 1965. GS: Martin Landau, Trevor Bardette, Mort Mills, Chris Alcaide. Shenandoah heads into Indian territory to search for the fugitive who may have a clue to his identity, but he will have to find him before a bounty hunter, who plans to shoot the wanted man on sight.

101.11 *The Reward.* Nov. 29, 1965. GS: Kevin Hagen, Karen Steele, Lloyd Bochner, Hank Patterson, Walter Sande, Kate Murtagh, Lyle Sudrow. After someone takes a shot at him, Shenandoah learns there is a price on his head—$500 dead or alive.

101.12 *Special Talent for Killing.* Dec. 6, 1965. GS: Madlyn Rhue, George Kennedy, James Frawley, Willard Sage. Shenandoah gets a hostile reception in El Dorado, a nearly deserted gold mining town.

101.13 *The Siege.* Dec. 13, 1965. GS: Charles Aidman, Malcolm Atterbury, Hal Baylor, George Mitchell. Shenandoah is confronted by an angry innkeeper who says he once skipped out on a large hotel bill.

101.14 *The Bell.* Dec. 20, 1965. GS: Nehemiah Persoff, Arthur Batanides, Robert Sorrells, Jim Boles, Meg Wyllie. A Spanish priest asks Shenandoah to help him transport a huge bell across desert country to his village.

101.15 *The Young Outlaw.* Dec. 27, 1965. GS: John Dehner, Bob Random, John Milford, Myron Healey. Shenandoah is held up by a teenager who has decided to pursue the life of an outlaw.

101.16 *The Accused.* Jan. 3, 1966. GS: Albert Salmi, Fay Spain, Gregory Walcott, Russell Collins. A local marshal informs Shenandoah and his drovers that their pay hasn't arrived, and that he will hold Shenandoah responsible for any trouble that might result.

101.17 *Run, Killer, Run.* Jan. 10, 1966. GS: Sally Kellerman, Leonard Nimoy, Sandy Kenyon, Roy Barcroft, James Seay. While bossing stevedores in Galveston, Texas, Shenandoah becomes the target of a killer hired by a very frightened hotel owner.

101.18 *Rope's End.* Jan. 17, 1966. GS: Michael Ansara, Susan Oliver, L.Q. Jones, Russell Thorson, Vic Perrin. Shenandoah is waiting at a stage stop for Judge Harvey, who may have a clue to his identity. Also waiting are a pair of gunmen, who have business with the judge.

101.19 *The Lost Diablo.* Jan. 24, 1966. GS: Robert Loggia, James Gregory, Than Wyenn, Susan Bay. The key to a safe deposit box leads Shenandoah to a town he doesn't remember, a treasure map, and his former partner, who once tried to kill him for the treasure.

101.20 *A Long Way Home.* Jan. 31, 1966. GS: Geraldine Brooks, Lyle Bettger, Ron Hayes, William Quinn, John D. Reilly, Quentin Sondergaard. Fleeing bank robber Jamie Brewster recognizes and tries to kill Shenandoah, even though the attempt jeopardizes his efforts to escape.

101.21 *End of a Legend.* Feb. 7, 1966. GS: Gail Kobe, Karl Swenson, J.D. Cannon, Alfred Shelly, John Damler. Shenandoah wants to find aging gunfighter Jason Brewster. But the sheriff doesn't want Brewster bothered by strangers, especially young gunslingers trying to build a reputation.

101.22 *Run and Hide.* Feb. 14, 1966. GS: Andrew Duggan, Lynn Loring, Frank Marth, Lane Bradford, Berkeley Harris. Shenandoah tries to find the killer of town boss Harley Kern's son before Kern's bloodthirsty posse does.

101.23 *The Riley Brand.* Feb. 21, 1966. GS: Joanna Pettet, Warren Stevens, DeForest Kelley. Shenandoah may be the long-lost brother of wealthy ranch-owner Julia Riley, but her foreman says Shenandoah will never take over the Riley empire.

101.24 *Muted Fifes, Muffled Drums.* Feb. 28, 1966. GS: Norman Fell, Anne Helm, Michael Witney, John Cliff, Larry Thor, Gregory Morton. An old Army photograph identifies Shenandoah as Neal Henderson, a lieutenant who deserted his troops during an Indian attack.

101.25 *Plunder.* March 7, 1966. GS: Pat Hingle, Paul Fix, Mark Allen. Shenandoah tries to locate Sam Winters, an ex-convict who may have a clue to his past. But Winters is also being sought by lawmen, and by Winters' former partners in crime.

101.26 *Marlee.* March 14, 1966. GS: John Ireland, Nina Foch, Rikki Stevens, James Griffith. Shenandoah hopes that the woman shown in an old photograph will be able to identify him. But the woman, who lives in neurotic seclusion, is carefully shielded from the past by her husband, a small-town sheriff.

101.27 *The Death of Matthew Eldridge.* March 21, 1966. GS: Douglas V. Fowley, Louise Latham, Woodrow Parfrey, Gregory Walcott, Byron Morrow. Shenandoah wanders into steamy Eldridgeville, Louisiana, and into a four-year-old charge of murdering Matthew Eldridge, founder of the town.

101.28 *Aces and Kings.* March 28, 1966. GS: Antoinette Bower, Bert Freed, Steve Brodie, Strother Martin. Barmaid Lila Morgan shows great interest in Shenandoah's ring, and when he refuses her offer to buy it she asks cardsharp Gilbert Benteen to get it for her.

101.29 *The Imposter.* April 4, 1966. GS: Jay C. Flippen, Fred Beir, Juliet Mills, Ernest Sarracino. Shenandoah learns that he may be the disinherited son of Andrew O'Rourke, a wealthy cattleman who is dying.

101.30 *An Unfamiliar Tune.* April 11, 1966. GS: Diana Hyland, Harold J. Stone, Herb Vigran. Aging Jason Pruitt suspects that Shenandoah is his young wife's former boy friend.

101.31 *The Clown.* April 18, 1966. GS: Frank Gorshin, Arthur O'Connell, Paul Birch, Amber Flower, Chester Hayes. Otto, the clown in a traveling circus, reacts dramatically when he spots Shenandoah in the audience. He stops his act and flees.

101.32 *Requiem for the Second.* May 2, 1966. GS: Martin Milner, Ross Elliott, John Cliff, Maurine Dawson, Jason Wingreen. Shenandoah and fugitive hunter Jim Scully track down a former Army officer accused of desertion and who is determined not to be taken.

101.33 *Care of General Delivery.* May 9, 1966. GS: Jeanette Nolan, John McIntire, Charles Seel, James Doohan, Anne Loos, George Selk. In his search for identity, Shenandoah tries to locate Francis Xavier O'Connell whose forwarding address is Little Creek, Texas. When Shenandoah arrives in town, the postmistress says that she has never heard of the man.

101.34 *Macauley's Cure.* May 16, 1966. GS: Gary Merrill, Eduard Franz, Virginia Christine, Richard Cutting. Dr. Joshua Macauley, known for his work with the human mind, agrees to help Shenandoah, but the town's sheriff tells Macauley not to take the case.

102. Man from Blackhawk

ABC. 30 min. Broadcast history: Friday, 8:30-9:00, Oct. 1959–Sept. 1960.

Regular Cast: Robert Rockwell (Sam Logan).

Premise: Sam Logan, an investigator for the Chicago-based Blackhawk Insurance Company travels throughout the west settling claims and investigating attempts to defraud the company.

The Episodes

102.1 *Logan's Policy.* Oct. 9, 1959. GS: Beverly Garland, Richard Rust, King Calder, John Cason, Allen Pinson, Allen Jung. A woman in Galveston has taken out life insurance on Sam Logan. Two details trouble Sam. The lady is a total stranger and she has named herself as beneficiary.

102.2 *The Trouble with Tolliver.* Oct. 16, 1959. GS: Vaughn Taylor, Robert Bray, Henry Lascoe. Sam Logan is assigned to investigate the claim by Jenny Tolliver that unless her father, a newspaper editor, is protected from gambling boss Marcus Clagg, the Blackhawk company will have to pay his insurance premium.

102.3 *The New Semaria Story.* Oct. 23, 1959. GS: Karl Swenson, Paul Carr. A Blackhawk policy-holder is hanged for murder, and Sam Logan goes to settle the man's insurance policy with his wife. He learns that the wife has also died, and his search for the next-of-kin is hindered by the belligerent attitude of townspeople.

102.4 *The Man Who Stole Happiness.* Oct. 30, 1959. GS: Jean Willes, Robert Ellenstein. The Blackhawk Insurance Company sends agent Sam Logan to New Orleans to locate an embezzler. He discovers that the thief is about to fall victim to someone else's scheme.

102.5 *The Gypsy Story.* Nov. 6, 1959. GS: Frank Silvera, Marianne Stewart, William Roerick, Percy Helton. The sudden death of a Blackhawk policyholder, two days after taking out the insurance, brings Sam Logan to a Vermont town. Though the death seems natural, Logan learns that a Gypsy boy was lynched for murder.

102.6 *Station Six.* Nov. 13, 1959. GS: Mary LaRoche, Ralph Clanton, Mort Mills. Grace Arthur has been cleared of implication in the deaths of her two husbands. But Sam Logan still suspects that Grace murdered her husbands to collect their insurance.

102.7 *Vendetta for the Lovelorn.* Nov. 20, 1959. GS: Joe De Santis, Alan Reed, Joan Lora. Middle-aged Fidelio Pirozzi insures his young fiancee's arrival from Italy with the Blackhawk Company. But when her boat docks, the young lady can't be found.

102.8 *The Winthrop Woman.* Nov. 27, 1959. GS: Louis Jean Heydt. Agent Sam Logan is sent to investigate Mrs. Lettie Magwood's claim to her husband's insurance. Mrs. Magwood received an unusual letter telling her that her husband died in Mexico.

102.9 *Contraband Cargo.* Dec. 4, 1959. GS: John Sutton, Mara Corday. A ship's owner plots to victimize a group of Latin American revolutionaries and the Blackhawk Company. He intends to deliver a shipload of useless guns, then sink his ship and collect the insurance.

102.10 *A Matter of Conscience.* Dec. 11, 1959. GS: Bethel Leslie, Robert Burton, Mark Allen, Jimmy Baird. Notified of the death of an Alabama policyholder, the Blackhawk Insurance Company sent two claim forms to the beneficiary. Both forms were returned unsigned, and Sam Logan sets out for Alabama to find out why.

102.11 *Death Is the Best Policy.* Dec. 18, 1959. GS: Walter Burke, Virginia Christine, Ted Markland. Ambushed by two of the Schuler brothers, Martin Harris kills one in self-defense. Realizing that the remaining Schulers will be gunning for him, Harris asks Sam Logan to protect his young son Paul.

102.12 *The Legacy.* Dec. 25, 1959. GS: Ruta Lee, Joe di Reda, Charles Fredericks, Phil Chambers, Fred Sherman. Policyholder Cal Thompson is killed by a hired gun. Blackhawk agent Sam Logan suspects that someone is after the insurance money that will go to Thompson's daughter Ginnie.

102.13 *The Biggest Legend.* Jan. 1, 1960. GS: Joe Mantell, Arthur Hunnicutt, Susan Cummings, Brad Dexter, William Bryant. Publicist Wayne Weedy insures soprano Glory Vetal and asks the Blackhawk Insurance Company to provide a bodyguard for Glory during her tour of the West. Sam Logan is assigned to serve as Glory's protector.

102.14 *Death at Noon.* Jan. 8, 1960. GS: Charles McGraw, Jeanne Cooper, Harry Bellaver, Jack W. Harris, Wayne Davidson. Matt Clovis comes home from the war and, disapproving of his wife's job, leaves her and sets out for a small town. Aware that Matt is looking for trouble, his wife contacts the Blackhawk Insurance Company, which holds the insurance on his life.

102.15 *The Savage.* Jan. 15, 1960. GS: Sean McClory, Lonnie Blackman, Woody Strode, Malcolm Atterbury, Walter Coy, Mabel Rea, Ian MacDonald. Convicted of murdering a ship broker, Capt. John Goodhill is due to hang for the crime. Insurance agent Sam Logan is sent to investigate.

102.16 *The Hundred Thousand Dollar Policy.* Jan. 22, 1960. GS: Alan Hale, Jr., Barbara Lawrence, Robert J. Stevenson, Mike Lane, Judd Holdren, Herman E. West, Millie Stevens. A financier is murdered and actress Evelyn Marquis, his beneficiary, makes a hurried attempt to claim the benefits of his insurance. Then the dead man's business rival, also a friend of Evelyn's, begins to buy up the stocks that he controlled.

102.17 *Portrait of Cynthia.* Jan. 29, 1960. GS: Robert Lowery, Maria Winter, Morris Ankrum, Richard Angarola, Larry Hudson, Mike Masters. A portrait is reported stolen from Gordon Hull's home and Blackhawk insurance agent Sam Logan is sent to recover it. Hull's wife Cynthia tells Logan that her husband is holding her prisoner and asks him to help her escape.

102.18 *El Patron.* Feb. 5, 1960. GS: Eduardo Noriega, William Edmonson, Pitt Herbert, Laurie Mitchell. Blackhawk insurance agent Sam Logan is sent to recover a medallion that was stolen from a museum. Logan learns that the thief was caught, escaped and has stolen the medallion again.

102.19 *Drawing Account.* Feb. 12, 1960. GS: Judson Pratt, Kathie Browne, Ron Hagerthy. A New York cartoonist takes out a life insurance policy, and none too soon. His political cartoons have badly damaged Boss Tweed's ring. Sam Logan, as the insurance company's trouble-shooter, sets himself up in the cartoonist's home to protect him.

102.20 *The Ghost of Lafitte.* Feb. 26, 1960. GS: Tommy Rettig, Amanda Randolph, Richard Miles, Robert Foulk. Since the death of his parents, Francois Lafitte has been taking care of his younger brothers and sisters. But Francois is not of age, and Blackhawk agent Sam Logan must turn the insurance money over to an adult. Logan asks Hoag Lafitte, the children's only adult relative, to handle the family finances.

102.21 *Execution Day.* March 4, 1960. GS: Pamela Lincoln, Sam Buffington, Karl Lukas, Bart Burns, Jim Hayward. A worker on a Tennessee chain-gang thinks his son is a potential murderer. He asks insurance agent Logan to avert trouble.

102.22 *Destination Death.* March 11, 1960. GS: Robert H. Harris, Billy Curtis. The midget star of a traveling show is heavily insured. When he gets an anonymous death threat Sam Logan goes along as his bodyguard.

102.23 *Diamond Cut Diamond.* March 18, 1960. GS: Robert F. Simon, Dean Stanton, O.Z. Whitehead. A fortune in diamonds has been stolen from a stage attacked by Indians. But the Redskins don't seem to have the loot. Sam Logan suspects the local sheriff.

102.24 *Death by Northwest.* March 25, 1960. GS: Forrest Lewis, Hollis Irving, Artie Lewis, Doug DeCosta. Logan is assigned to guard a valuable statue. Then the carving and a coffin disappear from the same train.

102.25 *The Last Days of Jessie Turnbull.* April 1, 1960. GS: Virginia Gregg, Chubby Johnson, Tom Reese, John Gentry. The last days of Jessie Turnbull are spent on a series of drunken sprees. His long-suffering daughter can't do a thing about her father's shenanigans, but the girl's suitor has an eye to the future. He takes out a policy on Jessie's life.

102.26 *The Search for Cope Borden.* April 15, 1960. GS: Sandra Knight, George Neise, Kenneth MacDonald. Hunting the leader of a gang of bank robbers, Logan takes on an assistant—a young lady who would like to see him dead.

102.27 *The Sons of Don Antonio.* April 22, 1960. GS: Jacques Aubuchon, Gustavo Rojo, Johnny Seven, Nacho Galindo. The sons of Don Antonio threaten Sam Logan when he investigates the burning of their barn. But threats don't work on the man from Blackhawk. He is even more suspicious of foul play.

102.28 *Incident at Tupelo.* April 29, 1960. GS: Betsy Jones-Moreland, George Milan, Charles Watt, Ken Becker. The people in the little town of Tupelo are in a hanging mood, and their target is Henry Thornton. Desperate for help, Mrs. Thornton wires her insurance company—the Blackhawk.

102.29 *The Harpoon Story.* May 6, 1960. GS: Gil Rankin, Rebecca Welles, Gregg Palmer, Lou Krugman, Walter Burke. In a New England seacoast town, Logan senses something fishy in the death of a ship's chandler. The man was accidentally injured by a harpoon.

102.30 *The Montreal Story.* May 13, 1960. GS: Marie Aldon, Robert Eyer. The Blackhawk hears from the widow of an Army deserter. She has had word that her husband is still alive — somewhere in Montreal.

102.31 *In His Steps.* May 20, 1960. GS: Nita Talbot, Richard Shannon, Duane Grey, Robert J. Stevenson. Logan heads for New York City's Bowery district to help a fellow agent investigate the death of a policy holder. When Sam arrives, his colleague is dead.

102.32 *Trial by Combat.* May 27, 1960. GS: Robert Brubaker, Russell Thorson, Fredd Wayne. Claflin Pryor sues the Blackhawk for withholding payment on his brother's police. There is reason for the delay. Logan suspects Pryor of murder.

102.33 *The Man Who Wanted Everything.* June 3, 1960. GS: Patricia Donahue, Denver Pyle, Andy Clyde. Sam Logan visits Laura White to pay her late husband's insurance policy. The he learns that the man's body was never recovered and Laura doesn't seem too eager to answer questions.

102.34 *The Money Machine.* June 10, 1960. GS: John Anderson, Oliver McGowan, Jean Willes, Leslie Barrett. An anonymous donor sends a large sum in cashier's checks to the Blackhawk's Chicago office. There is no explanation attached, but Logan suspects the checks add up to past or present fraud.

102.35 *The Lady in Yellow.* June 17, 1960. GS: Neil Hamilton, Regis Toomey, Bethel Leslie, Kem Dibbs. A Boston collector reports the theft of an authentic Velasquez, heavily insured by Blackhawk. But Sam Logan suspects that the painting was nothing more than a clever forgery.

102.36 *Gold Is Where You Find It.* June 24, 1960. GS: Logan Field, Lyn Thomas, Lewis Charles, William Kendis, Francis De Sales, S. John Launer. An Arizona bandit finds gold in a heavily insured shipment headed for the Denver mint. Sam Logan tries to learn how news of the secret shipments leaked out to the thief.

102.37 *Remember Me Not.* Sept. 9, 1960. GS: Peter Adams, Joanna Barnes, Bernard Fein, Robert Vaughn, Eleanor Audley. Harrison Elwood is slated to die for the murder of his wife, but the body has never been found. Logan hunts for new evidence.

103. *Man Without a Gun*

Syndicated. 30 min. Broadcast history: Various, Nov. 1957–Sept. 1959.

Regular Cast: Rex Reason (Adam MacLean), Mort Mills (Marshal Frank Tallman), Harry Harvey, Sr. (Mayor George Dixon), Forrest Taylor (Doc Brannon).

Premise: Adam MacLean is a newspaper editor in the town of Yellowstone in the Dakota Territory of the 1880s. He uses the paper to help bring law and order to the town.

The Episodes

103.1 *The Seven Killers.* Nov. 8, 1957. A group of strangers arrive in Yellowstone and obtain jobs. Adam MacLean hires one of the men to work on his newspaper, unaware that the man belongs to a gang that plans to rob the bank.

103.2 *Decoy.* Nov. 13, 1957. GS: Robert Foulk, Jean Willes, Myron Healey, Sam Flint, James Philbrook. Adam takes the place of the seriously wounded owner of the local freight line as part of a trap of catch the person who shot him.

103.3 *The Fugitive.* Nov. 21, 1957. GS: Dayton Lummis, Gary Gray, John Doucette, Helen Thurston. An article about a local rancher printed by MacLean in his newspaper brings an out-of-town lawman to Yellowstone.

103.4 *High Iron.* Nov. 28, 1957. The railroad is being built through Dakota, but according to the plan it will bypass Yellowstone. The townspeople feel that this will ruin the town.

103.5 *Man Missing.* Dec. 5, 1957. GS: Dorothy Provine. Lucy Mae Brown arrives in town in search of her lost brother.

103.6 *Teen-Age Idol.* Jan. 10, 1958. GS: Chris Alcaide. When the young lads of Yellowstone are impressed by a killer who is in town, Adam MacLean runs an editorial in his newspaper telling the outlaw to get out of town.

103.7 *Silent Town.* March 7, 1959. The mayor of Yellowstone feels he cannot run for re-election because his opponent knows he has served a prison term for murder.

103.8 *Shadow of a Gun.* Jan. 20, 1958. GS: Denver Pyle. Will and Roy Hatterson are the biggest ranchers in Yellowstone. But it is not until the brothers use their influence to prevent the townspeople from attending church that the people realize the power of the Hattersons.

103.9 *The Sealed Envelope.* Jan. 24, 1958. A man gives Adam MacLean an envelope, the contents of which are to be published one week after his death.

103.10 *The Thin Wall.* Jan. 29, 1958. Five outlaws rob the town bank. Jessie Hamilton, owner of the local cafe, kills one of them, unaware that he is the son of her old sweetheart. The boy's father confronts Adam MacLean, and demands to know who killed his son.

103.11 *Wanted.* Feb. 6, 1958. Adam investigates the apparent reappearance of Marshal Frank Tallman's nephew, who was believed to have been killed with his regiment in a Sioux massacre.

103.12 *The Gun from Boot Hill.* Feb. 11, 1958. GS: Val Benedict. Billy John Wells has been shot by Jud Haimes. Billy's father asks Adam MacLean to collect his son's belongings, and he learns that the slain boy's gun had been tampered with.

103.13 *Indian Fury.* Feb. 14, 1958. GS: Lewis Charles, Carl Milletaire, Dennis Cross. Jed Keogh takes silver trinkets from the burial grounds of the Dakota Indians. Fearing that war will break out between the Indians and the settlers, Adam MacLean attempts to act as a go-between and prevent a war.

103.14 *Guilty.* Feb. 19, 1958. GS: Adrienne Marden, John Baer, Frank Gerstle, Joseph Perry, Stanley Farrar. Adam tries to settle a feud between two ranchers, one of whom needs milk from the other's cow for his baby.

103.15 *Dark Road.* Feb. 24, 1958. GS: James Griffith. A man who was blinded by a horse thief's bullet becomes a gunman, goes after the outlaw who blinded him, and wrongly identifies Adam's voice as that of his target.

103.16 *Reward.* March 5, 1958. GS: Christopher Dark, Stacy Harris, Harry Shannon. Adam becomes involved with a near-bankrupt farmer who decides to impersonate a dangerous outlaw and turn himself in so that his wife will get the reward money.

103.17 *Danger.* March 10, 1958. GS: Phillip Pine, Kem

Dibbs, Ziva Rodann, Fred Graham. Adam frantically searches for a doctor to treat the stranger who was wounded saving him from an Indian attack.

103.18 *The Last Hunt.* March 13, 1958. GS: Francis J. McDonald. Two buffalo hunters are robbed of their bullets. Adam MacLean has bought the bullets, not knowing where they originally came from. Trouble brews when the hunters come into town.

103.19 *The Day the West Went Wild.* March 18, 1958. GS: Jane Nigh, Ray Teal, Stuart Bradley, Fred Graham. Adam learns that some fun-loving townsmen are planning a fake bank robbery to impress a girl from Boston who has come West looking for excitement.

103.20 *Peril.* April 1, 1958. Thieves steal the safe from the Bismark Express Company. Unable to open it, they arrange to have a notorious safe cracker break out of jail.

103.21 *Trap Line.* April 4, 1958. Adam tries to prove the innocence of the man to whom all the evidence points in the murder of a trapper.

103.22 *Night of Violence.* April 9, 1958. GS: Diane Jergens. Adam MacLean tries to help a young couple get married even though the girl's father opposes the marriage.

103.23 *Lady from Laramie.* April 14, 1958. Adam becomes involved with a woman who is determined to murder the man who killed her husband.

103.24 *The Dream Weaver.* April 17, 1958. A ten-year-old orphan is cared for by the townspeople until his wealthy Uncle Mark comes to town. Adam is suspicious when a man comes to town claiming to be her uncle.

103.25 *The Law of the Land.* April 22, 1958. Settlers are threatened with the loss of their homesteads when a representative of the Government Land Office arrives in Yellowstone.

103.26 *No Heart for Killing.* April 25, 1958. Adam tries to stop a troubled young man who has come to Yellowstone intent on killing his brother.

103.27 *Buried Treasure.* April 30, 1958. GS: Robert J. Wilke, Leonard Bell. Adam MacLean inherits a coded treasure map that leads to the loot from an old robber. He finds trouble when the dead thief's living partners hunt for the treasure too.

103.28 *The Quiet Strangers.* May 5, 1958. GS: Jacqueline de Wit. At Adam MacLean's request, Senator Armitage visits Yellowstone while evaluating the Dakotas as a potential state.

103.29 *The Claim Jumpers.* May 8, 1958. Adam MacLean receives a threatening letter from a man he helped to imprison.

103.30 *Jailbreak.* May 13, 1958. GS: Lillian Bronson, Don Gordon, Wayne Taylor, Greta Granstedt, Mitchell Kowal. The Halley family, led by Ma Halley, plans to free her son Lee before he can be hanged.

103.31 *The Kidder.* May 16, 1958. GS: Doug McClure, Charles Fredericks, Benny Baker, Richard Collier, Constance Collier. Adam tries to help a simple farm boy who has been sold a worthless silver mine by a practical joker.

103.32 *Lissie.* May 21, 1958. After the daughter of a killer is caught trying to rob a store, Adam sets out to teach the uncouth girl to act and speak like a lady.

103.33 *Aftermath.* May 26, 1958. GS: Robert F. Simon, James Drury, Whit Bissell, Walter Maslow, Robert Simpson, Herb Vigran, Robert O'Connor. Adam encounters a former Army officer who is being hunted by three vengeful men because his cowardice was responsible for a troop massacre.

103.34 *The Last Bullet.* May 29, 1958. GS: Judith Ames. Two men whose original duel was interrupted by the law plan to stage the duel again — this time in Yellowstone.

103.35 *Special Edition.* June 4, 1958. GS: Patrick McVey. Adam goes after a man who is threatening homesteaders and buying their property for a small price.

103.36 *Headline.* June 9, 1958. GS: Christine White, Bruce Gordon, John Banner, Frank Sully. Doc Brannon is followed by a gunslinger when he refuses to tell the gunslinger the whereabouts of his ex-wife.

103.37 *The Mine.* June 17, 1958. A young woman cares for a wounded stagecoach robber in a deserted mine. Trouble arises when the owner of the mine decides to dig for gold.

103.38 *Invisible Enemy.* June 24, 1958. GS: Peter Hansen, Ricky Kelman, Tom Masters, Aline Towne, Robert Karnes. Adam tries to keep the situation under control when rancher Ben Telford buys a few head of cattle and lets them mingle with his herd, unaware that the new cattle are infected with hoof and mouth disease.

103.39 *Wire's End.* June 29, 1958. GS: Trevor Bardette, Steve Terrell. Adam MacLean is assigned a story on the progress being made by the crew stringing the line across the Dakota territory. Among the members of the crew is a young man who carries the reputation of a coward.

Season Two

103.40 *Face of the Moon.* May 27, 1959.

103.41 *Eye Witness.* June 1, 1959. GS: Virginia Christine, John Anderson, Kenneth Becker, Hal K. Dawson, Stanley Farrar, Tiger Fafara, Paul Jasmin. Adam tries to help when Marshal Tallman resigns his office and leaves town after evidence indicates the innocence of a local boy hanged for murder on Tallman's testimony.

103.42 *The Hero.* June 4, 1959. GS: Chris Alcaide. Marshal Tallman receives a letter from an old friend and former lawman stating his intention of settling in Yellowstone.

103.43 *Witness in Terror.* June 9, 1959. A maid caught a fleeting glimpse of her employer's murderer.

103.44 *Man with the Wrong Face.* June 12, 1959. When a newlywed couple arrive in Yellowstone, the wife finds an impostor claiming to be her husband.

103.45 *The Last Holdup.* June 17, 1959. GS: Lloyd Corrigan, Francis McDonald, John Close, Jason Wingreen. An old man decides to sell his ranch and retire to the poor farm.

103.46 *Daughter of the Dragon.* June 22, 1959. GS: Maria Tsien, Victor Sen Yung, Frances Morris, Olan Soule, Roy Barcroft, Raymond Guth. Adam MacLean risks his life when he befriends two Chinamen who have escaped from a slave labor camp.

103.47 *The Shaving Mug.* June 25, 1959. GS: Will J. White. A barber pretends that his criminal son is a brilliant lawyer.

103.48 *Devil's Acres.* June 30, 1959. GS: Carol Ohmart, Anthony Jochim, Paul Maxey, Gordon Clark, Earle Hodgins, Larry Chance, Victor Rodman, Hugh Langtry. A man dies willing his property to the devil. When his daughter visits, she finds her father very much alive, and he holds her captive.

103.49 *Accused*. July 3, 1959. GS: Cathy O'Donnell, Peter Leeds, Leonard Bell, Patrick Hawley. A young widow seeks revenge on the man responsible for the lynching of her husband.

103.50 *Hangtree Inn*. Sept. 2, 1959. GS: Michael Quinn, Jack Easton, Jr., Peggy Webber, Dabbs Greer, Terry Frost, Jerry Oddo, George Brenlin, Tommy Cook. A marshal whose fiancee was killed by bank robbers resigns his post to hunt down the criminals.

103.51 *The Giant*. Sept. 10, 1959. GS: Michael Lane, Russ Bender, Eddy Waller, Vic Perrin, Richard Cleary, Cyril Delevanti. The partners of Adam MacLean and Mayor Dixon in a silver mine accuse Griff Hagen, a giant of a man, of murder.

103.52 *Stolen Stage*. Sept. 16, 1959. Adam unsuspectingly boards a stagecoach in which a murderer is traveling.

104. The Marshal of Gunsight Pass

ABC. 30 min. Broadcast history: Saturday, 6:30-7:00, March 1950–Sept. 1950.

Regular Cast: Russell Hayden (Marshal), Eddie Dean (Marshal Eddie Dean), Roscoe Ates (Deputy Roscoe), Jane Adrian (Ruth).

Premise: This live-action series depicted the adventures of singing cowboy Eddie Dean and his sidekick Deputy Roscoe in the old West.

105. Maverick

ABC. 60 min. Broadcast history: Sunday, 7:30-8:30, Sept. 1957–Sept. 1961; Sunday, 6:30-7:30, Sept. 1961–July 1962.

Regular Cast: James Garner (Bret Maverick) 57-61, Jack Kelly (Bart Maverick), Roger Moore (Beau Maverick) 60-61, Robert Colbert (Brent Maverick) 1961.

Premise: This series depicted the exploits of Bret and Bart Maverick, two gamblers and con men who travelled the old West in the 1880s.

The Episodes

105.1 *The War of the Silver Kings*. Sept. 22, 1957. GS: Edmund Lowe, John Litel, Leo Gordon, Carla Merey, John Hubbard, Fred Sherman, Paul Baxley, Robert Griffin, Bob Steele, Donald Kirke, Frank Sutton. In a poker game with Phineas King, a rich mine owner, Bret Maverick wins by bluffing. Enraged, King tries to run Maverick out of town. But Maverick decides to stay after he learns that King and his henchmen have control of the town. He plans to fight the crooked syndicate by getting a former judge, Joshua Thayer, re-elected to office, and in doing so endangers his life.

105.2 *Point Blank*. Sept. 29, 1957. GS: Michael Connors, Karen Steele, Richard Garland, Benny Baker, Robert Foulk, John Harmon, Peter Brown, Zon Murray, Mitchell Kowal. A couple makes friends with Bret Maverick, planning to make use of him in an embezzling scheme without his knowledge. They plan to kill Maverick after stealing the money, and make it appear that he is the thief.

105.3 *According to Hoyle*. Oct. 6, 1957. GS: Diane Brewster, Ted de Corsia, Leo Gordon, Jay Novello, Tol Avery, Esther Dale, Tyler McVey, Walter Reed, Robert Carson. When Bret Maverick gets into a card game with a beautiful girl, he loses all his money. Bankrupt, Maverick agrees to go into partnership on a gambling hall with the girl. Then he learns that his new partner intends to double-cross him.

105.4 *Ghost Riders*. Oct. 13, 1957. GS: Joanna Barnes, Rhodes Reason, Willard Sage, Stacy Keach, Edd Byrnes, Dan Sheridan, Charles Tannen, John Cliff. Bret Maverick befriends a young widow in a small western town. He takes her to her room and even lends her his coat. But the woman mysteriously disappears and Maverick finds a lonely grave with his jacket hanging on the tombstone. Refusing to believe her dead, he begins an investigation and almost loses his life.

105.5 *The Long Hunt*. Oct. 20, 1957. GS: Richard Webb, Joan Vohs, Richard Crane, Tommy Farrell, Richard Reeves, Harry Harvey, Sr., Stanley Andrews. Bret Maverick sets out to prove the innocence of a man serving a life sentence for homicide. He encounters obstacles when he learns that the prisoner's wife has a jealous suitor who wants to be sure that the man remains in prison.

105.6 *Stage West*. Oct. 27, 1957. GS: Erin O'Brien, Ray Teal, Edd Byrnes, Peter Brown, Chubby Johnson, Jim Bannon, Michael Dante, Howard Negley, Fern Barry. A young woman arrives in the West to meet her husband, who has written her that he has discovered a valuable mine in Indian territory. She does not know that her husband has been murdered by the renegade Fallon family, and that they intend to persuade her to lead them to the mine. Bret Maverick comes to the young woman's assistance.

105.7 *Relic of Fort Tejon*. Nov. 3, 1957. GS: Maxine Cooper, Fredd Wayne, Sheb Wooley, Dan Tobin. Bret Maverick accidentally becomes the possessor of an affectionate Army camel. While trying to avoid the animal, he runs into an old friend, Donna Selly. Her jealous boy friend, a gambler, forces Maverick into a gun fight.

105.8 *Hostage!* Nov. 10, 1957. GS: Laurie Carroll, Stephen Bekassy, Mickey Simpson, Don Durant, Wright King, Trevor Bardette. The Maverick brothers, Bret and Bart, are stranded in New Orleans without money. They attempt to book passage on a new, luxurious river boat to play poker against some of the wealthy passengers. Devereaux, the owner of the boat, refuses to let them aboard. But when the man's daughter is kidnaped, the brothers decide to rescue her to gain free passage.

105.9 *Stampede*. Nov. 17, 1957. GS: Efrem Zimbalist, Jr., Pamela Duncan, Pat Comiskey, Mike Lane, Joan Shawlee, Chris Alcaide. Bret Maverick and his pal Dandy Jim talk backwoods boy Noah Perkins into challenging Battling Krueger to a boxing match. Bret and Jim plan to win money by wagering on Noah, but things go wrong, and Bret himself is forced to fight the muscleman Krueger.

105.10 *The Jeweled Gun*. Nov. 24, 1957. GS: Kathleen Crowley, Stehpen Coit, Miguel Landa, Roy Barcroft, Terrence de Marney, Edwin Bruce, James Parnell, Alfred Hopson, Ezelle Poule, Tom McKee, Norman Frederic. Bart Maverick agrees to pose as the husband of pretty Daisy Harris to escort her through the Badlands. Daisy tells him that she was forced to shoot her former escort in self-defense. When Bart expresses his doubt about her story, he finds his own life in danger.

105.11 The Wrecker. Dec. 1, 1957. GS: Patric Knowles, Karl Swenson, Bartlett Robinson, Thomas B. Henry, Maurice Manson, Alfred Kramer, Barry Brooks, Murvyn Vye. During an auction, curiosity causes Bret and Bart Maverick to outbid a man for the cargo of a ship, mysteriously beached on Midway Island in the South Pacific. When they attempt to claim the ship and its cargo, the find themselves opposed by a gang of opium smugglers.

105.12 The Quick and the Dead. Dec. 8, 1957. GS: Gerald Mohr, Marie Windsor, John Vivyan. Bret Maverick loses a fortune to the famous gambler Doc Holliday. Later, he encounters John Stacey, the only man who can prove Bret did not commit a robbery of which he has been accused. Then Bret learns that Holliday is gunning for Stacey.

105.13 Naked Gallows. Dec. 15, 1957. GS: Michael Connors, Sherry Jackson, Fay Spain, Ed Kemmer, Jeanne Cooper, Morris Ankrum, Bing Russell, Forrest Lewis. Bart Maverick meets Clete Overton, who tells him of his escape from jail after being convicted of murder on circumstantial evidence. Bart, believing Overton innocent, attempts to clear his name.

105.14 Comstock Conspiracy. Dec. 29, 1957. GS: Werner Klemperer, Oliver McGowan, Ed Prentiss, Ruta Lee, Percy Helton, Arthur Batanides, Terry Frost. Bret Maverick tries to help a mining engineer in his fight to get mine owners to improve working conditions for their men.

105.15 The Third Rider. Jan. 5, 1958. GS: Dick Foran, Barbara Nichols, Frank Faylen, Michael Dante, Kasey Rodgers. Bart Maverick helps two exhausted travelers who have only one horse between them. They reward his kindness by stealing his horse and framing him for a bank robbery they have committed.

105.16 A Rage for Vengeance. Jan. 12, 1958. GS: John Russell, Catherine McCleod, Gage Clarke, Russ Conway, S. Newton Anderson, Lewis Martin, Jonathan Hole, William Forrest. An attractive widow asks Bret Maverick to accompany her on a journey to deposit a large sum of money in a Montana bank. The woman is afraid that the man responsible for her husband's death will try to rob her. Maverick his happy to oblige, until he discovers that the money is counterfeit.

105.17 Rope of Cards. Jan. 19, 1958. GS: Tol Avery, Joan Marshall, William Reynolds, Will Wright, Hugh Sanders, Frank Cady, Don Beddoe, Harry Cheshire, Harry Harvey, Sr., George O'Hanlon, Donald Kirke. A young man is convicted of slaying a rancher and is brought to trial. The jury is certain of the accused man's guilt even before the trial begins. Bret Maverick decides to take a desperate chance in order to help the young man.

105.18 Diamond in the Rough. Jan. 26, 1958. GS: William Forrest, Jacqueline Beer, Fred Wayne, Otto Waldis, Lili Valenti, Sig Ruman, Carlyle Mitchell, Terrence de Marney, I. Stanford Jolley, Patrick Whyte. Bart Maverick attempts to expose a wealthy San Franciscan as a diamond swindler.

105.19 Day of Reckoning. Feb. 2, 1958. GS: Russell Thorson, Jean Willes, Virginia Gregg, Mort Mills, Tod Griffin, Willard Sage, Jon Lormer, Murvyn Vye, James McCallion. In a small cowtown, Maverick is threatened by two cowboys. When the local marshal comes to his aid, the two cowboys gun the marshal down.

105.20 The Savage Hills. Feb. 9, 1958. GS: Diane Brewster, Peter Whitney, Stanley Andrews, Thurston Hall, John Dodsworth. A charming swindler, Samantha Crawford, persuades Bart Maverick to help her take a set of plates used in printing counterfeit money from a government agent. She has convinced Maverick that she is the real government agent and that their victim is an impostor.

105.21 Trail West to Fury. Feb. 16, 1958. GS: Efrem Zimbalist, Jr., Gene Nelson, Aline Towne, Charles Fredericks, Paul Fierro, Don Kelly, Russ Bender, Mike Ragan. Bret and Bart Maverick take jobs as trail bosses on a cattle drive through Texas. When a hired gunman from a rival ranch threatens them, they are forced to shoot him. Then they become fugitives from the law.

105.22 The Burning Sky. Feb. 23, 1958. GS: Gerald Mohr, Joanna Barnes, Whitney Blake, Douglas Kennedy, Phillip Terry. Bart Maverick is aboard a stagecoach that is ambushed by Apaches on the desert. The other passengers decide that Maverick should try to elude the Indians and bring help for them.

105.23 The Seventh Hand. March 2, 1958. GS: Diane Brewster, Sam Buffington, James Philbrook, Myrna Dell, Joe Perry. Samantha Crawford meets up with Bret Maverick and stakes him in a no-limit poker game. When Bret wins he is accused of cheating and he finds that Samantha has disappeared. To clear his name he must find her, but she has gone into Indian territory.

105.24 Plunder of Paradise. March 9, 1958. GS: Joan Weldon, Leo Gordon, Ruta Lee, Jay Novello, Eugene Iglesias, Nacho Galindo, Jorge Moreno, Rico Alaniz. A widow tells Bart Maverick and his friend Big Mike McComb of a fortune in gold in Mexico, and offers to lead them to the cache. But a Mexican bandit and a Mexican government agent are also interested in the gold.

105.25 Black Fire. March 16, 1958. GS: Hans Conried, Jane Darwell, Will Wright, Theona Bryant, Charles Bateman, John Vivyan, Dan Sheridan, George O'Hanlon, Edith Leslie, Emory Parnell, Harry Harvey, Sr. Hoping to gain a share of a rich relative's estate, a man persuades Bret Maverick to pose as the old man's nephew. When a murder is committed, Bret's deception endangers his life.

105.26 Burial Ground of the Gods. March 30, 1958. GS: Claude Akins, Nancy Gates, Charles Cooper, Robert Lowery, Sandra Edwards, Raymond Hatton. Cheated by an extortionist, Bart Maverick follows the man to Denver. There he finds his quarry attempting to cheat a woman who believes her husband was killed in an Indian raid.

105.27 Seed of Deception. April 13, 1958. GS: Joi Lansing, Adele Mara, Myron Healey, Bing Russell, Frank Ferguson, Frances Morris, Gerald Mohr, Ron Hayes, Guy Wilkerson. A pretty girl plans to divert the sheriff's attention while a gang of bandits robs the bank. Bret and Bart Maverick risk their lives in an attempt to stop the robbery.

Season Two

105.28 The Day They Hanged Bret Maverick. Sept. 21, 1958. GS: Whitney Blake, Ray Teal, Jay Novello, Robert Griffin, John Cliff, Burt Mustin, Roy Erwin. A Wells Fargo agent is killed and the company's office is robbed. The killer, who is dressed like Bret Maverick, makes his escape.

105.29 Lonesome Reunion. Sept. 28, 1958. GS: Joanna Barnes, Richard Reeves, John Russell, John Qualen, Claire Carleton, Byron Foulger, Robert Carson. In the lobby of a Denver hotel, Bret Maverick meets Abigail Taylor. She offers to pay him to keep a suspicious character who has been following her, from stealing her hatbox. Abigail tells Bret that the box contains valuable papers.

105.30 Alias Bart Maverick. Oct. 5, 1958. GS: Richard Long, Eurlyne Howell, I. Stanford Jolley, Richard Reeves, Charlie Riggs, Jack Lomas. Bart Maverick makes friends with Gentleman Jack Darby, unaware that Darby is wanted for embezzlement. Darby enlists the aid of a pretty girl and swaps identities with Maverick.

105.31 The Belcastle Brand. Oct. 12, 1958. GS: Reginald Owen, Joan Elan, Seymour Green. In order to repay a debt, Bret Maverick agrees to take three Britishers on a bear hunt. But the party is ambushed by bandits who take their guns, horses and supplies and leave them to die in the desert. The Britishers decide to cast a vote on what they should do and disregard Maverick's advice that they follow the bandits.

105.32 High Card Hangs. Oct. 19, 1958. GS: Martin Landau, Efrem Zimbalist, Jr,. Frank Ferguson, Charles Fredericks, Dan Sheridan, Lilyan Chauvin. While working in a gold-mining camp in South Dakota, Bart Maverick and his friend Dandy Jim Buckley meet an old prospector who has a large sum of money saved up. Bart and the prospector get into a poker game with two other miners and the prospector ends up winning. Later the old man is found dead and Maverick and the other two card players are accused of murder.

105.33 Escape to Tampico. Oct. 26, 1958. GS: Gerald Mohr, Barbara Lang, John Hubbard, Paul Picerni, Louis Mercier, Ralph Faulkner. Bret Maverick is offered a large sum of money to go to Tampico and bring back a man wanted for murder. The culprit, a U.S. citizen, now operates a tourist camp in Mexico.

105.34 The Judas Mask. Nov. 2, 1958. GS: John Vivyan, Anna-Lisa, Mel Welles, Richard Garland, Nico Minardos, Robert Jordan, Rosa Turich. Bart Maverick decides to go into a business partnership with Walter Osbourne and invests a large sum. Then a beautiful Spanish dancer steals the money and Bart pursues her to Mexico.

105.35 The Jail at Junction Flats. Nov. 9, 1958. GS: Patrick McVey, Jean Allison, Efrem Zimbalist, Jr., John Harmon, Bert Remsen. Bret Maverick's friend Dandy Jim Buckley borrows $2000 from Bret for a horse-trading enterprise. Later, Bret learns that Buckley has swindled the residents of a small town and is being held in the local jail. Bret decides to free Buckley in an effort to regain his money.

105.36 The Thirty-Ninth Star. Nov. 16, 1958. GS: Bethel Leslie, John Litel, Sam Buffington, Mark Tapscott, William Phipps, Roy Barcroft. Judge Somervell suspects that Bart Maverick has stolen his traveling bag to gain possession of the important documents it contains.

105.37 Shady Deal at Sunny Acres. Nov. 23, 1958. GS: Regis Toomey, Richard Long, Arlene Howell, John Dehner, Diane Brewster, Karl Swenson, Efrem Zimbalist, Jr., Leo Gordon, Joan Young. Bret Maverick is robbed of $15,000 by a crafty banker who denies that the money was ever deposited in his bank. Bret calls on his brother Bart for help.

105.38 Island in the Swamp. Nov. 30, 1958. GS: Arlene Howell, Erin O'Brien, Edgar Buchanan, Lance Fuller, Richard Reeves, Doye O'Dell, Albert Carrier, Roy Engel. Bret Maverick is set adrift in a rowboat which finds its way to an island inhabited by swamplanders. They believe that Bret is a government agent sent to spy on them and promptly take him prisoner.

105.39 Prey of the Cat. Dec. 7, 1958. GS: Wayne Morris, Patricia Barry, Yvette Dugay, Barry Kelley, William Gordon, William Bryant, Syd Saylor. Bart Maverick rests at the Stillmans' ranch while his broken leg heals. Caring for him, Stillman's wife Kitty falls in love with Bart, and suggests a plot to get rid of her husband.

105.40 The Spanish Dancer. Dec. 14, 1958. GS: Richard Long, Adele Mara, Slim Pickens, Tony Romano, Ben Morris, Mark Tapscott. Bart and his partner Gentleman Jack Darby visit a mining town where they meet a beautiful Spanish dancer. Both attracted to the girl, the men become involved in a fist fight, and Bart soon finds himself accused of murder.

105.41 Holiday at Hollow Rock. Dec. 28, 1958. GS: William Reynolds, Saundra Edwards, Tod Griffin, Emile Meyer, Guy Wilkerson. When Bret loses a large sum in a crooked poker game, he decides to use his knowledge of horse-racing odds to recover his money.

105.42 Game of Chance. Jan. 4, 1959. GS: Roxanne Berard, Marcel Dalio, Lou Krugman, Jonathan Hole, Fred Essler, Terrence de Marney. Bart accepts an expensive necklace from the beautiful Countess de Barot as security for a loan. When Bart learns that the necklace is worthless, he and Bret join forces in an attempt to outwit the countess and her uncles.

105.43 Gun-Shy. Jan. 11, 1959. GS: Ben Gage, Marshall Kent, Walker Edmiston, Kathleen O'Malley, Reginald Owen, Gage Clarke, Andra Martin, Roscoe Ates, Doodles Weaver, Irene Tedrow, William Fawcett, Iron Eyes Cody. In a parody of "Gunsmoke", Bret Maverick matches wits and six-gun skill with the incomparable Marshal Mort Dooley, who owns 37 1/2 percent of the Weeping Willow Saloon in Ellwood, Kansas.

105.44 Two Beggars on Horseback. Jan. 18, 1959. GS: Ray Teal, Patricia Barry, John Cliff, Clem Bevans, Will Wright. Bret and Bart Maverick become rivals for the affection of a beautiful adventuress. The three members of the triangle, however, have one objective in common — to cash money drafts at a remote express office which hasn't been informed that its parent company has gone bankrupt.

105.45 The Rivals. Jan. 25, 1959. GS: Patricia Crowley, Roger Moore, Neil Hamilton, Dan Tobin, Barbara Jo Allen, Sandra Gould. Bret Maverick becomes involved in a romantic scheme of mixed identities.

105.46 Duel at Sundown. Feb. 1, 1959. GS: Clint Eastwood, Abby Dalton, Edgar Buchanan, James Griffith, Dan Sheridan. Bret Maverick agrees to help Jed Christiansen break up his daughter's romance with young Red Hardigan. Jed hopes that Bret will be able to prove that Red is a coward. Red, however, is reputed to be the fasted gun around, and Bret is in no hurry to get involved in a fight in which he might be the loser. He conceives a plan which requires his brother Bart to masquerade as the infamous gunslinger John Wesley Hardin.

105.47 Yellow River. Feb. 8, 1959. GS: Patricia Breslin, Robert Conrad, Sam Buffington, Mike Lane, Robert Richards, Harry Hines. Bart Maverick is employed by a beautiful blonde to act as trail boss of a cattle drive. During the first two days of the drive two cowhands meet with death.

105.48 *The Saga of Waco Williams.* Feb. 15, 1959. GS: Wayde Preston, Louise Fletcher, R.G. Armstrong, Brad Johnson, Ken Mayer, Hank Patterson, Lane Bradford. Bret and gun-happy Waco Williams arrive in Bent City together. Bret tries to bring about a peaceful settlement of differences between the cattlemen and the homesteaders, but finds his efforts being undermined by Waco.

105.49 *The Brasada Spur.* Feb. 22, 1959. GS: Hope Summers, Julie Adams, Patrick McVey, Ken Lynch, Ralph Neff, James Lydon, Robert Griffin, Gertrude Flynn, Fred Kruger. Bart Maverick meets beautiful and wealthy Belle Morgan, who gets him into an exclusive poker game. Bart wins stock in the Brasada Spur Railroad, which he discovers is no bargain.

105.50 *Passage to Fort Doom.* March 8, 1959. GS: Nancy Gates, Diane McBain, Arlene Howell, Fred Beir, John Alderson, Sheila Bromley, Charles Cooper, Alan Caillou, Thomas B. Henry. Working as a member of a stagecoach crew, Bart Maverick spots a familiar passenger—his old girl friend Cindy Lou Brown. The trip to Fort Doom, however, isn't a smooth one when marauders attack the stagecoach.

105.51 *Two Tickets to Ten Strike.* March 15, 1959. GS: Connie Stevens, Adam West, Andrea King, William D. Gordon. Riding the stage from Tucson to Ten Strike, Bret Maverick meets charming Frankie French, a former saloon dancer who has been invited to Ten Strike by an unknown benefactor. Arriving in Ten Strike, Bret is strongly urged to leave town and Frankie is jailed for the murder of her benefactor.

105.52 *Betrayal.* March 22, 1959. GS: Patricia Crowley, Ruta Lee, Morgan Jones, Don "Red" Barry. Traveling on a stagecoach, Bart Maverick is charmed by pretty Ann Saunders, who is on her way west to live with her cousin. When the stage is held up by two robbers, Bart notices that Ann apparently knows one of the outlaws.

105.53 *The Strange Journey of Jenny Hill.* March 29, 1959. GS: William Schallert, Peggy King, Sig Ruman, Leo Gordon, George Keymas, K.L. Smith, Mark Tapscott. Singer Jenny Hill combines a concert tour with a search for her outlaw husband. Bret Maverick, too, is looking for Jenny's husband, but he finds it hard to concentrate on his mission when he falls in love with the songstress.

Season Three

105.54 *Pappy.* Sept. 13, 1959. GS: Henry Daniell, Adam West, Troy Donahue, Virginia Gregg, Mike Forest, Kaye Elhardt. Bret and Bart learn that their Pappy is about to be married. When the boys are told that the bride to be is eighteen years old, they set out for the wedding in New Orleans.

105.55 *Royal Four-Flush.* Sept. 20, 1959. GS: David Frankham, Roxane Berard, Arch Johnson, Roberta Shore, Jimmy Baird. Arriving in Virginia City, Bart Maverick is delighted to encounter Captain Fitzgerald, who owes him a large sum of money from a poker game and now appears to be well-heeled. But though Fitzgerald is employed by a beautiful countess, he claims he is broke. Suspecting that currency may soon change hands, Bart decides to stay around and collect his share.

105.56 *The Sheriff of Duck 'n' Shoot.* Sept. 27, 1959. GS: Peggy McCay, Chubby Johnson, Jack Mather, Don "Red" Barry. During a brawl, a horse's kick knocks out the town bully, but townspeople insist on giving Bret Maverick, an innocent bystander, the credit. They think that Bret would be an ideal choice for sheriff.

105.57 *You Can't Beat the Percentage.* Oct. 4, 1959. GS: Karen Steele, Gerald Mohr, Ray Daley, Tim Graham. In the town of Arroyo, Bart Maverick takes a job protecting gambling-hall owner Dave Lindell from a vengeful young cowboy named Brazos. When someone kills Brazos, Maverick takes a shot at the killer, but the assassin gets away.

105.58 *Cats of Paradise.* Oct. 11, 1959. GS: Mona Freeman, Lance Fuller, Buddy Ebsen, Wendell Holmes, Richard Deacon, Murvyn Vye, Robert Griffin, Earl Hansen. Bret Maverick and Modesty Blaine enter in partnership to sell cats to a mining camp overrun by rats. After Bret and Modesty buy the cats with Bret's money, Bret disappears. Upon his return, Bret searches for Modesty to get back his money.

105.59 *A Tale of Three Cities.* Oct. 18, 1959. GS: Patricia Crowley, Ed Kemmer, Ben Gage, Barbara Jo Allen, Ray Teal, Frank Richards. Bart Maverick travels to three cities and seems fated to encounter Stephanie Malone in each one. In Gold Flats, the first city, Stephanie points a gun at Bart and takes off with all of his money.

105.60 *Full House.* Oct. 25, 1959. GS: Robert Lowery, Joel Grey, Kelly Thordsen, Gregory Walcott, William Shaw, Jean Willes, Gordon Jones. A convention of notorious gunmen mistake Bret Maverick for outlaw Foxie Smith, who has sent word that he has planned the greatest theft in history. Not to be outfoxed, Bret tells them that the plan is to rob the Denver Mint, confident that these experienced gunmen will ridicule the idea. But the outlaws agree to pull off the job.

105.61 *The Lass with the Poisonous Air.* Nov. 1, 1959. GS: Howard Petrie, Joanna Moore, John Reach, Carole Wells, Stacy Keach. On his way to Denver, Bart Maverick rescues a young lady on a runaway horse. Charmed by the woman, Bart makes a date and rides into Denver, where he discovers that news of his skill as a poker player has preceded him.

105.62 *The Ghost Soldiers.* Nov. 8, 1959. GS: James Westerfield, Ted Otis, Paul Clarke, Chuck Wassil, Stuart Randall. When the soldiers pull out of an Army fort, Chief Running Horse decides to move in. But the fort is not completely uninhabited—three men remain, one of them Bret Maverick.

105.63 *Easy Mark.* Nov. 15, 1959. GS: Nita Talbot, Wynn Pearce, Edgar Buchanan, Pippa Scott, Douglas Kennedy, Hanley Stafford, Frank Ferguson. Bart Maverick agrees to pose as wealthy Cornelius Van Rensselaer Jr., on his way to an important meeting in St. Louis. Maverick hopes to trap some man who wants to prevent Van Rensselaer from attending the meeting.

105.64 *A Fellow's Brother.* Nov. 22, 1959. GS: Adam West, Gary Vinson, Diane McBain, Wally Brown, Robert Foulk, Bing Russell. Gunslinger Henry Arnett leaves town to avoid paying a gambling debt. His departure coincides with the arrival of Bret Maverick. Young Smoky Vaughn thinks that Maverick's coming provoked Arnett's flight, and Smoky is smitten with a severe case of hero worship for Maverick.

105.65 *Trooper Maverick.* Nov. 29, 1959. GS: Herbert Rudley, Joe Sawyer, Charles Cooper, Suzanne Lloyd, Myron Healey, Mark Tapscott. Caught gambling on an Army post, Bart Maverick is sentenced to the stockade. To avoid serving time, Maverick agrees to become an Army undercover agent.

105.66 *Maverick Springs.* Dec. 6, 1969. GS: King Donovan, Kathleen Crowley, Doris Packer, Tol Avery, Leslie Barrett. Bret Maverick is employed by Kate Dawson to bring her wandering brother Mark back home. Bret finds Mark in Saratoga, where Melanie Blake is busy relieving Mark of his money. Bret calls in brother Bart, and the two Mavericks devise a plot to trap the girl.

105.67 *The Goose-Drownder.* Dec. 13, 1959. GS: Richard Long, Fay Spain, Will Wright, H.M. Wynant, Robert Nichols, Clarke Alexander, Billy M. Greene. Bart Maverick and Gentleman Jack Darby take shelter from a rainstorm in a town inhabited by one man. As the three men begin to tire of each other, a stagecoach arrives carrying four men, one an infamous gunman, and a woman.

105.68 *A Cure for Johnny Rain.* Dec. 20, 1959. GS: William Reynolds, Dolores Donlon, John Vivyan, Thomas B. Henry, Kenneth MacDonald, Bud Osborne. On a stagecoach heading for the town of Apocalypse, Bret Maverick is drawn into a game of blackjack by a tinhorn gambler. The game is interrupted by the arrival of an affable young man who efficiently hijacks the stage's cargo. Maverick is impressed with the bandit's polite manner and intrigued by the vividly decorated bandana which hides his face.

105.69 *The Marquesa.* Jan. 3, 1960. GS: Adele Mara, Jay Novello, Edward Ashley, Rodolfo Hoyos, Morris Ankrum, Carlos Romero, Raymond Hatton, Lane Chandler. Sitting at a poker table, Bart Maverick wins the title to the Lucky Lady saloon in Santa Leora. When Bart arrives in Santa Leora, he is confronted by the Marquesa Luisa de Ruisoner and her cohorts, who claim to own the entire town.

105.70 *Cruise of the Cynthia B.* Jan. 10, 1960. GS: Mona Freeman, Jack Livesy, Karl Webber, Maurice Manson, Gage Clarke, Irene Tedrow. Sight unseen, Bret Maverick buys a riverboat from Scotsman Gillespie MacKenzie. Bret soon learns that MacKenzie has sold the same boat to six other people. The seven owners decide to take the boat to Memphis to resell it.

105.71 *Maverick and Juliet.* Jan. 17, 1960. GS: Steve Terrell, Carole Wells, Michael Garrett, Jack Mather, Sarah Selby, Rhys Williams. Every since a Montgomery killed a Carteret to avenge the loss of land in a card game, the two families have been feuding. Bret Maverick is discovered helping Juliet Carteret and Sonny Montgomery elope, and he is held by the Carterets. Bret suggests that they settle the dispute at the card table and offers to play on behalf of Juliet's clan.

105.72 *The White Widow.* Jan. 24, 1960. GS: Julie Adams, Richard Webb, Ross Elliott, Don Kennedy, Pilar Seurat, Charles Alvin Bell, Charles S. Buck. Bart Maverick turns detective to find the author of some poison pen letters and a robber. Bank president Wilma White has been receiving the letters, and the thief has made off with a large sum of money Bart placed in a hotel safe.

105.73 *Guatemala City* (A.K.A. "Tropical City"). Jan. 31, 1960. GS: Suzanne Storrs, Linda Dangcil, Patric Knowles, Tudor Owen, Charles Watts, John Holland, Robert Carson, Nacho Galindo, Mousie Garner. Though she insists on calling him Bert, Bret Maverick falls for Ellen Johnson. When Ellen and some stolen diamonds disappear, Bret heads south of the border to find the girl and the jewels.

105.74 *The People's Friend.* Feb. 7, 1960. GS: R.G. Armstrong, John Litel, Merry Anders, Walter Sande, Francis DeSales, John Zaremba. Bart Maverick agrees to run for the state senate. The campaign promises of Bart's opponent are a bit disconcerting — he promises that Maverick will die if he wins the election.

105.75 *A Flock of Trouble.* Feb. 14, 1960. GS: Myrna Fahey, George D. Wallace, Tim Graham, Armand Alzamora. At the poker table, Bret Maverick wins a large herd of sheep. Caught in the middle of a range war, he assumes the role of a federal inspector as he tries to find a buyer for his sheep.

105.76 *The Iron Hand.* Feb. 21, 1960. GS: Susan Morrow, Edward Ashley, Anthony Caruso, Anthony Eustrel, Joan Elan, Robert Redford, Lane Bradford, Lane Chandler, John Zaccaro. Bart Maverick is employed by pretty Connie Coleman to protect her cattle drive on its way to Abilene. While Bart is chasing Indians, Connie sells the herd and is paid in counterfeit bills. Bart, paid for his services in useless paper, decides to exchange it for legal tender.

105.77 *The Resurrection of Joe November.* Feb. 28, 1960. GS: Nita Talbot, Charles Maxwell, Joanna Barnes, Roxanne Berard, Donald "Red" Barry, Kelly Thordsen, Harry Cheshire. At cards Bret loses a pile of money to lovely Felice De Lassignac. Her husband offers him double his losses to deliver a casket, supposedly containing the remains of an old family employee. On the way, Bret meets another lady who claims to be Felice De Lassignac.

105.78 *The Misfortune Teller.* March 6, 1960. GS: Alan Mowbray, Kathleen Crowley, Ben Gage, Emory Parnell, Mickey Simpson, William Challee, Chubby Johnson. Accused of killing the mayor, Bret Maverick is jailed to await his trial. All hopes seems lost when Bret learns that his defense attorney's practice of law is based on an astrology chart.

105.79 *Greenbacks Unlimited.* March 13, 1960. GS: Wendell Holmes, John Dehner, Roy Engle, Gage Clarke, Jonathan Hole, Robert Nichols, Patrick Westwood, Ray Walker. Big Ed Murphy and his cohorts have a bad habit. They keep trying to rob Colonel Dutton's bank. Bret Maverick prescribes a cure. Whenever Murphy gets the urge to pull a bank heist, Maverick and Forsquare Foley get to the bank first and make off with the money.

Season Four

105.80 *Bundle from Britain.* Sept. 18, 1960. GS: Robert Douglas, Robert Casper, Diana Crawford, Laurie Main, Clancy Cooper, Mickey Simpson. Bart Maverick's cousin Beau from England joins Bart in the West. He joins right in on the Maverick tradition by impersonating Freddie Bugnor, scion of an old, and rich, English family.

105.81 *Hadley's Hunters.* Sept. 25, 1960. GS: Clint Walker, Ty Hardin, Will Hutchins, Peter Brown, John Russell, Edd Byrnes, Edgar Buchanan, Robert J. Wilke, Andra Martin, Robert Colbert, Howard McNear, Herb Vigran, George Kennedy, James Gavin, Roscoe Ates, Gregg Barton, Harry Harvey, Sr. Bart turns bounty hunter to clear himself of a trumped-up charge hung on him by the sheriff of Hadley. On the way, Maverick meets some prominent lawmen.

105.82 *The Town That Wasn't There.* Oct. 2, 1960. GS: Merry Anders, Richard Hale, John Astin, Craig Duncan, Forrest Lewis, Lane Chandler, Jon Lormer. Railroad agent Wilbur

Shanks is trying to buy land, at unfair prices, from the people of Silver Hill. Cousin Beau hits on a scheme to outwit him.

105.83 *Arizona Black Maria.* Oct. 9, 1960. GS: Joanna Barnes, Donald "Red" Barry, Alan Hale, Jr., Gary Murray, John Holland, Terrence DeMarney, Art Stewart, Harry Swoger, Charles Stevens. When Capt. Jim Pattishal is wounded in an Indian attack, Bart is made responsible for keeping four prisoners under control. But one of the prisoners is Daphne Tolliver, who turns on all her charm.

105.84 *Last Wire from Stop Gap.* Oct. 16, 1960. GS: Robert Cornthwaite, Don Harvey, Olive Sturgess, Tol Avery, Stephen Coit, Lane Bradford. Bart and Beau win a lot of money in a poker game, and wire it to a bank in Denver. The boy's get to Denver, but the money doesn't.

105.85 *Mano Nera.* Oct. 23, 1960. GS: Gerald Mohr, Myrna Fahey, Frank Wilcox, Anthony Caruso, John Beradino, Paul Bryar, Nesdon Booth, Arthur Marshall. During the Mardi Gras in New Orleans, Bart sees a costumed killer murder a wine merchant named Agostino. Bart discovers, when the police question him, that there may be a "Black Hand" involved.

105.86 *A Bullet for the Teacher.* Oct. 30, 1960. GS: Kathleen Crowley, Brad Johnson, Arch Johnson, Joan Tompkins, Sammy Jackson, Henry Brandon, Carol Nicholson, Max Baer, Jr., John Harmon, Tom London. Beau wins half ownership in a gambling casino, but that's where his luck stops. Flo, a dance hall girl, kills his partner and then leaves town. Beau is accused of the crime.

105.87 *The Witch of Hound Dog.* Nov. 6, 1960. GS: Wayde Preston, Anita Sands, William B. Corrie, Sheldon Allman, Phil Tully. Bart rides into Hound Dog looking for some money that belongs to him. Instead he finds Nancy, a witch with a romantic pitch, and her two not-so-romantic brothers.

105.88 *Thunder from the North.* Nov. 13, 1960. GS: Robert Warwick, Andra Martin, Richard Coogan, Janet Lake. Chief Standing Bull helps Beau escape from Fort Casper where he has been framed for the murder of an Indian brave. The chief chooses Maverick to marry his daughter, Pale Moon, and Beau is overjoyed, until he learns that the wedding will be the death of him.

105.89 *The Maverick Line.* Nov. 20, 1960. GS: Buddy Ebsen, Will Wright, Peggy McCay, Chubby Johnson. Uncle Micah wills his stagecoach line to Bart and Bret. But they soon discover that where there's a will there may not be a way to settle their debt.

105.90 *Bolt from the Blue.* Nov. 27, 1960. GS: Richard Hale, Fay Spain, Will Hutchins, Owen Bush, Tim Graham, Percy Helton, Charles Fredericks, George Cleveland. A jury convicts Beau of horse theft. There's just one thing wrong with the verdict — they think his name is Benson January.

105.91 *Kiz.* Dec. 4, 1960. GS: Kathleen Crowley, Peggy McCay, Tristram Coffin, Whit Bissell, Claude Stroud, Max Baer, Jr., Thomas B. Henry, Emory Parnell, Don Beddoe. Kiz is a madcap young lady who suspects she is going to be murdered. Beau suspects she is merely out of her mind.

105.92 *Dodge City or Bust.* Dec. 11, 1960. GS Diana Millay, Peter Whitney, Med Flory, Howard McNear. Bart wanders into town just as a bullet is about to do away with wealthy Miss Diana Dangerfield. He saves her, but she's certain he faked the whole thing just to meet her. Then she spots the bullet hole in her purse.

105.93 *The Bold Fenian Men.* Dec. 18, 1960. GS: Arthur Shields, Herb Vigran, Arch Johnson, Sharon Hugueny, Jack Livesy, Lane Bradford, James O'Hara. A group of Irishmen plan to capture a bit of British-owned land in Canada. Col. Gaylord Summers would like to stop the plot and, when he catches Beau gambling on Dakota City property, he offers him a choice of jail or a mission as a government spy.

105.94 *Destination Devil's Flat.* Dec. 25, 1960. GS: Peter Breck, Merry Anders, Frank Ferguson, Richard Reeves, Patrick Westwood, Chubby Johnson, Helen Mayon. Not-so-honest Sheriff Dan Trevor plans to hijack a suitcase filled with gold. But Bart replaces the gold with stones.

105.95 *A State of Siege.* Jan. 1, 1961. GS: Ray Danton, Lisa Gaye, Joe De Santis. Don Felipe's hacienda is surrounded by a band of guerrilla fighters. It is the visit of Don Felipe's fiancee, Soledad, and her father, that is causing the trouble.

105.96 *Family Pride.* Jan. 8, 1961. GS: Karl Swenson, Anita Sands, Robert Cornthwaite, Denver Pyle, Dorothea Lord, Wallace Rooney, Olan Soule. Beau's got a lot of money in his pockets that Jerry O'Brien gave him for safekeeping. But it doesn't look like Beau's going to have it much longer when two con men arrive with useless land to sell.

105.97 *The Cactus Switch.* Jan. 15, 1961. GS: Peter Hansen, Fay Spain, Edgar Buchanan, Tom Gilson, Carolyn Komant. Bart has cleaned up in a card game and come away from the table with several thousand dollars. Thinking all's well with the world, he goes to his hotel room — only to meet Lana Cane, a woman down the hall who wants to commit suicide.

105.98 *Dutchman's Gold.* Jan. 22, 1961. GS: Mala Powers, Jacques Aubuchon. In a poker game, Beau wins part ownership in Charlotte Simmons' saloon. He soon discovers he hasn't won much — the place is in bad financial shape.

105.99 *The Ice Man.* Jan. 29, 1961. GS: Andrew Duggan, Shirley Knight, James Seay, Bruce Gordon, Virginia Gregg, John Kellogg, Nelson Olmstead, Clyde Howdy. Bart has lost all his money at the card tables again, so he takes a job on Cal Powers' ranch, hauling ice from the nearby mountains. It is a pretty solid job until Bart discovers the body of a dead man sealed up in the ice.

105.100 *Diamond Flush.* Feb. 5, 1961. GS: Roxane Berard, Dan Tobin, Ann Lee, Carl Esmond, Sig Ruman. Danielle de Lisle is lovely, and so is her expensive diamond. The Fergusons, the couple who sold her the stone, say it is a fake, they have the real thing, and wish to make up for past misdeeds.

105.101 *Last Stop: Oblivion.* Feb. 12, 1961. GS: Suzanne Lloyd, Buddy Ebsen, Maurice Manson, Hampton Fancher, Virginia Christine, Donald "Red" Barry. Bart has got some interesting company on the stage to Denver. There is a young woman, Laura Nelson, who is looking for her missing fiance. There is a gunman named Tate McKenna and a very friendly undertaker named Bascombe Sunday. A town called Oblivion is where they make an overnight stop.

105.102 *Flood's Folly.* Feb. 19, 1961. GS: Marlene Willis, Jeanne Cooper, Alan Baxter, Michael Pate. A bad snowstorm drives Beau Maverick and Judge Scott, his traveling companion, to a broken-down hotel. There they meet a lovely young woman accused of being insane by the aunt who lives with her. Beau believes the aunt, until he himself begins to hear strange voices.

105.103 *Maverick at Law.* Feb. 26, 1961. GS: Tol Avery, Gage Clarke, Kem Dibbs, Dolores Donlon, James Anderson, Ken Mayer. When part of the loot from a bank robbery turns up in Bart's saddlebags, the real thieves accuse him of hiding the balance. Stalked by law and outlaw alike, Bart tries to prove his hunch that the bank owner has the missing money.

105.104 *Red Dog.* March 5, 1961. GS: John Carradine, Mike Road, Evan McCord, Lee Van Cleef, Sherry Jackson. Out in the Montana hinterland, searching for a warm, dry refuge, Beau wanders into a cave that turns out to be the meeting place for a band intent on bank robbery.

105.105 *Deadly Image.* March 12, 1961. GS: Jack Kelly, Gerald Mohr, Dawn Wells, Robert Ridgely, Bartlett Robinson, Abraham Sofaer, Kelly Thordsen, Harvey Johnson. Bart looks just like outlaw Rod Claxton, a coincidence which may put his head in a hangman's noose. Bart needs his freedom to prove his identity, but he is locked up in an escape-proof guardhouse.

105.106 *Triple Indemnity.* March 19, 1961. GS: Alan Hewitt, Peter Breck, Charity Grace, Laurie Mitchell, J. Edward McKinley, Don Beddoe. George Parker, business tyrant of Parkersville, fails to pay a poker debt to Bart. Bart ingeniously retaliates. First he buys a life-insurance policy from Parker's company, then he hints that he may be killed in a gunfight, an event that would throw Parker into bankruptcy.

105.107 *The Forbidden City.* March 26, 1961. GS: Lisa Montell, Nina Shipman, Vladimir Sokoloff, Jack Mather, Jeff De Benning, Thomas B. Henry, Robert Foulk, Gertrude Flynn. Bart and his younger brother Brent are enjoying a traveling card game when their stagecoach stops at Sunburst, a nice, clean little town. So clean, in fact, that the presiding sheriff throws Brent, the owner of the cards, into jail.

105.108 *Substitute Gun.* April 2, 1961. GS: Walter Sande, Carlos Romero, Robert Rockwell, Coleen Gray, Joan Marshall. After Sheriff Coleman saves him from a professional gunman, Bart feels he owes him a favor. Since Coleman suspects that saloon owner Tom Blauvelt is about to kill a rival, Bart obligingly hires out as Blauvelt's card dealer.

105.109 *Benefit of Doubt.* April 9, 1961. GS: Elizabeth Macrae/Burstyn, Randy Stuart, George D. Wallace, Trevor Bardette. Brent and his friends see a band of thieves attempting to hold up the mail office. Sheriff Holly appears, dutifully shoots the would-be robbers, and helps himself to the stolen cash.

105.110 *The Devil's Necklace* Part One. April 16, 1961. GS: John Dehner, Steve Brodie, Sharon Hugueny, John Hoyt, John Archer, Kasey Rogers, Rita Lynn, Michael Forest, Rayford Barnes. At an isolated Army post, Bart buys a wagonload of wares sight unseen from peddler Luther Cannonbaugh. When Bart examines his purchase, he finds that it includes a cache of illegal liquor, and a kidnaped Indian girl named Tawney.

105.111 *The Devil's Necklace* Part Two. April 23, 1961. GS: John Dehner, Steve Brodie, Sharon Hugueny, John Hoyt, John Archer, Kasey Rogers, Rita Lynn, Michael Forest, Rayford Barnes. Bart has been captured by the Apaches, and so has crooked peddler Luther Cannonbaugh. The latter earns his freedom by giving the chief a "magic" necklace, while the Indian maid Tawney comes to Bart's rescue. Bart and the girl ride to alert the fort of an impending Indian attack.

Season Five

105.112 *Dade City Dodge.* Sept. 18, 1961. GS: Kathleen Crowley, Mike Road, Robert Burton, Gage Clarke, Charles Arnt, Guy Wilkerson. Con man Pearly Gates cheats Bart out of a large sum, jilts his fiancee Marla, and flees town. Bart and Marla join forces to track slippery Pearly down.

105.113 *The Art Lovers.* Oct. 1, 1961. GS: Jack Cassidy, James Westerfield, Leon Belasco, Maurine Dawson. A combine of San Francisco investors is putting the financial squeeze on railroad owner Paul Sutton. Bart decides to help Sutton raise enough money to keep the line by engaging the investors in a game of cards.

105.114 *The Golden Fleecing.* Oct. 8, 1961. GS: John Qualen, Paula Raymond, Oliver Sturgess, J. Edward McKinley, Myron Healey. Bart is anxious to help farmer Henry Albright set up a gold-mining company. To do so, Bart switches from gambling at the poker table, and takes a whirl at gambling on the stock market.

105.115 *Three Queens Full.* Nov. 12, 1961. GS: Jim Backus, Merry Anders, Kasey Rogers, Don Kennedy, Frank Ferguson, Allyson Ames, Evan McCord, Jake Sheffield, Harry Lauter, Willard Waterman. Joe Wheelwright, proud owner of the Subrosa Ranch, figures it is about time his sons, Moose, Henry and Small Paul, got hitched. He imports three pretty girls from San Francisco, but he needs an upright citizen to chaperone them before the wedding. His choice is Bart Maverick.

105.116 *A Technical Error.* Nov. 26, 1961. GS: Reginald Owen, Peter Breck, Frank De Kova, Jolene Brand, Frank London, Nick Pawl. Bart feels like a million when he wins a bank, building and all, in a poker game. But there is one thing that nobody mentioned—the bank is on the brink of ruin.

105.117 *Poker Face.* Jan. 7, 1962. GS: Carlos Rivas, Rudolph Acosta, Tol Avery, William Fawcett. Traveling on a stagecoach, Bart is being ostracized by the other passengers because he is a gambler. But then a group of bandits hold up the stage, and make a deal with Bart. If he can beat them in poker, they will spare the lives of the passengers.

105.118 *Mr. Muldoon's Partner.* Jan. 14, 1962. GS: Mickey Shaughnessy, Janet Lake. Mr. Muldoon tells Bart that he is a genuine leprechaun and to prove it, he grants Bart five wishes. Bart, who is naturally skeptical, makes his first wish a tough one. He wants the exact amount of money taken during a recent robbery.

105.119 *Epitaph for a Gambler.* Feb. 11, 1962. GS: Robert J. Wilke, Dan Haggerty, Marie Windsor, Fred Beir, Joyce Meadows, Adam Williams, Frank Albertson. During a poker game, Bart wins a partnership in Diamond Jim Malone's casino. Then he discovers that he has also won something he hadn't bargained on—Malone's blackmail payments to Lucky Matt Elkins.

105.120 *The Maverick Report.* March 4, 1962. GS: Ed Nelson, Lloyd Corrigan, George Neise, Jo Morrow, Patricia Crest, Kem Dibbs, Peter Breck. In a poker game, Bart wins ownership of a newspaper from a man named Jonesy. But the paper isn't quite the prize it appears because there is a libel suit against it, instigated by Senator Porter and his aide Gary Harrison.

105.121 *Marshal Maverick.* March 11, 1962. GS: John Dehner, Peter Breck, Gail Kobe, Earl Hammond. Bart's latest gambling debt brings him into contact with a new character in town named Archie Walker, the funniest, if not the fastest, gun in the West. Walker poses as first one, then another, feared gunman.

105.122 *The Troubled Heir.* April 1, 1962. GS: Mike Road, Alan Hale, Jr., Kathleen Crowley, Chick Chandler, Gordon Jones. Bart's poker game is broken up at gun point by Pearly Gates, who needs the money so he and his gal Marla can get hitched. Bart's sorry too, but another player, Big Jim Watson, is downright mad, and plans to find Pearly and kill him.

105.123 *The Money Machine.* April 8, 1962. GS: Kathy Bennett, Andrew Duggan, Patrick Westwood, Ted de Corsia, Henry Corden. Bart's cousin Jacqueline Sutton has a large sum of money which she intends to use to repay a family debt. But Big Ed Murphy convinces her that a delay won't hurt, especially when the loan of her money will bring handsome returns out of the money-making machine he is going to buy with it.

105.124 *One of Our Trains Is Missing.* April 22, 1962. GS: Kathleen Crowley, Peter Breck, Alan Hewitt. Modesty Blaine is a very handsome woman in search of a husband, but Bart resists her overtures. Then Modesty does an about face, and accuses him of being a murderer.

106. The Men from Shiloh

NBC. 90 min. Broadcast history: Wednesay, 7:30-9:00, Sept. 1970–Sept. 1971.

Regular Cast: James Drury (the Virginian), Stewart Granger (Colonel Alan MacKenzie), Doug McClure (Trampas), Lee Majors (Roy Tate),

Premise: A sequel to *The Virginian*, set ten years later in the 1890s, this series continues the exploits of the Virginian in Medicine Bow, Wyoming.

The Episodes

106.1 *The West vs. Colonel MacKenzie.* Sept. 16, 1970. GS: Martha Hyer, Elizabeth Ashley, Don DeFore, John Larch, John McLiam, Bobby Eilbacher. Col. Alan MacKenzie, an Englishman who bought the Shiloh, stirs up trouble when he investigates the bizarre hanging of a neighbor.

106.2 *The Best Man.* Sept. 23, 1970. GS: Desi Arnaz, Katy Jurado, James Farentino, Mario Alcaide, Susana Miranda. In Mexico, Trampas stumbles into a romantic triangle. Two of his friends have proposed to Teresa Zaragosa, and while Teresa ponders the matter, Trampas tries to keep the men from killing each other.

106.3 *Jenny.* Sept. 30, 1970. GS: Janet Leigh, Charles Drake, John Ireland, Jo Ann Harris, Lew Brown, Christopher Dark, Myron Healey. Jenny, the Virginian's old flame, asks the Virginian for protection from three mysterious men after a stagecoach ambush.

106.4 *With Love, Bullets, and Valentines.* Oct. 7, 1970. GS: Art Carney, Tom Ewell, Deborah Walley, Jack Albertson, Ben Cooper, Gene Evans, Ed Faulkner. An old rascal named Skeet loses his paddle-wheel riverboat to Trampas in a poker game. Since the Nancy Belle is a floating woodpile, Skeet figures he can buy it back for a song. Unfortunately, Trampas is after a higher price. Outlaws Hoy and Billy Valentine also have their eyes on the creaky paddle-wheeler. Now that they are about to retire, the Valentines want to bow out with a spectacular crime and use the Nancy Belle for their getaway.

106.5 *The Mysterious Mr. Tate.* Oct. 14, 1970. GS: Robert Webber, Dane Clark, Annette O'Toole, John McLiam, Dent Hales, John Rayner, Ken Renard. Roy Tate is traveling aboard a train that also carries Colonel MacKenzie and the daughter of a Chicago millionaire. Also on board are two ex-convicts who are intent on kidnaping the girl.

106.6 *Gun Quest.* Oct. 21, 1970. GS: Anne Francis, Neville Brand, Brandon de Wilde, Agnes Moorehead, Joseph Cotten, Rod Cameron, Monte Markham, John Smith. The Virginian is wrongly accused of murder, and hunts down the real killer.

106.7 *Crooked Corner.* Oct. 28, 1970. GS: Susan Strasberg, Kurt Kasznar, Brock Peters, Walter Koenig, Lloyd Battista. Tate and Colonel MacKenzie come to the aid of German immigrants who are being terrorized by a hired gun and night riders.

106.8 *Lady at the Bar.* Nov. 4, 1970. GS: Greer Garson, E.G. Marshall, James Whitmore, Jay Robinson, Kenneth Tobey, Bill Zuckert, Ron Soble, Paul Fix, Arthur Hunnicutt. Lawyer Frances Finch is defending Trampas on a murder charge. It is an uphill battle as the judge and his bailiff want a quick conviction so they can go on a fishing trip.

106.9 *The Price of the Hanging.* Nov. 11, 1970. GS: Jane Wyatt, Lew Ayres, Edward Binns, Tom Tryon, Patricia Harty, Bo Svenson, Lincoln Demyan, Howard Culver. Tate is drawn into a murder case while trying to get medical aid for the injured Colonel MacKenzie. The only doctor in town is a convicted murderer, and he refuses to operate unless Tate tries to clear his name.

106.10 *Experiment at New Life.* Nov. 18, 1970. GS: Ralph Meeker, Vera Miles, Michael McGreevey, Chris Robinson, Rex Holman. The Virginian attempts to rescue two women who are being held prisoner because they oppose the idea of multiple marriage.

106.11 *Follow the Leader.* Dec. 2, 1970. GS: Anthony Franciosa, Frank Gorshin, Kate Woodville, Noah Beery, Jr., Ross Elliott, Steve Sandor, Harry Carey, Jr. The head of a dull-witted backwoods clan murders his cousin and pins the crime on Trampas.

106.12 *Last of the Comancheros.* Dec. 9, 1970. GS: Ricardo Montalban, Beth Brickell, Carlos Romero, James Gregory, Anthony Caruso, Lenore Stevens, Richard Van Vleet, Del Moore, Parley Baer, William Fawcett. Sosentes is the leader of a community of former outlaws. He kidnaps a lady reporter whose story triggered a raid on his livestock. He demands $25,000 in ransom and MacKenzie is forced to gather it.

106.13 *Hannah.* Dec. 30, 1970. GS: Lisa Gerritsen, Susan Culver, Warren Stevens, J.D. Cannon, Peter Breck, Bartlett Robinson, Kay Stewart, Sally Marr, Lorraine Gary, Dan White, Sid Clute, Gregg Palmer, Leo Gordon. Hannah Carson is a little girl who has come West with her dying father. To save Hannah from an orphanage, Trampas tries to locate her mother, a woman of dubious reputation who deserted her family years before.

106.14 *Nan Allen.* Jan. 6, 1971. GS: Diane Baker, E.G. Marshall, Tom Skerritt, Eric Christmas, Arch Johnson, Read Morgan, Jon Lormer, Pitt Herbert, Lou Wagner. When a romance develops between Nan Allen and MacKenzie, he becomes suspicious about her jealous brother Bobby and the two dead men in Nan's past.

106.15 *The Politician.* Jan. 13, 1971. GS: John Ericson, William Windom, Diana Muldaur, Jean Hale, Denny Miller, Jim Davis, Carl Ballantine. The Virginian becomes involved in a web of intrigue and death surrounding Senatorial appointee Foster Bonham, his alcoholic brother and his ambitious wife.

106.16 *The Animal.* Jan. 20, 1971. GS: Rudy Ramos, Scott Brady, Katherine Crawford, Andy Devine, Chuck Connors, James Wainwright, Leon Ames, Jack Ging, Ed Byrnes, Shug Fisher. A deaf-mute Indian boy is accused of murder. Roy Tate risks his life to insure that the boy receive a fair trail in a town with hanging fever.

106.17 *The Legacy of Spencer Flats.* Jan. 27, 1971. GS: Ann Sothern, Carolyn Jones, Bradford Dillman, Edgar Buchanan. Two dimwitted sisters have mistaken Trampas for an escaped convict, and imprison him in a ghost town while they decide his fate.

106.18 *The Angus Killer.* Feb. 10, 1971. GS: Dina Merrill, Van Johnson, Ruth Roman, Andrew Parks, Chill Wills, Stephen McNally, Slim Pickens. A run of bad luck is forcing widow Laura Duff to sell her ranch despite the protests of her seventeen-year-old son who is determined to prove that their bad luck is no accident.

106.19 *Flight from Memory.* Feb. 17, 1971. GS: Burgess Meredith, Robert Fuller, Tisha Sterling, Roger Cudney. A hermit joins MacKenzie in an effort to help a frightened amnesia victim being stalked by a lone rider.

106.20 *Tate, Ramrod.* Feb. 24, 1971. GS: Michael Burns, Sally Ann Howes, Craig Stevens, Joan Harris, Alan Hale, Jr., Peter Mark Richman, Mickey Caruso, John Lupton, Rex Allen. Tate, temporarily in charge of a widower's ranch, has a passel of problems—a dispute over the use of barbed wire, two rambunctious teenagers, and the unexpected arrival of the widower's bride-to-be.

106.21 *The Regimental Line.* March 3, 1971. GS: John Saxon, Eric Christmas, Eddie Little Sky, Bert Freed, Randolph Mantooth, Terry Wilson. Colonel MacKenzie becomes the hunted hunter. He is tracking the man he believes responsible for his brother's death, and being stalked by a band of scalp-hunting Indians.

106.22 *The Town Killer.* March 10, 1971. GS: Peter Lawford, Howard Duff, Lloyd Bochner, Brenda Benet, Bill Fletcher, Leonard Stone. Ben Hunter is the gentlemanly leader of a protection racket. His challenger is the Virginian, whose efforts to arouse the cowed townspeople range from simple persuasion to an all-out, one-man war.

106.23 *Wolf Track.* March 17, 1971. GS: Julie Harris, Pernell Roberts, Clint Howard, Arthur O'Connell. While hunting for a killer wolf that seems possessed of almost human cunning, MacKenzie requires the aid of Jenny, an impoverished homesteader.

106.24 *Jump-Up.* March 24, 1971. GS: John McGiver, Madlyn Rhue, John Astin, Guy Raymond, Rick Jason, George Mitchell, Jan Sterling. John Timothy Driscoll is an unethical character who is out to own a town. In his determination he takes full advantage of Tate's presence, by framing him for the murder of a troublesome gambler.

107. The Monroes

ABC. 60 min. Broadcast history: Wednesday, 8:00–9:00, Sept. 1966–Aug. 1967.

Regular Cast: Michael Anderson, Jr. (Clayt Monroe), Barbara Hershey (Kathy Monroe), Keith Schultz (Jefferson "Big Twin" Monroe), Kevin Schultz (Fenimore "Little Twin" Monroe), Tammy Locke (Amy Monroe), Ron Soble (Jim), Liam Sullivan (Major Mapoy), James Westmoreland (Ruel Jaxon), Ben Johnson (Sleeve).

Premise: This series follows the five orphaned Monroe children as they struggle to survive in the Wyoming territory during the 1870's.

The Episodes

107.1 *The Intruders.* Sept. 7, 1966. GS: John Doucette, Russ Conway, Marilyn Moe, James Murdock, Rance Howard. After their parents are lost, eighteen-year-old Clayt Monroe becomes the head of the family, leading his sisters, twin brothers and an Indian friend to the land their father staked out years before. The orphaned youngsters face their first crisis when little Amy is felled by a high fever.

107.2 *Night of the Wolf.* Sept. 14, 1966. GS: James Gammon, Richard Bakalyan. Bounty hunters searching for wolves used one of Major Mapoy's cows for bait, but the major's men suspect that Clayt is responsible.

107.3 *Ride with Terror.* Sept. 21, 1966. GS: Jeanne Cooper, James Stacy, Claude Akins, Peter Leeds, Michael Ragan, Tap Canutt, Joe Canutt. Saloon owner Mae Duvall offers Clayt $50 to take a wagonload of her household goods to another town, but she doesn't mention that he will also be carrying a fortune in miners gold.

107.4 *The Forest Devil.* Sept. 28, 1966. GS: Warren Oates, Ralph Moody. The Forest Devil is a vicious wolverine that moves Jim to react with unnatural fear. The superstitious Indian warns the Monroes to stay inside the cabin, and then rides off for help.

107.5 *Wild Dog of the Tetons.* Oct. 5, 1966. GS: Albert Salmi. The twins find a huge white dog seriously wounded, and try to persuade Clayt to doctor the animal, known throughout the Tetons as a vicious killer.

107.6 *Incident at Hanging Tree.* Oct. 12, 1966. GS: Robert Middleton, James Brolin, Tim O'Kelly, Lisa Jak. A fiery old man and his two tough sons, who claim the Monroes are setting on their land, launch a barrage of fire arrows to drive them out of the cabin.

107.7 *Ordeal by Hope.* Oct. 19, 1966. GS: Edward Faulkner, John Bryant, Jack Williams, Rico Alaniz. Little Twin is bitten by a rock chuck, an animal that Major Mapoy's men suspect is carrying rabies.

107.8 *The Hunter.* Oct. 26, 1966. GS: James Whitmore, Roy Jenson, Rex Holman, Sean McClory, Bing Russell, Bea Tomkins, John J. Cooke. Jim is rescued from a lynch mob by a Cavalry officer, but the Indian seems more afraid of the officer than the mob.

107.9 *War Arrow.* Nov. 2, 1966. GS: Anna Navarro, Morgan Woodward, Steve Gravers, Dub Taylor, James Almanzar. The Monroes take refuge at Major Mapoy's headquarters after a bloodless Indian attack which seems senseless to everyone except one of the Major's cowboys.

107.10 *The Friendly Enemy.* Nov. 9, 1966. GS: Harry Townes. The Monroes lose their dog to backwoods trapper Joe Smith, who intends to use the huge family pet to replace his runaway pack mule.

107.11 *Court Martial.* Nov. 16, 1966. GS: Robert Fuller, John McLiam, Burt Douglas, James J. Griffith, Warren Kemmerling, William Bryant. Jim's mysterious past intrudes on his happy life with the Monroes when the former Army scout is arrested and brought before a frontier court-martial. The charge is murder.

107.12 *Silent Night, Deathly Night.* Nov. 23, 1966. GS: Robert Middleton, James Brolin, Tim O'Kelly, Ray Teal, Hampton Fancher. Clayt must find a way to prove his innocence to brutish Barney Wales, who has sentenced the young homesteader to death for wounding his mute daughter.

107.13 *Lost in the Wilderness.* Nov. 30, 1966. GS: Noah Beery, Jr., George "Shug" Fisher. A playful raft ride leads to a night of terror for Big Twin and Amy. Lost in strange country, the children encounter a kindly prospector and his murderous partner, who is determined to silence the young Monroes before they can reveal the location of a mine.

107.14 *Gold Fever.* Dec. 14, 1966. GS: Dan Duryea, Alan Baxter, Hank Brandt, Hardie Albright. Clayt, seeking a better life for his brothers and sisters, becomes a victim of gold fever. The youthful head of the Monroe clan joins a prospector to mine a gold vein, a venture that may be cut short by two murderous claim jumpers.

107.15 *Range War.* Dec. 21, 1966. GS: Robert Middleton, James Brolin, Tim O'Kelly, Gordon Westcourt. The Monroe cabin becomes a battle site with the return of brutish Barney Wales. The bull-headed horse breeder and his boys force Clayt to take sides in a showdown with Major Mapoy for control of the valley.

107.16 *Pawnee Warrior.* Dec. 28, 1966. GS: Alejandro Rey. The Monroe cabin becomes the site of an Indian battle when the Pawnee chief who swore vengeance against Ruel Jaxon finds him with the Monroes.

107.17 *Mark of Death.* Jan. 4, 1967. GS: Robert Middleton, James Brolin, Mario Alcaide, Tim O'Kelly, Savannah Bentley. Barney Wales and his brood threaten to destroy the herd of cattle Clayt is protecting for a Basque herdsman, who brought the healthy animals from a plague-infested area.

107.18 *To Break a Colt.* Jan. 11, 1967. GS: Buck Taylor, Fredd Wayne, Elisha Cook, Jr., Charles Berger, Casey Tibbs. Wanting money and experience, Clayt joins a Mapoy cattle drive over dangerous terrain. Bradford, the trail boss, is soon pushing the young homesteader harder than the cattle.

107.19 *Race for the Rainbow.* Jan. 18, 1967. GS: James Wilder, Buck Taylor, Lisa Jak. The handsome owner of a prize horse brings romance into Kathy's life. The Monroe girl cheers for the slick Michael Duquesne as he races against Mapoy's top riders, who include a rival for Kathy's affections.

107.20 *Gun Bound.* Jan. 25, 1967. GS: Nick Adams, John Dehner, Michael Greene. The twins respect for big brother Clayt is challenged when bank robbers capture the Monroes. Clayt seems too afraid to fight the outlaws.

107.21 *Killer Cougar.* Feb. 1, 1967. GS: Robert Walker, Jr., Robert J. Wilke, Rance Howard. Clayt and Jim go after a mean cougar with a price on its head. The danger grows when they clash with two professional killers who have no use for competition.

107.22 *Wild Bull.* Feb. 15, 1967. GS: Jeffrey Hunter, Stanley Adams, Med Florey, Dub Taylor. The Monroes dream of owning a herd begins to come true when Clayt acquires five head of cattle. But a drifter claims prior ownership and he is ready to back up his claim with bullets.

107.23 *Trapped.* Feb. 22, 1967. After surviving the tornado that ravaged the Monroe cabin, Clayt and Little Twin again face death. While hunting for food, the boys get trapped in a mine with a vicious bear.

107.24 *Manhunt.* March 1, 1967. GS: Robert Lansing, Billie Hayes, Martin Wyler. A flash of lightning reveals a figure at the Monroes' cabin window. Clayt investigates, but finds nothing. Other strange incidents occur. The Monroe livestock are restless, and Clayt is nearly crushed by a falling boulder. After learning that a rustler has been stealing Major Mapoy's best beef, Clayt is relieved. He is certain that no rustler would bother with the small Monroe herd, until he is ambushed by a sniper.

107.25 *Teach the Tigers to Purr.* March 8, 1967. GS: Ronny Howard, Clint Howard, Kay Ann Kemper, Eddie Sallia, Sofia Marie, Jody Carter, Rance Howard, Carolyn Conwell, Ann Ayers, Ben Miller. Kathy becomes a schoolmarm and converts the cabin into a classroom for the homesteaders' children. Her biggest headache is Major Mapoy's ward Timothy, who is infecting his classmates with the thought of playing hooky.

107.26 *Ghosts of Paradox.* March 15, 1967. GS: Michael Dunn, Richard Kiel, Anna Capri, Jack Bailey, Buck Taylor, X Brands, Johnny Cardos, Bob Gunderson. In the nearly deserted town of Paradox, the Monroes celebrate Clayt's birthday with a strange trio: a young schoolmarm, a circus dwarf, and a gigantic strongman. Meanwhile, Indians who have been trailing the Monroes slip into town.

108. My Friend Flicka

CBS. 30 min. Broadcast history: Friday, 7:30–8:00, Sept. 1955–June 1956.

Regular Cast: Johnny Washbrook (Ken McLaughlin), Gene Evans (Rob McLaughlin), Anita Louise (Nell McLaughlin), Frank Ferguson (Gus), Pamela Beaird (Hildy Broeberg), Sydney Mason (Sheriff Downey), Robert Adler (Ben).

Premise: This series depicted the adventures of Ken McLaughlin and his horse, Flicka, at his parents ranch in Montana.

The Episodes

108.1 *One Man's Horse.* Sept. 30, 1955. GS: Hugh Beaumont, Don Harvey, Joe Haworth, Hugh Sanders, Forrest Lewis. When Ken discovers the identity of a dangerous outlaw, the criminal abducts Flicka and threatens to kill her if Ken reveals the truth to the authorities.

108.2 *Blind Faith.* Oct. 7, 1955. GS: Wilton Graff, Phil Chambers. After tumbling down a steep incline, Flicka begins to show signs of blindness. Grief-striken, Ken must draw on the power of faith while trying to ease his horse back to health.

108.3 *A Case of Honor.* Oct. 14, 1955. GS: Craig Duncan, Peter Whitney, Phil Chambers. There is trouble when a sheep herder moves into the valley. Cattle ranchers and sheepmen feud over rights to the grazing land, and Ken's father is accused of poisoning a water hole.

108.4 *A Good Deed.* Oct. 21, 1955. GS: Butch Bernard, Dan Riss. Ken and his faithful Flicka try to help a crippled boy overcome his fear of horses.

108.5 *Cavalry Horse.* Oct. 28, 1955. GS: Tudor Owen, John Cliff, Charles Evans, William Henry. Sgt. Tim O'Gara, who soldiered with Ken's father in the old days, is distraught over the fate in store for his old horse. O'Gara cannot prove ownership of the horse, who is then sold to a glue factory.

108.6 *The Accident.* Nov. 4, 1955. GS: Don Beddoe. An accident occurs when Ken and Flicka are out riding the range. Ken is thrown and can't walk. Then a cougar begins to stalk him.

108.7 *The Stranger.* Nov. 11, 1955. GS: Jeff Morrow, Frank Ferguson, Pamela Beaird, Sydney Mason. A desperate escaped convict takes Ken hostage in his escape from the law. When the posse arrives to help Ken, the outlaw offers to trade his own freedom for Ken's life.

108.8 *The Wild Horse.* Nov. 18, 1955. GS: Guinn Williams, Charles Cane, Denver Pyle, Tyler McVey. Two suspicious-looking characters try to buy Flicka from Ken, who refuses to sell. The next morning Flicka is missing from her stall.

108.9 *Rogue Stallion.* Nov. 25, 1955. GS: John Doucette, Claude Akins. Ken's father and a rival rancher both want to capture a beautiful wild horse. Ken agrees to let his father take Flicka with him when he goes to round up the horse.

108.10 *The Little Secret.* Dec. 2, 1955. GS: Louis Jean Heydt, Robert Foulk, Jack Littlefield, Serena Sande, Claude Akins, Craig Duncan. When a frightened young Indian woman turns her sick baby over to Ken for treatment by a white doctor, an unscrupulous Indian agent tries to arrest Ken's father.

108.11 *Act of Loyalty.* Dec. 8, 1955. GS: Paul Campbell, Robert Anderson. Flicka, having a reputation for being a one-man horse, gets Ken into trouble when a young man escapes from the local jail. Flicka is known to have helped the fugitive escape, causing the townspeople to believe Ken had a hand in it.

108.12 *Silver Saddle.* Dec. 16, 1955. GS: Herbert Rudley, Bill Chapin. Ken is accused of deliberately letting a trained show-horse escape so that his own Flicka could win the competition for a silver saddle.

108.13 *The Phantom Herd.* Dec. 23, 1955. GS: Roy Roberts, George Eldredge, Carol Coombs. Ken is brokenhearted when his father decides to sell the ranch. The elder McLaughlin seems to have no choice—the entire herd of horses has run away to join a wild stallion.

108.14 *Little Visitor.* Dec. 30, 1955. GS: Peter Votrian, Frank Ferguson, Lowell Gilmore, Herbert Deans. The spoiled son of a friend of Ken's father's manages to get into trouble during his visit to the McLaughlin ranch. The boy panics when an old mine caves in.

108.15 *The Golden Promise.* Jan. 6, 1956. GS: Stanley Adams, J. Steven Darrell, Mason Curry. Both Ken and Gus the hired hand neglect their duties at the ranch to hunt for gold. An irate Rob attempts to take care of the ranch without their help but breaks his leg.

108.16 *Black Dust.* Jan. 13, 1956. GS: Ann Lee, John Doucette. The McLaughlin ranch is endangered when a construction crew reopens a mine using methods which contaminate the water and block the way to the grazing pastures.

108.17 *Night Rider.* Jan. 20, 1956. GS: Richard Crane, Walter Sande. When Ken and Flicka trail a ghostly night rider, they help to solve a ten-year-old mystery.

108.18 *The Settler.* Jan. 27, 1956. GS: Lurene Tuttle, Trevor Bardette, Lonnie Thomas. En route to Oregon, a man's horse bolts and the man and his family take shelter with the McLaughlins. Young Ken McLaughlin sets out to try to find the man's horse.

108.19 *Wind from Heaven.* Feb. 3, 1956. GS: John Pickard, Steve Conte, Stephen Wootton, James Anderson, Donald McDonald, Buzzy Bookman. Even though Ken's father and the rest of the ranchers are at war with a family of nesters, Ken befriends one of the youngsters.

108.20 *The Whip.* Feb. 10, 1956. GS: Herbert Rudley. Ken uses kindness to tame a wild stallion who attacked his trainer. The man believed that the use of fear was the only way to train an animal.

108.21 *The Runaways.* Feb. 17, 1956. GS: Minerva Urecal. Flicka runs away from the McLaughlin ranch to join a wild stallion that Ken's father had been breaking. The stallion is mistaken for an albino killer.

108.22 *The Cameraman.* Feb. 24, 1956. GS: John Carradine. A traveling photographer tries to photograph a herd of wild horses. The horses stampede and head directly for the cameraman.

108.23 *Old Danny.* March 2, 1956. GS: Sandy Descher, Ann Doran, Robert G. Anderson. Hank Miller, a neighbor of the McLaughlins, decides to get rid of a mongrel dog, Danny, because he objects to his niece's affection for the animal. The child runs away with Danny to protect him. Nell's election to a school committee is endangered by a neighbor asking her to intercede in the family quarrel.

108.24 *The Royal Carriage.* March 16, 1956. GS: Guinn Williams, Richard Garrick.

108.25 *Mister Goblin.* March 23, 1956. GS: Jane Darwell, Philip Tonge, Tiger Fafara, Wesley Hudman. Ken finds a stray white colt, and since no one seems to know who the colt belongs to, he takes it back to the ranch with him.

108.26 *Rebels in Hiding.* March 30, 1956. GS: Jim Baird, Roy Engel, Francis J. McDonald. Ken comes upon two Indians, an old man and his grandson, who have left the reservation to keep the child out of the white man's school. They treat Flicka's hoof, burnt in an accident, and in return Ken promises not to reveal their hiding place.

108.27 *Lock, Stock and Barrel.* April 6, 1956. GS: Roy Barcroft, Jean Howell, Claude Akins, Craig Hill, Tudor Owen. Ken disobeys his father by not turning Flicka out to range, fearing she will be hurt. The youngster hides the horse in a vacant barn and nearly loses Flicka when the barn is sold lock, stock and barrel.

108.28 *The Unmasking.* April 13, 1956. GS: Sheb Wooley, Jeanne Bates, Clarence Straight, Forrest Taylor. A man forced by circumstances to turn thief is befriended by Ken and also by a spinster who is looking for a husband.

108.29 *Refuge for the Night.* April 20, 1956. GS: Paul Campbell, Craig Duncan, Florence Lake, Gregg Barton, Kenne

Duncan, Donald Kennedy. Nell and Ken are alone at the ranch when an escaped criminal forces his way in to seek refuge from the law.

108.30 *Against All Odds.* April 27, 1956. GS: Phil Chambers. A puppy, found in one of Ken's rabbit snares, disrupts the McLaughlin hosehold.

108.31 *The Old Champ.* April 4, 1956. GS: Mike Mazurki, Thomas B. Henry. In desperate need of money for the foreman on the McLaughlin ranch, Ken puts up his horse Flicka against a cash prize in a wrestling match between his father and a professional wrestler.

108.32 *The Medicine Man.* May 11, 1956. GS: Blossom Rock, James Macklin, Charles Hicks, Ward Wood. Ken's mother is ill, and the only doctor available is Mark Hak, a young Indian. But prejudiced neighbors try to prevent him from treating her.

108.33 *When Bugles Blow.* May 18, 1956. GS: Tudor Owen, Craig Hill, Raymond Bailey. Even though he has spent years building up his ranch, Rob McLaughlin is prompted to re-enlist in the Cavalry after a visit with an old Army friend.

108.34 *The Recluse.* May 25, 1956. GS: Erin O'Brien-Moore, Doug Evans, Barry Froner, Tiger Fafara. Ken and two of his friends make cruel fun of an eccentric woman who lives alone.

108.35 *The Foundlings.* June 1, 1956. GS: Guinn Williams, Ray Ferrell, Jimmy Karath, Kenneth MacDonald Ken realizes he has made a mistake in running away from home. He meets two young orphan boys whose only ambition is to be part of a family.

108.36 *Growing Pains.* June 8, 1956. GS: Reba Waters. A little girl who pays a visit to the McLaughlin ranch learns that a prize bull can be quite unpredictable.

108.37 *Lost River.* June 15, 1956. GS: Forrest Taylor, Don C. Harvey, John Parris, Sammee Tong. The McLaughlins run into a series of mishaps while digging a well to alleviate the water shortage at the ranch. Ken tries not to believe, as others do, that a new Mongolian pony with a Chinese bad-luck symbol on his head is responsible.

108.38 *Big Red.* June 22, 1956. GS: Denver Pyle, Jean Byron, Terry Frost. A valuable show horse, frightened by a fire, escapes into wild and rugged range country. Ken and Rob try to get to the horse before a trigger-happy cowhand does.

109. *Nakia*

ABC. 60 min. Broadcast history: Saturday, 10:00-11:00, Sept. 1974–Dec. 1974.

Regular Cast: Robert Forster (Deputy Nakia Parker), Arthur Kennedy (Sheriff Sam Jericho), Gloria DeHaven (Deputy Irene James), Taylor Lacher (Deputy Hubbel Martin), John Tenorio, Jr. (Half Cub).

Premise: Nakia Parker, a deputy sheriff of Navaho Indian heritage, helped maintain the law in a modern New Mexico city.

The Episodes

109.1 *Nakia.* April 17, 1974. GS: Linda Evans, Chief George Clutesi, Maria-Elena Cordero, Taylor Lacher, Stephen McNally, George Nader, Robert Donner. Nakia tries to settle a dispute between his tribe and a housing developer who wants to destroy an historic mission.

Season One

109.2 *The Non-Person.* Sept. 21, 1974. GS: A. Martinez, Elizabeth Chauvet, Edward Bell, Victor Jory, Sandra Smith. Nakia Parker helps a young Indian accused of murder.

109.3 *The Quarry.* Sept. 28, 1974. GS: Burr DeBenning, Beth Brickell, Gale Sondergaard, Crawford MacCallum, Ray Greenway, Claudia Baca, Robert Vigil. Nakia becomes involved with a fugitive's family while trying to learn what turned the kind, loving farmer into a murderous wild man.

109.4 *The Sand Trap.* Oct. 5, 1974. GS: Jan Clayton, Jo Ann Harris, Marianna Hill, Richard Kelton, David Huddleston, Robert Ginty. A country boy who married into high society is murdered at an elegant party, and his widow is the leading suspect.

109.5 *The Hostage.* Oct. 12, 1974. GS: Kay Lenz, David Huffman, Jeanne Stein, Emmett S. Robbins, Michael C. Eiland. An unlikely bond develops between a tough bank robber and the mentally retarded young woman he takes hostage.

109.6 *No Place to Hide.* Oct. 19, 1974. GS: Gabriel Dell, Ray Danton, Gwen Van Dam, Marc Singer. A new resident of Concord is trying to get a fresh start, but his former colleagues in the syndicate feel that if he lives he might talk.

109.7 *A Beginning in the Wilderness.* Oct. 26, 1974. GS: Greg Mabrey, Joanne Linville, Cameron Mitchell, Robert Urich. Nakia is forced to call upon his knowledge of nature when he single-handedly tries to save a kidnaped boy.

109.8 *The Driver.* Nov. 2, 1974. GS: Geoffrey Deuel, Tim O'Connor, Todd Armstrong, Robert Doyle, Victoria Racimo, Harry Basch, Peter Prouse. Nakia is concerned that a naive young friend is unknowingly becoming involved in criminal activities.

109.9 *The Moving Target.* Nov. 9, 1974. GS: Marjoe Gortner, John Bennett Perry, Conny Van Dyke, Robin Mattson, Philip L. Mead. Nakia is afraid that an old friend, a country-western star, may be the prospective target of a sharpshooter's revenge.

109.10 *The Dream.* Nov. 23, 1974. GS: Michael Ansara, Richard Hatch, Kent Lane, Betty Ann Carr, Judson Morgan. An Indian doctor is marked for death by a student he committed to psychiatric treatment years earlier, and who now is the prime suspect in a series of crimes.

109.11 *Roots of Anger.* Nov. 30, 1974. GS: Pernell Roberts, Barbara Rhoades, Steve Sandor, Richard Young. Nakia is forced to clear his name when a local troublemaker dies soon after the deputy hits him in a barroom brawl.

109.12 *A Matter of Choice.* Dec. 7, 1974. GS: Charles Aidman, Pat Carroll, Farley Granger, Jared Martin, Susan Richardson, Kipp Whitman. A seasoned deputy intensifies his personal crusade to bust a dope-peddling ring after a young informant disappears.

109.13 *Pete.* Dec. 21, 1974. GS: Johnny Doran, George Maharis, Shirley Knight, Carmen Zapata. Ignoring Jericho's warning to go by the book, Nakia uses his native acumen to deal with a couple on a robbery spree, and with the son they have abandoned.

109.14 *The Fire Dancer.* Dec. 28, 1974. GS: Anthony Caruso, Victor Jory, Burr Smidt, Thomas J. Conlan. Ben Redfearn is hospitalized after a bear claws him, but insists on undergoing an Indian cure requiring nine days on a mountaintop.

110. Ned Blessing: The Story of My Life and Times

CBS. 60 min. Broadcast history: Wednesday, 9:00-10:00, Aug. 1993–Sept. 1993.

Regular Cast: Brad Johnson (Ned Blessing), Luis Avalos (Crecencio), Tim Scott (Sticks Packwood), Wes Studi (One Horse), Richard Riehle (Judge Longley), Brenda Bakke (the Wren), Bill McKinney (Verlon Borgers), Jeremy Roberts (Hugh Bell Borgers), Rob Campbell (Roby Borgers), Rusty Schwimmer (Big Emma), Richard Jones (Leopole Siddons).

Premise: Outlaw Ned Blessing, now an old man waiting to be hanged, remembers back to the days he was a sheriff in the town of Plum Creek.

The Episodes

110.1 *Return to Plum Creek.* Aug. 18, 1993. GS: Gregory Scott Cummings, Donzaleigh Abernathy, Julius Tennon, Tony Genero, Jill Parker-Jones. Ex-bandit Ned Blessing returns to his small Texas hometown and takes on the lawless Borgers family that has taken control of the town.

110.2 *A Ghost Story.* Aug. 25, 1993. GS: Tony Genero, Margaret Bowman, Jesse Shephard, Brent Bratton, Bill Wittliff. Ned and Crecencio get some help from the hereafter when Big Emma and Ned's Mexican adversary, General Pelo Blanco, team up to finish them off.

110.3 *The Smink Brothers.* Sept. 1, 1993. GS: Sage Allen, John Dennis Johnston, Marianne Muellerleile, William Sanderson, Nik Hagler, Jerry Swindell. When the notorious Smink Brothers ride into Plum Creek and harass One Horse, Ned arrests them, unaware that he is their real target.

110.4 *Oscar.* Sept. 8, 1993. GS: Stephen Fry, Jill Parker-Jones, Jerry Biggs, Joe Stevens, Don Stroud. Irish writer Oscar Wilde visits Plum Creek and invites the Wren to travel to Europe with him, forcing Ned to realize the depths of his feelings for her.

111. The New Land

ABC. 60 min. Broadcast history: Saturday, 8:00-9:00, Sept. 1974–Oct. 1974.

Regular Cast: Scott Thomas (Christian Larsen), Bonnie Bedelia (Anna Larsen), Todd Lookinland (Tuliff Larsen), Debbie Lytton (Annaliese Larsen), Kurt Russell (Bo Larsen), Donald Moffat (Lundstrom), Gwen Arner (Molly Lundstrom), Lew Frizzell (Murdock).

Premise: This series told of the hardships faced by a family of young Scandinavian immigrants who settle in the wilderness of Minnesota in the late 1850s.

The Episodes

111.1 *The Word Is: Persistence.* Sept. 14, 1974. GS: James Olson, Mike Farrell, Sally Carter. The immigrant Larsen family lose their livestock in a fire. They can replace the animals in one of two ways — by accepting charity from a self-righteous neighbor, or by trading land to a Mormon family, a move opposed by the community.

111.2 *The Word Is: Growth.* Sept. 21, 1974. GS: Ed Lauter, Ellen Geer, June Dayton. After a tornado destroys his farm, the Larsens' friend Nils decides to leave Minnesota. His departure poses a problem for the women of Solna since Nils' wife is the only midwife in the area.

111.3 *The Word Is: Acceptance.* Sept. 28, 1974. Bo has been grievously injured by a bear, and young Tuliff is haunted by his friend's misfortune.

111.4 *The Word Is: Mortal.* Oct. 5, 1974. GS: Salome Jens, Don Dubbins, Lin McCarthy, Robert Emhardt, Maxine Stuart. A cholera epidemic threatens the community when an entire family is stricken with the contagious disease. While Anna and Molly risk infection to nurse the victims, Bo sets out on a two-day journey to the nearest doctor.

111.5 *The Word Is: Alternative.* Oct. 12, 1974. GS: Belinda J. Montgomery, Paul Sorenson, Keith Atkinson. Romantic complications arise when Bo meets a young immigrant who has come to Solna to marry a man she has never met, the Larsens' pious neighbor Johansen.

111.6 *The Word Is: Celebration.* Oct. 19, 1974. GS: Wendell Wellman, Tenaya Torres, Charles Wagenheim. Unexpected dangers await the Larsens on a three-day journey to their first taste of frivolity — a dance in a neighboring town.

112. Nichols

NBC. 60 min. Thursday, 9:00-10:00, Thursday, Sept. 1971–Nov. 1971; Tuesday, 9:30-10:30, Nov. 1971–Aug. 1972.

Regular Cast: James Garner (Nichols), Neva Patterson (Ma Ketcham), Margot Kidder (Ruth), John Beck (Ketcham), Stuart Margolin (Mitchell), Paul Hampton (Johnson), M. Emmet Walsh (Gabe McCutcheon), Alice Ghostley (Bertha), Richard Bull (Judge Thatcher), John Harding (Salter).

Premise: Nichols returns to his hometown of Nichols, Arizona, in 1914, where he is blackmailed by powerful matriarch Ma Ketcham into serving as sheriff.

The Episodes

112.1 *Pilot.* Sept. 16, 1971. GS: John Quade, Jesse Wayne, Florence Lake. Nichols, an eighteen-year Army veteran leaves the service to get away from guns, only to wind up as the reluctant sheriff of a rowdy Arizona town.

112.2 *The Siege.* Sept. 23, 1971. GS: Ricardo Montalban, Armand Alzamora, Stefan Gierasch, Wayne Heffley, Barbara Collentine. Easy-going Sheriff Nichols faces his first uptight situation when Mexican rebel troops are holding the townsfolk incommunicado while their leader undergoes extensive dental surgery.

112.3 *The Indian Giver.* Sept. 30, 1971. GS: Michael Tolan, James Greene, Judson Pratt. Nichols gets a chance to get back at rancher Ma Ketcham, who conned him into his job as sheriff, by backing an Indian who claims to own the Ketcham spread.

112.4 *Culley vs. Hansen.* Oct. 7, 1971. GS: Robert Gist, Charles McGraw, Joe Brown, Emmet Walsh. Two old gunfighters who, after twenty years of almost legendary feuding, are being goaded into a final showdown.

112.5 *The Paper Badge.* Oct. 14, 1971. GS: John Rubinstein, Joyce Van Patten, Tracey Bogart, Ray Reinhardt, Richard Ryal. Nichols' young, correspondence-trained deputy has crossed path with the town's dumb, but dangerous, bully.

112.6 *Deer Crossing.* Oct. 21, 1971. GS: Ray Danton, Gene Evans, William Bramley, Claudio Martinez, Ted Gehring, Joanie Larson, James Lee Reeves. An Apache is hunting a 12-point buck out of season. Ketcham gets up in arms as he wants to bag the beauty himself.

112.7 *The Specialists.* Oct. 28, 1971. GS: Ralph Waite, Don Keefer, Michael Baseleon, Henry Beckman, Charles Dierkop, Robert F. Simon, Poupee Bocar. A motley crew storms an outlaw redoubt in Mexico. Joining Nichols and Ketcham are a safe-cracker, a butterfingered demolitions man, a hatchet-happy Indian and a befuddled ex-Army scout.

112.8 *Peanuts and Crackerjacks.* Nov. 4, 1971. GS: Med Florey, Wayne Heffley, Don Newcombe, Art Paserella, Richard Bull, William Christopher. A heavily-wagered game of baseball between an Army team and Nichols' Nuggets causes problems.

112.9 *Ketcham Power.* Nov. 11, 1971. GS: Alan Oppenheimer, Clifford David, Hoke Howell, E.J. Andre, Don Pedro Colley. Ma Ketcham's loutish son is sworn in as a deputy and soon begins to abuse his authority.

112.10 *The One Eyed Mule's Time Has Come.* Nov. 23, 1971. GS: Kristoffer Tabori, Roy Jenson, Walter Burke, Rayford Barnes, Jerry Summers, Lillian Bronson, Edith Leslie.

112.11 *Where Did Everybody Go?* Nov. 30, 1971. GS: Nira Barab/Caitlin Adams, Jesse Vint, Bill Vint, Alan Vint, Bennie Dobbins. Nichols is caught between a fun-loving spitfire and her watchdogs—a brutish boy friend and his three mean-tempered brothers.

112.12 *Away the Rolling River.* Dec. 7, 1971. GS: Steve Forrest, Richard Yniguez, John Day, William Patterson. Sam Yeager is an aging hell-raiser who tries to enlist Nichols in his ultimate escapade—robbing a money train.

112.13 *The Marrying Fool.* Dec. 28, 1971. GS: Tom Skerritt, Gerald S. O'Loughlin, Susan Tyrell. Wedding bells are chiming for Ruth the barmaid. The problem is that her groom's obscure past is about to see daylight, thanks to a wild-eyed stranger who is out to kill him.

112.14 *Eddie Joe.* Jan. 4, 1972. GS: Paul Winfield, Warren Vanders, Eric Laneuville, James Daris, Lou Frizzell, James Beard, Napoleon Whiting. A black fugitive is pursued by an unrelenting white enemy, a razor-happy ex-prison mate bent on seeing him dead.

112.15 *Zachariah.* Jan. 11, 1972. GS: Strother Martin, Marc Lawrence, Barry Cahill, Edward Faulkner, Barbara Collentine. Nichols' con-man uncle matches with with him in a heated battle over a hidden $32,000.

112.16 *The Unholy Alliance.* Jan. 18, 1972. GS: Noam Pitlik, Jennifer Gan, Orwin Harvey, Chuck Hicks, Liam Dunn, William Christopher. Nichols is pressured by thieves who think he is an ace safe-cracker, and will kill him if he bungles a job.

112.17 *Bertha.* Jan. 25, 1972. GS: Karl Lukas, Gale Dixon, Eva Bruce, Maria Gahva, Sandy Brown Wyeth. Nichols' temporarily replaces Bertha as saloonkeeper.

112.18 *Sleight of Hand.* Feb. 1, 1972. GS: Bo Hopkins, Dabbs Greer, Jonathan Lippe. Nichols' townsolk are victimized by a mining swindle using fool's gold.

112.19 *Wings of an Angel.* Feb. 8, 1972. GS: Val Avery, John Crawford, Chuck Hicks. Orv, a daredevil pilot, is pressed into Nichols' search for killers.

112.20 *About Jesse James.* Feb. 15, 1972. GS: Jack Elam, Charles McGraw, Vincent Van Patten, Fran Ryan, Dort Clark, Rance Howard, John Bunzel. A con man joins Nichols to follow up a lead about Jesse James that could be worth a fortune in reward money.

112.21 *Fight of the Century.* Feb. 22, 1972. GS: H.B. Haggerty, Ray Young, Ed Flanders, Richard Stahl, Sid Kane, Florence Lake. Nichols becomes involved in a rousing boxing match against a professional fighter.

112.22 *Man's Best Enemy.* Feb. 29, 1972. GS: Lou Wagner, Kelly Thordsen, Iler Rasmussen, James Lee Reeves. Keeping a killer-escape artist locked up proves no easy task for Nichols, thanks to a mangy mutt that is becoming the center of distraction.

112.23 *Wonder Fizz Flies Again.* March 7, 1972. GS: Ramon Bieri, Priscilla Garcia, Jay Varela, Allyn Ann McLerie, Val Avery, Rayford Barnes, Douglas Dirkson. Mexico holds unknown dangers for Nichols and a biplane pilot, who are flying to the rescue of an Army captain's kidnaped daughter.

112.24 *All in the Family.* March 14, 1972. GS: Anthony Zerbe, Marge Redmond, John Quade, Ray Pourchot, Russ McCubbin. Nichols is killed and his lookalike brother sets out to avenge his twin's murder.

113. The Nine Lives of Elfego Baca

Regular Cast: Robert Loggia (Elfego Baca), Robert F. Simon (Sheriff Ed Morgan), Leonard Strong (Zangano), James Dunn (J. Henry Newman), Valerie Allen (Lucita Miranda), Ramon Novarro (Don Estevan Miranda), Skip Homeier (Ross Mantee), Rico Alaniz (El Sinverguenza), Brian Keith (Shadrock), Beverly Garland (Suzanna), Nestor Paiva (Justice of the Peace), Arthur Hunnicutt (Elias).

Premise: This series related the adventures of lawman turned lawyer Elfego Baca in Socorro County, New Mexico, in the late 1800s.

Notes: This series aired as segments of *Walt Disney Presents*.

The Episodes

113.1 *The Nine Lives of Elfego Baca.* Oct. 3, 1958. GS: Lisa Montell. Baca enters the town of Frisco, New Mexico, and finds the townspeople terrorized by a drunken cowboy.

113.2 *Four Down and Five Lives to Go.* Oct. 17, 1958. GS: Linc Foster, Lisa Montell. Elected Sheriff of Socorro County, New Mexico, Baca is particularly disturbed when he learns that the bandit and killer, El Sinverguenza ("The Shameless One") has entered Baca's territory. Alone, he trails the killer through dangerous Apache country and into old Mexico.

113.3 *Elfego — Lawman or Gunman.* Nov. 28, 1958. GS: Joe Maross. While studying law under J. Henry Newman of Santa Fe, Baca learns of a scheme to take away the lands belonging to Don Esteban Miranda, a Spanish-American ranch owner. He goes to confer with Miranda and finds the rancher besieged by a band of cowboys.

113.4 *Law and Order, Incorporated.* Dec. 12, 1958. Elfego Baca, intending to shed his guns permanently, joins with attorney J. Henry Newman in forming the law firm of Newman and Baca. Baca realizes the dangers of his new way of life when he again meets gunman Ross Mantee.

113.5 *Elfego Baca, Attorney at Law.* Feb. 6, 1959. GS: Edward Colmans, Annette Funicello, Lynn Bari. When a Santa Fe bank is robbed, Elfego's friend Fernando Bernal is identified as one of the bandits. Because of his prison record, Bernal's plea of innocence is ignored by everyone except Elfego, who originally had obtained a parole for him.

113.6 *The Griswold Murder.* Feb. 20, 1959. GS: Patric Knowles, Audrey Dalton. Elfego Baca is again forced to strap on his guns as he battles in and out of court for the lives of an English couple accused of murder. In court he must face his former partner, J. Henry Newman, and outside he must protect his clients from the dead man's family.

113.7 *Move Along, Mustangers.* Nov. 13, 1959. GS: Barry Kelley, James Coburn, Robert Hoy. Elfego Baca defends a group of persecuted nomads, who want to end their Gypsy existence and settle on newly opened Government land. The local ranchers, resenting this intrusion, attempt to drive the new settlers away.

113.8 *Mustang Man, Mustang Maid.* Nov. 20, 1959. GS: Barry Kelley, James Coburn, Robert Hoy. Although the Mustangers have established themselves on their homesteads, the local ranchers still consider them worthless nomads and attempt to drive them out. When town merchants refuse to sell the necessities of life to the new settlers, Baca uses his legal knowledge, and his guns, to protect his clients' rights.

113.9 *Friendly Enemies at Law.* March 18, 1960. GS: Barton MacLane, John Kerr, Ray Teal, Pat Crowley, Robert Lowery. Gun-toting attorney Elfego Baca is out to prove that a cattle-baron is stealing a rancher's cattle. When a search warrant isn't honored, Baca tries less orthodox methods.

113.10 *Gus Tomlin Is Dead.* March 25, 1960. GS: Howard Negley, Richard Garland, Paul Birch, Alan Hale, Jr., Coleen Gray, Brian Corcoran. Chasing an elusive murderer, Baca learns that the son of one of the killer's victims may beat him to the punch.

114. *Northwest Passage*

NBC. 30 min. Sunday, 7:30–8:00, Sept. 1958–Jan. 1959; Friday, 7:30–8:00, Jan. 1959–July 1959.

Regular Cast: Keith Larsen (Major Robert Rogers), Buddy Ebsen (Sgt. Hunk Marriner), Don Burnett (Ensign Langdon Towne), Philip Tonge (General Amherst).

Premise: This adventure series was based on the characters created by Kenneth Roberts in his historical novel of the French and Indian War. The series depicted the adventures of members of an outfit of colonials known as Rogers' Rangers.

The Episodes

114.1 *Fight at the River.* Sept. 14, 1958. GS: Rayford Barnes, Stuart Wade, Harry Lauter, Denny Miller, Hal Riddle. A wounded Ranger makes his way back to Fort Crown Point and brings the news that the French are using captured Rangers to build fortifications. Maj. Rogers selects some men and sets out with a cannon to do battle with the French.

114.2 *The Red Coat.* Sept. 21, 1958. GS: Patrick Macnee, Roger Til, Alan Hale, Jr., Phillip Tonge, William Boyette, Norman DuPont. A British officer is assigned to accompany Maj. Roberts and the Rangers in an attempt to capture a French general. The Britisher insists on wearing his uniform, and his bright red coat places the entire company in danger.

114.3 *The Gunsmith.* Sept. 28, 1958. GS: Lisa Davis, Larry Chance, Lisa Gaye, Pat Hogan, Jim Hayward. When the Indian chief Black Wolf begins making raids on the colonists. Maj. Rogers suspects that someone is acting as a spy for the chief and the French. He decides to go out on a map-making and scouting expedition and kidnaps a new recruit who has been paying too much attention to Rogers' sweetheart.

114.4 *Surprise Attack.* Oct. 5, 1958. GS: Larry Chance, Lisa Gaye, Phillip Tonge. Langdon Towne, the Rangers' mapmaker, is kidnaped by the Indians and help prisoner. Major Roberts tries to rescue Towne.

114.5 *The Bound Women.* Oct. 12, 1958. GS: Angie Dickinson, Rebecca Welles, Emile Meyer, Irene Tedrow. According to colonial custom, women prisoners were often placed in bondage as servants. But one man with several women in bondage to him begins selling them illegally to frontiersmen. One young woman escapes and Maj. Rogers hears of her plight.

114.6 *Break Out.* Oct. 19, 1958. Maj. Rogers and Rangers Hunk Marriner and Langdon Towne are taken prisoner by the French forces and imprisoned in a stockade. In an effort to conceal Rogers' identity, all the prisoners in the camp take the name of Smith. Then Rogers and his men begin the slow process of digging a tunnel out of the stockade in an effort to escape.

114.7 *Court Martial.* Oct. 26, 1958. GS: Richard Ney, Louis Jean Heydt. Two rangers, Hunk Marriner and Adam Pierce, are charged with desertion by a British officer. The two deny the charges and Maj. Rogers comes to the prisoners' defense.

114.8 *The Hostage.* Nov. 2, 1958. GS: Bobby Clark, Kelly Thordsen, Lillian Gillespie, Ivan Triesault. During a cleanup operation among the ruins in Montreal, Maj. Rogers falls through a floor and is held prisoner by five children. Rogers is afraid that the children may turn him over to the French.

114.9 *Sorrow Song.* Nov. 9, 1958. Maj. Rogers arrives at an Indian camp for a powwow and learns that the chief's infant son has disappeared. Rogers declares a temporary truce and begins a search for the child.

114.10 *The Assassin.* Nov. 16, 1958. GS: Carol Ohmart, Paul Cavanaugh, Jacques Aubuchon, Pernell Roberts. Col. George Clayton and his daughter Nora are being held prisoner by the French. A French officer promises them their freedom if they will carry a message to Maj. Robert Rogers.

114.11 *The Long Rifle.* Nov. 23, 1958. GS: Dean Harens, Jeanne Baird, Douglas Kennedy, Phillip Tonge, Gavin Muir, Hugh Sanders. Maj. Rogers asks Hunk Marriner to test a new gunpowder. Marriner suddenly finds himself very popular with a man who wants him to say that the new gunpowder is inferior to the kind now used by the Rangers.

114.12 *War Sign.* Oct. 30, 1958. GS: Joe Maross, Peter Votrian, Mary Lawrence. A thirteen-year-old boy tells Maj. Rogers that he wants to join the Rangers. When Rogers returns the youngster to his home, he learns that the boy ran away because his father threatened to whip him.

114.13 *The Traitor.* Dec. 7, 1958. GS: Lewis Martin. An English officer who desperately needs money for his sick wife, has been selling information to the French. Then he recognizes a newly arrived British officer as a French spy and discovers a plot to kill Major Rogers.

114.14 *Vengeance Trail.* Dec. 21, 1958. GS: Paul Fix, Rod Dana, Joe Vitale. Maj. Roberts hears a report from bounty hunter Joe Waters that an Indian attack is in preparation. Although Roberts doesn't believe Walter's story, he investigates the report.

114.15 *The Vulture.* Dec. 28, 1958. GS: Bruce Cowling. Sir Martin Stanley, envious of Maj. Rogers' popularity, and fearing it will hinder his colonial ambitions, devises a way to get rid of Rogers.

114.16 *The Counterfeiters.* Jan. 2, 1959. Maj. Rogers, Hunk Marriner and Langdon Towne are three very embarrassed men. After spending some time in Portsmoth, N.H., they are confronted with the fact that the money they have been spending, their military pay, is counterfeit.

114.17 *The Secret of the Cliff.* Jan. 9, 1959. GS: Taina Elg, Philip Tonge, Maurice Marsac, Albert Carrier. Attempting to discover the secret entrance to a cave, Maj. Rogers, Hunk Marriner and Langdon Towne don disguises and enter Quebec. Rogers is surprised to discover that his contact in the city is a very pretty young lady.

114.18 *Dead Reckoning.* Jan. 16, 1959. GS: John Carlyle, Ben Wright, Morris Ankrum.

114.19 *Death Rides the Wind.* Jan. 23, 1959. GS: Murvyn Vye, DeForest Kelley. Two criminals escape the Crown Point stockade and head for Portsmouth, N.H., unaware that they are carrying smallpox. The Rangers begin a frantic search for the men.

114.20 *The Fourth Brother.* Jan. 30, 1959. GS: Gene Nelson, Marcia Henderson, Grant Withers, Lee Van Cleef. One of four outlaw brothers decides to reform, and leaves the family fold. He goes to see his girl friend, but finds that the girl's father holds his past against him.

114.21 *The Ambush.* Feb. 6, 1959. GS: Jean Moorehead, Anne Gwynne, George N. Neise, John Cliff, Robert Foulk. While escorting a young woman to Portsmouth, Maj. Rogers and Sgt. Marriner are joined by a bailiff and his prisoner and an unhappily married couple.

114.22 *The Witch* (A.K.A. "Witchcraft"). Feb. 13, 1959. GS: Edith Barrett, Philip Tonge, Robert E. Griffith, Marsha Wentworth, Wendy Stuart, Kay Stuart. Maj. Rogers arrives in town just as the townspeople are about to throw in the river a woman they claim is a witch.

114.23 *Stab in the Back.* Feb. 20, 1959. GS: Philip Tonge, Lisa Montell, Luis Van Rooten. Four Rangers are the victims of a mysterious prowler who has taken their uniforms. Gen. Amherst suspects that spies plan to pose as Rangers in order to intercept an important messenger.

114.24 *The Deserter.* Feb. 27, 1959. GS: Carole Mathews, John Beradino, Burt Douglas, Carolyn Craig. Army private Tom Jason, worried about his wife and baby, unable to get a leave, deserts from Fort Crown Point. Arriving home, Tom asks his father for money and his ordered to leave. When his father is murdered, Tom is suspected of the crime.

114.25 *Trial by Fire.* March 6, 1959. GS: Peter Whitney, Connie Buck, Richard Karlan, X Brands. During a frontier dispute between the French and the Indians, a Frenchman named Daumier, who is married to an Indian, remains neutral. As a result he and his wife are threatened by both the French and the Indians.

114.26 *The Killers.* March 13, 1959. GS: Karen Clarke, Christopher Dark, John Russell, Claire Kelly. Mary Clark comes to the frontier as a young bride and learns that her role in Colonial life differs from what she had expected.

115. *The Oregon Trail*

NBC. 60 min. Broadcast history: Wednesday, 9:00-10:00, Sept. 1977–Oct. 1977.

Regular Cast: Rod Taylor (Evan Thorpe), Andrew Stevens (Andrew Thorpe), Tony Becker (William Thorpe), Gina Marie Smika (Rachel Thorpe), Darleen Carr (Margaret Devlin), Charles Napier (Luther Sprague).

Premise: Evan Thorpe is a widower with three children and the responsibility of getting a wagon train to Oregon in 1842.

The Episodes

115.1 *Hard Ride Home* & *The Last Game.* Sept. 21, 1977. GS: Hoke Howell, John Vernon, Carole Tru Foster, Wilford Brimley. Thorpe's twelve-year-old son inadvertently defiles Indian burial ground.

115.2 *The Waterhole.* Sept. 28, 1977. GS: Kim Hunter, Lonny Chapman, Jean Rasey, William Phipps. A sudden dust storm contributes to the pioneers' desperation as they trek across the desert in search of a water hole.

115.3 *Trapper's Rendezvous.* Oct. 12, 1977. GS: Claude Akins, Ted Gehring. The Thorpes befriend a crusty mountain man, unaware that he is leading a pack of trappers planning deadly revenge on an ex-comrade, wagon scout Luther.

115.4 *The Army Deserter.* Oct. 19, 1977. GS: Kevin McCarthy, Clu Gulager, Nicholas Hammond. The Thorpes take in an injured young man claiming to be the sole survivor of an Indian massacre, unaware that he is an Army deserter and his wounds are self-inflicted.

115.5 *Hannah's Girls.* Oct. 26, 1977. GS: Stella Stevens, Denise Galik, Billy Green Bush, Mills Watson, Maxine Olmsted, Suzanne Hunt, Roy Gaintner. Prostitutes pose as mail-order brides to join the wagon train and elude their procurer.

115.6 *The Scarlet Ribbon.* Nov. 30, 1977. GS: Bill Bixby, Donna Mills, William Shatner, Richard Jaeckel, Damon Douglas, Harry G. Adams. Evan tangles with a gunrunner and his moll who are smuggling Army rifles to a tribe of bloodthirsty Indians.

116. The Outcasts

ABC. 60 min. Broadcast history: Monday, 9:00–10:00, Sept. 1968–Sept. 1969.

Regular Cast: Don Murray (Earl Corey), Otis Young (Jemal David).

Premise: A Virginia aristocrat-turned-gunfighter and a freed slave team up as bounty hunters to track down wanted criminals in the post–Civil War West.

The Episodes

116.1 *The Outcasts.* Sept. 23, 1968. GS: Slim Pickens, Burr De Benning, Gino Conforti, Warren Finnerty. Earl Corey, an uprooted Virginia aristocrat, is forced into an unwilling partnership with ex-slave Jemal David, an unabashed bounty hunter. Their first quarry is a killer who must be smoked out of a cavalry wagon train.

116.2 *A Ride to Vengeance.* Sept. 30, 1968. GS: Charles McGraw, Diana Muldaur, Ken Lynch, Erik Holland, Frank Marth, Gene Shane. A wary bond between Virginian and ex-slave strengthens as they grapple with a mystery that endangers Jemal's life. A $1000 reward has been offered for Jemal, who is wanted dead or alive for murder in the Dakota Territory, where he has never been.

116.3 *Three Ways to Die.* Oct. 7, 1968. GS: James Gregory, Paul Langton, Christopher Stone. Corey moves to avert a double tragedy when Jemal is framed for the murder of a man who knew too much about the past of an embittered lawman.

116.4 *The Understanding.* Oct. 14, 1968. GS: William Mims, Nico Minardos, Jorge Moreno. While fighting over a windfall of gold pesos, the bounty hunters are seized and sentenced to death on a false charge of gunrunning in Mexico. A scheming Mexican officer frees Corey, promising Jemal's release when the gold is returned. But Corey is unaware that the gold has been taken from its hiding place by Jemal.

116.5 *Take Your Lover in the Ring.* Oct. 28, 1968. GS: Gloria Foster, John Dehner, Walter Coy, Virginia Gregg. In a poker game with a sly Southern colonel, Earl Corey wins $600 and the queen of hearts—a beautiful serving girl who is the colonel's prize possession. Next morning, Corey and Jemal are both suffering loss and betrayal.

116.6 *The Heroes.* Nov. 11, 1968. GS: Royal Dano, Michael Margotta, James Westerfield. Corey and Jemal face double jeopardy when they assume the unwanted roles of gunslingers for Walt Madsen, who is being squeezed off his land. Their presence inflames a smoldering hostility between Madsen and his restless son, who idolizes the bounty hunters.

116.7 *My Name Is Jemal.* Nov. 18, 1968. GS: James Edwards, Arthur Franz, John Marley, Charles Dierkop, James Michelle, Walter Brooke, Roy Jenson. Jemal is shanghaied and put in a prison wagon in place of a Negro marked for execution. Miles from the scene, Corey begins a search when a stage arrives with a murdered driver and a passenger who gives a description of Jemal as the killer.

116.8 *The Night Riders.* Nov. 25, 1968. GS: Steve Ihnat, Larry Gates, Joan Hotchkis, Isabelle Cooley, Jeff Pomerantz. The bounty hunters confront the bitterness of the reconstruction era during a tragic incident at a remote way station. Jemal is shot and Corey confronted by a band of black-hooded night riders who want him to lead their violent anti-Union activities.

116.9 *The Heady Wine.* Dec. 2, 1968. GS: William C. Watson, Kay Reynolds, Logan Ramsey, Lou Frizzell, Jan Burrell. A strange turn of events leaves Jemal acting sheriff with a murder to solve, and Corey as his deputy. The black man's handling of unaccustomed power and unplumbed prejudices soon jeopardizes an investigation already hobbled by lies, conspiracy and threats.

116.10 *The Man from Bennington.* Dec. 16, 1968. GS: Fritz Weaver, Michael Conrad, Kenneth Tobey, Hayden Rorke, Gerald Michenaud, Richard Tate, Don Keefer. Corey wages a battle of nerves to expose a killer. A solid wall of opposition, including Jemal's, frustrates his efforts to prove that a man wanted for wartime atrocities is not only on the scene, but has killed again to protect his new identity.

116.11 *The Bounty Children.* Dec. 23, 1968. GS: Michael Burns, Charles Aidman, Dan Tobin, Linda Sue Risk. Corey and Jemal face a moral dilemma after taking two children under their wing. Found alone on a wagon trail, the youngsters are being stalked by two other bounty men hunting a man with a price on his head—the children's father.

116.12 *They Shall Rise Up.* Jan. 6, 1969. GS: William Bramley, Sean McClory, Mort Mills, Frank Ramirez. Jemal is dragooned back into slavery by a sinister cabal working a clandestine mine operation. Narrowly escaping the same fate, Corey worms his way into the murderous group, and finds Jemal suffering under concentration camp conditions.

116.13 *Alligator King.* Jan. 20, 1969. GS: Paul Mantee, William Wintersole, John Lawrence, Jerry Daniels, John War Eagle. In Oklahoma, Corey and Jemal clash over Jemal's involvement in a crisis of the Creek nation. A chief has disgraced himself by being cheated out of tribal land by greedy whites. Jemal's persistence in setting matters aright leads to bloodshed and a death sentence.

116.14 *The Candidates.* Jan. 27, 1969. GS: Susan Howard, Grant Williams, Madeleine Sherwood, Bill Walker, Edward Faulkner, Art Metrano. The bounty hunters' attempt to smoke out a fugitive who has assumed another identity sparks an emotional upheaval for Corey. The mayoralty candidates of a bustling Western community are their prime suspects, and one of them is married to Corey's lost love.

116.15 *The Glory Wagon.* Feb. 3, 1969. GS: Jack Elam, Ezekial Williams, Bing Russell, Nick Cravat, Mudcat Grant. Corey, Jemal and a treacherous prisoner set out on a death-defying errand of mercy, transporting nitroglycerin across the desert to rescue twelve miners trapped in a cave-in. As their tempers, and cargo, inch toward explosion, the men are met by a Negro boy desperately trying to reach his trapped father.

116.16 *Act of Faith.* Feb. 10, 1969. GS: Brock Peters, Robert F. Simon, Karl Swenson, Ron Soble, Wright King, Susan Brown. Jemal bridles at the job of bringing in a Negro murder suspect who swears he was framed by his rancher boss. After talking Ben Pritchard into standing trial, the bounty hunters discover they have thrown Ben to the lions.

116.17 *The Thin Edge.* Feb. 17, 1969. GS: Ida Lupino, Paul Fix, Harry Carey, Jr., George Clifton, Ross Hagen. The shock of accidentally killing a young girl makes Corey a danger to himself and to Jemal. Ravaged by guilt, Corey returns to the scene of the tragedy where the girl's angelic memory, and her enigmatic mother, intensify his remorse.

116.18 Gideon. Feb. 24, 1969. GS: Roscoe Lee Browne, Robert J. Wilke, Howard Caine, Lonny Chapman, Rayford Barnes, Charles Maxwell. Already clashing with two other bounty hunters over a hunted outlaw, Corey and Jemal add a bitter personal quarrel. Trouble begins when Corey renews a friendship with one of his former slaves, a treacherous Uncle Tom Jemal distrusts on sight.

116.19 And Then There Was One. March 3, 1969. GS: Harvey Jason, Alejandro Rey, John Cullum, James Davidson, Arthur Hunnicutt. Tragicomic misfortunes befalls the bounty hunters as they try to deliver a wagonload of prisoners. Transpiring at every turn is lots of trouble, from senseless violence to a poignant shotgun wedding.

116.20 Hung for a Lamb. March 10, 1969. GS: Tammy Grimes, Mike Road, Kevin Hagen, John Zaremba, Ed Peck. Corey is being driven nuts by a pussyfooting parade of townsfolk, and a sheriff, who think he is a robber's accomplice.

116.21 A Time of Darkness. March 24, 1969. GS: A Martinez. Submerged antagonisms rush to the surface when Corey and Jemal are trapped in a dark Indian burial cave. White and black reach their boiling points when Jemal becomes hamstrung by a morbid fear of defiling the sacred place, while Corey defiantly burns holy relics to stay warm.

116.22 The Town That Wouldn't. March 31, 1969. GS: Ruth Roman, Pippa Scott, Tom Palmer, Robert F. Lyons, Hilarie Thompson, Leo V. Gordon, John Dennis, Michael Michaelian, Dennis Cross. Mystery and terror shroud the desolate town where Corey and Jemal track a desperado. But their quarry, and the sheriff died in a shootout, and the townspeople await an attack by the outlaw's avenging friends.

116.23 The Stalking Devil. April 7, 1969. GS: William Windom, Rodolfo Acosta, Robert Phillips. Corey and Jemal capture a fanatic who paints himself black to slaughter red men. Capable of rationalizing any atrocity, he soon seizes on the grim logic presented by Jemal's black skin and a band of avenging Indians.

116.24 Give Me Tomorrow. April 21, 1969. GS: Nancy Malone, Dick Sargent, John Hoyt, William Traylor, Rodolfo Hoyos. Corey is the catalyst in fomenting explosion as he escorts a family of Virginia aristocrats to a new settling place. Tensions multiply as he becomes trusted confidant to the secretive father, enemy of the alienated son, and a rival of the daughter's lowborn fiance.

116.25 The Long Ride. April 28, 1969. GS: William Bassett, J. Pat O'Malley, Ted de Corsia, Barbara Morrison. The bounty hunters capture an outlaw, and are soon besieged by enraged Indians who have been hunting the man for murdering Apache women.

116.26 How Tall Is Blood? May 5, 1969. GS: H.M. Wynant, Phil Bruns, Parley Baer, Lilyan Chauvin, Rex Holman. The leader of peaceful Navajos has begun to equate manhood with the brutality his people has suffered from whites. Hiring Corey and Jemal as gunslingers is his first step in a disastrous plan to regain his honor.

117. The Outlaws

NBC. 60 min. Broadcast history: Thursday, 7:30-8:30, Sept. 1960-Sept. 1962.

Regular Cast: Barton MacLane (U.S. Marshal Frank Caine) 60-61, Don Collier (Deputy Marshal Will Forman), Jock Gaynor (Deputy Marshal Heck Martin) 60-61, Bruce Yarnell (Deputy Marshal Chalk Breeson) 61-62, Slim Pickens (Slim) 61-62, Judy Lewis (Connie Masters) 61-62.

Premise: The outlaws of the Oklahoma Territory tell their own stories as each 19th century badman shows how he got his start and how he was brought to justice by Marshal Frank Caine and Deputies Will Foreman and Heck Martin.

The Episodes

117.1 Thirty a Month. Sept. 29, 1960. GS: Steve Forrest, Robert Culp, Warren Oates, Garry Walberg. Hardworking trail boss Rance Hollister has been saving for years to buy acreage in a beautiful valley. But his money is stole, and he vows to get it back any way he can.

117.2 Ballad for a Badman. Oct. 6, 1960. GS: Cliff Robertson, Madlyn Rhue, Charles Aidman, Paul Hartman, Patricia Breslin, Jerome Cowan, James Dobson, Grandon Rhodes, Onslow Stevens. Chad Burns robs the rich and gives to the poor. Because of his charm and generosity, and a supply of alibis, he manages to elude the law.

117.3 Beat the Drum Slowly. Oct. 20, 1960. GS: Vic Morrow, Dean Jones, Ray Walston. Joe and Danny Cannon want to get back some money they think is rightfully theirs. Their plan is to rob a casino that boasts it can't be robbed.

117.4 Rape of Red Sky. Oct. 27, 1960. GS: Skip Homeier, Gerald Mohr, Jackie Coogan, Leo Gordon, William Bryant, Eugene Iglesias, Patricia Barry. Gabe Cutter has sworn to make the town of Red Sky pay for lynching his brother, who was innocent of murder.

117.5 Shorty. Nov. 3, 1960. GS: Alfred Ryder, Hampton Fancher, Edward Binns, Vivi Janiss, Robert Harland. Killer Jack Duane is sour on life because of his size. He won't let neighboring ranchers use the right-of-way on his land. And when one does, he shoots him in the back.

117.6 Last Chance. Nov. 10, 1960. GS: Jack Mullaney, John Larch, Ellen Willard, Phillip Pine, Bruce Gordon. Oklahoma bandit Harry Gannon decides to settle down with his sweetheart and go straight.

117.7 Starfall Part One. Nov. 24, 1960. GS: William Shatner, David White, Jack Warden, Adam Williams, Paul Richards, Edgar Buchanan, Pippa Scott, Ken Lynch, John Anderson, John Hoyt, Cloris Leachman. The Oklahoma Territory is torn apart by a range war, and the Government tires to quell dissension. But four men can't abide the law or the lawful.

117.8 Starfall Part Two. Dec. 1, 1960. GS: William Shatner, David White, Jack Warden, Adam Williams, Paul Richards, Edgar Buchanan, Pippa Scott, Ken Lynch, John Anderson, John Hoyt, Cloris Leachman. Peace has been restored to the Oklahoma Territory, and the participants in the range war have agreed to sign an amnesty. But four men involved in the feud find that hate and prejudice are not easily forgotten.

117.9 *The Fortune Stone.* Dec. 15, 1960. GS: Gerald Mohr, Dianne Foster, Edward Atienza. A jeweler named Fescu, in possession of a valuable gem, is a passenger when a stage is held up. To keep the robbers from getting the stone, Fescu flips it out onto the road.

117.10 *The Quiet Killer.* Dec. 29, 1960. GS: Gene Evans, Phyllis Thaxter, Carleton Young, Fuzzy Knight, J. Pat O'Malley, Dan Frazer, Clegg Hoyt, Johnny Washbrook. Marshal Tom Doan brought many cattle rustlers to trial, but lost his respect for the law when juries failed to convict them. He finds a better way to bring the thieves to justice.

117.11 *The Waiting Game.* Jan. 19, 1961. GS: Alan Hale, Jr., Edward Andrews, Larry Gates, Fred Beir, Constance Ford. A gang of robbers holds up the Topeka bank and makes off with a huge haul. They plan to hide the money for a number of years before dividing it among themselves, and devise an ingenious way of preventing any one of them from getting the money ahead of time.

117.12 *The Daltons Must Die* Part One. Jan. 26, 1961. GS: Larry Pennell, Robert Lansing, Joan Evans, Chris Robinson, Charles Carlson, Bill Tannant. Five brothers, all deputy marshals, turn away from the law. The brothers are after a dangerous killer named Red Buck and his two sidekicks.

117.13 *The Daltons Must Die* Part Two. Feb. 2, 1961. GS: Larry Pennell, Robert Lansing, Joan Evans, Chris Robinson, Charles Carlson, Bill Tannant. Embittered because a jury has failed to convict their brother's killers, the four Daltons take the law into their own hands.

117.14 *Assassin.* Feb. 9, 1961. GS: Dean Stockwell, Kevin Hagen, Jennifer West, Edmon Ryan. One of Caine's deputies has been murdered, and the marshal goes on an all-out campaign against crime. He starts by closing down some of town boss McKinnon's more dubious establishments, and McKinnon retaliates by hiring Billy Joe Minden to kill Caine.

117.15 *Culley.* Feb. 16, 1961. GS: Henry Hull, James Coburn, John Milford, Sue Ane Langdon, Judson Pratt, Vito Scotti, James Griffith. Caught in an ambush, Jeb Wood's son is murdered, and Jeb himself is blinded. The only witness, a young stranger named Culley, decides to take advantage of the wealthy old man by impersonating his son.

117.16 *The Bill Doolin Story.* March 2, 1961. GS: Joe Maross, Jacques Aubuchon, Wright King, Jean Allison, Jim Beck. When railroad interests force ranchers out of business, cowhand Bill Doolin takes up a gun and turns badman.

117.17 *The Bell.* March 9, 1961. Simon Oakland, Jack Lord, John Howard. Foreman, taking killer Neil Gwinner back to prison, is joined on the road by ex-convict Jim Houston. Gwinner offers Houston money to help him escape.

117.18 *No More Pencils — No More Books.* March 16, 1961. GS: David Wayne, Tom Gilson, Patricia Barry. Red McCool's curriculum never included crime, but when he revisits his old schoolteacher Darius Woodley, he is a confirmed outlaw. Woodley enlivens his own bookish life by lying to a posse when they pursue his ex-student.

117.19 *Blind Spot.* March 30, 1961. GS: Gary Merrill, Roger Mobley, V.J. Ardwin. Thirteen-year-old Davey's father has been killed by an outlaw known only as the Weasel. Gunman Frank Denton prepares the boy to avenge his father's murder.

117.20 *Outrage at Pawnee Bend.* April 6, 1961. GS: Paul Ford, Frank McHugh, Jonathan Harris. A routine, and unsuccessful, holdup of the afternoon train occurs each time there is a money shipment. Sam and John, long-time railway employees, have had time to witness the flawless record of the Pickham Agency in preventing the attempted robberies. They have also had time to prepare a perfect theft themselves.

117.21 *The Avenger.* April 13, 1961. GS: Vic Morrow, Martin Landau, Randy Sparks, Jeanette Nolan. Sheriff Dodge is lynched by a band of desperadoes disguised as Confederate soldiers. His son Tommy searches for his father's murderers.

117.22 *The Sooner.* April 27, 1961. GS: Cesare Danova, Stacy Harris, James Chandler, Joan Tetzel, Robert Carricart, Joseph Ruskin, Henry Rowland. Into the quiet frontier lives of trapper Grigor Zacod and his wife Jane ride three Eastern badmen. They believe Zacod knows the hiding place of a former member of their gang who gave them the doublecross.

117.23 *Sam Bass.* May 4, 1961. GS: Jack Chaplain, Dennis Patrick, Walter Burke, Cal Bolder, Gregg Palmer, Margarita Cordova. In his dreams, young Sam Bass is an awesome guntoter, but in the Denton City Saloon he just pushes a broom. Sam's social status suffers another setback when he inadvertently alerts a wanted gunman to the presence of the local sheriff, and the lawman is killed as a result.

117.24 *The Brothers.* May 11, 1961. GS: Richard Rust, Charles Briggs, Christine White, Jim Davis. When Jim Kelly kills a gambler in cold blood during a saloon card game, the other patrons become incensed and subject him to a savage beating. Foreman arrives, helps to rescue Kelly from his attackers, and places him under arrest.

117.25 *The Little Colonel.* May 18, 1961. GS: Ralph Manza, Craig Curtis, Rafael Campos, Ted Markland, Anna Navarro. Cass, Ben and Valdez are three bandits who escape across the Mexican borer after robbing a train. Foreman and Caine go after them in hot pursuit — only to be arrested by a fiery Mexican colonel.

117.26 *Return to New March.* June 22, 1961. GS: Julie Adams, Preston Foster. The town of New March might be a ghost town before too long. The Great Plains Railroad is planning to bypass it and build a company town two miles away. Some irate citizens of New March kill a railroad employee, and Foreman, who was raised in the town, is assigned to investigate.

Season Two

117.27 *Chalk's Lot.* Oct. 5, 1961. GS: David White, Cindy Robbins, Robert Karnes, Tom Symonds. Businessman Charlie Peal has his eye on a choice piece of land owned by Slim, and manages to cheat the old man out of it. Chalf talks Foreman into pulling a series of legal maneuvers to help Slim regain his land.

117.28 *The Connie Masters Story.* Oct. 12, 1961. GS: Cliff Robertson, Charles Fredericks, Lincoln Demyan. Connie Masters, employed by the Wells Fargo Bank, thinks her husband Jack is dead. But one day Jack shows up and wants to make a deal. He will tell Connie the whereabouts of her long-lost son if she will help him rob the bank.

117.29 *My Friend, the Horse Thief.* Oct. 19, 1961. GS: Brian Keith. Chalk Breeson's childhood friend, a cowboy called Whip, arrives in town. Everybody likes the newcomer, but

The Outlaws [1960]

Foreman, investigating a series of horse rustlings, finds that Whip has been near the scene of every crime.

117.30 *The Cutups*. Oct. 26, 1961. GS: Ray Walston, Bruce Gordon, Joan Camden, Dale Hill, Garth Benton. Two city slickers called Willie and Skinner dupe Slim into committing a robbery by telling him that the whole scheme is a practical joke. But Slim isn't laughing when he finds himself in jail.

117.31 *Night Riders*. Nov. 2, 1961. GS: Robert J. Wilke, Dick York, Jena Engstrom. A man named Meder heads a band of hooded criminals who are terrorizing the town of Stillwater. When Slim stands up to the gang, Meder sends his mob out to get him.

117.32 *The Brathwaite Brothers*. Nov. 9, 1961. GS: Lonny Chapman, Conlan Carter, Harry Raybould. Immediately after the Brathwaite Brothers, Silas, Perry and Levi, deposit their life savings in the Stillwater Bank, the bank is robbed of everything except their money. When the boys are told they can't withdraw their deposit, they decide to pull a bank robbery of their own.

117.33 *Walk Tall*. Nv. 16, 1961. GS: Paul Carr, Nina Shipman, Katharine Warren, Joe Brown, Robert Fortier, Stephen Joyce, Charles Hradilac. Young Jan Batory was born on the wrong side of the tracks, but he is determined to come up in the world by becoming a first-class thief.

117.34 *Roly*. Nov. 23, 1961. GS: David Wayne, Dianne Foster, Barbara Stuart. A holdup man, carrying a large sum of money, dies on Roly McDonough's farm. Rather than report the matter to the sheriff, Roly decide to spend the money on his wife.

117.35 *No Luck on Friday*. Nov. 30, 1961. GS: Vic Morrow, Gerald Mohr, Wright King. Everyone is positive that a certain payroll shipment is impossible to rob, everyone but crafty Leonard Lopez. He is sure he can pull it off, and chooses two very unlikely sorts to help him, dirt farmer Tim Sawyer and young Charlie Sondberg.

117.36 *The Outlaw Marshals*. Dec. 14, 1961. GS: Myron McCormick, Emile Meyer, Ken Lynch, Jack Elam, Pat McCaffrie, William Fawcett. Murder suspect Logan Henry is captured, and he begs Foreman to protect him. Marshals Root, Slater and Diamond threaten to use force if Logan isn't turned over to them.

117.37 *Masterpiece*. Dec. 21, 1961. GS: Walter Slezak, Howard I. Smith, Harry Townes. Bank owner Sam Porter doesn't like artist Martin Hall's portrait of him and he refuses to pay for it. Hall and locksmith Jerry Rome try to think of a really good way to hurt Porter's feelings—like robbing his bank.

117.38 *The Verdict*. Dec. 28, 1961. GS: Russell Thorsen, Carleton Young, Jan Merlin, Pippa Scott. Wealthy Titus Holbrook's son is killed in the theft of a money shipment. Foreman is called in to investigate the murder, and finds that he has one prime suspect in Chalk Breeson, his deputy.

117.39 *The Dark Sunrise of Griff Kincaid*. Jan. 4, 1962. GS: Cliff Robertson, Elisha Cook, Jr., Robert H. Harris, Joyce Jameson, Edward Asner. Blind Griff Kincaid comes to Stillwater to help the farmers, who are being exploited by a land syndicate. Griff wins the trust of most of the populace, but Foreman has some doubts about his motives.

117.40 *The Bitter Swede*. Jan. 18, 1962. GS: Brian Keith, Erika Peters, Myron Healey, Ken Drake. Sven Johannsen has one ambition in life: to remain a bachelor. Hulda Christianson, Sven's childhood sweetheart, has an equally powerful desire: to marry Sven. Foreman and Breeson watch as Hulda plots an all-out campaign to trap Sven.

117.41 *Buck Breeson Rides Again* (A.K.A. "The Old Man"). Jan. 25, 1962. GS: Lloyd Nolan, Bruce Gordon, John Abbott. Chalk Breeson is delighted when his father, Buck, comes to Stillwater for a visit. But when Buck joins up with a gang of swindlers and tries to drag his son in as an accomplice, Chalk wishes daddy had stayed at home.

117.42 *A Bit of Glory*. Feb. 1, 1962. GS: Eli Wallach, Jerome Cowan, Larry Chance, Dean Harens, Joan O'Brien, Dee Pollock. An outlaw named Spangler has escaped the law and Sheriff Ned Canvers is determined to track him down. Danvers has a special interest in the case. The aging sheriff's re-election depends on capturing Spangler.

117.43 *Horse of a Similar Color*. Feb. 8, 1962. GS: Tony Tery, Ron Trujillo. Slim makes a deal with two Indians called Fair Child and Bloody Claw to trade several ponies for a fast horse they own. But the Indians have neglected to tell Slim just how unusual their horse is.

117.44 *The Sisters*. Feb. 15, 1962. GS: Olive Sturgess, Gina Gillespie, Jackie Coogan, Arthur Hunnicutt, Carl Crow. Ruth and Bridget Durant wander into town, looking worn and bedraggled, but loaded down with spending money. Foreman learns they are the daughters of outlaw Ed Durant, a man he has been after for a long time.

117.45 *A Day to Kill*. Feb. 22, 1962. GS: Alejandro Rey, Mario Alcaide, Harry Townes, Vincent Padula. The Cuban ambassador is going to pass through Stillwater, and Foreman and Breeson are expected to guard him. Cuban refugees Carlos and Frank Vincente are planning a special greeting for the ambassador—they intend to assassinate him.

117.46 *No More Horses*. March 1, 1962. GS: Richard Long, John Fielder, Mike Kellin. Ludlow Pratt introduces his latest invention, an automobile, to Stillwater. Morgan Mayberry sees great possibilities for Pratt's pride and joy as the getaway car for a bank job he is planning.

117.47 *Ride the Man Down*. March 8, 1962. GS: Henry Jones. Chalk Breeson's search for a fugitive criminal leads him to the town of Sanctuary. The place is aptly named. It is crawling with killers and thieves and there is no law enforcement.

117.48 *Farewell Performance*. March 15, 1962. GS: Myron McCormick, Ruta Lee, Myron Healey, George Kennedy. Thomas Healy, head of a traveling Shakespearean troupe, arrives in Stillwater and talks Slim and Breeson into appearing in his show. This leaves only Foreman on duty.

117.49 *Charge!* March 22, 1962. GS: Claude Akins, Frank DeKova, Jay Lanin, Christopher King. Three Cavalry sergeants named Ben Thompson, Frank Burling and Myles Ree are trotting along a few miles out of Stillwater when they chance upon some Indians. To the sergeants' dismay, these particular Redmen apparently are dead set against coexistence and have a Gatling gun.

117.50 *All in a Day's Work*. May 10, 1962. GS: Alan Hewitt, Gene Lyons. Keenan, a man Foreman sent to prison, is out on parole. Foreman learns that Keenan has vowed to kill him.

118. Outlaws

CBS. 60 min. Broadcast History: Saturday, 8:00-9:00, Jan. 1987–May 1987.

Regular Cast: Rod Taylor (John Grail), William Lucking (Harland Pike), Charles Napier (Wolfson "Wolf" Lucas), Richard Roundtree (Isaiah "Ice" McAdams), Patrick Houser (Billy Pike), Christine Belford (Lt. Maggie Randall).

Premise: Texas Sheriff John Grail and the outlaw gang led by Harland Pike are caught in a freak storm in 1899 and find themselves in hurtling through time to Texas of the 1980s. They settle their differences and form the Double Eagle Detective Agency to bring justice to the modern Southwest.

The Episodes

118.1 *Outlaws.* Dec. 28, 1986. GS: Lewis Van Bergen, Wendy Girard, Grand L. Bush, Judd Omen, Ron Joseph, Roger Aaron Brown, Shannen Doherty. Four desperadoes and a sheriff are struck by a bolt from the blue and transported from 1899 Texas to modern-day Houston. There Grail and Pike's gang take the law into their own hands after a run-in with a ruthless gang.

118.2 *Tintype.* Jan. 3, 1987. GS: Leigh Taylor-Young, Barry Sattels, Brandon Call, Al Ruscio, Jack Hogan, William Riley. Maggie asks the boys to help a friend who is being held captive in her own house by her mobster husband.

118.3 *Primer.* Jan. 10, 1987. GS: Mary-Margaret Humes, Evan Richards, Thomas F. Duffy, James Hong, Juan Fernandez, Michael Horsley, Julius Harris. Grail and the boys are hired by merchants being victimized by local hoods.

118.4 *Orleans.* Jan. 17, 1987. GS: Lynne Moody, Andrew Masset, Sandy McPeak, Candi Brough, Randi Brough, Toby Norton, Denny Miller. Ice's moneymaking plans take the boys to New Orleans to find a buried treasure. Once there, they lock horns with the descendant of a man Ice once killed in a duel.

118.5 *Hymn.* Jan. 31, 1987. GS: Samantha Eggar, Grand L. Bush, Anthony James, Gregory Wagrowski, MacKenzie Allen. The boys ride to the aide of a television evangelist whose life is being threatened by a religious fanatic.

118.6 *Madrid.* Feb. 7, 1987. GS: Lew Ayres, Ben Piazza, Gertrude Flynn, Rex Ryon, Jeff MacKay, Claudia Christian, Robert Feero. Grail and the boys end up on opposite sides when a land developer attempts to take over a ghost town.

118.7 *Potboiler.* Feb. 28, 1987. GS: Aubrey Morris, Marshall Teague, Randi Brooks, Irwin Keyes, Gary Armagnac, Patrick Dollaghan. A Western writer who claims to know about the boys' past hires them at twice their normal fee on the pretext of collecting information for future projects.

118.8 *Pursued.* March 7, 1987. GS: Lar Park Lincoln, Mike Preston, Lee de Broux, Robin Dearden, Hoke Howell, Carl Bressler, Ben Kronen. While searching for a runaway girl, the boys lock horns with mobsters.

118.9 *Independents.* March 21, 1987. GS: Judith Chapman, Frank Annese, Tammy Lauren, Richard Brose. When mobsters put the squeeze on an independent cab company, the owner's daughter hires the Double Eagle detective agency.

118.10 *Hardcase.* March 28, 1987. GS: Richard Coca, Gerald Prendergast, Bob Giovane. The boys get roped into being guardians for a young boy who is mixed up with the hoods they are trying to track down.

118.11 *Jackpot.* April 4, 1987. GS: Ethan Phillips, Barbra Horan, Anthony Eisley. The boys head to Vegas for a vacation courtesy of a satisfied client, but the festivities get put on hold when they run into some ladies of the evening who are being abused by a mysterious pimp.

118.12 *Birthday.* May 2, 1987. Things look grim when the boys are trapped in their house by some sharpshooters, and Maggie takes a bullet in the head.

119. The Overland Trail

NBC. 60 min. Broadcast history: Sunday, 7:00-8:00, Feb. 1960–Sept. 1960.

Regular Cast: William Bendix (Fred Thomas), Doug McClure (Frank "Flip" Flippen).

Premise: A former Civil War engineer attempts to establish a route for the Overland Stage Lines from Missouri to California in the late 1860s.

The Episodes

119.1 *Perilous Passage.* Feb. 7, 1960. GS: Lynn Bari, Robert J. Wilke, Harry Guardino. Kelly and Flip make a stagecoach run with a very special passenger, outlaw Cole Younger, who has been taken prisoner. They stop at a relay station where the notorious Belle Starr is waiting with a scheme to free Younger.

119.2 *The O'Mara's Ladies.* Feb. 14, 1960. GS: Sean McClory, Maggie Pierce, Della Sharman, Nola Thorp, Heather Ames. Kelly and Flip agree to supply a gambler and his four female card dealers with transportation to Carson City. The trip is far from quiet, as Kelly and Flip are forced to keep the stage free from outlaws and would-be suitors.

119.3 *West of Boston.* Feb. 21, 1960. GS: Caroline Craig, Guy Mitchell, Arthur Hunnicutt, Earl Hodgins, Ken Mayer. Kelly promises to get a job as a teacher for Flip's fiancee if Flip will open a branch office in Mesa Flats. The trip to Mesa Flats, however, causes the young lady from Boston to question her decision to settle in the west.

119.4 *High Bridge.* Feb. 28, 1960. GS: Whitney Blake, Robert McQueeney, John Anderson, George Wallace. The stage is conveying a lovely and dangerous lady outlaw to her own hanging. Sensing Flip's qualms about a woman in irons, she makes a play for his sympathy.

119.5 *Westbound Stage.* March 6, 1960. GS: Suzanne Lloyd, Barbara Woodell, Edward Kemmer, Dodie Heath, George Keymas, Edward C. Platt. Kelly and Flip know that the overland jaunt is going to be hazardous—it takes them through hostile Indian country. During the journey, they learn their passengers' reasons for making the risky trip.

119.6 *All the O'Mara's Horses.* March 13, 1960. GS: Sean McClory, Karen Sharpe, Kelly Thorsden, Dan Sheridan. A man calls himself The O'Mara and has appointed himself sheriff of gold rush territory where Kelly and Flip intend to open a branch office. With gunslingers for deputies, The O'Mara is collecting tolls on all roads.

119.7 *Daughter of the Sioux.* March 20, 1960. GS:

Frank Ferguson, Jean Ingram, Mario Alcaide, Martin Eric, Gil Rankin. Kelly and Flip want a new relay station in South Dakota, but they need an OK from a local trapper. He offers them a deal. He will give the go-ahead if they escort his half-breed daughter to a St. Louis finishing school.

119.8 *Lawyer in Petticoats.* March 27, 1960. GS: Diane Foster, Barton MacLane, George Tobias, Walter Sande, John Qualen, Denver Pyle. A female lawyer hears that Flip has inherited some shares in a mine. She plots to do him out of them.

119.9 *Vigilantes of Montana.* April 3, 1960. GS: Werner Klemperer, Walter Coy, Myrna Fahey, Sherwood Price, Charles Maxwell, Gregg Palmer. An outlaw gang is running rampant, robbing stagecoaches of their gold. Kelly and Flip pose as bandits and try to infiltrate the gang.

119.10 *Fire in the Hole.* April 17, 1960. GS: Claude Akins, Susan Cummings, Robert Bray, Dan O'Kelly, John Pickard. Kelly and Flip are blasting through a mountain for their stage line. Trouble brews when the crew boss demands a saloon at the tunnel entrance.

119.11 *Mission to Mexico.* April 24, 1960. GS: Robert Loggia, Barbara Lord, Barbara Luna. Kelly is making a chivalrous attempt to help Emperor Maximilian's niece escape from Mexico. But revolutionary Porfirio Diaz has other ideas. Taking advantage of Flip's well-known interest in women, he uses a pretty girl to bait a trap.

119.12 *First Stage to Denver.* May 1, 1960. GS: Sue George, Peter Whitney, Judson Pratt, Wendell Holmes, Peter Brocco, Kay E. Kuter. The first stage to Denver will win the contract to carry the mail. It is Kelly and Flip's American-built stage vs. Calamity Jane's European one.

119.13 *Sour Annie.* May 8, 1960. GS: Mercedes McCambridge, Richard Devon, Andrew Prine, Slim Pickens, Harry Carey, Jr. Sour Annie is a gambler and gold-miner. On her way to file a gold claim, she is badly injured and the stage must halt in the middle of the desert.

119.14 *The Baron Comes Back.* March 15, 1960. GS: Lucy Marlowe, Gerald Mohr, Denver Pyle, Dolores Donlan, Ken Lynch. James Addison Reaves, a reformed con man who once worked the Arizona Territory, is traveling by stage. Before his trip is completed he is tempted to return to his former ways.

119.15 *Escort Detail.* May 22, 1960. GS: David Wayne, James Best, Miriam Colon, Lorin Tindall. A Indian princess who has just signed a peace treaty in Washington is traveling back to her reservation. Renegade Indians attack the stage and her Army escort must subordinate his hatred for all Indians to his duty to protect his charge.

119.16 *The Reckoning.* May 29, 1960. GS: Monica Lewis, John Carradine, Harold J. Stone, Dennis Miller. Fighting off a holdup of an overland stage, Flip manages to shoot one of the attackers. The gunman dies clutching a locket that bears the faded portrait of a woman.

119.17 *The Most Dangerous Gentleman.* June 6, 1960. GS: Ron Randell, John McIntire, Jeff Donnell, Onslow Stevens, Robert Emhardt, Lang Jeffries. Kelly is hired to help protect a railroad line against a professional killer. The gunman's target is President Ulysses S. Grant.

120. *Paradise*

CBS. 60 min. Broadcast history: Thursday, 9:00-10:00, Oct. 1988–March 1989; Saturday, 8:00-9:00, April 1989–Sept. 1990; Friday, 8:00-9:00, Jan. 1991–June 1991.

Regular Cast: Lee Horsley (Ethan Allen Cord), Jenny Beck (Claire Carroll Cord), Matthew Newmark (Joseph Cord), Brian Lando (Benjamin Cord), Michael Patrick Carter (George Cord), Sigrid Thornton (Amelia Lawson), Dehl Berti (John Taylor), Bert Rosario (Mendez), Mack Dryden (Scotty), John Miranda (Baxter), John Bloom (Tiny), Michael Ensign (Mr. Axelrod) 89-91, Will Hunt (Carl) 89-91, Benjamin Lum (Mr. Lee), James Crittenden (Charlie) 88-90, John Terlesky (Dakota) 90-91.

Premise: Professional gunfighter Ethan Cord becomes guardian of his late sister's four young children in the frontier mining town of Paradise, California, in the 1890s.

Note: This series was also known as *Guns of Paradise* during its third, and final, season.

The Episodes

120.1 *The News from St. Louis.* Oct. 27, 1988. GS: Tim Choate, Marilyn Jones, Kathryn Leigh Scott, Charles Young, Branscombe Richmond. Ethan Allen Cord is a hired gun in the town of Paradise who is suddenly saddled with the responsibility of caring for his dying sister's four children.

120.2 *The Holstered Gun* (A.K.A. "Too Far"). Nov. 3, 1988. GS: Bert Kramer, Jim Beaver, John C. Cooke, Don W. Lewis, Robert Harland, Gary Lee. For the children's sake, Ethan hangs up his guns to try ranching, which sits just fine with three new troublemakers in town.

120.3 *Founder's Day.* Nov. 10, 1988. GS: Nicolas Surovy, William Smith, Charles Tyner, Scott Coffee, Julianna McCarthy, Andrew Lowery. Amelia kills a young bank robber, whose family vows revenge.

120.4 *Ghost Dance.* Nov. 24, 1988. GS: Nicolas Surovy, Dennis A. Pratt, Dave Alverson, Mack Dryden, Andrew Prine, Lee de Broux, Lewis Arquette, Charles Tyner. Hanging fever grips Paradise after John Taylor is falsely accused of killing a hotheaded cowboy who had been harassing him.

120.5 *Devil's Canyon.* Dec. 1, 1988. GS: Nicolas Surovy, Martin Bright, Mitch Carter, Ross Harris, Mimi Rose. While Ethan is away tending his disease-threatened livestock, Claire is abducted by a trapper and his son.

120.6 *Stray Bullet.* Dec. 8, 1988. GS: Nicolas Surovy, Sherry Hursey, Stephen Godwin, Robert O'Reilly, Paul Tuerpe, Robert Keith. Amelia's life and the children's future hang in the balance after Ethan is jailed for inadvertently wounding her while firing at a rampaging drunk.

120.7 *The Promise.* Dec. 15, 1988. GS: Ted Hayden, Al Fleming. On their way home for Christmas, Ethan, George and Ben promise a dying woman they will get her newborn son safely to Paradise, but they lose their water and horses before crossing the desert.

120.8 *Childhood's End.* Dec. 29, 1988. GS: Irene Miracle, Milla Jovovich, Larry Hankin, Matthew Faison, V.C. Dupree, Tony Epper. Claire delightedly befriends a girl her age, whose tales of glamorous life mask a seamier existence with her mother's traveling social club.

120.9 *A Private War.* Jan. 5, 1989. GS: Nicolas Surovy, Lewis Arquette, Kenny Lao, Stanley Kamel, Joe Colligan, Christopher Fong. No holds are barred when the mine manager sets out to buy up the town's businesses and recapture two young, indentured runaways.

120.10 *Hard Choices.* Jan. 12, 1989. GS: Tuck Milligan, Dennis Hayden, Robert Keith, John Beck, Julianna McCarthy, Jerry Tullos. A ranger arrives to take Ethan back to Texas to stand trial for a killing Ethan claims was committed in self-defense.

120.11 *Crossroads.* Jan. 26, 1989. GS: Kris Kamm, Stacy Galina, Brad Michael Pickett, Lance Gilbert, Julianna McCarthy, Gay Hagen, Rebecca Balding. After breaking a grocer's window, Joseph lands in jail and falls in with a gang of fugitive teenagers.

120.12 *The Traveler.* Feb. 2, 1989. GS: Hunter Von Leer, Rhoda Gemignani, Terrence Evans, F. William Parker, Julianna McCarthy. Ethan and Amelia befriend a traveler who has lost his memory in a stagecoach accident, but slowly comes to realize that he was hired to kill Ethan.

120.13 *The Secret.* Feb. 8, 1989. GS: Carl Gant, Rebecca Balding, Julianna McCarthy, Candice J. Hincks, Randy Crowder, Kenny Lao, Christopher Fong. Ethan reluctantly turns murder investigator after everyone gratefully assumes that he is the one who gunned down the town bully.

120.14 *A House Divided.* Feb. 16, 1989. GS: Don Stroud, Don Swayze, Royce D. Applegate, Robert Dean, Len Wayland, Eric Lawson. Murderous robbers seize the hotel, shoot one hostage and threaten to kill the rest if their own wounded man isn't saved.

120.15 *The Last Warrior.* Feb. 23, 1989. GS: Nancy Paul, George McDaniel, Chip Heller, Richard Bull, Marshall Bell. John Taylor attempts to stop a lumber company from building a road over land he claims is his.

120.16 *Vengeance.* March 16, 1989. GS: Lance LeGault, Charles Boswell, William Jordan, Marl Balou, Jimmy Burke, Gary Epper. Nothing can dissuade Ethan from seeking out a man he has wanted to kill for twenty years, not even consideration for Claire, who is in love with the man's son.

120.17 *A Matter of Honor* Part One. April 8, 1989. GS: Chuck Connors, Nancy Lenehan, Michael McManus, Chris McDonald, Dennis Patrick, Brooks Gardner, Stephen Lee, James Hardie. A powerful rancher starts a range war over water rights when he hires a notorious gunslinger, Ethan's old saddle pal, who is now a falling-down drunk.

120.18 *A Matter of Honor* Part Two. April 15, 1989. GS: Chuck Connors, Nancy Lenehan, Michael McManus, Chris McDonald, Dennis Patrick, Brooks Gardner, Stephen Lee, James Hardie. After being sobered up by Ethan, gunslinger Gideon McKay turns on him to lead an escalating water-rights war against the small ranchers, which culminates in a showdown.

120.19 *Hour of the Wolf.* April 29, 1989. GS: Randy Crowder, Jonathan Perpich, F. William Parker, James Tartan, Chuck Lindsly, Gay Hagen. After Ethan and Claire are bitten by a wolf that was foaming at the mouth, they can only wait and hope as John Taylor rides to Reno in a desperate effort to obtain medical help.

120.20 *Treasure.* May 6, 1989. GS: Gary Grubbs, Ann Dusenberry, Mark Dornan. Ben and George go into the mountains hunting for the fabled Chinaman's treasure while following a map found on a dead man. They are being followed by the pair who shot him.

120.21 *Squaring Off.* May 13, 1989. GS: John Beck, David Haskell, Barbara Howard, Buck Taylor, Ron Soble, Blake Gibbons, Ginny Wohland, Armand Asselin, William Forward. Ethan rescues from the hangman the Texas ranger who once rescued him, but enrages the police chief who framed the ranger.

120.22 *Long Lost Lawson.* May 20, 1989. GS: Randy Crowder, Ted Shackelford, Charles Frank, Warren Munson, B.J. Turner, Jim Ingersoll, Gay Hagen. Amelia has good reason to suspect the motives of her long-lost husband, a charming scoundrel who is back in town.

Season Two

120.23 *A Gather of Guns.* Sept. 10, 1989. GS: Gene Barry, Jack Elam, Charles Frank, Charles Napier, Hugh O'Brian, John Schneider, Ray Walston, Rawley Valverde, Mark Herrier, Johnny Crawford. Bat Masterson and Wyatt Earp join Pat Garrett for a last crusade to spring Ethan from an infamous prison from which no one has ever escaped.

120.24 *Home Again.* Sept. 16, 1989. GS: Hugh O'Brian, Robert Fuller, Mark Herrier, Summer Thomas, John Maynard Pennell, Richard Lineback. After the great prison escape, Ethan is followed home by Wyatt Earp, and by a reporter who wants to know why.

120.25 *Common Good.* Sept. 23, 1989. GS: Craig Bierko, David Anthony Marshall, F. William Parker, Warren Munson, Craig Stark. Paradise needs a marshal now that a vicious outlaw's gang is preparing to break him out of jail. Ethan is the obvious choice, but he isn't interested, not even if it costs him his ranch.

120.26 *Dead Run.* Oct. 7, 1989. GS: Jonathan Gries, Todd Bryant, Christopher Bradley, Michael McGrady, Robert Dean, Noel Conlon. Five laid-off miners strike gold when they ambush Ethan and Amelia on their way to Virginia City to deposit $50,000.

120.27 *All the Pretty Little Horses.* Oct. 14, 1989. GS: Olivia Brown, Caryn Ward, Michael Champion, H. Richard Greene, Warren Munson, Jane Kean. A woman wages an unrelenting war against the railroad she blames for the loss of her husband, son and farm, regardless of the cost to her and her surviving daughter.

120.28 *Orphan Train.* Oct. 28, 1989. GS: Warren Munson, Cliff Osmond, Dean Hill, Michael John Burns, Crystal McKellar, Edward Penn, David Knell, Jane Kean. Ethan defies the law to help a fugitive orphan who was forcibly, but legally, separated from his sister.

120.29 *The Burial Ground.* Nov. 4, 1989. GS: Geoffrey Lewis, Nick Ramus, Michael Horse, Trent Bross, Ray Oriel, Warren Munson, Spencer Garrett. Former Indian fighter Ethan attempts to forge peace between an old foe on the warpath and an old friend in the cavalry.

120.30 *A Proper Stranger.* Nov. 11, 1989. GS: Crystal Bernard, Macon McCalman, Steve Rankin, Tony Epper, Jimmy Booth. While Ethan keeps watch on the cemetery for a mysterious graverobber, Amelia keeps watch on the children's new live-in teacher, a pretty rival she doesn't know is wanted by the law.

Paradise

120.31 *Boomtown.* Nov. 18, 1989. GS: Randy Crowder, John Shearin, Warren Munson, Gary Lee Davis, Hank H. Woessner, Tom Kendall, Gay Hagen, Tom Reese. A gold strike on Ethan's land is no bonanza. It transforms Paradise into an avaricious boom town.

120.32 *The Return of Johnny Ryan.* Dec. 2, 1989. GS: Craig Bierko, Marc Alaimo, David Hayward, Burke Byrnes, Warren Munson, Alan Stock. Johnny Ryan, the killer whose gang once sprang him from the Paradise jail, makes good on his word to return for revenge on the man who humiliated him, Ethan Cord.

120.33 *The Plague.* Dec. 9, 1989. GS: Nancy Warren, Rebecca Balding, F. William Parker, Louis R. Plante, John Thornton, Christopher Fong. An outbreak of smallpox tests the character of the townsfolk, especially Ethan, when George is stricken.

120.34 *The Gates of Paradise.* Jan. 6, 1990. GS: Jerry Hardin, Patrick Laborteaux, Joseph Campanella, Christian Jacobs, Randy Crowder, Patrick Day, Ronnie Rondell. A black-clad horseman spooks Ethan's horse on a mountain trail, causing Ethan to tumble into a deep abandoned mine. The stranger then rides off, leaving Ethan trapped. Ethan is helped to safety by young Jerome, who accompanies him back to Paradise.

120.35 *Devil's Escort.* Jan. 13, 1990. GS: P.L. Brown, Patrick Dollaghan, R.D. Call, Dave Adams, Daniel Beer, Terry Beaver, Gil Combs. The accused killer Ethan is escorting back to Paradise for trial is a raging bull dead set on killing him, if pursuing vigilantes don't get the man first.

120.36 *Dangerous Cargo.* Jan. 20, 1990. GS: John Beck, Olivia Burnette, Mako, Alex Courtney, Robert Dryer, William Shockley, Bill Saito. Ethan's old friend Matthew Grady persuades him to join in a well-paying but dangerous job — hauling the opium that mine owners use to keep their Chinese workers in a state of virtual enslavement.

120.37 *Till Death Do Us Part.* Feb. 3, 1990. GS: Stacy Galina, Barry Jenner, James Sloyan, Wayne Arrants, Jimmie Booth. Joseph's tomboy friend Frankie returns to Paradise, now elegantly attired and married to a possessive, abusive judge who has the power to extradite Ethan to Texas on a murder warrant.

120.38 *Avenging Angel.* Feb. 10, 1990. GS: Gregg Henry, Gay Hagen. Just about everyone is willing to give a second chance to the new preacher, a paroled murderer who claims he has seen the light. Only Ethan, who testified against him, is an unbeliever.

120.39 *A Gathering of Guns.* Feb. 17, 1990. GS: Chuck Connors, Johnny Crawford, John Lehne, Bibi Besch, Charles Lucia, David Sherrill, Steve Boyum, Norman Howell. The son of Ethan's old pal Gideon volunteers them as guns in a range war.

120.40 *Shadow of a Doubt.* March 3, 1990. GS: Patrick Laborteaux, Randy Crowder, Brian Patrick Clark, Paige Pengra, Ben Rawnsley, Doug Sloan. A jury debates the fate of gentle, slow-witted Jerome, accused of strangling a girl who rejected him.

120.41 *The Coward.* April 7, 1990. GS: Patrick Laborteaux, Matthew Laborteaux, K.T. Oslin, Bruce Newbold, Steven Hovack, Read Morgan, Marcia Solomon. Ethan harbors a young deserter wanted by the Army for cowardice and by a rifle-toting mother who blames him for her son's death.

120.42 *The Chase.* April 14, 1990. GS: Bonnie Burroughs, Gregory Webb. Amelia takes it personally when a con woman sells her on trolleys for the town and then takes everyone for a ride, by looting the place while they are away partying.

120.43 *Dust on the Wind.* April 28, 1990. GS: James Hampton, Rebecca Balding, Keone Young, Don Sparks, F. William Parker, Julianna McCarthy. Ethan and Amelia decide to tie the knot, but a closure of the mine unravels everything, triggering a mass exodus from the town.

Season Three

120.44 *Out of Ashes.* Jan. 4, 1991. GS: Robert Fuller, H. Richard Greene, Bruce Wright, Christopher Crabb, Leah Remini. A new marshal is hired, who is as short on scruples as he is long on greed.

120.45 *The Bounty.* Jan. 11, 1991. GS: H. Richard Green, Aeryk Egan, Patrick Kilpatrick, Tom O'Rourke, Peter Vogt, Joshua Harris, Chuck Sloan, Jan Merlin. In his new role as marshal, Ethan pursues a bank robber who has a price on his head that attracts Dakota as well. Meanwhile, Ben battles bullies, and George dyslexia.

120.46 *The Women.* Jan. 25, 1991. GS: Cathy Podewell, Carol Huston, Jeffrey Josephson, Betsy Randle, Buck Taylor, Billy Ray Sharkey. Ethan and Dakota ride escort for a wagon train of women harassed by outlaws who shot their men and now want their money.

120.47 *Bad Blood.* Feb. 1, 1991. GS: Christopher Curry, Todd Allen, Barbara Rush, Kristen Meadows, Joe Dorsey, Gregory Scott Cummins, Hoke Howell, Ed Hooks. Ethan returns to Texas to settle matters with a powerful matriarch whose son he killed, and who won't rest until Cord has had a proper hanging.

120.48 *The Valley of Death.* Feb. 8, 1991. GS: Susan Diol, Brooks Gardner, F. William Parker, Tom O'Rourke, Julie Payne, Mitch Pileggi. It's high noon for Ethan, whose wedding plans are shot down by outlaws, and who may be gunned down himself by Dakota, in the belief that Ethan killed his father.

120.49 *A Bullet Through the Heart.* Feb. 15, 1991. GS: George DiCenzo, Aeryk Egan, Kim Landkford, Pat Skipper, Joshua Harris, Janet Gunn, Doug Sloan. His hands tied for lack of proof, Ethan is unable to arrest a cold-blooded killer, and even must protect him from a mob.

120.50 *See No Evil.* Feb. 22, 1991. GS: Stephen Burleigh, Brett Porter, Pat Skipper, Richardson Morse, Randy Crowder, Graham Jarvis, Laurence Haddon. Ethan has mixed feelings about a specialist called to Paradise to battle a mysterious epidemic when he also starts courting Amelia.

120.51 *Birthright.* March 8, 1991. GS: Edward Albert, Janet Gunn, Gay Hagen, Dell Yount. The children's father returns. He is a lying, cheating charmer who ran out on their mother but who, she told them, died a hero.

120.52 *A Study in Fear.* March 29, 1991. GS: Janet Gunn, Dell Yount, Jack Kehler, Pat Skipper, Michael J. Pollard, Julie Payne, Lisa Toothman. A serial killer terrorizes the young women of Paradise.

120.53 *The Search for K.C. Cavanaugh.* April 5, 1991. GS: Mary Crosby, David Graf, Dean Smith. Ethan brings in a spunky bank robber, who has served her time but faces the noose for killing a lawman — she says in self-defense.

120.54 *Shield of Gold.* April 12, 1991. GS: Rod Arrants, Will MacMillan, Michael Milhoan, Randy Boffman, Russ McCubbin. John Taylor repossesses a golden shield that was treasured by his people, from a traveling Government exhibition.

120.55 *Twenty-Four Hours.* May 3, 1991. GS: Nicollette Sheridan, Irene Arranga, Maggie Roswell, Aeryk Egan, Louis R. Plante, Greg Collins, Marcia Solomon. This episode recounts twenty-four hours in the hectic life of Marshal Cord.

120.56 *Unfinished Business.* May 10, 1991. GS: Brian Libby, Bob Swain. Reflecting on his years as a family man, Ethan sends the children away before facing the gunman who once left him for dead, and has returned to finish the job.

121. *Pistols 'n' Petticoats*

CBS. 30 min. Broadcast history: Saturday, 8:30–9:00, Sept. 1966–Jan. 1967; Saturday, 9:30–10:00, Jan. 1987–Aug. 1987.

Regular Cast: Ann Sheridan (Henrietta Hanks), Ruth McDevitt (Grandma Hanks), Douglas V. Fowley (Andrew "Grandpa" Hanks), Carole Wells (Lucy Hanks), Gary Vinson (Harold Sikes), Robert Lowery (Buss Courtney), Lon Chaney, Jr. (Chief Eagle Shadow), Marc Cavell (Gray Hawk), Alex Henteloff (Little Bear).

Premise: This Western comedy dealt with the humorous exploits of the fast-drawing Hanks family in the town of Wretched, Colorado, in the 1870s.

The Episodes

121.1 *A Crooked Line.* Sept. 17, 1966. GS: Pat Buttram, Murray MacLeod, Nancy Andrews, Butch Patrick, Walker Edmiston, Jay Ripley, Bill Quinn, Howard Wright, Gail Bonney. Kenny Turner tells the Hanks he doesn't want to become a thief, even though it means breaking a family tradition.

121.2 *No Sale.* Sept. 24, 1966. GS: Morgan Woodward, Stanley Adams, Eleanor Audley, Francine Pyne, Gil Lamb. A ruthless land grabber, backed by hired gunslingers, is buying up the entire town of Wretched, but the Hanks would rather shoot than sell.

121.3 *Title Unknown.* Oct. 1, 1966. GS: Jack Albertson, Julie Parrish, Tina Menard. The Hanks invite Chief Eagle Shadow to tea in an attempt to learn the whereabouts of a lovely Irish colleen, kidnaped years earlier by Indians.

121.4 *Title Unknown.* Oct. 8, 1966. GS: Patrick Horgan, John Wright, Eleanor Audley, Robert Pine, Stanley Adams. The Hanks think that a visiting British poet is a helpless dude, unaware that the smooth-talking gent masterminded an attempted stagecoach robbery.

121.5 *Title Unknown.* Oct. 15, 1966. GS: Jay Silverheels, Willis Bouchey. The Hanks host a peace powwow in hopes of preventing an intertribal war.

121.6 *The Triangle.* Oct. 22, 1966. GS: Charlie Ruggles, Clinton Sundberg, Read Morgan, Joe Quinn. Orville Snip, Grandma's old beau, is on his way to Wretched to marry his supposedly widowed sweetheart.

121.7 *Title Unknown.* Oct. 29, 1966. GS: John Hoyt, Gil Lamb. Wretched's bachelors are up in arms. Their mail order brides have been kidnaped by the scoundrels from Sorry Water.

121.8 *Title Unknown.* Nov. 5, 1966. GS: Beverly Garland, Stacy Harris, Hal Baylor, Richard Reeves, George Taylor. Grandma and Hank unwittingly rent a spare room to a lovely lady bank robber.

121.9 *Title Unknown.* Nov. 12, 1966. GS: Leo Gordon, Simon Scott, Gerald Mohr, G.D. Spradlin, Burt Mustin, Dee Cooper, Foster Hood. Suspected of selling guns to the Indians, Grandma and Hank set out to prove their innocence by becoming hostesses at the saloon headquarters of gunrunner Cyrus Breech.

121.10 *Title Unknown.* Nov. 19, 1966. GS: Grant Woods. Landgrabber Buss Courtney, who is after the Hanks' ranch, is sneak enough to throw the clan in jail. The Hanks will have to be just as sneaky to bust out and foil Courtney's scheme.

121.11 *Title Unknown.* Nov. 26, 1966. The Hanks have trouble keeping peace in the valley when acting chief Gray Hawk announces plans to go on the warpath.

121.12 *Title Unknown.* Dec. 3, 1966. GS: Roy Engel, Don Beddoe, Charles Maxwell, Stuart Margolin, Bruce Watson. The town gets its own wacky version of the gunfight at the OK Corral. Sheriff Sikes, who must face the murderous Blanton boys, is getting help from Wyatt Earp and Doc Holliday, but the aging gunfighters aren't as quick as they used to be.

121.13 *Title Unknown.* Dec. 10, 1966. GS: Lurene Tuttle. The Hanks look for a diplomatic way to get rid of their obnoxious house guest, the prime and patronizing headmistress of Lucy's finishing school.

121.14 *Title Unknown.* Dec 17, 1966. GS: Johnny Haymer, Mickey Simpson, John Mitchum, Frank Wilcox, Robert Buckingham, John Fox. The Hanks are rewarded for a life-saving rescue with the services of a finicky French valet, who is determined to please the hardy frontier family in spite of Grandpa's insults.

121.15 *Title Unknown.* Dec. 24, 1966. GS: Ron Russell, Robert Carraway, Harry Hickox. Bad guy Buss Courtney tells sharpshooter Curly Bigelow that the retired gunslinger Curly wants to gun down is none other than town sheriff Harold Sikes, alias Willie the Kid.

121.16 *Title Unknown.* Dec. 31, 1966. GS: Robert Easton, James McCallion, Eleanor Audley. Grandma is forced into helping a couple of bank robbers, after the outlaws threaten to harm the Hanks' pet wolf Bowser.

121.17 *Title Unknown.* Jan. 7, 1967. GS: Judy Canova, Harry Raybould, Bill Oberlin, Bob Lyons. Grandma doesn't cotton to gun-wielding Daisy, who finds Grandpa's mean disposition mighty attractive.

121.18 *Title Unknown.* Jan. 14, 1967. GS: Lee Bergere, Eleanor Audley. Everyone gets into the act, including the Indians, when a silver-tongued actor arrives in Wretched with a scheme to fleece the local gentry.

121.19 *Title Unknown.* Jan. 21, 1967. GS: Donald "Red" Barry, George Keymas, Jay Silverheels, Phil Arnold, Peter Virgo, Jr. The Hanks have to bail Little Bear out of big trouble. Conniving Buss Courtney has turned the whole town against the honest Injun with a phony charge of cattle rustling.

121.20 *Title Unknown.* Jan. 28, 1967. GS: William Schallert, Ken Mayer, Lou Krugman, William Fawcett. A fortuneteller says that Hank will marry the first man who comes to visit. But the prediction goes haywire with the arrival of a

Bostonian land grabber, a passel of Indians and a gunslinger named Dirty Dan.

121.21 *Title Unknown.* Feb. 4, 1967. GS: Royal Dano, Timothy Scott, Robert Sorrells. Three desperadoes take over the Hanks' ranch and hold Lucy hostage.

121.22 *Title Unknown.* Feb. 11, 1967. GS: Pat Buttram, Judy Canova, Philip Bourneuf. Con man Jake Turner was all set to go straight after a hitch in prison, but he may revert to his old ways when a well-heeled Easterner has come shopping for a gold mine.

121.23 *Title Unknown.* Feb. 18, 1967. GS: Jonathan Daly, Jan Arvan. The Hanks try to make an Indian out of Dr. John Fire String, a true Kiowa brave who studies medicine in Boston. John is so civilized that his tribe won't accept him.

121.24 *Title Unknown.* Feb. 25, 1967. GS: John Doucette, Margaret Lindsey, Ross Elliott, Vinton Hayworth. Hank and Grandma set out to save Sorry Water, a town taken over by outlaws. Grandpa must take over the clean-up job when gunmen capture the women.

121.25 *Title Unknown.* March 3, 1967. GS: Michael Evans. The Hanks are being held prisoner by Rodney's Raiders, a bedraggled company of Confederate soldiers who don't know the Civil War is over and who are planning a raid on Wretched.

121.26 *Title Unknown.* March 11, 1967. GS: Joan Staley, Chubby Johnson, Joe Dougherty, Jan A. Johnston. A look-alike outlaw impersonates the sheriff to set up a robbery. Everyone is fooled by the masquerade, including girlfriend Lucy, who is astounded by the sheriff's new-found boldness.

122. *Pony Express*

Syndicated. 30 min. Broadcast history: Various, Oct. 1959–May 1960.

Regular Cast: Grant Sullivan (Brett Clark), Bill Cord (Tom Clyde), Don Dorell (Donovan).

Premise: This series related the exploits of Pony Express troubleshooter Brett Clark in the West of the 1860s.

The Episodes

122.1 *Wrong Rope.* Oct. 7, 1959. Brett and Donovan are after a couple of mail-robbing brothers.

122.2 *The Deadly Sniper.* Oct. 14, 1959. An Express rider is shot, and before he dies he tells Brett he knows the mysterious marksman's next victim — Brett himself.

122.3 *Justice for Jenny.* Oct. 21, 1959. Brett plays Cupid to a young Express rider and his girl. But he needs the sharp end of his arrow for a sadistic stepfather.

122.4 *The Treaty.* Oct. 28, 1959. A government surveyor has been tortured. Dying, he tells Brett his maps and papers must get to Washington to prevent an Indian massacre.

122.5 *Message rom New Orleans.* Nov. 4, 1959. An Express rider is heir to his grandfather's fortune.

122.6 *The Good Samaritan.* Nov. 11, 1959. GS: Whitney Blake. There is a land-grab plot on Pony Express holdings. The plotter is a beautiful and vicious woman.

122.7 *The Peace Offering.* Nov. 18, 1959. GS: Wesley Lau, Lisa Gaye. The Paiute Indians demand tribute, or they will leave their reservation for an uprising.

122.8 *The Wrong Man.* Nov. 25, 1959. Ex-convict Emmet Saunders has been hired by the Pony Express. When a station is robbed and the stationkeeper killed, Saunders is accused of the crime.

122.9 *The Reluctant Bride.* Dec. 2, 1959. Clark and a lady geologist are captured by an Indian.

122.10 *Lady's Choice.* Dec. 9, 1959. A gang holds the daughter of a Pony Express official for ransom.

122.11 *Token Payment.* Dec. 16, 1959. A rider is lured from the trail by a Gypsy. Then her band kills him and steals from the mail pouches.

122.12 *We Ourselves.* Dec. 23, 1959. Suspected of being an informer, a man wants to get out of town in a hurry.

122.13 *Showdown at Thirty Mile Ridge.* Dec. 30, 1959. GS: Douglas Fowley. A girl hires a gunman to kill a Pony Express stationkeeper she thinks murdered her father.

122.14 *Bandido.* Jan. 6, 1960. A desperado is taken in by stagecoach passengers during an Indian attack.

122.15 *Princess of Crazy Creek.* Jan. 13, 1960. A Japanese princess and her samurai escort are attacked while traveling in a stagecoach.

122.16 *The Theft.* Jan. 20, 1960. GS: Ross Elliott. A theft comes off, but the thief is the victim of a double cross. Then one of the double-crossers is double-crossed.

122.17 *Duel at Devil's Canyon.* Jan. 27, 1960. Brett's job is to convince some Indians that the Express is good medicine.

122.18 *Vendetta.* Feb. 3, 1960. GS: Steve Brodie. The five brothers of Jed Branson, who was wrongly accused and hanged for the murder of a Pony Express rider, wage a war of vengeance on the Express.

122.19 *Mail for a Male.* Feb. 10, 1960. Brett Clark is compelled to stop a stage.

122.20 *The Breadwinner.* Feb. 17, 1960. GS: Jennifer Raine. Posing as a man, teenage Tracy Holland lands a job with the Pony Express. The girl is unaware that her uncle plans to rob the stage on which she is riding.

122.21 *The Golden Circle.* Feb. 24, 1960. GS: Nancy Hadley. Brett Clark and Senator Orion Rivington are passengers aboard a stage, not realizing that Belle Terry, a fellow rider, heads a gang of desperadoes.

122.22 *The Station Keeper's Bride.* March 2, 1960. GS: Bill Cord, Judy Bamber, Donald Murphy. A bride, fed up with frontier life, complicates an attempt to trap two crooks.

122.23 *The Story of Julesburg.* March 9, 1960. GS: James Best, Helen Westcott, Sebastian Cabot. Brett's assistant complains of boredom. He is told the story of his predecessor, a self-appointed lawman who cleaned up the town single-handed.

122.24 *The Pendant.* March 16, 1960. GS: Paul Wexler, Natalie Trundy. A pendant is stolen from a mail pouch by a dim-witted renegade named Big Dipper. When the loot becomes a present to a teenage sweetheart, Brett's plan for its recovery takes a new turn.

122.25 *The Killer.* March 23, 1960. GS: John Lawrence, Mark Allen. Clark is ordered to capture a cold-blooded killer who murdered a Pony Express rider. But he is blocked by an uncooperative marshal and a reward hungry couple.

122.26 *Replacement.* March 30, 1960. GS: Tom Sidell, Bob Anderson. Clark is sent by Pony Express headquarters to fire a division agent who has overstepped his authority.

122.27 *The Last Mile.* April 6, 1960. GS: Madlyn Rhue, Hugh Sanders. Brett Clark is forced to take a stage on its entire run, risking an Indian attack at any moment.

122.28 *Payoff.* April 13, 1960. GS: Douglas Kennedy, Paul Carr, Charles Cane. Two marshals hunt for a criminal. But one, believing the desperado is his son, plans to outwit the other so the boy can have a second chance.

122.29 *Special Delivery.* April 20, 1960. GS: Denver Pyle. An express station keeper gets a ransom note for the return of his wife and children.

122.30 *The Wedding of Big Zack.* April 27, 1960. GS: Richard Wessel. Clark is faced with the task of bringing Big Zack, a professional hunter, to justice.

122.31 *The Renegade.* May 3, 1960. GS: Don Dorrell, Richard Karlan. On the trail of killers and horse thieves, Brett has reason to doubt the loyalty of his new assistant.

122.32 *Trial by Fury.* May 10, 1960. GS: Robert Gist. Brett Clark is confronted by a trio of outlaws who are holding a station-keeper and his wife prisoner.

122.33 *Reclaim.* May, 17, 1960. GS: Don Dorrell. In a plan to get guns, outlaws rife a mail pouch and replace a genuine letter with a fake.

123. The Quest

NBC. 60 min. Broadcast history: Wednesday, 10:00-11:00, Sept. 1976–Dec. 1976.

Regular Cast: Kurt Russell (Morgan Beaudine), Tim Matheson (Quentin Beaudine).

Premise: The two young Beaudine brothers for search their sister, who was captured years earlier by the Cheyenne Indians, in the West during the 1890s.

The Episodes

123.1 *The Captive.* Sept. 22, 1976. GS: Susan Dey, Christopher Connelly, Richard Egan, Russ Tamblyn, Dennis Cole, Royal Dano, Bill Fletcher. The Beaudines rescue a captive white woman from the Indians only to deliver her into an unsympathetic, provincial frontier society.

123.2 *The Buffalo Hunters.* Sept. 29, 1976. GS: Alex Cord, Linda Moon Redfern, John Quade, Ray Young, Lee de Broux, James Griffith, Bob Hoy, Walter Wyatt. The Beaudine brothers are taken captive by a band of ruthless buffalo hunters marked for massacre by a vengeful Indian.

123.3 *Shanklin.* Oct. 13, 1976. GS: Don Meredith, Ned Romero, John Anderson, Eric Server, Armando Silvestre, Mariette Hartley, Phillip Pine, John Steadman. A fanatical Texas Ranger persuades the Beaudines to help him track a bloodthirsty bandit to his sanctuary in Mexico.

123.4 *Day of Outrage.* Oct. 27, 1976. GS: Amanda Blake, Pamela Sue Martin, George Gaynes, James Keach, Don Matheson, Mills Watson, Severn Darden. The Beaudine brothers encounter Miss Sally, who runs a bawdy ranch house where they find shelter during a windstorm. They soon grow attached to the strong-willed woman and involve themselves in her cause of helping ranchers and homesteaders in their fight against corrupt cattle barons.

123.5 *Seventy-Two Hours.* Nov. 3, 1976. GS: Cameron Mitchell, Howard Keel, Aldo Ray, Mitch Vogel, Jacques Aubuchon, Marie-Elena Cordero, Frank Rayn, Patti Jerome. The Beaudines' revel in a lusty cattle town is abruptly halted when a friend is struck down by a stray bullet fired by a drunk.

123.6 *Prairie Woman.* Nov. 10, 1976. GS: Ty Hardin, Laraine Stephens, Jim Davis, Tom Reese, Francine York, Michael Bell. Morgan tracks a killer who knows the whereabouts of their sister, while Quentin ministers to the dying baby of a lonely settler.

123.7 *Welcome to America, Jade Snow.* Nov. 24, 1976. GS: Gary Collins, Jerry Douglas, Irene Yeh-Ling Sun, Jason Wingreen, Richard Loo, Frank Aletter. The Beaudines become involved with a young Chinese girl who has just arrived in the West.

123.8 *The Longest Drive* Part One. Dec. 1, 1976. GS: Dan O'Herlihy, Erik Estrada, Keenan Wynn, John Rubinstein, Woody Strode, Gary Lockwood, Sander Johnson, Cooper Huckabee, Angela May. The Beaudines help a gritty, aging rancher who is having trouble hiring hands for a cattle drive because of his reputation as a jinx.

123.9 *The Longest Drive* Part Two. Dec. 8, 1976. GS: Dan O'Herlihy, Erik Estrada, Keenan Wynn, John Rubinstein, Woody Strode, Gary Lockwood, Sander Johnson, Cooper Huckabee, Angela May. Superstition and harsh elements plague the Beaudines as they drive cattle through the Colorado badlands for a reputedly jinxed trail boss.

123.10 *Portrait of a Gunfighter.* Dec. 22, 1976. GS: Andrew Stevens, John Ireland, Frank Marth, Ivor Francis, Arthur Franz, Robert Phillips, June Whitley Taylor. Quentin begins to regret teaching marksmanship to an orphaned teenager when the youth develops a passion for gunslinging.

123.11 *The Freight Train Rescue.* Dec. 29, 1976. GS: Monte Markham, Jon Cedar, Jack Hogan, Alan Fudge, Bruce M. Fischer, Jack O'Leary, Frank McRae. A gritty group of teamsters drive their mule train 300 miles into primitive territory to rescue a party of bushwhacked surveyors who were left to starve.

124. The Range Rider

Syndicated. 30 min. Broadcast history: Various, Dec. 1950–June 1953.

Regular Cast: Jock Mahoney (the Range Rider), Dick Jones (Dick West).

Premise: The Range Rider and his young sidekick, Dick West, defend justice during the pioneering years of the Old West.

The Episodes

124.1 *Six Gun Party.* Dec. 28, 1950. GS: Elaine Riley, Earle Hodgins, Denver Pyle, Dick Curtis, Wes Hudman, Al Wyatt. The Range Rider and his young sidekick Dick West run up against an unscrupulous rancher who will stop at nothing to gain possession of a neighboring spread.

124.2 *The Secret Lode.* Dec. 28, 1950. GS: Anne Nagel, Tommy Ivo, Leonard Penn, Harry Cheshire, Bill Kennedy, Gregg Barton, Frank Matts. The Range Rider and Dick West help a married couple when their young son is kidnapped by

The Range Rider

outlaws who demand as ransom the gold the parents discovered on their homesetead.

124.3 *The Range Rider.* Dec. 28, 1950. GS: Anne Nagel, Leonard Penn, Kenneth MacDonald, Bill Kennedy, Harry Cheshire, Gregg Barton, Frank Matts. The Range Rider and Dick West try to save a man unjustly accused of manslaughter from a life of crime.

124.4 *Stage to Rainbow's End.* Dec. 28, 1950. GS: Jim Bannon, Raymond Hatton, Eve Miller, Kenne Duncan, Tom Monroe, Bob Woodward. The Range Rider and Dick West come to the aid of a young woman stageline owner whose crooked partner's schemes have forced her to drive her coaches herself.

124.5 *Gunslinger in Paradise.* Feb. 19, 1951. GS: Elaine Riley, Dick Curtis, Jerry Hunter, Earle Hodgins, Denver Pyle, Al Wyatt. The murder of the O'Neals and the attempted abduction of their eleven-year-old son, Denny, reveal a plot to gain an inheritance.

124.6 *Right of Way.* Feb. 19, 1951. GS: Margaret Field, Dick Curtis, Kenne Duncan, Denver Pyle, Robert Wilke, Wes Hudman. Range Rider and his pal come to the aid of Beth Harper, when she unwillingly decides to sell the Bar-H.

124.7 *The Crooked Fork.* Feb. 19, 1951. GS: Raymond Hatton, Eve Miller, Jim Bannon, Kenne Duncan, Tom Monroe. A sheriff and his daughter, who are looking for raiders of a freight line, mistake the Range Rider and Dick for the outlaws.

124.8 *Gun Point.* Feb. 19, 1951. The Range Rider and Dick West go after the outlaws who stole gold ore from the Preston mine and left a young summer visitor unconscious in the shaft as part of a scheme to salt a worthless claim.

124.9 *The Baron of Broken Bow.* Feb. 1, 1951. GS: Leonard Penn, Patricia Michon, Hal K. Dawson, Don C. Harvey, Frank Hagney, Jack Ingram, Tom London, Wes Hudman. The Range Rider and Dick West find themselves opposing Dick's father, cattleman Lance West, when his attempts to drive the sheepmen out of Cedar Valley lead to murder.

124.10 *Western Fugitive.* March 8, 1951. GS: Margaret Field, Dick Curtis, Denver Pyle, Kenne Duncan, Harry Mackin, Robert Wilke. When a gunman who held him up is killed, the Range Rider takes the dead man's place in order to infiltrate the gang the gunman was about to join and to solve the mystery behind a murder and a forged ranch deed.

124.11 *Bad Medicine.* March 8, 1951. GS: Alan Hale, Jr., Edgar Dearing, Marshall Reed, Francis McDonald, Bob Woodward. After stopping a group of renegades in the act of rustling horses, Range Rider discovers that the outlaws have just killed a bank teller.

124.12 *Pack Rat.* March 8, 1951. GS: Alan Hale, Jr., J. Farrell MacDonald, Stanley Andrews, Edgar Dearing, Marshall Reed, Francis McDonald. When Ben Brown is suspected of the murder of Joe Harris, a pack rat helps the Range Rider discover the real criminal.

124.13 *The Grand Fleece.* March 8, 1951. GS: Steve Clark, Jonathan Hale, Wanda McKay, Richard Powers, Harry Harvey, Sr., Riley Hill, Fred Graham, Al Wyatt. When Range Rider and Dick West spot a group of masked and robed men entering an isolated cabin, Range Rider joins the group.

124.14 *The Flying Arrow.* April 8, 1951. GS: Mary Young, James Griffith, Douglas Evans, Dick Alexander, Alan Bridge. When a man is found murdered by an arrow, the Range Rider and Dick West search for his partner, an expert archer who has disappeared.

124.15 *The Hawk.* April 8, 1951. GS: Louise Lorimer, Barbara Ann Knudson, Denver Pyle, Gregg Barton, Tom London, John Cliff, Bill Hale. After an express office is robbed and the agent murdered, the Range Rider and Dick West help the local sheriff track down the outlaw known as the Hawk who has been terrorizing the town.

124.16 *Dead Man's Shoes.* April 8, 1951. GS: Louise Lorimer, Sherry Jackson, Denver Pyle, Gregg Barton, Tom London, Francis McDonald, John Cliff, Bill Hale. The Range Rider and Dick West stop a runaway wagon and find inside a dying man who asks them to deliver the map to his gold mine to his niece. A word code between a youngster and her uncle reveals the location of the hidden gold mine.

124.17 *The Golden Peso.* April 8, 1951. GS: Wanda McKay, Jonathan Hale, Harry Harvey, Sr., Steve Clark, Riley Hill, Fred Graham, Al Wyatt. The town assayer is suspicious of the first sample of ore he takes from Dick's mine. When he returns for a secret sample, he is shot. The Range Rider is charged with the murder, which is connected with a salted-mine scheme.

124.18 *Hidden Gold.* June 25, 1951. GS: Douglas Evans, Dick Alexander, Alan Bridge. A group of outlaws force Range Rider to lead them to a supposedly fabulous mine.

124.19 *Diablo Pass.* June 25, 1951. GS: Joan Baxter, Alan Hale, Jr., William Fawcett, Stanley Andrews, Leonard Penn, Pat O'Malley, Kenne Duncan. When a wagon belonging to Jim Harris and his daughter is stolen by outlaws, the Range Rider and Dick West take up the trail and learn that the revamped wagon was later purchased by another settler.

124.20 *Last of the Pony Express.* Aug. 6, 1951. GS: William Fawcett, Alan Hale, Jr., Stanley Andrews, Leonard Penn, Pat O'Malley, Kenne Duncan. The Range Rider finally succeeds in reconciling the advocates of the pony express and those of the stage line.

124.21 *Marked for Death.* Aug. 6, 1951. GS: Harry Lauter, Jim Bannon, Stanley Andrews, Alan Bridge. Piney Baker, owner of the adjoining ranch, accuses Verne Underhill of the murder of his foreman because the two were seen quarreling. Although Range Rider is instrumental in bringing Verne into custody, he does so only to keep him safe until he has a chance to clear him.

124.22 *Ten Thousand Reward.* Aug. 6, 1951. GS: Alan Hale, Jr., Harry Lauter, Steve Conte, Jim Bannon, Dennis Moore, Alan Bridge, John Cason. When the Apache Kid is turned in by one of his own gang, Range Rider and Dick West ride to the scene of the supposed capture and come to the conclusion that the Kid's captor is lying.

124.23 *Indian Sign.* Aug. 6, 1951. GS: Elaine Riley, Minerva Urecal, John Doucette, Edgar Dearing, House Peters, Jr., Kenneth MacDonald. The Range Rider and Dick West pursue a gunman who has murdered an Indian chief in his quest for a rug in which a valuable message is hidden.

124.24 *False Trail.* Aug. 6, 1951. GS: Elaine Riley, John Doucette, Edgar Dearing, House Peters, Jr., Kenneth MacDonald. While helping a friend's daughter, who with her fiance claims to be fleeing from outlaws, the Range Rider and Dick West find themselves trapped by a sheriff's posse.

124.25 *The Ghost of Poco Loco.* Aug. 6, 1951. GS:

Donna Martell, Gloria Winters, Dick Curtis, James Griffith, Robert Peyton, John Cliff, Bud Osborne, Al Wyatt, Earle Duane. By pretending she is the Ghost of Poco Loco, a young Spanish girl conducts an underground railroad for outlaws, until the Range Rider interferes with her plans.

124.26 *Harsh Reckoning.* Sept. 10, 1951. GS: Donna Martell, Dick Curtis, James Griffith, Robert Peyton, John Cliff, Bud Osborne, Al Wyatt, Earle Duane. The Range Rider and his pal come upon two men, one a rancher, the other a squatter, who have apparently shot each other to death in a quarrell. He uncovers a malicious plot to obtain possession of oil properties.

Season Two

124.27 *Sealed Justice.* Nov. 29, 1951. GS: Barbara Stanley, Marshall Reed, Terry Frost, Chief Yowlachie, Steve Clark, Pat O'Malley, Kermit Maynard, Al Wyatt. Range Rider and Dick West answer a call for help from a sheriff who is murdered before their arrival. The last words the sheriff spoke were the names of the friends that were coming to help him, but the townspeople believed them to be the names of his killers.

124.28 *Marked Bullets.* Nov. 29, 1951. GS: Christine McIntyre, Don C. Harvey, Harry Cheshire, George DeNormand, Edmund Cobb, Al Wyatt. A gunman masquerades as a respectable citizen while he plans to rob a bank. After the robbery, Range Rider tracks the criminal to a deserted island and retrieves the loot buried there. Later Range Rider must reveals to Dick West that his uncle is mixed up in the bank robbery.

124.29 *The Fatal Bullet.* Dec. 28, 1951. GS: James Griffith, Lois Hall, Mike Ragan, John Parrish, Edgar Dearing, Mickey Simpson, Tom London, Sandy Sanders. An ex-convict and lawyer kills an erstwhile blackmailer and frames his client, rancher Jim Harrison, for the murder. A few days before his execution, Harrison's daughter discovers the bullet used in the murder and saves her father from being hanged.

124.30 *Dim Trail.* Dec. 28, 1951. GS: William Fawcett, Harry Lauter, House Peters, Jr., Rand Brooks, Mickey Simpson, Wade Crosby. The Range Rider pretends to turn outlaw and stages a fight with Dick West in order to win the confidence of a gang of counterfeiters who have killed a government courier and stolen the currency plates he was carrying.

124.31 *Red Jack.* Dec. 28, 1951. GS: Christine McIntyre, Don C. Harvey, Harry Cheshire, Steve Clark, George De Normand, Edmund Cobb, Stanley Blystone, Al Wyatt. When a red jack playing card is left at the scenes of several murders, the townspeople blame a redheaded ex-convict named Jack and are about to lynch him when the Range Rider and Dick West step in and try to prove he has been framed.

124.32 *Gunman's Game.* Dec. 28, 1951. GS: Barbara Stanley, Ruth Robinson, Terry Frost, Marshall Reed, Kermit Maynard, Al Wyatt. Dick West has sent a picture of Range Rider to a young girl he has been writing to. Unknown to him, escaped convicts are using the girl's ranch for a hideout.

124.33 *Big Medicine Man.* Dec. 28, 1951. GS: Sandra Valles, Denver Pyle, Chief Yowlachie, Ewing Mitchell, Alan Bridge, Duke York. Range Rider comes to the aid of the Navajo Indians and destroys a professional hideout for gunmen in an area where the Indians gather colored sand for their ceremonies.

124.34 *Blind Trail.* Jan. 24, 1952. GS: Lois Hall, James Griffith, John Parrish, Mike Ragan, Edgar Dearing, Tom London, Mickey Simpson, Sandy Sanders. Near the town of Sunrise, Range Rider and his saddle-pal rescue young Judy Harper from thugs in the employ of Starky Shaw, the town's crooked mayor.

124.35 *Rustler's Range.* Jan. 24, 1952. GS: Ruth Brady, Sandra Valles, Denver Pyle, Ewing Mitchell, Duke York, Alan Bridge, Al Wyatt. A murdered wrangler and an unconscious little girl lying on a lonely trail involve the Range Rider and his sidekick, Dick West, in a baffling horse-rustling mystery.

124.36 *Shotgun Stage.* Jan. 24, 1952. GS: Elaine Riley, William Fawcett, Harry Lauter, Rand Brooks, House Peters, Jr., Mickey Simpson. To gain the transportation monopoly, a stageline operator kidnaps the man who has inherited the line. Range Rider thwarts a kidnaper, exposes an imposter and saves the Shotgun Stage.

124.37 *Blind Canyon.* Jan. 31, 1952. GS: Gloria Winters, B.G. Norman, Pierre Watkin, Stanley Blystone, William Haade, Marshall Reed, Frank Jaquet, Red Morgan. A courageous blind boy regains his sight and helps the Range Rider to capture a diabolical outlaw and his brutal gang.

124.38 *Trail of the Lawless.* Dec. 23, 1951. The Range Rider's twin brother is faced with the choice of helping his outlaw friends or saving his brother's life when the Range Rider is hired to recover stolen money.

124.39 *Fight Town.* Jan. 31, 1952. GS: James Griffith, Darryl Hickman, Lois Hall, Mike Ragan, Mickey Simpson, Sandy Sanders, Bob Woodward. When ange Rider and Dick West ride into Fight Town, they discover a crooked fight promoter planning to rob the townspeople by first losing a little money to them in a set-up fight and then holding a fixed rematch to recoup.

124.40 *Secret of the Red Raven.* Feb 12, 1952. GS: Sherry Jackson, Denver Pyle, Steve Clark, Ewing Mitchell, Gregg Barton, Kermit Maynard, Robert Wilke. The Range Rider and Dick West interrupt a holdup and chase the masked bandit to a cabin where the outlaw kills another man and tricks the Range Rider into believing he is the murderer himself.

124.41 *Pale Horse.* Feb. 12, 1952. GS: Jane Frazee, Phyllis Coates, Don C. Harvey, Duke York, Edmund Cobb, Red Morgan. While trying to solve a killing and track down a gang of Border smugglers, the Range Rider and Dick run afoul of an ancient Indian legend and curse.

124.42 *Jimmy the Kid.* Feb 12, 1952. GS: Wendy Waldron, Denver Pyle, Steve Clark, Gregg Barton, Kermit Maynard, Ewing Mitchell, Robert Wilke, Boyd Stockman. Dick West's resemblance to a stagecoach robber forces the Range Rider into a dangerous adventure in order to track down the real culprit and prove Dick's innocence.

124.43 *The Bandit Stallion.* Feb. 18, 1952. GS: Gloria Winters, Pierre Watkin, B.G. Norman, William Haade, Marshall Reed, Red Morgan, Molly Bee. While the Range Rider is judging horses at a stock show, a wild stallion trained by bandits breaks into the exhibition area so that his owners can escape with two stolen horses in the confusion. The Range Rider and Dick West track the human thieves and their equine accomplice to a barn.

124.44 *Renegade Ranch.* Feb. 18, 1952. GS: Wendy Waldron, Patricia Michon, Steve Clark, Gregg Barton, Ewing

Mitchell, Don Mahin, Red Morgan. Strange tracks left at the scene of a brutal killing set the Range Rider and Dick West on the trail of a gunman who uses soft-nosed bullets and help them save a young woman's ranch from the murderer.

124.45 *Outlaw Masquerade.* Feb. 18, 1952. GS: Steve Clark, Patric Mitchell, Christine McIntyre, Gregg Barton, Robert Wilke, Kermit Maynard, Red Morgan, Boyd Stockman. While trailing a gang of outlaws wearing Halloween masks, the Range Rider and Dick West discover a runaway boy who helps them rescue a man the gang caught spying on them.

124.46 *Law of the Frontier.* March 3, 1952. GS: Lois Hall, Dub Taylor, Harry Lauter, Stanley Andrews, George J. Lewis, Ewing Mitchell, Mickey Simpson. After the mysterious deaths of three judges in a lawless frontier town, Range Rider poses as a judge to investigate the crimes.

124.47 *Let 'er Buck.* March 3, 1952. GS: Lois Hall, Harry Lauter, George J. Lewis, Dub Taylor, Ewing Mitchell, Mickey Simpson, Rush Williams. U.S. Marshal Glenn Allen is trailing recent robberies that seem to follow a Wild West show, so the Range Rider joins the show to get the evidence needed.

124.48 *Gold Fever.* March 3, 1952. GS: Lois Hall, Louise Lorimer, Harry Lauter, Ewing Mitchell, Stanley Andrews, Dub Taylor, George J. Lewis, Mickey Simpson, Rush Williams. The Range Rider and Dick West search for a prospector who was captured on his way to register a claim and is being pistolwhipped by the vicious woman owner of a halfway house to make him turn over his map.

124.49 *Silver Blade.* March 26, 1952. GS: Francis McDonald, Charlita, George J. Lewis, Myron Healey, Earle Hodgins, Gregg Barton, Dick Alexander, Stuart Whitman. The Range Rider and his partner, Dick West, trailing an outlaw named Silver Blade, receive an urgent call for help from a friend who has been ambushed by the outlaw after receiving a warning from him.

124.50 *Romeo Goes West.* March 26, 1952. GS: Eilene Janssen, Myron Healey, Earle Hodgins, George J. Lewis, Mickey Little, Gregg Barton, Dick Alexander, Francis McDonald. On the outskirts of a ghost town, the Range Rider and Dick West meet a traveling troupe of Shakespearean actors and borrow their costumes in order to trap some outlaws.

124.51 *Peace Pipe.* March 26, 1952. GS: Paul Fierro, Monte Blue, James Kirkwood, Gloria Saunders, Louis Lettieri, Robert Wilke, Mike Ragan, Henry Rowland, Frank Jaquet. When a young Navajo doctor returns to practice medicine among his people, the Range Rider and Dick West help him fight the gunmen who are trying to force the Indians off their tribal land.

124.52 *Border Trouble.* March 26, 1952. GS: Gloria Saunders, Muriel Landers, Henry Rowland, Mike Ragan, Robert Wilke, Paul Fierro, Red Morgan. The Range Rider and Dick West fidn a murdered trapper, follow hoofprints from the corpse to an old barn, and join forces with the Canadian Mounties to trap the outlaws responsible.

Season Three

124.53 *Greed Rides the Range.* Nov. 13, 1952. GS: Gail Davis, Stanley Andrews, Kenneth MacDonald, Lee Van Cleef, Kenne Duncan, Keith Richards, Riley Hill, Fred Krone. The Range Rider and his saddle pal smash a gold-mining feud and save a town from total ruin.

124.54 *Gold Hill.* Nov. 13, 1952. GS: John Hamilton, Myron Healey, William Fawcett, Gloria Talbott, Eula Morgan, David Coleman, Edward Coch, Sandy Sanders. A clergyman receives letters threatening his life if he doesn't sell his land. A group of broken vases, the handiwork of Laurette, a Mexican beauty, help th reverend and the Range Rider discover why the land is so valuable.

124.55 *Outlaw's Double.* Nov. 13, 1952. GS: Gail Davis, Keith Richards, Stanley Andrews, Lee Van Cleef, Kenneth MacDonald, Kenne Duncan, Bob Woodward, Fred Krone. An outlaw holds up Range Rider, steals his clothes adn leaves him for dead. Range Rider is mistaken for the outlaw.

124.56 *Feud at Friendship City.* Dec. 16, 1952. GS: John Hamilton, Myron Healey, William Fawcett, Bob Woodward, Lee Phelps, Steve Clark, Tom London, Sandy Sanders. When Range Rider and Dick West ride into a cattle town, they find themselves in the midst of a war between ranchers.

124.57 *The Secret of Superstition Peak.* Dec. 16, 1952. GS: Pamela Blake, Cecil Elliott, Tom Monroe, Lyle Talbot, Lane Chandler, Francis McDonald, Steve Clark. Range Rider and his pal Dick West ride down the deserted street of a ghost town. They have no idea they are headed into an adventure in which a lovely girl, a missing man and a hidden treasure are intermingled with an incomplete map, a ghost cougar, an eerie blue flame and a whistling pile of rocks on Superstition Peak, the bleak mountain that frowns over the town.

124.58 *Ambush in Coyote Canyon.* Dec. 16, 1952. GS: Clayton Moore, Harry Lauter, Nan Leslie, Lane Chandler, Judd Holdren, Fred Krone, Rocky Shahan. When Clay Matthews, a secret agent for Wells Fargo, is injured on his way to investigate gold thefts, he asks Range Rider to take his place.

124.59 *Indian War Party.* Jan. 29, 1953. GS: Rodd Redwing, Gloria Saunders, Glenn Strange, Denver Pyle, Gregg Barton, Pierce Lyden. A tribe of Indians goes on the warpath because a new land survey excludes an area rich in copper ore from their reservation. Range Rider becomes a blood-brother of the tribe and discovers the Indians covet the land because it is the burial grounds of a sacred ancestral chief.

124.60 *The Badmen of Rimrock.* Jan. 29, 1953. GS: Jim Bannon, Gloria Barton, Stanley Andrews, Gloria Eaton, Minerva Urecal, Mickey Simpson. An eccentric old man, who owns most of the land on which Rimrock is built, is killed by gamblers. When the old man's sister, a rawboned old spinster, arrives to take over the property, an attempt is made on her life.

124.61 *The Saga of Silver Town.* Jan. 29, 1953. GS: Nan Leslie, Gloria Saunders, Harry Lauter, Clayton Moore, William Fawcett, Lane Chandler, John Phillips, Judd Holdren, Edward Colmans. An organized gang is driving a silver-maker out of business by stealing his shipments of bullion. The Range Rider and Dick West help out the silversmith.

124.62 *Cherokee Round-Up.* Feb. 2, 1953. GS: Gloria Saunders, Glenn Strange, William Fawcett, Denver Pyle, Rodd Redwing, Gregg Barton, Pierce Lyden. An Indian agent holds a trial at which a Cherokee chief is convicted as a horse thief and sentenced to hang. The chief's son captures the Range Rider and threatens to kill him if the chief isn't released.

124.63 *The Treasure of Santa Dolores.* Feb. 2, 1953.

GS: Laurette Luez, Lee Van Cleef, Sheb Wooley, Charles Stevens, Erville Alderson, Rush Williams. When two bandits break out of jail, one shoots the other for the possession of a treasure map. After some vicious battles the Range Rider discovers the treasure in plain sight.

124.64 *The Holy Terror.* Feb. 20, 1953. GS: Stanley Andrews, Peter Votrian, Steve Darrell, Alan Bridge, John Pickard, Paul McGuire, Fred Krone. A kidnaper poses as a dumb camp cook for the young man he plans to kidnap. Range Rider and Dick West become involved in the case when they visit the boy's camp just before he is kidnaped.

124.65 *Border City Affair.* March 16, 1953. GS: Myron Healey, Jean Willes, Fred Krone, John Doucette, Brad Johnson. When an outlaw is discovered posing as a murdered sheriff, Range Rider and Dick West are framed for the killing.

124.66 *The Black Terror.* March 16, 1953. GS: Jim Bannon, Regina Gleason, I. Stanford Jolley, Jeanne Bates, Ella Ethridge, B.G. Norman, Lee Phelps, Ewing Mitchell, Emil Sitka. As Range Rider and Dick ride into town to visit the sheriff, a man is killed and his slayer escapes. Range Rider learns that this was one in a series of recent murders, committed for no apparent reason.

124.67 *Marshal from Madero.* April 17, 1953. GS: Margaret Field, Harry Lauter, Stanley Andrews, Terry Frost, Gregg Barton, Bob Woodward. The Range Rider and Dick West use a clever ruse to capture an outlaw gang, and their leader disguises himself to free his men.

124.68 *Bullets and Badmen.* April 17, 1953. GS: John Doucette, Brad Johnson, Ella Ethridge, Myron Healey, Alan Bridge, Steve Clark. The Range Rider and Dick West try to rescue the town doctor, who has been kidnapped by an outlaw gang with a wounded leader.

124.69 *West of Cheyenne.* April 17, 1953. GS: Pamela Blake, Tom Monroe, Lyle Talbot, House Peters, Jr., William Haade, John Phillips, William Bailey, Harold Farren, Boyd Stockman. While helping to complete a telegraph line, the Range Rider and Dick West are held up by a gang of masked men who are determined to stop the line from being finished.

124.70 *Western Edition.* May 21, 1953. GS: Elizabeth Harrower, Lyle Talbot, Annie Carroll, George Meader, Sam Flint, Tom Monroe, Marshall Reed, Francis McDonald. During a flurry of gunfire following his wedding, a newspaper editor is killed. The Range Rider and Dick West agree to help the young widow.

124.71 *Convict at Large.* May 21, 1953. GS: Margaret Field, Harry Lauter, Stanley Andrews, Terry Frost, House Peters, Jr., Kenneth MacDonald, Gregg Barton, Ewing Mitchell, Bob Woodward, Fred Krone. When a stagecoach guard who had served a prison sentence is suspected of helping a former cellmate pull a holdup, the Range Rider and Dick West risk their lives to clear the man.

124.72 *Hideout.* May 21, 1953. GS: Regina Gleason, Jim Bannon, I. Stanford Jolley, Ewing Mitchell, Bud Osborne, Fred Krone. The Range Rider has to rescue Dick West when his young sidekick's infatuation with a beautiful adventuress makes him the unwitting tool of a robber gang.

124.73 *The Buckskin.* May 21, 1953. GS: Pamela Blake, Tom Monroe, William Haade, Lyle Talbot, Lonnie Burr, John Phillips, Fred Krone. When the Range Rider's horse is stolen by three Cavalry soldiers, he and his buddy go to the fort to protest, only to learn that the thieves are bogus soldiers who are using Army clothes.

124.74 *The Chase.* May 21, 1953. GS: Karen Sharpe, Stanley Andrews, Steve Darrell, Alan Bridge, Paul McGuire, Fred Krone. A beautiful and clever woman, adept at disguising herself, almost prevents Range Rider from capturing an outlaw gang.

124.75 *Old Timer's Trail.* June 12, 1953. GS: Elaine Riley, Stanley Andrews, Sheb Wooley, Erville Alderson, Rush Williams, Charles Stevens, Dee Cooper. While pursuing the Diamond Hitch gang, the Range Rider and Dick West meet hotel owner Owen Barth, who claims to be a victim of amnesia, and help him regain his memory while chasing the outlaws.

124.76 *Two-Fisted Justice.* June 12, 1953. GS: Sheb Wooley, Kathleen Case, Stanley Andrews, George J. Lewis, Francis McDonald, Richard Avonde, Sam Flint, George DeNormand, Robert Brunner, Bob Woodward. The Range Rider and Dick West try to help some ranchers who have been illegally evicted from their land by the owner of a railroad.

124.77 *Outlaw Territory.* June 12, 1953. GS: Jim Bannon, Minerva Urecal, Stanley Andrews, Richard Emory, Brad Johnson, Mickey Simpson, Gregg Barton, Edward Coch, Fred Krone. The Range Rider and Dick West help a woman trading post owner against outlaws who oppose her call for a referendum to annex certain lands into the state of Texas.

124.78 *Outlaw Pistols.* June 12, 1953. GS: Sheb Wooley, George J. Lewis, Stanley Andrews, Kathleen Case, John McKee, Bob Woodward, George DeNormand, Jack Ingram, Boyd Stockman. A packing company hires Range Rider and Dick West to investigate the murder and robbery of three cattle buyers, and to capture a notorious bandit. After the bandit's capture, he escapes and sets out to get revenge on Range Rider.

125. Rango

ABC. 30 min. Friday, 9:00-9:30, Jan. 1967–Sept. 1967.

Regular Cast: Tim Conway (Rango), Norman Alden (Captain Horton), Guy Marks (Pink Cloud).

Premise: This comedy Western depicted the misadventures of a bumbling Texas Ranger who finds ways of getting into trouble at the Deep Wells Ranger Station, supposedly the quietest station in the state.

The Episodes

125.1 *Rango the Outlaw.* Jan. 13, 1967. GS: Ned Romero, Ted DeCorsia, John Cliff, Herbie Faye, Michael Carr. The Texas Rangers plan to trap Butch Durham and his gang by staging an ambush at the bank in Gopher Gulch. To insure the scheme's success, the Rangers must get Rango out of the way, so they send him on a mission to Plainview. Unfortunately, that is where the Durham gang really is.

125.2 *The Daring Holdup of the Deadwood Stage.* Jan. 20, 1967. GS: Parley Baer, Leo Gordon, Kent Taylor, Roxanne Arlen, Troy Melton, Ernie Anderson. Ranger Rango plays a wild hunch while investigating the daring robbery of the Deadwood Stage.

125.3 *The Town Tamer.* Jan. 27, 1967. GS: Paul Richards, Robert Strauss. It appears that bumbling Rango has tamed an outlaw town. But brawling bandits are just waiting for the right moment to steal a big gold shipment.

125.4 *Gunfight at the K.O. Saloon.* Feb. 3, 1967. GS: Joan Staley, Howard Caine, Dabbs Greer. Confusion reigns when Captain Horton uses Rango's resemblance to a debonair thief to locate hidden loot.

125.5 *The Spy Who Was Out Cold.* Feb. 10, 1967. GS: Paul Mantee, John Harmon. Rango tries out the latest detective methods to bust up a gang of gunrunners. The fumbling Ranger comes up with two prime suspects — Captain Horton and a Government undercover agent.

125.6 *What's a Nice Girl Like You Doing Holding Up a Place Like This?* Feb. 17, 1967. GS: Carolyn Jones, Richard Deacon, Peter Leeds, Ruben Moreno, Michael Carr. Rango blithely believes that a lovely lady robber is the governor's daughter, and he is helping her to case the town bank.

125.7 *Requiem for a Ranger.* Feb. 24, 1967. GS: Billy DeWolfe, Larry Pennell, Larry D. Mann. Rango plays dead in an attempt to smoke out the varmint who made off with a gold shipment worth $25,000.

125.8 *Diamonds Look Better Around Your Neck Than a Rope.* March 3, 1967. GS: Mike Mazurki, Linda Foster. It is a case of law and disorder when Rango tries to unravel a jewel robbery and murder.

125.9 *My Teepee Runneth Over.* March 10, 1967. GS: Jesse White, Michael Pate, Walter Sande, Grace Lee Whitney, Bill Foster. Rango becomes a peddler of pots and pans as he tries to find and rescue Pink Cloud, who has been captured by decidedly unfriendly Indians.

125.10 *The Not So Great Train Robbery.* March 17, 1967. GS: Myrna Fahey, William Mims. Rango's troubles get rolling when he boards a train with his lady prisoner and mistakes a disguised Captain Horton for one of the girl's cohorts.

125.11 *Viva Rango.* March 24, 1967. GS: Vito Scotti, Toian Matchinga. A little white lie leads to big trouble when a lovesick Rango is ordered to guard his girl friend's jewels They don't exist, but some bandits think they do.

125.12 *It Ain't the Principle, It's the Money.* March 31, 1967. GS: Robert J. Wilke, Henry Beckman, Don Wilbanks, Tol Avery. Rango and Pink Cloud infiltrate a robbery gang by pretending to be a notorious outlaw and his sinister sidekick.

125.13 *Shootout at Mesa Flats.* April 7, 1967. GS: Lane Bradford, Jonathan Hole. A wounded Captain Horton has only one man's help as he guards a notorious outlaw. Unfortunately, Rango is the man.

125.14 *In a Little Mexican Town.* April 14, 1967. GS: Don Haggerty, Mike de Anda, Rodolfo Hoyos, Pedro Gonzalez Gonzalez. One blunder leads to another as Rango and Pink Cloud go south of the border to capture an elusive Mexican bandit.

125.15 *If You Can't Take It with You, Don't Go.* April 21, 1967. GS: Tom Stern, Martin West, Herbie Faye, Barry Kelley, Don Gazzaniga. Rango triumphs, briefly, by jailing two robbers. But he may not be smiling for long. The prisoners are secretly tunneling through the cell to a safe next door.

125.16 *You Can't Scalp a Bald Indian.* April 28, 1967. GS: Anthony Caruso, Muriel Landers. Rango masquerades as an Indian to capture Chief Angry Bear. Once inside the Indian camp, Rango can't get out when Angry Bear's daughter wants to marry him.

125.17 *The Rustlers.* May 5, 1967. GS: Ellen Corby, Walter Burke. Rango stumbles through a series of setbacks to prove that a family of sheepherders are really rustlers.

126. Rawhide

CBS. 60 min. Broadcast history: Friday, 8:00–9:00, Jan. 1959–April 1959; Friday, 7:30–8:30, May 1959–Sept. 1963; Thursday, 8:00–9:00, Sept. 1963–Sept. 1964; Friday, 7:30–8:30, Sept. 1964–Sept. 1965; Tuesday, 7:30–8:30, Sept. 1965–Jan. 1966.

Regular Cast: Eric Fleming (Gil Favor) 59–65, Clint Eastwood (Rowdy Yates), Jim Murdock (Mushy) 59–65, Paul Brinegar (Wishbone), Steve Raines (Quince), Rocky Shahan (Joe Scarlett) 59–65, Sheb Wooley (Pete Nolan) 61–65, Robert Cabal (Hey Soos) 62–65, John Ireland (Jed Colby) 65–66, David Watson (Ian Cabot) 65–66, Raymond St. Jacques (Simon Blake) 65–66.

Premise: This western series depicted the exploits of a cattle drive from San Antonio, Texas, to Sedalia, Kansas, in the 1880s.

The Episodes

126.1 *Incident of the Tumbleweed Wagon.* Jan. 9, 1959. GS: Terry Moore, Tom Conway, Frank Wilcox, John War Eagle, Val Dufour, John Larch, Bob Steele, David Whorf, Maurice Manson. During a cattle drive, Gil Favor and Rowdy Yates make camp with a marshal and his deputy who are escorting prisoners to trial. The prisoners fail in an escape attempt but kill the lawmen, leaving Gil and Rowdy the responsibility of taking them to trial.

126.2 *Incident at Alabaster Plain.* Jan. 16, 1959. GS: Suzanne Lloyd, Mark Richman, Martin Balsam, Troy Donahue, Joe DeSantis, Peter Mamakos, Myron Healey. Stopping at a mission during their cattle drive, Gil Favor, Rowdy Yates and the cowhands are invited to attend a wedding. The wedding celebration turns into a brutal showdown when the bride's brother, an outlaw, arrives.

126.3 *Incident with an Executioner.* Jan. 23, 1959. GS: Dan Duryea, Marguerite Chapman, Jan Shepard, Martin Milner, Stafford Repp, James Drury, William Schallert, Glenn Gordon. Driving their cattle North, Gil Favor and Rowdy Yates come upon a stagecoach accident. The two men soon learn that the stagecoach passengers are living in fear of one man, a gunman who has not as yet revealed his victim.

126.4 *Incident of the Widowed Dove.* Jan. 30, 1959. GS: Sally Forrest, Jay C. Flippen, Harry Lauter, Harry Shannon, Vic Perrin, Fred Graham, Harry Harvey, Sr., Dick Ryan, Henry Wills. Deciding that his cowhands need a day of relaxation, Gil Favor stops his cattle drive in a small trail town. While there, Rowdy Yates becomes involved with a dance-hall girl and a gun-happy marshal.

126.5 *Incident on the Edge of Madness.* Feb. 6, 1959. GS: Lon Chaney, Jr., Marie Windsor, Alan Marshall, Ralph Reed, Duane Grey, Fay Roope, George Hickman, Jester Hairston. Driving their cattle north from Texas, Gil Favor and Rowdy Yates are deserted by their cowhands, who are still bitter about the Civil War. A Southern aristocrat has persuaded the men to leave the cattle drive and help him set up a new Confederate empire. Attempting to get their men back, Gil and Rowdy learn that a woman is behind this movement.

126.6 *Incident of the Power and the Plow.* Feb. 13, 1959. GS: Brian Donlevy, Michael Pate, Dick Van Patten, Rudolfo Acosta, Jack Williams, Malcolm Atterbury, Jeanne Bates, Carol Thurston, Robert Gist, Sandy Kenyon. While driving their cattle North, Gil Favor and Rowdy Yates run afoul of a cattle baron.

126.7 *Incident at Barker Springs.* Feb. 20, 1959. GS: Paul Richards, June Lockhart, Richard Gilden, DeForest Kelley, Bill Hale. While the drive is passing through Barker Springs, one of Gil Favor's trail hands suddenly leaves the drive. Soon afterward he is found shot to death. His brother, who has joined the drive, vows to avenge his death.

126.8 *Incident West of Lano.* Feb. 27, 1959. GS: Martha Hyer, Abby Dalton, Nancy Hadley, Jacqueline Mayo, Robert H. Harris, James Anderson, Ron Soble, K.L. Smith. Gil Favor and the men of his cattle drive come across four sisters taking refuge in their broken-down show wagon. Gil promises the young ladies protection until they reach safe territory.

126.9 *Incident of the Town in Terror.* March 6, 1959. GS: Margaret O'Brien, Harry Townes, Don Harvey, Pat O'Moore, Russ Conway, Kem Dibbs, Dan White, James Gavin, Gary Walberg. Some of Gil Favor's cattle are stricken with a fatal disease. Gil seeks help in a nearby town, but the townspeople turn him away because his sidekick Rowdy Yates also has contracted the disease. Only one person, the pharmacist's daughter, tries to help him.

126.10 *Incident of the Golden Calf.* March 13, 1959. GS: Macdonald Carey, John Pickard, Charles Gray, Richard Shannon, Chuck Roberson, Clem Fuller. Gil Favor runs up against a rival trail boss who is plotting to take over Gil's herd of cattle.

126.11 *Incident of the Coyote Weed.* March 20, 1959. GS: Rick Jason, Buzz Martin, Jorge Moreno, Gary Walberg. Trail boss Gil Favor and his ramrod Rowdy Yates find their cowhands and cattle threatened by a gang of outlaws.

126.12 *Incident at Chubasco.* April 3, 1959. GS: George Brent, John Ericson, Olive Sturgess, Noah Beery, Jr., Stacy Harris. Sally Devereaux leaves her tyrannical husband and, with another man, seeks protection in Gil Favor's cattle drive. When Sally's husband demands that she return home, Gil refuses to turn her away.

126.13 *Incident of the Curious Street.* April 10, 1959. GS: Mercedes, McCambridge, James Westerfield, Whitney Blake, Dennis Cross, Ralph Moody. Searching for some stray cattle, Gil Favor and Rowdy Yates come upon a woman and her daughter who are being held by outlaws in an abandoned town.

126.14 *Incident of the Dog Days.* April 17, 1959. GS: Don Dubbins, Addison Richards, John Vivyan, Ross Elliott, R.G. Armstrong, Craig Dean, Milan Smith, Hal Roth. Gil Favor risks his herd and his reputation as he attempts to take his cattle drive across dry plains. Soon thirst and the pressure of the drive begin to tell on the trail hands.

126.15 *Incident of the Calico Gun.* April 24, 1959. GS: Gloria Talbott, Myron Healey, Steve Mitchell, Jack Lord, Gene Collins, Damian O'Flynn. A burning cabin confronts Gil Favor and his trail hands as they are taking a herd to market. They manage to rescue a pretty girl, the only survivor of the fire, but a short while later they are caught and held captive by three outlaws.

126.16 *Incident of the Misplaced Indians.* May 1, 1959. GS: Kim Hunter, Lyle Talbot, Virginia Gregg, Richard Hale, Robert Carson, Milan Smith, Rodd Redwing. Outside a cabin there are a slew of Indian corpses, inside, sits an unruffled young woman with no explanation.

126.17 *Incident of Fear in the Streets.* May 8, 1959. GS: Gary Merrill, Robert Driscoll, Corey Allen, Guy Stockwell, Ed Faulkner, Morris Ankrum, Don Haggerty, Eleanor Ayer, Ed Nelson, Olan Soule, Bob Steele, Amzie Strickland, Len Hendry. When Pete Nolan is injured by a steer, Gil Favor and Rowdy Yates ride to a nearby town for a doctor. Once in town, however, they are forced to join the townspeople as the prisoners of Jed Mason and his sons.

126.18 *Incident Below the Brazos.* May 15, 1959. GS: Leslie Nielsen, Martin Landau, Kathleen Crowley, Irene Tedrow, William Joyce, John Craven, Alan Reynolds. Trail boss Gil Favor and Rowdy Yates are driving their cattle through Paradise Valley. They are confronted by a group of armed farmers who tell the cattlemen to stay off their land.

126.19 *Incident of the Dry Drive.* May 22, 1959. GS: Victor Jory, Jean Inness, Ron Hagerthy, Chris Alcaide, Paula Winslowe. On a drive across a dry range, the herd is endangered by a lack of water. Gil Favor finds a plentiful water supply on Jess Hode's property, but the embittered man refuses to let the cattle drink.

126.20 *Incident of the Judas Trap.* June 5, 1959. GS: Nina Foch, Phyllis Coates, Jane Nigh, Gerald Mohr, Hugh Sanders, John Bleifer, Larry Thor, Paul McGuire, Rush Williams, Rick Arnold, Milan Smith. When their cattle drive is attacked by wolves, trail boss Gil Favor, Rowdy Yates, and their hands turn to rancher Madrina Wilcox for help.

126.21 *Incident in No Man's Land.* June 12, 1959. GS: Brian Keith, Phyllis Avery, Reed Hadley, Adam Williams, Mary Beth Hughes, Don Megowan, Dee J. Thompson, Shirley Knight, Ron Foster, Larry J. Blake. Gil Favor and Rowdy Yates leave the cattle drive to find the source of explosions that threaten to stampede their cattle. They come upon a settlement inhabited by the wives and girl friends of convicts who are working with dynamite in a nearby prison.

126.22 *Incident of a Burst of Evil.* June 26, 1959. GS: Linda Cristal, Elisha Cook, Jr., H.M. Wynant, Charles Bateman, Eve McVeagh, Russ Bender, Kenneth MacDonald, Ralph Votrian, Jean Tatum, Dick Nelson. The trail hands bring in a wild-looking man who has been prowling near camp. The man tells of his escape from the Comancheros who he says intend to attack the cattle drive.

126.23 *Incident of the Roman Candles.* July 10, 1959. GS: Beverly Garland, Richard Eyer, Bill Henry, Gerald Milton, Zon Murray, David McMahon, Will Wright, Robert Ellenstein, Robert Griffin, William Tannen, Don Wilbanks. Trail boss Gil favor, Rowdy Yates and scout Pete Nolan come across young Davey Colby wandering alone on the prairie, carrying Roman candles. They is unaware that the boy is attempting to save his father's life from ambush.

Season Two

126.24 *Incident of the Day of the Dead.* Sept. 18, 1959.

GS: Viveca Lindfors, Alexander Scourby, Nancy Hadley, Ron Soble, Carlos Romero, Claire Carleton, William Fawcett, Helen Westcott, Alex Montoya, Connie Buck, Maurice Jara, Julian Rivero. In town to pick up the mail for the members of the cattle drive, Rowdy Yates stops a runaway horse. Rancher Luisa Hadley, who watched Rowdy's act of heroism, tries to lure him to her ranch to work with a difficult horse.

126.25 *Incident at Dangerfield Dip.* Oct. 2, 1959. GS: Phillip Pine, Douglas Kennedy, Alan Baxter, Bert Remsen, Pitt Herbert, Gregg Barton, Dorothy Morris. Gil Favor and the other members of the cattle drive are startled by the arrival at their camp of a woman who has been critically wounded. She dies, and the mystery deepens when Gil and Rowdy Yates come across her baby. Later, rounding up some stray cattle, the encounter a cowboy who claims to be the baby's father.

126.26 *Incident of the Shambling Man.* Oct. 9, 1959. GS: Victor McLaglen, Anne Francis, Gene Nelson, Robert Lowery, Harry Carey, Jr., Earle Hodgins, Robert Karnes, Ed Faulkner, Stephen Joyce, Pamela Duncan. Harry Wittman, a retired bare-knuckle fighter, is tormented by his ruthless daughter-in-law, who want to rid herself of the burden of caring for him. She schemes to have him declared insane and goads him to violence. Gill Favor and Rowdy Yates become innocently involved in her scheme.

126.27 *Incident at Jacob's Well.* Oct. 16, 1959. GS: David Brian, Patricia Medina, Jean Allison, Henry Rowland, Mason Curry, Kathleen O'Malley, Dean Williams. When trail boss Gil Favor tells drought-stricken farmers he can't spare them any horses to help them, a farmwife devises a plan to steal the horses.

126.28 *Incident of the Thirteenth Man.* Oct. 23, 1959. GS: Edward C. Platt, Richard Shannon, Paul Fix, Jerome Cowan, Robert Anderson, Grant Richards, Terry Becker, Robert Cornthwaite, Russell Thorson, Mike Ragan, Harry Antrim, Iron Eyes Cody, John Hart, Charles Tannen. Rowdy and Wishbone ride into the town of Blanton so that Wishbone can see a dentist. The sheriff insists that the strangers serve on the jury in a murder trial. Talking with the other jurors, Rowdy and Wishbone learn that the trial is fixed.

126.29 *Incident at the Buffalo Smokehouse.* Oct. 30, 1959. GS: Vera Miles, Leif Erickson, Gene Evans, Allison Hayes, John Agar, J. Pat O'Malley, Karl Swenson, Lane Bradford, Dean Stanton, Harry Swoger, Jack Weston. Looking for a good place for the herd to cross the river, Gil Favor stops to get information from Mr. and Mrs. Jeremiah Walsh. Then outlaw Wes Thomas and his gang ride up and take the three of them hostage.

126.30 *Incident of the Haunted Hills.* Nov. 6, 1959. GS: John Barrymore, Jr., Kent Smith, Strother Martin, Charles Gray, Marya Stevens, Clarke Gordon, Harry Lauter, Ron Hayes, Glenn Strange, Moody Blanchard. When the need for water arises, Tasunka, an Indian with the cattle drive, knows where to find some—in hostile Indian country.

126.31 *Incident of the Stalking Death.* Nov. 13, 1959. GS: Cesar Romero, Mari Blanchard, Regis Toomey, Martin Garralaga, Scott Davey, Marilyn Winston, Doug Wilson. Gil Favor and Rowdy Yates come upon a dead steer that was killed by a wild puma. Gil succeeds in wounding the wild animal, but is injured in his attempt to kill it. Then the enraged beast kills Margarita Colinas' young son and Gil and Rowdy go on a puma hunt.

126.32 *Incident of the Valley in Shadow.* Nov. 20, 1959. GS: Rick Jason, Fay Spain, Leo Gordon, Arthur Batanides. Gil Favor hires bounty hunters as extra hands on the drive. As they travel through Indian country, the bounty hunters ask the cowboys to help look for a white girl who they say is being held by the Indians.

126.33 *Incident of the Blue Fire.* Dec. 11, 1959. GS: Skip Homeier, Joe de Santis, Eddie Little Sky. The threat of an electric storm has made the cattle uneasy and the weird, superstitious stories told by a wrangler have upset the cowhands. Then Lucky Markley rides up and one of the stories begins to come true.

126.34 *Incident at Spanish Rock.* Dec. 18, 1959. GS: Elena Verdugo, Jacques Aubuchon, Pepe Hern, Frank DeKova, Wolfe Barzell, Roberto Contreras, Jorge Moreno, Vincent Padula. Gil Favor and Rowdy Yates encounter a troop of Mexican soldiers, who demand custody of Frank Volaro, one of the cowhands. The soldiers claim that Volaro is the son of a revolutionary leader.

126.35 *Incident of the Druid's Curse.* Jan. 8, 1960. GS: Luana Patten, Byron Foulger, Claude Akins, Stanley Adams, Don Keefer. Along the trail Gil Favor encounters an archaeologist and his niece looking for ruins of an ancient civilization. Later, outlaws capture the pair.

126.36 *Incident at Red River Station.* Jan. 15, 1960. GS: James Dunn, Robert F. Simon, Stanley Clements, William Tannen, Peter Adams, Frances Morris, Glen Gordon, Earle Hodgins, Kim Hector. Dr. Solomon Flood wants to keep a few cases of smallpox from turning into an epidemic by giving vaccinations. He meets opposition from a brutal man named Junkin. When Junkin learns that Gil Favor has been exposed to the disease, he forces Gil to stay in a room with smallpox victims.

126.37 *Incident of the Devil and His Due.* Jan. 22, 1960. GS: Neville Brand, John Pickard, Louis Jean Heydt, Sheila Bromley, James Griffith, Ralph Reed, Tudor Owen, Fred E. Sherman, Peter Mamakos, Ken Mayer, Hank Worden, Barbara Morrison, Lindsay Workman. Looking for a way to see his cattle drive around a landslide, Gil Favor finds a murdered man in a farmhouse. The cattleman is charged with the killing.

126.38 *Incident of the Wanted Painter.* Jan. 29, 1960. GS: Steve Brodie, Arthur Franz, Robert Lowery, Dennis Cross, Charles Maxwell, Frank Wolfe, Rex Holman, Norman Winston. Along the trail, Gil Favor and his men find an artist badly wounded. The man tells them his attackers attempted to steal a sketch of a town. Later, Favor learns that his commanding officer during the Civil War is awaiting execution in the town depicted in the sketch.

126.39 *Incident at Tinker's Dam.* Feb. 5, 1960. GS: Anthony Dexter, Regis Toomey, Monte Blue, Ron Soble, Robert Chadwick, Russ Conklin, Jeanne Bates, Ray Montgomery, Herbert Patterson. T.J. Wishbone, twin brother of the cattle drive's cook, is chased by Indians and is wounded just as he reaches the drive camp. To confuse T.J.'s pursuers, the cowboys hold a mock funeral.

126.40 *Incident of the Night Horse.* Feb. 19, 1960. GS: George D. Wallace, Judy Nugent, Madeline Holmes. Gil Favor and Rowdy Yates find some of their cattle caught in mustang traps. Jed Carst, intent on catching a certain wild stallion, has covered the area with the traps and refuses to let the cattle pass through.

126.41 *Incident of the Sharpshooter.* Feb. 26, 1960. GS: Jock Mahoney, Hugh Sanders, Stafford Repp, Raymond Greenleaf, Harry Ellerbe, Norman Leavitt, Olan Soule, Morgan Jones, Kenne Duncan, Fred Lerner, Terry Loomis. As Gil and Rowdy approach the town of Prairie Springs with the cattle drive, they meet an outlaw posing as a respectable lawyer. Later, a murder is committed in town and Rowdy is the prime suspect.

126.42 *Incident of the Dust Flower.* March 4, 1960. GS: Margaret Phillips, Arthur Shields, Tom Drake, Frances Bavier, Doreen Lang, Len Hendry, Don Happy. Heading West, an Easterner and his spinster daughter meet with an accident. Aided by Pet Nolan and friends, they go on. Complications occur when the girl mysteriously disappears.

126.43 *Incident at Sulphur Creek.* March 11, 1960. GS: John Dehner, Jan Shepard, Charles Aidman, Ross Ford, Howard Wendell, Duane Grey, James Gavin, Joe Vitale, K.L. Smith, X Brands. Horse thieves go to work on Gil Favor and his men. The huge herd is at a standstill while Pete Nolan scouts for new steeds.

126.44 *Incident of the Champagne Bottles.* March 18, 1960. GS: Hugh Marlowe, Patricia Barry, Lane Bradford, John Hart. The cattle drive is still moving. On the road, too, is an innocent-looking wagon, loaded with nitroglycerin. Gil and Rowdy's boys are keeping their distance.

126.45 *Incident of the Stargazer.* April 1, 1960. GS: Buddy Ebsen, Dorothy Green, Richard Webb, Marya Stevens, Kelton Garwood, Ted De Corsia, Jonathan Hole, Tom Fadden, Clem Fuller. Nolan escorts an astronomer's wife back home to an observatory in the midst of a desolate plain. They're greeted by an Indian maid and a man who claims he's the astronomer.

126.46 *Incident of the Dancing Death.* April 8, 1960. GS: Kipp Hamilton, Mabel Albertson, Anthony Caruso, Paul Picerni, Warren Oates, Michael Mark. A stolen horse reappears, with the body of a Gypsy prince. The Gypsies accuse the drovers of murder.

126.47 *Incident of the Arana Sacar.* April 22, 1960. GS: Cloris Leachman, Chris Alcaide, Russell Arms, Charles Fredericks. The drovers encounter an aptly named Pagan who talks them into heading en masse for the liquid refreshments at a nearby trading post. When Gil and Rowdy return, the herd has disappeared.

126.48 *Incident of the Deserter.* April 29, 1960. GS: Sheila Bromley, William Tannen, Michael Granger, Bob Steele, Walter Burke, Rush Williams, Bob Steele. Whiskery Wishbone is tired of all the jokes about his cooking. He leaves the cattle drive in a huff—for romance and a restaurant of his own.

126.49 *Incident of the One Hundred Amulets.* May 6, 1960. GS: Argentina Brunetti, R.G. Armstrong, Whit Bissell, Vaughn Taylor, Pat Michon, Richard Reeves, Ed Nelson, Carol Seflinger, Alex Montoya, Virginia Christine, Peter Whitney. Wrangler Hey Soos rides into town to buy some groceries for his mother, and is stoned by frightened and superstitious townsfolk. They think his mother is bewitched.

126.50 *Incident of the Murder Steer.* May 13, 1960. GS: James Franciscus, Whitney Blake, Howard Petrie, Paul Lukather, Stephen Joyce, Robert Jordan. A rash of mysterious killings all have on thing in common. A steer with the word "murder" branded on it appears after each death.

126.51 *Incident of the Music Maker.* May 20, 1960. GS: Lili Kardell, Werner Klemperer, Peter Whitney, Robert Boon, Jerry Barclay, Norman Winston, John Duran, X Brands. Gunsmith Anton Zwahlen, traveling with his family by wagon, devises a plan to rustle part of the herd from the cattle drive. His plans call for tampering with the drover's guns.

126.52 *Incident of the Silent Web.* June 3, 1960. GS: Don Haggerty, Reba Waters, William Thourlby, Charles Maxwell, Paul Langton, Carlos Romero, Joseph Patridge, Stephen Ellsworth, John War Eagle. An escaped convict comes upon a burned-out encampment and the sole survivor, a little girl, who's been struck dumb by fear. Posing as her father, he asks for the cattle drive's protection.

126.53 *Incident of the Last Chance.* June 10, 1960. GS: John Kerr, Roxane Berard, John Marley, Kathryn Card, Jon Lormer, Dick Elliott, William D. Gordon, Hank Patterson, Bob Hopkins. A pair of Eastern newlyweds join the cattle drive after a flash flood carries away their wagon. The groom is a mild-mannered dude, until his bride runs into some drunken Indians.

126.54 *Incident in the Garden of Eden.* June 17, 1960. GS: John Ireland, Debra Paget, Robert Coote, John Hoyt, J. Pat O'Malley, Pat O'Moore, Gregory Walcott, Adrienne Marden, Charles Davis, John Cole. Rowdy Yates is sent to buy some cattle. He finds some, owned by Englishman Sir Richard Ashley, but learns they are not for sale. Then he meets Sir Richard's daughter, who promises to work out a deal.

Season Three

126.55 *Incident at Rojo Canyon.* Sept. 30, 1960. GS: Julie London, Bobby Troup, Frank Maxwell, John Pickard, Stanley Clements, Bill Wellman, Jr., Robert Easton, Nelson Welch, Len Hendry, Linden Chiles. Singer Anne Danders and her accompanist Nelson Hoyt join up with the cattle drive. They're trying to trace Anne's father, but they can find only his burned-out farmhouse.

126.56 *Incident of the Challenge.* Oct. 14, 1960. GS: Lyle Bettger, Michael Pate, Ann Robinson, Ann Doran, Orville Sherman, John Hart, Vici Raaf, Harry Ellerbe. Mitla, a Mexican peasant, saves Gil Favor from a ravaging dust storm. Grateful, Favor joins Mitla in his search for Julia Garcia, a girl who is said to have mystic powers over poverty and death.

126.57 *Incident at Dragoon Crossing.* Oct. 21, 1960. GS: Dan O'Herlihy, Ralph Thomas, Garry Walberg, Duane Grey, John Irwin. Favor gets sick and asks John Cord to take over. But Yates resents the new leader and suspected he is tied up with an outlaw gang that's trying to collect a toll at a river crossing.

126.58 *Incident of the Night Visitor.* Nov. 4, 1960. GS: Dane Clark, Tommy Nolan, Harold J. Stone, John Irwin, Mark Nolan. Joey Gardner creeps into the drovers' camp one night, but runs away when Jeff Barkley sees him. When Jeff gives chase, Joey nicks him with a wild gun-shot.

126.59 *Incident of the Slavemaster.* Nov. 11, 1960. GS: Peter Lorre, John Agar, Lisa Gaye, Theodore Newton, Ernest Sarracino, K.T. Stevens, Roy Glenn, James Gavin, Andy Albin. Favor and Nolan are off the trail scouting for water. They stumble across a man named Somers, who tells them an incredible tale. He and a group of his former Union Army buddies have been held as slaves for eight years.

126.60 *Incident on the Road to Yesterday.* Nov. 18,

Rawhide

1960. GS: Frankie Laine, Chester Morris, Robert Gist, Nan Grey, King Calder, Stephen Joyce, Shirley O'Hara, Charles Tannen, Connie Buck. Ralph Bartlet stole some money when he was a youth, and now he is trying to repay his victims, one of whom was Gil Favor. The drovers escort Bartlet to the town where he is to make further restitution, and where he is wanted for robbery and murder.

126.61 *Incident at Superstition Prairie.* Dec. 2, 1960. GS: Rodolfo Acosta, Michael Pate, Carlos Romero, Connie Buck. Wishbone stumbles across a secret Comanche burial ground. He is mighty surprised to find that someone there is still alive, an old brave named Sankeno.

126.62 *Incident at Poco Tiempo.* Dec. 9, 1960. GS: Gigi Perreau, Agnes Moorehead, Stewart Bradley, Carolyn Hughes, Gregory Walcott, Frank Puglia, Lew Gallo, Ken Mayer, Allen Nixon, Henry Wills. Rowdy and Quince lose their mounts in a landslide. While looking for replacements, they are accused of murdering a priest, and are put on a stagecoach with two nuns who seem to know something about him.

126.63 *Incident of the Captive.* Dec. 16, 1960. GS: Mercedes McCambridge, Albert Salmi, Joe De Santis, Dan Sheridan, Robert Driscoll, Kathryn Card, Vic Perrin, Hank Worden, Bud Osborne, Russ Bender, Allen Jaffe. Martha Mushgrove, Mushy's mother, has arrived at camp. She wants her son to quit as Cook's helper and come home to take over her late husband's barber shop.

126.64 *Incident of the Buffalo Soldier.* Jan. 1, 1961. GS: Woody Strode, Ray Montgomery, Roy Glenn, Rupert Crosse, Charles Stevens. Rowdy and Quince are met on the trail by Cpl. Gabe Washington who has been sent to help them hurry a small drive of cattle to an Army post. The cattle are meant as a peace offering to the Indians, but the Redskins also meet them on the trail, and want their beef right now.

126.65 *Incident of the Broken Word.* Jan. 20, 1961. GS: E.G. Marshall, Dick York, Gloria Talbott, Morris Ankrum, Ross Elliott, Howard Petrie, Frank Gerstle, John Hart, Don Diamond. Ben Foley approaches Gil Favor and arranges to sell his cattle. What he doesn't tell Gil is that the herd is infected with anthrax.

126.66 *Incident at the Top of the World.* Jan. 27, 1961. GS: Robert Culp, Jan Sheppard, Les Tremayne, Paul Carr, Ronald Foster, Bill Cutler. A story threatens the drive, and Favor decides to put on an extra hand. He hires Craig Kern, unaware that the man has just been released from an Army hospital where he was convalescing from an emotional disturbance.

126.67 *Incident Near the Promised Land.* Feb. 3, 1961. GS: Mary Astor, Hugh Sanders, Stafford Repp, Frank Wilcox, John Harmon, Bert Remsen, Michael Ford. The drive reaches the market at Sedalia, Missouri, but Favor learns that a panic has knocked the bottom out of cattle prices. The only thing to do is to scout up some grazing land and wait out the decline, and Emma Cardwell just happens to have a nice grassy pasture available.

126.68 *Incident of the Big Blowout.* Feb. 10, 1961. GS: Mari Blanchard, Myron Healey, Hugh Sanders, John Alvin, Len Hendry, Bert Remsen, Charles Tannen, Dabbs Greer, Frank Cady. The drovers are celebrating the end of the cattle drive at Sedalia, but the celebration is disrupted when Rowdy is attacked by a bounty hunter and forced to shoot him.

126.69 *Incident of the Fish Out of the Water.* Feb. 17, 1961. GS: Dorothy Green, Candy Moore, Barbara Beaird, George D. Wallace, Jock Gaynor, Fred Graham, Max Mellinger. In Philadelphia to visit his two young daughters, Favor decides to retire as cattle boss and help his sister-in-law Eleanor Bradley raise the children. This brings Wishbone and Pete to the city in an attempt to make him reconsider.

126.70 *Incident on the Road Back.* Feb. 24, 1961. GS: Gene Evans, Jeanne Cooper, Arch Johnson, Adrienne Hayes, Brian Hutton, Mark Tapscott, Lane Bradford, Dick Elliott, Len Hendry. Favor is rounding up his crew of drovers for the trek back to Texas. Then he is arrested for horse theft, and the money from the cattle sale is confiscated by the sheriff.

126.71 *Incident of the New Start.* March 3, 1961. GS: John Dehner, Burt Douglas, Jan Harrison, William Erwin, John Hart, Robert Bice, Robert B. Williams, Henry Wills, Bill Cutler, Jack Perkins. In San Antonio it is time to begin a new drive to Sedalia, but the Cattlemen's Association names Jubal Wade as trail boss, putting Favor second in command. Just before the start the trek, Favor receives a letter from the Association explaining his new duties.

126.72 *Incident of the Running Iron.* March 10, 1961. GS: Darryl Hickman, Frank Wilcox, William Schallert, Kenneth MacDonald, Addison Richards, John Litel, William Foster. Quince is chasing a cattle rustler when a posse, out on the same mission, mistakes him for the thief. Taken back to town, he is sentenced to be hanged.

126.73 *Incident Near Gloomy River.* March 17, 1961. GS: John Cassavetes, Leif Erickson, John Ericson, Rosemary DeCamp, Anne Helm. Dan Fletcher and his crew drive their herd to a normally full-running stream, and find only a dry riverbed. Dan decides to investigate.

126.74 *Incident of the Boomerang.* March 24, 1961. GS: James Drury, Patricia Medina, Woody Strode, Michael Pate, Frank DeKova, Charles Stevens. Gil and Pete run into a rancher named Goffage and his fiancee Ruthanne Harper. The drovers try to warn them that they are right in the middle of Indian territory, but they are not impressed, until they get a visit from Chief Tawyawp and his braves.

126.75 *Incident of His Brother's Keeper.* March 31, 1961. GS: Jack Lord, Susan Oliver, Jeff Richards, Viola Harris, Alan Reynolds, Norman Leavitt, Fenton G. Jones. Invalid rancher Paul Evans thinks his good-looking wife Laurie should go out and have some fun. When the couple meet Pete and Wishbone at the cattle market, Evans prods Pete into taking his wife to a local dance.

126.76 *Incident in the Middle of Nowhere.* April 7, 1961. GS: Cecil Kellaway, Fay Spain, George Keymas, X Brands, Olan Soule, Elisha Cook, Jr., Charles Fredericks, James Griffith, Ralph Smiley. Gil and Rowdy are scouring the prairie in search of water for the herd. They halt in disbelief at the sight which greets them—a ballet troupe, in full performance.

126.77 *Incident of the Phantom Burglar.* April 14, 1961. GS: Jock Mahoney, Vaughn Taylor, Kathie Browne, Hardie Albright, Ken Mayer, Richard Wolf, Jr., Bill Cutter. Problems abound for Favor and Yates. First, they can't find the mysterious bugler whose nocturnal trumpeting is unnerving the drovers. Then they meet more trouble at a river crossing—an outlaw band demands a toll charge.

126.78 *Incident of the Lost Idol.* April 28, 1961. GS:

Claude Akins, Jean Engstrom, Doug Lambert, K.L. Smith, Ted de Corsia, David McMahon, Ken Curtis. The drovers happen upon Mrs. Manson and her children in the desert, and they realize that the woman is dying. Favor and his men make plans to take care of the youngsters, only to learn that their outlaw father has just escaped from prison.

126.79 *Incident of the Running Man.* May 5, 1961. GS: Lloyd Corrigan, Robert J. Wilke, Donald "Red" Barry, Robert Donner, Luana Anders, Walter Coy, Peter Mamakos, Peter Adams, Russ Conway, Lew Brown, James Anderson, Gregg Martel, Terry Frost, Reg Parton. Yates is accosted by a frenzied figure who caps his tale of an outlaw attempt to commandeer a nearby Army camp by handcuffing himself to Yates. Events take a further turn for the bizarre when the man is shot by pursuing killers.

126.80 *Incident of the Painted Lady.* May 12, 1961. GS: Marie Windsor, David Brian, Ed Nelson, Raymond Guth, Herbert Patterson, Paul Barselow, Harry Lauter, Ted Stanhope, Byron Morrow. The drive is stopped in Kansas by a sheriff, George Harms, accompanied by a grim posse. Harms tells Favor the local citizens have been cheated by another Texas drover named Thad Clemens, and Favor must make up for their loss or have his cattle impounded.

126.81 *Incident Before Black Pass.* May 19, 1961. GS: Zachary Scott, Robert Armstrong, Cathy Downs, Joan Taylor, Arthur Batanides, Leonard Nimoy, Dennis Cross, Robert Sampson, Reg Parton. Nolan and Yates have fallen into the hand of the warlike Kiowa Indians, and the Army tells Favor there is still a chance of rescuing them. But a newly arrived drover named Gypsy tells them it is not in the cards. He says the two men are dead.

126.82 *Incident of the Blackstorms.* May 26,1961. GS: Stephen McNally, Robert Crawford, Jr., Bern Hoffman, Virginia Christine, Dee Pollack, Harry Shannon, Milton Parsons, Anthony Dexter, Richard Reeves, Val Avery. Young Danny Blackstorm lives quietly in River City with his Aunt, Ada Covey, and doesn't know he is the son of notorious outlaw Sky Blackstorm. Then Sky captures Mushy and sends him to River City with a message. He wants his son, and is coming to get him.

126.83 *Incident of the Night on the Town.* June 2, 1961. GS: Harry Townes, James Drury, Maggie Hayes, Don Haggerty, Anne Whitfield, Ralph Dumke, Norman Leavitt, Grady Sutton, Ralph Smiley, Allan Nixon. The cattle drive is halted by a lawyer named Lewis Lewis who intends to take Favor into court. Lewis' client, a Mrs. North, claims that a large number of the drive's cattle belong to her.

126.84 *Incident of the Wager on Payday.* June 16, 1961. GS: Stephen Joyce, Ford Rainey, Ken Mayer, Charley Watts, Lurene Tuttle, Mark Tapscott, Percy Helton, Kathie Brown, Hank Patterson, Jonathan Hole, Dick Ryan, Larry Kent, Henry Wills. Sidney Porter, son of the town's bank president, thinks it would be a good joke to hold up his father's bank. But it seems that Sidney's accomplice, Joe Stapp, is in the scheme for more than laughs.

Season Four

126.85 *Incident at Rio Salado.* Sept. 29, 1961. GS: Tom Tully, Edward Andrews, Carlos Romero, Alex Montoya, John Pickard, Jan Arvan, Bert Remsen, Michael Davis, Tyler McVey, Penny Santon, Len Hendry. Rowdy and Hey Soos arrive at Rio Salado where the drovers are gathering to start another drive. As they take a breather in the local saloon, Rowdy and his friends hear a belligerent old trail bum insult Hey Soos, and are shocked to learn that he is Rowdy's father, who had been presumed dead.

126.86 *The Sendoff.* Oct. 6, 1961. GS: Darren McGavin, Claude Akins, Lillian Bronson, Stacy Harris, Edward Colmans, John Hart, Charles Tannen, George Chalk. Favor comes across the burned-out remains of a raided wagon train. Not far away, some of the drovers find wagonmaster Jed Hadley, who has been living like a hermit for two years since the raid took place.

126.87 *The Long Shakedown.* Oct. 13, 1961. GS: Skip Homeier, Lew Gallo, Jay Douglas, Ed Faulkner, Kelly Dobson. The drive is three days out of Laredo, and Favor is bearing down on his men, trying to drive the town fever out of their systems. A drover named Haskell is the first to crack under the discipline.

126.88 *Judgment at Hondo Seco.* Oct. 20, 1961. GS: Ralph Bellamy, Anne Whitfield, Burt Douglas, Jean Inness, Roy Barcroft, Richard Wessel, Kathie Browne, Ray Teal, Robert Bice, George Petrie, Robert Donner. Quince asks Favor for some time off to take care of personal business in Hondo Seco. Favor gives Quince the go-ahead.

126.89 *The Lost Tribe.* Oct. 27, 1961. GS: Abraham Sofaer, Sonya Wilde, Larry Chance, John Hart, Elizabeth Furedi, Bob Swimmer. A stampeded begins in the middle of the night and thousands of cattle scatter into the brush. A local sheriff says the stampede was caused by Indians — Cheyenne Indians wandering a thousand miles from their home grounds.

126.90 *Inside Man.* Nov. 3, 1961. GS: Chris Alcaide, Anne Helm, Lane Bradford. A likeable young drover named Clay Forrester asks Favor if he can join the drive, and Gil obliges, unaware that Forrester's employer, Roy Craddock, plans to take over the herd.

126.91 *The Black Sheep.* Nov. 10, 1961. GS: Richard Basehart, Will Wright, Hardie Albright, James Anderson, Clarke Gordon, Fred Graham. Cattle drovers just naturally don't like sheepherders, and shepherd Ted Stone naturally dislikes cattlemen. Stone seems to have the advantage as his flock is ahead of the cattle herd, and sheep don't leave much food behind them.

126.92 *The Prairie Elephant.* Nov. 17, 1961. GS: Lawrence Dobkin, Gloria Talbott, Britt Lomond, Billy Barty, Laurie Mitchell, Mickey Morton, Maxine Gates. The cattle and horses seem to be unusually restless and when Mushy goes to do the dishes in a nearby stream, he finds the reason. There is an elephant out somewhere in the wilderness.

126.93 *The Little Fishes.* Nov. 24, 1961. GS: Burgess Meredith, Phyllis Coates, Richard Webb, Richard Reeves, Russell Bender, Leake Bevil. Scientist Tom Gwynn intends to stock the rivers of California with shad, and wants Favor to help him get there before the fish he has with him die. But Favor is in a hurry to get his herd to market.

126.94 *The Blue Sky.* Dec. 8, 1961. GS: Phyllis Thaxter, Lyle Bettger, George D. Wallace, Charles Aidman, Harry Lauter, Reg Parton, Guy Cain. No one believes Nolan's story about coming upon a bunch of Indians running around in strange costumes. Then Pauline Wakefield stumbles into camp and tells of an Indian attack on her theatrical wagon.

126.95 *The Gentleman's Gentleman.* Dec. 15, 1961. GS: Brian Aherne, John Sutton, Sheila Bromley, Richard Shannon, Russell Thorson, Kathryn Card, Jay Silverheels, Paul Barselow, Tim Graham. Lord Ashton is shot while on a hunting expedition out West. It is his dying wish that his servant Woolsey go to work for Favor, who soon becomes the only trail boss in the West with an English valet.

126.96 *Twenty-five Santa Clauses.* Dec. 22, 1961. GS: Ed Wynn, Anne Seymour, Rafael Lopez, John Hart, Guy Cain, Theodore Newton. Mushy is looking out across the Texas trail with the hot August sun burning down on him. In fact he may be getting too much, for he sees Santa Claus with his bag of toys coming toward him.

126.97 *The Long Count.* Jan. 5, 1962. GS: Bethel Leslie, Kevin Hagen, Robert Cornthwaite, Harry Shannon, Charles Maxwell, Cheerio Meredith, Milton Frome, Vito Scotti. This story tells how Clay Forrester became a member of Gil Favor's group. When Forrester first rides into town he says that he is a Government census taker and needs Favor's help, but Favor thinks he had better get the stranger's number first.

126.98 *The Captain's Wife.* Jan. 12, 1962. GS: Barbara Stanwyck, John Howard, Robert Lowery, Nestor Paiva, Eugene Martin, Dennis Cross, Bill Walker, John Hart. Nora Holloway, an ambitious army wife, wants to be sure that her officer-husband's mission to put down a Comanchero uprising is a success. Faking some orders from her husband, she sends all but a skeleton squad into the field, leaving the fort nearly defenseless.

126.99 *The Peddler.* Jan. 19, 1962. GS: George Kennedy, Shelley Berman, Vitina Marcus, William Tannen, Hal Jon Norman, Don Beddoe, I. Stanford Jolley. Gil Favor and his drovers discover peddler Mendel J. Sorkin single-handedly trying to drive a small herd of cattle. Mendel explains that he wants to sell the cattle in the next town and use the money to return to his native country.

126.100 *Incident of the Woman Trap.* Jan. 26, 1962. GS: Robert Gist, Alan Hale, Jr., Maria Palmer, Karen Steele, Rayford Barnes, Marion Ross, Dorothy Dells, Ray Montgomery, Carol Byron. Favor and his drovers come upon an unlikely sight, a wagon filled with girls who claim to be mail-order brides. And somewhere there is going to be a town full of angry eligible men unless they can fix their broken axle.

126.101 *The Bosses' Daughter.* Feb. 2, 1962. GS: Paul Richards, Dorothy Green, Candy Moore, Barbara Beiard, Byron Morrow, Harry Fleer, Vici Raaf, Red Morgan. Favor and his men find their drive stopped by a fence at Vance Caldwell's ranch and are told they will have to wait until Caldwell returns from the east to get permission to pass. The fence isn't Favor's only problem, as his daughters are about to join him on the trail.

126.102 *Deserter's Patrol.* Feb. 9, 1962. GS: Jock Gaynor, Russell Arms, Don Megowan, Robert Dix, Conlan Carter, Dan Stafford, Edward Faulkner, Harry Carey, Jr., Russ Conway, John Hart, Hal Needham. Favor and his drovers are warned by two soldiers that hostile Crow Indians are in the area. When Pete is out searching for signs of the Indians, he meets Ogalla, chief of the Crows, and talks him into surrendering.

126.103 *The Greedy Town.* Feb. 16, 1962. GS: Mercedes McCambridge, Diana Millay, Jim Davis, Kathleen Freeman, Ross Elliott, J. Pat O'Malley, Roy E. Glenn, William Phipps, Dean Fredericks, Addison Richards, Jim Galante, Chuck Hicks. A man named Joshua shows up in the drover's camp bearing an odd message. Someone in the town of Dry Rock will pay Clay Forrester a large amount just to come into town.

126.104 *Grandma's Money.* Feb. 23, 1962. GS: Josephine Hutchinson, Frank Maxwell, Jonathan Hole, Frank Wilcox, Harry Ellerbe, Carol Ann Daniels, Thomas B. Henry, James Gavin, Daniel M. White, Norman Leavitt, Olan Soule, Everett Glass. Rowdy, Clay and Wishbone deliver some cattle to Colonel Agee's ranch, only to find that they can't collect because the colonel has gone off on a honeymoon. Rowdy decides to ride out and find him.

126.105 *The Pitchwagon.* March 2, 1962. GS: Buddy Ebsen, Joan O'Brien, Hugh Marlowe, Jack Elam, Nick Paul, Dan Grayam, Edward Foster, Clancy Cooper, John Hart, Bud Osborne, Gail Bonney. Patent-medicine pitchman George Simpson manages to get out of town one jump ahead of the law. George heads for the prairie, and finds that now there are some Indians in hot pursuit.

126.106 *The Hostage Child.* March 9, 1962. GS: Debra Paget, James Coburn, Jimmy Baird, Edward Kemmer, Naomi Stevens, Alan Reynolds, Joe Brooks. Mushy and Wishbone, moving ahead of the drive, begin to get the feeling that someone has been following them. They soon find out who it is. A young Indian named Arnee collapses from hunger soon after he catches up with them.

126.107 *The Immigrants.* Ma. 16, 1962. GS: Maria Palmer, John Van Dreelan, Robert Boon, John Mauldin, Jim Galante, Don Hight. Clay, Wishbone and Quince encounter an unusual party near their drive. A group of German immigrants are making their way West, led by a former Prussian officer named Ulrich, who exacts typical Prussian discipline.

126.108 *The Child Woman.* March 23, 1962. GS: Cesar Romero, Jena Engstrom, Dorothy Morris, Julian Burton, John Hart, Coke Willis, Dick Winslow, Jack Perkins. All the drovers are getting slicked up for a big night on the town, but Mushy is going to extraordinary lengths. He is shaving. It seems that Mushy's actress cousin, LaVerne Mushgrove, is appearing at the Longhorn theater and he is going to pay his glamorous relative a visit.

126.109 *A Woman's Place.* March 30, 1962. GS: Gail Kobe, Mala Powers, Eduard Franz, Jacques Aubuchon, Charles Maxwell, Herbert Patterson, Robert B. Williams, John Close, John Alvin, Reg Parton. When one of the drovers is injured, Gil and Rowdy rush to a nearby town for a doctor. But the medical community there is limited to a medicine man and only one real physician, and that one is a woman.

126.110 *The Reunion.* April 6, 1962. GS: Darryl Hickman, Walter Pidgeon, Sheb Wooley, Anthony Caruso, Eugene Iglesias, Judson Pratt, William Wellman, Jr., John Hart. Rowdy and Gil are engaged in a desperate search for water when they come upon a strange sight on the prairie. Someone has planted a marker flying the flag of Texas and an arrow pointing toward a nearby rise. The boys follow the arrow's direction and come upon a cool, brimming waterhole.

126.111 *The House of the Hunter.* April 20, 1962. GS: Robert F. Simon, Rosemary De Camp, Paula Raymond, Lester Matthews, Peter Adams, Lane Bradford, Harry Shannon, Hal Jon Norman, John Hart. Hey Soos says he can tell fortunes while playing cards, and Clay volunteers himself as a subject. The prediction is that death is near at hand.

126.112 *Gold Fever.* May 4, 1962. GS: Victor Jory, Karen Sharpe, Marion Ross, Adam Williams, Davey Davison, Logan Field, Charles Tannen, Quentin Sondergaard, Glen Gordon. Hosea Brewer, an old prospector, rides into the drovers' camp and talks Wishbone into selling his pick and shovel. Hosea pays in gold dust, creating the impression that maybe the old boy has finally made a strike.

126.113 *The Devil and the Deep Blue.* May 11, 1962. GS: Coleen Gray, Ted DeCorsia, Tod Andrews, Harry Lauter, John Pickard, Len Hendry, John Hart, George Hickman, Larry Kent. Nearing Abilene, Favor decides to stop and let the herd grave for a few days before going into market. Then Clay rides in to report that there is another herd coming and it is only a few days behind.

126.114 *Abilene.* May 18, 1962. GS: Audrey Totter, Ken Lynch, John Pickard, Bing Russell, Richard Collier, James Secrest, Gracy Graham, John Hart, E.J. Andre, Kent Hays, Dick Winslow, Guy Teague. The herd finally arrives in Abilene, the end of a long hard drive. While most of the drovers plan to spend their pay painting the town, Favor has a few other ideas. He is going to buy some land and get out of the cattle business.

Season Five

126.115 *Incident of the Hunter.* Sept. 28, 1962. GS: Mark Stevens, Gregory Walcott, Hal Baylor. A new man joins the drive and Rowdy recognizes him as John Shepard, a former Confederate officer. But Clay says he knows Shepard as a bounty hunter named Rankin.

126.116 *Incident of the Portrait.* Oct. 5, 1962. GS: John Ireland, Nina Shipman, Ted de Corsia, Emile Meyer. Blind Marion Curtis temporarily joins the drive after her father is murdered by an unknown assailant. Favor assigns the job of driving Marion's wagon to a new drover named Trask, who happens to be the man who murdered Marion's father.

126.117 *Incident at Cactus Wells.* Oct. 12, 1962. GS: Keenan Wynn, Ron Hagerthy, Henry Wills, Don Haggerty. For days a mysterious stranger has been following the drive and the drovers are getting edgy. Finally the man rides into camp and says that his name is Simon Royce. He claims that he is just looking for a job.

126.118 *Incident of the Prodigal Son.* Oct. 19, 1962. GS: Carl Reindel, Gene Evans, Frank Wilcox. On the open prairie, the drovers come across a young man dying of thirst and exposure. The youth reveals that he is Benjamin Paine Whitney IV, the scion of a very wealthy family.

126.119 *Incident of the Four Horsemen.* Oc. 26, 1962. GS: Robert J. Wilke, Ron Hayes, Jena Engstrom, Edward Faulkner, Claude Akins, John Dehner, I. Stanford Jolley. The Justice of the Peace has just joined Frank Louden and Amy Gault in wedlock when Amy's brother Carl, who opposed the marriage, bursts into the courthouse.

126.120 *Incident of the Lost Woman.* Nov. 2, 1962. GS: Fay Spain, R.G. Armstrong, Dean Stanton, Hampton Fancher, Roy Engel. On the open desert, Favor finds a woman and her baby near death from exposure. She says that she is Lissa Hobson and that her husband was killed in a wagon accident.

126.121 *Incident of the Dogfaces.* Nov. 9, 1962. GS: James Whitmore, John Doucette, Steve Brodie, Ford Rainey, Robert J. Stevenson, James Beck, William Wellman, Jr., Kathleen O'Malley. Rowdy, Clay and Quince rescue three Union soldiers from a small Comanche raiding party. The Indians flee but soon return with plenty of reinforcements.

126.122 *Incident of the Wolvers.* Nov. 16, 1962. GS: Dan Duryea, Patty McCormack, Paul Carr, Jack Grinnage. There is big trouble on the drive when the herd is menaced by a large wolf pact. Then Rowdy receives a visit from a man named Cannon, who reveals that he makes his living by hiring out to kill wolves.

126.123 *Incident at Sugar Creek.* Nov. 23, 1962. GS: Beverly Garland, Everett Sloane, John Larch, John Litel, Charles Herbert, Arthur Franz. Drover Sam Garrett, injured on the trail, is going to die if Rowdy doesn't get medical aid in nearby Sugar Creek. It looks like Sam is doomed when Dr. Harper refuses to help when he learns the patients name is Sam Garrett.

126.124 *Incident of the Reluctant Bridegroom.* Nov. 30, 1962. GS: Ruta Lee, Ed Nelson, Arch Johnson, Jack Kosslyn, Rodney Bell, Harry Lauter, Edward Foster, Richard Bartell. Favor sends Rowdy and Wishbone into town to pick up supplies, but Rowdy finds time to pick up something else — a wife.

126.125 *Incident of the Querencias.* Dec. 7, 1962. GS: Edward Andrews, Herbert Patterson, Hal Baylor. Favor takes time out from the drive to visit an old friend, cattleman Lije Crowning. But he finds Lije in trouble. He has lost his ranch and all that remains of his herd are a few head of cattle.

126.126 *Incident at Quivira.* Dec. 14, 1962. GS: Royal Dano, Claude Akins, Donald Losby, William Henry, Robert Kline, John Dierkes. An old prospector named Monty Fox staggers into camp and insists that he has found Quivira, Coronado's legendary city of treasure. All of the drovers think that Fox is a little off, except for Mushy.

126.127 *Incident of Decision.* Dec. 28, 1962. GS: Carlos Romero, Doug Lambert, Hugh Sanders, Sheila Bromley, Michael de Anda. When Rowdy, Quince and Hey Soos stop at the Calvin Ranch, teenager Johnny Calvin begs them to take him on the drive. The boy is determined to be a drover, despite the fact that he is crippled.

126.128 *Incident of the Buryin' Man.* Jan. 4, 1963. GS: King Donovan, Constance Ford, Richard Devon. While crossing Indian country, Favor and Rowdy find undertaker Poke Tolliver's broken-down hearse. But Poke has undertaken another endeavor. He has a small print shop that turns out fresh counterfeit money.

126.129 *Incident at the Trail's End.* Jan. 11, 1963. GS: Harold J. Stone, George Brenlin, Dwayne Spratt, King Calder. Favor meets up with his old trail boss, Harry Maxton, and asks him to join the drive. Maxton accepts, but he doesn't mention that a doctor has just told him that he is going blind.

126.130 *Incident at Spider Rock.* Jan. 18, 1963. GS: Susan Oliver, Lon Chaney, Jr., James Best, Mary Beth Hughes, Peggy Ann Garner. The drovers are taking a welcome break at the town of High Divide, but they don't like it when they find that their drinks have been watered down. The Rowdy overhears one of the saloon girls make a remark which indicates that the whole town is out to make suckers of them.

Rawhide

126.131 *Incident of the Mountain Man.* Jan. 25, 1963. GS: Patricia Crowley, Robert Middleton, Robert J. Wilke. Scout Josh Green has been accused of murder, and the members of his wagon train plan to hold a necktie party for him. Green's daughter Sara is looking for someone to help her stop the lynching.

126.132 *Incident at Crooked Hat.* Feb. 1, 1963. GS: James Gregory, Jeanne Cooper, Arch Johnson, Jan Merlin, Robert J. Stevenson, Walter Sande. Gunslinger Jack Jennings has decided to turn over a new leaf. He has changed his name to Owen Spencer and is working for Favor as a drover. But Little Sam Talbot is anxious to build up a reputation and when he recognizes Jennings he forces a showdown.

126.133 *Incident of Judgment Day.* Feb. 8, 1963. GS: Claude Rains, John Dehner, John Kellogg, Richard Carlyle, Howard Dayton, Gail Kobe. Rowdy is brought to a ghost town by some of his old Confederate Army buddies who plan to hold him for trial. He is charged with betraying their attempted escape from a Union prison.

126.134 *Incident of the Gallows Tree.* Feb. 22, 1963. GS: Beverly Garland, Judson Pratt, Gregory Walcott, Edward Faulkner, William Henry, Mike Ragan. A posse arrests Quince on a charge of murder. While he was on a drinking spree in a nearby town, he threatened to kill someone, who was later shot in the back.

126.135 *Incident of the Married Widow.* March 1, 1963. GS: Patricia Barry, Dabbs Greer, Sheila Bromley, Don Haggerty, Roy Engel. In town for supplies, Rowdy, Wishbone and Mush run into a saloon hostess named Abigail, who claims to be Gil Favor's widow.

126.136 *Incident of the Pale Rider.* March 15, 1963. GS: Albert Salmi, Fredd Wayne, Chubby Johnson, Jack Searl, I. Stanford Jolley, Russell Thorson, Daniel White. Rowdy thinks he is seeing ghosts when he meets the new drover, who is the image of John Day, a man he was forced to kill in self-defense.

126.137 *Incident of the Comanchero.* March 22, 1963. GS: Robert Loggia, Virginia Gregg, Nina Shipman, Christopher Dark, Than Wyenn, Joseph Perry. Chappala, a Comanchero left to die by his colleagues, is rescued by two nuns. But his former friends aren't through with him yet.

126.138 *Incident of the Clown.* March 29, 1963. GS: Eddie Bracken, Harry Lauter, Ted de Corsia, Richard Hale, X Brands, Joey Russo. Morris G. Stevens is quite a character. He is a scholar, he is a former circus clown, he is accident prone and, when the drovers meet up with him on the trail, he is possessed of an idea for bringing about peaceful coexistence between white men and Indians. His method is to compile a Comanche-English dictionary. Unfortunately, the Comanches are not thinking in terms of peace. Their chief has only one word on his mind, and the word is war.

126.139 *Incident of the Black Ace.* April 12, 1963. GS: Walter Slezak, Karen Sharpe, Robert Strauss. Gypsy Lazio Tzgorni, who has joined the drive, tells Wishbone's fortune. Unless the cook leaves now, he will die.

126.140 *Incident of the Hostages.* April 19, 1963. GS: Suzanne Cupito/Morgan Brittany, Tony Haig, Leslie Wales, Michael Davis, Rodolfo Acosta, Joseph Perry. Rowdy gives a band of Indians forty heads of cattle in exchange for three white children they are holding captive.

126.141 *Incident of the White Eyes.* May 3, 1963. GS: Nita Talbot, Nehemiah Persoff, John Vivyan, Diana Millay, William Schallert, William Henry, Guy Teague. Favor halts a runaway stagecoach and escorts the passengers to a relay station, but a band of renegade Apaches shows up and they are out to get one of the passengers.

126.142 *Incident at Rio Doloroso.* May 10, 1963. GS: Michael Ansara, Cesar Romero, Madlyn Rhue, Carlos Romero, Ernest Sarracino. Rowdy and Wishbone gets into a fight with the Maldenado brothers, who claim that a fee must be paid before the herd crosses their property.

126.143 *Incident at Alkali Sink.* May 24, 1963. GS: Russell Johnson, Ruta Lee, Roy Barcroft, Judson Pratt, I. Stanford Jolley. Lorraine Stanton ran away from home to marry, but her father is determined to bring her back.

Season Six

126.144 *Incident of the Red Wind.* Sept. 26, 1963. GS: Neville Brand. A new drover named Lou Bowdark convinces Favor he knows a way to drive the thirsty heard through the desert, but Rowdy doesn't like Bowdark's plan.

126.145 *Incident of Iron Bull.* Oct. 3, 1963. GS: James Whitmore, Michael Ansara, Judson Pratt, Ralph Moody, Daniel M. White, Richard X. Slattery. Rowdy hires a Comanche named Joseph as a drover, but he is going to run into trouble with John Macklin, an Indian-hating Army colonel.

126.146 *Incident at El Crucero.* Oct. 10, 1963. GS: Elizabeth Montgomery, Gene Evans, Parley Baer, L.Q. Jones, Buddy Baer, John Craig, Mike Ragan, Richard Simmons, Joi Lansing. Rose Cornelius refuses to let the cattle cross her land, and she has a dozen brothers to back her up.

126.147 *Incident of the Travellin' Man.* Oct. 17, 1963. GS: Simon Oakland, Robert Middleton, James Sikking, Robert Donner. A river is no place to be wearing leg irons, and Bolivar Jagger might have drowned if the drovers hadn't saved him. Jagger claims Matt Harger was keeping him as a slave, and Matt says Jagger is a killer.

126.148 *Incident at Paradise.* Oct. 24, 1963. GS: Burgess Meredith, Patty McCormack, Beau Bridges, Arch Johnson, Neil Nephew, Peter Helm. Rowdy comes to the aid of Matthew Higgins, a stubborn little nester who does not intend to move off his land just because rancher Harry Johanson wants him to.

126.149 *Incident at Farragut Pass.* Oct. 31, 1963. GS: Frankie Avalon, Glenda Farrel, Tommy Farrell, Dee Pollock, John Pickard, William Henry. Elizabeth Farragut will allow the herd to cross her land on one condition. Favor must hire her rebellious grandson Billy as a drover, and teach him some discipline in the bargain.

126.150 *Incident at Two Graves.* Nov. 7, 1963. GS: Bill Travers, Steve Brodie, Don Haggerty, Dennis Cross. Jeremiah O'Neal, the new drover, was kicked out of town for throwing a fight with Rowdy.

126.151 *Incident of the Rawhiders.* Nov. 14, 1963. GS: Denver Pyle, Nina Shipman, James Best, Wright King, John Mitchum. Rowdy spares Brock Quade's life, and Brock returns the favor by giving Rowdy his fiancee, Valley Rose, whom Rowdy must now marry.

126.152 *Incident of the Prophecy.* Nov. 21, 1963. GS: Dan Duryea, Warren Oates, James Griffith, Raymond Guth,

Dean Stanton. Brother William, a gunman-turned-preacher, foretells death for Rowdy and a fellow drover after one of them accidentally kills his brother.

126.153 *Incident at Confidence Creek.* Nov. 28, 1963. GS: Dick York, Barbara Eden, Harry Lauter, J. Pat O'Malley, Byron Foulger, Richard Wessel, Roy Roberts, Norman Leavitt, Roy Barcroft. Magician Elwood Gilroy plays a dirty trick on the drovers. He poses as Favor and sells the herd.

126.154 *Incident of the Death Dancer.* Dec. 5, 1963. GS: Forrest Tucker, Med Florey. Mushy is attacked by an escape circus lion. It is the same lion that Dan Carlock has been tracking for several years.

126.155 *Incident of the Wild Deuces.* Dec. 12, 1963. GS: Barbara Stuart, George Chandler, Ken Lynch, Robert B. Williams, W.J. Vincent, Sandra Giles. Mushy gets into a small-town poker session and wins a bundle when he calls for deuces wild.

126.156 *Incident of the Geisha.* Dec. 19, 1963. GS: Miyoshi Umeki, Joseph Perry. Knocked unconscious when he falls from his horse, Hey Soos awakens to find himself being cared for by a young Japanese girl.

126.157 *Incident at Ten Trees.* Jan. 2, 1964. GS: Susan Kohner, Royal Dano, Michael Pate, Iron Eyes Cody. On the prairie, the drovers encounter Abbie Bartlett, wearing Indian paint and babbling nonsense.

126.158 *Incident of the Rusty Shotgun.* Jan. 9, 1964. GS: Marie Windsor, Claude Akins, Don Megowan, Kelly Thordsen, Herbert Anderson, Don Beddoe, Jonathan Hole. After Wishbone settles a dispute between a lady storekeeper and a salesman, the lady's three burly brothers decide Wishbone would make a fine mate for her.

126.159 *Incident of the Midnight Cave.* Jan. 16, 1964. GS: Edward Kemmer. On the trail, Wishbone slips, falls off a cliff and is saved by Rowdy and Favor, who discover Wishbone has been blinded by the fall.

126.160 *Incident of the Dowry Dundee.* Jan. 23, 1964. GS: Hazel Court, Lyle Bettger. While looking for stray cattle, Rowdy and Quince find a stray girl, who has wandered all the way from Scotland

126.161 *Incident at Gila Flats.* Jan. 30, 1964. GS: Gene Evans, Harry Lauter, Rodolfo Acosta, Leslie Wales, Michael Keep, Joseph Vitale, L.Q. Jones, Mike Ragan, Edward Faulkner. While helping the Army deliver cattle to an Apache tribe, Favor, Wishbone and Quince run into a band of renegade Indians determined to stop them.

126.162 *Incident of the Pied Piper.* Feb. 6, 1964. GS: Eddie Bracken, Arch Johnson, Everett Sloane, Duane Grey, Rodney Bell, Butch Patrick, Jenny Lynn. An orphanage operator sells off some of Favor's strays.

126.163 *Incident of the Swindler.* Feb. 20, 1964. GS: John Dehner, Peter Leeds, Sally Forrest, Richard Reeves, William Fawcett, Vici Raaf. Wishbone stuns his fellow drovers by holding them at gunpoint to help a thief escape.

126.164 *Incident of the Wanderer.* Feb. 27, 1964. GS: Nehemiah Persoff, Gregory Walcott, Daniel White. After a heavy thunderstorm, a stranger wanders into camp, evidently untouched by the rain.

126.165 *Incident at Zebulon.* March 5, 1964. GS: Robert Cornthwaite, John Lupton, Patricia Huston, Ron Foster, Jack Searl, I. Stanford Jolley, Herbert Patterson, Kelly Thordsen. The black-hooded Regulators ride into camp and whisk away drover Johnny Larkin, whom they accuse of murder.

126.166 *Incident at Hourglass.* March 12, 1964. GS: Jay C. Flippen, John Anderson, Elizabeth MacRae, Kent Smith, Russell Arms, William Wellman, Jr. An Army captain's wife murders her lieutenant boy friend, and then accuses Favor of the crime.

126.167 *Incident at the Odyssey.* March 26, 1964. GS: Mickey Rooney, Carole Matthews, Raymond Guth, Norman Leavitt, Robert B. Williams, John Pickard. A happy, childlike wanderer becomes friendly with the drovers.

126.168 *Incident of the Banker.* April 2, 1964. GS: Allyn Joslyn, Lola Albright, Virginia Gregg, Marjorie Bennett. Banker Albert Ashton-Warner longs to be an outdoor man like Favor, who has just asked for a loan, so he agrees to okay the loan, if Favor will temporarily take charge of the bank while he takes over as the trail boss.

126.169 *Incident at El Toro.* April 9, 1964. GS: James Best, Hal Baylor, John Cole, Brad Morrow. Favor's got troubles. The cattle drive is a week behind schedule, there aren't enough drovers, and a wild bull is frightening the herd.

126.170 *Incident at Dead Horse* Part One. April 16, 1964. GS: Broderick Crawford, Burgess Meredith, Chill Wills, Robert Middleton, Paul Carr, Hampton Fancher II. Judd Hammerklein has been sentenced to hang for murder, but he is the most popular and powerful man in town, and no one really believes that the sentence will be carried out.

126.171 *Incident at Dead Horse* Part Two. April 23, 1964. GS: Broderick Crawford, Burgess Meredith, Chill Wills, Robert Middleton, Paul Carr, Hampton Fancher II. The hangman is preparing to execute Jud Hammerklein, who is still confident that he will never be hanged.

126.172 *Incident of the Gilded Goddess.* April 30, 1964. GS: Dina Merrill, Herbert Rudley, Robert J. Stevenson, George Van Wort, John McKee. Dazed Lisa Temple wanders into camp suffering from exposure, and Rowdy, who knows that she once ran a crooked gambling house, learns she is running from the law.

126.173 *Incident at Seven Fingers.* May 7, 1964. GS: William Marshall, Harry Townes, Hari Rhodes, Ken Johnson, Don Marshall. Rowdy befriends Sam Turner, gets him a job on the drive, and then the Army arrests Turner as a deserter.

126.174 *Incident of the Peyote Cup.* May 14, 1964. GS: James Gregory, Pilar Seurat, Ted de Corsia, Richard Hale, Hal Jon Norman. The drovers encounter hostile Indians.

Season Seven

126.175 *The Race.* Sept. 25, 1964. GS: Warren Oates, William Bryant, Emil Genest, Joe Breen, L.Q. Jones, Jacque Shelton, Barry Brooks, Hal Needham. After an argument with Favor, Rowdy quits his job and signs on as trail boss for another drive. He intends to get his herd to market ahead of Favor's.

126.176 *The Enormous Fist.* Oct. 2, 1964. GS: Brenda Scott, Mark Slade, Lee Van Cleef, James Anderson. Favor gets involved in fist fight in self defense. The fight results in the death of the father of four children.

126.177 *Piney.* Oct. 9, 1964. GS: Ed Begley, Elisha

Cook, Jr., J.D. Cannon, Lee Van Cleef. Piney, an old friend of Favor's, is digging for dollars by digging a tunnel beneath a bank.

126.178 *The Lost Herd.* Oct. 16, 1964. GS: Bill Williams, Harry Townes, Royal Dano, Leo Gordon, Peter Bourne. Favor tries to beat another drive to market by taking a dangerous pass, but loses his herd in a stampede over a cliff.

126.179 *A Man Called Mushy.* Oct. 23, 1964. GS: Paul Comi, Mike Kellin, Sondra Kerr, Jonathan Kidd, Michael Pataki, John McLiam, John Hubbard. Four Gypsies talk dim-witted Mushy into giving them the drive's wagons and saddle horses.

126.180 *Canliss.* Oct. 30, 1964. GS: Dean Martin, Laura Devon, Michael Ansara, Scott Marlowe, Theodore Bikel, Ramon Novarro. Against his wife's wishes, gunman Gurd Canliss hires out for one last killing.

126.181 *Damon's Road* Part One. Nov. 13, 1964. GS: Fritz Weaver, Sean McClory, Barbara Eden, Paul Comi, Robert Sorrells. Railroad boss Jonathan Damon has a problem. He has to get more track laid, but his crew has walked off the job because they haven't been paid. Damon decides to get Favor's drovers to do the job, by hook or by crook.

126.182 *Damon's Road* Part Two. GS: Fritz Weaver, Sean McClory, Barbara Eden, Paul Comi, Robert Sorrells. An enraged Gil Favor is behind bars and Damon has accomplished his task—getting the drovers to lay the track for his railroad.

126.183 *The Backshooter.* Nov. 27, 1964. GS: Louis Hayward, Slim Pickens, Terry Becker, Joseph Hoover, Holly McIntire, Bob Yuro, Steve Gravers. Rowdy brings in the body of an outlaw, shot from behind, and asks for the reward money.

126.184 *Corporal Dasovik.* Dec. 4, 1964. GS: John Barrymore, Jr., Nick Adams, G.B. Atwater, Sherwood Price, Howard Caine, Ron Soble. Corporal Dasovik has always shunned responsibility, but now, with the sudden death of his commanding officer, he reluctantly finds himself in command of a squad of soldiers escorting Indian prisoners to a reservation.

126.185 *The Photographer.* Dec. 11, 1964. GS: Eddie Albert, Morgan Woodward, Ben Cooper, Richard X. Slattery, Christopher Dark, William O'Connell, Frank Richards. Photographer Taylor Dickson's presence on the drive is turning out to be disastrous. His continual picture snapping is playing havoc with the routine and annoying Favor.

126.186 *No Dogs or Drovers.* Dec. 18, 1964. GS: Philip Abbott, Dabbs Greer, Gilbert Green, Zeme North, Bryan O'Byrne, Olan Soule. No dogs or drovers are welcome in Junction City, and while Favor is being entertained by cattleman Ben Dennis, his men are receiving shabby treatment from the townspeople.

126.187 *The Meeting.* Dec. 25, 1965.

126.188 *The Book.* Jan. 8, 1965. GS: Pat Hingle, J.D. Cannon, Leonard Strong, Ziva Rodann, Valentine de Vargas, Timothy Carey. Pop Starke trains gunfighters and then matches them in gunfights on which he wagers heavily. But Pop has just lost a match as well as a gunfighter, and Rowdy Yates is his choice as a replacement.

126.189 *Josh.* Jan. 15, 1965. GS: Albert Dekker, Jay C. Flippen, John Doucette, John Pickard, Ann Shoemaker, Fletcher Fist, Ottola Nesmith. The drive has been having bad luck and Favor takes out his frustration by firing Mushy's friend Josh, a proud old drover.

126.190 *A Time for Waiting.* Jan. 22, 1965. GS: George Grizzard, Lisabeth Hush, Lin McCarthy, Ken Berry. Although it was Rowdy's testimony that helped convict his friend Captain Ballinger of murder, the captain asks Rowdy to come see him before the execution.

126.191 *Moment in the Sun.* Jan. 29, 1965. GS: Gene Evans, Pat Conway, Billy Gray, Sherry Jackson. Over the years outlaw Reed McCuller has become a Western Robin Hood by lending a helping hand to some of the local farmers. But although McCuller is still a wanted man, no one wants to see him get locked up, except for Marshal Royal Shaw.

126.192 *Texas Fever.* Feb. 5, 1965. GS: Royal Dano, Frank Maxwell, Judi Meredith. Trail drive scout Pete Nolan is about to be lynched for a murder he didn't commit.

126.193 *Blood Harvest.* Feb. 12, 1965. GS: Tom Tully, Michael Petit, Richard X. Slattery. A man and his young son, picked up on the trail, join the cattle drive.

126.194 *The Violent Land.* March 5, 1965. GS: Michael Forest, Davey Davison, Gregg Palmer, Lew Brown, Paul Sorensen. In the midst of hostile Indian country, one of the drovers is keeping a sharp lookout for a white girl captured by the red men. The girl's father has offered a large reward for her return.

126.195 *The Winter Soldier.* March 12, 1965. GS: Robert Blake, Brooke Bundy, Liam Sullivan. Irresponsible, devil-may-care soldier Hap Johnson has been thinking of deserting, and when he hears that the Comanches are on the warpath, his mind is made up.

126.196 *Prairie Fire.* March 19, 1965. GS: Michael Conrad, Anthony Caruso, Vic Perrin. A dying friend asks Wishbone to get his herd to market and see that his daughter receives the money from the cattle sale. But the rancher's three drovers have other ideas.

126.197 *The Retreat.* March 26, 1965. GS: John Anderson, Steve Ihnat, John Lasell, Keith McConnell, Ford Rainey. A bitter Army major who is about to retires decides to steal the post payroll as his last official act.

126.198 *The Empty Sleeve.* April 2, 1965. GS: Everett Sloane, Burt Douglas, Nancy Rennick. After being without water for several days, the drive finally reaches a river, but the cattle refuse to drink.

126.199 *The Diehard* (A.K.A. "The Last Order"). April 9, 1965. GS: Efrem Zimbalist, Jr., Lawrence Dobkin, Harry Lauter. After some ex-Confederate soldiers hold up a stagecoach, one of them staggers mortally wounded into the drovers' camp with the stolen strongbox.

126.200 *Mrs. Harmon.* April 16, 1965. GS: Barbara Barrie, Paul Lambert. Wishbone comes to the aid of Elizabeth Harmon and her three children after Mrs. Harmon is beaten up by her drunken husband.

126.201 *The Calf Women.* April 30, 1965. GS: Julie Harris, Betty Conner, Roger Ewing, Karl Lukas, Kelly Thordsen. Both Rowdy and Mush have problems. Rowdy, as acting trail boss, has to deal with hostile buffalo hunters who don't want cattle grazing on buffalo land, and Mushy has the unpleasant task of getting ride of tome tiny calves that are slowing down the drive.

126.202 *The Spanish Camp.* May 7, 1965. GS: John Ireland, Brock Peters. A man named Merritt and his men are digging for Spanish treasure, and in the process they have dammed up a stream, cutting off the herd's water supply.

126.203 *El Hombre Bravo.* May 14, 1965. GS: Frank Silvera, Malachi Throne, Henry Corden, Manuel Padilla, Carmelita Acosta. In revolution-torn Mexico, Favor and Mushy encounter an old man and a group of children fleeing from federal troops.

126.204 *The Gray Rock Hotel.* May 21, 1965. GS: Lola Albright, Steven Hill, Vic Tayback, Strother Martin, Rex Holman. Stricken with a mysterious illness, the drovers stagger into a deserted town where they encounter a beautiful but peculiar lady named Lottie.

Season Eight

126.205 *Encounter at Boot Hill.* Sept. 14, 1965. GS: Simon Oakland, Peter Haskell, Timothy Carey, Malcolm Atterbury, Dal Jenkins, Jeff Corey. Two of the drovers are gunned down while trying to stop a lynching.

126.206 *Ride a Crooked Mile.* Sept. 21, 1965.

126.207 *Six Weeks to Bent Fork.* Sept. 28, 1965. GS: James Gregory, R.G. Armstrong, Roy Roberts, Vaughn Taylor. A cattle owner offers Rowdy and the drovers and unusual deal. If they can get his herd to market in six weeks, he will pay them an extraordinary fee, but if they fail they will receive no pay at all.

126.208 *Walk into Terror.* Oct. 5, 1965. GS: Claude Akins, Bruce Dern, Roy Barcroft. Simon and an injured Quince are trapped in a mine cave-in.

126.209 *Escape to Doom.* Oct. 12, 1965. GS: Rip Torn, Christopher Dark. Rowdy and the crew are worried. A band of Indians has been following them for several days.

126.210 *Hostage for Hanging.* Oct. 19, 1965. GS: Mercedes McCambridge, Robert Blake, Sharon Farrell, Warren Oates, Hal Baylor. Rowdy is kidnaped and held for ransom by Ma Gufler and her unscrupulous mountain brood.

126.211 *The Vasquez Woman.* Oct. 26, 1965. GS: Cesar Romero, Carol Lawrence, Malachi Throne. In Mexico, a revolutionary leader called Colonel Vasquez forces Jed to accept worthless money in payment for a herd of cattle.

126.212 *Clash at Broken Bluff.* Nov. 2, 1965. GS: Warren Stevens, Nancy Gates, Ron Randell, Elisabeth Fraser, Lyn Edgington. Mal Thorner, mayor of Broken Bluff, asks Rowdy's men to vote for him when they get to town. Thorner says that his opposition candidate plans to clean up th wide-open hamlet.

126.213 *The Pursuit.* Nov. 9, 1965. GS: Ralph Bellamy, Jim Davis. Jed is the target for sniper fire from a man who later identifies himself as a U.S. marshal.

126.214 *Duel at Daybreak.* Nov. 16, 1965. GS: Charles Bronson, Jill Haworth, Brendon Boone, Larry Gates, Joe di Reda. Rowdy, who has contracted to deliver a herd of cattle for rancher Mason Woodruff, want to call off the driver. There is bad blood between Woodruff's foreman and one of the drovers.

126.215 *Brush War at Buford.* Nov. 23, 1965. GS: Richard Carlson, Robert Middleton, Skip Homeier, Tim McIntire. Rowdy agrees to transport cattle belonging to Major Buford, unaware that he is becoming involved in a feud between the Southerner Buford and a cattle rancher who fought for the North.

126.216 *The Testing Post.* Nov. 30, 1965. GS: Rory Calhoun, Dick Foran, Burt Brinckerhoff, K.L. Smith, Eddie Firestone. Rowdy may soon have the Army after him for shooting an arrogant lieutenant who tried to forcibly requision some cattle.

126.217 *Crossing at White Feather.* Dec. 7, 1965. GS: Johnny Crawford, Albert Dekker, G.B. Atwater. Rowdy's new scout turns out to be an unreliable loafer and a drunk.

127. The Rebel

ABC. 30 min. Broadcast history: Sunday, 9:00-9:30, Oct. 1959–Sept. 1961.

Regular Cast: Nick Adams (Johnny Yuma).

Premise: The series depicted the adventures of Johnny Yuma, a former Confederate soldier, who travels the West after the Civil War.

The Episodes

127.1 *Johnny Yuma.* Oct. 4, 1959. GS: John Carradine, Dan Blocker, Strother Martin, Jeanette Nolan. Johnny Yuma returns home after the truce at Appomattox and finds his father dead and the town in the hands of outlaws. Johnny vows to avenge his father's death.

127.2 *Judgment.* Oct. 11, 1959. GS: Sue Randall, Bob Steele, J. Pat O'Malley. In his attempt to flee from a posse, Will Randall tries to take Johnny Yuma's horse, but Yuma captures him and turns him over to the posse. Randall's daughter later tells Johnny that her father is being framed.

127.3 *Yellow Hair.* Oct. 18, 1959. GS: Royal Dano, Rodolfo Acosta, Perry Lopez, Carol Nugent. At an abandoned Army post, Johnny Yuma finds a strange man babbling insanely. He tells Johnny he is just acting like a madman to keep the Indians from killing him. Suddenly, the Indians reappear.

127.4 *Vicious Circle.* Oct. 25, 1959. GS: George Macready, Eddie Ryder, Ed Nelson, William Foster. Johnny Yuma is beaten up by two ex-Union soldiers who want to know the whereabouts of a two-million dollar cache of gold. But Johnny knows nothing at all about it.

127.5 *Panic.* Nov. 1, 1959. GS: Karl Swenson, J. Pat O'Malley, Allen Kramer, Edith Claire, Laurie Perreau. Johnny Yuma comes upon a squatter family in need of help. The townspeople fear that the squatters have diphtheria.

127.6 *The Scavengers.* Nov. 8, 1959. GS: James Westerfield, Olive Sturgess. A band of murderous pillagers besiege a homesteader family intent on taking over their home for the winter. The scavengers run out of ammunition and try to trick the family into giving them some.

127.7 *School Days.* Nov. 15, 1959. GS: Fintan Meyler, Warren Oates, Dick Rush, Olan Soule. Johnny Yuma agrees to act temporarily as schoolmaster. But he runs into difficulty with one of his students, who is sore because his sweetheart has a crush of Johnny.

127.8 *Dark Secret.* Nov. 22, 1959. GS: Tyler McVey, N.J. Davis, Edith Claire, Johnny Eimen, Bobby Beekman. Embittered Sime Trask goads Johnny Yuma into a gunfight. Trask is killed, and Yuma and the Sheriff go to explain his death to the widow.

127.9 *Misfits.* Nov. 29, 1959. GS: Hampton Fancher, Hal

The Rebel

Stalmaster. Three young boys ambush Johnny Yuma. The youths then tell Yuma of their bold plan to rob a bank.

127.10 *In Memoriam.* Dec. 6, 1969. GS: Agnes Moorehead, Madlyn Rhue. Johnny Yuma fulfills a promise made to a dying Union soldier. He rides into Lassiter City to return a keepsake medal to the boy's family. The mother proudly receives the medal and then asks Yuma to stay on as a cowhand.

127.11 *The Vagrants.* Dec. 20, 1959. GS: Robert Foulk, Wright King, K.L. Smith, Kelton Garwood. Johnny is arrested by a corrupt sheriff on a trumped-up charge of vagrancy, and forced to join a gang of slave laborers.

127.12 *Gun City.* Dec. 27, 1959. GS: Otto Kruger, Dan Sheridan. Yuma goes to see the newspaper editor in a frontier town. The editor tells Yuma that the city is trying a new approach to law and order by assuring that everyone in disarmed.

127.13 *The Death of Gray.* Jan. 3, 1960. GS: Harry Townes, Johnny Cash, Steven Marlo. Two men in Confederate uniforms attack Johnny Yuma and force him to come to their hideout. Yuma learns that the men are members of a group who refuse to acknowledge the end of the Civil War.

127.14 *Angry Town.* Jan. 10, 1960. GS: Perry Cook, Jose Sanchez, Jose Gonzales Gonzales, Ian MacDonald, Jim Giles. Johnny Yuma comes to town for supplies and discovers that he is the victim of a conspiracy. No one will sell to him and he will starve unless he can break the boycott.

127.15 *Gold Seeker.* Jan. 17, 1960. GS: John Sutton, Eddie Little Sky, Henry Brandon. Johnny Yuma tangles with a man who intends to mine gold in Indian territory, despite laws prohibiting it. Yuma pursues the man into the territory.

127.16 *Glory.* Jan. 24, 1960. GS: Marie Windsor, Jenifer Lea, William Bryant. In the desert, Johnny Yuma encounters a girl who has been stranded and left to die. Yuma learns that the girl's romance was broken up the hate of her fiance's sister.

127.17 *The Unwanted.* Jan. 31, 1960. GS: Trevor Bardette, Carleton Young, Henry Rowland, Buck Young. Johnny Yuma tries to befriend old man Amister. But townspeople warn that the man has been behaving strangely.

127.18 *The Crime.* Feb. 7, 1960. GS: Walter Sande, Paul Clarke, Richard Devon. Townspeople hurl charges of robbery at Johnny Yuma, but the rebel proves his innocence. The anxious citizens then turn their accusations on an equally innocent Mexican.

127.19 *Noblesse Oblige.* Feb. 14, 1960. GS: Robert Vaughn, Gail Russell. On a visit to his old commanding officer, Johnny Yuma discovers that the major is planning to hang an apparently innocent man.

127.20 *Land.* Feb. 21, 1960. GS: Rudolph Anders, Ralph Moody, Rick Rich, Ross Elliott. Johnny Yuma is called on to testify in a trial involving some prairie land. But after his appearance, Johnny learns that he has unwittingly helped pull off a big land swindle.

127.21 *He's Only a Boy.* Feb. 28, 1960. GS: Robert Blake, Michael Vandever, Donald Woods, George Becwar. His father has been called a coward, and young Virgil Morse intends to defend the family honor. Johnny Yuma has a letter that would disprove the accusation, but Virgil, unaware of this, tries to shoot him.

127.22 *Take Dead Aim.* March 6, 1960. GS: Edgar Barrier, Mala Powers. Bianco and Cassie are a husband-and-wife shooting team. Yuma finds himself right in their line of fire.

127.23 *The Rattler.* March 13, 1960. GS: Martha Vickers, Tommy Haig, Keith Richards. When a rattler bites Johnny Yuma, Tom Weed comes to his aid. But Weed is another kind of snake in the grass and plans to use Johnny in a scheme to take over the town.

127.24 *You Steal My Eyes.* March 20, 1960. GS: Cathy O'Donnell, William Bryant, Russ Sturlin, George Graham. Johnny Yuma rescues a trapper who was caught in his own snare. But Hump, the trapped trapper, has enemies who would just as soon he was left in the trap.

127.25 *Fair Game.* March 27, 1960. GS: James Drury, Patricia Medina, Jim Chandler, Stacy Harris, Mickey Finn. A bounty hunter is murdered while escorting outlaw Belle Kenyon to justice. Johnny Yuma takes charge of Belle and stalks the killer.

127.26 *Unsurrendered Sword.* April 3, 1960. GS: Jay Novello, Paul Picerni, Peggy Webber, Mary Gregory. Johnny Yuma goes to Mexico to retrieve a sword. He has promised to bring it back to Juanita, the widow of a Confederate general.

127.27 *The Captive of Tremblor.* April 10, 1960. GS: Robert Brubaker, John Pickard, James Seay, Mimi Gibson, Lillian Adams. A doctor who saved Johnny's life is in jail, but he has never been convicted of a crime.

127.28 *Blind Marriage.* April 17, 1960. GS: Lisa Lu, Philip Ahn, Victor Buono, Wyatt Cooper. Four larcenous characters are about to bamboozle a wealthy Chinese family. Though the odds are against him, Yuma tries to smash the scheme.

127.29 *Absolution.* April 24, 1960. GS: Gloria Talbott, Barry Atwater, John Maxwell, Natalie Masters, Laura Wood. Johnny hurries to the bedside of a dying young woman. His mission evokes the memory of an earlier time during the Civil War, when he and the girl were in love.

127.30 *A Grave for Johnny Yuma.* May 1, 1960. GS: Fred Beir, John Brinkley, Bruno Ve Sota, Mike Mikler, Ross Sterling, Olan Soule. Concealing his true identity, Johnny Yuma joins forces with a stranger who's trailing a man he intends to kill—Johnny Yuma.

127.31 *In Memory of a Son.* May 8, 1960. GS: Harry Bartell, Jack Hogan, Richard Evans, Marjorie Stapp, James Giles. Charlie Burton, in memory of a son lost during the Civil War, wills his valuable property to four of his son's wartime buddies.

127.32 *Paint a House with Scarlet.* May 15, 1960. GS: Clu Gulager, Maggie Mahoney, John Anderson. Johnny Yuma makes a brief stop at the farmhouse of a young widow, a former dance hall girl. He learns that she is being maliciously persecuted by a self-righteous neighbor.

127.33 *Grant of Land.* May 22, 1960. GS: Paul Richards, Ruta Lee, Ed Nelson, Jimmy Lee Cook, Ben Wright. A former Northern soldier has settled on a small piece of land in the South, and townspeople make it known that he is not welcome.

127.34 *Night on a Rainbow.* May 29, 1960. GS: James Best, Gail Kobe, Perry Cook, Jon Lormer. Johnny learns that an old friend from his Army days has become a drug addict.

127.35 *Lady of Quality.* June 5, 1960. GS: Joanna Moore, Edward Kemmer, Bart Burns. Johnny comes upon the burned-out remains of a fine old home. In the midst of the wreckage he finds a deranged young woman, oblivious to her surroundings and playing a pump organ.

127.36 *The Earl of Durango.* June 12, 1960. GS: Patricia Medina, John Sutton, George Tobias, L.Q. Jones, Jody Lawrence, Nick Dennis, Victor Buono, Bruno Ve Sota. Johnny is hired as bodyguard for the head of an investment company. He reports for duty just seconds too late and his employer has been shot.

Season Two

127.37 *Johnny Yuma at Appomattox.* Sept. 18, 1960. GS: George Macready, Ed Nelson, William Bryant, J. Pat O'Malley, Andrew J. Fenady, Teddy Rooney. General Grant pays a postwar visit to the South and Johnny tells young Jimmy the story of Lee's surrender.

127.38 *The Bequest.* Sept. 25, 1960. GS: Elisha Cook, Jr., John Carradine, Natalie Masters, John Pickard, Russ Sturlin, Robert Swan. Johnny Yuma, after the reward money on killer Jeremy Hake, returns to his home town. But Johnny's old buddies turn their backs on him for becoming just another bounty hunter.

127.39 *The Champ.* Oct. 2, 1960. GS: Michael Ansara, Edward Kemmer, Chuck Hicks, William Harlow, Eric Alden. Yuma runs into Docker Mason, an old Army buddy who is now a broken-down prizefighter. It seems that Docker is taking the punches but Jake Wiley, his manager, is taking most of the purse for himself.

127.40 *The Waiting.* Oct. 9, 1960. GS: Claude Akins, Joan Evans, Harry Whisner, Russ Sturlin, William Bryant. Yuma enters a saloon and finds three people inside: Mike the bartender, a bounty hunter named Tom Hall, and Cassie, a barmaid whose fugitive husband is the man Hall is looking for.

127.41 *To See the Elephant.* Oct. 16, 1960. GS: Mark Goddard, Ron Soble, Ken Mayer, Judith Rawlings, Ellen Corby. Rancher Bull Hollingsworth commissions Yuma to make a man out of his sheltered son, Seldon. Among other things, Seldon gets lessons in gunplay.

127.42 *Deathwatch.* Oct. 23, 1960. GS: James Best, Frank Silvera, Rocky Ybarra, Don Carlos. Looking for water, Johnny stumbles into the desert camp of sheepman Abel Waares. The two of them are joined by three Mexicans who tell Waares they want his sheep off the range by dawn.

127.43 *Run, Killer, Run.* Oct. 30, 1960. GS: Richard Jaeckel, Ed Nelson, John Pickard, William Harlow. Riding through brush country, Yuma is confronted by a fugitive named Traskel, who pulls his gun and makes Johnny trade horses.

127.44 *The Hunted.* Nov. 6, 1960. GS: Leonard Nimoy, Arline Sax, Yale Wexler, Dorothy Adams, Nick Dennis, Morgan Sha'an, Joe Dominguez, Len Weinrib, Tina Menard. Jim Colburn, sentenced to hang for murder, escapes from jail and a posse sets out to get him. Meanwhile, a telegram arrives, proving him innocent.

127.45 *The Legacy.* Nov. 13, 1960. GS: Jon Lormer, James Chandler, Paul Picerni, Robert Hutton. Yuma gets framed on a murder charge, but that is not the half of it. The man who set up the frame is the trial judge, the prosecutor and sheriff are his sons, and so is the defense lawyer.

127.46 *Don Gringo.* Nov. 20, 1960. GS: Gigi Perreau, Rosa Turich, Eugene Iglesias, Edgar Barrier, Ed Coch. Senorita Demetria is being escorted to meet her prospective bridegroom, Don Rolando, but Indians ambush the party and Demetris is the sole survivor. Yuma comes along and offers to escort her to Yuma.

127.47 *Explosion.* Nov. 27, 1960. GS: L.Q. Jones, Denny Niles, Douglas Spencer, Ross Elliott. A bandit named Roy shoots a man down while looting a stagecoach. But Roy doesn't get away, Yuma catches him in the act.

127.48 *Vindication.* Dec. 4, 1960. GS: James Drury, Martha Vickers, William Bryant, Dan Sheridan. Yuma loses his horse and gear in an Indian attack, but is picked up by a passing stage and taken to a relay station. There Capt. Paul Travers, a blind man, tells Johnny he was attacked at the same spot.

127.49 *The Scalp Hunter.* Dec. 11, 1960. GS: John Dehner, Earl Parker, Hal Needham, Ross Sturlin. Uncle John Sims arrives in time to save Johnny from a couple of Apache bandits. Then Sims asks Johnny's help. He believes a renegade Indian named Masi slew his wife, and he is out to track him down.

127.50 *Berserk.* Dec. 18, 1960. GS: Tom Drake, Dan Barton, Arthur Peterson, Jr., K.T. Stevens, George Becwar. Yuma is passing through a frontier town and decides to pay a visit to Sheriff Matt Dunsen, his old Army C.O. Matt shows up with two bodies—one of them his son Garth.

127.51 *The Hope Chest.* Dec. 25, 1960. GS: William Demarest, Soupy Sales, Cathy O'Donnell, William Harlow. Ulysses Bowman is rescued from an ambush by Yuma's timely arrival. He is so grateful, he even says that Johnny can marry his daughter.

127.52 *The Liberators.* Jan. 1, 1961. GS: Nico Minardos, Joan Vohs, Jody Warner, Nick Dennis. Yuma comes into a small town and finds it deserted. It looks like a hasty evacuation. The saloon is empty and half-consumed drinks are still on the bar.

127.53 *The Guard.* Jan. 8, 1961. GS: Ed Nelson, Dee Pollock, William Phipps, Allen Kramer. Clint Mowbree is all shook up when he learns that Yuma's coming to town. When Yuma was a prisoner of war, Clint had tortured him.

127.54 *The Promise.* Jan. 15, 1961. GS: Gigi Perreau, Peter Whitney, Richard Hartunian, John Gentry, Victor Izay. Yuma has some belongings to give to Laurie, the daughter of a deceased war buddy. Yuma finds her, but she is now a bonded servant, scheduled to marry gunslinger Billy Joe Kincaid against her wishes.

127.55 *Jerkwater.* Jan. 22, 1961. GS: John Dehner, John Marley, George Becwar, Charles Cason. In a small town, Yuma gets into an argument about the Civil War. The next thing he knows, he is shooting in self-defense. When the smoke clears, George Campbell, son of the town's leading citizen, lies dead, and Johnny is badly wounded.

127.56 *Paperback Hero.* Jan. 29, 1961. GS: Virginia Gregg, Robert Palmer, Daniel White, Robert Diamond. Newspaperwoman Emily Stevens becomes impressed when Johnny Yuma turns the tables on a bully named Jack Slater.

127.57 *The Actress.* Feb. 5, 1961. GS: Virginia Field, Sandra Knight, Vic Perrin, Robert L. Hickman. Johnny Yuma moseys into town one day and meets actress Lotta Langley. Lotta offers Johnny a part in her play.

127.58 *The Threat.* Feb. 12, 1961. GS: Aladdin Pallante,

Trevor Bardette, Richard Bakalyan, Red Morgan, Charles Heart, Ben Wright. Yuma visits the cattle town of Rescue, New Mexico, and finds the townsfolk paralyzed by fear. They've been told by Bart Vogan and his henchmen that Indians will shortly attack.

127.59 *The Road to Jericho.* Feb. 19, 1961. GS: Robert Middleton, Warren Stevens. Yuma finds a man named Sutro staked to an ant hill in the desert. After he frees the poor wretch, Johnny discovers Sutro's personal code calls from his to serve Yuma until he has repaid the debt.

127.60 *The Last Drink.* Feb. 26, 1961. GS: Tom Drake, Jack Chaplain. Yuma's teenage cousin Eddie years to be a gunslinger. Seeking vocational guidance, he starts hanging around with a professional gunman named Dawes.

127.61 *The Burying of Sammy Hart.* March 5, 1961. GS: Iron Eyes Cody, George D. Wallace, Eugene Martin, Peggy Stewart. Aaron Wallace's son Billy has disappeared into the hills with and old Redskin named Sammy Hart. Aaron is heading for town to report the kidnaping when he meets Johnny Yuma.

127.62 *The Pit.* March 12, 1961. GS: Olive Sturgess, Myron Healey, Sheldon Allman, Ralph Reed. A Woman named Charity engages Yuma to escort her and her infant son to a village where she hopes to find her missing husband. When Johnny inquires among the townspeople about the man, he is greeted with complete silence.

127.63 *Shriek of Silence.* March 19, 1961. GS: Tommy Noonan, Yvette Vickers, Jack Lester, Anna Karen, Frank de Kova. Yuma tries to care for the mute son of a man he killed in a fair fight. But the boy retains a natural hostility toward his father's slayer.

127.64 *Two Weeks.* March 26, 1961. GS: Frank Overton, Jaime Farr, Shirley Ballard. Yuma plays poker for curious stakes. If he loses, he becomes John Galt's prisoner for two weeks.

127.65 *Miz Purdy.* April 2, 1961. GS: Patricia Breslin, Jason Evers, Ken Mayer, Red Morgan, Russ Sturlin. Liz Purdy levels a shotgun at Johnny when he rides up to request a drink of water. It seems there have been some raids by outlaws in the area, and she thinks that he is one of the gang.

127.66 *The Ballad of Danny Brown.* April 9, 1961. GS: Tex Ritter, Gail Kobe, Stephen Joyce, William Bryant. Johnny Yuma arrives in Shady Grove to find the citizens preparing a hostile welcome home for ex-convict Danny Brown. Figuring that Brown has paid his debt to society, Johnny decides to join Danny's girl Emily in a friendlier greeting.

127.67 *The Proxy.* April 16, 1961. GS: Vic Damone, Royal Dano. Yuma and two volunteers named Wilkers and Crowe are hot after a banker who went south of the border with his depositors' savings. Johnny seems to be the only one interested in justice as Wilkers wants to kill the man and Crowe is after the money.

127.68 *Decision at Sweetwater.* April 23, 1961. GS: Yvette Vickers, William Phipps, Sally Bliss, Donald Losby, Donald Buka, Herman Rudin, Bruno Ve Sota. Out to waylay a gold shipment, Jess Galt and his henchmen hold up a stage on which Yuma is a passenger. Finding no gold, the frustrated outlaws don't want to leave empty handed, so they decide to kidnap a passenger.

127.69 *Helping Hand.* April 30, 1961. GS: Leif Erickson, Jack Elam, Eddie Ryder. Yuma and his mount are looking forward to a cool drink at the water hole. But two gents named Dave and Uncle Luce are having a knock-down, drag-out battle.

127.70 *The Uncourageous.* May 7, 1961. GS: George Dolenz, Eugene Iglesias, Penata Vanni, Maria Val. Yuma is on a round up in Mexico when he accidentally shoots young Felipe Amontillo. As he tends the boy's wound, Johnny learns he is the son of a famous matador, Juan Amontillo, and the Felipe is in disfavor at home because he can't match his father's bravery.

127.71 *Mission — Varina.* May 14, 1961. GS: Frieda Inescort, William Schallert. After the Civil War, Jefferson Davis is released from prison, and his wife Varina asks Yuma and three other ex-Rebel soldiers to escort him to Richmond. At the rendezvous point, Yuma finds that two of the men haven't shown up and the third intends to assassinate Davis.

127.72 *The Calley Kid.* May 21, 1961. GS: Richard Bakalyan, Michael Vanderver. Bushwacked on the trail, Yuma awakens to discover his attacker has stripped him of his horse, guns and personal belongings. Tracking the mysterious assailant, Yuma runs across a dying lawman who says he was shot by the notorious Calley Kid.

127.73 *Ben White.* May 28, 1961. GS: Mary Murphy, Charles Aidman, Bruno Ve Sota, William Henry. U.S. Marshal Ab Jason deputizes Yuma to take one member of an outlaw gang to jail while he goes after the others. Yuma's prisoner is a girl known only as T, and she doesn't intend to go to jail.

127.74 *The Found.* June 4, 1961. GS: Peggy Campbell, Karl Held, George Sawaya. Yuma comes upon a girl named Sally who is alone and about to give birth to a child. Yuma helps deliver the baby, and then finds himself held at gunpoint by Danny, the child's father.

127.75 *The Hostage.* June 11, 1961. GS: Lon McCallister, Jean Innes, Corey Allen, Stephen Joyce, Edward Kemmer, Aladdin. Frank Dagget is in jail and sentenced to hang, but his brother Yancey has a plan to free him. Yancey kidnaps Jess Wilks, the sheriff's brother, and proposes and exchange of prisoners.

127.76 *The Executioner.* June 18, 1961. GS: Terry Moore, Barry Atwater, Ken Mayer, Charles Aidman, Arthur Peterson. Two of Chief Leblanc's braves have been killed and the chief has three hostages he plans to kill in reprisal. Yuma points out that three for two is not a fair exchange, and the chief readily agrees. He tells Yuma to select the two who are to die.

128. *Redigo*

NBC. 30 min. Broadcast history: Tuesday, 8:30–9:00, Sept. 1963–Dec. 1963.

Regular Cast: Richard Egan (Jim Redigo), Roger Davis (Mike), Rudy Solari (Frank Martinez), Elena Verdugo (Gerry), Mina Martinez (Linda Martinez).

Premise: The series depicted the exploits of Jim Redigo, the owner and operator of a small ranch in the modern Southwest.

Note: This series was a sequel to the previous season's *Empire.*

The Episodes

128.1 *Lady War-Bonnet.* Sept. 24, 1963. GS: Mary

Murphy, Ed Ames, Byron Morrow. Laura McAdams, one of Jim's ranching neighbors, runs for councilwoman and loses, not only the election but her father too.

128.2 *The Blooded Bull.* Oct. 1, 1963. GS: Peter Brown, Richard Evans, Kay E. Kuter, Don Diamond, Nesdon Booth. With the future of his ranch hanging in the balance, Redigo sets out to find the rustlers that swiped his prize bull.

128.3 *Boy from the Rio Bravo.* Oct. 8, 1962. GS: Michael Davis. Redigo has his hands full fighting a contagious horse disease when a runaway Mexican boy named Carlos shows up. He wants to stay permanently and learn to be a cowboy.

128.4 *Prince Among Men.* Oct. 15, 1963. GS: Nico Minardos, Tim Graham, Don Diamond. Luis Guardino, son of a Latin American dictator, learns of his father's murder while on Redigo's ranch and asks to say on as a hand.

128.5 *The Crooked Circle.* Oct. 22, 1963. GS: Pippa Scott, Richard Anderson, Don Haggerty, Robert Armstrong. Redigo sends for old friend Pat Royal to do a dynamiting job, but the Pat who arrives is Royal's daughter Patricia.

128.6 *Little Angel Blue Eyes.* Oct. 29, 1963. GS: Kathie Browne, James Best, William Woodson. Angel Carr may look sweet and innocent, but Redigo has his reasons for not confusing her with Little Red Riding Hood.

128.7 *Man in a Blackout.* Nov. 5, 1963. GS: Albert Salmi, Evans Evans, Harry Carey, Jr., Dort Clark, Don Spruance, Don Diamond. Redigo is struck a glancing blow by a truck and wakes up an amnesia victim.

128.8 *Papa-San.* Nov. 12, 1963. GS: Anita Loo, Chad Everett, Ed Peck, Robert Anderson, Jan and Dean. Papa-San is Redigo's name during the visit of Sada, a Korean orphan that Redigo's unit adopted during the war. Jim is happy to see her but sad to hear that she has fallen for a local yokel whose most obvious characteristic is rudeness.

128.9 *Horns of Hate.* Nov. 19, 1963. GS: John Anderson, Diana Millay, Claude Johnson. Rancher Lee Cresco finds the body of a contagiously diseased deer on his ranch, panics and dumps the carcass on Redigo's land.

128.10 *Shadow of the Cougar.* Nov. 26, 1963. GS: Kathleen Crowley, Mike Connors. There is a big cougar prowling the foothills, and Redigo's house guest Jack Marston would like to hunt it down.

128.11 *The Thin Line.* Dec. 3, 1963. GS: Ray Danton, Jim Drum. Redigo hires Jeff Burton, an ex-convict trying for a new start, and learns that Jeff and Gerry were once very much in love and may still be.

128.12 *Hostage Hero Riding.* Dec. 10, 1963. GS: Ed Nelson, Elinor Donahue, Brian Keith, Tyler McVey. Redigo's old friend Danny Kilpatrick took big chances in the war and became a hero, a role he wants to continue, chances and all.

128.13 *Privilege of a Man.* Dec. 17, 1963. GS: Arch Johnson, Peggy McCay. Stuart Graham, novelist and outdoorsman, looks forward to some vigorous activity during his visit to Redigo's ranch, ignoring the fact that his health is failing.

128.14 *The Black Rainbow.* GS: Gordon Wescourt, Susan Seaforth. Redigo and his ranch hand are held hostage by gun-toting Gussie Leonard and Bert Baker.

128.15 *The Hunters.* Dec. 31, 1963. GS: Perry Lopez, Walter Sande, Don Diamond. An Indian named Afraid of His Own Horses decides to feed his family by hunting, even though it is not hunting season, and the game is on someone else's land.

129. The Restless Gun

NBC. 30 min. Broadcast history: Monday, 8:00–8:30, Sept. 1957–Sept. 1959.

Regular Cast: John Payne (Vint Bonner).

Premise: This series depicted the exploits of ex-gunfighter Vint Bonner, who roamed the West aiding people in need of help.

The Episodes

129.1 *Duel at Lockwood.* Sept. 23, 1957. GS: Vic Morrow, Olive Carey, Walter Coy. Vint Bonner meets an elderly woman who asks him to do something about her grandson. The young man has already killed two men and has vowed to add Vint Bonner to the list.

129.2 *Trail to Sunset.* Sept. 30, 1957. GS: Jack Elam. Vint Bonner meets five men who have just come from a lynching. He confronts them with evidence that they have killed an innocent man.

129.3 *Revenge at Harness Creek.* Oct. 7, 1957. A young man, angered by his brother's constant domination, takes out his bitterness on a friend of his. When he becomes violent, the friend is forced to shoot him in self-defense.

129.4 *Rink.* Oct. 14, 1957. GS: Peter Votrian, Denver Pyle, George Keymas, Fred Kruger, Tony Hughes. Vint Bonner meets a teenage boy who is seeking his father's killer. The boy is determined to exact revenge.

129.5 *Jenny.* Oct. 21, 1957. GS: Veda Ann Borg, Walter Reed, Stuart Randall. Vint Bonner joins up with a posse on the trail of an outlaw. They learn he has taken refuge in the outlying ranch home of a woman who lives alone.

129.6 *The Shooting of Jett King.* Oct. 28, 1957. GS: John Larch, Leon Askin, Nesdon Booth, Whit Bissell. An outlaw notoriously fast on the draw, is finally caught after a bank robbery and brought in by the posse. He claims it was Vint Bonner who beat him to the draw, but Vint denies it and refuses to accept the reward money.

129.7 *Jody.* Nov. 4, 1957. GS: Rip Torn, Dan Blocker, Luana Anders, Jeanne Bates, Martin Garralaga, Paul Fix. A reckless youth, ambitious to become a gunfighter, becomes a prime target for revenge when he kills a man in self-defense. The hulking brother and father of the victim set out to avenge the death.

129.8 *General Gilford's Widow.* Nov. 11, 1957. GS: Lurene Tuttle, Paul Birch, Harry Shannon, Howard Negley, Hal K. Dawson. On his way to town to sell cattle, Vint Bonner takes the wrong turn and seeks directions at an isolated ranch. Recognizing Vint as a former soldier, the woman invites him in for a visit with her husband, Gen. Gilford. But Vint knows that the general was killed five years earlier in an Indian raid. When he arrives in town Vint learns that the people there intend to send the widow Gilford to a mental home, by force, if necessary.

129.9 *The New Sheriff.* No. 18, 1957. GS: Lloyd Corrigan, Henry Brandon, Stacy Harris, William Fawcett, Gregg

The Restless Gun

Martell, Frank Marlowe, John Merrick. Doc Cross railroads Vint Bonner into the job of Sheriff. Vint is forced much against his will into a showdown with a trio of toughs.

129.10 *Man and Boy.* Nov. 25, 1957. GS: Emile Meyer. Vint helps a stern sheriff trail a youthful killer who they believe is the lawman's son.

129.11 *Cheyenne Express.* Dec. 2, 1957. GS: Royal Dano, Dan Riss, Chris Randall, Anthony Ray, Harry Fleer, Tim Graham. A cowardly gunman shoots his gang leader in the back, then runs to Vint Bonner for protection. Vint struggles with his conscience over whether he should protect the spineless killer.

129.12 *Thicker Than Water.* Dec. 9, 1957. GS: Claude Akins, Lars Henderson, Frank Richards, Ted de Corsia, Penny Edwards, Jack Lomax. A notorious gambler learns that the wife he deserted has died, and decides to return now to claim his young son. Vint Bonner, however, feels that it is more important to keep the boy from learning a gambler's life.

129.13 *Silver Threads.* Dec. 16, 1957. GS: Chuck Connors, John Patrick, Sean McClory, Steve Firstman. A rancher is robbed and fatally shot by a stranger in the territory. Vint Bonner's only clue is a song which the killer was heard to sing.

129.14 *The Child.* Dec. 23, 1957. GS: Dan Blocker, Carlos Arevalo, James Gleason, Anthony Caruso, Elizabeth Garcia. Vint Bonner tracks down a fugitive in the snow country and captures him. During a blizzard Bonner, and his prisoner seek shelter at a monastery, where the prisoner is chained in a cell.

129.15 *The Gold Buckle.* Dec. 30, 1957. GS: Roy Roberts, Claude Akins, Madge Blake, Jerry Brown, Fred Graham, Terry Frost. Two men hold up a stagecoach, shoot and kill an elderly gentleman passenger and then head for the border. Vint Bonner takes out after them and along the way meets two strangers who profess to be pursuing the killers for the reward.

129.16 *The Coward.* Jan. 6, 1958. GS: Gene Evans, John Dehner, John Mitchum, Carol Henry, Marilyn Saris, Lane Bradford. A range baron who dislikes the cowardly attitude of a farmer, determines to drive him off his land. Vint Bonner intervenes when he learns that the farmer's cattle have been poisoned and his fences cut.

129.17 *Friend in Need.* Jan. 13, 1958. GS: Harry Fleer, Corey Allen, Mark Dana, Emile Meyer, Arthur Space, Irene Tedrow. Two former friends have accused each other of murder. Vint Bonner decides to look into the truth of the matter.

129.18 *Strange Family in Town.* Jan. 20, 1958. GS: Jacques Aubuchon, Patrick McVey, Jeanne Bates, Ricky Klein, Virginia Christine. A family of peaceful Quakers newly arrived in the territory find themselves objects of their neighbors' scorn. The ranchers and even the children mistake the Quaker's pacifistic beliefs for cowardice.

129.19 *Hang and Be Damned.* Jan. 27, 1958. GS: Gloria Talbot, Joe Maross, Ray Teal, Charles Wagenheim. Vint Bonner arrests a killer and begins the journey to the next town and the nearest jail. The prisoner's girl friend, Valya, follows them. On the way they meet a band of drunken Apaches, who agree to spare Bonner and his prisoner if they will turn Valya over to them.

129.20 *Quiet City.* Feb. 3, 1958. GS: John Dehner, William Joyce, Reed Howes, Austin Green, Lyle Talbot. A veteran sheriff of a now peaceful, law-abiding town glories in memories of the past when he fought gunmen and outlaws. Then he begins to imagine that the whole town is plotting against him.

129.21 *Hornitas Town.* Feb. 10, 1958. GS: Peggie Castle, John Larch, Millicent Patrick, Jack Elam, Glenn Strange. A very devout young girl who hates violence makes a strange request of Vint Bonner. She wants him to subdue a crooked sheriff who rules his town by terror, but she asks Vint not to use his gun.

129.22 *Imposter for a Day.* Feb. 17, 1958. GS: Kent Taylor, Angie Dickinson, Robert Rourke, Gene Roth, Harry Hines, Lane Chandler, Lou Krugman. A young gunslinger, under orders from an older man, adopts Vint Bonner's identity and terrorizes the townspeople. Vint is forced into a showdown with the boy.

129.23 *Pressing Engagement.* Feb. 24, 1958. GS: Fay Spain, Peter Hansen, Edith Evanson, Iron Eyes Cody, Larry Blake. Pretty Helen Rockford has been receiving letters from an ardent admirer who signs himself Vint Bonner. But when Vint rides into town he is taken aback by the many congratulations concerning his upcoming wedding to Helen. Vint disclaims all knowledge of both the letters and the wedding.

129.24 *The Woman from Sacramento.* March 3, 1958. GS: Kathleen Crowley, Will Wright, H.M. Wynant, Rosa Turich, Gregg Barton. Vint Bonner's employer, an elderly rancher who is dying, receives word that his daughter is coming to see him for the first time in many years. Because the old man owns a large ranch, he believes that the girl is not his daughter, but an opportunist.

129.25 *Sheriff Billy.* March 10, 1958. GS: Tom Tryon, Harold J. Stone, Joyce Meadows, Hank Patterson. A town employs Bill Riddle, a serious young man, as its sheriff. Bill is determined to find his father, who disappeared many years ago. When a dangerous outlaw appears in the town, Bill is surprised to find in his possession a locket that his mother once wore.

129.26 *The Hand Is Quicker.* March 17, 1958. GS: John Ericson, Gregg Palmer, Ray Teal, Hank Faber, Tyler McVey. A young widower asks Vint Bonner's help in becoming a fast gunman. The young man, Henry Wilson, tells Vint he is the potential target of a vicious killer who was in love with Wilson's recently deceased wife.

129.27 *The Suffragette.* March 24, 1958. GS: Ellen Corby, John Dierkes, Don Beddoe. Emma Birch has organized the women of the town into a determined suffragette group. The men rebel and attempt to put the women in their place. Vint Bonner becomes the reluctant liaison man.

129.28 *The Whip.* March 31, 1958. GS: Diane Brewster, John Stephenson, Harvey Stephens. An old suitor turns the town against the wife of an accused killer

129.29 *The Crisis at Easter Creek.* April 7, 1958. GS: Frank Wilcox, Amzie Strickland, Marshall Bradford, John Larch, Henry Corden. Rev. Broome prevails upon Vint Bonner to help solicit funds for a new organ for the Easter Creek Church. After small success in the town, Vint decides to try his luck at a nearby settlement notorious for its thieves, gamblers and desperadoes.

129.30 *Aunt Emma.* April 14, 1958. GS: Connie Gilchrist, Edgar Buchanan, Stuart Randall, William Fawcett, Paul Grant, Lane Bradford, Mauritz Hugo. While attempting to track down the Drake brothers, dangerous bank robbers, Vint Bonner is wounded. He is nursed back to health by his elderly aunt, who tries to prevent him from continuing his search for the robbers after he recovers.

129.31 *The Outlander.* April 21, 1958. GS: George Dolenz, Gloria Talbott, Reed Hadley, George Keymas, Mitchell Kowal, Stanley Farrar, Paul Sorensen. Vint Bonner arrives in a Kansas town and finds that it has been taken over by a band of renegade Texans. A Count Von Gilsa stands up to the ruffians, and they attempt to drag him out of town.

129.32 *The Battle of Tower Rock.* April 28, 1958. GS: Irene Ryan, Lillian Bronson, Lloyd Corrigan, Don Beddoe, Dan Riss, James F. Stone, Tim Graham. Vint Bonner rides into town and finds the town split by a bitter feud. After an investigation, Vint finds that two sisters and some strawberry preserves are responsible for the feud.

129.33 *The Torn Flag.* May 5, 1958. GS: Kristine Miller, Alan Baxter, Paul Birch, Fred Kohler. Riding into town, Vint Bonner finds the body of a man draped with a torn Confederate flag. He learns Confederate patriots have banded together to plan retaliation against the Union, and suspects the man was murdered by one of the fanatics.

129.34 *Hiram Grover's Strike.* May 12, 1958. GS: Will Wright, Trevor Bardette, Lane Bradford, John Mitchum, Pierre Watkin. After 45 years of prospecting, Hiram Grover finally hits a vein of gold. On his way to town to have the find assayed, he is jumped by two gunmen. But Vint Bonner happens onto the scene and saves Hiram's life and his gold. Vint then accompanies Hiram into town, not realizing that the gunmen are planning another attack on the old man.

129.35 *The Gold Star.* May 19, 1958. GS: Edgar Buchanan, Sandy Sanders, Dick Elliot, I. Stanford Jolley, James Anderson, Craig Duncan, Rankin Mansfield, Frank Sully. After many years of service, the town's sheriff is retiring. Because he has grown bitter toward the townspeople, who have become rich while he remained poor. the sheriff plans a bank robbery while the mayor and the people are gathered at a ceremony in his honor.

129.36 *More Than Kin.* May 26, 1958. GS: John Carradine, Veda Ann Borg, Max Hartman, Ken Hooker, Emmett Lynn. The rugged frontier town of Virtue City has little use for Archibald Plunkette and his company of Shakespearean players. When Archibald has an opportunity to audition for the great P.T. Barnum, he enlists the aid of Vint Bonner to keep order in the audience.

129.37 *The Manhunters.* June 2, 1958. GS: Tom Pittman, Kay Stewart, Carlyle Mitchell, John Cason, Robert Swan, Morgan Woodward, Dennis Moore, Harry Hines. Vint Bonner goes to visit an old lawyer friend who has been made bitter by the death of his only son. While in the town, Bonner sees the three Cotterman brothers goad a younger man into a gun fight. The shooting ends with the death of one of the Cottermans, and when the young man escapes, the brothers swear to track him down and kill him. Bonner appeals to his friend to help the young fugitive, but he refuses.

129.38 *The Peddler.* June 9, 1958. GS: Eduard Franz, Olive Carey, Bob Morgan, Bob La Varre, Bert Nelson. While an elderly peddler is showing Osa Carpenter some of his wares, Duke Ballinger and two of his cronies ride up. The three men, who have been drinking, begin maliciously to tease the peddler. Osa becomes enraged and drives the attackers away. But before they leave, Duke threatens to get even with the peddler.

129.39 *Gratitude.* June 1, 1958. GS: John Litel, Jeanne Bates, Johnny Crawford. While fixing territorial borders for the government, Vint Bonner clashes with landowner McClelland Burke. While attempting to force Bonner of his land, Burke loses control of his horse and is thrown.

Season Two

129.40 *Jebediah Bonner.* Sept. 22, 1958. GS: John Payne, Dennis Holmes, James Best, Carlyle Mitchell, Edith Evanson, Read Morgan. Vint Bonner tells a young boy about an incident involving his grandfather, Marshal Jeb Bonner. Jeb Bonner has come home to settle down and retire. But on his arrival he is met by Jim Kenyon, the son of an outlaw that Bonner was once forced to kill. Kenyon is determined to needle the old man into a gunfight.

129.41 *Dragon for a Day.* Sept. 29, 1958. GS: Allen Breneman, Frank De Kova, Alan Reynolds, Felipe Turich, Juney Ellis, Leslie Bradley, Joel Ashley, Harry Fleer. After fourteen-year-old John Fletcher's mother and father are murdered and their ranch is burned by a band of renegade Indians, the youngster plots revenge. Despite Vint Bonner's warnings, John sneaks away from town with a borrowed rifle and many rounds of ammunition to find the Indians.

129.42 *Mercyday.* Oct. 6, 1958. GS: Gloria Talbott, Veda Ann Borg, Dean Stockwell, Dan Blocker. To satisfy the dying wish of a mountaineer friend, Vint Bonner promises to look after the man's daughter and to help make a lady out of the wild young girl.

129.43 *Thunder Valley.* Oct. 13, 1958. GS: John Larch, Robert Black, Marya Stevens, Sergio Virell. A ruthless bounty hunter, interested only in money, poses as a sheriff while tracking down a Mexican bandit who robbed a stagecoach. The bounty hunter asks Vint Bonner to help him, and Bonner agrees, thinking the man is actually a sheriff.

129.44 *The Nowhere Kid.* Oct. 20, 1958. GS: Steven Terrell, Luana Patten, Rusty Lane, Ralph Sanford, Tyler McVey, Lenny Geer, Paul Marcus. In an attempt to impress his girl, Johnny Smith challenges Vint Bonner to a horse race. After Bonner wins the race, Johnny is caught attempting to steal Bonner's horse. Instead of turning Johnny over to the law, Vint tries to help him by getting the youngster a job.

129.45 *Bonner's Squaw.* Nov. 3, 1958. GS: Daria Massey, Joe Vitale, Ewing Mitchell, Paul Keast, Frances Morris, Frank Scannell, Charles Briggs. Vint Bonner discovers a shy Indian girl sleeping on the floor of his hotel room. The girl's chief insists that Vint must live up to Indian law and marry the girl, or else there will be an Indian attack.

129.46 *Tomboy.* Nov. 10, 1958. GS: Judi Meredith, Don C. Harvey, Leon Tyler, Jack Grinnage, Gene Roht. Pretty Lettie Belknap is jealous because her father gives all his attention to her brother George. She decides that she will prove to her father that she can do anything better than George can. Lettie stages a holdup, and her victim turns out to be Vint Bonner.

129.47 *Remember the Dead.* Nov. 17, 1958. GS: Frank Ferguson, Bartlett Robinson, Joe Flynn, Rickie Sorenson, Sandra Wright, Selmer Jackson, John Dennis. Vint Bonner discovers that he has arrived in town too late with evidence that would have saved his friend from being hanged for murder. The townspeople resent Bonner's presence because he reminds them of the terrible mistake they made, but Bonner refuses to leave until he has located the real murderer.

129.48 *No Way to Kill.* Nov. 24, 1958. GS: Henry Corden, Jeanne Bates, Ronald Sorensen, Don Grady, Don Kennedy, Ben Johnson, Austin Green. A one-armed gunman escapes prison to seek vengeance on the bounty hunters who crippled him eight years earlier.

129.49 *Take Me Home.* Dec. 1, 1958. GS: Mala Powers, Peter Breck, Jeff Daley, Sheldon Allman, Jean Harvey. Vint Bonner meets the daughter of some friends when he travels to a far-off Quaker settlement to deliver a set of schoolbooks. The girl has taken up with a brutal saloon owner. Vint tries to persuade her to return home.

129.50 *Multiply One Boy.* Dec. 8, 1958. GS: Jimmy Baird, Jim Reppert, Ricky Klein, Kay Stewart, Clark Howat. Vint Bonner brings a young Southern boy, orphaned during the Civil War, to live with his Northern relatives. But the youngster is bitter and proves difficult to manage because of his resentment toward his uncle, whom he thinks of as a traitor.

129.51 *Peligroso.* Dec. 15, 1958. GS: Marcia Henderson, Trevor Bardette, Robert Fuller, Ashley Cowan, Ted Markland, Dabbs Greer. Vint Bonner is the intended target of a hired gunman. The would-be assassin was hired by a beautiful but vindictive young woman.

129.52 *A Bell for Santo Domingo.* Dec. 22, 1958. GS: John Litel, Arline Sax, Sarah Selby, Hal Jon Norman, Ronny Mann. Vint Bonner is acting as guide for two nuns and a priest who want to locate a mission that hasn't been heard from for a long time. The journey takes Vint and his party through dangerous Indian country.

129.53 *Take Me Home.* Dec. 29, 1958. GS: Dan Blocker, James Coburn, Stuart Randall, Morgan Woodward, Bek Nelson, Voorhies J. Ardoin. Vint Bonner steps in when a mercenary pair of men and a saloon hostess attempt to bilk an unsuspecting farm boy of his life savings.

129.54 *The Painted Beauty.* Jan. 5, 1959. GS: Ruta Lee, Charles Cooper, William Hudson, Jeff Daley, Roscoe Ates, Paul Dubov. When Lucy agrees to pose for a picture to be placed over the bar of a local saloon, her tough boy friend makes matters uncomfortable for Vint Bonner and the artist.

129.55 *Shadow of a Gunfighter.* Jan. 12, 1959. GS: Robert Fuller, Douglas Kennedy, John Goddard, John Milford, Mara Corday. Ex-gunfighter Cal Winfield comes out of retirement to find the man who killed his only son. Cal has been told that his old pal Vint Bonner is responsible for his boy's death.

129.56 *The Lady and the Gun.* Jan. 19, 1959. GS: Mala Powers, Lloyd Corrigan, Evelyn Scott, Charles Irwin. Vint Bonner is angry when he discovers that a woman he has never met has borrowed his horse for a morning ride.

129.57 *The Red Blood of Courage.* Feb. 2, 1959. GS: Lee Farr, J. Carrol Naish, Alex Talton, Gregg Barton, Charles Keane. While Vint Bonner is a guest at the ranch of a cattle baron, Maj. Quint Langley, Langley's foreman plots to take over all of his employer's property.

129.58 *Better Than a Cannon.* Feb. 9, 1959. GS: Herbert C. Lytton, Bern Hoffman, Wilhelm Augustus, Jeanne Bates, Shirley Knight. U.S. Marshal Gavin Brandon asks Vint Bonner to help him solve a problem. Wilhelm Augustus Von Ritter has recently inherited the title of baron and feels he has the authority to set up a toll gate on his property, blocking a road that everyone uses. The marshal wants to settle the matter without violence.

129.59 *The Dead Ringer.* Feb. 16, 1959. GS: John Payne, Walter Coy, Richard Cutting, Michael Lipton, George Eldredge, Roy Engel, Richard Attlinger. Outlaw Nick Dawson sees Vint Bonner riding into town and is shocked at the strong resemblance between Bonner and Dawson's boss. Later the local bank is robbed and a man is killed. Witnesses swear that the man who did the killing was Vint.

129.60 *The Last Grey Man.* Feb. 23, 1959. GS: Henry Hull, Robert H. Barratt, William Joyce, Chris Roberts. The Army traces a shipment of gold, missing since the Civil War, to the shack of a stubborn old Confederate soldier. But the old man refuses to give the gold up without a fight. Vint Bonner decides to visit him.

129.61 *Melany.* March 2, 1959. GS: Mayra Stevens, Craig Palmer, Claude Akins, Alan Reynolds. Vint Bonner goes to visit an old friend whose husband is crippled as a result of a gunfight. Vint becomes suspicious that the man's injury is more mental than physical.

129.62 *Ricochet.* March 9, 1959. GS: Robert H. Harris, John Lupton, Mary Webster, Abel Fernandez. Pete Garrick, a schoolteacher bored with his way of life, decides to move West with his wife and become a rancher. But ranching proves very difficult, and Garrick becomes despondent. They he becomes friendly with gangsters.

129.63 *Dead Man's Hand.* March 16, 1959. GS: Henry Hull, Charles Cooper, James Griffith, David Leland, Charles R. Keane. Vint Bonner encounters an old acquaintance, Doc Kemmer, who makes his living by selling patent medicine. Doc gets in trouble when he sells his cure-all, which has a high alcohol content, to a man with heart trouble who has been warned not to drink.

129.64 *The Sweet Sisters.* March 23, 1959. GS: Edith Evanson, Jeanette Nolan, Frank Wilcox. Elizabeth and Abigail, the elderly Sweet sisters, abhor the slaughter of animals and begin rustling cattle to save them. The local ranchers, however, blame nearby homesteaders for the trouble.

129.65 *Incident at Bluefield.* March 30, 1959. GS: Alan Hale, Jr., Morgan Woodward, John Litel, William Lundmark, Goovy Von Eur, Dan Seymour, Dan Hix. Vint Bonner rides into the town of Bluefield and finds that his best friend has been shot to death. This episode is told, through a flashback, by an old man whose grandson has asked him to tell a story of the Old West.

129.66 *The Pawn.* April 6, 1959. GS: James Coburn, Julie Payne, Onslow Stevens, Denver Pyle, Tyler McVey, Robert Foulk, Howard McLeod. Down on his luck, Peggy McGiven's father joins a gang of cattle rustlers in a desperate attempt to provide for his deaf-mute daughter.

129.67 *Four Lives.* April 13, 1959. GS: John Ericson, Gregg Palmer, Mary Murphy, Robert Griffin. Vint Bonner helped raise Bud Rainey from childhood, and Bud is known as a likable young man. But it is learned that he has murdered a woman.

129.68 *One on the House.* April 20, 1959. GS: Henry Hull, Whitney Blake, Roy Engel, Howard Wendell, Kenneth

MacDonald. Old Matt Harper has served a long jail sentence for bank robbery. The government discovers that Matt is innocent, frees him and offers him a sum of money as indemnity. But he refuses the money, claiming that the government owes him the privilege of committing an actual bank robbery.

129.69 Code for a Killer. April 27, 1959. GS: Floyd Simmons, Lane Bradford, Jean Howell, Edgar Stehli. Vint Bonner goes to Dorado for the wedding of his friend, Sheriff Dave Regan. When he arrives he finds that Regan has been killed and the suspect, a known gunslinger, has left town.

129.70 Mme. Brimstone. May 4, 1959. GS: Bea Benaderet, Don Grady, Leslie Bradley, Nacho Galindo, Alan Roberts, Don Harvey. A blustering lady ranch-owner asks Vint Bonner to teach the ways of the West to her ten-year-old grandson who is arriving from Boston. The youth, Sylvester Cromwell III, provides Bonner with a harrowing experience.

129.71 Lady by Law. May 11, 1959. GS: Peggie Castle, Stewart Bradley, S. John Launer, Paul Baxley, Douglas Kennedy. A footloose young miss is ordered out of town by the sheriff, but Vint Bonner takes pity on her and intercedes. The judge allows the girl to remain — in Bonner's custody.

129.72 Ride with the Devil. May 18, 1959. GS: Jan Arvan, Rafael Campos, Sergio Virell, Paul Vera. Don Tomas Verdes, a Mexican ranch owner, calls on Vint Bonner to help dissuade his son from riding with a bandit gang. Bonner decides to join the outlaws in order to bring the boy to his sense.

129.73 A Trial for Jenny May. May 25, 1959. GS: Kasey Rogers, Ellen Corby, Guinn "Big Boy" Williams, Nancy DeCarl, John Collier, Scotty Morrow, George Sawaya, Paul Lukather. Because she works in a saloon, a woman is accused of being an unfit mother for her three children. Vint Bonner comes to her defense when the townspeople begin to torment the family.

129.74 The Cavis Boy. June 1, 1959. GS: Don Grady, Wilton Graff, Baynes Barron, Charles Maxwell. Bob Cavis, though innocent of any wrongdoing, is sentenced to hang. His twelve-year-old son strives to help his father, feeling that any measures are justified in his attempt to right the wrong.

129.75 The Englishman. June 8, 1959. GS: Lyle Talbot, Lester Fletcher, Frank Albertson, John Milford, Dale Johnson, Jeff Daley, Dale Allen. Mort Askins plans to play a practical joke on his friend Vint Bonner. He enlists the aid of a unique Englishman, and the two of them plot a daring robbery.

129.76 A Very Special Investigator. June 15, 1959. GS: Andy Clyde, Reed Hadley, Fay Spain, Don Kelly. Newspaper editor Aldrick Newton prints the story that a special investigator is coming to town. At the same time he invites his friend Vint Bonner to come for a visit, and Vint's arrival leads to some desperate activity on the party of several shady citizens.

129.77 The Hill of Death. June 22, 1959. GS: Regis Toomey, John Dehner, Fernando Lusk, Jerry Brent, Harry Hines, Dorothea Lord, Dick Jeffries. While Vint Bonner is visiting his old friend Dr. Lem Shepherd, a young boy is left on the doctor's doorstep. The boy is badly beaten and near death. Since the sheriff is away Bonner takes on the responsibility of finding the boy's assailants.

129.78 The Way Back. July 13, 1959. GS: James Coburn, Dan Blocker, Stuart Randall, Morgan Woodward, Mala Powers, Peter Breck, Bek Nelson, Sheldon Allman, Bill George, Jean Harvey, Jeff Daley, Voorhies J. Ardoin. Vint Bonner steps in when a mercenary pair of men and a saloon hostess attempt to bilk an unsuspecting army boy of his life's savings.

130. The Rifleman

ABC. 30 min. Broadcast history: Tuesday, 9:00-9:30, Sept. 1958–Sept. 1960; Tuesday, 8:00-8:30, Sept. 1960–Sept. 1961; Monday, 8:30-9:00, Oct. 1961–July 1963.

Regular Cast: Chuck Connors (Lucas McCain), Johnny Crawford (Mark McCain), Paul Fix (Marshal Micah Torrance), Bill Quinn (Sweeney, the bartender), Hope Summers (Hattie Denton), Joan Taylor (Millie Scott) 60-62, Patricia Blair (Lou Mallory) 62-63.

Premise: Rancher Lucas McCain, a widower and expert shot with a rifle, tries to bring up his young son, Mark, in the town of North Fork, New Mexico, in the late 1880s.

The Episodes

130.1 The Sharpshooter. Sept. 30, 1958. GS: Leif Erickson, Dennis Hopper, Sidney Blackmer, R.G. Armstrong, Charles Arnt, Mickey Simpson, Kathleen Mulqueen, Victoria Aldridge. Lucas and Mark see a sign offering a ranch for sale. To raise the money to buy the ranch, Lucas decides to enter a local turkey shoot. *Note*: This episode is a re-edited version of the pilot, which originally aired on *Dick Powell's Zane Grey Theater* on March 7, 1958.

130.2 Home Ranch. Oct. 7, 1958. GS: Lee Farr, Steve Rowland, Harold J. Stone, Rodolfo Hoyos, Don Kennedy. Cattle baron Oat Jackford orders his two cowboys to run Lucas McCain and his son off their ranch. Jackford feels that the range belongs to him. When McCain refuses to leave, the two cowboys set fire to his house.

130.3 End of a Young Gun. Oct. 14, 1958. GS: Michael Landon, Charles Cooper, Jo Haworth, Carolyn Craig, Mel Carter. Young Mark McCain gets caught on a mountain ledge. A young outlaw risks his life to rescue Mark and breaks his leg doing so. Lucas McCain has to decide whether to care for the injured outlaw or to turn him over to the law.

130.4 The Marshal. Oct. 21, 1958. GS: James Drury, Warren Oates, Robert J. Wilke. The notorious Sheltin brothers ride into the town of North Fork to take revenge on an elderly marshal who is now crippled and working for Lucas McCain. They ride on to McCain's ranch looking for the old man and intent on killing him.

130.5 The Brother-in-Law. Oct. 28, 1958. GS: Jerome Courtland, Charles Watts, Fay Roope, Karl Lukas. Johnny Gibbs, Lucas McCain's brother-in-law, visits the McCain ranch. Gibbs, a rodeo rider wanted by the law, begins stirring up trouble.

130.6 Eight Hours to Die. Nov. 4, 1958. GS: George Macready, Russell Collins, Marilee Phelps, Irving Mitchell, Bud Osborne, Bobby Crawford. An elderly judge is convinced that Lucas McCain is responsible for the death of his son who was hanged. He tells Lucas that he will kill Mark, Lucas's son, in revenge.

130.7 Duel of Honor. Nov. 11, 1958. GS: Cesare Danova, Jack Elam, Glenn Strange, John Dierkes, Joe Bassett, John

Harmon. A stagecoach breaks down and an Italian nobleman, Count Di Montova, is stranded overnight in North Fork. Several of the town's drifters, led by Sim Groder, make fun of the elegantly dressed nobleman and when Groder insults the count he is challenged to a duel.

130.8 *The Safe Guard.* Nov. 18, 1958. GS: Claude Akins, Marc Lawrence, Sidney Blackmer, Harlan Warde, Dennis Cross, Mel Carter, Fritz Ford. A gunman is hired as a guard at the first bank opened in North Fork. The banker attempts to persuade the townspeople to deposit their money, and at the same time a band of outlaws plans to rob the bank.

130.9 *The Sister.* Nov. 25, 1958. GS: Sherry Jackson, Dan Blocker, Mort Mills, Lance Fuller, David Tyrell, Michael Morgan, John Dierkes. Mark McCain introduces his father to pretty Rebecca Snipe, who had just arrived in North Fork. But Rebecca's two tough brothers Josh and Pete don't believe that Lucas's intentions are honorable.

130.10 *New Orleans Menace.* Dec. 2, 1958. GS: Akim Tamiroff, Michael Pate, Jerry Oddo, Harlan Warde, Galvan DeLeon. A gambling czar, fleeing from New Orleans, stops at the McCain ranch with his following of bodyguards, henchmen and gamblers. He tells Lucas McCain that he will buy his ranch and when Lucas refuses, warns him that he will be run off his property.

130.11 *The Apprentice Sheriff.* Dec. 9, 1958. GS: Robert Vaughn, Edward Binns, Russell Collins, Grant Richards, Fritz Ford, Elyse Gordon, Steven Gardner. Acting Marshal Dan Willard tries to show a band of Texas cowhands that he is the boss of the town, and he decrees that all guns must be checked by the cowboys. But the new ordinance leads to a killing. Finally Lucas McCain tries to help Willard.

130.12 *Young Englishman.* Dec. 16, 1958. GS: Ted De Corsia, Allen Case, James Coburn, Dick Rich. Lucas McCain accuses the foreman of a neighboring ranch of rustling one of his calves. Although the foreman and his men whip Lucas, he remains determined to prove the rustling charge.

130.13 *The Angry Gun.* Dec. 23, 1958. GS: Vic Morrow, Leo Gordon, Gregory Walcott, Harry Hickox, Joe Quinn, Kathleen Mulqueen. Lucas McCain and his son are robbed during a stagecoach trip. Determined to get his rifle back, Lucas sets out after the three robbers.

130.14 *The Gaucho.* Dec. 30, 1958. GS: Perry Lopez, Chana Eden, Lawrence Dobkin, Stuart Randall, Harlan Warde, Dennis Cross, Bobby Crawford, Morris Lippert, Montie Montana, Lauren Janes. Manolo Argentez, his father and his sister arrive in North Fork ready to work the ranch that Manolo has bought. The children of North Fork, however, along with rancher Curge Palmer find fault with their new neighbors.

130.15 *The Pet.* Jan. 6, 1959. GS: Robert J. Wilke, Edgar Buchanan, Bill Erwin, Hal Jon Norman. Ward Haskins, fearing that Lucas McCain knows he is a wanted man, threatens the rifleman's life. To complicate matters, Haskins' horse, stricken with anthrax, bites both Mark and Haskins.

130.16 *The Sheridan Story.* Jan. 13, 1959. GS: Frank Wilcox, Bill Meigs, Lawrence Dobkin, Royal Dano, Stephen Chase, Fritz Ford. Lucas McCain hires embittered Confederate veteran Frank Blandon to work on his ranch. Lucas and Mark try to strike up a friendship with Blandon, but to no avail. When Gen. Phil Sheridan and his staff spend a night at the ranch, Lucas realizes that Blandon's bitterness threatens to bring about trouble.

130.17 *The Retired Gun.* Jan. 20, 1959. GS: Robert Webber, Eileen Harley, Jack Kruschen, Duke Snider, John Anderson, Herman Rudin, Joe Mell. Wes Carney, noted for his skill with a gun, settles in North Fork with his wife, to live a quiet life. The town bullies, however, refuse to leave Carney alone, trying to taunt him into using his gun. When the marshal suggests that the Carneys leave town, they turn to Lucas McCain for help.

130.18 *The Photographer.* Jan. 27, 1959. GS: John Carradine, Sidney Blackmer, Raymond Bailey, Robert Ellenstein. Photographer Abel Goss, a former prisoner of war, prepares to take a picture of Mark McCain. As Goss is taking the picture, the commander of the camp where Goss was held prisoner arrives on the scene. The two men engage in gunplay.

130.19 *Shivaree.* Feb. 3, 1959. GS: Luana Anders, Paul Carr, Morris Ankrum, John Anderson, Olive Carey, Edgar Dearing, William Bryant. Two young men are traveling with Aaron Pelser's wagon train. Pelser discovers that one of them is really a girl.

130.20 *The Deadeye Kid.* Feb. 10, 1959. GS: Douglas Spencer, Kip King, Jason Johnson, Glenn Strange. Lucas McCain befriends Donnel O'Mahoney, a tough young man who is traveling West. He arranges for the lad to travel on a wagon owned by two men named Jackson and Cramer. Later, Jackson accuses the young man of shooting Cramer.

130.21 *The Indian.* Feb. 17, 1959. GS: Michael Ansara, Herbert Rudley, Lewis Charles, Frank DeKova, Mickey Simpson, Lenny Geer, Robert Chadwick. U.S. Marshal Sam Buckhart arrives in North Fork to look for Indians who are suspects in the brutal murder of a Ranger and his family. Buckhart is welcomed by the townspeople until they learn that he too is an Indian.

130.22 *The Boarding House.* Feb. 24, 1959. GS: Katy Jurado, Alan Baxter, Harlan Warde, Sarah Selby, Kay Cousins, Peggy Maley, Charles Fredericks, Charles Seel. Julia Massini, a reformed gambler, runs a respectable boarding house in North Fork. Gambler Sid Fallon tries to get Julia to let him use her house as a gambling hall and saloon, threatening to reveal her past if she doesn't cooperate.

130.23 *The Second Witness.* March 3, 1959. GS: Michael Pate, Edgar Buchanan, Robert Foulk, Bill Catching, Bill Meigs, Robert Crawford. Investigation reveals that Lucas McCain has information that can aid the prosecution in a murder case. Lucas is asked to help the law, even though one witness was killed before testifying and the killer has not been apprehended.

130.24 *The Trade.* March 10, 1959. GS: Paul Richards, Chris Alcaide, Katherine Bard, Edgar Buchanan, Dan Sheridan, Michael Fox, John Harmon. Sam Morley, a man wanted by the law, falls in love with Beth Landis, a sick young woman. Sam asks his friend Lucas McCain to turn him in and give the reward money to Beth to pay for the medical help that she needs.

130.25 *One Went to Denver.* March 17, 1959. GS: Richard Anderson, Jack Kruschen, John Goddard, Ben Morris, Lewis Charles, John Harmon. Bank robber Tom Birch and his gang arrive in North Fork. Birch takes time off to visit his old friend Lucas McCain.

130.26 *The Deadly Wait.* March 24, 1959. S: Lee Van Cleef, Edgar Buchanan. Dan Mowry, released from Yuma prison, arrives in North Fork intent on getting even with Marshal Torrance, who helped send him to jail.

130.27 *The Wrong Man.* March 31, 1959. GS: Lyle Bettger, Gordon Jones, Robert H. Harris, Frank Sully. Jay Jefferson, a gunslinging lawman, arrives in North Fork in search of an outlaw. Marshal Torrance and Lucas McCain will have little to do with Jefferson, but Mark decides to help him find his man.

130.28 *The Challenge.* April 7, 1959. GS: Adam Williams, Les Tremayne, John Durran, Harlan Warde, John Maxwell, Mel Carter, Mike Harris, Ian Murray. Arriving in North Fork, three escaped convicts decide to hold up the general store. During the holdup the outlaws take Marshal Torrance and storekeeper Hattie Denton hostage.

130.29 *The Hawk.* April 14, 1959. GS: Patrick McVey, John Anderson. Mark McCain succeeds in capturing a hawk, but his life is endangered by a rattlesnake. A stranger observes his plight and saves the boy. Grateful, Mark brings the man home with him.

130.30 *Three-Legged Terror.* April 21, 1959. GS: Dennis Hopper, John Hoyt, Patricia Barry, Robert Foulk. Teenager Johnny Clover wrecks a classroom in the North Fork School. Lucas McCain, who is on the school board, asks Johnny's uncle to pay for the damage.

130.31 *The Angry Man.* April 28, 1959. GS: George Mathews, Edgar Buchanan, Kim Charney, Fritz Ford. Rancher Abel MacDonald homesteads next to Lucas McCain. A bitter man, MacDonald tells Lucas to say off his land and refuses to allow his son and Mark McCain to become friends.

130.32 *The Woman.* May 5, 1959. GS: Patricia Barry, Paul Carr, Mel Carter, James Westerfield, David Leland, Fern Barry, Glenn Strange, Jack Younger. Schoolteacher Adele Adams is an outspoken supporter of women's suffrage. When a rumor about her spreads through North Fork, some of the townspeople decide to run her out of town.

130.33 *The Money Gun.* May 12, 1959. GS: Bert Freed, William Phipps, John Dehner, Jason Johnson, Earl Hodgins, Harlan Warde. A rancher suspects his bookkeeper, Asa Manning, of embezzlement. When Manning learns that his thefts are known, he tries to contact a professional gunman.

130.34 *A Matter of Faith.* May 19, 1959. GS: Royal Dano, Parley Baer, Bing Russell. During a drought at North Fork, cowhands try to earn a living by working on a railroad-construction project. Then an old timer announces that there is a new water source available, and the railroad officials fear that the workers will desert them.

130.35 *Blood Brothers.* May 26, 1959. GS: Rhys Williams, Ian Murray, Richard Devon, Max Wagner. Lucas McCain brings a wounded man to North Fork for medical attention. Marshal Torrance's odd behavior toward the man surprises McCain. Then three men from a nearby town appear and demand custody of the stranger.

130.36 *Stranger at Night.* June 2, 1959. GS: Thomas Gomez, Jack Hogan. Mark McCain's discovery of a murder victim starts Lucas McCain, his friend Artemus Quarles and Marshal Torrance on a search for the killer.

130.37 *The Raid.* June 9, 1959. GS: Michael Ansara, Mike Forest, Robert Foulk, Pat Hogan, Mark Goddard, Clancy Cooper, Robert Dix. When a band of Apache Indians wound Lucas McCain and kidnap his son Mark, Marshal Torrance and special U.S. Marshal Sam Buckhart head up a posse to bring back the boy.

130.38 *Outlaw's Inheritance.* June 16, 1959. GS: William Bishop, Harlan Warde, Bartlett Robinson, Robert Foulk, Dabbs Greer. When an outlaw dies and leaves Lucas McCain a large sum of money, the leading citizens of North Fork request that he resigns as the town's representative in an impending railroad deal.

130.39 *Boomerang.* June 23, 1959. GS: Harlan Warde, Lee Kinsolving, Dabbs Greer. Soon after a banker forecloses on Sam Elder's ranch, the rancher dies. His son believes the banker's actions were responsible for his father's death.

130.40 *The Mind Reader.* June 30, 1959. GS: John Carradine, Sue Randall, Michael Landon, Charles Seel, William Schallert, James Chandler, Steve Hatch, John Harmon. A wealthy rancher is killed and Lucas McCain helps Marshal Torrance look for the murderer. Acting upon Mark's suggestion, Lucas consults a mind reader.

Season Two

130.41 *The Patsy.* Sept. 29, 1959. GS: Whit Bissell, John Anderson, Steve Marlo, Dan Grady, Dennis Cross. Sully Hobbs, Doke Marvin and Lafe Oberly arrive in North Fork with a plan to take over the town. Their plot makes use of barber Sam Barrows to get rid of Lucas McCain and Marshal Torrance.

130.42 *Bloodlines.* Oct. 6, 1959. GS: Denver Pyle, Warren Oates, Christopher Dark, Buddy Hackett, John Durren, Rhys Williams. Daniel Malakie, father of three sons, arrives in North Fork. Determined to break two of his boys out of jail, Malakie also seeks revenge against Lucas McCain and Marshal Torrance. He holds them responsible for his third son's death.

130.43 *The Blowout.* Oct. 13, 1959. GS: Hugh Sanders, John Dehner, Howard Ledig, John Milford, Glenn Strange, George Brenlin, James Parnell. A few days after his arrival in North Fork, gunslinger Al Walker throws a big party at the saloon. Since Marshal Torrance is out of town, Ben Waller, who has taken over the marshal's duties, is kept busy. When Lucas and Mark McCain return from a trip, Lucas attempts to get Walker to end his party.

130.44 *Obituary.* Oct. 20, 1959. GS: Alexander Scourby, Joanna Moore, Chris Alcaide, Byron Hutton, Steven Darrell, Ian Murray. A story by newspaperman Byron Claremont was responsible for an old-time marshal's death. The reporter, who write in glowing terms about famous gun handlers, decides to do a story on Lucas McCain.

130.45 *Tension.* Oct. 27, 1959. GS: Dean Stanton, Robert H. Harris, Gregory Walcott, Jack Elam, Sydna Scott, Jeff Connors, Ted Stanhope. Gavin and Ezra Martin are convinced that Lucas McCain took part in a train robbery and killed Ezra's son Clemmie. Lucas decides to hand the situation in his own way and refuses to discuss it with the Martins.

130.46 *Eddie's Daughter.* Nov. 3, 1959. GS: Gloria DeHaven, John Harmon, Peter Whitney, Ray Teal, Jeff Daley, Kathleen Mulqueen. Two outlaws threaten Lil Halstead's life soon after her arrival in North Fork. Lucas McCain, a friend of Lil's father, decides to help the Halsteads find the reason for the threats.

The Rifleman

130.47 *Panic.* Nov. 10, 1959. GS: Enid Janes, Dabbs Greer, Bill Joyce, Fay Roope, Charles Watts, Lynn Cartier. Brett Conway, a town character, learns that a sick couple in the North Fork area are suffering from yellow fever knowing that Lucas McCain found the couple, Conway threatens to inform the townspeople unless Lucas pays him off.

130.48 *Ordeal.* Nov. 17, 1959. GS: Hank Stohl. Lucas McCain and his son Mark are crossing a desert when their wagon breaks down.

130.49 *The Spiked Rifle.* Nov. 24, 1959. GS: Harlan Warde, Richard Devon, Jack Lambert, Baynes Barron, Virginia Christine, Glenn Strange, Charles Conrad, Fay Roope, John Harmon. The North Fork bank is ready to send off a shipment of money, but the man hired to guard it has not yet arrived. Banker John Hamilton asks Lucas McCain to take the missing man's place.

130.50 *Letter of the Law.* Dec. 1, 1959. GS: Vic Morrow, Milton Parsons, Ken Lynch, Michael Fox, Paul Carr, John Goddard, Rhys Williams, Harlan Warde. Lucas McCain assumes Marshal Torrance's duties in North Fork while the marshal transports a prisoner to another town. En route, the marshal and his charge are ambushed.

130.51 *The Legacy.* Dec. 8, 1959. GS: James Franciscus, James Barton, Jack Grinnage, Paul Jasmin, Denver Pyle, Harry Harvey, Sr., Lillian Bronson, John Harmon. Fulfilling a promise to a dying man, Lucas McCain sends East for the man's son Philip. Arriving in North For, Phillip, a Boston lawyer, learns that his father died a derelict.

130.52 *The Baby Sitter.* Dec. 15, 1959. GS: Phyllis Avery, John Dehner, Lillian Bronson, Henry Rowland. Leona Bartell, a young mother, asks Lucas McCain to care for her baby. Leona fears that her estranged husband will take the baby away.

130.53 *The Coward.* Dec. 22, 1959. GS: Carleton Carpenter, Steve Rowland, John Milford, Robert Bice, Don Elson. Lucas and Mark McCain show some kindness toward George Collins, a trail cook who has been driven out of a camp. Later, two cowhands from the camp ride into town.

130.54 *Surveyors.* Dec. 29, 1959. GS: Mike Kellin, Lin McCarthy, Ted Otis, Harlan Warde. His friendship with three surveyors leads Mark McCain into a rift with his father. Upset, the lad decides to leave home.

130.55 *Day of the Hunter.* Jan. 5, 1960. GS: John Anderson, Dick Elliott. Famed hunter Cass Callicot challenges Lucas McCain to use his repeater rifle in a shooting match against Callicot and his buffalo gun.

130.56 *Mail Order Groom.* Jan. 12, 1960. GS: Peter Whitney, Alice Backes, John Anderson, Sandy Kenyon, Monte Montana. Shortly after his arrival in North Fork, John Jupiter is taunted and beaten by Jess and Jim Prophet.

130.57 *A Case of Identity.* Jan. 19, 1960. GS: Royal Dano, Herbert Rudley, Chris Alcaide, Jim Brenaman, Rhys Williams. Aaron Wingate arrives in North Fork and tells Lucas McCain that he believes Mark McCain to be his missing son. Wingate then tells Lucas that he will employ every means possible to gain custody of the boy.

130.58 *The Visitors.* Jan. 26, 1960. GS: Michael Pate, Christine White, June Vincent, John Harmon, Ralph Moody. Ann Dodd arrives in North Fork to assume ownership of her dead uncle's ranch, but two people plot to kill her.

130.59 *The Hero.* Feb. 2, 1960. GS: Robert Culp, Frank Ferguson, Lynn Cartier, Dennis Cross, Dick Keene. By killing a notorious gunman, young stablehand Colly Vane seems to have done the community a favor, and himself one as well, as there is a large reward involved. But Colly finds the townspeople not only reluctant to give him the prize money, they are downright belligerent about it.

130.60 *The Horse Traders.* Feb. 9, 1960. GS: James Kirkwood, John Milford, Clegg Hoyt, Chubby Johnson, Fern Barry. Colonel Bourbon, a horse trader, stops in North Fork. Two saddle tramps attempt to con him out of his prize stallion.

130.61 *The Spoiler.* Feb. 16, 1960. GS: Skip Homeier, Chubby Johnson, Ellen Corby, Malcolm Cassell, Ralph Moody. An escaped convict hides out in the home of an elderly couple. Mark learns of the convict's whereabouts but realizes that if he tells, he will surely endanger the couple's lives.

130.62 *Heller.* Feb. 23, 1960. GS: Gigi Perreau, Peter Whitney, Don Grady, K.T. Stevens, Sid Gilman. Heller Chase is caught breaking into the local general store. Lucas McCain tries to uncover what turned the youngster into a robber.

130.63 *The Grasshopper.* March 1, 1960. GS: Richard Devon, Arthur Hunnicutt, Stuart Randall, James Anderson, Arthur Space, Joe Bassett, Ronny McEvoy, Joe Haworth. Escorted by a marshal, convicted killer Walt Ryerson is traveling by train to his hanging. With the help of two pals, Ryerson kills the marshal, takes command of the train and holds Mark McCain hostage.

130.64 *A Time for Singing.* March 8, 1960. GS: Chris Alcaide, Robert Knapp, Patricia Barry, John Milford, Robert Osterloh. Planning an unusual robbery, two members of an outlaw gang pose as a minister and his wife.

130.66 *The Deserter.* March 15, 1960. GS: Ron Haggerthy, Robert Cornthwaite, Harry Carey, Jr., Baynes Barron. Unwilling to take his punishment, a wounded soldier flees from the guardhouse and takes refuge in Lucas McCain's house. When the Army comes to take him back, Lucas and Marshal Torrance side with the young man and request lighter punishment.

130.66 *The Vision.* March 22, 1960. GS: Marian Seldes, Milton Parsons, Karl Swenson, Natividad Vacio, Jeanne Wood, Dennis Cross, John Abbott. Young Mark contracts typhoid fever. Lucas is worried because the boy doesn't seem to care about getting well.

130.67 *The Lariat.* March 29, 1960. GS: Richard Anderson, Steve Conte, Harlan Warde, Dayton Lummis, George Macready, James Flavin. Lariat Jones has returned to North Fork and, much to Lucas disgust, is entering into a new business venture — partnership with a dishonest gambler.

130.68 *Smoke Screen.* April 5, 1960. GS: Paul Carr, Jenifer Lea, Douglas Kennedy, Warner Jones, George Neise, William Benedict, Dick Alexander, Johnny Collier. Two young men are fighting for Marge Crandell's affections, when along comes a third candidate and takes the girl away. Then she is murdered and he is the prime suspect.

130.69 *Shotgun Man.* April 12, 1960. GS: John Anderson, John Harmon, Paul Mazursky, Jack Elam. Rifleman Lucas McCain has another encounter with Shotgun Man John Beaumont, who's out to get him for sending him to prison.

130.70 *Sins of the Father.* April 19, 1960. GS: Richard Evans, George Wallace, Eugene Martin, Kelton Garwood, Dick

Wilson, Rhys Williams. Andy Moon shoots a man in self-defense. Realizing that the dead man's brother will want revenge, he heads for McCain's protection.

130.71 *The Prodigal.* April 26, 1960. GS: Kevin Hagen, Josephine Hutchinson, Warren Oates, Rodolfo Hoyos, Rhys Williams, Lee Van Cleef. An outlaw forces his way into the McCain household and installs his invalid mother as a resident. Then he makes Lucas play the role of a hired hand and gives Mark the part of the woman's grandson.

130.72 *The Fourflusher.* May 3, 1960. GS: Whit Bissell, James Westerfield, K.T. Stevens. Sharecropper Gabe Fenway enters his colt in a race, hoping to win enough money to buy his farm. The farm's owner has bet on another colt, one owned by Mark McCain.

130.73 *The Jailbird.* May 10, 1960. GS: Dabbs Greer, Karl Swenson, Molly Dodd, Charles Briggs, Charles Tannen. Lucas hires as ex-convict to work on the ranch. When there is a killing in the area, the ex-convict feels the pinch of his past. He's the first man under suspicion.

130.74 *Meeting at Midnight.* May 17, 1960. GS: Claude Akins, Chris Alcaide, John Milford, Frank DeKova, Ian Murray. Lucas' former Army captain arrives in North Fork, and it appears that he has joined an outlaw band.

130.75 *Nora.* May 24, 1960. GS: Julie Adams, Murvyn Vye, Michael Fox, Michael Stefani, John Carpenter. Nora Sanford returns to North Fork. Taking a liking to the lady, young Mark thinks his father should court her.

130.76 *The Hangman.* May 31, 1960. GS: Denver Pyle, Whit Bissell, Richard Deacon, Michael Fox, Ralph Moody, Betty Lou Gerson, Ian Murray, Amanda Ames. A local man is murdered and the prime suspect, his ex-convict employee, is put under protective custody. The enraged townspeople cry out for a quick hanging.

Season Three

130.77 *Trail of Hate.* Sept. 27, 1960. GS: Harold J. Stone, Harvey Johnson, Marc Lawrence, Jack Kruschen, Harlan Warde. Mark is held hostage by Benjamin Stark and his gang to make sure Lucas doesn't upset their bank robbery plans. But the boy is hurt and Lucas is out for blood.

130.78 *Woman from Hog Ridge.* Oct. 4, 1960. GS: Dee J. Thompson, Jan Stine, Lane Bradford, Jim Hurst, Robert Hoy, Charles Tannen. McCain shoots a would-be horse thief, a member of the Boyle clan. So Ma Boyle decides that a feud has just begun.

130.79 *Seven.* Oct. 11, 1960. GS: Dan Megowan, Bing Russell, Hal Jon Norman, Paul Sorenson, Helen Beverly. Seven prisoners on their way to the gallows break away from their guard. They take over the town of North Fork.

130.80 *The Pitchman.* Oct. 18, 1960. GS: Bob Sweeney, Danny Richards, John Milford, Paul Wexler. Speedy Sullivan tries to sell Lucas a spiffy new lightning rod. Later, Mark finds a piece of gold ore on the McCain property and Speedy returns, this time to buy.

130.81 *Strange Town.* Oct. 25, 1960. GS: Claude Akins, Peter Whitney, William Schallert, Milton Parsons, Joe Higgins. Luke trails gunman Bletch Droshek to a strange town, only to find that the place is controlled by his quarry's brother.

130.82 *Baranca.* Nov. 1, 1960. GS: Cesare Danova, John Milford, Larry Peron, Linda Dangcil, Henry Amargo, Jack Kruschen. Outlaw leader Baranca plans to get Torrance out of town so he and his cohorts can string up Hadley, a townsman who killed one of their gang.

130.83 *The Martinet.* Nov. 8, 1960. GS: John Hoyt, Don Dubbins, Richard Alexander. Capt. Josiah Perry comes to North Fork, determined to punish the man who killed his son in a gun fight. Mark lets it slip out that it was Lucas who killed young Perry.

130.84 *Miss Milly.* Nov. 15, 1960. GS: Warren Oates, Richard Devon, Michael Fox, Charles Tannen. Milly Scott comes to North Fork to take over as storekeeper. Milly's infuriated that practically everyone in town owes the store money, including Lucas McCain.

130.85 *Dead Cold Cash.* Nov. 22, 1960. GS: Ed Nelson, Chris Alcaide, Steven Darrell, Sara Taft, Harlan Warde. According to Sara Carruther's will, if Lucas McCain died within a week of her death, the citizens of North Fork will be the beneficiaries of her fortune.

130.86 *The Schoolmaster.* Nov. 29, 1960. GS: Arnold Moss, Jimmy Fields, Pamela Cole. Stevan Griswold is North Fork's new schoolmaster. He is also too stern to suit young Mark, who decides that the best way is to play hooky.

130.87 *The Promoter.* Dec. 6, 1960. GS: Dabbs Greer, Denny Miller, Ollie O'Toole, Robert Hoy, Jack Lester. Gambler Jack Tully tries to provoke Reuben Miles, a youth with a fast draw, into drawing on McCain. Tully tells Miles that McCain's been saying things behind his back.

130.88 *The Illustrator.* Dec. 13, 1960. GS: Richard Whorf, Ed Nelson, Midge Ware, Dayton Lummis, Joe Perry, Ian Murray. Jake Shaw has imported Jeremiah Crownley, an Eastern portrait painter, to do a picture of his daughter. Then Crownley turns out to be a light worker and a heavy drinker.

130.89 *The Silent Knife.* Dec. 20, 1960. GS: Brad Weston, Richard Devon, Robert B. Williams, Amanda Ames, James Chandler. There's a new boy in North Fork, and Mark sets out to investigate. He finds that the newcomer is an orphan, a mute, and his name is also Mark.

130.90 *Miss Bertie.* Dec. 27, 1960. GS: Agnes Moorehead, Richard Anderson, Glenn Strange, Mel Allen, Leonard Stone. A sweet little lady, Miss Bertie, arrives in the wicked West. She tries to talk outlaw Duke Jennings into letting her turn him in. The reason is that she needs the bounty money.

130.91 *Six Years and a Day.* Jan. 3, 1961. GS: John Larch, James Gavin, Regina Gleason, Ralph Moody, Hal K. Dawson, Ron Hayes. Traveler Lee Marston stops at McCain's ranch for help. Marston's wife Sarah is expecting a child soon, and she has just been badly hurt in a fall.

130.92 *Flowers by the Door.* Jan. 10, 1961. GS: Patricia Breslin, Richard Anderson, Jean Allison. McCain notices a prowler near his ranch. He goes out after him, but loses him in the dark. Returning home, Luke remembers that the Seevers' ranch is near by, and that Cora Seevers is home alone.

130.93 *Long Trek* (A.K.A. "Escort for a Killer"). Jan. 17, 1961. GS: Lonny Chapman. McCain and Torrance are escorting a renegade named Stanley back to justice. Stanley picks the right moment to drive his captors' horses off, leaving the men in the desert and short of water.

130.94 *The Actress.* Jan. 24, 1961. GS: Diana Millay, Morris Ankrum, Ralph Moody, Herb Armstrong, Charles Tan-

The Rifleman

nen, Kathleen Mulqueen, Joe E. Benson. McCain rides to far-off Willow Springs to bring Beth Black to the side of her suddenly stricken husband, Jacob. But Beth doesn't want to go.

130.95 *Face of Yesterday.* Jan. 31, 1961. GS: Ben Cooper, John Anderson, K.T. Stevens. Rancher Hank Clay is jealous of McCain's high standing in the community. He tries to goad Lucas into a brawl with his young stepson Simon Lee — who is very fast with a six-gun.

130.96 *The Wyoming Story* Part One. Feb. 7, 1961. GS: Kent Taylor, Enid Janes, Dabbs Greer, Russell Thorson, Chris Alcaide, Joe Higgins. McCain's cattle are destroyed when an epidemic of hoof-and-mouth disease hits North Fork. Lucas is resigned to becoming a dirt farmer, but Marshal Torrance tells him about a job as a Government secret agent in the Wyoming Territory.

130.97 *The Wyoming Story* Part Two. Feb. 14, 1961. GS: Kent Taylor, Enid Janes, Dabbs Greer, Russell Thorson, Chris Alcaide, Joe Higgins. Lucas has left to work as an undercover agent in Wyoming. He is on the trail of a gang that is illegally selling weapons to the Indians. But Mark worries when his Pa is gone so long and figures something has happened to him.

130.98 *Closer than a Brother.* Feb. 21, 1961. GS: Berry Kroeger, Kelly Thordsen, Rex Ingram, Jack Wells. Marshal Torrance won the respect of his fellow townsmen when he overcame the drinking habit, but now he has fallen off the wagon. McCain doesn't understand why Torrance has slipped, and becomes more puzzled when the marshal turns in his badge.

130.99 *The Lost Treasure of Canyon Town.* Feb. 28, 1961. GS: William Fawcett, Robert Foulk, Mickey Finn. Marshal Torrance takes Lucas and Mark to see his one-time home, now a ghost town. Upon arriving however, they discover considerable unrest in the spirit world. The very much alive Newman family is there and on the prowl.

130.100 *Dark Day at North Fork.* March 7, 1961. GS: John Milford, Joe Higgins, Ralph Moody. McCain is blinded in an explosion, and Doc Burrage tells him the injury may be permanent. Into this situation rides Jack Solby, an old enemy, who is gunning for McCain.

130.101 *The Prisoner.* March 14, 1961. GS: John Dehner, Adam Williams. Two former Confederate officers, Major Aaron King and Captain Trock, recognize Lucas from the time he served as a guard at the camp where they were prisoners of war. They blame him for all their troubles in prison and since, and plan revenge.

130.102 *Assault.* March 21, 1961. GS: Linda Lawson, Bob Sweeney, Danny Richards, Jr., King Calder, Paul Mantee. Speed Sullivan, a hot-shot salesman, needs all his persuasive powers to convince King Croxton that he is not the bounder who gave Croxton's daughter Vashti a black eye. So far, Lucas appears to be the only one who believes that Speed did not strike the girl.

130.103 *Short Rope for a Tall Man.* March 28, 1961. GS: Bert Freed, Hal Baylor, William Schallert, Joe Higgins, Charlie Briggs, Norman Leavitt. Lucas finds himself in a strange town, and in big trouble. He is accused of being a horse thief.

130.104 *The Clarence Bibs Story.* April 4, 1961. GS: Buddy Hackett, Lee Van Cleef, John Milford, Denver Pyle, X Brands. Good old Clarence Bibbs, a local janitor, meets a gunfighter named Longden in the middle of the street. Clarence's gun goes off, and Longden falls dead, leading Clarence to believe he is now the fastest gun in the West.

130.105 *The Score Is Even.* April 11, 1961. GS: Adam Williams, Kelly Thordsen, Joe Benson. On a hunting trip, Lucas witnesses the murder of an old prospector. When he attempts to interfere he is shot down by the two killers, Jax and Andy, and left for dead.

130.106 *The Mescalero Curse.* April 18, 1961. GS: Michael Pate, Charles Watts, Larry Chance, Ralph Moody, Jack Searl, Joe Brown. A curse is put on Lucas by a renegade Apache medicine man named Mogollan. Lucas is marked for death because he was the foreman of the jury which convicted Mogollan's son of murder.

130.107 *Stopover.* April 25, 1961. GS: Adam West, Bethel Leslie, Gordon Jones, Joe Higgins. A sudden blizzard forces a stagecoach to stop for shelter at McCain's ranch. Trouble brews when Medford, a whiskey salesman who has been sampling his own wares, and a gunman named Rolf, both take a fancy to Tess, a pretty fellow passenger.

130.108 *The Lonesome Ride.* May 2, 1961. GS: Joan Shawlee, Kay E. Kuter, Lincoln Demyan. Drifters Charve and Kelly Banner regard the practical joke as the last word in humor. Out for a few laughs, they write to St. Louis for a mail-order bride, and sign McCain's name to the letter.

130.109 *Death Trap.* May 9, 1961. GS: James Drury, Philip Carey, Gigi Perreau, John Pickard, Larry Perron, Steve Pendleton, Hank Stohl, William Kendis. A cowboy named Stark has been wounded by cowhands. Lucas' call for a physician produces Dr. Simon Battle, a one-time gunslinger he fought years ago.

130.110 *The Queue.* May 16, 1961. GS: Victor Sen Yung, Peter Whitney, Paul Wexler, Dick Kay Hong. Wang Chi and his son Wang Lee have come to start a laundry business in North Fork, but Vince Fergus and Les Foster have fixed ideas about foreigners coming to live in their town.

Season Four

130.111 *The Vaqueros.* Oct. 2, 1961. GS: Martin Landau, Ziva Rodann, Pepe Hern, Than Wyenn, Vladimir Sokoloff, Roberto Contreras. Lucas and Mark go to Mexico to buy a bull for the ranch. Before they reach their destination they are captured by a bandit named Miguel.

130.112 *First Wages.* Oct. 9, 1961. GS: Ed Nelson, Troy Melton, Joe Higgins, David M. Rodman, Glen Ryle. Lucas returns from a trip to find Mark working as a stable boy at Harmon's livery. Lucas is surprised and puzzled. He has always given Mark all the money that he needs.

130.113 *Sheer Terror.* Oct. 16, 1961. GS: Charles Macauley, Tommy Cook, Harlan Warde, Paul Wexler, Bruce Hayward. Lucas is asked to stand guard while a large cash shipment is transferred from a stage to the local bank. A former bank clerk named Sloan has also made some plans. He and two pals hide out in Milly's store and await their chance at the shipment.

130.114 *The Stand-In.* Oct. 23, 1961. GS: Dabbs Greer, Richard Devon, Charles Cooper. Gus Potter and Bert Taylor, a pair of prison guards, are transporting killer Rudy Croft to Yuma for hanging, and enlivening the journey with frequent swigs from a bottle. During one of their stops, Croft escapes. To solve their problem the guards take Lucas prisoner and plan to let him hang in the killer's place.

130.115 *The Journey Back.* Oct. 30, 1961. GS: John Anderson, John Milford, Chris Alcaide, Harry Carey, Jr., Mel Carter. Searching the brush country for a runaway calf, Lucas and Mark encounter a man named Will Temple. The stranger's appearance is disquieting. His face is a mass of scars, and his behavior is mystifying. He offers Mark a job on his ranch.

130.116 *The Decision.* Nov. 6, 1961. GS: Hampton Fancher, Denver Pyle, Kevin Hagen, Richard Kiel, Henry Howell, Jim Stewart, Arlyne Lampshire. Lucas is working his south forty when he sees Corey Hazlett gun another man down. Later, when he is captured, Hazlett maintains that he didn't commit the murder, even though Lucas was an eyewitness.

130.117 *Knight Errant.* Nov. 13, 1961. GS: Lawrence Dobkin, Sean McClory, Jack Elam, Charles Reade. One of Lucas' old friends, Don Chimera del Laredo, rides into the ranch one day. Lucas is amused by Don Chimera's Old World manner and his references to knighthood and chivalry, until he learns that the man is serious about doing battle with another old friend, Colonel Black.

130.118 *Honest Abe.* Nov. 20, 1961. GS: Royal Dano, K.T. Stevens, Charles Cooper, Steve Warren, Rex Morgan, Pam Smith, Pick Temple, Joe Higgins. A harmless soul named Lincoln, whose first name is Able, insists that he is the Great Emancipator himself. The citizens of North Fork are willing to humor him, except for Matt Yorty, who won't go along with the gag.

130.119 *The Long Goodbye.* Nov. 27, 1961. GS: Edgar Buchanan, Teddy Rooney, Virginia Christine, Bill Zuckert. Among Lucas McCain's duties as head of the town council is getting young Woody Fogarty to attend school. But Woody's grandpa has little use for education, and no use at all for strangers who try to meddle in family affairs.

130.120 *The Shattered Idol.* Dec. 4, 1961. GS: Kevin McCarthy, Jack Elam, John Harmon, Bud Osborne, Mary Jo Tierney. The stage breaks down on the McCain ranch, and Mark quickly recognizes a passenger named Clemens as the famous writer, Mark Twain. Young Mark approaches with some eager questions, but Twain gruffly tells the boy not to bother him.

130.121 *Long Gun from Tucson.* Dec. 11, 1961. GS: Peter Whitney, Whit Bissell, William Hughes, John Harmon, Joe Higgins, Brian G. Hutton. John Holliver was ridden out of North Fork on a rail, five years earlier. Now he is back to take his revenge, and Lucas has the job of stopping him.

130.122 *The High Country.* Dec. 18, 1961. GS: James Coburn, Booth Colman, Ellen Corby, Jan Stine, Valora Noland. Lucas catches a pair of mountaineers named Gorwin and Ambrose trying to steal his rifle. There is a struggle, the gun goes off, and Gorwin is killed.

130.123 *A Friend in Need.* Dec. 25, 1961. GS: Parley Baer, Lee Farr, Tom Snyder, Harlan Warde. Mark is on his way home from town when he runs into gunman Carl Avery. Avery won't say exactly where he is going, but he does say Mark should go with him, because Lucas will be killed if he doesn't.

130.124 *Skull.* Jan. 1, 1962. GS: Lyle Bettger, Thomas Brown, John Alvin, Lewis Charles, George Willeford, Don Drysdale. Mark has been injured on a hunting trip and Lucas is going for help when he is captured by riders from the notorious Skull Ranch. They say Lucas must join their gang, or else.

130.125 *The Princess.* Jan. 8, 1962. GS: Annie Farge, Michel Petit, Robert Burton, Stephen Bekassy, Ron Penford. A girl named Jennifer and her young brother Charles find the McCain ranch a welcome haven when Charles develops a case of measles. Then Jennifer develops a crush on Lucas.

130.126 *Gunfire.* Jan. 15, 1962. GS: Lon Chaney, Jr., Ross Elliott, William Bryant, Grant Richards, Preston Price, Joe Higgins. Killer Charlie Gordo is locked up tight in the North Fork jail waiting to be picked up by the Federal marshal. But Gordo tells Marshal Torrance that when he leaves it will be with his own men.

130.127 *The Quiet Fear.* Jan. 22, 1962. GS: Patrick McVey, Enid Janes, Richard Rust, Dennis Cross. Lucas' old Army pal Jake Striker has come to North Fork with his daughter Abbey to settle as a rancher. Abbey arouses the curiosity of some of the local citizens, as she is a deaf-mute.

130.128 *Sporting Chance.* Jan. 29, 1962. GS: Arthur Malet, James Luisi, Al Collins. Englishman Jeremy Pennebroke steps from the stage at North Fork with a special custom-made rifle under his arm. Marshal Torrance extends a welcome and inquires about the handsome weapon, which Pennebroke explains he intends to use to kill Lucas McCain.

130.129 *A Young Man's Fancy.* Feb. 5, 1962. GS: Cheryl Holdridge, Dick Evans, Paul Richards. When Sally Walker comes to visit her Aunt Milly, Mark takes one look and it's love at first sight. But Sally is only interested in young Bruce Henry, and she asks Mark to take a message to him.

130.130 *The Man from Salinas.* Feb. 12, 1962. GS: Robert Culp, Jack Hogan, Ralph Moody, Harlan Warde, Joe Higgins, Fred Sherman. Banker John Hamilton is closing up for the day when cowboy Rudy Gray persuades him to stay open for one more transaction. Rudy wants to draw out some money — at gunpoint.

130.131 *Two Ounces of Tin.* Feb. 19, 1962. GS: Sammy Davis, Jr., Johnny Ginger. A stranger creates quite a sensation in North Fork with his six-gun agility. He says he is Tip Corey, son of a man who was murdered in the town by a mob.

130.132 *Deadly Image.* Feb. 26, 1962. GS: Leonard Stone, Robert Bice, Gloria Morland. North Fork citizens are thrown off stride when Earl Bantry rides into tow. Earl looks just like Lucas McCain. But Bantry proves that is where the resemblance ends when he gets tough with bartender Sweeney and starts to make a shambles of his place.

130.133 *The Debit.* March 5, 1962. GS: Keith Andes, Hank Patterson. Marshal Torrance is escorting a prisoner to another town to be executed when Lucas and Mark ride up with a message. Mark takes one look at the prisoner, and is shocked to find that he is the man who once saved his life.

130.134 *The Tinhorn.* March 12, 1962. GS: Grant Richards, Grace Lee Whitney, Larry Thor, Stephen Wooton, Barbara Eiler, Jim Hayward, Gary Gadson. When a boy named Willie says something about Lucas that Mark doesn't like, a scuffle ensues and Mark finds himself on the loosing end. Then Willie leads him to the rear window of a hotel to prove that he wasn't lying and Mark sees Lucas is really playing poker.

130.135 *None So Blind.* March 19, 1962. GS: Cliff Osmond, Jeff York. Mark stops to water his horse and strikes

The Rifleman

up a conversation with a banjo-playing singer named Lafayette Bly, who is camping by a stream. Mark notes that Bly has a very acute sense of hearing, and then learns that the man is blind.

130.136 *Jealous Man.* March 26, 1962. GS: Mort Mills, Diana Brewster. Lucas and Mark visit their new neighbors, the Owens, and ride up just in time to save Fay Owens from a rearing stallion. Lucas says it looks as though the animal was recently beaten.

130.137 *Guilty Conscience.* April 2, 1962. GS: Lee Patrick, Tommy Nolan, Argentina Brunetti, Chubby Johnson, Bill Cerone, Billy Paul Fix. Leota Carraway arrives in North Fork and claims that Marshal Torrance is her long-lost husband and the father of her child.

130.138 *Day of Reckoning.* April 9, 1962. GS: Royal Dano, Warren Oates, L.Q. Jones, Billy Hughes. The town council has voted approval of a new town preacher named Reverend Jamison. This is fine with Lucas, until he recognizes Jamison as a former outlaw.

130.139 *The Day a Town Slept.* April 16, 1962. GS: Lawrence Dobkin, James Best, John Harmon, Joe Higgins. Lucas and Mark arrive back in North Fork after a trip to find that Marshal Torrance has been defeated in the election, and a smooth-talking Ben Judson has taken over.

130.140 *Milly's Brother.* April 23, 1962. GS: Richard Anderson, Joe Higgins. Milly takes quite a shine to newcomer Harry Chase. She feels even closer to him when he reveals he was her late brother's commanding officer during the Civil War.

130.141 *Outlaw Shoes.* April 30, 1962. GS: Michael Greene, Paul Wexler, Tom Gilson, Roy Barcroft, William Woodson, Mel Carter, Stanley Adams, Jim Galante, Donald Elson. Lucas finally revives after being shot and left for dead by the notorious outlaw George Vale, and finds that he is wearing a gun engraved "George Vale."

130.142 *The Executioner.* May 7, 1962. GS: Adam Williams, Michael Pate, John Davis Chandler, Amanda Ames. Lucas doesn't know it but there is a trespasser on his property named Russell Gannaway. And Gannaway isn't anxious to have anyone find him their either, including the two badmen on his trail.

Season Five

130.143 *The Wanted Man.* Sept. 25, 1962. GS: John Anderson, Adam Williams, Rex Holman, Arthur Batanides, Joe Higgins.

130.144 *Waste* Part One. Oct. 1, 1962. GS: Vito Scotti, Pepe Hern, Tony Rosa, Alex Montoya, Sara Taft, Enid Janes. After a cattle sale, Marshal Torrance, Lucas and Mark are traveling home through desolate border country. When the old lawman disappears, Lucas and his son pick up his trail in a nearby Mexican ghost town.

130.145 *Waste* Part Two. Oct. 8, 1962. GS: Vito Scotti, Pepe Hern, Tony Rosa, Alex Montoya, Sara Taft, Enid Janes. After Alphonso's wife gives birth, the bandits relax their guard. Lucas and Mark escape, free Marshal Torrance, and carry the wounded lawman to the ghost town's saloon.

130.146 *Lou Mallory.* Oct. 15, 1962. GS: Peter Whitney, Conlan Carter, Mel Carter, Thom Carney, Charles La Franchise. Soon after red-haired Lou Mallory arrives in North Fork, she arouses the suspicions of the townspeople

130.147 *Quiet Night, Deadly Night.* Oct. 22, 1962. GS: Ed Ames, Maurine Dawson, Carol Leigh, Ralph Moody, Charles Harrison, Joe Higgins. A couple of girls are coming in on the Denver stage to work at Lou Malloy's new hotel. When the stage arrives, Lou finds that one girl is very sick.

130.148 *Death Never Rides Alone.* Oct. 29, 1962. GS: Lee Van Cleef, Rex Holman, Joe Higgins, Mel Carter, John Rayborn. Hard-bitten gunman Johnny Drako rides into North Fork and lets it be known that he is looking for Lucas McCain. Lucas agrees to meet Drako in his hotel alone.

130.149 *I Take This Woman.* Nov. 5, 1962. GS: Sean McClory, Charles Cooper, Joe Higgins. It seems that Lou's father made Dennis O'Flarrety a promise just before he died. He said that Lou would marry him. Now Dennis is in town to collect his bride.

130.150 *The Assailants.* Nov. 12, 1962. GS: Edward Platt, John Milford, Steve Marlo, Noam Pitlik, William Bryant, Benny Carle, Henry Allin, Joe Higgins. Four cavalrymen, lugging a large crate, ride into North Fork and register at the hotel. Inside the create is a Gatling gun that they have carried to town with which they plan to assassinate Senator Jim Borden.

130.151 *Mark's Rifle.* Nov. 19, 1962. GS: Mark Goddard, Ralph Moody, Eddie Quillan. Mark is quite impressed with the sharpshooting ability of Marty Blair, a drifter who has come to North Fork with the circus. Marty suggests that Mark talk Lucas into getting him a rifle of his very own.

130.152 *The Most Amazing Man.* Nov. 26, 1962. GS: Sammy Davis, Jr., Richard Devon, Pat Henry. A self-styled fast-draw artist named Wade Randall is recounting his gun-slinging feats to a North Fork crowd.

130.153 *Squeeze Play.* Dec. 3, 1962. GS: Gerald Mohr, Chris Alcaide, Dean Fredericks, Henry Madden. Lucas is the only rancher holding out on land speculator Willard Prescott, who wants his property for resale to the railroad. When Lucas remains stubborn about selling, Prescott brings in a few gunslingers to persuade him.

130.154 *Gun Shy.* Dec. 10, 1962. GS: Peter Whitney, Pat Goldin, Jimmy Carter, Jay Nelson, Bob Hall, Darryl Richard. Mark's young pal Charlie is killed when Lucas' rifle is accidentally fired by another boy. Mark is so stricken by the accident, and by the sight of his dad's rifle, that he decides to leave home.

130.155 *The Anvil Chorus.* Dec. 17, 1962. GS: Norm Alden, Steven Marlo, Joe Higgins, Adam Williams, William Meigs, Michael Morris, Olan Soule. When Micah has to leave town, Nils the blacksmith is the only man available to act as deputy. But the blacksmith immediately displays his new authority by forging a law that the citizens must turn in the shootin' irons.

130.156 *Conflict.* Dec. 24, 1962. GS: Rhodes Reason, Eddie Quillan, Ralph Moody. A rifle shot by Lucas frightens away a cougar which is about to attack Mark, but Lucas is angry because he missed the animal. He decides that there is something wrong either with the rifle or with him.

130.157 *Incident at Line Shack Six.* Jan. 7, 1963. GS: John Anderson, Paul Mantee, Raymond Guth, Ray Kellogg, Dale Wright, Claude Hall. It is pay day at the railroad camp, but Mr. Gangling, the boss, wants one man's money back and shoots him to get it. Just then, an Apache named Johnny Wing comes on to the murder scene, and Gangling frames him for the killing.

130.158 *Suspicion.* Jan. 14, 1963. GS: Kevin McCarthy, Joe Higgins, William Fawcett. Traveling peddler Winslow Quince comes to North Fork and impresses the townsfolk with his pleasant manner. But, after his arrival, there are some killings in the area, and several of the citizens connect Quince with the rising death rate.

130.159 *The Sidewinder.* Jan. 21, 1963. GS: Billy Hughes, Jr., Joe Higgins. Teenager Gridley Mau comes to North Fork gunning for Lucas, who killed his father during an attempted bank robbery. Gridley wants to force a showdown and Lucas, patient as he is, can't find a way to prevent it.

130.160 *The Sixteenth Cousin.* Jan. 28, 1963. GS: John Mamo, Vito Scotti, Charles Maxwell, Paul Sorensen. The railroad comes to North Fork and on the first train into town are Lucas, Mark, Japanese nobleman Hikaru Yamanaka and his servant Soto. When Soto is ridiculed by a couple of local yokels, Yamanaka demands satisfaction — Oriental style.

130.161 *Hostages to Fortune.* Feb. 4, 1963. GS: Maurice Dallimore, Paul Mazursky, I. Stanford Jolley, Andy Martin, Rusty Stevens, Daniel White. At Halloween time in North Fork, a pair of genuine rustlers take advantage of the seasonal disguises to make off with some cattle, and the ranchers lose their holiday spirit.

130.162 *And the Devil Makes Five.* Feb. 11, 1963. GS: Lonny Chapman. When Mark goes to wake his father, he finds Lucas isn't sleeping — a rattlesnake has crawled into his bedroll and, if he moves, the serpent may strike.

130.163 *End of the Hunt.* Feb. 18, 1963. GS: Jeff Morrow, K.T. Stevens, Joe Higgins, John C. Gilbert, Harry Finley. When Lucas McCain's old enemy Reef Jackson arrives in town, Micah locks Lucas in a jail cell, to keep his friend from becoming a murderer.

130.164 *The Bullet.* Feb. 25, 1963. GS: Richard Anderson, Harold J. Stone, Asa Maynor, Harry Lauter, Gene Tyburn, Norman Leavitt, Reg Parton, Dal McKennon. On his way to Las Cruces, Lucas stops a gambler named Griff from committing murder. But when he turns Griff over to the marshal in Las Cruces, the lawman releases him.

130.165 *Requiem at Mission Springs.* March 4, 1963. GS: George Lindsey, Dal Jenkins, Dean Fredericks, Ralph Moody, Joe E. Benson. Mark is paralyzed after a fall from his horse, and Lucas and Lou start out with him for a ghost town once noted for its heating mineral waters, praying the boy will live to reach the springs.

130.166 *The Guest.* March 11, 1963. GS: Cesare Danova, Walter Sande. Mario Arsatti, a new arrival in North Fork, gets real chummy with Lucas. But it is just pleasure before business. He has been hired to kill the Rifleman.

130.167 *Old Man Running.* March 18, 1963. GS: John Anderson, Adam Williams, Rex Holman. Lucas refuses to help Mark's grandfather, Sam Gibbs, who rides into North Fork ahead of three gunmen who are out to kill him. Lucas still blames the old man for his wife's death.

130.168 *Which Way'd They Go?* April 1, 1963. GS: Peter Whitney, Conlan Carter, Mickey Manners, John Craig, Vito Scotti, Leo Gordon, Dal McKennon, Beatrice Kay. The Jackman boys don't like to work very hard but they may have to. Their mortgage has just been foreclosed.

130.169 *Old Tony.* April 8, 1963. GS: Stefan Schnable, Karen Sue Trent, Martin Kosleck. Mary and his girl friend Lorrie are taken prisoner by a hermit called Old Tony when he catches them trespassing on his land.

Rin Tin Tin see ***The Adventures of Rin Tin Tin***

131. Riverboat

NBC. 60 min. Broadcast history: Sunday, 7:00–8:00, Sept. 1959–Jan. 1960; Monday, 7:30–8:30, Feb. 1960–Jan. 1961.

Regular Cast: Darren McGavin (Grey Holden), Burt Reynolds (Ben Frazer) 59-60, Noah Beery, Jr. (Bill Blake) 60-61, Dick Wessel (Carney), Jack Lambert (Joshua), Mike McGreevey (Chip), John Mitchum (Pickalong), Bart Patton (Terry).

Premise: This series related the exploits of Grey Holden, captain of the riverboat Enterprise, which travelled the Mississippi and Missouri rivers during the 1840s.

The Episodes

131.1 *Payment in Full.* Sept. 13, 1959. GS: Nancy Gates, Aldo Ray, Louis Hayward, Barbara Bel Geddes, William Bishop, John Larch. For a price, simple-minded Hunk Farber is only to happy to reveal the whereabouts of his boss Monte, who accidentally killed a senator's son. The reward in his pocket, Hunk heads for Captain Holden's riverboat. He is eager to impress a particular young lady aboard the Enterprise.

131.2 *The Barrier.* Sept. 20, 1959. GS: Elizabeth Montgomery, John Kerr, William Bendix, Read Morgan. Young Jefferson Carruthers has been assigned to a new post as Indian agent. He and his wife board the Enterprise to travel to their new home. Also on board is Vance Muldoon, who plans to offer Carruthers money if he will help smuggle liquor to the Indians.

131.3 *About Roger Mowbray.* Sept. 27, 1959. GS: Robert Vaughn, Vera Miles, Cameron Prud'homme, Madlyn Rhue, John Hoyt, Hank Patterson, Sandy Kenyon. Wealthy Roger Mowbray's marriage is threatened when an old sweetheart intimates that Roger married for money. Because he really loves his wife, Roger is doubly upset to discover that his father seems to be involved in the scheme to break up the marriage.

131.4 *Race to Cincinnati.* Oct. 4, 1959. GS: Anne Baxter, Monica Lewis, Robert Lowery, Lloyd Corrigan, Don Haggerty. John Jenkins has placed a large down payment on land owned by three ruthless farmers. Jenkins is planning to deliver a shipment of peaches, via the Enterprise, to Cincinnati as final payment for the land. But the farmers plot to block the boat so the shipment of peaches will be spoiled.

131.5 *The Unwilling.* Oct. 11, 1959. GS: Eddie Albert, Debra Paget. Riverboat pilot John Murrell plans to hijack a shipment from rival pilot Dan Sampson. Murrell arranges to have Lela Candida take a job on Sampson's boat as a dancing girl so that she can signal his raiders when to attack.

131.6 *The Fight Back.* Oct. 18, 1959. GS: John Ireland,

Riverboat

Karl Swenson, Joan O'Brien, William D. Gordon. Ansel Torgin hires the Enterprise for his daughter's wedding. Captain Grey Holden recognizes the bridegroom as a drifter he once threw off the riverboat.

131.7 *Escape to Memphis.* Oct. 25, 1959. GS: Jeanne Crain, Claude Akins, Philip Reed, Richard Wessel. Laura Sutton is forced to kill her husband in self-defense. Laura's brother-in-law, Jarrett Sutton, witnesses the shooting and tries to blackmail her.

131.8 *Witness No Evil.* Nov. 1, 1959. GS: Vincent Price, Barbara Lawrence. Otto Justin, dealer in wild animals, is escorting a shipment of his captured beasts to St. Louis aboard the Enterprise. Widow Aby Saunders and her young son Paddy are both impressed with Justin's manner.

131.9 *A Night at Trapper's Landing.* Nov. 8, 1959. GS: Ricardo Montalban, Peter Whitney, Judson Pratt. French playboy Andre Devereaux has become an American Army lieutenant. Assigned to lead some troops into Indian country, he finds that the normally peaceful Indians have been provoked to violence.

131.10 *The Faithless.* Nov. 22, 1959. GS: Richard Carlson, Bethel Leslie, Bert Freed, William Phipps, Jeanne Bates. Prisoner Paul Drake is being returned to custody by a prison guard. Because Drake has already tricked him once, the guard shackles his prisoner to a deckhouse of the Enterprise.

131.11 *The Boy from Pittsburgh.* Nov. 29, 1959. GS: Tommy Nolan, Mona Freeman, Robert Emhardt. Tommy Jones, a young stowaway, is discovered aboard the Enterprise. Also on board are a pair of thieves who plan to blow up the boat to collect insurance on some diamonds they are shipping to St. Louis.

131.12 *Jessie Quinn.* Dec. 6, 1959. GS: Mercedes McCambridge, Clu Gulager, Richard Gardner. Lt. Perry Quinn, an officer in Sam Houston's Texas Army, hires the Enterprise to deliver a cargo of lead down river. Captain Grey Holden is warned that Santa Ana's agent's may try to sabotage the shipment.

131.13 *Strange Request.* Dec. 13, 1959. GS: Jan Sterling, Rhys Williams, Lawrence Dobkin, Peter Lazer, Richard Wessel, William D. Gordon, Lee Van Cleef, Glenn Thompson. Actress Lorna Langton wants to charter the enterprise and a skeleton crew for a trip from St. Louis. The actress has been told that her young son, kidnaped some years before, is being held in another town.

131.14 *Guns for Empire.* Dec. 20, 1959. GS: George Macready, Gena Rowlands, Dennis Patrick. Antony Lorrimer charters the Enterprise to deliver a cargo of farm machinery to his thriving community of Lorrimer City. Captain Grey Holden is unaware that the cargo is actually arms and ammunition.

131.15 *Face of Courage.* Dec. 27, 1959. GS: Joanna Moore, Tom Drake, Doug McClure, Tracey Roberts, Paul Birch. The Enterprise steams up river with a cargo of arms and recruits for the Fort Union outpost. At Atkins Landing, Grey Holden is told by Homer Atkins that the Sioux have been watching the boat and are planning an uprising.

131.16 *Tampico Raid.* Jan. 3, 1960. GS: Patricia Crowley, Edward Colmans. A group of volunteer teachers who have gone to the island of Diablo Corozan off the coast of Tampico are imprisoned when Spain conquers the island. The corrupt Spanish officials allow Joan Marchand, one of the teachers, to return to the United States to raise ransom for the rest.

131.17 *Landlubbers.* Jan. 10, 1960. GS: Gloria Talbott, Richard Devon, Kay E. Kuter, Arthur Batanides, Jerry O'Sullivan, Frank Warren. The Enterprise, tied up overnight, is boarded and hijacked by a vicious crew, who kill the three men left to guard the boat. Captain Grey Holden and Ben Fraser return to the scene in time to see their craft heading down the river. They set out overland to head it off.

131.18 *The Blowup.* Jan. 17, 1968. GS: Whitney Blake, Dean Harens, Carlos Romero, James R. Scott, John Day. Captain Grey Holden and his crew get into a street brawl over Martha Crane and land in jail. Martha agrees to bail them out on the condition that Grey will transport a supply of gun powder up river to her father.

131.19 *Forbidden Island.* Jan. 24, 1960. GS: Miguel Landa, Patricia Michon, Bruce Gordon, Patrick Westwood. While the Enterprise makes a stop for wood, a group of Cajuns board the vessel and hijack part of the cargo. Two people are shot during the incident.

131.20 *Salvage Pirates.* Jan. 31, 1960. GS: Judi Meredith, Richard Garland, Bern Hoffman, Johnstone White. Louise Harrison and her boy friend, the only survivors of a boat tragedy, do some quick thinking. Realizing that a fortune in jewels went down with the ship, they appeal to their rescuer, Grey Holden, to help them retrieve Louise's dowry.

131.21 *Path of the Eagle.* Feb. 1, 1960. GS: Dianne Foster, Dayton Lummis, Myron Healey, Wilton Graff, Grant Richards. A trip to Independence, Missouri, brings back memories of a bitter adventure to Grey Holden. Holden tells the story to Chip and Joshua.

131.22 *The Treasure of Hawk Hill.* Feb. 8, 1960. GS: Kent Taylor, Richard Hale. Bank robbers have a falling-out over some hidden loot. One of the men manages to give a map of th hiding place to his son before he is killed, and the boy heads up river on a raft to deliver it to his uncle.

131.23 *Fight at New Canal.* Feb. 22, 1960. GS: Charles Aidman, Jean Allison, John Maxwell, John Archer. Grey Holden is chosen to represent riverboat captains in seeking a Government-subsidized canal. Preliminary surveys and work must be completed before Congress will approve and opponents of the canal set out to sabotage the project.

131.24 *The Wichita Arrows.* Feb. 29, 1960. GS: Dan Duryea, Betty Lou Keim, Don Haggerty. Brad Turner, temporary captain of the Enterprise, finds the bodies of two brothers. The only clue to the killer's identity is that he was wearing moccasins and buckskin trousers.

131.25 *Fort Epitaph.* March 7, 1960. GS: Dan Duryea, Joan Camden, Brad Weston, Charles Cooper, Mark Allen, Stuart Randall, Ronnie Rondell, Jr. After an Indian siege, Fort Wilson's commander expects more trouble. Captain Turner and the rivermen are pressed into Army service.

131.26 *Three Graves.* March 14, 1960. GS: Beverly Garland, Robert Bray, John McKee, Harry Ellerbe, Will White. The crew has planned a big night on the town. But when they dock, they find the place completely deserted except for three new graves.

131.27 *Hang the Men High.* March 21, 1960. GS: Stephen McNally, Karen Steele, Walter Sande, Dallas Mitchell, Ray Hamilton. A young passenger on the Enterprise has been accused of murder by his dying father. An aroused posse light out to drag him off the riverboat and serve up their own brand of justice.

131.28 *The Night of the Faceless Men*. March 28, 1960. GS: Hugh Downs, Patricia Medina, Jocelyn Brando, Charles Gray, Douglas Kennedy. The Enterprise makes a wood stop at a small river town. But there is no wood for sale to strangers.

131.29 *The Long Trail*. April 4, 1960. GS: Perry Lopez, Abraham Sofaer, Anthony Caruso, Harry Lauter. An Army colonel wants the Cherokee to take the long trail to a new settling place. Pillagers burn the Indian village to make sure the Cherokees have no reason to stay.

131.30 *The Quick Noose*. April 11, 1960. GS: Nan Leslie, Ed Nelson, Jack Mather. A noose is about to tighten around Carney's neck. Visiting his brother in Wingate, the riverboater is charged with murder.

131.31 *The Sellout*. April 18, 1960. GS: Frank Overton, Barbara Stuart, Bartlett Robinson. The Enterprise is badly in need of repairs and Holden's got to accept Nick Logan's offer. He will repair the boat if, afterward, he and his partner can use it.

Season Two

131.32 *End of a Dream*. Sept. 19, 1960. GS: Cliff Robertson, Susan Cummings, Robert J. Wilke, June Vincent, Ben Wright. Fast-talking Martinus Van der Brig persuades Holden and Bill Blake, the riverboat's new pilot, to transport a group of pioneers to some new territory, recently purchased from Mr. Van Der Brig.

131.33 *The Taylor Affair*. Sept. 26, 1960. GS: Arlene Dahl, Robert Ellenstein, Stanley Adams, Paul Fix, Gil Rankin, Milton Frome. Holden and Blake have an idea for making the Enterprise famous by shanghaiing President Zachary Taylor. They get some help from a girl named Lucy Belle.

131.34 *The Two Faces of Grey Holden*. Oct. 3, 1960. GS: Suzanne Pleshette, Thomas Gomez, Celia Lovsky, Lillian Buyeff, Nico Minardos, Herb Ellis, Lomax Study. To Captain Holden, his romance with Marie Tourette was just a pleasant interlude, but Marie has taken him seriously. Now that it is time for him to leave, her father want's Grey to marry her.

131.35 *River Champion*. Oct. 10, 1960. GS: Dennis O'Keefe, George Kennedy, Slim Pickens, Norma Crane, Ralph Reed, Jack Hogan. Gentleman Dan Muldoon is backing Dublin Boy against Gunner Stagle for the bare-knuckle championship of the river. Before th fight, Dublin Boy proves to have a glass jaw when flattened by Grey Holden.

131.36 *No Bride on the River*. Oct. 24, 1960. GS: Sandy Kenyon, Hayden Rorke, Pat Michon, Denver Pyle, Bartlett Robinson, Tyler McVey. There was no bridge on the river to Grey's knowledge, but someone has gone and built a railroad trestle, and the Enterprise rams into its pilings. Holden sues for damages and finds himself in court, face to face with a young lawyer named Abe Lincoln.

131.37 *Trunk Full of Dreams*. Oct. 31, 1960. GS: Raymond Massey, Bethel Leslie, Willard Waterman, Mary Tyler Moore, Hugh Sanders, Jody Fair. Sir Oliver Garrett and Juliet, his young companion, are a couple of shipwrecked actors. Captain Holden fishes them out of the river, and books them as entertainers aboard the Enterprise.

131.38 *The Water of Gorgeous Springs*. Nov. 7, 1960. GS: Buddy Ebsen, Sherry Jackson, Barry Atwater, Jocelyn Brando, Gregory Walcott, Dody Heath. The feuding families of Jennings and Cox are going to a fair, and Holden unwittingly books both families on the Enterprise. Now he has got to act as peacemaker or have the riverboat wrecked by gunfire.

131.39 *Devil in Skirts*. Nov. 21, 1960. GS: Gloria Talbott, Frank Silvera, Brad Weston, Arthur Batanides. If Grey will lure a belle named Lucinda away from Colonel Ashley's son Tony, the Colonel will provide a profitable cotton cargo for the Enterprise. Unfortunately, Lucinda overhears the proposition.

131.40 *The Quota*. Nov. 28, 1960. GS: Gene Evans, James Griffith, Ron Hagerthy, Tom Gilleran, Stuart Randall. Army Sgt. Dan Phillips is trying to recruit new members for his platoon. Using a convincing argument — a bop on the head — he has filled all but two sports in his quota. And he has his eye on Phelan, one of Grey's crewmen, for one of those spots.

131.41 *Chicota Landing*. Dec. 5, 1960. GS: Joe De Santis, Connie Hines, John McLiam. The Enterprise arrives at Chicota Landing with a cargo of gunpowder for the Army. Before they can unload the stuff, the boat is taken over by a gang of Mexican bandits led by Juan Cortilla.

131.42 *Duel on the River*. Dec. 12, 1960. GS: Fay Spain, Claude Akins, Robert Emhardt, Edgar Buchanan. Brian Cloud monopolizes all the cotton crop in the area, and Laurie Rawlins, the wife of a cotton planter, doesn't like being under Cloud's thumb.

131.43 *Zigzag*. Dec. 26, 1960. GS: Charles Bronson, Stella Stevens, William Fawcett, Don O'Kelly, John Milford, Ray Teal, Tom Fadden, Phil Tully. In town to have an aching tooth removed, Carney stops at the saloon for a bolstering snort. This makes him late for the dentist's, so Blake undertakes to separate Carney from his tooth.

131.44 *Listen to the Nightingale*. Jan. 2, 1961. GS: Jeanne Bal, Jack Albertson, DeForest Kelley, Paul Stader, Hal Needham, Claire Carleton, John Warburton. Norwegian songbird Julie Lang wants to take her troupe to New Orleans for an engagement, but she has no money. Grey finally agrees to take the troupe aboard the Enterprise, for an IOU against their New Orleans receipts.

132. The Road West

NBC. 60 min. Broadcast history: Monday, 9:00–10:00, Sept. 1966–Aug. 1967.

Regular Cast: Barry Sullivan (Ben Pride), Andrew Prine (Tim Pride), Brenda Scott (Midge Pride), Charles Seel (Grandpa Pride), Kelly Corcoran (Kip Pride), Kathryn Hays (Elizabeth Reynolds), Glenn Corbett (Chance Reynolds).

Premise: Benjamin Pride and his family travel from Springfield, Ohio, to the Kansas Territory after the end of the Civil War.

The Episodes

132.1 *This Savage Land* Part One. Sept. 12, 1966. GS: George C. Scott, John Drew Barrymore, Roy Roberts, Katherine Squire, Charles Gray, Rex Holman. A band of terrorizing

The Road West

vigilantes, led by ex-Confederate officer Jud Barker, warns the Pride family that homesteaders aren't welcome in Kansas.

132.2 *The Savage Land* **Part Two.** Sept. 19, 1966. GS: George C. Scott, John Drew Barrymore, Roy Roberts, Katherine Squire, Charles Gray, Rex Holman. Jud Barker is angered by Stacey Daggart's cold-blooded murder of Elizabeth's father, but he is even more upset by the continued presence of the homesteading Prides, who refuse to move on.

132.3 *The Gunfighter.* Sept. 26, 1966. GS: James Daly, James Gammon, John Wright, Jonathan Lippe, James Nusser, Bern Hoffman, Leonard Yorr, Brett Pearson. Veteran cowboy Andy Benteen, who has seen Tim in a scuffle with some drovers, insists that the young man will have to learn to handle a gun if he is going to survive.

132.4 *The Lean Years.* Oct. 3, 1966. GS: Charles Aidman, Robert P. Leib, Elva Miler, Willard Sage. Chance and Tim head for town to spend a sociable evening at the local saloon.

132.5 *This Dry and Thirsty Land.* Oct. 10, 1966. GS: Anthony Caruso, Jess Pearson, George Furth. The Prides build a primitive irrigation system in the hopes of saving their drought-stricken corn crop.

132.6 *Long Journey to Leavenworth.* Oct. 17, 1966. GS: Geoffrey Horne, Robert F. Simon, E.J. Andre, Don Dubbins, Ron Russell, Hal Baylor, John Pickard, Sam Edwards. During Ben and Tim's absence, Midge invites a friendly stranger into the house, unaware that the man has just robbed the Lawrence bank.

132.7 *Ashes and Tallow and One True Love.* Oct. 24, 1966. GS: Robert Walker, Jr., Adam Roarke, Kelly Thordsen, Harlan Warde, Clyde Howdy, Deanna Lund. Midge falls for the charming young Cavalry officer who rescued her from a band of renegade Indians.

132.8 *Piece of Tin.* Oct. 31, 1966. GS: Wendell Corey, William Smithers, John McLiam, Hampton Fancher. Ben is asked to run against town-council boss Sam Gaskins. The corrupt official has filled the post of town marshal with a gunman who refuses to enforce anything except Gaskins' power politics.

132.9 *Lone Woman.* Nov. 7, 1966. GS: Lonny Chapman, George Wallace, Mickey Sholdar, Eddie Little Sky, Jack Chapman, Ted Jordan, Tina Mangosing. When a horse-stealing Arapaho murders an orphan boy, the usually compassionate Elizabeth insists that Ben find and kill the boy's murderer.

132.10 *Shaman.* Nov. 14, 1966. GS: Elisha Cook, Jr., Henry Wilcoxon, David Astor, Anne Meacham, Christopher Cary, Rodd Redwing, Larry Ward, Len Wayland. The terror-stricken citizens of a small town, believing that an old hermit is possessed by evil spirits, organize a posse to hunt down the recluse, whom the Indians revere as a medicine man.

132.11 *To Light a Candle.* Nov. 28, 1966. GS: Katharine Ross, Mike Constantine. Tim incurs the anger of a clannish religious sect when he hides young runaway Rachel Adams, who says that she has suffered brutal treatment at the hands of her father.

132.12 *Pariah.* Dec. 5, 1966. GS: Barbara Anderson, Tom Drake, Donnelly Rhodes, Phyllis Hill, John Mitchum, Stuart Nisbet, Gail Bonney. Susan Douglass, wife of an Indian named Red Eagle, plans to raise her child in the white man's world, despite her relatives' bigotry, and threats from Red Eagle, who demands the return of his son.

132.13 *Have You Seen the Aurora Borealis?* Dec. 12, 1966. GS: Dan O'Herlihy, Jackie Russell. Young Midge falls for the Prides' house guest, forty year old poet Seamas O'Flaherty. The infatuated girl, ignoring her father's objections, sets out to help the hard-drinking Seamas regains his poetic skill.

132.14 *Power of Fear.* Dec. 26, 1966. GS: John Dehner, Joseph Campanella, Barbara Werle, Gary Walberg, John Hoyt, William Fawcett, Kim Hector, William Phipps. A surgeon educated in Europe comes to Lawrence, where his brusque manner and revolutionary use of chloroform create a distrust among the people and promote a murder threat from the brother of a patient who died while under the new anesthetic.

132.15 *Reap the Whirlwind.* Jan. 9, 1966. GS: James Farentino, Lauri Peters, Richard X. Slattery, John Lodge, William Phipps. Ben takes up the search for the man who wounded Midge. The fugitive wanted for murder, is also being hunted by a band of vigilantes, who are more interested in bounty money than justice.

132.16 *Beyond the Hill.* Jan. 16, 1967. GS: Victor Jory, Gena Rowlands. The Prides ask for trouble when they allow a sharp-tongued old squatter and his young wife to camp on their land. Chance is soon infatuated with the woman, unaware that her husband killed the last man who came near her.

132.17 *The Predators.* Jan. 23, 1967. GS: Tony Bill, John Marshall, Lane Bradford, Willard Sage. Midge is trapped by her growing love for fugitive Andy Wilkins. The young man is being hunted by vengeful Judith Devery, who accuses Wilkins of murdering her father.

132.18 *A Mighty Hunter Before the Lord.* Jan. 30, 1967. GS: Lloyd Nolan, Strother Martin, Jack Dodson. A salty old hunter is too proud to change his way of life. The frontier is fast disappearing and so is the wildlife that afforded men like Jed Daniell a decent living.

132.19 *No Sanctuary.* Feb. 6, 1967. GS: Jan Shepard, Keenan Wynn, Warren Vanders, John Litel, Wynn Pearce. The Prides invite trouble when they offer refuge to widowed Ellen Brewster. The woman's love-crazed brother-in-law is determined to take her for himself, even if it means killing her protectors.

132.20 *The Insider.* Feb. 13, 1967. GS: Jason Evers, Colin Wilcox, Myron Healey, Ross Hagen, Tyler McVey. Ben Pride tries to save a small town from disaster. Ben's warning that the acting sheriff is a gunslinger goes unheeded, even when his gang shows up.

132.21 *Road to Glory.* Feb. 20, 1967. GS: John Anderson, Emile Genest, Bonnie Beecher. Continuing their westward trek, the Prides join a wagon train plagued by renegade Indians and internal strife. Stern wagonmaster Sewell Trask blames the trouble on the scout, a tormented ex-Army officer who has been brought to the breaking point by Trask's continual harassment.

132.22 *Fair Ladies of France.* Feb. 27, 1967. GS: Signe Hasso, Kim Darby, Svea Grunfeld, Gerry Gaylor, Richard Hale. Chance takes on the job of escorting four nuns who are determined to head north-west to an old mission, despite the continuing threat of Indian attack.

132.23 *Never Chase a Rainbow.* March 6, 1967. GS: Kevin McCarthy, Jack Carter, Barbara Anderson. Tim and Chance stay on after helping Barbara Plummer find her long-lost father. The boys are concerned about the young woman's welfare, and her life savings. Barbara's father is a compulsive gambler deep in debt.

132.24 *Eleven Miles to Eden.* March 13, 1967. GS: Jan Sterling, Michael Burns, Tisha Sterling. Tim receives a legacy of violence when he helps the family of a man he killed in self-defense. The late Harry Meagen owed money to three men who have come to collect the debt, or wipe out the family.

132.25 *Charade of Justice.* March 27, 1967. GS: Kurt Russell, Jay C. Flippen, Melodie Johnson, Tom Tryon, Roy Barcroft, Ted H. Jordan, Robert B. Williams, Jan Murphy. A judge sentences a boy to hang for stealing Ben's horse. Ben is determined to save the lad, even though he testified against him.

132.26 *The Eighty-Seven Dollar Bride.* April 3, 1967. GS: Gavin MacLeod, Cloris Leachman, William Bramley, Lou Antonio. Midge succeeds as a matchmaker between a saloon singer and an immigrant farmer, but the jealous saloon owner takes violent steps to kill a romance.

132.27 *A War for the Gravediggers.* April 10, 1967. GS: Michael Ansara, Joe De Santis. In a Mexican town, Ben and Tim are caught up in a conflict between an old general and a young firebrand, the leaders of a revolutionary army.

132.28 *The Agreement.* April 24, 1967. GS: Virginia Gregg, James Gammon, Barbara Werle, Dan Frazer, Jason Wingreen. Chance is caught up in a clash between a vengeful woman and an honorable lawman. Sheriff Lyle Saunders is holding Chance for the murder of Tom Bishop, whose mother is determined to act as judge, jury and executioner.

132.29 *Elizabeth's Odyssey.* May 1, 1967. GS: Albert Salmi, Dabbs Greer, Peggy Lipton, Amzie Strickland, Bill Zuckert. Elizabeth and Chance undertake a two-day wagon trip to help an injured farmer, a mission that soon becomes a journey into terror.

133. The Rough Riders

ABC. 30 min. Broadcast history: 9:30–10:00, Thurday, Oct. 1958–Sept. 1959.

Regular Cast: Kent Taylor (Captain Jim Flagg), Jan Merlin (Lt. Kirby), Peter Whitney (Sgt. Buck Sinclair).

Premise: Two Union Army veterans and an ex-Confederate officer join forces after the end of the Civil War as they journey west.

The Episodes

133.1 *The Murderous Sutton Gang.* Oct. 2, 1958. GS: John Doucette, Joan Young, Dan Sheridan. After their discharge from the service, Union Army Capt. Jim Flagg, Confederate Army Lt. Kirby and Union Army Sergeant Buck Sinclair decide to join forces on their long trek West. They stop at a farmhouse and the farmer tells them that the notorious Sutton gang has kidnaped his daughter. The three men try to rescue the girl.

133.2 *Breakout.* Oct. 9, 1958. GS: Robert H. Harris, Douglas Kennedy, Robert Brubaker, Craig Duncan. The Rough Riders find a Union prison camp and learn that the commander has falsified records in order to hold Confederate prisoners even though peace has been signed. The three friends plan to rescue the prisoners.

133.3 *The Maccabites.* Oct. 16, 19589. GS: Trevor Bardette, Kaye Ebhardt, Mark Tapscott, Keith Vincent, Preston Hanson, Ray Kellogg. Capt. Flagg, Sgt. Sinclair and Lt. Kirby take on a big job when they assume the defense of a religious group against an attack by a band of renegades. The principles of the group forbid their defending themselves.

133.4 *The Duelists.* Oct. 23, 1958. GS: Stephen Bekassy, Jeanne Vaughn, Patrick Waltz, Jason Wingreen. A young woman comes to the Rough Riders and asks their aid. Her brother has been challenged to a duel by a politician known to enjoy killing. He gets rid of all of his opponents and enemies by challenging them to duels and then killing them unfairly.

133.5 *The Imposters.* Oct. 30, 1958. GS: Yvette Vickers, Leo Gordon, John Parrish. The Rough Riders try to help a young lady collect on an Army requisition for a cow. They uncover a plot to steal the Army payroll.

133.6 *The Governor.* Nov. 6, 1958. GS: Carlyle Mitchell, Joan Marshall, Russ Bender, William Conrad. A pretty girl asks the Rough Riders to help rescue her father, the governor, who is being held hostage by a band of outlaws. The outlaws will release the Governor in return for a member of the band who is imprisoned.

133.7 *Blood Feud.* Nov. 13, 1958. GS: Kathleen Crowley, Larry Pennell, Carol Thurston, Charles Fawcett, Troy Melton. The Rough Riders loan a horse to a pretty girl and find that their good deed has involved them in a feud between two mountain families.

133.8 *The Nightbinders.* Nov. 20, 1958. GS: DeForest Kelley, Jean Allison, Jack Hogan. While riding west the rough Riders are stopped by hooded vigilantes. They learn that the leader of the vigilantes is using his men for purely selfish motives.

133.9 *Shadow of the Past.* Nov. 27, 1958. GS: Patrick McVey, Mitchell Kowal, Mary-Robin Redd, Ed Hinton. Capt. Flagg, Lt. Kirby and Sgt. Sinclair find a group of deserters from the Union Army. The fugitives have set up an outlaw settlement and are holding prisoner an Army officer.

133.10 *Killers at Chocktaw Valley.* Dec. 4, 1958. GS: Robert J. Stevenson, Ted Jacques, Connie Buck. While journeying West, Capt Flagg, Lt. Kirby and Sgt. Sinclair skirt the edge of Indian territory. When a chief's son is killed, the three men are blamed for the murder.

133.11 *The Counterfeiters.* Dec. 11, 1958. GS: John Vivyan, Nancy Hadley, House Peters, Jr., George Eldredge. The Rough Riders come upon four men who are redeeming Union Army script with counterfeit money.

133.12 *Strand of Wire.* Dec. 18, 1958. GS: Roy Barcroft, Keith Richards, Maurice Wells, Aline Towne. A telegraph lineman's death leads to the discovery of a plot to disrupt communications.

133.13 *The Electioners.* Jan. 1, 1959. GS: Don Haggerty, Jack Wagner, Carlyle Mitchell, Yvette Vickers. Flagg, Kirby and Sinclair take special interest in a coming election. For one thing, voters are being prevented from registering. For another, one candidate is a former Army officer reputed to have sacrificed his troops for personal glory.

133.14 *The Scavengers.* Jan. 8, 1959. GS: Ronald Foster, Karen Kadler, Harlen Warde, Mauritz Hugo. While searching for a missing husband, Flagg, Kirby and Sinclair stumble on an organized gang that is engaged in shanghaiing wanderers for sea duty.

The Rough Riders

133.15 *An Eye for an Eye.* Jan. 15, 1959. GS: Lon Chaney, Jr., Allison Hayes, Richard Emory, Lane Bradford, Earl R. Sands, Carol Henry. Flagg, Kirby and Sinclair find themselves confronted with a man and his three sons who are bent on avenging their hatred of rebels on Kirby.

133.16 *Double Cross.* Jan. 22, 1959. GS: Jean Willes, John Reach, Walter Barnes. Flagg, Kirby and Sinclair help a woman who is being pursued by outlaws. Soon after, they learn that the woman they saved is none other than the infamous lady gunslinger, Belle Starr.

133.17 *Wilderness Trace.* Jan. 29, 1959. GS: Kenneth MacDonald, Michael Connors, Karen Sharpe. Flagg, Kirby and Sinclair accidentally come upon the hideout of a gang of outlaws and meets its inhabitants. Soon, the three men find themselves caught in a struggle between two factions—law-minded citizens and the outlaws.

133.18 *The Plot to Assassinated President Johnson.* Feb. 5, 1959. GS: Broderick Crawford, Barbara Woodell, Keith Richards, Don Gordon. Flagg, Kirby and Sinclair accidentally learn of a plot to assassinate President Andrew Johnson. The men planning the assassination are led by the infamous William Quantrill.

133.19 *The End of Nowhere.* Feb. 12 1959. GS: John Carradine, John Panish, Eugenia Paul, Richard Garland. Flagg, Kirby and Sinclair run into a unusual group of tax collectors—they are collecting taxes for an independent nation. The Rough Riders learn that a well-meaning visionary is behind the movement, but that some of his followers are pocketing the money.

133.20 *A Matter of Instinct.* Feb. 19, 1959. GS: Steve Brodie, Penny Edwards, Gary Vinson. Flagg, Kirby and Sinclair encounter a plot to induct farmers into slave-labor gangs. When the three men try to foil the plot, they find themselves trapped by it.

133.21 *Witness Against the Judge.* Feb. 26, 1959. GS: Oliver McGowan, Harvey Stephens, Jack Edwards, Joel Riordan, Owen Cameron. Flagg, Kirby and Sinclair, traveling through a valley, are arrested and imprisoned by local troops. The three rangers learn that the troops are controlled by a land-hungry judge.

133.22 *End of Track.* March 5, 1959. GS: John Anderson, Joan Granville, Clancy Cooper. Flagg, Kirby and Sinclair come across a frontier town where the marshal has been killed, leaving its citizens at the mercy of outlaws. The three riders decide to take over the enforcement of the law.

133.23 *Death Sentence.* March 12, 1959. GS: Kasey Rogers, John Larch, Robert Lynn. The three riders come upon a mountain settlement controlled by Ed Mackin and his gang, who have murdered the sheriff and are about to hang four townspeople.

133.24 *The Double Dealers.* March 19, 1959. GS: Paula Raymond, Charles Maxwell, Tyler McVey. Capt. Flagg is assigned the job of apprehending a glamorous female spy, but is not permitted to tell Kirby or Sinclair about his mission.

133.25 *Lesson in Violence.* March 26, 1959. GS: Dorothy Provine, James Seay, Carole Mathews, Veda Ann Borg. When Mayor Thackeray sets out to harm schoolteacher Holly Morrow's reputation, his wife Dora decides to help the teacher.

133.26 *The Promise.* April 2, 1959. GS: Barbara Woodell, Stuart Randall, Joyce Taylor, Dehl Berti, Charles Fredericks. Lt. Kirby promises his aunt that he won't become involved in settler-rancher disputes. But he finds that because of his neutrality he has been labeled a coward.

133.27 *The Injured.* April 9, 1959. GS: Gerald Mohr, Ken Mayer, Bill Masters. Kirby and Flagg, injured during an ambush, send Sinclair to find the outlaws who attacked them and to bring back medical help.

133.28 *Paradise Gap.* Apr, 16, 1959. GS: Jeanette Nolan, Claudia Barrett, Helen Kleeb, Richard Devon, Dabbs Greer. Three nuns run into opposition when they try to claim a property inheritance for charity. Lieutenant Kirby meets the nuns and hearing of their difficulty, offers to help them.

133.29 *Hired Gun.* April 23, 1959. GS: Wendell Holmes, Joyce Meadows, John Beradino, Walter Coy. Lt. Kirby parts company with his pals and sets out for Three Rivers to visit his cousin Sam Hanks. When he gets there, Kirby finds them a gambler has set his sights on Sam's freight line.

133.30 *Gunpoint Persuasion.* April 30, 1959. GS: Lynn Bernay, Leonard Nimoy, Harry Lauter, Robert Tetrick. Margaret Tolen, anxious to get married so that she can claim an inheritance, sets her sights on an unwilling Lt. Kirby.

133.31 *The Rifle.* May 7, 1959. GS: Dorothy Ford, Judson Pratt, Warren Oates, Mickey Simpson. Poker Kate Jones is engaged in a squabble with crooked Marshal Jack McCoy. Sgt. Sinclair lends her a helping hand by posing as her missing husband Rifle Jones.

133.32 *Forty-Five Calibre Law.* May 14, 1959. GS: James Westerfield, Ted de Corsia, Douglas Henderson, Paul Langton. An outlaw gang plans to ambush a government official and secure a judicial post for one of the members of the gang.

133.33 *Deadfall.* May 21, 1959. GS: Will Wright, Marjorie Hellen, James Coburn, Wayne Heffley. An outlaw gang, controlled by Adam Bunch and his family, make the town of Deadfall their headquarters. A short time after a bounty hunter's murder. Lieutenant Kirby rides into Deadfall.

133.34 *The Highgraders.* May 28, 1959. GS: Aline Towne, Richard Reeves, Russ Conway, K.L. Smith. An old friend of Captain Flagg's becomes the victim of an outlaw gang headed by a woman. The band has been terrorizing prospectors, and Flagg calls on some other miners to help him capture the crooks.

133.35 *The Wagon Raiders.* June 4, 1959. GS: Frank Faylen, Joan Banks, Mimi Gibson, Bill Mims. The Rough Riders hunt for the men who raided and burned a wagon. They suspect that Indians committed the crime.

133.36 *Ransom of Rita Renee.* June 11, 1959. GS: Susan Cummings, Jack Kruschen, John Anderson, Tom Gilson, Roberto Contreras. Lieutenant Kirby's horse breaks a leg and he is forced to travel by stagecoach. On the stage, Kirby is accompanied by French singer Rita Renee and her unprincipled manager Tully.

133.37 *Reluctant Hostage.* June 18, 1959. GS: Joanna Moore, Joe Maross, Sam Buffington, William Tannen. Lieutenant Kirby is asked to take an unwilling girl witness to save an innocent man's life. On the way, the two are ambushed by a group of men led by the girl's boy friend.

133.38 *The Holdout.* June 25, 1959. GS: Jackie Blanchard, Dennis Moore, Bill Henry, Craig Duncan, Ted Mapes. Lieutenant Kirby, Captain Flagg and Sergeant Sinclair come upon a girl who is waging a fight against a group of men seeking control of all the horse-breeding in the area.

133.39 *The Last Rebel.* July 16, 1959. GS: George Macready, Joyce Meadows, Michael Lane, Lori March. The Rough Riders come upon a wagon train carrying arms and munitions. They learn that the munitions are for Confederate Colonel Miller, who will not accept the fact that the war is over.

134. The Rounders

ABC. 30 min. Broadcast history: Tuesday, 8:30–9:00, Sept. 1966–Jan. 1967.

Regular Cast: Ron Hayes (Ben Jones), Patrick Wayne (Howdy Lewis), Chill Wills (Jim Ed Love), Bobbi Jordan (Ada), Janis Hansen (Sally), Jason Wingreen (Shorty Dawes), J. Pat O'Malley (Vince), Walker Edmiston (Regan).

Premise: This Western comedy depicted the adventures of two fun-loving cowpokes who work as hired hands for Texas cattle ranch owner Jim Ed Love.

The Episodes

134.1 *Title Unknown.* Sept. 6, 1966. GS: Harry Carey, Jr., Marianne Gordon, Jennifer Billingsley, Robert G. Anderson, Buzz Henry. Jim Ed plans to buy unpredictable Old Fooler and make a fortune selling the cantankerous critter to a rodeo, but the horse has other ideas about the transaction.

134.2 *Title Unknown.* Sept. 13, 1966. GS: Robert B. Williams. Jim Ed is using a remote-controlled dogie as a training device in hopes of tuning the ranch plugs into first-class cutting horses and ending Old Fooler's cow-horse career.

134.3 *Title Unknown.* Sept. 20, 1966. GS: John Smith, Charles Wagenheim. Jim Ed hires Noble Vestry, the world's best cowboy, to show Ben and Howdy what cowpunching really means.

134.4 *Title Unknown.* Sept. 27, 1966. GS: Walker Edmiston, Meg Wyllie, Ellen Atterbury. Jim Ed begins his job as temporary sheriff by trying to smash a moonshiner's illegal still.

134.5 *Title Unknown.* Oct. 4, 1966. Ben and Howdy stand to make a tidy sum if they can find, and corral, a buffalo for Jim Ed.

134.6 *Title Unknown.* Oct. 11, 1966. GS: Zsa Zsa Gabor, Virginia Wood, Dodie Marshall, Sharyn Hillyer, Joy Harmon, Tom Hayden. Ben and Howdy are literally lassoed off the J.L. Ranch and into a job at near-by Velvet Haven, an exclusive health resort for women.

134.7 *Title Unknown.* Oct. 18, 1966. GS: G.D. Spradlin, Robert B. Williams, John Cliff, Hal Smith. Jim Ed wants to buy Howdy's remarkable effective good-luck piece, but some things just aren't for sale.

134.8 *Title Unknown.* Oct. 25, 1966. GS: Margaret Teele, Clyde Howdy, Walter Sande. Disgusted with life on the ranch, Ben gives Old Fooler to Howdy and takes over the operation of a one-pump gas station.

134.9 *Title Unknown.* Nov. 1, 1966. GS: Hal Smith, Bill Quinn. Jim Ed wants to be named Man of the Year in Texas so the ornery tightwad makes a painful effort to change his image.

134.10 *Title Unknown.* Nov. 15, 1966. GS: Casey Tibbs, Dick Haynes, Barbara Barrett. Jim Ed has bought a trailer from Howdy, but the merchandise might not arrive in A-1 condition. Howdy and Ben are throwing a party for the whole darned community in the trailer.

134.11 *Title Unknown.* Nov. 22, 1966. Jim Ed promises a handsome sum if Ben and Howdy will haul his new boat to Lake Love. Leave it to the two cowpokes to foul up a simple job.

134.12 *Title Unknown.* Nov. 29, 1966. GS: Andy Devine, Strother Martin, Linda Lorimer. A cutting-horse contest finds Howdy and Jim Ed backing different entrants and using all the sneaky tricks in the book to win their bets.

134.13 *Title Unknown.* Dec. 6, 1966. GS: Jay C. Flippen. Howdy and Ben plan to use Old Fooler to fool old Jim Ed. The two cowhands are out to convince their tightwad employer that the stubborn nag is a valuable polo pony.

134.14 *Title Unknown.* Dec. 13, 1966. GS: Mabel Albertson, Strother Martin. Jim Ed's sneaky, low-down tricks are nothing compared to those of Abbey Marstow, a wily woman rancher who is out to outfox foxy Jim Ed in the annual horse race.

134.15 *Title Unknown.* Dec. 20, 1966. GS: Andy Devine, Josephine Hutchinson. Jim Ed's former fourth-grade teacher, Martha Frobish, descends on the ranch like an avenging angel and soon throws everything out of whack.

134.16 *Title Unknown.* Dec. 27, 1966. GS: Melodie Johnson. Jim Ed hires a saucy female efficiency expert to bring progress to the ranch, where she soon puts a burr under the saddles of Jim Ed's two laziest cowpokes.

134.17 *Title Unknown.* Jan. 3, 1967. GS: Benny Rubin, G.D. Spradlin. It is pretty hard to hide an elephant, but that is just what Ben and Howdy are doing. The two conniving cowpokes are using the runaway pachyderm to do their chores for Jim Ed.

135. The Roy Rogers Show

NBC. 30 min. Broadcast history: Sunday, 6:30–7:00, Dec. 1951–June 1957.

Regular Cast: Roy Rogers (Roy Rogers), Dale Evans (Dale Evans), Pat Brady (Pat Brady), Harry Harvey, Sr. (Sheriff Potter), The Sons of the Pioneers.

Premise: This series depicted the adventures of ranchers Roy Rogers and Dale Evans who, with sidekick Pat Brady, help maintain law and order in the contemporary Western community of Mineral City.

The Episodes

135.1 *Jailbreak.* Dec. 30, 1951. GS: Rand Brooks, Nan Leslie, Steve Clark, Terry Frost, Riley Hill, Douglas Evans, Gregg Barton. Someone attempts to kill young Tom Lee, who is in prison for the murder of banker Joe Walton during a recent bank robbery. Roy and Dale suspect that Tome was framed and that the person responsible is also behind the murder attempt.

135.2 *Doc Stevens' Traveling Store.* Jan. 6, 1952. GS: Ferris Taylor, Wheaton Chambers, Peggy Stewart, Zon Murray,

The Roy Rogers Show

Stanley Andrews, Boyd "Red" Morgan. Doc Stevens seems to be mixed up in the lawless goings on in Eagle Rock. The unscrupulous publisher of the Eagle Rock newspaper tries to take the law into his own hands.

135.3 *The Set-Up.* Jan. 20, 1952. GS: Hallene Hill, Wheaton Chambers, Zon Murray, Boyd "Red" Morgan. A fur-trapping grandma is unaware that her life is in danger because she has refused to sell her lands.

135.4 *The Treasure of Howling Dog Canyon.* Jan. 27, 1952. GS: Carl Switzer, Don Harvey, Dorothy Crider, Denver Pyle, Boyd "Red" Morgan, Chief Yowlachie. Roy and Dale come to the aid of a young man whose evil step-parents are willing to commit murder to obtain the young man's half of a map leading to a cursed treasure.

135.5 *The Train Robbery.* Feb. 3, 1952. GS: Reed Howes, William Fawcett, Robert J. Wilke, Mike Ragan, Charles M. Heard. Two men dynamite a train and rob the mails. Pat and Dale give aid to the blast victims while Roy tries to head off the thieves.

135.6 *Badman's Brother.* Feb. 10, 1952. GS: Minerva Urecal, Harry Mackin, Robert Hyatt, Francis McDonald, Riley Hill, Sandy Sanders, Harry Harvey. A young boy who worships his older brother, an outlaw, is part of a gang which captures Roy and Pat.

135.7 *The Outlaw's Girl.* Feb. 17, 1952. GS: Brett King, John Crawford, Tom Tyler, Bill Tannen, Rocky Stanton, Art Dillard. It seems as if Roy, Pat and Dale will never be able to convince a young girl that she is wrong in loving a notorious bank robber.

135.8 *The Desert Fugitive.* Feb. 24, 1952. GS: Rand Brooks, Stephen Chase, Virginia Carroll, Terry Frost, Gregg Barton, Riley Hill, Chuck Roberson. A robber who had taken secret documents for the Sheldon gang escapes from prison and tries to regain his loot. The Sheldon gang has other plans for him.

135.9 *Outlaws' Town.* March 1, 1952. GS: Reed Howes, Ferris Taylor, William Tannen, John Crawford, Tom Tyler, Hank Patterson, Art Dillard, Brett King. Roy is deputized to pose as a fugitive and join a gang of outlaws holed up in a town in no man's land which the law can't reach.

135.10 *The Unwilling Outlaw.* March 8, 1952. GS: I. Stanford Jolley, Sherry Jackson, Dale Van Sickel, George J. Lewis, Reed Howes, William Fawcett. After supposedly embezzling funds from the bank, Jed Collins joins an outlaw gang. Roy and Dale try to find him and learn the reason for his new life of crime.

135.11 *Dead Men's Hills.* March 15, 1952. GS: Forrest Taylor, Richard Emory, Larry Hudson, George Slocum, Steve Raines, Stuart Whitman, Sandy Sanders. Roy and Dale join a posse besieging a gang of outlaws hiding in a ghost town next to an abandoned mine.

135.12 *The Minister's Son.* March 23, 1952. GS: Keith Richards, Raymond Hatton, Riley Hill, Terry Frost, Stephen Chase, Chuck Roberson, Gregg Barton, Douglas Evans, Ferris Taylor, Lonnie Burr. Dale brings a counterfeit ring into the open when she unwittingly passes a phoney bill given to her by an old miner. A minister's son is suspected to be a member of the gang.

135.13 *Ghost Gulch.* March 30, 1952. GS: Peggy Stewart, Zelda Cleaver, William Fawcett, George J. Lewis, Dale Van Sickel, Reed Howes, I. Stanford Jolley. A young lady comes to Roy with news that outlaws are trying to take away her land. he land grabbers have already kidnaped her husband.

135.14 *Ride in the Death Wagon.* April 6, 1952. GS: Forrest Taylor, George Slocum, Richard Emory, Bee Humphries, Larry Hudson. Two murderers posing as legitimate businessmen make off with a large fund intended to start a clinic for crippled children.

135.15 *Peril from the Past.* April 13, 1952. GS: John Doucette, Pierre Watkin, Ann Doran, Lee Roberts, Bill Catching, Paul Fierro, Russ Scott. Roy and Dale try to protect a bank clerk whose past has been threatened with exposure unless he helps an outlaw and his Indian sidekick rob the Mineral City bank.

135.16 *The Ride of the Ranchers.* April 20, 1952. GS: Pedro Regas, Tina Mendard, Millicent Patrick, Fred Cummins, Jim Diehl, Steve Raines, Russ Scott, Augie Gomez. While Roy and the other men of Paradise Valley are taking part in the annual Ride of the Ranchers, Dale and a handful of women are besieged in a hacienda by outlaws.

135.17 *Shoot to Kill.* April 27, 1952. GS: Carl "Alfalfa" Switzer, Lee Roberts, John Doucette, Dick Reeves, Sandy Sanders. Roy and Dale try to rescue a bumptious young newcomer who falsely claims that he has taken a photograph of a notorious outlaw. Roy intercepts the notorious Opal gang in their attempt to hold up a stagecoach.

135.18 *The Hermit's Secret.* May 4, 1952. GS: Evelyn Finley, Fred Graham, Gloria Winters, Hank Patterson, Henry Wills, James Kirkwood, Stanley Blystone. A supposed invalid is a murderer and has framed an innocent man. But he is not really and invalid after all, and Roy and Dale must get the evidence to prove he is a killer.

135.19 *Haunted Mine of Paradise Valley.* May 18, 1952. GS: Hank Patterson, Jean Harvey, Frank Jacquet, Fred Graham, Henry Wills, Buff Brady, Sandy Sanders, Nolan Leary, Tommy Coleman. A prospector tells Roy with his dying gasp that the map of his gold mine has been stolen.

135.20 *Ghost Town Gold.* May 25, 1952. GS: Tom London, Don C. Harvey, Marshall Reed, Sandy Sanders, Jeanne Dean, Harry Harvey, Sr., Rand Brooks, Russ Scott. Pat has bought Ghost Town, and when the sounds of shots are heard ringing through its empty streets, Roy rides out with him to investigate.

135.21 *The Doublecrosser.* June 1, 1952. GS: Harry Lauter, Dorothy Vaughan, Denver Pyle, Don C. Harvey, Boyd "Red" Morgan. Roy and Dale go to Eagle Rock on the pretext of seeking advice for a land purchase, when they really are there to investigate a sudden breakdown in law enforcement.

135.22 *Carnival Killer.* June 8, 1952. GS: Rand Brooks, Tom London, Don C. Harvey, Marshall Reed, Jeanne Dean, Russ Scott. Roy and Dale become involved when a carnival owner is murdered and the chief suspects are the trick marksman and the bullwhip expert, who had fought over the dead man's daughter.

135.23 *Flying Bullets.* June 15, 1952. GS: Herman Levitt, Steve Pendleton, George Douglas, Denver Pyle, Harry Harvey, Russ Scott. When Kentucky mountaineer Cliff Miller, whose storehouse has burned down, is showing the ruins to Roy, he is shot at by a masked gunman.

135.24 *Death Medicine.* Sept. 7, 1952. GS: Ray Bennett,

Rory Mallinson, Bill George, Fred Graham, Burt LeBaron, Bill McCormick. Roy and Dale need assistance from Bullet as they trail a gang of kidnapers and their hostage. The old man the kidnappers hold will die unless he takes the proper medicine.

135.25 *Outlaw's Return.* Sept. 28, 1952. GS: Myron Healey, Steve Pendleton, John Doucette, Tom London, Fred Graham, Russ Scott. Roy gives a job on his ranch to an ex-convict whom he had once sent to prison, but then learns that his new hand matches the description of the man who recently held up a stagecoach and a bank.

135.26 *Huntin' for Trouble.* Oct. 5, 1952. GS: John Doucette, Myron Healey, Steve Pendleton, Tom London, Kim Walker, Richard Eyer, Russ Scott. Roy is captured by the fugitive Wolf Gang who try to force him to lead them to safety.

135.27 *The Feud.* Nov. 16, 1952. GS: Sydney Mason, William Fawcett, Ed Hinkle, Stuart Whitman, Gloria Eaton, Pierce Lyden, Ruth Lee, Russ Scott. Roy and Dale become entangled in a family feud when a bridegroom postpones his wedding in order to shoot the cousin he blames for his father's murder.

135.28 *Go for Your Gun.* Nov. 23, 1952. GS: Carl "Alfalfa" Switzer, James Diehl, Robert J. Wilke, Reed Howes, Michael Ragan, George J. Lewis, William Fawcett. Roy is upset to learn that Dale's nephews idolize a local gunman. He is determined to expose the outlaw as the leader of a robber gang.

135.29 *The Mayor of Ghost Town.* Nov. 30, 1952. GS: Lane Bradford, Zon Murray, Frances Conley, Hal Price, Boyd "Red" Morgan, James Diehl, Russ Scott. Roy, Pat and Dale help Peter Arnold, an eccentric mining engineer, retain title to Red Dog, a ghost town, against the claim of a crooked lawyer.

135.30 *Blind Justice.* Dec. 14, 1952. GS: James Kirkwood, William Tannen, Terry Frost, Stanley Blystone, Russ Scott. Bullet is wounded and a prospector killed as Roy tries to prevent the bushwhackers from jumping a gold claim.

135.31 *The Knockout.* Dec. 28, 1952. GS: Sarah Padden, Charles Bronson, Leonard Penn, Wally West, Frank Jenks, Roy Brent. Pat gets a little more than information when Roy sets him to spying on a boxing instructor with a link to a gang of bank robbers.

135.32 *The Run-a-Round.* Feb. 22, 1953. GS: Sydney Mason, Ed Hinkle, Stuart Whitman, Pierce Lyden. Roy and his men are on the trail of a gang of confidence men who made Dale sign her name to a phony bill of sale. The outlaws are off on another bit of dirty work, one of them posing as a T-Man.

135.33 *Phantom Rustlers.* April 5, 1953. GS: Robert Hyatt, Francis McDonald, Minerva Urecal, Riley Hill, Harry Mackin, Sandy Sanders. Roy and Dale help their Paradise Valley neighbors fight off a gang of hit-and-run rustlers who killed a rancher during a raid.

135.34 *Loaded Guns.* April 12, 1953. GS: Evan Loew, George Douglas, Denver Pyle, Steve Pendleton, Lyle Talbot, Russ Scott. Roy and Dale pursue a vicious killer who makes use of other people's guns tries to frame a young cowpoke.

135.35 *The Silver Fox Hunt.* April 19, 1953. GS: Leonard Penn, Frank Lackteen, Herbert Wyndham, Roy Brent, Wally West, Russ Scott, Augie Gomez. An Indian chief, who suspects a merchant of high grading the ore from mines owned by the Tribe is murdered. Roy and Bullet seek the killers.

135.36 *The Mingo Kid.* April 26, 1953. GS: Bill Tannen, Terry Frost, Stanley Blystone, Russ Scott. Roy is knocked out by the fugitive Mingo Kid, who swaps clothes with him. Then some outlaws about to pull a big robbery mistake Roy for Mingo, and Roy plays along in order to trap the gang.

135.37 *The Long Chance.* May 24, 1953. GS: Henry Rowland, Myron Healey, Robert J. Wilke, Sandy Sanders, William Fawcett. Pete Grundy and his gang terrorize Paradise alley when they stage a series of robberies and rustlings. Roy and Dale get on the gang's trail after Pete's boys steal the school fund.

135.38 *Money to Burn.* June 28, 1953. GS: Dub Taylor, Harry Harvey, Jr., John L. Cason, Jack O'Shea, Boyd "Red" Morgan, Russ Scott. Two thieves hide a lot of money in an old stove. Its owner, not knowing of the stove's valuable contents, sells it to Dale. Roy and Dale are in trouble when the thieves come for their money.

Season Two

135.39 *The Milliner from Medicine Hat.* Oct. 11, 1953. GS: Frances Conley, Hal Price, James Diehl, Zon Murray, Boyd "Red" Morgan, Lane Bradford, Russ Scott. A pretty milliner and her grandfather comes to Mineral City and has all the boys aflutter. Roy and Dale are suspicious of the newcomers and investigate.

135.40 *Pat's Inheritance.* Nov. 1, 1953. G. : Mary Ellen Kaye, Tom London, Terry Frost, Myron Healey, Gregg Barton. Pat and a pretty young miss inherit the Merryweather Ranch, but a gang of outlaws seem determine to keep them from taking over the property.

135.41 *Outlaws of Paradise Valley.* Nov. 8, 1953. GS: Rick Vallin, Pamela Duncan, Pierre Watkin, Jack O'Shea, Sandy Sanders, Richard Avonde, Rusty Wescoatt, Russ Scott, Cheryl Rogers. Outlaws who plan to rob the Mineral City Bank, take as hostages members of an archaeological expedition from the State University who are on a hunt for Indian ruins.

135.42 *Bullets and a Burro.* Nov. 15, 1953. GS: Raymond Hatton, Chuck Roberson, Norman Leavitt, Terry Frost, Gregg Barton. Bullet and Trigger help Roy escape from the jail where he was locked up by the sheriff's renegade brother and his gang, who are after an old prospector's gold.

135.43 *Gun Trouble.* Nov. 22, 1953. GS: John L. Cason, Harry Harvey, Jr., Dub Taylor, Boyd "Red" Morgan, Russ Scott. An outlaw evolves a plan to get rid of Roy Rogers. He persuades his young cohort to get into the cowboy's confidence, and then gun him down.

135.44 *M Stands for Murder.* Dec. 6, 1953. GS: Myron Healey, Robert J. Wilke, Henry Rowland, Sydney Mason. Roy and Dale investigate the superstition that whoever sees the ghost of One Arm Johnny will die when a man who claims to have seen the ghost if found dead.

135.45 *The Peddler from the Pecos.* Dec. 13, 1953. GS: Ray Whitley, Dub Taylor, Rusty Wescoatt, Dick Reeves, Jack O'Shea, Russ Scott. Two brothers seek vengeance upon a government agent who refuses them permission to shoot beavers in Paradise Valley. Roy hunts down the trappers when the game warden is murdered and Dale is taken hostage.

135.46 *Bad Company.* Dec. 27, 1953. GS: Jim Hayward, Fred Sherman, Dick Reeves, Mike Ragan, Wally West, Jack O'Shea. Roy goes to Dale's rescue when she is held hostage by a gang of robbers who want to steal the gold that Roy has hidden in the shipping office.

135.47 *Little Dynamite.* Jan. 3, 1954. GS: Dick Reeves, Rusty Wescoatt, Russ Scott, Dub Taylor, Ray Whitley, Little Doe Rogers. A gang of crooks steal the tax funds from city hall. A baby is kidnaped by mistake when the bandits make a getaway in the wrong wagon.

135.48 *The Kid from Silver City.* Jan. 17, 1954. GS: Charles Tannen, William Tannen, Francis MacDonald, Ray Whitley, Richard Avonde, Russ Scott. Roy and Dale go after a young hoodlum and his gang, who have shot the marshal on their trail and are now planning to rob the Mineral City bank.

135.49 *The Secret of Indian Gap.* Jan. 24, 1954. GS: B.G. Norman, Harry Strang, Myron Healey, Russ Scott. Roy befriends a little orphan boy when he discovers that high grade gold is being dug out of government land.

135.50 *The Deputy Sheriff.* Feb. 7, 1954. GS: Myron Healey, Tom London, Gregg Barton, Terry Frost. The sheriff of Mineral City is wounded when he sets out to get a posse to catch rustlers. His deputy is lax in forming the posse in his place

135.51 *The High-Graders of Paradise Valley.* Feb. 28, 1954. Myron Healey, Harry Strang, Ruth Lee, Russ Scott, Jack O'Shea. Mart Woodward is accused by his partner of stealing gold ore. Pat Brady gets himself into serious trouble when he accidentally discovers there are gold smugglers operating in Paradise Valley.

135.52 *The Land Swindle.* March 14, 1954. GS: Fred Sherman, Gloria Talbott, Sam Flint, Dick Reeves, Mike Ragan, Jim Hayward. An editor dares to quote a rancher who claims he is being swindled out of his land. The editor is kidnaped when he refuses to spring a retraction.

Season Three

135.53 *The Lady Killer.* Sept. 12, 1954. GS: Peter Votrian, Pamela Duncan, Bill Tannen, Charles Tannen, Richard Avonde, Francis McDonald, Russ Scott. Roy finds out that ranchers who borrow from the local bank pay off their loans both with interest and terror.

135.54 *The Young Defenders.* Oct. 3, 1954. GS: B.G. Norman, Noralee Norman, Barry Regan, John Cason, Rex Lease, Russ Scott, Hank Patterson. Two children become pawns in the attempts of two renegades to get their father's batch of furs. After their father has been kidnaped, the children help Roy in his attempt to find their missing parent.

135.55 *Backfire.* Oct. 10, 1954. GS: John Doucette, Sydney Mason, Henry Rowland, Bradley Morrow, Helen Burnett. While chasing the outlaws who shot a minister and stole the payroll he was carrying, Roy and Dale and the minister's two children become suspicious of a stranger they meet who claims to be a traveling evangelist.

135.56 *The Last of the Larrabee Kid.* Oct. 17, 1954. GS: Bill George, Sarah Padden, Don Harvey, John Cason, John Merton, Jack O'Shea, Fred Sherman. Roy is on the trail of a holdup man who makes it a practice to relieve fellow thieves of their stolen loot.

135.57 *The Hijackers.* Oct. 24, 1954. GS: Fred Graham, Forrest Taylor, James Diehl, Steve Raines, Wally West, Russ Scott. Dale comes to Roy's rescue after Pat Brady takes money from a fur trappers' association in return for Roy's services in catching a gang of fur hijackers.

135.58 *Hard Luck Story.* Oct. 31, 1954. GS: John Cason, Rex Lease, Bert LeBaron, Don Harvey, Barry Regan, Virginia Carroll. In his effort to help the victim of an illegal insurance racket, Roy finds himself in jail as a suspect in a robbery.

135.59 *Boys' Day in Paradise Valley.* Nov. 7, 1954. When the offices of the law are turned over to students in honor of Boys' Day, young Bob Miner is named sheriff for the day. He deputizes Roy and joins in the search for the man responsible for shooting a rancher.

135.60 *Bad Neighbors.* Nov. 21, 1954. GS: Alan Wells, Jean Howell, Forrest Taylor, Rayford Barnes. Homesteaders and ranchers feud when the farmers dam up a creek in order to irrigate their land. The ranchers depend on the creek for water for their cattle.

135.61 *Strangers.* Dec. 5, 1954. GS: John Doucette, David Bair, Henry Rowland, Russ Scott, Francis McDonald, Wally West. A gang of outlaws attempts to victimize an artist and his father who have recently arrived in Paradise Valley.

135.62 *Hidden Treasure.* Dec. 19, 1954. GS: Harry Lauter, William Fawcett, Dub Taylor, Rusty Wescoatt. Outlaws hear Roy tell an old prospector that the key to a treasure is in the Bible. Misunderstanding the meaning of Roy's words, the men kidnap the prospector.

135.63 *Outcasts of Paradise Valley.* Jan. 9, 1955. GS: Rayford Barnes, Alan Wells, Forrest Taylor, Margaret Bert, Jack O'Shea. Two unsuccessful prospectors turn to stealing in order to get food. After imposing on a homesteading couple, one brash prospector decides to rob the bank.

135.64 *The Big Chance.* Jan. 23, 1955. GS: Harry Lauter, Rusty Wescoatt, Dub Taylor. Pat Brady is kidnaped in his own jeep by a gang of outlaws who try to get him to pose as the crook's representative and collect a huge sum of money.

135.65 *Uncle Steve's Finish.* Feb. 3, 1955. GS: Bill Tannen, Virginia Carroll, Myron Healey, Louis Lettieri, Earle Hodgins. Roy and Dale suspect they must teach a schoolteacher a few things about the law when clues implicating him are left at the scene of a stage robbery.

135.66 *Dead End Trail.* Feb. 20, 1955. GS: Harry Hickox, Carl Switzer, Don C. Harvey, Russ Scott. Roy Rogers is faced with the problem of a sixteen-year-old boy who shows hero worship for a desperado. The young boy tries his best to keep Roy from finding the outlaw, wanted for highway robbery assault and murder.

135.67 *Born Fugitive.* Feb. 27, 1955. GS: Don C. Harvey, Frances Karath, Harry Hickox, Jean Harvey. Dale and Roy are afraid that the little daughter of an outlaw is going to follow in her father's footsteps. The child is caught stealing.

135.68 *Quick Draw.* March 20, 1955. GS: Don C. Harvey, Virginia Carroll, Louis Lettieri, Carl Switzer, Russ Scott. Roy Rogers lectures ill-tempered rancher Marv Hanley on his quickness to use a gun. They are only just in time to keep him from shooting a little boy's dog.

135.69 *The Ginger Horse.* March 27, 1955. GS: Don C. Harvey, Frances Karath, Harry Hickox. Roy finds himself implicated in a case of fraud and robbery when he tries to recover a little girl's stolen ginger horse.

Season Four

135.70 *The Showdown.* May 22, 1955. GS: Claudia Barrett, Ewing Mitchell, Ralph Sanford, Fred Coby. Roy is alerted when Wayne Cordink, a man who served a long prison term for robbery, returns to town. The ex-convict never revealed the name of his partner-in-crime. Now Ray fears that this silent partner will kill to insure his secret.

135.71 *And Sudden Death.* Oct. 9, 1955. GS: Gene Roth, Myron Healey, Louis Lettieri, Carl "Alfalfa" Switzer, Russ Scott, William Tannen. Roy becomes involved in politics and murder when a candidate in the mayoralty election of Paradise Valley is found knifed to death.

135.72 *Ranch War.* Oct. 23, 1955. GS: Harry Harvey, Jr., Claudia Barrett, Ralph Sanford, Fred Coby, Russ Scott, Ewing Mitchell. A man and his wife returning to Paradise Valley are fired upon when they try to reclaim their ranch and the wife is kidnaped.

135.73 *Violence in Paradise Valley.* Nov. 2, 1955. GS: Ray Bennett, Bill George, Rory Mallinson, Fred Graham, Bert LeBaron, Bill McCormick. Roy and Dale lead the fight against four escaped criminals who try to dominate Paradise Valley.

135.74 *The Brothers O'Dell.* Nov. 20, 1955. GS: Robert Bice, Dan Barton, Reed Howes, Henry Rowland, Paul Harvey, Dennis Moore, George Eldredge. A fortunate change of heart by the leader of a gang of outlaws leads to a happy reunion for the Brothers O'Dell.

135.75 *The Scavenger.* Nov. 27, 1956. GS: Rand Brooks, Wayne Mallory, Britt Wood. Old Mose, the scavenger, finds a roll of phony money that has been dumped by counterfeiters. He adds it to his hoard of savings and unknowingly puts his own life in danger.

135.76 *Treasure of Paradise Valley.* Dec. 11, 1955. GS: Britt Wood, Claudia Barrett, Rand Brooks, Bud Osborne, Tom London, Wayne Mallory, Jack O'Shea. A pair of outlaws learns that an old prospector has found treasure. Then Roy learns that the prospector is wanted in five states for swindling.

135.77 *Three Masked Men.* Dec. 18, 1955. GS: Reed Howes, Robert Bice, Henry Rowland, Dennis Moore, Paul Harvey, Louise Venier, John Hamilton, Dusty Rogers. Roy uncovers a plot by outlaws to kidnap the governor of the state and hold him hostage until their gang leader is released from jail.

135.78 *Ambush.* Jan. 15, 1956. GS: Paul Harvey, Dan Barton, Dennis Moore, Henry Rowland, Rosemary Bertrand, Bob Bice. Hired gunmen shoot a prospector, but do not succeed in their attempt at murder. Roy tries to track down the would-be killers.

135.79 *Money Is Dangerous.* Jan. 29, 1956. GS: Lucien Littlefield, John Truax, Craig Duncan, James Macklin. Roy discovers that a rancher thought to be a miser is not so stingy after all when he is robbed by his bodyguard.

135.80 *False Faces.* Feb. 5, 1956. GS: Harry Shannon, Keith Richards, Ralph Moody, Joe Bassett, Dorothy Andre, Wally West. When the body of a murdered man is discovered in an old Indian burial ground, it appears that renegade Indians are responsible for the crime.

135.81 *Horse Crazy.* Feb. 26, 1956. GS: John Truax, Craig Duncan, James Macklin. Roy tangles with three wanted criminals when he is kidnaped in order to help a gang leader track down his lost horse.

135.82 *Smoking Guns.* March 3, 1956. GS: Harry Shannon, Ralph Moody, Keith Richards, Joe Bassett, Jack O'Shea, Russ Scott. An agent is sent from Washington to investigate trouble on a formerly peaceful Indian reservation. The murder of an Indian agent is involved with the theft of gold ore.

135.83 *Empty Saddles (A.K.A. "Cattle Drive").* March 10, 1956. GS: Troy Melton, John Cason, Steve Pendleton, William Hudson, Bill Catching. A group of settlers are being stopped from taking their cattle to market by a band of rustlers.

135.84 *Sheriff Missing.* March 18, 1956. GS: Helen Spring, Howard Negley, Keith Richards, Troy Melton, Russ Scott. Roy uncovers a plot by a pair of would-be gamblers to smear the reputation of the local sheriff.

135.85 *The Horse Mixup.* March 25, 1956. GS: Howard Negley, Harry Harvey, Jr., Keith Richards, Troy Melton, George Eldredge, Steve Raines, Russ Scott. A schemer destroys the papers proving ownership of a valuable horse. When the horse's former owner disappears, Roy begins an intense investigation.

Season Five

135.86 *Head for Cover.* Oct. 21, 1956. GS: Ellen Corby, Byron Foulger, Robert Knapp, Troy Melton, Les Mitchell, Harry Strang. A bank robber runs out on his cohorts with all the money and heads for Mineral City. Roy and Dale protect an elderly couple who have wound up with the loot.

135.87 *Fishing for Fingerprints.* Oct. 28, 1956. GS: Francis McDonald, Steve Pendleton, Fred Sherman, John McKee, Russ Scott. Roy Rogers switches vehicles when he leaves Trigger on shore and takes off in a motorboat after some outlaws who have been stealing from fishermen.

135.88 *Mountain Pirates.* Nov. 4, 1956. GS: Steve Pendleton, Fred Sherman, John McKee, Russ Scott. Roy and Dale combat a gang of outlaws, led by a man posing as a vacationing tourist, who plan to steal fish from a lake near Mineral City.

135.89 *His Weight in Wildcats.* Nov. 11, 1956. GS: House Peters, Jr., Steve Stevens, Pierce Lyden, John L. Cason, I. Stanford Jolley, Virginia Carroll, Russ Scott, Wally West. Roy comes to the aid of a research professor when outlaws make off with half a map which shows the location of a buried express box.

135.90 *Paleface Justice.* Nov. 18, 1956. GS: Bobby Blake, Robert Knapp, Troy Melton, John War Eagle, Bob Bice, Les Mitchell, Russ Scott, Anna Marie Majalca, Jack O'Shea. An influential rancher accuses a young Indian of murdering the town blacksmith.

135.91 *Tossup.* Dec. 2, 1956. GS: Gay Goodwin, House Peters, Jr., Charles Anthony Hughes, George DeNormand, George Mather, Bill Catching, Steve Raines, Russ Scott, Wally West, Jack Trent. A little orphan girl is the pawn in a family feud over ownership of a sliver mine.

135.92 *Fighting Sire.* Dec. 16, 1956. GS: Harry Landers, John Meek, Robert Knapp, Troy Melton, Les Mitchell, Bob Bice. A former boxing champion's life is threatened by gangsters who know him to be the sole witness to a murder.

135.93 *Deadlock at Dark Canyon.* Jan. 6, 1957. GS: John L. Cason, Nolan Leary, Troy Melton, Steve Pendleton. A greedy ranch foreman tries to frighten away ranchers and so that he can take over their land.

135.94 *End of the Trail.* Jan. 27, 1957. GS: Gregg Barton, Terry Frost, Troy Melton, Harry Tyler, Wally West, Russ Scott. Roy faces censure of the townspeople when it appears that he is permitting an escaped convict to roam the countryside.

135.95 *Junior Outlaw.* Feb. 10, 1957. GS: Speer Martin, Scotty Morry, Roy "Dusty" Rogers, Jr., Mel Stevens, Terry Frost, Rusty Wescoatt, Bob Bice, Russ Scott, Jack O'Shea. A young delinquent visits Roy's summer camp. he youngster causes trouble by tipping off a gunman that Roy knows his identity.

135.96 *High Stakes.* Feb. 24, 1957. GS: Bob Bice, Ed Hinton, J. Harris Howell, Bill Catching, Harry Tyler, Helen Brown. A boy is the only living witness able to identify members of a notorious holdup gang. Roy is suspicious of the marshal sent to escort the youngster to the trial.

135.97 *Accessory to Crime.* March 3, 1957. GS: Harry Harvey, Jr., Bob Bice, Ewing Mitchell, Bill George, Bill Catching, Loann Morgan, Wally West. Roy and Dale come to the rescue when Pat Brady unwittingly buys a belt which is being used to smuggle diamonds into the country.

135.98 *Portrait of Murder.* March 17, 1957. GS: House Peters, Jr., Ed Dearing, Ewing Mitchell, Norman Wescoatt. A mute painter is the prime suspect in the murder of a doctor. The doctor had accused the painter of theft shortly before he was found shot to death.

135.99 *Brady's Bonanza.* March 31, 1957. GS: Dick Rich, Harry Tyler, Rick Vallin, Gregg Barton, Troy Melton. Pat Brady believes he has found uranium. When claim jumpers try to take over his claim, Pat fights them off.

135.100 *Johnny Rover.* June 9, 1957. GS: Dan Barton, Paul Harvey, Dennis Moore, Henry Rowland, Robert Bice. A newly-appointed deputy sheriff tries to hide his past reputation for getting into trouble. But he is victimized by local gangsters who threaten to expose him unless he released their leader from jail.

136. *The Saga of Andy Burnett*

ABC. 60 min. Broadcast history: Wednesday, 7:30-8:30, Oct. 1957–March 1958.

Regular Cast: Jerome Courtland (Andy Burnett), Jeff York (Joe Crane), Andrew Duggan (Jack Kelly), Slim Pickens (Old Bill Williams), Robert J. Wilke (Ben Tilton), Iron Eyes Cody (Mad Wolf), Abel Fernandez (Kiasax), John War Eagle (Chief Matosuki), Ralph Valencia (Small Eagle).

Premise: Young farmer Andy Burnett travels west to Missouri in the 1820s.

Note: This series aired as segments of *Walt Disney Presents*.

The Episodes

136.1 *Andy's Initiation.* Oct. 2, 1957. Andy is a young backwoods farmer in 1820 on his way west to buy a farm in Missouri for himself and his grandmother. She is the widow of Gail Burnett, partner of Daniel Boone. Along the way Andy meets a mountain man, Joe Crane, who comes to Andy's aid when three thugs try to take his rifle and money.

136.2 *Andy's First Chore.* Oct. 9, 1957. Andy and Joe Crane, one of his trapper friends, are trying to buy supplies for their trip west. But a rival group bribes the blacksmith into refusing to sell supplies to Andy and his friend.

136.3 *Andy's Love Affair.* Oct. 16, 1957. Andy and his friends are on their way to deliver an important letter to Santa Fe when they are stopped by the Spanish border patrol. The patrol insists that only Kelly proceed.

136.4 *The Land of Enemies.* Feb. 26, 1958. Andy makes his first trip into unmapped wilds of the Rocky Mountain region where he goes fur-trapping with his friends Joe Crane, Jack Kelly and Old Bill. They are attacked by a band of Snake Indians.

136.5 *White Man's Medicine.* March 5, 1958. Andy and his friends are captured by Blackfoot Indians. Andy amazes his captors by pretending to evoke the powers of the Sun God, using a telescope as a burning glass.

136.6 *The Big Council.* March 12, 1958. Captured by the Blackfoot Indians, Andy and his friends await the decision of the Big Council as to their fate. Although they have friends in the tribe, the jealous medicine man Mad Wolf is working to have them executed.

137. *Sara*

CBS. 60 min. Broadcast history: Friday, 8:00-9:00, Feb. 1976–July 1976.

Regular Cast: Brenda Vaccaro (Sara Yarnell), Bert Kramer (Emmet Ferguson), Albert Stratton (Martin Pope), William Wintersole (George Bailey), Mariclare Costello (Julia Bailey), Louise Latham (Martha Higgins), William Phipps (Claude Barstow), Kraig Metzinger (Georgie Bailey), Debbie Lytton (Debbie Higgins), Hallie Morgan (Emma Higgins).

Premise: Sara is a feisty Eastern schoolteacher who moves West, determined to make her mark on a Colorado frontier town.

The Episodes

137.1 *Title Unknown.* Feb. 13, 1976. GS: Jerry Hardin, Bill McKinney, Patricia Ganem, Michael LeClaire. Sara battles prejudiced townspeople who refuse to allow their children to attend class with a ten-year-old half-breed.

137.2 *Title Unknown.* Feb. 20, 1976. GS: Lance Kerwin, Robert Mandan, Jerry Hardin, Michael LeClaire, Stephen Manley. Newly enrolled in Sara's class, an educated, wealthy boy has already managed to alienate his schoolmates. They dislike him not only for flaunting his schooling, but for having a father who unjustly fires employees.

137.3 *Title Unknown.* Feb. 27, 1976. GS: Jean Rasey, Richard Dysart, Harry Townes. When an epidemic sweeps the community while the doctor is away, Sara's star pupil, a girl with some knowledge of medicine, is the only one left to tend the stricken.

137.4 *Title Unknown.* March 5, 1976. GS: Inga Swenson, Don Collier, Joseph A. Goodwin, Jeff Jones. Sara persuades a cultured, reclusive woman to venture among her neighbors for the unveiling of the town's first piano.

137.5 *Title Unknown.* March 12, 1976. GS: Richard Stanley, Ron Soble, Kim Richards. A seventeen-year-old steals his employer's horse and sets out to find the father who ran out on him.

137.6 *Title Unknown.* March 19, 1976. GS: Henry Darrow, Joe DeSantis, Kevin Hagen, Raymond Singer.

137.7 *Title Unknown.* March 26, 1976. GS: Sam Groom, Robert Donner, Christain Grey, Raymond Singer. An eligible, wealthy Easterner is courting Sara to her delight and the school board's dismay. They are worried she will leave her teaching post if she marries.

137.8 *Title Unknown.* April 2, 1976. GS: Melinda Dillon, Megan Sullivan, John Carter, John Harkins. Believing an insane asylum escapee to be perfectly sane, Sara sets out to help the woman, committed by her husband for her outspokenness.

137.9 *Title Unknown.* April 9, 1976. GS: Shannon Terhune, Tom Skerritt, Gaye Nelson, Ford Rainey. Sara withdraws the attention she had been lavishing on one of her favorite pupils, leaving the girl feeling hurt and rejected.

137.10 *Title Unknown.* April 23, 1976. GS: Victor French, Richard Yniguez, Larry Ward. With classes over, everyone thinks that Sara has taken off for Denver, not realizing that she has been kidnaped by an illiterate trapper and taken to his mountain hideaway.

137.11 *Title Unknown.* May 7, 1976. GS: Kristie McNichol. Sara has her hands full with a strong-willed teenager left in her custody after the girl's only living relative dies.

The Secret Empire see Cliffhangers

138. *Sergeant Preston of the Yukon*

CBS. 30 min. Broadcast history: Thursday, 7:30–8:00, Sept. 1955 — Sept. 1958.

Regular Cast: Richard Simmons (Sgt. Preston).

Premise: Sergeant Preston of the Northwest Canadian Mounted Police, aided by his malamute dog, Yukon King, and his horse, Rex, brought law and order to Canada's Yukon during the Gold Rush of the 1890s.

The Episodes

138.1 *Vindication of Yukon.* Sept. 29, 1955. GS: Paul McGuire, Hal K. Dawson, Carol Henry, Pitt Herbert. Yukon King is blamed for the death of a man and branded a killer. Sgt. Preston sets out to find the real murderer and clear his dog's name.

138.2 *Rebellion in the North.* Oct. 6, 1955. GS: Sid Cassell, Thom Carney, Joe Granby, Lane Bradford, John Pickard, Charles Stevens, Bob Swan. Greedy for the riches of the Yukon, a renegade white man stirs up trouble by leading a band of Eskimos in rebellion against the crown. Sgt. Preston sets out to suppress the uprising.

138.3 *Trouble at Hogback.* Oct. 13, 1955. GS: Frank Fenton, Leonard Penn, Steven Ritch, Iron Eyes Cody, Robert Sheldon, Martin Greene, Babe London. When Sergeant Preston investigates a series of mysterious mine accidents, he learns they are actually not accidents at all.

138.4 *Incident at Gordon Landing.* Oct. 20, 1955. GS: Francis de Sales, Robert Lynn, Lewis Charles, Donna Jo Gribble. A trader is paid an unwelcome visit by his ex-convict brother and a crony. They want the gold dust the traders holds in safekeeping for miners.

138.5 *Bad Medicine.* Oct. 27, 1955. GS: Charles Stevens. A jealous Indian medicine man obstructs Sgt. Preston's efforts to get medical aid for a diphtheria epidemic endangering an Indian tribe.

138.6 *Hidden Gold.* Nov. 3, 1955. GS: Vernon Rich, Cheryl Calloway. Gold is stolen from a trader's safe by two Klondike desperadoes. They try to make it appear that an ex-convict is guilty of the theft. The irate miners form a lynching party and go after the man accused of stealing the gold.

138.7 *Last Mail from Last Chance.* Nov. 10, 1955. GS: Jack Rutherford, Gregg Barton, Fred Sherman, Phyllis Cole. Sgt. Preston makes a desperate race against time to recover a fortune in gold dust before the oncoming Arctic winter isolates an entire community.

138.8 *The Assassins.* Nov. 17, 1955. GS: Terry Frost, Paul McGuire, Coleman Francis. A crooked land commissioner conspires to turn over gold-rich government lands to four miners in exchange for half of their diggings.

138.9 *Golden Gift.* Nov. 24, 1955. GS: Larry Chance, Douglas Henderson, George Nader, Jack Hill, Hazel Franklyn, Richard Powers. Two desperadoes learn that the secret to a coded message naming the location of a fortune in gold dust lies in the Scriptures. Sgt. Preston races against time to foil their plot.

138.10 *Cry Wolf.* Dec. 1, 1955. Sergeant Preston, assigned to escort a gold shipment, barely escapes with his life.

138.11 *Girl from Vancouver.* Dec. 8, 1955. GS: Patti Gallagher, Kirk London, Douglas Henderson. Three killers murder a miner in order to gain possession of his mine. Then then try to pin the crime on the dead man's partner.

138.12 *Treasure of Fifteen Mile Creek.* Dec. 15, 1955. GS: George Mather, Jack Rutherford, Gregg Barton. Thieves unwittingly reunite father and son when they attempt to steal a violin containing the map of a rich gold strike.

138.13 *The Boy Nobody Wanted.* Dec. 22, 1955. GS: Jeanne Wood, Harvey Grant, Judd Holdren, Reed Howes. A renegade plots with his brother to steal a fortune in bank notes and smuggle them out of the Yukon.

138.14 *The Mad Wolf of Lost Canyon.* Dec. 29, 1955. Don Kohler, Charmienne Harker, Dave Weichman. Preston is snubbed by a Scotland Yard detective when he offers to help the investigator search for a murderer.

138.15 *One Bear Too Many.* Jan. 5, 1956. GS: Lyn Thomas. A newspaper photographer seeking adventure finds more than he bargained for in his trip to the Yukon.

138.16 *Crime at Wounded Moose.* Jan. 12, 1956. GS: Edmund Cobb, George Lewis, Thayer Roberts, Glen Kilburn, Almira Sessions, Mason Curry. An ex-convict is unjustly accused of being involved in some gold thefts. Sgt. Preston gives the man a dangerous assignment to help clear him.

138.17 *Dog Race.* Jan. 19, 1956. GS: Wayne Mallory, Edward Dearing, Jason Johnson, Tom Carney, William Tannen. A gambling syndicate tries to fix the outcome of a dog-sled race by poisoning the favored team's lead dog.

138.18 *Phantom of Phoenixville.* Jan. 26, 1956. GS: Maggie Magennis, Don Durant, Terry Frost, Ted Jacques. A young American married couple arrive in the Yukon from the U.S. to take over the ghost town they have inherited. Unknown

Sergeant Preston of the Yukon

to them, a pair of dangerous gold robbers are making their headquarters there.

138.19 *Trapped*. Feb. 2, 1956. GS: Lyn Thomas, Jay Douglas, Francis DeSales, Robert Paqin, Edward Foster. A desperado who is nursed back to health by the wife of a prospector, repays the family's kindness by trying to take over its new gold claim.

138.20 *Justice at Goneaway Creek*. Feb. 9, 1956. GS: Linda Leighton, Dehl Berti, Jack Reynolds, Bill Phillips, Craig Duncan, Arnold Daly, Jack Woody. The paw prints of a husky dog give Sgt. Preston his first lead in tracking down the real murderer before an innocent man is condemned to death by a kangaroo court.

138.21 *Skagway Secret*. Feb. 16, 1956. GS: Chuck Webster, Lane Bradford, Mark Sheeler, Lyn Thomas, Richard Avonde, Richard Powers. Sgt. Preston's life is endangered by the chief of a gold-smuggling gang. The U.S. Marines stationed in the Yukon join forces with Preston to bring the gang to justice.

138.22 *Relief Train*. Feb. 23, 1956. GS: George Eldredge, Virginia Wave, Coleman Francis, John Damler, John Marshall, Bill Fox. Two greedy renegades bargain with a band of Yukon newcomers who struck it rich, but are unable to get food. The renegades offer them food at a high price — a pound of food for a pound of gold.

138.23 *Totem Treasure*. March 1, 1956. GS: Dirk London, Stanley Fraser, Mason Curry, Iron Eyes Cody, John Carpenter, J.W. Cody. A white renegade posing as an Indian totem spirits, holds two scientists captive. He believes the legends and learns where Indians have hidden a fortune in gold. The tribe of Indians, at the urging of the renegade whites, sets upon Sgt. Preston when they become convinced he is seeking a cache of gold belonging to the tribe. The warriors plan to burn him at the stake.

138.24 *One Good Turn*. March 8, 1956. GS: John Irving, Casey MacGregor, Francis DeSales, Jerry Eskow, Lee Sharon. The partner of an Englishman is killed after the two make a rich find. With a reputation as a marksman, the Englishman is the prime suspect.

138.25 *The Cache*. March 15, 1956. Sergeant Preston joins the search for a missing cache of gold.

138.26 *Cinderella of the Yukon*. March 22, 1956. GS: Maureen Cassidy, Robert Malcolm, Karen Scott, Joseph Downing, Lewis Charles. A secret will, hidden in a child's rag doll, is the clue by which Sgt. Preston discovers that a young wife plots to claim the title to a gold mine.

138.27 *Go Fever*. Ma. 29, 1956. GS: Betty Farrington, George Crise, William Boyett, John Mitchum. When a pair of Klondike desperados plans to rob a general store, the young son of the woman owner seeks to distract them by running away with the cash.

138.28 *The Fancy Dan*. April 5, 1956. GS: Rusty Wescoatt, Alan Welles, Barry Truex, Joseph Downing, Douglas Henderson, I. Stanford Jolley, John Lehman. After using foul tactics to win a prize fight, a Yukon fighter and his gang make off with the purse. Sgt. Preston sets out to track them down.

138.29 *The Coward*. April 12, 1956. GS: Edmund Cobb, Wayne Mallory, Don Kent, Thayer Roberts. The son of a newspaper editor tries to live down his reputation as a coward. He volunteers to join Sgt. Preston in a showdown with members of a gang whose operation of a mine threatens to ruin a town.

138.30 *Father of the Crime*. April 19, 1956. GS: Jimmy Dobson, John Dennis, Joan Granville, Norman Willis, Robert Roark, Carol Henry. In an effort to make good his gambling debts, a man robs his father. But this is only the beginning of tragedy for the son.

138.31 *Remember the Maine*. Apr, 26, 1956. GS: Edward Hinton, Linda Brent, John Pickard, Robert Carson. News of the sinking of the battleship Maine in Havana reaches the Klondike. The residents donate a fortune in gold dust to help those involved in the disaster. But the funds are stolen and Sgt. Preston is called in to track down the thieves.

138.32 *Love and Honor*. May 3, 1956. GS: Charles Braswell, Alena Murray, Wade Cagle, Steve Mitchell. The wedding ceremony of a Mountie is interrupted by news of a bank robbery, committed by the brother of the bride.

138.33 *All Is Not Gold*. May 10, 1956. GS; Sherman Sanders, Marjorie Bennett, Dennis Moore, Robert Christopher, Bob Paquin, Leo Curley. A town character nicknamed Windy because of his constant gossiping, inadvertently causes Sgt. Preston to be ambushed while escorting a gold shipment.

Season Two

138.34 *Limping King*. Sept. 13, 1956. GS: George Selk, Don Durant, Jack Reynolds, Pierce Lyden. An veterinarian, who has been swindled out of his life savings, vows revenge on anyone who approaches a mountain pass near him. He mounts guard over the important pass with a shotgun. Sgt. Preston uses Yukon King to distract the doctor's attention.

138.35 *The Rookie*. Sept. 20, 1956. GS: Edward Foster, Steve Warren, Mary Adams, Edward Hinton. A young Mountie does not realize that the man he is after is his own father.

138.36 *Pack Ice Justice*. Sept. 27, 1956. GS: Weaver Levy, Ralph Ness, Terry Frost, Joy Lee, Robert Cabal. A gang of white renegades raids a tribe of Eskimos. They steal the winter fur catch, setting the Eskimos against the white men. Sergeant Preston nearly becomes the target for lethal Eskimo harpoons.

138.37 *Revenge*. Oct. 4, 1956. GS: John Lehman, Fred Cavens, Francis DeSales, Harrison Lewis. After several years in prison, a psychopathic criminal is released. He swears vengeance on Sergeant Preston.

138.38 *Littlest Rookie*. Oct. 11, 1956. GS: Paul Engle, Helen Jay, Gregg Palmer, Arnold Daly. Sgt. Preston sets out after a ten-year-old boy who has been kidnaped. The child finds a surprising way to help his rescuers reach him.

138.39 *Lost Patrol*. Oct. 18, 1956. GS: Ted Jacques, Pat Whyte, Bill Tischer, Michael Loring, Pat Coleman. Sergeant Preston searches desperately or a lost patrol. He hopes to get to the men before they run out of food or are killed.

138.40 *King of Herschel Island*. Oct. 25, 1956. GS: Lane Bradford, John Pickard, Charles Stevens, Robert Cabal. Ruthless sailors from an ice-bound whaling ship in the northern part of the Yukon enslave the local Eskimos.

138.41 *Ghost of the Anvil*. Nov. 1, 1956. GS: Leo Curley, Pierce Lyden, Charles Fredericks, Ed Foster. Sgt. Preston and Yukon King embark on a trip into the wild Arctic wilderness to investigate reports of fantastic and dangerous creatures.

138.42 *Eye of Evil.* Nov. 8, 1956. GS: Dirk London, Jan Shepard, Sydney Mason, Thayer Roberts. The pursuit of a stolen black pearl almost cost Sergeant Preston his life.

138.43 *Luck of the Trail.* Nov. 15, 1956. GS: Paul McGuire. Sergeant Preston comes to the aid of some men who are having trouble with their sled. Paul McGuire.

138.44 *Return Visit.* Nov. 22, 1956. GS: Walter Reed, Douglas Henderson, Paul Ringle, Virginia Wave. A bank robber, who defies the Northwest Mounted Police, surrenders to a little boy who has faith in him. The youngster is the man's son.

138.45 *The Tobacco Smugglers.* Nov. 29, 1956. GS: William Haade, Carol Henry, Richard Wilson, Don Kent. On the trail of stolen goods, Sgt. Preston follows the tobacco smugglers to their hideout. Then he finds he has walked into a trap.

138.46 *Turnabout.* Dec. 6, 1956. GS: Paul McGuire, Murvyn Vye, Thom Carney. On a lonely Arctic trail, Sgt. Preston comes upon a group of men who are stranded. He tries to help them, but finds his own life is in danger at their hands.

138.47 *Emergency on Scarface Flat.* Dec. 13, 1956. GS: Walter Reed, Elaine Williams, Les Mitchell. A convict breaks out of jail when he learns that his cellmate has hidden a large sum of stolen money in Yukon territory.

138.48 *The Williwaw.* Dec. 20, 1956. GS: James Lydon, Ted Jacques. Sergeant Preston, with an injured leg, reaches the safety of an isolated cabin just in time to avoid a dread Arctic blizzard and to share quarters with a homicidal maniac.

138.49 *Border Action.* Dec. 27, 1956. GS: Ed Dearing, Barry Curtis, Charles Conrad, Kenne Duncan, Coleman Francis. Sgt. Preston helps an elderly friend who is being victimized. A gang of smugglers is trying to gain control of his freight line.

138.50 *The Black Ace.* Jan. 3, 1957. GS: Richard Emory, Bill Hunt, Don Durant. A young trapper is suspected of the murder of his brother because of very strong circumstantial evidence. But Sgt. Preston tries to find evidence of the man's innocence.

138.51 *Scourge of the Wilderness.* Jan. 11, 1957. GS: Russ Conklin, House Peters, Jr., John Cravens, Robert Carson, Harry Tyler. Sgt. Preston tries to prevent bloodshed when an Indian chief goes on the warpath. The chief resents the intrusion of a lumber camp on the tribe's hunting grounds.

138.52 *Blind Justice.* Jan. 17, 1957. GS: Don Lawton, Alma Lawton, Harvey Grant, Jack Harris, Richard Warren, Joe Abdullah. Sergeant Preston teams a blind Husky dog with Yukon King to track down a pair of killers.

138.53 *The Stolen Malamute.* April 4, 1957. GS: Frank Richards, Grant Richards, Rickey Murray, Tom London, Zon Murray. A boy intends to sell his valuable Husky dog in order to help pay medical expenses for his sick mother. But thieves abduct the dog and head for the border.

138.54 *The Devil's Roost.* April 11, 1957. GS: George Lynn, Robert Cunningham, Robert Whitesides, Jo Ann Wade, Belle Mitchell. An old Indian woman has a dream that everyone laughs at except Sgt. Preston. The dream gives the mountie a clue to a plot by two renegades.

138.55 *Ten Little Indians.* April 18, 1957. GS: Billy Miller, Dennis Moore, David Leonard, Don Barry. Sgt. Preston gets aid from an Indian boy named Napoleon in trying to capture a gold thief.

138.56 *Underground Ambush.* April 25, 1957. GS: Kasey Rogers, Will White, Dan Blocker, Frank Scannell, John Ayres. Sergeant Preston adopts the disguise of a sourdough to investigate the activities of a counterfeiting gang. The trail leads to an abandoned mine, the headquarters of their operation.

Season Three

138.57 *Old Ben's Gold.* Oct. 3, 1957. GS: Harry Strang, Philip Greisman, Mauritz Hugo, John Pickard, Michael Mark, Jack Littlefield. An old prospector, who has told his grandson exaggerated tales of his bravery, loses the boy's respect when he meekly hands over his cache of gold to a gang of thieves.

138.58 *The Rebel Yell.* Oct. 10, 1957. GS: Guy Kingsford, Richard Devon, Fred Graham, Lionel Ames, Ruell Shayne. An elderly Southerner, who is now a prospector, is attacked by a band of gunmen. He uses the rebel yell in a desperate bid for help.

138.59 *The Mark of Crime.* Oct. 17, 1957. GS: Coleman Francis, Barbara Woodell, Charles Brasswell, John Close, George Diestel. A pair of bank robbers are posing as respectable citizens in a Hudson Bay post. When Sgt. Preston and Yukon King pay an unofficial visit to the community, the thieves become worried.

138.60 *Storm the Pass.* Oct. 24, 1967. GS: Glenn Turnbull, Dori Simmons, Hal Gerard, Bill Hale, Freeman Lusk. A Yukon renegade tries to sell a greenhorn the deed to a valuable goldmine claim for much less than the mine is worth. Sgt. Preston is suspicious.

138.61 *Old Faithful.* Oct. 31, 1957. Sgt. Preston attempts to locate the source of thousands of counterfeit ills being smuggled into the U.S. The gang of counterfeiters hires a thug to take care of Preston.

138.62 *The Skull in the Stone.* Nov. 7, 1957. GS: Paul Cavanagh, Pat Aherne, Robert La Varre, Gene Roth, Ben Frommer. Sgt. Preston runs up against superstition when he takes up the trail of a would-be murderer who uses tiny stone skulls to cause seeming accidents and near-disasters. Friendly Eskimos refuse to help Preston.

138.63 *Ghost Mine.* Nov. 14, 1957. GS: Rand Brooks, Margaret Stewart, Ralph Sanford, Charles Wagenheim, Charles Hayes. Two robbers plot to steal a valuable gold mine and murder the owner. Sgt. Preston enlists the aid of a ghost to help capture the criminals.

138.64 *The Jailbreaker.* Nov. 21, 1957. GS: Pierre Watkins, Lane Bradford, Dick Wilson. A giant-size ex-convict who was jailed by Sergeant Preston manages to escape, intending to wreak vengeance on the Mountie. When the criminal kills one of Preston's best friends, the Mountie's determined search for the fugitive leads him into a trap.

138.65 *Out of the Night.* Nov. 28, 1957. GS: Syd Saylor, Gene Walker, Bill Henry, Gilbert Frye, Barbara Knudsen, Charles J. Conrad, Ewing Mitchell. It looks like an inside job when the store clerk and the contents of a safe disappear at the same time. Preston and Yukon King trail the thieves to an abandoned gold mine.

138.66 *Three Men in Black.* Dec. 5, 1957. A trio of hooded bandits add a murder to their list of crimes. When one bandit panics and attempts to confess to Preston, he too is killed.

138.67 *Lost River Roundup.* Dec. 12, 1957. GS: Robert Bice, Tyler MacDuff, X Brands, Nancy Kilgas, Pat Lawless, Bob Swan. A ruthless gunman goes into business for himself after forcibly taking over a trading post from a young woman and her ailing father.

138.68 *The Old Timer.* Dec. 19, 1957. GS: George Milan, Carol Hill. A young store clerk disappears and is suspected of robbing the store safe. The real thieves have kidnaped him.

138.69 *Battle at Bradley's.* Dec. 26, 1967. GS: Herbert C. Lytton, Larry Hudson. Sgt. Preston is wounded in a gunfight with a gang of gold thieves. He seeks refuge in an empty cabin but the outlaws learn of his whereabouts and set out to kill him.

138.70 *The Generous Hobo.* Jan. 2, 1958. GS: Betty Benson, Tim Graham, Guy Williams. Two ex-convicts learn that the manager of the company store is an old prison mate of theirs. They take the man's daughter and her fiance as hostages to force him to turn over the company money.

138.71 *Follow the Leader.* Jan. 9, 1958. GS: Dick Wilson, Gene Roth, Ralph Neff, Ed Deering. A blinding snowstorm prevents Sergeant Preston and Yukon King from following two desperate criminals who have fled in Preston's dog sled.

138.72 *Gold Rush Patrol.* Jan. 16, 1958. GS: John Ayres, Bill Cassaday, Tom Noel, Harry Lauter, I. Stanford Jolley. Sgt. Preston warns a youth not to divulge the location of his gold strike until Mounties can patrol the area to prevent claim jumping. But in his excitement the boy tells the news, giving two thieves plenty of clues to the whereabouts of the treasure.

138.73 *Grizzly.* Jan. 23, 1958. Preston trails two fur thieves to a cabin where the lone occupant refuses to tell the Mountie where the thieves are hiding. Then he learns that the men have harmed his dog.

138.74 *The Diamond Collar.* Jan. 30, 1958. GS: Ann Cornell, John Bryant, Myron Cook. An entertainer named Anita Varden has three men interested in her—a rich Texan, a cafe owner and a prospector who owns a valuable diamond. Then the prospector is attacked by an unknown assailant, and Preston advises him to place the necklace in a safe place.

138.75 *Escape to the North.* Feb. 6, 1958. GS: George Eldredge, Jenifer Lea, John Compton, Allan Nixon, Paul Henderson. A pair of holdup men needing medical attention force an ex-convict to shelter them and get them a doctor. When the man's future son-in-law visits the cabin to announce news of a gold strike, the holdup men take him prisoner too.

138.76 *Outlaw in Uniform.* Feb. 13, 1958. A Mountie companion of Sergeant Preston is wounded by three outlaws. Then the criminals seek refuge in the home of the wounded Mountie and hold his parents as hostages.

138.77 *Boy Alone.* Feb. 20, 1958. GS: James Bronte, George Pelling, Paul Playdon, Larry Blake, Dick Warren, Zon Murray, Eddie Foster, Paul McGuire. A crafty Englishman comes to the Yukon to find and do away with his young cousin in the hope of inheriting a vast fortune.

138.78 *The Criminal Collie.* Feb. 27, 1958. GS: William Fawcett, Jody McCrea, John Ayres, George Baxter, Jim Bannon. A collie dog is the only witness to the murder of his master, an elderly prospector. When the prospector's son hears of the murder he tries to get the dog to lead him to the killer. The dog is brought to town, where he attacks a well-known citizen.

139. Shane

ABC. 60 min. Broadcast history: Saturday, 7:30-8:30, Sept. 1966–Dec. 1966.

Regular Cast: David Carradine (Shane), Jill Ireland (Marian Starett), Christopher Shea (Joey Starett), Tom Tully (Tom Starett), Sam Gilman (Sam Grafton), Bert Freed (Rufe Ryker).

Premise: This western series, set in the late 1800s, concerns Shane, a wandering ex-gunman, who takes the side of homesteaders in their battle against cattlemen in the quest for land.

The Episodes

139.1 *The Distant Bell.* Sept. 10, 1966. GS: Diane Ladd, Larry D. Mann, Owen Bush, Karl Lukas, Del Ford. A teacher has arrived in the valley, and a barn is being prepared for her classes. But cattleman Rufe Ryker warns the homesteaders that he won't allow the school to open.

139.2 *The Hant.* Sept. 17, 1966. GS: John Qualen, Carl Reindel, John Garfield, Jr., Sam Melville, Ned Romero, Claude Hall. Shane doesn't believe in ghosts, but he must admit to having seen some strange sights. He has seen a face pressed against his window at night, a man in a buggy, who appears, then suddenly disappears, and a shabby old stranger, who calls Shane by name and then vanishes.

139.3 *The Wild Geese.* Sept. 24, 1966. GS: William Smithers, Don Gordon, Bill Fletcher, Allen Jaffe. The Staretts face possible starvation. Cholera has killed their hogs and Ryker is threatening to destroy the winter wheat crop.

139.4 *An Echo of Anger.* Oct. 1, 1966. GS: Warren Oates, Cliff Osmond, Richard Evans, Charles Kuenstle. Mountaineer Kemp Spicer tells Marian that he and his kinfolk have come to the valley to kill Shane.

139.5 *The Bitter, the Lonely.* Oct. 8, 1966. GS: Steve Ihnat, Ned Romero, Owen Bush, Lawrence Mann. The Staretts' new hired hand, a destitute cowboy named R.G. Posey, is the same man who gave Shane a brutal beating.

139.6 *Killer in the Valley.* Oct. 15, 1966. GS: Joseph Campanella, George Keymas, Paul Grant, Robert Hoy, Owen Bush. A sick stranger asks Shane and Marian to help his wife, but the woman is already dead, and the man lives just long enough to expose them to a deadly disease.

139.7 *Day of the Hawk.* Oct. 22, 1966. GS: James Whitmore, Jason Wingreen, Gregory Walcott, Dee Pollack, Ned Romero. Circuit preacher Harry Himber's pleas for peace go unheeded by a bereaved homesteader bent on taking vengeance against Ryker's men, whom he blames for the death of his young wife.

139.8 *The Other Image.* Oct. 29, 1966. GS: Robert Brown, Owen Bush, Larry D. Mann. The arrival of State Senator Warren Eliot, Marian's old beau from the East, forces the frontier widow to make a choice between two worlds.

139.9 *Poor Tom's A-Cold.* Nov. 5, 1966. GS: Robert Duvall, Phyllis Love, Claire Wilcox, Joey Wilcox. Tom Gary becomes deranged when his cattle die at a water hole that has gone bad. Insisting that Ryker is responsible, Tom begins treating the other homesteaders like enemies when they try to tell him otherwise.

139.10 *High Road in Viator.* Nov. 12, 1966. GS: X Brands, Anne Morrell. Shane and the Starett family head for the annual dance at Viator, but the pleasant three-day journey soon becomes a dangerous ordeal.

139.11 *The Day the Wolf Laughed.* Nov. 19, 1966. GS: Skip Homeier, J.D. Cannon, Larry D. Mann, Clyde Ventura. Shane heads for a showdown with his friend Reno. The outlaw and his gang are trapped in the saloon, where they are holding Marian as hostage.

139.12 *The Silent Gift.* Nov. 26, 1966. GS: Jack Ging, J. Pat O'Malley, Claude Hall. Shane faces Ryker's harsh brand of frontier justice when two of the cattle baron's hired hands accuse him of stealing a pony.

139.13 *The Big Fifty.* Dec. 10, 1966. GS: Joanne Linville, Bill Fletcher, Owen Bush, Larry D. Mann. The arrival of Easterner Lydia Montgomery forces Tom Starett to relive a painful past. The revenge-bent woman is planning to kill Tom, once a hard-drinking judge who sentenced her husband to death.

139.14 *The Great Invasion* Part One. Dec. 17, 1966. GS: Bradford Dillman, Constance Ford, Archie Moore, Ross Hagen, Frank Marth, Tim O'Kelly, Hal Lynch, Larry Thor, Bill Quinn, Charles Grodin, E.J. Andre. A former Army major is organizing a campaign to clear the landowners out of the valley with the aid of newspaper propaganda, hired killers and a Gatling gun.

139.15 *The Great Invasion* Part Two. Dec. 24, 1966. GS: Bradford Dillman, Constance Ford, Archie Moore, Ross Hagen, Frank Marth, Tim O'Kelly, Hal Lynch, Larry Thor, Bill Quinn, Charles Grodin, E.J. Andre. A mercenary army is preparing to wipe out everyone in the valley, ranchers and homesteaders alike. Shane, who has learned the plan of attack, pleads with Ryker and the others to form a defensive alliance against the terrorists.

139.16 *A Man'd Be Proud.* Dec. 31, 1966. GS: Owen Bush, Larry D. Mann. Shane is suspicious of cattleman Rufe Ryker's surprising bid for Marian's hand, and more than a little upset that Marian is giving serious consideration to their old enemy.

140. Shotgun Slade

Syndicated. 30 min. Broadcast history: Various, Oct. 1959–June 1961.

Regular Cast: Scott Brady (Shotgun Slade).

Premise: This series depicted the exploits of Shotgun Slade, a lawman in the 1860s, who used a double-barreled shotgun in his efforts to maintain law and order in the West.

The Episodes

140.1 *The Missing Train.* Oct. 24, 1959. GS: Frank Watkins. Slade tries to return a carload of stolen gold to the authorities.

140.2 *The Salted Mine.* Oct. 26, 1959. GS: Ernie Kovacs. Swindlers spray a mine with gold dust to make it seem valuable.

140.3 *Lady and the Piano.* Nov. 2, 1959. A piano player, scorned by a beautiful singer, threatens to kill her. When she is found murdered, he sends for Slade.

140.4 *Omar the Sign Maker.* Nov. 3, 1959.

140.5 *Safe Cracker.* Nov. 7, 1959. Shotgun Slade is retained by the Rocky Mountain Bankers Association to combat safe crackers.

140.6 *The Stalkers.* Nov. 9, 1959. The girl friend of a man who has embezzled money helps Slade to trap the crook.

140.7 *Freight Line.* Nov. 14, 1959. GS: Jane Nigh, Chris Alcaide, Gregg Palmer. Shotgun Slade aids a lady in distress. Her freight line is beset by bandits, and she is losing her clients.

140.8 *Marked Money.* Nov. 16, 1959. GS: John Hart. A lawyer pays Shotgun Slade to clear the name of a banker who is said to have committed suicide after his bank was robbed.

140.9 *Bob Ford.* Dec. 19, 1959. Bob Ford, the man who shot Jesse James, is defended by Slade and seeks to return the favor.

140.10 *Gunnar Yensen.* Dec. 21, 1959. When a Swedish carpenter arrives in town to set up trade he is threatened by protection racketeers. Shotgun Slade attempts to give him the protection he really needs.

140.11 *Plate of Death.* Dec. 26, 1959.

140.12 *Mesa of Missing Men.* Dec. 28, 1959. Shotgun Slade disguises himself as a criminal and invades a den of treacherous outlaws when he tries to reform a man running from the law.

140.13 *The Blue Dogs.* Jan. 2, 1960.

140.14 *Major Trouble.* Jan. 4, 1950. GS: Ed Kemmer.

140.15 *Barbed Wire.* Jan. 9, 1969. GS: Roy Barcroft.

140.16 *The Marriage Circle.* Jan. 11, 1960.

140.17 *Treasure Trap.* Jan. 12, 1960. Slade goes to Mesa City for an insurance company to investigate a bank robbery.

140.18 *The Deadfall.* Feb. 2, 1960. After his horse and shotgun are stolen, Slade stops at a ranch and discovers that a murder has been committed.

140.19 *Pool Shark.* Feb. 23, 1960. A friendly game of pool turns into murder.

140.20 *Street of Terror.* Feb. 23, 1960. After being nicked by a sniper's bullet, Slade makes up his mind to help a young woman find the person who shot her father.

140.21 *Too Smart to Live.* March 1, 1960. A bank president sends for Slade to investigate a robbery.

140.22 *Shotgun Trial.* March 1, 1960. Slade is hired to protect the key witness in a murder trial.

140.23 *The Deadly Key.* March 8, 1960. GS: Glenn Dixon, Vito Scotti. An ancient key spells death for four people.

140.24 *The Swindle.* March 8, 1960. GS: Charlie Briggs. A gang of outlaws learn that Slade is to receive a shipment of money.

140.25 *The Smell of Money.* April 8, 1960.

140.26 *Donna Juanita.* April 15, 1960.

140.27 *The Golden Tunnel.* April 22, 1960. GS: Mary Webster. A mine-owner wants Slade to find out what's wrecking his profits.

140.28 *Flower for Jenny.* April 29, 1960. GS: Ludwig Stossel. A singer due to appear at the Deadwood saloon arrives in town and sends for Slade. She claims that someone is trying to kill her.

140.29 *The Fabulous Fiddle.* May 6, 1960. GS: Ludwig Stossel. Slade tries to protect a Stradivarius violin for an insurance company.

140.30 *Crossed Guns.* May 13, 1960. GS: Barry Atwater,

Rick Turner, Sue Ane Langdon. A gunslinger with a hook instead of a hand claims that Slade is responsible for the injury.

140.31 *Sudden Death.* May 20, 1960. GS: Beverly Tyler. Slade gets himself a job as bouncer for the Square Chance casino in hopes of meeting the author of an anonymous plea for help.

140.32 *The Spanish Box.* May 27, 1960.

140.33 *Backtrack.* May 28, 1960. GS: King Donovan, Connie Hines, Warren Kemmerling, Tom Gilson. Slade boards a train with an embezzler as his prisoner, unaware that outlaws are seeking out their friend and the loot.

140.34 *Ring of Death.* June 3, 1960. GS: Bethel Leslie. A vicious killer and a young woman wait for her fiance to stop by her house with an engagement ring.

140.35 *Killer's Brand.* June 4, 1960. GS: Ruta Lee. Slade gets a letter from a rancher who suspects his horses have been stolen and his foreman murdered.

140.36 *A Flower on Boot Hill.* June 11, 1960. GS: Shirley Ballard. Though the bandits have been arrested, the stolen money is still missing.

140.37 *Charcoal Bullet.* July 1, 1960. GS: Jacqueline Holt, Ned Glass, George Keymas. An alcoholic drifter who witnessed a bank robbery offers to sketch the likeness of the three holdup men.

140.38 *Lost Gold.* July 5, 1960. GS: Alan Hale, Jr., Stacy Keach. Owners of the Gold Run Mining Company discover that quantities of high-grade ore are mysteriously vanishing.

140.39 *Murder in Gingham.* July 8, 1960.

Season Two

140.40 *Skyfire.* Sept. 30, 1960.
140.41 *Gold.* Oct. 3, 1961. GS: Tex Ritter.
140.42 *Ghost of Yucca Flats.* Oct. 7, 1960.
140.43 *The Laughing Widow.* Oct. 14, 1960.
140.44 *Dead Man's Tale.* Oct. 21, 1960.
140.45 *Mountain Murderess.* Oct. 28, 1960.
140.46 *The Vengeance.* Nov. 4, 1960.
140.47 *The Traveling Trunk.* Nov. 11, 1960.
140.48 *Railhead at Rampart.* Nov. 18, 1960.
140.49 *Turkey Shoot.* Nov. 21, 1960.
140.50 *Hang Him Twice.* Dec. 2, 1960.
140.51 *Little Sister.* Dec. 9, 1960.
140.52 *Mystery of Black River.* Dec. 1, 1960.
140.53 *Impatient Bullet.* Dec. 23, 1960.
140.54 *Secret Gold.* Jan. 1, 1961.
140.55 *Legend of a Hero.* Jan. 8, 1961.
140.56 *The Copper Cylinder.* Jan. 10, 1961.
140.57 *Valley of the Shadow.* Jan. 17, 1961.
140.58 *Mother Six-Gun.* Jan. 26, 1961.
140.59 *Misplaced Genius.* Jan. 29, 1961.
140.60 *Horse for Hurley.* Feb. 5, 1961.
140.61 *School Ma'am.* Feb. 15, 1961.
140.62 *Widow of El Dorado.* Feb. 26, 1961.
140.63 *The Silver Queen.* Feb. 28, 1961.
140.64 *The Lost Herds.* March 12, 1961.
140.65 *Skinner's Rainbow.* March 19, 1961.
140.66 *A Grave for San Gallo.* March 26, 1961.
140.67 *Yankee Spy.* April 2, 1961.
140.68 *Search for Susan.* April 9, 1961.
140.69 *The Phantom Horse.* April 16, 1961.
140.70 *Madame Vengeance.* April 23, 1961.
140.71 *The Silent Man.* April 30, 1961.
140.72 *Friends No More.* May 5, 1961.
140.73 *Five Graves.* May 19, 1961.
140.74 *The Payrollers.* May 26, 1961.
140.75 *A Gun and a Prayer.* June 2, 1961.
140.76 *The Ranch Ghost.* June 9, 1961.
140.77 *Something to Die For.* June 16, 1961.
140.78 *The Missing Dog.* June 18, 1961.
140.79 *The Woman from Wyoming.* June 25, 1961.

141. Sky King

ABC/CBS. 30 min. Broadcast history: Various, April 1952–March 1959.

Regular Cast: Kirby Grant (Schuyler J. "Sky" King), Gloria Winters (Penny), Ron Hagerthy (Clipper), Ewing Mitchell (Mitch), Norman Olmstead (Bob Carey), Gary Hunley (Mickey).

Premise: Sky King, the owner and operator of the Flying Crown Ranch, used his twin-engined Cessna, The Songbird, to bring order to Grover City, Arizona.

The Episodes

141.1 *Operation Urgent.* April 5, 1952. GS: John Banner, Todd Karns, Rand Brooks, Pierre Watkin. Sky King intercepts as SOS from an air force pilot who is lost in a storm and out of fuel.

141.2 *Carrier Pigeon.* April 19, 1952. GS: Morgan Farley. Penny finds an injured carrier pigeon and discovers a rare ruby attached to its leg. Sky and the Mexican police investigate.

141.3 *Stagecoach Robbers.* May 3, 1952. GS: Stephen Chase, Emmett Lynn, Glenn Strange, Robert J. Wilke, Mike Ragan, Richard Powers, Gregg Barton. Sky flies to the rescue in hisplane, the Songbird, when Penny is taken captive by a crooked express agent who plans to steal gold from his company by faking a holdup.

141.4 *Deadly Cargo.* May 17, 1952. GS: Gene Roth, Myron Healey, John Cason. Sky investigates the accidental crash of a feeder line's transport plane and runs into a gang of gold smugglers and their cargo.

141.5 *Jim Bell's Triumph.* May 31, 1952. GS: Chubby Johnson, Emmett Vogan, Maurice Jara, Fred Libby, Richard Powers, Tony Dante. Sky sets out to expose the corrupt county clerk and winds up having to help his terrified foreman land the Songbird by remote control.

141.6 *Designing Woman.* June 14, 1952. GS: Angela Greene, Robert Shayne, Frank Dae, Evan Loew. Sky, Penny and Clipper are returning from an aerial survey when a woman flags down the plane. She turns out to be the daughter of a rancher who died mysteriously.

141.7 *One for the Money.* June 28, 1952. GS: John Doucette, Steven Clark, Dale Van Sickel, Charles Horvath, Dorothy Vaughan, Monte Blue. Returning from a trip, Penny picks up the wrong suitcase by mistake. When she opens it, she finds it full of money — all counterfeit.

141.8 *Danger Point.* July 12, 1952. GS: Keith Richards, Darryl Hickman, John Eldredge, Stanley Andrews, Monte Blue, Joseph Crehan, Mickey Simpson, Jack Shea, Joe Haworth. An elderly rancher disinherits his nephew in favor of his young son. When the rancher is murdered, the son is blamed.

141.9 *Desperate Character.* July 26, 1952. GS: Chubby Johnson, Bob Arthur, House Peters, Jr., Frank Fenton, Greta Granstedt, Gordon Wynne, Steve Dunhill. A mysterious young hitchhiker who has escaped from a reformatory. He won't tell who he is, where he's been or where he is going. Sky sets out to discover the boy's identity.

141.10 *The Man Who Forgot.* Aug. 9, 1952. GS: Earle Hodgins, James Brown, Dorothy Patrick, David Bruce, Mickey Simpson, George Pembroke, Monte Blue. A young rancher is blamed for the murder of a crook who was trying to foreclose his mortgage. Sky thinks there's another explanation for the rancher's sudden disappearance.

141.11 *The Threatening Bomb.* Aug. 23, 1952. GS: Anthony Warde, Stanley Andrews, Mira McKinney, George Lynn, Frank Richards, Monte Blue. A group of ranchers appeal to Sky for help when some Eastern gangsters move into the area and offer protection.

141.12 *Speak No Evil.* Sept. 6, 1952. GS: Richard Gaines, Raymond Greenleaf, Ross Elliott, Dana McGraw, Hal K. Dawson, Ben Welden, Alan Ray, Ted Jordan. Sky delivers a drug needed to save a sick man's life but stays to give more help when in his delirium the man confesses to his doctor that he is a former criminal who has gone straight since breaking out of prison years ago.

141.13 *Two-Gun Penny.* Sept. 20, 1952. GS: Chubby Johnson, Nestor Paiva, Steven Geray, Jill Oppenheim, Frederic Brune, John Hart. Sky King's niece Penny captures the agents who've taken a refugee professor prisoner.

141.14 *Formula for Fear.* Oct. 4, 1952. GS: Hayden Rorke, Fred Essler, David Leonard, Sarah Selby, Lee Van Cleef. Driving into town, Penny sees a many trying to escape from a doctor. She stops and is told that the man is a mental patient.

141.15 *The Giant Eagle.* Oc. 18, 1952. GS: John Alvin, William Vedder, Monte Blue, Hugh Prosser, Russell Trent, Murray Alper, Tom Tyler, Robert Forrest. Three payroll robberies are successfully pulled off in one month, and there's one really strange aspect of the cast. The bandits disappear from the scene of the crime, right into thin air.

141.16 *Blackmail.* Nov. 8, 1952. GS: Don Beddoe, Gene Roth, John Gallaudet, Mary Newton, Connie Marshall, James Flavin. The local banker, a highly respected citizen of the town, is visited by two blackmailers who can link him to a 23-year-old crime.

141.17 *Wings of Justice.* Nov. 22, 1952. GS: Fay Baker, Douglas Evans, Pierre Watkins, Maude Wallace, James Flavin. Sky is suspicious of an Eastern couple visiting a dude ranch. They claim to be on a hunting trip, but there's a uranium deposit on the property.

141.18 *Destruction from the Sky.* Dec. 6, 1952. GS: Chubby Johnson, Janna de Loss, Hugh Sanders, David Bond, Bob Carson, Emmett Lynn, Pete Kooy. Military intelligence enlists Sky's help to look for the saboteur who has blown up a secret project.

141.19 *The Porcelain Lion.* Dec. 20, 1952. GS: Grandon Rhodes, Johnny Downs, Robert Rockwell, James Parnell, James Flavin, George Eldredge. When a pilot reports that engine trouble force him to bail out of a plane that in fact never left the ground, Sky investigates and becomes involved in the theft of a valuable porcelain lion.

Season Two

141.20 *The Neckerchief.* Jan. 2, 1956. GS: Leonard Mazzola, Gil Frye, Dennis Moore. A young parolee is sent to Sky King's ranch for a visit. Soon after his arrival two criminals from the boy's past are known to be in the vicinity. When the local bank is robbed and an article of clothing resembling the young parolee's is left behind, trouble begins.

141.21 *Man Hunt.* Jan. 2, 1956. GS: Dick Beymer, Kathleen Mulqueen, Craig Duncan, Gary Conway, Richard Denby, Mark Sather. Young Joe Beldon thinks he killed another boy during a fight. Driven by fear, he takes a gun and heads for Mexico.

141.22 *The Plastic Ghost.* Jan. 9, 1956. GS: I. Stanford Jolley, Myron Healey, Frank Richards, Fred Krone. While flying over a ghost town in the desert, Sky King sees a distress signal. He lands and begins a search of the decaying buildings for signs of someone in need of help. Finally, he comes face to face with a dangerous criminal who is holding a plastic surgeon as a hostage.

141.23 *The Rainbird.* Jan. 9, 1956. GS: Charles Stevens, Russ Conklin, Harry Mackin. Village Indians give their medicine-man and rainmaker two days to bring an end to the dry spell that has parched their land, or they will kill him.

141.24 *The Crystal Trap.* Jan. 30, 1956. GS: Dennis Moore, Gilbert Frye, Eddie Erwin, Leonard Mazzola, Hal Taggart. Prospectors await the posting of a uranium map. They wait in vain, as the map has been stolen. The map's theft brings on a dangerous aerial chase.

141.25 *The Red Tentacle.* Jan. 30, 1956. GS: James Hong, Sammee Tong, Gene Roth, W.T. Chang, Weaver Levy. Several Chinese living near the town of Grover have suffered severe beatings, but none will tell why or by whom.

141.26 *Boomerang.* Feb. 6, 1956. GS: Steven Geray, Don C. Harvey, Bill Kennedy, June Burt, George DeNormand. Enemy agents try to blackmail an important refugee scientist now working for the U.S. government. They are trying to get the secret of a new electronic device.

141.27 *The Geiger Detective.* Feb. 6, 1956. GS: William Henry, Bill Hale, Joe Conway. Some bandits steal a payroll and escape into the hills. They hold a uranium prospector as hostage. Sky King uses the Geiger detective to help track down the bandits in an exciting chase.

141.28 *The Golden Burro.* Feb. 27, 1956. GS: Eugenia Paul, Stanley Andrews, Kenne Duncan, Nesdon Booth, Gregg Barton. Penny discovers an old prospector almost dead of thirst on the desert. With him are three burros whose saddle bags are full of gold ore.

141.29 *Rustlers on Wheels.* March 5, 1956. GS: Bill Lechner, Kenne Duncan, Stanley Andrews, Nesdon Booth, Gregg Barton, Chuck Slay, Hal Conrad. When sixty cattle vanish from the herd of a yough neighbor who is new to the west, Sky tries to help and discovers that the animals were taken away in a truck with diamond-shaped tire treads.

Sky King

141.30 *The Silver Grave.* March 5, 1956. GS: Baynes Barron, Effie Laird, Sam Flint, I. Stanford Jolley. Sky King tries to help a man claiming to be an expert on Western lore. The man appears particularly interested in an old gang whose loot was never found.

141.31 *Uninvited Death.* March 12, 1956. GS: Brad Trumball, Gloria Moore, Mauritz Hugo, Don Brodie. Sky and Penny tour an Army special-projects plant, unaware that an enemy agent has tampered with their car, planting a time bomb in it.

141.32 *Fish Out of Water.* March 19, 1956. GS: Sam Flint, Baynes Barron, Effie Laird, I. Stanford Jolley. An escaped convict heads for the town of Grover to get revenge upon the judge who was responsible for his prison sentence. The judge is on a fishing trip with Sky King and Penny takes a desperate chance to warn them of their danger.

141.33 *Diamonds on a Sky-Hook.* March 26, 1956. GS: Ralph Neff, Hal K. Dawson, Rusty Wescoatt, Nick Prizant, Charlie Hayes. Fred Watson, old-time prospector, has gotten an order for a fortune in diamonds. But his mine is small, the time is short, and the early snows may block the road to the mine.

141.34 *Flood of Fury.* April 2, 1956. GS: John Cason, Joe Conway, Rusty Wescoatt, John Frank. When Riverdale is flooded, Sky saves three men from drowning in the river. Then he learns that the are escaped convicts bent on robbing the local bank.

141.35 *Rocket Story.* April 2, 1956. GS: Dennis Moore, Don Marlowe, Scott Douglas, Robert Malcolm. At dawn the government experiment station near Sky's ranch will end up a new rocket to relay vital information back to Earth. Sky learns that one of the guests at his ranch is an enemy agent.

141.36 *Rodeo Roundup.* April 23, 1956. GS: Rhodes Reason, Bill Hale, Harrison Lewis, Red Morgan. The yearly rodeo in the town of Grover has everything, including a mock holdup. But this year two strangers arrive in town with a clever scheme to make off with the money for the new hospital.

141.37 *Showdown.* April 23, 1956. GS: John Cason, Dennis Moore, George Milan, Don Brodie. Penny and Bob Carey set out on horseback to track down thieves who stole four of Sky's best horses. Bob ends us seriously hurt.

141.38 *Land o' Cotton.* April 30, 1956. GS: Harvey Dunn, Larry Gelbman, Bill Vaughan, Orlando Rodriguez, Carol Thurston, Gilbert Frye, Jack O'Shea. Sky King learns of a Southerner's attempt to irrigate part of the desert to plant cotton. Then he meets a Mexican family on the desert and finds that they are fleeing from the Southerner. He decides to investigate and disguises himself as a peon.

141.39 *Dust of Destruction.* April 30, 1956. GS: Bill Lechner, Rhodes Reason, Bill Hale, Harrison Lewis. A young man, recently discharged from the Navy, has inherited his uncle's ranch. But he is in trouble because of a debt he owes to a neighboring rancher who is anxious to gain possession of the property. When his alfalfa crop is ready he feels sure he will be able to pay his debt.

Season Three

141.40 *Mystery Horse.* Dec. 29, 1957. GS: Richard Vath, Rick Vallin, Joseph Turkel. Sky is forced to take drastic action to save the life of a famous race horse trapped in a canyon.

141.41 *Double Trouble.* Dec. 29, 1957. GS: Alan Ray, Mauritz Hugo, Harry Fleer, Rand Brooks, Wally Walker, Ed Erwin. When a man who looks like Sky King steals the Songbird and attempts to blow up a Navy missile center. Sky borrows a jet to chase him.

141.42 *Note for a Dam.* Jan. 5, 1958. GS: Jack Tesler, Paul Donovan, Al Ferguson, Troy Patterson, Charlie Hayes. Sky learns from an old friend that a dam is to be dynamited. Sky flies to the rescue, only to be held captive by a madman.

141.43 *Bad Actor.* Jan. 5, 1958. GS: Ted Wedderspoon, Michael Carr, Fred Krone, Alan Ray, Rusty Wescoatt. Penny becomes stage-struck when she and Sky King go on location with a movie outfit.

141.44 *Fight for Oil.* Jan. 12, 1958. GS: Jack Lomas, Travis Bryan, Paul Farber, Robert Swan, Jim Lake, Paul Sickner, Robert Tetrick. Sky's old friend Willie McNair owns an oil well which looks like a gusher. But Willie may not be around to enjoy his riches.

141.45 *Lost Boy.* Jan. 12, 1958. GS: Gordon Barnes, Lettie Lovell, Ricky Allen, Michael Hale. Sky King, flying his new Songbird, searches for a boy whose life is endangered.

141.46 *The Brain and the Brawn.* Jan. 26, 1958. GS: Malcolm Steen, William Vaughan, Austin Green, Karl Davis, Edmund Cobb, Rusty Wescoatt, Graig Karr. Sky King and Penny encounter a wicked hypnotist and investigate a crime wave at a county fire.

141.47 *The Feathered Serpent.* Jan. 26, 1958. GS: Milano Kay, William Flaherty, Terry Frost, Henry Rowland, Audley Anderson, Howard Dayton. A homing pigeon alights on Sky King's property. When he finds an emerald attached to its leg, Sky becomes suspicious and releases the bird to see where it will lead him.

141.48 *The Circus Clown Mystery.* Feb. 22, 1958. GS: Dave Tomack, Frank Scannell, Larry Johns, Gloria Marshall, Nick Nicholson. Sky and Penny go to the circus to find a thief. The culprit is described in the police bulletin as over seven feet tall.

141.49 *Dead Man's Will.* Feb. 22, 1958. GS: Steve London, Joe Partridge, Nick Thompson, Frederic Welch, Jack George. Dr. Dan Vickers has succeeded in setting up a clinic for poverty-stricken Indians. But a man named Sam Driver says he has proof that the land the clinic is built on belongs to him. Sky King comes to the aid of the young doctor.

141.50 *Cindy, Come Home.* March 9, 1958. GS: Bill Hudson, Darcy Hinton, Bruce Kay, Dayle Rodney, Elizabeth Harrower, Harvey B. Dunn. The doctor says that nothing can revive little Mary's will to live, except a visit from her father, who can't be found. Sky King searches the mining country for the little girl's father.

141.51 *Rodeo Decathalon.* March 9, 1958. GS: Gary Clarke, John Cason, Paul Donovan, Tex Foster, Gordon Terry, Dick Elliott. Stoney Harrison wants to win enough money in the rodeo to go to college. But he is hurt during the first event and Sky decides to take his place. He enters the bulldogging, roping and shooting contests.

141.52 *Abracadabra.* March 9, 1958. GS: Norman Nazarr, Gloria Pall, William Keene, Dirk Evans, Jack Reynolds. Sky and Penny go to a Hollywood party and meet a magician. The fun ceases when a precious diamond is reported missing.

141.53 *Triple Exposure.* March 9, 1958. GS: Barbara Ann Knudsen, Sam Scar, Mary Newton, Phil Van Zandt, Lomax Study, Frank Richards. Newspaper photographer Gloria Blane helps Sky and Penny track down a valuable stamp collection.

141.54 *The Haunted Castle.* March 16, 1958. GS: Robert Roark, Gail Bonney, Robert Gunderson, Curt Barrett. Sky and Penny are asked to investigate stories about a strange house out on a lonely prairie. The meet some very curious people when they arrive there.

141.55 *Danger at the Sawmill.* March 16, 1958. GS: Larry Scruggs, Henry Kulky, Rex Mann, Walter Kray, Ed Hinton, Chuck Stanaker. Sky King and Penny are almost run down by a lumber truck. An investigation shows that local lumbermen are being victimized.

141.56 *Sleight of Hand.* March 23, 1958. GS: Terry Kelman, Marc Platt, Walter Maslow, Frankie Van, Jack LeMaire, Irvin Ashkenazy, Joseph Conway. After flying Songbird to Center City, Sky and young Davey fall into a trap laid by crooked gamblers.

141.57 *The Runaway.* March 23, 1958. GS: Terry Kelman, Gregg Palmer, Bob LaVarre, Britt Wood. Pursued by gunmen, twelve-year-old Davey Wilson runs away to Phantom Mountain. Sky and Penny join in the search for him.

141.58 *Stop That Train.* March 30, 1958. GS: Terry Kelman, Edward Foster, William Hale, Pierre Watkin, George Mather, Elmore Vincent. Penny is captured by three men who plan to dynamite a train. Sky and his young friend Davey race to the rescue.

Season Four

141.59 *The Wild Man.* Dec. 28, 1958. GS: Buddy Baer, Nick Nicholson, I. Stanford Jolley, Henry Rowland, Tom Daly. When the payroll of a logging company is stolen and its paymaster injured in an auto crash, the obvious suspect is a man with a grudge against the loggers.

141.60 *Sky Robbers.* Dec. 28, 1958. GS: Dwight Brooks, Bill Catching, Vic Marlo, Pat Miller. Greg Nelson, an entrant in an air race, uses his flight to make off with the funds from the town's Community Chest.

141.61 *A Dog Named Barney.* Dec. 28, 1958. GS: Harvey Grant, Buck Bradley, Keith Richards. A blind newsboy receives a German-shepherd dog called Barney from the townspeople of Grover. The boy and his dog are present during a holdup and Barney follows the bandit.

141.62 *Bullet Bait.* Dec. 28, 1958. GS: James Dobson, Jacquelyn Revell, Don C. Harvey, Boyd Stockman, Joe Hamilton. At the Flying Crown Ranch everybody's ready for a wedding but Joe Halliday, the bridegroom, who doesn't show up. He ran out of gas, and a couple of hijackers ambushed him.

141.63 *Money Has Wings.* Jan. 4, 1959. GS: Rand Brooks, Will J. White, George Mather, John Alvin, Charlene Brooks. The operator of Wellman Air Freight lines loses four pilots during his first month as conveyor of a large payroll. Investigating, Sky poses as a security guard.

141.64 *Frog Man.* Jan. 4, 1959. GS: Mason Alan Dinehart, Emlen Davies, Jerry Oddo, Jim Beck, Dennis Moore. A phone call warns Sky that the son of a ranch hand is in trouble. Sky flies to Reno to investigate.

141.65 *Terror Cruise.* Feb. 1, 1959. GS: Leslie Bradley, Daria Massey, Paul Fierro, David Renard, Edmund Hashim. Sky leaves Penny with some friends aboard a cruising yacht, unaware that three escaped convicts are watching his departure.

141.66 *Runaway Truck.* Feb. 1, 1959. GS: Clark Smith, Richard Clayton, William Meigs, Jeanne Bates, Robert Dix. Sky learns that a neighbor, driving some children home from a picnic, has accidentally taken an overdose of sleeping pills.

141.67 *Bounty Hunters.* Feb. 1, 1959. GS: Michael Hinn, Robert Swan, George Becwar, Wayne Heffley. Coyotes have killed some cattle on the Flying Crown Ranch, so Sky hires two professional hunters, Al Collier and Max Wilson, to wipe out the animals.

141.68 *A Mickey for Sky.* Feb. 22, 1959. GS: Gary Hunley, John Mylong. A young boy named Mickey is flying to visit Sky. On the plane he overhears a conversation that portends danger for another passenger.

141.69 *Dead Giveaway.* March 1, 1959. GS: Gary Hunley, Robert Clarke, Glenn Strange, Bill Hale. Sky's visitor, Mickey, goes exploring on his pony. He is taken prisoner by the thugs in charge of some stolen cars.

141.70 *Ring of Fire.* March 1, 1959. GS: Clark Smith, Antony George, Jan Arvan, Walter Reed, Rusty Wescoatt. Sky flies to help ailing Indian Chief Lone Cloud when the old man refuses to go to a hospital for medical treatment. He believes that he is about to die, and wants to do so on his own land.

141.71 *Mickey's Birthday.* March 8, 1959. GS: Larry Chance, Gary Hunley, Joe Patridge, John Mitchum, William Bakewell. Sky and Penny take Mickey to an amusement park for his birthday. The youngster becomes an unwitting tool of a pair of smugglers.

142. Stagecoach West

ABC. 60 min. Broadcast history: Tuesday, 9:00-10:00, Oct. 1960–Sept. 1961.

Regular Cast: Wayne Rogers (Luke Perry), Robert Bray (Simon Kane), Richard Eyer (David Kane), James Burke (Zeke Bonner).

Premise: This series depicted the exploits of the men who drove the stage from Missouri to California during the 1860s.

The Episodes

142.1 *High Lonesome.* Oct. 4, 1960. GS: Jane Greer, James Best, Robert F. Simon, Paul Engle, Stafford Repp, Norman Leavitt. Bad weather forces the coach to stop at a way station. There Kane meets Les Hardee, who has been hired to kill him.

142.2 *The Land Beyond.* Oct. 11, 1960. GS: Gigi Perreau, Bob Harland, Richard Anderson, John Litel, Don Kennedy. Lin and Sarah Lou Proctor sign up for the long trip West. Luke and Simon discover that the couple has eloped and that they are being followed. A man named Cole Dawson has been hire to see that their marriage doesn't last.

142.3 *Dark Return.* Oct. 18, 1960. GS: Billy Gray, John Kellogg, Jim Hyland, Frank Wilcox. Young Frankie Niles returns from a tour of duty at sea and beds down in Stanley Culver's livery stable. He sees Stanley and his brother Jed Culver arguing over money matters. There is a fight and Stanley is killed.

142.4 *The Unwanted.* Oct. 25, 1960. GS: Tammy Marihugh, Bethel Leslie, Gerald Mohr, Richard Crane, John Litel. Luke makes an unscheduled stop to take a lame horse out of the lead spot. But Johnny Kelly accuses Luke of making the passengers sitting ducks for road agents. He pulls a gun and doesn't live to regret it.

142.5 *A Fork in the Road.* Nov. 1, 1960. GS: Jack Warden, Jack Elam, Richard Devon, Joe Perry. Simon and Davey are driving West with one passenger — a corpse. When they pick up Stacey Gibbs, a stranger, he is more than interested in the contents of the coffin.

142.6 *A Time to Run.* Nov. 15, 1960. GS: Cesar Romero, Barbara Nichols, William Schallert, Than Wyenn, Richard Coogan, Guy Wilkerson. Luke picks up Manola Lalanda, a wounded fugitive from the Mexican government, and plans to turn him over to the authorities in the next town. Then he is overtaken by a group of bounty hunters who announce that Lalanda is just the man they are looking for.

142.7 *Red Sand.* Nov. 22, 1960. GS: Dean Jones, Harold J. Stone, Diana Millay, Edgar Buchanan, Guy Stockwell, John Damler, Warren Vanders. Kane picks up two lost travelers in a sandstorm. He learns they have robbed a bank and would kill for a well-packed till.

142.8 *The Saga of Jeremy Boone.* Nov. 29, 1960. GS: Marti Stevens, Steve Brodie, Ben Cooper, John Litel, Hugh Sanders, Sheila Pinkham. Handsome Jeremy Boone, carrying a handsome sum of money, is a passenger on Luke's stage to Timberline. Also a passenger is Felicia Sparks, who likes men and money.

142.9 *Life Sentence.* Dec. 6, 1960. GS: Virginia Grey, Bruce Gordon, Harry Townes, Robert J. Stevenson. Toby Reese and Leo Calloway have sworn to kill each other, but Simon Kane hopes to end the feud.

142.10 *The Storm.* Dec. 13, 1960. GS: Beverly Garland, Tom Drake, J. Pat O'Malley, Robert J. Stevenson. Doc Apperson and Luke fight the driving snow in the storm to get to Halfway House where Zeke Bonner is seriously ill. They are stopped en route by a man and woman who take over the stage, but leave Luke and Doc.

142.11 *Three Wise Men.* Dec. 20, 1960. GS: Dick York, Ellen Clark, Denver Pyle, Arthur Batanides, Harry Lauter. Webb Crawford, a fugitive wanted for robbery, is dying of leukemia and has one last wise. To be with his wife and children on Christmas Eve.

142.12 *By the Deep Six.* Dec. 27, 1960. GS: Ashley Cowan, Mort Mills, Walter Sande, Ross Elliott, Catherine McLeod, Gina Gillespie, Joan Elan, Joseph Ruskin. Kane and his passengers have been ambushed by outlaws, and it looks like murder's in the offing. Then Kane finds out that the would-be murderers think they are saving all concerned from a fate worse than death.

142.13 *Object: Patrimony.* Jan. 3, 1961. GS: Pippa Scott, George Neise, Robert Vaughn, Dennis Patrick, Warren Oates, Than Wyenn, T.M. McBride. Susan McLord and her fiance Lionel Chambers try to elope on Luke's stage. But a band or renegades intercept the coach, killing Chambers and kidnaping Susan.

142.14 *Come Home Again.* Jan. 10, 1961. GS: James Coburn, Lisa Kirk, Reba Waters, John Litel, Joyce Jameson. Deborah Cotton and her daughter Abigail are passengers on Kane's stage to Outpost. A private eye hired by Deborah's family is hot on their trail. The Cotton family insists Deborah is kidnaping her own daughter.

142.15 *The Brass Lily.* Jan. 17, 1961. GS: Jean Hagen, John Litel, Robert Strauss, Robert J. Wilke. Singer Lilly de Milo comes to Outpost to fill a singing engagement. But before she gets a chance to sing, she is shot in the side.

142.16 *Finn McColl.* Jan. 24, 1961. GS: Sean McClory, Hazel Court, John Sutton, Denny Miller. Finn McColl makes overtures to Mrs. Robert Allison on Simon Kane's stage. Kane doesn't like this sort of carrying on, so he challenges McColl to a fist fight.

142.17 *Image of a Man.* Jan. 31, 1961. GS: Thomas Mitchell, John Dehner, DeForest Kelley. Alcoholic lawyer Ethan Blount is forced to prosecute a man named Clay for murder. He doesn't really want the case, especially since Clay's brother, a shady politician, has told him he had better lose the case.

142.18 *Not in Our Stars.* Feb. 7, 1961. GS: Lon Chaney, Jr., Jay C. Flippen, Karen Green. Kane offers shelter to Ben Wait, a man who is trying to dodge a vengeful blow from Aaron Sutter. Sutter insists that Wait murdered his daughter.

142.19 *The Arsonist.* Feb. 14, 1961. GS: James Dunn, Adele Mara, James Best, Olan Soule. The stage bogs down in a wooded area, and Davey rides to Halfway House for help. When he returns, he finds the coach threatened by a forest fire.

142.20 *Songs My Mother Told Me.* Feb. 21, 1961. GS: Arthur O'Connell, Richard Devon, Harry Lauter, John Damler, Rachel Ames. Luke and Simon's suspicions are aroused when Davey begins to slip out with packages of food and clothing. They discover he has befriended Matt Dexter, a murder witness who has taken refuge in the hills. The killers would like to make Matt their next victim.

142.21 *The Root of Evil.* Feb. 28, 1961. GS: Philip Carey, Rachel Ames, Don Haggerty, Linda Lawson, John Dehner. Major Barnes' honeymoon is off to an ominous start. His bride points out that they are being followed, so Barnes forces a showdown with the man and shoots him.

142.22 *The Outcasts.* March 7, 1961. GS: Don Dubbins, Joanna Barnes, Stacy Harris, Hollis Irving, Lyle Talbot, Olan Soule. Ken Rawlins fires after a fleeing holdup gang. One of the men he kills is his own brother.

142.23 *The Remounts.* March 14, 1961. GS: Richard Devon, Mort Mills, Don Burnett, James Beck, James Griffith, Chris Alcaide. Davey is taken hostage by two men who plan to steal a herd of wild horses. Simon and Luke see only one way to get Davey back — assist the horse thieves with their scheme.

142.24 *House of Violence.* March 21, 1961. GS: Jack Lord, Robert J. Stevenson, Olan Soule. Luke's stagecoach is stopped by outlaw Russ Doty and the passengers are seized as hostages. Luke is sent for supplies, but is warned that the passengers will be killed if he contacts the law.

142.25 *The Butcher.* March 28, 1961. GS: Rodolfo Hoyos, John Dehner, Jack Lord, Dody Heath, Christopher Dark, Frank Ferguson. The Mexican bandit Domingo is determined to kill passenger Sam Carlin, even if it means slaughtering Simon and his other passengers.

142.26 *Fort Wyatt Crossing.* April 4, 1961. GS: Steven

Terrell, Madlyn Rhue, Alvy Moore. When he sees a body sprawled across the road, Luke stops the stage and finds Julian Tibbs, a badly wounded soldier. While Luke tries to revive him, one of the passengers finds Julian's wagon, filled with Army gold.

142.27 *A Place of Still Waters.* April 11, 1961. GS: Darren McGavin, Edward Binns, Chuck Robertson. Weary gunman Pierce Martin wants only to forget his past. But a brash upstart challenges him to draw, and he is forced to shoot in self-defense. Once more a wanted killer, Martin rides to the town of Outpost in search of Jim Hallett, his only friend.

142.28 *Never Walk Alone.* April 18, 1961. GS: William Campbell, Lee Van Cleef, Karen Sharpe. Train robber Cole Eldridge is pardoned by the governor and released from prison. He hops a train and discovers that Hyatt, a member of his old gang, is aboard. Hyatt wants to rob the train.

142.29 *The Big Gun.* April 25, 1961. GS: Cesar Romero, Barbara Luna, DeForest Kelley. Luke is carrying a Gatling gun in his stage for delivery to an Army post. He is intercepted by Francisco Martinez and his band, followers of Juarez in the war against Maximillian. Martinez rides off with the gun, and takes Luke along for good measure.

142.30 *The Dead Don't Cry.* May 2, 1961. GS: James Best, Tod Lasswell, King Calder, Harry Lauter. Luke rides into Tucson to see his brother Sam. He learns that Sam, unjustly accused of murder, has left town, and Mike Pardee, a shrewd bounty hunter, is stalking him.

142.31 *The Raider.* May 9, 1961. GS: Henry Silva, Jan Shepard, James Lydon, Norman Leavitt. Emily Prince and her homesteader fiance Gil Soames are to meet at Halfway House. But killer Mel Harney, who was once engaged to Emily, arrives there before eight of them.

142.32 *Blind Man's Bluff.* May 16, 1961. GS: James Drury, Ruta Lee, Whit Bissell. Della Bell's former suitor Stace threatens to kill Della and her husband Harmony. The couple decide to leave Outpost, and run for their lives.

142.33 *The Bold Whip.* May 23, 1961. GS: John Kellogg, Carolyn Kearney, Olan Soule. Luke and Simon are taking their first run on a new stagecoach when they are attacked by Cheyennes. The stage carries an Army payroll and Rupe Larned, a man whom Luke and Simon suspect of being a good friend of the Cheyenne chief.

142.34 *The Orphans.* May 30, 1961. GS: Robert Cabal, Linda Dangcil, John Milford. Jaime and Angela Toreno come over from Spain to join their father, who is working as a sheepherder. The children find him dead.

142.35 *The Guardian Angels.* June 6, 1961. GS: Casey Adams, Malcolm Atterbury, Steve Brodie, Walter Kinsella. Among the passengers on Luke's stage are a dude, a preacher and a gambler. When the coach is attacked by Indians, Luke has more trouble with the passengers than with the redskins.

142.36 *The Swindler.* June 13, 1961. GS: Dennis Patrick, John Litel. Hollis Collier offers the citizens of Outpost a chance to invest their money in a gold mine. Simon thinks Collier is up to no good, but David is convinced of the man's honesty.

142.37 *The Renegades.* June 20, 1961. GS: Richard Devon, Warren Oates, Edward Kemmer. A group of renegade soldiers, headed by Ed Bush and Tom Lochlin, are headed for the Canadian border. To be less conspicuous, they decide they need a stagecoach.

142.38 *The Marker.* June 27, 1961. GS: Mort Mills, Ruta Lee, Olan Soule. Luke is helping Jenny Forbes hide from her former boy friend, a gambler called Mingo. When Mingo learns of this, he send Luke a present — a tombstone.

143. *Steve Donovan, Western Marshal*

Syndicated. 30 min. Broadcast history: Various, Sept. 1955–June 1956.

Regular Cast: Douglas Kennedy (Marshal Steve Donovan), Eddy Waller (Rusty Lee).

Premise: Marshal Steve Donovan maintains law and order in the West in the 1890s.

The Episodes

143.1 *The Midnight Election.* Sept. 24, 1955. Hoping the new Wyoming territory woman's suffrage law will help her get elected, a pretty girl runs for mayor. The election commissioner, however, is strongly opposed to females in politics and connives to prevent the women from voting.

143.2 *The Deputy.* Oct. 1, 1955. A debt-ridden deputy marshal tries to settle his gambling accounts by allowing the gambler's partner to escape from jail.

143.3 *Plague Town.* Oct. 8, 1955. When a town is hit by an epidemic, outlaws attempt to gain control over the community by seizing the only available serum.

143.4 *Crooked Star.* Oct. 15, 1955. Marshal Donovan and Rusty discover that an outlaw is posing as a local sheriff.

143.5 *Special Delivery.* Oct. 22, 1955. Steve and Rusty, assigned to transfer a notorious gang leader to prison, must choose one of two routes — one patrolled by the man's gang and the other through Indian territory.

143.6 *Terror Town.* Oct. 29, 1955. A meek newspaper editor accidentally witnesses a murder, and although he realizes how much this knowledge can mean to the welfare of the town, he refuses to tell his story.

143.7 *The School Teacher.* Nov. 5, 1955. A land speculator attempts to implicate the local schoolteacher in mail robberies. Steve and Rusty are assigned to investigate.

143.8 *Sketch Artist.* Nov. 12, 1955. A local artist helps solve the mystery of the Grandma stagecoach robberies, committed under the instigation of an elderly woman.

143.9 *Ghost Town.* Nov. 19, 1955. Marshal Donovan and Rusty seek refuge from a storm in a ghost town shack, where they find themselves facing the wrong end of a gun.

143.10 *Journey into Danger.* Nov. 26, 1955. Rather than risk riding through dangerous Indian territory with their prisoner, Marshal Donovan and Rusty decide to use a road which is being guarded by the prisoner's gang.

143.11 *The People's Choice.* Dec. 3, 1955. An outlaw running for mayor attempts to force his only opponent out of the race by kidnaping the man's daughter.

143.12 *Outlaw Actor.* Dec. 10, 1955. A practiced impersonator executes a successful bank robbery by posing as a telegraph operator.

143.13 *Napoleon's Eagle.* Dec. 17, 1955. While checking a report of trouble between immigrants and natives in the Southwest, Marshal Donovan and Rusty uncover a foreign plot to overthrow the United States Government.

143.14 *Two Men Out.* Dec. 24, 1955. While on the trail of two convicts, Steve and Rusty find a woman who has left her husband and has been robbed on her way to the station. Suspecting that the robbers are the convicts, Steve and Rusty escort the woman safely back to her husband.

143.15 *Mystery Canyon.* Dec. 31, 1955. Marshal Donovan and Rusty are called in to round up a band of outlaws who always manage to elude their pursuers by riding into a canyon and mysteriously disappearing. Steve and Rusty solve the mystery, but the tables are turned at the last minute and they almost meet an untimely end.

143.16 *Crisis at Canyonville.* Jan. 7, 1956. By law, Marshal Steve Donovan and Rusty Lee are unable to arrest a murderer without being asked to do so by the local sheriff, and the sheriff refuses.

143.17 *The Comanche Kid.* Jan. 14, 1956. When one of their friends is murdered by the mysterious Comanche Kid, Steve and Rusty set out to track down the man who is terrorizing local settlers.

143.18 *Journey to Justice.* Jan. 21, 1956. A murderer, handcuffed to Marshal Donovan, knocks out Rusty Lee and draws a gun on the Marshal.

143.19 *The Medicine Man.* Jan. 28, 1956. An embittered doctor, unjustly deprived of his license, retaliates by leading the outlaws he was accused of aiding. Part of his gang is captured and his own men turn against him, believing he has double-crossed them. Steve and Rusty have no proof of the doctor's identity until an innocent young man is wounded and needs immediate medical attention.

143.20 *Unbranded.* Feb. 4, 1956. When Steve and Rusty open a U.S. marshal office in a lawless frontier town, they encounter opposition from several of the townspeople.

143.21 *Decision at Noon.* Feb. 11, 1956. Steve has to protect a sullen young thief from his cohorts, his family and an avenging Indian tribe.

143.22 *Missouri Outlaws.* Feb. 18, 1956. Steve Donovan and his partner Rusty are blocked in their attempt to capture the notorious Cantrell gang. The citizens in a small Texas cattle town are protecting the criminals because they believe they plan no harm. Steve, representing the law, antagonizes the residents, so Rusty, posing as a wealthy cattle buyer, tries to trick the Cantrells into revealing their true identity.

143.23 *Stone River.* Feb. 25, 1956. Assigned to investigate a counterfeiting gang in a southwest border town, Steve Donovan and Rusty discover an innocent widow running a dry goods store as a front for the counterfeiting activities.

143.24 *A Pair of Jacks.* March 3, 1956. Steve and Rusty are caught in a barrage of gunfire while protecting two outlaws from a lynch mob. A crooked mine owner is trying to pin the murder of his partner on the outlaws, who are guilty only of robbing the miners. Steve and Rusty believe the outlaws' story, but while taking them to the county jail, they are intercepted by the mob, which has been stirred up by the mine owner.

143.25 *Crystal Gazers.* March 10, 1956. Rusty has been studying ventriloquism, which he puts to a practical use with the help of the sister of a presumably murdered man. The man responsible for the murder realizes the setup is a trap and tries to escape.

143.26 *The Imposters.* March 17, 1956. Four white men, disguised as Indians, raid an Army wagon. Steve and Rusty try to avert an all-out Indian war.

143.27 *Outlaw's Boy.* March 24, 1956. When Steve and Rusty succeed in capturing the notorious Yarbo Gang, they find themselves responsible for a sixteen-year-old boy.

143.28 *The Hope Chest.* March 31, 1956. When a young boy's father dies, the lad finds a mail sack crammed with money among his father's possessions.

143.29 *The Coward.* April 7, 1956. A notorious killer breaks out of jail and sets out to kill the two men responsible for his imprisonment — Steve Donovan, who captured him, and Lou Park, who testified against him. Donovan heads for Park's home to warn him, not knowing that the murderer has already planted a time bomb in Park's house.

143.30 *Gunfighter's Return.* April 14, 1956. Steve Donovan tries to persuade a young gunman to give up his life of crime. The youth thinks his strength is greater than that of the law, but when a notorious gunman arrives in own, the boy gets to see which force is the strongest.

143.31 *Widow's Warrant.* April 21, 1956. A widow rancher has never believed in paying her taxes. Steve and Rusty are assigned to serve eviction papers on her. They find that her foreman has been helping her resist tax payments because he wants her evicted.

143.32 *Green Star.* April 28, 1956. A greenhorn marshal trying to live down a reputation for bad blood hits a rough trail when he rides out with Steve and Rusty.

143.33 *White Cloud.* May 5, 1956. Some peaceful Indians ask fo a loan to fiance land irrigation, but the banker refuses their application.

143.34 *The General.* May 12, 1956. In an attempt to sabotage government peace negotiations with the Apaches, a greedy land speculator plots to have the general in charge of the Office of Indian Affairs killed.

143.35 *Shadow of Fear.* May 19, 1956. Marshal Donovan and Rusty determine to revenge the murder of a fellow United States marshal and find themselves dealing with a woman outlaw who has terrorized an entire town.

143.36 *The Border Shift.* May 26, 1956. Cattlemen rout a gang of rustlers from their town, but refuse to help Marshal Donovan when the thieves relocate their operations across the border.

143.37 *Shadow Gold.* June 2, 1956. A young man, injured while rescuing some children from a runaway horse, suffers brain damage. Steve Donovan and Rusty Lee battle ignorance and prejudice when they try to arrange a vital brain operation for their friend.

143.38 *Poison Trail.* June 9, 1956. Marshal Donovan and Rusty find a half-dead youth who tells him that he has been framed for robbery and poisoned.

143.39 *Trail of the Dude.* June 16, 1956. Steve and Rusty trail a newly released convict on the hope that he will lead them to the gang he plans to join. But he is killed on his way to tie up with the new gang.

144. Stoney Burke

ABC. 60 min. Broadcast history: Monday, 9:00–10:00, Oct. 1962–Sept. 1963.

Regular Cast: Jack Lord (Stoney Burke), Bruce Dern (E.J. Stocker), Warren Oates (Ves Painter), Robert Dowdell (Cody Bristal), Bill Hart (Red).

Premise: This series depicted the exploits of rodeo rider Stoney Burke and his quest to win the Gold Buckle, the trophy awarded to the best saddle bronco buster in the world.

The Episodes

144.1 *The Contender.* Oct. 1, 1962. GS: Philip Abbott, Ruby Lee, Kate Manx. Stoney's ambitions to win the Gold Buckle, the trophy given to the world's champion saddle bronc rider, suffer a setback when he draws the meanest bronc in the rodeo and the horse throws him.

144.2 *Fight Night.* Oct. 8, 1962. GS: Alan Bunce, Edgar Buchanan, George Mitchell, Claudia Bryar, Bill Zuckert. The afternoon performance is over and the rodeo is ready to move on to Cade City. But a couple of thugs beat up Cody and issue a warning. There is only room enough in Cade City that night for one big event, and it is a prize fight and not a rodeo.

144.3 *Child of Luxury.* Oct. 15, 1962. GS: Judson Laire, Ina Balin, Eduard Franz, Charles Carlson, Dee J. Thomson. Wealthy young Sutton Meade, accustomed to getting what she wants, has her eye on Stoney. But it takes two to tango, and when the cowboy turns down her invitation to dance he has to face the music.

144.4 *Point of Honor.* Oct. 22, 1962. GS: Scott Marlowe, Patricia Breslin, Dean Stanton, Ben Johnson, Lew Brown, Ian Wolfe, Bill Millikin, Casey Tibbs. Local boy Soames Hewitt signs up to ride a Brahma at the rodeo, but Stoney and E.J. stop him when the notice that he is drunk. Soames regards this as an insult to his honor, so he sets out with a pistol to demand satisfaction.

144.5 *The Mob Riders.* Oct. 29, 1962. GS: Michael Parks, Bill Gunn, Gene Lyons, Ford Rainey, Denise Alexander. Clyde Lampert says that he wants Stoney to put on a rodeo, and offers to renovate the old town stadium for the event. But the teenage stock-car drives, who have been using the arena for auto races, claim that Lampert and the town council are just out to get them.

144.6 *A Matter of Pride.* Nov. 5, 1962. GS: William Windom, Ben Piazza, Jena Engstrom, Conrad Janis, Virginia Christine, George Mitchell. Everything is a matter of pride for Miller Hill, who insists on lashing himself so tightly to a mean Brahma bull that the animal kills him. Hill's son Dayton and the rest of the family are just as proud. They won't accept the money Stoney has collected to help tide them over.

144.7 *Sidewinder.* Nov. 12, 1962. GS: Edward Binns, Mark Miller, Strother Martin. Stoney is set to do some bronc-busting aboard a critter called Sidewinder, but the bronc does all the busting, crashing through a safety fence and into the crowd. Spectator Loreen Julian is injured and before Stoney knows it, he is slapped with a lawsuit.

144.8 *The Scavenger.* Nov. 19, 1962. GS: John Kellogg, Shirley Ballard, Paul Comi, Enoch Gates, Ray Glenn. The police arrest Ves and he admits that he got garage owner Howard Foley drunk, but not to rob him. Then the officers reveal that the charge is not robbery after all, but murder.

144.9 *Spin a Golden Web.* Nov. 26, 1962. GS: Robert Webber, Salome Jens, John Anderson, Ken Lynch, James Callahan, Mary Munday. Stoney and Bruce Austin are tied for first place in the saddle bronc event. Two of the spectators, land investors Roy Hazelton and Lyle Sweet, are so interested in the match that they make a wager of several million dollars on the outcome.

144.10 *The Wanderer.* Dec. 3, 1962. GS: Albert Salmi, Jacqueline Scott, Milton Selzer, Roy Engle, Lex Connelly, John Graham. Expectant mother Leora Dawson collapses on the rodeo grounds and tells Stoney that she won't go to the hospital. She insists that her husband be present when their child is born, but she doesn't know where he is.

144.11 *Five by Eight.* Dec. 10, 1962. GS: Ed Nelson, William Schallert, Bennye Gatteys, Joseph Perry, Mary Jackson, John McLiam. Nick Martin plans to escape from prison when the rodeo comes to entertain the convicts. A friend of Nick's on the outside has planted a gun in Stoney's gear and, while the cowboys are busting broncos, Nick plans to bust out of jail.

144.12 *Bandwagon.* Dec. 17, 1962. GS: Mariette Hartley, Larry Gates, Len Lesser, James Bell, Joan Chambers, Jean Carson. Stoney gets on the political bandwagon when Senator Lockridge, an old family friends asks him to make a few informal campaign speeches in his behalf. During a rally, Paul Grayson accuses the Senator of larceny and murder.

144.13 *Cousin Eunice.* Dec. 24, 1962. GS: Cloris Leachman, Jim Davis, George Mitchell, Jon Newton, Jo Marie Ward. E.J.'s ornery cousin Eunice, a far cry from a lady, suddenly demands that he help her become of the rodeo's glamorous feminine trick riders.

144.14 *Gold-Plated Maverick.* Jan. 7, 1963. GS: Michael Anderson, Jr., John Larch, Joe Maross, Maxine Stuart, S. John Launer, Buck Taylor. Wealthy Byron Latimer needs someone else's help to tame his wild teenage son David, and he thinks that Stoney is the man for the job. Stoney is willing, but it soon becomes clear that his manliness will not be enough to do the trick.

144.15 *Death Rides a Pale Horse.* Jan. 14, 1963. GS: Steve Cochran, Dyan Cannon, Geraldine Brooks, Ken Patterson. Mal Torrance is one bronc rider who wants to stand in the way of Stoney's advance toward the championship. But Stoney doesn't realize that Mal is actually emotionally disturbed.

144.16 *King of the Hill.* Jan. 21, 1963. GS: John Dehner, Leora Dana, Ted DeCorsia, Phil Chambers, Hugh Sanders, Allyson Ames, Dave Weaver. Former bronc rider Zack Mundorf and his wife Ellen invite Stoney for a visit to their home. Zack is in a boyish mood and wants to Indian wrestle, but Stoney realizes that Zack means to prove that he is champion of more than just these childhood games.

144.17 *A Matter of Percentage.* Jan. 28, 1963. GS: Jack Weston, Elizabeth MacRae, Robert Emhardt, Vito Scotti. Two gamblers, Sam Marigold and Harry Marsh, bet heavily on Stoney's match with a bronc buster named Trig. But Marsh likes a sure thing, so he asks Stoney to throw the match.

144.18 *Image of Glory.* Feb. 4, 1963. GS: Simon Oakland, Carol Rossen, Richard Evans, Dabbs Greer. Sam Hagen wants his son Jess to win the rodeo's All-Around Cowboy title at all costs, but Stoney knows that the boy has injured his knee, and one more fall may cripple him.

144.19 *Cat's Eyes*. Feb. 11, 1963. GS: Fay Spain, Robert Doyle, Breena Howard, Kathleen O'Malley, William Phipps. Young rodeo performer Doyle Yates has a terrible fear of Libby Ferris. He claims that she is a witch and that her enchantments caused his brothers accidental death.

144.20 *Webb of Fear*. Feb. 18, 1963. GS: Carroll O'Connor, Jeanne Cooper, Ted DeCorsia, John Milford, Hal Needham. Ves thinks that a series of accidents which have befallen Stoney are not accidental. When Stoney starts getting threatening phone calls, Ves' fears are confirmed.

144.21 *Point of Entry*. March 4, 1963. GS: Cesare Danova, Antoinette Bower, William Smith, Stefan Geirasch, Ben Wright. In Mexico for a rodeo, Stoney provides an alibi for lovely Erna Bremen, who has been arrested for the assassination of a mysterious European visitor. Now all he has to do is convince the police that he is telling the truth.

144.22 *To Catch the Kaiser*. March 11, 1963. GS: Diana Hyland, John Anderson, Jack Pearlman, Don LeMond, Bing Russell. Stoney receives two offers to catch the Kaiser, the wild stallion that crippled horsewoman Eileen Fowler. Eileen wants the stallion captured, but her father will double Stoney's fee if the horse is destroyed.

144.23 *Joby*. March 18, 1963. GS: Robert Duvall, Frank Overton, Joyce Van Patten, John Karlen, David Kent. Cowboy Joby Pierce heroically stops a robbery at the rodeo office. But when newsmen arrive, Joby appeals to Stoney. He doesn't want his name in the papers.

144.24 *Forget Me More*. March 25, 1963. GS: Laura Devon, William Sargent, Noah Keen, Lee Orlano, Kenneth Tobey. Stacy Morgan follows the rodeo wherever it goes in her search for her father, although she was a witness to his death several years ago.

144.25 *Color Him Lucky*. April 1, 1963. GS: Charles Robinson, Lin McCarthy, Judson Pratt, Frank Behrens, Tom Palmer. Brad Cullman is found innocent of a crime for which he has been serving a prison term and, after his release, he returns to the rodeo as a bronc-buster. But city officials won't let him participate, because he is a former convict.

144.26 *The Weapons Man*. April 8, 1963. GS: J.D. Cannon, Henry Silva, Pilar Seurat, William Douglas, Philip Ahn, James McCallion. At the rodeo archery exhibition, a Government official is fatally wounded by a stray arrow from the bow of Indian Matt Elder, who claims that it was an accident. Mark Vickers, an authority on the use of weapons, launches an investigation.

144.27 *Kelly's Place*. April 15, 1963. GS: Elizabeth Allen, Joe Maross, Vic Weber, Joan Staley, Diane Strom. Ves and the boys celebrate Stoney's birthday at a club called Kelly's Place, and Kelly, the bistro's half-owner and singing star, tells Stoney her troubles.

144.28 *Kincaid*. April 22, 1963. GS: Dick Clark, David Winters, Sarah Marshall, David Macklin, Gerald Trump, Craig Curtis, Mario Roccuzzo, Casey Tibbs, Harley May, Buck Taylor. Socialite Diane Banner wants youth worker Andy Kincaid to get his boys to sell charity tickets for the rodeo, but Andy says that it is up to the boys to decide.

144.29 *A Girl Named Amy*. April 29, 1963. GS: June Harding, Chris Robinson, Donald Woods, Peter Helm, Jack Grinnage. Stoney gladly accepts an invitation from his friend Dave Jenson to judge a college rodeo, but he runs into trouble. Jenson's 18-year-old daughter mistakes Stoney's affection toward her for romantic interest.

144.30 *Tigress by the Tail*. May 6, 1963. GS: Elizabeth Ashley, Edward Asner, Lex Connelly, Harry Carey, Jr., Michael Mikler, Schuyler Hayden. After the death of her father, Donna Weston assumes an attitude of reckless abandon which Stoney attributes to grief. Ves thinks it is just the real Donna showing through.

144.31 *The Test*. May 13, 1963. GS: Richard Eyer, Ivan Dixon, James Coburn, J. Pat O'Malley, Christine Burker. After he is trampled by a wild horse, Stoney can't move his legs. But the doctors can find no medical reason for his paralysis.

144.32 *The Journey*. May 20, 1963. GS: Mark Richman, Harry Swoger, Willis Bouchey. Stoney's injured hand takes him off the rodeo circuit, but Mr. Redmond offers him a chance to make some money by helping purchase stock for the slaughterhouse.

145. *Stories of the Century*

Syndicated. 30 min. Broadcast history: Various, Jan. 1954–March 1955.

Regular Cast: Jim Davis (Matt Clark), Mary Castle (Frankie Adams), Kristine Miller (Jonsey Jones).

Premise: This series depicted the exploits of Matt Clark, a detective for the Southwestern Railroad, in the West of the 1890s.

The Episodes

145.1 *Belle Starr*. Jan. 23, 1954. GS: Marie Windsor, Ric Roman, Steve Darrell, Stuart Randall. When a herd of U.S. Cavalry horses is stolen, rail detective Matt Clark is summoned to solve the crime. He learns that the leader of the outlaws is a woman with a fancy plumed hat.

145.2 *Billy the Kid*. Jan. 30, 1954. GS: Richard Jaeckel, Richard Travis, Alex Montoya, John Cason, Duane Thorsen, Fred Coby. Matt Clark and Frankie Adams set out on the trail of cattle rustlers led by one of the West's youngest and most notorious outlaws.

145.3 *Frank and Jesse James*. Feb. 7, 1954. GS: Lee Van Cleef, Richard Travis, Frank Dae, Tyler McVey, Rand Brooks, Tyler MacDuff. The vengeful James brothers wage a retaliative war against the law for the death of their half-brother, killed in a police ambush.

145.4 *Geronimo*. Feb. 14, 1954. GS: Chief Yowlachie, Pat Hogan, Brett King, Emile Meyer, Robert Shayne. It is rail detective Clark's job to take a night watchman, who was attacked during a freight-car robbery, to identify the Apaches captured for the crime.

145.5 *Quantrill and His Raiders*. Feb. 21, 1954. GS: Bruce Bennett, Ric Roman, Steve Darrell, Bill Hudson, Lyle Talbot, Al Bridge. Matt Clark, serving with the Union Army as a spy, is assigned to obtain information about Quantrill, the guerrilla-band leader who claims to be for the Confederate Army.

145.6 *Cattle Kate*. Feb. 28, 1954. GS: Jean Parker, James

Seay, Tom Monroe, Herbert Heyes, Francis McDonald, Gil Harman. Rail detective Matt Clark poses as a crooked trail boss in his efforts to elicit a confession of murder from Wyoming's notorious cattle rustler, Cattle Kate.

145.7 *Sam Bass.* March 4, 1954. GS: Don Haggerty, Denver Pyle, Dennis Moore, James Anderson, Alan Wells, Earle Hodgins, Don Harvey, Larry Hudson, Chris Mitchell, Stuart Whitman. When Sam Bass and his gang steal $60,000 in a robbery, rail detective Matt Clark follows the robbers into the swampland.

145.8 *Johnny Ringo.* March 11, 1954. GS: Donald Curtis, Harry Lauter, Emlyn Davies, Gregg Barton, Ralph Sanford, Lee Roberts. When a construction payroll of 10,000 silver dollars is stolen from Southwest Railroad, Matt Clark is called in.

145.9 *The Dalton Gang.* March 18, 1954. GS: Myron Healey, Fess Parker, Robert Bray, John Mooney, James F. Stone, Robert Foulk, Keith Richards, George Selk. When the Dalton brothers turn in their badges and shift from the side of the law to lawlessness, railroads, banks and stagelines are in danger.

145.10 *Doc Holliday.* March 25, 1954. GS: Kim Spalding, Frank Richards, Harry Harvey, George Eldredge, James Craven. Holliday leads a double life as friend and foe of the law. Matt Clark and his assistant attempt to end Doc's two-faced, two-fisted, career.

145.11 *The Younger Brothers.* April 2, 1954. GS: Sheb Wooley, George Wallace, Louise Beavers, John Merrick, Paul McGuire, Clarence Straight, Roy Gordon, Gregory Walcott, Ken Carlton. Rail detective Matt Clark and his assistant try to get proof of the Younger Brothers' participation in a bank robbery. Frankie Adams poses as a country cousin from Virginia when she pays a visit to the Younger Brothers' home.

145.12 *John Wesley Hardin.* April 9, 1954. GS: Richard Webb, Howard Negley, Paul Keast, John Pickard, Robert Karnes, John Eldredge, Abel Fernandez. At 25, John Wesley Hardin had killed forty men. His fabulous life carried him from lawlessness to a career as a respected lawyer. But Hardin couldn't resist the outlaw's life. Matt Clark is called in after a cattle theft and a murder are committed in Abilene.

145.13 *Joaquin Murieta.* April 16, 1954. GS: Rick Jason, Bob Anderson, Charlita, John Gifford. Joaquin Murieta, the outlaw scourge of the California goldfields, kills men in cold blood, but has a weakness for girls. Matt Clark and his assistant, Frankie Adams, set out to capture him.

145.14 *Tiburcio Vasquez.* April 23, 1954. GS: Anthony Caruso, Lillian Molieri, Glenn Strange, Edward Colmans, Eddie Parker, Frank Hagney. Tiburcio Vasquez follows the vengeance trail and kills Americanos, because brawling Americans were responsible for his sister's death.

145.15 *Chief Crazy Horse.* April 30, 1954. GS: George Keymas, Chubby Johnson, John Holland, Alma Beltran. A Sioux chief leads a massive uprising in the Nebraska area. Matt Clark is called in after the U.S. Army, local Indian agents and the government have failed to subdue the Sioux.

145.16 *Black Bart.* May 6, 1954. GS: Arthur Space, Frank Sully, Sammy Ogg, I. Stanford Jolley, William Tannen, Victor Sen Yung, Frank Jaquet. A notorious gentleman-outlaw always rides alone on his missions of robbery and murder. Rail detective Matt Clark is sent to find the dangerous dandy.

145.17 *Henry Plummer.* May 13, 1954. GS: John Dehner, Bill Kennedy, Lane Bradford, Mike Ragan, Kristine Miller, Hal Baylor, George D. Barrows. Henry Plummer is elected sheriff on his promise of honesty and law enforcement. Little do the people realize that, in the space of eight months, he and his outlaw gang will be responsible for the deaths of 103 people.

145.18 *Bill Longley.* May 20, 1954. GS: Douglas Kennedy, Marlo Dwyer, Fred Coby, John Halloran, Harry Hayden. Bill Longley escapes from jail after conviction for robbery and murder. His loot has been railroad moneyh, so Matt Clark is assigned to the case. Matt knows of Bill's love for a circus trapeze artist. Find her and they may find Longley and his loot.

145.19 *Harry Tracy.* May 27, 1954. GS: Steve Brodie, Richard Avonde, Helen Wallace, Edward Clark, Gene Roth. A member of his own gang tips off rail detective Clark as to the whereabouts of psychopathic killer Harry Tracy. Even his former friends can't stand his brutality and needless killings.

145.20 *Wild Bunch of Wyoming.* June 3, 1954. GS: Joe Sawyer, Slim Pickens, Lane Chandler, Bob Carney. A jokester alerts Matt Clark to his activities when he signs the names of past and present greats to $30,000 worth of stolen bank notes.

145.21 *The Doolin Gang.* June 10, 1954. GS: Leo Gordon, Joan Shawlee, Kenneth MacDonald, Don Kennedy, Pat Waltz, Ken Chryson. Frankie thoroughly confuses outlaw leader Bill Doolin with her pose as the widow of one of his slain men.

145.22 *Little Britches.* June 17, 1954. GS: Robert Livingston, Gloria Winters, James Best, Tyler McVey, Bruce Payne, Norman Field. A girl turns outlaw in order to follow her outlaw lover in Oklahoma.

145.23 *Black Jack Ketchum.* June 24, 1954. GS: Jack Elam, Michael Hall, Mitchell Kowal, Jean Inness, Zon Murray, Otis Garth, Charles Horvath. A mother's fears for her son, who has run off to join the notorious Ketchum gang, help Matt Clark track down the outlaws.

145.24 *Tom Horn.* July 1, 1954. GS: Louis Jean Heydt, Stanley Andrews, Harry Woods, Michael Whalen, Walter Coy, Chuck Courtney, Clay Randolph. Matt Clark and Frankie tackle the case of a color-blind cattle detective who turns killer during a Wyoming range war.

145.25 *Ben Thompson.* July 8, 1954. GS: Richard Simmons, Howard Wright, Claire Carleton, Mauritz Hugo, Douglas Evans. A baby-faced gunman starts the biggest fire that Texas ever had as part of a gigantic wheatfield swindle.

145.26 *Clay Allison.* July 15, 1954. GS: Jack Kelly, Paul Farber, Fred Sherman, Willard Sage, George Taylor, Frank Fenton. Clay Allison andhis brother John, Confederate soldiers in whom Yankee defeat breeds a desire for revenge, terrorize the Southwest.

Season Two

145.27 *Burt Alvord.* Jan. 2, 1955. GS: Christian Drake, Howard Wright, Kathleen Mulqueen, Fran Bennett, Paul Sorenson. A notorious outlaw manages to cover up his crimes because he is the son of a sheriff until Matt Clark gets on his trail.

145.28 *The Apache Kid.* Jan. 9, 1955. GS: Kenneth Alton, Kenneth MacDonald, Pilar del Rey. An Indian youth, who has been trained and trusted by the U.S. Army Chief of Scouts, embarks on a path of crime and destruction.

145.29 *Tom Bell.* Jan. 16, 1955. GS: Glen Gordon, Robert Malcolm, John Beradino, Jeanne Dean, Edythe Elliott, Rankin Mansfield, George Meader, Stanley Blystone, Stuart Whitman. While helping a mother find her long-lost doctor son, Matt and Jonesy come upon the trail of a famous gunman.

145.30 *Kate Bender.* Jan. 23, 1955. GS: Veda Ann Borg, Kay E. Kuter, Peter Brocco, Hal K. Dawson, Butler Hixson, Corey Allen, Slim Pickens. Kate Bender and her half-witted brother go undetected as they lure victims to their farmhouse, and rob and kill them.

145.31 *Augustine Chacon.* Jan. 30, 1955. GS: Rodolfo Hoyos, Alan Reynolds, Keith Richards, Laurette Luez, Will White, Felipe Turich, Tony Roux, Dehl Berti. A handsome Mexican bandit conducts a crime-rampage without interruption until he starts to use the rails to dispose of his victims.

145.32 *Cherokee Bill.* Feb. 1, 1955. GS: Pat Hogan, Robert Burton, Frank Sully, Brad Johnson, Lisa Fusaro, Pierre Watkin, Dennis Moore, Chris Mitchell, James F. Stone. A young Oklahoma half-breed with a deep hatred for white men, embarks on a life of crime after he is expelled from college on suspicion of petty thievery. Railroad-detective Matt Clark and his female assistant Jonesy go after him when he tries to rob a wagon train.

145.33 *Nate Champion.* Feb. 6, 1955. GS: Henry Brandon, Lisa Daniels, Damian O'Flynn, Robert B. Williams, Don Kennedy, Gene Roth, Paul E. Burns. An embezzling Englishman, his criminally trained young daughter and a cattle rustler combine forces to wreak havoc upon Wyoming cattle ranches.

145.34 *Sontag and Evans.* Feb. 8, 1955. GS: John Smith, Howard Negley, Morris Ankrum, Claudia Barrett, Carl Christian. Two men wage a campaign of robbery and sabotage against the railroads of California's San Joaquin Valley.

145.35 *Rube Burrows.* Feb. 15, 1955. GS: Paul Picerni, Jean Willes, Norman Leavitt, Terry Frost, Ralph Sanford, Earle Hodgins, Bob Carney, Frank Jaquet, Watson Downs. Matt and Jonesy are assigned to track down Rube Burrows, a thief with dramatic flair who has pulled off a daring rail robbery, and try to locate him through his favorite girlfriend.

145.36 *Jim Courtright.* Feb. 22, 1955. GS: Robert Knapp, Rory Mallinson, Vernon Rich, Fred Sherman, Daniel White, Wally Cassell, Lee Roberts. Matt Clark comes to Fort Worth, Texas, to investigate a gunslinging ex-marshal who kills those who refuses his offers of protection.

145.37 *Milt Sharp.* Feb. 28, 1955. GS: Don Barry, William Tannen, Harry Antrim, Harry Woods, George Taylor, Edith Evanson, Willa Pearl Curtis. An escaped highwayman and a fellow convict, a murderer, stop a stagecoach and kidnap a banker riding in it. Because the coach was a connection between railroads, the case falls under the jurisdiction of Matt Clark.

145.38 *Jack Slade.* March 4, 1955. GS: Elaine Riley, Gregg Palmer, Harry Harvey, Jr., Paul Newlan, Pierce Lyden, George Eldredge. A man tops his life of crime by getting a job with the Pony Express. There, he can get information on shipments of cash and bullion. When the information leads him to a shipment of railroad money, Matt and his assistant are assigned to find him and the loot.

145.39 *Musgrove.* March 11, 1955. GS: John Archer, Rod Williams, James Craven, Jack Shea, Charles Evans, Jack Daly. A clever and unscrupulous manipulator develops a huge fortune with his plans for wholesale cattle thievery. Matt Clark is assigned to investigate him when horses are found missing from the railroad's corral.

146. *Sugarfoot*

ABC. 60 min. Broadcast history: Tuesday, 7:30–8:30, Sept. 1957–Sept. 1960, Monday, 7:30–8:30, Oct. 1960–July 1961.

Regular Cast: Will Hutchins (Tom Brewster).

Premise: This series chronicled the adventures of Tom Brewster, who is known as Sugarfoot, a nickname denoting one grade lower than a tenderfoot.

Notes: *Sugarfoot* alternated with *Cheyenne* during its first two seasons. It alternated with *Bronco* as part of the *Cheyenne Show* during its third season, and alternated with both *Bronco* and *Cheyenne* during its final season.

The Episodes

146.1 *Brannigan's Boots.* Sept. 17, 1957. GS: Dennis Hopper, Merry Anders, Arthur Hunnicutt, Chubby Johnson. Tom Brewster heads for the town of Bluerock in search of a post office. But in Bluerock he finds a local celebration going on and enters a shooting contest. His aim is so bad that the crooked politicians decide Tom is a likely replacement for their late sheriff and promptly pin a badge on him. Tom, however, takes the job seriously and walks into the sheriff's office to look things over. Now that he has a job he needs a new pair of boots and he spies a pair standing against the wall. He puts them on and feels he is all set for the job of sheriff. But a pretty girl who has been watching him calls him a Sugarfoot, and says he's not man enough to fill her late father's boots. In an attempt to prove her wrong, Tom finds himself on the trail of her father's killer.

146.2 *Reluctant Hero.* Oct. 1, 1957. Sugarfoot takes a job with a rancher, unaware that his new employer is involved in a range war. Then he learns that the owner of the rival ranch is an attractive young lady.

146.3 *The Strange Land.* Oct. 15, 1957. GS: Morris Ankrum, Rhodes Reason, Jan Chaney. An elderly rancher, bitter at the world, uses a gunman as a means of avenging himself. Sugarfoot attempts to stop the gunman's reign of terror, but first must talk to the old man.

146.4 *Bunch Quitter.* Oct. 29, 1957. GS: Ray Danton. When a trail boss is shot by outlaws, Sugarfoot is appointed to lead a cattle drive to a secret destination. The cattle-owner's daughter reveals this destination to a charming cowboy who then joins the rustlers in an ambush.

146.5 *Trail's End.* Nov. 12, 1957. GS: Venetia Stevenson, Chris Alcaide. Reunited with his childhood sweetheart, Sugarfoot is disappointed to learn that she is now a dance-hall queen. She tells Sugarfoot that she is trying to break away from this life, but a ruthless cattle baron intends to force her to marry him.

146.6 *Quicksilver.* Nov. 26, 1957. GS: John Litel, Fay Spain, Frank Wilcox, Nestor Paiva, Richard Crane. Sugarfoot comes to the aid of a silver-mine owner who can't meet his payroll because he has been robbed.

146.7 *Misfire.* Dec. 10, 1957. GS: Connie Stevens, Frank

Albertson, Eve Brent, Pernell Roberts. Mercy Preston schemes to use Sugarfoot to dispose of two men who stand between her and the possession of a rich mine. Her sister Patience attempts to help Sugarfoot.

146.8 *The Stallion Trail.* Dec. 24, 1957. GS: Paul Birch, Patrick Waltz, Will Wright, Carol Kelly. While out in the mountains Sugarfoot captures a wild horse. Later the horse is stolen from him and sold to a rancher. Sugarfoot takes a job as a stablehand in order to take care of the animal and to expose the horse thief.

146.9 *Small War at Custer Junction.* Jan. 7, 1958. GS: Jean Carson, Reba Waters, Karl Swenson. Sugarfoot rescues a girl after claim jumpers kill her miner father.

146.10 *Bullet Proof.* Jan. 21, 1958. GS: Joi Lansing, Gregory Walcott, Guinn Williams, Donald "Red" Barry, Richard Reeves, Dick Rich. In an attempt to trap the robbers, Sugarfoot pretends to know the whereabouts of a haul made in a bank robbery.

146.11 *Deadlock.* Feb. 4, 1958. GS: Herbert Heyes, John Vivyan, William Schallert, Oliver McGowan. Sugarfoot, who has been studying law by correspondence, is tricked into serving as a juror in a crime case in which his own employer is the plaintiff. As the trial progresses, Sugarfoot comes to the realization that some of the evidence being presented is phony.

146.12 *Man Wanted.* Feb. 18, 1958. GS: Anna-Lisa, Charles Bronson, Pernell Roberts, Mort Mills. A friend of Sugarfoot's decides to write to Sweden for a mail-order bride. Convinced that he isn't good-looking enough to attract a young lady, he sends along Sugarfoot's picture instead of his own.

146.13 *The Dead Hills.* March 4, 1958. GS: Ruta Lee, Veda Ann Borg, Michael Dante, Lane Bradford, Duane Grey. Sugarfoot's boss, Lucy Barron, tells him that there is a large sum of money owing on her ranch and that it's threatened with foreclosure. Sugarfoot determines to protect his employer's interest.

146.14 *A Wreath for Charity Lloyd.* March 18, 1958. GS: Erin O'Brien, Charles Cooper, James Philbrook, Mike Monahan, Harry Harvey, Sr. Sugarfoot, as acting sheriff, is asked to help find a woman's missing husband. When he finds the man, he realizes that he is a wanted outlaw who must be taken into custody.

146.15 *Hideout.* April 1, 1958. GS: Paul Fix, Anita Gordon, Peter Brown. A group of teenagers decide to become bandits. Sugarfoot tries to help the sister of one of the youngsters who wants to keep her brother from a life of crime.

146.16 *Guns for Big Bear* (A.K.A. "Contraband Cargo"). April 15, 1958. GS: Lisa Montell, Ted de Corsia, Gerald Mohr, Bing Russell. A pretty Indian girl guides Sugarfoot as he drives a wagonload of supplies to a Pawnee village. But he doesn't realize just what cargo he's carrying.

146.17 *Price on His Head.* April 29, 1958. GS: Patrick McVey, Dorothy Green, Karl Swenson, Venetia Stevenson, Virginia Gregg. Four stagecoach passengers are kidnaped by masked bandits and held hostage. Sugarfoot is dispatched to raise the ransom money.

146.18 *Short Range.* May 13, 1958. GS: Erin O'Brien, Myron Healey, Olive Sturgess, Sammy Jackson, Stephen Ellsworth, Anna Maria Nanasi, Lane Chandler, Slim Pickens, George O'Hanlon. Sugarfoot is on the trail of a renegade who is selling guns to the Indians. Learning that his quarry is connected with a traveling puppet show, Sugarfoot joins the show.

146.19 *The Bullet and the Cross.* May 27, 1958. GS: Charles Bronson, Stuart Randall, Robert Wark. After a mine cave-in, Sugarfoot is trapped with a half-breed Indian who has been accused of murder. The man tells Sugarfoot that he has been wrongly accused and that he hid in the mine to escape from the lawmen hunting him.

146.20 *Mule Team.* June 10, 1958. GS: Don Haggerty, Elaine Janssen. When Sugarfoot inherits a mine and a mule team he is hard put to realize any value from them. He begins to build a railroad spur to work the mine but is blocked by a man who wants to gain control of the mine.

Season Two

146.21 *Ring of Sand.* Sept. 16, 1958. GS: John Russell, Edward Byrnes, Will Wright. An elderly frontiersman becomes embittered when his only son is killed by bandits. He forces Sugarfoot to help him lead the gunmen into the desert in search of a non-existent waterhold.

146.22 *Brink of Fear.* Sept. 30, 1958. GS: Jerry Paris, Venetia Stevenson, Allen Case, Harry Antrim, Lane Chandler, Don Gordon. An old friend of Sugarfoot's is paroled from prison and Sugarfoot tries to help him. Then the deputy marshal, jealous because Sugarfoot's friend is winning the affections of the prettiest girl in town, decides to frame him.

146.23 *The Wizard.* Oct. 14, 1958. GS: Efrem Zimbalist, Jr., Norma Moore, Edward Kemmer, Paul Keast, Oliver McGowan, Jon Lormer, Beverly Gowan. A traveling magician, who is also an accomplished hypnotist, hypnotizes his assistant and orders her to set fire and to name Sugarfoot as the arsonist. After the fire the irate townspeople, hearing Sugarfoot is responsible for the blaze, decide to lynch him.

146.24 *The Ghost.* Oct. 28, 1958. GS: Tommy Rettig, Edward Kemmer, Gail Kobe, Michael Pate. Sugarfoot is given the assignment of taking a teenager to Missouri to collect the boy's inheritance. Enroute, Sugarfoot learns that the boy is violent and is also suspected of a murder.

146.25 *The Canary Kid.* Nov. 11, 1958. GS: Frank Albertson, Lonie Blackman, Saundra Edwards, Donald "Red" Barry, Yvonne Shubert, Stuart Randall. A notorious gunman learns that he and Sugarfoot are almost doubles. He kidnaps Sugarfoot and prepares to impersonate him in order to carry out a bank robbery.

146.26 *The Hunted.* Nov. 25, 1958. GS: Michael Lane, Sue George, R.G. Armstrong, Francis DeSales. Sugarfoot makes friends with a wounded soldier. He does not know that the man is mentally unbalanced and is being sought by lawmen as a killer.

146.27 *Yampa Crossing.* Dec. 9, 1958. GS: Harold J. Stone, Brian Hutton, Roger Smith, Sam Buffington, Earle Hodgins. Sugarfoot sets out to find a notorious outlaw whose signature is wanted by a Kansas City law firm. Sugarfoot finds the outlaw, but soon learns that there are other men in the area who want to capture him for the price on his head.

146.28 *Devil to Pay.* Dec. 23, 1958. GS: Tol Avery, Grace Raynor, John Carradine, H.M. Wynant. Sugarfoot's life is threatened when he discovers the secret behind a strange Indian ritual.

Sugarfoot

146.29 *The Desperadoes.* Jan. 6, 1959. GS: Jack Kruschen, Anthony George, Abby Dalton, Richard Garland, Eugene Martin, Neyle Morrow. While visiting his friend Padre John at a mission school in Texas, Sugarfoot learns of a plot to kill Mexico's President Benito Juarez.

146.30 *The Extra Hand.* Jan. 20, 1959. GS: Karl Swenson, Anthony Caruso, Jack Lambert. In exchange for a horse and provisions, Sugarfoot agrees to travel with Alex Sharlakov, a former Russian seaman. After reaching Kansas, Sharlakov takes Sugarfoot to a ghost mining town, where the Russian looks for two men who had attempted to kill him.

146.31 *The Return of the Canary Kid.* Feb. 3, 1959. GS: Wayde Preston, Saundra Edwards, Donald "Red" Barry, Doye O'Dell, Richard Reeves. Tom Brewster and Christopher Colt joins forces in an attempt to capture a gang of outlaws. Brewster disguises himself as the infamous Canary Kid and makes contact with the outlaws. Then the real Kid escapes from prison and heads for the gang's hideout.

146.32 *The Mysterious Stranger.* Feb. 17, 1959. GS: Adam West. While working in a mine office as a clerk, Tom learns that the mine owner's lawyer is in collusion with the superintendent in swindling the firm and workers.

146.33 *The Giant Killer.* March 3, 1959. GS: R.G. Armstrong, Patricia Barry, Jay North, John Litel, Jonathan Kidd, Joan Camden, Dorothy Provine. A young widow, angered by a rumor which links her to the town's political boss, threatens to blow up a hotel. Sugarfoot tries to disprove the rumors in order to save the hotel and its occupants.

146.34 *The Royal Raiders.* March 17, 1959. GS: Helmut Dantine, Jacqueline Beer, Joe de Santis, Dennis Patrick, Betty Lynn. Attractive French emissary Yvette Marveux entrusts Sugarfoot with a fortune in diamonds. Traveling by train, the two find their trip interrupted by a group of European military men who want the diamonds.

146.35 *The Mountain.* March 31, 1959. GS: Don Dubbins, Miranda Jones, Rosa Rey. Tom Brewster searches for Vic Bradley and his Indian wife, who are hiding out in a mountain area that is supposed to be haunted. Brewster has evidence which may clear Bradley of a murder charge.

146.36 *The Twister.* April 14, 1959. GS: Don Dubbins, Stephen Talbot, Fred Beir, Betty Lynn, Wendy Winkelman, Robin Warge, Tom Brown. Bank robber Sid Garvin has forced his brother, a schoolteacher, to hold money he has stolen. When Garvin comes to collect his money, he holds Sugarfoot and three schoolchildren as hostages.

146.37 *The Vultures.* April 28, 1959. GS: Faith Domergue, Alan Marshall, Richard Long, Philip Ober, Roy Engel. Along the trail, Sugarfoot comes upon a young woman wandering in a daze and takes her to a nearby fort. Sugarfoot finds that the fort has recently been attacked by Indians and its sole inhabitant is an officer who had been jailed on charges of desertion.

146.38 *The Avengers.* May 12, 1959. GS: Steve London, Luana Anders, Richard Cutting, Vito Scotti, Dorothy Provine, Edgar Stehli. Tom Brewster and a convicted murderer called Pike are passengers on the same stagecoach when a sudden storm forces all the travelers to take shelter. While the travelers wait in a deserted cathedral, Pike's guard is shot. Sugarfoot traces the sniper to an abandoned mine shaft.

146.39 *Small Hostage.* May 26, 1959. GS: Robert Warwick, Gary Hunley, Jay Novello, Rodolfo Acosta, Joan Lora. Sugarfoot travels with Col. Cyrus Craig toward Mexico, where they are to claim the corpse of the colonel's son. En route, they are stopped by a gang of blackmailers.

146.40 *Wolf.* June 9, 1959. GS: Wright King, Judy Nugent, Virginia Gregg, Ted de Corsia, William Fawcett, Frank Ferguson. Sugarfoot is working as a ranch foreman for a widow. When some of the cattle are stolen and evidence point to Wolf Wilkes, Tom comes to Wolf's defense.

Season Three

146.41 *The Trial of the Canary Kid.* Sept. 15, 1959. GS: Wayde Preston, Peter Brown, Ty Hardin, Frances Bavier, Adam West, Lisa Gaye, Donald "Red" Barry. The Canary Kid, Sugarfoot's cousin and bitter enemy, is charged with murder and is in need of legal advice. Sugarfoot's Aunt Nancy uses a gun to force him to take the case.

146.42 *The Wild Bunch.* Sept. 29, 1959. GS: Ray Danton, Connie Stevens, Troy Donahue. Sugarfoot rides into Morgan's Ford, a seemingly quiet and friendly town, and takes a job as schoolteacher. He soon learns that the townspeople are fighting over water rights and living in fear of a gang of young toughs who are his pupils.

146.43 *MacBrewster the Bold.* Oct. 13, 1959. GS: Myron Healey, Robin Hughes, Tudor Owen, Alan Caillou. The citizens of a rough frontier town appoint Tom Brewster as sheriff. The same day three of Tom's relatives arrive to heap another honor on the unsuspecting cowboy. Dougal, Angus and Wee Rabbie MacBrewster have traveled from Scotland to proclaim Tom chief of their clan. When Ben Cadigan and his gang attempt to hold up the bank, Sugarfoot's visiting relatives come to the aid of the chief.

146.44 *The Gitanos.* Oct. 27, 1959. GS: Suzanne Lloyd, Henry Lascoe. Tom Brewster rescues a Gypsy girl and soon finds that the young lady has marriage on her mind. The Gypsy chief looks on Tom with disfavor and the cowboy must contend with a vengeful Gypsy rival.

146.45 *The Canary Kid, Inc.* Nov. 10, 1959. GS: Wayde Preston, Fredd Wayne. Government agent Chris Colt suspects that recent prison breaks have been supervised by the Canary Kid, an imprisoned outlaw. Colt asks Sugarfoot to take the Kid's place in prison.

146.46 *Outlaw Island.* Nov. 24, 1959. GS: Merry Anders, Gerald Mohr, Lisa Montell, Henry Lascoe, Robert Bray, William Bryant, Jon Lormer, Francis de Sales, Martin Garralaga, Paul Fierro. Tom Brewster wants to free Sally Ormand, who is a prisoner of the Baron, ruler of an island. Learning that the islanders are ready to revolt, Tom sparks the uprising.

146.47 *Apollo with a Gun.* Dec. 8, 1959. GS: Mari Blanchard, Joe Sawyer, Clinton Sundberg, Ken Clark, Billy M. Greene, Eric Sinclair, Frank Nechero. Tom Brewster is caught between a famous actress' request that he find her lost stallion, and a killer's promise of death if he does.

146.48 *The Gaucho.* Dec. 22, 1959. GS: Carlos Rivas, Lori Nelson, Richard Rust. Tom Brewster meets Curro Santiago, who is romancing Ellen Conway, despite her brother's opposition. When Santiago is held for a murder that he didn't commit, Tom tries to help his new friend.

146.49 *Journey to Provision.* Jan. 5, 1960. GS: Mort Mills, Maurice Manson. A mayor and a sheriff offer Tom Brewster a bribe to leave town. Tom, realizing that he has been taken for a government investigator, attempts to discover what the two men are so eager to hide.

146.50 *The Highbinder.* Jan. 19, 1960. GS: H.T. Tsiang, James Hong, Don Haggerty, Judy Dan, Larry Blake, William Yip. An elderly Chinese asks Tom Brewster to help him deliver an urn containing his son's ashes to San Francisco. But the urn holds more than ashes, it's also got the map of a gold mine also.

146.51 *Wolf Pack.* Feb. 2, 1960. GS: Richard Coogan, Susan Crane, Richard Garland. A pack of wolves kill three people, one of them a friend of Tom Brewster's. Perplexed by the incident, Tom moves in with his dead friend's family.

146.52 *Fernando.* Feb. 16, 1960. GS: Pat Comiskey, Nico Minardos, Merritt Bohn, Harry Bellaver. If he defeats the boxing champ, Fernando will use his winnings to save an old mission. But Fernando and his trainer find they've taken on more than just a bout—a local gambler is after the land the mission is built on.

146.53 *Blackwater Swamp.* March 1, 1960. GS: Robert Colbert, George Wallace, Kasey Rogers, Chuck Essegian. Tom Brewster tries to bring an estranged father and son together. His efforts, however, ar undermined by the father's new wife, who is willing to commit murder to get control of her husband's property.

146.54 *Return to Boot Hill.* March 15, 1960. GS: Gary Vinson, Alan Hewitt, Diane McBain, Hanley Stafford. Mayor Plummer agrees to help Tom Brewster clear a young man of a murder charge. But Tom gets suspicious when he learns about the mayor's connection with the defendant's sister.

146.55 *Vinegaroom.* March 29, 1960. GS: Richard Devon, Frank Ferguson, Ric Roman, Eugene Iglesias, Brad Weston, Don C. Harvey. Townsfolk welcome Tom Brewster to town by charging him with murder and sentencing him to the gallows. But Judge Roy Bean is a fan of actress Lily Langtry, and Tom tries to take advantage of this to save his neck.

146.56 *The Corsican.* April 12, 1960. GS: Mala Powers, Harry Shannon, Paul Picerni. Tom Brewster helps a New Englander and his daughter take a wounded Corsican to the trading post for help. But there is no assistance waiting, only a warlike band of Sioux.

146.57 *Blue Bonnet Stray.* April 26, 1960. GS: Alan Baxter, Janet De Gore, Wynn Pearce, Dolores Donlon, Douglas Kennedy, Charles Fredericks. As the train pulls out, Tom Brewster notices that an infant is on board, but its mother is still in the station. He returns the child, unaware that he is bringing it closer to death.

146.58 *The Long Dry.* April 10, 1960. GS: Jennifer West, Francis J. McDonald, Robert Armstrong, John McCann. Jericho Dooley's town is plagued by drought. But he is determined to float off in his ark, taking Tom Brewster and Anne Carmody with him.

146.59 *Funeral at Forty Mile.* May 24, 1968. GS: Donald May, Kent Taylor, John Qualen, Louise Fletcher. Tom Brewster arrives in town to help his cousin fun for office. Soon, some strange things start happening. The local hanging tree is struck by lightning, and an empty coffin is left in the middle of the street.

146.60 *The Captive Locomotive.* June 7, 1960. GS: Jeanne Cooper, Horace MacMahon, Rex Reason, Dan Sheridan. As Sugarfoot comes on the scene, a railroad is gobbling up land in a Western valley, forcing out the landowners.

Season Four

146.61 *Shadow Catcher.* Sept. 26, 1960. Sugarfoot becomes involved with an army officer who is trying to provoke a war with the Indians to get land that is rich in gold.

146.62 *A Noose for Nora.* Oct. 24, 1960. GS: Madlyn Rhue, Robert Colbert, Charles Arnt, Tristram Coffin. Tom "Sugarfoot" Brewster sees Nora Sutton shoot down a wealthy landowner. But Judge Lawson names Brewster to be her defense attorney.

146.63 *Man from Medora.* Nov. 21, 1960. GS: Albert Carrier, Peter Breck, Ray Walker, Jean Blake, Dorothea Lord, John Milford, Mickey Simpson, Roscoe Ates. When Jake Sloane can't take the measure of a dude named Theodore in a barbershop brawl, Sugarfoot decides to find out more about the dude. One thing he finds out is that his last name is Roosevelt.

146.64 *Welcome Enemy.* Dec. 26, 1960. GS: Glenn Strange, Suzanne Lloyd, J. Edward McKinley, Hal Torey, Gregg Palmer, Janet Lake, Bruce Gordon, Bob Wiensko, Grady Sutton. Chief Red Wing of the Sioux Indians is on his way to Chicago for a conference with President Grant. Sugarfoot has been hired to accompany the chief to see that he doesn't get assassinated.

146.65 *Toothy Thompson.* Jan. 16, 1961. GS: Jack Elam, John Marley, Stephen Courtleigh, Gregory Morton. John Brice is in town to investigate charges of corruption. When someone tries to murder Brice, Toothy Thompson, a long-time troublemaker, is jailed as a suspect.

146.66 *Shepherd with a Gun.* Feb. 6, 1961. GS: Raoul De Leon, Regis Toomey, Rafael Campos, Don Haggerty, Nancy Hadley. John Peel, a greedy rancher, tries to use grazing land belonging to a shepherd named Joachin. The shepherd can't defend his property, but his son Pablo can, and he's got a gun to help him.

146.67 *Angel.* March 6, 1961. GS: Ty Hardin, Cathy O'Donnell, Jack Elam, Bruce Gordon, John Pickard, Frank Albertson, Ann Robinson, Percy Helton, Max Baer, Charles Fredericks, John Cason. Sugarfoot and his pal Toothy Thompson don't mind helping out Sheriff Boyce with a gang of killers, but they would like to know just who the leader of the gang is.

146.68 *Stranger in Town.* March 27, 1961. GS: Jacques Aubuchon, Stephen Lander, Erika Peters. Sugarfoot loads the bodies of two murderers onto a horse and brings them into town. Although the killers shot each other, the townspeople are convinced that Sugarfoot is the fast gun who got them both.

146.69 *Trouble at Sand Springs.* April 17, 1961. GS: Suzanne Storrs, Craig Hill, Tommy Rettig, Ross Elliott, Dayton Lummis. Jimmy and Rance Benbow are accused of murder, and Sugarfoot is appointed their defense counsel. He knows he has got a tough case when he sees that the prosecuting attorney is Rhonda Rigsby, the daughter of the murdered man.

147. *Tales of the Texas Rangers*

CBS/ABC. 30 min. Broadcast history: Various, Aug. 1955–Dec. 1958.

Tales of the Texas Rangers

Regular Cast: Willard Parker (Jace Pearson), Harry Lauter (Clay Morgan).

Premise: This series depicted the adventures of Texas Rangers Jace Pearson and Clay Morgan from the 1830s through the 1950s.

The Episodes

147.1 *Ransom Flight.* Aug. 27, 1955. GS: Jan Shepard, Paul Maxey, John Pickard, Jack Littlefield, William Boyett, Peter Dane. The Rangers use a flock of carrier pigeons in their efforts to locate a band of kidnapers.

147.2 *Carnival Criss-Cross.* Sept. 3, 1955. GS: Gordon Mills, Jean Willes, Peter Ronan, Hy Anzel, John Hamilton, Harvey Dunn, Robert Roark. Belle and Duke Bishop rob and murder a gas-station owner. Though they disclaim all knowledge of the crime, the Texas Rangers are suspicious and begin an investigation.

147.3 *Shorty Sees the Light.* Sept. 10, 1955. GS: Kim Charney, Stanley Andrews, Tom Murray, Michael Granger. Ten-year-old Shorty Lassiter recognizes one of the bandits holding up his grandfather's stage coach. The outlaws warn the boy not to tell and Shorty is torn between fear and the desire to help the Texas Rangers.

147.4 *West of Sonora.* Sept. 17, 1955. GS Robert E. Griffin, Cheryl Callaway, I. Stanford Jolley. A child's gold claim inheritance is threatened by a feud which develops between her two grandfathers.

147.5 *Blood Trail.* Sept. 24, 1955. GS: Mel Welles, Harry Hickok, Joseph Hamilton, Mauritz Hugo, Antonio Roux. The Rangers suspect a ranch owner of murdering a doctor and a cowhand.

147.6 *Uranium Pete.* Oct. 1, 1955. GS: Dick Elliott, Chris Alcaide, K.L. Smith, Almira Sessions, Bernie Rich, Rhodes Reason. An old-time prospector has gone through the gold rush, the silver rush and now the uranium rush without hitting pay dirt. Rangers Jace and Clay stake the old man to one last chance and find it well worth their while.

147.7 *Double Edge.* Oct. 8, 1955. GS: Barbara Wooddell, John Hart, John Phillips. When two masked gunmen hold up the Midland Bank, one is shot and killed, the other escapes with the loot. Rangers Jace Pearson and Clay Morgan set out to uncover the identity of the masked bandit.

147.8 *The Shooting of Sam Bass.* Oct. 15, 1955. GS: John Hart, John Phillips, William Haade, Stanley Andrews. An outlaw, killed in a holdup, is mistakenly identified as the desperado Sam Bass. Bass, hearing of this, decides to reform.

147.9 *Home in San Antone.* Oct. 22, 1955. GS: Burt Mustin, William Boyett, Kay Bell, Jack Lomas. After stealing a fortune in diamonds, outlaws escape to their hideout, only to be robbed by a harmless old kleptomaniac. Rangers Pearson and Morgan are attracted to the spot by the shots fired at the fleeing old man.

147.10 *Jail Bird.* Oct. 2, 1955. GS: Dorothy Crider, Kay Bell, William Boyett, Jack M. Lomas. A notorious Hackett gang holds up a stagecoach and escapes. Ranger Jace Pearson poses as an outlaw and sets out to apprehend the gang.

147.11 *Tornado.* Nov. 5, 1955. GS: Barry Brooks, Michael Garth, Jerry Hartleben. Rangers Pearson and Morgan seek a gang that looted the town of Stardale after it was hit by a tornado.

147.12 *Prairie Raiders.* Nov. 12, 1955. GS: Sandy Descher, Rand Brooks. Working for a ruthless land baron, two henchmen rustle cattle, beat a young man and claim his land. Rangers Pearson and Morgan investigate.

147.13 *The Atomic Trail.* Nov. 19, 1955. GS: Harry Cody, Paul Engle, Joel Ashley. Two gunmen hold up an Army truck and, after killing a sergeant, make off with a capsule containing a new fuel vital to the country's defense.

147.14 *Return of the Rough Riders.* Nov. 26, 1955. GS: Kim Charney, Tom McKee, Don C. Harvey. A ranch owner and his gang are using electronic rays to destroy government rockets. They kill another rancher, who accidentally uncovers the plot, but find it harder to stop the Texas Rangers.

147.15 *Blazing Across the Pecos.* Dec. 3, 1955. GS: Baynes Barron, Lane Bradford. Asa Brockway learns that the railroad intends to buy land owned by trading-post operator Matt Carter. He plans to force Carter to sell his land to him.

147.16 *The Rough, Tough West.* Dec. 10, 1955. GS: Roger Broaddus, Baynes Barron, Lane Bradford, John Cason, Ed Hinton. An ex-ranger opens a gambling hall and saloon in a mining town. His unscrupulous dealings soon lead to lawlessness, and Rangers Pearson and Morgan are sent in to restore law and order.

147.17 *Hail to the Rangers.* Dec. 17, 1955. GS: Myron Healey, Harry Hickok, Chris Alcaide, Rhodes Reason. The Texas Rangers are disbanded because of lack of funds. When order begins to break down in Texas, ex-Rangers Jace Pearson and Clay Morgan try to persuade the State Senate to reinstate the law-enforcement agency.

147.18 *Singing on the Trail.* Dec. 24, 1955. GS: Ken Christy, Herb Vigran. A man plots the murder of his partner in order to gain full control of their oil company. But Texas Rangers Pearson and Morgan learn of the plot.

147.19 *The Black Eyes of Texas.* Dec. 31, 1955. GS: Stanley Andrews, Bobby Clark, Robert Bice. A former Texas Ranger is wounded during a robbery at the bank where he is employed as a guard. When his young grandson comes home with black eyes as a result of defending his grandfather's name, he puts on his gun belt and goes after the outlaws.

147.20 *The Devil's Deputy.* Jan. 7, 1956. Ron Hagerthy, Richard Avonde, Allan Nixon, Mildred Von Hollen, Gloria Grant. A man steals money to pay for his wife's emergency operation, then is manhandled by a gang of thugs who want to take the money from him.

147.21 *Horseman of the Sierras.* Jan. 14, 1956. GS: Gregg Barton, George Lynn, Alan Wells, Patricia Parsons. Two members of feuding families decide to marry and the long-standing argument is almost forgotten. But an outsider decides to start the feud up again.

147.22 *The Man from Sundown.* Jan. 21, 1956. GS: Bernie Rich, Allan Nixon, Edwin Parker. Rangers Jace Pearson and Clay Morgan set out to find the Mackinson gang, which held up a stagecoach and made off with the payroll.

147.23 *The Hobo.* Jan, 28, 1956. GS: Pat Walter, Robert Bice, Paul Brinegar, Stanley Andrews, Tom Black. An old hobo is shot and wounded in an abandoned house. When Rangers Pearson and Morgan investigate they find an old gold coin which a newspaperman identifies as part of a buried treasure.

147.24 *Buckaroo from Powder River.* Feb. 4, 1956. GS: Henry Rowland, Rush Williams, Chuck Courtney, Bill Hale. Three outlaws who have been plaguing Texas with robberies for years fear exposure when the stepson of one of them rebels at being forced into a life of crime. They decide to kill the young man.

147.25 *Last Days of Boot Hill.* Feb. 11, 1956. GS: William Tannen, William Boyett, Barry Brooks, Harry Strang, Daniel White. While tracking down the murderer of a government employee, Rangers Pearson and Morgan are ambushed by a group of foreign agents.

147.26 *Bandits of the El Dorado.* Feb. 18, 1956. GS: Jack Lomas, Frank Fenton, Edward Colmans. A number of notorious outlaws mysteriously disappear. The Rangers decide to find out what happened to them.

Season Two

147.27 *Panhandle.* Sept. 22, 1957. GS: J. Anthony Hughes, Bek Nelson, Gregg Palmer, Zon Murray, Dennis Moore, Kim Charney. An outlaw leader is determined to keep homesteaders from settling in the Texas strip he considers his own property. The Rangers are sent to capture the outlaw after a land agent is murdered.

147.28 *Key Witness.* Sept. 29, 1957. GS: Nicky Blair, Gloria Grant, Ken Mayer, Mickey Finn. A photographer who has entered the U.S. illegally, after escaping from an Iron Curtain country, witnesses a homicide and photographs the killer. He hesitates to go to the police for fear of deportation, but then learns that the killer is on his trail.

147.29 *Quarter Horse.* Oct. 6, 1957. GS: Thurston Hall, Stanley Clements, Jack Bassett, Jack Lomas, John Reach. Rangers Pearson and Morgan investigate the death of a young jockey. A race-track exercise boy admits that he quarreled with the jockey and during the struggle a gun went off. The Rangers, while they believe the boy's story, are convinced he is holding something back.

147.30 *Whirlwind Raiders.* Oct. 13, 1957. GS: James Gavin, Ewing Mitchell, X Brands, Paul Sorensen, Ron Hargrave, Tom Dillon. After the Civil War, the Texas Rangers are disbanded. An ex-Ranger, Tom Weldon, and a Mexican undercover agent learn that the state police captain is in alliance with a gang of outlaws.

147.31 *Both Barrels Blazing.* Oct. 20, 1957. GS: Wally Vernon, Grant Richards, John Merrick, Dick Elliott, Jett Roberts, Jack Harris. An actor disguises himself as an old woman and robs a train carrying a shipment of gold coins. Rangers Pearson and Morgan set out to trail the actor.

147.32 *A Texas Million.* Oct. 27, 1957. GS: Glenn Turnball, Willard Sage. An outlaw breaks out of jail and sets out to get his share of the loot from a robbery. The fugitive swaps his getaway car for a truck owned by a rodeo rider. Rangers Pearson and Morgan find the rodeo rider in the outlaw's car.

147.33 *Hardrock's Dilemma.* Nov. 3, 1957. GS: Andy Clyde, Gregg Barton. In his will, Charley Brent names Hardrock Sturgis his beneficiary. When Charley is knocked unconscious by a tramp, his nephews murder the tramp and attempt to blame the killing on Hardrock and inherit their uncle's money.

147.34 *Trail Herd.* Nov. 10, 1957. GS: Morris Ankrum, Chris Alcaide, Irving Bacon, John Truax. Colonel Bryson is hated by small ranchers because of the high prices he forces them to pay for driving their cattle to market. Bryson causes the death of a cattleman and uses forgery to cover-up his guilt.

147.35 *The Kid from Amarillo.* Nov. 17, 1957. GS: Richard Karlan, Ward Wood, Don Kennedy. Two Treasury men are killed while investigating the smuggling of silver from Mexico into Texas. Texas Ranger Clay Morgan poses as a professional boxer to find the men responsible.

147.36 *Gypsy Boy.* Nov. 24, 1957. GS: Paul Picerni, Louis Lettieri, Richard Benedict, Baynes Barron. Two roughnecks order Philip Conzog, a Gypsy, and his son Julio off the land where they have camped outside of town. Conzog leaves his knife behind, and it is picked up in a fight and used as a murder weapon.

147.37 *Riders of the Lone Star.* Dec. 1, 1957. GS: Diana Darrin, Dickie Belle, Bill Henry, William Boyett, Rusty Westcoatt. An outlaw, reported dead, is said to have hidden his stolen loot in a mine. Sandra Clark, a uranium prospector, buys the mine. While she is talking to the outlaw's son and his friend at the site, masked gunmen approach.

147.38 *Streamlined Rustlers.* Dec. 8, 1957. GS: Dirk London, Jacquelyn Park. When Joe Stuart's herd of horses is raided by rustlers, his young friend Rusty suggests the animals were transported by truck. Rangers Pearson and Morgan follow this theory in their investigation.

147.39 *Double Reward.* Dec. 15, 1957. GS: Andy Clyde, Darleen Fields, William Bryant, Gregg Barton, Larry Chance. An ex-marine is suspected of a bank robbery and the shooting of the cashier.

Season Three

147.40 *Traitor's Gold.* Oct. 2, 1958. GS: Keith Richards, Joe Bassett, Harry Harvey, Jr., Richard Powers, Steve Pendleton. Two Union soldiers, Jim Rhodes and Sam Devers, murder a Union lieutenant and a private during the Battle of Nashville in 1864. The killers escape with $150,000 from the paymaster's wagon.

147.41 *Warpath.* Oct. 9, 1958. GS: James Lydon, Patrick Whyte, Raymond Hatton, Edmund Hashim, Louis Lettieri. Jace and Clay go as scouts with Lt. Evans, who is to negotiate a treaty with a Comanche chief. Instead of submitting to Evans' ultimatum to surrender at Gila Flats, the Indians attack the town and massacre the inhabitants.

147.42 *Texas Kewpie.* Oct. 16, 1958. GS: Stacy Harris, Richard Benedict. Rangers Jace Pearson and Clay Morgan are assigned to track down a diamond-smuggling gang. Prior to their assignment, a treasury agent who was working on the case was shot and killed.

147.43 *Edge of Danger.* Oct. 23, 1958. GS: Michael Dante, Linda Lawson, Larry Perron, Donald Lawton, Vince Barnett. Killer Johnny Ryan escapes from prison and heads for Mexico, where he intends to kill a famous bullfighter and his wife.

147.44 *Cattle Drive.* Oct. 30, 1958. GS: Grant Withers, Stanley Adams, Kelley Thordsen. Rangers Pearson and Morgan, guarding a cattle drive to Abilene, suspect that the cook is in league with the Comanches in a plot to stampede the herd.

147.45 *Deadfall.* Nov. 6, 1958. GS: Frank Ferguson,

Joseph Turkel, Bud Doty, Richard Newton. Pursued by Rangers Jace and Clay, the Dembrow gang plunge into a river. The Rangers, convinced that the outlaws have drowned, tell the story to their friend Joe Taylor, unaware that he is one Dembrow son who has tried to live within the law.

147.46 *The Steel Trap.* Nov. 13, 1958. GS: Clark Howat, Nancy English, Olan Soule, Eddie Featherstone. After a pyromaniac escapes from a psychopathic ward, a series of fires breaks out. Jace and Clay learn that all of the burned buildings were insured by the same company.

147.47 *Desert Fury.* Nov. 20, 1958. GS: Leo Gordon, Rayford Barnes, Harry Cheshire. Rangers Jace and Clay trail two bank robbers to their desert hideout. In the ensuing gun battle the robbers are captured.

147.48 *Texas Flyer.* Nov. 28, 1958. GS: Leslie Bradley, Joe Kelsey, Denver Pyle, Milton Frome. Looking for a herd of horses, Rangers Jace and Clay come across a homemade glider and decide to use it. But they meet resistance. A local citizen has convinced the populace that it is against nature for man to fly.

147.49 *Jace and Clay.* Dec. 5, 1958. GS: George Cisar, Edwin Parker, Ken Becker. New Ranger Jace Pearson is assigned to round up the raiders of Rubyville. Attacked by an outlaw named Tucker, Pearson's life is saved by a stranger named Clay Morgan.

147.50 *Kickback.* Dec. 12, 1958. GS: Anthony Eisley, Laurie Carroll, Charles Tannen, Paul McGuire. Racketeer Arnie Sears is arrested because of the testimony of one witness, Jack Carr. To dissuade Carr from telling his story to the grand jury, the racketeer's friends kidnap Carr's wife.

147.51 *The Fifth Plague.* Dec. 19, 1958. Lisa Lu, George Keymas, Dub Taylor, Manuel Lopez, Robert Riordan, Guy Teague. Rangers Jace and Clay go to Gulf City to pick up an American criminal being extradited by the South American country. Before they can take him into custody, he escapes into the city. Then the Rangers learn that the criminal has smallpox.

147.52 *Ambush.* Dec. 26, 1958. GS: Marjorie Stapp, Ted DeCorsia, Russell Thorson. Rangers Jace and Caly come upon a burning wagon train and find only one survivor, a woman named Stacey Walker. On their way to a nearby settlement they encounter another wagon train being attacked by Indians.

148. *Tales of Wells Fargo*

NBC. 30/60 min. Broadcast history: Monday 8:30–9:00, March 1957–Sept. 1961; Saturday, 7:30–8:30, Sept. 1961–Sept. 1962.

Regular Cast: Dale Robertson (Jim Hardie), Jack Ging (Beau McCloud) 61-62, William Demarest (Jeb Gaine) 61-62, Virginia Christine (Ovie) 61-62, Mary Jane Saunders (Mary Gee) 61-62, Lory Patrick (Tina) 61-62.

Premise: This series depicted the adventures of Wells Fargo troubleshooter Jim Hardie in the West of the 1860s.

The Episodes

148.1 *The Thin Rope.* March 18, 1957. GS: Chuck Connors, George D. Wallace, Robert Burton, Russell Thorson, Jacqueline Holt. Jim Hardie starts an investigation into a stagecoach holdup in which the driver was killed and a guard wounded. He accompanies the guard to headquarters in Sacramento. En route, the guard gets into a poker game which gives Jim a vital clue.

148.2 *The Hasty Gun.* March 25, 1957. GS: Leo V. Gordon, John Merrick, Rusty Lane. The town marshal jeopardizes his job when he accidentally kills a youth at the scene of a robbery. Wells Fargo agent Jim Hardie starts an investigation of his own when he realizes that the town's lawless elements want to be rid of the marshal.

148.3 *Alder Gulch.* April 8, 1957. GS: Lee Van Cleef, John Doucette, Tom McKee, Tim Graham, Hugh Sanders, George Travino, Nesdon Booth, Russ Thorson. Wells Fargo sends Jim Hardie to Alder Gulch, Montana, when the office there reports a series of stagecoach robberies. Alder Gulch is a town that has had over 100 murders in three months.

148.4 *The Bounty.* April 15, 1957. GS: Gerald Milton, Richard Shannon, Anthony George, Jean Howell, Paul Bryar. Jim Hardie is sent to Moose County, Canada, for the task of identifying the body of a wanted outlaw. A man is claiming the reward money due, but Hardie suspects foul play.

148.5 *A Time to Kill.* April 22, 1957. GS: Robert Rockwell, Judith Ames, Brad Morrow. On the trail of stolen money, Jim Hardie is led to the home of a man who recently died. Both his sister and young son are certain the dead man had nothing to do with the robbery. The boy is determined to vindicate his father's name.

148.6 *Shotgun Messenger.* May 7, 1957. GS: Michael Landon, Kem Dibbs, Kevin Hagen, John Pickard, Eilene Janssen. Jim Hardie is seeking a man to hire as a shotgun messenger for a new branch on the Wells Fargo line. He decides on young Tad Cameron, even though the youth's father was once fired from Wells Fargo.

148.7 *The Lynching* (A.K.A. "Manuel"). May 13, 1957. GS: Victor Millan. Jim Hardie prevents angry townspeople from lynching a shepherd accused of kidnaping a six-year-old girl. The man, who is unable to speak English, was unable to explain to them his story of what happened.

148.8 *Renegade Raiders.* May 20, 1957. GS: Francis McDonald, George Chandler, Denver Pyle, Morgan Woodward, Dan Blocker, Paul Brinegar, Rick Vallin. Jim Hardie heads for St. Joseph, Missouri, after hearing a report that renegade Indians are getting their supplies of guns and ammunition from there.

148.9 *Rio Grande.* June 3, 1957. GS: Diane Brewster, Joe De Santis, Russell Johnson, Rico Alaniz, Luis Gomez, Lisa Montell. Jim Hardie is given the task of transporting a million dollars across the Mexican border where bandits have been operating. Complications arise when transportation is cut off and, accompanied by two tourists, Jim travels the Rio Grande by mule and canoe.

148.10 *Sam Bass.* June 10, 1957. GS: Chuck Connors, Pat Hogan, Ric Roman, Michael Landon, Ray Teal, Howard Negley, Tom McDonough. Disguised as an outlaw Jim Hardie heads for Texas on the trail of Sam Bass, who has eluded the law for many years. Hardie comes close to his quarry when he joins a band of desperadoes.

148.11 *The Hijackers.* June 17, 1957. GS: Terry Frost, Alan Reynolds, Jack Elam, Jacqueline Holt, Harry Harvey, Jr.,

Glenn Strange, Fred Carson. Jim Hardie is called back from his vacation to check on the whereabouts of an overdue stage carrying as passengers a wealthy young man and his fiancee. Hardie suspects outlaws are holding them.

148.12 *Stage to Nowhere.* June 24, 1957. GS: Walter Coy, Bobby Clark, Barbara Eiler, Lyle Talbot, Henry Rowland. Aboard a stagecoach, Jim Hardie joins a group of passengers that includes a woman and her son, an outlaw, and a reporter.

148.13 *Jesse James.* July 1, 1957. GS: Hugh Beaumont, Olive Carey, Jesse Griffith, Bobby Jordan, Chris Drake, Henry Ellis. A Wells Fargo office in a small Missouri town is robbed and a messenger killed. Suspecting that Jesse James and his gang were responsible, Jim Hardie disguises himself as a photographer-writer and heads for Missouri.

148.14 *The Silver Bullets.* July 8, 1957. GS: Douglas Kennedy, James Seay, Pamela Duncan, Jim Hayward, John Eldredge. A Wells Fargo agent dies under mysterious circumstances. Jim Hardie takes on the guise of a dealer in a gambling house in an attempt to gain a clue to the murder and to $15,000 missing from the agent's office.

Season Two

148.15 *Belle Star.* Sept. 9, 1957. GS: Jeanne Cooper, George Keymas, Edmund Hashim, Harry Ivans. Jim Hardie is sent on the trail of Belle Starr and her gang when they stage a train robbery. In an attempt to bring in the elusive woman bandit, Hardie challenges her to a race.

148.16 *Two Cartridges.* Sept. 16, 1957. GS: Jim Davis, James Burke, Harry Harvey, Sr., Horst Ehrhardt, Tom McDonough, Kit Carson. Jim Hardie captures a stagecoach robber and begins the three-day trek back to town. En route they are attacked by a band of Indians, and Jim must fight off the attackers and hold on to his prisoner as well.

148.17 *Apache Gold.* Sept. 23, 1957. Jim Hardie sets out for Hidden Valley, which is part of the Apache territory. He is in search of a teenager who has run away from home to search for gold in the valley. Jim is afraid that the youngster will be killed by the Indians, as they consider the land sacred.

148.18 *John Wesley Hardin.* Sept. 30, 1957. GS: Lyle Bettger, Frank Ferguson, Robert Foulk, Dick Forester. After Jim Hardie witnesses a robbery and murder, a hired gunman rides into town. His quarry is Jim Hardie. Jim tries to learn who has hired the gunslinger, and almost loses his life.

148.19 *The Target.* Oct. 7, 1957. After Stan Blake, a pony express rider, is killed, Jim Hardie takes over his run. He sets himself up as a human target in the hope that the outlaws will follow him and betray themselves.

148.20 *The Feud.* Oct. 14, 1957. GS: King Donovan, Jackie Blanchard, Ted de Corsia, Don Haggerty, House Peters, Jr. Jim Hardie finds himself in the middle of a feud between two families when he sets out to gain permission for Wells Fargo to use the road across their properties.

148.21 *Billy the Kid.* Oct. 21, 1957. GS: Robert Vaughn, Addison Richards, Aline Towne. Jim Hardie begins an investigation of a stagecoach robbery in which two Wells Fargo men are killed. A few people in the territory try to place the blame on Billy the Kid. But a woman injured in the melee claims Bill risked his life to help her.

148.22 *The Auction.* Oct. 28, 1957. GS: Edgar Buchanan, Margaret Stewart. Jim Hardie attends the annual Wells Fargo auction of unclaimed express packages. A girl and a man compete for a battered suitcase, with bids reaching over $200. The man wins it, but he is later struck on the head, and the mysterious package is stolen.

148.23 *Chips.* Nov. 4, 1957. GS: Gregg Palmer, Penny Edwards, Don Biddle, Craig Duncan, Alan Wells. Outlaws stop a stagecoach, taking nothing but a dog named Hank. Jim Hardie questions Jeff Anderson, to whom the dog was being sent, and finds that the dog's original owner was Anderson's brother, who was recently killed when he fell down a shaft in his gold mine.

148.24 *Man in the Box.* Nov. 11, 1957. GS: Beverly Wells, Robert Jordan, Lane Bradford, Sheb Wooley, Nelson Casey, Jr. The Wells Fargo office receives an anonymous note warning that there will be a railroad holdup that night, so Jim Hardie and his men stake out the train. But in spite of their surveillance, the strongbox disappears. Hardie suspects that a harmless-looking elderly woman may have been responsible for the theft.

148.25 *The Kid.* Nov. 18, 1957. GS: Michael Landon, John Pickard, Eilene Janssen, Monte Blue. Young Tad Cameron, hired by Jim Hardie as a messenger, is charged with murder when he is found standing over a body with a gun in his hand. Convinced that the boy is innocent, Hardie tries to clear him.

148.26 *Barbara Coast.* Nov. 25, 1957. GS: Paul Newland, Jean Willes, Robert Swan. Jim Hardie is sent to the rugged Barbary Coast area in San Francisco to keep his eye on a jade shipment from the Orient. But the agent guarding the shipment is stabbed to death and the ship captain is jailed. Believing the captain innocent, Hardie tangles with the nefarious Sydney Ducks, a ruthless gang who stop at nothing.

148.27 *Ride with the Killer.* Dec. 2, 1957. GS: Robert Jordan, Bob Woodward, Lane Bradford, Claudia Barrett. Jim Hardie has a dual assignment. He must find a gunman wanted for a holdup, and put a new Wells Fargo employee to the test at the same time.

148.28 *The Inscrutable Man.* Dec. 9, 1957. GS: Carolyn Craig, Will J. White, Barry Kelley, Kathleen Mulqueen, Fay Roope, Robert Roark, Morgan Sha'an. Hardie is out to find the man who killed a messenger in a Wells Fargo stagecoach robbery. He learns that townsfolk disapprove of the stage driver who identified the outlaw.

148.29 *The General.* Dec. 16, 1957. GS: Jane Nigh. Jim Hardie accompanies an intolerant general on an assignment to settle a Sioux uprising. They are delayed on their mission when outlaws attack them.

148.30 *Laredo.* Dec. 23, 1957. GS: Rodolfo Hoyos, Louis Zito, Robert Bice, Carlos Vera. Jim Hardie sets out after a ring which is smuggling guns into Mexico from Laredo.

148.31 *The Witness.* Dec. 30, 1957. GS: William Henry, Tyler McDuff, Paul Engel, Gloria Henry. After a Wells Fargo safe is robbed and an innocent bystander murdered a man comes to Jim Hardie claiming to be an eyewitness to the crime. Later the man admits he made up the story to collect the reward offered for information concerning the robbery.

148.32 *Doc Bell.* Jan. 6, 1958. GS: Edward Platt, Jim Bannon, Richard Reeves. After a suspected robber is captured, Wells Fargo agent Jim Hardie poses as a fellow prisoner to learn where the robber has hidden the stolen money.

Tales of Wells Fargo

148.33 *Stage West.* Jan. 13, 1958. GS: Darlene Fields, Stafford Repp, John Casson, Craig Duncan, Mauritz Hugo. Jim Hardie is assigned to escort a young lady by stagecoach to San Francisco. The girl's evidence is needed in the trail of a man accused of a political swindle.

148.34 *Hoss Tamer.* Jan. 20, 1958. GS: Chuck Courtney, Walter Coy. Agent Jim Hardie befriends a young man in need of a job and helps him find employment. Later, Jim's new friend is able to help Jim solve a Wells Fargo office robbery.

148.35 *Hide Jumpers.* Jan. 27, 1958. GS: Jimmy Gavin, Guy Wilkerson, Don Megowan. Jim Hardie goes after a gang of hijackers who have stolen a shipment of buffalo hides. He sets a trap for the outlaws that almost causes him to lose his life.

148.36 *Walking Mountain.* Feb. 3, 1958. After a gold strike is reported from a mine on Walking Mountain, Jim Hardie is sent to investigate the claim. There is suspicion that the ore is being hijacked from Wells Fargo wagons and that news of the strike is a cover-up for the robberies.

148.37 *Bill Longley.* Feb. 10, 1958. GS: Steve McQueen, Jacqueline Holt, Steve Rowland, Ken Christy. Jim Hardie learns that a notorious outlaw, Bill Longley, is searching for the man who has stolen a large sum of money from Wells Fargo.

148.38 *The Prisoner.* Feb. 17, 1958. GS: Harvey Stephens, Edgar Buchanan, Robert Armstrong, Norman Willis, Clarence Straight, Keith Richards, Johnny Western. When a U.S. Senator and former judge is kidnaped by the two outlaws he once jailed, Jim Hardie seeks the aid of a one-time outlaw to track down the criminals.

148.39 *Dr. Alice.* Feb. 23, 1958. GS: Diane Brewster, Richard Devon, Boyd Stockman. A band of outlaws kidnap a woman doctor and order her to treat their wounded leader. Wells Fargo agent Jim Hardie tries to rescue the young woman.

148.40 *The Sooners.* March 3, 1958. GS: Jeff Daley, Eddie Coch, Ed Hinton. In order to enable Wells Fargo to take out a claim to Oklahoma, Jim Hardie delivers a fast-running horse to the man commissioned to make the claim. But the claim is not made and both man and horse disappear.

148.41 *Alias Jim Hardie.* March 10, 1958. GS: Kent Taylor, Rush Williams, Terry Frost, Lionel Ames, Phyllis Coates, Paul Keast. Three outlaws kidnap agent Jim Hardie and steals his identification papers. One of them impersonates Hardie and robs the Wells Fargo office in a nearby town.

148.42 *The Johnny Ringo Story.* March 17, 1958. Wells Fargo agent Jim Hardie finally tracks down the famous gun fighter Johnny Ringo. But Johnny asks Jim to wait three days before taking him in. The reason is Johnny's sister, who doesn't suspect that her brother is an outlaw, is dying, and Johnny wants to see her.

148.43 *The Newspaper.* March 24, 1958. GS: Claire DuBrey, Sue George, Tyler MacDuff, Carlyle Mitchell, Robert Osterloh. Jim Hardie arrives in the small town of Madden to investigate sabotage against Wells Fargo coaches. He learns that a ruthless woman, Effie Sutton, not only owns and runs the whole town, but has started an independent stage line.

148.44 *Special Delivery.* March 31, 1958. GS: Robert Lowery, Bing Russell, Jason Johnson, Judith Ames, Clark Howat, Ken Mayer, Steven Ritch, Fred Sherman, Frank Hagney. Jim Hardie is assigned to see that the passengers aboard a Wells Fargo stagecoach reach their destination without interference from hostile Indians. Among the passengers is a baby girl, and an Army major who is to be tried for the massacre of an Indian village.

148.45 *Deadwood.* April 7, 1958. GS: Mari Aldon, Richard Crane, Roy Barcroft, Stewart Bradley, Fred Graham, Robert Hinkle, Kit Carson. A Wells Fargo stagecoach is robbed, and two men are killed. Evidence at the scene of the crime points to former outlaw Billy Reno, but Jim Hardie believes that Reno is being framed.

148.46 *The Gun.* April 14, 1958. GS: Jeanette Nolan, Laurie Carroll, Clay Randolph, Morgan Sha'an. Agent Jim Hardie becomes an outcast when townspeople become convinced that he shot an innocent man during a Wells Fargo stagecoach holdup. The other two men involved in the holdup claim the dead man was not one of their gang. Despite rising resentment, Hardie stays in the town to clear his name.

148.47 *The Reward.* April 21, 1958. GS: Marcia Henderson, Allan "Rocky" Lane, Otto Waldis, Charles Tannen, Hank Worden, Bill Catching, Earl L. Sands. Jim Hardie has prevented the holdup of a Wells Fargo stage. But when he tries to collect the reward, he encounters suspicion and hostility. Seems the man who was to deliver it to him has been murdered.

148.48 *The Pickpocket.* April 28, 1958. GS: James Fairfax, Carole Mathews, Renny McEvoy, John Harmon, Jack Lomas. On the trail of train robbers, Hardie takes a train to Emigrant Pass. When the train is robbed he finds himself without cash on his arrival at Emigrant Pass. A fellow passenger gives Hardie a watch to pawn. Hardie becomes suspicious when he is offered a large sum of money for the timepiece.

148.49 *Scapegoat.* May 5, 1958. GS: Bruce Bennett, Johnny Mack Brown, Paul Engle, Ricky Klein, Arthur Space. A Wells Fargo agent is killed in a robbery, and the townspeople jump to the conclusion that Clyde Bender, a former outlaw turned teacher, is guilty. Jim Hardie won't accept the townspeople's accusations and refuses to arrest Bender.

148.50 *The Renegade.* May 12, 1958. GS: John Anderson, Walter Maslow, John Doucette, Frank Gerstle. Charles Mason, a newly hired Wells Fargo messenger, is not trusted by the company, and Jim Hardie is sent out to investigate the man's background. He learns Mason belongs to a family of notorious outlaws.

148.51 *The Break.* May 19, 1958. GS: Steven Terrell, Jack Littlefield, Richard Travis, Jack Ingram, Mike Masters, Tom Monroe, Gene Roth. Jim Hardie poses as outlaw Jesse James and joins a band of renegades. He is trying to find a man who has killed a Wells Fargo agent and pulled off a series of gold robberies.

148.52 *The Sniper.* May 26, 1958. GS: Robert Williams, Harold J. Stone, Shirley Whitney, Olan Soule, Bill Tennan. Jim Hardie comes to town to investigate a gold robbery. But when the Wells Fargo manager is killed, Hardie stays in the town to solve the murder of his friend.

Season Three

148.53 *The Gambler.* Sept. 8, 1958. GS: Tom Pittman, Wilton Graff, Richard Deacon. Young Bill Dowd, a gambler, has just been released from prison. Even though the townspeople are suspicious of the bitter young man, Wells Fargo Agent Jim Hardie decides to trust Dowd and tries to help him.

148.54 *The Manuscript.* Sept. 15, 1958. GS: Edgar Buchanan, Charles Wagenheim, Dan White, Roy Engel, Shary Layne, Robert Brubaker, Jay Jostyn. A former outlaw, who is on parole in the custody of Jim Hardie, boasts to the townspeople that many of them will appear in the memoirs he is writing. Later, when the outlaw is jailed for shooting a man during a gun fight, Hardie becomes suspicious. He discovers that his parolee's manuscript is missing.

148.55 *White Indian.* Sept. 22, 1958. GS: Dick Evans, Neil Hamilton, Elizabeth Harrower, Howard Negley. Jim Hardie tries to establish the real identity of a white boy living with an Indian tribe. Several years earlier a little boy traveling via Wells Fargo to his parents disappeared during a stage robbery, and was never found.

148.56 *The Golden Owl.* Sept. 29, 1958. GS: Elaine Edwards, Willis Bouchey, Clarence Lung, Harold Fong. Jim Hardie is assigned to deliver a solid gold statue of an owl to Virginia City. During the trip he discovers that his life is in danger as long as the statue is in his possession.

148.57 *Faster Gun.* Oct. 6, 1958. GS: Tom Neal, William Bakewell, Robert J. Wilke, Frances De Sales. In a showdown with stagecoach robber Johnny Reno, Jim Hardie is beaten to the drawn and wounded by the outlaw. This is the first time anyone has beaten Hardie to the draw, and he turns down a suggestion from Wells Fargo that he take a desk job. Hardie is determined to go after Reno to prove that he hasn't lost his nerve.

148.58 *Butch Cassidy.* Oct. 13, 1958. GS: Charles Bronson, James Coburn, Barbara Pepper, Murvyn Vye. Jim Hardie investigates when a gang of desperadoes rob a train. Butch Cassidy, a former gunman who has gone straight, insists on riding along with Hardie when he trails the outlaws. Cassidy figures they intend to set a trap for Hardie.

148.59 *End of the Trail.* Oct. 20, 1958. GS: Mickey Finn, Don C. Harvey, William Benedict, Jerry Summers. Attacks by the Pawnee Indians halt work on a Wells Fargo road through the Dakotas. Jim Hardie is sent to investigate when the workers threaten to quit.

148.60 *A Matter of Honor.* Nov. 3, 1958. GS: Mark Damon, King Calder, Peter Coe, Joe Vitale. Jim Hardie hires an Indian to drive for Wells Fargo despite protests from the townspeople. When the stagecoach is robbed, the Indian is suspected of the crime.

148.61 *The Most Dangerous Man Alive.* Nov. 10, 1958. GS: Claude Akins, Patricia Powell, Frank McGrath, Ana Maria Majalca. While Jim Hardie is waiting to stop two outlaws at the Mexican border, he unexpectedly meets John Leslie Nagel, a notorious gunfighter. Nagel is desperate because there is a large reward for his capture, so he makes Hardie his prisoner in an effort to escape the law.

148.62 *The Gunfighter.* Nov. 17, 1958. GS: Lyle Bettger, Jan Harrison, Joe Abdullah, John Goddard. Jim Hardie is assigned to check on two outlaws. While Carrying out this assignment, Hardie becomes involved with gunfighter John Hardin and a renegade sheriff.

148.63 *The Deserter.* Nov. 24, 1958. GS: Charles Cooper, Jennifer Lea, Monte Hale, Don Sheridan. Jim Hardie is on the trail of an Army deserter turned outlaw. Hardie is aided by an Army colonel who also wants to locate the desperado.

148.64 *The Killer.* Dec. 1, 1958. GS: Paul Burke, Paul Fix, Addison Richards, George Keymas, Harry Strang. Hardie is assigned to protect a U.S. Senator in danger of assassination by a professional gunman. The killer has been hired by a group of ranchers who object to a bill proposed by the senator which would infringe on their range lands.

148.65 *The Counterfeiters.* Dec. 8, 1958. GS: John Beradino, Don Kennedy, Patricia Donahue, Milton Frome, Robert Bice, Neil Grant. Jim Hardie travels to El Paso, Texas. He believes that the headquarters of a gang of counterfeiters of Wells Fargo travelers' checks is located there.

148.66 *Cow Town.* Dec. 15, 1958. GS: Jack Lambert, John Alvin, Guinn Williams, Don Riss. A Texas trail driver, posing as a bandit, steals his own money being sent via Wells Fargo. Jim Hardie sets out to investigate the thief's identity.

148.67 *The Happy Tree.* Dec. 22, 1958. GS: John Merrick, Bob Steele, Alan Reynolds, Brad Morrow, Kay Stewart. At Christmastime a condemned prisoner asks Jim Hardie to look after his son who is in an orphanage. Jim places the boy with a family, but the boy refuses to overcome his belligerence toward his benefactors.

148.68 *The Dealer.* Dec. 29, 1958. GS: Vic Perrin, Jeanne Bates, Michael De Carlo, Johnny Crawford. Jim Hardie, attempting to locate a pair of stage bandits, enlists the aid of a gambler. During a lucky streak, the gambler wins money which later proves to have been stolen.

148.69 *Showdown Trail.* Jan. 5, 1959. GS: Will Wright, Stanley Clements, Myron Healey, Frank Watkins, Gloria Talbott. Jim Hardie is confronted by an entire family of outlaws — a father, three sons and a girl.

148.70 *Wild Cargo.* Jan. 19, 1959. GS: Adele Mara, Dorothy Partington, Monica Lewis, Nancy Kilgas, Cliff Ketchum, Henry Corden, Brad Johnson. Assigned to guard a valuable cargo being transported via Wells Fargo, Jim Hardie is surprised to learn that the shipment consists of four very beautiful women.

148.71 *The Cleanup.* Jan. 26, 1959. GS: James Bell, Julie Van Zandt, Harry Fleer, Ken Dibbs, L.Q. Jones. A Wells Fargo agent is murdered in a town which has given a lot of trouble to the stage line. Jim Hardie begins an investigation.

148.72 *Fort Massacre.* Feb. 2, 1959. GS: Walter Stocker, Lane Bradford, Charmienne Harker, Pete Dunn. Jim Hardie tries to help the Army hold a fort against an Indian attack. Because of a cowardly commanding officer, the odds are against the Army.

148.73 *The Town That Wouldn't Talk.* Feb. 9, 1959. GS: Linda Leighton, Charles Hayes, Sydney Mason, William Erwin. Investigating the death of a Wells Fargo stage driver, Jim Hardie discovers that several other people in the same town have died under similar circumstances. A mysterious funeral for a dead cow leads Hardie to believe that an epidemic may be threatening the entire community.

148.74 *Lola Montez.* Feb. 16, 1959. GS: Rita Moreno, Robert Anderson, Chubby Johnson, Ralph Reed, Hank Patterson. After capturing an outlaw, Jim Hardie must deliver his prisoner to Tucson, Arizona. During the stagecoach trip to Tucson Hardie encounters the resentment of his fellow passengers.

148.75 *The Branding Iron.* Feb. 23, 1959. GS: Ann Rutherford, Willard Sage, J. Edward McKinley, Earl Robie,

Tales of Wells Fargo

Terry Burnham. Jim Hardie goes to the aid of the widow and family of a friend who has been killed. Jim soon finds himself very close to acquiring a wife and family of his own.

148.76 *The House I Enter.* March 2, 1959. GS: Michael Hinn, Alan Baxter. Wells Fargo agent Jim Hardie is trying to track down two men who have stolen a large sum of money and killed a Wells Fargo agent. Hardie loses the trail and stops at the home of a doctor to ask for assistance. But the doctor seems very bitter and refuses to aid him.

148.77 *The Legacy.* March 9, 1959. GS: William Joyce, Sandra Knight, Will Wright, Emile Meyer. A recluse dies and bequeaths his ranch to a young Easterner. The young man comes West to claim his inheritance and runs into a range war.

148.78 *The Rawhide Kid.* March 16, 1959. GS: Troy Donahue, Roy Barcroft, Jackie Russell. A series of shootings leads Hardie to suspect that the Rawhide Kid, an outlaw who dropped out of sight many years before, may be back in circulation. The victims were all former members of the Kid's gang.

148.79 *Toll Road.* March 23, 1959. GS: Frank Ferguson, Loren Tindall, Elmore Vincent, Will White. Jim Hardie inadvertently becomes involved in violence between a sheriff and a gunslinger who is wanted for a shooting.

148.80 *The Tired Gun.* March 30, 1959. GS: Nick Adams, Penny Edwards, Harry Shannon. Outlaws Ira Watkins and his gang rob a Wells Fargo bank. Wells Fargo agent Jim Hardie goes after them.

148.81 *Terry.* April 6, 1959. GS: Steven Ritch, Judi Meredith, John Culwell, Trevor Bardette. Jim Hardie, sent to investigate the theft of some horses from a Wells Fargo relay station, finds the agent more concerned about his tomboy daughter than the stolen horses.

148.82 *The Last Stand.* April 13, 1959. GS: Eddy Waller, John Harmon, Richard Crane, Jon Locke, Terry Frost. Outlaws ask a shiftless former lawman to help them stage a robbery.

148.83 *Bob Dawson.* April 20, 1959. GS: Edgar Buchanan, James Bannon, Mel Pogue, Marx Hartman. Outlaw Bob Dawson is paroled from prison because he did a favor for Wells Fargo. Agent Jim Hardie is assigned as Dawson's parole officer.

148.84 *The Tall Texan.* April 27, 1959. GS: John Reach, Merry Anders, Clay Randolph. Wells Fargo agent Jim Hardie learns that a gang of outlaws is planning to rob a train. Hardie decides to visit the town where the robbery is supposed to take place and investigate.

148.85 *Doc Holliday.* May 4, 1959. GS: Martin Landau, Whitney Blake, Henry Hunter. Jim Hardie suspects that gambler Doc Holliday is connected with a recent stagecoach robbery. But Holliday insists that he is innocent.

148.86 *Kid Curry.* May 11, 1959. GS: Phillip Pine. Hardie is on the trail of outlaw Kid Curry.

148.87 *The Little Man.* May 18, 1959. GS: Walter Burke, Read Morgan, Steve Mitchell, Kate Manx, Quentin Sondergaard. Wells Fargo agent Jim Hardie tries to track down a suspect in a stagecoach robbery. His best lead is the information that the suspect is known as "the little man."

148.88 *The Daltons.* May 25, 1959. GS: Don Kelly, Harry Harvey, Jr., John Milford. Agent Jim Hardie risks a visit to ex-lawman Bob Dalton and his outlaw gang in an attempt to get them to surrender peacefully. His appeal is rejected violently and he is left handcuffed to a tree.

148.89 *The Bounty Hunter.* June 1, 1959. GS: Darryl Hickman, Mort Mills, Betty Lynn. Don Francis, a young outlaw, is pursued by Wells Fargo agent Jim Hardie. Unknown to either Hardie or Francis, a ruthless bounty hunter is also on Francis' trail.

148.90 *Clay Allison.* June 15, 1959. GS: Warren Stevens, Jeanne Cooper, Barry Kelley, Baynes Barron. Gunman Clay Allison plans to open a saloon and gambling parlor, but his equipment is stolen. He and Wells Fargo agent Jim Hardie join forces to track down the thieves.

Season Four

148.91 *Young Jim Hardie.* Sept. 7, 1959. GS: Walter Sande, John Dehner, Robert Nicholas, Kelly Thordsen, Vito Scotti. A newspaperman seeking information about Jim Hardie's background learns of Hardie's early career in a lawless Texas town. In those days, young Jim was associated with outlaws.

148.92 *Desert Showdown.* Sept. 14, 1959. GS: Gregory Walcott, Armand Alzamora, Al Wyatt, George Wallace, Dick Rich, Miriam Colon. Jim Hardie is assigned by Wells Fargo to help a cavalry patrol bring a prisoner to the small town where he will be tried for murder and robbery. Hardie joins the small patrol and they begin their journey across the desert.

148.93 *The Warrior's Return.* Sept. 21, 1959. GS: Don Megowan, Marie Windsor, Gregg Palmer. Townspeople have accused tough Soldier O'Malley of murder. Acting on a hunch, Jim Hardie stands up in defense of O'Malley.

148.94 *The Jackass.* Sept. 28, 1959. GS: Kathleen Crowley. Assigned to investigate three recent stagecoach robberies, Jim Hardie becomes curious about a mysterious old lady he meets. He feels sure that she knows something about the robberies, despite her innocent appearance.

148.95 *The Stage Line.* Oct. 5, 1959. GS: Carolyn Craig, James Franciscus, Wally Richard, John Pickard. Wells Fargo agent Jim Hardie is puzzled to find that Joe Braddock, owner of an apparently successful stage line, wants to sell out at a low price. It seems that robberies are forcing him out of business.

148.96 *The Train Robbery.* Oct. 12, 1959. GS: Jeanne Bates, John Doucette, Al Wyatt, Kay E. Kuter, Bing Russell, Mara Corday, Richard Shannon, Dan Sheridan. Wells Fargo agent Jim Hardie is trying to find the man behind a train robbery. He finds little to help him until he meets the embittered wife of the thief.

148.97 *Double Reverse.* Oct. 19, 1959. GS: Judith Evelyn, Joe Sullivan, Denver Pyle. Wells Fargo agent Jim Hardie is assigned to find out whether a company employee, Ann Rawlins, is honest. Company officials suspect she is secretly working with her outlaw husband, who left her a year before.

148.98 *Tom Horn.* Oct. 26, 1959. GS: Les Johnson, Gil Rankin, Gregory Walcott, Anthony Caruso, Charles McClellan. Tom Horn, a man with a long criminal record, has saved Jim Hardie from the Apaches. Then a lynching party overtakes Horn and Hardie tells a lie to save him.

148.99 *The Quiet Village.* Nov. 2, 1959. GS: Katherine Squire, Tom Laughlin, Jack Lester, John Anderson. Agent Jim Hardie's search for outlaw Jess Walton leads him to a widow's ranch. Hardie is surprised to find that Wilson, who knows he is a wanted man, is not running from the law.

148.100 *Home Town.* Nov. 16, 1959. GS: Ben Cooper, Jacqueline Holt, Craig Duncan, Leroy Johnson. Wells Fargo agent Jim Hardie offers a job as a stagecoach driver to a former outlaw who says he is trying to go straight.

148.101 *End of a Legend.* Nov. 23, 1959. GS: Philip Coolidge, John Larch, Vivi Janiss, Ward Wood. A gun found at the scene of a shooting is inscribed with the name of Johnny Caine, an old-time outlaw. Old John, the town bum, confesses that he is Caine, but Jim Hardie is not convinced. He begins a search for the real Johnny Caine.

148.102 *Return of Doc Bell.* Nov. 30, 1959. GS: Edward C. Platt, Logan Field, Bobby Hall, William Keene. Former outlaw Doc Bell is trying to live down his past. But his old companions pull a train robbery and Doc is suspected of aiding them.

148.103 *Woman with a Gun.* Dec. 7, 1959. GS: Madelyn Rhue, William Forrester. After Jim Hardie kills a man in self-defense, the dead man's self-righteous sister threatens revenge. Then the Wells Fargo agent discovers that the woman was involved in a crime.

148.104 *Long Odds.* Dec. 14, 1959. GS: Mary LaRoche, Russ Conway, Roscoe Ates. Dangler, a former outlaw, is suspected of reverting to his old ways. But Wells Fargo agent Jim Hardie thinks Dangler is going straight and gives him a chance to prove it.

148.105 *Wanted: Jim Hardie.* Dec. 21, 1959. GS: Beverly Tyler, Richard Shannon, Bing Russell, Duane Cress, Robert Carricart. The outlaw Donlan gang offer a reward for Wells Fargo agent Jim Hardie. The reward is good if Hardie is brought in dead.

148.106 *Relay Station.* Dec. 28, 1959. GS: Lori Nelson, Wynn Pearce. Jim Hardie has temporarily taken charge of a relay station. He learns that outlaws plan to hold up a stagecoach scheduled to arrive at the station.

148.107 *Cole Younger.* Jan. 4, 1960. GS: Royal Dano, Patty Ann Garrity, George Keymas. While Wells Fargo agent Jim Hardie is baby-sitting with a seven year old girl, the house is invaded by outlaw Cole Younger and his gang.

148.108 *The Easterner.* Jan. 11, 1960. GS: Gerald Mohr, Joanna Moore, Dick Rich, Jason Johnson. Wells Fargo agent Jim Hardie believes that Dan Mulvaney is an honest man. But after a stagecoach robbery attempt, Hardie begins to have doubts.

148.109 *The Governor's Visit.* Jan. 18, 1960. GS: Wendell Holmes, Tom McKee, Mari Blanchard, Mari Lynn. Jim Hardie is assigned to protect the governor of Wyoming from outlaws. Hardie precedes the governor into the town of Powder River and finds it almost deserted.

148.110 *The Journey.* Jan. 25, 1960. GS: Robert Cornthwaite, Coleen Gray, Britt Lomond. Wells Fargo agent Jim Hardie is assigned to guard a valuable shipment of jewels. During the trip, the jewels vanish.

148.111 *The Canyon.* Feb. 1, 1960. GS: Bruce Gordon, Jean Ingram, Harry Bartell. Jim Hardie is looking for evidence which could clear a man convicted of robbing a Wells Fargo stagecoach. Posing as an outlaw, Jim Hardie hunts for a man named Fred Kimball.

148.112 *Red Ransom.* Feb. 8, 1960. GS: Nancy Crawford, Frank de Kova. Apaches are holding the daughter of a Wells Fargo agent as ransom for one of their tribesmen who is in jail for murder. Anxious citizens think that the Indian out to be freed despite his guilt.

148.113 *The English Woman.* Feb. 15, 1960. GS: Adrienne Reys, Wesley Lau, Gene Roth. Jim Hardie is investigating the mysterious death of a woman, and he asks the daughter of the victim to help him. Narrowing the suspects to four, Hardie devises a scheme to trick the murderer into revealing himself.

148.114 *Forty-Four Forty.* Feb. 29, 1960. GS: Chris Alcaide, Roy Barcroft, Peter Whitney. Forty-Four forty is the calibre of a notched bullet found at the scene of the crime as Jim Hardie investigates the murder of a stage driver.

148.115 *The Late Mayor Brown.* March 7, 1960. GS: Gail Kobe, John Stephenson, George Mitchell, Charles Cooper, Vic Perrin. Mayor Brown was shot with an unusual gun. With this clue, Hardie finds it easy to trace the killer. The trouble is that he is dead too.

148.116 *Black Trail.* March 14, 1960. GS: Diane Foster, Ron Robel, Maury Hill, Virginia Eiler. Jim Hardie locates a killer's hideout by following the outlaw's girl friend.

148.117 *The Great Bullion Robbery.* March 21, 1960. GS: Edward Kemmer, Joyce Taylor, George Ramsey, Jan Merlin. A Wells Fargo agent is murdered for a fortune in gold. Hardie narrows the suspects to three, two elusive strangers and an ex-convict.

148.118 *The Outlaw's Wife.* March 28, 1960. GS: Bob Strong, Cassie Case, John Archer, Patricia Huston. An outlaw's wife is bothered by blackmail. Her husband gives Hardie a proposition — get rid of the blackmailers in return for some missing loot.

148.119 *The Town.* April 4, 1960. GS: Mary Webster, Rhys Williams, Bert Remsen. The town of Wolf Creek has been deeded to Lucy Potter by her father, but there are others who want control, and Lucy is told to give it up or die.

148.120 *The Trading Post.* April 11, 1960. GS: Mort Mills, Paul Langton, X Brands. Hardie is looking for the heir to a fortune. The search gets more difficult when he learns that his man is going under an assumed name and is wanted for murder.

148.121 *Dead Man's Street.* April 18, 1960. GS: Barney Phillips, Wallace Ford, Robert Bray, Buddy Ebsen. The Ferguson brothers have the citizens of a small Texas town completely buffaloed. Hardie offers to tame the Fergusons.

148.122 *Threat of Death.* April 25, 1960. GS: Robert Middleton, William Campbell, Elizabeth Allen, King Calder. Hardie's prisoner faces trial for robbery and murder, and Jim is escorting him to the county seat. But there is unexpected opposition from local citizens who fear reprisals from the outlaw's gang.

148.123 *Dealer's Choice.* May 2, 1960. GS: Patricia Barry, Robert Lowery, Robert Carson, Arthur Space. It is Jim Hardie's job to deliver a diamond pendant to Sacramento. But Miss Phyllis Randolph has other ideas about its future.

148.124 *Pearl Hart.* May 9, 1960. GS: Beverly Garland, Michael Pate, Boyd Stockman, Stafford Repp, Jean Inness. Pearl Hart, a notorious outlaw, makes plans to hold up a Wells Fargo stagecoach. But she picks the wrong stage because riding on the coach is Jim Hardie.

148.125 *Vasquez.* May 16, 1960. GS: Cesare Danova, Barbara Luna, Rodolfo Hoyos, Jack Reitzen, Hal Jon Norman. Jim Hardie holds up a stage, is captured and thrown in jail. It

Tales of Wells Fargo

is all part of an elaborate plot to win the confidence of an outlaw.

148.126 *Kid Brother.* May 23, 1960. GS: Larry Pennell, Lucy Marlow, Richard Avonde. Jim Hardie's kid brother envies the romantic life he thinks Jim leads. Bored with the routine on the farm, he sets out to follow his brother's hazardous path.

148.127 *Man for the Job.* May 30, 1960. GS: Harold J. Stone, Ken Lynch, Dennis Cross, Regis Toomey, Al Wyatt. Hardie arrives in Goldfield to interview prospective guards for the Wells Fargo line. He decides to trust a former employee who was suspected of taking part in a robbery.

148.128 *Long Odds.* June 27, 1960. GS: Mary La Roche, Russ Conway, Roscoe Ates. Dangler used to be an outlaw and maybe he is again. Hardie doubts it and gives him a chance to prove he is still on the straight and narrow.

Season Five

148.129 *Day of Judgement.* Sept. 5, 1960. GS: John Dehner, John Lupton, Doris Dowling, Kit Carson. Hardie is following Eli Fisher, who is wanted for murder. But a man named Cather is also on the trail and he is following Hardie.

148.130 *Doc Dawson.* Sept. 19, 1960. GS: Edgar Buchanan, Don Haggerty, Douglas Spencer. Hardie finds a missing freight wagon and the dead body of its driver. But only dental equipment has been stolen and there is a new dentist in town.

148.131 *The Kinfolk.* Sept. 26, 1960. GS: Richard Jaeckel, Dan Riss, Robert Burton, Logan Field. Jim Hardie finds a dead man in the woods, and brings the body into town. The Lassiter family insists that Jim is the murderer.

148.132 *All That Glitters.* Oct. 24, 1960. GS: Ken Lynch, Barbara Stuart, Robert P. Lieb, Ron Harper. Hardie investigates a theft from the Wells Fargo office safe. His suspect is Marshal Joe Brass, a safe-cracker before he became a lawman.

148.133 *Run for the River.* Nov. 7, 1960. GS: Ron Hayes, John Dehner, Bruce Gordon, Forrest Taylor, Ann Morrison. Hardie is escorting prisoner Ira Kyle to Santa Fe to stand trial, but they are detained on the way. Red Bluff's Marshal Haig wants to hang Kyle for the murder of a local man.

148.134 *Leading Citizen.* Nov. 14, 1960. GS: Wesley Lau, Robert Carricart, Robert Middleton. A missing stage has turned up in the wide open border town of San Tomas. Hardie, who has come to investigate, is immediately drawn into a gunfight with Morgan Bates. The result is the Hardie loses his gun for disturbing the peace.

148.135 *The Killing of Johnny Lash.* Nov. 21, 1960. GS: Jean Allison, Anne Helm, Dennis Patrick, Howard Negley, Rodney Bell, Mastin Smith, Austin Green. Wells Fargo has acquired a gambling casino and Hardie is assigned to sell it. But he no sooner arrives in town when he learns that the casino's manager has just been murdered.

148.136 *The Wade Place.* Nov. 28, 1960. GS: Robert J. Wilke, Vaughn Taylor, Russell Thorson. Jim has been tipped off about a holdup at the Wade place. He arrives to find company rival Mike Ross, who says he can handle any trouble without Hardie's help.

148.137 *Jeff Davis' Treasure.* Dec. 5, 1960. GS: John Dehner, John McLiam, Leo Gordon, Lennie Geer. Some time ago a Wells Fargo stage was robbed by two bandits, one of whom disappeared with a fortune in gold. When Birely, the bandit who was captured, winds up his jail term, Jim trails him.

148.138 *The Bride and the Bandit.* Dec. 12, 1960. GS: Jan Clayton, Dabbs Greer, Myron Healey, Ellen Corby, Terry Frost. Mail-order bride Ellen Stevens is aboard a Wells Fargo Stage when a bandit holds it up. She recognizes the man as Tip Rollins.

148.139 *Escort to Santa Fe.* Feb. 19, 1960. GS: Gregory Walcott, Alex Montoya, Linda Lawson, Stephen Chase. Hardie rides to El Paso to meet a Major Barclay. But Barclay doesn't make it because he has been ambushed by Ortega, one of Kyle Gentry's boys. Gentry comes into El Paso disguised as Barclay.

148.140 *Frightened Witness.* Dec. 26, 1960. GS: John Milford, Michael Burns, Gary Walberg, Penny Edwards, Jason Johnson, Robert J. Stevenson, Julian Burton, Keith Richards. Walt Corbin faces trial for murder, but Corbin is all smiles. He claims that witnesses Frazier and Matson are going to suffer a lapse of memory.

148.141 *The Border Renegade.* Jan. 2, 1961. GS: Ernest Sarracino, Elaine Davis, John Beradino, Alberto Morin. Jim intercepts an illegal shipment of guns, and captures Virgil McCready, the wagon driver. Then they go on to the original destination.

148.142 *Captain Scoville.* Jan. 9, 1961. GS: William Tannen, John Craig, Pat Michon, DeForest Kelley. Hardie is looking for Cole Scoville, who is wanted for robbery, murder and Army desertion. Cole has had a loss of memory from a head injury, and Susan Kellogg is nursing him at her ranch when Hardie turns up.

148.143 *The Has-Ben.* Jan. 16, 1961. GS: Adam West, J. Pat O'Malley, Charles Tannen. Jim is riding shotgun on a stage which stops in the ghost town of Tubac. One of the passengers is Cedric Mannning, an entertainer who made his last appearance here with his late wife.

148.144 *Town Against a Man.* Jan. 23, 1961. GS: Val Avery, Casey Tibbs, Lurene Tuttle. Jim is on his way to visit rancher Tony Crandall, who is to be married soon. When Jim arrives, he learns that Tony has been drowned.

148.145 *The Barefoot Bandit.* Jan. 30, 1961. GS: Tom Hennesy, John Marshall, Don Harvey. The Barefoot Bandit kills a Wells Fargo employee and make off with some money. It looks like an open and shut case because prize fighter Miller Sledge runs around bare-footed, and now has skipped town.

148.146 *The Hand That Shook the Hand.* Feb. 6, 1961. GS: Vito Scotti, Claude Akins, I. Stanford Jolley. The stage is met by Hardie and the sheriff who have had word there is a troublesome brute on board. When Jim finds the man has been drinking, he hauls him away to sleep it off. The next morning he finds out that the bruiser is none other than John L. Sullivan, en route to a fight.

148.147 *That Washburn Girl.* Feb. 13, 1961. GS: Jack Nicholson, Mari Aldon, John Archer, Anne Whitfield, Morris Ankrum, Gene Roth. Wells Fargo sub-agent Nora Washburn gets upset when her brother Tom tells her he is getting married. The fiancee is Ruby Coe, daughter of former outlaw Jonas Coe, and Coe hates Tom Washburn.

148.148 *The Diamond Dude.* Feb. 27, 1961. GS: Robert Middleton, James Milhollin, Grant Sullivan, Bill Hale. Hardie is assigned to protect an Eastern diamond salesman named

Leroy Finch and his small fortune in diamonds. Finch, however, doesn't appreciate Hardie's close guard on him, especially when he tries to show the diamonds to an old friend.

148.149 *A Show from Silver Lode.* March 6, 1961. GS: Patrice Wymore, Jerry O'Sullivan, John Lasell, Thomas B. Henry. Glamorous Pearl Harvey arrives to entertain the miners of Silver Lode, but refuses to go on when she discovers her dog Poochie is missing. It looks like a sad day for the eager miners, and a sad day for Wells Fargo — they had insured Poochie for a large sum.

148.150 *Fraud.* March 13, 1961. GS: Earl Hansen, Michael Whalen, Sue Ane Langdon, Steve Brodie. Blazing Rock's Fargo agent is found dead with a gun in his hand. Marshal Williams says it is suicide, but Hardie believes otherwise.

148.151 *Stage from Yuma.* March 20, 1961. GS: Brad Dexter, Harry Harvey, Jr., Joan Evans. Outlaw Bud Pierce hires gunslinger Clint Carpenter to help his gang hold up the stage from Yuma. Carpenter has more than a casual interest in the job as he is Jim Hardie in disguise.

148.152 *Prince Jim.* March 27, 1961. GS: Norma Leavitt, J. Pat O'Malley, Gina Gillespie, Kristine Miller. When highwaymen rob the stagecoach to Danton, little Carol Butler isn't too upset until they take her doll. Hardie promises Carol to catch the dollnappers.

148.153 *The Remittance Man.* April 3, 1961. GS: David Frankham, Yvonne Craig, William Mims, Ron Soble. Badman Tim Flaherty has succumbed to an occupational disease — gunfire. Opportunist Gabe Adams fired the shot, planning to make off with the loot from Flaherty's latest caper. But when Hardie suddenly appears Adams decides to settle for the reward money, only to discover that Flaherty's body has vanished.

148.154 *The Jealous Man.* April 10, 1961. GS: Faith Domergue, Ed Nelson, John Zaremba. Kitty Thorpe told her jail-bound husband Andy that their marriage was all washed up, and he reacted by threatening to kill her. Now Andy has escaped from prison, and Kitty asks Hardie to protect her.

148.155 *Something Pretty.* April 17, 1961. GS: Peter Whitney, Margo Lorenz, Dennis Moore, James Seay, Leonard Nimoy, William Giorgio. While fleeing from the law, a bandit throws a stolen diamond bracelet into the brush. Moose Gilliam, the slow-witted town handyman, stumbles upon the valuable gems, but is afraid to tell anyone about him.

148.156 *Lady Trouble.* April 24, 1961. GS: Josephine Hutchinson, Robert Armstrong, Robert Richards, Barry Cahill. Agatha Webster, wealthy owner of a mining company, arrives in Saddle Ridge to give the Wells Fargo service there the once-over. She will award them the contract for handling her firm's shipments, once Hardie has proven the company's mettle.

148.157 *Moment of Glory.* May 1, 1961. GS: Bryan Russell, Eddy Waller, Edith Evanson. Travelers aren't exactly dying to book passage on the Mountain Stage Line, but they will certainly be dead if they don't. Owner Bart Dillon's hired gunmen coerce Wells Fargo passengers into transferring to his line and Hardie is sent to restore a sense of fair competition.

148.158 *The Lobo.* May 8, 1961. GS: Jim Davis, Betsy Hale. Sam Horne, wanted for a Wells Fargo robbery and murder, is wounded in a gunfight with Boyd and Bevoe Sawyer. Fargo agent Hi Walker hears of Sam's plight and offers Hardie a huge reward out of his own pocket to bring Horne in, preferable Dead. But Hardie wants to know Horne's side of the story.

148.159 *Rifles for Red Hand.* May 15, 1961. GS: Ziva Rodann, Harp McGuire, Carleton G. Young, Edmund Hashim, Stanley Adams, J. Anthony Hughes. The Army suspects that comely gambling-hall owner Leah Harper is selling guns to the Indians, and shipping her merchandise via Wells Fargo. Captain Rawlings of the Cavalry asks Hardie to help him investigate.

148.160 *Gunman's Revenge.* May 22, 1961. GS: Harry Carey, Jr., Robert Foulk, Ollie O'Toole, Roy Wright, Larrian Gillespie, Jimmy Gaines, Jenny Lynn. Rocky Nelson is being released from prison, and the rumor is that he is aiming to take revenge on the four men who convicted him. Hardie, who is on the list, tries to warn the other three.

148.161 *The Repentant Outlaw.* May 29, 1961. GS: Edgar Buchanan, Lew Gallo, Leonard Bell, John Dennis. Hardie escorts an Army payroll into Mesa City, but finds the soldiers won't be by to pick it up for two more days. Since the Sheriff is leaving town, Jim can do nothing but allow himself to be deputized and protect the money himself.

148.162 *A Quiet Little Town.* June 5, 1961. GS: John Dehner, Shirley Ballard, Bill Henry, Stephen Courtleigh. Marshal David Prescott has cleaned up the town of Warburg, and manages to keep it that way, until he is murdered.

148.163 *Bitter Vengeance.* June 12, 1961. GS: Tom Gilson, Nina Shipman, Lillian Bronson, Phyllis Coates, Richard Hale, Edgar Dearing. Sarah Martin is desperately in need of money. When Hardie recovers a lot of loot from captured outlaw Joe Snyder, Sarah sees her chance to get some of it by helping Snyder to escape.

148.164 *John Jones.* June 26, 1961. GS: Justice Watson, Donna Martell. An elderly passenger has been kidnaped from the Wells Fargo stage. Called in to investigate Hardie questions a gypsy girl named Zita who was riding with Jones at the time.

148.165 *The Dowry.* July 10, 1961. GS: Lisa Gaye, Alan Napier, Wynn Pearce, George Chandler, Bob Anderson. Hardie starts out on a carefree riverboat trip to New Orleans, but he soon acquire responsibilities. He is hired to keep an eye on Michelle Bovarde and her dowry, a fortune in jewels and securities.

Season Six

148.166 *Casket 7.3.* Sept. 30, 1961. GS: Howard Keel, Suzanne Lloyd, Torin Thatcher. In New Orleans, a group of ex-Confederates raid a steamer and steal a casket.

148.167 *The Dodger.* Oct. 7, 1961. GS: Claude Akins, Philip Carey, Steven Darrell, Jon Lormer, Paul Barselow. Jay Squire, a man Hardie helped send to jail ten years earlier, is out of prison and seeking revenge. He is passing out leaflets offering a big reward to the man who gets Hardie, and the leaflets specify dead only.

148.168 *Treasure Coach.* Oct. 14, 1961. GS: Robert Vaughn, Pat Crowley, J. Pat O'Malley, Jocelyn Brando, Shari Lee Bernath, Tol Avery. Hardie and Beau set a trap for bandit Billy Brigode whom they expect to try to rob the stage when it stops in Cinnabar. But Brigode fails to show and the agents must continue the run, risking attack by both Brigode and renegade Indians.

148.169 *Death Raffle.* Oct. 21, 1961. GS: Gary Clarke, Bennye Gatteys, Kelly Thordsen, Gregg Palmer, Grant Sullivan, Paul Bryar. Ex-safecracker Davie Hewitt is stranded in Gloribee where, it just so happens, a large shipment of money is being held in the bank. Jim decides to keep a close watch on Hewitt, and is berated for it by a girl named Jessamie, who thinks he is picking on a former outlaw.

148.170 *Tanoa.* Oct. 18, 1961. GS: Pat Michon, Richard Hale, Rudolph Acosta, Ricky Branson, Charles Watts. Hardie and Beau meet with Chief Pochalo to negotiate a new stage route through Indian territory. Pochalo is satisfied with the results of the meeting but his cousin Red Knife is itching to get back on the warpath.

148.171 *Mr. Mute.* Nov. 4, 1961. GS: Vito Scotti, Lyle Bettger, Lane Bradford, Ron Soble. A pair of crooks named LaPorte and Hull hijack a Wells Fargo money shipment, board a train and hide their loot in the trunk of a circus clown named Mr. Mute.

148.172 *Jeremiah.* Nov. 11, 1961. GS: Nancy Gates, Albert Salmi, Margarita Cordova, Bryan Russell, Jennifer Gillespie, Joseph Ruskin, Joe Brown, Steve Warren. Jeremiah Logart was once a friend of Jim Hardie's, but now they are on opposite sides of the law. When Jeremiah tries to rob a Wells Fargo office, Hardie is waiting for him.

148.173 *A Fistful of Pride.* Nov. 18, 1961. GS: Eddie Albert, Ed Nelson, Gina Gillespie, Barbara Stuart, David White. Bonzo Croydon, a boxer who has hit the skids, gets involved in a legal fight with his estranged wife over custody of their daughter Cindy. To prove he can take care of Cindy, Bonzo gets involved in an even tougher fight with a young boxer called the Frisco Kid.

148.174 *Defiant at the Gate.* Nov. 25, 1961. GS: Tom Tully, Gloria Talbot, Nesdon Booth, Frank Ferguson, L.Q. Jones, Joe Forte. Old outlaw Matt Blackner decides to pay a final visit to his family in the town of Rimfire. But Blackner's return is not a happy one — his wife is dead, his daughter denies him and his old gang wants a cut from his last robbery.

148.175 *Man of Another Breed.* Dec. 2, 1961. GS: Debra Paget, Robert Middleton, Tom Gilson, Dee Pollack, Wright King, Willis Bouchey. Jim and Beau set out to visit station agent Frank Dane, who is due for retirement. But Dave isn't going to retire, he's murdered shortly after Jim and Beau arrive.

148.176 *Kelly's Clover Girls.* Dec. 9, 1961. GS: Virginia Field, Dawn Wells, Lisa Gaye, Michael Pate, Hank Patterson, Glenn Strange, Earl Hansen. Three dance-hall girls are being transported to Nevada as witnesses in a murder trial. But a man named Kalo is trying to prevent them from reaching their destination, and for a good reason — he was the murderer.

148.177 *A Killing in Calico.* Dec. 16, 1961. GS: Dean Jones, John Larch, George Brenlin, Patricia Breslin, Byron Foulger, Herb Vigran. There is a large reward for information leading to the arrest of any members of the infamous Morgan gang. Jamie Coburn, one of Morgan's gunslingers, tells Hardie he will surrender provided he gets the reward money and can pay a last visit to his mother before he goes to prison.

148.178 *New Orleans Trackdown.* Dec. 23, 1961. GS: Tina Louise, Wilton Graff, Henry Brandt. A pair of gunmen try to rob the stage of a small package, but Beau, with the help of passenger Roger Montclair, manages to thwart them. Montclair then shows his true colors. He clobbers Beau and makes off with the package himself.

148.179 *Trackback.* Dec. 30, 1961. GS: Richard Rust, Leo Gordon, John Cliff, Morgan Woodward, Steven Darrell, Ed Mallory. Outlaw Frank Lambert is not pleased when his younger brother Wally rides into his hideout. Frank is afraid Hardie may be following. But Wally isn't upset, even though Frank is right.

148.180 *Moneyrun.* Jan. 6, 1962. GS: Michael Ansara, George Dolenz, Anna Navarro, Rodolfo Hoyos, Baynes Barron, Larry Chance, Vinton Hayworth, Frank Gerstle. Mexico has fallen under the hand of the Emperor Maximilian, so former Governor Rafael De Lopa and his ward Carla decide it might be safer across the border. They make a dash for Gloribee with Maximilian's soldiers right behind them.

148.181 *Return to Yesterday.* Jan. 13, 1962. GS: Dianne Foster, Addison Richards, Lew Gallo, Yvette Vickers, Phil Chambers, Steven Darrell, Phil Tully. Noted concert singer Ella Congreve arrives in town and her father asks Hardie to guard his daughter and her jewelry collection. But Hardie is reluctant. He remembers Ella when she was an unknown and his girl friend.

148.182 *Reward for Gaine.* Jan. 20, 1962. GS: John Doucette, John War Eagle, Brad Weston, John Anderson, Robert Osterloh, Loyal "Doc" Lucas, Linda Dangcil, Steven Terrell, Robert Karnes, Kit Carson, Dean Smith, Allen Pinson. Sergeant Gaine learns from three condemned soldiers that their plight is the fault of their commanding officer, Colonel Bledsie, who attacked some Indians without provocation. An Indian scout named Kill Eagle, who witnessed the raid, might have vindicate them, but Kill Eagle wasn't allowed to testify.

148.183 *Assignment in Gloribee.* Jan. 27, 1962. GS: Rod Cameron, Patricia Owens, George Kennedy, Stafford Repp, Lenny Geer, Steven Darrell. Writer Katherine Anne Murdock, on her way to Gloribee to do a story about the West, meets gunman Nathan Chance on the train. Just as they are about to get better acquainted, bounty hunter Jeelo Curran gets the drop on them and Nathan kills him.

148.184 *Incident at Crossbow.* Feb. 3, 1962. GS: Robert Sampson, Dara Howard, Sean McClory, Dan Sheridan, Hal Baylor, Allen Jaffe, Michael Forest, Russell Thorson, Robert B. Williams. A San Francisco-bound stage carrying Hardie pulls up at the Crossbow way station, but manager Jug Perry seems to be missing. Suddenly he appears, escorted by bank robber Con Toole and his well-armed companions Hondo and Case.

148.185 *Portrait of Teresa.* Feb. 10, 1962. GS: Arthur Franz, Simon Oakland, Georgette Duval, George Keymas, Rico Alaniz, Roberto Contreras, Bill Catching, Rankin Mansfield, William Fawcett, Boyd Stockman, Hal Needham, Red Morgan. A wealthy Mexican named Poderio is looking for American Mel Akin. Mel is a portrait painter, but Poderio doesn't want a picture of himself. He just wants Mel to return his fiancee, Teresa.

148.186 *Hometown Doctor.* Feb. 17, 1962. GS: Richard Long, Nina Shipman, Ken Scott, George Wallace, Emerson Treacy. Hardie must wait for the veterinarian to arrive and inspect Tom Rogers' herd before he can accept delivery for Wells Fargo. But the drovers are a restless lot and they soon kick up enough ruckus to make the citizens of Gloribee wonder if Hardie isn't observing the law too strictly.

148.187 *The Traveler.* Feb. 24, 1962. GS: Jack Warden, Ken Mayer, Warren Kemmerling, Tyler McVey, Chuck Roberson, Phil Chambers, Dorothy Lovett. No one knows why, but respected schoolteacher Brad Axton has suddenly decided to quit his job and head for Gloribee. And Brad doesn't know that two tough customers named Sunderman and Morgan have decided to follow him.

148.188 *Winter Storm.* March 3, 1962. GS: Dan Duryea, R.G. Armstrong, Eddie Firestone, Jim Beck, Gale Garnett, Boyd Stockman. Caught in the middle of a raging snow storm, Hardie, Jeb and Tina are forced to look for temporary refuge. Their search leads them to what appears to be a ghost town, and then they notice lights in the supposedly deserted hotel.

148.189 *Chauncey.* March 17, 1962. GS: Burt Brinckerhoff, Andy Albin, Phil Chambers, Donald Elsom. Tina finds that she and young Chuck Evans share an interest in the cultured things in life. And it is not long before she finds him interesting in other ways. He may be just the man to help her escape her life as a schoolteacher.

148.190 *Who Lives by the Gun.* March 24, 1962. GS: Burt Patton, Judith Evelyn, Paul Birch, Rex Holman, Kathie Browne, Howard Wright, John Alderson, John Archer, John Mitchum, Kit Carson. Hardie and Sheriff Maxon have cornered robbers Tolly Sherman and Jeff Callan in a cabin. Then Callan makes a break for it and Hardie wounds him, only to discover that Jeff is a young boy and his gun isn't loaded.

148.191 *To Kill a Town.* March 31, 1962. GS: Buddy Ebsen, Joan Staley, Russell Johnson, Peter Helm, Harry Lauter. Hardie is delivering outlaw Lou Reese to prison, and when they camp for the night a voice calls out of the darkness with a proposition. It is a man named Normalie and he would like Hardie to let him hang Reese.

148.192 *End of a Minor God.* April 7, 1962. GS: Eileen Ryan, Lin McCarthy, Jan Merlin, Robert J. Stevenson, William Schallert, Hank Patterson, Steven Darrell. Badman Billy Trent buys a ticket out of Gloribee on the Wells Fargo stage. Then Hardie learns that someone is gunning for Trent, and begs Billy not to endanger the other passengers by taking the trip.

148.193 *Remember the Yazoo.* April 14, 1962. GS: Jason Evers, James Westerfield, Robert Cornthwaite, Jonathan Kidd, Alan Napier. Gunman Sam Heffridge is bailed out of jail by a stranger named Anthony Boaz, who only wants a small favor in return, Sam's help in robbing the Wells Fargo office in New Orleans.

148.194 *The Angry Sky.* April 21, 1962. GS: Arch Johnson, Fay Spain, James Griffith, Robert Colbert, Anne Barton, Gabrielle desEnfants. Swede Lowell is assigned to accompany his friend Jim Hardie with a shipment of diamond drills. Two outlaws named Jensen and Rossi set in motion their plans to steal the drills by kidnaping Lowell's wife and daughter.

148.195 *Royal Maroon.* April 28, 1962. GS: Kathleen Crowley, Harold J. Stone, Frank Ferguson, Ron Foster, Rush Williams, Charles Seel. A stagecoach driver named Sedge is known as a man who won't stop his coach for anything except a pretty girl. So when he spots lovely Royal Maroon, naturally he stops and, naturally, he gets robbed.

148.196 *The Gold Witch.* May 5, 1962. GS: Ron Randall, Diana Millay, Alan Hale, Jr., Whit Bissell. People are amazed at Arthur Reardon's hypnotism act. Under one of Arthur's trances, his wife seems to know everything about everybody in town.

148.197 *Don't Wake a Tiger.* May 12, 1962. GS: Royal Dano, Jim Davis, Gary Clarke, Kelly Thordsen, Marjorie Reynolds, Harp McGuire, William Tannen, Tom Greenway, Hank Patterson, Charles Briggs. The revenge bent Sawyers have been looking for a man named Mapes for a long time. When they find Mapes running a Wells Fargo relay station they stage a kidnaping and imprison him in a barbed-wire enclosure.

148.198 *The Wayfarers.* May 19, 1962. GS: James Coburn, Roxane Berard, Hugh Marlowe, June Vincent, Robert Ellenstein, Robert Bray, Paul Fierro. Having just robbed a Wells Fargo office, Ben Crider and Ada Parker are heading for Mexico. Only miles from the border, they find that Hardie is waiting for them.

148.199 *Vignette of a Sinner.* June 2, 1962. GS: Jeff Morrow, Edward C. Platt, Joyce Taylor, William Mims, James Craig. Banker Les Caldwell has a plan to make himself really wealthy. The trouble is that a Wells Fargo safe gets cleaned out in the process.

149. The Tall Man

NBC. 30 min. Broadcast history: Saturday, 8:30-9:00, Sept. 1960–Sept. 1962.

Regular Cast: Clu Gulager (Billy Kid), Barry Sullivan (Sheriff Pat Garrett).

Premise: This series depicted the relationship between outlaw Billy the Kid and Sheriff Pat Garrett in Lincoln County, New Mexico, in the late 1870s.

The Episodes

149.1 *Garrett and the Kid.* Sept. 10, 1960. GS: Robert Middleton, Denver Pyle, King Donovan, Hank Patterson, Ray Kellogg. Gambler Paul Mason is trying to take over Lincoln County, and it looks like he might succeed. He has bought off everyone except Pat Garrett.

149.2 *Forty-Dollar Boots.* Sept. 17, 1960. Ron Soble, Ken Lynch, Jim Davis, Ford Rainey, Tom London. Jerry Evers offers Billy the Kid a handsome new pair of boots if he well help drive a herd of stolen cattle out of the county. Billy can't resist the bait.

149.3 *Bad Company.* Sept. 24, 1960. GS: Otto Waldis, Ralph Votrian, Jason Johnson, Guy Wilkerson, Adele Lamont. Karl Nagel accuses Billy the Kid of leading his son astray and causing his death. He wants Pat Garrett to make an arrest.

149.4 *The Shawl.* Oct. 1, 1960. GS: Frank Killmond, Gregory Walcott, Daria Massey, Linda Dangcil, Will J. White. The Roberts brothers are gunning for Billy, but they kill his sweetheart Maria by mistake. Meanwhile, Billy is heading home with a fancy Spanish shawl as a gift for his girl.

149.5 *The Lonely Star.* Oct. 8, 1960. GS: Jim Davis, Ken Lynch, Ford Rainey, Henry Norell, Russ Bender, Walter Lawrence. Sheriff Brady is shot on election eve, and his dying request is that Deputy Garrett run for the office. But Bob Orringer, Brady's opponent is out to win the election any way he can.

149.6 *A Bounty for Billy.* Oct. 5, 1960. GS: Leonard Nimoy, Ray Dale, Marianne Hill, Robert Patten, Malcolm Atterbury, Robert J. Stevenson, Charles Seel, Bob Adler. Pat Garrett has just been elected sheriff, but his enemies don't seem

The Tall Man

to waste much time. The express office is robbed, and Pat is shot from ambush. Deputy Johnny Smith has evidence that the guilty party is Billy the Kid.

149.7 *The Parson.* Oct. 29, 1960. GS: Harold J. Stone, Robert Shawley, Richard Devon, Ed Prentiss. Ben Myers and his son Jubal are looking for the men who blinded Ben. They go into a saloon where somebody is preaching a sermon, and Ben recognizes the voice of the man they are looking for.

149.8 *Night Train to Tularosa.* Nov. 5, 1960. GS: Claude Akins, Robert McQueeney, Norman Pabst, Jr., Doye O'Dell, Howard McLeod. Garrett is taking killer Dan Rees to prison board the night train to Tularosa and, so far as he is concerned, justice has never been sweeter. Rees had married and caused the death of the girl Pat loved.

149.9 *Larceny and Young Ladies.* Nov. 12, 1960. GS: Cindy Robbins, Judy Nugent, Steven Darrell, Andy Clyde, John Cliff, Phil Chambers. Teenagers May and June McBean steal some horses, but they manage to convince Garrett that the herd is theirs. Then the girls go on step further and steal Garrett's horse.

149.10 *Counterfeit Law.* Nov. 19, 1960. GS: George Macready, Lane Bradford, Harry Harvey, Jr., George Mitchell, Ralph Neff. Roy Barlow is the law around Gunsite. Billy goes to Barlow's place to collect money for some cows he sold. He is beaten, robbed and thrown into Barlow's jail.

149.11 *And the Beast.* Nov. 26, 1960. GS: Ellen Willard, Regis Toomey, Marianna Hill. Garrett gets word of trouble at the Corbin Ranch and when he gets there, sure enough the Corbins are dead. But Agatha Evans, the hired girl, tells Pat that the killer was really after her.

149.12 *Bitter Ashes.* Dec. 3, 1960. GS: Narda Onyx, R.G. Armstrong, Don Kennedy, Paul Baxley, Ernesto Zambrano. It is a few days before the wedding and Garrett rides out to visit his fiancee, Teresa Oberon. He arrives to find the ranch in flames, Teresa's father dead and neighbor Neal Bailey and his men chasing the terrified girl.

149.13 *McBean Rides Again.* Dec. 10, 1960. GS: Judy Nugent, Olive Sturgess, Andy Clyde, Patrick Waltz, Iron Eyes Cody. Tomboys June and May McBean learn that Garrett thinks their pa is selling firewater to the Indians. Pa is innocent, but the prankish juveniles decide to help Garrett prove his suspicions.

149.14 *Tiger Eye.* Dec. 17, 1960. GS: Richard Bakalyan, Paul Bryar, Michael Hinn, Rex Holman, Joe Yrigoyen. An Apache youth has killed his girl, and his tribe ties him to a stake on an anthill. Billy rescues the boy and gets him a job sweeping the saloon, but the townspeople don't like him any better than his tribesmen did.

149.15 *Billy's Baby.* Dec. 24, 1960. GS: Marianna Hill, K.L. Smith, Pedro Regas. Billy and his girl Rita are whooping it up in the local tavern, and along comes a tough guy named Hartman who insults Rita.

149.16 *One of One Thousand.* Dec. 31, 1960. GS: George Wallace, Harry Carey, Jr., Jack Mather, Craig Duncan, Loyal T. Lucas, Tom Jackson. Garrett is the winner in a rifle shoot, and his prize is a dandy new Winchester. But when it is time to collect the award, the gunsmith has been murdered and the rifle is missing.

149.17 *First Blood.* Jan. 7, 1961. GS: Jan Merlin, Robert Montgomery, Jr., Ken Lynch, Red Morgan. Hendry Grant has shot down fifteen men, but he still can't match Billy the Kid's record. Grant figures the only thing to do is to make Billy his next victim.

149.18 *A Gun Is for Killing.* Jan. 14, 1961. GS: Gregg Palmer, Leonard Nimoy, Mary Webster, George Orrison, Robert E. Griffin. A hard-living rancher named Blanchard and his gang hit town, intent on painting it red. When Deputy Johnny Swift tries to contain the rowdies, Swift gets killed for his trouble.

149.19 *The Grudge Fight.* Jan. 21, 1961. GS: Richard Jaeckel, Jerry Summers. A fight may go to the death. Billy and a young man named Denver have sworn to kill each other.

149.20 *The Best Policy.* Jan. 28, 1961. GS: James Coburn, Ron Harper. Cattleman John Miller adds a few of his branded animals to a herd belonging to Pat and Billy Then Miller accuses the boys of rustling.

149.21 *The Reversed Blade.* Feb. 4, 1961. GS: John Archer, Jeanne Cooper, Murray Matheson. Ben Webster plans to rob John Tundall by remote control. He sends his wife Elmira to do the dirty work. Elmira is reluctant since Tundall is her former husband.

149.22 *Dark Moment.* Feb. 11, 1961. GS: Martin Landau, Mimi Gibson, Adelina Pedroza, Justice Watson, Charles Webster. Francisco, a tenant farmer, accidentally shoots his landlord to death during an argument. Judy, the landlord's daughter and the only witness, is also wounded. When Garrett arrives, Judy is near death and is only able to point out Francisco as the killer.

149.23 *The Reluctant Bridegroom.* Feb. 18, 1961. GS: Judy Nugent, Olive Sturgess, Andy Clyde, Ellen Corby. The mischievous McBean girls are back. They think it is time for their Pa to get married again, so they send a letter of proposal to widow Hannah Blossom, signing Pa's name, but enclosing Garrett's picture.

149.24 *Maria's Little Lamb.* Feb. 25, 1961. GS: Pat Michon, Martin Garralaga, James Westerfield, Robert Hoy. Billy goes or Maria in a big way. Her father, however, is a sheep rancher, which traditionally means trouble with the local cattlemen. Torn between Maria and Garrett, who is aligned with the cattlemen, Billy isn't sure which side he will take if it comes to a showdown.

149.25 *Big Sam's Boy.* March 4, 1961. GS: Russell Collins, Paul Carr, Lew Gallo, John Damler, Henry Hunter, Don Ross. A pair of schemers named Jarrico and Clegg decide to capitalize on the death of Lonnie, an Army buddy who was the long-lost son of wealthy Sam Masters. Jarrico and Clegg talk a third man into posing as Lonnie.

149.26 *The Last Resource.* March 11, 1961. GS: Robert J. Wilke, Marianne Hill. In a gunfight, Billy accidentally kills an innocent bystander, the young daughter of Marshal Ben Hartley. Garrett puts Billy in jail.

149.27 *Rovin' Gambler.* March 18, 1961. GS: Faith Domergue, Robert Lansing, X Brands, Tom London, George Hickman, Charles Watts. Kate Elder, who tips the bottle occasionally, witnesses a murder and puts the blame on her former boy friend, Doc Holliday.

149.28 *Hard Justice.* March 25, 1961. GS: Lyle Bettger, Steve Warren, Steve Raines, Mike Masters, Mark Tapscott, Jack Hogan, Bruno VeSota. Vince Ober is supposed to be buying cattle for the Army, but he is really trying to arrange a deal that will profit only himself. He asks Billy to rustle some cattle and, when Billy refuses, sends a couple of killers to gun him down.

149.29 *The Legend and the Gun.* April 1, 1961. GS: Michael Pate, Jocelyn Brando, Tom Gilson, Gene Roth, Buzz Martin. Billy's stepfather, Bill Antrim, is attacked and killed by a trio of gunmen. When the news reaches town, Billy vows vengeance on the murderers and, despite Garrett's warning, takes the law into his own hands.

149.30 *A Kind of Courage.* April 8, 1961. GS: James Griffith, Tommy Ivo, David Kent. Ex-lawman Clint Latimer has a passion for invoking parental discipline and he has the impression that his son Jody is learning to be a gunslinger from Billy the Kid.

149.31 *Millionaire McBean.* April 15, 1961. GS: Judy Nugent, Olive Sturgess, Andy Clyde. Tomboys June and May McBean are up to their old tricks. The girls figure that if people thought their Pa was rich, they might land a husband, so they plant some gold in the old man's mine.

149.32 *A Scheme of Hearts.* April 22, 1961. GS: Kathleen Hughes, John Lassell, Raymond Hatton, Ralph Votrian, Joanne Moriarity. Nita Jardine wants to get rid of her husband Ben. Toward this end she makes a play for both Pat and Billy, hoping Ben will become jealous enough to take one of them on in a gunfight.

149.33 *The Cloudbusters.* April 29, 1961. GS: Sue George, Frank de Kova, Gregory Morton, George Keymas. Henrietta Russell is a rainmaker hired by the citizens of Lincoln County to break a long drought. But one man stands to lose by this deal, Mike Gray Eagle, an Apache who has been selling water to the white men.

149.34 *Ransom of a Town.* May 6, 1961. GS: Michael Forest, Michael Burns, Eduardo Ciannelli, Stephen Ellsworth. An outlaw named Ledall kidnaps the local padre, figuring that everyone in town will chip in to help meet his ransom. While Garrett is trying to figure a way to save the good father, Billy decides to borrow the ransom money from the bank.

149.35 *Ladies of the Town.* May 20, 1961. GS: Monica Lewis, Wesley Lau, Claire Carleton, John Harmon, Fred Sherman. The ladies of the town decide to take things into their own hands and clean up the community. They start by demanding that Sal, the dance-hall hostess, leave town.

149.36 *Death or Taxes.* May 27, 1961. GS: Alan Baxter, Joe De Santis, James Seay, Will Wright. A railroad land purchaser named Fallon has secured the right-of-way through town. But he refuses to pay the required taxes and backs us his stand with a gang of gunmen.

149.37 *The Great Western.* June 3, 1961. GS: Connie Gilchrist, Frank Ferguson, Howard Negley, Ron Starr, Robert Tafur. Garrett thinks it would be a good idea to clean up the town before Territorial Governor Lew Wallace arrives. He plans to run out a saloonkeeper named Big Mamacita. Her plans are to stay right where she is.

Season Two

149.38 *Full Payment.* Sept. 9, 1961. GS: Rory Mallinson, Jim Boles, William Phipps, Alice Frost, Harry Von Zell, Jack Spain. Jack Barron has vowed to kill Billy, and he shows up in Lincoln County demanding that the Kid be turned over to him. Garrett refuses, despite townsmen's fears that Barron will enforce his request by bringing his gang into town.

149.39 *The Liberty Belle.* Sept. 16, 1961. GS: Patricia Donahue, Chris Alcaide, Wally Brown, Hal K. Dawson, Alan Carney. Elena, Garrett's old heartthrob, returns to town, and Pat is almost oblivious to the fact that she is accompanied by gun-toting Joe Durango, the man she left Pat to join three years earlier.

149.40 *Where Is Sylvia?* Sept. 23, 1961. GS: Patricia Barry, Stanley Kohn, Jeff DeBenning, Tom Monroe, Wallace Rooney. Garrett and Billy take in a poker session in El Paso, and take their opponents to the cleaners. Then a woman named Sylvia approaches and pleads with Pat and the Kid to return her husband's losses.

149.41 *The Female Artillery.* Sept. 30, 1961. GS: Nan Leslie, Joan Evans, Susan Crane. Billy is wounded by Apaches, and seeks refuge in an abandoned Army fort while the Indians regroup for another attack. In the fort, Billy finds three women huddled together, two with babies and the third one expecting.

149.42 *Shadow of the Past.* Oct. 7, 1961. GS: Charles Aidman, Nancy Davis, Barbara Perkins, Mark Tapscott. When Ben Wiley and his family arrive in Lincoln County, Pat thinks he recognizes the man as someone out of his past. He gets a chance to confirm his suspicions when the Wileys invite him and Billy for dinner.

149.43 *An Item for Auction.* Oct. 14, 1961. GS: Sandy Kenyon, Jena Engstrom, Charles Fredericks, Frank Sully. Town ne'er-do-well Sam Nayfack is offering an item for sale at the local saloon. When Garrett learns that the merchandise is Nayfack's young daughter Susan, he decides to intervene.

149.44 *The Judas Palm.* Oct. 21, 1961. GS: Edgar Buchanan, Vincent Padula, Marianna Hill, Craig Duncan, Dallas MacKennon. Drifter Archie Keogh holds up a saloon in Lincoln and then makes it look as though Billy pulled the job. Garrett jails Billy even though he knows he isn't the guilty party.

149.45 *The Woman.* Oct. 28, 1961. GS: Don Harvey, Kay E. Kuter, Coleen Gray, Julie Sommars. Garrett shoots down a horse thief, and finds himself in a dilemma. Jeboriah Henry, brother of the dead man, demands that Pat marry his victim's widow or die.

149.46 *Trial by Hanging.* Nov. 4, 1961. GS: George Kennedy, Walter Kinsella, Richard Carlyle. Billy goes to work for a rancher named Jake Newton, unaware that his new employer is wanted for murder. A lynch mob shows up looking for Newton and, unable to find its quarry, turns its menacing attentions to Billy.

149.47 *The Leopard's Spots.* Nov. 11, 1961. GS: Paul Birch, Bennye Gatteys, Don Megowan, Frank Watkins, John Halloran. Billy wants to impress a gentle girl named Charity, so he stops wearing his guns. Then a couple of hired killer's show up and they are out to get Bill.

149.48 *Petticoat Crusade.* Nov. 18, 1961. GS: Mona Freeman, Harry Von Zell, Cecil Smith, Herbert C. Lytton. Suffragette Amy Dodds throws a brick through Pat Garrett's window and demands to be arrested. Garrett refuses, so she goes on down the street to Murphy's saloon and throws some more bricks.

149.49 *Time of Foreshadowing.* Nov. 25, 1961. GS: Vic Morrow, Judi Meredith, Robert Foulk, Larry Perron. Billy encounters Skip Farrell, who once saved his life, and it looks like Billy has a chance to repay the favor. Skip is fleeing a posse and Billy agrees to help him to safety.

149.50 *Fool's Play.* Dec. 2, 1961. GS: Paul Comi, Phyllis Love, Mark Tapscott, Fredric deWilde. Billy has a job riding shotgun on Bert Wilson's stage. It looks like a pretty routine run until they are surprised by a bandit named Pollitt.

149.51 *Legend of Billy.* Dec. 9, 1961. GS: Berry Kroeger, Emile Meyer, Mark Tapscott, Harry Antrim. New York writer Dean Almond shows up in Lincoln and writes a first hand story on Billy the Kid. The article also includes some references to Sheriff Garrett and the state legislature investigates Garrett because of it.

149.52 *A Tombstone for Billy.* Dec. 16, 1961. GS: Howard McNear, Natividad Vacio, Russell Collins, Herbert C. Lytton, Don Kennedy. Cyrus Skinner, the town skinflint, has purchased his tombstone. But Fate seems to have other plans as the headstone mysteriously appears over the grave of Maria Gonzales, whose husband Juan was too poor to afford one.

149.53 *Sidekick.* Dec. 23, 1961. GS: Rafael Lopez, Earl Hansen, Alma Beltran, Stafford Repp, Joseph Conway, Tim Graham, Lennie Geer. Billy rides onto the scene just in time to prevent a wagon driver named Sledge from bullwhipping a Mexican boy named Fosforito. Then Billy learns that Sledge considers Fosforito his property, purchased from the boy's mother for a few dollars.

149.54 *Apache Daughter.* Dec. 30, 1961. GS: Sherry Jackson, J. Pat O'Malley, Anthony Hall, Ralph Moody. An Apache girl named White Moon is found to be Sally Bartlett, a white girl captured years ago by the Indians. Garrett arranges for her return to her family, and he and Billy ride out to escort her home.

149.55 *Substitute Sheriff.* Jan. 6, 1962. GS: Andy Clyde, Cindy Robbins, Judy Nugent, Bob Hastings. The railroad line is coming through and that means eviction for the McBean family. But May and June McBean get an idea. Pa can stp the process server if he poses as Sheriff Pat Garrett.

149.56 *The Girl from Paradise.* Jan. 13, 1962. GS: Pippa Scott, Kelly Thordsen, Frank Logan, Andy Albin. Sheriff Rafe Tollinger frames Billy on a murder charge and loads him onto a wagon with another killer to be taken out and hanged. Billy manages to find some small consolation in his companion, a pretty girl named Anne.

149.57 *St. Louis Woman.* Jan. 20, 1962. GS: Jan Clayton, Russ Conway, Roger Mobley, Larry Chance. Widow Harper and her son David arrive in Lincoln, where she is to marry Garrett's friend Tom Davis. Then Mrs. Harper begins seeing a lot of Pat, and soon she isn't sure she chose the right man.

149.58 *The Hunt.* Jan. 27, 1962. GS: Richard Ney, Madge Kennedy, Hal K. Dawson, Mark Tapscott, Hank Patterson. Wealthy Edward Van Doren and his wife Elizabeth have come out West to hunt big game. Van Doren knows just the person he wants for his guide is Billy the Kid.

149.59 *The Impatient Brides.* Feb. 3, 1962. GS: Joan O'Brien, Hollis Irving, Beverly Wills, Jane Dulo, Tom Fadden, Adam Stewart. A stagecoach carrying four mail-order brides is forced to stop in Lincoln when the Apaches go on the warpath. The housing situation is desperate, so the girls turn to Garrett and demand that he put them in jail.

149.60 *Rio Doloroso.* Feb. 10, 1962. GS: Dennis Patrick, Alex Montoya, Julia Montoya, Jose Gonzalez Gonzalez. Garrett is traveling with a prisoner named Curtis when the heat of the desert forces them to stop in the town of Rio Doloroso. The poverty-stricken inhabitants offer to share what they have, and apparently expect Garrett to do the same.

149.61 *An Hour to Die.* Feb. 17, 1962. GS: Pamela Duncan, Don Hamner, Edward Mallory, Harry Swoger, Harry Antrim. Billy is attempting to break a wild stallion when he is thrown and suffers a head injury. He comes to and starts behaving as though he is deranged.

149.62 *Property of the Crown.* Feb. 24, 1962. GS: Mark Miller, Miriam Colon, Katharine Warren. Angelita Sanchez has an old Spanish land grant she thinks is valuable. Garrett agrees that it shows that Angelita owns half of Lincoln Country.

149.63 *Night of the Hawk.* March 3, 1962. GS: John Anderson, Hal Jon Norman, David McCally. Army Major Jud Randolph, stern-mannered and unbending, isn't exactly the ideal type for his current mission to obtain the surrender of the hostile Indian chief Chatto.

149.64 *Three for All.* March 10, 1962. GS: George Kennedy, Tom Gilson, Irene Tedrow, Edgar Dearing, Allan Ray. Maw Killgore and her boys, Hyram and Dwig, meander down from the hills for a little fun in town, which consists of smashing up the local saloon.

149.65 *Quarantine.* March 17, 1962. GS: Gary Clarke, Don Beddoe, Susan Silo, I. Stanford Jolley, Mark Tapscott. Garret has taken Bob Kelso, a wounded prisoner, to Doc Beckett's office for treatment. Kelso tries to catch the eye of Beckett's daughter Amy, who used to be his girl, hoping that she might still love him enough to help him escape.

149.66 *The Four Queens.* March 24, 1962. GS: Monica Lewis, Gaylor Cavallaro, Joyce Bullifant. Showman Jacques Montreaux and his four lovely song-and-dance girls arrive in town, and Jacques stops off to show Garrett a letter from the mother of one of the girls, asking that plans to kill Billy the Kid be abandoned.

149.67 *The Long Way Home.* March 31, 1962. GS: Doris Dowling, Harp McGuire, Clancy Cooper, John McKee, Paul Theodore. A tired Billy is taking a snooze during a train ride and misses some interesting action. A marshal uncovers an illegal gun shipment and is shot by the conductor.

149.68 *A Time to Run.* April 7, 1962. GS: Sandra Knight, John Fiedler, Charles Watts, Ted Jacques. Abner Moody walks into the Lincoln jailhouse and demands that Garrett arrest him for grand theft. And in case Garrett has any doubt, Abner has a valise full of stolen cash to prove it.

149.69 *Trial by Fury.* April 14, 1962. GS: Robert Emhardt, Barbara Lawrence, James Griffith, Fuzzy Knight. Billy, Sadie Wren and Jason Cutter all have one thing in common. Each has been acquitted at one time or another of a murder charge in Judge Oliver Cromwell's court and much to Cromwell's displeasure. Now the judge has definite plans to correct these verdicts with his own private brand of justice.

149.70 *The Frame.* April 21, 1962. GS: Lori March, Harry Townes, Mark Tapscott, Hal K. Dawson, Stewart Bradley. Isobel Stewart is a very beautiful woman with a very jealous husband named Henry. Henry doesn't like it one bit when Isobel meets an old schoolmate of hers, Pat Garrett.

149.71 *The Runaway Groom.* April 28, 1962. GS:

Roberta Shore, Gary Vinson, William Bramley, Peter Miller, Bernie Fein. Garret encounters Bart and Luke Tugwell who are engaged in a grim manhunt. The quarry is their sister's husband, who ran off leaving her with a baby.

149.72 *The Black Robe.* May 5, 1962. GS: Martin Landau, Russell Thorson, Slim Pickens, Vincent St. Cyr, Chief Yowlachie. Garrett is called in to investigate when it becomes apparent that the Mescalero Apaches are getting guns and ammunition illegally.

149.73 *The Woman in Black.* May 12, 1962. GS: Gregory Morton, Adele Mara, Robert Vera, Valentin de Vargas. There was a time when Don Diego wanted to marry Rosa, but now all he wants is to see her dead. He believes that she put a curse on him.

149.74 *Doctor on Horseback.* May 19, 1962. GS: Ed Nelson, Mabel Albertson, June Kenney, Paul Hartman, Richard Reeves. When old Doc Baines passes away and young Dr. Wade Parsons tries to take his place, the local citizens regard him with mistrust.

149.75 *Phoebe.* May 26, 1962. GS: George Macready, Floy Dean Smith, Cyril Delevanti, Jon Lormer, Eve McVeagh, Clegg Hoyt, Lorna Thayer. When Phoebe Canfield runs away, her father Cyrus is furious. And Cyrus is determined to teacher her a lesson as soon as he catches her.

150. Tate

NBC. 30 min. Broadcast history: Wednesday, 9:30–10:00, June 1960–Sept. 1960.

Regular Cast: David McLean (Tate).

Premise: An ex-gunfighter who lost the use of his left arm during the Civil War, wanders the West and fights against injustice.

The Episodes

150.1 *Home Town.* June 8, 1960. GS: Royal Dano, James Coburn, Sandra Knight, Don Wilbanks, Jim Hayward. Tate returns to the town of his boyhood to repay a debt to a friend.

150.2 *Stopover.* June 15, 1960. GS: King Calder, Bill Tennant, Peggy Ann Garner. Tate is forced to shoot Ben Tracy, who is known as the fastest gun. Then he faces the wrath of young Will Smith, who wanted to launch his own gunfighting career by outdrawing Tracy.

150.3 *The Bounty Hunter.* June 22, 1960. GS: Robert Culp, Louise Fletcher, Robert Redford, Robert Warwick. Tom Sandee believes that Tate is a fugitive from justice and he goes after him.

150.4 *Voices of the Town.* July 6, 1960. GS: Paul Richards, William Mims, George Mitchell, Don Wilbanks, Gail Bonney, Bob January, Wendy Winkelman. Out to capture Frank Turner, Tate is caught in an ambush by Mrs. Turner and forced to shoot her. Angry townsfolk rise up in protest.

150.5 *A Lethal Pride.* July 20, 1960. GS: Ronald Nicholas, Marianna Hill, Gregory Morton, Jack Orrison. Manuel Arriega hires Tate to track down a fugitive from justice. Bent on revenge, Arriega wants the man killed on sight, but Tate insists on bringing him in alive.

150.6 *Tigero.* Aug. 3, 1960. GS: Martin Landau, Ted Markland, Mark Norton. Tate is escorting murderer John Chess to jail. But the Towey brothers have other plans for the prisoner.

150.7 *Comanche Scalps.* Aug. 10, 1960. GS: Frank Overton, Robert Redford, Leonard Nimoy, Lane Bradford, Anne Whitfield. Lucy was engaged to Amos Dundee, and she got married. There was just one small change in plans, the bridegroom was Amos' brother Tad. And now Amos plans to kill his brother.

150.8 *Before Sunup.* Aug. 17, 1960. GS: Robert Boon, Jean Allison, Warren Oates, Peter Whitney, William Challee, Morgan Sha'an. A cold-blooded gang of outlaws seriously wound Otto, then bet on how long he'll live. Tate guards the wounded man from Clay Sedon who wants to insure his bet.

150.9 *The Reckoning.* Aug. 24, 1960. GS: Phyllis Avery, Crahan Denton, Bing Russell. Stalking a killer named Abel King, Tate falls ill. He is nursed back to health by King's daughter Lulie.

150.10 *The Gunfighters.* Aug. 31, 1960. GS: Jack Hogan, Elizabeth Perry, Alan Reynolds, Fay Roope, Ken Mayer. Keefer, a rancher, owes his employees their year's wage of two head of cattle each. They hire Tate to help them collect. Soon Tate and the ranch hands are faced with an ambush.

150.11 *Quiet After the Storm.* Sept. 7, 1960. GS: Cathy O'Donnell, Hampton Fancher, Rusty Lane, Don Wilbanks. A girl is shot by a jealous suitor named Coley, and Tate takes after the man, hoping to reach him before a lynch mob does. He tracks him to his home and meets Jesse, Coley's aged father.

150.12 *The Return of Jessica Jackson.* Sept. 14, 1960. GS: Jock Gaynor, John Kellogg, Patricia Breslin, Henry Corden, Lilian Buyeff, Donald Losby, Jon Lormer. Tate is hired by frontiersman Milo Jackson to find his wife Jessica, who has been abducted by the Paiute Indians.

150.13 *The Mary Hardin Story.* Sept. 21, 1960. GS: Julie Adams. Tate gets a plea for help from a pretty widow. A man named Tetlow is trying to force her into giving up her land.

151. Temple Houston

NBC. 60 min. Broadcast history: Thursday, 7:30–8:30, Sept. 1963–Sept. 1964.

Regular Cast: Jeffrey Hunter (Temple Houston), Jack Elam (George Taggart).

Premise: Temple Houston, the son of Sam Houston, is a circuit-riding attorney in the early southwest. He is assisted by George Taggart, a gunslinger turned lawman.

The Episodes

151.1 *The Twisted Rope.* Sept. 19, 1963. GS: Victor Jory, Collin Wilcox, Richard Evans, Anthony Call. Dorrie Chevenix wants Temple to defend her two brothers accused of killing a sheriff. Temple must act hastily, as an irate mob wants the prisoners at the end of a rope.

151.2 *Find Angel Chavez.* Sept. 26, 1963. GS: Herbert Rudley, Rafael Campos, Gene Evans, Linda Dangcil, Anna Navarro, Woodrow Parfrey. Taggart has killed a man in a gunfight, but he may have trouble proving self-defense. Some-

Temple Houston

one has made it appeared that he gunned down an unarmed man.

151.3 Letter of the Law. Oct. 3, 1963. GS: Brenda Scott, Victor French, James Anderson, Jan Stine, Crahan Denton, Hayden Rorke, H.M. Wynant. Houston agrees to defend the Harrod brothers on criminal charges, although he believes that one of the trio is guilty.

151.4 Toll the Bell Slowly. Oct. 17, 1963. GS: Susan Kohner, Noah Beery, Jr., Everett Sloane, Leo Gordon, Royal Dano, Walter Burke, Robert Foulk, Rusty Lane, James Bell. Before Houston can clear a client, he has to clear the client's chief witness, who is scheduled to hang for murder.

151.5 The Third Bullet. Oct. 24, 1963. GS: Frank Sutton, Anne Helm, Hampton Fancher, Parley Baer, Don Beddoe, George Petrie. Convicted killer Jim Stocker finds he has two improbable allies—Houston, who is interested in winning a new hearing on the case, and Taggart, who is interested in winning Stocker's fiancee.

151.6 Gallows in Galilee. Oct. 31, 1963. GS: Robert Lansing, Ralph Reed, Jacqueline Scott, Dabbs Greer, Elisha Cook, Jr., Tol Avery, Bob Steele, Richard Grant. Roy Julian is up for murder before a hanging judge, but Julian is innocent, and the murder was an accident.

151.7 The Siege at Thayer's Bluff. Nov. 7, 1963. GS: William Reynolds, E.J. Andre, Robert Bray, Russell Thorson, Nina Shipman, John Cliff, Shug Fisher. Miner Paul Bannerman and his wife Mary are determined to maintain squatters rights to Thayer's Bluff, despite Red Gilman and his hired guns.

151.8 Jubilee. Nov. 14, 1963. GS: Peter Whitney, Virginia Gregg, Morgan Woodward, Eddie Firestone, William Bramley, Dub Taylor, Paul Birch, Ian Wolfe. Houston and Taggart save Tobe Gillard from a lynch mob, but Houston's not so happy he interfered when he finds out that Tobe is accused of killing a good friend of his.

151.9 Thunder Gap. Nov. 21, 1963. GS: Diana Millay, Robert Colbert, Richard Garland, Brad Weston, Harry Lauter. Marcey Bannister refuses to believe her husband is an outlaw, even when he and a pal try to run off with the stage she is on.

151.10 Billy Hart. Nov. 28, 1963. GS: Philip Ober, Russ Conway, Audrey Dalton, Ron Hayes, Pat Cardi, Jon Lormer, Rhys Williams, Len Lesser, Jim Nusser. In his will, Amy Hart's husband stipulated that all his property, and the custody of their child, must be turned over to his foreman.

151.11 Seventy Times Seven. Dec. 5, 1963. GS: Susanne Cramer, Steve Ihnat, Karl Swenson, Charles Radilac, Simon Scott, Dan Stafford, Sam Edwards, Tom Holland, James Almanzar, Robert Rothwell, Marshall Bradford. Pacifist Gustav Bergen and his family won't fight back against bullying Ben Wade and his gang. Houston gets a court order naming Taggart as the family's official protector.

151.12 Fracas at Kiowa Flats. Dec. 12, 1963. GS: Kathie Browne, Barry Kelley, Dayton Lummis, J. Pat O'Malley, Chubby Johnson, Jean Willes, James Best, Jonathan Hole, Ralph Neff, Robert Phillips. Houston and Taggart try to stop a feud between Col. Jim Shepard and Col. Bob Grainger, who have been fighting the Civil War for some twenty years.

151.13 Enough Rope. Dec. 19, 1963. GS: John Dehner, John Harmon, Ruta Lee, Ron Soble, Walter Sande, Tim Graham, Steve Condit, Ed Prentiss, Kenneth MacDonald. Mayoralty candidate Houston intends to give incumbent Benedict Williams, who is conducting a smear campaign, enough rope to hang himself.

151.14 The Dark Madonna. Dec. 26, 1963. GS: Constance Ford, Don Collier, Johnny Seven, Stacy Harris, Penny Santon, Nick Alexander. A padre asks Temple to defend a youth accused of a shotgun murder. But Lily Lamont and her pals are determined to see the young man convicted.

151.15 The Guardian. Jan. 2, 1964. GS: Robert Emhardt, Julie Parrish, Greg Irvin, Sammy Jackson, John Archer. Fatally wounded, Adam Ballard asks Houston to take care of his fiery daughter and to carry on the fight against Owen Judd, a tyrannical rancher.

151.16 Thy Name Is Woman. Jan. 9, 1964. GS: Charles Lane, Mary Wickes, Patricia Blair, Frank Ferguson, Georgia Goode. Houston enlists the aid of a lady lawyer in his defense of a saloon hostess, who claims she shot a man in self-defense.

151.17 The Law and Big Annie. Jan. 16, 1964. GS: Norman Alden, Mary Wickes, Carol Byron. Taggart happily pays off a large freight and feed bill for some livestock he inherited, but his inheritance turns out to be a hungry, four-ton elephant.

151.18 Sam's Boy. Jan. 23, 1964. GS: Douglas Fowley, Kenneth Tobey, William Fawcett, Charles Seel, Frank Ferguson, Herb Vigran, William Bryant, Don Kennedy, Kenneth MacDonald. Three spry old-timers want Houston to lead their plot to rearrange the State of Texas, just as Sam Houston did years before.

151.19 Ten Rounds for Baby. Jan. 30, 1964. GS: Anne Francis, Van Williams, Zeme North, Dave Willock, William Phipps, Hal Baylor. Joey Baker is a good man with his fists in a barroom, and Kate Fitzpatrick wants him to take on a professional boxer.

151.20 The Case for William Gotch. Feb. 6, 1964. GS: Ray Danton, James Best, Mary Wickes, Richard Jaeckel, Denver Pyle, Gordon Wescourt, Chubby Johnson, Erin O'Donnell. Houston agrees to help a rancher who claims that gambler Martin Royale cheated him out of his spread. Houston enlists the aid of a bumbling horse thief to outwit the card sharp.

151.21 A Slight Case of Larceny. Feb. 13, 1964. GS: Vito Scotti, Charles Watts, Carol Byron. Penniless Pancho Blanca is living off the credit he has established with the townspeople by bragging that he was responsible for a gold robbery.

151.22 Last Full Moon. Feb. 27, 1964. GS: Abraham Sofaer, Larry Ward, Vaughn Taylor, Pilar Seurat, John Alonzo, Frank Ferguson, Charles Lane, Edward Colmans, Charles Bateman, Karen Noel. When his prospective son-in-law is accused of horse theft, Chief Last Full Moon decides to take a case to the courts, instead of paying the usual bribe to the Indian agent.

151.23 The Gun That Swept the West. March 5, 1964. GS: Michael Pate, John Dehner, Sherwood Price, Mary Wickes. Inventor Jed Dobbs brings his double-barreled cannon to town for an Army test, only to have it stolen by a pair of crooks who plan to sell it to the Indians.

151.24 Do Unto Others, Then Gallop. March 19, 1964. GS: Mary Wickes, James Best, Frank Ferguson, Chubby Johnson, Adam Williams, Grace Lee Whitney, Robert McQueeney, Paul Smith, Ken Mayer, Claude Stroud, William Bramley. A whispering campaign blames the murder of an unarmed man on Houston.

151.25 *The Town That Trespassed.* March 26, 1964. GS: Robert Conrad, Parley Baer, Connie Stevens, Walter Sande, Dave Willock, Claude Stroud, Sheldon Allman, Martin West, Dal Jenkins, Richard Collier, Robert Adler. Charity Simpson has a valid deed proving that she owns all the property in Houston's old home town.

151.26 *Miss Katherina.* April 2, 1964. GS: Paula Raymond, John Baer, Richard X. Slattery, Anthony Costello, Simon Scott, John Lupton, Sammy Jackson, Donald Losby, Robert Phillips, David McMahon. Miss Katherina, the town spinster, lost her heart to suave Frank McGuire, so much so that she won't reveal his plot to steal a gold shipment.

152. The Texan

CBS. 30 min. Broadcast history: Monday, 8:00-8:30, Sept. 1958–Sept. 1960.

Regular Cast: Rory Calhoun (Bill Longley).

Premise: Bill Longley is the Texan, who travels from place to place in the years after the Civil War helping people in distress.

The Episodes

152.1 *Law of the Gun.* Sept. 29, 1958. GS: Neville Brand, John Larch, Helen Wallace, Reggie Parton, Howard Wright, Carl Thayler, Fred Krone, Karl Swenson, Ralph Moody. Bill Longley rides into a Western town looking for his friend Les Torbert. The two fought side by side at Vicksburg. He learns that Torbert is in the local jail, about to be hanged for shooting a young girl.

152.2 *The Man with the Solid Gold Star.* Oct. 6, 1958. GS: Thomas Gomez, Bruce Bennett, Robert Burton, Alan Wells, Steve Terrell. A former sheriff, losing money in a poker game, borrows from Bill Longley and gives him his gold sheriff's badge as security. But the man continues to lose money and finally the Texan is forced to protect his investment.

152.3 *The Troubled Town.* Oct. 13, 1958. GS: James Drury, William Schallert, Greg Palmer, Walter Sande, Andy Clyde, Kathryn Card, Dean Stanton, Harry Harvey, Sr., Pat Conway. Johnny Kaler, brother of one of the fastest guns in the West, is killed in a street fight. The brother believes that Bill Longley is the one who killed Johnny and sets out to get revenge.

152.4 *The First Notch.* Oct. 20, 1958. GS: J. Carrol Naish, Ron Hagerthy, Peggie Castle, Dan Sheridan, Dick Rich. A young man who believes he is a fast gun, is anxious to kill a man so he can put a notch in his gun. In an effort to demonstrate his prowess, he almost kills the Texan.

152.5 *The Edge of the Cliff.* Oct. 27, 1958. GS: Sidney Blackmer, Barbara Baxley, Norman Leavitt, Michael Connors. Orin McKnight, a middle-aged rancher, blames himself for his son's death and his wife's suicide. Although McKnight has since remarried he feels that he is too old for his young wife and a crisis develops when his wife's former fiance comes to visit her. Bill Longley tries to help McKnight.

152.6 *Jail for the Innocents.* Nov. 3, 1958. GS: Ray Ferrell, Vaughn Taylor, Grant Richards, John Milford, Herbert Rudley, Elaine Riley, Frank Marlow. Bill Longley saves a little boy from being kidnaped by two men. But he finds that the boy remains terrified and begins an investigation to find out why.

152.7 *A Tree for Planting.* Nov. 10, 1958. GS: Martin Garralaga, James Westerfield, Paul Fix, Lurene Tuttle, John Cliff, Clarke Gordon, James Parnell, Ruby Goodwin. An elderly Mexican is distressed when a group of cattle ranchers chop down the peach tress he has planted. The Texan tries to help the Mexican and runs into trouble from the cattlemen, who are determined to keep the land uncluttered by orchards.

152.8 *The Hemp Tree.* Nov. 17, 1958. GS: Michael Landon, Susan Anderson, Stacy Harris, Stuart Randall, S. John Launer, Charles Meredith, John Maxwell, Allan Lurie, Joe McGuinn. Bill Longley has just delivered some cattle and collects several thousand dollars for his work. White at the bank he is robbed of his hard-earned money by two bandits who hold up the bank.

152.9 *The Widow of Paradise.* Nov. 24, 1958. GS: Alan Hale, Jr., Marilyn Hanold, Russell Thorson, Charles Watts, Ricky Allen, Gary Allen, Kem Dibbs, Len Lesser, Shirley Collins. Bill Longley kills a drunken cowhand in self-defense and learns that under an ancient Montana law he must provide for the man's widow and her children. He tries to get the lady married off, but she prefers Longley to any other man in town.

152.10 *Desert Passage.* Dec. 1, 1958. GS: Jon Locke, R.G. Armstrong, Mae Clarke, Fay Roope, Wright King, Robert Foulk, Gregg Barton, John Reach, George Barrows, Howard Negley, Frank Harding. While escorting to prison the leader of a notorious gang, a sheriff and his deputy are attacked by the gang. Bill Longley helps to fight off the outlaws and aids the wounded sheriff and deputy in taking the outlaw to jail. Then the outlaws threaten the entire town.

152.11 *No Tears for the Dead.* Dec. 8, 1958. GS: Beverly Washburn, Michael Pate, Carole Mathews, Ray Teal, William Challee. A young girl holds a gun on Bill Longley and forces him to help her father, who is mortally wounded. The dying man extracts a promise from Longley that he will look after the girl.

152.12 *The Easterner.* Dec. 15, 1958. GS: Donald Harron, Fay Spain, Natividad Vacio, Jack Elam, Jim Drake, Tom Hardison. Bill Longley agrees to guide a pair of Philadelphia newlyweds on their first venture into the West. Bill soon realizes that they are not a happy couple, the wife believing her husband married her for her money, and the husband determined to prove his bravery on this trip.

152.13 *A Time of the Year.* Dec. 22, 1958. GS: George Macready, Suzanne Lloyd, Michael Macready, Peggy Maley, Howard Wendell, William Challee. The Texan meets a young married couple aboard a stagecoach. During the trip the coach is attacked and the husband is killed. Bill escorts the wife into town, only to find that her father-in-law has closed the town to them.

152.14 *The Lord Will Provide.* Dec. 29, 1958. GS: Ric Roman, Ellen Corby, Ross Elliott, Murvyn Vye, Francis MacDonald, Milton Frome, William Newell. Too many preachers have been killed or have fled town. As a result, no congregation has been started. In an effort to remedy the situation, Bill Longley disguises himself as a clergyman.

152.15 *The Duchess of Denver.* Jan. 5, 1959. GS: Gerald Mohr, Dolores Donlon, Mason Alan Dinehart, Emory Parnell,

The Texan

Robert Carson. Bill Longley brings the first herd of Texas cattle to Colorado, where he sells it to gambling queen Gay Brewster. Once there, however, Bill is confronted with the fact that Gay, who has known and idolized him since childhood, is still fond of him. Her partner, Col. Garson, is jealous.

152.16 *A Quart of Law.* Jan. 12, 1959. GS: Edgar Stehli, Robert Lowery, Charles Cooper, Theona Bryant, Billy M. Greene, Don Kelly, Mike Ragan. Longley supports Winthrop Davis, an alcoholic lawyer, in his battle against Sheriff Coy Benner. The issue is whether balloting should be secret.

152.17 *Outpost.* Jan. 19, 1959. GS: Les Tremayne, Harry Swoger, Patrick McVey, Christopher Dark, Scott Peters, Robert Karnes, Jim Lake. A wounded doctor is the sole survivor of a massacre at a stagecoach relay station. Bill Longley and the doctor set out to track down the killers.

152.18 *The Peddler.* Jan. 26, 1959. GS: Lou Jacobi, Elissa Palfi, Chris Alcaide, James Bell, Irene Tedrow, Steve Conte, John Francis, Nick Paul, Ed Hice. A newspaper editor has sworn to use his paper to bring an outlaw gang to justice. But the editor is killed and a travelling peddler witnesses the murder. Bill Longley intervenes when the outlaw and his men terrorize the peddler and his wife.

152.19 *Return to Friendly.* Feb. 2, 195. GS: James Philbrook, Mary Webster, John Harmon, John Alderson, Anthony Warde. On their way to the territorial prison, Bill Longley and his prisoner are pursued by outlaws. Confronted by a blinding snowstorm, Longley is forced to take refuge in a ghost town as the outlaws close in.

152.20 *The Man Behind the Star.* Feb. 9, 1959. GS: Brian Donlevy, Richard Jaeckel, Jean Willes, Russell Simpson, Robert E. Griffin. Sheriff Gleason's son has killed a woman rancher. When Bill Longley arrives to apprehend the lad, Gleason is torn between his respect for the law and his feelings as a father.

152.21 *The Ringer* (A.K.A. "The Imposter"). Feb. 16, 1959. GS: Reggie Parton, Adam Williams, Grant Withers, Daniel White, Olive Sturgess, Paul Brinegar, Ron Hayes, Mel Welles, Vito Scotti. A man who looks very much like Bill Longley goes on a drunken binge, terrorizing the town. Bill soon realizes that his reputation and his life are in danger.

152.22 *The Eyes of Captain Wylie.* Feb. 23, 1959. GS: Chill Wills, Lane Bradford, Tudor Owen, Bruce Cowling, Mack Williams. A sea captain comes home to claim a ranch he has inherited. He meets opposition in the form of a hired gun, and asks Bill Longley to help him assert his claim.

152.23 *The Marshal of Yellow Jacket.* March 2, 1959. GS: Robert J. Wilke, John Beradino, Anne Neyland, Kathryn Card, Harry Harvey, Sr., Richard Adams, Kenneth MacDonald, Henry Rowland, Red Morgan. Bart Pannock digs deep into the lawbooks to find reasons for fining the townspeople of Yellow Jacket.

152.24 *No Love Wasted.* March 9, 1959. GS: Lon Chaney, Jr., Marian Seldes, Eugene Martin, Ken Mayer, Richard Adams, William Gould, Tom London. Wylie has sent his mail-order bride a picture of his friend Bill Longley instead of his own. But before he can meet his bride. Wylie is killed in a saloon brawl.

152.25 *A Race for Life.* March 16, 1959. GS: Frank Ferguson, Douglas Fowley, Bart Bradley, Kelly Thordsen, Kem Dibbs, Ralph Moody, Harry Harvey, Sr. An elderly rancher enters a horse in a race, and bets all his money. Bill Longley learns that the rancher's horse is to race against a gambler's thoroughbred.

152.26 *Letter of the Law.* March 23, 1959. GS: Trevor Bardette, Richard Hale, Cathy Case, Ralph Dumke, R.G. Armstrong, Ron Soble, Stuart Randall, Richard Reeves. Bill Longley comes upon an ambush. Outlaws want to kill a circuit judge before he can try their boss for murder.

152.27 *Private Account.* April 6, 1959. GS: Jesse White, Karen Sharpe, Joe Di Reda, Konstantin Shayne, Fred Kohler, Maudie Prickett. Bill Longley is accidentally knocked down and pinned beneath a tree. An outlaw fleeing from a posse sees Bill's plight and helps free him. Bill feels that he is now obligated to the outlaw.

152.28 *Caballero.* April 13, 1959. GS: Cesar Romero, Whit Bissell, Mari Blanchard, Fred Graham, Abel Fernandez, Jim Hayward. It comes to Bill Longley's attention that an American trader is supplying Indians in Mexico with guns and ammunition. Longley enlists the aid of a Mexican official to try to put an end to the trader's ruthless activities.

152.29 *Blood Money.* April 20, 1959. GS: Ralph Meeker, Dorothy Provine, Charles Maxwell, Robert J. Wilke, Mike Forest, William Vaughn, Than Wyenn, Charles Gray. Bill Longley discovers the corpse of a young man lying near a shack. Immediately two men ride up who claim to be older brothers of the dead man. They accuse Longley of killing their brother and threaten to hang him.

152.30 *No Place to Stop.* April 27, 1959. GS: Chuck Wassil, Sally Fraser, Robert Burton, Strother Martin, Denver Pyle, Charles Arnt, James Anderson, Dehl Berti. A greedy old desperado and his sons devise a plan by which they hope to provoke a law-abiding ex-convict into violating the terms of his parole.

152.31 *Reunion.* May 4, 1959. GS: Bethel Leslie, Christopher Dark, Richard Carlyle, Robert F. Simon, Clarence Straight, Norman Leavitt, Steve Carruthers. Bill Longley is one of a group of ex-officers attending a reunion five years after the end of the Civil War. He finds that the lives of his two closest friends have taken.

152.32 *Badlands.* May 11, 1959. GS: Stephen McNally, Judith Ames, Myron Healey, Michael Galloway, Fintan Meyler. Bill Longley sets out to stop bounty hunter Clay Thompson. Thompson is search for Frank Kincaid, unaware that Kincaid is no longer wanted for murder.

152.33 *South of the Border.* May 18, 1959. GS: Jack Elam, John Doucette, Joyce Meadows, Leslie Wenner, Peter Mamakos, Duane Grey. Sheriff Ben Carter is prohibited from crossing the Mexican border. So Longley goes after some outlaws alone.

152.34 *The Smiling Loser.* May 25, 1959. GS: Eddie Quillan, Rusty Lane, John McKee, Harry Lauter, Boyd "Red" Morgan. A cheating cardsharp is found out by a pair of drunken cattle ranchers, who decide to hang the man. Bill Longley stops the lynching but finds his own life in jeopardy.

152.35 *The Sheriff of Boot Hill.* June 1, 1959. GS: Reed Hadley, Denver Pyle, Charles Maxwell, Chuck Bail, Chick Bilyeau. Bill Longley learns of plans to murder a sheriff. Working fast he is able to thwart the attempt, but the outlaws turn their attention to Longley.

152.36 *The Gunfighter.* June 8, 1959. GS: Dick Kallman, John Pickard, Kristine Miller, Nancy Valentine, Robert Bice, Rick Rodman. Seeking to qualify himself for membership in an outlaw band, a young gunslinger turns to drink to bolster his courage. He then brashly challenged Bill Longley to a duel.

152.37 *The Man Hater.* June 15, 1959. GS: Lori Nelson, William Tannen, Henry Brandon, Tom London, Charles Horvath, Henry Kulky. Bill Longley encounters a young lady in distress and offers aid. He learns that she is being pursued by dangerous outlaws but he is unable to find out why.

Season Two

152.38 *No Way Out.* Sept. 14, 1959. GS: Helen Wallace, Stuart Randall, Lucien Littlefield, James Griffith, Gerald Milton, Kem Dibbs, Joseph Turkel, Tom Hardison. Seeking protection from a storm, Bill Longley stops at a way station. There he meets an old friend, a lawman with two killers in his custody. But Longley's friend is unable to leave the station because a mob is waiting to ambush him and free the prisoners.

152.39 *Image of Guilt.* Sept. 21, 1959. GS: Richard Travis, Chris Alcaide, Stephen Hammer, Don Haggerty, Selene Walters. While the townspeople are watching a draw-and-shoot contest, a photographer friend of Bill Longley's is killed by bank robbers. Longley discovers that the photographer's small son can recognize the killers even though he has never seen them.

152.40 *Cattle Drive.* Sept. 28, 1959. GS: Claude Akins, Whitney Blake. Bill Longley is hired to go into Mexico to buy cattle. After purchasing the cattle Bill is arrested for passing counterfeit money. He insists that he was framed, but the authorities don't believe him.

152.41 *The Dishonest Posse.* Oct. 5, 1959. GS: Henry Rowland, William Merwin, Peter Whitney, Nestor Paiva, Bing Russell, Jack Lambert, Chick Bilyeau. Members of a posse capture a bank robber, split his loot and become a bandit gang. Bill Longley is the only man who stands in their way.

152.42 *Blue Norther.* Oct. 12,1 959. GS: Dan Barton, John Beradino, Eddy Waller, Dean Stanton, Hal Baylor, James Turley, Parley Baer, Ned Wever. Robbers ambush Bill Longley and steal his horse. Forced to take a stagecoach, Longley encounters a passenger named Pony Sloan, who is wanted for robbery and murder. The Texan soon realizes that he is in the middle of a deadly private feud.

152.43 *Traildust.* Oct. 19, 1959. GS: Brian Donlevy, Chuck Henderson, Addison Richards, Nan Peterson, Mike Ragan, Lane Bradford, John Milford. Sam Gallup is hired to rid a town of an outlaw gang. Texan Bill Longley arrives in town with the news that the outlaws are preparing to attack.

152.44 *The Telegraph Story.* Oct. 26, 1959. GS: Denver Pyle, Edward Ashley, Barbara Pepper, Richard Adams, Charles Horvath, Harry Fleer, Tom Trout, Fred Graham. Bill Longley is foreman of a telegraph work crew which unknowingly comes upon an outlaw gang's hideout. Fearing disclosure, the crooks pose as gold miners and plan to attack the work camp.

152.45 *Stampede.* Nov. 2, 1959. GS: Michael Dante, Shirley Knight, Mario Alcaide, Pedro Gonzalez-Gonzalez, Red Morgan, Roy Barcroft. Bill Longley accepts a job to drive a herd of cattle to Abilene, Kansas. After the drive begins, Longley realizes that another outfit will stop at nothing to beat him to the cattle market.

152.46 *Showdown at Abilene.* Nov. 9, 1959. GS: Michael Dante, Shirley Knight, Mario Alcaide, Barbara Luna, Pedro Gonzalez-Gonzalez, Roy Barcroft. While bossing a cattle drive across land owned by rancher Carl Maynor, Bill Longley is told by a pretty girl that Maynor is trying to force her to marry him.

152.47 *The Reluctant Bridegroom.* Nov. 16, 1959. GS: Michael Dante, Mario Alcaide, Barbara Luna, Pedro Gonzalez-Gonzalez, Rodolfo Acosta, Ralph Moody. Texan Bill Longley is kidnaped from his job as boss of the cattle drive and taken to a Camanche Indian village. Chief White Cloud informs Longley that he must fight a warrior named Black Eagle for the hand of the chief's daughter.

152.48 *Trouble on the Trail.* Nov. 23, 1959. GS: Michael Dante, Mario Alcaide, Pedro Gonzalez-Gonzalez, Kay E. Kuter, Joan Taylor, Tod Griffin. Bill Longley's cattle drive is being harassed by Indians hired by a rival drive. Longley's Indian tracker and the Indian's girl friend are kidnaped, and the Texan attempts to rescue them.

152.49 *Cowards Don't Die.* Nov. 30, 1959. GS: Karl Swenson, Sally Fraser, Robert Wilke, Mac Tyler, Bern Hoffman, Hal Baylor. Outlaw Pete Torrey torments Sam Maitland, a former marshal who has become gun-shy. Maitland's daughter refuses help from Bill Longley, who knows that Torrey will not stop until he has killed Maitland.

152.50 *Border Incident.* Dec. 7, 1959. GS: Duncan Lamont, Kipp Hamilton, Alan Hale, Jr., Claude Akins, Whitney Blake, Douglas Kennedy, Alan Roberts, Natividad Vacio, Rodolfo Hoyos. A railroad construction company is trying to build a railroad, but it encounters constant delays. Bill Longley is hired to find out who is causing the trouble.

152.51 *Dangerous Ground.* Dec. 14, 1959. GS: Duncan Lamont, Kipp Hamilton, Alan Hale, Jr., Harry Shannon, Dick Kallman, Robert Foulk, Wendell Holmes, Reg Parton. Rancher Jay Howell warns engineer David MacMorris and Bill Longley that the railroad will have to steer clear of his land. Soon after, a railroad worker is wounded by a sniper.

152.52 *End of Track.* Dec. 21, 1959. GS: Duncan Lamont, Kipp Hamilton, Alan Hale, Jr., Michael Pate, Bern Hoffman, Richard Adams, Don Harvey, Harry Fleer, Reg Parton. Texan Bill Longley's work train is pressed from service to take some convicted killers to prison. On the way, the prisoners kill the crew and attempt an escape.

152.53 *Rough Track to Payday.* Dec. 28, 1959. GS: Stacy Harris, Myrna Dell, Neeley Edwards, Gregg Barton, Reg Parton, Mary Melrose, James Anderson. Outside interests seek to take over the railroad for which Bill Longley works. Abel Crowder, the spokesman for this group, claims that the railroad is broke and can't meets the payroll.

152.54 *Friend of the Family.* Jan. 4, 1960. GS: John Dehner, Steve Terrell, Roger Perry, James Coburn, Bob Terhune, Reg Parton. A man who was a comrade of Bill Longley's during the Civil War asks Longley to let his son ride the trail with him. The Texan soon learns that the young man hates his father and is a troublemaker.

152.55 *The Taming of Rio Nada.* Jan. 11, 1960. GS: Valerie Allen, Barbara Stuart, Reed Hadley, Bern Hoffman, James Griffith, Mason Alan Dinehart, Richard Devon, Tom Fadden. In the town of Rio Nada, Bill Longley is appointed special deputy to rid the town of corruption. His first job is to find the unidentified outlaw leader who controls the town.

152.56 Sixgun Street. Jan. 18, 1960. GS: Valerie Allen, Barbara Stuart, Mason Alan Dinehart, Reed Hadley, Richard Devon, Tom Fadden. To stop Bill Longley's attempt to clean up Rio Nada, gamblers hire outlaws to ambush the Texan. When Longley foils this plot, the gamblers import a pair of professional gunmen.

152.57 The Terrified Town. Jan. 25, 1960. GS: Valerie Allen, Barbara Stuart, Mason Alan Dinehart, Reed Hadley, Richard Devon, Tom Fadden. As Bill Longley presses his search for the bandit leader known as El Sombro, gambling queen Poker Alice saves Longley from an ambush by her own partner Tim Craven.

152.58 Thirty Hours to Kill (A.K.A. "The Ambushers"). Feb. 1, 1960. GS: Mort Mills, Katherine Squire, Ron Soble, Malcolm Atterbury, Morris Ankrum. In a forced gunfight, Longley kills his man and is marked for revenge by the dead man's brother.

152.59 Quarantine. Feb. 8, 1960. GS: Lita Baron, Frank Ferguson, Duncan Lamont, Andy Clyde, Alan Hale, Jr., Kem Dibbs, James Drake. A rich land baron, accustomed to getting his way, comes to see Bill Longley at the railroad construction camp. He has brought a fistful of money to arrange a detour of the track through one of his towns.

152.60 Buried Treasure. Feb. 15, 1960. GS: Lita Baron, Frank Ferguson, Andy Clyde, Duncan Lamont, Don Beddoe, Dick Rich, Douglas Kennedy. Violence and threats fail to intimidate Bill Longley's construction crew, so a rival outfit sends an old prospector into the Texan's camp with news of a gold strike, hoping that the men will desert to hunt for gold.

152.61 Captive Crew. Feb. 22, 1960. GS: Lita Baron, Andy Clyde, Alan Hale, Jr., Kem Dibbs, Duncan Lamont, Kipp Hamilton, Michael Pate. Longley's work train is used to take some convicted killers to prison.

152.62 Showdown. Feb. 29, 1960. GS: Kipp Hamilton, Alan Hale, Jr., Duncan Lamont, Anthony Caruso, Hugh Sanders, Ron Hayes. Job completed, Bill Longley is about to leave the railroad construction outfit when a disreputable ex-crewman show up. The man, who was fired for being a troublemaker, is now an agent for the company with which the railroaders hope to land a new contract.

152.63 Borrowed Time. March 7, 1960. GS: Ann Robinson, John Pickard, Russ Conway, Raymond Greenleaf, James Drake, George Keymas. A gang busy robbing stagecoaches also kills its victims, leaving as a result no witnesses.

152.64 The Governor's Lady. March 14, 1960. GS: Lita Baron, Richard Travis, Frank Puglia, Mark Dana, Myron Healey. Bill Longley prevents the ambush of a special governor's agent who is carrying a list of tax-evading cattle barons.

152.65 Town Divided. March 21, 1960. GS: Walter Coy, June Blair, Steve Terrell, Morgan Woodward, Robert Foulk. Young Ken Crowley thinks his doctor deliberately crippled his arm. Bill Longley tries to stall the young man's revenge.

152.66 The Guilty and the Innocent. March 28, 1960. GS: Robert F. Simon, Bud Slater, Helen Wallace, Denver Pyle, Percy Helton, Don C. Harvey. Bill Longley and an angry mob are both after the same man. Longley has an order for a new trial, but the mob has a noose.

152.67 Presentation Gun. April 4, 1960. GS: Robert Brubaker, Ron Starr, Gary Judas, Chris Alcaide, Stafford Repp, Harry Harvey, Sr. Bill Longley rides down to the jail to see his friend the sheriff, who has been locked up on a murder charge. There is a confession and an eyewitness, but Longley still has his doubts.

152.68 Ruthless Woman. April 11, 1960. GS: Joyce Meadows, Bob Hopkins, Francis MacDonald, Ken Mayer, Joyce Staigg. On the prairie, Bill Longley finds a badly beaten cowhand and takes him to the nearest ranch for help. But the ranch foreman is the man who administered the beating.

152.69 The Nomad. April 18, 1960. GS: Danny Scholl, Cindy Ames, Bob Anderson, Nesdon Booth, Larry Chance, Edward Earle, William Fawcett. Longley rescues a shiftless stranger who is being worked over in the local saloon. Taking the poor fellow in tow he tries to teach him self-respect.

152.70 Killer's Road. April 25, 1960. GS: Robert J. Wilke, James Best, Harry Fleer, Lane Bradford. Bill Longley sets out on a nerve-racking trip to the state prison. He is escorting a killer whose gang is due to show up any minute.

152.71 Lady Tenderfoot. May 9, 1960. GS: Claire Kelly, Emory Parnell, Jack Elam, Pedro Gonzalez-Gonzalez, Jim Drake, Billy M. Greene. An Eastern horse breeder and his daughter come West to capture a wild stallion. They've got a letter of introduction to Bill Longley.

152.72 The Invisible Noose. May 16, 1960. GS: Elaine Edwards, Charles Maxwell, Reg Parton, Bill Erwin, Gregg Barton, Paul Keast, Anthony Brand, James Anderson. Riding into town to attend a wedding, Bill Longley is disarmed by bandits, who force him to accompany them while they rob a bank.

152.73 The Mountain Man. May 23, 1960. GS: Charles Arnt, Duncan Lamont, Ken Mayer, Sam Edwards, Hal Smith, Reg Parton, Bud Osborne. Longley runs into an old buddy, an elderly frontiersman, who brags about his prospects for a stake. Later Longley learns that the take came through a payroll robbery

152.74 Johnny Tuvo. May 30, 1960. GS: Ron Haggerty, Mary Webster, Myron Healey, Dehl Berti, Frank Wilcox, Jack Carr. Bill Longley joins the town's best horsemen in a friendly race for $1000. While the men are riding, a pair of gunmen make an unsportsmanlike play for even higher stakes.

152.75 The Accuser. June 6, 1960. GS: Fay Roope, Kristine Miller, Don Haggerty, Harry Cheshire, Jim Hayward, James Lydon, Reg Parton, Mike Mazurski. Longley spots two men fleeing a band of horsemen and rides over to help them out. Too late he learns that the pair are bank robbers and their pursuers are a posse.

152.76 Mission to Monteray. June 13, 1960. GS: Eduardo Noriega, Richard Carlyle, Jewell Lain, Raymond Bailey, Lane Bradford. The United States Consul in Monterrey asks Longley's help. A gang from the States is printing counterfeit American money in Mexico and smuggling it across the border into Texas.

152.77 Badman. June 20, 1960. GS: Tod Griffin, Beverly Washburn, Celia Lovsky, Anthony Warde, John Harmon, John Alderson, Gil Rankin. Marshal Roy Adams is wounded and can't deliver an outlaw to Pueblo to face a Federal charge. He asks his friend Bill Longley to take over the job.

152.78 Twenty-four Hours to Live. Sept. 5, 1960. GS: Charles Cooper, Barbara Kelly, Paul Birch, Wendell Holmes, Harry Bartell, Richard Norris, Burt Mustin. A love triangle always means trouble. And this time it may mean hanging for Steve Murrow, who has been convicted of murder. Bill Longley gets a message that he will be killed if he tries to help his friend.

153. *Texas John Slaughter*

ABC. 60 min. Broadcast history: Friday, 8:00–9:00, Sept. 1958–Sept. 1959; Friday, 7:30–8:30, Sept. 1959–Sept. 1960; Sunday, 6:30–7:30, Sept. 1960–Sept. 1961.

Regular Cast: Tom Tryon (Texas John Slaughter), Betty Lynn (Viola Slaughter), Brian Corcoran (Willie Slaughter), Harry Carey, Jr. (Ben Jenkins), Annette Gorman (Addie), Onslow Stevens (General Miles), Pat Hogan (Geronimo), R.G. Armstrong (Billy Soto), Stafford Repp (Sheriff Hatch), Ross Martin (Cesario Lucero), Jim Beck (Burt Alvord), Norma Moore (Adeline Harris).

Premise: This series depicted the exploits of lawman John Slaughter in Friotown, Texas, in the 1880s.

Note: This series aired as segments of *Walt Disney Presents*.

The Episodes

153.1 *Texas John Slaughter.* Oct. 31, 1958. GS: Robert Middleton. Texas Ranger John Slaughter attempts a seemingly impossible ride in order to break the alibi of an outlaw suspected of having killed another ranger.

153.2 *Ambush in Laredo.* Nov. 14, 1958. GS: Robert Middleton. Slaughter and his Texas Ranger partner Ben Jenkins trail outlaw Frank Davis to the town of Laredo in the hope of obtaining some conclusive evidence against him. Unknown to Slaughter, Davis and his outlaw friends are planning an ambush.

153.3 *Killers from Kansas.* Jan. 9, 1959. GS: Beverly Garland, Lyle Bettger, Christopher Dark, Judson Pratt. As Slaughter and a fellow Ranger ar transacting business in a bank, they are attacked by Mrs. Barko and her bang of bank robbers.

153.4 *Showdown at Sandoval.* Jan. 23, 1959. GS: Dan Duryea, Robert Foulk. After breaking up the Barko Gang, Texas John Slaughter tries to outwit the outlaw Dan Trask. Slaughter and his fiancee pose as Bark and Mrs. Barko and, with several disguised rangers, head for the rendezvous with Trask and his men.

153.5 *The Man from Bitter Creek.* March 6, 1959. GS: Stephen McNally, Bill Williams, Grant Williams. Slaughter, after marrying and resigning from the Texas Rangers, buys a herd of cattle in Mexico, intending to drive it to market in New Mexico. To reach the market he must pass through outlaw territory.

153.6 *The Slaughter Trail.* March 20, 1959. GS: Harold J. Stone, Bill Williams. Convinced that his cattle would die on the long, dry Chisholm Trail, Slaughter opens a new and shorter trail. On the new trail, Slaughter faces attacks of raiding Comanche Indians and attempts by cattle baron John Chisholm to hang him as a Texas gunfighter.

153.7 *The Robber Stallion.* Dec. 4, 1959. GS: Barton MacLane, Darryl Hickman, John Vivyan, Jean Innes. Slaughter is talked into going on a wild horse roundup, but before he can capture any of the horses, he must overcome an outlaw and a spirited stallion.

153.8 *Wild Horse Revenge.* Dec. 11, 1959. GS: Darryl Hickman, John Vivyan, Bill Phipps. Pursuing the leader of a herd of wild horses, Slaughter is on the verge of capturing him when Carstairs lets him get away.

153.9 *Range War at Tombstone.* Dec. 18, 1959. GS: Darryl Hickman, James Westerfield, Nora Marlowe, Regis Toomey. Texas John Slaughter drives a herd to Tombstone, Arizona, and establishes a ranch on open land. But cattle baron Ike Clanton thinks that the property is part of his private territory.

153.10 *Desperado from Tombstone.* Feb. 12, 1960. Texas John Slaughter is baffled when his two young children, whom he has rejoined after years of separation, regard him as a frightening stranger. His problem seems solved when a neighbor offers to care for them, but then he learns that her ranch has been taken over by cattle rustler Loco Crispin, an old enemy of his.

153.11 *Apache Friendship.* Feb. 19, 1960. GS: Jay Silverheels, Nora Marlowe, Regis Toomey. Texas John Slaughter's prospective mother-in-law tells him that his marriage to Viola Howell is off, unless he gives up wearing guns. John reluctantly agrees and so becomes easy prey for a horse thief.

153.12 *Kentucky Gunslick.* Feb. 26, 1960. GS: Darryl Hickman, James Edwards, Allan Lane. Ashley Carstairs brings Texas John Slaughter the two Kentucky thoroughbreds he had promised him. John notices that young Ashley has a quick temper and a pride in his speed to the draw.

153.13 *Geronimo's Revenge.* April 4, 1960. GS: Darryl Hickman, Jay Silverheels. Repeated attacks by the Apache renegade Geronimo provoke Texas John Slaughter to challenge Geronimo to single combat to the death.

153.14 *The End of the Trail.* Jan. 29, 1961. The Apaches are on the warpath, but their leader, Geronimo, is nowhere to be found. General Miles gets Slaughter to track him down.

153.15 *A Holster Full of Law.* Feb. 5, 1961. Rustler Billy Soto has been stealing cattle from Texas John's ranch, so Slaughter reports the dirty business to Sheriff Hatch. But Hatch seems to do nothing about it, and Slaughter gets it into his head that he himself ought to be sheriff.

153.16 *A Trip to Tucson.* April 16, 1961. GS: Joe Maross. Slaughter is criticized for his conduct as sheriff of Tombstone. It seems he uses a gun more readily than the outlaws he is after. Slaughter isn't about to change when he learns that a stage has been robbed and the driver murdered by the cold-blooded renegade.

153.17 *Frank Clell Is in Town.* April 23, 1961. GS: Ralph Meeker, Raymond Bailey. The local saloon keeper's idea of livening up the town of Tombstone is to make it accessible to hard-drinking outlaws. The plan necessitates the murder of Sheriff Slaughter, and results in the sudden appearance of professional killer Frank Clell.

154. *Tomahawk*

Syndicated. 30 min. Broadcast history: Various, Oct. 1957–Jan. 1958.

Regular Cast: Jacques Godin (Pierre Radisson), Rene Caron (Medard).

Premise: This adventure series depicted the exploits of pioneers Pierre Radisson and Medard, who explored the American Northwest of the 1700s.

The Episodes

154.1 *Capture.* Oct. 6, 1957. Voyageur Pierre Esprit Radisson goes on the warpath after two friends on a hunting trip are killed by the Iroquois.

154.2 *Feast of the Gluttons.* Oct. 20, 1957. Radisson reluctantly agrees to accompany a Jesuit missionary to a small mission in the heart of Iroquois country.

154.3 *The Old and the New.* Oct. 27, 1957. On a visit to France, Radisson is horrified to discover that the French government considers Canada merely a source of revenue.

154.4 *Lake Winnipeg.* Nov. 10, 1957. En route to Lake Winnipeg, Radisson and his friend Medard come to the aid of the Hurons.

154.5 *Iroquois Blockade.* Nov. 17, 1957. While traveling with a group of friendly Hurons, Radisson is surrounded by Iroquois.

154.6 *The Adam Dollars Massacre.* Nov. 24, 1957. Radisson and his party travel downriver in the middle of Iroquois territory.

154.7 *Fear and Fireworks.* Dec. 1, 1957. Radisson and Medard plan a voyage to the north.

154.8 *Race Against Time.* Dec. 8, 1957. On their northern expedition, Radisson and his group are caught by the approach of winter. Radisson orders hunting parties to trap enough animals to feed them all for the coming season, but the Indians disagree with his concern over their food supply.

154.9 *The Famine.* Dec. 15, 1957. While Radisson, Medard and the Hurons are on a strict rationing system to make their supplies last the winter, they are visited by a party of starving Ottawa Indians begging for food.

154.10 *The Sea to the North.* Jan. 5, 1958. After a long journey, Radisson and the Hurons finally reach the destination of their northern trek.

154.11 *The Mighty Hunter.* Jan. 12, 1958. Scornful of Radisson's fur-trapping ability, the Huron chief sets out alone into the woods to prove his own skill at trapping beaver.

154.12 *Seizers of the Wilderness.* Jan. 19, 1958. A blizzard confines Radisson and the Hurons to their cabin, and after three weeks Radisson comes close to losing his sanity.

155. *Tombstone Territory*

ABC/Syndicated. 30 min. Broadcast history: Wednesday, 8:30-9:00, Oct. 1957–Sept. 1958; Friday, 9:00-9:30, March 1959–Oct. 1959; Various, Oct. 1959–July 1960.

Regular Cast: Pat Conway (Sheriff Clay Hollister), Richard Eastham (Harris Claybourne), Gil Rankin (Deputy Charlie Riggs).

Premise: Set in Tombstone ("the town too tough to die"), Arizona, in the 1880s, this series depicted the adventures of Sheriff Clay Hollister and Tombstone Epitaph editor Harris Clayton and their attempt to establish law and order in the territory.

The Episodes

155.1 *Gunslinger from Galeville.* Oct. 16, 1957. GS: Robert Foulk, Brett King, Thomas B. Henry. Sheriff Clay Hollister rides out to collect the county taxes. He is determined to make the outlaws pay their taxes too and decides upon a daring scheme. He goes to Curly Bill, a notorious outlaw, and makes him a deputy to help him collect the taxes.

155.2 *Reward for a Gunslinger.* Oct. 23, 1957. GS: Ken Drake, Bobbie Collentine, Michael Whalen, Dennis Moore. Sheriff Clay Hollister tracks down Frank Masters, accused of terrorizing the residents of Tombstone and killing a stagecoach driver. Hollister heads for Tombstone with his prisoner, but runs into two bounty hunters intent on killing the sheriff to claim the reward for Masters.

155.3 *Ride Out at Noon.* Oct. 30, 1957. GS: Dan Sheridan. A young deputy sheriff kills a cattleman's son in a gunfight. The citizens of Tombstone Territory demand that Sheriff Hollister fire the deputy, but he refuses. The dead boy's father vows vengeance on Hollister and swears that he will destroy Tombstone.

155.4 *Revenge Town.* Nov. 6, 1957. GS: James Seay, Robert J. Wilke, Jean Howell, Morris Ankrum, Nestor Paiva. Sheriff Clay Hollister kills a man during a gunfight and then learns he was a prominent citizen of the town of Galeno. He is tricked into riding into Galeno, where the enraged citizens take the law into their own hands and put him on trial for murder.

155.5 *A Bullet for an Editor.* Nov. 13, 1957. GS: Stephen Bekassy, Allison Hayes. A smooth-talking Frenchman arrives in Tombstone and quickly charms all the ladies in town. Sheriff Clay Hollister is suspicious of the newcomer. Editor Harris Claibourne exposes the Frenchman as a cardsharp and fortune hunter and he is challenged to a duel.

155.6 *Killer without a Conscience.* Nov. 20, 1957. GS: Bruce Gordon, Thomas B. Henry. Jake Hoyt, a stranger in town, kills a gunman who is about to shoot Sheriff Clay Hollister in the back. But Hoyt has an ulterior motive.

155.7 *Guns of Silver.* Nov. 27, 1957. GS: Leo Gordon, Mike Ragan, Pamela Duncan, Bing Russell. Two miners discover silver while they are burying a dead partner. The heirs of the dead man demand a cut of the treasure.

155.8 *Desert Survival.* Dec. 4, 1957. GS: John Vivyan, Jack Reitzen, Michael Fox. Three outlaws capture Sheriff Clay Hollister, and force him to lead them across the desert to Mexico. For appearances' sake, they permit him to carry his gun unloaded.

155.9 *Apache Vendetta.* Dec. 11, 1957. GS: Peter Whitney, Arthur Batanides, Mike Forest. Sheriff Clay Hollister attempts to give an Indian accused of homicide a fair trial, angering the town of Tombstone.

155.10 *Ambush at Gila Gulch.* Dec. 18, 1957. GS: Rhodes Reason, Dabbs Greer. Nate Crandall murders a wealthy Mexican to rob him of a huge sum. He finds too late that the money is in the hands of Sheriff Clay Hollister, who has deposited it in a safe. Crandall gets young Jim Edwards to aid him in robbery.

155.11 *Sermons and Six Guns.* Dec. 25, 1957. GS: Christopher Dark. A clergyman attempts to bring religion to a town dominated by a ruthless gunman. Sheriff Hollister rides out to save the preacher when he learns that the gunman has sworn to kill him.

155.12 *The Youngest Gun.* Jan. 1, 1958. GS: Ralph Reed, Brad Trumbull, Tom Holland. Clay Hollister tries to befriend the son of an outlaw whom he was forced to shoot. He is unaware that the young man has sworn to kill him.

155.13 *Shoot Out at Dark.* Jan. 8, 1958. GS: John Beradino, Rayford Barnes, Harry Fleer, Morgan Jones, Robin Riley, Mary Anderson. After serving time for killing a man, Frank Leslie comes back to Tombstone to marry the man's widow. But the dead man's four brothers have sworn they will kill Leslie on sight, and Clay Hollister learns that Leslie has now hung up his guns.

155.14 *The Rebels' Last Charge.* Jan. 15, 1958. GS: Harry Lauter, Richard Reeves, Kay Elhardt, Wayne Heffley. A group of renegade Civil War veterans rides in an terrorizes the small town of Osage in Arizona. The townspeople evacuate the town only to be pursued by the raiders. Tombstone Sheriff Clay Hollister and editor Harris Claibourne, who are visiting the town, decide on a desperate maneuver to rout the marauders.

155.15 *Gun Fever.* Jan. 22, 1958. GS: William Phipps. When Neal Weaton, a deputy sheriff, shoots a man, Clay Hollister believes he was too quick to use his gun and fires him. Weaton then gets a job as a guard in a saloon in town and soon gains a reputation as a fast gun. Hollister decides Weaton must leave Tombstone to avoid further killing.

155.16 *Mexican Bandito.* Jan. 29, 1958. GS: Anthony Caruso, Michael Morgan, Fred King, Jose Gonzales, Bob Shield, Ollie O'Toole. On the trail of a Mexican bandit, Sheriff Clay Hollister disguises himself as an outlaw in order to cross the border and bring his quarry back to Tombstone.

155.17 *Tong War.* Feb. 5, 1958. GS: Frances Fong. The Chinese residents of Tombstone are thrown into a panic when men from the Society of Death, a Chinese outlaw gang, arrive in Tombstone. Sheriff Clay Hollister learns that the Society is intent on killing a local man who has broken one of the organization's rules.

155.18 *Postmarked for Death.* Feb. 12, 1958. GS: Edmund Cobb, Virginia Gregg, Robert Brubaker, William Vaughan, Ken Mayer, Bob Shield, Rand Brooks, Harry Woods. Three desperados shoot the postmaster to draw Sheriff Clay Hollister out of town so that they can rob the mine payroll.

155.19 *Johnny Ringo's Last Ride.* Feb. 19, 1958. GS: Myron Healey, Bob Bice, Ann Diamond, Jack Mann, James Winslow. When the outlaw Johnny Ringo is arrested on a minor charge, he is released on bail. Then an ambitious judge decides to arrest Johnny again on a technicality and during the scuffle a member of the posse is shot.

155.20 *The Epitaph.* Feb. 26, 1958. GS: Andrew Duggan, Sam Buffington. A cattle broker who buys stolen cattle learns that his supply has been cut off because of the activities of Sheriff Clay Hollister. Hollister, with the help of Editor Harris Claibourne, has turned public opinion against the broker.

155.21 *Geronimo.* March 5, 1958. GS: John Doucette, Angie Dickinson, George Gilbreath, Tom Greenway. The Apache war chief Geronimo goes on the warpath and kills a dozen people in Tombstone. Then he takes over a pool hall in the town and his braves stand guard while he plays pool. Sheriff Clay Hollister decides to go in after the chief.

155.22 *The Return of the Outlaw.* March 12, 1958. GS: Norma Moore, William Talman. The leader of a gang of outlaws is pursued by Sheriff Clay Hollister and a posse. Wounded, the outlaw seeks refuge in the Danbury ranch house.

155.23 *Guilt of a Town.* March 19, 1958. GS: James Best, Kathleen Crowley, Jan Merlin. Mitt Porter, anxious to prove his bravery to his older brother, helps in a holdup. Later he arrives in Tombstone with a pretty nurse and tries to establish an alibi for the time of the robbery.

155.24 *Cave-In.* March 26, 1958. GS: Robert J. Stevenson, Margaret Hayes, Ruthie Robinson. A miner falls in love with a mercenary dance-hall girl. To cater to her greed he secretly mines a vein of silver running under the main street of Tombstone.

155.25 *Skeleton Canyon Massacre.* April 2, 1958. GS: Rodolfo Hoyos, Karl Lukas, Dennis Moore. Sheriff Hollister is accused by a prominent Mexican of being the leader of a gang that has hijacked Mexican pack trains on the American side of the border. The Mexican decides to take the law into his own hands and sends for an armed band from Mexico.

155.26 *Strange Vengeance.* April 9, 1958. GS: Dan Barton, Jean Willes, Don Gardner, Grant Richards, Francis McDonald. An elderly man is accused of killing a large number of cattle with poison he has used to kill wolves. Protesting his innocence, the old man blames the two Beaumont brothers.

155.27 *The Tin Gunman.* April 16, 1958. GS: Neil Grant, Hal Smith, Patrick Waltz, Paul Lambert, Lisa Gaye, Dennis Moore, Charles Seel. A vaudeville artist arrives in town claiming that he is the world's fastest gun, and offers to prove his claim against all comers. Sheriff Hollister and editor Harris Claibourne try to warn the man against making the offer, but the showman ignores them.

155.28 *The Outcasts.* April 23, 1958. The citizens of Tombstone are violently opposed to members of a religious sect who have camped on the edge of town. Sheriff Hollister feels they should be expelled to prevent a riot, while editor Claibourne contends that as Americans they are entitled to settle where the choose.

155.29 *Doc Holliday in Durango.* April 30, 1958. GS: Gerald Mohr, Mark Tapscott, Len Hendry. Sheriff Clay Hollister meets up with Doc Holliday, one of the fastest guns in the West. Hollister is tracking a fugitive who killed his deputy, while Holliday is tracking the same man to kill him for personal reasons.

155.30 *Triangle of Death.* May 7, 1958. GS: Peter Hansen, Bartlett Robinson, Cathy Downs. A blackmailer and his victim go gunning for each other in Tombstone. Sheriff Hollister, trying to avert violence, gets caught in the cross fire.

155.31 *Pick up the Gun.* May 14, 1958. GS: Fay Spain, Patrick McVey, Thomas Pittman, Pernell Roberts, Paul Comi, Max Cutler. A young girl is ordered by her strict father to marry a miner. But the girl falls in love with a cowboy and runs away from home. Sheriff Clay Hollister tries to bring about a reunion between the girl and her father, but finds himself in the middle of a feud between a group of miners and cowboys.

155.32 *The Assassin.* May 21, 1958. GS: Larry Pennell, Cece Whitney, Gail Kobe. Bill Doolin, a gunman recently released from prison, attempts to kill Sheriff Clay Hollister.

Tombstone Territory

Hollister, believing that there is more to the attempted murder than appears on the surface, lets Doolin go free.

155.33 *The Lady Gambler.* May 28, 1958. GS: Diane Brewster, Peter Breck, Peggy Maley, Carlyle Mitchell, Ollie O'Toole. A pretty blonde woman arrives in Tombstone and soon makes it known that she is a former socialite who is now a faro dealer. She goes to work at Val Slater's Oriental saloon and business booms. But Sheriff Clay Hollister is intrigued by the fact that the woman meets every incoming stagecoach. She says she is seeking her brother.

155.34 *Fight for a Fugitive.* June 4, 1958. GS: Joe Haworth, Joan Marshall, Jeff De Benning, William Boyett, William Bakewell, Dennis Moore, Billy Nelson, Keene Duncan. A man is convicted of murder and sent to Yuma Prison. He escapes and his friend, editor Harris Claibourne, hides him while he tries to prove his innocence. But the escaped man panics, and runs away from Tombstone, and Sheriff Clay Hollister begins a search for him.

155.35 *Legacy of Death.* June 11, 1958. GS: Anthony George, Joe De Santis, Perry Lopez. A group of men who love freedom oppose a cruel Mexican despot, Commandante Nexor. The commandante wipes out the group, and the leader, who is dying, seeks sanctuary in Tombstone Territory. Sheriff Clay Hollister finds him and brings the dying man's brother to see him.

155.36 *Outlaw's Bugle.* Aug. 6, 1958. GS: Andrew Duggan, Sam Buffington. A cattle broker who buys stolen cattle learns that his supply has been cut off because of the activities of Sheriff Clay Hollister. Hollister, with the help of editor Harris Claibourne, has turned public opinion against the broker.

155.37 *The Gatling Gun.* Aug. 27, 1958. GS: Douglas Kennedy, Ed Kemmer, Maggie Mahoney. Sam Colby, former resident of Tombstone, still loves a local girl. When the girl becomes engaged to Lt. Crane, whose job is to guard the Army payroll, Colby hatches a unique plot.

155.38 *The Black Marshal from Deadwood.* Sept. 3, 1958. GS: Lon Chaney, Jr., John Close, Fredric Gavlin, David Whorf. Dagett, a famed lawman, arrives in Tombstone and retires to a small ranch after warning editor Harris Claibourne not to print anything concerning his whereabouts. Sheriff Hollister does some investigating and learns that Dagett's wrist has been shattered in a gunfight and that he can't draw very fast. Hollister is sure Dagett's enemies will seek him out.

155.39 *Thicker Than Water.* Sept. 10, 1958. GS: Paul Richards, Steve Terrell. While returning to Tombstone with Milo Wade, a notorious gunman, Sheriff Clay Hollister is attacked by Wade's brother and tied to a tree in the burning sun. Wade and his brother ride off and the fugitive is sure that Hollister will die.

155.40 *Rose of the Rio Bravo.* Sept. 17, 1958. GS: Kathy Nolan, Michael Landon. The son of an Eastern publisher comes to Tombstone to learn the newspaper business from Editor Harris Claibourne. He promptly falls in love with Rose, a beautiful girl who has a record of lawlessness and cruelty. Sheriff Clay Hollister and Claibourne try to warn the young man against the girl.

Season Two

155.41 *Whipsaw.* March 13, 1959. GS: Myron Healey, Warren Oates. Hollister sets out to bring in a prisoner and encounters an Indian ambush.

155.42 *Marked for Murder.* March 20, 1959. GS: Lloyd Corrigan, Roy Engel, Dehl Berti. A citizen of Tombstone is aware that newspaper editor Harris Claibourne knows of his shady past. Afraid that the editor may reveal all he knows, he hires a professional gunman to kill Claibourne.

155.43 *Payroll to Tombstone.* March 27, 1959. GS: Peggy Knudson, John Reach, Robert Shayne, Hugh Sanders. As the stage from Tucson comes to a stop in front of a Tombstone store, a man flees from the store pursued by the proprietor, carrying a gun. When the excitement subsides, it is discovered that a dispatch case belonging to a stagecoach passenger is missing.

155.44 *Day of the Amnesty.* April 3, 1959. GS: Jack Elam, Patrick McVey, Ron Hayes, Joyce Meadows. Because of a recently declared amnesty, Sheriff Clay Hollister is unable to arrest two hired gunmen.

155.45 *Trail's End.* April 10, 1959. GS: Harry Harvey, Jr., Olive Carey, Jeff De Benning, Joe Hamilton. Sheriff Clay Hollister goes after a young murderer who shot a miner in the back.

155.46 *The Black Diamond.* April 17, 1958. GS: Jean Willes, Burt Mustin, Pierre Watkin. As the silver-miners of Tombstone have been realizing a profit from their labors, crooks have been coming into town. Sheriff Clay Hollister discovers a method of protecting the miners.

155.47 *The Man from Brewster.* April 24, 1959. GS: Michael Landon, Richard Reeves, Tom London. Chris Anderson, a young stagecoach driver, comes to Sheriff Clay Hollister for help. Anderson, who is wanted for robbery in Brewster Flats, tells Clay that the sheriff of Brewster Flats and one of his men were involved in the crime.

155.48 *Gun Hostage.* May 1, 1959. GS: Lee Van Cleef, Pamela Duncan, Bill Henry, Raymond Hatton. Deputy Marshal Bledsoe and his prisoner Sam Carver are traveling to Chicago by train. As the train nears Tombstone, Carver makes his escape, still wearing leg irons. Sheriff Clay Hollister plays a hunch and pays a visit to Carver's sister, who lives in the area.

155.49 *Warrant for Death.* May 8, 1959. GS: Russ Conway, Mary Webster, Wright King. Two outlaws stop a stagecoach in which Sheriff Clay Hollister is traveling. Hollister soon realizes that the men are not ordinary robbers, but killers who are out to get him.

155.50 *Surrender at Sunglow.* May 15, 1959. GS: John Doucette, Cathy Downs, Billy Nelson, Mark Tapscott. An outlaw gang has gradually gained control of the town of Sunglow. Hollister and Claibourne, in town on a visit, are captured and thrown in jail by the gangsters.

155.51 *Grave Near Tombstone.* May 22, 1959. GS: Robert J. Wilke, Lisa Gaye. C.J. Cooley's niece Nancy comes to Tombstone to find her uncle. Cooley's partner tells Nancy that the old man has gone prospecting. But Nancy finds this hard to believe, and she asks Sheriff Hollister for help in locating him.

155.52 *Death Is to Write About.* May 29, 1959. GS: John Sutton, Jack Hogan, Ken Mayer, John Wengraf. While he is visiting Tombstone, an author's room is broken into by an outlaw. Sheriff Hollister suspects that there is more to the outlaw's action than robbery.

155.53 *Red Terror of Tombstone.* Oct. 9, 1959. GS:

Harvey Stephens, John Vivyan, Allison Hayes. The townspeople of Tombstone are divided into two groups — those who want the county seat moved to Benson, a nearby town, and those who will risk a war between the two towns to retain this honor.

Season Three

155.54 *The Gunfighter.* Oct. 16. 1959. GS: James Coburn, Ron Hagerthy. A rancher hires a gunfighter to protect him from impetuous young Jeff Harper, whose family had fought a bloody feud with the rancher. Sheriff Hollister tries to keep the peace with Harper tells him that he comes to seek a truce with the rancher.

155.55 *Stolen Loot.* Oct. 23, 1959. Sheriff Hollister arrests Anita Torreon as a receiver of loot for a holdup gang and takes her to Prescott to stand trial. Aboard the stagecoach making the trip, violence erupts as disguised gunmen suddenly appear to rescue Anita and recover the loot.

155.56 *The Writer.* Oct. 30, 1959. GS: Allison Hayes, Don Kennedy. Beautiful Elizabeth Blythe comes from New York to Tombstone to write a story about the town. She promptly finds herself in mortal danger while riding unescorted into wilderness territory. She is captured by outlaw Ed Chandler and Sheriff Hollister must face the gunman in an attempt to save Miss Blythe.

155.57 *Payroll Robbery.* Nov. 6, 1959. GS: Morris Ankrum. Released from prison together, Jake Conroy and Hobe Jones become partners in a scheme to rob a rich mine owner. Conroy gets a job with the miner and Jones stages a great display of honesty in order to win the assignment of transporting the payroll from town to mine. With the cash in their control, the thieves head out to Mexico.

155.58 *The Horse Thief.* Nov. 13, 1959. GS: Leonard Nimoy, Jack LaRue. Hollister stops gunman Jess Buckhorn from shooting Little Hawk, who denies stealing horses from a mission. Attorney Fred Griffin, the gunman's secret employer, plots to discredit the Indians so he can gain title to their land cheaply.

155.59 *The Legend.* Nov. 20, 1959. GS: Britt Lomond, Michael Morgan. Writer Jay Pell sets out to create a new legendary badman for his readers. He persuades Sam Crane to hold up a stagecoach in order to write an eyewitness story. The stage driver is killed and Crane is wounded. Pell subsequently betrays the outlaw when he learns about Sheriff Hollister being a true hero and attempts to get another eyewitness story of the sheriff gunning down the badman.

155.60 *Premature Obituary.* Nov. 27, 1959. GS: Philip Baird, Ike Cobb. Ron Browning learns that his fiancee is arriving from London. Not wanting her to find him a broken-down failure, he begs the Tombstone Epitaph's editor to run his obituary. When the editor refuses Ron tries to shoot himself, but fails. When he is locked up by the sheriff for his own protection he is taken as hostage when another prisoner breaks out of jail. This crisis soon restores Browning's self respect when he saves the life of the sheriff.

155.61 *Dangerous Romance.* Dec. 4, 1959. GS: Page Slattery, Joan Connors. Young cowhand Paul Hayden is baited into a fight with three wild brothers and wounds one. Sheriff Hollister arrests Paul and paroles him in the custody of Editor Claibourne. Paul meets and falls in love with Karen Thomas, sister of the three assailants.

155.62 *Self-Defense.* Dec. 11, 1959. GS: Roy Barcroft. When Sheriff Hollister is forced to gun down the son of wealthy rancher Flint Anson in self-defense, Anson offers a reward for Clay's death.

155.63 *The Marked Horseshoe.* Dec. 18, 1959. GS: Robert J. Wilke, Gene Roth. A wealthy rancher is killed and robbed of the range payroll and Sheriff Hollister sets out to find the killer with his only clue a horseshoe print.

155.64 *The Noose That Broke.* Dec. 25, 1959. GS: Paul Richards, Don Devlin. Reed Barker is sentenced to hang for a holdup and murder. His brother Seth concocts a scheme to free Reed, resulting in the rope breaking during the hanging. Under territorial law, this leaves Reed a free man.

155.65 *Mine Disasters.* Jan. 1, 1960. GS: Donald Murphy. Sheriff Hollister is angered over several recent mine disasters and campaigns for mine safety legislation.

155.66 *Eyewitness.* Jan. 8, 1960. GS: Elisha Cook, Jr. Oriental Saloon handyman Adam Kirby witnesses a murder at the livery stable. He becomes a target of the killer, even though he cannot identify the assailant.

155.67 *The Capture.* Jan. 15, 1960. GS: Chuck Couch, William Phipps. When a U.S. marshal is ambushed while bringing in outlaw Kyle Dodge, he turns his captive over to Hollister just before he dies. Hollister uses the prisoner to lure a ruthless gang into the open.

155.68 *State's Witness.* Jan. 22, 1960. GS: Mark Tobin. In order to trap an outlaw gang, the Epitaph reports that a gang member, left behind in a getaway, is turning state's witness.

155.69 *The Target.* Jan. 29, 1960. GS: Warren Oates, Liam Sullivan. The editor of the Epitaph witnesses a murder and identifies Vic Reel as the killer. Claibourne becomes a target when the gang leader sends killers to try and silence him.

155.70 *The Bride.* Feb. 5, 1960. GS: Byron Morrow, Edson Stroll, Linda Lawson. Rancher Bert Magraw returns from Denver with his young bride. When he returns he is baited into a fight with a gunslinger as part of a plot to steal his ranch and money.

155.71 *Female Killer.* Feb. 12, 1960. GS: Mala Powers, Donald Harvey. Renee Carter is being taken to Yuma prison for robbing a miner. When the miner dies she must return to Tombstone to stand trial for murder. Sheriff Hollister believes she is protecting someone.

155.72 *The Lady Lawyer.* Feb. 19, 1960. GS: Kathie Browne, James Westerfield, Regis Toomey. Sheriff Hollister prevents a gunfight between mine owner Big Jim Gerson and his manager Feeny Spindler. Gerson suspects Spindler of mismanaging the mine, so the manager hires a lady lawyer, who with the help of Hollister and Claibourne, find some surprising facts.

155.73 *Silver Killers.* Feb. 26, 1960. GS: Constance Ford. Clay Hollister investigates a series of mysterious deaths among the silver miners. The evidence implicates philanthropist Lily Murdock.

155.74 *Holcomb Brothers.* March 4, 1960. GS: Harry Carey, Jr. Marshal Vern Fawcett turns in his badge after accidentally shotting outlaw Brade Holcomb in the back. Sheriff Hollister tries to prevent a feud when Holcomb's vengeful brothers ride into Tombstone.

155.75 *Young Killer.* March 11, 1960. GS: Robert Ivers, Kay Elhardt. Young Eddie Casper attempts to kill Sheriff Hollister and is seriously wounded. He takes the young man to the home of a nurse, who is kidnapped with the dying boy by the Gayleville gang.

155.76 *Coded Newspaper.* March 18, 1960. Fragments of the Tombstone Epitaph's front page found at the scene of a robbery and also on the body of a known killer. Sheriff Hollister and Sheriff Claibourne find a strange code in the help wanted ads.

155.77 *Memory.* March 25, 1960. GS: Allison Hayes. Sheriff Hollister supervises the transfer of a shipment of bank cash from a stage coach to the Wells Fargo office safe. Beautiful Liz Dolthan uses her amazing memory to learn the combination of the safe and steal its contents.

155.78 *Revenge.* April 1, 1960. A brother and sister come to Tombstone to avenge Sheriff Hollister's killing of their father, outlaw Jonas Bell.

155.79 *The Hostage.* April 8, 1960. GS: Anthony Ray, Keith Larsen. When Sheriff Hollister tries to hang murderer Sam Edwards, his brother John engineers an escape and takes Editor Claibourne as hostage.

155.80 *Stolen Loot.* April 15, 1960. GS: Patrick Waltz, Jean Allison. Three holdup men rob the Tombstone Bank and hide the money at Dan Jensen's farm. Jensen is kidnapped when his wife brings the stolen loot to Sheriff Hollister.

155.81 *The Kidnapping.* April 22, 1960. Outlaw chief Frank Banta's gang kidnaps the territorial governor in order to save the life of his brother, who is scheduled to hang.

155.82 *Girl from Philadelphia.* April 29, 1960. GS: Erin O'Brien. Isabelle Reed comes to Tombstone from Philadelphia, looking for excitement. She falls in love with gambler-gunman Ben Quaid who is wanted for murder.

155.83 *The Fortune.* May 6, 1960. On the road outside Tombstone, Clay encounters three escaped criminals who have discovered a fortune in silver. The plan to kill the sheriff to protect their secret.

155.84 *The Innocent Man.* May 13, 1960. GS: John Doucette. Sheriff Eli Parsons asks Hollister to help track down convicts, one of whom is an innocent man.

155.85 *The Siesta Killer.* May 20, 1960. GS: Harold Peary. The mysterious Siesta Killer goes from town to town killing throughout the Southwest during the Siesta hours. Sheriff Hollister attempts to capture the killer when his trail leads to Tombstone.

155.86 *The Return of Kansas Joe.* May 27, 1960. Hollister receives word that Kansas Joe Barton has been released from Yuma Prison. He has sworn vengeance on the territorial governor, who was once the judge who convicted him. When an attempt is made on the governor's life, Barton seems like the main suspect.

155.87 *Betrayal.* June 3, 1960. Sheriff Hollister captures outlaw Lafe Jackson while trying to rendezvous with his gang to divide the loot from a robbery. Jackson and Hollister soon find themselves fighting at each other's side when the gang decides to kill both men.

155.88 *The Treaty.* June 10, 1960. While General Crook and Geronimo are negotiating a treaty with the Apaches, a fanatic brave of the tribe challenges Geronimo's leadership and starts a series of bloody massacres in the territory. Hollister devises a trap for the renegade to save the town of Tombstone.

155.89 *The Outlaw.* June 17, 1960. Claibourne follows up a report that a notorious outlaw is living in Tombstone as a respected citizen. Sheriff Hollister tries to find the man before Claibourne, and both find themselves in grave danger when the get an answer to the mystery.

155.90 *The Injury.* June 24, 1960. Clay takes a vacation in Tucson after his gun-arm is badly wounded. He encounters the brother of a killer he once captured and is provoked into a gunfight where he is forced to shoot left-handed.

155.91 *Crime Epidemic.* July 1, 1960. GS: Ralph Taeger. Sheriff Hollister tries to learn the identity of the leader behind and epidemic of crimes in the territory.

155.92 *Juan Diega.* July 8, 1960. Sheriff Hollister learns that Mexican bandit chief Juan Diega plans a bank robbery in Tombstone. Hollister takes the identity of a member of the bandit gang in order to foil their plans.

156. Trackdown

CBS. 30 min. Broadcast history: Friday, 8:00-8:30, Oct. 1957–Jan. 1959; Wednesday, 8:30-9:00, Feb. 1959–Sept. 1959.

Regular Cast: Robert Culp (Hoby Gilman).

Premise: This series concerned the adventures of Texas Ranger Hoby Gilman in the West of the 1870s.

The Episodes

156.1 *Marple Brothers.* Oct. 4, 1957. GS: James Best, Don House, James Griffith, Jan Merlin, Gail Kobe, Tom Pittman. Hoby Gilman follows the trail of the notorious Marple Brothers to Stockton. He finds that the gang is holding women and children as hostages and is barricaded in the local church. He must take the Marple Brothers without endangering the townspeople's lives.

156.2 *Law in Lampasas.* Oct. 11, 1957. GS: Frank Ferguson, James Lydon, Vaughn Taylor, John Cliff, Fintan Meyler. A man accused of killing the newspaper publisher in a small town faces an angry mob determined to lynch him. Ranger Hoby Gilman tries to see that justice is done.

156.3 *The San Saba Incident.* Oct. 18, 1957. GS: Rex Reason, Margaret Hayes, Mort Mills, Guy Wilkerson. Texas Ranger Hoby Gilman sets out for th state penitentiary at San Saba with a wagonload of prisoners, one of them a beautiful woman who has been convicted of manslaughter. The Ranger suddenly finds that the wagon is being followed, and he prepares to defend his captives.

156.4 *Easton, Texas.* Oct. 25, 1957. GS: Dabbs Greer, Larry Kelly, Gale Robbins, Dee Carroll, Robert Foulk, Ned Glass. Texas Ranger Hoby Gilman goes to Easton, to solve a robbery. He finds two dead men, a wounded station agent and a dynamited safe.

156.5 *Like Father.* Nov. 1, 1957. GS: William Talman, Malcolm Brodrick, James Seay, James Nolan, Don Diamond. Texas Ranger Hoby Gilman captures a vicious criminal and then must deal with the man's rebellious teenage son.

156.6 *Sweetwater, Texas.* Nov. 8, 1957. GS: Valerie French, Ray Danton, Paul Richards, Paul Birch, Arthur Space.

Gilman comes upon a stagecoach that has been robbed, with all the passengers dead except for a baby. His only clue is the phonograph of a woman which he finds on the scene.

156.7 *Alpine, Texas.* Nov. 15, 1957. GS: Ian MacDonald, Virginia Christine, Robin Raymond, Robert Griffin, Dick Wessel, Paul Engle. Hoby Gilman is assigned to investigate the death of a fellow Texas Ranger. He enters a lawless town that despises the Rangers.

156.8 *Self-Defense.* Nov. 22, 1957. GS: Constance Ford, Stacy Harris, Eve Miller, Richard Webb, Helen Jay. Sharpshooting Polly Webster arranges a showdown when the man who shot her husband is acquitted. She swears she will shoot it out with Duke Kinkaid the moment he steps out of jail. Texas Ranger Hoby Gilman attempts to prevent any more bloodshed.

156.9 *End of an Outlaw.* Nov. 29, 1957. GS: John Anderson, Willard Sage, John Baer, DeForest Kelley, James Gavin, Mario Siletti. Jim Murphy, member of an outlaw gang headed by Sam Bass, informs Hoby Gilman and Dick Wade that Bass plans to rob a bank in Round Rock. Gilman and Wade set up an ambush, but a self-important deputy tips off Bass.

156.10 *Look for the Woman.* Dec. 6, 1957. GS: William Phipps, Phyllis Avery, Larry Dobkin, Ross Elliot, Ray Teal. During a gun battle, Hoby Gilman fatally wounds the criminal Bud Crome. Just before Crome dies, he asks Gilman to find his sister Charlotte, the only other person who knows the identity of his accomplices.

156.11 *The Town.* Dec. 13, 1957. GS: Lee Van Cleef, Stuart Whitman, Gloria Saunders, Richard Reeves, Roy Barcroft, Ric Roman, Richard Hale. Hoby Gilman trails a killer to a small mining town. There Gilman is captured by outlaws.

156.12 *Man and Money.* Dec. 27, 1957. GS: Vic Morrow, Victor Millan, Anna Navarro, Don Diamond. Texas Ranger Hoby Gilman sets out to apprehend a bank robber who has stolen $50,000. He finds the fugitive near death from a bullet wound, and conceals his identity in an effort to find out the location of the money.

156.13 *The Reward.* Jan. 3, 1958. GS: Virginia Christine, Pernell Roberts, Jay Novello, Russ Bender, John Doucette, Robin Raymond, Val Dufour. A man who can identify the persons who committed a robbery goes into hiding. Ranger Hoby Gilman sets out to find him.

156.14 *The Farrand Story.* Jan. 10, 1958. GS: Carole Mathews, Judith Ames, Grant Richards, Richard Webb, Richard Crane. Hoby Gilman sets out to trace a missing person. He uncovers a murder motivated by jealousy.

156.15 *Right of Way.* Jan. 17, 1958. GS: Dan Barton, Robert Cornthwaite, Edward Platt, Harry Harvey, Jr., Barbara Wilson. Texas Ranger Hoby Gilman tries to help a young man about to be executed for murder. The Ranger has only a slim clue with which to establish the man's innocence.

156.16 *The Witness.* Jan. 24, 1958. GS: Jacques Aubuchon, Harold J. Stone, Sam Edwards, Joe Perry, Malcolm Atterbury, Dabbs Greer. Hoby Gilman, investigating the murder of a small-town storekeeper, follows a suspicious-looking fur trapper into the wilderness. He comes upon a blind man, the only witness to the murder, who is half-crazed in his fear of being followed by the killer.

156.17 *The Toll Road.* Jan. 31, 1958. GS: Will Wright, Trevor Bardette, Bill Erwin, Parley Baer, John Cliff. Hoby Gilman views all the townspeople of Garrison Flats as suspects in a murder case. The dead man was hated by everyone.

156.18 *The Young Gun.* Feb. 7, 1958. GS: Corey Allen, Karen Sharpe, Bill Henry, Christopher Dark, Robert Anderson, Norman Leavitt. A young man who needs money to get married, teams up with two notorious outlaws to stage a bank robbery. The outlaws make their escape after the holdup, but the young man is captured. Ranger Hoby Gilman decides on a daring plan to learn the whereabouts of the escapees.

156.19 *The Wedding.* Feb. 14, 1958. GS: Virginia Gregg, June Vincent, Robert Burton, John Harmon, Frank Cady, Kem Dibbs. Ranger Hoby Gilman is sent to a town in Texas to investigate a strange death. The man, who was about to be married, is found dead just before the wedding.

156.20 *The Trail.* Feb. 28, 1958. GS: Harry Bellaver, Elisha Cook, Jr., Didi Ramati, Ted de Corsia, Thomas B. Henry, Rodolfo Hoyos. After capturing a train robber in Mexico, Hoby Gilman sets out to escort his prisoner back to Texas. But on the way Hoby is bitten by a rattlesnake and his prisoner leaves him to die on the trail.

156.21 *The Bounty Hunter.* March 7, 1958. GS: Steve McQueen, Jean Willes, Barbara Fuller, Kenneth McDonald, George Neise. Ranger Hoby Gilman decides to investigate a man with a reputation for capturing wanted criminals and collecting the rewards offered for them.

156.22 *The Judge.* March 14, 1958. GS: Steve Terrell, John Litel, James Griffith, Ellen Corby, Norman Leavitt, Kasey Rogers. Ranger Hoby Gilman arrests a young man who has killed another in an argument. Then Gilman learns that the prisoner's father is the judge and insists that the judge must preside at the trail and determine the fate of his son.

156.23 *The House.* March 21, 1958. GS: Jacques Aubuchon, Judith Ames, Gail Kobe, James Griffith, Ellen Corby, Norman Leavitt. Ranger Hoby Gilman helps a blind girl search for her mother, who has disappeared from her home. Gilman traces the woman to a lonely farmhouse.

156.24 *The Boy.* March 28, 1958. GS: John Crawford, Gail Kobe, James Griffith, King Donovan, Larry Dobkin, Norman Leavitt. A young boy witnesses a murder and goes to Ranger Hoby Gilman for help. Gilman starts hunting for the murderer and uncovers a peculiar motive for the crime.

156.25 *The Pueblo Kid.* April 4, 1958. GS: Michael Landon, George Brenlin, James Griffith, Ellen Corby, Gail Kobe, Sally Fraser. A young man returns to his home town with a reputation as one of the fastest guns in the territory. He has the whole town terrified, and Texas Ranger Hoby Gilman tries to avert a gun battle.

156.26 *The Winter Boys.* April 11, 1958. GS: Tom Pittman, James Griffith, Ellen Corby, Norman Leavitt, Nick Adams, Doris Singleton. An outlaw turns over the wanted Winter brothers to ranger Hoby Gilman. Afraid that his key witness will be killed before the Winter brothers are brought to trial, Hoby Gilman hides the outlaw in a hotel in a small Western town.

156.27 *The Mistake.* April 18, 1958. GS: James Best, James Griffith, Bruce Gordon, Joseph Mell, Rusty Wescoatt, Roy Engel. When Hoby Gilman helps to get a man acquitted of murder, the local townspeople turn against him. Later, Hoby learns that the man is really guilty of the murder and his mistake troubles his conscience.

Trackdown

156.28 *The Deal.* April 25, 1958. GS: James Westerfield, Johnny Crawford, James Griffith, Norman Leavitt, Bert Stevens. A cowboy threatens to kill a small boy unless Ranger Hoby Gilman gives him the money from the town's bank. Knowing that the cowboy would carry out his threat, Gilman devises a plan which he hopes will save the boy's life and the money.

156.29 *The Jailbreak.* May 2, 1958. GS: DeForest Kelley, John Litel, James Griffith, Ellen Corby, Norman Leavitt, I. Stanford Jolley, Nolan Leary, Ned Glass. A prisoner facing execution overpowers his jailer and holds three men at his mercy. He tells Ranger Hoby Gilman that unless he is allowed to escape, he will kill the three men.

156.30 *The End of the World.* May 9, 1958. GS: Larry Dobkin, Richard Hale, Claudia Barrett, Dabbs Greer, Neyle Morrow. Walter Trump, a confidence man, puts on a long robe and holds a tent meeting in the town of Talpa. He tells the townspeople that a cosmic explosion will rain fire on the town and that he is the only one that can save them from death. Ranger Hoby Gilman attempts to prove Trump is a fraud.

156.31 *The Brothers.* May 16, 1958. GS: Steve McQueen, Rebecca Welles, Richard Devon, Ian MacDonald, Tim Graham. Texas Ranger Hoby Gilman is assigned to take a murderer into custody. While traveling to pick up the wanted man, Gilman is ambushed and his gun and identification papers are taken from him. Reaching his destination, he finds identical twins who answer the wanted man's description.

156.32 *The Governor.* May 23, 1958. GS: Frank Wilcox, Robert E. Griffith, Amzie Strickland, B.G. Norman, Terry Frost, Robert Gothie, Wilbur Mack. Ranger Hoby Gilman learns of a plot to assassinate the governor of Texas at a civic celebration. He tries to warn the governor, who refuses to cancel his appearance at the event. Gilman makes plans to try to avert the murder.

Season Two

156.33 *Killer Take All.* Sept. 5, 1958. GS: Nancy Gates, Ellen Corby, Whit Bissell, Don Durant, Forrest Lewis. Texas Ranger Hoby Gilman conducts an investigation when a professional gambler is killed. He learns that the dead man had made an unusual wager and lost.

156.34 *Outlaw's Wife.* Sept. 12, 1958. GS: Diane Brewster, Richard Crane, Ellen Corby, James Griffith, Lurene Tuttle, Norman Leavitt, Marjorie Bennett, Kathryn Card, Dorothy Adams. Abigail Duke comes back to her home town which she left some time before to elope with a wanted outlaw. The women of the town demand that Texas Ranger Hoby Gilman tell Abigail to get out of town, but Gilman refuses.

156.35 *Chinese Cowboy.* Sept. 19, 1958. GS: Keye Luke, Don Megowan, Ellen Corby, Norman Leavitt, Don Gordon, Fred Sherman, Rusty Wescoatt. A kindly Chinese man arrives in the town of Porter and opens a laundry. He is ignored by all the townspeople except the town bully, Les Morgan. Morgan and his friends harass the laundryman and finally Texas Ranger Hoby Gilman offers his protection. But the protection is refused.

156.36 *The Set Up.* Sept. 26, 1958. GS: James Griffith, Ellen Corby, Norman Leavitt, Douglas Fowley, King Donovan, Jan Arvan. Texas Ranger Hoby Gilman begins an investigation of a bank robbery. The man he suspects of the crime has a convincing alibi.

156.37 *A Stone for Benny French.* Oct. 3, 1958. GS: Wallace Ford, Strother Martin, Richard Devon, Gordon Polk, James Goodwin. While bringing in a wanted man, Hoby Gilman is held up by a backwoodsman and his two sons. They try to force Gilman to give up his prisoner.

156.38 *Trapped.* Oct. 10, 1958. GS: Virginia Grey, Ross Elliot. Texas Ranger Hoby Gilman, seeking shelter from a blinding snowstorm, stumbles into an abandoned stagecoach station. There he finds a woman wanted for murder, and her wounded companion, hiding from the law.

156.39 *Matter of Justice.* Oct. 17, 1958. GS: Steve Brodie, Regis Toomey, Bob Nichols, Larry White, Virginia Christine, Ellen Wells, Kasey Rogers. Texas Ranger Hoby Gilman brings in a wanted man who is placed in the town's prison. The townspeople, afraid of reprisals from the prisoner's gang, want Gilman to release the outlaw.

156.40 *Tenner Smith.* Oct. 24, 1958. GS: Phil Leeds, George Brenlin, Walter Sande, Bob Tetrick, Ellen Corby, Norman Leavitt. A professional gambler is accused of cheating a young cowboy in a card game. Texas Ranger Hoby Gilman tries to protect the gambler and give him a fair trial, but the townspeople order Gilman to turn the gambler over to them.

156.41 *The Avenger.* Oct. 31, 1958. GS: George Neise, Barbara Lawrence, Marjorie Owens, Dennis Moore, Orville Sherman. After a payroll robbery Texas Ranger Hoby Gilman begins an investigation. Then the man he suspects of the robbery is murdered.

156.42 *The Schoolteacher.* Nov. 7, 1958. GS: Robert Cornthwaite, Harold J. Stone, Jean Howell, Ellen Corby, Peter Leeds, Norman Leavitt. A schoolteacher attempts to give the children of a Texas town a good education, but his efforts are balked by a gunslinger who believes schools are unnecessary. The schoolteacher is determined to run the gunman out of town even if it means losing his life.

156.43 *Deadly Decoy.* Nov. 14, 1958. GS: Ed Kemmer, Chris Alcaide, Than Wyenn, Tom Fadden, Tom McKee. Afraid that Texas Ranger Hoby Gilman will prevent them from committing a crime, a band of outlaws use the body of a man as a decoy. Gilman believes that the dead man is the leader of the gang.

156.44 *Sunday's Child.* Nov. 21, 1958. GS: James Best, Gail Kobe, Peter Leeds, Ellen Corby, Norman Leavitt, William Fawcett. Texas Ranger Hoby Gilman is forced to comply with a court order and help a gunslinger take custody of his small child. But the child's mother refuses to surrender the infant.

156.45 *Day of Vengeance.* Nov. 28, 1958. GS: Michael Landon, Jean Allison, Francis J. McDonald, Peter Leeds, Ellen Corby, George Keymas. After his release from prison, a young man goes home intent on avenging his brother's death. Texas Ranger Hoby Gilman tries to reach the killer of the dead youth before the ex-convict does.

156.46 *Three Legged Fox.* Dec. 5, 1958. GS: Henry Hull, Ray Teal, Hank Patterson, Ellen Corby, Norman Leavitt, Robert Armstrong, Peter Brocco, Sam Flint, Jason Johnson. Texas Ranger Hoby Gilman learns that there is a band of gunmen in his territory. He investigates and is surprised that the band consists of six once famous bandits who plan to strike again.

156.47 *The Kid.* Dec. 12, 1958. GS: Jack Kruschen, Vivi Janiss, Ellen Corby, Addison Richards, Dabbs Greer, Jonathan Hole, Joe Mell. Texas Ranger Hoby Gilman shoots a teenager fleeing from the scene of a robbery. The townspeople rise up in anger against Gilman.

156.48 *Guilt.* Dec. 19, 1958. GS: Ted de Corsia, Regis Toomey, Don Gordon, Forrest Lewis, David Post. Hoby Gilman tells the townspeople that a convicted killer is returning to town. Three witnesses who testified against the man fear that the killer is returning to seek revenge.

156.49 *Every Man a Witness.* Dec. 26, 1958. GS: Edward C. Platt, Kasey Rogers, Walter Coy, Kenneth MacDonald, Dick Ryan, Joan Lora. A prisoner in the local jail refuses to confess to the crime he is accused of. Finally a group of men decide to take matters into their own hands.

156.50 *McCallin's Daughter.* Jan. 2, 1959. GS: Anna Marie Nanasi, Russ Conway, Barbara Eiler, Ellen Corby, Norman Leavitt. Ranger Hoby Gilman learns of a forthcoming robbery from the prospective robber's little daughter.

156.51 *Bad Judgment.* Jan. 28, 1959. GS: Mort Mills, Warren Oates, Lee Farr, Jean Howell. Texan Ranger Hoby Gilman tries to persuade a witness to testify against a killer even though his testimony will endanger his family.

156.52 *Terror.* Feb. 4, 1959. GS: Addison Richards, Adrienne Marden, Peter Leeds, Frank Ferguson, Karl Swenson, Jan Shepard. Texas Ranger Hoby Gilman sets out to find a typhoid carrier. Gilman's only clue to the whereabouts of the unidentified person is the trail of fear and sickness he leaves behind.

156.53 *The Feud.* Feb. 11, 1959. GS: Lillian Bronson, Charles Cooper, James Lydon, Gary Gray, Ellen Corby, Norman Leavitt, Trevor Bardette, Helen Wallace. A dying woman returns to her home town, where she wants to be buried after her death. Her arrival in town revives an old feud and Hoby Gilman must try to use reason to combat the townspeople's deep prejudice.

156.54 *The Samaritan.* Feb. 18, 1959. GS: Rita Moreno, Chill Wills, Charles Aidman. Ranger Hoby Gilman, injured and unarmed, joins two strangers on a wilderness trail. They are menaced by a desperate killer.

156.55 *The Gang.* Feb. 25, 1959. GS: Nick Adams, George Brenlin, Gordon Polk, Addison Richards, Michael Fox, Peter Leeds. Texas Ranger Hoby Gilman must cope with a band of young saddle tramps who have overrun the town and taken a hostage.

156.56 *The Threat.* March 4, 1959. GS: Lloyd Corrigan, Peter Leeds, Norman Leavitt, Michael Fox. An odd little man threatens to blow up the town with homemade bombs if he doesn't receive a large sum of money from the bank.

156.57 *Hard Lines.* March 11, 1959. GS: James Coburn, Bevely Garland, DeForest Kelley. A Civil War soldier, accused of deserting during battle, returns to his home town. Texas Ranger Hoby Gilman places his own life in danger as he attempts to save the accused man from an angry mob.

156.58 *Fear.* March 18, 1959. GS: Harold J. Stone, Gordon Polk, Peter Leeds, Warren Oates. Texas Ranger Hoby Gilman tries to stop four trigger-happy brothers from terrorizing the area. He soon learns that the brothers have picked him as their next target.

156.59 *Stranger in Town.* March 25, 1959. GS: Peter Leeds, Ellen Corby, Norman Leavitt, John Hackett, James Drury, Paul Carr. From a man he doesn't know, Texas Ranger Hoby Gilman receives a letter predicting his death.

156.60 *The Protector.* April 1, 1959. GS: Richard Jaeckel, Grace Raynor, Paul Brinegar, Russell Thorson, John Harmon, Sid Clute, Jason Johnson. Trailing an outlaw, Texas Ranger Hoby Gilman enters a quiet town and soon discovers that it is the ideal place for a criminal to reside.

156.61 *False Witness.* April 8, 1959. GS: Peter Leeds, Ellen Corby, Norman Leavitt, Bethel Leslie, Addison Richards, Pat Donahue, James Lydon. A girl claims that she witnessed a murder for which a man has already been convicted and sentenced to hang. Because of the girl's statement Ranger Hoby Gilman reopens the murder case.

156.62 *The Trick.* April 15, 1959. GS: Edgar Buchanan, Nick Adams, Peter Leeds, Rusty Wescoatt, Norman Leavitt, Ellen Corby. A young man persistently attempts to provoke Tenner Smith, a friend of Ranger Hoby Gilman, into a gunfight. Smith can't understand why the boy wants to fight him until it is discovered that he was hired for that purpose.

156.63 *The Eyes of Jerry Kelson.* April 22, 1959. GS: Addison Richards, Jonathan Hole, Carleton Carpenter, Norman Leavitt, Judith Braun, Edward C. Platt. Pearl Madson agrees to go away with a traveling salesman, even though her father violently opposes the plan. But the salesman is found dead before Pearl can leave him.

156.64 *Gift Horse.* April 29, 1959. GS: Michael Fox, Will Wright, James Burke, Norman Leavitt, James Collier. Two schemers arrive in town claiming to be long-lost relatives of a bank employee who is all alone in the world. They explain that they want to make up for all his lonely years.

156.65 *The Vote.* May 6, 1959. GS: Ellen Corby, Norman Leavitt, Peter Leeds, James Seay, Barbara Eiler, Gregory Walcott, Rodney Bell, Bruce MacFarland. A couple of smooth operators arrive in Porter, Texas, and start a campaign for women's suffrage. The men of the town don't like the idea of being pushed into it so fast.

156.66 *The Unwanted.* May 13, 1959. GS: Dorothy Adams, Rhys Williams, Walter Brooke, Paul Engel, Hal K. Dawson, Tom Wilde, Robert La Varre, Roy Barcroft. Ranger Hoby Gilman investigates a series of strange occurrences in a small town. Townspeople charge that members of a religious sect have been practicing witchcraft.

156.67 *Toss Up.* May 20, 1959. GS: Scott Forbes, Jean Howell, Lee Farr, John Anderson. A woman comes to Hoby Gilman for help after she learns that her feuding husband and brother are plotting to kill each other.

156.68 *Back to Crawford.* Sept. 9, 1959. GS: Nancy Asch, Peggy Webber, King Calder, Charles Seel, Warren Oates, Donald A. Losby, Jr. After receiving an urgent message from his sister, Hoby Gilman prepares to leave for his home town. His sister is frightened because of recent threats on her life.

156.69 *Blind Alley.* Sept. 16, 1959. GS: Robert Driscoll, Susan Oliver, Dennis Cross, Richard Devon, Norman Leavitt, Addison Richards, DeForest Kelley. Texas Ranger Hoby Gilman goes on the trail of an escaped convict. Gilman learns that the convict is stalking a blind boy he has sworn to kill.

156.70 *Quiet Night in Porter.* Sept. 23, 1959. GS: Helen Kleeb, Don Durant, DeForest Kelley. Two sons follow their senile mother on a petty thievery excursion and land in some trouble of their own.

157. The Travels of Jaimie McPheeters

ABC. 60 min. Broadcast history: Sunday, 7:30-8:30, Sept. 1963–March 1964.

Regular Cast: Kurt Russell (Jaimie McPheeters), Dan O'Herlihy (Doc Sardius McPheeters) Michael Witney (Coulter), Donna Anderson (Jenny), James Westerfield (Murrel), Charles Bronson (Murdock), Mark Allen (Matt Kissel), Meg Wyllie (Mrs. Kissel), the Osmond Brothers (the Kissel Boys), Sandy Kenyon (Baggott), Hedley Mattingly (Coe), Vernett Allen (Othello).

Premise: This adventure series related the exploits of twelve-year-old Jaimie McPheeters as he traveled by wagon train to California in 1849.

The Episodes

157.1 *The Day of Leaving.* Sept. 15, 1963. GS: Sandy Kenyon, Jena Engstrom. Scatting out of Paducah just ahead of his creditors, Doc grabs Jaimie and boards a river boat to St. Louis. But Jaimie lands in the drink and is held for ransom by a trio of captivating thugs.

157.2 *The Day of the First Trail.* Sept. 22, 1963. GS: John Chandler. Some new people come aboard the wagon train taking Doc and Jaimie west. It is smooth going for all, until some Indians show up.

157.3 *The Day of the First Suitor.* Sept. 29, 1963. GS: Warren Oates, Albert Salmi, Karl Swenson, Charles Seel, Hope Summers. Jenny is surprised to get a marriage proposal from Frank Furnter, whom she hardly knows. Eavesdropping is Eldon Bishop, who thinks Jenny is more his type.

157.4 *The Day of the Golden Fleece.* Oct. 6, 1963. GS: James Whitmore, Andrew Duggan. While gathering herbs for his father, Jaimie stumbles on, and is dragged into, a dark cave.

157.5 *The Day of the Last Bugle.* Oct. 13, 1963. GS: Charles Robinson, Vernett Allen, III. The Beaver Company comes across Lt. Reid Beecher, who has just lost his entire six-man patrol to an Indian raiding party. Wounded, the officer mumbles that he is not to blame.

157.6 *The Day of the Skinners.* Oct. 20, 1963. GS: Diana Millay, Pete Whitney. Wandering away from the wagon train, Jaimie comes upon a ragged band of buffalo skinners. The skinners take him back and one of them, a girl named Tassie, wants to stay with the wagon train.

157.7 *The Day of the Taboo Man.* Oct. 26, 1963. GS: Frank Silvera, Michael Keep, Norman Alden. Disregarding a taboo, Doc rescues an old medicine man whom the Indians planned to sacrifice.

157.8 *The Day of the Giants.* Nov. 3, 1963. GS: Dean Harens, Don Megowan, Len Lesser. Coulter's old neighbors, Ed Matlock and his loutish kin, were never the friendly type, but after being kicked out of one wagon train they decide to travel with the Beaver Company.

157.9 *The Day of the Long Night.* Nov. 10, 1963. GS: George Kennedy, Collin Wilcox, Katy Sweet. Jaimie, Lucy Ann and her dog sneak off to a dark and foggy swamp where they are trapped by Angus, a bear of a man with the mind of a child.

157.10 *The Day of the Killer.* Nov. 17, 1963. GS: Martin Landau. At a river ford, the Beaver Company comes upon the remains of a gunfight. Two dead pistoleros and scarred, thick-muscled Linc Murdock stumbling through the brush with a pistol in his hand.

157.11 *The Day of the Flying Dutchman.* Dec. 1, 1963. GS: Lloyd Corrigan, Norma Varden, Dick Reeves. While Jaimie is sick, Doc reads him the legend of the Flying Dutchman, and soon Jaimie's imagination pictures a phantom ship sailing across the Nebraska prairie.

157.12 *The Day of the Homeless.* Dec. 8, 1963. GS: John Williams, Antoinette Bower, Jimmy Baird, Slim Pickens. While Doc and Murdock are off to a nearby town, Jaimie has three visitors — a scrawny runaway boy and two men from an orphanage who are tracking him.

157.13 *The Day of the Misfits.* Dec. 15, 1963. GS: Mariette Hartley, Henry Hull, Lee Van Cleef. Two men sneak into camp one night in search of a midwife, and kidnap Doc.

157.14 *The Day of the Pawnees* Part One. Dec. 22, 1963. GS: Howard Caine, Kathy Garver, Hank Worden, Sheldon Alman, Danny Bravo, Ed Ames. Jaimie is captured by Indians who intended to trade him for horses.

157.15 *The Day of the Pawnees* Part Two. Dec. 29, 1963. GS: Howard Caine, Kathy Garver, Hank Worden, Sheldon Alman, Danny Bravo, Ed Ames. After escaping from the Pawnees, Jaimie is recaptured by Murrel and Baggott, and all three are surrounded by the Indians.

157.16 *The Day of the Toll Takers.* Jan. 5, 1964. GS: Leif Erickson, Mary Anderson, Nick Georgiade, Michael Petit. At a river crossing, the travelers learn that Sugar Bob Devlin has the only barge and he is charging a stiff toll.

157.17 *The Day of the Wizard.* Jan. 12, 1964. GS: Burgess Meredith, Joan Tompkins, Crahan Denton, Vitina Marcus. Saracen, a traveling oracle, predicts that Jaimie will kill his own father.

157.18 *The Day of the Search.* Jan. 19, 1964. GS: David McCallum, Keenan Wynn, Charles McGraw, Karl Swenson, Susan Seaforth. A wailing sound from a rocky draw leads Jaimie to Sam Parks, chained and crouching behind a rock, Dan Carver, armed and trapped under a fallen tree, and a dead man.

157.19 *The Day of the Haunted Trail.* Jan. 26, 1964. GS: Royal Dano, John Harmon, Paul Baxley, Abel Fernandez. Beaver Company has some problems. There is no pass through the mountains, there is no water and they have encountered a ten foot ghost that looks like a monk.

157.20 *The Day of the Tin Trumpet.* Feb. 2, 1964. GS: Wallace Ford, Arch Johnson, Antoinette Bower, Rodolfo Acosta, Doodles Weaver. Beaver Company picks up three unprepossessing passengers: a drunken braggart, a killer passing himself off as the marshal he just shot, and a wounded half-breed.

157.21 *The Day of the Lame Duck.* Feb. 9, 1964. GS: Joe Mantell, Ruta Lee, Paul Langton. Jaimie encounters Piggy Trewblood just as the political has-been is attempting suicide.

157.22 *The Day of the Picnic.* Feb. 16, 1964. GS: Robert Miller Driscoll, Paul Fix, Gina Gillespie, John Chandler, James Griffith, Richard Hale. Jaimie tells a young companion about an early incident on the trip when Billy Slocum was to be hanged for horse stealing.

157.23 *The Day of the 12 Candles.* Feb. 23, 1964. GS: Joan Freeman, Paul Carr, Frank de Kova, John Harmon. Jaimie finds a murdered Indian squaw, and he decides to bring her papoose back to the wagon train.

157.24 *The Day of the Pretenders.* March 1, 1964. GS: Michael Petit, Steve Geray, Carl Esmond, Nick Georgiade, James Griffith. A trace of Old World aristocracy distinguishes Beaver Company newcomer Anton Berg and his twelve-year-old nephew Paul, as well as the uniformed men who are trailing them.

157.25 *The Day of the Dark Deeds.* March 8, 1964. GS: Barbara Nichols, Harold J. Stone, Anthony Caruso. A money pouch that Doc delivers is found to contain only a brick wrapped in newspaper, and Doc is arrest for theft.

157.26 *The Day of the Reckoning.* March 15, 1964. GS: Susan Oliver, John Fiedler, Douglas V. Fowley, Ron Hagerthy, Rayford Barnes, Jan Merlin, Robert Carricart. Linc Murdock thought he was responsible for the death of an old flame five years earlier, but now she turns up working in a shabby small-town saloon.

158. *26 Men*

Syndicated. 30 min. Broadcast history: Various, Oct. 1957–June 1959.

Regular Cast: Tris Coffin (Captain Tom Rynning), Kelo Henderson (Ranger Clint Travis).

Premise: This series related the exploits of the Arizona Rangers, who upheld justice in the Arizona Territory in the early 1900s.

The Episodes

158.1 *The Recruit.* Oct. 15, 1957. GS: Don Haggerty. Captain Tom Rynning and Ranger Clint Travis answer a request for help sent out by a newspaper editor in the town of Wilcox. They arrive to find the editor hanging from a tree.

158.2 *Trouble at Pinnacle Peak.* Oct. 22, 1957. Pursuing a group of viscous outlaws, Rynning and Travis enlist the help of an Indian tracker.

158.3 *The Wild Bunch.* Oct. 29, 1957. GS: Norma Ward, Hal Hopper, Dusty Walker, Jack Riggs, Bud Brown, Jim Norman, Ed Morgan, Bill Gillis, Dot Johnson, Robin Jewel, Joe Angel, Walter Crane, Bob Pollard. Ranger Clint Travis is fired when a member of the notorious Wild Bunch escapes his custody. Feeling he was responsible for the escape, the ranger matches guns with the entire gang.

158.4 *Border Incident.* Nov. 5, 1957. GS: Rico Alaniz, Arthur Palmer, Lane Bradford, Allegra Varron, Joe Angel, Ron Hansen, Ed Morgan, Jack Martin, Jay Orent. Disguised as a gunrunner, Clint Travis attempts to foil the plan of Juan Morales to overthrow the Mexican government.

158.5 *Destination Nowhere.* Nov. 12, 1958. GS: Lane Bradford, Joe Angel, Gloria Rhodes, Walter Crane, Bloyce Wright, Bob Pollard, Rico Alaniz, Ronnie Hansen. Capt. Tom Rynning and Ranger Clint Travis are called upon to help immigrations officials track down a gang smuggling Chinese coolies into the United States from Mexico.

158.6 *Incident at Yuma.* Nov. 19, 1957. GS: Steve Conte, Gregg Barton, Philip Tonge, Jack Riggs, Ed Morgan, Marjorie Stapp, Ronnie Hansen, Bloyce Wright, Bud Brown, John Carr. Ranger Captain Tom Rynning has difficulty gathering men to help him capture a group of convicts who have escaped from prison.

158.7 *The Slater Brothers.* Nov. 26, 1957. GS: Walter Crane, Stanley Andrews, Monte Blue, Richard Garland, George Ross, Bud Brown, Bill Hall, Jim Norman, Jack Riggs, Ed Morgan, Bill Gillis. Ranger Clint Travis is falsely accused of murder. He is sent by Capt. Tom Rynning into the Galioro Mountains of Arizona to prove his innocence and to find a group of cattle rustlers.

158.8 *Dead Man at Tucson.* Dec. 3, 1957. GS: Steve Conte. Ranger Clint Travis pursues diabolical escaped convict Cain Devers, who has robbed a bank in Yuma and is using counterfeit plates as part of a scheme to destroy his father and younger brother.

158.9 *Man on the Run.* Dec. 10, 1957. GS: George Ross, Bob Pollard, Richard Garland, Stanley Andrews, Monte Blue, Jeanne Wood, Ronnie Hansen, Bill Gillis. An Arizona Ranger resigns, with no explanation. Captain Rynning discovers that the man is trying to hide a terrible secret. He gets a clue to the mystery from an escaped bank robber who tries to kill the Ranger.

158.10 *The Big Rope.* Dec. 17, 1957. GS: Lyn Thomas. Three men are mysteriously hanged and the Arizona Rangers enter the case after receiving an anonymously signed telegram. Ranger Clint Travis journeys alone to the town of Galeyville and discovers sullen townspeople, a cowardly sheriff and a missing preacher.

158.11 *Valley of Fear.* Dec. 24, 1957. GS: William Forrest, Jim Conino, Mickey Simpson, Tim Graham, Norman MacDonald, Phil Munch, Michael Ivor, Art Palmer. Ranger Clint Travis, posing as an outlaw, tries to solve the mysterious disappearance of a U.S. Marshal in a seemingly peaceful valley.

158.12 *Indian Gunslinger.* Dec. 31, 1957. GS: Tony Russo, Mickey Simpson, Norma Ward, Tim Graham, Phil Munch, Johnny Silvers, Norman MacDonald, Jack Lang, Walter Crane, Joe Angel. Rynning and Travis stand between an Apache who has inherited land and some ranchers who don't want an Indian neighbor.

158.13 *Trail of Darkness.* Jan. 7, 1958. GS: Paul Sorensen, Rayford Barnes, Mary Newton, Dorothy Johnson, Ron Hanson. Rynning and Travis ride into a town that is enraged over the murders of two women.

158.14 *Trade Me Deadly.* Jan. 14, 1958. The Texas Rangers join with the Arizona Rangers in an attempt to save the daughter of the governor of Texas.

158.15 *Violent Land.* Jan. 28, 1958. After trailing two wanted men across the desert, Tom Rynning and Clint Travis overtake and capture them at a coral near Winona. They turn their prisoners over to Winona's sheriff. The sheriff sees a chance to make some crooked money.

158.16 *Panic at Bisbee.* Feb. 4, 1958. GS: I. Stanford Jolley, Norma Ward, John Cole, Bob Pollard, Fred Shryer, Bloyce Wright, Hal Hopper, Tom Monroe, Paul Sorensen, Rayford Barnes, Bud Brown. Ranger Clint Travis and a rancher's beautiful daughter shoot their way through dangerous badlands to bring financial aid to a surrounded bank in Bisbee.

158.17 *Insurrection.* Feb. 11, 1958. GS: Walter Kelly. An

Arizona Ranger suddenly resigns to accept a better paying job which would give him plenty of money for his forthcoming marriage. Capt. Tom Rynning and Ranger Clint Travis discover that the activities of the former ranger could provoke a war between Mexico and Arizona.

158.18 *Slaughter Trail.* Feb. 18, 1958. GS: Joe Pierce, Britt Lomond, Fred Graham, Laurie Carroll, Rodney Bell, Frank Richards, Alex Montoya, Walter Kelly, Danny Gamboa. The Rangers oppose a ruthless cattle baron who is determined to drive his herds through the planted fields of the homesteaders.

158.19 *Gun Hand.* Feb. 25, 1958. GS: Paul Picerni, Raymond Hatton, John Redmond, Barbara Bestar, Robert Swan, John James, Joseph Crehan, Alan Wells, Don C. Harvey, Riley Hill, Jim Norman, Frank Mullen. An Arizona Ranger is doing an able job of holding down lawlessness in Cochise County despite the pleadings of his fiance to give up the dangerous business of law enforcement. Capt. Tom Rynning is called upon to aid a wounded lawman when hijackers threaten the mining industry.

158.20 *Cattle Embargo.* March 4, 1958. GS: Tom Hennessey, Penny Edwards, Oliver Palmer, Steve Mitchell, Mauritz Hugo, Alex Montoya, Kim Spalding. A ranger tries to prevent three cowboys from running illegal cattle and is shot and left to die. One of the cowmen refuses to let the lawman die and brings him into town for care. Then he vanishes.

158.21 *Badge to Kill.* March 11, 1958. GS: Clarence Beaty, Paul Picerni, Robert Swan, Barbara Bestar, John James, Carole Campbell, Alan Wells, Joseph Crehan, Ralph Quita. Ranger Carl Hubbard is ambushed and wounded while escorting a shipment of Mexican gold through the Arizona territory.

158.22 *Montezuma's Cave.* March 18, 1958. GS: Robert Foulk, Joe Pierce, Phil Turich, Bill Henry, Don Diamond, Jim Norman, Louis Lettieri, Danny Zapien, Tony Chavez. Rynning's Rangers and Mexican mounted police pursue a famed Mexican bandit and his lieutenant into Arizona where they trap and kill the lieutenant but wrongly identify him as the bandit leader.

158.23 *Sundown Decision.* March 25, 1958. GS: Penny Edwards, Clarence Beaty, Kim Spalding, Harry Strang, Mauritz Hugo, Claire Dubrey, Steve Mitchell, Rev. George Ray, J.M. Brown, Frank Weidner. The Rangers encounter a physically and mentally crippled rancher who is trying to murder his brother and frame his neighbor for the crime.

158.24 *The Parrish Gang.* April 1, 1958. GS: Robert Lowery, Gregg Barton, Johnny Carpenter, Joe Pierce, Anabel Shaw, Joe Kelsay, Hal Hopper. Posing as a member of a gang of bank robbers, Ranger Clint Travis leads the Arizona Rangers to the gang's hide out.

158.25 *Hoax at Globe.* April 8, 1958. GS: Oliver Parmer, Bill Henry, Robert Foulk, Don Diamond, Robert Casino, Bob Pollard, Bill Gillis, Grizzly Green. A crooked candidate for sheriff of the town of Globe tries to use the Arizona Rangers to guarantee his election.

158.26 *Bounty Hunter.* April 15, 1958. GS: Gregg Barton, Robert Lowery, Tommy Ivo, John Redmond, Harry Fleer. A young man asks Arizona Ranger Tom Rynning to help him prove the innocence of his convicted brother-in-law by capturing the real criminal.

158.27 *Apache Water.* April 22, 1958. Ranger Tom Rynning is called upon to help persuade members of a religious group camped on Apache land to move.

158.28 *Legacy of Death.* April 29, 1958. GS: Roy Barcroft, Clarence Beaty, Don Haggerty, Lynne Carter, Helen Begam, Peter Adams, Ewing Mitchell. At the reading of rancher Bart Evans will, Rynning learns that Evans hired someone to kill him.

158.29 *Chain Gang.* May 6, 1958. GS: Lash LaRue, Glenn Strange, Lane Bradford, Oliver Parmer, Gregg Palmer, Dan Riss, Hal Hopper, Art Palmer, Norman McDonald, Bob Pollard. An ex-convict reports to the Governor of the Territory of Arizona that the guards at the prison labor camps are killing and stealing from the prisoners.

158.30 *The Bells of St. Thomas.* May 13, 1958. GS: Roy Barcroft, Jim Davis, Pierce Lyden, Jack Beutel, John Redmond, Dave Robard, Jack Riggs, Ewing Mitchell. Three outlaws elude their pursuers after robbing a bank and killing a guard and take refuge in an Indian school.

158.31 *Hondo Man.* May 20, 1958. GS: Oliver Parmer, Gregory Walcott, Ophelia Barron, Fred Kohler, Jr., Mickey Simpson, Milton Frome, Herb Vigran, Ed Morgan. On the way to the town of Contention with his niece, Jim Graves finds the body of an Arizona Ranger.

158.32 *The Vanquisher.* May 27, 1958. GS: Gregg Palmer, John Redmond, Jacqueline Holt, Mickey Simpson, Herb Vigran, Milton Frome, Jack Austin. Hearing reports that a group of outlaws have taken over his home town. Ranger Andrew Shoreham sets out alone to rid the town of the gang.

158.33 *The Ranger and the Lady.* June 3, 1958. Rynning and Travis are called into the town of Bisbee when trouble arises after women launch a campaign to secure the vote.

158.34 *Idol in the Dust.* June 10, 1958. Ranger Clint Travis sets out to investigate an outlaw who has hired a famous lawman anxious for financial security in his old age as a hired gunman.

158.35 *Runaway Stage.* June 17, 1958. GS: Gregg Palmer, Jackie Loughery, Joe Pierce, Baynes Barron, Ralph Neff, Bloyce Wright, Jack Austin, Jack Riggs. When outlaws attack a gold-carrying stage, Ranger Andy Shoreham is thrown off and knocked unconscious. When he returns to town, people don't believe his story.

158.36 *Wayward Gun.* June 24, 1958. GS: Jim Canino, Jack Beutel, Clarence Beaty, William Fawcett, William Haade, Gail Ganley, Hal Baylor, Doug McClure, Ken Becker. Much to the dismay of the Arizona Rangers, Bud Larch, a runt of a man, turns killer to compensate for his lack of height.

158.37 *Hole Up.* July 1, 1958. GS: John Redmond, Gregg Palmer, James Gavin, Paul Burns, Ophelia Barron, Baynes Barron, Jack Austin. While taking an Indian prisoner to headquarters, Clint Travis learns that a railroad depot was robbed. He enlists the aid of his prisoner to help rescue a girl held hostage by two outlaws.

158.38 *Unholy Partners.* July 8, 1958. Trailing a young hijacker to his hideout, Clint Travis attempts to capture the hijacking gang singlehanded.

158.39 *Killer's Trail.* July 15, 1958. GS: Robert Lowery, John Redmond, Mason Alan Dinehart, William Haade, George Keymas, Paul Burns, William Fawcett, Gail Ganley, Claire Carleton, Ann Daniels. The Arizona Rangers set up a dragnet after four criminals escape prison and throw the Arizona territory into a panic.

Season Two

158.40 *The Glory Road.* Oct. 7, 1958. GS: Don Haggerty, Charles Tannen, Eve Brent, Hal Hopper, William Tannen, Frank Weidner, Frank Mullen. A preacher who was once indicted for manslaughter is blackmailed into helping a killer escape from prison. In the break, an innocent man is killed and the preacher sets out to recapture the criminals.

158.41 *Shadow of a Doubt.* Oct. 14, 1958. GS: Chuck Courtney. A Ranger accused of cowardice by his fellow Rangers is put in charge of a patrol assigned to rescue a girl held captive by Indians.

158.42 *Man in Hiding.* Oct. 21, 1958. GS: Elaine Riley, Gregory Walcott. A miner informs the Rangers that a wanted killer is hiding out in the frontier town of Arbuckle.

158.43 *Cross and Double Cross.* Oct. 27, 1958. GS: Blackie Austin, Edgar Buchanan, Ron Hayes, Ed Morgan, Frank Mullen, Milo Bejarano. The Rangers persuade an outlaw to help them trap a notorious band of thieves, but when the trap is set, the outlaw deserts.

158.44 *The Last Rebellion.* Nov. 4, 1958. GS: Tony Dexter, Roy Barcroft, Dub Taylor, Jean Carmen, Robert Swan, Billy Dix, Blackie Austin, Dan Zapien. Apaches attempt to try an Apache farmer for murder according to tribal ritual even though the man has already been acquitted in court.

158.45 *Brief Glory.* Nov. 11, 1958. GS: Robert Foulk, Maudie Prickett, Forrest Lewis, Jason Johnson, Reg Browne, Charles L. Lassell, Jim Hurley, Ted Gilbert, John Graff, Al Overend. A timid bankteller tries to make himself seem important by confessing to a robbery he didn't commit.

158.46 *Dog Eat Dog.* Nov. 18, 1958. GS: Steve Pendleton, Gary Gray, James Seay, Darlene Fields, Hal Hopper, Bob Pollard, Blu Wright. The citizens of a frontier town are tyrannized by both their sheriff and their marshal.

158.47 *Judge Not.* Nov. 25, 1958. GS: Myron Healey, Rebecca Welles, Jason Johnson, Bob Johnson, Harry Mitchell, Jim Hurley, Jack Riggs. Released from a mental institution, a man sets out to find revenge against the people who sent him there.

158.48 *My Brother's Keeper.* Dec. 2, 1958. GS: I. Stanford Jolley. After learning that his son and nephew were killed in the Spanish-American War, a man allows most of his land to be purchased for back taxes.

158.49 *Run No More.* Dec. 9, 1958. GS: David Cross, Joseph Waring, Leo Gordon, Terry Frost, Eugenia Paul. The Rangers become involved when an old man is hanged for murder on perjured testimony and his vengeful son encounters the real killers at the house of a witness.

158.50 *Manhunt.* Dec. 16, 1958. GS: Richard Crane, Morris Ankrum, Ted DeCorsia, Richard Cutting, Guy Prescott, Connie Buck, Robert Noe. Captain Rynning arrests a man for murder and then learns that he has arrested the killer's twin brother.

158.51 *The Avenger.* Dec. 23, 1958. GS: Dale Cummings, Karl Davis, Gates Brown, Thomas Cain, Mark Williams. A young boy joins the Rangers to become an expert gunslinger.

158.52 *False Witness.* Dec. 30, 1958. GS: Ted DeCorsia, Morris Ankrum, Richard Cutting, Guy Prescott, Connie Buck. A crooked town boss attempts to silence the father of the man he killed by threatening to harm the old man's daughter.

158.53 *The Torch.* Jan. 6, 1958. GS: Grant Withers, Dale Cummings, Karl Davis, Paul Lukather, Gates Brown, Lynne Reetz, John Schifeling, Mark Williams. Captain Tom Rynning is ordered to solve the town of Jerome's education problems when teacher after teacher is run out of town.

158.54 *Trail of Revenge.* Jan. 13, 1959. GS: DeForest Kelley, Leonard Nimoy, Montie Montana, Arthur Space, Bill Henry, Jeanne Baird, Vera Costello. An escaped convict returns to his ranch and finds his wife has disappeared. He forces another man to hunt for her while he hides out from the authorities.

158.55 *The Hellion.* Jan. 20, 1959. GS: Doug McClure, Robert Shayne, Ann Daniels, Rayford Barnes, Hal Baylor, Vera Costello, Rex Lease, Dusty Walker, Mark Williams, Bob Taylor, Bob Johnson. The Rangers go after a young outlaw who has killed the woman he loves and is trying to frame both the murder and a robbery on his rival for the dead girl's affection.

158.56 *Ranger Without a Badge.* Jan. 27, 1959. GS: Orville Sherman, Bill Henry, Charlita, Arthur Space. A gambler helps Captain Rynning and Ranger Clint Travis capture the leader of a gang of rustlers. The three men are forced to take refuge in a jail when a band of killers ride out to free the imprisoned bandit.

158.57 *Showdown.* Feb. 3, 1959. GS: Leo Gordon, David Cross, George Douglas, Terry Frost, Robert Pollard, James Hurley, Jack Riggs. A young man plots to make use of the double jeopardy clause in the Constitution to escape punishment for the murder of his father.

158.58 *Long Trail Home.* Feb. 10, 1959. GS: Leonard Nimoy, Walter Maslow, Richard Carlyle, Barbara Bestar, Gates Brown, Stuart Wade. A gang of murderers invades the Arizona territory just when an ex-member of the band breaks out of prison. Fearing that the convict's wife will reveal their hideout to the authorities, the gang kills her.

158.59 *Death in the Dragoons.* Feb. 17, 1959. GS: Robert Shayne, Jeanne Dean, Rayford Barnes, Rex Lease, Hal Baylor, Bob Taylor, Tom Cain, Mark Williams, Kenneth Kennedy. Captain Rynning rescues a young woman rancher from a gun battle with three men and then learns that the woman is wanted for murder.

158.60 *Ricochet.* Feb. 24, 1959. Richard Carlyle, Gates Brown, Leonard Nimoy, Barbara Bestar, Jack Mather, Stuart Wade, Walter Maslow, Mitzi Meade, Bob Pollard, Paul Raymond. Three wild brothers return to their home town after a three-year absence to warn the townspeople of an impending outlaw attack. But a bullet from one of the boy's guns accidentally kills a citizen, and the town refuses to believe that the death was accidental.

158.61 *House Divided.* March 3, 1959. GS: George Keymas, Robert Dix, Daria Massey, Hal Hopper, William Swan. A rancher, whose father was slain by Indians, discovers that his brother has taken an Indian wife, and he determines to separate them.

158.62 *Profane Masquerade.* March 30, 1959. GS: Eve Brent, Patricia Michon, George Keymas, Patrick Waltz, Jack

Riggs. The girlfriend of a gangster borrows a nun's habit in an effort to disguise herself and avoid capture by the Rangers.

158.63 *Dead or Alive.* March 17, 1959. GS: Gregg Barton, Steve Darrell. Capt. Tom Rynning tries to solve a three-year-old robbery involving a crooked sheriff and a repentant marshal.

158.64 *The Has-Been.* March 24, 1959. GS: Mike Forest, Roy Barcroft, Jon Locke, Blu Wright, Bob Corrigan. The Territorial government calls on Captain Rynning to investigate a boxing racket involving heavyweight champ Duke Bristol. The Rangers find there is nothing actually illegal about the racket, which is filching the dollars of hundreds of honest men.

158.65 *The Unwanted.* March 31, 1959. GS: Mason Alan Dinehart, James Canino, Nancy Kilgas, Chuck Courtney, James Seay, Robert Armstrong. A group of young people journey to the territory of Arizona to seek their fortune. Arizona Ranger Captain Tom Rynning assigns Ranger Tex Fallan to take time off from his regular duties to try to help his young friends.

158.66 *Live and Let Die.* April 7, 1959. GS: Jon Locke, Bob Taylor. An outlaw returns from the dead to seek revenge against his wife and another man.

158.67 *Trial at Verde River.* April 14, 1959. GS: Richard Crane. A lawyer returns to handle a case for the Verde River Water Company and incurs the wrath of his friends and neighbors.

158.68 *Scorpion.* April 21, 1959. GS: Lane Bradford. Ranger Clint Travis races against time to return a captured outlaw to headquarters before he succumbs to the poison from a scorpion bite.

158.69 *The Last Kill.* April 28, 1959. GS: Richard Garland, Patsy Kelly, Virginia Stefan, William Fawcett, James Hyland, Ted Stanhope. A man with only a few days to live rides into Yuma after spending five years in prison on a manslaughter charge for killing a young boy.

158.70 *Redskin.* May 5, 1959. GS: I. Stanford Jolley. Cincioni, a decorated war hero but an Indian, returns to the territory to find that his people will have nothing to do with him.

158.71 *Cave-In.* May 12, 1959. GS: Richard Garland, William Fawcett, Virginia Stefan, James Hyland, Todd Lasswell, Rex Dunn. An Arizona Ranger and the new owner of a small newspaper join forces to try to expose a crooked mining outfit.

158.72 *Terror in Paradise.* May 19, 1959. GS: Johnnie Westmore, I. Stanford Jolley, Gregg Palmer, Robert Karnes, Wendy Wilde, James Hayward, Bob Taylor, Stirling Welker, James Dugan. Two dancehall girls witness a cold-blooded murder, and agree to testify against the killer. But their civic-mindedness melts when they face the muzzle of a gun.

158.73 *Fighting Man.* May 26, 1959. GS: Grant Withers, Denver Pyle, Lance Fuller, Carol Thurston, Richard Reeves, Harry Shannon, Bill Baucom, Blackie Austin, Bud Brown, Stirling Welker. A touch marshal has his integrity tested when his girl is accidentally injured.

158.74 *Tumbleweed Ranger.* June 2, 1959. SP: Tap Canutt, Roy Barcroft, Lyn Thomas, Bob Taylor. The Arizona Rangers take on the unusual assignment of protecting a shipment of prospective brides.

158.75 *The Tiger.* June 9, 1959. A gang of American outlaws descends on the small Mexican village of San Felipe and kills three policemen, as the first step in a plan to take over the settlement.

158.76 *Abandoned.* June 16, 1959. GS: Richard Reeves. Arizona Rangers launch a posse on a desperate journey into Indian country.

158.77 *Bandit Queen.* June 23, 1959. GS: Jackie Blanchard, Tap Canutt, Bob Johnson, Stirling Welker, Ed Scarla. After outwitting scores of sheriffs and marshals a beautiful bandit queen is sought by the Rangers.

158.78 *Refuge at Broken Bow.* June 30, 1959. A young boy must decide between devotion to his two outlaw uncles or respect for the law.

159. Two Faces West

Syndicated. 30 min. Broadcast history: Various, Oct. 1960–July 1961.

Regular Cast: Charles Bateman (Dr. Ben January/Rick January), Joyce Meadows (Stacy), Francis DeSales (Sheriff Maddox), Paul Comi (Deputy Johnny Evans).

Premise: The Western series related the exploits of twin brothers, Ben January, a doctor, and Rick January, a saddle tramp, in the town of Gunnison during the 1860s.

The Episodes

159.1 *Hot Water.* Oct. 17, 1960. GS: Richard Reeves, Guy de Vestel. Rick and Dr. Ben go on a hazardous errand.

159.2 *Prognosis: Death.* Oct. 24, 1960. GS: Kathie Browne, James Callahan. Laurie Parks summons Dr. Ben to aid her brother, really a disguised outlaw.

159.3 *Sheriff of the Town.* Oct. 31, 1960. GS: Paul Comi, Walter Coy, Diane Cannon. Rich and Dr. Ben try to help Sheriff Johnny Evans, a war hero, overcome his horror of gunplay.

159.4 *The Challenge.* Nov. 7, 1960. GS: Barbara Stuart, Charles Maxwell. Ex-convict Frank Turner returns to Gunnison. The townspeople fear he is plotting to kill Rick January, the man who brought him to trial.

159.5 *The Operation.* Nov. 14, 1960. GS: Willard Sage, John Milford, Michael Stefani. Rick and Dr. Ben are held by a wounded criminal and his gang. Ben refuses to give medical aid unless Rick is allowed to escape.

159.6 *Fallen Gun.* Nov. 21, 1960. GS: DeForest Kelley, James Gavin. Rick saves an unknown man from an Indian ambush. He learns that the stranger is an outlaw.

159.7 *The Man in 204.* Dec. 5, 1960. GS: Henry Beckman, Warren Kemmerling. Hatred drives the Evans brothers to kidnap Duvall.

159.8 *The Hanging.* Dec. 12, 1960. GS: Robert Patton, Ken Mayer, Rex Holman. Jim Evers is sentenced to death for murder.

159.9 *The Last Man.* Dec. 19, 1960. GS: John Pickard, L.Q. Jones. Laird Willoughby is the last man of a murderous gang whose other members have been captured. Sheriff Tromp wants to get him, but Rick believes he is innocent.

159.10 *The Proud Man.* Dec. 26, 1960. GS: Dabbs Greer, Robert Anderson. Willie Medord refuses to allow Amos

Johnson's entry on his land. But Amos's cattle need water and he intends to get it for them.

159.11 *The Trespasser.* Jan. 2, 1961. GS: William Bryant, Pamela Grey. Rick looks for stole cattle on Dani Borden's ranch and is forced to get off.

159.12 *The Drought.* Jan. 9, 1961. GS: Walter Burke, Lou Krugman. A rainmaker will relieve a drought in Gunnison for a large sum of money.

159.13 *The Avengers.* Jan. 16, 1961. GS: Don Spruance, Paul Birch, Jay Strong. J.C. Wilkes tries to shoot Rick in the back, but Rick gets him first.

159.14 *The Witness.* Jan. 12, 1961. GS: Julian Barton, Marianna Hill. Leopold Inyo, a Gypsy, is shot because he knew too much about a murder.

159.15 *Performance Under Fire.* Jan. 30, 1961. GS: Lew Brown, Ron Soble. At the Baker Ranch, the Januarys meet Bray and Collins, two gunmen they once beat in a fight.

159.16 *The Prisoner.* Feb. 6, 1961. GS: Chris Alcaide, David Manley. Outlaws bent on freeing a killer named Willis bound the sheriff who is guarding him.

159.17 *The Trigger.* Feb. 13, 1961. GS: Ron Haggerty, Don Harvey. Lucas Garret locks himself in a house filled with gunpowder and threatens to blow the town of Gunnison off the map.

159.18 *The Return.* Feb. 20, 1961. GS: James Griffith, Dehl Berti. Gunslinger Verne Cleary wants revenge on Rick January.

159.19 *The Accused.* Feb. 27, 1961. GS: Jon Lormer, Joseph Turkel. Rick is at the scene of the crime when Harry Bright is shot. The people of Gunnison accuse him of the murder.

159.20 *The Crisis.* March 6, 1961. GS: Rick Marlow, Joseph Ruskin. Coley Wade is very ill and two drifters hear him talking about some hidden gold. They decide to cash in on a good thing.

159.21 *Portrait of Bravery.* March 13, 1961. GS: Grace Raynor, Arvid Nelson. The owner of a photography studio is badly beaten.

159.22 *The Stilled Gun.* March 20, 1961. Richard Shannon, Joyce Meadows. Buchanan, a renowned gunfighter, gets badly hurt when he attempts to stop a robbery.

159.23 *The Wayward.* March 27, 1961. GS: Chris Robinson, James Stapleton. A hoodlum robs and murders an elderly prospector.

159.24 *Hand of Vengeance.* April 3, 1961. GS: John Marley, Denver Pyle. Josiah Brady, wounded in a gunfight, trains his son to avenge his honor.

159.25 *The Decision.* April 10, 1961. GS: John Cliff, Gil Rankin. A gang of outlaws kidnaps a young girl. They won't free her unless Rick and Ben release a member of their gang from prison.

159.26 *The $10,000 Reward.* April 17, 1961. Walter Kray, Dennis Cross, Roxanne Brooks. Cole Burnet, half-dead and with a price on his head, is put under the care of Dr. Ben January.

159.27 *Trail to Indian Wells.* April 24, 1961. GS: Don Megowan, John McLiam. Rick and Ben follow three Army deserters who have stolen horses.

159.28 *Double Action.* May 8, 1961. GS: Kelton Garwood, Lisabeth Hush. Davis Flagg and his three rowdy sons ride into Gunnison with one purpose in mind — to start trouble.

159.29 *The Noose.* May 15, 1961. GS: Joyce Meadows, L.Q. Jones, Victor French. Rick is left alone to guard the Sundown Kid, in jail for robbing the payroll of the Triangle B Ranch.

159.30 *The Lesson.* May 22, 1961. GS: Joyce Meadows, Robert Anderson. Rick is taking care of a young boy who is gravely ill.

159.31 *The Vials.* May 29, 1961. GS: Howard Caine, Robert Brubaker. Ben learns that serum needed to check an epidemic of anthrax has been stolen from a stagecoach.

159.32 *Doctor's Orders.* June 5, 1961. GS: Joyce Meadows, Leonard Nimoy, Ryan O'Neal. Rick and Ben fulfill a dying woman's last request — to see her outlaw son one more time.

159.33 *The Trophy Hunter.* June 19, 1961. GS: Jackie Russell, Richard Reeves, Jack Mather. Frederick Caldwell is in Dr. Ben's infirmary being treated for a wound he got while hunting. Outside the door two men wait to kill him.

159.34 *The Coward.* June 26, 1961. GS: Paul Pepper, Mike Ragan, Laurie Mitchell, George Brenlin. Charlie Baker and his two partners plan to kill Toby Grant to get his share of the gold mine.

159.35 *The Sure Thing.* July 3, 1961. GS: Robert J. Stevenson, Gary Walberg, Baynes Barron. Ben suggests that Connelly's horse Molly is too sick to run in Gunnison's big race. The townspeople cal Ben a liar when Molly is entered and wins.

159.36 *Day of Violence.* July 10, 1961. GS: Willard Sage, John Seven, Kay E. Kuter. Sheb and Riley don't like the plans their new partner Ben has for improving the ranch they own. Their solution is to murder Ben.

159.37 *Music Box.* July 17, 1961. GS: Ron Hayes, Sue George.

159.38 *The Dead Ringer.* July 24, 1961. GS: Gregg Palmer, Paul Pepper.

160. Union Pacific

Syndicated. 30 min. Broadcast history: Various, Sept. 1958–June 1959.

Regular Cast: Jeff Morrow (Bart McClelland), Judson Pratt (Bill Kincaid), Susan Cummings (Georgia).

Premise: This adventure series related the exploits of Bart McClelland, operations head of the Union Pacific Railroad, in his quest to complete the link between Omaha in the East and Cheyenne in the West.

The Episodes

160.1 *The Black Hills Incident.* Sept. 27, 1958. Rugged terrain and obstinate politicians are just two of the obstacles encountered in trying to forge a railroad through the Black Hills.

160.2 *Deadline.* Oct. 4, 1958. GS: Raymond Bailey. A federal inspector is late with important funds for the railroad.

160.3 *Yesterday's Killer.* Oct. 11, 1958. A large consignment of logs, needed by the railroad for ties, disappears without a trace.

160.4 *Payroll to Cheyenne.* Oct. 18, 1958. Troops are not available to protect the payroll coming from Omaha to Cheyenne.

160.5 *The Challenge.* Oct. 25, 1958. A gambler and gunman defies Bart McClelland's order to leave town.

160.6 *The Surveyor.* Nov. 1, 1958. During and idle period in the building of the railroad, a group of local troublemakers tries to rough up the crewmen.

160.7 *Indian Treaty.* Nov. 8, 1958. The railroad's graders are cut off from the supply line during bitter-cold weather.

160.8 *The Bridge at Devil's Canyon.* Nov. 15, 1958. Bart McClelland attempts to clear a stationmaster accused of murder.

160.9 *DeKett Territory.* Nov. 22, 1958. A young surveyor is jailed on a phony murder charge. He is threatened with hanging if the railroad comes through the territory belonging to a tyrant.

160.10 *End of Track.* Nov. 29, 1958. A U.S. Senator is shocked at the goings on in the gambling hall in the end-of-track town.

160.11 *The Dale Incident.* Dec. 6, 1958. Animosity between the townspeople of Dale, Wyoming, and the railroad workmen threatens to develop into open warfare.

160.12 *The Haunted Hills.* Dec. 13, 1958. A mysterious sniper threatens the life of Bart McClelland. The uncanny gunman can ricochet bullets off the engine bell.

160.13 *The Challenger.* Dec. 20, 1958. A gambler and gunman defies Bart McClelland's order to leave town.

160.14 *The Impractical Joker.* Dec. 27, 1958. One of the railroad crewmen, a practical joker, is accused of causing a serious accident to the road and the men.

160.15 *Incident at Bitter Creek.* Jan. 3, 1959. After a stationmaster is killed, an Indian comes to town dressed in the murdered man's clothes.

160.16 *The Roadblock.* Jan. 10, 1959. A wealthy landowner dies before signing a right-of-way agreement. Bart tries to get his young daughter, heir to the property, to sign the document.

160.17 *Patterns for Revenge.* Jan. 17, 1959. A series of unexplained deaths cause the men to panic.

160.18 *Iron West.* Jan. 24, 1959. GS: J.M. Kerrigan. When a Senate committee sets an early deadline for completing the railroad, the men threaten to quit.

160.19 *Railroad Doctor.* Jan. 31, 1959. A young medical student, working on the railroad to earn money for his education, is tormented by one of the camp bullies.

160.20 *Prison Camp.* Feb. 7, 1959. Two men pose as cavalry men and order the road to halt operations.

160.21 *Pawnee Bill.* Feb. 14, 1959. A stubborn old man hates the railroad for bringing civilization to the West.

160.22 *Nineteen to Cheyenne.* Feb. 21, 1959. Bart McClelland faces almost impossible odds in trying to bring off the first run of a train from Omaha to Cheyenne.

160.23 *Lost Boy.* Feb. 28, 1959. GS: Trevor Bardette. The railroad is prevented from going through town by the mayor and hostile stage line interests.

160.24 *The Charming Rustler.* March 7, 1959. Kyle Sutherland promises the Indians 250 head of cattle in exchange for a right of way.

160.25 *Counterfeit Lady.* March 14, 1959. Finding a package of counterfeit Union Pacific Railroad certificates makes Bart and Georgia think that an old lady from Boston might be implicated.

160.26 *Supply Train.* March 21, 1959. A supply train is attacked by a band of renegade Cheyennes.

160.27 *The Choice.* March 28, 1959. A missing wagonload of dynamite halts work on the railroad.

160.28 *The Bullock Incident.* April 4, 1959. Two railroaders try to get Bart out of difficulties with the head office.

160.29 *The Cheyenne Incident.* April 11, 1959. Bart's aide, Billy Kincaid, is suspected of robbery and murder. Bart tries to clear his friend's name by trapping the guilty parties.

160.30 *Runaway.* April 18, 1959. A surveyor whose wife has just died meets a young orphan who changes his life.

160.31 *The Wedding.* April 25, 1959. Susan, the sister of Georgia, the dance hall owner, and her fiance arrive in town. The young man's mother disapproves of Georgia.

160.32 *The Trestle.* May 2, 1959. Floods threaten to demolish a trestle and halt work on the railroad.

160.33 *Women with Guns.* May 9, 1959. To alleviate the men's homesickness, Bart decides to bring out some of the men's wives.

160.34 *Ten to a Rail.* May 16, 1959. Work on the railroad is slowed down because of an open conflict between the crewmen and the townspeople.

160.35 *Ring of Iron.* May 23, 1959. Bart McClelland accepts a dinner invitation from a Quaker family who expect him to marry their daughter.

160.36 *The Glass Bullet.* May 30, 1959. A headstrong lady journalist and her photographer come to do a story on the railroad.

160.37 *Cave-In.* June 6, 1959. Several of McClelland's men are caught in a cave-in while blasting a roadbed.

160.38 *To the Death.* June 13, 1959. GS: John Doucette. Bart is harassed by an express rider whose family and livelihood are affected by the railroad.

161. The Virginian

NBC. 90 min. Broadcast history: Wednesday, 7:30-9:00, Sept. 1962–Sept. 1970.

Regular Cast: James Drury (the Virginian), Doug McClure (Trampas), Lee J. Cobb (Judge Henry Garth) 62-66, Roberta Shore (Betsy Garth) 61-65, Pippa Scott (Molly Wood) 62-64, Gary Clarke (Steve) 62-64, Randy Boone (Randy Garth) 63-66, L.Q. Jones (Andy Belden) 64-67, Harlan Warde (Sheriff Brannon) 64-66, Roy Engel (Barney Wingate) 63-67, John Bryant (Dr. Spaulding) 63-68, Clu Gulager (Deputy Ryker) 64-68, Diane Roter (Jennifer) 65-66, John Dehner (Starr) 65-66, Charles Bickford (John Grainger) 66-67, Don Quine (Stacy Grainer) 66-68, Sara Lane (Elizabeth Grainger) 66-70, Ross Elliott (Sheriff Abbott) 66-70, John McIntire (Clay Grainger) 67-70, Jeanette Nolan (Holly Grainger) 68-70, David Hartman (David Sutton) 68-69, Tim Matheson (Jim Horn) 69-70.

Premise: Based on Owen Wister's novel, this series depicted events during the 1880s as experienced by the Virginian, the foreman of the Shiloh Ranch in Medicine Bow, Wyoming.

Note: The series became *The Men from Shiloh* in the final 1970-71 season.

The Episodes

161.1 *The Virginian*. July 6, 1958. GS: Robert Burton, Stephen Joyce, Jeanette Nolan, Robert Gist, Dan Blocker, Andrew Duggan. The Virginian arrives at the ranch of a retired judge to work as the foreman. He investigates a series of accidents that are delaying the judge's attempts to build a railroad spur to his ranch.
Note: This unsuccessful 30 minute pilot was aired as a segment of *Decision*.

Season One

161.2 *The Executioners*. Sept. 19, 1962. GS: Hugh O'Brian, Colleen Dewhurst, John Larch, Richard Bull, Barry Brooks, Arnold Lessing, Jeanne Wood, Audrey Swanson, Tony Maxwell, John Francis. Paul Taylor is a strange one. A new arrival in town, he charms everyone, including schoolteacher Celia Ames. Yet he keeps asking some very searching questions.

161.3 *Woman from White Wing*. Sept. 26, 1962. GS: Barry Sullivan, Robert Sampson, Tom Reese, Parley Baer, George Dunn, Jan Stine, Arnold Lessing, Darrell Howe, Brendan Dillon. When Judge Garth returns home from a trip East, he learns that the Virginian has expressed some interest in the town of White Wing. Later he tells about his connection with the town and explains why a man named Frank Dawson is waiting for him there.

161.4 *Throw a Long Rope*. Oct. 3, 1962. GS: Jack Warden, Jacqueline Scott, John Anderson, Ted Knight, Roger Mobley, Lew Brown, Richard Bull, Charles Briggs, Arnold Lessing, Hal Bokar, Michael James. Judge Garth and the other cattle men are threatened by homesteaders moving on their land, and now one of the sod busters has been accused of cattle rustling.

161.5 *The Big Deal*. Oct. 10, 1962. GS: Ricardo Montalban, William Zuckert, Brendan Dillon, Orville Sherman, George Cisar, Jason Johnson, Dal McKennon, Martin Eric. Enrique Cuellar arrives in town intent on selling a section of inherited land lying within the boundaries of Judge Garth's ranch. The Judge makes a reasonable offer, which Cuellar refuses when he learns that the property contains a valuable cattle trail.

161.6 *The Brazen Bell*. Oct. 17, 1962. GS: George C. Scott, Ann Meacham, Royal Dano, John Davis Chandler, Michael Fox, William Challee, Lennie Geer, Kay Stewart, Robert J. Stevenson, Justin Smith, Lester Maxwell. Arthur Lilley and his domineering wife Sarah arrive in Medicine Bow, where Arthur is to become the schoolmaster. His meekness leads the townfolk to believe that Lilley will be ineffectual in disciplining some of the older students.

161.7 *Big Day, Great Day*. Oct. 24, 1962. GS: Aldo Ray, Mickey Shaughnessy, Carolyn Kearney, Dennis Patrick, Dan Sheridan, Rosemary Murphy, Paul Barselow, Dorothy Neumann, Richard Shannon, Barry McGuire. Judge Garth, in town with Steve and Trampas, meets his old friend Frank Krause, who says that today is going to be a big day.

161.8 *Riff-Raff*. Nov. 7, 1962. GS: Ray Danton, Don Durant, Karl Swenson, Judson Pratt, Jan Stone, Rod Daniels, Bing Russell, Tom Hernandez, Hal Needham. When Molly returns from a trip, she is all excited about the Spanish-American War. The Virginian argues that herding beef is part of the war effort, but a recruiting poster convinces Trampas that Uncle Sam needs him.

161.9 *Impasse*. Nov. 14, 1962. GS: Eddie Albert, Jim McMullen, Tom Skerritt, Robert Colbert, William Phipps, Denise Alexander, Quinn Redecker, Leonard P. Geer, Jeff Lerner, Jimmy Lee Cook, Jerry Summers. While the Virginian and his hands are rounding up some wild horses, they incur the wrath of a family of squatters named Kroeger. The Kroegers regard the animals as their property, and they will fight to protect their squatters' rights.

161.10 *It Tolls for Thee*. Nov. 21, 1962. GS: Lee Marvin, Albert Salmi, Ron Soble, Warren Kemmerling, Brendan Dillon, Jan Stine, John Zaremba, Michael Mikler, Francis DeSales, Wayne Heffley. During a cattle roundup, ex-convict Martin Kalig rounds up Judge Garth and demands a large ransom for him.

161.11 *West*. Nov. 28, 1962. GS: Claude Akins, Steve Cochran, James Brown, Allen Case, Russell Thorson, Richard Reeves, Leo Gordon, Raymond Guth, William Gordon, James Anderson. In Medicine Bow, Trampas runs into carefree Jamie Dobbs and his two fun-loving pals Lump and Lucky. Jamie's stories about the life he and his pals have found in the real West interest Trampas, and he decides to join them on the trail.

161.12 *The Devil's Children*. Dec. 5, 1962. GS: Charles Bickford, Joan Freeman, Burt Brinckerhoff, Carl Reindel, Charles Aidman, Vivi Janiss, Katherine Squire, Ed Prentiss, Pitt Herbert, Russell Thorson, Russell Bender, Dan White. Rancher Tucker McCallum refuses to believe that his daughter Tabby and son Bruce are anything but perfect, even when Tabby becomes a very frisky kitten. She sets a little fire and then gets her young friend Dan Flood accused of arson.

161.13 *Fifty Days to Moose Jaw*. Dec. 12, 1962. GS: Brandon de Wilde, James Gregory, Frank Overton, Charles Briggs, H.M. Wynant. The Virginian has his job cut out for him. He has been ordered to move several thousand head of cattle to Moose Jaw. To fill out his crew for the drive, he hires some new men, including a weathered veteran named Slim Jessup, and Mike Flynn, a hero-worshiping youth, who wants to pattern his life after Jessup.

161.14 *The Accomplice*. Dec. 19, 1962. GS: Bette Davis, Lin McCarthy, Gene Evans, Woodrow Parfrey, Noah Keen, Byron Morrow, Ken Mayer, Jerry Summers, Brian O'Byrne, Christopher Dark, Harold Gould, Alice Backes, Victor French. After two men rob the local bank, teller Delia Miller identifies Trampas as one of the outlaws. Actually, Delia is telling her own version of the incident as a means of blackmailing one of the real robbers.

161.15 *The Man from the Sea*. Dec.26, 1962. GS: Tom Tryon, Shirley Knight, Carol Lynley, Larry J. Blake, Jan Arvan, Russ Whiteman, John McKee, Dick Wilson. Retired sailor Kevin Doyle, who is looking for a wife, is captivated by the Morrow Twins, Judith and Susan. Doyle is more entranced by Judith, but she insists that she will never leave her sister.

161.16 *Duel at Shiloh*. Jan. 2, 1963. GS: Geraldine Brooks, Brian Keith, Ben Johnson, Christopher King, DeForest Kelley, Russell Thorson, Mort Mills, Roy Engel, Lew Brown, Richard Garland. Drifter Johnny Wade and his boss, ranch-owner Georgia Price, insist that the rangelands remain open. When Judge Garth and the other ranchers decide to put up fences, Johnny and Georgia threaten to start a range war.

161.17 *The Exiles.* Jan. 9, 1963. GS: Tammy Grimes, Ken Lynch, Brad Weston, Frank Cady, Ed Nelson, Herbert Rudley, Addison Richards, Herb Vigran, Ben Wright, Don Harvey, Stafford Repp, Francis DeSales, Allyson Ames. Judge Garth's claim that he killed a neighbor in self-defense isn't going to stand up in court. There were not witnesses, and the sheriff finds that the dead man was unarmed.

161.18 *The Judgment.* Jan. 16, 1963. GS: Clu Gulager, Patricia Barry, Conlan Carter, John Kerr, David McLean, Gilbert Green, Regis Toomey, Wilton Graff, Steve Harris. Judge Garth is asked to run for district judge, which prompts him to recall his earlier days on the bench. Garth was trying a man named Carewe, but it was Carewe's brother Jake that menaced the town and the judge.

161.19 *Say Goodbye to All That.* Jan. 23, 1963. GS: Charles McGraw, Fabian, Royal Dano, Katherine Crawford, Robert Brubaker, Roy Engel, Paul Langton, John Bryant, James Best, Meg Wyllie, Howard Wendell. Young Martin Belden is out to avenge his father, wounded by Trampas in a gunfight. Martin, who has been thoroughly coached by his father, feels that by killing Trampas he can prove that he is a man.

161.20 *The Man Who Wouldn't Die.* Jan. 30, 1963. GS: Vera Miles, Jeff Morrow, Walter Brooke, James Doohan, Pat McCaffrie, Brendan Dillon, E.J. Andre, David White, Anne Loos, Ollie O'Toole. Judge Garth is in San Francisco to find the woman who disappeared after he hired her to tutor Betsy. The Judge is attacked and kills his assailant in self-defense, but when he reports the incident to the police, they can't find the body and the man's business partner denies that he is dead.

161.21 *If You Have Tears.* Feb. 13, 1963. GS: Robert Vaughn, Phyllis Avery, Dana Wynter, Nancy Sinatra, Britt Lomond, Gene Lyons, John Milford, Frank Ferguson, Tol Avery, Stacy Harris, Bill McLean, Guy Wilkerson. The Virginian is eager to help Kyle Lawson prove that he is innocent of a murder charge, until he meets the person Kyle accuses, the victim's widow, beautiful Leona Kelland.

161.22 *The Small Parade.* Feb. 20, 1963. GS: David Wayne, R.G. Armstrong, J. Pat O'Malley, Barbara Barrie, George Brenlin, Curtis Haymore, Gregor Vigen, Tane McClure, Morgan Woodward, Roy Barcroft, Dal McKennon, Ford Rainey, William Fawcett, John Banner, Alan Dexter, Claudia Bryar. After vegetarian Martin Reese gives a very badly-received lecture in the carnivorous cattle town of Coyote Wells, the Virginian advises him to leave. Then Reese's toughest heckler, Jack Brandon, is found dead, and the citizens think it is the work of the mad vegetarian.

161.23 *Vengeance Is the Spur.* Feb. 27, 1963. GS: Nina Foch, Michael Rennie, Denver Pyle, Edward Kemmer, Adam Hill, John Bryant, Dan Barton, Kathryn Card, Jon Lormer, Gil Perkins, Paul Sorensen. Judge Garth agrees to help Carol Frances find the outlaw band of Michael O'Rourke, as a means of locating her husband.

161.24 *The Money Cage.* March 6, 1963. GS: Steve Forrest, Bethel Leslie, Ronald Foster, Dayton Lummis, Joanna Moore, Harry Carter, Rusty Lane, John Harmon, Cyril Delevanti, King Calder, Jim Brown. On their way to Medicine Bow, Will Martin impresses Lydia Turner, the banker's daughter, with his gallantry and his talk of oil investments. But he is just telling her a tale.

161.25 *The Golden Door.* March 13, 1963. GS: Karl Boehm, Robert Duvall, Ilze Taurins, Russell Thorson, John Hoyt, Paul Carr, Lew Brown, Donald "Red" Barry, S. Newton Anderson, Bobs Watson, Henry Hunter. The rifle of a murder victim is discovered in the possession of immigrant Karl Rilke. He claims he bought it, but the seller can't be found.

161.26 *A Distant Fury.* March 20, 1963. GS: Howard Duff, Ida Lupino, Joey Heatherton, John Ewing, Bobs Watson, Francis DeSales, Ken Paterson, Willis Bouchey, Roy Engel, Jonathan Hole, Paul Carr. Released after serving three years for robbery, Ed Frazer returns to Medicine Bow, and Steve, whose testimony helped to convict him, fears that he is seeking revenge.

161.27 *Echo from Another Day.* March 27, 1963. GS: Bradford Dillman, John Dehner, Edward Asner, Francis J. MacDonald, Joe Maross, John Mitchum, Grace Lee Whitney, Russell Thorson, Frank Watkins, Frank Sully. There is a $50,000 cache of stolen gold, and two men who want it. Trampas' friend Sam Harder, who wants to return the loot, and George Bleeck, Harder's accomplice in the robbery, who has a somewhat different plan in mind.

161.28 *Strangers at Sundown.* April 3, 1963. GS: Harry Morgan, Skip Homeier, Paul Richards, Arthur Hunnicutt, Evans Evans. A group of stagecoach passengers, besieged by outlaws at a way station, receive an ultimatum. If they don't turn over stool pigeon Jed Carter, they will all die.

161.29 *The Mountain of the Sun.* April 17, 1963. GS: Jeanette Nolan, Dolores Hart, Amzie Strickland, George D. Wallace, Rodolfo Acosta, Joe De Santis, Rico Alaniz, Alex Montoya, King Calder, Clancy Cooper, Carlos Romero, K.L. Smith. The Virginian falls in love with Cathy Maywood, one of three widows who insist on continuing their husbands' missionary work among the hostile Yaqui Indians. He reluctantly agrees to guide them to Redskins' territory.

161.30 *Run Away Home.* April 24, 1963. GS: Russ Conway, Jeannine Riley, Karl Swenson, Crahan Denton, Fred Coby, Michael Vandever, Ann Doran, Steve Brodie, Kevin Hagen, Robert B. Williams, I. Stanford Jolley, Don Harvey, Alvy Moore. The Virginian's job of transferring $40,000 to a distant bank is complicated by a family of angry farmers out to retrieve their lost life savings, and by a freight hopping blonde out to see the world.

161.31 *The Final Hour.* May 1, 1963. GS: Jacques Aubuchon, Ulla Jacobsson, Myron Healey, Bert Freed, Don Galloway, Dean Fredericks, Dan Sheridan, Murvyn Vye, Whit Bissell, Ted Knight, Peter Mamakos, Richard Garland. Rancher Milo Henderson opposes Judge Garth's importation of Polish immigrants to mine coal on the Shiloh, and when the group arrives, a complicated romantic situation develops which leads to the death of Milo's son.

Season Two

161.32 *Ride a Dark Trail.* Sept. 18, 1963. GS: Sonny Tufts, Charles Fredericks, Hal Baylor, Stuart Randall. In this tail of how Trampas came to the Shiloh Ranch, Judge Garth is forced to kill Frank Trampas in self-defense. Young Trampas sets out to locate and kill the man who slayed his father.

161.33 *To Make This Place Remember.* Sept, 25, 1963. GS: Joan Blondell, Sunny Jordan, John Dehner, Jocelyn Brando, William Bramley, Catherine McLeod, Jack Easton, Jr., John Hoyt. When the vigilantes caught Rosanna Dobie's son, suspected of murder, they hanged him without a trial. Now the aging dancehall queen wants Judge Garth to arrange for a legal trial so she can clear the boy's name. At a special hearing, flashbacks and conflicting testimony recreate the events surrounding the girl's death.

161.34 *No Tears for Savannah.* Oct. 2, 1963. GS: Everett Sloane, Stephen McNally, Gena Rowlands, Arthur Franz, Joanna Moore, Robert Coleman, Vaughn Taylor, Don Wilbanks. The Virginian, trailing a swindler named Madden, runs into his old flame, Savannah, who is Madden's girl friend.

161.35 *A Killer in Town.* Oct. 9, 1963. GS: Broderick Crawford, Arch Johnson, Bill Smith, Jim Boles, Roy Engel. Bounty hunter George Wolfe knows that someone in Medicine Bow has a price on his head, and Wolfe thinks that Trampas might be that someone.

161.36 *The Evil That Men Do.* Oct. 16, 1963. GS: Robert Redford, Patricia Blair, L.Q. Jones, Simon Scott, Don O'Kelley. Betsy becomes attracted to Matthew Cordell, a bitter convict who has been paroled in Judge Garth's custody. Afraid of jeopardizing his parole, and unable to cope with freedom, Cordell masks his fear with hostility as he shuns offers of friendship.

161.37 *It Takes a Big Man.* Oct. 23, 1963. GS: Lloyd Nolan, Chris Robinson, Ryan O'Neal, Pamela Austin, Bobs Watson, Robert Cornthwaite. Wade Anders wants his unruly son Hank to get straightened out, so he asks Judge Garth to take the young man in at the Shiloh ranch.

161.38 *Brother Thaddeus.* Oct. 30, 1963. GS: Albert Salmi, Joe Maross, Kathie Browne, Richard Devon, Christopher Dark, Bronwyn FitzSimons, Ann Ayars. Brother Thaddeus used to be outlaw Willy Cain, but he returns to Medicine Bow in monk's robes and claims he has given up his life of crime in favor of religion.

161.39 *A Portrait of Marie Valonne.* Nov. 6, 1963. GS: Madlyn Rhue, Mark Richman, Skip Homeier, Marge Redmond, Oscar Beregi, Ken Lynch, Adam Roarke. The Virginian falls hard for Louisiana beauty Marie Valonne, but Marie belongs to political boss Johnny Madrid.

161.40 *Run Quiet.* Nov. 13, 1963. GS: Clu Gulager, Gail Kobe, L.Q. Jones, Slim Pickens, Don "Red" Barry, Lew Gallo. Steve befriends an embittered deaf-mute named Judd and gets him a job at the Shiloh ranch.

161.41 *Stopover in a Western Town.* Nov. 27, 1963. GS: Dick York, Joan Freeman, Lillian Bronson, Warren Oates, Robert F. Simon. Wealthy visitor Caroline Witman sets her sights on the Virginian, and Jeff Tolliver sets his sights on her.

161.42 *The Fatal Journey.* Dec. 4, 1963. GS: Robert Lansing, David McLean, Steve Ihnat, John Milford, William Bakewell. The Virginian tries to hunt down the killers of his friend Molly Dodd, editor of the local newspaper.

161.43 *A Time Remembered.* Dec. 11, 1963. GS: Yvonne DeCarlo, Melinda Plowman, Paul Comi, John Bryant, William Zuckert. Judge Garth renews his friendship with an old flame, an opera singer named Elena.

161.44 *Siege.* Dec. 18, 1963. GS: Philip Carey, Elinor Donahue, Joseph Campanella, Ron Hayes, Nestor Paiva, Myron Healey, Thomas Bellin, Ed Faulkner. Trampas finds his home town is being terrorized by outlaws.

161.45 *Man of Violence.* Dec. 25, 1963. GS: Michael Pate, Leonard Nimoy, Peggy McCay, DeForest Kelley, William Bryant, Ann Gardner. Trampas sets out after the men who killed his close friend during a robbery.

161.46 *The Invaders.* Jan. 1, 1964. GS: Ed Begley, Beverly Owen, James McMullan, Rees Vaughn, Bing Russell, Roy Engel. Wealthy Mike Tyrone, a newcomer to Medicine Bow, plans to force local ranchers to sell out.

161.47 *Roar from the Mountain.* Jan. 8, 1964. GS: Jack Klugman, Joyce Bulifant, Emile Genest, Blair Davies. After two weeks on the trail of a killer mountain lion, Steve takes refuge in the mountain cabin of Charles Mayhew and his young wife Nancy.

161.48 *The Fortunes of J. Jimerson Jones.* Jan. 15, 1964. GS: Pat O'Brien, Jeanne Cooper, Peter Adams, Ann Doran, David Macklin. Prospector J. Jimerson Jones strikes it rich and heads for Chicago, where his old pal Judge Garth helps him get settled, and where con artist Julia Montgomery sets her sights on Jones' fortune.

161.49 *The Thirty Days of Gavin Heath.* Jan. 22, 1964. GS: Leo Genn, Brendon Dillon, Ina Victor, Don Hammer. Wealthy Gavin Heath, bitten by a dog thought to have rabies, decides to live it up in the short time he has left.

161.50 *The Drifter.* Jan. 29, 1964. GS: Leif Erickson, Michael Forest, Mariette Hartley, Rex Holman, Calvin Bartlett, Gregg Palmer. This episode recalls the Virginian's arrival in Medicine Bow, when he was hired by rancher Miles Peterson who is carrying on a range war against Judge Garth.

161.51 *First to Thine Own Self.* Feb. 12, 1964. GS: Claire Wilcox, Mary La Roche, Frank Maxwell, Jan Merlin, Bruce Dern. Randy, a young wanderer, is accused of murdering a prospector who struck it rich.

161.52 *A Matter of Destiny.* Feb. 19, 1964. GS: Peter Graves, Richard Jaeckel, Jean Hale, Roy Engel. Wealthy Chicago financier Robert Gaynor wants the Virginian to go to work for him as foreman of his new ranch. And there is something else he wants — Trampas' girl friend Janet.

161.53 *Smile of a Dragon.* Feb. 26, 1964. GS: Richard Carlson, Miyoshi Umeki, Frank Overton, Kam Tong, Buck Taylor, Phyllis Coates, Stephen Price. Shot during a stagecoach robbery, Trampas is taken prisoner by Sheriff Marden, who accuses him of being one of the outlaws.

161.54 *The Intruders.* March 4, 1964. GS: Darren McGavin, Hugh Marlowe, David Macklin, David Carradine, Iron Eyes Cody, Mickey Simpson, Larry Perron. Because he stands to profit by an Indian war, outlaw Mark Troxel plans to kill the Sioux chief who is coming to talk peace with the Army.

161.55 *Walk in Another's Footsteps.* March 11, 1964. GS: John Agar, Sheree North, Peter Mamakos, John Mitchum, John Drury, Dennis Holmes. The Virginian vows to capture the bank robbers who killed his friend.

161.56 *Rope of Lies.* March 25, 1964. GS: Diana Millay, Peter Breck, Henry Hunter. Steve quits his job at the Shiloh to become foreman at pretty Alva Lowell's new ranch.

161.57 *The Secret of Brynmar Hall.* April 1, 1964. GS: Jane Wyatt, Mark Goddard, Brooke Bundy, Tom Skerritt. The secret of Brynmar Hall is explored by Sarah Brynmar, who has

The Virginian

invited Betsy and three other young people to her old mansion in the hope of finding out who murdered her daughter.

161.58 *The Long Quest.* April 8, 1964. GS: Patricia Breslin, Ruta Lee, Joseph Campanella, Casey Peters, J. Pat O'Malley, Whit Bissell. Judith Holly and a private detective plan to take custody of widow Mary Ann Martin's son.

161.59 *A Bride for Lars.* April 15, 1964. GS: Peter Whitney, Katherine Crawford, Ricks Falk, Stewart Bradley. Lars Holstrum is injured, so he sends Trampas to fetch his mail-order bride, with a warning to bring her back safe, or else.

161.60 *Dark Destiny.* April 29, 1964. GS: Brenda Scott, Robert J. Wilke, Ed Faulkner, Bill Smith. After the Virginian aids in the capture of a band of cattle rustlers, he is given temporary custody of the gang leader's tomboy daughter.

161.61 *A Man Called Kane.* May 6, 1964. GS: Dick Foran, Jeremy Slate, Merry Anders, Mauritz Hugo. It seems Randy has run into some luck. First he finds a cache of money in a cave, and then his long-lost brother shows up at the ranch.

Season Three

161.62 *Ryker.* Sept. 16, 1964. GS: Anne Helm, Leslie Nielsen, Jan Merlin, Russ Conway. Emmett Ryker, a man with a reputation as a fast gun, turns down a cash offer to murder a prominent rancher. But someone else does the job, and Ryker becomes the chief suspect.

161.63 *The Dark Challenge.* Sept. 23, 1964. GS: Victor Jory, Katharine Ross, Joan O'Brien, Chris Robinson, Than Wyenn, Larry Pennell, Louis Quinn, John Bryant, Frank Sully. Trampas is a mighty embarrassed cowpoke. He tried to force newcomer Jenny Hendricks to dance with him, and then learned she couldn't because she is lame. He makes a play for the crippled girl whose overprotective brother intensely dislikes the Shiloh hand.

161.64 *The Black Stallion.* Sept. 30, 1964. GS: Robert Culp, Jena Engstrom, Donald "Red" Barry, Roy Engel, Paul Baxley. Randy finds a black stallion, a wild, dangerous thoroughbred that has escaped from its brutal owner, a man named Slaughter.

161.65 *The Hero.* Oct. 7, 1964. GS: Steve Forrest, Warren Stevens, Steve Ihnat, Brad Weston. Debonair Eastern newspaperman James Templeton arrives at the Shiloh to do a feature story on Judge Garth, and he makes quite a hit with Betsy.

161.66 *Felicity's Springs.* Oct. 14, 1964. GS: Katherine Crawford, Carl Benton Reid, Mariette Hartley, Dean Harens, Jennie Lynn, Casey Peters, L.Q. Jones, Frank Sully. Certain that he has found the perfect woman, the Virginian proposes marriage to schoolteacher Felicity Andrews, despite disturbing warnings from her family.

161.67 *The Brazos Kid.* Oct. 21, 1964. GS: Barbara Eden, Skip Homeier, J.B. Brown, George Petrie, Alvy Moore. The Brazos Kid is an outlaw who is supposed to be dead, but newspaperwoman Samantha Fry knows better. She writes a series of articles about him that brings bounty hunters to Medicine Bow.

161.68 *Big Image ... Little Man.* Oct. 28, 1964. GS: Slim Pickens, Linden Chiles, Olive Sturgess, Paul Birch, Roger Torrey, Vincent Cobb. The Virginian, leading a cattle drive through desert country, comes across a strange sight. Wandering in a daze is a man wearing a velvet robe and leather slippers. He is Paul Leland, an arrogant Eastern millionaire who reluctantly joins the cowboys, but refuses to sacrifice his comfort in the wilderness.

161.69 *A Father for Toby.* Nov. 4, 1964. GS: Rory Calhoun, Kurt Russell, Joanna Moore. Young Toby Shea, a resident of Medicine Bow's orphanage, adopts Trampas as a father. But Toby's real father isn't dead, he has just been released from prison and has set out to find his son.

161.70 *The Girl from Yesterday.* Nov. 11, 1964. GS: Mark Richman, Ruta Lee, Don Collier, L.Q. Jones, Charles Bateman, Barry Kelley. Marshal Cass suspects that Steve's old girl friend, Jane Carlyle, is now working with an outlaw gang.

161.71 *Return a Stranger.* Nov. 18, 1964. GS: Leif Erickson, Peter Brown, Whit Bissell, William Fawcett, Robert Colbert. Fresh out of college with an engineering degree, young Craig Ryan returns home to Medicine Bow determined to make his father's old silver mine pay off.

161.72 *All Nice and Legal.* Nov. 25, 1964. GS: Anne Francis, Ellen Corby, Paul Comi, John Kellogg, Judson Pratt, Jeff Cooper, Robert Gothie. Medicine Bow's new lady lawyer wants to rent some office space from Garth, but the Virginian's highly dubious about her chances for professional success.

161.73 *A Gallows for Sam Horn.* Dec. 2, 1964. GS: John Lupton, Edward Binns, George Kennedy, Laurel Goodwin, Buck Taylor. Railroad magnate John Briscoe shipped his son Scott off to Europe to keep him from marrying Peg Dineen. Now Scott is in Medicine Bow involved in a land dispute, and he once again meets up with Peg.

161.74 *Portrait of a Widow.* Dec. 9, 1964. GS: Vera Miles, John Gavin, Ann Doran, Michael Forest, Roy Engel, Pitt Herbert, David McMahon, Audrey Swanson, Nancy Gates. Charming Claude Boulanger, a portrait artist with a lot of gambling debts and a clientele of wealthy women, has decided to get away from it all. He is accompanying Betsy and the Widow Benken, a prospective client, to Medicine Bow.

161.75 *The Payment.* Dec. 16, 1964. GS: Lloyd Nolan, Bruce Dern, Lisbeth Hush, Ed Peck, Robert Ivers, Med Flory. Ryker's stepfather, Abe Clayton, is out of prison and in Medicine Bow, and Ryker wants him to say on good terms with the law, but the old man has other ideas.

161.76 *Man of the People.* Dec. 23, 1964. GS: James Dunn, Martin West, Roy Engel, Alvy Moore, Arthur Space, Brendan Dillon, A.G. Vitanza, Hal Baylor, Robert Boon, Pitt Herbert. Garth and the Virginian find homesteaders camped on the cattlemen's grazing lands, and then learn the sod busters are there legally, through the manipulations of Congressman "Honest Mack" Cosgrove.

161.77 *The Hour of the Tiger.* Dec. 30, 1964. GS: Tom Tully, Cely Carrillo, Leo Gordon. Garth's cattle are trapped by a landslide, and the only way out is to drive the herd across rancher Junius Antlow's land. But the crippled Antlow nurses a bitter hatred toward Garth, and he refuses to let the cattle pass.

161.78 *Two Men Named Laredo.* Jan. 6, 1965. GS: Fabian, Ford Rainey, Elizabeth MacRae, Paul Comi, John Bryant, Rayford Barnes, Thomas Bellin, Walter Woolf King. Eddie Laredo is a quiet, shy, poetry-reading young cowboy, but he has another side to him that is dangerously violent.

161.79 *Hideout.* Jan. 13, 1965. GS: Forrest Tucker, Andrew Prine, Douglas Fowley, John Bryant, Walter Woolf King. Martin and Clint Evers aren't the least bit happy when

Betsy discovers the mountain domain where the two have been corralling valuable wild broncs.

161.80 *Six Graves at Cripple Creek.* Jan. 27, 1965. GS: John Doucette, Sheilah Wells, Walter Reed, Paul Birch, Harry Lauter, Catherine McLeod, Robert Pine. During a bank robbery, Ryker guns down one of two killers he has been after for a long time, and the wounded outlaw gives Ryker a clue to the whereabouts of the other man.

161.81 *Lost Yesterday.* Feb. 3, 1965. GS: Shirley Knight, Monica Lewis, Simon Scott, John Kellogg, John Bryant, Don Wilbanks, Stuart Randall, Sam Edwards. Clara Malone loses her memory after a stagecoach accident, and among the things she doesn't remember is that two killers are looking for her.

161.82 *A Slight Case of Charity.* Feb. 10, 1965. GS: Kathryn Hays, Les Tremayne, Jerome Courtland, Kathryn Givney, Harry Harvey, Sr., E.J. Andre. Charity is a very pretty and very crafty young lady who has stolen the money that Trampas obtained from the sale of some cattle.

161.83 *You Take the High Road.* Feb. 17, 1965. GS: Richard Beymer, Diana Lynn, Roy Engel, Myron Healey, Robert B. Williams, Edward Faulkner. On a cattle drive, rancher Peggy Shannon is confronted with the trouble that has developed between her young brother Mark and hardened trail boss Slauson.

161.84 *Shadows of the Past.* Feb. 24, 1965. GS: Jack Warden, Marilyn Erskine, John Milford, James Beck, Jackie Russell, Frank Sully, Diane Lee Quinn. Ryker has two growing concerns. Two outlaw brothers have threatened him, and a close friend is marrying a younger woman he has known only briefly.

161.85 *Legend for a Lawman.* March 3, 1965. GS: Adam West, Ford Rainey, William Mims, John Litel, Michael Macready, Adrienne Ellis, Ken Mayer, Shug Fisher, Bill McLean, Walker Edmiston, William Stevens, John Hubbard. Randy, tricked into helping some bank robbers, finds himself facing charges of robbery and murder.

161.86 *Timberland.* March 10, 1965. GS: Martin Milner, Joan Freeman, William Smith, Arch Johnson, Russell Thorson, William Bramley, Roy Engel, Norman Leavitt. A feud has broken out between the Medicine Bow ranchers and the Daniels Lumber Company. The lumbermen are planning to cut down timber which would leave the ranchers' grazing land exposed to mudslides.

161.87 *Dangerous Road.* March 17, 1965. GS: Simon Oakland, Tom Simcox, Marilyn Wayne, Robert Pine, Ben Johnson, Tom Reese, Frank Gerstle. Trampas is deputized to deliver young Bob Coulter to his home town, where he is wanted for the slaying of a woman.

161.88 *Farewell to Honesty.* March 24, 1965. GS: Kathleen Crowley, Richard Carlson, Harold Gould, Herbert Voland, Dorothy Green, Douglas Henderson, Richard Crane, John Lodge, Harry Swoger. The Virginian rides into the town of Honesty, Wyoming, with a warrant to arrest the towns wealthiest and most prominent citizen on charges of fraud.

161.89 *The Old Cowboy.* March 31, 1965. GS: Franchot Tone, Billy Mumy, Alan Baxter, Adam Williams. A proud old cowboy named Murdock feels he is as good as any younger man, but the Virginian doesn't see it that way. He refuses to hire him.

161.90 *The Showdown.* April 14, 1965. GS: Michael Ansara, Peter Whitney, Tom Skerritt, Leonard Nimoy, Barry Kelley, Leslie Perkins, Edward Faulkner, Calvin Bartlett, Dabbs Greer. The Virginian arrives in a town to complete a cattle deal, and finds himself on the wrong side of the law. The men he has come to see are bitter foes of Marshal Merle Frome.

161.91 *We've Lost a Train.* April 21, 1965. GS: Ida Lupino, Fernando Lamas, William Smith, Rhonda Fleming, Philip Carey, Neville Brand, Peter Brown, L.Q. Jones, Carol Bryon, Hal Baylor, George Sawaya, Alberto Morin, Teresa Terry, Priscilla Garcia, Ruben Moreno. Trampas is sent to Mexico on an errand and, in the border town of Laredo, he gets into brawls with three Texas Rangers.

Note: This episode served as a pilot for the *Laredo* series and was later released as the feature film *Backtrack*.

Season Four

161.92 *The Brothers.* Sept. 15, 1965. GS: Robert Lansing, Andrew Prine, Jan Shepard, Kurt Russell, Hal Baylor, Stuart Randall, Brad Weston, Loyal T. "Doc" Lucas, Bill Quinn. Matt Denning has broken his brother Will out of an Army stockade, and Ryker, Matt's close friend, sets out to capture them.

161.93 *Day of the Scorpion.* Sept. 22, 1965. GS: John Anderson, Maura McGiveney, John McLiam, Jon Locke, Sean McClory, Tim Donnelly, Harold Gould, Edward Faulkner. A range war threatens with the presence of Australian shepherds led by Adam Tercell, a man with a hot-headed son and a daughter the Virginian finds very attractive.

161.94 *A Little Learning....* Sept. 29, 1965. GS: Albert Salmi, Susan Oliver, Bruce Dern, Harry Townes, Craig Hundley, Alice Frost, Dub Taylor, George Kirgo. Big Rafe Simmons, who wants to learn to read and write, quits his job at the Shiloh and asks schoolteacher Martha Perry for permission to join her class.

161.95 *The Claim.* Oct. 6, 1966. GS: William Shatner, Strother Martin, Donald "Red" Barry, Jackie Russell, Darlene Enlow. Trampas, fed up with the life of a cowhand, runs into his old friend Luke Milford, a drifter who seems to live pretty well without holding a steady job.

161.96 *The Awakening.* Oct. 13, 1965. GS: Glenn Corbett, John Doucette, Virginia Christine, Jack Lambert, Ford Rainey. Betsy has taken a liking to a barefoot stranger, and the local miners are protesting their unsafe working conditions.

161.97 *Ring of Silence.* Oct. 27, 1965. GS: Earl Holliman, Joyce Van Patten, Royal Dano, Peggy Lopez, Joe De Santis, Edward Binns, Pepe Calahan, John Hoyt, Guy Wilkerson, Heather Ames. The passengers of a stagecoach, including Ryker and an insulting, unsavory character named Wiley, discover that they are being followed by a small army of Mexicans.

161.98 *Jennifer.* Nov. 3, 1965. GS: James MacArthur. Judge Garth's orphaned niece Jennifer comes to Shiloh Ranch, unaware that the young man she met on the stage is a killer.

161.99 *Nobility of Kings.* Nov. 10, 1965. GS: Charles Bronson, Lois Nettleton, George Kennedy, Vito Scotti, Bob Random, Edward Faulkner, Robert P. Lieb, James Sikking, John Mitchum, Charles McDaniel, Davis Roberts. Because of past failures, embittered Ben Justin is determined to make a success of his modest cattle ranch, and he plans to do it without any help from neighborly people like the Virginian.

The Virginian

161.100 *Show Me a Hero.* Nov. 17, 1965. GS: Richard Beymer, Leonard Nimoy, Sherry Jackson, Douglas V. Fowley, Lee Patterson. The sixty hard-pressed settlers of a former ghost town are surprised when gunmen ride into town bearing money. They would like to buy their way into the town, and turn it into a wide-open gambling hole.

161.101 *Beyond the Border.* Nov. 24, 1965. GS: Thomas Gomez, Joan Staley, Joe Mantell, Michael Forest, Gregg Palmer, Jimmy Lee Cook. In Mexico, the Virginian is stricken with fever and Trampas is forced to leave him at an isolated cantina with only a saloon girl to care for him.

161.102 *The Dream of Stavros Karas.* Dec. 1, 1965. GS: Michael Constantine, Louise Sorel, Anthony Hayes, Russ Conway, Vicki Malkin, Joey Russo. An immigrant Greek widower sends home for a wife to help care for his two children, but he receives quite a shock. Instead of the middle-aged woman he was expecting, his future bride turns out to be young and attractive.

161.103 *The Laramie Road.* Dec. 8, 1965. GS: Leslie Nielsen, Claude Akins, Harold J. Stone, Margaret Blye, Berkeley Harris, Marge Redmond, Rory Stevens. The outraged citizens of Medicine Boy want to lynch two hobos suspected of murder.

161.104 *The Horse Fighter.* Dec. 15, 1965. GS: Harry Guardino, Kelly Thordsen, Don Dubbins, Stuart Anderson, Nolan Leary. Bronco buster Sam Willock is after more than work when he signs on at the Shiloh ranch. He wants to steal the ranch payroll.

161.105 *Letter of the Law.* Dec. 22, 1965. GS: Simon Oakland, James Best, Davey Davison, Don Stewart, Ron Soble, David McLean, Bryan O'Byrne. The Virginian shoots a train robber, who dies after confessing to a robbery which another man has been imprisoned for.

161.106 *Blaze of Glory.* Dec. 29, 1965. GS: Leif Erickson, Joan Freeman, Karl Swenson, Michael Sarrazin, Rayford Barnes, Hal Bokar, Noam Pitlik, Jim Boles, John Mitchum. Trampas is fond of Judy King, who is encountering financial problems at home. Her father can't get an extension on his loan and is about to have the mortgage on his ranch foreclosed.

161.107 *Nobody Said Hello.* Jan. 5, 1966. GS: Virginia Grey, James Whitmore, Steve Carlson, Peter Whitney, Wesley Lau. Photographer Ansel Miller, who blames former Confederate prison commander Piper Pritikin for the loss of his arm, becomes bitter and vindictive when he learns that Pritikin has been released from prison and is coming to Medicine Bow.

161.108 *Men with Guns.* Jan. 12, 1966. GS: Telly Savalas, Robert F. Simon, Brenda Scott, Buck Taylor, Douglas Kennedy, Coleen Gray, Peter Coe. In the desert town of New Hope to pick up some horses from wealthy Colonel Bliss, Trampas and Randy learn that the greedy millionaire has been evicting settlers from land he sold them.

161.109 *Long Ride to Wind River.* Jan. 19, 1966. GS: Michael Burns, Pilar Seurat, John Cassavetes, Dub Taylor, Richard Devon, Quinn Redeker, Robert Karnes, Maggie Mitchell. Benjy Davis threatened to kill Hobey Kendall, who has made advances toward Benjy's wife. When Hobey is found murdered, Benjy's plea of innocence doesn't stand up very well in court.

161.110 *Chaff in the Wind.* Jan. 26, 1966. GS: Ed Begley, Tony Bill, Linda Lawson, Lonny Chapman, John Pickard. Booted out of Laramie, the conniving Ellis clan descend on the Shiloh Ranch, where they receive a warm welcome from Jennifer and Randy.

161.111 *The Inchworm's Got No Wings at All.* Feb. 2, 1966. GS: Stacey Maxwell, Lou Antonio, Anthony Caruso, Angela Clarke, Jack Dodson, Ed Deemer, Michael Stanwood, Gregg Palmer, Robert Petersen. Outlaw Henry Brodie murders his partner and hides the money from a holdup, unaware that he is being watched by a retarded teenage girl.

161.112 *Morgan Starr.* Feb. 9, 1966. GS: Peggie Castle, George Mitchell, Buck Young, Brad Weston, Ken Mayer, Edward Faulkner, Paul Birch, James Hurst, Pitt Herbert. After his appointment as territorial governor of Wyoming, Judge Garth passes over the Virginian and bring in a man named Morgan Starr to run Shiloh ranch.

161.113 *Harvest of Strangers.* Feb. 16, 1966. GS: Geoffrey Horne, John Anderson, Barbara Turner, Jan Shepard, Val Avery, Emile Genest, Fabrizio Mioni, Willard Sage, Robert P. Lieb, Stuart Nisbet. The citizens of Medicine Bow are alarmed when a band of heavily armed French-Canadians arrive in town.

161.114 *Ride a Cock-Horse to Laramie Cross.* Feb. 23, 1966. GS: Nita Talbot, Clint Howard, Ken Lynch, Steven Gravers, Harry Harvey, Sr., Alex Montoya, Rance Howard, John Harmon, William Tannen. Trampas tries to help a boy and his infant sister reach Laramie to join their mother. But a gang of gunfighters is planning to return the children to their grandfather, a powerful Mexican landowner.

161.115 *One Spring Like Long Ago.* March 2, 1966. GS: Eduard Franz, Warren Oates, Clive Clerk, Martine Bartlett, Garry Walberg. An old Indian prophecy comes true. After many years, the buffalo return to the area near a reservation, and Chief Two Hawks believes that this means his tribesmen will now be able to free themselves of the white man's rule.

161.116 *The Return of Golden Tom.* March 9, 1966. GS: Victor Jory, Linden Chiles, Jean Inness, Kelly Thordsen, Dee Pollock, Dee Carroll, Don Keefer, Larry J. Blake, Carole Kane, Med Flory, Kimberly Beck, Ross Hagen. The return of Tom Brant after 35 years in prison sparks mixed emotions in Medicine Bow. Brant took part in the town's biggest gunfight.

161.117 *The Wolves Up Front, The Jackals Behind.* March 23, 1966. GS: James Farentino, Jay C. Flippen, Michael J. Pollard, Peggy Lipton, Jack Ragotzy, Donnelly Rhodes, Harlan Warde, Bing Russell. Randy and his friend Georgie Sam are both taken with young Dulcie Colby, but the return of her brother Frank has left Dulcie a very troubled girl.

161.118 *That Saunders Woman.* March 30, 1966. GS: Sheree North, Liam Sullivan, Victoria Albright, Stephen Roberts, Stuart Anderson, Douglas Henderson, Tol Avery, Stuart Randall. Released from prison, Della Saunders starts a new life in Medicine Bow, where she opens a dress shop. But one of the townsfolk knows the facts about Della's past, and he plans to make use of them.

161.119 *No Drums, No Trumpets.* April 6, 1966. GS: Julie Adams, Leslie Nielsen, Hans Gudegast/Eric Braeden, Richard Devon, Eduardo Ciannelli. A U.S. senator and a Mexican governor are scheduled to sign a trade agreement in the Mexican town of Gato Rojo, but a group of hired gunmen have arrived in town to make certain that the treaty is never signed.

161.120 *A Bald-Faced Boy.* April 13, 1966. GS: Andrew

Prine, Royal Dano, Andrew Duggan, Karen Jensen, Michael Stanwood, Kay E. Kuter, Barry O'Hara, Ken McWhirter, Jeff Scott, Harold Fong, Jimmy Lee Cook. Randy's brother, uncle and cousins arrive in Medicine Bow with the express purpose of protecting the boy from ex-convict Brett Benton, who is also due in town. Randy's testimony helped put Benton behind bars.

161.121 *The Mark of a Man.* April 20, 1966. GS: Harold J. Stone, Brooke Bundy, Barry Primus, John McLiam, Irene Tedrow, Jean Willes, Richard LePore, Bill Quinn, Stuart Nisbet. Hopping mad after he is fired from his job in a saloon, Johnny Younce goes on a rampage, breaking windows and setting fires.

Season Five

161.122 *Legacy of Hate.* Sept. 14, 1966. GS: Jo Van Fleet, Jeremy Slate, Ed Prentiss, Troy Melton, Robert Hoy, Elizabeth Harrower, Clyde Howdy, Dennis McCarthy. Rancher John Grainger, the Shiloh's new owner, has already got problems. His grandson Stacy spent his first night in Medicine Bow in jail, and cattle from an adjoining ranch have been found wearing the Shiloh brand.

161.123 *Ride to Delphi.* Sept. 21, 1966. GS: Harold J. Stone, Angie Dickinson, Warren Oates, Bernie Hamilton, Ron Russell. The Virginian's search for stolen cattle leads him to a stubborn sodbuster who refuses to relinquish the rustled beef, and to an old girl friend who pretends she doesn't know him.

161.124 *The Captive.* Sept. 28, 1966. GS: Susan Strasberg, Don Hanmer, Gus Trikonis, Than Wyenn, Virginia Vincent, Tina Menard. The Graingers agree to board a young girl raised by the Arapahoes until the sheriff can find her real parents, but the hostile girl refuses to admit that she is not an Indian.

161.125 *An Echo of Thunder.* Oct. 5, 1966. GS: Jason Evers, Linden Chiles, Indus Arthur, Mark Miranda, John Anderson, Barbara Werele, Brendan Boone, Les Tremayne, Shug Fisher. On a cattle drive south, Trampas gets sidetracked when he investigates the murder of an old friend.

161.126 *Jacob Was a Plain Man.* Oct. 12, 1966. GS: Aldo Ray, Peter Duryea, Alfred Ryder, Robert Pine, Edward Faulkner, Larry J. Blake. The Virginian agrees to hire a nameless deaf mute, unaware that the hard-working man is wanted for murder.

161.127 *The Challenge.* Oct. 19, 1966. GS: Barbara Anderson, Dan Duryea, Michael Burns, Don Galloway, Ed Peck, Bing Russell, Hal Bokar, Grant Woods, Byron Keith, Lew Brown, Clyde Howdy. Trampas, half conscious and badly injured, staggers to a near-by farm, where his loss of memory makes him a prime suspect in a recent murder and stage robbery.

161.128 *Outcast.* Oct. 26, 1966. GS: Fabian, Milton Selzer, George Wallace, Carole Kane, Marvin Brody, Quentin Sondergaard. Stacy doesn't like the idea of newly hired Charley Ryan paying so much attention to Elizabeth, and Stacy would like it even less if he knew that Ryan is an escaped prisoner who has been charged with murder.

161.129 *Trail to Ashley Mountain.* Nov. 2, 1966. GS: Martin Milner, Hugh Marlowe, Steve Carlson, Raymond St. Jacques, Gene Evans, Judi Meredith. With the help of a man named Case, Trampas sets out to clear a friend of murder, unaware that Case is the real killer.

161.130 *Dead Eye Dick.* Nov. 9, 1966. GS: Alice Rawlings, William Schallert, June Vincent, David Macklin, Patricia Donahue. Young Easterner Marjorie Hammond isn't paying much attention to the dude who is wooing her. The pretty sixteen-year-old, whose image of the West comes from a romantic dime novel, is set on lassoing the Virginian, her dream hero come to life.

161.131 *High Stakes.* Nov. 16, 1966. GS: Terry Moore, Jack Lord, Michael Ansara, Dirk Rambo, Harry Hickox, Mark Tapscott, William Fawcett, Walter Reed, Robert Carson. The Virginian poses as a law-breaker to capture his friend's killer in a ghost town controlled by the killer's brother and his outlaw band.

161.132 *Beloved Outlaw.* Nov. 23, 1966. Elizabeth is determined to tame the beautiful wild stallion Grandfather Grainger bought at an auction, despite her grandfather's warnings.

161.133 *Linda.* Nov. 30, 1966. GS: Diane Baker, Frank McGrath, Clifton James, Bill Fletcher, James Bowen Brown. The Virginian is caught between outlaws and the law when he becomes involved with Linda Valence, a beautiful actress who is working as the courier for a robbery ring.

161.134 *Long Journey Home.* Dec. 14, 1966. GS: Pernell Roberts, Michael Burns, Noah Beery, Jr., Jan Shepard, Jay Ripley, Don Stroud. The Virginian finds himself rivaled by Jim Boyer, a hard-luck cowboy who is trying to win back the family he deserted. Boyer's son thinks the Virginian is a better man than his father, a sentiment that Boyer Sr. is determined to shatter.

161.135 *Girl on the Glass Mountain.* Dec. 28, 1966. GS: Tom Tryon, Hugh Beaumont, Pamela Austin, Dorothy Green, Brian Avery, Michael Greene, John Archer, Steve Raines, Ed Prentiss, Laurie Mitchell. Howie Sheppard, a former Shiloh hand turned businessman, is trying to live up to his city-bred wife's expectations. Sheppard's saddle shop and his marriage are both threatened when he is drawn into a poker game by his former cronies.

161.136 *Vengeance Trail.* Jan. 4, 1967. GS: Ron Russell, Mary Ann Mobley, Ben Hammer, Wesley Lau, William Bramley, Jeff Scott, Barbara Eiler, Noah Keen, Warren Hammack, John Zaremba. A man in search of his brother's murderer joins a Shiloh trail drive, unaware that the killer is his friend Stacy, who was forced to shoot in self-defense.

161.137 *Sue Ann.* Jan. 11, 1967. GS: Patty Duke, Edward Binns, Paul Carr, Tim McIntire, Rita Lynn, Kirk Travis, Kerry MacLane, Roy Barcroft. Young farm girl Sue Ann MacRae leaves home for the excitement of a job as a saloon hostess in Medicine Bow. Meanwhile, her disapproving boy friend signs on at the Shiloh to keep an eye on the girl.

161.138 *Yesterday's Timepiece.* Jan. 18, 1967. GS: Audrey Totter, Stuart Erwin, Pat O'Brien, Andy Devine, Bruce Bennett, Kelly Jean Peters, Robert F. Simon. A mysterious watch and a recurring nightmare spur Stacy into leaving Shiloh to investigate the murder of his parents, who were killed during Stacy's childhood.

161.139 *Requiem for a Country Doctor.* Jan. 25, 1967. GS: Cloris Leachman, Debbie Watson, John Doucette, Coleen Gray, Dick Foran, Ford Rainey, Morgan Woodward, Tom

The Virginian

Baker, Raymond Guth, Dee Carroll, Tim Graham. Stacy will stand on the gallows unless the Virginian proves him innocent of murdering a town's beloved doctor. The grim foreman, probing the doc's past, is running into strong opposition from the townsfolk.

161.140 *The Modoc Kid.* Feb. 1, 1967. GS: John Saxon, Harrison Ford, Paul Fix. Terror comes to the Shiloh in the form of an outlaw band. The crazed leader is holding the young folks at gunpoint while Grandpa goes after medical aid for a wounded gang member.

161.141 *The Gauntlet.* Feb. 8, 1967. GS: Mark Richman, Marian Moses, Stefan Arngrim, Harry Lauter, Tony Young, Robert B. Williams, Calvin Brown, Fred Carson, Pitt Herbert, Bruce Bennett. At a sprawling Texas ranch, the Virginian becomes an unwitting accomplice in a lonely woman's plan to leave her callous husband and return East with their son.

161.142 *Without Mercy.* Feb. 15, 1967. GS: James Gregory, Katherine Walsh, Lonny Chapman, Warren Hammack. Grainger goes to work on a murder case. The suspect is Stacy, who is known to have argued violently with the murdered man.

161.143 *Melanie.* Feb. 22, 1967. GS: Susan Clark, Victor Jory, Clint Howard. Wealthy Melanie Kohler, an Eastern-bred beauty, falls in love with Trampas, and the feeling is mutual. The ranch hand has no inkling that his wish to marry the girl is doomed from the start.

161.144 *Doctor Pat.* March 1, 1967. GS: Jill Donahue, John Bryant, Mari Blanchard, Donald "Red" Barry, Jean Inness, Walter Coy. A doctor fights to gain the confidence of the people in Medicine Bow, but they are reluctant to accept the newcomer, a lady fresh out of medical school.

161.145 *Nightmare at Fort Killman.* March 8, 1967. GS: James Daly, Johnny Seven, Les Crane, Don Mitchell, Wally Strauss. Two unscrupulous sergeants have shanghaied Stacy Grainger into the Cavalry. One brutal incident leads to another as the pair hold Stacy prisoner to prevent him from seeing the fort's commander.

161.146 *Bitter Harvest.* March 15, 1967. GS: Whitney Blake, Larry Pennell, John Lupton, Russ Conway, Michael Shea. The Virginian is thrust into hostilities between a struggling rancher and determined homesteaders. While the Shiloh foreman tries to arbitrate the conflict, a hot-headed farmer drums up support for a range war.

161.147 *The Welcoming Town.* March 22, 1967. GS: Robert Fuller, Jocelyn Brando, Lynda Day, Frank Overton, Carole Wells. Trampas delves into the past to clear the name of a dead friend, who was accused of assaulting a young girl. The friend was killed by a mob, and Trampas soon learns that the girl's family profited from his death.

161.148 *The Girl on the Pinto.* March 29, 1967. GS: Valora Noland, R.G. Armstrong, Vivi Janiss, Warren Stevens. An aura of mystery surrounds lovely Amanda Harley, but an infatuated Trampas is determined to break thorugh her barrier of aloofness.

161.149 *Lady of the House.* April 5, 1967. GS: Myrna Loy, L.Q. Jones. Mrs. Miles is a graceful and cunning widow. Grainger hires the lady to run his house, where she soon imposes her genteel manners on the ranch family, and alienates Stacy and Elizabeth, who believe that Grainger wants to marry the devious woman.

161.150 *The Strange Quest of Claire Bingham.* April 12, 1967. GS: Andrew Prine, Sandra Smith. Ryker befriends a nurse who believes that an accused murderer is her long-lost brother. But lawman and lady clash when the prisoner escapes, and Ryker sets out in pursuit, unaware that the nurse is helping the wounded fugitive.

Season Six

161.151 *Reckoning.* Sept. 13, 1967. GS: Dick Foran, Charles Bronson, Miriam Colon, Charles Grodin. The Virginian is in a Texas border town buying cattle. He is soon engaged in a desperate transaction, freeing Elizabeth from an outlaw who has an old score to settle with him.

161.152 *The Deadly Past.* Sept. 20, 1967. GS: Darren McGavin, Linden Chiles, Mary-Robin Redd, Bing Russell, Alan Baxter, Robert Strauss, Gregg Martell, Jan Inness, Eve McVeagh, John Rubenstein. Trampas joins a hard-drinking gunslinger and a sheriff's wife to search for the mysterious person who has sent them all death notes.

161.153 *The Lady from Witchita.* Sept. 27, 1967. GS: Joan Collins, Harry Lauter, Rose Marie, Ann Doran. Two saloon girls inherit a ranch in Medicine Bow. Pleased with their new-found status, the ladies decide to remain in town, hoping their past won't catch up with them.

161.154 *Star Crossed.* Oct. 4, 1967. GS: Tom Tryon, Lisabeth Hush, Kiel Martin, Brian Nash. Deputy Ryker sidesteps the law to help an old friend make a new start. Andrew Hiller, wanted for robbery, is well on the way to reforming, until he encounters a blackmailing Shiloh ranch hand.

161.155 *Johnny Moon.* Oct. 11, 1967. GS: Tom Bell, Ben Johnson, Michael Higgins, Bo Hopkins, Cliff Potter, George Brenlin, John Bryant, Norman Leavitt. Johnny Moon, recovering from a bullet wound at the Shiloh ranch, is a Canadian Mountie wanted for desertion. The Virginian faces a tough decision. Turn Moon in or help him pursue a gang of murderous wolves.

161.156 *The Masquerade.* Oct. 18, 1967. GS: Lloyd Nolan, David Hartman, Diana Muldaur, Bobby Buntrock, Ed Prentiss, Harry Hickox, Norman Leavitt. All of Medicine Bow helps timid bank clerk George Foster masquerade as the sheriff. The pose is being staged to impress Foster's visiting father, a former lawman.

161.157 *Ah Sing vs. Wyoming.* Oct. 25, 1967. GS: Edmond O'Brien, Aki Aleong, Lloyd Bochner, Robert Ellenstein, Jill Donohue, Gilbert Green, John Hoyt, Bartlett Robinson, Roy Engel. A civil rights court battle takes place in Medicine Bow. The defendant is former Shiloh cook Ah Sing, who landed in jail after he opened a restaurant in defiance of a bigoted official.

161.158 *Bitter Autumn.* Nov. 1, 1967. GS: John Anderson, Richard X. Slattery, Steve Carlson, Virginia Gregg, Shelly Novack, Dabbs Greer, Craig Hundley, John Bryant, Russell Thordsen. Overseeing the Shiloh in his brother's absence, Clay Grainger contends with a herd of diseased cattle and an ex-marshal seeking revenge against the young drover who shot his wife.

161.159 *A Bad Place to Die.* Nov. 8, 1967. GS: Victor Jory, Susanne Benton, Myron Healey, Henry Beckman, John Milford, Parley Baer. Trampas awaits hanging for murder as the

Virginian and Clay Grainger rush to save his life. When all else looks hopeless, Trampas desperately agrees to break jail with an old convict.

161.160 *Paid in Full.* Nov. 22, 1967. GS: James Whitmore, Don Stroud, Douglas Kennedy, Robert Yuro, Hal Baylor, Robert Karnes, Ed Prentiss. Ex-convict Frank Hollis' return to the Shiloh sparks nothing but trouble. Young Hollis has an obsessive resentment of Trampas and Clay, whom he blames for the crippled condition of his father, a veteran Shiloh wrangler.

161.161 *To Bear Witness.* Nov. 29, 1967. GS: William Windom, Joanna Moore, Malachi Throne, Paul Carr. Trampas becomes the target of hatred and abuse when he implicates the town doctor in a murder case tainted with scandal.

161.162 *The Barren Ground.* Dec. 6, 1967. GS: Jay C. Flippen, Collin Wilcox, Byron Mabe, Christopher Horne, Noah Keen, Michael Vandever, Charles Seel, John Harmon, Harry Harvey, Sr., Dee Carroll. After killing an outlaw, the Virginian becomes involved with the dead man's father. While caring for the old man, the Virginian tries to grant a last wish to bring home his daughter, who has lived for many years with the Shoshone.

161.163 *Execution at Triste.* Dec. 13, 1967. GS: Sharon Farrell, Robert Lansing, Kelly Thordsen, Burt Douglas, Cyril Delevanti, Steve Raines, Nate Esformes, Philip Chapin, Percy Helton, Bert Freed. In the nearly deserted town of Triste, Trampas is greeted by a death threat from an obsessed gunfighter. The man, known as the Executioner and dressed all in black, intends to goad the Shiloh hand into a showdown.

161.164 *A Small Taste of Justice.* Dec. 20, 1967. GS: Susan Oliver, Peter Brown, John Lupton, Virginia Christine, Vaughn Taylor, Bert Freed, James Gammon, Judson Pratt, Stephen Coit, Quentin Sondergaard, Stuart Nisbet. The Virginian joins the citizens of Three Falls to settle a score with an arrogant rancher and his men, who started a gun battle that left a small child critically wounded.

161.165 *The Fortress.* Dec. 27, 1967. GS: Leslie Nielsen, Kipp Hamilton, Barbara Bouchet, Willard Sage, H.M. Wynant, Paul Picerni. In a Canadian town, the Virginian matches wits with a polished thief named Winthrop, who stole $100,000 of Shiloh money. The foreman is determined to retrieve the cash, even though Winthrop controls the town and its citizens, and knows the Virginian's every move.

161.166 *The Death Wagon.* Jan. 3, 1968. GS: Albert Salmi, Michael Constantine, Tim McIntire, Ken Swofford, Bill Baldwin, Jeff Malloy, Nicolas Beauvy, Adam O'Neil. Trampas joins two veteran soldiers on a dangerous search for an escaped prisoner who poses a double threat. The fugitive is armed, and they are certain that he has scarlet fever.

161.167 *Jed.* Jan. 10, 1968. GS: Steve Ihnat, Brenda Scott, Sammy Jackson, Stuart Margolin, Ken Swofford, Walter Coy, Lew Brown, Victor Creatore, Jill Jenkins. Gunman Jed Matthews is planted at the Shiloh during an impending range war to sabotage Grainger's attempts at a peaceful settlement. But Matthews finds himself questioning his loyalties when he renews and old friendship with Trampas, and meets a young farm girl.

161.168 *With Help from Ulysses.* Jan. 17, 1968. GS: Hugh Beaumont, J. Pat O'Malley, Jill Donohue, Barbara Rhoades, Eileen Wesson, June Vincent, Warren Hammack, David Farrow, Clyde Howdy, Peter Leeds, Brenda Robin. A shaggy mutt, appropriately named Ulysses, helps Trampas search for an old prospector's long-lost niece, who can be identified by a birthmark just above her knee.

161.169 *The Gentle Tamers.* Jan. 24, 1968. GS: Antony Call, Darwin Joston, Wesley Lau, Don Pedro Colley, James Griffith, William Fawcett, Gail Bonney, Paul Comi, Jean Peloquin. Grainger accepts three prison inmates for the Shiloh labor force. The misfits soon use the rehabilitation experiment as a chance to make quick money at poker, and rustling.

161.170 *The Good-Hearted Badman.* Feb. 7, 1968. GS: Peter Deuel, Anthony Zerbe, John Larch, K.L. Smith, Jim Boles, Stuart Nisbet, John Stevens, Robert Rothwell. Wounded outlaw leader Jim Dewey's stay at the Shiloh causes grave concern. Elizabeth is infatuated with the young man, who is being tracked by a bounty hunter closing in for the kill.

161.171 *The Hell Wind.* Feb. 14, 1968. GS: Patricia Crowley, Ford Rainey, Woodrow Parfrey, Kiel Martin. A sandstorm leaves Trampas, Elizabeth and Stacy stranded in an old shack, which also becomes the refuge of a sick banker and his young wife. Distrust develops in the marooned group after the Shiloh hands find a fortune in gold stashed nearby.

161.172 *The Crooked Path.* Feb. 21, 1968. GS: Tom Skerritt, Kevin Coughlin, John Marley, Ellen Moss. The Virginian has a devil of a time keeping order at the Shiloh. He has hired a boastful teenager, whose arrogant behavior is sparking bitter feelings among the veteran cowhands.

161.173 *Stacey.* Feb. 28, 1968. GS: Robert H. Harris, Lee Kroeger, Barbara Werle, John Bryant, Jean Peloquin, Dick Shane. When his arm is severely injured, young Stacey suffers both mental and physical anguish. He fears that the arm may be permanently paralyzed.

161.174 *The Handy Man.* March 6, 1968. GS: Mel Torme, Tom Simcox, Paul Mantee, William Bramley, Noam Pitlik. Rumored to be an infamous gunfighter, the handy man becomes the storm center in a clash between the Grainger and a hot-headed neighbor.

161.175 *The Decision.* March 13, 1968. GS: Steve Carlson, Kenneth Tobey, Monica Lewis, Ben Murphy, Lawrence Dane, Than Wyenn, Chuck Courtney, Harper Flaherty. To save his marriage, veteran sheriff Dan Porter abandons the badge for a job as a Shiloh hand. The lawman undergoes severe strain due to age, inexperience, and a rekindled conflict with Trampas.

161.176 *Seth.* March 20, 1968. GS: Michael Burns, Kevin Hagen, Richard LePore, Rusty Lane, Harper Flaherty, Dick Shane, Jay Clark, William Fawcett, Mark Tapscott. Trampas appointed himself foster father to an itinerant teenager. After getting young Seth a job at the Shiloh, Trampas teaches him the ranch hand's trade, unaware that the boy is tied in with outlaws.

Season Seven

161.177 *The Saddle Warmer.* Sept. 18, 1968. GS: Ralph Bellamy, Tom Skerritt, Quentin Dean, Chris Robinson, Jean Peloquin, The Irish Rovers. Greenhorn David Sutton hires on at the Shiloh. He gets a bittersweet introduction to the West when he tries to help a runaway farm girl.

161.178 *Silver Image.* Sept. 25, 1968. GS: Geraldine

Brooks, James Daly, William Smith, Bob Random, Harry Harvey, Sr., Harper Flaherty, Tim Graham, Donald "Red" Barry. Tempers flare in Medicine Bow as widow Della Price ponders a decision that could ruin the cattle business. Despite the Virginian's protests, she wants to sell her ranch to an oil speculator, a move that would flood the range with wildcatters.

161.179 *The Orchard.* Oct. 2, 1968. GS: William Windom, Burgess Meredith, Brandon de Wilde, Ben Wright, William Phipps, Lee Brown, Ben Murphy, Jean Peloquin. An old cattleman, trying to rebuild a ranch is caught in a clash between his sons. One wants to farm the land, the other prefers gambling and rustling.

161.180 *Vision of Blindness.* Oct. 9, 1968. GS: John Saxon, Ben Johnson, The Irish Rovers. Blinded in a stagecoach accident, Elizabeth is forced to rely on a young ex-convict. As the pair hike over rugged terrain toward the Shiloh, the helpless girl is also blind to the man's plan to murder Trampas.

161.181 *The Wind of Outrage.* Oct. 16,1968. GS: Ricardo Montalban, Lois Nettleton, Lawrence Dane. In a Minnesota border town, the Virginian and Trampas become embroiled in the intrigue surrounding an exiled Canadian revolutionary. The man's comrades want him to lead a new revolt, a move that would mean forsaking his fiancee and risking execution.

161.182 *Image of an Outlaw.* Oct. 23, 1968. GS: Don Stroud, Amy Thomson, Sandy Kenyon, Ed Prentiss, Walter Reed, John Cliff, Warren Hammack, Dennis McCarthy. Shiloh hand Rafe Judson has become a mistaken target of the law and bounty hunters because of his amazing resemblance to a notorious outlaw. When financial ruin threatens, Judson decides to turn that liability into an asset.

161.183 *The Heritage.* Oct. 30, 1968. GS: Buffy Sainte-Marie, Ned Romero, Jim Davis, Karl Swenson, Jay Silverheels. A Shoshone girl returns from an Eastern school with serious doubts about rejoining her tribe. Caught between cultures, the girl seeks advice from the Graingers as her beleaguered people face threats from a land-greedy cattleman.

161.184 *Ride the Misadventure.* Nov. 6, 1968. GS: Joseph Campanella, Katherine Justice, Joe Maross, Barbara Werle, Harry Dean Stanton, John Aniston, Robert Donner, Virginia Gregg, Ken Swofford. Time is of the essence as the Virginian and David join forces with a bounty hunter to track an outlaw gang. The thieves robbed a stage cargo, which included anthrax vaccine meant for the Shiloh ranch.

161.185 *The Storm Gate.* Nov. 13, 1968. GS: Burr DeBenning, Susan Oliver, Scott Brady, Robert F. Simon, Roy Jenson, Ted Gehring, Mitch Vogel, Charles H. Radilac. In River Oaks, Trampas is forced to question the motives of an old friend who is working on a grandiose dam project. Jason Crowder's determination becomes an obsession as he tries to gain control of farming land, and avoid the gun of a vengeful enemy from his past.

161.186 *Dark Corridor.* Nov. 27, 1968. GS: Judy Lang, Paul Winchel, Paul Smith. In a remote mountainous region, the Virginian and an old recluse become the guardians of a frightened, speechless young girl. Unable to get medical help, the men try to bring the girl back to reality, hoping to uncover the cause of her withdrawal.

161.187 *The Mustangers.* Dec. 4, 1968. GS: John Agar, James Edwards, Don Knight, Chuck Daniel, William Bruns, Marjorie Bennett, Grace Lee Whitney, Mina Martinez. Desperate for horses, the Virginian and David head up a mustang hunt. Plagued by their own inexperience, the men also fight horse thieves and the alienation between two members of their skeleton crew, an aging bronc buster and his young son.

161.188 *Nora.* Dec. 11, 1968. GS: Anne Baxter, Hugh Beaumont, Tim McIntire, Ken Renard, Harry Lauter, Pilar Seurat, Steve Raines, Mark Tapscott, Ron Burke, Tom Basham, John Bryant. Nora Carlton is a conniving Army wife visiting the Shiloh with her husband, an officer frequently passed over for promotion. Word of an Indian uprising cuts short the visit, but kindles a scheme to advance her husband's career.

161.189 *Big Tiny.* Dec. 18, 1968. GS: Roger Torrey, Dick Foran, Julie Sommars, Mabel Albertson, David Sutton. In Durango, the Shiloh hand agrees to be the make-believe fiance of a young woman trying to discourage a suitor. David learns too late that he is competing with Tiny Morgan, a giant of a man whose persistence is surpassed only by his strength.

161.190 *Stopover.* Jan. 8, 1969. GS: Jay C. Flippen, Herb Jeffries, Douglas Henderson, Kevin Hagen, John Kellogg, Jan Shepard, William Fawcett, John McLiam, Frances Spanier, Stuart Nisbet. The arrival of gunman Frank Hammel creates an atmosphere of fearful expectation in Medicine Bow. As the uneasy mood heightens, several citizens dredge up past deeds that could make them the killer's target.

161.191 *Death Wait.* Jan. 15, 1969. GS: Harold J. Stone, Sheila Larkin, Murray MacLeod, Conlan Carter, Clyde Ventura, Rachel Ames, Ed Faulkner. David's self-defense killing of a young rancher makes him the target of a vengeful family. Waiting in Medicine Bow are the dead man' father and brother, a gunfighter who intends to goad David into a showdown.

161.192 *Last Grave at Socorro Creek.* Jan. 22, 1969. GS: Kevin Coughlin, Steve Ihnat, Lonny Chapman, Ellen McRae, Larry Ward, James Wainwright, Jocelyn Brando, Don Keefer, Mills Watson, Walter Coy. The Virginian matches wits with a sadistic killer while investigating the lynching of an old friend. In the thick of it is the dead man's son, insisting vengeance is his alone.

161.193 *Crime Wave at Buffalo Springs.* Jan. 29, 1969. GS: Carrie Snodgrass, Tom Bosley, Yvonne DeCarlo, James Brolin, Ann Prentiss, Gary Vinson, Angie Love, The Irish Rovers. David and Trampas get embroiled in a mishmash of mistaken identities, barroom brawls and bumbling robberies in a town plagued by a power struggle between a lady saloonkeeper and a stuffy banker.

161.194 *The Price of Love.* Feb. 12, 1969. GS: Peter Deuel, James Gregory, Skip Homeier. The Graingers welcome Denny Todd, a drifter who lived with them years before. The couple's affection for the young man blinds them to his troubled personality which includes fits of violence and threats against any who opposed the Graingers on their ranch.

161.195 *The Ordeal.* Feb. 19, 1969. GS: Robert Pine, Michael Masters, Jennifer Gan. The Virginian struggles with Eastern dandy Scott Austin, trying to turn him into a Shiloh hand. But the troublesome apprentice prefers romancing Elizabeth to doing his job.

161.196 *The Land Dreamer.* Feb. 26, 1969. GS: Don Francks, James Olson, Cloris Leachman, Ford Rainey, John Daniels. The Virginian, Trampas and David pursue a farmer accused of wounding the sheriff and killing a land baron.

Awaiting the fugitive in Medicine Bow is a jail cell and the vengeful brother of the dead man.

161.197 *Eileen.* March 5, 1969. GS: Debbie Watson, Richard Van Vleet, Donald "Red" Barry. Elizabeth becomes the confidante of young Eileen Linden, who has been sent West to forget a forbidden romance. Eileen's personal crisis intensifies when her suitor follows her to Shiloh, demanding that they marry immediately.

161.198 *Incident at Diablo Crossing.* March 12, 1969. GS: Gary Collins, Kiel Martin, Lee Kroeger, Bernie Hamilton. Trampas and his fellow stagecoach passengers face a dangerous delay at a ferry crossing. The boat has been destroyed and the operator killed. The stranded travelers must now brace themselves for an attack from an unknown enemy.

161.199 *Storm Over Shiloh.* March 19, 1969. GS: Harper Flaherty. The Virginian, Trampas and the Graingers team up to rescue Elizabeth, who is trapped in a deserted mine. They have established voice contact with her, but their rescue attempts could cause another cave-in.

161.200 *The Girl in the Shadows.* March 26, 1969. GS: Jack Albertson, Brenda Scott, Greg Mullavey, Larry Chance, Stuart Nisbet, Ken Swofford, Eddie Quillan. Doc Watson and Miss Claire, partners in a mind-reading act, attract Grainger's special attention. There is reason to believe the girl is Granger's long-lost niece.

161.201 *Fox, Hound, and the Widow McCloud.* April 2, 1969. GS: Troy Donahue, Jean Inness, Victor Jory, Dennis McCarthy, Clyde Howdy, Harper Flaherty, Stuart Randall, Mark Tapscott. Trampas shelters a fugitive who helped him escape from prisoner years before, and who is now being tracked by a bounty hunter moving in for the kill.

161.202 *The Stranger.* April 9, 1969. GS: Shelley Novack, John Doucette, Michael Conrad. The standoffish behavior of a new Shiloh hand ironically gets him involved in a Medicine Bow murder. The loner becomes the prime suspect, and the Virginian is the only one to champion his claim of innocence.

Season Eight

161.203 *The Long Ride Home.* Sept. 17, 1969. GS: Leslie Nielsen, Lonny Chapman, Joyce Jameson, Patrick Tovatt, Jester Hairston, Lynn Youngreen, Pete Kellett. The free life and close friendship of teenage cowhand Jim Horn and an itinerant wrangler are threatened when the two sign on at the Shiloh. Jim takes a shine to his new surroundings, and to Elizabeth.

161.204 *A Flash of Darkness.* Sept. 24, 1969. GS: James Whitmore, Pamela McMyler. Blinded in a fall, the Virginian faces a torturous test of survival in remote, rugged territory.

161.205 *Halfway Back from Hell.* Oct. 1, 1969. GS: John Dehner, Susan Howard, William Windom. Trampas becomes the teaching foreman for a group of prisoners selected to start a rehabilitation ranch in Arizona. The men's biggest hurdle is overcoming the hotbed of fear and hostility that exists in a neighboring town.

161.206 *The Power Seekers.* Oct. 8, 1969. GS: Barry Sullivan, Andrew Prine. Clay Grainger gets an enlightening course in power politics when he runs for territorial representative. Amidst a cross fire of vested interests and uneasy loyalties, the Shiloh rancher attempts to beat his opponent, a young businessman with a slick campaign for civic progress.

161.207 *Family Man.* Oct. 15, 1969. GS: Frank Webb, Darleen Carr, John Pickard, Quinn Redeker. Young Jim Horn gets deeply involved in the trouble-plagued life of a teenage couple. After the husband flees from the law, Jim steps in to aid the pregnant wife, acting as farm hand, midwife and an increasingly infatuated friend.

161.208 *The Runaway Boy.* Oct. 22, 1969. GS: Guy Stockwell, Johnny Whitaker, Peter Whitney, Jan Shepard. The Graingers act as stand-in parents for a runaway boy who bears the emotional and physical scars of his days in an orphanage. As the couple's attachment deepens, the boy's brutish keeper heads for Medicine Bow with the papers to take him back.

161.209 *A Love to Remember.* Oct. 29, 1969. GS: Diane Baker, Fred Beir, George Murdock. The usually stoic Virginian is swept into a romance with a lovely lady reporter from Boston. Complicating the affair is the lady's persistent meetings with merchant Ord Glover, an Easterner whom she vaguely associates with a tragedy in her past.

161.210 *The Substitute.* Nov. 5, 1969. GS: Dennis Cooney, Beverly McKinsey, Ken Lynch, Karl Swenson, Harry Cooper. Trampas' two-week vacation takes a nightmarish turn when the cowhand is jailed in a small town. The cards are viciously stacked against him. He is charged with murdering a beloved doctor, there is an eyewitness accuser, and a lynching mood is gaining ground.

161.211 *The Bugler.* Nov. 19, 1969. GS: Michael Burns, Morgan Woodward, Alan Hale, Jr. The divisive issue between a man and his son is the military. The father, a veteran officer, sends a search party for his son, an embittered youth who has deserted the Army and taken refuge at the Shiloh.

161.212 *Home to Methuselah.* Nov. 26, 1969. GS: Audrey Totter, John Anderson, Timothy Carey, Anthony Call, G.D. Spradlin. The Virginian joins veteran lawman Seth James on a hunting expedition, and finds himself involved in an obsessive search. The pair are deep in the Tetons when the foreman learns that James is hunting the two surviving members of an outlaw gang he has tracked for a year.

161.213 *A Touch of Hands.* Dec. 3, 1969. GS: Belinda Montgomery, Michael Constantine. Trampas becomes involved in a bittersweet romance with young Peg Halstead, whose father strongly opposes the match. As the relationship deepens, Halstead, an old farmer with a serious heart condition, steps up the pressure to stop it.

161.214 *Journey to Scathelock.* Dec. 10, 1969. GS: Burr DeBenning, Anne Helm, Frank Campanella, Lawrence Dane. In North Dakota to purchase ponies, young Jim Horn becomes the target for a pair of sharp operators who are carefully plotting the theft of his $4000 bank roll.

161.215 *A Woman of Stone.* Dec. 17, 1969. GS: Bethel Leslie, Charles Drake, Tim Holt. The Shiloh people unwittingly stir up the painful past when they give shelter to the son and white widow of a Shoshone chief. Complicating the situation is the fact that the woman has relatives living in Medicine Bow.

161.216 *Black Jade.* Dec. 31, 1969. GS: William Shatner, Jill Townsend, James A. Watson. Trampas takes a side trip into danger when he goes to High Time, a ghost town where black recluse Cobey Jade is the sole inhabitant. The two men form an alliance for survival when they are visited by a seedy outlaw gang, whose leader, a Southern gambler, is a vicious bigot.

161.217 You Can Lead a Horse to Water. Jan. 7, 1970. GS: Ellizabeth Hubbard, Strother Martin, Noah Beery, Jr. Mary Charles Marshall, a proper Southern lady, has come West to marry. The wedding must wait, however, while Mary, and helpers Trampas and old Luther, pursue stage robbers who made off with her dowry.

161.218 Nightmare. Jan. 21, 1970. GS: Joan Crawford, Steve Sandor, Warren Kemmerling, Michael Conrad, Rachel Rosenthal. Smoldering jealousies surface with the arrival of Stephanie White, new wife of a prominent Medicine Bow businessman. The lady faces deep, and dangerous, resentment from her husband's son, the housekeeper and a business associate.

161.219 The Shiloh Years. Jan. 28, 1970. GS: Anthony Franciosa, Harold J. Stone. The Graingers face disaster when Clay joins his fellow cattlemen in openly opposing an Eastern combine. Night raiders burn down the Shiloh ranch, leaving Clay one slim hope against total ruination — getting a herd to Denver in record time.

161.220 Train of Darkness. Feb. 4, 1970. GS: Dennis Weaver, Charlotte Stewart, Barbara Werle, John Larch, Gerald S. O'Loughlin, Kaz Garas, Patrick Tovatt. A train trip from Cheyenne to Medicine Bow holds unforeseen danger for travelers Clay, Elizabeth and Jim. A vengeful, gun-toting family is waiting in ambush to abduct a passenger, the person who killed their kinsman.

161.221 A Time of Terror. Feb. 11, 1970. GS: Joseph Cotten, Shelly Novack, Phillip Alford, Pamela Murphy, Virginia Gregg. Two young men and a girl turn the Shiloh ranch into an arena of terror. The trio is holding the Graingers at gunpoint while they set a trap for Judge Will McMasters, Clay's close friend.

161.222 No War for the Warrior. Feb. 18, 1970. GS: Henry Jones, Charles Robinson, Charles Aidman, David Sheiner, Patricia Hyland. A fugitive Indian is caught between his Kiowa heritage and the demands of a white world. The man signs on with a Shiloh cattle drive, inadvertently leading the wranglers to danger in a small, bigoted town.

161.223 A King's Ransom. Feb. 25, 1970. GS: Jackie DeShannon, Patrick Macnee, Don Knight, Michael Pate. Tragedy strikes the Shiloh when Clay Grainger is kidnaped by a ruthless gang from Australia. They're holding the cattleman in an abandoned mine and demanding $20,000 ransom.

161.224 The Sins of the Father. March 4, 1970. GS: Robert Lipton, Tim McIntire, William Lucking, Stuart Nisbet, Harper Flaherty, Bob Gravage. Mystery and fear surround the hiring of gunfighter Adam Randall as a Shiloh hand. Despite his trouble-making ways, Randall is backed by the Virginian, whose life he saved, and Clay Grainger, for an unrevealed reason.

161.225 Rich Man, Poor Man. March 11, 1970. GS: Jack Elam, Patricia Morrow, Michael Larrain, Tom Basham, Kenneth Tobey, Russell Thorson, Arthur Hanson, Robert Brubaker, Bud Walls. Harve Yost is a poor farmer who suddenly comes into money. His spending spree is getting out of hand as he gives large parties, amasses luxury items, and takes on a ranch hand too big for his experience and bank account.

161.226 The Gift. March 18, 1970. GS: Tab Hunter, Julie Gregg, Frank Marth, Walter Burke. A saloon singer may be the key to a Medicine Bow robbery and murder. The crime involves one clue and several people — Shiloh hands Trampas and Jim, a thief, the sheriff and a zealous railroad detective.

162. Wagon Train

NBC/ABC. 60/90 minutes. Broadcast history: Sept. 1957-Sept. 1962, Wednesday, 7:30-8:30 (NBC); Sept. 1962-Sept. 1963, Wednesday, 7:30-8:30 (ABC); Sept. 1963-Sept. 1964, Monday, 8:30-10:00 (ABC); Sept. 1964–Sept. 1965, Sunday, 7:30-8:30 (ABC).

Regular Cast: Ward Bond (Major Seth Adams) 57-61, Robert Horton (Flint McCullough) 57-62, Terry Wilson (Bill Hawks), Frank McGrath (Charlie Wooster), Scott Miller (Duke Shannon) 61-64, John McIntire (Christopher Hale) 61-65, Michael Burns (Barnaby West) 63-65, Robert Fuller (Cooper Smith) 63-65.

Premise: This series recounted the adventures of a group of pioneers traveling in covered wagons from the Midwest to California in the early 1870s. Wagonmaster Seth Adams and guide Flint McCullough lead the wagon train and its passengers through hostile Indian territory.

The Episodes

162.1 The Willy Moran Story. Sept. 18, 1957. GS: Ernest Borgnine, Marjorie Lord, Beverly Washburn, Andrew Duggan, Donald Randolph, Richard Hale, John Harmon. Seth Adams rescues a man from a street brawl and is surprised to find that he is Willy Moran, under whom Adams served in the Civil War. Moran, once a great fighter, is now an alcoholic, unable to fight or to earn an honest living. Adams offers Moran a job with the wagon train, but warns him to stay away from liquor during the trip. A widow traveling with the train is attracted to Moran and tries to help him. She is confident that Moran has conquered his craving for liquor, even though the others members of the wagon train try to tell her otherwise.

162.2 The Jean LeBec Story. Sept. 25, 1957. GS: Ricardo Montalban, Joanna Moore, Grant Withers, Bill Phipps. A young aristocrat from New Orleans is asked by a family friend to escort his daughter to San Francisco. LeBec and the girl join the wagon train.

162.3 The John Cameron Story. Oct. 2, 1957. GS: Carolyn Jones, Michael Rennie, Claude Akins, William Boyett, Henry Wills, Francis J. McDonald. John Cameron and his pretty young wife start the trek westward in hopes of beginning a new life. Cameron's wife Julie has promised to settle down and give up her flirtatious ways. But when the three Tacker brothers join the wagon train in Kansas City, Julie gives them her entire attention. Convinced that Cameron is a wealthy man, the three men decide to kidnap her and hold her for ransom.

162.4 The Ruth Owens Story. Oct. 9, 1957. GS: Shelley Winters, Dean Stockwell, Kent Smith. Ruth Owens, with her daughter and new husband, journeys in the wagon train, headed for California. Her brother, who overtakes the wagon train in search of her, overhears a derogatory remark about his sister, and in the ensuing fight, kills the man. Facing a murder charge, he refuses to defend himself when he learns the man's remark about his sister was true.

162.5 The Les Rand Story. Oct. 16, 1957. GS: Sterling Hayden. Les Rand is released from prison after serving seven years for murder. He returns to his small home town in the Midwest to avenge the death of his Indian bride. He believes that his father, the town's only doctor, is responsible for the tragedy. His arrival coincides with that of Flint McCullough, guide and scout of the wagon train, who has come for the doctor to attend a seriously injured member of the train's party.

162.6 *The Nels Stack Story.* Oct. 23, 1957. GS: Mark Stevens, Joanne Dru, Kevin Hagen, Charles Stevens, Irene Corlett, Dale Van Sickle. Nels Stack, on his way to California with the wagon train, is a quiet, unassuming man. But his mild manner leads the other travelers to call him a coward. He succeeds in antagonizing them even further by befriending an Indian.

162.7 *The Emily Rossiter Story.* Oct. 30, 1957. GS: Mercedes McCambridge, Susan Oliver, John Dehner, Bill Phipps, Robert McQueeney. When her husband is killed on the way to California, Emily Rossiter decides to remarry to provide a home for her daughter Judy. Her second husband is a ruthless leader of bandits who robs the wagon train of a California land deed.

162.8 *The John Darro Story.* Nov. 6, 1957. GS: Eddie Albert, Margo, Kim Charney, Edgar Buchanan, Don Durant. John and Aline Darro are on their way west in a wagon train with their son. The boy keeps singing a ballad about a legendary wagonmaster who refused to fight when his wagon was attacked by Indians. Darro and his wife are trying to keep part of Darro's past from their son, but a tramp whom Darro once knew during a similar Indian attack threatens to expose John Darro's secret to his son.

162.9 *The Charles Avery Story.* Nov. 13, 1957. GS: Farley Granger, Chuck Connors, Susan Kohner, Bing Russell, Mack Williams, Nico Minardos, Henry Brandon, Abel Fernandez. Charles Avery, an officer in the Union Army, is assigned to deliver a peace treaty to a formerly hostile Indian chief. Accompanying him are the chief's daughter and frontier scout Flint McCullough, whom wagonmaster Seth Adams has sent to insure the safe delivery of the treaty. But McCullough suspects that Avery's determination to reach the village involves more than the peace treaty.

162.10 *The Mary Halstead Story.* Nov. 20, 1957. GS: Agnes Moorehead, Tom Laughlin, Vaughn Taylor, Tom Pittman, Walter Coy, Gregg Palmer, Jack Lambert, Robert Patten, Terry Wilson, Frank McGrath. Mary Halstead is prodded by her guilty conscience to find the son she deserted years before. She joins the wagon train to search for him. On its way West, the train picks up a wounded young man who killed an outlaw leader in a skirmish with bandits.

162.11 *The Zeke Thomas Story.* Nov. 27, 1957. GS: Gary Merrill, Janice Rule, K.T. Stevens. Zeke Thomas and his wife Maggie are traveling with a wagon train which becomes stranded near a small western town. The town leaders are reluctant to furnish the train with water at a reasonable price. Zeke is also confronted with a startling problem when he sees in the saloon his first wife, whom he presumed died.

162.12 *The Riley Gratton Story.* Dec. 4, 1957. GS: Guy Madison, Karen Steele, Jeannie Carson, James Westerfield, Gregory Walcott, Gregg Palmer, Malcolm Atterbury. A con man sells worthless land to immigrants aboard the wagon train. Only after the handsome young man slips out of camp does wagonmaster Seth Adams realize what's happened, and he sets out to recover the money.

162.13 *The Clara Beauchamp Story.* Dec. 11, 1957. GS: Nina Foch, Shepperd Strudwick, Richard Garland, Robert Swan, Irene Windust, Ellen Hardies, Robert Roark, John Merrick, Monte Blue, Mike Ragan, Will White. The wife of a frontier-fort commander longs to be back among her Eastern society friends. Her husband, Col. Beauchamp, invites an Indian chief to the fort, hoping to avert a war with the tribe. His wife insults the chief, making war inevitable. Her plan is that her husband will win the battle so triumphantly that he will be sent back East for a promotion.

162.14 *The Julia Gage Story.* Dec. 18, 1957. GS: Anne Jeffreys, Robert Sterling, Don Megowan, Jimmie Komack, Esther Dale. An independent girl on the wagon train to California refuses to admit she needs a man's help to drive her wagon. Wagonmaster Seth Adams persuades a reluctant young man to volunteer.

162.15 *The Cliff Grundy Story.* Dec. 25, 1957. GS: Dan Duryea, Russell Johnson. When Cliff Grundy, traveling with the wagon train, is trampled by a buffalo and believed to be mortally injured, scout Clint McCullough volunteers to stay behind with the dying man. Another member of the train also volunteers to stay with Grundy in an attempt to learn the location of a gold mine.

162.16 *The Luke O'Malley Story.* Jan. 1, 1958. GS: Keenan Wynn, Cesar Romero, Mary Murphy, Reba Waters. A gambler, fleeing from a notorious Mexican bandit, disguises himself as a parson and joins the wagon train. He deceives Seth Adams for a while, but later his masquerade is discovered. In vain, he tries to convince the members of the train that he is not a member of the Mexican's band.

162.17 *The Jessie Cowan Story.* Jan. 8, 1958. GS: George Montgomery, James Burke, Olive Carey, Malcolm Atterbury, Clarence Straight. A Civil War veteran rides out after the wagon train to revenge himself on the people he holds responsible for the death of his parents.

162.18 *The Gabe Carswell Story.* Jan. 15, 1958. GS: James Whitmore, Scott Marlowe, Thomas B. Henry, Sondra Rodgers, Norman Willis. An old Indian scout and trapper gives all his affection to his half-Indian son, a bitter young man who hates all white men. The old man faces a difficult decision when his son wants to lead hostile Indians against the wagon train making its way through their territory.

162.19 *The Honorable Don Charlie Story.* Jan. 22, 1958. GS: Cesar Romero, Virginia Crane, Diane Brewster, Lela Bliss, Hal Baylor, Ray Kellogg, Ken Christy, Jack Lomas. During a stopover at Dobe Flats, Wagonmaster Seth Adams suspects trouble when a local Lothario focuses his attentions on Julie Wharton, a young lady traveling with the wagon train to San Francisco.

162.20 *The Dora Gray Story.* Jan. 29, 1958. GS: Linda Darnell, John Carradine, Dan Blocker. Flint McCullough runs across the ruins of a farmhouse which has been attacked by Indians. He learns that the inhabitants have been killed with bullets and not arrows and decides to scout ahead of the wagon train. Then he runs into a man named Doc who is traveling with a girl. He soon learns that Doc is the illegal gun runner he has been seeking.

162.21 *The Annie MacGregory Story.* Feb. 5, 1958. GS: Jeannie Carson, Richard Long, Tudor Owen, Kevin Hagen, Chet Stratton, Isaac Jones, William Lee, Maxwell Smith, Robert Stevens, Thurl Ravenscroft. A band of Scottish settlers

Wagon Train

traveling with the wagon train cause problems with the other members by playing their bagpipes and practicing their country's customs. A further conflict develops when the clan chief's daughter falls in love with an American settler also traveling west.

162.22 The Bill Tawnee Story. Feb. 12, 1958. GS: Macdonald Carey, Joy Page, Morgan Woodward, Dee Pollock, John Mitchum, Edith Evanson, Frank Cady. A Sioux Indian who fought in the Civil War is traveling west with the wagon train. The other members of the train are afraid of the Indian, and when wagonmaster Seth Adams defends his passenger, the settlers begin agitating to have a new wagonmaster.

162.23 The Mark Hanford Story. Feb. 26, 1958. GS: Tom Tryon, Onslow Stevens, Kathleen Crowley, I. Stanford Jolley, Paul Fix, Perry Ivins, Steven Ritch, Susan White, Frances Morris, Charles Stevens. Young Mark Hanford rides out to meet the wagon train, which is carrying a young woman who has come from the East to marry his father. Bitter at his father's betrayal of his dead Indian mother, the youth plans revenge.

162.24 The Bernal Sierra Story. March 12, 1958. GS: Gilbert Roland, Charlita Regis, Louis Jean Heydt, Dorothy Adams, Lane Bradford, James Dobson. Bernal Sierra, a follower of Juarez, joins the wagon train on his way West. He is searching for two thieves who murdered a guard and stole a large cache of gold needed for Juarez' fight for freedom. The Sierra recognizes the thieves among the passengers in the wagon train.

162.25 The Marie Dupree Story. March 19, 1958. GS: Debra Paget, Nick Adams, Robert Lowery, Raymond Greenleaf, Nicky Blair, Grazia Narcisco. A pretty girl traveling with the wagon train flirts with several of the men. When she turns her attentions to a young Sicilian immigrant, a tragedy seems imminent.

162.26 A Man Called Horse. March 26, 1958. GS: Ralph Meeker, Joan Taylor, Michael Pate, Anthony Numkena, Jorie Wyler, Jacqueline Mayo, Owen Cunningham. Seth Adams encounters a white man garbed in Indian's clothing who goes by the name of Horse. Seth is curious about the man's background, and his unusual story.

162.27 The Sarah Drummond Story. April 2, 1958. GS: June Lockhart, William Talman, Gene Evans, Debby Hengen, Claudia Drake. Flint McCullough seeks lodging in the home of Jeb and Sarah Drummond, and becomes involved in a bitter feud between the Drummonds and their bigoted neighbors.

162.28 The Sally Potter Story. April 9, 1958. GS: Jocelyn Brando, Lyle Bettger, Vanessa Brown, Brad Dexter, Johnny Crawford, Martin Milner, King Donovan, Larry Thor. Sally Potter, a newcomer to Seth Adams' wagon train causes a stir among the men. Joe Trumbull and his nephew Matt are taken with pretty Sally. But as the two men begin to fall in love with her, their regard for one another slowly turns to hate.

162.29 The Daniel Barrister Story. April 16, 1958. GS: Charles Bickford, Roger Smith, Peg Hillias, Allan Lane, Kay Cousins, Sarah Selby, Arthur Space, Anthony Lawrence. When Ralph Barrister's wife is critically injured in an accident, her husband will not allow any treatment for her except prayer. Finally, when the woman asks for a doctor, McCullough rides out to find one.

162.30 The Major Adams Story Part One. April 23, 1958. GS: Virginia Grey, Douglas Kennedy, Irene Windust, Ben Morris, Kay Stewart, Craig Duncan, Renny McEvoy, Bob Bryant. After many years, Seth meets his first love again when she joins his wagon train heading for Arizona. Seth and Ranie had been in love, but before they could be married, he left to fight in the Civil War. Believing that Seth had been killed, Ranie then married another.

162.31 The Major Adams Story Part Two. April 30, 1958. GS: Virginia Grey, Douglas Kennedy, Irene Windust, Ben Morris, Kay Stewart, Craig Duncan, Renny McEvoy, Bob Bryant. Learning that his sweetheart Ranie has married someone else during the Civil War, Seth Adams decides to become head of a wagon train. It is some years later that Ranie, now widowed, joins his wagon train and they are reunited. Seth is eager to begin his life again with Ranie, but she seems reluctant.

162.32 The Charles Maury Story. May 7, 1958. GS: Charles Drake, Wanda Hendrix, George Keymas, House Peters, Jr., Steve Rowland, Freida Inescort. Seth and Flint are worried about a possible attack from Maury's Marauders, a band of renegade Confederates who prey on unprotected wagon trains. When a group of Union soldiers offers to accompany the wagon train, Seth is only too glad to accept. But he soon becomes suspicious of their intentions. The leader is overly friendly with a woman passenger, who has already made known her dislike for Yankees.

162.33 The Dan Hogan Story. May 14, 1958. GS: Jock Mahoney, John Larch, Judith Ames, Richard Cutting, Tom Greenway. The wagon train stops in the town of Sweet Sabbath. Wagonmaster Seth Adams recognizes a man, Dan Hogan, as a fighter he once managed. Hogan has just turned down the job of deputy sheriff, as he refuses to wear a gun. Later, in a barroom brawl, he knocks down a bully, who later threatens his life.

162.34 The Ruttledge Munroe Story. May 21, 1958. GS: Jon Barrymore, Jr., Mala Powers, Jack Grinnage, William Tannen, Tom Monroe, George Eldredge, Helen Brown. Seth Adams takes young Ruttledge Munroe into the wagon train when he learns that the youth has lost his horse. After Munroe shoots down two men attempting to rob the train, he offers to give protection to young passenger Ruth Hadley and her baby. But Ruth is terrified of Munroe.

162.35 The Rex Montana Story. May 28, 1958. GS: James Dunn, Forrest Tucker, Kristine Miller, Joe Vitale, Maggie Mahoney, Peter Whitney, Butch Bernard, Myron Healey, Frank Scannell, Ralph Reed, Rodd Redwing. Western hero Rex Montana and his Wild West show join Seth Adams' wagon train. Montana has a reputation for bravery, but Seth and Flint soon have reason to suspect that Montana can't live up to his reputation.

162.36 The Cassie Tanner Story. June 4, 1958. GS: Marjorie Main, George Chandler, Harry Hines. Flint McCullough rescues tough, outspoken Cassie Tanner from an Indian attack while she is heading West alone. After her narrow escape Cassie decides to accept Flint's invitation to continue her journey with the wagon train. Once she sees Seth Adams, headstrong Cassie makes up her mind that he is the man for her.

162.37 The John Wilbot Story. June 11, 1958. GS: Dane Clark, Robert Vaughn, Audrey Dalton, Tyler McVey, Virginia Aldridge, Tharon Crigler, Roy Engel. In an attempt to settle an argument about who works harder, Flint McCullough and Seth

Adams temporarily switch jobs. During the trip. Flint has to appease the members of the wagon train when an ardent Abolitionist violently accuses a limping schoolmaster of being John Wilkes Booth, the assassin of Abraham Lincoln.

162.38 *The Monte Britton Story.* June 18, 1958. GS: Ray Danton, Mona Freeman. Seth Adams sends Flint McCullough ahead of the wagon train to find a water hole because the train's water supply is diminishing rapidly. When Adams finally catches up with Flint, he finds the young man delirious, and the water hole poisoned. The last hope is a nearby Army camp, but when Seth approaches the only man who knows the location of the camp, the man refuses to go for help.

162.39 *The Sacramento Story.* June 25, 1958. GS: Dan Duryea, Margaret O'Brien, Linda Darnell, Marjorie Main, Harry Stephens, Reed Hadley, George Chandler, Roscoe Ates. Major Adams, Flint McCullough and the wagon train reach their final destination, Sacramento, California. Flint accompanies ailing Maxwell Revere and his daughter Julie, who have traveled from the East to locate the ranch Revere bought several years ago and will now see for the first time. Flint discovers Revere has been victimized and that the land is a swamp. Rather than reveal this to Revere, Flint directs the dying man to an area of fertile land, and then seeks out the swindler.

Season Two

162.40 *Around the Horn.* Oct. 1, 1958. GS: William Bendix, Ernest Borgnine, Osa Massen, Sandy Descher, Marc Lawrence, Patrick Westwood, Harold Fong, Angela Greene, Gil Perkins, Ethel Shutta. Looking for a good time in San Francisco, Seth Adams, Wooster and Hawks are shanghaied aboard a schooner headed for New Orleans by way of South America. Also aboard ship, presided over by ruthless Captain Cobb, are his young daughter, Pat, and her pretty schoolteacher, Minnie Jellison.

162.41 *The Juan Ortega Story.* Oct. 8, 1958. GS: Dean Stockwell, Robert F. Simon, Robert Osterloh, Lillian Bronson, Paul Langton, Vic Perrin, Larry Blake. Adams and McCullough come across a Mexican youth, Juan Ortega, deep in shock after seeing his father lynched by three strangers. Taking the youth with them, they find a victim of Indian torture, near death, along the route of the wagon train. The boy's knowledge of native herbs saves the man's life. But Adams discovers this is one of the conspirators who murdered Juan's father.

162.42 *The Jennifer Churchill Story.* Oct. 15, 1958. GS: Rhonda Fleming, Andy Clyde, Eddy Waller, Paul Maxey. Beautiful Jennifer Churchill joins Seth Adams' wagon train to run away from her father and escape a marriage that she doesn't want. When Flint McCullough discovers that the girl's father has offered a large reward for her return, Flint tries to help her escape, knowing that she will be prey to bounty hunters.

162.43 *The Tobias Jones Story.* Oct. 22, 1958. GS: Lou Costello, Beverly Washburn, Harry Von Zell, June Clayworth, Peter Breck, Morris Ankrum. Midge, a young orphan girl, appoints herself as guardian to Tobias Jones, a homeless drifter. Together they stow away on Seth Adams' wagon train. Seth discovers the pair and puts them to work to earn their way during the trip. But the other passengers are distrustful of Tobias, and their suspicions seem confirmed when one of the passengers is found murdered with Tobias Jones's knife.

162.44 *The Liam Fitzmorgan Story.* Oct. 28, 1958. GS: Cliff Robertson, Audrey Dalton, Rhys Williams, David Leland, Terence DeMarney, Sean Meaney, Michael Rye, Reggie Dvorak. Liam Fitzmorgan has been ordered by Ireland's freedom fighters to find a traitor who caused the execution of several of their followers. Liam gets a tip that the man he is looking for is a member of Seth Adams' wagon train, so he joins the train. A group of Irish settlers already with the train become very suspicious of the newcomer.

162.45 *The Doctor Willoughby Story.* Nov. 5, 1958. GS: Jane Wyman, Alan Marshal, Orville Sherman, Tony Rock, Ethel Shutta, Dick Wilson. To carry out her assignment to practice medicine in a Western town, Dr. Carol Willoughby joins Seth Adams' wagon train. During the trip a badly injured Indian chief is brought to the doctor, and she must save his life or his tribe will attack the wagon train.

162.46 *The Bije Wilcox Story.* Nov. 19, 1958. GS: Chill Wills, Onslow Stevens, Lawrence Dobkin, Abraham Sofaer, Chuck Roberson, Richard Evans. Francis Mason joins the wagon train in an effort to locate his long-missing brother. He tells Seth Adams that a man named Bije Wilcox has written him, telling him he has information as to his brother's whereabouts. Mason is to meet Wilcox at the end of the trip.

162.47 *The Millie Davis Story.* Nov. 26, 1958. GS: Nancy Gates, Evelyn Rudie, Eleanor Audley, Whit Bissell, Irving Bacon, Chubby Johnson, Harry Hines, Amzie Strickland, James Coburn. While passing through a town ahead of the wagon train, Flint McCullough sees his friends Millie Davis and Penny, whom Millie adopted and raised from infancy. Later a stagecoach arrives in the town with a woman aboard who claims that she is Penny's maternal grandmother. Afraid that the woman will take Penny away from her, Millie tells her that she and Flint are the parents of the little girl.

162.48 *The Sakae Ito Story.* Dec. 3, 1958. GS: Sessue Hayakawa, Robert Kino, James Griffith, Jack Lambert, Henry Rowland, Dennis Moore, Steven Ritch. Seth Adams finds two Japanese along the trail, a Samurai warrior and his servant. They are on their way to San Francisco, carrying a large urn with them. Suspecting that the urn contains gold, three men steal it and run away.

162.49 *The Tent City Story.* Dec. 10, 1958. GS: Wayne Morris, Audrey Totter, Slim Pickens, Dennis McCarthy, Yvonne White, Juney Ellis, Peter Coe, Bill Henry, Earl Hansen, Carol Henry. Adams and McCullough argue about a member of the wagon train who shot a buffalo while passing through Indian hunting grounds. Flint disapproves of Seth's action in placing the hunter in chains, and McCullough leaves the train. Later, when the wagon train pull into Tent City, Seth learns that Flint is the new town marshal.

162.50 *The Beauty Jamison Story.* Dec. 17, 1958. GS: Virginia Mayo, Russell Johnson, Ken Mayer, Frank Gerstle, Phil Chambers, Charles Tannen, May Lee, Pete Dunn, Jim Bannon. A woman ranch-owner controls the largest land area in the territory, and is attempting to wrest land from all the surrounding smaller ranchers as well. She refuses McCullough permission to let the wagon train cross her land, claiming that he is sympathetic to the ranchers who are stubbornly holding out against her.

162.51 *The Mary Ellen Thomas Story.* Dec. 24, 1958. GS: Patty McCormack, Jenny Hecht, Claudia Bryar, Dick

Wagon Train

Cutting, Vernon Rich, Barbara Pepper, Clifford Botelho. Mary Ellen Thomas, an orphan girl who is traveling west to join distant relatives, is rejected by Wagon Train members because of her unhappy disposition. Sally Mayhew, a girl of Mary Ellen's age who is fatally ill with consumption, finally makes friends with the lonely young girl.

162.52 *The Dick Richardson Story.* Dec. 31, 1958. GS: John Ericson, Lyle Talbot, Betty Lynn, Aline Towne, Dennis Holmes, Daniel White, Jack Lomas, Jeanne Bates, Ethel Shutta. Seth Adams entrusts Richardson with money from an emergency fund. Richardson is to ride on to the next town to replace the wagon train horses wiped out by disease. Adams has reason to regret giving Richardson the money, however, when his companions riderless horse returns to the train.

162.53 *The Kitty Angel Story.* Jan. 7, 1959. GS: Anne Baxter, Henry Hull, Vivi Janiss, Kathleen Freeman, Ben Morris, David Leland, Ethel Shutta, Steve Warren, Abel Fernandez. Kitty Angel, a woman of questionable character, is ostracized by the indignant wives of the men traveling with the wagon train. But Kitty is the only one who has the compassion to befriend an orphaned Indian baby. When the infant contracts smallpox, members of the wagon train put pressure on Major Adams to leave Kitty and the child behind to avoid an epidemic.

162.54 *The Flint McCullough Story.* Jan. 14, 1959. GS: Everett Sloane, Rebecca Welles, Charles Cooper, Theodore Newton, Milton Frome, Logan Field, Buzz Martin, Joel Ashley. Riding ahead of the wagon train, scout Flint McCullough arrives at Fort Bridger, which is home town to him. His homecoming, however, is spoiled when he learns that Jase Taylor, a former Confederate colonel, is living at the fort. McCullough had once sworn to kill the colonel.

162.55 *The Hunter Malloy Story.* Jan. 21, 1959. GS: Lloyd Nolan, Terence de Marney, Luana Patten, Troy Donahue, Theodore Newton, Bill Erwin, Joseph Abdullah. While with the wagon train, Hunter Malloy and his partner devise a plan to rob a young married couple of their life savings. But before they can commit the theft, Malloy discovers gold along the wagon train trail. Set Adams warns his passengers that they must move on before they are trapped by snow storms, but no one will heed Adams' warning.

162.56 *The Ben Courtney Story.* Jan. 28, 1959. GS: Stephen McNally, Kay Stewart, John Larch, Darryl Glenn, Roger Mobley, Phillip Pine, Judith Ames, Richard Hale, Arthur Space, Tom McKee. Flint McCullough escorts two families from the wagon train to Bitter Springs, a small settlement. One family includes two adopted children, one of them a young Negro boy named Daniel. At Bitter Springs, the sheriff refuses to let them join the settlement unless they give up Daniel.

162.57 *The Ella Lindstrom Story.* Feb. 4, 1959. GS: Bette Davis, Cindy Robbins, Robert Fuller, Alex Gerry, Norman Leavitt, Harold Daye, Terry Kelman, Susan Henning, Jamie Matt, Terry Burnham, Bobby Buntrock. En route to California, Ella Lindstrom's husband dies, leaving her to care for their seven children, one of them a deaf-mute. She must decide whether to continue the journey.

162.58 *The Last Man.* Feb. 11, 1959. GS: Dan Duryea, Judi Meredith, Damian O'Flynn, Wilton Graff. Scout Flint McCullough finds a tattered stranger along the trail. A diary found among the debris of an earlier wagon train indicates that the stranger's survival cost the lives of other travelers. Distrusted by everyone else, the stranger is befriended by Ellen Emerson, who fiance was on the ill-fated wagon train.

162.59 *The Old Man Charvanaugh Story.* Feb. 18, 1959. GS: J. Carrol Naish, Dorothy Green, Bernadette Withers, Ricky Klein, L.Q. Jones, Jeff Daley, Mickey Finn, Quentin Sondergaard. Posing as a concertina-playing wanderer, old man Charvanaugh forces his company on Helen Lerner and her two children while they are being escorted by Flint McCullough to a settlement off the wagon-train trail.

162.60 *The Annie Griffith Story.* Feb. 25, 1959. GS: Jan Sterling, John Dehner, Clem Bevans, Robert Anderson. Guest Looking for a pass in the snow-covered mountains, Flint McCullough is ambushed and badly wounded by some Indians. A rugged, unkempt woman finds Flint and nurses him back to health. After Flint is well enough to travel, the woman tells him that she is going to turn him over to the Indians in hope that they will help her get back to civilization.

162.61 *The Jasper Cato Story.* March 4, 1959. GS: Brian Donlevy, Allen Case. Bostonian Joseph Cato joins Maj. Seth Adams' wagon train. Adams becomes suspicious when he discovers that the stranger is anxious to find Jim Collins, a small-town newspaper editor and friend of the Major's. Adams tries to reach Collins before Cato can.

162.62 *The Vivian Carter Story.* March 11, 1959. GS: Lorne Greene, Phyllis Thaxter, Patric Knowles, Jane Darwell. Vivian Carter is traveling with the wagon train to join her fiance in a small Western town. Although she is engaged, another traveler falls in love with her.

162.63 *The Conchita Vasquez Story.* March 18, 1959. GS: Anna Maria Alberghetti, Carlos Romero, Joyce Meadows, William Lundmark, Alan Reynolds, John Goddard. Conchita Vasquez, a Spanish-Indian girl, lures scout Flint McCullough into a trap so that her people can capture him and hold him for ransom. But after Flint's capture, Conchita decides to help him escape

162.64 *The Sister Rita Story.* March 25, 1959. GS: Vera Miles, Sylvia Marritt, Frances Bavier, Lalo Rios. On their way to Nevada to start an Indian mission school, three nuns are aided by Flint McCullough. They find the ways of the scout quite strange. McCullough finds the nuns equally strange to him, but an unusual camaraderie develops as they move west.

162.65 *The Matthew Lowry Story.* April 1, 1959. GS: Richard Anderson, Cathleen Nesbitt, John Pickard, Ronny Anton, Dorothy Provine. Matthew Lowry, a Quaker who has only one arm, is constantly ridiculed by Jed Otis. Because of Matthew's pacifist beliefs, he is suspected of cowardice by his young brother.

162.66 *The Swift Cloud Story.* April 8, 1959. GS: Rafael Campos, Johnny Washbrook, Henry Brandon, Lee Papel, Alan Baxter, Otto Waldis, Edmund Hashim. During an Indian attack on the wagon train, Maj. Seth Adams spares the life of Swift Cloud, crippled son of the Indian chief. Adams is shocked to learn that Swift Cloud's condition is a result of a vicious assault by a half-breed.

162.67 *The Vincent Eaglewood Story.* April 15, 1959. GS: Wally Cox, Gail Kobe, Read Morgan, Guinn Williams, Robert Eyer, Karen Sue Trent, Mary Gregory, Felix Locher, William Riggs. Hired as the schoolteacher for the children traveling with the wagon train, meek Vincent Eaglewood takes his job very seriously. So seriously, in fact, that he worries Major Adams. Eaglewood takes his pupils away from the wagon train on nature hikes, and Adams knows that there are hostile Indians roaming the territory.

162.68 *The Clara Duncan Story.* April 22, 1959. GS: Angie Dickinson, Eduardo Ciannelli, William Reynolds, Robert Clarke, Myron Healey, Rusty Lane, Robert Easton. The fiancee and the father of Claude Soriano, a missing artist, are on their was West to find him. Scout Flint McCullough and a newspaperman discover a painting by Soriano which leads them to believe that the artist's life is in danger.

162.69 *The Duke LeMay Story.* April 29, 1959. GS: Cameron Mitchell, Edward C. Platt, Joan Evans, Terry Kelman. Duke LeMay, an escaped convict, joins the wagon train in an effort to escape from justice. But he is trailed by a deputy sheriff from the East. Frightened when the sheriff rides up, LeMay shoots him and then flees from the wagon train.

162.70 *The Kate Parker Story.* May 6, 1959. GS: Robert Fuller, Virginia Grey, Warren Stevens, Royal Dano, Ruta Lee. While traveling with the wagon train, young Evie Finley is seriously injured. Kate Parker offers to stay behind with Evie and Evie's husband while the wagon train goes to the next town for a doctor. After the wagon train leaves, Kate's husband Jonas decides to kill Kate and the Finleys and steal the gold that his wife has been carrying during the trip.

162.71 *The Steve Campden Story.* May 13, 1959. GS: Ben Cooper, Torin Thatcher. An early snow blocks the advance of the wagon train. Scout Flint McCullough meets Steve Camden and his son, and the three of them decide to climb a peak and look for an open passage. During the ascent they are forced to seek refuge in a cave.

162.72 *Chuck Wooster, Wagonmaster.* May 20, 1959. GS: Douglas Kennedy, Harry Carey, Jr., Jean Inness. After the wagon train is halted by a raging blizzard, Maj. Seth Adams, scout Flint McCullough and several others mysteriously disappear. Chuck Wooster, the train's cook, takes charge in an effort to lead the rest of the group to safety.

162.73 *The Jose Maria Moran Story.* May 27, 1959. GS: Robert Loggia, Audrey Dalton, Kim Laughlin, Tudor Owen. The wagon train comes upon a man staked out and left to die by the Shoshone Indians. Maj. Seth Adams learns that he is Jose Maria Moran, a Spanish-Irish renegade who has lived with the Pawnees for some years. Then the Shoshones discover that he has been saved and the threaten to attack the caravan unless Moran is turned over to them.

162.74 *The Andrew Hale Story.* June 3, 1959. GS: John McIntire, Jane Darwell, James Best, Louise Fletcher, Fintan Meyler, Jack Beutel, Clu Gulager. In a shooting accident, preacher Andrew Hale kills one of his church members. Dazed by the incident, Hale disappears into the desert where he is found by the wagon train.

162.75 *The Rodney Lawrence Story.* June 10, 1959. GS: Dean Stockwell, Frank de Kova, Cindy Robbins. The wagon train comes upon a band of wandering Indians, among whom is a young white man they have raised from childhood. Ocheo, the boy's foster father, sees an opportunity for the young man to return to his own way of life and urges him to join the wagon train.

162.76 *The Steele Family.* June 17, 1959. GS: Lee Patrick, Lori Nelson, Barbara Eiler, Dan Tobin. The mother of four marriageable daughters decides it's time to find husbands for the girls. She gets Major Seth Adams to point out some likely prospects.

162.77 *The Jenny Tannen Story.* June 24, 1959. GS: Ann Blyth, Chuck Henderson, William Hunt, Jean Harvey. Young Phoebe Tannen joins the wagon train in order to go to San Francisco to locate her mother. During the journey she has an accident and is threatened with blindness. Maj. Seth Adams promises to help Phoebe find her mother when they arrive.

Season Three

162.78 *The Stagecoach Story.* Sept. 30, 1959. GS: Debra Paget, Clu Gulager, Abraham Sofaer, Lalo Rios. After a gala night in San Francisco, Maj. Seth Adams and his friends Wooster and Hawks buy stagecoach tickets to return to St. Louis. They are dismayed to learn that their driver will be none other than scout Flint McCullough, but the appearance of a lovely Mexican dancer on the coach brightens their spirits.

162.79 *The Greenhorn Story.* Oct. 7, 1959. GS: Mickey Rooney, Ellen Corby, Daria Massey, Byron Foulger, Jerry Hauser, James Burke, Ronnie Dapo. Samuel T. Evans, a young man from the East, signs up to travel with Maj. Seth Adams' wagon train. At first Seth is amused at the young man's obvious naivete. But later he grows concerned and is moved to caution.

162.80 *The C.L. Harding Story.* Oct. 14, 1959. GS: Claire Trevor, Amzie Strickland, Theodore Newton. A woman newspaper reporter is assigned to travel with Seth Adams' wagon train. Once aboard the train, the reporter begins a women's suffrage movement among the wives.

162.81 *The Estaban Zamora Story.* Oct. 21, 1959. GS: Ernest Borgnine, Leonard Nimoy, Phillip Pine, Robert Armstrong, Stuart Randall, James Griffith, David McMahon, Jeanne Bates. Immigrant Estaban Zamora joins Seth Adams' wagon train to travel West, where his three sons are working for a sheep farmer. Upon his arrival, he discovers that his youngest son was killed and he vows revenge.

162.82 *The Elizabeth McQueeney Story.* Oct. 28, 1959. GS: Bette Davis, Maggie Pierce, Robert Strauss, Barney Biro, Lynn Bernay, Meg Wyllie, Danielle Aubrey, Marjorie Bennett, Joseph Mell, Phil Arnold. Elizabeth McQueeney joins Seth Adams' wagon train with a group of lovely young girls as her charges. She tells the people of the train that she is taking the girls west to begin a finishing school.

162.83 *The Martha Barham Story.* Nov. 4, 1959. GS: Ann Blyth, Dayton Lummis, Read Morgan, Mike Road, Henry Brandon, Warren Oates, Larry Blake, John Damler. Flint McCullough arrives at an Army fort with a Sioux companion, and the daughter of the fort's commander accuses Flint of being a renegade. Then the girl's fiance is captured by Indians, and she asks McCullough to help her rescue him.

162.84 *The Cappy Darrin Story.* Nov. 11, 1959. GS: Ed Wynn, Tommy Nolan, Rodd Redwing, Robert Burton, Tyler McVey, Bill Foster. Cappy Darrin, an elderly riverboat captain, joins the wagon train with his grandson Tuck Hardy. As the wagon train nears Cappy's destination, he and the boy decide to leave the train and strike out on their own for California.

162.85 *The Felizia Kingdom Story.* Nov. 18, 1959. GS: Dame Judith Anderson, Larry Perron. Scout Flint McCullough goes to the ranch of Felezia Kingdom to ask permission for the

Wagon Train

wagon train to cross her land. McCullough disarms a ranch hand who holds a gun on him but is taken captive by the strong willed woman.

162.86 *The Jess MacAbbee Story.* Nov. 25, 1959. GS: Andy Devine, Glenda Farrell, Carol Byron, Karen Green, Terry Burnham, Tammy Marihugh, Ray Teal, Bill St. John. Flint McCullough comes upon the ranch home of Jess MacAbbee, who appears to be trying to hid something. McCullough discovers that MacAbee has five beautiful daughters he doesn't want the scout to know about.

162.87 *The Danny Benedict Story.* Dec. 2, 1959. GS: Brandon de Wilde, Onslow Stevens, Walter Reed, Melinda Plowman, Herbert Lytton. Young Danny Benedict is unhappy with the strict military life his father, Col. Daniel Benedict, has planned for him. After his father threatens to punish the boy in public, Danny runs away.

162.88 *The Vittorio Bottecelli Story.* Dec. 16, 1959. GS: Gustavo Rojo, Elizabeth Montgomery, Anthony Caruso. Italian Duke Vittorio Bottecelli attempts to charm some of the wagon train's married women. Major Seth Adams warns the duke to stop his romancing before some angry husband comes after him.

162.89 *The St. Nicholas Story.* Dec. 23, 1959. GS: Edward Vargas, Robert Emhardt, Johnny Bangert, Elizabeth Fraser, J.M. Kerrigan, Fintan Meyler, Sue Randall, Henry Brandon, Vito Scotti, Kay Stewart, Richard Cutting. On Christmas Eve, the wagon train stops to make camp. Young Jimmy Sherman wanders away from the train and meets Little Eagle, an Indian boy.

162.90 *The Ruth Marshall Story.* Dec. 30, 1959. GS: Luana Patten, Mike Keene, Fred Sherman, Bob Bice, Sam Capuano. Scout Flint McCullough agrees to search for a girl who was captured by Indians many years ago.

162.91 *The Lita Foladaire Story.* Jan. 6, 1960. GS: Diane Brewster, Tom Drake, Kent Smith, Richard Crane, Evelyn Brent, Jay Novello, Paul Birch, Lurene Tuttle. Along the wagon trail, Maj. Seth Adams finds a woman unconscious and near death. He discovers that she is the wife of his friend Jess Foladaire. The girl dies, and Adams sets out to hunt down the person responsible.

162.92 *The Colonel Harris Story.* Jan. 13, 1960. GS: John Howard, James Best, Nestor Paiva, Ken Mayer, Irene Windust, Jacqueline DeWitt. On his way to Fort Harris, Scout Flint McCullough is eagerly anticipating a visit with some old friends. Arriving at the fort, he is distressed to learn that his two closes friends are on the verge of starting a senseless war with one another.

162.93 *The Marie Brant Story.* Jan. 20, 1960. GS: Jean Hagen, Edward Platt, Richard Eyer, Claudia Bryant, Ronnie Sorensen, Johnny Eimen. Wagon train passenger Orobio Da Costa meets a beautiful widow who apparently distrusts all men and has taught her teen-age son to hold the weak and helpless in contempt. Da Costa attempts to learn why the woman is so bitter.

162.94 *The Larry Hanify Story.* Jan. 27, 1960. GS: Tommy Sands, Gene Roth, Cindy Robbins, Wally Moon, Orville Sherman, Olan Soule, Edith Evanson, Dan Riss, Joseph Mell. Before he dies, Joe Hanify asks Flint McCullough to take care of his son Larry. McCullough agrees, though he is warned that Larry is a liar and a thief.

162.95 *The Clayton Tucker Story.* Feb. 10, 1960. GS: Jeff Morrow, James Best, Dorothy Breen, Louis Jean Heydt, Aline Towne, Bobby Beekman, Robert Hensley, Dwight Marfield, Terry Ann Ross. A small party of travelers are making their way through the desert to a rendezvous with Seth Adams' wagon train. When their scout dies from a snake bite, the party must rely on one of their own group to lead them over the right trail.

162.96 *The Benjamin Burns Story.* Feb. 17, 1960. GS: James Franciscus, J. Carrol Naish, Olive Sturgess, Jack Lambert. A dried-up river leaves the wagon train short of water, so Flint McCullough takes a party on a search for a legendary mountain spring. The men soon return with the news that their guide, mountaineer Benjamin Burns, has been killed.

162.97 *The Ricky and Laura Bell Story.* Feb. 24, 1960. GS: June Lockhart, James Gregory, Ann Doran, Theodore Newton. Ricky Bell is moving West with his family to seek a new life. It becomes obvious that Ricky is jealous of the attention his wife showers on their infant son.

162.98 *The Tom Tuckett Story.* March 2, 1960. GS: Robert Middleton, Ben Cooper, Josephine Hutchinson, Louise Fletcher, Don Keefer, Frank DeKova, Ralph Moody, Frank Wilcox. A hunted traitor risks capture to see a youth who once helped him escape.

162.99 *The Tracy Sadler Story.* March 9, 1960. GS: Elisha Cook, Jr., Elaine Stritch, Carl Benton Reid, Eugene Martin, Ted Mapes, Butch Hengen. Tracy's son was born while she was in prison. Searching for him after her release, she learns he may be with the wagon train.

162.100 *The Alexander Portlass Story.* March 16, 1960. GS: Peter Lorre, Morgan Woodward, Sherwood Price, Bern Hoffman. An English archaeologist, searching for Aztec treasure, teams up with an outlaw gang. Needing a guide through the desert, they kidnap Flint McCullough.

162.101 *The Christine Elliot Story.* March 23, 1960. GS: Henry Daniell, Phyllis Thaxter, Donald Woods, Kathryn Card, Harry Harvey, Sr., Don Grady, Todd Farrell, Scotty Morrow, Anthony Maxwell. Slated for an orphanage, a dozen boys run off from a state agency to join the wagon train. Christine is willing to help them escape, but an agency man is in close pursuit.

162.102 *The Joshua Gilliam Story.* March 30, 1960. GS: Dan Duryea, Bethel Leslie, Irene Tedrow, Betsy Brooks, Pitt Herbert. On the trail, Adams finds Joshua Gilliam, who's been beaten and left for dead. Joshua, a con man, smells a new opportunity. He offers to be schoolteacher in return for passage.

162.103 *The Maggie Hamilton Story.* April 6, 1960. GS: Susan Oliver, Les Tremayne, Sylvia Marriott, Orville Sherman, Frank Wolff, Leonard Nimoy. A spoiled young lady, a passenger on the wagon train, runs off and hides in the nearby hills. She plans on sulking until someone comes to find her.

162.104 *The Jonas Murdock Story.* April 13, 1960. GS: Noah Beery, Jr., Joseph Barnett, Bernadette Withers, Lyle Talbot, Gail Bonney. Jonas is a rabbit-hunting mountain man who gets the wagon trainers into a stew by defying the no-hunting edict of a local Indian chief.

162.105 *The Amos Gibbon Story.* April 20, 1960. GS: Arthur Shields, Francis J. McDonald, Charles Aidman, Bob Hopkins, William Schallert, John Ashley, Darlene Fields, Mickey Finn. Amos Gibbon and his men have been taking prisoners wholesale and forcing them into slave labor. But they've got the wrong man when they capture Flint McCullough. He tries to talk his fellow prisoners into escaping.

162.106 *Trial for Murder* **Part One.** April 27, 1960. GS: Henry Daniell, Henry Hull, Marshall Thompson, Dianne Foster, Melinda Plowman, Murvyn Vye, Connie Gilchrist, John Locke, Claire Carleton, William Schallert, Ethel Shutta. A member of the wagon train has been clubbed to death, and overwhelming evidence points to the guilt of Brad Mason, a surly, friendless drunkard.

162.107 *Trial for Murder* **Part Two.** May 4, 1960. GS: Henry Daniell, Henry Hull, Marshall Thompson, Dianne Foster, Melinda Plowman, Murvyn Vye, Connie Gilchrist, John Locke, Claire Carleton, William Schallert, Ethel Shutta. When Brad Mason was accused of murder, many wanted to lynch him. But Seth Adams insisted on a trail. Then Mason blurted out a confession and his conviction seemed certain. Now the defense counsel produces a surprise witness, the dead man's wife.

162.108 *The Countess Baranof Story.* May 11, 1960. GS: Taina Elg, Simon Oakland, Peter Leeds, Ann B. Davis, Roy Engel, Ethel Shutta. The wagon train is too slow for the Countess Baranof, who is in a hurry to reach Alaska before its rumored sale to the United States. She urges Flint McCullough to desert and guide her over a swifter route.

162.109 *The Dick Jarvis Story.* May 18, 1960. GS: Tommy Nolan, Vivi Janiss, Bobby Diamond, Richard Reeves, Vaughn Meadows. Seth Adams takes a kindly interest in Dick, who is fatherless and crippled. Then a runaway orphan youth joins the train, and Dick feels his friendship with Adams is threatened.

162.110 *The Dr. Swift Cloud Story.* May 25, 1960. GS: Rafael Campos, Phillip Pine, Brad Morrow, Henry Brandon, Francis MacDonald, Dabbs Greer. Swift Cloud comes home from medical school to discover his tribesmen attacking the wagon train. The travelers refuse to accept his medical aid, and his own people think he's a traitor.

162.111 *The Luke Grant Story.* June 1, 1960. GS: Donald Woods, Joan O'Brien, James Bell, Marlene Willis, Kay Elhardt, Wende Wagner, Rodd Redwing. A tribe of friendly Mojaves find Luke Grant in the desert and bring him to the wagon train. A singer recognizes the dying man as a minister she once knew.

162.112 *The Charlene Brenton Story.* June 8, 1960. GS: Sean McClory, Jean Willes, Raymond Bailey, Harry Harvey, Sr. A stage coach arrives in Apache Flats. Its only passengers are a dead woman and her infant daughter, still very much alive.

162.113 *The Sam Livingston Story.* June 15, 1960. GS: Charles Drake, Onslow Stevens, Barbara Eiler, James Lydon, Anna-Lisa. Sam Livingston arrives in Carson City with his pet pig, a fortune in gold and a plot for revenge. He's out to get the town banker, once his partner in a mining claim.

162.114 *The Shad Bennington Story.* June 22, 1960. GS: David Wayne, Maggie Pierce, Charles Herbert, Laurie Mitchell, Claire Carleton, Steven Darrell, Henry Hunter. On the last lap of a cross country trip, an itinerant medicine man joins the wagon train. In his wagon is a remarkable traveling companion, a performing lion.

Season Four

162.115 *Wagons Ho!* Sept. 28, 1960. GS: Mickey Rooney, Ellen Corby, Olive Sturgess. As Adams and Flint prepare to leave San Francisco on their way back to Missouri, they meet newsman Sam Evans, who made the trip west with them the year before.

162.116 *The Horace Best Story.* Oct. 5, 1960. GS: George Gobel, Ken Curtis, Joe Flynn, Otto Waldis, Allen Jenkins, Mary Field. Horace Best is Major Adams' distant cousin, but it seems like he just isn't cut from the same sturdy stock. But he wants to learn to be a wagon master anyway.

162.117 *The Albert Farnsworth Story.* Oct. 12, 1960. GS: Charles Laughton, James Fairfax, Terence De Marney, Kathleen O'Malley, Gina Gillespie, Robert Brown, Orville Sherman, Quentin Sondergaard, Jan Arvan. Colonel Farnsworth is a British Army surgeon traveling with the wagon train. He's convinced that the British way of life is the only way.

162.118 *The Allison Justis Story.* Oct. 19, 1960. GS: Gloria De Haven, Michael Burns, Edward G. Robinson, Jr., Gregg Stewart, Ken Hooker, Dan Tobin. Flint guns down a horse thief named Justis. Then he learns that his victim was the husband of one of his old girl friends.

162.119 *The Jose Morales Story.* Oct. 26, 1960. GS: Lee Marvin, Lon Chaney, Jr., Clark Howat, Aline Towne, Charles Herbert, Stevan Darrell, Gregg Palmer. Three wagons, with Hawks in charge, are crossing Sioux territory. There's no trouble from Indians, but quite a bit from Jose Morales and his Mexican bandidos.

162.120 *Princess of a Lost Tribe.* Nov. 2, 1960. GS: Linda Lawson, Raymond Massey, Ed Mallory, Raymond Greenleaf, Frank Jenks, Chet Stratton. The tribesmen are descendants of the Aztecs, and they live in a hidden city, ruled by a namesake of the fabulous Montezuma. Flint McCullough and his companions, when they discover the city, are told they aren't prisoners, they just can't leave.

162.121 *The Cathy Eckhardt Story.* Nov. 9, 1960. GS: Susan Oliver, Martin Landau, Ron Hayes, Vivi Janiss, John Larch, Gregg Walcott, Brad Johnson, Claire Carleton. Adams is planning to skirt a certain pass where several wagon trains have recently been attacked by Indians. But four alternate routes appear to be equally dangerous.

162.122 *The Bleymier Story.* Nov. 16, 1960. GS: Dan Duryea, Ellen Willard, James Drury, John McLiam, Juney Ellis, David McMahon. Flint and a small party of settlers on the way to Dakota homesteads are bogged down by torrential rains. Samuel Bleymier says that the raging skies are an omen of catastrophe.

162.123 *The Colter Craven Story.* Nov. 23, 1960. GS: John Carradine, Carleton Young, Anna Lee, Paul Birch, John Wayne, Ken Curtis, Jack Pennock, Hank Worden, Charles Seel, Willis Bouchey, Cliff Lyons. Major Adams and the train come across the disabled wagon of Dr. Colter Craven and his wife. Though Craven appears to be an alcoholic, Adams decides to give him a chance to become a useful member of the westbound party.

162.124 *The Jane Hawkins Story.* Nov. 30, 1960. GS: Myrna Fahey, Edgar Buchanan, Kathie Browne, Sherwood Price, Whit Bissell, Kay Stewart, Nestor Paiva. Jane Hawkins is shot by Jesse, a hired gun for town dictator Ben Mattox.

162.125 *The Candy O'Hara Story.* Dec. 7, 1960. GS: Teddy Rooney, Jim Davis, Joan O'Brien, Edith Evanson,

Wagon Train

Richard Cutting, Fred Sherman, Robert Lowery, Lane Bradford. Recently a widower, Gabe Henry is eager to remarry and provide a mother for his boy Luther. Gabe can't find anyone to suit him, but little Luther can. He spots Candy O'Hara on the streets of Aurora.

162.126 *The River Crossing.* Dec. 14, 1960. GS: Michael Keep, Charles Aidman, X Brands, Robert J. Wilke, Ron Harper, Marshall Reed, Claudia Bryar, Colette Jackson, Allen Jaffe. The wagon train comes up against a dangerously swollen river, but that's only half of the problem. The party is also threatened by Comanches.

162.127 *The Roger Bigelow Story.* Dec. 21, 1960. GS: Robert Vaughn, Audrey Dalton, Claude Akins, Ronnie Rondell. Clergyman Roger Bigelow is on his way to California with his bride Nancy and his life savings, intent on establishing a new church. The wagon encounters wounded bandit Wes Varney, and the Bigelows offer his refuge and medical attention, despite Adams' warning that he is dangerous.

162.128 *The Jeremy Dow Story.* Dec. 28, 1960. GS: Leslie Nielsen, James Lydon, Michael Burns, Mari Aldon, Morgan Woodward, John War Eagle, Dal McKennon. Drifter Jeff Durant is hired to drive the Millikans' wagon west. Clete Millikan's stepson Bruce begins telling Durant about his real father and the drifter grows very uneasy.

162.129 *The Earl Packer Story.* Jan. 4, 1961. GS: Ernest Borgnine, Edward Binns, Rex Holman, Jane Burgess. Sheriff Bill Strode has a reputation for facing the toughest of hombres. That is why Flint is puzzled when Strode tries to elude a bounty hunter named Earl Packer.

162.130 *The Patience Miller Story.* Jan. 11, 1961. GS: Michael Ansara, Rhonda Fleming, E.J. Andre, Terry Burnham, Henry Brandon, Morgan Woodward, Charlotte Fletcher, Bart Bradley, Jason Robards, Sr. The Millers, Quaker missionaries, are traveling to the Arapahoe Indian mission when they are attacked by Indians and the husband is slain. Patience Miller vows to take her husband's place and help the tribe.

162.131 *The Sam Elder Story.* Jan. 18, 1961. GS: Everett Sloane, Ray Stricklyn, Walter Coy, Roberta Shore, Roger Mobley, Adrienne Marden. Former Army captain Sam Elder asks if he and his group of orphaned boys can join the train on their way to California. Hawks agrees, but soon finds the rest of the wagon party is up in arms. They have discovered something they don't like about Elder's Civil War record.

162.132 *Weight of Command.* Jan. 25, 1961. GS: Tommy Rettig, Dan Riss, Jeanne Bates, Richard Crane, Nancy Rennick, Dana Dillaway, Wilton Graff, Clancy Cooper, Jan Arvan. Hawks and a couple of young men from the train, Dan Foster and Billy Gentry, go to investigate the ruins of an adobe hut. The trio is attacked by a band of renegade Cheyennes.

162.133 *The Prairie Story.* Feb. 1, 1961. GS: Beulah Bondi, Jan Clayton, John Archer, Virginia Christine, Diane Jergens, Mickey Sholder, Ilana Dowding, Jack Beutel. The wagons roll West and cross the threshold of the arid, Indian-infested prairieland. It soon becomes apparent that one of the passengers, Charity Kirby, is unwilling to face the dangers of the crossing.

162.134 *Path of the Serpent.* Feb. 8, 1961. GS: Paul Burke, Noah Beery, Jr., Melinda Plowman, Jay Silverheels, Robert Harland, Clay Taylor, Paul Birch. Penelope, a young passenger, learns that her father is dying in a village just beyond an area of Indian uprisings. Mountaineer Ruddy Blaine offers to take Penelope and a party through the danger zone.

162.135 *The Odyssey of Flint McCullough.* Feb. 15, 1961. GS: Henry Hull, Michael Burns, Dana Dillaway, Suzi Carnel, Tony Maxwell, Bryan Russell, Clay Randolph, Laurie Main. On a scouting mission, Flint runs across the survivors of an Indian raid. He decides to guide them out of the hostile territory.

162.136 *The Beth Pearson Story.* Feb. 22, 1961. GS: Virginia Grey, Johnny Washbrook, Del Moore. Widow Beth Pearson and her son Ronald join the west-bound train, and Major Adams is strangely shaken by their presence. Beth closely resembles Ranie Webster, a woman Seth once loved.

162.137 *The Jed Polke Story.* March 1, 1961. GS: John Lasell, Joyce Meadows, Willard Waterman, Ron Hayes, Dennis Holmes, Perry Lopez, Frank Gerstle, Juney Ellis. McCullough finds Jed and Rheba Polke near death in the desert. Dr. Day is traveling with the train, but for some reason he won't treat Polk.

162.138 *The Nancy Palmer Story.* March 8, 1961. GS: Elisha Cook, Jr., Audrey Meadows, Jack Cassidy, Vivi Janiss, Jeanne Bates, Roger Mobley, Rory Stevens, Harry Lauter, Med Florey, Bern Hoffman. The wagon train folk don't cotton to newcomer Dan Palmer and his prickly disposition. But Dan's wife Nancy, with her charm and acts of kindness, does much to help offset her husband's shortcomings. Then a theft is discovered and the members of the train suspect Dan.

162.139 *The Christopher Hale Story.* March 15, 1961. GS: Lee Marvin, L.Q. Jones, Nancy Rennick, Claire Carleton, Wesley Lau, Charles Horvath, Red Morgan. Flint meets retired wagonmaster Chris Hale, who is overcome with grief following the massacre of his family by marauding Indians. Meanwhile, the company that owns the wagon train has employed a new wagonmaster, Jud Benedict, who arrives to put thing in order, with the aid of four gun-toting associates.

162.140 *The Tiburcio Mendez Story.* March 22, 1961. GS: Nehemiah Persoff, Leonard Nimoy, Lisa Gaye, Russell Collins, David Garcia. Hawks leaves the main train with four wagons and heads southwest toward Los Angeles. On the way, he is halted by Tiburcio Mendez and his band of renegades, and is told that strangers are not welcome in California.

162.141 *The Nellie Jefferson Story.* April 5, 1961. GS: Janis Paige, H.M. Wynant, Don Megowan, Dennis Rush, Don Harvey. Flint and new wagonmaster Chris Hale are perturbed by the demands of actress Nellie Jefferson, who has joined the train. But Wooster, taken with Nellie's beauty, begins to wait on her hand and foot.

162.142 *The Saul Bevins Story.* April 12, 1961. GS: Rod Steiger, Charles Herbert, Vivi Janiss, Rachel Ames, Willard Waterman, Charles Carlson, I. Stanford Jolley. Saul Bevins, who is blind, must prove he is capable of caring for his son Job and his sister Martha during their planned trip to California. Turned down by several other wagonmasters, Bevins gets Chris Hale to give him a chance.

162.143 *The Joe Muharich Story.* April 19, 1961. GS: Robert Blake, Akim Tamiroff, Susan Silo, Tris Coffin, Doodles Weaver, Kelton Garwood, Stacy Harris. Joe, Muharich, a kindly Polish immigrant who has joined the train, notices that young Johnny Kamen is carrying a chip on his shoulder and a fast gun in his holster. He decides to tame the boy before they arrive in the land of gunslingers.

162.144 *The Duke Shannon Story.* April 26, 1961. GS: Frank McHugh, James Griffith, John Cason, Leonard Geer, Maudie Prickett. Duke Shannon's grandfather, prospector Henry Shannon, has a map for a lost gold mine. When he meets the wagon train, he talks Wooster into joining him in recovering the treasure. Three shady characters overhear the plan, decide to trail the pair, and take the money for themselves.

162.145 *The Will Santee Story.* May 3, 1961. GS: Dean Stockwell, Millie Perkins, Virginia Christine, Barbara Beaird, Jocelyn Brando, Harry Von Zell, John Crawford, Dal McKennon. Will Sheridan, his mother Amanda, and his sister Wendy join the wagon train. Because their consciences are bothering them, they confide in Hale that their real name is Santee, and they are using an alias because Will's brother was involved in a scandal.

162.146 *The Jim Bridger Story.* May 10, 1961. GS: Karl Swenson, John Doucette, Jackie Russell, Hank Brandt, Barbara Woodell, Nestor Paiva, Francis DeSales. McCullough, left in temporary command of the wagons, is approached by Army General Jameson. The general orders him to take the train back into hostile Indian territory and help to rescue a trapped cavalry garrison.

162.147 *The Eleanor Culhane Story.* May 17, 1961. GS: Felicia Farr, John Lasell, Russell Thorson, Orville Sherman, Renata Vanni, Hank Patterson. Flint goes to visit Eleanor Culhane, an old girl friend, and finds that she is now the widow of a notorious gunman. Flint's love for Eleanor begins to return, but so does her supposedly dead husband.

162.148 *The Chalice.* May 24, 1961. GS: Lon Chaney, Jr., Richard Jaeckel, Argentina Brunetti, Harold Heifetz, Edward Colmans. The Canevaris are going to California to plant a new vineyard, and they need help in transporting water to keep the young grapevines alive during the trek. Two men named Carstairs and Barker offer the use of their wagon, but the gesture isn't exactly unselfish, as they are wondering what they can take from the Canevaris to pay for their services.

162.149 *The Janet Hale Story.* May 31, 1961. GS: Jeanette Nolan, Bethel Leslie, Charles Aidman, Bobby Hyatt, Richard Cutting, Claudia Bryar. In a flashback, Chris Hale's duties as wagonmaster require him to temporarily leave his family in their prairie home. His truce with Red Cloud reassures him that there won't be any danger of Indian raids, as long as the tribe's braves keep their chief's promise.

162.150 *Wagon to Fort Anderson.* June 7, 1961. GS: Albert Salmi, Carol Rossen, Don Rickles, Candy Moore, Lou Webb, Hal Needham. Flint comes upon Fay and Sue Ellison, the only survivors off an Indian massacre, and he starts to guide them back to the wagon train. Suddenly they are overtaken by Joe Carder and his brother George, a pair of Army deserters, who tell the girls that McCullough is only pretending to lead them to safety.

162.151 *The Ah Chong Story.* June 14, 1961. GS: Arnold Stang, Jess Kirkpatrick, Frank Ferguson. Wooster has developed a take it or leave it attitude about his cooking lately, and Hale and Hawks decide to leave it. They tell the cook that they would rather eat the offerings of his Chinese helper, Ah Cong, and promote the underling to chief cook for the wagon train.

162.152 *The Don Alvarado Story.* June 21, 1961. GS: Andrea Martin, Vladimir Sokoloff, Michael Forest, Ed Nelson, Ken Terrell, David Faulkner, Jerry Lazarre, Armand Alzamora. A group of Mexican settlers in California are becoming unsettled by Donovan and Hayes, two men who want the land at any cost. Under the terms of an old Spanish land grant, the property belongs to one Don Alvarado, if he claims it.

Season Five

162.153 *The Captain Dan Brady Story.* Sept. 27, 1961. GS: Joseph Cotten, Paul Comi, David Faulkner, Dawn Wells, Russell Thorson, Mauritz Hugo, Edward Colmans. Wagonmaster Chris Hale finds himself faced with a dilemma. If he hires Dan Brady, who is demanding to be taken on as trail scout, he will probably lose Flint McCullough. If he doesn't, he will lose a Government mail contract that is necessary to finance the wagon train.

162.154 *The Kitty Allbright Story.* Oct. 4, 1961. GS: Polly Bergen, Jocelyn Brando, Morgan Woodward, Kathleen Freeman, Eleanor Audley, Howard Wendell, Arlen Stuart. Nurse Allbright joins the wagon train and soon becomes concerned about the poor sanitation habits of her fellow travellers. When she tries to do something about it, she finds they also have some strange notions about the nursing profession.

162.155 *The Maud Frazer Story.* Oct. 11, 1961. GS: Barbara Stanwyck, Nora Marlowe, Renee Godfrey, Russ Conway. Flint runs across a most unusual group heading west—an all-woman wagon train led by wagonmistress Maud Frazer. He tries to dissuade Maud from leading her defenseless ladies into hostile Indian country. She refuses, but asks him to leave his own train and come with hers.

162.156 *The Selena Hartnell Story.* Oct. 18, 1961. GS: Jan Sterling, Claude Akins, Billy Hughes. Female bounty hunter Selena Hartnell catches up with the wagon train and asks Hale to make the formal arrest of her quarry. The man she points out happens to be Will Cotrell, the beloved leader of a band of pacifists.

162.157 *The Clementine Jones Story.* Oct. 25, 1961. GS: Ann Blyth, Dick York, Willard Waterman, Roger Mobley, Nestor Paiva, Henry Corden, Frank Wilcox. Although Clementine is a popular attraction at the Cinnibar Saloon, certain righteous citizens feel that she is a blight on the community, and ask the mayor to boot her out of town. Fortunately for her, the wagon train is passing through, and Hale offers the girl passage west.

162.158 *The Jenna Douglas Story.* Nov. 1, 1961. GS: Carolyn Jones, John Lupton, Charles Briggs, Andy Green. The wagon train comes upon a woman stumbling along the trail, and Hale takes her aboard as a passenger. She tells him she is Jenna Douglas, but she doesn't tell him that she has just escaped from a mental hospital.

162.159 *The Artie Matthewson Story.* Nov. 8, 1961. GS: Rory Calhoun, Jane Darwell, Joyce Meadows, House Peters, Jr. Flint discovers that his foster brother Artie has been elected mayor of a boom town. He suspects that opportunistic Artie is up to no good, but no one in town will believe him.

162.160 *The Mark Miner Story.* Nov. 15, 1961. GS: Brandon de Wilde, Michael Burns, Robert Cornthwaite, Barbara Parkins. Passengers on the wagon train suspect a thief when some of their belongings begin to disappear. The evidence points to Duke Shannon as the thief.

162.161 *The Bruce Saybrook Story.* Nov. 22, 1961. GS: Brian Aherne, Antoinette Bower, Liam Sullivan. British nobleman Lord Bruce Saybrook, escorting a party through the American Wild West, is taking the adventure as a lark. McCullough meets the group and warns them that they are right in the middle of hostile Indian territory.

162.162 *The Lizabeth Ann Calhoun Story.* Dec. 6, 1961. GS: Dana Wynter, Richard Crane, Raymond Bailey, Peter Whitney. Lizabeth Ann Calhoun wants to join the wagon train, and begins flirting alternately with Hawks and Shannon. Soon a jealous rivalry develops between the two friends.

162.163 *The Traitor.* Dec. 13, 1961. GS: Nick Adams, Jeanne Cooper, Myron Healey, Stacy Keach, Alex Montoya, Anthony Caruso. Flint McCullough, mixed up in a horse theft, is tried and found guilty by wagonmaster Chris Hale. The sentence is a whipping and banishment from the wagon train.

162.164 *The Bettina May Story.* Dec. 20, 1961. GS: Bette Davis, Ron Hayes, Joby Baker, Asa Maynor. Chris Hale isn't too happy with the new additions to the wagon train, Bettina May and her large brood. It is going to be a tough trip and Chris doesn't think Bettina's pampered progeny can take it.

162.165 *Clyde.* Dec. 27, 1961. GS: Harry von Zell, Nora Marlowe, Lenore Kingston, Mike McGreevey, Frank de Kova. Clyde is a captured buffalo that has been turned over to Wooster for safe-keeping. Wooster develops quite an attachment for the beast, just as the train is faced with a meat shortage.

162.166 *The Martin Onyx Story.* Jan. 3, 1962. GS: Jack Warden, Sherwood Price, Morgan Woodward. Legendary lawman Martin Onyx answers a plea for help when citizens of a prairie village are plagued by outlaws. McCullough, who happens to be in town, is surprised when he hears the news because he thought Onyx was dead.

162.167 *The Dick Pederson Story.* Jan. 10, 1961. GS: James MacArthur, Anne Helm, Alice Frost. Orphan Dick Pederson resents the other young people on the wagon train, particularly Janey Cutler, because they all have families. But Janey's four younger sisters take Dick under their wing, and he soon warms to them.

162.168 *The Hobie Redman Story.* Jan. 17, 1962. GS: Lin McCarthy, Arch Johnson, Barbara Eiler, Parley Baer, Amzie Strickland, Ann Jillian. Hale sends Shannon to guide three wagons waiting to join the train. But Duke finds a balky customer among the newcomers. Hobie Redman refuses to come along because his family died on the same trail a few years earlier.

162.169 *The Malachi Hobart Story.* Jan. 24, 1962. GS: Franchot Tone, Irene Ryan, Wally Brown, Steven Darrell. Duke finds that while Malachi Hobart may say he is a traveling preacher, he is actually a confidence man. In an effort to expose him, Duke lets himself be talked into one of Hobart's schemes.

162.170 *The Dr. Denker Story.* Jan. 31, 1962. GS: Theodore Bikel, Michael Burns, George Keymas, Kathleen O'Malley, James Lydon. Flint comes upon young Billy Latham, who is paralyzed with fear and unable to talk after witnessing the murder of his father.

162.171 *The Lonnie Fallon Story.* Feb. 7, 1962. GS: Frank Overton, Gary Clarke, Lynn Loring, Alan Hale, Jr., Stacy Harris, Paul Birch, Angela Greene. Young cowboy Lonnie Fallon is smitten with pretty Kathy Jennings but her father disapproves of the match. Jennings is taking Kathy to California, and he warns Lonnie that if he attempts to follow the wagon train, he will shoot him.

162.172 *The Jeff Hartfield Story.* Feb. 14, 1962. GS: Jack Chaplain, Roger Mobley, Dennis Rush, Michael Forest, House Peters, Jr., Jackie Loughery, Ross Elliott, Mary Gregory. Teenager Jeff Hartfield's father is in prison awaiting execution. Jeff, who thinks it is his duty to save his father, plans to run away from the wagon train.

162.173 *The Daniel Clay Story.* Feb. 21, 1962. GS: Claude Rains, Fred Beir, Maggie Pierce, Peter Helm, Frances Reid, Jack Mather, Hal Smith, Orville Sherman. Judge Daniel Clay has a reputation for handing down extremely harsh sentences. Now the judge is taking his family West on the wagon train, and the other passengers form an immediate dislike for the man.

162.174 *The Lieutenant Burton Story.* Feb. 28, 1962. GS: Dean Jones, Charles McGraw, Ray Stricklyn, Ray Baumann, Jenny Maxwell, Brett King, Robert Reiner. Riding ahead of the wagon train, Chris Hale is suddenly shot down from ambush by a Cavalry patrol looking for deserters. The order to fire was given by Sergeant Kile, who believes in shooting first and asking questions later.

162.175 *The Charley Shutup Story.* March 7, 1962. GS: Dick York, R.G. Armstrong, Dorothy Green, Anita Sands. Hale and Duke are escorting an advance group from the wagon train who need to reach California in time to lay claim to a gold mine. They reach the rugged snowy mountain country when Duke suddenly breaks his ankle, and Hale and the others are forced to leave him.

162.176 *The Amos Billings Story.* March 14, 1962. GS: Jon Locke, Paul Fix, Dennis Patrick. While scouting ahead for the wagon train, Flint is stopped by a man named Amos Billings. Billings says he and his son Gabe have blasted a road through a dead-end canyon, and it will save the wagons two weeks if they detour through this new passage.

162.177 *The Baylor Crowfoot Story.* March 21, 1962. GS: Robert Culp, John Larch, Joyce Taylor. Jethro Creech and his daughter Ruth join the wagons along the trail. Creech, a stern disciplinarian, catches schoolteacher Baylor Crofoot exchanging glances with Ruth, and warns Crofoot to leave her alone.

162.178 *The George B. Hanrahan Story.* March 28, 1962. GS: Lee Tracy, Frank De Kova, Harry Carey, Jr., Douglas Jones, Brett King, Dennis McCarthy. When Indian medicine man Running Bear incurs the wrath of his fellow tribesmen, he gets the chance to live up to his name. Duke rescues him from the pursuing mob and takes him back to the wagon train, where the Indian soon makes friends with an emigrating politician named George B. Hanrahan. Hanrahan thinks they will make a great team at conning the public.

162.179 *Swamp Devil.* April 4, 1962. GS: Philip Bourneuf, Otto Waldis, Richard Cutting, Kay Stewart, Robert Bice. With Flint as a guide, Otto Burger and his followers strike out on their own and soon arrive at the edge of a swamp. A friendly Indian chief advises them to detour, because an evil spirits dwells in the marshes ahead.

162.180 *The Cole Crawford Story.* April 11, 1962. GS:

James Drury, Diana Millay, Robert Colbert, Fay Wray. Newlyweds Cole and Helen Crawford join the wagon train, and it's not long before things start getting complicated. A former suitor of Helen's, Blake Dorty, rides up and demands that she go away with him.

162.181 *The Levi Hale Story.* April 18, 1962. GS: John McIntire, Trevor Bardette, Hugh Sanders, Daniel M. White, Myron Healey. Chris Hale journeys to the Wyoming Territorial Prison to meet his older brother Levi, who is being released. Chris thinks that Levi has a pardon from the governor, until the warden tells him that Levi is actually being released on the condition that he get out of the Territory.

162.182 *The Terry Morrell Story.* April 25, 1962. GS: Henry Jones, David Ladd, Vivi Janiss, Paul Langton, Lane Bradford, Eve McVeagh. Ben Morrell and his son Terry join the wagon train and quickly establish themselves as two very antisocial types. Terry doesn't even seem to like his own father.

162.183 *The Jud Steele Story.* May 2, 1962. GS: Arthur Franz, Edward Binns, Mary La Roche, Robert J. Wilke, Cliff Osmond, Joe Turkel, Tim Graham, Fred Sherman. Fleeing gunman Jud Steele and his pal show up at the wagon train, asking for fresh horses. Steele is displeased when Hawks says no.

162.184 *The Mary Beckett Story.* May 9, 1962. GS: Anne Jeffreys, Lee Bergere, Carole Wells, Jocelyn Brando, Whit Bissell, Joe Maross. Frenchman Alex Lamont's suave manner has produced mixed reactions around the wagon train. The men think he is a phony, but the women adore him.

162.185 *The Nancy Davis Story.* May 16, 1962. GS: Keith Richards, Lory Patrick, Cloris Leachman, Russell Collins, George Keymas, Bob Anderson, Sam Edwards, Kay Stewart, Don Gazzaniga. Flint, Wooster and Hawks are in a local saloon when the barkeep happens to mention a man called Lace Andrews. Flint has been looking for Lace for eight years—to kill him.

162.186 *The Frank Carter Story.* May 23, 1962. GS: Albert Salmi, Frances Reid, Gloria Talbott, Edward Platt, Norman Leavitt, Jeanne Bates, William Fawcett. Duke is a dead ringer for a gambler named Jason Carter. In fact, many people are easily convinced that Duke is Jason, including someone who is out to kill the gambler.

162.187 *The John Turnbull Story.* May 30, 1962. GS: Henry Silva, Steven Geray, Warren Stevens, Dayton Lummis, John War Eagle, I. Stanford Jolley, Tim Frawley, Frank Wilson. White settlers are up to their old tricks and are attempting to force the Indians off their lands. But this time they are faced with a new and unfamiliar kind of opposition: legal barriers initiated by two attorneys named Jacob Solomon and John Turnbull, who returned from the East to help his fellow Indians.

162.188 *The Hiram Winthrop Story.* June 6, 1962. GS: Eduard Franz, Ron Soble, Barbara Woodell, Art Lund, Frank Gerstle, Claudia Bryar, Aline Towne. Indian Agent Hiram Winthrop wants to establish a welfare program in his district, but he needs help to do it. He persuades Shannon to give up his job as scout for the wagon train and join him as an administrator.

162.189 *The Heather Mahoney Story.* June 13, 1962. GS: Jane Wyatt, Nellie Burt, John Emery, Cyril Delevanti, Harry Holcombe. The wagon train finally reaches the end of the line when it pulls into Sacramento. But it may be a beginning rather than an end as far as Hale is concerned. He has taken an interest in widow Heather Mahoney.

Season Six

162.190 *The Wagon Train Mutiny.* Sept. 19, 1962. GS: Dan Duryea, Jane Wyman, Jose de Vega, Peter Helm. The wagon train comes across a devastated wagon party where they find Renaldo, a wounded member of the attacking Comancheros who was left to die.

162.191 *The Caroline Casteel Story.* Sept. 26, 1962. GS: Barbara Stanwyck, Charles Drake, Roger Mobley, Robert F. Simon, Alice Frost, Richard Cutting, Dennis Rush. Many years earlier, Caroline Casteel was captured by Indians. Her husband Frank has long since given up hope that she may be alive, but now a man named Schofield claims that he has managed to trade her away from the savages.

162.192 *The Madame Sagittarius Story.* Oct. 3, 1962. GS: Thelma Ritter, Doug Lambert, Zeme North, Murvyn Vye, Robert Ryan, John Bernard, Perry Lopez. When the other passengers snub Mme. Sagittarius, a con woman, Charley takes pity on her and the two soon develop a very close relationship.

162.193 *The Martin Gatsby Story.* Oct. 10, 1962. GS: Fred Clark, Virginia Christine, James McCallion, Jocelyn Brando. Martin Gatsby doesn't care about other people. He wants to get the wagons moving and, since Cabel Lefton is causing the delays, Gatsby tells Hale that the Leftons will have to leave the wagon train.

162.194 *The John Augustus Story.* Oct. 17, 1962. GS: Joseph Cotten, Nobu McCarthy, Meg Wyllie, Allen Jung. John Augustus plays cards with Chinese merchant Din Pau Yee and comes out a winner. The prize turns out to be a beautiful Chinese girl named Mayleen.

162.195 *The Mavis Grant Story.* Oct. 24, 1962. GS: Ann Sheridan, Parley Baer, Anna Karen, Mary Jayne Saunders. Hale's wagon train is in desperate need of water and Grant's Well is the only nearby source. Well owner Mavis Grant offers them all the water they need, as long as they pay her price.

162.196 *The Lisa Raincloud Story.* Oct. 31, 1962. GS: Dana Wynter, George Keymas, Gregg Barton, Dal McKennon, Ken Mayer. Hawks has been badly wounded and taken prisoner by Indians who intend to execute him as soon as he recovers. But during his convalescence Hawks and the Indian princess Lisa Raincloud fall in love.

162.197 *The Shiloh Degnan Story.* Nov. 7, 1962. GS: Nancy Gates, Russell Johnson, Lorence Kerr, Barry Morse, Peter Whitney, R.G. Armstrong, James Gavin. A badly wounded soldier is found near the wagon train's campsite and Hale recognizes him as Major Dan Marriott. Just before Marriott dies he accuses Shiloh Degnan, his commander officer and a national hero, of murder by sending him to certain death in a battle with Indians.

162.198 *The Levy-McGowan Story.* Nov. 14, 1962. GS: Liam Redmond, Lee Fuchs, Lory Patrick, Gary Vinson, Nora Marlowe. What began as a peaceful game of checkers has turned into a feud between passengers Simon Levy and Patrick McGowan. And the hostilities are making it difficult for Patrick McGowan's son Sean to carry on his romance with Levy's daughter Rachel.

162.199 *The John Bernard Story.* Nov. 21, 1962. GS:

Wagon Train

Robert Ryan, Perry Lopez, Doris Kemper, Cliff Osmond, Beau Bridges, William Fawcett, Herbert C. Lytton, Jack Grinnage. Indians kidnap Mrs. Budgen from the wagon train. In her place they leave Mitsina, an Indian youth who is seriously ill. The Indians promise to return Mrs. Budgen when Mitsina is cured.

162.200 *The Kurt Davos Story.* Nov. 28, 1962. GS: Eddie Albert, Frances Reid, Arthur Space, Amzie Strickland, Karl Lukas. Wagon train passenger Florence Hastings is terribly afraid of dogs, and for this reason she avoids fellow passenger Kurt Davos and his bulldog. But when a wild bull charges Florence, it is Kurt and his dog who come to her rescue.

162.201 *The Eve Newhope Story.* Dec. 5, 1962. GS: Ann Blyth, Tudor Owen, Jim Davis, George Kane, Richard Reeves, Slim Pickens. Patrick O'Shaughnessy has come West to pay a surprise visit to his daughter Eve, whom he believes to be a respectable married woman. But Patrick is the one who is going to be surprised. His daughter isn't married, and to make ends meet, she is running a saloon.

162.202 *The Orly French Story.* Dec. 12, 1962. GS: Peter Fonda, Sharon Farrell, John Doucette, Gil Perkins, Robert Cornthwaite. Jason Hartman is now a marshal, and he has also become deeply religious. When Hartman catches up with young bank robber Orly French, he tries his best to lead the boy along the same path toward faith that he himself traveled.

162.203 *The Donna Fuller Story.* Dec. 19, 1962. GS: Jeanne Cooper, Simon Oakland, Elvia Allman, Sandra Gould. Soon after temperance crusader Donna Fuller and her flock of female followers join the wagon train, Donna becomes romantically interested in Alonzo Galezio. But Donna his distressed when she learns that Alonzo is a wine maker.

162.204 *The Sam Darland Story.* Dec. 26, 1962. GS: Art Linkleter, Rusty Stevens, Nancy Davis/Reagan, Tommy Nolan, Billy Mumy, Steven Ritch, X Brands. In the middle of Indian country, the wagon train runs into Sam Darland and his group of orphan boys. Darland has started a home for these youngsters in an abandoned ghost town and he is doing his best to provide the unwanted children with proper guidance.

162.205 *The Abel Weatherly Story.* Jan. 2, 1963. GS: J.D. Cannon, John Ashley, Valerie Varda, William Fawcett, Chane Kelle. Hawks and Wooster come across an overturned wagon on the prairie and give aid to injured driver, sea captain Abel Weatherly. But during the night, for no apparent reason, Weatherly goes into a violent rage and tries to kill Hawks.

162.206 *The Davey Baxter Story.* Jan. 9, 1963. GS: Tommy Sands, Jeannine Riley, Charles Herbert, Sam Edwards, Louise Arthur. Young Davey Baxter loses his mother in a wagon accident which also badly mangles his arm. The doctor is away, and Hale is forced to make a terrible decision. He will have to amputate Davey's arm in order to save his life.

162.207 *The Johnny Masters Story.* Jan. 16, 1963. GS: Anthony George, Robert J. Wilke, Harry Hickox, William Mims. Duke rescues Indian-turned-soldier Johnny Masters from a war party and continues on to Fort David, where he hopes to pick up a military escort for the wagons. But the troopers are on patrol and only a small garrison is left to guard the fort.

162.208 *The Naomi Kaylor Story.* Jan. 30, 1963. GS: Joan Fontaine, Natalie Trundy, Dick Sargent, Fred Beir. Naomi Kaylor takes the news of her husband's death quite calmly, until she learns that he left most of his estate to their daughter.

162.209 *The Hollister John Garrison Story.* Feb. 6, 1963. GS: Charles Drake, Gary Cockrell, Evans Evans, Peter Whitney. Bitter ex-Confederate soldier Stevenson Drake develops a strong dislike for John Hollister when he learns that Hollister, a Southerner, didn't fight for the Confederacy.

162.210 *The Lily Legend Story.* Feb. 13, 1963. GS: Susan Oliver, Richard Jaeckel, Trevor Bardette, Frank Cady. Sheriff Lund is escorting a woman prisoner who is going to be hanged and Duke recognizes her as Lily Legend, his childhood sweetheart.

162.211 *Charlie Wooster — Outlaw.* Feb. 20, 1963. GS: Jeanette Nolan, L.Q. Jones, Morgan Woodward, Mickey Sholdar, Frank Ferguson. Hoping to find out about a gold shipment which the wagon train is supposed to be carrying bandit leader Bella McKavitch tells her outlaw sons to kidnap Hale, but her boys get mixed up and grab Wooster instead.

162.212 *The Sara Proctor Story.* Feb. 27, 1963. GS: Jean Hagen, Chris Robinson, Holly McIntire. The other passengers believe that Sarah Proctor has mutilated some dolls belonging to children on the wagon train, and they also believe that Sarah is mentally ill.

162.213 *The Emmett Lawton Story.* March 6, 1963. GS: Dennis Hopper, Frances Reid, Richard Devon, Ric Roman, Stanley Adams, Philip Bourneuf, Rusty Lane. Scout Duke Shannon rides into the town of High Times, which is being terrorized by gunmen, one of whom Duke kills in self-defense during a fist fight.

162.214 *The Annie Duggan Story.* March 13, 1963. GS: Arthur Franz, Carolyn Kearney, Katie Sweet, Donny Carter, Sally Bliss, Gregory Irvin. An elderly couple on the wagon train dies of typhoid fever, and their servant, Annie Duggan, is quarantined, much to the annoyance of Dan Highet, who has fallen in love with her.

162.215 *The Michael McGoo Story.* March 20, 1963. GS: Jocelyn Brando, John Doucette, Cathleen Cordell, Roger Mobley, Donald Losby. Charlie wants to adopt the four Hooper boys, whose parents were killed by Indians, so he proposes to Ada Meyers.

162.216 *The Adam MacKenzie Story.* March 27, 1963. GS: Michael Ansara, Peter Brown, Danny Bravo, William Mims. Esteban Perez and his family are run off their land by an angry mob, which accuses their daughter Juana of being a witch.

162.217 *The Tom Tuesday Story.* April 3, 1963. GS: Brian Keith. Outlaw Tom Tuesday has an important rendezvous to keep, but he is going blind from a gunshot wound, so he kidnaps Duke to act as a guide for him.

162.218 *Heather and Hamish.* April 10, 1963. GS: Anne Helm, Michael Parks, Liam Redmond, Meg Wyllie. Scotsman Samuel MacIntosh wants to marry off his daughter Heather to farmer Hamish Browne, and after persuading Hamish to take the girl, sight unseen, he makes him sign a marriage contract to insure the deal.

162.219 *The Blane Wessels Story.* April 17, 1963. GS: Juanita Moore, Robert Colbert, Lory Patrick, Virginia Christine. During an Indian attack, a gent named Blane Wessels saves Duke Shannon and three women he is escorting to the wagon train, but the Redskins will be back, and one of the ladies is about to have a baby.

162.220 *The Tom O'Neal Story.* April 24, 1963. GS:

Peter Helm, Brenda Scott, Les Tremayne, Myron Healey, Aline Towne. Two young passengers on the wagon train fall in love and, because of their parents' opposition, they decide that they will have to run away to get married.

162.221 *The Clarence Mullins Story.* May 1, 1963. GS: Clu Gulager, Carleton Young, I. Stanford Jolley, James McMullan, Lisa Seagram. Duke and Charlie decide to enter dangerous Indian country in an attempt to locate their old friend Clarence Mullins, a minister who was ousted from the Army because he refused to fight Indians, and who is now preaching among them.

162.222 *The David Garner Story.* May 8, 1963. GS: Randy Boone, Susan Silo, Peter Whitney, Harry Harvey. Hale has been entrusted with a strongbox full of cash, which young David Garner is determined to steal, despite the objections of her girl friend Susan.

162.223 *Alias Bill Hawks.* May 15, 1963. GS: Joan Freeman, Jeanne Bal, Arthur Space, Ed Nelson, Hal Baylor, Cliff Osmond, Ralph Leabow, Dennis McCarthy. Bill Hawks rides into a prairie town to look up an Indian friend, but he soon discovers that strangers aren't welcome. The townspeople are drilling for water on the Indian's property, and they refuse to give Bill any information as to his whereabouts.

162.224 *The Antone Rose Story.* May 22, 1963. GS: Trevor Bardette, Judi Meredith, Charles Robinson, Charles Herbert. Invalid cattle rancher Henry Ludlow is determined that his daughter Judy will not marry her fiance, sheepherder Antone Rose. He is so determined that he sells his land and makes plans to take Judy West on the wagon train.

162.225 *The Jim Whitlow Story.* May 29, 1963. John Kerr.

162.226 *The Barnaby West Story.* June 5, 1963. GS: Michael Burns, Stuart Erwin, Brad Morrow, Amzie Strickland, Dennis McCarthy, Renee Godfrey, Richard Reeves. Bill Hawks befriends Barnaby West, a thirteen-year-old boy who has come West by himself in an attempt to find his father.

Season Seven

162.227 *The Molly Kincaid Story.* Sept. 16, 1963. GS: Barbara Stanwyck, Ray Danton, Fabian, Brenda Scott, Pamela Austin, Harry Carey, Jr., Richard Reeves, Myron Healey, William Challee, Carolyn Jones. Molly Kincaid is seeking vengeance on the man whose cowardice resulted in her capture by the Indians.

162.228 *The Fort Pierce Story.* Sept. 23, 1963. GS: Ronald Reagan, Ann Blyth, John Doucette, Kathie Browne, Robert J. Wilke, Berkeley Harris. With the wagon train headed for Indian country, Hale asks Colonel Lathrop for an escort. Lathrop turns him down, but provides a new passenger, the wife of Captain Winters, whom Lathrop has ordered to leave the fort.

162.229 *The Gus Morgan Story.* Sept. 30, 1963. GS: Peter Falk, Tommy Sands, Harry Swoger, Ken Mayer, Harlan Warde, Tim Graham. To find the best route for Gus Morgan's railroad, Hale accompanies Gus and his brother Ethan on a snowy mountain expedition.

162.230 *The Widow O'Rourke Story.* Oct. 7, 1963. GS: Robert Fuller, Carol Lawrence, Richard Loo, Linda Ho, Tanigoshi, Peter Mamakos, H.T. Tsiang. Cooper sets out to look for Duke and Wooster, who are prisoners of Princess Mei Ling, matriarch of a hidden Chinese empire.

162.231 *The Robert Harrison Clarke Story.* Oct. 14, 1963. GS: Michael Rennie, Brian Keith, Henry Silva, Royal Dano, Randy Boone, George Keymas. English newspaperman Clarke thinks that the wagon train would be a good place to learn all about the wild, woolly and uncivilized West, so off he goes.

162.232 *The Myra Marshall Story.* Oct. 21, 1963. GS: Suzanne Pleshette, Charles Drake, Rex Reason, Jack Lambert, Beverly Owens, Stanley Clements, Read Morgan, I. Stanford Jolley, Norman Leavitt, Dayton Lummis. Grace Marshall heads West on the wagon train to take her sister Myra away from an unhappy marriage.

162.233 *The Sam Spicer Story.* Oct. 28, 1963. GS: Clu Gulager, Ed Begley, Frank Cady, Jean Inness, Jon Locke, Frank Mitchell, Mark Tapscott, Dennis McCarthy. Outlaw Sam Spicer and Reno Sutton flee after robbing a bank, and they take Barnaby along as a hostage.

162.234 *The Sam Pulaski Story.* Nov. 4, 1963. GS: Ross Martin, Annette Funicello, Jocelyn Brando, Stanley Adams, Richard Bakalyan. Brooklyn hoodlum Sam Pulaski joins the wagon train along with his mother and his sister Rose. Cooper, attracted to Rose, remembers Sam as the leader of a band of thugs who once robbed him in New York.

162.235 *The Eli Bancroft Story.* Nov. 11, 1963. GS: Leif Erickson, Bruce Dern, David Carradine, Randy Boone, Carl Reindel, Diane Mountford, Nestor Paiva, Rachel Ames, Parley Baer, Elizabeth Fraser, Larry J. Blake. Cooper and a small party of travelers are left stranded in the wilderness by outlaw Eli Bancroft and his sons.

162.236 *The Kitty Pryer Story.* Nov. 17, 1963. GS: Diana Hyland, Bradford Dillman, Don Durant, Jeanne Cooper, Milton Frome, John Dennis, Jack Bighead, Dal McKennon. Pretty Kitty Pryer marries Victor Harpe, only to find that he is already married to a wealthy woman named Martha.

162.237 *The Sandra Cummings Story.* Dec. 2, 1963. GS: Rhonda Fleming, Cynthia Pepper, Michael Conrad, John Archer, Jason Johnson, Brett King, Paul Baxley, K.L. Smith. Singer Sandra Cummings objects to Cooper's attention toward her daughter.

162.238 *The Bleeker Story.* Dec. 9, 1963. GS: Joan Blondell, Ruta Lee, Ed Nelson, Tim McIntire, Holly McIntire, Tudor Owen, Brooke Bundy, John McKee, Tyler McVey. Ma Bleeker and her gang, disguised as farm folk, join the wagon train near Fort Bridger, where the Army has a large deposit of gold bullion.

162.239 *The Story of Cain.* Dec. 16, 1963. GS: Ron Hayes, Anne Helm, Allen Joseph, Frank Overton, Lane Bradford. Prospector John Cain, found half-dead in the desert, has recovered enough to begin selling shares in his gold mine to the travelers.

162.240 *The Cassie Vance Story.* Dec. 23, 1963. GS: Laraine Day, Richard Carlson, Kevin Corcoran, Robert Strauss, Eve McVeagh, John Harmon, Adrienne Marden, Beverly Washburn, Eleanor Audley, Harry Holcombe. Cassie Vance is a happily married woman with a hidden past. She once did time in prison.

162.241 *The Fenton Canaby Story.* Dec. 30, 1963. GS:

Wagon Train

Jack Kelly, Barbara Bain, Virginia Gregg, Robert Cornthwaite, Jon Locke, Dee Carroll, John Hoyt, George E. Dunn, I. Stanford Jolley, Walter Reed, Kelly Thordsen. Wagon master Fenton Canaby is accused of deserting his wagon train and leaving his passengers to die of thirst.

162.242 *The Michael Malone Story.* Jan. 6, 1964. GS: Michael Parks, Dick York, Joyce Bulifant, Judi Meredith, Nellie Burt, Armand Alzamora, Tim Graham, John Bryant, Chuck Courtney. Juli Holland falls in love with wagon driver Michael Malone, a troubled man with a hidden past.

162.243 *The Jed Whitmore Story.* Jan. 13, 1964. GS: Les Tremayne, Neville Brand, Karl Swenson, William Mims, Jan Clayton, Lois Roberts, Burt Mustin, Michael Ross, Byron Morrow. Ex-convict Harry Whitmore has a story for newspaperman William Carr. Harry claims that Sheriff Frank Lewis is really his brother Jed Whitmore, a wanted outlaw.

162.244 *The Geneva Balfour Story.* Jan. 20, 1964. GS: Sherry Jackson, Robert Lansing, Peter Brown, Archie Moore, E.J. Andre, Jack Grinnage, Byron Foulger, Kate Murtagh, Kathleen Freeman, William Challee, James Griffith. In the desert, Boston matron Geneva Balfour, an expectant mother, destroys the food supplies, in an attempt to force the wagon train to return to safety.

162.245 *The Kate Crawley Story.* Jan. 27, 1964. GS: Barbara Stanwyck, Noah Beery, Jr., Richard Reeves, Charles Carlson, Juney Ellis, Bill Baldwin, Karen Flynn, Margaret Sheridan. Romance blossoms between Hale and rough-mannered, independent Kate Crawley.

162.246 *The Grover Allen Story.* Feb. 3, 1964. GS: Burgess Meredith, Nancy Gates, Marshall Thompson, Byron Foulger, Scott Lane, Lillian Bronson, Charles Morton, Paul E. Burns. In flight after murdering his tyrannical employer, Grover Allen joins the wagon train with his daughter-in-law and grandson.

162.247 *The Andrew Elliott Story.* Feb. 10, 1964. GS: Everett Sloane, Dick Sargent, Alfred Ryder, Skip Homeier, Myron Healey, Grace Lee Whitney, Robert Osterloh. The Army holds Duke for questioning in the disappearance and possible murder of a senator's son.

162.248 *The Melanie Craig Story.* Feb. 17, 1964. GS: Myrna Fahey, Jim Davis, John Craig, Tony Young, Roger Torrey, Terry Burnham, Amzie Strickland, Elvia Allman, Bobby Diamond, Marjorie Bennett. Four eligible bachelors, including Duke, are vying for the attentions of widow Melanie Craig.

162.249 *The Pearlie Garnet Story.* Feb. 24, 1964. GS: Sharon Farrell, Marilyn Maxwell, Hugh Beaumont, H.M. Wynant, Aline Towne, Laurie Mitchell, Lane Chandler, Ralph Leabow, Ken Mayer, Lennie Geer, David McMahon. Wooster suspects that pretty Pearlie Garnet is the thief who has been looting a number of wagons.

162.250 *The Trace McCloud Story.* March 2, 1964. GS: Larry Pennell, Audrey Dalton, Rachel Ames, Stanley Adams, John Lupton, Charlie Briggs, Paul Newland, James McCallion, Nora Marlowe, Richard Cutting. Because there have been a number of unsolved murders in Bedrock, some of the townsfolk decide to join the wagon train, including the murderer.

162.251 *The Duncan McIvor Story.* March 9, 1964. GS: Ron Hayes, Chris Robinson, Joanna Moore, John Larkin, Gene Evans, James Griffith, L.Q. Jones, Mike Mazurki, Dennis McCarthy, Ashley Cowan. Duke and Hawks are saved from hostile Indians by Duncan McIvor, an Army officer who is investigating recent thefts of military property.

162.252 *The Ben Engel Story.* March 16, 1964. GS: Clu Gulager, Katherine Crawford, John Doucette, Whit Bissell, J. Pat O'Malley, I. Stanford Jolley, Darby Hinton, Frances Morris, Dick Winslow, Elisha Cook, Jr., Frank Ferguson. Ruthless Harry Diel might have been lynched if it hadn't been for kindly Ben Engel, who has helped Harry out of tough scrapes before.

162.253 *The Whipping.* March 23, 1964. GS: Martin Balsam, Jeanne Cooper, William Fawcett, John Litel, Ann Staunton, Mike Smith, Harold Goodwin. Hawks thinks that Barnaby has been getting out of line a little too much lately, and he threatens to give him a whipping.

162.254 *The Santiago Quesada Story.* March 30, 1964. GS: Joseph Wiseman, Edward Binns, Perry Lopez, Jena Engstrom, Morgan Woodward, Walter Coy, George Keymas, Nina Roman, Kay Stewart, William Phipps. Indian Lance Starbuck is in love with Kim Case, whose uncle nurses a hatred for all Indians.

162.255 *The Stark Bluff Story.* April 6, 1964. GS: Ray Danton, Jean Hale, Peter Whitney, Hari Rhodes, Stanley Adams, Carmen D'Antonio, Chester Hayes, Leonard Thomas. In the town of Stark Bluff, Duke learns that a friend of his died in a fire, and that the man's widow is now working for a ruthless saloon owner.

162.256 *The Link Cheney Story.* April 13, 1964. GS: Charles Drake, Yvonne Craig, Pippa Scott, Will Kuluva, Tom Simcox, Alice Backes, Harry Von Zell, Paul Stader, Paul Baxley. Gambler Euchre Jones encounters former protege Link Cheney on the wagon train, but it isn't a happy reunion.

162.257 *The Zebedee Titus Story.* Arp. 20, 1964. GS: Neville Brand, Angela Dorian, Robert Santon, Harry Harvey, Sr., Sid Clute, Dallas McKinnon. Elderly frontier scout Zebedee Titus was having a hard time making a living until Hale gave him a job as scout for the wagon train.

162.258 *The Last Circle Up.* April 27, 1964. GS: Joe De Santis, Naomi Stevens, Karen Green, Tim McIntire, Arthur Space, Kay Stewart, Tom Skerritt, J. Pat O'Malley, Valora Noland, Myron Healey, Lane Bradford. The wagon train is nearing the end of the trail and, when Hale pays off his men, they immediately engage in some off-beat gambling contests.

Season Eight

162.259 *The Bob Stuart Story.* Sept. 20, 1964. GS: Robert Ryan, Vera Miles, Tommy Sands, Andrew Prine, Bill Smith, Stacy Harris. Ex-lawman Bob Stuart gets into a fight on his wedding day with an old enemy.

162.260 *The Hide Hunters.* Sept. 27, 1964. GS: Chris Robinson, Morgan Woodward, Charla Doherty, Ted White, Mickey Finn. Cooper and Barnaby set out to stalk buffalos with a group of hide hunters, one of whom delights in taunting young Barnaby.

162.261 *The John Gillman Story.* Oct. 4, 1964. GS: Bobby Darin, Betsy Hale, Whit Bissell, Virginia Gregg, James McCallion, Elisabeth Fraser. Embittered outlaw John Gillman doesn't want any friends, but like it or not he has one, a little orphan girl named Abigail.

162.262 *The Race Town Story.* Oct. 11, 1964. GS: Dan Duryea, Allyson Ames, Cheryl Holdridge, Hal Needham.

Cooper and Barnaby escort young Annabelle to Sam Race's tent city of honkytonks and con games, where Annabelle is dismayed to learn that Race hired her as a saloon girl, not as an entertainer.

162.263 *The Barbara Lindquist Story.* Oct. 18, 1964. GS: Dana Wynter, G.B. Atwater, Dave Perna, Walter Woolf King. Cooper goes to the aid of a stagecoach being fired on by bandits, and discovers that the sole surviving passenger is Bostonian Barbara Lindquist.

162.264 *The Brian Conlin Story.* Oct. 25, 1964. GS: Leslie Nielsen, Audrey Dalton, Paul Fix, Jodi Pearson, Eileen Baral, Patricia Lyon, Dick Miller. Delirious and dust-covered, Irishman Brian Conlin stumbles into the wagon train encampment and falls unconscious. The leader of an immigrant band that has been victimized at every turn, Conlin sees no reason to trust Chris Hale.

162.265 *The Alice Whitetree Story.* Nov. 1, 1964. GS: Diane Baker, Ken Lynch, Chuck Courtney, John Hoyt. Coop finds himself becoming involved with a half-breed Indian girl he found wandering in the wilderness.

162.266 *Those Who Stay Behind.* Nov. 8, 1964. GS: Lola Albright, Bruce Dern, Peter Brown, Jay North, Dennis Holmes, Gale Berber, Walter Coy, Willa Pearl Curtis. Hale hasn't room on the wagon train for a group of people. Among them is ex-convict Ben Campbell, whose life has been threatened by his former partner in crime.

162.267 *The Nancy Styles Story.* Nov. 22, 1964. GS: Deborah Walley, Ryan O'Neal, James Griffith, Marilyn Wayne, Rex Holman, Olan Soule. Wealthy young Nancy Styles is determined to get to Denver, despite Hale's edict that the train will by-pass the mile-high city.

162.268 *The Richard Bloodgood Story.* Nov. 29, 1964. GS: Guy Stockwell, Reta Shaw, William Smith, David Foley, Johnny Tuohy, Janet Hamill, John Crowther, Ralph Leabow, Glenn Yarbrough. Coop's boyhood blood brother, now blind, joins the wagon train with one purpose, to kill Coop.

162.269 *The Clay Shelby Story.* Dec. 6, 1964. GS: Richard Carlson, Celia Kaye, Dwayne Hickman, Mort Mills, Berkeley Harris, Gail Bonney. The wagon train is in trouble. Hawks is ill, Coop has been wounded and a band of hostile Indians are preparing to attack.

162.270 *Little Girl Lost.* Dec. 13, 1964. GS: Eileen Baral, John Doucette, Richard Cutting. A little girl's cries are heard during the night, but Wooster is the only one who catches a glimpse of her before she vanishes.

162.271 *The Story of Hector Heatherington.* Dec. 20, 1964. GS: Tom Ewell, Kim Darby, Jeanne Cooper. Wagon train passenger Hector Heatherington is a cobbler by trade, but an inventor by instinct. Hector believes that man will someday fly, and his enthusiasm infects Wooster and Barnaby, who join him in an attempt to launch a flying machine. Among the obstacles are the law of gravity and the iron will of Hector's wife Harriet, who insists that he abandon his scheme. Hector, who cannot get his mind out of the clouds, continues to work on the project secretly with Wooster and Barnaby.

162.272 *The Echo Pass Story.* Jan. 3, 1965. GS: Jack Lord, James Caan, Diane Brewster, Susan Seaforth. An outlaw gang whose members include two women, shoot Wooster and force Coop to lead them to water.

162.273 *The Chottsie Gubenheimer Story.* Jan. 10, 1965. GS: Jeanette Nolan, Paul Stewart, John Doucette, Buck Taylor, Claire Carleton, Gail Bonney. A scuffle between Chottsie Gubenheimer and gambler Jim Brannan is broken up by Chris Hale, Chottsie's old sweetheart.

162.274 *The Wanda Snow Story.* Jan. 17, 1965. GS: Marta Kristin, Arthur O'Connell, Dabbs Greer, Donnelly Rhodes, Ken Mayer. Traveler Wanda Snow has a premonition. She is sure that Coop's life is in danger.

162.275 *The Isaiah Quickfox Story.* Jan. 31, 1965. GS: Andrew Prine, Frank De Kova, John Doucette, Nancy Rennick, Jan Clayton. Coop and Charlie ride into a town that appears completely deserted and, from the look of things, everyone left in a big hurry.

162.276 *Herman.* Feb. 14, 1965. GS: Charles Ruggles, Tim McIntire, Linda Evans, Lane Bradford. Old-timer Jamison Hershey has been able to pass safely through hostile Indian country because the red men are in awe of his giant horse Herman, a Clydesdale, nineteen hands high and weighing 3000 pounds.

162.277 *The Bonnie Brooke Story.* Feb. 21, 1965. GS: Katharine Ross, Lee Philips, Robert Emhardt, James Davidson. Expectant parents Don and Bonnie Brooke are in desperate need of money. Don, already deep in debt, has to have case for Bonnie's medical care.

162.278 *The Miss Mary Lee McIntosh Story.* Feb. 28, 1965. GS: Bethel Leslie, Jack Warden, Kevin O'Neal, David McMahon, Dennis McCarthy, Jack Bighead, Eddie Little Sky. Willful spinster Mary Lee McIntosh, refusing to pay what she considers an outlandish fee to join the wagon train, plans to follow the travelers in her lone wagon.

162.279 *The Captain Sam Story.* March 21, 1965. GS: Robert Santon, Cathy Lewis, Leslie Perkins. Captain Sam, a woman ferryboat skipper, receives a pleasant surprise when the wagon train brings her two visitors, her sailor son Johnny and his bride Mary Anne.

162.280 *The Betsy Blee Smith Story.* March 28, 1965. GS: Jennifer Billingsley, Joel McCrea, Peter Whitney, Meg Wyllie. Coop goes to visit an old girl friend named Eloise, and ends up being recruited to pose as the husband of Eloise's twin sister Betsy.

162.281 *The Katy Piper Story.* April 11, 1965. GS: Virginia Christine, Frances Reid. Barnaby is guilt stricken because the masked bandit he killed turns out to be a boy his own age.

162.282 *The Indian Girl Story.* April 18, 1965. GS: Ernest Borgnine, Bruce Dern, Maggie Pierce, Michael Pate, John Lupton. The wagon train encounters an Indian girl on the trail.

162.283 *The Silver Lady.* April 25, 1965. GS: Vera Miles, Michael Burns, Arthur O'Connell, Henry Silva, Don Galloway, Don Collier. Coop tells Hawks the story of the Silver Lady, about the famed Earp brothers and a lady who perished in the wreck of a stagecoach hauling a cargo of silver.

162.284 *The Jarbo Pierce Story.* May 2, 1965. GS: Rory Calhoun, Tom Simcox, Arthur Hunnicutt, Lee Philips, Stanley Adams, Angela Dorian, Mort Mills, Morgan Woodward, Bern Hoffman, Lane Bradford, Mickey Finn. Charlie Wooster tells about his younger days in Pierce's Bend when he worked for a rugged, trading-post operator named Jarbo Pierce.

163. Walker, Texas Ranger

CBS. 60 min. Saturday, 10:00-11:00, April 1993–May 1993, Sept. 1993–Current.

Regular Cast: Chuck Norris (Cord Walker), Clarence Gilyard (Jimmy Trivette), Sherre J. Wilson (Alex Cahill), Noble Willingham (C.D. Parker), Floyd Red Crow Westerman (Uncle Ray Firewalker) 93-94.

Premise: Cordell Walker is a Texas Ranger who sometimes bends the law, to the dismay of Fort Worth prosecutor Alex Cahill.

The Episodes

163.1 *One Riot, One Ranger.* April 21, 1993. GS: Gailard Sartain, Marshall Teague, Marco Perella, Woody Watson, Debbie Slaboda. Walker's new partner Jimmy Trivette shares a past with a suspect in a bank robbery that took the life of another Ranger.

163.2 *Borderline.* April 24, 1993. GS: Leon Rippy, Mark Walters, Jonathan Hayes, Ray Lykins. Alex gets a veiled threat from the first man she sent to prison, but she has no proof he is the same man who is stalking her.

163.3 *A Shadow in the Night.* May 1, 1993. GS: Andrew Robinson, Aki Aleong, Patty Toy, Danny Kamekona. Walker and Trivette must protect a Congressman whose connection with a murder in the Japanese underworld has made him a target of an old friend of Walker's.

Season Two

163.4 *Bounty.* Sept. 25, 1993. GS: Bruce McGill, Ned Vaughn, Melora Walters. Walker tracks a bounty hunter who is after a bail jumper who has $250,000

163.5 *Storm Warning.* Oct. 2, 1993. GS: Patricia Charbonneau, Richard Norton, Luis Guzman, Mike Norris. An undercover Trivette is forced to go along with a hostage-taking incident after convicts en route to prison escape during a violent storm.

163.6 *In the Name of God.* Oct. 30, 1993. GS: Franc Luz, Suzanne Ventulett, Rick Le Ribeus, Steve Shearer, David Sheldon. Alex is taken prisoner while visiting a religious cult at the request of a man seeking to free his daughter.

163.7 *Crime Wave Dave.* Nov. 6, 1993. GS: R.D. Call, Tom Hodges, Patrick St. Esprit, Dave Kilmer. Armored-car robbers are found to have the same tough parole officer, who will stop at nothing to find another parolee, a friend of Walker's.

163.8 *End Run.* Nov. 13, 1993. GS: Troy Beyer, Gregory Scott Cummins, Cylk Cozart, Larry Manetti. New Orleans is the destination as the Rangers escort a captured gang member, who is sure her boyfriend will sprig her, but she is unaware that he is no longer the gang leader and that the new leader wants her dead.

163.9 *Family Matters.* Nov. 20, 1993. GS: Benjamin Mouton, Brian Thompson, Judith Hoag, Brady Bluhm. Alex bows to pressure from upstairs and orders the release of two armed robbers, one of whom shot a man and claims he is invincible because his sister is in the wintess protection program. Meanwhile, Walker befriends a bullied youth.

163.10 *She'll Do to Ride the River With.* Nov. 24, 1993. GS: Cali Timmins, Tristan Rogers, M.C. Gainey, Ken Kercheval. The mysterious deaths of animals coincide with the death of a veterinarian, whose daughter suspects foul play connected with his research.

163.11 *Unfinished Business.* Nov. 27, 1993. GS: Kim Myers, Sam Jones, Joe Stevens, Lou Hancock. Suspects sought by Walker are being killed by a vigilate who is calling himself a Texas Ranger, and criticizing Walker for being too soft.

163.12 *An Innocent Man.* Dec. 4, 1993. GS: Don Fischer, Leo Burmester, Scott Parkin, Alissa Alban. A drug dealer's tip leads the Rangers to suspect that the wrong man is scheduled to be executed for serial killings, but the condemned man sticks to his confession.

163.13 *Night of the Gladiator.* Dec. 11, 1993. GS: Michael Beach, Kasi Lemmons, Topm Atkins, Jeep Swenson. Trivett's old friend, involved in illegal bare-knuckle boxing matches, is led by his boss to believe that he accidentally killed an opponent.

163.14 *The Legend of Running Bear.* Jan. 8, 1994. GS: Gregg Rainwater, Kamala Dawson, Eugene Robert Glazer, Brummett Echohawk. The Rangers learn that a missing Native American is hiding after witnessing a robbery and murder, but the FBI says he is a suspect.

163.15 *Something in the Shadows* Part One. Jan. 15, 1994. GS: Jeff Kober, Giovanni Ribisi, Bill Bolander, Tom Virtue, John Fertitta, Ellen Dolan, David Beecroft, John S. Davies. A drug supplier targets Walker, who suspects there is a serial rapist on the campus where Alex teaches.

163.16 *Something in the Shadows* Part Two. Jan. 22, 1994. GS: Jeff Kober, Giovanni Ribisi, Bill Bolander, Tom Virtue, John Fertitta, Ellen Dolan, David Beecroft, John S. Davies. Walker's frind Tony is caught delivering drugs. Meanwhile, the Rangers consider two suspects in the campus rapes.

163.17 *On Deadly Ground.* Jan. 29, 1994. GS: Carmen Argenziano, Yul Vasquez, Fabiana Udenio, Alberto Vazquez, Gary Cervantes. Walker goes south of the border to rescue a kidnapped DEA agent who once saved his life.

163.18 *Right Man, Wrong Time.* Feb. 5, 1994. GS: Mary Elizabeth McGlynn, Wings Hauser, Molly Orr, Brad Leland. Walker becomes smitten while protecting a country singer who is being stalked by her ex-husband.

163.19 *The Prodigal Son.* March 5, 1994. GS: Tobey Maguire, Rick Aiello, Tony Di Benedetto, Frank Vincent. After unwittingly stealing heroin from traffickers, a teen crosses paths with Walker, who is blaming himself for the recent shooting of another teen in a hostage situation.

163.20 *The Committee.* March 12, 1994. GS: Kim Johnston Ulrich, Marco St. John, Mitchell Ryan, Alex Hyde-White. Walker builds a reputation for using excessive force in order to infiltrate a vigilante group of law-enforcement officials.

163.21 *Deadly Vision.* March 26, 1994. GS: Susan Blakely, Mark Metcalf, Shea Smillie, Rose Mari Rountree, Bryan Cranston. A woman hires a psychic to help find her abducted child, but the psychic's television appearance makes her a target of the abductor.

163.22 *Skyjacked.* April 2, 1994. GS: Patrick Kilpatrick, Earl Billings, Ely Pouget, Dennis O'Neill. The Rangers escort a cop killer on a plane back to Texas, and the killer's cohorts are also on board.

163.23 *The Long Haul.* April 9, 1994. GS: Michael Nickles, Lanel Pena, Jordan Lund, Debbie Barker, Marco Perella. A plan to catch truck hijackers puts Trivette in a crash course to learn big-rig driving.

163.24 *Rampage.* April 30, 1994. GS: Lise Cutter, Ian Ogilvy, Lindsey Ginter, Mark Walters. A gang of brothers shoots an undercover man arranging to buy its stolen firearms, and later kidnaps a woman who IDs two of them as her attackers.

163.25 *The Reunion.* May 14, 1994. GS: Stuart Whitman, Ben Masters, Jonathan Banks, William Prince, Alexia Robinson, Maggie Baird, Blue Deckert. A retired Texas Ranger brings a hidden agenda to a national pistol competition, where a group plans to assassinate a U.S. Senator.

163.26 *Stolen Lullaby.* May 21, 1994. GS: Danica McKellar, Ray Wise, Gregg Henry, Mary Chris Wall. The man who arranged an illegal adoption for a mayoral candidate tries to silence an unwed mother who claims the child is her stolen baby.

Season Three

163.27 *Badge of Honor.* Sept. 24, 1994. GS: Geoffrey Lewis, Hill Harper, Derek McGrath, Brad Leland. The Rangers run into a small-town sheriff who rules with an iron fist and doesn't discourage racism among his deputies.

163.28 *Branded.* Oct. 1, 1994. GS: Scott Plank, Joe Stephens, Mark Walters, Gil Glasgow. The Rangers try to pick up the trail after finding the body of a cattle-brand inspector killed by rustlers who think they have made the death look like an accidental stampede.

163.29 *Silk Dreams.* Oct. 8, 1994. GS: Kent Broadhurst, Cliff Stephens, Barry Jenner, David Harrod, Shannon Sturges. Alex is tempted to deal with a devil to find a designer-drug distributor. But then Walker gets his own lead, which turns into a dead end.

163.30 *Mustangs.* Oct. 15, 1994. GS: Sylvia Short, Woody Watson, Matthew Glave, James Morrison. A man is murdered as he tries to give Alex evidence of a plan to exterminate a protected herd of wild mustangs.

163.31 *Till Death Do Us Part.* Oct. 22, 1994. GS: Kirk Sisco, Suzy Blaylock, Spencer Prokop, Jerry Biggs. While Trivette seeks the reckless driver who put Walker in a coma, C.D. and Alex keep a bedside vigil, and recall memories that include Alex and Walker's first meeting and first kiss.

163.32 *Rainbow Warriors.* Nov. 5, 1994. GS: August Schellenberg, Frederick Coffin, Blue Deckert, Larry Sellers. Walker searches for his Native American blood brother, who is planning a showdown with the oil-company rep he blames for his father's accidental death.

163.33 *The Road to Black Bayou.* Nov. 19, 1994. GS: Mike Norris, Jo Champa, Glenn Walker Harris, Carl Fontana. A concussion gives Walker flashbacks of Vietnam and a forced vacation. But a fishing trip to the Louisiana bayou brings no respite for the ranger, who suspects the presence of a drug factor.

163.34 *Line of Fire.* Nov. 26, 1994. GS: John Calvin, Sean Hennigan, Joe Colligan, Lisa Peterson. Alex and Walker are tripped to a coke theft from a police-evidence room, but their source is silence permanently by a dirty cop, who is now after them.

163.35 *Payback.* Dec. 10, 1994. GS: William Smithers, Cindy Hogan, Ryan Slater, Marco Perella. Someone's put a million-dollar contract out on Walker, who is more concerned with recovering a carjacked van that is specially equipped for a handicapped boy.

163.36 *Tiger's Eye.* Dec. 17, 1994. GS: George K. Cheung, James Lew, Audrea Lynn Ulmer, David Ackroyd. A Japanese-mob vendetta comes to Texas where a former Japanese policeman refuses help from the Rangers when his wealthy boss's daughter is kidnapped.

163.37 *The Big Bing Bamboozle.* Jan. 7, 1995. GS: Doris Roberts, Robert Foster, Garrett Warren, Diamond Farnsworth. The witness against a drug-money launderer makes repeated attempts to escape from protective-custody.

163.38 *Money Train.* Jan. 14, 1995. GS: Morgan Margolis, Sharisse Baker, Gene Butler, Garrett Warren, Colleen Keegan. As technical advisors on a movie, the Rangers work with a pair of stuntmen who are in a group planning a heist of a Federal Reserve cash shipment. And Trivette tries writing a script based on his Ranger experiences, only slightly exaggerated.

163.39 *Mean Streets.* Jan. 28, 1995. GS: Eileen Brennan, John Terlesky, Sam Williamson, Todd Terry. A witness helps Walker go undercover to bust a gang of wealthy teenagers, who are beating up homeless men.

163.40 *Cowboy.* Feb. 4, 1995. GS: Wayne Pere, Sean McGraw, Eleese Lester, David Denney. Alex is taken hostage during the kidnapping of an oil executive, but her hidden cellular phone provides a trail for the Rangers.

163.41 *War Zone.* Feb. 11, 1995. GS: Wilford Brimley, Tim Thomerson, Susan Diol, Ian Bohen, Buck Taylor. A gang of serial robbers is responsible for the death of Walker's ex-partner, who is survived by a rebellions teenage son and a policewoman-daughter, who wants in on the investigation.

163.42 *Trust No One.* Feb. 18, 1995. GS: Robert Culp, Dirk Blocker, Charles Frank, Crystal Chappell, Michael Crabtree. Five-million dollars in counterfeit bills disappears during a bust and a television reporter points the finger at Trivette, who is suspended from field duty.

163.43 *Blue Movies.* Feb. 25, 1995. GS: Howard Keel, Cathy Podewell, Sherman Howard, Tim Wrightman, Barri Murphy. A judge's murderer finges a prominent businessman as the one who ordered the hit, but when the killer is killed, Walker must follow a different lead to nail the exec.

163.44 *On Sacred Ground.* March 11, 1995. GS: Adam Beach, August Schellenberg, Jacob Witkin, Nick Ramus. Walker recognizes the leader of a Native American group that has been raiding art galleries to recover artifacts stolen from sacred burial grounds.

163.45 *Case Closed.* April 29, 1995. GS: Abbi Lambert, Leah Kalish, Dirk Benedict, Roy Thinnes. Walker investigates encounters with UFOs in a small Texas town and tries to prove the residents have been deceived for the past forty years.

163.46 *Flashback.* May 6, 1995. GS: Martin Kove, Kevin Quigley, Fritz Sperberg, Tim Helms, Russ Marker, Woody Watson. The tale of a legendary ranger and a buffalo soldier parallels Walker and Trivette's pursuit of killers seeking a gold cache thought to have been stolen by the Ranger a century ago.

163.47 *Standoff.* May 13, 1995. GS: Robin Sachs, Efrain Figueroa, Gregory Sierra, Scott Allan Campbell, Juan Fernandez. After Walker thwarts an attempt on the life of a Mexican official, the would-be assassin assembles a team to execute a more elaborate plan that includes taking hostages.

Season Four

163.48 *Blown Apart.* Sept. 23, 1995. GS: Ed O'Ross, Marta DuBois, Lisa Wilhoit, Bari Hochwald. An escaped bomber targets those who helped put him away, including his ex-wife, Alex, who testified against him, and Walker.

163.49 *Deep Cover.* Sept. 30, 1995. GS: Kathy Long, Andrew Divoff, Calvin Lane, Amanda Wyss. Walker is undercover in Miami as a coke dealer. His assignment is to bust a drug kingpin and rescue a hostage cop.

163.50 *The Guardians.* Oct. 7, 1995. GS: Steve Railsback, Geoff Koch, Alex Cord, Don Stroud, Don Swayze. Walker goes undercover on an oil rig in the Gulf of Mexico to keep tabs on a radical environmentalist purportedly bent on sabotage.

163.51 *Collision Course.* Oct. 14, 1995. GS: Brian Krause, Shannon Fill, Paul Williams. C.D.'s niece is kidnapped by an ex-boyfriend who sees her as Bonnie to his Clyde and forces her to accompany him on a bank-robbery spree across Texas.

163.52 *Point After.* Oct. 21, 1995. GS: Leah Kalish, Adam Mayfield, Brandon Smith, Brandy Sanders, Robert Prentiss, Darlene Mann. Blackmail and high-stakes gambling underscore a scenario in which a suspect in the murder of a small-town high-school football coach dies while in custody.

163.53 *Evil in the Night.* Nov. 4, 1995. GS: Billy Drago, Frank Sotonoma Salsedo, Leah Kalish, John Lansing, Efrain Figueroa, Patrick Amos, Gary Ragland. A witness claims that ghosts were present when two teenagers were killed at a construction site on a sacred Indian burial ground. And later on, the Rangers experience a similar sight.

163.54 *Final Justice.* Nov. 11, 1995. GS: John Vernon, Karen Person, Clu Gulager, Geoff Mead. A convict claims that the killer of Walker's parents, who was presumed to be dead, is still alive. hat leads the Ranger to a witness to the murders who has knowledge of the killer's involvement in gunrunning.

163.55 *The Lynching.* Nov. 18, 1995. GS: Eric Bruskotter, Ritch Brinkley, Cliff Stephens, Sam Williamson. Vigilantes in a small town demand instant justice against a murder suspect, a mentally challenged man who was involved in a previous death that was ruled to have been accidental.

163.56 *Whitewater* Part One. Nov. 25, 1995. GS: Bruce McKinnon, James Hardy, Jonah Blechman, Carrie Hamilton. Alex and Walker set out on a relaxing rafting trip, and wind up being dogged by a vicious, escaped killer.

163.57 *Whitewater* Part Two. Dec. 2, 1995. GS: Bruce McKinnon, James Hardy, Jonah Blechman, Carrie Hamilton. Briscoe takes full control of the rafting party, while Trivette and C.D. battle time and dwindling fuel as they search for the rafters from the air.

163.58 *The Covenant.* Dec. 9, 1995. GS: Demetrius Navarro, Boris Cabrera, Roland Rodriguez, Art Chudabala. A young hood, who tries to shake down C.D., wants one of Walker's karate students to help his gang in a turf war.

163.59 *Rodeo.* Jan. 6, 1996. GS: Patrick Dollaghan, Joseph Campanella, Joe Inscoe. As a murderer's trial approaches, all the witnesses to the crime has been rubbed out except for a rodeo rider who was once personally involed with Alex and who bucks protective custody.

163.60 *Flashpoint.* Jan. 13, 1996. GS: Sarah Buxton, Michael Beck, Paul Jenkins, Billy Jayne. IRA terrorists vow to rescue a compatriot who is captured when Walker foils their attempted assassination of an Irish peacemaker.

163.61 *Break-In.* Jan. 20, 1996. GS: Anthony Zerbe, William Lucking, Joe Unger, Ed Brigadier. In a maximum-security prison, Walker goes undercover as a notorious hitman, while Trivette poses as a guard, in order to get evidence on an incarcerated racketeer who has had a key witness, and two Rangers, eliminated.

163.62 *The Return of LaRue.* Feb. 3, 1996. GS: Wayne Pere, John Davies, Gail Cronauer. The killer-kidnapper Alex helped put behind bars hs been released on a technicality, and is staying within the confines of the law as he stalks Alex.

163.63 *The Juggernaut.* Feb. 10, 1996. GS: Patrick St. Esprit, Jamie Austin, Khadijah Kariem. An abusive husband tracks down his wife at Alex's support group, and when he learns she wants a divorce, he again loses control, putting everyone in danger.

163.64 *El Coyote* Part One. Feb. 17, 1996. GS: Efrain Figueroa, Issabela Camil, Clifton Gonzalez-Gonzalez, Valerie Wildman, Rick Prieto. In Mexico, Walker poses as a peasant to track the path of slave-labor smugglers, whose abuses make it difficult for him to maintain his cover.

163.65 *El Coyote* Part Two. Feb. 24, 1996. GS: Efrain Figueroa, Issabela Camil, Clifton Gonzalez-Gonzalez, Valerie Wildman, Rick Prieto. Walker's Rebellious actions net him positive attention from the slave-operation kingpin, who promotes him. But Jesse is recognized by a man he once arrested.

163.66 *The Avenger.* March 2, 1996. GS: Michael Parks, Todd Terry, Michael Costello. An international mercenary leader kidnaps Walker after the ranger kills the man's younger brother during an illegal weapons bust.

163.67 *Behind the Badge.* March 23, 1996. GS: Shari Headley, Tara Karsian, Matt Maples. A tabloid-television crew follows Trivette in his dogged search for a most-wanted fugitive. But the lawman is continually upstaged by Walker, who is where the action is along with the mayor's nephew.

163.68 *Blackout.* April 6, 1996. GS: Julie Condra, Gil Segel, Cosie Costa, Scott Colomby. Walker awakens in a room wearing a tuxedo, holding a gun, lying near a dead boy and having no idea how he got there, or who he is. But a lovely casino dealer provides a clue.

163.69 *Deadline.* April 13, 1996. GS: Robert Englund, Josh Taylor, Jessie Robertson, Gabriel Folse. A wealthy state senator proposes disbanding the Rangers to save money. But that is before his daughter is kidnapped.

163.70 *The Siege.* April 27, 1996. GS: Lewis Van Bergen, Ashley Wood, Dean Lindsay. Heroin smugglers lay siege to a fishing lodge that is housing a vacationing Walker and his friends, one of whom is criticallly wounded by the felons.

163.71 *The Moscow Connection.* May 4, 1996. GS: Elya Baskin, Peter Lucas, Morgan Hunter. A Moscow policeman, who is anxious to impress, comes to Dallas to help the Rangers nail a Russian mobster who is ruthlessly trying to take over a local crime operation.

163.72 *Miracle at Middle Creek.* May 11, 1996. GS: Tony Becker, Trenton Terrell, James Horan. A little boy trapped in a drain pipe sidetracks Walker from his pursuit of bank robbers, among them the youngster's father, who was forced to participate in the crime.

163.73 *Hall of Fame.* May 18, 1996. GS: Lenny von Dohlen, Lori Huering, Jennifer Cain. After eleven years, a serial killer resurfaces to mar C.D.'s impending induction into the Texas Rangers Hall of Fame. It is the only case he never solved.

Season Five

163.74 *High Power.* Sept. 21, 1996. Walker takes on a formidble foe for the freedom of a boy who has been reincarnated as the spirit of a renowned Buddhist monk.

163.75 *Patriot.* Sept. 28, 1996. GS: John Savage, Lynne Moody, Tyreese Allen, Mike Alton, Manning Mpinduzi-Mott. Trivette's military cousin discovers weapons thefts by a white-supremacist group, whose hostages include Alex when they try to free their imprisoned leader.

163.76 *Ghost Rider.* Oct. 5, 1996. GS: Brian Keith, Eric Scott Woods, Art Evans. A developer's ne'er-do-well son is suspected after a skeleton found at a building site reveals the murder of a Native American teen eight years earlier.

163.77 *The Brotherhood.* Oct. 12, 1996. GS: Jameson Parker, John Beck. A trio of cops are dispatching deadly vigilante justice to criminals released on technicalities. Meanwhile, a young man Walker helped get out of gang life is wrongly accused of a rape.

163.78 *Plague.* Oct. 19, 1996. GS: Robert Vaughn, Wilbur Fitzgerald, Frank Sotonoma Salsedo. A biological emergency erupts at Walker's former Cherokee reservation. But the agricultural conglomerate that is responsible is more interested in containing information than containing the spreading virus.

163.79 *Redemption.* Oct. 26, 1996. GS: Rod Taylor, Stephen McHattie, Keith Szarabajka, Joseph Stephens. Alex and her estranged alcoholic father are headed for court. He is defending the crime boss she is prosecuting.

163.80 *Codename: Dragonfly.* Nov. 2, 1996. GS: Marshall Teague, Reni Santoni, George Del Hoyuo. A state-of-the-art military helicopter with stealth capabilities is stolen for use by a drug cartel, and the thief is an ex-marine who left Walker for dead twenty years earlier in Vietnam.

163.81 *A Silent Cry.* Nov. 9, 1996. GS: Yelba Osorio, Rosana DeSoto, Mark Rolston, Timothy Vahle. The Blackout Rapists, a trio using the date-rap drug Rohypnol, claim as their latest victim Walker's 21-year-old friend.

163.82 *Swan Song.* Nov. 16, 1996. GS: Dave Jensen, Newell Alexander, Anthony Leger. In a Utah woodland, a trio of opportunists tails Alex, Walker and two forest rangers to the remote site of a plane that crashed eight years earlier, with $3 million in stolen loot on board.

163.83 *Cyclone.* Nov. 23, 1996. GS: Edward Albert, Eamonn Roche, Tyrees Allen, Rafael Tamayo. Tornado activity in the area complicates mattes, yet provides a clue after commandos kidnap a busload of school kids.

163.84 *Lucky.* Nov. 30, 1996. Walker relies on the help of a homeless man's dog while investigating the death of a priest. Meanwhile, Alex and C.D. plan a charitable Thanksgiving dinner.

163.85 *The Deadliest Man Alive.* Dec. 14, 1996. GS: Kai Wulff, Martin Jarvis, Maud Adams. An Interopl agent asks the Rangers' help in finding an international assassin who has eluded him for twenty-five years. The killer may be in Dallas to target an Israeli ambassador.

163.86 *A Ranger Christmas.* Dec. 21, 1996. GS: William Sanderson, John Dennis Johnston, Laurie O'Brien, Byron Chief-Moon. Walker tells a group of orphans a story set in 1876 about Ranger Hayes Cooper, whose Christmas spirits is renewed in his quest to recover a kidnapped baby from a gang of robbers.

164. *Wanted: Dead or Alive*

CBS. 30 min. Broadcast history: Saturday, 8:30–9:00, Sept. 1958–Sept. 1960; Wednesday, 8:30–9:00, Sept. 1960–March 1961.

Regular Cast: Steve McQueen (Josh Randall), Wright King (James Nicholas) 1960.

Premise: This Western series concerned the adventures of Josh Randall, bounty hunter, who tracked down wanted men and brought them in — dead or alive — to collect the rewards offered for them.

The Episodes

164.1 *The Martin Poster.* Sept. 6, 1958. GS: Michael Landon, Nick Adams, Jenifer Lea, Dabbs Greer, Vaughn Taylor, John Cliff. Two outlaws shoot down the sheriff of a small Western town and their crime is witnessed by Josh Randall. The outlaws escape and a reward is offered for their capture. Josh Randall sets out after the fugitives.

164.2 *Fatal Memory.* Sept. 13, 1958. GS: Gloria Talbott, Russell Thorson, Ralph Moody, Vic Perrin, Joan Banks, Kem Dibbs, Mike Ragan. Josh Randall learns that a counterfeit poster, proclaiming that his former Army commander is a wanted man, has been printed and distributed. Randall tries to outwit other bounty hunters and learn the identity of the people who have distributed the counterfeit posters.

164.3 *The Bounty.* Sept. 2, 1958. GS: Mort Mills, Jean Howell, Francis McDonald, James Burkes, Dennis Cross. Josh Randall finds a man with an old murder charge against him, living in a deserted Indian village. Then a sadistic bounty hunter, Clark Daimier, arrives in the village determined to bring the murder suspect in for the reward.

164.4 *Dead End.* Sept. 27, 1958. GS: Joe De Santis, Robert Griffin, Anna Navarro. Josh Randall hunts a young man charged with murder. But the killer prepares a trap for Randall that almost costs the bounty hunter his life.

164.5 *Shawnee Bill.* Oct. 4, 1958. GS: Alan Hale, Jr., Lewis Charles. Josh Randall decides to accept a stranger's offer to lead him to a wanted fugitive. The stranger asks to collect half of the reward.

164.6 *The Giveaway Gun.* Oct. 11, 1958. GS: Everett Sloane, Lurene Tuttle, Frank Faylen, Richard Devon. Josh Randall goes in search of a gunman wanted for robbery and murder. The only way he will recognize his quarry is by the odd way he draws his gun.

164.7 *Ransom for a Nun.* Oct. 18, 1958. GS: Claire Griswold, Lillian Bronson, George Brenlin, Hugh Sanders, Terry Frost. Bounty hunter Josh Randall offers to escort a killer to Tucson for safekeeping. Although the killer is in prison the sheriff fears that the man's gang will try to rescue him.

164.8 *Miracle at Pot Hole.* Oct. 25, 1958. GS: Jay C. Flippen, Paul Wexler, Steve Brodie, John Dierkes, Frank Marlowe, Helen Jay, Claire Carleton. Bounty hunter Josh Randall tracks down a wanted murderer and then turns his captive over to a sheriff. Later Randall learns that the sheriff is crooked and begins to have doubts about the wanted man's guilt.

164.9 *The Fourth Headstone.* Nov. 1, 1958. GS: Mona Freeman, Rusty Lane, Russ Conway. Josh Randall is deputized to bring in a woman wanted for murder. After meeting the woman, Josh is convinced that she is innocent of the crime.

164.10 *Til Death Do Us Part.* Nov. 8, 1958. GS: Mala Powers, Gerald Mohr. A pretty girl is wanted for murder, but bounty hunter Josh Randall learns that the victim is very much alive. He tries to clear the girl of the murder charge.

164.11 *The Favor.* Nov. 15, 1958. GS: Skip Homeier, Sam Buffington, Joe Perry, Douglas Kennedy. Josh Randall begins a dangerous journey when he escorts a murder suspect back to justice.

164.12 *Ricochet.* Nov. 22, 1958. GS: Ross Elliot, Tom Drake, Jean Willes, J. Carrol Naish, Onslow Stevens, Barbara Eller, Regis Toomey. A woman asks Josh Randall to track down her missing husband, a doctor. Josh soon learns that the woman plans to kill her husband once he is found.

164.13 *Sheriff of Red Rock.* Nov. 29, 1958. GS: Joe Mantell, Frank Silvera, James Best, Gordon Polk, John Litel. When bounty hunter Josh Randall brings in a man suspected of murder, he is thrown in jail. He learns that the sheriff has teamed up with two murderers in a scheme to make money by jailing innocent people and claiming they are wanted outlaws.

164.14 *Die by the Gun.* Dec. 6, 1958. GS: John Wilder, Warren Oates, Ray Teal, Russ Bender, John Larch, Forrest Lewis. Bounty hunter Josh Randall is bringing in a prisoner wanted for robbery when the two are ambushed by a pair of killers.

164.15 *Rawhide Breed.* Dec. 13, 1958. GS: George Macready, Charles Cooper, Steve Rolland, John Schefering. Josh Randall and Jefferson Klingsmith are the only passengers who escape death when the stagecoach in which they are riding is attacked by marauding Indians. Among the dead is a prisoner Randall was bringing to justice. The two survivors attempt to escape further attention from the Indians only to be hounded by the prisoner's two brothers who are out gunning for Randall.

164.16 *Eight Cent Record.* Dec. 20, 1958. GS: Jay North, Virginia Gregg, Mort Mills, Lloyd Corrigan, John Cliff, Sam Buffington, Robert Foulk, Richard Reeves, James Bell. A little boy gets the notion of retaining Josh Randall to bring in Santa Clause.

164.17 *Drop to Drink.* Dec. 27, 1958. GS: Joe Maross, John Cliff, Alan Wells, Victor Rodman, Dabbs Greer, Willis Bouchey, Kenneth MacDonald. Bounty hunter Josh Randall is hired by a Pony Express company to resolve the mystery surrounding a murdered express rider and a stolen ring.

164.18 *Rope Law.* Jan. 3, 1959. GS: Richard Arlen, Darryl Hickman, Sidney Blackmer, Robert Strauss, Virginia Christine, Herb Vigran, David Whorf. Bounty hunter Josh Randall undertakes a big job as he sets out to prevent the hanging of his prisoner, despite the fact that circumstantial evidence links the prisoner with the murder of his young stepdaughter.

164.19 *Six-Up to Bannack.* Jan. 10, 1959. GS: James Best, Stacy Harris, Sam Buffington. Josh Randall rides with his prisoner on a stagecoach in a race against time to reach the town of Bannach and prevent the hanging of an innocent man. The stage, however, is carrying dynamite, and is therefore unable to travel fast.

164.20 *The Spur.* Jan. 17, 1959. GS: Betsy Drake, Don Durant, Dick Foran, Robert Ellenstein, Bob Nichols, Jonathan Hole, Mel Gaines. Josh Randall refuses to believe reports that the bank robber he is trailing has been murdered, and decides to continue his search for the man.

164.21 *Reunion for Revenge.* Jan. 24, 1959. GS: Ralph Meeker, Alan Wells, James Coburn, Judith Braun, Ed Kemmer, Michael Fox, Alan Reynolds, Frank Cardell. Josh Randall is bringing in a man who is wanted not only by the law but also by a group of escaped convicts. The convicts feel that Randall's prisoner was responsible for their going to jail, and they intend to square matters.

164.22 *Competition.* Jan. 31, 1959. GS: Lee Farr, Charles Aidman, Patricia Crowley, King Calder, Charles Seel, Lindsay Workman. Josh Randall rides into Abilene for a vacation and a whirl at the casinos. While he is visiting his friend Sheriff Neely, a pair of bounty hunters ride up with a dead man tied across a horse. The corpse is identified as a man named Wilson, a local farmer who had a reputation for gentleness and kindliness. Randall becomes suspicious when he notes that Wilson was shot in the back.

164.23 *Call Your Shot.* Feb. 7, 1959. GS: James Dunn, Steve Brodie, Luana Patten, Robert Burton, Louise Lormer, James Burke, John Milford, William Schallert, Rusty Wescoatt, Dale Van Sickle. Bounty hunter Josh Randall is hired by Gabe Henshaw, a local drunk, to locate his son.

164.24 *Secret Ballot.* Feb. 14, 1959. GS: John Lupton, Wayne Morris, Bethel Leslie, Mary Beth Hughes, DeForest Kelley, Troy Melton, Bill Catching. Josh Randall attempts to aid the political campaign of a friend who is running for mayor. Josh suddenly finds himself accused of murder.

164.25 *The Corner.* Feb. 21, 1959. GS: William Phipps, Don Gordon, James Dobson, John Damler, Arthur Space, Alan Reynolds, Judith Ames, Nolan Leary, John Litel, Dean Cromer. Accused of killing a friend, Josh Randall tries to prove himself innocent.

164.26 *Eager Man.* Feb. 28, 1959. GS: Toni Geary, John Hackett, Richard Devon, Walter Sande, Olan Soule, Craig Duncan. A fugitive is willing to surrender if he is assured that his wife will get a share of the reward money. Josh Randall agrees to help him, but another bounty hunter is also on the fugitive's trail

164.27 *The Legend.* March 7, 1959. GS: Victor Jory, Michael Landon, Nan Leslie, Warren Oates, Kenneth Tobey, Roy Barcroft. Rancher Sam McGarrett hires Josh Randall to help him to find some hidden gold. Two desperadoes are also searching for the treasure.

164.28 *Railroaded.* March 14, 1959. GS: Edgar Buchanan, Mort Mills, Buzz Martin, Jack Kruschen, Kasey Rogers, James Nolan, Jon Lormer. When a young boy is accused of killing a Pinkerton detective, Josh Randall attempts to prove the lad innocent.

164.29 *Double Fee.* March 21, 1959. GS: June Vincent, Diane Brewster, Christopher Dark, Robert H. Harris, Peggy

Maley, John Harmon, Penny McEvoy, Robert Lynn. Josh Randall is hired by an opera star to deliver the ransom money asked by a kidnaper who is holding her sister.

164.30 *The Kovack Affair.* March 28, 1959. GS: Jacques Aubuchon, Jean Willes, James Coburn, Alan Wells, Lester Dorr, Bobby Clark, Mel Carter, Olan Soule, Mike Steele. Under pressure from a gambler to give up his control in a hotel, a man turns to his friend Josh Randall for help.

164.31 *Bounty for a Bride.* April 4, 1959. GS: Lori Nelson, Michael Pate, Patrick McVey, Joe Perry, Than Wyenn. A man hires Josh Randall to persuade his daughter to come back home. The girl, who was kidnaped by Indians years before, refuses to return because she feels that the Indians are now her people.

164.32 *Crossroads.* April 11, 1959. GS: John McIntire, Clu Gulager, Hugh Sanders. On the trail of an escaped murderer, Josh Randall finds that he has to contend with the elusive fugitive's father.

164.33 *Angels of Vengeance.* April 18, 1959. GS: John Dehner, Judith Ames, Eduard Franz, Bob Nichols, Bob Griffin, Donald Cook. Josh Randall is forced to kill a youth in self-defense and finds himself the target of an unusual vengeance.

164.34 *Littlest Giant.* April 25, 1959. GS: Sarah Selby, Anna Marie Nanasi, William Schallert, Anthony Caruso, William Fawcett, Marian Collier. Josh Randall finds it very difficult to refuse the earnest pleas of a ten-year-old girl. The little girl firmly believes that her father, reportedly dead, is still alive and she wants Randall to find him.

164.35 *The Conquerers.* May 2, 1959. GS: Paul Carr, Than Wyenn, Michael Pate, John Eldridge, John Dehner, Joe Perry, Steve Darrell. The son of a wealthy banker runs away and joins a band of marauders. The banker, anxious to find his son, hires bounty hunter Josh Randall to help him.

164.36 *Amos Carter.* May 9, 1959. GS: Arthur Hunnicutt, Willis Bouchey, Edgar Buchanan, Warren Oates, Olan Soule. Two families have been engaged in a reckless feud that has reached dangerous proportions. Bounty hunter Josh Randall attempts to solve the differences.

Second Season

164.37 *Montana Kid.* Sept. 5, 1959. GS: Richard Eyer, Steve Brodie, Jean Willes, Richard Devon, Clancy Cooper. The Montana Kid is released from jail without knowing that bounty hunter Josh Randall paid his bail. Randall is trying to locate card sharp Johnny Deuce, and he believes the Kid will lead him to the gambler.

164.38 *The Healing Woman.* Sept. 12, 1959. GS: Mort Mills, John Collier, Virginia Gregg, James Westerfield, Paul Engle, Helen Kleeb. Rejecting orthodox medicine, a desperate father takes his seriously ill son to an old medicine woman. Bounty hunter Josh Randall attempts to take the boy from the raving medicine woman and angry father so that a doctor can operate.

164.39 *The Matchmaker.* Sept. 19, 1959. GS: Royal Dano, Fay Spain, Kasey Rogers, Virginia Christine, Steven Talbot, Clegg Hoyt, Mauritz Hugo. Charlie Wright, a good friend of Josh Randall's, has been tagged the ugliest man in town. Charlie is eager to get married but he doesn't think anyone would marry him. Josh takes pity on his friend and offers to find a bride for him.

164.40 *Breakout.* Sept. 26, 1959. GS: Phillip Pine, Mona Freeman, Richard Carlyle, William Phipps, Walter Coy. Josh Randall is hired to trace a large sum of stolen money. In order to find it, Randall helps a convict involved in the theft escape from jail. He then discovers that some unscrupulous government agents are also trying to locate the loot.

164.41 *Estralita.* Oct. 3, 1959. GS: Rita Lynn, Robert J. Wilke, Charles Aidman, Chris Alcaide, Jeff de Benning. Josh Randall is hunting a murderer in hopes of collecting the reward money. As he gets closer to his quarry, he discovers that an angry mob is anxious to locate the murderer too.

164.42 *The Hostage.* Oct. 10, 1959. GS: Lon Chaney, Jr., Jack Kruschen, DeForest Kelley, Olan Soule. Tracing a murderer, Josh Randall encounters a sheriff who provides him with a lead. Randall soon discovers that his own life is in danger.

164.43 *The Empty Cell.* Oct. 17, 1959. GS: Lee Van Cleef, Alexander Scourby, Marcia Henderson, Joe Conley, Tyler McVey. Josh Randall delivers a prisoner to jail, but he must wait a day to receive his reward. The next day Josh discovers that the prisoner is gone, and the sheriff is not the same man Randall met the day before.

164.44 *Bad Gun.* Oct. 24, 1959. GS: King Donovan, Harry Bellaver, Jacqueline Russell, Steve Darrell, Jeff Daley, Rodney Bell. A gun salesman realizes he has sold a defective gun to a man. The salesman hires bounty hunter Josh Randall to find the man before any damage is done.

164.45 *The Tyrant.* Oct. 31, 1959. GS: R.G. Armstrong, Frank Albertson, Vaughn Taylor, Russ Conway, Dick Garner. Josh Randall is hired to bring in an Army deserter. Randall tracks the man to a town, where he finds him held prisoner by the town marshal.

164.46 *Reckless.* Nov. 7, 1959. GS: Everett Sloane, Les Johnson, Ron Hayes, Jean Allison, Mark Allen, Joseph Ruskin. During an argument over a girl, a young man is shot. The victim's father hires Josh Randall to capture the killer.

164.47 *Desert Seed.* Nov. 14, 1959. GS: Carlos Romero, Rafael Campos, Miriam Colon, Tom Gilson, Bing Russell. Juan Gomez shoots a man in self-defense and then runs away. Josh Randall goes after him.

164.48 *Twelve Hours to Crazy Horse.* Nov. 21, 1959. GS: John Dehner, James Lydon, Dabbs Greer. Josh Randall is bringing an accused murderer to trial. But the brother of the murder victim wants to mete out his own brand of justice.

164.49 *No Trail Back.* Nov. 28, 1959. GS: Wright King, Robert J. Wilke, Howard Petrie, Forrest Lewis, Blackie Austin, Guy Teague. Josh Randall goes on the trail of a pair of bank robbers who have bungled the job. Randall catches up with them and discovers that one of the men has been bitten by a rabid dog.

164.50 *Man on Horseback.* Dec. 5, 1959. GS: Jay Silverheels, Fred Beir, Jeanne Cooper, James T. Chandler, Howard Negley, Alan Wells. Charley Red Cloud, an Apache accused of murder, flees into wild Indian country. Josh Randall decides that the high bounty offered for Charley is worth the risk of tracking him down.

164.51 *Chain Gang.* Dec. 12, 1959. GS: Dave Willock, Ted de Corsia, Laurie Mitchell, Chris Alcaide, James Burke. While camping on the trail one night, Josh Randall is confronted by a sheriff, who arrests the bounty hunter on a false charge. He is then turned over to a mine owner to work in a chain gang.

164.52 *Vanishing Act.* Dec. 26, 1959. GS: Lawrence Dobkin, Dyan Cannon, Steven Darrell, Ken Mayer, Brad Weston. Bartolo the Baffler, a magician, draws the townspeople to his performance outside the city. While he awes the crowd, outlaws enter the bank in the deserted town.

164.53 *Mental Lapse.* Jan. 2, 1960. GS: Harry Townes, Jan Shepard, Ed Prentiss, Paul Dubov, John Parris, Billy Halop. A man tacks up a poster requesting information about himself. Josh Randall learns that the man is an amnesia victim.

164.54 *Angela.* Jan. 9, 1960. GS: Fay Spain, Richard Bakalyan, Joe Partridge, Warren Oates, Wayne Rogers, Howard Petrie, Earl Hodgins. After witnessing her father's murder, Angela Prior is determined to bring the killer to the gallows. But Josh Randall, who has been hunting the man in connection with another crime, wants to postpone the killer's execution.

164.55 *The Monsters.* Jan. 16, 1960. GS: Martin Landau, Eugene Martin, Bek Nelson, Ned Glass, Russell Thorson, William Fawcett. An elephant trainer is using an elephant to frighten people away from their villages so that he can plunder the towns. Bounty hunter Josh Randall decides to put an end to the man's activities.

164.56 *The Most Beautiful Woman.* Jan. 23, 1960. GS: Arthur Franz, Mort Mills, Gordon Polk, Owen Bush, Grace Albertson, James Parnell. John Garth, an Easterner, offers Josh Randall $100 a day to find his fiancee. He refuses to believe she is dead. The people of a frontier town are unwilling to tell Randall anything about the girl.

164.57 *Jason.* Jan. 30, 1960. GS: Sean McClory, Barry Kelley, Frank Krieg, Bill Catching, Lennie Geer, Orville Sherman, Pierre Watkin. While tracing an elusive desperado, Josh Randall encounters a deputy sheriff who begs to join the manhunt. Randall reluctantly agrees.

164.58 *The Partners.* Feb. 6, 1960. GS: Robert Morris, Elaine Riley, Leslie Bradley, Richard Farnsworth, Wayne Heffley. Josh Randall is accustomed to working alone, but young Jason Nichols, a deputy sheriff talks him into forming a partnership.

164.59 *Tolliver Bender.* Feb. 13, 1960. GS: Douglas Fowley, Gloria Talbott, John Carradine, Ken Becker, Percy Helton, Howard Negley, Frank Sully, Robert Stephenson. Josh Randall and his new partner Jason Nichols save a man from the gallows so that he can testify at a trial. But the citizens demand a hostage to insure his return.

164.60 *A House Divided.* Feb. 20, 1960. GS: Don Gordon, Eduard Franz, Stafford Repp, Helen Wescott, Jan Arvan, Fred Sherman, Raymond Hatton, Murray Parker. Josh Randall and Jason Nichols become involved in a dangerous family dispute.

164.61 *Triple Vise.* Feb. 27, 1960. GS: Chana Eden, Bing Russell, Jose Gonzalez Gonzalez, Nestor Paiva, Salvador Baguez, Carlos Rivera, William Phipps. Josh and Jason chase a killer to Mexico, where Josh meets a barmaid who has a few new angles on bounty hunting.

164.62 *Black Belt.* March 19, 1960. GS: Robert Kino, Richard Crane, Stuart Randall, Chubby Johnson. Josh and Jason are hired to track a murderer. They don't know that their employer is the real killer.

164.63 *The Parish.* March 26, 1960. GS: Don Dubbins, Susan Oliver, Rhys Williams. Josh agrees to keep an eye on the son of an old friend, but he's tempted to break his promise. The young man has deliberately withheld the town's medical supplies.

164.64 *Vendetta.* April 9, 1960. GS: Arthur Batanides, Harry Townes, Willis Bouchey, Bert Remsen, Fred Colby, Joe Haworth. Josh is all set to collect the bounty on a killer. Then he learns that his prisoner's been hired to start an Indian war, and the man who hired him may start it alone.

164.65 *Death, Divided by Three.* April 23, 1960. GS: Mara Corday, Richard Garland, John Harmon, Walter Sande, Mark Allen. The bounty hunters trap their man in a stable. Then the killer's wife takes a hand in the proceedings and she kills her own husband.

164.66 *The Inheritance.* April 30, 1960. GS: John Litel, Edward Kemmer, Don Kennedy, John Anderson, Maxine Cooper, Thomas B. Henry, George Eldredge. Blind and dying, the owner of the biggest ranch west of the Missouri asks Randall to find his only son. The boy left home years before.

164.67 *Prison Trail.* May 14, 1960. GS: Beverly Garland, Brad Dexter, Claude Akins, Joe Di Reda, Bill Tannen. Josh and Jason are taking three men and a girl to jail. The girl is terrified when she spots a stranger along the way.

164.68 *Payoff at Pinto.* May 21, 1960. GS: Philip Ahn, Barry Kelley, Addison Richards, Harlan Warde, Than Wyenn. The bank of Pinto is robbed, and the town panics. Fearing for his life, the bank owner summons Josh Randall for help.

Season Three

164.69 *The Trial.* Sept. 21, 1960. GS: Paul Burke, James Coburn, John Pickard, Edwin Mills, Bob January. Josh is hired to capture Daniel Trenner, a former Union officer. His employer, a man named Howard Catlett, claims to be a representative of the law.

164.70 *The Cure.* Sept. 28, 1960. GS: Harold J. Stone, Claudia Bryar, Thomas B. Henry, Charles P. Thompson. Spinster Emily Kendrick sees a chance to reform hard-drinking Harry Simmons. She hires Josh Randall to keep Harry Respectable long enough for a visit from his long-lost brother, and maybe long enough for a trip to the altar.

164.71 *Journey for Josh.* Oct. 5, 1960. GS: Lisa Gaye, Jason Wingreen. A girl named Susan is wanted in Allenton as an accomplice in a holdup. Josh is taking her into town, but he has a tough adversary — his own heart.

164.72 *The Looters.* Oct. 12, 1960. GS: Dennis Patrick, Tom Gilson, John Alderman, Gloria Blondell, Dave Willock. Josh is on his way to River City to pick up a trio of desperadoes in the custody of River City's sheriff. But a tornado beats him to town, and the crooks escape.

164.73 *The Twain Shall Meet.* Oct. 19, 1960. GS: Michael Lipton, Mary Tyler Moore, Howard Ledig, Allen Jaffe. Arthur Pierce Madison, a Boston newspaper reporter, is after an exclusive story. He wants to join Josh on a real bounty-hunting trip in the Wild West.

164.74 *The Showdown.* Oct. 26, 1960. GS: Tom Drake, June Dayton, Jackie Loughery, Walter Sande, Mark Allen, William Vaughn. Johnny Haywood once saved Josh Randall's life. Now he's in jail on a murder charge and he wants Josh to help him escape.

164.75 *Surprise Witness.* Nov. 2, 1960. GS: Sara Price, Argentine Brunetti, Bill Quinn, Lee Bergere, Sam Hearn, Robert W. Kenneally. One of Josh's friends is murdered by some hired gunslingers. But when Josh tries to find out who did the hiring, the whole town clams up. It seems everybody has been threatened with the same fate.

164.76 *To the Victor.* Nov. 9, 1960. GS: Frank Albertson, Suzanne Storrs, Susan Crane, Jan Stine, Olan Soule, Hal K. Dawson. The men in Coronado are wrecking the town with their gunplay. The women leave town, and wont' come back until the guns are put away.

164.77 *Criss Cross.* Nov. 16, 1960. GS: Mark Rydell, Vaughn Taylor, John Craven, Patricia King, Robert Nash. Josh doggedly tracks a robber and finally gets his man. But when he brings him in, there's another problem. The sheriff says it's the wrong man.

164.78 *The Medicine Man.* Nov. 23, 1960. GS: John Baer, J. Pat O'Malley, Cloris Leachman, Ted de Corsia, Dick Bartell, Ben Morris. A large sum of money is missing from the bank and so is bank teller Jim Lansing. But a friend of Josh's, a medicine man called Doc, says Lansing is innocent.

164.79 *One Mother Too Many.* Dec. 7, 1960. GS: Joyce Meadows, Bryan Russell, Betty Lou Gerson, Raymond Greenleaf, Lewis Charles. Beth Morrison has just become a widow. Fearing she will lose custody of her son unless she acquires a father for him, Beth proposes to Josh.

164.80 *The Choice.* Dec. 14, 1960. GS: Maxine Stuart, Dick Foran, Burt Douglas, Barbara Hines, Chuck Hayward. Jane Koster's husband Frank is a bounty hunter too, but Jane hires Josh to find him before he's killed. It seems he is after outlaw Stacy Lenz, who has already shot him once.

164.81 *Three for One.* Dec. 21, 1960. GS: Richard Anderson, Adam Becker, Harry Landers, Gloria Talbott, Leonard Bell, Kasey Rogers. Josh has captured a crook named Tom, who has a couple of buddies that go to considerable lengths to set him free. These buddies, Lafe Martin and Ben Farrell, take three innocent townspeople as hostages.

164.82 *Witch Woman.* Dec. 28, 1960. GS: Victor Millan, Julio Montoya, Rodolfo Hoyos, Jeanette Nolan. Rafael Guerra doesn't believe in the powers of La Curandera, a local conjure woman, she he hires Josh to make sure the old crone stays away from his expectant wife. But Don Emilio, Guerra's father-in-law, insists that La Curandera should help his daughter.

164.83 *Baa-Baa.* Jan. 4, 1961. GS: Dave Willock, Hollis Irving, Stuart Randall, Gerald Milton, Robert Easton, Judith Rawlins, Wally Brown, Frank Gerstle. Josh has been hired to track down some strange characters in his time, but now George Goode wants him to find his wife's pet ewe.

164.84 *The Last Retreat.* Jan. 11, 1961. GS: Constance Ford, Ross Elliot, Warren Oates, John Cliff, William Hudson. Sarah Lawton's testimony clinches a murder conviction against Clem Robinson, but Robinson hasn't been transferred to the territorial prison yet. So lawyer Jim Lawton hires Josh to protect his wife from Robinson's revenge.

164.85 *Bounty on Josh.* Jan. 25, 1961. GS: Jean Allison, Mike Green, Jay Adler, Rhys Williams. A cash offer lures Josh to a small town. When he tries to find the man who hired him and learn what he is supposed to do, someone takes a shot at him.

164.86 *Hero in the Dust.* Feb. 1, 1961. GS: Nick Bon Tempi, Paul Bon Tempi, Audrey Clarke-Caire, Ralph Bell. It's no good being a twin when your brother has a price on his head. Fearing for his own life, Harry Weaver begs Josh to find his brother Pete, a fugitive from a murder charge.

164.87 *Epitaph.* Feb. 8, 1961. GS: Richard Anderson, Lewis Charles, Enid Janes, Bart Burns, Jim Sommers, Jim Drake. Sheriff Jim Kramer robs the local bank and Josh is asked to hunt him down. Josh's job isn't easy because Kramer was once his close friend.

164.88 *The Voice of Silence.* Feb. 15, 1961. GS: Roy Barcroft, Carolyn Kearney, Dick Rich, Vince Deadrick, Chuck Ball, Herman Rudin. Frank Hagen hires Josh to guard his deafmute daughter Carol while he is gone on business.

164.89 *El Gato.* Feb. 22, 1961. GS: Olan Soule, Noah Beery, Jr., Steven Marlo, Roberto Contreras, Linda Cordova. Archie Warner has traveled all the way from New York to a small Mexican border town, and he wants Josh to help him find a notorious bandit named El Gato. Warner's errand is to snap the desperado's picture.

164.90 *Detour.* March 1, 1961. GS: Howard Morris, Jane Brooks, Howard Smith, Melinda Plowman. City man Clayton Armstrong is in love with Jane Fairweather, a small-town girl. Afraid of the girl's father, Clayton hires Josh to help him elope with her.

164.91 *Monday Morning.* March 8, 1961. GS: Richard Carlyle, Bill Quinn, Ralph Bell, David Manley. Clerk Charlie Glover, with two accomplices, robs his employer Porter Fairchild. Then Charlie has a change of heart, but he is afraid his buddies won't want to return the money.

164.92 *The Long Search.* March 15, 1961. GS: Linda Wong, Dale Ishimoto, William Eben Stephens, Robert W. Kenneally, Stanley Clements. Bill Timmons promised to marry a geisha-girl named Yoshika, but he never returned to Japan. Yoshika comes to the United States and hires Josh to find her delinquent suitor.

164.93 *Dead Reckoning.* March 22, 1961. GS: James Lydon, Jan Brooks, Chuck Hayward, John Alderman, Roy Engel, Leonard Bell. Paul Brecker is on the run. The Taggert boys want to even the score with him for killing their brother. But Decker's wife tells Josh the killing was done in self-defense, and he rides after the hunted man hoping to find him before the avenging Taggerts do.

164.94 *Barney's Bounty.* March 29, 1961. GS: Noah Berry, Jr., Jan Arvan, Jonathan Bolt, Bill Quinn, Vince Deadrick, Al Austin, William Hart. Josh is about to rent a couple of horses from Barney Durant when the two gunmen in his custody escape with Barney's horses. So Barney decides to become a bounty hunter himself.

Wells Fargo see *Tales of Wells Fargo*

165. The Westerner

NBC. 30 min. Broadcast history: Friday, 8:30-9:00, Sept. 1960–Dec. 1960.

Whispering Smith

Regular Cast: Brian Keith (Dave Blassingame), John Dehner (Burgundy Smith).

Premise: This series depicted the exploits of cowboy Dave Blassingame near the Mexican border in the 1890s.

The Episodes

165.1 *Jeff*. Sept. 30, 1960. GS: Diana Millay, Geoffrey Toone, Charles Horvath, Warren Oates, Wayne Tucker, Michael Green, Marie Selland, William Sharon.

165.2 *School Days*. Oct. 7, 1960. GS: R.G. Armstrong, John Anderson, Richard Rust, Maggie Mahoney, William Tracy, Frank Hagney, James Anderson, Dub Taylor, Bill Quinn, William Mims. Blassingame arrives on the scene of a murder, just in time to be accused of committing it. Fleeing from a posse eager to string him up, Dave turns himself over to a deputy sheriff. But the weak-willed lawman won't stop the lynch mob from taking him.

165.3 *Brown*. Oct. 21, 1960. GS: John Dehner, Harry Swoger, Victor Izay, Conlan Carter, Henry A. Gobble, Chris Carter, Michael T. Mikler, Rudy Dolan, Jimmy Lee Cook. Burgundy Smith, a fast-talking gent from the Yukon Territory, wants to buy Dave's dog, Brown. Dave says no sale, but agrees to have a friendly drink.

165.4 *Mrs. Kennedy*. Oct. 28, 1960. GS: Paul Richards, Jean Allison, Wendell Holmes. Mrs. Kennedy takes a shine to her husband's new hired hand, Dave Blassingame. Marsh Kennedy demonstrates his disapproval.

165.5 *Dos Pinos*. Nov. 4, 1960. GS: Red Morgan, Malcolm Atterbury, Adam Williams, Jean Willes, Marie Selland, Michael T. Mikler, Marianna Hill. Blassingame rides into the town of Dos Pinos to find a trio of trail bums plaing a weird game. They have shot rancher Red Coons and are betting he will die before morning.

165.6 *The Courting of Libby*. Nov. 11, 1960. GS: Joan O'Brien, John Dehner, John Apone, Rudy Dolan, Henry Gobble, Jimmy Lee Cook, Barney Brown, Marie Selland.

165.7 *Treasure*. Nov. 18, 1960. GS: Malcolm Atterbury, Arthur Hunnicut, Victor Izay, Henry A. Gobble, Leonard P. Geer, Michael Morgan.

165.8 *The Old Man*. Nov. 25, 1960. GS: Sam Jaffe, Robert J. Wilke, Michael Forest, Dee Pollack, Frank Ferguson, Michael Mikler, Jimmy Lee Cook, Marie Selland, Earle Hodgins, Ryan Hayes.

165.9 *Ghost of a Chance*. Dec. 2, 1960. GS: Katy Jurado, Joseph Wiseman, Pepe Callahan, Roberto Contreras, Julio Alejos Corona, Irene Calvillo.

165.10 *Line Camp*. Dec. 9, 1960. GS: Robert Culp, Slim Pickens, Carl Swenson, Hari Rhodes, Hank Patterson, Jimmy Lee Cook.

165.11 *Going Home*. Dec. 16, 1960. GS: Mary Murphy, Virginia Gregg, Jack Kruschen, John Brinkley, Michael T. Mikler, Rudy Dolan, Jimmy Lee Cook.

165.12 *Hand on the Gun*. Dec. 23, 1960. GS: Michael Ansara, Ben Cooper, John Pickard, Wayne Tucker, Hank Gobble.

165.13 *The Painting*. Dec. 30, 1960. GS: John Dehner, Hank Gobble, Paul Sorensen, Waddie Waddle, Tom Steele, Charles La Rocca.

166. *Whispering Smith*

NBC. 30 min. Broadcast history: Monday, 9:00–9:30, May 1961–Sept. 1961.

Reagular Cast: Audie Murphy (Tom "Whispering" Smith), Guy Mitchell (George Romack), Sam Buffington (Chief John Richards).

Premise: This series depicted the exploits of police detective Tom "Whispering" Smith in Denver in the 1870s.

The Episodes

166.1 *The Blind Gun*. May 8, 1961. GS: Jan Merlin, Earl Hansen, Robert Osterloh. Bandit Thad Janeck, sightless as the result of a gunfight in which he was captured, agrees to turn over his booty in exchange for reward money, which he intends to spend for an operation on his eyes.

166.2 *The Grudge*. May 15, 1961. GS: Robert Redford, June Walker, Gloria Talbott. Revenge has a long memory, as Smith seems destined to learn when Ma Gates, widow of an outlaw he once brought to justice, arrives in town with a plan to kill him. To this end, Ma enlists her trigger-happy son Johnny and her daughter Cora in the plan, with Cora as the bait for her lethal trap.

166.3 *The Devil's Share*. May 22, 1961. GS: Clu Gulager, Rosemary Day, James Lydon, Otto Waldis, Kathie Browne. Frank Whalen has just proposed to Marjanne Gaul, a gesture which nettles his brother Jeff, a one-time suitor of Marjanne's. Jeff, in fact, works himself up into such a state that he kills his brother.

166.4 *Stakeout*. May 29, 1961. GS: John Cliff, Troy Melton, Joyce Taylor. Detective Romack is approached by a couple of old friends, outlaws Garrity and Duggan. They remind him that he was once a member of their gang, and if he wants to keep that little secret from his present employer, he had better play along on a robbery they have lined up.

166.5 *Safety Value*. June 5, 1961. GS: Della Sharman, Les Tremayne, Harry Carey, Jr. Several Army officers were shot in the back during skirmishes with the Indians, but there were no Indians behind them, only their own men.

166.6 *Stain of Justice*. June 12, 1961. GS: Richard Chamberlain, Patric Knowles, Nancy Valentine. Judge Wilbur Harrington puts an end to Stella Dean's blackmailing — permanently. But shortly after he leaves Stella's house, his son Chris comes calling, and when Smith arrives there it is Chris holding the murder weapon.

166.7 *The Deadliest Weapon*. June 19, 1961. GS: Aline Towne, Paul Lees, Bartlett Robinson, Don Keefer. Businessman Ralph Miller get an unexpected reaction to his announcement that he is issuing some gold-mine stock — a death threat. Smith and Romack get the job of determining who would profit from Miler's death.

166.8 *The Quest*. June 26, 1961. GS: Ellen Willard, John Harmon, Kay Stewart. Charlotte Laughlin comes to Denver, searching for her mother. The missing matron was quite well known at one time as a dance hall singer.

166.9 *Three for One*. July 3, 1961. GS: Richard Crane, Ken Mayer, Roscoe Ates, Pamela Duncan, K.L. Smith, Tom P. Dillon, Claire Meade. Denver City prisoner Ralph Malone is placed in the custody of two deputies named Lucas and Carter, who supposedly take him back to Phoenix for trial. Then a telegram arrives saying that the two men were imposters.

166.10 *Death at Even Money.* July 10, 1961. GS: Marc Lawrence, Robert Lowery, John Day, Sandy Sanders, Sherwood Price, Herbert C. Lytton. Gambler Frankie Wisdom can't seem to win at ordinary games of chance with Dave Markson. So he proposes a unique wager. He bets that Markson can't prevent him from causing Smith's death.

166.11 *The Hemp Reeger Case.* July 17, 1961. GS: James Best, Patricia Medina, Edward C. Platt, John Craven. Smith finally gets outlaw Hemp Reeger locked up in Sheriff Aiken's jail. But Aiken doesn't like Smith, and it would please him no end if he could help Reeger escape.

166.12 *The Mortal Coil.* July 24, 1961. GS: Henry Brandon, Hugh Sanders. Smith, positive that Claude Denton murdered his twin brother Rex, decides to use an amateur production of "Hamlet" as a means to trap the killer.

166.13 *Cross Cut.* July 31, 1961. GS: Audrey Dalton, Colin Male, Jim Hayward. Smith thinks of April as a sweet young thing spellbound by the charms of an outlaw called Dakota. But April's ambition is to get Dakota and Smith to kill each other in a fight, so she can run off with Dakota's loot.

166.14 *Double Edge.* Aug. 7, 1961. GS: Myron Healey, Lori Nelson, Red Morgan. Venetia Molloy and bandit Jim Conley fall madly in love. There is only one thing that might mar their happiness — Venetia's husband.

166.15 *The Trademark.* Aug. 14, 1961. GS: Marie Windsor, Donald Buka, Andrew Winberg, Forrest Tucker. When a widow, Maple Gray, offers a large sum of money for revenge on the six men who lynched her husband, ex-convict Fred Gavin sets out to collect it. But what he forgets is that murder makes news, and a newspaper has recorded his trademark.

166.16 *The Jodie Tyler Story.* Aug. 21, 1961. GS: Rachel Foulger, Read Morgan, Jimmy Carter. A grocery store owner is murdered and robbed of a large sum of money by Hob Tyler, a notorious gunman. When his sister Jodie pays exactly the same amount to buy the dead man's store, the local citizens get suspicious.

166.17 *Poet and Peasant Case.* Aug. 28, 1961. GS: Alan Mowbray, Jack Catron, Yvonne Adrian, Paul Keast, Dean Williams. Lord Hillary, a famous English poet touring America, is robbed and his stagecoach driver is murdered. Another Englishman, Carruthers comes under suspicion. The two men had met previously in a Denver bar and it was obvious they didn't hit it off.

166.18 *Dark Circle.* Sept. 4, 1961. GS: E.J. Andre, Diana Millay, Carleton Young, Adam Williams. A lawyer named Philo likes to drink, but he hates Fender, the local saloonkeeper. When Fender gets killed it looks as if Philo had something to do with it, even though the lawyer claims he was dead drunk at the time.

166.19 *Swift Justice.* Sept. 11, 1961. GS: Monte Burkhart, Minerva Urecal, William Tannen. The MacDonalds and the Campbells, always feuding, decide that the way to settle which clan is bet is to arrange a horse race. The whole town bets on the outcome, but there is something they don't bargain on. When a Campbell steed takes the lead, the rider gets shot.

166.20 *The Idol.* Sept. 18, 1961. GS: Joan O'Brien, Alan Hale, Jr., John Stephenson, Larry Perron, Marjorie Reynolds. Ole Brindessen sees swindler Edie Royce commit murder, but refuses to go to the police. His reason is that Ole's girl friend, Marilyn, is in love with Royce.

167. *Wichita Town*

NBC. 30 min. Broadcast history: Wednesday, 10:30–11:00, Sept. 1959–April 1960.

Regular Cast: Joel McCrea (Marshal Mike Dunbar), Jody McCrea (Deputy Ben Matheson), Carlos Romero (Deputy Rico Rodriguez), Bob Anderson (Aeneas MacLinahan), George Neise (Nat Wyndham), Robert Foulk (Joe Kingston).

Premise: Marshal Mike Dunbar attempts to maintain law and order in Wichita Town, Kansas, in the 1870s.

The Episodes

167.1 *The Night the Cowboys Roared.* Sept. 30, 1959. GS: Tony Montenaro, Frank Ferguson, Chuck Hayward. A band of boisterous cowboys ride into Wichita and begin playfully to shoot up the town. An overenthusiastic cowhand shoots a young boy. When the cowboy is jailed, his friends swear they will get him out.

167.2 *Wyndham's Way.* Oct. 7, 1959. Marshal Mike Dunbar is surprised to see a doctor ride into Wichita. The town has been without a doctor, and Dunbar tries to persuade the stranger to stay. But the doctor loses interest when a band of hostile Indians make an attempt on his life.

167.3 *Bullet for a Friend.* Oct. 14, 1959. GS: Robert J. Wilke, Carlos Romero, James Griffith. During the absence of Marshal Dunbar, gunman Rico Rodriguez comes to Wichita. Despite Rico's warning Johnny Burke vows to kill Vic Parker, a man who once double-crossed him.

167.4 *They Won't Hang Jimmy Relson.* Oct. 21, 1959. GS: Vic Morrow, Carlos Romero, Dave Willock. A hanging is scheduled for Wichita, and despite the guilty man's protests Marshal Dunbar prepares for the execution. But Jimmy Relson, the condemned man, laughs at Dunbar's precautions and swears that the hanging will never happen.

167.5 *Drifting.* Oct. 28, 1959. GS: John Larch, John McIntire, Benny Niles, L.Q. Jones. A gunman named Gant comes to Wichita looking for a Frank Matheson. Ben Matheson suddenly realizes that the hired killer is seeking his father, who had deserted the Matheson family and disappeared twelve years before.

167.6 *Man on the Hill.* Nov. 4, 1959. GS: Mort Mills, Don Grady, Virginia Gregg, Jan Shepard, Jenifer Lea, William Schallert. Pete Bennett, a Wichita farmer, goes on a killing spree and threatens the life of young Arnie Slocum. Marshal Dunbar and his deputy realize they must outsmart a madman in order to save Arnie's life.

167.7 *Day of Battle.* Jan. 18, 1959. GS: Robert Foulk, Carlos Romero, Nan Leslie, Harry Lauter, Jean Willes, John Stephenson. Marshal Mike Dunbar learns about an illicit romance in Wichita. Afraid that trouble may result, the Marshal decides to intervene.

167.8 *Compadre.* Nov. 25, 1959. GS: Carlos Romero, Robert Foulk, Victor Millan. Rafael is constantly ridiculed and taunted by two fellow cowhands. One night in a bar, Rafael's tormentors set out to get him drunk.

167.9 *Passage to the Enemy.* Dec. 2, 1959. GS: Robert Vaughn, Jean Inness, Ben Cooper. Marshal Mike Dunbar decides to allow accused murderer Frank Warren to see his dying mother. But Frank must be smuggled past the brother and father of his murder victim who have sworn revenge.

167.10 *Out of the Past.* Dec. 9, 1959. GS: Skip Homeier, Robert H. Harris, Jan Stine. A bounty hunter rides into Wichita looking for a man who committed a crime some years past. It is discovered that the guilty man is a German immigrant who is a skilled gunsmith.

167.11 *Death Watch.* Dec. 16, 1959. GS: Howard Negley, Phillip Pine, Tina Carver, John Dehner. During a furious Kansas cyclone Marshal Mike Dunbar, Deputy Ben Matheson and Doc Wyndham take a wounded man into a storm cellar. They are unaware that the man's assailant is also in the cellar.

167.12 *The Devil's Choice.* Dec. 23, 1959. GS: Robert Bray, Richard Coogan, Bob Swan, Carlos Romero, Dave Willock, Earl Hodgins, Dabbs Greer, Arthur Space, Fred Sherman. Marshal Dunbar and his deputy discover the dead body of a federal agent who was escorting two killers. Three men with the body all claim to be Rev. Nichols, but Dunbar knows that two of the men are murderers.

167.13 *Biggest Man in Town.* Dec. 30, 1959. GS: Don Dubbins, Yvonne Lime, Ron Hagerthy, Bill Catching. Outlaw Ab Singleton is beating an old man when mild-mannered Petey McGlasson happens on the scene. Petey fires his gun wildly and a shot hits the outlaw.

167.14 *Ruby Dawes.* Jan. 6, 1960. GS: Marilyn Erskine, Charles Aidman, Jock Gaynor, Gregg Walcott. Pretty Ruby Dawes brings outlaw Wes Barker to Wichita in search of a doctor. Marshal Dunbar is strongly attracted to the girl.

167.15 *Bought.* Jan. 13, 1960. GS: Robert Middleton, Enid Janes, Rodney Bell, Cliff Field. Sam Buhl claims that he bought a young Indian squaw for several bottles of whisky. Ben Matheson tries to protect the young girl, and this makes Sam furious.

167.16 *The Long Night.* Jan. 20, 1960. GS: Charles Seel, Sherwood Price, Peter Leeds, Richard Keene, Angus Duncan, Joe McGuinn. Mike Dunbar learns that he has helped convict an innocent man of murder. He attempts to notify prison officials, but circumstances delay the message and the man is hanged.

167.17 *Seed of Hate.* Jan. 2,7 1960. GS: Keith Larsen, Francis J. McDonald, Harry Harvey, Jr., Ben Chadwick, Armand Alzamora, Larry Chance. During a tribal ritual, Blue Raven gets drunk and reams that he must slay a white man wearing a badge. The Indian brave picks Deputy Ben Matheson as the victim.

167.18 *The Avengers.* Feb. 3, 1960. GS: Emile Meyer, Tom Gilson, Paul Carr, John Milford. Mike Dunbar is kidnaped by the three brothers of a man he shot during the war. They tell Mike that their Pa, who was wounded at the same time, is waiting for him.

167.19 *Brothers of the Knife.* Feb. 10, 1960. GS: Anthony Caruso, Abraham Sofaer, David Whorf, Jay Novello, Robert Carricart. The black hand of the Mafia reaches into Wichita when one of its bosses forces a citizen to exact large cash tributes from Sicilian-born families. The man won't heed his son's plea to reveal the plot to Marshal Dunbar.

167.20 *Afternoon in Town.* Feb. 17, 1960. GS: Dick Sargent, James Coburn, Suzanne Lloyd. Scotty and Wally, a couple of cowhands, head for town on their day off. Scotty says he is tired of wine, women and gambling and wants to meet a nice respectable girl, but Wally ridicules him.

167.21 *The Frontiersman.* March 2, 1960. GS: Gene Evans, Frank Kilmond. An itinerant schoolmaster applies for work. Hard-headed town councilmen agree to let him have the job provided he releases balances the city's books and teaches a surly prisoner to read in three days.

167.22 *The Hanging Judge.* March 9, 1960. GS: Frank Lovejoy, Carl Benton Reid, Yale Wexler, Phil Chambers, William Leslie, Suzi Crandall. Marshal Dunbar and his prisoner are greeted by the sight of six men stretched on the gallows when the ride into town.

167.23 *Second Chance.* March 16, 1960. GS: Tom Drake, Robert F. Simon, Charles Herbert, Jane Nigh, Carlos Romero, Dennis Cross, John Pickard. Walt's son Rafe has turned out to be a failure and the old man doesn't want the same thing to happen to Rafe's son. He buys the boy from Rafe.

167.24 *Paid in Full.* March 23, 1960. GS: John McIntire, I. Stanford Jolley, Richard Cutting. Annoyed with Mike, Deputy Ben Matheson ignores an order, and Mike gets shot.

167.25 *The Legend of Tom Horn.* March 30, 1960. GS: Nancy Gates, Michael Pate, Denver Pyle, Bob Bice, Joe Patridge. Unknown rustlers have ruined local ranchers with their slick work. Marshal Dunbar is baffled, so Laurie Carter turns to a legendary stranger to protect her ranch.

167.26 *Sidekicks.* April 6, 1960. GS: Alan Hale, Jr., Ron Hayes, Suzanne Lloyd, Dub Taylor. Wally and Scotty have been sidekicks for a long time, but now Scotty plans to get married and break up the range-riding partnership. Wally has other ideas.

168. *The Wide Country*

NBC. 60 min. Broadcast history: Thursday, 7:30–8:30, Sept. 1962–Sept. 1963.

Regular Cast: Earl Holliman (Mitch Guthrie), Andrew Prine (Andy Guthrie).

Premise: In this series Mitch Guthrie, a champion rodeo rider, has less trouble handling a bronco than settling a difference of opinion with his kid brother, Andy.

The Episodes

168.1 *The Royce Bennett Story.* Sept. 20, 1962. GS: Steve Forrest, Jacqueline Scott, Bill Mumy, Sandy Kenyon, Lennie Geer. Royce Bennett's wife Ella is worried about him. His recent work has not been up to par.

168.2 *A Guy for Clementine.* Sept. 27, 1962. GS: Joyce Bulifant, Noah Beery, Jr., Rosemary Murphy, James McMullan, Edward Holmes. Mitch and Andy meet a girl named Clemmie, who is looking for her father, a veteran rodeo performer. Clemmie claims she hasn't seen her dad since childhood, and now she wants to make sure he attends her wedding.

168.3 *Journey Down a Dusty Road.* Oct. 4, 1962. GS: Wallace Ford, Nellie Burt, Sam Edwards, Roger Mobley, Nesdon Booth. While hitchhiking to the next rodeo, Mitch gets a lift with the Perrys, a family of itinerant farmers. Years earlier, they say, a flood ruined their farm and since then the family has been traveling around, trying to save up enough to buy another place.

168.4 *Who Killed Edde Gannon?* Oct. 11, 1962. GS: Ed Nelson, Russell Johnson, Charles Aidman, Eddie Ryder, Alejandro Rey, Stanley Adams, Shirley Ballard, Joyce Van Patten, Ella Ethridge. Eddie Gannon was killed in action during the Korean War. One of his buddies, Paul Corbelo, charges that Eddie died because of the cowardice of one of the other soldiers.

168.5 *What Are Friends For?* Oct. 18, 1962. GS: Jay Novello, James Westerfield, Hal Baylor, Jerome Cowan. It took some doing, but policeman Burt Carter finally jails Julio Perez for drunken driving and resisting arrest. And Carter hasn't heard the last of Julio. He finds himself charged with brutality.

168.6 *Straight Jacket for an Indian.* Oct. 25, 1962. GS: Claude Akins, Howard McNear, Ray Teal, Edmund Vargas, Lory Patrick, Alvy Moore, Johnny Coons. Mitch decides to buy some horses from an Indian reservation and sell them to the rodeo. His Indian friend Bullriver is supposed to deliver the animals.

168.7 *Our Ernie Kills People.* Nov. 1, 1962. GS: Irene Hervey, Richard Jordan, Don Collier, John Litel, Barbara Parkins, Ted de Corsia, Frank Wilcox, Willis Bouchey. Andy is relaxing at a drive-in restaurant late one night when he is approached by some surly teenagers. The gang is looking for kicks and Andy is a convenient target.

168.8 *A Devil in the Chute.* Nov. 8, 1962. GS: Michael Ansara, Coleen Gray, Donald Losby, Ray Teal. Mitch and Andy give a lift to crippled Jay Brenner, who has just been beaten up and robbed. But the boys learn that Brenner himself hasn't always been on the right side of the law, in fact he has just been released from prison.

168.9 *The Girl in the Sunshine Smile.* Nov. 15, 1962. GS: Anne Helm, Ray Walston, Peter Leeds, Russ McCubbin, Lyle Talbot, Donald Barry, I. Stanford Jolley. Andy has really flipped over carnival dancer Jenny Callan.

168.10 *Tears on a Painted Face.* Nov. 29, 1962. GS: Dan Duryea, Charles Robinson, Carole Wells, Slim Pickens. When a bull catches up with rodeo clown Willie Xeno, it becomes obvious that his legs are giving out. But Willie won't consider retirement. He needs the paycheck to support his son Chris.

168.11 *The Bravest Man in the World.* Dec. 6, 1962. GS: Ray Danton, Ford Rainey, Peggy McCay, Yvonne Craig, Bob Steele, Harold Fong, Jerry Gatlin. Andy is really impressed with a book which purports to be the life story of adventurer Warren Price. When Andy meets Price and strikes up a friendship with him, he is overwhelmed by all of the exciting things Price has done, or, at least, by all of his stories about them.

168.12 *Good Old Uncle Walt.* Dec. 13, 1962. GS: Edgar Buchanan, Walter Burke, Lurene Tuttle, Read Morgan, Alan Hale, Jr., Stacy King, Theona Bryant, Patty Mains. When Mitch and Andy run into Uncle Walt, whom they haven't seen in years, they find him engaged in his favorite pastime, cheating people out of their money.

168.13 *My Candle Burns at Both Ends.* Dec. 20, 1962. GS: Laura Devon, Roy Roberts, David McMahon, Clyde Howdy. The Guthrie Brothers meet up with beautiful Valerie Moore, who seems to find Mitch very attractive. But Valerie's life is a battle against time she is dying of leukemia.

168.14 *Memory of a Filly.* Jan. 3, 1963. GS: Ronnie Haran, Richard Hale, Slim Pickens, Harry Raybould, Olan Soule, Elizabeth Thompson. During an argument Slim Walker's sister disagrees with him rather violently. In fact, she pushes him down a flight of stairs and Slim is hospitalized with a broken leg.

168.15 *Step Over the Sky.* Jan. 10, 1963. GS: Victor Jory, Diane Ladd, Robert Brubaker. Johnny Prewitt, an oldtime rodeo rider, has only one ambition in life, to capture and ride a wild stallion named Santanas, the animal that crippled him years before.

168.16 *A Cry from the Mountain.* Jan. 17, 1963. GS: Jacques Aubuchon, James Caan, Tony Ray, Diane Sayer, Karyn Kupcinet, Brad Weston. Mitch and Andy's light airplane gets caught in a bad storm and crashes into a mountain. Mitch is badly hurt and Andy is forced to leave his brother on the desolate mountainside while he goes for help.

168.17 *Don't Cry for Johnny Devlin.* Jan. 24, 1963. GS: James McMullan, R.G. Armstrong, Jody Fair, Slim Pickens, Lyle Talbot, Paul Harmon, Paul Birch. Mitch has lost his lead in the rodeo standings to Johnny Devlin, a young man from his home town. But Mitch won't be counted out. He bets Devlin that he will regain the lead.

168.18 *Speckle Bird.* Jan. 31, 1963. GS: Forrest Tucker, Chris Robinson, Maggie Lou, Slim Pickens, Ted de Corsia, Ray Teal, Ray Montgomery, Kenneth MacDonald, Henry Hunter, Madie Norman. Wealthy Lynn Horn, a rugged ex-rodeo performer, considers his son a weakling. The boy would rather draw pictures than ride bronc.

168.19 *The Man Who Ran Away.* Feb. 7, 1963. GS: John Doucette, Mala Powers, Jay Lanin, Frank Ferguson, Quinn Redeker, Katie Sweet, Olan Soule. Andy's car matches the description of a hit-and-run auto, and the girl who was struck picks him out of a police lineup as the driver who hit her and ran.

168.20 *Whose Hand at My Throat?* Feb. 14, 1963. GS: Eduard Franz, Erika Peters, John Qualen, Paul Newlan, Virginia Gregg. Dr. Carl Lukins, brilliant foreign surgeon, can't obtain a license to practice in America and is working as a veterinarian instead.

168.21 *The Judas Goat.* Feb. 21, 1963. GS: Eddie Albert, Kent Smith, Christine White, Bert Freed, Doodles Weaver, Jack Cassidy. Newspaper publisher John Edgecomb is looking for an attractive gubernatorial candidate to help him overthrow the political bosses. His secretary Angel suggest her husband Duke Donovan, a popular singing cowboy.

168.22 *To Cindy, with Love.* Feb. 28, 1963. GS: Patty Duke, Lonny Chapman, Vaughn Taylor, Noah Keen, Dorothy Green, Barbara Pepper, Willa Pearl Curtis. When Cindy Hopkins' horse Becky suffers a bad fall, the regular vet says that the animal will have to be destroyed, but Chuck Martin, a vet who has lost all confidence in himself, says that the mare can be saved.

168.23 *The Quest for Jacob Blaufus.* March 7, 1963. GS: Peter Whitney, David Macklin, Marjorie Reynolds, Diane Mountford, Norman Leavitt, Conlan Carter, Art Lewis, John Banner, James Bannon. Amish farm boy Jacob Blaufus is making his father unhappy. The boy is more interested in science than he is in farming. When Jacob buys a set of encyclopedias, his father puts them in storage at the bottom of the river.

168.24 *Farewell to Margarita.* March 21, 1963. GS: Barbara Luna, Vito Scotti, Frank Puglia, Mario Magana. When Mitch is struck by a hit-and-run driver in a Mexican town, cabaret dancer Margarita Diaz takes him to her home to care for him. She warns him to conceal her job from her grandfather. He believes that she is a secretary.

168.25 *The Girl from Nob Hill.* March 28, 1963. GS: Kathryn Hays, Olive Sturgess, Carol Byron, Frank Aletter, Gene Blakely, Les Tremayne, Rayford Barnes, Jonathan Hole, Doris Lloyd. Lila Never is a pretty socialite and she and Mitch have developed a strong attraction for each other. Lila met Mitch by capturing him on a scavenger hunt in which she was supposed to bring in a cowboy.

168.26 *Yanqui, Go Home!* April 4, 1963. GS: Henry Corden, Miguel Landa, Ellen Madison, Don Durant, Than Wyenn, Allegra Varron, David Renard, Ralph Manza. A sign greets Mitch and Andy when they arrive in a small town in Mexico to ride in a charity rodeo. A Communist group is trying to stir up big trouble.

168.27 *The Lucky Punch.* April 18, 1963. GS: Bruce Yarnell, Audrey Dalton, Gene Lyons. In a small-town bar, Mitch knocks out Tom Kidwell with one punch, and then discovers that Kidwell is a ranking contender for the world heavyweight championship.

168.28 *The Care and Handling of Tigers.* April 25, 1963. GS: Anthony George, Teddy Eccles, Barbara Mansell, William Bramley, Brendan Dillon. Manager Edward Garner's decision to close down the Marshfield Lumber Mill puts a lot of people out of work and Garner's young son David finds that he is not very well liked anymore.

169. Wild Bill Hickok

Syndicated. 30 min. Broadcast history: Various, April 1951–May 1958.

Regular Cast: Guy Madison (U.S. Marshal James Butler "Wild Bill" Hickok), Andy Devine (Jingles B. Jones).

Premise: This series recounted the exploits of legendary Western lawman Wild Bill Hickok in the 1870s.

The Episodes

169.1 *Behind Southern Lines* (A.K.A. "Civil War Story"). April 15, 1951. Bill McKenzie, Park MacGregor, Bill Ruhl, Rand Brooks, George Sanders, Murray Alper, Jonathan Hale. Wild Bill and Jingles meet for the first time at the close of the Civil War while Bill is on an undercover mission.

169.2 *The Rock Springs Rustlers.* April 22, 1951. GS: Robin Winans, Sharyne Payne, M'Liss McClure, James Craven, Lane Bradford, Zon Murray. Bill and Jingles pursue some rustlers, but Jingles nearly winds up with his neck in a noose.

169.3 *Lady Mayor* (A.K.A. "The Spinster Mayor"). April 29, 1951. GS: Dick Curtis, Fred Libby, Isa Ashdown, Francis Morris, David Sharpe, John Carpenter. A vigorous lady mayor teams up with Bill and Jingles to solve a murder mystery centered around the local gambling casino.

169.4 *The Dog Collar Story* (A.K.A. "Trap of Diamonds"). May 6, 1951. GS: Lois Hall, Marshall Reed, Tommy Ivo, Gregg Barton, Byron Foulger, Bill Fawcett. Wild Bill and Jingles try to solve the puzzle of a kindly barber and a dunking that lead to the plundering and murdering of settlers.

169.5 *The Silver Mine Protection Story* (A.K.A. "The Western Shakedown"). May 13, 1951. GS: Milburn Stone, Lee Phelps, Bill Meade, Duke York, Robert Shayne, Orley Lindgren. Paid gunmen are swindling the local miners in a protection racket until they tangle with Wild Bill.

169.6 *Indian Bureau Story* (A.K.A. "The Pawnee Treaty", "Indian Pony Express", "The Osage Incident"). May 20, 1951. GS: Monte Blue, Raymond Hatton, Terry Frost, Jack Reynolds, Steve Pendleton, Neyle Morrow, Wendy Waldron. Bill and Jingles try to clear an Indian tribe accused of cattle rustling.

169.7 *Indian Pony Express.* May 27, 1951. GS: Rory Mallinson, Wendy Waldron, Anthony Sydes, Francis Ford, Ferris Taylor, Dick Rich, Tom Steele, Dave Sharpe, Tito Renaldo, Rodd Redwing. Indian arrows kill two men, but Wild Bill tries to prove Indians didn't shoot the arrows.

169.8 *The Tax Collecting Story* (A.K.A. "The Brimstone Taxes"). June 3, 1951. GS: Margery Bennett, Roy Bennett, Sam Flint, Gordon Jones, Mike Ragan, Billy Bletcher, Joe Greene, James Guilfoyle. Bill and Jingles enlist Curly Wolf and his gang to rustlers as tax collectors in order to lure them into a trap.

169.9 *The Widow Muldane* (A.K.A. "Branding Iron Trail"). June 10, 1951. GS: Christine Larson, Kenne Duncan, Edward Clark, Helen Van Tuyle. Bill and Jingles become concerned about a branding iron in the wrong hands.

169.10 *Ghost Town Story* (A.K.A. "Ghost Town Adventure", "Deserted Town", "New Ghost Town"). June 17, 1951. GS: John Doucette, Betty Davison, Russell Simpson. A half-crazy prospector leads Bill and Jingles into an encounter with what seems to be ghosts.

169.11 *Yellow Haired Kid* (A.K.A. "Double Identity"). Aug. 28, 1951. GS: David Bruce, Alice Rolph, Bill Phipps, Marcia Mae Jones, Wade Crosby, Tom Hubbard. Two bandits pose as Wild Bill and Jingles and stage several holdups, throwing a bad light on the marshal and his deputy.

169.12 *Johnny Deuce* (A.K.A. "Bitter Creek Masquerade"). July 1, 1951. GS: Alan Hale, Jr., Riley Hill, Tommy Ivo, Emory Parnell, Tom Tyler, Renie Riano. Dishonest city officials help a dangerous gunman to escape from jail in order to set a trap for Wild Bill.

169.13 *Homer Atchison* (A.K.A. "Kansas Kid"). July 8, 1951. GS: George Lewis, Fred Kohler, Carol Brannon, Tris Coffin, Larry Hudson, John Baer, Carol Henry, Mickey Simpson, George Eldredge. Bill and Jingles encounter an outlaw gang led by a killer with the dignified name of Homer Atchison, who prefers to be known as the Kansas Kid.

Season Two

169.14 *Border City Election.* Oct. 14, 1951. GS: Lyle Talbot, Gloria Saunders, Fred Hoose, Zon Murray, Robert Bice, Dave Sharpe, Jim Connell. A newspaper editor is killed just before an election. Wild Bill and Jingles track down the murderer.

169.15 *Pony Express vs. Telegraph.* Oct. 21, 1951. GS: Don Haydon, Mike Vallon, Peggy Stewart, Park MacGregor,

Fred Kohler, Tom Steele. A young pony express rider, suspected of killing a telegraph company lineman in order to keep the telegraph firm from taking away pony express business, almost gets lynched.

169.16 *The Lady School Teacher.* Oct. 28, 1951. GS: Rory Mallinson, Pat Mitchell, Isa Ashdown, Almira Sessions, Sam Flint, Tom Steele. Bill and Jingles help homesteaders protect a valley of precious grazing ground against outlaw squatters.

169.17 *Outlaw Flats.* Nov. 4, 1951. GS: Kristine Miller, Richard Avonde, John Crawford, Bobby Jordan, Tris Coffin, Ed Clark, William Haade. A crooked cattle buyer secretly leads a band of hooded terrorists to steal back the money he has paid the men who sold him large herds. Wild Bill and his side man Jingles try to catch the crook.

169.18 *Silver Stage Holdup.* Nov. 11, 1951. GS: Jane Adams, Bill Haade, Lennie Geer, Wade Crosby, Reed Howes, Riley Hill. Bill and Jingles deal with the owner of a silver smelting mill who attempts to hold up and steal his own stagecoach shipments.

169.19 *Mexican Rustlers Story.* Nov 18, 1951. GS: Carol Thurston, Roland Varno, Don Harvey, Leonard Penn, Chad Mallory, Eddy Kane, Dennis Moore, Mike Ragan. Bill pretends to turn outlaw and kill the chief marshal in order to win the confidence of a holdup gang.

169.20 *Masked Riders.* Oct. 30, 1951. GS: Tom Steele, Ted Stanhope, John Carpenter, Norman Bishop, Ferris Taylor, Belle Mitchell, Jim Diehl. A greedy landowner connives to gain control of the mortgages of local merchants and settlers.

169.21 *Hepsibah.* Dec. 2, 1951. GS: Isabel Randolph, George Eldredge, Robert Bice, Douglas Evans, Billy Griffith, Larry Johns. Bill and Jingles team up with the sharp-tongued woman mayor of Green Springs to solve a murder centering around the local gambling casino.

169.22 *Border City.* Dec. 9, 1951. GS: Don Turner, Steve Pendleton, George Lewis, Murray Alper, Gloria Talbott, Isabel Randolph, George Eldredge, Robert Bice. Bill and Jingles arrange to fake their own murders as part of a plan to trap an outlaw gang.

169.23 *Ex-Convict Story* (A.K.A. "The Innocent Cowpoke"). Dec. 16, 1951. GS: Bruce Edwards, Gregg Barton, Jo Carroll Dennison, Rex Lease, John Carpenter, Pierce Lyden. After serving a prison term for a crime he did not commit, a cowhand is accused of killing the judge who convicted him. Wild Bill and Jingles try to expose the real killer.

169.24 *Papa Antonelli* (A.K.A. "Jingles' Disguise"). Dec. 23, 1951. GS: Mike Vallon, Pamela Duncan, Alan Foster, Francis McDonald, Elizabeth Harrower, Irene Martin. Attempting to solve the robbery of a Wells Fargo stagecoach, Bill has Jingles disguise himself as a peddler's wife.

169.25 *The Slocum Family* (A.K.A. "Education and Brawn"). Dec. 30, 1951. GS: Raymond Hatton, Carole Mathews, Minerva Urecal, Richard Tyler, Frankie Darro, Sara Haden. Wild Bill teaches a lesson to a father and his two sons who believe that education spoils a man's courage.

169.26 *Lost Indian Mine* (A.K.A. "The Evil Assayer"). Jan. 6, 1952. GS: David Sharpe, Don Turner, Anthony Sydes, Guy Beach, John Eldredge, James Bush, Bob Osborn. A crooked assayer schemes to deprive an old prospector of his rich gold strike by convincing him that the claim is worthless.

Season Three

169.27 *Civilian Clothes.* Jan. 27, 1952. GS: Norma Eberhardt, John Merton, Pat Mitchell, Leonard Penn, Fred Kelsey, Ric Vallin, Tris Coffin, Bill Hale. A dishonest clerk tries to buy out the bank with money he has stolen from gold shipments. Wild Bill and Jingles become suspicious and start to investigate.

169.28 *Medicine Show.* Feb. 3, 1952. GS: Ralph Sanford, Fred Kohler, Jr., Tom Monroe, Larry Hudson, Peter McCabe, Bill Coontz, George Sherwood. Bill and Jingles go after a gunman whose hideout is the coffin a magician uses in his act.

169.29 *Blacksmith Story.* Feb. 10, 1952. GS: Carole Mathews, Sam Flint, Robert Livingston, Richard Alexander, William McCormick. Wild Bill matches wits with a burly and brutal blacksmith who has been beating up local ranchers in order to drive them out of the territory.

169.30 *Mexican Gun Running Story.* Feb. 17, 1952. GS: Theodora Lynch, Sujata, Rand Brooks, Murray Alper, Tom Tyler, Bob Woodward, Neyle Morrow, Charles Stevens. While investigating arms smugglers, Bill and Jingles encounter a young woman disguised as a man who comes to their rescue and saves Bill's life.

169.31 *Schoolteacher Story.* Feb. 24, 1952. GS: Anne Carroll, Rory Mallinson, Emory Parnell, Steve Pendleton, Don Harvey, Peter Votrian, Jim Flowers. Bill and Jingles go after a group of conspirators who are out to gain control of an underground spring.

169.32 *Vigilante Story* (A.K.A. "Brave Lash Corby"). March 3, 1952. GS: Tom Neal, William Ruhl, George Lewis, Shannon O'Neill, Jim Parnell, Roland Varno, Perry Ivins. Bill and Jingles enlist a brave citizen to help them expose a band of hooded terrorists.

169.33 *The Professor's Daughter* (A.K.A. Flashy Sweetwater Singer"). March 10, 1952. GS: Martha Hyer, Byron Foulger, Bobby Blake, James Bush, Bud Osborne, Henry Rowland. Wild Bill and his deputy deceive a strait-laced professor about the fact that his daughter sings in a dance hall.

169.34 *Photographer Story.* March 17, 1952. GS: Dorothy Patrick, John Ridgely, I. Stanford Jolley, Ferris Taylor, William Fawcett, John Parrish, Dick Rich, Bob Cason. Mysterious prowlers steal photographs from the town studio. Wild Bill and Jingles start an investigation.

169.35 *The Outlaw's Son.* March 24, 1952. GS: Anne Kimball, Steve Darrell, Dan White, Ralph Reed. Bill and Jingles encounter a holdup man who would rather kill his son than see him become an outlaw like himself.

169.36 *Savvy, the Smart Little Dog.* March 31, 1952. GS: Jeanne Dean, George Eldredge, William Haade, Howard Negley, Francis Ford, Steve Clark. Wild Bill and Jingles start out on a search for an old prospector, his dog, and a stolen map.

169.37 *Ghost Rider.* April 7, 1952. GS: Paul Bryar, Steve Pendleton, Hank Patterson, William Vedder, Ethan Laidlaw. Jingles plays ghost and rides to the Banshee City burial grounds to help Wild Bill trap a clever gang of criminals.

169.38 *Wild White Horse* (A.K.A. "Rustling Stallion", "Smart Stallion"). April 14, 1952. GS: Bobby Hyatt, Guy Wilkerson, Frank Fenton, Pierce Lyden, Fred Kelsey, Wes Hudman. Wild Bill and Jingles refuse to believe the story they are told about a wild stallion that helps other horses to break out of their corral.

169.39 *Lumber Camp Story.* April 21, 1952. GS: Frances Charles, George Barrows, Kenne Duncan, Harry Lauter. Wild Bill and Jingles go after a man who conspired to defraud his own niece. Wild Bill poses as a woodsman. He does not realize that he is in danger of being shot by a sharpshooter.

169.40 *The Trapper Story.* April 28, 1952. GS: Jeanne Cagney, Clayton Moore, Hal Gerard, James Bell, Jack Reynolds, Marshall Reed. Wild Bill and Jingles pose as trappers to get evidence against a gang of fur thieves.

169.41 *The Boy and the Bandit.* May 5, 1952. GS: Henry Blair, John Merton, Bruce Edwards, Buddy Roosevelt, Edmund Cobb, Mike Vallon. Bill and Jingles take along a teenage boy in their search for a criminal. They want the boy to realize the nature of the man he has been hero-worshiping.

169.42 *A Joke on Sir Anthony.* May 12, 1952. GS: Dick Cavendish, Dick Elliott, Gerald O. Smith, Park MacGregor, Russ Whiteman, I. Stanford Jolley, Guy Teague, Marshall Reed. Bill and Jingles help out a visiting British diplomat, en route to a post in China, who makes the mistake of boasting to American bandits about the martial arts skills he acquired in Asia.

169.43 *Wrestling Story.* May 19, 1952. GS: Karl Davis, Douglas Fowley, Rand Brooks, Lyle Talbot, House Peters, Jr., Fred Sherman, Henry Kulky. In order to foil a bank robbery, Bill persuades Jingles to challenge a champion wrestler.

169.44 *Jingles Becomes a Baby Sitter.* May 26, 1952. GS: Raymond Hatton, Toni Jerry, Roy Parsons, Elfie Laird, Al Bridge, Riley Hill. Wild Bill sets out to expose a land-grabbing scheme and leaves Jingles behind to guard a besieged homestead and take care of the baby.

169.45 *The Fortune Telling Story* (A.K.A. "Ghost Breakers"). June 9, 1952. GS: Elizabeth Harrower, Charles Hatton, Florence Auer, Marvin Press, Reed Howes. While trying to solve a series of robberies, wild Bill and Jingles run into a fortune teller. Jingles has his fortune told, and Wild Bill is left to battle the outlaws alone.

169.46 *A Close Shave for the Marshal* (A.K.A. "Close Shave"). June 16, 1952. GS: Robert Filmer, Byron Foulger, Harry Harvey, Steve Brodie, Burt Wenland. Wild Bill disguises himself as a notorious outlaw and joins a band of looters. He wants to bring the gang to justice.

169.47 *Prairie Flats Land Swindle* (A.K.A. "The Swindlers"). June 23, 1952. GS: Bobby Hyatt, Irving Bacon, Douglas Evans, Fred Libby, Terry Frost, Sam Flint, Fred Kelsey. The career of Abilene's marshal, Wild Bill Hickok, almost ends when he is knocked unconscious and thrown off a cliff into a lake. A young boy's quick thinking helps Wild Bill and Jingles round up the outlaws responsible for the attack.

169.48 *Marriage Feud of Ponca City* (A.K.A. "The Feuding Westerners"). June 30, 1952. GS: Ann Carrol, Robert Jordan, Nelson Leigh, Forrest Taylor, Louise Lorimer, Ed Cassidy, Paul McGuire. After the wedding of two young people from feuding families, a man is murdered. Wild Bill and Jingles try to find the killer.

Season Four

169.49 *Grandpa and Genie.* Sept. 13, 1953. GS: George Cleveland, Isa Ashdown, Will Wright, Almira Sessions, Pierre Watkin, Guy Teague. Grandpa Quenley doesn't realize how valuable his property really is. Bill and Jingles do some sharpshooting to protect the rights of the old man and his granddaughter.

169.50 *The Nephew from Back East.* Sept. 20, 1953. GS: Douglas Fowley, B.G. Norman, Edmund Cobb, Bob Woodward, Boyd Stockman. Jingles' Eastern-reared nephew Horace comes West for a visit but his uncle thinks he is a sissy until he helps Bill and Jingles track down some thieves.

169.51 *Wagon Wheel Trail.* Sept. 27, 1953. GS: Robert S. Carson, Morgan Jones, Sandy Sanders, Burt Wenland, Howard Wright. With a broken wagon wheel as their clue, Bill and Jingles try to recover a friend's money which has been stolen and hidden in a can of axle grease.

169.52 *Heading for Trouble.* Oct. 4, 1953. GS: James Millican, John Merton, Riley Hill, Joan Diener. While trailing some thieves, Bill and Jingles encounter three men who offer to help, but what the marshals don't realize is that these three are themselves the thieves.

169.53 *The Young Witness.* Oct. 11, 1953. GS: Steve Brodie, Gregg Barton, Charles Halton, Gordon Gebert, Buzz Henry, Harry Harvey, Sr., Wheaton Chambers. A youngster sees a deputy sheriff and his companion attack an aged prospector. Bill and Jingles try to save the life of the boy.

169.54 *Chain of Events.* Oct. 18, 1953. GS: Gloria Winters, Chuck Courtney, Ewing Mitchell, Terry Frost, Harry Cording, Harry Strang. Wild Bill sets a trap for a crooked mine owner who schemes to get paid twice for his ore.

169.55 *The Doctor's Story.* Oct. 25, 1953. GS: Tom Hubbard, Pamela Duncan, Nadene Ashdown, Bill Hale, William Tannen, Mike Ragan. Wild Bill and Jingles become involved with a doctor in the Old West.

169.56 *The Indians and the Delegates.* Nov. 1, 1953. GS: John Aldredge, Tris Coffin, Henry Kulky, William Wilkerson. Wild Bill and Jingles match their marksmanship against that of thieving gamblers.

169.57 *The Sheriff Was a Redhead.* Nov. 8, 1953. GS: Veda Ann Borg, Jim Bannon, Keith Richards, Henry Rowland, Frank Hagney, George Slocum. Accused of murder, Wild Bill and Jingles are at the mercy of a lynch mob.

169.58 *Hands Across the Border.* Nov. 15, 1953. GS: Alan Hale, Jr., Steve Pendleton, Denver Pyle, Rory Mallinson, John Crawford, William Fawcett. A case of mistaken identity brings Wild Bill and the Canadian Mounties to the aid of a man accused of robbery and murder.

169.59 *The Avenging Gunman.* Nov. 22, 1953. GS: Joan Arnold, Rosa Turich, Carol Henry, Tom Moore, James Millican, Sandy Sanders, Monte Blue, Rand Brooks. While escorting a prisoner to the state penitentiary, Bill and Jingles learn that the man's brother is on the prowl and determined to free him.

169.60 *The Right of Way.* Nov. 29, 1953. GS: Lyle Talbot, Allan Nixon, Guy Teague, Buzz Henry, Frank Jenks, Theodore Von Eltz. Bill and Jingles try to stop the violence when two factions start fighting over the route for a new railroad.

169.61 *The Monster in the Lake.* Dec. 6, 1953. GS: Bill Henry, Tony Hughes, Bobby Hyatt, Hal Gerard, Read Morgan, Richard Avonde, Bobby Haade, William Haade. Bill and Jingles investigate reports of a monster coming up from the depths of Medicine Lake and terrorizing the people along the shore.

Season Five

169.62 *The Maverick.* Nov. 21, 1954. GS: Gordon Wynn, Bill Evandell, Marshall Reed, Gloria Eldridge, Bill Tannen, Tommy Cook, Sally Mansfield, Bill Crandall. A young man courts a girl on the promise that he will soon be rich from gold mining interests. Wild Bill and Jingles suspect that his riches will be from robbing banks.

169.63 *The Kid from Red Butte.* Nov. 28, 1954. GS: Sam Flint, Charles Fredericks, Murray Alper, Alice Rolph, Isabelle Dawn, Art Dillard, Henry Rowland, Gordon Gebert. A young boy who got a bad start in life because of his stagecoach robber father is taught a lesson by Wild Bill and Jingles.

169.64 *Masquerade at Moccasin Flats.* Dec. 5, 1954. GS: Elizabeth Harrower, John Damler, Ken Acton, Tom Hubbard, Wes Hudman, Robert Bray, Ella Ethridge. Mrs. Turtledove's traveling emporium is disrupted when a gang of crooks learn that one of their men has hidden plates for printing counterfeit money on the premises.

169.65 *Stolen Church Funds.* Dec. 12, 1954. GS: Bill George, Sam Flint, John Eldredge, Rory Mallinson, Louis Lettieri. Two men, one a bank teller, the other a crook, plan to steal the proceeds of a charity bazaar. Neither man knows of the other's plans.

169.66 *Ol' Pardner Rides Again.* Dec. 19, 1954. GS: Raymond Hatton, I. Stanford Jolley, Don Harvey, Bill Fawcett, Bill Coontz, Chad Mallory, Fred Gabourie. The owner of a country store blames the town loafer's aged horse because it was not fast enough to capture a gang of pilferers who have ransacked his store. Wild Bill and Jingles try to stop the storekeeper's one-man crusade against the old horse.

169.67 *The Gorilla of Owl Hoot Mesa.* Dec. 26, 1954. GS: John Carradine, George Barrows, Rand Brooks, Terry Frost, Paul McGuire, Reed Howes, Pete Kellett, Chad Mallory. There are two gorillas at large from a traveling circus. One has escaped from a traveling circus, the other is actually a killer masquerading as a gorilla.

169.68 *Superstition Stage.* Jan. 2, 1955. GS: Lucien Littlefield, Jackie Parks, Tom Hubbard, Zon Murray, William Pullen, John Damler, James Diehl. Wild Bill Hickok and Jingles attempt to solve the mysterious tomahawk slayings of Jed Walker's stagecoach drivers.

169.69 *Cry Wolf.* Jan. 9, 1955. GS: Don Haggerty, Edward Norris, Brad Morrow, Virginia Carroll, Larry Chance, Joel Allen. Wild Bill and his pal Jingles set off for a quiet fishing holiday. Instead, they run into a gang of fur thieves.

169.70 *The Boy and the Hound Dog.* Jan. 16, 1954. GS: Elisha Cook, Jr., Douglas Fowley, Tris Coffin, Rick Vallin, Mickey Little, Jack Mulhall, Fred Kelsey. A notorious claim jumper and his gang attempt to take a hidden gold mine away from its rightful owner. Bill and Jingles enlist the owner's young son and his dog to help stop the gang.

169.71 *The Sheriff's Secret.* Jan. 23, 1955. GS: Patricia Lynn, Alan Wells, Rudy Lee, Carleton Young, Mauritz Hugo, Bill Haade, Ralph Sanford, Harry Hayden. A secret from the past of the sheriff of Powder Springs prevents him from taking action against two desperadoes who invade the town.

169.72 *To the Highest Bidder.* Jan. 30, 1955. GS: Joi Lansing, Steve Wyman, Kem Dibbs, Fred Libby, Almira Sessions, Art Dillard. Wild Bill and Jingles can't understand why a gang of thieves wants to get hold of Jingles' trick shaving mirror. The murder of an auctioneer and several attempts to steal the mirror lead Bill and Jingles to a stolen army payroll.

169.73 *Sundown Valley.* Feb. 6, 1955. GS: Dorothy Patrick, William Bryant, Dan White, Brad Morrow, Fred Sherman, Frank Christie, Jack Reynolds, John Cason. The peace of Sundown Valley is disturbed by the misdeeds of the Colton gang who rob the Cattleman's Association offices and stage a jailbreak. Wild Bill and Jingles try to restore order.

169.74 *Sagebrush Manhunt.* Feb. 13, 1955. GS: Jill Richards, Lewis Martin, Gregg Barton, Richard Thorne, Kenne Duncan, Tony Hughes, John Morlas. Wild Bill and Jingles trail an Army renegade who has stolen a payroll pouch. His tracks lead to a lonely desert cottage where their quarry is posing as a homesteader.

Season Six

169.75 *Outlaw's Portrait.* Sept. 4, 1955. GS: Bernadette Withers, Tris Coffin, Robert Hutton, Sandy Sanders, Michael Dale. When Jingles takes up painting as a hobby, his attempt to do a portrait of a gun-toting bandit unexpectedly helps Bill track the man down.

169.76 *Buckshot Comes Home.* Sept. 11, 1955. GS: Paula Kent, Don C. Harvey, John Damler, Rayford Barnes, Bobby Hyatt, Iron Eyes Cody. Bill's horse Buckshot helps him prove the innocence of an Indian friend accused of murdering the sheriff.

169.77 *The Music Teacher.* Sept. 18, 1955. GS: Richard Karlan, William Ching, Don Garrett, Kem Dibbs, Ginny Jackson, Burt Wenland, Keith Richards. Bill and Jingles confront an outlaw, posing as a music teacher, who plans to loot a gold shipment.

169.78 *The Golden Rainbow.* Sept. 25, 1955. GS: Raymond Hatton, Tom Monroe, John Beradino, Lucien Littlefield, Park MacGregor, Liz Slifer. Bill and Jingles are deceived by an old professor who claims to have rediscovered a lost gold mine.

169.79 *Old Cowboys Never Die.* Oct. 2, 1955. GS: Dick Foran, Raymond Hatton, Fuzzy Knight, Robert Filmer, Charles Fredericks, J.P. Catching. Suffering from a minor illness that convinces him he is at death's door, Jingles suddenly develops a tiger's courage and dashes into battle with Bill against an outlaw gang.

169.80 *Blake's Kid.* Oct. 9, 1955. GS: Guinn "Big Boy" Williams, Tommy Ivo, Bill Pullen, John Merton, Tim Sullivan, G. Pat Collins, Ann Staunton, Barbara Woodell. Because he doesn't like his new stepmother, a youngster gets mixed up with a band of rogues.

169.81 *Treasure Trail.* Oct. 16, 1955. GS: Linda Dansen, Wayne Mallory, Thom Carney, Harry Lauter, Ray Walker, Keith Richards, Bert Bradley. Bill puts on a Cavalry uniform and attends a costume ball in order to find out why hired thugs are terrorizing a local rancher who is giving away a worthless tract of land for a water project.

169.82 *Battle Line.* Oct. 23, 1955. GS: Don Mathers, William Haade, Fuzzy Knight, Earl Hodgins, Major James S. Wilson. Wild Bill and Jingles try to protect the mining prop-

Wild Bill Hickok

erty of two old Civil War veterans who are in danger of being cheated.

169.83 *Ambush.* Oct. 30, 1955. GS: Charles Chaplin, Jr., David Cross, Jonathan Seymour, Sam Flint, Robert Bice, Joseph Greene, John Eldredge, Stanley Andrews. Bill and Jingles commandeer a wagonload of barrels to protect their prisoner from a bloodthirsty mob.

169.84 *The Hideout.* Nov. 6, 1955. GS: Philip Van Zandt, Henry Rowland, Terry Frost, Joel Smith, Frank Hagney. Wild Bill and Jingles find their lives in danger when they trail a desperado to an out-of-the-way frontier town. They find that the U.S. Government's authority is not recognized there and they can't arrest him.

169.85 *Ghost Town Lady.* Nov. 13, 1955. GS: Earl Ross, Burt Wenland, Isa Ashdown, John Damler, Jim Alexander, Robert Homan. Strange thing begin to happen to Josh Boone, who lives alone in a ghost town with the memory of an old girl friend. Wild Bill and Jingles attempt to prevent harm from coming to Boone.

169.86 *The Mountain Men.* Nov. 20, 1955. GS: Claudia Barrett, Bill Bryant, Henry Kulky, Paul Sorenson, Donald Kerr, Charles Wilcox. Young Jeff Stratton wants to join a group calling themselves the Mountain Men, but must prove his worth at the annual games of the trappers and hunters. Wild Bill and Jingles attend the meet to assist him.

169.87 *Return of Chief Red Hawk.* Nov. 27, 1955. GS: Frank Scannell, George Chandler, Larry Chance, Allan Wells, Don Marlowe, G. Pat Collins, Billy Rhodes, David Street. An Indian attempts to avenge himself on a side-show sharpie who held him prisoner in his show tent. Wild Bill is faced with the problem of bringing the man in for trial.

Season Seven

169.88 *Halley's Comet.* Sept. 2, 1956. GS: Rolfe Sedan, Tris Coffin, Lillian Bronson, Dennis Moore, Robin Hughes, Wayne Mallory, Donald Kerr. Bill and Jingles visit a small town with a party of scientists studying the imminent return of Halley's Comet, but they run into a thief who is planning a gold robbery during the excitement of the comet's reappearance.

169.89 *Blind Alley.* Sept. 9, 1956. GS: Mel Stevens, Pierce Lyden, Jim Alexander, Don Harvey, Sam Flint. Bill and Jingles try to save an Indian child who has been bitten by a rabid dog and whose pet deer is threatened with death unless he brings ammunition to a hunted criminal.

169.90 *The Great Obstacle Race.* Sept. 16, 1956. GS: Billy Nelson, Janet Harding, Damian O'Flynn, Paul McGuire, Terry Frost, Gregg Barton, Kenne Duncan. Wild Bill and Jingles set out to find the reason why the U.S. Cavalry won't buy horses from their friend. They arrange with the colonel to test the stamina of the horses with field trials.

169.91 *The Kangaroo Kaper.* Sept. 23, 1956. GS: Mauritz Hugo, Frank Scannell, Larry Gelbman, John Goddard, Ken Christy, Fred Gabourie, Casey MacGregor. Bill becomes involved with the owner of a traveling carnival, who uses his boxing kangaroo to trick Jingles out of some money he is carrying for a stage line.

169.92 *The Missing Diamonds.* Sept. 30, 1956. GS: Byron Foulger, Richard Valdespine, Rick Vallin, John Merrick, Pierre Watkin, Alma Beltran. On the trail of valuable jewelry that was stolen from a traveling salesman, Bill and Jingles stop to help a Mexican boy worried about his sick mother and run smack into the jewel thieves.

169.93 *Jingles Gets the Bird.* Oct. 7, 1956. GS: Raymond Hatton, Rory Mallinson, Frank Sully, George Cisar. A retired sea captain and his pet parrot are trailed by two suspicious-looking characters. The outlaws believe that the bird can tell them the hiding place of a store of buried treasure.

169.94 *Wild Bill's Odyssey.* Oct. 14, 1956. GS: Lyle Talbot, Barbara Woodell, Ralph Neff, Wayne Mallory, Alan MacAteer, Scott Morrow, Tom McKee, Hank Patterson. Bill has to call on his knowledge of Greek mythology when an unsigned telegram brings him and Jingles to Rapid Mills to find out why a well-known rancher disappeared.

169.95 *The Bold Raven Rodeo.* Oct. 21, 1956. GS: Mary Jane Saunders, Elizabeth Harrower, Julia Montoya, Orlando Rodriguez, Iron Eyes Cody. Bill and Jingles stage a rodeo in order to break up a feud between Indian and white parents that resulted from a fight between their children.

169.96 *The Rainmaker.* Oct. 28, 1956. GS: Frank Fenton, William Haade, Emory Parnell, Morgan Jones, Earle Hodgins. A phony rainmaker attempts to swindle destitute ranchers stricken by drought. The people take sides as to whether or not they should pay for his services.

169.97 *The Iron Major.* Nov. 4, 1956. GS: Audrey Conti, Irving Bacon, Leonard Penn, King Donovan, Edward Foster. An unscrupulous rancher tries to prevent a surveyor from mapping land between an Indian reservation and a rowdy frontier town.

169.98 *Jingles Wins a Friend.* Nov. 11, 1956. GS: Philip Ahn, Harry Lauter, King Donovan, Edward Foster, Larry Chance, Terry Frost. Wild Bill and Jingles investigate a polluted brook that is poisoning a rancher's cattle and discover that the water is full of cyanide.

169.99 *The Gatling Gun.* Nov. 18, 1956. GS: Michael Bryant, Joe Breen, Stanley Andrews, Victor Millan, Donald E. Sullivan, George Baxter, John Damler. A bandit's success in robbing travelers leads people to believe he is assisted by a small army of thieves. Wild Bill finds a different answer.

169.100 *The Steam Wagon.* Nov. 25, 1956. GS: Lucien Littlefield, Richard M. Wessel, Don C. Harvey, Brad Morrow, Donald Kerr, Louis Lettieri, George Eldredge. When Grandpaw Crank takes his newly-invented steam wagon on a trial run, patent-seekers attempt to sabotage the vehicle. They plan to convince the old man his invention is worthless and then take over the plans themselves.

Season Eight

169.101 *Marvin's Mix-Up.* Feb. 19, 1958. GS: Bill Henry, Donna Drew, Buzz Henry, Bud Osborne, Fred Sherman, Forrest Stanley. Wild Bill and Jingles find that a mail-order bride plays a vital part in their search for a mysterious robber, the Highlander, who wears a Scottish costume and speaks with an accent.

169.102 *Spurs for Johnny.* Feb. 26, 1958. GS: Johnny Crawford, Harry Hickok, Ted Lehmann, Florence Lake, Gil Perkins, Guy Teague. Johnny, a little boy from the East who has come to live with his uncle, Matt Hendricks, is taught the way of the West by Wild Bill. Soon Johnny's training comes in handy.

169.103 *Monkeyshines.* March 5, 1958. GS: Michael Vallon, Larry Chance, Lela Bliss, Ken Mayer, Rube Schaffer. A monkey leads Wild Bill and Jingles to the aid of Luigi Pastore who was kidnaped by outlaws when he discovered a hidden stream in a drought area.

169.104 *The Runaway Wizard.* March 12, 1958. GS: Pamela Beaird, Monte Hale, Bill Hale, George Ross, William Newell, Paul Hahn. Mary Lou Stanton, a child genius, is duped by an outlaw into figuring out a perfect bank robbery for him.

169.105 *Meteor Mesa.* March 19, 1958. GS: Bill Catching, Gil Frye, Harry Antrim, Robert Swan, Sam Flint. When a scientist makes important discoveries on an Indian reservation, an outlaw tries to frighten the Indians into giving up the land.

169.106 *Town Without Law.* March 26, 1958. GS: Carol Nugent, Emmett Lynn, Stanley Adams, George Barrows, Jack V. Littlefield, John Truax. Wild Bill disguises himself as a saddle tramp to break up a gang of outlaws, the sole inhabitants of a frontier town.

169.107 *The Sheriff of Buckeye.* April 2, 1958. GS: Robert Clarke, Dorothy Neumann, Byron Foulger, Patrick Whyte, Baynes Barron, Fred Kohler, William Benedict. When outlaws attempt to defraud the state of a large sum of money intended for a mountain highway, a newspaper editor brings Wild Bill and Jingles in to help trap the criminals.

169.108 *Clem's Reformation.* April 9, 1958. GS: William Bryant, Gay Goodwin, Lonnie Thomas, Frank Scannell, Duane Grey, William Justine. Ex-convict Clem Orton, who his determined to hide his prison record from his young daughter, joins Wild Bill in stopping a gang of thieves who plan to hijack a gold shipment before it leaves the mine.

169.109 *Jingles on the Jailroad.* April 16, 1958. GS: Richard Karlan, Leonard Penn, Syd Saylor, Roy Erwin, Ben Welden, Bob Stratton, Richard Farnsworth, Robert Jordan. Wild Bill must transport the outlaw Slade to prison by train. He handcuffs Jingles to the prisoner, disguising him as an outlaw to learn of any plans Slade has made to escape.

169.110 *The Daughter of Casey O'Grady.* April 23, 1958. GS: Harry Tyler, Jacquelyn Park, Mike Lane, Michael Forest, Frank Lackteen. Bill and Jingles try to save retired army officer Casey O'Grady, who has devoted his life to raising an orphaned Indian girl but is marked for death by a Cheyenne chief because of a massacre he once took part in.

169.111 *The Angel of Cedar Mountain.* April 30, 1958. GS: Rosetta Duncan, Gregg Barton, Chuck Courtney, Chuck Callaway, Wayne Davidson. Bill and Jingles go after a bank robber who has forced lovable old Ma Malone to give him shelter.

169.112 *The Good Indian.* May 9, 1958. GS: Charles Stewart, John Reach, Dehl Berti, Rush Williams, Lane Chandler, Joseph A. Vitale, Michael Carr. The captain of a cavalry troop, who hates Indians and trusts a crooked scout, unjustly accuses an Indian of murder, and Wild Bill and Jingles try to save him.

169.113 *Counterfeit Ghost.* May 16, 1958. GS: Iris Adrian, Earle Hodgins, William Keene, Rusty Wescoatt, Robert Nash. Bill tries to help Jingles when he and two other people inherit a rundown hotel with the reputation of being haunted by a pirate's ghost.

170. Wild Wild West

CBS. 60 min. Broadcast history: Friday, 7:30–8:30, Sept. 1965–Sept. 1969.

Regular Cast: Robert Conrad (James West), Ross Martin (Artemus Gordon), Charles Aidman (Jeremy Pike) 68–69.

Premise: This Western adventure series depicted the exploits of Secret Service agents James T. West and Artemus Gordon in the 1870s as they foiled diabolical plots against the United States government.

The Episodes

170.1 *The Night of the Inferno.* Sept. 17, 1965. GS: Victor Buono, Suzanne Pleshette, Nehemiah Persoff, James Gregory, Walter Woolf King, Bebe Louie, Alberto Morin, Chet Stratton. West and Artemus travel to the Southwest frontier to sabotage the efforts of Juan Manolo, a bandit chieftain intent on claiming U.S. territory as his own.

170.2 *Night of the Deadly Bed.* Sept. 24, 1965. GS: J.D. Cannon, Danica D'Hondt, Barbara Luna, Anna Shin, Bob Herron, Bill Catching, Don Diamond. In Mexico, West searches for a man named Florey, whose henchmen murdered a Secret Service agent.

170.3 *The Night the Wizard Shook the Earth.* Oct. 1, 1965. GS: Michael Dunn, Leslie Parrish, Richard Kiel, Phoebe Dorin, Sigrid Vladis, Harry Bartell, William Mims, Mike Masters. In an effort to safeguard the life of Professor Nielsen, a demolitions expert, West assumes the professor's identity, but the hoax proves unsuccessful when the real Nielsen is killed.

170.4 *The Night of the Sudden Death.* Oct. 8, 1965. GS: Robert Loggia, Julia Payne, Antoinette Bower, Harlan Warde, Elisa Ingram, Sandy Kenyon, Henry Hunter, Don Gazzaniga, Bill Cassady, Joel Fluellen. West and Artemus head for the U.S. Mint because what the papers reported as a gas explosion was really the cover for a gang that has stolen currency plates.

170.5 *The Night of the Casual Killer.* Oct. 15, 1965. GS: John Dehner, Ruta Lee, Bill Williams, Charles Davis, Len Lesser, Mort Mills, Curtis Taylor, Ed Gilbert, Dub Taylor. West and Artemus are sent to do what the Army couldn't — penetrate the stronghold of a corrupt political boss and return him to Washington to stand trial.

170.6 *The Night of a Thousand Eyes.* Oct. 22, 1965. GS: Jeff Corey, Diane McBain, Donald O'Kelly, Barney Phillips, Linda Ho, Janine Gray, Jeanne Vaughn, Jack Searl, Victor French, Celeste Yarnell. A gang of river pirates, wreaking havoc on Mississippi shipping, have killed four Government agents. West has only one clue to their whereabouts, a gambling chip found on the body of a dead agent.

170.7 *The Night of the Glowing Corpse.* Oct. 29, 1965. GS: Kipp Hamilton, Phillip Pine, Charles Horvath, Marion Thompson, Ron Whelan, Oscar Beregi, Jr., Ralph Roberts, Frank Delfino, Jayne Massey, Louise Lawson. As the Franco-Prussian War rages in Europe, West tries, and fails, to safeguard an important canister of radioactive material that both combatants want very much.

170.8 *The Night of the Dancing Death.* Nov. 5, 1965. GS: Mark Richman, Ilze Taurins, Leslie Brander, Arthur Batanides, Booth Colman, Byron Morrow, Francoise Ruggieri,

Wild Wild West

Wolfe Barzell, Eva Soreny, Lynn Carey. When West and Artemus learn that the princess they are guarding is an impostor, they set out to find the real ruler.

170.9 *The Night of the Double-Edged Knife.* Nov. 12, 1965. GS: Leslie Nielsen, John Drew Barrymore, Charles Davis, Katharine Ross, Elisha Cook, Jr., Tyler McVey, Harry Townes, Vaughn Taylor, Ed Peck, Orrin Cobb. An Indian demand for $500,000 in gold must be met, or the Indians will kill five railroad workers a day until they are paid.

170.10 *The Night That Terror Stalked the Town.* Nov. 19, 1965. GS: Michael Dunn, Richard Kiel, Phoebe Dorin, Jean Hale, Joe Hooker, Jordan Shelley, Chuck O'Brien. West again matches wits with the diabolical Dr. Miguelito Loveless. This time in a ghost town peopled with lively sounds and lifelike dummies.

170.11 *The Night of the Red-Eyed Madmen.* Nov. 26, 1965. GS: Martin Landau, Joan Huntington, Shary Marshall, Gregg Martell, Toian Matchinga, Marianna Case, Ted Markland, Nelson Olmsted, Don Rizzan, Ray Kellogg. In Mars, California, to join a secret army of fanatics dedicated to overthrowing the Government, West has no problem joining up, but anyone attempting to leave the premises will be shot.

170.12 *The Night of the Human Trigger.* Dec. 3, 1965. GS: Burgess Meredith, Kathie Browne, Gregg Palmer, Mike Masters, Virginia Sale, Hank Patterson, James Jeter, Robert Phillips, Robert L. McCord, William Henry, Lindsay Workman, Dick Winslow, Vernon Scott. West and Artemus head toward Ellenville, the town that's next in line to experience an earthquake, courtesy of a demented geologist.

170.13 *The Night of the Torture Chamber.* Dec. 10, 1965. GS: Alfred Ryder, Henry Beckman, Sigrid Valdis, Viviane Ventura, H.M. Wynant, Mike Abelar, Nadia Sanders. Ordered to aid Governor Bradford, West is unaware the he is being briefed by the governor's double since the real Bradford has been kidnaped.

170.14 *The Night of the Howling Light.* Dec. 17, 1965. GS: Sam Wanamaker, Scott Marlowe, Ralph Moody, Linda Marsh, E.J. Andre, Ottola Nesmith, Clancy Cooper, Roy Barcroft, Don Kennedy, Robert Bice, Dan Riss, Kay E. Kuter. West is held captive by Dr. Arcularis, who plans to turn the Government agent into an assassin.

170.15 *The Night of the Fatal Trap.* Dec. 24, 1965. GS: Ron Randell, Joanna Moore, Joseph Ruskin, Don Briggs, Charles Davis, Walker Edmiston, Rodolfo Hoyos, Alan Sues, Dal Jenkins, Christian Anderson. To put a marauding band of Mexican bandits out of business, West disguises himself as a wanted outlaw.

170.16 *The Night of the Steel Assassin.* Jan. 7, 1966. GS: John Dehner, Sue Ane Landon, Allen Jaffe, Sara Taft, John Pickard, Arthur Malet, Roy Engel, Bruno VeSota. At the scene of a murder, West encounters a formidable opponent, a former Army officer whose injured body has been mended with steel, and who is systematically murdering the officers who served with him.

170.17 *The Night the Dragon Screamed.* Jan. 14, 1966. GS: Pilar Seurat, Ben Wright, Beulah Quo, Richard Loo, Philip Ahn, Benson Fong, Guy Lee, Michael Sung, Nancy Hsueh, Vince Elder, Paul King. Opium and alien Chinese are being smuggled into San Francisco, and West's only clues are a Tong insignia and a fortune cookie.

170.18 *The Night of the Grand Emir.* Jan. 28, 1966. GS: Yvonne Craig, Robert Middleton, Richard Jaeckel, Don Francks, James Lanphier, Tom Palmer, Arthur Gould-Porter, Ralph Gary, Phyllis Davis. West is taken prisoner when he pursues two men who tried to assassinate a Middle eastern ruler visiting America.

170.19 *The Night of the Flaming Ghost.* Feb. 4, 1966. GS: John Doucette, Karen Sharpe, Lynn Loring, Robert Ellenstein, Harry Bartell, Charles Wagenheim. While investigating the disappearance of Government copper and kerosene, West is told that the theft was engineered by abolitionist John Brown, who was pronounced dead in 1859.

170.20 *The Night of the Whirring Death.* Feb. 18, 1966. GS: Michael Dunn, Jesse White, Norman Fell, Pamela Austin, Richard Kiel, Phoebe Dorin, Barbara Nichols, Val Avery, Jason Wingreen, Sam Flynn, Richard Reeves. West and Artemus are transferring a wealthy citizen's millions to the state treasury when an explosion occurs. The diabolical Dr. Loveless, who engineered the blast, makes off with the money.

170.21 *The Night of the Puppeteer.* Feb. 25, 1966. GS: Lloyd Bochner, Imalda de Martin, John Hoyt, Nelson Olmsted, Sara Taft, Janis Hansen, Len Rogel, Jack Tygett, Wayne Albritton, Walter Painter. West has trouble convincing a Supreme Court justice that his life is in danger, until a puppet show marionette fires a gun at the jurist.

170.22 *The Night of the Bars of Hell.* March 4, 1966. GS: Arthur O'Connell, Indus Arthur, Elisha Cook, Jr., Paul Genge, Chet Stratton, Milton Parsons, Jenie Jackson, Bob Herron, Roy Sickner, Shawn Michaels. Posing as a prison inspector, West hunts for clues to a pillaging outlaw band, and two attempts on his life convince West that he is on the right track.

170.23 *The Night of the Two-Legged Buffalo.* March 11, 1966. GS: Dana Wynter, Nick Adams, Robert Emhardt, Paul Comi, Al Wyatt, Clint Ritchie, Lindsay Workman. West is assigned to protect a pleasure-loving prince who is determined to visit a plush spa, where assassins eagerly await his arrival.

170.24 *The Night of the Druid's Blood.* March 25, 1966. GS: Don Rickles, Ann Elder, Bartlett Robinson, Rhys Williams, Don Beddoe, Simon Scott, Sam Wade, Susan Browning, Emanuel Thomas. West is furious when his superiors refuse him permission to investigate the murder of a close friend who was burned to death before his eyes.

170.25 *The Night of the Freebooters.* April 1, 1966. GS: Keenan Wynn, Maggie Thrett, William Campbell, Andre Philippe, James Gammon, Robert Matek, James Connell, John Sterling. West poses as an escaped convict and Artemus impersonates a corrupt Mexican Army colonel to gain admittance to the stronghold of renegade army leader Thorwald Wolfe.

170.26 *The Night of the Burning Diamond.* April 8, 1966. GS: Robert Drivas, Christine Schmidtmer, Dan Tobin, Calvin Brown, Vito Carbonara, Whitey Hughes, Chuck O'Brien. An explosion occurs while West is trying to convince a Serbian official that the famed Kara Diamond should be moved for safekeeping. When the diamond disappears, West is blamed.

170.27 *The Night of the Murderous Spring.* April 15, 1966. GS: Michael Dunn, Jenie Jackson, Phoebe Dorin, Bill McLean, Leonard Falk, Tod Garrett, William Fawcett. West again faces his old nemesis, Dr. Miguelito Loveless, who is plotting to drive West insane.

170.28 *The Night of the Sudden Plague.* April 22, 1966. GS: Theo Marcuse, Nobu McCarthy, Harvey Levine, H.M. Wynant, Elliott Reid, Robert Phillips, Eddie Durkin. A mysterious epidemic has brought life to a standstill in several communities, paralyzing the townsfolk for 48 hours, and allowing outlaws to execute their robberies without opposition.

Season Two

170.29 *The Night of the Eccentrics.* Sept. 16, 1966. GS: Victor Buono, Richard Pryor, Anthony Eisley, Paul Wallace, Le Grande Mellon, Roy Jenson, Harry Ellerbe, Frank Sorrells, Mike Masters. West finds anything but amusement in the Echo Amusement Park, headquarters for the Eccentrics, a group of assassins hired to dispose of Mexican President Juarez.

170.30 *The Night of the Golden Cobra.* Sept. 23, 1966. GS: Boris Karloff, Simon Scott, James Westmoreland, Audrey Dalton, Jose de Vega, Morgan Farley, Michael York, John Alonzo, John Mountanto, Sugata Osaka. A maharajah who has built a palace in Oklahoma, kidnaps West to tutor his assassin sons in the ways of Western combat.

170.31 *The Night of the Raven.* Sept. 30, 1966. GS: Michael Dunn, Phyllis Newman, Phoebe Dorin, Howard Hoffman, Sandy Josel, Bill Catching. The Indians threaten a massacre unless West returns an Indian girl kidnaped by the evil Dr. Loveless.

170.32 *The Night of the Big Blast.* Oct. 7, 1966. GS: Ida Lupino, Mala Powers, Patsy Kelly, Robert Miller Driscoll, Rita Damico, Melville Ruick, Bruce Manning. A mad lady scientist sends a robot-like West to a meeting with the President's Cabinet.

170.33 *The Night of the Returning Dead.* Oct. 14, 1966. GS: Sammy Davis, Jr., Peter Lawford, Hazel Court, Ken Lynch, Alan Baxter, Frank Wilcox. West and Artemus try to unravel the riddle of the ghostly night rider who wears a Confederate Army uniform and is impervious to bullets fired at point blank range.

170.34 *The Night of the Flying Pie Plate.* Oct. 21, 1966. GS: William Windom, Ford Rainey, Leslie Parrish, Woodrow Chambliss, Pitt Herbert, Arlene Charles, Cindy Taylor. A glowing disc crashes near the gold-mining town of Morning Glory, Arizona, where West and startled spectators see a green girl emerge from the craft.

170.35 *The Night of the Poisonous Posey* (A.K.A. "The Night of the Situation Normal"). Oct. 28, 1966. GS: Delphi Lawrence, Percy Rodriguez, Eugene Iglesias, Shug Fisher, George Keymas, Michael Masters, H.M. Wynant, Andre Philippe, Christopher Cary, Hal Lynch. Vacationing agents West and Artemus learn that the town of Justice, Nevada, is playing host to an international convention of criminals.

170.36 *The Night of the Bottomless Pit.* Nov. 4, 1966. GS: Theo Marcuse, Joan Huntington, Tom Drake, Mabel Albertson, Steve Franken, Fred Carson, Seymour Green, Chuck O'Brien, Gregg Martell, Ernie Misco. West goes undercover as a prisoner at Devil's Island. His assignment is to rescue a secret agent who has been marked for execution by the prison's bestial commandant.

170.37 *The Night of the Watery Death.* Nov. 11, 1966. GS: John Van Dreelan, Jocelyn Lane, John Ashley, Forrest Lewis, James Galante. West is kidnaped by a madman named La Mer, who is planning to blow up a Naval vessel carrying the famous Admiral Farragut.

170.38 *The Night of the Green Terror.* Nov. 18, 1966. GS: Michael Dunn, Anthony Caruso, Paul Fix, Phoebe Dorin, Peggy Rea. The mad Dr. Loveless again tries to establish a Utopia of evil. This time, he promises a life without toil to a tribe of Indians, provided they obey his orders and kill James West.

170.39 *The Night of the Ready-Made Corpse.* Nov. 25, 1966. GS: Carroll O'Connor, Alan Bergman, Karen Sharpe, Patricia Huston, Jack Perkins, Daniel Ades, Paul Comi, Gene Tyburn, Andi Garrett. The assassination of a Latin American dictator leads West to the grave of the murderer, and to the suspicion that the man in the coffin is really a look-alike corpse.

170.40 *The Night of the Man-Eating House.* Dec. 2, 1966. GS: Hurd Hatfield, William Talman. West and Artemus witness eerie phenomena when they take refuge with sheriff and his prisoner in an abandoned bayou mansion.

170.41 *The Night of the Skulls.* Dec. 16, 1966. GS: Donald Woods, Lisa Gaye, Douglas Henderson, Francis de Sales, Sebastian Tom, Madame Spivy, Michael Masters, Calvin Browne. West gains entry to an exclusive band of murderers who are being groomed for a high-level assassination.

170.42 *The Night of the Infernal Machine.* Dec. 23, 1966. Ed Begley, Bill Zuckert, Elaine Dunn, Will Kuluva, Vito Scotti, Jon Lormer, William Gwinn, Michael Pate, John Harmon. Judge M'Guigan is one of the Federal judges at a convention in Denver, where the distinguished assembly is threatened by an ex-convict in possession of stolen dynamite.

170.43 *The Night of the Lord of Limbo.* Dec. 30, 1966. GS: Ricardo Montalban, Dianne Foster, Felice Orlandi, Gregory Morton, Ed Prentiss. A legless madman, maimed in the Civil War, claims he can enter the fourth dimension. He invites West and Artemus to accompany him back in time to the battle of Vicksburg.

170.44 *The Night of the Tottering Tontine.* Jan. 6, 1967. GS: Harry Townes, Robert Emhardt, Lisa Pera, Michael Road, Henry Darrow, Arthur Space, William Wintersole. West acts as bodyguard for a scientist who belongs to a group of investors Their rules call for the surviving member to inherit all the cash, but someone is cashing in early by murdering his fellow investors.

170.45 *The Night of the Feathered Fury.* Jan. 13, 1967. GS: Victor Buono, Michele Carey, Perry Lopez, George Murdock, Hiedo Imamura, Oliver McGowan. West and Artemus are trying to figure out why Count Manzeppi is so anxious to get his hands on a toy chicken.

170.46 *The Night of the Gypsy Peril.* Jan. 20, 1967. GS: Arthur Batanides, Ruta Lee, Ronald Long, Mark Slade, Johnny Seven, Charles Horvath. Agents West and Artemus turn their talents to the search for a kidnaped white elephant. The Old West game of hid-and-seek leads them to a holdup gang, a Gypsy circus troupe and the full fury of an outraged, sultan, owner of the purloined pachyderm.

170.47 *The Night of the Tartar.* Feb. 3, 1967. GS: John Astin, Malachi Throne, Susan Odin, Andre Philippe, Martin Blaine, Walter Sande, Larry Anthony, Michael Panaiv, Chubby Johnson, Loila Bell. West's head will roll unless he can lead the mad Count Sazanov to five million dollars extorted by the count's late cousin.

Wild Wild West

170.48 *The Night of the Vicious Valentine.* Feb. 10, 1967. GS: Agnes Moorehead, Diane McBain, Henry Beckman, Sherry Jackson, J. Edward McKinley, Walter Sande, Sherman Menchen, Mitzi Evans, Quinn Cunningham. West investigates the deaths of three wealthy Americans who had one thing in common. They met their wives at parties thrown by a regal Washington hostess.

170.49 *The Night of the Braine.* Feb. 17, 1967. GS: Edward Andrews, Brioni Farrell, Allen Jaffe. West clashes with a madman who is bent on conquering the world, and making West his second in command.

170.50 *The Night of the Deadly Bubble.* Feb. 24, 1967. GS: Alfred Ryder, Judy Lang, Lou Krugman, Nelson Welch, Nacho Galindo, Kai Hernandez. A lady scientist helps West investigate the death of her employer, an oceanographer who was killed before divulging information about a series of tidal waves that hit the Pacific Coast.

170.51 *The Night of the Surreal McCoy.* March 3, 1967. GS: Michael Dunn, John Doucette, Ivan Triesault, John Alonzo, Quentin Sondergaard, Jose Moreno. Pint-sized madman Dr. Miguelito Loveless returns to hold West captive while awaiting the arrival of a hired executioner, gunman Kid McCoy.

170.52 *The Night of the Colonel's Ghost.* March 10, 1967. GS: Kathie Browne, Lee Bergere, Alan Hewitt, Walker Edmiston, Arthur Hunnicutt, Roy Engel. West rides into nearly deserted Gibsonville, where strange incidents foretell a dangerous reception for President Grant. Gibsonville's few remaining citizens are tearing up the town in search for buried gold.

170.53 *The Night of the Deadly Blossom.* March 17, 1967. GS: Nehemiah Persoff, Miiko Taka, Pitt Herbert, Reggie Valencia, George Keymas, Lee Staley. In San Francisco, West joins forces with a lovely Japanese agent to prevent the murder of the King of Hawaii. Their adversary is a madman out to gain control of the islands.

170.54 *The Night of the Cadre.* March 24, 1967. GS: Donald Gordon, Richard Jaeckel, Sheilah Wells, Vince Howard, Val Avery, Ken Drake. West poses as a mad killer to join an army of assassins bent on murdering President Grant.

170.55 *The Night of the Wolf.* March 31, 1967. GS: Joseph Campanella, John Marley, Lori Scott, Jonathan Lippe, Eddie Fontaine, Michael Shillo, Charles Radilac, Jimmy Booth. In a nearly deserted mining town, West fights to protect the heir to a foreign throne. His adversary is a sinister Old World medicine man who commands a pack of wolves.

170.56 *The Night of the Bogus Bandits.* April 7, 1967. GS: Michael Dunn, Marianna Hill, Grace Gaynor, Walter Sande, Patsy Kelly, Donald "Red" Barry, Roland La Starza. A charred hundred-dollar bill propels West into a fresh encounter with the mad master of crime, Dr. Miguelito Loveless.

Season Three

170.57 *Night of the Bubbling Death.* Sept. 8, 1967. GS: Harold Gould, Madlyn Rhue, William Schallert, Timmy Brown, Val Avery, A.G. Ventana, John Mathews. West and Artemus are matched against a latter-day conquistador and his lovely accomplice. The schemers plot to hold the curator of the U.S. Archives prisoner, along with the priceless original of the U.S. Constitution, until the Government cedes them land for a private domain.

170.58 *The Night of the Firebrand.* Sept. 15, 1967. GS: Pernell Roberts, Lana Wood, Paul Lambert, Paul Prokop, Russ McCubbin, Zack Banks, Len Wayland, Walter Sande. West and Artemus grapple with a double-edged emergency. Canadian conspirators are out to topple the Crown. To mount their revolution, they have stripped a U.S. fort and left it helpless before an imminent Indian attack.

170.59 *The Night of the Assassin.* Sept. 22, 1967. GS: Robert Loggia, Frank Sorrells, Conlan Carter, Donald Woods, Ramon Navarro, Nina Roman, Phyllis Davis, Carlos Ramirez, Nate Esformes, Juan Talvera. West and Artemus match wits with Mexican authorities and a mysterious senorita. They are investigating an attempted assassination of President Juarez designed to incriminate the United States.

170.60 *The Night Dr. Loveless Died.* Sept. 29, 1967. GS: Michael Dunn, Susan Oliver, Robert Ellenstein, Anthony Caruso, Chubby Johnson, Jonathan Hole, Peter Hale, Lew Brown, Debra Lee, Marta Kopenhafer. The mad mini-genius of crime, Dr. Miguelito Loveless, is dead. West is assigned to protect his uncle and heir Dr. Liebknicht.

170.61 *The Night of the Jack O'Diamonds.* Oct. 6, 1967. GS: Frank Silvera, Mario Alcaide, James Alexander, David Renard, Maria Gomez, Ref Sanchez, Rico Aláñiz, Louis Massad. In Mexico, West and Artemus tangle with Mexican bandits and French imperialists. The agents are trying to recover and Arabian stallion, a gift from President Grant to Mexican President Juarez.

170.62 *The Night of the Samurai.* Oct. 13, 1967. GS: Paul Stevens, Irene Tsu, Thayer David, Khigh Dhiegh, John Hubbard, Jane Betts, Jerry Fujikawa, Anders Andelius, Candy Ward, Helen Funai. West and Artemus seek a faceless enemy on San Francisco's Barbary Coast. Their search for a stolen Samurai sword, vital symbol of Japanese-American friendship, hinges on a rendezvous with a mysterious middleman called the Dutchman.

170.63 *The Night of the Hangman.* Oct. 20, 1967. GS: John Pickard, Martin Brooks, Ahna Capri, Sarah Marshall, Harry Dean Stanton, Paul Fix. West and Artemus begin their own investigation when the murder suspect they captured is hastily sentenced to hang.

170.64 *The Night of Montezuma's Hordes.* Oct. 27, 1967. GS: Ray Walston, Jack Elam, Edmund Hashim, Roy Monsell, Roland La Starza, Hal Jon Norman, Carla Borelli. To protect Mexico's rights to a priceless Aztec hoard, West and Artemus strike out on a treasure hunt. Their companions are a gringo-hating Mexican officer and a cabal of Americans willing to kill to get the golden artifacts.

170.65 *The Night of the Circus of Death.* Nov. 3, 1967. GS: Phil Bruns, Joan Huntington, Paul Comi, Arlene Martel, Florence Sundstrom, Arthur Millay, Dort Clark, Sharon Kentran, Ashley LaRue, Mary Ashley, Red West. A spate of superbly counterfeited money sends West and Artemus to Denver, where the agents confront an improbably triangle connecting the U.S. Mint, a flamboyant circus troupe and the lingerie department of the Denver Emporium.

170.66 *The Night of the Falcon.* Nov. 10, 1967. GS: Robert Duvall, Lisa Gaye, Kurt Kreuger, John Alderson, George Keymas, Joseph Ruskin, Douglas Henderson, Edward

Knight, Gene Tyburn, Warren Hammack, William Phipps, Lynn Wood, Michael Shea, Michelle Tobin. West and Artemus have to stop a giant cannon, whose location is unknown, before it pulverizes Denver. The first clue leads them to Sinful, Colorado, where the creator of the grotesque weapon plans to hear competitive bidding from four villainous foreigners.

170.67 *The Night of the Cut Throats.* Nov. 17, 1967. GS: Bradford Dillman, Beverly Garland, Walter Burke, Shug Fisher, Jackie Coogan, Eddie Quillan, Harry Swoger, Lou Fraly, Quentin Sondergaard, Red West. Agents West and Artemus find murder and mystery as they investigate the mass exodus of townspeople from New Athens, Wyoming. An army of cutthroats has gathered on the town's outskirts, coincidental with the return of outcast Mike Trayne.

170.68 *The Night of the Legion of Death.* Nov. 24, 1967. GS: Kent Smith, Anthony Zerbe, Donnelly Rhodes, Karen Jensen, James Nusser, Toian Matchinga, Alex Gerry, Walter Brooke, Robert Terry, Eli Behar, Bill Erwin, Doug Rowe. The agents juggle a political powder keg as they try to topple an iron-fisted territorial governor without igniting Civil War II. To maintain his rule, the dictator is ready to pit his black-shirted legions against the United States.

170.69 *The Night of the Turncoat.* Dec. 1, 1967. GS: John McGiver, Marj Dusay, Bebe Louie, Douglas Henderson, Warren Edmiston, Brad Trumbull, Noel Swan, Andy Davis, Jim Driscoll, Rae Cousins, John Armand, Frederick Combs. Dismissed in disgrace from the Secret Service, James West searches for the mastermind who engineered a sophisticated campaign of character assassination to get him fired.

170.70 *The Night of the Iron Fist.* Dec. 8, 1967. GS: Mark Lenard, Ford Rainey, Bill Fletcher, Ross Hagen, Lisa Pera, William von Homburg, Bo Hopkins, James Gavin, Red West, Whitey Hughes, Fred Stromsoe, Troy Melton, Wayne Heffley, Craig Shreve. Agents West and Artemus grapple with bounty hunters and hired gunmen as they try to insure that a criminal is returned to his homeland for trial.

170.71 *The Night of the Running Death.* Dec. 15, 1967. GS: Jason Evers, Dub Taylor, T.C. Jones, Maggie Thrett, Ken Swofford, Karen Arthur, Oscar Beregi, Jr., John Pickard, Laurie Burton, Dante DePaulo, Tony Gage, Whitey Hughes, Don Reisen. To find a hired killer the agents join a wagon train peopled by bizarre characters and fraught with recurring violence.

170.72 *The Night of the Arrow.* Dec. 29, 1967. GS: Robert J. Wilke, Jeannine Riley, Robert Phillips, Frank Martin, William Bassett, Roy Engel, Logan Field, Paul Sorenson, William Massey. West and Artemus investigate a plot to steamroll an ambitious general into the Presidency. The frontier hero threatens to blaze a path to the White House over the bodies of American Indians.

170.73 *The Night of the Headless Woman.* Jan. 5, 1968. GS: Richard Anderson, Dawn Wells, Theo Marcuse, John McLiam, Pepe Callahan, Sandra Wells, Don Rizzan, Harry Lauter, Marlene Tracy, Steve Mitchell, Mary Ann Chin, Quentin Sondergaard. West and Artemus combat a weird conspiracy designed to reduce the U.S. to a have-not nation. An Egyptian syndicate, smuggling boll weevils cross-country, is breeding a super race of the bugs to devour American food crops.

170.74 *The Night of the Vipers.* Jan. 12, 1968. GS: Donald Davis, Nick Adams, Sandra Smith, Red West, Johnny Haymer, Richard O'Brien, Gwen Tolford, Clay Hodges. The agents track the dread Viper gang to Freedom, Kansas, a Western town spared from attack apparently because of the town's saintly mayor and no-nonsense sheriff.

170.75 *The Night of the Underground Terror.* Jan. 19, 1968. GS: Jeff Corey, Nehemiah Persoff, Sabrina Scharf, Douglas Henderson, Kenya Colbern, Red West, Greg Martell, Whitey Hughes, Dick Ainge, Terry Leonard, Louise Lawson. The agents plunge into the maelstrom of Mardi Gras to protect the bestial ex-commandant of a Civil War prison camp. Wanted by the Government, the fugitive is close to being captured by the half-human survivors of the camp.

170.76 *The Night of the Death Masks.* Jan. 26, 1968. GS: Milton Selzer, Patty McCormack, Louis Quinn, Bill Quinn, Douglas Henderson, Judy McConnell, Bobbie Jordan, Sam Edwards, Chuck Courtney, Dick Chauncey, Jerry Laverone. A kidnaped West is taken to the illusory town of Paradox, a hellish limbo of spectral sights and disembodied sounds. The phantasmagoria and its ephemeral cast of characters are the work of a madman out to destroy West and Artemus.

170.77 *The Night of the Undead.* Feb. 2, 1968. GS: Hurd Hatfield, John Zaremba, Priscilla Morrill, Joan Delaney, Roosevelt Grier, Kai Hernandez, David Fresco, Marvin Brodie, Rhys Williams, Joseph Perry, Hal DeWitt. West and Artemus grope through a voodoo world in search of a vanished scientist. The perilous trail leads the agents to a confrontation with a satanic biologist and his zombie cult.

170.78 *The Night of the Amnesiac.* Feb. 9, 1968. GS: Edward Asner, Sharon Farrell, Kevin Hagen, Gil Lamb, George Petrie, John Kellogg, Jim Nolan, Jack Rainey. West loses a crucial supply of smallpox vaccine, and his memory, when he is bushwhacked by bandits. While Artemus searches for the missing serum, West faces continued danger as he tries to find out who he is.

170.79 *The Night of the Simian Terror.* Feb. 16, 1968. GS: Dabbs Greer, Grace Gaynor, John Abbott, Felice Orlandi, H.M. Wynant, Chubby Johnson, Peter Hale, Jonathan Hole. Gothic horrors unfold as agents West and Artemus probe a senator's refusal to leave his heavily guarded home. With an enormous beast prowling the premises, the spooked household conspires to keep its terrible family secret.

170.80 *The Night of the Death-Maker.* Feb. 23, 1968. GS: Wendell Corey, Angel Tompkins, J. Pat O'Malley, Arthur Batanides, Roy Engel, Michael Fox, Nick Blair. A bad vintage wine provides the clue that leads the agents to a monastery where a would-be Presidential assassin is readying a paramilitary group to seize California after he has murdered President Grant.

Season Four

170.81 *The Night of the Big Blackmail.* Sept. 27, 1968. GS: Harvey Korman, William von Homburg, Roy Engel, Ron Rich. At a Washington embassy, West and Artemus work feverishly to squelch the framing of President Grant as an international conspirator.

170.82 *The Night of the Doomsday Formula.* Oct. 4, 1968. GS: Kevin McCarthy, E.J. Andre, Melinda Plowman, Gail Billings, Vince Howard, Fred Stromsoe, Tom Huff, Red

West, Dick Gangey. The disappearance of a Government scientist pits West and Artemus against General Walter Kroll, an ex-cavalry officer who has opened a deadly private business with foreign powers.

170.83 *The Night of the Juggernaut.* Oct. 11, 1968. GS: Simon Scott, Floyd Patterson, Peter Hale, Gloria Calamie, Byron Foulger, Bart LaRue, Wild Bill Reynolds, Irving Mosley. West and Artemus battle a reign of terror that is driving homesteaders off their land, spearheaded by a monstrous machine that belches fire and crushes everything in its path.

170.84 *The Night of the Sedgewick Curse.* Oct. 18, 1968. GS: Richard Hale, Jay Robinson, Arthur Space, Sharon Acker, Lee Weaver, Maria Leonard, Frank Campanella, Arthur Adams, Robert McCord, Anthony Jochim, Red West. In a bizarre and Gothic tale, the agents probe sinister disappearances at a health spa. The trail left by men who vanished leads to the Sedgewick family, who live under a terrible curse.

170.85 *The Night of the Gruesome Games.* Oct. 25, 1968. GS: William Schallert, Robert Ellenstein, Sherry Jackson, Helen Page Camp, Astrid Werner, Ken Drake, Jacqueline Hyde, Greg Palmer, Lee Cleem, Red West. West and Artemus are fighting time to keep a stolen plague virus from causing an epidemic. The setting is a gala, who's eccentric host is running his guests through a gamut of childish, and cruel, mirthless merriment.

170.86 *The Night of the Kraken.* Nov. 1, 1968. GS: Jason Evers, Ford Rainey, Ted Knight, Marj Dusay, Anthony Caruso, Brent Davis. The grotesque murder of a navy lieutenant in a coastal fishing village spurs the agents into a water investigation. The port and its naval personnel have been paralyzed by fatal encounters with a gigantic sea monster.

170.87 *The Night of the Fugitives.* Nov. 8, 1968. GS: Simon Oakland, Susan Hart, Charles McGraw, J.S. Johnson, Mickey Hargitay. The town of Epitaph proves to be an enemy camp when West and Artemus try to get a prisoner out of the place. The man holds the key to the growing crime syndicate that owns Epitaph—lock, stock and citizenry.

170.88 *The Night of the Egyptian Queen.* Nov. 15, 1968. GS: Sorrell Booke, Morgan Early, Tom Troup, Walter Brooke, William Marshall, Penny Gaston, Gene Tyburn, Cindy Hunter. The agents grapple with assassins and a maze of Egyptology in their quest of an archaeological treasure stole from a San Francisco museum. West and Artemus find themselves in deadly competition with two bands of cut-throats for possession of an ancient ruby.

170.89 *The Night of Fire and Brimstone.* Nov. 22, 1968. GS: Charles Macaulay, Robert Phillips, Dabbs Greer, John Crawford, Bill Quinn, Leslie Charleson, Ken Mayer, Fred Stromsoe, Dick Gangey, Red West. West and Artemus keep murderous predators at bay in an abandoned min that holds an undisclosed discovery. The man with the key to the mystery lies gravely wounded in a tunnel, guarded by a wild-eyed, tattered relic of the Confederacy.

170.90 *The Night of the Camera.* Nov. 29, 1968. GS: Pat Buttram, Barry Atwater, Fuji, Rico Cattani, Victor Sen Yung, Julio Medina, Ken Mendosa. A disbelieving West is saddled with Bosley Cranston, a greenhorn agent with a photographic memory and a missionary zeal to give his all, such as it is, to crack an opium ring.

170.91 *The Night of the Avaricious Actuary.* Dec. 6, 1968. GS: Harold Gould, Emily Banks, Ross Elliott, Jenny Maxwell, Judy Sherwin, Tol Avery, Fritz Feld, Barbara Hemingway, Frank Somenetti, Lou Krugman, Joseph Durkin, Bennett King, Red West. West and Artemus try to nab the fiendish mastermind of a bizarre insurance racket. Prospective clients of the Cyclops Insurance Company are assured that if they do not sign, their homes will be leveled by sound waves from a titanic tuning fork.

170.92 *The Night of Miguelito's Revenge.* Dec. 13, 1968. GS: Michael Dunn, Susan Seaforth, Byron Morrow, Douglas Henderson, Linda Chandler, Jim Shane, Johnny Silver, Percy Helton, Arthur Batanides, Don Pedro Colley, Walter Corey, Wendy Douglas, Paul Barselow, Dort Clark. Dr. Miguelito Loveless is motivated by revenge and working behind the gaudy facade of a circus. The tiny ringmaster directs the abduction of seven people, giving West one tantalizing clue—the legend a Thursday's child has far to go.

170.93 *The Night of the Pelican.* Dec. 27, 1968. GS: Khigh Dhiegh, Francine York, Lou Cutell, Andre Philippe, Debbie Wong, Ella Edwards, Buck Kartalian, James Shen, John Cremer, Jonathan Brooks, Vincent Beck, John Quey, Lorna Darnell, Linda Ho, Holly Mascott. The search for outlaw Din Chang leads West and Jeremy into clamorous New Years festivities in San Francisco's Chinatown. Baffling possibilities arise when the agents detect a grotesque connection between Chang, Alcatraz prison and a Government warehouse full of high explosives.

170.94 *The Night of the Spanish Curse.* Jan. 3, 1969. GS: Thayer Davis, Tolan Matchinga, Richard Angarola, Edward Colman, Pepe Callahan, Gil Serna, Ted de Corsia, Jon Lormer. West and Artemus plumb unknown reaches of Mexico in search of a spectral horde of conquistadors. After raids north of the border, the ghostly quarry disappears into a fabled Mexican valley where human sacrifice is made to the Spirit of Cortez.

170.95 *The Night of the Winged Terror* **Part One.** Jan. 17, 1968. GS: William Schallert, Christopher Cary, Michele Carey, Jackie Coogan, Bernard Fox, Robert Ellenstein, Roy Engel, Frank Sorrells, Valentine de Vargas, John Harding, Vic Perrin, Rico Alaniz. The U.S. and Mexico join forces to stop a grotesque subversion of their governments. Men in the public trust are going berserk, with inexplicable acts of wanton criminality. West's only clues are an omnipresent raven, and weird eyeglasses being dispensed by an itinerant oculist.

170.96 *The Night of the Winged Terror* **Part Two.** Jan. 24, 1968. GS: William Schallert, Christopher Cary, Michele Carey, Jackie Coogan, Bernard Fox, Robert Ellenstein, Roy Engel, Frank Sorrells, Valentine de Vargas, John Harding, Vic Perrin, Rico Alaniz. Under the hypnotic spell of the subversive Raven organization, West shoots the Mexican ambassador. To forestal international calamity, his assistant, disguised as an arch villain, pursues West into the madmen's lair.

170.97 *The Night of the Sabatini Death.* Feb. 7, 1969. GS: Ted de Corsia, Jill Townsend, Alan Hale, Jr., Douglas Henderson, Ben Wright, Jim Backus, Tom Geas, Bethel Leslie, Donald "Red" Barry, Eddie Quillan, Red West. Bizarre revelations by the weird inhabitants propel the agent toward the solution to the twelve-year-old robbery that made Calliope a ghost town.

170.98 *The Night of the Janus.* Feb. 15, 1969. GS: Jack

Carter, Anthony Eisley, Jackie DeShannon, Gail Billings, Arthur Malet, Nicky Blair, Benny Rubin, Red West, Tony Gangey, Bob Dodson. A Secret Service man is murdered and a song written by the victim contains a clue that sends West and Jeremy to the Service training center — and the killer.

170.99 *The Night of the Pistoleros.* Feb. 21, 1969. GS: Edward Binns, Robert Pine, Henry Wilcoxon, Perry Lopez, Richard O'Brien, Eugene Iglesias, William O'Connell, John Pickard, Jay Jostyn. West and Artemus probe a threatened territorial take-over near Mexico. Signs of conspiracy between men of the local Army garrison and Mexican outlaws are coupled with the outlaws' ominous interest in Artemus.

170.100 *The Night of the Diva.* March 7, 1969. GS: Patrice Munsel, Patrick Horgan, Beverly Todd, Patricia Dunne, Martin Kosleck, Lester Fletcher, Douglas Henderson. After preventing a tempestuous prima donna's kidnaping from a New Orleans opera house, West and Artemus discover that two previous stars of "Lucia de Lammermoor" have vanished, and that the mysterious Order of Lucia is linked to the affair.

170.101 *The Night of Bleak Island.* March 14, 1969. GS: John Williams, Gene Tyburn, Robert H. Harris, Beverly Garland, Richard Erdman, Jana Tyler, James Westerfield, Yvonne Schubert, Lorna Lewis, Jon Lormer. West and a British detective attend the reading of a will at a desolate estate. Murder stalks the gathering, pitting the sleuths against such spooky goings-on as a storm-lashed manor house, a howling hound, and an unseen presence.

170.102 *The Night of the Cossacks.* March 21, 1969. GS: Guy Stockwell, Nina Foch, Donnelly Rhodes, Jennifer Douglas, Alicia Gur, Oscar Beregi, Jr. Murderous interference plagues West and Artemus as they escort a Russian prince and his royal caravan to New Petersburg. Pretenders to the throne menace the prince as he seeks to reclaim a spiritually symbolic royal icon.

170.103 *The Night of the Tycoons.* March 28, 1969. GS: Jo Van Fleet, Steve Carlson, Tol Avery, Joanie Sommers, Richard O'Brien, E.A. Sirianni, Lee Duncan, Milton Parsons, Virginia Peters, Nelson Wells, Maria Garcia, Mike Mahoney, Biff Brody, Jerry Mann. West locks horns with an autocratic, and vindictive, lady board chairman. Although her directors are being murdered one by one, she mysteriously refuses to let West go after the killer.

170.104 *The Night of the Plague.* April 4, 1969. GS: Lana Wood, William Bryant, James Lanphier, John Hoyt, Bill Zuckert, Douglas Henderson, Red West, Eddie Firestone, Cliff Norton, Pilar Del Rey, Flora Plumb, Jacqueline Saylis, Tyler McVey, Steve Raines, Wayne Cochran. West is after a gang of theatrical thieves, and Artemus is after West. A crook West captured has since died of a contagious disease that kills within a few days.

171. *Wildside*

ABC. 60 min. Broadcast history: Thurday, 8:00-9:00, March 1985–April 1985.

Regular Cast: William Smith (Brodie Hollister), J. Eddie Peck (Sutton Hollister), Howard E. Rollins, Jr. (Bannister Sparks), Terry Funk (Prometheus Jones), John Di Aquino (Varges De La Cosa), Sandy McPeak (Governor J.W. Summerhayes), Meg Ryan (Cally Oaks), Jason Hervey (Zeke), Tommy Lamey (Parks Ritche).

Premise: Set in the late 1800s in Northern California, this series deals with an elite law-enforcement unit who preserve peace in Wildside Territory. The unit consists of Brodie Hollister, the leader and fast gun; his son, Sutton Hollister, who is also quick on the draw; explosives expert Bannister Sparks; Varges de la Cosa, a master of knives; and trick rope artist and wildman Prometheus Jones.

The Episodes

171.1 *Pilot.* March 21, 1985. GS: Jack Starrett. A renegade Confederate general is tearing up small towns looking for gold.

171.2 *Delinquincy of Miners.* March 28, 1985. Zeke is lured to a gold mine by an ad promising a chance to strike it rich, but the mother lode turns out to be coal and unsuspecting fortune hunters are the slave labor to mine it.

171.3 *The Crime of the Century.* April 4, 1985. Renegade British soldiers claiming to be members of the Light Brigade are terrorizing Wildside County, but the Governor refuses to let Brodie and the boys get involved.

171.4 *Title Unknown.* April 11, 1985. GS: Robin Hoff. Brodie tries to snap Bannister out of a severe depression over the sudden death of his fiancee before a notorious outlaw and his gang descend on the town.

171.5 *Title Unknown.* April 18, 1985. GS: James Cromwell, Alejandro Rey, Gerald Hiken, Dee Dee Rescher. A man posing as Buffalo Bill Cody brings his phony Wild West Show into Wildside to avenge his imprisonment in Cuba at the hands of the Spanish ambassador, who is secretly staying at Bannister's.

171.6 *Until the Fat Lady Signs.* April 25, 1985. GS: Geoffrey Lewis. Brodie is lured into a trap by an old nemesis who is anxious to settle a score with him.

172. *Wrangler*

NBC. 30 min. Broadcast history: Thursday, 9:30-10:00, Aug. 1960–Sept. 1960.

Regular Cast: Jason Evers (Pitcairn).

Premise: This series related the exploits of Pitcairn, a cowboy who wandered the Western frontier of the 1880s assisting people in need.

The Episodes

172.1 *Incident at the Bar M.* Aug. 4, 1960. GS: Susan Oliver, Bing Russell. Helen McQueen, a gorgeous blonde, has a problem with her ranch, so she hires Pitcairn to give her a hand.

172.2 *A Time for Hanging.* Aug. 11, 1960. GS: Robert Middleton, Joseph Bassett, Paul Carr, John Marley. Riding through the Circle J Ranch, Pitcairn is attacked, accused of cattle rustling and hauled off to the hanging tree.

172.3 *Affair at the Trading Post.* Aug. 18, 1960. GS: Suzanne Lloyd, Warren Oates, Bern Hoffman, Al Ruscio. Pitcairn gets lucky in a poker game and wins an Indian girl named Monacita.

172.4 *The Affair with Browning's Woman.* Aug. 25, 1960. GS: Julie Adams, William Redfield, Richard Cowl, Michael Burns. Pitcairn is on his way to the Texas panhandle and a job as ranch foreman when he gets involved with the Browning's woman. Alerted by a scream, he rides off the trail and finds a young woman struggling desperately to escape a man's embrace.

172.5 *Incident of the Wide Lop.* Sept. 1, 1960. GS: Harry Townes, Don Spruance, Pat Michon, Forrest Lewis, Michael Keel. Pitcairn is hired to drive a herd of cattle to market. But Cole Barton, a competing rancher, wants to make sure the Wangler doesn't reach his destination.

172.6 *Encounter at Elephant Butte.* Sept. 15, 1960. GS: Robert Emhardt, Robert Carricart, Hal K. Dawson, Leonard Bell, Al Hopson. Pitcairn is beaten and robbed by a crooked sheriff. Then he is delivered to a construction company, and forced to work with a chain gang.

Wyatt Earp see *The Life and Legend of Wyatt Earp*

173. *Yancy Derringer*

CBS. 30 min. Broadcast schedule: Thursday, 8:30-9:00, Oct. 1958–Sept. 1959.

Regular Cast: Jock Mahoney (Yancy Derringer), X Brands (Pahoo-Ka-Ta-Wha), Kevin Hagen (John Colton), Frances Bergen (Mme. Francis).

Premise: Yancy Derringer, a riverboat gambler, tries to help establish law and order in New Orleans during the 1880s.

The Episodes

173.1 *Return to New Orleans.* Oct. 2, 1958. GS: Julie Adams. Yancy Derringer tries to raise enough money to return to New Orleans, his native city. In a poker game with three men, Derringer wins, but the players try to rob him of the money. He escapes to a river boat he once owned.

173.2 *Gallatin Street.* Oct. 9, 1958. GS: John Qualen, Claude Akins, Paula Raymond. Sven Larsen, a sea captain, leaves his boat and goes to New Orleans to have a good time. He loses all his money in a saloon on notorious Gallatin Street and Yancy Derringer tries to help him recoup his losses.

173.3 *Ticket to Natchez.* Oct. 23, 1958. GS: Marie Windsor, Bill Williams. Yancy Derringer is given an Army payroll and told to take it to Natchez on the river boat Sultana. Aboard the Sultana an attempt is made to steal the payroll.

173.4 *An Ace Called Spade.* Oct. 30, 1958. GS: Ray Danton, Joan Taylor, Lisa Lu. Yancy Derringer is shocked when he reads in a local newspaper that John Colton, the Civil Administrator of New Orleans, has been killed. He decides to check the report and learns that Colton is very much alive but faces death in a forthcoming duel.

173.5 *A Bullet for Bridget.* Nov. 6, 1958. GS: Maggie Mahoney. An Irish girl in New Orleans is determined to find a husband. When she sees Yancy Derringer she is convinced that he is the man for her.

173.6 *The Belle from Boston.* Nov. 13, 1958. GS: Noreen Nash. A member of a gang of desperadoes is caught and hanged by John Colton, the civil administrator. Soon after, Colton's sister is menaced by the hoodlums, who are bent on exacting revenge.

173.7 *The Loot from Richmond.* Nov. 20, 1958. A civil war general sends his secretary with a message to John Colton, civil administrator of New Orleans. But the secretary is killed before he can deliver the message.

173.8 *The Saga of Lonesome Jackson.* Nov. 27, 1958. GS: Gene Evans, Maggie Hayes. A rich man goes to New Orleans in an attempt to find a wife. He meets Yancy Derringer and asks for his help.

173.9 *Memo to a Firing Squad.* Dec. 4, 1958. A man is sentenced to die before a firing squad. Although a Presidential pardon has arrived, a vengeful Army officer tries to stop the pardon from going into effect.

173.10 *Three Knaves from New Haven.* Dec. 11. 1958. GS: Maggie Mahoney. Local shop owners are receiving offers from three men for the sale of their shops. The offers, however, carry with them threats of violence if the owners do not sell. Bridget Malone receives an offer for her hat shop coupled with a proposal of marriage.

173.11 *Marble Fingers.* Dec. 18, 1958. GS: Kathleen Crowley, Kasey Rogers. Derringer attempts to discover the identities of some grave-robbers.

173.12 *Old Dixie.* Dec. 25, 1958. GS: Louise Fletcher, Lester Mathews, Bill Walker. Yancy's dog old Dixie narrowly escapes an untimely death after the Derringer will is made known. Yancy's father buried the Derringer fortune on the grounds of the plantation prior to the Civil War. According to the will, only old Dixie holds the clue to the location of the treasure.

173.13 *Two of a Kind.* Jan. 1, 1959. GS: Dick Foran. Yancy and Pahoo, blamed for a wave of crimes, are arrested and ordered executed.

173.14 *Nightmare on Bourbon Street.* Jan. 8, 1959. GS: Mary La Roche. A mysterious little old man kills a guard, breaks into a government warehouse and steals dynamite. Terror strikes New Orleans when the fanatic "Mr. D" leaves notes threatening to blow up the entire city.

173.15 *The Fair Freebooter.* Jan. 15, 1959. GS: Beverly Garland. A band of Mississippi river pirates nearly set off an international incident when they steal a valuable necklace from the Mexican government. The leader of the band is a beautiful woman, and Yancy decides to employ an unusual approach to retrieve the stolen goods.

173.16 *Mayhem at the Market.* Jan. 22, 1958. GS: Mari Aldon, Raymond Bailey. A ruthless protection racket develops in New Orleans. Frightened merchants refuse to cooperate with Yancy and Pahoo, despite the fact that there have been killings.

173.17 *The Night the Russians Landed.* Jan. 29, 1959. GS: Nick Adams. A Russian duke with an eye for women and a taste for vodka visits New Orleans. It soon becomes apparent that the duke is a target for murder.

173.18 *A Game of Chance.* Feb. 5, 1959. GS: Karen Sharpe. The winner of a New Orleans lottery dies before she can collect. Yancy suspects that this was more than pure coincidence.

173.19 *Panic in Town.* Feb. 12, 1959. GS: Peggy Stewart,

Donald Randolph. Several prominent New Orleans women have been murdered by a man dressed as a clown. A group of citizens are impatient because the civil authorities have failed to stop the killings, and they take matters into their own hands.

173.20 *Hell and High Water.* Feb. 19, 1959. GS: Charles Bronson, Patricia Cutts. When the Mississippi River reaches flood stage, Lady Charity's estate is threatened. To save it from devastation, the Lady and her friend Rogue Donovan devise a devious plot.

173.21 *The Louisiana Dude.* Feb. 26, 1959. GS: Hillary Brooke, Addison Richards. On a visit to Virginia City, Yancy gets involved in a poker game and wins half interest in a silver mine. He is pleased, but startled, to discover that his new partner is a beautiful woman.

173.22 *Longhair.* March 5, 1959. GS: Grant Williams. Gen. George Custer, famed Indian fighter, pays a visit to New Orleans. Yancy discovers that the general is being stalked by an Indian seeking revenge.

173.23 *Thunder on the River.* March 12, 1959. GS: Patricia Barry, Oliver McGowan. Yancy comes to the aid of the pretty owner of a fleet of river boats. Her boats are being sabotaged by a rival faction which hopes to monopolize river-boat service on the Mississippi.

173.24 *The Gun That Murdered Lincoln.* March 19, 1959. GS: Willard Sage, Bert Remsen, Robert McCord III, Tom McKee. Yancy is accused of having sold the assassination weapon to John Wilkes Booth.

173.25 *Collector's Item.* March 26, 1959. GS: Claude Akins, Richard Devon, Robert Cornthwaite. Yancy becomes friendly with a widow who is attempting to aid the orphans of New Orleans. To help the young lady commit what he considers to be a justifiable crime, Yancy enlists the aid of Mathew Brady, the famous photographer.

173.26 *Fire on the Frontier.* April 2, 1959. GS: Kelly Thordsen, Noreen Nash, Dan Tobin, Charles Fredericks, Robert Carricart. The Pawnee Indians threaten war because they feel that their rights are being violated. Pahoo-Ka-Ta-Wah, Yancy Derringer's Pawnee companion, becomes a statesman in an effort to prevent the uprising.

173.27 *Duel at the Oaks.* April 9, 1959. GS: Robert McCord III, Richard Devon, Charleen James, Hugh Sanders, John Vivyan. Yancy Derringer engages in a duel at New Orleans' famous field of honor and suddenly finds himself sentenced to hang.

173.28 *The Wayward Warrior.* April 16, 1959. GS: Beverly Garland, Karl Lukas, Mickey Simpson, William Pullen, Harry Jackson, Larry Blake. Trying to pick up some information on Mississippi gunrunners, Yancy encounters a river queen and a boxing champion.

173.29 *A State of Crisis.* April 30, 1959. GS: Richard Arlen, John Lupton, Walter Coy, Larry Blake, Charles Bateman. Gen. Hugh Morgan arrives in New Orleans bearing orders for the promotion of Civil Administrator John Colton to a post in Washington. Gen. Morgan assumes the job of Administrator and boasts that he is going to break up a huge counterfeiting ring in the city.

173.30 *Outlaw at Liberty.* May 7, 1959. GS: Kelly Thordsen, Lee Van Cleef, Kel Elhardt, John Anderson, Brett King. Wayne Raven, a wartime friend of Yancy's, is charged with murder by Marshal Ike Melton. Derringer goes to see Raven in answer to his appeal for help and discovers that the marshal is not the Ike Melton he knows.

173.31 *V As in Voodoo.* May 14, 1959. GS: Virginia Gray, Judi Meredith, Brad Dexter, Bill Walker, Naaman Brown. The city of New Orleans is plagued by a series of unfortunate incidents which seem to be the result of Voodoo magic. It is learned that a mysterious "cat woman" is terrorizing the city.

173.32 *The Quiet Firecracker.* May 21, 1959. GS: Lisa Lu, Jean Willes, Richard Devon, Lee Kendall, Mickey Morton. Yancy's friend, Miss Mandarin, owner of the Sazerac in New Orleans, is arrested for opium smuggling. It is charged that the opium was brought into the city in firecrackers which she received from her uncle in San Francisco.

173.33 *Gone but Not Forgotten.* May 28, 1959. GS: Kelly Thordsen, Joyce Jameson, Charles Gray, Luke Saucier, Dayton Lummis. Yancy is pleased at the news that his silver mine in Virginia City is beginning to pay off. But he becomes concerned when his friend Colorado Charlie comes to New Orleans with a report that Yancy's name is gracing a tombstone in a Virginia City graveyard.

173.34 *Two Tickets to Promontory.* June 4, 1959. GS: Jim Davis, Lee Kendall, John Larch, Rita Lynn. Two segments of a transcontinental railroad are joined and Yancy Derringer receives tickets to ride the train to the junction point, where a big celebration is planned. On board, Yancy encounters a strange fellow passenger.

174. *Young Dan'l Boone*

CBS. 60 min. Broadcast history: Monday, 8:00-9:00, Sept. 1977; Tuesday, 8:00-9:00, Oct. 1977.

Regular Cast: Rick Moses (Dan'l Boone), Devon Ericson (Rebecca Bryan), Ji-Tu Cumbuka (Hawk), John Joseph Thomas (Peter).

Premise: This adventure series depicted the exploits of Kentucky frontiersman Daniel Boone as a young man.

The Episodes

174.1 *The Trail Blazer.* Sept. 12, 1977. GS: Len Birman, Jeremy Brett, Jimmy Sangster. Dan'l battles hostile Indians and a hired killer while blazing a trail to Kentucky during the French and Indian War.

174.2 *The Pirate.* Sept. 19, 1977. GS: Paul Shenar, Clive Revill, William Watson, David Adamson. Dan'l is ambushed by a pack of thieves who make off with the pelts that would buy freedom for Hawk.

174.3 *The Salt Licks.* Sept. 26, 1977. GS: John Devlin, Jerry Rushing, Cal Bellini, Manu Toupou, Daniel S. Zapien. Shawnees capture Dan'l and a group of settlers to obtain firearms and instruction in their use for an uprising against the white man.

174.4 *The Game.* Oct. 10, 1977. Norman Alden, Kurt Kasznar, Virgil Frye, Richard Kiel. Dan'l guides trappers who want to set up trading posts in a wilderness inhabited by hostile Indians and haunted by a legendary beast.

175. Young Maverick

CBS. 60 min. Broadcast history. Wednesday, 8:00-9:00, Nov. 1979-Jan. 1980.

Regular Cast: Charles Frank (Benjamin Maverick), Susan Blanchard (Neil McGarrahan), John Dehner (Marshal Edge Troy).

Premise: This series followed the adventures of Ben Maverick, the son of Beau Maverick, and cousin to Bret and Bart Maverick. Ben is an Ivy League dropout who follows in the footsteps of his illustrious family as a card-sharp and con-man.

The Episodes

175.1 The New Maverick. Sept. 3, 1978. GS: James Garner, Jack Kelly, Susan Sullivan, Eugene Roche, George Loros, Woodrow Parfrey, Gary Allen, Helen Page Camp, Jack Garner, Graham Jarvis. Card-sharps Bret and Bart Maverick link up with their young kin Ben Maverick, the son of cousin Beau. The trio attempt to turn the tables on outlaws who are selling Gatling guns.

Season One

175.2 Clancy. Nov. 28, 1979. GS: Denny Miller, Dick O'Neill, Burton Gilliam, Joanne Nail, James Garner, Morgan Woodward, Dave Cass, Warren Berlinger. Ben sees fast-money potential in an oversized Irish immigrant, who must might hold his own against a barnstorming boxer.

175.3 A Fistful of Oats. Dec. 5, 1979. GS: J. Pat O'Malley, Clifton James, Vito Scotti, Noble Willingham, William Boyett, Med Flory, Arch Johnson. Nell's bibulous uncle finds himself sentenced to the gallows after he inadvertently spooks the horse of a hanging judge.

175.4 Hearts o'Gold. Dec. 12, 1979. GS: Bill McKinney, Audrey Landers, Robert Hogan, Douglas Dirkson, Severn Darden, Barney Phillips, Gene Tyburn. Ben's pursuit of a man who welshed on a gambling debt takes him to a small town about to fall prey to bank robbers.

175.5 Dead Man's Hand Part One. Dec. 26, 1979. GS: Howard Duff, James Woods, John McIntire, Donna Mills, George Dzundza, Alan Fudge, Harry Dean Stanton, Betsey Slade. Ben is bequeathed a pat hand in a high-stakes poker game by a tinhorn who died before he could play his cards.

175.6 Dead Man's Hand Part Two. Jan. 2, 1980. GS: Howard Duff, James Woods, John McIntire, Donna Mills, George Dzundza, Alan Fudge, Harry Dean Stanton, Betsey Slade. Ben plays out the hand of the tinhorn who died during a high-stakes poker game.

175.7 Makin' Tracks. Jan. 9, 1980. GS: Victor Jory, John Hillerman, Morgan Fairchild, Ray Tracey, Andrew Robinson, Regis Cordic, Vernon Weddle, Miriam Byrd Nethery. An 80-year-old Indian cardsharp tells railroad officials they'll have to win the right of way through his land in a poker game.

175.8 Have I Got a Girl for You. Jan. 16, 1980. GS: Richard B. Shull, Patch MacKenzie, Gary Grubbs, Bruce M. Fischer. Ben and Nell plan to bridle a crooked marriage broker.

175.9 Half-Past Noon. Jan. 30, 1980. GS: Howard Platt, Dennis Burkley, Jerry Hardin, Vincent Schiavelli, Guy Raymond, Cliff Norton, Lisa Cori, Richard Landin, Jim B. Smith, Robin G. Eisenmann. Ben enjoys the red-carpet treatment of a small town, unaware that he is being set up by the townsfolk for a duel with a fast gun.

176. The Young Pioneers

ABC. 60 min. Broadcast history: Sunday, 7:00-8:00, April 1976.

Regular Cast: Linda Purl (Molly Beaton), Roger Kern (David Beaton), Robert Hays (Dan Gray), Robert Donner (Mr. Peters), Mare Winningham (Nettie Peters), Michelle Stacy (Flora Peters), Jeff Cotler (Charlie Peters).

Premise: This is the tale of young newlyweds, Molly and David Beaton, who endure the hardships of the Dakota Territory in the early 1870s.

The Episodes

176.1 The Young Pioneers. March 1, 1976. GS: Shelly Jutner, Frank Marth, Arnold Soboloff, Brendon Dillon, Charles Tyner, Jonathan Kidd, Bernice Smith, Janis Famison, Dennis Fimple. This pilot tele-film told the story of teenage newlyweds, Molly and David Beaton, who try and build a life in the Dakota frontier of the 1870s.

176.2 The Young Pioneers' Christmas. Dec. 17, 1976. GS: Kay Kimler, Sherri Wagner, Brian Melrose, Britt Leach, Arnold Soboloff, Brendon Dillon, Rand Bridges. In the second pilot tele-film Molly and David Beaton try to extend friendship to their neighbors in the Dakota wilderness during the Christmas season.

Season One

176.3 Episode One. April 2, 1978. GS: David Huddleston, A Martinez, Cynthia Avila, Guillermo San Juan, Geno Silva. Molly and David befriend a stricken Indian family reluctant to accept their aid.

176.4 Episode Two. April 9, 1978. GS: E.J. Andre, Jeffrey Altman, Ellen Blake, Britt Leach. Young Charlie contracts diphtheria and may die unless the aging town doctor's untried assistant is allowed to operate.

176.5 Episode Three. April 16, 1978. GS: Charles Tyner, Betty Jinnette. The elder Beatons visit, but joy departs when Molly falls down a well during a dust story, leaving her bedridden and downcast.

177. Young Riders

ABC. 60 min. Broadcast history: Thursday, 9:00-10:00, Sept. 1989-Sept. 1990; Saturday, 8:00-9:00, Sept. 1990-Aug. 1991; Saturday, 9:00-10:00, Sept. 1991-Jan. 1992; Thursday, 8:00-9:00, May 1992-July 1992.

Regular Cast: Anthony Zerbe (Teaspoon Hunter), Ty Miller (the Kid), Stephen Baldwin (Billy Cody), Josh Brolin (Jimmy Hickok), Travis Fine (Ike McSwain), Gregg Rainwater (Buck Cross), Yvonne Suhor (Lou McCloud), Melissa Leo (Emma Shannon) 89-90, Brett Cullen (Marshal Sam Cain), Clare Wren (Rachel), Don Franklin (Noah Dixon), Don Collier (Tompkins) 91-92.

Premise: This series depicted the adventures of teenage orphans who join the pony express in the Dakota territory of the 1860s, working the line from Sweetwater.

The Episodes

177.1 *Pilot.* Sept. 20, 1989. GS: David Marshal, Eric Christmas, David Dunard, Jim Beaver, Ace Mask. The young riders are tutored by their wily supervisor, Teaspoon, and tested by a ruthless bandit.

177.2 *Gunfighter.* Sept. 21, 1989. GS: Jay O. Sanders, Wayne Northrop, G.W. Lee, George Dobbs, Bing Blenman, Glynn Williams. Hickok projects the demons of his childhood onto a bullying hired gun and decides only a showdown with the gunslinger will exorcise them.

177.3 *Speak No Evil.* Sept. 28, 1989. GS: Michael Wren, Don Collier, Semu Huaute, Nick Young. With the Kiowas on the warpath, Buck must choose between his allegiance to the pony express and his kinship with the tribe.

177.4 *Home of the Brave.* Oct. 5, 1989. GS: Albert Salmi, Larry Soller, Earle W. Smith, Henry Max Kendrick, Richard Sugarman. Ike witnesses a stagecoach massacre and turns the leader over to the marshal, but the robber's gang seeks to silence Ike permanently before he can testify.

177.5 *Bad Blood.* Oct. 12, 1989. GS: Jon De Vries, Robert Prentiss, George K. Sullivan, Kristina Betts, Toby Goodwin. Lou returns to the orphanage to retrieve her younger brother and sister, but her estranged father, a gunrunner, gets to them first.

177.6 *Black Ulysses.* Oct. 26, 1989. GS: Stan Shaw, Tim Thomerson, Austin J. Judson, Gabriel Folse, Peppi Sanders. The riders stand up for a runaway slave who is pursued by Missouri state militiamen committed to bringing down the fugitive.

177.7 *Ten-Cent Hero.* Nov. 2, 1989. GS: M.C. Gainey, Gerrit Graham, Billy Jacoby, Brad Leland, Don Collier. A dime novelist creates the legendary gunslinger Wild Bill Hickok, and Hickok faces the consequences when a gunfighter arrives for a showdown with the fastest gun in the West.

177.8 *False Color.* Nov. 8, 1989. GS: Page Mosely, Tony Noakes, Ed Adams, Sanford Gibbons, Don Baker. Kid enjoys a reunion with his brother Jed, who seems to have found a niche in the Army, but is really leading a gang that is posing as cavalry to steal gold for the budding Confederacy.

177.9 *Good Day to Die.* Nov. 16, 1989. GS: Bob Estes, J. Kenneth Campbell, Tommy Townsend, Sanford Gibbons, Bob Hoy. Kid finds a young warrior at the scene of a way-station massacre and, although the warrior denies any wrongdoing, Kid hauls him back through Indian territory to face justice in Sweetwater.

177.10 *End of Innocence.* Nov. 30, 1989. GS: James Sutorius, Lenny Von Dohlen, Dennis Creaghan, Frederick Lopez. Hickok discovers hidden feelings for Emma on a venture to an Army outpost commanded by a captain with a passion for cruelty.

177.11 *Blind Love.* Dec. 7, 1989. GS: Ely Pouget, Macon McCalman, Casey Biggs, William J. Fisher. Hickok's heart is lassoed by a mysterious woman, but he is caught in a dangerous tangle when he discovers that she is bound to another man.

177.12 *The Keepsake.* Dec. 14, 1989. GS: Ted Shackelford, Gary Bell, Mel Coleman, Lori Ann Kalos. Teaspoon is given claim to a small fortune, but he may lose it to a young woman he thinks is his lost daughter, and to a crooked gambler willing to kill for the cash.

177.13 *Fall from Grace.* Jan. 4, 1990. GS: Robin Strasser, Tony Longo, Brion James, Raymond Bieri, Tanya Kush. Hickok has a falling-out with Teaspoon, and he falls in with a gang of outlaws who are after a store of Army guns and ammunition.

177.14 *Hard Time.* Jan. 11, 1990. GS: Mark Rolston, Robert Clohessy, Cassie Yates. Kid is sentenced to hard time on a trumped-up charge by a small-town sheriff carrying out the policies of the sadistic man who keeps the town under a cloud of fear.

177.15 *Lady for a Night.* Jan. 18, 1990. GS: Roger Rees, Steven Hartley, Daniel O'Haco, Travis Shepard, Don Collier, Craig Reay. Dressed as a lady for a night, Lou meets a vicious brute who develops an obsession for her, while he masterminds a series of heists in the territory.

177.16 *Unfinished Business.* Feb. 1, 1990. GS: Cliff De Young, Frederick Coffin, Chip Campbell, Ana Auther, Paul Threlkeld. After surviving a massacre of wealthy settlers near Salt Lake, Emma's estranged husband arrives in Sweetwater looking for shelter from Emma, and raising the suspicions of Sam and the riders.

177.17 *Decoy.* Feb. 8, 1990. GS: Meg Foster, Doug Seus, James Poslof. On a wild ride to deliver a top-secret Government message, Cody helps a mortally wounded mountain man, who asks Cody to care for his pet bear. Meanwhile, back in Sweetwater, the other riders look after an abandoned baby.

177.18 *Daddy's Girl.* Feb. 15, 1990. GS: Lloyd Bochner, Alice Adair, Scott Kraft, Heather McNair, Greg Doty. A new girl in town has Buck in her sights, but he is caught in the cross-fire between her, her tyrannical father and her cruel suitor.

177.19 *Bull Dog.* Feb. 22, 1990. GS: Fisher Stevens, William Kiehl, Jay Bernard, Jim Newcomer. An Eastern college boy arrives with dreams of meeting his Western idol, Hickok, but he is used as an unwitting accomplice in a scheme that endangers all the riders.

177.20 *Matched Pair.* March 8, 1990. GS: H.M. Wynant, Leilani Sarelle, Mark Shaughnessy. Hickok helps a friendly rival search for their gunfighting mentor's kidnapped daughter, who actually has escaped with evidence of her dad's corruption.

177.21 *Man Behind the Badge.* March 22, 1990. GS: Patrick John Hurley, Eddie Jones, Bill T. Middleton, Earl W. Smith, Catherine Gilman, Sonny Skyhawk. Sam finds himself on the wrong side of the law in his own town when the man responsible for the murder of Sam's wife takes over Sweetwater.

177.22 *Then There Was One.* April 5, 1990. GS: Noble Willingham, Michael J. Pollard, Barbara Luna, Tommy Townsend, Ben Zeller, Dick Belerue. Teaspoon sets out for Texas with an old comrade in arms to warn three other veterans that someone has been murdering the last men who truly remember the Alamo.

177.23 *Gathering Clouds* Part One. April 30, 1990. GS: David Soul, Jason Adams, Franc Luz, Martha Byrne, Michael F. Woodson, John Phildin, Cynthia Nixon. The tension between the North and the South reaches crisis proportions, and Kid is recruited to infiltrate a band of Southern guerrillas led by a charismatic Robin Hood called the Hawk.

177.24 *Gathering Clouds* **Part Two.** May 7, 1990. GS: David Soul, Jason Adams, Franc Luz, Martha Byrne, Michael F. Woodson, John Phildin, Cynthia Nixon. Kid escapes the noose but Hawk's raiders are still on the loose, so Hickok works his way into the gang, which hangs any pretense of civility to pursue its violent purpose.

Season Two

177.25 *Born to Hang.* Sept. 22, 1990. Della Reese, Barry Culliton, Ron Phillips, Elijah N. Carne, Francesca Jarvis. Hickok meets a freeborn black man named Noah, and the two ride along with Stagecoach Sally, a woman who saved Noah when he was a child and is now on a mission to take freed slaves to Africa.

177.26 *Ghosts.* Sept. 29, 1990. GS: David Carradine, James Healy, James Lancaster, Jeff Bennett, Mark Jeffreys, Jay Bernard. A tragic incident from the past haunts Rachel, who forms a special bond with Lou. Meanwhile, a fearsome outlaw stalks Teaspoon.

177.27 *Dead Ringer.* Oct. 6, 1990. GS: John Slattery, William Shockley, David Richards, Ken Bridges. Thanks to a boastful impersonator, there is a price on Hickok's head for bank robbery, and a bushwhacking bounty hunter poised to kill him.

177.28 *Blood Moon.* Oct. 13, 1990. George Hearn, Doug Hutchison, Seth Foster, Travis Middleton. A cholera outbreak threatens Sweetwater, but fear among the townspeople may be a bigger problem than the spread of the deadly disease.

177.29 *Pride and Prejudice.* Oct. 27, 1990. GS: Jenny O'Hara, Amy O'Neill, Joaquin Martinez, Joseph Runningfox, Richard Comeau. After guiding the cavalry to a Sioux camp, Buck returns to Sweetwater with a surprise for Tompkins — his wife and daughter, who were seized years earlier but managed to live within the tribe.

177.30 *The Littlest Cowboy.* Nov. 3, 1990. GS: Judith Hoag, John Christian Graas, George O. Petrie, Kathy Fitzgerald, Tom Noga. Embittered by his handicap, silent Ike lashes out, but his life converges with that of a terminally ill youngster, who has a lust for life and a desire to meet the Pony Express riders.

177.31 *Blood Money.* Nov. 10, 1990. GS: Sherman Howard, John Nesci, Pierrette Grace, George Dobbs, Billy Joe Patton. The riders investigate a corrupt marshal after a murder suspect turned in by Kid hangs himself under questionable circumstances.

177.32 *Requiem for a Hero.* Nov. 17, 1990. GS: Pernell Roberts, Norm Skaggs, Travis Middleton, Don Pendergrass, George Salazar. Cody meets his Western idol Hezekiah Horn, a writer disgusted by development of the West and disturbed by the violence of the Indian police. Meanwhile, Lou and Kid's hemming and hawing seems to be coming to an end.

177.33 *Bad Company.* Dec. 1, 1990. GS: Michelle Joyner, Stephen Root, Karen Person, Hank Fletcher, William J. Fisher. Hickok accidentally kills an innocent woman during a gunfight, triggering troubling feelings about all his violent deeds.

177.34 *Star Light, Star Bright.* Dec. 15, 1990. GS: Brian Keith, Richard Zobel, Jaime Lyn Bauer, Craig Reay, Ed Adams. With Christmas approaching, the riders fall under the spell of a con man, who promises them a half share in a gold mine.

177.35 *The Play's the Thing.* Dec. 29, 1990. GS: Tammy Grimes, Rebecca Staab, Grant James, Dane Christopher. A wide-eyed Cody joins a traveling acting troupe, unaware that its members are Confederates intent on assassinating General Fremont.

177.36 *Judgment Day.* Jan. 5, 1991. GS: Patrick Massett, James Lashly, Park Overall, David Richards, Monty Stuart. Cody falls in with bounty hunters who may be worse than their quarry. Meanwhile, a vivacious woman puts a spell on Teaspoon, and Lou and Kid consider commitment.

177.37 *Kansas.* Jan. 12, 1991. GS: Richard Roundtree, Barry Culliton, Andre Marcellous, Ric San Nicholas, Jason Kenny. A heated Noah heads into slave territory, where he stakes his life to help his old teacher. Meanwhile, Rachel tangles with a card sharp.

177.38 *The Peacemakers.* Jan. 19, 1991. GS: Steve Railsback, James Cromwell, Brenda Bakke, Joe Sikorra, Alan McRae, Blake Conway. Hickok defends a religious group called the Peacemakers against the hostile town in which they intend to settle. Meanwhile, a vengeful soul has a less-than-peaceful aim as he tries to rehabilitate a fast gun, now a broken-down drunk, to send after Wild Bill.

177.39 *Daisy.* Feb. 2, 1991. GS: William Russ, Lexi Randall, Robert F. Hoy, Sydney Warner, Gerry Glombecki. On the run from a dangerous riverboat gambler, a small-time hustler and his precocious daughter storm into Sweetwater to see Rachel, his old flame. Meanwhile, Lou does a slow burn over Kid's irksome protectiveness.

177.40 *Color Blind.* Feb. 9, 1991. GS: Nancy Valen, Olivia Virgil Harper, David Patrick Wilson, Seth Foster. After the breakup, Kid is sweet on Sweetwater's new schoolteacher, who has brought many secrets to town. Meanwhile, Lou joins Hickok on a ride, and their friendship grows.

177.41 *Old Scores.* Feb. 16, 1991. GS: George Deloy, Brian Bonsall, Daniel Martine, Peppi Sanders, Gary Clarke. Ike is convinced he has seen one of the men responsible for the murder of his family, but the suspected killer is now a family man himself. Meanwhile, the other riders try to track down a mysterious beast that is terrorizing the town.

177.42 *The Talisman.* Feb. 23, 1991. GS: Jim Haynie, Valerie Mahaffey, Julian Reyes, Robert Sonne Browne, Fredrick Lopez. After a missionary priest calls on him for help, Teaspoon takes Hickok, Kid, Noah and Cody on a mission to save a farming village being terrorized by murderous bandits.

177.43 *The Noble Chase.* March 9, 1991. GS: William Shockley, Tony Maggio, David Adams, Mark Lang, Ed Beimfohr. Hickok reluctantly teams with rival Jake Colter to chase down a bank robber who has a price on his head, but who also has a heart of gold.

177.44 *Face of the Enemy.* April 6, 1991. GS: Timothy Carhart, Steve Arlen, Richard Comeau, Bob Cota. When Teaspoon's war-hero friend orders an attack upon a Sioux delegation, Indians threaten to retaliate.

177.45 *The Exchange.* May 4, 1991. GS: Jeffrey Nordling, Tony Acierto, Peter Phelps, Sue-Ann Leeds, Robert Knott. When Teaspoon arranged for the hanging of a bank robber, the man's brother kidnaps Teaspoon's would-be daughter, precipitating a massive showdown.

Season Three

177.46 *A House Divided.* Sept. 28, 1991. GS: William Smith, Darrell Larson, Frances Fisher, Charles Benton. Kid and Hickok set out to rebuild an Express station apparently destroyed by abolitionists near the Nebraska Territory town of Cross Creek, which lies on the border of slave and free territory.

177.47 *Jesse.* Oct. 5, 1991. GS: James Gleason, John Schuck, Mark Davenport, Warner McKay. The riders befriend a young man named Jesse, who seeks vengeance against a gang of outlaws that kills his guardian.

177.48 *The Blood of Others.* Oct. 12, 1991. GS: James Gammon, William Lucking, Tanya Kush, Neal Thomas. Lou, Hickok and Kid are to deliver a long-sought outlaw to his hanging, but en route discover that the man's more honorable than ornery.

177.49 *Between Rock Creek and a Hard Place.* Oct. 25, 1991. GS: Gloria Reuben, Eugene Byrd, Richard Glover, Tim DeZarn, Gary Clarke. Noah tangles with an unlikable Army recruiter who winds up murdered, and Noah becomes the prime suspect.

177.50 *The Presence of Mine Enemies.* Nov. 9, 1991. GS: Kelli Williams, Michael Harris, Buck Taylor, Robert L. Lee, Brett Marston. Fate plays a hand when Ike meets a young woman whose gambler father clashes with a dangerous cardsharp dandy.

177.51 *Survivors.* Nov. 16, 1991. GS: Margaret Reed, Gregot Hesse, Brian Burke, Laurie Allyn, Jonathan Mincks. Cody befriends a boy whose widowed mother makes Cody's heart race, but she is forced to be involved with gun-running outlaws.

177.52 *The Initiation.* Nov. 25, 1991. GS: Jamie Walters, Leo Burmester, Robert Knott, Steven Schwartz-Hartley, Stacy Keach, Sr. Hickok rounds up a bank robber who is related to Jesse. The young man's name is Frank James.

177.53 *Just Like Old Times.* Nov. 30, 1991. GS: Tim Quill, Kim Myers, Jake Walker, Ted Parks, Jarrod Wilson. A childhood girlfriend of Kid brings back memories, but her husband, another old acquaintance, brings nothing but trouble. Meanwhile, the riders want to take part in a cowboy competition.

177.54 *Spirits.* Dec. 7, 1991. GS: Stephen Meadows, Jeff L. O'Haco, Daniel O'Haco, Forrie J. Smith. A charismatic division agent's problem with alcohol spills over onto Rachel, who falls off the wagon when she starts to fall for him.

177.55 *A Tiger's Tale.* Dec. 28, 1991. GS: Stephen Meadows, Claudette Nevins, Georgia Emelin, Jim Cody Williams. Cody and Noah bite off more than they can chew trying to deliver a tiger to St. Joseph while protecting nuns and a noviate they meet en route. Meanwhile, Jesse is bitten by the love bug.

177.56 *Good Night Sweet Charlotte.* Jan. 4, 1992. GS: Christopher Pettiet, Jennifer Hetrick, John De Lancie, Randolph Messersmith, George Salazar. A former prostitute arrives in Rock Creek hoping to start a new life, but her presence brings back bitter memories for Lou. Meanwhile, Hickok befriends a wounded Lakota Indian out on the trail.

177.57 *Song of Isiah.* Jan. 18, 1992. GS: James Handy, Sydney Walsh, Ric San Nichols, Lalita Lauren. On a visit to his sister's, Hickok becomes affected by her and her husband's cause, and finds himself riding with a band of vigilante abolitionists led by a zealous man wanted for murder.

177.58 *Spies.* Jan. 25, 1992. GS: Krystyne Haje, Gary Sandy, Sandy Elias, Michael F. Woodson, Danny Ray. With war possible, Kid gets mixed up in espionage involving a charming spy. Meanwhile, Teaspoon plans to make Rachel the new schoolteacher.

177.59 *Shadowmen.* May 21, 1992. GS: Art LaFleur, Greta Lambert, Sean C. Robinson, Scott Frederick. The young riders have to deal with the arrival of an overzealous Pinkerton agent in Rock Creek on the trail of a murderous bank robber, and the appearance of a damsel in distress who distracts Teaspoon.

177.60 *Mask of Fear.* May 28, 1992. GS: Mimi Maynard, Paul Rossilli, Randy Crowder, Barney McFadden. Mob mentality grips Rock Creek after a Polish immigrant convicted of killing his wife is released from prison and returns to town.

177.61 *Dark Brother.* June 4, 1992. GS: Sam Vlahos, John Stockwell, Megan Gallivan, Phil Mead, Suzi List. Buck sets out on a journey to save the life of a stricken friend, a white girl who was raised by the Kiowas.

177.62 *The Road Not Taken.* June 11, 1992. GS: Joseph Bottoms, Dey Young, Benjamin Stewart, Justin Rigney. Jesse tags along with Hickok, who has personal reasons for nailing the killer he is tracking. Meanwhile, Cody's published story about the Pony Express is taken very personally by the other riders.

177.63 *The Sacrifice.* June 25, 1992. GS: Mel Winkler, Justin Whalin, Grant James, David Lagle. Teaspoon and Hickok set out to restore order to a town besieged by outlaws, which also happens to be where Kid thinks he can spend some time with Lou.

177.64 *Lessons Learned.* July 9, 1992. GS: Wings Hauser, Mitchell Ryan, Leigh Taylor-Young, Douglas Freimuth, Jim Newcomer, Heather McNair. A slippery killer whose conviction has been overturned arrives seeking vengeance. Meanwhile, Teaspoon's ex-wife slides into town as the new saloon owner.

177.65 *The Debt.* July 16, 1992. GS: William Sanderson, Ed Adams, Elizabeth Hanley, Michael Roddy. Hickok is hot on the trail of a new rider who disappeared in a town overrun by bad guys. Meanwhile, Lou saddles up with cold feet to buy a wedding dress in another town.

177.66 *'Til Death Do Us Part.* July 22, 1992. GS: Sydney Walsh, Frederick Forrest, Jesse Vint, Tim Hiser. Tension rides high as Lou and Kid prepare to solidify their blessed union in marriage just as the national Union is beginning to dissolve.

178. *Zane Grey Theater*

CBS. 30 min. Broadcast history: Friday, 8:30-9:00, Oct. 1956–July 1957, Thursday, 9:00-9:30, Oct. 1958–Sept. 1960, Thursday, 8:30-9:00, Oct. 1960–July 1961; Thursday, 9:30-10:00, April 1962–Sept. 1962.

Regular Cast: Dick Powell (Host).

Premise: This series was an anthology of western dramas.

Zane Grey Theater

The Episodes

178.1 *You Only Run Once.* Oct. 5, 1956. GS: Robert Ryan, Cloris Leachman, John Hoyt, Howard Petrie, Stuart Randall. A cattle rancher unknowingly hires two ranch hands who are wanted criminals. A vigilante mob accuses him of being an accomplice to a killing and he is marched off to be lynched.

178.2 *The Fearful Courage.* Oct. 12, 1956. GS: James Whitmore, Ida Lupino, Michael Pate, Paul Hahn, Robert Karnes. A woman flees from her ranch after she learns that a gunfighter has been paid to get the deed to her land, by violence if necessary. She takes refuge in what she believes is a deserted cabin, but finds it is occupied by a man who wants no part of anyone else's fight.

178.3 *The Long Road Home.* Oct. 19, 1956. GS: Dick Powell, Ray Collins, Ainslie Pryor, Jean Willes, Conrad Janis. A man returns to his Texas home with his mind set on accomplishing two things. He wants to avenge his brother's death and also settle a long-standing feud between two families.

178.4 *The Unrelenting Sky.* Oct. 26, 1956. GS: Lew Ayres, Phyllis Avery, Willis Bouchey, Walter Sande, Steven Geray. A rancher and his wife run into more hardship than happiness as they struggle to settle on their Arizona homesite. The rancher joins two neighbors in trying to obtain water from a merciless old man who refuses to share his supply during a drought.

178.5 *The Lariat.* Nov. 2, 1956. GS: Jack Palance, Constance Ford, Addison Richards, Robert Anderson, Michael Garrett, Guy Teague, Buff Brady. A man sentenced to prison for killing a man with his lariat in a saloon fight returns five years later. He intends to even the score with the judge who passed sentence on him and finds the means for his revenge when he meets the judge's pretty daughter. Despite the man's threats, the judge tries to help rehabilitate the outlaw.

178.6 *Death Watch.* Nov. 9, 1956. GS: Lee J. Cobb, Bobby Driscoll, John Larch, John Alderson, Abel Fernandez. Four ragged survivors of a frontier regiment, cut off from an Army troop in an Apache-infested desert, tensely await help. They fear the Indians will discover their hiding place.

178.7 *Stage to Tucson.* Nov. 16, 1956. GS: Eddie Albert, John Ericson, Mona Freeman, Rusty Lane, Ian MacDonald, Jaclynne Greene, DeForest Kelley. A Tucson-bound stagecoach stops for a short rest at an isolated depot. The local sheriff is waiting to identify one of the travelers as a bank robber.

178.8 *A Quiet Sunday in San Ardo.* Nov. 23, 1956. GS: Wendell Corey, Peggie Castle, Gerald Mohr, Harry Lauter, Morgan Woodward, Tim Graham, Robert Burton, Sam Flint. A small Western town is jolted from its serenity by the murder of its marshal. A local rancher is accused of cowardice when he refuses to fill the post because of his strong desire for a quiet and peaceful life.

178.9 *Vengeance Canyon.* Nov. 30, 1956. GS: Walter Brennan, Ben Cooper, Sheb Wooley, Robert Griffin. Clint Harding sets out to exact revenge on his father for deserting his mother years ago. Learning that the old man lives on the other side of Comanche territory, he starts out to cross the canyon and falls in with three bank robbers.

178.10 *Return to Nowhere.* Dec. 7, 1956. GS: John Ireland, Stephen McNally, Audrey Totter, Jimmy Baird, Ralph Moody, Don Riss. A gunslinger, believed dead, returns to his home town years later to find his wife has married the marshal. He determines to win her back, even if it means a showdown with the marshal.

178.11 *Courage Is a Gun.* Dec. 14, 1956. GS: Dick Powell, Robert Vaughn, Beverly Garland, James Westerfield, Claude Akins, Leonard Penn. A gunslinger is wounded by the marshal in a shooting while waiting to settle a feud with an enemy. He then plots to kill the marshal as well.

178.12 *Muletown Gold Strike.* Dec. 21, 1956. GS: Rory Calhoun, Barbara Eiler. A Confederate veteran, embittered by his war experiences, takes a job as a schoolteacher. He is annoyed with one of his pupils who dreams of finding gold in their poor community.

178.13 *Stars Over Texas.* Dec. 28, 1956. GS: Ralph Bellamy, Beverly Washburn, Gloria Talbott, James Garner. In the early 1800's the young bride of a pioneer encourages the attentions of a young cavalry lieutenant because he saved their wagon train from attackers.

178.14 *The Three Graves.* Jan. 4, 1956. GS: Jack Lemmon, Nan Leslie, Frank Ferguson, James Best, Terry Frost, Don Kennedy. A gunman moves into a sleepy Western town with the intention of taking it over for himself. But a pretty young woman sets her sights on him as a prospective husband. He places himself in a precarious situation by challenging a strange law enforced by the town.

178.15 *No Man Living.* Jan. 11, 1957. GS: Frank Lovejoy, Margaret Hayes, Judson Pratt, Russ Conway, Peter Whitney, James Anderson. A sheriff gives up his badge to take personal revenge. The criminal he is seeking has carefully disguised himself as a law-abiding citizen.

178.16 *Time of Decision.* Jan. 18, 1957. GS: Lloyd Bridges, Diane Brewster, Walter Sande, Bill Erwin, Jean Howell, Trevor Bardette, Mort Mills. A lawyer in a small Western town is torn between defending a man accused of murder, and the powerful group of cattle ranchers who threaten violence.

178.17 *Until the Man Dies.* Jan. 25, 1957. GS: Stuart Whitman, Carolyn Jones, John Payne, Steve Darrell, Dick Rich, Stuart Randall, Gregg Barton, James Seay, Richard Newton. A cattle rancher saves a criminal from a lynching, determined not to allow mob rule to deprive Nevada of her chance for statehood. He decides to escort the outlaw to the marshal's office himself.

178.18 *Back Trail.* Feb. 1, 1957. GS: Dick Powell, James Anderson, Emile Meyer, Catherine McLeod, Kim Charney, Robert Crosson, Raymond Bailey, John Pickard. A rich cattleman hires a gunfighter to drive the farmers out of his territory.

178.19 *Dangerous Orders.* Feb. 8, 1957. GS: Mark Stevens, Jack Elam, Willis Bouchey, Robert Cornthwaite, William Leicester, Thomas B. Henry, John Eldredge, Simon Scott. A Southerner serving in the Union Army finds his loyalty subject to question when he is given important orders to deliver.

178.20 *The Necessary Breed.* Feb. 15, 1957. GS: Sterling Hayden, Jean Willes, James Griffith, Strother Martin, Carlyle Mitchell, Roy Barcroft, Frank Scannell, Gregory Walcott, Bill Henry, Bill Fawcett, Fred Sherman. A gunman attempts to win back the love of his former sweetheart. She refuses to marry him because he makes his living seeking and killing wanted men for the reward men.

178.21 *The Hanging Tree.* Feb. 22, 1957. GS: Robert Ryan, Cloris Leachman, John Hoyt, Howard Petrie, Stuart Randall. A cattle rancher unknowingly hires two ranch hands who are wanted criminals. A vigilante mob accuses him of being an accessory to a killing and he is marched off to be lynched.

178.22 *Village of Fear.* March 1, 1957. GS: David Niven, George D. Wallace, Ross Elliott, Peter Hanson, DeForest Kelley, Don Diamond, Harry Lauter, Dan Barton, Anne Barton, Bill Catching, Troy Melton. A traveling book salesman is greeted by a dead man hanging in an alley when he arrives in a deserted Western town. The frightened townspeople are the victims of a terrorizing campaign by a gang of outlaws.

178.23 *Black Creek Encounter.* March 8, 1957. GS: Ernest Borgnine, Jan Merlin, Norma Crane, Billy Chapin, Lou Krugman, Howard Negley. A man is faced with a difficult decision when challenged by a gunman who has searched for him for many years. To accept the challenge would mean almost certain death. To decline would mean shaming himself in the eyes of his son.

178.24 *They Were Four.* March 15, 1957. GS: Dean Jagger, John Derek, David Janssen, Dick Rich, James Gavin, Grant Withers, Kenneth MacDonald, Jimmie Kovack. A young man vows to get revenge on a wealthy rancher. He uses lawless methods, because he regards an outlaw he knows as a hero. These methods, however, result in his being involved ina rustling scheme which he hadn't anticipated.

178.25 *A Fugitive.* March 22, 1957. GS: Eddie Albert, Celeste Holm, Peter Votrian, Richard Shannon. Fleeing from Union soldiers, an ex-Confederate is helped by a young widow who believes that he, like the rest of the community, is a Union man. The soldier soon realizes he has fallen in love with his pretty nurse, but he does not dare tell her which side he belongs to.

178.26 *Lariat.* March 29, 1957. GS: Jack Palance, Constance Ford, Addison Richards, Robert Anderson. A man sentenced to prison for a saloon fight in which he killed a man with his lariat, returns five years later. He intends to even the score with the judge who passed sentence and finds the means for his revenge when he meets the judge's pretty daughter.

178.27 *A Time to Live.* April 5, 1957. GS: Ralph Meeker, Julie London, Forrest Lewis, Ken Lynch, John Larch, Walter Barnes, Alan Wells. A dance-hall singer tries to dissuade the man she loves from seeking revenge on a man who shot him and left him for dead.

178.28 *Black Is for Grief.* April 12, 1957. GS: Mary Astor, Tom Tryon, Beulah Bondi, Chester Morris, Mala Powers, Tom Tully, Skip Homeier, Richard Anderson. A young man returning from the Civil War learns that his wife has been murdered. His attempts to find her killers lead him to several people with good reason to want her dead. In trying to find the killer he learns a strange story.

178.29 *Badge of Honor.* May 3, 1957. GS: Robert Culp, Gary Merrill, Tom Tully, Peggy Webber, Dick Gardner, Mike Ragan, Walter Coy, Bill Henry, Bill Leicester, Richard Devon. A young man just returned from service in the Civil War wants no part of violence and bloodshed. He is discouraged to find his home town in the hands of a greedy colonel who allows only limited power to the sheriff.

178.30 *Decision at Wilson's Creek.* May 17, 1957. GS: John Forsythe, Marjorie Lord, John Dehner, Bart Burns, Willis Bouchey, Harry Lauter, Joe diReda, John Wilder, William Swan. A Confederate soldier quits the Army to return to his northern wife, supposedly to protect her from a possible Confederate attack. But neighbors suspect the man's motive.

178.31 *A Man on the Run.* June 21, 1957. GS: Scott Brady, Eve Miller, Hugh Sanders, Mort Hall, Adam Kennedy, Nancy Hale. Accused of a crime he did not commit, a man flees and seeks refuge at a ranch. There he finds a girl held prisoner by her sister and brother-in-law.

Season Two

178.32 *The Deserters.* Oct. 4, 1957. GS: Dick Powell, Margaret Hayes, Tom Pittman, Joe de Santis, Larkin Ford, Charles Gray, Patrick Clement. A U.S. Army sergeant is assigned to track down deserters in the Arizona territory. He has no compassion for the men he captures, and returns them to the U.S. Army authorities. Then he meets John Harris, who he suspects is a deserter, and his pretty traveling companion.

178.33 *Blood in the Dust.* Oct. 11, 1957. GS: Claudette Colbert, Jeff Morrow, Barry Atwater, Denver Pyle, Kelly Thordsen. A Northern rancher and his wife resettle after the Civil War in a south-western frontier town. A Yankee-hating gunman tries to bait the man into a gunfight. The rancher's wife, knowing her husband cannot handle a gun, pleads with the townsfolk to stop the fight. When they refuse, she decides to take matters into her own hands.

178.34 *A Gun Is for Killing.* Oct. 18, 1957. GS: Edmond O'Brien, Robert Vaughn, Marsha Hunt, Paul Engle, James Maloney, Michael Hinn, Walter Reed, John Brinkley. Russell Andrews promises his wife that he will never again use a gun. Then his son is killed in a gunfight with the son of a neighboring rancher, and Andrews is powerless to take revenge.

178.35 *Proud Woman.* Oct. 25, 1957. GS: Hedy Lamarr, Paul Richards, Roy Roberts, Edward Colmans, Iphigenie Castiglioni, Val Avery. When Consuela Bowers arrives in the West, she hires a man to work on her father's ranch. She does not know that he is a professional gunman involved in a plot to steal a valuable horse.

178.36 *Ride a Lonely Tail.* Nov. 2, 1957. GS: Walter Brennan, Val Dufour, Richard Keith, John Zaremba, Russell Thorson. An elderly sheriff refuses to retire even though the townspeople consider him too old for the job. Then a prospector is shot down and the sheriff sets out alone, across the desert, to track down the murderer.

178.37 *The Promise.* Nov. 8, 1957. GS: Gary Merrill, Tommy Sands, Whitney Blake, Carl Benton Reid. A dying rancher forces his restless young son Jace to promise he will remain on the ranch with his older brother Noah. But the discord between the brothers grows when Noah comes to suspect Jace of attempt to steal his wife. When the will is read, it turns out that Jace receives the better half of the ranch.

178.38 *Episode in Darkness.* Nov. 15, 1957. GS: Dewey Martin, Anne Bancroft, Phillip Pine, John Anderson. Traveling cattleman Ethan Boyan is framed in a frontier town for the slaying of a woman in a stagecoach holdup. The only person present when the crime was committed was Isabelle Rutledge, an embittered blind woman.

178.39 *The Open Cell.* Nov. 22, 1957. GS: Dick Powell,

Zane Grey Theater

Marshall Thompson, Steve Terrell, Frances Robinson, Maurice Manson. A frontier sheriff attempts to save young Jess Bolin from leading the life of a gunslinger. Jess is sentenced to prison for shooting a man in a saloon brawl, but the sentence is suspended when the sheriff agrees to accept responsibility for the young man. Then Jess is bullied into a gun fight by a deputy.

178.40 *A Man to Look Up To.* Nov. 29, 1957. GS: Lew Ayres, Diane Brewster, Will Wright, Willis Bouchey, Robert Gothie, Jess Kirkpatrick, K.L. Smith, Ron Brogan. Jud Lester is a cowardly man who draws his courage from drink and the strength of his wife. In a last attempt to be a man, he sets up a law office in a wild frontier town.

178.41 *The Bitter Land.* Dec. 6, 1957. GS: Dan O'Herlihy, Peggy Wood. A determined woman is willing to sacrifice her family in a range war to build a cattle empire.

178.42 *Gift from a Gunman.* Dec. 13, 1957. GS: Howard Keel, John Dehner, Jean Willes, Michael Landon. Gunman Will Gorman is shot in a gun duel and decides to reform. He visits an old friend whose restless wife and gun-eager son threaten to make him resume his life as a gunslinger.

178.43 *A Gun for My Bride.* Dec. 27, 1957. GS: Eddie Albert, Jane Greer, Onslow Stevens, Chris Alcaide. The daughter of a wealthy cattleman elopes with one of her father's ranch hands. Then she learns that her new husband is a fugitive from justice.

178.44 *Man Unforgiving.* Jan. 3, 1958. GS: Joseph Cotten, Johnny Crawford, Claude Akins, Mary Shipp, Joel Ashley, Val Benedict, John Valvo, William Vaughan, S. John Launer, Dan Blocker. Ben Harper, a stranger passing through a frontier town, becomes the target of the sheriff. The lawman believes Ben is the doctor who amputated his leg during the Civil War.

178.45 *Trial by Fear.* Jan. 10, 1958. GS: Robert Ryan, David Janssen, Harold J. Stone, Ed Platt, Raymond Bailey. A gunslinger is placed on trial for murder. Although the rest of the jury believes the man is guilty, one juror believes him innocent. But before the jury can return its verdict, the gunman escapes.

178.46 *The Freighter.* Jan. 17, 1958. GS: Barbara Stanwyck, Robert H. Harris, John Archer, James Bell, Jason Johnson, Bill Catching, Thomas Peters, Robert Hoy, Charles Tannen. The lady owner of an Arizona freight line tries to keep a family from muscling in on her company. She relies on an old Indian trick to scare them off.

178.47 *This Man Must Die.* Jan. 24, 1958. GS: Dan Duryea, Carole Mathews, Karl Swenson, Than Wyenn, Walter Coy, Joseph Sargent, Tom Vize, Michael Ragan, Chuck Hayward. A man sentenced to hang escapes and returns to his home town to kill the witness whose false testimony convicted him. Hunted by a posse and forced into hiding, the fugitive enlists the aid of his girl friend and his business partner to track down the witness.

178.48 *Wire.* Jan. 31, 1958. GS: Lloyd Bridges, David Opatoshu, June Vincent, Edward Binns, James Drury, John Wilder. A man who has spent his life working on other people's property, vows to own his own land.

178.49 *License to Kill.* Feb. 7, 1958. GS: Macdonald Carey, John Ericson, Jacques Aubuchon, Stacy Harris, Richard Devon, Peter Whitney. A frontier sheriff finds he is unable to cope with a group of trouble-making trailherders when he breaks his arm. Then his younger brother arrives in town and the sheriff swears him in as his deputy. But the older man learns that his brother's idea of law enforcement is to kill any lawbreaker, regardless of the crime.

178.50 *Sundown at Bitter Creek.* Feb. 14, 1958. GS: Dick Powell, Cathy O'Donnell, Nick Adams, Tex Ritter, Jeanne Cooper, Dennis Cross, Peter Breck, Bill Guyman. A man arrives in the town of Bitter Creek. Though he is trying to live down his past as a gunfighter, the stranger learns that his appearacne has a decided effect on three of the town's inhabitants.

178.51 *The Stranger.* Feb. 28, 1958. GS: Mark Stevens, Dan Barton, Denver Pyle, Walter Barnes, Judith Ames, William Schallert. A man arrives in a frontier town seeking to buy a ranch. He witnesses a robbery and murder and attempts to stop the fleeing gunman. But the townspeople believe he is the guilty man and want to lynch him.

178.52 *The Sharpshooter.* March 7, 1958. GS: Chuck Connors, Leif Erickson, Dennis Hopper, Sidney Blackmer. A rifleman and a fast-drawing gunman decide on a shooting match to see who is the better sharpshooter. The crooked town boss backs the gunman and is determined, if necessary, to have the rifleman killed so he will not win the competition.

178.53 *Man of Fear.* March 14, 1958. GS: Dewey Martin, Arthur Franz, Julie Adams. The famed gunman Doc Holliday visits a young married couple who are friends of his. He learns that the wife holds her husband in contempt because he is paying protection money to a gang of thieves in order to keep his home and ranch safe.

178.54 *The Doctor Keeps a Promise.* March 21, 1958. GS: Cameron Mitchell, Carolyn Kearney, Ken Lynch, Forrest Taylor, Peter Breck. A doctor in a frontier town is called out to treat a man for gunshot wounds. He learns the man stole some money to buy seed for his farm after an unscrupulous cattle baron had let his herd ruin the man's crop.

178.55 *Three Days to Death.* April 4, 1958. GS: Michael Rennie. An Easterner learns that his brother has been killed out West and sets out to find the murderers. He learns that the killer's identity is known, but that the law does not have the men to go after him.

178.56 *Shadow of a Dead Man.* April 11, 1958. GS: Barry Sullivan, Carl Benton Reid, Whitney Blake, DeForest Kelley, Richard Shannon. An outlaw is captured and is being returned to justice. When the man's captor is bitten by a rattlesnake, the outlaw must choose between leaving him to die or escaping to freedom.

178.57 *Debt of Gratitude.* April 18, 1958. GS: Steve Cochran, James Whitmore. Marshal Cam Tolby faces the enmity of the townspeople when he tries to take an outlaw to Prescott, Arizona, to stand trial for robbery and murder. His difficulties increase when the outlaw, despite handcuffs, manages to save a group of schoolchildren from disaster.

178.58 *A Handful of Ashes.* May 2, 1958. GS: Thomas Mitchell, June Lockhart. A man who was once a fast gun has become a drunkard. Knowing that his friends are skeptical of his professed speed and accuracy with a gun, the old man tries to prove his skill when a desperado rides into town.

178.59 *Threat of Violence.* May 23, 1958. GS: Lyle Bettger, Cesar Romero, Chris Alcaide, Jorja Curtright, Harry Lauter, Alex Gerry, Bruce Cowling, Jess Kirkpatrick, Jason Johnson. A gunman, tired of violence, hangs up his guns and tries to make a new life of himself as an attorney. But he finds that his reputation as a gunman hinders him. Then he takes the case of a man whose past record makes him the suspect in a murder case.

178.60 *Utopia, Wyoming.* June 6, 1958. GS: Gary Merrill, Joanne Gilbert, Pernell Roberts, Robert Gothie, Myron Healey, Walter Coy, Henry Oliver, Charles Horvath, Ray Ferrell. Seeking shelter during a violent storm, two cowboys come upon a long-forgotten ghost town. This ghost town is inhabited, however, and the inhabitants try desperately to remain hidden from the intruders.

Season Three

178.61 *Trail to Nowhere.* Oct. 2, 1958. GS: David Janssen, Barbara Stanwyck, Paul Genge. Julie Holman swears vengeance when her husband is murdered. Suspecting Carl Benson, a man with whom her husband has quarreled, Julie rides out to his ranch. She finds that Benson has disappeared and she sets out to track him down.

178.62 *The Scaffold.* Oct. 9, 1958. GS: Dick Powell, Paul Richards, Virginia Christine. An embittered man who is hated by the townspeople, shoots and kills one of the town's leading citizens. The sheriff insists that the man be brought to trial, but the townspeople prepare for a lynching.

178.63 *The Homecoming.* Oct. 23, 1958. GS: Lloyd Nolan, Judith Ames. Adam Larkin has spent many years trying to make a living from his land, he has only met with failure. When his wife tells him she is expecting a child, Larkin goes to the bank and asks for a loan, but the bank refuses. Larkin decides to take what he needs.

178.64 *The Accuser.* Oct. 30, 1958. GS: David Niven, Gail Kobe, Malcolm Brodrick, Chris Alcaide, George D. Wallace, DeForest Kelley, Ross Elliott, Peter Hansen, Don Diamond, Harry Lauter, Dan Barton, Troy Melton, Bill Catching, Gary Hanley. After discovering the body of a rancher who has been murdered, Milo Brant tries to comfort the grieving widow. The widow's son, however, distrusts Brant and resents the man's attentions to his mother.

178.65 *Legacy of a Legend.* Nov. 6, 1958. GS: Lee J. Cobb, John Dehner, J. Pat O'Malley, Frank Ferguson, John Pickard, Joan Banks, Robert Carson, Tyler McVey, Maudie Prickett. A drifter arrives in a small Western town claiming to be a famous lawman who had lived there years before. The townspeople, who remember the lawman as a young and vigorous man, refuse to believe him.

178.66 *To Sit in Judgment.* Nov. 13, 1958. GS: Robert Ryan, John Washbrook, Dean Stanton, Betsy Jones-Moreland, Michael Pate. Sheriff Parney hangs a local badman. Later the dead man's two sons vow to kill Parney in revenge.

178.67 *The Tall Shadow.* Nov. 20, 1958. GS: John Ericson, Julie Adams, Steve Darrell, Brad Dexter, Sean McClory, Don Durand. Linc Hardaway's father is one of the wealthiest men in the West. In his efforts to prove that he can do anything as well as his father, Linc encounters one failure after another, until even the girl he loves loses respect for him. Then Hardaway's father is murdered and he is suspected of the crime.

178.68 *The Vaunted.* Nov. 27, 1958. GS: Eddie Albert, Jane Greer, Mickey Braddock, Kathryn Card. Ellie Matson's husband Jess is a wanted outlaw. When she realizees that their son admires Jess, Ellie decides to show him just what kind of man his father is.

178.69 *Pressure Point.* Dec. 4, 1958. GS: Walter Pidgeon, Walter Sande, Raymond Bailey, Pernell Roberts. Jess Clark is an ex-lawman who has lost his sight. Determined to shoot accurately, Jess is learning to shoot at sounds, when a man who has sworn to kill him comes into town ready for a gunfight.

178.70 *Bury Me Dead.* Dec. 11, 1958. GS: Barry Sullivan, Joan Tetzel, John Beradino. A wanted criminal disrupts the serenity of ranch life for Kathy and Jed Lorimer. Fleeing from justice, the criminal decides to take Kathy with him.

178.71 *Let the Man Die.* Dec. 18, 1958. GS: Marsha Hunt, Dick Powell, Ralph Reed, R.G. Armstrong, Brent King, Frank Ferguson. Dr. Reynolds is faced with a major decision. To let his patient die would insure his son's future, but he doesn't know if he can let the patient die.

178.72 *Medal for Valor.* Dec. 25, 1958. GS: Richard Basehart, June Dayton, Richard Anderson, Paul Fix. David Manning, returning from the Civil War, seeks out Adam Stewart. Manning wishes to obtain a deposition from Stewart stating that he served in Stewart's place during the war. But Manning is opposed by Stewart's father, who hires someone to run him out of town.

178.73 *Living Is a Lonesome Thing.* Jan. 1, 1959. GS: Michael Rennie, Michael Landon, Walter Sande. Grant Coburn learns that his son has been hired as a professional gunslinger. He is faced with a choice between saving an innocent man's life or shooting down his own son.

178.74 *Day of the Killing.* Jan. 8, 1959. GS: Paul Douglas, Peter Breck, John Litel, Jonathan Hole, Ricky Murray, Lane Bradford, Jason Johnson. Blacksmith Jonas Sutton is elected sheriff. After he takes office townsfolk pressure him into hunting down a murderer who previously saved Sutton's son.

178.75 *Hang the Heart High.* Jan. 15, 1959. GS: Barbara Stanwyck, David Janssen, Paul Richards, Lane Bradford, Margarita Cordova, Frank Harding. Regan Moore, discontented with her marriage, attracts the love of a gunman. Feeling sure of the gunman's love, she tries to persuade him to kill her husband.

178.76 *Welcome Home a Stranger.* Jan. 15, 1959. GS: Dick Powell, Torin Thatcher, Frank Albertson, James Drury, Loren Grey. Folowing the Civil War lawman Ben Sanderson returns to his home in the South only to be greeted by angry former friends bearing drawn guns.

178.77 *Trail Incident.* Jan. 2, 1959. GS: Cameron Mitchell, John Ericson, Tim Considine, Dennis Cross, Paul Jasmin, Michael Hinn, Quentin Sondergaard, Michael Forest. During a cattle drive, cowhands find a young boy wandering along the trail. They pick up the youngster, who turns out to be a spoiled brat and seems to resent his rescuers.

178.78 *Make It Look Good.* Feb. 5, 1959. GS: Arthur Kennedy, Parley Baer, Jacqueline Scott, Robert F. Simon, Edwin Jerome, Meg Wyllie, Ed Nelson, Richard Rust. When Sam Cartner refuses to accept his share of stolen money, he inadvertently places his wife Jenny's life in jeopardy. Cartner's companions in crime suspect that he has informed on them.

178.79 *A Thread of Respect.* Dec. 12, 1959. GS: Danny Thomas, James Coburn, Nick Adams, Denver Pyle, Tommy Cook, Chuck Courtney. Gino Pelleti, an Italian immigrant tai-

Zane Grey Theater

lor, opens a shop in Yucca City. Although he and his son George are subjected to cruel pranks, Gino refuses to defend himself, telling George that he doesn't believe in violence.

178.80 *Deadfall.* Feb. 19, 1959. GS: Van Johnson, Bing Russell, Harry Townes, Grant Withers, Paul Langton, John Zaremba, Jan Stine. Frank Gillette, a notorious gunman just out of prison, is framed for a bank robbery. Convicted of the charge, Gillettte is on his way to prison, accompanied by the sheriff and his deputy, when gunmen kill the sheriff and take Gillette and the deputy to a hideout.

178.81 *The Last Raid.* Feb. 26, 1959. GS: Fernando Lamas, Rita Moreno, William Reynolds, Michael Davis, Abel Fernandez, Peter Coe. During a bank raid Miguel and his gang get away with several thousand pesos in gold. But Miguel is betrayed by one of his men, who steals the gold, takes Miguel's woman and her younger brother and escapes to a hiding place in the mountains.

178.82 *Man Alone.* March 5, 1959. GS: Thomas Mitchell, Marilyn Erskine, Scott Forbes. Derelict Cason Thomas is held in contempt by most of his fellow townspeople. When the new sheriff befriends him and offers to make him a deputy, the old man feels he has an opportunity to gain new respect.

178.83 *Hanging Fever.* March 12, 1959. GS: Frank Lovejoy, Patrick McVey, Beverly Garland. A murder is committed and the chief suspect flees from town. Sam Walston leads a band of vigilantes in pur suit of the man.

178.84 *Trouble at Tres Cruces.* March 26, 1959. GS: Brian Keith, Neville Brand, Michael Pate. After many years away from his family, Dave Blasingame is asked to return home. Dave makes the trip, unaware that his only relative has been killed and his family's land has been seized by a ruthless tyrant.

178.85 *Heritage* (A.K.A. "Loyalty"). April 2, 1959. GS: Edward G. Robinson, Edward G. Robinson, Jr., John Hackett, Robert Blake, Dan Barton, Lew Gallo. Victor Bers becomes bitter when his son deserts their farm to join the Confederate Army. They are suddenly reunited when the young soldier, attempting to evade a Union patrol, seeks refuge at the farm.

178.86 *Checkmate.* April 30, 1959. GS: James Whitmore, Marsha Hunt, Mark Miner, Dabbs Greer. Joel Begley, who was crippled in a mine accident, is now a bank teller. He is sitting in a restaurant across from the bank when the bank president is killed and the mine payroll taken.

178.87 *Mission to Marathon.* May 14, 1959. GS: John McIntire, Stephen McNally, Mark Richman, Robert Cornthwaite, Alan Dexter. Gil Durand, dishonorably discharged from the Army, is asked by the government to take an undercover position. His job is to locate a missing Army major.

178.88 *The Law and the Gun.* June 4, 1959. GS: Michael Ansara, Lyle Bettger, Paul Carr. John Welker, a lawman embittered by the death of his fiancee, and Fitzgerald, a calculating bounty hunter, are both trailing a fleeing outlaw and his girl.

Season Four

178.89 *Interrogation.* Oct. 1, 1959. GS: Robert Ryan, Harry Townes, Alexander Scourby, Don Diamond, Rodolfo Hoyos. During the Mexican-American war in 1847, Captain Kraig's reputation for bravery was well known. He and Corporal Dubin are taken prisoner by the enemy and face severe interrogation and torture. Kraig pleads with his corporal not to submit to the enemy.

178.90 *Lone Woman.* Oct. 8, 1959. GS: Barbara Stanwyck, Martin Balsam, George Keymas, Joel Crothers. Leona Butler, a frontier mother, is overcome with grief when her son is accidentally killed by an Indian. Believing that the death was not accidental, Leona refuses to forgive the Indian.

178.91 *Confession.* Oct. 15, 1959. GS: Dick Powell, Charles Aidman, Walter Burke. Watson Cooke, New York newspaper reporter, comes to the West to do a story on Sheriff Agate Slade. The reporter forms an immediate dislike for the Sheriff and he sets out to ruin Slade's reputation.

178.92 *The Lonely Gun.* Oct. 22, 1959. GS: Barry Sullivan, Wayne Rogers, Patricia Donahue, Paul Birch. Embittered and lonely, gunman Clint Shannon rides into Del Rio to see his nephew. Shannon finds the young man under the thumb of a scheming girl.

178.93 *Hand on the Latch.* Oct. 29, 1959. GS: Anne Baxter, Charles Gray, Paul Richards. Laura Fletcher's husband, a Union Army purchasing agent, has been given money to obtain supplies for rebel prisoners. But he intends to keep the money for himself, and orders Laura not to revel his intentions.

178.94 *Shadows.* Nov. 5, 1959. GS: Frank Lovejoy, Paul Carr, Stacy Harris, Alan Dexter, Diane Cannon. Loy Bannister is the town's most powerful figure because of his political and economic influence. In a wild bid to gain Bannister's admiration, young Branch Neeley agrees to stand trial for a murder he didn't commit.

178.95 *Mission.* Nov. 12, 1959. GS: Sammy Davis, Jr., James Edwards, Abraham Sofaer. The Army wants to get an Indian chief to sign a peace treaty. A young corporal is given command of a cavalry unit and ordered to bring the Indian to the fort.

178.96 *Lonesome Road.* Nov. 19, 1959. GS: Edmond O'Brien, Rita Lynn, Tom Gilson. Marshal Ben Clark is accustomed to the danger and excitement of the Western frontier. Settling in a small Kansas town, he finds it hard to adjust to the tranquil atmosphere he finds there.

178.97 *King of the Valley.* Nov. 26, 1959. GS: Walter Pidgeon, Leora Dana, Karl Swenson. Cattle baron Dave King, who has tremendous land holdings, is suddenly faced with the loss of everything he owns when the bottom drops out of the cattle market. Citizens who have resented King's success are elated over his misfortune.

178.98 *Rebel Ranger.* Dec. 3, 1959. GS: Joan Crawford, Scott Forbes, Don Grady. Stella Faring, widowed by the Civil War, is anxious to regain the house she was forced to abandon during the war.

178.99 *Death in a Wood.* Dec. 17, 1959. GS: Dick Powell, Simon Oakland, Don Grady, William Boyett. Two Confederate soldiers are sent into the woods on a reconnaissance mission. They suddenly discover that a Yankee has spotted them.

178.100 *The Grubstake.* Dec. 24, 1959. GS: Cameron Mitchell, Ben Piazza, John Milford, Joseph Sullivan. Released after a long prison term, prospector Jim Goad is ready to resume panning for gold, and he plans to take his son with him. But the boy, who was raised by friends of Jim's has fallen in with a bad crowd.

178.101 *The Ghost.* Dec. 31, 1959. GS: Mel Ferrer, Alex Davion, Cathy Case, Henry Brandon. Marshal Monty Elstrode is captured by an outlaw gang who are planning to organize a new Confederate Army. Elstrode is shocked to learn that the leader of the group is the supposedly dead murderer of President Lincoln.

178.102 *Miss Jenny.* Jan. 7, 1960. GS: Vera Miles, Adam Williams, Ben Cooper, Jack Elam, Tony Haig, Linda Bennett. Jenny Breckenridge is accompanying her meek husband on a journey to the West. At an outpost, a stranger threatens them.

178.103 *The Reckoning.* Jan. 14, 1960. GS: Stephen McNally, Cesar Romero, Robert Harland, Ed Nelson, Jeff Morris. Mace, a cattleman, hates sheepherders because he believes that sheep ruin good grazing land. He takes a liking to a young man and sets out to train him as a good cattleman.

178.104 *Wayfarers.* Jan. 21, 1960. GS: James Whitmore, Felicia Farr, Robert B. Williams. Cassie, a forlorn young woman, has come to a strange and hostile frontier village to tell her husband, who has been working there, that she is expecting a child. Cassie learns that her husband was killed the day before.

178.105 *Picture of Sal.* Jan. 28, 1960. GS: Rod Taylor, Carolyn Jones, Richard Shannon, J. Pat O'Malley, Louis Mercier, Diane Dubois, Rene Godfrey. Sal, the owner of the Rue Royuale gambling house, is a hard-hearted young woman who seems to have a chip on her shoulder. One day, Jed Harper rides into town carrying a picture of a girl who looks very much like Sal.

178.106 *Never Too Late.* Feb. 4, 1960. GS: Ginger Rogeres, Richard Eastham, Melinda Byrd, Alan Reed, Jr., Roy Barcroft, Wendell Holmes. Angie Cartwright wants to buy some land that is being offered for sale by the railroad. She hires Jim Amber, an ex-gunslinger to help her carry out her plans.

178.107 *Man in the Middle.* Feb. 11, 1960. GS: Richard Jaeckel, Michael Rennie, Louis Jean Heydt, Jason Johnson, Jim Anderson, Michael Mikler. An Indian agent has double trouble. He has to convince townspeople that a young fellow deserves punishment for shooting an Indian. Then he must arrest the culprit, who is his best friend's son.

178.108 *Guns for Garibaldi.* Feb. 18, 1960. GS: Fernando Lamas, Mary La Roche. Townspeople are disappointed when Giulio Mandati comes to Indian Creek to take over his brother's gold claim. They had hoped that the gold would be used to pay for a much needed dam. What they don't know is that Guilio is an imposter who plans to use the riches to finance Garibaldi's Italian revolt.

178.109 *The Sunday Man.* Feb. 25, 1960. GS: Brian Donleavy, Dean Jones, Leif Erickson. Sheriff Walt Devlin and his brother, Deputy Bill Devlin, are alike in name only. Walt is a letter of the law man who believes the end does not justify the means. Bill's methods are sometimes questionable, and certain citizens suspect that he is a law man purely for the thrill of gunslinging.

178.110 *Setup.* March 3, 1960. GS: Steve Forrest, Phyllis Kirk, Robert Gist. Seeking vengeance, Mike Bagley returns to the ranch he lost five years earlier when he was forced to marry a girl and turn over his property to her guardian, then driven off the land as a trespasser.

178.111 *A Small Town That Died.* March 10, 1960. GS: Beverly Garland, Henry Hull, Dick Powell, Denver Pyle. An ex-convict hears about a good straight ranch job. Arriving he finds the rancher murdered and a suspect lynched.

178.112 *Killer Instinct.* March 17, 1960. GS: Wendell Corey, Marc Lawrence, Robert Harland, Howard Petrie, Ann Barton. Citizens doubt their marshal's talents when he fails to squelch a town troublemaker.

178.113 *Sundown Smith.* March 24, 1960. GS: Jack Carson, Simon Oakland, Ray Ferrell, George D. Wallace. Sundown Smith is a cowboy with a resemblance to a wanted killer. The killer, with a pack of hounds on his trait, meets Sundown and forces him to exchange boots.

178.114 *Calico Bait.* March 31, 1960. GS: Robert Culp, Inger Stevens, Burt Douglas, DeForest Kelley, Paul Sorensen, Luis Gomez. A fleeing felon leaves his sweetheart behind, promising to meet her later. On the killer's trail, a deputy finds the girl and decides to use her to bait his trap.

178.115 *Seed of Evil.* April 7, 1960. GS: Raymond Massey, Cara Williams, Charles Maxwell, Myron Healey, Marion Ross. Malachi West is seething with hate for a Union Secret Service man who hanged his son during the war. Then he learns that the man has come to the area to start a private detective business.

178.116 *Deception.* April 14, 1960. GS: Bary Nelson, Peggy Ann Garner, Jack Elam. Stage line operators aim for deception by posting no guard with a huge gold shipment. They suspect that robbers have been spotting the big-money cargos by watching for special guards.

178.117 *Stagecoach to Yuma.* May 5, 1960. GS: Dewey Martin, Jane Greer, Tom Drake, Stacy Harris, J. Pat O'Malley. One-eyed Marshal Dave Harmon heads for Yuma to end the lawless reign of a notorious woman. He doesn't know that his brother is her right-hand man.

178.118 *The Sunrise Gun.* May 19, 1960. GS: Dennis Hopper, Everett Sloane, Ben Cooper, Frank Faylen, Karl Swenson, Bill Henry. Bitter memories plague Johnny Sunrise, one time gunslinger. Though he is now old and crippled, he plans a day of reckoning for a former enemy.

Season Five

178.119 *A Gun for Willie.* Oct. 6, 1960. GS: Ernest Borgnine, Paul Birch, Nancy Valentine, Dub Taylor, Paul Sorensen, Ralph Moody, Ken Patterson, George Robotham, Read Morgan. Willie is a poverty stricken farmer without a friend in the world until he accidentally kills a horse thief and gets the reward money.

178.120 *Desert Flight.* Oct. 13, 1960. GS: Dick Powell, James Coburn, Ben Cooper, John Pickard, Robert Hoy, Buzz Henry, Rand Brooks, Fred Krone. Brenner, Doyle and Sandy are a trio of bank robbers who have come up with a really slick plan. But Brenner, the mastermind, hasn't taken Doyle's itchy trigger-finger into account.

178.121 *Cry Hope! Cry Hate!* Oct. 20, 1960. GS: June Allyson, Paul Fix, Brett King, Robert Crawford, Jr. Stella made a mistake when she ran off with a trail bum a few years earlier. Now she has come home, bringing a young son, but her father says he wants nothing to do with her.

178.122 *The Ox.* Nov. 3, 1960. GS: Burl Ives, Whit Bissell, Edward Platt, Kay Stewart, Jacklyn O'Donnell, Andy

Zane Grey Theater

Albin, William Erwin, Karen Norris, Patrick Hector, Gregory Irvin, Fred Krone, Rudy Dolan, Stuffy Singer. A former Confederate soldier who has spent some long years in prison. Ox has only one thing in mind — revenge on his old commanding officer for putting him behind bars.

178.123 *So Young the Savage Land.* Nov. 20, 1960. GS: Claudette Colbert, John Dehner, Chris Robinson, Dean Stanton, Roy Barcroft, Lee Kross, Perry Cook. Beth and Jim Brayden have struggled to keep their ranch, but Beth has had her fill of the West and wants to go back home to the genteel South.

178.124 *Ransom.* Nov. 17, 1960. GS: Lloyd Bridges, Claude Akins, Aneta Corsaut, Ed Nelson, Michael Hinn, Michael Parks, Frank Griffin. Comanche Indians raid a shepherd's camp, killing all the hands except an itinerant cowboy named Dundee. He doesn't have to wait long before he learns why he was spared. The Indians plan to torture him in a tribal ceremony.

178.125 *The Last Bugle.* Nov. 24, 1960. GS: Robert Cummings, Michael Pate, Rodd Redwing, Jerry Oddo, Michael Hinn, Michael Keep, Robert Warwick, Robert Carricart, Rodolfo Hoyos. Geronimo and his renegades are on the warpath again. Gatewood, an American Army officer, heads for the Mexican Sierras with two Apache prisoners. His purpose is to talk the ruthless leader into surrender.

178.126 *The Black Wagon.* Dec. 1, 1960. GS: Esther Williams, Larry Pennell, Joseph Sargent, Ken Patterson, Ryan Hayes, Karen Norris. Sarah Harmon is traveling in a wagon train that halts at the scene of an Apache raid. The only survivors are some cholera victims locked in a black barred wagon.

178.127 *Knife of Hate.* Dec. 8, 1960. GS: Lloyd Nolan, Susan Oliver, Robert Harland, Vladimir Sokoloff, Michael Mikler. Though Jack Hoyt has been badly wounded in a gun fight, Dr. Pittman refuses to treat him. There has been a big conflict between the two as the doctor tried every way to keep Hoyt from seeing his daughter.

178.128 *The Mormons.* Dec. 15, 1960. GS: Stephen McNally, Tuesday Weld, Mark Goddard, Michael Hinn, Joe Perry, Bing Russell, Robert Griffin, Carl Dickinson. A trail-weary Mormon group, led by Adam Lawson, finds a suitable area for settling. But rancher Matt Rowland, hearing that the Mormons have been hit by cholera, orders them to leave.

178.129 *The Man from Yesterday.* Dec. 22, 1960. GS: Wendell Corey, Marsha Hunt, Cubby O'Brien, John Anderson, Duke Norton, William Idelson, Paul Stader, Chuck Hayward. An old-time gunslinger named Mapes gets out of prison and returns to track down John Duncan, the man who framed him many years earlier. But he can't find Duncan, and the wild frontier town is now a peaceful village.

178.130 *Morning Incident.* Dec. 29, 1960. GS: Robert Culp, Martha Hyer, Robert Garland, Kevin Jones, Fiona Hale. Laurie Pritchard dreams of a knight in shining armor who will whisk her away from the dull prospect of marriage to Lucas, a plodding farmer. Alone one morning, Laurie finds handsome Shad Hudson flying wounded in the barn.

178.131 *Ambush.* Jan. 5, 1961. GS: Dick Powell, Don Dubbins, Jack Elam, Arch Johnson, Dean Stanton, Conlan Carter, Charles Fredericks. Union Army Colonel Blackburn commands a squad of mercenary soldiers whose current mission is to get vital papers through Confederate lines. There is an air of mutiny as the mercenaries complain about the dangerous duty.

178.132 *One Must Die.* Jan. 12, 1961. GS: Joan Crawford, Philip Carey, Carl Benton Reid, Ben Wright, Ted Stanhope. John Baylor comes West to handle the will of his old friend Thad Hobbes. Baylor thinks the will is a little odd, as Hobbes plans to leave all his property to his daughter Sarah and nothing to his other daughter Melanie.

178.133 *The Long Shadow.* Jan. 19, 1961. GS: Ronald Reagan, Nancy Davis, Scott Marlowe, Roberta Shore, Walter Sande, John Pickard, Bill Brauer. Widow Amy Lawson's son, a cavalry officer, is killer in action. Amy blames Major Sinclair for her son's death. The major isn't just the cavalry commander, he is also Amy's fiance.

178.134 *Blood Red.* Jan. 29, 1961. GS: Carolyn Jones, Paul Richrads, Iron Eyes Cody, Sterling Holloway, Charlie Briggs, Sam Edwards, Rhoda Williams, Mary Patton, Hal Torey, Eddie Little Sky, Chief Yowlachie, Charlotte Knight. Julie Whiting is half French and half Cherokee Indian. And the mixed blood is very becoming, except to a Comanche who has sworn to kill all the members of Julie's tribe.

178.135 *Honor Bright.* Feb. 2, 1961. GS: Danny Thomas, Marlo Thomas, Ed Nelson, Robert Warwick, Grace Lee Whitney. Ex-convict Ed Dubro has reluctantly agreed to his daughter's marriage to Vince Harwell. But on the wedding day, Laurie learns that Vince is already married.

178.136 *The Broken Wing.* Feb. 9, 1961. GS: Arthur O'Connell, David Ladd, John Larch, K.T. Stevens. Lyman, now a cripple, years ago tried to fly through the air under his own power. Now Lyman's nephew Thalian is determined to try.

178.137 *The Silent Sentry.* Feb. 16, 1961. GS: Don Taylor, Dick Powell. During the Civil War in the cold and bleak mountain country of the West, neither Union nor Confederacy bothered to muster troops. But both sides posted a solitary picket to protect their interests. One windy day, the two men decide to head for a nearby cabin for warmth.

178.138 *The Bible Man.* Feb. 23, 1961. GS: Art Linkletter, Jack Linkletter, Peter Whitney, Alvy Moore. Albert Pierce, a successful circuit-riding preacher, is confronted by his grown son, Jimmy, whom he hasn't seen for years. Jimmy still blames his father for his mother's death.

178.139 *The Scar.* March 2, 1961. GS: Lew Ayres, Mort Mills, Patricia Barry, Alan Hale, Jr., Patrick Martin. Jesse Martin was in a prison camp during the Civil War. Now he has taken a job with a railroad construction outfit and the foreman brings back memories of camp guards' brutality.

178.140 *Knight of the Sun.* March 9, 1961. GS: Dan Duryea, Constance Towers. Henry Jacob Hanley, a drunken desert rat, is just making himself at home in a deserted fort when he acquires some company. Beth Woodfield arrives on a mission taken over from her dead father, delivering the new Gatling gun to the troops in Mexico.

178.141 *A Warm Day in Heaven.* March 23, 1961. GS: Lon Chaney, Jr., Thomas Mitchell, Hank Patterson, Bill Erwin. Heaven is a peaceful Arizona community until Nick Finn enters it. Trader Michael Peters is about to sell a horse, when Nick puts something in a water trough. Soon afterwards, the horse dies.

178.142 *The Empty Shell.* March 30, 1961. GS: Jean

Hagen, Jan Murray, Denver Pyle, Dub Taylor. Anne Madden goads her husband Cletis into bidding for a ranch against tough Nat Sledge. Madden decides he needs something to back up his bid so he hocks his wife's engagement ring.

178.143 *The Atoner.* April 6, 1961. GS: Herbert Marshall, Edward Binns, Britt Lomond, Virginia Gregg, Alan Reed, Jr. New Bethlehem, Arizona, has no saloons or gambling halls because of the House of Matthew religious sect which inhabits it. But now the new owner of the livery stable plans to install a saloon on the premises.

178.144 *Man from Everywhere.* April 13, 1961. GS: Burt Reynolds, Cesar Romero, King Calder, Peter Whitney, Ruta Lee. Sheriff Morgan is worried about his prisoner, Tom Bowdry, because the local gentry seems to be getting lynch fever. Morgan hires guide Branch Taylor to hustle Bowdry to the nearby town of Borrego.

178.145 *The Release.* April 27, 1961. GS: Gary Merrill, Cesare Danova, Lee Kinsolving, Howard St. John, Bill Quinn. Jailed gunslinger Lee DuVal can win his freedom by making a deal with the governor of Texas, who offers him a chance to use his talents against the bandits who are making things hot near the Louisiana border.

178.146 *Storm Over Eden.* May 4, 1961. GS: John Derek, Nancy Gates, Robert Middleton, Dean Stanton, Roberto Contreras. The marriage plans of Chet Loring and Elen Gaynor receive a setback. Chet is forced to kill Ellen's brother in self-defense.

178.147 *Image of a Drawn Sword.* May 11, 1961. GS: Lloyd Bridges, Beau Bridges, Susan Oliver, Royal Dano. Union Lieutenant Sam Kenyon informs the citizens of an isolated Rebel community that some rookie troops will be camping near there for a few days. For the sake of their own health, he offers the townspeople a warning — don't taunt the young soldiers.

178.148 *Jericho.* May 18, 1961. GS: Guy Madison, Beverly Garland, Claude Akins, Les Tremayne. Amy Schroeder is convicted of killing her husband and sentenced to die. A man comes to see the condemned woman, supposedly about buying her land. Then he reveals himself as an agent for the Attorney General.

179. Zorro

ABC. 30 min. Broadcast history: Thursday, 8:00-8:30, Oct. 1957–Sept. 1959.

Regular Cast: Guy Madison (Don Diego de la Vega/Zorro), George J. Lewis (Don Alejandro de la Vega), Gene Sheldon (Bernardo), Henry Calvin (Sergeant Garcia), Britt Lomond (Captain Monastario), Don Diamond (Corporal Reyes), Jolene Brand (Anna Maria Verdugo) 58-59.

Premise: This series concerned the exploits of Don Diego de la Vega, who became the masked avenger Zorro to defend the weak and oppressed in Monterey, California in the 1820s.

The Episodes

179.1 *Presenting Senor Zorro.* Oct. 10, 1957. Don Diego returns to Monterey at the request of his father to help end the reign of the evil Spanish commandant, Monastario.

179.2 *Zorro's Secret Passage.* Oct. 17, 1957. GS: Romney Brent. Zorro's servant Bernardo brings news that Monastario has posted a reward for the capture of Zorro and that a great manhunt has begun. Using his secret passage, Zorro makes an unexpected appearance.

179.3 *Zorro Rides to the Mission.* Oct. 24, 1957. GS: Romney Brent, Jan Arvan. Zorro sets out to aid a political fugitive who is fleeing from the tyrannical Captain Monastario.

179.4 *The Ghost of the Mission.* Oct. 31, 1957. GS: Jan Arvan. Zorro attempts to protect the escaped political prisoner Torres, who is hiding in an old mission, from recapture by the military tyrant Captain Monastario. He takes advantage of the superstitious nature of Monastario's men to spread a rumor that the mission is haunted.

179.5 *Zorro's Romance.* Nov. 7, 1957. GS: Eugenia Paul, Jan Arvan. Captain Monastario plans to capture the escaped political prisoner Torres, and claim his daughter Elena as his bride. But Don Diego learns of the plot and rides to warn the Torres family.

179.6 *Zorro Saves a Friend.* Nov. 14, 1957. Monastario arrests a woman whose husband is an escaped prisoner, and her daughter. He hopes to force Zorro to try to free them. Monastario posts extra guards around the cell.

179.7 *Monastario Sets a Trap.* Nov. 21, 1957. Zorro's father visits captive Dona Luisa and Elena Torres, and is greatly angered by the treatment Captain Monastario has given them. He gathers a party to ride to Monastario's headquarters and free the ladies.

179.8 *Zorro's Ride into Terror.* Nov. 28, 1957. Don Diego returns home for instruments to remove a bullet from his wounded father. He finds that Captain Monastario and his men are seeking to capture his father, and put Don Diego under house arrest.

179.9 *A Fair Trail.* Dec. 5, 1957. GS: Sebastian Cabot. Don Diego visits his father and Torres where they are imprisoned pending trial on charges of treason. Diego suspects that Captain Monastario plans to convict them without a fair trial.

179.10 *Garcia's Sweet Mission.* Dec. 12, 1957. GS: Jan Arvan. Captain Monastario strips Garcia of his rank and discharges him, hoping he can mingle with Zorro's friends and learn of his whereabouts.

179.11 *Double Trouble for Zorro.* Dec. 19, 1957. GS: Tony Russo. In a plan to disgrace Zorro, Captain Monastario directs one of his men to masquerade as Zorro as rob the commandante's dinner guests.

179.12 *The Luckiest Swordsman Alive.* Dec. 26, 1957. GS: Tony Russo. In an attempt to discredit Zorro, Monastario arranges for a man to impersonate Zorro and execute a jewel robbery. Don Diego learns of the plot and is forced into a duel with the robber.

179.13 *The Fall of Monastario.* Jan. 2, 1958. GS: John Dehner, Lisa Gaye, Than Wyenn. Monastario jails Don Diego as the masked avenger, Zorro. Then a chance visit from the King's viceroy prompts the commandant to release all the prisoners but Diego, to prove a point.

179.14 *Shadow of Doubt.* Jan. 9, 1958. GS: Peter Damon, Robin Hughes, Charles Stevens, Myrna Fahey. After the new commandante of Los Angeles is assassinated, Zorro sets out to catch the murderer. Then a beggar is arrested and charged with the killing. Zorro believes the man innocent.

179.15 *Garcia Stands Accused.* Jan. 16, 1958. GS: Henry

Zorro [1957]

Willis, Myrna Fahey. Zorro sets out to help his enemy, Sgt. Garcia, when Garcia is framed for the theft of the garrison payroll.

179.16 *Slaves of the Eagle.* Jan. 23, 1958. GS: Charles Korvin, Myrna Fahey, Vinton Hayworth, Ray Teal, John Doucette. An imposter passes himself off as the king's tax collector and imposes heavy taxes. Those who can't pay the taxes are forced into slavery. Zorro begins an investigation to learn the real identity of the imposter.

179.17 *Sweet Face of Danger.* Jan. 30, 1958. GS: Charles Korvin, Julie Van Zandt, Henry Wills, Vinton Hayworth. Don Diego learns that Magdalena, daughter of the king's magistrate, is marked for death. He makes plans to save her life.

179.18 *Zorro Fights His Father.* Feb. 6, 1958. GS: Charles Korvin, Julie Van Zandt, Peter Brocco, John Shayne. The landowners decide to trap Zorro, feeling that his capture will restore law and order to the area. Don Diego is told of the trap by his father.

179.19 *Death Stacks the Deck.* Feb. 13, 1958. GS: Charles Korvin, Joan Shawley, Jim Bannon. A stranger arrives in the area with a scheme to force the rancheros from their lands. After a young man has lost his ranch through gambling with the stranger, Zorro decides to challenge him to a game of cards.

179.20 *Agent of the Eagle.* Feb. 20, 1958. GS: Charles Korvin, Anthony Caruso, Vinton Hayworth, George Keymas, Anthony George, Sandy Livingstone. An outlaw leader known as the Eagle, orders members of his gang to extort cash from the frightened citizens to aid the unscrupulous magistrate of Los Angeles. Zorro decides to unmask the outlaw.

179.21 *Zorro Springs Trap.* Feb. 27, 1958. GS: Charles Korvin, Vinton Hayworth, Anthony Caruso, George Keymas. Ortega captures Zorro's horse Tornado and offers him for auction. He hopes that the masked avenger will show himself in an attempt to rescue the animal.

179.22 *The Unmasking of Zorro.* March 6, 1958. GS: Charles Korvin, Anthony Caruso, Sandy Livingstone, Eugenia Paul, George Keymas, Vinton Hayworth. Commandante Juan Ortega tries to kill a girl from Monterey who can expose him as an impostor. Zorro comes to her aid but is unmasked in his duel with Ortega.

179.23 *The Secret of the Sierra.* March 13, 1958. GS: Laurie Carroll, Rudolfo Acosta. A Gypsy girl arrives in Los Angeles and tries to sell some gold nuggets. Henchman of the crooked magistrate force her to reveal where she got them. Zorro tries to help the girl.

179.24 *The New Commandante.* March 20, 1958. GS: Peter Adams, Suzanne Lloyd, Anthony George, Vinton Hayworth. A new commandante arrives in Los Angeles and refuses to go along with the unscrupulous Magistrate Galindo. The magistrate decides to get rid of the new commandante.

179.25 *The Fox and the Coyote.* March 26, 1958. GS: Peter Adams, Suzanne Lloyd, Anthony George, Vinton Hayworth. The forth-coming horse race in Los Angeles, sponsored by Magistrate Galindo, features all the soldiers from the garrison. Zorro learns that the race is planned by Galindo to enable him to steal the supplies of gunpowder and use them for an insurrection. Gathering a band of lancers, Zorro rides to the scene of the planned theft.

179.26 *Adios, Senor Magistrado.* April 3, 1958. GS: Vinton Hayworth, Peter Adams, Suzanne Lloyd. Two prisoners held by Galindo are put to death. Zorro believes the magistrate ordered the men killed so that his part in a recent insurrection would not be disclosed. Galindo accuses the new Commandante of conspiracy against the people of Los Angeles and proposes to deal with him without even a trial. Zorro learns of Galindo's plot and decides to help thwart it.

179.27 *The Eagle's Brood.* April 10, 1958. GS: Charles Korvin, Michael Pate, Suzanne Lloyd. El Aguila plans to smuggle gunpowder into Los Angeles. Zorro decides to foil the man's plot.

179.28 *Zorro by Proxy.* April 17, 1958. GS: Charles Korvin, Michael Pate, Suzanne Lloyd, Peter Mamakos. A beautiful girl teams up with The Eagle in a scheme to track down Zorro. She decides to choose someone at random and accuse him of being Zorro, and singles out Don Diego as her victim.

179.29 *Quintana Makes a Choice.* April 24, 1958. GS: Charles Korvin, Michael Pate, Suzanne Lloyd, Ted de Corsia. Sgt. Garcia uncovers a plot to steal gunpowder form the Los Angeles arsenal. When Zorro learns that Garcia's life is in danger, he tries to save him.

179.30 *Zorro Lights a Fuse* (A.K.A. "Conspiracy"). May 1, 1958. GS: Charles Korvin, Michael Pate, Suzanne Lloyd, Ted de Corsia. Zorro leans that a group of conspirators plan to overthrow the government. He decides to expose them.

179.31 *The Man with the Whip.* May 8, 1958. GS: Kent Taylor, Steve Stevens, Myrna Fahey. Don Rodolfo Martinez is vexed when another man begins to annoy his sweetheart. When he objects, the other man demands a duel. Zorro, knowing Martinez has no knowledge of fencing, tries to prevent the duel.

179.32 *The Cross of the Andes.* May 15, 1958. GS: Steve Stevens, Kent Taylor, Myrna Fahey. When his servant Bernardo is attacked by one of Eagle's men, Zorro goes to his rescue. In the skirmish with the assailant, Zorro is unmasked.

179.33 *The Deadly Bolas* (A.K.A. "The Missing Jewels"). May 22, 1958. GS: Paul Picerni, Mary Wickes. Don Diego disguises his servant Bernardo as Zorro and sends him to search a tannery for some missing jewels. Two agents of the Eagle, an outlaw, bring Bernardo down with South American weapons called bolas.

179.34 *The Well of Death.* May 29, 1958. GS: Paul Picerni, Mary Wickes, Bobby Crawford, Jr. Two of the Eagle's henchmen conceal a batch of stolen gems in a tannery. Zorro and Sgt. Garcia surprise the two men, and a fight ensues.

179.35 *The Tightening Noose.* June 5, 1958. GS: Charles Korvin, Jay Novello. A new administrator, Jose Sebastian de Varga, comes to take command of Los Angeles. His first act is to seize the hacienda of Don Alejandro. While lurking in a hidden passage of the hacienda, Zorro learns the identity of his enemy the Eagle.

179.36 *The Sergeant Regrets.* June 12, 1958. GS: Charles Korvin, Jay Novello. Sgt. Garcia is sent with a warning to the citizens of an ambush by the Eagle. But Garcia lingers too long over a meal and the Eagle succeeds in capturing one of the rancheros.

179.37 *The Eagle Leaves the Nest.* June 19, 1958. GS: Charles Korvin, Jay Novello. The Eagle, posing as Senor Varga, takes over the home of Don Alejandro while he is away. Don Alejandro is determined to fight a duel to the death with the

Eagle and Don Diego decides to appear as Zorro to save his father's life.

179.38 *Bernardo Faces Death.* June 26, 1958. GS: Charles Korvin, Henry Rowland. The Eagle plans to use a cannon in an uprising against the government.

179.39 *Day of Decision.* July 3, 1958. GS: Charles Korvin, Jay Novello, Henry Rowland. The Eagle starts a full-scale rebellion against the government of Spanish California. He takes over the government headquarters and imprisons Alejandro, Don Diego and Bernardo.

Season Two

179.40 *Welcome to Monterey.* Oct. 9, 1958. GS: Eduard Franz, Carlos Romero, Wolfe Barzell, Joe Conway, Lee Van Cleef. Don Diego and Bernardo travel to Monterey and are accorded a mixed reception in the mission city. They are attacked by two ruffians who believe that Don Diego is carrying a large sum of money.

179.41 *Zorro Rides Alone.* Oct. 16, 1958. GS: Carlos Romero, Eduard Franz, Joe Conway, Kem Dibbs, Joseph Waring, Ken Lynch. Zorro believes that Gregorio Verdugo has hired bandits to steal gold shipments and decides to set a trap for him. He tells Verdugo that the gold will be taken along a different route.

179.42 *Horse of Another Color.* Oct. 23, 1958. GS: Carlos Romero, Eduard Franz, Joe Conway, Mike Forest, Ken Lynch. Gregorio Verdugo and his daughter Anna Maria set out for San Francisco, carrying with them a fortune in gold. Verdugo is unaware that the leader of the party they are traveling with is a member of a bandit gang.

179.43 *The Senorita Makes a Choice.* Oct. 30, 1958. GS: Carlos Romero, Eduard Franz, Joe Conway, Ken Lynch. Gregorio Verdugo is kidnaped by a band of outlaws who demand that Verdugo's daughter, Anna Maria, turn over a large amount of gold that has been collected to buy supplies for blockaded California. Don Diego pleads with Anna Maria to demand proof that her father is alive before turning over the gold.

179.44 *Rendezvous at Sundown.* Nob. 6, 1958. GS: Carlos Romero, Eduard Franz, Joe Conway, Ken Lynch. The bandits who are holding Gregorio Verdugo release him after taking his daughter Anna Maria as their captive instead. They instruct Verdugo to return with ransom money for the girl or they will kill her.

179.45 *The New Order.* Nov. 13, 1958. GS: Barbara Luna, Al Ruscio, Perry Lopez. The acting governor of California orders the peons to remove their vending stands from the public square of Monterey. One young lady, who operates a tamale stand, reacts violently to the order and is imprisoned.

179.46 *An Eye for an Eye.* Nov. 20, 1958. GS: Barbara Luna, Danny Lopez, John Litel, Ric Roman, Frank Wilcox. Joaquin Castenada, the rebel, leads a raid in the city of Monterey. One member of his band only fourteen years old is killed, and Castenada vows to kill two of the governors in revenge.

179.47 *Zorro and the Flag of Truce.* Nov. 27, 1958. GS: Barbara Luna, Danny Lopez, John Litel, Al Ruscio, Ric Roman, Frank Wilcox. The governor of Monterey returns and his aide urges that the governor discuss peace terms with the rebel leader Joaquin Castenada. Don Diego and his father Alejandro are given the task of finding Castenada.

179.48 *Ambush.* Dec. 4, 1958. GS: Barbara Luna, Danny Lopez, John Litel, Ric Roman, Frank Wilcox. Joaquin Castenada is captured during a foray into Monterey. Castenada, who claims he was fired on during a truce, holds the governor responsible. When he is offered his freedom on condition that he take part in a plot to assassinate the governor, Castenada agrees.

179.49 *The Practical Joker.* Dec. 11, 1958. GS: Richard Anderson. Charmed by Anna Maria, Don Diego's visiting friend Ricardo devises a series of pranks to eliminate Don Diego as a competitor fo her affections. But he goes too far. The result is that when he tries to warn everyone of a payroll-robbery plot he's heard about, no one believes him.

179.50 *The Flaming Arrow.* Dec. 18, 1958. GS: Richard Anderson, Whit Bissell, Yvette Dugay. To put Zorro at a disadvantage in Anna Maria's eyes, Ricardo Del Amo disguises himself as Zorro, and sets out to serenade Anna Maria's cousin. Captured by Sgt. Garcia, Ricardo finds his disguise is too good.

179.51 *Zorro Fights a Duel.* Dec. 25, 1958. GS: Richard Anderson, Joseph La Cava. Still attempting to win Anna Maria's affection, Ricardo Del Amo challenges Zorro to a duel. Diego, unable to persuade Ricardo to call the duel off, becomes concerned when he sees Ricardo's skill in handling weapons.

179.52 *Amnesty for Zorro.* Jan. 1, 1959. GS: Richard Anderson, John Litel. The authorities tell Zorro that they will forget his past actions if he will surrender and unmask. Zorro decides to take the big step and reveal his identity.

179.53 *The Runaways.* Jan. 8, 1959. GS: Tom Pittman, John Hoyt, Gloria Castillo, Arthur Batanides. Two servants find their wedding plans opposed by one of their masters. Don Diego, learning that the master who so bitterly opposes the marriage will kill one or both of the young lovers to prevent the marriage, decides to help them.

179.54 *The Iron Box.* Jan. 15, 1959. GS: Rebecca Welles, Mark Damon, Harold J. Stone, Tige Andrews. Moneta, a barmaid, is also leader of a gang which plans to steal the strongbox containing the Los Angeles tax collection. She befriends a locksmith's son as part of the burglary scheme.

179.55 *The Gay Caballero.* Jan. 22, 1959. GS: Cesar Romero, Patricia Medina, Howard Wendell. Don Diego's uncle Estevan de la Cruz, a suave confidence man, arrives unexpectedly in Los Angeles for a visit. In town only a short time, Estevan charms Margarita Cotazar and her father into taking part in one of his get-rich-quick schemes.

179.56 *Tornado Is Missing.* Jan. 29, 1959. GS: Cesar Romero, Patricia Medina. Don Diego discovers that Tornado, the black horse he rides when masquerading as Zorro, is missing from his secret stable. Diego's uncle Estevan tells him that he has found a black horse and is going to enter it in a race. Diego realizes that he must recover Tornado before the race.

179.57 *Zorro Versus Cupid.* Feb. 5, 1959. GS: Cesar Romero, Patricia Medina. Don Diego's uncle, Estevan de la Cruz, who is after Margarita Cortazar's money, decides to propose marriage to her. Diego's father tries to discourage Estevan, telling him that Zorro will consider him a thief.

179.58 *The Legend of Zorro.* Feb. 12, 1959. GS: Cesar Romero, Patricia Medina. Estevan knows that his marriage to Margarita will not take place so long as Zorro questions his intentions. Estevan decides to announce that he no longer wishes to marry her, though he plans a secret elopement.

179.59 *Spark of Revenge.* Feb. 19, 1959. GS: Neil Hamilton, Robert Vaughn. A drought causes Miguel Roverto to steal water from his neighbor. This act leads to dire consequences for Miguel.

179.60 *The Missing Father.* Feb. 26, 1959. GS: Annette Funicello, Carlos Rivas, Penny Santon, Arthur Space, Wendell Holmes. Anita Cabrillo travels from Spain to Los Angeles, to be with her father. She is, however, unable to find him immediately and Don Diego invites her to stay at his hacienda.

179.61 *Please Believe Me.* March 5, 1959. GS: Annette Funicello, Carlos Rivas, Penny Santon, Arthur Space, Wendell Holmes. Anita tries to locate her father, who she believes is in Los Angeles. Since nobody has heard of the man, all except Don Diego refuse to believe her story.

179.62 *The Brooch.* March 12, 1959. GS: Annette Funicello, Carlos Rivas, Penny Santon, Arthur Space, Wendell Holmes. Anita Cabrillo wears a brooch which Don Alejandro recognizes as one he gave to a church auction in Los Angeles years ago. Anita tells him that she received it from her father.

179.63 *The Mountain Man.* March 19, 1959. GS: Jeff York, Jonathan Harris, Paul Richards. Joe Crane, a bold, carefree trapper, arrives in Los Angeles. His unorthodox actions soon provoke the wrath of Don Carlos Fernandez.

179.64 *The Hound of the Sierras.* March 26, 1959. GS: Jeff York, Jean Willes, Jonathan Harris, Paul Richards. Zorro helps trapper Joe Crane escape from jail. Once free, Joe realizes that his furs are still imprisoned and decides to try to reclaim them.

179.65 *Manhunt.* April 2, 1959. GS: Jeff York, Jean Willes, Jonathan Harris, Paul Richards. Don Carlos Fernandez uses impounded furs to set a death trap for Joe Crane.

179.66 *The Man from Spain.* April 9, 1959. GS: Everett Sloane, Robert J. Wilke, Gloria Talbott, Edgar Barrier. Andres Felipe Basilio and his right-hand man Mendoza arrive in Los Angeles to sell Spanish war bonds. The two visitors quickly succeed in annoying the townspeople.

179.67 *Treasure for the King.* April 16, 1959. GS: Everett Sloane, Robert J. Wilke, Gloria Talbott, Edgar Barrier. Andres Basilio and his cohort Captain Mendoza decide to keep the money they have collected selling Spanish bonds. They devise a plot that involves blowing up a ship in order to cover up their crime.

179.68 *Exposing the Tyrant.* April 23, 1959. GS: Everett Sloane, Robert J. Wilke, Gloria Talbott, Edgar Barrier. A visitor from Spain, Andres Basilio, sets his sights on Don Cornelio Esperon's home. Basilio charges Esperon with treason against the king.

179.69 *Zorro Takes a Dare.* April 30, 1959. GS: Everett Sloane, Robert J. Wilke, Gloria Talbott, Edgar Barrier. Andres Basilio holds Sgt. Garcia prisoner at the fort. While his troops prepare an ambush, Basilio dares Zorro to come to Garcia's rescue.

179.70 *An Affair of Honor.* May 7, 1959. GS: Tony Russo, Booth Colman. Master swordsman Pedro Avila attempts to trick the evasive Don Diego into a duel.

179.71 *The Sergeant Sees Red.* May 14, 1959. GS: Joseph Calleia, Richard Reeves. Carlos, servant of Padre Simeon, steals a chalice from the priest. Locking Padre Simeon in the house, the boy posts a quarantine notice on the door and flees.

179.72 *Invitation to Death.* May 21, 1959. GS: John Litel, Joan Evans, George Neise. The governor of California, convalescing from an accident, is attacked by a mysterious assailant. Although Zorro knows that the governor is widely disliked, his suspicions are aroused when he hears that the deputy governor left no guard with the invalid.

179.73 *The Captain Regrets.* May 28, 1959. GS: John Litel, Joan Evans, George Neise, Myron Healey, Douglas Kennedy. Captain Arrellano joins the rebel Don Gabriele Luna in his plot to assassinate the Governor of California. As the first step, the conspirators attempt to drug the governor's bodyguards.

179.74 *Masquerade for Murder.* June 4, 1959. GS: John Litel, Joan Evans, George Neise, Douglas Kennedy, Don Haggerty. The governor's aide is a member of a secret society which is plotting to assassinate the governor during a masquerade party.

179.75 *Long Live the Governor.* June 11, 1959. GS: John Litel, Joan Evans, George Neise, Douglas Kennedy. Captain Arrellano and the Rebatos plot once more to kill the governor. This time they plan to have everyone leave the governor alone and unprotected in the De la Vega Hacienda.

179.76 *The Fortune Teller.* June 18, 1959. GS: Roxanne Berard, Paul Dubov, Kay E. Kuter, Max Mellinger, Lou Krugman, William Hunt, Alex Gerry. Don Alejandro gives Sergeant Garcia a large sum of money to hold for him. When Lupita, a Gypsy, learns that Garcia has the money, she tells the sergeant a story devised to make him easy prey for a robber.

179.77 *Senor China Boy.* June 25, 1959. GS: James Hong, Richard Deacon, Charles Horvath. A Chinese lad who doesn't speak English arrives in Los Angeles. Later, a sailor arrives in port and charges the boy with murder and deserting the ship.

179.78 *Finders Keepers.* July 2, 1959. GS: Fenton Meyler, Rodolfo Hoyos, Richard Garland. When Celesta Villagrana accuses Bernardo of robbery and attempted murder, Don Diego sets out to find the real culprit.

Season Three

Note: The following episodes aired as segments of *Walt Disney Presents*.

179.79 *El Bandito.* Oct. 30, 1960. GS: Gilbert Roland, Rita Moreno. El Cuchillo, a handsome bandit, decides to rob a stagecoach. But Chulita, a shapely barmaid temporarily forces him to change his plans.

179.80 *Adios El Cuchillo.* Nov. 6, 1960. GS: Gilbert Roland, Rita Moreno. El Chuchillo plans to capture a wagonload of treasures and Zorro is determined to stop him.

179.81 *The Postponed Wedding.* Jan. 1, 1961. GS: Annette Funicello, Mark Damon. Zorro believes that Miguel Serrano is just a rogue who is after lovely Constancia's largte dowry. When the couple decides to elope, Zorro decides to stop them.

179.82 *Auld Acquaintance.* April 2, 1961. GS: Ricardo Montalban, Suzanne Lloyd, Ross Martin. The rogue Ramon Castillo plans to steal an army payroll. He fears that Don Diego may foil his plot.

180. Zorro

Family Channel. 30 min. Broadcast history: Jan. 1990–June 1993. 88 episodes.

Regular Cast: Duncan Regehr (Don Diego de la Vega/Zorro), Efrem Zimbalist, Jr. (Don Alejandro Sebastian de la Vega) 1990, Henry Darrow (Don Alejandro Sebastian de la Vega), Patrice Cahmi Martinez (Victoria Scalanti), James Victor (Sgt. Hymen Mendoza), Michael Tylo (Luis Ramone/the Alcalde) 90-91, John Hertzler (Ignacio DeSoto/the Alcalde) 91-94, Juan Diego Botto.

Premise: This series recounted the adventures of Zorro, the masked avenger of the oppressed in Spanish California.

181. Zorro and Son

CBS. 30 min. Broadcast history: Wednesday, 8:00-8:30, April 1983–June 1983.

Regular Cast: Henry Darrow (Don Diego de la Vega/Zorro), Paul Regina (Don Carlos), Bill Dana (Bernardo), Gregory Sierra (Captain Paco Pico), Richard Beauchamp (Sergeant Sepulveda), John Moschitta, Jr. (Corporal Cassette), Barney Martin (Brother Napa/Brother Sonoma).

Premise: This comedic series related the adventures of Don Carlos de la Vega, who takes his aging father's role as Zorro, the masked defender of old California.

The Episodes

181.1 *Title Unknown.* April 6, 1983. The elder Zorro's manservant sends for the son who has been studying abroad and knows nothing of his father's identity or his need to help to save a monk accused of selling a wine before its time.

181.2 *Title Unknown.* April 13, 1983. Captain Pico poses as Zorro and embarks on a crime spree.

181.3 *Title Unknown.* April 20, 1983. GS: Gina Gallego, Vic Dunlop. Zorro Jr. clicks with a flamenco dancer seeking political asylum.

181.4 *Title Unknown.* April 27, 1983. Zorro continues to confound Captain Pico.

181.5 *Title Unknown.* May 4, 1983. Zorro seeks to free a political prisoner unjustly jailed by Captain Pico.

181.6 *Title Unknown.* June 1, 1983. GS: Dick Gautier, H.B. Haggerty. Don Diego and Pico form an unlikely alliance to combat a common enemy—the Butcher of Barcelona, an old nemesis of Zorro's assigned to replace Pico as commandante.

Storyline Index

In this brief index are found the names of characters (by first name), the names of historical persons, tribes, companies and institutions that figure in the storylines, fictional places and institutions, indications of time frame (e.g., "1870s"), real locations (including battles), and significant subjects or objects bearing on the premise of the story.

Adam Cartwright 14
Adam MacLean 103
Africa 36
Alex Cahill 163
American Northwest 154
Andy Burnett 136
Annie Oakley 6
Annie O'Connell 22
anthology 43, 54, 61, 178
Apache Indians 20
Arizona 141
Arizona Rangers 158
Arizona Territory 15, 19, 20, 44, 71, 72, 79, 155, 158
Arlo Pritchard 24
Artemus Gordon 170
Audra Barkley 12

Baca, Elfego 113
Bannister Sparks 171
Bar 20 Ranch 73
Barbary Coast 7
Barkley family 12
Barrett Fears 11
Bart McClelland 160
Bart Maverick 105, 175
Bat Masterson 8
Battle of Bitter Creek 17
Battle of the Little Big Horn 38
Beau Maverick 175
Ben Calhoun 76
Ben Cartwright 14
Ben January 159
Ben Maverick 175
Ben Newcomb 22
Ben Wiley 23
Beth Purcell 29
Betty Ann Sundown 24
Biff O'Hara 3
Big Tim Champion 31
Bill Longley 152
Bill Winter 37
Billy the Kid 149
Blackhawk Insurance Company 102
Boston 48
bounty hunters 116, 164
Bowie, Jim 42, 78
Brady Hawkes 59

Brave Eagle 18
Bret Maverick 19, 105, 175
Brett Clark 122
Brisco County, Jr. 1
Brodie Hollister 171
Broken Wheel Ranch 57
Bronco Layne 21
Buddhist Monk 83
Buffalo Bill, Jr. 23
Bustedluck 42
Butch Cavendish 97

Calamity 23
California 8, 12, 24, 28, 35, 43, 47, 40, 62, 84, 119, 120, 121, 142, 157, 179
California Joe Milner 38
Canada 16, 138
Canadian Mounties 16
Candy 14
Cannon family 71
Carlos de la Vega 181
Carson, Kit 81
Cartwright family 14
Casablanca 27
Cash Conover 7
cattle drive 126
Cessna 141
Chad Cooper 86
Champion, the Wonder Horse 2, 60
Charlie Wooster 162
Chester B. Goode 65
Cheyenne Bodie 27
Cheyenne Indians 18, 123
Chicago 102
China 83
Chingachgook 67, 68
Chisholm family 28
Christopher Colt 34
Christopher Hale 162
Cimarron City, Oklahoma 29
Cincinatus 41
circus 31, 55
Cisco Kid 32
Clay Culhane 13
Clay Hollister 155
Clay McCord 44
Clay Morgan 147
Clive Bennett 16

Cochise 20
Colorado 26, 74, 137
Colorado Territory 48, 166
comedy 5, 10, 50, 52, 125, 134
contemporary West 24, 135
Cord 64
Cordell Walker 163
Corky 31
Crazy Horse 38
Culhane 49
Curtis Wells 100
Custer, George Armstrong 38
Cyrus Pike 47

Dakota Territory 39, 53, 103, 176, 177
Dan Troop 89
Daniel Best 10
Dave Blassingame 165
David Beaton 176
Deep Wells Ranger Station 125
Denver 166
Diablo 6
Dick West 124
Doc Adams 65
Doc Jerome Kullens 10
Dodge City 65, 93
Don Diego de la Vega 179
Double Bar M Ranch 58
Double Eagle Detective Agency 118
Duell McCall 45
Dulcey Coppersmith 30
Dundee 49
Dusty Rhoades 14

Earp, Wyatt 93
1800s 97; late 1800s 43, 94, 113, 139, 171
1820s 136, 179
1830s 147
1832 115
1840s 131
1849 157
1850s 25, 77, 111
1860s 21, 27, 46, 65, 92, 101, 122, 140, 142, 159, 177; late 1860s 48, 119
1865 10
1869 72
1870s 7, 15, 17, 20, 37, 53, 66, 70, 74, 84, 89, 91, 93, 96, 107, 121, 156, 162, 166, 167, 169, 170;

early 1870s 76; late 1870s 12, 149
1876 38
1880 22, 33
1880s 2, 3, 8, 16, 29, 30, 34, 35, 42, 44, 50, 55, 81, 85, 88, 103, 105, 153, 155, 161, 172, 173; late 1880s 130
1887 95
1890s 5, 23, 82, 106, 120, 123, 138, 143, 145, 165; early 1890s 1; late 1890s 4; "late 1800s" 43, 94, 113, 139, 171
1899 118
eighteenth century see 17XXs [seventeen…]
El Toro 81
Elvira Best 10
Enterprise 131
Ernest Pratt 91
Evan Thorpe 115

Fantan 4
fantasy 1
Festus Haggen 65
Fifth Cavalry 15
Fink, Mike 42
Flicka 108
Flint McCullough 162
Flying Crown Ranch 141
Fort Apache 3
Fort Laramie, Wyoming 28
Fort Worth, Texas 163
Francis Wilde 30
Frank Caine 117
Frank Ragan 39
Friotown, Texas 153
Frog 10
Fury 57

George Taggart 151
Geronimo, Chief 96.79
Gib Scott 13
Gil Favor 126
Gold Buckle 144
Gold Rush 4, 82, 138
Golden Gate Casino 7
Great Overland Mail Stage Lines 85
Grey Holden 131
Griff King 14
Grizzly Adams 94
Grover City, Arizona 141
Gunnison 159
Guns of Paradise 120

Hank Brackett 9
Hanks family 121
Hannibal Heyes 5
Harland Pike 118
Harris Clayton 155
Harrison Destry 46
Hawaii 11
Hawkeye 67, 68
Heath Barkley 12
Hec Ramsey 69
Heck Martin 117
Hickok, Wild Bill 169
High Chaparral Ranch 71
Hole in the Wall Gang 97
Hondo Lane 72
Hop Sing 14
Hopalong Cassidy 73
horse 2, 57, 60, 108
Hoss Cartwright 14
Hotel de Paree 74
Houston, Temple 151

Illinois 102

J.J. Jackson 24
Jace Pearson 147

Jack Craddock 16
Jack McGivern 25
Jackson 53
Jaimie McPheeters 157
James Bustard 38
James T. West 170
Jamie Hunter 14
January brothers 159
Jarrod Barkley 12
Jason Bolt 70
Jason McCord 17
Jeff Cable 7
Jeff Durain 82
Jeremy Bolt 70
Jeremy Pitt 25
Jess Harper 85
Jim Crown 30
Jim Donner 33
Jim Ed Love 134
Jim Hardie 148
Jim Newton 57
Jim Redigo 128
Jim Sinclair 36
Jocko 42
Jody O'Connell 22
Joe Riley 86
Joey Newton 57
John Bly 1
John Grail 118
John Henry 36
John Reid 97
Johnny McKay 89
Johnny Reach 9
Johnny Yuma 127
Josh Randall 164
Joshua Bolt 70
Joshua Smith 5
Jubilee 77

Kansas 167
Keke 11
Ken McLaughlin 108
Kentucky 40, 41, 174
Kid Curry 5
King's Row 27
Kwai Chang Caine 83

Lancer Ranch 84
Lane Temple 29
Langtry, Texas 80
Laramie, Wyoming 89
Laredo, Texas 86
lawyer 13, 49
Lazy Ace Ranch 19
Lincoln County, New Mexico 149
Little Joe Cartwright 14
Lofty Craig 6
Lord Bowler 1
Lucas McCain 130

Ma Ketcham 112
Macahan family 75
Madrid County, California 24
Marie Dumont 16
Mark McCain 130
Martha McGivern 25
Mary Lou Springer 19
Massachusetts 48
Masterson, Bat 93
Matt Clark 145
Matt Dillon 65
Matthew Rockfort 29
Matthew Wayne 25
Medard 154
Medicine Bow, Wyoming 106, 161
Mexican border 165
Mexico 32

Michaela Quinn 48
Mike Dunbar 167
Mike Halliday 82
Mineral City 135
Mingo 41
mini-series 26, 28, 59, 99
Minnesota 95, 96, 111
Mississippi River 131
Missouri 92, 119, 136, 142
Missouri River 131
Mitch Fears 11
Mitch Guthrie 168
Molly Beaton 176
Montana 22, 99, 108
Monterey, California 179
Moose Moran 7
Morning Star 18
Mushy 126
Myles Keogh 38

Nakia Parker 109
Navaho Indian 109
Ned Blessing 110
Nevada 14, 43
New Mexico 32, 51, 109, 113, 130, 149
New Mexico Territory 37, 49, 88
New Orleans 78, 173
New York 67, 68
Newly O'Brian 65
newspaper 77, 103
Newt Dobbs Call 99
Nick Barkley 12
Nicodemus Legend 91
Nifty Cronin 4
Nightlinger 37
1900s (early) 56, 158
1914 9, 112
1930s 78
1950s 147
1970s 26
1980s 118
nineteenth century see 18XXs [eighteen…]
Nora Travers 13
North Fork, New Mexico 130
Northern California 171
Northwest Canadian Mounted Police 138

Ohio 132
Oklahoma Territory 29, 30, 69, 117
Old California 181
Omaha 160
Oregon 115

Paladin 66
Pancho 32
Paradise, California 120
Paradise Ranch 11
Parker Tillman 10
Pat Gallagher 35
Philo Sandine 19
Pierre Radisson 154
Pitcairn 172
Plum Creek 110
Plumb Creek, Minnesota 95
Ponderosa Ranch 14
Pony Express 122
Prometheus Jones 171

Quake City, California 62
Quint Asper 65

Randy Booney 3
Range Rider 124
Red Ox saloon 19
Reese Bennett 86
Reno McKee 4
Rex 138

Storyline Index

Rick January 159
Ricky North 2
Rin Tin Tin 3
Ringo, Johnny 79
Rip Masters 3
Robin Hood of the West 32
Rocky Shaw 4
rodeo 144, 168
Rogers' Rangers 114
Rowdy Yates 126
Roy Coffee 14
Rudy Davilo 24
Rusty 3

Sally Fergus 47
Sam Best 10
Sam Brennan 25
Sam Buckhart 88
Sam Cade 24
Sam Colt, Jr. 34
Sam Houston 151
Sam Logan 102
Samson 36
San Antonio, Texas 126
San Francisco 7, 25
San Francisco Gold Rush 25
San Joaquin Valley 12, 84
Sandy North 2
Sara 137
Scandinavian immigrants 111
science fiction 1, 33
Seattle 70
Secret Service 170
Seth Adams 162
1700s 154
1750s 26, 67, 68
Shane 139
Shank Adams 15
Shenandoah 101
Sheriff Powers 2
Shiloh Ranch 161

Shotgun Slade 140
Silky Harris 4
Silver City, Arizona 44
Simon Fry 44
singing cowboy 60, 104
Slim Sherman 85
Smitty 27
Socorro County, New Mexico 113
Socrates Poole 1
The Songbird 141
The Sons of the Pioneers 135
Southwest 2, 9, 13, 55, 60
Southwestern Railroad 145
Spanish California 180
Springfield, Ohio 132
stallion 2
Stockton, California 12
Stutz Bearcat 9
Sugarfoot 21, 27, 146
Sully 48
Sundance Kid 74
Sutton Hollister 171
Sweetwater, Arizona 19

Tagg Oakley 6
Tara 33
Teaspoon Hunter 177
Temple Houston 151
Terlesky, John 120
Tetons 75
Texas 21, 23, 80, 86, 126, 153, 163
Texas Rangers 86, 97, 125, 147, 163
Thimbelrig 42
Thorval 33
Tom Brewster 146
Tom Guthrie 19
Tom Jeffords 20
Tom Sellers 22
Tombstone 93
Tombstone, Arizona 155
Tombstone Epitaph 155

Tonto 97
Trampas 161
Tucson, Arizona 20, 71

Union Pacific Railroad 160

Varges de la Cosa 171
Velardi, Arizona 79
Victoria Barkley 12
vigilantes 25
Vint Bonner 129
Virginia 28, 116
Virginia City, Nevada 14
Virginian, The 106

wagon train 50, 115, 157, 162
Walnut Grove, Minneosta 96
Washington 70
Wells Fargo 148
Whispering Smith 166
Wichita, Kansas 167
Wildside Territory 171
Wileyville, Texas 23
Will Calhoun 2
Will Foreman 117
Will Sonnett 63
William Colton 98
Wilton Parmenter 52
Wishbone 126
Wretched, California 121
Wyoming 28, 33, 76, 89, 106, 161
Wyoming territory 107

Yadkin 41
Yellowstone 103
Yukon King 138
Yukon Territory 138

Zeb Macahan 75
Zorro 179, 181

Personnel Index

Aaker, Lee 3, 97.150
Aames, Willie 65.554, 65.582, 96.60
Abbott, John 14.80, 46.8, 65.14, 65.176, 66.83, 76.45, 86.12, 117.41, 130.66, 170.79
Abbott, Mark 67.9, 67.17
Abbott, Philip 13.14, 14.139, 51.20, 65.128, 65.309, 74.25, 96.106, 126.186, 144.1
Abdullah, Joe 138.52, 148.62, 162.55
Abelar, Michael 76.36, 170.13
Abellira, Remi 11
Abernathy, Donzaleigh 110.1
Abrahams, Doug 67.18
Ace, Rosemary 43.89, 43.97
Acierto, Tony 177.45
Acker, Sharon 5.11, 24.6, 65.546, 69, 84.31, 170.84
Ackerman, Bettye 14.270, 65.587
Ackroyd, David 163.36
Acosta, Carmelita 126.203
Acosta, Rodolfo 12.11, 14.181, 14.216, 14.371, 21.38, 24.4, 27.53, 27.59, 27.87, 41.39, 41.63, 43.289, 43.299, 43.321, 61.1, 61.2, 66.7, 66.9, 66.70, 66.141, 71, 76.7, 77.8, 86.47, 105.117, 116.23, 126.6, 126.61, 126.140, 126.161, 127.3, 146.39, 148.170, 152.47, 157.20, 161.29, 179.23
Acton, Ken 169.64
Adair, Alice 45.3, 177.18
Adam, Darren 67.13
Adams, Arthur 36.8, 36.20, 170.84
Adams, Ashby 1.5, 1.11, 1.15
Adams, Caitlin 112.11
Adams, Casey 65.85, 142.35
Adams, Dave 53.1, 120.35, 177.43
Adams, Dorothy 6.38, 65.40, 81.40, 81.49, 88.4, 127.44, 156.34, 156.66, 162.24
Adams, Ed 90.20, 91.5, 177.8, 177.34, 177.65
Adams, Evan 67.8
Adams, Harry G. 115.6
Adams, Jack 81.8
Adams, Jane 32.1, 81.38, 169.18
Adams, Jason 177.23, 177.24
Adams, Jason Leland 48, 48.38, 48.64
Adams, Joan 98.24
Adams, Julie 4.10, 12.37, 12.81, 14.48, 27.63, 27.64, 105.49, 105.72, 117.26, 130.75, 150.13, 161.119, 172.4, 173.1, 178.53, 178.67
Adams, Kathy 65.5
Adams, Lillian 12.69, 127.27
Adams, Madeleine 47.9
Adams, Mary 3.66, 65.22, 138.35
Adams, Maud 163.85
Adams, Nick 29.4, 72.6, 72.16, 107.20, 126.184, 127, 148.80, 156.26, 156.55, 156.62, 162.25, 162.163, 164.1, 170.23, 170.74, 173.17, 178.50, 178.79
Adams, Paige 66.146
Adams, Peggy 51.31
Adams, Peter 38.16, 64.10, 93.33, 102.37, 126.36, 126.79, 126.111, 158.28, 161.48, 179.24, 179.25, 179.26
Adams, Richard 152.23, 152.24, 152.44, 152.52
Adams, Stanley 14.157, 43.352, 44.72, 65.45, 65.51, 65.377, 66.188, 84.44, 86.27, 92.14, 107.22, 108.15, 121.1, 121.4, 126.35, 130.141, 131.33, 147.44, 148.159, 162.213, 162.234, 162.250, 162.255, 162.284, 168.4, 169.106
Adams, Ted 32.16, 32.22, 32.37, 35.20, 97.47
Adamson, David 174.2
Addams, Dorothy 54.15
Adderley, Julian "Cannonball" 83.55
Ades, Daniel 65.420, 71.23, 170.39
Adiarte, Patrick 14.403
Adler, Jay 164.85
Adler, Luther 69.7
Adler, Nathan 96.109
Adler, Robert 14.135, 41.119, 41.124, 65.278, 66.189, 84.1, 85.96, 108, 149.6, 151.25
Adrian, Iris 169.113
Adrian, Jane 104
Adrian, Yvonne 166.17
Agar, John 8.104, 17.28, 43.256, 72.9, 89.156, 126.29, 126.59, 161.55, 161.187
Aguilar, George 94.10
Aherne, Brian 126.95, 162.161
Aherne, Pat 138.62
Ahn, Philip 3.162, 14.77, 14.162, 25.25, 66.31, 77.5, 83, 86.49, 89.10, 127.28, 144.26, 164.68, 169.98, 170.17
Aidman, Charles 7.1, 13.17, 13.27, 14.60, 25.37, 25.55, 34.30, 57.96, 65.124, 65.182, 65.218, 65.477, 65.486, 66.35, 66.98, 66.117, 69.9, 69.10, 71.20, 79.32, 83.62, 85.75, 96.65, 101.13, 109.12, 116.11, 117.2, 126.43, 126.94, 127.73, 127.76, 131.23, 149.42, 156.54, 161.12, 161.222, 162.105, 162.126, 162.149, 164.22, 164.41, 167.14, 168.4, 170, 178.91
Aiello, Rick 163.19
Ainge, Dick 170.75
Airlie, Andrew 67.13
Akey, Lisa 91.10
Akins, Claude 4.32, 8.28, 12.14, 14.23, 14.36, 14.66, 14.105, 17.2, 21.1, 27.52, 39.16, 41.17, 43.189, 44.75, 46.1, 51.4, 51.29, 54.14, 55.12, 59.4, 61.1, 61.2, 63.1, 65.3, 65.49, 65.102, 65.254, 65.279, 65.353, 65.373, 65.410, 65.436, 65.559, 66.3, 69.4, 72.15, 78.64, 82.6, 85.19, 85.31, 85.92, 85.122, 86.20, 86.22, 86.52, 86.54, 86.56, 88.22, 92.18, 101.6, 105.26, 107.3, 108.9, 108.10, 108.27, 115.3, 117.49, 119.10, 126.35, 126.78, 126.86, 126.119, 126.126, 126.158, 126.208, 127.40, 129.12, 129.15, 129.61, 130.8, 130.74, 130.81, 131.7, 131.41, 148.61, 148.146, 148.167, 149.8, 152.40, 152.50, 161.11, 161.103, 162.3, 162.127, 162.156, 164.67, 168.6, 173.2, 173.25, 178.11, 178.44, 178.124, 178.148
Alaimo, Marc 59.3, 65.618, 120.32
Alaniz, Rico 3.57, 3.87, 12.32, 12.33, 14.163, 14.357, 21.60, 23.28, 43.37, 65.315, 65.316, 65.460, 65.466, 66.84, 71.1, 71.15, 71.52, 71.89, 81.1, 81.7, 93, 93.3, 93.21, 93.31, 93.49, 93.68, 93.78, 93.85, 93.98, 93.103, 93.107, 93.109, 93.117, 93.129, 93.130, 93.135, 93.175, 97.149, 105.24, 107.7, 113, 148.9, 148.185, 158.4, 158.5, 161.29, 170.61, 170.95, 170.96
Alaska 4, 82
Alban, Alissa 163.12
Albee, Josh 65.554, 65.571
Alberghetti, Anna Maria 162.63
Alberghetti, Carla 44.59
Albert, David 27.2
Albert, Eddie 55.5, 83.40, 85.2, 126.185, 131.5, 148.173, 161.9, 162.8, 162.200, 168.21, 178.7, 178.25, 178.43, 178.68
Albert, Edward 48.23, 67.12, 83.40, 120.51, 163.83
Albert, Susan 41.112
Albert, Susan Lee 92.2
Albert, Wil 96.66
Alberti, Mercedes 76.36
Albertson, Frank 14.136, 21.30, 21.54, 25.54, 27.70, 34.59, 46.6, 89.32, 105.119, 129.75, 126.25, 146.7, 146.67, 164.45, 164.76, 178.76
Albertson, Grace 31.26, 164.56
Albertson, Jack 5.18, 12.107, 14.285, 14.425, 32.70, 32.81, 32.121, 41.157, 43.282, 65.493, 65.558, 65.609, 66.8, 66.121, 70.10, 82.7, 89.155, 106.4, 121.3, 131.44, 161.200
Albertson, Mabel 21.60, 25.16, 41.86, 65.239, 65.306, 66.81, 126.46, 134.14, 149.74, 161.189, 170.36
Albin, Andy 8.16, 14.138, 44.75, 65.315, 65.316, 65.419, 93.169, 93.208, 126.59, 148.189, 149.56, 178.122
Albin, Dolores 96.155
Albright, Hardie 64.7, 65.274, 65.397, 76.3, 85.72, 107.14, 126.77, 126.91

Personnel Index

Albright, Lola 14.189, 14.253, 17.19, 17.47, 17.48, 30.11, 65.13, 86.18, 126.78, 126.204, 162.226
Albright, Victoria 161.118
Albritton, Wayne 170.21
Alcaide, Chris 2.1, 2.6, 6.1, 6.10, 6.25, 12.44, 12.66, 12.93, 13.23, 14.25, 14.133, 14.262, 15.1, 17.34, 20.5, 20.56, 21.13, 23.12, 25.26, 27.101, 39.5, 41.2, 41.50, 43.274, 44.38, 46.9, 65.29, 65.82, 65.129, 65.22, 66.21, 66.171, 66.220, 72.12, 81.62, 81.74, 81.94, 81.95, 82.17, 85.19, 85.98, 88.6, 88.14, 88.27, 89.51, 89.114, 101.10, 103.6, 103.42, 105.9, 126.19, 126.47, 126.90, 130.24, 130.44, 130.57, 130.64, 130.74, 130.85, 130.96, 130.97, 130.115, 130.153, 140.8, 142.23, 146.5, 147.6, 147.17, 147.34, 148.114, 149.39, 152.18, 152.39, 152.67, 156.43, 159.16, 164.41, 164.51, 178.43, 178.59, 178.64
Alcaide, Mario 14.129, 41.27, 61.6, 65.430, 66.61, 86.2, 106.2, 107.17, 117.45, 119.7, 152.45, 152.46, 152.47, 152.48, 170.61
Alda, Anthony 41.109
Alden, Eric 97.10, 177.39
Alden, Norman 3.143, 3.164, 12.67, 14.41, 14.74, 24.7, 31.46, 39.18, 63.16, 65.450, 65.452, 65.485, 65.597, 76.45, 83.12, 89.118, 93, 93.222, 93.224, 93.226, 125, 130.155, 151.17, 157.7, 174.4
Alderman, John 65.119, 76.30, 164.72, 164.93
Alders, James 41.91
Alderson, Erville 97.27, 124.63, 124.75
Alderson, John 13.24, 15, 25.22, 25.24, 25.36, 27.11, 34.40, 36.21, 43.298, 43.341, 43.345, 43.353, 63.21, 63.23, 65.11, 65.62, 65.291, 66.172, 66.216, 85.8, 96.20, 96.38, 105.50, 148.190, 152.19, 152.77, 170.66, 178.6
Aldon, Mari 14.232, 44.26, 85.26, 102.30, 148.45, 148.147, 162.128, 173.16
Aldredge, Charles 97.196
Aldredge, John 169.56
Aldridge, Victoria 130.1
Aldridge, Virginia 27.45, 162.37
Alejandro, Miguel 71.89
Aleong, Aki 25.6, 93.177, 161.157, 163.3
Aletter, Frank 123.7, 168.25
Alexander, Clarke 66.75, 105.67
Alexander, Denise 144.5, 161.9
Alexander, Dick 6.53, 23.24, 60.15, 60.18, 96.119, 97.26, 97.41, 97.126, 124.14, 124.18, 124.49, 124.50, 130.68
Alexander, George 25.11
Alexander, Jeff 43.81
Alexander, Jim 169.85, 169.89, 170.61
Alexander, Newell 96.168, 163.82
Alexander, Nick 151.14
Alexander, Richard 130.83, 169.29
Alexander, Tommy 65.350
Alford, Phillip 161.221
Ali, Hadji 43.94
Alish, Ben 70.21
Allan, Lane 39.5
Allen, Barbara Jo 105.45, 105.59
Allen, Chad 48
Allen, Corey 39.16, 65.99, 66.29, 89.127, 98.14, 126.17, 127.75, 129.17, 145.30, 156.18
Allen, Dale 129.75
Allen, David 28.1
Allen, Elizabeth 71.45, 144.27, 148.122
Allen, Gary 152.9, 175.1
Allen, Joel 169.69
Allen, Jonelle 48
Allen, MacKenzie 118.5
Allen, Mark 14.17, 51.14, 65.207, 83.2, 84.18, 101.25, 102.10, 122.25, 131.25, 157, 164.46, 164.65, 164.74
Allen, Marty 12.92
Allen, Mel F. 12.37, 130.90
Allen, Rex 56, 106.20
Allen, Ricky 141.45, 152.9

Allen, Sage 110.3
Allen, Sian Barbara 5.22, 14.421, 65.551, 65.552, 65.553
Allen, Ta-Ronce 83.17, 83.62
Allen, Todd 120.47
Allen, Tyreese 163.75, 163.83
Allen, Valerie 8.90, 14.169, 65.263, 113, 152.55, 152.56, 152.57
Allen, Vernett 157, 157.6
Alley, Jack 96.149
Allin, Henry 130.150
Allison, Jean 4.26, 4.36, 8.98, 14.26, 21.25, 21.33, 21.62, 25.37, 25.55, 65.510, 65.604, 66.20, 69.6, 79.16, 85.85, 88.3, 88.12, 89.23, 93.208, 105.35, 117.16, 126.27, 130.92, 131.23, 133.8, 148.135, 150.8, 155.80, 156.45, 164.46, 164.85, 165.4
Allman, Elvia 162.203, 162.248
Allman, Sheldon 14.152, 21.54, 27.76, 27.78, 39.19, 41.62, 41.116, 43.198, 43.317, 65.143, 65.290, 65.317, 65.362, 65.463, 65.475, 85.121, 89.93, 89.112, 89.130, 96.30, 96.31, 105.87, 127.62, 129.49, 129.78, 151.25
Allport, Christopher 28.4
Allyn, Laurie 177.51
Allyn, William 78.50
Allyson, Beverly 98.26
Allyson, June 178.121
Allyson, Mark 49.1
Alman, Sheldon 157.14, 157.15
Almanzar, James 30.7, 65.401, 65.416, 65.439, 65.461, 65.492, 65.525, 70.1, 70.3, 70.6, 70.19, 71.16, 71.17, 71.25, 76.6, 76.17, 107.9, 151.11
Alonzo, John 27.81, 27.83, 46.9, 151.22, 170.30, 170.51
Alper, Murray 141.15, 169.1, 169.22, 169.30, 169.63
Alpert, David 6.28, 6.36
Altman, Jeffrey 176.4
Alton, Kenneth 65.45, 66.10, 145.28
Alton, Mike 163.75
Alu, Al 24.12
Alvar, John 41.70
Alvarado, Don 73.39
Alvarado, Gina 24.11
Alvarez, Abraham 1.14
Alverson, Dave 120.4
Alvin, John 21.47, 73.31, 97.14, 97.35, 97.50, 97.74, 97.93, 126.68, 126.109, 130.124, 141.15, 141.63, 148.66
Alyn, Kirk 6.19, 6.32, 23.39, 23.40
Alzamora, Amanda 43.101
Alzamora, Armand 14.16, 20.37, 51.14, 89.134, 92.22, 93.160, 105.75, 112.2, 148.92, 162.152, 162.242, 167.17
Amargo, Henry 130.82
Ameche, Don 5.25
Amendola, Tony 90.7
American Horse, George 59.3
Ames, Allyson 65.327, 105.115, 144.16, 161.17, 162.262
Ames, Amanda 130.76, 130.89, 130.142
Ames, Cindy 152.69
Ames, Ed 41, 65.640, 128.1, 130.147, 157.14, 157.15
Ames, Florenz 20.11, 65.65
Ames, Heather 8.70, 119.2, 161.97
Ames, Joyce 65.510
Ames, Judith 20.1, 25.4, 25.57, 29.21, 93.119, 103.34, 148.5, 148.44, 152.32, 156.14, 156.23, 162.33, 162.56, 164.25, 164.33, 178.51, 178.63
Ames, Leon 106.16
Ames, Lionel 138.58, 148.41
Ames, Rachel 85.43, 93.167, 142.20, 142.21, 161.191, 162.142, 162.235, 162.250
Amos, John 14.431
Amos, Patrick 163.53
Amsterdam, Morey 65.95, 66.54, 78.56
Anakorita 14.357, 41.164
Andelius, Anders 170.62

Andelman, Julie 83.33
Anders, Dusty 25.53, 93.171
Anders, James 31.9
Anders, Luana 29.15, 89.74, 96.56, 126.79, 129.7, 130.19, 146.38
Anders, Merry 20.44, 21.39, 21.44, 27.30, 27.70, 43.239, 43.253, 65.542, 65.543, 105.74, 105.82, 105.94, 105.115, 146.1, 146.46, 148.84, 161.61
Anders, Richard 9.11, 71.67
Anders, Rudolph 74.29, 127.20
Anderson, Anne 21.11, 89.35
Anderson, Audley 141.47
Anderson, Barbara 14.431, 86.50, 132.12, 132.23, 161.127
Anderson, Bill 5.33
Anderson, Bridgette 62
Anderson, Christian 14.311, 170.15
Anderson, Dame Judith 162.85
Anderson, Deke 1.11
Anderson, Donna J. 65.340, 157
Anderson, Ernie 125.2
Anderson, Herbert 41.112, 65.336, 126.158
Anderson, James 3.48, 14.134, 17.18, 17.37, 25.61, 32.107, 32.114, 32.134, 32.143, 34.9, 34.37, 39.18, 51.3, 55.16, 60.43, 60.45, 63.5, 65.12, 65.248, 65.345, 65.384, 65.416, 65.442, 65.443, 65.457, 66.133, 66.142, 73.35, 76.10, 77.11, 85.19, 85.34, 85.65, 85.75, 85.105, 85.113, 89.83, 89.112, 92.6, 93.224, 105.103, 108.19, 126.8, 126.79, 126.91, 126.176, 129.35, 130.63, 145.7, 151.3, 152.30, 152.53, 152.72, 161.11, 165.2, 178.15, 178.18
Anderson, Jim 178.107
Anderson, Joel 48.69
Anderson, John 8.87, 9.12, 12.3, 12.13, 13.20, 14.75, 14.137, 14.332, 19.12, 21.36, 24.5, 25.45, 27.88, 30.7, 43.199, 43.286, 49.10, 55.5, 65.96, 65.124, 65.163, 65.288, 65.392, 65.395, 65.396, 65.428, 65.498, 65.502, 65.532, 65.584, 66.12, 66.35, 66.53, 66.79, 69.5, 69.8, 70.23, 70.33, 76.34, 79.33, 83.4, 83.34, 84.2, 85.36, 85.83, 85.101, 88.8, 88.16, 88.28, 89.64, 89.98, 92.30, 93, 93.100, 93.195, 93.202, 93.223, 93.224, 93.225, 93.226, 96.28, 101.2, 102.34, 103.41, 117.7, 117.8, 119.4, 123.3, 126.166, 126.197, 127.32, 128.9, 130.17, 130.19, 130.29, 130.41, 130.55, 130.56, 130.69, 130.95, 130.115, 130.143, 130.157, 130.167, 132.21, 133.22, 133.36, 144.9, 144.22, 148.50, 148.99, 148.182, 149.63, 156.9, 156.67, 161.4, 161.93, 161.113, 161.125, 161.158, 161.212, 164.66, 165.2, 173.30, 178.38, 178.129
Anderson, Loni 59.5
Anderson, Mabel 14.235
Anderson, Mary 25.52, 89.152, 155.13, 157.16
Anderson, Melissa Sue 96
Anderson, Merry 14.29
Anderson, Michael, Jr. 92.3, 107, 144.14
Anderson, Richard 5.14, 12.30, 12.68, 12.80, 12.94, 12.104, 14.279, 24.1, 30.2, 41.133, 43.319, 65.350, 65.504, 65.614, 65.615, 88.29, 128.5, 130.25, 130.67, 130.90, 130.92, 130.140, 130.164, 142.2, 162.65, 164.81, 164.87, 170.73, 178.28, 178.72, 179.49, 179.50, 179.51, 179.52
Anderson, Richard Dean 91
Anderson, Robert G. "Bob" 8.9, 21.57, 27.73, 27.94, 41.14, 41.81, 43.342, 43.425, 51.32, 52.4, 54.22, 54.25, 65.1, 65.197, 66.73, 77.13, 92.24, 98.89, 93.116, 101.6, 108.11, 108.23, 122.26, 126.98, 128.8, 134.1, 145.13, 148.74, 148.165, 152.69, 156.18, 159.10, 159.30, 162.60, 162.185, 167 178.5, 178.26
Anderson, S. Newton 14.219, 14.220, 14.323, 33, 105.16, 161.25
Anderson, Sam 1.19
Anderson, Stuart 14.276, 86.37, 161.104, 161.118
Anderson, Susan 152.8
Anderson, Warner 43.171

Personnel Index

Andes, Keith 17.16, 41.75, 41.76, 43.307, 65.590, 66.164, 130.133
Andre, Annette 63.24
Andre, Dorothy 135.80
Andre, E.J. 12.58, 14.136, 14.368, 28.11, 39.16, 41.56, 43.371, 65.463, 65.571, 71.81, 76.4, 84.26, 86.42, 92.33, 96.35, 96.45, 96.66, 96.156, 96.157, 96.172, 112.9, 126.114, 132.6, 139.14, 139.15, 151.7, 161.20, 161.82, 162.130, 162.244, 166.18, 170.14, 170.82, 176.4
Andre, Tommy 21.16
Andrece, Alyce 14.324
Andrece, Rhae 14.324
Andres, Stanley 141.11
Andrews, Ben 41.101
Andrews, Brian 83.14
Andrews, Edward 5.2, 7.7, 14.116, 14.393, 27.3, 55.24, 63.18, 65.386, 94.25, 117.11, 126.85, 126.125, 170.49
Andrews, Mark 85.85
Andrews, Nancy 121.1
Andrews, Stanley 3.46, 3.61, 3.101, 3.163, 6.9, 6.15, 6.26, 6.28, 6.36, 6.40, 6.56, 6.64, 6.73, 6.77, 6.81, 23.7, 23.12, 23.18, 23.24, 23.37, 23.38, 31.5, 31.11, 32.28, 32.34, 35.3, 35.3, 35.12, 43, 57.9, 60.7, 60.8, 60.23, 60.24, 60.62, 60.64, 60.66, 60.70, 60.76, 60.78, 73.40, 80.24, 81.11, 81.17, 93.32, 97.10, 97.24, 97.59, 97.75, 97.87, 97.89, 97.150, 105.5, 105.20, 124.12, 124.19, 124.20, 124.21, 12.46, 124.48, 124.53, 124.55, 124.60, 124.64, 124.67, 124.71, 124.74, 124.75, 124.76, 124.77, 124.78, 135.2, 141.8, 141.28, 141.29, 145.24, 147.3, 147.8, 147.19, 147.23, 158.7, 158.9, 169.83, 169.99
Andrews, Tige 7.9, 12.46, 49.6, 65.59, 65.460, 179.54
Andrews, Tod 43.193, 43.385, 55.6, 65.231, 126.113
Andriane, Marayat 12.56
Angarola, Richard 14.120, 30.5, 41.107, 41.117, 43.159, 43.444, 65.510, 71.8, 75.2, 102.17, 170.94
Angel, Heather 63.26, 89.107
Angel, Joe 158.3, 158.4, 158.5, 158.12
Angela, Mary 65.508, 70.15, 70.20
Angell, Christopher 80.6, 80.34
Angelo, Jody 34.25
Angus, Forbes 67.3, 67.13
Aniston, John 161.184
Ankers, Evelyn 27.46
Ankrum, Morris 3.32, 3.138, 3.140, 3.143, 15.3, 21.50, 27.6, 27.49, 27.75, 35.16, 35.18, 35.36, 43.146, 56.17, 65.192, 66.36, 73.9, 73.38, 78.19, 93.14, 102.17, 105.13, 105.69, 114.18, 126.17, 126.65, 130.19, 130.94, 145.34, 146.3, 146.34, 148.147, 152.58, 155.4, 155.57, 158.50, 158.52, 162.43
Anna-Lisa 13, 14.44, 21.7, 43.343, 65.197, 85.38, 105.34, 146.12, 162.113
Annese, Frank 118.9
Annie O'Connell 22
Ansara, Michael 3.78, 7.1, 17.5, 20, 26, 36.26, 41.53, 41.69, 56.8, 65.401, 65.431, 68.1, 70.15, 71.53, 76.14, 84.86, 88, 97.74, 97.80, 101.18, 109.10, 126.142, 126.145, 126.180, 127.39, 130.21, 130.37, 132.27, 148.180, 161.90, 161.131, 162.130, 162.216, 165.12, 168.8, 178.88
Anthony, Bob G. 53.30
Anthony, Joseph 1.11
Anthony, Larry 170.47
Anthony, Lee 43.114
Anthony, Mark 43.356, 43.366
Anthony, Wayne 65.640
Anton, Ronny 162.65
Antonio, Jim 5.26, 96.141
Antonio, Lou 14.296, 24.19, 65.390, 65.448, 65.469, 65.481, 65.484, 66.124, 70.35, 70.47, 132.26, 161.111

Antrim, Harry 6.41, 34.4, 66.116, 89.79, 89.83, 126.28, 145.37, 146.22, 149.51, 149.61, 169.105
Anzel, Hy 147.2
Apesanahkwat 65.640
Apone, John 65.184, 165.6
Applegate, Christine 53.4
Applegate, Fred 48.98
Applegate, Royce D. 26, 94.34, 96.164, 120.14
Aragon, Tita 3.87, 6.71, 78.62
Arana, Tomas 90.15
Arau, Alfonso 14.408, 65.556
Arbizu, Linda 94.37
Arbus, Allan 19.5, 70.31
Archer, Anne 5.26, 96.16
Archer, John 14.88, 14.245, 14.290, 20.61, 25.11, 25.27, 27.27, 27.69, 34.54, 85.8, 105.110, 105.111, 131.23, 145.39, 148.118, 148.147, 148.190, 149.21, 151.15, 161.135, 162.133, 162.237, 178.46
Archibek, Ben 41.135
Arco, Victor 83.19
Arden, Eve 86.11
Ardoin, Voorhies J. 129.53, 129.78
Ardwin, V.J. 117.19
Arevalo, Carlos 129.14
Argenziano, Carmen 163.17
Ari, Ben 17.29, 17.30
Arin, Christian 91.9
Arizona 3, 15, 19, 20, 44, 56, 71, 79, 112, 141, 155
Arlen, Richard 8.44, 8.88, 17.7, 24.9, 89.20, 89.52, 89.103, 164.18, 173.29
Arlen, Roxanne 27.94, 125.2
Arlen, Steve 177.44
Armagnac, Gary 1.24, 118.7
Armand, John 170.69
Arms, Russell 22.36, 65.212, 66.65, 66.158, 126.47, 126.102, 126.166
Armstrong, Dick 96.77
Armstrong, Herb 19.16, 51.24, 65.568, 130.94
Armstrong, R.G. 5.27, 8.97, 12.8, 13.4, 14.8, 14.76, 14.234, 21.3, 25.26, 27.68, 27.77, 30.4, 38.6, 41.77, 41.105, 43.420, 55.11, 63.12, 65.243, 65.296, 65.368, 65.403, 65.449, 66.38, 69.1, 70.26, 71.83, 77.3, 84.4, 85.39, 85.53, 85.75, 85.102, 89.17, 89.25, 93.209, 105.48, 105.74, 126.14, 126.49, 126.120, 126.207, 130.1, 146.26, 146.33, 148.188, 149.12, 152.10, 152.26, 153, 161.22, 161.148, 162.175, 162.197, 164.45, 165.2, 168.17, 178.71
Armstrong, R.L. 65.611, 83.61
Armstrong, Robert 4.34, 20.8, 27.6, 29.25, 66.43, 85.48, 89.56, 89.88, 126.81, 128.5, 146.58, 148.38, 148.156, 156.46, 158.65, 162.81
Armstrong, Todd 65.461, 65.470, 109.8
Armstrong, Vaughn 1.15
Arnaz, Desi 106.2
Arner, Gwen 111
Arness, James 65, 65.636, 65.637, 65.638, 65.639, 65.640, 75, 97.33
Arness, Jenny Lee 65.319, 65.354
Arness, Virginia 65.13
Arngrim, Allison 95.8, 96
Arngrim, Stefan 65.405, 70.4, 161.141
Arnold, Bert 81.10, 97.43, 97.61, 97.62
Arnold, Danny 65.600
Arnold, Joan 169.59
Arnold, Lane 97.23
Arnold, Larry 54.9
Arnold, Phil 12.47, 35.1, 35.2, 35.5, 35.8, 35.9, 35.11, 35.12, 35.13, 35.16, 35.19, 35.23, 35.24, 35.27, 35.28, 35.30, 35.31, 35.32, 35.35, 35.36, 35.38, 121.19, 162.82
Arnold, Rick 126.20
Arnt, Charles 13.9, 25.50, 105.112, 130.1, 146.62, 152.30, 152.73
Arquette, Cliff 52.64
Arquette, Lewis 120.4, 120.9
Arranga, Irene 120.55

Arrants, Rod 120.54
Arrants, Wayne 120.37
Arroya, Roger 14.146
Arthur, Indus 161.125, 170.22
Arthur, Jean 65.365
Arthur, Karen 170.71
Arthur, Louise 43.20, 93.25, 162.206
Arthur, Maureen 17.19
Arthur, Robert 97.45, 97.79, 97.86, 141.9
Arthurs, Douglas H. 100.9
Arvan, Jan 3.90, 3.106, 3.136, 3.145, 20.43, 38.5, 51.7, 54.17, 64.7, 65.116, 71.6, 77.14, 81.15, 84.31, 86.22, 121.23, 126.85, 129.71, 141.70, 156.36, 161.15, 162.117, 162.132, 164.60, 164.94, 179.3, 179.4, 179.5, 179.10
Arvin, William 43.300, 61.6, 65.341
Asch, Nancy 156.68
Ashdown, Isa 6.18, 169.3, 169.16, 169.49, 169.85
Ashdown, Nadene 97.156, 169.55
Ashe, Eve Brent 10.4
Ashe, Martin 12.69, 14.312, 76.18
Ashely, Joel 41.80
Ashkenazy, Irvin 42, 141.56
Ashley, Edward 14.27, 78.52, 97.135, 105.69, 105.76, 152.44
Ashley, Elizabeth 106.1, 144.30
Ashley, Joel 3.70, 6.47, 6.80, 13.10, 15.14, 15.18, 32.138, 32.141, 65.25, 65.34, 65.50, 65.154, 65.208, 66.50, 66.86, 77.12, 97.201, 129.41, 147.13, 162.54, 178.44
Ashley, John 43.218, 44.2, 56.34, 77.1, 162.105, 162.205, 170.37
Ashley, Mary 170.65
Ashley, Peter 65.264
Ashton, Joseph 48.87
Askew, Luke 9.12, 14.388, 71.42, 75.21, 83.63
Askin, Leon 41.142, 129.6
Asner, Edward 24.23, 65.349, 65.417, 70.14, 70.34, 76.46, 101.7, 117.39, 144.30, 161.27, 170.78
Assan, Ratna 46.13
Asselin, Armand 120.21
Astin, John 1.1, 1.3, 1.5, 1.8, 1.13, 1.26, 1.27, 14.346, 43.392, 46.12, 65.445, 105.28, 106.24, 170.47
Astor, David 132.10
Astor, Mary 126.67, 178.28
Aten, Laurence 65.420
Ates, Roscoe 3.93, 6.56, 6.66, 22.29, 32.73, 89.24, 89.26, 89.54, 104, 105.43, 105.81, 129.54, 146.63, 148.104, 148.128, 162.39, 166.9
Atherton, William 26
Atienza, Edward 117.9
Atkins, Suanne 53.10
Atkins, Tom 163.13
Atkinson, Keith 111.5
Atterbury, Ellen 66.169, 134.4
Atterbury, Malcolm 14.14, 14.230, 41.70, 57.51, 63.34, 65.1, 65.18, 65.41, 65.55, 65.242, 65.267, 65.549, 66.83, 86.50, 96.125, 101.13, 102.15, 126.6, 126.205, 142.35, 149.6, 152.58, 156.16, 162, 162.17, 165.5, 165.7
Attlinger, Richard 129.59
Atwater, Barry 8.11, 13.11, 13.18, 21.16, 27.63, 27.64, 51.15, 54.4, 54.9, 65.17, 65.143, 65.178, 65.499, 66.18, 83.33, 84.18, 89.155, 127.29, 127.76, 131.38, 140.30, 170.90, 178.33
Atwater, Edith 14.362, 92.10, 92.11
Atwater, G.B. 14.214, 126.184, 126.217, 162.263
Aubrey, Danielle 14.224, 85.99, 162.82
Aubuchon, Jacques 7.9, 8.18, 27.76, 41.18, 52.41, 65.35, 65.43, 65.367, 65.635, 66.66, 66.114, 66.170, 74.18, 79.21, 83.56, 83.57, 83.58, 83.59, 86.20, 86.52, 88.17, 102.27, 105.98, 114.10, 117.16, 123.5, 126.34, 126.109, 129.18, 146.68, 156.16, 156.23, 161.31, 164.30, 168.16, 178.49
Audley, Eleanor 12.14, 66.95, 66.170, 66.211, 78.12, 102.37, 121.2, 121.4, 121.16, 121.18, 162.47, 162.154, 162.240

Personnel Index

Auer, Florence 169.45
August, Adele 27.2
Augustein, Ira 84.46
Augustus, Wilhelm 129.58
Austin, Al 164.94
Austin, Blackie 158.43, 158.44, 158.73, 164.49
Austin, Carmen 27.59, 65.460
Austin, Jack 158.32, 158.33, 158.35
Austin, Jamie 163.63
Austin, Pamela 89.154, 161.37, 161.135, 162.227, 170.20
Auther, Ana 91.8, 177.16
Autry, Gene 60
Avalon, Frankie 126.149
Avalos, Luis 110
Avenetti, Phillip 14.430
Avery, Brian 161.135
Avery, Phyllis 20.41, 41.90, 44.22, 66.182, 85.35, 85.110, 126.21, 130.52, 150.9, 156.10, 161.21, 178.4
Avery, Tol 14.100, 14.114, 14.149, 14.282, 14.360, 21.2, 21.65, 34.21, 34.40, 43.349, 43.360, 52.42, 76.11, 81.52, 81.57, 89.23, 105.3, 105.17, 105.66, 105.84, 105.103, 105.117, 125.12, 146.28, 148.168, 151.6, 161.21, 161.118, 170.91, 170.103
Avery, Val 14.41, 41.34, 65.91, 65.370, 65.432, 65.495, 66.143, 84.6, 86.41, 112.19, 112.23, 126.82, 148.144, 161.113, 170.20, 170.54, 170.57, 178.35
Avila, Cynthia 176.3
Avonde, Richard 3.84, 18.18, 31.16, 32.83, 43.26, 60.82, 60.87, 73.23, 78.15, 78.23, 81.41, 81.90, 81.98, 93.61, 97.101, 97.113, 97.125, 97.179, 124.76, 135.41, 135.48, 135.53, 138.21, 145.19, 147.20, 148.126, 169.17, 169.61
Axton, Hoyt 14.195, 45.3, 76.4
Ayars, Ann 107.25, 161.38
Ayer, Eleanor 126.17
Ayres, John 138.56, 138.72, 138.78
Ayres, Lew 12.68, 12.89, 65.441, 70.18, 83.51, 85.102, 95.3, 106.9, 118.6, 178.4, 178.40, 178.139

Babatunde, Obba 1.15
Babcock, Barbara 10.13, 48
Baca, Claudia 109.3
Baccala, Donna 12.106, 30.23, 41.139, 65.457, 71.55
Backes, Alice 65.162, 65.332, 65.394, 84.44, 88.5, 130.56, 161.14, 162.256
Backman, George 41.30, 41.75, 41.76, 41.143
Backus, Jim 5.34, 41.102, 65.630, 105.115, 170.97
Bacon, Irving 85.25, 147.34, 162.47, 169.47, 169.97
Bacon, Margaret 65.467, 65.560
Baddeley, Hermione 96.67, 96.70, 96.107
Baer, Buddy 27.30, 31.35, 65.88, 66.8, 126.146, 141.59
Baer, John 57.71, 65.581, 103.14, 151.26, 156.9, 164.78, 169.13
Baer, Max 27.78, 27.79, 97.213, 146.67
Baer, Max, Jr. 105.86, 105.91
Baer, Parley 13,5, 14.62, 14.158, 14.225, 43.324, 52.14, 53.28, 55.17, 57.3, 63.39 ,66.89, 66.184, 66.193, 75.3, 83.5, 85.94, 86.55, 96.39, 96.133, 106.12, 116.26, 116.26, 125.2, 126.146, 130.34, 130.123, 151.5, 151.25, 152.42, 156.17, 161.3, 161.159, 162.168, 162.195, 162.235, 178.78
Bagdad, William 71.72
Baguez, Salvador 14.52, 14.229, 25.18, 32.69, 73.39, 97.77, 164.61
Bail, Chuck 8.61, 12.13, 12.20, 12.38, 12.42, 12.45, 14.320, 14.339, 65.234, 71.42, 71.50, 83.3, 152.35, 164.88
Bailes, Fred 80.9
Bailey, Blake 1.17
Bailey, G.W. 91.3
Bailey, Jack 65.433, 65.498, 107.26
Bailey, Mark 41.85

Bailey, Raymond 8.84, 13.7, 14.15, 14.100, 21.22, 65.11, 65.112, 66.57, 66.91, 85.68, 85.84, 108.33, 130.18, 152.76, 153.17, 160.2, 162.112, 162.162, 173.16, 178.18, 178.45, 178.69
Bailey, William 124.69
Bailey-Gates, Charles 1.21
Bain, Barbara 51.26, 162.241
Bain, Sherry 9.1
Baine, Enid 93.141
Baines, Walter 53.24
Bair, David 135.61
Baird, Jeanne 14.145, 114.11, 158.54
Baird, Jimmy 57, 89.35, 89.49, 97.197, 102.10, 105.55, 108.26, 126.106, 129.50, 157.12, 178.10
Baird, Maggie 163.25
Baird, Phillip 8.48, 155.60
Baird, Sharon 43.27
Bairtow, Scott 99, 100
Bakalyan, Richard 8.12, 17.24, 30.12, 44.10, 65.424, 65.498, 74.6, 79.22, 85.117, 89.131, 107.2, 127.58, 127.72, 149.14, 162.234, 164.54
Baker, Benny 27.32, 52.6, 52.19, 52.34, 89.125,103.31, 105.2
Baker, Diane 12.17, 14.258, 14.395, 106.14, 161.133, 161.209, 162.265
Baker, Don 177.8
Baker, Ed 49.8, 83.38, 83.39
Baker, Elsie 32.131, 32.137
Baker, Fay 66.57, 78.45, 93.88, 141.17
Baker, James 100.2
Baker, Joby 43.366, 52.46, 55.20, 65.269, 98.12, 162.164
Baker, Joe Don 12.103, 14.307, 65.409, 65.483, 71.95, 84.1, 84.32
Baker, Roy 89.34
Baker, Sharisse 163.38
Baker, Simon 67.8, 67.17
Baker, Tom 76.40, 161.139
Baker, Virginia 47.13, 65.117, 65.593
Bakewell, William 14.269, 32.58, 32.64, 42, 141.1, 148.57, 155.34, 161.142
Bakey, Ed 12.64, 12.79, 14.312, 14.331, 14.418, 30.22, 50.9, 63.15, 63.47, 65.450, 65.485, 65.566, 71.75, 71.82, 84.44
Bakke, Brenda 1.21, 110, 177.38
Bakken, Vicki 78.18
Bakkum, Andrea 48, 48.70
Bal, Henry K. 96.119
Bal, Jeanne 14.130, 131.44, 162.223
Balaban, Bob 91.9
Balaski, Belinda 37.12
Balding, Rebecca 120.11, 120.13, 120.33, 120.43
Balduzzi, Dick 70.1, 70.3, 70.7, 70.13, 70.28
Baldwin, Bill 161.166, 162.245
Baldwin, Janit 65.608
Baldwin, Stephen 91.2, 177
Baldwin, Walter 25.52, 65.430, 84.10
Balfour, Eric 48.21, 48.37
Balin, Ina 5.29, 14.208, 98.16, 144.3
Balk, Martin 3.130, 77.9
Ball, Betty 73.12
Ball, Robert 14.305, 14.349
Ballantine, Carl 86.52, 106.15
Ballard, Ray 4.36, 8.79, 86.22
Ballard, Shirley 14.58, 43.236, 127.64, 140.36, 144.8, 144.162, 168.4
Ballentine, Barbara 96.154
Ballew, Robert 65.397, 65.418
Balou, Marl 120.16
Balsam, Martin 66.40, 66.122, 126.2, 162.253, 178.90
Balson, Allison 95, 96
Bambara, Susan 48.40
Bamber, Judy 122.22
Bancheri, Christine 43.409
Bancroft, Anne 178.38
Bandit, Sierra 65.626

Bane, Holly 97.21, 97.35, 97.50
Bane, Laurence 96.158, 96.159
Bangert, Johnny 162.89
Bank, Douglas 66.85
Banke, Richard 40
Banks, Carl 1.27
Banks, Emily 36.6, 43.429, 170.91
Banks, Joan 133.35, 164.2, 178.65
Banks, Jonathan 96.128, 163.25
Banks, Zack 170.58
Banner, Jill 24.16, 24.17
Banner, John 3.148, 5.36, 29.1, 97.39, 103.36, 141.1, 161.22, 168.23
Bannon, Jack 41.93, 41.106, 41.125, 70.37, 84.2
Bannon, Jim 2, 3.109, 6.66, 6.67, 8.11, 22.16, 43.321, 57.66, 57.68, 60.16, 60.17, 60.71, 60.76, 77.6, 81.29, 93.82, 93.121, 97.37, 97.72, 97.201, 97.212, 97.218, 105.6, 124.4, 124.7, 124.21, 124.22, 124.60, 124.66, 124.72, 124.77, 138.78, 148.32, 148.83, 162.50, 168.23, 169.57, 179.19
Barab, Nira 112.11
Baragrey, John 29.23
Baral, Eileen 12.63, 14.209, 84.45, 162.264, 162.270
Barash, Olivia 96.152, 96.153
Barclay, Jered 14.119, 21.63, 34.66, 39.4, 89.114, 126.51
Barcroft, Roy 2.19, 2.25, 6.1, 6.10, 6.51, 6.58, 6.59, 6.61, 6.68, 6.72, 14.207, 14.222, 30.2, 31.23, 35.29, 35.33, 43.106, 43.315, 43.363, 44.7, 51.7, 55.2, 55.8, 57.16, 64.1, 65.199, 65.206, 65.216, 65.286, 65.323, 65.350, 65.361, 65.365, 65.375, 65.431, 65.440, 65.469, 65.482, 66.5, 66.28, 66.73, 66.77, 66.139, 66.146, 66.163, 66.173, 66.207, 66.224, 73.36, 76.37, 81.54, 81.64, 85.55, 85.60, 86.9, 86.12, 89.137, 93.15, 93.91, 93.114, 97.182, 97.200, 97.215, 101.17, 103.46, 105.10, 105.36, 108.27, 126.88, 126.143, 126.153, 126.208,130.141, 132.25, 133.12, 140.15, 148.45, 148.78, 148.114, 152.45, 152.46, 155.62, 156.11, 156.66, 158.28, 158.30, 158.44, 158.64, 158.74, 161.22, 161.137, 164.27, 164.88, 170.14, 178.20, 178.106, 178.123
Bard, Katherine 12.8, 65.113, 130.24
Bardette, Trevor 14.106, 14.139, 20.4, 20.35, 21.58, 27.10, 27.23, 27.86, 27.87, 27.102, 54.17, 65.159, 65.198, 65.439, 65.450, 65.527, 66.97, 66.120, 66.153, 74.3, 78.71, 85.80, 93, 93.26, 93.54, 93.109, 93.114, 93.151, 93.152, 93.153, 93.155, 93.156, 93.157, 93.161, 93.164, 93.170, 93.174, 93.176, 93.178, 93.179, 93.180, 93.181, 93.183, 93.187, 93.188, 93.189, 93.190, 93.194, 93.195, 93.200, 93.204, 93.206, 93.208, 93.209, 93.211, 93.213, 93.216, 93.219, 93.222, 97.203, 97.209, 101.10, 103.39, 105.8, 105.109, 108.18, 127.17, 127.58, 129.34, 129.51, 133.3, 148.81, 152.26, 156.17, 156.53, 160.23, 162.181, 162.210, 162.224, 178.16
Bari, Lynn 21.19, 43.290, 88.21, 113.5, 119.1
Barjac, Sophie 16
Barker, Bob 14.38
Barker, Debbie 163.23
Barkley, Lucille 43.45
Barnes, George 68.31
Barnes, Gordon 35.10, 81.10, 141.45
Barnes, Joanna 5.17, 5.29, 27.41, 27.54, 34.19, 51.24, 66.205, 85.78, 85.93, 102.37, 105.4, 105.22, 105.29, 105.77, 105.83, 142.22
Barnes, Phil 54.24
Barnes, Rayford 1.1, 1.12, 3.147, 3.163, 8.91, 12.47, 12.79, 12.93, 14.429, 30.8, 30.19, 34.5, 41.67, 43.372, 44.1, 57.34, 63.2, 63.40, 65.175, 65.217, 65.222, 65.260, 65.313, 65.324, 65.344, 65.493, 65.562, 66.46, 66.53, 66.125, 66.138, 66.158, 66.224, 71.19, 71.60, 76.12, 83.33, 84.2, 85.6, 85.48, 85.63, 85.91, 86.21, 88.5, 93, 93.190, 93.200, 93.211, 93.223, 93.224, 93.225, 93.226,

96.54, 105.110, 105.111, 112.10, 112.23, 114.1, 116.18, 126.100, 135.60, 135.63, 147.47, 155.13, 157.26, 158.13, 158.16, 158.55, 158.59, 161.78, 161.106, 168.25, 169.76
Barnes, Walter 5.10, 8.18, 14.338, 14.354, 14.378, 14.392, 21.4, 27.44, 24.6, 43.124, 65.114, 65.123, 66.32, 71.81, 83.27, 133.16, 178.27, 178.51
Barnett, Griff 73.31, 97.131
Barnett, Joseph 162.104
Barnett, Vince 30.12, 147.43
Baron, Lita 43.339, 43.392, 56.30, 152.59, 152.60, 152.61, 152.64
Barondes, Elizabeth 1.14
Barratt, Robert H. 129.60
Barreto, Gil 35.7
Barrett Fears 11
Barrett, Barbara 134.10
Barrett, Claudia 23.5, 23.11, 25.16, 32.90, 32.128, 34.57, 35.9, 35.19, 43.63, 43.137, 57.26, 73.14, 97.102, 97.144, 133.28, 135.70, 135.72, 135.76, 145.34, 148.27, 156.30, 169.86
Barrett, Curt 141.54
Barrett, Edith 114.22
Barrett, Katie 14.126
Barrett, Leslie 102.34, 105.66
Barrett, Majel 14.87, 14.224, 70.7
Barrett, Stan 72.6
Barrett, Toni 3.115
Barrett, Tony 3.41
Barrey, Christopher 65.331
Barrie, Barbara 126.200, 161.22
Barrier, Edgar 20.11, 127.22, 127.46, 179.66, 179.67, 179.68, 179.69
Barrier, Ernestine 8.37, 34.16
Barrier, Michael 65.265
Barringer, Stephen 85.85, 85.101
Barron, Baynes 3.91, 6.47, 6.63, 6.65, 6.80, 14.261, 31.34, 43.57, 65.455, 77.21, 81.6, 81.28, 85.26, 97.210, 97.211, 129.74, 130.49, 130.65, 141.30, 141.32, 147.15, 147.16, 147.36, 148.90, 148.180, 158.33, 158.35, 159.35, 169.107
Barron, Jim 68.33
Barron, Ophelia 158.31, 158.35
Barron, Richard 32.65, 32.66
Barrows, George 52.38, 55.9, 97.144, 97.206, 145.17, 152.10, 169.39, 169.67, 169.106
Barry, Betty 8.97
Barry, Don "Red" 7.13, 8.49, 14.182, 14.238, 21.18, 21.61, 27.54, 30.21, 34.13, 34.18, 34.52, 34.54, 41.132, 50.3, 52.2, 65.285, 65.580, 66.46, 85.9, 85.117, 86.45, 89.33, 89.65, 89.98, 89.122, 92.28, 96.53, 96.71, 96.100, 96.101, 96.103, 96.108, 105.52, 105.56, 105.77, 105.83, 105.101, 121.19, 126.79, 138.55, 145.37, 146.10, 146.25, 146.31, 146.41, 161.25, 161.40, 161.64, 161.95, 161.144, 161.178, 161.197, 168.9, 170.56, 170.97
Barry, Eleanor 43.167
Barry, Fern 105.6, 130.32, 130.60
Barry, Gene 8, 59.4, 120.23
Barry, Ivor 14.233, 41.64, 41.92, 41.125, 53.15, 86.43
Barry, Joe 78.72
Barry, Patricia 5.22, 21.32, 46.5, 55.14, 63.17, 65.102, 65.200, 65.509, 71.12, 76.29, 85.5, 105.39, 105.44, 117.4, 117.18, 126.44, 126.135, 130.30, 130.32, 130.64, 146.33, 148.123, 149.40, 161.18, 173.23, 178.139
Barrymore, John Blythe 83.56, 83.57, 83.58, 83.59
Barrymore, John Drew 49.1, 65.359, 65.378, 83.30, 132.1, 132.2, 170.9
Barrymore, John, Jr. 126.30, 126.184, 162.34
Barselow, Paul 53.13, 65.370, 126.80, 126.95, 148.167, 161.7, 170.92
Bart, Anthony 39.3
Bartell, Dick 164.78
Bartell, Harry 17.4, 65.29, 65.63, 65.295, 65.306,

65.337, 65.375, 65.401, 66.50, 66.79, 85.17, 127.31, 148.111, 152.78, 170.3, 170.19
Bartell, Richard 65.250, 126.124
Bartlett, Bennie 32.70, 32.104, 65.605
Bartlett, Bonnie 96, 96.4, 96.8, 96.13, 96.29, 96.120
Bartlett, Calvin 96.177, 161.50, 161.90
Bartlett, Martine 12.13, 161.115
Bartley, Bart 66.39
Bartold, Norman 65.585
Barton, Anne 13.9, 30.12, 44.51, 65.33, 65.133, 65.337, 65.346, 66.64, 85.25, 148.194, 178.22, 178.112
Barton, Dan 3.43, 27.37, 43.139, 66.110, 97.208, 127.50, 135.74, 135.78, 135.100, 152.42, 155.26, 156.15, 161.23, 178.22, 178.51, 178.64, 178.85
Barton, David 47.11
Barton, Dorie 90.17
Barton, Gloria 124.60
Barton, Gregg 2.9, 2.14, 6.2, 6.3, 6.7, 6.19, 6.28, 6.36, 6.52, 6.53, 6.63, 6.65, 6.66, 23.9, 23.19, 23.28, 23.29, 32.108, 32.115, 34.25, 35.16, 35.24, 25.39, 43.342, 57.72, 60.2, 60.3, 60.4, 60.6, 60.25, 60.26, 60.28, 60.30, 60.43, 60.45, 60.48, 60.51, 60.62, 60.66, 60.67, 60.68, 60.72, 60.73, 60.74, 60.77, 60.78, 60.88, 60.89, 60.90, 73.23, 77.14, 81.26, 81.53, 81.69, 81.90, 81.98, 85.50, 85.53, 85.84, 85.87, 93.31, 93.47, 93.110, 93.137, 97.59, 97.71, 97.166, 97.187, 97.194, 97.216, 105.81, 108.29, 124.2, 124.5, 124.15, 124.16, 124.40, 124.42, 124.44, 124.45, 124.49, 124.50, 124.59, 124.62, 124.67, 124.71, 124.77, 126.25, 129.24, 129.57, 135.1, 135.8, 135.12, 135.40, 135.42, 135.50, 135.94, 135.99, 138.7, 138.12, 141.3, 141.28, 141.29, 145.8, 147.21, 147.33, 147.39, 152.10, 152.53, 152.72, 158.6, 158.24, 158.26, 158.63, 162.196, 169.4, 169.23, 169.53, 169.74, 169.90, 169.111, 178.17
Barton, Irene 43.14, 43.119
Barton, James 55.23, 74.7, 130.51
Barton, Julian 159.14
Barton, Larry 65.422, 65.563
Barty, Billy 31.1, 31.2, 50.13, 95.5, 96.117, 126.92
Barzell, Wolfe 14.219, 14.220, 66.154, 126.34, 170.8, 179.40
Basch, Harry 41.120, 65.433, 109.8
Basehart, Richard 65.531, 75.5, 75.6, 75.7, 96.40, 126.91, 178.72
Baseleon, Michael 24.14, 70.35, 70.47, 71.88, 112.7
Basham, Tom 14.379, 161.188, 161.225
Baskin, Elya 163.71
Baskin, Tiny 17.37
Bass, Bobby 5.17, 7.3
Bassett, Jack 147.29
Bassett, Joseph 43.196, 44.48, 65.111, 66.9, 66.65, 93.217, 130.7, 130.63, 135.80, 135.82, 147.40, 172.2
Bassett, William H. 14.357, 24.23, 70.15, 70.26, 116.25, 170.72
Baster, George 93.97
Batanides, Arthur 14.31, 14.52, 30.5, 34.22, 41.160, 43.343, 44.29, 61.8, 65.345, 65.382, 101.14, 105.14, 126.32, 126.81, 130.143, 131.17, 131.39, 142.11, 155.9, 164.64, 170.8, 170.46, 170.80, 170.92, 179.53
Bateman, Charles 7.8, 14.166, 41.44, 43.315, 105.25, 126.22, 151.22, 159, 161.70, 173.29
Bateman, Jason 96
Bates, Jeanne 22.5, 28.11, 29.15, 65.6, 65.7, 66.56, 85.32, 93.197, 97.187, 108.28, 124.66, 126.6, 126.39, 129.7, 129.18, 129.39, 129.48, 129.58, 131.10, 141.66, 148.68, 148.96, 162.52, 162.81, 162.132, 162.138, 162.186
Batson, Susan 65.503
Battaglia, Rudy 72.17
Battista, Lloyd 14.341, 106.7
Baucom, Bill 6.58, 23.42, 804, 80.20, 80.30, 93.113, 158.73

Bauer, Jaime Lyn 177.34
Baumann, Ray 162.174
Baur, Elizabeth 41.161, 84
Baur, Marc 67.19
Bavier, Frances 97.159, 126.42, 146.41, 162.64
Baxley, Barbara 66.28, 66.112, 152.5
Baxley, Paul 22.33, 86.9, 105.1, 129.71, 149.12, 157.19, 161.64, 162.237, 162.256
Baxter, Alan 4.8, 14.298, 14.335, 17.29, 17.30, 21.23, 27.70, 34.56, 41.67, 44.28, 65.239, 65.307, 66.204, 92.23, 93.201, 98.7, 105.102, 107.14, 126.25, 129.33, 130.22, 146.57, 148.76, 149.36, 161.89, 161.152, 162.66, 170.33
Baxter, Anne 12.102, 36.5, 98.5, 131.4, 161.188, 162.53, 178.93
Baxter, George 93.68, 138.78, 169.99
Baxter, Joan 124.19
Baxter, John 8.52, 93.137, 93.166, 93.181
Bay, Susan 101.19
Bayati, Saadoren 71.58
Baylor, Hal 4.26, 7.6, 7.10, 8.73, 12.52, 14.24, 14.41, 14.84, 14.130, 14.179, 14.228, 14.244, 14.280, 14.300, 25.50, 25.69, 27.23, 27.67, 39.3, 41.9, 43.231, 43.349, 43.403, 44.61, 57.41, 63.4, 63.34, 64.10, 65.26, 65.330, 65.451, 65.576, 65.591, 65.616, 66.30, 66.210, 74.13, 77.22, 85.12, 85.50, 85.80, 85.110, 86.1, 86.18, 89.20, 89.150, 93.1, 93.2, 93.3, 93.103, 93.105, 93.107, 93.114, 97.54, 97.66, 97.70, 97.136, 97.142, 101.13, 121.8, 126.115, 126.125, 126.129, 126.210, 130.103, 132.6, 145.17, 148.184, 151.19, 152.42, 152.49, 158.34, 158.55, 158.59, 161.32, 161.76, 161.91, 161.92, 161.160, 162.19, 162.223, 168.5
Beach, Adam 99.8, 163.44
Beach, Guy 169.26
Beach, Michael 163.13
Beach, Richard 97.56
Beacham, Stephanie 91.1
Beaird, Barbara 43.144, 126.69, 126.101, 162.145
Beaird, Pamela 31.38, 57.30, 78.30, 108, 108.7, 169.104
Beal, John 4.27, 14.8
Bean, Orson 48
Bean, Roy 80
Beard, Betsy 91.1
Beard, James 112.14
Bearpaw, Cody 5.42
Beatty, Ned 65.626
Beaty, Clarence 158.21, 158.23, 158.28, 158.34
Beauchamp, Richard 181
Beaudine, Deka 48.6
Beaudine brothers 123
Beaumont, Chris 14.400
Beaumont, Hugh 73.5, 97.99, 108.1, 148.13, 161.135, 161.168, 161.188, 162.249
Beauvy, Nicolas 14.418, 161.166
Beaver, Jim 65.638, 65.639, 120.2, 177.1
Beaver, Terry 120.35
Beavers, Louise 145.11
Beban, Gary 12.102
Becher, John C. 93.123
Beck, Billy 17.48, 65.399
Beck, Bob 38.6
Beck, James 14.70, 14.102, 14.161, 17.36, 65.143, 72.6, 72.8, 79.21, 85.81, 85.99, 85.104, 117.16, 126.121, 141.64, 142.23, 148.188, 153, 161.84
Beck, Jennifer 53.12, 53.31, 120
Beck, John 14.340, 14.360, 65.510, 65.533, 65.633, 75.23, 84.41, 84.48, 112, 120.10, 120.21, 120.36, 163.77
Beck, Kimberly 161.116
Beck, Michael 163.60
Beck, Stanley 76.39
Beck, Steven 30.8
Beck, Vincent 5.6, 14.239, 14.240, 41.45, 65.390, 76.16, 170.93
Becker, Adam 164.81

Personnel Index

Becker, Ken 14.29, 65.250, 74.12, 89.36, 89.74, 102.28, 103.41, 147.49, 158.34, 164.59
Becker, Oliver 67.8, 67.21
Becker, Terry 14.104, 29.18, 65.25, 126.28, 126.183
Becker, Tony 96.103, 115, 163.72
Beckman, Henry 14.305, 14.386, 38.16, 43.371, 65.270, 65.281, 65.609, 65.614, 65.615, 66.197, 70, 76.46, 85.89, 94.28, 112.7, 124.12, 159.7, 161.159, 170.13, 170.48
Becwar, George 127.21, 127.50, 127.55, 141.67
Beddoe, Don 4.16, 14.101, 20.16, 20.17, 21.15, 27.60, 31.25, 34.25, 43.40, 43.162, 52.40, 653.58, 66.100, 66.154, 66.172, 85.42, 85.81, 86.55, 89.35, 89.99, 96.178, 96.179, 97.47, 97.92, 97.116, 97.136, 97.140, 105.17, 105.91, 105.106, 108.6, 121.12, 126.99, 126.158, 129.27, 129.32, 141.16, 149.65, 151.5, 152.60, 170.24
Bedelia, Bonnie 14.330, 14.416, 36.19, 65.437, 65.438, 71.36, 111
Bee, Molly 124.43
Beech, Adam 91.5
Beecher, Bonnie 132.21
Beecher, Robert 86.39
Beecroft, David 163.15, 163.16
Beekman, Bobby 43.66, 127.8, 162.95
Beer, Daniel 120.35
Beer, Ingrid 48.76
Beer, Jacqueline 4.20, 21.48, 21.64, 41.45, 105.18, 146.34
Beery, Bucklind 14.374
Beery, Noah, Jr. 5.21, 14.198, 14.290, 17.18, 31, 43.261, 61.1, 61.2, 65.321, 65.401, 71.76, 72, 84.26, 86.31, 106.11, 107.13, 126.12, 131, 151.4, 161.134, 161.217, 162.104, 162.134, 162.245, 164.89, 164.95, 168.2
Begam, Helen 158.28
Beggs, Hagan 36.13, 70.14, 70.28
Beggs, James 65.397
Beggs, Malcolm 73.9
Begley, Ed 14.206, 14.238, 51.2, 65.382, 65.462, 71.30, 126.177, 161.46, 161.110, 162.233, 170.42
Behar, Eli 170.68
Behrens, Bernard 96.72
Behrens, Frank 144.25
Beimfohr, Ed 177.43
Beir, Fred 7.6, 12.38, 14.35, 21.50, 44.6, 83.15, 101.29, 105.50, 105.119, 117.11, 127.30, 146.36, 161.209, 162.173, 162.208, 164.50
Bejarano, Milo 158.43
Bekassy, Stephen 8.26, 8.52, 105.8, 130.125, 133.4, 155.5
Belasco, Leon 96.80, 105.113
Belford, Christine 5.43, 59.1, 118
Bel Geddes, Barbara 41.138, 131.1
Bell, Charles Alvin 89.80, 105.72
Bell, Dan 90.10
Bell, Edward 109.2
Bell, Gary 177.12
Bell, Ivan 52
Bell, James 14.114, 14.175, 27.65, 34.57, 44.33, 66.210, 67.18, 81.99, 89.15, 144.12, 148.71, 151.4, 152.18, 162.111, 164.16, 169.40, 178.46
Bell, Jeff 55.24
Bell, Kay 147.9, 147.10
Bell, Leonard 78.55, 103.27, 103.49, 148.161, 164.81, 164.93
Bell, Loila 170.47
Bell, Marshall 120.15
Bell, Michael 12.100, 70.11, 123.6
Bell, Ralph 164.86, 164.91
Bell, Rodney 126.124, 126.162, 148.135, 156.65, 158.18, 164.44, 167.15
Bell, Tobin 90.11
Bell, Tom 161.155
Bell, Vanessa 45.2
Bell, William 21.67
Bellamy, Ann 93.206

Bellamy, Ned 53.29, 65.637
Bellamy, Ralph 43.253, 65.451, 95.12, 126.88, 126.213, 161.177, 178.13
Bellaver, Harry 41.101, 102.14, 146.52, 156.20, 164.44
Belle, Dickie 147.37
Bellerue, Dick 91.6, 91.9, 91.10, 177.22
Bellflower, Nellie 65.609
Bellin, Thomas 161.44, 161.78
Bellini, Cal 11.2, 37.11, 83.43, 174.3
Bellis, Dick 27.70
Bellucci, John 1.9
Bellwood, Pamela 11.6
Beltran, Alma 14.16, 34.7, 84.17, 145.15, 149.53, 169.92
Ben Ali, Booker 97.149
Ben-Victor, Paul 1.23
Benaderet, Bea 129.70
Bender, Don 23.29
Bender, Russ 14.141, 14.173, 20.29, 20.50, 27.62, 30.7, 65.392, 66.145, 74.23, 74.28, 78.31, 85.108, 93.62, 93.124, 103.51, 105.21, 126.22, 126.63, 126.93, 133.6, 149.5, 156.13, 161.12, 164.14
Bendien, Mia 65.534
Bendix, William 119, 131.2, 162.40
Bendixsen, Mia 96.69
Benedict, Dirk 163.45
Benedict, Greg 89.146
Benedict, Nick 5.9
Benedict, Richard 31.30, 78.13, 93.207, 97.215, 147.36, 147.42
Benedict, Steve 14.427
Benedict, Val 65.107, 103.12, 178.44
Benedict, William 5.25, 17.47, 65.429, 72.6, 72.8, 130.68, 148.59, 169.107
Benesch, Lynn 65.633, 96.127
Benet, Brenda 41.66, 43.434, 53.15, 71.52, 76.22, 106.22
Benet, Vicki 66.187
Beneveds, Robert 43.99
Benjamin Pride 132
Bennett, Bruce 17.20, 85.25, 145.4, 148.49, 152.2, 161.138, 161.141
Bennett, Fran 23.24, 34.10, 145.27
Bennett, Jeff 177.26
Bennett, Kathy 27.100, 105.123
Bennett, Linda 51.9, 178.102
Bennett, Margery 169.8
Bennett, Marjorie 22, 22.35, 25.67, 52.25, 126.168, 138.33, 156.34, 161.187, 162.82, 162.248
Bennett, Mark 43.64, 57.34
Bennett, Nigel 100.4
Bennett, Raphael 2.22, 32.45, 32.52, 60.27
Bennett, Ray 60.1, 60.29, 65.49, 97.9, 97.23, 97.49, 135.24, 135.73
Bennett, Roy 169.8
Benoit, Suzanne 65.365
Benson, Betty 138.70
Benson, Carl 66.27, 71.85, 93.177
Benson, Joe E. 130.94, 130.105, 130.165
Benson, Lucille 14.410, 24.2, 96.133
Benson, Roy 84.42
Bentley, Savannah 107.17
Benton, Anne 14.89, 88.4
Benton, Charles 177.46
Benton, Garth 117.30
Benton, Gene 65.209
Benton, Susanne 65.635, 161.159
Beradino, John 6.71, 6.74, 20.22, 20.62, 21.14, 29.9, 32.119, 32.123, 32.146, 32.150, 34.2, 66.59, 77.25, 89.83, 97.184, 97.186, 97.189, 105.85, 114.24, 133.29, 145.29, 148.65, 148.141, 152.23, 152.42, 155.13, 169.78, 178.70
Berard, Roxane 21.65, 34.31, 44.19, 66.81, 66.118, 66.167, 79.22, 105.42, 105.55, 105.77, 105.100, 126.53, 148.198, 179.76

Berber, Gale 162.266
Berdahl, Donn 48.11
Beregi, Oscar 8.58, 43.328, 43.347, 66.107, 66.133, 161.39
Beregi, Oscar, Jr. 170.7, 170.71, 170.102
Berg, Bryce 96.69
Bergen, Frances 173
Bergen, Polly 162.154
Berger, Charles 107.18
Berger, Ion 14.383
Berger, Mel 14.183
Berger, Melissa 1.19
Bergerac, Jacques 41.97
Bergere, Lee 4.27, 14.97, 43.396, 121.18, 162.184, 164.75, 170.52
Bergman, Richard 53
Bergmann, Alan 12.54, 14.233, 14.316, 71.10, 170.39
Berkeley, George 3.34
Berkeley, Xander 1.6
Berkes, Johnny 97.10
Berle, Milton 12.63, 52.39
Berlinger, Warren 65.452, 175.2
Berman, Shelley 126.99
Bermudez, Richard 22.20, 66.174
Bernard, Arthur 30.4, 84.51
Bernard, Barry 31.34
Bernard, Butch 108.4, 162.35
Bernard, Crystal 120.30
Bernard, Jay 177.19, 177.26
Bernard, John 162.192
Bernard, Joseph 70.36
Bernard, Ralph 66.201
Bernard, Tom 32.70
Bernardi, Hershel 14.67
Bernath, Shari Lee 148.168
Bernay, Lynn 133.30, 162.82
Berrigan, Christian 96.103
Berry, Eleanor 43.222, 43.266
Berry, Fern 93.193
Berry, Ken 52, 94.3, 96.117, 126.190
Berry, Michael 67.1, 67.2, 67.20
Berryman, Michael 59.3
Bert, Margaret 135.63
Berti, Dehl 3.90, 3.92, 3.98, 3.134, 3.138, 8.39, 8.101, 24.16, 24.17, 31.21, 65.274, 72.22, 84.32, 93.166, 120, 133.26, 138.20, 145.31, 152.30, 152.74, 155.42, 159.18, 169.112
Bertrand, Rosemary 135.78
Besch, Bibi 48.89, 75.20, 120.39
Besser, Joe 60.79
Best, James 2.13, 2.21, 6.25, 6.26, 8.4, 8.80, 13.16, 14.52, 14.288, 21.68, 23.6, 26, 27.98, 27.99, 41.21, 43.48, 43.244, 43.282, 43.300, 46.7, 54.12, 54.28, 60.68, 60.72, 63.8, 63.41, 65.296, 65.319, 65.496, 66.134, 66.135, 73.34, 75.25, 76.3, 81.93, 84.49, 85.6, 85.20, 85.80, 97.177, 119.15, 122.23, 126.130, 126.151, 126.169, 127.34, 127.42, 128.6, 129.40, 130.139, 142.1, 142.19, 142.30, 145.22, 151.12, 151.20, 151.24, 152.70, 155.23, 156.1, 156.27, 156.44, 161.19, 161.105, 162.74, 162.92, 162.95, 164.13, 164.19, 166.11, 178.14
Bestar, Barbara 2.13, 43.39, 81.26, 81.62, 81.74, 93.9, 93.76, 93.218, 158.19, 158.21, 158.58, 158.60
Bethune, Ivy 53, 83.2, 83.62
Bethune, Zina 65.602, 84.41
Betten, Mary 65.604
Bettger, Lyle 14.89, 14.236, 30.14, 41.82, 41.127, 43.279, 44.40, 65.327, 85.14, 85.52, 85.76, 85.89, 85.100, 88.2, 101.20, 126.56, 126.94, 126.160, 130.27, 130.124, 148.18, 148.62, 148.171, 149.28, 153.3, 162.28, 178.59, 178.88
Bettin, Sandra Gale 21.46
Betts, Jack 14.114
Betts, Jane 170.62

Personnel Index

Betts, Kristina 177.5
Betz, Carl 65.59
Beutel, Jack 80, 158.30, 158.34, 162.74, 162.133
Bevans, Clem 3.89, 42, 55.7, 65.116, 105.44, 162.60
Beverley, Scotch 48.9
Beverly, Helen 130.79
Bevil, Leake 126.93
Beyer, Troy 163.8
Beymer, Richard 43.389, 141.21, 161.83, 161.100
Bezaleel, Khalil 36.5
Biberman, Abner 69.2
Bice, Robert 2.21, 3.85, 6.29, 32.25, 32.33, 32.38, 32.75, 35.2, 35.5, 35.6, 35.23, 35.31, 43.373, 57.91, 60.47, 60.50, 60.91, 64.7, 65.308, 65.326, 65.337, 66.13, 73.10, 73.33, 81.23, 81.50, 81.71, 81.73, 93.222, 97.34, 97.77, 97.78, 97.137, 126.71, 126.88, 130.53, 130.132, 135.74, 135.77, 135.78, 135.90, 135.92, 135.95, 135.96, 135.97, 135.100, 138.67, 147.19, 147.23, 148.30, 148.65, 152.36, 155.19, 162.90, 162.179, 167.25, 169.14, 169.21, 169.22, 169.83, 170.14
Bick, Stewart 1.20
Bickford, Charles 161, 161.12, 162.29
Biddle, Don 148.23
Bieheller, Robert 84.12
Bieri, Ramon 5.11, 5.42, 14.380, 14.429, 19, 41.158, 65.472, 65.488, 65.541, 65.562, 65.567, 65.613, 75.22, 83.25, 84.35, 96.1, 112.23, 177.13
Bierko, Craig 120.25, 120.32
Bigelow, Ben 44.5
Biggs, Casey 177.11
Biggs, Jerry 110.4, 163.31
Bighead, Jack 4.30, 14.156, 14.184, 14.219, 14.220, 86.19, 162.236, 162.278'
Biheller, Robert 14.177, 14.265, 65.346, 70, 70.29
Bikel, Theodore 65.362, 74.1, 96.43, 126.180, 162.70
Bill, Tony 14.246, 24.16, 24.17, 98.1, 132.17, 161.110
Billings, Earl 163.22
Billings, Gail 170.82, 170.98
Billingsley, Jennifer 30.18, 65.311, 134.1, 162.280
Billingsley, Neil 53.16
Billingsley, Peter 96.169
Bilson, Tom 89.124
Bilyeau, Chick 152.35, 152.41
Binns, Edward 14.347, 39.1, 41.28, 43.272, 44.60, 65.84, 86.53, 98.19, 101.3, 106.9, 117.5, 130.11, 142.27, 144.7, 161.73, 161.97, 161.137, 162.129, 162.183, 162.254, 170.99, 178.48, 178.143
Birch, Paul 3.41, 4.30, 13.35, 14.8, 14.217, 20.15, 21.46, 27.36, 43.158, 43.229, 43.278, 46.7, 51.5, 61.8, 65.257, 66.43, 66.68, 66.203, 73.29, 85.57, 85.87, 97.103, 97.150, 101.31, 113.10, 129.8, 129.33, 131.15, 146.8, 148.190, 149.47, 151.8, 152.78, 156.6, 159.13, 161.68, 161.80, 161.112, 162.91, 162.123, 162.134, 162.171, 168/17. 178.92, 178.119
Birk, Raye 1.26
Birman, Len 36.20, 174.1
Biro, Barney 162.82
Bishop, John 94.4, 94.15, 94.22, 94.32
Bishop, John Glenn 48.29
Bishop, Larry 83.10
Bishop, Mary 85.69
Bishop, Mel 8.49
Bishop, Norman 169.20
Bishop, Wes 71.85
Bishop, William 130.38, 131.1
Bisoglio, Val 14.307
Bissell, Whit 7.13, 14.98, 25.29, 27.67, 39.14, 40.2, 41.21, 44.71, 66.12, 66.33, 66.214, 76.44, 78.54, 82.3, 86.20, 89.4, 89.109, 89.121, 89.149, 93.131, 97.143, 97.163, 97.177, 98.1, 101.4, 103.33, 105.73, 126.49, 129.6, 130.41, 130.72, 130.76, 130.121, 142.32, 148.196, 152.28, 156.33, 161.31, 161.58, 161.71, 162.47, 162.124, 162.184, 162.252, 162.261, 178.122, 179.50

Bixby, Bill 76.23, 115.6
Black, Ian 67.3
Black, Karen 12.59, 76.46
Black, Robert 129.43
Black, Tom 147.23
Blackburn, Ward 97.29, 97.35, 97.60, 97.73
Blackman, Joan 65.400
Blackman, Lonie 8.66, 102.15, 126.25
Blackmer, Sidney 14.64, 14.291, 25.15, 41.78, 78.62, 78.63, 78.67, 130.1, 130.8, 130.18, 152.5, 164.18, 178.52
Blackwell, William 42
Blackwood, Steve 48.39
Blaine, Martin 14.300, 65.345, 170.47
Blair, Henry 169.41
Blair, Janet 46.4
Blair, June 8.43, 8.84, 152.65
Blair, Nicky 147.28, 162.25, 170.80, 170.98
Blair, Patricia 14.148, 41, 130, 151.16, 161.36
Blair, Wally 55.14
Blake, Amanda 65, 65.636, 123.4
Blake, Bobby 135.90, 169.33
Blake, Ellen 65.626, 176.4
Blake, Geoffrey 1.13, 48.86
Blake, Jean 8.79, 34.56, 146.63
Blake, Larry J. 12.24, 12.48, 20.51, 41.9, 65.169, 65.335, 65.348, 66.71, 82.2, 83.13, 83.46, 89.78, 89.117, 93.124, 96.39, 97.56, 97.67, 97.72, 97.81, 97.171, 126.21, 129.23, 138.77, 146.50, 161.15, 161.116, 161.126, 162.41, 162.83, 162.235, 173.28, 173.29
Blake, Madge 129.15
Blake, Michael 14.427
Blake, Michael Francis 83.46
Blake, Oliver 3.137, 3.161
Blake, Pamela 32.4, 32.9, 32.12, 124.57, 124.69, 124.73
Blake, Robert 8.97, 13.7, 20.64, 25.50, 32.74, 32.81, 43.353, 66.118, 66.125, 66.196, 85.72, 126.195, 126.210, 127.21, 162.143, 178.85
Blake, Robin 65.398
Blake, Sondra 65.607
Blake, Whitney 17.37, 21.41, 21.47, 27.43, 27.65, 31.19, 44.7, 65.145, 65.595, 65.596, 86.40, 92.22, 105.22, 105.28, 119.4, 122.6, 126.13, 126.50, 129.68, 131.18, 148.85, 152.40, 152.50, 161.146, 178.37, 178.56
Blakely, Gene 168.25
Blakely, Susan 163.21
Blakeney, Olive 65.140
Blakesley, Marshal 65.400
Blanch, Jewel 14.375, 14.397
Blanchard, Jackie 133.38, 148.20, 158.77
Blanchard, Mari 21.35, 64.7, 82, 85.21, 126.31, 126.68, 146.47, 148.109, 152.28, 161.144
Blanchard, Moody 8.16, 126.30
Blanchard, Susan 175
Blatchford, Edward 1.9
Blaylock, Suzy 163.31
Blayne, Jack 85.113
Blechman, Jonah 163.56, 163.57
Bleifer, John 43.174, 96.103, 126.20
Blenman, Bing 65.640, 177.2
Blessing, Ned 110
Bletcher, Billy 97.27, 169.8
Bliss, Lela 162.19, 169.103
Bliss, Sally 127.68, 162.214
Bliss, Ted 73.39
Blocker, Dan 14, 27.26, 29, 34.2, 65.39, 65.123, 77.17, 127.1, 129.7, 129.14, 129.42, 129.53, 129.78, 130.9, 138.56, 148.8, 161.1, 162.20, 178.44
Blocker, Dirk 14.432, 14.433, 45.1, 96.9, 163.42
Blodgett, Michael 7.12, 14.275, 41.75, 41.76
Blom, Dan 1.17
Blondell, Gloria 164.72
Blondell, Joan 14.166, 43.261, 63.15, 70, 161.33, 162.238

Bloom, Charles 96.131
Bloom, John 120
Bloom, Verna 14.332, 48.1
Blue, Monte 3.92, 3.156, 3.164, 6.66, 6.67, 93.78, 97.9, 97.58, 97.69, 97.83, 97.92, 97.124, 124.51, 126.39, 141.7, 141.8, 141.10, 141.11, 141.15, 148.25, 158.7, 158.9, 162.13, 169.6, 169.59
Bluhm, Brady 163.9
Bluhm, Brandon 1.6
Bly, Margaret 65.341, 65.363, 161.103
Blystone, Stanley 2.10, 32.47, 73.8, 73.26, 97.43, 97.113, 97.122, 124.31, 124.37, 135.18, 135.30, 135.36, 145.29
Blystone, Susan 97.121
Blyth, Ann 162.77, 162.83, 162.157, 162.201, 162.228
Boardman, Nan 78.62
Boaz, Charles 8.20
Bocar, Poupee 112.7
Bochner, Lloyd 7.4, 12.64, 14.263, 17.28, 38.9, 41.55, 41.100, 41.103, 41.159, 43.356, 65.606, 69.3, 92.2, 101.11, 106.22, 161.157, 170.21, 177.18
Bodeen, Robert 96.41
Boehm, Karl 161.25
Boffman, Randy 120.54
Bogart, Tracy 24.19, 112.5
Bogert, William 26
Bohen, Ian 48.61, 163.41
Bohn, Merrit 34.62, 146.52
Bokar, Hal 65.603, 161.4, 161.106, 161.127
Bolander, Bill 163.15, 163.16
Bolder, Cal 14.46, 14.232, 30.18, 41.62, 46.10, 65.262, 117.23
Bolding, Bonnie 27.37, 66.44
Bolender, Bill 1.1
Boles, Jim 12.10, 12.23, 12.66, 14.165, 21.68, 27.87, 49.7, 63.14, 65.538, 65.539, 65.574, 66.126, 83.45, 96.51, 96.52, 101.14, 149.38, 161.35, 161.106, 161.170
Boles, Michael 5.3
Bolger, Ray 96.93, 96.94, 96.105
Bolger, Robert 71.16
Bolling, Tiffany 14.325, 94.23
Bolt, Jonathan 164.94
Bolton, Tim 43.214
Bon Tempi, Nick 164.86
Bon Tempi, Paul 164.86
Bonar, Ivan 14.426, 66.205, 96.61, 96.62, 96.140
Bond, Alicia 71.46
Bond, David 141.18
Bond, Eric 43.87
Bond, Lillian 25.19
Bond, Raymond 81.11, 81.39
Bond, Rex 30.2
Bond, Rudy 51.32
Bond, Ward 162
Bondi, Beulah 47.8, 162.133, 178.28
Bonilla, Michelle 48.99
Bonn, Walter 97.102
Bonne, Shirley 14.252
Bonney, Gail 12.68, 14.154, 32.74, 39.7, 65.581, 89.98, 89.139, 121.1, 126.105, 132.12, 141.54, 150.4, 161.169, 162.104, 162.269, 162.273
Bonsall, Brian 177.41
Booke, Sorrell 5.47, 65.572, 83.30, 96.82, 170.88
Bookman, Buzzy 108.19
Boomer, Linwood 96, 96.87, 96.88
Boon, Robert 4.11, 86.16, 96.171, 126.51, 126.107, 150.8, 161.76
Boone, Brendon 14.234, 65.494, 126.214, 161.125
Boone, Daniel 40, 51, 174
Boone, Peter 66.132, 66.195
Boone, Randy 14.245, 30, 65.633, 72.1, 72.2, 83.61, 161, 162.222, 162.231, 162.235
Boone, Richard 30.8, 54.23, 66, 69
Boonesborough, Kentucky 41
Booth, Billy 89.129

Personnel Index

Booth, Carol 12.64
Booth, James 14.405, 65.638, 120.30, 120.37, 170.55
Booth, Nesdon 46.10, 65.269, 105.85, 128.2, 129.6, 141.28, 141.29, 148.3, 148.174, 152.69, 168.3
Borden, Fred 83.61
Borden, Lynn 26
Borelli, Carla 170.64
Borg, Veda Ann 14.52, 25.54, 129.5, 129.36, 129.42, 133.25, 145.30, 146.13, 169.57
Borgnine, Ernest 85.3, 85.34, 96.13, 162.1, 162.40, 162.81, 162.129, 162.282, 178.23, 178.119
Bosley, Tom 14.309, 14.337, 161.193
Bosson, Barbara 5.45
Boston, Michael 1.21
Boswell, Charles 45.2, 120.16
Botelho, Clifford 162.51
Botto, Juan Diego 180
Bottoms, Joseph 65.638, 177.62
Bouchet, Barbara 161.165
Bouchey, Willis 3.111, 8.31, 8.32, 20.26, 21.57, 22.6, 25.16, 27.65, 34.34, 39.9, 44.20, 52.3, 65.389, 65.454, 66.5, 85.85, 85.94, 89.30, 121.5, 144.32, 148.56, 148.175, 161.26, 162.123, 164.17, 164.36, 164.64, 168.7, 178.4, 178.19, 178.30, 178.40
Bourne, Peter 126.178
Bourneuf, Philip 12.36, 65.47, 65.101, 69.4, 121.22, 162.179, 162.213
Boutin, Judi 78.16
Boutwell, John 60.91
Bowen, Michael 1.10
Bowen, Roger 47.3, 96.59
Bower, Antoinette 12.91, 14.311, 36.1, 36.25, 61.7, 66.164, 76.13, 84.30, 101.28, 144.21, 157.12, 157.20, 162.161, 170.4
Bowles, Billy 65.373
Bowles, Jim 51.19
Bowman, Jessica 48
Bowman, Margaret 110.2
Boxleitner, Bruce 59.1, 5.2, 59.3, 59.5, 65.635, 65.640, 75
Boyd, Blake 65.637
Boyd, Guy 48.1
Boyd, William 73
Boyer, John 65.411
Boyett, William 32.82, 32.89, 43.38, 43.89, 43.216, 64.9, 65.372, 66.85, 85.92, 85.108, 114.2, 138.27, 147.1, 147.9, 147.10, 147.25, 147.37, 155.34, 162.3, 175.3, 178.99
Boyle, Ray 43.28, 65.3
Boyum, Steve 120.39
Bracken, Eddie 126.138, 126.62
Bracken, Jimmy 65.481
Bradbury, Lane 5.46, 65. 390, 65.427, 65.458, 65.467, 65.481, 65.497, 66.64, 76.19, 83.5, 126.90
Braddock, Martin 43.169
Braddock, Mickey 31, 178.68
Bradford, Lane 2.12, 3.28, 3.42, 3.87, 3.104, 6.6, 6.8, 6.27, 6.39, 6.56, 6.62, 6.76, 6.77, 8.65, 13.9, 14.34, 14.134, 14.202, 14.260, 14.309, 14.382, 17.38, 20.49, 20.59, 20.65, 23.2, 23.8, 23.10, 23.15, 23.41, 23.42, 27.22, 27.39, 30.13, 32.110, 32.116, 32.147, 32.152, 34.42, 35.1, 35.17, 39.11, 41.19, 41.64, 43.43, 43.142, 43.353, 43.437, 43.442, 44.15, 56.2, 57.70, 57.98, 60.60, 60.84, 65,138, 65.179, 65.201, 65.270, 65.278, 65.331, 65.352, 65.489, 65.544, 65.548, 65.563, 71.3, 71.32, 73.3, 73.18, 74.24, 76.34, 77.7, 78.17, 80.4, 80.12, 80.13, 82.14, 85.84, 85.86, 85.102, 86.22, 88.14, 88.19, 89.78, 93.8, 93.61, 93.85, 93.169, 93, 192, 97.4, , 97.19, 97.44, 97.58, 97.64, 97.71, 97.76, 97.84, 97.105, 97.111, 97.133, 97.138, 97.187, 97.197, 97.216, 98.5, 101.22, 105.48, 105.76, 105.84,105.93, 125.13,
126.29, 126.44, 126.70, 126.111, 129.16, 129.30, 129.34, 129.69, 130.78, 132.17, 133.15, 135.29, 135.39, 138.2, 138.21, 138.40, 138.64, 145.17, 146.13, 147.15, 147.16, 148.24, 148.27, 148.72, 148.171, 149.10, 150.7, 152.22, 152.43, 152.70, 152.76, 158.4, 158.5, 158.29, 158.68, 162.24, 162.125, 162.182, 162.239, 162.258, 162.276, 162.284, 169.2, 178.74, 178.75
Bradford, Marshall 2.23, 6.44, 6.46, 32.67, 32.71, 32.85, 93.1, 93.155, 97.18, 97.73, 97.89, 97.157, 97.177, 97.178, 129.29, 151.11
Bradford, Richard 65.400, 71.85
Bradley, Bart 4.13, 152.25, 162.130, 169.81
Bradley, Bea 41.62, 86.20
Bradley, Buck 141.61
Bradley, Christopher 65.639, 65.640, 120.26
Bradley, Leslie 34.10, 93.171, 129.41, 129.70, 141.65, 147.48, 164.58
Bradley, Stewart 8.72, 39.3, 43.291, 51.19, 65.203, 66.112, 74.22, 78.56, 84.7, 84.51, 89.17, 93.186, 103.19, 126.62, 129.71, 148.45, 149.70, 161.59
Bradshaw, Terry 1.26, 1.27
Brady, Buff 8.74, 52.4, 92.1, 98.25, 135.19, 178.5
Brady, Marshall 97.37
Brady, Pat 135
Brady, Robert 169.64
Brady, Ruth 124.35
Brady, Scott 47.1, 65.493, 65.577, 65.597, 71.83, 84.44, 106.16, 140, 161.185, 178.31
Brady, Zoltan 67.10
Braeden, Eric 7.3, 9.2, 24.24, 65.534, 65.551, 65.552, 65.553, 65.606, 75.13, 75.15, 161.119
Braithwaite, Beryl 68.31
Bralver, Robert 83.10
Bramhall, Mark 1.9
Bramley, William 7.2, 14.98, 14.375, 14.418, 30.1, 30.16, 39.3, 43.314, 46.11, 51.32, 65.253, 65.273, 65.398, 65.411, 65.434, 65.437, 65.473, 65.489, 65.547, 65.583, 76.15, 76.45, 85.92, 86.46, 112.6, 116.12, 132.26, 149.71, 151.8, 151.24, 161.33, 161.86, 161.136, 161.174, 168.28
Brand, Anthony 152.72
Brand, Jolene 21.66, 27.90, 43.157, 105.116, 179
Brand, Neville 5.26, 5.35, 7.1, 14.42, 14.372, 14.400, 41.91, 43.234, 46.1, 65.383, 86, 106.6, 126.37, 126.144, 152.1, 161.91, 162.243, 162.257, 178.84
Brand, Sharon 23.25
Brander, Leslie 170.8
Brando, Jocelyn 22.34, 55.5, 85.29, 85.45, 96.20, 131.28, 131.38, 148.168, 149.29, 161.33, 161.147, 161.192, 162.28, 162.145, 162.154, 162.184, 162.193, 162.215, 162.234
Brandon, Henry 20.5, 21.36, 41.47, 44.10, 64.11, 65.194, 65.224, 64.11, 66.14, 66.58, 78.39, 86.24, 89.44, 89.57, 105.86, 127.15, 129.9, 145.33, 152.37, 162.9, 162.66, 162.83, 162.89, 162.110, 162.130, 166.12, 178.101
Brandon, Jane Alice 96.22
Brandon, John 65.487
Brands, X 3.80, 3.87, 3.139, 5.34, 5.48, 6.54, 6.55, 6.72, 8.65, 9.6, 14.184, 20.58, 23.27, 23.30, 23.41, 23.42, 27.81, 35.32, 35.33, 41.69, 65.391, 65.459, 65.494, 65.521, 65.522, 65.595, 65.596, 65.625, 70.26, 71.1, 71.16, 71.91, 80.1, 80.3, 80.5, 80.6, 80.7, 80.8, 80.11, 80.12, 80.13, 80.15, 80.20, 80.21, 80.22, 80.24, 80.25, 81.101, 85.86, 86.4, 93.214, 107.26, 114.25, 126.43, 126.51, 126.76, 126.138, 130.104, 138.67,139.10, 147.30, 148.120, 149.27, 162.126, 162.204, 173
Brandt, Hank 12.38, 41.107, 65.457, 65.489, 65.512, 65.515, 65.622, 65.623, 107.14, 148.178, 162.146
Brannon, Carol 169.13
Bransh, Marion 65.20
Branson, Ricky 148.170
Branton, Alban 96.129

Braswell, Charles 138.32, 138.59
Bratton, Brent 110.2
Brauer, Bill 178.133
Braun, Judith 77.16, 156.63, 164.21
Bravo, Annette 5.47
Bravo, Danny 157.14, 157.15, 162.216
Bray, Robert 27.55, 35.11, 35.12, 35.30, 35.37, 54.19, 65.289, 74.17, 77.18, 81.39, 85.26, 85.111, 93.8, 97.84, 97.98, 97.125, 97.137, 97.146, 97.163, 102.2, 119.10, 131.26, 142, 145.9, 146.46, 148.121, 148.198, 151.7, 167.12
Breck, Peter 5.6, 12, 13, 14.153, 17.8, 17.9, 17.10, 21.47, 27.90, 27.102, 27.103, 33, 65.119, 65.303, 66.45, 89.116, 89.154, 105.94, 105.106, 105.116, 105.120, 105.121, 105.124, 106.13, 129.49, 129.78, 146.63, 155.33, 161.56, 162.43, 178.50, 178.54, 178.74
Breen, Dorothy 162.95
Breen, John 65.437, 65.438
Breen, Joseph 14.127, 14.138, 65.421, 126.175, 169.99
Breen, Mike 65.177
Breeze, Michelle 65.388, 65.437, 65.438, 65.480
Bremen, Lennie 43.160
Brenaman, Jim 130.57
Brendel, El 3.95, 35.1, 35.17, 35.29, 35.33, 46.8
Breneman, Allen 129.41
Brenlin, George 14.130, 25.46, 44.57, 65.84, 103.50, 126.129, 130.43, 148.177, 156.25, 156.40, 156.55, 159.34, 161.22, 161.155, 164.7
Brennan, Claire 65.611
Brennan, Eileen 163.39
Brennan, John H. 16
Brennan, Walter 5.16, 5.30, 5.36, 63, 178.9, 178.36
Brennan, Walter, Jr. 66.9
Brenner, Eve 48.57
Brent, Eve 8.24, 146.7, 158.40, 158.62
Brent, Evelyn 162.91
Brent, George 126.12
Brent, Jerry 129.77
Brent, Linda 43.67, 138.31
Brent, Paul 17.13
Brent, Romney 78.75, 179.2, 179.3
Brent, Roy 135.31, 135.35
Breslin, Patricia 14.100, 74.31, 105.47, 117.2, 127.65, 130.92, 144.4, 148.177, 150.12, 161.58
Bressler, Carl 118.8
Brett, Jeremy 174.1
Brewster, Carol 17.31, 43.317, 92.5
Brewster, Diane 8.31, 8.32, 27.6, 27.17, 27.22, 27.103, 29.17, 39.8, 43.76, 43.304, 51.32, 56.23, 105.3, 105.20, 105.23, 105.37, 129.28, 130.36, 148.9, 148.39, 155.33, 156.34, 162.19, 162.91, 162.272, 164.29, 178.16, 178.40
Brian, David 17.40, 17.41, 17.42, 30.23, 39.8, 41.5, 43.276, 65.475, 65.527, 65.616, 69.4, 72.12, 76.9, 85.106, 86.6, 126.27, 126.80
Brian, Fletcher 65.430
Brickell, Beth 5.4, 14.328, 14.376, 65.594, 106.12, 109.3
Bridge, Alan 6.2, 6.19, 60.62, 60.66, 124.14, 124.18, 124.21, 124.22, 124.33, 124.35, 124.64, 124.68, 124.74, 145.5, 169.44
Bridge, Loie 23.15
Bridges, Beau 14.252, 17.37, 30.2, 65.398, 98.21, 98.22, 126.148, 162.199, 178.147
Bridges, Cindy 98.23
Bridges, Jeff 98.15
Bridges, Ken 177.27
Bridges, Lloyd 61.4, 75.4, 75.5, 75.6, 75.7, 98, 178.16, 178.48, 178.124, 178.147
Bridges, Rand 65.592, 176.2
Bridges, Todd 96.63
Brien, Joan 8.40
Brigadier, Ed 163.61
Briggs, Charlie 5.7, 12, 12.36, 14.91, 27.74, 27.97, 41.8, 43.325, 44.19, 63.35, 65.298, 65.310,

84.49, 85.38, 88.26, 89.49, 89.131, 89.147, 117.24, 129.45, 130.73, 130.103, 140.24, 148.197, 161.4, 161.13, 162.158, 162.250, 178.134
Briggs, Don 14.321, 65.355, 84.19, 170.15
Briggs, Harlan 97.59
Briggs, Jack 97.57, 97.60
Bright, Martin 120.5
Brightman, Larry 66.172
Briles, Charles 14.340
Brill, Charles 20.58
Brimley, Wilford 75.21, 83.54, 115.1, 163.41
Brin, Suzannah 83.61
Brinckerhoff, Burt 65.357, 85.98, 126.216, 148.189, 161.12
Brindle, Eugene 42
Brinegar, Paul 1.1, 1.4, 7.5, 27.23, 41.86, 43.348, 43.352, 59.4, 63.26, 76.27, 84, 93, 93.35, 93.36, 93.37, 93.38, 93.39, 93.40, 93.42, 93.43, 93.65, 93.67, 93.71, 93.73, 93.76, 93.77, 93.81, 93.83, 93.86, 93.88, 93.89, 93.101, 93.102, 93.106, 93.108, 93.110, 93.111, 94.19, 96.55, 97.140, 126, 147.23, 148.8, 152.21, 156.60
Brinkley, John 127.30, 165.11, 178.34
Brinkley, Ritch 163.55
Britt, Leo 23.9, 97.129
Brittain, Jim 60.40
Brittany, Morgan 17.48, 41.4, 65.302, 126.140
Britton, Pamela 64.8
Broadhurst, Kent 163.29
Broadus, Roger 57.28, 147.16
Brocco, Peter 5.20, 66.5, 66.188, 88.25, 119.12, 145.30, 156.46, 179.18
Brock, Heinie 65.25
Broderick, James 65.311, 65.346
Brodie, Don 31.30, 141.31, 141.37
Brodie, Kevin 93.220
Brodie, Marvin 170.77
Brodie, Steve 4.21, 14.126, 14.168, 14.293, 21.54, 27.83, 27.100, 34.51, 39.11, 44.34, 65.235, 65.555, 85.81, 93, 93.194, 93.204, 93.205, 93.208, 93.210, 93.216, 93.223, 93.225, 93.226, 97.103, 97.120, 101.28, 105.110, 105.111, 122.18, 126.38, 126.121, 126.150, 133.20, 142.8, 142.35, 145.19, 148.150, 156.39, 161.30, 164.8, 164.23, 164.37, 169.46, 169.53
Brodrick, Malcolm 156.5, 178.64
Brody, Biff 170.103
Brody, Marvin 41.22, 41.48, 41.65, 161.128
Brogan, Ben 66.97
Brogan, Ron 178.40
Brolin, James 65.639, 107.6, 107.12, 107.15, 107.17, 161.193
Brolin, Josh 177
Brolly, Clark 1.19, 65.640
Bromfield, John 54.6
Bromfield, Valri 10
Bromilow, Peter 1.1, 36.2, 41.93, 41.144
Bromley, Sheila 3.55, 89.103, 105.50, 126.37, 126.48, 126.95, 126.127, 126.135
Bronson, Charles 12.9, 14.180, 34.9, 51.1, 65.28, 65.74, 65.125, 66.2, 66.42, 66.160, 66.165, 66.209, 85.23, 85.53, 92.25, 126.214, 131.43, 135.31, 146.12, 146.19, 148.58, 157, 161.99, 161.151, 173.20
Bronson, Lillian 3.135, 27.94, 55.31, 66.101, 66.171, 66.154, 103.30, 112.10, 126.86, 129.32, 130.51, 130.52, 148.163, 156.53, 161.41, 162.41, 162.246, 164.7, 169.88
Bronte, James 25.31, 93.137, 138.77
Brooke, Hillary 89.34, 173.21
Brooke, Walter 5.48, 9.9, 11.5, 12.79, 14.175, 14.303, 14.349, 14.372, 21.65, 27.85, 37.6, 43.303, 43.440, 51.19, 65.156, 43.284, 71.20, 71.44, 84.21, 95.6, 95.7, 96.47, 96.48, 116.7, 156.66, 161.20, 170.68, 170.88
Brookfield, Fred 69.6
Brooks, Alan 91.3

Brooks, Barry 85.80, 85.98, 88.10, 105.11, 126.175, 147.11, 147.25, 161.2
Brooks, Betsy 162.102
Brooks, Charlene 65.22, 141.63
Brooks, Charlie 63.11
Brooks, David 48.4
Brooks, Donna 66.120
Brooks, Doyle 3.130
Brooks, Dwight 141.60
Brooks, Foster 65.270, 65.524
Brooks, Geraldine 14.65, 14.241, 41.16, 65.397, 66.106, 71.11, 83.8, 85.119, 101.20, 144.15, 161.16, 161.178
Brooks, Jan 65.298, 164.93
Brooks, Jane 164.90
Brooks, Jay 31.8
Brooks, Joe 52, 126.106
Brooks, Joel 48.50
Brooks, Jonathan 170.93
Brooks, Maggie 79.30
Brooks, Martin E. 7.8, 65.432, 98.24, 170.63
Brooks, Norma 80.36
Brooks, Peter 65.372
Brooks, Rand 3, 8.51, 14.243, 31.13, 32.77, 60.15, 60.16, 60.17, 65.232, 65.292, 77.19, 81.54, 81.64, 93.139, 97.9, 97.23, 97.91, 97.111, 97.149, 97.182, 97.183, 97.193, 97.205, 124.30, 124.36, 135.1, 135.8, 135.20, 135.22, 135.75, 135.76, 138.63, 141.1, 141.1, 141.41, 141.63, 147.1, 155.18, 169.1, 169.30, 169.43, 169.59, 169.67, 178.120
Brooks, Randi 118.7
Brooks, Roxanne 159.26
Brooks, Walter 43.331
Brophy, Edward S. 31.33
Brophy, Sallie 22, 54.5, 54.11, 61.3
Brose, Richard 118.9
Bross, Trent 120.29
Brothers, Jamie 66.190
Brough, Candi 118.4
Brough, Randi 118.4
Brown, Barney 165.6
Brown, Barry 65.526
Brown, Bud 158.3, 158.6, 158.7, 158.16, 158.73
Brown, Calvin 12.2, 161.141, 170.26, 170.41
Brown, Carlos 10.21
Brown, Dwier 45.3
Brown, Ewing 60.55, 60.61
Brown, Gates 158.51, 158.53, 158.58, 158.60
Brown, George Stanford 70.40
Brown, Helen 6.66, 23.40, 34.1, 43.40, 57.18, 135.96, 162.34
Brown, J.B. 41.12, 161.67
Brown, J.M. 158.23
Brown, James 141.10, 161.11, 161.24, 161.133
Brown, James L. 3, 7.9, 65.292, 97.82
Brown, Jeannine 14.385
Brown, Jeremy 48.4
Brown, Jerry 65.540, 129.15
Brown, Jim 85.62
Brown, Joe 112.4, 117.33, 130.106, 148.172
Brown, Johnny Mack 148.49
Brown, Lee 161.179
Brown, Les, Jr. 52.36, 65.391
Brown, Lew 5.3, 30.2, 30.16, 43.304, 43.345, 43.425, 43.427, 51.18, 65.39, 65.153, 65.161, 65.186, 65.213, 65.228, 65.165, 65.429, 65.439, 65.440, 65.468, 65.527, 65.559, 65.572, 65.609, 66.187, 71.92, 85.101, 96.20, 106.3, 126.79, 126.194, 144.4, 159.15, 161.4, 161.16, 161.25, 161.127, 161.167, 170.60
Brown, Mark Robert 84.8
Brown, Mina 89.129
Brown, Mitch 37
Brown, Naaman 173.31
Brown, Olivia 120.27
Brown, P.L. 120.35
Brown, Pepe 65.487

Brown, Peter 27.44, 27.47, 27.50, 27.104, 34.1, 86, 86.43, 89, 105.2, 105.6, 105.81, 128.2, 146.15, 146.41, 161.71, 161.91, 161.164, 162.216, 162.244, 162.266
Brown, Phil 14.362
Brown, Reb 26
Brown, Robert 14.96, 70, 139.8, 162.117
Brown, Roger Aaron 118.1
Brown, Susan 43.364, 43.376, 43.442, 116.16
Brown, Thomas 130.124
Brown, Tim 65.156
Brown, Timmy 170.57
Brown, Timothy 24.3
Brown, Tom 30.14, 31.29, 65, 66.53, 78.72, 93.20, 93.91, 97.145, 97.196, 97.221, 146.36
Brown, Vanessa 162.28
Brown, Vivian 96.79
Brown, Wally 14.71, 29, 43.131, 79.18, 85.12, 105.64, 149.39, 162.169, 164.83
Browne, Kathie 12.91, 14.54, 14.82, 14.144, 14.153, 14.166, 17.40, 17.41, 17.42, 21.55, 24.19, 55.26, 65.91, 66.194, 66.203, 72, 85.100, 85.107, 86.39, 89.142, 102.19, 126.77, 126.84, 126.88, 128.6, 148.190, 151.12, 155.72, 159.2, 161.38, 162.124, 162.228, 166.3, 170.12, 170.52
Browne, Reg 80.31, 80.32, 80.33, 158.45
Browne, Robert Sonne 177.42
Browne, Roscoe Lee 14.411, 116.18
Browning, Norman 67.15
Browning, Susan 76.9, 170.24
Broyles, Robert 71.92
Brubaker, Robert 14.239, 14.240, 14.272, 14.300, 20.27, 27.103, 41.72, 44.59, 65. 124, 65.135, 65.139, 65.147, 65.151, 65.185, 65.200, 65.272, 65.455, 65.484, 65.494, 65.505, 65.599, 65.603, 65.624, 83.41, 102.32, 127.27, 133.2, 148.54, 152.67, 155.18, 159.31, 161.19, 161.225, 168.15
Bruce, David 32.14, 32.23, 32.24, 73.16, 97.25, 97.63, 97.177, 141.10, 169.11
Bruce, Ed 19
Bruce, Edwin 105.10
Bruce, Eva 112.17
Bruck, Bella 43.395, 52.3
Brull, Pamela 33
Brundin, Bo 26
Brune, Frederic 141.13
Brunetti, Argentina 44.43, 65.392, 71.55, 73.10, 78.23, 97.153, 126.49, 130.137, 162.148, 164.75
Brunner, Robert 124.76
Bruns, Philip 7.11, 75.22, 116.26, 170.65
Bruns, William 161.187
Bruskotter, Eric 163.55
Bryan, Marvin 65.2
Bryan, Travis 34.18, 141.44
Bryant, Bob 82.1, 162.30, 162.31
Bryant, Claudia 162.93
Bryant, Fletcher 65.512
Bryant, Jan 32.93, 32.97
Bryant, John 78.7, 97.94, 97.180, 107.7, 138.74, 161, 161.19, 161.23, 161.43, 161.63, 161.78, 161.79, 161.81, 161.144, 161.155, 161.173, 161.188, 162.242
Bryant, Joshua 19.6, 30.16, 65.478, 70.51, 90.15, 96.78
Bryant, Lee 75.19
Bryant, Michael 23.28, 23.29, 93.41, 169.99
Bryant, Theona 27.55, 43.239, 79.34, 105.25, 152.16, 168.12
Bryant, Todd 120.26
Bryant, William 3.52, 5.18, 7.9, 14.278, 14.300, 14.322, 17.8, 17.9, 17.10, 17.35, 17.40, 17.41, 17.42, 17.44, 17.45, 24, 21, 28.12, 43.253, 50.14, 51.16, 53.21, 54.21, 56.6, 65.64, 65.154, 65.282, 65.421, 65.516, 65.562, 65.618, 66.91, 74.9, 75.19, 84.8, 84.9, 84.15, 84.28, 85.5, 85.65, 85.99, 85.120, 93.7, 93.98, 102.13, 105.39, 107.11, 117.4, 126.175, 127.16, 127.24, 127.37, 127.40,

Personnel Index

127.48, 127.66, 130.19, 130.126, 130.150, 146.46, 147.39, 151.18, 159.11, 169.73, 169.86, 169.108, 170.104
Bryar, Claudia 5.5, 12.65, 14.137, 14.282, 22.8, 43.171, 63.8, 65.579, 86.26, 89.110, 93.137, 144.2, 161.22, 162.51, 162.126, 162.149, 162.188, 164.70
Bryar, Paul 14.121, 25.14, 43.208, 65.488, 71.14, 78.6, 83.4, 97.130, 105.85, 148.4, 148.169, 149.14, 169.37
Bryon, Carol 161.91
Buchan, Judith 99.14
Buchanan, Buck 76.43
Buchanan, Edgar 8.73, 14.43, 14.66, 21.39, 24, 25.33, 25.67, 29.7, 44.14, 65.251, 65.301, 66.204, 73, 78.61, 80, 82.13, 85.27, 85.30, 85.47, 85.96, 89.15, 89.33, 105.38, 105.46, 105.63, 105.81, 105.97, 106.17, 117.7, 117.8, 129.30, 129.35, 130.15, 130.23, 130.24, 130.26, 130.31, 130.119, 131.42, 142.7, 144.2, 148.22, 148.38, 148.54, 148.83, 148.130, 148.161, 149.44, 156.62, 158.43, 162.8, 162.124, 164.28, 164.36, 168.12
Buchholz, Horst 75.4, 75.5
Buck, Charles S. 105.72
Buck, Connie 8.62, 13.28, 65.164, 114.25, 126.24, 126.60, 126.61, 133.10, 158.50, 158.52
Buckingham, Robert 121.14
Buffington, Sam 13.14, 13.21, 65.150, 102.21, 105.23, 105.36, 105.47, 133.37, 146.27, 155.20, 155.36, 164.11, 164.16, 164.19, 166
Buka, Donald 34.31, 71.65, 88.7, 89.16, 89.45, 127.68, 166.15
Bukich, Rudy 12.37
Bulifant, Joyce 14.355, 46.7, 51.20, 65.281, 84.19, 149.66, 161.47, 162.242, 168.2
Bull, Richard 14.339, 14.422, 43.443, 43.448, 46.12, 65.574, 70.34, 76.1, 95, 95.22, 95.23, 95.24, 96, 112, 112.8, 120.15, 161.2, 161.4
Bumatai, Ray 1.2, 1.21
Bunce, Alan 144.2
Bundy, Brooke 12.50, 14.203, 14.272, 14.273, 36.15, 41.114, 53.19, 53.20, 65.317, 65.394, 84.13, 84.32, 126.195, 161.57, 161.121, 162.238
Bunker, Rodney 68.25, 68.28
Buntrock, Bobby 161.156, 162.57
Bunzel, John 112.20
Buono, Victor 41.88, 127.28, 127.36, 170.1, 170.29, 170.45
Burchett, Kevin 14.331, 43, 428, 43.433, 65.408, 65.532, 71.53
Burdette, Sunny 35.17
Burdoff, James 48.10
Burgess, Jane 162.129
Burgess, Rick 67.1, 67.2
Burk, Jim 50.11, 84.51
Burke, Brian 177.51
Burke, Delta 28
Burke, James 142, 148.16, 156.64, 162.17, 162.79
Burke, Jimmy 120.16
Burke, Paul 13.44, 43.182, 61.7, 66.86, 74.26, 97.168, 148.64, 162.134, 164.69
Burke, Ron 86.2, 161.188
Burke, Stoney 144
Burke, Walter 4.3, 4.31, 4.37, 12.41, 12.68, 12.80, 12.112, 13.17, 13.18, 13.21, 14.51, 14.221, 14.442, 17.15, 43.286, 43.357, 51.18, 63.28, 63.32, 65.145, 65.177, 65.257, 65.315, 65.316, 65.361, 65.502, 66.75, 66.137, 82.11, 86.54, 88.9, 89.86, 92.34, 94.31, 102.11, 102.29, 112.10, 117.23, 125.17, 126.48, 148.87, 151.4, 159.12, 161.226, 168.21, 170.67, 178.91
Burker, Christine 144.31
Burkes, James 164.3
Burkette, Madeleine 32.77
Burkhart, Monte 166.19
Burkley, Dennis 175.9

Burleigh, Stephen 120.50
Burmester, Leo 163.12, 177.52
Burnett, Don 14.76, 114, 142.23
Burnett, Helen 135.55
Burnette, Olivia 120.36
Burnham, Terry 148.75, 162.57, 162.86, 162.130, 162.248
Burns, Bart 65.289, 83.35, 86.13, 98.18, 102.21, 127.35, 164.87, 178.30
Burns, Brendan 48.27
Burns, J.P. 12.4, 12.27, 12.38, 12.46
Burns, John 8.86, 8.99
Burns, Michael 12.43, 12.85, 14.227, 14.265, 36.18, 41.98, 49.7, 65.456, 65.465, 65.513, 92.32, 101.9, 106.20, 116.11, 132.24, 148.140, 149.34, 161.109, 161.127, 161.134, 161.176, 161.211, 162, 162.118, 162.128, 162.135, 162.60, 162.70, 162.226, 162.283, 172.4
Burns, Michael John 120.28
Burns, Paul E. 6.1, 6.10, 6.41, 6.53, 6.73, 34.5, 57.37, 73.20, 85.88, 145.33, 158.35, 158.39, 162.246
Burns, Phil 70.5
Burns, Ronnie 44.20
Burns, Timothy 65.513, 65.535
Burr, Lonnie 124.73, 135.12
Burr, Raymond 26
Burr, Robert 65.583
Burrell, Jan 65.598, 116.9
Burroughs, Bonnie 120.42
Burrows, Bob 65.498, 65.518, 65.530
Burson, Wayne 8.6
Burstyn, Elizabeth 105.109
Burstyn, Ellen 27.87, 65.542, 65.543, 85.109
Burstyn, Neil 49.2
Burt, June 141.26
Burt, Nellie 51.16, 65.298, 84.34, 162.189, 162.242, 168.3
Burton, Hal 14.429
Burton, Jeff 36.22
Burton, Julian 70.41, 126.108, 148.140
Burton, Laurie 170.71
Burton, Norman 65.385
Burton, Robert 3.6, 3.27, 14.109, 20.22, 25.24, 25.37, 25.55, 44.70, 54.14, 57.112, 65.70, 97.190, 97.194, 97.197, 97.216, 102.10, 105.112, 130.125, 145.32, 148.1, 148.131, 152.2, 152.30, 156.19, 161.1, 162.84, 164.23, 178.8
Burton, Tony 19.14, 19.15
Burton, Wendell 83.12
Busey, Gary 14.424, 65.633, 71.92, 83.16
Bush, Billy Green 5.15, 7.14, 14.354, 47.4, 65.598, 115.5
Bush, Grand L. 118.1, 118.5
Bush, James 169.26, 169.33
Bush, Owen 1.5, 12.68, 14.151, 14.243, 65.463, 76.15, 105.90, 139.1, 139.5, 139.6, 139.8, 139.13, 139.16, 164.56
Bush, Tony 19
Busk, Lori 24.20
Buster, Budd 23.5, 60.78
Butler, Dean 95, 95.22, 95.24, 96
Butler, Gene 163.38
Butler, John A. 97.31, 97.58
Butterfield, Herb 54.10
Buttons, Red 43.178, 55.21, 96.18
Buttram, Pat 5.38, 53.28, 60, 121.1, 121.22, 170.90
Buxton, Sarah 163.60
Buyeff, Lillian 131.34, 150.12
Buzzi, Ruth 62.5
Byington, Spring 85
Byles, Bobby 43.346, 43.391, 63.45
Byrant, William 161.45
Byrd, David 96.34
Byrd, Eugene 177.49
Byrd, Melinda 178.106
Byrne, Barbara 10.14

Byrne, Martha 177.23, 177.24
Byrnes, Bara 41.69
Byrnes, Burke 120.32
Byrnes, Edd 5.45, 27.32, 27.45, 34.20, 89.1, 89.79, 105.4, 105.6, 105.81, 106.16, 146.21
Byron, Carol 65.307, 86.1, 126.100, 151.17, 151.21, 162.86, 168.25
Byron, Jean 3.39, 27.36, 27.57, 27.72, 27.93, 57.17, 77.6, 85.91, 85.101, 108.38
Byron, Keith 43.106, 89.31
Byron, Melinda 3.140, 97.217
Bystrom, Steve 97.128

Caan, James 43.267, 43.273, 162.272, 168.16
Cabal, Robert 6.54, 6.55, 12.7, 20.19, 25.28, 32.58, 32.64, 73.22, 93.211, 126, 138.36, 138.40, 142.34
Cabello, Luis 78.20
Cabot, Bruce 14.175, 41.21
Cabot, Ceil 63.16, 70.23
Cabot, Sebastian 14.21, 27.40, 65.10, 65.67, 74.7, 122.23, 179.9
Cabot, Susan 66.19, 66.73
Cabrera, Boris 163.58
Cade, Michael 1.19
Cadiente, David 41.2
Cady, Frank 4.25, 20.40, 65.354, 82.6, 105.17, 126.68, 156.19, 161.17, 162.22, 162.210, 162.233
Cagle, Wade 138.32
Cagney, Jeanne 169.40
Cahill, Barry 5.49, 14.94, 65.225, 66.2, 66.6, 66.14, 66.99, 66.163, 70.1, 70.3, 85.101, 92.31, 112.15, 148.156
Cahill, Margaret 32.134
Caillou, Alan 14.107, 14.349, 21.33, 25.64, 27.76, 41.84, 41.106, 41.144, 43.260, 66.85, 71.88, 105.50, 146.43
Cain, Guy 126.94, 126.96
Cain, Jennifer 163.73
Cain, Thomas 158.51, 158.59
Caine, Howard 19.9, 25, 65.174, 71.69, 89.19, 116.18, 125.4, 126.184, 157.14, 157.15, 159.31
Caine, Richard 83.27
Calahan, Pepe 161.97
Calamie, Gloria 170.83
Calder, King 8.49, 8.104, 21.9, 44.72, 66.30, 66.79, 89.76, 89.96, 89.129, 102.1, 126.60, 126.129, 130.103, 142.30, 148.60, 148.122, 150.2, 156.68, 161.24, 161.29, 164.22, 178.144
Calhoun, Rory 5.23, 14.172, 38.12, 43.270, 43.339, 65.375, 69.3, 84.50, 126.216, 152, 161.69, 162.159, 162.284, 178.12
Calia, Hank 80.39
Call, Anthony 14.204, 39.12, 65.427, 151.1, 161.169, 161.212
Call, Brandon 118.2
Call, Ed 65.604
Call, R.D. 96.178, 96.179, 120.35, 163.7
Callahan, James 24.3, 25.66, 51.23, 66.180, 95.22, 144.9, 159.2
Callahan, Pepe 12.19, 14.306, 43.434, 65.528, 65.551, 65.552, 65.553, 165.9, 170.73, 170.94
Callaway, Bill 65.513
Callaway, Cheryl 22.3, 138.6, 147.4
Callaway, Chuck 169.111
Calleia, Joseph 66.40, 179.71
Calomee, Gloria 36.10, 65.503
Calvert, Charles 8.50
Calvert, Jim 10.18
Calvillo, Irene 165.9
Calvin, Henry 179
Calvin, John 24.5, 163.24
Cambell, Laura 75.22
Camden, Joan 13.5, 20.17, 117.30, 131.25, 146.33
Cameron, Dave 8.85
Cameron, Keith 48.33
Cameron, Michael 83.8

Personnel Index

Cameron, Owen 133.21
Cameron, Rod 5.34, 5.40, 9.5, 14.219, 14.220, 17.38, 72.11, 76.5, 85.40, 85.61, 85.69, 85.97, 85.117, 106.6, 148.183
Cameron, Todd 65.577
Camil, Issabela 163.64, 163.65
Camlin, Peter 6.54
Camp, Hamilton 14.323, 14.360
Camp, Helen Page 65.582, 65.594, 70.5, 170.85, 175.1
Campanella, Frank 69.7, 161.214, 170.84
Campanella, Joseph 5.11, 7.8, 12.36, 12.56, 65.465, 65.572, 84.26, 120.34, 132.14, 139.6, 161.44, 161.58, 161.184, 163.59, 170.55
Campbell, Alexander 25.58, 77.26
Campbell, Beverly 97.48
Campbell, Bruce 1
Campbell, Carole 158.21
Campbell, Charles L. 28
Campbell, Chip 177.16
Campbell, J. Kenneth 177.9
Campbell, J. Marvin 48.39
Campbell, Lauren 9.6
Campbell, Paul 60.16, 60.17, 97.72, 97.206, 108.11, 108.29
Campbell, Peggy 127.74
Campbell, Rob 110
Campbell, Scott Allan 163.47
Campbell, William 14.291, 49.12, 65.251, 65.625, 69.9, 142.28, 148.122, 170.25
Campeau, Jerry 46.13
Campo, Wally 8.94
Campos, Rafael 12.72, 17.43, 26, 43.172, 65.381, 65.413, 66.84, 66.202, 72.17, 85.78, 117.25, 129.72, 146.66, 151.2, 162.66, 162.110, 164.47
Campos, Victor 24, 71.55, 84.49
Canadian Mounties 16
Canale, Cosmo 1.23
Canary, David 5.28, 5.47, 9.4, 14, 30.18, 49.5, 65.437, 65.438, 83.27
Cane, Charles 73.24, 108.8, 122.28
Cane, Michael 78.71
Canino, Jim 158.34, 158.65
Cannon, Dyan 8.41, 8.88, 65.354, 144.15, 159.3, 164.52, 178.94
Cannon, J.D. 5.4, 5.15, 5.24, 5.33, 5.38, 5.39, 14.332, 30.14, 63.14, 65.351, 65.501, 76.47, 84.2, 101.21, 106.13, 126.177, 126.188, 139.11, 144.26, 162.205, 170.2
Cannon, Kathy 9.8, 24.12, 53, 65.699
Canon, Peter 96.91
Canova, Judy 121.17, 121.22
Canty, Katie 48.30
Canutt, Joe 3.90., 41.29, 107.3
Canutt, Tap 107.3, 158.74, 158.77
Capers, Virginia 41.67, 66.159
Capps, Henry 17.36
Capri, Anna 17.29, 17.30, 21.66, 27.84, 63.22, 76.40, 86.36, 107.26, 170.63
Capuano, Sam 162.90
Carbonara, Vito 170.26
Carbone, Anthony 14.163
Card, Kathryn 20.4, 77.6, 97.151, 126.53, 126.63, 126.95, 152.3, 152.23, 156.34, 161.23, 162.101, 178.68
Cardell, Frank 164.21
Cardenas, Elsa 66.89
Cardi, Pat 17.31, 65.370, 65.388, 65.429, 151.10
Cardinal, Lorne 67.4, 99.1, 99.2, 99.3
Cardinal, Tantoo 48.14, 48.18, 48.19, 48.29, 48.64, 65.636
Cardona, Annette 14.408, 65.528, 71.30
Cardos, Johnny 41.110, 41.116, 71.14, 107.26
Carey, Harry, Jr. 14.34, 14.187, 14.259, 17.2, 20.66, 30.19, 55.24, 65.159, 65.212, 65.270, 65.278, 65.305, 65.367, 65.453, 65.474, 65.540, 65.551, 65.552, 65.553, 65.608, 66.42, 66.46, 66.82, 66.102, 66.128, 66.130, 66.139, 66.158, 66.191, 66.194, 66.218, 66.224, 66.225, 74.26, 85.55, 85.78, 85.97, 85.102, 89.148, 92.12, 96.138, 97.174, 106.11, 116.17, 119.13, 126.26, 126.102, 128.7, 130.65, 130.115, 134.1, 144.30, 148.160, 149.16, 153, 155.74, 162.72, 162.178, 162.227, 166.5
Carey, Leonard 31.25
Carey, Lynn 170.8
Carey, Macdonald 17.8, 17.9, 17.10, 41.17, 126.10, 162.22, 178.49
Carey, Michelle 5.8, 47.1, 65.557, 170.45, 170.95, 170.96
Carey, Olive 29.26, 66.173, 85.70, 88.11, 89.147, 129.1, 129.38, 130.19, 148.13, 155.45, 162.17
Carey, Philip 21.64, 27.94, 27.107, 30.18, 38.5, 41.83, 65.546, 86, 89.137, 96.119, 130.109, 142.21, 148.167, 161.44, 161.91, 178.132
Carey, Timothy 12.19, 30.20, 35.3, 35.7, 36.19, 41.115, 65.117, 65.421, 73.32, 83.61, 126.188, 126.205, 161.212
Carhart, Timothy 177.44
Carillo, Elpidia 90.16
Carle, Benny 130.150
Carleton, Claire 29, 60.75, 73.13, 93.8, 93.125, 97.192, 105.29, 126.24, 131.44, 145.25, 149.35, 158.39, 162.106, 162.107, 162.114, 162.121, 162.139, 162.273, 164.8
Carlile, David 92.1, 93.199
Carlin, Lynn 65.572
Carlos, Don 127.42
Carlsle, Spence 89.55
Carlson, Charles 117.12, 117.13, 144.3, 162.142, 162.245
Carlson, Karen 14.429, 26, 43.435, 43.436, 70.1, 70.7, 70.12, 70.15
Carlson, Richard 14.286, 84.34, 126.215, 131.10, 161.53, 161.88, 162.240, 162.269
Carlson, Robert 14.217
Carlson, Steve 65.515, 161.107, 161.129, 161.158, 161.175, 170.103
Carlton, Ken 145.11
Carlye, Richard 164.40
Carlyle, John 39.19, 114.18
Carlyle, Richard 4.32, 43.178, 61.3, 65.359, 101.7, 126.133, 149.46, 152.31, 152.76, 158.58, 158.60, 164.91
Carmel, Roger C. 71.93
Carmen, Jean 158.44
Carmichael, Hoagy 85
Carnagin, James 96.139
Carne, Elijah N.177.25
Carne, Judy 5.12, 12.70, 12.71, 14.140, 24.13, 65.394
Carnegie, Robert 10.15
Carnell, Cliff 3.45, 3.49
Carnell, Suzi 27.91, 51.29, 66.144, 66.161, 162.135
Carney, Alan 41.86, 66.172, 149.39
Carney, Art 106.4
Carney, Bob 145.20, 145.35
Carney, Thom 3.131, 8.89, 65.3, 92.19, 93.173, 130.146, 138.2, 138.17, 138.46, 169.81
Caron, Rene 154
Carpenter, Carlton 29.14, 130.53, 156.63
Carpenter, Edgar 73.12
Carpenter, John 80.6, 80.7, 80.8, 80.10, 80.14, 80.15, 130.75, 138.23, 158.24, 169.3, 169.20, 169.23
Carr, Betty Ann 24, 94.9, 109.10
Carr, Darleen 5.48, 19, 115, 161.207
Carr, Jack 152.74
Carr, John 158.6
Carr, Michael 3.30, 3.132, 3.133, 5.5, 5.14, 34.29, 63.5, 65.271, 66.52, 93.78, 93.107, 93.109, 93.160, 125.1, 125.6, 141.43, 169.112
Carr, Paul 5.21, 13.30, 14.32, 30.11, 65.240, 65.392, 66.48, 79.24, 85.102, 85.113, 101.5, 102.3, 117.33, 122.28, 126.66, 126.122, 126.170, 126.171, 130.19, 130.32, 130.50, 130.68, 149.25, 156.59, 157.23, 161.25, 161.26, 161.137, 161.161, 164.35, 167.18, 172.2, 178.88, 178.94
Carr, Stephen 35.11, 35.13, 35.28, 35.30
Carradine, Bruce 83.29, 83.54
Carradine, Calista 83.63
Carradine, David 30.5, 59.4, 65.537, 83, 83.63, 139, 161.54, 162.235, 177.26
Carradine, John 8.22, 12.109, 14.68, 17.8, 17.9, 17.10, 17.44, 17.45, 17.48, 27.33, 29.15, 37.4, 41.104, 43.227, 65.13, 65.157, 66.39, 72.9, 79.9, 83.3, 83.37, 83.61, 86.29, 89.152, 92.27, 93.160, 105.104, 108.22, 119.16, 127.1, 127.38, 129.36, 130.18, 130.40, 133.19, 146.28, 162.20, 162.123, 164.59, 169.67
Carradine, Keith 83.1
Carradine, Robert 37, 83.3
Carraway, Robert 121.15
Carrera, Barbara 26
Carricart, Robert 12.61, 14.123, 27.73, 43.308, 66.134, 66.135, 66.148, 66.168, 71.15, 117.22, 148.105, 148.134, 157.26, 167.19, 173.26, 178.125
Carrier, Albert 41.23, 41.42, 43.133, 105.38, 114.17, 146.63
Carrillo, Cely 161.77
Carrillo, Leo 32
Carroll, Angela 65.510
Carroll, Ann 43.200, 51.29, 169.31, 169.48
Carroll, Annie 124.70
Carroll, Brandon 65.489
Carroll, Dee 14.142, 41.49, 65.519, 65.540, 69.8, 89.121, 156.4, 161.116, 161.139, 161.162, 162.241
Carroll, Diahann 99.1, 99.2, 99.3, 99.20
Carroll, John 72.7
Carroll, Laurie 3.139, 20.62, 43.115, 43.132, 43.158, 105.8, 147.50, 148.46, 158.18, 179.23
Carroll, Leo G. 27.9
Carroll, Lucia 73.5
Carroll, Pat 109.12
Carroll, Virginia 81.87, 81.93, 135.8, 135.58, 135.65, 135.68, 135.89, 169.69
Carrott, Ric 47.11
Carruthers, Ben 65.130
Carruthers, Steve 152.31
Carry, Julius 1
Carson, Chuck 32.125
Carson, David 94.34
Carson, Fred 17.24, 41.52, 81.99, 148.11, 161.141, 170.36
Carson, Jack 14.9, 178.113
Carson, Jean 43.126, 144.12, 146.9
Carson, Jeannie 162.12, 162.21
Carson, John 77.17
Carson, Kit 148.16, 148.45, 148.129, 148.182, 148.190
Carson, Robert S.35.9, 71.22, 86.24, 93.90, 93.137, 93.215, 97.17, 97.73, 97.91, 97.96, 97.138, 97.177, 101.7, 105.3, 105.29, 105.73, 126.16, 138.31, 138.51, 141.18, 148.123, 152.15, 161.131, 169.51, 178.65
Carter, Chris 165.3
Carter, Conlan 5.5, 12.93, 12.107, 14.170, 14.289, 43.438, 46.12, 65.204, 65.237, 65.465, 65.478, 117.32, 126.102, 130.146, 130.168, 161.18, 161.191, 165.3, 168.23, 170.59, 178.131
Carter, Dixie 10.19, 19.8, 59.5
Carter, Donny 162.214
Carter, Harry 61.8, 161.24
Carter, Jack 24.20, 132.23, 170.98
Carter, Jimmy 4.23, 130.154, 166.16
Carter, Jody 107.25
Carter, John 12.57, 14.312, 43.431, 65.436, 96.56, 137.8
Carter, June 78.48, 78.53
Carter, Lynda 67
Carter, Lynne 158.28

Personnel Index

Carter, Mel 130.3, 130.8, 130.28, 130.32, 130.115, 130.141, 130.146, 130.148, 164.30
Carter, Michael Patrick 91.6, 120
Carter, Mitch 5.31, 75.23, 120.5
Carter, Sally 111.1
Cartier, Lynn 130.47, 130.59
Cartwright, Veronica 41, 43.437
Caruso, Anthony 14.4, 14.39, 14.105, 14.182, 20.18, 22.33, 31.3, 31.22, 40, 43.130, 43.141, 43.443, 44.29, 47.9, 57.7, 61.1, 61.2, 63.25, 64.3, 65.86, 65.200, 65.250, 65.290, 65.305, 56.329, 65.338, 65.500, 65.535, 65.547, 65.569, 65.602, 65.627, 66.4, 66.64, 66.98, 66.158, 71.13, 71.32, 71.39, 71.45, 84.1, 85.14, 85.89, 93.190, 97.162, 105.76, 105.85, 106.12, 109.14, 125.16, 126.46, 126.110, 126.196, 129.14,131.29, 132.5, 145.14, 146.30, 148.98, 152.62, 155.16, 157.25, 161.111, 162.88, 162.163, 164.34, 167.19, 170.38, 170.60, 170.86, 179.20, 179.21, 179.22
Caruso, Mickey 106.20
Carver, Mary 13.4, 65.34, 65.122, 65.182, 65.302
Carver, Tina 34.8, 167.11
Cary, Christopher 12.40, 132.10, 170.35, 170.95, 170.96
Casabian, Dan 20.36
Case, Allen 21.1, 34.31, 44, 65.140, 65.335, 65.414, 66.59, 66.69, 89.29, 92, 130.12, 146.22, 161.11, 162.61
Case, Cassie 148.118
Case, Cathy 44.50, 152.56, 178.101
Case, Kathleen 73.20, 81.40, 81.49, 124.76, 124.78
Case, Kathy 43.127
Case, Marianna 170.11
Casey, Bernie 24.16, 24.17
Casey, Chick 38.14
Casey, Claude R. 92.21
Casey, Lawrence 7.5, 14.329, 24.23, 65.418
Casey, Lee J. 24.7
Casey, Nelson, Jr. 148.24
Casey, Sue 65.287
Casey, Taggart 97.161, 97.178
Cash, Johnny 44.73, 48.4, 48.22, 48.51, 96.46, 127.13
Cash, June Carter 48.22, 48.51, 96.46
Casino, Robert 158.25
Cason, Bob 60.8, 60.9, 60.10, 60.26, 60.82, 60.87, 81.17, 97.6, 97.27, 97.64, 97.66, 97.132, 97.146, 97.162, 169.34
Cason, Chuck 23.41, 32.131, 81.48, 97.170, 127.55
Cason, John 2.19, 2.25, 3.6, 6.11, 6.16, 6.44, 32.42, 32.58, 32.59, 32.96, 32.101, 32.106, 32.113, 35.10, 35.11, 35.15, 35.24, 35.26, 35.30, 35.31, 35.33, 35.38, 35.39, 57.41, 73.6, 80.27, 80.28, 80.31, 80.33, 80.37, 81.8, 81.12, 81.13, 81.37, 81.38, 81.39, 81.48, 93.66, 97.95, 97.108, 102.1, 124.22, 129.37, 135.38, 135.43, 135.54, 135.56, 135.58, 135.83, 135.89, 135.93, 141.4, 141.34, 141.37, 141.51, 145.2, 146.67, 147.16, 162.144, 169.73
Casper, Mike 91.9
Casper, Robert 95.21, 95.24, 105.80
Cass, Dave 59.5, 70.35, 71.94, 175.2
Cass County Boys 60.2, 6.74, 60.81, 60.85, 60.86, 60.88, 60.89, 60.90, 60.91
Cassady, Bill 93.68, 93.98, 93.124, 93.127, 93.135, 93.138, 93.141, 93.142, 93.143, 138.72, 170.4
Cassavetes, John 92.7, 126.73, 161.109
Cassel, Seymour 86.3
Cassell, Cindy 41.4
Cassell, Malcolm 130.61
Cassell, Sid 57.108, 78.42, 138.2
Cassell, Wally 65.26, 145.36
Cassidy, David 14.353
Cassidy, Edward 31.28, 81.6, 97.6, 97.43, 169.48
Cassidy, Jack 5.17, 14.395, 21.55, 21.63, 65.117, 105.113, 162.138, 168.21
Cassidy, Maureen 32.130, 78.74, 138.26

Cassidy, Ted 14.357, 41.102, 86.53
Cassmore, Judy 70.1
Casson, John 148.33
Castiglioni, Iphigenie 66.173, 78.75, 178.35
Castillo, Gloria 65.14, 179.53
Castle, Dolores 32.44, 32.51
Castle, Mary 27.27, 56.24, 145
Castle, Peggy 27.12, 27.34, 65.66, 89, 129.21, 129.71, 152.4, 161.112, 178.8
Castle, Richard 32.131, 32.137
Catching, Bill 8.10, 8.54, 14.79, 14.174, 17.47, 32.80, 32.83, 32.87, 32.90, 32.96, 32.99, 32.100, 32.101, 32.136, 43.80, 65.159, 65.355, 65.492, 65.505, 65.546, 77.4, 83.42, 85.108, 88.7, 93.113, 130.23, 135.15, 135.83, 135.91, 135.96, 135.97, 141.60, 148.47, 164.24, 164.57, 167.13, 169.105, 170.2, 170.31, 178.22, 178.46, 178.64
Catching, J.P. 169.79
Catron, Jack 63.4, 166.17
Catron, Jerry 8.92
Cattani, Rico 71.59, 170.90
Cattrall, Kim 75.27
Caulfield, Joan 27.109, 71.1
Caulfield, Maxwell 48.41, 90.6
Cavallero, Gaylord 66.171, 149.66
Cavanagh, Paul 66.105, 114.10, 138.62
Cavanaugh, Michael 48.7
Cavanaugh, Tom 67.19
Cavell, Marc 27.41, 41.55, 65.427, 121
Cavendish, Dick 169.42
Cavens, Albert 66.148
Cavens, Fred 138.37
Cavett, Dick 5.30
Cedar, Jon 123.11
Cerone, Bill 130.137
Cervantes, Gary 163.17
Ceyon, Connie 3.18
Chadwick, Ben 167.17
Chadwick, Robert 126.39, 130.21
Chalk, Gary 67.9, 99.1, 99.2, 99.3
Chalk, George 126.86
Challee, William 14.225, 65.255, 65.536, 66.134, 66.135, 76.43, 78.66, 82.6, 85.71, 89.56, 93.92, 97.25, 97.106, 97.153, 97.165, 97.169, 97.175, 97.183, 97.185, 97.193, 105.78, 150.8, 152.11, 152.13, 161.6, 162.227, 162.244
Challes, Morgan 30.2
Chamberlain, Richard 26, 44.62, 65.192, 166.6
Chambers, Joan 144.12
Chambers, Phil 8.20, 12.53, 14.108, 14.135, 14.1137, 14.162, 14.178, 14.189, 14.199, 14.251, 14.269, 14.322, 41.63, 43.442, 65.205, 66.97, 83.18, 88.13, 93.1, 97.147, 98.20, 102.12, 108.2, 108.3, 108.30, 144.16, 148.181, 148.187, 148.189, 149.9, 162.50, 167.22
Chambers, Richard 92.21
Chambers, Steve 83.15, 83.19, 83.22
Chambers, Wheaton 73.13, 73.18, 97.8, 135.2, 135.3, 169.53
Chambliss, Woodrow 8.56, 30.11, 47.10, 65, 170.34
Champa, Jo 163.33
Champion, Michael 120.27
Chan, Spencer 35.2, 73.21
Chance, Larry 3.94, 3.144, 3.154, 6.17, 6.18, 14.44, 21.36, 41.5, 41.66, 86.44, 103.48, 114.3, 114.4, 117.42, 126.89, 130.106, 138.9, 141.71, 147.39, 148.180, 149.57, 152.69, 161.200, 167.17, 169.69, 169.87, 169.98, 169.103
Chandler, Chick 14.251, 14.319, 14.331, 14.343, 14.369, 14.397, 41.60, 43.270, 55.12, 97.133, 97.145, 105.122
Chandler, Frontis 43.439
Chandler, George 5.11, 14.269, 31.5, 44.62, 57.34, 81.54, 81.64, 86.17, 93.26, 97.142, 126.155, 148.8, 148.165, 162.36, 162.39, 169.87

Chandler, James 14.418, 17.27, 30.15, 51.7, 65.534, 65.563, 65.576, 65.604, 117.22, 127.25, 127.45, 130.40, 130.89, 164.50
Chandler, John 157.2, 157.22
Chandler, John Davis 51.22, 65.609, 71.8, 101.2, 130.142, 161.6
Chandler, Lane 6.34, 25.7, 27.29, 27.79, 32.15, 32.18, 32.21, 32.121, 60.53, 60.60, 65.212, 65.275, 65.352, 66.92, 66.113, 66.165, 81.50, 81.71, 81.73, 93.58, 93.134, 97.8, 97.20, 97.50, 97.61, 105.69, 105.76, 105.82, 124.57, 124.58, 124.61, 129.22, 145.20, 146.18, 146.22, 162.249, 169.112
Chandler, Linda 170.92
Chandler, Patricia 5.23
Chandler, Tanis 32.17, 32.19, 32.26
Chaney, Jan 146.3
Chaney, Lon, Jr. 8.75, 44.68, 51.26, 66.61, 66.215, 68, 79.22, 82.17, 89.135, 121, 126.5, 126.130, 130.26, 133.15, 142.18, 152.24, 155.38, 162.119, 162.148, 164.42, 178.141
Chaney, Thomas Leon 48.32
Chang, Jane 55.9, 66.77
Chang, W.T. 4.32, 141.25
Chang, Wilbur 83.40
Chao, Rosalind 75.26, 83.6
Chapin, Billy 25.24, 57.21, 57.103, 108.12, 178.23
Chapin, Lauren 27.39
Chapin, Michael 97.49
Chapin, Philip 161.163
Chaplain, Jack 14.98, 14.214, 44.65, 65.471, 85.80, 85.113, 117.23, 127.60, 162.172
Chaplin, Charles, Jr. 169.83
Chapman, David 65.28
Chapman, Helen 35.18
Chapman, Jack 132.9
Chapman, Judith 118.9
Chapman, Leigh 76.6
Chapman, Lonny 12.55, 12.75, 14.229, 14.364, 24.13, 43.367, 49.9, 63.6, 63.33, 65.299, 65.390, 65.408, 76.36, 86.15, 98.25, 115.2, 116.18, 117.32, 130.93, 130.162, 132.9, 161.110, 161.142, 161.192, 161.203, 168.22
Chapman, Marguerite 85.51, 126.3
Chappel, John 91.2, 91.9
Chappell, Crystal 163.42
Charbonneau, Patricia 45.5, 163.5
Charles, Annie 67.4
Charles, Arlene 170.34
Charles, Frances 169.39
Charles, Leon 66.89, 96.90, 96.91, 96.93, 96.94, 96.100, 96.101
Charles, Lewis 12.25, 14.165, 78.23, 93.48, 98.24, 102.36, 103.13, 130.21, 130.25, 130.124, 138.4, 138.26, 164.5, 164.79, 164.87
Charleson, Leslie 83.54, 170.89
Charlita 3.87, 27.29, 35.24, 35.39, 64.3, 81.23, 81.29, 81.84, 97.131, 124.49, 145.13, 158.56
Charney, Kim 27.52, 89.87, 130.31, 147.3, 147.14, 147.27, 162.8, 178.18
Charone, Irwin 47.1
Chartoff, Melanie 59.3
Chase, Barrie 14.186, 66.47
Chase, Duane 12.39
Chase, Eric 70
Chase, Stephen 21.17, 22.20, 32.1, 32.32, 32.39, 34.43, 43.114, 43.116, 43.138, 43.205, 65.134, 81.10, 97.41, 97.55, 97.71, 97.84, 97.104, 97.112, 130.16, 135.8, 135.12, 141.3, 148.139
Chastain, Don 12.47, 12.56, 12.72, 12.98, 28.10, 34.60, 65.473
Chatton, Charlotte 48.79, 48.81, 48.86, 48.90, 48.98
Chau, Francois 1.24
Chauncey, Dick 170.76
Chauvet, Elizabeth 109.2
Chauvin, Lilyan 25.20, 41.73, 78.15, 105.32, 116.26

Personnel Index

Chaves, Richard 59.3
Chavez, Gloria 84.46
Chavez, Jose 65.466
Chavez, Tony 158.22
Cheathem, Marie 65.527
Checco, Al 14.349, 83.56, 83.57, 83.58, 83.59
Chen, Tina 83.6
Chepovetsky, Dmitry 67.14
Chesebro, George 97.1, 97.2, 97.3, 97.73
Cheshire, Harry 6.34, 6.45, 23, 60.19, 60.21, 89.2, 89.12, 89.98, 89.100, 89.138, 89.150, 97.90, 97.123, 105.17, 105.77, 124.2, 124.5, 124.28, 124.31, 147.47, 152.75
Chesis, Eileen 14.111, 14.137, 46.4
Chester, Colby 5.19
Chester, George 78.20, 78.24
Cheung, George K.163.36
Chew, Sam 24.16, 24.17
Cheyenne Indians 18, 123
Chiang, George 83.47, 83.48
Chief-Moon, Byron 67.6, 163.86
Chien, Richard 83.25
Childers, Isa 54.18
Chiles, Linden 65.296, 84.18, 126.55, 161.68, 161.116, 161.125, 161.152
Chin, Mary Ann 170.73
Ching, William 25.34, 78.37, 169.77
Choate, Tim 65.639, 120.1
Chong, Rae Dawn 99.11
Chow, David 83.1, 83.23
Chrane, Calvin 24.5
Christi, Frank 84.48, 169.73
Christian, Carl 145.34
Christian, Claudia 118.6
Christie, Shannon 5.23
Christine, Virginia 12.4, 14.116, 14.182, 22.16, 41.112, 41.161, 44.67, 65.89, 65.367, 78.2, 84.24, 86.29, 93.124, 97.215, 101.34, 102.11, 103.41, 105.101, 126.49, 126.82, 129.18, 130.49, 130.119, 144.6, 148, 156.7, 156.13, 156.39, 161.96, 161.164, 162.133, 162.145, 162.193, 162.219, 162.281, 164.18, 164.39, 178.62
Christmas, Eric 14.344, 24.7, 95.18, 106.14, 106.21, 177.1
Christofer, Michael 65.614, 65.615
Christopher, Dane 177.35
Christopher, Eunice 65.483
Christopher, Robert 14.72, 138.33
Christopher, William 112.8, 112.16
Christopherson, Stefanianna 70.9
Christy, Ken 6.62, 8.13, 20.23, 20.36, 43.62, 85.61, 93.26, 147.18, 148.37, 145.21, 162.19, 169.91
Chudabala, Art 163.58
Ciannelli, Eduardo 66.23, 66.78, 149.34, 161.119, 162.68
Cioffi, Charles 14.409, 96.110
Cisar, George 4.37, 20.56, 34.40, 66.67, 66.178, 85.81, 147.49, 161.5, 169.93
Civil War 10, 13, 38, 64, 98, 127, 132, 133, 150, 152
Claire, Edith 127.5, 127.8
Clancy, Tom 53.4, 96.102, 96.132
Clanton, Ralph 31.48, 66.101, 102.6
Clark, Bill 14.143, 14.170, 14.180, 14.191, 14.205, 14.287, 14.378, 14.417
Clark, Bobby E. 65.466, 65.535, 83.42, 84.3, 114.8, 147.19, 148.12, 164.30
Clark, Brian Patrick 120.40
Clark, Dane 24.9, 106.5, 126.58, 162.37
Clark, Davison 32.70, 81.7
Clark, Dick 144.24
Clark, Dort 41.96, 51.31, 112.20, 128.7, 170.65, 170.92
Clark, Edward 6.17, 6.18, 32.57, 32.63, 32.78, 32.108, 60.80, 73.6, 73.19, 97.77, 97.93, 145.19, 169.9, 169.17

Clark, Ellen 65.165, 66.97, 142.11
Clark, Eugene A. 100.18
Clark, Fred 14.285, 52.58, 86.13, 162.193
Clark, Gordon 32.67, 32.71, 93.61, 103.48
Clark, Helen 96.17
Clark, J.R. 65.592
Clark, Jason 94.3
Clark, Jay 161.176
Clark, Ken 43.107, 146.47
Clark, Ken, Jr. 34.33
Clark, Marlene 14.380
Clark, Matt 14.335, 43.378, 49.4, 59.3, 83.27, 96.17, 96.111, 100.15
Clark, Paul 44.31, 66.89
Clark, Robin 95.24
Clark, Roydon 14.417
Clark, Steve 6.52, 6.53, 32.16, 32.22, 32.27, 32.30, 32.36, 32.79, 32.86, 32.93, 32.97, 32.141, 32.147, 43.39, 60.44, 60.46, 73.34, 97.12, 97.24, 97.29, 97.32, 97.38, 97.42, 97.56, 97.77, 97.82, 124.13, 124.17, 124.27, 124.31, 124.40, 124.42, 124.44, 124.45, 124.56, 124.57, 124.68, 135.1, 141.7, 169.36
Clark, Susan 161.143
Clark, Wallis 81.53, 81.69
Clarke, Angela 5.9, 14.200, 14.347, 41.61, 43.309, 43.342, 49.2, 65.270, 65.297, 65.336, 71.26, 161.111
Clarke, Ernestine 8.7
Clarke, Gage 21.21, 46.5, 65.40, 65.41, 65.56, 65.66, 65.93, 65.191, 65.203, 65.220, 65.238, 65.261, 65.263, 66.30, 85.81, 85.104, 105.16, 105.43, 105.70, 105.79, 105.103, 105.112
Clarke, Gary 72, 85.68, 141.51, 148.169, 148.197, 149.65, 161, 162.171, 177.41, 177.49
Clarke, John 43.187, 43.291, 43.412, 43.336, 43.405, 65.165, 65.286, 65.298, 88.28
Clarke, Karen 114.26
Clarke, Mae 20.33, 35.25, 52.11, 93.133, 152.10
Clarke, Michael 43.336
Clarke, Paul 105.62, 127.18
Clarke, Robert 27.74, 32.94, 32.102, 85.24, 97.80, 141.69, 162.68, 169.107
Clarke-Caire, Audrey 164.86
Clary, Robert 71.44
Clay, Juanin 53.13
Clayton, Homer 43.71
Clayton, Jan 43.355, 44.24, 65.33, 65.372, 109.4, 148.138, 149.57, 162.133, 162.243, 162.275
Clayton, Ken 57.112
Clayton, Melissa 48.61
Clayton, Richard 141.66
Clayworth, June 162.43
Cleary, Richard 103.51
Cleaver, Zelda 135.13
Cleem, Lee 170.85
Clemenson, Christian 1
Clement, Patrick 178.32
Clements, Stanley 3.63, 20.70, 30.13, 41.65, 43.55, 57.22, 64.6, 65.176, 65.482, 65.524, 65.578, 76.29, 93.154, 93.255, 97.132, 126.36, 126.55, 147.29, 148.69, 162.232, 164.92
Clemons, Maryellen 6.58, 6.59
Clerk, Clive 71.28, 161.115
Cleveland, George 105.90, 169.49
Clexx, Harry 8.81, 44.48
Cliff, John 2.22, 3.51, 3.124, 8.21, 20.68, 27.37, 27.91, 32.145, 34.6, 34.14, 38.10, 54.13, 57.16, 78.24, 83.7, 85.67, 86.4, 89.103, 93.63, 93.104, 97.41, 97.51, 97.75, 97.115, 97.148, 97.185, 97.193, 97.205, 101.24, 101.32, 105.4, 105.28, 105.44, 108.5, 114.21, 114.15, 124.16, 124.25, 124.26, 125.1, 134.7, 148.179, 149.9, 151.7, 152.7, 156.2, 156.17, 159.25, 161.182, 164.1, 164.16, 164.17, 164.84, 166.4
Clifford, Jack 97.1, 97.2, 97.3
Clifton, George 70.29, 116.17

Clinton, Steve 43.225
Clohessy, Robert 177.14
Close, John 3.97, 8.10, 8.102, 14.65, 60.81, 60.86, 65.179, 65.201, 66.118, 74.14, 93.49, 93.134, 97.81, 103.45, 126.109, 138.59, 155.38
Clothier, Robert 100.2
Clute, Chester 32.39
Clute, Sidney 5.20, 65.44, 76.44, 106.13, 156.60, 162.257
Clutesi, George 109.1
Clyde, Andy 3.48, 3.66, 3.109, 3.129, 22.29, 31.2, 31.18, 31.31, 34.46, 57.22, 57.91, 65.132, 65.259, 77.16, 93.203, 102.33, 129.76, 147.33, 147.39, 149.9, 149.13, 149.23, 149.31, 149.55, 152.3, 152.59, 152.60, 152.61, 162.42
Clyde, Jeremy 86.19
Coates, Phyllis 13.4, 32.14, 32.20, 32.23, 32.24, 43.301, 54.7, 64.10, 65.101, 65.339, 97.124, 97.125, 97.166, 124.41, 126.20, 126.93, 148.41, 148.163, 161.53
Coates, Robert 97.125
Cobb, Edmund 8.55, 31.36, 32.1, 32.7, 32.40, 32.73, 32.99, 32.103, 32.120, 60.54, 60.58, 97.33, 97.53, 97.61, 97.62, 97.71, 97.77, 97.105, 124.28, 124.31, 124.41, 138.16, 138.29, 141.46, 155.18, 169.41, 169.50
Cobb, Ike 155.60
Cobb, Julie 47.13, 65.597, 65.624, 96.20
Cobb, Lee J. 65.624, 161, 178.6, 178.65
Cobb, Orrin 170.9
Cobb, Vincent 161.68
Coburn, James 8.33, 8.56, 13.10, 14.11, 14.56, 14.98, 21.20, 21.29, 25.67, 25.69, 27.84, 43.188, 44.29, 66.93, 66.105, 79.1, 82, 85.51, 89.53, 89.88, 93.161, 93.163, 113.7, 113.8, 117.15, 126.106, 129.53, 129.66, 129.78, 130.12, 130.122, 133.33, 142.14, 144.31, 148.58, 148.198, 149.20, 150.1, 152.54, 155.54, 156.57, 162.47, 164.21, 164.30, 164.69, 167.20, 178.79, 178.120
Coburn, Sheldon 96.61, 96.62
Coby, Fred 23.9, 30.7, 57.72, 65.268, 65.321, 65.365, 65.422, 65.432, 65.470, 65.475, 65.508, 65.528, 85.36, 85.67, 85.100, 85.107, 97.115, 97.143, 135.70, 135.72, 145.2, 145.18, 161.30
Coca, Richard 118.10
Coch, Edward 124.54, 124.77, 127.46, 148.40
Cochran, Steve 14.194, 43.284, 144.15, 161.11, 178.57
Cochran, Wayne 170.104
Cockrell, Gary 162.209
Cockrum, Dennis 1.20
Codee, Ann 78.9
Cody, Harry 32.130, 43.30, 147.13
Cody, Iron Eyes 3.151, 3.161, 14.287, 17.13, 32.82, 32.89, 50.10, 65.469, 93.52, 105.43, 126.28, 126.157, 127.61, 129.23, 136, 138.3, 138.23, 149.13, 161.54, 169.76, 169.95, 178.134
Cody, J.W. 138.23
Cody, Kathleen 7.2, 47.14, 65.588, 65.659, 65.610, 65.627
Coe, Barry 14.101
Coe, Peter 3.65, 3.73, 3.108, 20.38, 32.44, 32.51, 32.95, 32.100, 41.3, 41.40, 66.9, 66.76, 93.214, 148.60, 161.108, 162.49, 178.81
Coe, Vickie 14.182
Coffee, Scott 120.3
Coffin, Frederick 163.32, 177.16
Coffin, Tristram 2.3, 2.7, 4.33, 8.60, 14.127, 21.47, 32.17. 32.19, 32.26, 32.41, 32.47, 32.95, 32.100, 32.133, 32.135, 34.53, 35.16, 35.18, 35.36, 43.341, 43.343, 43.351, 43.447, 43.449, 80.1, 80.3, 80.5, 80.34, 80.35, 80.38, 81.26, 81.51, 81.81, 81.84, 92.7, 93.14, 93.52, 97.1, 97.16, 97.54, 97.200, 97.215, 105.91, 146.62, 158, 162.143, 169.13, 169.17, 169.27, 169.56, 169.70, 169.75, 169.88

Personnel Index

Coffin, Winifred 14.201, 14.210, 43.349, 84.42
Cogan, Rhodie 65.603
Coghlan, Phyllis 65.453
Cohoon, Patti 47.2, 65.546, 65.554, 65.564, 65.565, 65.572, 65.606, 70
Coit, Stephen 21.19, 105.10, 105.84, 161.164
Colbern, Kenya 170.75
Colbert, Claudette 178.33, 178.123
Colbert, Robert 4.16, 4.35, 5.30, 14.210, 21.28, 21.35, 2.40, 21.62, 27.73, 34.59, 34.63, 34.66, 43.262, 43.305, 43.449, 85.123, 89.132, 105, 105.81, 146.53, 146.62, 148.194, 151.9, 161.9, 161.71, 162.180, 162.219
Colby, Barbara 65.618, 83.37
Colby, Fred 65.404, 65.440, 164.64
Cole, Ariana 43.56
Cole, Dennis 9, 84.21, 123.1
Cole, John 14.76, 126.54, 126.169, 158.16
Cole, Michael 65.410
Cole, Pamela 130.86
Cole, Phyllis 138.7
Coleman, Dabney 14.314, 14.343, 49.6, 76.45
Coleman, David 124.54
Coleman, Dick 60.57
Coleman, Mel 177.12
Coleman, Pat 138.39
Coleman, Robert 161.34
Coleman, Tommy 135.19
Coley, Thomas 43.196, 65.80, 65.173
Colicos, John 65.631, 71.68
Colin, Joel 44.2
Collentine, Barbara 112.15, 155.2
Colley, Don Pedro 30.22, 41.110, 41.115, 41.120, 41.126, 70.9, 96.63, 112.9, 161.169, 170.92
Collier, Constance 103.31
Collier, Don 14.34, 14.113, 14.187, 14.242, 14.406, 17.29, 17.30, 43.255, 43.274, 43.302, 43.355, 65.605, 65.640, 71, 91.6, 95.19, 96.39, 117, 137.4, 151.14, 161.70, 162.283, 168.7, 177, 177.3, 177.7, 177.15
Collier, James 156.64
Collier, John 129.73, 130.68, 164.38
Collier, Lois 27.10
Collier, Marion 66.42, 85.28, 164.34
Collier, Richard 4.37, 12.38, 14.65, 20.61, 86.12, 96.42, 103.31, 126.114, 151.25
Collier, Sue 65.437, 65.438
Colligan, Joe 120.9, 163.64
Collins, Al 130.128
Collins, G. Pat 169.80, 169.87
Collins, Gary 76, 123.7, 161.198
Collins, Gene 126.15
Collins, Georgie 99.15
Collins, Greg 120.55
Collins, Jack 14.333, 14.359, 14.363, 47.7
Collins, Joan 161.153
Collins, Joel 43.78
Collins, Lisa 1.22
Collins, Patrick 96.162
Collins, Ray 178.3
Collins, Roberta 24.11, 70.44
Collins, Russell 14.63, 66.127, 101.16, 130.6, 130.11, 149.25, 149.52, 162.140, 162.185
Collins, Sheldon 41.104, 41.128
Collins, Shirley 152.9
Collison, Frank 48
Colman, Booth 5.7, 5.16, 7.12, 14.179, 14.239, 14.240, 20.11, 20.53, 25.65, 41.25, 41.26, 41.75, 41.76, 43.244, 65.287, 65.562, 66.203, 78.3, 78.5, 78.13, 83.21, 130.122, 17.8, 179.70
Colman, Edward 170.94
Colmans, David 81.30, 81.55
Colmans, Edward 3.63, 15.12, 32.65, 32.66, 35.7, 43.107, 43.396, 64.11, 65.556, 66.84, 71.86, 73.12, 73.38, 78.24, 81.30, 81.78, 97.153, 113.5, 124.61, 126.86, 131.16, 145.14, 147.26, 151.22, 162.148, 162.153, 178.35

Colomby, Scott 163.68
Colon, Alex 26
Colon, Miriam 14.339, 21.33, 44.29, 61.1, 61.2, 65.254, 65.289, 65.466, 65.496, 65.516, 65.564, 65.565, 65.606, 66.216, 71.30, 92.16, 119.15, 148.92, 149.62, 161.151, 164.47
Colt, Steve 66.40
Colti, Tony 14.354, 14.373, 14.156
Comar, Richard 16, 99.19
Combs, Frederick 170.69
Combs, Gary 65.492, 65.535
Combs, Gil 120.35
Comeau, Richard 177.29, 177.44
Comer, Anjanette 7.12, 14.156, 65.313
Comi, Paul 12.23, 12.32, 12.33, 12.54, 89.78, 126.179, 126.181, 126.182, 144.8, 149.50, 155.31, 159, 159.3, 161.43, 161.72, 161.78, 161.169, 162.153, 170.23, 170.39, 170.65
Comiskey, Pat 105.9, 146.52
Compton, Forrest 57.103
Compton, John 32.140, 32.144, 57.84, 57.107, 65.97, 78.74, 138.75
Compton, Joyce 78.58
Conde, Rita 81.2
Condit, Steve 151.13
Condra, Julie 163.68
Conforti, Gino 71.59, 94.14, 116.1
Conino, Jim 158.11
Conklin, Russell 3.140, 74.6, 97.34, 97.45, 126.39, 138.51, 141.23
Conlan, Thomas J. 109.14
Conley, Darlene 65.520, 96.162
Conley, Frances 41.109, 135.39
Conley, Joe 65.348, 78.9, 164.43
Conlon, Noel 120.26
Connell, Jim 169.14, 170.25
Connelly, Christopher 14.351, 41.148, 65.338, 65.593, 123.1
Connelly, Lex 144.10, 144.30
Connelly, Norma 96.8
Conner, Betty 65.348, 126.201
Connery, Phillip 91.7
Connors, Chuck 10.13, 17, 36, 54.18, 59.4, 65.30, 78.67, 78.68, 106.16, 120.17, 120.18, 120.39, 129.13, 130, 148.1, 148.10, 162.9, 178.52
Connors, Jeff 130.45
Connors, Joan 155.61
Connors, Michael 21.16, 25.68, 27.54, 29.6, 54.2, 65.48, 66.6, 77.26, 78.6, 89.12, 93.12, 105.2, 105.13, 128.10, 133.17, 152.5
Conrad, Charles 65.66, 130.49, 138.49, 138.65
Conrad, Hal 141.29
Conrad, Michael 5.43, 14.232, 36.16, 36.17, 41.33, 65.349, 65.395, 65.396, 65.415, 75.11, 75.13, 75.15, 75.16, 86.23, 96.74, 116.10, 126.196, 161.202, 161.218, 162.237
Conrad, Robert 26, 34.34, 89.25, 105.47, 151.25, 170
Conrad, William 8.4, 8.94, 66.182, 66.193, 71.81, 133.6
Conried, Hans 25.48, 41.109, 42, 66.168, 78.70, 105.25
Considine, Charlotte 65.464
Considine, David 96.82
Considine, John 43.224, 43.447
Considine, Tim 3.3, 3.86, 14.213, 27.58, 65.521, 65.522, 79.13, 91.7, 178.77
Constantine, Michael 39.4, 43.307, 43.336, 49.1, 65.459, 76.32, 132.11, 161.102, 161.166, 161.213
Conte, John 14.199
Conte, Richard 55.19
Conte, Steve 2.26, 3.23, 20.7, 20.23, 20.68, 23.33, 23.34, 27.3, 43.54, 43.99, 57.21, 60.49, 60.52, 60.54, 60.58, 60.80, 60.84, 73.20, 108.19, 124.22, 130.67, 152.18, 158.6, 158.8
Conti, Audrey 43.65, 43.91, 43.117, 169.97
Contreras, Luis 1.16

Contreras, Roberto 12.45, 37.6, 66.76, 66.148, 71, 83.52, 86.3, 93.162, 126.34, 130.111, 133.36, 148.185, 164.89, 165.9, 178.146
Converse, Frank 5.43
Conway, Blake 177.38
Conway, Curt 15.13, 2.27, 14.197, 98.19
Conway, Gary 34.58, 41.107, 141.21
Conway, Joe 141.27, 141.34, 141.56, 149.53, 179.40, 179.41, 179.42, 179.43, 179.44
Conway, Melora 14.147, 21.40, 51.16
Conway, Pat 14.207, 14.276, 14.306, 17.5, 51.21, 65.5, 65.97, 65.128, 65.580, 72.3, 76.14, 85.74, 98.17, 126.191, 152.3, 155
Conway, Russ 14.54, 14.275, 14.308, 17.4, 21.13, 27.50, 32.94, 32.102, 39.9, 41.46, 41.121, 57.4, 57.111, 66.9, 73.30, 74.12, 89.109, 97.22, 97.104, 97.106, 97.167, 98.10, 105.16, 107.1, 126.9, 126.79, 126.102, 133.34, 148.104, 148.128, 149.57, 151.10, 152.63, 155.49, 156.50, 161.30, 161.62, 161.102, 161.146, 162.155, 164.9, 164.45, 178.15
Conway, Tim 125
Conway, Tom 27.38, 126.1
Conwell, Carolyn 12.53, 12.85, 107.25
Conwell, John 57.105
Coogan, Jackie 5.25, 5.35, 5.48, 35, 47.12, 65.614, 65.615, 82.10, 117.4, 117.44, 170.67, 170.95, 170.96
Coogan, Richard 14.55, 21.29, 25, 27.68, 65.307, 85.41, 85.50, 85.63, 85.78, 85.88, 85.109, 105.88, 142.6, 146.51, 167.12
Coogan, Robert 41
Cook, Carole 41.74
Cook, Christopher 6.7, 6.19
Cook, Donald 164.33
Cook, Edwin 17.28
Cook, Elisha, Jr. 8.1, 8.39, 14.235, 14.364, 30.6, 39.19, 44.74, 46.3, 65.118, 65.167, 65.349, 65.366, 79.8, 85.58, 93.65, 107.18, 117.39, 126.22, 126.76, 126.177, 127.38, 132.10, 151.6, 155.66, 156.20, 162.99, 162.138, 162.252, 169.70, 170.9, 170.22
Cook, Jimmy Lee 127.33, 161.9, 161.101, 161.120, 165.3, 165.6, 165.8, 165.10, 165.11
Cook, Myron 138.74
Cook, Perry 8.50, 63.1, 63.1, 65.190, 66.66, 66.82, 66.117, 66.121, 66.153, 66.159, 66.181, 88.30, 127.14, 127.34, 178.123
Cook, Ron 67.18
Cook, Tommy 66.93, 93.14, 93.103, 93.105, 93.107, 93.136, 103.50, 130.113, 169.62, 178.79
Cooke, John C. 120.2
Cooke, John J. 107.8
Cooley, Isabelle 116.8
Coolidge, Philip 65.129, 65.251, 65.359, 66.72, 66.173, 148.101
Coombs, Carol 108.13
Cooney, Dennis 70.39, 76.47, 161.210
Coons, Johnny 168.6
Coontz, Bill 93.132, 169.28, 169.66
Cooper, Ben 14.33, 14.76, 43.429, 65.244, 65.366, 65.374, 79.21, 83.38, 83.39, 85.84, 85.103, 106.4, 126.185, 130.95, 142.8, 148.100, 162.71, 162.98, 165.12, 167.9, 178.9, 178.102, 178.118, 178.120
Cooper, Charles 14.8, 21.12, 21.35, 34.17, 34.55, 43.263, 43.304, 43.342, 44.16, 53, 65.114, 65.134, 79.22, 89.24, 96.98, 105.26, 105.50, 105.65, 129.54, 129.63, 130.3, 130.114, 130.118, 130.149, 131.25, 146.14, 148.63, 148.115, 152.16, 152.78, 156.53, 162.54, 164.15
Cooper, Clancy 3.39, 3.90, 3.94, 20.27, 22.18, 44.52, 65.76, 88.11, 89.40, 89.47, 89.54, 93.162, 93.168, 93.184, 93.212, 97.15, 97.140, 105.80, 126.105, 130.37, 133.22, 149.67, 161.29, 162.132, 164.37, 170.14
Cooper, Dee 121.9, 124.75
Cooper, George 60.25

Personnel Index

Cooper, Harry 161.210
Cooper, Jackie 69.8
Cooper, Jackie, Jr. 35.28
Cooper, James Fenimore 67, 68
Cooper, Jeanne 12.3, 12.29, 14.113, 14.135, 17.4, 21.16, 21.29, 27.44, 27.96, 27.101, 30.18, 39.3, 41.48, 41.81, 43.34, 43.54, 65.314, 66.208, 77.10, 81.54, 81.64, 84.11, 86.53, 98.3, 101.2, 102.14, 105.13, 105.102, 107.3, 126.70, 126.132, 144.20, 146.60, 148.15, 148.90, 149.21, 161.48, 162.163, 162.203, 162.236, 162.253, 162.271, 164.50, 178.50
Cooper, Jeff 161.72
Cooper, Keene 60.13
Cooper, Kevin 65.473
Cooper, Maxine 105.7, 164.66
Cooper, Melville 22.15, 25.13
Cooper, Stuart 61.9, 61.10
Cooper, Tamar 20.16, 54.16
Cooper, Wyatt 127.28
Coote, Robert 126.54
Copperman, Stephane 91.1
Coppola, Alicia 90.6
Corbeil, Luc 67.3
Corbett, Glenn 5.30, 5.43, 14.211, 14.387, 65.352, 65.541, 65.602, 92.30, 132, 161.96
Corbett, Gretchen 7.10, 65.613
Corbett, Lois 78.70
Corby, Ellen 3.104, 12.69, 14.19, 14.121, 27.97, 41.13, 46.10, 55.4, 63.30, 71.31, 78.45, 84.28, 86.39, 93.50, 125.17, 127.41, 129.27, 129.73, 130.61, 130.122, 135.86, 148.138, 149.23, 152.14, 156.22, 156.23, 156.25, 156.26, 156.29, 156.33, 156.34, 156.35, 156.36, 156.40, 156.42, 156.44, 156.45, 156.46, 156.47, 156.50, 156.53, 156.59, 156.61, 156.62, 156.65, 161.72, 162.79, 162.115
Corcoran, Billy 41.89, 41.160
Corcoran, Brian 40.2, 113.10, 153
Corcoran, Hugh 22.20
Corcoran, Kelly 12.101, 132
Corcoran, Kevin 40, 162.240
Corcoran, Noreen 12.14, 31.27, 65.332
Cord, Alex 17.1, 65.574, 123.2, 163.50
Cord, Bill 27.62, 93.186, 122, 122.22
Corday, Mara 81.12, 81.23, 85.43, 102.9, 129.55, 148.96, 164.65
Cordell, Cathleen 162.215
Cordell, Melinda 96.112
Corden, Henry 41.64, 65.117, 66.107, 105.123, 126.203, 129.29, 129.48, 148.70, 150.12, 162.157, 168.26
Cordero, Maria Elena 83.20, 109.1, 123.5
Cordic, Regis J. 65.566, 65.575, 65.585, 65.622, 65.623, 83.11, 175.7
Cording, Harry 73.2, 97.22, 169.54
Cordova, Anthony 65.528
Cordova, Linda 66.196, 164.89
Cordova, Margarita 12.61, 12.108, 17.44, 17.45, 27.92, 65.495, 65.506, 71.82, 117.23, 148.172, 178.75
Core, Natalie 41.128
Core, Virginia 78.38, 93.98
Corey, Jeff 5.46, 14.248, 14.376, 65.485, 76.33, 96.108, 96.154, 126.205, 170.6, 170.75
Corey, Walter 170.92
Corey, Wendell 17.8, 17.9, 17.10, 63.4, 132.8, 170.80, 178.8, 178.112, 178.129
Corey, Will 65.292, 66.192
Cori, Lisa 175.9
Corlett, Irene 162.6
Cornell, Ann 138.74
Corner, Sally 54.20, 65.14, 97.95
Cornthwaite, Robert 7.13, 12.18, 12.58, 14.360, 20.9, 25.8, 25.20, 25.39, 41.124, 41.159, 43.335, 46.4, 65.85, 65.536, 71.43, 78.3, 78.19, 78.24, 83.35, 84.9, 85.104, 86.14, 86.31, 89.107, 105.84, 105.96, 126.28, 126.97, 126.165, 130.65, 148.110,

148.193, 156.15, 156.42, 161.37, 162.160, 162.202, 162.241, 173.25, 178.19, 178.87
Corona, Julio Alejos 165.9
Corrie, William B. 105.87
Corrigan, Bob 158.64
Corrigan, Lloyd 14.157, 14.196, 43.166, 43.229, 64.9, 65.317, 66.177, 78.49, 93.16, 93.57, 93.82, 93.120, 93.161, 93.196, 103.45, 105.120, 126.79, 129.9, 129.32, 129.56, 131.4, 155.42, 156.56, 157.11, 164.16
Corrigan, Mary Elizabeth 96.127
Corsaro, Franco 20.55
Corseaut, Aneta 13.25, 14.124, 43.245, 43.307, 43.331, 43.333, 65.370, 65.436, 79.27, 178.124
Corsentino, Frank 65.541, 65.602
Corsi, Ron 21.49
Cort, William 17.12, 50, 96.13
Cortez, Ricardo 14.16
Cory, Steve 14.301, 43.443
Cos, Vickie 65.331
Costa, Cosie 163.68
Costello, Anthony 41.150, 43.306, 43.340, 43.344, 65.523, 65.537, 151.26
Costello, Lou 162.43
Costello, Mariclaire 96.141, 137
Costello, Michael 163.66
Costello, Vera 158.54, 158.55
Costello, Ward 96.141
Cota, Bob 177.44
Cotler, Jeff 176
Cotsworth, Staats 14.422
Cotten, Joseph 30.9, 61.1, 61.2, 106.6, 161.221, 162.153, 162.194, 178.44
Cotton, Heather 65.540
Couch, Chuck 66.176, 66.189, 155.67
Coughlin, Kevin 14.301, 65.482, 65.492, 65.524, 65.587, 65.631, 161.172, 161.192
Coulouris, George 49.9
Court, Hazel 14.27, 76.14, 126.160, 142.16, 170.33
Courtland, Jerome 3.94, 43.310, 130.5, 136, 161.82
Courtleigh, Stephen 14.38, 41.1, 89.4, 146.65, 148.162
Courtney, Alex 120.36
Courtney, Chuck 3.147, 3.149, 23.4, 77.3, 85.88, 85.108, 89.9, 92.32, 97.22, 97.51, 97.111, 97.113, 97.141, 97.148, 97.151, 97.154, 97.158, 97.161, 97.164, 97.166, 97.169, 97.170, 145.24, 147.24, 148.34, 158.41, 158.65, 161.175, 162.242, 162.265, 169.54, 169.111, 170.76, 178.79
Courtney, James 97.165
Cousins, Brian 1.13
Cousins, Kay 130.22, 162.29
Cousins, Rae 170.69
Covarrubias, Robert 1.22, 65.637
Covelli, Gene 32.132
Cowan, Jerome 4.8, 5.12, 8.31, 8.32, 8.52, 14.160, 41.62, 46.3, 74.21, 82.11, 117.2, 117.42, 126.28, 168.5
Cowen, Ashley 14.191, 25.35, 93.114, 93.141, 129.51, 142.12, 162.251
Cowl, Richard 172.4
Cowling, Bruce 3.72, 27.29, 57.23, 66.31, 97.127, 97.134, 97.156, 97.163, 114.15, 152.22, 178.59
Cox, Richard 91.4
Cox, Ronny 14.420, 94.4
Cox, Victor 32.15, 32.18, 32.21
Cox, Wally 5.33, 14.283, 14.309, 162.67
Coy, Walter 8.71, 12.44, 12.103, 14.62, 14.138, 21.3, 21.15, 27.42, 27.74, 29.7, 41.101, 54, 54.3, 66.63, 74.18, 85.27, 89.25, 93.34, 93.144, 93.191, 97.149, 102.15, 116.5, 119.9, 126.79, 129.1, 129.59, 133.29, 145.24, 148.12, 148.34, 152.67, 156.49, 159.3, 161.144, 161.167, 161.192, 162.10, 162.131, 162.254, 162.266, 164.40, 173.29, 178.29, 178.47, 178.60
Cozart, Cylk 163.8
Crabb, Christopher 120.44

Crabtree, Michael 163.42
Craig, Carolyn 6.50, 6.79, 23.39, 25.5, 25.46, 44.58, 85.94, 93.102, 93.121, 93.192, 114.24, 119.3, 130.3, 148.28, 148.95
Craig, Dana 1.25
Craig, Donald 53.5, 53.6
Craig, James 20.24, 38.6, 43.176, 66.26, 148.199
Craig, Janet 67.8
Craig, John 96.83, 126.146, 130.168, 148.142, 162.248
Craig, Melanie 84.46
Craig, Yvonne 12.16, 85.96, 148.153, 162.256, 168.11, 170.18
Crain, Jeanne 131.7
Cramer, Susanne 14.195, 39.12, 63.47, 151.11
Crandall, Bill 6.9, 6.15, 169.62
Crandall, Suzi 167.22
Crandall, Will 60.88, 60.89, 60.90
Crane, Chilton 67.15
Crane, Frederick 89.79, 89.87
Crane, John 166.11
Crane, Les 161.145
Crane, Norma 12.42, 44.69, 63.45, 65.142, 65.234, 66.17, 66.56, 66.80, 66.152, 131.35, 178.23
Crane, Richard 43.148, 73.13, 93.205, 97.47, 97.65, 97.85, 97.103, 97.116, 97.128, 97.157, 97.199, 97.202, 97.211, 105.5, 108.17, 142.4, 146.6, 148.45, 148.82, 156.14, 156.34, 158.50, 158.67, 161.88, 162.91, 162.132, 162.162, 164.62, 166.9
Crane, Susan 4.37, 27.82, 43.218, 146.51, 149.41, 164.76
Crane, Virginia 162.19
Crane, Walter 158.3, 158.5, 158.7, 158.12
Cranshaw, Patrick 10.2, 10.11
Cranston, Bryan 163.21
Cranston, Joe 6.49, 6.78
Cravat, Nick 42, 116.15
Craven, James 60.28, 60.30, 60.35, 60.37, 81.41, 81.50, 81.71, 81.73, 97.135, 145.10, 145.39, 169.2
Craven, John 12.9, 93.28, 126.18, 138.51, 164.77
Crawford, Bobby 65.402, 130.6, 130.14
Crawford, Bobby, Jr. 179.34
Crawford, Broderick 5.32, 8.2, 24.11, 30.21, 46.1, 126.170, 126.171, 133.18, 161.35
Crawford, Diana 8.68, 66.71, 105.80
Crawford, Edward 14.411
Crawford, Joan 161.218, 178.98, 178.132
Crawford, John 3.72, 12.98, 12.108, 14.350, 31.11, 32.98, 32.104, 41.43, 41.48, 41.70, 63.49, 65.161, 65.262, 65.289, 65.375, 65.473, 65.476, 65.500, 65.504, 65.534, 65.551, 65.552, 65.553, 65.591, 65.613, 73.2, 73.11, 73.19, 97.97, 97.116, 97.127, 112.19, 135.7, 135.9, 156.24, 162.145, 169.17, 169.58, 170.89
Crawford, Johnny 17.7, 24.11, 59.2, 59.4, 66.15, 84.7, 96.55, 97.187, 120.23, 120.39, 126.217, 129.39, 130, 148.68, 156.28, 162.28, 169.102, 178.44
Crawford, Katherine 46.6, 61.6, 70.38, 106.16, 161.19, 161.59, 161.66, 162.252
Crawford, Lee 53.21
Crawford, Nancy 148.112
Crawford, Robert 25.69, 27.57, 130.23
Crawford, Robert, Jr. 27.89, 85, 126.82, 178.121
Craxton, Dee 96.81
Crayne, Dani 27.25
Creach, Everett L. 83.22
Creamer, Patrick 92.24
Creatore, Victor 161.167
Creghan, Dennis 177.10
Crehan, Joseph 8.90, 97.5, 97.30, 97.158, 97.199, 141.8, 158.19, 158.21
Cremer, John 170.93
Crenna, Richard 26, 27.35, 44.30, 54.14
Cress, Duane 43.87, 44.53, 148.105

Personnel Index

Crest, Patricia 21.62, 105.120
Crider, Dorothy 135.4, 147.10
Crigler, Tharon 22.5, 162.37
Crino, Isa 41.24
Crise, George 138.27
Cristal, Linda 14.403, 24.10, 71, 76.26, 126.22
Crittenden, James 120
Crockett, Davy 42
Crockett, Luther 32.2, 32.6, 32.11, 32.13, 97.26
Crockett, Polly 42
Croft, Bill 67.15
Cromer, Dean 164.25
Cromwell, James 7.5, 53.25, 53.26, 67.21, 171.5, 177.38
Cronauer, Gail 163.62
Cronin, Dermot 89.65
Crosby, Denise 1.3, 48.91
Crosby, Gary 72.14
Crosby, Mary 120.53
Crosby, Wade 6.21, 35.34, 60.8, 97.15, 124.30, 169.11, 169.18
Cross, Bill 96.131
Cross, David 158.49, 158.57, 169.83
Cross, Dennis 12.1, 12.19, 12.23, 12.42, 13.20, 13.37, 30.5, 41.52, 43.224, 43.322, 43.325, 44.34, 63.30, 63.39, 65.18, 65.41, 65.178, 65.297, 65.451, 65.483, 66.31, 74.23, 76.13, 77.15, 92.4, 103.13, 116.22, 126.13, 126.38, 126.81, 126.98, 126.150, 130.8, 130.14, 130.41, 130.59, 130.66, 130.127, 148.127, 156.69, 159.26, 164.3, 167.23, 178.50, 178.77
Cross, Jimmy 65.116, 65.389
Cross, Roger R. 67.17
Cross, Yvonne 43.52
Crosse, Rupert 14.366, 36.3, 66.163, 126.64
Crosson, Robert 85.58, 97.212, 178.18
Crothers, Joel 43.198, 66.153, 178.90
Crothers, Scatman 14.67
Crow, Carl 117.44
Crowder, Randy 120.13, 120.19, 120.22, 120.31, 120.34, 120.40, 120.50, 177.60
Crowley, Kathleen 2.25, 8.21, 8.78, 14.28, 14.129, 14.303, 17.17, 21.5, 21.61, 27.42, 29.12, 34.16, 44.43, 71.47, 85.23, 97.145, 105.10, 105.66, 105.78, 105.86, 105.91, 105.112, 105.122, 105.124, 126.18, 128.10, 129.24, 133.7, 148.94, 148.195, 155.23, 161.88, 162.23, 173.11
Crowley, Patricia 5.29, 14.122, 21.21, 27.60, 105.45, 105.52, 105.59, 113.9, 126.131, 131.16, 148.168, 161.171, 164.22
Crowther, John 162.268
Cruz, Brandon 65.568, 83.2
Cubitt, David 99.1, 99.2, 99.3, 99.5
Cudney, Roger 106.19
Cullen, Brett 28, 59.5, 177
Cullen, William Kirby 75
Culliton, Barry 177.25, 177.37
Culliton, Patrick 12.15
Cullum, John 116.19
Cully, Zara 36.10
Culp, Robert 14.72, 43.222, 48.8, 51.18, 61.6, 65.349, 99.1, 99.2, 99.3, 117.1, 126.66, 130.59, 130.130, 150.3, 156, 161.64, 162.177, 163.42, 165.10, 178.29, 178.114, 178.130
Culver, Howard 65, 106.9
Culver, Susan 106.13
Culwell, John 148.81
Cumbuka, Ji-Tu 41.157, 83.56, 83.57, 83.58, 83.59, 174
Cummings, Dale 158.51, 158.53
Cummings, Robert 70.43, 178.125
Cummings, Susan 8.3, 8.44, 8.82, 27.83, 65.201, 79.32, 85.52, 93.201, 102.13, 119.10, 131.32, 133.36, 160
Cummins, Fred 135.16
Cummins, Gregory Scott 110.1, 120.47, 163.8
Cunningham, Bob 78.22, 93.64, 138.54

Cunningham, Owen 162.26
Cunningham, Quinn 170.48
Cupito, Suzanne *see* Brittany, Morgan
Curley, Leo 138.33, 138.41
Curran, Pamela 17.27, 85.77, 85.85, 85.99
Currie, Red 65.545
Curry, Anne E. 96.161
Curry, Christopher 120.47
Curry, Howard 25.32
Curry, Kristen 94.1
Curry, Mason 25.31, 65.20, 65.43, 108.15, 126.27, 138.16, 138.23
Curtis, Barry 2, 6.47, 6.80, 23.41, 138.49
Curtis, Billy 14.146, 32.60, 65.578, 97.154, 102.22
Curtis, Craig 14.111, 14.213, 65.455, 117.25, 144.28
Curtis, Dick 60.23, 60.24, 60.31, 60.33, 97.20, 97.33, 97.66, 124.1, 124.5, 124.6, 124.10, 124.25, 124.26, 169.3
Curtis, Donald 6.64, 6.81, 56.28, 93.40, 145.8
Curtis, Ken 43.279, 65, 65.138, 65.149, 65.186, 65.190, 65.280, 65.307, 66.82, 66.92, 66.119, 66.155, 66.190, 75.21, 94.37, 126.78, 162.116, 162.123
Curtis, Willa Pearl 162.266, 168.22
Curtiz, Gabor 6.47, 6.80, 97.212
Curtwright, Jorja 14.229, 65.36, 76.22, 178.59
Cutell, Lou 170.93
Cutler, Bill 126.66, 126.71
Cutler, Max 155.31
Cutrona, Ryan 1.19
Cutter, Bill 126.77
Cutter, Lise 45.1, 45.3, 45.4, 163.24
Cutting, Richard 4.33, 14.9, 22.19, 22.39, 23.1, 39.13, 43.144, 44.41, 73.34, 77.13, 92.7, 92.29, 101.34, 129.59, 146.38, 158.50, 158.52, 162.33, 162.51, 162.89, 162.125, 162.149, 162.179, 162.191, 162.250, 162.270, 167.24
Cutts, Patricia 173.20
Cypher, Charles 95.22
Cypher, Jon 14.413, 48.104
Czingland, John 70.46

Dae, Frank 141.6, 145.3
Daggett, Jensen 1.9
Dahl, Arlene 131.33
Dahlgren, Tom 1.12
Dale, Esther 105.3, 162.14
Dale, Fred 65.422, 76.3
Dale, Michael 169.75
Dale, Ray 149.6
Dale, Virginia 6.66, 23.25, 81.5, 81.27, 93.83
Daley, Jeff 129.49, 129.54, 129.75, 129.78, 130.46, 148.40, 162.59, 164.44
Daley, Ray 14.22, 14.72, 34.62, 43.238, 55.22, 105.57
Dalio, Marcel 43.170, 105.42
Dallas, Johnny 2.4
Dallimore, Maurice 130.161
Dalton, Abby 66.48, 77.24, 105.46, 126.8, 146.29
Dalton, Audrey 8.9, 8.37, 8.101, 12.9, 12.24, 14.83, 39.19, 43.259, 65.285, 86.13, 113.6, 151.10, 162.37, 162.44, 162.73, 162.127, 162.250, 162.264, 166.13, 168.27, 170.30
Dalton, Darren 48.11
Dalton, Timothy 26
Daly, Arnold 8.52, 138.20, 138.38
Daly, Jack 2.24, 23.1, 23.22, 23.30, 31.16, 43.47, 60.80, 60.81, 60.86, 145.39
Daly, James 38.2, 65.434, 132.3, 161.145, 161.178
Daly, Jonathan 121.23
Daly, Tom 141.59
D'Amico, Rita 76.30, 170.32
Damison, Larry 43.280
Damler, John 2.26, 6.34, 6.45, 32.74, 32.91, 43.54, 66.206, 81.98, 97.85, 97.101, 97.117, 97.156, 98.7, 101.21, 138.22, 142.7, 149.25, 162.83, 164.25, 169.64, 169.68, 169.76, 169.85, 169.99

Damon, Les 66.201
Damon, Mark 148.60, 179.54, 179.81
Damon, Peter 179.14
Damone, Vic 127.67
Dan, Judy 32.86, 35.2, 97.192, 146.50
Dana, Bill 181
Dana, Leora 144.16, 178.97
Dana, Mark 2.19, 2.25, 43.69, 43.127, 66.57, 73.40, 85.62, 85.110, 93.23, 93.79, 93.125, 93.162, 129.17, 152.64
Dana, Rod 114.14
Dana, Rudi 3.129
Dane, Lawrence 14.318, 84.13, 161.175, 161.181, 161.214
Dane, Peter 43.59, 147.1
Dangcil, Linda 17.43, 24.4, 70.25, 72.17, 105.73, 130.82, 142.34, 148.182, 149.4, 151.2
Dangler, Anita 96.81
Daniel, Chuck 161.187
Daniell, Henry 25.12, 25.60, 25.68, 105.54, 162.101, 162.106, 162.107
Daniels, Ann 25.47, 93.135, 158.39, 158.55
Daniels, Carol Ann 78.21, 126.104
Daniels, Elaine 94.16
Daniels, J.D. 48.54
Daniels, Jerry 24.11, 71.49, 116.13
Daniels, John 12.82, 98.25, 161.196
Daniels, Lisa 145.33
Daniels, Rod 161.8
Daniels, William 7.7
Dano, Richard 65.639
Dano, Royal 5.5, 12.22, 12.44, 12.66, 12.100, 14.87, 14.213, 14.264, 30.3, 30.11, 36.25, 39.15, 41.57, 41.94, 43.309, 43.326, 43.395, 43.435, 43.437, 55.9, 63.7, 63.28, 64.1, 65.5, 65.30, 65.330, 65.343, 65.358, 65.394, 65.442, 65.443, 65.445, 65.491, 65.513, 65.531, 65.540, 66.140, 72.8, 74.3, 75.1, 75.2, 76.15, 79.27, 83.8, 92.9, 96.124, 96.152, 96.153, 116.6, 121.21, 123.1, 126.126, 126.157, 126.178, 126.192, 127.3, 127.67, 129.11, 130.16, 130.34, 130.57, 130.118, 130.138, 148.107, 148.197, 150.1, 151.4, 157.19, 161.6, 161.19, 161.97, 161.120, 162.70, 162.231, 164.39, 178.147
Danova, Cesare 14.185, 41.25, 41.26, 41.73, 50.13, 117.22, 130.7, 130.82, 130.166, 144.21, 148.125, 178.145
Dansen, Linda 169.81
Dante, Michael 3.157, 12.91, 14.205, 27.43, 34.3, 34.24, 38, 41.137, 43.151, 89.15, 105.6, 105.15, 146.13, 147.43, 152.45, 152.46, 152.47, 152.48
Dante, Tony 141.5
Dantine, Helmut 146.34
Danton, Ray 4, 8.35, 12.84, 21.2, 21.46, 27.74, 34.64, 43.281, 51.15, 85.94, 89.40, 89.82, 105.95, 109.6, 112.6, 128.11, 146.4, 146.42, 151.20, 156.6, 161.8, 162.38, 162.227, 162.255, 168.11, 173.4
D'Antonio, Carmen 41.14, 162.255
Dapo, Ronnie 27.94, 162.79
Darby, Kim 14.278, 65.432, 65.442, 65.443, 132.22, 162.271
D'Arcy, Alexander 41.57
Darden, Severn 5.14, 7.9, 14.400, 41.122, 123.4, 175.4
Dare, Doreen 43.83
Darfler, Gene 65.305
Darin, Bobby 24.10, 162.261
Daris, James 41.119, 112.14
Dark, Christopher 14.20, 14.141, 14.279, 20.9, 20.18, 34.16, 41.54, 43.184, 44.5, 54.22, 54.24, 55.21, 65.274, 66.65, 66.215, 71.38, 71.49, 71.63, 73.32, 76.28, 85.6, 85.62, 86.24, 88.25, 92.17, 97.139, 97.176, 103.16, 106.3, 114.26, 126.137, 126.185, 126.209, 130.42, 142.25, 152.17, 152.31, 153.3, 155.11, 156.18, 161.14, 161.38, 164.29
Darnell, Cliff 18.15
Darnell, Linda 29.7, 162.20, 162.39

Darnell, Lorna 170.93
Darnell, Robert 53.31, 95.21
Darr, Larry 8.92
Darrell, Steve 6.11, 6.14, 6.16, 8.68, 20.42, 20.54, 27.9, 27.42, 34.11, 41.87, 44.55, 60.2, 60.4, 60.6, 65.379, 73.5, 81.93, 81.99, 85.24, 85.58, 89.44, 93.148, 97.88, 97.119, 97.123, 98.24, 108.15, 124.64, 124.74, 130.44, 130.85, 145.1, 145.5, 148.167, 148.179, 148.181, 148.183, 148.192, 149.9, 158.63, 162.114, 162.119, 162.169, 164.35, 164.44, 169.35, 164.52, 178.17, 178.67
Darren, Diana 14.90, 88.30, 147.37
Darro, Frankie 8.46, 80.35, 80.38, 169.25
Darrow, Barbara 34.34
Darrow, Henry 9.11, 14.257, 26, 41.86, 65.424, 65.436, 71, 76.7, 83.20, 137.6, 170.44, 180, 181
Darrow, Susannah 70.33, 71.49
Darvi, Andrea 43.271, 65.332
Darwell, Jane 3.57, 22.22, 31.17, 105.25, 108.25, 162.62, 162.74, 162.159
Dash, Darien 53.16
Da Silva, Howard 83.26, 98.26
Davalos, Ellen 14.327, 65.460
Davalos, Elyssa 75.4, 75.5, 75.6, 75.21
Davalos, Richard 14.43, 75.27, 85.69
Davenport, Havis 78.7
Davenport, Mark 177.47
Davenport, Ned 73.23
Davey, Scott 126.31
David, Brad 65.506
David, Clifford 12.112, 112.9
David, Jeff 75.22
David, Michael 126.85
David, Thayer 170.62
Davidson, James 14.214, 14.254, 14.300, 30.22, 41.114, 70.45, 116.19, 162.277
Davidson, John 41.132, 41.153
Davidson, Wayne 102.14, 169.111
Davies, Blair 161.47
Davies, Emlen 93.4, 93.51, 97.134, 97.154, 141.64, 145.8
Davies, John S. 163.15, 163.16, 163.62
Davion, Alex 38.1, 43.154, 43.213, 66.115, 178.101
Davis, Andy 170.69
Davis, Ann B. 162.108
Davis, Bette 65.412, 161.14, 162.57, 162.82, 162.164
Davis, Brent 170.86
Davis, Charles 5.10, 43.176, 66.114, 126.54, 170.5, 170.9, 170.15, 170.74
Davis, Elaine 43.193, 148.141
Davis, Gail 6, 32.5, 32.10, 32.13, 32.55, 32.59, 43.18, 60.7, 60.8, 60.10, 60.15, 60.18, 60.31, 60.33, 60.35, 60.38, 60.39, 60.40, 60.41, 60.63, 60.65, 60.76, 81.41, 97.25, 97.38, 97.77, 97.89, 124.52, 124.55
Davis, Gary Lee 120.31
Davis, George 32.32, 32.39, 93.64
Davis, Harry 65.387, 65.481
Davis, Jeff 66.188
Davis, Jim 14.59, 14.198, 14.299, 17.13, 17.23, 17.44, 17.45, 30.9, 35.9, 35.19, 35.35, 35.37, 41.72, 41.89, 41.141, 43.255, 43.277, 43.291, 43.297, 43.350, 43.365, 43.396, 63.25, 64.12, 65.229, 65.395, 65.396, 65.406, 65.413, 65.459, 65.466, 65.472, 65.527, 65.535, 65.585, 65.604, 66.208, 71.75, 72.7, 83.7, 83.17, 85.16, 85.95, 85.111, 85.122, 86.9, 106.15, 117.24, 123.6, 126.103, 126.213, 144.13, 145, 148.16, 148.158, 148.197, 149.2, 149.5, 158.30, 161.183, 162.125, 162.201, 162.248, 173.34
Davis, Karl 6.20, 6.22, 21.13, 32.45, 32.52, 89.26, 141.46, 158.51, 158.53, 169.43
Davis, Kristin 48.51
Davis, Lindy 98.8
Davis, Lisa 114.3
Davis, Michael 12.32, 12.33, 14.134, 51.27, 65.388, 89.105, 126.140, 128.3, 178.81

Davis, N.J. 82.11, 127.8
Davis, Nancy 149.42, 162.204, 178.133
Davis, Ossie 14.326
Davis, Phyllis 170.18, 170.59
Davis, Roger 5, 12.51, 14.245, 14.378, 128
Davis, Rufe 97.7
Davis, Sammy, Jr. 55.11, 89.102, 130.131, 130.152, 170.33, 178.95
Davis, Susan 66.96, 66.169
Davis, Thayer 170.94
Davis, Tony 41.160, 65.452, 65.528, 76.24, 84.23
Davis, Walt 5.12, 5.35, 5.40
Davis, Wee Willie 32.41
Davison, Betty 169.10
Davison, Bruce 69.5
Davison, Davey 14.138, 14.275, 51.21, 65.357, 126.112, 126.194, 161.105
Davison, James 43.337
Davitt, Theodora 27.46
Dawn, Isabelle 27.50, 169.63
Dawson, Hal K. 2.3, 6.70, 20.16, 23.15, 23.28, 23.29, 32.67, 32.71, 44.70, 57.65, 60.21, 81.95, 82.4, 85.80, 85.95, 89.96, 93.206, 97.81, 97.123, 103.41, 124.9, 129.8, 130.91, 138.1, 141.12, 141.33, 145.30, 149.39, 149.58, 149.70, 156.66, 164.76
Dawson, Kamala 163.14
Dawson, Maurine 101.32, 105.113, 130.147
Dawson, Nancy Juno 83.33
Dawson, Peter 86.33
Day, Dennis 43.239
Day, John 2.7, 34.2, 97.12, 97.22, 97.42, 97.67, 112.12, 131.18, 166.10
Day, Laraine 162.240
Day, Patrick 120.34
Day, Rosemary 166.3
Daye, Harold T. 43.118, 162.57
Dayton, Howard 25.12, 66.112, 126.133, 141.47
Dayton, June 43.165, 43.197, 43.314, 43.445, 65.107, 65.333, 65.350, 65.526, 72.12, 84.4, 84.31, 96.27, 111.2, 164.74, 178.72
Deacon, Richard 14.28, 65.54, 105.58, 125.6, 130.76, 148.53, 179.77
Deadrick, Vincent 65.504, 164.88, 164.94
Deale, Nancy 14.32
Dean, Crag 126.14
Dean, Eddie 104
Dean, Fabian 71.60, 86.35
Dean, Jeanne 32.28, 32.34, 32.100, 73.19, 135.20, 135.22, 145.29, 158.59, 169.36
Dean, Jimmy 41, 41.82, 41.103, 41.105
Dean, Phil 8.78, 57.105
Dean, Quentin 12.74, 71.46, 84.35, 161.177
Dean, Rick 1.1
Dean, Robert 120.14, 120.26
De Anda, Miguel 12.1, 12.24, 14.272, 14.283, 14.408, 66.140, 71.1, 71.5, 71.40, 71.59, 92.16, 125.14, 126.127
Deans, Herbert 108.14
Dearden, Robin 118.8
Dearing, Edgar 2.12, 6.69, 6.70, 6.72, 23.28, 23.39, 23.40, 60.16, 60.17, 60.69, 73.14, 73.19, 124.11, 124.12, 124.23, 124.24, 124.29, 124.34, 130.19, 135.98, 138.17, 138.49, 148.163, 149.64
De Benning, Burr 7.8, 14.352, 24.9, 30.15, 38.8, 41.156, 53.1, 53.19, 53.20, 76.1, 84.17, 96.73, 109.3, 116.1, 161.185, 161.214
De Benning, Jeff 8.3, 14.86, 27.95, 70.25, 89.95, 93.189, 105.107, 149.40, 155.34, 155.45, 164.41
DeBriac, Jean 97.6
De Broux, Lee 5.7, 14.403, 65.444, 65.457, 65.470, 65.474, 65.499, 65.626, 75.23, 118.8, 120.4, 123.2
De Camp, Rosemary 43.330, 43.335, 70.21, 126.73, 126.111
De Camp, Valerie 43.406, 43.425
DeCarl, Nancy 129.73
De Carlo, Michael 148.68

DeCarlo, Yvonne 14.1, 38.16, 43.202, 161.43, 161.193
Deckert, Blue 163.25, 163.32
De Closs, Jim 89.127
DeCoit, Dick 96.77
de Cordova, Luis 71.52
de Cordova, Pedro 97.13, 97.22
de Corsia, Ted 8.31, 8.32, 8.53. 20.1, 20.2, 25.8, 39.8, 41.25, 41.26, 41.137, 41.151, 43.340, 44.63, 54.28, 54.30, 56.32, 63.42, 65.254, 65.405, 66.13, 71.88, 77.26, 78.48, 85.26, 85.66, 89.11, 89.33, 89.111, 97.164, 105.3, 105.123, 116.25, 125.1, 126.45, 126.78, 126.113, 126.116, 126.138, 126.174, 129.12, 130.12, 133.32, 144.16, 144.20, 146.16, 146.40, 147.52, 148.20, 156.20, 156.48, 158.50, 158.52, 164.51, 164.78, 168.7, 168.18, 170.94, 170.97, 179.29, 179.30
DeCosta, Doug 102.24
Deebank, Felix 21.48
Deemer, Ed 161.111
Deering, Ed 138.71
Deering, John 73.7, 73.24
DeFore, Don 106.1
De Gore, Janet 14.249, 17.1, 146.57
De Groot, Myra 70.25
DeHart, Wayne 90.20
De Haven, Carter, Jr. 88.11
de Haven, Gloria 65.603, 79.11, 109, 130.146, 162.118
Dehner, John 4.3, 4.6, 4.12, 4.37, 7.12, 8.38, 8.90, 11, 12.16, 13.7, 13.42. 14.34, 14.152, 17.13, 21.10, 27.36, 29.4, 51.11, 52.12, 54.12, 54.27, 65.2, 65.22, 65.75, 65.79, 65.106, 65.204, 65.240, 65.271, 65.290, 65.331, 65.371, 65.455, 66.8, 71.49, 71.64, 75.1, 75.2, 81.48, 85.20, 88.12, 89.140, 101.15, 105.37, 105.79, 105.110, 105.111, 105.121, 107.20, 116.5, 126.43, 126.71, 126.119, 126.133, 126.163, 127.49, 127.55, 129.16, 129.20, 129.77, 130.33, 130.43, 130.52, 130.101, 132.14, 142.17, 142.21, 142.25, 144.16, 145.17, 148.97, 148.129, 148.133, 148.137, 148.162, 151.13, 151.23, 152.54, 161, 161.27, 161.33, 161.205, 162.7, 162.60, 164.33, 164.35, 164.48, 165, 165.3, 165.6, 165.13, 167.11, 170.5, 170.16, 175, 178.30, 178.42, 178.65, 178.123, 179.1
De Hubp, Barbara Turner 41.58, 41.59
Deitt, Hal 170.77
Dekker, Albert 14.298, 126.189, 126.217
de Kova, Frank 3.110, 3.114, 4, 13.8, 22.23, 25.48, 27.51, 27.59, 27.85, 27.104, 39.19, 41.7, 41.24, 43.431, 44.3, 52, 55.10, 64.12, 65.49, 65.57, 65.65, 65.120, 65.157, 71.39, 74.21, 85.3, 85.72, 85.114, 89.89, 96.103, 96.119, 105.116, 117.49, 126.34, 126.74, 127.63, 129.41, 130.21, 130.74, 148.112, 149.33, 157.23, 162.75, 162.98, 162.165, 162.178, 162.275
DeKoven, Roger 71.7
De Lain, Marguerite 96.173
de Lancie, John 91, 177.56
Del Conte, Ken 41.31, 43.362
De Leon, Raoul 27.92, 66.122, 146.66
Del Hoyuo, George 163.80
de Loss, Janna 141.18
Del Rey, Pilar 41.121, 66.62, 73.22, 81.23, 145.28, 170.104
Del Rio, Dolores 17.43
Del Stark 39
Del Val, Jean 14.120
Delaney, Joan 170.77
Delaney, Lawrence 65.557
Delano, Mike 24.3
Delany, Pat 12.111, 70.2
DeLeon, Galvan 130.10
Delevanti, Cyril 3.129, 41.34, 65.15, 65.48, 65.356, 65.397, 77, 103.51, 149.75, 161.24, 161.163, 162.189
Delfino, Frank 14.146, 170.7

Personnel Index

Delgado, Luis 19
Dell, Gabriel 109.6
Dell, Myrna 78.33, 105.23, 152.53
Della, Jay 86.38
Dells, Dorothy 66.104, 66.177, 66.191, 66.195, 66.218, 86.2, 126.100
DeLongis, Anthony 67.14
DeLorenzo, Michael 1.4
Deloy, George 177.41
Demarest, William 14.121, 14.178, 127.51, 148
de Marney, Terence 3.82, 14.9, 66.87, 66.122, 79, 105.10, 105.18, 105.42, 105.83, 162.44, 162.55, 162.117
de Martin, Imalda 170.21
Demetrio, Anna 32.37
DeMetz, Danielle 66.81
de Meyer, Margie 65.473
Demyan, Lincoln 14.299, 14.327, 83.46, 106.9, 117.28, 130.108
Denaszody, Alex 68.5
Denby, Richard 141.21
Dengate, Mike 97.165
Denn, Marie 96.124
Dennehy, Elizabeth 90.1, 90.2
Denney, David 163.40
Denney, Michael 1.7
Denning, Richard 27.7, 27.16
Dennis, John 44.27, 44.57, 83.24, 92.8, 116.22, 129.47, 138.30, 148.161, 162.236
Dennis, Matt 79.24
Dennis, Nick 43.240, 66.16, 78.42, 89.79, 127.36, 127.44, 127.52
Dennis, Peter 1.15, 1.24
Dennis-Leigh, Pat 65.545
Dennison, Jo Carroll 81.48, 169.23
De Normand, George 32.1, 32.2, 32.3, 32.8, 32.9, 32.10, 35.6, 35.23, 124.31, 124.28, 124.76, 124.78, 135.91, 141.26
Denton, Crahan 14.63, 65.244, 65.291, 65.217, 66.132, 66.179, 66.191, 66.218, 150.9, 151.3, 157.17, 161.30
Denton, Doby 43.318
Denver, Bob 50
DePaulo, Dante 170.71
Derek, John 55, 178.24, 178.146
Dern, Bruce 12.20, 12.26, 12.31, 12.72, 12.97, 14.284, 14.356, 17.33, 65.381, 65.388, 65.412, 65.484, 71.82, 84.6, 84.35, 86.5, 98.26, 101.7, 126.208, 144, 161.51, 161.75, 161.94, 162.235, 162.266, 162.282
Derringer, Yancy 173
DeSales, Francis 14.299, 34.12, 44.32, 44.40, 61.6, 77.22, 93.140, 93.143, 93.175, 120.36, 105.74, 138.4, 138.19, 138.24, 138.37, 146.26, 146.46, 148.57, 159, 161.10, 161.17, 161.26, 162.146, 170.41
De Santis, Joe 14.92, 14.270, 14.357, 17.3, 27.59, 27.72, 41.15, 61.8, 64.4, 65.59, 65.460, 65.464, 66.21, 71.86, 84.12, 86.30, 88.18, 102.7, 105.95, 126.2, 126.33, 126.63, 131.41, 132.27, 137.6, 146.34, 148.9, 149.36, 155.35, 161.29, 161.97, 162.258, 164.4, 178.32
DeSautels, Val 97.100
Descher, Sandy 108.23, 147.12, 162.40
desEnfants, Gabrielle 148.194
DeShannon, Jackie 161.223, 170.98
de Silva, Nico 71.80
Desjarlais, Jules 48.38
DeSoto, Rosana 163.81
Desti, Maria 43.440
Determann, Jeanne 14.201
Deuel, Geoffrey 71.16, 109.8
Deuel, Peter 5, 161.170, 161.194
Devane, William 65.584
De Vargas, Valentin 14.185, 20.69, 34.13, 41.43, 43.299, 43.311, 43.429, 43.443, 61.7, 65.429, 65.490, 71.80, 71.93, 83.56, 83.57, 83.58, 83.59, 126.188, 149.73, 170.95, 170.96

De Vega, Jose 14.218, 17.43, 43.241, 71.22, 162.190, 170.30
de Vestel, Guy 159.1
Devi, Kamala 17.8, 17.9, 17.10, 17.44, 17.45, 36.14
Devine, Andy 5.33, 14.285, 65.491, 106.16, 134.11, 134.15, 161.138, 162.86, 169
DeVita, Noreen 14.113
Devlin, Don 3.149, 3.162, 155.64
Devlin, John 174.3
De Vol, Gordon 14.305, 70.9, 70.30
Devon, Laura 12.38, 126.180, 144.24, 168.13
Devon, Richard 3.35, 3.75, 12.3, 12.96, 14.174, 14.253, 34.46, 41.5, 41.46, 41.68, 41.118, 41.145, 43.234, 46.6, 63.19, 65.305, 65.314, 71.4, 74.19, 76.21, 79.5, 84.17, 85.27, 85.103, 86.12, 86.23, 88.1, 88.26, 93.72, 93.127, 101.1, 119.13, 126.28, 127.18, 130.35, 130.49, 130.63, 130.84, 130.89, 130.114, 130.152, 131.17, 133.28, 138.58, 142.5, 142.20, 142.23, 142.37, 146.55, 148.39, 149.7, 152.55, 152.56, 152.56, 156.37, 156.69, 161.38, 161.109, 161.119, 162.213, 164.6, 164.26, 164.37, 173.25, 173.27, 173.32, 178.29, 179.49
De Vries, Jon 177.5
Devry, Elaine 14.189
Dew, Eddie 6.35, 6.37, 23.6, 23.12
Dewey, Brian 69
Dewhurst, Colleen 12.43, 161.2
de Wilde, Brandon 106.6, 161.13, 161.179, 162.87, 162.160
deWilde, Fredric 149.50
de Witt, Alan 86.36
DeWitt, Jacqueline 103.28, 162.92
DeWolfe, Billy 125.7
Dexter, Alan 34.42, 65.112, 65.308, 66.110, 71.96, 85.22, 161.22, 178.87, 178.94
Dexter, Anthony 8.70, 71.9, 126.39, 126.82
Dexter, Brad 8.57, 21.28, 29.19, 34.46, 43.258, 66.36, 77.16, 102.13, 148.151, 158.44, 162.28, 164.67, 173.31, 178.67
Dey, Susan 123.1
DeYoung, Cliff 26, 177.16
DeZarn, Tim 48.11, 48.26, 48.31, 48.38, 177.49
Dhiegh, Khigh 83.11, 83.22, 83.47, 83.48, 170.62, 170.93
D'Hondt, Danica 170.2
Diamond, Ann 155.19
Diamond, Bobby 57, 162.109, 162.248
Diamond, Don 12.29, 31.4, 31.40, 51.15, 51.27, 52, 63.3, 71.59, 81, 93.49, 93.66, 93.162, 97.7, 126.65, 128.2, 128.4, 128.7, 128.15, 156.5, 156.12, 158.22, 158.25, 170.2, 178.22, 178.64, 178.89, 179
Diamond, Jack 3.159, 65.44, 93.137, 97.166
Diamond, Robert 127.56
Di Aquino, John 171
Diaz, Rudy 5.2, 5.29, 5.41, 7.10, 50.5
Dibbs, Kem 14.6, 20.7, 25.9, 78.1, 78.8, 78.9, 78.30, 85.39, 93.2, 93.3, 93.72, 93.220, 97.170, 102.35, 103.17, 105.103, 105.120, 126.9, 148.6, 148.71, 152.9, 152.25, 152.38, 152.59, 152.61, 156.19, 164.2, 169.72, 169.77, 179.41
Di Benedetto, Tony 163.19
Di Cenzo, George 65.599, 65.628, 75.25, 83.43, 120.49
Dick, Douglas 14.151, 21.8, 93.76, 93.98
Dickerson, George 96.140
Dickinson, Angie 20.11, 23.6, 27.28, 34.24, 43.43, 65.56, 66.5, 69.7, 93.28, 114.5, 129.22, 155.21, 161.123, 162.68
Dickinson, Carl 178.128
Diehl, Jim 32.28, 32.34, 73.7, 81.87, 97.164, 135.16, 135.28, 135.29, 135.39, 135.57, 169.20, 169.68
Diehl, John 6.32, 90.1, 90.2
Diener, Joan 169.52
Dierkes, John 3.24, 14.9, 43.16, 65.43, 65.59, 65.549, 65.601, 126.126, 129.27, 130.7, 130.9, 164.8

Dierkop, Charles 5.28, 5.46, 14.332, 14.379, 14.420, 24.8, 30.15, 38.9, 41.124, 65.398, 65.420, 65.600, 83.19, 84.2, 84.26, 84.44, 112.7, 116.7
Diestel, George 138.59
Dillard, Art 60.20, 60.22, 60.27, 60.29, 135.7, 135.9, 169.63, 169.72
Dillaway, Dana 65.453, 162.132, 162.135
Dillaway, Don 12.32, 12.33, 93.122
Dillman, Bradford 5.31, 12.45, 12.69, 14.397, 75.24, 106.17, 139.14, 139.15, 161.27, 162.236, 170.67
Dillon, Brendan 12.6, 14.128, 39.17, 161.3, 161.5, 161.10, 161.20, 161.49, 161.76, 168.28, 176.1, 176.2
Dillon, Melinda 14.337, 137.8
Dillon, Seth 48.8
Dillon, Thomas 25.52, 147.30, 166.9
Dilworth, Gordon 14.316
Dimmitt, Joseph 66.176
Dimster, Dennis 96.151
Dinehart, Mason Alan, III 43.148, 80.24, 93, 93.1, 93.2, 93.3, 93.4, 93.33, 93.34, 93.44, 93.45, 93.46, 93.47, 93.48, 93.49, 93.50, 93.51, 93.55, 93.58, 93.59, 93.60, 93.63, 93.67, 93.72, 93.86, 93.87, 93.91, 93.94, 93.95, 93.96, 93.100, 93.101, 93.103, 93.105, 93.107, 93.109, 93.130, 93.133, 93.135, 93.144, 97.162, 141.64, 152.15, 152.55, 152.56, 152.57, 158.39, 158.65
Diol, Susan 120.48, 163.41
Dion Patrick 25
di Reda, Joe 4.5, 34.41, 39.18, 65.256, 65.574, 102.12, 126.214, 152.27, 164.67, 178.30
Dirkson, Douglas 14.421, 65.612, 75.19, 83.24, 96.16, 112.23, 175.4
DiStefano, James 1.8
Divoff, Andrew 1.7, 163.49
Dix, Billy 158.44
Dix, Robert 43.134, 56.33, 65.239, 65.243, 126.102, 130.37, 141.66, 158.61
Dixon, Gale 112.17
Dixon, Glenn 5.14, 140.23
Dixon, Ivan 61.7, 66.138, 85.92, 144.31
Dizon, Jesse 83.31, 83.53
Dobbins, Bennie 65.560, 83.30, 112.11
Dobbs, George 177.2, 177.31
Dobkin, Lawrence 12.98, 19.3, 21.34, 46.9, 51.30, 65.31, 65.60, 65.202, 66.3, 66.106, 66.205, 78.52, 78.58, 82.15, 88.19, 89.37, 126.92, 126.199, 130.14, 130.16, 130.117, 130.139, 131.13, 156.10, 156.24, 156.30, 162.46, 164.52
Dobson, James 15.14, 15.25, 41.91, 65.81, 117.2, 138.30, 141.62, 162.24, 164.25
Dobson, Kelly 126.87
Dobson, Michael 67.19
Dobson, Peter 1.23
Dodd, Molly 130.73
Dodson, Bob 84.9, 170.98
Dodson, Jack 132.18, 161.111
Dodsworth, John 105.20
Doff, Millie 3.28, 31.7
Doherty, Charla 17.7, 162.260
Doherty, Charles 63.4
Doherty, Shannon 53.5, 53.6, 95, 95.24, 118.1
Dolan, Bill 89.76
Dolan, Ellen 163.15, 163.16
Dolan, Joan 70.14
Dolan, John 65.467
Dolan, Rudy 165.3, 165.6, 165.11, 178.122
Dolan, Trent 21.44
Dolenz, Coca 31.26
Dolenz, George 14.120, 29.25, 44.74, 127.70, 129.31, 148.180
Dolenz, Mickey 31
Dollaghan, Patrick 65.639, 118.7, 120.35, 163.59
Dollarhide, Jessica 48.23
Dollier, Don 65.335
Doman, John 48.77

Personnel Index

Domasin, Debra 14.313
Domasin, Larry 41.38
Domergue, Faith 14.70, 14.163, 21.38, 27.59, 34.55, 66.197, 66.223, 146.37, 148.154, 149.27
Dominguez, Joe 27.53, 32.143, 93.222, 97.77, 127.44
Dominquez, Bob 60.60
Domsin, Larry 12.37
Donahue, Elinor 48.23, 48.67, 66.214, 101.8, 128.12, 161.44
Donahue, Jill 161.144
Donahue, Patricia 8.6, 8.50, 13.36, 14.37, 25.23, 43.74, 88.22, 93.173, 102.33, 148.65, 149.39, 156.61, 161.130, 178.92
Donahue, Troy 4.30, 21.15, 21.26, 34.44, 89.70, 105.54, 126.2, 146.42, 148.78, 161.201, 162.55
Donaldson, Gil 81.40, 81.49, 97.98, 97.144
Donat, Richard 96.125
Donath, Ludwig 14.124, 17.31
Donigan, Satenio 66.217
Donlan, Dolores 119.14
Donlevy, Brian 74.2, 126.6, 152.20, 152.43, 162.61, 178.109
Donley, Robert 83.37
Donlon, Dolores 25.66, 66.105, 66.168, 105.68, 105.103, 146.57, 152.15
Donnell, Jeff 41.127, 119.17
Donnelly, Tim 92.19, 161.93
Donner, Jack 66.205
Donner, Robert 5.14, 5.27, 5.46, 14.342, 14.359, 41.55, 41.86, 63.21, 63.35, 65.463, 65.626, 71.74, 71.90, 83.6, 91, 95.14, 109.1, 126.79, 126.88, 126.147, 137.7, 161.184, 176
Donohue, Jill 161.157, 161.168
Donovan, King 8.1, 12.25, 54.1, 74.9, 74.27, 78.22, 105.66, 126.128, 140.33, 148.20, 149.1, 156.24, 156.36, 162.28, 164.44, 169.97, 169.98
Donovan, Marshal Steve 143
Donovan, Paul 43.98, 141.42, 141.51
Donovan, Warde 93.215
Doohan, James 14.145, 41.149, 51.23, 65.270, 86.3, 101.33, 161.20
Dooley, Jeb 97.37
DoQui, Robert 26, 36.20, 63.28, 65.482, 65.487, 71.37
Doran, Ann 2.24, 5.49, 14.245, 14.307, 20.21, 34.33, 34.51, 53.17, 56.27, 60.67, 60.73, 63.20, 92, 96.23, 97.91, 97.119, 108.23, 126.56, 135.15, 161.30, 161.48, 161.74, 161.153, 162.97
Doran, Johnny 96.72, 109.13
Dore, Anne 8.17
Doremus, David 14.427
Dorian, Angela 12.32, 12.33, 27.107, 43.377, 46.9, 162.257, 162.284
Dorin, Phoebe 170.3, 170.10, 170.20, 170.27, 170.31, 170.38
Dornan, Mark 120.20
Dorough, Robert 66.93
Dorr, Lester 93.115, 93.186, 97.80, 164.30
Dorrell, Don 40.2, 122, 122.31, 122.33
D'Orsay, Fifi 14.141
Dorsey, Joe 120.47
Dotson, Ernie 57.8, 57.56
D'Ottoni, Wanda 78.25
Doty, Bud 147.45
Doty, Greg 177.18
Doucette, Jeff 1.25
Doucette, John 6.31, 6.43, 8.36, 8.67, 12.84, 14.108, 14.208, 14.288, 20.61, 23.8, 23.15, 25.11, 27.42, 32.80, 32.87, 34.28, 60.9, 60.10, 60.48, 60.51, 60.55, 60.61, 66.25, 75.27, 81.51, 83.7, 85.104, 89.2, 89.22, 93.126, 97.14, 97.31, 97.46, 97.60, 97.76, 97.98, 97.131, 97.140, 97.150, 97.178, 97.181, 98.21, 98.22, 103.3, 107.1, 108.9, 108.16, 121.24, 124.23, 124.24, 124.65, 124.68, 126.121, 126.189, 133.1, 135.15, 135.17, 135.25, 135.26, 135.55, 135.61, 141.7, 148.3, 148.50,
148.96, 148.182, 152.33, 155.21, 155.50, 155.84, 156.13, 160.38, 161.80, 161.96, 161.139, 161.202, 162.146, 162.202, 162.215, 162.228, 162.252, 162.270, 162.273, 162.275, 168.19, 169.10, 170.19, 170.51, 179.16
Dougherty, Joe 121.26
Douglas, Brandon 48.82, 48.93, 48.94, 48.106
Douglas, Burt 13.41, 14.55, 14.64, 21.20, 43.331, 51.25, 65.131, 65.216, 65.232, 65.348, 65.626, 89.32, 89.66, 107.11, 114.24, 126.71, 126.88, 126.198, 161.163, 164.80, 178.114
Douglas, Damon 115.6
Douglas, Diana 37, 83.23
Douglas, Don 8.79, 17.16
Douglas, George 44.47, 97.98, 135.23, 135.34, 158.57
Douglas, James 43.167, 93.141
Douglas, Jay 126.87, 138.19
Douglas, Jennifer 14.329, 84.29, 170.102
Douglas, Jerry 51.22, 65.378, 123.7
Douglas, Jim 43.153
Douglas, John Jay 14.288
Douglas, Mark 22.26
Douglas, Paul 178.74
Douglas, Robert 26, 105.80
Douglas, Scott 141.35
Douglas, Warren 27.97, 65.445, 97.69
Douglas, Wendy 170.92
Douglas, William 144.26
Dourif, Brad 45.4
Dowd, Mel 78.37
Dowdell, Robert 144
Dowding, Ilana 162.133
Dowling, Doris 27.5, 66.77, 148.129, 149.67
Downey, John 97.80
Downey, Marvin J. 12.100.
Downey, Michelle 96.97
Downing, David 96.63
Downing, Frank 60.14
Downing, Joseph 138.26, 138.28
Downs, Cathy 8.20, 8.64, 97.94, 126.81, 155.30, 155.50
Downs, Frederick 5.11, 5.33, 5.45, 43.223, 51.2, 51.21, 65.414, 65.425, 84.6, 96.63
Downs, Hugh 131.28
Downs, Johnny 141.19
Downs, Watson 32.58, 97.182, 145.35
Doyce, Ron 96.139
Doyle, David 24.10
Doyle, Robert 14.247, 14.411, 38.13, 65.271, 84.5, 84.27, 92.31, 109.8, 144.19
Doyle, Ron 43.359, 95.15
Dozier, Deborah 65.598
Drago, Billy 1.1, 1.2, 1.8, 1.12, 1.17, 1.20, 28.4, 163.53
Drake, Betsy 164.20
Drake, Charles 41.108, 41.118, 46.11, 52.65, 85.35, 85.71, 66.1, 93.41, 93.88, 93.115, 106.3, 161.215, 162.32, 162.113, 162.191, 162.209, 162.232, 162.256
Drake, Christian 97.24, 97.137, 97.168, 145.27, 148.13
Drake, Claudia 32.32, 162.27
Drake, Colin 53.9
Drake, James 17.28, 65.321, 152.12, 152.59, 152.63, 152.71, 164.87
Drake, Ken 8.9, 8.78, 8.95, 12.19, 12.45, 14.160, 14.288, 14.314, 14.327, 30.20, 46.3, 51.24, 61.6, 65.445, 65.469, 71.10, 71.95, 88.22, 93.209, 98.4, 117.40, 155.2, 170.54, 170.85
Drake, Pauline 93.146
Drake, Tom 4.19, 14.214, 17.12, 17.17, 27.84, 29.19, 39.11, 65.500, 69.9, 85.22, 89.41, 89.59, 89.83, 126.42, 127.50, 127.60, 131.15, 132.12, 142.10, 162.91, 164.12, 164.74, 167.23, 170.36, 178.117
Draper, David 70.39
Drayton, Noel 8.22, 61.8

Dreier, Alex 36.18
Dressler, Lieux 65.542, 65.543, 65.562, 65.588, 65.589
Drew, Donna 21.52, 43.61, 169.101
Drexel, Steve 34.65
Dreyfuss, Richard 12.48, 65.587
Driscoll, Bobby 178.6
Driscoll, Jim 170.69
Driscoll, Robert Miller 41.84, 126.17, 126.63, 156.69, 157.22, 170.32
Driskill, Jim 12.44
Drivas, Robert 14.289, 170.26
Dru, Joanne 162.6
Drum, James 98.13, 128.11
Drury, James 1.1, 1.21, 5.1, 5.39, 13.17, 20.63, 21.8, 27.61, 43.161, 59.4, 65.13, 65.149, 65.160, 65.221, 66.60, 89.26, 103.33, 106, 126.3, 126.74, 126.83, 127.25, 127.48, 130.4, 130.109, 142.32, 152.3, 156.59, 161, 162.122, 162.180, 178.48, 178.76
Drury, John 161.55
Drury, Tom 41.120, 41.128, 41.138
Dryden, Mack 120, 120.4
Dryer, Robert 120.36
Drysdale, Don 36.22, 89.56, 130.124
Duane, Earle 124.25, 124.26
Dubbins, Don 4.16, 12.93, 14.29, 24.18, 61.8, 63.48, 65.158, 65.242, 65.246, 65.321, 79.23, 83.13, 88.25, 96.56, 111.4, 126.14, 130.83, 132.6, 142.22, 146.35, 146.36, 161.104, 164.63, 167.13, 178.131
Dubin, Gary 70.9
DuBois, Diane 43.170, 178.105
DuBois, Marta 163.48
Dubov, Paul 8.17, 8.106, 14.48, 20.59, 20.65, 27.59, 44.22, 65.30, 65.63, 93.70, 93.115, 129.54, 164.53, 179.76
Du Brey, Claire 20.23, 25.65, 148.43, 158.23
Dubrey, Gabriel 81.17
Duff, Howard 5.26, 14.5, 83.30, 83.42, 106.22, 161.26, 175.5, 175.6
Duffy, Thomas F. 118.3
Dufour, Val 65.16, 65.20, 65.189, 65.247, 74.15, 78.11, 78.23, 126.1, 156.13, 178.36
Dugan, James 158.72
Dugan, Yvette 27.63, 27.64, 21.16, 31.36, 56.38, 78.6, 97.176, 105.39, 179.50
Duggan, Andrew 7.5, 12.2, 12.51, 14.148, 27.20, 27.26, 27.56, 27.79, 27.98, 27.109, 30.4, 30.8, 30.22, 34.1, 39.2, 52.21, 61.9, 61.10, 65.46, 65.71, 65.372, 77.5, 83.6, 84, 89.95, 89.146, 101.22, 105.99, 105.123, 136, 155.20, 155.36, 157.4, 161.1, 161.120, 162.1
Dukakis, John 96.138
Duke, John 3.128, 8.87, 31.40, 51.18, 65.272, 66.43
Duke, Patty 161.137, 168.22
Duke, Stan 36.12
Dukes, David 75.22
Dullaghan, John 65.528, 65.546
Dullea, Keir 14.117, 51.14
Dulo, Jane 65.423, 149.59
Dumbrille, Douglas 8.68, 25.24, 25.34, 85.22
Dumke, Ralph 126.83, 152.26
Dunard, David 177.1
Dunbar, Olive 12.106, 96.8
Duncan, Angus 5.18, 65.575, 167.16
Duncan, Ann 32.156
Duncan, Archie 4.7, 13.44, 34.55, 79.10, 89.55
Duncan, Craig 3.150, 8.63, 8.102, 14.135, 14.144, 27.93, 61.8, 65.105, 65.209, 66.71, 66.152, 79.27, 93.94, 105.82, 108.3, 108.10, 108.29, 129.54, 133.2, 133.38, 135.79, 135.81, 138.20, 141.21, 148.23, 148.33, 148.100, 149.16, 149.44, 162.30, 162.31, 164.26
Duncan, John B. 32.148, 32.153
Duncan, Kenne 2.14, 6.20, 6.37, 6.58, 6.69, 6.70,

Personnel Index

23.7, 23.18, 31.4, 32.17, 32.19, 32.26, 60.11, 60.13, 60.19, 60.21, 60.62, 60.66, 60.74, 60.77, 60.89, 60.90, 81.88, 81.89, 97.19, 97.32, 97.97, 97.164, 108.29, 124.4, 124.6, 124.7, 124.10, 124.19, 124.20, 124.53, 124.55, 126.41, 138.49, 141.28, 141.29, 155.34, 169.9, 169.39, 169.74, 169.90
Duncan, Lee 170.103
Duncan, Pamela 3.38, 8.41, 34.60, 34.67, 35.11, 35.31, 43.107, 43.147, 43.165, 78.76, 81.78, 85.22, 93.32, 93.138, 105.9, 126.26, 135.41, 135.53, 148.14, 149.61, 155.7, 155.48, 166.9, 169.24, 169.55
Duncan, Rita 93.206
Duncan, Rosetta 169.111
Duncan, Sandy 14.389
Dundee, Jimmy 97.11, 97.45
Dunhill, Peter 86.45
Dunhill, Steve 93.73, 97.43, 97.161, 141.9
Dunlap, Al 92.19
Dunlap, Bob 27.79
Dunlap, Pamela 65.500, 65.521, 65.522, 70.13, 71.64
Dunlap, Robert 43.403
Dunlop, Vic 181.3
Dunn, Eddie 97.40
Dunn, Elaine 170.42
Dunn, George 4.7, 29.8, 29.11, 29.16, 78.72, 89.140, 161.3, 162.241
Dunn, Greg 65.213, 66.83
Dunn, Harvey 32.74, 44.47, 141.38, 141.50, 147.2
Dunn, James 14.86, 17.11, 49.10, 61.1, 61.2, 113, 126.36, 142.19, 161.76, 162.35, 164.23
Dunn, Liam 5.5, 65.555, 112.16
Dunn, Michael 14.347, 107.26, 170.3, 170.10, 170.20, 170.27, 170.31, 170.38, 170.51, 170.56, 170.60, 170.92
Dunn, Peter 29.11, 29.16, 65.355, 72.16, 81.87, 86.16, 148.72, 162.50
Dunn, Rex 158.71
Dunne, Irene 55.4
Dunne, Patricia 170.100
Du Pois, Starletta 96.150
DuPont, Norman 114.2
Dupree, V.C. 120.8
Dupuis, Art 32.2, 32.10, 32.11
Dupuis, Joan 66.149
Duran, Darryl 27.32, 57.36
Duran, John 126.51
Duran, Larry 65.569
Durant, Don 79, 85, 105.8, 138.18, 138.34, 138.50, 156.33, 156.70, 161.2, 162.8, 162.236, 164.20, 168.26, 178.67
Durkin, Eddie 170.28
Durkin, Joseph 170.91
Durkin, Mike 65.471, 65.495
Durning, Charles 59.3, 71.74
Durran, John 130.28
Durrell, Nick 25.16
Durrell, Steven 27.47
Durren, John 27.87, 130.42
Duryea, Dan 14.35, 14.173, 29.2, 41.18, 55.10, 85.1, 85.36, 85.67, 98.18, 107.14, 126.3, 126.122, 126.152, 132.24, 132.25, 148.188, 153.4, 161.127, 162.15, 162.39, 162.58, 162.102, 162.122, 162.190, 162.262, 168.10, 178.47, 178.140
Duryea, Peter 41.18, 161.126
Dusay, Marj 5.14, 14.294, 14.333, 19.4, 19.14, 19.15, 19.17, 30.14, 41.142, 170.69, 170.86
Dusenberry, Ann 120.20
Dutchison, Lawrence 66.144
Duval, Georgette 25.18, 148.185
Duvall, Juan 97.33
Duvall, Robert 30.8, 139.9, 144.23, 161.25, 170.66
Dvorak, Reggie 162.44
Dwan, Isabelle 60.86
Dwyer, Marlo 145.18

Dyer, Eddy C. 96.168
Dynarski, Gene 12.13, 83.61
Dysart, Richard 137.3
Dzundza, George 83.33

Eager, Jean 66.108
Earle, Edward 6.2, 44.28, 152.69
Early, Morgan 170.88
Earp, Wyatt 93
East, Jeff 75.18
East, Stewart 66.114, 66.139, 66.149, 66.162, 66.163, 66.166, 66.217
Eastham, Richard 8.92, 14.261, 14.429, 24.13, 36.15, 155, 178.106
Easton, Jack, Jr. 103.50, 161.33
Easton, Robert 3.146, 5.27, 5.48, 6.57, 23.1, 43.302, 65.12, 121.16, 126.55, 162.68, 164.83
Easton, Sheena 1.12
Eastwood, Clint 43.82, 105.46, 126
Eaton, Gloria 124.60, 135.27
Eaton, Marjorie 97.30
Eberg, Victor 65.529
Eberhardt, Norma 169.27
Ebert, Joyce 12.67
Ebhardt, Kaye 133.3
Ebsen, Buddy 5.37, 5.40, 13.38, 14.406, 21.42, 42, 64.8, 65.210, 65.238, 65.550, 66.147, 66.166, 79.29, 105.58, 105.89, 105.101, 114, 126.45, 126.105, 131.38, 148.121, 148.191
Eccles, Aimee 83.9
Eccles, Teddy 12.52, 41.89, 41.123, 41.151, 61.9, 61.10, 63.48, 84.34, 168.28
Echohawk, Brummett 163.14
Eddy, Duane 65.306, 66.157, 66.207
Eden, Barbara 65.87, 126.153, 126.181, 126.182, 161.67
Eden, Chana 4.34, 8.35, 14.15, 66.160, 130.14, 164.61
Edgington, Lyn 14.243, 65.409, 126.212
Edmiston, Walker 12.2, 12.28, 12.52, 41.56, 65.511, 65.533, 65.582, 65.594, 66.155, 96.49, 96.92, 96.151, 105.43, 121.1, 134, 134.4, 161.85, 170.15, 170.52
Edmiston, Warren 170.69
Edmonds, Scott 65.534
Edmonson, William 102.18
Edwards, Bill 11.1
Edwards, Bruce 97.100, 169.23, 169.41
Edwards, Cliff 8.28
Edwards, Don 14.125
Edwards, Elaine 34.22, 34.61, 81.51, 97.180, 148.56, 152.72
Edwards, Ella 170.93
Edwards, Gerald G. 36
Edwards, Guy 36.25
Edwards, Jack 133.21
Edwards, James 36.21, 43.299, 116.7, 153.12, 161.187, 178.95
Edwards, Jennifer 43.438
Edwards, Julie 86.33
Edwards, Mary Ann 35.1
Edwards, Neeley 152.53
Edwards, Penny 4.16, 25.48, 27.14, 29.25, 43.110, 43.227, 93.140, 129.12, 133.20, 148.23, 148.80, 148.140, 158.20, 158.23
Edwards, Sam 9.4, 13.43, 65.114, 65.133, 65.387, 65.490, 65.501, 82.1, 85.11, 86.4, 95, 96.124, 96.164, 96.174, 96.175, 132.6, 151.11, 152.73, 156.16, 161.81, 162.185, 162.206, 168.3, 170.76, 178.134
Edwards, Saundra 4.36, 27.68, 89.84, 105.26, 105.41, 126.25, 146.31
Edwards, Vince 44.38, 85.26
Egan, Aeryk 120.45, 120.49, 120.55
Egan, Richard 51, 123.1, 128
Egan, Will 48.26
Eggar, Samantha 118.5

Ego, Sandra 24.12
Ehrhardt, Horst 148.16
Eiland, Michael C. 109.5
Eilbacher, Bob 65.531, 106.1
Eilbacher, Cindy 5.20, 36.5, 63.38, 86.5
Eilbacher, Lisa 5.20, 14.427, 65.584, 65.635
Eiler, Barbara 27.15, 97.174, 130.134, 148.12, 156.50, 156.65, 161.136, 162.76, 162.113, 162.168, 178.12
Eiler, Virginia 148.116
Eimen, Johnny 66.80, 66.149, 127.8, 162.93
Einer, Robert 20.53
Eisenmann, Ike 65.571, 65.581, 65.604, 83.14, 96.43, 96.96
Eisenmann, Robin G. 175.9
Eisley, Anthony 19.4, 84.42, 118.11, 147.50, 170.29, 170.98
Eitner, Dan 8.15, 71.10, 92.19
Elam, Jack 5.38, 14.49, 14.253, 14.374, 14.432, 14.433, 21.1, 27.81, 27.96, 27.97, 30.20, 39, 41.18, 43.216, 52.6, 53.5, 53.6, 54.10, 63.7, 64.2, 65.138, 65.164, 65.183, 65.215, 65.339, 65.348, 65.380, 65.386, 65.407, 65.461, 65.503, 65.535, 65.554, 65.564, 65.565, 66.70, 66.177, 71.35, 72.17, 75.3, 82.14, 83.21, 84.28, 85.58, 85.103, 89.1, 89.33, 89.63, 89.118, 89.141, 92.1, 94.30, 97.137, 97.180, 99.12, 112.20, 116.15, 117.36, 120.23, 126.105, 127.69, 129.2, 129.21, 130.7, 130.45, 130.69, 130.117, 130.120, 142.5, 145.23, 146.65, 146.67, 148.11, 151, 152.12, 152.33, 152.71, 155.44, 161.225, 170.64, 178.19, 178.102, 178.116, 178.131
Elan, Joan 8.25, 66.175, 105.31, 105.76, 142.12
Elcar, Dana 5.9, 5.50, 14.331, 14.422, 26, 65.521, 65.522, 83.8, 83.18
Elder, Ann 43.331, 43.340, 170.24
Elder, Vince 170.17
Eldredge, George 3.99, 3.158, 8.23, 8.100, 31.45, 32.41, 32.46, 32.47, 35.21, 35.32, 65.218, 78.2, 93.14, 108.13, 129.59, 133.11, 135.74, 135.85, 138.22, 138.75, 141.19, 145.10, 145.38, 162.34, 164.66, 169.13, 169.21, 169.22, 169.36, 169.100
Eldredge, John 6.14, 35.8, 35.9, 35.19, 35.22, 35.35, 43.20, 81.23, 81.30, 81.55, 97.18, 97.36, 97.65, 141.8, 145.12, 148.14, 164.35, 169.26, 169.65, 169.83, 178.19
Eldridge, Gloria 169.62
Elfego Baca 113
Elg, Taina 114.17, 162.108
Elhardt, Kaye 8.71, 21.51, 34.46, 105.54, 155.14, 155.75, 162.111
Elhardt, Kel 173.30
Elias, Louie 65.562
Elias, Sandy 177.58
Eliot, Rosemary 63.15
Eliott, Ross 14.62
Elizondo, Hector 19.17
Elkins, Richard 36.11
Ellenstein, Robert 12.51, 12.99, 14.223, 25.14, 43.441, 65.33, 78.64, 102.4, 126.23, 130.18, 131.33, 148.198, 161.157, 164.20, 170.19, 170.60, 170.85, 170.95, 170.96
Eller, Barbara 78.3, 164.12
Ellerbe, Harry 64.10, 126.41, 126.56, 126.104, 131.26, 170.29
Ellin, Robert 39.1
Elliot, Sam 65.563, 84.14, 84.20, 84.40
Elliott, Beverly 67.7, 67.21
Elliott, Biff 14.418, 85.76, 88.27
Elliott, Cecil 6.35, 124.57
Elliott, Dick 3.131, 6.25, 6.74, 23.6, 23.8, 81.74, 97.101, 97.150, 126.53, 126.70, 129.35, 130.55, 141.51, 147.6, 147.31, 169.42
Elliott, Edythe 145.29
Elliott, Laura 54.2, 97.161
Elliott, Ross 14.227, 20.2, 27.22, 27.68, 27.83, 34.56, 39.12, 43.163, 57.17, 65.173, 65.188, 78.5,

78.7, 83.5, 85.33, 85.63, 85.73, 86.1, 93, 93.149, 93.150, 97.90, 97.104, 101.32, 105.72, 106.11, 121.24, 122.16, 126.14, 126.65, 126.103, 127.20, 127.47, 130.126, 141.12, 142.12, 146.69, 152.14, 156.10, 156.38, 161, 162.172, 164.12, 164.84, 170.91, 178.22, 178.64
Elliott, Scott 97.133
Elliott, Stephen 75.15, 75.16, 95.9
Ellis, Adrienne 161.85
Ellis, Bob 93.52
Ellis, Georgia 82.4
Ellis, Henry 148.13
Ellis, Herb 54.24, 131.34
Ellis, Juney 12.16, 41.63, 86.26, 129.41, 162.49, 162.122, 162.137, 162.245
Ellis, Robert 43.136, 97.178
Ellison, Bob 68.12
Ellison, Trudy 8.98, 14.218
Ellsworth, Stephen 8.87, 43.206, 65.93, 89.96, 126.52, 146.18, 149.34
Ellwand, Greg 99.11
Elson, Donald 65.581, 130.53, 130.141, 148.189
Elston, Robert 43.192
Ely, Richard 65.624
Ely, Ron 67.8, 93.185
Emelin, Georgia 177.55
Emerson, Allen 65.71, 65.415
Emerson, Hope 43.123
Emery, John 66.75, 162.189
Emery, Matt 65.448, 65.484, 65.531, 84.10
Emhardt, Robert 14.123, 14.309, 14.337, 41.98, 61.6, 65.172, 65.470, 66.134, 66.135, 66.183, 66.211, 76.23, 83.4, 85.48, 98.18, 111.4, 119.17, 131.11, 131.42, 144.17, 149.69, 151.15, 162.89, 162.227, 170.23, 170.44
Emmett, Michael 15.12, 43.132, 43.146, 65.52, 93.25, 93.100, 93.119, 93.173
Emmich, Cliff 19.9, 96.92
Emory, Richard 3.9, 8.20, 31.23, 32.15, 32.18, 32.21, 60.63, 124.77, 133.15, 135.11, 135.14, 138.50
Encinas, James 48.13
Enery, Woody 96.149
Engel, Roy 8.19, 13.19, 14.53, 14.97, 14.108, 14.113, 14.133, 14.147, 14.163, 13.352, 32.118, 34.51, 43.134, 43.194, 43.297, 43.299, 43.331, 43.333, 43.426, 43.435, 65.33, 65.55, 65.145, 65.395, 65.396, 65.521, 65.522, 65.571, 66.51, 66.144, 66.161, 66.170, 70.32, 84.7, 93.221, 105.38, 105.79, 108.26, 121.12, 126.120, 126.135, 129.59, 129.68, 144.10, 146.37, 148.54, 155.42, 156.27, 161, 161.16, 161.19, 161.26, 161.35, 161.46, 161.52, 161.64, 161.74, 161.76, 161.83, 161.86, 161.157, 162.37, 162.108, 164.93, 170.16, 170.52, 170.72, 170.80, 170.81, 170.95, 170.96
Engel, William 70.29
England, Hal 52.19, 52.64, 70.24
England, Jan 93.56
England, Sue 20.3, 20.35, 32.140, 36.26, 41.43, 85.24, 85.63, 85.84, 97.42
Engle, Page 31.48
Engle, Paul 27.21, 34.26, 44.6, 57.114, 65.101, 65.125, 97.183, 97.185, 97.205, 97.214, 138.38, 142.1, 147.13, 148.31, 148.49, 156.7, 156.66, 164.38, 178.34
English, Nancy 147.46
Englund, Robert 91.7, 163.69
Engstrom, Jena 14.68, 14.110, 43.223, 43.350, 51.29, 55.20, 64.2, 65.242, 65.265, 66.140, 66.143, 66.157, 66.181, 66.196, 85.76, 85.98, 117.31, 126.78, 126.108, 126.119, 144.6, 149.43, 151.7, 161.64, 162.254
Enlow, Darlene 161.95
Enriquez, Rene 26
Ensign, Michael 120
Ensley, Harold 65.358
Epper, Gary 83.27, 120.16

Epper, John Anthony 41.123
Epper, Tony 30.12, 71.77, 72.16, 83.30, 120.8, 120.30
Erdman, Richard 170.101
Eric, Martin 85.106, 89.82, 119.7, 161.5
Erickson, Brett 96.79
Erickson, John 7.6
Erickson, Lee 23.29, 54.3, 57.94, 57.115, 78.34, 93.15
Erickson, Leif 14.55, 14.216, 17.38, 41.36, 41.72, 61.3, 65.425, 71, 74.4, 101.9, 126.29, 126.73, 127.69, 130.1, 157.16, 161.50, 161.71, 161.106, 162.235, 178.52, 178.109
Ericson, Devon 28, 174
Ericson, John 14.41, 14.256, 65.478, 106.15, 126.12, 126.73, 129.26, 129.67, 162.52, 178.7, 178.49, 178.67, 178.77
Ermey, R. Lee 1.1
Erskine, Marilyn 86.52, 161.84, 167.14, 178.82
Erwin, Bill 13.18, 39.18, 65.240, 65.333, 65.444, 65.461, 65.468, 65.492, 65.514, 65.562, 70.17, 70.51, 88.9, 126.71, 130.15, 148.73, 152.72, 156.17, 162.55, 170.68, 178.16, 178.141
Erwin, Eddie 141.24, 141.41
Erwin, Roger 43.436
Erwin, Roy 3.18, 3.101, 3.135, 80.9, 105.28, 169.109
Erwin, Stuart 12.70, 12.71, 14.224, 65.397, 161.138, 162.226
Erwin, William 178.122
Escandon, Fernando 83.20
Escondas, Fernando 5.29
Esformes, Nate 7.6, 12.111, 71.80, 83.29, 161.163, 170.59
Eskow, Jerry 3.100, 3.106, 138.24
Esmond, Carl 12.70, 12.71, 27.12, 44.52, 105.100, 157.24
Esparza, Ernesto, III 50.8
Essay, Christopher 89.75
Essegian, Chuck 146.53
Essler, Fred 97.108, 105.42, 141.14
Estelita 86.6
Estes, Bob 177.9
Estrada, Erik 123.8, 123.9
Ethan Cord 120
Ethridge, Ella 35.28, 43.16, 43.47, 124.66, 124.68, 168.4, 169.64
Etienne, Roger 78.12
Euringer, Fred 68.4
Eustral, Anthony 78.22, 78.45, 20.30, 105.76
Evandell, Bill 169.62
Evans, Art 163.76
Evans, Charles 3.156, 93.56, 93.132, 97.91, 108.5, 145.39
Evans, Dale 135
Evans, Dick 130.129, 148.55
Evans, Dirk 141.52
Evans, Douglas 32.3, 32.8, 93.29, 93.119, 97.83, 97.105, 97.124, 108.34, 124.14, 124.18, 135.1, 135.12, 141.17, 145.25, 169.21, 169.47
Evans, Evan 43.269, 65.237, 128.7, 161.28, 162.209
Evans, Gene 5.33, 14.20, 14.142, 14.368, 17.5, 30.6, 38.8, 41.16, 41.143, 43.282, 47.3, 64.6, 65.315, 65.316, 65.444, 65.461, 65.521, 65.522, 65.541, 65.573, 65.606, 65.616, 76.5, 79.16, 92.6, 97.37, 97.49, 97.73, 106.4, 108, 112.6, 117.10, 126.29, 126.70, 126.118, 126.146, 126.161, 126.191, 129.16, 131.40, 151.2, 161.14, 161.129, 162.27, 162.251, 167.21, 173.8
Evans, Jacqueline 41.58, 41.59
Evans, Joan 27.56, 85.74, 117.12, 117.13, 127.40, 148.151, 149.41, 162.69, 279.72, 179.73, 179.74, 179.75
Evans, Linda 12, 59.2, 59.4, 109.1, 162.276
Evans, Mary Beth 53.31
Evans, Maurice 12.110, 41.92
Evans, Michael 86.38, 121.25

Evans, Mitzi 170.48
Evans, Monica 70.48
Evans, Richard 4.26, 12.79, 14.206, 14.261, 14.360, 21.30, 27.86, 51.20, 63.34, 65.179, 65.379, 65.393, 65.441, 71.25, 75.27, 76.13, 84.28, 85.54, 89.77, 89.146, 127.31, 128.2, 130.70, 139.4, 144.18, 151.1, 162.46
Evans, Terence 96.144, 120.12
Evanson, Edith 34.39, 65.329, 93.134, 129.23, 129.40, 129.64, 145.37, 148.157, 162.22, 162.94, 162.125
Evelyn, Judith 148.97, 148.190
Everett, Chad 17.11, 21.42, 21.57, 26, 27.96, 39, 89.119, 128.8
Everhart, David 99.12
Evers, Jason 12.5, 12.91, 14.57, 14.256, 17.3, 27.72, 27.88, 43.320, 55.22, 63, 65.256, 65.273, 65.353, 69.9, 85.55, 85.67, 85.90, 89.111, 127.65, 132.20, 148.193, 161.125, 170.71, 170.86, 172
Evers, Juanita 22.9
Everson, Corey 1.3, 1.13
Ewell, Tom 5.12, 10, 106.4, 162.271
Ewing, Bill 96.112
Ewing, Diana 12.109, 65.501, 84.45
Ewing, John 161.26
Ewing, Roger 65, 65.362, 65.380, 126.201
Eyer, Richard 65.166, 126.23, 135.26, 142, 144.31, 162.93, 164.37
Eyer, Robert 102.30, 162.67

Fabares, Shelley 6.76, 24.23, 41.132, 84.21
Faber, Hank 129.26
Fabian 41.41, 161.19, 161.78, 161.128, 162.227
Fabray, Nanette 85.2
Factory Rock Quartet 52.57
Fadden, Tom 12.16, 20.1, 20.2, 20.3, 20.4, 20.66, 29.1, 41.114, 65.519, 84.11, 85.68, 86.20, 92.3, 126.45, 131.43, 149.59, 152.55, 152.56, 152.57, 156.43
Fafara, Tiger 3.74, 3.121, 93.84, 103.41, 108.25, 108.34
Faherty, Mike 91.5
Fahey, Myrna 4.33, 34.27, 41.19, 65.111, 85.97, 86.6, 105.75, 105.85, 119.9, 125.10, 162.124, 162.248, 179.14, 179.15, 179.16, 179.31, 179.32
Fair, Jody 131.37, 168.17
Fairchild, Margaret 83.24
Fairchild, Morgan 175.7
Fairfax, James 78.17, 78.44, 148.48, 162.117
Fairman, Michael 1.26, 1.27
Faison, Matthew 120.8
Faith, Dolores 66.216
Falk, Leonard 170.27
Falk, Peter 66.126, 162.229
Falk, Ricks 161.59
Falk, Tom 24.20, 65.584
Falkenberg, Kort 1.8, 48.9
Fallman, Gil 97.167
Falvo, John 8.12
Famison, Janis 176.1
Fancher, Hampton 13.2, 13.16, 14.235, 27.75, 41.84, 41.97, 65.210, 65.277, 65.367, 66.40, 66.86, 66.102, 89.113, 105.101, 107.12, 117.5, 126.120, 126.170, 126.171, 127.9, 130.116, 132.8, 150.11, 151.5
Faraci, Richard 67.10
Farber, Arlene 83.33
Farber, Paul 141.44, 145.26
Farentino, James 86.3, 106.2, 132.15, 161.117
Farge, Annie 130.125
Farina, Dennis 14.433
Farley, Morgan 12.32, 12.33, 141.2, 170.30
Farmer, Mimsy 86.17, 86.43
Farmer, Richard 73.18
Farnon, Shannon 84.33
Farnsworth, Diamond 163.37
Farnsworth, Richard 14.378, 14.406, 14.411, 30.4, 45.4, 71.61, 164.58, 169.109

Personnel Index

Farnum, Franklyn 32.46
Farnum, Shannon 14.282
Farr, Felicia 14.120, 162.147, 178.104
Farr, Jaime 127.64
Farr, Lee 14.110, 14.329, 66.68, 84.29, 85.97, 89.17, 93.200, 129.57, 130.2, 130.123, 156.51, 156.67, 164.22
Farrar, Stanley 8.69, 81.10, 97.20, 103.14, 103.41, 129.31
Farrell, Brioni 9.11, 14.231, 14.313, 41.117, 43.406, 84.13, 170.49
Farrell, Glenda 14.157, 29.9, 55.20, 126.149, 162.86
Farrell, Mike 14.424, 111.1
Farrell, Ray 93.146
Farrell, Sharon 43.275, 51.14, 65.296, 65.312, 65.336, 76.18, 126.210, 161.163, 162.202, 162.249, 170.78
Farrell, Todd 162.101
Farrell, Tommy 3.47, 3.106, 3.107, 3.108, 3.114, 3.117, 3.139, 3.151, 27.52, 65.115, 105.5, 126.149
Farren, Harold 124.69
Farrington, Betty 138.27
Farrow, David 41.121, 71.54, 161.168
Fast, Lou 96.97
Faulkner, David 162.152, 162.153
Faulkner, Edward 9.7, 14.74, 14.158, 14.242, 30.16, 46.2, 65.144, 65.182, 65.550, 65.575, 66.46, 66.106, 66.155, 66.163, 66.166, 66.175, 66.207, 74.24, 86.50, 98.3, 106.4, 107.7, 112.15, 116.14, 126.17, 126.26, 126.87, 126.102, 126.119, 126.134, 126.161, 161.44, 161.60, 161.83, 161.90, 161.93, 161.99, 161.112, 161.126, 161.191
Faulkner, Ralph 105.33
Faustino, David 96.140
Fawcett, Charles 133.7
Fawcett, William 3.10, 3.44, 3.58, 3.89, 3.115, 6.5, 6.13, 6.21, 6.28, 6.36, 6.51, 6.61, 8.56, 12.9, 14.38, 14.162, 21.67, 23.17, 23.20, 23.22, 23.35, 23.36, 27.79, 27.83, 31.21, 32.73, 32.84, 32.91, 32.100, 32.130, 32.151, 32.155, 35.16, 39.9, 41.8, 43.440, 44.49, 46.1, 57, 60.27, 60.29, 60.36, 60.42, 60.53, 60.60, 60.62, 60.67, 60.68, 60.71, 60.72, 60.73, 60.76, 65.169, 65.313, 65.350, 65.370, 65.495, 65.506, 65.517, 66.3, 73.11, 73.27, 81.12, 81.98, 81.99, 85.19, 85.39, 85.88, 85.98, 85.102, 88.26, 89.19, 89.81, 89.123, 89.143, 97.108, 97.207, 97.214, 97.220, 105.43, 105.117, 106.12, 117.36, 121.20, 124.19, 124.20, 124.30, 124.36, 124.54, 124.56, 124.61, 124.62, 126.24, 126.163, 129.9, 129.30, 129.30, 130.99, 130.158, 131.43, 132.14, 135.5, 135.10, 135.13, 135.27, 135.28, 135.37, 135.62, 138.78, 146.40, 148.185, 151.18, 152.69, 156.44, 158.34, 158.39, 158.69, 158.71, 161.22, 161.71, 161.131, 161.169, 161.176, 161.190, 162.186, 162.199, 162.205, 162.253, 164.34, 164.55, 169.4, 169.34, 169.58, 169.66, 170.27, 178.20
Fax, Jesslyn 30.20, 65.286
Faye, Herbie 125.1, 125.15
Faylen, Frank 105.15, 133.35, 164.6, 178.118
Featherstone, Eddie 147.46
Feero, Robert 118.6
Fein, Bernie 4.30, 89.84, 102.37, 149.71
Fein, Doren 48.63
Feinberg, Ronald 36.16, 36.17, 70.26, 70.39, 70.46, 71.61, 83.9
Feld, Fritz 170.91
Feliciano, Jose 83.55
Fell, Norman 94.7, 101.24, 170.20
Fellows, Edith 53.29
Fenady, Andrew J.127.37
Fennelly, Parker 66.34, 66.123
Fenton, Frank 2.10, 3.93, 6.54, 6.55, 6.63, 6.65, 6.69, 6.70, 81.68, 93.62, 97.27, 97.91, 97.120, 97.130, 97.136, 138.3, 141.9, 145.26, 147.26, 169.38, 169.96
Ferdin, Pamelyn 17.31, 65.477, 71.51, 71.53, 92.34

Ferens, Sandra 67.7
Ferguson, Al 141.42
Ferguson, Frank 4.2, 4.30, 5.38, 8.48, 8.75, 14.149, 21.6, 21.44, 27.65, 34.17, 34.36, 44.30, 46.10, 65.351, 66.151, 73.6, 82.8, 83.38, 83.39, 85.3, 89.79, 89.107, 89.133, 89.154, 93.218, 97.147, 97.149, 97.173, 97.178, 105.27, 105.32, 105.63, 105.94, 105.115, 108, 108.7, 108.14, 119.7, 129.47, 130.59, 142.45, 146.40, 146.55, 147.45,148.18, 148.79, 148.174, 148.195, 149.37, 151.16, 151.18, 151.22, 151.24, 152.25, 152.59, 152.60, 156.2, 156.52, 161.21, 162.151, 162.211, 162.252, 165.8, 167.1, 168.19, 178.14, 178.65, 178.71
Ferguson, Myles 67.15
Fernandez, Abel 3.50, 3.65, 3.67, 3.132, 41.25, 41.26, 41.30, 41.38, 41.78, 65.45, 65.160, 66.13, 76.8, 78.20, 129.62, 136, 145.12, 152.28, 157.19, 162.9, 162.53, 178.6, 178.81
Fernandez, Emilio 83.20
Fernandez, Juan 118.3, 163.47
Fernetz, Charlene 67.18
Ferracane, Rusty 91.2
Ferrante, Joseph 84.23
Ferrara, Al 20.42
Ferrell, Ray 57.64, 108.35, 152.6, 178.60, 178.113
Ferrente, Joe 8.10.
Ferrer, Mel 75.5, 178.101
Ferris, Michael 43.44, 43.53, 66.110
Ferrone, Dan 12.49, 14.396, 14.425, 24.7, 30.23, 65.456, 65.459, 65.487, 65.498, 65.588, 65.589
Ferrone, Laurie 5.47
Fertitta, John 163.15, 163.16
Fetty, Darrell 7.4
Fickett, Mary 14.321, 41.151, 66.156, 84.9, 84.50
Fieberling, Hal 97.54
Fiedler, John 14.132, 43.385, 46.8, 47.12, 53.24, 65.355, 65.582, 66.143, 149.68, 157.26
Field, Cliff 43.54, 167.15
Field, Daphne 65.513
Field, Darlene 25.3
Field, Grace 2.9, 6.37, 6.60, 6.75, 23.21
Field, Lillian 14.391
Field, Logan 14.30, 102.36, 126.112, 148.102, 148.131, 162.54, 170.72
Field, Margaret 60.70, 60.75, 97.19, 124.6, 124.10, 124.67, 124.71
Field, Mary 43.105, 65.175, 65.257, 162.116
Field, Norman 145.22
Field, Sally 5.25, 5.42
Field, Virginia 76.9, 127.57, 148.176
Fielder, John 117.46
Fielding, Elaine 70.4
Fielding, Joy 65.474
Fields, Charlie 59.2
Fields, Darlene 27.73, 31.25, 147.39, 148.33, 158.46, 162.105
Fields, Edith 1.25
Fields, Izack 36.5, 36.20, 71.37
Fields, Jimmy 130.86
Fields, Lyndsey 48.32, 48.37
Fierro, Paul 3.76, 8.71, 8.79, 21.60, 27.22, 32.134, 32.143, 51.24, 71.75, 71.82, 78.61, 84.1, 93.108, 93.172, 97.77, 97.79, 97.91, 105.21, 124.51, 124.52, 135.15, 141.65, 146.46, 148.198
Figueroa, Efrain 163.47, 163.53, 163.64, 163.65
Figueroa, Laura 65.515
Fill, Shannon 163.51
Filmer, Robert 60.20, 60.22, 97.118, 169.46, 169.79
Filpi, Carmen 1.9
Fimple, Dennis 1.13, 5.7, 5.10, 5.16, 5.32, 5.34, 5.41, 24.3, 50.2, 70.21, 83.34, 176.1
Fine, Ray 84.19
Fine, Travis 177
Finley, Evelyn 135.18
Finley, Harry 130.163

Finley, Larry 65.531, 65.585
Finn, John 65.508
Finn, Mickey 8.101, 66.46, 86.7, 86.10, 88.19, 127.25, 130.99, 147.28, 148.59, 162.59, 162.105, 162.260, 162.284
Finnerty, Warren 14.388, 116.1
Firestone, Eddie 12.70, 12.71, 13.12, 13.33, 14.54, 14.196, 14.210, 14.325, 30.13, 42.231, 43.427, 43.432, 49.4, 63.46, 65.402, 65.437, 65.438, 65.465, 65.575, 65.551, 65.552, 65.553, 70.32, 71.43, 83.21, 92.4, 126.216, 148.188, 151.8, 170.104
Firstman, Steve 129.13
Fischer, Bruce M. 10.8, 53.28, 65.629, 123.11, 175.8
Fischer, Corey 41.78
Fischer, Don 163.12
Fischler, Patrick 1.12
Fisher, Frances 177.46
Fisher, George C. 41.51
Fisher, Shug 14.303, 14.371, 30.1, 30.23, 41.25, 41.26, 41.31, 65.262, 65.263, 65.265, 65.334, 65.358, 65.394, 65.414, 65.430, 65.463, 65.472, 65.476, 65.497, 65.520, 65.533, 65.542, 65.543, 65.582, 65.614, 65.615, 66.158, 66.195, 66.209, 86.34, 86.53, 92.12, 106.16, 107.13, 151.7, 161.85, 161.125, 170.35, 170.67
Fisher, William J. 177.11, 177.33
Fist, Fletcher 12.42, 126.189
Fitch, Louise 14.325
Fitzgerald, Kathy 177.30
Fitzgerald, Wilbur 163.78
Fitzpatrick, Aileen 96.149
Fitzpatrick, Paul 6.64
FitzSimons, Bronwyn 161.38
Fix, Billy Paul 130.137
Fix, Paul 5.16, 5.23, 5.50, 12.10, 12.50, 12.99, 14.283, 14.375, 21.5, 34.20, 41.61, 41.129, 43.355, 63.1, 63.30, 65.53, 65.340, 65.380, 65.430, 65.442, 65.443, 66.214, 70.34, 71.10, 71.24, 75.3, 88.13, 89.29, 97.53, 101.25, 106.8, 114.14, 116.17, 126.28, 129.7, 130, 131.33, 146.15, 148.64, 152.7, 157.22, 161.140, 162.23, 162.176, 162.264, 170.38, 170.63, 170.72, 178.121
Flaherty, Harper 84.4, 161.175, 161.176, 161.178, 161.199, 161.201, 161.224
Flaherty, William 43.212, 141.47
Flanagan, Fionnula 14.417, 48.30, 65.568, 69.10, 75, 91.3
Flanders, Ed 9.4, 24.23, 30.8, 41.145, 83.25, 112.21
Flannery, Susan 43.320
Flavin, James 20.56, 22.19, 85.104, 97.29, 130.67, 141.16, 141.17, 141.19
Fleer, Harry 8.17, 8.106, 17.7, 44.72, 66.95, 85.71, 93.57, 93.95, 93.120, 126.101, 129.11, 129.17, 129.41, 141.41, 148.71, 152.44, 152.52, 152.70, 155.13, 158.26
Fleming, Al 120.7
Fleming, Arthur 25
Fleming, Carolyn 84.19
Fleming, Eric 14.222, 14.239, 14.240, 126
Fleming, Rhonda 43.255, 83.61, 86.1, 161.91, 162.42, 162.130, 162.237
Fletcher, Aaron 96.160
Fletcher, Bill 5.14, 5.26, 5.35, 5.45, 14.244, 14.255, 14.275, 30.5, 41.84, 71.40, 75.26, 83.12, 83.52, 106.22, 123.1, 139.3, 139.13, 161.133, 170.70
Fletcher, Charlotte 162.130
Fletcher, Hank 177.33
Fletcher, Jay 53.28
Fletcher, Lester 129.75, 170.100
Fletcher, Louise 8.10, 89.16, 93.219, 105.48, 146.59, 150.3, 162.74, 162.98, 173.12
Fletcher, Page 100.13
Flinn, John 65.520
Flint, Sam 2.24, 3.66, 6.5, 6.9, 6.15, 6.45, 6.48,

Flippen, Jay C. 14.147, 65.332, 70.43, 79.17, 101.29, 126.4, 126.166, 126.189, 132.25, 134.13, 142.18, 161.117, 161.162, 161.190, 164.8
Flippen, Lucy Lee 96, 96.113, 96.114, 96.162
Florek, Dave 65.637
Flores, Erika 48
Flores, Melissa 48, 48.42
Flory, Med 5.13, 14.56, 14.130, 14.390, 21.68, 30.8, 39.14, 41.40, 41.110, 41.119, 41.134, 41.159, 41.164, 46.7, 52.51, 65.529, 65.613, 89.88, 89.108, 89.143, 96.138, 105.92, 107.22, 112.8, 126.154, 161.75, 161.116, 162.138, 175.3
Flower, Amber 65.384, 101.31
Flower, Danny 14.176, 43.303
Flowers, George "Buck" 1.5
Flowers, Jim 169.31
Fluellen, Joel 30.3, 30.5, 41.146, 43.327, 76.2, 76.47, 78.13, 170.4
Flynn, Dan 65.555
Flynn, Dan, Jr. 65.548
Flynn, Gertrude 65.169, 65.405, 65.451, 66.164, 105.49, 105.107, 118.6
Flynn, Joe 5.23, 65.144, 65.277, 86.56, 129.47, 162.116
Flynn, Karen 162.245
Flynn, Sam 170.20
Foch, Nina 14.267, 65.492, 101.26, 126.20, 161.23, 162.13, 170.102
Foley, Brian 65.531
Foley, David 162.268
Folse, Gabriel 163.69, 177.6
Fonda, Henry 44
Fonda, Peter 161.202
Fong, Benson 14.162, 43.153, 49.2, 66.103, 83.1, 83.4, 83.20, 83.51, 83.63, 170.17
Fong, Brian 83.47, 83.48
Fong, Christopher 120.9, 120.13, 120.33
Fong, Frances 83.41, 83.54, 89.10, 155.17
Fong, Harold 66.31, 148.56, 161.120, 162.40, 168.11
Fontaine, Eddie 7, 170.55
Fontaine, Joan 162.208
Fontaine, Lili 68.1
Fontana, Carl 163.33
Foo, Lee Tung 97.39
Foot, Hallie 65.640
Foote, Dick 93.150
Foote, Fred 3.7
Foran, Dick 14.316, 27.108, 31.49, 34.6, 39.7, 41.60, 41.135, 43.237, 43.256, 43.275, 43.319, 44.58, 65.296, 66.48, 85.43, 85.57, 85.74, 85.99, 89.145, 105.15, 126.216, 161.61, 161.139, 161.151, 161.189, 164.20, 164.80, 169.79, 173.13
Forbes, Scott 13.10, 54.1, 54.4, 54.20, 54.23, 78, 156.67, 178.82, 178.98
Ford, Constance 8.27, 8.63, 39.2, 44.60, 55.19, 65.52, 65.260, 66.21, 88.25, 117.11, 126.128, 139.14, 139.15, 151.14, 155.73, 156.8, 164.84, 178.5, 178.26
Ford, Del 139.1
Ford, Dorothy 133.31
Ford, Francis 60.9, 60.10, 97.31, 169.7, 169.36
Ford, Frederick 6.48, 6.57, 43.90, 66.21
Ford, Fritz 6.56, 130.8, 130.11, 130.16, 130.31
Ford, Glenn 24
Ford, Harrison 65.574, 65.583, 83.34, 161.140
Ford, Larkin 66.65, 178.32
Ford, Michael 126.67
Ford, Paul 117.20
Ford, Peter 24
Ford, Ross 60.55, 60.61, 65.51, 81.13, 97.9, 97.38, 97.70, 97.89, 97.108, 126.43

Ford, Wallace 44, 82.5, 148.121, 156.37, 157.20, 168.3
Forest, Denis 1.3, 1.14
Forest, Michael 3.132, 8.34, 8.63, 14.4, 14.196, 14.271, 17.39, 21.20, 27.85, 41.87, 43.25, 55.13, 65.288, 65.353, 65.368, 66.46, 70.16, 70.36, 85.84, 85.111, 85.115, 86.52, 105.54, 105.110, 105.111, 126.94, 129.194, 130.37, 148.184, 149.34, 152.29, 155.9, 158.64, 161.50, 161.74, 161.101, 162.152, 162.172, 165.8, 169.110, 178.77, 179.42
Forester, Dick 148.18
Forman, Carol 32.15, 32.18, 32.21
Forrest, Frederick 177.66
Forrest, James 41.23
Forrest, Robert 97.93, 141.15
Forrest, Sally 126.4, 126.163
Forrest, Steve 5.30, 14.277, 14.339, 30.3, 30.19, 43.259, 43.293, 65.480, 65.512, 65.575, 65.592, 65.636, 71.71, 112.12, 117.1, 161.24, 161.65, 168.1, 178.110
Forrest, William 3.20, 3.77, 3.92, 3.93, 3.106, 21.29, 97.142, 97.159, 105.16, 105.18, 158.11
Forrester, William 148.103
Forster, Robert 66.63, 109
Forsyth, Rosemary 7.4, 24.22, 83.41
Forsythe, John 178.30
Forte, Joe 32.43, 32.49, 32.50, 148.174
Fortier, Robert 14.79, 34.18, 65.282, 65.335, 117.33
Forward, Robert 96.66
Forward, William 120.21
Foster, Alan 169.24
Foster, Bill 162.84
Foster, Buddy 5.43, 72
Foster, Carole Tru 115.1
Foster, Dianne 12.34, 14.36, 44.42, 65.256, 66.137, 85.57, 117.9, 117.34, 119.8, 131.21, 148.116, 148.181, 162.106, 162.107, 170.43
Foster, Donald 14.24
Foster, Edward 44.35, 126.105, 126.124, 138.19, 138.35, 138.41, 138.77, 141.58, 169.97, 169.98
Foster, Gloria 116.5
Foster, Jodie 14.413, 41.163, 65.502, 65.554, 65.559, 83.11
Foster, Linc 113.2
Foster, Linda 14.261, 52.34, 65.355, 125.8
Foster, Maralee 70.3
Foster, Meg 14.383, 70.46, 177.17
Foster, Preston 64, 117.26
Foster, Robert 163.37
Foster, Ronald 8.56, 8.106, 14.169, 14.222, 14.236, 14.271, 34.64, 43.100, 65.226, 65.245, 71.24, 85.108, 93.173, 126.66, 126.165, 126.21, 133.14, 148.195, 161.24
Foster, Ruth 96.12
Foster, Seth 177.28, 177.40
Foster, Tex 20.72, 141.51
Foster, Wayne 83.18
Foster, William 63.8, 63.42, 89.81, 93.154, 93.183, 125.9, 126.72, 127.4
Foulger, Byron 3.97, 3.165, 14.155, 32.1, 32.104, 35.27, 35.28, 41.75, 41.76, 60.83, 65.277, 65.424, 66.178, 73.2, 80.30, 86.31, 86.36, 97.26, 97.45, 97.103, 97.220, 105.29, 126.35, 126.153, 135.86, 148.177, 162.79, 162.244, 162.246, 169.4, 169.33, 169.46, 169.92, 169.107, 170.83
Foulger, Rachel 166.16
Foulk, Robert 7.2, 8.66, 14.24, 14.67, 14.126, 14.201, 14.231, 14.247, 14.267, 14.287, 20.19, 27.41, 27.78, 27.104, 30.21, 31.12, 34.24, 34.35, 34.62, 37.7, 41.2, 44.73, 57.28, 57.91, 63.15, 65.6, 70.51, 77.10, 77.18, 78.1, 83.7, 84.13, 97.87, 97.111, 97.138, 97.159, 101.1, 102.20, 103.2, 105.2, 105.64, 105.107, 108.10, 114.21, 127.11, 129.66, 130.23, 130.30, 130.37, 130.38, 130.99, 145.9, 148.18, 148.160, 149.49, 151.4, 152.10, 152.51, 152.65, 153.4, 155.1, 156.4, 158.22, 158.25, 158.45, 164.16, 167, 167.7, 167.8

Fountain, John 48.12
Fowler, Danny 65.370
Fowler, Jean 24.1
Fowler, Porter 70.45
Fowley, Douglas 3.55, 3.144, 7.14, 14.186, 27.9, 41.53, 43.182, 43.396, 49.5, 53.9, 63.40, 65.582, 76.43, 77.10, 83.18, 86.8, 93, 93.6, 93.10, 93.12, 93.16, 93.17, 93.18, 93.21, 93.22, 93.30, 93.31, 93.66, 93.67, 93.69, 93.71, 93.72, 93.75, 93.77, 93.80, 93.81, 93.83, 93.138, 93.141, 93.151, 93.152, 93.153, 93.154, 93.155, 93.156, 93.158, 93.163, 93.169, 93.170, 93.171, 93.172, 93.173, 93.174, 93.179, 93.180, 93.182, 93.183, 93.185, 93.187, 93.189, 93.191, 93.192, 93.193, 93.194, 93.195, 93.199, 122.13, 93.200, 93.202, 93.204, 93.206, 93.207, 93.210, 93.213, 93.214, 93.216, 93.217, 93.219, 93.220, 93.221, 93.222, 93.224, 93.225, 93.226, 101.27, 121, 151.18, 152.25, 156.36, 157.26, 161.79, 161.100, 164.59, 169.43, 169.50, 169.70
Fox, Bernard 7.11, 41.148, 47.1, 52.3, 62.1, 70.28, 170.95, 170.96
Fox, Bill 138.22
Fox, Craig 65.182
Fox, John 43.425, 121.14
Fox, John J. 12.65, 12.83, 47.6, 71.90
Fox, Michael 12.2, 51.5, 65.313, 65.399, 65.445, 73.32, 79.30, 86.46, 130.24, 130.50, 130.75, 130.76, 130.84, 155.8, 156.55, 156.56, 156.64, 161.6, 164.21, 170.80
Foxworth, Robert 45.2, 69.10, 83.29, 90.11
Fraim, Tracy 48.52, 48.53
Fraly, Lou 170.67
Franciosa, Anthony 106.11, 161.219
Francis, Anne 43.288, 65.569, 83.33, 106.6, 126.26, 151.19, 161.72
Francis, Coleman 138.8, 138.22, 138.49, 138.59
Francis, Ivor 14.344, 50, 70.37, 83.35, 96.78, 123.10
Francis, John 152.18, 161.2
Francis, Missy 96
Francis, Paul 48.86
Francis, Stan 68.3
Francisco, Charles 12.20, 43.321, 65.411
Francisco, James 66.38
Franciscus, James 13.43, 43.162, 44.44, 126.50, 130.51, 148.95, 162.96
Francks, Don 84.38, 161.196, 170.18
Franco, Abel 71.7
Frank, Ben 83.10
Frank, Charles 28, 120.22, 120.23, 163.42, 175
Frank, Eddie 84.36
Frank, John 73.8, 141.34
Frank, Tony 90.20
Franken, Steve 12.93, 170.36
Frankfather, William 1.18
Frankham, David 43.120, 105.55, 148.153
Franklin, Don 177
Franklin, Pamela 14.427
Franklyn, Camille 43.71, 43.80, 93.41
Franklyn, Hazel 138.9
Franz, Arthur 4.32, 14.91, 38.5, 43.201, 43.233, 44.56, 65.195, 84.26, 97.13, 116.7, 123.10, 126.38, 126.123, 148.185, 161.34, 162.183, 162.215, 164.56, 178.53
Franz, Eduard 29.26, 43.235, 44.9, 65.23, 65.621, 66.148, 101.34, 126.109, 129.38, 144.3, 161.115, 162.188, 164.33, 164.60, 168.20, 179.40, 179.41, 179.42, 179.43, 179.44
Fraser, Duncan 67.5, 67.9, 67.13
Fraser, Elisabeth 126.212, 162.261, 162.89, 162.235
Fraser, Sally 2.22, 6.69, 6.70, 20.22, 27.24, 32.129, 60.85, 60.91, 93.133, 152.30, 152.49, 156.25
Fraser, Stanley 138.23
Frasher, Jim 60.1, 60.3, 60.19
Frawley, James 65.348, 101.12

Personnel Index

Frawley, Tim 162.187
Frazee, Jane 60.45, 97.44, 124.41
Frazer, Dan 117.10, 132.28
Frazer, Elizabeth 65.403
Frazier, James 60.11
Frazier, Roger 28.4
Frederic, Norman 27.11, 27.36, 27.52, 105.10
Frederick, John 14.142
Frederick, Scott 177.59
Fredericks, Charles 4.37, 8.23, 8.82, 20.29, 20.58, 21.5, 21.49, 27.46, 34.5, 34.37, 34.61, 43.309, 44.10, 64.4, 65.129, 65.135, 65.194, 65.282, 65.492, 77.25, 79.21, 82.5, 85.110, 89.78, 93.38, 93.42, 93.49, 93.117, 93.157, 93.158, 102.12, 103.31, 105.21, 105.32, 105.90, 117.28, 126.47, 126.76, 130.22, 133.26, 138.41, 146.57, 146.67, 149.43, 161.32, 169.63, 169.79, 173.26, 178.131
Fredericks, Dean 21.43, 40, 44.18, 85.23, 89.85, 126.103, 130.153, 130.165, 161.31
Fredericks, Norman 65.67
Fredric, Norman 3.40, 3.45, 3.49, 3.76, 3.110, 31.10
Freed, Bert 12.24, 12.34, 12.59, 12.95, 14.27, 14.291, 39.9, 63.20, 65.144, 65.384, 71.50, 76.18, 84.29, 88.13, 98.13, 101.28, 106.21, 130.33, 130.103, 131.10, 139, 161.31, 161.163, 161.164, 168.21
Freeman, Arny 66.164
Freeman, Joan 14.194, 14.274, 39.4, 65.276, 85.122, 93.23, 98.2, 157.23, 161.12, 161.41, 161.86, 161.106, 162.223
Freeman, Kathleen 14.268, 14.354, 22.9, 22.13, 22.31, 41.117, 71.39, 84.36, 85.87, 86.47, 89.121, 126.103, 162.53, 162.154, 162.244
Freeman, Leonard 97.112
Freeman, Matt 53.16
Freeman, Mona 17.36, 79.19, 105.58, 105.70, 131.11, 149.48, 162.38, 164.9, 164.40, 178.7
Frees, Paul 78.25
Freidman, David 95.24
Freimuth, Douglas 177.64
French, Bill 80.24, 80.29, 80.30, 80.33, 80.35
French, Marinda 41.106
French, Susan 95.5, 96.125
French, Ted 65.428, 65.491
French, Valerie 4.28, 66.90, 66.115, 156.6
French, Victor 14.287, 14.342, 14.359, 14.389, 30.10, 39.8, 41.88, 41.134, 41.159, 41.164, 43.341, 52.58, 65.399, 65.409, 65.425, 65.442, 65.443, 65.446, 65.458, 65.467, 65.469, 65.474, 65.510, 65.546, 65.561, 65.568, 65.587, 65.590, 65.620, 65.635, 76.25, 83.16, 84.25, 95, 95.22, 95.23, 95.24, 96, 96.4, 96.8, 96.13, 96.17, 96.22, 96.120, 96.165, 137.10, 151.3, 159.29, 161.14, 170.6
French and Indian War 67, 68, 114
Fresco, David 65.488, 92.19, 93.205, 170.77
Frey, Leonard 10
Friebus, Florida 65.591
Friedkin, Joel 97.15
Friedman, David 95
Frizzel, Lou 14, 14.316, 14.351, 14.359, 14.363, 14.366, 26, 71.56, 71.57, 111, 112.14, 116.9
Frome, Milton 5.19, 8.6, 39.7, 64.8, 82.11, 126.97, 131.33, 147.48, 148.65, 152.14, 158.31, 158.32, 162.54, 162.236
Frommer, Ben 138.62
Froner, Barry 3.96, 6.49, 6.78, 32.152, 57.42, 108.34
Frost, Alice 14.136, 65.187, 74.9, 149.38, 161.94, 162.167, 162.191
Frost, Terry 2.12, 3.88, 3.104, 6.23, 6.24, 6.60, 6.66, 6.75, 8.53, 20.52, 23.3, 23.27, 23.30, 27.76, 32.31, 32.37, 32.125, 32.129, 32.133, 32.135, 32.146, 32.150, 60.39, 60.41, 60.56, 60.59, 60.62, 60.63, 60.65, 60.66, 60.74, 60.77, 60.81, 60.86, 65.416, 73.27, 81.26, 81.90, 81.93, 81.95, 93.48, 93.121, 97.120, 97.125, 97.145, 97.160, 97.176, 103.50, 105.14, 108.38, 124.27, 124.32, 124.67, 124.71, 126.79, 129.16, 135.1, 135.8, 135.12, 135.30, 135.36, 135.40, 135.42, 135.50, 135.94, 135.95, 138.8, 138.18, 138.36, 141.47, 145.35, 148.11, 148.41, 148.82, 148.138, 156.32, 158.49, 158.57, 164.7, 169.6, 169.47, 169.54, 169.67, 169.84, 169.90, 169.98, 178.14
Frothingham, Diana 43.355
Fry, Stephen 110.4
Frye, Gilbert 71.14, 138.65, 141.20, 141.24, 141.38, 169.105
Frye, Sean 96.105
Frye, Virgil 14.334, 174.4
Fuchs, Lee 162.198
Fudge, Alan 65.555, 83.28, 96.20, 123.11, 175.5, 175.6
Fuji 66.103, 66.185, 170.90
Fujikawa, Jerry 83.27, 83.53, 170.62
Fujima, Kansuma 83.50
Fujioka, John 83.44, 83.49, 83.56, 83.57, 83.58, 83.59, 83.60
Fujiwara, Tom 11.2
Fulkerson, Elaine 65.612
Fuller, Barbara 156.21
Fuller, Clem 65.131, 65.161, 126.10, 126.45
Fuller, Erwin 53.2, 53.4
Fuller, Kathryn 96.162
Fuller, Lance 8.12, 8.67, 8.88, 34.35, 89.125, 105.38, 105.58, 130.9, 158.73
Fuller, Robert 1.1, 1.4, 3.149, 12.63, 14.431, 22.5, 25.29, 29.20, 69.5, 85, 89.39, 93.140, 106.19, 107.11, 120.24, 120.44, 129.51, 129.55, 161.47, 162, 162.57, 162.70, 162.230
Fuller, Roy 83.1
Fulton, Rad 85.20
Funai, Helen 170.62
Funicello, Annette 72.16, 113.5, 162.234, 179.60, 179.61, 179.62, 179.81
Funk, Terry 1.1, 171
Furedi, Elizabeth 126.89
Furth, George 14.334, 48.3, 48.36, 52.49, 86.56, 96.36, 132.5
Fusaro, Lisa 145.32

Gabay, Eli 67.4, 99.13
Gabel, Martin 66.118, 66.167
Gabor, Zsa Zsa 14.268, 52.24, 134.6
Gabourie, Fred 169.66, 169.91
Gabriel, John 12.44
Gackle, Kathleen 83.4
Gadson, Gary 130.134
Gage, Ben 46.3, 52.25, 105.43, 105.59, 105.78
Gage, Tony 170.71
Gagnier, Holly 1.10.
Gahva, Maria 112.17
Gail, Max 90.18
Gaines, Jimmy 148.160
Gaines, Mel 65.416, 164.20
Gaines, Richard 88.5, 141.12
Gainey, M.C. 1.1, 1.12, 163.10, 177.7
Gains, Courtney 91.6
Gaintner, Roy 115.5
Galante, Jim 51.28, 126.103, 126.107, 130.141, 170.37
Gale, Eddra 71.93
Galik, Denise 115.5
Galina, Stacy 120.11, 120.37
Galindo, Jose Hector 41.57
Galindo, Nacho 23.9, 44.63, 65.466, 78.76, 97.141, 102.27, 105.24, 105.73, 129.70, 170.50
Gallagher, Mel 63.45, 65.356, 71.71
Gallagher, Patti 138.11
Gallaudet, John 8.46, 25.19, 84.31, 93.166, 93.169, 141.16
Gallego, Gina 181.3
Gallendo, Silvana 26

Gallery, James 96.127, 96.155
Gallison, Joseph 51.25
Gallivan, Megan 48.20, 177.61
Gallo, Jacques 78.10
Gallo, Lew 12.24, 39.3, 43.161, 44.50, 57.104, 64.5, 65.125, 65.165, 65.399, 65.434, 74.18, 76.23, 89.19, 126.62, 126.87, 148.161, 148.181, 149.25, 161.40, 178.85
Galloway, Don 94.6, 161.31, 161.127, 162.283
Galloway, Michael 20.72, 152.32
Gamboa, Danny 158.18
Gammon, James 14.264, 50.3, 65.407, 65.599, 71.82, 83.37, 84.3, 84.27, 107.2, 132.3, 132.28, 161.164, 170.25, 177.48
Gampu, Ken 36.9, 41.96
Gan, Jennifer 112.16, 161.195
Ganem, Patricia 137.1
Gange, Tony 41.156
Gangey, Dick 170.82, 170.89
Gangey, Tony 170.98
Ganley, Gail 158.34, 158.39
Gant, Carl 120.13
Garas, Kaz 7.13, 48.77, 65.489, 71.94, 161.220
Garcia, David 162.140
Garcia, Elizabeth 129.14
Garcia, Joe 28
Garcia, Kenny 3.43, 3.44
Garcia, Maria 170.103
Garcia, Priscilla 14.394, 112.23, 161.91
Garcia, Stella 65.556
Gardenia, Vincent 12.1, 12.47, 65.433
Gardiner, Reginald 85.120
Gardner, Ann 161.45
Gardner, Brooks 120.17, 120.18, 120.48
Gardner, Dick 178.29
Gardner, Don 32.145, 32.149, 65.14, 155.26
Gardner, Hunter 32.50
Gardner, Jack 43.65
Gardner, Richard 89.118, 131.12
Gardner, Steven 130.11
Garfield, Allen 14.399, 65.628
Garfield, John, Jr. 139.2
Garland, Beverly 39.16, 53.8, 65.303, 65.454, 65.479, 65.508, 75.27, 83.55, 84.26, 85.27, 86.2, 98.23, 101.1, 102.1, 113, 121.8, 126.23, 126.123, 126.134, 131.26, 142.10, 148.124, 153.3, 156.57, 164.67, 170.67, 170.101, 173.15, 173.28, 178.11, 178.83, 178.111, 178.148
Garland, Richard 21.48, 27.49, 27.53, 27.60, 34.3, 34.22, 34.63, 44.27, 53.12, 53.21, 57.64, 81.51, 81.87, 81.101, 89.75, 93.85, 93.117, 113.10, 105.2, 105.34, 131.20, 133.19, 146.29, 146.51, 151.9, 158.7, 158.9, 158.69, 158.71, 161.16, 161.31, 162.13, 164.65, 179.78
Garland, Robert 178.130
Garner, David 66.202
Garner, Dick 164.45
Garner, Don 97.182
Garner, Jack 5.5, 41.138, 65.512, 65.524, 84.5, 175.1
Garner, James 19, 27.1, 27.7, 27.15, 27.16, 105, 112, 175.1, 175.2, 178.13
Garner, Mousie 105.73
Garner, Peggy Ann 14.60, 66.176, 126.130, 150.2, 178.116
Garnett, Gale 14.105, 66.211, 148.188
Garon, Richard 48.76
Garr, Eddie 31.3
Garralaga, Martin 31.10, 43.37, 65.460, 66.1, 71.47, 71.52, 78.76, 81.23, 97.142, 126.31, 129.7, 146.46, 149.24, 152.7
Garrett, Andi 170.39
Garrett, Don 3.78, 97.155, 169.77
Garrett, Gary 32.42, 35.37
Garrett, Leif 24.10, 65.574
Garrett, Mike 6.58, 6.59, 23.28, 23.29, 44.73, 93.29, 105.71, 178.5

Garrett, Pat 149
Garrett, Spencer 48.33, 120.29
Garrett, Todd 70.13, 170.27
Garrett, Tru 85.79, 85.97, 85.121
Garrick, Rian 21.59
Garrick, Richard 108.24
Garrison, Sean 5.11, 12.4, 27.48, 33, 34.21, 49, 65.400
Garrity, Patty Ann 148.107
Garroway, Dave 5.33, 5.39
Garson, Greer 106.8
Garth, Annabel 43.300
Garth, Michael 43.60, 147.11
Garth, Otis 145.23
Garver, Kathy 12.105, 43.313, 43.346, 157.14, 157.15
Garvie, Parker 43.75
Garwood, John 61.8
Garwood, Kelton 12.40, 51.11, 65.233, 65.277, 65.408, 66.91, 66.109, 74.6, 126.45, 127.11, 130.70, 159.28, 162.143
Gary, Lorraine 69.3, 106.13
Gary, Paul 93.50, 93.150
Gary, Ralph 170.18
Gaston, Penny 170.88
Gates, Enoch 144.8
Gates, Larry 14.37, 30.3, 116.8, 117.11, 126.214, 144.12
Gates, Maxine 60.85, 126.92
Gates, Nancy 14.226, 65.266, 85.19, 98.8, 105.50, 105.26, 126.212, 131.1, 148.172, 156.33, 161.74, 162.47, 162.197, 162.246, 167.25, 178.146
Gates, Rick 65.550, 71.95
Gatlin, Jerry 14.369, 14.378, 14.429, 53.17, 65.564, 65.565, 65.592, 66.189, 66.204, 168.11
Gatteys, Bennye 65.297, 85.111, 144.11, 148.169, 149.47
Gautier, Dick 181.6
Gavin, James 12.4, 12.46, 12.49, 12.51, 12.55, 27.20, 30.9, 57.70, 65.116, 66.76, 71.44, 101.7, 105.81, 126.9, 126.43, 126.59, 126.104, 130.91, 147.30, 148.35, 156.9, 158.35, 159.6, 162.197, 170.70, 178.24
Gavin, John 46, 161.74
Gavlin, Fredric 155.38
Gay, Gregory 39.10, 80.31, 80.33
Gay, Linda 31.46
Gaye, Lisa 6.53, 8.17, 8.36, 8.105, 13.3, 21.63, 25.51, 27.67, 27.71, 34.36, 43.178, 43.216, 43.299, 43.322, 43.325, 43.358, 43.395, 43.405, 43.426, 66.16, 66.29, 78.5, 78.23, 85.77, 105.95, 114.3, 114.4, 122.7, 126.59, 146.41, 148.165, 148.176, 155.27, 155.51, 162.140, 164.71, 170.41, 170.66, 179.13
Gayle, Monica 37.7
Gaylor, Gerry 96.30, 96.31, 132.22
Gaynes, George 14.291, 27.106, 51.15, 123.4
Gaynor, Grace 14.84, 170.56, 170.79
Gaynor, Jock 27.75, 34.57, 64.10, 76.5, 76.24, 85.114, 93.184, 117, 126.69, 126.102, 150.12, 167.14
Gaynor, Steven 65.332
Gazinga, Dick 71.12
Gazzaniga, Don 125.15, 162.185, 170.4
Geary, Paul 85.89
Geary, Toni 164.26
Geas, Tom 170.97
Gebert, Gordon 6.38, 64.53, 169.53, 169.63
Geer, Ellen 83.63, 111.2
Geer, Leonard P. "Lennie" 8.10, 13.10, 85.53, 85.78, 85.101, 85.108, 86.34, 93.196, 93.208, 93.223, 98.23, 129.44, 130.21, 148.137, 148.183, 149.53, 161.6, 161.9, 162.144, 162.249, 164.57, 165.7, 168.1, 169.18
Geer, Will 5.19, 14.329, 14.370, 14.402, 24.2, 41.147, 65.468, 70.20, 83.16
Gehring, Ted 5.31, 5.45, 12.12, 14.284, 14.325,
14.338, 14.361, 14.366, 14.390, 14.412, 24.15, 30.12, 37.12, 43.445, 43.450, 65.406, 65.418, 65.441, 65.451, 65.585, 65.618, 71.18, 71.54, 71.95, 83.31, 83.56, 83.57, 83.58, 83.59, 84.16, 84.18, 96, 96.20, 96.26, 96.42, 112.6, 115.3, 161.185
Geirasch, Stefan 144.21
Gelbman, Larry 141.38, 169.91
Gell, Sherwood 35.34
Gemignani, Rhoda 120.12
Genero, Tony 110.1, 110.2
Genest, Emile 41.6, 65.304, 65.339, 76.36, 85.99, 86.16, 126.175, 132.21, 161.47, 161.113
Genge, Paul 14.217, 170.22, 178.61
Genn, Leo 161.49
Gentry, John 102.25, 127.54
Gentry, Race 3.118, 31.32
Gentry, Robert 65.627
George, Anthony 3.54, 27.34, 43.145, 141.70, 146.29, 148.4, 155.35, 162.207, 168.28, 179.20, 179.24, 179.25
George, Bill 32.40, 32.46, 32.50, 32.110, 32.116, 60.52, 129.78, 135.24, 135.56, 135.73, 135.97, 169.65
George, Chief Dan 14.403, 24.24, 26, 71.61, 83.16
George, Douglas 6.78
George, Gladys 73.32
George, Jack 32.44, 32.51, 141.49
George, Lynda Day 7.1, 14.300, 36.4, 70.52, 83.32, 84.12, 161.147
George, Sue 25.39, 27.32, 77.9, 93.89, 119.12, 146.26, 148.43, 149.33, 159.37
Georgetown, Colorado 74
Georgiade, Nick 157.16, 157.24
Gerard, Gil 96.70
Gerard, Hal 93.48, 93.79, 138.60, 169.40, 169.61
Geray, Steven 14.97, 25.9, 78.2, 141.13, 141.26, 157.24, 162.187, 178.4
Germaine, Elizabeth 65.466
Gerritsen, Lisa 14.395, 65.473, 65.478, 65.519, 65.530, 84.20, 106.13
Gerrity, Dan 1.1
Gerry, Alex 31.45, 40.1, 40.2, 88.18, 162.57, 170.68, 178.59, 179.76
Gerry, Antoinette 73.13
Gerry, Toni 20.58, 34.3, 93.60
Gerson, Betty Lou 130.76, 164.79
Gerstle, Frank 8.55, 14.102, 14.275, 25.4, 27.85, 34.63, 43.111, 43.125, 77.13, 84.27, 85.109, 89.99, 93.138, 93.168, 93.193, 98.20, 103.14, 126.65, 148.50, 148.180, 161.87, 162.50, 162.137, 162.188, 164.83
Ghazio, Anthony, Sr. 36.6
Ghostley, Alice 112
Giambalvo, Louis 1.23
Gibbons, Ayllene 92.4
Gibbons, Blake 48.18, 120.21
Gibbons, Robert 66.187, 96.56
Gibbons, Sanford 177.8, 177.9
Gibbs, Charles 97.92
Gibbs, Timothy 53
Gibson, Harriet 96.117
Gibson, Henry 7.11, 52.18, 52.48, 86.14
Gibson, Mimi 127.27, 133.35, 149.22
Gierasch, Stefan 14.335, 14.399, 51.16, 65.415, 83.38, 83.39
Gifford, Alan 65.115
Gifford, John 145.13
Gift, Robert 65.101
Giftos, Elaine 14.350, 14.351, 24.3
Gilbert, Ed 70.41, 170.5
Gilbert, Helen 43.64, 68.30, 93.45
Gilbert, Jo 81.11
Gilbert, Joanne 21.6, 178.60
Gilbert, John 99.1, 99.2, 99.3, 130.163
Gilbert, Jonathan 95, 96
Gilbert, Lance 120.11

Gilbert, Lauren 51.30
Gilbert, Marcus 90.20
Gilbert, Melissa 65.567, 95, 95.22, 95.24, 96
Gilbert, Nancy 23, 60.90
Gilbert, Paul 44.61
Gilbert, Ted 158.45
Gilbreath, George 155.21
Gilchrist, Connie 3.119, 41.25, 41.26, 129.30, 149.37, 162.106, 162.107
Gilden, Richard 3.141, 43.79, 43.176, 43.343, 43.338, 65.9, 65.401, 76.5, 126.7
Giles, James 127.31
Giles, Jerry 48.37
Giles, Jim 127.14
Giles, Sandra 126.155
Gilford, Gwynne 65.533
Gilgreen, John 71.87
Gillerman, Tom 14.397, 131.40
Gillespie, Gina 85.91, 86.28, 88, 117.44, 142.12, 148.152, 148.173, 157.22, 162.117
Gillespie, Jean 43.234
Gillespie, Jennifer 148.172
Gillespie, Larrian 14.111, 148.160
Gillespie, Lillian 114.8
Gilliam, Burton 10.3, 75.17, 175.2
Gillis, Bill 158.3, 158.7, 158.9, 158.25
Gilman, Catherine 177.21
Gilman, Sam 12.76, 63.16, 65.410, 65.433, 65.451, 66.35, 93.180, 96.80, 139, 130.62
Gilmore, Jonathan 14.19, 89.52
Gilmore, Lowell 25.4, 108.14
Gilmour, Nancy 48.37
Gilson, Tom 8.80, 27.68, 27.87, 89.28, 89.78, 89.96, 89.147, 105.97, 117.18, 130.141, 133.36, 140.33, 148.163, 148.175, 149.29, 149.64, 164.47, 164.72, 167.18, 178.96
Gilstrap, Suzy 96.143
Gilyard, Clarence 163
Ging, Jack 8.43, 8.75, 13.36, 14.290, 44.50, 65.419, 93.192, 95.20, 96.21, 106.16, 139.12, 148
Ginger, Johnny 130.131
Ginter, Lindsey 67.10, 163.24
Ginty, Robert 109.4
Giorgio, William 148.155
Giovane, Bob 118.10
Girard, Hal 93.14
Girard, Wendy 118.1
Girardin, Ray 65.630
Giroux, Lee 31.44
Gist, Robert 13.4, 43.171, 65.10, 65.121, 66.38, 66.83, 66.96, 66.141, 66.187, 74.28, 79.3, 112.4, 122.32, 126.6, 126.60, 126.100, 161.1, 178.110
Givney, Kathryn 161.82
Glasgow, Gil 163.28
Glass, Everett 32.65, 32.66, 126.104
Glass, Ned 13.2, 65.64, 65.67, 65.108, 65.184, 65.203, 65.320, 65.488, 66.7, 66.9, 66.146, 70.43, 77.10, 84.32, 88.17, 140.37, 156.4, 156.29, 164.55
Glass, Seamon 7.6, 65.583
Glave, Matthew 163.30
Glazer, Eugene Robert 163.14
Gleason, James 1.12, 27.6, 129.14, 177.47
Gleason, Regina 14.242, 43.26, 43.81, 66.118, 66.167, 124.66, 124.72, 130.91
Gleason, Tom 65.71
Glenn, Darryl 162.56
Glenn, Ray 144.8
Glenn, Roy E., Jr. 30.6, 126.59, 126.64, 126.103
Gless, Sharon 26
Glombecki, Gerry 177.39
Glover, Bruce 9.7, 12.98, 14.360, 63.45, 65.492, 65.568
Glover, Edmund 22.27, 66.91
Glover, Richard 177.49
Glover, William 83.18
Gobble, Henry A. 165.3, 165.6, 165.7, 165.12, 165.13

Personnel Index

Gobel, George 41.24, 43.269, 52.20, 162.116
Goddard, John 29.19, 41.114, 93.90, 129.55, 130.25, 130.50, 148.62, 162.63, 169.91
Goddard, Mark 65.341, 79, 127.41, 130.37, 130.151, 161.57, 178.128
Godfrey, Renee 23.35, 23.36, 55.20, 162.155, 162.226, 178.105
Godin, Jacques 154
Godwin, Stephen 120.6
Goff, John 12.13
Gold, Harvey 84.32
Gold, Missy 75.24
Gold, Tracy 53.11
Golden, Bob 65.534
Golden, Larry 14.416, 96.66, 96.128
Goldin, Pat 130.154
Goldyn, Miriam 66.202
Golomb, Sheldon 12.5
Golonka, Arlene 12.70, 12.71
Gomes, Thomas 161.101
Gomez, Augie W. 32.65, 32.66, 135.16, 135.35
Gomez, Luis 66.21, 148.9, 178.114
Gomez, Marie 71.4, 71.20, 71.38, 71.48, 72.10, 76.36, 170.61
Gomez, Thomas 65.556, 86.44, 130.36, 131.34, 152.2
Gonzales Gonzales, Jose 6.75, 14.16, 32.95, 32.100, 80.2, 80.15, 80.23, 127.14, 149.60, 155.16, 164.61
Gonzalez Gonzalez, Clifton 163.64, 163.65
Gonzalez Gonzalez, Pedro 12.32, 12.33, 17.25, 17.26, 27.92, 56.30, 71.15, 71.72, 86.22, 86.47, 125.14, 152.45, 152.46, 152.47, 152.48, 152.71
Goode, Georgia 151.16
Goodwin, Gay 135.91, 169.108
Goodwin, Harold 41.33, 41.38, 41.63, 41.94, 65.171, 73.5, 97.31, 162.253
Goodwin, James 53.13, 70.35, 86.31, 86.40, 96.30, 96.31, 156.37
Goodwin, Joseph A. 137.4
Goodwin, Laurel 161.73
Goodwin, Robert 5.28
Goodwin, Ruby 78.74, 152.7
Goodwin, Toby 177.5
Gordien, Fortune 32.124
Gordin, Charles 139.14, 139.15
Gordon, Anita 43.130, 146.15
Gordon, Bruce 8.40, 14.9, 14.202, 14.363, 25.58, 43.213, 65.97, 65.118, 65.205, 66.6, 66.58, 74.20, 77.4, 79.2, 85.28, 103.36, 105.99, 117.6, 117.30, 117.41, 131.19, 142.9, 146.64, 146.67, 148.111, 148.133, 155.6, 156.27
Gordon, Clarke 5.8, 5.32, 5.48, 14.409, 17.15, 51.17, 65.108, 126.30, 126.91, 152.7
Gordon, Don 44.35, 51.28, 103.30, 133.18, 139.3, 146.22, 156.35, 156.48, 164.25, 164.60, 170.54
Gordon, Elyse 130.1
Gordon, Gerald 66.169, 66.171
Gordon, Glen 8.87, 97.143, 126.3, 126.36, 126.112, 145.29
Gordon, Leo 3.2, 3.40, 3.61, 5.19, 7.1, 8.8, 8.74, 14.2, 14.110, 14.289, 20.12, 21.24, 21.61, 27.5, 27.19, 27.93, 31.1, 41.40, 43.260, 43.316, 44.25, 51.8, 53.10, 53.20, 61.4, 65.26, 65.207, 65.555, 65.582, 65.604, 66.4, 66.75, 66.133, 66.142, 71.18, 86.2, 86.36, 88.24, 89.108, 93.217, 96.121, 105.1, 105.3, 105.24, 105.37, 105.53, 106.13, 116.22, 117.4, 121.9, 125.2, 126.32, 126.178, 130.12, 130.168, 133.5, 145.21, 147.47, 148.2, 148.137, 148.179, 151.4, 155.7, 158.49, 158.57, 161.11, 161.77
Gordon, Marianne 86.4, 134.1
Gordon, Mary 32.13
Gordon, Roy 3.99, 43.93, 43.101, 6.43, 60.45, 97.17, 145.11
Gordon, Susan 65.223
Gordon, William D. 5.44, 88.1, 105.39, 105.51, 126.53, 131.6, 131.13, 161.11

Gordon-Levitt, Joseph 48.16
Goritsas, Demetri 67.14
Gorman, Annette 153
Gorman, Patrick T. 67.18
Gorshin, Frank 51.7, 56.15, 71.48, 101.31, 106.11
Gorss, Saul 44.47, 85.96, 98.14
Gortner, Marjoe 109.9
Gossett, Lou, Jr. 5.27, 14.380, 24.12, 36.8, 36.20, 96.41
Gothie, Robert 93.188, 156.32, 161.72, 178.40, 178.60
Gough, Lloyd 30.19, 65.406, 76.31, 98.7
Gould, Graydon 12.36, 71.30
Gould, Harold 12.60, 12.86, 12.105, 41.103, 47.13, 51.14, 59.1, 59.2, 65.346, 65.614, 65.615, 70.41, 71.86, 84.9, 84.48, 161.14, 161.88, 161.93, 170.57, 170.91
Gould, Sandra 105.45, 162.203
Gould, William 97.25, 152.24
Gould-Porter, Arthur 170.18
Goulet, Robert 12.53
Gowan, Beverly 126.23
Gozier, Bernie 20.20
Graas, John Christian 48.80, 90.1, 90.2, 177.30
Grace, Charity 25.63, 88.17, 105.106
Grace, Pierrette 177.31
Grace, Wayne 48.19, 90
Grady, Don 22.20, 66.123, 88.14, 129.48, 129.70, 129.74, 130.41, 130.62, 162.101, 167.6, 178.98, 178.99
Graf, David 120.53
Graf, Dick 21.55
Graff, John 158.45
Graff, Wilton 20.49, 43.195, 65.19, 78.69, 108.2, 129.74, 131.21, 148.53, 148.178, 161.18, 162.58, 162.132
Graham, Fred 20.46, 20.48, 43.352, 81.29, 85.83, 88.27, 97.7, 97.48, 97.148, 103.17, 103.19, 124.13, 124.17, 126.4, 126.69, 126.91, 129.15, 135.18, 135.19, 135.24, 135.25, 135.57, 135.73, 138.58, 148.45, 152.28, 152.44, 158.18
Graham, George 74.14, 127.24
Graham, Gerrit 177.7
Graham, Gracy 126.114
Graham, John 144.10
Graham, Scott 43.337, 43.441
Graham, Tim 4.35, 22.31, 27.79, 34.50, 3.8, 41.12, 65.12, 65.66, 73.14, 89.110, 89.151, 97.20, 97.48, 105.57, 105.75, 105.90, 126.95, 128.4, 129.11, 129.32, 138.70, 148.3, 149.53, 151.13, 156.31, 158.11, 158.12, 161.139, 161.178, 162.183, 162.229, 162.242, 178.8
Grahame, Gloria 41.153, 76.23
Granby, Joe 138.2
Granby, Joseph 32.25, 32.33, 32.38
Grange, Douglas 6.49
Granger, Dorothy 43.95
Granger, Farley 72.6, 109.12, 162.9
Granger, Michael 20.17, 65.21, 66.10, 126.48, 147.3
Granger, Philip 99.10
Granger, Stewart 106
Granstedt, Greta 97.18, 97.66, 97.75, 97.104, 103.30, 141.9
Grant, Barra 65.592
Grant, Gillian 96.151
Grant, Gloria 31.34, 81.10, 147.20, 147.28
Grant, Harvey 3.39, 31.7, 138.13, 138.52, 141.61
Grant, Kirby 141
Grant, Lee 12.58
Grant, Mudcat 116.15
Grant, Neil 148.65, 155.27
Grant, Paul 129.30, 139.6
Grant, Richard 151.6
Grant, Rodney A. 67, 91.9
Grant, Saginaw 90.10
Grant, Shelby 71.18
Granville, Joan 8.62, 65.408, 133.22, 138.30

Grassle, Karen 65.617, 95.23, 96
Gravage, Robert 65.287, 65.238, 65.486, 84.41, 161.224
Gravers, Steve 5.15, 5.29, 5.34, 5.45, 66.55, 70.44, 82.8, 88.12, 98.6, 101.1, 107.9, 126.183, 161.114
Graves, Anne 64.4
Graves, Gayla 27.73
Graves, Joel 95.24
Graves, Peter 17.44, 17.45, 29.21, 41.65, 57, 61.9, 61.10, 86.19, 161.52
Gray, Beatrice 60.5, 60.16
Gray, Billy 27.39, 38.9, 44.63, 60.5, 60.17, 126.191, 142.3
Gray, Bruce 91.8
Gray, Charles H. 5.20, 5.43, 13.3, 14.406, 43.208, 64, 65.15, 65.35, 65.127, 65.325, 66.96, 71.20, 71.37, 76.3, 86.10, 126.10, 126.30, 131.28, 132.1, 132.2, 152.29, 173.33, 178.32, 178.93
Gray, Christopher 65.217, 65.232, 100.13
Gray, Coleen 14.290, 17.22, 39.15, 44.30, 53.12, 66.165, 89.104, 105.108, 113.10, 126.113, 148.110, 149.45, 161.108, 161.139, 168.8
Gray, Gary 6.30, 93.176, 103.3, 156.53, 158.46
Gray, Janine 98.6, 170.6
Gray, Linda 11.3, 14.432, 59.3
Gray, Maralou 43.100
Gray, Ralph 8.69
Gray, Virginia 173.31
Gray-Stanford, Jason 67.13
Grayam, Dan 126.105
Grayson, Philip 43.192
Greavers, Steve 43.322
Green, Andy 162.158
Green, Austin 78.36, 129.20, 129.48, 141.46, 148.135
Green, Bernard 5.9
Green, Dorothy 14.5, 14.106, 14.198, 25.21, 27.89, 41.105, 64.12, 65.199, 65.249, 65.331, 73.16, 85.76, 93.90, 93.118, 93.220, 126.45, 126.69, 126.101, 146.17, 161.88, 161.135, 162.59, 162.175, 168.22
Green, Earl 12.40
Green, Gilbert 12.110, 14.219, 14.220, 43.262, 43.284, 43.315, 43.335, 43.378, 51.2, 65.259, 126.186, 161.18, 161.157
Green, Grizzly 158.25
Green, Karen 43.194, 57.92, 142.18, 162.86, 162.258
Green, Lawrence 65.81
Green, Michael 12.16, 39, 79.14, 164.85, 165.1
Green, Seymour 105.31, 170.36
Green, William E. 97.57
Greenbush, Lindsay 96
Greenbush, Sidney 96
Greene, Angela 27.79, 56.29, 89.155, 93.23, 93.187, 141.6, 162.40, 162.171
Greene, Barry 67.5
Greene, Billy M. 4.33, 14.155, 21.36, 105.67, 146.47, 152.16, 152.71
Greene, Bradley 96.17
Greene, Graham 99.1, 99.2, 99.3
Greene, H. Richard 120.27, 120.44, 120.45
Greene, Jaclynne 34.9, 34.25, 34.28, 178.7
Greene, James 1.7, 1.11, 1.13, 112.3
Greene, Joe 23.30, 169.8, 169.83
Greene, Karen 3.7
Greene, Lorne 14, 21.17, 27.63, 27.64, 162.62
Greene, Martin 138.3
Greene, Michael 27.96, 65.411, 65.463, 65.545, 65.639, 83.10, 83.50, 86.48, 107.20, 130.141, 161.135
Greene, Otis 51.19
Greene, Ronald 66.59
Greene, Sam 65.453
Greenfield, Darwyn 6.5
Greenleaf, Raymond 14.93, 85.68, 97.84, 97.117, 126.41, 141.12, 152.63, 162.25, 162.120, 164.79

Personnel Index

Greenway, Ray 109.3
Greenway, Tom 8.100, 14.111, 65.66, 65.88, 65.125, 65.209, 66.65, 85.86, 101.7, 148.197, 155.21, 162.33
Greer, Dabbs 8.38, 12.73, 13.13, 14.72, 14.129, 14.272, 14.324, 14.360, 14.384, 30.12, 43.174, 46.2, 51.16, 57.44, 65, 65.37, 65.135, 66.171, 84.29, 85.87, 86.41, 88.4, 89.94, 89.155, 93.1, 95, 95.22, 96, 96.13, 96.15, 96.57, 96.176, 97.83, 103.50, 112.18, 125.4, 126.68, 126.135, 126.186, 129.51, 130.38, 130.39, 130.47, 130.73, 130.87, 130.96, 130.97, 130.114, 132.29, 133.28, 144.18, 148.138, 151.6, 155.10, 156.4, 156.16, 156.30, 156.47, 159.10, 161.90, 161.158, 162.110, 162.274, 164.1, 164.17, 164.48, 167.12, 170.79, 170.89, 178.86
Greer, Jane 142.1, 178.43, 178.68, 178.117
Greet, Janet 14.6
Gregg, George 35.9, 35.19, 35.30, 35.35
Gregg, Julie 65.534, 76.27, 161.226
Gregg, Virginia 5.35, 8.92, 12.50, 14.173, 34.4, 41.104, 44.45, 51.23, 63.7, 65.105, 65.225, 65.229, 65.268, 65.276, 65.400, 65.478, 66.47, 66.180, 69.4, 77.14, 82.3, 89.141, 92.1, 102.25, 105.19, 105.54, 105.99, 116.5, 126.16, 126.137, 126.168, 127.56, 132.28, 146.17, 146.40, 151.8, 155.18, 156.19, 161.158, 161.184, 161.221, 162.241, 162.261, 164.16, 164.38, 165.11, 167.6, 168.20, 178.143
Gregg, Walter 49.4
Gregory, Fabian 65.556
Gregory, James 12.35, 12.62, 12.86, 12.108, 14.179, 14.270, 14.322, 24.4, 30.5, 36.8, 41.96, 51.12, 52.32, 52.62, 55.1, 65.376, 65.391, 65.454, 71.25, 84.5, 85.11, 85.115, 98.20, 101.19, 106.12, 116.3, 126.132, 126.174, 126.207, 161.13, 161.142, 161.194, 162.97, 170.1
Gregory, Mary 65.18, 66.99, 66.181, 127.26, 162.67, 162.172
Gregory, Michael 65.634
Greisman, Philip 138.57
Grey, Christian 137.7
Grey, Duane 3.103, 5.2, 6.73, 14.319, 14.327, 43.352, 51.8, 63.35, 64.10, 65.279, 65.295, 66.77, 71.54, 76.10, 76.43, 84.21, 102.31, 126.5, 126.43, 126.57, 126.162, 146.13, 152.33, 169.108
Grey, Joel 21.30, 89.68, 89.81, 89.120, 105.60
Grey, Loren 178.76
Grey, Nan 126.60
Grey, Pamela 159.11
Grey, Virginia 14.103, 21.39, 142.9, 156.38, 161.107, 162.30, 162.31, 162.70, 162.136
Grey, Zane 178
Gribble, Donna Jo 138.4
Griego, Sandra 28
Grier, Roosevelt 170.77
Gries, Jonathan 120.26
Grieve, Russ 83.36
Griffeth, Simone 19.14, 19.15
Griffin, Bob 164.33
Griffin, Frank 43.55, 178.124
Griffin, Robert E. 3.118, 13.12, 14.26, 14.53, 25.6, 34.27, 43.25, 43.155, 44.64, 65.68, 65.170, 73.25, 77.9, 79.26, 82.4, 105.1, 105.28, 105.49, 105.58, 126.23, 129.67, 147.4, 149.18, 152.20, 156.7, 164.4, 178.9, 178.128
Griffin, Stephanie 27.10
Griffin, Tod 27.82, 44.24, 105.19, 105.41, 152.48, 152.77
Griffith, Andy 10.4, 26
Griffith, Billy 32.58, 32.64, 169.21
Griffith, James 6.44, 6.46, 7.12, 12.18, 14.45, 14.272, 21.59, 22.30, 23.2, 23.10, 27.26, 27.79, 27.109, 41.6, 41.31, 41.66, 41.83, 43.21, 44.1, 51.3, 53.3, 53.24, 60.20, 60.22, 61.4, 63.40, 65.8, 65.94, 65.292, 65.326, 65.459, 66.178, 66.219, 73.4, 76.17, 77.20, 82.12, 83.3, 84.11,
84.33, 84.37, 85.50, 85.99, 89.154, 93.221, 94.18, 96.22, 96.177, 97.32, 97.54, 97.87, 97.110, 97.153, 97.175, 97.204, 101.6, 101.26, 103.15, 105.46, 107.11, 123.2, 124.14, 124.25, 124.26, 124.49, 124.34, 124.39, 126.37, 126.76, 126.152, 129.63, 131.40, 12.23, 148.194, 149.30, 149.69, 152.38, 152.55, 156.1, 156.22, 156.23, 156.24, 156.25, 156.26, 156.27, 156.28, 156.29, 156.34, 156.36, 157.22, 157.24, 159.18, 161.169, 162.48, 162.81, 162.144, 162.244, 162.251, 162.267, 167.3, 178.20
Griffith, Jesse 148.13
Griffith, Raymond 43.450
Griffith, Robert E. 114.22, 156.32
Griffith, William 3.91, 31.39
Grimes, Gary 65.453
Grimes, Tammy 46.1, 116.20, 161.17, 177.35
Grimm, Maria 14.408
Grinnage, Jack 65.141, 65.205, 65.211, 65.400, 126.122, 129.46, 130.51, 144.29, 162.34, 162.199, 162.244
Griswold, Claire 14.263, 51.11, 89.113, 164.7
Grizzard, George 126.190
Grodin, Charles 12.76, 63.2, 76.18, 161.151
Groom, Sam 65.555, 65.601, 137.7
Gross, Robert 17.31
Grossfeld, Sid 24.14
Grossinger, Fred 65.159
Grubbs, Gary 120.20, 175.8
Gruber, John 24.13
Gruner, David 5.33, 5.44
Grunfeld, Svea 66.87, 132.22
Guard, Kit 81.48
Guardino, Harry 119.1, 161.104
Guardino, Joe 8.40
Guerin, Lenmana 21.44
Guild, Lyn 93.70
Guilford, Margot 81.5
Guilfoyle, James 97.66, 97.73, 169.8
Guilfoyle, Paul 65.200
Guillermo, Kuthie 96.79
Gulager, Clu 13.2, 14.423, 44.4, 44.37, 59.1, 66.71, 83.4, 85.4, 115.4, 127.32, 131.12, 149, 161, 161.18, 161.40, 162.74, 162.78, 162.221, 162.233, 162.252, 163.54, 164.32, 166.3
Gunderson, Robert 64.11, 93.165, 107.26, 141.54
Gunn, Adam 96.82
Gunn, Anna 90.12
Gunn, Bill 144.5
Gunn, Janet 120.49, 120.51, 120.52
Gunn, Moses 37, 53, 83.14, 96.76, 96.100, 96.101, 96.108, 96.150
Gunning, Charles 48.9
Gur, Alizia 12.9, 41.43, 170.102
Guth, Raymond 5.5, 14.140, 14.147, 14.319, 24.2, 43.189, 43.445, 64.2, 65.268, 65.314, 66.197, 71.19, 85.105, 103.46, 126.80, 126.152, 126.167, 130.157, 161.11, 161.139
Guthrie, Tani Phelps 65.527, 65.550, 69.8, 71.9565.527
Guyman, Bill 178.50
Guzman, Luis 163.5
Gwinn, Bill 43.378, 43.447, 43.449, 170.42
Gwynne, Anne 43.91, 114.21
Gwynne, Michael C. 24.18

Haade, Bobby 169.61
Haade, William 60.7, 60.8, 73.31, 81.28, 97.48, 97.56, 97.79, 97.102, 97.140, 124.37, 124.43, 124.69, 124.73, 138.45, 147.8., 158.34, 158.39, 169.17, 169.18, 169.36, 169.61, 169.71, 169.82, 169.96
Haas, Hugo 14.31
Haas, Peter 96.35
Hack, Herman 60.59
Hack, Steven 48.4
Hackett, Buddy 12.31, 130.42, 130.104

Hackett, Joan 5.15, 14.185, 14.405, 41.139, 51.31, 61.3, 65.258
Hackett, John 93.184, 156.59, 164.26, 178.85
Hackman, Gene 76.37
Haddock, Julie Anne 96.92
Haddon, Laurence 43.343, 70.34, 120.50
Haden, Sara 169.25
Hadley, Nancy 8.8, 14.99, 51.25, 54.21, 66.53, 77.25, 93.86, 93.186, 122.21, 126.8, 126.24, 133.11, 146.66
Hadley, Reed 8.3, 44.59, 72.13, 126.21, 129.31, 129.76, 152.35, 152.55, 152.56, 152.57, 162.39
Hagan, Molly 91.11
Hagen, Anna 99.10
Hagen, Claire 70.44
Hagen, Gay 120.11, 120.19, 120.22, 120.31, 120.38, 120.51
Hagen, Jean 142.15, 162.93, 162.212, 178.142
Hagen, Kevin 8.101, 12.4, 12.42, 12.65, 12.77, 12.94, 12.102, 14.80, 14.117, 14.142, 14.256, 14.279, 17.19, 27.91, 30.21, 37.2, 41.15, 41.118, 41.140, 44.26, 63.47, 65.137, 65.211, 65.260, 65.303, 65.324, 65.454, 66.34, 66.88, 66.134, 66.135, 66.196, 71.6, 74.31, 84.7, 85.8, 85.53, 85.74, 89.134, 89.148, 95, 95.22, 95.23, 95.24, 96, 101.11, 116.20, 117.14, 126.97, 130.71, 130.116, 137.6, 148.6, 161.30, 161.176, 161.190, 162.6, 162.21, 170.78, 173
Hagen, Michael 66.52
Hagen, Paul 97.104
Hagen, Ross 12.43, 19.11, 63.18, 65.427, 65.468, 65.538, 65.539, 70.26, 70.33, 83.8, 84.21, 84.43, 116.17, 132.20, 139.14, 139.15, 161.116, 170.70
Hagerthy, Ron 3.66, 3.101, 6.68, 6.72, 34.51, 43.129, 56.28, 64.6, 64.12, 65.38, 65.99, 66.50, 71.3, 73.15, 77.24, 93.91, 97.184, 97.186, 102.19, 126.19, 126.117, 131.40, 130.65, 141, 147.20, 152.4, 152.74, 155.54, 157.26, 159.17, 167.13
Haggard, Merle 26
Haggerty, Dan 25.19, 34.57, 43.269, 94, 105.119
Haggerty, Don 3.96, 8.41, 14.114, 14.241, 14.280, 14.309, 21.47, 25.59, 27.65, 27.86, 27.95, 41.77, 43.226, 43.247, 43.276, 43.295, 43.299, 43.300, 43.336, 43.349, 43.357, 43.374, 43.427, 43.432, 46.1, 55.24, 56.33, 63.19, 65.308, 65.312, 66.67, 89.115, 92.9, 93, 93.4, 93.6, 93.8, 93.11, 93.13, 93.15, 93.16, 93.17, 93.18, 93.21, 93.22, 93.23, 93.30, 93.123, 93.222, 97.11, 97.33, 97.57, 97.152, 97.218, 125.14, 126.17, 126.52, 126.83, 126.117, 126.135, 126.150, 128.5, 131.4, 131.24, 133.13, 142.21, 145.7, 146.20, 146.50, 146.66, 148.20, 148.130, 152.39, 152.75, 158.1, 158.28, 158.40, 169.69, 179.74
Haggerty, H.B. 112.21, 181.6
Haggerty, Teddy 48.12
Hagler, Nik 110.3
Haglund, Dean 100.1
Hagney, Frank 32.99, 32.103, 41.70, 41.78, 73.21, 81.2, 97.156, 124.9, 145.14, 148.44, 165.2, 169.57, 169.84
Hahn, Paul 32.147, 65.192, 169.104, 178.2
Haid, Charles 65.603, 83.62
Haig, Sid 5.7, 5.16, 19.13, 41.102, 65.419, 65.479, 65.495, 65.501, 70.41, 76.13, 86.42
Haig, Tommy 127.23
Haig, Tony 57.106, 65.370, 65.395, 65.396, 66.126, 126.140, 178.102
Hairston, Jester 65.14, 126.5, 161.203
Haje, Krystyne 177.58
Hakim, Fred 66.176, 66.217
Haldeman, Tim 83.3, 83.29, 83.38, 83.39
Hale, Alan, Jr. 4.23, 5.5, 6.6, 6.8, 8.15, 14.7, 21.23, 21.58, 27.43, 27.72, 34.33, 43.224, 44.36, 51.32, 55.18, 57.25, 60.2, 60.4, 60.6, 60.16, 60.17, 60.19, 60.21, 60.39, 60.41, 65.225, 65.423, 65.577, 70.37, 72.13, 85.116, 102.16, 105.122,

Personnel Index

105.83, 106.20, 113.10, 114.2, 117.11, 124.11, 124.12, 124.19, 124.20, 124.22, 126.100, 129.65, 140.38, 148.196, 152.9, 152.50, 152.51, 152.52, 152.59, 152.61, 152.62, 161.211, 162.171, 164.5, 166.20, 167.26, 168.12, 169.12, 169.58, 170.97, 178.139
Hale, Barbara 38.11
Hale, Bernadette 65.378
Hale, Betsy 65.327, 66.172, 148.158, 162.261
Hale, Bill 3.115, 3.118, 3.120, 3.121, 32.74, 44.68, 65.35, 81.11, 124.15, 124.16, 126.7, 138.60, 141.27, 141.36, 141.39, 141.58, 141.69, 147.24, 148.148, 169.27, 169.55, 169.104
Hale, Chanin 14.320, 65.537, 65.586, 92.7
Hale, Fiona 88.6, 178.130
Hale, Jean 14.307, 92.20, 98.20, 106.15, 161.52, 162.255, 170.10
Hale, John 63.49
Hale, Jonathan 32.3, 32.8, 35.3, 35.37, 93.119, 124.13, 124.17, 169.1
Hale, Michael 141.45
Hale, Monte 65.155, 65.467, 148.63, 169.104
Hale, Nancy 6.24, 6.64, 6.81, 27.7, 27.16, 27.23, 32.122, 43.24, 43.33, 43.119, 81.53, 81.69, 93.39, 93.132, 97.133, 97.168, 178.31
Hale, Peter 170.60, 170.79, 170.83
Hale, Richard 12.6, 14.219, 14.220, 14.256, 14.271, 20.30, 21.36, 21.42, 27.90, 37.11, 39.1, 46.5, 63.43, 63.44, 65.461, 65.504, 65.555, 70.51, 72.15, 76.7, 76.34, 78.63, 78.67, 89.67, 105.82, 105.90, 126.16, 126.138, 126.174, 131.22, 132.22, 148.163, 148.170, 152.26, 156.11, 156.30, 157.22, 162.1, 162.56, 168.14, 170.84
Hale, Scott 30.2, 65.407, 65.437, 65.438, 65.444, 65.485
Hales, Dent 106.5
Hales, Fiona 65.141
Halferty, James 65.273
Hall, Anthony 43.252, 149.54
Hall, Bill 158.7
Hall, Bob 130.154
Hall, Bobby 8.6, 8.52, 65.501, 66.56, 70.49, 148.102
Hall, Claude 12.16, 14.224, 17.6, 17.23, 41.60, 63.35, 130.157, 139.2, 139.12
Hall, Ellen 32.16, 32.22, 32.27
Hall, Gordon 8.73
Hall, Lois 6.39, 32.40, 32.46, 32.50, 53.5, 53.6, 97.80, 97.112, 124.29, 124.34, 124.39, 124.46, 124.47, 124.48, 169.4
Hall, Michael 23.18, 23.24, 145.23
Hall, Mort 178.31
Hall, Richard 25.19
Hall, Thad 65.613
Hall, Thurston 3.91, 31.42, 73.11, 73.20, 97.171, 105.20, 147.29
Hall, Zooey 70.51
Hallahan, Charles 19.3
Halliday, Jack 81.38
Halloran, John 32.145, 60.31, 60.33, 73.10, 97.69, 145.18, 149.47
Halop, Billy 32.81, 32.88, 65.407, 65.431, 65.449, 164.53
Halper, David 44.12
Halsey, Brett 5.7, 5.46, 8.18, 65.21, 78.71
Halton, Charles 78.57, 97.152, 169.53
Hamill, Janet 162.268
Hamill, Mary 96.125
Hamilton, Bernie 30.17, 69.5, 161.123, 161.198
Hamilton, Big John 14.141
Hamilton, Bruce 97.38
Hamilton, Carrie 163.56, 163.57
Hamilton, Dran 65.605
Hamilton, George 3.153, 29.18
Hamilton, Jean 78.60
Hamilton, John 32.68, 32.72, 32.76, 60.63, 60.65, 65.52, 81.5, 124.54, 124.56, 135.77, 147.2
Hamilton, Joseph 22.38, 65.219, 65.264, 65.319, 66.96, 141.62, 147.4, 155.45

Hamilton, Kim 41.67
Hamilton, Kipp 126.46, 152.50, 152.51, 152.52, 152.61, 152.62, 161.165, 170.7
Hamilton, Lynn 65.487, 65.503
Hamilton, Margaret 65.582, 85.100
Hamilton, Murray 19.10, 65.66, 65.101, 65.126, 66.20
Hamilton, Neil 34.35, 55.19, 102.35, 105.45, 148.55, 179.59
Hamilton, Ray 8.93, 131.27
Hamilton, Richard 19
Hamilton, Ted 66.121
Hammack, Warren 161.136, 161.142, 161.168, 161.182, 170.66
Hammer, Ben 14.319, 161.136
Hammer, Stephen 57.110, 57.115, 152.39
Hammond, Earl 21.65, 105.121
Hammond, Nicholas 47.14, 65.588, 65.589, 65.616, 115.4
Hammond, Reid 43.201
Hampton, Adrienne 1.12
Hampton, James 26, 30.6, 43.283, 52, 65.304, 65.318, 65.364, 120.43
Hampton, Jan 43.31
Hampton, Paul 112
Hancock, Lou 163.11
Handy, James 177.57
Hanek, John 65.320
Hanket, Arthur 90.6
Hankin, Larry 120.8
Hanley, Bridget 24.18, 70, 75.3, 76.30
Hanley, Elizabeth 177.65
Hanley, Gary 178.64
Hanley, Katie 28.2
Hanley-Creore, Katie 53.22
Hanlon, Tom 57.110
Hanmer, Don 43.272, 65.415, 65.472, 70.46, 83.38, 83.39, 149.61, 161.49, 161.124
Hanneford, Grace 32.53
Hanneford, Poodles 32.53
Hanold, Marilyn 66.70, 152.9
Hansen, Al 94.31
Hansen, Earl 44.1, 105.58, 148.150, 148.176, 149.53, 162.49, 166.1
Hansen, Janice 43.409
Hansen, Janis 12.90, 12.107, 14.213, 134, 170.21
Hansen, Peter 8.13, 43.209, 43.227, 78.8, 78.11, 78.20, 78.29, 78.59, 97.145, 97.155, 97.159, 97.171, 97.173, 103.38, 105.97, 129.23, 155.30, 178.64
Hansen, Ron 77.21, 158.4, 158.5, 158.6, 158.9, 158.13
Hansen, Ross 14.356
Hansen, William 24.22
Hanson, Arthur 20.30, 161.225
Hanson, Bert 43.96
Hanson, Peter 178.22
Hanson, Preston 93.183, 133.3
Hantley, Kate 28
Happy, Don 65.399, 65.444, 65.488, 65.491, 126.42
Haran, Ronnie 27.99, 43.251, 168.14
Harbaugh, Jim 1.27
Harden, Jack 73.6
Harden, Sasha 21.27
Hardie, James 120.17, 120.18
Hardies, Ellen 162.13
Hardin, Jerry 28, 48.18, 48.83, 48.84, 53.19, 53.20, 65.605, 96.111, 120.34, 137.1, 137.2, 175.9
Hardin, Melora 95.22, 96.158, 96.159
Hardin, Ty 21, 27.76, 105.81, 123.6, 146.41, 146.67
Harding, Frank 8.52, 152.10, 178.75
Harding, Janet 169.90
Harding, John 14.189, 68.28, 112, 170.95, 170.96
Harding, June 49.13, 144.29
Hardison, Tom 152.12, 152.38
Hardt, Eloise 43.204, 89.149, 98.25

Hardy, James 163.56, 163.57
Hardy, Robert 22.27
Hardy, Sarah 65.489
Hare, Lumsden 3.33
Harens, Dean 8.10, 8.47, 13.31, 14.200, 14.242, 43.180, 65.107, 66.44, 76.19, 84.18, 114.11, 117.42, 131.18, 157.8, 161.66
Harewood, Dorian 48.33
Harford, Betty 12.30, 65.183
Harget, Link 65.425
Hargitay, Mariska 59.5
Hargitay, Mickey 170.87
Hargrave, Ron 147.30
Harker, Charmienne 34.26, 43.66, 138.14, 148.72
Harker, Wiley 96.172
Harkins, John 137.8
Harlan, Scott 1.19
Harland, Richard 88.20
Harland, Robert 88, 93.215, 117.5, 120.2, 142.2, 162.134, 178.103, 178.112, 178.127
Harley, Amanda 12.43
Harley, Eileen 130.17
Harlow, James 1.9
Harlow, William 127.39, 127.43, 127.51
Harman, Gil 145.6
Harmon, John 3.138, 12.3, 12.14, 12.48, 12.60, 14.119, 22.22, 27.73, 37.5, 43.174, 47.13, 65.257, 66.215, 77.12, 84.26, 84.43, 85.88, 86.21, 86.37, 105.2, 105.35, 105.86, 125.5, 126.67, 130.7, 130.24, 130.25, 130.40, 130.46, 130.49, 130.51, 130.58, 130.69, 130.120, 130.121, 130.139, 148.48, 148.82, 149.35, 151.13, 152.19, 152.77, 156.19, 156.60, 157.19, 157.23, 161.24, 161.114, 161.162, 162.1, 162.240, 164.29, 164.65, 166.8, 170.42
Harmon, Joy 134.6
Harmon, Mark 26
Harmon, Paul 168.17
Harolde, Ralf 44.59
Harp, Ken 43.65
Harper, Hill 163.27
Harper, John 65
Harper, Jonathan 65.455, 65.464, 65.493
Harper, Olivia Virgil 177.40
Harper, Paul 83.2, 83.3, 83.33
Harper, Rand 65.174
Harper, Robert 83.63
Harper, Ron 12.99, 44.54, 85.42, 85.116, 148.132, 149.20, 162.126
Harrell, James 28
Harrington, Pat 24.5
Harrington, Pat, Jr. 52.22, 70.42
Harrington, Vicki 43.337, 41.23
Harris, Ben 57.90
Harris, Berkeley 65.332, 65.385, 101.22, 161.103, 162.228, 162.269
Harris, Bob 14.63
Harris, Don 14.426
Harris, Glenn Walker 163.33
Harris, Holly 93.79
Harris, Jack W. 31.24, 102.14, 138.52, 147.31
Harris, Jo Ann 65.492, 71.66, 106.3, 109.4
Harris, Joan 106.20
Harris, Jonathan 14.136, 84.15, 117.20, 179.63, 179.64, 179.65
Harris, Joshua 120.45, 120.49
Harris, Julie 12.96, 14.295, 41.113, 86.5, 106.23, 126.201
Harris, Julius 118.3
Harris, Michael 12.22, 12.25, 12.34, 72.8, 90.9, 130.28, 177.50
Harris, Phil 52.54
Harris, Richard 12.38
Harris, Robert H. 14.88, 14.145, 65.40, 65.57, 66.26, 66.115, 102.22, 117.39, 126.8, 129.62, 130.27, 130.45, 133.2, 161.173, 164.29, 167.10, 170.101, 178.46
Harris, Rosemary 28

Personnel Index

Harris, Ross 120.5
Harris, Rossie 96.149
Harris, Stacy 3.121, 3.132, 13.23, 14.18, 14.69, 14.138, 14.184, 14.214, 22.2, 23.27, 23.30, 23.39, 23.40, 38.12, 41.42, 56.7, 65.531, 66.111, 85.19, 85.32, 85.99, 86.16, 93, 93.61, 93.155, 93.157, 93.163, 93.170, 93.175, 93.181, 93.182, 93.186, 93.198, 93.206, 93.209, 93.211, 93.212, 93.216, 93.219, 93.220, 93.221, 93.225, 93.226, 103.16, 117.22, 121.8, 126.12, 126.86, 127.25, 129.9, 142.22, 147.42, 151.14, 152.8, 152.53, 156.8, 161.21, 162.143, 162.171, 162.259, 164.19, 178.49, 178.94, 178.117
Harris, Steve 14.154, 161.18
Harris, Viola 126.75
Harrison, Charles 130.147
Harrison, Gregory 26
Harrison, James 32.75, 60.23, 60.24, 97.40
Harrison, Jan 8.45, 8.93, 43.205, 65.119, 65.131, 65.188, 65.211, 89.27, 126.71, 148.62
Harrison, Jane 94.7
Harrison, John 88.11
Harrison, Susan 14.31
Harrod, David 163.29
Harrold, Chuck 84.21
Harron, Donald 152.12
Harrower, Elizabeth 6.7, 60.83, 65.566, 65.606, 93.26, 93.54, 93.135, 124.70, 141.50, 148.55, 161.122, 169.24, 169.45, 169.64, 169.95
Hart, Bill 10.4, 65.400, 65.494, 65.560, 98.25, 144
Hart, Bret 99, 100
Hart, Buddy 57.95
Hart, Dolores 161.29
Hart, John 3.148, 8.31, 8.32, 8.50, 57.20, 68, 97, 97.34, 97.46, 126.28, 126.44, 126.56, 126.65, 126.71, 126.86, 126.89, 126.96, 126.98, 126.102, 126.105, 126.108, 126.110, 126.111, 126.113, 126.114, 140.8, 141.13, 147.7, 147.8
Hart, Susan 43.367, 85.84, 170.87
Hart, Tommy 65.23
Hart, William 164.94
Hartford, Dee 65.290
Hartleben, Jerry 147.11
Hartley, Mariette 14.192, 14.312, 14.352, 14.399, 24.7, 30.20, 41.122, 41.152, 43.333, 43.378, 43.389, 43.406, 65.286, 65.351, 65.541, 65.567, 65.606, 92.34, 96.42, 123.3, 144.12, 157.13, 161.50, 161.66
Hartley, Steve 177.15
Hartman, David 161, 161.156
Hartman, Ena 14.164
Hartman, Marx 148.83
Hartman, Max 129.36
Hartman, Paul 66.166, 92.19, 117.2, 149.74
Hartunian, Richard 127.54
Harty, Patricia 14.393, 38.11, 106.9
Harushi 83.60
Harvey, Charles 35.34
Harvey, Don C. 3.85, 2.13, 2.21, 6.9, 6.15, 6.24, 6.44, 6.46, 13.32, 14.49, 23.7, 23.13, 32.7, 34.30, 43.77, 43.85, 51.23, 56.4, 57.19, 60.12, 60.14, 60.19, 60.21, 60.31, 60.33, 60.44, 60.46, 60.54, 60.58, 64.10, 73.15, 81.53, 81.81, 81.84, 85.70, 85.82, 85.97, 85.102, 93.1, 93.25, 93.48, 93.116, 93.193, 97.134, 97.143, 97.158, 97.204, 97.208, 105.84, 108.1, 108.37, 124.9, 124.28, 124.31, 124.41, 126.9, 129.46, 129.70, 135.4, 135.20, 135.21, 135.22, 135.56, 135.58, 135.66, 135.67, 135.68, 135.69, 141.26, 141.62, 145.7, 146.55, 147.14, 148.59, 148.145, 149.45, 152.52, 152.66, 158.19, 159.17, 161.17, 161.30, 162.141, 169.19, 169.31, 169.66, 169.76, 169.89, 169.100
Harvey, Donald 155.71
Harvey, Harry 60.11, 60.38, 60.40, 60.64, 60.78, 60.85, 73.15, 84.13, 93.32, 93.52, 97.8, 97.41, 97.95, 97.133, 97.151, 97.163, 135.6, 135.23, 145.10, 162.222, 169.46

Harvey, Harry, Jr. 3.124, 6.2, 20.9, 20.39, 32.75, 85.53, 93.141, 97.136, 135.38, 135.43, 135.72, 135.85, 135.97, 145.38, 147.40, 148.11, 148.88, 148.151, 149.10, 155.45, 156.15, 167.17
Harvey, Harry, Sr. 2.4, 5.30, 6.20, 6.22, 6.32, 17.17, 17.39, 30.3, 30.16, 34.48, 41.65, 60.13, 60.91, 63.9, 65.447, 65.456, 65.470, 65.519, 65.551, 65.552, 65.553, 81.68, 81.87, 81.101, 84.23, 86.38, 89.152, 97.66, 97.72, 97.100, 97.112, 103, 105.5, 105.17, 105.25, 105.81, 124.13, 124.17, 126.4, 130.51, 135, 135.20, 146.14, 148.16, 152.3, 152.22, 152.25, 152.67, 161.82, 161.114, 161.162, 161.178, 162.101, 162.112, 162.257, 169.53
Harvey, Jean 93.114, 129.49, 129.78, 135.19, 135.67, 162.77
Harvey, Orwin 41.125, 112.16
Harvey, Paul 135.74, 135.77, 135.78, 135.100
Hasfal-Schou, Topaz 67.17
Hashim, Edmund 3.20, 18.18, 65.402, 65.424, 65.439, 65.454, 65.479, 65.496, 97.188, 97.198, 141.65, 147.41, 148.15, 148.159, 162.66, 170.64
Haskell, David 120.21
Haskell, Peter 12.23, 12.83, 12.97, 43.301, 53.24, 76.35, 126.205
Haslett, Elaine 31.15, 31.27
Hasso, Signe 14.123, 132.22
Hastings, Bob 65.240, 65.269, 149.55
Hatch, Richard 109.10
Hatch, Richard Lawrence 83.9
Hatch, Steve 130.40
Hatfield, Hurd 14.413, 170.40, 170.77
Hathaway, Michael 43.23
Hatton, Barbara 158.19
Hatton, Charles 169.45
Hatton, Raymond 6.60, 6.75, 8.15, 27.46, 31.4, 32.3, 32.8, 32.54, 32.61, 32.111, 32.117, 43.109, 44.28, 60.25, 60.26, 65.179, 66.112, 66.116, 66.139, 73.30, 81.41, 82.15, 105.26, 105.69, 124.4, 124.7, 135.12, 135.42, 147.41, 149.32, 155.48, 164.60, 169.6, 169.25, 169.44, 169.66, 169.78, 169.79, 169.93
Hauser, Jerry 162.79
Hauser, Wings 163.18, 177.64
Hawkes, John 1.10
Hawkes, Terri 99.12
Hawkins, Jimmy 6
Hawley, Pat 12.16, 93.185
Hawley, Patrick 103.49
Haworth, Jill 14.381, 126.214
Haworth, Jo 130.3
Haworth, Joe 5.30, 5.42, 6.28, 6.36, 6.43, 14.237, 30.12, 65.439, 65.490, 65.555, 79.16, 81.101, 85.101, 97.115, 97.139, 108.1, 130.63, 141.8, 155.34, 164.64
Hayakawa, Sessue 162.48
Hayden, Dennis 120.10
Hayden, Don 93.88
Hayden, Harry 73.37, 145.18, 169.71
Hayden, Nora 14.61, 65.249
Hayden, Russell 35, 60.22, 80, 104
Hayden, Sandra 80.6, 80.34
Hayden, Schuyler 144.30
Hayden, Sterling 162.5, 178.20
Hayden, Ted 48.42, 120.7
Hayden, Tom 134.6
Haydn, Richard 14.324, 86.26
Haydon, Don 169.15
Hayes, Adrienne 41.28, 41.101, 43.278, 126.70
Hayes, Allison 4.5, 8.8, 8.16, 8.29, 8.54, 8.61, 8.69, 8.78, 43.90, 76.28, 85.68, 126.29, 133.15, 155.5, 155.53, 155.56, 155.77
Hayes, Anthony 161.102
Hayes, Bernadene 80.7, 80.24, 80.25, 80.26
Hayes, Bill 24.21
Hayes, Billie 107.24
Hayes, Byron 48.4

Hayes, Charlie 2.9, 2.25, 6.47, 6.58, 6.64, 6.81, 23.9, 23.31, 23.32, 23.35, 23.38, 138.63, 141.33, 141.42, 148.73
Hayes, Chester 101.31, 162.255
Hayes, Gabby 58
Hayes, James 41.22
Hayes, Joanna 93.100
Hayes, Jonathan 163.2
Hayes, Maggie 14.75, 27.24, 126.83, 173.8
Hayes, Margaret 93, 93.37, 93.42, 93.43, 155.24, 156.3, 178.15, 178.32
Hayes, Philip 67.9, 99.12
Hayes, Ron 8.29, 8.61, 8.76, 8.105, 14.23, 14.55, 14.127, 14.248, 14.274, 14.328, 21.6, 43.191, 44.28, 46.10, 65.179, 65.219, 65.221, 65.272, 65.295, 65.506, 65.521, 65.522, 71.27, 71.50, 74.15, 75.20, 82.16, 85.95, 85.106, 101.20, 105.27, 126.30, 126.119, 130.91, 134, 148.133, 151.10, 152.21, 152.62, 155.44, 158.43, 159.37, 161.44, 162.121, 162.137, 162.164, 162.239, 162.251, 164.46, 167.26
Hayes, Ryan 65.388, 165.8, 178.126
Haymer, Johnny 65.470, 121.14, 170.74
Haymes, Dick 5.19, 55.26, 69.9, 71.66, 134.10
Haymore, Curtis 161.22
Haynes, Lloyd 84.3, 84.5
Haynes, Roberta 13.28
Haynie, Jim 90.7, 177.42
Hays, Kathryn 9.11, 14.171, 17.12, 24.20, 70.16, 71.31, 132, 161.82, 168.25
Hays, Kent 126.114
Hays, Robert 176
Hayward, Brooke 14.85
Hayward, Bruce 130.113
Hayward, Chuck 65.138, 65.234, 66.120, 83.17, 96.27, 164.80, 164.93, 167.1, 178.47, 178.129
Hayward, David 28, 120.32
Hayward, Jim 3.53, 31.5, 57.3, 57.4, 89.80, 89.117, 97.109, 97.113, 102.21, 114.3, 130.134, 135.46, 135.52, 148.14, 150.1, 152.28, 152.75, 158.72, 166.13
Hayward, Louis 126.183, 131.1
Haywood, George 93.124
Haywood, Lenice 43.245
Hayworth, Joe 57.14
Hayworth, Vinton 12.76, 39.19, 65.27, 65.81, 65.336, 85.17, 85.45, 85.70, 85.117, 89.48, 89.69, 89.80, 89.93, 89.116, 89.123, 89.133, 89.139, 89.151, 121.24, 148.180, 179.16, 179.17, 179.21, 179.22, 179.24, 179.25, 179.26
Haze, Jonathan 29.2
Headley, Shari 163.67
Healey, Michael 34.7, 93.76
Healey, Myron 2.4, 3.18, 3.36, 3.63, 4.28, 6.2, 6.3, 6.7, 6.19, 6.35, 6.37, 6.48, 6.50, 6.57, 6.79, 8.27, 8.37, 14.182, 14.266, 14.286, 14.288, 21.9, 21.28, 22.5, 23.14, 23.21, 24.1, 27.4, 27.17, 27.41, 27.77, 27.79, 29.17, 32.29, 32.35, 32.69, 32.106, 32.113, 34.24, 35.20, 37.9, 39.18, 41.41, 41.65, 41.137, 43.204, 44.42, 46.4, 60.35, 60.37, 60.48, 60.51, 60.56, 60.59, 60.62, 60.64, 60.66, 60.78, 60.80, 60.82, 60.84, 60.87, 63.4, 63.33, 65.262, 65.270, 71.6, 71.96, 73.20, 76.38, 78.50, 80.17, 80.19, 80.23, 80.26, 81.29, 81.50, 81.71, 81.73, 81.88, 81.89, 83.24, 85.33, 85.73, 85.85, 85.100, 86.11, 86.18, 86.33, 86.57, 93, 93.38, 93.104, 93.106, 93.108, 93.110, 93.111, 93.125, 93.127, 93.129, 93.145, 93.147, 93.148, 93.150, 97.55, 97.92, 97.135, 97.207, 97.214, 97.217, 97.220, 101.15, 103.2, 105.27, 105.65, 105.114, 106.3, 117.40, 117.48, 124.49, 124.50, 124.54, 124.56, 124.65, 124.68, 126.2, 126.15, 126.68, 127.26, 131.21, 132.20, 135.25, 135.26, 135.37, 135.40, 135.44, 135.49, 135.50, 135.51, 135.65, 135.71, 141.4, 141.22, 145.9, 146.18, 146.43, 147.17, 148.69, 148.138, 152.32, 152.64, 152.74, 155.19, 155.41, 158.47, 161.31, 161.44, 161.83,

Personnel Index

161.159, 162.35, 162.68, 162.163, 162.181, 162.220, 162.227, 162.247, 162.258, 166.14, 178.60, 178.115, 179.73
Healy, Christine 48.88
Healy, James 177.26
Heard, Charles MacDonald 8.11, 135.5
Heard, Charlie 43.70
Hearn, George 177.28
Hearn, Guy E. 97.123
Hearn, Sam 164.75
Heart, Charles 127.58
Heath, Dody 34.49, 89.56, 119.5, 131.38, 142.25
Heath, Ed 35.12
Heath, Emily 43.26
Heath, Luise 75.27
Heatherton, Joey 161.26
Heatherton, May 65.267
Heaton, Tom 43.378, 76.33, 101.18
Hebert, Gordon 57.116
Hecht, Jenny 162.51
Heckart, Eileen 65.368, 65.499, 96.105
Hector, Jay 65.196
Hector, Kim 85.43, 86.5, 126.36, 132.14
Hector, Patrick 178.122
Hedison, David 59.2
Heffley, Wayne 14.233, 34.34, 51.11, 65.283, 66.36, 74.18, 74.25, 83.24, 84.18, 96.11, 96.19, 96.20, 96.23, 112.8, 133.33, 141.67, 155.14, 161.10, 164.58, 170.70
Heflin, Van 61
Heifetz, Harold 162.148
Heigh, Helene 3.131, 3.165, 93.143
Heinberg, Sarah Kim 1.7, 48.27
Heinz, Kurt 27.17
Heitgert, Don 44.61, 44.64
Held, Christopher 30.11
Held, Karl 12.10, 39.10, 127.74
Hellen, Marjorie 133.33
Heller, Chip 120.15
Hellerman, John 96.96
Hellman, Les 8.7, 8.55, 8.80
Hellstrom, Gunnar 51.25, 65.455
Helm, Anne 12.6, 12.84, 14.210, 14.301, 21.51, 41.29, 43.238, 51.32, 55.13, 64.12, 65.216, 65.359, 85.106, 101.24, 126.73, 126.90, 148.134, 151.5, 161.62, 161.214, 162.167, 162.218, 162.239, 168.9
Helm, Frances 44.70, 65.238
Helm, Peter 14.208, 92.21, 126.148, 144.29, 148.191, 162.173, 162.190, 162.220
Helmond, Katherine 65.567
Helmore, Tom 66.13
Helms, Tim 163.46
Helton, Jo 65.299
Helton, Percy 3.89, 3.137, 3.161, 14.5, 14.121, 14.145, 14.255, 30.2, 31.12, 34.62, 39.6, 41.63, 41.102, 43.62, 43.123, 63.45, 65.172, 65.262, 65.395, 65.396, 73.32, 78.57, 85.66, 88.23, 89.46, 97.148, 102.5, 105.14, 105.90, 126.84, 146.67, 152.66, 161.163, 164.59, 170.92
Hemingway, Barbara 170.91
Hemmings, Wayne 99.15
Hemphill, Ray 14.12, 14.213
Hendershott, Adam 1.25
Henderson, Chuck 152.43, 162.77
Henderson, Douglas 14.214, 14.255, 14.276, 41.68, 43.42, 133.32, 138.9, 138.11, 138.28, 138.44, 161.88, 161.118, 161.190, 170.41, 170.66, 170.69, 170.75, 170.76, 170.92, 170.97, 170.100, 170.104
Henderson, Kelo 158
Henderson, Lars 57.89, 129.12
Henderson, Marcia 8.2, 8.48, 34.23, 44.18, 114.20, 129.51, 148.47, 164.43
Henderson, Paul 138.75
Hendrix, Elaine 1.23

Hendrix, Wanda 8.85, 44.55, 162.32
Hendry, Len 8.27, 65.170, 126.17, 126.42, 126.55, 126.68, 126.70, 126.85, 126.113, 155.29
Hengen, Butch 162.99
Hengen, Debby 89.36, 162.27
Hennesey, Tom 65.250, 65.262, 66.194, 148.145, 158.20
Hennigan, Sean 163.34
Henning, Susan 162.57
Henry, Bill 2.13, 2.21, 3.126, 3.149, 3.165, 6.29, 6.40, 6.56, 6.64, 6.71, 6.74, 6.77, 6.81, 8.2, 8.7, 8.59, 17.24, 20.69, 22.6, 22.11, 23.5, 23.11, 23.18, 23.24, 23.33, 23.34, 32.16, 32.22, 32.27, 32.72, 32.76, 32.85, 32.92, 32.99, 32.103, 34.4, 57.19, 57.64, 60.12, 60.14, 60.57, 65.320, 73.3, 73.25, 73.37, 80.4, 80.12, 80.13, 81.88, 81.89, 93.20, 93.83, 93.112, 97.194, 97.197, 98.25, 126.23, 133.38, 138.65, 147.37, 148.162, 155.48, 156.18, 158.22, 158.25, 158.54, 158.56, 162.49, 169.61, 169.101, 178.20, 178.29, 178.118
Henry, Buzz 2.19, 2.25, 6.51, 6.61, 20.32, 23.20, 89.146, 134.1, 169.53, 169.60, 169.101, 178.120
Henry, Carl 66.123
Henry, Carol 6.27, 6.35, 32.4, 32.9, 32.12, 81.40, 81.49, 129.16, 133.15, 138.1, 138.30, 138.45, 162.49, 169.13, 169.59
Henry, Emmaline 14.346
Henry, Gloria 148.31
Henry, Gregg 120.38, 163.26
Henry, O. 32
Henry, Pat 130.152
Henry, Thomas B. 14.47, 31.24, 105.11, 105.50, 105.68, 105.91, 105.107, 108.31, 126.104, 148.149, 155.1, 155.6, 156.20, 162.18, 164.66, 164.70, 178.19
Henry, Tom Browne 12.5, 41.30, 41.69
Henry, William 65.355, 65.380, 84.26, 89.2, 93.53, 108.5, 126.126, 126.134, 126.141, 126.149, 127.73, 141.27, 148.31, 170.12
Hensley, Robert 162.95
Henteloff, Alex 83.11, 83.45, 121
Herbert, Charles 82.10, 126.123, 162.114, 162.199, 162.142, 162.206, 162.224, 167.23
Herbert, Percy 30
Herbert, Pitt 44.44, 63.9, 65.19, 65.154, 66.213, 89.139, 93.186, 102.18, 106.14, 126.25, 138.1, 161.12, 161.74, 161.76, 161.112, 161.141, 162.102, 170.34, 170.53
Herbert, Tim 14.257
Herbsleb, John 96.65
Herbst, Becky 90.9
Herd, Richard 1.20, 1.27, 48.23
Herman, Brad 55.2
Hermensen, Tina 98.3
Hern, Pepe 12.11, 12.22, 12.32, 12.33, 14.163, 20.5, 20.54, 65.315, 65.316, 73.10, 126.34, 130.111, 130.144, 130.145
Hernandez, Kai 170.50, 170.77
Hernandez, Robert 71.9
Hernandez, Tom 27.12, 161.8
Herrera, Joe 80.15
Herrick, Frederick 65.612
Herrick, Virginia 32.41, 32.47, 35.20
Herrier, Mark 120.23, 120.24
Herrin, William 40
Herron, Bob 65.463, 65.531, 83.3, 170.2, 170.22
Herschberger, Gary 48.19
Hershey, Barbara 41.93, 71.24, 83.47, 83.48, 107
Hertzler, J.G. 1.16
Hertzler, John 180
Hervey, Irene 31.14, 168.7
Hervey, Jason 171
Hess, James 53.22
Hesse, Gregot 177.51
Hetrick, Jennifer 177.56

Hewitt, Alan 52.1, 69.3, 76.44, 105.106, 105.125, 117.50, 146.54, 170.52
Heydt, Louis Jean 57.21, 102.8, 108.10, 114.7, 126.37, 145.24, 162.24, 162.95, 178.107
Heyes, Herbert 97.174, 145.6, 146.11
Hi, Don 22.9
Hice, Eddie 65.342, 65.373, 152.18
Hickman, Bill 17.12
Hickman, Darryl 6.14, 65.151, 65.157, 93.60, 97.75, 97.123, 124.39, 126.72, 126.110, 141.8, 148.89, 153.7, 153.8, 153.9, 153.12, 153.13, 164.18
Hickman, Dwayne 97.75, 97.158, 162.269
Hickman, George 126.5, 126.113, 149.27
Hickman, James J. 97.11
Hickman, Robert L. 127.57
Hickman, William 82.5
Hickox, Harry 3.53, 3.158, 5.4, 5.18, 14.125, 14.305, 31.14, 31.47, 35.24, 35.33, 35.39, 69.6, 71.31, 77.1, 77.9, 84.33, 86.2, 86.17, 121.15, 130.13, 135.66, 135.67, 135.69, 147.5, 147.17, 161.131, 161.156, 162.207, 169.102
Hicks, Chuck 5.48, 27.97, 76.36, 83.55, 108.32, 112.16, 112.19, 126.103, 127.39
Hicks, Russell 32.13, 97.92
Higgins, Joe 12.7, 12.14, 12.25, 12.29, 12.40, 12.56, 65.430, 65.490, 92.7, 130.81, 130.96, 130.97, 130.100, 130.103, 130.107, 130.112, 130.118, 130.121, 130.126, 130.130, 130.139, 130.140, 130.143, 130.147, 130.148, 130.149, 130.150, 130.155, 130.158, 130.159, 130.163
Higgins, Joel 10
Higgins, Joey 66.206
Higgins, Michael 65.294, 65.327, 161.155
Hight, Don 126.107
Hiken, Gerald 171.5
Hildred, Robin 67.15
Hildreth, Mark 67.18
Hill, Adam 161.23
Hill, Arthur 84.17, 96.51, 96.52
Hill, Carol 66.76, 138.68
Hill, Craig 43.83, 43.91, 108.27, 108.33, 146.69
Hill, Dale 117.30
Hill, Dean 28.1, 120.28
Hill, Hallene 135.3
Hill, Hick 38, 84.3
Hill, Hickman 65.329
Hill, Jack 138.9
Hill, Lois 81.27
Hill, Marianna 14.149, 41.156, 43.298, 65.318, 71.58, 83.35, 109.4, 149.6, 149.11, 149.15, 149.26, 149.44, 150.5, 159.14, 165.5, 170.56
Hill, Maurice 5.10
Hill, Maury 148.116
Hill, Phyllis 14.265, 43.171, 132.12
Hill, Ramsay 78.16
Hill, Riley 32.2, 32.5, 32.10, 32.11, 32.43, 32.49, 32.79, 35.15, 35.26, 60.28, 60.30, 60.40, 81.6, 81.17, 97.52, 97.78, 124.13, 124.17, 124.53, 135.1, 135.6, 135.8, 135.12, 135.33, 158.19, 169.12, 169.18, 169.44, 169.52
Hill, Stephanie 55.22, 76.1
Hill, Steven 126.204
Hillaire, Marcel 41.117, 70.48
Hillerman, John 175.7
Hillias, Peg 25.8, 25.32, 64.53, 65.90, 66.12, 162.29
Hillman, Les 8.105
Hills, Beverly 71.7
Hillyer, Sharyn 134.6
Hincks, Candice J. 120.13

Personnel Index

Hindle, Art 99.15
Hindy, Joseph 65.587, 65.612
Hines, Barbara 164.80
Hines, Connie 14.335, 21.21, 131.41, 140.33
Hines, Harry 27.68, 73.16, 105.47, 129.22, 129.37, 129.77, 162.36, 162.47
Hingert, Maureen 43.102
Hingle, Pat 7.2, 14.336, 30.3, 41.14, 65.644, 65.545, 65.547, 65.548, 65.549, 65.550, 65.638, 69.5, 71.27, 83.7, 84.37, 98.21, 98.22, 101.25, 126.188
Hinkle, Ed 60.43, 60.45, 135.27, 135.32
Hinkle, Robert 6.79, 55.16, 65.48, 65.270, 148.45
Hinn, Michael 14.363, 15, 20.70, 65.43, 65.58, 65.105, 65.159, 65.208, 79.27, 79.29, 88.6, 88.21, 141.67, 148.76, 149.14, 178.34, 178.77, 178.124, 178.125, 178.128
Hinton, Darby 12.48, 41, 141.50, 162.252
Hinton, Ed 2.5, 2.11, 3.31, 3.39, 3.69, 23.37, 23.38, 31.18, 31.44, 31.48, 32.107, 32.114, 93.91, 93.122, 97.36, 97.69, 97.152, 97.156, 133.9, 135.96, 138.31, 138.35, 141.55, 147.16, 148.40
Hiona, Sam 83.47, 83.48
Hirt, Christianne 99
Hiser, Tim 177.66
Hix, Dan 129.65
Hix, Don 55.16
Hixon, Butler 93.59, 145.30
Ho, Linda 162.230, 170.6, 170.93
Hoag, Judith 1.5, 163.9, 177.30
Hoag, Mitzi 5.9, 14.224, 14.423, 65.299, 65.453, 70, 70.50, 96.65
Hobart, Rose 65.463
Hobbie, Duke 65.462
Hobbs, Peter 12.77, 14.404, 96.145, 96.146, 96.154
Hoby Gilman 156
Hochwald, Bari 48.54, 163.48
Hodge, Kate 90.9
Hodges, Clay 170.74
Hodges, Eddie 14.215, 30.20, 65.428
Hodges, Tom 163.7
Hodgins, Earle 32.5, 32.11, 32.13, 32.40, 32.69, 32.105, 32.112, 32.120, 32.139, 32.142, 32.155, 60.82, 65.74, 65.241, 65.270, 65.294, 66.3, 66.33, 66.59, 66.117, 66.17, 73.29, 80.17, 80.19, 80.26, 80.29, 80.30, 80.39, 88.10, 97.10, 97.24, 97.41, 97.72, 97.135, 97.170, 103.48, 119.3, 124.1, 124.5, 124.49, 124.50, 126.26, 126.36, 130.33, 135.65, 141.10, 145.7, 145.35, 146.27, 164.54, 165.8, 167.12, 169.82, 169.96, 169.113
Hoff, Robin 171.4
Hoffman, Bern 12.34, 14.125, 14.134, 14.141, 14.152, 14.160, 14.169, 14.217, 22.18, 34.27, 43.349, 44.67, 47.9, 51.24, 55.1, 84.14, 86.2, 86.34, 126.82, 129.58, 131.20, 132.3, 152.49, 152.52, 152.55, 162.100, 162.138, 162.284, 172.3
Hoffman, Howard 170.31
Hoffman, Pato 48.8, 48.21, 91.4
Hoffman, Robert 96.2
Hogan, Cindy 163.35
Hogan, Jack 8.37, 8.98, 14.59, 20.55, 27.89, 34.50, 38.2, 44.39, 66.51, 89.79, 89.117, 89.141, 118.2, 123.11, 127.31, 130.36, 130.130, 131.35, 133.8, 149.28, 150.10, 155.52
Hogan, Pat 20.18, 41.14, 42, 65.23, 114.3, 130.37, 145.4, 145.32, 146.10, 153
Hogan, Paul 32.31, 32.37, 97.41
Hogan, Robert 14.333, 21.67, 27.95, 65.344, 65.551, 65.552, 65.553, 175.4
Hoiseck, Ronald F. 10.16
Hokanson, Mary Alan 29.1
Holchak, Victor 65.525, 65.558
Holcomb, Kathryn 75
Holcombe, Harry 14.328, 14.333, 14.341, 14.361, 14.375, 14.383, 14.385, 14.415, 14.424, 27.80, 43.196, 43.304, 43.338, 162.189, 162.240

Holdren, Judd 97.81, 97.94, 97.110, 97.117, 102.16, 124.58, 124.61, 138.13
Holdridge, Cheryl 130.129, 162.262
Hole, Jonathan 8.21, 14.64, 14.179, 27.45, 57.104, 63.15, 66.3, 78.44, 83.51, 86.18, 93.79, 105.16, 105.42, 105.79, 125.13, 126.45, 126.84, 126.104, 126.158, 151.12, 156.47, 156.63, 161.26, 164.20, 168.25, 170.60, 170.79, 178.74
Holiday, Hope 66.159
Holland, Bert 5.20, 97.146
Holland, Bruce 65.33
Holland, Buck 65.472
Holland, Edna 2.5, 2.11, 6.45, 97.125
Holland, Erik 5.15, 10.16, 14.236, 63.47, 116.2
Holland, Jack 65.33
Holland, John 20.39, 22.17, 27.60, 43.97, 43.140, 52.3, 66.83, 66.183, 105.73, 105.83, 145.15
Holland, Joseph 21.15
Holland, Kristina 70.8
Holland, Tina 70.19, 86.24
Holland, Tom 32.43, 151.11, 155.12
Hollander, David 96.140
Holliday, Clive 25.37
Holliday, Doc 93
Holliday, Fred 12.10
Holliman, Earl 5.1, 5.16, 14.187, 61.5, 65.495, 65.514, 65.580, 65.636, 74, 161.97, 168
Holloway, Sterling 3.75, 3.93, 3.135, 31.15, 31.37, 31.44, 52.47, 178.134
Holly, Mark 5.43
Holm, Celeste 178.25
Holman, Rex 9.3, 12.24, 12.42, 12.62, 14.119, 30.1, 36.18, 41.95, 41.124, 43.319, 43.336, 44.38, 63.1, 63.14, 63.29, 65.198, 65.207, 65.238, 65.386, 65.417, 65.439, 65.466, 65.484, 65.500, 65.523, 65.542, 65.543, 65.569, 65.604, 66.222, 71.27, 74.31, 76.3, 76.41, 83.21, 84.24, 84.47, 85.46, 86.11, 86.32, 89.101, 92.28, 106.10, 107.8, 116.26, 126.38, 126.204, 130.143, 130.148, 130.167, 132.1, 132.2, 148.190, 149.14, 159.8, 161.50, 162.129, 162.267
Holmes, Bill 32.28, 32.34
Holmes, Dennis 44.69, 85, 129.40, 161.55, 162.52, 162.137, 162.266
Holmes, Edward 168.2
Holmes, Hal 84.43
Holmes, Madeline 64.7, 126.40
Holmes, Taylor 56.10
Holmes, Wendell 14.35, 25.25, 65.141, 89.48, 105.58, 105.79, 119.12, 133.29, 148.109, 152.51, 152.78, 165.4, 178.106, 179.60, 179.61, 179.62
Holt, Jacqueline 140.37, 148.1, 148.11, 148.37, 148.100, 158.32
Holt, Tim 161.215
Holztman, Glen 93.183
Homan, Robert 169.85
Homeier, G.V. 17.7
Homeier, Skip 14.237, 43.292, 43.317, 44.8, 55.24, 75.18, 76.15, 77.11, 89.35, 98.21, 98.22, 113, 117.4, 126.33, 126.87, 126.215, 130.61, 139.11, 161.28, 161.39, 161.67, 161.194, 162.247, 164.11, 167.10, 178.28
Homel, Bob 41.52
Hong, Dick Kay 130.110
Hong, James 1.1, 1.17, 1.24, 3.162, 8.37, 14.35, 25.60, 66.185, 76.2, 76.30, 83.6, 83.21, 83.35, 83.36, 83.41, 83.42, 83.46, 83.60, 91.11, 118.3, 141.25, 146.50, 179.77
Hood, Foster 121.9
Hooker, Joe 170.10
Hooker, Joey 3.69, 3.74
Hooker, Ken 129.36, 162.118
Hooks, David 95.6, 95.7, 96.89, 96.90, 96.97, 96.100, 96.101
Hooks, Ed 120.47
Hoose, Fred 169.14
Hootkins, William 19.5
Hoover, Joseph 41.71, 51.26, 65.402, 126.183

Hopkins, Bo 14.335, 63.35, 65.445, 112.18, 161.155, 170.70
Hopkins, Bob 14.65, 44.23, 63.18, 65.177, 66.106, 93.90, 126.53, 152.68, 162.105
Hopkins, John 66.139
Hopkins, Kaitlin 48.58
Hopper, Dennis 12.55, 12.73, 14.165, 27.6, 27.11, 27.25, 39.7, 63.14, 65.359, 92.22, 130.1, 130.30, 146.1, 162.213, 178.52, 178.118
Hopper, Hal 3.40, 3.57, 3.63, 3.73, 3.78, 3.84, 3.89, 3.92, 3.97, 3.118, 3.142, 31.15, 80.1, 80.17, 80.19, 80.26, 80.30, 80.36, 80.38, 80.39, 158.3, 158.16, 158.24, 158.29, 158.40, 158.46, 158.61
Hopper, William 57.13, 65.38
Hopson, Alfred 105.10
Horan, Barbra 118.11
Horan, James 163.72
Horgan, Patrick 30.18, 36.21, 63.23, 71.2, 121.4, 170.100
Horino, Tad 83.9, 83.23, 83.40, 83.49, 83.50, 83.60
Horne, Christopher 161.162
Horne, Chuck 63.39, 63.43, 63.44
Horne, Geoffrey 65.595, 65.596, 132.6, 161.113
Hornsby, Peter 77.19
Horse, Michael 67.15, 120.29
Horsey, Martin 41.106
Horsley, Lee 67, 120
Horsley, Michael 118.3
Horton, Edward Everett 52
Horton, Robert 97.142, 101, 162
Horvath, Charles 3.100, 3.114, 12.30, 17.19, 17.33, 20.33, 25.22, 27.21, 30.23, 41.21, 41.35, 41.58, 41.59, 65.67, 66.41, 71.15, 71.42, 76.36, 86.17, 89.86, 97.64, 141.7, 145.23, 152.37, 152.44, 162.139, 165.1, 170.7, 170.46, 178.60, 179.77
Hossack, Allison 99.9
Hotchkis, Joan 54.26, 76.39, 116.8
Hotton, Donald 96.145, 96.146
House, Billy 25.55
House, Don 156.1
Houser, Patrick 118
Houston, Paula 32.144
Hovack, Steven 120.41
Hover, Robert 27.30
Hovey, Tim 29.11
Hovis, Joan 97.179
Howard, Barbara 120.21
Howard, Breena 98.3, 144.19
Howard, Clint 14.216, 37, 65.535, 84.40, 86.45, 106.23, 107.25, 161.114, 161.143
Howard, Dara 148.184
Howard, Dennis 96.169
Howard, Gregory 57.48
Howard, Jennifer 27.26
Howard, John 21.52, 27.69, 64.6, 89.53, 92.28, 96.37, 117.17, 126.98, 162.92
Howard, Judy 79.25
Howard, Ken 14.422
Howard, Nancy 43.359
Howard, Rance 8.30, 14.409, 65.530, 65.621, 70.24, 83.26, 96.58, 107.1, 107.21, 107.25, 112.20, 161.114
Howard, Ron 79.3
Howard, Ronald 36
Howard, Ronny 12.12, 14.418, 41.136, 65.496, 84.8, 84.25, 107.25
Howard, Sherman 163.43, 177.31
Howard, Susan 70.15, 76.23, 76.38, 116.14, 161.205
Howard, Vince 170.54, 170.82
Howard Hayes 36
Howat, Clark 8.18, 43.51, 43.62, 93.195, 129.50, 147.46, 148.44, 162.119
Howden, Mike 65.465
Howdy, Clyde 14.222, 14.263, 27.80, 27.91, 30.12, 43.430, 43.432, 65.415, 65.440, 105.99, 132.7, 134.8, 161.122, 161.127, 161.168, 161.201, 168.13

Personnel Index

Howe, Darrell 161.3
Howe, David 43.201
Howe, Eileen 43.43
Howell, Arlene 21.27, 105.37, 105.38, 105.50
Howell, Eurlynne 105.30
Howell, Henry 130.116
Howell, Hoke 14.231, 65.426, 70, 83.62, 112.9, 115.1, 118.8, 120.47
Howell, J. Harris 135.96
Howell, Jean 3.133, 6.25, 6.26, 20.12, 20.48, 43.133, 55.4, 60.79, 60.83, 63.38, 65.192, 78.49, 81.28, 81.68, 93.59, 93.122, 108.27, 129.69, 135.60, 148.4, 155.4, 156.42, 156.51, 156.67, 164.3, 178.16
Howell, Kay 95.15, 96.131, 96.147
Howell, Norman 120.39
Howes, Basil 78.58
Howes, Reed 6.48, 20.48, 22.6, 25.45, 32.28, 32.34, 32.85, 32.92, 60.20, 60.22, 60.25, 60.27, 60.87, 81.12, 81.39, 97.176, 129.20, 135.5, 135.9, 135.10, 135.13, 135.28, 135.74, 135.77, 138.13, 169.18, 169.45, 169.67
Howes, Sally Ann 106.20
Howland, Beth 96.37
Howlin, Olin 25.65, 31.1, 73.2, 78.65
Hoy, Elizabeth 53.13
Hoy, Robert 7.1, 9.6, 17.22, 24.20, 37.1, 59.2, 71, 83.2, 83.15, 85.109, 86.7, 86.47, 96.22, 113.7, 113.8, 123.2, 130.78, 130.87, 139.6, 149.24, 161.122, 177.9, 177.39, 178.46, 178.120
Hoyos, Rodolfo 14.46, 14.163, 34.53, 43.139, 65.516, 71.89, 78.54, 83.20, 86.15, 93.222, 105.69, 116.24, 125.14, 130.2, 130.71, 142.25, 145.31, 148.30, 148.125, 148.180, 152.50, 155.25, 156.20, 164.82, 170.15, 178.89, 178.125, 179.78
Hoyos, Rudolfo, Jr. 3.26, 3.26, 78.38
Hoyt, Clegg 12.10, 14.136, 14.146, 14.178, 14.247, 22.33, 27.16, 51.22, 65.44, 65.45, 65.349, 66.146, 88.10, 117.10, 130.60, 149.75, 164.39
Hoyt, David 97.30
Hoyt, John 3.1, 4.16, 12.21, 12.32, 12.33, 14.112, 39.18, 41.51, 41.64, 43.186, 44.35, 46.4, 54.18, 56.14, 64.8, 65.64, 65.207, 66.100, 66.198, 78.19, 85.9, 85.118, 86.20, 86.35, 88.19, 89.10, 89.71, 97.146, 98.1, 105.110, 105.111, 116.24, 117.7, 117.8, 121.7, 126.54, 130.30, 130.83, 131.3, 132.14, 161.25, 161.33, 161.97, 161.157, 162.241, 162.265, 170.21, 170.104, 178.1, 178.21, 179.53
Hoyt, Richard 41.88
Hradilac, Charles 117.33
Hsueh, Nancy 4.32, 170.17
Huaute, Semu 177.3
Hubbard, Elizabeth 161.217
Hubbard, John 14.161, 14.169, 14.197, 14.204, 14.282, 21.4, 27.78, 31.7, 34.26, 65.373, 89.50, 89.151, 93.110, 97.157, 105.1, 105.33, 126.179, 161.85, 170.62
Hubbard, Tom 169.11, 169.55, 169.64, 169.68
Hubley, Season 83.40
Hubley, Whip 45.4
Huckabee, Cooper 96.40, 123.8, 123.9
Huddleston, David 14.392, 14.424, 47.14, 65.537, 65.592, 65.611, 65.621, 75.2, 83.25, 83.54, 109.4, 176.3
Hudgkins, Ken 65.272, 66.222
Hudkins, John "Bear" 65.463
Hudman, Wesley 32.58, 35.13, 43.46, 57.13, 60.5, 60.10, 60.11, 60.12, 60.13, 60.14, 60.15, 60.16, 60.17, 60.18, 60.25, 60.74, 81.5, 93.41, 108.25, 124.1, 124.6, 124.9, 169.38, 169.64
Hudson Valley 67, 68
Hudson, Dawn 48.39
Hudson, Gary 1.18, 1.26, 1.27
Hudson, John 65.323
Hudson, Larry 2.26, 8.65, 57.13, 60.53, 60.60, 73.21, 73.38, 81.95, 93.145, 97.93, 97.171, 102.17, 135.11, 135.14, 138.69, 145.7, 169.13, 169.28

Hudson, Rochelle 17.8, 17.9, 17.10
Hudson, William 43.34, 43.92, 43.104, 129.54, 135.83, 141.50, 145.5, 164.84
Huering, Lori 163.73
Huff, Tom 170.82
Huffman, David 95.11, 109.5
Huggard, John 65.383
Hughes, Billy 65.242, 65.280, 130.138, 162.156
Hughes, Billy, Jr. 130.159
Hughes, Carolyn 126.62
Hughes, Charles Anthony 135.91
Hughes, J. Anthony 147.27, 148.159
Hughes, Kathleen 74.8, 149.32
Hughes, Mary Beth 3.155, 22.17, 34.10, 44.46, 56.11, 126.21, 126.130, 164.24
Hughes, Robin 98.9, 146.43, 169.88, 179.14
Hughes, Roy 78.66
Hughes, Sally 93.99
Hughes, Tony 129.4, 169.61, 169.74
Hughes, Whitey 65.577, 170.26, 170.70, 170.71, 170.75
Hughes, William 130.121
Hugo, Mauritz 2.10, 12.106, 14.10, 23.3, 23.36, 32.35, 32.33, 32.38, 43.75, 43.148, 46.6, 81.93, 81.99, 93.51, 93.89, 97.121, 97.122, 97.204, 129.30, 133.14, 138.57, 141.31, 141.41, 145.25, 147.5, 148.33, 158.20, 158.23, 161.61, 162.153, 164.39, 169.71, 169.91
Hugueny, Sharon 34.63, 89.85, 105.93, 105.110, 105.111
Hules, Endre 48.4
Hull, Cynthia 70
Hull, Henry 14.19, 14.34, 85.42, 85.123, 117.15, 129.60, 129.63, 129.68, 156.46, 157.13, 162.53, 162.106, 162.107, 162.135, 178.111
Human, Robert 65.225
Humes, Mary-Margaret 91.6, 118.3
Humphrey, Dee 78.51
Humphrey, Tom 23.23
Humphreys, Chris 67.6
Humphreys, Peter 68.20, 68.30
Humphries, Bee 135.14
Hundley, Chris 65.503, 65.397, 84.8, 83.62, 84.24, 84.25, 161.94, 161.158
Hunley, Gary 141, 141.68, 141.69, 141.71, 146.39
Hunnicutt, Arthur 13.6, 14.12, 14.126, 14.168, 14.344, 27.19, 41.65, 61.9, 61.10, 65.536, 85.49, 85.72, 85.111, 86.9, 102.13, 106.8, 113, 116.19, 116.44, 119.3, 130.63, 146.1, 161.28, 162.284, 164.36, 165.7, 170.52
Hunt, Allan 65.307
Hunt, Bill 138.50
Hunt, Heidy 70.6
Hunt, Marsha 65.319, 85.3, 178.34, 178.71, 178.86, 178.129
Hunt, Suzanne 115.5
Hunt, Will 53.10, 120
Hunt, William 65.304, 162.77, 179.76
Hunter, Cindy 170.88
Hunter, Craig 32.40
Hunter, Henry 63.47, 148.85, 149.25, 161.25, 161.56, 162.114, 168.18, 170.4
Hunter, Jeffrey 41.70, 43.245, 92.32, 107.22, 124.5, 151
Hunter, Kim 14.288, 65.545, 69.7, 115.2, 126.16
Hunter, Morgan 1.25, 163.71
Hunter, Tab 161.226
Hunter, Thomas 65.492
Hunter, Tod 43.328
Hunter, William 4.37
Huntington, Joan 14.183, 17.29, 17.30, 76.25, 86.42, 170.11, 170.36, 170.65
Hurlbut, Gladys 78.55
Hurley, Jim 158.45, 158.47, 158.58
Hurley, Patrick John 177.21
Hursey, Sherry 48.37, 120.6
Hurst, James 27.70, 130.78, 161.112

Hurst, Richard 96.3
Hush, Lisabeth 14.112, 65.384, 55.22, 76.17, 86.43, 126.190, 159.28, 161.75, 161.154
Hussey, Olivia 99.10, 99.13
Huston, Brick 84.3
Huston, Carol 1.9, 120.46
Huston, Martin 84.44
Huston, Patricia 27.74, 39.5, 41.15, 43.252, 43.271, 43.365, 43.381, 65.140, 126.165, 170.39
Hutchins, Charles 1.6
Hutchins, Will 21.47, 27.76, 65.291, 105.81, 105.90, 146
Hutchinson, Josephine 14.370, 44.44, 65.160, 65.436, 96.6, 126.104, 130.71, 134.15, 148.156, 162.98
Hutchison, Doug 177.28
Hutton, Betty 65.373
Hutton, Brian 13.22, 55.6, 65.42, 66.113, 85.100, 88.5, 126.70, 130.121, 146.27
Hutton, Byron 130.44
Hutton, Robert 43.16, 93.187, 127.45, 169.75
Hyatt, Bobby 25.9, 135.6, 135.33, 162.149, 169.38, 169.47, 169.61, 169.76
Hyde, Jacquelyn 17.40, 17.41, 17.42, 170.85
Hyde-White, Alex 91.4, 163.20
Hyde-White, Wilfrid 41.106, 53.18
Hyer, Martha 44.17, 97.17, 106.1, 126.8, 169.33, 178.130
Hyke, Ray 32.32, 32.39
Hyland, Diana 5.7, 65.580, 76.1, 101.30, 144.22, 162.236
Hyland, Jim 65.30, 142.3, 158.69, 158.71
Hyland, Patricia 14.281, 161.222
Hylands, Scott 26, 83.4, 83.22
Hyman, Charles H. 1.6

Idelson, William 178.129
Iglesias, Eugene 14.185, 20.8, 31.19, 39.14, 44.59, 72.17, 78.62, 85.77, 105.24, 117.4, 126.110, 127.46, 127.70, 146.55, 170.35, 170.99
Ihnat, Steve 5.9, 12.19, 14.195, 14.295, 14.384, 24.18, 30.5, 41.42, 43.294, 49.13, 65.371, 65.398, 65.413, 65.433, 65.489, 65.530, 70.29, 70.50, 76.1, 76.35, 116.8, 126.197, 139.5, 151.11, 161.42, 161.65, 161.167, 161.192
Imamura, Hideo 70.25, 170.45
Indrisano, John 14.125, 72.17
Inescort, Frieda 127.71, 162.32
Infuhr, Teddy 32.45, 32.57, 60.32
Ing, Alvin 75.26
Ingersoll, Jim 120.22
Ingram, Elisa 170.4
Ingram, Jack 6.33, 23.17, 23.22, 32.4, 32.9, 32.12, 32.53, 32.60, 32.110, 32.116, 35.11, 60.7, 60.25, 60.26, 73.39, 81.13, 81.48, 97.52, 97.115, 124.9, 124.78, 148.51
Ingram, Jean 65.206, 119.7, 148.111
Ingram, Rex 13.3, 17.34, 36.26, 65.487, 130.98
Inness, Jan 161.152
Inness, Jean 12.99, 14.100, 14.239, 14.240, 51.28, 65.16, 65.194, 66.192, 79.26, 97.140, 126.19, 126.88, 127.75, 145.23, 148.124, 153.7, 161.116, 161.155, 161.201, 162.72, 162.233, 167.9
Innocent, Harold 65.252, 66.107
Inscoe, Joe 163.59
Ireland, Ian 41.154
Ireland, Ira 70.30
Ireland, Jill 41.145, 139
Ireland, John 14.259, 14.431, 17.6, 17.47, 41.87, 65.419, 65.442, 65.443, 76.23, 96.57, 96.91, 101.26, 106.3, 123.10, 126, 126.54, 126.116, 126.202, 131.6, 178.10
Irish, Tom 32.125, 32.129, 81.90, 81.98, 97.46
Irish Rovers, The 161.177, 161.180, 161.193
Irvin, Gregory 57.113, 151.15, 162.214, 178.122
Irving, Charles 14.136, 14.225, 14.245, 14.298, 39.18, 84.27, 84.28

Personnel Index

Irving, Hollis 102.24, 142.22, 149.59, 164.83
Irving, John 138.24
Irwin, Charles 3.137, 129.56
Irwin, John 126.57, 126.58
Ishimoto, Dale 83.11, 83.49, 83.60, 164.92
Islas, Armando 71.29, 71.53
Isobel, Katharine 99.18
Itkin, Paul Henry 75.22
Ito, Robert 75.26, 83.1, 83.18, 83.31
Ivans, Harry 148.15
Ivar, Stan 95, 95.23
Ivens, Terri 1.17
Ivers, Robert 8.59, 8.96, 65.153, 155.75, 161.75
Ives, Burl 5.2, 5.31, 5.35, 5.41, 41.127, 41.134, 96.55, 178.122
Ivins, Perry 13.23, 44.31, 65.185, 66.101, 162.23, 169.32
Ivo, Tommy 3.111, 60.4, 73.7, 97.169, 124.2, 149.30, 158.26, 169.4, 169.12, 169.80
Ivor, Michael 158.11
Izay, Victor 17.27, 30.14, 65.379, 65.384, 65.416, 65.523, 65.525, 65.545, 65.591, 65.603, 65.616, 65.639, 127.54, 165.3, 165.7

Jackson, Al 97.165
Jackson, Anne 65.561
Jackson, Bradford 3.73, 3.93, 31.11, 43.73, 43.84, 97.219
Jackson, Colette 162.126
Jackson, General Andrew 42
Jackson, Ginny 169.77
Jackson, Harry 173.28
Jackson, Jenie 170.22, 170.27
Jackson, Kate 14.415
Jackson, Mary 84.24, 84.33, 144.11
Jackson, Michael 36.16, 36.17
Jackson, Sam 3.163
Jackson, Sammy 24.7, 105.86, 146.18, 151.15, 151.26, 161.167
Jackson, Selmer 3.114, 6.43, 93.35, 93.40, 93.45, 93.46, 93.58, 129.47
Jackson, Sherry 7.3, 17.38, 43.346, 60.36, 60.42, 65.249, 65.271, 105.13, 105.104, 124.16, 124.40, 126.191, 130.9, 131.38, 135.10, 149.54, 161.100, 162.244, 170.48, 170.85
Jackson, Thomas E. 98.14
Jackson, Tom 66.116, 149.16
Jackson, Tommy 44.62
Jacobi, Lou 152.18
Jacobs, Bruce 41.47
Jacobs, Christian 120.34
Jacobsson, Ulla 161.31
Jacoby, Billy 177.7
Jacques, Ted 8.36, 92.30, 133.10, 138.18, 138.39, 138.48, 149.68
Jacquet, Frank 60.54, 73.6, 97.35, 124.37, 124.51, 135.19, 145.16, 145.35
Jaeckel, Richard 11.7, 14.177, 14.274, 29.10, 39.8, 55, 65.294, 65.395, 65.396, 65.627, 66.200, 89.102, 96.41, 96.152, 96.153, 115.6, 127.43, 145.2, 148.131, 149.19, 151.20, 152.20, 156.60, 161.52, 162.148, 162.210, 170.18, 170.54, 178.107
Jaffe, Allan 8.50, 8.74, 8.84, 8.92, 12.2, 17.7, 39.4, 43.196, 43.214, 63.40, 64.5, 65.363, 65.378, 65.380, 65.387, 65.417, 65.447, 65.501, 65.515, 70.5, 76.47, 98.15, 126.63, 139.3, 148.184, 162.126, 164.73, 170.16, 170.49
Jaffe, Sam 5.6, 5.8, 5.38, 14.225, 41.41, 165.8
Jagger, Dean 5.50, 14.382, 83.3, 178.24
Jak, Lisa 84.1, 107.6, 107.19
Jalbert, Pierre 38.7
James, Anthony 12.66, 12.110, 14.373, 30.14, 65.445, 65.458, 65.467, 65.469, 65.481, 65.497, 65.499, 65.634, 71.7, 118.5
James, Brion 45.4, 59.2, 96.177, 177.13
James, Charleen 173.27
James, Clifton 30.10, 65.122, 65.368, 65.416, 65.521, 65.522, 161.133, 175.3

James, Debbie 91.5
James, Frank 92
James, Grant 177.35, 177.63
James, Hawthorne 1.18
James, Jeri 81.39
James, Jesse 92
James, John 158.19, 158.21
James, Kyle 32.73
James, Lisa 86.54
James, Michael 161.4
James, Ralph 24.1, 65.477, 65.486
James, Scott 84.25
James, Ward C. 32.130, 32.148, 32.153
Jameson, Adair 86.9
Jameson, Joyce 5.24, 7.6, 12.51, 32.146, 32.150, 52.61, 65.262, 117.39, 142.14, 161.203, 173.33
Jamison, Richard L. 28.4
Jan and Dean 128.8
Janes, Enid 66.224, 79.33, 88.17, 88.29, 93.188, 130.47, 130.96, 130.97, 130.127, 130.44, 130.145, 164.87, 167.15
Janes, Lauren 130.14
Janes, Loren 32.130
Janis, Conrad 144.6, 178.3
Janiss, Vivi 65.55, 66.174, 85.34, 89.24, 117.5, 148.101, 156.47, 161.12, 161.148, 162.53, 162.109, 162.121, 162.138, 162.142, 162.182
Jann, Gerald 83.49
Janos Bartok 91
Janssen, David 26, 43.205, 178.24, 178.45, 178.61, 178.75
Janssen, Eileen 60.24, 60.55, 124.50, 146.20, 148.6, 148.25
Janti, David 66.107
January, Bob 150.4, 164.69
Jara, Maurice 14.44, 20.15, 43.37, 89.67, 97.92, 97.149, 97.201, 126.24, 141.5
Jarman, Claude 26
Jarmyn, Jill 20.36, 27.31, 43.19, 43.141
Jarrett, Kirk 67.3
Jarrett, Renne 71.73
Jarvis, Francesca 71.38, 96.122, 177.25
Jarvis, Graham 53.7, 65.635, 120.50, 175.1
Jarvis, Martin 163.85
Jasmin, Paul 66.34, 93.184, 103.41, 130.51, 178.77
Jason, Harvey 36.24, 116.19
Jason, Peter 30.23, 41.131, 48.28, 65.506, 65.520, 65.586, 70.19
Jason, Rick 106.24, 126.11, 126.32, 145.13
Jauregui, Ed 14.378
Javis, Sam 12.27, 71.85
Jay, Helen 138.38, 156.8, 164.8
Jay, Tony 1.9
Jayne, Billy 163.60
Jean, Gloria 6.44, 6.46, 43.27
Jeffcoat, Donnie 48.61
Jefferson, Brenden 48.79, 48.82
Jeffreys, Anne 14.230, 162.14, 162.184
Jeffreys, Mark 177.26
Jeffries, Dick 129.77
Jeffries, Herb 161.190
Jeffries, Lang 119.17
Jellison, Bob 8.18, 66.169
Jenckes, Joe 41.95, 41.121
Jenkins, Allen 162.116
Jenkins, Dal 14.175, 24.3, 46.9, 70.33, 76.3, 84.36, 92.10, 126.205, 130.165, 151.25, 170.15
Jenkins, Jill 161.167
Jenkins, Ken 91.3
Jenkins, Mark 24.16, 24.17, 43.439
Jenkins, Mike 71.61
Jenkins, Paul 163.60
Jenks, Frank 31.33, 32.77, 60.79, 85.107, 135.31, 162.120, 169.60
Jenks, Si 97.138
Jenner, Barry 120.37, 163.29
Jenoff, Art 41.120

Jens, Salome 14.365, 65.531, 65.586, 111.4, 144.9
Jensen, Dave 163.82
Jensen, Johnny 17.2, 41.140
Jensen, Karen 161.120, 170.68
Jenson, Marlowe 65.182
Jenson, Roy 12.66, 14.147, 14.205, 14.326, 14.416, 19.6, 30.2, 30.23, 41.35, 41.58, 41.59, 41.141, 53.1, 65.411, 65.454, 65.472, 65.508, 65.525, 65.624, 71.30, 71.71, 75.27, 83.13, 96.54, 107.8, 112.10, 116.7, 161.185, 170.29
Jergens, Diane 40, 93.217, 103.22, 162.133
Jeris, Nancy 65.597
Jerome, Edwin 25.37, 78.51, 178.78
Jerome, Patti 123.5
Jerry, Toni 169.44
Jeter, James 14.140, 14.318, 14.323, 65.580, 65.604, 96.11, 96.47, 96.48, 170.12
Jetton, Jodee 94.18
Jewel, Robin 158.3
Jewell, Isabelle 65.361
Jillian, Ann 162.168
Jinnette, Betty 176.5
Jochim, Anthony 3.128, 103.48
Joe, Jeanne 83.60
Joel, Dennis 44.48
Johansson, Paul 99
Johns, Larry 3.139, 43.143, 44.21, 97.56, 141.48, 169.21
Johnson, Arch 8.70, 12.57, 12.102, 14.103, 14.159, 14.272, 14.273, 21.37, 27.96, 30.3, 41.1, 41.75, 41.76, 41.133, 43.391, 51.21, 52.60, 65.260, 65.355, 65.413, 65.519, 83.35, 85, 86.19, 88.23, 89.80, 89.127, 89.138, 96.39, 105.55, 105.86, 105.93, 106.14, 126.70, 126.124, 126.132, 126.148, 126.162, 128.13, 148.194, 157.20, 161.35, 161.86, 162.168, 175.3, 178.131
Johnson, Arte 46.8, 55.7
Johnson, Bayn 84.38
Johnson, Ben 14.93, 14.327, 14.378, 14.432, 14.433, 17.36, 65.300, 65.421, 65.550, 66.120, 66.162, 66.195, 85.25, 85.43, 85.63, 107, 129.48, 144.4, 161.16, 161.87, 161.155, 161.180
Johnson, Bob 158.47, 158.55, 158.77
Johnson, Brad 3.42, 3.72, 6, 27.69, 31.27, 32.36, 35.9, 35.15, 35.19, 35.26, 35.35, 43.137, 43.142, 43.168, 65.440, 93.63, 93.105, 97.213, 105.48, 105.86, 110, 124.65, 124.68, 124.77, 145.32, 148.70, 162.121
Johnson, Carter 43.303
Johnson, Chal 65.275
Johnson, Chubby 3.68, 3.150, 12.12, 14.84, 14.193, 14.251, 14.283, 22.13, 31.26, 43.395, 43.428, 44.73, 65.352, 65.355, 65.481, 78.55, 89.112, 97.121, 97.122, 102.25, 105.6, 105.56, 105.78, 105.89, 105.94, 121.26, 126.136, 130.60, 130.61, 130.137, 141.5, 141.9, 141.13, 141.18, 145.15, 146.1, 148.74, 151.12, 151.20, 152.24, 162.47, 164.62, 170.47, 170.60, 170.79
Johnson, Claude 14.68, 41.93, 41.120, 65.350, 128.9
Johnson, Dale 34.40, 93.223, 129.75
Johnson, Don 11.1, 83.22
Johnson, Dorothy 8.53, 158.13
Johnson, Dot 158.3
Johnson, Edmund 66.42
Johnson, Georgann 48.23, 48.67, 48.93, 48.94
Johnson, Harvey 51.31, 105.105, 130.77
Johnson, Haylie 48.5, 48.6, 48.25, 48.37, 48.70, 48.89
Johnson, Howard 17.11
Johnson, J.S. 14.320, 170.87
Johnson, Janet 5.50
Johnson, Jason 12.66, 14.179, 31.26, 51.23, 65.98, 65.384, 74.10, 78.72, 85.106, 97.215, 130.20, 130.33, 138.17, 148.44, 148.108, 148.140, 149.3, 156.46, 156.60, 158.45, 158.47, 161.5, 162.237, 178.46, 178.59, 178.74, 178.107

Personnel Index

Johnson, Ken 96.69, 126.173
Johnson, King 12.17
Johnson, Kyle 36.12
Johnson, Lamont 12.42, 65.441
Johnson, Larry 97.187
Johnson, Leroy 148.100
Johnson, Les 148.98, 164.46
Johnson, Linda 32.57, 32.63, 32.78, 97.59
Johnson, Melodie 86.38, 132.25, 134.16
Johnson, Rafer 41.33
Johnson, Russell 3.54, 12.76, 13, 25.43, 31.5, 39.3, 43.209, 44.76, 51.27, 65.60, 65.142, 65.484, 65.570, 77.6, 85.56, 85.77, 85.85, 85.99, 89.16, 97.181, 126.143, 148.9, 148.191, 162.15, 162.50, 162.197, 168.4
Johnson, Ryan Thomas 1.20
Johnson, Sander 123.8, 123.9
Johnson, Tim 32.137
Johnson, Van 106.18, 178.80
Johnston, Jan A. 121.26
Johnston, John Dennis 10.15, 19.17, 91.10, 96.178, 96.179, 110.3, 163.86
Johnston, Shaun 67.21
Joiner, Pat 43.58
Jolley, I. Stanford 2.10, 4.7, 6.14, 12.69, 14.140, 14.159, 14.222, 14.322, 17.27, 21.29, 27.81, 27.83, 27.85, 32.15, 32.18, 32.21, 32.41, 32.47, 32.83, 32.90, 32.109, 32.122, 32.127, 41.17, 43.61, 43.93, 43.138, 57.65, 60.16, 60.17, 60.71, 60.76, 65.313, 65.389, 65.448, 65.464, 65.483, 65.490, 65.512, 65.526, 66.65, 71.12, 73.27, 86.10, 89.7, 89.93, 93.48, 93.130, 93.158, 93.187, 93.220, 97.34, 97.68, 97.97, 97.98, 97.119, 105.18, 105.30, 124.66, 124.72, 126.99, 126.119, 126.136, 126.143, 126.165, 129.35, 130.161, 135.10, 135.13, 135.89, 138.28, 138.72, 141.22, 141.30, 141.32, 141.59, 145.16, 147.4, 148.146, 149.65, 156.29, 158.16, 158.48, 158.70, 158.72, 161.30, 162.23, 162.142, 162.187, 162.221, 162.232, 162.241, 162.252, 167.24, 168.9, 169.34, 169.42, 169.66
Jones, Ashley 48.2
Jones, Carolyn 55.16, 106.17, 125.6, 162.3, 162.158, 162.227, 178.17, 178.105, 178.134
Jones, Chester 78.30
Jones, Christopher 92
Jones, Claude Earl 26, 95.16, 96.171
Jones, Dean 14.74, 117.3, 142.7, 148.177, 162.174, 178.109
Jones, Dick 6.20, 6.22, 6.30, 6.38, 23, 60.15, 60.23, 60.32, 60.34, 60.41, 60.44, 60.51, 60.66, 60.70, 60.75, 97.5, 97.40, 124
Jones, Douglas 162.178
Jones, Eddie 177.21
Jones, Fenton G. 126.75
Jones, Gordon 20.44, 34.56, 43.11, 55.3, 55.22, 57.24, 60.32, 60.34, 66.203, 78.42, 89.20, 93.18, 105.60, 105.122, 130.27, 130.107, 169.8
Jones, Henry 5.16, 12.54, 14.181, 14.412, 41.98, 41.125, 55.15, 62, 63.29, 65.449, 65.508, 65.555, 69.5, 70.22, 101.8, 117.47, 161.222, 162.182
Jones, Isaac 162.21
Jones, Ivy 65.579, 96.60
Jones, Jay 14.348, 71.65, 83.54
Jones, Jeff 137.4
Jones, Jeffrey 59.3
Jones, Keith 86.13
Jones, Kevin 43.175, 178.130
Jones, L.Q. 5.9, 5.48, 6.51, 6.61, 12.26, 12.54, 12.57, 12.62, 12.80, 13.13, 17.4, 24.9, 27, 30.4, 30.9, 51.32, 65.309, 65.352, 65.369, 65.487, 65.509, 65.524, 65.557, 66.171, 66.211, 72.13, 77.16, 79.17, 82.2, 82.3, 82.4, 83.5, 83.62, 84.27, 85.10, 85.49, 85.66, 85.88, 85.92, 85.95, 85.119, 86.1, 89.144, 93.209, 101.18, 126.146, 126.161, 126.175, 127.36, 127.47, 130.138, 148.71, 148.174, 159.9, 159.29, 161, 161.36, 161.40, 161.66, 161.70, 161.91, 161.149, 162.59, 162.139, 162.211, 162.251, 167.5
Jones, Marcia Mae 169.11
Jones, Marianne 67.11
Jones, Marilyn 120.1
Jones, Marsha 32.43, 32.49
Jones, Mickey 53.11, 65.636
Jones, Miranda 8.52, 65.278, 66.59, 66.104, 89.14, 89.95, 89.153, 146.35
Jones, Morgan 2.22, 8.65, 41.93, 43.53, 43.118, 65.397, 80.27, 80.28, 80.37, 96.38, 105.52, 126.41, 155.13, 169.51, 169.96
Jones, Richard 110
Jones, Sam 163.11
Jones, Sonny 70.34
Jones, Stanley 54.6
Jones, T.C. 170.71
Jones, Warner 130.68
Jones-Moreland, Betsy 14.129, 65.306, 66.126, 66.150, 102.28, 178.66
Jonson, James 22.24
Jordan, Bobbi 7, 134
Jordan, Bobbie 170.76
Jordan, Bobby 148.13, 169.17
Jordan, Richard 51.5, 51.16, 69.7, 168.7
Jordan, Robert 3.128, 105.34, 126.50, 148.24, 148.27, 169.48, 169.109
Jordan, Sunny 161.33
Jordan, Ted 17.18, 65, 72.12, 132.9, 132.25, 141.12
Jordan, Tom 65
Jordan, William 7.10, 14.274, 14.323, 71.37, 120.16
Jory, Victor 14.219, 14.220, 51.4, 52.29, 61.6, 65.360, 71.24, 76.5, 83.45, 92.26, 98.25, 109.2, 109.14, 126.19, 126.112, 132.16, 151.1, 161.63, 161.116, 161.143, 161.159, 161.201, 164.27, 168.15, 175.7
Josel, Sandy 170.31
Joseph, Allen 5.28, 5.48, 162.239
Joseph, Jackie 52.17
Joseph, Ron 118.1
Josephson, Jeffrey 120.46
Joslin, Warren 66.209, 66.226
Joslyn, Allyn 4.1, 52.16, 65.187, 66.140, 74.10, 126.168
Joslyn, Sandra 65.251
Joston, Darwin 161.169
Jostyn, Jay 17.12, 17.31, 64.8, 78.35, 148.54, 170.99
Jovovich, Milla 120.8
Joyce, Bill 130.47
Joyce, Elaine 70.1, 70.4
Joyce, Patricia 65.326
Joyce, Peggy 74.8
Joyce, Stephen 14.63, 21.33, 39.4, 117.33, 126.26, 126.50, 126.60, 126.84, 127.66, 127.75, 161.1
Joyce, Susan 14.397
Joyce, William 66.95, 89.142, 126.18, 129.20, 129.60, 148.77
Joyner, Michelle 48.97, 177.33
Juan, Simon 67.18
Judas, Gary 152.67
Judson, Austin J. 53.3, 177.6
Julian, Mike 68.21
Jump, Gordon 24.5, 41.21, 70.1
Jung, Allen 65.514, 66.103, 102.1, 162.194
Jung, Nathan 83.36
Jurado, Katy 5.41, 43.242, 106.2, 130.22, 165.9
Justason, David 67.15
Justice, Katherine 9.3, 12.27, 65.498, 65.525, 65.551, 65.552, 65.553, 65.574, 76.20, 84.36, 161.184
Justine, William 169.108
Jutner, Shelly 176.1

Kaase, Walter 65.636
Kabott, Frankie 12.67, 41.81
Kadler, Karen 27.12, 133.14
Kahn, Sajid 12.105
Kakoano, Kim 11.1
Kalish, Leah 163.45, 163.52, 163.53
Kallman, Dick 25.63, 152.36, 152.51
Kalos, Lori Ann 177.12
Kamekona, Danny 163.3
Kamel, Stanley 120.9
Kamen, Milt 24.13
Kamm, Kris 59.5, 120.11
Kane, Carole 161.116, 161.128
Kane, Eddy 169.19
Kane, George 162.201
Kane, Ken 70.39, 70.49
Kane, Margo 67.7, 67.16
Kane, Patti 34.35
Kane, Sid 112.21
Kanet, Margo 67.8
Kansas 5, 8, 65, 126
Kansas Territory 132
Karath, Frances 3.55, 23.25, 135.67, 135.69
Karath, Jimmy 57.11, 108.35
Kardell, Lili 6.52, 6.53, 126.51
Karen, Anna 65.421, 76.24, 77.20, 127.63, 162.195
Karen, James 14.433, 95.23
Kariem, Khadijah 163.63
Kark, Raymond 70.17
Karlan, Richard 22.8, 54.10, 57.68, 114.25, 122.31, 146.35, 169.77, 169.109
Karlan, Robert 57.12
Karlen, John 144.23
Karloff, Boris 170.30
Karnes, Robert 8.58, 8.82, 12.9, 12.32, 12.33, 12.39, 14.101, 14.166, 14.281, 20.66, 25.24, 30.12, 44.44, 63.14, 63.35, 65.70, 65.146, 65.179, 65.228, 65.233, 65.264, 65.478, 65.485, 65.502, 66.4, 66.49, 66.56, 66.137, 66.145, 66.159, 82.13, 83.17, 103.38, 117.27, 126.26, 145.12, 152.17, 148.182, 158.72, 161.109, 161.160, 178.2
Karns, Todd 97.109, 141.1
Karpf, Jason 14.407
Karr, Graig 141.46
Karras, Alex 26, 41.149
Karsian, Tara 163.67
Kartalian, Buck 70.1, 70.2, 70.6, 70.9, 70.19, 70.20, 17.93
Kasday, David 57.5
Kashfi, Anna 21.43, 44.25
Kastner, Peter 30.7
Kasznar, Kurt 106.7, 174.4
Katch, Kurt 3.82
Katcher, Aram 41.142
Katt, William 83.16
Kattrell, Kaye 48.39
Kaufman, Davis 53.29
Kavadas, Andrew 67.3
Kay, Beatrice 4.9, 14.71, 130.168
Kay, Bruce 141.50
Kay, Mary Ellen 6.48, 6.57. 31.10, 97.196, 97.221
Kay, Milano 141.47
Kaye, Bruce 43.102
Kaye, Celia 76.25, 96.3, 162.269
Kaye, Mary Ellen 135.40
Kazann, Zitto 7.3
Keach, James 83.18, 123.4
Keach, Stacy 27.80, 34.8, 44.21, 97.160, 97.161, 97.168, 105.4, 105.61, 140.38, 162.163
Keach, Stacy, Sr. 14.422, 25.13, 25.15, 48.97, 177.52
Keale, Moe 11
Kean, Jane 120.27, 120.28
Keane, Charles 129.57, 129.63
Keane, Edward 32.29, 32.35
Keane, Kerrie 83.63
Keane, Robert Emmett 97.12
Kearney, Carolyn 14.128, 22.1, 22.21, 51.10, 55.9, 142.33, 161.7, 162.214, 164.88, 178.54
Kearns, Joe 65.112

Keast, Paul 3.43, 3.66, 31.24, 35.26, 97.143, 97.154, 97.159, 97.175, 129.45, 145.12, 146.23, 148.41, 152.72, 166.17
Keats, Norman 97.150
Kee, John 60.22
Keefer, Don 5.10, 14.400, 30.15, 39.17, 49.5, 63.19, 65.68, 65.212, 65.257, 65.300, 65.371, 65.382, 65.423, 65.520, 65.593, 66.4, 66.52, 66.124, 7.181, 74.30, 76.30, 83.45, 83.56, 83.57, 83.58, 83.59, 98.10, 112.7, 116.10, 126.35, 161.116, 161.192, 162.98, 166.7
Keegan, Colleen 163.38
Keel, Howard 43.263, 123.5, 148.166, 164.43, 178.42
Keel, Michael 172.5
Keen, Noah 12.16, 12.97, 14.263, 14.297, 51.5, 51.30, 66.161, 66.167, 71.23, 101.1, 144.24, 161.14, 161.136, 161.162, 168.22
Keene, Dick 130.59
Keene, Mike 21.26, 21.41, 25.69, 93.159, 162.90
Keene, Richard 167.16
Keene, Robert 65.9
Keene, Tom 80.15
Keene, Valley 80.36
Keene, William 14.103, 14.325, 25.49, 65.97, 93.184, 141.52, 148.102, 169.113
Keener, Hazel 73.36, 80.5
Keenleyside, Eric 67.1, 67.2
Keep, Michael 14.139, 14.321, 14.324, 17.3, 17.25, 17.26, 21.46, 37.9, 41.44, 43.265, 43, 295, 43.300, 43.318, 43.375, 43.431, 43.432, 65.270, 65.360, 66.209, 71.28, 72.44, 71.72, 71.76, 71.96, 86.52, 126.161, 157.7, 162.126, 178.125
Kehler, Jack 120.52
Keim, Betty Lou 44, 131.24
Keith, Brian 26, 28, 55.2, 59.4, 75.4, 75.5, 85.9, 113, 117.29, 117.40, 126.21, 128.12, 161.16, 162.217, 162.231, 163.76, 165, 177.34, 178.84
Keith, Byron 3.42, 21.52, 161.127
Keith, Ian 3.36
Keith, Richard 43.95, 65.42, 178.36
Keith, Robert 1.15, 48.22, 57.43, 120.6, 120.6
Keith, Sherwood 66.106
Kelamis, Peter 67.5
Kellard, Bob 97.21, 97.25, 97.27, 97.40, 97.66, 97.72
Kellaway, Cecil 79.10, 126.76
Kelle, Chane 162.205
Kellerman, Sally 14.235, 14.355, 26, 27.97, 49.5, 92.23, 101.17
Kellett, Pete 17.5, 17.11, 65.418, 65.423, 65.428, 65.467, 65.481, 65.492, 65.504, 65.507, 65.548, 161.203, 169.67
Kelley, Barry 8.98, 14.107, 21.15, 21.27, 27.57, 27.103, 39.17, 43.316, 52.1, 65.87, 66.131, 66.144, 66.206, 85.83, 86.30, 89.14, 89.120, 97.139, 105.39, 113.7, 113.8, 125.15, 148.28, 148.90, 151.12, 161.70, 161.90, 164.57, 164.68
Kelley, DeForest 8.97, 13.28, 14.69, 14.112, 14.219, 14.220, 15.14, 37.1, 39.13, 43.237, 43.266, 43.346, 44.64, 65.23, 66.208, 85.103, 86.29, 89.60, 89.96, 97.4, 97.27, 97.117, 101.23, 114.19, 126.7, 131.44, 133.8, 142.17, 142.29, 148.142, 156.9, 156.29, 156.57, 156.69, 156.70, 158.54, 159.6, 161.16, 161.45, 164.24, 164.42, 178.7, 178.22, 178.56, 178.64, 178.114
Kellin, Mike 13.28, 65.422, 66.52, 66.137, 66.145, 66.167, 117.46, 126.179, 130.54
Kellogg, John 5.9, 5.37, 5.47, 13.41, 14.140, 14.158, 14.173, 14.272, 14.306, 39.4, 41.52, 41.149, 65.259, 65.314, 65.395, 65.396, 65.454, 65.486, 84.6, 86.18, 89.104, 89.126, 97.12, 105.99, 126.133, 142.3, 142.33, 144.8, 150.12, 161.72, 161.81, 161.190, 170.78
Kellogg, Ray 8.5, 8.58, 25.7, 44.71, 84.7, 84.16, 84.43, 86.21, 88.23, 93.31, 93.41, 93.57, 93.166, 93.198, 130.157, 133.3, 149.1, 162.19, 170.11

Kellogg, Roy 57.109, 93.28
Kelly, Barbara 152.78
Kelly, Barry 21.21, 43.283
Kelly, Bebe 41.22, 43.338, 75.3
Kelly, Carol 44.15, 146.8
Kelly, Christopher Keene 48.4, 48.28
Kelly, Claire 3.123, 114.26, 152.71
Kelly, Don 13.19, 20.61, 43.72, 54.22, 54.25, 89.4, 89.27, 105.21, 129.76, 148.88, 152.16
Kelly, Jack 5.23, 19.17, 54.26, 54.29, 54.30, 59.4, 65.78, 71.8, 76.43, 86.28, 86.51, 105, 145.26, 162.241, 175.1
Kelly, Karolee 32.115
Kelly, Kitty 14.143
Kelly, Larry 156.4
Kelly, Patsy 14.285, 85.18, 158.69, 170.32, 170.56
Kelly, Sean 14.418, 37, 84.37, 96.40
Kelly, Tom 36.16, 36.17
Kelly, Walter 158.17, 158.18
Kelman, Peter 96.111
Kelman, Rickey 22.13, 22.19, 22.39, 65.259, 103.38
Kelman, Sandy 22.19, 22.39
Kelman, Terry 141.56, 141.57, 141.58, 162.57, 162.69
Kelsay, Joe 158.24
Kelsey, Fred 169.27, 169.38, 169.47, 169.70
Kelsey, Joe 147.48
Kelsey, Tamsin 67.6
Kelton, Richard 24.10, 37.3, 65.521, 65.522, 65.545, 65.567, 65.579, 75.21, 83.44, 109.4
Kelton, Roy 7.5
Kemmer, Ed 4.26, 21.6, 27.63, 27.64, 34.60, 43.228, 65.111, 74.16, 85.28, 105.13, 105.59, 119.5, 126.106, 126.159, 127.35, 127.39, 127.75, 140.14, 142.37, 146.23, 146.24, 148.117, 155.37, 156.43, 161.23, 164.21, 164.66
Kemmerling, Warren 14.115, 14.257, 14.339, 14.417, 24.10, 41.112, 46.3, 65.231, 65. 237, 65.422, 65.551, 65.552, 65.553, 65.597, 71.90, 75.7, 75.11, 75.12, 75.15, 85.82, 86.25, 86.34, 89.92, 89.152, 107.11, 140.33, 148.187, 159.7, 161.10, 161.218
Kemp, Dan 5.3, 14.336, 14.381, 65.527, 71.89, 71.67
Kemp, Sally 14.428, 65.588, 65.589
Kemper, Doris 162.199
Kemper, Kay Ann 107.25
Kendall, Arthur 44.44
Kendall, Lee 173.32, 173.34
Kendall, Tom 120.31
Kendis, William 65.95, 102.36, 130.109
Kendrick, Hank 94.1
Kendrick, Henry Max 177.4
Kenneally, Phil 14.232, 14.422, 24.23
Kenneally, Robert W. 96.87, 96.88, 164.75, 164.92
Kennedy, Adam 25, 55.16, 65.8, 65.189, 178.31
Kennedy, Arthur 178.78
Kennedy, Bill 23.3, 32.14, 32.20, 32.23, 32.24, 32.106, 32.113, 43.38, 43.39, 60.25, 60.26, 60.32, 60.34, 97.21, 97.44, 97.59, 97.148, 97.154, 124.2, 124.5, 141.26, 145.17
Kennedy, Dennis 28
Kennedy, Don 6.24, 8.38, 8.44, 25.53, 39.16, 43.31, 54.24, 70.4, 73.33, 85.40, 85.107, 85.109, 93.95, 93.166, 105.72, 105.115, 108.29, 129.48, 130.2, 142.2, 145.21, 145.33, 147.35, 148.65, 149.12, 149.52, 151.18, 155.56, 164.66, 170.14, 178.14
Kennedy, Douglas 6.44, 6.46, 8.16, 12.2, 12.45, 12.61, 14.215, 14.246, 14.270, 14.298, 21.4, 24.6, 27.34, 29.7, 34.36, 44.39, 65.190, 65.195, 65.409, 66.102, 73.30, 76.20, 77.24, 78.38, 85.11, 92.10, 92.11, 93.150, 97.41, 97.82, 97.86, 97.101, 97.136, 97.161, 105.22, 105.63, 114.11, 122.28, 126.25, 129.55, 129.71, 130.68, 131.28,

133.2, 43, 145.18, 146.57, 148.14, 152.50, 152.60, 155.37, 161.108, 161.160, 162.30, 162.31, 162.72, 164.11, 179.73, 179.74, 179.75
Kennedy, George 8.101, 12.21, 14.61, 14.174, 27.62, 34.43, 41.40, 43.231, 59.3, 65.197, 65.217, 65.222, 65.567, 65.338, 65.343, 65.404, 66.120, 66.130, 66.153, 66.156, 66.160, 66.180, 66.220, 82.12, 85.22, 86.14, 92.20, 99.5, 101.12, 105.81, 117.28, 126.99, 131.35, 148.183, 149.46, 149.64, 157.9, 161.73, 161.99
Kennedy, Jo Nell 1.18
Kennedy, Kenneth 158.59
Kennedy, Lindsay 95, 95.23
Kennedy, Madge 93.174, 149.58
Kennedy, Mary Jo 70.22, 71.21, 84.31
Kennedy, Phyllis 97.39
Kennedy, Ron 93.52
Kennedy, Sarah 47.7
Kenneth, Arthur 109
Kenney, Jack 97.46
Kenney, June 14.61, 149.74
Kenny, J. Andrew 96.91
Kenny, Jason 177.37
Kenopka, Ken 65.287, 65.308
Kent, Carole 74.23
Kent, David 65.215, 144.23, 149.30
Kent, Don 43.71, 138.29, 138.45
Kent, Eleanor 54.17
Kent, Larry 126.84, 126.113
Kent, Marshall 96.58, 105.43
Kent, Paul 5.3
Kent, Paula 169.76
Kent, Robert 97.34, 97.68
Kent, Sandra 65.576
Kentran, Sharon 170.65
Kenyon, Sandy 17.7, 4.176, 34.27, 64.4, 65.124, 65.222, 65.295, 65.376, 65.475, 66.104, 66.121, 66.226, 83.28, 101.17, 126.6, 130.56, 131.3, 131.36, 149.43, 157, 157.1, 161.182, 168.1, 170.4
Kercheval, Ken 163.10
Kern, Roger 176
Kerns, Hubie 25.24
Kerr, Billy 19.1
Kerr, Donald 82.5, 169.86, 169.88, 169.100
Kerr, John 5.50, 65.253, 71.9, 113.9, 126.53, 131.2, 161.18, 162.225
Kerr, Lorence 162.197
Kerr, Sondra 65.241, 92.23, 126.179
Kerrigan, J.M. 54.15, 160.18, 162.89
Kershaw, Doug 28
Kerwin, Brian 28
Kerwin, Lance 65.628, 96.3, 137.2
Ketchum, Cliff 65.195, 148.70
Kevin, James 65.105
Kevin, Sandy 14.145, 24.10, 24.14, 65.442, 65.443, 76.30
Keyes, Irwin 118.7
Keymas, George 3.50, 3.77, 3.81, 3.152, 3.161, 5.39, 13.20, 14.105, 14.234, 31.41, 34.25, 41.125, 43.186, 43.280, 47.14, 54.4, 65.221, 65.259, 65.305, 65.322, 65.401, 65.569, 65.602, 71.21, 73.36, 78.63, 79.34, 84.9, 84.33, 85.48, 85.63, 85.84, 86.8, 86.45, 88.29, 93.201, 93.211, 105.53, 119.5, 121.19, 126.76, 129.4, 129.31, 139.6, 140.37, 145.15, 147.51, 148.15, 148.64, 148.107, 148.185, 149.33, 152.63, 156.45, 158.39, 158.61, 158.62, 162.32, 162.170, 162.185, 162.196, 162.231, 162.254, 170.35, 170.53, 170.66, 178.90, 179.20, 179.21, 179.22
Keys, Alan 81.7
Keys, Robert 3.61, 65.58
Khan, Kubla 31.35
Khouth, Sam 100.5
Kidd, Jonathan 65.373, 98.8, 126.179, 146.33, 148.193, 176.1
Kidder, Margot 112
Kiehl, William 177.19

Personnel Index

Kiel, Richard 7, 41.142, 82.9, 107.26, 130.116, 170.3, 170.10, 170.20, 174.4
Kilburn, Glen 81.87, 138.16
Kiley, Richard 14.367, 65.518, 65.547, 65.566, 65.593, 65.637
Kilgas, Nancy 138.67, 148.70, 158.65
Killian, Victor 65.619
Killmond, Frank 43.144, 149.4
Kilmer, Dave 163.7
Kilmond, Frank 167.21
Kilpatrick, Lincoln 9.7
Kilpatrick, Patrick 48.90, 48.92, 48.93, 48.94, 91.8, 120.45, 163.22
Kim, Evan C. 83.53
Kimball, Anne 32.68, 32.76, 81.93, 81.99, 169.35
Kimbley, Bill 60.21
Kimbrough, Clint 76.20
Kimler, Kay 176.2
Kimmell, Leslie 78.28
King, Andrea 4.3, 4.37, 27.21, 105.51
King, Bennett 170.91
King, Brent 178.71
King, Brett 8.16, 8.77, 43.165, 65.27, 65.93, 65.282, 79.16, 79.28, 82.11, 85.118, 89.27, 93.121, 93.207, 135.7, 135.9, 145.4, 155.1, 162.174, 162.178, 162.237, 173.30, 178.121
King, Chris 66.210
King, Christopher 117.49, 161.16
King, Evelyn 71.1
King, Fred 155.16
King, Jean Paul 8.16, 8.62
King, Kip 130.20
King, Megan 65.223
King, Michael 65.223
King, Patricia 164.77
King, Paul 170.17
King, Peggy 105.53
King, Rip 65.223
King, Robert 99.9
King, Stacy 168.12
King, Walter Woolf 12.10, 12.37, 57.22, 161.78, 161.79, 162.263, 170.1
King, Wright 15.3, 21.55, 27.31, 27.50, 64.4, 65.86, 65.170, 65.223, 65.233, 65.278, 65.324, 65.384, 66.16, 66.68, 66.117, 66.150, 66.168, 79.28, 84.22, 105.8, 116.16, 117.16, 117.35, 126.151, 127.11, 146.40, 148.175, 152.10, 155.49, 164, 164.49
King, Zalman 14.223, 30.9, 41.150, 65.381, 65.407, 65.412, 65.427, 65.450, 92.8, 98.16
Kingsford, Guy 138.58
Kingsley, Martin 65.19
Kingston, Lenore 162.165
Kingston, Ralph 80.3, 80.14, 80.17, 80.19, 80.24, 80.26, 80.29, 80.30, 80.32, 80.35
Kinkade, Brendan 91.7
Kino, Lloyd 83.54
Kino, Robert 85.64, 162.48, 164.62
Kinsella, Walter 142.35, 149.46
Kinskey, Leonid 4.34, 66.175
Kinsolving, Lee 13.13, 65.340, 66.72, 130.39, 178.145
Kirby, Bruce 14.305, 14.349
Kirgo, George 161.94
Kirk, Lisa 142.14
Kirk, Phyllis 178.110
Kirk, Tommy 25.11, 54.15, 65.40
Kirke, Donald 105.1, 105.17
Kirkpatrick, Jess 17.16, 57.109, 65.46, 65.52, 65.79, 65.107, 65.261, 65.313, 76.47, 88.20, 88.24, 162.151, 178.40, 178.59
Kirkwood, James 32.40, 32.46, 32.50, 97.52, 124.51, 130.60, 135.18, 135.30
Kirkwood, James, Jr. 89.18
Kirzinger, Ken 67.12
Kizzier, Heath 48.22
Kleeb, Helen 54.12, 65.38, 65.110, 65.346, 65.566, 70.25, 71.34, 95.12, 133.28, 156.70, 164.38

Klein, Ricky 129.18, 129.50, 148.49, 162.59
Klemperer, Werner 4.15, 39.12, 65.100, 66.85, 66.154, 105.14, 119.9, 126.51
Kline, James 85.122
Kline, Robert 126.126
Klugman, Jack 65.96, 161.47
Klyn, Vincent 1.10
Knapp, Robert 13.36, 14.3, 20.45, 27.108, 43.165, 65.250, 65.301, 65.306, 65.424, 65.479, 65.516, 65.532, 73.28, 73.37, 85.14, 85.118, 130.64, 135.86, 135.90, 135.92, 145.36
Knapp, Wilfred 65.11, 65.17
Knell, David 10.8, 19, 120.28
Kneuer, Cameo 1.3, 1.13
Knight, Charlotte 178.134
Knight, Christopher 65.473
Knight, Don 12.87, 12.108, 14.325, 14.398, 14.426, 53.11, 83.12, 84.51, 96.3, 161.187, 161.223
Knight, Ed 61.4
Knight, Edward 170.66
Knight, Fuzzy 60.23, 60.24, 60.25, 60.26, 89.101, 117.10, 149.69, 169.79, 169.82
Knight, Gladys 45.1
Knight, Sandra 85.40, 85.69, 102.26, 127.57, 148.77, 149.68, 150.1
Knight, Shirley 5.45, 21.9, 21.45, 22, 89.110, 105.99, 109.13, 126.21, 129.58, 152.45, 152.46, 161.15, 161.81
Knight, Ted 14.222, 65.153, 89.58, 161.4, 161.31, 170.86
Knobeloch, Jim 48
Knoll, R.J. 48.70
Knott, Robert 177.45, 177.52
Knowles, Patric 66.90, 66.129, 66.219, 82.16, 105.11, 105.73, 113.6, 162.62, 166.6
Knox, Mickey 97.148
Knox, Ronnie 51.19
Knudsen, Peggy 8.15, 8.87, 93.94, 155.43
Knudson, Barbara 6.50, 41.48, 43.30, 57.64, 60.80, 73.25, 97.183, 97.193, 124.15, 138.65, 141.53
Knudson, Harlan 91.6
Kobayashi, Tsuruko 55.18
Kobe, Gail 25.54, 27.20, 27.52, 30.11, 41.118, 41.154, 51.16, 65.103, 65.367, 65.422, 65.486, 66.222, 85.103, 85.111, 88.2, 101.21, 105.121, 126.109, 126.133, 127.34, 127.66, 146.24, 148.115, 155.32, 156.1, 156.23, 156.24, 156.25, 156.44, 161.40, 162.67, 178.64
Kober, Jeff 90.16, 163.15, 163.16
Kobi, Michi 25.6, 25.25, 25.60
Koch, Geoff 163.50
Koenig, Walter 106.7
Kohler, Don 138.14
Kohler, Fred 31.40, 129.33, 152.57, 169.13, 169.15, 169.107
Kohler, Fred, Jr. 32.2, 32.4, 32.5, 32.6, 32.9, 32.10, 32.11, 32.12, 32.13, 80.30, 80.39, 97.5, 158.31, 169.28
Kohn, Stanley 149.40
Kohner, Susan 126.157, 151.4, 162.9
Komack, Jimmie 162.14
Komant, Carolyn 89.115, 105.97
Konrad, Dorothy 14.341, 65.307, 89.118, 96.98
Koock, Guich 28.8
Koons, Robert 65.636
Kooy, Pete 141.18
Kopcha, Michael 20.54
Kopenhafer, Marta 170.60
Korens, Angela 52.24
Korita, Ana 65.573
Korman, Harvey 51.10, 52.37, 170.81
Korn, Iris 96.118
Korvin, Charles 179.16, 179.17, 179.18, 179.19, 179.20, 179.21, 179.22, 179.27, 179.28, 179.29, 179.30, 179.35, 179.36, 179.37, 179.38, 179.39
Kosh, Pamela 48.23, 48.27

Kosleck, Martin 130.169, 170.100
Koslo, Paul 9.1, 19.10, 59.2, 65.621, 75.19
Kosslyn, Jack 126.124
Kosterman, Mitch 67.3
Kotto, Yaphet 12.41, 12.75, 14.305, 35.3, 41.120, 41.130, 43.372, 45.1, 65.525, 71.37
Koufax, Sandy 34.51
Kovack, Jimmie 178.24
Kovacs, Ernie 140.2
Kovacs, Jonathan Hall 95.6, 95.7, 95.21
Kove, Martin 59.5, 65.621, 163.46
Kowal, Jon 65.384, 65.449, 65.575, 76.2
Kowal, Mitchell 32.119, 32.123, 97.59, 103.30, 105.2, 129.31, 133.9, 145.23
Kozak, Heidi 48.1, 48.5, 48.17
Kraft, Scott 90.16, 177.18
Kramer, Alfred 105.11
Kramer, Allen 127.5, 127.53
Kramer, Bert 96.104, 120.2, 137
Kramer, Stepfanie 33
Krangle, Iris 68.10, 68.35
Krause, Brian 163.51
Kray, Walter 41.61, 141.55, 159.26
Kreig, Frank 89.89
Krest, Pat 85.94
Kreuger, Kurt 170.66
Krieg, Frank 164.57
Krieger, Lee 12.40, 12.51, 65.353, 65.441
Kriesa, Christopher 48.5, 48.8, 48.12
Kristen, Linda 96.64
Kristin, Marta 162.274
Kroeger, Berry 14.65, 21.22, 41.85, 41.101, 130.98, 149.51
Kroeger, Lee 161.173, 161.198
Krohn, Don 85.123
Krone, Fred 23.9, 23.37, 23.38, 71.42, 79.25, 86.47, 93.201, 124.53, 124.55, 124.58, 124.64, 124.65, 124.71, 124.72, 124.73, 124.74, 124.77, 141.22, 141.43, 152.1, 178.120, 178.122
Kronen, Ben 118.8
Kross, Lee 178.123
Kruger, Fred 44.48, 105.49, 129.4
Kruger, Otto 14.117, 55.3, 127.12
Krugman, Lou 3.136, 52.33, 65.109, 65.150, 66.90, 93.153, 97.170, 97.175, 98.1, 102.29, 105.42, 121.20, 129.22, 159.12, 170.50, 170.91, 178.23, 179.76
Kruschen, Jack 8.34, 14.231, 14.262, 14.313, 41.138, 43.181, 65.51, 88.12, 95.11, 94.37, 96.163, 130.17, 130.25, 130.77, 130.82, 133.36, 146.29, 156.47, 164.28, 164.42, 165.11
Kruse, William 93.193
Kuenstle, Charles 65.318, 65.407, 65.416, 65.439, 65.445, 65.468, 65.478, 65.490, 65.501, 65.540, 65.561, 66.192, 139.4
Kulik, Jennifer 24.24
Kulky, Henry 14.178, 97.141, 141.55, 152.37, 169.43, 169.56, 169.86
Kuluva, Will 14.110, 43.339, 43.342, 84.31, 86.34, 162.256, 170.42
Kunze, Steve 96.16
Kupcinet, Karyn 168.16
Kuperman, Alvin 96.103
Kurtzman, Katy 75.23, 96.64, 96.82
Kusatsu, Clyde 1.19, 83.9, 83.36, 83.40, 83.53
Kush, Tanya 177.13, 177.48
Kushida, Beverly 83.18
Kuter, Kay E. 36.14, 65.569, 65.604, 78.30, 78.66, 83.40, 83.61, 86.29, 119.12, 128.2, 130.108, 131.11, 145.30, 148.96, 149.45, 152.48, 159.36, 161.120, 170.14, 179.76
Kwan, Nancy 83.38, 83.39

LaBelle, Yvan 67.20
Laborteaux, Matthew 96, 96.51, 96.52, 96.82, 120.41

Personnel Index

Laborteaux, Patrick 96, 96.71, 96.138, 120.34, 120.40, 120.41
La Cava, Joseph 179.51
Lacher, Taylor 24, 50.1, 53.10, 75.18, 95.9, 109, 109.1
Lachman, Stanley 43.93, 43.94
Lackteen, Frank 3.145, 73.22, 135.35, 169.110
Lacy, Tom 65.632
Ladd, David 14.30, 65.385, 162.182, 178.136
Ladd, Diana 41.46, 12.48, 48.1, 48.27, 65.342, 65.394, 65.434, 139.1, 168.15
LaDue, Lyzanne 98.3
Lafferty, Marcy 7.5, 11.5
LaFleur, Art 19.11, 177.59
La Franchise, Charles 130.146
Lagle, David 177.63
Laidlaw, Ethan 93.198, 169.37
Lail, Leah 91.3
Lain, Jewell 152.76
Laine, Frankie 126.60
Laird, Effie 31.35, 60.64, 141.30, 141.32, 169.44
Laird, Monte 5.36, 5.40, 5.48
Laire, Judson 144.3
Lake, Florence 35.8, 35.29, 35.36, 97.213, 97.216, 97.219, 108.29, 112.1, 112.21, 169.102
Lake, Janet 14.74, 35.64, 66.158, 93.215, 105.88, 105.118, 146.64
Lake, Jim 141.44, 152.17
Lally, William 31.12, 34.36
Lamarr, Hedy 178.35
Lamas, Fernando 5.7, 71.15, 72.10, 75.27, 86.1, 86.25, 161.91, 178.81, 178.108
Lamb, Gil 65.287, 121.2, 121.7, 170.78
Lambert, Abbi 163.45
Lambert, Douglas 12.65, 4.92, 66.187, 126.78, 126.127, 162.192
Lambert, George 65.256
Lambert, Greta 177.59
Lambert, Jack 3.76, 8.21, 8.91, 14.33, 17.24, 25.56, 25.66, 34.36, 41.55, 41.75, 41.76, 41.97, 43.328, 43.360, 44.3, 55.10, 56.19, 65.152, 65.224, 65.285, 65.305, 65.471, 65.483, 65.508, 66.109, 89.11, 98.14, 130.49, 131, 146.30, 148.66, 152.41, 161.96, 162.10, 162.48, 162.96, 162.232
Lambert, Jane 83.17
Lambert, Lee 65.468
Lambert, Lee Jay 14.334. 14.365, 41.126
Lambert, Paul 8.22, 8.52, 8.76, 12.88, 12.106, 14.314, 25.38, 64.7, 65.41, 65.57, 70.37, 76.32, 126.200, 155.27, 170.58
Lambert, Tex 66.117
Lambie, Joe 96.162
Lamey, Tommy 171
Lamont, Adele 149.3
Lamont, Duncan 93.168, 152.50, 152.51, 152.52, 152.59, 152.60, 152.61, 152.62, 152.73
Lamphier, James 43.283, 93.59
Lampkin, Charles 36.12, 53.21
Lampshire, Arlyne 130.116
Lamson, Rick 14.345
Lancaster, James 177.26
Lancaster, Stuart 17.39
Land, Charles 12.27
Landa, Miguel 3.157, 8.60, 20.31, 34.53, 65.315, 65.316, 71.57, 71.69, 78.53, 105.10, 131.19, 168.26
Landau, Martin 12.11, 14.59, 17.34, 65.119, 65.411, 79.33, 83.63, 89.5, 101.10, 105.32, 117.21, 126.18, 130.111, 148.85, 149.22, 149.72, 150.6, 157.10, 162.121, 164.55, 170.11
Lander, Stephen 146.68
Landers, Audrey 175.4
Landers, Harry 13.39, 66.14, 76.16, 79.14, 88.19, 135.92, 164.81
Landers, Muriel 60.86, 124.52, 125.16
Landfield, Jerome 31.34
Landin, Richard 175.9
Landis, Monte 71.76

Landkford, Kim 120.49
Lando, Brian 120
Lando, Joe 48
Landon, Leslie 95, 95.23, 95.24, 96.116
Landon, Michael 14, 27.49, 56.15, 78.4, 78.15, 95.1, 95.22, 95.23, 96, 130.3, 130.40, 148.6, 148.10, 148.25, 152.8, 155.40, 155.47, 156.25, 156.45, 164.1, 164.27, 178.42, 178.73
Landon, Michael, Jr. 14.431, 14.432, 14.433
Landon, Sue Ane 170.16
Lane, Abbe 52.22
Lane, Allan 14.47, 34.52, 65.108, 65.204, 65.227, 148.47, 153.12, 162.29
Lane, Calvin 163.49
Lane, Charles 52.38, 89.149, 95.3, 151.16, 151.22
Lane, Elizabeth 5.26
Lane, Jocelyn 170.37
Lane, Kent 109.10
Lane, Michael 17.19, 41.130, 65.569, 74.13, 102.16, 103.51, 105.9, 105.47, 133.39, 146.26, 169.110
Lane, Randy 41.128
Lane, Robert Bruce 5.14
Lane, Rusty 4.17, 14.74, 14.272, 17.37, 21.30, 22.28, 43.266, 65.378, 65.387, 65.518, 65.562, 65.598, 66.40, 129.44, 148.2, 150.11, 151.4, 152.34, 161.24, 161.176, 162.68, 162.213, 164.9, 178.7
Lane, Sara 161
Lane, Scott 162.246
Laneuville, Eric 112.14
Lang, Barbara 43.50, 43.71, 43.73, 89, 105.33
Lang, Doreen 47.10, 65.584, 83.29, 126.42
Lang, Jack 158.12
Lang, Judy 161.186, 170.50
Lang, Katherine Kelly 100.21
Lang, Mark 177.43
Lang, Perry 75.20
Langan, Glenn 72.7, 72.11
Langdon, Sue Ane 14.73, 14.193, 65.252, 117.15, 140.30, 148.150
Langton, Paul 8.73, 20.43, 20.51, 27.86, 65.120, 65.171, 65.229, 88.29, 89.9, 97.131, 97.181, 116.3, 126.52, 133.32, 148.120, 157.21, 161.19, 162.41, 162.182, 178.80
Langtry, Hugh 41.92, 103.48
Lanin, Jay 14.132, 65.274, 65.337, 117.49, 168.19
Lannom, Les 26, 28.8, 83.7
Lannon, Jimmy 7.10.
Lanphier, James 3.113, 44.24, 170.18, 170.104
Lansing, John 163.53
Lansing, Joi 8.39, 82, 105.27, 126.146, 146.10, 169.72
Lansing, Robert 14.58, 14.348, 14.417, 17.40, 17.41, 17.42, 30.16, 41.44, 65.384, 65.490, 71.13, 98.19, 107.24, 117.12, 117.13, 149.27, 151.6, 161.42, 161.92, 161.163, 162.244
Lao, Kenny 120.13, 120.9
Lapp, Richard 14.306, 30.6, 65.510, 65.521, 65.522, 71.63, 76.2
Lara, Joe 65.637
Larch, John 5.5, 8.29, 11.2, 13.9, 14.3, 20.28, 41.99, 44.46, 65.7, 65.89, 65.154, 65.166, 65.181, 65.227, 65.238, 66.43, 66.121, 77.2, 79.18, 85.17, 85.81, 88.15, 96.138, 106.1, 117.6, 126.1, 126.123, 129.6, 129.21, 129.29, 129.43, 130.91, 131.1, 133.23, 144.14, 148.101, 148.177, 152.1, 161.2, 161.170,161.220, 162.33, 162.56, 162.121, 162.177, 164.14, 167.5, 173.34, 178.6, 178.27, 178.136
Largay, Raymond 97.33, 97.83
Larkin, Audrey 14.225
Larkin, John 14.115, 65.284, 162.251
Larkin, Sheila 14.279, 65.490, 65.573, 161.191
La Rocca, Charles 165.13
La Roche, Mary 13.15, 65.300, 65.309, 77.19, 102.6, 148.104, 148.128, 161.51, 162.183, 173.14, 178.108
Larrain, Michael 65.501, 161.225

Larsen, Keith 18, 114, 155.79, 167.17
Larson, Christine 32.3, 32.8, 32.85, 32.92, 97.52, 97.70, 169.9
Larson, Darrell 65.570, 90.16, 177.46
Larson, Ham 96.149
Larson, Joanie 112.6
Larson, Wolf 1.17
LaRue, Ashley 170.65
LaRue, Bart 14.334, 24.19, 70.51, 170.83
LaRue, Jack 27.41, 56.22, 155.58
LaRue, Lash 80.20, 80.23, 80.24, 80.25, 80.29, 80.30, 80.39, 87, 93, 93.156, 93.157, 93.165, 93.174, 93.179, 93.181, 93.188, 158.29
LaRue, Walt 71.14
LaRusso, Adrianna 26
Lascoe, Henry 14.7, 102.2, 146.44, 146.46
Lasell, John 65.236, 126.197, 148.149, 162.137, 162.147
La Shelle, Happy 53.24
Lashly, James 177.36
Lasky, Gil 43.136
Lassell, Charles L.158.45
Lassell, John 149.32
Lasswell, Tod 142.30, 158.71
La Starza, Roland 170.56, 170.64
Latham, Louise 14.247, 14.383, 65.474, 65.482, 65.494, 65.502, 65.520, 65.610, 69.5, 101.27, 137
Latimer, Cherie 14.296, 63.9
Lau, Wesley 12.9, 13.6, 13.39, 14.23, 14.226, 65.134, 65.168, 65.197, 66.72, 79.23, 86.17, 86.46, 88.26, 89.8, 93.198, 122.7, 148.113, 148.134, 149.35, 161.107, 161.136, 161.169, 162.139
Laughlin, Kim 162.73
Laughlin, Tom 44.6, 148.99, 162.10
Laughton, Charles 162.117
Launer, S. John 14.11, 14.103, 24.14, 65.17, 65.89, 65.309, 66.34, 102.36, 129.71, 144.14, 152.8, 178.44
Lauren, Lalita 177.57
Lauren, Tammy 95.4, 118.9
Lauter, Ed 75.11, 75.15, 75.16, 111.2
Lauter, Harry 2.12, 5.19, 6.6, 6.8, 6.25, 6.26, 6.27, 6.39, 6.49, 6.54, 6.55, 6.63, 6.65, 6.78, 8.61, 12.103, 14.77, 17.25, 17.26, 23.1, 23.6, 23.12, 23.19, 23.26, 23.41, 23.42, 24.16, 24.17, 27.65, 30.9, 30.23, 34.32, 34.51, 35.15, 35.26, 43.135, 43.136, 43.186, 43.396, 44.55, 57.14, 57.100, 60.7, 60.8, 60.19, 60.32, 60.34, 60.44, 60.46, 60.53, 60.60, 60.67, 60.71, 60.73, 60.76, 60.79, 60.83, 63.30, 63.43, 63.44, 65.174, 65.188, 65.199, 65.314, 65.351, 65.375, 65.453, 65.470, 66.130, 71.91, 73.21, 77.14, 78.34, 81.36, 81.68, 82.8, 85.8, 85.18, 85.53, 85.70, 85.74, 85.91, 85.116, 89.122, 93.19, 97.5, 97.26, 97.55, 97.67, 97.129, 97.154, 97.174, 97.181, 97.188, 97.191, 97.198, 105.115, 114.1, 124.21, 124.22, 124.30, 124.36, 124.46, 124.47, 124.48, 124.58, 124.61, 124.67, 124.71, 126.4, 126.30, 126.80, 126.94, 126.113, 126.124, 126.138, 126.153, 126.161, 126.199, 130.164, 131.29, 133.30, 135.21, 135.62, 135.64, 138.72, 142.11, 142.20, 142.30, 147, 148.191, 151.9, 152.34, 155.14, 161.80, 161.141, 161.153, 161.188, 162.138, 167.7, 169.39, 169.81, 169.98, 170.73, 178.8, 178.22, 178.30, 178.59, 178.64
La Varre, Robert 129.38, 138.62, 141.57, 156.66
Laverone, Jerry 170.76
Lawford, Peter 106.22, 170.33
Lawless, Patrick 25.52, 97.218, 138.67
Lawrence, Anthony 162.29
Lawrence, Ashley 91.4
Lawrence, Barbara 8.74, 14.40, 27.15, 29.2, 78.65, 102.16, 131.8, 149.69, 156.41
Lawrence, Carol 83.44, 126.211, 162.230
Lawrence, Delphi 65.429, 170.35
Lawrence, Hugh 51.28

Personnel Index

Lawrence, Jodean 96.89, 96.90
Lawrence, Jody 127.36
Lawrence, John 86.30, 96.165, 116.13, 122.25
Lawrence, Marc 14.358, 21.37, 44.57, 89.97, 112.15, 130.8, 130.77, 162.40, 166.10, 178.112
Lawrence, Mary 114.12
Lawrence, Mitchell 3.38
Lawrence, Peter 70.30
Lawrence, Tony 43.79
Lawrence, Walter 149.5
Lawson, Carol 14.347, 14.370, 14.425
Lawson, Eric 120.14
Lawson, Linda 14.43, 14.197, 34.51, 66.86, 130.102, 142.21, 147.43, 148.139, 155.70, 161.110, 162.120
Lawson, Louise 86.35, 170.7, 170.75
Lawton, Alma 138.52
Lawton, Don 138.52
Lawton, Donald 147.43
Layne, Shary 148.54
LaZarre, Jerry 44.76, 162.152
Lazer, Peter 131.13
Le, Chief Geronimo Kuth 71.49
Lea, Jennifer 34.47, 65.370, 66.113, 127.16, 130.68, 138.75, 148.63, 164.1, 167.6
Lea, Nicholas 100.13
Leabow, Ralph 162.223, 162.249, 162.268
Leach, Britt 176.2, 176.4
Leachman, Cloris 12.55, 55.5, 63.13, 65.47, 65.231, 84.19, 84.38, 85.90, 101.4, 117.7, 117.8, 126.47, 132.26, 144.13, 161.139, 161.196, 162.185, 164.78, 178.1, 178.21
Learned, Michael 65.590, 65.595, 65.596, 65.637
Leary, Nolan 57.15, 66.103, 73.15, 81.26, 85.87, 97.14, 135.19, 135.93, 156.29, 161.104, 164.25
Leary, Timothy 1.22
Lease, Rex 2.6, 77.5, 93.57, 93.73, 93.86, 93.118, 97.78, 135.54, 135.58, 158.55, 158.59, 169.23
Leavitt, Norman 3.37, 14.33, 14.47, 14.226, 14.267, 30.21, 41.27, 55.4, 63.15, 64.7, 85.50, 85.65, 85.74, 85.85, 85.95, 85.99, 85.105, 86.8, 93.204, 93.212, 126.41, 126.75, 126.83, 126.104, 126.153, 126.167, 130.103, 130.164, 135.42, 142.1, 142.31, 145.35, 148.152, 152.5, 152.31, 156.18, 156.22, 156.23, 156.24, 156.26, 156.28, 156.29, 156.34, 156.35, 156.36, 156.40, 156.42, 156.44, 156.46, 156.50, 156.53, 156.56, 156.59, 156.61, 156.62, 156.63, 156.64, 156.65, 156.69, 161.86, 161.155, 161.156, 162.57, 162.186, 162.232, 168.23
LeBaron, Bert 135.24, 135.58, 135.73
Lebeau, Mikey 65.640
LeBell, Gene 24.23
Lechner, Bill 141.29, 141.39
Leckner, Brian 14.432, 14.433
LeClair, Michael 26, 65.627, 96.54, 137.1, 137.2
Ledig, Howard 14.94, 34.48, 130.43, 164.73
Lee, Ann 105.100, 108.16
Lee, Anna 41.23, 65.451, 162.123
Lee, Anthony 48.82
Lee, Billy 23.31
Lee, Brandon 83.63
Lee, Bruce 70.25
Lee, Cajan 73.3, 73.38
Lee, Carl 7.4
Lee, Christopher 75.4
Lee, Debra 170.60
Lee, G.W. 177.2
Lee, Gary 120.2
Lee, Gracia 96.37
Lee, Guy 14.20, 14.210, 170.17
Lee, Jack 97.43
Lee, Jennifer Ann 83.49
Lee, Joanna 43.140
Lee, John G. 65.16
Lee, Johnny 5.3, 14.391, 78.16, 96.19
Lee, Joy 138.36
Lee, May 162.50
Lee, Michele 5.35, 5.36, 5.38

Lee, Robert L. 177.50
Lee, Ruby 144.1
Lee, Rudy 169.71
Lee, Ruta 4.11, 4.17, 14.125, 27.108, 34.66, 63.42, 65.115, 65.272, 85.66, 102.12, 105.14, 105.24, 105.52, 117.48, 126.124, 126.143, 127.33, 129.54, 140.35, 142.32, 142.38, 146.13, 151.13, 157.21, 161.58, 161.70, 162.70, 162.238, 170.5, 170.46, 178.144
Lee, Ruth 8.28, 25.57, 135.27, 135.51
Lee, Scott 35.10
Lee, Sheryl 48.31
Lee, Stephen 120.17, 120.18
Lee, Tommy 83.36, 83.53
Lee, Virginia 6.17, 6.18, 43.48, 42.103, 43.124
Lee, William 162.21
Lee-Sung, Richard 83.49
Leeds, Maureen 27.94, 79.29
Leeds, Peter 14.32, 14.289, 32.68, 32.72, 32.76, 52.50, 63.45, 66.97, 103.49, 107.3, 125.6, 126.163, 156.42, 156.44, 156.45, 156.52, 156.55, 156.56, 156.58, 156.59, 156.61, 156.62, 156.65, 156.40, 161.168, 162.108, 167.16, 168.9
Leeds, Sue-Ann 177.45
Lees, Paul 166.7
LeGault, Lance 7.4, 59.1, 65.613, 75.23, 120.16
Leger, Anthony 163.82
Lehman, John 138.28, 138.37
Lehman, Trent 65.497
Lehmann, Ted 50.9, 88.19, 169.102
Lehne, Fredric 75.20
Lehne, John 120.39
Lei, Linda 19.4
Leib, Robert P. 132.4
Leicester, William 4.33, 20.44, 89.68, 178.19, 178.29
Leigh, Carol 44.3, 78.24, 130.147
Leigh, Erin 66.164
Leigh, Janet 106.3
Leigh, Leatrice 8.79
Leigh, Nelson 14.239, 14.240, 32.4, 32.9, 32.12, 73.8, 169.48
Leighton, Linda 138.20, 148.73
Leland, Brad 163.18, 163.27, 177.7
Leland, David 22.31, 66.31, 129.63, 130.32, 162.44, 162.53
Lelliott, Jeremy 90.12
LeMaire, Jack 141.56
LeMat, Paul 99.1, 99.2, 99.3, 99.15, 100.1, 100.19
Lemmon, Jack 178.14
Lemmons, Kasi 163.13
LeMond, Don 144.22
Lenard, Mark 5.3, 30.23, 33, 65.456, 70, 76.30, 170.70
Lenehan, Nancy 120.17, 120.18
Lennert, Roy 39.13
Lennox, Doug 100.1
Lenz, Kay 65.605, 75.13, 75.14, 75.16, 109.5
Lenz, Richard 69
Leo, Melissa 177
Leon, Peggie 3.98
Leonard, David 60.84, 97.13, 97.77, 138.55, 141.14
Leonard, Maria 170.84
Leonard, Terry 170.75
Leong, Dalton 83.36
Leong, John 83.1
Leopold, Thomas 65.610
LePore, Richard 55.13, 161.121, 161.176
Le Ribeus, Rick 163.6
Lerigny, Mathew 99.15
Lerner, Fred 83.22, 83.30, 126.41
Lerner, Jeff 161.9
Le Roy, Gloria 48.89, 65.614, 65.615
Lesko, Jennifer 37.3
Leslie, Bethel 8.38, 14.88, 41.4, 43.180, 51.8, 55.1, 65.262, 65.353, 66.21, 71.51, 83.35, 98.17, 102.10, 102.35, 105.36, 126.97, 130.107, 131.10,

131.37, 140.34, 142.4, 152.31, 156.61, 161.24, 161.215, 162.102, 162.149, 162.278, 164.24, 170.97
Leslie, Edith 3.23, 35.9, 93.217, 105.25, 112.10
Leslie, John 17.6
Leslie, Nan 3.72, 3.84, 3.85, 6.27, 25, 31.30, 32.84, 32.91, 32.106, 32.113, 32.121, 57, 60.23, 60.25, 60.26, 60.86, 73.23, 81.50, 81.71, 81.73, 81.78, 97.14, 97.47, 97.68, 97.81, 97.110, 97.118, 97.143, 97.175, 124.58, 124.61, 131.30, 135.1, 149.41, 164.27, 167.7, 178.14
Leslie, William 3.53, 57.84, 167.22
Lesser, Len 7.3, 8.71, 14.358, 14.417, 61.4, 74.18, 86.26, 144.12, 151.10, 152.9, 157.8, 170.5
Lessing, Arnold 161.2, 161.3, 161.4
Lester, Bill 97.7
Lester, Buddy 5.25
Lester, Eleese 163.40
Lester, Jack 8.73, 14.38, 127.63, 130.87, 148.99
Lester, Ketty 70.40, 95, 96.76, 96.105, 96.106, 96.109, 96.111, 96.118, 96.145, 96.146, 96.156, 96.157, 96.173
Lester, Terry 7.1
Lester, Tom 96.168
Letscher, Matthew 48.35
Lettier, Anthony 65.378
Lettieri, Louis 3.61, 3.77, 3.156, 20.40, 20.41, 23.32, 31.10, 57.7, 78.37, 97.188, 124.51, 135.65, 135.68, 135.71, 147.36, 147.41, 158.22, 169.65, 169.100
Letuli, Fred 31.9
Leversee, Loretta 14.398, 41.163, 70.4
Levine, Harvey 170.28
Levitt, Herman 135.23
Levitt, Steve 53.8
Levy, Mark 12.27
Levy, Weaver 70.25, 138.36, 141.25
Lew, James 163.36
Lew, Jocelyne 83.36
Lewis, Al 10.5, 10.6
Lewis, Art 168.23
Lewis, Artie 102.24
Lewis, Cathy 43.279, 51.3, 52.30, 162.279
Lewis, David 14.280, 39.6, 76.33
Lewis, Derrick 71.16
Lewis, Don W. 120.2
Lewis, Forrest 34.42, 52.4, 78.66, 78.69, 82.2, 93.183, 102.24, 105.13, 105.82, 108.1, 156.33, 156.48, 158.45, 164.14, 164.49, 170.37, 172.5, 178.27
Lewis, Geoffrey 5.9, 5.27, 5.44, 14.363, 19.8, 24.3, 26, 59.5, 62, 65.576, 65.637, 83.10, 95.14, 96.54, 120.29, 163.27, 171.6
Lewis, George J. 2.3, 2.7, 3.69, 6.4, 6.12, 6.71, 6.74, 20.32, 23.6, 23.12, 23.35, 23.36, 41.14, 60.1, 60.3, 60.5, 60.15, 60.18, 60.27, 60.29, 60.38, 60.40, 60.80, 60.84, 86.22, 93.14, 93.44, 97.1, 97.2, 97.28, 97.31, 97.74, 97.189, 124.46, 124.47, 124.48, 124.49, 124.50, 124.76, 124.78, 135.10, 135.13, 135.28, 138.16, 169.13, 169.22, 169.32, 179
Lewis, Harrison 66.169, 66.184, 89.89, 89.100, 138.37, 141.36, 141.39
Lewis, Jean 6.41, 43.46, 80.1
Lewis, Judy 117
Lewis, Lorna 170.101
Lewis, Louise 97.203, 97.209
Lewis, Monica 7.12, 44.31, 85.55, 86.57, 119.16, 131.4, 148.70, 149.35, 149.66, 161.81, 161.175
Lewis, Robert 67.5, 67.19
Lewis, Robert Q. 17.8, 17.9, 17.10, 17.46
Lewis, Virginia 65.279
Libby, Brian 120.56
Libby, Fred 23.16, 35.2, 35.21, 97.58, 97.68, 97.71, 97.110, 97.118, 97.145, 97.164, 141.5, 169.3, 169.47, 169.72
Libertini, Richard 19.14, 19.15

Personnel Index

Lieb, Robert P. 5.31, 14.164, 14.284, 25.32, 43.270, 44.40, 52.22, 77.3, 148.132, 161.99, 161.113
Lilburn, James 43.44
Lime, Yvonne 167.13
Lincoln, Lar Park 118.8
Lincoln, Pamela 21.4, 66.79, 102.21
Lincoln, Scott 1.4
Lind, Brit 75.1, 75.3
Linder, Alfred 65.41
Lindfors, Viveca 14.201, 126.24
Lindgren, Orley 169.5
Lindheim, Richard 48.20
Lindsay, Dean 163.70
Lindsay, Margaret 22.4
Lindsey, George 41.1, 65.318, 65.349, 65.374, 65.403, 65.426, 65.561, 130.165
Lindsey, Margaret 121.24
Lindsly, Chuck 120.19
Lineback, Richard 120.24
Linkletter, Art 162.204, 178.138
Linkletter, Jack 178.138
Linn, Rex 1.16
Linville, Albert 65.133
Linville, Joanne 14.248, 51.6, 65.235, 65.274, 65.470, 66.122, 74.30, 84.34, 85.71, 109.7, 139.13
Linville, Lawrence 14.332, 70.41
Lippe, Jonathan 14.365, 30.9, 65.397, 65.409, 65.431, 65.466, 65.479, 65.490, 65.512, 65.547, 65.551, 65.552, 65.553, 65.569, 65.590, 65.609, 71.77, 71.92, 112.18, 132.3, 170.55
Lippert, Morris 130.14
Lipscomb, Dennis 48.49, 96.177
Lipton, Michael 22, 129.59, 164.73
Lipton, Peggy 132.29, 161.117
Lipton, Robert 161.224
List, Suzi 177.61
Lister, Chez 53, 96.165
Litel, John 14.5, 14.79, 17.2, 21.39, 27.57, 29.7, 34.19, 66.165, 93.174, 105.1, 105.36, 105.74, 126.72, 126.123, 129.39, 129.52, 129.65, 132.19, 142.2, 142.4, 142.8, 142.14, 142.15, 142.36, 146.6, 146.33, 156.22, 156.29, 161.85, 162.253, 164.13, 164.25, 164.66, 168.7, 178.74, 179.46, 179.47, 179.48, 179.52, 179.72, 179.73, 179.74, 179.75
Little, Mickey 6.28, 60.78, 124.50, 169.70
Little Sky, Dawn 65.227, 66.209
Little Sky, Eddie 17.13, 41.28, 41.140, 43.433, 50.8, 61.1, 61.2, 64.11, 65.100, 65.156, 65.265, 65.295, 65.455, 65.461, 65.499, 65.525, 65.601, 66.94, 66.127, 72.18, 86.24, 106.21, 126.33, 127.15, 132.9, 162.278, 178.134
Littlefield, Jack V. 3.145, 3.146, 3.148, 3.164, 32.148, 108.10, 138.57, 147.1, 148.51, 169.106
Littlefield, Lucien 11.47, 97.32, 97.53, 97.126, 135.79, 152.38, 169.68, 169.78, 169.100
Littlefield, Ralph 97.1, 97.2
Liu, Frank Michael 83.4, 83.49
Lively, Jason 65.638
Livermore, Paul 32.55, 32.59
Livesy, Jack 105.70, 105.93
Livingston, Princess 86.22
Livingston, Robert 32.2, 32.5, 32.6, 32.10, 32.11, 32.13, 32.80, 32.87, 60.3, 60.5, 97.85, 97.133, 145.22, 169.29
Livingstone, Sandy 179.20, 179.22
Lloyd, Christopher 10.1, 10.3, 10.14
Lloyd, Doris 168.25
Lloyd, George 60.10, 97.12, 97.55
Lloyd, Jimmy 97.37
Lloyd, Josie 66.207
Lloyd, Kathleen 48.49
Lloyd, Kathy 9.1
Lloyd, Susan 65.157
Lloyd, Suzanne 8.60, 14.50, 21.22, 22.24, 34.50, 65.219, 66.111, 85.116, 88.4, 88.28, 89.66, 93.200, 105.65, 105.101, 119.5, 126.2, 146.44,

146.64, 148.166, 152.13, 167.20, 167.26, 172.3, 179.24, 179.25, 179.26, 179.27, 179.28, 179.29, 179.30, 179.82
Locher, Felix 17.40, 17.41, 17.42, 65.461, 78.63, 93.160, 162.67
Locke, Jon 14.18, 41.74, 41.106, 47.1, 55.4, 65.567, 86.10, 148.82, 152.10, 158.64, 158.66, 161.93, 162.106, 162.107, 162.176, 162.233, 162.241
Locke, Sandra 83.42
Locke, Sharyl 14.224
Locke, Tammy 107
Lockhart, Anne 48.23
Lockhart, June 17.2, 29.5, 43.313, 43.328, 65.90, 65.103, 66.12, 66.35, 126.7, 162.27, 162.97, 178.58
Lockwood, Alexander 12.23, 12.24, 65.45, 65.258
Lockwood, Gary 65.395, 65.396, 92.17, 123.8, 123.9
Lodge, John 14.290, 14.296, 41.87, 85.109, 132.15, 161.88
Loew, Evan 135.34, 141.6
Logan, Frank 149.56
Logan, Pete 41.118
Logan, Robert 41.29
Loggia, Robert 12.95, 38.7, 65.360, 71.36, 71.88, 95.4, 101.19, 113, 119.11, 126.137, 162.73, 170.4, 170.59
Lohman, Glase 6.1, 6.10
Loiseaux, Mayo 25.29
Loken, Duane 75.19
Lomas, Jack 3.119, 3.162, 20.48, 43.135, 89.29, 105.30, 129.12, 141.44, 147.9, 147.10, 147.26, 147.29, 148.48, 162.19, 162.52
Lomond, Britt 6.72, 27.27, 34.45, 43.76, 43.131, 82.11, 93, 93.190, 93.192, 93.200, 93.216, 126.92, 148.110, 155.59, 158.18, 161.21, 178.143, 179
Lonaker, Rachel 96.59
London, Babe 138.3
London, Dick 65.182
London, Dirk 3.76, 93, 93.19, 93.71, 93.126, 93.148, 93.149, 93.150, 93.189, 93.193, 93.195, 93.202, 93.204, 93.223, 93.224, 93.225, 93.226, 138.23, 138.42, 147.38
London, Frank 105.116
London, Julie 12.88, 85.31, 126.55, 178.27
London, Keith 14.213
London, Kirk 138.11
London, Steve 141.49, 146.38
London, Tom 6.4, 6.12, 6.30, 6.59, 6.74, 8.15, 8.85, 20.44, 32.56, 32.62, 35.14, 57.64, 60.2, 60.4, 60.6, 60.14, 60.63, 60.65, 60.66, 73.6, 81.2, 81.49, 81.98, 85.52, 93.116, 93.143, 97.103, 97.126, 97.130, 105.86, 124.9, 124.15, 124.16, 124.29, 124.34, 124.56, 135.20, 135.22, 135.25, 135.26, 135.40, 135.50, 135.76, 138.53, 149.2, 149.27, 152.24, 152.37, 155.47
Long, Ed 14.307, 14.329, 14.417, 65.470, 65.512
Long, Kathy 163.49
Long, Richard 12, 66.22, 89.34, 105.30, 105.37, 105.40, 105.67, 117.46, 146.37, 148.186, 162.21
Long, Ronald 14.381, 170.46
Longet, Claudine 5.13
Longmire, Adele 97.114
Longo, Tony 177.13
Lontoc, Leon 14.349, 70.42
Loo, Anita 128.8
Loo, Richard 14.77, 39.16, 70.25, 83.1, 83.2, 83.3, 83.23, 83.36, 83.47, 83.48, 83.49, 123.7, 162.230, 170.17
Lookinland, Todd 53.27, 65.554, 65.607, 65.624, 111
Loomis, Terry 43.191, 126.41
Loos, Anita 85.64
Loos, Ann 65.331, 101.33, 161.20
Lopez, Danny 179.46, 179.47, 179.48
Lopez, Frederick 177.10, 177.42
Lopez, Manuel 88.7, 93.222, 147.51

Lopez, Peggy 161.97
Lopez, Perry 14.119, 66.145, 69.2, 72.3, 78.28, 127.3, 128.15, 130.14, 131.29, 155.35, 162.137, 162.192, 162.199, 162.254, 170.45, 170.99, 179.45
Lopez, Rafael 43.212, 98.7, 126.96, 149.53
Lo Presti, Joe 43.196
Lora, Joan 34.61, 102.7, 146.39, 156.49
Lord, Barbara 65.239, 119.11
Lord, Dorothea 22.9, 105.96, 129.77, 146.63
Lord, Jack 14.17, 65.92, 66.1, 71.19, 86.18, 98.2, 117.17, 126.15, 126.75, 142.24, 142.25, 144, 161.131, 162.272
Lord, Marjorie 73.40, 81.17, 97.35, 97.155, 162.1, 178.30
Lorde, Athena 14.397, 30.11, 65.387
Lorenz, Margo 148.155
Lorimer, Linda 134.11
Lorimer, Louise 23.37, 23.38, 60.29, 60.69, 93.142, 97.16, 14.267, 124.15, 124.16, 124.48, 164.23, 169.48
Loring, Lynn 12.15, 14.236, 41.2, 65.318, 84.4, 84.39, 101.22, 162.171, 170.19
Loring, Michael 138.39
Lormer, Jon 5.7, 5.18, 5.34, 12.50, 12.90, 14.174, 14.286, 14.298, 14.307, 14.352, 17.8, 17.9, 17.10, 17.18, 47.5, 51.28, 65.134, 65.181, 65.527, 65.544, 65.546, 65.562, 84.2, 86.21, 89.21, 96.118, 105.19, 105.82, 106.14, 126.53, 127.34, 127.45, 146.23, 146.46, 148.167, 149.75, 150.12, 151.10, 159.19, 161.23, 164.28, 170.42, 170.94, 170.101
Loros, George 175.1
Lorre, Peter 126.59, 162.100
Losby, Donald 14.88, 41.137, 44.67, 61.5, 65.371, 65.417, 126.126, 127.68, 150.12, 151.26, 162.215, 168.8
Losby, Donald A., Jr. 156.68
Losley, Dawn 68.25
Losley, Donald 41.4
Lou, Maggie 168.18
Loughery, Jackie 8.104, 14.144, 32.144, 52.24, 80, 158.33, 162.172, 164.74
Louie, Bebe 170.1, 170.69
Louise, Anita 108
Louise, Margaret 71.76
Louise, Tina 14.277, 83.30, 148.178
Love, Angie 161.193
Love, Phyllis 44.64, 65.226, 65.346, 66.134, 66.135, 85.33, 139.9, 149.50
Love, Victor 45.2
Lovejoy, Frank 167.22, 178.15, 178.83, 178.94
Lovell, Lettie 141.45
Lovett, Dorothy 148.187
Lovsky, Beverly 152.77
Lovsky, Celia 12.44, 64.11, 131.34
Lowe, Edmund 105.1
Lowe, Kevin 1.13, 1.20
Lowe, Stanja 65.381
Lowe, Tom 84.31
Lowe, Tom Roy 53.17, 96.178, 96.179
Lowell, Tom 12.57, 14.219, 14.220, 41.123, 65.306, 65.339, 98.4
Lower, Geoffrey 48
Lowery, Andrew 120.3
Lowery, Robert 3.85, 3.118, 3.150, 4.31, 21.11, 27.71, 29.24, 31, 34.38, 35.3, 35.7, 35.11, 35.30, 35.31, 43.23, 55.26, 60.63, 60.65, 65.275, 74.29, 80.2, 80.5, 93.10, 93.82, 102.17, 105.26, 105.60, 113.9, 121, 126.26, 126.38, 126.98, 131.4, 148.44, 148.123, 152.16, 158.24, 158.26, 158.39, 162.25, 162.125, 166.10
Lowry, Michael 1.11
Loy, Myrna 161.149
Lozoff, Josh 1.7
Lu, Lisa 8.94, 12.82, 12.90, 14.77, 27.104, 29.24, 66, 66.103, 127.28, 147.51, 173.4, 173.32
Lucas, Karl 65.418

Personnel Index

Lucas, Loyal "Doc" 17.7, 66.144, 148.182, 149.16, 161.92
Lucas, Peter 163.71
Lucas, Sharon 32.96
Lucas, Shirley 32.96, 32.101
Lucia, Charles 120.39
Luckinbill, Laurence 14.382
Lucking, William 11, 65.612, 70.38, 71.90, 75.22, 83.14, 83.63, 84.21, 90.13, 118, 161.224, 163.61, 177.48
Ludwig, Howard 65.63
Luez, Laurette 124.63, 145.31
Luisi, James 14.126, 14.168, 24.6, 65.614, 65.615, 130.128
Lukas, Karl 7.11, 14.409, 44.15, 65.349, 70.4, 96.27, 102.21, 112.17, 126.201, 130.5, 139.1, 155.25, 162.200, 173.28
Lukather, Paul 8.89, 14.194, 22.7, 66.32, 85.122, 126.50, 129.73, 158.53
Luke, Keye 6.33, 19.4, 23.31, 65.10, 75.26, 83, 83.63, 156.35
Lum, Benjamin 120
Lumbly, Carl 90.3
Lumley, Terry 96.3
Lummis, Dayton 14.25, 14.63, 14.145, 14.204, 22.11, 27.86, 39.16, 43.169, 43.200, 51.13, 51.24, 65.629, 78.32, 85.46, 88, 97.108, 103.3, 130.67, 130.88, 131.21, 146.69, 151.12, 161.24, 162.83, 162.187, 162.232, 173.33
Luna, Barbara 12.78, 14.16, 30.2, 43.185, 64.11, 65.254, 71.15, 83.52, 84.51, 86.35, 119.11, 142.29, 148.125, 152.47, 168.24, 170.2, 177.22, 179.45, 179.46, 179.47, 179.48
Lunan, Deryle 91.9
Lund, Art 38.4, 65.282, 65.599, 69.8, 70.31, 96.20, 162.188
Lund, Deanna 98.19, 132.7
Lund, Jordan 163.23
Lunda, Barbara 152.46
Lundigan, William 43.211
Lundin, Richard 65.581, 65.590
Lundin, Vic 65.154
Lundmark, William 22.7, 129.65, 162.63
Lundy, Rocky 57.66
Lung, Clarence 148.56
Lupino, Ida 5.37, 14.7, 43.188, 86.1, 116.17, 161.26, 161.91, 170.32, 178.2
Lupino, Richard 61.9, 61.10
Lupper, Kenneth 36.12
Lupton, John 13.25, 20, 41.35, 43.154, 43.206, 43.254, 65.206, 65.352, 83.56, 83.57, 83.58, 83.59, 85.56, 85.86, 106.20, 126.165, 129.62, 148.129, 151.26, 161.73, 161.146, 161.164, 162.158, 162.250, 162.282, 164.24, 173.29
Lurie, Allen 65.145, 152.8
Lusier, Robert 71.34
Lusk, Fernando 129.77
Lusk, Freeman 22.24, 22.30, 22.32, 93.226, 138.60
Luster, Robert 65.478
Luz, Franc 163.6, 177.23, 177.24
Lyden, Pierce 8.15, 32.28, 32.34, 32.145, 32.149, 35.20, 35.25, 60.54, 60.58, 60.71, 60.76, 73.12, 73.24, 80.2, 80.3, 80.5, 81.88, 81.89, 93.194, 97.203, 97.206, 97.209, 124.59, 124.62, 135.27, 135.32, 135.89, 138.34, 138.41, 145.38, 158.30, 169.23, 169.38, 169.89
Lydon, James 21.40, 24.11, 34.12, 34.38, 65.461, 74.30, 93.216, 105.49, 138.48, 142.31, 147.41, 152.75, 156.2, 156.53, 156.61, 162.113, 162.128, 162.170, 164.48, 164.93, 166.3
Lykins, Ray 163.2
Lyn, Dawn 65.574, 65.588, 65.589
Lynch, Hal 12.28, 12.30, 14.307, 38.12, 65.384, 65.435, 98.14, 139.14, 139.15, 170.35
Lynch, Ken 5.21, 8.24, 12.4, 12.14, 12.19, 12.25, 14.109, 14.128, 14.142, 14.260, 14.294, 14.322, 21.25, 21.55, 21.62, 25.23, 25.45, 46.8, 65.64, 65.104, 65.119, 65.212, 65.215, 65.234, 65.521, 65.522, 65.580, 65.591, 65.86, 66.55, 66.104, 66.128, 74.13, 76.35, 83.2, 85.112, 86.26, 86.37, 89.90, 89.115, 94.24, 101.6, 105.49, 116.2, 117.7, 117.8, 117.36, 119.14, 126.114, 126.155, 130.50, 144.9, 148.127, 148, 132, 149.2, 149.5, 149.17, 161.17, 161.39, 161.114, 161.210, 162.265, 170.33, 178.27, 178.54, 179.41, 179.42, 179.43, 179.44
Lynch, Theodora 169.30
Lynde, Paul 52.35
Lynley, Carol 12.93, 161.15
Lynn, Betty 21.9, 89.4, 96.6, 146.34, 146.36, 148.89, 153, 162.52
Lynn, Dani 85.69
Lynn, Diana 161.83
Lynn, Emmett 3.164, 25.27, 60.71, 60.76, 97.4, 97.7, 97.28, 97.53, 97.67, 97.74, 97.105, 97.134, 97.172, 129.36, 141.3, 141.18, 169.106
Lynn, George 3.55, 44.57, 81.30, 81.55, 97.28, 97.83, 138.54, 141.11, 147.21
Lynn, Jennie 161.66
Lynn, Jenny 126.162, 148.160
Lynn, Mari 148.109
Lynn, Patricia 169.71
Lynn, Rita 12.44, 14.261, 25.68, 66.23, 66.114, 77.4, 78.13, 78.14, 93.10, 93.196, 105.110, 105.111, 161.137, 164.41, 173.34, 178.96
Lynn, Robert 8.15, 8.85, 57.17, 78.10, 133.23, 138.4, 164.29
Lyon, Charles 60.8
Lyon, Lisa 96.28
Lyon, Patricia 162.264
Lyon, Therese 32.30
Lyons, Cliff 162.123
Lyons, Colette 93.5, 93.22, 93.126, 93.127
Lyons, Gene 14.228, 39.15, 43.322, 65.211, 65.333, 66.80, 66.153, 117.50, 144.5, 161.21, 168.27
Lyons, Robert F. 14.262, 65.446, 76.6, 116.22, 121.17
Lysen, Kitty 80.23
Lytton, Debbie 111, 137
Lytton, Herbert C. 14.42, 14.137, 44.18, 65.15, 65.42, 65.105, 65.291, 73.5, 73.18, 97.78, 97.121, 97.122, 129.58, 138.69, 149.48, 149.52, 162.87, 162.199, 166.10

Ma, Tzi 1.24
Mabe, Byron 14.384, 14.428, 65.563, 83.11, 83.54, 161.162
Mabrey, Greg 109.7
McAdams, Heather 53.25, 53.26
Macae, Elizabeth 65.330
McArthur, Alex 45
MacArthur, Charles 78.69
MacArthur, James 14.281, 17.35, 43.382, 65.404, 72.8, 161.98, 162.167
McAsh, Braun 67.12
MacAteer, Alan 169.94
Macaulay, Charles 7.2, 46.4, 65.572, 65.586, 130.113, 170.89
McBain, Diane 4.22, 7.8, 89.71, 105.50, 105.64, 146.54, 170.6, 170.48
McBeath, Tom 67.3
McBride, Dan 96.83
McBride, T.M. 142.13
McBroom, Amanda 65.630
McCabe, Gregg 43.149
McCabe, Peter 169.28
McCaffrie, Pat 44.54, 117.36, 161.20
McCall, Marty 14.425
McCalla, Irish 66.210
McCallion, James 5.27, 12.3, 14.354, 24.14, 38.10, 63.14, 63.45, 65.17, 65.472, 65.557, 70.14, 105.19, 121.16, 144.26, 162.193, 162.250, 162.261
McCallister, Lon 127.75
MacCallum, Crawford 109.3

McCallum, David 61.9, 61.10, 157.18
McCally, David 149.63
McCalman, Macon 1.26, 10, 59.2, 120.30, 177.11
McCambridge, Mercedes 14.83, 14.353, 39.4, 65.540, 119.13, 126.13, 126.63, 126.103, 126.210, 131.12, 162.7
McCann, Chuck 14.412, 96.11
McCann, John 34.44, 34.54, 41.129, 86.7, 89.83, 146.58
McCarroll, Frank 32.17, 32.19, 32.26
McCart, Mollie 23.13
McCarthy, Dennis 13.36, 29.16, 29.22, 29.24, 29.26, 161.122, 161.182, 161.201, 162.49, 162.178, 162.223, 162.226, 162.233, 162.251, 162.278
McCarthy, Devlni 65.10
McCarthy, Julianna 120.3, 120.10, 120.11, 120.12, 120.13, 120.43
McCarthy, Kevin 9.5, 63.11, 71.35, 92.34, 115.4, 130.120, 130.158, 132.23, 170.82
McCarthy, Lin 43.156, 65.607, 84.16, 85.66, 85.121, 111.4, 126.190, 130.54, 144.25, 148.192, 161.14, 162.168
McCarthy, Nobu 83.18, 85.64, 162.194, 170.28
McCauley, Tom 65.406
McCay, Peggy 14.392, 61.9, 61.10, 65.516, 65.547, 78.39, 78.55, 85.117, 89.108, 105.56, 105.89, 105.91, 128.13, 161.45, 168.11
McClamon, Zahn 90.10
McClarndon, Zahn 48.29, 48.38
McCleister, Tom 1.21
McClellan, Charles 148.98
McClelland, Scott 100.10
McCleod, Catherine 34.52, 105.16
McClory, Sean 14.82, 14.146, 20.5, 21.55, 25, 39.15, 41.21, 41.114, 43.313, 43.442, 54.2, 63.43, 63.44, 65.506, 65.604, 66.52, 71.45, 76.4, 78.22, 78.41, 84.1, 85.89, 93.218, 96.39, 102.15, 107.8, 116.12, 119.2, 119.6, 126.181, 126.182, 129.13, 130.117, 130.149, 142.16, 148.184, 161.93, 162.112, 164.57, 178.67
MacCloskey, Ysabel 96.105
McClure, Doug 7, 43.93, 43.98, 59.4, 78.71, 86.1, 103.31, 106, 119, 131.15, 158.34, 158.55
McClure, M'Liss 169.2
McClure, Tane 161.22
McClure, Tipp 8.78
McColm, Matt 1.21
McConnell, Judy 170.76
McConnell, Keith 126.197
McCord, Evan 21.51, 21.59, 21.62, 27.80, 27.87, 89.106, 89.118, 89.147, 105.104, 105.115
McCord, Robert, III 173.24, 173.27
McCord, Robert L. 170.12, 170.85
McCormack, Eric 99, 100
McCormack, Patty 43.199, 84.24, 126.122, 126.148, 162.51, 170.76
McCormick, Bill 135.24, 135.73
McCormick, Myron 117.36, 117.48
McCormick, Pat 62
McCormick, William M. 32.31, 32.37, 169.29
McCoy, Tony 3.84
McCracken, Bob 48.80
McCrea, Ann 13.39, 27.51, 43.68, 43.179, 43.249, 44.36
McCrea, Jody 138.78, 167
McCrea, Joel 162.280, 167
McCready, Ed 14.323, 17.19, 30.8, 65.387, 65.391, 65.421, 65.444, 65.453, 65.562, 70.20, 72.16, 83.26
McCubbin, Russ 17.46, 41.29, 41.44, 41.53, 41.98, 76.2, 86.23, 112.24, 120.54, 168.9, 170.58
McCue, Matthew 65.225
McCulloch, Jack 96.40
McDaniel, Charles 161.99
McDaniel, George 120.15
McDermott, Keith 75.18
McDevitt, Ruth 65.620, 96.6, 121

McDonald, Chris 120.17, 120.18
MacDonald, Donald 54.19, 57.3
McDonald, Donald 108.19
McDonald, Francis 2, 6.3, 6.16, 8.79, 20.38, 20.51, 20.25, 32.87, 57.37, 57.72, 60.7, 60.8, 60.28, 60.30, 60.49, 60.52, 60.74, 60.78, 60.91, 66.1, 81.62, 81.74, 81.81, 81.84, 85.79, 88.19, 89.38, 93.64, 93.131, 93.205, 97.13, 97.151, 97.196, 97.200, 97.201, 103.18, 103.45, 108.26, 124.11, 124.12, 124.16, 124.49, 124.50, 124.57, 124.70, 124.76, 135.6, 135.33, 135.53, 135.61, 135.87, 145.6, 146.58, 148.8, 155.26, 156.45, 162.3, 162.105, 164.3, 167.17, 169.24
MacDonald, Francis 32.80, 44.58, 135.48, 152.14, 152.68, 161.27, 162.110
MacDonald, Ian 3.44, 65.103, 102.15, 127.14, 156.7, 156.31, 178.7
McDonald, Ian 93.68, 97.124
MacDonald, J. Farrell 124.12
McDonald, Jennifer 1.3
McDonald, Jet 65.240
MacDonald, Kenneth 6.13, 6.21, 8.26, 27.24, 32.108, 32.115, 32.121, 32.124, 32.128, 34.2, 34.12, 34.15, 35.14, 41.37, 44.63, 56.29, 60.15, 60.18, 73.16, 81.2, 81.37, 81.38, 85.9, 85.72, 93.209, 97.8, 97.56, 97.164, 97.173, 102.26, 105.68, 108.35, 124.5, 124.23, 124.24, 124.53, 124.55, 124.71, 126.22, 126.72, 129.68, 133.17, 145.21, 145.28, 151.13, 151.18, 152.23, 156.49, 164.17, 168.18, 178.24
McDonald, Kenneth 35.16, 81.8, 156.21
MacDonald, Norman 158.11, 158.12
McDonald, Norman 158.29
McDonell, Arch 68.8
McDonough, Eileen 65.629
McDonough, Tom 88.7, 148.10, 148.16
McDougall, Alistair 14.432
McDougall, Fred 65.227, 65.428
MacDuff, Tyler 6.51, 6.61, 6.69, 6.70, 65.453, 89.113, 97.182, 97.194, 97.216, 138.67, 145.3, 148.43
McDuff, Tyler 43.67, 148.31
McEachin, James 36.6
McEndree, Maurice 86.3
McEntire, Reba 59.4
McEvoy, Penny 164.29
McEvoy, Renny 14.238, 20.56, 76.21, 130.63, 148.48, 162.30, 162.31
Mcey, Tyler 162.238
McFadden, Barney 26, 75.20, 177.60
McFadden, Tom 65.562
MacFarlane, Bruce 89.104, 156.65
McFee, Bruce 100.19, 100.21
McGavin, Darren 24.1, 30.2, 38.9, 43.215, 65.370, 65.389, 65.415, 126.86, 131, 142.27, 161.54, 161.152
McGhee, Gloria 65.37, 65.69, 65.284, 80.36
McGier, John 106.24
McGill, Bruce 163.4
McGiveney, Maura 161.93
McGiver, John 5.8, 5.49, 14.81, 46.5, 71.34, 170.69
McGivney, Maura 43.431, 86.32
McGlynn, Mary Elizabeth 163.18
McGonagle, Richard 1.22
McGough, John 65.52
McGowan, Molly 43.119, 43.146
McGowan, Oliver 51.1, 51.16, 51.23, 51.24, 65.249, 74.22, 74.25, 85.78, 102.34, 105.14, 133.21, 146.11, 146.23, 170.45, 173.23
McGrady, Michael 120.26
McGrail, Walter 32.77, 35.12
McGrath, Derek 163.27
McGrath, Frank 12.55, 148.61, 161.133, 162, 162.10
McGraw, Ali 65.639
McGraw, Charles 14.93, 14.330, 44.31, 46.9, 65.333, 65.448, 65.549, 72.5, 74.9, 85.51, 93.175, 101.5, 102.14, 112.4, 112.20, 116.2, 157.18, 161.19, 162.174, 170.87
McGraw, Dana 141.12
McGraw, Sean 163.40
McGreevey, Michael 13.27, 106.10, 131, 162.165
MacGregor, Casey 138.24, 169.91
MacGregor, Katherine 95, 96
MacGregor, Park 169.1, 169.15, 169.42, 169.78
MacGregor, Warren 35.12
McGregor, Warren 35.10
McGuinn, Joe 60.61, 92.4, 93.191, 152.8, 167.16
McGuire, Barry 65.103, 65.139, 74.32, 161.7
McGuire, Betty 96.177
McGuire, Biff 65.619
McGuire, Harp 34.64, 65.229, 148.159, 148.197, 149.67
McGuire, John 97.20, 97.77
McGuire, Paul 6.3, 43.73, 81.29, 81.81, 93.177, 124.64, 124.74, 126.20, 138.1, 138.8, 138.43, 138.46, 138.77, 145.11, 147.50, 169.48, 169.67, 169.90
McHale, Mike 81.57
McHattie, Stephen 26, 90.4, 163.79
Machon, Karen 5.17
Macht, Stephen 11.3
McHugh, Frank 52.34, 84.18, 117.20, 162.144
McHugh, Matt 97.29
McIntire, Holly 65.321, 126.183, 162.212, 162.238
McIntire, James 96.128
McIntire, John 14.50, 14.244, 29.24, 41.22, 41.39, 47.1, 49.5, 85.6, 85.44, 101.33, 119.17, 161, 162, 162.74, 162.181, 164.32, 167.5, 167.24, 175.5, 175.6, 178.87
McIntire, Peggy 97.39
McIntire, Tim 12.30, 14.173, 14.217, 14.244, 43.323, 43.326, 65.379, 76.18, 83.5, 83.17, 83.56, 83.57, 83.58, 83.59, 92, 126.215, 161.37, 161.166, 161.188, 161.224, 162.238, 162.258, 162.276
MacIntosh, Jay 14.406, 26, 65.573
McIntyre, Christine 124.28, 124.31, 124.45
McIntyre, Stephen 99.15
Mack, Cactus 32.32, 32.39, 32.55
Mack, Wilbur 156.32
McKay, Allison 70.37
MacKay, David 67.1, 67.2, 67.17
McKay, David 67.4
McKay, Gardner 15, 43.115, 77.15
MacKay, Jeff 118.6
McKay, Peggy 65.106
McKay, Wanda 32.32, 32.39, 97.67, 97.74, 124.13, 124.17
McKay, Warner 177.47
McKee, John 2.18, 30.22, 37.6, 44.4, 71.66, 76.47, 124.78, 126.172, 131.26, 135.87, 135.88, 149.67, 152.34, 161.15, 162.238
McKee, Tom 3.65, 3.77, 3.119, 3.149, 3.155, 8.3, 8.20, 27.41, 31.19, 44.35, 105.10, 147.14, 148.3, 148.109, 156.43, 162.56, 169.94, 173.24
McKeever, Jacqueline 21.28
McKellar, Crystal 120.28
McKellar, Danica 163.26
McKellar, Lorne 84.4
MacKenna, Kenneth 14.45
MacKennon, Dallas 65.269, 149.44
McKennon, Dallas 12.1, 14.246, 41, 49.11, 65.241, 85.87, 85.103, 130.164, 130.168, 161.5, 161.22, 162.128, 162.145, 162.196, 162.236, 162.257
McKenzie, Bill 169.1
McKenzie, Fred 67.17
MacKenzie, Patch 175.8
McKeon, Doug 26
Mackin, Harry 3.57, 6.36, 6.52, 6.70, 43.70, 60.54, 124.10, 135.6, 135.33, 141.23
Macklin, David 7.2, 14.47, 63.12, 65.350, 76.17, 84.34, 144.28, 161.48, 161.54, 161.130, 168.23
Macklin, James 35.13, 35.27, 35.28, 108.32, 135.79, 135.81

McKinley, J. Edward 14.164, 14.197, 191.6, 21.67, 22.27, 34.64, 44.74, 65.253, 65.258, 65.497, 89.99, 92.28, 105.106, 105.114, 146.64, 148.75, 170.48
McKinney, Bill 5.7, 5.10, 5.34, 19.1, 90.9, 110, 137.1, 175.4
McKinney, Mira 60.23, 60.44, 60.46, 60.74, 60.77, 97.24, 97.46, 97.70, 97.76, 97.108, 97.138, 141.11
McKinnon, Bruce 163.56, 163.57
McKinnon, Ray 91.6
McKinsey, Beverlee 43.438, 161.210
McLaglen, Victor 66.25, 126.26
McLain, David 14.328
McLaine, John 44.58
MacLane, Barton 13.12, 27.8, 31.29, 65.401, 65.433, 72.15, 85.23, 85.82, 85.108, 85.122, 113.9, 117, 119.8, 153.7
MacLane, Kerry 37, 83.40, 161.137
McLaren, John 67.3
McLaren, Wayne 65.587
McLarty, Gary 9.4, 83.2
McLaughlin, Mac 36.19
McLean, Bill 83.3, 83.25, 65.223, 161.21, 161.85, 170.27
McLean, David 14.355, 41.158, 43.257, 43.289, 43.311, 43.441, 43.446, 65.478, 84.19, 84.33, 84.47, 85.83, 85.100, 85.120, 150, 161.18, 161.42, 161.105
McLeod, Catherine 14.67, 54.27, 65.68, 65.300, 66.188, 74.27, 89.25, 89.70, 89.105, 89.129, 142.12, 161.33, 161.80, 178.18
McLeod, Duncan 13.29, 17.25, 17.26, 53.5, 53.6, 92.24
MacLeod, Gavin 12.53, 12.89, 12.104, 43.385, 76.41, 84.30, 132.26
McLeod, Howard 129.66, 149.8
MacLeod, Murray 14.421, 41.161, 70.26, 71.21, 83.12, 121.1, 161.191
McLeod, Murray 43.437
McLerie, Allyn Ann 14.358, 112.23
McLiam, John 12.6, 14.352, 19.1, 24.2, 41.11, 41.51, 41.71, 43.337, 43.445, 43.450, 51.19, 65.222, 65.351, 65.407, 65.408, 65.459, 65.469, 66.161, 84.44, 92.33, 95.13, 96.61, 96.62, 96.81, 106.1, 106.5, 107.11, 126.179, 131.41, 132.8, 144.11, 148.137, 159.27, 161.93, 161.121, 161.190, 162.122, 170.73
McLiam, John, Jr. 65.423
McMahon, David 89.82, 97.60, 97.72, 126.23, 126.78, 151.26, 161.74, 162.81, 162.122, 162.249, 162.278, 168.13
MacMahon, Horace 4.29, 21.40, 146.60
McManus, Don 65.639
McManus, Michael 120.17, 120.18
MacMichael, Florence 65.163
McMickle, Billy 65.538, 65.539
McMillan, Linda 96.81
MacMillan, Will 120.54
McMullan, Jim 12.22, 26, 41.115, 41.117, 41.158, 46.10, 55.24, 76.46, 85.96, 85.100, 161.9, 161.46, 162.221, 168.2, 168.17
McMullen, Dennis 65.160, 79.20
MacMurray, Fred 29.1
McMyler, Pamela 65.555, 65.620, 161.204
McNab, Mercedes Alicia 1.19
McNair, Heather 177.18, 177.64
McNally, David 99.12
McNally, Edward 77.4
McNally, Stephen 12.44, 17.21, 63.10, 65.432, 76.8, 85.32, 106.18, 109.1, 126.82, 131.27, 152.32, 153.5, 161.34, 162.56, 178.10, 178.87, 178.103, 178.128
McNally, Terrence 48.6
McNamara, John 25.27, 25.67
McNear, Howard 55.17, 65.24, 65.169, 65.176,

Personnel Index

65.271, 65.354, 66.131, 78.35, 82.13, 105.81, 105.92, 149.52, 168.6
McNeely, Howard 60.77
MacNee, Patrick 5.10, 13.3, 59.4, 114.2, 161.223
MacNeil, Evan 8.49
MacNeil, Peter 100.3
McNeil, Scott 67.13
McNichol, Kristie 137.11
MacNiven, David 67.4, 67.14, 67.15
McPeak, Sandy 11.5, 19.9, 26, 96.81, 118.4, 171
McPeters, Cactus 81.38
McPeters, Taylor 65.246
MacPherson, Shannon 48.32
McQuade, Arlene 43.448, 66.129
McQuain, Robert 65.277
McQueen, Steve 148.37, 156.21, 156.31, 164
McQueeney, Robert 4.29, 14.60, 14.212, 14.254, 14.275, 21.53, 21.61, 27.61, 27.80, 27.99, 34.31, 34.43, 65.87, 89.42, 89.61, 89.70, 89.128, 92.1, 119.4, 149.8, 151.24, 162.7
McRae, Alan 177.38
MacRae, Elizabeth 14.293, 65.253, 65.280, 65.323, 65.361, 126.166, 144.17, 161.78
McRae, Ellen 12.59, 65.260, 76, 85.109, 161.192
McRae, Frank 123.11
MacRae, Meredith 5.21
MacRae, Michael 65.621
McRaney, Gerald 5.46, 65.583, 65.593, 65.631, 75.25
Macready, George 8.86, 14.1, 39.3, 55.22, 65.127, 66.110, 84.36, 85.73, 127.4, 127.37, 130.6, 130.67, 131.41, 133.39, 149.10, 149.75, 152.13, 164.15
Macready, Michael 89.23, 152.13, 161.85
McVeagh, Eve 5.44, 41.20, 41.43, 52.25, 66.177, 89.58, 126.22, 149.75, 161.152, 162.182, 162.240
McVey, Patrick 8.2, 13.16, 14.5, 15, 27.33, 27.50, 27.84, 65.292, 66.201, 89.7, 103.35, 105.35, 105.49, 129.18, 130.29, 130.127, 133.9, 146.17, 152.17, 155.31, 155.44, 164.31, 178.83
McVey, Tyler 6.56, 8.3, 8.102, 14.108, 14.291, 14.338, 20.29, 22.30, 34.58, 41.155, 43.220, 43.235, 44.51, 64.8, 65.26, 65.33, 65.55, 65.87, 65.103, 65.179, 66.32, 71.83, 82.7, 88.19, 93.97, 93.99, 93.123, 93.193, 97.132, 105.3, 108.8, 126.85, 127.8, 128.12, 128.12, 129.26, 129.44, 129.66, 131.36, 132.20, 133.24, 145.3, 145.22, 148.187, 162.37, 162.84, 164.43, 170.9, 170.104, 178.65
McWhirter, Ken 161.120
Madden, Ed 65.301
Madden, Henry 130.153
Madden, Patrick 67.13, 67.21
Maddern, Victor 14.136
Mader, Ilse 32.35
Madison, Ellen 76.35, 168.26
Madison, Guy 43.195, 162.12, 169, 178.148, 179
Madrid, Bert 65.528
Maffei, Robert 14.40
Magana, Mario 168.24
Magana, Victor 78.20
Magana, Victor, Jr. 25.62
Magenniss, Maggie 138.18
Maggart, Brandon 1.2, 1.17
Maggio, Tony 177.43
Maguire, Tobey 163.19
Mahaffey, Valerie 177.42
Maharis, George 24.8, 109.13
Mahin, Dan 97.96
Mahin, Don 32.58, 124.44
Mahoney, Jock 43.32, 64.5, 83.26, 85.45, 85.65, 124, 126.41, 126.77, 162.33, 173
Mahoney, Maggie 14.217, 89.114, 127.32, 155.37, 162.35, 165.2, 173.5, 173.10
Mahoney, Mike 170.103
Mahoney, Sharon 65.639
Maier, Tim 96.133

Main, Laurie 41.23, 41.31, 41.66, 41.83, 41.154, 63.21, 76.36, 96.167, 105.80, 162.135
Main, Marjorie 162.36, 162.39
Mains, Patty 168.12
Majalca, Ana Maria 27.92, 34.13, 135.90, 148.61
Majors, Lee 5.31, 12, 65.352, 99.21, 106
Majulin, John 31.32
Makaj, Steve 67.22
Makee, Blaisdell 13.25, 76.24
Mako 12.82, 52.52, 83.6, 83.63, 120.36
Malcolm, James 65.213
Malcolm, Robert 138.26, 141.35, 145.29
Male, Colin 65.574, 166.13
Malet, Arthur 14.310, 46.12, 63.28, 65.357, 84.42, 130.128, 170.16, 170.98
Maley, Peggy 77.18, 130.22, 152.13, 155.33, 164.29
Malil, Shelley 1.22
Malinda, Jim 5.6
Malinger, Ross 48.37
Malis, Sy 66.61
Malkin, Vicki 161.102
Mallinson, Rory 27.81, 27.83, 32.29, 32.35, 32.81, 32.84, 32.88, 32.91, 32.122, 60.68, 60.72, 97.84, 97.137, 135.24, 135.73, 145.36, 149.38, 169.7, 169.16, 169.31, 169.58, 169.65, 169.93
Mallory, Chad 169.19, 169.66, 169.67
Mallory, Ed 43.219, 148.179, 149.61, 162.120
Mallory, Wayne 32.132, 32.136, 43.46, 135.75, 135.76, 138.17, 138.29, 169.81, 169.88, 169.94
Malloy, Jeff 161.166
Malls, Cy 66.45
Malone, Dorothy 29.9, 43.225
Malone, Nancy 12.101, 14.255, 72.4, 116.24
Maloney, James 34.28, 65.84, 65.104, 65.228, 66.151, 178.34
Maloney, Patty 91.11
Malooly, Maggie 19.12, 65.627
Mamakos, Peter 3.146, 20.13, 20.35, 32.140, 32.144, 41.31, 41.66, 41.157, 44.21, 65.116, 78.18, 78.21, 78.27, 78.54, 81.1, 81.78, 93.110, 93.142, 93.185, 93.205, 97.23, 97.50, 97.61, 97.62, 97.106, 97.118, 97.149, 97.156, 97.181, 126.2, 126.37, 126.79, 152.33, 161.31, 161.55, 162.230, 179.28
Mamo, John 83.9, 83.26, 130.160
Manay, Maria 97.189
Mandan, Robert 137.2
Mando, Peggy 86.44
Mandrell, Barbara 48.98
Manetti, Larry 163.8
Mangosing, Tina 132.9
Manley, David 14.79, 159.16, 164.91
Manley, Louise 32.54, 32.61
Manley, Stephen 83.52, 83.54, 96.163, 137.2
Mann, Darlene 163.52
Mann, Dolores 70.2, 70.11, 73.30
Mann, Jack 65.82, 155.19
Mann, Jerry 170.103
Mann, Larry D. 12.10, 39.10, 63.35, 65.446, 65.466, 65.474, 65.498, 65.588, 65.589, 68.30, 70.6, 70.23, 71.81, 76.15, 92.10, 125.7, 139.1, 139.8, 139.11, 139.13, 139.16
Mann, Lawrence 139.5
Mann, Rex 141.55
Mann, Ronny 129.52
Manners, Mickey 130.168
Manning, Bruce 170.32
Manning, Jack 5.48
Manon, Gloria 41.40
Manos, Gloria 96.163
Mansell, Barbara 168.28
Mansfield, John 81.15, 97.158
Mansfield, Rankin 32.102, 81.57, 129.35, 145.29, 148.185
Mansfield, Sally 43.16, 60.88, 60.89, 60.90, 169.62
Manson, Maurice 27.77, 34.29, 65.20, 65.31, 85.73, 85.93, 89.112, 105.11, 105.70, 105.101, 126.1, 146.49, 178.39

Mantee, Paul 14.300, 30.22, 41.164, 86.26, 116.13, 125.5, 130.102, 130.157, 161.174
Mantell, Joe 98.19, 102.13, 157.21, 161.101, 164.13
Mantley, Jon Jason 65.538, 65.539, 65.540
Mantley, Maria 65.538, 65.539, 65.540, 65.524
Mantooth, Randolph 5.9, 106.21
Manx, Kate 144.1, 148.87
Manza, Ralph 65.455, 71.82, 80.10, 86.12, 86.23, 86.57, 95.15, 117.25, 168.26
Mapes, Ted 32.42, 32.48, 32.54, 32.61, 32.111, 32.117, 60.62, 73.6, 73.13. 81.37, 81.83, 133.38, 162.99
Maples, Matt 163.67
Mara, Adele 3.53, 3.69, 8.1, 27.4, 27.13, 27.56, 85.17, 93.108, 93.223, 105.27, 105.40, 105.69, 142.19, 148.70, 149.73
Mara, Ralph 70.16
Marandi, Evi 49.6
Marcellous, Andre 177.37
March, Linda 14.317
March, Lori 133.39, 149.70
Marcus, Bernie 97.43
Marcus, Paul 129.44
Marcus, Vitina 64.11, 65.240, 65.283, 126.99, 157.17
Marcuse, Theodore 4.9, 14.40, 41.107, 65.55, 66.1, 66.62, 86.15, 170.23, 170.36, 170.73
Marden, Adrienne 14.158, 14.208, 83.3, 83.44, 89.97, 103.14, 126.54, 156.52, 162.131, 162.240
Marfield, Dwight 162.95
Margetts, Monty 4.7
Margo 162.8
Margolese, E.M. 96.148
Margolin, Stuart 17.15, 19, 65.579, 65.602, 112, 121.12, 161.167
Margolis, Morgan 163.38
Margotta, Michael 43.437, 116.6
Mariani, Josanna 78.50
Marie, Sofia 107.25
Marihugh, Tammy 142.4, 162.86
Marin, Paul 70.30
Marin, Russ 14.403, 19.2
Marion, Paul 32.58, 32.83, 32.90, 73.21, 81.6, 81.15
Mark, Flip 12.76, 66.170
Mark, Michael 32.36, 126.46, 138.57
Marker, Preshy 43.161
Marker, Russ 163.46
Markes, Tony 96.74
Markham, Monte 5.21, 19.12, 70.14, 71.87, 76.28, 106.6, 123.11
Markland, Ted 14.433, 22.23, 53.22, 66.66, 71, 102.11, 117.25, 129.51, 150.6, 170.11
Markoff, Diane 33
Markov, Margaret 24.4
Marks, Garnett A. 32.31
Marks, Guy 125
Marley, John 13.39, 14.305, 17.2, 17.27, 27.59, 44.67, 61.7, 65.381, 70.6, 76.33, 86.3, 88.7, 92.11, 116.7, 126.53, 127.55, 146.65, 159.24, 161.172, 170.55, 172.2
Marlo, Steven 14.237, 14.261, 17.8, 18.9, 17.10, 43.318, 61.5, 79.30, 88.23, 127.13, 130.41, 130.150, 130.155, 164.89
Marlo, Vic 141.60
Marlow, Ric 14.42, 89.124, 159.20
Marlowe, Don 141.35, 169.87
Marlowe, Frank 73.36, 97.34, 129.9, 152.6, 164.8
Marlowe, Hugh 126.44, 126.105, 148.198, 161.54, 161.129
Marlowe, Lucy 65.149, 119.14, 148.126
Marlowe, Nora 12.30, 24.3, 65.17, 65.356, 65.478, 65.533, 70.25, 74.6, 82.11, 88, 153.9, 153.11, 162.155, 162.165, 162.198, 162.250
Marlowe, Scott 14.161, 21.3, 24.19, 27.66, 65.308, 65.349, 65.365, 65.402, 66.43, 66.91, 66.148,

74.14, 84.44, 88.24, 126.180, 144.4, 162.18, 170.14, 178.133
Marno, Marc 55.18, 66.185
Maross, Joe 14.25, 55.26, 65.98, 65.257, 65.360, 71.33, 76.41, 77.12, 83.55, 113.3, 114.12, 117.16, 129.19, 133.37, 144.14, 144.27, 153.16, 161.27, 161.38, 161.184, 162.184, 164.17
Marquis, Kristopher 75.6
Marr, Eddie 31.1
Marr, Sally 106.13
Marriott, Sylvia 162.64, 162.103
Mars, Bruce 14.214, 14.232
Mars, Kenneth 65.431
Marsac, Maurice 41.25, 41.26, 41.117, 78.4, 78.13, 78.14, 78.59, 114.17
Marsden, Jason 1.8
Marsell, Lita 66.223
Marsh, Linda 5.30, 12.102, 41.158, 43.327, 65.556, 65.566, 70.8, 76.32, 170.14
Marsh, Mae 14.8
Marsh, Michele 65.630, 65.617, 95.4
Marsh, Myra 73.1
Marsh, Tiger Joe 7.11, 86.29, 86.38
Marsh, Tony 81.5
Marsha, Sandra 43.220
Marshal, David 177.1
Marshal, Helen 43.49
Marshal, Jack 66.160
Marshall, Alan 22.10, 126.5, 146.37, 162.45
Marshall, Arthur 51.18, 105.85
Marshall, Connie 141.16
Marshall, David Anthony 120.25
Marshall, Dodie 36.2, 134.6
Marshall, Don 126.173
Marshall, Donald James 96.161
Marshall, E.G. 106.8, 106.14, 126.65
Marshall, Gary 97.186
Marshall, Gloria 35.14, 43.32, 141.48
Marshall, Helene 6.19, 6.47, 6.80, 31.13, 97.205
Marshall, Herbert 178.143
Marshall, Joan 8.4, 14.264, 21.40, 21.45, 21.49, 65.260, 86.20, 89.69, 105.17, 105.108, 133.6, 155.34
Marshall, John 93.92, 132.17, 138.22, 148.145
Marshall, Kenneth 75.24
Marshall, Linda 52.7
Marshall, Liz 65.474, 65.535
Marshall, Marion 66.67
Marshall, Nancy 65.421
Marshall, Nora 88.1
Marshall, Peter 11.1
Marshall, Sarah 41.37, 41.86, 41.108, 52.18, 144.28, 170.63
Marshall, Sean 83.14
Marshall, Shary 43.316, 43.323, 46.10, 65.282, 65.329, 170.11
Marshall, Timothy 14.425
Marshall, William 14.164, 41.80, 126.173, 170.88
Marsic, Bob 96.78
Marston, Brett 177.50
Marston, Joel 32.54, 32.61
Marta, Lynn 65.579
Martel, Arlene 65.625, 70.47, 76.16, 170.65
Martell, Donna 8.14, 14.139, 20.31, 27.69, 54.10, 60.28, 60.30, 73.10, 81.6, 81.15, 124.25, 124.26, 148.164
Martell, Gregg 126.79, 129.9, 161.152, 170.11, 170.36, 170.75
Marth, Frank 10.5, 10.6, 12.18, 12.24, 12.41, 12.58, 12.91, 14.336, 36.1, 65.470, 65.493, 65.511, 65.611, 76.21, 84.9, 84.33, 96.74, 101.22, 116.2, 123.10, 139.14, 139.15, 161.226, 176.1
Martin, Andra 4.22, 4.25, 4.35, 21.12, 27.63, 27.64, 34.32, 34.58, 89.31, 105.43, 105.81, 105.88, 162.152
Martin, Andy 130.161
Martin, Barney 181

Martin, Buzz 21.56, 34.41, 44.50, 66.131, 66.186, 126.11, 149.29, 162.54, 164.28
Martin, Charles 43.68, 93.45
Martin, Chris-Pin 97.42
Martin, Daniel F. 5.33
Martin, Dean 126.180
Martin, Dewey 40, 43.287, 85.119, 178.38, 178.53, 178.117
Martin, Eugene 8.81, 14.127, 20.27, 38.14, 77, 126.98, 127.61, 130.70, 146.29, 152.24, 162.99, 164.55
Martin, Florence 66.94
Martin, Frank 170.72
Martin, Irene 169.24
Martin, Jack 158.4
Martin, Jared 75.14, 75.16, 75.17, 109.12
Martin, Kiel 65.568, 83.14, 161.154, 161.171, 161.198
Martin, Lewis 44.46, 57.105, 66.74, 66.109, 66.190, 73.33, 78.61, 105.16, 114.13, 169.74
Martin, Margarita 97.14
Martin, Marion 97.41
Martin, Nan 1.14, 84.49
Martin, Pamela Sue 123.4
Martin, Patrick 178.139
Martin, Pepper 5.50, 9.5, 14.315, 63.23
Martin, Ross 8.9, 14.134, 65.106, 65.126, 85.43, 153, 162.234, 170, 179.82
Martin, Speir 78.24, 135.95
Martin, Strother 12.37, 12.53, 13.11, 14.160, 14.210, 14.336, 14.373, 14.412, 20.15, 20.52, 39.11, 41.150, 43.287, 43.302, 43.344, 43.361, 54.22, 54.24, 63.6, 63.31, 65.14, 65.27, 65.104, 65.154, 65.214, 65.248, 65.275, 65.324, 65.522, 65.623, 66.5, 66.8, 66.93, 66.171, 74, 76.6, 76.31, 77.23, 78.57, 89.41, 92.20, 101.28, 112.15, 126.30, 126.204, 127.1, 132.18, 134.11, 134.14, 144.7, 152.30, 156.37, 161.95, 161.217, 178.20
Martin, Todd 5.43, 7.1, 14.327, 36.12, 71.75, 92.27
Martin, Tony 43.240
Martine, Daniel 177.41
Martinez, A 14.367, 26, 37, 83.44, 109.2, 116.21, 176.3
Martinez, Claudio 65.634, 112.6
Martinez, Joaquin 5.13, 26, 43.446, 49.9, 65.515, 65.637, 71.2, 71.82, 75.27, 177.29
Martinez, Mina 128, 161.187
Martinez, Patrice 65.636, 180
Martinez, Tony 52.19
Marvin, Frankie 60.2, 60.5, 60.6, 60.8, 60.9, 60.11, 60.12, 60.13, 60.15, 60.19, 60.21, 60.43, 60.45, 60.50, 60.57, 60.63, 60.65, 60.66, 60.68, 60.70, 60.74, 60.76, 60.77, 60.80, 60.83
Marvin, Lee 14.94, 161.10, 162.119, 162.139
Mascott, Holly 170.93
Masen, Osa 162.40
Mask, Ace 177.1
Maslow, Walter 34.54, 57.90, 93.103, 93.105, 93.107, 93.112, 93.113, 103.33, 141.56, 148.50, 158.58, 158.60
Mason, Big Foot 42
Mason, Eric 24.11
Mason, Margaret 43.306
Mason, Marlyn 12.23, 12.66, 14.154, 14.188, 46.12, 86.8, 86.19
Mason, Morgan 41.73
Mason, Sydney 31.39, 32.138, 32.141, 32.152, 6.82, 60.87, 77.21, 97.183, 97.185, 97.193, 97.208, 108, 108.7, 135.27, 135.32, 135.44, 135.55, 138.42, 148.73
Mason, Tom 90.5
Mason, Vivian 32.25
Massad, Louis 170.61
Massengale, Joseph 53.22
Masset, Andrew 118.4
Massett, Patrick 177.36
Massey, Daniel 14.381

Massey, Daria 29.26, 43.88, 43.92, 129.45, 141.65, 149.4, 158.61, 162.79
Massey, Jayne 170.7
Massey, Raymond 131.37, 162.120, 178.115
Massey, William 170.72
Masters, Bill 133.27
Masters, Daryl 68.12
Masters, Michael 9.1, 17.6, 86.39, 102.17, 148.51, 149.28, 161.195, 170.3, 170.12, 170.29, 170.35, 170.41
Masters, Natalie 22.14, 65.399, 65.509, 79.25, 97.169, 127.29, 127.38
Masters, Tom 22.3, 22.14, 103.38
Masterson, Christopher 48.37
Mastes, Ben 163.25
Matchett, Christie 70.11
Matchinga, Toian 12.62, 76.11, 125.11, 170.11, 170.68, 170.94
Matek, Robert 170.25
Mather, George 80.10, 80.14, 97.191, 135.91, 138.12, 141.58, 141.63
Mather, Jack 3.139, 4.26, 14.9, 21.38, 34.41, 43.164, 85.5, 105.56, 105.71, 105.107, 131.30, 149.16, 158.60, 159.33, 162.173
Mathers, Don 32.156, 169.82
Matheson, Don 43.377, 123.4
Matheson, Murray 69.2, 85.42, 149.21
Matheson, Tim 14, 14.419, 14.420, 75.5, 75.6, 75.7, 83.24, 123, 161
Mathews, Carmen 5.22
Mathews, Carole 25, 32.56, 32.62, 43.226, 78.32, 114.24, 126.167, 133.25, 148.48, 152.11, 156.14, 169.25, 169.29, 178.47
Mathews, George 43.63, 51.2, 65.261, 66.93, 66.198, 130.31
Mathews, Hrothgar 67.13
Mathews, Lester 14.122, 126.111, 173.12
Mathias, Stefany 67.16
Matra, Leo V. 41.75, 41.76
Matt, Jamie 162.72
Matthews, John 14.154, 51.26, 66.203, 170.57
Matthews, Junius 60.83, 66.42
Matthews, Zook 100.3
Mattingly, Hedley 43.304, 43.345, 157
Matts, Frank 32.3, 3.8, 32.15, 32.18, 32.21, 60.15, 124.2, 124.5
Mattson, Denver 96.75
Mattson, Robin 41.165, 109.9
Mauck, Jack 23.28
Mauldin, John 66.133, 126.107
Maunder, Wayne 38, 83.1, 84
Maurer, Ralph 41.87
Maxey, Jean R. 25.31
Maxey, Paul 97.47, 103.48, 147.1, 162.42
Maxwell, Anthony 162.101
Maxwell, Charles 8.1, 8.14, 8.102, 14.3, 14.37, 14.89, 14.175, 14.242, 14.281, 14.305, 14.322, 14.353, 14.398, 17.5, 17.22, 32.135, 32.151, 32.155, 65.132, 65.151, 65.373, 65.479, 71.27, 71.37, 71.94, 85.104, 89.155, 105.77, 116.18, 119.9, 121.12, 126.38, 152.52, 126.97, 126.109, 130.160, 133.24, 152.29, 152.35, 152.72, 159.4, 178.115
Maxwell, Frank 5.16, 13.26, 24.15, 44.54, 65.131, 126.55, 126.104, 126.192, 161.51
Maxwell, James 51.12
Maxwell, Jenny 43.306, 162.174, 170.91
Maxwell, John 14.33, 79.33, 93.165, 93.173, 97.205, 127.29, 130.28, 131.23, 152.8
Maxwell, Lester 66.200, 161.6
Maxwell, Marilyn 17.16, 65.193, 162.249
Maxwell, Paul 21.30
Maxwell, Stacey 161.111
Maxwell, Tony 161.2, 162.135
May, Angela 123.8, 123.9
May, Donald 27.70, 34, 146.59
May, Harley 144.28
May, Lenora 96.83

Personnel Index

Mayana, Miko 52.52
Mayer, Ken 3.120, 3.153, 5.6, 8.62, 8.100, 12.5, 12.30, 14.27, 14.38, 14.97, 14.200, 14.234, 14.267, 14.323, 17.31, 21.19, 21.68, 27.76, 39.10, 41.69, 43.176, 43.238, 43.346, 43.372, 43.428, 43.429, 46.1, 46.3, 56.38, 65.62, 65.113, 65.209, 65.358, 65.435, 65.451, 65.515, 65.524, 65.545, 65.557, 65.578, 66.45, 71.48, 71.89, 76.40, 77.26, 79.18, 86.24, 88.22, 92.12, 93.215, 105.48, 105.103, 119.3, 121.20, 126.37, 126.62, 126.77, 126.84, 127.41, 127.65, 127.76, 133.27, 147.28, 148.44, 148.187, 150.10, 151.24, 152.24, 152.68, 152.73, 155.18, 155.52, 159.8, 161.14, 161.85, 161.112, 162.50, 162.92, 162.196, 162.229, 162.249, 162.274, 164.52, 166.9, 169.103, 170.89
Mayfield, Adam 163.52
Maynard, Kermit 32.45, 32.52, 32.57, 32.63, 32.78, 32.101, 32.108, 32.115, 32.125, 60.20, 60.22, 60.27, 60.29, 60.47, 60.50, 60.54, 81.78, 97.19, 97.64, 124.27, 124.32, 124.40, 124.42, 124.45
Maynard, Mimi 177.60
Maynor, Asa 89.79, 130.164, 162.164
Mayo, Jacqueline 126.8, 66.34, 162.26
Mayo, Raymond 65.463, 71.88, 89.152
Mayo, Virginia 162.50
Mayon, Helen 105.94
Mazurki, Mike 14.303, 14.344, 41.45, 42, 52.17, 65.546, 66.17, 66.119, 66.180, 78.14, 83.13, 86.14, 98.24, 108.31, 125.8, 152.75, 162.251
Mazursky, Paul 130.69, 130.161
Mazzola, Leonard 141.20, 141.24
Meacham, Anne 132.10, 161.6
Mead, Geoff 163.54
Mead, Philip L. 109.9, 177.61
Meade, Bill 169.5
Meade, Claire 166.9
Meade, Mitzi 158.60
Meader, George 3.63, 32.148, 97.29, 124.70, 145.29
Meadows, Audrey 162.138
Meadows, Jayne 70.30
Meadows, Joyce 27.85, 79.24, 89.100, 89.124, 105.119, 129.25, 133.29, 133.39, 152.33, 152.68, 155.44, 159, 159.22, 159.29, 159.30, 159.32, 162.63, 162.137, 162.159, 164.79
Meadows, Kristen 120.47
Meadows, Stephen 177.54, 177.55
Meadows, Vaughn 6.50, 162.109
Meaney, Colm 48.1
Meaney, Sean 162.44
Medin, Harriet 14.312
Medina, Hazel 65.487
Medina, Julie 9.1, 65.385, 65.528, 65.556
Medina, Julio 71.55, 71.89, 83.20, 83.52, 170.90
Medina, Patricia 13.31, 14.21, 17.39, 25.38, 66.49, 66.62, 66.212, 74.23, 126.27, 126.74, 127.25, 127.36, 131.28, 166.11, 179.55, 179.56, 179.57, 179.58
Meek, John 135.92
Meeker, Ralph 7.5, 38.3, 49.7, 51.6, 71.11, 106.10, 152.29, 153.17, 162.26, 164.21, 178.27
Meerbaum, Nora 96.121
Megowan, Dan 130.79
Megowan, Debbie 13.40, 93.220
Megowan, Don 14.10, 14.125, 17.16, 25.52, 27.13, 27.43, 27.54, 27.58, 27.78, 27.89, 29.2, 29.8, 34.11, 36.14, 41.9, 42, 43.42, 43.150, 43.311, 43.363, 43.364, 43.448, 44.45, 65.174, 65.276, 65.238, 65.604, 65.631, 66.30, 66.53, 66.74, 66.79, 83.27, 85.12, 85.30, 89.84, 93.142, 97.138, 101.8, 126.21, 126.102, 126.158, 148.35, 148.93, 149.47, 156.35, 157.8, 159.27, 162.14, 162.141
Meigs, William 66.45, 130.16, 130.23, 130.155, 141.66
Mele, Toni 96.128

Melendez, Ron 48.27
Mell, Joseph 43.391, 65.35, 65.46, 65.217, 65.220, 82.10, 130.17, 156.27, 156.47, 162.82, 162.94
Mellinger, Max 66.209, 126.69, 179.76
Mellini, Scott 53
Mellon, Le Grande 170.29
Melocchi, Vince 1.21, 48.51
Melrose, Brian 176.2
Melrose, Mary 152.53
Melton, Gerald 65.69
Melton, Roy 86.9
Melton, Troy 8.4, 12.47, 14.174, 14.200, 14.229, 14.242, 14.296, 14.306, 24.20, 32.81, 32.84, 32.88, 32.94, 32.95, 32.104, 65.423, 65.431, 65.432, 65.434, 65.457, 65.470, 65.490, 65.531, 65.563, 65.570, 81.13, 82.12, 93.217, 93.223, 96.74, 125.2, 130.112, 133.7, 135.83, 135.84, 135.85, 135.86, 135.90, 135.92, 135.93, 135.94, 135.99, 161.122, 164.24, 166.4, 170.70, 178.22, 178.64
Melville, Sam 12.47, 43.447, 49.13, 63.6, 65.435, 65.450, 65.487, 65.501, 65.504, 65.524, 65.551, 65.552, 65.553, 70.13, 76.37, 139.2
Melvin, Allan 51.17, 83.54
Melvoin, Don 14.352, 71.70
Menard, Tina 14.108, 14.366, 65.172, 121.3, 127.44, 135.16, 161.124
Menchen, Sherman 170.48
Mendenhall, James 96.95
Mendosa, Ken 170.90
Menken, Shep 12.64
Menzies, Heather 5.5, 14.369, 71.66
Mercer, Mae 83.17, 83.62
Merchant, Cathie 85.94
Mercier, Louis 14.42, 105.33, 178.105
Meredith, Burgess 14.280, 17.46, 41.129, 86.2, 98.13, 106.19, 126.93, 126.148, 126.170, 126.171, 157.17, 161.179, 162.246, 170.12
Meredith, Charles 78.51, 78.57, 97.16, 97.133, 97.160, 152.8
Meredith, Cheerio 3.115, 14.86, 21.7, 126.97
Meredith, Don 123.3
Meredith, Judi 14.108, 14.266, 29.14, 43.366, 65.261, 66.151, 66.199, 66.219, 74, 85.40, 126.192, 129.46, 131.20, 148.81, 149.49, 161.129, 162.58, 162.224, 162.242, 173.31
Meredith, Madge 35.6, 35.22, 35.23, 35.32, 80.37, 97.150
Merey, Carla 105.1
Meriwether, Lee 52.13, 76.43
Merkel, Una 46.3
Merlin, Jan 8.82, 14.84, 17.35, 20.31, 24.18, 54.16, 54.26, 65.342, 85.33, 85.47, 85.90, 85.92, 85.110, 92.12, 93.56, 96.7, 117.38, 120.45, 126.132, 133, 148.117, 148.192, 149.17, 155.23, 156.1, 157.26, 161.51, 161.62, 166.1, 178.23
Merrick, Doris 32.43, 32.49
Merrick, John 43.149, 54.17, 129.9, 145.11, 147.31, 148.2, 148.67, 162.13, 169.92
Merrick, Virginia 60.11
Merrill, Dina 14.239, 14.240, 41.44, 106.18, 126.172
Merrill, Gary 17.29, 17.30, 29.5, 72.1, 83.31, 85.13, 101.34, 117.19, 126.17, 162.11, 178.29, 178.37, 178.60, 178.145
Merrow, Jane 5.24, 9.5
Merton, John 32.31, 32.37, 32.79, 32.86, 73.22, 97.6, 97.63, 135.56, 169.27, 169.42, 169.52, 169.80
Merwin, William 152.41
Messersmith, Randolph 177.56
Metcalf, Mark 163.21
Metcalfe, Burt 43.157, 57.115
Metcalfe, Vince 67.14
Metchik, Aaron Michael 48.32
Metrango, Leo V. 17.46
Metrano, Art 14.358, 26, 116.14

Metzinger, Kraig 96.95, 137
Meurer, Raymond 97.150, 97.157
Meyer, Emile 6.37, 8.19, 8.46, 14.357, 20.48, 34.23, 43.52, 60.89, 60.90, 85.55, 89.65, 92.19, 105.41, 114.5, 117.36, 126.116, 129.10, 129.17, 145.4, 148.77, 149.51, 167.18, 178.18
Meyers, Dick 71.78, 74.22, 74.28
Meyler, Fintan 14.23, 65.50, 65.168, 65.189, 66.24, 66.107, 66.180, 74.17, 127.7, 152.32, 156.2, 162.74, 162.89, 179.78
Micale, Paul 5.6, 5.31, 14.241, 65.502
Michael, Frank 83.43
Michaelian, Michael 116.22
Michaels, Beverly 27.8
Michaels, Corrine 96.69
Michaels, Dolores 85.92
Michaels, Janna 48.78
Michaels, Joseph 23.16, 23.23, 60.81
Michaels, Shawn 66.184, 170.22
Michaels, Susan 70.3
Michaels, Toby 14.131
Michell, Cameron 109.7
Michell, Laurie 164.51
Michelle, Donna 12.21
Michelle, James 116.7
Michenaud, Gerald 116.10
Michener, James 26
Michon, Pat 14.20, 14.63, 25.50, 81.10, 81.37, 85.56, 124.44, 124.9, 126.49, 131.19, 131.36, 148.142, 148.170, 149.24, 158.62, 172.5
Middlebrooks, Harry 65.625
Middleton, Bill T. 177.21
Middleton, Ray 69.1
Middleton, Robert 5.27, 5.36, 8.1, 12.49, 12.82, 14.32, 14.155, 14.269, 41.49, 65.3, 65.32, 65.277, 83.35, 107.6, 107.12, 107.15, 107.17, 126.131, 126.147, 126.170, 126.171, 126.215, 127.59, 148.122, 148.134, 148.148, 148.175, 149.1, 153.1, 153.2, 162.98, 167.15, 170.18, 172.2, 178.146
Middleton, Travis 177.28, 177.32
Midthunder, David Paul 90.14
Mikler, Michael T. 5.47, 14.138, 14.380, 30.7, 51.18, 65.204, 65.282, 65.287, 76.11, 127.30, 144.30, 161.10, 165.3, 165.5, 165.8, 165.11, 178.107, 178.127
Milan, George 102.28, 138.68, 141.37
Milan, Lita 66.33, 77.8, 78.27
Milanesa, James 65.637
Miler, Elva 132.4
Miles, Bob 14.143
Miles, Joanna 7.3
Miles, Marc 90.11
Miles, Peter 34.27, 97.215
Miles, Richard 102.20
Miles, Robert, Jr. 14.35, 65.428
Miles, Sherry 71.76
Miles, Vera 5.20, 14.243, 14.386, 55.3, 65.519, 75.6, 75.7, 75.8, 85.33, 95.18, 106.10, 126.29, 131.3, 161.20, 161.74, 162.64, 162.259, 162.283, 178.102
Milford, John 12.2, 12.31, 12.68, 12.90, 14.118, 14.317, 22.32, 27.100, 30.4, 30.19, 41.141, 46.11, 51.25, 57.97, 63.47, 65.209, 65.363, 65.440, 65.508, 65.521, 65.522, 65.606, 66.125, 66.138, 76.10, 84.5, 85.105, 88.18, 92, 93, 93.129, 93.153, 93.159, 93.164, 93.178, 93.188, 93.189, 96.68, 101.15, 117.15, 129.55, 129.75, 130.43, 130.53, 130.60, 130.64, 130.74, 130.80, 130.82, 130.100, 130.104, 130.115, 130.150, 131.43, 142.34, 144.20, 146.63, 148.88, 148.140, 152.6, 152.43, 159.5, 161.21, 161.42, 161.84, 161.159, 164.23, 167.18, 179.100
Milhil, Billy 20.19
Milhoan, Michael 120.54
Milhollin, James 148.148
Miljan, John 54.16, 78.21
Millan, Art 93.58

Millan, Lynne 25.11, 93.65
Millan, Victor 6.71, 6.74, 12.78, 14.44, 20.19, 20.54, 23.42, 73.2, 73.28, 76.36, 81.1, 83.19, 148.7, 156.12, 164.82, 167.8, 169.99
Millard, Harry 89.30
Millard, Helene 32.48
Millay, Arthur 170.65
Millay, Diana 14.64, 65.232, 85.87, 93.193, 105.92, 126.103, 126.141, 128.9, 130.94, 142.7, 148.196, 151.9, 157.6, 161.56, 162.180, 165.1, 166.18
Miller, Ben 107.25
Miller, Billy 3.105, 23.28, 138.55
Miller, Cheryl Lynn 24.15
Miller, Dennis 85.30, 119.16
Miller, Denny 43.400, 44.68, 48.843, 48.84, 65.548, 66.122, 71.39, 85.39, 99.13, 99.15, 106.15, 114.1, 118.4, 130.87, 142.16, 175.2
Miller, Dick 14.125, 17.37, 162.264
Miller, Eve 6.41, 6.63, 6.65, 124.4, 124.7, 156.8, 178.31
Miller, Frederick 66.48
Miller, Jesse Dillon 48.40
Miller, Kenneth 32.138
Miller, Kristine 129.33, 145, 145.17, 148.152, 152.36, 152.75, 162.35, 169.17
Miller, Mark 65.145, 83.30, 144.7, 149.62
Miller, Marvin 8.103
Miller, Michael T. 43.300
Miller, Pat 141.60
Miller, Peter 93.163, 149.71
Miller, Roger 41.140
Miller, Sarah 96.155
Miller, Scott 162
Miller, Stephen 99.1, 99.2, 99.3
Miller, Ty 177
Milletaire, Carl 20.40, 32.31, 89.37, 103.13
Millican, James 169.52, 169.59
Millicano, Pat 1.22
Milligan, Spencer 7.14, 53.1, 65.630
Milligan, Tuck 120.10
Millikin, Bill 144.4
Mills, Alley 48.23, 48.67, 48.93, 48.94
Mills, Brooke 7
Mills, Donna 65.595, 65.596, 84.43, 115.6, 175.5, 175.6
Mills, Edwin 41.94, 61.6, 66.106, 164.69
Mills, Gordon 147.2
Mills, John 49
Mills, Juliet 5.10, 101.29
Mills, Mort 4.13, 5.48, 8.42, 12.4, 12.5, 12.24, 14.13, 14.100, 14.116, 14.260, 20.21, 20.38, 21.5, 21.42, 27.14, 32.93, 32.97, 32.132, 32.136, 41.93, 41.121, 42, 63.43, 63.44, 65.15, 65.31, 65.86, 65.148, 65.347, 65.450, 66.70, 73.23, 76.11, 81.69, 85.52, 85.69, 85.93, 88.9, 89.120, 93.61, 93.197, 97.172, 101.10, 102.6, 103, 105.19, 116.12, 130.9, 130.136, 142.12, 142.23, 142.38, 146.12, 146.49, 148.89, 148.120, 152.58, 156.3, 156.51, 161.16, 162.269, 162.284, 164.3, 164.16, 164.28, 164.38, 164.56, 167.6, 170.5, 178.16, 178.139
Milner, Jessamine 65.598
Milner, Martin 74.3, 86.4, 97.28, 101.32, 126.3, 161.86, 161.129, 162.28
Milo, Christopher 38.14, 92.31
Milton, George 20.70
Milton, Gerald 8.33, 8.66, 8.77, 44.10, 66.7, 66.185, 77.6, 126.23, 148.4, 152.38, 164.83
Mims, William 5.4, 5.35, 12.36, 12.46, 14.50, 14.179, 14.415, 21.36, 27.71, 36.7, 41.54, 41.97, 43.191, 51.31, 65.538, 65.539, 66.90, 66.206, 83.11, 83.61, 84.45, 89.94, 89.144, 93.196, 93.212, 116.4, 125.10, 133.35, 148.153, 148.199, 150.4, 161.85, 162.207, 162.216, 162.243, 165.2, 170.3
Minardos, Nico 5.13, 5.29, 12.36, 17.29, 17.30, 20.26, 55.17, 72.5, 105.34, 116.4, 127.52, 128.4, 131.34, 146.52, 162.9

Mincks, Jonathan 177.51
Miner, Mark 178.86
Mines, Steven 12.42
Minner, Kathryn 65.481
Minotto, James 65.533
Minzies, Liza 79.12
Mioni, Fabrizio 12.61, 14.190, 21.38, 43.243, 71.42, 161.113
Miracle, Irene 120.8
Miranda, Claudio 5.41
Miranda, John 120
Miranda, Mark 41.121, 161.125
Miranda, Susana 106.2
Misco, Ernie 170.36
Misura, Nick 67.8
Mitchell, Belle 2.24, 60.38, 60.40, 73.22, 138.54, 169.20
Mitchell, Cameron 5.35, 14.18, 24.6, 34.23, 41.51, 41.68, 43.185, 59.2, 65.618, 71, 75.5, 123.5, 162.69, 178.54, 178.77, 178.100
Mitchell, Carlyle 8.93, 14.15, 27.37, 27.74, 105.18, 129.37, 129.40, 133.6, 133.13, 148.43, 155.33, 178.20
Mitchell, Chris 145.7, 145.32
Mitchell, Dallas 30.22, 34.30, 34.39, 65.167, 65.220, 66.92, 131.27
Mitchell, Don 161.145
Mitchell, Ewing 2, 6.50, 6.73, 6.79, 23.5, 23.11, 43.122, 60.28, 60.30, 60.35, 60.37, 60.40, 60.56, 60.59, 81.41, 93.64, 97.201, 97.218, 124.33, 124.35, 124.40, 124.42, 124.44, 124.47, 124.48, 124.66, 124.71, 124.72, 129.45, 135.70, 135.72, 135.97, 135.98, 138.65, 141, 147.30, 158.28, 158.30, 169.54
Mitchell, Frank 89.91, 162.233
Mitchell, George 14.19, 14.81, 14.311, 25.57, 43.25, 43.155, 43.251, 43.280, 55.14, 65.163, 65.205, 66.45, 66.131, 84.15, 85.21, 85.45, 88.9, 101.13, 106.24, 144.2, 144.6, 144.13, 148.115, 149.10, 150.4, 161.112
Mitchell, Guy 119.3, 166
Mitchell, Hamilton 91.7, 91.10
Mitchell, Harry 158.47
Mitchell, Irving 74.18, 130.6
Mitchell, Keith 62, 96.150
Mitchell, Laurie 14.40, 14.155, 21.65, 44.25, 102.18, 105.106, 126.92, 159.34, 161.135, 162.114, 162.249
Mitchell, Les 135.86, 135.90, 135.92, 138.47
Mitchell, Maggie 161.109
Mitchell, Minga 44.50
Mitchell, Pat 60.73, 169.16, 169.27
Mitchell, Patric 124.45
Mitchell, Paula 14.349
Mitchell, Sharren J. 1.3
Mitchell, Steve 6.7, 8.81, 23.18, 23.24, 44.25, 64.5, 66.2, 97.107, 126.15, 138.32, 148.87, 158.20, 158.23, 170.73
Mitchell, Thomas 85.10, 142.17, 178.58, 178.82, 178.141
Mitchlll, Scoey 70.27
Mitchum, James 66.193, 71.54
Mitchum, John 3.100, 14.91, 14.145, 14.172, 17.23, 46.6, 52, 65.62, 65.108, 65.154, 65.294, 66.175, 76.36, 80.28, 80.37, 86.4, 92.2, 93.63, 96.41, 121.14, 126.151, 129.16, 129.34, 131, 132.12, 138.27, 141.71, 148.190, 161.27, 161.55, 161.99, 161.106, 162.22
Mobley, Mary Ann 38.1, 76.21, 161.136
Mobley, Roger 22.22, 27.93, 27.99, 39.17, 43.273, 46.11, 51.12, 55.20, 57, 65.236, 117.19, 149.57, 161.4, 162.56, 162.131, 162.138, 162.157, 162.172, 162.191, 162.215, 168.3
Mock, Laurie 30.61, 61.9, 61.10, 65.506, 71.26
Moe, Marilyn 107.1
Moede, Titus 66.184

Moffat, Donald 111
Moffat, Katherine 91.1
Moffatt, Donald 14.350, 14.397. 28.7, 28.9, 45.1, 65.605, 70.30, 71.73, 84.43, 96.83
Mohr, Gerald 4.15, 8.30, 8.93, 12.111, 14.40, 14.209, 14.285, 21.5, 21.45, 21.68, 27.9, 27.75, 43.342, 44.26, 76.29, 79.11, 86.57, 105.12, 105.22, 105.27, 105.33, 105.57, 105.85, 105.105, 117.4, 117.9, 117.35, 119.14, 121.9, 126.20, 130.153, 133.27, 142.4, 146.16, 146.46, 148.108, 152.15, 155.29, 164.10, 178.8
Molen, Annette 84.49
Molieri, Lillian 32.151, 73.2, 81.1, 81.36, 145.14
Moll, Richard 10.2, 48.48, 75.19
Moloney, Janel 1.7
Moloney, Jim 97.108
Monahan, Mike 146.14
Monay, Maria 23.28
Mondo, Peggy 89.150
Monroe, Alfred 35.11, 35.30, 35.31
Monroe, Del 39.10, 65.407, 65.550, 65.593, 84.7, 84.17, 84.48, 92.15, 93.181
Monroe, Michael 43.53
Monroe, Tom 6.27, 6.39, 12.43, 23.16, 23.23, 32.58, 32.64, 35.2, 35.9, 35.19, 35.21, 35.22, 35.25, 35.32, 35.35, 60.20, 60.22, 60.28, 60.30, 80.29, 80.30, 80.39, 93.29, 93.55, 93.95, 93.122, 93.173, 124.4, 124.7, 124.57, 124.69, 124.70, 124.73, 124.6, 148.51, 149.40, 158.16, 162.34, 169.28, 169.78
Monroe, Vaughn 14.90
Monsell, Roy 170.64
Monsour, Nyra 43.120
Montaigne, Lawrence 9.9, 14.410, 41.33, 41.80, 70.39, 72.7, 86.49
Montalban, Ricardo 14.39, 41.74, 43.181, 61.1, 61.2, 65.516, 71.23, 71.40, 75.4, 75.5, 106.12, 112.2, 131.9, 161.5, 161.181, 162.2, 170.43, 179.82
Montana, Monte 56.24, 130.14, 130.56, 158.54
Montana, Monte, Jr. 65.272
Monte, Albert 71.52
Montell, Jovan 88.23
Montell, Lisa 8.51, 20.15, 27.4, 27.66, 34.7, 44.66, 60.82, 66.84, 78.59, 105.107, 113.1, 113.2, 114.23, 146.16, 146.46, 148.9
Montenaro, Tony 167.1
Montgomery, Belinda J. 5.16, 75.25, 111.5, 161.213
Montgomery, Bryan 5.18
Montgomery, C. Elliott 5.12
Montgomery, Elizabeth 29.6, 55.6, 126.146, 131.2, 162.88
Montgomery, George 5.18, 14.223, 29, 162.17
Montgomery, John D. 29.11
Montgomery, Lee H. 69.2
Montgomery, Missy 29.11
Montgomery, Ralph 14.159, 14.226
Montgomery, Ray 41.40, 57.30, 93.19, 97.55, 97.68, 97.127, 97.157, 126.39, 126.64, 126.100, 168.18
Montgomery, Robert, Jr. 43.194, 44.23, 149.17
Montgomery, Tom 8.49
Montoya, Alex 14.119, 20.30, 25.28, 65.315, 65.316, 65.460, 71.5, 71.33, 71.34, 81.23, 126.24, 126.49, 126.85, 130.144, 130.145, 145.2, 148.139, 149.60, 158.18, 158.20, 161.29, 161.114, 162.163
Montoya, Julia 34.53, 73.39, 71.42, 149.60, 169.95
Montoya, Julio 164.82
Monty, Eva 92.19
Moody, Jeanne 54.25, 78.2, 78.15, 78.36
Moody, King 14.303, 71.9, 96.96
Moody, Lynne 118.4, 163.75
Moody, Ralph 3.35, 3.65, 3.80, 3.88, 3.103, 3.154, 8.24, 13.22, 13.27, 14.147, 14.160, 14.218, 14.390, 20.46, 20.64, 27.12, 31.6, 31.9, 31.23, 31.41, 41.7, 43.303, 44.33, 61.6, 65.156, 65.192, 65.283, 65.322, 66.63, 66.146, 78.64, 82.15, 88.10, 89.145, 89.148, 97.8, 97.40, 97.44, 107.4, 126.13,

Personnel Index

126.145, 127.20, 130.58, 130.61, 130.76, 130.91, 130.94, 130.100, 130.106, 130.130, 130.147, 130.151, 130.156, 130.165, 135.80, 135.82, 149.54, 152.1, 152.25, 152.47, 162.98, 164.2, 170.14, 178.10, 178.119
Moody, Ron 65.591
Moon, Wally 162.94
Mooney, John 145.9
Moore, Alvy 41.24, 43.250, 43.310, 79.18, 79.31, 92.15, 142.26, 161.30, 161.67, 161.76, 168.6, 178.138
Moore, Archie 139.14, 139.15, 162.244
Moore, Candy 126.69, 126.101, 162.150
Moore, Clayton 6.14, 60.55, 60.61, 60.73, 73.14, 97, 124.58, 124.61, 169.40
Moore, Constance 85.18
Moore, Del 14.268, 52.20, 106.12, 162.136
Moore, Dennis 3.104, 6.29, 6.40, 8.15, 8.38, 8.50, 8.93, 22.9, 22.17, 23.5, 23.11, 23.18, 23.24, 23.28, 23.39, 32.16, 32.22, 32.27, 32.32, 32.39, 32.105, 32.112, 32.126, 57.94, 60.31, 60.33, 60.43, 60.45, 60.87, 80.20, 80.24, 80.25, 81.83, 93.67, 93.104, 97.146, 97.192, 97.200, 97.213, 97.219, 124.22, 129.37, 133.38, 135.74, 135.77, 135.78, 135.100, 138.33, 138.55, 141.20, 141.24, 141.35, 141.37, 141.64, 145.7, 145.32, 147.27, 148.155, 155.2, 155.25, 155.27, 155.34, 156.41, 162.48, 169.19, 169.88
Moore, Gloria 141.31
Moore, Henrietta 65.277
Moore, Joanna 8.42, 8.47, 36.2, 39.10, 41.56, 51.13, 65.185, 65.195, 65.375, 71.62, 76.44, 105.61, 127.35, 130.44, 131.15, 133.37, 148.108, 161.24, 161.34, 161.69, 161.161, 162.2, 162.251, 170.15
Moore, Juanita 83.56, 83.57, 83.58, 83.59, 162.219
Moore, Mary Tyler 21.27, 44.51, 131.37, 164.73
Moore, Michael 43.24, 43.50
Moore, Norma 146.23, 153, 155.22
Moore, Roger 4, 105, 105.45
Moore, Terry 14.367, 51, 126.1, 127.76, 161.131
Moore, Tom 169.59
Moorehead, Agnes 38.14, 84.35, 106.6, 126.62, 127.10, 130.90, 162.10, 170.48
Moorehead, Jean 43.101, 114.21
Moran, Eric 65.554
Moran, Erin 9.4, 43.428, 43.429, 65.548
Moran, Johnny 48.69, 48.70
Moran, Margie 32.131
Moran, Pat 93.219
Moran, Patsy 32.103
Morante, Milburn 32.42, 32.44, 32.48, 32.51
Moray, Dean 55.2
Moreland, Sherry 32.42, 32.48, 81.7
Morell, Ann 17.18, 65.247
Moreno, Jorge 65.460, 65.515, 71.1, 71.33, 71.45, 105.24, 116.4, 126.11, 126.34
Moreno, Jose 170.51
Moreno, Rita 29.25, 69.6, 148.74, 156.54, 178.81, 179.79, 179.80
Moreno, Ruben 12.62, 14.382, 28.11, 43.375, 43.446, 50.5, 63.16, 65.460, 84.1, 93.222, 125.6, 161.91
Morgan, Alexandra 65.601
Morgan, Bob 36.16, 36.17, 65.124, 129.38
Morgan, Boyd "Red" 5.11, 6.31, 30.16, 32.84, 32.91, 41.53, 46.7, 60.68, 65.531, 66.167, 71.42, 89.132, 93.214, 124.37, 124.41, 124.43, 124.44, 124.45, 124.52, 126.101, 127.58, 127.65, 135.2, 135.3, 135.4, 135.21, 135.29, 135.38, 135.39, 135.43, 141.36, 148.185, 149.17, 152.23, 152.34, 152.45, 162.139, 165.5, 166.14
Morgan, Ed 158.3, 158.4, 158.6, 158.7, 158.31, 158.43
Morgan, Eula 97.26, 124.54
Morgan, George 14.342, 14.359

Morgan, Hallie 137
Morgan, Harry 65.526, 65.572, 65.630, 66.50, 66.213, 69, 161.28
Morgan, Henry 65.617
Morgan, John 97.70
Morgan, Judson 109.10
Morgan, Lee 32.146, 32.150, 32.156, 35.12, 60.35, 60.37
Morgan, Loann 135.97
Morgan, Mae 97.191
Morgan, May 80.31
Morgan, Michael 64.11, 96.77, 130.9, 155.16, 155.59, 165.7
Morgan, Paula 43.44
Morgan, Read 5.24, 14.186, 30.13, 38.14, 44, 44.5, 65.136, 65.369, 65.512, 65.519, 65.545, 65.559, 65.564, 65.565, 65.572, 65.591, 74.20, 85.9, 85.14, 85.29, 106.14, 120.41, 121.6, 129.40, 131.2, 148.87, 162.67, 162.83, 162.232, 166.16, 168.12, 169.61, 178.119
Morgan, Rex 130.118
Morgan, Stacy 55.12, 85.84
Morgan, Stafford 41.138
Morgan, Tracy 84.2, 98.3
Moriarity, Joanne 149.32
Morick, Dave 5.36, 5.44, 41.75, 41.76
Morin, Alberto 86.1, 148.141, 161.91, 170.1
Morison, Patricia 66.54
Morita, Pat 83.61
Morland, Gloria 130.132
Morlas, John 169.74
Morley, Fay 32.109, 32.120, 32.153
Morley, Jay 97.43
Morley, Karen 83.12
Morley, Kay 32.30, 32.36, 97.5
Morphy, Louis 60.11, 60.13
Morrell, Anne 139.10
Morrill, Priscilla 19.2, 19.4, 19.6, 19.9, 170.77
Morris, Aubrey 118.7
Morris, Bea 96.16
Morris, Ben 22.14, 105.40, 130.25, 162.30, 162.31, 162.53, 164.78
Morris, Chester 30.22, 126.60, 178.28
Morris, Dorothy 126.25, 126.108
Morris, Eric 89.28
Morris, Frances 44.27, 103.46, 105.27, 126.36, 129.45, 162.23, 162.252, 169.3
Morris, Greg 17.25, 17.26
Morris, Howard 164.90
Morris, Jeff 7.2, 14.320, 14.379, 14.411, 43.291, 178.103
Morris, Michael 130.155
Morris, Phyllis 97.63
Morris, Robert 88.13, 164.58
Morris, Rusty 43.36, 43.52
Morris, Wayne 8.19, 21.18, 34.2, 65.103, 89.13, 105.39, 162.49, 164.24
Morriseau, Renae 67.15
Morrison, Ann 65.223, 66.193, 148.133
Morrison, Barbara 116.25, 126.37
Morrison, Bob 76.18
Morrison, Brian 65.554, 65.559
Morrison, Hollis 70.3, 70.7, 70.15
Morrison, James 163.30
Morrison, Shelley 65.403, 86.4, 86.12. 86.23, 86.57
Morriss, Ann 34.42
Morrow, Brad 23.35, 23.36, 60.87, 78.7, 93.40, 93.99, 97.202, 126.169, 135.44, 148.5, 148.67, 162.110, 162.226, 169.69, 169.73, 169.100
Morrow, Byron 8.100, 12.99, 14.239, 14.240, 14.282, 14.313, 19.6, 43.345, 51.25, 64.8, 70.37, 84.15, 101.27, 126.80, 126.101, 128.1, 155.70, 161.14, 162.243, 170.8, 170.92
Morrow, Jeff 14.69, 27.93, 41.74, 41.113, 44.42, 54.5, 76.9, 108.7, 130.163, 148.199,160, 161.20, 162.95, 178.33

Morrow, Jo 85.121, 89.144, 105.120
Morrow, Neyle 23.33, 146.29, 156.30, 169.6, 169.30
Morrow, Patricia 65.524, 161.225
Morrow, Scott 22.9, 22.21, 22.33, 31.26, 129.73, 162.101, 169.94
Morrow, Susan 4.15, 21.31, 65.61, 65.65, 89.65, 105.76
Morrow, Vic 14.26, 14.79, 43.236, 79.12, 117.3, 117.21, 117.35, 129.1, 130.13, 130.50, 149.49, 156.12, 167.4
Morry, Scotty 135.95
Morse, Barry 162.197
Morse, Freeman 93.141
Morse, Richardson 120.50
Morse, Robert 5.16
Morton, Charles 162.246
Morton, Gregory 41.1, 41.40, 43.215, 101.24, 146.65, 149.33, 149.73, 150.5, 170.43
Morton, Judee 14.133, 61.9, 61.10
Morton, Mickey 8.94, 65.268, 70.34, 126.92, 173.32
Morton, Randy 53.12
Morton, Rob 67.13
Moschitta, John, Jr. 181
Mosely, Page 177.8
Mosely, Roger 83.32
Moses, Marian 86.25, 161.141
Moses, Rick 174
Mosley, Irving 170.83
Mosley, Roger 94.29
Moss, Arnold 14.296, 41.86, 86.35, 130.86
Moss, Bill 14.177
Moss, Ellen 14.393, 161.172
Moss, Jesse 67.7
Moss, Mary Dean 32.45, 32.52
Moss, Michael 91.2
Moss, Stewart 14.219, 14.220, 14.432, 24.24, 65.639, 98.16
Mossley, Robin 67.9
Mott, Zachary 1.15
Mountanto, John 170.30
Mountfort, Diane 14.80, 57.83, 65.269, 162.235, 168.23
Mouton, Benjamin 163.9
Movita 81.13
Mowbray, Alan 105.78, 166.17
Mower, Jack 97.63
Mowery, Helen 25.33
Mpinduzi-Mott, Manning 163.75
Mueller, John 1.12
Muellerleile, Marianne 110.3
Muir, Gavin 8.25, 114.11
Muldaur, Diana 5.6, 14.308, 65.430, 69.4, 83.27, 106.15, 116.2, 161.156
Mulhall, Jack 2.21, 81.8, 81.99, 169.70
Mulhare, Edward 36.13, 38.15, 41.23, 41.30, 41.100
Mulhern, Matt 65.638
Mullaney, Jack 117.6
Mullavey, Greg 5.17, 12.100, 14.294, 14.415, 26, 65.545, 161.200
Mullen, Frank 158.19, 158.40, 158.43
Mullen, Virginia 32.79
Mulligan, Richard 14.388, 14.396, 65.452, 96.44
Mullins, Michael 96.83
Mulqueen, Kathleen 130.1, 130.13, 130.46, 130.94, 141.21, 145.27, 148.28
Mummert, Danny 73.15
Mumy, Billy 51.16, 70.41, 84.29, 161.89, 162.204, 168.1
Munch, Phil 158.11, 158.12
Munday, Mary 13.32, 13.40, 44.58, 65.218, 65.325, 66.147, 66.190, 144.9
Muneko, Yaski 4.32
Munro, Lochlyn 67
Munroe, Tom 89.138
Munsel, Patrice 170.100

Munson, Warren 12.44, 53, 70.21, 120.22, 120.25, 120.27, 120.28, 120.29, 120.31, 120.32
Murcelo, Karmin 26
Murdoch Lancer 84
Murdock, Alec 65.618
Murdock, George 14.304, 14.365, 24.22, 30.18, 43.321, 46.7, 65.426, 65.451, 65.559, 65.618, 65.420, 76.28, 96.60, 161.209, 170.45
Murdock, James 107.1
Murdock, Jim 126
Murdock, Kermit 5.28, 71.95, 83.4
Murdock, Minerva 31.25
Murnik, Peter 65.637
Murphey, Michael Martin 99.9
Murphy, Audie 166
Murphy, Barri 163.43
Murphy, Ben 5, 28, 48.6, 48.58, 161.175, 161.179
Murphy, Bill 65.155, 80.1
Murphy, Bob 65.279
Murphy, Donald 8.61, 54.17, 89.68, 93.78, 93.113, 93.145, 122.22, 155.65
Murphy, Jan 132.25
Murphy, Jimmy 6.30., 22.28, 41.98, 93.201
Murphy, Mary 43.373, 85.59, 86.51, 127.73, 128.1, 129.67, 162.16, 165.11
Murphy, Maura 6.4, 6.12, 43.125, 54.20, 54.23, 73.11
Murphy, Melissa 14.315, 14.335, 14.424, 65.511, 65.558, 65.563, 84.27
Murphy, Michael 5.2, 14.287, 14.288, 70.6
Murphy, Pamela 161.221
Murphy, Rosemary 48.17, 161.7, 168.2
Murphy, William 65.453, 65.470, 65.475, 65.538, 65.539
Murray, Alena 138.32
Murray, Don 75.1, 75.2, 75.3, 116
Murray, Fred 97.16
Murray, Gary 105.83
Murray, Guy 97.210
Murray, Ian 32.152, 130.28, 130.35, 130.44, 130.74, 130.76, 130.88
Murray, Jan 36.16, 36.17, 178.142
Murray, Ken 43.207, 43.280
Murray, Rick 65.319
Murray, Ricky 97.134, 138.53, 178.74
Murray, Tom 147.3
Murray, Zon 3.68, 14.150, 32.17, 32.19, 32.25, 32.43, 32.49, 32.53, 32.60, 32.105, 32.122, 32.127, 32.139, 32.142, 44.45, 60.11, 60.13, 64.5, 73.36, 81.36, 93.43, 93.94, 93.209, 97.28, 97.97, 97.134, 97.207, 97.214, 105.2, 126.23, 135.2, 135.3, 135.29, 135.39, 138.53, 138.77, 145.23, 147.27, 169.2, 169.14, 169.68
Murrill, Milton 67.17
Murtagh, Kate 41.72, 101.11, 162.244
Mustin, Burt 3.21, 5.14, 14.130, 14.210, 14.247, 30.14, 30.20, 46.10, 65.458, 65.467, 81.12, 97.152, 105.28, 121.9, 147.9, 152.78, 155.46, 162.243
Myer, Martha 17.28
Myers, Kim 163.11, 177.53
Myers, Paulene 65.487, 78.32
Myhers, John 71.87
Mylong, John 13.5, 141.68

Nader, George 85.38, 109.1, 138.9
Naehrlich, John 48.39
Nagel, Anne 31.49, 124.2, 124.5
Nagel, Conrad 8.17, 65.266
Nail, Joanne 175.2
Nairne, Richmond 68.12
Naish, J. Carrol 14.302, 29.10, 129.57, 152.4, 162.59, 162.96, 164.12
Naismith, Laurence 14.334, 84.10
Nakopoulou, Aspa 71.78
Nanasi, Anna Maria 3.107, 22.9, 31.49, 146.18, 156.50, 164.34

Napier, Alan 41.25, 41.26, 41.42, 86.13, 148.165, 148.193
Napier, Charles 115, 118, 120.23
Napier, John 14.225
Napier, Paul 96.141
Naranjo, Ivan 50.10, 65.595, 65.596, 83.38, 83.39
Narcisco, Grazia 81.51, 162.25
Nardini, Tom 9.5, 24.6, 30.6, 36, 43.311, 65.392, 83.51
Narita, Richard 83.43, 83.47, 83.48
Nash, Bob 74.15
Nash, Brian 161.154
Nash, Eddie 32.47
Nash, Jennifer 90.11
Nash, Marilyn 73.9
Nash, Noreen 73.8, 97.105, 173.6, 173.26
Nash, Robert 93.189, 164.77, 169.113
Nathan, Stephen 14.428
Natoli, Ric 41.90, 70.32, 86.48
Natwick, Mildred 14.320
Navarro, Anna 8.96, 14.257, 14.286, 14.371, 25.34, 25.45, 25.62, 32.135, 32.143, 43.79, 65.424, 71.10, 73.39, 81.52, 81.57, 93.160, 107.9, 117.25, 148.180, 151.2, 156.12, 164.4
Navarro, Demetrius 163.58
Navarro, Ramon 170.59
Naylor, B. 60.15
Naylor, Cal 65.409, 65.446
Nazarr, Norman 141.52
Neal, Patricia 83.40, 96.30, 96.31
Neal, Tom 60.11, 60.13, 148.57, 169.32
Nealson, John 30.22, 38.10
Nechero, Frank 20.43, 146.47
Needham, Hal 30.4, 65.494, 66.92, 66.95, 66.97, 66.110, 66.112, 66.123, 66.128, 66.136, 66.139, 66.149, 66.163, 66.166, 66.176, 66.189, 66.199, 66.207, 66.216, 66.217, 126.102, 126.175, 127.49, 131.44, 144.20, 148.185, 161.8, 162.150, 162.262
Needham, Leo 8.19, 14.34, 32.148, 32.153
Neely, Mark 26, 96.81
Neff, Ralph 43.198, 65.506, 105.49, 138.71, 142.33, 149.10, 151.12, 158.33, 169.94
Negley, Howard J. 2.9, 2.14, 20.39, 44.30, 73.3, 73.23, 81.52, 93.18, 93.153, 105.6, 113.10, 129.8, 135.84, 135.85, 145.12, 145.34, 148.10, 148.55, 148.184, 149.37, 152.10, 164.50, 164.59, 167.11, 169.36, 178.23
Neil, Robert 97.107, 97.118
Neill, Noel 32.7, 97.69
Neise, George 8.29, 21.67, 27.27, 43.137, 43.445, 66.105, 97.179, 102.26, 105.120, 114.21, 130.68, 142.13, 156.21, 156.41, 167, 179.72, 179.73, 179.74, 179.75
Nelkin, Stacey 28
Nelson, Arvid 13.2, 159.21
Nelson, Barry 178.116
Nelson, Bek 8.95, 14.2, 22.36, 44.32, 89, 129.53, 129.78, 147.27, 164.55
Nelson, Bert 129.38
Nelson, Billy 43.105, 155.34, 155.50, 169.90
Nelson, Burt 93.116
Nelson, David 72.16
Nelson, Dick 126.22
Nelson, Ed 5.44, 8.20, 8.105, 13.20, 13.25, 14.100, 19.6, 39.11, 43.246, 44.53, 65.148, 65.168, 65.234, 65.266, 65.329, 66.70, 66.74, 66.87, 79.24, 83.15, 85.57, 85.64, 85.108, 93.199, 105.120, 126.17, 126.49, 126.80, 126.124, 127.4, 127.33, 127.37, 127.43, 127.53, 128.12, 130.85, 130.88, 130.112, 131.30, 144.11, 148.154, 148.173, 149.74, 161.17, 162.152, 162.223, 162.238, 168.4, 178.78, 178.103, 178.124, 178.135
Nelson, Felix 43.18
Nelson, Gaye 47.10, 137.9
Nelson, Gene 8.23, 13.40, 65.155, 65.164, 65.199, 66.62, 88.30, 105.21, 114.20, 126.26
Nelson, Herbert 83.28, 96.68

Nelson, Jay 130.154
Nelson, Lloyd 65.545, 65.562, 65.573, 65.585, 65.613
Nelson, Lori 85.59, 146.48, 148.106, 152.37, 162.76, 164.31, 166.14
Nelson, Ned 65.281
Nelson, Nels 14.146
Nelson, Ricky 72.9
Nelson, Willie 48.103
Nephew, Neil 61.4, 126.148
Nervik, Rik 65.213
Nesbitt, Cathleen 51.10, 162.65
Nesbitt, Chance 21.30
Nesci, John 177.31
Nesmith, Ottola 27.68, 126.189, 170.14
Ness, Ralph 138.36
Nethery, Miriam Byrd 175.7
Nettleton, Lois 14.239, 14.240, 26, 41.119, 65.245, 65.431, 83.56, 83.57, 83.58, 83.59, 161.99, 161.181
Neumann, Dorothy 14.164, 14.264, 21.44, 65.251, 65.509, 65.558, 161.7, 169.107
Nevins, Claudette 177.55
Newbold, Bruce 120.41
Newby, Pat 66.207
Newcombe, Don 112.8
Newcomer, Jim 177.19, 177.64
Newell, William 65.205, 74.21, 152.14, 169.104
Newlan, Paul 22.35, 42, 46.10, 55.21, 65.16, 65.51, 145.38, 148.26, 162.250, 168.20
Newman, Andrew Hill 1.26, 91.6, 91.10
Newman, Melissa 14.386
Newman, Phyllis 170.31
Newman, William 48.72
Newmar, Julie 52.41
Newmark, Matthew 120
Newton, Christopher 67.5
Newton, John 13.35, 13.43, 65.243, 65.309, 79.33, 88.11, 144.13
Newton, Mary 14.137, 21.44, 97.197, 141.16, 141.53, 158.13
Newton, Richard 79.18, 147.45, 178.17
Newton, Theodore 25.19, 64.5, 89.104, 126.59, 126.96, 162.54, 162.55, 162.80, 162.97
Newton, Wayne 14.230, 14.250
Ney, Richard 66.159, 74.19, 114.7, 149.58
Neyland, Anne 152.23
Ng, Craig Ryan 1.24
Nicholas, Barbara 86.8, 142.6
Nicholas, Bob 156.39
Nicholas, Michele 14.400
Nicholas, Robert 5.38, 148.91
Nicholas, Ron 12.8, 150.5
Nicholas, Thomas Ian 48.25
Nichols, Arizona 112
Nichols, Barbara 105.15, 157.25, 170.20
Nichols, Janet 65.607
Nichols, Robert 12.67, 12.88, 14.28, 65.555, 93.24, 93.106, 93.161, 105.67, 105.79, 164.20, 164.33
Nichols, Taylor 48.2
Nicholson, Carol 27.95, 105.86
Nicholson, Jack 21.54, 148.147
Nicholson, Nick 8.52, 51.21, 85.103, 141.48, 141.59
Nickel, Earl 12.83
Nickles, Michael 163.23
Nielsen, Erik 57.9
Nielsen, Leslie 9.10, 12.109, 14.255, 28.11, 30.11, 41.11, 65.479, 83.56, 83.57, 83.58, 83.59, 98.4, 126.18, 161.62, 161.103, 161.119, 161.165, 161.203, 162.128, 162.264, 170.9
Nielsen, Lily 91.2
Nigh, Jane 34.48, 103.19, 126.20, 140.7, 148.29, 167.23
Niles, Benny 167.5
Niles, Denny 127.47
Niles, Wendell 31.13
Nilsson, Norma Jean 3.101

Personnel Index

Nimoy, Leonard 14.46, 14.433, 34.39, 41.46, 43.318, 65.247, 65.268, 65.295, 65.406, 85.84, 101.17, 126.81, 127.44, 133.30, 148.155, 149.6, 149.18, 150.7, 155.58, 158.54, 158.58, 158.60, 159.32, 161.45, 161.90, 161.100, 162.81, 162.103, 162.140
Nipar, Yvette 1.5, 1.7, 1.8
Nisbet, Stuart 14.64, 51.15, 86.26, 132.12, 161.113, 161.121, 161.164, 161.170, 161.190, 161.200, 161.224
Niven, David 178.22, 178.64
Niven, Kip 75.19
Nix, Martha 96.106
Nixon, Allan 80.8, 80.9, 80.11, 126.62, 126.83, 138.75, 147.20, 147.22, 169.60
Nixon, Cynthia 177.23, 177.24
Noakes, Tony 177.8
Noe, Robert 14.385, 158.50
Noel, Frank 28.7
Noel, Jimmy 93.124, 93.169
Noel, Karen 151.22
Noel, Tom 23.30, 138.72
Noga, Tom 177.30
Nogulich, Natalija 90
Nolan, James 34.6, 65.31, 77.71, 93.196, 156.5, 164.28, 170.78
Nolan, Jeanette 8.96, 13.14, 14.244, 24.19, 47, 52.31, 55.15, 65.83, 65.109, 65.215, 65.354, 65.538, 65.539, 65.554, 65.558, 66.29, 66.124, 66.179, 66.181, 69.5, 70.51, 74, 82.6, 85.112, 86.9, 86.25, 86.55, 89.27, 101.33, 117.21, 127.1, 129.64, 133.28, 148.46, 161, 161.1, 161.29, 162.149, 162.221, 162.273, 164.82
Nolan, Kathleen 12.25, 20.14, 38.8, 65, 269, 65.238, 65.599
Nolan, Kathy 155.40
Nolan, Lloyd 14.24, 41.19, 61.1, 61.2, 85.5, 85.70, 85.93, 117.41, 132.18, 161.37, 161.75, 161.156, 162.55, 178.63, 178.127
Nolan, Mark 126.58
Nolan, Tommy 22, 65.499, 71.31, 126.58, 130.137, 131.11, 162.84, 162.109, 162.204
Noland, Charles 1.1
Noland, Valora 85.99, 130.122, 161.148, 162.258
Nolte, Nick 65.620
Nomkeena, Keena 18
Nono, Claire 83.33, 83.60
Noonan, Barbara 70.44
Noonan, Sheila 65.73
Noonan, Tommy 127.63
Nordling, Jeffrey 177.45
Norell, Henry 149.5
Noriega, Eduardo 102.18, 152.76
Norman, B.G. 32.75, 32.112, 60.67, 97.48, 97.84, 97.93, 124.37, 124.43, 124.66, 135.49, 135.54, 156.32, 169.50
Norman, Bruce 60.43, 60.45
Norman, Hal Jon 14.44, 41.34, 41.48, 71.38, 126.99, 126.111, 126.174, 129.52, 130.15, 130.79, 148.125, 149.63, 170.64
Norman, Jim 158.3, 158.7, 158.19, 158.22
Norman, Maidie 43.327, 83.56, 83.57, 83.58, 83.59, 96.63, 168.18
Norman, Noralee 81.17, 135.54
Norman, Waldon 41.66
Norris, Chuck 163
Norris, Edward 169.69
Norris, Karen 178.122, 178.126
Norris, Mike 163.5, 163.33
Norris, Richard 152.78
Norsworthy, Robert 100.14
North, Jay 146.33, 162.266, 164.16
North, Sheree 5.33, 12.39, 61.4, 65.307, 69.8, 70.5, 76.15, 83.15, 98.14, 161.55, 161.118
North, Zeme 14.181, 17.33, 92.11, 126.186, 151.19, 162.192
Northrop, Wayne 177.2
Northrup, Harry E. 5.10

Norton, Cliff 43.391, 170.104, 175.9
Norton, Duke 93.201, 178.129
Norton, Ken, Jr. 1.27
Norton, Mark 150.6
Norton, Richard 163.5
Norton, Toby 118.4
Norwick, Natalie 15.3, 43.53, 66.63, 66.110, 66.132, 66.155, 66.189, 66.226, 88.27
Nova, Lou 73.27
Novack, Shelly 24.19, 65.518, 83.7, 83.37, 161.158, 161.202, 161.221
Novak, John 67.5
Novarro, Anna 14.348, 65.315, 65.316
Novarro, Ramon 14.205, 71.26, 113, 126.180
Novello, Jay 3.111, 3.133, 8.72, 14.185, 14.337, 21.2, 34.5, 34.43, 43.308, 43.375, 54.12, 52.46, 63.3, 63.49, 66.174, 66.192, 89.156, 105.3, 105.24, 105.28, 105.69, 127.26, 146.39, 156.13, 162.91, 167.19, 168.5, 179.35, 179.36, 179.37, 179.39
Novis, Donald 73.28, 80.1
Nozick, Bruce 48.54
Nuell, Fay 66.11
Nugent, Carol 43.99, 60.37, 127.3, 169.106
Nugent, Judy 6.11, 97.115, 126.40, 146.40, 149.9, 149.13, 149.23, 149.31, 149.55
Numkena, Anthony 162.26
Nunez, Daniel 61.8
Nunn, Alice 5.48
Nusser, Jim 20.17, 30.10, 65, 65.21, 132.3, 151.10, 170.68
Nutter, Mayf 65.445, 71.87
Nuyen, France 65.401, 65.415, 83.41

Oakie, Jack 14.250, 41.62
Oakland, Simon 4.10, 12.101, 13.11, 14.131, 14.282, 14.323, 1.5, 21.32, 24.18, 30.11, 41.32, 41.85, 41.131, 49.6, 65.46, 65.116, 65.168, 65.389, 66.39, 85.24, 117.17, 126.147, 126.205, 144.18, 148.185, 161.87, 161.105, 162.108, 162.203, 170.87, 178.99, 178.113
Oates, Warren 3.149, 8.27, 8.99, 12.10, 12.40, 13.10, 14.99, 17.17, 22.32, 30.4, 30.12, 49.1, 65.132, 65.198, 65.215, 65.246, 65.248, 65.326, 65.361, 65.381, 65.413, 65.439, 66.34, 66.126, 76.38, 79.31, 84.23, 84.47, 85.54, 89.87, 101.3, 107.4, 117.1, 126.46, 126.152, 126.175, 126.210, 127.7, 130.4, 130.42, 130.71, 130.84, 130.138, 133.31, 139.4, 142.13, 142.37, 144, 150.8, 155.41, 155.69, 156.51, 156.58, 156.68, 157.3, 161.41, 161.115, 161.123, 162.83, 164.14, 164.27, 164.36, 164.54, 164.84, 165.1, 172.3
Ober, Philip 8.90, 14.133, 43.219, 51.24, 76.6, 146.37, 151.10
Oberdiear, Karen 65.628
Oberlin, Bill 121.17
O'Brian, Hugh 59.4, 65.637, 93, 120.23, 120.24, 161.2
O'Brien, Chuck 170.10, 170.26, 170.36
O'Brien, Clay 37, 65.564, 65.565, 65.594, 96.29
O'Brien, Cubby 178.129
O'Brien, Devon 1.19
O'Brien, Edmond 24.15, 71.95, 85.7, 161.157, 178.34, 178.96
O'Brien, Erin 8.58, 8.103, 27.40, 34.1, 43.183, 85.75, 85.89, 105.6, 105.38, 108.34, 146.14, 146.18, 155.82
O'Brien, Joan 4.31, 8.14, 8.79, 21.38, 27.75, 44.41, 117.42, 126.105, 131.6, 149.59, 161.63, 162.111, 162.125, 165.6, 166.20
O'Brien, Kenneth 83.6, 83.16, 83.45, 96.112
O'Brien, Kim 65.616
O'Brien, Laurie 90.5, 163.86
O'Brien, Margaret 126.9, 162.39
O'Brien, Pat 5.26, 17.27, 161.48, 161.138
O'Brien, Richard 12.20, 12.28, 12.39, 12.89, 12.104, 14.392, 19.6, 26, 30.9, 30.20, 65.478, 65.575, 65.609, 84.25, 96.79, 170.74, 170.99, 170.103

O'Brien, Rory 14.96, 41.89, 41.160
O'Byrne, Bryan 12.48, 41.64, 65.545, 76.41, 98.15, 126.186, 161.14, 161.105
O'Byrne, Maggie 97.204
Ocean, Ivory 48.1
O'Connell, Arthur 5.38, 12.5, 14.391, 51.13, 101.31, 106.23, 142.20, 162.274, 162.283, 170.22, 178.136
O'Connell, J.P. 3.45
O'Connell, Susan 12.98, 84.17
O'Connell, William 41.37, 41.151, 41.160, 65.508, 126.185, 170.99
O'Connor, Carroll 14.133, 43.258, 49.8, 61.8, 65.416, 65.446, 144.20, 170.39
O'Connor, Glynnis 28
O'Connor, Larry 68.19
O'Connor, Peggy 43.84
O'Connor, Robert 103.33
O'Connor, Robert Emmett 6.1, 6.10
O'Connor, Rod 57.11
O'Connor, Tim 41.165, 65.342, 65.526, 65.567, 84.45, 109.8
O'Conor, Irene 96.139
O'Crotty, Peter 14.430
O'Dell, Doye 21.62, 51.32, 105.38, 146.31, 149.8
Oddo, Jerry 14.40, 25.34, 25.62, 103.50, 130.10, 141.64, 178.125
Odetta 66.163
Odin, Susan 170.47
Odney, Doug 43.140, 65.36, 89.95
O'Donnell, Cathy 14.148, 25.28, 103.49, 127.24, 127.51, 146.67, 150.11, 178.50
O'Donnell, Erin 14.200, 71.1, 151.20
O'Donnell, Gene 12.43, 43.98, 65.48, 65.444
O'Donnell, J.P .32.118, 93.7
O'Donnell, Jacklyn 178.122
Offerman, George 8.20, 32.30, 32.36
O'Flynn, Damian 6.15, 20.16, 43.45, 93, 93.34, 93.48, 93.53, 93.58, 93.77, 93.83, 93.84, 93.88, 93.96, 93.106, 93.110, 93.111, 93.129, 93.132, 93.140, 93.147, 93.151, 93.153, 93.154, 93.155, 93.157, 93.168, 93.169, 93.170, 93.171, 93.184, 93.191, 93.193, 93.198, 93.199, 93.201, 93.203, 93.206, 93.210, 93.212, 93.221, 9.225, 126.15, 145.33, 162.58, 169.90
Ogden, Morry 41.125
Ogg, Jimmy 20.45, 97.22
Ogg, Sammy 6.42, 23.2, 57.11, 60.88, 60.89, 60.90, 145.16
Ogilvy, Ian 1.16, 163.24
Oglesby, Randy 91.2
O'Grady, Lani 71.54
Oh, Sandra 100.7
Oh, Soon-Taik 43.439, 75.26, 83.9, 83.35, 83.49
O'Haco, Daniel 177.15, 177.54
O'Haco, Jeff 48.38, 48.90, 177.54
O'Halloran, Jim 10.18
O'Hanlon, George 105.17, 105.25, 146.18
O'Hara, Barry 161.120
O'Hara, James 41.44, 65.414, 105.93
O'Hara, Jenny 19.7, 177.29
O'Hara, Pat 43.75
O'Hara, Shirley 14.428, 65.184, 65.224, 65.312, 66.73, 66.136, 66.160, 126.60
O'Herlihy, Dan 12.47, 14.103, 51.9, 71.7, 72.14, 123.8, 123.9, 126.57, 132.13, 157, 178.41
Ohio 132
Ohmart, Carol 8.30, 8.56, 17.46, 21.15, 93.142, 103.48, 114.10
Ojala, Arvo 84.4, 84.32
Okazaki, Bob 66.185, 83.53
O'Keefe, Dennis 131.35
O'Kelly, Dan 119.10
O'Kelly, Don 4.14, 4.19, 8.69, 8.81, 8.99, 14.148, 39.8, 44.49, 65.364, 66.95, 85.22, 89.61, 131.43, 161.36, 170.6

O'Kelly, Tim 12.34, 30.3, 63.27, 65.397, 65.454, 107.6, 107.12, 107.15, 107.17, 139.14, 139.15
Olandt, Ken 65.636
O'Leary, Jack 123.11
Olek, Henry 65.599, 65.612, 96.6
Oleynik, Larisa 48.14
Oliphant, Peter 41.38
Oliver, Henry 178.60
Oliver, Susan 5.13, 12.104, 14.17, 44.40, 46.13, 65.571, 85.79, 101.18, 126.75, 126.130, 156.69, 157.26, 161.94, 161.164, 161.185, 162.7, 162.103, 162.121, 162.210, 164.63, 170.60, 172.1, 178.127, 178.147
Olken, Gerald 32.137
Olmstead, Norman 141
Olmsted, Maxine 115.5
Olmsted, Nelson 14.349, 105.99, 170.11, 170.21
O'Loughlin, Gerald S. 24.16, 24.17, 30.19, 65.370, 112.13, 161.220
Olsen, Chris 27.37
Olsen, Merlin 53, 83.8, 96, 96.124
Olsen, Susan 65.471, 65.495
Olsen, Tracy 14.227
Olson, Eric 96.65
Olson, James 14.318, 14.421, 65.570, 66.32, 83.46, 84.14, 96.122, 111.1, 161.196
Olson, Nancy 12.12, 65.560
O'Mahoney, Mora 25.22
O'Malley, J. Pat 5.4, 12.14, 12.48, 13.6, 13.8, 13.14, 13.19, 13.20, 13.21, 14.57, 14.132, 14.381, 17.22, 17.24, 25.52, 41.128, 43.344, 43.409, 46.8, 55.4, 55.6, 55.14, 55.18, 55.20, 63.1, 65.121, 65.153, 65.283, 65.283, 65.582, 65.583, 66.80, 66.121, 72.13, 74.24, 82.9, 86.21, 88.1, 88.16, 88.29, 89.30, 89.74, 92.22, 116.25, 117.10, 126.29, 126.54, 126.103, 126.153, 127.2, 127.5, 127.37, 134, 139.12, 142.10, 144.31, 148.143, 148.152, 148.168, 149.54, 151.12, 161.22, 161.58, 161.168, 162.252, 162.258, 164.78, 170.80, 175.3, 178.65, 178.105, 178.117
O'Malley, John 65.192, 66.51
O'Malley, Kathleen 14.127, 21.15, 65.417, 65.519, 85.11, 92.4, 105.43, 126.27, 126.121, 144.19, 162.117, 162.170
O'Malley, Pat 6.18, 81.81, 81.88, 85.68, 124.19, 124.20, 124.27
Omen, Judd 118.1
O'Moore, Patrick 41.95, 43.440, 65.24, 126.9, 126.54
O'Neal, Anne 60.34, 65.65, 97.15
O'Neal, Bob 3.65
O'Neal, Kevin 41.143, 44.55, 65.416, 162.278
O'Neal, Patrick 5.28
O'Neal, Ryan 51, 159.32, 161.37, 162.267
O'Neal, William 43.42, 43.110
O'Neall, Kevin 84.32
O'Neil, Adam 161.166
O'Neil, Kevin 92.26
O'Neil, Sherry 43.346
O'Neil, Tricia 11.2
O'Neill, Amy 177.29
O'Neill, Dennis 163.22
O'Neill, Dick 175.2
O'Neill, Shannon 169.32
Ontkean, Len 68.10
Onyx, Narda 66.131, 78.11, 149.12
O'Pace, Leslie 73.30
Opatoshu, David 41.100, 41.162, 96.87, 96.88, 98.11, 178.48
Oppenheim, Jill 141.13
Oppenheimer, Alan 14.379, 14.408, 14.414, 70.24, 70.48, 71.92, 84.20, 112.9
Opper, Don Keith 1.25
Orchard, John 12.21, 30.15, 41.42, 41.82, 41.93, 41.145, 65.569
O'Rear, James 65.11
O'Reilly, Don 89.109

O'Reilly, James D. 28.1
O'Reilly, Robert 1.7, 45.5, 53.29, 120.6
Orend, Jack R.1.9
Orent, Jay 158.4
Oriel, Ray 120.29
Oringer, Annie 90.9
Orlandi, Felice 24.23, 65.460, 71.79, 170.43, 170.79
Orlano, Lee 144.24
O'Ross, Ed 163.48
O'Rourke, Donald 41.2
O'Rourke, Tom 120.45, 120.48
Orr, Molly 163.18
Orr, Owen 27.91
Orrison, George 85.107, 149.18
Orrison, Jack 65.240, 150.5
Ortega, Francisco 61.8
Osaka, Sugata 170.30
Osborn, Bob 169.26
Osborn, Lyn 78.39, 78.64
Osborne, Bud 3.91, 3.134, 6.6, 6.8, 14.23, 32.24, 32.28, 32.34, 32.67, 32.71, 60.9, 60.10, 66.97, 66.186, 73.8, 73.35, 81.26, 88.5, 93.93, 97.51, 97.63, 97.78, 97.96, 105.68, 124.25, 124.26, 124.72, 126.63, 126.105, 130.6, 130.120, 135.76, 152.73, 169.33, 169.101
Osborne, Robert 25.46
O'Shea, Jack 135.38, 135.41, 135.45, 135.46, 135.51, 135.56, 135.63, 135.76, 135.82, 135.90, 135.95, 141.38
Oslin, K.T. 120.41
Osmond, Cliff 36.22, 39.5, 65.454, 65.465, 65.502, 65.511, 65.538, 65.539, 66.216, 86.4, 86.32, 120.28, 130.135, 139.4, 162.183, 162.199, 162.223
Osmond, Dayton 32.119
Osmond, Ken 6.59, 31.23
Osmond Brothers 157
Osorio, Yelba 163.81
Ossetynski, Leonidas 4.16
Osterloh, Robert 44.12, 44.51, 44.74, 65.110, 85.25, 88.16, 92.14, 130.64, 148.43, 148.182, 162.41, 162.247, 166.1
Ostos, George 71.34, 84.8, 84.46
O'Sullivan, Gungarie 67.6
O'Sullivan, James 95.9
O'Sullivan, Jerry 131.17, 148.149
Otis, Joyce 89.58
Otis, Ted 43.173, 105.62, 130.54
O'Toole, Annette 47.11, 65.526, 99.17, 106.5
O'Toole, Ollie 8.20, 14.7, 14.320, 14.339, 31.18, 41.114, 41.117, 65.271, 65.326, 65.373, 66.151, 66.159, 66.170, 66.184, 71.81, 93.218, 130.87, 148.160, 155.16, 155.33, 161.20
Outerbridge, Peter 100.16
Over, Josie 11
Overall, Park 59.4, 177.36
Overbey, Kellie 90.14
Overend, Al 158.45
Overland Stage Line 119
Overton, Frank 13.30, 14.85, 14.266, 44.75, 51.8, 85.82, 85.118, 89.114, 127.64, 131.31, 144.23, 150.7, 161.13, 161.53, 161.147, 162.171, 162.239
Owen, Beverly 161.46, 162.232
Owen, Patricia 65.337
Owen, Reginald 105.31, 105.43, 105.116
Owen, Tudor 3.82, 82.14, 97.19, 97.184, 97.186, 97.189, 97.192, 105.73, 108.5, 108.27, 108.33, 126.37, 146.43, 152.22, 162.21, 162.73, 162.201, 162.238
Owens, Grant 53.9
Owens, Marjorie 20.9, 54.24, 65.15, 93.93, 156.41
Owens, Patricia 148.183

Pabst, Norman, Jr. 149.8
Pace, Judy 83.32
Packer, Doris 105.66

Padden, Sarah 32.4, 32.13, 97.49, 135.31, 135.56
Padilla, Manuel 14.394, 84.46, 126.203
Padilla, Manuel, Jr. 65.466, 65.499, 65.505, 65.546
Padilla, Robert 14.311, 14.360, 75.2
Padula, Vincent 3.157, 78.38, 117.45, 126.34, 149.44
Page, Harrison 83.46
Page, Harry 14.326
Page, Joy 27.40, 27.53, 162.22
Page, Ray 97.99
Paget, Debra 29.18, 79.14, 126.54, 126.106, 131.5, 148.175, 162.25, 162.78
Pagett, Gary 65.378
Paige, Janis 19.1, 62, 91.11, 162.141
Paige, Mabel 6.7
Painter, Walter 170.21
Paiva, Nestor 3.22, 3.98, 14.26, 14.149, 27.22, 27.31, 27.92, 41.38, 43.141, 60.79, 65.363, 66.224, 78.10, 89.39, 97.51, 97.141, 113, 126.98, 141.13, 146.6, 152.41, 155.4, 161.44, 162.92, 162.124, 162.146, 162.157, 162.235, 164.61
Palance, Holly 19.5
Palance, Jack 178.5, 178.26
Palfi, Elissa 152.18
Pall, Gloria 141.52
Pallante, Aladdin 127.58, 127.75
Palmer, Arthur 158.4, 158.11, 158.29
Palmer, Byron 89.34
Palmer, Craig 129.61
Palmer, Gregg 2.12, 5.36, 12.7, 14.331, 14.334, 17.28, 20.46, 22.18, 27.79, 29.13, 30.1, 30.14, 30.23, 43.80, 43.86, 43.90, 43.103, 43.126, 43.145, 43.150, 43.307, 43.319, 43.382, 43.430, 44.37, 56.4, 65.174, 65.276, 65.291, 65.303, 65.364, 65.384, 65.387, 65.388, 65.403, 65.454, 65.455, 65.465, 65.471, 65.515, 65.529, 65.547, 65.562, 65.633, 66.85, 66.102, 66.104, 66.206, 71.21, 74.13, 77.19, 77.19, 85.96, 85.121, 86.9, 89.91, 92.19, 93.210, 93.219, 93.224, 93.225, 97.147, 98.1, 102.29, 106.13, 119.9, 117.23, 126.194, 129.26, 129.67, 138.38, 140.7, 141.57, 145.38, 146.64, 147.27, 148.23, 148.93, 148.169, 149.18, 152.3, 158.29, 158.32, 158.33, 158.35, 158.72, 159.38, 161.50, 161.101, 161.111, 162.10, 162.12, 162.119, 162.170, 170.85
Palmer, Jeff 65.422
Palmer, Maria 25.69, 73.4, 126.100, 126.107
Palmer, Max 8.7
Palmer, Oliver 158.20
Palmer, Peter 38, 84.15, 84.51
Palmer, Robert 21.43, 43.220, 65.289, 89.115, 127.56
Palmer, Tex 2.11
Palmer, Tom 14.225, 30.5, 43.160, 61.6, 65.72, 66.115, 93.70, 93.118, 93.171, 116.22, 144.25, 170.18
Palter, Lew 65.464, 71.72
Paluzzi, Luciana 14.97, 66.86
Panaiv, Michael 170.47
Panish, John 133.19
Papel, Lee 162.66
Paqin, Robert 73.32, 138.19, 138.33
Parady, Hersha 96, 96.51, 96.52, 96.71, 96.124
Parfrey, Woodrow 5.11, 14.228, 14.265, 14.319, 14.409, 24.18, 39.18, 41.144, 43.344, 51.29, 65.284, 66.210, 71.95, 76.1, 76.14, 76.29, 76.42, 83.13, 84.23, 86.5, 92.11, 96.83, 101.27, 151.2, 161.14, 161.171, 175.1
Paris, Jerry 4.21, 34.14, 43.254, 146.22
Park, Jacquelyn 6.56, 32.107, 32.114, 60.80, 147.38, 169.110
Parker, Andrea 1.11, 1.15
Parker, Brett 37.2
Parker, Brook Susan 1.3
Parker, Earl 65.135, 65.138, 66.49, 66.136, 93.133, 127.49

Personnel Index

Parker, Eddie 145.14
Parker, Edwin 23.19, 23.26, 32.10, 32.69, 32.108, 32.115, 32.120, 34.2, 73.11, 73.13, 81.2, 147.22, 147.49
Parker, F. William 120.12, 120.19, 120.25, 120.33, 120.43, 120.48
Parker, Fess 6.17, 6.18, 41, 42, 43.33, 43.231, 46.2, 145.9
Parker, Jameson 19.14, 19.15, 163.77
Parker, Jean 35.36, 35.38, 145.6
Parker, Judy 14.280
Parker, Lara 83.2
Parker, Lew 52.42
Parker, Monica 100.10
Parker, Murray 164.60
Parker, Sunshine 14.319, 95.14
Parker, Warren 66.2, 66.57
Parker, Willard 147
Parker-Jones, Jill 110.1, 110.4
Parkin, Scott 163.12
Parkins, Barbara 85.108, 162.160, 168.7
Parks, Andrew 106.18
Parks, Jackie 169.68
Parks, Michael 65.267, 144.5, 162.218, 162.242, 163.66, 178.124
Parks, Ted 91.4, 177.53
Parmer, Oliver 158.25, 158.29, 158.31
Parnell, Emory 4.30, 4.37, 8.90, 27.67, 82.15, 89.26, 89.36, 89.39, 89.74, 97.129, 105.25, 105.78, 105.91, 152.15, 152.71, 169.12, 169.31, 169.96
Parnell, James 4.36, 8.66, 14.25, 32.56, 32.62, 32.109, 44.18, 66.4, 97.80, 97.85, 97.98, 97.135, 97.186, 105.10, 130.43, 141.19, 152.7, 164.56, 169.32
Parrio, Barbara 14.326
Parrish, Helen 35.35
Parrish, John 2.12, 6.52, 43.132, 97.7, 108.37, 124.29, 124.34, 133.5, 164.53, 169.34
Parrish, Julie 14.237, 43.371, 65.338, 121.3, 151.15
Parrish, Leslie 8.69, 8.83, 9.6, 12.83, 24.16, 24.17, 76.47, 170.3, 170.34
Parsons, Milton 39.7, 83.38, 83.39, 89.85, 89.153, 96.50, 126.82, 130.50, 130.66, 130.81, 170.22, 170.103
Parsons, Patricia 147.21
Parsons, Roy 169.44
Part, Brian 96.30, 96.31, 96.50
Partington, Dorothy 89.20, 148.70
Parton, Reggie 7.6, 17.5, 126.79, 126.81, 126.94, 126.109, 130.164, 152.1, 152.21, 152.51, 152.52, 152.53, 152.54, 152.72, 152.73, 152.75
Partridge, Joe 14.55, 34.50, 78.76, 126.52, 141.49, 141.71, 164.54
Paserella, Art 112.8
Pastko, Earl 100.10
Pataki, Michael 14.407, 24.15, 49.7, 53.1, 53.10, 83.38, 83.39, 96.73, 96.115, 126.179
Pate, Christopher 65.417
Pate, Michael 3.160, 13.15, 17.40, 17.41, 17.42, 20.1, 20.2, 20.3, 27.40, 27.107, 39.6, 41.7, 41.61, 43.232, 43.270, 43.354, 55.10, 65.69, 65.147, 65.155, 65.345, 66.7, 66.162, 66.183, 72, 85.28, 85.77, 85.86, 88.20, 89.124, 105.102, 125.9, 126.6, 126.56, 126.61, 126.74, 126.157, 130.10, 130.23, 130.58, 130.106, 130.142, 146.24, 148.124, 148.176, 149.29, 151.23, 152.11, 152.52, 152.61, 161.45, 161.223, 162.26, 162.282, 164.31, 164.35, 167.25, 170.42, 178.2, 178.66, 178.84, 178.125, 179.27, 179.28, 179.29, 179.30
Paterson, Ken 161.26
Patrick, Butch 14.147, 41.128, 43.271, 65.322, 65.426, 121.1, 126.162
Patrick, Cynthia 43.213
Patrick, Dennis 7.10, 12.80, 12.96, 12.107, 14.37, 22.34, 38.15, 39.9, 44.9, 51.20, 65.126, 85.29, 85.47, 85.61, 85.68, 85.79, 85.107, 85.120, 101.2, 117.23, 120.17, 120.18, 131.14, 142.13, 142.36, 146.34, 148.135, 149.60, 161.7, 162.176, 164.72
Patrick, Dorothy 35.27, 35.33, 97.128, 141.10, 169.34, 169.73
Patrick, John 6.32, 65.22, 65.43, 129.13
Patrick, Jon 14.7
Patrick, Lee 31.25, 89.22, 89.80, 130.137, 162.76
Patrick, Lori 85.112
Patrick, Lory 14.256, 43.283, 148, 162.185, 162.198, 162.219, 168.6
Patrick, Millicent 85.75, 129.21, 135.16
Patridge, Joe 167.25
Patten, Luana 14.242, 29.4, 52.42, 126.35, 129.44, 162.55, 162.90, 164.23
Patten, Robert 14.288, 24.21, 65.115, 93.125, 149.6, 162.10
Patterson, Elizabeth 78.45
Patterson, Floyd 41.141, 170.83
Patterson, Hank 2.10, 2.24, 4.1, 6.14, 6.81, 8.11, 8.86, 20.41, 21.17, 23.13, 23.19, 23.26, 30.6, 32.17, 32.19, 32.26, 32.68, 32.72, 32.113, 41.22, 41.94, 41.119, 43.16, 43.161, 51.29, 60.75, 63.9, 65, 65.197, 66.41, 66.86, 66.101, 66.124, 66.147, 66.169, 66.175, 66.225, 73.34, 82.14, 85.88, 86.26, 89.77, 92.24, 93.55, 93.103, 97.4, 97.27, 101.11, 105.48, 126.53, 126.84, 129.25, 130.133, 131.3, 135.9, 135.18, 135.19, 135.54, 148.74, 148.176, 148.192, 148.197, 149.1, 149.58, 156.46, 162.147, 165.10, 169.37, 169.94, 170.12, 178.141
Patterson, Herbert 66.98, 126.39, 126.80, 126.109, 126.125, 126.165
Patterson, James 12.4, 14.317
Patterson, Kenneth 13, 13.17, 79.34, 81.40, 81.49, 97.138, 144.15, 17.119, 178.126
Patterson, Lee 4.22, 4.34, 14.290, 44.32, 161.100
Patterson, Melody 52
Patterson, Neva 19.7, 112
Patterson, Pat 63.15
Patterson, Troy 141.42
Patterson, William 112.12
Patton, Bart 131
Patton, Billy Joe 177.31
Patton, Burt 148.190
Patton, Mary 65.269, 178.134
Patton, Robert 93.92, 96.169, 159.8
Paul, Dick 4.5
Paul, Don Michael 1.13
Paul, Eugenia 20.49, 31.9, 43.37, 60.84, 78.62, 78.67, 97.210, 122.19, 141.28, 158.49, 179.5, 179.22
Paul, Jarrad 91
Paul, Lee 45.3, 69.5, 83.19
Paul, Nancy 120.15
Paul, Nick 34.42, 126.105, 152.18
Paul, Taffy 8.102
Paulin, Scott 59.5
Paull, Morgan 9.10, 26, 65.602, 65.625
Paulson, Albert 55.6, 71.93
Paulson, George 43.450
Pawl, Nick 8.106, 105.116
Paxton, Dick 65.3
Payne, Brad 65.138
Payne, Bruce 32.55, 32.59, 32.154, 81.62, 97.119, 145.22
Payne, Joan 65.418
Payne, John 24.11, 65.520, 129, 129.40, 178.17
Payne, Julie 12.4, 120.48, 120.52, 129.66, 170.4
Payne, Sally 81.40, 81.81, 81.84
Payne, Sharyne 169.2
Payton-Wright, Pamela 14.410, 65.560
Peabody, Richard 12.74, 14.221, 24.2, 41.132, 41.149, 50.1, 65.276, 65.459, 70.36, 84.44
Peach, John 3.99
Peaker, E.J. 24.11
Pearce, Wynn 4.15, 14.51, 27.65, 65.166, 89.90, 105.63, 132.19, 146.57, 148.106, 148.165
Pearcy, Patricia 95.24
Pearlman, Jack 144.22
Pearson, Brett 38.15, 41.80, 132.3
Pearson, Jess 14.320, 43.288, 43.325, 43.338, 43.409, 43.435, 61.5, 63.39, 132.5
Pearson, Jodi 162.264
Pearson, Stephen 3.154
Peary, Hal 31.33
Peary, Harold 98.9, 155.85
Peck, Charles 11.4
Peck, Ed 14.331, 39.6, 41.11, 41.62, 43.221, 43.359, 65.270, 65.344, 66.161, 66.179, 71.43, 86.54, 98.4, 98.24, 116.20, 128.8, 161.75, 161.127, 170.9
Peck, J. Eddie 171
Peck, Steven 44.56
Pedroza, Adeline 44.29, 149.22
Peel, David 41.74, 41.106
Peel, Richard 71.76
Peeler, Tina 91.7
Pegg, Ann Warn 100.2
Peine, Josh 43.238
Pelish, Thelma 47.12
Pelling, George 138.77
Peloquin, Jean 161.169, 161.173, 161.177, 161.179
Pelot, Matt 8.49
Peluce, Meeno 10
Pemberton, James 78.69
Pembroke, George 6.23, 35.34, 60.43, 60.49, 60.52, 60.57, 60.69, 81.53, 97.36, 97.50, 141.10
Pena, Lanel 163.23
Pendergrass, Don 177.32
Pendleton, Steve 6.2, 6.3, 6.32, 23.22, 32.29, 32.35, 60.36, 60.42, 73.26, 89.75, 93.51, 93.68, 93.114, 93.178, 93.179, 93.183, 93.188, 93.189, 93.216, 97.127, 130.109, 135.23, 135.25, 135.26, 135.34, 135.83, 135.87, 135.88, 135.93, 147.40, 158.46, 169.6, 169.22, 169.31, 169.37, 169.58
Penford, Ron 130.125
Pengra, Paige 120.40
Penn, Edward 120.28
Penn, Leonard 2.9, 2.14, 6.62, 6.76, 23.14, 23.21, 32.42, 32.48, 32.54, 32.61, 32.109, 32.124, 32.128, 43.75, 60.12, 60.14, 60.32, 60.34, 60.49, 60.52, 60.88, 60.89, 60.90, 66.126, 73.35, 80.10, 80.14, 93.10, 93.56, 93.96, 97.6, 124.2, 124.5, 124.9, 124.19, 124.20, 135.31, 135.35, 138.3, 169.19, 169.27, 169.97, 169.109, 178.11
Pennel, Jon 91.1
Pennell, John Maynard 120.24
Pennell, Larry 4.31, 8.106, 12.52, 17.20, 29.12, 30.14, 38.4, 43.190, 65.462, 65.608, 66.73, 82.7, 96.66, 117.12, 117.13, 125.7, 133.7, 148.126, 155.32, 161.163, 161.146, 162.250, 178.126
Penney, Edward 57.5
Pennock, Jack 162.123
Penrose, Jameson 3.21
Pepper, Barbara 66.177, 148.58, 152.44, 162.51, 168.22
Pepper, Barry 100.18
Pepper, Cynthia 162.237
Pepper, Paul 159.34, 159.38
Pera, D. Martin 67.7, 67.16
Pera, Lisa 36.7, 96.43, 170.44, 170.70
Pera, Radames 83, 96.45, 96.68
Perak, John 14.341, 14.413
Peralta, Lou 5.41
Perch, John 14.310
Pere, Wayne 163.40, 163.62
Pereira, Fernando 71.53
Perella, Marco 163.1, 163.23, 163.35
Perez, Jose 1.11
Perez, Miguel 1.4
Perez, Tony 24.5
Perkins, Barbara 149.42
Perkins, Gil 14.108, 14.263, 25.24, 34.25, 86.10, 161.23, 162.40, 162.202, 169.102
Perkins, Jack 65.537, 65.558, 65.593, 70.21, 70.25, 84.11, 126.71, 126.108, 170.39

Personnel Index

Perkins, Larry 49.9
Perkins, Leslie 161.90, 162.279
Perkins, Millie 47.4, 162.145
Perna, David 8.61, 86.28, 92.31, 162.263
Perpich, Jonathan 120.19
Perreau, Gigi 65.352, 76.28, 85.37, 126.62, 127.46, 127.54, 130.62, 130.109, 142.2
Perreau, Laurie 127.5
Perrin, Vic 13.12, 44.9, 51.1, 54.19, 65.15, 65.70, 65.226, 65.330, 65.335, 66.4, 66.9, 66.90, 66.99, 66.114, 66.144, 78.61, 83.15, 84.10, 84.29, 101.18, 103.51, 126.4, 126.63, 126.196, 127.57, 148.68, 148.115, 162.41, 164.2, 170.95, 170.96
Perron, Larry 20.63, 85.64, 130.82, 130.109, 147.43, 149.49, 161.54, 162.85, 166.20
Perry, Barbara 41.68, 93.143
Perry, Elizabeth 14.204, 61.8, 65.376, 150.10
Perry, Felton 1.9, 70.28, 70.41
Perry, Harvey 52.6
Perry, Joan Bennett 7.9
Perry, John 43.367
Perry, John Bennett 83.55, 96.74, 109.9
Perry, Joseph 13.2, 4.411, 17.15, 20.52, 41.10, 41.124, 43.159, 43.357, 43.448, 65.20, 65.60, 65.194, 65.288, 65.378, 66.40, 66.54, 66.87, 70.32, 76.27, 79.29, 84.4, 84.20, 84.47, 88.30, 103.14, 105.23, 126.137, 126.40, 126.156, 130.88, 142.5, 144.11, 156.16, 164.11, 164.31, 164.35, 170.77, 178.128
Perry, Lila 41.67
Perry, Roger 5.21, 72.9, 84.25, 152.54
Perryman, Lloyd 65.619
Persoff, Nehemiah 12.32, 12.33, 55.25, 65.381, 65.387, 65.457, 65.482, 65.603, 65.634, 71.89, 92.16, 96.85, 101.14, 126.141, 126.164, 162.140, 170.1, 170.53, 170.75
Person, Karen 163.54, 177.83
Persons, Philip 48.42
Petal, Erica 14.78, 65.503, 70.11
Peters, Brock 41.10, 65.487, 65.585, 98.10, 106.7, 126.202
Peters, Casey 161.58, 161.66
Peters, Erika 117.40, 146.68, 168.20
Peters, Gus 96.98
Peters, House 97.211
Peters, House, Jr. 2.4, 6.4, 6.12, 6.62, 6.76, 8.40, 20.64, 22.25, 23.20, 23.25, 23.31, 23.32, 32.56, 32.62, 34.33, 57.15, 60.1, 60.5, 65.143, 65.218, 73.20, 89.116, 93.6, 93.7, 93.8, 97.23, 97.40, 97.64, 97.72, 97.74, 97.128, 97.129, 97.132, 97.164, 97.199, 97.202, 124.23, 124.24, 124.30, 124.36, 124.69, 124.71, 133.11, 135.89, 135.91, 135.98, 138.51, 141.9, 148.20, 162.32, 162.159, 162.172, 169.43
Peters, Jan 65.373, 65.488, 66.184, 92.26
Peters, Kay 96.59
Peters, Kelly Jean 14.404, 65.436, 65.448, 65.476, 76.6, 83.14, 96.44, 161.138
Peters, Laurie 65.325, 65.347, 132.15
Peters, Lyn 41.95
Peters, Ralph 93.102, 97.16, 97.48, 97.89
Peters, Scott 12.29, 65.154, 93.150, 152.17
Peters, Thomas 14.360, 43.348, 43.449, 178.46
Peters, Virginia 170.103
Petersen, Chris 96.80
Petersen, Pat 75.9, 75.10, 75.13, 75.14
Petersen, Robert 161.111
Peterson, Alan C. 100.22
Peterson, Amanda 53.18
Peterson, Arthur 14.284, 14.296, 14.354, 14.372, 43.371, 63.8, 65.241, 65.247, 65.423, 65.502, 76.19, 127.50, 127.76
Peterson, Hank 8.54
Peterson, Lisa 163.34
Peterson, Nan 13.37, 65.181, 89.32, 89.40, 152.43
Peterson, Paul 12.94, 38.7, 52.30, 76.40
Peterson, William 24.18

Petes, Brock 116.16
Petit, Michael 14.179, 17.21, 65.358, 126.193, 130.125, 157.16, 157.24
Petlock, John 48.42
Petrie, Donald 96.145, 96.146
Petrie, George O. 7.14, 21.57, 65.511, 75.20, 126.88, 151.5, 161.67, 170.78, 177.30
Petrie, Howard 8.50, 8.51, 8.67, 8.74, 20.15, 25.29, 27.20, 27.51, 34.47, 43.177, 65.18, 66.101, 79.25, 89.41, 93.190, 93.193, 105.61, 126.50, 126.65, 164.49, 164.54, 178.1, 178.21, 178.112
Petruzzi, Jack 82.17
Pettet, Joanna 101.23
Pettiet, Christopher 177.56
Peyton, Robert 35.34, 60.35, 60.37, 81.12, 81.27, 124.25, 124.26
Pfeifer, Constance 96.141
Pflug, Jo Ann 5.50, 12.49
Phalen, Robert 26
Phelps, Lee 32.1, 32.7, 60.15, 60.18, 97.30, 124.56, 124.66, 169.5
Phelps, Marilee 130.6
Phelps, Peter 177.45
Phelps, Tani *see* Guthrie, Tani Phelps
Philbin, Regis 12.86
Philbrook, James 14.95, 20.69, 103.2, 105.23, 146.14, 152.19
Phildin, John 177.23, 177.24
Philippe, Andre 14.78, 14.302, 170.25, 170.35, 170.47, 170.93
Philips, Lee 43.196, 98.8, 162.277, 162.284
Phillips, Barney 13.14, 13.29, 14.419, 24.5, 24.8, 24.13, 24.24, 43.228, 65.43, 65.143, 65.147, 65.222, 66.63, 66.94, 66.99, 66.125, 93.193, 93.203, 93.217, 148.121, 170.6, 175.4
Phillips, Carmen 44.50, 46.12, 85.71, 86.22
Phillips, Ethan 118.11
Phillips, Jeff 1.18, 1.23, 1.24, 1.25, 1.26, 1.27, 14.433
Phillips, John 57.8, 97.93, 97.179, 124.61, 124.69, 124.73, 147.7, 147.8
Phillips, Margaret 126.42
Phillips, Robert 14.254, 30.17, 50.7, 65.524, 69.1, 71.17, 83.43, 86.16, 98.4, 116.23, 123.10, 151.12, 151.26, 170.12, 170.28, 170.72, 170.89
Phillips, Ron 177.25
Phillips, William 70.30, 73.27, 138.20
Phipps, William 2.25, 3.39, 6.41, 6.50, 6.79, 8.16, 17.32, 20.12, 20.38, 27.82, 29.12, 30.18, 31.48, 32.99, 32.103, 34.7, 41.19, 41.117, 49.7, 65.143, 65.167, 65.266, 65.313, 65.523, 66.86, 79.27, 85.26, 86.15, 92.2, 93, 93.46, 93.55, 93.71, 93.89, 93.113, 93.145, 93.163, 93.170, 93.189, 93.190, 93.216, 93.219, 93.222, 93.224, 93.226, 105.36, 115.2, 126.103, 127.53, 127.68, 130.33, 131.10, 132.14, 132.15, 137, 144.19, 149.38, 151.19, 153.8, 155.15, 155.67, 156.10, 161.9, 161.179, 162.2, 162.7, 162.254, 164.25, 164.40, 164.61, 169.11, 170.66
Piazza, Ben 28.9, 28.12, 65.631, 118.6, 144.6, 178.100
Picardo, Robert 1.2
Piccaro, Steven 66.201
Picerni, Paul 3.152, 12.41, 14.21, 15.9, 20.36, 20.46, 31.36, 34.11, 34.38, 34.62, 57.89, 57.107, 65.432, 65.447, 65.593, 65.611, 84.7, 93.136, 105.33, 126.46, 127.26, 127.45, 145.35, 146.56, 147.36, 158.19, 158.21, 161.165, 179.33, 179.34
Pickard, John 3.2, 3.67, 3.99, 12.60, 14.322, 15, 17.2, 17.11, 17.23, 17.40, 17.41, 17.42, 30.13, 32.75, 32.118, 41.19, 41.91, 43.125, 43.295, 43.300, 43.333, 43.349, 43.381, 43.403, 43.427, 49.7, 55.26, 57.23, 57.97, 64, 65.180, 65.209, 65.285, 65.397, 65.420, 65.432, 65.483, 65.572, 65.595, 65.596, 65.628, 71.6, 71.41, 73.28, 74.10, 76.8, 76.12, 79.14, 81.90, 83.7, 85.3, 85.15, 85.30, 85.38, 85.73, 85.123, 88.5, 89.31, 93.65, 93.71, 93.150, 97.79, 97.94, 97.126,

97.158, 97.169, 97.196, 97.221, 98.10, 108.19, 119.10, 124.64, 126.10, 126.37, 126.55, 126.85, 126.113, 126.114, 126.149, 126.167, 126.189, 127.27, 127.38, 127.43, 130.109, 132.6, 138.2, 138.31, 138.40, 138.57, 145.12, 146.67, 147.1, 148.6, 148.25, 148.95, 152.36, 152.63, 159.9, 161.110, 161.207, 162.65, 164.69, 165.12, 167.23, 170.16, 170.63, 170.71, 170.99, 178.18, 178.65, 178.120, 178.133
Pickens, James, Jr. 90.5
Pickens, Slim 5.3, 5.10, 5.16, 5.47, 6.60, 6.68, 6.72, 6.75, 10.2, 14.118, 14.155, 14.310, 14.360, 23.35, 23.36, 30.16, 31.8, 38, 41.47, 41.60, 56.19, 65.323, 65.394, 65.525, 65.564, 65.565, 75.9, 75.10, 75.11, 75.12, 75.13, 83.29, 92.33, 94.10, 97.184, 97.192, 105.40, 106.18, 116.1, 117, 119.13, 126.183, 131.35, 136, 145.20, 145.30, 146.18, 149.72, 157.12, 161.40, 161.68, 162.49, 162.201, 165.10, 168.10, 168.14, 168.17, 168.18
Pickett, Bobby 14.325
Pickett, Brad Michael 120.11
Pidgeon, Walter 41.12, 126.110, 178.69, 178.97
Pierce, Joe 158.18, 158.22, 158.24, 158.33
Pierce, Lonnie 4.36
Pierce, Maggie 8.75, 21.67, 39.9, 85.123, 88.13, 119.2, 162.82, 162.114, 162.173, 162.282
Pierce, Preston 14.175, 65.395, 65.396
Pietro, Don 60.13
Pilato, Josep 1.7
Pilavin, Barbara 1.8
Pileggi, Mitch 120.48
Pillar, Gary 70.16
Pine, Phillip 7.13, 14.145, 14.232, 43.354, 44.20, 63.46, 65.72, 66.78, 82.8, 85.17, 93.9, 93.124, 96.127, 103.17, 117.6, 123.3, 126.25, 148.86, 162.56, 162.81, 162.110, 164.40, 167.11, 170.7, 178.38
Pine, Robert 14.329, 63.39, 65.464, 65.485, 65.520, 65.585, 71.73, 121.4, 161.80, 161.87, 161.126, 161.195, 170.99
Pinkard, Fred 53.21
Pinkham, Sheila 142.8
Pinsent, Gordon 99.14
Pinson, Allen 5.37, 32.55, 102.1, 148.182
Pisani, Remo 14.340, 14.349
Pitlik, Noam 63.23, 65.370, 70.34, 76.27, 112.16, 130.150, 161.106, 161.174
Pitt, Ingrid 49.7
Pitti, Carl 96.21, 96.75
Pittman, Tom 22.4, 27.18, 29.15, 65.32, 65.83, 129.37, 148.53, 155.31, 156.1, 156.26, 162.10, 178.32, 179.53
Pitts, Carl 14.350
Place, Martin 65.400
Plank, Scott 163.28
Plante, Louis R. 120.33, 120.55
Platt, Alma 65.404
Platt, Edward C. 8.21, 14.17, 14.89, 14.115, 21.57, 43.199, 44.66, 65.7, 65.60, 66.56, 119.5, 126.28, 130.150, 148.32, 148.102, 148.199, 156.15, 156.49, 156.63, 162.69, 162.93, 162.186, 166.11, 178.45, 178.122
Platt, Howard 175.9
Platt, Marc 74.30, 93.100, 141.56
Plaughter, Wilbur 41.159
Playdon, Paul 78.17, 78.19, 78.21, 78.30, 78.34, 78.44, 138.77
Pleasence, Donald 26
Pleshette, Suzanne 13.23, 14.413, 30.10, 65.518, 66.65, 131.34, 162.232, 170.1
Plowman, Melinda 2.3, 2.7, 6.28, 6.36, 14.243, 32.133, 60.78, 161.43, 162.87, 162.106, 162.107, 162.134, 164.90, 170.82
Plumb, Eva 12.44, 65.481, 84.11
Plumb, Flora 24.2, 170.104
Podewell, Cathy 120.46, 163.43
Pogue, Mel 148.83

Personnel Index

Point, Inez 67.21
Pointer, Priscilla 71.90
Polic, Henry, II 62.4
Polk, Gordon 13.18, 66.87, 66.127, 74.30, 79.17, 156.37, 156.55, 156.58, 164.13, 164.56
Pollack, Dean 76.22
Pollack, Dee 14.150, 14.222, 60.71, 64, 79.26, 81.5, 85.118, 88.9, 97.104, 117.42, 126.82, 126.149, 127.53, 139.7, 148.175, 161.116, 162.22, 165.8
Pollack, Sydney 44.70, 66.134, 66.135
Pollard, Bob 158.3, 158.5, 158.9, 158.16, 158.25, 158.29, 158.46, 158.57, 158.60
Pollard, Michael J. 17.29, 17.30, 30.6, 65.341, 120.52, 161.117, 177.22
Pollick, Teno 14.274, 65.383, 65.407, 84.36
Pollis, Eunice 65.326
Pollock, Channing 14.401, 41.46, 61.8
Pomerantz, Jeff 41.93, 65.476, 65.573, 71.30, 70.23, 116.8
Ponti, Sal 34.47
Poole, Roy 49.4
Poppe, Herman 1.2, 65.533, 65.617, 65.638
Popwell, Albert 36.10, 36.16, 36.17
Porter, Brett 120.50
Porter, Don 24.22
Porter, J. Robert 65.456
Porter, Lillian 35.5, 80.2
Porter, Lulu 17.22
Porter, R.J. 12.15
Porter, Robert 12.4
Porter, Robie 41.93
Poslof, James 177.17
Posner, Stephen 48.28
Post, Clayton 65.51, 65.80
Post, David 25.49, 156.48
Postil, Adam 53.30
Poston, Richard 12.19
Poston, Tom 48.20
Potash, Paul 12.10.
Potter, Cliff 161.155
Potts, Cliff 11, 19.13, 69.10
Potts, Maria 26
Pouget, Ely 1.26, 1.27, 163.22, 177.11
Poule, Ezelle 32.72, 32.76, 105.10
Pourchot, Ray 112.24
Powell, Addison 65.139
Powell, Dick 178, 178.3, 178.11, 178.32, 178.39, 178.50, 178.62, 178.71, 178.76, 178.91, 178.99, 178.111, 178.120, 178.131, 178.137
Powell, Lillian 22.17
Powell, Patricia 8.18, 148.61
Powell, Randolph 53.13
Powell, Sandye 65.578
Power, Udana 7.14
Powers, Mala 14.8, 21.35, 27.68, 27.84, 40, 41.79, 70.37, 89.111, 105.98, 126.109, 127.22, 129.49, 129.56, 129.78, 146.56, 155.71, 162.34, 164.10, 168.19, 170.32, 178.28
Powers, Richard 23.17, 23.22, 73.33, 80.6, 80.7, 80.15, 124.13, 138.9, 138.21, 141.3, 141.5, 147.40
Powers, Stefanie 14.141, 83.45, 84.15, 84.28
Powers, Tom 97.75
Prange, Laurie 65.540, 75.24, 83.26
Pratt, Dennis A. 120.4
Pratt, Judson 14.62, 14.118, 41.4, 41.46, 43.301, 43.312, 63.47, 65.69, 65.75, 66.1, 66.39, 74.16, 76.44, 77.25, 82.4, 83.5, 102.19, 112.3, 117.15, 119.12, 126.110, 136.134, 126.145, 131.9, 133.31, 144.25, 153.3, 160, 161.8, 161.72, 161.164, 178.15
Pratt, Kevin 85.35
Pratt, Robert 5.23, 65.579, 69.1
Preece, Michael 65.433
Prendergast, Gerald 118.10
Prentiss, Ann 14.342, 14.359, 14.401, 161.193
Prentiss, De 20.63
Prentiss, Ed 14.143, 21.42, 27.44, 27.76, 39.6, 44.53, 52.21, 78.74, 85.34, 85.63, 85.79, 85.103, 85.119, 105.14, 149.7, 151.13, 161.12, 161.122, 161.135, 161.156, 161.160, 161.182, 164.53, 170.43
Prentiss, Robert 1.6, 163.52, 177.5
Prescott, Guy 8.45, 43.74, 43.93, 65.250, 158.80, 158.52
Press, Marvin 93.20, 169.45
Pressman, Lawrence 48.83, 48.84
Preston, J.A. 28.12, 96.173
Preston, Mike 118.8
Preston, Robert 28
Preston, Sergeant 138
Preston, Wayde 14.144, 34, 105.48, 105.87, 146.31, 146.41, 146.45
Price, Allen 47.4
Price, Annabella 1.25
Price, Gerald 66.174
Price, Hal 97.11, 97.21, 97.97, 135.29, 135.39
Price, Preston 130.126
Price, Sara 164.75
Price, Sherwood 12.6, 12.37, 12.78, 14.25, 14.45, 14.63, 14.150, 14.238, 27.77, 27.81, 27.100, 43.350, 65.380, 66.206, 76.41, 89.149, 93.195, 119.9, 126.184, 151.23, 162.100, 162.124, 162.166, 166.10, 167.16
Price, Stanley 23.10
Price, Stephen 161.53
Price, Vincent 41.128, 52.56, 66.54, 131.8
Prickett, Carl 65.298
Prickett, Maudie 41.9, 47.9, 57.77, 57.112, 65.405, 73.3, 81.48, 152.27, 158.45, 162.144, 178.65
Priest, Pat 43.315
Prieto, Rick 163.64, 163.65
Primus, Barry 161.121
Prince, Michael 96.84
Prince, William 163.25
Prine, Andrew 7.3, 14.200, 41.112, 48.10, 48.11, 61.3, 65.266, 65.282, 65.310, 66.128, 66.141, 83.28, 84.11, 84.43, 119.13, 120.4, 132, 161.79, 161.92, 161.120, 161.150, 161.206, 162.259, 162.275, 168
Pritchard, David 14.236
Prizant, Nick 141.33
Procopio, Lou 92.21
Proctor, Philip 41.161
Prohaska, Janos 50.6, 50.14
Prokop, Paul 170.58
Prokop, Spencer 163.31
Prosser, Hugh 32.40, 32.46, 32.50, 60.39, 60.41, 97.48, 97.96, 97.100, 97.102, 97.116, 97.119, 141.15
Prouse, Peter 109.8
Provendie, Zine 65.110
Provine, Dorothy 4, 21.20, 29.13, 34.30, 89.12, 103.5, 133.25, 146.33, 146.38, 152.29, 162.65
Prud'homme, Cameron 131.3
Pryor, Ainslie 27.41, 65.7, 65.29, 65.37, 65.82, 178.3
Pryor, Nicholas 48.49, 95, 95.1, 95.2
Pryor, Richard 170.29
Puglia, Frank 34.13, 71.27, 88.23, 126.62, 152.64, 168.24
Puglia, John 65.538, 65.539
Pugliese, Al 1.5
Pullen, William 14.13, 32.134, 32.143, 43.82, 93.51, 93.117, 93.187, 169.68, 169.80, 173.28
Purcell, Lee 14.364, 59.1
Purdy, Constance 97.74
Purl, Linda 176
Purves-Smith, Esther 100.5
Pyle, Denver 6.11, 6.16, 8.20, 8.89, 14.68, 14.104, 14.133, 14.134, 14.154, 14.308, 14.365, 14.419, 20.50, 21.46, 21.50, 21.52, 23.5, 23.11, 27.99, 30.13, 32.43, 32.49, 35.14, 43.265, 43.279, 43.297, 43.349, 44.4, 44.65, 47.5, 51.1, 54.13, 57.8, 60.28, 60.30, 60.38, 60.40, 60.48, 60.51, 60.67, 60.70, 60.73, 60.75, 63.25, 65.52, 65.77, 65.142, 65.208, 65.280, 65.303, 65.324, 65.345, 65.358, 65.405, 65.411, 65.426, 65.453, 65.580, 66.11, 66.22, 66.55, 66.82, 66.115, 66.123, 66.132, 70.49, 71.10, 72.14, 73.10, 73.31, 74.26, 75.19, 77.25, 78.18, 78.21, 81.62, 81.74, 81.78, 83.16, 83.34, 85.33, 85.62, 85.66, 85.105, 88.21, 89.37, 89.153, 93, 93.1, 93.2, 93.3, 93.17, 93.53, 93.108, 93.128, 93.167, 93.199, 94, 97.71, 97.76, 97.120, 97.131, 97.166, 97.187, 97.190, 102.33, 103.8, 105.96, 108.8, 108.38, 119.8, 119.14, 122.29, 124.1, 124.5, 124.6, 124.10, 124.15, 124.16, 124.33, 124.35, 124.40, 124.42, 124.59, 124.62, 126.151, 129.4, 129.66, 130.42, 130.51, 130.76, 130.104, 130.116, 131.36, 135.4, 135.21, 135.23, 135.34, 142.11, 145.7, 147.48, 148.8, 148.97, 149.1, 151.20, 152.30, 152.35, 152.44, 152.66, 158.73, 159.24, 161.23, 167.25, 169.58, 178.33, 178.51, 178.79, 178.111, 178.142
Pyne, Francine 86.15, 121.2
Pyper-Ferguson, John 1.1, 1.4, 1.5, 1.6, 1.22, 1.24, 1.26, 1.27, 91.5, 100.3

Quade, John 14.310, 24.8, 50.2, 71.45, 83.42, 112.1, 112.24, 123.2
Qualen, John 4.5, 14.68, 21.22, 25.27, 25.61, 27.29, 82.14, 85.95, 89.91, 89.111, 89.153, 105.29, 105.114, 119.8, 139.2, 146.59, 168.20, 173.2
Quarry, Robert 56.9, 97.143
Quey, John 170.93
Quigley, Kevin 163.46
Quill, Tim 177.53
Quillan, Eddie 4.7, 14.112, 30.10, 41.56, 41.64, 41.106, 43.207, 43.221, 53.28, 63.13, 88.5, 95.19, 96.73, 96.75, 96.110, 96.120, 96.144, 130.151, 130.156, 152.34, 161.200, 170.67, 170.97
Quine, Don 84.4, 161
Quinlivan, Charles 27.55
Quinn, Ariane 65.421
Quinn, Ben 170.76
Quinn, Bill 5.11, 5.35, 5.45, 12.10, 12.18, 12.37, 12.40, 14.13, 14.131, 14.144, 14.286, 25.34, 51.24, 76.43, 86.38, 96.41, 98.2, 101.20, 121.1, 130, 134.9, 139.14, 139.15, 161.92, 161.121, 164.75, 164.91, 164.94, 165.2, 170.89, 178.145
Quinn, Diane Lee 161.84
Quinn, Joe 121.6, 130.13
Quinn, Louis 161.63, 170.76
Quinn, Michael 103.50
Quinn, Teddy 14.249, 84.8
Quita, Ralph 158.21
Quo, Beulah 66.185, 83.4, 83.44, 83.60, 170.17

Raaf, Vici 25.31, 34.5, 65.334, 93.53, 126.56, 126.101, 126.163
Racimo, Victoria 28, 48.83, 48.84, 83.49, 109.8
Raciti, Joe 65.365
Radilac, Charles 151.11, 161.185, 170.55
Rae, Peggy 65.390, 66.117
Rafferty, Chips 12.27, 65.405
Raffetto, Michael 82.17, 88.8
Ragan, Mike 2.23, 6.29, 6.40, 6.71, 6.74, 14.21, 14.34, 14.101, 14.149, 14.162, 14.213, 23.3, 23.23, 23.33, 32.14, 32.20, 32.23, 32.24, 32.54, 32.61, 32.93, 32.97, 34.51, 34.59, 41.36, 41.74, 55.2, 57.98, 60.8, 60.25, 60.26, 60.79, 65.268, 76.46, 85.31, 86.10, 86.23, 92.24, 93.24, 93.50, 93.72, 93.97, 93.178, 93.179, 97.57, 97.70, 97.83, 97.198, 105.21, 107.3, 124.29, 124.34, 124.39, 124.51, 124.52, 126.28, 126.134, 126.146, 126.161, 135.1, 135.28, 135.46, 135.52, 141.3, 145.17, 152.16, 152.43, 155.7, 159.34, 162.13, 164.2, 169.8, 169.19, 169.55, 178.29, 178.47
Ragin, John S. 5.22, 86.43
Ragland, Gary 163.53
Ragotzy, Jack 161.117
Railsback, Steve 163.50, 177.38
Raine, Jennifer 25.64, 122.20

Raines, Cristina 26
Raines, Steve 14.221, 14.285, 60.81, 65.144, 65.419, 65.428, 65.455, 65.465, 65.467, 65.469, 65.478, 65.493, 65.525, 65.530, 71.3, 71.67, 71.83, 76.6, 93.217, 126, 135.11, 135.16, 135.57, 135.85, 135.91, 149.28, 161.135, 161.163, 161.188, 170.104
Rainey, Ford 5.3, 5.14, 5.32, 5.34, 5.43, 12.6, 14.66, 14.96, 14.127, 14.203, 14.254, 14.281, 14.327, 14.391, 14.402, 30.2, 35.10, 41.3, 41.123, 41.151, 51.10, 63.2, 63.36, 65.268, 65.362, 65.616, 76.15, 81.10, 83.13, 85.110, 96.25, 126.84, 126.121, 126.197, 137.9, 144.5, 149.2, 149.5, 161.22, 161.78, 161.85, 161.96, 161.139, 161.171, 161.196, 168.11, 170.34, 170.70, 170.86
Rainey, Jack 170.78
Rains, Claude 126.133, 162.173
Rainwater, Gregg 163.14, 177
Raitt, John 43.175
Ralph, Sheryl Lee 59.4
Ramati, Didi 156.20
Rambo, Dack 47, 63, 65.526, 65.538, 65.539
Rambo, Dirk 161.131
Rambo, Norman 76.30
Ramirez, Caesar 96.60
Ramirez, Carlos 170.59
Ramirez, Frank 65.583, 71.46, 116.2
Ramondetta, John 21.53, 27.79, 27.87
Ramos, Rudy 71, 106.16
Ramsay, Logan 5.12, 5.22, 12.110, 70.17, 70.43, 83.21, 116.9
Ramsey, George 98.23, 148.117
Ramsey, Jeff 48.17
Ramus, Nick 26, 28.6, 48.29, 48.55, 48.64, 65.606, 96.79, 120.29, 163.44
Rand, Edwin 73.29, 97.14, 97.96, 97.117
Randal, Glen, Jr. 65.494
Randal, Stuart 161.92
Randall, Anne 24.23
Randall, Chris 129.11
Randall, Lexi 177.39
Randall, Ron 148.196
Randall, Stuart 5.25, 12.79, 14.148, 29, 34.4, 41.29, 46.6, 54.8, 71.73, 85, 93.105, 93.109, 93.136, 93.158, 97.61, 97.62, 97.147, 97.152, 105.62, 129.5, 129.30, 129.53, 129.78, 130.14, 130.63, 131.25, 131.40, 133.26, 145.1, 146.19, 146.25, 152.8, 152.26, 152.38, 161.32, 161.81, 161.118, 161.201, 162.81, 164.62, 164.83, 178.1, 178.17, 178.21
Randall, Sue 8.77, 14.76, 14.211, 21.1, 39.13, 43.274, 43, 293, 43.305, 43.338, 65.209, 65.242, 66.83, 66.95, 93.195, 127.2, 130.40, 162.89
Randell, Ron 14.201, 65.123, 119.17, 126.212, 170.15
Randle, Betsy 120.46
Randolph, Amanda 102.20
Randolph, Clay 21.30, 43.117, 145.24, 148.46, 148.84, 162.135
Randolph, Donald 12.78, 20.1, 25.66, 65.131, 66.37, 66.142, 78.58, 78.76, 162.1, 173.19
Randolph, Isabel 12.17, 93.95, 169.21, 169.22
Randolph, John 10.10, 14.304, 14.382, 14.425, 19.2
Random, Bob 30.16, 41.20, 41.40, 65.388, 65.394, 65.413, 65.456, 65.485, 65.509, 65.535, 76, 76.22, 92.1, 101.15, 161.99, 161.178
Rangno, Terry 8.53, 21.1, 54.13
Rankin, Gil 4.24, 20.19, 27.39, 27.84, 51.30, 54.24, 65.385, 65.397, 65.416, 66.90, 85.9, 102.29, 119.7, 131.33, 148.98, 152.77, 155, 159.25
Rankin, Steve 1.8, 120.30
Rapp, Anthony 90.8
Rasey, Jean 115.2, 137.3
Rasmussen, Iler 112.22
Ratchford, Jeremy 99.15
Ravenscroft, Thurl 162.21
Rawley, James 14.340
Rawlings, Alice 161.130

Rawlings, Robert 93.176
Rawlins, Judith 8.85, 127.41, 164.83
Rawls, Lou 12.100.
Rawnsley, Ben 120.40
Ray, Alan 141.12, 141.41, 141.43
Ray, Aldo 14.171, 14.419, 41.35, 55.1, 123.5, 131.1, 161.7, 161.126
Ray, Allan 149.64
Ray, Anthony 129.11, 155.79
Ray, Araceli 25.50
Ray, Clark 91.5
Ray, Danny 177.58
Ray, Jane 65.72
Ray, Joey 32.105
Ray, The Rev. George 158.23
Ray, Tony 168.16
Rayborn, John 12.24, 130.148
Raybould, Harry 41.65, 65.275, 65.532, 76.31, 117.32, 121.17, 168.14
Rayden, Eddie 96.12
Raye, Tisch 96.142
Raymond, Gene 72.11, 79.15, 86.36
Raymond, Guy 5.15, 65.224, 65.238, 65.418, 70.42, 106.24, 175.9
Raymond, Jory 34.39
Raymond, Paul 126.111, 158.60
Raymond, Paula 8.26, 8.55, 8.81, 25.35, 27.69, 43.281, 44.16, 66.108, 93.162, 105.114, 133.24, 151.26, 173.2
Raymond, Robin 83.7, 156.7, 156.13
Rayn, Frank 123.5
Rayner, John 12.27, 14.259, 106.5
Raynor, Grace 21.8, 25.43, 66.42, 146.28, 156.60, 159.21
Rea, Mabel 43.93, 102.15
Rea, Peggy 14.375, 43.427, 65.265, 65.453, 65.469, 65.540, 66.67, 66.163, 66.213, 170.38
Reach, John 3.72, 3.133, 4.19, 31.11, 77.21, 105.61, 133.16, 147.29, 148.84, 152.10, 155.43, 169.112
Reade, Charles 8.61, 8.66, 8.82., 82.2, 130.117
Reagan, Nancy see Davis, Nancy
Reagan, Ronald 43, 43.303, 43.312, 43.314, 43.316, 43.321, 43.323, 43.327, 43.328, 162.228, 178.133
Reagan, Tony 66.113
Reardon, Don 43.112
Reason, Rex 2.11, 4.18, 4.24, 4.33, 4.36, 21.35, 103, 146.60, 156.3, 162.232
Reason, Rhodes 2.5, 12.55, 21.22, 21.33, 27.24, 27.67, 34.65, 41.13, 41.48, 43.61, 43.359, 54.21, 56.28, 105.4, 130.156, 141.36, 141.39, 146.3, 147.6, 147.17, 155.10
Reay, Craig 177.15, 177.34
Redd, Ivalou 43.430, 43.333
Redd, Jana 43.433
Redd, Mary-Robin 53.27, 133.9, 161.152
Redding, Glenn 65.519
Redeker, Quinn 14.139, 70.48, 85.116, 161.9, 161.109, 161.207, 168.19
Redfern, Gene 65.355
Redfern, Linda Moon 123.2
Redfield, Dennis 65.611, 65.630, 83.12
Redfield, William 65.213, 172.4
Redford, Robert 44.31, 105.76, 150.3, 150.7, 161.36, 166.2
Redgrave, Lynn 26
Reding, Judi 12.72
Reding, Julie 17.5
Redmond, John 158.19, 158.26, 148.30, 158.32, 158.35, 158.39
Redmond, Liam 41.38, 65.263, 162.198, 162.218
Redmond, Marge 112.24, 161.39, 161.103
Redondo, Anthony 65.437, 65.438, 84.10
Redwing, Rodd 6.20, 23.1, 23.32, 32.32, 32.124, 38.12, 54.13, 93, 93.3, 93.21, 93.49, 93.78, 93.85, 93.103, 124.59, 124.62, 126.16, 132.10, 162.35, 162.84, 162.111, 169.7, 178.125

Reed, Alan 66.78, 78.51, 88.21, 102.7
Reed, Alan, Jr. 39.7, 43.163, 43.309, 65.162, 65.258, 178.106, 178.143
Reed, Margaret 177.51
Reed, Marshall 6.5, 6.21, 8.59, 8.79, 14.48, 32.15, 32.18, 32.21, 32.53, 32.60, 32.70, 32.96, 32.101, 32.107, 32.111, 32.114, 32.117, 32.138, 32.141, 35.8, 35.20, 35.22, 35.32, 43.426, 43.435, 60.19, 60.21, 60.31, 60.33, 60.57, 60.69, 65.278, 73.14, 73.25, 81.26, 81.62, 81.74, 89.135, 97.88, 97.126, 97.163, 124.11, 124.12, 124.27, 124.32, 124.37, 124.43, 124.70, 135.20, 135.22, 162.126, 169.4, 169.40, 169.42, 169.62
Reed, Maxwell 14.57, 41.37
Reed, Philip 131.7
Reed, Ralph 66.151, 89.7, 93.62, 93.121, 93.190, 93.204, 93.224, 93.225, 126.5, 126.37, 127.62, 131.25, 148.74, 151.6, 155.12, 162.35, 169.35, 178.71
Reed, Richard 66.224
Reed, Robert 21.31, 72.4, 89.64
Reed, Walter 1.8, 2.24, 3.99, 6.30, 6.38, 6.47, 6.60, 6.71, 6.74, 6.75, 6.80, 22.11, 23.2, 23.10, 23.16, 23.23, 23.31, 23.32, 27.73, 57.2, 57.88, 65.62, 66.3, 73.9, 74.17, 89.109, 93.31, 93.202, 97.95, 97.118, 97.154, 105.3, 129.5, 138.44, 138.47, 141.70, 161.80, 161.131, 161.182, 162.87, 162.241, 178.34
Rees, Danny 41.128
Rees, Jed 67
Rees, Lanny 97.88
Rees, Roger 177.15
Reese, Della 177.25
Reese, Dorothy 22.36
Reese, Larry 99.15
Reese, Sam 65.426, 76.25, 88.10
Reese, Tom 14.22, 14.180, 14.234, 17.36, 30.13, 46.12, 61.4, 63.8, 65.189, 65.196, 65.214, 65.219, 65.256, 65.322, 65.371, 65.389, 65.402, 65.421, 65.437, 65.438, 65.474, 65.625, 71.34, 72.11, 76.2, 83.40, 86.9, 88.28, 102.25, 120.31, 123.6, 161.3, 161.87
Reese, Tony 66.124
Reese, Walter 41.52
Reetz, Lynne 158.53
Reeves, James Lee 83.25, 112.6, 112.22
Reeves, Lisa 96.68
Reeves, Richard 4.19, 6.17, 6.18, 6.68, 6.72, 8.12, 14.7, 52.25, 55.14, 55.21, 57.12, 65.177, 66.164, 73.16, 77.14, 78.70, 81.52, 81.75, 86.6, 86.31, 89.60, 92.8, 93.165, 93.205, 97.80, 97.166, 97.167, 105.5, 105.29, 105.30, 105.38, 105.94, 121.8, 126.49, 126.82, 126.93, 126.163, 133.34, 135.17, 135.45, 135.46, 135.47, 135.52, 146.10, 146.31, 148.32, 149.74, 152.26, 155.14, 155.47, 156.11, 157.11, 158.73, 158.76, 159.1, 159.33, 161.11, 162.109, 162.201, 162.226, 162.227, 162.245, 164.16, 170.20, 179.71
Regan, Barry 135.54, 135.58
Regan, Ellen 96.106
Regan, Patty 52.45
Regas, Pedro 24.16, 24.17, 65.516, 135.16, 149.15
Regehr, Duncan 180
Reger, John 48.29
Regina, Paul 181
Regis, Charlita 162.24
Reid, Carl Benton 14.11, 14.99, 44.47, 55.14, 65.136, 85.14, 85.65, 91.66, 162.99, 167.22, 17.37, 178.56, 178.132
Reid, Elliott 170.28
Reid, Frances 162.173, 162.186, 162.200, 162.213, 162.281
Reilly, Elizabeth 48.9
Reilly, Jennifer 92.24
Reilly, John 43.325, 65.610, 65.617, 101.20
Reindel, Carl 14.109, 14.282, 14.369, 27.100, 43.341, 43.343, 65.264, 65.268, 65.310, 65.358, 85.111, 126.118, 139.2, 161.12, 162.235

Personnel Index

Reiner, Robert 162.174
Reinhardt, Ray 112.5
Reinhold, Judge 99.4
Reiplinger, Rep 11.7
Reischl, Geri 65.531
Reisen, Don 170.71
Reiser, Fred 65.414
Reitzen, Jack 8.8, 8.47, 8.86, 27.71, 148.125, 155.8
Rekert, Winston 99.18
Remar, James 45.4
Remini, Leah 120.44
Remsen, Bert 1.1, 77.23, 105.35, 126.25, 126.67, 126.68, 126.85, 148.119, 164.64, 173.24
Renaldo, Duncan 32
Renaldo, Tito 3.130, 169.7
Renard, David 12.32, 12.33, 12.54, 14.408, 20.62, 30.19, 43.392, 65.429, 65.460, 65.529, 65.556, 71.24, 71.35, 141.65, 168.26, 170.61
Renard, Ken 14.164, 30.2, 30.17, 36.10, 41.49, 41.65, 41.137, 50.10, 65.383, 65.401, 65.632, 69.4, 106.5, 161.188
Renell, Andreas 1.15
Renella, Pat 4.35, 71.94
Rennick, Nancy 14.127, 14.143, 43.116, 43.243, 43.310, 65.191, 126.198, 162.132, 162.139, 162.275
Rennie, Michael 14.191, 17.23, 41.7, 41.64, 72.2, 76.24, 161.23, 162.3, 162.231, 178.55, 178.73, 178.107
Renschler, George 70.8
Renteria, Joe 24.24, 83.42
Repp, Stafford 14.40, 14.74, 25.61, 27.21, 37.7, 44.61, 64.3, 65.72, 65.108, 65.370, 65.576, 83.19, 126.3, 126.41, 126.67, 142.1, 148.33, 148.124, 148.183, 149.53, 152.67, 153, 161.17, 164.60
Reppert, Jim 129.50
Rescher, Dee Dee 171.5
Retey, Elaine 97.31
Rettig, Tommy 43.251, 89.77, 102.20, 146.24, 146.69, 162.132
Reuben, Gloria 177.49
Revell, Jacquelyn 141.62
Revill, Clive 26, 174.2
Revink, George 88.17
Rey, Alejandro 5.42, 36.16, 36.17, 41.57, 43.260, 65.551, 65.552, 65.553, 71.80, 76.26, 83.52, 107.16, 116.19, 117.45, 168.4, 171.5
Rey, Araceli 65.515
Rey, Rosa 23.33, 89.14, 146.35
Reyes, Julian 177.42
Reynolds, Adeline deWalt 66.36
Reynolds, Alan 14.294, 21.52, 34.65, 126.18, 126.75, 126.106, 129.41, 129.61, 145.31, 148.11, 148.67, 150.10, 162.63, 164.21, 164.25
Reynolds, Burt 17.18, 65, 79.32, 131, 178.144
Reynolds, Gene 6.43, 97.18
Reynolds, Jack 32.25, 32.33, 32.38, 138.20, 138.34, 141.52, 169.6, 169.40, 169.73
Reynolds, Kay 116.9
Reynolds, Marjorie 148.197, 166.20, 168.23
Reynolds, Ray 12.15
Reynolds, Sammie 81.27
Reynolds, Wild Bill 170.83
Reynolds, William 21.9, 21.12, 43.94, 105.17, 105.41, 105.68, 151.7, 162.68, 178.81
Reys, Adrienne 148.113
Rhoades, Barbara 5.11, 109.11, 161.168
Rhoades, Jennifer 96.169
Rhodes, Billy 169.87
Rhodes, Bob 36.14
Rhodes, Donnelly 14.34, 28.13, 30.20, 38.13, 49.2, 70.31, 86.5, 86.30, 132.12, 161.117, 162.274, 170.68, 170.102
Rhodes, Gloria 158.5
Rhodes, Grandon 14.154, 14.167, 14.191, 14.202, 14.218, 14.221, 14.226, 14.228, 14.229, 14.257, 14.261, 14.269, 14.274, 44.18, 85.49, 86.11, 89.33, 117.2, 141.19
Rhodes, Hari 66.125, 126.173, 162.255, 165.10
Rhodes, Jennifer 71.96
Rhodes, Jordan 14.427, 53.7
Rhodes, Lee 43.81
Rhodes, Lou 93.48
Rhue, Madlyn 4.24, 13.19, 14.39, 27.62, 36.23, 41.13, 63.32, 65.171, 66.38, 66.60, 74.15, 76.10, 85.15, 86.30, 101.12, 106.24, 117.2, 122.27, 126.142, 127.10, 131.3, 142.26, 146.62, 148.103, 161.39, 170.57
Rhys-Davies, John 45.5
Riano, Renie 169.12
Ribisi, Giovanni 163.15, 163.16
Rice, Bob 8.95, 8.103
Rice, Dorothy 98.25
Rice, Jack 14.65
Rich, Adam 62
Rich, Allan 96.84
Rich, Bernie 147.6, 147.22
Rich, Christopher 1.15
Rich, Dick 4.17, 21.36, 27.85, 32.29, 32.35, 34.43, 44.30, 60.81, 60.86, 65.94, 65.110, 65.151, 65.182, 66.74, 66.109, 73.35, 74.14, 81.69, 89.75, 97.128, 130.12, 135.99, 146.10, 148.92, 148.108, 152.4, 152.60, 164.88, 169.7, 169.34, 178.17, 178.24
Rich, Rick 127.20
Rich, Ron 170.81
Rich, Vernon 22.21, 138.6, 145.36, 162.51
Richard, Darryl 74.12, 130.154
Richard, David 92.22
Richard, Dawn 27.35, 34.20
Richard, Devon 156.31
Richard, Wally 148.95
Richards, Addison 3.158, 14.76, 14.123, 20.8, 22.24, 25.46, 29, 44.36, 44.37, 44.38, 44.43, 44.46, 64.4, 78.18, 78.50, 85.72, 85.88, 89.138, 97.173, 126.14, 126.72, 126.103, 148.21, 148.64, 148.181, 152.43, 156.47, 156.52, 156.55, 156.61, 156.63, 156.69, 161.17, 164.68, 173.21, 178.5, 178.26
Richards, Beah 12.3, 12.31, 12.38
Richards, Danny 130.80
Richards, Danny, Jr. 130.102
Richards, David 92.27, 92.31, 177.27, 177.36
Richards, Evan 118.3
Richards, Frank 6.66, 6.67, 32.131, 42, 43.102, 44.21, 57.16, 97.100, 97.106, 97.121, 97.122, 97.139, 105.59, 126.185, 129.12, 138.53, 141.11, 141.22, 141.53, 145.10, 158.18
Richards, Gordon 3.70, 3.107, 93.39
Richards, Grant 14.102, 22.13, 29.18, 43.192, 78.29, 78.60, 79.19, 85.10, 93.96, 126.28, 130.11, 130.126, 130.134, 131.21, 138.53, 147.31, 152.6, 155.26, 156.14
Richards, Jeff 77, 85.41, 126.75
Richards, Jill 169.74
Richards, Keith 2.10, 3.89, 3.155, 4.27, 6.20, 6.22, 6.34, 6.52, 6.53, 6.73, 14.53, 21.52, 21.56, 23.4, 23.33, 23.34, 32.41, 32.47, 32.57, 32.63, 32.78, 32.79, 32.85, 32.86, 32.96, 32.101, 32.109, 32.125, 32.129, 32.154, 57.9, 60.36, 60.42, 60.80, 60.84, 73.1, 73.12, 73.34, 80.16, 80.21, 80.22, 81.28, 85.93, 89.105, 93.49, 93.93, 93.133, 97.13, 97.99, 97.111, 97.161, 97.202, 124.53, 124.55, 127.23, 133.12, 133.18, 135.12, 135.80, 135.82, 135.84, 135.85, 141.8, 141.61, 145.9, 145.31, 147.40, 148.38, 148.140, 162.185, 169.57, 169.77, 169.81
Richards, Kim 96.7, 137.5
Richards, Kyle 96.30, 96.31, 96.49, 96.110, 96.120
Richards, Lorrie 55.10
Richards, Paul 3.45, 3.49, 8.31, 8.32, 8.84, 13.8, 14.70, 14.258, 14.310, 20.25, 43.252, 54.12, 54.20, 54.23, 63.5, 63.37, 65.1, 65.37, 65.95, 65.460, 66.68, 66.197, 73.22, 73.24, 77.15, 79.26, 98.5, 117.7, 117.8, 125.3, 126.7, 126.101, 127.33, 130.24, 130.129, 150.4, 155.39, 155.64, 156.6, 161.28, 165.4, 178.35, 178.62, 178.75, 178.93, 178.134, 179.63, 179.64, 179.65
Richards, Robert 105.47, 148.156
Richards, Tommy 65.355
Richardson, Duncan 2.18
Richardson, George 66.49
Richardson, James G. 69.6
Richardson, Susan 109.12
Richer, Daniel 67.7
Richman, Josh 1.13
Richman, Peter Mark 14.317, 14.431, 41.90, 65.462, 74.5, 76.26, 84.19, 98.23, 106.20, 126.2, 144.32, 161.39, 161.70, 161.141, 170.8, 178.87
Richmond, Bill 89.33
Richmond, Branscombe 120.1
Richmond, Deon 45.4
Richter, Caroline 14.66, 14.283
Richter, Debi 26
Rick, Dick 65.50
Rickles, Don 52.5, 162.150, 170.24
Riddle, Hal 96.95, 114.1
Ridgely, John 169.34
Ridgely, Robert 14.66, 14.196, 21.41, 21.41, 83.38, 83.39, 89.92, 105.105
Rieffel, Lisa 48.30
Riehl, Kay 97.220
Riehle, Richard 59.5, 110
Riggle, Jess 71.37
Riggs, Charlie 105.30
Riggs, Jack 158.3, 158.6, 158.7, 158.30, 158.33, 158.47, 158.57, 158.62
Riggs, William 162.67
Rigney, Justin 177.62
Riha, Bobby 14.287, 65.445, 71.95
Riley, Elaine 32.138, 32.141, 57.15, 60.48, 60.50, 60.51, 73.31, 97.172, 124.1, 124.5, 124.23, 124.24, 124.36, 124.75, 145.38, 152.6, 158.42, 164.58
Riley, Jack 83.28
Riley, Jeannine 50, 161.30, 162.206, 170.72
Riley, Patrick 88.9
Riley, Robin 8.75, 29.3, 74.10, 155.13
Riley, Skip 37.12, 83.24
Riley, William 118.2
Ringle, Paul 138.44
Rings, Mary 48.38, 65.532
Rings, Tracy 48.52, 48.53
Rio, Mark Adair 91
Rio, S.J. 48.99
Riordan, Joel 8.16, 133.21
Riordan, Robert 25.25, 61.6, 89.48, 93.171, 147.51
Rios, Lalo 65.227, 71.14, 86.17, 162.64, 162.78
Rios, Maraida 1.4
Ripley, Jay 14.196, 65.374, 121.1, 161.134
Rippy, Leon 163.2
Rising Springs, Arizona 56
Risk, Linda Sue 14.311, 70.3, 116.11
Riss, Dan 14.102, 14.147, 14.199, 25.37, 25.63, 34.22, 57.13, 57.14, 65.63, 93.184, 97.142, 108.4, 129.11, 129.32, 148.66, 148.131, 158.29, 162.94, 162.132, 170.14, 178.10
Ritch, Steve 3.50, 3.77, 3.132, 3.158, 20.23, 20.38, 20.42, 20.46, 20.48, 20.55, 20.64, 20.72, 44.1, 97.157, 97.199, 97.211, 138.3, 148.44, 148.81, 162.23, 162.48, 162.204
Ritchie, Clint 26, 41.129, 170.23
Ritter, Fred 6.29
Ritter, Tex 127.66, 140.41, 178.50
Ritter, Thelma 55.7, 162.192
Rivas, Carlos 14.306, 17.44, 17.45, 27.14, 39.14, 41.146, 41.152, 65.429, 71.2, 105.117, 146.48, 179.60, 179.61, 179.62
Rivera, Carlos 12.11, 44.35, 93.222, 164.61
Rivero, Jorge 26

Rivero, Julian 20.17, 23.20, 23.42, 24.5, 24.8, 25.51, 27.4, 81.36, 97.153, 126.24
Rivers, Victor 1.27
Rizzan, Don 170.11, 170.73
Roach, Daryl 96.76
Road, Mike 4.17, 4.24, 5.8, 5.26, 21.46, 21.67, 22, 22.7, 24.12, 24.14, 27.101, 34.48, 34.52, 65.196, 65.351, 89.43, 89.73, 89.103, 105.104, 105.112, 105.122, 116.20, 162.83, 170.44
Roark, Bob 97.203, 90.209
Roark, Gary 57.111
Roark, Robert 138.30, 141.54, 147.2, 148.28, 162.13
Roarke, Adam 132.7, 161.39
Roat, Richard 69.2
Robard, Dave 158.30
Robards, Jason, Sr. 20.50, 29.1, 29.3, 29.7, 34.15, 44.76, 85.35, 162.130
Robb, Larry 83.37
Robb, Lou 39.11, 70.48
Robbins, Cindy 117.27, 149.9, 149.55, 162.57, 162.75, 162.94
Robbins, Emmett S. 109.5
Robbins, Gale 65.423, 156.4
Robbins, Peter 52.53
Robbins, Rudy 41.47
Robel, Ron 148.116
Roberson, Chuck 35.12, 41.58, 41.59, 41.66, 43.189, 48.86, 60.15, 60.18, 60.23, 60.24, 65.156, 65.190, 65.278, 66.130, 66.155, 66.165, 84.1, 85.50, 97.11, 126.10, 135.8, 135.12, 135.42, 148.187, 162.46
Roberson, Lou 17.17
Roberts, Alan 20.41, 129.70, 152.50
Roberts, Austin E. 76.23
Roberts, Chris 22.10, 22.23, 129.60
Roberts, Davis 17.25, 17.26, 36.20, 65.487, 75.23, 161.99
Roberts, Doris 163.37
Roberts, Jeremy 1.3, 1.14, 110
Roberts, Jett 147.31
Roberts, John Todd 41.118
Roberts, Kenneth 114
Roberts, Lee 3.33, 3.70, 3.103, 3.143, 20.66, 32.68, 32.72, 32.76, 32.85, 32.92, 32.111, 32.117, 35.1, 36.17, 35.20, 35.23, 73.12, 73.29, 97.54, 97.117, 135.15, 135.17, 145.8, 145.36
Roberts, Lenore 43.203, 89.90
Roberts, Lois 65.436, 162.243
Roberts, Luanne 41.129
Roberts, Lynne 60.16, 60.17, 93.11
Roberts, Mark 15.3, 27.29, 65.63
Roberts, Pernell 5.3, 5.30, 12.60, 12.90, 14, 21.14, 22.37, 26, 29.23, 45.1, 65.449, 66.31, 84.34, 89.23, 106.23, 109.11, 114.10, 146.7, 146.12, 155.31, 156.13, 161.134, 170.58, 177.32, 178.60, 178.69
Roberts, Ralph 65.436, 170.7
Roberts, Randolph 65.592, 65.624
Roberts, Roy 3.3, 3.86, 14.104, 14.267, 27.105, 43.293, 44.53, 65, 66.187, 86.27, 86.37, 89.142, 93.11, 97.162, 108.13, 126.153, 126.207, 129.15,132.1, 132.2, 168.13, 178.35
Roberts, Stephen 13.19, 25.59, 27.77, 43.301, 44.71, 66.64, 66.146, 66.151, 74.30, 97.130, 98.1, 161.118
Roberts, Thayer 32.122, 32.127, 43.212, 93.99, 138.16, 138.29, 138.42
Roberts, Tracey 3.126, 44.76, 131.15
Robertson, Chuck 142.27
Robertson, Cliff 117.2, 117.28, 117.39, 131.32, 162.44
Robertson, Dale 43, 43.426, 43.434, 43.440, 76, 148
Robertson, Dennis 5.11, 14.427, 43.313, 65.331, 95.23
Robertson, Jessie 163.69
Robertson, Steven 94.37

Robie, Earl 43.119, 148.75
Robin, Brenda 161.168
Robinson, Alexia 163.25
Robinson, Andrew 163.3, 175.7
Robinson, Andy 14.416, 83.34
Robinson, Ann 27.1, 27.29, 57, 93.203, 126.56, 146.67, 152.63
Robinson, Bartlett 14.259, 14.355, 27.47, 39.12, 57.110, 63.4, 63.48, 64.53, 65.105, 65.122, 65.141, 65.159, 65.181, 83.37, 85.21, 85.42, 85.44, 85.110, 93.203, 105.11, 105.105, 106.13, 129.47, 130.38, 131.31, 131.36, 155.30, 161.157, 166.7, 170.24
Robinson, Charles 24.11, 65.441, 71.31, 85.70, 85.99, 36.6, 144.25, 157.5, 161.222, 162.224, 168.10
Robinson, Chris 34.65, 38.2, 39.2, 51.3, 65.287, 106.10, 117.12, 117.13, 144.29, 159.23, 161.37, 161.63, 161.177, 162.212, 162.251, 162.260, 168.18, 178.123
Robinson, Edward G. 178.85
Robinson, Edward G., Jr. 85.42, 162.118, 178.85
Robinson, Frances 31.24, 178.39
Robinson, Jay 33, 106.8, 170.84
Robinson, Ruth 23.17, 124.32, 155.24
Robinson, Sean C. 177.59
Robotham, George 5.37, 14.108, 178.119
Roccuzzo, Mario 144.28
Roche, Eamonn 163.83
Roche, Eugene 175.1
Roche, Sean Thomas 75.21
Rock, Blossom 108.32
Rock, Tony 162.45
Rockwell, Robert 21.66, 43.212, 65.146, 97.48, 97.65, 97.71, 97.72, 97.79, 102, 105.108, 141.19, 148.5
Rodann, Ziva 14.52, 43.173, 66.107, 103.17, 126.188, 130.111, 148.159
Rodd, Marcia 19.4
Roddy, Michael 177.65
Roden, Molly 14.65
Rodgers, Kasey 105.15
Rodgers, Sondra 32.44, 32.51, 162.18
Rodman, David M. 130.112
Rodman, Ric 66.60, 152.36
Rodman, Victor 103.48, 164.17
Rodney, Dayle 141.50
Rodney, John 14.122, 27.88
Rodriguez, Orlando 80.19, 141.38, 169.95
Rodriguez, Percy 170.35
Rodriguez, Roland 163.58
Roeder, Charlita 73.28
Roehn, Franz 3.67, 78.17
Roerick, William 102.5
Rogel, Len 170.21
Rogers, Cheryl 135.41
Rogers, Dusty 135.77, 135.95
Rogers, Elizabeth 14.191, 65.418, 96.166
Rogers, Fred 48.85
Rogers, Ginger 178.106
Rogers, Gregg 97.61, 97.62
Rogers, John 78.27
Rogers, Kasey 8.13, 8.65, 8.80, 34.87, 34.38, 34.59, 89.42, 93.44, 89.216, 105.110, 105.111, 105.115, 129.73, 133.23, 138.56, 146.53, 156.22, 156.39, 156.49, 164.28, 164.39, 164.81, 173.11
Rogers, Kenny 48.17, 59
Rogers, Little Doe 135.47
Rogers, Richard 89.136
Rogers, Rita 83.22
Rogers, Roy 135
Rogers, Shorty 70.22
Rogers, Suzanne 96.132
Rogers, Tristan 163.10
Rogers, Wayne 12.92, 43.318, 65.170, 65.250, 65.382, 66.211, 79.29, 84.12, 88.2, 88.14, 88.23, 142, 164.54, 178.92

Rojas, Manuel 20.17, 20.43
Rojo, Gustavo 21.36, 88.3, 89.72, 102.27, 162.88
Roland, Gilbert 14.207, 43.271, 55.14, 65.315, 65.316, 71.93, 83.19, 162.24, 179.79, 179.80
Rolfes, Andrew A. 1.3
Rolin, Judi 14.228
Rolland, Steve 164.15
Rollins, Howard E., Jr. 171
Rolofson, Bobby 96.110
Rolph, Alice 169.11, 169.63
Rolston, Mark 90.14, 163.81, 177.14
Roman, Greg 20.43
Roman, Leticia 12.70, 12.71, 52.46
Roman, Nina 65.381, 65.383, 65.576, 65.608, 162.254, 170.59
Roman, Ric 12.21, 20.68, 41.15, 65.177, 65.353, 86.3, 86.50, 89.59, 89.94, 97.52, 97.187, 97.190, 145.1, 145.5, 146.44, 148.10, 152.14, 156.11, 162.213, 179.46, 179.47, 179.48
Roman, Ruth 14.10, 65.492, 65.542, 65.543, 69.6, 83.30, 106.18, 116.22
Romano, Andy 70.1, 70.7, 85.95
Romano, Tony 105.45
Romero, Carlos 3.151, 12.32, 12.33, 20.63, 21.17, 21.38, 25.51, 27.59, 41.45, 43.371, 51.18, 63.43, 63.44, 64.7, 66.223, 66.226, 71.12, 83.29, 86.3, 105.69, 105.108, 106.12, 126.24, 126.52, 126.61, 126.85, 126.127, 126.142, 131.18, 161.29, 162.63, 164.47, 167, 167.3, 167.4, 167.7, 167.12, 167.23, 179.40, 179.41, 179.42, 179.43, 179.44, 179.56
Romero, Cesar 5.2, 5.31, 5.41, 14.190, 17.8, 17.9, 17.10, 41.45, 41.85, 41.146, 43.151, 126.31, 126.108, 126.142, 126.211, 142.6, 142.29, 152.28, 162.16, 162.19, 178.59, 178.103, 178.144, 179.55, 179.57, 179.58
Romero, Ned 14.296, 43.441, 43.446, 71.38, 83.38, 83.39, 83.56, 83.57, 83.58, 83.59, 84.32, 94.32, 123.3, 125.1, 139.2, 139.5, 139.7, 161.183
Ronan, Frank 1.4
Ronan, Peter 147.2
Rondell, Ronnie 120.34, 162.127
Rondell, Ronnie, Jr. 131.25
Rooney, Mickey 55.17, 59.4, 126.167, 162.79, 162.115
Rooney, Teddy 127.37, 130.119, 162.125
Rooney, Wallace 39.13, 65.269, 65.278, 65.281, 65.282, 105.96, 149.40
Roope, Fay 25.5, 65.144, 65.148, 66.28, 66.69, 78.24, 93.104, 97.133, 126.5, 130.5, 130.47, 130.49, 148.28, 150.10, 152.10, 152.75
Roosevelt, Buddy 169.41
Root, Juan 68.31
Root, Stephen 177.33
Rorex, Tony 97.50
Rorke, Hayden 20.33, 21.56, 27.18, 39.13, 54.4, 97.90, 97.125, 116.10, 131.36, 141.14, 151.3
Rosa, Tony 130.144, 130.145
Rosales, Tomas 19.12, 48.16
Rosario, Bert 120
Rosato, Tony 99.12
Rose, Bob 81.55
Rose, Bobby 66.112
Rose, Mimi 120.5
Rose, Peegen 68.20
Rose, Ralph 65.423
Rose Marie 65.94, 78.56, 161.153
Rosemont, Romy 1.14
Rosenthal, Rachel 161.218
Rosenthal, Sandy 71.50, 71.73, 71.76
Rosmini, Richard 14.72
Rosqui, Tom 96.122
Ross, Dennis 97.106, 97.114
Ross, Don G. 65.381, 65.446, 149.25
Ross, Earl 169.85
Ross, Gene 96.165
Ross, George 8.61, 20.68, 158.7, 158.9, 169.104
Ross, Katharine 12.7, 65.343, 65.368, 98.7, 132.11, 161.63, 162.277, 170.9

Personnel Index

Ross, Manning 3.134, 3.157, 31.17, 31.46, 78.35, 78.65
Ross, Marion 22.11, 43.212, 43.363, 61.3, 97.139, 126.100, 126.112, 178.115
Ross, Michael 31.3, 97.8, 162.243
Ross, Naomi 96.61, 96.62
Ross, Robert C. 44.65, 65.73
Ross, Terry Ann 162.95
Rossen, Carol 17.15, 144.18, 162.150
Rossilli, Paul 177.60
Rosson, Pat 39.12
Rossovich, Rick 59.4
Roswell, Maggie 120.55
Rotblatt, Janet 1.11
Rote, Edward 48.28
Roter, Danielle 72.6
Roter, Diane 86.33, 161
Roth, Gene 8.13, 8.70, 27.41, 32.149, 39.10, 43.310, 66.1, 66.48, 66.115, 85.69, 85.104, 93.214, 97.8, 97.21, 97.34, 97.45, 97.73, 97.111, 97.144, 129.22, 129.46, 135.71, 138.62, 138.71, 141.4, 141.16, 141.25, 145.19, 145.33, 148.51, 148.113, 148.147, 149.29, 155.63, 162.94
Roth, Hal 126.14
Roth, Suzanne 24.20
Rothhaar, Michael 48.73
Rothwell, Robert 14.215, 65.437, 65.438, 65.505, 65.519, 155.11, 161.170
Rouges, Michael 96.55
Roundtree, Richard 14.433, 118, 177.37
Rountree, Rose Mari 163.21
Rourke, Robert 129.22
Rousseau, Marcel 78.31
Roux, Antonio "Tony" 73.38, 145.31, 147.5
Rowan, Kelly 100
Rowe, Doug 170.68
Rowe, Douglas 91.8, 91.10
Rowe, Eileen 35.34
Rowe, Red 65.363
Rowland, Henry 2.23, 3.71, 6.20, 6.22, 6.34, 6.45, 6.63, 6.65, 20.42, 23.4, 23.26, 23.33, 23.34, 32.67, 32.71, 32.105, 32.112, 32.119, 32.123, 44.48, 57.41, 60.62, 60.66, 60.67, 60.70, 60.73, 60.75, 65.336, 73.1, 73.17, 77.17, 81.68, 81.78, 85.78, 93.24, 93.46, 93.54, 93.97, 93.190, 93.194, 97.49, 97.190, 117.22, 124.51, 124.52, 126.27, 127.17, 130.52, 135.37, 135.44, 135.55, 135.61, 135.74, 135.77, 135.78, 135.100, 141.4, 141.59, 147.24, 148.12, 152.23, 152.41, 162.48, 169.33, 169.57, 169.63, 169.84, 179.38, 179.39
Rowland, Oscar G. 94.16
Rowland, Steve 14.13, 73.14, 93, 93.57, 93.159, 93.161, 93.164, 93.176, 93.190, 93.211, 93.213, 130.2, 130.53, 148.37, 162.32
Rowlands, Gena 14.135, 85.8, 131.14, 132.16, 161.34
Roy, Andre 99.14
Royal, Allan 48.42, 48.60
Royce, Frosty 32.139, 32.142
Roylance, Pamela 95
Rubin, Benny 3.71, 18.17, 65.507, 134.17, 170.98
Rubin, Brady 19.6
Rubinstein, John 7.14, 112.5, 123.8, 123.9, 161.152
Rubinstein, Zelda 59.4
Rucker, Dennis 5.28, 5.47, 69, 69.8, 96.74
Rudie, Evelyn 89.59, 162.47
Rudin, Herman 43.184, 43.338, 43.343, 127.68, 130.17, 164.88
Rudley, Herbert 15.5, 21.34, 25, 65.50, 65.76, 66.25, 85.26, 85.93, 89.46, 105.65, 108.2, 108.12, 126.172, 130.21, 130.57, 151.2, 152.6, 161.17
Ruggieri, Francoise 170.8
Ruggles, Charles 14.237, 46.8, 55.13, 86.31, 121.6, 162.276
Ruhl, William 97.36, 97.51, 169.1, 169.32
Ruick, Melville 17.7, 86.38, 98.17, 170.32

Rule, Janice 66.1, 162.11
Ruman, Sig 41.9, 89.22, 105.18, 105.53, 105.100
Rumsey, Bert 32.155, 65.141
Runningfox, Joseph 177.29
Rupert, Michael 5.50.
Rupp, Debra Jo 1.22
Ruscio, Al 14.42. 14.69, 66.212, 118.2, 172.3, 179.45, 179.47
Rush, Barbara 24.21, 38.15, 55.2, 86.24, 120.47
Rush, Dennis 44.15, 162.141, 162.172, 162.191
Rush, Dick 127.7
Rush, Sarah 19.13
Rushin, Jerry 174.3
Rushton, Jared 48.7
Ruskin, Joseph 34.62, 39.17, 43.266, 65.255, 65.419, 71.62, 88.8, 89.90, 89.138, 117.22, 142.12, 148.172, 159.20, 164.46, 170.15, 170.66
Russ, William 1.5, 91.5, 177.39
Russek, Jorge 71.35, 71.52
Russel, Jackie 161.95
Russel, Tony 71.79
Russell, Bill 36.9
Russell, Bing 4.14, 12.21, 12.39, 12.60, 13.7, 13.23, 14.98, 14.118, 14.121, 14.131, 14.206, 14.241, 14.264, 14.265, 14.266, 14.276, 14.277, 14.279, 14.299, 14.309, 14.327, 14.328, 14.339, 14.347, 14.374, 14.381, 14.396, 14.397, 14.404, 17.12, 17.32, 21.17, 21.49, 34.19, 34.28, 43.225, 43.270, 43.396, 43.430, 49.7, 63.20, 65.37, 65.127, 65.202, 65.235, 65.428, 65.606, 66.199, 85.20, 85.30, 85.115, 93.90, 101.7, 105.13, 105.27, 105.64, 107.8, 116.15, 126.114, 130.34, 130.79, 144.22, 146.16, 148.44, 148.96, 148.105, 150.9, 152.41, 155.7, 161.8, 161.46, 161.117, 161.127, 161.152, 162.9, 164.47, 164.61, 172.1, 178.80, 178.128
Russell, Brian 88.12
Russell, Bryan 148.157, 148.172, 162.135, 164.79
Russell, Don 65.250
Russell, Gail 127.19
Russell, George 42
Russell, Jackie 5.34, 14.40, 65.452, 65.631, 132.13, 148.78, 159.33, 161.84, 162.146
Russell, Jacqueline 164.44
Russell, Jane 43.189
Russell, John 5.35, 5.46, 5.49, 27.48, 27.54, 41.15, 65.618, 89, 105.16, 105.29, 105.81, 114.26, 146.21
Russell, Kurt 41.16, 41.19, 41.81, 41.131, 41.147, 65.342, 65.608, 69.9, 71.71, 86.21, 92.18, 111, 123, 132.25, 157, 161.69, 161.92
Russell, Monte 1.6
Russell, Neil 5.31, 96.35
Russell, Ron 86.36, 121.15, 132.6, 161.123, 161.136
Russo, Joey 126.138, 161.102
Russo, Tony 20.54, 158.12, 179.11, 179.12, 179.70
Russom, Leon 90.10
Rust, Richard 13.20, 13.38, 14.143, 21.39, 22.29, 65.161, 65.199, 66.100, 66.151, 66.186, 79.26, 88.13, 89.49, 102.1, 117.24, 130.127, 146.48, 148.179, 165.2, 178.78
Ruth, Marshall 97.81
Rutherford, Ann 148.75
Rutherford, Gene 14.271, 65.439, 70.43
Rutherford, Jack 138.7, 138.12
Rutherford, Kelly 1.1, 1.2, 1.4, 1.6, 1.11, 1.15, 1.23, 1.24
Rutherford, Lori 65.577
Ruud, Michael 91.10
Ruysdael, Basil 13.3, 42
Ryal, Richard 112.5
Ryan, Dick 8.75, 126.4, 126.84, 156.49
Ryan, Edmon 27.85, 117.14
Ryan, Eileen 14.90, 14.427, 96.11, 148.192
Ryan, Fran 41.134, 65.563, 65.617, 65.630, 65.632, 65.634, 65.636, 112.20
Ryan, Frank 53.11
Ryan, Irene 129.32, 162.169

Ryan, John P .1.10.
Ryan, Meg 171
Ryan, Mitchell 28, 59.2, 71.70, 163.20, 177.64, 162.192, 162.199, 162.259, 178.1, 178.21, 178.45, 178.66, 178.89
Ryan, Sheila 6.32, 60.2, 60.4, 60.12, 60.14, 60.57, 60.58, 60.64, 60.69, 60.78, 97.7, 97.51
Ryan, Ted 14.303
Rydell, Mark 164.77
Ryder, Alfred 14.388, 65.136, 69.8, 84.40, 86.46, 117.5, 161.126, 162.247, 170.13, 170.50
Ryder, Eddie 14.61, 14.272, 14.336, 65.575, 70.47, 127.4, 127.69, 168.4
Rye, Michael 3.131, 162.44
Ryker, Ed 43.281
Ryle, Lawrence 6.33, 6.42
Ryon, Rex 118.6

Saber, David 20.19, 57.44, 60.84
Sabinson, Lee 65.253
Sachs, Robin 163.47
Sadle, Barry 71.38
Sadoff, Fred 24.12, 83.13
Safren, Dennis 12.46, 71.22
Sage, Willard 12.85, 13.31, 14.212, 14.261, 14.429, 17.14, 17.17, 17.35, 17.36, 34.8, 41.53, 43.330, 43.336, 43.347, 51.26, 51.28, 65.98, 65.347, 65.379, 65.393, 66.58, 71.34, 71.87, 76.46, 92.4, 93.209, 101.12, 105.4, 105.19, 132.4, 132.17, 145.26, 147.32, 148.75, 156.9, 159.5, 159.36, 161.113, 161.165, 173.24
Sages, Joanna 14.9
St. Clair, Michael 36.21, 41.36
St. Cyr, Vincent 51.5, 149.72
Saint Duval, Mallia 14.408
St. Espirit, Patrick 48.52, 48.53, 163.7, 163.63
St. Jacques, Raymond 41.67, 96.76, 126, 161.129
St. James, David 48.23
Saint James, Susan 5.1
St. John, Bill 162.86
St. John, Howard 178.145
St. John, Jill 12.21
St. John, Marco 14.419, 65.576, 65.611, 163.20
St. Onge, Guylaine 100.12
Sainte-Marie, Buffy 161.183
Sais, Marin 97.52
Saito, William 76.2, 83.51, 83.60, 120.36
Sakai, Set 11.4
Sakal, Richard 89.110
Salazar, George 177.32, 177.56
Sale, Virginia 170.12
Salem, Kario 26
Sales, Soupy 127.51
Sali, Richard 67.1, 67.2
Sallia, Eddie 107.25
Salmi, Albert 12.20, 12.75, 14.45, 14.286, 14.410, 14.421, 30.13, 38.13, 41, 46.5, 65.393, 65.435, 65.529, 66.133, 69.9, 71.96, 74.32, 83.1, 83.8, 83.45, 86.12, 92.23, 101.16, 107.5, 126.3, 126.136, 128.7, 132.29, 144.10, 148. 172, 157.3, 161.10, 161.38, 161.94, 161.166, 162.150, 162.186, 177.4
Salsedo, Frank Sotonoma 163.53, 163.78
Sampson, Robert 12.100, 14.93, 14.105, 55.9, 65.440, 93.198, 126.81, 148.184, 161.3
San Juan, Guillermo 176.3
San Nicholas, Ric 177.37, 177.57
Sanchez, Jaime 14.371
Sanchez, Jose 127.14
Sanchez, Marco 65.639
Sanchez, Ref 14.300, 84.1, 170.61
Sand, Paul 48.27
Sande, Serena 108.10
Sande, Walter 4.28, 12.99, 13.6, 14.112, 14.204, 21.45, 29.9, 43.310, 55.8, 65.232, 65.368, 65.491, 65.498, 65.551, 65.552, 65.553, 78.1, 79.34, 85.15, 85.44, 85.79, 85.97, 97.1, 97.2, 97.3, 97.28, 97.46, 97.54, 97.76, 97.93, 101.11,

105.74, 105.108, 108.17, 119.8, 125.9, 126.132, 127.18, 128.15, 130.166, 131.27, 134.8, 142.12, 148.91, 151.13, 151.25, 152.3, 156.40, 164.26, 164.65, 164.74, 170.47, 170.48, 170.56, 170.58, 178.4, 178.16, 178.69, 178.73, 178.133
Sandee, Darrell 53.1
Sanders, Brandy 163.52
Sanders, George 41.48, 169.1
Sanders, Henry G. 48
Sanders, Hugh 4.22, 8.51, 14.32, 14.151, 14.159, 14.186, 20.66, 21.20, 21.35, 34.9, 34.31, 44.21, 64.7, 74.9, 82.10, 85.87, 85.98, 89.18, 97.99, 97.104, 07.137, 97.140, 97.151, 97.180, 105.17, 108.1, 114.11, 122.27, 126.20, 126.41, 126.67, 126.68, 126.127, 130.43, 131.37, 141.18, 142.8, 144.16, 148.3, 152.62, 155.43, 162.181, 164.7, 164.32, 166.12, 173.27, 178.31
Sanders, Jay O. 177.2
Sanders, Nadia 70.44, 170.13
Sanders, Peppi 177.6, 177.41
Sanders, Sandy 23.14, 23.21, 32.77, 32.107, 32.114, 32.120, 32.154, 60.3, 60.36, 60.39, 60.41, 60.42, 60.47, 60.55, 60.56, 60.59, 60.61, 73.11, 81.26, 97.4, 97.66, 124.29, 124.34, 124.39, 124.54, 124.56, 129.35, 135.6, 135.11, 135.17, 135.19, 135.20, 135.33, 135.37, 135.41, 166.10, 169.51, 169.59, 169.75
Sanders, Shepherd 70.47
Sanders, Sherman 93.218, 138.33
Sanders, Steve 65.431
Sanderson, William 19.8, 110.3, 163.86, 177.65
Sandor, Steve 5.26, 65.468, 106.11, 109.11, 161.218
Sands, Anita 14.49, 27.77, 85.49, 85.82, 105.87, 105.96, 162.175
Sands, Earl L. 148.47
Sands, Earl R. 133.15
Sands, Lee 66.102, 66.118
Sands, Serena 3.50.
Sands, Tommy 14.203, 17.14, 85.122, 162.94, 162.206, 162.229, 162.259, 178.37
Sandy, Gary 177.58
Sanford, Garwin 67
Sanford, Ralph 6.3, 25.21, 60.2, 60.83, 93, 93.34, 93.73, 93.97, 93.112, 93.118, 93.120, 93.123, 93.125, 93.127, 93.132, 93.135, 93.137, 93.139, 93.140, 93.144, 93.147, 93.149, 97.94, 97.203, 129.44, 135.70, 135.72, 138.63, 145.8, 145.35, 169.28, 169.71
Sangster, Jimmy 174.1
Sansom, Ken 24.18
Santell, Boyd 30.22
Santon, Penny 14.92, 14.231, 14.313, 71.26, 78.42, 93.172, 126.85, 151.14, 179.60, 179.61, 179.62
Santon, Robert 162.257, 162.279
Santoni, Reni 163.80
Santos, Bert 5.47, 24.4, 70.15, 84.4
Santos, Joe 83.52
Sardo, Cosmo 14.72
Sarelle, Leilani 177.20
Sargent, Joseph 65.61, 65.152, 97.217, 178.47, 178.126
Sargent, Mike 21.36
Sargent, Richard 4.20, 41.47, 41.79, 43.207, 65.252, 116.24, 162.208, 162.247, 167.20
Sargent, William 27.82, 144.24
Saris, Marilyn 32.147, 43.60, 78.10, 129.16
Sarracino, Ernest 3.60, 3.79, 3.80, 3.138, 3.145, 21.62, 64.4, 65.528, 78.18, 89.134, 101.29, 126.59, 126.142, 148.141
Sarrazin, Michael 161.106
Sartain, Gailard 163.1
Sather, Mark 141.21
Satra, Sonja 14.433
Sattels, Barry 118.2
Saucier, Luke 17.47, 173.33
Saulsberry, Rodney 48.28
Saunders, Gloria 32.58, 32.64, 54.17, 56.12, 60.66,
93.70, 124.51, 124.52, 124.59, 124.61, 124.62, 156.11, 169.14
Saunders, J. Jay 45.2
Saunders, Lori 50
Saunders, Mark 67.9
Saunders, Mary Jane 2.21, 41.20, 148, 162.195, 169.95
Saunders, Nancy 78.29
Saunders, Ray 97.165
Savage, Ann 43.19
Savage, John 24.6, 48.62, 163.75
Savage, Paul 27.44
Savage, Tracie 96, 96.10
Savalas, Telly 14.197, 30.4, 39.13, 51.27, 161.108
Sawa, Devon 100.2
Sawatsky, Sara 67.19
Sawaya, George 8.90, 20.59, 20.65, 86.1, 127.74, 129.73, 161.91
Sawyer, Connie 11.5, 14.323
Sawyer, Joe 3, 56.8, 105.65, 145.20, 146.47
Sax, Arline 43.184, 64.9, 66.136, 127.44, 129.52
Saxon, Aaron 97.171
Saxon, John 14.254, 14.272, 14.319, 30.1, 65.369, 65.391, 65.417, 65.447, 65.625, 83.2, 106.21, 161.140, 161.180
Sayer, Diane 39.19, 70.1, 70.3, 70.15, 168.16
Saylis, Jacqueline 170.104
Saylor, Syd 3.66, 3.69, 3.70, 3.71, 3.74, 3.75, 3.97, 3.131, 3.137, 23.27, 23.30, 57.106, 93.59, 97.84, 105.39, 138.65, 169.109
Sayre, Bigelow C.44.62
Scannell, Frank 4.36, 6.75, 8.16, 8.55, 12.15, 12.17, 77.18, 93.66, 93.102, 93.116, 97.183, 129.45, 138.56, 141.48, 162.35, 169.87, 169.91, 169.108, 178.20
Scannell, Kevin 10.9
Scar, Sam 141.53
Scarfe, Alan 65.640
Scarfe, Jonathan 67.9
Scarla, Ed 158.77
Schaaf, Edward 14.314
Schaal, Wendy 96.117
Schaech, Jonathan 1.16
Schaffer, Rube 81.10, 81.48, 169.103
Schallert, William 8.54, 8.85, 13.32, 14.92, 43.55, 43.158, 43.182, 43.237, 51.28, 63.21, 64.10, 65.94, 65.133, 65.302, 65.477, 65.509, 65.590, 66.10, 66.172, 66.221, 70.4, 70.27, 77.12, 78.27, 78.31, 78.37, 78.57, 78.60, 79.3, 83.12, 89.62, 96.43, 96.118, 105.53, 121.20, 126.3, 126.72, 126.141, 127.71, 130.40, 130.81, 130.103, 142.6, 144.11, 146.11, 148.192, 152.3, 161.130, 162.105, 162.106, 162.107, 164.23, 164.34, 167.6, 170.57, 170.85, 170.95, 170.96, 178.51
Scharf, Sabrina 41.70, 65.490, 170.75
Schatter, Wayne 97.181
Schefering, John 164.15
Schellenberg, August 99.8, 163.32, 163.44
Schiavelli, Vincent 175.9
Schifeling, John 158.53
Schiller, Norbert 65.24, 71.40
Schilling, Gregg 65.208
Schmidt, Georgia 95.16, 96.23
Schmidtmer, Christine 170.26
Schnable, Stefan 130.169
Schneider, John 48.9, 120.23
Schneider, Joseph 5.32, 65.447
Schoeler, Jill 95.10
Scholl, Danny 152.69
Schone, Reiner 91.9
Schott, Paul 5.30, 5.38, 5.49
Schreck, Vicki 75
Schreiber, R. Leo 48.7
Schrum, Pete 91.1
Schubert, Yvonne 170.101
Schuck, John 14.376, 24.16, 24.17, 65.492, 65.513, 177.47

Schulman, John 53.17
Schulman, Russell 14.346
Schultz, Keith 65.453, 107
Schultz, Kevin 107
Schumacher, Phil 93.65
Schuster, E.J. 14.340
Schuyler, Dorothy 65.12, 65.22, 65.39, 65.67
Schwartz, Sam 65.43
Schwartz-Hartley, Steven 177.52
Schweig, Eric 67.11
Schwimmer, Rusty 110
Scoggins, Tracy 100
Scollay, Fred J.49.12, 65.385, 65.434
Scott, Brenda 5.49, 14.184, 24.8, 65.293, 70.31, 84.10, 84.47, 126.176, 132, 151.3, 161.60, 161.108, 161.167, 161.200, 162.220, 162.227
Scott, Dan 14.401
Scott, Evelyn 14.131, 65.22, 65.24, 129.56
Scott, Geoffrey 33
Scott, George C. 132.1, 132.2, 161.6
Scott, Jacqueline 8.33, 14.82, 14.170, 14.215, 63.48, 65.137, 65.273, 65.334, 65.417, 65.449, 65.471, 65.495, 65.559, 66.36, 66.55, 66.85, 66.127, 66.215, 70.26, 85.95, 85.108, 85.115, 93.205, 144.10, 151.6, 161.4, 168.1, 178.78
Scott, Jacques 78.3, 78.22
Scott, James R. 131.18
Scott, Jeff 38.16, 161.120, 161.136
Scott, Joey 14.122
Scott, Judson 1.3
Scott, Karen 80.33, 138.26
Scott, Kathryn Leigh 96.104, 120.1
Scott, Ken 5.8, 5.25, 41.56, 43.268, 43.290, 43.333, 65.361, 86.44, 148.186
Scott, Linda Gaye 14.379
Scott, Lori 12.36, 170.55
Scott, Mark 57.26
Scott, Martha 30.9
Scott, Mel 36.2
Scott, Pippa 4.34, 24.2, 37.7, 52.53, 65.243, 65.549, 66.154, 84.46, 105.63, 116.22, 117.7, 117.8, 117.38, 128.5, 142.13, 149.56, 161, 162.256
Scott, Russ 135.15, 135.16, 135.20, 135.22, 135.23, 135.25, 135.26, 135.27, 135.29, 135.30, 135.34, 135.35, 135.36, 135.38, 135.39, 135.41, 135.43, 135.45, 135. 47, 135.48, 135.49, 135.51, 135.53, 135.54, 135.57, 135.61, 135.66, 135.68, 135.71, 135.72, 135.82, 135.84, 135.85, 135.87, 135.88, 135.89, 135.90, 135.91, 135.94, 135.95
Scott, Simon 7.1, 7.8, 13.21, 14.13, 14.216, 14.291, 24.4, 43.327, 65.610, 76.39, 101.8, 121.9, 151.11, 151.26, 161.36, 161.81, 170.24, 170.30, 170.83, 178.19
Scott, Sydna 130.45
Scott, Timothy 12.74, 41.52, 70.48, 95.14, 110, 121.21
Scott, Vernon 170.12
Scott, Walter 65.598
Scott, Zachary 126.81
Scotti, Vito 14.62, 14.70, 21.25, 21.62, 25.63, 27.71, 41.88, 44.33, 44.36, 44.37, 55.1, 65.389, 65.447, 65.493, 65.529, 86.3, 117.15, 125.11, 126.97, 130.144, 130.145, 130.160, 130.168, 140.23, 144.17, 146.38, 148.91, 148.146, 151.21, 152.21, 161.99, 162.89, 168.24, 170.42, 175.3
Scourby, Alexander 14.6, 41.20, 126.14, 130.44, 164.43, 178.89
Scribner, Ronnie 59.1, 96.104
Scruggs, Larry 141.55
Scudero, Joe 65.38
Scully, Frank 89.20
Seaforth, Susan 14.165, 21.68, 27.95, 27.98, 43.291, 93.54, 128.14, 157.18, 162.272, 170.92
Seagram, Lisa 162.221
Seamon, Helen 97.171
Searl, Jack 8.83, 46.10, 51.22, 63.42, 64.7, 65.269, 65.481, 71.19, 71.44, 89.135, 126.136, 126.165, 130.106, 170.6

Personnel Index

Sears, Pamela 99.15
Seay, James 8.63, 8.80, 23.35, 23.36, 27.46, 27.72, 29.14, 31.27, 32.77, 32.151, 32.155, 35.13, 35.24, 35.27, 35.28, 35.29, 43.297, 43.328, 43.447, 57, 65.332, 73.35, 86.6, 93, 93.52, 93.155, 93.160, 93.170, 93.171, 93.173, 93.183, 93.184, 93.187, 93.188, 93.193, 93.198, 93.204, 93.205, 93.206, 93.216, 93.221, 93.223, 93.225, 101.17, 105.99, 127.27, 133.25, 145.6, 148.14, 148.155, 149.36, 155.4, 156.5, 156.65, 158.46, 158.65, 178.17
Sebastian, John 81.15
Secrest, James 126.114
Sedalia, Kansas 126
Sedan, Rolfe 83.34, 169.88
Seel, Charles 8.12, 14.102, 14.326, 30.9, 44.26, 44.28, 63.2, 65, 70.33, 73.6, 85.98, 92.15, 101.33, 130.22, 130.40, 132, 148.195, 149.6, 151.18, 155.27, 156.68, 157.3, 161.162, 162.123, 164.22, 167.16
Seffinger, Carol 4.35, 65.269, 126.49
Segel, Gil 163.68
Seifers, Joey 96.122
Selby, Sarah 14.124, 14.218, 21.20, 43.278, 65, 79.23, 89.156, 93.191, 105.71, 129.52, 130.22, 141.14, 162.29, 164.34
Seldes, Marian 17.21, 65.45, 66.6, 66.27, 130.66, 152.24
Selk, George 65.80, 65.84, 65.93, 85.107, 101.33, 138.34, 145.9
Selland, Marie 165.1, 165.5, 165.6, 165.8
Selleck, Tom 84.14
Sellers, Larry 48, 48.1, 48.42, 48.64, 48.67, 67.16, 163.32
Selles, Scott 65.587
Selzer, Milton 41.49, 65.175, 65.293, 65.318, 65.509, 66.167, 66.184, 71.60, 76.8, 96.138, 101.3, 144.10, 161.128, 170.76
Seman, Darryl 70.10
Sen Yung, Victor 14, 20.67, 43.128, 83.1, 83.12, 83.21, 83.31, 83.47, 83.48, 83.50, 97.192, 103.46, 130.110, 145.16, 170.90
Sentry, Frank 14.44, 65.227
Sepulveda, Carl 60.16, 60.17
Serna, Gil 170.94
Serna, Pepe 83.19
Server, Eric 83.34, 123.3
Servis, Helen 60.39
Sessions, Almira 6.43, 27.25, 32.65, 32.66, 32.90, 60.52, 73.26, 97.22, 97.47, 138.16, 147.6, 169.16, 169.49, 169.72
Seurat, Pilar 14.408, 41.27, 71.14, 105.72, 126.174, 144.26, 151.22, 161.109, 161.188, 170.17
Seus, Doug 177.17
Seven, Johnny 7.10, 8.85, 14.183, 43.248, 44.23, 65.245, 65.378, 70.48, 84.10, 102.27, 151.14, 159.36, 161.145, 170.46
Severinsen, Doc 14.412
Severn, Maida 51.31
Sexton, John 48.17
Seymour, Anne 12.39, 14.414, 24.16, 24.17, 51, 65.158, 65.208, 83.62, 126.96
Seymour, Dan 78.70, 129.65
Seymour, Harry 14.6
Seymour, Jane 48
Seymour, Jonathan 169.83
Sha'an, Morgan 43.101, 127.44, 148.28, 148.46, 150.8
Shackelford, Ted 11.2, 120.22, 177.12
Shackleton, Dick 23.15
Shaffe, Edmund L. 48.76
Shahan, Rocky 65.54, 66.4, 124.58, 126
Shalet, Diane 14.373, 14.396, 65.571, 65.628, 96.143
Shane, Dick 76.15, 161.173, 161.176
Shane, Gene 71.54, 116.2
Shane, Jim 170.92

Shank, John 65.445, 70.32
Shanks, Don 28, 94
Shannon, Bill 24.21, 37.2, 71.50
Shannon, Harry 3.119, 8.99, 27.14, 27.89, 34.66, 39.10, 43.129, 43.205, 65.218, 66.1, 66.36, 89.49, 89.87, 103.16, 126.4, 126.82, 126.97, 126.111, 129.8, 135.80, 135.82, 146.56, 148.80, 152.51, 158.73
Shannon, Richard 13.20, 43.156, 43.248, 44.2, 44.69, 65.275, 66.23, 66.51, 66.54, 66.69, 66.100, 66.181, 66.191, 66.218, 74.27, 85.15, 85.111, 102.31, 126.10, 126.28, 126.95, 148.4, 148.96, 148.105, 159.22, 161.7, 178.25, 178.56, 178.105
Shannon, Wanda 43.190
Sharan, Ron 97.154
Sharkey, Billy Ray 120.46
Sharman, Della 119.2, 166.5
Sharny, Suzanne 7.11
Sharon, Lee 138.24
Sharon, William 165.1
Sharp, Alex 8.62, 14.65, 27.97, 32.73, 65.76, 65.234, 65.274, 65.295, 65.301, 65.455, 65.580
Sharp, Clint 14.228, 17.17, 84.6
Sharpe, Dave 32.1, 32.7, 71.44, 169.3, 169.7, 169.14, 169.26
Sharpe, Karen 14.46, 39.6, 43.14, 65.62, 65.320, 79, 85.73, 119.6, 124.74, 126.112, 126.139, 133.17, 142.28, 152.27, 156.18, 170.19, 170.39, 173.18
Sharpe, Lester 97.15
Shatner, William 7, 12.18, 24.7, 65.421, 75.7, 75.8, 83.41, 115.6, 117.7, 117.8, 161.95, 161.216
Shaughnessy, Mark 177.20
Shaughnessy, Mickey 5.16, 86.14, 92.22, 105.118, 161.7
Shaw, Anabel 158.24
Shaw, Bill 66.72
Shaw, Hal 65.348
Shaw, Paula 96.68
Shaw, Reta 162.268
Shaw, Stan 177.6
Shaw, Steve 96.112
Shaw, Victoria 43.449
Shaw, William 105.60
Shawlee, Joan 105.9, 130.108, 145.21, 179.19
Shawley, Robert 149.7
Shay, John 77.2
Shayne, Cari 90.10
Shayne, John 179.18
Shayne, Konstantin 152.27
Shayne, Robert 56.32, 97.109, 97.144, 141.6, 145.4, 155.43, 158.55, 158.59, 169.5
Shayne, Ruell 138.58
Shea, Christopher 14.284, 70.26, 139
Shea, Dan 67.15
Shea, Don 67.19
Shea, Eric 65.449, 65.477, 65.486, 70.3, 96.36
Shea, Jack 4.36, 141.8, 145.39
Shea, Michael 161.146, 170.66
Shear, Pearl 41.27
Shearer, Steve 163.6
Shearin, John 19, 96.161, 120.31
Sheeler, Mark 138.21
Sheen, Martin 24.3, 84.22
Sheffield, Jake 83.40, 105.115
Sheffield, Jay 52.1
Sheffield, Jeanne 70.1
Sheffield, Reginald 78.37
Sheiner, David 12.25, 12.41, 12.73, 14.400, 65.542, 65.543, 76.1, 76.29, 101.4, 161.222
Sheldon, Bill 43.49
Sheldon, David 163.6
Sheldon, Gene 179
Sheldon, James 97.10
Sheldon, Jerome 81.90, 97.128
Sheldon, Kathryn 23.15
Sheldon, Robert 138.3

Shelley, Jordan 170.10
Shelley, Norman 66.95
Shelly, Alfred 101.21
Shelton, Abagail 14.72, 14.196
Shelton, Jacque 65.353, 126.175
Shelton, Laura 43.214, 43.302
Shelton, Robert 91
Sheltop, Abbey 22.34
Shelyne, Carol 70
Shen, James 170.93
Shenar, Paul 174.2
Shepard, Jan 3.163, 8.91, 14.223, 31.17, 43.28, 64.5, 65.214, 65.221, 65.322, 65.433, 71.9, 71.40, 81.95, 85.60, 85.75, 85.101, 89.137, 93.18, 97.177, 126.3, 126.43, 132.19, 138.42, 142.31, 147.1, 156.52, 161.92, 161.113, 161.134, 161.190, 161.208, 164.53, 167.6
Shepard, Travis 177.15
Shephard, Jesse 110.2
Shepodd, John 65.5
Sheppard, Jan 126.66
Sheppard, Jim 12.44, 65.516
Sheppard, W. Morgan 65.636
Shera, Mark 65.634
Sheridan, Ann 121, 162.195
Sheridan, Chick 65.422, 65.428
Sheridan, Dan 8.13, 14.75, 27.57, 34.29, 65.85, 65.131, 65.154, 77.17, 88.17, 89, 89.40, 89.82, 93.203, 105.4, 105.25, 105.32, 105.46, 119.6, 126.63, 127.12, 127.48, 130.24, 133.1, 146.60, 148.63, 148.96, 148.184, 152.4, 155.3, 161.7, 161.31
Sheridan, Margaret 162.245
Sheridan, Nicollette 120.55
Sheriff, Paul 44.19
Sherman, Allan 98.9
Sherman, Bobby 24.21, 70
Sherman, Fred 2.18, 23.37, 29, 44.15, 73.24, 78.25, 89.104, 93.89, 93.93, 102.12, 105.1, 126.37, 130.130, 135.46, 135.52, 135.56, 135.87, 135.88, 138.7, 145.26, 145.36, 148.44, 149.35, 156.35, 162.90, 162.125, 162.183, 164.60, 167.12, 169.43, 169.73, 169.101, 178.20
Sherman, Orville 5.2, 22.7, 22.10, 22.16, 22.19, 22.39, 27.77, 41.27, 41.30, 41.31, 41.33, 41.51, 41.55, 41.63, 65.297, 65.310, 65.332, 65.410, 93.160, 93.179, 126.56, 156.41, 158.56, 161.5, 162.45, 162.94, 162.103, 162.117, 162.147, 162.173, 164.57
Sherrill, David 120.39
Sherwin, Judy 170.91
Sherwood, George 169.28
Sherwood, Madeleine 14.375, 116.14
Shibuya, Kinji 83.23, 83.41
Shieh, K.C. 83.25
Shield, Bob 8.14, 155.16, 155.18
Shields, Arthur 8.31, 8.32, 43.213, 105.93, 126.42, 162.105
Shields, Eugene 5.36
Shields, Sonny 5.43, 5.46
Shigeta, James 83.46, 83.53, 96.61, 96.62
Shillo, Michael 170.55
Shimada, Teru 66.185, 85.64
Shimada, Yuki 12.12, 83.9, 83.36, 83.41, 83.47, 83.48
Shimerman, Armin 90.13
Shin, Anna 170.2
Shinn, Margaret 14.233
Shipman, Nina 14.99, 21.59, 41.9, 63.26, 76.5, 84.42, 89.96, 93.199, 101.9, 105.107, 117.33, 126.116, 126.137, 126.151, 148.163, 148.186, 151.7
Shipp, Mary 178.44
Shirley, Mercedes 65.248, 97.214
Shockley, Sallie 5.9, 5.37
Shockley, William 48, 120.36, 177.27, 177.43
Shoemaker, Ann 126.189
Sholdar, Mickey 14.137, 51.8, 65.326, 132.9, 162.133, 162.211

Personnel Index

Shore, Dinah 29.11
Shore, Roberta 85.88, 89.120, 105.55, 149.71, 161, 162.131, 178.133
Short, Judy 31.8
Short, Robin 2.19, 2.25, 32.140, 32.144, 43.57, 97.69
Short, Sylvia 163.30
Showalter, Max 51.9
Shreve, Craig 170.70
Shriver, William 65.600
Shryer, Fred 158.16
Shubert, Lynn 3.134, 65.98
Shubert, Yvonne 126.25
Shull, Richard B. 175.8
Shumski, John 1.6
Shumway, Lee 97.32, 97.64, 97.110
Shumway, Walter 97.47
Shutta, Ethel 162.40, 162.45, 162.52, 162.53, 162.106, 162.107, 162.108
Sibbald, Laurie 52.15
Sibbett, Jane 1.25
Sickner, Paul 141.44
Sickner, Roy 72.16, 92.3, 170.22
Sidell, Tom 122.26
Siemaszko, Casey 1.21
Sierra, Gregory 5.13, 45.5, 48.49, 59.2, 65.588, 65.589, 65.631, 71.67, 83.14, 163.47, 181
Sifuentes, Kevin 65.637
Sikking, James 14.259, 14.284, 24.3, 45.5, 70.29, 70.47, 96.61, 96.62, 126.147, 161.99
Sikorra, Joe 48.11, 177.38
Silbersher, Marvin 70.12
Siler, Russ 65.446
Siletti, Mario 27.89, 156.9
Silo, Jon 30.15, 66.129
Silo, Susan 14.185, 51.7, 65.484, 66.222, 70.30, 149.65, 162.143, 162.222
Silva, Geno 28, 176.3
Silva, Henry 9.3, 30.1, 41.32, 71.14, 74.32, 86.49, 142.31, 144.26, 162.187, 162.231, 162.283
Silveira, Ruth 96.177
Silver, Jeff 27.1, 65.18
Silver, Joe 65.575
Silver, Johnny 8.12, 14.237, 170.92
Silver, Rick 165.103
Silvera, Frank 8.35, 14.52, 14.163, 41.27, 49.2, 65.393, 71, 79.34, 102.5, 126.203, 127.42, 131.39, 157.7, 164.13, 170.61
Silverheels, Jay 17.3, 24.6, 41.20, 41.43, 64.6, 85.86, 97, 121.5, 121.19, 126.95, 153.11, 153.13, 161.183, 162.134, 164.50
Silverman, Mitchell 65.550
Silvern, Bea 96.148
Silvers, Johnny 158.12
Silvestre, Armando 41.58, 41.59, 41.140, 41.146, 123.3
Simcox, Tom 14.206, 65.317, 65.320, 65.363, 65.387, 65.414, 65.444, 65.498, 65.608, 86.29, 161.87, 161.174, 162.256, 162.284
Simmons, Dori 138.60
Simmons, Floyd 129.69
Simmons, Georgia 52.4
Simmons, Richard 43.308, 43.354, 43.374, 43.426, 81.83, 126.146, 138, 145.25
Simmons, Tom 1.2
Simms, Bill 93.181
Simms, George 70.10
Simon, Robert F. 8.84, 13.22, 14.29, 14.349, 20.23, 27.31, 27.62, 38, 39.12, 41.1, 55.16, 61.8, 63.49, 65.71, 65.83, 65.130, 65.329, 65.350, 65.362, 65.413, 66.11, 66.48, 66.116, 66.177, 79.12, 82.13, 85.3, 86.10, 86.50, 88.9, 89.39, 89.113, 92.13, 102.23, 103.33, 112.7, 113, 116.19, 126.36, 126.111, 132.6, 142.1, 152.31, 152.66, 161.41, 161.108, 161.138, 161.185, 162.41, 162.191, 167.23, 178.78
Simons, Doris 80.9, 80.11

Simpson, Alan 41.23
Simpson, Mickey 4.8, 6.5, 6.23, 6.24, 8.77, 14.18, 21.17, 21.58, 27.27, 27.85, 27.97, 32.45, 32.52, 32.105, 32.139, 32.142, 34.33, 39.13, 44.6, 57.42, 65.50, 66.67, 89.57, 89.86, 97.59, 97.63, 97.71, 97.89, 97.104, 97.117, 97.123, 97.141, 97.161, 97.184, 97.189, 105.8, 105.78, 105.80, 121.14, 124.29, 124.30, 124.34, 124.36, 124.39, 124.46, 124.47, 124.48, 124.60, 124.77, 130.1, 130.21, 133.31, 141.8, 141.10, 146.63, 158.11, 158.12, 158.31, 158.32, 161.54, 169.13, 173.28
Simpson, O.J. 24.22
Simpson, Robert 103.33
Simpson, Russell 97.120, 152.20, 169.10
Sinatra, Frank, Jr. 5.39
Sinatra, Nancy 161.21
Sinatra, Richard 65.170
Sinclair, Eric 146.47
Sinclair, Mary 85.78
Singer, Marc 109.6
Singer, Raymond 137.6, 137.7
Singer, Sally 66.99
Singer, Stuffy 6.29, 6.40, 6.62, 57.18, 178.122
Singleton, Doris 65.275, 156.26
Singleton, Penny 43.275
Sinutko, Shane 96.33
Sipes, Stacy 96.131
Sirianni, E.A. 170.103
Sirola, Joseph 19.11, 43.309, 65.305, 65.334
Sisco, Kirk 163.31
Sitka, Emil 31.29, 124.66
Skagen, Peter 99.12
Skaggs, Norm 177.32
Skagway, Alaska 82
Skarstedt, Vance 8.13
Skerritt, Tom 14.172, 14.430, 30.18, 43.277, 43.295, 43.329, 43.351, 65.387, 65.412, 65.422, 65.517, 65.577, 84.22, 85.109, 106.14, 112.13, 137.9, 161.9, 161.57, 161.90, 161.172, 161.177, 162.258
Skinner, Edna 41.2
Skipper, Pat 1.2, 48.105, 120.49, 120.50, 120.52
Skyhawk, Sonny 177.21
Slaboda, Debbie 163.1
Slack, Bill 97.103, 97.120
Slade, Betsey 175.5, 175.6
Slade, Mark 14.247, 71, 94.33, 126.176, 170.46
Slade, Shotgun 140
Slate, Jeremy 8.43, 9.12, 14.95, 14.264, 14.308, 44.19, 51.17, 65.249, 65.255, 65.313, 65.376, 65.395, 65.396, 65.471, 65.542, 65.543, 66.147, 161.61, 161.122
Slater, Bud 66.116, 152.66
Slater, Ryan 163.35
Slattery, John 177.27
Slattery, Page 8.71, 8.73, 155.61
Slattery, Richard X. 5.20, 14.280, 30.6, 41.75, 41.76, 52.44, 65.325, 65.506, 71.48, 76.20, 84.22, 84.29, 84.48, 126.145, 126.185, 126.193, 132.15, 151.26, 161.158
Slaughter, John 153
Slavin, Brad 97.52
Slay, Chuck 141.29
Slezak, Walter 117.37, 126.139
Slifer, Lizz 6.68, 43.109, 169.78
Sloan, Chuck 120.45
Sloan, Doug 120.40, 120.49
Sloane, Everett 14.22, 14.192, 29.22, 39.10, 65.312, 65.370, 85.1, 126.123, 126.162, 126.198, 151.4, 161.34, 162.54, 162.131, 162.247, 164.6, 164.46, 178.118, 179.66, 179.67, 179.68, 179.69
Slocum, George 60.53, 97.14, 97.48, 97.83, 135.11, 135.14, 169.57
Sloyan, James 26, 48.55, 48.90, 120.37
Small, Peg 28.2
Smaller, Debbie 14.331
Smidt, Burr 109.14

Smika, Gina Marie 115
Smile, Ted 66.149
Smiley, Ralph 78.18, 126.76, 126.83
Smillie, Shea 163.21
Smith, Bernice 176.1
Smith, Bill 43.439, 161.35, 161.60, 162.259
Smith, Brandon 163.52
Smith, Brian A. 14.431
Smith, Cecil 79.16, 149.48
Smith, Charles Martin 94.8
Smith, Clark 141.66, 141.70
Smith, Dean 66.177, 92.22, 120.53, 148.182
Smith, Drake 35.15
Smith, Earl T. 36.10, 94.7
Smith, Earle W. 177.4, 177.21
Smith, Elizabeth 11
Smith, Floy Dean 44.62, 149.75
Smith, Forrie J.177.54
Smith, Gerald O. 169.42
Smith, Glenn 80.34, 80.35, 80.38
Smith, Hal 14.10, 20.13, 20.70, 30.12, 43.362, 65.193, 66.3, 66.116, 77.1, 77.3, 77.7, 77.11, 77.14, 85.74, 96.178, 96.179, 134.7, 134.9, 152.73, 155.27, 162.173
Smith, Howard 39.1, 117.37, 164.90
Smith, J. Brennan 96.166
Smith, J.L. 8.91
Smith, Jim 67.21
Smith, Jim B. 175.9
Smith, Joe 41.106
Smith, Joel 20.72, 32.147, 32.152, 35.12, 169.84
Smith, John 29, 34.4, 34.23, 54.1, 72.1, 85, 106.6, 134.3, 145.34
Smith, Juney 48.14
Smith, Justin 14.158, 39.16, 89.141, 161.6
Smith, K.L. 8.1, 12.5, 13.1, 20.47, 21.9, 27.71, 30.20, 34.44, 54.20, 57.108, 65.21, 65.50, 65.110, 65.282, 74.6, 85.64, 85.93, 86.14, 86.21, 86.32, 86.37, 89.128, 105.53, 126.8, 126.43, 126.78, 126.216, 127.11, 133.34, 147.6, 149.15, 161.29, 161.170, 162.237, 166.9, 178.40
Smith, Karen 5.36
Smith, Kent 21.59, 41.84, 61.1, 61.2, 61.6, 65.294, 65.319, 66.10, 66.137, 66.186, 89.126, 101.4, 126.30, 126.166, 162.4, 162.91, 168.21, 170.68
Smith, Kirby 31.27
Smith, Lou 6.35
Smith, Martin 77.2
Smith, Mastin 148.135
Smith, Maxwell 162.21
Smith, Melanie 1.20
Smith, Mike 162.253
Smith, Milan 126.14, 126.16, 126.20
Smith, P.L. 66.220
Smith, Pam 14.87, 130.118
Smith, Patricia 14.331, 65.96, 65.230
Smith, Paul 151.24, 161.186
Smith, Queenie 96.24, 96.44, 96.46, 96.73
Smith, Reid 28
Smith, Roger 146.27, 162.29
Smith, Sandra 12.52, 12.77, 14.306, 14.343, 65.462, 65.473, 65.573, 76.12, 109.2, 161.150, 170.74
Smith, Savannah 19.10
Smith, Shawn 93.109
Smith, Sue 6.35
Smith, Sydney 14.136, 14.205, 27.25, 92.26
Smith, William 5.44, 9.11, 38.11, 41.101, 41.121, 43.448, 63.19, 63.37, 65.576, 65.631, 70.15, 83.19, 86, 120.3, 144.21, 161.86, 161.91, 161.178, 162.268, 171, 177.46
Smithers, William 24.14, 132.8, 139.3, 163.35
Smoyer, Montana 96.78
Smyth, Brian 68.22, 68.35
Smythe, Kit 65.424
Snedeker, Michael 11.5
Snider, Duke 130.17

Personnel Index

Snodgrass, Carrie 161.193
Snyder, Arlen Dean 19.16
Snyder, Tom 130.123
Soble, Ron 30.18, 41.147, 43.287, 44.23, 64.2, 65.613, 66.108, 83.31, 89.29, 98.2, 106.8, 107, 116.16, 120.21, 126.8, 126.24, 126.39, 126.184, 127.41, 137.5, 148.153, 148.171, 149.2, 151.13, 152.26, 152.58, 159.15, 161.10, 161.105, 162.188
Sobolewski, Simon Juan 67.18
Soboloff, Arnold 176.1, 176.2
Sofaer, Abraham 41.12, 41.39, 43.252, 65.180, 65.248, 66.15, 71.30, 78.52, 86.33, 105.105, 126.89, 131.29, 151.22, 162.46, 162.78, 167.19, 178.95
Sofia-Marie 72.6
Sokoloff, Vladimir 4.21, 66.16, 89.91, 105.107, 130.111, 162.152, 178.127
Solari, Rudy 12.32, 12.33, 51.15, 65.194, 66.122, 128
Soldani, Charles 32.32
Soller, Larry 177.4
Solomon, Marcia 120.41, 120.55
Solway, Larry 68.11
Somars, Julie 161.189
Somenetti, Frank 170.91
Somers, Brett 66.126, 66.220
Somers, Esther 97.20, 97.107
Somers, Jimsey 43.206
Sommars, Julie 14.161, 26, 43.306, 43.336, 49.6, 61.5, 65.337, 65.369, 65.387, 65.412, 84.25, 149.45
Sommers, Jim 164.87
Sommers, Joanie 170.103
Sondergaard, Gale 26, 109.3
Sondergaard, Quentin 8.80, 14.243, 14.328, 44.1, 66.97, 101.20, 126.112, 148.87, 161.128, 161.164, 162.59, 162.117, 170.51, 170.67, 170.73, 178.77
Sonessa, Joseph 93.172
Song, Arthur 83.60
Sooter, Rudy 65.382, 65.387, 65.425, 65.437, 65.438, 65.442, 65.443
Sorel, Guy 97.173
Sorel, Louise 7.9, 14.212, 41.92, 76.3, 161.102
Sorensen, Linda 99.16
Sorensen, Paul 3.32, 5.8, 6.49, 12.13, 12.21, 12.37, 12.46, 12.60, 13.44, 30.7, 43.430, 43.432, 44.45, 52.38, 57.23, 63.12, 65.594, 65.619, 66.67, 66.82, 66.88, 70.32, 71.67, 76.2, 76.15, 77.5, 79.16, 84.44, 88.27, 111.5, 126.194, 129.31, 130.79, 130.160, 145.27, 147.30, 158.13, 158.16, 161.23, 165.13, 169.86, 170.72, 178.114, 178.119
Sorensen, Ricky 44.65, 129.47
Sorensen, Ronald 129.48
Sorensen, Ronnie 162.93
Soreny, Eva 170.8
Sorrells, Frank 170.29, 170.59, 170.95, 170.96
Sorrells, Robert 14.146, 14.181, 14.210, 14.298, 14.344, 30.1, 30.23, 41.8, 41.149, 43.438, 65.244, 65.319, 65.366, 65.380, 65.386, 65.412, 65.420, 65.444, 65.466, 65.527, 65.551, 65.552, 65.553, 65.627, 83.43, 84.16, 101.14, 121.21, 126.181, 126.182
Sorrentino, John 43.89
Sothern, Ann 5.28, 92.14, 106.17
Soto, Rosana 83.21
Soul, David 65.630, 70, 177.23, 177.24
Soule, Olan 8.10, 12.14, 14.53, 14.183, 14.270, 14.272, 14.292, 30.23, 41.128, 44.57, 46.2, 65.391, 65.482, 66.31, 66.97, 66.107, 66.152, 66.184, 66.194, 85.68, 85.95, 85.103, 103.46, 105.96, 126.17, 126.41, 126.76, 126.104, 126.186, 127.7, 127.30, 130.155, 142.19, 142.22, 142.24, 142.33, 142.38, 147.46, 148.52, 162.94, 162.267, 164.26, 164.30, 164.36, 164.42, 164.76, 164.89, 168.14, 168.19
Space, Arthur 6.11, 6.16, 8.30, 12.11, 12.39, 14.114, 20.16, 20.53, 21.62, 24.2, 34.19, 34.52, 34.67, 41.52, 43.35, 43.146, 43.158, 60.68, 60.72, 60.82, 60.87, 66.99, 70.2, 93.1, 93.152, 96.53, 129.17, 130.63, 145.16, 148.49, 148.123, 156.6, 158.54, 158.56, 161.76, 162.29, 162.56, 162.200, 162.223, 162.258, 164.25, 167.12, 170.44, 170.84, 179.60, 179.61, 179.62
Spaeth, Merrie 92.12
Spain, Fay 4.21, 4.27, 8.22, 14.14, 27.18, 41.9, 43.359, 44.49, 64.1, 65.85, 65.247, 65.452, 66.8, 76.41, 85.22, 85.41, 85.105, 101.16, 105.13, 105.67, 105.90, 105.97, 126.32, 126.76, 126.120, 129.23, 129.76, 131.42, 144.19, 146.6, 148.194, 152.12, 155.31, 164.39, 164.54
Spain, Jack 149.38
Spalding, Kim 44.22, 97.53, 97.78, 97.103, 145.10, 158.20, 158.23
Spang, Laurette 5.50.
Spanier, Frances 84.45, 161.190
Sparks, Adrian 1.8, 48.1
Sparks, Don 120.43
Sparks, Randy 34.51, 117.21
Spaulding, George 73.18
Speare, Matthew 48.16
Spears, Aries 1.22
Spell, George 14.326, 83.17, 83.62
Spelling, Aaron 65.35
Spencer, Diana 79.30
Spencer, Douglas 14.19, 27.43, 127.47, 130.20, 148.130
Spencer, Robert 93.1, 97.113
Spencer, Sundown 14.340, 84.34
Sperberg, Fritz 91.4, 163.46
Sperdakos, George 30.22
Spielberg, David 7.4
Spivy, Madame 170.41
Spivy, Mme.41.101
Spooner, Cecil 97.30
Spradley, Jon 48.11
Spradlin, G.D. 5.49, 14.304, 14.368, 83.16, 121.9, 134.7, 134.17, 161.212
Spratt, Dwayne 126.129
Spring, Helen 3.148, 25.44, 135.84
Springer, Thais 1.3
Spruance, Don 128.7, 159.13, 172.5
Squire, Katherine 132.1, 132.2, 148.99, 152.58, 161.12
Staab, Rebecca 177.35
Stacy, James 30.15, 65.354, 65.442, 65.443, 65.560, 65.594, 66.204, 84, 107.3
Stacy, Michelle 176
Stader, Paul 131.44, 162.256, 178.129
Stafford, Bucko 6.47, 57.116
Stafford, Dan 43.291, 65.237, 65.296, 66.156, 126.102, 151.11
Stafford, Hanley 27.78, 105.63, 146.54
Stafford, Tim 14.221
Stagg, Alex 20.55, 78.56
Stahl, Richard 112.21
Staigg, Joyce 152.68
Stait, Brent 99.13
Staley, James 1.10, 19.14, 19.15
Staley, Joan 14.24, 86.7, 121.26, 125.4, 144.27, 148.191, 161.101
Staley, Lee 170.53
Stalmaster, Hal 127.9
Stanaker, Chuck 141.55
Standing, Eugene George 94.16
Standingbear, Chief 28.5
Standish, Phyllis 22.26
Stang, Arnold 14.73, 162.151
Stanhope, Ted 73.35, 81.69, 81.93, 126.80, 130.45, 158.69, 169.20, 178.132
Stanley, Barbara 60.5, 60.49, 124.27, 124.32
Stanley, Forrest 65.116, 169.101
Stanley, Helen 42
Stanley, Helene 66.81
Stanley, Richard 96.68, 137.5
Stanton, Harry Dean 3.141, 3.142, 8.24, 12.26, 14.56, 14.124, 30.10, 41.8, 51.28, 63.8, 65.102, 65.235, 65.267, 65.309, 65.238, 65.347, 65.476, 66.58, 66.178, 71.18, 79.25, 85.10, 85.49, 85.81, 85.107, 101.5, 102.23, 126.29, 126.120, 126.152, 130.45, 144.4, 152.3, 152.42, 161.184, 170.63, 175.5, 175.6, 178.66, 178.66, 178.123, 178.131, 178.146
Stanton, Rochelle 60.68, 60.72
Stanton, Rocky 135.7
Stanwood, Michael 70.33, 161.111, 161.120
Stanwyck, Barbara 12, 126.98, 162.155, 162.191, 162.227, 162.245, 178.46, 178.61, 178.75, 178.90
Stapleton, James 51.21, 159.23
Stapp, Marjorie 93.101, 127.31, 147.52, 158.6
Starett, Michael 96.85
Stark, Craig 120.25
Starke, Anthony 1.10.
Starr, Don 71.37, 71.38
Starr, Ron 14.165, 44.43, 149.37, 152.67
Starr, Sam 96.80
Starrett, Charles 65.188
Starrett, Jack 24.8, 171.1
Starrett, Valerie 43.209
Staten, Max 14.65
Statten, Lynn 4.18, 4.35
Stauffer, Jack 75.23
Staunton, Ann 98.7, 162.253, 169.80
Steadman, John 123.3
Steele, Bob 25.24, 25.60, 27.23, 52, 74.9, 74.13, 93.14, 93.15, 105.1, 126.1, 126.17, 126.48, 127.2, 148.67, 151.6, 168.11
Steele, Don 70.50
Steele, George 60.13, 60.22
Steele, Karen 4.14, 4.19, 4.29, 8.34, 14.79, 17.20, 21.53, 44.34, 51.25, 77.7, 85.48, 85.83, 89.72, 101.11, 105.2, 105.57, 126.100, 131.27, 162.12
Steele, Mike 66.61, 164.30
Steele, Robert 66.19
Steele, Tom 6.72, 65.424, 165.13, 169.7, 169.15, 169.16, 169.20
Steen, Malcolm 141.46
Stefan, Virginia 158.69, 158.71
Stefani, Michael 130.75, 159.5
Stehli, Edgar 22.32, 27.58, 65.54, 129.69, 146.38, 152.16
Stehpens, Larraine 86.29
Steiger, Rod 45.3, 162.142
Stein, Jeanne 109.5
Steindler, Maureen 28
Stenberg, Helen 96.56
Stennette, Shera 43.95
Stephani, Michael 14.313, 14.231
Stephens, Chris 65.446, 163.29, 163.55
Stephens, Harry 44.7, 162.39
Stephens, Harvey 8.9, 8.40, 14.131, 14.216, 34.21, 129.28, 133.21, 148.38, 155.53
Stephens, Joe 163.28
Stephens, Johnny 14.142
Stephens, Joseph 163.79
Stephens, Laraine 24.3, 86.18, 123.6
Stephens, Norm 83.10
Stephens, William Eben 164.92
Stephenson, John 52.8, 97.141, 129.28, 148.115, 166.20, 167.7
Stephenson, Maureen 43.42
Stephenson, Robert 164.59
Sterling, Jack 6.8
Sterling, Jan 14.47, 83.42, 96.51, 96.52, 106.24, 131.13, 132.24, 162.60, 162.156
Sterling, John 170.25
Sterling, Robert 162.14
Sterling, Ross 127.30
Sterling, Tisha 14.292, 106.19, 132.24
Stern, Tom 65.471, 98.6, 125.15
Sterne, Morgan 14.355
Stevens, Andrew 115, 123.10

Personnel Index

Stevens, Angela 31.20, 43.149
Stevens, Bert 156.28
Stevens, Bill 14.392
Stevens, Charles 3.68, 3.98, 3.129, 4.30, 4.32, 20.41, 81.28, 81.30, 81.36, 81.55, 88.29, 97.44, 97.114, 97.188, 97.191, 97.198, 105.83, 124.63, 124.75, 126.64, 126.74, 138.2, 138.5, 138.40, 141.23, 162.6, 162.23, 169.30, 179.14
Stevens, Connie 27.58, 105.51, 146.7, 146.42, 151.25
Stevens, Craig 5.29, 97.35, 106.20
Stevens, Fisher 177.19
Stevens, Harmon 97.107
Stevens, Inger 14.3, 51.30, 178.114
Stevens, Jack Ray 48.8
Stevens, Joe 110.4, 163.11
Stevens, John 161.170
Stevens, K.T. 12.20, 12.47, 76.12, 96.38, 126.59, 127.50, 130.62, 130.72, 130.95, 130.118, 130.163, 162.11, 178.136
Stevens, Lenore 106.12
Stevens, Mark 126.115, 162.6, 178.19, 178.51
Stevens, Marti 142.8
Stevens, Marya 8.100, 20.59, 20.65, 126.30, 126.45, 129.43, 129.61
Stevens, Mel 135.95, 169.89
Stevens, Millie 102.16
Stevens, Naomi 12.7, 51.31, 66.16, 66.188, 126.106, 162.258
Stevens, Onslow 3.143, 13.1, 14.12, 27.5, 44.5, 65.148, 66.7, 85.46, 117.2, 119.17, 129.66, 153, 162.23, 162.46, 162.87, 162.113, 164.12, 178.43
Stevens, Oren 14.320
Stevens, Paul 47.10, 65.546, 65.587, 65.595, 65.596, 170.62
Stevens, Rikki 101.26
Stevens, Robert 162.21
Stevens, Rory 14.145, 41.127, 92.4, 161.103, 162.138
Stevens, Rusty 130.161, 162.204
Stevens, Scott 65.150
Stevens, Stella 14.45, 55.12, 69.2, 79.23, 115.5, 131.43
Stevens, Steve 65.289, 135.89, 179.31, 179.32
Stevens, Warren 4.23, 12.29, 14.186, 14.263, 14.284, 14.371, 39.6, 41.50, 41.75, 41.76, 43.360, 65.93, 65.235, 65.293, 66.14, 66.220, 66.226, 71.3, 76.39, 85.10, 89.57, 92.22, 98.11, 101.23, 106.13, 126.212, 127.59, 148.90, 161.65, 161.148, 162.70, 162.187
Stevens, William 44.67, 66.41, 66.181, 161.85
Stevenson, Parker 65.610
Stevenson, Robert J. 8.64, 14.6, 14.78, 14.122, 14.199, 44.42, 51.29, 65.255, 65.262, 66.99, 66.142, 66.190, 66.207, 66.218, 66.226, 77, 85.34, 102.16, 102.31, 126.121, 126.132, 126.172, 133.10, 142.9, 142.10, 142.24, 148.140, 148.192, 149.6, 155.24, 159.35, 161.6
Stevenson, Venetia 34.18, 89.8, 146.5, 146.17, 146.22
Stewart, Adam 149.59
Stewart, Alana 99.12
Stewart, Art 8.83, 27.85, 65.479, 105.83
Stewart, Benjamin 177.62
Stewart, Charles 169.112
Stewart, Charlotte 14.341, 14.390, 24.9, 65.512, 96, 96.50, 161.220
Stewart, David J. 66.145
Stewart, Don 86.5, 161.105
Stewart, Elaine 8.76
Stewart, Gregg 65.171, 162.118
Stewart, Hayes 94.7
Stewart, Jim 130.116
Stewart, Kay 12.15, 13.42, 29.4, 43.35, 43.303, 43.376, 92.33, 106.13, 129.37, 129.50, 148.67, 161.6, 162.30, 162.31, 162.56, 162.89, 162.124, 162.179, 162.185, 162.254, 162.258, 166.8, 178.122

Stewart, Malcolm 67.18
Stewart, Margaret 97.206, 138.63, 148.22
Stewart, Marianne 14.18, 22.25, 65.59, 102.5
Stewart, Mel 96.150
Stewart, Paul 65.515, 162.273
Stewart, Peggy 32.2, 32.6, 32.11, 32.67, 41.40, 60.22, 65.146, 65.193, 65.239, 65.348, 662, 66.166, 74.18, 93.104, 93.139, 127.61, 135.2, 135.13, 169.15, 173.19
Stewart, Wendy 65.146
Stine, Jan 13.6, 64.6, 82.7, 89.145, 130.78, 130.122, 151.3, 161.3, 161.10, 164.76, 167.10, 178.80
Stine, Jean 89.93
Stirling, Linda 81.18, 81.87, 81.101, 93.30
Stock, Alan 120.32
Stock-Poynton, Amy 65.637, 65.638, 65.639, 65.640
Stocker, Walter 148.72
Stockman, Boyd 60.17, 50.23, 60.25, 63.39, 81.29, 81.40, 81.49, 81.64, 81.83, 85.86, 124.42, 124.45, 124.69, 124.78, 141.62, 148.39, 148.124, 148.185, 148.188, 169.50
Stockwell, Dean 14.340, 29.7, 59.3, 117.14, 129.42, 162.4, 162.41, 162.75, 162.145
Stockwell, Guy 14.169, 14.338, 14.432, 65.207, 65.209, 75.18, 84.23, 89.136, 126.17, 142.7, 161.208, 162.268, 170.102
Stockwell, John 177.61
Stohl, Hank 130.48, 130.109
Stokey, Michael 24.4
Stoll, Frank 5.46
Stone, Arthur 97.59
Stone, Carol 93, 93.66, 93.72, 93.77, 93.80, 93.81, 93.83, 93.84, 93.111
Stone, Christopher 24.15, 70.5, 70.24, 70.29, 116.3
Stone, George E. 66.30
Stone, Harold J. 4.17, 8.25, 12.19, 14.170, 24.21, 27.45, 27.92, 29.9, 41.4, 51.20, 65.73, 65.122, 65.150, 65.236, 65.339, 65.349, 65.377, 66.5, 66.16, 66.142, 69.10, 76.40, 85.37, 92.32, 93.197, 101.30, 119.16, 126.58, 126.129, 129.25, 130.2, 130.77, 130.164, 142.7, 146.27, 148.52, 148.127, 148.195, 149.7, 153.6, 156.16, 156.42, 156.58, 157.25, 161.103, 161.121, 161.123, 161.191, 161.219, 164.70, 178.45, 179.54
Stone, James 66.101, 129.32, 145.9, 145.32
Stone, Jan 161.8
Stone, Jeffrey 25.21, 25.33, 43.203
Stone, Leonard 30.15, 51.13, 51.16, 65.360, 65.585, 65.593, 65.619, 71.34, 72.11, 84.42, 106.22, 130.90, 130.132
Stone, Milburn 65, 169.5
Stone, Sandra 93.146
Stoner, Sherri 95.20, 95.21, 95.22
Stoney Crockett 35
Storch, Larry 62, 94.20
Storey, Ruth 65.90, 66.12
Storm, Debi 12.53, 84.25, 84.42
Storm, James 83.29
Storm, Wayne 14.335, 71.71, 83.18
Storrs, Suzanne 89.76, 105.73, 146.69, 164.76
Story, Larry 5.39
Stossel, Ludwig 140.28, 140.29
Stowe, Madeline 96.141
Straight, Clarence 73.9, 97.49, 97.73, 97.137, 108.28, 145.11, 148.38, 152.31, 162.17
Straler, Lucia 11
Strang, Harry 3.101, 3.117, 3.146, 3.147, 3.149, 3.162, 3.165, 31.15, 32.88, 43.108, 81.49, 97.204, 97.208, 97.217, 135.49, 135.51, 135.86, 138.57, 147.25, 148.64, 158.23, 169.54
Strange, Glenn 2.9, 2.14, 2.23, 3.94, 6.62, 6.76, 23.16, 23.23, 32.126, 32.154, 34.63, 43.111, 56.1, 60.81, 60.91, 65, 73.4, 80.16, 80.21, 80.22, 80.34, 80.35, 80.38, 81.2, 93.23, 93.80, 93.200, 97.1, 97.2, 97.3, 97.30, 97.95, 97.121, 97.122, 97.132, 97.160, 124.59, 124.62, 126.30, 129.21,

130.7, 130.20, 130.32, 130.43, 130.49, 130.90, 141.3, 141.69, 145.14, 146.64, 148.11, 148.176, 158.29
Strangis, Judy 7.13
Strasberg, Susan 5.3, 12.65, 14.302, 84.6, 92.17, 106.7, 161.124
Strasser, Robin 177.13
Stratton, Albert 137
Stratton, Bob 169.109
Stratton, Chet 14.324, 20.17, 25.37, 46.13, 66.51, 66.105, 66.143, 162.21, 162.120, 170.1, 170.22
Strauss, Robert 8.83, 14.111, 125.3, 126.39, 142.15, 161.152, 162.82, 162.240, 164.18
Strauss, Wally 161.145
Street, David 169.87
Street, Elliot 24.15, 83.21
Strickland, Amzie 5.3, 12.49, 13.13, 30.9, 43.352, 52.65, 53.9, 65.6, 65.49, 65.345, 65.519, 78.49, 126.17, 129.29, 132.29, 156.32, 161.29, 162.47, 162.80, 162.168, 162.200, 162.226, 162.248
Strickland, Gail 48
Strickler, Jerry 84.43
Stricklyn, Ray 14.20, 14.222, 20.4, 20.21, 21.24, 27.82, 78.32, 89.97, 162.131, 162.174
Stritch, Elaine 162.99
Strode, Woody 41.62, 102.15, 123.8, 123.9, 126.64, 126.74
Stroll, Edson 155.70
Strom, Diane 144.27
Stromsoe, Fred 65.531, 65.546, 170.70, 170.82, 170.89
Strong, Bob 148.118
Strong, Harry 3.66, 22.28
Strong, Jay 159.13
Strong, Leonard 4.32, 97.16, 97.31, 113, 126.188
Strong, Michael 12.77, 30.1, 65.410, 65.584
Strong, Robert 32.142, 65.47
Stroud, Claude 82.11, 105.91, 151.24, 151.25
Stroud, Don 1.6, 48.10, 65.585, 65.613, 69.4, 83.45, 110.4, 120.14, 161.134, 161.160, 161.182, 163.50
Strudwick, Sheppard 25.24, 66.94, 162.13
Stuart, Arlen 162.154
Stuart, Barbara 5.19, 34.29, 46.2, 55.6, 76.30, 77.2, 77.9, 83.15, 89.4, 117.34, 126.155, 131.31, 148.132, 148.173, 152.55, 152.56, 152.57, 159.4
Stuart, Chad 86.19
Stuart, Gilchrest 27.17
Stuart, Kay 114.22
Stuart, Maxine 111.4, 144.14, 164.80
Stuart, Monty 177.36
Stuart, Randy 14.57, 21.37, 27.49, 27.52, 27.73, 27.88, 34.14, 89.71, 89.94, 93, 93.145, 93.151, 93.152, 93.153, 93.154, 93.155, 93.158, 93.164, 93.167, 93.168, 93.171, 93.180, 93.181, 93.182, 93.186, 93.188, 105.109
Stuart, Wendy 114.22
Studi, Wes 110
Study, Lomax 131.34, 141.53
Sturges, Mark 65.402
Sturges, Shannon 163.29
Sturges, Solomon 30.15, 63.20, 71.81
Sturgess, Olive 14.104, 22.38, 27.47, 46.8, 66.68, 85.20, 89.31, 105.84, 105.114, 117.44, 126.12, 127.6, 127.62, 146.18, 149.13, 149.23, 149.31, 152.21, 161.68, 162.96, 162.115, 168.25
Sturgis, Norman 8.53, 65.170, 177.36
Sturlin, Ross 66.111, 66.136, 127.24, 127.38, 127.40, 127.49, 127.65
Stuthman, Fred 53.28, 96.65
Subkoff, Tar 48.32
Sublette, Linda 65.617
Sudrow, Lyle 101.11
Sues, Alan 170.15
Sugarman, Richard 177.4
Suhor, Yvonne 177
Sujata 169.30

Personnel Index

Sullivan, Barry 14.2, 14.273, 71.84, 71.90, 83.1, 83.34, 96.123, 98.12, 132, 149, 161.3, 161.206, 178.56, 178.70, 178.92
Sullivan, Billy L. 48.72, 48.78
Sullivan, Brad 10.1
Sullivan, Brick 65.84
Sullivan, Buck 93.119
Sullivan, Donald E. 169.99
Sullivan, George K. 177.5
Sullivan, Grant 122, 148.148, 148.169
Sullivan, Jenny 96.110
Sullivan, Joseph 148.97, 178.100
Sullivan, Liam 8.89, 14.217, 27.63, 27.64, 41.134, 41.153, 43.66, 65.58, 65.421, 66.131, 92.24, 96.127, 107, 126.195, 155.69, 161.118, 162.161
Sullivan, Megan 137.8
Sullivan, Patrick 71.71
Sullivan, Susan 175.1
Sullivan, Tim 169.80
Sully, Frank 3.34, 85.75, 97.55, 103.36, 129.35, 130.27, 145.16, 145.32, 149.43, 161.27, 161.63, 161.66, 161.84, 164.59, 169.93
Summers, Bunny 86.46
Summers, Hope 57.109, 65.133, 65.210, 65.308, 88.5, 96.46, 105.49, 130, 157.3
Summers, Jerry 3.149, 6.55, 14.263, 14.326, 65.469, 66.141, 66.220, 66.225, 112.10, 148.59, 149.19, 161.9, 161.14
Summers, Neil 65.573, 65.590
Summers, Tom 48.12
Sumper, William L. 65.446
Sun, Irene Yeh-Ling 123.7
Sun Chief, Duke 80.19
Sundberg, Clinton 66.13, 86.8, 89.150, 121.6, 146.47
Sundstrom, Florence 14.132, 170.65
Sung, Michael 170.17
Surovy, Nicolas 1.18, 12.15, 90.10, 120.3, 120.4, 120.5, 120.6, 120.9
Sussman, Todd 96.164
Sutherland, Victor 78.64
Sutorius, James 177.10
Sutton, David 161.189
Sutton, Dolores 65.287
Sutton, Frank 43.272, 51.22, 65.236, 65.252, 65.283, 66.179, 105.1, 151.5
Sutton, Grady 89.80, 89.116, 89.120, 89.126, 93.28, 126.83, 146.64
Sutton, John 8.27, 8.47, 25.44, 102.9, 126.95, 127.15, 127.36, 142.16, 155.52
Sutton, Tom 65.504, 65.505, 65.560
Svenson, Bo 41.139, 70, 71.60, 83.22, 84.13, 106.9
Svensson, Monica 65.594
Swain, Bob 48.32, 48.37, 120.56
Swan, Michael 28.12
Swan, Noel 170.69
Swan, Robert 2.23, 8.7, 8.49, 8.61, 8.93, 17.36, 65.515, 65.526, 80.17, 80.19, 80.26, 93.184, 93.150, 96.4, 97.188, 97.198, 127.38, 129.37, 138.2, 183.67, 141.44, 141.67, 148.26, 158.19, 158.21, 158.44, 162.13, 167.12, 169.105
Swan, William 66.17, 158.61, 178.30
Swanson, Audrey 161.2, 161.74
Swayze, Don 120.14, 163.50
Sweeney, Bob 130.80, 130.102
Sweeney, Pepper 48.51
Sweet, Dolph 96.102
Sweet, Katie 14.144, 14.166, 14.167, 61.5, 157.9, 162.214, 168.19
Swenson, Carl 165.10
Swenson, Inga 14.95, 14.142, 137.4
Swenson, Jeep 163.29
Swenson, Karl 8.10, 12.7, 12.30, 12.46, 13.29, 14.2, 14.39, 14.215, 21.13, 21.20, 30.3, 30.6, 30.11, 30.12, 30.16, 30.18, 31.44, 34.26, 39.5, 43.305, 63.22, 65.89, 65.158, 65.220, 65.265, 65.342, 65.404, 65.420, 65.490, 65.537, 66.36, 66.47,
66.69, 66.141, 66.147, 66.150, 74.22, 77.13, 78.59, 82.1, 82.12, 85.83, 85.90, 85.119, 96.42, 96.93, 96.94, 101.21, 102.3, 105.11, 105.37, 105.96, 116.16, 126.29, 127.5, 130.66, 130.73, 131.6, 146.9, 146.17, 146.30, 151.11, 152.1, 152.49, 156.52, 157.3, 157.18, 161.8, 161.30, 161.106, 161.183, 161.210, 162.146, 162.243, 178.47, 178.97, 178.118
Swift, Joan 43.96, 85.104
Swift, Susan 28
Swift, Thad 21.30
Swimmer, Bob 126.89
Swindell, Jerry 110.3
Swit, Loretta 14.414, 24.1, 65.505, 65.521, 65.522
Switzer, Carl 135.4, 135.17, 135.28, 135.66, 135.68, 135.71
Swofford, Ken 12.43, 30.12, 41.107, 37.9, 59.2, 65.452, 65.465, 65.475, 65.490, 65.514, 65.537, 65.557, 65.597, 65.632, 65.638, 70.28, 70.35, 75.25, 83.33, 83.42, 84.45, 161.166, 161.167, 161.184, 161.200, 170.71
Swoger, Harry 4.32, 12.6, 12.23, 12.50, 12.70, 12.71, 12.85, 14.45, 14.73, 14.152, 63.18, 63.49, 65.162, 65.185, 65.204, 65.209, 74.10, 74.28, 76.1, 84.9, 84.39, 88.1, 92.34, 105.83, 126.29, 144.32, 149.61, 152.17, 161.88, 162.229, 165.3, 170.67
Sydes, Anthony 73.26, 97.135, 169.7, 169.26
Sylvester, William 14.348, 14.426, 71.51, 71.66
Symonds, Tom 117.27
Szabo, Sandor 14.314
Szabo, Valrie 17.1
Szarabajka, Keith 163.79
Szold, Bernard 60.56, 60.59

Tabor, Joan 66.174, 85.61
Tabori, Kristoffer 112.10
Taeger, Ralph 8.66, 72, 82, 155.91
Ta Fel, Suzanne 81.90, 81.98
Taft, Sara 65.299, 130.85, 130.144, 130.145, 170.16, 170.21
Tafur, Robert 9.2, 17.43, 43.56, 43.77, 65.413, 78.29, 149.37
Taggart, Hal 31.17, 31.19, 141.24
Taka, Miiko 170.53
Takei, George 43.329
Talbot, Gloria 148.174
Talbot, Lyle 3.21, 3.74, 6.66, 6.67, 14.48, 22.30, 23.8, 23.15, 29.17, 32.82, 32.89, 32.95, 34.32, 35.5, 35.6, 35.23, 60.53, 50.56, 60.59, 73.17, 81.28, 81.78, 86.11, 89.130, 92.6, 97.45, 97.45, 97.108, 97.146, 97.154, 97.182, 124.57, 124.69, 124.70, 124.73, 126.16, 129.20, 129.75, 135.34, 142.22, 145.4, 148.12, 162.54, 162.104, 168.9, 168.17, 169.14, 169.43, 169.60, 169.94
Talbot, Nita 14.282, 41.53, 65.126, 65.191, 102.31, 105.63, 105.77, 126.141, 161.114
Talbot, Stephen 88.15, 89.24, 146.36, 164.39
Talbot-Martin, Elizabeth 14.349
Talbott, Gloria 6.5, 8.11, 8.72, 14.25, 21.60, 29.23, 32.80, 32.87, 35.13, 43.287, 43.319, 43.217, 54.14, 55.21, 60.59, 65.4, 65.250, 65.288, 73.18, 85.25, 85.44, 85.65, 85.104, 88.26, 93.1, 93.2, 93.221, 124.54, 126.15, 126.65, 126.92, 127.29, 129.19, 129.31, 129.42, 131.17, 131.39, 135.52, 148.69, 162.186, 164.2, 164.59, 164.81, 166.2, 169.22, 178.13, 179.66, 179.67, 179.68, 179.69
Talboy, Tara 47.4
Talman, William 29.3, 65.308, 66.125, 66.138, 155.22, 156.5, 162.27, 170.40
Talton, Alix 66.13, 129.57
Talton, Reedy 44.65
Talvera, Juan 170.59
Tamayo, Rafael 163.83
Tamblyn, Russ 24.20, 65.377, 76.25, 94.35, 123.1
Tamiroff, Akim 79.20, 130.10, 162.143
Tannen, Bill 135.7, 135.36, 135.53, 135.65, 164.67, 169.62

Tannen, Charles 14.24, 14.46, 34.12, 64.2, 66.45, 77.18, 82.10, 89.115, 105.4, 126.28, 126.60, 126.68, 126.86, 126.112, 130.73, 130.78, 130.84, 130.94, 135.48, 135.53, 147.50, 148.47, 148.143, 158.40, 162.50, 178.46
Tannen, William 2.1, 2.6, 3.72, 3.91, 6.31, 6.33, 6.42, 6.43, 6.48, 6.57, 8.10, 8.54, 8.83, 8.100, 14.133, 14.182, 14.214, 35.50, 30.14, 32.82, 32.89, 32.118, 34.12, 36.24, 41.63, 41.69, 41.78, 43.291, 64.8, 65.456, 65.490, 71.6, 71.18, 71.19, 71.43, 81.6, 81.13, 81.41, 85.18, 93, 93.38, 93.41, 93.43, 94.53, 93.56, 93.59, 93.62, 93.64, 93.70, 93.84, 93.85, 93.87, 93.88, 93.89, 93.90, 93.95, 93.101, 93.103, 97.20, 97.191, 126.23, 126.36, 126.48, 126.99, 133.37, 135.9, 135.30, 135.48, 135.71, 138.17, 145.16, 145.37, 147.25, 148.142, 148.197, 152.37, 158.40, 161.114, 162.34, 166.19, 169.55
Tanner, Clay 12.54, 14.219, 14.220, 14.234, 65.546, 83.5, 83.16, 83.44, 86.50
Tapscott, Mark 12.40, 12.93, 12.100, 13.10, 14.313, 14.354, 43.433, 44.7, 66.60, 71.58, 71.83, 74.3, 84.46, 105.36, 105.40, 105.53, 105.65, 126.70, 126.84, 133.3, 149.28, 149.42, 149.50, 149.51, 149.58, 149.65, 149.70, 155.29, 155.50, 161.131, 161.176, 161.188, 161.201, 162.233
Taranto, Glenn 1.6
Tarbuck, Barbara 96.156, 96.157
Tarkington, Rockne 9.8, 36.10, 71.21
Tartan, James 30.14, 120.19
Tate, Kevin 92.31
Tate, Lincoln 84.6
Tate, Richard 116.10
Tatro, Richard 27.85
Tatum, Jean 126.22
Taurins, Ilze 14.190, 161.25, 170.8
Taxier, Arthur 48.63
Tayback, Vic 14.358, 22.4, 30.5, 52.4, 65.436, 65.484, 65.534, 65.570, 70.1, 70.42, 84.26, 84.32, 126.204
Taylor, Bob 158.55, 158.59, 158.66, 158.72, 158.74
Taylor, Buck 1.4, 14.170, 17.35, 41.71, 43.426, 45.4, 65, 65.443, 65.443, 65.636, 66.208, 92.2, 107.18, 107.19, 107.26, 120.21, 120.46, 144.14, 144.28, 161.53, 161.73, 161.108, 162.273, 163.41, 177.50
Taylor, Cindy 170.34
Taylor, Clay 162.134
Taylor, Curtis 170.5
Taylor, Don 178.137
Taylor, Dub 3.115, 5.13, 12.31, 12.80, 14.251, 14.283, 14.342, 14.359, 14.389, 14.401, 19.17, 24.9, 30.23, 43.233, 43.357, 43.374, 49.9, 53.28, 59.4, 63.21, 65.398, 65.425, 65.426, 65.437, 65.438, 65.468, 65.510, 71.31, 71.62, 84.9, 84.28, 86.4, 86.20, 96.134, 96.135, 96.140, 96.154, 98.9, 107.9, 107.22, 124.46, 124.47, 124.48, 135.38, 135.43, 135.45, 135.47, 135.62, 135.64, 147.51, 151.8, 158.44, 161.94, 161.109, 165.2, 167.26, 170.5, 170.71, 178.119, 178.142
Taylor, Ferris 22.9, 32.16, 32.27, 32.55, 32.127, 60.69, 81.48, 97.100, 135.2, 135.9, 135.12, 169.7, 169.20, 169.34
Taylor, Forrest 6.11, 6.16, 32.2, 32.5, 32.9, 32.10, 32.11, 32.13, 32.70, 32.85, 32.92, 60.68, 60.72, 73.38, 93.32, 93.55, 103, 108.28, 108.37, 135.11, 135.14, 135.57, 135.60, 135.63, 148.133, 169.48, 178.54
Taylor, George 121.8, 145.26, 145.37
Taylor, Joan 21.58, 34.49, 65.134, 126.81, 130, 152.48, 162.26, 173.4
Taylor, Josh 163.69
Taylor, Joyce 8.57, 14.107, 89.18, 133.26, 148.117, 148.199, 162.177, 166.4
Taylor, Jud 3.160, 65.91

Personnel Index

Taylor, June Whitley 123.10
Taylor, Kent 8.60, 21.25, 21.49, 34.8, 85.18, 125.2, 129.22, 130.96, 130.97, 131.22, 133, 146.59, 148.41, 179.31, 179.32
Taylor, Mary Lou 65.379, 65.445
Taylor, Michael 6.66, 6.67, 57
Taylor, Robert 43, 43.347, 43.363, 43.364, 43.367, 43.373, 43.376, 43.384, 43.406, 72.1, 72.2
Taylor, Rod 9, 27.3, 115, 118, 163.79, 178.105
Taylor, Tom 28
Taylor, Vaughn 5.7, 5.16, 13.13, 14.247, 14.272, 14.273, 14.352, 21.14, 21.47, 27.50, 27.105, 34.29, 34.59, 41.56, 41.149, 43.312, 63.11, 64.2, 65.98, 65.169, 65.469, 66.53, 71.4, 84.3, 84.28, 85.55, 86.54, 92.26, 102.2, 126.49, 126.77, 126.207, 148.136, 151.22, 152.6, 156.2, 161.34, 162.10, 164.1, 164.45, 164.77, 168.22, 170.9
Taylor, Wayne 103.30
Taylor-Young, Leigh 118.2, 177.64
Tead, Phil 20.48, 31.42, 73.36, 97.35, 97.39, 97.43, 97.117, 97.127, 97.143, 97.147, 97.168
Teague, Guy 57.16, 65.145, 81.23, 126.114, 126.141, 147.51, 164.49, 169.42, 169.49, 169.60, 169.102, 178.5
Teague, Marshall 118.7, 163.1, 163.80
Teal, Ray 4.11, 8.39, 8.74, 14, 20.7, 20.42, 21.11, 21.26, 25.45, 27.2, 27.7, 27.71, 27.109, 31.16, 34.67, 51.8, 54.8, 65.115, 82.1, 85.2, 89.110, 97.30, 97.132, 97.160, 97.175, 103.19, 105.6, 105.28, 105.54, 105.59, 107.12, 113.9, 126.88, 129.19, 129.26, 130.46, 131.43, 148.10, 152.11, 156.10, 156.46, 162.86, 164.14, 168.6, 168.8, 168.18, 179.16
Tedrow, Irene 14.96, 14.304, 14.346, 26, 37.12, 43.313, 43.346, 43.436, 49.7, 77.15, 83.38, 83.39, 105.43, 105.70, 114.5, 126.18, 129.17, 149.64, 152.18, 161.121, 162.102
Teed, Jill 67.4
Teele, Margaret 134.8
Tegge, Shirley 32.103
Temple, Pick 130.118
Tennant, Bill 85.62, 117.12, 117.13, 148.52, 150.2
Tennon, Julius 110.1
Tenorio, John, Jr. 109
Terhune, Bob 41.47, 41.58, 41.59, 152.54
Terhune, Max 6.23, 97.57
Terhune, Shannon 137.9
Terlesky, John 120, 163.39
Terman, Hy 14.67
Terranova, Dan 65.470
Terrell, Kenneth 32.110, 32.116, 32.126, 162.152
Terrell, Steven 8.43, 14.15, 14.49, 43.197, 65.73, 65.181, 66.5, 103.39, 105.71, 129.44, 142.26, 148.51, 148.182, 152.2, 152.54, 152.65, 155.39, 156.22, 178.39
Terrell, Trenton 163.72
Terry, Gordon 141.51
Terry, Michael 67.21
Terry, Philip 25.56, 89.107, 105.22
Terry, Robert 170.68
Terry, Teresa 161.91
Terry, Tex 60.70, 60.75, 65.131, 66.59
Terry, Todd 163.39, 163.66
Tery, Tony 117.43
Tesler, Jack 141.42
Tessier, Robert 26, 83.50, 96.21, 14.30, 133.30, 141.44
Tetrick, Bob 156.40
Tetzel, Joan 65.78, 117.22, 178.70
Teuber, Andreas 12.75
Tgo, Sandra 14.381
Thaddeus Jones 5
Thatcher, Torin 14.65, 36.4, 41.86, 41.126, 46.13, 63.24, 65.430, 148.166, 162.71, 178.76
Thaxter, Phyllis 14.323, 84.7, 117.10, 126.94, 162.62, 162.101

Thayer, Lorna 3.46, 13.19, 25.30, 31.47, 66.88, 66.94, 66.119, 66.190, 78.19, 78.73, 93.108, 149.75
Thayler, Carl 152.1
Theimann, Seeley Ann 96.80
Theiss, Manuela 43.403
Theodore, Paul 149.67
Thinnes, Roy 65.282, 65.304, 163.45
Thomas, Danny 178.79, 178.135
Thomas, Emanuel 170.24
Thomas, Gretchen 25.52
Thomas, John Joseph 174
Thomas, Lance 65.519
Thomas, Leonard 162.255
Thomas, Lonnie 108.18, 169.108
Thomas, Lyn 32.25, 32.33, 32.38, 34.11, 43.22, 43.72, 77.3, 93.214, 102.36, 138.15, 138.19, 138.21, 158.10, 158.74
Thomas, Marlo 14.162, 178.135
Thomas, Michael 73.20
Thomas, Neal 177.48
Thomas, Powys 68.31
Thomas, Ralph 79.31, 126.57
Thomas, Richard 14.364
Thomas, Scott 14.325, 111
Thomas, Summer 120.24
Thomerson, Tim 62, 91.1, 163.41, 177.6
Thompson, Brian 163.9
Thompson, Carl 36.9
Thompson, Charles P. 14.328, 14.331, 14.356, 65.140, 65.476, 164.70
Thompson, Dee J. 65.25, 65.364, 126.21, 130.78, 144.3
Thompson, Elizabeth 168.14
Thompson, Evan 8.70.
Thompson, Glenn 131.13
Thompson, Hal H.93.115
Thompson, Hilarie 65.494, 69.9, 116.22
Thompson, Marion 76.8, 170.7
Thompson, Marshall 21.25, 26, 43.294, 65.113, 69.7, 162.106, 162.107, 162.246, 178.39
Thompson, Mort 97.76
Thompson, Nick 141.49
Thompson, Pat 65.474
Thompson, Paul 78.17
Thompson, Peter 43.72, 43.88, 93.163, 93.187, 97.166
Thompson, Susanna 48.78
Thompson, Tiger 26, 94.18
Thompson, Tina 93.80
Thompson, Tod 96.126
Thompson, Victoria 5.12, 63.34
Thomsen, Greg 1.17
Thomson, Amy 12.103, 161.182
Thor, Jerome 41.56, 44.67
Thor, Larry 93.121, 101.24, 126.20, 130.134, 139.14, 139.15, 162.28
Thordsen, Kelly 4.37, 12.38, 14.104, 14.129, 14.164, 14.189, 14.204, 14.283, 21.20, 25.9, 25.60, 27.88, 30.2, 34.41, 37.4, 41.11, 41.83, 41.95, 41.119, 44.12, 51.7, 65.85, 65.379, 65.441, 69.7, 70.32, 71.25, 71.32, 83.37, 85.45, 85.71, 85.105, 89.7, 92.33, 93.154, 96.9, 96.24, 101.9, 105.60, 105.77, 105.105, 112.22, 114.8, 119.6, 126.158, 126.165, 126.201, 130.98, 130.105, 132.7, 147.44, 148.91, 148.169, 148.197, 149.56, 152.25, 161.104, 161.116, 161.163, 162.241, 173.26, 173.30, 173.33, 178.33
Thordsen, Russell 161.158
Thorne, Richard 169.74
Thornton, Evans 9.1, 71.61, 71.94
Thornton, John 120.33
Thornton, Sigrid 120
Thorp, Nola 119.2
Thorsen, Duane 2.18, 2.24, 3.46, 6.25, 6.26, 43.47, 43.68, 63.65, 73.24, 73.38, 81.50, 81.55, 145.2

Thorsen, Rex 32.126, 81.83, 97.145
Thorson, Russell 3.141, 12.112, 14.82, 14.307, 14.424, 27.43, 30.16, 43.308, 51.23, 65.21, 65.34, 65.318, 65.362, 66.14, 77.14, 84.8, 84.27, 89.7, 89.17, 101.18, 102.32, 105.19, 117.38, 126.28, 126.95, 126.136, 130.96, 130.97, 147.52, 148.1, 148.3, 148.136, 148.184, 149.72, 151.7, 152.9, 156.60, 161.11, 161.12, 161.16, 161.25, 161.27, 161.86, 161.225, 162.147, 162.153, 164.2, 164.55, 178.36
Thourlby, William 93.214, 126.52
Threlkeld, Paul 177.16
Thrett, Maggie 49.10, 170.25, 170.71
Throne, Malachi 12.1, 12.29, 12.35, 71.58, 76.2, 86.37, 126.203, 126.211, 161.161, 170.47
Thundercloud, Chief 23.1, 60.12
Thursby, David 8.37
Thurston, Carol 43.43, 54.1, 54.23, 66.4, 66.76, 81.30, 81.40, 81.55, 93.34, 93.64, 93.85, 93.129, 93.151, 93.152, 93.153, 93.154, 93.156, 93.161, 93.163, 93.164, 93.170, 93.176, 93.180, 93.213, 97.13, 97.61, 97.62, 126.6, 133.7, 141.38, 158.73, 169.19
Thurston, Helen 103.3
Thye, John 8.30, 66.116
Tibbs, Casey 107.18, 134.10, 144.4, 144.28, 148.144
Tiernan, Michael 67.19
Tiernan, Patricia 27.19, 32.126
Tierney, Mary Jo 130.120
Tigar, Kenneth 1.19
Til, Roger 78.17, 114.2
Tiliesas, Ken 65.317
Tilles, Ken 70.45
Timmins, Cali 163.10
Tindall, Lorin 119.15, 148.79
Tinney, Cal 8.30.
Tipton, Kathleen 48.23
Tischer, Bill 138.39
Tnigoshi 162.230
Tobey, Kenneth 5.18, 5.49, 8.54, 14.286, 21.41, 24.21, 41.77, 42, 54.28, 54.30, 55.22, 65.203, 65.323, 65.488, 65.573, 66.149, 76.42, 77.22, 83.11, 89.73, 89.131, 96.38, 97.38, 106.8, 116.10, 144.24, 151.18, 161.175, 161.225, 164.27
Tobias, George 44.33, 85.18, 119.8, 127.36
Tobin, Dan 14.51, 14.308, 14.372, 65.298, 65.423, 105.7, 105.45, 105.100, 116.11, 162.76, 162.118, 170.26, 173.26
Tobin, Mark 155.68
Tobin, Michele 14.295, 170.66
Tochi, Brian 83.6, 83.50
Tochi, Wendy 83.53
Todd, Beverly 170.100
Todd, James 97.96, 97.115, 97.174
Todd, Sally 79.30
Toeves, Robert 91.8
Toigo, Al 65.64
Tolan, Michael 112.3
Tolford, Gwen 170.74
Tolsky, Susan 70
Tom, David 48.14, 48.20
Tom, Sebastian 170.41
Tomack, Dave 141.48
Tomack, Sid 57.24
Tomaren, Peter 33
Tomarken, Jason 53.14
Tompkins, Angel 14.362, 70.4, 170.80
Tompkins, Bee 65.294, 71.35, 107.8
Tompkins, Joan 14.321, 25.47, 96.53, 96.108, 105.86, 157.17
Tone, Franchot 14.38, 161.89, 162.169
Toner, Tom 71.81
Tong, Kam 12.49, 12.81, 14.210, 25.25, 66, 161.53
Tong, Sammee 25.60, 80.16, 108.37, 141.25
Tonge, Philip 108.25, 114, 114.2, 114.4, 114.11, 114.17, 114.22, 114.23, 158.6
Toomey, Bill 5.32

Personnel Index

Toomey, Regis 20.72, 21.31, 27.8, 27.35, 27.105, 43, 218, 44.28, 78.48, 89.64, 92.26, 102.35, 105.37, 126.31, 126.39, 129.77, 146.66, 148.127, 149.11, 153.9, 153.11, 155.72, 156.39, 156.48, 161.18, 164.12
Toone, Geoffrey 165.1
Toothman, Lisa 120.52
Tootoosis, Gordon 99.1, 99.2, 99.3
Toovey, Shawn 48
Torey, Hal 34.65, 43.314, 78.73, 89.92, 146.64, 178.134
Torme, Mel 161.174
Torn, Rip 14.398, 55.5, 61.8, 126.209, 129.7
Torres, Tenaya 111.6
Torrey, Roger 14.125, 19.2, 53.12, 65.325, 65.377, 65.564, 65.565, 76, 95.23, 161.68, 161.189, 162.248
Torti, Robert 96.163
Totino, Frank M. 65.636
Totten, Heather 96.34
Totten, Robert 47.11, 65.482, 65.484, 65.514, 65.520, 65.531, 65.536, 65.562, 65.586
Totter, Audrey 14.238, 25.12, 27.48, 29, 126.114, 161.138, 161.212, 162.49, 178.10
Toupou, Manu 174.3
Toussaint, Beth 91.8
Tovatt, Patrick 161.203, 161.220
Towers, Constance 178.140
Towers, Richard 57.34
Towne, Aline 34.8, 73.26, 93.58, 97.97, 97.197, 103.38, 105.21, 133.12, 133.34, 148.21, 162.52, 162.95, 162.199, 162.188, 162.220, 162.249, 166.7
Townes, Harry 12.81, 14.36, 14.107, 17.32, 24.20, 39.17, 43.164, 44.29, 65.51, 65.121, 65.162, 65.309, 65.374, 65.386, 65.548, 66.21, 79.28, 83.5, 85.21, 101.7, 107.10, 117.37, 117.45, 126.9, 126.83, 126.173, 126.178, 127.13, 137.3, 142.9, 149.70, 161.94, 164.53, 164.64, 170.9, 170.44, 172.5, 178.80, 178.89
Townes, Stuart 54.13
Townsend, Isabelle 90, 90.22
Townsend, Jill 14.334, 30, 161.216, 170.97
Townsend, Tommy 177.9, 177.22
Toy, Patty 163.3
Tozere, Frederic 97.35
Tracey, Ray 26, 75.9, 75.10, 75.11, 175.7
Tracy, John 14.339
Tracy, Lee 162.178
Tracy, Marlene 170.73
Tracy, Steve 96, 96.134, 96.135
Tracy, William 93.218, 165.2
Travanty, Dan 65.603, 65.624, 70.8, 84.12
Travers, Bill 126.150
Travino, George 148.3
Travis, Gary 41.63
Travis, Kirk 161.137
Travis, Richard 29.13, 35.1, 35.8, 35.17, 35.22, 35.32, 35.38, 57.9, 60.47, 60.50, 73.13, 92.2, 93.1, 93.2, 93.3, 97.134, 97.155, 97.165, 145.2, 145.3, 148.51, 152.39, 152.64
Travis, William 42
Traylor, William 83.31, 96.139, 116.24
Treacy, Emerson 22.2, 22.8, 73.21, 89.23, 97.89, 97.102, 148.186
Treadway, Wayne 8.84
Treen, Mary 14.99, 60.47, 60.50
Trekilis, Michael 51.17
Tremayne, Les 3.130, 3.138, 3.141, 3.145, 3.152, 3.155, 3.156, 3.158, 3.161, 14.91, 14.353, 39.18, 126.66, 130.28, 152.17, 161.82, 161.125, 162.103, 162.220, 162.243, 166.5, 168.25, 178.148
Tremko, Anne 1.1
Trent, Jack 135.91
Trent, Karen Sue 130.169, 162.67
Trent, Lee 31.28
Trent, Russell 12.12, 97.68, 97.72, 141.15
Trevor, Claire 162.80

Triesault, Ivan 14.294, 78.13, 78.16, 78.23, 114.8, 170.51
Trikonis, Gus 49.10, 76.25, 161.124
Trinka, Paul 12.29
Triolo, Lori Ann 67.19
Tripp, Paul 51.1, 66.196
Tristan, Dorothy 65.614, 65.615
Tritt, Travis 48.80
Troster, Gavin 28.1
Troughton, Patrick 88.21
Troup, Bobby 126.55
Troup, Ronne 41.135
Troupe, Tom 7.12, 89.89, 170.88
Trout, Tom 25.58, 152.44
Troy, Dennis 52.45
Troy, Louise 49.8, 76.34
Truax, John 86.32, 135.79, 135.81, 147.34, 169.106
Truex, Barry 93.26, 138.28
Truex, Ernest 14.176
Trujillo, Raoul 100.12
Trujillo, Ronald 71.6, 117.43
Trumbull, Brad 65.170, 65.209, 65.256, 66.77, 74.29, 141.31, 155.12, 170.69
Trump, Gerald 144.28
Trundy, Natalie 14.38, 39.1, 122.24, 162.208
Trusel, Lisa 53
Tryon, Tom 12.28, 54.7, 106.9, 129.25, 132.25, 153, 161.15, 161.135, 161.154, 162.23, 178.28
Tsiang, H.T. 65.415, 146.50, 162.230
Tsien, Maria 25.17, 103.46
Tsu, Irene 24.9, 86.49, 170.62
Tuck, Jessica 1.10.
Tucker, Duane 1.9
Tucker, Forrest 5.1, 14.403, 24.12, 41.88, 41.124, 43.277, 50, 52, 65.356, 65.379, 65.440, 65.504, 65.529, 65.560, 72.9, 94.20, 96.23, 126.154, 161.79, 162.35, 166.15, 168.18
Tucker, Wayne 79.17, 88.10, 88.17, 165.1, 165.12
Tuerpe, Paul 120.6
Tufts, Sonny 98.15, 161.32
Tullos, Jerry 120.10
Tully, Phil 44.31, 44.41, 44.52, 44.53, 44.66, 105.87, 131.43, 148.181
Tully, Tom 14.204, 14.278, 51.5, 63.10, 63.39, 71.44, 92.15, 98.13, 126.85, 126.193, 139, 148.174, 161.77, 178.28, 178.29
Tuohy, Johnny 162.268
Turich, Felipe 13.8, 37.6, 71.89, 83.20, 129.41, 145.31
Turich, Phil 158.22
Turich, Rosa 32.82, 84.4, 97.54, 105.34, 127.46, 129.24, 169.59
Turkel, Joseph 3.89, 3.101, 8.8, 8.68, 14.151, 20.21, 24.22, 77.16, 93.43, 97.153, 97.180, 141.40, 147.45, 152.38, 159.19, 162.183
Turley, Jack 84.36
Turley, James 152.42
Turman, Glynn 26
Turnbeaugh, Brenda 96
Turnbeaugh, Wendi 96
Turnbull, Glenn 51.11, 93.80, 138.60, 147.32
Turner, B.J. 120.22
Turner, Barbara 161.113
Turner, Dan C. 96.106
Turner, Dave 7
Turner, Don 169.22, 169.26
Turner, Frank C. 100.5
Turner, Moira 65.237
Turner, Rick 140.30
Tuttle, Lurene 14.252, 20.20, 22.6, 25.28, 25.53, 34.9, 34.60, 37.4, 65.211, 65.579, 66.32, 76.30, 78.36, 89.35, 89.101, 96.34, 96.45, 108.18, 121.13, 126.84, 129.8, 148.144, 152.7, 156.34, 162.91, 164.6, 168.12
Twa, Kate 67.4
Tweddell, Frank 78.44
Twitchell, Archie 35.14, 81.51

Twogood, Mark 1.1
Tyburn, Gene 7.13, 14.156, 14.232, 65.390, 65.572, 70.18, 130.164, 170.39, 170.66, 170.88, 170.101, 175.4
Tygett, Jack 170.21
Tyler, Beverly 14.53, 21.2, 43.69, 140.131, 148.105
Tyler, Harry O. 22.18, 57.9, 57.35, 85.44, 135.94, 135.96, 135.99, 138.51, 169.110
Tyler, Jana 170.101
Tyler, Leon 129.46
Tyler, Mac 152.49
Tyler, Richard 169.25
Tyler, Tom 32.14, 32.20, 32.23, 32.24, 35.14, 60.49, 60.52, 60.53, 60.60, 97.39, 135.7, 135.9, 141.15, 169.12, 169.30
Tylo, Michael 180
Tyne, George 52.36
Tyner, Charles 5.29, 12.74, 53, 53.14, 71.43, 75.20, 83.11, 95.16, 120.3, 120.4, 176.1, 176.5
Tyrell, Ann 81.53, 81.69
Tyrell, David 130.9
Tyrrell, Susan 14.391, 112.13
Tyson, Cicely 36.11, 65.525, 70.40

Udenio, Fabiana 163.17
Udy, Helen 48, 99.7
Ulmer, Audrea Lynn 163.36
Ulrich, Kim Johnston 163.20
Umeki, Miyoshi 126.156, 161.53
Underwood, Hank 5.15
Unger, Joe 163.61
Upton, Julian 60.54, 60.58
Urecal, Minerva 60.4, 78.8, 78.14, 78.29, 97.29, 97.145, 108.21, 124.23, 124.60, 124.77, 135.6, 135.33, 166.19, 169.25
Urich, Robert 65.634, 83.4, 90, 109.7
Urton, Frank 60.14

Vaccaro, Brenda 137
Vachon, Jean 80.26
Vachon, Joseph Dean 48.97
Vacio, Natividad 3.117, 30.4, 34.42, 65.528, 71.33, 71.75, 97.55, 130.66, 149.52, 152.12, 152.50
Vahle, Timothy 163.81
Val, Maria 127.70
Valdespine, Richard 169.92
Valdis, Sigrid 170.13
Valen, Nancy 177.40
Valencia, Ralph 136
Valencia, Reggie 170.53
Valentine, John 48.73
Valentine, Nancy 44.33, 89.73, 152.36, 166.6, 178.119
Valenty, Lili 14.31, 14.120, 14.190, 14.302, 96.86, 105.18
Vallee, Rudy 5.25, 5.32, 43.384
Valles, Sandra 124.33, 124.35
Vallin, Rick 2.5, 2.11, 3.90, 6.9, 6.15, 6.25, 6.26, 6.41, 6.58, 6.59, 6.69, 6.70, 8.103, 18.13, 23.14, 23.21, 23.37, 23.38, 29.1, 31.19, 35.5, 35.6, 35.7, 35.13, 35.16, 35.18, 35.23, 35.28, 35.38, 41.50, 60.57, 60.69, 60.74, 60.77, 73.9, 73.27, 73.38, 77.7, 80.31, 80.32, 80.33, 81.38, 81.53, 81.69, 93.6, 93.47, 93.169, 97.157, 97.217, 135.41, 135.99, 141.40, 148.8, 169.27, 169.70, 169.92
Vallon, Michael 3.136, 6.9, 32.45, 32.52, 43.57, 85.42, 93.56, 93.142, 169.15, 169.24, 169.41, 169.103
Valverde, Rawley 120.23
Valvo, John 178.44
Van, Frankie 141.56
Van Ark, Joan 7.6, 14.218, 63.49, 65.491
Van Bergen, Lewis 118.1, 163.70
Van Cleef, Lee 4.21, 6.34, 6.45, 13.40, 14.47, 17.24, 17.40, 17.41, 17.42, 21.47, 21.63, 23.7, 23.13, 27.84, 29.25, 34.15, 34.67, 39.5, 43.247, 44.34, 46.2, 56.11, 60.64, 60.78, 65.193, 65.371,

Personnel Index

65.407, 66.208, 66.224, 74.17, 81.54, 81.64, 81.87, 81.101, 85.38, 85.56, 85.105, 85.119, 86.27, 88.12, 89.1, 89.37, 89.75, 89.81, 97.82, 97.114, 97.124, 105.104, 114.20, 124.53, 124.55, 124.63, 126.176, 126.177, 130.26, 130.71, 130.104, 130.148, 131.13, 141.14, 142.28, 145.3, 148.3, 155.48, 156.11, 157.13, 164.43, 173.30, 179.40
Vance, Vivian 44.13
Van Dam, Gwen 109.6
Vanders, Warren 5.46, 12.89, 14.184, 14.219, 14.220, 14.284, 14.380, 30.2, 30.3, 41.49, 41.129, 41.136, 41.137, 41.141, 46.10, 51.17, 65.252, 65.402, 65.421, 65.432, 65.439, 65.454, 65.466, 65.485, 65.490, 65.502, 65.591, 75.10, 76.9, 76.32, 83.10, 83.32, 92.5, 96.59, 112.14, 132.19, 142.7
Vanderveen, Joyce 31.40, 43.140, 78.12, 78.17, 78.19, 78.21, 78.30, 78.34, 78.44
Vandever, Michael 14.316, 39.11, 65.378, 65.392, 65.419, 65.460, 86.46, 88.6, 127.21, 127.72, 161.30, 161.162
Van Dien, Casper 48.44, 48.45
Vandis, Titos 75.22
Van Dreelan, John 65.230, 89.99, 126.107, 170.37
Van Dyke, Barry 62
Van Dyke, Conny 7.7, 109.9
Van Dyke, Phillip 48.105
Van Fleet, Jo 14.350, 14.385, 55.15, 161.122, 170.103
Van Lynn, Vincent 12.51, 86.8
Vanni, Renata 65.515, 127.70, 162.147
Van Orman, Gary 5.15, 5.21, 5.26, 5.50
Van Patten, Dick 69.1, 126.6
Van Patten, Jimmy 28, 65.598
Van Patten, Joyce 65.293, 76.45, 98.21, 98.22, 112.5, 144.23, 161.97, 168.4
Van Patten, Vincent 14.361, 14.423, 47.2, 65.566, 65.591, 71.81, 75.18, 112.20
Van Rooten, Luis 25.30, 65.110, 114.23
Van Sickel, Dale 14.34, 81.50, 81.71, 81.73, 93.217, 135.10, 135.13, 141.7, 162.6, 164.23
Van Tuyl, Helen Marr 93.135
Van Tuyle, Helen 169.9
Van Vleet, Richard 106.12, 161.197
Van Wort, George 126.172
Van Zandt, Julie 65.57, 89.132, 93.25, 148.71, 179.17, 179.18
Van Zandt, Phil 3.71, 20.16, 31.25, 43.100, 57.35, 73.10, 141.53, 169.84
Vara, Sarita 43.215, 64.3
Varady, Brien 48.29
Varda, Valerie 162.205
Varden, Norma 14.90, 157.11
Vardi, Sara 71.32, 71.53
Varela, Jay 112.23
Varela, Nina 23.21, 44.39, 65.99, 65.177
Vargas, Edmund 65.295, 168.6
Vargas, Edward 162.89
Vargas, John 1.14
Vari, John 65.270
Varno, Roland 169.19, 169.32
Varron, Allegra R.80.2, 158.4, 168.26
Vasquez, Albert 1.4
Vasquez, Yul 163.17
Vath, Richard 43.143, 141.40
Vaughan, Dorothy 135.21, 141.7
Vaughn, Heidi 24.1, 43.443, 65.505, 71.45
Vaughn, Jean 65.79
Vaughn, Jeanne 66.152, 89.125, 93.185, 133.4, 170.6
Vaughn, Mina 89.58, 89.86
Vaughn, Ned 163.4
Vaughn, Ondine 12.97
Vaughn, Rees 65.297, 161.46
Vaughn, Robert 14.106, 21.12, 26, 45.1, 51.19, 54.29, 56.31, 65.27, 65.87, 77.20, 85.37, 88.10, 88.11, 102.37, 127.19, 130.11, 131.3, 142.13, 148.21,

148.168, 161.21, 162.37, 162.127, 163.78, 167.9, 178.11, 178.34, 179.59
Vaughn, William 3.131, 8.1, 8.81, 32.156, 64.12, 65.23, 66.78, 71.67, 84.23, 86.4, 93.184, 93.196, 141.38, 141.46, 152.29, 155.18, 164.74, 178.44
Vazquez, Alberto 163.17
Vedder, William 32.113, 97.49, 97.55, 97.109, 141.15, 169.37
Vegas, Pedro 65.515
Vejar, Harry 81.6
Velez, Olga 65.460, 71.44
Venetoulis, Nick 20.7
Venier, Louise 135.77
Venner, Obie 34.24
Ventana, A.G. 170.57
Ventulett, Suzanne 48.79, 163.6
Ventura, Clyde 12.36, 43.371, 49.10, 139.11, 161.191
Ventura, Viviane 98.12, 170.13
Venture, Richard 1.10
Venus, Brenda 83.50
Vera, Carlos 57.114, 97.219, 148.30
Vera, Paul 129.72
Vera, Ricky 20.10, 31.36, 66.76
Vera, Robert 149.73
Verbois, Jack 48.16
Verdugo, Elena 76.20, 88.11, 126.34, 128
Verne, Karen 21.27
Vernon, Glen 22.16, 30.7, 47.1, 97.47
Vernon, Irene 97.79
Vernon, John 7.1, 9.1, 14.315, 65.628, 68.23, 71.43, 83.44, 83.56, 83.57, 83.58, 83.59, 115.1, 163.54
Vernon, Lou 65.6, 65.9
Vernon, Valerie 35.21
Vernon, Wally 147.31
Ve Sota, Bruno 14.223, 14.229, 14.290, 14.303, 14.309, 17.46, 41.70, 127.30, 127.36, 127.68, 127.73, 149.28, 170.16
Vetri, Victoria 43.377
Vickers, Martha 127.23, 127.48
Vickers, Yvette 8.12, 127.63, 127.68, 133.5, 133.13, 148.181
Victor, Carlos 80.22
Victor, Ina 161.49
Victor, Inva 55.17
Victor, James 83.55, 180
Viespi, Alex 55.8, 85.67
Vigen, Gregor 161.22
Vigil, Robert 109.3
Vigran, Herb 3.146, 14.28, 14.247, 31.35, 39.7, 65.526, 65.548, 65.554, 65.555, 65.558, 65.562, 65.582, 65.595, 65.596, 65.600, 65.610, 65.628, 85.73, 89.123, 101.30, 103.33, 105.81, 105.93, 147.18, 148.177, 151.18, 158.31, 158.32, 161.17, 164.18
Viharo, Robert 30.6, 65.574, 71.65
Vil, Lester 93.173
Villani, Fred 93.165
Vincent, Billy 97.68, 97.87, 97.123
Vincent, Elmore 141.58, 148.79
Vincent, Frank 163.19
Vincent, Jan-Michael 14.299, 14.330, 65.545
Vincent, June 61.6, 66.7, 66.11, 66.144, 66.149, 83.31, 130.58, 131.32, 148.198, 156.19, 161.130, 161.168, 164.29, 178.48
Vincent, Keith 133.3
Vincent, Sailor 97.14
Vincent, Steve 84.13
Vincent, Virginia 65.477, 161.124
Vincent, W.J. 126.155
Vincent, William 97.46
Vinson, Gary 4.25, 4.30, 8.7, 21.4, 21.26, 21.45, 34.56, 34.67, 44.2, 50.7, 85.86, 89.8, 89.153, 105.64, 121, 133.20, 146.54, 149.71, 161.193, 162.198
Vint, Alan 14.339, 24.2, 26, 71.66, 112.11
Vint, Bill 84.49, 96.178, 96.179, 112.11
Vint, Jesse 19.11, 26, 112.11, 177.66

Vint, William 69.1, 71.66
Virell, Sergio 129.43, 129.72
Virgo, Peter, Jr. 121.19
Virtue, Danny 67.17
Virtue, Tom 163.15, 163.16
Vitale, Joseph 3.134, 3.151, 31.41, 51.15, 93.90, 97.157, 97.189, 97.192, 97.213, 114.14, 126.43, 126.161, 129.45, 148.60, 162.35, 169.112
Vitanza, A.G. 161.76
Vitina, Dolores 66.57
Vivyan, John 8.26, 8.77, 34.13, 41.12, 43.202, 43.241, 51.24, 93.34, 93.144, 105.12, 105.25, 105.34, 105.68, 126.14, 126.141, 133.11, 146.11, 153.7, 153.8, 155.8, 155.53, 173.27
Vize, Tom 178.47
Vladis, Sigrid 170.3
Vlahos, Sam 65.637, 177.61
Vogan, Emmett 43.57, 73.7, 141.5
Vogel, Carol 65.629, 75.23
Vogel, Michael 14.307
Vogel, Mitch 14, 43.428, 49.11, 65.527, 65.597, 70.50, 96.5, 96.22, 123.5, 161.185
Vogt, Peter 120.45
Vohs, Joan 34.15, 54.9, 105.5, 127.52
Voight, Jon 30.22, 65.420, 65.448, 65.488
Voland, Herbert 14.304, 76.1, 161.88
Von Beltz, Brad 57.112, 66.71, 66.94, 66.114, 89.39
von Dohlen, Lenny 163.73, 177.10
Von Eltz, Theodore 169.60
Von Eur, Goovy 129.65
von Franckenstein, Clement 1.16
von Furstenberg, Betsy 66.24
von Holland, Mildred 3.27, 3.46, 3.52, 3.70, 3.74, 3.91, 3.142
Von Hollen, Mildred 85.5, 147.20
Von Homburg, Wilhelm 65.335, 170.70, 170.81
Von Leer, Hunter 24.16, 24.17, 120.12
Von Zell, Harry 149.38, 149.48, 162.43, 162.145, 162.165, 162.256
Vosper, John 35.2, 35.21, 35.25
Votrian, Peter 20.50, 23.26, 31.38, 54.3, 57.40, 57.87, 60.74, 60.79, 60.89, 60.90, 65.6, 65.45, 108.14, 114.12, 124.64, 129.4, 135.53, 169.31, 178.25
Votrian, Ralph 13.7, 126.22, 149.3, 149.32
Vultaggio, Lisa 100.5
Vuolo, Tito 23.34
Vye, Murvyn 8.2, 8.7, 14.28, 22.38, 44.56, 66.13, 88.30, 89.19, 89.62, 105.11, 105.19, 105.58, 114.19, 130.75, 138.46, 148.58, 152.14, 161.31, 162.106, 162.107, 162.192

Waddle, Waddie 165.13
Wade, Ernestine 78.16
Wade, Jo Ann 138.54
Wade, Sam 170.24
Wade, Stuart 114.1, 158.58, 158.60
Wagenheim, Charles 5.2, 12.29, 14.9, 14.223, 30.5, 65, 84.45, 93.176, 93.221, 97.202, 111.6, 129.19, 134.3, 138.63, 148.54, 170.19
Waggner, Lia 65.228
Waggoner, Lyle 62.3, 65.399
Wagner, Jack 8.7, 133.13
Wagner, Lou 5.8, 106.14, 112.22
Wagner, Max 32.94, 32.102, 32.156, 46.2, 130.35
Wagner, Mike 12.83, 43.359, 71.48, 86.38
Wagner, Sherri 176.2
Wagner, Wende 162.111
Wagrowski, Gregory 118.5
Wainwright, Anna 76.40
Wainwright, James 5.18, 36.13, 41.129, 41.136, 41.145, 41.159, 43.374, 63.13, 63.33, 65.468, 83.44, 84.8, 94.15, 96.69, 106.16, 161.192
Waite, Ralph 112.7
Walberg, Garry 43.238, 46.13, 65.150, 65.229, 65.246, 65.247, 65.265, 65.279, 65.294, 65.345, 65.595, 65.596, 71.43, 71.73, 71.85, 84.24,

Personnel Index

88.12, 117.1, 126.9, 126.11, 126.57, 132.14, 148.140, 159.35, 161.115
Walcott, Gregory 5.29, 8.55, 8.104, 12.39, 14.32, 14.116, 14.257, 14.319, 13.343, 14.369, 14.419, 37.5, 39.5, 41.90, 44.72, 56.1, 71.51, 71.77, 85.40, 85.59, 85.98, 85.106, 93.191, 96.27, 101.16, 101.27, 105.60, 126.54, 126.62, 126.115, 126.134, 126.164, 130.13, 130.45, 131.38, 139.7, 145.11, 146.10, 148.92, 148.98, 148.139, 149.4, 156.65, 158.31, 158.42, 162.12, 162.121, 167.14, 178.20
Walcutt, John 1.7
Walden, Robert 26
Waldis, Otto 3.67, 31.8, 64.12, 66.150, 73.4, 89.100, 105.18, 148.47, 149.3, 162.66, 162.116, 162.179, 166.3
Waldron, Wendy 60.9, 60.10, 60.27, 60.29, 60.53, 60.60, 124.42, 124.44, 169.6, 169.7
Wales, Leslie 14.96, 126.140, 126.161
Walker, Bill 8.30, 21.65, 31.14, 39.16, 68.5, 68.14, 68.17, 86.4, 116.14, 126.98, 173.12, 173.31
Walker, Clint 26, 27, 59.4, 105.81
Walker, Dusty 158.3, 158.55
Walker, Gene 138.65
Walker, Jake 90.20, 177.53
Walker, June 166.2
Walker, Kim 1.14, 135.26
Walker, Marcy 45.2
Walker, Matthew 99.12
Walker, Peter 3.140, 43.115, 78.16
Walker, Ray 57.44, 73.37, 105.79, 146.63, 169.81
Walker, Robert, Jr. 12.8, 14.276, 107.21, 132.7
Walker, Rock 83.22
Walker, Scott 14.369, 65.572, 65.607
Walker, Wally 141.41
Wall, Geraldine 70.41, 97.88
Wall, Mary Chris 163.26
Wallace, George D. 4.8, 1.33, 14.357, 21.18, 27.91, 40.2, 41.73, 43.179, 44.52, 65.26, 65.310, 65.563, 73.7, 73.8, 73.29, 73.39, 81.81, 81.84, 85.60, 85.70, 85.87, 85.99, 89.38, 89.98, 93.210, 93.219, 93.224, 93.225, 96.102, 105.75, 105.109, 119.4, 126.40, 126.69, 126.69, 126.94, 127.61, 130.70, 132.9, 145.11, 146.53, 148.1, 148.92, 148.186, 149.16, 161.29, 161.128, 178.22, 178.64, 178.113
Wallace, Helen 20.10, 65.16, 65.39, 65.257, 145.19, 152.1, 152.38, 152.66, 156.53
Wallace, Jack 28.2
Wallace, Maude 141.17
Wallace, Paul 170.29
Wallace-Rhodes, Laura 53.7
Wallach, Eli 117.42
Waller, Eddy 14.101, 20.14, 32.110, 32.116, 40, 51.9, 57.14, 78.37, 85, 85.3, 85.12, 85.31, 85.54, 85.65, 85.94, 93.134, 97.118, 97.169, 97.170, 103.51, 143, 148.82, 148.157, 152.42, 162.42
Walley, Deborah 106.4, 162.267
Wallis, Shani 65.588, 65.589
Walls, Bud 161.225
Walmsley, Jon 41.104
Walsh, Edward 83.36
Walsh, Joey 65.473
Walsh, Katherine 161.142
Walsh, Kathryn 41.71
Walsh, M. Emmet 96.165, 112, 112.4
Walsh, Sydney 45.1, 177.57, 177.66
Walsh, William 68.19, 68.30
Walston, Ray 38.8, 48.102, 96.121, 117.30, 120.23, 168.9, 170.64
Walter, Jessica 5.28
Walter, Pat 147.23
Walter, Tracey 1.3, 1.14, 10
Walters, Jamie 177.52
Walters, Mark 163.2, 163.24, 163.28
Walters, Melora 163.4
Walters, Selene 152.39

Walton, Jess 63.41, 65.581
Walton Walker, Peggy 19.12
Waltson, Ray 117.3
Waltz, Patrick 8.5, 8.53, 31.40, 43.97, 133.4, 146.8, 145.21, 149.13, 155.27, 155.80, 158.62
Wanamaker, Sam 65.408, 170.14
Wanderman, Walter 94.24
War Eagle, John 2.23, 3.51, 6.54, 6.55, 23.14, 65.383, 76.16, 83.5, 83.45, 94.17, 116.13, 126.1, 126.52, 135.90, 136, 148.182, 162.128, 162.187
Warburton, John 25.53, 65.366, 80.4, 80.8, 80.9, 80.12, 80.13, 80.27, 80.28, 80.37, 131.44
Ward, Bill 97.34, 97.44, 97.45
Ward, Candy 170.62
Ward, Caryn 120.27
Ward, Dave "Squatch" 67.7, 67.8, 67.10, 67.17
Ward, Jo Marie 86.15, 144.13
Ward, Larry 14.315, 14.366, 14.405, 27.96, 39, 65.284, 65.377, 65.424, 66.199, 89.138, 98.6, 132.10, 137.10, 151.22, 161.192
Ward, Lyman 14.401
Ward, Norma 43.84, 158.3, 158.12, 158.16
Ward, Sandy 5.5, 96.126
Ward, Skip 41.119
Warde, Anthony 78.13, 93.182, 141.11, 152.19, 152.77
Warde, Harlan 12.5, 12.25, 12.37, 12.46, 12.50, 12.67, 14.282, 14.298, 14.369, 15.37, 34.3, 39.17, 41.156, 57.11, 57.70, 57.71, 73.31, 76.46, 85.104, 93.213, 97.88, 130.8, 130.10, 130.14, 130.22, 130.28, 130.33, 130.38, 130.39, 130.49, 130.50, 130.54, 130.67, 130.77, 130.85, 130.113, 130.123, 130.130, 132.7, 133.14, 161, 161.117, 162.229, 164.68, 170.4
Warden, Hugh 96.155
Warden, Jack 14.4, 117.7, 117.8, 142.5, 148.187, 161.4, 161.84, 162.166, 162.278
Ware, Midge 64, 130.88
Warfield, Chris 25.50, 34.25, 43.141
Warfield, Emily 14.432, 14.433
Warfield, Marlene 96.161
Warge, Robin 146.36
Waring, Joseph 3.108, 73.29, 93.59, 93.126, 158.49, 179.41
Wark, Robert 146.19
Warner, David 1.11, 45.1
Warner, Jody 14.33, 127.52
Warner, Sandra 14.174
Warner, Sydney 177.39
Warno, Helen 93.61
Warren, Anne 65.6
Warren, Dick 138.77
Warren, Frank 8.10, 8.40, 8.69, 131.17
Warren, Garrett 163.37, 163.38
Warren, Gil 81.51
Warren, Katherine 14.49, 85.38, 85.49, 85.111, 97.160, 117.33, 149.62
Warren, Lance 65.6
Warren, Lesley Ann 65.404
Warren, Nancy 120.33
Warren, Richard 14.35, 44.64, 93.175, 138.52
Warren, Ruth 6.41
Warren, Sonia 66.113
Warren, Stefani 70.14
Warren, Steve 8.62, 31.23, 65.227, 66.154, 85.77, 130.118, 138.35, 148.172, 149.28, 162.53
Warrick, Ruth 41.164, 65.379
Warwick, Robert 3.113, 3.118, 3.122, 3.152, 3.156, 20.2, 20.64, 21.1, 21.10, 21.43, 31.38, 34.10, 44.14, 78.56, 88.27, 105.88, 146.39, 150.3, 178.125, 178.135
Washbrook, John 178.66
Washbrook, Johnny 108, 117.10, 162.66, 162.136
Washburn, Beverly 57.15, 152.11, 152.77, 162.1, 162.43, 162.240, 178.13
Washington, Chester 36.9, 36.14
Washington, Dino 41.157

Wassil, Chuck 27.62, 105.62, 152.30
Wasson, Craig 48.34
Waterfield, Chris 43.227
Waterman, Willard 8.28, 8.53, 14.61, 27.87, 31.42, 78.11, 85.59, 89.50, 105.115, 131.37, 162.137, 162.142, 162.157
Waters, Ethel 41.155
Waters, James 39.11, 89.104
Waters, Reba 23.27, 108.36, 126.52, 142.14, 146.9, 162.16
Waters, Tom 5.35, 65.470, 65.535, 83.26
Watkin, Pierre 3.37, 3.117, 6.37, 6.65, 8.50, 32.4, 32.9, 32.12, 34.16, 57.7, 60.47, 60.50, 73.25, 81.52, 81.57, 97.44, 97.71, 97.89, 97.110, 97.135, 97.167, 124.37, 124.43, 129.34, 135.15, 135.41, 138.64, 141.1, 141.17, 141.58, 145.32, 155.46, 164.57, 169.49, 169.92
Watkins, Carlene 10, 33
Watkins, Frank 89.136, 140.1, 148.69, 149.47, 161.27
Watkins, Linda 14.350, 14.382, 27.40, 43.25, 65.140, 65.210, 65.236, 65.277, 65.347, 65.580, 78.73
Watson, Bobby 3.21
Watson, Bobs 161.25, 161.26, 161.37
Watson, Bruce 14.334, 65.473, 121.12
Watson, David 41.116, 41.139, 41.161, 126
Watson, Debbie 161.139, 161.197
Watson, James A.161.216
Watson, James A., Jr. 83.22
Watson, Justice 44.64, 148.164, 149.22
Watson, Mills 5.2, 5.12, 5.38, 5.42, 14.338, 47.4, 65.457, 65.464, 65.468, 65.474, 65.491, 65.512, 65.527, 65.551, 65.552, 65.553, 65.559, 65.578, 65.602, 65.638, 70.7, 70.28, 70.50, 71.39, 71.75, 75.35, 83.2, 84.41, 115.5, 123.4, 161.192
Watson, William C. 14.411, 30.12, 65.425, 65.505, 65.622, 65.623, 71.79, 116.9, 174.2
Watson, Woody 163.1, 163.30, 163.46
Watt, Jock C. 6.79
Watts, Charles 14.54, 14.181, 32.25, 32.33, 32.38, 32.99, 43.147, 57.10, 65.298, 93.206, 78.14, 93.226, 97.49, 97.60, 97.67, 102.28, 105.73, 126.84, 130.5, 130.47, 130.106, 148.170, 149.27, 149.68, 151.21, 152.9
Wave, Virginia 138.22, 138.44
Waxman, Stanley 84.1
Way, Jacqueline 57.7
Wayland, Len 12.1, 65.377, 65.432, 96.156, 96.157, 120.14, 132.10, 170.58
Wayne, Billy 57.24
Wayne, David 11.7, 24.14, 65.597, 65.632, 117.18, 117.34, 119.15, 161.22, 162.114
Wayne, Fredd 4.14, 24.21, 41.144, 65.44, 66.134, 66.135, 102.32, 105.7, 105.18, 107.18, 126.136, 146.45
Wayne, Harte 73.17
Wayne, Jerry 66.152
Wayne, Jesse 112.1
Wayne, John 162.123, 72
Wayne, Marilyn 161.87, 162.267
Wayne, Patrick 17.8, 17.9, 17.10, 66.111, 94.32, 134
Wayne, Steve 32.73
Wead, Timothy 96.125
Weatherford, Jeff 48.27
Weatherill, James 83.3, 83.28, 83.38, 83.39
Weathers, Carl 83.56, 83.57, 83.58, 83.59
Weaver, Dave 144.16
Weaver, Dennis 26, 65, 97.162, 99.1, 99.2, 99.3, 99.8, 99.15, 161.220
Weaver, Doodles 14.268, 21.65, 41.65, 41.86, 57.113, 66.201, 85.73, 86.11, 86.15, 89.60, 89.69, 89.73, 10.43, 157.20, 162.143, 168.21
Weaver, Fritz 12.72, 12.106, 65.429, 83.31, 116.10, 126.181, 126.182
Weaver, Jackson 12.36
Weaver, Lee 24.9, 170.84

Personnel Index

Weaver, Rickie 65.223, 65.584
Weaver, Robby 26, 65.223, 65.223
Webb, Amanda 22.20
Webb, Bruce 68.15
Webb, Frank 14.332, 71.91, 161.207
Webb, Gregory 120.42
Webb, Lou 162.150
Webb, Richard 4.33, 17.48, 27.73, 27.95, 27.108, 34.15, 41.80, 43.270, 43.276, 63.25, 65.406, 65.431, 77.10, 105.5, 105.72, 126.45, 126.93, 145.12, 156.8, 156.14
Webber, Karl 21.19, 105.70
Webber, Peggy 27.11, 54.13, 65.71, 85.81, 88.15, 103.50, 127.26, 156.68, 178.29
Webber, Robert 19.14, 19.15, 106.5, 130.17, 144.9
Weber, Dewey 1.2
Weber, Vic 144.27
Webster, Byron 14.328
Webster, Chuck 8.102, 65.36, 76.6, 82.12, 138.21, 149.22
Webster, Mary 22.27, 34.37, 43.162, 129.62, 140.27, 148.119, 149.18, 152.19, 152.74, 155.49
Wedderspoon, Ted 141.43
Weddle, Vernon 175.7
Wedemeyers, Hans 41.111
Weeks, Claire 43.62
Weichman, Dave 138.14
Weidner, Frank 158.23, 158.40
Weil, Bruce 3.52
Weinrib, Lennie 86.39, 127.44
Welch, Frederic 141.49
Welch, Nelson 126.55, 170.50
Weld, Tuesday 30.17, 178.128
Welden, Ben 17.43, 23.7, 23.13, 57.68, 60.1, 60.3, 60.35, 60.37, 97.75, 97.87, 97.101, 97.138, 97.196, 141.12, 169.109
Weldon, Joan 27.38, 34.21, 66.22, 105.24
Weldon, Tim 84.30
Welker, Stirling 158.72, 158.73, 158.77
Welles, Alan 138.28
Welles, Diana 32.149
Welles, Mel 3.136, 44.12, 66.45, 97.181, 105.34, 147.5, 152.21
Welles, Rebecca 8.23, 15.12, 21.18, 25.36, 25.65, 65.72, 102.29, 114.5, 156.31, 158.47, 162.54, 179.54
Wellman, Wendell 111.6
Wellman, William, Jr. 65.152, 66.82, 66.88, 66.109, 66.185, 85.82, 126.55, 126.110, 126.121, 126.166
Wells, Alan 2.23, 3.113, 6.13, 27.42, 32.128, 43.50, 73.19, 93.24, 93.101, 93.200, 97.95, 97.102, 97.130, 97.200, 135.60, 135.63, 145.7, 147.21, 148.23, 152.2, 158.19, 158.21, 164.17, 164.21, 164.30, 164.50, 169.71, 169.87, 178.27
Wells, Beverly 148.24
Wells, Billy 8.94, 34.42
Wells, Carole 57.116, 85.103, 105.61, 105.71, 121, 161.147, 162.184, 168.10
Wells, Dawn 14.106, 14.287, 14.288, 85.113, 89.136, 105.105, 148.176, 162.153, 170.73
Wells, Dud 5.37
Wells, Ellen 156.39
Wells, Eric Briant 48.26
Wells, Jack 130.98
Wells, Maurice 133.12
Wells, Nelson 170.103
Wells, Sandra 170.73
Wells, Sheilah 14.285, 14.387, 86.25, 161.80, 170.54
Wells, Stanley 19.16
Welsh, Kenneth 99.6
Wendel, David 41.123
Wendell, Howard 12.39, 14.18, 14.183, 44.35, 65.314, 65.332, 65.344, 78.83, 86.32, 93.30, 93.58, 93.119, 126.43, 129.68, 152.13, 161.19, 162.154, 179.55

Wendland, Burt 169.51
Wendley, Richard 12.12
Wengraf, John 8.34, 14.23, 34.61, 155.52
Wenland, Burt 169.46, 169.77, 169.85
Wenner, Leslie 152.33
Wentworth, Marsha 114.22
Werber, Vic 14.126, 14.168
Werle, Barbara 86.8, 86.45, 86.51, 132.14, 132.28, 161.125, 161.173, 161.184, 161.220
Werner, Astrid 170.85
Wertimer, Ned 65.501
Wescoatt, Norman 135.98
Wescoatt, Rusty 3.67, 23.23, 31.33, 60.63, 60.65, 65.76, 73.18, 81.27, 81.50, 81.71, 89.143, 92.98, 97.92, 135.41, 135.45, 135.47, 135.62, 135.64, 135.95, 138.28, 141.33, 141.34, 141.43, 141.46, 141.70, 147.37, 156.27, 156.35, 156.62, 164.23, 169.113
Wescott, Helen 164.60
Wescourt, Gordon 14.223, 107.15, 128.14, 151.20
Wessel, Richard 20.4, 41.24, 57.5, 65.375, 85.62, 97.164, 122.30, 126.88, 126.153, 131, 131.7, 131.13, 156.7, 169.100
Wessen, Eugene 97.113
Wesson, Eileen 161.168
West, Adam 5.33, 12.87, 14.50, 21.22, 27.57, 34.27, 34.37, 34.42, 65.290, 85.45, 85.107, 89.36, 105.51, 105.54, 105.64, 130.107, 146.32, 146.41, 148.143, 161.85
West, Herman E. 102.16
West, Jennifer 21.30, 22.17, 65.514, 70.3, 70.42, 117.14, 146.58
West, Judi 65.537
West, Martin 14.259, 65.409, 66.151, 66.190, 125.15, 151.25, 161.76
West, Parker 5.28
West, Red 170.65, 170.67, 170.70, 170.74, 170.75, 170.82, 170.85, 170.89, 170.91, 170.97, 170.98, 170.104
West, Tegan 1.3
West, Wally 18.15, 23.1, 135.31, 135.35, 135.46, 135.57, 135.61, 135.80, 135.89, 135.91, 135.94, 135.97
West, Wayne 65.233
Westcott, Helen 14.20, 14.115, 77.17, 122.23, 126.24
Westerfield, James 4.5, 8.6, 12.94, 14.43, 14.351, 25.20, 39.17, 41.8, 41.102, 44.6, 65.2, 65.128, 65.293, 65.497, 78.60, 78.73, 79.13, 85.46, 88.30, 89.119, 97.139, 105.62, 105.113, 116.6, 126.13, 127.6, 130.32, 130.72, 133.32, 148.193, 149.24, 152.7, 153.9, 155.72, 156.28, 157, 162.12, 164.38, 168.5, 170.101, 178.11
Westerman, Floyd Red Crow 163
Western, Johnny 15.12, 66.12, 66.35, 148.38
Westman, Nydia 14.176, 84.15
Westmore, Johnnie 158.72
Westmoreland, James 63.9, 107, 170.30
Weston, Brad 17.4, 27.80, 27.108, 44.11, 46.7, 65.411, 66.96, 66.104, 66.145, 66.161, 85.31, 85.35, 85.101, 130.89, 131.25, 131.39, 146.55, 148.182, 151.9, 161.17, 161.65, 161.92, 161.112, 164.52, 168.16
Weston, Ellen 14.338
Weston, Jack 65.100, 65.376, 66.108, 66.126, 86.25, 86.42, 126.29, 144.17
Westward, Patrick 4.7, 22.10, 105.79, 105.94, 125.123, 131.19, 162.40
Wever, Ned 12.15, 152.42
Wexler, Paul 4.37, 43.58, 50.11, 63.2, 65.56, 65.74, 65.481, 93.194, 122.24, 130.80, 130.110, 130.113, 130.141, 164.8
Wexler, Yale 127.44, 167.22
Whalen, Michael 32.30, 32.36, 32.98, 32.104, 97.10, 97.50, 97.147, 97.163, 97.179, 145.24, 148.150, 155.2
Whaley, Bert 12.20

Whalin, Justin 177.63
Wheeler, Andrew 67.16
Wheeler, Bert 18
Wheeler, John L. 14.304, 65.632
Whelan, Ron 170.7
Whinnery, Barbara 10.8
Whisner, Harry 127.40
Whitaker, Steve 12.22
Whitcomb, Dennis 43.383
White, Betty 10.16
White, Bill, Jr. 65.31, 65.39
White, Christine 14.35, 66.25, 66.46, 103.36, 117.24, 130.58, 168.21
White, Dan 8.57, 8.95, 14.26, 14.123, 14.133, 25.58, 31.26, 32.98, 32.104, 32.108, 44.53, 65.191, 65.532, 71.83, 73.25, 85.98, 93.212, 97.107, 106.13, 126.9, 126.104, 126.136, 126.145, 126.154, 127.56, 130.161, 145.36, 147.25, 148.54, 152.21, 161.12, 162.52, 162.181, 169.35, 169.73
White, David 46.2, 61.6, 61.8, 66.86, 66.88, 66.144, 66.203, 74.29, 117.7, 117.8, 117.27, 148.173, 161.20
White, Jesse 4.6, 14.160, 31.42, 97.165, 125.9, 152.27, 170.20
White, Johnstone 131.20
White, Jonathan 68.15
White, Larry 156.39
White, Lucas 65.510
White, Naomi 53.1
White, Ron 99.22
White, Susan 162.23
White, Ted 4.36, 41.17, 41.35, 41.38, 41.39, 41.47, 41.118, 41.151, 83.33, 162.260
White, Tony 36.12
White, Will J. 14.145, 14.266, 43.124, 93.95, 97.160, 103.47, 131.26, 138.56, 141.63, 145.31, 148.28, 148.79, 149.4, 162.13
White, Yvonne 162.49
Whitecloud, Joel 81.55
Whitehead, O.Z. 14.28, 65.127, 74.28, 102.23
Whiteman, Frank 83.24
Whiteman, Russ 57.110, 161.15, 169.42
Whiteside, Ray 42
Whitesides, Robert 138.54
Whitfield, Ann 14.5, 27.8, 27.86, 39.7, 65.419, 85.102, 126.83, 126.88, 148.147, 150.7
Whiting, Margaret 34.62
Whiting, Napoleon 12, 112.14
Whitley, June 97.156
Whitley, Ray 135.45, 135.47, 135.48
Whitman, Gayne 23.39, 23.40
Whitman, Kip 30.15, 65.479, 65.496, 83.24, 109.12
Whitman, Stuart 1.1, 30, 66.20, 69.6, 124.49, 135.11, 135.27, 135.32, 145.7, 145.29, 156.11, 163.25, 178.17
Whitmore, James 12.22, 12.37, 12.65, 12.79, 14.297, 36.18, 38.14, 65.369, 65.385, 65.588, 65.589, 98.21, 98.22, 106.8, 107.8, 126.121, 126.145, 139.7, 157.4, 161.107, 161.160, 161.204, 162.18, 178.2, 178.57, 178.86, 178.104
Whitmore, James, Jr. 19.9
Whitney, CeCe 14.56, 65.263, 65.503, 155.32
Whitney, Crane 73.7
Whitney, Grace Lee 8.96, 12.85, 30.18, 43.248, 43.391, 65.256, 125.9, 130.134, 151.24, 161.27, 161.187, 162.247, 178.135
Whitney, Michael 14.211, 14.300, 65.388, 76.27
Whitney, Peter 4.20, 4.35, 12.73, 14.34, 14.294, 25.13, 25.35, 27.49, 27.61, 27.70, 27.90, 34.18, 41.10, 43.210, 43.298, 43.306, 43.334, 43.340, 57.105, 63.5, 65.9, 65.56, 65.161, 65.237, 65.357, 65.385, 66.20, 66.129, 70.36, 74.6, 76.42, 78.39, 79.8, 85.94, 88.4, 88.10, 88.18, 89.67, 89.122, 92.5, 97.152, 105.20, 105.92, 108.3, 114.25, 119.12, 126.49, 126.51, 127.54, 130.46, 130.56, 130.62, 130.81, 130.110, 130.121,

Personnel Index

130.146, 130.154, 130.168, 131.9, 133, 148.114, 148.155, 150.8, 151.8, 152.41, 155.9, 157.6, 161.59, 161.90, 161.107, 161.208, 162.35, 162.162, 162.197, 162.209, 162.222, 162.255, 162.280, 168.23, 178.15, 178.49, 178.138, 178.144
Whitney, Russell 32.133
Whitney, Ruth 35.27
Whitney, Shirley 148.52
Whitney, Susan 8.14
Whitsett, Ann 14.396, 24.5
Whittaker, Johnnie 14.295, 65.431, 65.542, 65.543, 84.24, 161.208
Whittinghill, Dick 65.283
Whittington, Dick 5.49
Whorf, David 65.100, 66.40, 126.1, 155.38, 164.18, 167.19
Whorf, Richard 130.88
Whyte, Patrick 3.79, 3.80, 3.125, 3.152, 8.47, 25.52, 105.18, 138.39, 147.41, 169.107
Wickes, Mary 14.115, 14.250, 52.61, 151.16, 151.17, 151.20, 151.23, 151.24, 179.33, 179.34
Wickwire, Nancy 65.311
Widdoes, Kathleen 14.407, 70.2
Wiener, Sabrina 48.33
Wiensko, Bob 14.44, 21.37, 146.64
Wiggins, Russell 5.20, 65.600, 65.613, 69.8, 75.25
Wilbanks, Don 8.98, 14.81, 21.43, 27.93, 43.149, 46.7, 51.30, 63.35, 63.43, 63.44, 84.29, 84.31, 84.48, 93.223, 125.12, 126.23, 150.1, 150.4, 150.11, 161.34, 161.81
Wilcox, Charles 169.86
Wilcox, Claire 41.81, 41.136, 65.403, 71.21, 86.41, 139.9, 161.51
Wilcox, Collin 43.402, 61.5, 65.577, 96.73, 132.20, 151.1, 157.9, 161.162
Wilcox, Frank 8.40, 20.44, 20.45, 21.65, 32.83, 32.90, 43.239, 78.31, 83.11, 93.97, 93.150, 97.88, 97.105, 97.128, 97.176, 105.85, 121.14, 126.1, 126.67, 126.72, 126.104, 126.118, 129.29, 129.64, 130.16, 142.3, 146.6, 152.74, 156.32, 162.98, 162.157, 168.7, 170.33, 179.46, 179.47, 179.48
Wilcox, Joey 65.386, 139.9
Wilcox, Mary 30.13, 70.8
Wilcoxon, Henry 12.7, 30.6, 41.54, 65.518, 132.10, 170.99
Wilde, Sonja 14.42, 27.73, 43.176, 64.10, 126.89
Wilde, Tom 156.66
Wilde, Wendy 158.72
Wilder, James 107.19
Wilder, John 3.104, 20.58, 31.22, 164.14, 178.30, 178.48
Wilder, Kelly 7.12
Wilder, Laura Ingalls 95, 96
Wilder, Scott 3.47
Wildman, Valerie 163.64, 163.65
Wiles, Michael Shamus 48.7
Wiley, Sharon 65.251
Wilhoit, Lisa 163.48
Wilke, Robert J. 6.52, 6.59, 8.5, 8.43, 14.43, 14.159, 14.187, 14.293, 14.345, 21.62, 27.1, 27.18, 27.22, 27.39, 27.67, 30.4, 30.13, 32.57, 32.63, 32.78, 34.26, 35.15, 35.26, 39.6, 41.69, 41.108, 43.274, 43.318, 43.350, 44.1, 55.8, 60.9, 60.10, 60.44, 60.46, 63.17, 63.36, 65.118, 65.164, 65.174, 65.186, 65.254, 65.326, 65.440, 66.60, 66.92, 66.98, 66.213, 75.9, 75.10, 78.36, 83.5, 84.3, 85.8, 85.32, 85.43, 85.68, 85.87, 85.91, 85.120, 88.7, 89.8, 89.30, 89.48, 92, 97.17, 97.89, 97.127, 105.81, 105.119, 107.21, 116.18, 117.31, 119.1, 124.6, 124.10, 124.40, 124.42, 124.45, 124.51, 124.52, 125.12, 126.79, 126.119, 126.131, 130.4, 130.15, 131.32, 135.5, 135.28, 135.37, 135.44, 136, 141.3, 142.15, 148.77, 148.136, 149.26, 152.23, 152.29, 152.49, 152.70, 155.4, 155.51, 155.63, 161.60, 162.126, 162.183, 162.207, 162.228, 164.41, 164.49, 165.8, 167.3, 170.72, 179.66, 179.67, 179.68, 179.69

Wilkerson, Guy 32.62, 43.340, 43.362, 65.142, 89.89, 92.12, 105.27, 105.41, 105.112, 142.6, 148.35, 149.3, 156.3, 161.21, 161.97, 169.38
Wilkerson, William 169.56
Wilkes, Donna 53.19, 53.20
Wilkin, Brad 96.91
Wilkins, Barbara 12.76, 14.172
Wilkins, Pat 12.34
Willard, Ellen 65.277, 66.200, 66.217, 89.127, 117.6, 149.11, 162.122, 166.8
Willeford, George 130.124
Willes, Jean 8.1, 8.48, 14.152, 14.196, 14.292, 21.56, 25.15, 27.106, 34.21, 43.308, 44.27, 51.32, 54.29, 56.1, 63.16, 89.6, 89.106, 93.33, 102.4, 102.34, 103.2, 105.19, 105.60, 124.65, 133.16, 145.35, 147.2, 148.26, 151.12, 152.20, 155.26, 155.46, 156.21, 161.121, 162.112, 164.12, 164.30, 164.37, 165.5, 167.7, 173.32, 178.3, 178.20, 178.42, 179.64, 179.65
William, Sumner 43.147
Williams, Adam 13.15, 13.34, 14.12, 14.53, 14.205, 14.263, 27.107, 38.12, 41.3, 65.248, 66.68, 66.112, 71.22, 89.106, 101.2, 105.119, 117.7, 117.8, 126.21, 126.112, 130.28, 130.101, 130.105, 130.142, 130.143, 130.155, 130.167, 151.24, 152.21, 161.89, 165.5, 166.18, 178.102
Williams, Ann 92.31
Williams, Barry 70.16, 84.2
Williams, Bill 41.98, 65.586, 81. 85.11, 89.151, 126.78, 153.5, 153.6, 170.5, 173.3
Williams, Billy Dee 45.2, 99.1, 99.2, 99.3
Williams, Cara 178.115
Williams, Charles 6.35, 32.77
Williams, Chris 41.28
Williams, Dean 126.27, 166.17
Williams, Diahn 70.44
Williams, Elaine 81.36, 81.88, 89.89, 138.47
Williams, Esther 178.126
Williams, Ezekial 41.110, 41.120, 116.15
Williams, Glynn 177.2
Williams, Grant 14.25, 14.202, 65.142, 116.14, 153.5, 173.22
Williams, Guinn "Big Boy" 3.130, 27.38, 31, 65.61, 108.8, 108.24, 108.35, 129.73, 146.10, 148.66, 162.67, 169.80
Williams, Guy 14.159, 14.161, 14.163, 14.167, 97.172, 138.70
Williams, Hal 65.631, 83.17, 83.62
Williams, Jack 63.13, 84.22, 107.7, 126.6
Williams, Jim Cody 177.55
Williams, John 157.12, 170.101
Williams, Kelli 177.50
Williams, Mack 43.78, 97.16, 152.22, 162.9
Williams, Mark 158.51, 158.53, 158.55, 158.59
Williams, Mervin 35.12
Williams, Myron 53.3
WIlliams, Paul 163.51
Williams, Rhoda 178.134
Williams, Rhonda 12.18, 12.67
Williams, Rhys 8.62, 70.16, 105.71, 130.35, 130.42, 130.50, 130.57, 130.70, 130.71, 131.13, 148.119, 151.10, 156.66, 162.44, 164.63, 164.85, 170.24, 170.77
Williams, Robert B. 4.20, 5.7, 6.5, 6.13, 6.21, 12.9, 12.20, 14.228, 14.241, 14.266, 21.36, 27.93, 30.7, 30.14, 57.10, 57.11, 65.429, 65.433, 65.499, 65.536, 86.34, 89.21, 93.166, 97.85, 97.136, 97.168, 126.71, 126.109, 126.155, 126.167, 130.89, 132.25, 134.2, 134.7, 145.33, 148.52, 148.184, 161.30, 161.83, 161.141, 178.104
Williams, Rod 145.39
Williams, Rush 3.68, 14.158, 46.6, 65.470, 65.499, 71.3, 76.15, 93.150, 124.47, 124.48, 124.63, 124.75, 126.20, 126.48, 147.24, 148.41, 148.195, 169.112
Williams, Terry 65.635
Williams, Tiger 33

Williams, Tom 52.47
Williams, Van 12.82, 27.106, 34.32, 65.616, 89.28, 151.19
Williams, Vince 44.56
Williamson, Sam 163.39, 163.55
Willingham, Noble 59.1, 65.583, 163, 175.3, 177.22
Willis, Coke 126.108
Willis, Henry 179.15
Willis, Jerry 37.12
Willis, Marlene 105.102, 162.111
Willis, Norman 44.74, 97.4, 97.51, 97.172, 138.30, 148.38, 162.18
Willock, Dave 5.38, 14.71, 14.151, 14.179, 15, 22.34, 65.310, 65.352, 97.61, 97.62, 151.19, 151.25, 164.51, 164.72, 164.83, 167.4, 167.12
Willock, Margaret 94.11
Willowbird, Chief 35.34
Wills, Beverly 22.7, 149.59
Wills, Chill 5.34, 55, 60.20, 60.22, 65.278, 65.444, 65.463, 69.9, 106.18, 126.170, 126.171, 134, 152.22, 156.54, 162.46
Wills, Henry 14.44, 14.404, 70.33, 71.1, 71.70, 71.83, 71.91, 71.92, 83.27, 84.23, 86.2, 126.4, 126.62, 126.71, 126.84, 126.117, 135.18, 135.19, 162.3, 179.17
Wills, Jerry 71.87, 71.94
Wills, Lou 52.12, 52.29
Wilson, Barbara 156.15
Wilson, Betsy 43.29
Wilson, David Patrick 177.40
Wilson, Dick 8.87, 61.6, 93.168, 98.8, 130.70, 138.64, 138.71, 161.15, 162.45
Wilson, Don 43.152
Wilson, Doug 126.31
Wilson, Frank 162.187
Wilson, Jacqueline 66.217
Wilson, Jan 43.441
Wilson, Jarrod 177.53
Wilson, Major James S. 169.82
Wilson, Ned 53.12
Wilson, Regan 12.58
Wilson, Richard 138.45
Wilson, Robert Brian 65.637
Wilson, Rod 99.15
Wilson, Sherre J. 163
Wilson, Shirley 65.434, 65.444
Wilson, Terry 65.575, 72.13, 106.21, 162, 162.10
Wilson, Ty 41.163
Winans, Robin 169.2
Winberg, Andrew 166.15
Winchell, Paul 161.186
Windish, Ilka 14.140, 51.27, 65.371, 65.456
Windom, William 5.4, 14.292, 24.5, 27.90, 38.10, 49.11, 51.26, 65.245, 65.282, 65.567, 76.13, 84.20, 106.15, 116.23, 144.6, 161.161, 161.179, 161.205, 170.34
Windsor, Marie 4.8, 5.40, 8.5, 14.214, 17.14, 21.54, 25.7, 27.33, 27.39, 44.3, 46.5, 65.546, 69.3, 89.145, 92.7, 93.218, 105.12, 105.119, 126.5, 126.80, 126.158, 127.16, 145.1, 148.93, 166.15, 173.3
Windust, Irene 162.13, 162.30, 162.31, 162.92
Winfield, Paul 36.4, 71.41, 112.14
Wing, Hubert 83.36
Wingreen, Jason 7, 12.18, 14.124, 14.164, 14.424, 36.22, 65.563, 83.12, 84.7, 84.36, 84.45, 98.13, 101.32, 103.45, 123.7, 132.28, 133.4, 134, 139.7, 164.71, 170.20
Winkleman, Michael 97.212
Winkleman, Wendy 57.113, 146.36, 150.4
Winkler, Mel 177.63
Winningham, Mare 176
Winona, Kim 18
Winslow, Dick 14.244, 126.108, 126.114, 162.252, 170.12
Winslow, James 8.16, 65.98, 155.19

Winslow, Paula 93.207, 126.19
Winston, Edgar 43.343
Winston, Laura 26
Winston, Marilyn 126.31
Winston, Norman 126.38, 126.51
Winter, Maria 102.17
Winters, David 144.28
Winters, George 76.3
Winters, Gloria 56.39, 60.32, 80.36, 93.202, 97.39, 124.25, 124.37, 124.43, 135.18, 141, 145.22, 169.54
Winters, Isabel 20.50
Winters, Lee 65.154
Winters, Roland 20.20
Winters, Shelley 162.4
Wintersole, William 14.428, 24.18, 65.548, 70.35, 84.20, 84.40, 116.13, 137, 170.44
Wisden, Robert 67.17
Wise, Hank 65.502, 65.536
Wise, Ray 163.26
Wiseman, Joseph 92.29, 162.254, 165.9
Wiss, Doris 78.61
Wister, Owen 161
Withers, Bernadette 23.25, 162.59, 162.104, 169.75
Withers, Grant 27.21, 31.8, 31.38, 65.54, 65.90, 66.2, 66.12, 66.35, 93.72, 93.120, 114.20, 147.44, 152.21, 158.53, 158.73, 162.2, 178.24, 178.80
Withers, Mark 10.7
Withrow, Glenn 19.3
Witkin, Jacob 163.44
Witney, Michael 14.249, 14.394, 41.105, 43.316, 101.24, 157
Wittliff, Bill 110.2
Wixted, Michael-James 14.370, 41.155, 65.494, 84.39, 96.44
Wo, Brian 14.350
Woessner, Hank H. 120.31
Wohland, Ginny 120.21
Wolders, Robert 41.92
Wolf, Richard, Jr. 126.77
Wolf, Venita 65.436
Wolfe, Ian 7.3, 14.51, 14.73, 14.201, 17.22, 37.6, 69.4, 78.18, 84.9, 84.28, 84.37, 89.54, 97.11, 144.4, 151.8
Wolff, Frank 77.23, 126.38, 162.103
Wolff, Karen 70.2
Wolfington, Iggie 65.426
Wolmier, Bob 55.4
Wong, Anna May 93.177
Wong, Barbara Jean 23.31
Wong, Carey 83.23
Wong, Debbie 170.93
Wong, Jonathan 83.28
Wong, Linda 164.92
Wood, Allen 66.150
Wood, Ashley 163.70
Wood, Britt 32.132, 32.136, 97.91, 135.75, 135.76, 141.57
Wood, Douglas 97.52, 97.69
Wood, Gary 65.532
Wood, Jeanne 88.13, 130.66, 138.13, 158.9, 161.2
Wood, Lana 14.276, 170.58, 170.104
Wood, Larry 65.400
Wood, Laura 127.29
Wood, Lynn 50, 170.66
Wood, Napua 4.30
Wood, Peggy 178.41
Wood, Robert 32.30, 32.36
Wood, Virginia 134.6
Wood, Ward 3.92, 65.460, 66.57, 66.75, 108.32, 147.35, 148.101
Woodall, Jim 84.31
Woodell, Barbara 6.40, 6.42, 39.12, 97.93, 97.100, 119.5, 133.18, 133.26, 138.59, 147.7, 162.146, 162.188, 169.80, 169.94
Woods, Craig 6.33, 32.44, 32.51, 60.36, 60.42, 60.49, 60.52

Woods, Donald 5.34, 8.50, 14.262, 44.37, 72.3, 85.54, 127.21, 144.29, 162.101, 162.111, 170.41, 170.59
Woods, Eric Scott 163.76
Woods, Grant 38, 121.10, 161.127
Woods, Harry 8.93, 20.47, 23.42, 56.23, 65.73, 65.176, 81.51, 97.123, 145.24, 145.37, 155.18
Woods, James 175.5, 175.6
Woods, Lesley 14.312, 41.101
Woodson, Michael F. 177.23, 177.24, 177.58
Woodson, William 51.20, 52.17, 52.22, 66.177, 66.224, 82.7, 128.6, 130.141
Woodville, Katherine 83.28, 96.92, 106.11
Woodward, Bob 2.18, 6.3, 6.4, 6.6, 6.7, 6.8, 6.9, 6.10, 6.12, 6.15, 6.15, 6.17, 6.27, 6.28, 6.36, 6.38, 6.41, 6.44, 6.46, 6.47, 6.54, 6.63, 6.65, 6.69, 6.70, 6.73, 6.74, 6.76, 6.80, 23.12, 23.14, 23.18, 23.19, 23.21, 23.24, 23.32, 23.33, 23.34, 23.41, 23.42, 32.106, 32.113, 60.2, 60.9, 60.14, 60.16, 60.20, 60.27, 60.30, 60.33, 60.41, 60.46, 60.47, 60.48, 60.52, 60.53, 60.62, 60.63, 60.65, 60.66, 60.69, 60.77, 60.78, 60.83, 60.85, 60.89, 60.91, 66.139, 66.149, 66.208, 81.30, 81.54, 81.68, 93.148, 97.27, 97.29, 124.4, 124.11, 124.39, 124.55, 124.56, 124.67, 124.71, 124.76, 124.78, 148.27, 169.30, 169.50
Woodward, Morgan 1.16, 8.70, 9.9, 12.13, 14.32, 14.63, 14.139, 14.243, 14.301, 14.345, 14.394, 17.33, 20.70, 26, 30.8, 30.13, 30.17, 41.16, 41.43, 43.341, 43.345, 56.35, 63.42, 65.378, 65.382, 65.414, 65.417, 65.424, 65.442, 65.443, 65.450, 65.464, 65.475, 65.491, 65.514, 65.523, 65.563, 65.574, 65.595, 65.596, 65.612, 65.638, 66.204, 69.3, 71.37, 71.68, 71.92, 72.14, 75.17, 76.7, 83.9, 83.37, 84.20, 93, 93.1, 93.12, 93.13, 93.15, 93.16, 93.18, 93.20, 93.21, 93.22, 93.25, 93.26, 93.28, 93.29, 93.30, 93.31, 93.107, 93.132, 93.133, 93.136, 93.137, 93.138, 93.139, 93.140, 93.141, 93.142, 93.143, 93.146, 93.147, 93.155, 93.156, 93.158, 93.159, 93.161, 93.162, 93.163, 93.164, 93.165, 93.166, 93.167, 93.169, 93.170, 93.171, 93.173, 93.174, 93.176, 93.177, 93.179, 93.180, 93.181, 93.182, 93.183, 93.184, 93.185, 93.187, 93.188, 93.189, 93.191, 93.192, 93.193, 93.194, 93.195, 93.196, 93.197, 93.198, 93.200, 93.203, 93.204, 93.207, 93.208, 93.209, 93.210, 932.211, 93.212, 93.214, 93.215, 93.216, 93.217, 93.220, 107.9, 121.2, 126.185, 129.37, 129.53, 129.65, 129.78, 148.8, 148.179, 151.8, 152.65, 161.22, 161.139, 161.211, 162.22, 162.100, 162.128, 162.130, 162.154, 162.166, 162.211, 162.254, 162.260, 162.284, 175.2, 178.8
Woody, Jack 138.20
Wooley, Sheb 3.48, 27.25, 32.56, 32.62, 43.309, 81.52, 81.57, 81.98, 93.85, 97.116, 97.124, 97.133, 97.165, 105.7, 108.28, 124.63, 124.75, 124.76, 124.78, 126, 126.110, 145.11, 148.24, 178.9
Woolman, Claude 41.113, 86.54, 96.172
Woolvett, Jaimz 99.6
Wootton, Stephen 22.37, 25.30, 93.212, 108.19, 130.134
Worden, Hank 41.15, 76.43, 84.9, 97.126, 97.138, 97.179, 97.218, 126.37, 126.63, 148.47, 157.14, 157.15, 162.123
Workman, Lindsay 5.11, 9.6, 14.148, 14.189, 14.221, 14.256, 30.8, 34.45, 53.18, 65.298, 70, 74.6, 126.37, 164.22, 170.12, 170.23
Worley, Billie 1.10
Worsham, Marie 43.256
Worthington, Cathy 48.17
Wrather, Linda 97.219
Wray, Fay 162.180
Wren, Clare 1.16, 177
Wren, Michael 177.3
Wright, Ben 13.26, 13.38, 63.47, 65.104, 65.139, 65.173, 65.202, 65.285, 65.294, 65.322, 65.329, 65.420, 66.66, 66.75, 66.136, 66.150, 66.153,

72.8, 89.115, 114.18, 127.33, 127.58, 131.32, 144.21, 161.17, 161.179, 170.17, 170.97, 178.132
Wright, Bloyce 158.5, 158.6, 158.16, 158.33
Wright, Blu 158.46, 158.64
Wright, Bruce 90.13, 120.44
Wright, Dale 130.157
Wright, Howard 6.51, 8.11, 14.86, 14.121, 14.189, 43.346, 44.18, 65.280, 85.24, 93.1, 121.1, 145.25, 145.27, 148.190, 152.1, 169.51
Wright, John 121.4, 132.3
Wright, Patrick 94.3
Wright, Richard 5.30, 5.32, 75.17
Wright, Roy 44.76, 65.247, 65.252, 148.160
Wright, Sandra 129.47
Wright, Teresa 14.150, 84.16
Wright, Tom 90.7
Wright, Will 3.135, 8.19, 8.64, 8.91, 14.23, 14.52, 14.99, 21.11, 31.41, 57.12, 57.67, 65.3, 85.75, 85.80, 85.83, 89.9, 89.101, 97.156, 97.186, 105.17, 105.25, 105.44, 105.67, 105.89, 126.23, 126.91, 129.24, 129.34, 133.33, 146.8, 146.21, 148.69, 148.77, 149.36, 156.17, 156.64, 169.49, 178.40
Wrightman, Tim 163.43
Wrixon, Maris 32.29, 32.35
Wu, Ping 48.60
Wulff, Kai 163.85
Wyatt, Al 30.2, 60.23, 93.214, 97.174, 124.1, 124.5, 124.13, 124.17, 124.25, 124.26, 124.27, 124.28, 124.31, 124.32, 124.35, 148.92, 148.96, 148.127, 170.23
Wyatt, Jane 5.24, 70.52, 106.9, 161.57, 162.189
Wyatt, Walter 123.2
Wyenn, Than 12.32, 12.33, 43.133, 43.172, 65.12, 65.38, 65.78, 71.82, 77.8, 101.19, 126.137, 130.111, 142.6, 142.13, 152.29, 156.43, 161.63, 161.124, 161.175, 164.31, 164.35, 164.68, 168.26, 178.47, 179.13
Wyeth, Sandy Brown 112.17
Wyler, Josie 78.4, 78.20, 162.26
Wyler, Link 30.4, 65.446, 65.470, 65.504, 65.525, 65.540, 65.638, 83.26
Wyler, Martin 107.24
Wyles, Catherine 65.383
Wylie, Adam 1.7
Wyllie, Meg 5.12, 30.7, 43.157, 65.580, 66.48, 101.14, 134.4, 157, 161.19, 162.82, 162.194, 162.218, 162.280, 178.78
Wyman, Jane 48.3, 162.45, 162.190
Wyman, Steve 169.72
Wymore, Patrice 27.78, 44.47, 52.10, 52.65, 77.26, 148.149
Wynant, H.M. 8.14, 8.68, 9.6, 12.111, 17.8, 17.9, 17.10, 17.40, 17.41, 17.42, 20.62, 24.1, 27.53, 27.102, 41.121, 43.170, 43.179, 43.214, 44.46, 55.3, 65.203, 65.248, 65.301, 65.336, 65.363, 65.444, 65.555, 74.24, 105.67, 116.26, 126.22, 129.24, 146.28, 151.3, 161.13, 161.165, 162.141, 162.249, 170.13, 170.28, 170.35, 170.79, 177.20
Wyndham, Herbert 135.35
Wyner, Joel 100.4
Wynn, Ed 14.188, 126.96, 162.84
Wynn, Gordon 93.146, 93.214, 93.222, 97.87, 141.9, 169.62
Wynn, Keenan 5.9, 5.25, 5.44, 9.8, 14.151, 43.250, 69.6, 84.40, 94.27, 123.8, 123.9, 126.117, 132.19, 157.18, 162.16, 170.25
Wynne, Christopher 1.5
Wynter, Dana 49.12, 65.450, 161.21, 162.162, 162.196, 162.263, 170.23
Wyss, Amanda 65.638, 163.49

Yaconelli, Frank 78.18
Yamaji, Setsukuo 66.185
Yarbrough, Glenn 162.268
Yarbrough, Janice 63.8, 63.15
Yarnell, Bruce 14.160, 14.193, 117, 168.27

Personnel Index

Yarnell, Celeste 14.314, 170.6
Yashina, Momo 43.439
Yates, Cassie 177.14
Ybarra, Rocky 127.42
Yearwood, Trisha 48.54
Yeats, John Robert 96.121
Yip, William 65.237, 146.50
Yniguez, Richard 24.4, 14.400, 83.52, 112.12, 137.10
York, Chad 89.100
York, Dick 55.10, 117.31, 126.65, 126.153, 142.11, 161.41, 162.157, 162.175, 162.242
York, Duke 97.19, 97.43, 97.75, 124.33, 124.35, 124.41, 169.5
York, Elizabeth 65.167, 66.69, 66.72
York, Francine 7, 43.334, 47.3, 69.4, 123.6, 170.93
York, Jeff 4, 21.15, 25.45, 27.60, 41.63, 42, 76.22, 89.3, 89.36, 97.32, 97.36, 130.135, 136, 179.63, 179.64, 179.65
York, Michael 170.30
York, Teri 80.17, 80.27, 80.29
Yorr, Leonard 132.3
Yoshioka, Adele 83.53
Yothers, Tina 53.16
Young, Alan 43.247
Young, Blumen 48.32
Young, Buck 8.43, 41.56, 50.3, 65.192, 65.304, 65.349, 74.22, 84.17, 84.23, 93.140, 127.17, 161.112
Young, Carleton 6.47, 6.80, 23.20, 23.25, 44.24, 56.37, 73.26, 93.12, 93.31, 93.60, 93.122, 93.167, 117.10, 117.38, 127.17, 148.159, 162.123, 162.221, 166.18, 169.71

Young, Charles 94.7, 120.1
Young, Cletus 96.89, 96.90, 96.151
Young, David 19.7
Young, Dey 177.62
Young, J.S. 96.171
Young, Joan 105.37, 133.1
Young, Joe 96.112
Young, Keone 120.43
Young, Mary 6.8, 31.34, 52.38, 124.14
Young, Nick 177.3
Young, Otis 116
Young, Ray 65.526, 112.21, 123.2
Young, Richard 109.11
Young, Stan 43.200
Young, Tony 14.199, 21.63, 27.107, 43.264, 44.43, 57.100, 64, 76.16, 85.31, 89.47, 161.141, 162.248
Youngblut, Nancy 48.23
Younger, Jack 65.141, 130.32
Younggreen, Lynn 161.203
Youngs, Jennifer 48, 48.71
Yount, Del 120.51, 120.52
Youse, David 1.2, 1.16, 1.24
Yowlachie, Chief 3.71, 3.81, 23.17, 32.134, 97.6, 124.27, 124.33, 135.4, 145.4, 149.72, 178.134
Yrigoyen, Joe 14.59, 14.163, 44.44, 44.54, 65.439, 149.14
Yulin, Harris 75.9, 75.10, 75.11, 75.12, 75.13, 75.14, 75.15, 75.16, 96.19
Yune, Jon 83.46
Yuro, Robert 12.24, 14.310, 14.429, 43.326, 44.434, 71.26, 71.58, 86.21, 86.31, 86.47, 92.21, 126.183, 161.160

Zaccaro, John 65.201, 88.23, 105.76
Zacha, W.T. 19.13
Zacharias, Steffen 96.28
Zachary, Jane 14.270
Zambrano, Ernesto 149.12
Zapata, Carmen 14.367, 109.13
Zapien, Danny 158.22, 158.44, 174.3
Zaremba, John 14.286, 14.426, 24.7, 71.57, 84.12, 84.13, 96.115, 96.154, 105.74, 116.20, 148.154, 161.10, 161.136, 170.77, 178.36, 178.80
Zee, Eric Michael 48.42, 48.60, 48.77
Zeller, Ben 177.22
Zerbe, Anthony 12.13, 14.333, 24.13, 26, 28.1, 65.457, 65.528, 65.586, 75.1, 76.22, 83.26, 83.43, 95.6, 95.7, 112.24, 161.170, 163.61, 170.68, 177
Zika, Ann 32.31, 32.37
Zimbalist, Efrem, Jr. 4.14, 21.52, 105.9, 105.21, 105.32, 105.35, 105.37, 126.199, 126.23, 180
Zimbalist, Stephanie 26
Zito, Louis 43.96, 148.30
Zobel, Richard 177.34
Zonn, Alex 48.34
Zuckert, Robert 43.436
Zuckert, William 14.67, 14.117, 14.158, 14.343, 27.98, 30.12, 39.16, 43.271, 43.302, 43.303, 43.350, 43.438, 63.43, 63.44, 65.270, 65.295, 65.317, 65.358, 65.532, 70.3, 70.24, 70.35, 70.51, 76.33, 84.34, 89.128, 96.3, 98.7, 101.7, 106.8, 130.119, 132.29, 144.2, 161.5, 161.43, 170.42, 170.104
Zuroe, Heibi 96.168
Zwerling, Darrell 10.21, 96.61, 96.62